SO-ATU-761

Bill James presents. . .

STATS™
Minor League Handbook
1996

STATS, Inc.
and
Howe Sportsdata International

Published by STATS Publishing
A Division of Sports Team Analysis & Tracking Systems, Inc.
Dr. Richard Cramer, Chairman • John Dewan, President

This book is dedicated to
STATS' 1995 Co-Rookies of the Year:

Courtney Elizabeth Capuano
Philip Ignatius Henzler
Elena Sofia Palacios

Cover by John Grimwade and Excel Marketing

Photo of Derek Jeter courtesy of the Columbus Clippers

© Copyright 1995 by STATS, Inc.

All rights reserved. No information contained in this book nor any part of this book may be used, reproduced or transmitted for commercial use in any form without express written consent of STATS, Inc., 8131 Monticello, Skokie, Illinois 60076. (708) 676-3322. STATS is a trademark of Sports Team Analysis and Tracking Systems, Inc.

First Edition: November, 1995

Printed in the United States of America

ISBN 1-884064-18-3

Acknowledgments

Putting together three baseball books in about 10 days isn't easy, and we couldn't do it without the help, whether direct or indirect, of nearly every STATS employee.

Dick Cramer, founder and Chairman of the Board, lives in St. Louis but remains heavily involved in the company. John Dewan, President and CEO, somehow finds time in his hectic schedule to ensure the quality of each of our books.

The players make the numbers, but it takes our Systems Department to put them in formats we all find so useful. Sue Dewan oversees the Department, with the assistance of Mike Canter. Stefan Kretschmann was the "book man" who handled many of the details involved in getting the numbers on the page. Dave Mundo helped with both programming and with our publications software. David Pinto, Jeff Schinski and Madison Smith also contributed to the programming effort, and as always, Art Ashley made certain our hardware was running properly.

Jim Henzler, Scott McDevitt and Rob Neyer are my assistants in the Publicatons Department; Scott and Rob produced the prose sections of this book. Jim spends most of his time supplying ESPN with statistics and information.

The Marketing Department, headed by Ross Schaufelberger, sells STATS products and services. Ross' staff includes Kristen Beauregard, Drew Faust, Ron Freer, Chuck Miller and Jim Musso. Jim Capuano helps market our products and services in his post as Director of National Sales.

Steve Moyer heads the Operations Department, and is ably assisted by Ethan Cooperson, Mike Hammer, Kenn Ruby, Allan Spear and Peter Woelflein.

The Department of Finances and Human Resources, headed by Bob Mcycrhoff, processes the orders, handles the paperwork and makes sure our books get to you. Bob's staff consists of Brian Ersnberger, Ginny Hamill, Tim Harbert, Marge Morra, Betty Moy, Brynne Orlando, Jim Osborne, Pat Quinn and Leena Sheth. Stephanie Seburn is our Assistant Director of Marketing Support and Administration, and Buffy Cramer-Hammann serves as John Dewan's assistant.

Howe Sportsdata International is responsible for the collection of our minor league statistics, and we'd like to offer our thanks to President Jay Virshbo, Executive Vice President William Weiss, and the following people: Bob Townsend, Tom Graham, Jim Keller, Mike Walczak, John Foley, Vin Vitro, Paul La Rocca, Brian Joura, Bob Chaban and Dan Landesman. Special thanks go to Chris Pollari, who, as usual, was particularly helpful in the production of this book.

Last of all, thanks to Bill James for presenting this book, and for continuing to be the best friend STATS has ever had.

— Don Zminda, STATS Director of Publications

Table of Contents

Introduction

It's hard to believe that this is the fifth edition of the *STATS Minor League Handbook*—"the green book," as we like to call it. Like the minors themselves, this book gets a little more popular with each passing year. And like a dedicated minor leaguer, we work hard to keep improving it.

What's in this book? We begin with a complete career register for every player who performed in a Double- or Triple-A league last year, but who did not perform in the majors. Minor league stats for players who *did* perform in the majors are covered in our companion book, the *STATS Major League Handbook* ("the red book"). Check it out.

Next, the *Minor League Handbook* includes complete 1995 hitting and pitching data for all players who performed in the Class A or Rookie leagues last year. We continue with team statistics for every minor league in organized baseball last year, and then with leader boards for the Triple- and Double-A leagues.

The last three sections include the sort of unique numbers that only STATS and Howe Sportsdata can provide. First, there's park data for each minor league team—perfect for telling whose numbers were helped, or hindered, by their home yards. Next, we show you lefty/righty splits for 1995 Triple-A players.

Finally, we present "major league equivalencies" for the primary Double- and Triple-A hitters in each major league farm system. The MLE's, first developed by Bill James, show you how the player's 1995 numbers would have looked in a major league environment, after adjusting for home park and the level of competition. Take it from those who have studied the equivalencies over the years: they work!

We trust that you'll enjoy the *Minor League Handbook*. As always, we welcome your comments.

— Don Zminda

Career Stats

As in previous editions of the *Minor League Handbook*, any player who spent time at AAA and/or AA in 1995 and did not play in the majors gets a complete statistical profile in this section—which includes all major league stats and, with a few exceptions, all minor league stats. For a few players, complete minor league statistics prior to 1984 are unavailable.

Just like in the *Major League Handbook*:

Age is seasonal, based on July 1, 1996. This means the age listed is the player's age as of July 1. By choosing this particular date (very close to the middle of the major league season), we get the age for nearly all players at which they will play the majority of 1996.

TBB and **IBB** are Total Bases on Balls and Intentional Bases on Balls.

SB% is Stolen Base Percentage (stolen bases divided by attempts). **OBP** and **SLG** are On-Base Percentage and Slugging Percentage

BFP, **Bk**, and **ShO** are Batters Facing Pitcher, Balks, and Shutouts.

Andy Abad

Bats: Left **Throws:** Left **Pos:** OF   **Ht:** 6'1" **Wt:** 185 **Born:** 8/25/72 **Age:** 23

					BATTING											BASERUNNING				PERCENTAGES		
Year	Team	Lg	G	AB	H	2B	3B	HR	TB	R	RBI	TBB	IBB	SO	HBP	SH	SF	SB	CS	SB%	GDP	Avg	OBP	SLG
1993	Red Sox	R	59	230	57	9	2	1	73	24	28	25	0	27	2	2	4	2	2	.50	2	.248	.322	.317
1994	Sarasota	A	111	354	102	20	0	2	128	39	35	42	4	58	5	5	5	2	12	.14	9	.288	.367	.362
1995	Trenton	AA	89	287	69	14	3	4	101	29	32	36	2	58	3	6	3	5	7	.42	6	.240	.328	.352
	Sarasota	A	18	59	17	3	0	0	20	5	10	6	0	13	0	0	0	4	3	.57	0	.288	.354	.339
	3 Min. YEARS		277	930	245	46	5	7	322	97	105	109	6	156	10	13	12	13	24	.35	17	.263	.343	.346

Jeff Abbott

Bats: Right **Throws:** Left **Pos:** OF   **Ht:** 6'2" **Wt:** 190 **Born:** 8/17/72 **Age:** 23

					BATTING											BASERUNNING				PERCENTAGES		
Year	Team	Lg	G	AB	H	2B	3B	HR	TB	R	RBI	TBB	IBB	SO	HBP	SH	SF	SB	CS	SB%	GDP	Avg	OBP	SLG
1994	White Sox	R	4	15	7	1	0	1	11	4	3	4	0	0	0	0	0	2	1	.67	1	.467	.579	.733
	Hickory	A	63	224	88	16	6	6	134	47	48	38	1	33	1	1	1	2	1	.67	4	.393	.481	.598
1995	Pr. William	A	70	264	92	16	0	4	120	41	47	26	0	25	2	1	5	7	1	.88	8	.348	.404	.455
	Birmingham	AA	55	197	63	11	1	3	85	25	28	19	2	20	2	3	2	1	3	.25	3	.320	.382	.431
	2 Min. YEARS		192	700	250	44	7	14	350	117	126	87	3	78	5	5	8	12	6	.67	16	.357	.428	.500

Paul Abbott

Pitches: Right **Bats:** Right **Pos:** P   **Ht:** 6'3" **Wt:** 194 **Born:** 9/15/67 **Age:** 28

			HOW MUCH HE PITCHED						WHAT HE GAVE UP											THE RESULTS				
Year	Team	Lg	G	GS	CG	GF	IP	BFP	H	R	ER	HR	SH	SF	HB	TBB	IBB	SO	WP	Bk	W	L	Pct.	ShO	Sv	ERA
1985	Elizabethtn	R	10	10	1	0	35	172	33	32	27	3	1	0	0	32	0	34	7	1	1	5	.167	0	0	6.94
1986	Kenosha	A	25	15	1	7	98	462	102	62	49	13	3	2	2	73	3	73	7	0	6	10	.375	0	0	4.50
1987	Kenosha	A	26	25	1	0	145.1	620	102	76	59	11	5	6	3	103	0	138	11	2	13	6	.684	0	0	3.65
1988	Visalia	A	28	28	4	0	172.1	799	141	95	80	9	8	6	4	143	5	205	12	9	11	9	.550	2	0	4.18
1989	Orlando	AA	17	17	1	0	90.2	389	71	48	44	6	2	1	0	48	0	102	7	7	9	3	.750	0	0	4.37
1990	Portland	AAA	23	23	4	0	128.1	568	110	75	65	9	3	3	1	82	0	129	8	5	5	14	.263	1	0	4.56
1991	Portland	AAA	8	8	1	0	44	193	36	19	19	2	0	1	3	28	0	40	1	0	2	3	.400	1	0	3.89
1992	Portland	AAA	7	7	0	0	46.1	191	30	13	12	2	0	0	0	31	0	46	0	0	4	1	.800	0	0	2.33
1993	Charlotte	AA	4	4	0	0	19	91	25	16	14	4	3	1	0	7	0	12	3	0	0	1	.000	0	0	6.63
	Canton-Akrn	AA	13	12	1	0	75.1	315	71	34	34	4	1	0	1	28	2	86	6	0	4	5	.444	0	0	4.06
1994	Omaha	AAA	15	10	0	4	57.1	262	57	32	31	8	1	0	2	45	0	48	3	0	4	1	.800	0	0	4.87
1995	Iowa	AAA	46	11	0	7	115.1	498	104	50	47	12	4	1	0	64	4	127	12	0	7	7	.500	0	0	3.67
1990	Minnesota	AL	7	7	0	0	34.2	162	37	24	23	0	1	1	1	28	0	25	1	0	0	5	.000	0	0	5.97
1991	Minnesota	AL	15	3	0	1	47.1	210	38	27	25	5	7	3	0	36	1	43	5	0	3	1	.750	0	0	4.75
1992	Minnesota	AL	6	0	0	5	11	50	12	4	4	1	0	1	1	5	0	13	1	0	0	0	.000	0	0	3.27
1993	Cleveland	AL	5	5	0	0	18.1	84	19	15	13	5	0	0	0	11	1	7	1	0	0	1	.000	0	0	6.38
	11 Min. YEARS		222	170	14	18	1027	4560	882	552	481	83	31	21	16	684	14	1040	77	24	66	65	.504	4	0	4.22
	4 Maj. YEARS		33	15	0	6	111.1	506	106	70	65	11	8	5	2	80	2	88	8	0	3	7	.300	0	0	5.25

Todd Abbott

Pitches: Right **Bats:** Right **Pos:** P   **Ht:** 6'4" **Wt:** 200 **Born:** 9/13/73 **Age:** 22

			HOW MUCH HE PITCHED						WHAT HE GAVE UP											THE RESULTS				
Year	Team	Lg	G	GS	CG	GF	IP	BFP	H	R	ER	HR	SH	SF	HB	TBB	IBB	SO	WP	Bk	W	L	Pct.	ShO	Sv	ERA
1995	Sou. Oregon	A	17	5	0	2	48.2	199	39	22	16	3	1	1	0	18	0	41	2	1	2	3	.400	0	1	2.96
	Huntsville	AA	4	0	0	1	6.2	28	6	3	3	1	1	0	0	3	0	4	1	0	0	0	.000	0	0	4.05
	1 Min. YEARS		21	5	0	3	55.1	227	45	25	19	4	2	1	0	21	0	45	3	1	2	3	.400	0	1	3.09

Shawn Abner

Bats: Right **Throws:** Right **Pos:** DH   **Ht:** 6'1" **Wt:** 194 **Born:** 6/17/66 **Age:** 30

					BATTING											BASERUNNING				PERCENTAGES		
Year	Team	Lg	G	AB	H	2B	3B	HR	TB	R	RBI	TBB	IBB	SO	HBP	SH	SF	SB	CS	SB%	GDP	Avg	OBP	SLG
1984	Kingsport	R	46	183	50	8	0	10	88	32	35	10	1	24	2	0	2	9	6	.60	4	.273	.315	.481
	Little Fall	A	18	68	18	2	0	1	23	7	5	5	0	16	0	0	1	3	6	.33	0	.265	.311	.338
1985	Lynchburg	A	139	542	163	30	11	16	263	71	89	28	1	77	9	0	7	8	7	.53	14	.301	.341	.485
1986	Jackson	AA	134	511	136	29	8	14	223	80	76	23	1	76	7	2	7	8	6	.57	10	.266	.303	.436
1987	Las Vegas	AAA	105	406	122	14	11	11	191	60	85	26	2	68	8	2	5	11	11	.50	5	.300	.351	.470
1988	Las Vegas	AAA	63	252	64	16	2	4	96	35	34	11	0	39	1	0	4	0	1	.00	4	.254	.284	.381
1989	Las Vegas	AAA	56	223	60	11	2	8	99	31	31	17	0	53	1	2	1	3	3	.50	2	.269	.322	.444
1992	Vancouver	AAA	20	79	21	4	1	0	27	12	2	9	2	13	2	2	1	2	2	.50	3	.266	.352	.342
1993	Omaha	AAA	37	134	33	6	2	2	49	14	16	8	0	21	1	0	0	2	2	.50	4	.246	.294	.366
1995	Norfolk	AAA	11	31	8	0	0	0	8	3	1	1	0	7	0	0	0	0	0	.00	0	.258	.281	.258
1987	San Diego	NL	16	47	13	3	1	2	24	5	7	2	0	8	0	0	0	1	0	1.00	0	.277	.306	.511
1988	San Diego	NL	37	83	15	3	0	2	24	6	5	4	1	19	1	0	1	0	1	.00	1	.181	.225	.289
1989	San Diego	NL	57	102	18	4	0	2	28	13	14	5	2	20	0	0	1	1	0	1.00	1	.176	.213	.275
1990	San Diego	NL	91	184	45	9	0	1	57	17	15	9	1	28	2	2	1	2	3	.40	3	.245	.286	.310
1991	California	AL	41	101	23	6	1	2	37	12	9	4	0	18	0	0	0	1	2	.33	3	.228	.257	.366
	San Diego	NL	53	115	19	4	1	1	28	15	5	7	4	25	1	1	1	0	0	.00	3	.165	.218	.243
1992	Chicago	AL	97	208	58	10	1	1	73	21	16	12	2	35	3	2	3	1	2	.33	3	.279	.323	.351
	9 Min. YEARS		629	2429	675	120	37	66	1067	345	374	138	7	394	31	8	28	46	44	.51	46	.278	.321	.439
	6 Maj. YEARS		392	840	191	39	4	11	271	89	71	43	10	153	7	5	7	6	8	.43	14	.227	.269	.323

Bats: Left   Throws: Right   Pos: OF   # Bob Abreu   **Ht: 6'0"   Wt: 160   Born: 3/11/74   Age: 22**

					BATTING												BASERUNNING				PERCENTAGES		
Year Team	Lg	G	AB	H	2B	3B	HR	TB	R	RBI	TBB	IBB	SO	HBP	SH	SF	SB	CS	SB%	GDP	Avg	OBP	SLG
1991 Astros	R	56	183	55	7	3	0	68	21	20	17	0	27	1	2	3	10	6	.63	3	.301	.358	.372
1992 Asheville	A	135	480	140	21	4	8	193	81	48	63	1	79	3	0	3	15	11	.58	5	.292	.375	.402
1993 Osceola	A	129	474	134	21	17	5	204	62	55	51	1	90	1	1	3	10	14	.42	8	.283	.352	.430
1994 Jackson	AA	118	400	121	25	9	16	212	61	73	42	3	81	3	0	6	12	10	.55	2	.303	.368	.530
1995 Tucson	AAA	114	415	126	24	17	10	214	72	75	67	9	120	1	0	8	16	14	.53	6	.304	.395	.516
5 Min. YEARS		552	1952	576	98	50	39	891	297	271	240	14	397	9	3	23	63	55	.53	24	.295	.371	.456

Pitches: Right   Bats: Right   Pos: P   # Dave Adam   **Ht: 6'3"   Wt: 202   Born: 2/14/69   Age: 27**

			HOW MUCH HE PITCHED						WHAT HE GAVE UP										THE RESULTS					
Year Team	Lg	G	GS	CG	GF	IP	BFP	H	R	ER	HR	SH	SF	HB	TBB	IBB	SO	WP	Bk	W	L	Pct.	ShO	Sv	ERA
1990 Bellingham	A	19	7	4	7	69.1	269	40	13	11	0	4	0	4	22	1	76	6	1	4	4	.500	1	1	1.43
1992 San Bernrdo	A	26	26	0	0	155	702	178	110	97	17	3	10	4	64	1	112	16	3	7	12	.368	0	0	5.63
1993 Riverside	A	27	27	1	0	169	730	180	91	76	11	7	7	10	51	0	98	8	1	12	8	.600	0	0	4.05
1994 Jacksonville	AA	24	20	2	1	117.1	513	135	75	66	12	6	4	8	33	3	74	7	0	6	10	.375	0	0	5.06
1995 Port City	AA	31	13	0	9	112	492	107	58	54	10	4	0	11	48	1	85	5	1	6	10	.375	0	0	4.34
5 Min. YEARS		127	93	7	17	622.2	2706	640	347	304	50	24	21	37	218	6	445	42	6	35	44	.443	1	1	4.39

Bats: Right   Throws: Right   Pos: OF   # Tommy Adams   **Ht: 6'1"   Wt: 205   Born: 11/26/69   Age: 26**

					BATTING												BASERUNNING				PERCENTAGES		
Year Team	Lg	G	AB	H	2B	3B	HR	TB	R	RBI	TBB	IBB	SO	HBP	SH	SF	SB	CS	SB%	GDP	Avg	OBP	SLG
1991 Bellingham	A	46	150	39	12	0	3	60	27	18	34	2	39	5	0	1	7	2	.78	0	.260	.411	.400
1992 San Bernrdo	A	94	339	95	21	0	13	155	56	75	38	4	68	5	2	10	20	9	.69	6	.280	.352	.457
Jacksonville	AA	17	50	11	2	0	0	13	4	5	2	0	13	1	0	0	1	0	1.00	1	.220	.264	.260
1993 Jacksonville	AA	61	232	64	12	2	4	92	19	20	14	2	34	0	2	3	4	0	1.00	5	.276	.313	.397
1994 Riverside	A	8	30	7	0	0	0	7	5	3	6	0	3	1	0	0	2	2	.50	2	.233	.378	.233
Jacksonville	AA	71	251	58	12	1	8	96	31	19	23	1	55	1	2	1	8	8	.50	4	.231	.297	.382
1995 Riverside	A	69	251	72	17	4	8	121	46	40	28	0	40	7	1	3	12	4	.75	5	.287	.370	.482
Port City	AA	30	118	26	7	0	3	42	10	16	6	0	27	2	0	1	5	3	.63	1	.220	.268	.356
5 Min. YEARS		396	1421	372	83	7	39	586	198	196	151	9	279	22	7	19	59	28	.68	26	.262	.338	.412

Pitches: Right   Bats: Right   Pos: P   # Willie Adams   **Ht: 6'7"   Wt: 215   Born: 10/8/72   Age: 23**

			HOW MUCH HE PITCHED						WHAT HE GAVE UP										THE RESULTS					
Year Team	Lg	G	GS	CG	GF	IP	BFP	H	R	ER	HR	SH	SF	HB	TBB	IBB	SO	WP	Bk	W	L	Pct.	ShO	Sv	ERA
1993 Madison	A	5	5	0	0	18.2	84	21	10	7	2	1	1	0	8	0	22	1	1	0	2	.000	0	0	3.38
1994 Modesto	A	11	5	0	6	45.1	181	41	17	17	7	2	0	0	10	0	42	2	3	7	1	.875	0	2	3.38
Huntsville	AA	10	10	0	0	60.2	256	58	32	29	3	2	3	5	23	2	33	1	1	4	3	.571	0	0	4.30
1995 Huntsville	AA	13	13	0	0	80.2	330	75	33	27	8	2	1	2	17	0	72	1	1	6	5	.545	0	0	3.01
Edmonton	AAA	11	10	1	1	68	288	73	35	33	2	2	2	6	15	5	40	3	0	2	5	.286	0	0	4.37
3 Min. YEARS		50	43	1	7	273.1	1139	268	127	113	22	9	7	13	73	7	209	8	5	19	16	.543	0	2	3.72

Pitches: Left   Bats: Left   Pos: P   # Joel Adamson   **Ht: 6'4"   Wt: 180   Born: 7/2/71   Age: 24**

			HOW MUCH HE PITCHED						WHAT HE GAVE UP										THE RESULTS					
Year Team	Lg	G	GS	CG	GF	IP	BFP	H	R	ER	HR	SH	SF	HB	TBB	IBB	SO	WP	Bk	W	L	Pct.	ShO	Sv	ERA
1990 Princeton	R	12	8	1	3	48	204	55	27	21	2	1	0	3	12	1	39	6	7	2	5	.286	0	1	3.94
1991 Spartanburg	A	14	14	1	0	81	333	72	29	23	5	2	4	3	22	0	84	3	2	4	4	.500	1	0	2.56
Clearwater	A	5	5	0	0	29.2	125	28	12	10	1	2	1	1	7	0	20	2	1	2	1	.667	0	0	3.03
1992 Clearwater	A	15	15	1	0	89.2	378	90	35	34	4	2	3	7	19	0	52	0	1	5	6	.455	1	0	3.41
Reading	AA	10	10	2	0	59	255	68	36	28	10	3	1	0	13	1	35	3	0	3	6	.333	0	0	4.27
1993 Edmonton	AAA	5	5	0	0	26	125	39	21	20	5	1	1	0	13	0	7	0	1	1	2	.333	0	0	6.92
High Desert	A	22	20	6	1	129.2	571	160	83	66	13	3	4	4	30	0	72	5	7	5	5	.500	3	0	4.58
1994 Portland	AA	33	11	2	16	91.1	402	95	51	44	9	5	2	5	32	5	59	0	0	5	6	.455	2	7	4.34
1995 Charlotte	AAA	19	18	2	0	115	471	113	51	42	12	0	3	6	20	0	80	4	2	8	4	.667	0	0	3.29
6 Min. YEARS		135	106	15	20	669.1	2864	720	345	288	61	19	19	29	168	7	448	23	21	35	39	.473	7	8	3.87

Bats: Right   Throws: Right   Pos: SS   # Sharnol Adriana   **Ht: 6'1"   Wt: 185   Born: 11/13/70   Age: 25**

					BATTING												BASERUNNING				PERCENTAGES		
Year Team	Lg	G	AB	H	2B	3B	HR	TB	R	RBI	TBB	IBB	SO	HBP	SH	SF	SB	CS	SB%	GDP	Avg	OBP	SLG
1991 St. Cathrns	A	51	170	35	8	0	5	58	27	20	26	0	33	5	1	4	9	4	.69	6	.206	.322	.341
1992 Dunedin	A	69	210	58	6	3	0	70	25	18	31	1	43	0	4	0	9	4	.69	6	.276	.369	.333
1993 Knoxville	AA	64	177	38	3	1	0	43	19	18	24	2	59	2	2	2	9	8	.53	4	.215	.312	.243
1994 Syracuse	AAA	17	30	4	2	0	0	6	2	0	6	0	8	0	1	0	1	0	1.00	1	.133	.278	.200
Knoxville	AA	69	189	47	7	1	3	65	28	21	31	1	39	2	3	1	7	7	.50	5	.249	.359	.344
1995 Knoxville	AA	75	261	74	17	1	3	102	33	33	32	1	64	4	2	2	12	13	.48	6	.284	.368	.391
5 Min. YEARS		345	1037	256	43	6	11	344	134	110	150	5	246	13	13	9	47	36	.57	27	.247	.347	.332

Benny Agbayani

Bats: Right **Throws:** Right **Pos:** OF-DH   **Ht:** 5'11" **Wt:** 175 **Born:** 12/28/71 **Age:** 24

Year	Team	Lg	G	AB	H	2B	3B	HR	TB	R	RBI	TBB	IBB	SO	HBP	SH	SF	SB	CS	SB%	GDP	Avg	OBP	SLG
1993	Pittsfield	A	51	167	42	6	3	2	60	26	22	20	0	43	0	0	0	7	2	.78	4	.251	.332	.359
1994	St. Lucie	A	119	411	115	13	5	5	153	72	63	58	2	67	10	1	5	8	6	.57	9	.280	.378	.372
1995	St. Lucie	A	44	155	48	9	3	2	69	24	29	26	1	27	5	1	4	8	3	.73	6	.310	.416	.445
	Binghamton	AA	88	295	81	11	2	1	99	38	26	39	0	51	5	1	1	12	3	.80	6	.275	.368	.336
3 Min. YEARS			302	1028	286	39	13	10	381	160	140	143	3	188	20	3	10	35	14	.71	23	.278	.374	.371

Darrel Akerfelds

Pitches: Right **Bats:** Right **Pos:** P   **Ht:** 6'2" **Wt:** 218 **Born:** 6/12/62 **Age:** 34

Year	Team	Lg	G	GS	CG	GF	IP	BFP	H	R	ER	HR	SH	SF	HB	TBB	IBB	SO	WP	Bk	W	L	Pct.	ShO	Sv	ERA
1984	Madison	A	24	24	6	0	151	665	156	86	74	7	4	2	5	74	2	137	19	1	11	6	.647	1	0	4.41
1985	Huntsville	AA	17	17	1	0	96.1	418	75	42	37	12	2	3	1	64	0	56	4	0	9	6	.600	1	0	3.46
1986	Tacoma	AAA	25	24	2	0	150	656	158	91	79	12	3	7	6	62	3	91	10	2	8	12	.400	0	0	4.74
1987	Tacoma	AAA	19	19	3	0	129.2	549	117	52	51	9	2	3	4	57	1	84	9	1	10	3	.769	0	0	3.54
1988	Colo. Sprng	AAA	49	0	0	41	58	270	70	43	28	9	6	2	2	26	3	50	6	2	3	7	.300	0	6	4.34
1989	Okla. City	AAA	33	11	1	15	108	458	89	45	40	5	3	1	4	59	5	75	5	1	5	5	.500	0	4	3.33
1991	Scranton-Wb	AAA	11	11	0	0	52.2	239	52	37	37	9	3	1	0	39	0	36	5	1	3	3	.500	0	0	6.32
1992	Okla. City	AAA	24	1	0	5	33.2	172	48	28	26	7	6	3	5	19	1	18	0	1	3	4	.429	0	1	6.95
	Buffalo	AAA	24	0	0	5	32.1	147	34	22	15	3	2	2	0	17	2	14	3	0	0	2	.000	0	1	4.18
1993	Syracuse	AAA	40	1	0	15	64	285	68	36	31	5	3	1	5	30	2	34	8	0	3	4	.429	0	0	4.36
1995	Vancouver	AAA	9	9	0	0	48	216	60	24	24	5	3	3	4	19	1	27	3	1	3	3	.500	0	0	4.50
	Midland	AA	29	1	0	5	55	235	46	21	21	3	1	2	6	26	3	16	2	0	3	1	.750	0	0	3.44
1986	Oakland	AL	2	0	0	2	5.1	26	7	5	4	2	0	0	0	3	1	5	2	0	0	0	.000	0	0	6.75
1987	Cleveland	AL	16	13	1	0	74.2	347	84	60	56	18	2	4	7	38	1	42	7	0	2	6	.250	0	0	6.75
1989	Texas	AL	6	0	0	2	11	50	11	6	4	1	0	1	0	5	2	9	1	0	0	1	.000	0	0	3.27
1990	Philadelphia	NL	71	0	0	18	93	395	65	45	39	10	9	5	3	54	8	42	7	1	5	2	.714	0	3	3.77
1991	Philadelphia	NL	30	0	0	11	49.2	229	49	30	29	5	6	2	3	27	4	31	4	0	2	1	.667	0	0	5.26
10 Min. YEARS			304	118	13	86	978.2	4310	973	527	463	86	38	30	42	492	23	638	74	10	61	56	.521	2	12	4.26
5 Maj. YEARS			125	13	1	33	233.2	1047	216	146	132	36	17	12	13	127	16	129	21	1	9	10	.474	0	3	5.08

Israel Alcantara

Bats: Right **Throws:** Right **Pos:** 3B   **Ht:** 6'2" **Wt:** 165 **Born:** 5/6/73 **Age:** 23

Year	Team	Lg	G	AB	H	2B	3B	HR	TB	R	RBI	TBB	IBB	SO	HBP	SH	SF	SB	CS	SB%	GDP	Avg	OBP	SLG
1992	Expos	R	59	224	62	14	2	3	89	29	37	17	4	35	1	0	2	6	5	.55	8	.277	.328	.397
1993	Burlington	A	126	470	115	26	3	18	201	65	73	20	2	125	7	1	5	6	7	.46	5	.245	.283	.428
1994	W. Palm Bch	A	125	471	134	26	4	15	213	65	69	26	0	130	3	1	3	9	3	.75	6	.285	.324	.452
1995	Harrisburg	AA	71	237	50	12	2	10	96	25	29	21	1	81	2	1	1	1	1	.50	5	.211	.280	.405
	W. Palm Bch	A	39	134	37	7	2	3	57	16	22	9	0	35	2	2	1	3	0	1.00	0	.276	.329	.425
4 Min. YEARS			420	1536	398	85	13	49	656	200	230	93	7	406	15	5	12	25	16	.61	24	.259	.306	.427

Scott Aldred

Pitches: Left **Bats:** Left **Pos:** P   **Ht:** 6'4" **Wt:** 215 **Born:** 6/12/68 **Age:** 28

Year	Team	Lg	G	GS	CG	GF	IP	BFP	H	R	ER	HR	SH	SF	HB	TBB	IBB	SO	WP	Bk	W	L	Pct.	ShO	Sv	ERA
1987	Fayetteville	A	21	20	0	0	111	485	101	56	44	5	2	7	3	69	0	91	8	1	4	9	.308	0	0	3.57
1988	Lakeland	A	25	25	1	0	131.1	583	122	61	52	6	3	3	8	72	1	102	5	4	8	7	.533	1	0	3.56
1989	London	AA	20	20	3	0	122	513	98	55	52	11	3	3	5	59	0	97	9	2	10	6	.625	1	0	3.84
1990	Toledo	AAA	29	29	2	0	158	687	145	93	86	16	2	10	4	81	1	133	9	4	6	15	.286	0	0	4.90
1991	Toledo	AAA	22	20	2	2	135.1	581	127	65	59	7	8	3	4	72	1	95	4	0	8	8	.500	0	1	3.92
1992	Toledo	AAA	16	13	3	1	86	392	92	54	49	13	1	1	2	47	0	81	6	0	4	6	.400	0	0	5.13
1995	Lakeland	A	13	7	0	3	67.2	275	57	25	24	3	2	1	3	19	0	64	2	0	4	2	.667	0	2	3.19
	Jacksonville	AA	2	2	0	0	12	42	9	0	0	0	0	0	0	1	0	11	0	0	1	0	1.000	0	0	0.00
1990	Detroit	AL	4	3	0	0	14.1	63	13	6	6	0	2	1	1	10	1	7	7	0	1	2	.333	0	0	3.77
1991	Detroit	AL	11	11	1	0	57.1	253	58	37	33	9	3	2	0	30	2	35	3	1	2	4	.333	0	0	5.18
1992	Detroit	AL	16	13	0	0	65	304	80	51	49	12	4	3	3	33	4	34	1	0	3	8	.273	0	0	6.78
1993	Montreal	NL	3	0	0	1	5.1	25	9	4	4	1	0	0	0	1	0	4	1	0	1	0	1.000	0	0	6.75
	Colorado	NL	5	0	0	1	6.2	40	10	10	8	1	2	0	1	9	1	5	1	0	0	0	.000	0	0	10.80
7 Min. YEARS			148	136	11	6	823.1	3558	751	412	366	61	21	28	29	420	3	674	43	11	45	53	.459	2	3	4.00
4 Maj. YEARS			39	27	1	2	148.2	685	170	108	100	23	11	6	5	83	8	85	6	1	7	14	.333	0	0	6.05

Antonio Alfonseca

Pitches: Right **Bats:** Right **Pos:** P   **Ht:** 6'4" **Wt:** 160 **Born:** 4/16/72 **Age:** 24

Year	Team	Lg	G	GS	CG	GF	IP	BFP	H	R	ER	HR	SH	SF	HB	TBB	IBB	SO	WP	Bk	W	L	Pct.	ShO	Sv	ERA
1991	Expos	R	11	10	0	0	51	225	46	33	22	2	1	4	3	25	0	38	1	0	3	3	.500	0	0	3.88
1992	Expos	R	12	10	1	0	66	282	55	31	27	0	2	6	3	35	0	62	8	2	3	4	.429	1	0	3.68
1993	Jamestown	A	15	4	0	3	33.2	151	31	26	23	3	0	2	3	22	1	29	4	1	2	2	.500	0	1	6.15
1994	Kane County	A	32	9	0	7	86.1	361	78	41	39	5	2	3	2	21	1	74	14	0	6	5	.545	0	0	4.07
1995	Portland	AA	19	17	1	0	96.1	405	81	43	39	6	3	3	4	42	1	75	5	4	9	3	.750	0	0	3.64
5 Min. YEARS			89	50	2	10	333.1	1424	291	174	150	16	8	18	15	145	3	278	32	7	23	17	.575	1	1	4.05

Edgar Alfonzo

Bats: Right **Throws:** Right **Pos:** 2B-SS **Ht:** 6'0" **Wt:** 167 **Born:** 6/10/67 **Age:** 29

							BATTING										BASERUNNING				PERCENTAGES		
Year	Team	Lg	G	AB	H	2B	3B	HR	TB	R	RBI	TBB	IBB	SO	HBP	SH	SF	SB	CS	SB%	GDP	Avg	OBP	SLG
1985	Quad City	A	8	21	6	0	0	0	6	3	0	2	0	2	1	0	0	0	2	.00	0	.286	.375	.286
	Salem	A	56	209	57	10	2	4	83	29	25	17	0	28	2	2	2	0	3	.00	3	.273	.330	.397
1986	Quad City	A	67	219	47	8	1	1	60	21	12	22	0	42	2	6	0	1	1	.50	9	.215	.292	.274
1987	Palm Spring	A	36	92	28	4	0	1	35	13	15	13	0	21	0	3	1	1	1	.50	1	.304	.387	.380
	Quad City	A	51	198	50	9	3	4	77	25	25	12	0	35	2	3	3	3	7	.30	3	.253	.298	.389
1988	Palm Spring	A	5	9	1	0	0	0	1	0	2	1	0	3	0	0	0	0	0	.00	0	.111	.200	.111
	Quad City	A	102	406	83	12	2	2	105	36	36	23	1	58	6	8	6	5	5	.50	4	.204	.254	.259
1989	Palm Spring	A	77	242	58	10	2	3	81	31	27	40	0	37	3	3	3	8	3	.73	4	.240	.351	.335
1990	Edmonton	AAA	4	11	2	0	0	0	2	1	1	0	0	0	0	1	0	0	0	.00	1	.182	.182	.182
	Midland	AA	37	121	36	4	1	1	45	20	9	8	0	18	2	1	1	1	0	1.00	4	.298	.348	.372
	Palm Spring	A	57	203	56	4	2	2	70	44	12	30	0	37	0	5	2	5	4	.56	2	.276	.366	.345
1991	Palm Spring	A	81	292	81	11	4	4	112	43	38	38	3	32	1	10	2	5	7	.42	8	.277	.360	.384
	Midland	AA	26	83	23	1	1	4	38	13	13	2	0	7	1	2	0	0	0	.00	2	.277	.302	.458
1992	Palm Spring	A	65	257	92	18	2	3	123	52	42	31	3	25	2	0	3	1	4	.20	8	.358	.427	.479
	Midland	AA	61	220	65	9	1	4	88	39	30	26	0	30	5	1	0	2	2	.50	8	.295	.382	.400
1993	Bowie	AA	130	459	121	22	3	5	164	45	49	37	1	49	4	5	11	14	4	.78	15	.264	.317	.357
1994	Bowie	AA	124	463	143	35	1	11	213	75	73	40	2	63	4	3	6	13	8	.62	13	.309	.365	.460
1995	Orioles	R	6	18	3	0	0	0	3	1	1	0	0	0	1	0	0	0	0	.00	0	.167	.211	.167
	Bowie	AA	28	112	34	6	0	1	43	14	19	10	1	16	0	0	1	1	2	.33	2	.304	.358	.384
	Rochester	AAA	18	54	10	3	0	1	16	5	6	7	0	10	0	3	1	0	0	.00	3	.185	.211	.296
	11 Min. YEARS		1039	3689	996	166	25	51	1365	510	435	354	11	513	36	56	42	60	53	.53	90	.270	.336	.370

Jose Alguacil

Bats: Both **Throws:** Right **Pos:** SS **Ht:** 6'2" **Wt:** 175 **Born:** 8/9/72 **Age:** 23

							BATTING										BASERUNNING				PERCENTAGES		
Year	Team	Lg	G	AB	H	2B	3B	HR	TB	R	RBI	TBB	IBB	SO	HBP	SH	SF	SB	CS	SB%	GDP	Avg	OBP	SLG
1993	Giants	R	42	145	35	6	1	1	46	28	13	6	0	23	1	3	1	8	1	.89	3	.241	.275	.317
1994	Clinton	A	74	245	71	13	0	1	87	40	25	13	0	42	5	11	1	6	6	.50	2	.290	.337	.355
	Everett	A	45	169	36	7	0	0	43	24	7	10	1	41	8	3	0	18	4	.82	4	.213	.289	.254
1995	Burlington	A	38	136	30	2	0	0	32	15	5	7	0	27	2	3	0	13	1	.93	2	.221	.269	.235
	Shreveport	AA	1	4	1	0	0	0	1	1	0	0	0	1	0	0	0	1	0	1.00	0	.250	.250	.250
	San Jose	A	58	225	53	10	3	0	69	30	17	14	0	44	4	8	2	11	6	.65	2	.236	.290	.307
	3 Min. YEARS		258	924	226	38	4	2	278	138	68	50	1	178	20	28	4	57	18	.76	13	.245	.297	.301

Ed Alicea

Bats: Both **Throws:** Right **Pos:** 2B **Ht:** 5'10" **Wt:** 175 **Born:** 3/9/67 **Age:** 29

							BATTING										BASERUNNING				PERCENTAGES		
Year	Team	Lg	G	AB	H	2B	3B	HR	TB	R	RBI	TBB	IBB	SO	HBP	SH	SF	SB	CS	SB%	GDP	Avg	OBP	SLG
1988	Richmond	AAA	50	183	43	4	3	5	68	29	15	22	3	37	2	2	0	4	0	1.00	6	.235	.324	.372
1989	Greenville	AA	124	352	77	7	3	12	126	59	47	68	3	89	3	3	3	22	7	.76	3	.219	.347	.358
	Richmond	AAA	4	7	2	0	0	0	2	1	1	1	0	2	0	0	0	0	0	.00	0	.286	.375	.286
1990	Durham	A	113	370	103	28	0	13	170	55	49	68	3	79	4	6	4	14	8	.64	5	.278	.392	.459
1991	Miami	A	102	368	94	20	7	2	134	55	30	52	5	64	4	1	0	33	7	.83	2	.255	.354	.364
	Greenville	AA	13	42	14	3	0	1	20	6	5	6	1	5	0	0	0	1	0	1.00	0	.333	.417	.476
1992	Greenville	AA	102	315	74	13	8	5	118	49	33	47	4	55	1	2	4	13	10	.57	6	.235	.332	.375
1993	Greenville	AA	14	31	2	0	0	0	2	5	2	5	0	9	0	0	0	1	0	1.00	0	.065	.194	.065
	Central Val	A	12	49	15	2	0	1	20	5	5	2	0	5	0	1	0	0	2	.00	3	.306	.333	.408
	Colo. Sprng	AAA	67	205	69	8	4	1	88	44	23	20	3	30	0	3	1	3	5	.38	4	.337	.394	.429
1995	Norfolk	AAA	122	436	107	17	4	3	141	63	39	45	2	78	2	6	2	21	13	.62	11	.245	.318	.323
	7 Min. YEARS		723	2358	600	102	29	43	889	371	249	336	24	453	16	24	14	112	52	.68	40	.254	.349	.377

Miguel Alicea

Pitches: Right **Bats:** Right **Pos:** P **Ht:** 6'2" **Wt:** 192 **Born:** 11/10/59 **Age:** 36

			HOW MUCH HE PITCHED					WHAT HE GAVE UP									THE RESULTS					
Year	Team	Lg	G	GS	CG	GF	IP	BFP	H	R	ER	HR	SH	SF	HB	TBB	IBB	SO	WP	Bk	W	L	Pct.	ShO	Sv	ERA
1995	Albuquerque	AAA	7	0	0	5	6.2	31	6	5	3	0	2	0	0	4	1	0	3	0	1	1	.500	0	3	4.05

Jeff Alkire

Pitches: Left **Bats:** Right **Pos:** P **Ht:** 6'1" **Wt:** 200 **Born:** 11/15/69 **Age:** 26

			HOW MUCH HE PITCHED					WHAT HE GAVE UP									THE RESULTS					
Year	Team	Lg	G	GS	CG	GF	IP	BFP	H	R	ER	HR	SH	SF	HB	TBB	IBB	SO	WP	Bk	W	L	Pct.	ShO	Sv	ERA
1993	Savannah	A	28	28	0	0	171.2	711	143	56	47	10	5	3	11	68	0	175	8	0	15	6	.714	0	0	2.46
1994	Arkansas	AA	8	8	0	0	37.1	171	50	27	25	0	2	0	0	17	0	31	3	0	4	3	.571	0	0	6.03
	St. Pete	A	12	12	2	0	70	289	61	32	22	2	3	5	3	22	0	56	4	0	4	5	.444	0	0	2.83
1995	Arkansas	AA	2	0	0	0	3	13	4	1	1	0	1	0	0	0	0	2	1	0	0	0	.000	0	0	3.00
	St. Paul	IND	19	18	2	0	114.1	490	123	58	54	13	2	2	7	40	1	81	8	0	8	3	.727	0	0	4.25
	3 Min. YEARS		69	66	4	0	396.1	1674	381	174	149	25	13	10	21	147	1	345	24	1	31	17	.646	0	0	3.38

Matt Allen

Bats: Right **Throws:** Right **Pos:** C | **Ht:** 6'2" **Wt:** 190 **Born:** 12/25/69 **Age:** 26

Year	Team	Lg	G	AB	H	2B	3B	HR	TB	R	RBI	TBB	IBB	SO	HBP	SH	SF	SB	CS	SB%	GDP	Avg	OBP	SLG
1991	Jamestown	A	40	125	21	0	2	3	34	16	16	20	2	36	0	0	3	4	1	.80	0	.168	.277	.272
1992	Albany	A	16	51	10	2	0	0	12	6	2	5	0	17	1	0	0	0	0	.00	0	.196	.281	.235
	Jamestown	A	58	168	30	11	0	4	53	17	16	10	0	64	4	0	1	5	1	.83	2	.179	.240	.315
1993	W. Palm Bch	A	57	152	32	10	0	0	42	10	8	13	0	41	8	5	0	4	0	1.00	2	.211	.306	.276
1994	W. Palm Bch	A	44	110	24	1	0	1	28	14	17	21	0	31	2	0	3	3	3	.50	2	.218	.346	.255
1995	Harrisburg	AA	5	14	2	0	0	0	2	2	1	2	0	2	0	0	0	0	0	.00	0	.143	.250	.143
	Duluth-Sup.	IND	76	278	77	11	4	9	123	49	49	30	1	44	4	3	4	1	1	.50	3	.277	.351	.442
	5 Min. YEARS		296	898	196	35	6	17	294	114	109	101	3	235	19	8	11	17	6	.74	9	.218	.307	.327

Ronnie Allen

Pitches: Right **Bats:** Right **Pos:** P | **Ht:** 5'11" **Wt:** 185 **Born:** 5/10/70 **Age:** 26

Year	Team	Lg	G	GS	CG	GF	IP	BFP	H	R	ER	HR	SH	SF	HB	TBB	IBB	SO	WP	Bk	W	L	Pct.	ShO	Sv	ERA
1991	Batavia	A	8	7	0	1	46	171	33	18	16	5	1	1	1	7	0	39	2	2	3	3	.500	0	0	3.13
	Spartanburg	A	2	2	2	0	14	57	14	5	5	1	0	0	0	4	0	7	0	1	2	0	1.000	0	0	3.21
1992	Clearwater	A	15	15	1	0	91.1	372	87	36	29	6	3	2	1	24	0	49	1	3	6	6	.500	1	0	2.86
	Reading	AA	5	5	1	0	31	133	35	18	17	2	0	3	1	9	1	17	0	0	1	3	.250	0	0	4.94
1993	Scranton-Wb	AAA	5	5	0	0	24.1	110	30	15	14	3	1	2	1	8	1	12	1	0	2	2	.000	0	0	5.18
	Reading	AA	15	15	0	0	85	367	82	45	42	8	2	2	1	35	0	63	6	1	4	5	.444	0	0	4.45
1994	Clearwater	A	2	2	0	0	13.2	51	10	2	2	0	0	0	0	5	0	10	0	2	2	0	1.000	0	0	1.32
	Reading	AA	24	10	0	5	81.2	373	95	62	61	10	5	5	2	40	1	46	7	0	3	4	.429	0	0	6.72
1995	Jackson	AA	4	0	0	0	10.2	49	13	7	7	0	2	2	0	5	1	3	0	0	2	0	1.000	0	0	5.91
	5 Min. YEARS		80	61	4	6	397.2	1683	399	208	193	35	14	17	7	137	4	246	17	9	23	23	.500	1	0	4.37

Jermaine Allensworth

Bats: Right **Throws:** Right **Pos:** OF | **Ht:** 5'11" **Wt:** 180 **Born:** 1/11/72 **Age:** 24

Year	Team	Lg	G	AB	H	2B	3B	HR	TB	R	RBI	TBB	IBB	SO	HBP	SH	SF	SB	CS	SB%	GDP	Avg	OBP	SLG
1993	Welland	A	67	263	81	16	4	1	108	44	32	24	0	38	12	2	1	18	3	.86	2	.308	.390	.411
1994	Carolina	AA	118	452	109	26	8	1	154	63	34	39	0	79	11	5	3	16	14	.53	2	.241	.315	.341
1995	Carolina	AA	56	219	59	14	2	1	80	37	14	25	0	34	5	2	0	13	8	.62	4	.269	.357	.365
	Calgary	AAA	51	190	60	13	4	3	90	46	11	13	0	30	5	1	0	13	4	.76	3	.316	.375	.474
	3 Min. YEARS		292	1124	309	69	18	6	432	190	91	101	0	181	33	10	4	60	29	.67	11	.275	.351	.384

Carlos Almanzar

Pitches: Right **Bats:** Right **Pos:** P | **Ht:** 6'2" **Wt:** 166 **Born:** 11/6/73 **Age:** 22

Year	Team	Lg	G	GS	CG	GF	IP	BFP	H	R	ER	HR	SH	SF	HB	TBB	IBB	SO	WP	Bk	W	L	Pct.	ShO	Sv	ERA
1994	Medicne Hat	R	14	14	0	0	84.2	351	82	38	27	2	7	1	1	19	0	77	3	2	7	4	.636	0	0	2.87
1995	Knoxville	AA	35	19	0	7	126.1	546	144	77	56	10	3	6	3	32	1	93	4	1	3	12	.200	0	2	3.99
	2 Min. YEARS		49	33	0	7	211	897	226	115	83	12	10	7	4	51	1	170	7	3	10	16	.385	0	2	3.54

Garvin Alston

Pitches: Right **Bats:** Right **Pos:** P | **Ht:** 6'1" **Wt:** 175 **Born:** 12/8/71 **Age:** 24

Year	Team	Lg	G	GS	CG	GF	IP	BFP	H	R	ER	HR	SH	SF	HB	TBB	IBB	SO	WP	Bk	W	L	Pct.	ShO	Sv	ERA
1992	Bend	A	14	12	0	0	73	320	71	40	32	1	5	5	9	29	0	73	7	8	5	4	.556	0	0	3.95
1993	Central Val	A	25	24	1	0	117	538	124	81	71	11	6	6	8	70	0	90	10	2	5	9	.357	0	0	5.46
1994	Central Val	A	37	13	0	20	87	382	91	51	35	9	5	0	6	42	1	83	5	2	5	9	.357	0	0	3.62
	New Haven	AA	4	0	0	1	4.1	22	5	6	6	1	0	0	0	3	0	8	0	0	0	0	.000	0	1	12.46
1995	New Haven	AA	47	0	0	20	66.2	271	47	24	21	1	4	2	3	26	3	73	4	0	4	4	.500	0	6	2.84
	4 Min. YEARS		127	49	1	41	348	1533	338	202	165	23	20	13	26	170	4	327	26	12	19	26	.422	0	15	4.27

Clemente Alvarez

Bats: Right **Throws:** Right **Pos:** C | **Ht:** 5'11" **Wt:** 180 **Born:** 5/18/68 **Age:** 28

Year	Team	Lg	G	AB	H	2B	3B	HR	TB	R	RBI	TBB	IBB	SO	HBP	SH	SF	SB	CS	SB%	GDP	Avg	OBP	SLG
1987	White Sox	R	25	55	10	1	0	1	14	8	4	7	0	8	0	0	0	1	1	.50	1	.182	.274	.255
1988	South Bend	A	15	41	3	0	0	0	3	0	1	3	0	19	0	0	0	0	0	.00	2	.073	.136	.073
	Utica	A	53	132	31	5	1	0	38	15	14	11	0	36	2	4	1	5	2	.71	2	.235	.301	.288
1989	South Bend	A	86	230	51	15	0	0	66	22	22	16	0	59	0	9	1	4	1	.80	6	.222	.271	.287
1990	Sarasota	A	37	119	19	4	1	1	28	9	9	8	0	24	0	2	0	0	0	.00	5	.160	.213	.235
	South Bend	A	48	127	30	5	0	2	41	14	12	20	0	38	1	5	2	2	1	.67	1	.236	.340	.323
1991	Sarasota	A	71	194	40	10	2	1	57	14	22	20	0	41	4	7	1	3	2	.60	6	.206	.292	.294
1992	Birmingham	AA	57	169	24	8	0	1	35	7	10	10	0	52	2	3	0	1	1	.50	5	.142	.199	.207
1993	White Sox	R	2	5	0	0	0	0	0	0	0	1	0	2	0	0	0	0	1	.00	0	.000	.167	.000
	Nashville	AAA	11	29	6	0	0	0	6	1	2	0	0	4	0	2	0	0	0	.00	0	.207	.233	.207
	Birmingham	AA	35	111	25	4	0	1	32	8	8	11	0	28	1	1	1	0	4	.00	3	.225	.298	.288
1994	Nashville	AAA	87	223	48	8	1	3	67	18	14	17	0	48	2	12	2	0	2	.00	2	.215	.275	.300

Pitches: Right **Bats:** Right **Pos:** P

Kurt Archer

Ht: 6'4" **Wt:** 215 **Born:** 4/27/69 **Age:** 27

			HOW MUCH HE PITCHED						WHAT HE GAVE UP											THE RESULTS					
Year	Team	Lg	G	GS	CG	GF	IP	BFP	H	R	ER	HR	SH	SF	HB	TBB	IBB	SO	WP	Bk	W	L	Pct.	ShO	Sv	ERA
1990	Helena	R	10	0	0	9	19.2	83	19	9	8	0	0	0	2	3	2	23	0	1	0	2	.000	0	3	3.66
	Beloit	A	11	0	0	3	29.1	122	24	11	5	1	1	3	1	9	1	27	2	1	5	0	1.000	0	1	1.53
1991	Stockton	A	27	6	0	9	46.1	219	45	36	22	1	3	4	7	29	3	26	5	0	2	4	.333	0	1	4.27
1992	Stockton	A	55	0	0	42	76.2	317	60	19	16	2	5	3	5	32	8	49	2	0	11	3	.786	0	15	1.88
1993	El Paso	AA	54	5	0	28	104.2	457	129	63	57	10	6	6	8	38	8	50	6	0	9	8	.529	0	11	4.90
1994	Stockton	A	5	0	0	4	5	22	6	2	2	0	0	0	0	1	1	5	0	0	0	1	.000	0	2	3.60
	El Paso	AA	44	1	0	16	77	327	87	40	35	6	4	4	2	17	2	58	2	0	5	3	.625	0	9	4.09
1995	El Paso	AA	4	0	0	2	6	24	4	2	2	0	0	0	0	1	0	5	0	0	0	0	.000	0	1	3.00
	New Orleans	AAA	38	0	0	11	61	256	57	23	22	5	6	3	5	17	2	41	5	0	2	6	.250	0	2	3.25
	6 Min. YEARS		248	12	0	124	425.2	1827	431	205	169	25	25	23	30	147	27	284	22	2	34	27	.557	0	44	3.57

Pitches: Left **Bats:** Right **Pos:** P

Steve Arffa

Ht: 6'2" **Wt:** 195 **Born:** 1/26/73 **Age:** 23

			HOW MUCH HE PITCHED						WHAT HE GAVE UP											THE RESULTS					
Year	Team	Lg	G	GS	CG	GF	IP	BFP	H	R	ER	HR	SH	SF	HB	TBB	IBB	SO	WP	Bk	W	L	Pct.	ShO	Sv	ERA
1994	Pittsfield	A	14	14	1	0	88.1	372	91	46	35	5	1	5	4	13	1	56	4	1	6	5	.545	0	0	3.57
1995	Binghamton	AA	1	1	0	0	6	25	7	3	3	0	0	0	0	1	0	1	0	1	0	0	.000	0	0	4.50
	St. Lucie	A	32	10	1	2	88	373	99	46	42	8	0	4	3	22	3	46	8	1	5	5	.500	1	2	4.30
	2 Min. YEARS		47	25	2	2	182.1	770	197	95	80	13	1	9	7	36	4	103	12	3	11	10	.524	1	2	3.95

Bats: Both **Throws:** Right **Pos:** 2B

Amador Arias

Ht: 5'10" **Wt:** 160 **Born:** 5/28/72 **Age:** 24

			BATTING														BASERUNNING				PERCENTAGES		
Year	Team	Lg	G	AB	H	2B	3B	HR	TB	R	RBI	TBB	IBB	SO	HBP	SH	SF	SB	CS	SB%	GDP	Avg	OBP	SLG
1990	Reds	R	61	248	63	8	3	1	80	46	27	21	0	37	0	7	0	23	6	.79	4	.254	.312	.323
1991	Cedar Rapds	A	21	59	11	0	1	0	13	5	4	4	0	14	1	0	0	7	3	.70	0	.186	.250	.220
	Erie	A	52	200	46	14	2	2	70	24	17	18	1	42	0	1	2	13	5	.72	3	.230	.291	.350
1992	Charlstn-Wv	A	58	149	36	4	0	0	40	17	7	9	0	37	1	2	2	7	6	.54	3	.242	.286	.268
1993	Winston-Sal	A	58	179	47	3	0	0	50	25	12	7	0	28	0	4	1	5	6	.45	3	.263	.289	.279
	Chattanooga	AA	18	65	14	1	1	0	17	6	2	4	0	23	0	1	0	1	1	.50	0	.215	.261	.262
1994	Winston-Sal	A	75	193	46	7	0	2	59	25	15	11	0	33	1	3	1	7	6	.54	1	.238	.282	.306
1995	Indianaplis	AAA	5	15	6	0	0	0	6	2	1	2	0	1	0	0	0	1	0	1.00	0	.400	.471	.400
	Chattanooga	AA	71	108	24	3	1	0	29	17	4	6	0	15	0	1	0	3	2	.60	4	.222	.263	.269
	6 Min. YEARS		419	1216	293	40	8	5	364	167	89	82	1	230	3	19	6	67	35	.66	24	.241	.289	.299

Bats: Right **Throws:** Right **Pos:** 3B

George Arias

Ht: 5'11" **Wt:** 190 **Born:** 3/12/72 **Age:** 24

			BATTING														BASERUNNING				PERCENTAGES		
Year	Team	Lg	G	AB	H	2B	3B	HR	TB	R	RBI	TBB	IBB	SO	HBP	SH	SF	SB	CS	SB%	GDP	Avg	OBP	SLG
1993	Cedar Rapds	A	74	253	55	13	3	9	101	31	41	31	1	65	3	1	2	6	1	.86	6	.217	.308	.399
1994	Lk Elsinore	A	134	514	144	28	3	23	247	89	80	58	1	111	5	3	4	6	3	.67	9	.280	.356	.481
1995	Midland	AA	134	520	145	19	10	30	274	91	104	63	1	119	5	1	5	3	1	.75	11	.279	.359	.527
	3 Min. YEARS		342	1287	344	60	16	62	622	211	225	152	3	295	13	5	11	15	5	.75	26	.267	.348	.483

Pitches: Right **Bats:** Right **Pos:** P

Jamie Arnold

Ht: 6'2" **Wt:** 188 **Born:** 3/24/74 **Age:** 22

			HOW MUCH HE PITCHED						WHAT HE GAVE UP											THE RESULTS					
Year	Team	Lg	G	GS	CG	GF	IP	BFP	H	R	ER	HR	SH	SF	HB	TBB	IBB	SO	WP	Bk	W	L	Pct.	ShO	Sv	ERA
1992	Braves	R	7	5	0	2	20	85	16	12	9	0	0	2	4	6	0	22	0	2	0	1	.000	0	0	4.05
1993	Macon	A	27	27	1	0	164.1	692	142	67	57	5	3	4	16	56	0	124	13	2	8	9	.471	0	0	3.12
1994	Durham	A	25	25	0	0	145	656	144	96	75	26	3	1	14	79	4	91	8	4	7	7	.500	0	0	4.66
1995	Durham	A	15	14	1	0	80	347	86	42	35	5	4	1	9	21	0	44	4	0	4	8	.333	0	0	3.94
	Greenville	AA	10	10	0	0	56.2	266	76	42	40	8	0	2	7	25	1	19	6	0	1	5	.167	0	0	6.35
	4 Min. YEARS		84	81	2	2	466	2046	464	259	216	44	10	10	50	187	5	300	31	8	20	30	.400	0	0	4.17

Bats: Right **Throws:** Right **Pos:** SS

Ken Arnold

Ht: 6'1" **Wt:** 180 **Born:** 5/10/69 **Age:** 27

			BATTING														BASERUNNING				PERCENTAGES		
Year	Team	Lg	G	AB	H	2B	3B	HR	TB	R	RBI	TBB	IBB	SO	HBP	SH	SF	SB	CS	SB%	GDP	Avg	OBP	SLG
1992	Peoria	A	91	271	57	4	3	1	70	41	22	42	0	65	3	4	1	11	4	.73	11	.210	.322	.258
1993	Thunder Bay	IND	55	183	54	7	0	0	61	22	19	11	1	36	1	2	1	12	6	.67	4	.295	.337	.333
1994	Bowie	AA	86	228	61	8	1	5	86	29	27	23	0	48	1	9	1	4	5	.44	3	.268	.336	.377
1995	Bowie	AA	10	22	0	0	0	0	0	3	0	6	0	8	0	0	0	0	0	.00	1	.000	.214	.000
	Winnipeg	IND	85	322	74	12	1	1	91	43	32	20	1	73	2	5	2	6	3	.67	4	.230	.277	.283
	4 Min. YEARS		327	1026	246	31	5	7	308	138	100	102	2	230	7	20	5	33	18	.65	23	.240	.311	.300

Matt Arrandale

Pitches: Right **Bats:** Right **Pos:** P **Ht:** 6'0" **Wt:** 170 **Born:** 12/14/70 **Age:** 25

			HOW MUCH HE PITCHED						WHAT HE GAVE UP											THE RESULTS					
Year	Team	Lg	G	GS	CG	GF	IP	BFP	H	R	ER	HR	SH	SF	HB	TBB	IBB	SO	WP	Bk	W	L	Pct.	ShO	Sv	ERA
1993	Glens Falls	A	12	12	0	0	68.2	298	77	42	35	6	1	1	2	14	0	53	4	2	3	4	.429	0	0	4.59
	St. Pete	A	2	2	0	0	14	49	8	2	2	1	0	0	0	3	0	11	1	0	1	0	1.000	0	0	1.29
1994	Savannah	A	19	19	5	0	133.1	519	112	36	26	2	1	2	4	21	1	121	3	0	15	3	.833	0	0	1.76
	St. Pete	A	9	9	0	0	59	244	65	26	22	0	2	1	2	11	0	29	2	1	3	4	.429	0	0	3.36
1995	Arkansas	AA	47	3	0	23	68.2	296	72	28	25	1	2	2	1	22	4	28	1	0	3	5	.375	0	2	3.28
	3 Min. YEARS		89	45	5	23	343.2	1406	334	134	110	10	6	6	9	71	5	242	11	3	25	16	.610	0	2	2.88

Ivan Arteaga

Pitches: Left **Bats:** Right **Pos:** P **Ht:** 6'2" **Wt:** 220 **Born:** 7/20/72 **Age:** 23

			HOW MUCH HE PITCHED						WHAT HE GAVE UP											THE RESULTS					
Year	Team	Lg	G	GS	CG	GF	IP	BFP	H	R	ER	HR	SH	SF	HB	TBB	IBB	SO	WP	Bk	W	L	Pct.	ShO	Sv	ERA
1993	Burlington	A	20	20	2	0	127	549	114	57	40	7	2	5	7	47	1	111	10	4	6	5	.545	0	0	2.83
	W. Palm Bch	A	4	4	0	0	15.2	80	23	15	14	1	1	0	1	9	0	10	0	0	0	3	.000	0	0	8.04
1994	New Haven	AA	27	24	2	1	150	631	123	74	58	13	5	3	2	70	1	101	4	5	8	9	.471	0	0	3.48
1995	New Haven	AA	14	11	0	0	34	162	36	26	21	3	1	2	5	21	0	18	1	3	2	4	.333	0	0	5.56
	3 Min. YEARS		65	59	4	1	326.2	1422	296	172	133	24	9	10	15	147	2	240	15	12	16	21	.432	0	0	3.66

Scott Arvesen

Pitches: Right **Bats:** Right **Pos:** P **Ht:** 6'6" **Wt:** 210 **Born:** 7/15/68 **Age:** 27

			HOW MUCH HE PITCHED						WHAT HE GAVE UP											THE RESULTS					
Year	Team	Lg	G	GS	CG	GF	IP	BFP	H	R	ER	HR	SH	SF	HB	TBB	IBB	SO	WP	Bk	W	L	Pct.	ShO	Sv	ERA
1989	Welland	A	5	1	0	2	13.1	55	8	6	5	0	1	0	0	6	0	16	2	1	1	0	1.000	0	1	3.38
1990	Augusta	A	28	28	2	0	158.1	700	186	89	76	6	3	2	2	54	0	102	4	1	8	11	.421	1	0	4.32
1991	Augusta	A	8	8	0	0	44.2	204	46	25	14	1	2	1	3	20	0	33	3	1	2	2	.500	0	0	2.82
	Salem	A	19	19	4	0	119.1	526	141	75	62	13	3	5	5	35	3	73	8	0	5	10	.333	0	0	4.68
1995	Las Vegas	AAA	2	0	0	2	3	16	4	5	5	1	0	0	1	2	0	0	2	0	0	0	.000	0	0	15.00
	4 Min. YEARS		62	56	6	4	338.2	1501	385	200	162	21	9	8	11	117	3	224	19	3	16	23	.410	1	1	4.31

Neil Atkinson

Pitches: Left **Bats:** Left **Pos:** P **Ht:** 6'0" **Wt:** 190 **Born:** 1/14/71 **Age:** 25

			HOW MUCH HE PITCHED						WHAT HE GAVE UP											THE RESULTS					
Year	Team	Lg	G	GS	CG	GF	IP	BFP	H	R	ER	HR	SH	SF	HB	TBB	IBB	SO	WP	Bk	W	L	Pct.	ShO	Sv	ERA
1993	Eugene	A	23	4	0	7	47.2	217	50	28	23	2	1	3	3	26	7	43	5	0	2	3	.400	0	3	4.34
1994	Rockford	A	51	0	0	19	74.1	295	64	21	21	1	3	1	4	16	2	82	6	1	7	1	.875	0	5	2.54
1995	Wichita	AA	40	0	0	8	50.2	223	52	29	27	7	1	2	1	21	2	32	3	1	3	0	1.000	0	1	4.80
	Wilmington	A	8	0	0	5	22	93	21	7	7	1	2	0	1	6	3	20	3	0	1	1	.500	0	3	2.86
	3 Min. YEARS		122	4	0	39	194.2	828	187	85	78	11	7	6	9	69	14	177	17	2	13	5	.722	0	12	3.61

Derek Aucoin

Pitches: Right **Bats:** Right **Pos:** P **Ht:** 6'7" **Wt:** 226 **Born:** 3/27/70 **Age:** 26

			HOW MUCH HE PITCHED						WHAT HE GAVE UP											THE RESULTS					
Year	Team	Lg	G	GS	CG	GF	IP	BFP	H	R	ER	HR	SH	SF	HB	TBB	IBB	SO	WP	Bk	W	L	Pct.	ShO	Sv	ERA
1989	Expos	R	7	3	0	1	23.2	106	24	10	7	2	1	0	0	12	0	27	3	1	2	1	.667	0	1	2.66
1990	Jamestown	A	8	8	1	0	36.1	152	28	20	18	3	1	1	1	18	0	27	6	0	1	3	.250	0	0	4.46
1991	Sumter	A	41	4	0	8	90.1	408	85	55	43	5	4	2	10	44	3	70	6	1	3	6	.333	0	1	4.28
1992	Rockford	A	39	2	0	17	69	289	48	32	23	2	1	2	4	34	2	65	6	3	3	2	.600	0	3	3.00
1993	W. Palm Bch	A	38	6	0	6	87.1	387	89	48	41	5	6	2	0	44	3	62	8	2	4	4	.500	0	1	4.23
1994	W. Palm Bch	A	7	0	0	5	7.1	26	3	0	0	0	0	0	0	2	0	10	0	0	0	0	.000	0	2	0.00
	Harrisburg	AA	31	0	0	12	47	208	36	19	17	4	1	0	2	29	0	48	3	0	3	4	.429	0	4	3.26
1995	Harrisburg	AA	29	0	0	10	52.2	242	52	34	29	3	0	5	8	28	2	48	2	0	2	4	.333	0	1	4.96
	7 Min. YEARS		200	23	1	59	413.2	1818	365	218	178	24	14	12	25	211	10	357	34	7	18	24	.429	0	13	3.87

Don August

Pitches: Right **Bats:** Right **Pos:** P **Ht:** 6'3" **Wt:** 190 **Born:** 7/3/63 **Age:** 32

			HOW MUCH HE PITCHED						WHAT HE GAVE UP											THE RESULTS					
Year	Team	Lg	G	GS	CG	GF	IP	BFP	H	R	ER	HR	SH	SF	HB	TBB	IBB	SO	WP	Bk	W	L	Pct.	ShO	Sv	ERA
1985	Columbus	AA	27	27	4	0	176.1	752	183	77	58	11	1	7	3	49	4	78	9	1	14	8	.636	2	0	2.96
1986	Tucson	AAA	24	24	3	0	154.2	659	166	78	58	7	3	10	1	44	4	60	7	1	8	9	.471	0	0	3.38
	Vancouver	AAA	3	3	1	0	24.1	102	26	10	9	0	0	3	0	7	1	10	0	0	2	1	.667	0	0	3.33
1987	Denver	AAA	28	27	8	1	179.1	787	220	124	111	16	2	6	5	55	3	91	4	0	10	9	.526	0	0	5.57
1988	Denver	AAA	10	10	3	0	71.2	302	79	37	28	6	0	1	1	14	0	58	2	3	4	1	.800	0	0	3.52
1989	Denver	AAA	4	4	0	0	23.2	108	35	18	13	3	1	0	1	5	0	12	1	0	1	1	.500	0	0	4.94
1990	Denver	AAA	22	22	3	0	124	553	164	98	93	17	0	2	5	27	1	67	1	1	7	7	.500	1	0	6.75
1991	Denver	AAA	1	1	0	0	5	18	3	0	0	0	0	0	0	0	0	1	0	0	1	0	1.000	0	0	0.00
1992	London	AA	11	6	1	0	53	210	47	16	16	5	1	1	0	10	2	39	2	0	3	2	.600	1	0	2.72
	Toledo	AAA	5	3	0	2	14.2	75	25	17	14	2	0	1	0	7	0	6	1	0	0	2	.000	0	0	8.59
1993	Charlotte	AAA	14	5	0	0	44.1	195	57	29	27	9	2	0	1	10	0	24	1	0	3	1	.750	0	0	5.48
1994	Wichita	AA	4	0	0	0	11.2	57	18	7	5	1	0	0	0	5	1	7	1	0	0	0	.000	0	0	3.86
1995	Calgary	AAA	2	2	0	0	8	39	10	7	4	0	2	1	0	4	0	4	0	0	0	2	.000	0	0	4.50
1988	Milwaukee	AL	24	22	6	0	148.1	614	137	55	44	12	4	3	0	48	6	66	5	0	13	7	.650	1	0	3.09

Year	Team	Lg	G	GS	CG	GF	IP	BFP	H	R	ER	HR	SH	SF	HB	TBB	IBB	SO	WP	Bk	W	L	Pct.	ShO	Sv	ERA
1989	Milwaukee	AL	31	25	2	2	142.1	648	175	93	84	17	2	7	2	58	2	51	3	1	12	12	.500	1	0	5.31
1990	Milwaukee	AL	5	0	0	1	11	51	13	10	8	0	2	0	0	5	0	2	2	0	0	3	.000	0	0	6.55
1991	Milwaukee	AL	28	23	1	3	138.1	613	166	87	84	18	9	3	3	47	2	62	5	0	9	8	.529	1	0	5.47
	11 Min. YEARS		155	134	23	8	890.2	3857	1033	518	436	77	12	32	17	237	16	457	29	6	53	43	.552	4	0	4.41
	4 Maj. YEARS		88	70	9	6	440	1926	491	245	227	47	17	13	5	158	10	181	15	1	34	30	.531	3	0	4.64

Jake Austin

Bats: Left **Throws:** Right **Pos:** OF **Ht:** 6'0" **Wt:** 205 **Born:** 4/30/70 **Age:** 26

			BATTING														BASERUNNING				PERCENTAGES		
Year	Team	Lg	G	AB	H	2B	3B	HR	TB	R	RBI	TBB	IBB	SO	HBP	SH	SF	SB	CS	SB%	GDP	Avg	OBP	SLG
1992	Welland	A	9	33	12	2	0	0	14	4	4	1	0	2	0	0	1	3	1	.75	0	.364	.371	.424
	Augusta	A	62	221	51	9	3	1	69	19	23	22	3	44	5	0	2	4	1	.80	6	.231	.312	.312
1993	Augusta	A	123	449	132	24	4	7	185	71	54	32	4	85	9	6	1	14	7	.67	10	.294	.352	.412
1994	Salem	A	117	437	131	14	2	21	212	60	77	42	0	76	11	3	5	11	6	.65	11	.300	.372	.485
1995	Carolina	AA	102	352	83	19	2	4	118	29	40	17	4	51	2	2	3	5	3	.63	13	.236	.273	.335
	Lynchburg	A	18	74	20	6	0	1	29	7	11	3	0	8	0	0	2	0	3	.00	1	.270	.291	.392
	4 Min. YEARS		431	1566	429	74	11	34	627	190	209	117	11	266	27	11	14	37	21	.64	41	.274	.332	.400

James Austin

Pitches: Right **Bats:** Right **Pos:** P **Ht:** 6'2" **Wt:** 200 **Born:** 12/7/63 **Age:** 32

			HOW MUCH HE PITCHED						WHAT HE GAVE UP										THE RESULTS					
Year	Team	Lg	G	GS	CG	GF	IP	BFP	H	R	ER	HR	SH	SF	HB	TBB	IBB	SO	WP	Bk	W	L	Pct.	ShO	Sv	ERA
1986	Spokane	A	28	0	0	19	59.2	0	53	24	15	1	0	0	1	22	2	74	7	0	5	4	.556	0	5	2.26
1987	Charlstn-Sc	A	31	21	2	3	152	642	138	89	71	10	4	1	1	56	2	123	20	1	7	10	.412	1	0	4.20
1988	Riverside	A	12	12	2	0	80	333	65	31	24	5	2	3	0	35	0	73	2	0	6	2	.750	1	0	2.70
	Wichita	AA	12	12	4	0	73	313	76	46	39	9	2	3	0	23	0	52	10	0	5	6	.455	1	0	4.81
1989	Stockton	A	7	7	0	0	48.1	204	51	19	14	3	2	1	0	14	0	44	2	0	3	3	.500	0	0	2.61
	El Paso	AA	22	13	2	5	85	406	121	60	55	6	2	3	4	34	1	69	4	0	3	10	.231	0	1	5.82
1990	El Paso	AA	38	3	0	24	92.1	384	91	36	25	5	2	3	1	26	4	77	8	0	11	3	.786	0	6	2.44
1991	Denver	AAA	20	3	0	10	44	184	35	12	12	4	2	0	2	24	3	37	1	0	6	3	.667	0	3	2.45
1993	New Orleans	AAA	8	3	0	0	16	72	17	11	9	3	0	1	0	7	0	7	4	1	1	2	.333	0	0	5.06
1995	Buffalo	AAA	2	1	0	0	3	19	7	6	4	1	0	0	0	2	0	1	1	1	1	1	.500	0	0	12.00
1991	Milwaukee	AL	5	0	0	1	8.2	46	8	8	8	1	2	1	3	11	1	3	1	0	0	0	.000	0	1	8.31
1992	Milwaukee	AL	47	0	0	12	58.1	235	38	13	12	2	1	1	2	32	6	30	1	0	5	2	.714	0	1	1.85
1993	Milwaukee	AL	31	0	0	8	33	137	28	15	14	3	1	0	1	13	1	15	4	0	1	2	.333	0	0	3.82
	8 Min. YEARS		180	75	10	61	653.1	2557	654	334	268	47	16	15	9	243	12	557	59	2	48	44	.522	3	15	3.69
	3 Maj. YEARS		83	0	0	21	100	418	74	36	34	6	4	2	6	56	8	48	6	0	6	4	.600	0	3	3.06

Joe Aversa

Bats: Both **Throws:** Right **Pos:** SS-2B **Ht:** 5'10" **Wt:** 150 **Born:** 5/20/68 **Age:** 28

			BATTING														BASERUNNING				PERCENTAGES		
Year	Team	Lg	G	AB	H	2B	3B	HR	TB	R	RBI	TBB	IBB	SO	HBP	SH	SF	SB	CS	SB%	GDP	Avg	OBP	SLG
1990	Cardinals	R	9	34	8	1	0	0	9	5	4	8	0	8	1	0	0	2	3	.40	1	.235	.395	.265
	Johnson Cty	R	41	93	15	1	0	0	16	10	8	10	0	18	1	0	0	2	1	.67	2	.161	.250	.172
1991	Springfield	A	78	184	43	2	0	1	48	19	14	43	0	37	0	5	0	5	6	.45	2	.234	.379	.261
1992	St. Pete	A	25	44	7	1	0	0	8	4	3	8	0	8	0	0	1	0	1	.00	3	.159	.283	.182
	Arkansas	AA	49	106	25	4	1	0	31	16	3	21	0	20	0	2	0	3	2	.60	1	.236	.362	.292
1993	Arkansas	AA	95	199	36	4	2	0	44	23	5	17	0	34	1	2	3	3	1	.75	3	.181	.248	.221
1994	St. Pete	A	15	31	5	2	0	0	7	6	3	8	0	2	0	0	0	0	0	.00	0	.161	.333	.226
	Arkansas	AA	52	99	20	5	2	0	29	10	6	7	1	25	1	1	0	0	1	.00	2	.202	.262	.293
1995	Louisville	AAA	85	141	31	6	0	0	37	23	9	26	2	29	0	3	2	7	3	.70	1	.220	.337	.262
	6 Min. YEARS		449	931	190	26	5	1	229	116	55	148	3	181	4	13	4	22	18	.55	15	.204	.315	.246

Rolo Avila

Bats: Right **Throws:** Right **Pos:** OF **Ht:** 5'8" **Wt:** 170 **Born:** 8/10/73 **Age:** 22

			BATTING														BASERUNNING				PERCENTAGES		
Year	Team	Lg	G	AB	H	2B	3B	HR	TB	R	RBI	TBB	IBB	SO	HBP	SH	SF	SB	CS	SB%	GDP	Avg	OBP	SLG
1994	Bluefield	R	56	200	55	14	1	1	74	41	17	28	0	30	8	3	3	28	7	.80	0	.275	.381	.370
1995	High Desert	A	52	180	43	10	1	2	61	26	10	29	0	26	4	5	0	19	8	.70	0	.239	.357	.339
	Frederick	A	52	175	46	8	1	1	59	26	13	14	0	27	3	5	0	15	5	.75	2	.263	.328	.337
	Bowie	AA	16	43	10	2	0	0	12	8	4	6	0	8	0	1	1	2	2	.50	0	.233	.320	.279
	2 Min. YEARS		176	598	154	34	3	4	206	101	44	77	0	91	15	14	4	64	22	.74	2	.258	.354	.344

Bob Ayrault

Pitches: Right **Bats:** Right **Pos:** P **Ht:** 6'4" **Wt:** 235 **Born:** 4/27/66 **Age:** 30

			HOW MUCH HE PITCHED						WHAT HE GAVE UP										THE RESULTS					
Year	Team	Lg	G	GS	CG	GF	IP	BFP	H	R	ER	HR	SH	SF	HB	TBB	IBB	SO	WP	Bk	W	L	Pct.	ShO	Sv	ERA
1989	Reno	A	24	14	3	5	109.2	478	104	56	46	7	3	4	11	57	3	91	3	3	7	4	.636	1	0	3.78
	Batavia	A	4	3	2	1	26	93	13	5	4	2	1	0	2	7	0	20	0	0	2	1	.667	1	0	1.38
	Reading	AA	2	1	0	0	8.2	33	3	1	1	0	0	0	0	4	0	8	0	0	0	0	.000	0	0	1.04
1990	Reading	AA	44	9	0	29	109.1	432	77	33	28	4	3	5	2	34	1	84	2	2	4	6	.400	0	10	2.30
1991	Scranton-Wb	AAA	68	0	0	21	98.2	433	91	58	53	11	6	5	5	47	4	103	4	1	8	5	.615	0	3	4.83
1992	Scranton-Wb	AAA	20	0	0	14	25.1	110	19	15	14	4	3	2	1	15	3	30	0	0	5	1	.833	0	6	4.97
1993	Scranton-Wb	AAA	5	1	0	3	7.1	33	8	2	1	0	0	0	0	3	1	9	0	0	0	1	.000	0	0	1.23
	Calgary	AAA	3	0	0	2	4.1	22	8	5	5	0	0	0	0	2	0	3	0	0	0	0	.000	0	1	10.38

Year	Team	Lg	G	GS	CG	GF	IP	BFP	H	R	ER	HR	SH	SF	HB	TBB	IBB	SO	WP	Bk	W	L	Pct.	ShO	Sv	ERA
	Albuquerque	AAA	11	0	0	1	14.2	74	21	10	10	2	1	0	2	7	3	13	0	0	2	2	.500	0	0	6.14
1994	Edmonton	AAA	5	0	0	1	9.1	41	11	6	6	0	0	0	0	4	0	8	0	0	0	0	.000	0	0	5.79
1995	Calgary	AAA	6	0	0	3	7.1	35	7	4	4	0	0	1	1	4	1	3	0	0	0	0	.000	0	0	4.91
1992	Philadelphia	NL	30	0	0	7	43.1	178	32	16	15	0	4	3	1	17	1	27	0	0	2	2	.500	0	0	3.12
1993	Seattle	AL	14	0	0	6	19.2	80	18	8	7	1	1	2	0	6	1	7	0	0	1	1	.500	0	0	3.20
	Philadelphia	NL	10	0	0	3	10.1	59	18	11	11	1	0	0	1	10	1	8	1	0	2		1.000	0	0	9.58
	7 Min. YEARS		192	28	5	80	420.2	1784	362	195	172	30	17	17	24	184	16	372	9	6	28	20	.583	2	20	3.68
	2 Maj. YEARS		54	0	0	16	73.1	317	68	35	33	2	5	5	2	33	3	42	1	0	5	3	.625	0	0	4.05

Joe Ayrault

Bats: Right **Throws:** Right **Pos:** C **Ht:** 6'3" **Wt:** 190 **Born:** 10/8/71 **Age:** 24

						BATTING												BASERUNNING				PERCENTAGES		
Year	Team	Lg	G	AB	H	2B	3B	HR	TB	R	RBI	TBB	IBB	SO	HBP	SH	SF	SB	CS	SB%	GDP	Avg	OBP	SLG
1990	Braves	R	30	87	24	2	2	0	30	8	12	9	0	14	1	2	0	1	1	.50	1	.276	.351	.345
1991	Pulaski	R	55	202	52	12	0	3	73	22	27	13	0	49	0	2	0	0	0	.00	4	.257	.302	.361
1992	Macon	A	90	297	77	12	0	6	107	24	24	24	0	68	4	2	1	1	1	.50	7	.259	.322	.360
1993	Durham	A	119	390	99	21	0	6	138	45	52	23	0	103	7	8	3	1	4	.20	8	.254	.305	.354
1994	Greenville	AA	107	350	80	24	0	6	122	38	40	19	1	74	7	6	4	2	2	.50	6	.229	.279	.349
1995	Greenville	AA	89	302	74	20	0	7	115	27	42	13	5	70	3	7	3	2	4	.33	8	.245	.280	.381
	6 Min. YEARS		490	1628	406	91	2	28	585	164	197	101	6	378	22	27	11	7	12	.37	34	.249	.300	.359

Jesus Azuaje

Bats: Right **Throws:** Right **Pos:** 2B **Ht:** 5'10" **Wt:** 170 **Born:** 1/16/73 **Age:** 23

						BATTING												BASERUNNING				PERCENTAGES		
Year	Team	Lg	G	AB	H	2B	3B	HR	TB	R	RBI	TBB	IBB	SO	HBP	SH	SF	SB	CS	SB%	GDP	Avg	OBP	SLG
1993	Burlington	R	62	254	71	10	1	7	104	46	41	22	0	53	0	1	3	19	2	.90	4	.280	.333	.409
	Kinston	A	3	11	5	2	0	0	7	1	0	2	0	1	0	0	0	0	2	.00	0	.455	.538	.636
1994	Columbus	A	118	450	127	20	1	7	170	77	57	69	0	72	5	6	0	21	7	.75	6	.282	.384	.378
1995	Norfolk	AAA	5	14	6	1	0	0	7	1	0	2	0	2	0	0	0	1	1	.50	0	.429	.500	.500
	Binghamton	AA	24	86	17	5	0	0	22	10	8	11	0	25	2	3	0	1	1	.50	1	.198	.303	.256
	St. Lucie	A	91	306	73	5	1	2	86	35	20	36	1	55	7	11	0	14	9	.61	5	.239	.332	.281
	3 Min. YEARS		303	1121	299	43	3	16	396	170	126	142	1	208	14	21	3	56	22	.72	16	.267	.355	.353

Brett Backlund

Pitches: Right **Bats:** Right **Pos:** P **Ht:** 6'0" **Wt:** 195 **Born:** 12/16/69 **Age:** 26

			HOW MUCH HE PITCHED						WHAT HE GAVE UP										THE RESULTS						
Year	Team	Lg	G	GS	CG	GF	IP	BFP	H	R	ER	HR	SH	SF	HB	TBB	IBB	SO	WP	Bk	W	L	Pct.	ShO	Sv	ERA
1992	Augusta	A	5	4	0	1	25	91	10	3	1	1	1	0	0	4	0	31	1	1	3	0	1.000	0	0	0.36
	Carolina	AA	3	3	0	0	19	71	11	6	4	0	1	1	0	3	0	17	0	1	1	1	.500	0	0	1.89
	Buffalo	AAA	4	4	2	0	25	101	15	8	6	2	0	0	0	11	0	9	0	0	3	0	1.000	0	0	2.16
1993	Buffalo	AAA	5	5	0	0	21.1	109	30	25	25	5	3	1	2	14	0	10	0	0	0	4	.000	0	0	10.55
	Carolina	AA	20	20	0	0	106	457	115	66	54	22	1	4	2	28	3	94	7	2	7	5	.583	0	0	4.58
1994	Carolina	AA	25	25	4	0	147	627	147	81	59	14	5	7	7	47	0	86	7	0	5	13	.278	0	0	3.61
1995	Carolina	AA	22	14	0	1	93	388	81	46	37	10	4	3	5	35	2	80	2	0	5	6	.455	0	0	3.58
	Calgary	AAA	12	8	0	3	50	213	59	29	29	6	1	2	0	9	0	29	0	0	2	3	.400	0	0	5.22
	4 Min. YEARS		96	83	6	5	486.1	2057	468	264	215	60	16	18	16	151	5	356	17	4	26	32	.448	0		3.98

Mike Badorek

Pitches: Right **Bats:** Right **Pos:** P **Ht:** 6'5" **Wt:** 230 **Born:** 5/15/69 **Age:** 27

			HOW MUCH HE PITCHED						WHAT HE GAVE UP										THE RESULTS						
Year	Team	Lg	G	GS	CG	GF	IP	BFP	H	R	ER	HR	SH	SF	HB	TBB	IBB	SO	WP	Bk	W	L	Pct.	ShO	Sv	ERA
1991	Hamilton	A	13	11	1	1	63.1	282	56	33	19	2	1	1	3	30	0	48	9	0	2	5	.286	0	0	2.70
1992	Springfield	A	29	28	1	0	187.1	780	175	74	61	6	3	4	9	39	1	119	10	0	17	8	.680	0	0	2.93
1993	St. Pete	A	29	28	2	1	170	712	170	76	65	6	4	5	4	53	1	60	3	0	15	7	.682	0	0	3.44
1994	Arkansas	AA	40	15	2	4	123.1	528	119	61	43	8	5	2	3	36	4	95	4	0	8	8	.500	0	0	3.14
1995	Arkansas	AA	18	17	4	1	101.1	446	119	61	49	4	4	5	3	30	0	50	2	0	7	5	.583	2	1	4.35
	5 Min. YEARS		129	99	10	7	645.1	2748	639	305	237	26	17	17	22	188	6	372	28	0	49	33	.598	2	1	3.31

Kevin Baez

Bats: Right **Throws:** Right **Pos:** SS **Ht:** 5'11" **Wt:** 175 **Born:** 1/10/67 **Age:** 29

						BATTING												BASERUNNING				PERCENTAGES		
Year	Team	Lg	G	AB	H	2B	3B	HR	TB	R	RBI	TBB	IBB	SO	HBP	SH	SF	SB	CS	SB%	GDP	Avg	OBP	SLG
1988	Little Fall	A	70	218	58	7	1	1	70	23	19	32	1	30	2	2	3	7	3	.70	3	.266	.361	.321
1989	Columbia	A	123	426	108	25	1	5	150	59	44	58	3	53	6	9	3	11	9	.55	5	.254	.349	.352
1990	Jackson	AA	106	327	76	11	0	2	93	29	29	37	4	44	2	11	2	3	4	.43	7	.232	.313	.284
1991	Tidewater	AAA	65	210	36	8	0	0	44	18	13	12	1	32	4	5	4	0	1	.00	5	.171	.226	.210
1992	Tidewater	AAA	109	352	83	16	1	2	107	30	33	13	1	57	4	5	5	1	1	.50	9	.236	.267	.304
1993	Norfolk	AAA	63	209	54	11	1	2	73	23	21	20	1	29	1	2	1	0	2	.00	3	.258	.325	.349
1994	Rochester	AAA	110	359	85	17	1	2	110	50	42	40	0	52	2	5	5	2	7	.22	13	.237	.313	.306
1995	Toledo	AAA	116	376	87	13	2	4	116	30	37	22	1	57	1	10	2	1	6	.14	13	.231	.274	.309
1990	New York	NL	5	12	2	1	0	0	3	0	0	0	0	0	0	0	0	0	0	.00	2	.167	.167	.250
1992	New York	NL	6	13	2	0	0	0	2	0	0	0	0	0	0	0	0	0	0	.00	1	.154	.154	.154
1993	New York	NL	52	126	23	9	0	0	32	10	7	13	1	17	0	4	0	0	0	.00	1	.183	.259	.254
	8 Min. YEARS		762	2477	587	108	7	18	763	262	238	234	12	354	22	49	25	25	33	.43	58	.237	.306	.308
	3 Maj. YEARS		63	151	27	10	0	0	37	10	7	13	1	17	0	4	0	0	0	.00	4	.179	.244	.245

Jared Baker

Pitches: Right **Bats:** Left **Pos:** P **Ht:** 6'4" **Wt:** 220 **Born:** 3/25/71 **Age:** 25

		HOW MUCH HE PITCHED						WHAT HE GAVE UP										THE RESULTS					
Year Team	Lg	G	GS	CG	GF	IP	BFP	H	R	ER	HR	SH	SF	HB	TBB	IBB	SO	WP	Bk	W	L	Pct.	ShO	Sv	ERA
1992 Spokane	A	13	11	0	0	67	286	56	32	21	2	1	3	2	32	0	56	4	1	6	3	.667	0	0	2.82
Waterloo	A	2	2	0	0	12	54	10	7	6	2	1	0	1	7	0	19	1	0	0	2	.000	0	0	4.50
1993 Rancho Cuca	A	9	9	0	0	42	217	57	44	34	2	1	4	5	30	0	21	2	0	1	5	.167	0	0	7.29
Waterloo	A	15	15	2	0	81.1	370	82	60	51	13	5	2	3	54	2	62	6	3	6	7	.462	0	0	5.64
1994 Rancho Cuca	A	27	27	1	0	141.2	650	134	86	60	11	2	4	20	75	3	129	8	1	9	10	.474	0	0	3.81
1995 Memphis	AA	4	0	0	1	7.1	39	10	12	12	1	0	1	0	8	0	6	1	0	1	0	1.000	0	1	14.73
Rancho Cuca	A	31	15	1	3	101.1	442	98	57	50	9	3	4	8	49	1	98	3	1	7	2	.778	1	1	4.44
4 Min. YEARS		101	79	4	4	452.2	2058	447	298	234	40	13	18	39	255	6	391	25	6	30	29	.508	1	2	4.65

Scott Bakkum

Pitches: Right **Bats:** Right **Pos:** P **Ht:** 6'4" **Wt:** 205 **Born:** 11/20/69 **Age:** 26

		HOW MUCH HE PITCHED						WHAT HE GAVE UP										THE RESULTS					
Year Team	Lg	G	GS	CG	GF	IP	BFP	H	R	ER	HR	SH	SF	HB	TBB	IBB	SO	WP	Bk	W	L	Pct.	ShO	Sv	ERA
1992 Red Sox	R	4	1	0	2	11	52	19	11	11	0	1	1	0	5	0	8	0	1	0	1	.000	0	0	9.00
Winter Havn	A	5	4	2	0	27.2	109	19	9	9	1	3	1	1	10	0	10	0	0	1	3	.250	0	0	2.93
1993 Lynchburg	A	26	26	6	0	169.2	717	201	87	71	23	1	3	2	31	0	98	7	2	12	11	.522	4	0	3.77
1994 Sarasota	A	12	12	1	0	69	311	86	50	40	8	2	2	2	26	0	43	3	0	3	6	.333	0	0	5.22
New Britain	AA	3	3	0	0	15	68	20	8	8	1	1	1	0	9	0	7	0	0	0	2	.000	0	0	4.80
Lynchburg	A	11	8	0	1	44.2	206	58	39	35	3	1	1	0	18	0	37	1	0	1	6	.143	0	0	7.05
1995 Trenton	AA	28	0	0	10	47	181	31	12	7	4	1	1	2	9	2	24	1	0	6	4	.600	0	0	1.34
Pawtucket	AAA	15	0	0	4	26.1	114	21	13	5	3	0	1	2	7	0	15	4	0	1	0	1.000	0	2	1.71
4 Min. YEARS		104	54	9	17	410.1	1758	455	229	186	43	10	11	9	115	2	242	16	3	24	33	.421	4	2	4.08

Jeff Ball

Bats: Right **Throws:** Right **Pos:** 3B **Ht:** 5'10" **Wt:** 185 **Born:** 4/17/69 **Age:** 27

		BATTING																BASERUNNING				PERCENTAGES		
Year Team	Lg	G	AB	H	2B	3B	HR	TB	R	RBI	TBB	IBB	SO	HBP	SH	SF	SB	CS	SB%	GDP	Avg	OBP	SLG
1990 Auburn	A	70	263	76	18	1	5	111	40	38	22	1	35	4	3	5	20	5	.80	4	.289	.347	.422
1991 Osceola	A	118	392	96	15	3	5	132	53	51	49	4	74	10	3	4	20	8	.71	9	.245	.341	.337
1992 Jackson	AA	93	278	53	14	1	5	84	27	24	20	1	58	10	2	1	5	3	.63	9	.191	.269	.302
1993 Quad City	A	112	389	114	28	2	14	188	68	76	58	3	63	7	1	5	40	19	.68	11	.293	.390	.483
1994 Jackson	AA	111	358	113	30	3	13	188	65	57	34	3	74	5	5	3	9	8	.53	9	.316	.380	.525
1995 Tucson	AAA	110	362	106	25	2	4	147	58	56	25	3	66	7	4	5	11	5	.69	13	.293	.346	.406
6 Min. YEARS		614	2042	558	130	12	46	850	311	302	208	15	370	43	18	23	105	48	.69	55	.273	.349	.416

Brian Banks

Bats: Both **Throws:** Right **Pos:** OF **Ht:** 6'3" **Wt:** 200 **Born:** 9/28/70 **Age:** 25

		BATTING																BASERUNNING				PERCENTAGES		
Year Team	Lg	G	AB	H	2B	3B	HR	TB	R	RBI	TBB	IBB	SO	HBP	SH	SF	SB	CS	SB%	GDP	Avg	OBP	SLG
1993 Helena	R	12	48	19	1	1	2	28	8	8	11	0	8	0	0	1	1	2	.33	2	.396	.500	.583
Beloit	A	38	147	36	5	1	4	55	21	19	7	0	34	1	0	0	1	2	.33	1	.245	.284	.374
1994 Stockton	A	67	246	58	9	1	4	81	29	28	38	2	46	2	3	2	3	8	.27	8	.236	.340	.329
Beloit	A	65	237	71	13	1	9	113	41	47	29	5	40	2	1	4	11	1	.92	3	.300	.375	.477
1995 El Paso	AA	127	441	136	39	10	12	231	81	78	81	6	113	3	3	8	9	9	.50	10	.308	.413	.524
3 Min. YEARS		309	1119	320	67	14	31	508	180	180	166	13	241	8	7	15	25	22	.53	24	.286	.378	.454

Jim Banks

Pitches: Right **Bats:** Right **Pos:** P **Ht:** 6'0" **Wt:** 200 **Born:** 1/3/70 **Age:** 26

		HOW MUCH HE PITCHED						WHAT HE GAVE UP										THE RESULTS					
Year Team	Lg	G	GS	CG	GF	IP	BFP	H	R	ER	HR	SH	SF	HB	TBB	IBB	SO	WP	Bk	W	L	Pct.	ShO	Sv	ERA
1992 Sou. Oregon	A	24	0	0	22	28.2	125	20	11	9	1	1	0	1	17	0	40	3	0	3	2	.600	0	8	2.83
1993 Madison	A	44	0	0	23	55	253	39	24	16	1	2	1	1	46	8	66	6	1	4	1	.800	0	4	2.62
1994 Modesto	A	42	0	0	27	57	237	38	17	15	1	2	3	0	29	2	76	4	3	3	1	.750	0	15	2.37
1995 Huntsville	AA	44	1	0	19	66.2	305	72	39	35	5	3	4	3	40	3	52	7	0	3	2	.600	0	2	4.73
4 Min. YEARS		154	1	0	91	207.1	920	169	91	75	8	8	8	5	132	13	234	20	4	13	6	.684	0	29	3.26

Travis Baptist

Pitches: Left **Bats:** Both **Pos:** P **Ht:** 6'0" **Wt:** 190 **Born:** 12/30/71 **Age:** 24

		HOW MUCH HE PITCHED						WHAT HE GAVE UP										THE RESULTS					
Year Team	Lg	G	GS	CG	GF	IP	BFP	H	R	ER	HR	SH	SF	HB	TBB	IBB	SO	WP	Bk	W	L	Pct.	ShO	Sv	ERA
1991 Medicne Hat	R	14	14	1	0	85.1	379	100	52	39	5	2	2	1	21	0	48	4	1	4	4	.500	1	0	4.11
1992 Myrtle Bch	A	19	19	2	0	118	455	81	24	19	2	6	2	4	22	0	97	5	4	11	2	.846	1	0	1.45
1993 Knoxville	AA	7	7	0	0	33	139	37	17	15	2	2	3	2	7	0	24	3	0	1	3	.250	0	0	4.09
1994 Syracuse	AAA	24	22	1	0	122.2	539	145	80	62	20	3	4	0	33	2	42	6	2	8	8	.500	0	0	4.55
1995 Syracuse	AAA	15	13	0	0	79	356	83	56	38	12	2	3	2	32	2	52	4	1	3	4	.429	0	0	4.33
5 Min. YEARS		79	75	4	0	438	1868	446	229	173	41	15	14	9	115	4	263	22	8	27	21	.563	2	0	3.55

Don Barbara

Bats: Left   **Throws:** Left   **Pos:** 1B   **Ht:** 6'2"   **Wt:** 220   **Born:** 10/27/68   **Age:** 27

						BATTING												BASERUNNING				PERCENTAGES		
Year	Team	Lg	G	AB	H	2B	3B	HR	TB	R	RBI	TBB	IBB	SO	HBP	SH	SF	SB	CS	SB%	GDP	Avg	OBP	SLG
1990	Palm Spring	A	66	220	64	8	0	4	84	22	39	24	0	27	2	1	3	1	0	1.00	6	.291	.361	.382
1991	Quad City	A	66	226	65	15	2	5	99	29	48	59	10	49	0	0	6	2	1	.67	5	.288	.426	.438
	Midland	AA	63	224	81	13	0	10	124	43	40	37	6	45	0	0	1	0	0	.00	3	.362	.450	.554
1992	Edmonton	AAA	118	396	118	26	1	4	158	70	63	78	4	78	4	4	6	9	4	.69	11	.298	.413	.399
1993	New Orleans	AAA	84	255	75	10	1	4	99	34	38	42	2	38	1	1	6	1	3	.25	5	.294	.388	.388
1994	San Antonio	AA	8	30	11	3	0	1	17	4	10	5	0	8	0	0	0	0	0	.00	1	.367	.457	.567
	Albuquerque	AAA	81	168	59	14	1	12	111	37	37	32	1	22	0	0	2	1	0	1.00	5	.351	.450	.661
1995	Pawtucket	AAA	40	129	28	8	0	2	42	19	10	12	0	18	0	0	3	2	0	1.00	3	.217	.284	.326
	Long Beach	IND	61	221	74	16	1	5	107	31	48	35	6	15	3	0	7	7	2	.78	3	.335	.421	.484
	6 Min. YEARS		587	1869	575	113	6	47	841	289	333	324	29	300	10	6	31	23	10	.70	42	.308	.407	.450

Marc Barcelo

Pitches: Right   **Bats:** Right   **Pos:** P   **Ht:** 6'3"   **Wt:** 210   **Born:** 1/10/72   **Age:** 24

			HOW MUCH HE PITCHED						WHAT HE GAVE UP										THE RESULTS				
Year	Team	Lg	G	GS	CG	GF	IP	BFP	H	R	ER	HR	SH	SF	HB	TBB	IBB	SO	WP	Bk	W	L	Pct.	ShO	Sv	ERA
1993	Fort Myers	A	7	3	0	3	23	89	18	10	7	1	0	1	1	4	0	24	1	0	1	1	.500	0	0	2.74
	Nashville	AA	2	2	0	0	9.1	42	9	5	4	2	1	1	1	5	0	5	1	1	1	0	1.000	0	0	3.86
1994	Nashville	AA	29	28	4	0	183.1	760	167	74	54	11	5	2	9	45	0	153	8	0	11	6	.647	0	0	2.65
1995	Salt Lake	AAA	28	28	2	0	143	684	214	131	112	19	5	5	6	59	2	63	4	2	8	13	.381	0	0	7.05
	3 Min. YEARS		66	61	6	3	358.2	1575	408	220	177	33	11	9	17	113	2	245	14	3	21	20	.512	0	0	4.44

John Barfield

Pitches: Left   **Bats:** Left   **Pos:** P   **Ht:** 6'1"   **Wt:** 195   **Born:** 10/15/64   **Age:** 31

			HOW MUCH HE PITCHED						WHAT HE GAVE UP										THE RESULTS				
Year	Team	Lg	G	GS	CG	GF	IP	BFP	H	R	ER	HR	SH	SF	HB	TBB	IBB	SO	WP	Bk	W	L	Pct.	ShO	Sv	ERA
1986	Daytona Bch	A	3	3	0	0	17.1	69	14	9	8	0	1	0	1	1	0	13	0	0	1	1	.500	0	0	4.15
	Salem	A	13	11	0	0	56	250	71	43	31	7	2	0	1	22	0	39	3	1	2	5	.286	0	0	4.98
1987	Charlotte	A	25	25	3	0	153.2	654	145	75	63	3	1	8	3	55	0	79	6	3	10	7	.588	2	0	3.69
1988	Tulsa	AA	24	24	5	0	169	702	159	69	54	8	6	2	3	66	2	125	13	2	9	9	.500	0	0	2.88
1989	Okla. City	AAA	28	28	7	0	175.1	739	178	93	79	14	6	6	2	68	2	58	11	1	10	8	.556	3	0	4.06
1990	Okla. City	AAA	19	3	0	2	43.1	182	44	21	17	3	6	0	1	21	3	25	0	2	1	6	.143	0	1	3.53
1992	Charlotte	A	3	0	0	2	7	30	10	7	6	0	0	0	0	1	0	4	0	0	0	1	.000	0	1	7.71
	Okla. City	AAA	42	0	0	12	71.2	306	75	39	33	6	4	0	2	26	0	26	1	3	7	1	.875	0	2	4.14
1993	Birmingham	AA	13	5	1	5	42	185	57	24	18	1	2	1	1	5	0	18	0	1	5	2	.714	1	1	3.86
	Nashville	AAA	14	4	0	4	35	147	36	19	16	3	1	1	1	11	2	15	3	0	3	1	.750	0	1	4.11
1994	San Antonio	AA	51	0	0	24	73.1	298	63	27	22	3	8	2	3	24	6	45	4	2	6	5	.545	0	3	2.70
1995	Okla. City	AAA	4	0	0	0	7.1	26	4	2	0	0	0	0	0	1	0	2	0	0	0	0	.000	0	1	0.00
1989	Texas	AL	4	2	0	1	11.2	52	15	10	8	0	1	0	0	4	0	9	1	0	0	1	.000	0	0	6.17
1990	Texas	AL	33	0	0	10	44.1	178	42	25	23	2	3	4	1	13	3	17	1	1	4	3	.571	0	1	4.67
1991	Texas	AL	28	9	0	4	83.1	361	96	51	42	11	3	4	0	22	3	27	0	2	4	4	.500	0	1	4.54
	9 Min. YEARS		239	103	16	50	851	3588	856	428	347	48	36	20	18	301	15	449	41	15	54	46	.540	6	10	3.67
	3 Maj. YEARS		65	11	0	15	139.1	591	153	86	73	13	7	8	1	39	6	53	2	3	8	8	.500	0	2	4.72

Glen Barker

Bats: Right   **Throws:** Right   **Pos:** OF   **Ht:** 5'10"   **Wt:** 180   **Born:** 5/10/71   **Age:** 25

						BATTING												BASERUNNING				PERCENTAGES		
Year	Team	Lg	G	AB	H	2B	3B	HR	TB	R	RBI	TBB	IBB	SO	HBP	SH	SF	SB	CS	SB%	GDP	Avg	OBP	SLG
1993	Niagara Fal	A	72	253	55	11	4	5	89	49	23	24	0	71	4	2	3	37	12	.76	1	.217	.292	.352
1994	Fayetteville	A	74	267	61	13	5	1	87	38	30	33	0	79	9	2	1	41	13	.76	5	.228	.332	.326
	Lakeland	A	28	104	19	5	1	2	32	10	6	4	0	34	2	0	0	5	3	.63	2	.183	.227	.308
1995	Jacksonville	AA	133	507	121	26	4	10	185	74	49	33	0	143	9	12	1	39	16	.71	1	.239	.296	.365
	3 Min. YEARS		307	1131	256	55	14	18	393	171	108	94	0	327	24	16	5	122	44	.73	9	.226	.298	.347

Tim Barker

Bats: Right   **Throws:** Right   **Pos:** OF   **Ht:** 6'0"   **Wt:** 175   **Born:** 6/30/68   **Age:** 28

						BATTING												BASERUNNING				PERCENTAGES		
Year	Team	Lg	G	AB	H	2B	3B	HR	TB	R	RBI	TBB	IBB	SO	HBP	SH	SF	SB	CS	SB%	GDP	Avg	OBP	SLG
1989	Great Falls	R	59	201	63	9	6	5	99	54	36	37	0	55	2	1	1	25	9	.74	2	.313	.423	.493
1990	Bakersfield	A	125	443	120	22	6	8	178	83	62	71	1	116	5	4	4	33	14	.70	7	.271	.375	.402
1991	San Antonio	AA	119	401	117	20	4	2	151	70	46	80	2	61	6	8	5	32	13	.71	6	.292	.413	.377
1992	San Antonio	AA	97	350	95	17	3	1	121	47	26	33	2	91	5	6	1	25	9	.74	2	.271	.342	.346
1993	Harrisburg	AA	49	185	57	10	1	4	81	40	16	30	0	32	2	6	2	7	4	.64	1	.308	.406	.438
	Ottawa	AAA	51	167	38	5	1	2	51	25	14	26	0	42	3	7	1	5	3	.63	2	.228	.340	.305
1994	New Orleans	AAA	128	436	115	25	7	5	169	71	44	76	2	97	6	10	1	41	17	.71	6	.264	.380	.388
1995	New Orleans	AAA	80	264	68	9	5	1	90	44	24	29	0	39	4	8	1	10	8	.56	9	.258	.339	.341
	7 Min. YEARS		708	2447	673	117	33	28	940	434	268	382	7	533	33	50	16	178	77	.70	29	.275	.378	.384

15

Brian Barnes

Pitches: Left   Bats: Left   Pos: P   Ht: 5' 9"   Wt: 170   Born: 3/25/67   Age: 29

Year	Team	Lg	G	GS	CG	GF	IP	BFP	H	R	ER	HR	SH	SF	HB	TBB	IBB	SO	WP	Bk	W	L	Pct.	ShO	Sv	ERA
1989	Jamestown	A	2	2	0	0	9	33	4	1	1	0	0	0	0	3	0	15	1	1	1	0	1.000	0	0	1.00
	W. Palm Bch	A	7	7	4	0	50	187	25	9	4	0	3	1	0	16	0	67	4	0	4	3	.571	3	0	0.72
	Indianapols	AAA	1	1	0	0	6	24	5	1	1	0	0	0	0	2	0	5	0	0	1	0	1.000	0	0	1.50
1990	Jacksonville	AA	29	28	3	0	201.1	828	144	78	62	12	7	5	9	87	2	213	8	1	13	7	.650	1	0	2.77
1991	W. Palm Bch	A	2	2	0	0	7	27	3	0	0	0	0	0	0	4	0	6	3	0	0	0	.000	0	0	0.00
	Indianapols	AAA	2	2	0	0	11	44	6	2	2	0	1	0	1	8	0	10	0	0	2	0	1.000	0	0	1.64
1992	Indianapols	AAA	13	13	2	0	83	338	69	35	34	8	1	2	1	30	1	77	2	2	4	4	.500	1	0	3.69
1994	Charlotte	AAA	13	0	0	2	18.1	80	17	10	8	2	0	0	1	8	2	23	1	0	0	1	.000	0	1	3.93
	Albuquerque	AAA	9	9	0	0	47	221	57	38	33	9	0	1	1	23	2	44	1	0	5	1	.833	0	0	6.32
1995	Pawtucket	AAA	21	18	2	0	106.1	454	107	62	50	12	0	2	4	30	0	90	5	1	7	5	.583	0	0	4.23
1990	Montreal	NL	4	4	1	0	28	115	25	10	9	2	2	0	0	7	0	23	2	0	1	1	.500	0	0	2.89
1991	Montreal	NL	28	27	1	0	160	684	135	82	75	16	9	5	6	84	2	117	5	1	5	8	.385	0	0	4.22
1992	Montreal	NL	21	17	0	2	100	417	77	34	33	9	5	1	3	46	1	65	1	2	6	6	.500	0	0	2.97
1993	Montreal	NL	52	8	0	8	100	442	105	53	49	9	8	3	0	48	2	60	5	1	2	6	.250	0	3	4.41
1994	Cleveland	AL	6	0	0	0	13.1	67	12	10	8	2	0	1	0	15	2	5	0	0	0	1	.000	0	0	5.40
	Los Angeles	NL	5	0	0	1	5	29	10	4	4	1	0	0	0	4	1	5	2	0	0	0	.000	0	0	7.20
	6 Min. YEARS		99	82	11	2	539	2236	437	236	195	43	12	11	17	211	7	550	25	5	37	21	.638	5	1	3.26
	5 Maj. YEARS		116	56	2	13	406.1	1754	364	193	178	39	24	10	9	204	8	275	15	4	14	22	.389	0	3	3.94

Jon Barnes

Pitches: Right   Bats: Right   Pos: P   Ht: 6'1"   Wt: 175   Born: 4/11/73   Age: 23

Year	Team	Lg	G	GS	CG	GF	IP	BFP	H	R	ER	HR	SH	SF	HB	TBB	IBB	SO	WP	Bk	W	L	Pct.	ShO	Sv	ERA
1991	Padres	R	11	11	1	0	52	236	52	37	30	4	1	3	4	25	1	42	7	4	2	5	.286	0	0	5.19
1992	Charlstn-Sc	A	27	27	1	0	131.2	599	146	85	66	7	3	6	4	58	1	80	21	5	6	11	.353	0	0	4.51
1993	Waterloo	A	10	10	0	0	56.2	236	51	27	18	1	1	1	1	23	0	46	5	1	5	3	.625	0	0	2.86
	Rancho Cuca	A	14	13	0	0	79.1	372	88	60	50	10	0	5	3	54	0	59	9	0	5	5	.500	0	0	5.67
1994	Rancho Cuca	A	2	2	0	0	5.1	28	10	7	6	0	1	0	0	2	0	5	1	0	0	0	.000	0	0	10.13
1995	Memphis	AA	2	1	0	0	8.1	34	9	3	3	0	0	0	0	2	0	2	1	0	0	1	.000	0	0	3.24
	Rancho Cuca	A	5	1	0	3	10.2	39	6	3	2	0	0	0	0	2	0	10	0	0	0	0	.000	0	0	1.69
	5 Min. YEARS		71	65	2	3	344	1544	362	222	175	22	6	15	12	166	2	244	44	10	18	25	.419	0	0	4.58

Richard Barnwell

Bats: Right   Throws: Right   Pos: OF   Ht: 6'0"   Wt: 190   Born: 2/29/68   Age: 28

Year	Team	Lg	G	AB	H	2B	3B	HR	TB	R	RBI	TBB	IBB	SO	HBP	SH	SF	SB	CS	SB%	GDP	Avg	OBP	SLG
1989	Oneonta	A	69	256	74	17	5	2	107	58	29	33	1	57	6	4	2	39	9	.81	2	.289	.380	.418
1990	Ft. Laud	A	71	274	75	15	5	4	112	54	20	32	1	62	4	0	1	23	11	.68	3	.274	.357	.409
1991	Ft. Laud	A	86	298	86	15	3	5	122	50	37	43	2	76	9	6	0	29	7	.81	3	.289	.394	.409
	Albany-Colo	AA	5	19	5	0	0	0	5	4	0	1	0	6	0	0	0	2	0	1.00	0	.263	.300	.263
1992	Albany-Colo	AA	123	434	113	26	5	1	152	80	31	48	1	102	11	4	3	42	18	.70	5	.260	.347	.350
1993	Albany-Colo	AA	131	463	138	24	7	11	209	98	50	77	3	101	13	3	2	33	13	.72	6	.298	.411	.451
1994	Columbus	AAA	50	112	22	2	1	1	29	17	5	13	1	30	1	1	1	8	3	.73	3	.196	.283	.259
	Albany-Colo	AA	55	218	54	11	3	4	83	30	18	16	1	54	2	4	0	8	3	.73	6	.248	.305	.381
1995	Columbus	AAA	46	130	30	4	2	1	41	22	17	13	0	32	1	2	0	7	3	.70	4	.231	.306	.315
	7 Min. YEARS		636	2204	597	114	31	29	860	413	207	276	10	520	47	24	9	191	67	.74	34	.271	.363	.390

Tony Barron

Bats: Right   Throws: Right   Pos: OF   Ht: 6'0"   Wt: 185   Born: 8/17/66   Age: 29

Year	Team	Lg	G	AB	H	2B	3B	HR	TB	R	RBI	TBB	IBB	SO	HBP	SH	SF	SB	CS	SB%	GDP	Avg	OBP	SLG
1987	Great Falls	R	53	171	51	13	2	3	77	33	30	13	2	49	5	1	3	5	3	.63	1	.298	.359	.450
1988	Bakersfield	A	12	20	5	2	0	0	7	1	4	1	1	5	0	0	0	0	0	.00	1	.250	.286	.350
	Salem	A	73	261	79	6	3	9	118	54	38	25	1	75	10	6	0	36	7	.84	2	.303	.385	.452
1989	Vero Beach	A	105	324	79	7	5	4	108	45	40	17	1	90	4	2	3	26	12	.68	9	.244	.287	.333
1990	Vero Beach	A	111	344	102	21	3	6	147	58	60	30	1	82	7	2	5	42	7	.86	9	.297	.360	.427
1991	San Antonio	AA	73	200	47	2	2	9	80	35	31	28	2	44	3	0	1	8	3	.73	11	.235	.336	.400
1992	San Antonio	AA	28	97	39	4	1	7	66	18	22	6	1	22	2	0	1	7	3	.70	3	.402	.443	.680
	Albuquerque	AAA	78	286	86	18	2	6	126	40	33	17	1	65	2	2	0	6	4	.60	15	.301	.344	.441
1993	Albuquerque	AAA	107	259	75	22	1	8	123	42	36	27	1	59	2	2	2	6	5	.55	7	.290	.359	.475
1994	Jacksonville	AA	108	402	119	19	3	18	198	60	55	26	1	85	4	1	3	18	5	.78	19	.296	.343	.493
	Calgary	AAA	2	8	2	0	0	2	8	2	2	0	0	0	1	0	0	0	0	.00	1	.250	.250	1.000
1995	Tacoma	AAA	9	25	5	0	0	0	5	4	2	2	0	3	1	0	0	0	0	.00	0	.200	.286	.200
	Harrisburg	AA	29	103	30	5	0	10	65	20	23	10	0	21	2	0	0	0	0	.00	8	.291	.365	.631
	Ottawa	AAA	50	147	36	10	0	10	76	20	22	14	1	22	2	0	1	0	2	.00	3	.245	.317	.517
	9 Min. YEARS		838	2647	755	129	22	92	1204	432	398	216	13	622	44	16	19	154	51	.75	89	.285	.347	.455

Kimera Bartee

Bats: Right Throws: Right Pos: OF   Ht: 6'0" Wt: 180 Born: 7/21/72 Age: 23

Year	Team	Lg	G	AB	H	2B	3B	HR	TB	R	RBI	TBB	IBB	SO	HBP	SH	SF	SB	CS	SB%	GDP	Avg	OBP	SLG
1993	Bluefield	R	66	264	65	15	2	4	96	59	37	44	0	66	3	3	2	27	6	.82	0	.246	.358	.364
1994	Frederick	A	130	514	150	22	4	10	210	97	57	56	1	117	7	14	4	44	9	.83	7	.292	.367	.409
1995	Orioles	R	5	21	5	0	0	1	8	5	3	3	0	2	0	0	0	1	1	.50	0	.238	.333	.381
	Bowie		53	218	62	9	1	3	82	45	19	23	1	45	1	3	2	22	7	.76	1	.284	.352	.376
	Rochester	AAA	15	52	8	2	1	0	12	5	3	0	0	16	0	2	1	0	0	.00	0	.154	.151	.231
	3 Min. YEARS		269	1069	290	48	8	18	408	211	119	126	2	246	11	22	9	94	23	.80	8	.271	.351	.382

Mike Basse

Bats: Left Throws: Left Pos: OF   Ht: 6'0" Wt: 185 Born: 3/7/70 Age: 26

Year	Team	Lg	G	AB	H	2B	3B	HR	TB	R	RBI	TBB	IBB	SO	HBP	SH	SF	SB	CS	SB%	GDP	Avg	OBP	SLG
1991	Helena	R	55	218	80	15	4	3	112	55	26	29	1	43	5	0	3	16	9	.64	1	.367	.447	.514
1992	Stockton	A	115	407	110	16	3	2	138	77	37	62	1	87	3	4	2	36	15	.71	2	.270	.369	.339
1993	El Paso	AA	108	386	103	14	5	1	130	65	36	51	2	72	4	4	2	26	13	.67	7	.267	.357	.337
1994	New Orleans	AAA	75	238	68	6	7	2	94	44	28	46	2	52	3	3	5	23	7	.77	5	.286	.401	.395
	El Paso	AA	42	137	46	6	2	0	56	36	19	30	1	31	2	4	2	11	4	.73	1	.336	.456	.409
1995	New Orleans	AAA	121	381	94	14	2	0	112	49	35	58	3	62	3	7	6	15	9	.63	5	.247	.346	.294
	5 Min. YEARS		516	1767	501	71	23	8	642	326	181	276	10	347	20	22	20	127	57	.69	21	.284	.383	.363

Richard Batchelor

Pitches: Right Bats: Right Pos: P   Ht: 6'1" Wt: 195 Born: 4/8/67 Age: 29

Year	Team	Lg	G	GS	CG	GF	IP	BFP	H	R	ER	HR	SH	SF	HB	TBB	IBB	SO	WP	Bk	W	L	Pct.	ShO	Sv	ERA
1990	Greensboro	A	27	0	0	18	51.1	200	39	15	9	1	0	2	0	14	1	38	2	0	2	2	.500	0	8	1.58
1991	Ft. Laud	A	50	0	0	41	62	269	55	28	19	1	6	1	1	22	5	58	4	0	4	7	.364	0	25	2.76
	Albany-Colo	AA	1	0	0	1	1	9	5	5	5	0	1	0	0	1	0	0	0	0	0	0	.000	0	0	45.00
1992	Albany-Colo	AA	58	0	0	34	70.2	320	79	40	33	5	1	2	6	34	3	45	4	0	4	5	.444	0	7	4.20
1993	Albany-Colo	AA	36	0	0	32	40.1	162	27	9	4	1	1	0	1	12	0	40	3	0	1	3	.250	0	19	0.89
	Columbus	AAA	15	0	0	14	16.1	74	14	5	5	0	0	0	1	8	1	17	3	0	1	1	.500	0	6	2.76
1994	Louisville	AAA	53	0	0	13	81.1	347	85	40	32	7	5	3	3	32	6	50	7	0	1	2	.333	0	3	3.54
1995	Louisville	AAA	50	6	0	7	85	352	85	39	31	5	4	3	7	16	2	61	0	0	5	4	.556	0	0	3.28
1993	St. Louis	NL	9	0	0	2	10	45	14	12	9	1	1	2	0	3	1	4	0	0	0	0	.000	0	0	8.10
	6 Min. YEARS		290	6	0	160	408	1733	389	181	138	20	18	11	19	139	18	309	23	0	18	24	.429	0	65	3.04

Fletcher Bates

Bats: Both Throws: Right Pos: OF   Ht: 6'1" Wt: 193 Born: 3/24/74 Age: 22

Year	Team	Lg	G	AB	H	2B	3B	HR	TB	R	RBI	TBB	IBB	SO	HBP	SH	SF	SB	CS	SB%	GDP	Avg	OBP	SLG
1994	Mets	R	52	183	39	5	3	5	65	23	29	33	0	49	0	1	4	4	3	.57	1	.213	.327	.355
	St. Lucie	A	7	24	6	1	1	1	12	2	4	1	0	5	0	0	0	0	0	.00	0	.250	.280	.500
1995	Pittsfield	A	75	276	90	14	9	6	140	52	37	41	0	72	4	1	3	17	9	.65	1	.326	.417	.507
	Binghamton	AA	2	8	0	0	0	0	0	0	0	1	0	6	0	0	0	0	0	.00	0	.000	.111	.000
	2 Min. YEARS		136	491	135	20	13	12	217	78	70	76	0	132	4	2	7	21	12	.64	2	.275	.372	.442

Miguel Batista

Pitches: Right Bats: Right Pos: P   Ht: 6'0" Wt: 160 Born: 2/19/71 Age: 25

Year	Team	Lg	G	GS	CG	GF	IP	BFP	H	R	ER	HR	SH	SF	HB	TBB	IBB	SO	WP	Bk	W	L	Pct.	ShO	Sv	ERA
1990	Expos	R	9	6	0	1	40.1	167	31	16	9	0	1	2	1	19	0	22	1	1	4	3	.571	0	0	2.01
	Rockford	A	3	2	0	0	12.1	63	16	13	12	2	0	1	4	5	0	7	3	0	0	1	.000	0	0	8.76
1991	Rockford	A	23	23	2	0	133.2	592	126	74	60	1	6	8	6	57	0	90	12	2	11	5	.688	1	0	4.04
1992	W. Palm Bch	A	24	24	1	0	135.1	585	130	69	57	3	4	4	6	54	1	92	9	4	7	7	.500	0	0	3.79
1993	Harrisburg	AA	26	26	0	0	141	627	139	79	68	11	4	5	4	86	0	91	8	0	13	5	.722	0	0	4.34
1994	Harrisburg	AA	3	3	0	0	11.1	49	8	3	3	0	0	0	0	9	0	5	2	0	0	1	.000	0	0	2.38
1995	Charlotte	AAA	34	18	0	4	116.1	516	118	79	62	11	1	1	1	60	2	58	12	1	6	12	.333	0	0	4.80
1992	Pittsburgh	NL	1	0	0	1	2	13	4	2	2	1	0	0	0	3	0	1	0	0	0	0	.000	0	0	9.00
	6 Min. YEARS		122	102	3	5	590.1	2599	568	333	271	28	16	21	22	290	3	365	47	8	41	34	.547	1	0	4.13

Tony Batista

Bats: Right Throws: Right Pos: SS   Ht: 6'0" Wt: 180 Born: 12/9/73 Age: 22

Year	Team	Lg	G	AB	H	2B	3B	HR	TB	R	RBI	TBB	IBB	SO	HBP	SH	SF	SB	CS	SB%	GDP	Avg	OBP	SLG
1992	Athletics	R	45	167	41	6	2	0	51	32	22	15	0	29	2	5	0	1	1	1.00	4	.246	.315	.305
1993	Athletics	R	24	104	34	6	2	2	50	21	17	6	1	14	0	0	2	6	2	.75	1	.327	.357	.481
	Tacoma	AAA	4	12	2	1	0	0	3	1	1	1	0	4	1	0	0	0	0	.00	0	.167	.286	.250
1994	Modesto	A	119	466	131	26	3	17	214	91	68	54	1	108	4	5	2	7	7	.50	10	.281	.359	.459
1995	Huntsville	AA	120	419	107	23	1	16	180	55	61	29	0	98	2	6	3	7	8	.47	8	.255	.305	.430
	4 Min. YEARS		312	1168	315	62	8	35	498	200	169	105	2	253	9	16	7	21	17	.55	23	.270	.333	.426

Kim Batiste

Bats: Right   **Throws:** Right   **Pos:** 3B   **Ht:** 6' 0"   **Wt:** 193   **Born:** 3/15/68   **Age:** 28

							BATTING											BASERUNNING				PERCENTAGES		
Year	Team	Lg	G	AB	H	2B	3B	HR	TB	R	RBI	TBB	IBB	SO	HBP	SH	SF	SB	CS	SB%	GDP	Avg	OBP	SLG
1987	Utica	A	46	150	26	8	1	2	42	15	10	7	3	65	0	0	0	4	0	1.00	3	.173	.210	.280
1988	Spartanburg	A	122	430	107	19	6	6	156	51	52	14	1	101	1	5	1	16	9	.64	13	.249	.274	.363
1989	Clearwater	A	114	385	90	12	4	3	119	36	33	17	1	67	4	11	1	13	7	.65	7	.234	.273	.309
1990	Reading	AA	125	486	134	14	4	6	174	57	33	13	1	73	2	5	2	28	14	.67	11	.276	.296	.358
1991	Scranton-Wb	AAA	122	462	135	25	6	1	175	54	41	11	0	72	4	10	4	18	12	.60	5	.292	.312	.379
1992	Scranton-Wb	AAA	71	269	70	12	6	2	100	30	29	7	1	42	1	2	0	6	5	.55	8	.260	.282	.372
1995	Scranton-Wb	AAA	32	122	28	4	1	4	46	10	18	2	0	14	2	0	0	1	0	1.00	3	.230	.254	.377
	Bowie	AA	24	95	34	5	0	4	51	16	27	6	0	14	0	0	1	2	0	1.00	5	.358	.392	.537
	Rochester	AAA	122	477	135	22	2	11	194	57	74	16	0	55	3	1	2	7	8	.47	18	.283	.309	.407
1991	Philadelphia	NL	10	27	6	0	0	0	6	2	1	1	1	8	0	0	0	0	1	.00	0	.222	.250	.222
1992	Philadelphia	NL	44	136	28	4	0	1	35	9	10	4	1	18	0	0	3	0	0	.00	7	.206	.224	.257
1993	Philadelphia	NL	79	156	44	7	1	5	68	14	29	3	2	29	1	0	1	0	1	.00	3	.282	.298	.436
1994	Philadelphia	NL	64	209	49	6	0	1	58	17	13	1	0	32	1	1	2	1	1	.50	11	.234	.239	.278
	7 Min. YEARS		778	2876	759	121	30	39	1057	326	317	93	7	503	17	34	11	95	55	.63	73	.264	.290	.368
	4 Maj. YEARS		197	528	127	17	1	7	167	42	53	9	4	87	2	3	6	1	3	.25	21	.241	.253	.316

Matt Bauer

Pitches: Left   **Bats:** Left   **Pos:** P   **Ht:** 6'1"   **Wt:** 195   **Born:** 3/25/70   **Age:** 26

			HOW MUCH HE PITCHED						WHAT HE GAVE UP										THE RESULTS					
Year	Team	Lg	G	GS	CG	GF	IP	BFP	H	R	ER	HR	SH	SF	HB	TBB	IBB	SO	WP	Bk	W	L	Pct.	ShO	Sv	ERA
1991	Bristol	R	15	2	0	10	36.2	157	33	15	13	1	0	1	5	8	1	39	1	1	5	3	.625	0	4	3.19
	Fayetteville	A	4	0	0	1	10	38	7	2	2	0	0	0	0	3	0	9	0	0	2	0	1.000	0	0	1.80
1992	Lakeland	A	7	0	0	2	9.1	48	15	13	11	0	0	1	1	3	0	12	0	0	1	2	.333	0	0	10.61
	Niagara Fal	A	31	0	0	10	33	144	22	18	8	1	7	1	2	18	4	33	4	0	0	3	.000	0	2	2.18
1993	Fayetteville	A	40	0	0	16	62	268	57	30	20	2	6	1	3	23	1	81	4	0	6	5	.545	0	5	2.90
1994	Trenton	AA	14	0	0	9	25.1	99	17	4	3	0	0	0	0	13	0	30	0	0	2	0	1.000	0	3	1.07
	Toledo	AAA	37	0	0	13	36.1	172	29	25	22	3	3	1	2	34	5	24	2	0	2	1	.667	0	0	5.45
1995	Toledo	AAA	13	0	0	4	13	59	17	7	5	0	0	2	0	4	1	10	0	1	2	1	.667	0	0	3.46
	Jacksonville	AA	27	0	0	7	43.2	195	43	22	20	8	2	2	2	22	1	30	1	0	1	1	.500	0	2	4.12
	5 Min. YEARS		188	2	0	72	269.1	1180	240	136	104	15	18	9	15	128	13	268	12	2	21	16	.568	0	14	3.48

Juan Bautista

Bats: Right   **Throws:** Right   **Pos:** SS   **Ht:** 6'0"   **Wt:** 163   **Born:** 6/24/75   **Age:** 21

							BATTING											BASERUNNING				PERCENTAGES		
Year	Team	Lg	G	AB	H	2B	3B	HR	TB	R	RBI	TBB	IBB	SO	HBP	SH	SF	SB	CS	SB%	GDP	Avg	OBP	SLG
1993	Albany	A	98	295	70	17	2	0	91	24	28	14	0	72	7	3	4	11	3	.79	11	.237	.284	.308
1994	Orioles	R	21	65	10	2	2	0	16	4	3	2	0	19	1	1	0	3	1	.75	3	.154	.191	.246
1995	Bowie	AA	13	38	4	2	0	0	6	3	0	3	0	5	2	1	0	1	0	1.00	3	.105	.209	.158
	High Desert	A	99	374	98	13	4	11	152	54	51	18	0	74	7	6	3	22	9	.71	8	.262	.306	.406
	3 Min. YEARS		231	772	182	34	8	11	265	85	82	37	0	170	17	11	7	37	13	.74	25	.236	.283	.343

Bob Baxter

Pitches: Left   **Bats:** Right   **Pos:** P   **Ht:** 6'1"   **Wt:** 180   **Born:** 2/17/69   **Age:** 27

			HOW MUCH HE PITCHED						WHAT HE GAVE UP										THE RESULTS					
Year	Team	Lg	G	GS	CG	GF	IP	BFP	H	R	ER	HR	SH	SF	HB	TBB	IBB	SO	WP	Bk	W	L	Pct.	ShO	Sv	ERA
1990	Jamestown	A	13	13	2	0	74.1	321	85	44	32	4	2	1	0	25	1	67	4	0	5	4	.556	0	0	3.87
1991	Rockford	A	45	0	0	39	65	262	56	20	18	1	4	1	1	16	6	52	2	0	6	5	.545	0	19	2.49
	W. Palm Bch	A	1	0	0	0	1.1	8	4	3	3	0	0	0	0	0	0	1	0	0	0	0	.000	0	0	20.25
1992	W. Palm Bch	A	42	0	0	27	63.2	231	46	12	10	1	2	1	0	9	1	54	2	0	6	2	.750	0	7	1.41
1993	W. Palm Bch	A	33	0	0	18	59.1	232	55	20	15	1	4	4	0	5	1	29	2	1	2	2	.500	0	6	2.28
1994	Harrisburg	AA	40	11	0	6	105	451	107	61	49	10	3	3	0	32	0	56	4	0	11	3	.786	0	0	4.20
1995	Ottawa	AAA	39	13	0	10	101	426	125	51	44	6	4	5	0	25	1	39	3	0	5	5	.500	0	0	3.92
	6 Min. YEARS		213	37	2	100	469.2	1931	478	211	171	23	19	15	1	112	10	298	17	1	35	21	.625	0	32	3.28

Trey Beamon

Bats: Left   **Throws:** Right   **Pos:** OF   **Ht:** 6'3"   **Wt:** 195   **Born:** 2/11/74   **Age:** 22

							BATTING											BASERUNNING				PERCENTAGES		
Year	Team	Lg	G	AB	H	2B	3B	HR	TB	R	RBI	TBB	IBB	SO	HBP	SH	SF	SB	CS	SB%	GDP	Avg	OBP	SLG
1992	Pirates	R	13	39	12	1	0	1	16	9	6	4	1	0	0	0	0	1	0	.00	0	.308	.372	.410
	Welland	A	19	69	20	5	0	3	34	15	9	8	0	9	0	0	0	4	3	.57	6	.290	.364	.493
1993	Augusta	A	104	373	101	18	6	0	131	64	45	48	2	60	6	0	4	19	6	.76	12	.271	.360	.351
1994	Carolina	AA	112	434	140	18	9	5	191	69	47	33	4	53	5	4	3	24	9	.73	8	.323	.375	.440
1995	Calgary	AAA	118	452	151	29	5	5	205	74	62	39	4	55	2	2	3	18	8	.69	7	.334	.387	.454
	4 Min. YEARS		366	1367	424	71	20	14	577	231	169	132	11	177	13	6	10	65	27	.71	33	.310	.374	.422

Garrett Beard

Bats: Right   **Throws:** Right   **Pos:** C   **Ht:** 6'1"   **Wt:** 190   **Born:** 2/1/69   **Age:** 27

							BATTING											BASERUNNING				PERCENTAGES		
Year	Team	Lg	G	AB	H	2B	3B	HR	TB	R	RBI	TBB	IBB	SO	HBP	SH	SF	SB	CS	SB%	GDP	Avg	OBP	SLG
1989	Salem	A	75	274	66	11	2	6	99	38	54	31	1	58	4	0	3	6	4	.60	6	.241	.324	.361

18

Year	Team	Lg	G	AB	H	2B	3B	HR	TB	R	RBI	TBB	IBB	SO	HBP	SH	SF	SB	CS	SB%	GDP	Avg	OBP	SLG
1990	Vero Beach	A	6	16	4	1	0	0	5	1	3	2	0	2	0	0	0	0	0	.00	0	.250	.333	.313
	Yakima	A	60	232	63	13	1	5	93	29	39	17	2	30	4	1	10	5	6	.45	2	.272	.319	.401
	Bakersfield	A	5	15	3	2	1	0	7	2	3	1	0	2	0	0	0	0	0	.00	0	.200	.250	.467
1991	Bakersfield	A	48	152	42	14	0	6	74	22	30	27	0	30	2	5	1	0	1	.00	2	.276	.390	.487
1992	Modesto	A	98	348	94	12	2	10	140	55	59	51	1	84	9	4	5	4	6	.40	11	.270	.373	.402
1993	Huntsville	AA	18	61	16	3	1	0	21	8	6	6	0	13	1	0	1	1	1	.50	3	.262	.333	.344
	Modesto	A	83	284	76	17	2	6	115	46	33	63	0	55	3	3	3	3	2	.60	7	.268	.402	.405
	Tacoma	AAA	19	49	7	4	0	0	11	3	2	4	0	8	0	2	0	1	1	.50	3	.143	.208	.224
1994	Huntsville	AA	88	279	71	15	0	7	107	38	35	38	1	44	6	4	2	3	5	.38	5	.254	.354	.384
1995	Huntsville	AA	43	126	24	2	0	1	29	18	8	15	1	21	1	0	2	2	3	.40	4	.190	.278	.230
	Edmonton	AAA	22	61	14	2	0	0	16	5	10	3	0	7	2	1	2	0	0	.00	2	.230	.279	.262
	7 Min. YEARS		565	1897	480	96	9	41	717	265	282	258	6	354	32	20	29	25	29	.46	45	.253	.347	.378

Tony Beasley

Bats: Right **Throws:** Right **Pos:** 2B   **Ht:** 5'8" **Wt:** 165 **Born:** 12/5/66 **Age:** 29

			BATTING															BASERUNNING				PERCENTAGES		
Year	Team	Lg	G	AB	H	2B	3B	HR	TB	R	RBI	TBB	IBB	SO	HBP	SH	SF	SB	CS	SB%	GDP	Avg	OBP	SLG
1989	Erie	A	65	247	69	12	2	1	88	39	14	25	0	31	4	5	0	19	4	.83	4	.279	.355	.356
1990	Frederick	A	124	399	100	14	6	1	129	57	31	30	1	68	7	12	2	10	9	.53	6	.251	.313	.323
1991	Frederick	A	124	387	96	11	10	1	130	50	34	27	0	74	6	6	3	29	8	.78	6	.248	.305	.336
1992	Salem	A	72	237	62	10	2	7	97	34	25	16	0	44	3	2	1	12	4	.75	5	.262	.315	.409
	Carolina	AA	49	158	41	5	3	1	55	12	13	8	0	33	0	1	1	13	8	.62	0	.259	.293	.348
1993	Buffalo	AAA	30	95	18	3	0	0	21	9	8	4	0	17	2	4	1	1	0	1.00	0	.189	.235	.221
	Carolina	AA	82	252	51	7	3	4	76	39	13	23	2	52	0	3	1	11	6	.65	10	.202	.268	.302
1995	Carolina	AA	105	335	94	16	4	2	124	59	34	31	2	44	4	4	6	20	4	.83	6	.281	.343	.370
	6 Min. YEARS		651	2110	531	78	30	17	720	299	172	164	5	363	26	37	15	115	43	.73	37	.252	.311	.341

Blaine Beatty

Pitches: Left **Bats:** Left **Pos:** P   **Ht:** 6'2" **Wt:** 185 **Born:** 4/25/64 **Age:** 32

			HOW MUCH HE PITCHED						WHAT HE GAVE UP										THE RESULTS					
Year	Team	Lg	G	GS	CG	GF	IP	BFP	H	R	ER	HR	SH	SF	HB	TBB	IBB	SO	WP	Bk	W	L	Pct.	ShO	Sv	ERA
1986	Newark	A	15	15	8	0	119.1	475	98	37	28	6	5	2	1	30	3	93	6	0	11	3	.786	3	0	2.11
1987	Hagerstown	A	13	13	4	0	100	389	81	32	28	7	3	1	1	11	0	65	5	0	11	1	.917	1	0	2.52
	Charlotte	AA	15	15	3	0	105.2	438	110	38	36	2	1	4	1	20	2	57	4	0	6	5	.545	1	0	3.07
1988	Jackson	AA	30	28	12	1	208.2	824	191	64	57	13	12	6	0	34	3	103	3	7	16	8	.667	5	0	2.46
1989	Tidewater	AAA	27	27	6	0	185	764	173	86	68	14	4	8	1	43	0	90	3	2	12	10	.545	3	0	3.31
1991	Tidewater	AAA	28	28	3	0	175.1	750	192	86	80	18	7	4	5	43	6	74	0	1	12	9	.571	1	0	4.11
1992	Indianapols	AAA	26	12	2	3	94	412	109	52	45	8	4	4	1	24	3	54	4	1	7	5	.583	0	0	4.31
1993	Carolina	AA	17	13	2	1	94.1	378	67	42	30	8	3	0	2	35	0	67	4	0	7	3	.700	0	0	2.86
	Buffalo	AAA	20	4	0	5	36	168	51	25	22	2	2	2	2	8	0	14	3	0	2	3	.400	0	1	5.50
1994	Chattanooga	AA	27	26	6	1	196.1	770	146	66	52	15	6	3	8	43	0	162	4	0	14	7	.667	4	0	2.38
1995	Indianapols	AAA	20	8	0	1	67.1	293	80	33	27	7	4	1	2	16	0	37	3	2	7	1	.875	0	0	3.61
	Chattanooga	AA	8	8	1	0	52	225	60	22	20	2	3	3	1	17	2	34	2	1	3	2	.600	0	0	3.46
1989	New York	NL	2	1	0	0	6	25	5	1	1	1	0	0	0	2	0	3	0	0	0	0	.000	0	0	1.50
1991	New York	NL	5	0	0	1	9.2	42	9	3	3	0	1	1	0	4	1	7	1	0	0	0	.000	0	0	2.79
	9 Min. YEARS		246	197	47	12	1434	5886	1358	583	493	102	54	38	25	324	19	850	41	14	108	57	.655	18	1	3.09
	2 Maj. YEARS		7	1	0	1	15.2	67	14	4	4	1	1	1	0	6	1	10	1	0	0	0	.000	0	0	2.30

Kash Beauchamp

Bats: Right **Throws:** Right **Pos:** OF   **Ht:** 6'3" **Wt:** 165 **Born:** 1/8/63 **Age:** 33

			BATTING															BASERUNNING				PERCENTAGES		
Year	Team	Lg	G	AB	H	2B	3B	HR	TB	R	RBI	TBB	IBB	SO	HBP	SH	SF	SB	CS	SB%	GDP	Avg	OBP	SLG
1984	Kinston	A	130	463	123	23	9	8	188	63	58	51	0	92	1	1	3	10	9	.53	11	.266	.338	.406
	Knoxville	AA	3	10	4	0	0	1	7	3	3	1	0	2	0	0	0	1	0	1.00	0	.400	.455	.700
1985	Knoxville	AA	137	496	137	14	5	4	173	68	35	60	3	62	6	6	8	25	16	.61	10	.276	.356	.349
1986	Knoxville	AA	51	193	65	10	1	8	101	32	25	17	0	40	2	0	1	5	4	.56	0	.337	.394	.523
	Syracuse	AAA	55	198	52	11	1	7	86	23	21	13	0	44	1	1	0	6	4	.60	5	.263	.311	.434
1987	Knoxville	AA	59	188	56	10	2	5	85	28	24	24	0	39	3	1	2	3	5	.38	4	.298	.382	.452
1988	Knoxville	AA	8	28	4	1	0	0	5	2	3	5	0	9	0	0	0	0	0	.00	0	.143	.273	.179
	Greenville	AA	62	198	62	15	2	5	96	35	30	23	1	31	0	1	4	6	2	.75	2	.313	.378	.485
	Richmond	AAA	3	9	2	0	0	0	2	1	0	0	0	1	0	0	0	0	0	.00	0	.222	.222	.222
1989	Richmond	AAA	91	278	66	15	3	5	102	26	29	13	0	45	3	1	1	4	3	.57	2	.237	.278	.367
1990	Phoenix	AAA	55	121	34	4	2	1	45	12	15	7	1	21	1	0	1	2	3	.40	2	.281	.323	.372
	Shreveport	AA	38	141	45	11	0	5	71	15	18	8	0	16	2	1	1	7	2	.78	2	.319	.362	.504
1993	Rochester	IND	47	166	61	8	1	9	98	32	33	24	2	24	3	0	3	2	1	.67	1	.367	.449	.590
	Chattanooga	AA	18	60	24	6	1	5	47	16	15	10	0	9	2	1	0	1	1	.50	1	.400	.500	.783
1994	Albuquerque	AAA	6	18	4	2	1	0	8	3	0	0	0	5	0	0	0	0	1	.00	0	.222	.222	.444
	San Antonio	AA	82	224	57	13	1	6	90	30	28	26	2	44	2	1	5	2	2	.50	4	.254	.331	.402
1995	Edmonton	AAA	1	5	1	0	0	0	1	0	1	0	0	0	0	0	0	0	0	.00	0	.200	.200	.200
	10 Min. YEARS		846	2796	797	143	29	69	1205	389	338	282	9	484	26	14	29	74	53	.58	44	.285	.353	.431

Robbie Beckett

Pitches: Left **Bats:** Right **Pos:** P   **Ht:** 6'5" **Wt:** 235 **Born:** 7/16/72 **Age:** 23

Year	Team	Lg	G	GS	CG	GF	IP	BFP	H	R	ER	HR	SH	SF	HB	TBB	IBB	SO	WP	Bk	W	L	Pct.	ShO	Sv	ERA
1990	Padres	R	10	10	0	0	49.1	236	40	28	24	1	3	1	2	45	0	54	8	3	2	5	.286	0	0	4.38
	Riverside	A	3	3	0	0	16.2	76	18	13	13	0	1	0	0	11	0	11	1	1	2	1	.667	0	0	7.02
1991	Charlstn-Sc	A	28	26	1	0	109.1	545	115	111	100	5	1	8	3	117	0	96	20	2	2	14	.125	0	0	8.23
1992	Waterloo	A	24	24	1	0	120.2	578	77	88	64	4	1	1	6	140	0	147	20	4	4	10	.286	1	0	4.77
1993	Rancho Cuca	A	37	10	0	14	83.2	413	75	62	56	7	1	7	2	93	1	88	25	3	2	4	.333	0	4	6.02
1994	Wichita	AA	33	0	0	14	40	188	30	28	26	2	4	2	1	40	0	59	10	0	1	3	.250	0	2	5.85
	Las Vegas	AAA	23	0	0	11	23.2	134	27	36	31	4	0	3	0	39	0	30	7	0	0	1	.000	0	0	11.79
1995	Memphis	AA	36	8	2	11	86.1	400	65	57	46	3	2	3	10	73	4	98	19	0	3	4	.429	1	0	4.80
	6 Min. YEARS		194	81	4	50	529.2	2570	447	423	360	26	13	25	24	558	5	583	110	13	16	42	.276	2	6	6.12

Matt Beech

Pitches: Left **Bats:** Left **Pos:** P   **Ht:** 6'2" **Wt:** 190 **Born:** 1/20/72 **Age:** 24

Year	Team	Lg	G	GS	CG	GF	IP	BFP	H	R	ER	HR	SH	SF	HB	TBB	IBB	SO	WP	Bk	W	L	Pct.	ShO	Sv	ERA
1994	Batavia	A	4	3	0	1	18.2	80	9	4	4	0	1	0	4	12	0	27	0	0	2	1	.667	0	0	1.93
	Spartanburg	A	10	10	4	0	69.2	274	51	23	20	7	0	1	3	23	0	83	5	3	4	4	.500	1	0	2.58
1995	Clearwater	A	15	15	0	0	86	363	87	45	40	5	3	2	3	30	0	85	6	0	9	4	.692	0	0	4.19
	Reading	AA	14	13	0	0	79	345	67	33	26	7	6	2	6	33	1	70	4	1	2	4	.333	0	0	2.96
	2 Min. YEARS		43	41	4	1	253.1	1062	214	105	90	19	10	5	16	98	1	265	15	4	17	13	.567	1	0	3.20

Tim Belk

Bats: Right **Throws:** Right **Pos:** 1B   **Ht:** 6'3" **Wt:** 200 **Born:** 4/6/70 **Age:** 26

			BATTING															BASERUNNING				PERCENTAGES		
Year	Team	Lg	G	AB	H	2B	3B	HR	TB	R	RBI	TBB	IBB	SO	HBP	SH	SF	SB	CS	SB%	GDP	Avg	OBP	SLG
1992	Billings	R	73	273	78	13	0	12	127	60	56	35	0	33	4	0	6	15	2	.88	6	.286	.368	.465
1993	Winston-Sal	A	134	509	156	23	3	14	227	89	65	48	3	76	6	2	2	9	7	.56	8	.306	.372	.446
1994	Indianapols	AAA	6	18	2	1	0	0	3	1	0	1	0	5	0	1	0	1	0	.00	1	.111	.158	.167
	Chattanooga	AA	118	411	127	35	3	10	198	64	86	60	5	41	3	0	11	13	8	.62	7	.309	.392	.482
1995	Indianapols	AAA	57	193	58	11	0	4	81	30	18	16	0	30	2	1	0	2	5	.29	9	.301	.360	.420
	4 Min. YEARS		388	1404	421	83	6	40	636	244	225	160	8	185	15	4	19	39	23	.63	31	.300	.373	.453

Eric Bell

Pitches: Left **Bats:** Left **Pos:** P   **Ht:** 6'0" **Wt:** 165 **Born:** 10/27/63 **Age:** 32

Year	Team	Lg	G	GS	CG	GF	IP	BFP	H	R	ER	HR	SH	SF	HB	TBB	IBB	SO	WP	Bk	W	L	Pct.	ShO	Sv	ERA
1984	Hagerstown	A	3	1	0	0	3.2	23	6	4	4	0	0	1	1	5	0	6	0	0	0	0	.000	0	0	9.82
	Newark	A	15	15	4	0	102.1	424	82	40	28	6	2	2	2	26	0	114	8	1	8	3	.727	1	0	2.46
1985	Hagerstown	A	26	26	5	0	158.1	664	141	73	55	7	3	3	1	63	0	162	4	0	11	6	.647	2	0	3.13
1986	Charlotte	AA	18	18	6	0	129.2	539	109	49	44	7	3	1	1	66	0	104	5	0	9	6	.600	1	0	3.05
	Rochester	AAA	11	11	4	0	76.2	323	68	26	26	3	0	1	0	35	1	59	7	0	7	3	.700	0	0	3.05
1988	Rochester	AAA	7	7	0	0	36.1	148	28	10	8	0	3	1	0	13	0	33	1	2	3	1	.750	0	0	1.98
1989	Hagerstown	AA	9	7	0	1	43	170	32	11	9	3	1	0	1	11	1	35	0	1	4	2	.667	0	1	1.88
	Rochester	AAA	7	7	0	0	39.2	172	40	24	22	5	1	2	0	15	0	27	4	2	1	2	.333	0	0	4.99
1990	Rochester	AAA	27	27	3	0	148	667	168	90	80	16	4	8	9	65	0	90	11	1	9	6	.600	1	0	4.86
1991	Canton-Akrn	AA	18	16	1	0	93.1	402	82	47	30	1	3	5	2	37	1	84	6	0	9	5	.643	0	0	2.89
	Colo. Sprng	AAA	4	4	1	0	25.1	108	22	6	6	1	1	0	0	11	1	16	1	0	2	1	.667	1	0	2.13
1992	Colo. Sprng	AAA	26	18	5	8	137.2	575	161	64	57	10	5	4	0	30	1	56	6	2	10	7	.588	0	1	3.73
1993	Tucson	AAA	22	16	3	1	106.2	474	131	59	48	8	7	4	1	39	0	53	5	0	4	6	.400	1	0	4.05
1994	Tucson	AAA	30	29	0	1	171.1	769	209	112	85	12	7	11	6	60	1	82	4	2	8	8	.500	0	0	4.46
1995	Buffalo	AAA	28	24	3	1	161.1	687	177	76	70	18	1	4	7	47	0	86	3	0	13	9	.591	1	0	3.90
1985	Baltimore	AL	4	0	0	3	5.2	24	4	3	3	1	0	0	0	4	0	4	0	0	0	0	.000	0	0	4.76
1986	Baltimore	AL	4	4	0	0	23.1	105	23	14	13	4	1	1	0	14	0	18	0	0	1	2	.333	0	0	5.01
1987	Baltimore	AL	33	29	2	1	165	729	174	113	100	32	4	2	2	78	0	111	11	1	10	13	.435	0	0	5.45
1991	Cleveland	AL	10	0	0	3	18	61	5	2	1	0	0	0	1	5	0	7	0	0	4	0	1.000	0	0	0.50
1992	Cleveland	AL	7	0	0	2	15.1	75	22	13	13	1	1	1	1	9	0	10	1	0	0	1	.000	0	0	7.63
1993	Houston	NL	10	0	0	2	7.1	34	10	5	5	0	0	0	0	2	0	2	0	0	0	1	.000	0	0	6.14
	11 Min. YEARS		251	226	35	12	1433.1	6145	1457	691	572	97	41	47	31	523	6	1007	65	11	98	65	.601	7	2	3.59
	6 Maj. YEARS		68	34	2	11	234.2	1028	238	150	135	38	6	4	4	112	0	152	12	1	15	18	.455	0	0	5.18

Clay Bellinger

Bats: Right **Throws:** Right **Pos:** SS   **Ht:** 6'3" **Wt:** 195 **Born:** 11/18/68 **Age:** 27

			BATTING															BASERUNNING				PERCENTAGES		
Year	Team	Lg	G	AB	H	2B	3B	HR	TB	R	RBI	TBB	IBB	SO	HBP	SH	SF	SB	CS	SB%	GDP	Avg	OBP	SLG
1989	Everett	A	51	185	37	8	1	4	59	29	16	19	0	47	1	1	0	3	2	.60	4	.200	.278	.319
1990	Clinton	A	109	382	83	17	4	10	138	52	49	28	0	102	7	5	3	13	6	.68	5	.217	.281	.361
1991	San Jose	A	105	368	95	29	2	8	152	65	62	53	3	88	11	7	6	13	4	.76	3	.258	.363	.413
1992	Shreveport	AA	126	433	90	18	3	13	153	45	50	36	1	82	3	4	4	7	8	.47	15	.208	.271	.353
1993	Phoenix	AAA	122	407	104	20	3	6	148	50	49	38	4	81	4	7	5	7	7	.50	8	.256	.322	.364
1994	Phoenix	AAA	106	337	90	15	1	7	128	48	50	18	0	56	7	2	5	6	1	.86	8	.267	.315	.380
1995	Phoenix	AAA	97	277	76	16	1	2	100	34	32	27	1	52	2	2	3	3	2	.60	5	.274	.340	.361
	7 Min. YEARS		716	2389	575	123	15	50	878	323	307	219	9	508	35	28	24	52	30	.63	48	.241	.311	.368

Alonso Beltran

Pitches: Right **Bats:** Right **Pos:** P   **Ht:** 6'3" **Wt:** 180 **Born:** 3/4/72 **Age:** 24

Year	Team	Lg	G	GS	CG	GF	IP	BFP	H	R	ER	HR	SH	SF	HB	TBB	IBB	SO	WP	Bk	W	L	Pct.	ShO	Sv	ERA
1991	Blue Jays	R	14	3	0	7	33	126	26	9	7	0	1	3	1	7	0	30	1	1	2	0	1.000	0	3	1.91
1992	Medicne Hat	R	15	15	1	0	91.2	378	78	46	32	7	4	3	7	25	0	66	4	2	4	5	.444	0	0	3.14
1993	St. Cathrns	A	15	15	1	0	99	392	63	36	26	4	1	3	6	28	0	101	2	0	11	2	.846	1	0	2.36
1994	Dunedin	A	7	5	0	0	25.1	109	22	13	13	4	0	2	1	10	0	10	1	0	2	1	.667	0	0	4.62
1995	Knoxville	AA	28	6	0	7	87	399	111	60	55	8	3	4	5	32	0	54	6	2	3	6	.333	0	1	5.69
	5 Min. YEARS		79	44	2	14	336	1404	300	164	133	23	9	15	20	102	0	261	14	5	22	14	.611	1	4	3.56

Rigo Beltran

Pitches: Left **Bats:** Left **Pos:** P   **Ht:** 5'11" **Wt:** 185 **Born:** 11/13/69 **Age:** 26

Year	Team	Lg	G	GS	CG	GF	IP	BFP	H	R	ER	HR	SH	SF	HB	TBB	IBB	SO	WP	Bk	W	L	Pct.	ShO	Sv	ERA
1991	Hamilton	A	21	4	0	4	48	206	41	17	14	4	4	2	2	19	0	69	3	12	5	2	.714	0	0	2.63
1992	Savannah	A	13	13	2	0	83	316	38	20	20	4	1	0	4	40	0	106	8	6	6	1	.857	1	0	2.17
	St. Pete	A	2	2	0	0	8	30	6	0	0	0	1	0	0	2	0	3	0	0	0	0	.000	0	0	0.00
1993	Arkansas	AA	18	16	0	1	88.2	376	74	39	32	8	5	0	6	38	1	82	11	4	5	5	.500	0	0	3.25
1994	Arkansas	AA	4	4	1	0	28	95	12	3	2	2	1	0	0	3	0	21	0	0	4	0	1.000	1	0	0.64
	Louisville	AAA	23	23	1	0	138.1	624	147	82	78	15	7	7	5	68	2	87	18	5	11	11	.500	0	0	5.07
1995	Louisville	AAA	24	24	0	0	129.2	575	156	81	75	12	2	8	5	34	0	92	4	2	8	9	.471	0	0	5.21
	5 Min. YEARS		105	86	4	5	523.2	2222	474	242	221	45	21	17	22	204	3	460	44	29	39	28	.582	2	0	3.80

Freddie Benavides

Bats: Right **Throws:** Right **Pos:** SS   **Ht:** 6'2" **Wt:** 185 **Born:** 4/7/66 **Age:** 30

						BATTING													BASERUNNING				PERCENTAGES		
Year	Team	Lg	G	AB	H	2B	3B	HR	TB	R	RBI	TBB	IBB	SO	HBP	SH	SF	SB	CS	SB%	GDP	Avg	OBP	SLG
1987	Cedar Rapids	A	5	15	2	1	0	0	3	2	0	0	0	7	0	0	0	0	1	.00	1	.133	.133	.200
1988	Cedar Rapids	A	88	314	70	9	2	1	86	38	32	35	3	75	2	4	4	18	7	.72	7	.223	.301	.274
1989	Chattanooga	AA	88	284	71	14	3	0	91	25	27	22	0	46	2	2	3	1	4	.20	2	.250	.305	.320
	Nashville	AAA	31	94	16	4	0	1	23	9	12	6	0	24	0	1	0	0	0	.00	1	.170	.220	.245
1990	Chattanooga	AA	55	197	51	10	1	1	66	20	28	11	0	25	2	3	2	4	2	.67	4	.259	.302	.335
	Nashville	AAA	77	266	56	7	3	2	75	30	20	12	3	50	3	4	1	3	1	.75	2	.211	.252	.282
1991	Nashville	AAA	94	331	80	8	0	0	88	24	21	16	3	55	0	3	0	7	7	.50	10	.242	.277	.266
1993	Colo. Sprng	AAA	5	16	7	1	0	0	8	3	2	1	0	0	0	0	0	0	0	.00	0	.438	.471	.500
1995	Iowa	AAA	106	315	76	14	4	4	110	30	26	25	0	47	5	1	1	2	3	.40	12	.241	.306	.349
1991	Cincinnati	NL	24	63	18	1	0	0	19	11	3	1	1	15	1	1	1	1	0	1.00	1	.286	.303	.302
1992	Cincinnati	NL	74	173	40	10	1	1	55	14	17	10	4	34	1	2	0	0	1	.00	3	.231	.277	.318
1993	Colorado	NL	74	213	61	10	3	3	86	20	26	6	1	27	0	3	1	3	2	.60	4	.286	.305	.404
1994	Montreal	NL	47	85	16	5	1	0	23	8	6	3	1	15	1	0	1	0	0	.00	2	.188	.222	.271
	7 Min. YEARS		549	1832	429	68	13	9	550	181	168	128	9	329	14	18	11	35	25	.58	41	.234	.288	.300
	4 Maj. YEARS		219	534	135	26	5	4	183	53	52	20	7	91	3	6	3	4	3	.57	10	.253	.282	.343

Lou Benbow

Bats: Right **Throws:** Right **Pos:** SS   **Ht:** 6'0" **Wt:** 167 **Born:** 1/12/71 **Age:** 25

						BATTING													BASERUNNING				PERCENTAGES		
Year	Team	Lg	G	AB	H	2B	3B	HR	TB	R	RBI	TBB	IBB	SO	HBP	SH	SF	SB	CS	SB%	GDP	Avg	OBP	SLG
1991	St. Cathrns	A	54	147	26	0	0	0	26	13	4	18	0	40	6	9	0	6	7	.46	1	.177	.292	.177
1992	St. Cathrns	A	50	171	29	10	0	0	39	8	5	11	0	43	1	2	1	1	0	1.00	4	.170	.223	.228
1993	Hagerstown	A	71	193	32	5	2	1	44	22	12	13	0	47	2	2	2	2	1	.67	4	.166	.224	.228
1994	Dunedin	A	28	69	8	3	0	0	11	7	5	6	0	17	2	1	0	1	2	.33	4	.116	.208	.159
	St. Lucie	A	15	34	9	1	0	0	10	2	3	10	0	10	1	2	0	1	2	.33	0	.265	.444	.294
1995	Binghamton	AA	3	1	1	0	0	0	1	0	0	1	0	0	0	0	0	0	0	.00	0	1.000	1.000	1.000
	St. Lucie	A	12	33	12	2	0	0	14	4	2	1	1	7	1	1	0	0	1	.00	0	.364	.400	.424
	Durham	A	82	245	54	7	0	4	73	20	17	11	0	53	3	3	0	2	3	.40	8	.220	.263	.298
	5 Min. YEARS		315	893	171	28	2	5	218	76	48	71	0	217	16	20	3	13	16	.45	21	.191	.262	.244

Bill Bene

Pitches: Right **Bats:** Right **Pos:** P   **Ht:** 6'4" **Wt:** 205 **Born:** 11/21/67 **Age:** 28

Year	Team	Lg	G	GS	CG	GF	IP	BFP	H	R	ER	HR	SH	SF	HB	TBB	IBB	SO	WP	Bk	W	L	Pct.	ShO	Sv	ERA
1988	Great Falls	R	13	12	0	0	65.1	302	53	43	33	3	1	5	5	45	0	56	14	4	5	0	1.000	0	0	4.55
1989	Bakersfield	A	7	5	0	2	13.1	82	14	20	17	1	0	0	2	29	0	11	8	0	0	2	.000	0	0	11.48
	Salem	A	7	4	0	0	13.2	85	13	18	14	1	0	1	3	27	0	13	10	0	0	2	.000	0	0	9.22
1990	Vero Beach	A	17	14	0	2	56.2	307	49	55	44	3	1	2	6	96	0	34	23	1	1	10	.091	0	0	6.99
1991	Vero Beach	A	31	1	0	12	52	267	39	37	24	0	3	3	2	65	1	57	21	0	1	1	.500	0	0	4.15
1992	San Antonio	AA	18	1	0	5	32	144	19	15	11	1	2	1	0	34	1	25	10	1	0	2	.000	0	0	3.09
	Vero Beach	A	18	0	0	12	18	81	4	4	4	0	1	1	1	16	0	30	5	0	2	2	.500	0	0	2.00
1993	San Antonio	AA	46	0	0	12	70.2	313	50	43	38	3	3	5	4	53	1	82	15	2	5	6	.455	0	1	4.84
1994	Albuquerque	AAA	9	0	0	3	13.1	74	18	17	15	4	0	1	1	16	0	6	5	0	0	1	.000	0	0	10.13
	San Antonio	AA	20	0	0	8	37.1	176	34	23	19	4	3	0	2	33	3	34	7	1	1	0	1.000	0	0	4.58
1995	Chattanooga	AA	4	0	0	1	4	27	7	6	6	0	0	0	0	9	0	4	2	0	0	0	.000	0	0	13.50

						IP	BFP	H	R	ER	HR	SH	SF	HB	TBB	IBB	SO	WP	Bk	W	L	Pct.	ShO	Sv	ERA
Palm Spring	IND	18	12	0	3	70.2	333	61	55	36	1	1	1	9	54	0	80	15	0	3	4	.429	0	0	4.58
8 Min. YEARS		208	49	0	57	447	2192	368	336	261	23	15	20	35	477	6	432	134	9	18	30	.375	0	1	5.26

Bob Bennett

Pitches: Right Bats: Right Pos: P   Ht: 6'4" Wt: 205 Born: 12/30/70 Age: 25

		HOW MUCH HE PITCHED						WHAT HE GAVE UP												THE RESULTS					
Year Team	Lg	G	GS	CG	GF	IP	BFP	H	R	ER	HR	SH	SF	HB	TBB	IBB	SO	WP	Bk	W	L	Pct.	ShO	Sv	ERA
1992 Sou. Oregon	A	17	6	0	3	48	222	60	41	31	4	1	0	2	20	0	41	4	1	2	6	.250	0	2	5.81
1993 Madison	A	26	17	0	3	107	435	103	45	39	7	0	1	1	23	3	102	4	1	7	8	.467	0	1	3.28
1994 W. Michigan	A	6	4	0	1	24.2	103	23	8	6	1	2	0	2	6	0	23	0	0	0	2	.000	0	1	2.19
Modesto	A	20	10	0	4	80.2	332	75	31	27	2	1	0	1	25	0	71	5	1	8	2	.800	0	1	3.01
1995 Huntsville	AA	23	21	0	0	117.1	482	119	62	55	13	4	3	3	28	0	70	3	1	10	7	.588	0	0	4.22
4 Min. YEARS		92	58	0	11	377.2	1574	380	187	158	27	8	4	9	102	3	307	16	4	27	25	.519	0	4	3.77

Chris Bennett

Pitches: Right Bats: Right Pos: P   Ht: 6'6" Wt: 205 Born: 9/8/65 Age: 30

		HOW MUCH HE PITCHED						WHAT HE GAVE UP												THE RESULTS					
Year Team	Lg	G	GS	CG	GF	IP	BFP	H	R	ER	HR	SH	SF	HB	TBB	IBB	SO	WP	Bk	W	L	Pct.	ShO	Sv	ERA
1990 Jacksonville	AA	37	0	0	24	50	210	45	23	18	2	4	0	2	13	6	45	0	3	3	4	.429	0	9	3.24
Indianapolis	AAA	23	0	0	13	35	163	36	24	19	6	2	0	1	24	1	15	2	1	2	7	.222	0	3	4.89
1991 Indianapolis	AAA	6	0	0	1	11.1	45	12	10	10	3	0	1	1	1	0	5	0	1	1	0	1.000	0	0	7.94
Harrisburg	AA	28	9	0	7	74	320	82	36	26	5	1	5	2	22	1	35	3	1	5	6	.455	0	1	3.16
1993 Indianapolis	AAA	3	2	0	0	13	61	21	8	7	1	0	1	0	1	0	10	0	1	0	0	.000	0	0	4.85
1995 Calgary	AAA	4	0	0	1	7	35	11	7	4	0	0	2	0	1	0	7	0	0	0	0	.000	0	0	5.14
Carolina	AA	18	0	0	5	27	128	42	22	20	2	2	0	0	9	2	13	3	0	0	1	.000	0	1	6.67
4 Min. YEARS		119	11	0	51	217.1	962	249	130	104	19	9	9	6	71	10	130	8	7	11	18	.379	0	14	4.31

Joel Bennett

Pitches: Right Bats: Right Pos: P   Ht: 6'1" Wt: 161 Born: 1/31/70 Age: 26

		HOW MUCH HE PITCHED						WHAT HE GAVE UP												THE RESULTS					
Year Team	Lg	G	GS	CG	GF	IP	BFP	H	R	ER	HR	SH	SF	HB	TBB	IBB	SO	WP	Bk	W	L	Pct.	ShO	Sv	ERA
1991 Red Sox	R	2	2	0	0	10	38	6	2	2	0	0	1	1	4	0	8	2	1	0	0	.000	0	0	1.80
Elmira	A	13	12	1	0	81	325	60	29	22	3	3	1	6	30	0	75	7	0	5	3	.625	1	0	2.44
1992 Winter Havn	A	26	26	4	0	161.2	690	161	86	76	7	7	5	7	55	2	154	7	3	7	11	.389	1	0	4.23
1993 Lynchburg	A	29	29	3	0	181	754	151	93	77	17	7	9	4	67	6	221	18	0	7	12	.368	1	0	3.83
1994 New Britain	AA	23	23	1	0	130.2	560	119	65	59	9	2	2	4	56	0	130	10	0	11	7	.611	1	0	4.06
Pawtucket	AAA	4	4	0	0	21	91	19	16	16	8	0	0	1	12	0	24	1	0	1	3	.250	0	0	6.86
1995 Pawtucket	AAA	20	13	0	2	77	357	91	57	50	6	0	4	3	45	3	50	6	0	2	4	.333	0	0	5.84
5 Min. YEARS		117	109	9	2	662.1	2815	607	348	302	50	19	22	26	269	11	662	51	4	33	40	.452	3	0	4.10

Shayne Bennett

Pitches: Right Bats: Right Pos: P   Ht: 6'5" Wt: 200 Born: 4/10/72 Age: 24

		HOW MUCH HE PITCHED						WHAT HE GAVE UP												THE RESULTS					
Year Team	Lg	G	GS	CG	GF	IP	BFP	H	R	ER	HR	SH	SF	HB	TBB	IBB	SO	WP	Bk	W	L	Pct.	ShO	Sv	ERA
1993 Red Sox	R	2	1	0	1	7	25	2	1	1	1	0	0	0	1	0	4	1	0	0	0	.000	0	1	1.29
Ft. Laud	A	23	0	0	18	31.1	128	26	8	6	1	4	1	0	11	1	23	2	2	1	2	.333	0	6	1.72
1994 Sarasota	A	15	8	0	4	48.1	216	46	31	24	1	2	1	3	27	0	28	1	1	1	6	.143	0	3	4.47
1995 Sarasota	A	52	0	0	43	59.2	255	50	23	17	3	4	2	4	21	4	69	5	1	2	5	.286	0	24	2.56
Trenton	AA	10	0	0	6	10.2	48	16	6	6	0	3	1	0	3	0	6	1	0	0	1	.000	0	3	5.06
3 Min. YEARS		102	9	0	72	157	672	140	69	54	6	13	5	7	63	5	130	10	4	4	14	.222	0	37	3.10

Jeff Berblinger

Bats: Right Throws: Right Pos: 2B   Ht: 6'0" Wt: 190 Born: 11/19/70 Age: 25

		BATTING													BASERUNNING				PERCENTAGES		
Year Team	Lg	G	AB	H	2B	3B	HR	TB	R	RBI	TBB	IBB	SO	HBP	SH	SF	SB	CS	SB%	GDP	Avg	OBP	SLG
1993 Glens Falls	A	38	138	43	9	0	2	58	26	21	11	0	14	3	1	3	9	4	.69	2	.312	.368	.420
St. Pete	A	19	70	13	1	0	0	14	7	5	5	0	10	1	2	0	3	1	.75	1	.186	.250	.200
1994 Savannah	A	132	479	142	27	7	8	207	86	67	52	0	85	25	6	5	24	5	.83	8	.296	.390	.432
1995 Arkansas	AA	87	332	106	15	4	5	144	66	29	48	1	40	9	1	2	16	16	.50	2	.319	.417	.434
3 Min. YEARS		276	1019	304	52	11	15	423	185	122	116	1	149	38	10	10	52	26	.67	13	.298	.387	.415

Mike Berlin

Pitches: Right Bats: Right Pos: P   Ht: 6'1" Wt: 185 Born: 2/14/71 Age: 25

		HOW MUCH HE PITCHED						WHAT HE GAVE UP												THE RESULTS					
Year Team	Lg	G	GS	CG	GF	IP	BFP	H	R	ER	HR	SH	SF	HB	TBB	IBB	SO	WP	Bk	W	L	Pct.	ShO	Sv	ERA
1992 Bristol	R	4	1	0	0	11.2	47	11	4	4	0	0	0	0	5	1	10	0	0	1	1	.500	0	0	3.09
Niagara Fal	A	6	5	0	1	34	130	19	13	6	2	2	2	1	9	1	34	1	0	1	2	.333	0	0	1.59
Fayetteville	A	4	3	0	0	18	75	11	8	6	2	0	1	0	16	0	17	2	0	1	1	.500	0	0	3.00
1993 Fayetteville	A	18	5	1	6	58.1	257	50	29	21	1	0	3	2	28	1	44	6	0	4	2	.667	0	2	3.24
Lakeland	A	9	8	1	1	39	196	62	45	42	3	1	2	3	23	1	18	4	2	1	5	.167	1	0	9.69
1994 Fayetteville	A	6	1	0	1	13.1	47	8	1	0	0	0	0	2	2	0	9	2	0	1	0	1.000	0	1	0.00
Lakeland	A	27	5	0	8	81.2	350	80	35	29	4	6	0	5	34	2	55	8	0	6	5	.545	0	1	3.20
1995 Jacksonville	AA	3	0	0	1	3.2	14	3	1	1	0	1	0	0	0	0	1	1	0	0	0	.000	0	0	2.45

Lakeland	A	16	0	0	4	32.1	139	25	13	11	0	0	2	2	21	0	23	4	0	2	1	.667	0	1	3.06
4 Min. YEARS		93	28	2	22	292	1255	269	149	120	12	10	10	15	138	6	211	28	2	18	17	.514	1	4	3.70

Harry Berrios

Bats: Right **Throws:** Right **Pos:** OF

Ht: 5'11" **Wt:** 205 **Born:** 12/2/71 **Age:** 24

					BATTING											BASERUNNING				PERCENTAGES		
Year	Team	Lg	G	AB	H	2B	3B	HR	TB	R	RBI	TBB	IBB	SO	HBP	SH	SF	SB	CS	SB%	GDP	Avg	OBP	SLG
1993	Albany	A	46	145	30	5	1	3	46	16	16	18	1	20	5	0	2	2	0	1.00	3	.207	.312	.317
1994	Albany	A	42	162	54	12	2	6	88	42	35	18	1	23	9	0	1	14	0	1.00	4	.333	.426	.543
	Frederick	A	86	325	113	13	0	13	165	70	71	32	2	47	18	2	2	42	14	.75	6	.348	.432	.508
	Bowie	AA	1	4	1	1	0	0	2	1	0	0	0	1	0	0	0	0	0	.00	0	.250	.250	.500
1995	Frederick	A	71	240	50	5	2	10	89	33	28	32	3	66	4	0	2	10	6	.63	3	.208	.309	.371
	Bowie	AA	56	208	51	13	0	5	79	32	21	26	1	44	1	1	0	12	2	.86	6	.245	.332	.380
3 Min. YEARS			302	1084	299	49	5	37	469	194	171	126	8	201	37	3	7	80	22	.78	22	.276	.368	.433

Johnny Bess

Bats: Both **Throws:** Right **Pos:** OF

Ht: 6'1" **Wt:** 190 **Born:** 4/6/70 **Age:** 26

					BATTING											BASERUNNING				PERCENTAGES		
Year	Team	Lg	G	AB	H	2B	3B	HR	TB	R	RBI	TBB	IBB	SO	HBP	SH	SF	SB	CS	SB%	GDP	Avg	OBP	SLG
1992	Princeton	R	48	173	36	9	1	2	53	22	21	15	2	55	4	1	0	3	2	.60	0	.208	.286	.306
1993	Winston-Sal	A	11	33	8	0	0	2	14	4	7	6	1	7	0	0	0	2	1	.67	0	.242	.359	.424
	Charlstn-Wv	A	106	358	82	16	7	5	127	35	67	47	2	107	6	2	2	10	5	.67	4	.229	.327	.355
1994	Winston-Sal	A	58	186	56	7	0	8	87	41	29	34	1	51	2	3	2	8	6	.57	1	.301	.411	.468
	Chattanooga	AA	37	103	21	5	1	0	28	9	9	13	0	34	2	2	2	1	1	.50	1	.204	.300	.272
1995	Winston-Sal	A	88	246	46	10	2	4	72	35	21	30	4	83	8	2	0	12	4	.75	4	.187	.296	.293
	Indianapols	AAA	2	5	0	0	0	0	0	0	0	0	0	2	0	0	0	0	0	.00	0	.000	.000	.000
4 Min. YEARS			350	1104	249	47	11	21	381	146	154	145	10	339	22	10	6	36	19	.65	10	.226	.326	.345

Scott Bethea

Bats: Left **Throws:** Right **Pos:** SS

Ht: 5'11" **Wt:** 175 **Born:** 6/17/69 **Age:** 27

					BATTING											BASERUNNING				PERCENTAGES		
Year	Team	Lg	G	AB	H	2B	3B	HR	TB	R	RBI	TBB	IBB	SO	HBP	SH	SF	SB	CS	SB%	GDP	Avg	OBP	SLG
1990	Red Sox	R	43	161	38	4	0	0	42	24	8	31	0	20	2	1	1	6	3	.67	2	.236	.364	.261
	Winter Havn	A	5	15	6	0	0	0	6	0	1	2	0	2	0	1	0	0	0	.00	0	.400	.471	.400
1991	Lynchburg	A	112	336	81	6	1	1	92	46	28	50	0	47	1	12	3	8	8	.50	7	.241	.338	.274
1992	Pawtucket	AAA	7	15	1	0	0	0	1	1	2	4	0	3	0	0	1	0	0	.00	0	.067	.250	.067
	New Britain	AA	99	313	74	6	0	0	80	39	16	51	0	37	2	4	2	5	11	.31	3	.236	.345	.256
1993	New Britain	AA	117	395	90	13	1	0	105	47	30	32	4	48	2	8	4	3	4	.43	7	.228	.286	.266
1994	High Desert	A	107	373	111	21	3	2	144	65	47	44	3	51	4	4	6	13	10	.57	9	.298	.372	.386
1995	Arkansas	AA	11	34	6	1	0	0	7	6	4	2	0	5	0	2	1	1	0	1.00	0	.176	.216	.206
6 Min. YEARS			501	1642	407	51	5	3	477	228	136	216	7	213	11	32	18	36	36	.50	28	.248	.336	.290

Brian Bevil

Pitches: Right **Bats:** Right **Pos:** P

Ht: 6'3" **Wt:** 190 **Born:** 9/5/71 **Age:** 24

				HOW MUCH HE PITCHED					WHAT HE GAVE UP								THE RESULTS					
Year	Team	Lg	G	GS	CG	GF	IP	BFP	H	R	ER	HR	SH	SF	HB	TBB	IBB	SO	WP	Bk	W	L	Pct.	ShO	Sv	ERA
1991	Royals	R	13	12	2	1	65.1	262	56	20	14	0	1	0	2	19	0	70	3	3	5	3	.625	0	0	1.93
1992	Appleton	A	26	26	4	0	156	646	129	67	59	17	5	4	5	63	0	168	9	0	9	7	.563	2	0	3.40
1993	Wilmington	A	12	12	2	0	74.1	286	46	21	19	2	2	2	4	23	0	61	4	0	7	1	.875	0	0	2.30
	Memphis	AA	6	6	0	0	33	146	36	17	16	4	2	2	0	14	0	26	3	0	3	3	.500	0	0	4.36
1994	Memphis	AA	17	17	0	0	100	408	75	42	39	6	3	5	3	40	0	78	12	0	5	4	.556	0	0	3.51
1995	Omaha	AAA	6	6	0	0	22	119	40	31	23	7	1	0	3	14	1	10	2	0	1	3	.250	0	0	9.41
	Wichita	AA	15	15	0	0	74	334	85	51	48	7	0	3	3	35	0	57	6	0	5	7	.417	0	0	5.84
5 Min. YEARS			95	94	8	1	524.2	2201	467	249	218	43	14	16	20	208	1	470	39	3	35	28	.556	2	0	3.74

Joe Biasucci

Bats: Right **Throws:** Right **Pos:** DH

Ht: 5'11" **Wt:** 180 **Born:** 4/28/70 **Age:** 26

					BATTING											BASERUNNING				PERCENTAGES		
Year	Team	Lg	G	AB	H	2B	3B	HR	TB	R	RBI	TBB	IBB	SO	HBP	SH	SF	SB	CS	SB%	GDP	Avg	OBP	SLG
1990	Huntington	R	6	16	3	1	0	0	4	2	1	2	0	3	0	0	0	0	0	.00	0	.188	.278	.250
	Geneva	A	51	168	50	8	2	4	74	29	29	16	0	43	2	3	1	4	1	.80	4	.298	.364	.440
1991	Winston-Sal	A	67	211	58	10	3	1	77	35	34	30	0	58	4	4	3	2	3	.40	2	.275	.371	.365
	Charlotte	AA	24	50	11	2	0	0	13	4	2	6	0	18	0	0	1	2	0	1.00	0	.220	.298	.260
1992	Peoria	A	74	268	70	25	1	5	112	51	32	32	1	61	5	5	2	9	1	.90	1	.261	.349	.418
	Winston-Sal	A	30	93	22	6	2	1	35	13	9	9	0	22	1	2	0	1	1	.50	1	.237	.311	.376
1993	Springfield	A	119	398	115	30	3	26	229	76	86	62	3	111	7	4	5	15	5	.75	3	.289	.390	.575
1994	Arkansas	AA	112	355	90	18	1	15	155	45	48	50	4	98	3	3	1	1	7	.13	6	.254	.350	.437
1995	Canton-Akrn	AA	41	135	33	8	0	2	47	19	16	20	0	35	2	1	1	0	0	.00	2	.244	.348	.348
6 Min. YEARS			524	1694	452	108	12	54	746	274	257	227	8	449	24	22	14	34	18	.65	19	.267	.359	.440

Steve Bieser

Bats: Both **Throws:** Right **Pos:** C-OF **Ht:** 5'10" **Wt:** 170 **Born:** 8/4/67 **Age:** 28

Year Team	Lg	G	AB	H	2B	3B	HR	TB	R	RBI	TBB	IBB	SO	HBP	SH	SF	SB	CS	SB%	GDP	Avg	OBP	SLG
1989 Batavia	A	25	75	18	3	1	1	26	13	13	12	0	20	2	2	2	2	1	.67	1	.240	.352	.347
1990 Batavia	A	54	160	37	11	1	0	50	36	12	26	0	27	1	2	2	13	2	.87	3	.231	.339	.313
1991 Spartanburg	A	60	168	41	6	0	0	47	25	13	31	0	35	3	4	3	17	4	.81	4	.244	.345	.280
1992 Clearwater	A	73	203	58	6	5	0	74	33	10	39	3	28	9	8	0	8	8	.50	2	.286	.422	.365
Reading	AA	33	139	38	5	4	0	51	20	8	6	0	25	4	4	0	8	3	.73	3	.273	.322	.367
1993 Reading	AA	53	170	53	6	3	1	68	21	19	15	1	24	2	1	0	9	5	.64	2	.312	.374	.400
Scranton-Wb	AAA	26	83	21	4	0	0	25	3	4	2	0	14	1	1	0	3	0	1.00	0	.253	.279	.301
1994 Scranton-Wb	AAA	93	228	61	13	1	0	76	42	15	17	1	40	5	4	2	12	8	.60	2	.268	.329	.333
1995 Scranton-Wb	AAA	95	245	66	12	6	1	93	37	33	22	1	56	10	6	2	14	5	.74	5	.269	.351	.380
7 Min. YEARS		512	1471	393	66	21	3	510	230	127	170	7	269	37	32	11	86	36	.70	22	.267	.355	.347

Jeff Bigler

Bats: Left **Throws:** Left **Pos:** 1B **Ht:** 6'0" **Wt:** 190 **Born:** 9/13/69 **Age:** 26

Year Team	Lg	G	AB	H	2B	3B	HR	TB	R	RBI	TBB	IBB	SO	HBP	SH	SF	SB	CS	SB%	GDP	Avg	OBP	SLG
1992 Spartanburg	A	125	438	118	32	2	5	169	50	53	49	2	67	4	1	1	4	4	.50	4	.269	.348	.386
1993 Spartanburg	A	66	231	60	22	1	1	87	26	35	23	3	43	3	0	2	0	0	.00	3	.260	.332	.377
1994 Clearwater	A	104	366	103	21	1	5	141	41	49	54	3	47	1	0	4	1	1	.50	10	.281	.372	.385
1995 Reading	AA	13	44	4	1	0	0	5	4	2	6	2	10	1	1	1	0	0	.00	1	.091	.212	.114
Duluth-Sup.	IND	69	263	69	19	0	4	100	37	33	34	2	42	1	7	2	0	2	.00	4	.262	.347	.380
4 Min. YEARS		377	1342	354	95	4	15	502	158	172	166	12	209	10	9	10	5	7	.42	24	.264	.347	.374

Jeff Bittiger

Pitches: Right **Bats:** Right **Pos:** P **Ht:** 5'10" **Wt:** 175 **Born:** 4/13/62 **Age:** 34

Year Team	Lg	G	GS	CG	GF	IP	BFP	H	R	ER	HR	SH	SF	HB	TBB	IBB	SO	WP	Bk	W	L	Pct.	ShO	Sv	ERA
1984 Tidewater	AAA	24	23	3	0	134.2	571	124	72	58	14	4	5	2	53	1	70	5	0	8	8	.500	3	0	3.88
1985 Tidewater	AAA	24	24	2	0	131.2	566	131	62	54	14	4	7	1	52	2	66	2	1	11	7	.611	0	0	3.69
1986 Portland	AAA	27	26	6	0	171.1	730	181	83	79	15	2	14	5	58	3	101	3	2	13	8	.619	0	0	4.15
1987 Portland	AAA	26	24	9	2	180	755	171	84	68	13	3	9	2	57	2	94	9	1	12	10	.545	2	0	3.40
1988 Vancouver	AAA	7	7	5	0	52	195	35	9	6	2	1	1	1	6	0	49	0	1	4	1	.800	2	0	1.04
1989 White Sox	R	2	2	0	0	12	42	7	3	1	0	0	1	0	0	0	10	0	0	1	1	.500	0	0	0.75
Vancouver	AAA	17	17	6	0	123	488	93	31	29	5	6	3	4	40	0	122	3	0	9	5	.643	4	0	2.12
1990 Albuquerque	AAA	28	26	2	2	154	665	162	78	71	15	2	4	2	62	3	125	9	0	15	6	.714	0	0	4.15
1991 Colo. Sprng	AAA	27	27	2	0	147.2	670	158	89	64	12	3	6	6	83	0	93	13	1	9	12	.429	0	0	3.90
1992 Huntsville	AA	17	17	0	0	102	427	89	42	35	2	0	3	2	44	0	94	4	1	10	5	.667	0	0	3.09
Tacoma	AAA	9	9	0	0	46.1	209	51	15	14	2	0	2	2	28	1	24	3	0	3	3	.500	0	0	2.72
1993 Rochester	IND	12	12	3	0	66.1	289	68	38	33	6	4	0	3	27	1	67	2	0	5	4	.556	0	0	4.48
Memphis	AA	2	2	0	0	11.1	40	6	2	2	1	0	0	1	3	0	11	0	0	1	0	1.000	0	0	1.59
1994 Winnipeg	IND	14	14	3	0	85.2	347	70	32	29	3	1	2	1	33	0	100	1	0	9	4	.692	3	0	3.05
1995 Edmonton	AAA	6	1	0	0	15.1	70	17	10	9	1	1	2	0	7	0	10	3	0	2	0	1.000	0	0	5.28
Winnipeg	IND	20	20	3	0	124	536	131	65	55	13	7	5	4	46	0	106	4	0	8	5	.615	2	0	3.99
1986 Philadelphia	NL	3	3	0	0	14.2	68	16	10	9	2	1	0	1	7	1	8	2	2	1	1	.500	0	0	5.52
1987 Minnesota	AL	3	1	0	0	8.1	36	11	5	5	2	0	0	1	0	0	5	0	0	1	0	1.000	0	0	5.40
1988 Chicago	AL	25	7	0	9	61.2	268	59	31	29	11	4	4	0	29	2	33	3	2	2	4	.333	0	0	4.23
1989 Chicago	AL	3	1	0	1	9.2	41	9	7	7	2	0	0	0	6	0	7	1	0	0	1	.000	0	0	6.52
12 Min. YEARS		262	251	44	4	1557.1	6600	1494	715	607	118	38	64	36	599	13	1142	61	7	120	79	.603	16	0	3.51
4 Maj. YEARS		33	12	0	10	94.1	413	95	53	50	17	5	4	2	42	3	53	6	4	4	6	.400	0	0	4.77

Dirk Blair

Pitches: Right **Bats:** Right **Pos:** P **Ht:** 6'3" **Wt:** 215 **Born:** 5/19/69 **Age:** 27

Year Team	Lg	G	GS	CG	GF	IP	BFP	H	R	ER	HR	SH	SF	HB	TBB	IBB	SO	WP	Bk	W	L	Pct.	ShO	Sv	ERA
1991 Pulaski	R	18	0	0	10	45.2	197	47	21	17	2	1	2	0	15	0	41	5	4	8	1	.889	0	4	3.35
1992 Macon	A	41	0	0	22	67.1	279	66	25	17	1	3	2	2	12	1	60	2	1	2	1	.667	0	9	2.27
1993 Durham	A	44	0	0	23	81.1	340	78	32	29	7	2	2	3	17	1	69	3	1	4	5	.444	0	12	3.21
1994 Greenville	AA	49	0	0	21	86.2	370	93	38	34	6	6	3	3	18	6	59	5	1	8	3	.727	0	3	3.53
1995 Richmond	AAA	8	0	0	5	8.1	41	12	8	6	1	1	0	1	4	0	2	0	0	1	1	.500	0	0	6.48
Greenville	AA	40	0	0	19	62	261	69	29	29	7	3	0	3	11	2	38	1	0	2	2	.500	0	2	4.21
5 Min. YEARS		200	1	0	100	351.1	1488	365	153	132	24	16	9	12	77	10	269	16	7	25	13	.658	0	30	3.38

Mike Blais

Pitches: Right **Bats:** Right **Pos:** P **Ht:** 6'5" **Wt:** 226 **Born:** 10/2/71 **Age:** 24

Year Team	Lg	G	GS	CG	GF	IP	BFP	H	R	ER	HR	SH	SF	HB	TBB	IBB	SO	WP	Bk	W	L	Pct.	ShO	Sv	ERA
1993 Red Sox	R	22	0	0	17	26	99	15	6	4	0	1	2	2	8	0	22	2	0	3	1	.750	0	4	1.38
Ft. Laud	A	3	0	0	3	6	26	4	1	1	0	1	0	0	3	1	7	0	0	1	1	.500	0	1	1.50
1994 Lynchburg	A	25	10	0	6	77.1	354	99	66	57	12	2	2	1	18	0	46	3	1	1	6	.143	0	1	6.63
1995 Michigan	A	32	0	0	26	46	184	34	12	10	0	3	4	1	11	3	35	4	0	2	1	.667	0	10	1.96
Trenton	AA	13	0	0	7	25	96	19	8	7	1	1	2	1	7	0	20	0	0	2	0	1.000	0	0	2.52
3 Min. YEARS		95	10	0	59	180.1	759	171	93	79	13	8	10	5	47	4	130	9	1	9	9	.500	0	15	3.94

Henry Blanco

Bats: Right **Throws:** Right **Pos:** 3B **Ht:** 5'11" **Wt:** 168 **Born:** 8/29/71 **Age:** 24

					BATTING													BASERUNNING				PERCENTAGES		
Year	Team	Lg	G	AB	H	2B	3B	HR	TB	R	RBI	TBB	IBB	SO	HBP	SH	SF	SB	CS	SB%	GDP	Avg	OBP	SLG
1990	Dodgers	R	60	178	39	8	0	1	50	23	19	26	0	43	1	0	4	7	2	.78	6	.219	.316	.281
1991	Vero Beach	A	5	7	1	0	0	0	1	0	0	2	0	0	0	0	0	0	0	.00	0	.143	.333	.143
	Great Falls	R	62	216	55	7	1	5	79	35	28	27	0	39	1	2	3	3	6	.33	5	.255	.336	.366
1992	Bakersfield	A	124	401	94	21	2	5	134	42	52	51	3	91	9	10	9	10	6	.63	10	.234	.328	.334
1993	San Antonio	AA	117	374	73	19	1	10	124	33	42	29	0	80	4	2	1	3	3	.50	7	.195	.260	.332
1994	San Antonio	AA	132	405	93	23	2	6	138	36	38	53	2	67	2	5	3	6	6	.50	12	.230	.320	.341
1995	San Antonio	AA	88	302	77	18	4	12	139	37	48	29	2	52	4	0	0	1	1	.50	4	.255	.328	.460
	Albuquerque	AAA	29	97	22	4	1	2	34	11	13	10	1	23	0	1	2	0	0	.00	3	.227	.294	.351
	6 Min. YEARS		617	1980	454	100	11	41	699	217	240	227	8	395	21	20	22	30	24	.56	47	.229	.312	.353

Kent Blasingame

Bats: Left **Throws:** Left **Pos:** OF **Ht:** 6'0" **Wt:** 175 **Born:** 2/4/69 **Age:** 27

					BATTING													BASERUNNING				PERCENTAGES		
Year	Team	Lg	G	AB	H	2B	3B	HR	TB	R	RBI	TBB	IBB	SO	HBP	SH	SF	SB	CS	SB%	GDP	Avg	OBP	SLG
1994	Clearwater	A	106	395	100	12	7	6	144	61	37	29	2	90	9	6	3	18	16	.53	8	.253	.317	.365
1995	Reading	AA	86	195	40	4	2	1	51	38	17	29	0	43	5	5	2	9	7	.56	3	.205	.320	.262
	2 Min. YEARS		192	590	140	16	9	7	195	99	54	58	2	133	14	11	5	27	23	.54	11	.237	.318	.331

Ronald Blazier

Pitches: Right **Bats:** Right **Pos:** P **Ht:** 6'6" **Wt:** 215 **Born:** 7/30/71 **Age:** 24

				HOW MUCH HE PITCHED					WHAT HE GAVE UP												THE RESULTS				
Year	Team	Lg	G	GS	CG	GF	IP	BFP	H	R	ER	HR	SH	SF	HB	TBB	IBB	SO	WP	Bk	W	L	Pct.	ShO	Sv	ERA
1990	Princeton	R	14	1	1	1	78.2	331	79	46	39	10	1	3	1	29	1	45	3	1	3	5	.375	0	0	4.46
1991	Batavia	A	24	8	0	8	72.1	312	81	40	37	11	2	1	3	17	3	77	2	1	7	5	.583	0	2	4.60
1992	Spartanburg	A	30	21	2	6	159.2	640	141	55	47	10	2	5	5	32	0	149	4	0	14	7	.667	0	0	2.65
1993	Clearwater	A	27	23	1	1	155.1	663	171	80	68	8	4	4	6	40	5	86	1	1	9	8	.529	0	0	3.94
1994	Clearwater	A	29	29	0	0	173.1	715	177	73	65	15	4	6	9	36	1	120	2	2	13	5	.722	0	0	3.38
1995	Reading	AA	56	3	0	17	106.2	431	93	44	39	11	5	2	0	31	7	102	2	1	4	5	.444	0	1	3.29
	6 Min. YEARS		180	97	4	33	746	3092	742	338	295	65	18	21	24	185	17	579	14	6	50	35	.588	0	3	3.56

Greg Blosser

Bats: Left **Throws:** Left **Pos:** OF **Ht:** 6'3" **Wt:** 215 **Born:** 6/26/71 **Age:** 25

					BATTING													BASERUNNING				PERCENTAGES		
Year	Team	Lg	G	AB	H	2B	3B	HR	TB	R	RBI	TBB	IBB	SO	HBP	SH	SF	SB	CS	SB%	GDP	Avg	OBP	SLG
1989	Red Sox	R	40	146	42	7	3	2	61	17	20	25	1	19	1	0	2	3	0	1.00	7	.288	.391	.418
	Winter Havn	A	28	94	24	1	1	2	33	6	14	8	0	14	1	0	1	1	0	1.00	1	.255	.317	.351
1990	Lynchburg	A	119	447	126	23	1	18	205	63	62	55	3	99	1	0	1	5	4	.56	13	.282	.361	.459
1991	New Britain	AA	134	452	98	21	3	8	149	48	46	63	0	114	1	0	4	9	4	.69	16	.217	.312	.330
1992	New Britain	AA	129	434	105	23	4	22	202	59	71	64	9	122	1	0	3	0	2	.00	7	.242	.339	.465
	Pawtucket	AAA	1	0	0	0	0	0	0	0	1	0	1	0	0	0	0	0	0	.00	0	.000	1.000	.000
1993	Pawtucket	AAA	130	478	109	22	2	23	204	66	66	58	5	139	2	1	4	3	3	.50	4	.228	.312	.427
1994	Pawtucket	AAA	97	350	91	21	1	17	165	52	54	44	5	97	0	0	1	11	3	.79	9	.260	.342	.471
1995	Pawtucket	AAA	17	50	10	0	0	1	13	5	4	5	0	13	0	0	1	0	0	.00	0	.200	.268	.260
	Trenton	AA	49	179	44	13	0	11	90	25	34	13	0	42	0	1	3	3	2	.60	4	.246	.292	.503
1993	Boston	AL	17	28	2	1	0	0	3	3	1	2	0	7	0	0	0	1	0	1.00	1	.071	.133	.107
1994	Boston	AL	5	11	1	0	0	0	1	2	1	4	0	4	0	0	0	0	0	.00	0	.091	.333	.091
	7 Min. YEARS		744	2630	649	131	15	104	1122	342	371	336	23	659	7	2	20	35	18	.66	61	.247	.331	.427
	2 Maj. YEARS		22	39	3	1	0	0	4	3	2	6	0	11	0	0	0	1	0	1.00	0	.077	.200	.103

Jamie Bluma

Pitches: Right **Bats:** Right **Pos:** P **Ht:** 5'11" **Wt:** 195 **Born:** 5/18/72 **Age:** 24

				HOW MUCH HE PITCHED					WHAT HE GAVE UP												THE RESULTS				
Year	Team	Lg	G	GS	CG	GF	IP	BFP	H	R	ER	HR	SH	SF	HB	TBB	IBB	SO	WP	Bk	W	L	Pct.	ShO	Sv	ERA
1994	Eugene	A	26	0	0	23	36.1	133	19	5	4	0	1	1	0	6	0	35	0	0	2	1	.667	0	12	0.99
	Wilmington	A	7	0	0	7	9.2	34	7	2	1	0	0	0	0	0	0	5	0	0	4	0	1.000	0	2	0.93
1995	Wichita	AA	42	0	0	40	55.1	214	38	19	19	9	3	1	1	9	2	31	1	0	4	3	.571	0	22	3.09
	Omaha	AAA	18	0	0	10	23.2	101	21	13	8	1	3	3	0	14	4	12	3	0	0	0	.000	0	4	3.04
	2 Min. YEARS		93	0	0	80	125	482	85	39	32	10	7	5	1	29	6	83	4	0	10	4	.714	0	40	2.30

Todd Blyleven

Pitches: Right **Bats:** Right **Pos:** P **Ht:** 6'5" **Wt:** 230 **Born:** 9/27/72 **Age:** 23

				HOW MUCH HE PITCHED					WHAT HE GAVE UP												THE RESULTS				
Year	Team	Lg	G	GS	CG	GF	IP	BFP	H	R	ER	HR	SH	SF	HB	TBB	IBB	SO	WP	Bk	W	L	Pct.	ShO	Sv	ERA
1993	Angels	R	11	11	1	0	70	299	69	35	28	3	3	4		17	0	49	5	2	4	4	.500	0	0	3.60
1994	Boise	A	12	5	0	3	45.2	197	43	14	11	2	2	1	4	14	0	53	5	0	4	2	.667	0	0	2.17
	Lk Elsinore	A	8	6	0	0	42.1	182	38	20	14	4	0	4	2	17	0	33	2	0	1	2	.333	0	0	2.98
1995	Midland	AA	8	0	0	2	14.1	57	13	8	8	1	2	2	0	3	1	8	0	1	3	1	.750	0	0	5.02
	Lk Elsinore	A	6	0	0	0	8.1	44	12	9	4	2	0	2	2	5	0	8	1	0	0	1	.000	0	0	4.32

		G	GS	CG	GF	IP	BFP	H	R	ER	HR	SH	SF	HB	TBB	IBB	SO	WP	Bk	W	L	Pct.	ShO	Sv	ERA
Sioux City	IND	18	18	0	0	118	514	133	68	62	13	4	3	6	38	0	67	3	0	8	6	.571	0	0	4.73
3 Min. YEARS		63	40	1	5	298.2	1293	308	154	127	25	11	16	19	94	1	218	16	3	20	16	.556	0	0	3.83

Kurtiss Bogott

Pitches: Left **Bats:** Left **Pos:** P **Ht:** 6'4" **Wt:** 195 **Born:** 9/30/72 **Age:** 23

		HOW MUCH HE PITCHED						WHAT HE GAVE UP										THE RESULTS							
Year Team	Lg	G	GS	CG	GF	IP	BFP	H	R	ER	HR	SH	SF	HB	TBB	IBB	SO	WP	Bk	W	L	Pct.	ShO	Sv	ERA
1993 Red Sox	R	3	2	0	0	15	57	10	3	3	1	0	0	2	4	0	20	3	0	0	1	.000	0	0	1.80
Utica	A	13	10	0	0	56.2	260	64	37	28	4	2	1	3	23	0	53	8	3	1	7	.125	0	0	4.45
1994 Red Sox	R	3	2	0	0	13.2	49	7	1	1	0	0	0	1	3	0	12	2	0	1	0	1.000	0	0	0.66
Lynchburg	A	6	6	0	0	26.1	127	32	23	18	1	1	1	1	14	0	14	2	0	2	3	.400	0	0	6.15
1995 Sarasota	A	41	9	0	15	88.2	388	89	44	30	3	4	1	4	41	0	62	8	3	6	4	.600	0	0	3.05
Trenton	AA	2	0	0	2	3.1	13	3	1	1	1	0	0	0	1	0	2	0	0	0	1	.000	0	0	2.70
3 Min. YEARS		68	29	0	17	203.2	894	205	109	81	10	7	3	11	86	0	163	23	6	10	16	.385	0	0	3.58

Ben Boka

Bats: Right **Throws:** Right **Pos:** C **Ht:** 6'4" **Wt:** 215 **Born:** 1/9/73 **Age:** 23

		BATTING															BASERUNNING				PERCENTAGES		
Year Team	Lg	G	AB	H	2B	3B	HR	TB	R	RBI	TBB	IBB	SO	HBP	SH	SF	SB	CS	SB%	GDP	Avg	OBP	SLG
1992 Pirates	R	15	47	7	1	1	0	10	1	3	0	0	15	0	0	0	0	0	.00	0	.149	.149	.213
Welland	A	19	48	11	1	0	0	12	2	6	1	0	19	0	2	0	0	0	.00	1	.229	.245	.250
1993 Lethbridge	R	35	109	18	3	0	1	24	7	7	10	0	40	1	1	0	2	1	.67	0	.165	.242	.220
1994 Pittsfield	A	38	133	26	7	1	0	35	10	13	5	0	44	1	2	0	1	1	.00	2	.195	.230	.263
1995 Columbia	A	8	12	1	0	0	0	1	1	1	1	0	4	0	0	1	0	1	.00	1	.083	.143	.083
Norfolk	AAA	19	21	3	0	0	0	3	0	1	0	0	8	0	1	0	0	0	.00	0	.143	.143	.143
4 Min. YEARS		134	370	66	12	2	1	85	21	31	17	0	130	2	6	1	2	2	.50	4	.178	.218	.230

Frank Bolick

Bats: Both **Throws:** Right **Pos:** 3B **Ht:** 5'9" **Wt:** 190 **Born:** 6/28/66 **Age:** 30

		BATTING															BASERUNNING				PERCENTAGES		
Year Team	Lg	G	AB	H	2B	3B	HR	TB	R	RBI	TBB	IBB	SO	HBP	SH	SF	SB	CS	SB%	GDP	Avg	OBP	SLG
1987 Helena	R	52	156	39	8	1	10	79	41	28	41	1	44	3	1	0	4	0	1.00	3	.250	.415	.506
1988 Beloit	A	55	180	41	14	1	2	63	28	16	43	0	49	1	1	0	3	3	.50	3	.228	.379	.350
Brewers	R	23	80	30	9	3	1	48	20	20	22	0	8	0	0	3	1	0	1.00	0	.375	.495	.600
Helena	R	40	131	39	10	1	10	81	35	28	32	2	31	1	1	2	5	1	.83	2	.298	.434	.618
1989 Beloit	A	88	299	90	23	0	9	140	44	41	47	5	52	1	2	0	9	6	.60	3	.301	.404	.468
1990 Stockton	A	50	164	51	9	1	8	86	39	36	38	1	33	2	0	5	5	3	.63	0	.311	.435	.524
San Bernrdo	A	78	277	92	24	4	10	154	61	66	53	6	53	2	0	8	3	6	.33	2	.332	.432	.556
1991 Jacksonvlle	AA	136	468	119	19	0	16	186	69	73	84	3	115	5	2	7	5	4	.56	7	.254	.369	.397
1992 Jacksonvlle	AA	63	224	60	9	0	13	108	32	42	42	1	38	1	0	4	1	4	.20	3	.268	.380	.482
Calgary	AAA	78	274	79	18	6	14	151	35	54	39	2	52	1	1	4	4	4	.50	4	.288	.374	.551
1993 Ottawa	AAA	2	8	1	0	0	0	1	0	0	0	0	0	0	0	0	0	0	.00	0	.125	.125	.125
1994 Buffalo	AAA	35	95	25	6	0	2	37	18	8	27	3	29	2	1	2	0	1	.00	1	.263	.429	.389
New Haven	AA	85	301	76	13	0	21	152	53	63	41	3	57	3	1	2	2	2	.50	10	.252	.346	.505
1995 Colo. Sprng	AAA	23	68	16	3	1	2	27	8	7	8	0	14	0	1	0	0	0	.00	0	.235	.316	.397
Lubbock	IND	59	214	76	17	1	7	116	42	56	46	7	33	1	0	5	1	1	.50	5	.355	.462	.542
Buffalo	AAA	20	65	16	6	0	3	31	11	10	3	0	13	1	0	0	0	1	.00	3	.246	.290	.477
1993 Montreal	NL	95	213	45	13	0	4	70	25	24	23	2	37	4	0	2	1	0	1.00	4	.211	.298	.329
9 Min. YEARS		887	3004	850	188	19	128	1460	536	548	566	34	621	29	8	44	43	36	.54	46	.283	.397	.486

Tom Bolton

Pitches: Left **Bats:** Left **Pos:** P **Ht:** 6'2" **Wt:** 185 **Born:** 5/6/62 **Age:** 34

		HOW MUCH HE PITCHED						WHAT HE GAVE UP										THE RESULTS							
Year Team	Lg	G	GS	CG	GF	IP	BFP	H	R	ER	HR	SH	SF	HB	TBB	IBB	SO	WP	Bk	W	L	Pct.	ShO	Sv	ERA
1980 Elmira	A	23	1	1	15	56	237	43	26	15	4	1	1	0	22	0	43	0	0	6	2	.750	1	5	2.41
1981 Wintr Haven	A	24	0	0	3	92	420	125	62	46	5	2	3	3	41	0	47	7	1	2	3	.400	0	0	4.50
1982 Wintr Haven	A	28	25	4	1	163	682	161	67	54	3	6	4	2	63	0	77	7	4	9	8	.529	0	0	2.98
1983 New Britain	AA	16	16	2	0	99.2	416	93	36	32	7	1	0	1	41	0	62	5	0	7	3	.700	1	0	2.89
Pawtucket	AAA	6	6	0	0	29	144	33	26	21	4	1	0	1	25	0	20	1	1	0	5	.000	0	0	6.52
1984 New Britain	AA	33	9	0	11	87	380	87	54	40	5	2	3	4	34	3	66	6	2	4	5	.444	0	1	4.14
1985 New Britain	AA	34	10	1	14	101	437	106	53	48	3	5	3	2	40	1	74	3	2	5	6	.455	0	1	4.28
1986 Pawtucket	AAA	29	7	1	11	86	356	80	30	26	6	9	2	0	25	2	58	1	1	3	4	.429	0	2	2.72
1987 Pawtucket	AAA	5	4	0	1	21.2	93	25	14	13	0	0	0	0	12	1	8	1	0	2	1	.667	0	0	5.40
1988 Pawtucket	AAA	18	1	0	8	19.1	81	17	7	6	0	0	0	0	10	0	15	2	0	3	0	1.000	0	0	2.79
1989 Pawtucket	AAA	25	22	5	2	143.1	606	140	57	46	13	6	1	4	47	2	99	0	1	12	5	.706	2	1	2.89
1990 Pawtucket	AAA	4	2	0	1	11.2	50	9	6	5	2	0	1	0	7	0	8	2	0	1	0	1.000	0	0	3.86
1994 Rochester	AAA	16	0	0	7	20	76	13	5	5	1	0	0	0	8	0	16	2	1	2	0	1.000	0	0	2.25
1995 Nashville	AAA	19	17	1	1	101.2	433	106	52	50	10	0	1	3	31	0	82	3	2	5	7	.417	1	0	4.43
1987 Boston	AL	29	0	0	5	61.2	287	83	33	30	5	3	3	2	27	2	49	3	0	1	0	1.000	0	0	4.38
1988 Boston	AL	28	0	0	8	30.1	140	35	17	16	1	2	0	0	14	1	21	2	1	1	3	.250	0	1	4.75
1989 Boston	AL	4	4	0	0	17.1	83	21	18	16	1	0	1	0	10	1	9	1	0	0	4	.000	0	0	8.31
1990 Boston	AL	21	14	3	2	119.2	501	111	46	45	6	3	5	3	47	3	65	1	1	10	5	.667	0	0	3.38
1991 Boston	AL	25	19	0	4	110	499	136	72	64	16	2	4	1	51	2	64	3	0	8	9	.471	0	0	5.24
1992 Boston	AL	21	1	0	6	29	135	34	11	11	0	0	0	2	14	1	23	2	1	1	2	.333	0	0	3.41
Cincinnati	NL	16	8	0	3	46.1	210	52	28	27	1	1	1	2	23	0	27	3	1	3	3	.500	0	0	5.24

1993 Detroit	AL	43	8	0	9	102.2	462	113	57	51	5	7	2	7	45	10	66	5	1	6	6	.500	0	0	4.47
1994 Baltimore	AL	22	0	0	3	23.1	109	29	15	14	3	1	1	0	13	1	12	1	0	1	2	.333	0	0	5.40
13 Min. YEARS		280	120	15	75	1031.1	4411	1038	495	407	63	33	20	20	406	9	675	40	15	61	49	.555	5	12	3.55
8 Maj. YEARS		209	56	3	40	540.1	2426	614	297	274	46	19	18	17	244	23	336	21	5	31	34	.477	0	1	4.56

Rob Bonanno

Pitches: Right **Bats:** Right **Pos:** P **Ht:** 6'0" **Wt:** 178 **Born:** 1/5/71 **Age:** 25

		HOW MUCH HE PITCHED						WHAT HE GAVE UP												THE RESULTS					
Year Team	Lg	G	GS	CG	GF	IP	BFP	H	R	ER	HR	SH	SF	HB	TBB	IBB	SO	WP	Bk	W	L	Pct.	ShO	Sv	ERA
1994 Boise	A	6	6	0	0	39.2	155	23	11	6	1	0	0	2	10	0	41	2	0	5	0	1.000	0	0	1.36
Cedar Rapds	A	9	9	0	0	51	219	56	25	25	4	1	2	4	16	1	40	6	1	3	2	.600	0	0	4.41
1995 Midland	AA	3	3	0	0	13.1	68	24	16	14	5	0	1	0	6	0	6	0	0	1	1	.500	0	0	9.45
Lk Elsinore	A	17	17	4	0	112	455	112	49	38	10	2	4	3	16	0	72	0	0	8	4	.667	2	0	3.05
2 Min. YEARS		35	35	4	0	216	897	215	101	83	20	3	7	9	48	1	159	8	1	17	7	.708	2	0	3.46

James Bonnici

Bats: Right **Throws:** Right **Pos:** 1B **Ht:** 6'4" **Wt:** 230 **Born:** 1/21/72 **Age:** 24

		BATTING														BASERUNNING				PERCENTAGES		
Year Team	Lg	G	AB	H	2B	3B	HR	TB	R	RBI	TBB	IBB	SO	HBP	SH	SF	SB	CS	SB%	GDP	Avg	OBP	SLG
1991 Mariners	R	51	178	59	2	4	0	69	36	38	44	0	31	6	0	5	8	2	.80	1	.331	.468	.388
1992 Bellingham	A	53	168	44	6	1	4	64	13	20	22	2	54	2	1	0	5	2	.71	3	.262	.354	.381
1993 Riverside	A	104	375	115	21	1	9	165	69	58	58	2	72	9	3	1	0	0	.00	7	.307	.411	.440
1994 Riverside	A	113	397	111	23	3	10	170	71	71	58	0	81	18	0	3	1	2	.33	14	.280	.393	.428
1995 Port City	AA	138	508	144	36	3	20	246	75	91	76	15	97	9	0	3	2	2	.50	14	.283	.384	.484
5 Min. YEARS		459	1626	473	88	12	43	714	264	278	258	19	335	44	4	12	16	8	.67	39	.291	.399	.439

Aaron Boone

Bats: Right **Throws:** Right **Pos:** 3B **Ht:** 6'2" **Wt:** 190 **Born:** 3/9/73 **Age:** 23

		BATTING														BASERUNNING				PERCENTAGES		
Year Team	Lg	G	AB	H	2B	3B	HR	TB	R	RBI	TBB	IBB	SO	HBP	SH	SF	SB	CS	SB%	GDP	Avg	OBP	SLG
1994 Billings	R	67	256	70	15	5	7	116	48	55	36	3	35	3	0	6	6	3	.67	7	.273	.362	.453
1995 Chattanooga	AA	23	66	15	3	0	0	18	6	3	5	0	12	0	1	2	2	0	1.00	5	.227	.274	.273
Winston-Sal	A	108	395	103	19	1	14	166	61	50	43	7	77	9	4	2	11	7	.61	4	.261	.345	.420
2 Min. YEARS		198	717	188	37	6	21	300	115	108	84	10	124	12	5	10	19	10	.66	16	.262	.345	.418

Dean Borrelli

Bats: Right **Throws:** Right **Pos:** C **Ht:** 6'2" **Wt:** 210 **Born:** 10/20/66 **Age:** 29

		BATTING														BASERUNNING				PERCENTAGES		
Year Team	Lg	G	AB	H	2B	3B	HR	TB	R	RBI	TBB	IBB	SO	HBP	SH	SF	SB	CS	SB%	GDP	Avg	OBP	SLG
1988 Sou. Oregon	A	43	140	28	7	1	0	37	10	6	10	1	18	1	1	2	0	1	.00	5	.200	.255	.264
1989 Madison	A	20	59	9	1	0	1	13	2	6	4	0	18	0	0	0	0	0	.00	1	.153	.206	.220
Huntsville	AA	5	13	2	1	0	0	3	0	2	2	0	6	1	1	0	0	0	.00	0	.154	.313	.231
1990 Huntsville	AA	27	78	14	4	1	1	23	7	4	5	0	20	1	0	2	0	0	.00	4	.179	.233	.295
Modesto	A	52	148	34	9	1	1	48	22	11	24	0	25	7	1	0	0	2	.00	5	.230	.363	.324
1991 Huntsville	AA	64	184	35	4	1	0	41	9	7	15	0	45	3	4	1	1	1	.50	6	.190	.261	.223
1992 Huntsville	AA	85	238	48	5	0	1	56	20	23	26	0	45	2	3	2	3	3	.50	5	.202	.284	.235
1993 Tacoma	AAA	76	210	51	7	2	1	65	29	19	18	0	37	2	3	2	1	0	1.00	8	.243	.306	.310
1994 Tacoma	AAA	101	369	103	21	0	3	133	32	42	31	3	64	3	3	1	0	1	.00	8	.279	.339	.360
1995 Okla. City	AAA	54	185	37	9	1	2	54	17	17	18	0	50	2	0	2	0	1	.00	7	.200	.275	.292
8 Min. YEARS		527	1624	361	68	7	10	473	148	137	153	4	328	22	16	12	5	9	.36	49	.222	.296	.291

D.J. Boston

Bats: Left **Throws:** Left **Pos:** 1B **Ht:** 6'7" **Wt:** 230 **Born:** 9/6/71 **Age:** 24

		BATTING														BASERUNNING				PERCENTAGES		
Year Team	Lg	G	AB	H	2B	3B	HR	TB	R	RBI	TBB	IBB	SO	HBP	SH	SF	SB	CS	SB%	GDP	Avg	OBP	SLG
1991 Medcne Hat	R	59	207	58	12	0	1	73	34	25	33	0	33	2	1	1	4	8	.33	5	.280	.383	.353
1992 St. Cathrns	A	72	256	60	7	1	5	84	25	36	36	4	41	2	0	3	20	3	.87	2	.234	.330	.328
1993 Hagerstown	A	127	464	146	35	4	13	228	76	92	54	6	77	4	0	3	31	11	.74	10	.315	.389	.491
1994 Dunedin	A	119	433	125	20	1	7	168	59	52	55	2	65	0	2	5	19	9	.68	8	.289	.365	.388
1995 Knoxville	AA	132	479	117	27	1	11	179	51	71	47	1	100	2	2	3	12	8	.60	12	.244	.313	.374
5 Min. YEARS		509	1839	506	101	7	37	732	245	276	225	13	316	10	5	15	86	39	.69	37	.275	.355	.398

Daryl Boston

Bats: Left **Throws:** Left **Pos:** DH **Ht:** 6'3" **Wt:** 210 **Born:** 1/4/63 **Age:** 33

		BATTING														BASERUNNING				PERCENTAGES		
Year Team	Lg	G	AB	H	2B	3B	HR	TB	R	RBI	TBB	IBB	SO	HBP	SH	SF	SB	CS	SB%	GDP	Avg	OBP	SLG
1984 Denver	AAA	127	471	147	21	19	15	251	94	82	65	1	82	2	1	11	40	17	.70	10	.312	.390	.533
1985 Buffalo	AAA	63	241	66	12	1	10	110	45	36	33	0	48	4	2	1	15	5	.75	4	.274	.369	.456
1986 Buffalo	AAA	96	360	109	16	3	5	146	57	41	42	4	45	1	5	3	38	10	.79	3	.303	.374	.406
1987 Hawaii	AAA	21	77	23	3	0	5	41	14	13	10	1	10	1	0	0	10	0	1.00	3	.299	.386	.532
1995 Charlotte	AAA	18	64	12	5	0	1	20	7	2	6	0	12	0	0	0	0	1	.00	1	.188	.257	.313
Thunder Bay	IND	47	161	45	12	0	2	63	29	24	36	5	32	5	0	2	4	1	.80	0	.280	.422	.391
1984 Chicago	AL	35	83	14	3	1	0	19	8	3	4	0	20	0	0	0	6	0	1.00	0	.169	.207	.229
1985 Chicago	AL	95	232	53	13	1	3	77	20	15	14	1	44	0	1	1	8	6	.57	3	.228	.271	.332

Year	Team	Lg	G	AB	H	2B	3B	HR	TB	R	RBI	TBB	IBB	SO	HBP	SH	SF	SB	CS	SB%	GDP	Avg	OBP	SLG
1986	Chicago	AL	56	199	53	11	3	5	85	29	22	21	3	33	0	3	1	9	5	.64	4	.266	.335	.427
1987	Chicago	AL	103	337	87	21	2	10	142	51	29	25	2	68	0	4	3	12	6	.67	5	.258	.307	.421
1988	Chicago	AL	105	281	61	12	2	15	122	37	31	21	5	44	0	2	1	9	3	.75	5	.217	.271	.434
1989	Chicago	AL	101	218	55	3	4	5	81	34	23	24	3	31	0	4	1	7	2	.78	1	.252	.325	.372
1990	Chicago	AL	5	1	0	0	0	0	0	0	0	0	0	0	0	0	0	1	0	1.00	0	.000	.000	.000
	New York	NL	115	366	100	21	2	12	161	65	45	28	2	50	2	0	0	18	7	.72	7	.273	.328	.440
1991	New York	NL	137	255	70	16	4	4	106	40	21	30	0	42	0	0	1	15	8	.65	2	.275	.350	.416
1992	New York	NL	130	289	72	14	2	11	123	37	35	38	6	60	3	0	4	12	6	.67	5	.249	.338	.426
1993	Colorado	NL	124	291	76	15	1	14	135	46	40	26	1	57	2	0	1	1	6	.14	5	.261	.325	.464
1994	New York	AL	52	77	14	2	0	4	28	11	14	6	0	20	1	0	0	0	1	.00	0	.182	.250	.364
5 Min. YEARS			372	1374	402	69	23	38	631	246	198	192	7	229	13	8	17	107	33	.76	21	.293	.380	.459
11 Maj. YEARS			1058	2629	655	131	22	83	1079	378	278	237	23	469	8	14	13	98	50	.66	37	.249	.312	.410

Alan Botkin

Pitches: Left **Bats:** Left **Pos:** P **Ht:** 6'3" **Wt:** 204 **Born:** 10/6/67 **Age:** 28

			HOW MUCH HE PITCHED						WHAT HE GAVE UP											THE RESULTS					
Year	Team	Lg	G	GS	CG	GF	IP	BFP	H	R	ER	HR	SH	SF	HB	TBB	IBB	SO	WP	Bk	W	L	Pct.	ShO	Sv	ERA
1989	Johnson Cty	R	11	11	0	0	59	265	63	32	28	3	2	2	3	26	0	53	3	1	3	3	.500	0	0	4.27
1990	Springfield	A	6	5	0	1	23.1	112	27	23	16	3	0	2	1	12	1	20	2	0	0	4	.000	0	0	6.17
	Hamilton	A	13	13	4	0	87	343	66	26	15	1	6	4	1	26	0	72	12	0	7	4	.636	3	0	1.55
1991	Springfield	A	39	3	0	12	63.1	271	53	31	23	2	4	5	0	29	4	52	2	1	5	6	.455	0	0	3.27
1992	St. Pete	A	40	3	0	9	80	347	67	36	28	2	2	1	2	40	2	58	6	0	2	4	.333	0	0	3.15
1993	St. Pete	A	49	0	0	10	48.1	210	45	21	17	1	5	2	3	25	6	24	6	0	3	3	.500	0	0	3.17
1995	Harrisburg	AA	3	0	0	2	4.1	19	5	4	4	2	0	0	0	2	0	4	2	0	0	0	.000	0	1	8.31
	Albany	IND	15	11	3	1	77.2	318	79	32	26	1	1	2	2	14	0	56	1	0	7	3	.700	2	0	3.01
6 Min. YEARS			176	46	7	35	443	1885	405	205	157	15	20	18	12	174	13	339	34	2	27	27	.500	5	1	3.19

Kent Bottenfield

Pitches: Right **Bats:** Right **Pos:** P **Ht:** 6' 3" **Wt:** 237 **Born:** 11/14/68 **Age:** 27

			HOW MUCH HE PITCHED						WHAT HE GAVE UP											THE RESULTS					
Year	Team	Lg	G	GS	CG	GF	IP	BFP	H	R	ER	HR	SH	SF	HB	TBB	IBB	SO	WP	Bk	W	L	Pct.	ShO	Sv	ERA
1986	Expos	R	13	13	2	0	74.1	323	73	42	27	2	2	6	3	30	0	41	0	1	5	6	.455	0	0	3.27
1987	Burlington	A	27	27	6	0	161	706	175	98	81	12	3	3	2	42	0	103	9	2	9	13	.409	0	0	4.53
1988	W. Palm Bch	A	27	27	9	0	181	745	165	80	67	10	3	5	5	47	0	120	4	3	10	8	.556	4	0	3.33
1989	Jacksonvlle	AA	25	25	1	0	138.2	625	137	101	81	13	6	9	9	73	2	91	6	2	3	17	.150	0	0	5.26
1990	Jacksonvlle	AA	29	28	2	0	169	718	158	72	64	14	7	4	11	67	1	121	9	2	12	10	.545	1	0	3.41
1991	Indianapols	AAA	29	27	5	0	166.1	712	155	97	75	15	11	5	4	61	7	108	5	1	8	15	.348	2	0	4.06
1992	Indianapols	AAA	25	23	3	1	152.1	629	139	64	58	12	6	4	2	58	1	111	2	0	12	8	.600	1	0	3.43
1994	Colo. Sprng	AAA	5	4	1	0	31	135	35	19	17	6	3	0	1	11	0	17	1	0	1	2	.333	0	0	4.94
	Phoenix	AAA	8	5	1	0	35	143	30	13	10	3	0	0	3	11	1	11	0	0	2	1	.667	1	0	2.57
1995	Toledo	AAA	27	19	2	3	136.2	601	148	80	69	15	6	4	4	55	4	68	6	1	5	11	.313	1	1	4.54
1992	Montreal	NL	10	4	0	2	32.1	135	26	9	8	1	1	2	1	11	1	14	0	1	1	2	.333	0	1	2.23
1993	Montreal	NL	23	11	0	2	83	373	93	49	38	11	11	1	5	33	2	33	4	1	2	5	.286	0	0	4.12
	Colorado	NL	14	14	1	0	76.2	337	86	53	52	13	10	3	1	38	1	30	0	0	3	5	.375	0	0	6.10
1994	San Francisco	NL	1	0	0	0	1.2	9	5	2	2	1	0	0	0	0	0	0	0	0	0	0	.000	0	0	10.80
	Colorado	NL	15	1	0	3	24.2	112	28	16	16	1	1	0	2	10	0	15	2	0	3	1	.750	0	1	5.84
9 Min. YEARS			215	198	32	5	1245.1	5337	1215	666	549	102	47	40	44	455	16	791	42	12	67	91	.424	13	1	3.97
3 Maj. YEARS			63	30	1	7	218.1	966	238	129	116	27	23	6	9	92	4	92	6	1	9	13	.409	0	2	4.78

Denis Boucher

Pitches: Left **Bats:** Right **Pos:** P **Ht:** 6' 1" **Wt:** 195 **Born:** 3/7/68 **Age:** 28

			HOW MUCH HE PITCHED						WHAT HE GAVE UP											THE RESULTS					
Year	Team	Lg	G	GS	CG	GF	IP	BFP	H	R	ER	HR	SH	SF	HB	TBB	IBB	SO	WP	Bk	W	L	Pct.	ShO	Sv	ERA
1988	Myrtle Bch	A	33	33	1	0	196.2	809	161	81	62	11	7	6	8	63	1	169	15	21	13	12	.520	0	0	2.84
1989	Dunedin	A	33	28	1	1	164.2	675	142	80	56	6	3	8	6	58	2	117	13	8	10	10	.500	1	0	3.06
1990	Dunedin	A	9	9	2	0	60	226	45	8	5	1	0	0	2	8	0	62	4	0	7	0	1.000	2	0	0.75
	Syracuse	AAA	17	17	2	0	107.2	449	100	51	46	7	4	4	2	37	2	80	6	0	8	5	.615	1	0	3.85
1991	Syracuse	AAA	8	8	1	0	56.2	241	57	24	20	5	4	1	3	19	1	28	2	0	2	1	.667	0	0	3.18
	Colo. Sprng	AAA	3	3	0	0	14.1	59	14	8	8	1	0	1	0	2	0	9	0	0	1	0	1.000	0	0	5.02
1992	Colo. Sprng	AAA	20	18	6	1	124	497	119	50	48	4	3	4	2	30	1	40	7	2	11	4	.733	0	0	3.48
1993	Las Vegas	AAA	24	7	1	2	70	331	101	59	50	12	4	1	6	27	3	46	4	1	4	7	.364	0	1	6.43
	Ottawa	AAA	11	6	1	0	43	169	36	13	13	0	2	0	1	11	0	22	3	0	6	0	1.000	0	0	2.72
1994	Ottawa	AAA	18	18	0	0	114	480	110	52	47	10	3	3	2	37	1	49	1	1	7	6	.538	0	0	3.71
1995	Ottawa	AAA	14	11	0	1	55.1	254	65	39	35	1	3	3	0	31	0	22	4	0	2	3	.400	0	0	5.69
1991	Cleveland	AL	5	5	0	0	22.2	108	35	21	21	6	0	0	0	8	0	13	1	0	1	4	.200	0	0	8.34
	Toronto	AL	7	7	0	0	35.1	162	39	20	18	6	3	1	2	16	1	16	0	4	0	3	.000	0	0	4.58
1992	Cleveland	AL	8	7	0	0	41	184	48	29	29	9	1	3	1	20	0	17	1	0	2	2	.500	0	0	6.37
1993	Montreal	NL	5	5	0	0	28.1	111	24	7	6	1	0	3	0	3	1	14	0	1	3	1	.750	0	0	1.91
1994	Montreal	NL	10	2	0	3	18.2	84	24	16	14	6	2	1	0	7	0	17	1	0	0	1	.000	0	0	6.75
8 Min. YEARS			190	157	14	6	1006.1	4190	950	465	390	58	33	31	32	323	11	644	59	33	71	48	.597	4	1	3.49
4 Maj. YEARS			35	26	0	3	146	649	170	93	88	28	6	8	3	54	2	77	3	6	6	11	.353	0	0	5.42

Steven Bourgeois

Pitches: Right **Bats:** Right **Pos:** P   **Ht:** 6'1" **Wt:** 220 **Born:** 8/4/72 **Age:** 23

			HOW MUCH HE PITCHED						WHAT HE GAVE UP												THE RESULTS					
Year Team	Lg	G	GS	CG	GF	IP	BFP	H	R	ER	HR	SH	SF	HB	TBB	IBB	SO	WP	Bk	W	L	Pct.	ShO	Sv	ERA
1993 Everett	A	15	15	0	0	77	337	62	44	36	7	0	3	7	44	0	77	4	1	5	3	.625	0	0	4.21
1994 Clinton	A	20	20	0	0	106.1	464	97	57	43	16	4	2	7	54	0	88	11	0	8	5	.615	0	0	3.64
San Jose	A	7	7	0	0	36.2	167	40	22	22	4	1	1	1	22	0	27	5	0	4	0	1.000	0	0	5.40
1995 Shreveport	AA	22	22	2	0	145.1	604	140	50	46	8	4	5	4	53	1	91	11	1	12	3	.800	2	0	2.85
Phoenix	AAA	6	5	0	0	34.2	153	38	18	13	2	0	0	2	13	0	23	4	1	1	1	.500	0	0	3.38
3 Min. YEARS		70	69	2	0	400	1725	377	191	160	37	9	11	21	186	1	306	35	3	30	12	.714	2	0	3.60

Rafael Bournigal

Bats: Right **Throws:** Right **Pos:** SS   **Ht:** 5'11" **Wt:** 165 **Born:** 5/12/66 **Age:** 30

							BATTING									BASERUNNING				PERCENTAGES		
Year Team	Lg	G	AB	H	2B	3B	HR	TB	R	RBI	TBB	IBB	SO	HBP	SH	SF	SB	CS	SB%	GDP	Avg	OBP	SLG
1987 Great Falls	R	30	82	12	4	0	0	16	5	4	3	0	7	1	1	0	0	1	.00	1	.146	.186	.195
1988 Salem	A	70	275	86	10	1	0	98	54	25	38	0	32	0	6	2	11	6	.65	5	.313	.394	.356
1989 Vero Beach	A	132	484	128	11	1	1	144	74	37	33	0	21	3	5	3	18	13	.58	19	.264	.314	.298
1990 San Antonio	AA	69	194	41	4	2	0	49	20	14	8	0	24	0	7	2	2	1	.67	7	.211	.240	.253
1991 Vero Beach	A	20	66	16	2	0	0	18	6	3	1	0	3	0	1	1	2	1	.67	1	.242	.250	.273
San Antonio	AA	16	65	21	2	0	0	23	6	9	2	0	7	0	1	1	2	3	.40	2	.323	.338	.354
Albuquerque	AAA	66	215	63	5	5	0	78	34	29	14	1	13	0	8	4	4	1	.80	3	.293	.330	.363
1992 Albuquerque	AAA	122	395	128	18	1	0	148	47	34	22	5	7	5	10	4	5	3	.63	17	.324	.364	.375
1993 Albuquerque	AAA	134	465	129	25	0	4	166	75	55	29	1	18	3	8	5	3	5	.38	11	.277	.321	.357
1994 Albuquerque	AAA	61	208	69	8	0	1	80	29	22	9	1	9	0	2	1	2	3	.40	7	.332	.358	.385
1995 Albuquerque	AAA	15	31	4	1	0	0	5	2	1	1	0	2	1	0	0	0	0	.00	0	.129	.182	.161
Harrisburg	AA	29	95	21	3	1	0	26	12	7	11	0	8	1	6	1	1	0	1.00	2	.221	.306	.274
Ottawa	AAA	19	54	11	4	0	0	15	2	6	2	0	4	1	1	0	0	0	.00	2	.204	.246	.278
1992 Los Angeles	NL	10	20	3	1	0	0	4	1	0	1	0	2	1	0	0	0	0	.00	0	.150	.227	.200
1993 Los Angeles	NL	8	18	9	1	0	0	10	0	3	0	0	2	0	0	0	0	0	.00	0	.500	.500	.556
1994 Los Angeles	NL	40	116	26	3	1	0	31	2	11	9	1	5	2	5	0	0	0	.00	4	.224	.291	.267
9 Min. YEARS		783	2629	729	97	11	6	866	366	246	173	8	155	15	56	24	50	37	.57	79	.277	.323	.329
3 Maj. YEARS		58	154	38	5	1	0	45	3	14	10	1	9	3	5	0	0	0	.00	4	.247	.305	.292

Mike Bovee

Pitches: Right **Bats:** Right **Pos:** P   **Ht:** 5'10" **Wt:** 200 **Born:** 8/21/73 **Age:** 22

			HOW MUCH HE PITCHED						WHAT HE GAVE UP												THE RESULTS					
Year Team	Lg	G	GS	CG	GF	IP	BFP	H	R	ER	HR	SH	SF	HB	TBB	IBB	SO	WP	Bk	W	L	Pct.	ShO	Sv	ERA
1991 Royals	R	11	11	0	0	61.2	251	52	19	14	1	0	1	1	12	0	76	4	0	3	1	.750	0	0	2.04
1992 Appleton	A	28	24	1	0	149.1	618	143	85	59	8	4	9	3	41	1	120	13	3	9	10	.474	0	0	3.56
1993 Rockford	A	20	20	2	0	109	469	118	58	51	1	4	4	6	30	0	111	15	0	5	9	.357	0	0	4.21
1994 Wilmington	A	28	26	0	1	169.2	675	149	58	50	10	4	3	4	32	0	154	8	1	13	4	.765	0	0	2.65
1995 Wichita	AA	20	20	1	0	114	486	118	60	53	12	2	4	2	43	0	72	4	0	8	6	.571	0	0	4.18
5 Min. YEARS		107	101	4	1	603.2	2499	580	280	227	32	14	21	16	158	1	533	44	4	38	30	.559	0	0	3.38

Brent Bowers

Bats: Left **Throws:** Right **Pos:** OF   **Ht:** 6'3" **Wt:** 200 **Born:** 5/2/71 **Age:** 25

							BATTING									BASERUNNING				PERCENTAGES		
Year Team	Lg	G	AB	H	2B	3B	HR	TB	R	RBI	TBB	IBB	SO	HBP	SH	SF	SB	CS	SB%	GDP	Avg	OBP	SLG
1989 Medicne Hat	R	54	207	46	2	2	0	52	16	13	19	0	55	0	0	1	6	2	.75	5	.222	.286	.251
1990 Medicne Hat	R	60	212	58	7	3	3	80	30	27	31	0	35	1	1	0	19	8	.70	2	.274	.369	.377
1991 Myrtle Bch	A	120	402	101	8	4	2	123	53	44	31	1	76	2	9	4	35	12	.74	11	.251	.305	.306
1992 Dunedin	A	128	524	133	10	3	3	158	74	46	34	0	99	3	8	1	31	15	.67	4	.254	.302	.302
1993 Knoxville	AA	141	577	143	23	4	5	189	60	43	21	1	121	3	13	0	36	19	.65	5	.248	.278	.328
1994 Knoxville	AA	127	472	129	18	11	4	181	52	49	20	4	75	1	7	2	15	8	.65	8	.273	.303	.383
1995 Syracuse	AAA	111	305	77	16	5	5	118	38	26	10	0	57	1	1	1	5	1	.83	3	.252	.278	.387
7 Min. YEARS		741	2699	687	84	32	22	901	326	248	166	6	518	11	39	9	147	65	.69	38	.255	.299	.334

Jim Bowie

Bats: Left **Throws:** Left **Pos:** 1B   **Ht:** 6'0" **Wt:** 205 **Born:** 2/17/65 **Age:** 31

							BATTING									BASERUNNING				PERCENTAGES		
Year Team	Lg	G	AB	H	2B	3B	HR	TB	R	RBI	TBB	IBB	SO	HBP	SH	SF	SB	CS	SB%	GDP	Avg	OBP	SLG
1986 Bellingham	A	72	274	76	12	1	5	105	47	68	38	1	53	2	0	1	4	1	.80	6	.277	.357	.383
1987 Wausau	A	127	448	119	26	0	10	175	56	66	56	3	67	3	3	5	8	3	.73	14	.266	.348	.391
1988 San Bernrdo	A	139	529	154	28	0	15	227	76	102	58	5	84	1	1	10	8	5	.62	14	.291	.356	.429
1989 Calgary	AAA	100	336	90	12	0	4	114	28	37	17	0	45	2	0	4	2	2	.50	6	.268	.304	.339
Williamsprt	AA	11	42	11	5	0	0	16	3	1	5	0	7	0	0	0	0	0	.00	0	.262	.340	.381
1990 Williamsprt	AA	128	446	122	18	0	5	155	45	48	51	6	47	3	1	3	0	2	.00	15	.274	.350	.348
1991 Jacksonvlle	AA	123	448	139	25	0	10	194	51	67	36	2	67	0	1	6	3	3	.50	16	.310	.357	.433
Calgary	AAA	14	50	17	3	0	1	23	9	7	2	0	8	0	0	0	0	0	.00	1	.340	.365	.460
1992 Calgary	AAA	49	172	41	6	0	1	50	17	21	23	3	25	1	0	3	3	1	.75	6	.238	.320	.291
Jacksonvlle	AA	80	276	79	16	0	10	125	36	43	41	2	40	3	1	2	0	1	.00	8	.286	.382	.453
1993 Huntsville	AA	138	501	167	33	1	14	244	77	101	56	8	52	0	1	8	8	3	.73	17	.333	.395	.487
1994 Tacoma	AAA	109	411	129	24	2	8	181	66	66	51	5	38	2	0	6	2	2	.50	17	.314	.387	.440
1995 Edmonton	AAA	141	531	142	26	2	8	181	69	70	54	7	51	2	4	6	4	1	.80	19	.267	.334	.341

	Lg	G	AB	H	2B	3B	HR	TB	R	RBI	TBB	IBB	SO	HBP	SH	SF	SB	CS	SB%	GDP	Avg	OBP	SLG
1994 Oakland	AL	6	14	3	0	0	0	3	0	0	0	0	2	0	1	0	0	0	.00	1	.214	.214	.214
10 Min. YEARS		1231	4464	1286	234	6	86	1790	580	693	486	42	584	19	12	64	42	24	.64	139	.288	.356	.401

Tyrone Boykin

Bats: Right **Throws:** Right **Pos:** OF   **Ht:** 6'0" **Wt:** 195 **Born:** 4/25/68 **Age:** 28

		BATTING															BASERUNNING				PERCENTAGES		
Year Team	Lg	G	AB	H	2B	3B	HR	TB	R	RBI	TBB	IBB	SO	HBP	SH	SF	SB	CS	SB%	GDP	Avg	OBP	SLG
1991 Boise	A	52	162	34	8	2	4	58	26	22	33	0	54	0	1	2	4	1	.80	4	.210	.340	.358
1992 Quad City	A	119	383	87	18	1	7	128	77	43	93	1	108	4	2	6	20	12	.63	5	.227	.379	.334
1993 Palm Spring	A	77	286	93	13	1	3	117	48	40	51	0	52	0	2	3	22	8	.73	13	.325	.424	.409
Midland	AA	35	132	37	3	3	2	52	29	17	17	0	17	2	0	2	1	0	1.00	8	.280	.366	.394
1994 Midland	AA	119	426	100	21	3	5	142	67	63	73	1	78	1	5	8	9	10	.47	9	.235	.343	.333
1995 Midland	AA	62	210	57	11	3	7	95	34	25	21	1	36	0	1	3	2	1	.67	3	.271	.333	.452
5 Min. YEARS		464	1599	408	74	13	28	592	281	210	288	3	345	7	11	24	58	32	.64	42	.255	.367	.370

Marshall Boze

Pitches: Right **Bats:** Right **Pos:** P   **Ht:** 6'1" **Wt:** 212 **Born:** 5/23/71 **Age:** 25

		HOW MUCH HE PITCHED						WHAT HE GAVE UP									THE RESULTS					
Year Team	Lg	G	GS	CG	GF	IP	BFP	H	R	ER	HR	SH	SF	HB	TBB	IBB	SO	WP	Bk	W	L	Pct.	ShO	Sv	ERA
1990 Brewers	R	15	0	0	5	20.2	104	28	22	17	0	0	0	3	13	1	17	3	0	1	0	1.000	0	3	7.40
1991 Beloit	A	3	1	0	2	6.1	34	8	4	4	0	0	0	0	7	0	4	0	1	0	1	.000	0	0	5.68
Helena	R	16	8	0	1	56	271	59	49	43	3	2	3	3	47	0	64	6	2	3	3	.500	0	0	6.91
1992 Beloit	A	26	22	4	4	146.1	635	117	59	46	6	6	2	12	82	4	126	18	1	13	7	.650	1	0	2.83
1993 Stockton	A	14	14	0	0	88.1	379	82	36	26	4	2	4	7	41	2	54	6	0	7	2	.778	0	0	2.65
El Paso	AA	13	13	1	0	86.1	357	78	36	26	5	0	3	4	32	2	48	6	0	10	3	.769	0	0	2.71
1994 New Orleans	AAA	29	29	2	0	171.1	746	182	101	90	18	9	4	10	74	2	81	16	1	6	10	.375	0	0	4.73
1995 New Orleans	AAA	23	19	1	1	111.2	495	134	65	53	10	2	2	2	45	1	47	6	1	3	9	.250	0	1	4.27
6 Min. YEARS		139	106	8	13	687	3021	688	372	305	46	21	18	41	341	12	441	61	6	43	35	.551	1	4	4.00

Troy Bradford

Pitches: Right **Bats:** Right **Pos:** P   **Ht:** 6'2" **Wt:** 200 **Born:** 2/25/69 **Age:** 27

		HOW MUCH HE PITCHED						WHAT HE GAVE UP									THE RESULTS					
Year Team	Lg	G	GS	CG	GF	IP	BFP	H	R	ER	HR	SH	SF	HB	TBB	IBB	SO	WP	Bk	W	L	Pct.	ShO	Sv	ERA
1990 Geneva	A	7	7	1	0	45.1	167	27	9	9	2	0	1	0	14	0	54	1	1	5	0	1.000	0	0	1.79
Peoria	A	8	8	1	0	52.1	225	51	30	26	2	0	5	1	19	0	35	6	1	2	6	.250	0	0	4.47
1991 Winston-Sal	A	19	19	4	0	118	496	103	44	34	10	2	2	2	48	2	72	10	0	9	5	.643	2	0	2.59
1992 Peoria	A	6	6	0	0	39.1	167	33	19	13	1	2	1	0	20	0	31	4	0	2	2	.500	0	0	2.97
Charlotte	AA	2	2	0	0	11.1	50	16	5	4	0	0	0	0	3	0	8	1	0	1	1	.500	0	0	3.18
Winston-Sal	A	6	4	1	0	26.2	115	25	21	20	3	1	1	1	14	0	7	2	0	2	4	.333	0	0	6.75
1993 Daytona	A	11	10	0	0	53.2	243	58	35	33	7	1	3	3	27	1	39	3	0	3	5	.375	0	0	5.53
1994 Orlando	AA	18	13	1	2	72.1	323	74	45	40	8	5	2	1	42	4	48	4	0	3	9	.250	1	0	4.98
Daytona	A	9	9	0	0	40.1	191	45	31	28	3	1	2	1	26	0	23	6	0	1	3	.250	0	0	6.25
1995 Orlando	AA	4	4	0	0	22	92	22	13	12	3	1	0	1	9	0	6	4	0	1	1	.500	0	0	4.91
6 Min. YEARS		90	82	8	2	481.1	2069	454	252	219	39	13	17	10	222	7	323	41	2	29	36	.446	3	0	4.09

Derek Brandow

Pitches: Right **Bats:** Right **Pos:** P   **Ht:** 6'1" **Wt:** 200 **Born:** 1/25/70 **Age:** 26

		HOW MUCH HE PITCHED						WHAT HE GAVE UP									THE RESULTS					
Year Team	Lg	G	GS	CG	GF	IP	BFP	H	R	ER	HR	SH	SF	HB	TBB	IBB	SO	WP	Bk	W	L	Pct.	ShO	Sv	ERA
1992 St. Cathrns	A	22	2	0	9	58.1	249	51	16	6	3	3	2	2	26	0	74	5	1	5	2	.714	0	3	2.47
1993 Hagerstown	A	40	1	0	27	76.1	340	76	38	31	5	2	2	4	34	1	62	6	0	4	5	.444	0	6	3.66
1994 Dunedin	A	29	21	0	3	140.1	593	122	59	50	6	4	5	2	58	0	123	11	1	7	6	.538	0	1	3.21
1995 Knoxville	AA	25	21	1	1	107	466	95	60	51	13	1	8	6	50	1	106	9	0	5	6	.455	0	1	4.29
4 Min. YEARS		116	45	1	40	382	1648	344	180	148	30	10	18	14	168	2	365	31	2	21	19	.525	0	11	3.49

Cliff Brannon

Pitches: Right **Bats:** Right **Pos:** P   **Ht:** 6'6" **Wt:** 190 **Born:** 7/28/67 **Age:** 28

		HOW MUCH HE PITCHED						WHAT HE GAVE UP									THE RESULTS					
Year Team	Lg	G	GS	CG	GF	IP	BFP	H	R	ER	HR	SH	SF	HB	TBB	IBB	SO	WP	Bk	W	L	Pct.	ShO	Sv	ERA
1989 Hamilton	A	2	0	0	2	2	9	3	2	2	0	0	0	0	0	0	1	0	0	0	0	.000	0	0	9.00
1990 Savannah	A	6	0	0	5	6.1	28	5	2	2	0	0	0	0	5	0	7	0	0	0	0	.000	0	0	2.84
1991 Arkansas	AA	2	0	0	2	2.2	16	3	2	2	0	0	0	1	4	1	3	1	0	1	0	1.000	0	0	6.75
1995 Shreveport	AA	3	1	0	0	10	47	13	7	6	0	1	0	0	4	0	7	2	2	0	0	.000	0	0	5.40
4 Min. YEARS		13	1	0	9	21	100	24	13	12	0	1	0	1	13	1	18	3	2	1	0	1.000	0	0	5.14

Scott Bream

Bats: Both **Throws:** Right **Pos:** 2B   **Ht:** 6'1" **Wt:** 170 **Born:** 11/4/70 **Age:** 25

		BATTING															BASERUNNING				PERCENTAGES		
Year Team	Lg	G	AB	H	2B	3B	HR	TB	R	RBI	TBB	IBB	SO	HBP	SH	SF	SB	CS	SB%	GDP	Avg	OBP	SLG
1989 Padres	R	28	97	17	3	1	0	22	15	8	18	0	22	1	0	0	9	5	.64	2	.175	.310	.227
1990 Charlstn-Sc	A	4	14	1	0	0	0	1	2	0	4	0	7	0	1	0	1	0	1.00	0	.071	.278	.071
1991 Charlstn-Sc	A	52	174	24	2	1	0	28	17	7	20	0	61	1	1	1	10	6	.63	1	.138	.230	.161
Spokane	A	68	262	56	4	5	0	70	37	26	25	1	57	5	3	3	16	7	.70	5	.214	.292	.267
1992 Waterloo	A	124	392	90	9	6	1	114	50	29	33	2	126	2	4	0	17	9	.65	4	.230	.293	.291

1993 Rancho Cuca	A	113	405	114	15	6	4	153	70	52	74	3	85	2	4	3	30	14	.68	10	.281	.393	.378
1994 Wichita	AA	109	333	100	8	3	5	129	40	35	42	4	81	3	3	2	18	8	.69	4	.300	.382	.387
1995 Las Vegas	AAA	87	303	73	7	1	0	82	33	15	35	1	59	3	2	0	7	5	.58	7	.241	.326	.271
Iowa	AAA	29	82	13	1	0	2	20	10	9	11	0	20	0	3	0	1	0	1.00	1	.159	.258	.244
7 Min. YEARS		614	2062	488	49	23	12	619	274	181	262	9	518	17	21	9	109	54	.67	34	.237	.326	.300

Brent Brede

Bats: Left **Throws:** Left **Pos:** OF **Ht:** 6'4" **Wt:** 175 **Born:** 9/13/71 **Age:** 24

				BATTING												BASERUNNING				PERCENTAGES		
Year Team	Lg	G	AB	H	2B	3B	HR	TB	R	RBI	TBB	IBB	SO	HBP	SH	SF	SB	CS	SB%	GDP	Avg	OBP	SLG
1990 Elizabethtn	R	46	143	35	5	0	0	40	39	14	30	0	29	0	0	1	14	0	1.00	2	.245	.374	.280
1991 Kenosha	A	53	156	30	3	2	0	37	12	10	16	0	31	0	5	3	4	5	.44	8	.192	.263	.237
Elizabethtn	R	68	253	61	13	0	3	83	24	36	30	2	48	1	2	4	13	4	.76	7	.241	.319	.328
1992 Kenosha	A	110	363	88	15	0	0	103	44	29	53	1	77	4	4	3	10	12	.45	8	.242	.343	.284
1993 Fort Myers	A	53	182	60	10	1	0	72	27	27	32	3	19	1	2	0	8	4	.67	6	.330	.433	.396
1994 Fort Myers	A	116	419	110	21	4	2	145	49	45	63	3	60	0	3	1	18	4	.82	7	.263	.358	.346
1995 New Britain	AA	134	449	123	28	2	3	164	71	39	69	2	82	3	6	5	14	6	.70	13	.274	.371	.365
6 Min. YEARS		580	1965	507	95	9	8	644	266	200	293	11	346	9	22	17	81	35	.70	51	.258	.354	.328

Nevin Brewer

Pitches: Right **Bats:** Right **Pos:** P **Ht:** 6'4" **Wt:** 195 **Born:** 8/1/71 **Age:** 24

		HOW MUCH HE PITCHED						WHAT HE GAVE UP									THE RESULTS					
Year Team	Lg	G	GS	CG	GF	IP	BFP	H	R	ER	HR	SH	SF	HB	TBB	IBB	SO	WP	Bk	W	L	Pct.	ShO	Sv	ERA
1993 Eugene	A	10	8	0	0	37	148	26	7	4	0	0	0	0	17	0	31	3	0	3	0	1.000	0	0	0.97
1994 Rockford	A	44	0	0	40	64.1	250	43	9	7	2	2	1	3	19	0	69	3	0	7	1	.875	0	20	0.98
1995 Wilmington	A	17	0	0	13	29	120	19	4	3	0	3	0	1	15	2	20	3	0	1	1	.500	0	8	0.93
Wichita	AA	19	4	1	4	50	218	54	31	22	6	0	1	1	21	1	21	9	1	3	2	.600	1	0	3.96
3 Min. YEARS		90	12	1	57	180.1	736	142	51	36	8	5	2	5	72	3	141	18	1	14	4	.778	1	28	1.80

Rod Brewer

Bats: Left **Throws:** Left **Pos:** 1B **Ht:** 6'3" **Wt:** 218 **Born:** 2/24/66 **Age:** 30

				BATTING												BASERUNNING				PERCENTAGES		
Year Team	Lg	G	AB	H	2B	3B	HR	TB	R	RBI	TBB	IBB	SO	HBP	SH	SF	SB	CS	SB%	GDP	Avg	OBP	SLG
1987 Johnson Cty	R	67	238	60	11	2	10	105	33	42	36	5	40	3	0	2	2	2	.50	4	.252	.355	.441
1988 Springfield	A	133	457	136	25	2	8	189	57	64	63	7	52	5	1	4	6	4	.60	22	.298	.386	.414
1989 Arkansas	AA	128	470	130	25	2	10	189	71	93	46	3	46	7	0	3	2	3	.40	8	.277	.348	.402
1990 Louisville	AAA	144	514	129	15	5	12	190	60	83	54	7	62	9	0	6	0	2	.00	9	.251	.329	.370
1991 Louisville	AAA	104	382	86	21	1	8	133	39	52	35	1	57	6	0	1	4	0	1.00	10	.225	.300	.348
1992 Louisville	AAA	120	423	122	20	2	18	200	57	86	49	6	60	5	0	1	0	3	.00	8	.288	.368	.473
1995 Phoenix	AAA	15	45	11	4	0	1	18	8	8	3	0	10	5	0	2	1	1	.50	1	.244	.345	.400
Charlotte	AAA	69	236	76	15	1	9	120	31	55	33	3	45	5	0	5	0	0	.00	3	.322	.409	.508
1990 St. Louis	NL	14	25	6	1	0	0	7	4	2	0	0	4	0	0	0	0	0	.00	1	.240	.240	.280
1991 St. Louis	NL	19	13	1	0	0	0	1	0	1	0	0	5	0	0	0	0	0	.00	0	.077	.077	.077
1992 St. Louis	NL	29	103	31	6	0	0	37	11	10	8	0	12	1	0	1	0	1	.00	1	.301	.354	.359
1993 St. Louis	NL	110	147	42	8	0	2	56	15	20	17	5	26	1	1	2	1	0	1.00	5	.286	.359	.381
7 Min. YEARS		780	2765	750	136	15	76	1144	356	483	319	32	372	45	1	24	15	15	.50	65	.271	.353	.414
4 Maj. YEARS		172	288	80	15	0	2	101	30	33	25	5	47	2	1	3	1	1	.50	7	.278	.336	.351

Kary Bridges

Bats: Left **Throws:** Right **Pos:** 2B **Ht:** 5'10" **Wt:** 165 **Born:** 10/27/71 **Age:** 24

				BATTING												BASERUNNING				PERCENTAGES		
Year Team	Lg	G	AB	H	2B	3B	HR	TB	R	RBI	TBB	IBB	SO	HBP	SH	SF	SB	CS	SB%	GDP	Avg	OBP	SLG
1993 Quad City	A	65	263	74	9	0	3	92	37	24	31	1	18	2	1	3	15	10	.60	7	.281	.358	.350
1994 Quad City	A	117	447	135	20	4	1	166	66	53	38	3	29	3	8	4	14	11	.56	9	.302	.358	.371
1995 Jackson	AA	118	418	126	22	4	3	165	56	43	48	3	18	0	6	4	10	12	.45	12	.301	.370	.395
3 Min. YEARS		300	1128	335	51	8	7	423	159	120	117	7	65	5	15	11	39	33	.54	28	.297	.362	.375

Stoney Briggs

Bats: Right **Throws:** Right **Pos:** OF **Ht:** 6'2" **Wt:** 215 **Born:** 12/26/71 **Age:** 24

				BATTING												BASERUNNING				PERCENTAGES		
Year Team	Lg	G	AB	H	2B	3B	HR	TB	R	RBI	TBB	IBB	SO	HBP	SH	SF	SB	CS	SB%	GDP	Avg	OBP	SLG
1991 Medcne Hat	R	64	236	70	8	0	8	102	45	29	18	0	62	2	0	2	9	5	.64	2	.297	.349	.432
1992 Myrtle Bch	A	136	514	123	18	5	11	184	75	41	43	0	156	8	6	2	33	14	.70	6	.239	.307	.358
1993 Waterloo	A	125	421	108	15	5	9	160	57	55	30	1	103	12	4	5	21	8	.72	9	.257	.321	.380
1994 Rancho Cuca	A	121	417	112	22	2	17	189	63	76	54	1	124	9	2	7	14	13	.52	7	.269	.359	.453
1995 Memphis	AA	118	385	95	14	7	8	147	60	46	40	5	133	10	1	3	17	8	.68	13	.247	.331	.382
5 Min. YEARS		564	1973	508	77	19	53	782	300	247	185	7	578	41	13	19	94	48	.66	31	.257	.331	.396

Greg Briley

Bats: Left **Throws:** Right **Pos:** OF **Ht:** 5'9" **Wt:** 170 **Born:** 5/24/65 **Age:** 31

				BATTING												BASERUNNING				PERCENTAGES		
Year Team	Lg	G	AB	H	2B	3B	HR	TB	R	RBI	TBB	IBB	SO	HBP	SH	SF	SB	CS	SB%	GDP	Avg	OBP	SLG
1986 Bellingham	A	63	218	65	12	4	7	106	52	46	50	1	29	3	0	7	26	5	.84	1	.298	.424	.486
1987 Chattanooga	AA	137	539	148	21	5	7	200	81	61	41	0	58	2	2	8	34	14	.71	10	.275	.324	.371

Year	Team	Lg	G	AB	H	2B	3B	HR	TB	R	RBI	TBB	IBB	SO	HBP	SH	SF	SB	CS	SB%	GDP	Avg	OBP	SLG
1988	Calgary	AAA	112	445	139	29	9	11	219	74	66	40	5	51	3	2	7	27	10	.73	2	.312	.368	.492
1989	Calgary	AAA	25	94	32	8	1	4	54	27	20	13	1	10	2	0	0	14	2	.88	8	.340	.431	.574
1994	Charlotte	AAA	31	69	13	1	1	1	19	12	7	7	1	15	0	0	2	3	1	.75	1	.188	.256	.275
1995	Indianapols	AAA	46	146	34	8	0	3	51	17	17	22	3	34	0	1	0	9	2	.82	1	.233	.333	.349
	Jacksonvlle	AA	8	23	2	0	0	1	5	2	4	2	0	6	0	0	1	0	1	.00	0	.087	.154	.217
	Toledo	AAA	31	84	20	4	1	1	29	8	7	6	0	25	0	0	0	0	2	.00	3	.238	.289	.345
1988	Seattle	AL	13	36	9	2	0	1	14	6	4	5	1	6	0	0	1	0	1	.00	0	.250	.333	.389
1989	Seattle	AL	115	394	105	22	4	13	174	52	52	39	1	82	5	1	5	11	5	.69	9	.266	.336	.442
1990	Seattle	AL	125	337	83	18	2	5	120	40	29	37	0	48	1	1	4	16	4	.80	6	.246	.319	.356
1991	Seattle	AL	139	381	99	17	3	2	128	39	26	27	0	51	0	1	3	23	11	.68	7	.260	.307	.336
1992	Seattle	AL	86	200	55	10	0	5	80	18	12	4	0	31	1	0	2	9	2	.82	4	.275	.290	.400
1993	Florida	NL	120	170	33	6	0	3	48	17	12	12	0	42	1	1	1	6	2	.75	5	.194	.250	.282
	6 Min. YEARS		453	1618	453	83	21	35	683	273	228	181	11	228	10	5	25	113	37	.75	26	.280	.351	.422
	6 Maj. YEARS		598	1518	384	75	9	29	564	172	135	124	2	260	8	4	16	65	25	.72	31	.253	.310	.372

Brad Brink

Pitches: Right **Bats:** Right **Pos:** P   **Ht:** 6' 2" **Wt:** 208 **Born:** 1/20/65 **Age:** 31

			HOW MUCH HE PITCHED						WHAT HE GAVE UP										THE RESULTS					
Year	Team	Lg	G	GS	CG	GF	IP	BFP	H	R	ER	HR	SH	SF	HB	TBB	IBB	SO	WP	Bk	W	L	Pct.	ShO	Sv	ERA
1986	Reading	AA	5	4	0	0	23.2	107	22	12	10	2	3	1	1	20	2	8	0	0	0	4	.000	0	0	3.80
1987	Clearwater	A	17	17	2	0	94.1	418	99	50	40	5	4	5	2	39	2	64	1	0	4	7	.364	1	0	3.82
	Reading	AA	12	11	1	0	72	308	76	42	40	7	2	4	5	23	2	50	3	2	3	2	.600	1	0	5.00
1988	Maine	AAA	17	17	3	0	86	375	100	43	41	8	2	3	4	21	0	58	4	2	5	5	.500	1	0	4.29
1989	Scranton-Wb	AAA	3	3	0	0	11	49	11	7	5	0	1	1	0	6	0	3	0	0	0	1	.000	0	0	4.09
1991	Spartanburg	A	3	3	1	0	16.1	68	15	3	3	1	0	0	0	5	0	16	1	1	2	1	.667	0	0	1.65
	Clearwater	A	2	2	0	0	13	46	6	1	1	1	1	0	0	3	0	10	0	1	2	0	1.000	0	0	0.69
	Reading	AA	5	5	0	0	34	138	32	14	14	3	2	2	1	6	0	27	1	0	2	2	.500	0	0	3.71
1992	Reading	AA	3	3	0	0	13.2	59	14	6	5	0	1	0	0	3	0	12	0	0	1	1	.500	0	0	3.29
	Scranton-Wb	AAA	17	17	5	0	111.1	454	100	47	43	15	0	1	2	34	0	92	3	0	8	2	.800	2	0	3.48
1993	Scranton-Wb	AAA	18	18	2	0	106.2	445	104	53	50	10	6	0	5	27	1	89	0	0	7	7	.500	2	0	4.22
1994	Phoenix	AAA	23	22	0	0	128	543	140	68	59	16	4	9	3	41	3	79	2	0	7	5	.583	0	0	4.15
1995	Phoenix	AAA	11	9	0	0	44.2	215	55	35	35	3	1	4	2	30	0	33	1	0	2	5	.286	0	0	7.05
	Edmonton	AAA	9	3	0	4	24	112	24	20	13	2	0	1	2	16	3	15	1	0	0	1	.000	0	0	4.88
1992	Philadelphia	NL	8	7	0	0	41.1	187	53	27	19	2	1	0	1	13	2	16	0	0	0	4	.000	0	0	4.14
1993	Philadelphia	NL	2	0	0	1	6	24	3	2	2	1	0	0	0	3	0	8	1	0	0	0	.000	0	0	3.00
1994	San Francisco	NL	4	0	0	2	8.1	32	4	1	1	1	0	0	0	4	1	3	1	0	0	0	.000	0	0	1.08
	9 Min. YEARS		145	134	14	4	778.2	3337	798	401	359	73	27	31	27	274	11	556	17	6	43	43	.500	7	0	4.15
	3 Maj. YEARS		14	7	0	3	55.2	243	60	30	22	4	1	0	1	20	3	27	2	0	0	4	.000	0	0	3.56

Luis Brito

Bats: Both **Throws:** Right **Pos:** SS   **Ht:** 6'0" **Wt:** 155 **Born:** 4/12/71 **Age:** 25

			BATTING															BASERUNNING				PERCENTAGES		
Year	Team	Lg	G	AB	H	2B	3B	HR	TB	R	RBI	TBB	IBB	SO	HBP	SH	SF	SB	CS	SB%	GDP	Avg	OBP	SLG
1989	Martinsvlle	R	9	16	5	0	0	0	5	1	1	0	0	3	0	0	0	0	0	.00	0	.313	.313	.313
1990	Princeton	R	27	95	23	2	0	0	25	15	4	2	0	11	2	1	0	4	2	.67	1	.242	.273	.263
1991	Martinsvlle	R	31	123	33	5	0	0	38	17	9	5	0	21	2	1	2	5	2	.71	3	.268	.303	.309
	Batavia	A	22	76	24	2	1	0	28	13	10	6	0	8	0	2	0	9	3	.75	1	.316	.366	.368
1992	Spartanburg	A	34	105	23	1	1	0	26	11	9	4	0	17	0	1	0	7	8	.47	1	.219	.248	.248
	Clearwater	A	65	188	41	4	0	0	45	18	11	5	0	21	1	6	1	4	7	.36	0	.218	.241	.239
1993	Spartanburg	A	127	467	146	16	4	0	170	56	33	11	0	47	1	8	3	9	12	.43	12	.313	.328	.364
1994	Clearwater	A	31	108	35	4	3	1	48	18	13	2	0	3	0	1	1	2	1	.67	4	.324	.333	.444
	Reading	AA	86	284	63	6	2	3	82	33	21	13	0	38	2	4	2	4	4	.50	4	.222	.259	.289
1995	Reading	AA	2	3	1	0	0	0	1	1	1	0	0	0	0	0	0	1	0	1.00	0	.333	.333	.333
	Clearwater	A	109	383	105	14	3	3	134	42	41	17	0	35	1	5	3	12	5	.71	14	.274	.304	.350
	7 Min. YEARS		543	1848	499	54	14	7	602	225	153	65	0	204	9	29	12	57	44	.56	40	.270	.296	.326

Tilson Brito

Bats: Right **Throws:** Right **Pos:** SS   **Ht:** 6'0" **Wt:** 170 **Born:** 5/28/72 **Age:** 24

			BATTING															BASERUNNING				PERCENTAGES		
Year	Team	Lg	G	AB	H	2B	3B	HR	TB	R	RBI	TBB	IBB	SO	HBP	SH	SF	SB	CS	SB%	GDP	Avg	OBP	SLG
1992	Blue Jays	R	54	189	58	10	4	3	85	36	36	22	1	22	6	0	5	16	8	.67	5	.307	.387	.450
	Knoxville	AA	7	24	5	1	2	0	10	2	2	0	0	9	0	0	0	0	0	.00	0	.208	.208	.417
1993	Dunedin	A	126	465	125	21	3	6	170	80	44	59	0	60	10	10	3	27	16	.63	8	.269	.361	.366
1994	Knoxville	AA	139	476	127	17	7	5	173	61	57	35	2	68	8	9	7	33	12	.73	7	.267	.323	.363
1995	Syracuse	AAA	90	327	79	16	3	7	122	49	32	29	0	69	4	2	1	17	8	.68	6	.242	.310	.373
	4 Min. YEARS		416	1481	394	65	19	21	560	228	171	145	3	228	28	21	16	93	44	.68	26	.266	.340	.378

Chris Brock

Pitches: Right **Bats:** Right **Pos:** P   **Ht:** 6'0" **Wt:** 175 **Born:** 2/5/70 **Age:** 26

			HOW MUCH HE PITCHED						WHAT HE GAVE UP										THE RESULTS					
Year	Team	Lg	G	GS	CG	GF	IP	BFP	H	R	ER	HR	SH	SF	HB	TBB	IBB	SO	WP	Bk	W	L	Pct.	ShO	Sv	ERA
1992	Idaho Falls	R	15	15	1	0	78	333	61	27	20	3	3	2	3	48	0	72	12	8	6	4	.600	0	0	2.31
1993	Macon	A	14	14	1	0	80	333	61	37	24	3	1	0	2	33	0	92	8	1	7	5	.583	0	0	2.70
	Durham	A	12	12	1	0	79	335	63	28	22	7	1	2	5	35	0	67	6	0	5	2	.714	0	0	2.51
1994	Greenville	AA	25	23	2	0	137.1	576	128	68	57	9	4	4	5	47	0	94	8	3	7	6	.538	2	0	3.74

Year	Team	Lg	G	GS	CG	GF	IP	BFP	H	R	ER	HR	SH	SF	HB	TBB	IBB	SO	WP	Bk	W	L	Pct.	ShO	Sv	ERA
1995	Richmond	AAA	22	9	0	5	60	270	68	37	36	2	3	3	1	27	2	43	1	2	2	8	.200	0	0	5.40
	4 Min. YEARS		88	73	5	5	434.1	1847	381	197	159	24	12	11	16	190	2	368	35	14	27	25	.519	2	0	3.29

Russ Brock

Pitches: Right **Bats:** Right **Pos:** P **Ht:** 6'5" **Wt:** 210 **Born:** 10/13/69 **Age:** 26

			HOW MUCH HE PITCHED						WHAT HE GAVE UP												THE RESULTS					
Year	Team	Lg	G	GS	CG	GF	IP	BFP	H	R	ER	HR	SH	SF	HB	TBB	IBB	SO	WP	Bk	W	L	Pct.	ShO	Sv	ERA
1991	Sou. Oregon	A	8	8	1	0	43.1	180	37	19	15	2	1	0	1	12	1	48	4	1	4	0	1.000	1	0	3.12
	Modesto	A	4	4	0	0	27	111	25	15	12	3	1	0	1	6	0	12	1	0	1	2	.333	0	0	4.00
1992	Reno	A	25	23	0	0	90	414	109	61	44	10	1	3	5	34	3	72	3	0	3	10	.231	0	0	4.40
1993	Modesto	A	27	26	1	0	139.1	586	137	69	59	12	2	3	5	44	0	121	4	1	12	4	.750	0	0	3.81
1994	Huntsville	AA	10	9	1	0	64.2	269	58	27	21	4	3	2	2	23	3	49	1	1	2	3	.400	1	0	2.92
	Tacoma	AAA	19	18	1	0	119.2	514	115	61	50	13	2	1	3	54	0	85	0	0	6	8	.429	0	0	3.76
1995	Edmonton	AAA	18	8	0	2	55	266	75	44	42	6	0	3	3	31	4	44	2	1	1	8	.111	0	0	6.87
	5 Min. YEARS		111	96	4	2	539	2340	556	296	243	50	10	12	20	204	11	431	15	4	29	35	.453	2	1	4.06

Tarrik Brock

Bats: Left **Throws:** Left **Pos:** OF **Ht:** 6'3" **Wt:** 170 **Born:** 12/25/73 **Age:** 22

			BATTING													BASERUNNING				PERCENTAGES		
Year	Team	Lg	G	AB	H	2B	3B	HR	TB	R	RBI	TBB	IBB	SO	HBP	SH	SF	SB	CS	SB%	GDP	Avg	OBP	SLG
1991	Bristol	R	55	177	47	7	3	1	63	26	13	22	0	42	3	1	1	14	6	.70	3	.266	.355	.356
1992	Fayettevlle	A	100	271	59	5	4	0	72	35	17	31	1	69	4	5	1	15	10	.60	2	.218	.306	.266
1993	Fayettevlle	A	116	427	92	8	4	3	117	60	47	54	2	108	5	5	4	25	16	.61	5	.215	.308	.274
1994	Lakeland	A	86	331	77	17	14	2	128	43	32	38	2	89	2	2	2	15	6	.71	5	.233	.314	.387
	Trenton	AA	34	115	16	1	4	2	31	12	11	13	0	43	2	1	0	3	3	.50	2	.139	.238	.270
1995	Toledo	AAA	9	31	6	1	0	0	7	4	0	2	0	17	0	0	0	2	2	.50	0	.194	.242	.226
	Jacksonvlle	AA	9	26	3	0	0	0	3	4	2	3	0	14	1	1	0	2	0	1.00	0	.115	.233	.115
	Lakeland	A	28	91	19	3	0	0	22	12	5	12	0	32	0	1	0	5	3	.63	2	.209	.301	.242
	Visalia	A	45	138	31	5	2	1	43	21	15	17	0	52	4	2	0	11	1	.92	2	.225	.327	.312
	5 Min. YEARS		482	1607	350	47	31	9	486	217	142	192	5	466	21	18	8	92	47	.66	21	.218	.308	.302

Eric Brooks

Bats: Right **Throws:** Right **Pos:** C **Ht:** 6'2" **Wt:** 195 **Born:** 5/18/69 **Age:** 27

			BATTING													BASERUNNING				PERCENTAGES		
Year	Team	Lg	G	AB	H	2B	3B	HR	TB	R	RBI	TBB	IBB	SO	HBP	SH	SF	SB	CS	SB%	GDP	Avg	OBP	SLG
1988	St. Cathrns	A	47	152	34	3	1	1	42	10	9	29	0	49	2	0	1	2	5	.29	3	.224	.355	.276
1989	Myrtle Bch	A	75	270	70	7	0	1	80	33	35	32	0	48	2	2	2	2	1	.67	4	.259	.340	.296
1990	Myrtle Bch	A	68	213	56	8	0	3	73	26	22	44	1	34	2	1	1	1	1	.50	7	.263	.392	.343
1991	Dunedin	A	47	133	24	3	0	0	27	7	11	18	0	37	1	0	2	1	1	.50	6	.180	.278	.203
1992	Knoxville	AA	6	8	0	0	0	0	0	0	0	0	0	3	0	0	0	0	0	.00	0	.000	.000	.000
	Dunedin	A	30	82	19	3	0	1	25	7	6	6	1	16	1	0	0	0	0	.00	2	.232	.292	.305
1993	Dunedin	A	43	142	28	4	0	1	35	18	10	17	2	21	3	2	1	1	2	.33	4	.197	.294	.246
1994	Knoxville	AA	57	157	30	7	0	1	40	14	24	20	1	34	3	2	3	0	3	.00	7	.191	.290	.255
1995	Knoxville	AA	21	53	15	3	0	4	30	6	12	12	1	9	3	0	0	0	1	.00	0	.283	.441	.566
	Syracuse	AAA	47	120	23	3	1	0	28	12	5	12	0	27	0	1	0	0	2	.00	2	.192	.265	.233
	8 Min. YEARS		441	1330	299	41	2	12	380	133	134	190	6	278	16	10	7	7	16	.30	35	.225	.327	.286

Jerry Brooks

Bats: Right **Throws:** Right **Pos:** C-OF **Ht:** 6'0" **Wt:** 195 **Born:** 3/23/67 **Age:** 29

			BATTING													BASERUNNING				PERCENTAGES		
Year	Team	Lg	G	AB	H	2B	3B	HR	TB	R	RBI	TBB	IBB	SO	HBP	SH	SF	SB	CS	SB%	GDP	Avg	OBP	SLG
1988	Great Falls	R	68	285	99	21	3	8	150	63	60	24	0	25	4	0	9	7	4	.64	9	.347	.394	.526
1989	Bakersfield	A	141	565	164	39	1	16	253	70	87	25	0	79	6	0	8	9	6	.60	10	.290	.323	.448
1990	San Antonio	AA	106	391	118	19	0	9	164	52	58	26	4	39	4	1	5	5	8	.38	7	.302	.347	.419
1991	Albuquerque	AAA	125	429	126	20	7	13	199	64	82	29	5	49	6	1	4	4	3	.57	14	.294	.344	.464
1992	Albuquerque	AAA	129	467	124	36	1	14	204	77	78	39	1	68	4	0	7	3	2	.60	9	.266	.323	.437
1993	Albuquerque	AAA	116	421	145	28	4	11	214	67	71	21	2	44	2	3	7	3	4	.43	11	.344	.373	.508
1994	Albuquerque	AAA	115	390	125	23	1	16	198	76	79	31	3	34	5	0	3	4	1	.80	13	.321	.375	.508
1995	Indianapols	AAA	90	325	92	19	2	14	157	41	52	22	0	38	5	0	3	3	1	.75	16	.283	.335	.483
1993	Los Angeles	NL	9	9	2	1	0	1	6	2	1	0	0	2	0	0	0	0	0	.00	0	.222	.222	.667
	8 Min. YEARS		890	3273	993	205	19	101	1539	510	567	217	15	376	36	5	46	38	29	.57	89	.303	.349	.470

Wes Brooks

Pitches: Right **Bats:** Right **Pos:** P **Ht:** 6'3" **Wt:** 200 **Born:** 1/11/72 **Age:** 24

			HOW MUCH HE PITCHED						WHAT HE GAVE UP												THE RESULTS					
Year	Team	Lg	G	GS	CG	GF	IP	BFP	H	R	ER	HR	SH	SF	HB	TBB	IBB	SO	WP	Bk	W	L	Pct.	ShO	Sv	ERA
1992	Red Sox	R	14	11	1	1	71.1	307	78	40	28	1	0	6	2	21	0	57	1	2	3	5	.375	0	1	3.53
1993	Ft. Laud	A	19	18	4	0	127.1	536	124	62	55	7	4	2	2	42	0	85	4	1	8	5	.615	3	0	3.89
1994	Lynchburg	A	28	28	4	0	172.2	751	176	104	92	19	2	8	6	64	3	117	5	4	12	12	.500	1	0	4.80
1995	Trenton	AA	29	23	5	0	161.2	670	149	87	74	17	4	7	11	43	0	85	5	6	5	11	.313	0	0	4.12
	4 Min. YEARS		90	80	14	1	533	2264	527	293	249	44	10	23	21	170	3	344	15	13	28	33	.459	4	1	4.20

E.J. Brophy

Bats: Right Throws: Right Pos: C Ht: 6'3" Wt: 210 Born: 4/17/70 Age: 26

Year Team	Lg	G	AB	H	2B	3B	HR	TB	R	RBI	TBB	IBB	SO	HBP	SH	SF	SB	CS	SB%	GDP	Avg	OBP	SLG
1992 Martinsvlle	R	35	109	36	7	0	1	46	11	17	11	0	11	4	3	2	0	0	.00	4	.330	.405	.422
Spartanburg	A	25	81	19	0	0	0	19	3	6	2	0	14	3	4	0	0	2	.00	0	.235	.279	.235
1993 Spartanburg	A	51	162	30	4	0	2	40	12	14	12	0	27	4	3	0	0	1	.00	8	.185	.258	.247
1994 Clearwater	A	49	126	23	3	0	3	35	17	17	20	0	24	2	3	1	0	0	.00	3	.183	.302	.278
1995 Reading	AA	2	4	2	1	0	0	3	0	0	0	0	1	0	0	0	0	0	.00	0	.500	.500	.750
Scranton-Wb	AAA	34	65	13	2	0	1	18	7	6	8	1	15	0	3	0	0	0	.00	3	.200	.288	.277
4 Min. YEARS		196	547	123	17	0	7	161	50	60	53	1	92	13	16	3	0	3	.00	18	.225	.307	.294

Jason Brosnan

Pitches: Left Bats: Left Pos: P Ht: 6'1" Wt: 190 Born: 1/26/68 Age: 28

		HOW MUCH HE PITCHED						WHAT HE GAVE UP												THE RESULTS					
Year Team	Lg	G	GS	CG	GF	IP	BFP	H	R	ER	HR	SH	SF	HB	TBB	IBB	SO	WP	Bk	W	L	Pct.	ShO	Sv	ERA
1989 Great Falls	R	13	13	0	0	67	294	41	24	19	1	1	1	3	55	0	89	10	4	6	2	.750	0	0	2.55
1990 Bakersfield	A	26	25	0	0	136	607	113	63	47	4	3	4	7	91	1	157	7	2	12	4	.750	0	0	3.11
1991 San Antonio	AA	2	2	0	0	7.2	49	15	15	15	2	0	0	0	11	0	8	0	0	0	1	.000	0	0	17.61
Vero Beach	A	11	9	0	0	36.1	164	34	27	23	2	1	2	2	21	0	25	5	0	1	2	.333	0	0	5.70
1992 Albuquerque	AAA	8	0	0	3	8.2	44	13	9	8	2	1	0	1	4	0	12	2	0	0	0	.000	0	1	8.31
San Antonio	AA	8	8	0	0	32.1	163	44	33	28	9	2	2	1	21	1	27	4	0	1	7	.125	0	0	7.79
Vero Beach	A	18	8	2	3	58	255	69	32	30	2	2	1	2	26	2	51	11	1	3	4	.429	0	0	4.66
1993 Vero Beach	A	23	0	0	9	25.2	127	30	22	13	1	1	1	1	19	2	32	4	0	2	2	.000	0	1	4.56
Bakersfield	A	9	6	0	1	36.1	161	36	20	14	2	1	1	2	15	0	34	4	0	4	1	.800	0	0	3.47
San Antonio	AA	3	3	0	0	20.1	83	21	11	10	1	0	0	0	7	0	10	1	0	0	2	.000	0	0	4.43
1994 San Antonio	AA	17	1	0	8	30.2	141	34	16	12	3	0	1	2	12	1	29	3	0	2	3	.400	0	0	3.52
Albuquerque	AAA	24	7	0	5	61.2	275	75	36	36	4	2	1	0	30	0	43	3	2	2	4	.333	0	1	5.25
1995 Albuquerque	AAA	23	1	0	11	31	128	30	16	15	3	0	2	0	9	1	18	0	1	2	0	1.000	0	2	4.35
San Antonio	AA	19	0	0	7	22.2	94	24	9	9	1	1	0	0	4	0	21	1	0	1	0	1.000	0	0	3.57
7 Min. YEARS		204	83	2	47	574.1	2585	579	333	279	37	15	16	21	325	8	556	55	10	34	32	.515	0	8	4.37

Scott Brow

Pitches: Right Bats: Right Pos: P Ht: 6'3" Wt: 200 Born: 3/17/69 Age: 27

		HOW MUCH HE PITCHED						WHAT HE GAVE UP												THE RESULTS					
Year Team	Lg	G	GS	CG	GF	IP	BFP	H	R	ER	HR	SH	SF	HB	TBB	IBB	SO	WP	Bk	W	L	Pct.	ShO	Sv	ERA
1990 St. Cathrns	A	9	7	0	0	39.2	165	34	18	10	2	2	0	2	11	0	39	4	0	3	1	.750	0	0	2.27
1991 Dunedin	A	15	12	0	1	69.2	306	73	50	37	5	3	3	2	28	1	31	2	5	3	7	.300	0	0	4.78
1992 Dunedin	A	25	25	3	0	170.2	690	143	53	46	8	4	5	7	44	2	107	3	3	14	2	.875	1	0	2.43
1993 Knoxville	AA	3	3	1	0	19	74	13	8	7	1	1	0	0	9	0	12	2	0	1	2	.333	0	0	3.32
Syracuse	AAA	20	19	2	0	121.1	510	119	63	59	8	3	8	6	37	1	64	4	2	6	8	.429	0	0	4.38
1994 Syracuse	AAA	14	13	1	0	79.1	346	77	45	38	9	1	2	3	38	0	30	2	0	5	3	.625	1	0	4.31
1995 Syracuse	AAA	11	5	0	0	31	164	52	39	31	7	2	3	1	18	1	14	1	0	1	5	.167	0	0	9.00
1993 Toronto	AL	6	3	0	1	18	83	19	15	12	2	1	2	1	10	1	7	0	0	1	1	.500	0	0	6.00
1994 Toronto	AL	18	0	0	9	29	141	34	27	19	4	1	2	1	19	2	15	6	0	0	3	.000	0	2	5.90
6 Min. YEARS		97	84	7	2	530.2	2255	511	276	228	42	16	22	21	185	5	297	18	10	33	28	.541	2	0	3.87
2 Maj. YEARS		24	3	0	10	47	224	53	42	31	6	2	4	2	29	3	22	6	0	1	4	.200	0	2	5.94

Adam Brown

Bats: Left Throws: Right Pos: C Ht: 6'0" Wt: 203 Born: 8/10/66 Age: 29

Year Team	Lg	G	AB	H	2B	3B	HR	TB	R	RBI	TBB	IBB	SO	HBP	SH	SF	SB	CS	SB%	GDP	Avg	OBP	SLG
1986 Great Falls	R	64	209	63	13	1	8	102	30	41	37	1	62	4	0	3	6	5	.55	7	.301	.411	.488
1988 Bakersfield	A	92	318	112	18	3	9	163	66	80	54	4	50	8	3	8	5	2	.71	5	.352	.448	.513
San Antonio	AA	30	98	29	5	0	2	40	14	13	7	0	20	3	1	2	0	1	.00	5	.296	.355	.408
1989 San Antonio	AA	42	124	35	6	0	6	59	19	20	13	1	20	3	1	0	1	0	1.00	5	.282	.364	.476
1990 Albuquerque	AAA	5	11	4	0	0	0	4	2	1	0	0	1	0	0	0	0	0	.00	0	.364	.364	.364
San Antonio	AA	43	120	36	10	1	2	54	13	21	11	4	27	1	2	1	1	0	1.00	1	.300	.361	.450
1991 Vero Beach	A	58	183	52	10	1	6	82	26	35	25	4	29	3	0	3	1	1	.50	2	.284	.374	.448
San Antonio	AA	15	37	10	1	0	1	14	3	4	2	1	11	0	0	0	0	0	.00	0	.270	.308	.378
1992 San Antonio	AA	31	76	16	4	0	2	26	4	9	3	0	16	0	0	0	0	0	.00	2	.211	.241	.342
Albuquerque	AAA	6	9	4	1	0	1	8	3	3	0	0	1	0	0	0	0	0	.00	0	.444	.444	.889
1993 Daytona	A	36	109	31	8	0	4	51	17	23	15	1	21	0	0	3	0	1	.00	3	.284	.362	.468
Orlando	AA	2	6	3	1	0	0	4	0	1	0	0	0	0	0	0	0	0	.00	0	.500	.500	.667
1994 Orlando	AA	11	29	10	2	0	0	12	3	2	2	0	6	0	0	0	0	0	.00	1	.345	.387	.414
Iowa	AAA	60	133	32	8	1	5	57	14	18	5	1	23	1	1	2	0	1	.00	9	.241	.270	.428
1995 Chattanooga	AA	77	233	62	14	2	5	95	24	32	24	4	36	1	0	0	0	1	.00	9	.266	.336	.408
9 Min. YEARS		572	1695	499	101	9	51	771	238	303	198	21	324	24	8	23	14	11	.56	47	.294	.372	.455

Brant Brown

Bats: Left Throws: Left Pos: 1B Ht: 6'3" Wt: 220 Born: 6/22/71 Age: 25

Year Team	Lg	G	AB	H	2B	3B	HR	TB	R	RBI	TBB	IBB	SO	HBP	SH	SF	SB	CS	SB%	GDP	Avg	OBP	SLG
1992 Peoria	A	70	248	68	14	0	3	91	28	27	24	2	49	1	3	5	3	4	.43	4	.274	.335	.367
1993 Daytona	A	75	266	91	8	7	3	122	26	33	11	0	38	1	4	0	8	7	.53	5	.342	.371	.459

	Lg	G	AB	H	2B	3B	HR	TB	R	RBI	TBB	IBB	SO	HBP	SH	SF	SB	CS	SB%	GDP	Avg	OBP	SLG
Orlando	AA	28	110	35	11	3	4	64	17	23	6	1	18	4	0	1	2	1	.67	2	.318	.372	.582
1994 Orlando	AA	127	470	127	30	6	5	184	54	37	37	3	86	5	2	0	11	15	.42	10	.270	.330	.391
1995 Orlando	AA	121	446	121	27	4	6	174	67	53	39	2	77	3	11	3	8	5	.62	6	.271	.332	.390
4 Min. YEARS		421	1540	442	90	20	21	635	192	173	117	8	268	14	20	9	32	32	.50	27	.287	.341	.412

Chad Brown

Pitches: Left **Bats:** Left **Pos:** P   **Ht:** 6'0" **Wt:** 185 **Born:** 12/9/71 **Age:** 24

		HOW MUCH HE PITCHED						WHAT HE GAVE UP									THE RESULTS					
Year Team	Lg	G	GS	CG	GF	IP	BFP	H	R	ER	HR	SH	SF	HB	TBB	IBB	SO	WP	Bk	W	L	Pct.	ShO	Sv	ERA
1992 Medicne Hat	R	21	0	0	9	37	180	46	28	18	4	0	0	1	21	1	28	7	1	3	3	.500	0	1	4.38
1993 St. Cathrns	A	18	0	0	18	20.2	71	7	4	4	2	0	0	0	5	0	23	0	0	2	0	1.000	0	10	1.74
1994 Dunedin	A	52	0	0	20	78	326	59	29	28	1	4	3	0	41	1	56	3	2	6	7	.462	0	4	3.23
1995 Knoxville	AA	40	0	0	14	41.1	181	38	23	21	2	1	1	1	22	1	35	5	0	1	3	.250	0	1	4.57
Syracuse	AAA	11	0	0	5	22	106	21	11	8	1	2	2	0	20	3	14	4	0	1	1	.500	0	0	3.27
4 Min. YEARS		142	0	0	66	199	864	171	95	79	10	7	6	2	109	6	156	19	3	13	14	.481	0	16	3.57

Chris Brown

Bats: Right **Throws:** Right **Pos:** 3B   **Ht:** 6'2" **Wt:** 218 **Born:** 8/15/61 **Age:** 34

		BATTING															BASERUNNING			PERCENTAGES		
Year Team	Lg	G	AB	H	2B	3B	HR	TB	R	RBI	TBB	IBB	SO	HBP	SH	SF	SB	CS	SB%	GDP	Avg	OBP	SLG
1995 Indianapols	AAA	3	7	0	0	0	0	0	0	0	1	0	0	0	0	0	0	0	.00	0	.000	.125	.000

Dan Brown

Pitches: Right **Bats:** Right **Pos:** P   **Ht:** 6'5" **Wt:** 210 **Born:** 12/26/68 **Age:** 27

		HOW MUCH HE PITCHED						WHAT HE GAVE UP									THE RESULTS					
Year Team	Lg	G	GS	CG	GF	IP	BFP	H	R	ER	HR	SH	SF	HB	TBB	IBB	SO	WP	Bk	W	L	Pct.	ShO	Sv	ERA
1991 Martinsvlle	R	25	0	0	23	36.2	145	23	7	7	0	0	0	1	10	2	38	2	0	3	0	1.000	0	10	1.72
1992 Clearwater	A	6	0	0	2	7	29	5	2	2	0	1	0	1	3	0	4	0	0	0	1	.000	0	2	2.57
Spartanburg	A	16	0	0	4	30	131	26	16	8	1	1	1	3	10	3	30	1	1	0	2	.000	0	1	2.40
1993 Spartanburg	A	39	0	0	27	61	251	53	25	20	2	6	2	1	14	3	43	3	0	6	6	.500	0	3	2.95
1994 Clearwater	A	50	0	0	19	52	211	43	13	9	1	3	1	0	22	4	37	1	2	2	0	1.000	0	1	1.56
1995 Reading	AA	2	0	0	1	2.1	12	4	4	2	1	0	0	0	0	0	2	0	0	1	0	1.000	0	0	7.71
Sioux Falls	IND	7	0	0	4	10.1	56	22	10	10	2	1	0	1	4	1	11	1	0	0	1	.000	0	1	8.71
Mohawk Val	IND	20	0	0	8	41	157	24	9	9	0	2	2	2	11	6	37	1	0	4	1	.800	0	2	1.98
Mohawk Val	IND	29	0	0	13	53.2	225	50	23	21	3	3	2	3	15	7	50	2	0	5	2	.714	0	3	3.52
5 Min. YEARS		194	0	0	101	294	1217	250	109	88	10	17	8	12	89	26	252	11	3	21	13	.618	0	21	2.69

Dickie Brown

Pitches: Right **Bats:** Right **Pos:** P   **Ht:** 6'0" **Wt:** 160 **Born:** 8/13/70 **Age:** 25

		HOW MUCH HE PITCHED						WHAT HE GAVE UP									THE RESULTS					
Year Team	Lg	G	GS	CG	GF	IP	BFP	H	R	ER	HR	SH	SF	HB	TBB	IBB	SO	WP	Bk	W	L	Pct.	ShO	Sv	ERA
1990 Burlington	R	13	12	0	0	67.1	307	76	45	43	6	2	2	4	30	0	53	10	2	3	4	.429	0	0	5.75
1991 Columbus	A	27	26	1	1	152.1	678	167	111	92	11	4	4	10	61	2	109	6	1	8	11	.421	1	0	5.44
1992 Kinston	A	4	1	0	1	13.2	63	16	15	13	2	0	1	0	7	0	7	0	1	0	0	.000	0	0	8.56
Columbus	A	29	3	0	5	80	344	60	25	21	3	2	2	3	49	4	65	7	0	8	3	.727	0	0	2.36
1993 Kinston	A	31	8	0	7	82	366	77	40	30	6	4	2	7	42	0	62	5	0	4	3	.571	0	2	3.29
1994 High Desert	A	18	18	4	0	114.2	487	114	57	49	10	3	4	8	37	1	100	5	0	6	6	.500	1	0	3.85
Kinston	A	7	7	1	0	41	171	33	21	18	5	1	0	2	14	0	40	0	0	4	2	.667	0	0	3.95
1995 Canton-Akrn	AA	37	9	0	11	98.1	449	88	56	51	9	9	3	4	67	7	51	9	0	8	5	.615	0	3	4.67
6 Min. YEARS		166	84	6	25	649.1	2865	631	370	317	52	23	18	38	307	14	487	42	4	41	34	.547	2	5	4.39

Jeff Brown

Pitches: Left **Bats:** Left **Pos:** P   **Ht:** 6'0" **Wt:** 165 **Born:** 9/8/70 **Age:** 25

		HOW MUCH HE PITCHED						WHAT HE GAVE UP									THE RESULTS					
Year Team	Lg	G	GS	CG	GF	IP	BFP	H	R	ER	HR	SH	SF	HB	TBB	IBB	SO	WP	Bk	W	L	Pct.	ShO	Sv	ERA
1990 Padres	R	16	7	0	6	58.1	269	71	52	38	4	1	0	2	12	1	59	0	5	1	7	.125	0	1	5.86
1991 Charlstn-Sc	A	28	25	4	2	165	658	134	55	45	10	6	6	7	45	2	152	4	8	13	8	.619	2	1	2.45
1992 Waterloo	A	24	24	2	0	146.1	641	172	91	76	4	4	2	10	60	1	103	9	4	7	6	.538	2	0	4.67
High Desert	A	2	2	0	0	11.2	55	13	6	5	2	0	1	0	4	0	10	0	0	1	0	1.000	0	0	3.86
1993 Las Vegas	AAA	1	0	0	1	5	22	9	5	5	1	0	0	1	0	0	4	0	0	0	0	.000	0	0	9.00
Rancho Cuca	A	38	8	1	10	95	450	137	75	60	7	4	4	7	28	3	63	5	0	6	6	.500	0	0	5.68
1994 Marshall	IND	9	8	0	0	50	231	54	33	26	6	0	2	6	21	0	39	5	0	1	4	.200	0	0	4.68
1995 Richmond	AAA	12	0	0	6	22.1	94	23	10	8	1	1	0	1	5	3	12	1	0	1	2	.333	0	0	3.22
6 Min. YEARS		130	74	7	25	553.2	2416	613	327	263	35	16	15	34	175	10	442	24	17	30	33	.476	4	3	4.28

Keith Brown

Pitches: Right **Bats:** Both **Pos:** P   **Ht:** 6' 4" **Wt:** 215 **Born:** 2/14/64 **Age:** 32

		HOW MUCH HE PITCHED						WHAT HE GAVE UP									THE RESULTS					
Year Team	Lg	G	GS	CG	GF	IP	BFP	H	R	ER	HR	SH	SF	HB	TBB	IBB	SO	WP	Bk	W	L	Pct.	ShO	Sv	ERA
1986 Reds	R	7	7	1	0	47.1	179	29	15	5	0	2	1	2	5	1	26	3	0	4	1	.800	0	0	0.95
Billings	R	4	3	0	1	21.1		18	6	5	0	0	0	1	7	0	14	1	0	2	0	1.000	0	0	2.11
Vermont	AA	4	2	1	0	14	58	12	10	8	2	1	1	0	8	0	11	1	0	1	1	.500	0	0	5.14
1987 Cedar Rapds	A	17	17	3	0	124.1	481	91	28	22	5	2	1	3	27	0	86	3	0	13	4	.765	1	0	1.59
1988 Chattanooga	AA	10	10	2	0	69.2	273	47	11	11	3	2	1	4	20	1	34	1	0	9	1	.900	0	0	1.42

Year	Team	Lg	G	GS	CG	GF	IP	BFP	H	R	ER	HR	SH	SF	HB	TBB	IBB	SO	WP	Bk	W	L	Pct.	ShO	Sv	ERA
	Nashville	AAA	12	12	3	0	85.1	354	72	33	18	1	6	2	1	28	2	43	2	1	6	3	.667	1	0	1.90
1989	Nashville	AAA	29	27	4	0	161.1	695	171	99	86	13	10	4	1	51	2	85	5	2	8	13	.381	2	0	4.80
1990	Nashville	AAA	39	9	1	26	94.1	379	83	37	25	6	8	2	4	24	2	50	4	1	7	8	.467	0	9	2.39
1991	Nashville	AAA	47	1	0	32	62	274	64	26	24	3	5	2	2	32	4	53	5	0	2	5	.286	0	16	3.48
1992	Nashville	AAA	26	23	1	1	149.2	631	157	74	60	6	5	3	4	43	0	102	3	3	12	9	.571	0	0	3.61
1993	Omaha	AAA	26	25	1	1	148.2	636	166	85	80	25	2	4	3	36	0	98	3	1	13	8	.619	0	0	4.84
1994	Winnipeg	IND	3	0	0	1	3	14	3	2	2	1	0	0	0	2	0	5	0	0	0	0	.000	0	1	6.00
1995	Charlotte	AAA	4	0	0	2	7.1	31	6	3	2	1	0	0	1	2	0	3	1	0	0	1	.000	0	0	2.45
1988	Cincinnati	NL	4	3	0	1	16.1	63	14	5	5	1	0	0	0	4	0	6	1	0	2	1	.667	0	0	2.76
1990	Cincinnati	NL	8	0	0	2	11.1	46	12	6	6	2	1	0	0	3	0	8	0	0	0	0	.000	0	0	4.76
1991	Cincinnati	NL	11	0	0	3	12	56	15	4	3	0	1	0	0	6	1	4	1	0	0	0	.000	0	0	2.25
1992	Cincinnati	NL	2	2	0	0	8	37	10	5	4	2	0	0	0	5	0	5	0	0	0	1	.000	0	0	4.50
	10 Min. YEARS		228	136	17	64	988.1	4005	919	429	348	66	43	21	26	285	12	610	32	8	77	54	.588	4	26	3.17
	4 Maj. YEARS		25	5	0	6	47.2	202	51	20	18	5	2	0	0	18	1	23	2	0	2	2	.500	0	0	3.40

Kevin Brown

Bats: Right **Throws:** Right **Pos:** C   **Ht:** 6'2" **Wt:** 200 **Born:** 4/21/73 **Age:** 23

					BATTING												BASERUNNING				PERCENTAGES		
Year	Team	Lg	G	AB	H	2B	3B	HR	TB	R	RBI	TBB	IBB	SO	HBP	SH	SF	SB	CS	SB%	GDP	Avg	OBP	SLG
1994	Hudson Vall	A	68	232	57	19	1	6	96	33	32	23	0	86	4	0	6	0	1	.00	4	.246	.317	.414
1995	Charlotte	A	107	355	94	25	1	11	154	48	57	50	0	96	9	1	4	2	3	.40	9	.265	.366	.434
	Okla. City	AAA	3	10	4	1	0	0	5	1	0	2	0	4	0	0	0	0	0	.00	0	.400	.500	.500
	2 Min. YEARS		178	597	155	45	2	17	255	82	89	75	0	186	13	1	10	2	4	.33	13	.260	.350	.427

Kevin D. Brown

Pitches: Left **Bats:** Left **Pos:** P   **Ht:** 6'1" **Wt:** 185 **Born:** 3/5/66 **Age:** 30

				HOW MUCH HE PITCHED						WHAT HE GAVE UP											THE RESULTS				
Year	Team	Lg	G	GS	CG	GF	IP	BFP	H	R	ER	HR	SH	SF	HB	TBB	IBB	SO	WP	Bk	W	L	Pct.	ShO	Sv	ERA
1986	Idaho Falls	R	12	12	1	0	68	0	65	48	38	5	0	0	0	41	0	44	2	0	3	6	.333	0	0	5.03
1987	Sumter	A	9	9	0	0	56	232	53	14	12	2	2	1	1	19	0	45	5	0	7	1	.875	0	0	1.93
	Durham	A	13	12	1	1	72.2	330	78	46	42	6	0	1	0	42	0	48	5	2	4	4	.500	0	0	5.20
1988	Jackson	AA	5	5	1	0	32.2	129	24	9	8	1	1	2	0	11	0	24	2	0	1	2	.333	1	0	2.20
	St. Lucie	A	20	20	5	0	134	533	96	42	27	4	3	2	6	37	1	113	10	2	5	7	.417	1	0	1.81
1989	Jackson	AA	8	8	2	0	51.2	216	51	15	13	0	1	1	4	11	0	40	4	4	5	2	.714	2	0	2.26
	Tidewater	AAA	13	13	4	0	75	326	81	41	37	2	3	1	0	31	0	46	2	0	6	6	.500	0	0	4.44
1990	Tidewater	AAA	26	24	3	0	134.1	592	138	71	53	4	7	0	2	60	0	109	3	2	10	6	.625	0	0	3.55
1991	Denver	AAA	12	11	1	1	61.2	277	71	36	32	4	3	0	2	34	0	31	2	2	4	3	.571	0	0	4.67
1992	Calgary	AAA	32	20	4	0	150.2	660	163	97	81	13	4	3	4	64	2	49	5	2	6	10	.375	2	0	4.84
1993	Phoenix	AAA	23	20	0	0	120.1	540	134	74	66	12	8	3	2	60	2	75	5	2	6	10	.375	0	0	4.94
1995	Omaha	AAA	7	1	0	0	13	71	20	13	11	0	3	2	0	12	1	5	1	0	0	0	.000	0	0	7.62
	Corp.Chrsti	IND	10	5	0	2	25.2	124	42	24	17	1	1	4	1	8	0	19	2	0	1	3	.250	0	0	5.96
1990	Milwaukee	AL	5	3	0	1	21	87	14	7	6	1	1	1	1	7	1	12	2	0	1	1	.500	0	0	2.57
	New York	NL	2	0	0	1	2	9	2	0	0	0	0	0	0	1	0	0	0	0	0	0	.000	0	0	0.00
1991	Milwaukee	AL	15	10	0	0	63.2	285	66	39	39	6	5	1	1	34	2	30	6	0	2	4	.333	0	0	5.51
1992	Seattle	AL	2	0	0	0	3	15	4	3	3	1	0	0	0	3	0	2	0	0	0	0	.000	0	0	9.00
	9 Min. YEARS		190	160	22	8	995.2	4030	1016	530	437	54	36	20	22	430	6	648	48	16	58	60	.492	6	0	3.95
	3 Maj. YEARS		24	13	0	2	89.2	396	86	49	48	8	6	2	2	45	3	44	8	0	3	5	.375	0	0	4.82

Marty Brown

Bats: Right **Throws:** Right **Pos:** 3B   **Ht:** 6'1" **Wt:** 195 **Born:** 1/23/63 **Age:** 33

					BATTING												BASERUNNING				PERCENTAGES		
Year	Team	Lg	G	AB	H	2B	3B	HR	TB	R	RBI	TBB	IBB	SO	HBP	SH	SF	SB	CS	SB%	GDP	Avg	OBP	SLG
1985	Billings	R	68	248	84	21	3	10	141	50	45	50	3	44	0	2	4	11	3	.79	6	.339	.444	.569
1986	Cedar Rapds	A	139	508	152	19	8	18	241	85	83	58	4	100	4	1	6	58	20	.74	8	.299	.372	.474
1987	Vermont	AA	134	470	124	17	5	15	196	69	74	59	3	93	4	1	7	23	14	.62	10	.264	.346	.417
1988	Nashville	AAA	135	484	128	15	4	7	172	50	55	51	2	111	2	0	6	15	9	.63	6	.264	.333	.355
1989	Nashville	AAA	120	422	103	21	2	12	164	61	46	41	1	85	2	2	4	15	6	.71	11	.244	.311	.389
1990	Rochester	AAA	67	211	51	8	4	5	82	32	25	21	1	47	1	2	1	5	2	.71	10	.242	.312	.389
1991	Colo. Sprng	AAA	121	396	118	24	2	15	191	65	69	49	2	77	2	5	9	3	7	.30	13	.298	.371	.482
1995	Okla. City	AAA	30	101	17	5	0	3	31	12	12	8	1	25	2	0	1	0	0	.00	3	.168	.241	.307
1988	Cincinnati	NL	10	16	3	1	0	0	4	0	2	1	0	2	0	0	0	0	1	.00	0	.188	.235	.250
1989	Cincinnati	NL	16	30	5	1	0	0	6	2	4	4	0	9	0	0	1	0	0	.00	0	.167	.257	.200
1990	Baltimore	AL	9	15	3	0	0	0	3	1	0	1	0	7	0	0	0	0	0	.00	1	.200	.250	.200
	8 Min. YEARS		814	2840	777	130	28	85	1218	424	409	337	17	582	17	13	38	130	61	.68	67	.274	.350	.429
	3 Maj. YEARS		35	61	11	2	0	0	13	3	6	6	0	18	0	0	1	0	1	.00	1	.180	.250	.213

Matt Brown

Bats: Right **Throws:** Right **Pos:** C   **Ht:** 6'0" **Wt:** 195 **Born:** 4/4/69 **Age:** 27

					BATTING												BASERUNNING				PERCENTAGES		
Year	Team	Lg	G	AB	H	2B	3B	HR	TB	R	RBI	TBB	IBB	SO	HBP	SH	SF	SB	CS	SB%	GDP	Avg	OBP	SLG
1990	Elizabethtn	R	28	90	21	1	0	1	25	11	11	8	0	13	0	0	0	0	1	.00	1	.233	.296	.278
1991	Visalia	A	61	167	37	2	0	1	42	16	10	17	1	41	1	2	1	1	1	.50	9	.222	.296	.251
1992	Visalia	A	37	101	27	3	0	1	33	8	7	0	0	23	0	0	4	0	1	.00	4	.267	.267	.327
1993	Fort Myers	A	60	201	33	2	0	0	35	8	17	11	0	41	0	5	4	1	2	.33	6	.164	.204	.174

Year Team	Lg	G	AB	H	2B	3B	HR	TB	R	RBI	TBB	IBB	SO	HBP	SH	SF	SB	CS	SB%	GDP	Avg	OBP	SLG
1995 Trenton	AA	4	11	2	0	0	0	2	1	0	1	0	2	0	0	0	0	0	.00	0	.182	.250	.182
5 Min. YEARS		190	570	120	8	0	3	137	44	45	37	1	120	1	7	5	2	5	.29	20	.211	.258	.240

Michael Brown

Bats: Left **Throws:** Left **Pos:** 1B **Ht:** 6' 7" **Wt:** 235 **Born:** 11/4/71 **Age:** 24

		BATTING															BASERUNNING				PERCENTAGES		
Year Team	Lg	G	AB	H	2B	3B	HR	TB	R	RBI	TBB	IBB	SO	HBP	SH	SF	SB	CS	SB%	GDP	Avg	OBP	SLG
1989 Pirates	R	39	140	31	5	2	0	40	18	11	19	0	28	2	0	1	2	3	.40	2	.221	.321	.286
1990 Welland	A	66	194	57	7	0	2	70	23	32	22	4	35	1	0	1	4	3	.57	5	.294	.367	.361
1991 Augusta	A	94	314	73	13	4	3	103	24	34	47	1	77	3	0	6	12	6	.67	7	.232	.332	.328
1992 Augusta	A	102	322	82	11	9	2	117	34	33	37	5	69	1	4	5	11	5	.69	10	.255	.329	.363
1993 Salem	A	126	436	118	25	3	21	212	71	70	61	4	109	2	0	7	6	4	.60	15	.271	.358	.486
1994 Carolina	AA	117	377	94	24	2	7	143	49	45	44	8	94	3	1	0	3	1	.75	10	.249	.333	.379
1995 Carolina	AA	60	223	53	13	1	8	92	29	33	28	7	62	2	0	0	0	3	.00	1	.238	.328	.413
7 Min. YEARS		604	2006	508	98	21	43	777	248	258	258	29	474	14	5	20	38	25	.60	50	.253	.339	.387

Randy Brown

Bats: Right **Throws:** Right **Pos:** SS **Ht:** 5'11" **Wt:** 160 **Born:** 5/1/70 **Age:** 26

		BATTING															BASERUNNING				PERCENTAGES		
Year Team	Lg	G	AB	H	2B	3B	HR	TB	R	RBI	TBB	IBB	SO	HBP	SH	SF	SB	CS	SB%	GDP	Avg	OBP	SLG
1990 Elmira	A	74	212	50	4	0	1	57	27	8	17	0	47	4	9	0	17	4	.81	1	.236	.305	.269
1991 Red Sox	R	44	143	27	7	0	0	34	25	10	23	0	31	2	3	1	19	0	1.00	1	.189	.308	.238
Winter Havn	A	63	135	21	3	0	0	24	14	5	16	0	42	1	4	0	10	3	.77	2	.156	.250	.178
1992 Winter Havn	A	121	430	101	18	2	2	129	39	24	28	0	115	6	8	4	8	9	.47	1	.235	.288	.300
1993 Lynchburg	A	128	483	114	25	7	2	159	57	45	25	0	127	13	2	4	10	8	.56	6	.236	.290	.329
1994 New Britain	AA	114	389	87	14	2	8	129	51	30	30	0	102	5	7	4	9	5	.64	1	.224	.285	.332
1995 Pawtucket	AAA	74	212	53	6	1	2	67	27	12	10	0	53	4	4	2	5	1	.83	4	.250	.294	.316
6 Min. YEARS		618	2004	453	77	12	15	599	240	134	149	0	517	35	37	15	78	30	.72	19	.226	.289	.299

Tim Brown

Pitches: Right **Bats:** Right **Pos:** P **Ht:** 6'3" **Wt:** 185 **Born:** 9/16/68 **Age:** 27

		HOW MUCH HE PITCHED						WHAT HE GAVE UP												THE RESULTS				
Year Team	Lg	G	GS	CG	GF	IP	BFP	H	R	ER	HR	SH	SF	HB	TBB	IBB	SO	WP	Bk	W	L	Pct.	ShO	Sv	ERA
1988 St. Cathrns	A	15	8	1	1	72	299	58	33	24	5	3	1	2	22	1	37	4	5	1	3	.250	1	0	3.00
1989 Myrtle Bch	A	34	22	1	6	151	689	165	103	75	18	6	4	11	65	2	95	8	9	3	12	.200	1	0	4.47
1990 Dunedin	A	36	0	0	19	67	297	76	41	33	3	3	4	5	18	3	55	7	4	2	3	.400	0	1	4.43
1991 Dunedin	A	31	14	2	8	123	521	113	44	34	3	6	2	5	37	1	87	5	6	8	3	.727	0	1	2.49
1992 Knoxville	AA	24	24	2	0	152.1	646	159	77	63	10	4	10	13	32	0	82	6	6	8	11	.421	0	0	3.72
Syracuse	AAA	4	3	0	0	15.2	67	19	12	11	2	0	2	0	4	0	13	0	0	0	2	.000	0	0	6.32
1993 Syracuse	AAA	28	25	3	2	151	641	159	85	75	16	4	5	7	35	4	87	4	0	5	13	.278	1	0	4.47
1995 Syracuse	AAA	19	12	0	3	74.2	351	95	69	52	10	3	4	2	28	1	54	2	1	3	8	.273	0	0	6.27
7 Min. YEARS		191	108	9	39	806.2	3511	844	464	367	67	29	32	45	241	12	510	36	31	30	55	.353	2	3	4.09

Willie Brown

Pitches: Right **Bats:** Right **Pos:** P **Ht:** 6'4" **Wt:** 215 **Born:** 4/14/72 **Age:** 24

		HOW MUCH HE PITCHED						WHAT HE GAVE UP												THE RESULTS				
Year Team	Lg	G	GS	CG	GF	IP	BFP	H	R	ER	HR	SH	SF	HB	TBB	IBB	SO	WP	Bk	W	L	Pct.	ShO	Sv	ERA
1993 Boise	A	15	15	0	0	83.2	356	64	41	36	4	2	1	7	42	1	68	6	1	5	4	.556	0	0	3.87
1994 Cedar Rapds	A	27	27	5	0	176	728	158	89	74	6	6	4	12	45	2	129	4	6	6	9	.400	2	0	3.78
1995 Midland	AA	27	27	2	0	147.2	651	188	92	85	17	9	3	9	47	1	81	9	0	9	10	.474	0	0	5.18
3 Min. YEARS		69	69	7	0	407.1	1735	410	222	195	27	17	8	28	134	4	278	19	7	20	23	.465	2	0	4.31

Byron Browne

Pitches: Right **Bats:** Right **Pos:** P **Ht:** 6'7" **Wt:** 200 **Born:** 8/8/70 **Age:** 25

		HOW MUCH HE PITCHED						WHAT HE GAVE UP												THE RESULTS				
Year Team	Lg	G	GS	CG	GF	IP	BFP	H	R	ER	HR	SH	SF	HB	TBB	IBB	SO	WP	Bk	W	L	Pct.	ShO	Sv	ERA
1991 Brewers	R	13	11	0	0	58	312	68	65	52	2	0	4	5	67	1	68	14	2	1	6	.143	0	0	8.07
1992 Beloit	A	25	25	2	0	134.2	621	109	84	76	8	8	4	11	114	0	111	24	6	9	8	.529	0	0	5.08
1993 Stockton	A	27	27	0	0	143.2	661	117	73	65	9	7	6	11	117	1	110	13	0	10	5	.667	0	0	4.07
1994 Stockton	A	11	11	1	0	62	260	46	30	19	4	4	1	3	30	0	67	3	0	2	6	.250	0	0	2.76
El Paso	AA	5	5	0	0	29	124	26	11	8	3	0	1	0	13	0	33	1	0	2	1	.667	0	0	2.48
1995 El Paso	AA	25	20	2	3	126	540	106	55	48	7	3	9	6	78	2	110	7	0	10	4	.714	1	0	3.43
5 Min. YEARS		106	99	5	3	553.1	2518	472	318	268	33	22	25	36	419	4	499	62	8	34	30	.531	1	0	4.36

Mark Brownson

Pitches: Right **Bats:** Right **Pos:** P **Ht:** 6'2" **Wt:** 175 **Born:** 6/17/75 **Age:** 21

		HOW MUCH HE PITCHED						WHAT HE GAVE UP												THE RESULTS				
Year Team	Lg	G	GS	CG	GF	IP	BFP	H	R	ER	HR	SH	SF	HB	TBB	IBB	SO	WP	Bk	W	L	Pct.	ShO	Sv	ERA
1994 Rockies	R	19	4	0	6	54.1	224	48	18	10	2	2	2	3	6	0	72	2	2	4	1	.800	0	3	1.66
1995 Asheville	A	23	12	0	4	98.2	422	106	52	44	12	2	2	4	29	0	94	4	2	6	7	.462	0	1	4.01
New Haven	AA	1	1	0	0	6	24	4	2	1	1	0	0	0	1	0	4	0	0	0	0	.000	0	0	1.50
Salem	A	9	1	0	5	15.2	71	16	8	7	0	0	1	1	10	4	9	4	0	2	1	.667	0	1	4.02
2 Min. YEARS		52	18	0	15	174.2	741	174	80	62	15	4	5	8	46	4	179	10	4	12	9	.571	0	5	3.19

J.T. Bruett

Bats: Left **Throws:** Left **Pos:** OF   **Ht:** 5'11" **Wt:** 180 **Born:** 10/8/67 **Age:** 28

Year	Team	Lg	G	AB	H	2B	3B	HR	TB	R	RBI	TBB	IBB	SO	HBP	SH	SF	SB	CS	SB%	GDP	Avg	OBP	SLG
1988	Elizabethtn	R	28	91	27	3	0	0	30	23	3	19	0	15	0	0	0	17	4	.81	3	.297	.418	.330
	Kenosha	A	3	10	2	0	0	0	2	2	0	3	0	0	0	0	0	1	1	.50	0	.200	.385	.200
1989	Kenosha	A	120	445	119	9	1	3	139	82	29	89	2	64	0	2	1	61	27	.69	6	.267	.389	.312
1990	Portland	AAA	10	34	8	2	0	0	10	8	3	11	0	4	0	0	1	2	1	.67	0	.235	.413	.294
	Visalia	A	123	437	134	15	3	1	158	86	33	101	4	60	4	8	3	50	21	.70	8	.307	.439	.362
1991	Portland	AAA	99	345	98	6	3	0	110	51	35	40	1	41	3	9	0	21	9	.70	10	.284	.363	.319
1992	Portland	AAA	77	280	70	10	3	0	86	41	17	60	3	27	1	3	3	29	12	.71	5	.250	.381	.307
1993	Portland	AAA	90	320	103	17	6	2	138	70	40	55	3	38	3	10	3	12	11	.52	7	.322	.423	.431
1994	Salt Lake	AAA	46	151	42	8	0	3	59	25	29	29	1	18	2	2	1	7	5	.58	5	.278	.399	.391
	Charlotte	AAA	64	163	41	7	2	1	55	23	8	15	2	20	4	2	0	2	0	1.00	3	.252	.330	.337
1995	Omaha	AAA	44	129	36	6	1	2	50	20	14	17	1	19	1	5	3	6	4	.60	3	.279	.360	.388
1992	Minnesota	AL	56	76	19	4	0	0	23	7	2	6	1	12	1	1	0	6	3	.67	0	.250	.313	.303
1993	Minnesota	AL	17	20	5	2	0	0	7	2	1	1	0	4	1	0	0	0	0	.00	1	.250	.318	.350
	8 Min. YEARS		704	2405	680	83	19	12	837	431	211	439	17	306	18	41	15	208	95	.69	50	.283	.395	.348
	2 Maj. YEARS		73	96	24	6	0	0	30	9	3	7	1	16	2	1	0	6	3	.67	1	.250	.314	.313

Duff Brumley

Pitches: Right **Bats:** Right **Pos:** P   **Ht:** 6'4" **Wt:** 220 **Born:** 8/25/70 **Age:** 25

Year	Team	Lg	G	GS	CG	GF	IP	BFP	H	R	ER	HR	SH	SF	HB	TBB	IBB	SO	WP	Bk	W	L	Pct.	ShO	Sv	ERA
1990	Johnson Cty	R	12	11	0	0	55.2	263	61	48	40	4	0	3	3	29	0	43	2	1	2	6	.250	0	0	6.47
1991	Hamilton	A	15	15	0	0	89	384	90	49	36	7	1	4	5	24	0	80	5	2	2	6	.250	0	0	3.64
1992	Hamilton	A	9	9	2	0	59.2	234	38	19	18	3	1	3	2	21	0	83	0	1	6	0	1.000	0	0	2.72
	Savannah	A	5	5	0	0	31	128	17	9	6	1	1	2	0	14	0	46	2	2	2	1	.667	0	0	1.74
1993	St. Pete	A	8	8	0	0	56	203	26	5	4	2	2	0	2	13	0	67	1	0	5	1	.833	0	0	0.64
	Arkansas	AA	12	12	2	0	69.1	292	57	30	27	9	3	1	1	26	5	79	2	1	4	5	.444	1	0	3.50
	Tulsa	AA	6	6	0	0	41.1	165	30	13	9	4	1	1	2	9	1	42	2	0	3	2	.600	0	0	1.96
1994	Okla. City	AAA	29	15	0	11	101.1	470	107	71	62	9	5	12	8	64	0	100	8	1	3	6	.333	0	2	5.51
1995	Okla. City	AAA	3	0	0	0	5	24	6	4	3	0	1	0	0	2	0	3	0	0	1	1	.500	0	0	5.40
	Chattanooga	AA	25	0	0	9	48.1	193	31	11	9	0	3	2	2	16	2	60	3	2	5	1	.833	0	1	1.68
1994	Texas	AL	2	0	0	1	3.1	22	6	6	6	1	2	0	0	5	0	4	0	0	0	0	.000	0	0	16.20
	6 Min. YEARS		124	81	4	21	556.2	2356	463	259	214	39	18	28	25	218	8	603	25	10	33	29	.532	1	4	3.46

Julio Bruno

Bats: Right **Throws:** Right **Pos:** 3B   **Ht:** 5'11" **Wt:** 190 **Born:** 10/15/72 **Age:** 23

Year	Team	Lg	G	AB	H	2B	3B	HR	TB	R	RBI	TBB	IBB	SO	HBP	SH	SF	SB	CS	SB%	GDP	Avg	OBP	SLG
1990	Charlstn-Sc	A	19	75	17	1	1	0	20	11	5	1	0	21	0	1	1	0	0	.00	0	.227	.234	.267
	Spokane	A	68	251	63	7	2	2	80	36	22	25	1	78	2	0	0	7	5	.58	10	.251	.324	.319
1991	Waterloo	A	86	277	64	10	3	1	83	34	25	29	0	78	4	4	1	11	6	.65	8	.231	.312	.300
1992	High Desert	A	118	418	116	22	5	3	157	57	62	33	4	92	1	5	3	2	3	.40	8	.278	.330	.376
1993	Rancho Cuca	A	54	201	62	11	2	3	86	37	16	19	2	56	1	1	2	15	6	.71	7	.308	.368	.428
	Wichita	AA	70	246	70	17	1	3	98	34	24	11	3	46	2	1	1	3	5	.38	9	.285	.319	.398
1994	Rancho Cuca	A	6	25	14	2	1	2	24	11	7	4	0	4	1	0	0	2	0	1.00	0	.560	.633	.960
	Las Vegas	AAA	123	450	117	25	4	6	168	48	52	24	3	83	4	5	5	4	5	.44	15	.260	.300	.373
1995	Las Vegas	AAA	38	139	34	6	1	0	42	13	6	8	0	24	0	0	1	1	3	.25	6	.245	.284	.302
	Memphis	AA	59	196	53	6	3	2	71	16	25	8	0	35	2	3	2	3	2	.60	9	.270	.303	.362
	6 Min. YEARS		641	2278	610	107	23	22	829	297	244	162	13	517	17	20	16	48	35	.58	72	.268	.319	.364

William Brunson

Pitches: Left **Bats:** Left **Pos:** P   **Ht:** 6'4" **Wt:** 185 **Born:** 3/20/70 **Age:** 26

Year	Team	Lg	G	GS	CG	GF	IP	BFP	H	R	ER	HR	SH	SF	HB	TBB	IBB	SO	WP	Bk	W	L	Pct.	ShO	Sv	ERA
1992	Princeton	R	13	13	0	0	72.2	313	68	34	29	6	4	2	3	28	0	48	2	0	5	5	.500	0	0	3.59
1993	Charlstn-Wv	A	37	15	0	4	123.2	545	119	68	54	10	4	4	11	50	1	103	7	2	5	6	.455	0	0	3.93
1994	Winston-Sal	A	30	22	3	3	165	711	161	83	73	22	5	7	12	58	2	129	6	4	12	7	.632	0	0	3.98
1995	San Bernrdo	A	13	13	0	0	83.1	334	68	24	19	4	3	5	5	21	0	70	3	0	10	0	1.000	0	0	2.05
	San Antonio	AA	14	14	0	0	80	356	105	46	44	4	3	1	4	22	0	44	5	1	4	5	.444	0	0	4.95
	4 Min. YEARS		107	77	3	7	524.2	2259	521	255	219	46	19	19	35	179	3	394	23	7	36	23	.610	0	0	3.76

Pat Bryant

Bats: Right **Throws:** Right **Pos:** OF   **Ht:** 5'11" **Wt:** 182 **Born:** 10/27/72 **Age:** 23

Year	Team	Lg	G	AB	H	2B	3B	HR	TB	R	RBI	TBB	IBB	SO	HBP	SH	SF	SB	CS	SB%	GDP	Avg	OBP	SLG
1990	Indians	R	17	51	10	2	0	0	12	3	3	8	0	18	4	0	1	2	0	1.00	0	.196	.344	.235
	Burlington	R	17	50	5	0	0	1	8	3	2	7	0	23	0	0	0	7	1	.88	1	.100	.211	.160
1991	Columbus	A	100	326	68	11	0	7	100	51	27	49	0	108	7	2	4	30	6	.83	2	.209	.323	.307
1992	Columbus	A	49	151	33	14	2	2	57	36	19	30	2	52	7	2	0	10	2	.83	1	.219	.372	.377
	Watertown	A	63	220	58	13	1	7	94	41	30	33	1	61	5	1	1	35	8	.81	0	.264	.371	.427
1993	Columbus	A	121	483	127	26	2	16	205	82	61	43	1	117	13	0	2	43	11	.80	6	.263	.338	.424
1994	Canton-Akrn	AA	124	377	89	14	2	12	143	61	53	48	0	87	5	5	3	23	14	.62	4	.236	.328	.379

1995	Canton-Akrn	AA	127	421	109	22	3	17	188	60	59	52	0	116	4	5	3	16	8	.67	5	.259 .344 .447
	6 Min. YEARS		618	2079	499	102	10	62	807	337	254	270	4	582	45	15	12	166	50	.77	18	.240 .338 .388

Scott Bryant

Bats: Right **Throws:** Right **Pos:** DH-OF   **Ht:** 6'2" **Wt:** 215 **Born:** 10/31/67 **Age:** 28

						BATTING												BASERUNNING				PERCENTAGES		
Year	Team	Lg	G	AB	H	2B	3B	HR	TB	R	RBI	TBB	IBB	SO	HBP	SH	SF	SB	CS	SB%	GDP	Avg	OBP	SLG
1989	Cedar Rapids	A	49	186	47	7	0	9	81	26	39	30	0	46	0	1	1	2	4	.33	7	.253	.355	.435
1990	Cedar Rapids	A	67	212	56	10	3	14	114	40	48	50	5	47	1	0	3	6	4	.60	7	.264	.402	.538
	Chattanooga	AA	44	131	41	10	3	6	75	23	30	22	0	28	2	0	0	1	1	.50	5	.313	.419	.573
1991	Chattanooga	AA	91	306	93	14	6	8	143	42	43	34	1	77	3	0	2	2	3	.40	8	.304	.377	.467
1992	Charlotte	AA	6	20	3	1	1	1	9	3	2	1	0	9	0	0	0	0	0	.00	0	.150	.190	.450
	Iowa	AAA	98	315	79	22	3	18	161	35	49	25	2	73	3	2	2	0	2	.00	8	.251	.310	.511
1993	Ottawa	AAA	112	364	103	19	1	12	160	48	65	53	3	90	2	0	6	1	2	.33	11	.283	.372	.440
1994	Calgary	AAA	105	416	133	33	2	20	231	69	87	39	2	66	1	0	5	1	2	.33	12	.320	.375	.555
1995	Edmonton	AAA	119	406	117	33	3	10	186	58	69	49	3	87	6	0	5	1	3	.25	7	.288	.369	.458
	7 Min. YEARS		691	2356	672	148	23	98	1160	344	432	303	16	523	18	3	24	14	21	.40	65	.285	.368	.492

Shawn Bryant

Pitches: Left **Bats:** Right **Pos:** P   **Ht:** 6'3" **Wt:** 205 **Born:** 6/10/69 **Age:** 27

			HOW MUCH HE PITCHED						WHAT HE GAVE UP										THE RESULTS					
Year	Team	Lg	G	GS	CG	GF	IP	BFP	H	R	ER	HR	SH	SF	HB	TBB	IBB	SO	WP	Bk	W	L	Pct.	ShO	Sv	ERA
1990	Burlington	R	2	2	0	0	10.2	42	5	2	1	0	0	0	0	6	0	17	2	0	1	0	1.000	0	0	0.84
	Watertown	A	10	10	2	0	61.2	253	49	24	19	3	1	1	3	23	1	56	8	4	6	3	.667	0	0	2.77
	Kinston	A	2	2	0	0	8.2	43	10	6	5	0	0	0	0	7	0	13	1	2	1	1	.500	0	0	5.19
1991	Kinston	A	29	28	2	0	154.2	701	154	91	69	12	6	4	4	106	0	112	13	6	11	9	.550	1	0	4.02
1992	Kinston	A	27	27	3	0	167.2	713	152	85	71	8	7	6	5	69	0	121	15	8	10	8	.556	1	0	3.81
1993	Canton-Akrn	AA	27	27	0	0	172	740	179	80	71	11	7	4	7	61	3	111	11	7	10	5	.667	0	0	3.72
1994	Salt Lake	AAA	33	21	1	5	139.1	643	168	112	97	16	3	5	5	65	1	59	13	1	5	9	.357	0	2	6.27
1995	Salt Lake	AAA	31	0	0	8	48	221	62	31	26	1	3	0	2	16	2	27	1	2	4	1	.800	0	0	4.88
	6 Min. YEARS		161	117	8	13	762.2	3356	779	431	359	51	27	20	26	353	7	516	64	30	48	36	.571	2	2	4.24

Jim Buccheri

Bats: Right **Throws:** Right **Pos:** OF   **Ht:** 5'11" **Wt:** 165 **Born:** 11/12/68 **Age:** 27

						BATTING												BASERUNNING				PERCENTAGES		
Year	Team	Lg	G	AB	H	2B	3B	HR	TB	R	RBI	TBB	IBB	SO	HBP	SH	SF	SB	CS	SB%	GDP	Avg	OBP	SLG
1988	Sou. Oregon	A	58	232	67	8	1	0	77	42	17	20	0	35	4	0	3	25	7	.78	7	.289	.351	.332
1989	Madison	A	115	433	101	9	0	2	116	56	28	26	1	61	5	3	3	43	12	.78	5	.233	.283	.268
1990	Modesto	A	36	125	35	4	1	0	41	27	7	25	0	16	2	2	0	15	9	.63	2	.280	.408	.328
	Huntsville	AA	84	278	58	2	1	0	62	39	22	40	0	38	3	7	1	14	6	.70	5	.209	.314	.223
1991	Huntsville	AA	100	340	72	15	0	0	87	48	22	71	0	60	7	5	4	35	7	.83	5	.212	.355	.256
1992	Huntsville	AA	20	60	9	2	1	1	16	8	5	9	0	18	0	1	1	5	3	.63	2	.150	.257	.267
	Reno	A	63	259	95	14	2	4	125	65	38	56	3	40	2	2	2	33	13	.72	5	.367	.480	.483
	Tacoma	AAA	46	127	38	6	3	0	50	24	13	27	1	25	2	0	0	10	5	.67	2	.299	.429	.394
1993	Modesto	A	2	7	2	0	0	0	2	3	1	2	0	2	1	0	0	0	0	.00	1	.286	.500	.286
	Tacoma	AAA	90	293	81	9	3	2	102	45	40	39	1	46	2	10	1	12	9	.57	6	.276	.364	.348
1994	Tacoma	AAA	121	448	136	8	3	3	159	59	39	42	1	45	4	7	2	32	14	.70	8	.304	.367	.355
1995	Ottawa	AAA	133	470	126	16	4	0	150	64	30	49	5	58	3	11	2	44	11	.80	7	.268	.340	.319
	8 Min. YEARS		868	3072	820	93	19	12	987	480	262	406	12	444	35	48	19	268	96	.74	55	.267	.357	.321

Gary Buckels

Pitches: Right **Bats:** Both **Pos:** P   **Ht:** 6' 0" **Wt:** 185 **Born:** 7/22/65 **Age:** 30

			HOW MUCH HE PITCHED						WHAT HE GAVE UP										THE RESULTS					
Year	Team	Lg	G	GS	CG	GF	IP	BFP	H	R	ER	HR	SH	SF	HB	TBB	IBB	SO	WP	Bk	W	L	Pct.	ShO	Sv	ERA
1987	Salem	A	31	0	0	17	56	257	53	34	26	1	2	0	0	38	3	63	8	0	4	6	.400	0	0	4.18
1988	Quad City	A	46	0	0	25	79.2	334	66	32	28	3	3	3	2	29	1	109	6	5	14	3	.824	0	6	3.16
	Midland	AA	7	0	0	5	12.1	46	5	2	1	0	0	0	1	4	0	9	0	0	0	0	.000	0	1	0.73
1989	Midland	AA	32	0	0	25	36.2	141	24	7	6	0	0	0	0	14	2	32	3	0	2	1	.667	0	12	1.47
	Edmonton	AAA	24	0	0	18	24.1	116	29	23	23	4	1	2	1	19	2	14	2	0	0	3	.000	0	5	8.51
1990	Edmonton	AAA	53	0	0	29	67	290	66	38	34	8	4	4	0	32	7	61	3	0	2	7	.222	0	10	4.57
1991	Edmonton	AAA	51	0	0	21	56	244	66	27	26	5	3	1	0	20	5	34	6	0	5	3	.625	0	7	4.18
1993	Louisville	AAA	40	4	0	7	88	394	116	58	53	12	5	1	1	25	6	64	9	0	4	2	.667	0	1	5.42
1994	St. Pete	A	1	0	0	0	2	7	0	0	0	0	0	0	0	1	0	4	0	0	0	0	.000	0	0	0.00
	Louisville	AAA	48	0	0	11	77.1	313	69	32	28	4	3	1	1	21	1	69	9	0	7	2	.778	0	2	3.26
1995	Louisville	AAA	13	0	0	6	16.1	80	18	11	10	3	2	1	0	13	2	8	3	0	1	2	.333	0	5	5.51
	Toledo	AAA	31	0	0	7	46	193	37	14	11	2	1	1	0	20	2	38	10	0	2	2	.500	0	2	2.15
1994	St. Louis	NL	10	0	0	3	12	51	8	5	3	2	1	0	0	7	1	9	0	0	0	1	.000	0	0	2.25
	8 Min. YEARS		377	4	0	171	561.2	2415	549	278	246	42	24	14	6	236	31	505	59	5	41	31	.569	0	49	3.94

Travis Buckley

Pitches: Right **Bats:** Right **Pos:** P   **Ht:** 6' 4" **Wt:** 208 **Born:** 6/15/70 **Age:** 26

			HOW MUCH HE PITCHED						WHAT HE GAVE UP										THE RESULTS					
Year	Team	Lg	G	GS	CG	GF	IP	BFP	H	R	ER	HR	SH	SF	HB	TBB	IBB	SO	WP	Bk	W	L	Pct.	ShO	Sv	ERA
1989	Rangers	R	16	4	0	2	50.1	211	41	28	19	1	1	2	0	24	1	34	3	5	3	3	.500	0	0	3.40
1990	Gastonia	A	27	26	3	0	161.2	684	149	66	51	10	3	5	4	61	0	149	7	0	12	6	.667	0	0	2.84

Year	Team	Lg	G	GS	CG	GF	IP	BFP	H	R	ER	HR	SH	SF	HB	TBB	IBB	SO	WP	Bk	W	L	Pct.	ShO	Sv	ERA
1992	Quad City	A	4	0	0	3	7.1	33	9	2	2	0	0	0	0	3	0	7	1	0	0	0	.000	0	0	2.45
1993	Chattanooga	AA	31	1	0	14	48	189	33	21	19	2	2	4	2	14	4	35	4	0	2	2	.500	0	1	3.56
1994	Charlstn-Wv	A	8	4	0	4	35.1	135	31	5	5	2	1	1	1	2	0	26	1	0	3	0	1.000	0	1	1.27
	Winston-Sal		5	4	0	1	21.2	112	35	26	23	5	0	1	3	11	1	16	3	0	0	3	.000	0	0	9.55
	Chattanooga	AA	34	2	0	21	53.2	218	43	20	18	3	4	3	1	16	5	33	1	0	1	3	.250	0	3	3.02
1995	Chattanooga	AA	44	3	0	9	100.1	424	95	42	31	7	5	3	4	19	4	82	2	1	3	5	.375	0	0	2.78
	10 Min. YEARS		266	72	5	79	757.2	3171	708	336	278	46	29	35	20	244	25	528	34	9	36	35	.507	3	7	3.30

Alan Burke

Bats: Right **Throws:** Right **Pos:** 3B **Ht:** 6'0" **Wt:** 190 **Born:** 11/28/70 **Age:** 25

			BATTING														BASERUNNING				PERCENTAGES		
Year	Team	Lg	G	AB	H	2B	3B	HR	TB	R	RBI	TBB	IBB	SO	HBP	SH	SF	SB	CS	SB%	GDP	Avg	OBP	SLG
1992	Batavia	A	61	217	60	16	0	4	88	29	29	21	1	21	4	0	2	2	2	.50	8	.276	.348	.406
1993	Spartanburg	A	129	481	135	29	0	17	215	62	96	49	0	92	5	0	14	1	1	.50	9	.281	.344	.447
	Clearwater	A	8	27	3	0	0	1	6	2	3	2	0	7	0	0	0	0	0	.00	0	.111	.172	.222
1994	Clearwater	A	107	374	80	24	1	6	124	44	49	27	0	84	4	8	3	3	1	.75	7	.214	.272	.332
1995	Reading	AA	11	20	4	2	0	1	9	5	3	1	1	6	3	1	0	0	0	.00	0	.200	.333	.450
	Clearwater	A	3	9	2	0	0	1	5	2	2	0	0	2	0	0	0	0	0	.00	0	.222	.222	.556
	Long Beach	IND	86	331	97	12	0	5	124	47	48	24	0	38	7	2	3	5	2	.71	8	.293	.351	.375
	4 Min. YEARS		405	1459	381	83	1	35	571	191	230	124	2	250	23	11	22	11	6	.65	33	.261	.324	.391

John Burke

Pitches: Right **Bats:** Both **Pos:** P **Ht:** 6'4" **Wt:** 220 **Born:** 2/9/70 **Age:** 26

			HOW MUCH HE PITCHED						WHAT HE GAVE UP												THE RESULTS					
Year	Team	Lg	G	GS	CG	GF	IP	BFP	H	R	ER	HR	SH	SF	HB	TBB	IBB	SO	WP	Bk	W	L	Pct.	ShO	Sv	ERA
1992	Bend	A	10	10	0	0	41	173	38	13	11	3	1	0	0	18	0	32	0	3	2	0	1.000	0	0	2.41
1993	Central Val	A	20	20	2	0	119	521	104	62	42	5	7	2	3	64	0	114	8	1	7	8	.467	0	0	3.18
	Colo. Sprng	AAA	8	8	0	0	48.2	206	44	22	17	0	3	2	2	23	0	38	1	0	3	2	.600	0	0	3.14
1994	Colo. Sprng	AAA	8	0	0	3	11	72	16	25	24	0	0	1	2	22	0	6	5	0	0	0	.000	0	0	19.64
	Asheville	A	4	4	0	0	17	61	5	3	2	1	0	0	0	5	0	16	1	0	0	1	.000	0	0	1.06
1995	Colo. Sprng	AAA	19	17	0	1	87	376	79	46	44	7	2	3	1	48	0	65	5	1	7	1	.875	0	1	4.55
	4 Min. YEARS		69	59	2	4	323.2	1409	286	171	140	16	13	8	8	180	0	271	20	5	19	12	.613	0	1	3.89

Ben Burlingame

Pitches: Right **Bats:** Right **Pos:** P **Ht:** 6'5" **Wt:** 210 **Born:** 1/31/70 **Age:** 26

			HOW MUCH HE PITCHED						WHAT HE GAVE UP												THE RESULTS					
Year	Team	Lg	G	GS	CG	GF	IP	BFP	H	R	ER	HR	SH	SF	HB	TBB	IBB	SO	WP	Bk	W	L	Pct.	ShO	Sv	ERA
1991	Geneva	A	14	5	0	4	50.2	207	49	22	16	2	1	0	1	12	0	38	1	1	5	2	.714	0	1	2.84
1992	Winston-Sal	A	31	25	3	2	160.2	666	164	79	65	13	5	8	3	44	1	82	3	0	8	12	.400	0	0	3.64
1993	Daytona	A	8	1	0	2	17.1	85	27	16	15	4	0	2	2	9	0	10	0	0	0	1	.000	0	0	7.79
	Peoria	A	20	20	4	0	126.1	537	122	59	50	9	0	4	15	32	0	102	3	3	9	7	.563	1	0	3.56
1994	Orlando	AA	25	22	0	0	139	586	132	75	60	14	7	4	10	41	1	84	7	0	4	11	.267	0	0	3.88
1995	Orlando	AA	37	10	0	10	97	415	93	39	38	7	3	6	4	38	8	73	4	0	9	2	.818	0	1	3.53
	5 Min. YEARS		135	83	7	18	591	2496	587	290	244	49	16	24	35	176	10	389	18	4	35	35	.500	1	2	3.72

Roger Burnett

Bats: Right **Throws:** Right **Pos:** SS **Ht:** 6'1" **Wt:** 185 **Born:** 11/14/69 **Age:** 26

			BATTING														BASERUNNING				PERCENTAGES		
Year	Team	Lg	G	AB	H	2B	3B	HR	TB	R	RBI	TBB	IBB	SO	HBP	SH	SF	SB	CS	SB%	GDP	Avg	OBP	SLG
1991	Oneonta	A	62	232	64	6	2	4	86	36	28	17	0	40	8	0	2	3	4	.43	2	.276	.344	.371
1992	Pr. William	A	101	341	64	11	3	1	84	38	32	23	0	81	6	5	8	1	3	.25	9	.188	.246	.246
1993	Pr. William	A	18	53	10	1	0	2	17	3	7	6	0	7	1	1	0	1	0	1.00	3	.189	.283	.321
	San Bernrdo	A	72	245	70	15	0	6	103	34	33	25	1	39	2	4	1	3	2	.60	6	.286	.355	.420
1994	Tampa	A	6	20	2	0	0	1	5	2	4	2	0	8	0	0	1	0	1	.00	1	.100	.174	.250
	Albany-Colo	AA	74	196	42	8	2	0	54	19	9	16	0	43	3	7	1	0	4	.00	10	.214	.282	.276
1995	Norwich	AA	104	356	79	14	0	3	102	32	29	28	2	64	4	7	3	3	3	.50	9	.222	.284	.287
	5 Min. YEARS		437	1443	331	55	7	17	451	164	142	117	3	282	24	24	16	11	17	.39	40	.229	.295	.313

Darren Burton

Bats: Both **Throws:** Right **Pos:** OF **Ht:** 6'1" **Wt:** 185 **Born:** 9/16/72 **Age:** 23

			BATTING														BASERUNNING				PERCENTAGES		
Year	Team	Lg	G	AB	H	2B	3B	HR	TB	R	RBI	TBB	IBB	SO	HBP	SH	SF	SB	CS	SB%	GDP	Avg	OBP	SLG
1990	Royals	R	15	58	12	0	1	0	14	10	2	4	0	17	0	1	2	6	0	1.00	0	.207	.250	.241
1991	Appleton	A	134	532	143	32	6	2	193	78	51	45	4	122	1	3	6	37	12	.76	18	.269	.324	.363
1992	Baseball Cy	A	123	431	106	15	6	4	145	54	36	49	7	93	6	4	3	16	14	.53	7	.246	.329	.336
1993	Wilmington	A	134	549	152	23	5	10	215	82	45	48	1	111	1	13	4	30	10	.75	7	.277	.334	.392
1994	Memphis	AA	97	373	95	12	3	3	122	55	37	35	4	53	1	4	5	10	6	.63	5	.255	.316	.327
1995	Omaha	AAA	2	5	0	0	0	0	0	0	0	0	0	1	0	0	0	0	0	.00	0	.000	.000	.000
	Wichita	AA	41	163	39	9	1	1	51	13	20	12	0	27	1	9	0	6	6	.50	2	.239	.295	.325
	Orlando	AA	62	222	68	16	2	4	100	40	21	27	2	42	0	0	0	7	4	.64	5	.306	.382	.450
	6 Min. YEARS		608	2333	615	107	24	24	842	332	212	220	18	466	10	34	20	112	52	.68	44	.264	.327	.361

Essex Burton

Bats: Right **Throws:** Right **Pos:** 2B   **Ht:** 5'9" **Wt:** 155 **Born:** 5/16/69 **Age:** 27

Year	Team	Lg	G	AB	H	2B	3B	HR	TB	R	RBI	TBB	IBB	SO	HBP	SH	SF	SB	CS	SB%	GDP	Avg	OBP	SLG
1991	White Sox	R	50	194	54	5	2	0	63	37	17	26	0	27	1	3	0	21	7	.75	2	.278	.367	.325
	Utica	A	15	58	16	0	0	0	16	11	4	8	0	12	1	2	0	6	2	.75	1	.276	.373	.276
1992	South Bend	A	122	459	116	6	3	0	128	78	29	67	0	109	3	9	1	65	23	.74	1	.253	.351	.279
1993	South Bend	A	134	501	128	6	8	1	153	95	36	85	0	94	4	8	2	74	24	.76	3	.255	.367	.305
1994	Pr. William	A	131	503	143	22	10	3	194	94	50	67	1	88	5	6	6	66	19	.78	5	.284	.370	.386
1995	Birmingham	AA	142	554	141	15	2	1	163	95	43	80	4	79	5	15	2	60	22	.73	9	.255	.353	.294
	5 Min. YEARS		594	2269	598	54	25	5	717	410	179	333	5	409	19	43	11	292	97	.75	21	.264	.361	.316

Mike Busby

Pitches: Right **Bats:** Right **Pos:** P   **Ht:** 6'4" **Wt:** 215 **Born:** 12/27/72 **Age:** 23

Year	Team	Lg	G	GS	CG	GF	IP	BFP	H	R	ER	HR	SH	SF	HB	TBB	IBB	SO	WP	Bk	W	L	Pct.	ShO	Sv	ERA
1991	Cardinals	R	11	11	0	0	59	267	67	35	23	1	0	2	2	29	0	71	3	1	4	3	.571	0	0	3.51
1992	Savannah	A	28	28	1	0	149.2	665	145	96	61	11	1	7	17	67	0	84	16	1	4	13	.235	0	0	3.67
1993	Savannah	A	23	21	1	0	143.2	579	116	49	39	8	6	4	10	31	0	125	5	2	12	2	.857	1	0	2.44
1994	St. Pete	A	26	26	1	0	151.2	663	166	82	75	11	8	5	14	49	1	89	5	2	6	13	.316	0	0	4.45
1995	Arkansas	AA	20	20	1	0	134	565	125	63	49	8	3	3	6	35	1	95	5	0	7	6	.538	0	0	3.29
	Louisville	AAA	6	6	1	0	38.1	154	28	18	14	2	2	2	3	11	0	26	2	0	2	2	.500	0	0	3.29
	5 Min. YEARS		114	112	5	0	676.1	2893	647	343	261	41	20	23	52	222	2	490	36	6	35	39	.473	1	0	3.47

Homer Bush

Bats: Right **Throws:** Right **Pos:** 2B   **Ht:** 5'11" **Wt:** 180 **Born:** 11/11/72 **Age:** 23

Year	Team	Lg	G	AB	H	2B	3B	HR	TB	R	RBI	TBB	IBB	SO	HBP	SH	SF	SB	CS	SB%	GDP	Avg	OBP	SLG
1991	Padres	R	32	127	41	3	2	0	48	16	16	4	1	33	1	0	0	11	7	.61	2	.323	.348	.378
1992	Charlstn-Sc	A	108	367	86	10	5	0	106	37	18	13	0	85	3	0	2	14	11	.56	3	.234	.265	.289
1993	Waterloo	A	130	472	152	19	3	5	192	63	51	19	0	87	1	1	1	39	14	.74	10	.322	.349	.407
1994	Rancho Cuca	A	39	161	54	10	3	0	70	37	16	9	0	29	4	1	1	9	2	.82	2	.335	.383	.435
	Wichita	AA	59	245	73	11	4	3	101	35	14	10	0	39	3	1	0	20	7	.74	6	.298	.333	.412
1995	Memphis	AA	108	432	121	12	5	5	158	53	37	15	0	83	2	4	0	34	12	.74	6	.280	.307	.366
	5 Min. YEARS		476	1804	527	65	22	13	675	241	152	70	1	356	14	7	4	127	53	.71	29	.292	.323	.374

Chris Bushing

Pitches: Right **Bats:** Right **Pos:** P   **Ht:** 6'0" **Wt:** 183 **Born:** 11/4/67 **Age:** 28

Year	Team	Lg	G	GS	CG	GF	IP	BFP	H	R	ER	HR	SH	SF	HB	TBB	IBB	SO	WP	Bk	W	L	Pct.	ShO	Sv	ERA
1986	Bluefield	R	13	1	0	7	26.1	104	14	5	4	1	0	2	0	12	0	30	4	0	2	0	1.000	0	2	1.37
1987	Bluefield	R	20	0	0	11	37	157	27	20	15	2	1	0	1	18	0	51	1	1	2	0	1.000	0	6	3.65
1989	Peninsula	A	35	14	1	13	99.2	472	96	64	48	4	3	5	6	79	0	99	10	5	2	7	.222	1	3	4.33
1990	Rockford	A	46	0	0	32	79.2	344	62	38	29	5	8	2	2	38	6	99	3	0	3	6	.333	0	12	3.28
1991	W. Palm Bch	A	46	0	0	26	65	274	41	15	14	1	6	1	1	41	3	68	4	7	2	1	.667	0	9	1.94
	Harrisburg	AA	3	1	0	0	8.2	37	3	2	1	0	0	0	1	8	0	8	2	0	1	0	1.000	0	0	1.04
1992	Reading	AA	22	8	0	2	70.1	305	68	38	34	9	2	3	2	30	0	72	4	0	3	6	.333	0	1	4.35
	Nashville	AAA	5	0	0	1	10.1	42	8	4	4	1	1	1	0	6	0	6	0	0	1	0	1.000	0	0	3.48
1993	Chattanooga	AA	61	0	0	50	70	279	50	20	18	7	2	2	2	23	3	84	2	1	6	1	.857	0	29	2.31
1994	Nashville	AAA	9	0	0	0	12	55	12	7	6	1	1	1	0	9	3	16	0	0	0	1	.000	0	0	4.50
1995	Okla. City	AAA	3	0	0	2	1.1	10	5	2	2	2	0	1	0	0	0	2	0	0	0	0	.000	0	0	13.50
1993	Cincinnati	NL	6	0	0	2	4.1	25	9	7	6	1	0	1	0	4	0	3	2	0	0	0	.000	0	0	12.46
	9 Min. YEARS		263	24	1	144	480.1	2079	386	215	176	33	24	18	15	264	15	535	30	14	22	22	.500	1	62	3.28

Albert Bustillos

Pitches: Right **Bats:** Right **Pos:** P   **Ht:** 6'1" **Wt:** 230 **Born:** 4/8/68 **Age:** 28

Year	Team	Lg	G	GS	CG	GF	IP	BFP	H	R	ER	HR	SH	SF	HB	TBB	IBB	SO	WP	Bk	W	L	Pct.	ShO	Sv	ERA
1988	Dodgers	R	17	6	1	7	68	261	46	13	11	2	3	1	1	12	1	65	2	1	6	3	.667	0	2	1.46
1989	Vero Beach	A	7	7	1	0	43	183	42	19	14	4	2	0	1	11	0	30	4	1	2	4	.333	0	0	2.93
	Bakersfield	A	19	19	2	0	125	521	115	53	44	7	2	5	1	42	0	80	3	1	8	4	.667	1	0	3.17
1990	San Antonio	AA	5	0	0	1	8.1	38	8	6	6	0	1	1	0	5	0	6	1	1	0	1	.000	0	1	6.48
	Vero Beach	A	22	20	0	0	136	563	131	50	46	3	3	2	0	45	5	89	6	0	11	5	.688	1	0	3.04
1991	Bakersfield	A	11	5	1	4	42.2	176	31	15	7	2	2	1	1	16	0	37	5	0	2	3	.400	0	1	1.48
	San Antonio	AA	16	14	1	1	93	402	113	51	48	6	1	3	1	23	0	47	1	1	5	5	.500	0	0	4.65
1992	San Antonio	AA	6	0	0	2	13	52	8	3	1	0	1	0	0	3	0	10	0	0	1	0	1.000	0	2	0.69
	Albuquerque	AAA	26	0	0	13	37.2	164	41	20	20	4	4	1	0	16	5	23	2	0	1	2	.333	0	3	4.78
1993	Albuquerque	AAA	20	0	0	4	30.1	139	37	15	15	4	5	2	0	13	4	17	2	0	2	1	.667	0	2	4.45
1994	San Antonio	AA	16	8	0	3	65.2	272	75	28	23	3	2	2	0	16	2	34	0	2	5	2	.714	0	0	3.15
	Albuquerque	AAA	15	4	0	2	42.2	194	57	37	29	5	1	1	0	14	1	25	2	0	2	2	.500	0	1	6.12
1995	Colo. Sprng	AAA	34	19	0	2	132.2	572	155	82	68	15	4	2	4	33	0	77	8	0	8	4	.667	0	3	4.61
	8 Min. YEARS		214	102	8	42	838	3537	855	392	332	55	31	21	9	249	18	540	36	7	53	36	.596	2	16	3.57

43

Mike Butler

Pitches: Left **Bats:** Left **Pos:** P | **Ht:** 6'1" **Wt:** 195 **Born:** 12/14/70 **Age:** 25

Year Team	Lg	HOW MUCH HE PITCHED						WHAT HE GAVE UP												THE RESULTS					
		G	GS	CG	GF	IP	BFP	H	R	ER	HR	SH	SF	HB	TBB	IBB	SO	WP	Bk	W	L	Pct.	ShO	Sv	ERA
1991 Angels	R	11	7	0	2	50.1	221	50	29	23	2	1	3	1	26	0	57	5	2	2	1	.667	0	0	4.11
Boise	A	1	0	0	0	3.2	18	5	4	4	1	0	0	0	3	0	2	1	0	0	0	.000	0	0	9.82
1992 Boise	A	17	15	1	0	104.1	417	85	38	28	11	5	3	2	24	1	91	3	1	9	5	.643	0	0	2.42
1993 Palm Spring	A	27	27	4	0	179.1	783	197	112	92	11	6	9	4	61	1	123	5	0	8	10	.444	1	0	4.62
1994 Lk Elsinore	A	43	4	0	7	87.1	387	97	56	45	8	7	2	7	35	3	75	3	1	6	5	.545	0	2	4.64
1995 Vancouver	AAA	3	0	0	0	6	25	4	3	3	0	2	0	1	2	0	3	0	0	0	0	.000	0	0	4.50
Midland	AA	19	0	0	7	24	104	24	12	12	4	0	2	2	9	1	14	0	0	1	1	.500	0	0	4.50
5 Min. YEARS		121	53	5	16	455	1955	462	254	207	37	21	19	17	160	6	365	17	4	26	22	.542	1	2	4.09

Rich Butler

Bats: Left **Throws:** Right **Pos:** OF | **Ht:** 6'1" **Wt:** 180 **Born:** 5/1/73 **Age:** 23

Year Team	Lg	BATTING															BASERUNNING				PERCENTAGES		
		G	AB	H	2B	3B	HR	TB	R	RBI	TBB	IBB	SO	HBP	SH	SF	SB	CS	SB%	GDP	Avg	OBP	SLG
1991 Blue Jays	R	59	213	56	6	7	0	76	30	13	17	1	45	0	4	0	10	6	.63	0	.263	.317	.357
1992 Myrtle Bch	A	130	441	100	14	1	2	122	43	43	37	1	90	7	6	0	11	15	.42	6	.227	.297	.277
1993 Dunedin	A	110	444	136	19	8	11	204	68	65	48	10	64	3	1	4	11	13	.46	4	.306	.375	.459
Knoxville	AA	6	21	2	0	1	0	4	3	0	3	0	5	0	0	0	0	0	.00	0	.095	.208	.190
1994 Knoxville	AA	53	192	56	7	4	3	80	29	22	19	1	31	2	1	1	7	4	.64	1	.292	.360	.417
Syracuse	AAA	94	302	73	6	2	3	92	34	27	22	0	66	0	2	1	8	8	.50	6	.242	.292	.305
1995 Syracuse	AAA	69	199	32	4	2	2	46	20	14	9	0	45	0	1	1	2	3	.40	5	.161	.196	.231
Knoxville	AA	58	217	58	12	3	4	88	27	33	25	1	41	2	1	0	11	3	.79	5	.267	.348	.406
5 Min. YEARS		579	2029	513	68	28	25	712	254	217	180	14	387	14	16	7	60	52	.54	27	.253	.317	.351

Rob Butler

Bats: Left **Throws:** Left **Pos:** OF | **Ht:** 5'11" **Wt:** 185 **Born:** 4/10/70 **Age:** 26

Year Team	Lg	BATTING															BASERUNNING				PERCENTAGES		
		G	AB	H	2B	3B	HR	TB	R	RBI	TBB	IBB	SO	HBP	SH	SF	SB	CS	SB%	GDP	Avg	OBP	SLG
1991 St. Cathrns	A	76	311	105	16	5	7	152	71	45	20	5	21	2	6	3	31	15	.67	2	.338	.378	.489
1992 Dunedin	A	92	391	140	13	7	4	179	67	41	22	2	36	2	2	1	19	14	.58	7	.358	.394	.458
1993 Syracuse	AAA	55	208	59	11	2	1	77	30	14	15	2	29	3	3	2	7	5	.58	6	.284	.338	.370
1994 Syracuse	AAA	25	95	25	6	1	1	36	16	11	8	1	12	1	0	2	2	0	1.00	1	.263	.321	.379
1995 Scranton-Wb	AAA	92	327	98	16	4	3	131	46	35	24	2	39	6	4	4	5	8	.38	14	.300	.355	.401
1993 Toronto	AL	17	48	13	4	0	0	17	8	2	7	0	12	1	0	0	2	2	.50	0	.271	.375	.354
1994 Toronto	AL	41	74	13	0	1	0	15	13	5	7	0	8	1	4	2	0	1	.00	3	.176	.250	.203
5 Min. YEARS		340	1332	427	62	19	16	575	230	146	89	12	137	14	15	12	64	42	.60	30	.321	.366	.432
2 Maj. YEARS		58	122	26	4	1	0	32	21	7	14	0	20	2	4	2	2	3	.40	3	.213	.300	.262

Chris Butterfield

Bats: Both **Throws:** Right **Pos:** DH | **Ht:** 6'1" **Wt:** 193 **Born:** 8/27/67 **Age:** 28

Year Team	Lg	BATTING															BASERUNNING				PERCENTAGES		
		G	AB	H	2B	3B	HR	TB	R	RBI	TBB	IBB	SO	HBP	SH	SF	SB	CS	SB%	GDP	Avg	OBP	SLG
1989 Pittsfield	A	71	260	79	13	8	8	132	51	47	30	2	63	5	2	3	14	4	.78	3	.304	.383	.508
1990 St. Lucie	A	118	386	76	10	5	4	108	50	36	64	5	128	4	7	2	21	9	.70	6	.197	.316	.280
1991 St. Lucie	A	121	426	96	24	7	3	143	41	40	53	4	87	2	6	2	8	8	.50	5	.225	.313	.336
1992 Binghamton	AA	138	483	108	20	3	14	176	59	51	57	8	126	3	4	3	9	4	.69	4	.224	.308	.364
1993 Binghamton	AA	77	237	50	10	5	9	97	32	37	24	1	72	1	2	4	0	4	.00	2	.211	.282	.409
1994 Norfolk	AAA	24	66	12	3	0	2	21	4	9	4	0	29	0	0	0	0	1	.00	0	.182	.229	.318
Charlotte	AAA	22	39	9	2	0	2	17	5	7	5	1	11	0	0	0	1	0	1.00	1	.231	.318	.436
Canton-Akrn	AA	22	65	13	2	0	2	21	5	10	3	0	16	0	1	0	1	1	.50	0	.200	.235	.323
1995 San Antonio	AA	2	6	0	0	0	0	0	0	0	2	0	3	0	0	0	0	0	.00	0	.000	.250	.000
7 Min. YEARS		595	1968	443	84	28	44	715	247	237	242	21	535	15	22	14	54	31	.64	21	.225	.313	.363

John Byington

Bats: Right **Throws:** Right **Pos:** 3B | **Ht:** 5'8" **Wt:** 165 **Born:** 11/4/67 **Age:** 28

Year Team	Lg	BATTING															BASERUNNING				PERCENTAGES		
		G	AB	H	2B	3B	HR	TB	R	RBI	TBB	IBB	SO	HBP	SH	SF	SB	CS	SB%	GDP	Avg	OBP	SLG
1989 Beloit	A	44	149	31	7	2	1	45	14	14	14	2	26	3	0	2	0	3	.00	6	.208	.286	.302
1990 Beloit	A	127	438	115	23	1	17	191	75	89	49	2	68	8	2	7	2	4	.33	4	.263	.343	.436
1991 El Paso	AA	129	501	137	27	1	9	193	60	89	25	1	63	4	5	15	3	3	.50	17	.273	.305	.385
1992 El Paso	AA	130	468	143	39	4	4	202	60	64	32	2	54	7	1	11	5	9	.36	15	.306	.351	.432
1993 New Orleans	AAA	123	436	122	33	2	11	192	58	63	35	4	32	6	2	5	3	2	.60	17	.280	.338	.440
1994 New Orleans	AAA	134	506	157	32	4	9	224	71	86	36	3	29	8	0	5	8	2	.80	16	.310	.362	.443
1995 New Orleans	AAA	13	47	12	1	0	1	16	5	3	2	0	4	1	0	2	1	0	1.00	1	.255	.288	.340
Okla. City	AAA	109	390	101	15	2	2	126	44	29	19	2	37	4	4	4	6	2	.75	16	.259	.297	.323
7 Min. YEARS		809	2935	818	177	16	54	1189	387	437	212	16	313	41	14	51	28	25	.53	92	.279	.331	.405

Tony Byrd

Bats: Right **Throws:** Right **Pos:** OF   **Ht:** 5'11" **Wt:** 180 **Born:** 11/13/70 **Age:** 25

Year	Team	Lg	G	AB	H	2B	3B	HR	TB	R	RBI	TBB	IBB	SO	HBP	SH	SF	SB	CS	SB%	GDP	Avg	OBP	SLG
1992	Kenosha	A	46	150	35	5	3	0	46	15	10	12	0	35	0	3	0	7	1	.88	2	.233	.290	.307
1993	Fort Wayne	A	123	479	140	19	10	16	227	84	79	58	4	78	3	0	3	24	11	.69	6	.292	.370	.474
1994	Nashville	AA	132	512	121	25	6	7	179	62	38	37	0	114	3	4	3	28	10	.74	10	.236	.290	.350
1995	New Britain	AA	123	442	109	20	8	3	154	54	51	28	2	85	3	5	5	21	10	.68	13	.247	.293	.348
	4 Min. YEARS		424	1583	405	69	27	26	606	215	178	135	6	312	9	12	11	80	32	.71	31	.256	.316	.383

Clayton Byrne

Bats: Right **Throws:** Right **Pos:** OF   **Ht:** 6'1" **Wt:** 180 **Born:** 2/12/72 **Age:** 24

Year	Team	Lg	G	AB	H	2B	3B	HR	TB	R	RBI	TBB	IBB	SO	HBP	SH	SF	SB	CS	SB%	GDP	Avg	OBP	SLG
1991	Kane County	A	26	104	22	6	0	0	28	14	3	2	0	26	2	1	2	2	0	1.00	2	.212	.236	.269
	Bluefield	R	54	221	71	9	4	3	97	39	25	18	0	38	2	2	1	8	17	.32	2	.321	.376	.439
1992	Kane County	A	109	347	78	14	1	2	100	42	35	13	0	74	3	6	1	12	5	.71	7	.225	.258	.288
1993	Albany	A	122	457	126	26	3	6	176	64	55	42	0	69	3	0	4	23	11	.68	13	.276	.338	.385
1994	Rochester	AAA	3	2	0	0	0	0	0	0	0	0	0	2	0	0	0	0	0	.00	0	.000	.000	.000
	Frederick	A	77	290	83	20	2	8	131	48	39	19	0	45	3	2	3	14	6	.70	7	.286	.333	.452
	Bowie	AA	26	95	21	4	0	0	25	12	9	2	0	16	0	2	1	5	2	.71	1	.221	.235	.263
1995	Bowie	AA	14	55	12	2	1	1	19	5	6	4	0	8	0	2	2	2	1	.67	3	.218	.262	.345
	Frederick	A	35	136	31	7	0	3	47	16	13	5	0	29	0	0	0	3	4	.43	4	.228	.255	.346
	High Desert	A	54	199	47	10	2	1	64	24	19	7	0	36	3	0	0	7	5	.58	1	.236	.273	.322
	5 Min. YEARS		520	1906	491	98	13	24	687	264	204	112	0	343	16	15	14	76	51	.60	40	.258	.302	.360

Alexis Cabreja

Bats: Right **Throws:** Right **Pos:** OF   **Ht:** 6'1" **Wt:** 205 **Born:** 3/22/69 **Age:** 27

Year	Team	Lg	G	AB	H	2B	3B	HR	TB	R	RBI	TBB	IBB	SO	HBP	SH	SF	SB	CS	SB%	GDP	Avg	OBP	SLG
1993	Erie	A	46	159	36	9	2	1	52	23	27	9	0	36	1	0	1	5	2	.71	4	.226	.271	.327
1995	Norwich	AA	6	11	1	0	0	0	1	1	1	3	0	0	0	0	0	1	0	1.00	0	.091	.286	.091
	2 Min. YEARS		52	170	37	9	2	1	53	24	28	12	0	36	1	0	1	6	2	.75	4	.218	.272	.312

Francisco Cabrera

Bats: Right **Throws:** Right **Pos:** DH   **Ht:** 6'4" **Wt:** 195 **Born:** 10/10/66 **Age:** 29

Year	Team	Lg	G	AB	H	2B	3B	HR	TB	R	RBI	TBB	IBB	SO	HBP	SH	SF	SB	CS	SB%	GDP	Avg	OBP	SLG
1986	Ventura	A	6	12	2	1	0	0	3	2	3	0	0	4	0	0	0	1	0	1.00	0	.167	.167	.250
	St. Cathrns	A	68	246	73	13	2	6	108	31	35	16	1	48	4	1	1	7	4	.64	6	.297	.348	.439
1987	Myrtle Bch	A	129	449	124	27	1	14	195	61	72	40	6	82	3	0	6	4	2	.67	12	.276	.335	.434
1988	Dunedin	A	9	35	14	4	0	1	21	2	9	1	0	2	0	0	0	0	0	.00	0	.400	.417	.600
	Knoxville	AA	119	429	122	19	1	20	203	59	54	26	2	75	2	2	5	4	3	.57	13	.284	.325	.473
1989	Syracuse	AAA	113	428	128	30	5	9	195	59	71	20	2	72	3	1	7	4	4	.50	11	.299	.330	.456
	Richmond	AAA	3	6	2	1	0	0	3	0	1	0	0	0	0	0	1	0	0	.00	0	.333	.286	.500
1990	Richmond	AAA	35	132	30	3	1	7	56	12	20	7	0	23	1	0	2	2	0	1.00	3	.227	.268	.424
1991	Richmond	AAA	32	119	31	7	1	7	61	22	24	10	0	21	3	0	1	0	1	.00	6	.261	.331	.513
1992	Richmond	AAA	81	301	82	11	0	9	120	30	35	17	2	49	0	0	1	0	1	.00	6	.272	.310	.399
1995	Richmond	AAA	36	104	24	5	0	1	32	7	14	5	2	22	0	0	2	0	1	.00	4	.231	.261	.308
	Thunder Bay	IND	12	50	18	4	0	1	25	5	6	4	1	6	0	0	0	0	0	.00	1	.360	.407	.500
1989	Toronto	AL	3	12	2	1	0	0	3	1	0	1	0	3	0	0	0	0	0	.00	0	.167	.231	.250
	Atlanta	NL	4	14	3	2	0	0	5	0	0	0	0	3	0	0	0	0	0	.00	0	.214	.214	.357
1990	Atlanta	NL	63	137	38	5	1	7	66	14	25	5	0	21	0	0	1	1	0	1.00	4	.277	.301	.482
1991	Atlanta	NL	44	95	23	6	0	4	41	7	23	6	0	20	0	0	1	1	1	.50	5	.242	.284	.432
1992	Atlanta	NL	12	10	3	0	0	2	9	2	3	1	0	1	0	0	0	0	0	.00	0	.300	.364	.900
1993	Atlanta	NL	70	83	20	3	0	4	35	8	11	8	1	21	0	0	0	0	0	.00	2	.241	.308	.422
	8 Min. YEARS		643	2311	650	125	11	75	1022	290	344	146	16	404	16	4	26	22	16	.58	61	.281	.325	.442
	5 Maj. YEARS		196	351	89	17	1	17	159	32	62	21	1	69	0	0	2	2	1	.67	11	.254	.294	.453

Jolbert Cabrera

Bats: Right **Throws:** Right **Pos:** SS   **Ht:** 6'0" **Wt:** 177 **Born:** 12/8/72 **Age:** 23

Year	Team	Lg	G	AB	H	2B	3B	HR	TB	R	RBI	TBB	IBB	SO	HBP	SH	SF	SB	CS	SB%	GDP	Avg	OBP	SLG
1991	Sumter	A	101	324	66	4	0	1	73	33	20	19	0	62	4	4	2	10	11	.48	5	.204	.255	.225
1992	Albany	A	118	377	86	9	2	0	99	44	23	34	0	77	1	6	0	22	11	.67	8	.228	.294	.263
1993	Burlington	A	128	507	129	24	2	0	157	62	38	39	0	93	7	11	4	31	11	.74	13	.254	.314	.310
1994	W. Palm Bch	A	83	266	54	4	0	0	58	32	13	14	0	48	8	4	0	7	10	.41	4	.203	.264	.218
	San Bernrdo	A	30	109	27	5	1	0	34	14	11	14	0	24	0	4	2	2	2	.50	1	.248	.328	.312
	Harrisburg	AA	3	2	0	0	0	0	0	0	0	0	0	1	0	0	0	0	0	.00	0	.000	.000	.000
1995	W. Palm Bch	A	103	357	102	23	2	1	132	62	25	38	0	61	8	6	4	19	12	.61	3	.286	.364	.370
	Harrisburg	AA	9	35	10	2	0	0	12	4	1	1	0	3	0	2	0	3	1	.75	1	.286	.306	.343
	5 Min. YEARS		575	1977	474	71	7	2	565	251	131	159	0	369	28	37	12	94	58	.62	35	.240	.304	.286

45

Jose Cabrera

Pitches: Right **Bats:** Right **Pos:** P **Ht:** 6'0" **Wt:** 160 **Born:** 3/24/72 **Age:** 24

Year	Team	Lg	G	GS	CG	GF	IP	BFP	H	R	ER	HR	SH	SF	HB	TBB	IBB	SO	WP	Bk	W	L	Pct.	ShO	Sv	ERA
1992	Burlington	R	13	13	1	0	92.1	367	74	27	18	6	2	0	2	18	0	79	3	1	8	3	.727	0	0	1.75
1993	Columbus	A	26	26	1	0	155.1	624	122	54	46	8	2	4	1	53	2	105	8	4	11	6	.647	0	0	2.67
1994	Kinston	A	24	24	0	0	133.2	575	134	84	66	15	6	3	5	43	0	110	5	5	4	13	.235	0	0	4.44
1995	Canton-Akrn	AA	24	11	1	4	85	350	83	32	31	7	1	6	1	21	1	61	0	2	5	3	.625	1	0	3.28
	4 Min. YEARS		87	74	3	4	466.1	1916	413	197	161	36	11	13	9	135	3	355	16	12	28	25	.528	1	0	3.11

Greg Cadaret

Pitches: Left **Bats:** Left **Pos:** P **Ht:** 6'3" **Wt:** 215 **Born:** 2/27/62 **Age:** 34

Year	Team	Lg	G	GS	CG	GF	IP	BFP	H	R	ER	HR	SH	SF	HB	TBB	IBB	SO	WP	Bk	W	L	Pct.	ShO	Sv	ERA
1984	Modesto	A	26	26	6	0	171.1	0	162	79	58	7	0	0	1	82	0	138	14	2	13	8	.619	2	0	3.05
1985	Huntsville	AA	17	17	0	0	82.1	387	96	61	56	9	2	4	3	57	0	60	9	0	3	7	.300	0	0	6.12
	Modesto	A	12	12	1	0	61.1	0	59	50	40	4	0	0	0	54	0	43	10	0	3	9	.250	1	0	5.87
1986	Huntsville	AA	28	28	1	0	141.1	666	166	106	85	6	1	4	1	98	0	113	15	0	12	5	.706	0	0	5.41
1987	Huntsville	AA	24	0	0	21	40.1	172	31	16	13	1	1	0	0	20	3	48	6	1	5	2	.714	0	9	2.90
	Tacoma	AAA	7	0	0	4	13	57	5	6	5	1	2	0	0	13	1	12	0	0	1	2	.333	0	1	3.46
1995	Louisville	AAA	12	0	0	2	11.2	50	14	4	4	0	1	0	0	1	0	7	0	0	1	0	1.000	0	1	3.09
	Las Vegas	AAA	28	4	0	6	52	234	56	40	34	6	2	3	0	22	0	52	10	0	3	5	.375	0	0	5.88
1987	Oakland	AL	29	0	0	7	39.2	176	37	22	20	6	2	2	1	24	1	30	1	0	6	2	.750	0	0	4.54
1988	Oakland	AL	58	0	0	16	71.2	311	60	26	23	2	5	3	1	36	1	64	5	3	5	2	.714	0	3	2.89
1989	New York	AL	20	13	3	1	92.1	412	109	53	47	7	3	3	2	38	1	66	6	2	5	5	.500	1	0	4.58
	Oakland	AL	26	0	0	6	27.2	119	21	9	7	0	0	2	0	19	3	14	0	0	0	0	.000	0	0	2.28
1990	New York	AL	54	6	0	9	121.1	525	120	62	56	8	9	4	1	64	5	80	14	0	5	4	.556	0	3	4.15
1991	New York	AL	68	5	0	17	121.2	517	110	52	49	8	6	3	2	59	6	105	3	1	8	6	.571	0	3	3.62
1992	New York	AL	46	11	1	9	103.2	471	104	53	49	12	3	3	2	74	7	73	5	1	4	8	.333	1	1	4.25
1993	Kansas City	AL	13	0	0	3	15.1	62	14	5	5	0	1	0	1	7	0	2	0	0	1	1	.500	0	0	2.93
	Cincinnati	NL	34	0	0	15	32.2	158	40	19	18	3	3	0	1	23	5	23	2	0	2	1	.667	0	1	4.96
1994	Detroit	AL	17	0	0	9	20	91	17	9	8	0	0	0	0	16	3	14	3	0	1	0	1.000	0	2	3.60
	Toronto	AL	21	0	0	8	20	100	24	15	13	4	0	0	0	17	2	15	6	0	0	0	.000	0	0	5.85
	5 Min. YEARS		154	87	8	33	573.1	1566	589	362	295	34	9	11	6	347	4	473	64	3	41	38	.519	3	10	4.63
	8 Maj. YEARS		386	35	4	100	666	2942	656	325	295	50	34	20	11	377	34	486	45	7	37	30	.552	2	13	3.99

Tim Cain

Pitches: Right **Bats:** Both **Pos:** P **Ht:** 6'1" **Wt:** 180 **Born:** 10/9/69 **Age:** 26

Year	Team	Lg	G	GS	CG	GF	IP	BFP	H	R	ER	HR	SH	SF	HB	TBB	IBB	SO	WP	Bk	W	L	Pct.	ShO	Sv	ERA
1990	Rangers	R	16	1	0	4	36	146	27	22	15	1	0	0	5	6	0	38	2	2	0	3	.000	0	1	3.75
1991	Bend	A	17	6	0	4	58.1	267	65	49	37	2	0	1	4	25	0	59	8	0	1	3	.250	0	2	5.71
1993	Rochester	IND	20	12	2	1	102.1	428	76	37	27	4	7	1	13	28	0	73	3	1	4	4	.500	1	1	2.37
1994	Winnipeg	IND	6	6	1	0	43	167	30	11	11	2	1	0	1	6	0	50	1	0	5	1	.833	0	0	2.30
	New Britain	AA	10	10	0	0	50.2	226	65	39	32	8	2	0	3	18	0	37	1	1	2	4	.333	0	0	5.68
1995	Trenton	AA	29	1	0	8	50.2	215	46	25	21	1	4	0	6	17	3	45	3	0	4	3	.571	0	4	3.73
	Pawtucket	AAA	14	0	0	5	27.2	111	24	7	7	0	1	1	1	8	0	19	1	0	4	0	1.000	0	4	2.28
	5 Min. YEARS		112	36	3	22	368.2	1560	333	190	150	18	15	3	33	108	4	321	19	4	20	18	.526	1	12	3.66

Miguel Cairo

Bats: Right **Throws:** Right **Pos:** 2B **Ht:** 6'0" **Wt:** 160 **Born:** 5/4/74 **Age:** 22

Year	Team	Lg	G	AB	H	2B	3B	HR	TB	R	RBI	TBB	IBB	SO	HBP	SH	SF	SB	CS	SB%	GDP	Avg	OBP	SLG
1992	Dodgers	R	21	76	23	5	2	0	32	10	9	2	0	6	2	2	1	1	0	1.00	1	.303	.333	.421
	Vero Beach	A	36	125	28	0	0	0	28	7	7	11	0	12	0	3	1	5	3	.63	3	.224	.285	.224
1993	Vero Beach	A	89	343	108	10	1	1	123	49	23	26	0	22	7	10	0	23	16	.59	2	.315	.375	.359
1994	Bakersfield	A	133	533	155	23	4	2	192	76	48	34	3	37	6	15	4	44	23	.66	9	.291	.338	.360
1995	San Antonio	AA	107	435	121	20	1	1	146	53	41	26	0	31	5	4	4	33	16	.67	6	.278	.323	.336
	4 Min. YEARS		386	1512	435	58	8	4	521	195	128	99	3	108	20	34	10	106	58	.65	21	.288	.338	.345

Sergio Cairo

Bats: Right **Throws:** Right **Pos:** OF **Ht:** 6'1" **Wt:** 165 **Born:** 10/22/70 **Age:** 25

Year	Team	Lg	G	AB	H	2B	3B	HR	TB	R	RBI	TBB	IBB	SO	HBP	SH	SF	SB	CS	SB%	GDP	Avg	OBP	SLG
1989	Bluefield	R	57	207	55	13	2	2	78	30	40	13	0	19	2	1	2	1	7	.13	5	.266	.313	.377
1990	Wausau	A	111	333	80	8	4	3	105	31	29	25	0	49	3	2	3	12	7	.63	8	.240	.297	.315
1991	Frederick	A	90	299	94	20	2	3	127	38	40	47	2	39	0	1	2	4	7	.36	8	.314	.405	.425
1992	Hagerstown	AA	121	409	115	13	4	2	142	43	46	33	1	53	1	3	5	5	8	.38	11	.281	.333	.347
1993	Birmingham	AA	68	189	43	2	0	2	51	20	13	28	0	28	1	0	1	6	3	.67	6	.228	.329	.270
	Charlotte	A	34	122	45	4	1	5	66	15	25	15	0	11	2	2	0	3	4	.43	3	.369	.446	.541
1994	Tulsa	AA	123	454	124	24	1	14	192	48	76	40	1	88	2	2	3	1	3	.25	12	.273	.333	.423
1995	Ottawa	AAA	2	6	2	1	0	0	3	1	0	0	0	1	0	0	0	0	0	.00	0	.333	.333	.500
	Harrisburg	AA	4	13	0	0	0	0	0	0	0	1	0	2	1	0	0	0	0	.00	1	.000	.133	.000
	7 Min. YEARS		610	2032	558	85	14	31	764	226	269	202	4	290	12	11	16	32	39	.45	54	.275	.341	.376

Daniel Camacho

Pitches: Right **Bats:** Right **Pos:** P   **Ht:** 5'11" **Wt:** 190 **Born:** 11/11/73 **Age:** 22

			HOW MUCH HE PITCHED					WHAT HE GAVE UP												THE RESULTS					
Year	Team	Lg	G	GS	CG	GF	IP	BFP	H	R	ER	HR	SH	SF	HB	TBB	IBB	SO	WP	Bk	W	L	Pct.	ShO	Sv	ERA
1993	Great Falls	R	28	0	0	13	65.1	253	38	14	10	6	1	2	6	18	1	79	9	0	5	2	.714	0	5	1.38
1994	Bakersfield	A	10	0	0	4	22.1	86	9	3	3	0	0	1	0	15	1	25	5	0	0	0	.000	0	0	1.21
1995	San Antonio	AA	11	0	0	10	11.1	47	9	2	2	0	0	0	0	8	0	8	2	0	1	1	.500	0	2	1.59
	San Bernrdo	A	43	1	0	27	68.1	295	66	32	30	7	5	1	1	30	3	79	5	1	6	2	.750	0	9	3.95
	3 Min. YEARS		92	1	0	54	167.1	681	122	51	45	13	6	4	7	71	5	191	21	1	12	5	.706	0	16	2.42

Stanton Cameron

Bats: Right **Throws:** Right **Pos:** OF   **Ht:** 6'5" **Wt:** 195 **Born:** 7/5/69 **Age:** 26

			BATTING														BASERUNNING				PERCENTAGES		
Year	Team	Lg	G	AB	H	2B	3B	HR	TB	R	RBI	TBB	IBB	SO	HBP	SH	SF	SB	CS	SB%	GDP	Avg	OBP	SLG
1987	Kingsport	R	26	53	7	1	0	1	11	6	5	10	0	24	0	1	1	1	1	.50	1	.132	.266	.208
1988	Mets	R	51	171	40	10	1	1	55	24	15	25	0	33	3	1	0	10	5	.67	7	.234	.342	.322
1989	Pittsfield	A	71	253	65	13	1	10	110	35	50	41	2	71	4	1	1	7	2	.78	3	.257	.368	.435
1990	Columbia	A	87	302	90	19	1	15	156	57	57	52	1	68	4	0	7	3	2	.60	7	.298	.400	.517
1991	St. Lucie	A	83	232	43	7	0	2	56	25	26	46	0	82	4	3	1	1	1	.50	2	.185	.329	.241
1992	Frederick	A	127	409	101	16	1	29	206	76	92	90	3	121	11	2	5	2	3	.40	7	.247	.392	.504
1993	Bowie	AA	118	384	106	27	1	21	198	65	64	84	2	103	6	0	6	6	7	.46	11	.276	.408	.516
1994	Buffalo	AAA	38	139	24	4	0	4	40	10	14	8	1	29	2	0	0	3	0	1.00	5	.173	.228	.288
	Carolina	AA	88	327	102	28	3	11	169	58	56	34	2	74	2	0	4	10	2	.83	7	.312	.376	.517
1995	Calgary	AAA	7	24	5	4	0	0	9	8	4	4	0	4	0	0	0	0	0	.00	0	.208	.321	.375
	Okla. City	AAA	5	12	2	1	0	0	3	2	0	4	0	3	0	0	0	0	0	.00	0	.167	.375	.250
	Canton-Akrn	AA	35	82	21	8	0	1	32	11	12	10	0	18	4	2	2	1	0	1.00	1	.256	.357	.390
	9 Min. YEARS		736	2388	606	138	8	95	1045	377	395	408	11	630	40	10	27	44	23	.66	51	.254	.368	.438

Darrin Campbell

Bats: Right **Throws:** Right **Pos:** C   **Ht:** 5'9" **Wt:** 180 **Born:** 7/1/67 **Age:** 29

			BATTING														BASERUNNING				PERCENTAGES		
Year	Team	Lg	G	AB	H	2B	3B	HR	TB	R	RBI	TBB	IBB	SO	HBP	SH	SF	SB	CS	SB%	GDP	Avg	OBP	SLG
1988	South Bend	A	4	13	3	1	0	0	4	1	0	0	0	4	1	0	0	0	0	.00	0	.231	.286	.308
1989	Sarasota	A	29	89	20	6	0	0	26	10	3	4	0	23	2	2	0	0	0	.00	2	.225	.274	.292
1990	Birmingham	AA	3	11	2	0	0	0	2	0	0	1	0	3	1	0	0	0	0	.00	0	.182	.308	.182
	Sarasota	A	93	319	75	10	1	4	99	26	37	26	4	67	2	2	4	4	4	.50	5	.235	.293	.310
	Vancouver	AAA	2	7	1	0	0	0	1	0	0	0	0	1	0	0	0	0	0	.00	0	.143	.143	.143
1991	Birmingham	AA	94	289	64	7	3	7	98	39	32	27	0	94	7	1	3	0	1	.00	5	.221	.301	.339
1992	Vancouver	AAA	25	46	7	4	0	0	11	6	3	6	0	13	1	1	1	0	0	.00	1	.152	.259	.239
	Birmingham	AA	66	202	45	11	0	5	71	27	24	17	3	47	1	1	4	4	3	.57	4	.223	.281	.351
1993	Rochester	AAA	54	115	21	9	1	1	35	21	11	11	0	30	1	0	1	0	0	.00	3	.183	.258	.304
1995	Canton-Akrn	AA	2	7	0	0	0	0	0	1	0	0	0	1	0	0	0	0	0	.00	0	.000	.000	.000
	7 Min. YEARS		372	1098	238	48	5	17	347	131	110	92	7	283	16	7	13	8	8	.50	20	.217	.284	.316

Mike Campbell

Pitches: Right **Bats:** Right **Pos:** P   **Ht:** 6'3" **Wt:** 215 **Born:** 2/17/64 **Age:** 32

			HOW MUCH HE PITCHED					WHAT HE GAVE UP												THE RESULTS					
Year	Team	Lg	G	GS	CG	GF	IP	BFP	H	R	ER	HR	SH	SF	HB	TBB	IBB	SO	WP	Bk	W	L	Pct.	ShO	Sv	ERA
1985	Salinas	A	10	10	0	0	50	0	41	22	18	3	0	0	1	22	0	50	3	1	4	4	.500	0	0	3.24
1986	Chattanooga	AA	12	12	1	0	75	312	69	32	29	5	0	1	2	22	0	80	3	0	9	1	.900	1	0	3.48
	Calgary	AAA	1	1	0	0	3	12	1	3	3	1	0	0	0	2	0	3	0	0	0	1	.000	0	0	9.00
1987	Calgary	AAA	24	23	4	1	162.2	683	136	65	48	9	3	7	1	72	2	130	11	2	15	2	.882	1	0	2.66
1988	Calgary	AAA	10	10	3	0	70.1	303	80	35	35	7	3	0	0	26	1	38	2	1	4	4	.500	0	0	4.48
1989	Calgary	AAA	16	16	1	0	96	410	102	48	44	14	0	3	3	29	1	61	2	1	6	5	.545	0	0	4.13
	Indianapols	AAA	9	3	0	0	27	105	23	12	12	3	0	2	0	4	0	18	1	0	1	0	1.000	0	0	4.00
1990	Vancouver	AAA	21	8	0	5	66.1	297	76	45	43	6	2	5	1	30	1	50	0	0	4	5	.444	0	0	5.83
1991	Tulsa	AA	23	15	3	2	108.1	465	104	68	63	14	4	3	1	51	5	90	3	1	5	7	.417	0	1	5.23
	Okla. City	AAA	1	1	0	0	3.1	16	5	5	5	2	0	0	0	1	0	3	0	0	0	0	.000	0	0	13.50
1992	Okla. City	AAA	11	7	0	2	41	177	43	26	26	6	2	2	4	12	2	25	1	0	2	3	.400	0	0	5.71
1993	Rancho Cuca	A	2	0	0	1	4.2	18	1	1	1	1	0	0	0	4	0	4	0	0	1	0	1.000	0	0	1.93
	Las Vegas	AAA	21	0	0	9	31.2	142	39	20	19	9	0	4	0	9	2	24	6	0	2	1	.667	0	5	5.40
1994	Las Vegas	AAA	32	19	1	6	137	610	170	78	73	20	5	9	2	38	3	128	8	2	9	7	.563	0	0	4.80
1995	Iowa	AAA	21	15	0	2	102.2	419	93	31	28	10	4	4	3	29	5	88	2	0	9	3	.750	0	0	2.45
1987	Seattle	AL	9	9	1	0	49.1	215	41	29	26	9	2	3	2	25	2	35	1	1	1	4	.200	0	0	4.74
1988	Seattle	AL	20	20	2	0	114.2	507	128	81	75	18	2	5	0	43	1	63	4	4	6	10	.375	0	0	5.89
1989	Seattle	AL	5	5	0	0	21	103	28	22	17	4	0	0	0	10	0	6	0	0	1	2	.333	0	0	7.29
1992	Texas	AL	1	0	0	0	3.2	15	3	4	4	1	0	0	0	2	0	2	0	0	0	1	.000	0	0	9.82
1994	San Diego	NL	3	2	0	0	8.1	43	13	12	12	5	1	0	0	5	0	10	0	0	0	1	.500	0	0	12.96
	11 Min. YEARS		214	140	13	28	979	3969	983	491	447	110	23	40	18	351	22	792	42	6	71	43	.623	3	2	4.11
	5 Maj. YEARS		38	36	3	0	197	883	213	148	134	37	5	8	2	85	3	116	5	5	9	18	.333	0	0	6.12

George Canale

Bats: Left **Throws:** Right **Pos:** 1B **Ht:** 6' 1" **Wt:** 190 **Born:** 8/11/65 **Age:** 30

Year Team	Lg	G	AB	H	2B	3B	HR	TB	R	RBI	TBB	IBB	SO	HBP	SH	SF	SB	CS	SB%	GDP	Avg	OBP	SLG
1986 Helena	R	65	221	72	19	0	9	118	48	49	54	0	65	0	2	5	6	4	.60	2	.326	.450	.534
1987 Stockton	A	66	246	69	18	1	7	110	42	48	38	3	59	1	2	2	5	4	.56	8	.280	.376	.447
El Paso	AA	65	253	65	10	2	7	100	38	36	20	1	69	2	0	0	3	2	.60	4	.257	.316	.395
1988 El Paso	AA	132	496	120	23	2	23	216	77	93	59	5	152	2	0	2	9	3	.75	12	.242	.324	.435
1989 Denver	AAA	144	503	140	33	9	18	245	80	71	71	1	134	2	2	6	5	8	.38	3	.278	.366	.487
1990 Denver	AAA	134	468	119	18	6	12	185	76	60	69	4	103	1	3	3	12	5	.71	10	.254	.349	.395
1991 Denver	AAA	88	274	64	10	2	10	108	36	47	51	0	49	2	0	3	6	2	.75	6	.234	.355	.394
1992 Canton-Akrn	AA	54	194	59	10	1	15	116	47	49	30	1	37	1	0	1	2	1	.67	1	.304	.398	.598
Colo. Sprng	AAA	46	163	48	12	2	5	79	33	31	16	1	27	0	0	2	0	0	.00	2	.294	.354	.485
1993 Charlotte	AAA	73	208	45	8	0	6	71	32	27	26	3	47	0	0	1	1	1	.50	4	.216	.302	.341
Colo. Sprng	AAA	39	115	33	9	1	5	59	15	15	10	2	20	1	0	1	2	1	.67	1	.287	.346	.513
1994 Memphis	AA	114	426	98	25	2	12	163	54	51	51	8	79	0	0	2	7	1	.88	12	.230	.311	.383
1995 Carolina	AA	130	487	140	30	6	21	245	71	102	46	6	83	4	0	8	1	3	.25	15	.287	.349	.503
1989 Milwaukee	AL	13	26	5	1	0	1	9	5	3	2	0	3	0	1	0	0	1	.00	0	.192	.250	.346
1990 Milwaukee	AL	10	13	1	1	0	0	2	4	0	2	0	6	0	0	0	0	1	.00	0	.077	.200	.154
1991 Milwaukee	AL	21	34	6	2	0	3	17	6	10	8	0	6	0	0	0	2	0	.00	2	.176	.318	.500
10 Min. YEARS		1150	4054	1072	225	34	150	1815	649	679	541	35	924	16	9	36	59	35	.63	80	.264	.351	.448
3 Maj. YEARS		44	73	12	4	0	4	28	15	13	12	0	15	0	1	2	0	2	.00	5	.164	.276	.384

Willie Canate

Bats: Right **Throws:** Right **Pos:** OF **Ht:** 6' 0" **Wt:** 170 **Born:** 12/11/71 **Age:** 24

Year Team	Lg	G	AB	H	2B	3B	HR	TB	R	RBI	TBB	IBB	SO	HBP	SH	SF	SB	CS	SB%	GDP	Avg	OBP	SLG
1989 Indians	R	11	24	5	2	0	0	7	4	0	0	0	8	0	0	0	0	0	.00	0	.208	.208	.292
1990 Watertown	A	57	199	52	6	2	2	68	28	15	10	0	43	3	1	0	9	4	.69	6	.261	.307	.342
1991 Kinston	A	51	189	41	3	1	1	49	28	12	14	0	29	3	5	0	4	2	.67	5	.217	.282	.259
Columbus	A	62	204	49	13	2	4	78	32	20	25	0	32	4	7	3	14	5	.74	10	.240	.331	.382
1992 Columbus	A	133	528	167	37	8	5	235	110	63	56	3	66	10	3	6	25	9	.74	3	.316	.388	.445
1993 Indianapols	AAA	3	5	0	0	0	0	0	0	0	0	0	1	0	0	0	0	0	.00	0	.000	.000	.000
Knoxville	AA	9	37	10	2	0	1	15	8	4	5	0	2	0	0	0	2	1	.67	1	.270	.357	.405
Syracuse	AAA	7	24	6	0	0	2	12	3	5	5	0	3	0	0	0	0	2	.00	1	.250	.379	.500
1994 Syracuse	AAA	45	153	28	6	0	0	34	14	10	7	0	27	1	2	0	1	1	.50	1	.183	.224	.222
Knoxville	AA	85	326	80	12	1	0	94	39	28	22	0	52	4	2	5	16	7	.70	8	.245	.297	.288
1995 Syracuse	AAA	114	345	82	17	2	3	112	48	30	23	0	62	9	3	2	8	5	.62	9	.238	.301	.325
1993 Toronto	AL	38	47	10	0	0	1	13	12	3	6	0	15	1	2	1	1	1	.50	2	.213	.309	.277
7 Min. YEARS		577	2034	520	98	16	18	704	314	187	167	3	325	34	23	16	79	36	.69	44	.256	.320	.346

Casey Candaele

Bats: Both **Throws:** Right **Pos:** 2B **Ht:** 5' 9" **Wt:** 165 **Born:** 1/12/61 **Age:** 35

Year Team	Lg	G	AB	H	2B	3B	HR	TB	R	RBI	TBB	IBB	SO	HBP	SH	SF	SB	CS	SB%	GDP	Avg	OBP	SLG
1984 Jacksonvlle	AA	132	532	145	23	2	2	178	68	53	30	1	35	1	5	6	26	18	.59	13	.273	.309	.335
1985 Indianapols	AAA	127	390	101	13	5	0	124	55	35	44	2	33	0	11	1	13	10	.57	15	.259	.333	.318
1986 Indianapols	AAA	119	480	145	32	6	2	195	77	42	46	6	29	1	11	2	16	10	.62	8	.302	.363	.406
1988 Indianapols	AAA	60	239	63	11	6	2	92	23	36	12	0	20	0	1	7	5	1	.83	5	.264	.291	.385
Tucson	AAA	17	66	17	3	0	0	20	8	5	4	0	6	0	0	0	4	2	.67	5	.258	.300	.303
1989 Tucson	AAA	68	206	45	6	1	0	53	22	17	20	4	37	0	4	1	6	3	.67	7	.218	.286	.257
1990 Tucson	AAA	7	28	6	1	0	0	7	2	2	3	1	2	1	1	0	1	2	.33	1	.214	.313	.250
1993 Tucson	AAA	6	27	8	1	0	0	9	4	4	3	1	2	0	0	2	1	2	.33	2	.296	.367	.333
1994 Indianapols	AAA	131	511	144	31	7	4	201	66	52	32	4	65	0	3	4	8	6	.57	21	.282	.322	.393
1995 Albuquerque	AAA	12	27	7	0	0	0	7	2	2	4	0	4	0	1	1	0	1	.00	1	.259	.344	.259
Buffalo	AAA	97	364	90	10	7	4	126	50	38	22	1	42	2	4	7	9	2	.82	6	.247	.289	.346
1986 Montreal	NL	30	104	24	4	1	0	30	9	6	5	0	15	0	0	1	3	5	.38	3	.231	.264	.288
1987 Montreal	NL	138	449	122	23	4	1	156	62	23	38	3	28	2	4	2	7	10	.41	5	.272	.330	.347
1988 Houston	NL	21	31	5	3	0	0	8	2	1	1	0	6	0	1	0	0	1	.00	0	.161	.188	.258
Montreal	NL	36	116	20	5	1	0	27	9	4	10	1	11	0	2	0	1	0	1.00	7	.172	.238	.233
1990 Houston	NL	130	262	75	8	6	3	104	30	22	31	5	42	1	4	0	7	5	.58	4	.286	.364	.397
1991 Houston	NL	151	461	121	20	7	4	167	44	50	40	7	49	0	1	3	9	3	.75	5	.262	.319	.362
1992 Houston	NL	135	320	68	12	1	1	85	19	18	24	3	36	3	7	6	7	1	.88	5	.213	.269	.266
1993 Houston	NL	75	121	29	8	0	1	40	18	7	10	0	14	0	0	0	2	3	.40	0	.240	.298	.331
9 Min. YEARS		776	2870	771	131	34	14	1012	377	286	220	20	275	5	41	29	89	57	.61	84	.269	.319	.353
7 Maj. YEARS		716	1864	464	83	20	10	617	193	131	159	19	201	6	19	12	36	28	.56	29	.249	.308	.331

Jason Canizaro

Bats: Right **Throws:** Right **Pos:** 2B **Ht:** 5'10" **Wt:** 175 **Born:** 7/4/73 **Age:** 22

Year Team	Lg	G	AB	H	2B	3B	HR	TB	R	RBI	TBB	IBB	SO	HBP	SH	SF	SB	CS	SB%	GDP	Avg	OBP	SLG
1993 Giants	R	49	180	47	10	6	3	78	34	41	22	1	40	0	0	3	12	3	.80	4	.261	.337	.433
1994 San Jose	A	126	464	117	16	2	15	182	77	69	46	1	98	5	0	3	12	6	.67	7	.252	.324	.392
1995 Shreveport	AA	126	440	129	25	7	12	204	83	60	58	4	98	6	4	5	16	9	.64	9	.293	.379	.464
3 Min. YEARS		301	1084	293	51	15	30	464	194	170	126	6	236	11	4	11	40	18	.69	20	.270	.349	.428

Carmine Cappuccio

Bats: Left **Throws:** Right **Pos:** OF **Ht:** 6'3" **Wt:** 185 **Born:** 2/1/70 **Age:** 26

Year	Team	Lg	G	AB	H	2B	3B	HR	TB	R	RBI	TBB	IBB	SO	HBP	SH	SF	SB	CS	SB%	GDP	Avg	OBP	SLG
1992	Utica	A	22	87	24	4	2	0	32	15	13	6	0	10	1	0	1	5	0	1.00	3	.276	.326	.368
	South Bend	A	49	182	53	9	2	0	66	23	19	21	1	21	1	1	1	2	3	.40	4	.291	.366	.363
1993	Sarasota	A	24	90	17	2	2	1	26	9	12	4	1	10	0	0	0	3	0	1.00	1	.189	.223	.289
	South Bend	A	101	383	117	26	5	4	165	59	52	42	6	56	6	0	1	2	6	.25	11	.305	.382	.431
1994	Pr. William	A	101	401	117	30	1	12	185	71	60	25	1	53	9	2	4	8	4	.67	7	.292	.344	.461
1995	Birmingham	AA	65	248	69	13	3	4	100	34	38	22	4	21	2	3	2	2	2	.50	10	.278	.339	.403
	Nashville	AAA	66	216	59	14	0	5	88	30	24	29	4	26	1	1	1	0	2	.00	6	.273	.360	.407
	4 Min. YEARS		428	1607	456	98	15	26	662	241	218	149	17	197	20	7	10	22	17	.56	42	.284	.350	.412

Nick Capra

Bats: Right **Throws:** Right **Pos:** OF **Ht:** 5' 8" **Wt:** 165 **Born:** 3/8/58 **Age:** 38

Year	Team	Lg	G	AB	H	2B	3B	HR	TB	R	RBI	TBB	IBB	SO	HBP	SH	SF	SB	CS	SB%	GDP	Avg	OBP	SLG
1984	Okla. City	AAA	123	442	113	18	1	2	139	68	21	76	1	67	0	12	1	47	18	.72	4	.256	.364	.314
1985	Okla. City	AAA	97	353	96	17	1	0	115	53	27	68	1	45	4	2	1	25	16	.61	5	.272	.394	.326
1986	Buffalo	AAA	36	123	25	2	0	2	33	14	9	20	1	13	0	2	2	6	9	.40	2	.203	.310	.268
	Okla. City	AAA	72	283	80	16	2	5	115	54	22	46	0	36	2	6	2	26	6	.81	5	.283	.384	.406
1987	Okla. City	AAA	97	353	107	18	3	1	134	69	39	62	3	53	0	6	3	21	13	.62	6	.303	.404	.380
1988	Omaha	AAA	93	346	100	11	6	1	126	53	43	50	0	49	1	4	2	28	9	.76	9	.289	.378	.364
1989	Omaha	AAA	128	500	145	27	3	7	199	84	44	70	1	67	4	5	1	31	18	.63	8	.290	.381	.398
1990	Okla. City	AAA	122	451	125	26	3	5	172	80	45	68	0	61	3	7	1	34	14	.71	4	.277	.375	.381
1991	Okla. City	AAA	127	485	132	33	4	5	188	74	38	87	1	58	4	8	1	27	13	.68	7	.272	.386	.388
1992	Nashville	AAA	90	287	67	14	1	5	98	48	27	51	1	36	3	12	2	31	10	.76	3	.233	.353	.341
	Scranton-Wb	AAA	18	56	16	3	0	1	22	12	3	10	1	7	0	1	0	3	2	.60	0	.286	.394	.393
1993	Edmonton	AAA	106	389	108	19	4	7	156	71	44	58	0	42	2	4	4	20	13	.61	9	.278	.371	.401
1994	Edmonton	AAA	109	382	116	26	6	7	175	71	41	43	0	25	4	2	3	25	10	.71	7	.304	.377	.458
1995	Charlotte	AAA	119	406	104	17	1	9	150	60	51	54	0	45	1	2	2	22	12	.65	5	.256	.343	.369
1982	Texas	AL	13	15	4	0	0	1	7	2	1	3	0	4	1	0	0	2	1	.67	1	.267	.421	.467
1983	Texas	AL	8	2	0	0	0	0	0	2	0	0	0	0	0	0	0	0	0	.00	0	.000	.000	.000
1985	Texas	AL	8	8	1	0	0	0	1	1	0	0	0	0	0	0	0	0	0	.00	0	.125	.125	.125
1988	Kansas City	AL	14	29	4	1	0	0	5	3	0	2	0	3	0	0	0	1	0	1.00	3	.138	.194	.172
1991	Texas	AL	2	0	0	0	0	0	0	1	0	1	0	0	0	0	0	0	0	.00	0	.000	1.000	.000
	12 Min. YEARS		1337	4856	1334	247	35	57	1822	811	454	763	10	604	28	73	25	346	163	.68	74	.275	.375	.375
	5 Maj. YEARS		45	54	9	1	0	1	13	9	1	6	0	7	1	0	0	3	1	.75	4	.167	.262	.241

Johnny Cardenas

Bats: Right **Throws:** Right **Pos:** C **Ht:** 6'3" **Wt:** 210 **Born:** 7/23/70 **Age:** 25

Year	Team	Lg	G	AB	H	2B	3B	HR	TB	R	RBI	TBB	IBB	SO	HBP	SH	SF	SB	CS	SB%	GDP	Avg	OBP	SLG
1993	Bellingham	A	47	157	32	5	1	2	45	17	24	17	0	34	7	2	1	1	0	1.00	4	.204	.308	.287
1994	Riverside	A	58	178	37	3	0	1	43	16	13	14	1	36	3	3	1	0	1	.00	6	.208	.276	.242
1995	Port City	AA	57	195	44	9	0	0	53	17	17	9	1	45	0	1	1	1	3	.25	9	.226	.259	.272
	3 Min. YEARS		162	530	113	17	1	3	141	50	54	40	2	115	10	6	3	2	4	.33	19	.213	.280	.266

Paul Carey

Bats: Left **Throws:** Right **Pos:** 1B **Ht:** 6' 4" **Wt:** 215 **Born:** 1/8/68 **Age:** 28

Year	Team	Lg	G	AB	H	2B	3B	HR	TB	R	RBI	TBB	IBB	SO	HBP	SH	SF	SB	CS	SB%	GDP	Avg	OBP	SLG
1990	Miami	A	49	153	50	5	3	4	73	23	20	43	1	39	2	0	1	4	3	.57	2	.327	.477	.477
1991	Hagerstown	AA	114	373	94	29	1	12	161	63	65	68	8	109	4	2	5	5	4	.56	11	.252	.369	.432
1992	Frederick	A	41	136	41	6	0	9	74	24	26	28	5	22	2	0	1	0	1	.00	2	.301	.425	.544
	Rochester	AAA	30	87	20	4	1	1	29	9	7	6	0	16	2	0	1	0	0	.00	2	.230	.292	.333
	Hagerstown	AA	48	163	44	8	0	4	64	17	18	15	5	37	2	0	1	3	2	.60	4	.270	.337	.393
1993	Rochester	AAA	96	325	101	20	4	12	165	63	50	65	11	92	5	1	2	0	0	.00	10	.311	.431	.508
1994	Frederick	A	16	54	20	1	1	6	41	16	12	11	0	7	2	0	0	1	1	.00	2	.370	.493	.759
	Rochester	AAA	47	172	43	5	0	8	72	29	28	28	2	47	2	0	3	1	0	1.00	5	.250	.356	.419
1995	Rochester	AAA	89	284	67	13	0	9	107	39	50	40	5	68	5	1	5	1	2	.33	2	.236	.335	.377
1993	Baltimore	AL	18	47	10	1	0	0	11	1	3	5	0	14	0	0	0	0	0	.00	4	.213	.288	.234
	6 Min. YEARS		530	1747	480	91	10	65	786	283	276	304	37	437	26	4	19	14	13	.52	40	.275	.386	.450

Todd Carey

Bats: Left **Throws:** Right **Pos:** 3B **Ht:** 6'1" **Wt:** 180 **Born:** 8/14/71 **Age:** 24

Year	Team	Lg	G	AB	H	2B	3B	HR	TB	R	RBI	TBB	IBB	SO	HBP	SH	SF	SB	CS	SB%	GDP	Avg	OBP	SLG
1992	Elmira	A	54	197	40	7	2	0	51	18	19	9	1	40	0	1	3	0	4	.00	2	.203	.234	.259
1993	Ft. Laud	A	118	444	109	14	5	3	142	41	31	24	1	44	0	5	3	2	6	.25	10	.245	.282	.320
1994	Lynchburg	A	105	363	85	14	2	13	142	42	42	49	0	77	3	1	2	1	4	.20	5	.234	.329	.391
1995	Sarasota	A	25	85	26	6	0	4	44	15	19	9	0	17	0	0	2	2	1	.67	3	.306	.372	.518
	Trenton	AA	76	228	62	11	1	8	99	30	36	28	0	44	4	1	2	3	4	.43	2	.272	.359	.434
	4 Min. YEARS		378	1317	322	52	10	28	478	146	147	119	2	222	7	8	10	8	19	.30	22	.244	.308	.363

Dan Carlson
Pitches: Right **Bats:** Right **Pos:** P   **Ht:** 6'1" **Wt:** 185 **Born:** 1/26/70 **Age:** 26

			HOW MUCH HE PITCHED						WHAT HE GAVE UP												THE RESULTS					
Year	Team	Lg	G	GS	CG	GF	IP	BFP	H	R	ER	HR	SH	SF	HB	TBB	IBB	SO	WP	Bk	W	L	Pct.	ShO	Sv	ERA
1990	Everett	A	17	11	0	3	62.1	279	60	42	37	5	1	4	1	33	1	77	9	5	2	6	.250	0	0	5.34
1991	Clinton	A	27	27	5	0	181.1	740	149	69	62	11	3	3	2	76	0	164	18	5	16	7	.696	3	0	3.08
1992	Shreveport	AA	27	27	4	0	186	765	166	85	66	15	5	3	1	60	3	157	4	0	15	9	.625	1	0	3.19
1993	Phoenix	AAA	13	12	0	0	70	320	79	54	51	12	2	1	5	32	1	48	4	0	5	6	.455	0	0	6.56
	Shreveport	AA	15	15	2	0	100.1	397	86	30	25	9	4	4	0	26	3	81	5	0	7	4	.636	1	0	2.24
1994	Phoenix	AAA	31	22	0	2	151.1	665	173	80	78	21	3	9	1	55	1	117	10	0	13	6	.684	0	1	4.64
1995	Phoenix	AAA	23	22	2	1	132.2	582	138	67	63	11	7	7	3	66	0	93	6	1	9	5	.643	0	0	4.27
	6 Min. YEARS		153	136	13	6	884	3748	851	427	382	84	25	31	13	348	9	737	56	11	67	43	.609	5	1	3.89

Ken Carlyle
Pitches: Right **Bats:** Right **Pos:** P   **Ht:** 6'1" **Wt:** 185 **Born:** 9/16/69 **Age:** 26

			HOW MUCH HE PITCHED						WHAT HE GAVE UP												THE RESULTS					
Year	Team	Lg	G	GS	CG	GF	IP	BFP	H	R	ER	HR	SH	SF	HB	TBB	IBB	SO	WP	Bk	W	L	Pct.	ShO	Sv	ERA
1992	Niagara Fal	A	1	1	0	0	6	26	6	1	1	0	0	0	0	1	0	9	1	1	1	0	1.000	0	0	1.50
	Fayetteville	A	14	14	1	0	79.2	319	64	21	17	3	0	1	4	24	0	59	6	1	8	4	.667	1	0	1.92
1993	Toledo	AAA	15	14	1	0	75.2	339	88	59	54	13	2	2	1	36	1	43	4	2	2	10	.167	0	0	6.42
	London	AA	12	12	1	0	78	341	72	40	32	8	1	3	5	35	1	50	0	2	4	6	.400	0	0	3.69
1994	Trenton	AA	19	19	5	0	116.1	519	125	75	53	6	4	3	3	47	3	69	5	2	3	9	.250	1	0	4.10
	Toledo	AAA	12	1	0	3	24.1	104	23	13	11	2	1	2	2	8	0	12	1	0	1	0	1.000	0	1	4.07
1995	Toledo	AAA	32	20	0	0	124.2	541	139	65	60	10	2	5	4	44	2	63	7	0	8	8	.500	0	0	4.33
	4 Min. YEARS		105	81	8	3	504.2	2189	517	274	228	42	10	16	19	195	7	305	24	8	27	37	.422	2	1	4.07

Brian Carpenter
Pitches: Right **Bats:** Right **Pos:** P   **Ht:** 6'0" **Wt:** 220 **Born:** 3/3/71 **Age:** 25

			HOW MUCH HE PITCHED						WHAT HE GAVE UP												THE RESULTS					
Year	Team	Lg	G	GS	CG	GF	IP	BFP	H	R	ER	HR	SH	SF	HB	TBB	IBB	SO	WP	Bk	W	L	Pct.	ShO	Sv	ERA
1993	Savannah	A	28	28	0	0	154.1	629	145	55	49	8	2	5	2	41	0	147	2	1	10	8	.556	0	0	2.86
1994	St. Pete	A	26	20	0	3	131.2	572	152	76	70	16	2	5	7	38	1	76	2	1	12	7	.632	0	0	4.78
1995	St. Pete	A	16	7	0	2	59	226	40	17	14	4	1	1	0	11	0	51	4	0	5	3	.625	0	0	2.14
	Arkansas	AA	17	4	0	1	52.2	232	57	32	29	6	6	2	3	21	1	35	1	1	2	1	.667	0	0	4.96
	3 Min. YEARS		87	59	0	6	397.2	1659	394	180	162	34	11	13	12	111	2	309	9	3	29	19	.604	0	1	3.67

Bubba Carpenter
Bats: Left **Throws:** Left **Pos:** OF   **Ht:** 6'1" **Wt:** 185 **Born:** 7/23/68 **Age:** 27

			BATTING															BASERUNNING				PERCENTAGES		
Year	Team	Lg	G	AB	H	2B	3B	HR	TB	R	RBI	TBB	IBB	SO	HBP	SH	SF	SB	CS	SB%	GDP	Avg	OBP	SLG
1991	Pr. William	A	69	236	66	10	3	6	100	33	34	40	3	50	2	1	3	4	1	.80	7	.280	.384	.424
1992	Albany-Colo	AA	60	221	51	11	5	4	84	24	31	25	2	41	2	0	1	2	3	.40	8	.231	.313	.380
	Pr. William	A	68	240	76	15	2	5	110	41	41	35	2	44	1	1	6	4	4	.50	4	.317	.397	.458
1993	Albany-Colo	AA	14	53	17	4	0	2	27	8	14	7	0	4	0	0	1	2	2	.50	2	.321	.393	.509
	Columbus	AAA	70	199	53	9	0	5	77	29	17	29	3	35	3	0	1	2	2	.50	6	.266	.366	.387
1994	Albany-Colo	AA	116	378	109	14	1	13	164	47	51	58	5	65	3	3	3	9	5	.64	3	.288	.385	.434
	Columbus	AAA	7	15	4	0	0	0	4	0	2	2	0	7	0	0	0	0	0	.00	1	.267	.267	.267
1995	Columbus	AAA	116	374	92	12	3	11	143	57	49	40	2	70	1	2	3	13	6	.68	2	.246	.318	.382
	5 Min. YEARS		520	1716	468	75	14	46	709	239	239	234	15	316	12	7	18	36	23	.61	31	.273	.361	.413

Chris Carpenter
Pitches: Right **Bats:** Right **Pos:** P   **Ht:** 6'6" **Wt:** 220 **Born:** 4/27/75 **Age:** 21

			HOW MUCH HE PITCHED						WHAT HE GAVE UP												THE RESULTS					
Year	Team	Lg	G	GS	CG	GF	IP	BFP	H	R	ER	HR	SH	SF	HB	TBB	IBB	SO	WP	Bk	W	L	Pct.	ShO	Sv	ERA
1994	Medicne Hat	R	15	15	0	0	84.2	366	76	40	26	3	2	3	8	39	0	80	9	2	6	3	.667	0	0	2.76
1995	Dunedin	A	15	15	0	0	99.1	420	83	29	24	3	2	0	4	50	0	56	9	3	3	5	.375	0	0	2.17
	Knoxville	AA	12	12	0	0	64.1	287	71	47	37	3	1	4	1	31	1	53	9	0	3	7	.300	0	0	5.18
	2 Min. YEARS		42	42	0	0	248.1	1073	230	116	87	9	5	7	13	120	1	189	27	5	12	15	.444	0	0	3.15

Cris Carpenter
Pitches: Right **Bats:** Right **Pos:** P   **Ht:** 6'1" **Wt:** 198 **Born:** 4/5/65 **Age:** 31

			HOW MUCH HE PITCHED						WHAT HE GAVE UP												THE RESULTS					
Year	Team	Lg	G	GS	CG	GF	IP	BFP	H	R	ER	HR	SH	SF	HB	TBB	IBB	SO	WP	Bk	W	L	Pct.	ShO	Sv	ERA
1988	Louisville	AAA	13	13	1	0	87.2	359	81	28	28	7	2	1	0	26	0	45	1	0	6	2	.750	1	0	2.87
1989	Louisville	AAA	27	0	0	23	36.2	154	39	17	13	3	1	2	0	9	3	29	1	0	5	3	.625	0	11	3.19
1990	Louisville	AAA	22	22	2	0	143.1	591	146	61	59	16	6	5	6	21	2	100	1	1	10	8	.556	1	0	3.70
1995	Louisville	AAA	49	0	0	20	66.2	273	59	18	18	6	6	2	1	20	10	41	3	0	2	5	.286	0	5	2.43
1988	St. Louis	NL	8	8	1	0	47.2	203	56	27	25	3	1	4	1	9	2	24	1	0	2	3	.400	0	0	4.72
1989	St. Louis	NL	36	5	0	10	68	303	70	30	24	4	4	4	2	26	9	35	1	0	4	4	.500	0	0	3.18
1990	St. Louis	NL	4	0	0	1	8	32	5	4	4	2	0	0	0	2	1	6	0	0	0	0	.000	0	0	4.50
1991	St. Louis	NL	59	0	0	19	66	266	53	31	31	6	3	2	0	20	9	47	1	0	10	4	.714	0	1	4.23
1992	St. Louis	NL	73	0	0	21	88	355	69	29	29	10	8	3	4	27	8	46	5	0	5	4	.556	0	1	2.97
1993	Texas	AL	27	0	0	8	32	139	35	15	15	4	1	3	2	12	1	27	2	0	4	1	.800	0	1	4.22
	Florida	NL	29	0	0	9	37.1	154	29	15	12	1	1	1	2	13	2	26	5	0	0	1	.000	0	0	2.89

Year	Team	Lg																							
1994	Texas	AL	47	0	0	16	59	263	69	35	33	7	3	3	0	20	7	39	1	0	2	5	.286	0	5	5.03
4 Min. YEARS			111	35	3	43	334.1	1377	325	124	118	32	15	10	7	76	15	215	6	1	23	18	.561	2	16	3.18
7 Maj. YEARS			283	13	1	84	406	1715	386	186	173	37	21	20	11	129	39	250	16	0	27	22	.551	0	7	3.83

Jerry Carpenter

Bats: Right **Throws:** Right **Pos:** C   **Ht:** 6'0" **Wt:** 180 **Born:** 3/27/72 **Age:** 24

			BATTING													BASERUNNING				PERCENTAGES		
Year	Team	Lg	G	AB	H	2B	3B	HR	TB	R	RBI	TBB	IBB	SO	HBP	SH	SF	SB	CS	SB%	GDP	Avg	OBP	SLG
1994	Boise	A	24	55	14	2	0	1	19	5	9	3	0	16	0	2	0	1	0	1.00	2	.255	.293	.345
1995	Lk Elsinore	A	1	2	0	0	0	0	0	0	0	1	0	0	0	0	0	0	0	.00	1	.000	.333	.000
	Midland	AA	2	2	0	0	0	0	0	1	0	0	0	1	0	0	0	0	0	.00	0	.000	.000	.000
	Cedar Rapds	A	11	30	3	0	0	0	3	2	2	4	0	9	0	0	0	0	0	.00	0	.100	.206	.100
2 Min. YEARS			38	89	17	2	0	1	22	8	11	8	0	26	0	2	0	1	0	1.00	3	.191	.258	.247

Mark Carper

Pitches: Right **Bats:** Right **Pos:** P   **Ht:** 6'2" **Wt:** 200 **Born:** 9/29/68 **Age:** 27

			HOW MUCH HE PITCHED					WHAT HE GAVE UP									THE RESULTS					
Year	Team	Lg	G	GS	CG	GF	IP	BFP	H	R	ER	HR	SH	SF	HB	TBB	IBB	SO	WP	Bk	W	L	Pct.	ShO	Sv	ERA
1991	Frederick	A	26	9	1	5	87.2	401	92	59	42	5	3	3	2	51	1	49	3	2	3	8	.273	0	0	4.31
1992	Hagerstown	AA	11	9	0	1	59	258	59	23	22	2	2	2	1	37	0	38	4	1	4	3	.571	0	0	3.36
	Albany-Colo	AA	20	10	1	3	74.1	309	62	22	20	4	0	1	2	30	1	36	8	0	5	4	.556	0	0	2.42
1993	Albany-Colo	AA	25	25	0	0	155.1	667	148	96	78	9	5	6	4	70	3	98	17	4	7	10	.412	0	0	4.52
1994	Columbus	AAA	26	18	2	4	117.2	520	128	68	57	9	3	3	10	48	1	58	6	0	8	6	.571	1	1	4.36
1995	Norwich	AA	1	1	0	0	5	26	9	6	6	2	0	1	2	1	0	3	2	0	0	0	.000	0	0	10.80
	Columbus	AAA	33	14	0	3	106.1	478	114	61	57	10	2	2	7	55	0	61	10	0	8	9	.471	0	1	4.82
5 Min. YEARS			142	86	4	16	605.1	2659	612	335	282	41	15	18	28	292	6	343	50	7	35	40	.467	1	2	4.19

Glenn Carter

Pitches: Right **Bats:** Right **Pos:** P   **Ht:** 6'0" **Wt:** 175 **Born:** 11/29/67 **Age:** 28

			HOW MUCH HE PITCHED					WHAT HE GAVE UP									THE RESULTS					
Year	Team	Lg	G	GS	CG	GF	IP	BFP	H	R	ER	HR	SH	SF	HB	TBB	IBB	SO	WP	Bk	W	L	Pct.	ShO	Sv	ERA
1988	Bend	A	9	9	1	0	45	197	46	25	23	6	0	3	2	15	0	47	5	4	3	4	.429	0	0	4.60
1989	Quad City	A	25	25	5	0	166.2	646	109	48	38	10	2	2	2	57	1	190	4	8	15	6	.714	1	0	2.05
1990	Midland	AA	20	20	1	0	102.2	483	132	84	67	9	0	5	1	46	0	66	4	2	3	8	.273	0	0	5.87
1991	Midland	AA	8	8	0	0	40.1	214	69	46	37	5	2	1	0	26	1	13	3	1	1	6	.143	0	0	8.26
1992	El Paso	AA	15	14	2	1	78	340	91	47	41	7	2	5	4	23	2	40	5	1	6	5	.545	2	0	4.73
1993	El Paso	AA	18	9	0	4	63.1	270	65	44	36	10	3	3	2	22	1	47	2	1	3	5	.375	0	0	5.12
	New Britain	AA	12	12	2	0	80.1	331	67	31	28	5	2	2	1	35	0	55	6	2	5	4	.556	1	0	3.14
1994	New Britain	AA	5	5	1	0	31.2	130	30	11	8	3	0	2	1	9	0	20	2	0	2	2	.500	1	0	2.27
	Pawtucket	AAA	22	20	1	0	124	542	140	81	66	21	2	6	3	44	0	73	6	2	8	7	.533	0	0	4.79
1995	Trenton	AA	14	0	0	12	14.2	63	15	8	5	0	0	0	1	4	0	10	1	1	1	1	.500	0	1	3.07
8 Min. YEARS			148	122	13	17	746.2	3216	764	425	349	76	13	29	17	281	5	561	38	22	47	48	.495	5	8	4.21

Jeff Carter

Bats: Both **Throws:** Right **Pos:** 2B   **Ht:** 5'10" **Wt:** 160 **Born:** 10/20/63 **Age:** 32

			BATTING													BASERUNNING				PERCENTAGES		
Year	Team	Lg	G	AB	H	2B	3B	HR	TB	R	RBI	TBB	IBB	SO	HBP	SH	SF	SB	CS	SB%	GDP	Avg	OBP	SLG
1985	Everett	A	54	207	63	9	4	4	92	45	22	36	0	33	2	1	1	28	8	.78	2	.304	.411	.444
1986	Clinton	A	128	472	107	13	3	3	135	62	47	58	0	76	3	3	2	60	20	.75	2	.227	.314	.286
1987	Fresno	A	135	510	140	14	11	6	194	109	59	94	4	75	5	4	7	49	25	.66	6	.275	.388	.380
1988	Shreveport	AA	124	409	101	9	8	3	135	50	41	51	0	52	6	6	2	15	10	.60	6	.247	.338	.330
1989	Shreveport	AA	127	445	129	16	4	3	162	77	52	63	2	47	4	8	5	33	16	.67	4	.290	.379	.364
1990	Phoenix	AAA	123	435	127	21	9	2	172	80	63	63	1	81	5	2	2	28	11	.72	4	.292	.386	.395
1991	Phoenix	AAA	92	246	67	5	2	2	82	47	24	34	1	51	0	2	1	11	7	.61	2	.272	.359	.333
1992	Tacoma	AAA	123	379	102	14	5	1	129	60	36	70	0	63	5	9	5	22	9	.71	6	.269	.386	.340
1993	Portland	AAA	101	381	124	21	7	0	159	73	48	63	1	53	3	1	3	17	12	.59	7	.325	.422	.417
1994	Salt Lake	AAA	122	460	149	18	6	5	194	105	70	89	2	78	7	0	3	26	12	.68	14	.324	.438	.422
1995	Charlotte	AAA	124	428	115	20	3	0	141	78	22	62	0	86	5	9	1	22	10	.69	5	.269	.367	.329
11 Min. YEARS			1251	4372	1224	160	62	29	1595	786	475	683	11	695	45	45	32	311	140	.69	58	.280	.380	.365

John Carter

Pitches: Right **Bats:** Right **Pos:** P   **Ht:** 6'1" **Wt:** 195 **Born:** 2/16/72 **Age:** 24

			HOW MUCH HE PITCHED					WHAT HE GAVE UP									THE RESULTS					
Year	Team	Lg	G	GS	CG	GF	IP	BFP	H	R	ER	HR	SH	SF	HB	TBB	IBB	SO	WP	Bk	W	L	Pct.	ShO	Sv	ERA
1991	Pirates	R	10	9	0	0	41	179	42	20	15	0	0	0	5	13	0	28	5	2	5	4	.556	0	0	3.29
1992	Augusta	A	1	1	0	0	5	19	3	0	0	1	0	2	1	1	0	4	0	1	0	0	.000	0	0	0.00
	Welland	A	3	3	0	0	15.2	68	12	11	6	2	0	1	1	7	0	15	1	1	0	3	.000	0	0	3.45
	Watertown	A	13	11	3	0	63	269	55	36	29	2	0	3	2	32	0	39	4	4	4	4	.500	0	0	4.14
1993	Columbus	A	29	29	1	0	180.1	731	147	72	56	7	4	2	7	48	0	134	8	2	17	7	.708	0	0	2.79
1994	Canton-Akrn	AA	22	22	3	0	131	564	134	68	63	15	4	2	6	53	1	73	7	1	9	6	.600	1	0	4.33
1995	Canton-Akrn	AA	5	5	0	0	27.1	118	27	13	12	0	0	0	3	13	2	14	1	0	1	2	.333	0	0	3.95
5 Min. YEARS			83	80	7	0	463.1	1948	420	220	181	26	9	8	26	167	3	307	26	11	36	26	.581	1	0	3.52

51

Mike Carter

Bats: Right **Throws:** Right **Pos:** OF **Ht:** 5'9" **Wt:** 170 **Born:** 5/5/69 **Age:** 27

Year	Team	Lg	G	AB	H	2B	3B	HR	TB	R	RBI	TBB	IBB	SO	HBP	SH	SF	SB	CS	SB%	GDP	Avg	OBP	SLG
1990	Helena	R	61	241	74	11	3	0	91	45	30	16	0	20	6	2	5	22	7	.76	0	.307	.358	.378
1991	Beloit	A	123	452	126	24	4	2	164	62	40	26	5	42	4	2	3	46	13	.78	5	.279	.322	.363
1992	Stockton	A	67	252	66	9	1	3	86	38	26	17	1	26	2	3	5	31	8	.79	4	.262	.308	.341
	El Paso	AA	50	165	42	4	4	1	57	20	15	16	2	31	0	3	1	10	8	.56	3	.255	.319	.345
1993	El Paso	AA	17	73	27	4	1	2	39	16	16	3	0	7	0	0	0	6	4	.60	1	.370	.395	.534
	New Orleans	AAA	104	369	102	18	5	3	139	49	31	17	0	52	4	11	4	20	11	.65	6	.276	.312	.377
1994	Iowa	AAA	122	421	122	24	3	6	170	56	30	14	1	43	4	12	4	16	14	.53	7	.290	.316	.404
1995	Iowa	AAA	107	421	137	16	3	8	183	57	40	14	3	46	6	3	3	12	12	.50	5	.325	.354	.435
	6 Min. YEARS		651	2394	696	110	24	25	929	343	228	123	12	267	26	36	25	163	77	.68	31	.291	.329	.388

Steve Carter

Bats: Left **Throws:** Right **Pos:** OF **Ht:** 6'4" **Wt:** 205 **Born:** 12/12/64 **Age:** 31

Year	Team	Lg	G	AB	H	2B	3B	HR	TB	R	RBI	TBB	IBB	SO	HBP	SH	SF	SB	CS	SB%	GDP	Avg	OBP	SLG
1987	Watertown	A	66	242	75	18	1	0	95	50	30	33	2	37	4	0	3	24	8	.75	1	.310	.397	.393
1988	Harrisburg	AA	9	35	10	2	0	0	12	7	2	1	0	6	0	0	0	3	0	1.00	0	.286	.306	.343
	Augusta	A	74	278	83	18	6	3	122	47	43	31	5	59	2	1	4	22	8	.73	5	.299	.368	.439
	Salem	A	6	21	6	0	0	0	6	4	1	0	0	1	0	0	0	2	0	1.00	0	.286	.286	.286
1989	Buffalo	AAA	100	356	105	24	6	1	144	53	43	27	5	62	2	1	3	17	9	.65	4	.295	.345	.404
1990	Buffalo	AAA	120	426	129	19	12	8	196	62	45	25	3	61	9	2	0	10	10	.50	11	.303	.354	.460
1991	Iowa	AAA	136	519	149	31	11	8	226	79	67	36	3	77	15	6	2	11	11	.50	10	.287	.350	.435
1992	Toledo	AAA	130	470	141	22	2	9	194	56	58	25	2	66	4	0	4	12	5	.71	11	.300	.338	.413
1993	Indianapolis	AAA	68	212	57	13	0	3	79	21	22	10	4	27	3	1	0	5	0	1.00	2	.269	.311	.373
	Tucson	AAA	40	146	36	7	0	1	46	26	17	11	2	13	2	0	0	6	2	.75	2	.247	.308	.315
1995	Charlotte	AAA	24	72	18	0	0	3	27	9	15	7	0	6	0	0	1	0	0	.00	1	.250	.313	.375
1989	Pittsburgh	NL	9	16	2	1	0	1	6	2	3	2	1	5	0	0	0	0	0	.00	0	.125	.222	.375
1990	Pittsburgh	NL	5	5	1	0	0	0	1	0	0	0	0	1	0	0	0	0	0	.00	0	.200	.200	.200
	8 Min. YEARS		773	2777	809	154	38	36	1147	414	343	206	26	415	41	11	17	112	53	.68	47	.291	.347	.413
	2 Maj. YEARS		14	21	3	1	0	1	7	2	3	2	1	6	0	0	0	0	0	.00	0	.143	.217	.333

Tommy Carter

Pitches: Left **Bats:** Left **Pos:** P **Ht:** 6'8" **Wt:** 215 **Born:** 4/30/70 **Age:** 26

Year	Team	Lg	G	GS	CG	GF	IP	BFP	H	R	ER	HR	SH	SF	HB	TBB	IBB	SO	WP	Bk	W	L	Pct.	ShO	Sv	ERA
1991	Yankees	R	7	3	0	1	11	47	5	5	5	0	0	1	0	4	0	11	3	3	0	0	.000	0	0	4.09
1992	Ft. Laud	A	10	8	0	1	36.1	171	35	32	22	1	0	2	1	30	0	23	9	0	3	5	.375	0	0	5.45
	Greensboro	A	13	13	0	0	74.2	319	77	41	35	2	1	1	3	29	0	59	13	0	3	3	.500	0	0	4.22
1993	Pr. William	A	26	26	1	0	145.2	641	160	87	71	11	9	5	0	53	0	105	11	1	8	10	.444	0	0	4.39
1994	Albany-Colo	AA	24	15	0	4	92.2	431	128	66	61	8	3	4	4	28	1	73	11	2	2	8	.200	0	0	5.92
1995	Norwich	AA	28	15	0	2	97	467	128	69	60	4	3	4	3	47	3	65	10	0	3	7	.300	0	0	5.57
	5 Min. YEARS		108	80	1	8	457.1	2076	535	300	254	26	16	17	11	191	4	336	57	6	19	33	.365	0	0	5.00

Gino Caruso

Pitches: Left **Bats:** Left **Pos:** P **Ht:** 6'0" **Wt:** 185 **Born:** 7/20/69 **Age:** 26

Year	Team	Lg	G	GS	CG	GF	IP	BFP	H	R	ER	HR	SH	SF	HB	TBB	IBB	SO	WP	Bk	W	L	Pct.	ShO	Sv	ERA
1992	Athletics	R	7	1	0	4	17	79	15	14	9	1	1	2	1	12	0	22	1	3	1	1	.500	0	1	4.76
	Sou. Oregon	A	12	0	0	6	21.1	102	15	3	1	0	4	1	3	18	1	27	1	1	2	0	1.000	0	1	0.42
1993	Pocatello	R	16	14	7	0	110.2	481	83	52	39	8	3	2	12	58	0	163	13	1	7	5	.583	2	0	3.17
1994	Stockton	A	43	9	0	14	105.2	465	97	56	42	6	6	6	9	49	3	89	7	1	8	2	.800	0	4	3.58
1995	El Paso	AA	46	1	0	19	71	331	87	55	48	6	3	2	3	36	3	53	4	0	2	1	.667	0	2	6.08
	4 Min. YEARS		124	25	7	43	325.2	1458	297	180	139	21	17	13	28	173	7	354	26	10	20	9	.690	2	8	3.84

Joe Caruso

Pitches: Right **Bats:** Right **Pos:** P **Ht:** 6'3" **Wt:** 195 **Born:** 9/16/70 **Age:** 25

Year	Team	Lg	G	GS	CG	GF	IP	BFP	H	R	ER	HR	SH	SF	HB	TBB	IBB	SO	WP	Bk	W	L	Pct.	ShO	Sv	ERA
1991	Red Sox	R	2	0	0	0	6	24	6	3	3	0	0	0	0	4	0	4	0	0	2	0	1.000	0	0	4.50
	Elmira	A	21	4	0	7	66.2	289	56	23	21	2	4	2	5	29	2	68	4	0	2	1	.667	0	2	2.84
1992	Lynchburg	A	49	0	0	27	118	470	68	36	26	5	6	2	3	40	3	133	8	0	6	4	.600	0	15	1.98
1993	Pawtucket	AAA	36	17	2	6	122.1	562	138	82	71	15	0	3	7	68	0	65	5	1	5	10	.333	0	0	5.30
1994	New Britain	AA	56	2	0	28	91.2	413	93	47	37	6	3	2	4	45	3	76	6	1	7	4	.636	0	0	3.63
1995	Trenton	AA	11	0	0	5	12.2	64	21	16	16	1	0	0	2	8	0	8	2	0	1	1	.500	0	0	11.37
	Lynchburg	A	29	0	0	14	39.2	168	36	13	13	0	4	4	3	16	4	27	1	1	4	0	1.000	0	4	2.95
	5 Min. YEARS		204	23	2	87	457	1990	418	220	188	29	17	13	24	210	12	381	31	3	27	20	.574	0	21	3.70

Jovino Carvajal

Bats: Both **Throws:** Right **Pos:** OF **Ht:** 6'1" **Wt:** 160 **Born:** 9/2/68 **Age:** 27

Year	Team	Lg	G	AB	H	2B	3B	HR	TB	R	RBI	TBB	IBB	SO	HBP	SH	SF	SB	CS	SB%	GDP	Avg	OBP	SLG
1990	Oneonta	A	52	171	49	3	1	0	54	19	18	7	0	37	0	3	0	15	11	.58	1	.287	.315	.316
1991	Ft. Laud	A	117	416	96	6	9	1	123	49	29	28	5	84	0	3	1	33	17	.66	7	.231	.279	.296
1992	Ft. Laud	A	113	435	100	7	1	1	112	53	29	30	0	63	1	3	4	40	14	.74	6	.230	.279	.257
1993	Pr. William	A	120	445	118	20	9	1	159	52	42	21	1	69	1	8	3	17	13	.57	8	.265	.298	.357
1994	Cedar Rapds	A	121	503	147	23	8	6	204	82	54	40	3	76	1	3	1	68	25	.73	5	.292	.345	.406
1995	Midland	AA	79	348	109	13	5	2	138	58	23	18	2	42	1	5	2	39	21	.65	3	.313	.347	.397
	Vancouver	AAA	41	163	53	3	3	1	65	25	10	3	0	18	1	1	0	10	7	.59	6	.325	.341	.399
	6 Min. YEARS		643	2481	672	75	36	12	855	338	205	147	11	389	5	26	11	222	108	.67	36	.271	.312	.345

Papo Casanova

Bats: Right **Throws:** Right **Pos:** C **Ht:** 6'0" **Wt:** 192 **Born:** 8/24/72 **Age:** 23

Year	Team	Lg	G	AB	H	2B	3B	HR	TB	R	RBI	TBB	IBB	SO	HBP	SH	SF	SB	CS	SB%	GDP	Avg	OBP	SLG
1990	Mets	R	23	65	5	0	0	0	5	4	1	4	0	16	0	0	0	0	1	.00	2	.077	.130	.077
1991	Mets	R	32	111	27	4	2	0	35	19	9	12	0	22	2	1	1	3	0	1.00	4	.243	.325	.315
	Kingsport	R	5	18	1	0	0	0	1	0	0	1	0	10	0	0	0	0	0	.00	1	.056	.105	.056
1992	Columbia	A	5	18	3	0	0	0	3	2	1	1	0	4	0	0	0	0	0	.00	2	.167	.211	.167
	Kingsport	R	42	137	37	9	1	4	60	25	27	26	2	25	4	0	0	3	1	.75	7	.270	.401	.438
1993	Waterloo	A	76	227	58	12	0	6	88	32	30	21	2	46	1	5	0	0	1	.00	5	.256	.321	.388
1994	Rancho Cuca	A	123	471	160	27	2	23	260	83	120	43	2	97	9	0	3	1	4	.20	16	.340	.403	.552
1995	Memphis	AA	89	306	83	18	0	12	137	42	44	25	2	51	4	0	4	4	1	.80	7	.271	.330	.448
	6 Min. YEARS		395	1353	374	70	5	45	589	207	232	133	8	271	20	6	8	11	8	.58	44	.276	.348	.435

Mike Case

Bats: Right **Throws:** Right **Pos:** OF-1B **Ht:** 6'2" **Wt:** 185 **Born:** 12/26/68 **Age:** 27

Year	Team	Lg	G	AB	H	2B	3B	HR	TB	R	RBI	TBB	IBB	SO	HBP	SH	SF	SB	CS	SB%	GDP	Avg	OBP	SLG
1992	Bend	A	49	170	43	10	1	5	70	30	20	22	0	48	2	0	1	10	2	.83	7	.253	.344	.412
1993	Colo. Sprng	AAA	3	3	1	0	0	0	1	0	0	0	0	0	0	0	0	0	0	.00	0	.333	.333	.333
	Central Val	A	124	449	124	20	2	11	181	54	80	53	2	120	7	6	7	21	6	.78	8	.276	.357	.403
1994	New Haven	AA	118	369	96	20	2	7	141	47	39	39	1	100	1	3	2	10	4	.71	10	.260	.331	.382
1995	Colo. Sprng	AAA	7	14	4	1	0	0	5	2	0	0	0	4	0	0	0	1	1	.50	0	.286	.286	.357
	New Haven	AA	102	310	76	16	2	10	126	55	46	43	4	72	4	3	4	6	2	.75	6	.245	.341	.406
	4 Min. YEARS		403	1315	344	67	7	33	524	188	185	157	7	344	14	12	14	48	15	.76	31	.262	.343	.398

Gregg Castaldo

Bats: Right **Throws:** Right **Pos:** 2B-SS **Ht:** 6'0" **Wt:** 180 **Born:** 3/14/71 **Age:** 25

Year	Team	Lg	G	AB	H	2B	3B	HR	TB	R	RBI	TBB	IBB	SO	HBP	SH	SF	SB	CS	SB%	GDP	Avg	OBP	SLG
1992	Kane County	A	19	37	6	0	0	0	6	2	3	3	0	6	2	0	0	2	3	.40	0	.162	.262	.162
	Bluefield	R	12	29	9	0	0	0	9	7	2	5	0	5	1	0	1	0	1	.00	1	.310	.417	.310
1993	Frederick	A	75	208	45	8	0	0	53	23	13	27	0	61	5	8	2	2	3	.40	7	.216	.318	.255
1994	Frederick	A	83	232	61	5	6	8	102	39	32	27	0	51	7	6	3	2	0	1.00	8	.263	.353	.440
1995	Bowie	AA	104	265	62	12	3	2	86	37	26	39	0	61	9	7	2	5	3	.63	5	.234	.349	.325
	4 Min. YEARS		293	771	183	25	9	10	256	108	76	101	0	184	24	21	8	11	10	.52	21	.237	.341	.332

Vince Castaldo

Bats: Left **Throws:** Right **Pos:** 3B **Ht:** 6'0" **Wt:** 190 **Born:** 7/19/67 **Age:** 28

Year	Team	Lg	G	AB	H	2B	3B	HR	TB	R	RBI	TBB	IBB	SO	HBP	SH	SF	SB	CS	SB%	GDP	Avg	OBP	SLG
1990	Helena	R	62	236	79	19	2	8	126	53	47	29	1	36	4	3	2	10	5	.67	5	.335	.413	.534
1991	Stockton	A	131	478	119	28	4	13	194	80	74	80	7	96	7	3	2	25	9	.74	12	.249	.363	.406
1992	El Paso	AA	119	412	119	33	10	3	181	61	50	48	8	77	3	1	2	12	6	.67	13	.289	.366	.439
1993	Ottawa	AAA	77	241	58	9	1	2	75	22	45	29	2	49	3	0	7	0	4	.00	9	.241	.321	.311
1994	St. Paul	IND	79	301	95	22	1	15	164	60	66	43	3	65	7	1	2	12	6	.67	6	.316	.411	.545
1995	Charlotte	AAA	7	10	2	0	0	0	2	2	1	3	0	3	0	0	1	0	0	.00	0	.200	.357	.200
	St. Paul	IND	51	171	52	15	1	6	87	22	36	45	6	33	2	0	2	4	4	.50	4	.304	.450	.509
	6 Min. YEARS		526	1849	524	126	19	47	829	300	319	277	20	359	26	8	18	63	34	.65	49	.283	.381	.448

Hector Castaneda

Bats: Left **Throws:** Right **Pos:** C **Ht:** 6'2" **Wt:** 190 **Born:** 11/1/71 **Age:** 24

Year	Team	Lg	G	AB	H	2B	3B	HR	TB	R	RBI	TBB	IBB	SO	HBP	SH	SF	SB	CS	SB%	GDP	Avg	OBP	SLG
1992	Orioles	R	42	122	35	9	0	0	44	18	14	27	1	23	3	0	0	2	1	.67	3	.287	.428	.361
	Kane County	A	5	13	2	1	0	0	3	1	0	0	0	4	0	0	0	0	0	.00	1	.154	.154	.231
1993	Bluefield	R	22	56	10	4	0	0	14	8	8	9	0	12	0	1	0	0	0	.00	1	.179	.288	.250
1994	Albany	A	54	150	50	6	0	2	62	22	17	24	1	20	0	4	0	5	0	1.00	6	.333	.425	.413
1995	Frederick	A	17	47	10	1	1	0	13	6	4	6	0	9	0	2	1	0	0	.00	2	.213	.296	.277
	Bowie	AA	34	65	10	2	0	0	12	3	6	10	0	10	0	0	0	0	0	.00	1	.154	.263	.185
	4 Min. YEARS		174	453	117	23	1	2	148	58	49	76	2	78	3	7	3	7	1	.88	14	.258	.366	.327

Benny Castillo

Bats: Right   Throws: Right   Pos: OF   Ht: 6'1"   Wt: 192   Born: 7/15/66   Age: 29

Year	Team	Lg	G	AB	H	2B	3B	HR	TB	R	RBI	TBB	IBB	SO	HBP	SH	SF	SB	CS	SB%	GDP	Avg	OBP	SLG
1991	Salt Lake	R	67	277	90	29	5	6	147	62	64	43	4	43	6	0	1	28	8	.78	7	.325	.425	.531
1992	Charlotte	A	105	347	98	25	3	7	150	46	55	45	0	67	2	1	3	6	7	.46	6	.282	.365	.432
1993	Tulsa	AA	86	272	62	12	1	5	91	34	14	20	0	53	8	2	1	6	3	.67	5	.228	.299	.335
1994	St. Paul	IND	74	288	87	17	3	8	134	46	42	28	2	50	5	3	1	8	14	.36	4	.302	.373	.465
1995	Canton-Akrn	AA	32	116	26	7	2	2	43	15	15	11	0	23	1	0	1	1	2	.33	2	.224	.295	.371
	Sioux Falls	IND	71	297	94	29	1	10	155	51	60	25	1	54	2	0	5	6	4	.60	5	.316	.368	.522
5 Min. YEARS			435	1597	457	119	15	38	720	254	250	172	7	290	24	6	12	55	38	.59	29	.286	.362	.451

Felipe Castillo

Pitches: Right   Bats: Right   Pos: P   Ht: 6'3"   Wt: 161   Born: 8/23/66   Age: 29

| | | | HOW MUCH HE PITCHED | | | | | | WHAT HE GAVE UP | | | | | | | | | THE RESULTS | | | | | |
Year	Team	Lg	G	GS	CG	GF	IP	BFP	H	R	ER	HR	SH	SF	HB	TBB	IBB	SO	WP	Bk	W	L	Pct.	ShO	Sv	ERA
1986	Rangers	R	13	0	0	3	14.2	81	22	17	13	0	1	1	2	10	0	17	2	0	0	1	.000	0	0	7.98
1987	Gastonia	A	26	22	0	1	119.2	549	118	70	58	2	1	2	5	66	1	86	8	3	7	8	.467	0	0	4.36
1988	Gastonia	A	23	23	3	0	139	595	122	67	43	3	1	4	5	48	0	69	2	7	5	10	.333	1	0	2.78
	Charlotte	A	4	4	0	0	17	77	24	14	9	0	1	0	0	2	0	12	2	0	2	1	.667	0	0	4.76
1989	Charlotte	A	1	1	0	0	5	20	4	0	0	0	0	0	0	2	0	1	0	0	1	0	1.000	0	0	0.00
	Tulsa	AA	25	25	6	0	156.2	671	171	95	77	7	7	6	6	47	1	66	5	0	8	12	.400	2	0	4.42
1990	Tulsa	AA	20	0	0	6	46	199	41	13	12	2	2	3	3	26	1	39	7	1	6	1	.857	0	1	2.35
	Okla. City	AAA	20	1	0	6	28.2	137	40	19	11	0	0	0	1	10	0	12	4	0	1	3	.250	0	0	3.45
1995	Tulsa	AA	14	0	0	5	33	147	42	19	14	2	2	0	1	11	1	16	3	0	2	2	.500	0	0	3.82
6 Min. YEARS			146	76	9	21	559.2	2476	584	314	237	16	15	16	23	222	4	318	33	11	32	38	.457	3	1	3.81

Juan Castillo

Pitches: Right   Bats: Right   Pos: P   Ht: 6'5"   Wt: 205   Born: 6/23/70   Age: 26

| | | | HOW MUCH HE PITCHED | | | | | | WHAT HE GAVE UP | | | | | | | | | THE RESULTS | | | | | |
Year	Team	Lg	G	GS	CG	GF	IP	BFP	H	R	ER	HR	SH	SF	HB	TBB	IBB	SO	WP	Bk	W	L	Pct.	ShO	Sv	ERA
1988	Mets	R	9	3	0	3	19.2	97	28	19	14	2	0	1	1	9	0	16	1	3	0	2	.000	0	0	6.41
1989	Mets	R	14	13	2	0	84.1	370	84	41	27	1	3	5	7	29	0	59	13	3	4	7	.364	1	0	2.88
1990	Pittsfield	A	16	14	0	1	70.1	333	64	52	37	0	0	1	2	58	2	65	13	2	5	8	.385	0	0	4.73
1991	Columbia	A	28	27	3	1	157.2	698	148	82	67	6	3	10	9	89	0	144	15	6	12	9	.571	1	0	3.82
1992	St. Lucie	A	24	24	7	0	153.2	617	135	53	44	9	2	2	10	27	1	80	9	7	11	8	.579	3	0	2.58
1993	Binghamton	AA	26	26	2	0	165.2	716	167	93	84	27	6	2	13	55	1	118	6	1	7	11	.389	0	0	4.56
1994	Binghamton	AA	18	18	3	0	111.1	463	98	40	32	6	3	2	6	44	2	80	4	2	11	2	.846	0	0	2.59
	Norfolk	AAA	6	6	1	0	28.2	131	35	24	23	6	1	2	3	15	0	9	3	0	1	5	.167	0	0	7.22
1995	Tucson	AAA	11	10	0	1	40.1	206	66	51	49	4	1	3	5	27	0	21	5	0	0	4	.000	0	0	10.93
	Jackson	AA	12	12	0	0	67.1	301	68	39	30	5	2	1	7	27	0	38	4	0	4	4	.500	0	0	4.01
1994	New York	NL	2	2	0	0	11.2	54	17	9	9	2	2	0	0	5	0	1	0	0	0	0	.000	0	0	6.94
8 Min. YEARS			164	153	18	6	899	3932	893	494	407	66	21	29	63	380	6	630	73	24	55	60	.478	5	0	4.07

Mariano Castillo

Pitches: Right   Bats: Right   Pos: P   Ht: 6'0"   Wt: 168   Born: 3/17/71   Age: 25

| | | | HOW MUCH HE PITCHED | | | | | | WHAT HE GAVE UP | | | | | | | | | THE RESULTS | | | | | |
Year	Team	Lg	G	GS	CG	GF	IP	BFP	H	R	ER	HR	SH	SF	HB	TBB	IBB	SO	WP	Bk	W	L	Pct.	ShO	Sv	ERA
1992	San Jose	A	10	1	0	2	21	92	19	15	10	1	2	2	0	10	0	10	2	2	0	0	.000	0	0	4.29
	Clinton	A	13	0	0	5	19.1	88	23	15	13	1	1	0	2	5	1	15	1	0	1	3	.250	0	1	6.05
1993	Clinton	A	40	0	0	19	69	291	64	31	26	3	4	6	1	19	1	59	1	0	4	2	.667	0	6	3.39
1994	San Jose	A	45	0	0	15	106.2	448	106	49	41	10	9	2	2	27	2	81	5	0	10	7	.588	0	5	3.46
1995	San Jose	A	21	0	0	8	56.2	226	49	14	10	1	2	0	2	13	0	51	1	0	4	4	.500	0	3	1.59
	Shreveport	AA	22	0	0	4	37.1	161	38	17	13	4	4	0	0	13	3	31	0	0	3	1	.750	0	0	3.13
4 Min. YEARS			151	1	0	53	310	1306	299	141	113	20	22	10	7	87	7	247	10	2	22	20	.524	0	15	3.28

Kevin Castleberry

Bats: Left   Throws: Right   Pos: 2B   Ht: 5'10"   Wt: 170   Born: 4/22/68   Age: 28

Year	Team	Lg	G	AB	H	2B	3B	HR	TB	R	RBI	TBB	IBB	SO	HBP	SH	SF	SB	CS	SB%	GDP	Avg	OBP	SLG
1989	Burlington	A	64	224	55	8	0	1	66	27	20	20	1	32	0	2	2	14	8	.64	5	.246	.305	.295
1990	Durham	A	119	372	90	18	4	7	137	59	27	23	1	64	0	2	3	15	4	.79	3	.242	.288	.368
1991	Miami	A	20	64	14	4	2	0	22	12	4	9	0	9	0	2	1	8	1	.89	1	.219	.315	.344
	Birmingham	AA	1	1	0	0	0	0	0	0	0	0	0	0	0	0	0	0	0	.000	0	.000	.000	.000
	Sarasota	A	94	346	94	14	3	4	126	70	39	54	3	54	4	6	7	23	9	.72	4	.272	.370	.364
1992	Sarasota	A	24	98	28	4	0	0	32	16	10	14	0	12	2	1	1	8	3	.73	2	.286	.383	.327
	Birmingham	AA	104	382	98	9	5	2	123	57	26	48	1	59	3	0	1	13	10	.57	3	.257	.343	.322
1993	El Paso	AA	98	327	98	9	5	2	123	46	49	26	3	38	2	0	3	13	3	.81	9	.300	.352	.376
1994	El Paso	AA	74	251	69	6	8	1	94	44	35	26	1	50	3	2	0	12	7	.63	4	.275	.350	.375
1995	Ottawa	AAA	118	428	126	18	4	7	173	65	56	52	3	59	0	5	4	9	7	.56	5	.294	.368	.404
7 Min. YEARS			716	2493	672	90	31	24	896	396	266	272	13	377	16	21	20	115	52	.69	34	.270	.343	.359

Nelson Castro

Pitches: Right **Bats:** Right **Pos:** P   **Ht:** 6'1" **Wt:** 185 **Born:** 12/10/71 **Age:** 24

			HOW MUCH HE PITCHED					WHAT HE GAVE UP										THE RESULTS					
Year	Team	Lg	G	GS	CG	GF	IP	BFP	H	R	ER	HR	SH	SF	HB	TBB	IBB	SO	WP	Bk	W	L	Pct.	ShO	Sv	ERA
1990	Dodgers	R	10	10	0	0	55	233	65	30	26	2	1	0	0	7	0	35	1	5	3	1	.750	0	0	4.25
1991	Great Falls	R	14	14	1	0	75.1	325	81	51	44	7	0	4	5	13	0	63	2	4	7	4	.636	1	0	5.26
1993	Bakersfield	A	20	20	0	0	86.1	390	100	47	41	5	1	5	4	37	0	54	2	6	4	7	.364	0	0	4.27
	San Antonio	AA	5	5	0	0	27.1	117	35	16	15	2	1	2	1	4	0	15	0	3	2	1	.667	0	0	4.94
1994	San Antonio	AA	6	6	0	0	36	157	36	21	21	3	3	2	2	21	1	14	1	0	3	2	.600	0	0	5.25
	Bakersfield	A	22	12	0	4	91.1	409	96	57	36	8	3	7	5	45	1	74	5	0	7	5	.583	0	1	3.55
1995	San Antonio	AA	48	1	0	14	81.1	360	98	51	47	5	4	3	1	30	1	51	5	0	5	7	.417	0	3	5.20
	Albuquerque	AAA	2	0	0	2	2.1	7	0	0	0	0	0	0	1	0	0	2	1	0	0	0	.000	0	1	0.00
5 Min. YEARS			127	68	1	20	455	1998	511	273	230	32	13	23	19	157	3	308	17	18	31	27	.534	1	5	4.55

Frank Catalanotto

Bats: Left **Throws:** Right **Pos:** 2B   **Ht:** 6'0" **Wt:** 170 **Born:** 4/27/74 **Age:** 22

			BATTING														BASERUNNING				PERCENTAGES		
Year	Team	Lg	G	AB	H	2B	3B	HR	TB	R	RBI	TBB	IBB	SO	HBP	SH	SF	SB	CS	SB%	GDP	Avg	OBP	SLG
1992	Bristol	R	21	50	10	2	0	0	12	6	4	8	0	8	0	0	0	0	1	.00	0	.200	.310	.240
1993	Bristol	R	55	199	61	9	5	3	89	37	22	15	1	19	3	3	0	3	6	.33	3	.307	.364	.447
1994	Fayetteville	A	119	458	149	24	8	3	198	72	56	37	1	54	3	5	1	4	5	.44	4	.325	.379	.432
1995	Jacksonville	AA	134	491	111	19	5	8	164	66	48	49	4	56	9	6	4	13	8	.62	9	.226	.306	.334
4 Min. YEARS			329	1198	331	54	18	14	463	181	130	109	6	137	15	14	5	20	20	.50	16	.276	.343	.386

Mike Cather

Pitches: Right **Bats:** Right **Pos:** P   **Ht:** 6'2" **Wt:** 180 **Born:** 12/17/70 **Age:** 25

			HOW MUCH HE PITCHED					WHAT HE GAVE UP										THE RESULTS					
Year	Team	Lg	G	GS	CG	GF	IP	BFP	H	R	ER	HR	SH	SF	HB	TBB	IBB	SO	WP	Bk	W	L	Pct.	ShO	Sv	ERA
1993	Rangers	R	25	0	0	17	30.2	124	20	7	6	0	4	3	0	9	0	30	2	1	1	1	.500	0	4	1.76
1994	Charlotte	A	44	0	0	37	60.1	270	56	33	26	2	3	2	3	40	3	53	1	0	8	6	.571	0	6	3.88
1995	Tulsa	AA	18	0	0	12	21.2	90	20	11	8	0	4	1	1	7	5	15	0	0	0	2	.000	0	3	3.32
	Winnipeg	IND	27	0	0	24	31	123	18	6	5	1	2	0	0	12	3	35	2	0	4	2	.667	0	5	1.45
3 Min. YEARS			114	0	0	90	143.2	607	114	57	45	3	9	3	7	68	11	133	5	1	13	11	.542	0	18	2.82

Blas Cedeno

Pitches: Right **Bats:** Right **Pos:** P   **Ht:** 6'0" **Wt:** 165 **Born:** 11/15/72 **Age:** 23

			HOW MUCH HE PITCHED					WHAT HE GAVE UP										THE RESULTS					
Year	Team	Lg	G	GS	CG	GF	IP	BFP	H	R	ER	HR	SH	SF	HB	TBB	IBB	SO	WP	Bk	W	L	Pct.	ShO	Sv	ERA
1991	Bristol	R	14	2	0	6	45	202	47	36	19	7	0	3	2	18	1	37	3	4	1	4	.200	0	0	3.80
1992	Bristol	R	13	13	3	0	80.2	335	64	21	18	2	3	1	5	41	0	77	6	0	8	2	.800	2	0	2.01
	Fayetteville	A	2	1	1	1	9	32	3	3	3	0	0	0	0	4	0	12	0	0	1	0	1.000	0	1	3.00
1993	Fayetteville	A	28	22	1	3	148.2	621	145	64	52	11	5	3	11	55	0	103	6	0	6	6	.500	1	0	3.15
1994	Lakeland	A	5	0	0	3	14	52	9	3	2	1	1	1	0	4	0	16	1	0	1	0	1.000	0	1	1.29
	Trenton	AA	34	0	0	18	52.1	228	50	18	15	5	4	0	2	27	2	40	4	0	1	3	.250	0	3	2.58
1995	Jacksonville	AA	48	5	0	13	80.2	329	71	34	31	7	1	1	1	36	1	53	2	1	3	2	.600	0	0	3.46
5 Min. YEARS			144	43	5	44	430.1	1799	389	179	140	33	14	9	21	185	4	338	22	5	20	18	.526	3	4	2.93

Brett Cederblad

Pitches: Right **Bats:** Both **Pos:** P   **Ht:** 6'5" **Wt:** 195 **Born:** 3/6/73 **Age:** 23

			HOW MUCH HE PITCHED					WHAT HE GAVE UP										THE RESULTS					
Year	Team	Lg	G	GS	CG	GF	IP	BFP	H	R	ER	HR	SH	SF	HB	TBB	IBB	SO	WP	Bk	W	L	Pct.	ShO	Sv	ERA
1995	Sarasota	A	24	12	0	2	92.1	384	98	50	42	4	0	4	6	21	0	71	7	2	7	6	.538	0	0	4.09
	Trenton	AA	8	5	2	1	44.2	182	43	19	18	4	2	2	0	11	1	36	2	0	3	2	.600	1	0	3.63
1 Min. YEARS			32	17	2	3	137	566	141	69	60	8	2	6	6	32	1	107	9	2	10	8	.556	1	0	3.94

Henri Centeno

Bats: Both **Throws:** Right **Pos:** 2B   **Ht:** 5'11" **Wt:** 159 **Born:** 1/1/70 **Age:** 26

			BATTING														BASERUNNING				PERCENTAGES		
Year	Team	Lg	G	AB	H	2B	3B	HR	TB	R	RBI	TBB	IBB	SO	HBP	SH	SF	SB	CS	SB%	GDP	Avg	OBP	SLG
1991	Astros	R	31	85	27	4	0	0	31	12	7	5	0	10	3	4	0	4	4	.50	1	.318	.376	.365
1992	Asheville	A	126	461	115	15	1	1	135	62	24	37	0	65	16	6	2	14	7	.67	7	.249	.326	.293
1993	Quad City	A	102	296	74	5	3	1	88	42	24	30	0	50	8	4	3	23	9	.72	11	.250	.332	.297
1994	Tucson	AAA	4	9	1	1	0	0	2	0	0	1	0	2	0	0	0	0	0	.00	1	.111	.200	.222
	Osceola	A	49	175	49	8	1	0	59	21	29	20	0	24	1	2	1	11	1	.92	3	.280	.355	.337
	Jackson	AA	18	42	12	3	0	2	21	6	7	4	1	7	2	1	0	0	0	.00	0	.286	.375	.500
1995	Jackson	AA	92	172	44	3	1	2	55	24	12	24	2	31	3	3	2	6	4	.60	7	.256	.353	.320
5 Min. YEARS			422	1240	322	39	6	6	391	167	103	121	3	189	33	20	8	58	25	.70	30	.260	.340	.315

Tony Chance

Bats: Right **Throws:** Right **Pos:** OF   **Ht:** 6'1" **Wt:** 191 **Born:** 10/26/64 **Age:** 31

			BATTING														BASERUNNING				PERCENTAGES		
Year	Team	Lg	G	AB	H	2B	3B	HR	TB	R	RBI	TBB	IBB	SO	HBP	SH	SF	SB	CS	SB%	GDP	Avg	OBP	SLG
1984	Watertown	A	41	115	17	2	0	3	28	13	14	17	1	47	3	2	2	5	2	.71	1	.148	.270	.243

55

Year Team	Lg	G	AB	H	2B	3B	HR	TB	R	RBI	TBB	IBB	SO	HBP	SH	SF	SB	CS	SB%	GDP	Avg	OBP	SLG
Pirates	R	16	55	12	1	0	0	13	9	10	5	0	11	0	0	1	2	2	.50	3	.218	.279	.236
1985 Pirates	R	10	33	11	1	1	0	14	7	2	4	0	4	0	0	0	2	0	1.00	0	.333	.405	.424
Macon	A	6	17	2	0	0	0	2	3	1	2	0	10	0	0	0	1	0	1.00	0	.118	.211	.118
Gastonia	A	56	214	54	8	0	5	77	31	18	16	0	47	0	2	0	16	7	.70	3	.252	.304	.360
1986 Pr. William	A	19	60	14	1	2	2	25	5	11	3	0	15	0	0	0	4	2	.67	0	.233	.270	.417
Macon	A	108	366	85	12	3	17	154	52	55	38	3	99	3	5	5	18	2	.90	7	.232	.306	.421
1987 Salem	A	133	525	167	23	6	23	271	99	96	50	1	104	10	1	5	26	13	.67	15	.318	.385	.516
1988 Harrisburg	AA	56	196	43	8	2	3	64	26	10	20	0	48	2	1	0	9	4	.69	4	.219	.298	.327
Salem	A	54	207	44	7	0	5	66	25	26	9	0	51	3	2	1	3	3	.50	5	.213	.255	.319
1989 Augusta	A	5	22	3	1	1	1	9	3	5	0	0	5	0	0	0	0	0	.00	0	.136	.136	.409
Harrisburg	AA	4	14	2	1	0	0	3	1	2	0	0	4	0	0	0	0	0	.00	0	.143	.143	.214
Hagerstown	AA	67	246	66	15	4	8	113	34	44	14	0	65	5	0	2	11	3	.79	2	.268	.318	.459
1990 Rochester	AAA	130	454	122	17	4	14	189	55	75	41	2	115	1	1	3	14	9	.61	10	.269	.329	.416
1991 Rochester	AAA	111	355	89	14	3	14	151	61	55	41	0	98	2	2	0	4	3	.57	6	.251	.332	.425
1992 Iowa	AAA	131	434	117	23	1	11	175	60	52	34	1	100	4	4	3	5	3	.63	16	.270	.326	.403
1993 Iowa	AAA	101	294	83	23	0	16	154	50	46	38	2	73	1	2	4	5	5	.50	4	.282	.362	.524
1994 Charlotte	AAA	11	16	4	0	0	1	7	3	1	1	0	7	0	0	0	1	0	1.00	2	.250	.294	.438
1995 Okla. City	AAA	63	196	42	12	0	2	60	19	20	15	0	55	0	1	1	1	1	.50	5	.214	.269	.306
Long Beach	IND	41	170	59	12	1	10	103	40	42	14	3	32	0	0	4	4	2	.67	6	.347	.388	.606
12 Min. YEARS		1163	3989	1036	181	28	135	1678	596	585	362	13	990	34	23	31	131	61	.68	89	.260	.324	.421

Darrin Chapin

Pitches: Right Bats: Right Pos: P **Ht: 6' 0" Wt: 170 Born: 2/1/66 Age: 30**

Year Team	Lg	G	GS	CG	GF	IP	BFP	H	R	ER	HR	SH	SF	HB	TBB	IBB	SO	WP	Bk	W	L	Pct.	ShO	Sv	ERA
1986 Yankees	R	13	13	2	0	83.1	341	71	42	30	2	3	3	2	27	1	67	10	1	4	3	.571	2	0	3.24
1987 Oneonta	A	25	0	0	21	40	170	31	8	3	1	2	1	0	17	5	26	6	0	1	1	.500	0	12	0.68
1988 Albany-Colo	AA	3	0	0	3	4	26	11	7	5	0	0	0	1	2	0	4	0	0	0	0	.000	0	0	11.25
Ft. Laud	A	38	0	0	33	63	234	39	8	6	1	4	1	0	19	5	57	3	1	6	4	.600	0	15	0.86
1989 Albany-Colo	AA	7	0	0	7	8.2	32	5	0	0	0	0	0	0	1	1	16	2	0	1	0	1.000	0	3	0.00
Columbus	AAA	27	0	0	21	40	167	33	15	13	3	3	1	1	15	4	38	3	1	2	4	.333	0	5	2.93
1990 Columbus	AAA	6	0	0	5	8.2	41	10	8	7	0	0	0	0	6	0	8	1	0	0	1	.000	0	2	7.27
Albany-Colo	AA	43	0	0	40	52.2	223	43	20	16	2	1	4	1	21	1	61	4	0	3	2	.600	0	21	2.73
1991 Columbus	AAA	55	0	0	28	78.1	328	54	23	17	5	5	3	1	40	3	69	5	1	10	3	.769	0	12	1.95
1992 Scranton-Wb	AAA	40	0	0	16	61.2	291	72	39	35	5	2	3	0	33	5	67	7	0	5	4	.556	0	4	5.11
1993 Portland	AAA	47	0	0	35	56.1	244	58	28	27	5	3	1	1	24	2	43	6	0	5	2	.714	0	14	4.31
1994 Edmonton	AAA	53	2	0	17	91.1	421	110	72	63	13	1	6	5	41	1	64	5	0	3	2	.600	0	2	6.21
1995 Buffalo	AAA	6	0	0	3	8.2	42	12	10	8	2	2	1	0	2	1	4	1	0	0	1	.000	0	0	8.31
Canton-Akrn	AA	4	0	0	2	8	38	12	7	4	0	1	0	0	2	2	6	0	1	0	0	.000	0	0	4.50
1991 New York	AL	3	0	0	2	5.1	25	3	3	3	0	0	0	0	6	0	5	2	0	0	1	.000	0	0	5.06
1992 Philadelphia	NL	1	0	0	0	2	8	2	2	2	1	0	0	0	0	0	1	1	0	0	0	.000	0	0	9.00
10 Min. YEARS		367	15	2	231	604.2	2598	561	287	234	39	27	24	12	250	29	530	53	5	40	28	.588	2	90	3.48
2 Maj. YEARS		4	0	0	2	7.1	33	5	5	5	1	0	0	0	6	0	6	3	0	0	1	.000	0	0	6.14

Mark Charbonnet

Bats: Left Throws: Left Pos: OF **Ht: 6'1" Wt: 185 Born: 4/5/71 Age: 25**

Year Team	Lg	G	AB	H	2B	3B	HR	TB	R	RBI	TBB	IBB	SO	HBP	SH	SF	SB	CS	SB%	GDP	Avg	OBP	SLG
1989 Burlington	R	41	169	39	3	0	4	54	24	16	4	0	51	1	2	1	13	2	.87	0	.231	.251	.320
1990 Reno	A	9	27	2	0	0	0	2	1	1	0	0	5	0	0	0	0	0	.00	2	.074	.074	.074
Watertown	A	61	224	57	4	3	4	79	21	32	9	1	56	2	3	0	10	1	.59	4	.254	.289	.353
1991 Columbus	A	37	118	29	5	3	1	43	20	17	5	0	23	2	0	1	2	1	.67	2	.246	.286	.364
Watertown	A	47	174	49	4	2	4	69	18	19	5	1	31	3	1	2	12	4	.75	4	.282	.310	.397
1992 Columbus	A	122	416	115	14	6	13	180	55	64	14	2	86	4	7	1	10	4	.71	2	.276	.306	.433
1993 Kinston	A	96	319	78	13	5	7	122	35	34	11	0	89	3	3	1	8	8	.50	4	.245	.275	.382
1994 W. Palm Bch	A	103	323	86	18	6	1	119	44	32	25	2	69	3	3	2	7	7	.50	2	.266	.323	.368
1995 Harrisburg	AA	120	407	102	14	4	8	148	34	57	19	6	104	4	4	6	3	6	.33	12	.251	.287	.364
7 Min. YEARS		636	2177	557	75	29	42	816	252	272	92	12	514	22	23	14	65	39	.63	32	.256	.291	.375

Frank Charles

Bats: Right Throws: Right Pos: 1B **Ht: 6'4" Wt: 210 Born: 2/23/69 Age: 27**

Year Team	Lg	G	AB	H	2B	3B	HR	TB	R	RBI	TBB	IBB	SO	HBP	SH	SF	SB	CS	SB%	GDP	Avg	OBP	SLG
1991 Everett	A	62	239	76	17	1	9	122	31	49	21	0	55	1	0	1	1	2	.33	5	.318	.374	.510
1992 Clinton	A	2	5	0	0	0	0	0	1	0	0	0	3	0	0	0	0	0	.00	0	.000	.000	.000
San Jose	A	87	286	83	16	1	0	101	27	34	11	2	61	4	1	0	4	4	.50	12	.290	.326	.353
1993 St. Paul	IND	58	216	59	13	0	2	78	27	37	11	0	33	3	5	1	5	3	.63	9	.273	.316	.361
1994 Charlotte	A	79	254	67	17	1	2	92	23	33	16	1	52	3	5	2	2	3	.40	2	.264	.313	.362
1995 Tulsa	AA	126	479	121	24	3	13	190	51	72	22	0	93	4	1	4	1	0	1.00	19	.253	.289	.397
5 Min. YEARS		414	1479	406	87	6	26	583	160	225	81	3	297	15	12	8	13	12	.52	47	.275	.317	.394

Carlos Chavez

Pitches: Right **Bats:** Right **Pos:** P   **Ht:** 6'1" **Wt:** 200 **Born:** 8/25/72 **Age:** 23

				HOW MUCH HE PITCHED					WHAT HE GAVE UP									THE RESULTS					
Year	Team	Lg	G	GS	CG	GF	IP	BFP	H	R	ER	HR	SH	SF	HB	TBB	IBB	SO	WP	Bk	W	L	Pct.	ShO	Sv	ERA
1992	Bluefield	R	15	7	0	3	45.2	219	49	42	35	5	1	4	1	34	0	44	10	6	1	2	.333	0	1	6.90
1993	Albany	A	20	0	0	13	34	155	33	20	20	3	3	0	3	18	0	28	6	2	1	3	.250	0	3	5.29
	Bluefield	R	14	13	0	0	82	356	80	43	34	15	1	2	3	37	1	71	14	1	6	3	.667	0	0	3.73
1994	Albany	A	5	0	0	3	9.1	41	9	3	3	0	0	0	0	7	0	4	0	0	1	0	1.000	0	0	2.89
	Bluefield	R	13	13	2	0	85.2	346	58	38	28	11	2	5	6	32	0	92	12	1	7	5	.583	1	0	2.94
1995	Frederick	A	43	1	0	16	81.1	342	62	38	23	4	1	0	2	40	2	107	16	1	5	5	.500	0	6	2.55
	Rochester	AAA	1	0	0	0	1.2	11	3	2	2	0	0	1	0	3	0	1	2	0	0	0	.000	0	0	10.80
	Bowie	AA	1	0	0	0	2	6	0	0	0	0	0	0	0	1	0	2	0	0	0	0	.000	0	0	0.00
	4 Min. YEARS		112	34	2	35	341.2	1476	294	186	145	38	8	12	15	172	3	349	60	11	21	18	.538	1	10	3.82

Eric Chavez

Bats: Right **Throws:** Right **Pos:** 3B   **Ht:** 5'11" **Wt:** 212 **Born:** 9/7/70 **Age:** 25

						BATTING											BASERUNNING				PERCENTAGES		
Year	Team	Lg	G	AB	H	2B	3B	HR	TB	R	RBI	TBB	IBB	SO	HBP	SH	SF	SB	CS	SB%	GDP	Avg	OBP	SLG
1992	Bluefield	R	56	192	57	14	1	9	100	35	32	34	0	48	4	1	1	2	2	.50	3	.297	.411	.521
1993	Albany	A	139	476	119	38	2	18	215	74	74	79	6	124	5	2	4	3	3	.50	7	.250	.360	.452
1994	Frederick	A	124	388	103	26	3	23	204	75	82	65	0	100	3	2	8	3	2	.60	5	.265	.369	.526
1995	Bowie	AA	14	51	10	2	0	2	18	5	4	4	0	17	1	1	0	0	0	.00	1	.196	.268	.353
	High Desert	A	74	254	59	15	0	14	116	38	37	27	0	74	4	0	2	4	2	.67	4	.232	.314	.457
	4 Min. YEARS		407	1361	348	95	6	66	653	227	229	209	6	363	17	5	15	12	9	.57	20	.256	.358	.480

Raul Chavez

Bats: Right **Throws:** Right **Pos:** C   **Ht:** 5'11" **Wt:** 175 **Born:** 3/18/73 **Age:** 23

						BATTING											BASERUNNING				PERCENTAGES		
Year	Team	Lg	G	AB	H	2B	3B	HR	TB	R	RBI	TBB	IBB	SO	HBP	SH	SF	SB	CS	SB%	GDP	Avg	OBP	SLG
1990	Astros	R	48	155	50	8	1	0	60	23	23	7	0	12	2	2	1	5	3	.63	7	.323	.358	.387
1991	Burlington	A	114	420	108	17	0	3	134	54	41	25	1	64	10	3	4	1	4	.20	13	.257	.312	.319
1992	Asheville	A	95	348	99	22	1	2	129	37	40	16	1	39	4	1	4	1	0	1.00	6	.284	.320	.371
1993	Osceola	A	58	197	45	5	1	0	52	13	16	8	0	19	1	1	1	1	1	.50	12	.228	.261	.264
1994	Jackson	AA	89	251	55	7	0	1	65	17	22	17	3	41	2	2	1	1	0	1.00	5	.219	.273	.259
1995	Jackson	AA	58	188	54	8	0	4	74	16	25	8	1	17	3	4	2	0	4	.00	7	.287	.323	.394
	Tucson	AAA	32	103	27	5	0	0	32	14	10	8	0	13	2	1	1	0	1	.00	7	.262	.325	.311
	6 Min. YEARS		494	1662	438	72	3	10	546	174	177	89	6	205	24	14	14	9	13	.41	62	.264	.308	.329

Tony Chavez

Pitches: Right **Bats:** Right **Pos:** P   **Ht:** 5'10" **Wt:** 175 **Born:** 10/22/70 **Age:** 25

				HOW MUCH HE PITCHED					WHAT HE GAVE UP									THE RESULTS					
Year	Team	Lg	G	GS	CG	GF	IP	BFP	H	R	ER	HR	SH	SF	HB	TBB	IBB	SO	WP	Bk	W	L	Pct.	ShO	Sv	ERA
1992	Boise	A	14	0	0	2	16	75	22	13	7	0	0	0	0	4	2	21	3	0	1	1	.500	0	0	3.94
1993	Cedar Rapds	A	41	0	0	35	59.1	252	44	17	10	1	6	2	2	24	2	87	3	1	4	5	.444	0	16	1.52
	Midland	AA	5	0	0	3	8.2	41	11	5	4	1	0	1	0	4	1	9	3	0	0	0	.000	0	1	4.15
1994	Lk Elsinore	A	12	0	0	7	13.1	75	21	19	15	0	2	1	2	11	2	12	2	0	0	5	.000	0	1	10.13
	Cedar Rapds	A	39	1	0	34	50	227	48	33	24	0	3	2	2	28	4	52	7	0	4	3	.571	0	16	4.32
1995	Vancouver	AAA	8	0	0	5	12	46	7	4	2	0	1	0	0	4	0	8	0	0	2	0	1.000	0	1	1.50
	Midland	AA	7	0	0	6	9	42	13	9	8	1	0	0	1	1	0	4	1	0	0	1	.000	0	2	8.00
	Lk Elsinore	A	33	0	0	14	44.2	206	51	28	21	2	2	3	4	19	2	49	5	0	4	2	.667	0	0	4.23
	4 Min. YEARS		159	1	0	106	213	964	217	128	91	5	14	9	11	95	13	242	24	1	15	17	.469	0	37	3.85

Dan Chergey

Pitches: Right **Bats:** Right **Pos:** P   **Ht:** 6'2" **Wt:** 195 **Born:** 1/29/71 **Age:** 25

				HOW MUCH HE PITCHED					WHAT HE GAVE UP									THE RESULTS					
Year	Team	Lg	G	GS	CG	GF	IP	BFP	H	R	ER	HR	SH	SF	HB	TBB	IBB	SO	WP	Bk	W	L	Pct.	ShO	Sv	ERA
1993	Elmira	A	15	10	1	1	79.2	329	85	34	31	5	3	3	8	14	0	53	3	1	3	5	.375	0	0	3.50
1994	Edmonton	AAA	13	0	0	6	19.2	88	22	13	13	2	0	1	2	5	0	17	0	0	2	1	.667	0	0	5.95
	Brevard Cty	A	32	0	0	21	42	160	29	12	8	1	1	0	1	11	1	41	0	0	1	3	.250	0	9	1.71
1995	Portland	AA	55	0	0	27	80.1	331	62	35	31	7	7	2	3	26	6	75	2	0	6	7	.462	0	5	3.47
	3 Min. YEARS		115	10	1	55	221.2	908	198	94	83	15	11	6	14	56	7	186	5	1	12	16	.429	0	14	3.37

Bruce Chick

Bats: Right **Throws:** Right **Pos:** OF   **Ht:** 6'4" **Wt:** 210 **Born:** 3/7/69 **Age:** 27

						BATTING											BASERUNNING				PERCENTAGES		
Year	Team	Lg	G	AB	H	2B	3B	HR	TB	R	RBI	TBB	IBB	SO	HBP	SH	SF	SB	CS	SB%	GDP	Avg	OBP	SLG
1990	Red Sox	R	24	93	30	5	2	1	42	12	23	12	0	11	0	0	2	4	2	.67	4	.323	.393	.452
	Winter Havn	A	37	128	29	2	0	0	31	10	4	11	0	23	0	0	0	4	2	.67	4	.227	.288	.242
1991	Lynchburg	A	134	513	139	23	4	10	200	58	73	44	2	119	2	2	5	10	8	.56	11	.271	.328	.390
1992	New Britain	AA	128	436	96	19	0	9	142	52	51	28	3	122	2	3	5	8	5	.62	6	.220	.268	.326
1993	Ft. Laud	A	39	159	46	9	0	1	58	13	14	4	2	34	0	2	0	1	2	.33	3	.289	.307	.365
	Pawtucket	AAA	29	82	25	6	0	2	37	8	12	6	0	24	0	0	2	0	3	.00	1	.305	.348	.451
	New Britain	AA	55	193	50	8	1	3	69	20	14	8	0	39	1	2	2	2	3	.40	6	.259	.289	.358
1994	New Britain	AA	12	45	10	2	0	1	15	6	7	2	0	10	0	0	1	1	0	1.00	2	.222	.250	.333

57

	Lg	G	AB	H	2B	3B	HR	TB	R	RBI	TBB	IBB	SO	HBP	SH	SF	SB	CS	SB%	GDP	Avg	OBP	SLG
Central Val	A	50	196	73	12	2	3	98	29	31	12	1	24	2	2	3	3	5	.38	5	.372	.408	.500
New Haven	AA	13	39	7	1	1	0	10	3	1	0	0	12	0	0	0	1	0	1.00	1	.179	.179	.256
1995 Expos	R	15	51	12	5	0	1	20	4	9	5	0	8	1	0	0	1	2	.33	1	.235	.316	.392
W. Palm Bch	A	3	10	1	0	0	0	1	0	1	1	0	3	0	0	0	0	0	.00	1	.100	.182	.100
Harrisburg	AA	12	41	11	2	1	0	15	4	6	0	0	9	0	0	0	0	0	.00	1	.268	.268	.366
6 Min. YEARS		551	1986	529	94	11	31	738	219	246	133	8	438	8	13	19	35	32	.52	43	.266	.312	.372

Joel Chimelis

Bats: Right Throws: Right Pos: 1B Ht: 6' 0" Wt: 165 Born: 7/27/67 Age: 28

					BATTING												BASERUNNING				PERCENTAGES		
Year Team	Lg	G	AB	H	2B	3B	HR	TB	R	RBI	TBB	IBB	SO	HBP	SH	SF	SB	CS	SB%	GDP	Avg	OBP	SLG
1988 Sou. Oregon	A	61	225	62	8	0	1	73	40	28	31	1	35	1	1	2	14	7	.67	4	.276	.363	.324
1989 Modesto	A	69	211	40	1	0	1	44	18	14	33	0	41	3	3	1	2	3	.40	8	.190	.306	.209
1990 Reno	A	85	343	96	12	9	2	132	58	47	31	4	36	3	3	2	20	10	.67	17	.280	.343	.385
Modesto	A	46	188	65	14	1	2	87	29	23	18	0	20	0	3	1	10	5	.67	4	.346	.401	.463
1991 Huntsville	AA	68	238	51	10	2	1	68	26	16	18	0	30	0	7	3	4	3	.57	4	.214	.266	.286
San Jose	A	42	126	31	5	1	0	38	19	14	16	0	22	1	1	4	9	4	.69	3	.246	.327	.302
1992 Shreveport	AA	75	279	89	13	1	9	131	47	32	18	3	34	1	4	1	6	6	.50	4	.319	.361	.470
Phoenix	AAA	49	185	56	9	3	1	74	26	23	5	1	24	1	5	2	1	4	.20	3	.303	.321	.400
1993 Shreveport	AA	36	114	23	5	0	6	46	10	18	8	0	14	2	0	2	3	0	1.00	2	.202	.262	.404
Phoenix	AAA	80	262	81	14	3	13	140	40	46	22	1	41	3	1	2	4	3	.57	3	.309	.367	.534
1994 Shreveport	AA	127	478	141	43	1	10	216	74	72	41	2	58	13	1	5	8	6	.57	10	.295	.363	.452
1995 Phoenix	AAA	118	398	103	32	1	7	158	48	66	28	4	53	5	3	8	1	2	.33	7	.259	.310	.397
8 Min. YEARS		856	3047	838	166	22	53	1207	435	399	269	16	408	33	32	33	82	53	.61	69	.275	.337	.396

Steve Chitren

Pitches: Right Bats: Right Pos: P Ht: 6' 0" Wt: 180 Born: 6/8/67 Age: 29

			HOW MUCH HE PITCHED						WHAT HE GAVE UP											THE RESULTS					
Year Team	Lg	G	GS	CG	GF	IP	BFP	H	R	ER	HR	SH	SF	HB	TBB	IBB	SO	WP	Bk	W	L	Pct.	ShO	Sv	ERA
1989 Sou. Oregon	A	2	0	0	1	5	20	3	2	1	0	0	1	0	2	0	3	0	0	0	0	.000	0	0	1.80
Madison	A	20	0	0	18	22.2	85	13	3	3	1	0	2	2	4	1	17	0	0	2	1	.667	0	7	1.19
1990 Huntsville	AA	48	0	0	39	53.2	218	32	18	10	4	0	0	3	22	1	61	2	0	2	4	.333	0	27	1.68
Tacoma	AAA	1	0	0	1	0.2	3	1	0	0	0	0	0	0	0	0	2	0	0	0	0	.000	0	0	0.00
1992 Tacoma	AAA	29	7	0	3	62	296	64	53	47	5	5	3	10	46	5	37	4	2	4	7	.364	0	0	6.82
1993 Huntsville	AA	32	0	0	13	55.2	266	53	38	32	7	2	5	10	35	3	39	7	0	2	1	.667	0	1	5.17
Tacoma	AAA	14	0	0	6	24	107	21	9	8	0	0	0	1	14	2	27	2	0	1	0	1.000	0	1	3.00
1994 Bowie	AA	41	1	0	21	70	299	64	34	23	5	2	4	5	26	3	53	10	1	4	5	.444	0	2	2.96
1995 Rochester	AA	2	0	0	1	3.2	18	6	3	1	0	0	1	0	3	0	0	0	0	0	0	.000	0	0	2.45
Amarillo	IND	1	0	0	0	1.2	13	4	5	5	0	0	0	1	3	0	1	1	0	0	0	.000	0	0	27.00
1990 Oakland	AL	8	0	0	4	17.2	64	7	2	2	0	0	0	0	4	0	19	2	0	1	0	1.000	0	0	1.02
1991 Oakland	AL	56	0	0	20	60.1	271	59	31	29	8	4	2	4	32	4	47	2	1	1	4	.200	0	4	4.33
6 Min. YEARS		190	8	0	103	299	1325	261	165	130	22	9	16	32	155	14	240	26	3	15	18	.455	0	38	3.91
2 Maj. YEARS		64	0	0	24	78	335	66	33	31	8	4	2	4	36	4	66	4	1	2	4	.333	0	4	3.58

Dan Cholowsky

Bats: Right Throws: Right Pos: OF Ht: 6'0" Wt: 195 Born: 10/30/70 Age: 25

					BATTING												BASERUNNING				PERCENTAGES		
Year Team	Lg	G	AB	H	2B	3B	HR	TB	R	RBI	TBB	IBB	SO	HBP	SH	SF	SB	CS	SB%	GDP	Avg	OBP	SLG
1991 Hamilton	A	20	69	16	1	1	1	22	9	6	9	0	17	1	0	0	6	3	.67	0	.232	.329	.319
1992 Savannah	A	69	232	76	6	4	8	114	44	34	51	2	48	3	0	2	34	16	.68	1	.328	.451	.491
St. Pete	A	59	201	57	8	0	1	68	19	17	33	0	31	2	1	4	14	10	.58	8	.284	.383	.338
1993 St. Pete	A	54	208	60	12	0	2	78	30	22	20	2	54	2	0	0	6	8	.43	5	.288	.357	.375
Arkansas	AA	68	212	46	10	2	3	69	31	16	38	3	54	2	1	1	10	2	.83	7	.217	.340	.325
1994 Arkansas	AA	131	454	101	18	4	14	169	57	51	65	2	114	4	1	1	20	9	.69	9	.222	.324	.372
1995 Arkansas	AA	54	190	59	12	0	7	92	41	35	24	2	41	5	0	2	7	6	.54	2	.311	.398	.484
Louisville	AAA	76	238	52	9	1	7	84	27	25	36	0	64	5	0	6	10	4	.71	5	.218	.326	.353
5 Min. YEARS		531	1804	467	76	12	43	696	258	206	276	11	423	24	3	16	107	58	.65	37	.259	.362	.386

Bobby Chouinard

Pitches: Right Bats: Right Pos: P Ht: 6'1" Wt: 188 Born: 5/1/72 Age: 24

			HOW MUCH HE PITCHED						WHAT HE GAVE UP											THE RESULTS					
Year Team	Lg	G	GS	CG	GF	IP	BFP	H	R	ER	HR	SH	SF	HB	TBB	IBB	SO	WP	Bk	W	L	Pct.	ShO	Sv	ERA
1990 Bluefield	R	10	10	2	0	56	237	61	34	23	10	1	2	1	14	0	30	2	2	2	5	.286	1	0	3.70
1991 Kane County	A	6	6	1	0	33	147	45	24	17	3	0	3	2	5	0	17	3	1	2	4	.333	0	0	4.64
Bluefield	R	6	6	0	0	33.2	150	44	19	13	1	0	0	2	11	0	31	1	2	5	1	.833	0	0	3.48
1992 Kane County	A	26	26	9	0	181.2	735	151	60	42	4	9	7	6	38	3	112	13	5	10	14	.417	2	0	2.08
1993 Modesto	A	24	24	1	0	145.2	623	154	75	69	15	3	8	4	56	1	82	4	1	8	10	.444	0	0	4.26
1994 Modesto	A	29	20	0	5	145.2	599	147	53	42	5	8	2	8	32	1	74	5	1	12	5	.706	0	3	2.59
1995 Huntsville	AA	29	29	1	0	166.2	694	155	81	67	10	9	1	4	50	5	106	4	0	14	8	.636	1	0	3.62
6 Min. YEARS		130	121	14	5	762.1	3185	757	346	273	48	30	23	27	206	10	452	32	12	53	47	.530	4	3	3.22

Scott Christman

Pitches: Left **Bats:** Left **Pos:** P **Ht:** 6'3" **Wt:** 190 **Born:** 12/3/71 **Age:** 24

Year	Team	Lg	G	GS	CG	GF	IP	BFP	H	R	ER	HR	SH	SF	HB	TBB	IBB	SO	WP	Bk	W	L	Pct.	ShO	Sv	ERA
1993	White Sox	R	4	2	0	1	11.1	39	3	1	0	0	0	0	0	4	0	15	0	1	0	0	.000	0	1	0.00
	Sarasota	A	2	2	0	0	10.1	42	5	4	1	0	0	1	1	5	0	6	0	1	0	1	.000	0	0	0.87
1994	Pr. William	A	20	20	2	0	116	497	116	64	49	7	3	2	2	44	0	94	5	4	6	11	.353	0	0	3.80
1995	Birmingham	AA	12	12	0	0	62	284	76	49	44	6	2	4	3	24	1	37	6	0	2	5	.286	0	0	6.39
	Pr. William	A	13	13	1	0	85.1	346	83	38	34	7	1	6	2	19	2	56	3	0	4	4	.500	0	0	3.59
	3 Min. YEARS		51	49	3	1	285	1208	283	156	128	20	6	13	8	96	3	208	14	6	12	21	.364	0	1	4.04

Chris Christopher

Bats: Right **Throws:** Right **Pos:** OF **Ht:** 5'11" **Wt:** 175 **Born:** 11/16/71 **Age:** 24

Year	Team	Lg	G	AB	H	2B	3B	HR	TB	R	RBI	TBB	IBB	SO	HBP	SH	SF	SB	CS	SB%	GDP	Avg	OBP	SLG
1993	Johnson Cty	R	55	204	61	5	3	3	81	34	28	35	1	21	2	1	3	18	5	.78	4	.299	.402	.397
1994	Savannah	A	119	433	115	16	3	3	146	55	41	52	2	65	9	1	3	20	5	.80	11	.266	.354	.337
1995	Arkansas	AA	23	62	17	1	0	1	21	7	3	1	0	6	0	0	0	4	1	.80	2	.274	.286	.339
	3 Min. YEARS		197	699	193	22	6	7	248	96	72	88	3	92	11	2	6	42	11	.79	17	.276	.363	.355

Eric Christopherson

Bats: Right **Throws:** Right **Pos:** C **Ht:** 6'1" **Wt:** 190 **Born:** 4/25/69 **Age:** 27

Year	Team	Lg	G	AB	H	2B	3B	HR	TB	R	RBI	TBB	IBB	SO	HBP	SH	SF	SB	CS	SB%	GDP	Avg	OBP	SLG
1990	San Jose	A	7	23	4	0	0	0	4	4	1	3	0	6	0	0	0	0	0	.00	0	.174	.269	.174
	Everett	A	48	162	43	8	1	1	56	20	22	31	1	28	0	1	2	7	2	.78	2	.265	.379	.346
1991	Clinton	A	110	345	93	18	0	5	126	45	58	68	1	54	1	1	6	10	7	.59	10	.270	.386	.365
1992	Shreveport	AA	80	270	68	10	1	6	98	36	34	37	0	44	1	0	2	1	6	.14	5	.252	.342	.363
1993	Giants	R	8	22	9	1	1	0	12	7	4	9	0	1	0	0	0	0	0	.00	0	.409	.581	.545
	Shreveport	AA	15	46	7	2	0	0	9	5	2	9	0	10	0	0	0	1	1	.50	1	.152	.291	.196
1994	Shreveport	AA	88	267	67	22	0	6	107	30	39	42	4	55	0	1	2	5	1	.83	2	.251	.350	.401
1995	Phoenix	AAA	94	282	62	9	1	1	76	21	25	35	1	54	3	5	5	1	1	.50	12	.220	.308	.270
	6 Min. YEARS		450	1417	353	70	4	19	488	168	185	234	7	252	5	8	17	25	18	.58	32	.249	.354	.344

Joe Ciccarella

Pitches: Left **Bats:** Left **Pos:** P **Ht:** 6'3" **Wt:** 200 **Born:** 12/29/69 **Age:** 26

Year	Team	Lg	G	GS	CG	GF	IP	BFP	H	R	ER	HR	SH	SF	HB	TBB	IBB	SO	WP	Bk	W	L	Pct.	ShO	Sv	ERA
1992	Winter Havn	A	38	0	0	30	40.2	177	35	13	12	2	4	3	0	26	1	45	0	0	2	1	.667	0	12	2.66
1993	Pawtucket	AAA	12	0	0	2	17.2	89	27	13	11	2	0	0	2	12	0	8	0	0	0	1	.000	0	0	5.60
	New Britain	AA	30	0	0	30	31	151	31	19	15	1	1	1	1	23	4	34	5	0	0	4	.000	0	15	4.22
1994	New Britain	AA	31	18	0	1	113.2	524	134	68	53	11	5	3	7	54	0	95	5	2	6	6	.500	0	0	4.20
1995	Pawtucket	AAA	11	5	0	2	25.2	112	22	15	11	2	3	0	4	10	1	13	4	0	0	1	.000	0	0	3.86
	Trenton	AA	22	2	0	6	33	138	31	13	10	3	1	3	0	12	0	33	0	0	2	1	.667	0	0	2.73
	4 Min. YEARS		144	25	0	71	262.2	1191	280	141	112	21	14	10	14	137	6	228	14	2	10	14	.417	0	27	3.84

Frank Cimorelli

Pitches: Right **Bats:** Right **Pos:** P **Ht:** 6'0" **Wt:** 175 **Born:** 8/2/68 **Age:** 27

Year	Team	Lg	G	GS	CG	GF	IP	BFP	H	R	ER	HR	SH	SF	HB	TBB	IBB	SO	WP	Bk	W	L	Pct.	ShO	Sv	ERA
1989	Johnson Cty	R	12	12	1	0	65	286	78	40	33	2	1	1	3	17	1	36	3	3	2	4	.333	0	0	4.57
1990	Springfield	A	41	15	1	6	120.1	535	125	80	61	9	2	1	7	41	7	86	8	0	4	8	.333	0	4	4.56
1991	Springfield	A	29	29	3	0	191.2	825	203	94	73	12	4	8	9	51	1	98	10	1	8	14	.364	0	0	3.43
1992	Springfield	A	65	0	0	25	72.2	289	48	22	14	2	3	0	2	22	1	66	1	0	4	2	.667	0	9	1.73
1993	Arkansas	AA	37	0	0	9	56.2	232	44	20	16	3	4	1	3	23	5	36	2	0	1	1	.500	0	1	2.54
	Louisville	AAA	27	0	0	13	43	181	34	16	14	1	4	1	3	25	5	24	7	0	2	1	.667	0	2	2.93
1994	Louisville	AAA	48	0	0	17	60.2	267	64	30	27	6	4	3	5	20	1	46	7	0	5	3	.625	0	4	4.01
1995	Louisville	AAA	6	0	0	2	5	26	12	7	5	2	0	0	0	3	0	3	0	0	1	1	.500	0	0	9.00
	El Paso	AA	2	0	0	1	2	11	1	1	1	0	0	1	2	2	0	0	0	0	0	0	.000	0	0	4.50
1994	St. Louis	NL	11	0	0	2	13.1	73	20	14	13	0	1	2	2	10	2	1	2	0	0	0	.000	0	1	8.78
	7 Min. YEARS		267	56	5	72	617	2652	609	310	244	37	22	16	34	201	21	395	38	4	27	34	.443	0	16	3.56

Chris Clapinski

Bats: Both **Throws:** Right **Pos:** 3B **Ht:** 6'0" **Wt:** 165 **Born:** 8/20/71 **Age:** 24

Year	Team	Lg	G	AB	H	2B	3B	HR	TB	R	RBI	TBB	IBB	SO	HBP	SH	SF	SB	CS	SB%	GDP	Avg	OBP	SLG
1992	Marlins	R	59	212	51	8	1	1	64	36	15	49	2	42	4	3	2	5	6	.45	4	.241	.390	.302
1993	Kane County	A	82	214	45	12	1	0	59	22	27	31	0	55	1	8	4	3	8	.27	3	.210	.308	.276
1994	Brevard Cty	A	65	157	45	12	3	1	66	33	13	23	2	28	3	7	1	3	2	.60	2	.287	.386	.420
1995	Portland	AA	87	208	49	9	3	4	76	32	30	28	2	44	2	5	5	5	2	.71	4	.236	.325	.365
	4 Min. YEARS		293	791	190	41	8	6	265	123	85	131	6	169	10	23	12	16	18	.47	13	.240	.351	.335

Dera Clark

Pitches: Right Bats: Right Pos: P Ht: 6'1" Wt: 204 Born: 4/14/65 Age: 31

Year	Team	Lg	G	GS	CG	GF	IP	BFP	H	R	ER	HR	SH	SF	HB	TBB	IBB	SO	WP	Bk	W	L	Pct.	ShO	Sv	ERA
1987	Royals	R	21	0	0	8	56.1	230	42	20	14	1	3	1	1	17	5	51	3	0	3	4	.429	0	4	2.24
1988	Baseball Cy	A	34	0	0	13	79.2	335	73	28	24	2	3	4	1	31	6	46	9	2	5	2	.714	0	4	2.71
1989	Memphis	AA	30	13	1	5	106.1	459	103	63	52	11	2	5	8	29	0	93	15	2	5	5	.500	1	1	4.40
1990	Omaha	AAA	17	17	0	0	91.2	396	82	40	38	14	1	5	3	44	0	66	6	1	8	3	.727	0	0	3.73
1991	Omaha	AAA	25	23	0	1	129.2	577	126	76	65	10	5	6	4	74	0	108	17	0	6	9	.400	0	0	4.51
1992	Royals	R	2	1	0	0	8.2	40	7	4	2	0	0	1	0	2	0	13	2	0	0	0	.000	0	0	2.08
	Baseball Cy	A	3	3	0	0	16	63	15	3	3	0	0	0	0	3	0	7	0	0	2	0	1.000	0	0	1.69
	Omaha	AAA	9	9	0	0	43	197	57	39	38	9	1	3	1	16	0	32	3	0	1	6	.143	0	0	7.95
1993	Omaha	AAA	51	0	0	19	82.1	355	86	43	40	16	1	6	0	30	2	53	4	1	4	4	.500	0	5	4.37
1994	Richmond	AAA	8	0	0	1	10.1	48	9	8	7	1	1	0	2	7	0	11	0	1	0	0	.000	0	0	6.10
1995	Memphis	AA	23	0	0	13	26.1	111	18	7	7	1	0	0	0	14	3	29	5	0	2	2	.500	0	5	2.39
	9 Min. YEARS		223	66	1	60	650.1	2811	618	331	290	65	16	33	18	267	16	509	64	7	36	35	.507	1	19	4.01

Tim Clark

Bats: Left Throws: Left Pos: 1B Ht: 6'3" Wt: 210 Born: 2/10/69 Age: 27

Year	Team	Lg	G	AB	H	2B	3B	HR	TB	R	RBI	TBB	IBB	SO	HBP	SH	SF	SB	CS	SB%	GDP	Avg	OBP	SLG
1990	Beloit	A	67	219	57	13	1	4	84	27	44	31	1	45	3	2	3	3	4	.43	10	.260	.355	.384
1991	Stockton	A	125	424	116	19	4	9	170	51	56	57	4	60	8	1	5	9	7	.56	5	.274	.366	.401
1992	Salt Lake	R	69	272	97	25	2	11	159	57	53	28	1	36	3	1	4	1	2	.33	8	.357	.417	.585
1993	High Desert	A	128	510	185	42	10	17	298	109	126	56	3	65	4	0	13	2	5	.29	13	.363	.420	.584
1994	Portland	AA	135	486	129	30	0	14	201	63	65	50	0	112	3	0	4	3	7	.30	15	.265	.335	.414
1995	Portland	AA	134	499	135	34	2	8	197	62	88	59	12	86	3	0	7	0	5	.00	13	.271	.347	.395
	6 Min. YEARS		658	2410	719	163	19	63	1109	369	432	281	21	404	24	4	36	18	30	.38	64	.298	.372	.460

Marty Clary

Pitches: Right Bats: Right Pos: P Ht: 6'4" Wt: 190 Born: 4/3/62 Age: 34

Year	Team	Lg	G	GS	CG	GF	IP	BFP	H	R	ER	HR	SH	SF	HB	TBB	IBB	SO	WP	Bk	W	L	Pct.	ShO	Sv	ERA
1984	Greenville	AA	30	30	5	0	186.1	790	172	77	66	10	6	6	3	82	1	125	10	4	14	9	.609	2	0	3.19
1985	Richmond	AAA	26	25	0	1	156.2	688	155	81	73	7	8	6	5	77	1	76	9	1	8	12	.400	0	0	4.19
1986	Richmond	AAA	24	22	3	1	132.1	581	118	72	64	12	5	6	1	82	1	56	9	4	7	6	.538	1	0	4.35
1987	Richmond	AAA	26	26	5	0	178	768	180	86	74	13	5	5	4	75	2	91	10	0	11	10	.524	0	0	3.74
1988	Richmond	AAA	27	25	2	1	143.2	604	142	65	54	10	5	6	2	37	3	73	10	2	6	11	.353	1	0	3.38
1989	Richmond	AAA	15	15	4	0	101.2	408	87	33	23	3	5	4	2	28	0	70	2	0	7	5	.583	0	0	2.04
1991	Louisville	AAA	33	7	0	7	70.1	309	77	40	35	6	3	0	2	26	1	28	6	0	2	8	.200	0	1	4.48
	Buffalo	AAA	7	5	1	0	30	130	31	13	13	2	0	0	0	10	0	14	1	2	3	0	1.000	1	0	3.90
1994	Orlando	AA	13	6	0	4	52.2	202	46	23	20	4	4	0	0	9	1	27	3	0	4	3	.571	0	0	3.42
1995	Charlotte	AAA	9	4	0	5	19	86	26	16	10	1	1	4	2	1	0	8	1	0	2	2	.500	0	0	4.74
1987	Atlanta	NL	7	1	0	2	14.2	68	20	13	10	2	1	1	1	4	0	7	0	0	0	1	.000	0	0	6.14
1989	Atlanta	NL	18	17	2	0	108.2	452	103	47	38	6	4	3	1	31	3	30	5	0	4	3	.571	1	0	3.15
1990	Atlanta	NL	33	14	0	5	101.2	466	128	72	64	9	5	5	1	39	4	44	5	1	1	10	.091	0	0	5.67
	9 Min. YEARS		210	163	20	19	1070.2	4566	1034	506	432	68	42	37	21	427	10	568	61	13	64	66	.492	5	1	3.63
	3 Maj. YEARS		58	32	2	7	225	986	251	132	112	17	10	9	3	74	7	81	10	1	5	14	.263	1	0	4.48

Royal Clayton

Pitches: Right Bats: Right Pos: P Ht: 6'2" Wt: 210 Born: 11/25/65 Age: 30

Year	Team	Lg	G	GS	CG	GF	IP	BFP	H	R	ER	HR	SH	SF	HB	TBB	IBB	SO	WP	Bk	W	L	Pct.	ShO	Sv	ERA
1987	Oneonta	A	2	0	0	1	4	16	4	1	1	0	0	0	0	2	0	3	0	0	0	1	.000	0	0	2.25
	Yankees	R	3	1	0	2	10.1	44	12	5	4	0	0	1	0	2	1	5	0	0	0	2	.000	0	1	3.48
	Pr. William	A	9	4	0	4	37.1	181	49	25	19	4	0	0	0	17	0	20	1	2	2	1	.667	0	0	4.58
1988	Pr. William	A	22	11	3	8	91.1	372	81	31	24	2	3	1	2	25	1	44	1	2	5	5	.500	1	0	2.36
	Ft. Laud	A	6	6	5	0	43.2	166	38	10	7	2	0	0	0	3	0	16	1	0	4	2	.667	2	0	1.44
1989	Albany-Colo	AA	25	25	6	0	175	715	166	72	58	8	1	3	4	48	2	74	5	3	16	4	.800	0	0	2.98
1990	Columbus	AAA	4	4	0	0	26	111	33	12	11	1	0	0	0	7	0	15	1	0	1	2	.333	0	0	3.81
	Albany-Colo	AA	21	21	6	0	141.2	590	148	58	50	13	8	3	1	43	4	68	2	3	10	9	.526	2	0	3.18
1991	Columbus	AAA	32	19	1	2	150	650	152	76	64	15	2	4	2	53	1	100	2	1	11	7	.611	0	0	3.84
1992	Columbus	AAA	36	15	1	10	130.2	557	132	62	52	5	2	6	3	45	2	72	6	3	10	5	.667	1	1	3.58
1993	Columbus	AAA	47	11	0	21	117	489	119	56	46	12	5	3	2	31	3	66	3	0	7	6	.538	0	3	3.54
1994	Columbus	AAA	58	3	0	21	90	394	103	47	42	2	3	2	0	30	4	54	7	0	12	7	.632	0	5	4.20
1995	Phoenix	AAA	5	5	0	0	23	108	35	18	15	1	2	0	0	6	2	13	0	0	0	0	.000	0	0	5.87
	9 Min. YEARS		270	125	22	69	1040	4393	1072	473	393	65	26	23	14	312	20	550	29	14	78	53	.595	6	15	3.40

Jim Clinton

Bats: Right Throws: Right Pos: OF Ht: 6'2" Wt: 185 Born: 6/17/67 Age: 29

Year	Team	Lg	G	AB	H	2B	3B	HR	TB	R	RBI	TBB	IBB	SO	HBP	SH	SF	SB	CS	SB%	GDP	Avg	OBP	SLG
1989	Butte	R	60	137	30	7	0	0	37	14	15	12	2	37	2	0	0	3	3	.50	3	.219	.291	.270
1990	Gastonia	A	61	128	26	6	1	0	34	12	7	13	0	35	1	4	0	3	7	.30	1	.203	.282	.266
1991	Charlotte	A	86	244	47	12	1	1	64	19	17	16	0	63	3	4	0	16	8	.67	8	.193	.251	.262

Year	Team	Lg	G	AB	H	2B	3B	HR	TB	R	RBI	TBB	IBB	SO	HBP	SH	SF	SB	CS	SB%	GDP	Avg	OBP	SLG
1992	Charlotte	A	92	239	42	5	2	1	54	27	15	19	0	64	2	9	0	9	2	.82	7	.176	.242	.226
1993	Tulsa	AA	6	12	1	0	0	0	1	0	2	1	0	3	0	0	0	0	0	.00	0	.083	.154	.083
	Charlotte	AA	86	285	50	9	0	1	62	26	23	18	1	72	4	7	2	4	3	.57	9	.175	.233	.218
1994	Okla. City	AAA	6	22	4	1	0	0	5	1	2	0	0	4	0	0	0	1	0	1.00	0	.182	.182	.227
	Tulsa	AA	69	203	48	4	0	0	52	21	14	6	0	54	1	3	2	10	4	.71	3	.236	.259	.256
1995	Okla. City	AAA	8	13	0	0	0	0	0	0	0	1	0	0	0	0	0	0	0	.00	1	.000	.071	.000
	Tulsa	AA	28	57	11	2	0	1	16	6	7	7	0	16	1	3	1	2	0	1.00	3	.193	.288	.281
	7 Min. YEARS		502	1340	259	46	4	4	325	126	102	93	3	354	14	30	5	48	27	.64	35	.193	.252	.243

Alan Cockrell

Bats: Right **Throws:** Right **Pos:** OF **Ht:** 6'2" **Wt:** 210 **Born:** 12/5/62 **Age:** 33

Year	Team	Lg	G	AB	H	2B	3B	HR	TB	R	RBI	TBB	IBB	SO	HBP	SH	SF	SB	CS	SB%	GDP	Avg	OBP	SLG
1984	Everett	A	2	8	3	0	0	0	3	1	3	1	0	2	0	0	0	0	0	.00	0	.375	.444	.375
	Fresno	A	61	214	46	6	0	1	55	20	32	28	0	66	5	0	2	0	1	.00	10	.215	.317	.257
1985	Shreveport	AA	126	455	115	25	3	11	179	53	68	54	2	137	3	3	2	12	3	.80	16	.253	.335	.393
1986	Shreveport	AA	124	438	113	31	3	14	192	66	78	61	3	126	3	3	3	4	2	.67	11	.258	.350	.438
1987	Phoenix	AAA	129	432	111	23	5	11	177	82	72	69	4	131	3	5	4	7	3	.70	9	.257	.360	.410
1988	Phoenix	AAA	102	347	105	16	2	8	149	65	39	48	1	93	1	1	1	3	3	.50	6	.303	.388	.429
	Portland	AAA	18	63	15	1	1	2	24	9	8	5	0	25	0	0	0	1	0	1.00	0	.238	.294	.381
1989	Portland	AAA	127	433	116	15	3	11	170	60	61	57	0	127	2	5	6	8	5	.62	11	.268	.351	.393
1990	Portland	AAA	6	23	5	1	1	0	8	2	1	0	0	5	1	0	0	1	0	1.00	0	.217	.250	.348
	Colo. Sprng	AAA	113	352	116	23	4	17	198	75	70	50	2	68	2	0	3	5	3	.63	12	.330	.413	.563
1991	Calgary	AAA	117	435	126	27	2	11	190	77	81	45	1	74	4	1	3	7	4	.64	17	.290	.359	.437
1992	Colo. Sprng	AAA	82	259	61	6	2	7	92	31	38	22	1	51	4	2	2	0	2	.00	6	.236	.303	.355
1993	Charlotte	AAA	96	275	76	12	2	8	116	31	39	23	0	59	2	2	3	0	0	.00	6	.276	.333	.422
1994	New Haven	AA	12	43	13	4	0	1	20	6	8	3	1	6	1	0	1	2	0	1.00	1	.302	.354	.465
	Colo. Sprng	AAA	84	271	83	15	2	13	141	50	60	29	0	58	4	1	1	1	1	.50	6	.306	.380	.520
1995	Colo. Sprng	AAA	106	355	111	22	1	12	171	58	58	30	3	65	2	1	0	0	3	.00	8	.313	.370	.482
	12 Min. YEARS		1305	4403	1215	227	31	127	1885	686	716	525	18	1093	37	24	31	51	30	.63	122	.276	.356	.428

Kevin Coffman

Pitches: Right **Bats:** Right **Pos:** P **Ht:** 6'3" **Wt:** 206 **Born:** 1/19/65 **Age:** 31

Year	Team	Lg	G	GS	CG	GF	IP	BFP	H	R	ER	HR	SH	SF	HB	TBB	IBB	SO	WP	Bk	W	L	Pct.	ShO	Sv	ERA
1984	Anderson	A	7	7	0	0	32.2	155	37	23	17	1	0	0	0	26	0	23	8	3	1	4	.200	0	0	4.68
	Pulaski	R	11	7	0	2	48	215	41	26	22	4	1	0	1	33	1	41	5	0	1	4	.200	0	0	4.13
1985	Durham	A	3	0	0	2	4.1	28	4	5	5	0	1	1	1	11	2	1	2	0	0	1	.000	0	0	10.38
	Sumter	A	24	0	1	10	62.2	254	42	25	22	1	3	2	2	26	0	43	6	0	1	3	.250	0	3	3.16
1986	Durham	A	3	3	0	0	13.1	65	11	12	11	0	0	0	0	17	0	7	4	0	1	2	.333	0	0	7.43
	Sumter	A	18	18	3	0	114.1	505	99	66	30	2	1	2	7	64	0	120	10	0	10	0	.709	2	0	3.07
	Greenville	AA	8	8	0	0	48.2	223	43	24	24	4	1	1	4	30	0	43	6	0	3	4	.429	0	0	4.44
1987	Greenville	AA	30	30	1	0	181.2	818	162	102	89	9	5	4	6	130	3	153	21	1	11	11	.500	0	0	4.41
1988	Durham	A	8	0	0	7	10	46	12	6	5	0	1	2	0	3	0	10	1	0	1	1	.500	0	2	4.50
	Richmond	AAA	9	2	0	5	19.1	91	15	10	9	0	2	0	1	20	0	18	1	0	1	1	.500	0	0	4.19
1989	Charlotte	AA	7	4	0	1	21.2	106	15	15	9	0	1	1	2	26	2	12	5	1	0	3	.000	0	0	3.74
	Iowa	AAA	14	1	0	5	17.2	97	17	19	16	0	1	2	3	26	1	11	3	1	0	2	.000	0	0	8.15
	Winston-Sal	A	7	7	1	0	36	167	23	24	18	0	1	1	3	34	0	47	12	0	2	3	.400	0	0	4.50
1990	Charlotte	AA	14	14	5	0	93	399	77	28	21	10	2	1	0	54	0	84	14	0	7	3	.700	0	0	2.03
	Iowa	AAA	9	9	0	0	60.1	255	43	26	23	1	1	2	1	40	3	49	5	3	2	5	.286	0	0	3.43
1991	Jackson	AA	30	19	1	4	105.2	489	79	71	59	3	5	4	6	101	0	105	30	0	8	7	.533	1	1	5.03
1992	Greenville	AA	6	6	1	0	38	150	23	9	9	1	0	1	1	16	0	33	2	2	6	0	1.000	0	0	2.13
	Richmond	AAA	16	15	0	0	91.1	411	66	43	32	3	6	3	5	70	1	78	14	0	6	5	.545	0	0	3.15
1993	Mariners	R	4	0	0	0	7	28	3	4	1	0	0	0	0	5	0	6	1	0	0	0	.000	0	0	1.29
	Jacksonvlle	AA	10	10	0	0	50	228	33	33	30	0	1	2	4	47	0	45	19	0	1	7	.125	0	0	5.40
1995	Richmond	AAA	2	1	0	0	6	25	4	2	2	0	0	0	0	4	0	7	0	0	1	0	1.000	0	0	3.00
1987	Atlanta	NL	5	5	0	0	25.1	126	31	14	13	2	1	1	3	22	0	14	1	1	2	3	.400	0	0	4.62
1988	Atlanta	NL	18	11	0	2	67	311	62	52	43	3	3	4	4	54	2	24	11	1	2	6	.250	0	0	5.78
1990	Chicago	NL	8	2	0	0	18.1	100	26	24	23	0	2	1	0	19	0	9	4	0	0	2	.000	0	0	11.29
	11 Min. YEARS		240	165	13	36	1061.2	4755	849	563	463	39	32	28	45	783	13	936	177	11	63	70	.474	3	7	3.92
	3 Maj. YEARS		31	18	0	2	110.2	537	119	90	79	5	6	5	7	95	2	47	16	2	4	11	.267	0	0	6.42

Emmitt Cohick

Bats: Left **Throws:** Left **Pos:** OF **Ht:** 6'2" **Wt:** 175 **Born:** 8/8/68 **Age:** 27

Year	Team	Lg	G	AB	H	2B	3B	HR	TB	R	RBI	TBB	IBB	SO	HBP	SH	SF	SB	CS	SB%	GDP	Avg	OBP	SLG
1991	Quad City	A	112	350	96	22	9	11	169	52	53	56	3	97	5	2	3	8	4	.67	2	.274	.379	.483
1992	Palm Spring	A	117	402	121	17	6	8	174	69	78	49	2	91	3	2	7	15	12	.56	8	.301	.375	.433
1993	Midland	AA	105	356	96	18	5	11	157	59	53	35	2	91	5	9	2	6	2	.75	4	.270	.342	.441
1994	Midland	AA	96	330	86	25	5	8	145	41	62	32	1	99	4	2	3	3	4	.43	4	.261	.331	.439
1995	Midland	AA	56	153	35	13	2	2	58	25	23	33	1	45	2	2	3	3	2	.60	0	.229	.366	.379
	Vancouver	AAA	10	24	8	2	0	0	10	3	5	5	0	8	0	0	1	0	1	.00	1	.333	.433	.417
	5 Min. YEARS		496	1615	442	97	27	40	713	249	274	210	9	431	19	17	19	35	25	.58	19	.274	.360	.441

Craig Colbert

Bats: Right **Throws:** Right **Pos:** C **Ht:** 6' 0" **Wt:** 214 **Born:** 2/13/65 **Age:** 31

Year Team	Lg	G	AB	H	2B	3B	HR	TB	R	RBI	TBB	IBB	SO	HBP	SH	SF	SB	CS	SB%	GDP	Avg	OBP	SLG
1986 Clinton	A	72	263	60	12	0	1	75	26	17	23	1	53	3	0	1	4	1	.80	7	.228	.297	.285
1987 Fresno	A	115	388	95	12	4	6	133	41	51	22	2	89	4	3	5	5	5	.50	11	.245	.289	.343
1988 Clinton	A	124	455	106	19	2	11	162	56	64	41	0	100	1	2	2	8	9	.47	4	.233	.297	.356
1989 Shreveport	AA	106	363	94	19	3	7	140	47	34	23	5	67	0	2	2	3	7	.30	11	.259	.302	.386
1990 Phoenix	AAA	111	400	112	22	2	8	162	41	47	31	3	80	3	1	2	4	5	.44	8	.280	.335	.405
1991 Phoenix	AAA	42	142	35	6	2	2	51	9	13	11	2	38	0	0	1	0	1	.00	7	.246	.299	.359
1992 Phoenix	AAA	36	140	45	8	1	1	58	16	12	3	0	16	1	2	2	0	1	.00	4	.321	.336	.414
1993 Phoenix	AAA	13	45	10	2	1	1	17	5	7	0	0	11	1	0	1	0	0	.00	1	.222	.234	.378
1994 Charlotte	AAA	69	182	47	7	1	4	68	19	25	19	1	40	0	1	1	1	1	.50	9	.258	.327	.374
1995 Las Vegas	AAA	74	241	60	8	1	1	73	30	24	21	0	44	0	1	1	1	0	1.00	14	.249	.308	.303
1992 San Francisco	NL	49	126	29	5	2	1	41	10	16	9	0	22	0	2	2	1	0	1.00	8	.230	.277	.325
1993 San Francisco	NL	23	37	6	2	0	1	11	2	5	3	1	13	0	0	0	0	0	.00	0	.162	.225	.297
10 Min. YEARS		762	2619	664	115	17	42	939	290	294	194	14	538	13	12	18	26	30	.46	76	.254	.306	.359
2 Maj. YEARS		72	163	35	7	2	2	52	12	21	12	1	35	0	2	2	1	0	1.00	8	.215	.266	.319

Jim Cole

Pitches: Right **Bats:** Right **Pos:** P **Ht:** 6'2" **Wt:** 195 **Born:** 2/19/71 **Age:** 25

Year Team	Lg	G	GS	CG	GF	IP	BFP	H	R	ER	HR	SH	SF	HB	TBB	IBB	SO	WP	Bk	W	L	Pct.	ShO	Sv	ERA
1993 Helena	R	18	1	0	11	54.1	234	57	24	17	3	1	1	0	20	0	53	4	2	1	0	1.000	0	8	2.82
1994 Beloit	A	27	27	3	0	173.1	742	177	76	64	14	7	5	8	53	0	150	14	4	18	5	.783	1	0	3.32
1995 El Paso	AA	6	6	0	0	23.2	121	42	28	23	3	0	3	0	11	0	14	1	1	1	4	.200	0	0	8.75
Stockton	A	14	13	1	0	85.1	359	88	43	33	7	1	2	5	20	0	52	1	1	7	4	.636	0	0	3.48
3 Min. YEARS		65	47	4	11	336.2	1456	364	171	137	27	9	11	13	104	0	269	20	8	27	13	.675	1	8	3.66

Stu Cole

Bats: Right **Throws:** Right **Pos:** SS **Ht:** 6' 1" **Wt:** 175 **Born:** 2/7/66 **Age:** 30

Year Team	Lg	G	AB	H	2B	3B	HR	TB	R	RBI	TBB	IBB	SO	HBP	SH	SF	SB	CS	SB%	GDP	Avg	OBP	SLG
1987 Eugene	A	63	243	74	17	1	3	102	42	51	34	1	45	1	3	4	3	1	.75	3	.305	.387	.420
1988 Virginia	A	70	257	70	10	0	1	83	41	22	32	0	52	4	0	2	10	5	.67	6	.272	.359	.323
Baseball Cy	A	15	41	6	0	0	0	6	7	4	9	0	10	0	1	1	2	1	.67	4	.146	.294	.146
1989 Memphis	AA	90	299	64	8	3	6	96	30	32	25	0	67	0	4	2	11	3	.79	7	.214	.273	.321
1990 Memphis	AA	113	357	110	18	2	1	135	61	49	55	2	55	3	4	3	20	5	.80	8	.308	.402	.378
1991 Omaha	AAA	120	441	115	13	7	3	151	64	39	42	0	60	1	5	2	11	10	.52	12	.261	.325	.342
1992 Omaha	AAA	63	205	40	8	0	4	60	30	17	25	0	27	3	6	0	3	5	.38	5	.195	.292	.293
Memphis	AA	49	174	41	8	1	0	51	19	12	18	2	23	1	2	2	7	7	.50	7	.236	.308	.293
1993 Colo. Sprng	AAA	104	324	91	22	3	5	134	54	35	36	1	36	1	2	2	10	6	.63	14	.281	.353	.414
1994 Colo. Sprng	AAA	97	285	86	22	2	6	130	39	38	22	1	45	4	2	4	7	3	.70	9	.302	.356	.456
1995 Colo. Sprng	AAA	76	208	57	15	2	2	82	28	24	17	1	19	2	2	2	1	2	.33	8	.274	.332	.394
1991 Kansas City	AL	9	7	1	0	0	0	1	1	0	2	0	2	0	0	0	0	0	.00	0	.143	.333	.143
9 Min. YEARS		860	2834	754	141	21	31	1030	415	323	315	8	439	20	31	24	85	48	.64	83	.266	.341	.363

Victor Cole

Pitches: Right **Bats:** Both **Pos:** P **Ht:** 5'10" **Wt:** 160 **Born:** 1/23/68 **Age:** 28

Year Team	Lg	G	GS	CG	GF	IP	BFP	H	R	ER	HR	SH	SF	HB	TBB	IBB	SO	WP	Bk	W	L	Pct.	ShO	Sv	ERA
1988 Eugene	A	15	0	0	13	23.2	94	16	6	4	0	0	0	2	8	0	39	3	0	1	0	1.000	0	9	1.52
Baseball Cy	A	10	5	0	2	35	149	27	9	8	0	1	1	1	21	0	29	2	0	5	0	1.000	0	1	2.06
1989 Memphis	AA	13	13	0	0	63.2	303	67	53	45	4	4	1	5	51	1	52	4	1	1	9	.100	0	0	6.36
Baseball Cy	A	9	9	0	0	42	186	43	23	18	2	1	1	1	22	0	30	2	1	3	1	.750	0	0	3.86
1990 Memphis	AA	46	6	0	15	107.2	479	91	61	52	6	4	1	3	70	2	102	2	2	3	8	.273	0	4	4.35
1991 Omaha	AAA	6	0	0	1	13	54	9	6	6	1	0	0	0	8	1	12	0	0	1	1	.500	0	0	4.15
Carolina	AA	20	0	0	17	28.1	116	13	8	6	1	0	1	2	19	1	32	3	2	0	2	.000	0	12	1.91
Buffalo	AAA	19	1	0	9	24	115	23	11	10	2	0	1	1	20	0	23	3	0	1	2	.333	0	0	3.75
1992 Buffalo	AAA	19	19	3	0	115.2	498	102	46	40	8	3	3	4	61	0	69	8	0	11	6	.647	1	0	3.11
1993 Buffalo	AAA	6	6	0	0	26.1	134	35	25	25	5	2	1	0	24	0	14	1	0	1	3	.250	0	0	8.54
Carolina	AA	27	0	0	13	41	189	39	30	27	5	1	0	2	31	2	35	6	0	0	4	.000	0	8	5.93
New Orleans	AA	6	1	0	0	6	34	9	7	7	0	0	1	1	7	0	5	0	0	0	2	.000	0	0	10.50
1994 El Paso	AA	8	0	0	2	8	50	18	17	16	4	0	0	1	9	1	3	0	1	0	1	.000	0	0	18.00
Memphis	AA	6	6	0	0	35.2	162	32	22	19	3	0	4	0	23	0	22	2	0	2	1	.667	0	0	4.79
1995 Las Vegas	AAA	4	4	0	0	19.2	86	19	17	14	4	1	1	0	10	0	12	1	1	0	2	.000	0	0	6.41
Salinas	IND	4	4	0	0	22.2	104	25	16	9	0	2	2	0	13	0	22	2	0	1	1	.500	0	0	3.57
Memphis	AA	4	2	0	3	20	81	15	5	3	0	0	0	0	8	1	17	0	0	1	0	1.000	0	0	1.35
1992 Pittsburgh	NL	8	4	0	2	23	104	23	14	14	1	1	1	0	14	0	12	1	0	0	2	.000	0	0	5.48
8 Min. YEARS		226	76	3	75	632.1	2834	583	362	309	45	19	18	23	406	9	518	39	8	31	43	.419	1	34	4.40

Billy Coleman

Pitches: Right **Bats:** Right **Pos:** P   **Ht:** 6'1" **Wt:** 185 **Born:** 1/18/69 **Age:** 27

			HOW MUCH HE PITCHED				WHAT HE GAVE UP										THE RESULTS					
Year	Team	Lg	G	GS	CG	GF	IP	BFP	H	R	ER	HR	SH	SF	HB	TBB	IBB	SO	WP	Bk	W	L	Pct.	ShO	Sv	ERA
1991	Oneonta	A	18	5	0	4	52.2	230	44	22	17	1	2	2	1	30	0	36	4	1	2	3	.400	0	1	2.91
1992	Greensboro	A	56	0	0	25	73	336	59	39	27	4	4	2	6	52	3	67	14	1	3	5	.375	0	7	3.33
1993	Greensboro	A	59	0	0	41	70	290	54	24	20	5	3	5	3	23	4	82	5	0	5	3	.625	0	14	2.57
1994	Albany-Colo	AA	12	1	0	4	16.2	73	17	12	10	1	1	1	0	6	0	14	3	1	1	2	.333	0	2	5.40
	Tampa	A	14	0	0	8	16.2	72	13	10	3	1	1	2	0	6	1	21	2	0	2	2	.500	0	1	1.62
1995	Norwich	AA	46	0	0	12	73.1	335	56	52	33	5	3	4	4	57	5	64	12	1	6	4	.600	0	2	4.05
	5 Min. YEARS		205	6	0	94	302.1	1336	243	159	110	17	14	16	14	174	13	284	40	4	19	19	.500	0	27	3.27

Ken Coleman

Bats: Both **Throws:** Right **Pos:** 2B-3B   **Ht:** 5'10" **Wt:** 175 **Born:** 2/6/67 **Age:** 29

			BATTING												BASERUNNING				PERCENTAGES		
Year	Team	Lg	G	AB	H	2B	3B	HR	TB	R	RBI	TBB	IBB	SO	HBP	SH	SF	SB	CS	SB%	GDP	Avg	OBP	SLG
1989	Utica	A	27	90	16	0	0	0	16	16	4	14	0	17	1	0	1	9	2	.82	2	.178	.292	.178
	White Sox	R	22	76	33	6	2	0	43	23	13	13	0	7	3	1	1	18	6	.75	3	.434	.527	.566
1990	Sarasota	A	65	225	56	6	1	1	67	23	22	14	0	30	2	7	3	14	8	.64	3	.249	.295	.298
1991	South Bend	A	8	26	9	1	0	0	10	5	4	0	0	4	0	1	1	0	0	.00	0	.346	.333	.385
	Sarasota	A	44	118	33	6	1	1	44	15	15	20	0	21	1	0	2	5	3	.63	2	.280	.383	.373
1992	Sarasota	A	100	299	78	16	4	2	108	52	31	35	1	41	10	10	3	14	7	.67	7	.261	.354	.361
1993	Sarasota	A	11	32	6	0	0	0	6	4	2	6	0	4	0	0	1	1	1	.50	0	.188	.308	.188
	Birmingham	AA	50	129	30	3	0	0	33	11	14	13	0	25	1	3	2	2	1	.67	3	.233	.303	.256
1994	Nashville	AAA	5	16	5	2	1	1	12	5	3	3	0	1	1	0	0	0	0	.00	1	.313	.450	.750
	Birmingham	AA	75	188	36	6	0	0	66	30	26	37	0	88	5	4	0	4	4	.50	7	.191	.333	.253
1995	Orlando	AA	127	394	109	19	3	4	146	82	37	76	0	55	3	4	2	25	7	.78	16	.277	.396	.371
	7 Min. YEARS		534	1593	411	65	14	12	540	266	170	231	1	243	27	30	19	92	39	.70	44	.258	.358	.339

Cris Colon

Bats: Both **Throws:** Right **Pos:** 1B   **Ht:** 6' 2" **Wt:** 180 **Born:** 1/3/69 **Age:** 27

			BATTING												BASERUNNING				PERCENTAGES		
Year	Team	Lg	G	AB	H	2B	3B	HR	TB	R	RBI	TBB	IBB	SO	HBP	SH	SF	SB	CS	SB%	GDP	Avg	OBP	SLG
1987	Rangers	R	46	136	35	3	0	0	38	12	9	3	0	17	0	2	1	2	0	1.00	5	.257	.271	.279
1988	Gastonia	A	75	232	46	12	0	1	61	23	11	12	0	46	0	4	0	6	2	.75	5	.198	.238	.263
	Butte	R	49	190	37	3	4	1	51	21	19	3	0	34	0	1	1	3	0	1.00	4	.195	.206	.268
1989	Gastonia	A	125	473	107	9	8	3	141	58	49	10	0	95	2	11	4	8	5	.62	6	.226	.243	.298
1990	Gastonia	A	38	140	45	2	4	4	67	23	16	4	1	24	1	4	0	7	1	.88	2	.321	.345	.479
	Tulsa	AA	65	234	57	9	1	3	77	24	29	5	1	37	1	3	2	5	4	.56	6	.244	.260	.329
1991	Charlotte	A	66	249	78	9	5	3	106	33	27	9	2	44	3	5	0	4	5	.44	7	.313	.345	.426
	Tulsa	AA	26	102	40	6	2	3	59	20	28	4	0	11	0	1	3	0	1	.00	4	.392	.404	.578
1992	Tulsa	AA	120	415	109	16	3	1	134	35	44	16	3	72	0	3	5	7	4	.64	4	.263	.287	.323
1993	Tulsa	AA	124	490	147	27	3	11	213	63	47	13	0	76	5	4	5	6	3	.67	13	.300	.322	.435
1994	Iowa	AAA	123	434	118	31	2	12	189	53	55	14	3	68	7	3	3	2	2	.50	6	.272	.303	.435
1995	Iowa	AAA	106	366	95	18	1	4	127	35	36	17	4	51	4	3	1	1	0	1.00	5	.260	.299	.347
1992	Texas	AL	14	36	6	0	0	0	6	5	1	1	0	8	0	1	0	0	0	.00	2	.167	.189	.167
	9 Min. YEARS		963	3461	914	145	33	46	1263	400	370	110	14	575	23	44	25	51	27	.65	67	.264	.289	.365

Dennis Colon

Bats: Left **Throws:** Right **Pos:** 1B   **Ht:** 5'10" **Wt:** 165 **Born:** 8/4/73 **Age:** 22

			BATTING												BASERUNNING				PERCENTAGES		
Year	Team	Lg	G	AB	H	2B	3B	HR	TB	R	RBI	TBB	IBB	SO	HBP	SH	SF	SB	CS	SB%	GDP	Avg	OBP	SLG
1991	Astros	R	54	193	46	5	2	2	61	20	28	10	2	28	1	1	1	4	7	.36	4	.238	.278	.316
1992	Burlington	A	123	458	116	27	7	6	175	54	63	32	1	50	2	2	6	4	7	.36	9	.253	.301	.382
1993	Osceola	A	118	469	148	20	6	2	186	51	59	17	1	41	0	0	3	10	4	.71	12	.316	.337	.397
1994	Jackson	AA	118	380	105	17	6	5	149	37	52	18	5	43	0	4	5	8	5	.62	12	.276	.305	.392
1995	Jackson	AA	106	378	85	10	0	5	110	33	31	24	2	38	5	2	6	3	6	.33	8	.225	.276	.291
	5 Min. YEARS		519	1878	500	79	21	20	681	195	233	101	11	200	8	9	21	29	29	.50	45	.266	.303	.363

Felix Colon

Bats: Right **Throws:** Right **Pos:** 1B   **Ht:** 6'0" **Wt:** 176 **Born:** 9/15/70 **Age:** 25

			BATTING												BASERUNNING				PERCENTAGES		
Year	Team	Lg	G	AB	H	2B	3B	HR	TB	R	RBI	TBB	IBB	SO	HBP	SH	SF	SB	CS	SB%	GDP	Avg	OBP	SLG
1989	Red Sox	R	58	214	48	9	1	6	77	29	21	22	2	43	4	1	1	2	1	.67	4	.224	.307	.360
1990	Winter Havn	A	89	275	54	14	2	6	90	21	25	38	0	80	3	1	0	1	3	.25	2	.196	.301	.327
	Red Sox	R	29	108	30	11	0	1	44	22	22	16	1	21	2	0	2	0	0	.00	2	.278	.375	.407
1991	Elmira	A	63	205	51	8	0	12	95	32	41	32	1	56	3	0	1	0	2	.00	4	.249	.357	.463
1992	Winter Havn	A	97	339	83	14	3	5	118	33	40	36	2	75	5	0	1	1	1	.50	6	.245	.325	.348
1993	Lynchburg	A	97	319	102	22	0	16	172	52	58	45	0	65	1	2	7	0	1	.00	8	.320	.398	.539
1994	New Britain	AA	129	439	99	24	3	7	150	51	53	69	2	103	3	1	6	3	3	.50	9	.226	.331	.342
1995	Jacksonville	AA	31	81	21	7	0	2	34	5	8	13	0	13	2	0	0	0	0	.00	2	.259	.375	.420
	7 Min. YEARS		593	1980	488	109	9	55	780	245	268	271	8	456	23	5	18	7	11	.39	37	.246	.341	.394

Pat Combs

Pitches: Left **Bats:** Left **Pos:** P   **Ht:** 6' 4" **Wt:** 200 **Born:** 10/29/66 **Age:** 29

Year	Team	Lg	G	GS	CG	GF	IP	BFP	H	R	ER	HR	SH	SF	HB	TBB	IBB	SO	WP	Bk	W	L	Pct.	ShO	Sv	ERA
1989	Clearwater	A	6	6	0	0	41.2	165	35	8	6	0	3	0	1	11	0	24	0	1	2	1	.667	0	0	1.30
	Reading	AA	19	19	4	0	125	512	104	57	47	16	6	2	4	40	2	77	5	2	8	7	.533	0	0	3.38
	Scranton-Wb	AAA	3	3	2	0	24.1	94	15	4	1	0	0	1	0	7	0	20	1	0	3	0	1.000	1	0	0.37
1991	Scranton-Wb	AAA	6	6	1	0	27	132	39	23	20	0	2	3	0	16	0	14	1	0	2	2	.500	0	0	6.67
1992	Scranton-Wb	AAA	21	21	1	0	124.2	526	123	62	50	9	10	5	0	41	0	77	3	1	5	7	.417	0	0	3.61
1993	Scranton-Wb	AAA	15	15	1	0	83.2	372	97	57	45	8	4	2	4	27	1	60	7	0	0	9	.000	0	0	4.84
1994	Scranton-Wb	AAA	28	22	3	0	137.1	626	167	106	96	13	4	3	0	75	1	70	4	0	6	11	.353	0	0	6.29
1995	Scranton-Wb	AAA	22	6	0	7	56.1	251	71	37	34	6	2	2	1	25	3	36	1	0	4	4	.500	0	0	5.43
	New Orleans	AAA	12	2	0	5	15	78	19	11	9	1	0	1	1	13	0	10	5	0	1	1	.500	0	0	5.40
1989	Philadelphia	NL	6	6	1	0	38.2	153	36	10	9	2	2	0	0	6	1	30	5	0	4	0	1.000	1	0	2.09
1990	Philadelphia	NL	32	31	3	0	183.1	800	179	90	83	12	7	7	4	86	7	108	9	1	10	10	.500	2	0	4.07
1991	Philadelphia	NL	14	13	1	0	64.1	300	64	41	35	7	1	2	2	43	1	41	7	0	2	6	.250	0	0	4.90
1992	Philadelphia	NL	4	4	0	0	18.2	88	20	16	16	0	3	1	0	12	0	11	1	0	0	1	.500	0	0	7.71
	6 Min. YEARS		132	100	12	12	635	2756	670	365	308	53	31	19	11	255	7	388	27	4	31	42	.425	1	0	4.37
	4 Maj. YEARS		56	54	5	0	305	1341	299	157	143	21	13	10	6	147	9	190	22	1	17	17	.500	3	0	4.22

Jeff Conger

Bats: Left **Throws:** Left **Pos:** OF   **Ht:** 6'0" **Wt:** 185 **Born:** 8/6/71 **Age:** 24

Year	Team	Lg	G	AB	H	2B	3B	HR	TB	R	RBI	TBB	IBB	SO	HBP	SH	SF	SB	CS	SB%	GDP	Avg	OBP	SLG
1990	Pirates	R	46	120	22	3	1	0	27	19	6	18	0	52	1	1	0	3	1	.75	0	.183	.295	.225
1991	Pirates	R	15	37	12	0	0	0	12	5	4	4	0	8	0	0	0	7	2	.78	0	.324	.390	.324
	Welland	A	32	81	22	2	2	1	31	15	7	7	0	31	1	0	0	5	2	.71	0	.272	.337	.383
1992	Augusta	A	98	303	74	12	6	6	116	56	36	44	2	93	3	2	1	36	13	.73	1	.244	.345	.383
1993	Salem	A	110	391	90	12	1	4	116	40	31	31	2	125	1	7	1	24	10	.71	7	.230	.288	.297
1994	Salem	A	111	362	83	8	3	9	124	65	37	53	0	105	9	6	4	13	8	.62	5	.229	.339	.343
1995	Lynchburg	A	90	318	84	13	5	3	116	44	23	35	1	74	6	7	3	26	16	.62	1	.264	.345	.365
	Carolina	AA	39	128	37	6	1	1	48	15	17	18	2	31	1	2	1	8	2	.80	0	.289	.378	.375
	6 Min. YEARS		541	1740	424	56	19	24	590	259	161	210	7	519	22	25	10	122	54	.69	14	.244	.331	.339

Scott Conner

Pitches: Right **Bats:** Right **Pos:** P   **Ht:** 6'2" **Wt:** 182 **Born:** 3/22/72 **Age:** 24

Year	Team	Lg	G	GS	CG	GF	IP	BFP	H	R	ER	HR	SH	SF	HB	TBB	IBB	SO	WP	Bk	W	L	Pct.	ShO	Sv	ERA
1991	Orioles	R	12	7	0	4	48.2	210	49	33	29	0	2	2	3	18	0	35	6	0	1	4	.200	0	1	5.36
1992	Orioles	R	12	11	3	0	70	294	56	29	15	2	1	4	5	31	0	39	4	0	4	5	.444	1	0	1.93
1993	Albany	A	37	13	0	8	115.2	546	133	92	66	8	3	3	2	71	2	90	12	1	6	6	.500	0	0	5.14
1994	Frederick	A	53	0	0	22	73.1	325	65	34	29	5	4	1	5	49	2	61	8	0	2	1	.667	0	8	3.56
1995	Bowie	AA	44	0	0	9	82	378	57	43	38	7	4	7	10	74	2	82	13	2	5	1	.833	0	0	4.17
	5 Min. YEARS		158	31	3	43	389.2	1753	360	231	177	22	14	17	25	243	6	307	43	3	18	17	.514	1	9	4.09

Chris Connolly

Pitches: Left **Bats:** Left **Pos:** P   **Ht:** 6'2" **Wt:** 192 **Born:** 12/4/70 **Age:** 25

Year	Team	Lg	G	GS	CG	GF	IP	BFP	H	R	ER	HR	SH	SF	HB	TBB	IBB	SO	WP	Bk	W	L	Pct.	ShO	Sv	ERA
1991	Eugene	A	21	0	0	5	51	228	40	30	21	1	2	1	2	41	0	45	10	1	1	2	.333	0	2	3.71
1992	Appleton	A	20	0	0	5	22.2	109	28	16	13	0	1	1	2	14	0	12	1	0	0	0	.000	0	0	5.16
1993	Rockford	A	34	0	0	16	74.2	335	83	37	33	1	6	3	2	31	1	50	5	1	6	3	.667	0	3	3.98
1994	Wilmington	A	37	0	0	12	63	258	40	18	12	1	2	0	3	33	1	30	4	1	8	3	.727	0	2	1.71
1995	Wichita	AA	13	0	0	2	12.2	64	18	11	8	0	1	1	2	11	0	2	2	0	1	0	1.000	0	0	5.68
	Wilmington	A	27	0	0	13	44	196	38	23	17	2	1	1	5	23	2	29	10	1	5	2	.714	0	1	3.48
	5 Min. YEARS		152	0	0	53	268	1190	247	135	104	5	13	7	16	153	4	168	32	4	21	10	.677	0	8	3.49

Matt Connolly

Pitches: Right **Bats:** Right **Pos:** P   **Ht:** 6'8" **Wt:** 230 **Born:** 10/1/68 **Age:** 27

Year	Team	Lg	G	GS	CG	GF	IP	BFP	H	R	ER	HR	SH	SF	HB	TBB	IBB	SO	WP	Bk	W	L	Pct.	ShO	Sv	ERA
1991	Erie	A	19	0	0	9	41.2	188	39	23	20	1	1	2	2	25	1	43	5	1	2	1	.667	0	1	4.32
1992	Visalia	A	30	2	0	12	67.2	293	70	35	25	3	4	1	5	26	1	42	3	1	5	1	.833	0	0	3.33
1993	W. Palm Bch	A	6	0	0	0	14.2	67	14	9	8	0	2	0	1	9	0	8	0	0	1	1	.500	0	0	4.91
	Sioux City	IND	17	17	2	0	100.2	439	111	61	53	6	2	8	5	32	2	71	4	0	5	8	.385	0	0	4.74
1994	Sioux City	IND	16	16	2	0	108	468	117	51	43	9	1	4	1	34	0	107	6	1	7	1	.875	1	0	3.58
1995	Daytona	A	18	2	0	7	55.1	216	37	14	6	0	3	0	2	9	2	77	6	0	7	1	.875	0	2	0.98
	Orlando	AA	21	4	0	11	39.2	165	34	18	18	5	0	0	2	11	3	43	1	0	3	4	.429	0	2	4.08
	5 Min. YEARS		127	41	4	39	427.2	1836	422	211	173	24	13	15	18	146	9	391	25	3	30	17	.638	1	6	3.64

Chad Connors

Pitches: Right **Bats:** Right **Pos:** P Ht: 6'0" Wt: 200 Born: 10/18/71 **Age:** 24

Year	Team	Lg	G	GS	CG	GF	IP	BFP	H	R	ER	HR	SH	SF	HB	TBB	IBB	SO	WP	Bk	W	L	Pct.	ShO	Sv	ERA
1993	Billings	R	19	0	0	8	29.2	130	20	9	7	0	2	1	3	20	0	32	6	0	2	2	.500	0	5	2.12
1994	Charlstn-Wv	A	19	0	0	5	40	159	26	14	12	3	1	3	4	12	1	34	2	0	1	1	.500	0	0	2.70
	Winston-Sal	A	28	0	0	18	45.2	169	20	7	6	2	0	0	1	17	0	32	0	0	2	2	.500	0	11	1.18
1995	Chattanooga	AA	10	0	0	8	9.2	46	9	3	3	1	0	1	0	9	1	15	1	0	0	1	.000	0	0	2.79
	Winston-Sal	A	16	0	0	8	19.2	95	28	16	15	3	0	0	3	11	1	13	2	0	2	2	.500	0	2	6.86
	3 Min. YEARS		92	0	0	47	144.2	599	103	49	43	9	3	5	11	69	3	126	11	0	7	8	.467	0	18	2.68

Brian Conroy

Pitches: Right **Bats:** Both **Pos:** P Ht: 6'2" Wt: 185 Born: 8/29/68 **Age:** 27

Year	Team	Lg	G	GS	CG	GF	IP	BFP	H	R	ER	HR	SH	SF	HB	TBB	IBB	SO	WP	Bk	W	L	Pct.	ShO	Sv	ERA
1989	Red Sox	R	7	7	2	0	44	174	33	15	11	0	0	1	2	9	0	31	2	3	4	2	.667	0	0	2.25
	Winter Havn	A	8	6	2	1	39.2	172	38	19	13	3	1	1	4	11	0	30	3	2	3	3	.500	2	0	2.95
1990	Lynchburg	A	26	26	8	0	186.1	769	160	84	73	13	3	4	7	51	0	147	11	6	10	12	.455	4	0	3.53
	New Britain	AA	1	1	0	0	6	24	7	4	4	1	1	0	0	1	1	3	0	0	0	1	.000	0	0	6.00
1991	New Britain	AA	10	10	1	0	65.2	274	51	27	22	6	2	4	4	26	2	34	3	0	1	5	.167	1	0	3.02
	Pawtucket	AAA	17	16	1	1	98.1	431	95	60	50	13	3	8	2	51	1	66	3	1	6	4	.600	0	0	4.58
1992	New Britain	AA	11	11	3	0	75.1	303	70	33	32	9	1	3	0	17	0	40	1	0	4	6	.400	1	0	3.82
	Pawtucket	AAA	15	13	1	1	85.2	375	91	49	44	17	0	1	2	31	2	57	2	1	7	5	.583	1	0	4.62
1993	Pawtucket	AAA	19	19	0	0	106	478	126	74	69	24	1	3	2	40	0	64	6	0	5	7	.417	0	0	5.86
1994	Pawtucket	AAA	11	11	0	0	57.1	247	65	40	37	13	3	2	2	15	0	22	0	0	5	3	.625	0	0	5.81
	Colo. Sprng	AAA	16	15	1	0	87.2	411	121	80	70	22	2	2	2	30	0	40	0	1	8	3	.727	0	0	7.19
1995	Colo. Sprng	AAA	5	5	0	0	28	128	36	19	19	0	0	0	0	11	1	9	0	0	0	2	.000	0	0	6.11
	7 Min. YEARS		146	140	19	3	880	3786	893	504	444	121	17	29	28	292	10	545	31	14	53	53	.500	9	0	4.54

Andy Cook

Pitches: Right **Bats:** Right **Pos:** P Ht: 6'5" Wt: 205 Born: 8/30/67 **Age:** 28

Year	Team	Lg	G	GS	CG	GF	IP	BFP	H	R	ER	HR	SH	SF	HB	TBB	IBB	SO	WP	Bk	W	L	Pct.	ShO	Sv	ERA
1988	Oneonta	A	16	16	2	0	102	444	116	50	41	2	2	1	4	21	0	65	2	3	8	4	.667	0	0	3.62
1989	Pr. William	A	25	24	5	0	153	621	123	68	56	7	4	2	6	49	0	83	6	7	8	12	.400	1	0	3.29
1990	Albany-Colo	AA	24	24	5	0	156.2	648	146	69	60	12	4	5	4	52	2	53	5	4	12	8	.600	0	0	3.45
1991	Albany-Colo	AA	14	14	1	0	82	360	94	46	36	2	0	3	0	27	0	46	1	0	6	3	.667	0	0	3.95
	Columbus	AAA	13	13	2	0	79.1	338	63	34	31	0	5	3	4	38	1	40	1	1	5	5	.500	0	0	3.52
1992	Columbus	AAA	32	9	0	7	99.2	411	85	41	35	8	5	1	3	36	0	58	3	0	7	5	.583	0	2	3.16
1993	Columbus	AAA	21	20	0	0	118.1	543	149	91	86	14	6	5	7	49	3	47	4	3	6	7	.462	0	0	6.54
1994	Salt Lake	AAA	3	3	0	0	14.2	69	17	14	11	2	1	0	1	4	0	7	1	0	0	2	.000	0	0	6.75
	Columbus	AAA	34	8	0	5	80	341	86	36	33	6	3	1	4	26	2	49	2	0	3	5	.375	0	0	3.71
1995	Columbus	AAA	37	2	0	12	56.1	235	53	24	21	2	3	1	3	19	1	28	3	2	2	3	.400	0	0	3.36
1993	New York	AL	4	0	0	3	5.1	28	4	3	3	1	1	0	0	7	0	4	2	0	0	1	.000	0	0	5.06
	8 Min. YEARS		219	133	15	24	942	4010	932	473	410	55	33	22	36	321	9	476	28	20	57	54	.514	1	4	3.92

Steve Cooke

Pitches: Left **Bats:** Right **Pos:** P Ht: 6'6" Wt: 229 Born: 1/14/70 **Age:** 26

Year	Team	Lg	G	GS	CG	GF	IP	BFP	H	R	ER	HR	SH	SF	HB	TBB	IBB	SO	WP	Bk	W	L	Pct.	ShO	Sv	ERA
1990	Welland	A	11	11	0	0	46	188	36	21	18	2	1	1	2	17	0	43	6	1	2	3	.400	0	0	3.52
1991	Augusta	A	11	11	1	0	60.2	269	50	28	19	0	3	1	5	35	1	52	3	0	5	4	.556	0	0	2.82
	Salem	A	2	2	0	0	13	57	14	8	7	0	0	0	0	2	0	5	4	1	1	0	1.000	0	0	4.85
	Carolina	AA	9	9	1	0	55.2	223	39	21	14	2	1	1	4	19	0	46	5	0	3	3	.500	1	0	2.26
1992	Carolina	AA	6	6	0	0	36	143	31	13	12	1	0	1	3	12	1	38	1	0	2	2	.500	0	0	3.00
	Buffalo	AAA	13	13	0	0	74.1	325	71	35	31	2	5	3	4	36	2	52	5	1	6	3	.667	0	0	3.75
1995	Augusta	A	1	1	0	0	5	19	2	0	0	0	0	0	0	1	0	6	0	0	1	0	1.000	0	0	0.00
	Carolina	A	1	1	0	0	5	27	5	4	4	0	0	0	0	5	0	4	1	0	0	0	.000	0	0	7.20
1992	Pittsburgh	NL	11	0	0	8	23	91	22	9	9	2	0	0	0	4	1	10	0	0	2	0	1.000	0	1	3.52
1993	Pittsburgh	NL	32	32	3	0	210.2	882	207	101	91	22	13	6	3	59	4	132	3	3	10	10	.500	1	0	3.89
1994	Pittsburgh	NL	25	23	2	1	134.1	590	157	79	75	21	9	3	5	46	7	74	3	0	4	11	.267	0	0	5.02
	4 Min. YEARS		54	54	2	0	295.2	1251	248	130	105	7	10	7	18	127	4	246	25	3	20	15	.571	1	0	3.20
	3 Maj. YEARS		68	55	5	9	368	1563	386	189	175	45	22	9	8	109	12	216	6	3	16	21	.432	1	1	4.28

Mike Coolbaugh

Bats: Right **Throws:** Right **Pos:** 3B Ht: 6'1" Wt: 190 Born: 6/5/72 **Age:** 24

Year	Team	Lg	G	AB	H	2B	3B	HR	TB	R	RBI	TBB	IBB	SO	HBP	SH	SF	SB	CS	SB%	GDP	Avg	OBP	SLG
1990	Medicne Hat	R	58	211	40	9	0	2	55	21	16	13	0	47	1	1	2	3	2	.60	8	.190	.238	.261
1991	St. Cathrns	A	71	255	58	13	2	3	84	28	26	17	0	40	3	4	4	4	5	.44	1	.227	.280	.329
1992	St. Cathrns	A	15	49	14	1	1	0	17	3	2	3	0	12	0	2	0	0	2	.00	1	.286	.327	.347
1993	Hagerstown	A	112	389	94	23	1	16	167	58	62	32	5	94	3	4	4	4	3	.57	9	.242	.301	.429
1994	Dunedin	A	122	456	120	33	3	16	207	53	66	28	3	94	7	3	4	3	4	.43	14	.263	.313	.454
1995	Knoxville	AA	142	500	120	32	2	9	183	71	56	37	3	110	11	4	3	7	11	.39	13	.240	.305	.366
	6 Min. YEARS		520	1860	446	111	9	46	713	234	228	130	11	397	25	18	17	21	27	.44	46	.240	.296	.383

Gary Cooper

Bats: Right **Throws:** Right **Pos:** 3B   **Ht:** 6' 1" **Wt:** 200 **Born:** 8/13/64 **Age:** 31

Year Team	Lg	G	AB	H	2B	3B	HR	TB	R	RBI	TBB	IBB	SO	HBP	SH	SF	SB	CS	SB%	GDP	Avg	OBP	SLG
1986 Auburn	A	76	275	86	16	3	11	141	52	54	47	0	47	2	0	2	16	4	.80	5	.313	.414	.513
1987 Osceola	A	123	427	119	17	4	4	156	66	74	66	2	69	5	4	5	14	5	.74	12	.279	.378	.365
1988 Columbus	AA	140	474	128	25	7	7	188	65	69	87	0	87	4	4	7	13	7	.65	20	.270	.383	.397
1989 Tucson	AAA	118	376	102	23	3	1	134	51	50	48	2	69	4	1	5	5	7	.42	2	.271	.356	.356
1990 Osceola	A	8	26	4	4	0	0	8	4	2	3	0	3	1	0	1	0	0	.00	1	.154	.258	.308
Columbus	AA	54	160	42	7	0	8	73	29	30	30	0	32	1	0	1	1	2	.33	5	.263	.380	.456
1991 Tucson	AAA	120	406	124	25	6	14	203	86	75	66	5	108	3	2	5	7	8	.47	11	.305	.402	.500
1992 Tucson	AAA	127	464	139	31	3	9	203	66	73	47	0	86	3	3	7	8	6	.57	12	.300	.363	.438
1993 Buffalo	AAA	102	349	94	27	2	16	173	66	63	52	2	88	4	4	3	2	3	.40	12	.269	.368	.496
1994 Indianapols	AAA	76	226	73	19	3	10	128	43	36	37	0	57	4	2	0	7	3	.70	6	.323	.427	.566
1995 Jacksonville	AA	99	337	93	22	1	18	171	66	66	59	4	83	6	0	3	8	4	.67	11	.276	.390	.507
1991 Houston	NL	9	16	4	1	0	0	5	1	2	3	0	6	0	0	0	0	0	.00	0	.250	.368	.313
10 Min. YEARS		1043	3520	1004	216	32	98	1578	594	592	542	15	729	37	20	39	81	49	.62	97	.285	.383	.448

Rocky Coppinger

Pitches: Right **Bats:** Right **Pos:** P   **Ht:** 6'5" **Wt:** 245 **Born:** 3/19/74 **Age:** 22

Year Team	Lg	G	GS	CG	GF	IP	BFP	H	R	ER	HR	SH	SF	HB	TBB	IBB	SO	WP	Bk	W	L	Pct.	ShO	Sv	ERA
1994 Bluefield	R	14	13	0	1	73.1	302	51	24	20	5	0	3	2	40	0	88	5	0	4	3	.571	1	0	2.45
1995 Frederick	A	11	11	2	0	68.2	272	46	16	12	3	3	1	0	24	0	91	1	0	7	1	.875	1	0	1.57
Bowie	AA	13	13	2	0	83.2	352	58	33	25	7	0	4	3	43	0	62	4	1	6	2	.750	2	0	2.69
Rochester	AAA	5	5	0	0	34.2	140	23	5	4	2	0	2	1	17	0	19	0	0	1	0	1.000	0	0	1.04
2 Min. YEARS		43	42	4	1	260.1	1066	178	78	61	17	3	10	6	124	0	260	10	1	20	6	.769	3	0	2.11

Manuel Cora

Bats: Both **Throws:** Right **Pos:** 2B   **Ht:** 5'11" **Wt:** 165 **Born:** 12/20/73 **Age:** 22

Year Team	Lg	G	AB	H	2B	3B	HR	TB	R	RBI	TBB	IBB	SO	HBP	SH	SF	SB	CS	SB%	GDP	Avg	OBP	SLG
1991 Padres	R	49	198	71	8	5	0	89	38	32	17	0	27	3	1	4	12	10	.55	2	.359	.410	.449
1992 Charlstn-Sc	A	121	452	110	4	3	0	120	45	19	29	0	65	4	4	4	12	17	.41	7	.243	.292	.265
1993 Waterloo	A	22	73	24	4	0	1	31	8	11	5	0	6	0	0	0	1	1	.50	1	.329	.372	.425
1994 Riverside	A	115	411	124	13	9	0	155	50	46	17	0	49	1	11	2	7	5	.58	4	.302	.329	.377
1995 Port City	AA	80	261	59	8	3	0	73	17	15	8	0	38	0	0	1	1	6	.14	8	.226	.248	.280
5 Min. YEARS		387	1395	388	37	20	1	468	158	123	76	0	185	8	16	11	33	39	.46	22	.278	.317	.335

Archie Corbin

Pitches: Right **Bats:** Right **Pos:** P   **Ht:** 6' 4" **Wt:** 190 **Born:** 12/30/67 **Age:** 28

Year Team	Lg	G	GS	CG	GF	IP	BFP	H	R	ER	HR	SH	SF	HB	TBB	IBB	SO	WP	Bk	W	L	Pct.	ShO	Sv	ERA
1986 Kingsport	R	18	1	0	9	30.1	149	31	23	16	3	0	1	0	28	0	30	8	1	1	1	.500	0	0	4.75
1987 Kingsport	R	6	6	0	0	25.2	128	24	21	18	3	0	0	2	26	0	17	6	0	2	3	.400	0	0	6.31
1988 Kingsport	R	11	10	4	0	69.1	277	47	23	12	5	2	0	3	17	0	47	1	1	7	2	.778	1	0	1.56
1989 Columbia	A	27	23	4	3	153.2	664	149	86	77	16	4	4	5	72	0	130	2	0	9	9	.500	2	1	4.51
1990 St. Lucie	A	20	18	3	2	118	494	97	47	39	2	4	3	7	59	0	105	10	0	7	8	.467	0	0	2.97
1991 Memphis	AA	28	25	1	0	156.1	692	139	90	81	7	4	6	8	90	0	166	13	0	8	8	.500	0	0	4.66
1992 Memphis	AA	27	20	2	1	112.1	503	115	64	59	7	3	1	1	73	0	100	11	0	7	8	.467	0	0	4.73
Harrisburg	AA	1	1	0	0	3	11	2	0	0	0	0	0	0	1	0	3	0	0	0	0	.000	0	0	0.00
1993 Harrisburg	AA	42	2	0	21	73.1	314	43	31	30	0	1	5	2	59	1	91	5	1	5	3	.625	0	4	3.68
1994 Buffalo	AAA	14	1	0	3	22.2	99	14	13	12	0	1	1	1	18	0	23	2	0	0	0	.000	0	0	4.76
1995 Calgary	AAA	47	1	0	13	61	309	76	63	58	6	0	5	3	55	0	54	7	0	1	5	.167	0	1	8.56
1991 Kansas City	AL	2	0	0	0	2.1	12	3	1	1	0	0	0	0	2	0	1	0	1	0	0	.000	0	0	3.86
10 Min. YEARS		241	108	14	52	825.2	3640	737	461	402	49	19	26	32	498	2	766	65	3	47	47	.500	3	6	4.38

Ted Corbin

Bats: Both **Throws:** Right **Pos:** 2B-SS   **Ht:** 5'9" **Wt:** 150 **Born:** 4/27/71 **Age:** 25

Year Team	Lg	G	AB	H	2B	3B	HR	TB	R	RBI	TBB	IBB	SO	HBP	SH	SF	SB	CS	SB%	GDP	Avg	OBP	SLG
1992 Miracle	A	62	179	36	5	0	0	41	18	11	16	0	30	5	5	1	1	3	.25	3	.201	.284	.229
1993 Fort Myers	A	91	339	80	11	2	0	95	46	22	36	0	47	8	5	3	22	8	.73	9	.236	.321	.280
Nashville	AA	5	15	5	1	0	0	6	2	1	2	0	2	0	0	0	0	0	.00	0	.333	.412	.400
1994 Salt Lake	AAA	4	10	1	0	0	0	1	0	0	0	0	1	0	0	0	0	0	.00	0	.100	.100	.100
Nashville	AA	51	152	32	2	0	0	34	13	13	10	1	26	0	1	1	0	2	.00	3	.211	.258	.224
1995 Salt Lake	AAA	4	10	2	0	0	0	2	0	1	0	0	1	0	0	0	0	0	.00	1	.200	.200	.200
4 Min. YEARS		217	705	156	19	2	0	179	79	48	64	1	107	13	11	5	23	13	.64	17	.221	.296	.254

John Corona

Pitches: Left Bats: Left Pos: P Ht: 6'0" Wt: 185 Born: 5/28/69 Age: 27

Year Team	Lg	G	GS	CG	GF	IP	BFP	H	R	ER	HR	SH	SF	HB	TBB	IBB	SO	WP	Bk	W	L	Pct.	ShO	Sv	ERA
1989 Cardinals	R	28	0	0	18	38.1	181	48	25	22	1	3	1	1	14	4	31	0	0	0	1	.000	0	5	5.17
1990 Springfield	A	54	0	0	16	68	294	68	36	28	6	4	2	2	29	4	58	7	0	5	1	.833	0	1	3.71
1991 St. Pete	A	15	0	0	6	18.2	79	17	8	6	0	2	1	1	8	1	12	1	2	2	1	.667	0	0	2.89
Louisville	AAA	12	0	0	3	16.2	77	18	12	10	2	0	1	0	11	1	19	2	0	0	1	.000	0	0	5.40
Arkansas	AA	27	0	0	17	30.1	130	27	15	15	0	1	1	0	21	3	23	3	1	0	2	.000	0	0	4.45
1993 St. Pete	A	59	0	0	35	60.2	251	52	26	19	3	1	1	1	22	4	51	1	0	3	4	.429	0	16	2.82
1994 Arkansas	AA	33	0	0	11	40.1	181	41	19	13	4	3	0	2	23	3	37	4	1	3	1	.750	0	0	2.90
1995 Arkansas	AA	5	0	0	2	5	28	7	5	4	0	1	0	1	6	1	3	0	0	1	1	.500	0	0	7.20
Long Beach	IND	32	0	0	32	37.2	165	43	20	7	0	3	0	2	12	1	41	3	0	1	5	.167	0	17	1.67
6 Min. YEARS		265	0	0	140	315.2	1386	321	166	124	16	18	7	10	146	22	275	21	4	15	17	.469	0	39	3.54

Edwin Corps

Pitches: Right Bats: Right Pos: P Ht: 5'11" Wt: 180 Born: 11/3/72 Age: 23

Year Team	Lg	G	GS	CG	GF	IP	BFP	H	R	ER	HR	SH	SF	HB	TBB	IBB	SO	WP	Bk	W	L	Pct.	ShO	Sv	ERA
1994 San Jose	A	29	29	0	0	168.1	731	180	95	74	6	5	6	20	43	1	91	4	1	10	6	.625	0	0	3.96
1995 Shreveport	AA	27	27	2	0	165.2	712	195	80	71	16	2	6	8	41	2	53	4	2	13	6	.684	0	0	3.86
2 Min. YEARS		56	56	2	0	334	1443	375	175	145	22	7	12	28	84	3	144	8	3	23	12	.657	0	0	3.91

Ramser Correa

Pitches: Right Bats: Right Pos: P Ht: 6'5" Wt: 225 Born: 11/13/70 Age: 25

Year Team	Lg	G	GS	CG	GF	IP	BFP	H	R	ER	HR	SH	SF	HB	TBB	IBB	SO	WP	Bk	W	L	Pct.	ShO	Sv	ERA
1987 Helena	R	3	2	0	0	6	38	10	12	11	1	1	1	0	8	0	0	1	0	0	1	.000	0	0	16.50
1988 Helena	R	13	7	0	2	43.1	187	38	22	19	2	0	2	0	24	0	34	4	4	2	2	.500	0	0	3.95
1989 Helena	R	2	1	0	1	3	14	3	0	0	0	0	0	0	2	0	2	1	0	0	0	.000	0	0	0.00
1990 Beloit	A	4	4	0	0	24.2	105	24	8	6	1	0	0	0	9	0	30	1	0	3	0	1.000	0	0	2.19
1991 Stockton	A	10	8	0	0	33.2	147	31	14	11	1	1	1	2	20	0	21	2	0	2	1	.667	0	0	2.94
1992 Stockton	A	35	4	0	9	70.1	309	71	31	28	2	3	3	2	38	2	55	5	1	3	2	.600	0	1	3.58
1993 Stockton	A	21	10	0	6	67.2	304	78	38	34	2	1	5	1	30	1	32	2	1	4	3	.571	0	3	4.52
El Paso	AA	5	1	0	2	10.2	57	15	15	6	2	1	5	0	7	1	5	2	0	1	0	1.000	0	0	5.06
1994 Kinston	AA	4	4	0	0	18.1	87	14	11	9	3	0	0	0	19	0	17	1	1	2	1	.667	0	0	4.42
Canton-Akrn	AA	19	8	0	5	67.1	310	72	41	32	6	0	2	0	51	3	41	6	0	2	4	.333	0	0	4.28
1995 San Antonio	AA	42	0	0	32	49.2	221	54	29	25	5	0	2	0	21	0	34	4	0	1	4	.200	0	17	4.53
Albuquerque	AAA	2	0	0	0	4	16	5	0	0	0	0	0	0	1	1	3	0	0	0	0	.000	0	0	0.00
9 Min. YEARS		160	49	0	57	398.2	1795	415	221	181	25	7	21	5	230	8	274	29	7	20	18	.526	0	21	4.09

Jeff Cosman

Pitches: Right Bats: Right Pos: P Ht: 6'4" Wt: 197 Born: 2/8/71 Age: 25

Year Team	Lg	G	GS	CG	GF	IP	BFP	H	R	ER	HR	SH	SF	HB	TBB	IBB	SO	WP	Bk	W	L	Pct.	ShO	Sv	ERA
1993 Pittsfield	A	14	14	1	0	81.2	362	84	49	38	3	2	5	7	31	0	46	4	1	2	7	.222	0	0	4.19
1994 Columbia	A	20	20	3	0	136.1	557	125	52	42	4	4	0	10	34	0	120	16	2	9	7	.563	0	0	2.77
St. Lucie	A	7	7	2	0	48.1	203	42	14	11	1	4	0	3	20	2	31	0	0	3	2	.600	1	0	2.05
1995 St. Lucie	A	15	15	6	0	101	412	96	43	35	2	3	1	3	27	3	72	5	1	4	9	.308	2	0	3.12
Binghamton	AA	10	10	0	0	48.1	219	57	40	38	4	1	1	2	18	0	23	2	0	2	4	.333	0	0	7.08
3 Min. YEARS		66	66	12	0	415.2	1753	404	198	164	14	14	7	25	130	5	292	27	4	20	29	.408	4	0	3.55

Fred Costello

Pitches: Right Bats: Right Pos: P Ht: 6'4" Wt: 190 Born: 10/1/66 Age: 29

Year Team	Lg	G	GS	CG	GF	IP	BFP	H	R	ER	HR	SH	SF	HB	TBB	IBB	SO	WP	Bk	W	L	Pct.	ShO	Sv	ERA
1986 Astros	R	14	12	1	0	66.1	301	74	42	35	1	2	1	6	26	0	51	1	0	4	5	.444	1	0	4.75
1987 Astros	R	13	12	0	1	72.2	320	74	40	26	1	2	2	1	28	1	45	9	0	5	7	.417	0	0	3.22
1988 Asheville	A	51	0	0	37	76	329	76	34	30	5	9	1	3	31	2	65	2	1	6	7	.462	0	11	3.55
1989 Columbus	AA	30	0	0	17	54	220	39	22	20	5	1	1	0	21	1	39	5	0	4	5	.444	0	3	3.33
1990 Columbus	AA	35	5	0	20	45.1	214	54	31	21	4	3	1	1	23	3	39	6	2	0	5	.000	0	7	4.17
1991 Osceola	A	5	0	0	2	6	29	8	5	5	2	0	1	0	3	0	5	0	0	1	0	1.000	0	0	7.50
1992 Osceola	A	10	0	0	2	13.1	57	14	7	4	0	2	0	0	2	0	10	0	0	1	2	.333	0	1	2.70
Jackson	AA	36	0	0	10	53.1	215	51	22	16	3	1	2	0	13	3	35	2	0	2	2	.500	0	0	2.70
1993 Jackson	AA	12	12	0	0	60.2	248	57	24	19	2	4	1	3	13	0	45	1	1	8	3	.727	0	0	2.82
Tucson	AAA	14	14	0	0	83	370	92	42	34	6	2	2	6	33	1	36	1	0	6	2	.750	0	0	3.69
1994 Phoenix	AAA	34	14	0	10	113.2	512	141	80	67	10	5	5	4	39	2	52	7	1	7	10	.412	0	2	5.30
1995 Nashville	AAA	7	0	0	5	12.1	61	17	9	7	1	1	0	1	7	0	6	2	0	0	2	.000	0	0	5.11
10 Min. YEARS		261	69	1	104	656.2	2876	697	358	284	40	32	17	24	239	13	428	36	5	44	50	.468	1	24	3.89

Tim Costo

Bats: Right **Throws:** Right **Pos:** 1B **Ht:** 6' 5" **Wt:** 230 **Born:** 2/16/69 **Age:** 27

Year	Team	Lg	G	AB	H	2B	3B	HR	TB	R	RBI	TBB	IBB	SO	HBP	SH	SF	SB	CS	SB%	GDP	Avg	OBP	SLG
1990	Kinston	A	56	206	65	13	1	4	92	34	42	23	0	47	6	0	8	4	0	1.00	3	.316	.387	.447
1991	Canton-Akrn	AA	52	192	52	10	3	1	71	28	24	15	0	44	0	0	6	2	1	.67	10	.271	.315	.370
	Chattanooga	AA	85	293	82	19	3	5	122	31	29	20	0	65	4	0	2	11	4	.73	5	.280	.332	.416
1992	Chattanooga	AA	121	424	102	18	2	28	208	63	71	48	1	128	11	1	2	4	5	.44	10	.241	.332	.491
1993	Indianapols	AAA	106	362	118	30	2	11	185	49	57	22	1	60	5	1	1	3	2	.60	5	.326	.372	.511
1994	Indianapols	AAA	19	36	7	3	0	0	10	6	5	6	0	4	1	1	0	0	0	.00	0	.194	.326	.278
1995	Buffalo	AAA	105	324	80	11	2	11	128	41	60	27	0	65	8	3	7	2	0	1.00	7	.247	.314	.395
1992	Cincinnati	NL	12	36	8	2	0	0	10	3	2	5	0	6	0	0	1	0	0	.00	4	.222	.310	.278
1993	Cincinnati	NL	31	98	22	5	0	3	36	13	12	4	0	17	0	0	2	0	0	.00	1	.224	.250	.367
	6 Min. YEARS		544	1837	506	104	13	60	816	252	288	161	2	413	35	6	26	26	12	.68	40	.275	.341	.444
	2 Maj. YEARS		43	134	30	7	0	3	46	16	14	9	0	23	0	0	3	0	0	.00	5	.224	.267	.343

Henry Cotto

Bats: Right **Throws:** Right **Pos:** DH **Ht:** 6' 2" **Wt:** 180 **Born:** 1/5/61 **Age:** 35

Year	Team	Lg	G	AB	H	2B	3B	HR	TB	R	RBI	TBB	IBB	SO	HBP	SH	SF	SB	CS	SB%	GDP	Avg	OBP	SLG
1984	Iowa	AAA	8	30	6	2	0	0	8	3	0	2	0	3	1	0	0	1	2	.33	2	.200	.273	.267
1985	Columbus	AAA	75	272	70	16	2	7	111	38	36	19	0	61	2	1	3	10	4	.71	4	.257	.307	.408
1986	Columbus	AAA	97	359	89	17	6	7	139	45	48	19	1	53	4	1	1	16	6	.73	10	.248	.292	.387
1987	Columbus	AAA	34	129	39	13	2	3	65	26	20	10	0	16	1	0	1	14	2	.88	3	.302	.355	.504
1995	Nashville	AAA	17	61	8	1	0	1	12	4	4	1	0	20	0	0	0	0	1	.00	3	.131	.145	.197
1984	Chicago	NL	105	146	40	5	0	0	45	24	8	10	2	23	1	3	0	9	3	.75	1	.274	.325	.308
1985	New York	AL	34	56	17	1	0	1	21	4	6	3	0	12	0	1	0	1	1	.50	1	.304	.339	.375
1986	New York	AL	35	80	17	3	0	1	23	11	6	2	0	17	0	0	1	3	0	1.00	3	.213	.229	.288
1987	New York	AL	68	149	35	10	0	5	60	21	20	6	0	35	1	0	1	4	2	.67	7	.235	.269	.403
1988	Seattle	AL	133	386	100	18	1	8	144	50	33	23	0	53	2	4	3	27	3	.90	6	.259	.302	.373
1989	Seattle	AL	100	295	78	11	2	9	120	44	33	12	3	44	3	0	0	10	4	.71	4	.264	.300	.407
1990	Seattle	AL	127	355	92	14	3	4	124	40	33	22	2	52	4	6	3	21	3	.88	13	.259	.307	.349
1991	Seattle	AL	66	177	54	6	2	6	82	35	23	10	0	27	2	2	1	16	3	.84	7	.305	.347	.463
1992	Seattle	AL	108	294	76	11	1	5	104	42	27	14	3	49	1	3	1	23	2	.92	2	.259	.294	.354
1993	Seattle	AL	54	105	20	1	0	2	27	10	7	2	0	22	1	1	0	5	4	.56	0	.190	.213	.257
	Florida	NL	54	135	40	7	0	3	56	15	14	3	0	18	1	1	2	11	1	.92	3	.296	.312	.415
	5 Min. YEARS		231	851	212	49	10	18	335	116	108	51	1	153	8	2	5	41	15	.73	22	.249	.296	.394
	10 Maj. YEARS		884	2178	569	87	9	44	806	296	210	107	10	352	16	21	11	130	26	.83	49	.261	.299	.370

John Cotton

Bats: Left **Throws:** Right **Pos:** OF **Ht:** 5'11" **Wt:** 170 **Born:** 10/30/70 **Age:** 25

Year	Team	Lg	G	AB	H	2B	3B	HR	TB	R	RBI	TBB	IBB	SO	HBP	SH	SF	SB	CS	SB%	GDP	Avg	OBP	SLG
1989	Burlington	R	64	227	47	5	1	2	60	36	22	22	0	56	3	4	1	20	3	.87	5	.207	.285	.264
1990	Watertown	A	73	286	60	9	4	2	83	53	27	40	3	71	2	2	1	24	7	.77	4	.210	.310	.290
1991	Columbus	A	122	405	92	11	9	13	160	88	42	93	1	135	3	3	3	56	15	.79	6	.227	.373	.395
1992	Kinston	A	103	360	72	7	3	11	118	67	39	48	1	106	2	1	2	23	7	.77	3	.200	.296	.328
1993	Kinston	A	127	454	120	16	3	13	181	81	51	59	1	130	11	5	2	28	24	.54	3	.264	.361	.399
1994	Springfield	A	24	82	19	5	3	1	33	14	8	12	0	19	0	0	0	7	1	.88	0	.232	.330	.402
	Wichita	AA	34	85	16	4	0	3	29	9	14	13	3	20	1	0	2	2	0	1.00	3	.188	.297	.341
	Rancho Cuca	A	48	171	35	3	2	4	54	35	19	22	0	48	2	0	0	9	3	.75	3	.205	.303	.316
1995	Memphis	AA	121	407	103	19	8	12	174	60	47	38	0	101	4	6	4	15	6	.71	2	.253	.320	.428
	7 Min. YEARS		716	2477	564	79	33	61	892	443	269	347	9	686	28	21	15	184	66	.74	29	.228	.328	.360

Kevin Coughlin

Bats: Left **Throws:** Left **Pos:** OF **Ht:** 6'0" **Wt:** 175 **Born:** 9/7/70 **Age:** 25

Year	Team	Lg	G	AB	H	2B	3B	HR	TB	R	RBI	TBB	IBB	SO	HBP	SH	SF	SB	CS	SB%	GDP	Avg	OBP	SLG
1989	White Sox	R	24	74	19	2	0	0	21	11	13	12	0	8	0	0	0	9	2	.82	1	.257	.360	.284
1990	Utica	A	68	215	59	6	3	0	71	37	16	27	2	41	0	3	2	17	8	.68	4	.274	.352	.330
1991	South Bend	A	131	431	131	12	2	0	147	60	38	62	3	67	2	19	3	19	17	.53	6	.304	.392	.341
1992	White Sox	R	4	15	5	0	0	0	5	1	2	2	0	1	0	0	0	0	0	.00	0	.333	.412	.333
	Sarasota	A	81	291	79	7	1	1	91	39	28	22	1	51	2	8	1	14	4	.78	3	.271	.326	.313
1993	Sarasota	A	112	415	128	19	2	2	157	53	32	42	5	51	0	4	2	4	4	.50	9	.308	.370	.378
	Nashville	AAA	2	7	4	1	0	0	5	0	3	0	0	1	0	0	0	0	0	.00	0	.571	.571	.714
1994	Birmingham	AA	112	369	95	10	0	0	105	51	26	40	3	42	3	4	4	5	8	.38	9	.257	.332	.285
1995	Nashville	AAA	10	22	4	1	0	0	5	0	0	4	0	3	0	0	0	1	0	1.00	1	.182	.308	.227
	Birmingham	AA	96	327	126	29	2	3	168	56	49	34	7	43	5	8	2	5	2	.71	3	.385	.448	.514
	7 Min. YEARS		640	2166	650	87	10	6	775	308	207	245	21	308	12	46	14	73	46	.61	36	.300	.372	.358

Darron Cox

Bats: Right **Throws:** Right **Pos:** C **Ht:** 6'1" **Wt:** 205 **Born:** 11/21/67 **Age:** 28

Year	Team	Lg	G	AB	H	2B	3B	HR	TB	R	RBI	TBB	IBB	SO	HBP	SH	SF	SB	CS	SB%	GDP	Avg	OBP	SLG
1989	Billings	R	49	157	43	6	0	0	49	20	18	21	0	34	5	2	0	11	3	.79	1	.274	.377	.312

Year	Team	Lg	G	AB	H	2B	3B	HR	TB	R	RBI	TBB	IBB	SO	HBP	SH	SF	SB	CS	SB%	GDP	Avg	OBP	SLG
1990	Charlstn-Wv	A	103	367	93	11	3	1	113	53	44	40	2	75	7	4	3	14	3	.82	12	.253	.336	.308
1991	Cedar Rapds	A	21	60	16	4	0	0	20	12	4	8	0	11	4	1	0	7	1	.88	2	.267	.389	.333
	Chattanooga	AA	13	38	7	1	0	0	8	2	3	2	0	9	0	1	1	0	0	.00	1	.184	.220	.211
	Charlstn-Wv	A	79	294	71	14	1	2	93	37	28	24	0	40	2	1	7	8	4	.67	7	.241	.297	.316
1992	Chattanooga	AA	98	331	84	19	1	1	108	29	38	15	0	63	5	1	6	8	3	.73	7	.254	.291	.326
1993	Chattanooga	AA	89	300	65	9	5	3	93	35	26	38	2	63	3	7	1	7	4	.64	7	.217	.310	.310
1994	Iowa	AAA	99	301	80	15	1	3	106	35	26	28	4	47	4	3	0	5	2	.71	12	.266	.336	.352
1995	Orlando	AA	33	102	29	5	0	4	46	8	15	8	0	16	1	2	2	3	3	.50	3	.284	.336	.451
	Iowa	AAA	33	94	22	6	0	1	31	7	14	8	0	21	2	2	4	0	0	.00	0	.234	.296	.330
7 Min. YEARS			617	2044	510	90	11	15	667	238	216	192	8	379	33	24	24	63	23	.73	52	.250	.321	.326

Cobi Cradle

Bats: Left **Throws:** Left **Pos:** OF   **Ht:** 5'11" **Wt:** 165 **Born:** 7/7/71 **Age:** 24

Year	Team	Lg	G	AB	H	2B	3B	HR	TB	R	RBI	TBB	IBB	SO	HBP	SH	SF	SB	CS	SB%	GDP	Avg	OBP	SLG
1993	Princeton	R	27	105	25	4	4	1	40	21	11	14	1	15	1	3	1	7	2	.78	3	.238	.331	.381
	Charlstn-Wv	A	44	159	56	9	0	1	68	34	12	35	0	19	2	1	0	16	6	.73	4	.352	.474	.428
1994	Charlstn-Wv	A	112	412	114	19	5	1	146	80	28	60	3	59	6	6	4	43	12	.78	7	.277	.373	.354
	Princeton	R	17	61	19	3	2	1	29	17	6	16	1	12	3	1	0	14	4	.78	0	.311	.475	.475
1995	Winston-Sal	A	23	71	13	2	0	0	15	14	2	21	0	8	0	1	1	9	2	.82	0	.183	.366	.211
	Binghamton	AA	2	2	0	0	0	0	0	0	0	0	0	0	0	0	0	0	0	.00	0	.000	.000	.000
	St. Lucie	A	78	257	60	5	1	1	70	34	12	37	0	45	1	4	3	19	3	.86	1	.233	.329	.272
3 Min. YEARS			303	1067	287	42	12	5	368	200	71	183	5	158	13	16	9	108	29	.79	15	.269	.380	.345

Rickey Cradle

Bats: Right **Throws:** Right **Pos:** OF   **Ht:** 6'2" **Wt:** 180 **Born:** 6/20/73 **Age:** 23

Year	Team	Lg	G	AB	H	2B	3B	HR	TB	R	RBI	TBB	IBB	SO	HBP	SH	SF	SB	CS	SB%	GDP	Avg	OBP	SLG
1991	Blue Jays	R	44	132	28	4	3	1	41	16	6	24	1	37	3	1	1	4	5	.44	2	.212	.344	.311
1992	Medicne Hat	R	65	217	49	8	0	9	84	38	36	42	0	69	6	1	2	16	2	.89	5	.226	.363	.387
1993	Hagerstown	A	129	441	112	26	4	13	185	72	62	68	2	125	11	1	4	19	14	.58	5	.254	.365	.420
1994	Dunedin	A	114	344	88	14	3	10	138	65	39	59	0	87	9	0	1	20	10	.67	5	.256	.378	.401
1995	Knoxville	AA	41	117	21	5	1	4	40	17	13	17	0	29	3	1	1	3	3	.50	3	.179	.297	.342
	Dunedin	A	50	178	49	10	3	7	86	33	27	28	0	49	2	1	2	6	2	.75	2	.275	.376	.483
5 Min. YEARS			443	1429	347	67	14	44	574	241	183	238	3	396	34	5	11	68	36	.65	20	.243	.362	.402

Jay Cranford

Bats: Right **Throws:** Right **Pos:** 3B   **Ht:** 6'3" **Wt:** 175 **Born:** 4/7/71 **Age:** 25

Year	Team	Lg	G	AB	H	2B	3B	HR	TB	R	RBI	TBB	IBB	SO	HBP	SH	SF	SB	CS	SB%	GDP	Avg	OBP	SLG
1992	Welland	A	60	223	57	9	6	0	78	22	27	14	1	58	0	0	2	7	7	.50	0	.256	.297	.350
1993	Augusta	A	128	469	125	31	4	6	174	55	72	32	0	101	6	3	9	17	2	.89	6	.267	.316	.371
1994	Salem	A	110	417	110	27	4	13	184	66	53	23	0	97	6	0	3	6	6	.50	8	.264	.310	.441
	Carolina	AA	17	59	11	3	0	0	14	9	5	6	1	15	1	1	2	0	0	.00	1	.186	.265	.237
1995	Carolina	AA	93	288	66	12	1	5	95	30	42	52	1	67	4	2	7	3	4	.43	6	.229	.348	.330
4 Min. YEARS			408	1456	369	82	11	24	545	182	199	127	3	338	17	6	23	33	19	.63	21	.253	.316	.374

Carlos Crawford

Pitches: Right **Bats:** Right **Pos:** P   **Ht:** 6'1" **Wt:** 185 **Born:** 10/4/71 **Age:** 24

Year	Team	Lg	G	GS	CG	GF	IP	BFP	H	R	ER	HR	SH	SF	HB	TBB	IBB	SO	WP	Bk	W	L	Pct.	ShO	Sv	ERA
1990	Indians	R	10	9	0	0	53.2	257	68	43	26	0	0	2	8	25	0	39	6	4	2	3	.400	0	0	4.36
1991	Burlington	R	13	13	2	0	80.1	325	62	28	22	3	2	2	9	14	0	80	6	3	6	3	.667	1	0	2.46
1992	Columbus	A	28	28	6	0	188.1	805	167	78	61	7	5	4	12	85	4	127	3	2	10	11	.476	3	0	2.92
1993	Kinston	A	28	28	4	0	165	703	158	87	67	11	10	4	10	46	0	124	4	7	9	.438	1	0	3.65
1994	Canton-Akrn	AA	26	25	3	0	175	734	164	83	67	15	3	7	6	59	2	99	8	2	12	6	.667	0	0	3.45
1995	Buffalo	AAA	13	3	0	3	30.1	137	36	22	19	2	2	0	0	12	0	15	0	0	0	1	.000	0	0	5.64
	Canton-Akrn	AA	8	8	2	0	51.2	212	47	19	15	1	1	0	1	15	0	36	2	0	2	2	.500	0	0	2.61
6 Min. YEARS			126	114	17	3	744.1	3173	702	360	277	39	23	19	46	256	6	520	33	15	39	35	.527	5	1	3.35

Joe Crawford

Pitches: Left **Bats:** Left **Pos:** P   **Ht:** 6'3" **Wt:** 225 **Born:** 5/2/70 **Age:** 26

Year	Team	Lg	G	GS	CG	GF	IP	BFP	H	R	ER	HR	SH	SF	HB	TBB	IBB	SO	WP	Bk	W	L	Pct.	ShO	Sv	ERA
1991	Kingsport	R	19	0	0	16	32.1	118	16	5	4	0	0	0	1	8	0	43	3	1	0	0	.000	0	11	1.11
	Columbia	A	3	0	0	2	3	9	0	0	0	0	0	0	0	0	0	6	0	0	0	0	.000	0	0	0.00
1992	St. Lucie	A	25	1	0	16	43.2	174	29	18	10	1	1	3	0	15	3	32	1	3	3	3	.500	0	3	2.06
1993	St. Lucie	A	34	0	0	19	37	156	38	15	15	0	2	0	2	14	5	24	0	0	3	3	.500	0	5	3.65
1994	St. Lucie	A	33	0	0	15	42.2	155	22	8	7	1	1	2	2	9	2	31	1	0	1	1	.500	0	5	1.48
	Binghamton	AA	13	0	0	6	14.2	70	20	10	9	2	0	2	0	8	0	9	0	0	1	0	1.000	0	0	5.52
1995	Binghamton	AA	42	1	0	15	60.2	239	48	17	15	4	3	7	5	17	4	43	3	1	7	2	.778	0	0	2.23
	Norfolk	AAA	8	0	0	1	18.2	70	9	5	4	0	1	0	0	4	0	13	0	0	1	1	.500	0	0	1.93
5 Min. YEARS			177	2	0	90	252.2	991	182	78	64	8	8	14	10	75	14	201	8	5	16	10	.615	0	24	2.28

Ryan Creek

Pitches: Right **Bats:** Right **Pos:** P   **Ht:** 6'1" **Wt:** 180 **Born:** 9/24/72 **Age:** 23

			HOW	MUCH	HE	PITCHED		WHAT	HE	GAVE	UP									THE	RESULTS			
Year	Team	Lg	G	GS	CG	GF	IP	BFP	H	R	ER	HR	SH	SF	HB	TBB	IBB	SO	WP	Bk	W	L	Pct.	ShO	Sv	ERA
1993	Astros	R	12	11	2	1	69.1	291	53	22	18	0	1	5	4	30	0	62	6	0	7	3	.700	1	1	2.34
1994	Quad City	A	21	15	0	3	74	356	86	62	41	6	3	5	14	41	2	66	9	3	3	5	.375	0	0	4.99
1995	Jackson	AA	26	24	1	1	143.2	622	137	74	58	11	6	8	6	64	0	120	12	2	9	7	.563	1	0	3.63
	3 Min. YEARS		59	50	3	5	287	1269	276	158	117	17	10	18	24	135	2	248	27	5	19	15	.559	2	1	3.67

Felipe Crespo

Bats: Both **Throws:** Right **Pos:** 2B   **Ht:** 5'11" **Wt:** 190 **Born:** 3/5/73 **Age:** 23

						BATTING										BASERUNNING				PERCENTAGES		
Year	Team	Lg	G	AB	H	2B	3B	HR	TB	R	RBI	TBB	IBB	SO	HBP	SH	SF	SB	CS	SB%	GDP	Avg	OBP	SLG
1991	Medicne Hat	R	49	184	57	11	4	4	88	40	31	25	0	31	3	2	2	6	4	.60	2	.310	.397	.478
1992	Myrtle Bch	A	81	263	74	14	3	1	97	43	29	58	2	38	4	2	5	7	7	.50	1	.281	.412	.369
1993	Dunedin	A	96	345	103	16	8	6	153	51	39	47	3	40	4	5	2	18	5	.78	9	.299	.387	.443
1994	Knoxville	AA	129	502	135	30	4	8	197	74	49	57	3	95	2	4	1	20	8	.71	5	.269	.345	.392
1995	Syracuse	AAA	88	347	102	20	5	13	171	56	41	41	4	56	2	1	1	12	7	.63	5	.294	.371	.493
	5 Min. YEARS		443	1641	471	91	24	32	706	264	189	228	12	260	15	14	11	63	31	.67	22	.287	.377	.430

Andy Croghan

Pitches: Right **Bats:** Right **Pos:** P   **Ht:** 6'5" **Wt:** 205 **Born:** 10/26/69 **Age:** 26

			HOW	MUCH	HE	PITCHED		WHAT	HE	GAVE	UP									THE	RESULTS			
Year	Team	Lg	G	GS	CG	GF	IP	BFP	H	R	ER	HR	SH	SF	HB	TBB	IBB	SO	WP	Bk	W	L	Pct.	ShO	Sv	ERA
1991	Oneonta	A	14	14	0	0	78.1	352	92	59	49	6	1	1	2	28	0	54	5	0	5	4	.556	0	0	5.63
1992	Greensboro	A	33	19	1	3	122.1	544	128	78	61	11	2	9	3	57	0	98	9	0	10	8	.556	0	0	4.49
1993	Pr. William	A	39	14	1	19	105	455	117	66	56	9	4	4	3	27	0	80	6	0	5	11	.313	0	11	4.80
1994	Albany-Colo	AA	36	0	0	33	36.2	153	33	7	7	1	2	1	0	14	0	38	1	0	0	1	.000	0	16	1.72
	Columbus	AAA	21	0	0	17	24	110	25	11	11	6	5	0	0	13	1	28	3	0	2	2	.500	0	8	4.13
1995	Columbus	AAA	20	0	0	13	25	113	21	10	10	1	0	0	1	22	0	22	1	2	1	1	.500	0	4	3.60
	5 Min. YEARS		163	47	2	85	391.1	1727	416	231	194	34	14	15	9	161	1	320	25	2	23	27	.460	0	39	4.46

Nate Cromwell

Pitches: Left **Bats:** Left **Pos:** P   **Ht:** 6'1" **Wt:** 185 **Born:** 8/23/68 **Age:** 27

			HOW	MUCH	HE	PITCHED		WHAT	HE	GAVE	UP									THE	RESULTS			
Year	Team	Lg	G	GS	CG	GF	IP	BFP	H	R	ER	HR	SH	SF	HB	TBB	IBB	SO	WP	Bk	W	L	Pct.	ShO	Sv	ERA
1987	Medicne Hat	R	15	11	1	2	54.1	246	54	36	26	1	3	3	1	37	0	47	10	0	4	6	.400	0	0	4.31
1988	Myrtle Bch	A	21	20	1	1	124.1	513	88	47	40	6	6	2	8	67	2	86	8	6	8	8	.500	1	0	2.90
1989	Dunedin	A	31	30	0	1	151.2	665	136	70	61	5	2	1	4	84	0	161	25	4	12	6	.667	0	0	3.62
1990	Knoxville	AA	27	23	2	2	121.1	563	119	85	75	11	9	10	4	91	1	79	8	4	5	14	.263	0	0	5.56
1991	Knoxville	AA	16	16	0	0	80	363	73	53	44	6	1	3	5	53	0	61	8	4	2	9	.182	0	0	4.95
1992	Knoxville	AA	37	10	0	11	101	465	102	68	58	4	5	3	5	69	1	101	17	1	5	5	.500	0	0	5.17
1993	Knoxville	AA	6	1	0	3	9	52	15	13	11	2	0	0	1	10	0	11	1	0	0	1	.000	0	0	11.00
	Wichita	AA	21	11	1	2	89.1	389	90	49	41	9	4	2	4	38	4	86	8	3	3	5	.375	1	0	4.13
1994	Wichita	AA	31	20	0	2	132.2	588	130	78	60	9	10	4	5	61	3	126	12	0	9	5	.643	0	0	4.07
	Las Vegas	AAA	2	2	1	0	14.2	66	19	8	8	2	0	0	0	5	0	16	2	0	0	2	.000	0	0	4.91
1995	Las Vegas	AAA	9	3	0	3	15.1	94	35	27	23	5	1	0	1	14	1	11	0	0	0	2	.000	0	0	13.50
	Rancho Cuca	A	4	4	0	0	15.1	64	15	7	6	1	1	0	1	6	0	14	0	1	0	1	.000	0	0	3.52
	9 Min. YEARS		220	151	6	26	909	4068	876	541	453	61	42	28	39	535	12	799	99	23	48	64	.429	2	0	4.49

Chris Cron

Bats: Right **Throws:** Right **Pos:** 3B   **Ht:** 6'2" **Wt:** 200 **Born:** 3/31/64 **Age:** 32

						BATTING										BASERUNNING				PERCENTAGES		
Year	Team	Lg	G	AB	H	2B	3B	HR	TB	R	RBI	TBB	IBB	SO	HBP	SH	SF	SB	CS	SB%	GDP	Avg	OBP	SLG
1984	Pulaski	R	32	114	42	8	0	7	71	22	37	17	1	20	6	0	2	2	0	1.00	0	.368	.468	.623
1985	Sumter	A	119	425	102	20	0	7	143	53	59	51	2	98	18	0	1	5	2	.71	8	.240	.345	.336
1986	Durham	A	90	265	55	10	0	7	86	26	34	29	0	60	6	2	2	0	2	.00	2	.208	.298	.325
1987	Quad City	A	111	398	110	20	1	11	165	53	62	44	2	88	17	0	1	1	3	.25	5	.276	.372	.415
	Palm Spring	A	26	92	25	3	0	2	34	6	9	9	0	27	2	1	2	2	2	.50	3	.272	.343	.370
1988	Palm Spring	A	127	467	117	28	3	14	193	71	84	68	1	147	27	2	6	4	3	.57	10	.251	.373	.413
1989	Midland	AA	128	491	148	33	3	22	253	80	103	39	5	126	14	1	6	0	1	.00	10	.301	.365	.515
1990	Edmonton	AAA	104	401	115	31	0	17	197	54	75	28	1	92	5	1	5	7	5	.58	9	.287	.337	.491
1991	Edmonton	AAA	123	461	134	21	1	22	223	74	91	47	3	103	10	2	11	6	5	.55	12	.291	.361	.484
1992	Vancouver	AAA	140	500	139	29	0	16	216	76	81	94	12	111	17	2	3	12	4	.75	9	.278	.407	.432
1993	Nashville	AAA	126	460	118	27	0	22	211	69	68	61	5	114	8	3	4	2	1	.67	12	.257	.351	.459
1994	Charlotte	AAA	103	350	81	19	1	23	171	50	72	33	2	105	11	0	1	1	1	.50	10	.231	.316	.489
1995	Nashville	AAA	21	69	15	2	0	2	23	3	10	8	2	20	0	1	0	0	0	.00	2	.217	.299	.333
1991	California	AL	6	15	2	0	0	0	2	0	0	2	0	5	0	0	0	0	0	.00	0	.133	.235	.133
1992	Chicago	AL	6	10	0	0	0	0	0	0	0	0	0	4	0	0	0	0	0	.00	0	.000	.000	.000
	12 Min. YEARS		1250	4493	1201	251	9	172	1986	637	785	528	36	1111	141	15	44	42	29	.59	94	.267	.359	.442
	2 Maj. YEARS		12	25	2	0	0	0	2	0	0	2	0	9	0	0	0	0	0	.00	0	.080	.148	.080

Mike Crosby

Bats: Left **Throws:** Right **Pos:** C **Ht:** 6'1" **Wt:** 200 **Born:** 2/24/69 **Age:** 27

Year Team	Lg	G	AB	H	2B	3B	HR	TB	R	RBI	TBB	IBB	SO	HBP	SH	SF	SB	CS	SB%	GDP	Avg	OBP	SLG
1992 Columbus	A	53	149	25	3	0	0	28	14	13	6	0	32	4	2	2	0	1	.00	3	.168	.217	.188
1993 Kinston	A	72	203	44	9	0	3	62	20	17	7	0	45	3	4	2	1	2	.33	6	.217	.251	.305
1994 Canton-Akrn	AA	55	162	36	7	1	2	51	12	10	4	0	44	2	4	0	1	1	.50	3	.222	.250	.315
1995 Canton-Akrn	AA	75	224	37	5	1	5	59	18	20	10	0	60	3	7	1	1	1	.50	4	.165	.210	.263
4 Min. YEARS		255	738	142	24	2	10	200	64	60	27	0	181	12	17	5	3	5	.38	16	.192	.231	.271

Jim Crowley

Bats: Right **Throws:** Right **Pos:** 2B-3B **Ht:** 6'0" **Wt:** 190 **Born:** 10/16/69 **Age:** 26

Year Team	Lg	G	AB	H	2B	3B	HR	TB	R	RBI	TBB	IBB	SO	HBP	SH	SF	SB	CS	SB%	GDP	Avg	OBP	SLG
1991 Elmira	A	71	249	52	13	1	10	97	36	34	38	0	51	1	0	3	5	3	.63	4	.209	.313	.390
1992 Lynchburg	A	119	392	100	20	1	12	158	62	59	34	1	75	2	1	3	2	1	.67	6	.255	.316	.403
1993 Pawtucket	AAA	12	35	6	0	0	0	6	2	2	2	0	10	0	0	0	0	0	.00	2	.171	.216	.171
New Britain	AA	109	369	89	19	1	11	143	49	51	59	0	95	4	4	2	3	7	.30	6	.241	.350	.388
1994 Lynchburg	A	30	107	22	4	0	2	32	8	11	17	1	18	1	1	1	1	0	1.00	1	.206	.317	.299
New Britain	AA	76	220	42	2	1	7	67	25	24	27	1	57	1	3	2	2	3	.40	4	.191	.280	.305
1995 Bowie	AA	29	98	21	5	0	2	32	11	13	23	0	23	2	0	0	1	1	.50	0	.214	.374	.327
Rochester	AAA	34	98	17	3	0	1	23	7	6	7	0	21	4	1	0	0	1	.00	2	.173	.257	.235
5 Min. YEARS		480	1568	349	66	4	45	558	200	200	207	3	350	15	10	11	14	16	.47	25	.223	.317	.356

Brent Crowther

Pitches: Right **Bats:** Right **Pos:** P **Ht:** 6'4" **Wt:** 220 **Born:** 5/15/72 **Age:** 24

Year Team	Lg	G	GS	CG	GF	IP	BFP	H	R	ER	HR	SH	SF	HB	TBB	IBB	SO	WP	Bk	W	L	Pct.	ShO	Sv	ERA
1994 Bend	A	13	9	0	1	56	271	68	41	29	2	0	4	9	24	0	44	8	3	3	5	.375	0	0	4.66
1995 Asheville	A	15	15	3	0	98.2	393	79	31	25	4	0	1	3	25	0	72	11	1	12	3	.800	3	0	2.28
Salem	A	12	12	3	0	78.1	322	70	31	24	4	5	0	2	25	5	60	7	2	3	6	.333	1	0	2.76
Colo. Sprng	AAA	1	1	0	0	6	30	11	6	5	1	0	1	0	2	0	1	0	0	0	1	.000	0	0	7.50
2 Min. YEARS		41	37	6	1	239	1016	228	109	83	11	5	6	14	76	5	177	26	6	18	15	.545	4	0	3.13

Ivan Cruz

Bats: Left **Throws:** Left **Pos:** 1B **Ht:** 6'3" **Wt:** 210 **Born:** 5/3/68 **Age:** 28

Year Team	Lg	G	AB	H	2B	3B	HR	TB	R	RBI	TBB	IBB	SO	HBP	SH	SF	SB	CS	SB%	GDP	Avg	OBP	SLG
1989 Niagara Fal	A	64	226	62	11	2	7	98	43	40	27	4	29	3	0	1	2	0	1.00	2	.274	.358	.434
1990 Lakeland	A	118	414	118	23	2	11	178	61	73	49	3	71	5	2	4	8	1	.89	8	.285	.364	.430
1991 Toledo	AAA	8	29	4	0	0	1	7	2	4	2	0	12	1	0	0	0	0	.00	0	.138	.219	.241
London	AA	121	443	110	21	0	9	158	45	47	36	5	74	4	1	2	3	3	.50	12	.248	.309	.357
1992 London	AA	134	524	143	25	1	14	212	71	104	37	1	102	4	0	6	1	1	.50	16	.273	.322	.405
1993 Toledo	AAA	115	402	91	18	4	13	156	44	50	30	2	85	3	0	2	1	1	.50	5	.226	.284	.388
1994 Toledo	AAA	97	303	75	11	2	15	135	36	43	28	0	83	2	0	3	1	0	1.00	7	.248	.313	.446
1995 Toledo	AAA	11	36	7	2	0	0	9	5	3	6	0	9	0	0	1	0	0	.00	1	.194	.302	.250
Jacksonville	AA	108	397	112	17	1	31	224	65	93	60	15	94	0	0	3	0	0	.00	7	.282	.374	.564
7 Min. YEARS		776	2774	722	128	12	101	1177	372	457	275	30	559	22	3	22	16	6	.73	58	.260	.329	.424

Jake Cruz

Bats: Left **Throws:** Left **Pos:** OF **Ht:** 6'0" **Wt:** 175 **Born:** 1/28/73 **Age:** 23

Year Team	Lg	G	AB	H	2B	3B	HR	TB	R	RBI	TBB	IBB	SO	HBP	SH	SF	SB	CS	SB%	GDP	Avg	OBP	SLG
1994 San Jose	A	31	118	29	7	0	0	36	14	12	9	0	22	2	2	2	0	2	.00	6	.246	.305	.305
1995 Shreveport	AA	127	458	136	33	1	13	210	88	77	57	6	72	8	4	2	9	8	.53	15	.297	.383	.459
2 Min. YEARS		158	576	165	40	1	13	246	102	89	66	6	94	10	6	4	9	10	.47	21	.286	.367	.427

Calvain Culberson

Pitches: Right **Bats:** Right **Pos:** P **Ht:** 5'10" **Wt:** 195 **Born:** 11/14/66 **Age:** 29

Year Team	Lg	G	GS	CG	GF	IP	BFP	H	R	ER	HR	SH	SF	HB	TBB	IBB	SO	WP	Bk	W	L	Pct.	ShO	Sv	ERA
1989 Sumter	A	1	0	0	1	1	7	3	2	2	1	0	0	0	0	0	1	0	0	0	0	.000	0	0	18.00
1990 Charlstn-Wv	A	14	14	0	0	79	325	62	32	27	4	3	2	2	32	1	57	8	3	5	5	.500	0	0	3.08
1991 Cedar Rapds	A	18	14	1	1	88.1	396	82	54	41	4	2	5	3	54	3	68	4	1	6	8	.429	0	0	4.18
1992 Cedar Rapds	A	28	20	2	5	125.1	521	102	50	39	7	6	5	1	52	0	93	4	3	5	4	.556	2	0	2.80
1993 Indianapols	AAA	2	2	0	0	13	52	9	2	1	0	0	0	0	7	0	9	0	0	1	0	1.000	0	0	0.69
Chattanooga	AA	37	7	0	15	105.1	430	82	38	35	11	5	0	6	36	0	86	3	0	6	6	.500	0	1	2.99
1994 Chattanooga	AA	38	5	0	20	81	339	60	31	23	6	2	1	1	39	3	66	8	0	2	9	.182	0	9	2.56
1995 Pawtucket	AAA	6	0	0	1	12.2	65	18	12	9	0	0	3	0	11	0	4	1	0	0	0	.000	0	0	6.39
Mobile	IND	21	13	1	3	88	384	81	47	42	5	11	3	4	38	2	62	9	1	4	5	.444	1	0	4.30
7 Min. YEARS		165	75	4	46	593.2	2519	499	268	219	39	29	19	17	269	9	446	37	8	29	37	.439	1	12	3.32

Glen Cullop

Pitches: Right **Bats:** Right **Pos:** P **Ht:** 6'7" **Wt:** 180 **Born:** 10/4/71 **Age:** 24

Year Team	Lg	G	GS	CG	GF	IP	BFP	H	R	ER	HR	SH	SF	HB	TBB	IBB	SO	WP	Bk	W	L	Pct.	ShO	Sv	ERA
1992 Princeton	R	11	1	0	3	28.1	123	33	15	7	1	0	2	0	7	0	23	1	0	0	1	.000	0	2	2.22
1993 Winston-Sal	A	39	0	0	11	65	249	37	12	11	2	2	7	3	21	3	48	5	1	6	0	1.000	0	2	1.52
1994 Chattanooga	AA	40	0	0	8	59.1	267	54	28	25	2	5	2	4	36	2	41	8	1	3	3	.500	0	0	3.79
1995 Chattanooga	AA	8	0	0	3	13.2	63	15	13	12	1	1	2	0	7	1	8	0	0	0	0	.000	0	0	7.90
Winston-Sal	A	6	0	0	5	10	39	7	1	1	0	0	1	0	5	0	4	1	0	0	0	.000	0	0	0.90
4 Min. YEARS		104	1	0	30	176.1	741	146	69	56	6	8	14	7	76	6	124	15	2	9	5	.643	0	4	2.86

Will Cunnane

Pitches: Right **Bats:** Right **Pos:** P **Ht:** 6'2" **Wt:** 165 **Born:** 4/24/74 **Age:** 22

Year Team	Lg	G	GS	CG	GF	IP	BFP	H	R	ER	HR	SH	SF	HB	TBB	IBB	SO	WP	Bk	W	L	Pct.	ShO	Sv	ERA
1993 Marlins	R	16	9	0	4	66.2	290	75	32	20	1	3	0	0	8	0	64	2	1	3	3	.500	0	0	2.70
1994 Kane County	A	32	16	5	6	138.2	540	110	27	22	2	4	1	6	23	4	106	5	1	11	3	.786	4	1	1.43
1995 Portland	AA	21	21	1	0	117.2	497	120	48	48	10	3	0	5	34	1	83	2	0	9	2	.818	1	0	3.67
3 Min. YEARS		69	46	6	10	323	1327	305	107	90	13	10	1	11	65	5	253	9	2	23	8	.742	5	3	2.51

Chris Curtis

Pitches: Right **Bats:** Right **Pos:** P **Ht:** 6'2" **Wt:** 185 **Born:** 5/8/71 **Age:** 25

Year Team	Lg	G	GS	CG	GF	IP	BFP	H	R	ER	HR	SH	SF	HB	TBB	IBB	SO	WP	Bk	W	L	Pct.	ShO	Sv	ERA
1991 Butte	R	6	3	0	2	12.2	69	27	23	14	1	0	0	1	4	0	7	0	3	0	2	.000	0	0	9.95
Rangers	R	7	7	0	0	35	134	27	9	8	1	0	4	2	9	0	23	0	0	4	0	1.000	0	0	2.06
1992 Gastonia	A	24	24	1	0	147	590	117	60	43	3	1	5	6	54	0	107	6	7	8	11	.421	1	0	2.63
1993 Charlotte	A	27	26	1	0	151	637	159	76	67	6	4	2	8	51	0	55	4	5	8	8	.500	0	0	3.99
1994 Tulsa	AA	25	23	3	1	142.2	639	173	102	85	17	4	7	7	57	5	62	9	7	3	13	.188	1	0	5.36
1995 Okla. City	AAA	51	0	0	22	77.1	358	81	53	43	5	6	3	6	39	3	40	2	0	3	5	.375	0	5	5.00
5 Min. YEARS		140	83	5	25	565.2	2427	584	323	260	33	15	21	29	214	8	294	21	24	26	39	.400	2	5	4.14

Jim Czajkowski

Pitches: Right **Bats:** Both **Pos:** P **Ht:** 6'4" **Wt:** 215 **Born:** 12/18/63 **Age:** 32

Year Team	Lg	G	GS	CG	GF	IP	BFP	H	R	ER	HR	SH	SF	HB	TBB	IBB	SO	WP	Bk	W	L	Pct.	ShO	Sv	ERA
1986 Idaho Falls	R	16	13	3	1	88.2	0	90	44	36	5	0	0	3	16	0	46	3	0	7	5	.583	0	0	3.65
1987 Sumter	A	50	0	0	40	68.2	288	63	26	17	2	2	1	2	17	3	59	4	0	4	6	.400	0	20	2.23
1988 Durham	A	48	0	0	39	58.1	263	65	26	22	4	5	3	0	24	5	26	5	2	8	5	.615	0	17	3.39
1989 Durham	A	32	0	0	23	45.1	178	33	8	5	2	2	4	2	10	2	34	2	0	2	3	.400	0	14	0.99
Greenville	AA	17	4	0	3	34	161	39	31	21	4	1	2	1	16	0	18	0	0	1	6	.143	0	0	5.56
1990 Harrisburg	AA	9	0	0	4	14.2	67	17	7	7	1	0	1	1	6	0	6	1	0	0	0	.000	0	0	4.30
Salem	A	18	0	0	17	28	113	17	10	8	3	3	2	3	11	3	26	1	0	1	1	.500	0	6	2.57
Beloit	A	21	0	0	21	27.1	110	16	7	5	1	1	2	3	8	4	37	0	0	2	0	1.000	0	11	1.65
Stockton	A	2	0	0	1	2.2	10	1	0	0	0	1	0	0	2	0	2	0	0	0	0	.000	0	1	0.00
1991 El Paso	AA	43	0	0	32	78.1	366	100	54	43	5	4	2	3	29	4	69	5	1	5	2	.714	0	11	4.94
1992 El Paso	AA	57	2	0	29	79.1	351	92	44	43	8	4	1	7	26	4	62	1	0	5	7	.417	0	10	4.88
1993 Orlando	AA	10	0	0	4	19	76	15	7	6	0	0	1	1	3	1	16	0	1	1	2	.333	0	1	2.84
Iowa	AAA	42	0	0	18	70.1	304	64	31	30	3	4	3	3	32	2	43	4	0	7	5	.583	0	7	3.84
1994 Colo. Sprng	AAA	44	1	0	21	63	254	53	24	19	4	3	5	5	16	1	36	3	1	5	4	.556	0	8	2.71
1995 Colo. Sprng	AAA	60	0	0	44	83.2	382	90	54	47	8	6	8	2	52	7	56	4	0	3	10	.231	0	17	5.06
1994 Colorado	NL	5	0	0	2	8.2	42	9	4	4	2	1	0	3	6	1	2	1	0	0	0	.000	0	0	4.15
10 Min. YEARS		469	20	3	296	761.1	2923	755	373	309	50	36	35	36	268	36	536	33	5	51	56	.477	0	116	3.65

Mike D'Andrea

Pitches: Right **Bats:** Right **Pos:** P **Ht:** 5'10" **Wt:** 195 **Born:** 12/23/69 **Age:** 26

Year Team	Lg	G	GS	CG	GF	IP	BFP	H	R	ER	HR	SH	SF	HB	TBB	IBB	SO	WP	Bk	W	L	Pct.	ShO	Sv	ERA
1992 Pulaski	R	11	11	0	0	61.1	241	39	20	19	3	0	2	0	28	0	79	3	2	8	1	.889	0	0	2.79
1993 Macon	A	26	23	0	0	136.1	581	129	68	61	11	2	4	5	55	1	156	3	0	8	7	.533	0	0	4.03
1994 Durham	A	27	26	1	0	158	674	167	85	74	19	3	4	6	49	1	133	7	3	9	10	.474	0	0	4.22
1995 Greenville	AA	40	7	0	11	99.2	447	110	65	54	5	4	9	3	53	8	61	7	1	3	6	.333	0	2	4.88
4 Min. YEARS		104	67	1	12	455.1	1943	445	238	208	38	9	19	14	185	10	429	20	6	28	24	.538	0	2	4.11

Fred Dabney

Pitches: Left **Bats:** Right **Pos:** P **Ht:** 6'3" **Wt:** 190 **Born:** 11/20/67 **Age:** 28

Year Team	Lg	G	GS	CG	GF	IP	BFP	H	R	ER	HR	SH	SF	HB	TBB	IBB	SO	WP	Bk	W	L	Pct.	ShO	Sv	ERA
1988 Utica	A	19	13	1	3	87.2	382	83	40	26	1	2	0	1	41	1	69	2	5	9	4	.692	0	0	2.67
1989 South Bend	A	26	26	3	0	163.1	676	128	50	38	2	4	2	11	65	1	150	7	6	11	7	.611	0	0	2.09
1990 Sarasota	A	24	21	1	1	126.1	569	146	82	73	3	4	4	6	57	1	77	6	6	6	7	.462	0	0	5.20
1991 Sarasota	A	26	8	1	5	96.1	414	88	45	32	6	3	4	4	44	1	72	2	4	11	3	.786	1	1	2.99
1992 Birmingham	AA	25	14	0	5	105.1	460	116	57	45	9	5	7	1	41	1	86	6	1	2	8	.200	0	0	3.84
1993 Nashville	AAA	51	0	0	15	63	280	65	43	34	7	1	3	9	21	0	44	3	1	2	5	.286	0	3	4.86

Year	Team	Lg	G	GS	CG	GF	IP	BFP	H	R	ER	HR	SH	SF	HB	TBB	IBB	SO	WP	Bk	W	L	Pct.	ShO	Sv	ERA
1994	Canton-Akrn	AA	39	0	0	17	58	243	50	20	18	4	4	2	5	19	2	44	2	0	4	3	.571	0	2	2.79
1995	Iowa	AAA	33	1	0	4	56	262	68	42	37	8	5	3	3	29	3	33	5	0	4	6	.400	0	0	5.95
	Orlando	AA	13	0	0	4	17.1	78	13	9	4	0	2	0	2	10	4	9	1	1	2	1	.667	0	1	2.08
	8 Min. YEARS		256	83	6	54	773.1	3364	757	388	307	40	30	25	42	327	14	584	34	24	51	44	.537	1	7	3.57

Bob Daly

Bats: Right **Throws:** Right **Pos:** 1B   **Ht:** 6'2" **Wt:** 220 **Born:** 10/8/72 **Age:** 23

			BATTING															BASERUNNING				PERCENTAGES		
Year	Team	Lg	G	AB	H	2B	3B	HR	TB	R	RBI	TBB	IBB	SO	HBP	SH	SF	SB	CS	SB%	GDP	Avg	OBP	SLG
1992	Mets	R	50	181	49	8	2	0	61	17	18	12	0	12	1	1	2	1	0	1.00	4	.271	.316	.337
1993	Kingsport	R	62	239	72	16	2	6	110	47	32	24	1	23	1	3	1	1	2	.33	6	.301	.366	.460
1995	Pittsfield	A	76	303	89	22	3	3	126	43	60	22	1	28	1	0	7	4	1	.80	5	.294	.336	.416
	Binghamton	AA	1	4	0	0	0	0	0	1	0	1	1	1	0	0	0	0	0	.00	0	.000	.200	.000
	3 Min. YEARS		189	727	210	46	7	9	297	108	110	59	3	64	3	4	10	6	3	.67	15	.289	.340	.409

Eric Danapilis

Bats: Right **Throws:** Right **Pos:** OF   **Ht:** 6'2" **Wt:** 220 **Born:** 6/11/71 **Age:** 25

			BATTING															BASERUNNING				PERCENTAGES		
Year	Team	Lg	G	AB	H	2B	3B	HR	TB	R	RBI	TBB	IBB	SO	HBP	SH	SF	SB	CS	SB%	GDP	Avg	OBP	SLG
1993	Niagara Fal	A	65	208	71	9	1	3	91	35	28	33	0	36	6	0	1	8	4	.67	5	.341	.444	.438
1994	Fayettevlle	A	115	381	96	19	1	23	186	71	83	54	0	114	14	0	6	5	2	.71	12	.252	.360	.488
1995	Jacksonville	AA	129	415	107	24	1	10	163	47	63	61	6	100	9	0	3	3	3	.50	13	.258	.363	.393
	3 Min. YEARS		309	1004	274	52	3	36	440	153	174	148	6	250	29	0	10	16	9	.64	30	.273	.379	.438

Brad Dandridge

Bats: Right **Throws:** Right **Pos:** C   **Ht:** 6'0" **Wt:** 190 **Born:** 11/29/71 **Age:** 24

			BATTING															BASERUNNING				PERCENTAGES		
Year	Team	Lg	G	AB	H	2B	3B	HR	TB	R	RBI	TBB	IBB	SO	HBP	SH	SF	SB	CS	SB%	GDP	Avg	OBP	SLG
1993	Spokane	A	64	248	59	8	2	4	83	26	41	16	1	38	5	1	4	2	0	1.00	5	.238	.293	.335
1994	Ogden	R	43	171	63	11	1	2	82	41	45	17	2	15	3	1	5	6	2	.75	5	.368	.423	.480
	St. Paul	IND	19	67	14	4	0	0	18	4	6	8	0	22	0	2	0	0	1	.00	1	.209	.293	.269
1995	San Antonio	AA	3	12	5	0	0	0	5	1	1	0	0	1	0	0	0	0	1	.00	0	.417	.417	.417
	San Bernrdo	A	82	322	103	14	2	11	154	56	61	14	0	34	3	1	2	16	5	.76	11	.320	.352	.478
	3 Min. YEARS		211	820	244	37	5	17	342	128	154	55	3	110	11	5	11	24	9	.73	22	.298	.346	.417

Moe Daniels

Bats: Right **Throws:** Right **Pos:** OF   **Ht:** 6'2" **Wt:** 190 **Born:** 1/14/71 **Age:** 25

			BATTING															BASERUNNING				PERCENTAGES		
Year	Team	Lg	G	AB	H	2B	3B	HR	TB	R	RBI	TBB	IBB	SO	HBP	SH	SF	SB	CS	SB%	GDP	Avg	OBP	SLG
1992	Angels	R	40	152	43	6	5	1	62	33	22	20	0	32	0	2	1	12	6	.67	4	.283	.364	.408
1993	Cedar Rapds	A	110	367	89	7	2	7	121	53	36	54	1	113	2	3	0	25	8	.76	4	.243	.343	.330
1994	Lk Elsinore	A	79	237	62	6	3	7	95	55	36	49	0	85	1	5	0	18	6	.75	7	.262	.390	.401
1995	Lk Elsinore	A	39	151	46	8	2	0	58	26	11	18	0	35	1	0	0	6	4	.60	2	.305	.382	.384
	Midland	AA	25	84	17	5	0	1	25	9	4	14	0	22	2	0	0	2	4	.33	0	.202	.330	.298
	4 Min. YEARS		293	991	257	32	12	16	361	176	109	155	1	287	6	10	1	63	28	.69	17	.259	.363	.364

Jeff Darwin

Pitches: Right **Bats:** Right **Pos:** P   **Ht:** 6'3" **Wt:** 180 **Born:** 7/6/69 **Age:** 26

			HOW MUCH HE PITCHED						WHAT HE GAVE UP												THE RESULTS					
Year	Team	Lg	G	GS	CG	GF	IP	BFP	H	R	ER	HR	SH	SF	HB	TBB	IBB	SO	WP	Bk	W	L	Pct.	ShO	Sv	ERA
1989	Bellingham	A	12	12	0	0	64	286	73	42	35	3	1	3	3	24	0	47	4	0	1	7	.125	0	0	4.92
1990	Peninsula	A	25	25	1	0	150.1	651	153	86	67	12	6	2	4	57	0	89	6	9	8	14	.364	0	0	4.01
1991	San Bernrdo	A	16	14	0	1	74	323	80	53	51	14	2	4	4	31	1	58	1	1	3	9	.250	0	0	6.20
1992	Peninsula	A	32	20	4	9	139.2	583	132	58	52	13	5	3	4	40	5	122	6	5	5	11	.313	2	3	3.35
1993	Jacksonville	AA	27	0	0	22	36.1	159	29	17	12	1	1	0	3	17	3	39	0	0	3	5	.375	0	7	2.97
	Edmonton	AAA	25	0	0	14	30.2	151	50	34	29	5	1	2	0	10	2	22	1	0	2	2	.500	0	2	8.51
1994	Calgary	AAA	42	0	0	21	70.2	299	60	32	27	9	3	2	2	28	3	54	5	0	1	2	.333	0	11	3.44
1995	Tacoma	AAA	46	0	0	31	63.1	256	51	21	19	2	3	3	1	21	5	51	0	0	7	2	.778	0	12	2.70
1994	Seattle	AL	2	0	0	1	4	22	7	6	6	1	0	0	1	3	1	1	0	0	0	0	.000	0	0	13.50
	7 Min. YEARS		225	71	5	98	629	2708	628	343	292	59	22	19	21	228	19	482	23	15	30	52	.366	2	35	4.18

Doug Dascenzo

Bats: Both **Throws:** Left **Pos:** OF   **Ht:** 5'8" **Wt:** 160 **Born:** 6/30/64 **Age:** 32

			BATTING															BASERUNNING				PERCENTAGES		
Year	Team	Lg	G	AB	H	2B	3B	HR	TB	R	RBI	TBB	IBB	SO	HBP	SH	SF	SB	CS	SB%	GDP	Avg	OBP	SLG
1985	Geneva	A	70	252	84	15	1	3	110	59	23	61	4	20	2	1	4	33	9	.79	1	.333	.461	.437
1986	Winston-Sal	A	138	545	178	29	11	6	247	107	83	63	5	44	2	12	5	57	13	.81	9	.327	.395	.453
1987	Pittsfield	AA	134	496	152	32	6	3	205	84	56	73	5	38	1	7	5	36	7	.84	5	.306	.393	.413
1988	Iowa	AAA	132	505	149	22	5	6	199	73	49	37	4	41	2	7	5	30	14	.68	7	.295	.342	.394
1989	Iowa	AAA	111	431	121	18	4	4	159	59	33	51	3	41	0	9	2	34	21	.62	7	.281	.355	.369
1993	Okla. City	AAA	38	157	39	8	2	1	54	21	13	16	0	16	0	2	1	6	5	.55	7	.248	.316	.344
1994	Norfolk	AAA	68	246	68	13	1	4	95	30	27	22	3	23	0	4	1	5	7	.42	5	.276	.335	.386
1995	St. Paul	IND	9	38	11	2	0	0	13	8	7	8	0	2	0	0	1	2	2	.50	0	.289	.404	.342
	Charlotte	AAA	75	265	69	9	0	4	90	51	26	25	0	30	0	1	4	14	9	.61	7	.260	.320	.340

Year	Team	Lg	G	AB	H	2B	3B	HR	TB	R	RBI	TBB	IBB	SO	HBP	SH	SF	SB	CS	SB%	GDP	Avg	OBP	SLG
1988	Chicago	NL	26	75	16	3	0	0	19	9	4	9	1	4	0	1	0	6	1	.86	2	.213	.298	.253
1989	Chicago	NL	47	139	23	1	0	1	27	20	12	13	0	13	0	3	2	6	3	.67	2	.165	.234	.194
1990	Chicago	NL	113	241	61	9	5	1	83	27	26	21	2	18	1	5	3	15	6	.71	3	.253	.312	.344
1991	Chicago	NL	118	239	61	11	0	1	75	40	18	24	2	26	2	6	1	14	7	.67	3	.255	.327	.314
1992	Chicago	NL	139	376	96	13	4	0	117	37	20	27	2	32	0	4	2	6	8	.43	3	.255	.304	.311
1993	Texas	AL	76	146	29	5	1	2	42	20	10	8	0	22	0	3	1	2	0	1.00	1	.199	.239	.288
	8 Min. YEARS		775	2935	871	148	30	31	1172	492	317	356	24	255	7	43	28	217	87	.71	48	.297	.371	.399
	6 Maj. YEARS		519	1216	286	42	10	5	363	153	90	102	7	115	3	22	9	49	25	.66	14	.235	.294	.299

Jimmy Daspit

Pitches: Right **Bats:** Right **Pos:** P **Ht:** 6'7" **Wt:** 210 **Born:** 8/10/69 **Age:** 26

			HOW MUCH HE PITCHED						WHAT HE GAVE UP											THE RESULTS					
Year	Team	Lg	G	GS	CG	GF	IP	BFP	H	R	ER	HR	SH	SF	HB	TBB	IBB	SO	WP	Bk	W	L	Pct.	ShO	Sv	ERA
1990	Great Falls	R	14	9	0	1	51	222	45	26	23	0	3	2	5	30	0	40	1	0	5	2	.714	0	0	4.06
1991	Bakersfield	A	22	9	0	6	64.2	276	58	29	23	1	4	2	1	36	2	47	6	1	3	2	.600	0	2	3.20
1992	Vero Beach	A	26	25	0	0	149.1	625	135	67	57	10	6	3	7	57	1	109	7	1	6	12	.333	0	0	3.44
1993	Vero Beach	A	1	1	0	0	3	15	4	0	0	0	0	0	0	2	0	2	0	0	0	0	.000	0	0	0.00
	San Antonio	AA	15	15	0	0	81.1	363	92	48	40	5	4	4	8	33	0	58	5	0	3	8	.273	0	0	4.43
1994	Jackson	AA	28	10	1	7	71	274	48	22	18	1	2	0	2	23	0	74	3	0	5	1	.833	1	1	2.28
1995	Tucson	AAA	36	0	0	11	63	272	63	30	25	3	2	5	2	22	1	49	5	0	5	1	.833	0	1	3.57
	Edmonton	AAA	2	0	0	0	5	22	6	6	6	2	0	0	0	2	0	5	2	0	0	1	.000	0	0	10.80
	6 Min. YEARS		144	69	1	25	488.1	2069	451	228	192	22	21	16	25	205	4	384	29	2	27	27	.500	1	4	3.54

Brian Daubach

Bats: Left **Throws:** Right **Pos:** 1B **Ht:** 6'1" **Wt:** 201 **Born:** 2/11/72 **Age:** 24

			BATTING															BASERUNNING				PERCENTAGES		
Year	Team	Lg	G	AB	H	2B	3B	HR	TB	R	RBI	TBB	IBB	SO	HBP	SH	SF	SB	CS	SB%	GDP	Avg	OBP	SLG
1990	Mets	R	45	152	41	8	4	1	60	26	19	22	0	41	2	0	3	2	1	.67	2	.270	.363	.395
1991	Kingsport	R	65	217	52	9	1	7	84	30	42	33	5	64	6	1	2	1	3	.25	1	.240	.353	.387
1992	Pittsfield	A	72	260	63	15	2	2	88	26	40	30	2	61	3	1	4	4	0	1.00	5	.242	.323	.338
1993	Capital Cty	A	102	379	106	19	3	7	152	50	72	52	5	84	5	1	7	6	1	.86	14	.280	.368	.401
1994	St. Lucie	A	129	450	123	30	2	6	175	52	74	58	5	120	5	3	4	14	9	.61	3	.273	.360	.389
1995	Binghamton	AA	135	469	115	25	2	10	174	61	72	51	5	104	7	1	7	6	2	.75	5	.245	.324	.371
	Norfolk	AAA	2	7	0	0	0	0	0	0	0	2	1	0	0	0	0	0	0	.00	0	.000	.222	.000
	6 Min. YEARS		550	1934	500	106	14	33	733	245	319	248	23	474	28	7	27	33	16	.67	30	.259	.347	.379

Jack Daugherty

Bats: Both **Throws:** Left **Pos:** OF **Ht:** 6'0" **Wt:** 190 **Born:** 7/3/60 **Age:** 35

			BATTING															BASERUNNING				PERCENTAGES		
Year	Team	Lg	G	AB	H	2B	3B	HR	TB	R	RBI	TBB	IBB	SO	HBP	SH	SF	SB	CS	SB%	GDP	Avg	OBP	SLG
1984	Helena	R	66	259	104	26	2	15	179	77	82	52	10	48	2	0	2	16	3	.84	2	.402	.502	.691
1985	W. Palm Bch	A	133	481	152	25	3	10	213	76	87	75	11	58	0	0	5	33	6	.85	14	.316	.405	.443
1986	Jacksonville	AA	138	502	159	37	4	4	216	87	63	79	1	58	4	7	3	15	6	.71	14	.317	.412	.430
1987	Indianapols	AAA	117	420	131	35	3	7	193	65	50	42	5	54	1	2	4	11	0	1.00	12	.312	.373	.460
1988	Indianapols	AAA	137	481	137	33	2	6	192	82	67	56	4	50	1	7	7	18	6	.75	14	.285	.356	.399
1989	Okla. City	AAA	82	311	78	15	3	3	108	28	32	39	5	35	0	2	3	2	2	.50	9	.251	.331	.347
1991	Okla. City	AAA	22	77	11	2	0	0	13	4	4	8	2	14	0	1	0	1	0	1.00	1	.143	.224	.169
1992	Okla. City	AAA	9	18	5	2	0	0	7	3	2	3	0	3	0	0	0	0	0	.00	1	.278	.381	.389
1993	Tucson	AAA	42	141	55	9	2	2	74	23	29	26	2	12	3	0	2	1	0	1.00	1	.390	.488	.525
1994	Syracuse	AAA	47	149	50	12	0	3	71	19	21	27	1	16	0	1	0	0	0	.00	5	.336	.438	.477
1995	Phoenix	AAA	10	33	5	1	0	0	6	4	3	2	1	4	0	0	0	0	0	.00	1	.152	.194	.182
1987	Montreal	NL	11	10	1	1	0	0	2	1	1	0	0	3	0	2	0	0	0	.00	0	.100	.100	.200
1989	Texas	AL	52	106	32	4	2	1	43	15	10	11	0	21	1	0	3	2	1	.67	1	.302	.364	.406
1990	Texas	AL	125	310	93	20	2	6	135	36	47	22	0	49	2	2	3	0	0	.00	4	.300	.347	.435
1991	Texas	AL	58	144	28	3	2	1	38	8	11	16	1	23	0	4	3	1	0	1.00	3	.194	.270	.264
1992	Texas	AL	59	127	26	9	0	0	35	13	9	16	1	21	1	0	2	2	1	.67	3	.205	.295	.276
1993	Cincinnati	NL	46	59	13	2	0	2	21	7	9	11	0	15	0	0	1	0	0	.00	0	.220	.338	.356
	Houston	NL	4	3	1	0	0	0	1	0	0	0	0	0	0	0	0	0	0	.00	0	.333	.333	.333
	11 Min. YEARS		803	2872	887	197	19	50	1272	468	440	409	42	352	11	19	27	97	23	.81	74	.309	.394	.443
	6 Maj. YEARS		355	759	194	39	6	10	275	80	87	76	2	132	4	8	12	5	2	.71	10	.256	.322	.362

Phil Dauphin

Bats: Left **Throws:** Left **Pos:** OF **Ht:** 6'1" **Wt:** 180 **Born:** 5/11/69 **Age:** 27

			BATTING															BASERUNNING				PERCENTAGES		
Year	Team	Lg	G	AB	H	2B	3B	HR	TB	R	RBI	TBB	IBB	SO	HBP	SH	SF	SB	CS	SB%	GDP	Avg	OBP	SLG
1990	Geneva	A	73	233	55	8	1	12	101	47	47	51	1	45	7	8	3	8	6	.57	2	.236	.384	.433
1991	Peoria	A	120	426	126	27	5	11	196	74	49	72	9	66	4	4	7	15	7	.68	4	.296	.397	.460
1992	Charlotte	AA	136	515	131	24	3	10	191	83	43	55	2	71	6	6	4	17	10	.63	5	.254	.331	.371
1993	Orlando	AA	81	299	79	16	2	11	132	53	35	30	0	40	3	5	3	7	10	.41	3	.264	.334	.441
	Iowa	AAA	20	54	12	4	1	1	21	5	2	10	2	9	0	0	0	2	0	1.00	2	.222	.344	.389
	Indianapols	AAA	8	21	6	0	0	0	6	0	2	2	0	4	0	0	0	0	0	.00	0	.286	.348	.286
1994	Chattanooga	AA	1	4	2	0	0	0	2	1	1	1	0	1	0	0	0	0	0	.00	0	.500	.600	.500
	Harrisburg	AA	113	331	88	16	5	10	144	40	40	42	3	56	1	4	4	10	9	.53	2	.266	.347	.435
1995	Harrisburg	AA	111	398	97	20	2	5	136	53	38	43	8	61	2	3	7	17	7	.71	1	.244	.316	.342
	6 Min. YEARS		663	2281	596	115	19	60	929	356	257	306	25	353	23	30	28	76	49	.61	16	.261	.351	.407

74

Adell Davenport

Bats: Right **Throws:** Right **Pos:** OF   **Ht:** 5'11" **Wt:** 195 **Born:** 7/16/67 **Age:** 28

									BATTING										BASERUNNING				PERCENTAGES		
Year	Team	Lg	G	AB	H	2B	3B	HR	TB	R	RBI	TBB	IBB	SO	HBP	SH	SF	SB	CS	SB%	GDP	Avg	OBP	SLG
1988	Everett	A	61	229	54	14	1	5	85	40	29	31	1	65	5	0	0	0	0	.00	3	.236	.340	.371
1989	Clinton	A	128	436	103	16	2	14	165	50	65	35	2	98	13	5	4	1	4	.20	10	.236	.309	.378
1990	San Jose	A	132	495	124	20	5	17	205	76	66	46	3	108	16	2	3	3	6	.33	8	.251	.332	.414
1991	San Jose	A	67	242	70	16	0	6	104	34	42	40	1	61	10	0	1	1	3	.25	6	.289	.410	.430
	Shreveport	AA	59	165	38	3	0	7	62	19	24	14	0	44	6	3	1	0	1	.00	4	.230	.312	.376
1992	Shreveport	AA	124	441	127	31	5	19	225	54	88	28	6	78	8	1	2	2	4	.33	6	.288	.340	.510
1993	Phoenix	AAA	14	40	12	1	0	2	19	5	8	3	0	10	0	0	0	0	1	.00	0	.300	.349	.475
	Shreveport	AA	103	370	97	21	0	15	163	43	62	29	6	73	5	0	4	4	2	.67	6	.262	.321	.441
1994	Nashville	AA	123	457	108	20	0	20	188	55	71	27	3	111	8	2	5	1	1	.50	3	.236	.288	.411
1995	Canton-Akrn	AA	9	29	8	1	0	0	9	2	5	3	0	5	1	0	0	0	0	.00	0	.276	.364	.310
	Sioux Falls	IND	65	249	65	17	0	13	121	25	42	16	2	40	6	1	5	1	0	1.00	4	.261	.315	.486
8 Min. YEARS			885	3153	806	160	13	118	1346	403	502	272	24	693	78	14	25	13	22	.37	50	.256	.328	.427

Jackie Davidson

Pitches: Right **Bats:** Both **Pos:** P   **Ht:** 6'0" **Wt:** 175 **Born:** 9/20/64 **Age:** 31

				HOW MUCH HE PITCHED						WHAT HE GAVE UP										THE RESULTS					
Year	Team	Lg	G	GS	CG	GF	IP	BFP	H	R	ER	HR	SH	SF	HB	TBB	IBB	SO	WP	Bk	W	L	Pct.	ShO	Sv	ERA
1995	Tulsa	AA	2	2	0	0	7	42	21	18	17	1	0	0	0	1	0	5	0	0	0	2	.000	0	0	21.86

Clint Davis

Pitches: Right **Bats:** Right **Pos:** P   **Ht:** 6'3" **Wt:** 205 **Born:** 9/26/69 **Age:** 26

				HOW MUCH HE PITCHED						WHAT HE GAVE UP										THE RESULTS					
Year	Team	Lg	G	GS	CG	GF	IP	BFP	H	R	ER	HR	SH	SF	HB	TBB	IBB	SO	WP	Bk	W	L	Pct.	ShO	Sv	ERA
1991	Cardinals	R	21	0	0	9	26.2	130	35	23	17	0	2	3	3	12	0	25	1	2	3	3	.500	0	0	5.74
1992	Savannah	A	51	0	0	23	65	272	49	24	16	0	4	3	4	21	6	61	3	0	4	2	.667	0	1	2.22
1993	St. Pete	A	29	0	0	26	28	118	26	8	6	0	1	0	0	10	0	44	0	0	1	0	1.000	0	19	1.93
	Arkansas	AA	28	0	0	10	37	143	22	10	8	1	2	1	3	10	3	37	0	0	2	0	1.000	0	1	1.95
1995	Louisville	AAA	4	0	0	0	3.2	19	6	5	5	1	0	0	0	2	1	4	0	1	0	0	.000	0	0	12.27
	Rio Grande	IND	38	0	0	36	40	162	29	17	12	4	2	0	1	9	2	59	0	1	3	2	.600	0	21	2.70
4 Min. YEARS			171	0	0	104	200.1	844	167	87	64	6	11	7	11	64	12	230	4	4	13	7	.650	0	42	2.88

Jay Davis

Bats: Left **Throws:** Left **Pos:** OF   **Ht:** 6'0" **Wt:** 160 **Born:** 10/3/70 **Age:** 25

									BATTING										BASERUNNING				PERCENTAGES		
Year	Team	Lg	G	AB	H	2B	3B	HR	TB	R	RBI	TBB	IBB	SO	HBP	SH	SF	SB	CS	SB%	GDP	Avg	OBP	SLG
1989	Mets	R	52	195	48	6	5	0	64	26	18	12	0	33	2	0	2	7	11	.39	3	.246	.294	.328
1990	Kingsport	R	68	261	60	6	0	5	81	39	28	8	1	37	1	1	4	19	9	.68	8	.230	.252	.310
1991	Columbia	A	132	511	152	29	8	0	197	79	63	30	2	72	7	2	5	25	18	.58	14	.297	.342	.386
1992	St. Lucie	A	134	524	147	15	7	1	179	56	36	7	0	70	6	2	3	21	17	.55	15	.281	.296	.342
1993	Binghamton	AA	119	409	114	15	4	1	140	52	35	21	2	71	1	2	3	5	8	.38	8	.279	.313	.342
1994	Norfolk	AAA	6	14	3	1	0	0	4	3	0	1	0	1	0	0	0	0	0	.00	0	.214	.267	.286
	Binghamton	AA	105	325	107	15	3	5	143	51	42	14	4	39	3	3	2	9	3	.75	4	.329	.360	.440
1995	Norfolk	AAA	10	26	5	1	1	0	8	1	3	0	0	2	0	0	0	0	1	.00	1	.192	.192	.308
	Binghamton	AA	116	443	113	17	6	3	151	64	50	26	1	68	8	1	6	11	5	.69	7	.255	.304	.341
7 Min. YEARS			742	2708	749	105	34	15	967	371	275	119	10	393	28	11	25	97	72	.57	60	.277	.311	.357

Jeff Davis

Pitches: Right **Bats:** Right **Pos:** P   **Ht:** 6'0" **Wt:** 170 **Born:** 9/20/72 **Age:** 23

				HOW MUCH HE PITCHED						WHAT HE GAVE UP										THE RESULTS					
Year	Team	Lg	G	GS	CG	GF	IP	BFP	H	R	ER	HR	SH	SF	HB	TBB	IBB	SO	WP	Bk	W	L	Pct.	ShO	Sv	ERA
1993	Erie	A	27	0	0	24	37	155	32	18	15	3	2	2	4	10	2	41	2	0	0	5	.000	0	13	3.65
1994	Charlstn-Sc	A	45	0	0	43	49.2	214	53	25	22	3	0	1	2	11	0	72	2	1	2	3	.400	0	19	3.99
1995	Tulsa	AA	1	1	0	0	7	24	2	0	0	0	0	0	0	1	0	4	1	0	1	0	1.000	0	0	0.00
	Charlotte	A	26	26	0	0	165.1	691	159	74	53	10	6	2	11	37	0	105	6	2	12	7	.632	0	0	2.89
3 Min. YEARS			99	27	0	67	259	1084	246	117	90	16	8	5	17	59	2	222	11	3	15	15	.500	0	32	3.13

John Davis

Pitches: Right **Bats:** Right **Pos:** P   **Ht:** 6'7" **Wt:** 215 **Born:** 1/5/63 **Age:** 33

				HOW MUCH HE PITCHED						WHAT HE GAVE UP										THE RESULTS					
Year	Team	Lg	G	GS	CG	GF	IP	BFP	H	R	ER	HR	SH	SF	HB	TBB	IBB	SO	WP	Bk	W	L	Pct.	ShO	Sv	ERA
1984	Fort Myers	A	25	25	5	0	153	685	170	91	77	9	7	3	6	70	3	84	8	1	7	11	.389	0	0	4.53
1985	Memphis	AA	27	27	4	0	160.1	735	186	113	96	13	6	7	11	75	4	103	7	2	6	15	.286	0	0	5.39
1986	Memphis	AA	41	5	0	24	111.1	499	99	63	58	9	5	4	4	69	4	70	6	0	6	6	.500	0	8	4.69
	Omaha	AAA	2	0	0	2	2	10	2	1	1	0	0	1	1	1	0	1	0	0	0	0	.000	0	1	4.50
1987	Omaha	AAA	43	0	0	35	50.2	207	34	16	15	2	2	5	2	27	5	44	4	1	4	3	.571	0	7	2.66
1988	Vancouver	AAA	15	0	0	12	17.1	67	15	7	6	0	2	1	0	7	0	9	2	0	1	0	1.000	0	5	3.12
1989	Vancouver	AAA	35	0	0	27	49.1	215	33	24	13	2	1	1	3	33	2	57	8	1	4	3	.571	0	11	2.37
1990	Denver	AAA	6	0	0	4	4.1	25	4	7	6	0	0	2	0	8	2	3	2	0	1	3	.250	0	1	12.46
	Las Vegas	AAA	18	11	1	6	74.2	331	68	40	36	3	2	4	8	43	0	68	8	0	2	4	.333	0	0	4.34

Year	Team	Lg	G	GS	CG	GF	IP	BFP	H	R	ER	HR	SH	SF	HB	TBB	IBB	SO	WP	Bk	W	L	Pct.	ShO	Sv	ERA
1995	Nashville	AAA	4	0	0	3	3.1	16	3	2	0	0	0	0	0	3	1	0	0	0	1	1	.500	0	1	0.00
1987	Kansas City	AL	27	0	0	12	43.2	181	29	13	11	0	0	4	2	26	4	24	2	0	5	2	.714	0	2	2.27
1988	Chicago	AL	34	1	0	10	63.2	319	77	58	47	5	2	4	4	50	10	37	6	3	2	5	.286	0	1	6.64
1989	Chicago	AL	4	0	0	3	6	25	5	4	3	2	0	0	4	2	0	5	0	0	0	1	.000	0	1	4.50
1990	San Diego	NL	6	0	0	5	9.1	39	9	7	6	1	0	0	0	0	0	7	0	0	0	1	.000	0	1	5.79
	8 Min. YEARS		216	68	10	113	626.1	2790	614	364	308	38	25	26	35	336	21	439	45	5	32	46	.410	0	35	4.43
	4 Maj. YEARS		71	1	0	30	122.2	564	120	82	67	8	2	8	6	82	14	73	8	3	7	9	.438	0	4	4.92

Josh Davis

Bats: Right **Throws:** Right **Pos:** C **Ht:** 5'11" **Wt:** 170 **Born:** 6/13/76 **Age:** 20

			BATTING															BASERUNNING				PERCENTAGES		
Year	Team	Lg	G	AB	H	2B	3B	HR	TB	R	RBI	TBB	IBB	SO	HBP	SH	SF	SB	CS	SB%	GDP	Avg	OBP	SLG
1994	Padres	R	33	121	35	3	0	0	38	19	6	7	0	24	2	0	1	2	2	.50	4	.289	.336	.314
1995	Memphis	AA	1	2	1	0	0	0	1	0	0	1	0	1	0	0	0	0	0	.00	0	.500	.667	.500
	Clinton	A	8	15	3	0	0	0	3	2	1	1	0	5	0	0	0	1	0	1.00	0	.200	.250	.200
	Padres	R	37	128	26	4	1	0	32	20	7	14	0	35	3	2	0	3	3	.50	1	.203	.297	.250
	Idaho Falls	R	4	18	4	1	0	0	5	3	1	1	0	2	0	0	0	0	0	.00	1	.222	.263	.278
	2 Min. YEARS		83	284	69	8	1	0	79	44	16	24	0	67	5	2	1	6	5	.55	6	.243	.312	.278

Mark Davis

Pitches: Left **Bats:** Left **Pos:** P **Ht:** 6' 4" **Wt:** 215 **Born:** 10/19/60 **Age:** 35

			HOW MUCH HE PITCHED						WHAT HE GAVE UP												THE RESULTS				
Year	Team	Lg	G	GS	CG	GF	IP	BFP	H	R	ER	HR	SH	SF	HB	TBB	IBB	SO	WP	Bk	W	L	Pct.	ShO	Sv	ERA
1991	Omaha	AAA	6	6	0	0	35.2	142	27	11	8	1	0	2	1	9	0	36	1	0	4	1	.800	0	0	2.02
1995	Brevard Cty	A	3	0	0	1	5	16	2	0	0	0	0	0	0	0	0	4	0	0	0	0	.000	0	0	0.00
	Charlotte	AAA	9	0	0	0	9	44	13	8	5	0	0	1	1	1	0	5	2	0	0	0	.000	0	0	5.00
1980	Philadelphia	NL	2	1	0	0	7	30	4	2	2	0	0	0	0	5	0	5	0	0	0	0	.000	0	0	2.57
1981	Philadelphia	NL	9	9	0	0	43	194	49	37	37	7	2	4	0	24	0	29	1	1	1	4	.200	0	0	7.74
1983	San Francisco	NL	20	20	2	0	111	469	93	51	43	14	2	4	3	50	4	83	8	1	6	4	.600	2	0	3.49
1984	San Francisco	NL	46	27	1	6	174.2	766	201	113	104	25	10	10	5	54	12	124	8	4	5	17	.227	0	0	5.36
1985	San Francisco	NL	77	1	0	38	114.1	465	89	49	45	13	13	1	3	41	7	131	6	1	5	12	.294	0	7	3.54
1986	San Francisco	NL	67	2	0	20	84.1	342	63	33	28	6	5	5	1	34	7	90	3	0	5	7	.417	0	4	2.99
1987	San Diego	NL	43	0	0	17	62.1	265	51	26	22	5	4	0	2	31	7	47	2	0	5	3	.625	0	2	3.18
	San Francisco	NL	20	11	1	1	70.2	301	72	38	37	9	3	2	4	28	1	51	4	2	4	5	.444	0	0	4.71
1988	San Diego	NL	62	0	0	52	98.1	402	70	24	22	2	7	1	0	42	11	102	9	1	5	10	.333	0	28	2.01
1989	San Diego	NL	70	0	0	65	92.2	370	66	21	19	6	3	4	2	31	1	92	8	0	4	3	.571	0	44	1.85
1990	Kansas City	AL	53	3	0	28	68.2	334	71	43	39	9	2	2	4	52	3	73	6	0	2	7	.222	0	6	5.11
1991	Kansas City	AL	29	5	0	8	62.2	276	55	36	31	6	2	5	1	39	0	47	1	0	6	3	.667	0	1	4.45
1992	Kansas City	AL	13	6	0	4	36.1	176	42	31	29	6	1	4	0	28	0	19	1	0	1	3	.250	0	0	7.18
	Atlanta	NL	14	0	0	7	16.2	85	22	13	13	3	0	1	1	13	2	15	4	1	1	0	1.000	0	0	7.02
1993	Philadelphia	NL	25	0	0	4	31.1	154	35	22	18	4	1	0	1	24	1	28	1	0	1	2	.333	0	0	5.17
	San Diego	NL	35	0	0	3	38.1	173	44	15	15	6	3	1	0	20	6	42	1	1	0	3	.000	0	4	3.52
1994	San Diego	NL	20	0	0	3	16.1	81	20	18	16	4	1	0	0	13	1	15	0	0	0	0	.000	0	0	8.82
	2 Min. YEARS		18	6	0	1	49.2	202	42	19	13	1	0	3	2	10	0	45	3	0	4	1	.800	0	0	2.36
	14 Maj. YEARS		605	85	4	262	1128.2	4883	1047	572	520	125	59	44	27	529	63	993	63	12	51	84	.378	2	96	4.15

Ray Davis

Pitches: Right **Bats:** Right **Pos:** P **Ht:** 6'1" **Wt:** 170 **Born:** 2/6/73 **Age:** 23

			HOW MUCH HE PITCHED						WHAT HE GAVE UP												THE RESULTS				
Year	Team	Lg	G	GS	CG	GF	IP	BFP	H	R	ER	HR	SH	SF	HB	TBB	IBB	SO	WP	Bk	W	L	Pct.	ShO	Sv	ERA
1991	Cardinals	R	11	10	0	0	54.2	254	72	47	41	2	0	3	1	24	0	31	3	1	2	3	.400	0	0	6.75
1992	Cardinals	R	11	11	4	0	76	296	57	30	21	1	5	2	1	22	0	74	3	1	5	4	.556	4	0	2.49
1993	Savannah	A	26	26	1	0	131.1	569	141	73	53	10	4	4	3	53	0	120	7	1	9	7	.563	1	0	3.63
1994	Madison	A	27	27	1	0	167	691	149	68	55	9	5	5	7	58	2	127	2	3	12	10	.545	1	0	2.96
1995	Arkansas	AA	21	18	0	1	110	467	112	67	55	14	5	5	4	30	0	70	6	1	7	6	.538	0	0	4.50
	5 Min. YEARS		96	92	6	1	539	2277	531	285	225	36	19	19	16	187	2	422	21	7	35	30	.538	6	0	3.76

Storm Davis

Pitches: Right **Bats:** Right **Pos:** P **Ht:** 6' 4" **Wt:** 210 **Born:** 12/26/61 **Age:** 34

			HOW MUCH HE PITCHED						WHAT HE GAVE UP												THE RESULTS				
Year	Team	Lg	G	GS	CG	GF	IP	BFP	H	R	ER	HR	SH	SF	HB	TBB	IBB	SO	WP	Bk	W	L	Pct.	ShO	Sv	ERA
1979	Bluefield	R	10	10	3	-	58		44	34	25	3	-	-	2	30	0	54	4	0	4	4	.500	1	0	3.88
1980	Miami	A	25	25	7	-	151		157	85	59	3	-	-	0	55	0	90	13	4	9	12	.429	0	0	3.52
1981	Charlotte	AA	28	28	6	0	187		215	86	72	14	-	-	0	65	2	119	7	0	14	10	.583	2	0	3.47
1982	Rochester	AAA	4	4	0	0	26.2		25	13	11	1	-	-	0	7	0	27	1	0	2	1	.667	0	0	3.71
1986	Hagerstown	A	1	1	0	0	4	18	3	0	0	0	0	0	0	3	0	6	0	0	0	0	.000	0	0	0.00
	Hagerstown	A	1	1	0	0	4		3	0	0	0	-	-	0	3	0	6	0	0	0	0	.000	0	0	0.00
1987	Wichita	AA	1	1	0	0	4	17	4	3	0	0	2	0	0	0	0	2	0	0	0	1	.000	0	0	0.00
	Reno	A	1	1	0	0	5	22	2	2	2	0	0	0	0	6	0	5	0	0	0	0	.000	0	0	3.60
	Wichita	AA	1	1	0	0	4		4	3	0	0	0	0	0	0	0	2	0	0	0	1	.000	0	0	0.00
	Reno	A	1	1	0	0	5		2	2	2	0	0	0	0	6	0	5	0	0	0	0	.000	0	0	3.60
1995	Indianapolis	AAA	4	0	0	1	5.1	22	4	2	2	0	1	0	0	3	0	4	1	0	0	0	.000	0	0	3.38
1982	Baltimore	AL	29	8	1	9	100.2	412	96	40	39	8	4	6	0	28	4	67	2	1	8	4	.667	0	0	3.49
1983	Baltimore	AL	34	29	6	0	200.1	831	180	90	80	14	5	4	2	64	4	125	7	2	13	7	.650	1	0	3.59
1984	Baltimore	AL	35	31	10	3	225	923	205	86	78	7	7	9	5	71	6	105	6	1	14	9	.609	2	1	3.12

Year Team	Lg	G	GS	CG	GF	IP	BFP	H	R	ER	HR	SH	SF	HB	TBB	IBB	SO	WP	Bk	W	L	Pct.	ShO	Sv	ERA
1985 Baltimore	AL	31	28	8	0	175	750	172	92	88	11	3	3	1	70	5	93	2	1	10	8	.556	1	0	4.53
1986 Baltimore	AL	25	25	2	0	154	657	166	70	62	16	3	2	0	49	2	96	5	0	9	12	.429	0	0	3.62
1987 Oakland	AL	5	5	0	0	30.1	128	28	13	11	3	0	1	0	11	0	28	2	0	1	1	.500	0	0	3.26
San Diego	NL	21	10	0	5	62.2	292	70	48	43	5	2	2	2	36	6	37	7	1	2	7	.222	0	0	6.18
1988 Oakland	AL	33	33	1	0	201.2	872	211	86	83	16	3	8	1	91	2	127	16	2	16	7	.696	0	0	3.70
1989 Oakland	AL	31	31	1	0	169.1	733	187	91	82	19	5	7	3	68	1	91	8	1	19	7	.731	0	0	4.36
1990 Kansas City	AL	21	20	0	0	112	498	129	66	59	9	1	3	0	35	1	62	8	1	7	10	.412	0	0	4.74
1991 Kansas City	AL	51	9	1	22	114.1	515	140	69	63	11	6	4	1	46	9	53	1	0	3	9	.250	1	2	4.96
1992 Baltimore	AL	48	2	0	24	89.1	372	79	35	34	5	6	4	2	36	6	53	4	0	7	3	.700	0	4	3.43
1993 Detroit	AL	24	0	0	10	35.1	144	25	12	12	4	1	1	1	15	4	36	1	0	0	2	.000	0	4	3.06
Oakland	AL	19	8	0	2	62.2	284	68	45	43	5	1	2	2	33	2	37	2	0	2	6	.250	0	0	6.18
1994 Detroit	AL	35	0	0	10	48	212	36	23	19	3	3	1	0	34	7	38	10	0	2	4	.333	0	0	3.56
7 Min. YEARS		77	73	16	1	454	79	463	230	173	21	2	1	6	178	2	320	26	2	29	29	.500	3	0	3.43
13 Maj. YEARS		442	239	30	85	1780.2	7623	1792	866	796	136	50	57	20	687	59	1048	81	10	113	96	.541	5	11	4.02

Tommy Davis

Bats: Right **Throws:** Right **Pos:** 3B **Ht:** 6'1" **Wt:** 195 **Born:** 5/21/73 **Age:** 23

					BATTING												BASERUNNING				PERCENTAGES		
Year Team	Lg	G	AB	H	2B	3B	HR	TB	R	RBI	TBB	IBB	SO	HBP	SH	SF	SB	CS	SB%	GDP	Avg	OBP	SLG
1994 Albany	A	61	216	59	10	1	5	86	35	35	18	0	52	2	0	3	2	4	.33	6	.273	.331	.398
1995 Frederick	A	130	496	133	26	3	15	210	62	62	41	7	105	4	1	3	7	1	.88	14	.268	.327	.423
Bowie	AA	9	32	10	3	0	3	22	5	10	1	0	9	1	0	0	0	0	.00	1	.313	.353	.688
2 Min. YEARS		200	744	202	39	4	23	318	102	102	60	7	166	7	1	6	9	5	.64	21	.272	.329	.427

Lorenzo de la Cruz

Bats: Right **Throws:** Right **Pos:** OF **Ht:** 6'1" **Wt:** 199 **Born:** 9/5/71 **Age:** 24

					BATTING												BASERUNNING				PERCENTAGES		
Year Team	Lg	G	AB	H	2B	3B	HR	TB	R	RBI	TBB	IBB	SO	HBP	SH	SF	SB	CS	SB%	GDP	Avg	OBP	SLG
1993 Medicne Hat	R	62	208	62	11	6	11	118	44	43	23	0	59	7	3	2	5	1	.83	2	.298	.383	.567
St. Cathrns	A	6	16	0	0	0	0	0	2	0	3	0	5	0	1	0	0	0	.00	0	.000	.158	.000
1994 Hagerstown	A	125	457	111	20	4	19	196	72	62	30	1	152	6	1	0	12	8	.60	13	.243	.298	.429
1995 Knoxville	AA	140	508	139	20	12	8	207	63	61	36	3	129	15	1	0	11	11	.50	14	.274	.340	.407
3 Min. YEARS		333	1189	312	51	22	38	521	181	166	92	4	345	28	6	2	28	20	.58	29	.262	.330	.438

Rex De La Nuez

Bats: Right **Throws:** Right **Pos:** OF **Ht:** 5'10" **Wt:** 175 **Born:** 1/7/68 **Age:** 28

					BATTING												BASERUNNING				PERCENTAGES		
Year Team	Lg	G	AB	H	2B	3B	HR	TB	R	RBI	TBB	IBB	SO	HBP	SH	SF	SB	CS	SB%	GDP	Avg	OBP	SLG
1989 Elizabethtn	R	55	193	62	11	2	9	104	47	37	37	0	36	2	0	2	6	0	1.00	6	.321	.432	.539
1990 Kenosha	A	72	253	62	16	2	5	97	35	35	42	1	50	6	1	1	20	10	.67	5	.245	.364	.383
1991 Visalia	A	111	406	125	23	2	11	185	78	65	84	5	71	9	1	4	39	10	.80	2	.308	.433	.456
1992 Orlando	AA	132	437	117	34	2	12	191	70	59	69	0	88	12	6	8	13	10	.57	6	.268	.376	.437
1993 Nashville	AA	115	352	83	20	3	8	133	71	43	93	4	80	13	4	6	23	4	.85	7	.236	.407	.378
1994 Sioux Falls	IND	30	119	25	3	0	3	37	18	12	16	0	26	3	1	2	5	1	.83	0	.210	.314	.311
1995 Jacksonvlle	AA	111	331	87	22	1	9	138	47	41	49	3	74	8	8	3	10	6	.63	5	.263	.368	.417
7 Min. YEARS		626	2091	561	129	12	57	885	366	292	390	13	425	53	21	26	116	41	.74	25	.268	.392	.423

Francisco de la Rosa

Pitches: Right **Bats:** Both **Pos:** P **Ht:** 5'11" **Wt:** 185 **Born:** 3/3/66 **Age:** 30

		HOW MUCH HE PITCHED						WHAT HE GAVE UP												THE RESULTS					
Year Team	Lg	G	GS	CG	GF	IP	BFP	H	R	ER	HR	SH	SF	HB	TBB	IBB	SO	WP	Bk	W	L	Pct.	ShO	Sv	ERA
1985 Blue Jays	R	16	0	0	13	31	148	43	24	19	1	2	4	2	5	1	19	0	2	0	1	.000	0	1	5.52
1988 Hagerstown	A	29	1	0	16	41	182	34	21	21	2	1	2	1	29	4	47	0	2	3	4	.429	0	2	4.61
1989 Frederick	A	23	0	0	19	22.2	101	17	9	6	1	0	1	2	11	2	31	0	0	3	4	.429	0	5	2.38
Hagerstown	AA	18	0	0	15	29.2	133	27	15	15	1	3	1	1	20	0	34	0	0	1	1	.500	0	8	4.55
1990 Hagerstown	AA	23	20	2	2	131	531	97	42	30	5	3	4	4	51	0	105	1	1	9	5	.643	0	0	2.06
Rochester	AAA	2	0	0	1	0.2	4	0	0	0	0	0	0	0	1	0	1	0	0	0	0	.000	0	1	0.00
1991 Rochester	AAA	38	4	0	16	84.1	342	71	28	25	6	2	1	0	33	1	61	2	2	4	1	.800	0	3	2.67
1992 Columbus	AAA	48	0	0	18	55.2	230	47	26	23	5	0	0	2	18	1	43	2	0	6	1	.857	0	3	3.72
1993 Columbus	AAA	31	0	0	12	44.2	204	45	34	32	4	4	0	2	31	3	31	4	0	1	1	.500	0	1	6.45
1995 Louisville	AAA	28	19	1	1	115.1	483	104	56	52	15	2	3	2	38	4	66	2	1	2	5	.286	0	0	4.06
1991 Baltimore	AL	2	0	0	1	4	20	6	3	2	0	0	1	0	2	0	1	0	0	0	0	.000	0	0	4.50
8 Min. YEARS		256	44	3	113	556	2358	485	255	223	40	17	16	16	237	16	438	11	8	29	23	.558	0	24	3.61

Juan De La Rosa

Bats: Right **Throws:** Right **Pos:** OF **Ht:** 6'1" **Wt:** 190 **Born:** 12/1/68 **Age:** 27

					BATTING												BASERUNNING				PERCENTAGES		
Year Team	Lg	G	AB	H	2B	3B	HR	TB	R	RBI	TBB	IBB	SO	HBP	SH	SF	SB	CS	SB%	GDP	Avg	OBP	SLG
1986 St. Cathrns	A	6	21	5	0	0	0	5	0	0	0	0	5	0	0	0	0	0	.00	0	.238	.238	.238
Medicne Hat	R	51	182	41	8	2	0	53	19	15	4	0	46	0	1	0	5	3	.63	0	.225	.242	.291
1987 Medicne Hat	R	57	200	58	9	2	1	74	29	24	2	0	38	0	1	3	14	5	.74	3	.290	.293	.370
1988 Myrtle Bch	A	134	477	109	12	5	7	152	54	66	31	0	108	2	4	2	11	4	.73	14	.229	.277	.319
1989 Myrtle Bch	A	132	535	137	28	6	11	210	66	74	19	1	124	2	1	4	19	10	.66	11	.256	.282	.393
1990 Dunedin	A	131	529	136	19	8	10	201	57	76	19	2	98	3	0	7	9	3	.75	14	.257	.283	.380
1991 Knoxville	AA	122	382	82	11	1	4	107	37	33	17	0	95	3	3	2	17	11	.61	9	.215	.252	.280

Year	Team	Lg	G	AB	H	2B	3B	HR	TB	R	RBI	TBB	IBB	SO	HBP	SH	SF	SB	CS	SB%	GDP	Avg	OBP	SLG
1992	Knoxville	AA	136	508	167	32	12	12	259	68	53	15	0	94	8	2	5	16	12	.57	13	.329	.354	.510
1993	Syracuse	AAA	60	198	45	10	2	4	71	17	15	7	0	41	1	4	1	4	4	.50	6	.227	.256	.359
1994	Salt Lake	AAA	89	287	78	15	3	4	111	40	46	17	0	49	2	1	3	0	2	.00	9	.272	.314	.387
1995	Salt Lake	AAA	31	49	11	2	0	0	13	7	5	1	1	6	0	3	1	0	0	.00	2	.224	.235	.265
	Winnipeg	IND	34	134	44	7	1	4	65	27	13	12	0	16	2	0	0	4	3	.57	4	.328	.392	.485
	10 Min. YEARS		983	3502	913	153	42	57	1321	421	420	144	4	720	23	20	28	99	57	.63	89	.261	.292	.377

Maximo de la Rosa

Pitches: Right **Bats:** Right **Pos:** P   **Ht:** 5'11" **Wt:** 170 **Born:** 7/12/71 **Age:** 24

			HOW MUCH HE PITCHED						WHAT HE GAVE UP											THE RESULTS					
Year	Team	Lg	G	GS	CG	GF	IP	BFP	H	R	ER	HR	SH	SF	HB	TBB	IBB	SO	WP	Bk	W	L	Pct.	ShO	Sv	ERA
1993	Burlington	R	14	14	2	0	76.1	319	53	38	32	3	3	2	5	37	2	69	3	2	7	2	.778	1	0	3.77
1994	Columbus	A	14	14	0	0	75.1	310	49	33	28	2	1	1	10	38	0	71	5	2	4	2	.667	0	0	3.35
	Kinston	A	13	13	0	0	69.2	324	82	56	39	7	2	4	4	38	0	53	3	2	0	11	.000	0	0	5.04
1995	Canton-Akrn	AA	1	0	0	0	0.1	3	1	2	2	1	0	0	0	1	0	0	0	0	0	0	.000	0	0	54.00
	Kinston	A	43	0	0	21	61.2	266	46	23	15	0	5	2	4	37	3	61	7	1	5	2	.714	0	8	2.19
	3 Min. YEARS		85	41	2	21	283.1	1222	231	152	116	13	11	9	23	151	5	254	18	7	16	17	.485	1	8	3.68

Mariano De Los Santos

Pitches: Right **Bats:** Right **Pos:** P   **Ht:** 5'10" **Wt:** 200 **Born:** 7/13/70 **Age:** 25

			HOW MUCH HE PITCHED						WHAT HE GAVE UP											THE RESULTS					
Year	Team	Lg	G	GS	CG	GF	IP	BFP	H	R	ER	HR	SH	SF	HB	TBB	IBB	SO	WP	Bk	W	L	Pct.	ShO	Sv	ERA
1989	Pirates	R	13	4	0	6	37.1	172	41	27	24	2	1	5	2	19	0	24	5	0	2	2	.500	0	2	5.79
1991	Pirates	R	9	5	0	3	33.1	127	23	5	5	1	1	1	0	5	0	50	0	2	3	2	.600	0	1	1.35
	Welland	A	8	6	0	0	32.2	156	41	24	20	6	1	1	3	21	0	22	7	0	1	3	.250	0	0	5.51
1992	Augusta	A	52	1	0	28	96	390	75	33	24	2	4	4	6	38	2	103	4	3	7	8	.467	0	12	2.25
1993	Salem	A	18	18	2	0	99	429	90	46	37	8	5	0	5	41	0	80	8	5	9	5	.643	1	0	3.36
	Carolina	AA	8	8	0	0	40	181	49	24	21	1	1	3	4	15	1	34	2	0	1	2	.333	0	0	4.73
1994	Carolina	AA	14	14	1	0	76.1	322	77	34	31	7	3	3	8	24	0	57	2	0	7	2	.778	1	0	3.66
	Buffalo	AAA	9	9	0	0	48.2	208	46	27	26	5	2	2	4	17	0	26	0	0	2	6	.250	0	0	4.81
1995	Calgary	AAA	14	14	0	0	71.2	321	85	57	49	4	4	4	3	22	0	36	2	1	3	6	.333	0	0	6.15
	Carolina	AA	21	0	0	3	27.1	122	28	16	11	5	1	0	2	14	3	20	1	0	1	0	1.000	0	0	3.62
	6 Min. YEARS		166	79	3	40	562.1	2428	555	293	248	41	23	23	37	216	6	452	31	11	36	36	.500	2	15	3.97

Brian Deak

Bats: Right **Throws:** Right **Pos:** C   **Ht:** 6'0" **Wt:** 185 **Born:** 10/25/67 **Age:** 28

			BATTING															BASERUNNING				PERCENTAGES		
Year	Team	Lg	G	AB	H	2B	3B	HR	TB	R	RBI	TBB	IBB	SO	HBP	SH	SF	SB	CS	SB%	GDP	Avg	OBP	SLG
1986	Pulaski	R	62	197	64	15	2	12	119	45	43	49	0	57	3	0	3	12	2	.86	2	.325	.460	.604
1987	Sumter	A	92	252	51	6	0	15	102	50	49	68	2	89	2	0	5	7	1	.88	4	.202	.370	.405
1988	Burlington	A	119	345	85	19	1	20	166	58	59	79	1	130	10	0	4	3	4	.43	4	.246	.397	.481
1989	Durham	A	113	327	77	10	0	21	150	44	64	66	2	111	9	3	2	3	3	.50	6	.235	.376	.459
1990	Durham	A	43	133	25	3	1	3	39	14	16	23	2	41	3	1	0	2	0	1.00	2	.188	.321	.293
	Greenville	AA	66	188	41	13	0	3	63	24	26	43	1	47	4	2	3	2	2	.50	4	.218	.370	.335
1991	Greenville	AA	73	204	41	9	0	10	80	31	41	53	4	51	3	1	5	0	1	.00	4	.201	.366	.392
1992	Richmond	AAA	79	238	62	13	0	9	102	46	36	57	3	59	5	0	2	0	1	.00	4	.261	.411	.429
1993	Calgary	AAA	80	235	58	12	0	11	103	43	41	41	0	65	5	4	2	5	1	.83	5	.247	.367	.438
1994	Las Vegas	AAA	99	298	86	19	1	13	146	42	51	58	0	73	8	1	3	1	1	.50	11	.289	.414	.490
1995	Louisville	AAA	54	162	37	5	0	6	60	19	31	26	0	47	3	1	1	2	0	1.00	3	.228	.344	.370
	10 Min. YEARS		880	2579	627	124	5	123	1130	416	457	563	15	770	55	13	30	37	16	.70	49	.243	.386	.438

Darrell Deak

Bats: Both **Throws:** Right **Pos:** 1B-2B   **Ht:** 6'0" **Wt:** 180 **Born:** 7/5/69 **Age:** 26

			BATTING															BASERUNNING				PERCENTAGES		
Year	Team	Lg	G	AB	H	2B	3B	HR	TB	R	RBI	TBB	IBB	SO	HBP	SH	SF	SB	CS	SB%	GDP	Avg	OBP	SLG
1991	Johnson Cty	R	66	215	65	23	2	9	119	43	34	43	1	44	5	0	4	1	6	.14	2	.302	.423	.553
1992	Springfield	A	126	428	122	28	7	16	212	84	79	65	2	71	7	1	5	12	2	.86	9	.285	.384	.495
1993	Arkansas	AA	121	414	100	22	1	19	181	63	73	58	6	103	10	1	5	4	8	.33	8	.242	.345	.437
1994	Louisville	AAA	133	486	132	23	2	18	213	65	73	50	5	107	4	1	3	1	2	.33	15	.272	.343	.438
1995	Louisville	AAA	106	336	81	21	2	7	127	42	34	53	6	90	5	0	6	2	2	.50	5	.241	.348	.378
	5 Min. YEARS		552	1879	500	117	14	69	852	297	293	269	20	415	31	3	23	20	20	.50	39	.266	.363	.453

Joe DeBerry

Bats: Left **Throws:** Left **Pos:** 1B   **Ht:** 6'2" **Wt:** 195 **Born:** 6/30/70 **Age:** 26

			BATTING															BASERUNNING				PERCENTAGES		
Year	Team	Lg	G	AB	H	2B	3B	HR	TB	R	RBI	TBB	IBB	SO	HBP	SH	SF	SB	CS	SB%	GDP	Avg	OBP	SLG
1991	Billings	R	65	236	62	13	0	10	105	41	47	36	1	46	3	0	1	5	4	.56	4	.263	.366	.445
1992	Cedar Rapds	A	127	455	109	22	4	15	184	58	68	43	1	102	2	0	3	3	3	.50	5	.240	.306	.404
1993	Albany-Colo	AA	125	446	114	19	7	12	183	58	63	24	1	111	3	2	5	3	7	.30	6	.256	.295	.410
1994	Albany-Colo	AA	15	53	15	4	1	0	21	3	3	5	0	11	0	0	0	0	1	.00	2	.283	.345	.396
1995	Columbus	AAA	10	24	7	2	2	0	13	3	4	1	0	6	0	0	0	0	0	.00	1	.292	.320	.542
	Norwich	AA	2	4	0	0	0	0	0	0	0	0	0	2	0	0	0	0	0	.00	0	.000	.000	.000
	Greensboro	A	12	45	18	3	0	5	36	14	11	9	3	6	0	0	0	0	0	.00	1	.400	.500	.800
	Tampa	A	58	196	44	9	3	1	62	16	18	19	3	45	0	0	1	0	1	1.00	3	.224	.292	.316
	5 Min. YEARS		414	1459	369	72	17	43	604	193	214	137	9	329	8	2	10	12	15	.44	22	.253	.318	.414

Rob Deer

Bats: Right **Throws:** Right **Pos:** OF   **Ht:** 6' 3" **Wt:** 225 **Born:** 9/29/60 **Age:** 35

						BATTING													BASERUNNING				PERCENTAGES		
Year	Team	Lg	G	AB	H	2B	3B	HR	TB	R	RBI	TBB	IBB	SO	HBP	SH	SF	SB	CS	SB%	GDP	Avg	OBP	SLG
1984	Phoenix	AAA	133	449	102	21	1	31	218	88	69	96	4	175	2	2	2	9	3	.75	7	.227	.364	.486
1995	Vancouver	AAA	25	80	23	5	1	4	42	16	20	16	2	32	0	0	2	0	0	.00	1	.288	.398	.525
	Las Vegas	AAA	64	223	65	18	3	14	131	38	45	31	4	57	0	0	1	2	2	.50	3	.291	.376	.587
1984	San Francisco	NL	13	24	4	0	0	3	13	5	3	7	0	10	1	0	0	1	1	.50	0	.167	.375	.542
1985	San Francisco	NL	78	162	30	5	1	8	61	22	20	23	0	71	0	0	2	0	1	.00	0	.185	.283	.377
1986	Milwaukee	AL	134	466	108	17	3	33	230	75	86	72	3	179	3	2	3	5	2	.71	4	.232	.336	.494
1987	Milwaukee	AL	134	474	113	15	2	28	216	71	80	86	6	186	5	0	1	12	4	.75	4	.238	.360	.456
1988	Milwaukee	AL	135	492	124	24	0	23	217	71	85	51	4	153	7	0	5	9	5	.64	4	.252	.328	.441
1989	Milwaukee	AL	130	466	98	18	2	26	198	72	65	60	5	158	4	0	2	4	8	.33	8	.210	.305	.425
1990	Milwaukee	AL	134	440	92	15	1	27	190	57	69	64	6	147	4	0	3	2	3	.40	0	.209	.313	.432
1991	Detroit	AL	134	448	80	14	2	25	173	64	64	89	1	175	0	0	2	1	3	.25	3	.179	.314	.386
1992	Detroit	AL	110	393	97	20	1	32	215	66	64	51	1	131	3	0	1	4	2	.67	8	.247	.337	.547
1993	Boston	AL	38	143	28	6	1	7	57	18	16	20	0	49	2	0	0	2	0	1.00	2	.196	.303	.399
	Detroit	AL	90	323	70	11	0	14	123	48	39	38	1	120	3	0	3	3	2	.60	4	.217	.302	.381
	2 Min. YEARS		222	752	190	44	5	49	391	142	134	143	10	264	2	2	5	11	5	.69	11	.253	.371	.520
	10 Maj. YEARS		1130	3831	844	145	13	226	1693	569	591	561	27	1379	32	2	22	43	31	.58	37	.220	.323	.442

Rick DeHart

Pitches: Left **Bats:** Left **Pos:** P   **Ht:** 6'1" **Wt:** 180 **Born:** 3/21/70 **Age:** 26

			HOW MUCH HE PITCHED						WHAT HE GAVE UP												THE RESULTS					
Year	Team	Lg	G	GS	CG	GF	IP	BFP	H	R	ER	HR	SH	SF	HB	TBB	IBB	SO	WP	Bk	W	L	Pct.	ShO	Sv	ERA
1992	Albany	A	38	10	1	15	117	476	91	42	32	11	5	5	4	40	1	133	5	6	9	6	.600	1	3	2.46
1993	San Bernrdo	A	9	9	0	0	53.1	237	56	28	18	4	3	1	0	25	0	44	0	0	4	3	.571	0	0	3.04
	Harrisburg	AA	12	7	0	1	34	163	45	31	29	5	1	2	2	19	0	18	2	0	2	4	.333	0	0	7.68
	W. Palm Bch	A	7	7	1	0	42	175	42	14	14	0	1	1	1	17	0	33	2	0	1	3	.250	1	0	3.00
1994	W. Palm Bch	A	30	20	3	5	136.1	566	132	61	51	12	7	2	3	34	0	88	7	1	9	7	.563	2	0	3.37
1995	Harrisburg	AA	35	12	0	4	93	417	94	62	50	13	4	6	5	39	3	64	4	0	6	7	.462	0	0	4.84
	4 Min. YEARS		131	65	5	25	475.2	2034	460	238	194	45	21	17	15	174	4	380	20	11	31	30	.508	4	3	3.67

Bobby DeJardin

Bats: Both **Throws:** Right **Pos:** 2B   **Ht:** 5'11" **Wt:** 180 **Born:** 1/8/67 **Age:** 29

						BATTING													BASERUNNING				PERCENTAGES		
Year	Team	Lg	G	AB	H	2B	3B	HR	TB	R	RBI	TBB	IBB	SO	HBP	SH	SF	SB	CS	SB%	GDP	Avg	OBP	SLG
1988	Oneonta	A	69	289	85	8	4	1	104	45	27	33	1	47	0	4	3	15	6	.71	1	.294	.363	.360
1989	Pr. William	A	131	475	132	19	1	1	156	66	36	52	2	69	10	15	3	38	11	.78	11	.278	.359	.328
1990	Albany-Colo	AA	103	388	102	21	0	1	126	52	27	43	0	75	10	8	5	13	8	.62	5	.263	.348	.325
1991	Albany-Colo	AA	129	482	142	21	0	2	169	74	53	62	1	55	2	8	1	18	13	.58	9	.295	.377	.351
1992	Columbus	AAA	124	416	99	14	3	3	128	51	42	40	1	80	1	8	6	13	6	.68	13	.238	.302	.308
1993	Columbus	AAA	103	360	99	17	7	5	145	45	37	34	0	45	1	4	3	10	8	.56	8	.275	.337	.403
1994	Columbus	AAA	44	119	21	6	1	0	29	16	10	18	0	17	0	0	2	4	3	.57	1	.176	.281	.244
	Albany-Colo	AA	14	49	10	1	0	0	11	6	4	7	1	8	0	2	0	1	1	.50	1	.204	.304	.224
1995	Rochester	AAA	9	35	11	2	0	0	13	3	3	3	0	3	0	0	2	1	0	1.00	0	.314	.350	.371
	8 Min. YEARS		726	2613	701	109	16	13	881	361	239	292	6	399	24	49	25	113	56	.67	49	.268	.344	.337

Mike DeJean

Pitches: Right **Bats:** Right **Pos:** P   **Ht:** 6'2" **Wt:** 205 **Born:** 9/28/70 **Age:** 25

			HOW MUCH HE PITCHED						WHAT HE GAVE UP												THE RESULTS					
Year	Team	Lg	G	GS	CG	GF	IP	BFP	H	R	ER	HR	SH	SF	HB	TBB	IBB	SO	WP	Bk	W	L	Pct.	ShO	Sv	ERA
1992	Oneonta	A	20	0	0	19	20.2	78	12	3	1	1	0	0	0	3	0	20	0	0	0	0	.000	0	16	0.44
1993	Greensboro	A	20	0	0	18	18	87	22	12	10	1	1	1	0	8	2	16	1	0	2	3	.400	0	9	5.00
1994	Tampa	A	34	0	0	33	34	156	39	15	9	1	1	2	2	13	0	22	2	0	0	2	.000	0	16	2.38
	Albany-Colo	AA	16	0	0	10	24.2	110	22	14	12	1	4	1	2	15	3	13	6	0	0	2	.000	0	4	4.38
1995	Norwich	AA	59	0	0	40	78.1	323	58	29	26	5	2	3	5	34	2	57	4	1	5	5	.500	0	20	2.99
	4 Min. YEARS		149	0	0	120	175.2	754	153	73	58	9	8	7	9	73	7	128	13	1	7	12	.368	0	65	2.97

Javier DeJesus

Pitches: Left **Bats:** Left **Pos:** P   **Ht:** 5'11" **Wt:** 198 **Born:** 8/3/71 **Age:** 24

			HOW MUCH HE PITCHED						WHAT HE GAVE UP												THE RESULTS					
Year	Team	Lg	G	GS	CG	GF	IP	BFP	H	R	ER	HR	SH	SF	HB	TBB	IBB	SO	WP	Bk	W	L	Pct.	ShO	Sv	ERA
1992	Elizabethtn	R	2	0	0	0	2.1	12	3	3	2	0	0	0	0	3	0	3	1	0	0	0	.000	0	0	7.71
1993	Elizabethtn	R	12	12	0	0	78.1	323	55	27	26	9	3	1	3	36	0	79	5	0	9	0	1.000	0	0	2.99
1994	Fort Wayne	A	21	0	0	10	38.2	143	21	4	4	2	1	0	0	13	1	55	3	0	5	2	.714	0	2	0.93
	Nashville	AA	2	0	0	1	2	6	0	0	0	0	0	1	0	0	0	2	0	0	0	0	.000	0	0	0.00
1995	New Britain	AA	4	0	0	2	5.2	26	8	2	1	0	0	1	0	1	0	3	1	0	0	0	.000	0	0	1.59
	Alexandria	IND	1	0	0	0	3	19	8	7	4	0	0	0	0	1	0	3	0	0	0	0	.000	0	0	12.00
	Rio Grande	IND	17	1	0	10	26	110	17	14	10	4	1	2	1	14	0	21	1	0	1	2	.333	0	3	3.46
	4 Min. YEARS		59	14	0	23	156	639	112	57	47	15	5	4	4	68	1	166	11	0	15	4	.789	0	3	2.71

Jose DeJesus

Pitches: Right Bats: Right Pos: P Ht: 6' 5" Wt: 225 Born: 1/6/65 Age: 31

Year Team	Lg	G	GS	CG	GF	IP	BFP	H	R	ER	HR	SH	SF	HB	TBB	IBB	SO	WP	Bk	W	L	Pct.	ShO	Sv	ERA
1985 Fort Myers	A	27	26	3	0	129.2	563	119	70	62	9	1	4	7	59	0	94	4	3	8	10	.444	1	0	4.30
1986 Fort Myers	A	22	22	1	0	110	500	87	64	42	4	3	2	4	82	1	97	8	3	4	9	.308	0	0	3.44
1987 Memphis	AA	25	24	2	0	130.1	589	106	78	65	8	3	7	4	99	0	79	11	2	4	11	.267	0	0	4.49
1988 Memphis	AA	20	20	4	0	116	502	88	56	50	5	3	2	5	70	0	149	9	2	9	9	.500	1	0	3.88
Omaha	AAA	7	7	3	0	49.2	208	44	22	19	1	3	3	2	14	0	57	3	1	2	3	.400	0	0	3.44
1989 Omaha	AAA	31	21	2	7	145.1	638	112	78	61	9	4	6	6	98	1	158	11	2	8	11	.421	0	1	3.78
1990 Scranton-Wb	AAA	10	10	1	0	56	249	41	30	21	2	2	3	2	39	0	45	6	4	1	4	.200	0	0	3.38
1993 Clearwater	A	11	10	1	0	55.1	244	65	32	25	5	1	1	0	19	0	33	2	1	3	6	.333	0	0	4.07
1994 Omaha	AAA	30	2	0	10	58	254	51	29	26	6	4	1	4	37	1	54	3	1	4	4	.500	0	4	4.03
1995 Omaha	AAA	36	6	0	19	61.2	288	56	45	42	10	2	5	2	52	3	49	7	0	3	6	.333	0	10	6.13
1988 Kansas City	AL	2	1	0	0	2.2	19	6	10	8	0	0	0	0	5	1	2	0	0	0	1	.000	0	0	27.00
1989 Kansas City	AL	3	1	0	1	8	37	7	4	4	1	0	0	0	8	0	2	0	0	0	0	.000	0	0	4.50
1990 Philadelphia	NL	22	22	3	0	130	544	97	63	54	10	8	0	2	73	3	87	4	0	7	8	.467	1	0	3.74
1991 Philadelphia	NL	31	29	3	1	181.2	801	147	74	69	7	11	3	4	128	4	118	10	0	10	9	.526	0	1	3.42
1994 Kansas City	AL	5	4	0	0	26.2	112	27	14	14	2	1	0	0	13	0	12	3	0	3	1	.750	0	0	4.73
9 Min. YEARS		219	148	17	36	912	4035	769	504	413	59	26	34	36	569	6	815	64	19	46	73	.387	2	15	4.08
5 Maj. YEARS		63	57	6	2	349	1513	284	165	149	20	20	3	6	227	8	221	17	0	20	19	.513	1	1	3.84

Roland Dela Maza

Pitches: Right Bats: Right Pos: P Ht: 6'2" Wt: 195 Born: 11/11/71 Age: 24

Year Team	Lg	G	GS	CG	GF	IP	BFP	H	R	ER	HR	SH	SF	HB	TBB	IBB	SO	WP	Bk	W	L	Pct.	ShO	Sv	ERA
1993 Watertown	A	15	15	1	0	100	402	90	39	28	8	2	1	3	14	0	81	0	1	10	3	.769	0	0	2.52
1994 Columbus	A	21	21	1	0	112.2	473	102	59	37	13	5	4	6	25	0	97	3	2	13	2	.867	0	0	2.96
1995 Canton-Akrn	AA	7	7	0	0	37.1	162	35	19	17	5	0	0	2	18	0	27	1	0	2	1	.667	0	0	4.10
Kinston	A	26	12	0	5	110.1	445	99	31	29	13	7	0	3	28	3	100	3	0	6	0	1.000	0	1	2.37
3 Min. YEARS		69	55	2	5	360.1	1482	326	148	111	39	14	5	14	85	3	305	7	3	31	6	.838	0	1	2.77

Luis DeLeon

Pitches: Right Bats: Right Pos: P Ht: 6' 1" Wt: 160 Born: 8/19/58 Age: 37

Year Team	Lg	G	GS	CG	GF	IP	BFP	H	R	ER	HR	SH	SF	HB	TBB	IBB	SO	WP	Bk	W	L	Pct.	ShO	Sv	ERA
1984 Las Vegas	AAA	6	4	0	0	20.2	0	24	11	11	2	0	0	1	5	0	11	0	0	1	1	.500	0	0	4.79
1985 Las Vegas	AAA	9	3	0	3	23.1	0	27	14	14	3	0	0	2	8	1	19	0	0	2	1	.667	0	0	5.40
1986 Rochester	AAA	49	0	0	34	75	321	68	31	29	5	3	2	3	32	6	53	2	0	4	8	.333	0	13	3.48
1987 Rochester	AAA	33	2	0	20	47.1	206	41	17	14	3	4	1	3	22	7	47	2	0	3	3	.500	0	5	2.66
1988 Tucson	AAA	48	3	0	37	65.1	287	68	40	38	5	3	3	3	22	8	59	0	3	4	9	.308	0	14	5.23
1989 Calgary	AAA	33	5	0	13	71.2	331	83	50	41	6	2	6	4	36	4	63	2	3	4	4	.500	0	2	5.15
1990 Albuquerque	AAA	1	0	0	0	1.1	9	4	2	2	2	0	0	0	1	1	2	0	0	0	0	.000	0	0	13.50
1995 Iowa	AAA	2	0	0	1	2	12	6	3	3	0	0	0	0	0	0	3	0	1	0	1	.000	0	0	13.50
Orlando	AA	4	0	0	2	9	35	7	2	2	1	2	0	0	2	1	3	0	0	0	1	.000	0	0	2.00
1981 St. Louis	NL	10	0	0	2	15	59	11	4	4	1	1	0	0	3	2	8	0	0	0	1	.000	0	0	2.40
1982 San Diego	NL	61	0	0	41	102	390	77	25	23	10	8	1	1	16	9	60	0	0	9	5	.643	0	15	2.03
1983 San Diego	NL	63	0	0	34	111	442	89	34	33	8	7	9	1	27	7	90	1	0	6	6	.500	0	13	2.68
1984 San Diego	NL	32	0	0	10	42.2	191	44	34	26	12	2	1	4	12	2	44	1	0	2	2	.500	0	0	5.48
1985 San Diego	NL	29	0	0	13	38.2	163	39	18	18	6	3	1	3	10	4	31	1	0	0	3	.000	0	3	4.19
1987 Baltimore	AL	11	0	0	3	20.2	89	19	15	11	1	0	4	2	8	2	13	0	0	0	2	.000	0	1	4.79
1989 Seattle	AL	1	1	0	0	4	18	5	1	1	1	0	0	0	1	0	2	0	0	0	0	.000	0	0	2.25
8 Min. YEARS		185	17	0	110	315.2	1201	328	170	154	27	14	12	16	128	28	260	6	7	18	28	.391	0	34	4.39
7 Maj. YEARS		207	1	0	103	334	1352	284	131	116	39	21	16	12	77	26	248	3	0	17	19	.472	0	32	3.13

Roberto DeLeon

Bats: Right Throws: Right Pos: SS Ht: 5'10" Wt: 175 Born: 3/29/71 Age: 25

				BATTING											BASERUNNING				PERCENTAGES		
Year Team	Lg	G	AB	H	2B	3B	HR	TB	R	RBI	TBB	IBB	SO	HBP	SH	SF	SB	CS	SB%	GDP	Avg	OBP	SLG
1992 Spokane	A	42	119	25	4	1	1	34	10	7	9	0	25	1	2	1	7	4	.64	3	.210	.269	.286
1993 Waterloo	A	118	391	104	20	5	11	167	51	59	19	0	67	3	9	4	6	2	.75	10	.266	.302	.427
1994 Rancho Cuca	A	123	435	110	21	3	7	158	53	74	22	1	64	6	1	11	3	3	.50	8	.253	.291	.363
1995 Memphis	AA	73	236	63	10	0	7	94	24	34	12	0	32	2	1	1	2	2	.50	1	.267	.307	.398
4 Min. YEARS		356	1181	302	55	9	26	453	138	174	62	1	188	12	13	17	18	11	.62	22	.256	.296	.384

Alex Delgado

Bats: Right Throws: Right Pos: C Ht: 6'0" Wt: 160 Born: 1/11/71 Age: 25

				BATTING											BASERUNNING				PERCENTAGES		
Year Team	Lg	G	AB	H	2B	3B	HR	TB	R	RBI	TBB	IBB	SO	HBP	SH	SF	SB	CS	SB%	GDP	Avg	OBP	SLG
1988 R.S./Marinrs	R	34	111	39	10	0	0	49	11	22	6	0	5	1	3	2	2	4	.33	1	.351	.383	.441
1989 Winter Havn	A	78	285	64	7	0	0	71	27	16	17	0	30	1	5	0	7	3	.70	9	.225	.271	.249
1990 New Britain	AA	7	18	1	1	0	0	2	3	0	2	0	5	0	0	0	0	0	.00	1	.056	.150	.111
Winter Havn	A	89	303	68	9	2	1	84	37	25	37	0	37	3	5	3	10	4	.71	7	.224	.312	.277
1991 Lynchburg	A	61	179	38	8	0	0	46	21	17	16	0	19	2	1	1	2	1	.67	6	.212	.283	.257
1992 Winter Havn	A	56	167	35	2	0	2	43	11	12	16	0	11	1	4	1	1	1	.50	6	.210	.281	.257

Year Team	Lg	G	AB	H	2B	3B	HR	TB	R	RBI	TBB	IBB	SO	HBP	SH	SF	SB	CS	SB%	GDP	Avg	OBP	SLG
1993 Ft. Laud	A	63	225	57	9	0	2	72	26	25	9	1	21	5	7	1	2	2	.50	4	.253	.296	.320
New Britain	AA	33	87	16	2	0	1	21	10	9	4	0	11	4	4	2	1	1	.50	5	.184	.247	.241
1994 Red Sox	R	7	24	4	1	0	0	5	3	7	2	1	2	2	0	1	0	0	.00	0	.167	.276	.208
New Britain	AA	40	140	36	3	0	2	45	16	12	4	0	21	2	1	1	1	1	.50	7	.257	.286	.321
1995 Pawtucket	AAA	44	107	27	3	0	5	45	14	12	6	0	12	1	0	0	0	0	.00	4	.252	.298	.421
Trenton	AA	23	72	24	1	0	3	34	13	14	9	0	8	3	1	1	0	0	.00	2	.333	.424	.472
8 Min. YEARS		535	1718	409	56	2	16	517	192	171	128	2	182	25	31	13	26	17	.60	52	.238	.298	.301

Wilson Delgado

Bats: Both **Throws: Right** **Pos: SS** **Ht: 5'11"** **Wt: 165** **Born: 7/15/75** **Age: 20**

		BATTING															BASERUNNING				PERCENTAGES		
Year Team	Lg	G	AB	H	2B	3B	HR	TB	R	RBI	TBB	IBB	SO	HBP	SH	SF	SB	CS	SB%	GDP	Avg	OBP	SLG
1994 Mariners	R	39	149	56	5	4	0	69	30	10	15	0	24	1	0	0	13	5	.72	2	.376	.436	.463
Appleton	A	9	31	6	0	0	0	6	2	0	0	0	8	0	0	0	0	0	.00	2	.194	.194	.194
1995 Port City	AA	13	41	8	4	0	0	12	3	1	6	0	8	0	0	0	0	0	.00	0	.195	.298	.293
Wisconsin	A	19	70	17	3	0	0	20	13	7	3	0	15	0	2	0	3	0	1.00	5	.243	.274	.286
Burlington	A	93	365	113	20	3	5	154	52	37	32	1	57	2	2	1	9	9	.50	7	.310	.368	.422
San Jose	A	1	2	0	0	0	0	0	0	0	0	0	0	0	0	0	0	0	.00	0	.000	.000	.000
2 Min. YEARS		174	658	200	32	7	5	261	101	55	56	1	112	3	4	1	25	14	.64	17	.304	.361	.397

Rafael Delima

Bats: Left **Throws: Left** **Pos: OF** **Ht: 5'11"** **Wt: 175** **Born: 12/21/67** **Age: 28**

		BATTING															BASERUNNING				PERCENTAGES		
Year Team	Lg	G	AB	H	2B	3B	HR	TB	R	RBI	TBB	IBB	SO	HBP	SH	SF	SB	CS	SB%	GDP	Avg	OBP	SLG
1986 Kenosha	A	20	35	1	0	0	0	1	2	0	4	0	11	0	0	0	0	0	.00	0	.029	.128	.029
Elizabethtn	R	49	136	31	7	0	2	44	20	21	30	2	26	0	0	6	1	4	.20	2	.228	.355	.324
1987 Kenosha	A	131	494	135	24	9	9	204	75	67	86	5	77	1	1	2	12	9	.57	14	.273	.381	.413
1988 Orlando	AA	137	500	143	25	3	3	183	66	46	77	3	87	1	5	4	29	15	.66	10	.286	.380	.366
1989 Portland	AAA	127	464	127	19	3	3	161	54	33	37	0	79	2	2	0	18	15	.55	8	.274	.330	.347
1990 Portland	AAA	61	188	38	6	2	1	51	23	19	18	0	18	1	1	3	6	3	.67	4	.202	.271	.271
1991 Orlando	AA	122	394	98	14	4	4	132	45	46	47	1	56	1	3	3	13	7	.65	6	.249	.328	.335
1992 Orlando	AA	19	36	6	1	0	0	7	8	2	8	0	10	0	3	0	1	1	.50	1	.167	.318	.194
1995 Ottawa	AAA	10	27	7	0	0	0	7	4	3	5	0	3	0	1	0	2	0	1.00	2	.259	.375	.259
8 Min. YEARS		676	2274	586	96	21	22	790	297	237	312	11	367	6	16	18	82	54	.60	47	.258	.346	.347

Joe Dellicarri

Bats: Right **Throws: Right** **Pos: 2B** **Ht: 6'1"** **Wt: 178** **Born: 1/16/67** **Age: 29**

		BATTING															BASERUNNING				PERCENTAGES		
Year Team	Lg	G	AB	H	2B	3B	HR	TB	R	RBI	TBB	IBB	SO	HBP	SH	SF	SB	CS	SB%	GDP	Avg	OBP	SLG
1989 Pittsfield	A	7	24	9	1	0	0	10	3	5	4	0	4	0	0	0	1	0	1.00	0	.375	.464	.417
St. Lucie	A	44	107	28	3	0	4	43	17	18	14	0	18	2	4	1	1	3	.25	2	.262	.355	.402
1990 St. Lucie	A	40	126	26	1	2	0	31	16	13	17	0	34	3	0	3	5	2	.71	3	.206	.309	.246
Jackson	AA	49	120	33	7	3	1	49	18	9	15	0	34	1	1	0	1	3	.25	2	.275	.360	.408
1991 Williamsprt	AA	80	215	52	10	2	5	81	30	23	22	0	36	4	5	2	7	2	.78	4	.242	.321	.377
1992 Tidewater	AAA	5	16	4	0	0	1	7	1	1	1	0	3	0	0	0	0	0	.00	0	.250	.294	.438
Binghamton	AA	109	328	82	11	2	2	103	32	29	33	1	52	6	2	1	1	5	.17	6	.250	.329	.314
1993 Norfolk	AAA	7	13	1	0	0	0	1	0	1	2	0	5	0	0	0	1	0	1.00	1	.077	.200	.077
Binghamton	AA	85	252	63	16	1	1	84	37	19	30	2	49	3	6	2	2	1	.67	4	.250	.334	.333
1994 Trenton	AA	116	316	71	16	3	1	96	36	26	34	1	61	2	4	0	8	5	.62	8	.225	.304	.304
1995 Toledo	AAA	4	12	3	0	0	1	6	4	1	1	0	2	2	0	0	1	0	1.00	0	.250	.400	.500
7 Min. YEARS		546	1529	372	65	13	16	511	194	145	173	4	298	23	22	9	28	21	.57	30	.243	.328	.334

Nick Delvecchio

Bats: Left **Throws: Right** **Pos: 1B** **Ht: 6'5"** **Wt: 203** **Born: 1/23/70** **Age: 26**

		BATTING															BASERUNNING				PERCENTAGES		
Year Team	Lg	G	AB	H	2B	3B	HR	TB	R	RBI	TBB	IBB	SO	HBP	SH	SF	SB	CS	SB%	GDP	Avg	OBP	SLG
1992 Oneonta	A	68	241	66	12	1	12	116	43	35	35	3	76	8	1	0	0	1	.00	0	.274	.384	.481
1993 Greensboro	A	137	485	131	30	3	21	230	90	80	80	9	156	23	0	2	4	3	.57	9	.270	.397	.474
1994 Yankees	R	4	13	5	0	0	0	5	1	0	2	0	3	0	0	0	0	0	.00	0	.385	.467	.385
Tampa	A	27	95	27	3	0	7	51	17	18	11	0	20	1	0	1	0	0	.00	0	.284	.361	.537
1995 Norwich	AA	125	430	112	23	4	19	200	66	74	72	8	133	23	0	6	2	1	.67	6	.260	.390	.465
4 Min. YEARS		361	1264	341	68	8	59	602	217	207	200	20	388	55	1	9	6	5	.55	18	.270	.390	.476

Chris Demetral

Bats: Left **Throws: Right** **Pos: 2B** **Ht: 5'11"** **Wt: 175** **Born: 12/8/69** **Age: 26**

		BATTING															BASERUNNING				PERCENTAGES		
Year Team	Lg	G	AB	H	2B	3B	HR	TB	R	RBI	TBB	IBB	SO	HBP	SH	SF	SB	CS	SB%	GDP	Avg	OBP	SLG
1991 Yakima	A	65	226	64	11	0	2	81	43	41	34	2	32	1	6	0	4	3	.57	2	.283	.379	.358
1992 Bakersfield	A	90	306	84	14	1	4	112	38	36	33	7	45	1	4	3	7	8	.47	3	.275	.344	.366
1993 Vero Beach	A	122	437	142	22	3	5	185	63	48	69	2	47	2	6	3	6	6	.50	9	.325	.417	.423
1994 San Antonio	AA	108	368	96	26	3	6	146	44	39	34	5	44	1	11	4	5	2	.71	8	.261	.323	.397
1995 Albuquerque	AAA	87	187	52	7	1	3	70	34	19	24	2	28	0	3	0	1	6	.14	7	.278	.360	.374
5 Min. YEARS		472	1524	438	80	8	20	594	222	183	194	18	196	5	30	8	23	25	.48	29	.287	.368	.390

Drew Denson

Bats: Right **Throws:** Right **Pos:** DH **Ht:** 6' 5" **Wt:** 220 **Born:** 11/16/65 **Age:** 30

Year	Team	Lg	G	AB	H	2B	3B	HR	TB	R	RBI	TBB	IBB	SO	HBP	SH	SF	SB	CS	SB%	GDP	Avg	OBP	SLG
1984	Braves	R	62	239	77	20	3	10	133	43	45	17	0	41	3	0	1	5	2	.71	8	.322	.373	.556
1985	Sumter	A	111	383	115	18	4	14	183	59	74	53	3	76	4	0	4	5	3	.63	16	.300	.387	.478
1986	Durham	A	72	231	54	6	3	4	78	31	23	25	0	46	2	1	0	6	1	.86	10	.234	.314	.338
1987	Greenville	AA	128	447	98	23	1	14	165	54	55	33	1	95	11	1	2	1	2	.33	15	.219	.288	.369
1988	Greenville	AA	140	507	136	26	4	13	209	85	78	44	1	116	14	3	4	11	9	.55	11	.268	.341	.412
1989	Richmond	AAA	138	463	118	32	0	9	177	50	59	42	2	116	12	1	5	0	1	.00	4	.255	.330	.382
1990	Richmond	AAA	90	295	68	4	1	7	95	25	29	26	2	57	9	0	3	0	0	.00	9	.231	.309	.322
1992	Vancouver	AAA	105	340	94	7	3	13	146	43	70	36	3	58	7	0	0	1	0	1.00	12	.276	.358	.429
1993	Nashville	AAA	136	513	144	36	0	24	252	82	103	46	7	98	23	0	8	0	0	.00	22	.281	.361	.491
1994	Nashville	AAA	138	505	133	31	2	30	258	94	103	56	7	74	35	0	7	3	2	.60	13	.263	.371	.511
1995	Indianaplis	AAA	107	357	99	21	0	18	174	59	69	34	5	68	18	0	3	1	0	1.00	10	.277	.367	.487
1989	Atlanta	NL	12	36	9	1	0	0	10	1	5	3	0	9	0	0	0	1	0	1.00	0	.250	.308	.278
1993	Chicago	AL	4	5	1	0	0	0	1	0	0	0	0	2	0	0	0	0	0	.00	0	.200	.200	.200
	11 Min. YEARS		1227	4280	1136	224	21	156	1870	625	708	412	31	845	138	6	37	33	20	.62	130	.265	.346	.437
	2 Maj. YEARS		16	41	10	1	0	0	11	1	5	3	0	11	0	0	0	1	0	1.00	0	.244	.295	.268

Elmer Dessens

Pitches: Right **Bats:** Right **Pos:** P **Ht:** 6'0" **Wt:** 190 **Born:** 1/13/72 **Age:** 24

Year	Team	Lg	G	GS	CG	GF	IP	BFP	H	R	ER	HR	SH	SF	HB	TBB	IBB	SO	WP	Bk	W	L	Pct.	ShO	Sv	ERA
1995	Carolina	AA	27	27	1	0	152	638	170	62	42	10	11	4	3	21	3	68	7	2	15	8	.652	0	0	2.49

Chad Devereux

Pitches: Right **Bats:** Right **Pos:** P **Ht:** 6'2" **Wt:** 185 **Born:** 7/22/70 **Age:** 25

Year	Team	Lg	G	GS	CG	GF	IP	BFP	H	R	ER	HR	SH	SF	HB	TBB	IBB	SO	WP	Bk	W	L	Pct.	ShO	Sv	ERA
1992	Bluefield	R	4	1	0	1	9.1	38	5	5	3	2	1	0	1	3	0	12	1	0	1	1	.000	0	1	2.89
1993	Albany	A	27	1	0	9	62.1	269	69	38	30	6	1	3	1	15	0	48	1	2	3	2	.600	0	4	4.33
1994	Frederick	A	41	0	0	11	69	274	55	26	26	12	4	2	0	20	3	77	4	0	3	5	.375	0	2	3.39
1995	Bowie	AA	12	0	0	3	19	100	24	13	11	2	0	2	0	17	3	27	1	0	1	1	.000	0	0	5.21
	Thunder Bay	IND	18	16	0	1	110.1	468	113	50	50	12	4	3	2	33	5	89	3	0	4	6	.400	0	0	4.08
	4 Min. YEARS		102	18	0	25	270	1149	266	132	120	34	10	10	4	88	11	253	10	2	10	15	.400	0	4	4.00

Alfredo Diaz

Bats: Both **Throws:** Right **Pos:** 3B **Ht:** 5'11" **Wt:** 175 **Born:** 9/10/72 **Age:** 23

Year	Team	Lg	G	AB	H	2B	3B	HR	TB	R	RBI	TBB	IBB	SO	HBP	SH	SF	SB	CS	SB%	GDP	Avg	OBP	SLG
1992	Angels	R	14	37	10	3	0	0	13	6	4	5	0	7	0	2	1	3	1	.75	0	.270	.349	.351
1993	Boise	A	26	75	22	4	1	2	34	13	14	9	0	11	0	3	0	1	3	.25	0	.293	.369	.453
1994	Lk Elsinore	A	110	350	100	29	1	5	146	48	64	35	4	71	4	7	6	4	4	.50	5	.286	.352	.417
1995	Midland	AA	8	25	6	3	0	0	9	3	4	0	0	12	0	2	0	0	0	.00	1	.240	.240	.360
	Lk Elsinore	A	49	149	35	12	2	1	54	25	25	11	0	54	0	3	6	1	1	.50	6	.235	.277	.362
	4 Min. YEARS		207	636	173	51	4	8	256	95	111	60	0	155	4	17	13	9	9	.50	12	.272	.332	.403

Cesar Diaz

Bats: Right **Throws:** Right **Pos:** C **Ht:** 6'3" **Wt:** 185 **Born:** 7/12/74 **Age:** 21

Year	Team	Lg	G	AB	H	2B	3B	HR	TB	R	RBI	TBB	IBB	SO	HBP	SH	SF	SB	CS	SB%	GDP	Avg	OBP	SLG
1991	Kingsport	R	38	125	29	6	0	1	38	11	15	7	0	37	2	1	0	0	4	.00	1	.232	.284	.304
1992	Columbia	A	16	62	12	0	1	0	14	4	6	2	0	21	0	0	0	2	0	1.00	0	.194	.219	.226
	Pittsfield	A	66	226	47	9	4	5	79	32	25	27	2	86	4	0	4	4	1	.80	5	.208	.299	.350
1993	Kingsport	R	55	211	69	12	1	11	116	36	37	15	2	41	6	0	1	0	1	.00	2	.327	.386	.550
	Pittsfield	A	14	48	9	1	0	0	10	6	8	3	0	11	0	0	2	4	0	1.00	2	.188	.226	.208
1994	Columbia	A	66	225	55	13	1	7	91	26	27	21	0	46	5	0	2	3	2	.60	3	.244	.320	.404
1995	St. Lucie	A	102	360	84	17	2	6	123	33	40	19	1	91	2	3	1	0	5	.00	13	.233	.274	.341
	Norfolk	AAA	3	11	2	0	0	0	2	2	0	0	0	2	0	0	0	0	0	.00	0	.182	.182	.182
	Binghamton	AA	13	47	8	2	0	0	10	5	5	6	0	20	0	0	0	0	1	.00	3	.170	.264	.213
	5 Min. YEARS		373	1316	315	60	9	30	483	155	163	100	5	355	19	4	10	13	14	.48	31	.239	.300	.367

Eddy Diaz

Bats: Right **Throws:** Right **Pos:** SS-2B **Ht:** 5'10" **Wt:** 160 **Born:** 9/29/71 **Age:** 24

Year	Team	Lg	G	AB	H	2B	3B	HR	TB	R	RBI	TBB	IBB	SO	HBP	SH	SF	SB	CS	SB%	GDP	Avg	OBP	SLG
1991	Bellingham	A	61	246	68	14	1	3	93	48	23	24	1	33	1	3	2	9	2	.82	6	.276	.341	.378
1992	San Bernrdo	A	114	436	119	15	2	9	165	80	39	38	0	46	6	12	2	33	16	.67	11	.273	.338	.378
1993	Appleton	A	46	189	63	14	2	3	90	28	33	15	2	13	0	0	0	13	9	.59	7	.333	.382	.476
	Jacksonvlle	AA	77	259	65	16	0	6	99	36	26	17	1	31	2	7	4	6	3	.67	5	.251	.298	.382
1994	Jacksonvlle	AA	104	340	84	20	0	8	128	43	42	21	1	23	2	9	3	13	5	.72	8	.247	.292	.376
1995	Tacoma	AAA	11	36	12	2	0	0	14	5	5	4	0	2	0	0	0	0	0	.00	0	.333	.400	.389

Team	Lg	G	AB	H	2B	3B	HR	TB	R	RBI	TBB	IBB	SO	HBP	SH	SF	SB	CS	SB%	GDP	Avg	OBP	SLG
Port City	AA	110	421	110	22	0	16	180	66	47	40	3	39	8	1	4	9	7	.56	9	.261	.334	.428
5 Min. YEARS		523	1927	521	103	5	45	769	306	215	159	8	187	19	32	15	83	42	.66	44	.270	.330	.399

Edgar Diaz

Bats: Right **Throws:** Right **Pos:** SS **Ht:** 6' 0" **Wt:** 160 **Born:** 2/8/64 **Age:** 32

					BATTING												BASERUNNING				PERCENTAGES		
Year Team	Lg	G	AB	H	2B	3B	HR	TB	R	RBI	TBB	IBB	SO	HBP	SH	SF	SB	CS	SB%	GDP	Avg	OBP	SLG
1984 Stockton	A	123	419	108	1	7	0	123	58	35	46	1	54	0	11	1	8	6	.57	7	.258	.330	.294
1985 El Paso	AA	132	501	134	14	4	0	156	90	55	62	0	47	2	4	5	21	7	.75	11	.267	.347	.311
1986 Vancouver	AAA	108	346	109	2	4	0	119	44	43	44	0	27	1	3	5	12	7	.63	8	.315	.389	.344
1987 Denver	AAA	48	162	44	10	2	0	58	24	15	18	0	14	0	1	1	5	4	.56	8	.272	.343	.358
1988 Denver	AAA	79	278	65	7	0	0	72	44	21	40	0	36	1	1	4	8	2	.80	6	.234	.328	.259
1989 El Paso	AAA	23	78	24	0	0	0	24	16	6	15	0	7	0	0	0	3	2	.60	0	.308	.419	.308
Denver	AAA	105	316	68	8	1	1	81	29	22	44	1	29	1	6	3	4	2	.67	9	.215	.310	.256
1992 Nashville	AAA	11	42	8	2	0	0	10	5	3	4	1	3	0	2	0	0	0	.00	0	.190	.261	.238
Chattanooga	AA	129	472	122	11	2	0	137	72	45	71	2	45	3	6	7	7	3	.70	14	.258	.354	.290
1993 Memphis	AA	21	78	22	2	0	0	24	12	5	13	2	7	0	0	0	1	1	.50	2	.282	.385	.308
Omaha	AA	57	154	42	5	2	0	51	21	14	8	0	15	1	4	2	0	0	.00	10	.273	.309	.331
1995 Syracuse	AAA	15	43	13	0	1	0	15	5	2	7	0	6	1	1	0	0	0	.00	0	.302	.412	.349
1986 Milwaukee	AL	5	13	3	0	0	0	3	0	0	1	0	3	0	0	0	0	0	.00	0	.231	.286	.231
1990 Milwaukee	AL	86	218	59	2	2	0	65	27	14	21	0	32	1	5	0	3	2	.60	3	.271	.338	.298
9 Min. YEARS		851	2889	759	62	23	1	870	420	266	372	7	290	10	39	28	69	34	.67	75	.263	.346	.301
2 Maj. YEARS		91	231	62	2	2	0	68	27	14	22	0	35	1	5	0	3	2	.60	3	.268	.335	.294

Lino Diaz

Bats: Right **Throws:** Right **Pos:** 3B **Ht:** 5'11" **Wt:** 182 **Born:** 7/22/70 **Age:** 25

					BATTING												BASERUNNING				PERCENTAGES		
Year Team	Lg	G	AB	H	2B	3B	HR	TB	R	RBI	TBB	IBB	SO	HBP	SH	SF	SB	CS	SB%	GDP	Avg	OBP	SLG
1993 Eugene	A	53	183	46	7	1	1	58	19	23	13	0	25	3	2	4	6	2	.75	2	.251	.305	.317
1994 Rockford	A	127	414	131	23	1	4	168	57	44	32	4	33	14	2	5	11	6	.65	14	.316	.381	.406
1995 Wilmington	A	51	173	52	6	2	2	68	20	23	11	0	9	4	2	0	0	5	.00	2	.301	.356	.393
Wichita	AA	62	226	79	15	3	6	118	40	43	14	0	21	6	0	1	0	3	.00	5	.350	.401	.522
3 Min. YEARS		293	996	308	51	7	13	412	136	133	70	4	88	27	6	10	17	16	.52	23	.309	.367	.414

Ralph Diaz

Pitches: Right **Bats:** Right **Pos:** P **Ht:** 6'1" **Wt:** 175 **Born:** 12/12/69 **Age:** 26

			HOW MUCH HE PITCHED					WHAT HE GAVE UP									THE RESULTS					
Year Team	Lg	G	GS	CG	GF	IP	BFP	H	R	ER	HR	SH	SF	HB	TBB	IBB	SO	WP	Bk	W	L	Pct.	ShO	Sv	ERA
1989 Expos	R	11	8	1	1	54	225	62	27	22	1	1	0	1	9	0	50	3	2	2	8	.200	0	0	3.67
1990 Jamestown	A	24	4	0	14	41.2	174	33	18	14	2	2	0	2	15	2	39	2	0	4	3	.571	0	5	3.02
1991 Rockford	A	38	15	1	18	119.2	507	109	51	43	10	4	5	6	43	0	76	8	6	4	6	.400	1	3	3.23
1992 Indianapolis	AAA	1	1	0	0	4	17	3	2	2	0	0	1	1	3	0	2	0	0	0	0	.000	0	0	4.50
W. Palm Bch	A	24	12	3	5	119.2	460	88	34	29	5	3	4	3	24	0	77	2	1	8	4	.667	2	2	2.18
1993 Harrisburg	AA	31	8	0	7	91	394	86	46	36	4	1	3	5	31	1	62	8	1	5	4	.556	0	1	3.56
1994 Ottawa	AAA	7	5	0	0	28.2	135	41	25	20	5	0	1	0	15	1	14	3	0	0	4	.000	0	0	6.28
Harrisburg	AA	24	22	0	0	136.2	583	126	77	67	16	6	7	4	69	0	98	4	2	9	8	.529	0	0	4.41
1995 Ottawa	AAA	32	2	0	7	48	218	51	38	35	6	2	4	4	25	2	31	4	1	0	3	.000	0	0	6.56
Harrisburg	AA	11	1	0	2	19.1	83	17	13	12	3	2	0	1	9	2	16	1	0	2	2	.500	0	0	5.59
7 Min. YEARS		203	78	5	54	662.2	2796	616	331	280	52	21	25	27	243	8	465	35	13	34	42	.447	3	10	3.80

Mike Difelice

Bats: Right **Throws:** Right **Pos:** C **Ht:** 6'2" **Wt:** 205 **Born:** 5/28/69 **Age:** 27

					BATTING												BASERUNNING				PERCENTAGES		
Year Team	Lg	G	AB	H	2B	3B	HR	TB	R	RBI	TBB	IBB	SO	HBP	SH	SF	SB	CS	SB%	GDP	Avg	OBP	SLG
1991 Hamilton	A	43	157	33	5	0	4	50	10	15	9	0	40	1	0	0	1	5	.17	3	.210	.257	.318
1992 Hamilton	A	18	58	20	3	0	2	29	11	9	4	1	7	1	1	0	2	0	1.00	0	.345	.397	.500
St. Pete	A	17	53	12	3	0	0	15	0	4	3	0	11	0	0	2	0	0	.00	3	.226	.259	.283
1993 Springfield	A	8	20	7	1	0	0	8	5	3	2	0	3	1	0	0	0	1	.00	0	.350	.435	.400
St. Pete	A	30	97	22	2	0	0	24	5	8	11	1	13	1	2	2	1	0	1.00	4	.227	.306	.247
1994 Arkansas	AA	71	200	50	11	2	2	71	19	15	12	0	48	2	1	2	0	0	.00	9	.250	.296	.355
1995 Arkansas	AA	62	176	47	10	1	1	62	14	24	23	0	29	3	2	1	0	2	.00	13	.267	.360	.352
Louisville	AAA	21	63	17	4	0	0	21	8	3	5	0	11	0	0	0	1	0	1.00	4	.270	.324	.333
5 Min. YEARS		270	824	208	39	3	9	280	72	81	69	2	162	9	6	7	5	5	.36	36	.252	.315	.340

Tony Diggs

Bats: Both **Throws:** Right **Pos:** OF **Ht:** 6'0" **Wt:** 175 **Born:** 4/20/67 **Age:** 29

					BATTING												BASERUNNING				PERCENTAGES		
Year Team	Lg	G	AB	H	2B	3B	HR	TB	R	RBI	TBB	IBB	SO	HBP	SH	SF	SB	CS	SB%	GDP	Avg	OBP	SLG
1989 Helena	R	51	148	36	1	1	0	39	24	20	14	0	29	1	5	1	5	3	.63	0	.243	.311	.264
1990 Beloit	A	2	4	0	0	0	0	0	0	0	0	0	0	0	0	0	0	0	.00	0	.000	.000	.000
Helena	R	42	129	33	5	0	0	38	18	13	11	0	19	2	1	2	10	5	.67	1	.256	.319	.295
1991 Beloit	A	124	448	121	9	8	3	155	70	34	65	2	76	3	5	1	52	19	.73	6	.270	.366	.346
1992 El Paso	AA	107	281	61	6	3	0	73	47	20	29	2	48	3	7	3	31	8	.79	6	.217	.294	.260
1993 New Orleans	AAA	11	27	7	3	0	0	10	4	1	3	0	6	0	1	0	4	2	.67	0	.259	.333	.370
El Paso	AA	18	63	9	1	0	1	13	5	3	1	0	14	1	3	0	3	0	1.00	0	.143	.169	.206

Year Team	Lg	G	AB	H	2B	3B	HR	TB	R	RBI	TBB	IBB	SO	HBP	SH	SF	SB	CS	SB%	GDP	Avg	OBP	SLG
Stockton	A	81	285	84	14	3	1	107	48	31	43	2	34	3	1	3	31	11	.74	2	.295	.389	.375
1994 Arkansas	AA	105	288	62	13	4	0	83	33	13	20	4	36	3	4	0	7	6	.54	4	.215	.273	.288
1995 Arkansas	AA	78	235	63	9	8	2	94	33	21	35	5	41	2	2	1	7	6	.54	3	.268	.366	.400
Louisville	AAA	23	36	9	3	0	0	12	4	0	5	1	4	0	0	0	2	1	.67	1	.250	.341	.333
7 Min. YEARS		642	1944	485	64	27	7	624	286	156	226	16	307	18	29	11	152	61	.71	23	.249	.332	.321

Glenn Disarcina

Bats: Left **Throws:** Right **Pos:** DH **Ht:** 6'1" **Wt:** 180 **Born:** 4/29/70 **Age:** 26

				BATTING													BASERUNNING				PERCENTAGES		
Year Team	Lg	G	AB	H	2B	3B	HR	TB	R	RBI	TBB	IBB	SO	HBP	SH	SF	SB	CS	SB%	GDP	Avg	OBP	SLG
1991 Utica	A	56	202	51	9	1	0	62	27	27	22	0	30	0	2	0	11	2	.85	5	.252	.326	.307
1992 South Bend	A	126	467	123	29	6	1	167	60	50	44	4	105	0	3	6	12	5	.71	11	.263	.323	.358
Sarasota	A	1	4	0	0	0	0	0	0	0	0	0	1	0	0	0	0	0	.00	0	.000	.000	.000
1993 Sarasota	A	120	477	135	29	5	4	186	73	47	33	4	77	2	0	6	11	5	.69	7	.283	.328	.390
Birmingham	AA	3	5	2	0	0	0	2	1	1	2	0	2	0	0	1	1	0	1.00	0	.400	.500	.400
1994 Birmingham	AA	118	452	116	26	2	7	167	50	57	25	3	74	3	4	4	10	5	.67	12	.257	.298	.369
1995 White Sox	R	9	36	7	3	1	0	12	6	3	0	0	4	1	0	0	1	0	1.00	3	.194	.216	.333
Birmingham	AA	9	26	7	1	0	0	8	4	2	2	0	3	0	0	0	0	0	.00	0	.269	.321	.308
5 Min. YEARS		442	1669	441	97	15	12	604	221	187	128	11	296	6	9	17	46	17	.73	38	.264	.316	.362

Jamie Dismuke

Bats: Left **Throws:** Right **Pos:** 1B **Ht:** 6'1" **Wt:** 210 **Born:** 10/17/69 **Age:** 26

				BATTING													BASERUNNING				PERCENTAGES		
Year Team	Lg	G	AB	H	2B	3B	HR	TB	R	RBI	TBB	IBB	SO	HBP	SH	SF	SB	CS	SB%	GDP	Avg	OBP	SLG
1989 Reds	R	34	98	18	1	0	1	22	6	5	8	2	19	3	0	0	1	0	.00	0	.184	.266	.224
1990 Reds	R	39	124	44	8	4	7	81	22	28	28	5	8	5	0	2	3	3	.50	4	.355	.484	.653
1991 Cedar Rapds	A	133	492	125	35	1	8	186	56	72	50	3	80	4	2	9	4	2	.67	10	.254	.323	.378
1992 Charlstn-Wv	A	134	415	135	22	0	17	208	77	71	67	5	71	15	3	5	3	4	.43	15	.284	.386	.438
1993 Chattanooga	AA	136	497	152	22	1	20	236	69	91	48	6	60	14	0	4	4	2	.67	10	.306	.380	.475
1994 Indianapolis	AAA	121	391	104	22	0	13	165	51	49	47	6	52	7	2	2	1	0	1.00	13	.266	.353	.422
1995 Indianapolis	AAA	13	36	9	1	0	0	10	6	2	3	1	3	0	0	0	0	0	.00	1	.250	.308	.278
Chattanooga	AA	99	347	99	11	0	20	170	56	69	44	10	45	10	0	1	0	0	.00	11	.285	.381	.490
7 Min. YEARS		709	2460	686	122	6	86	1078	343	387	295	38	338	58	7	23	15	12	.56	64	.279	.366	.438

Colin Dixon

Bats: Right **Throws:** Right **Pos:** 1B **Ht:** 6'5" **Wt:** 215 **Born:** 8/27/68 **Age:** 27

				BATTING													BASERUNNING				PERCENTAGES		
Year Team	Lg	G	AB	H	2B	3B	HR	TB	R	RBI	TBB	IBB	SO	HBP	SH	SF	SB	CS	SB%	GDP	Avg	OBP	SLG
1989 Red Sox	R	24	87	24	2	1	1	31	10	7	8	0	10	3	0	0	0	1	.00	8	.276	.357	.356
Elmira	A	37	128	38	4	2	3	55	21	19	20	0	27	1	2	3	3	0	1.00	1	.297	.388	.430
1990 Winter Havn	A	117	414	102	19	0	1	124	35	39	31	1	64	9	1	3	4	1	.80	4	.246	.311	.300
1991 New Britain	AA	87	274	74	16	1	4	104	29	24	30	0	57	4	5	1	1	4	.20	5	.270	.350	.380
1992 Pawtucket	AAA	1	0	0	0	0	0	0	0	0	0	0	0	0	0	0	0	0	.00	0	.000	.000	.000
New Britain	AA	83	266	56	8	1	1	69	24	26	15	1	62	3	1	1	1	0	1.00	6	.211	.260	.259
1993 New Britain	AA	66	214	45	10	0	3	64	11	22	9	0	47	5	2	1	1	2	.33	1	.210	.258	.299
1994 San Bernrdo	A	126	477	134	31	1	19	224	79	79	39	0	92	16	7	4	4	2	.67	14	.281	.353	.470
1995 New Haven	AA	14	47	9	2	0	0	11	3	7	2	0	7	2	0	0	1	0	1.00	2	.191	.255	.234
Salem	A	57	220	64	13	1	5	94	25	30	13	1	30	5	0	2	0	0	.00	10	.291	.342	.427
7 Min. YEARS		612	2127	546	105	7	37	776	237	249	167	3	396	48	18	15	14	11	.56	55	.257	.323	.365

Steve Dixon

Pitches: Left **Bats:** Left **Pos:** P **Ht:** 6'0" **Wt:** 190 **Born:** 8/3/69 **Age:** 26

		HOW MUCH HE PITCHED						WHAT HE GAVE UP									THE RESULTS					
Year Team	Lg	G	GS	CG	GF	IP	BFP	H	R	ER	HR	SH	SF	HB	TBB	IBB	SO	WP	Bk	W	L	Pct.	ShO	Sv	ERA
1989 Johnson Cty	R	18	3	0	5	43.1	200	50	34	29	1	4	3	2	23	2	29	4	2	1	3	.250	0	0	6.02
1990 Savannah	A	64	0	0	21	83.2	355	59	34	18	1	8	0	4	38	5	92	4	0	7	3	.700	0	8	1.94
1991 St. Pete	A	53	0	0	23	64.1	269	54	32	27	3	7	4	0	24	1	54	2	2	5	4	.556	0	1	3.78
1992 Arkansas	AA	40	0	0	20	49	192	34	11	10	2	3	2	0	15	4	65	2	0	2	1	.667	0	2	1.84
Louisville	AAA	18	0	0	8	19.2	94	20	12	11	0	0	0	1	19	2	16	0	1	1	2	.333	0	2	5.03
1993 Louisville	AAA	57	0	0	41	67.2	292	57	38	37	8	4	2	4	33	7	61	2	0	5	7	.417	0	20	4.92
1994 Louisville	AAA	59	0	0	29	60.2	270	51	25	17	4	1	1	8	30	2	62	3	0	3	2	.600	0	11	2.52
1995 Iowa	AAA	53	0	0	19	41	176	34	13	13	4	0	2	5	19	4	38	2	0	6	3	.667	0	0	2.85
1993 St. Louis	NL	4	0	0	0	2.2	20	7	10	10	1	2	0	0	5	0	2	0	0	0	0	.000	0	0	33.75
1994 St. Louis	NL	2	0	0	0	2.1	18	3	6	6	0	0	1	0	8	0	1	0	0	0	0	.000	0	0	23.14
7 Min. YEARS		362	3	0	166	429.1	1848	359	202	162	23	27	14	24	201	27	417	19	5	30	25	.545	0	44	3.40
2 Maj. YEARS		6	0	0	0	5	38	10	16	16	1	2	1	0	13	0	3	0	0	0	0	.000	0	0	28.80

Robert Dodd

Pitches: Left **Bats:** Left **Pos:** P **Ht:** 6'3" **Wt:** 195 **Born:** 3/14/73 **Age:** 23

		HOW MUCH HE PITCHED						WHAT HE GAVE UP									THE RESULTS					
Year Team	Lg	G	GS	CG	GF	IP	BFP	H	R	ER	HR	SH	SF	HB	TBB	IBB	SO	WP	Bk	W	L	Pct.	ShO	Sv	ERA
1994 Batavia	A	14	7	0	2	52	209	42	16	13	0	2	1	2	14	1	44	4	0	2	4	.333	0	1	2.25
1995 Clearwater	A	26	26	0	0	151	636	144	64	53	4	3	6	1	58	0	110	3	7	8	7	.533	0	0	3.16
Reading	AA	1	0	0	0	1.1	5	0	0	0	0	0	0	0	2	0	0	0	0	0	0	.000	0	0	0.00
2 Min. YEARS		41	33	0	2	204.1	850	186	80	66	4	5	7	3	74	1	154	7	7	10	11	.476	0	1	2.91

Bo Dodson

Bats: Left **Throws:** Left **Pos:** 1B-DH   **Ht:** 6'2" **Wt:** 195 **Born:** 12/7/70 **Age:** 25

								BATTING									BASERUNNING				PERCENTAGES		
Year	Team	Lg	G	AB	H	2B	3B	HR	TB	R	RBI	TBB	IBB	SO	HBP	SH	SF	SB	CS	SB%	GDP	Avg	OBP	SLG
1989	Helena	R	65	216	67	13	1	6	100	38	42	52	2	52	4	1	3	5	1	.83	4	.310	.447	.463
1990	Stockton	A	120	363	99	16	4	6	141	70	46	73	2	103	3	1	1	1	1	.50	3	.273	.398	.388
1991	Stockton	A	88	298	78	13	3	9	124	51	42	66	7	63	4	0	2	4	2	.67	1	.262	.400	.416
1992	El Paso	AA	109	335	83	19	6	4	126	47	46	72	6	81	0	0	1	3	7	.30	7	.248	.380	.376
1993	El Paso	AA	101	330	103	27	4	9	165	58	59	42	4	69	6	0	2	1	6	.14	3	.312	.397	.500
1994	El Paso	AA	26	68	10	3	0	0	13	6	7	12	0	18	1	0	0	0	1	.00	2	.147	.284	.191
	New Orleans	AAA	79	257	67	13	0	2	86	41	29	42	2	44	2	3	1	2	3	.40	8	.261	.368	.335
1995	El Paso	AA	63	223	80	20	4	7	129	46	43	37	2	42	7	0	0	1	1	.50	6	.359	.464	.578
	New Orleans	AAA	62	203	57	5	1	9	91	29	34	36	6	42	0	0	5	0	0	.00	4	.281	.381	.448
	7 Min. YEARS		713	2293	644	129	23	52	975	386	348	432	31	499	27	5	15	17	22	.44	38	.281	.399	.425

Roger Doman

Pitches: Right **Bats:** Right **Pos:** P   **Ht:** 6'5" **Wt:** 185 **Born:** 1/26/73 **Age:** 23

			HOW MUCH HE PITCHED						WHAT HE GAVE UP											THE RESULTS					
Year	Team	Lg	G	GS	CG	GF	IP	BFP	H	R	ER	HR	SH	SF	HB	TBB	IBB	SO	WP	Bk	W	L	Pct.	ShO	Sv	ERA
1991	Blue Jays	R	13	10	0	0	50.1	214	54	29	27	2	0	1	2	17	0	28	9	1	2	2	.500	0	0	4.83
1992	St. Cathrns	A	15	14	0	1	68.2	316	70	47	35	3	3	2	2	47	0	53	12	1	2	7	.222	0	0	4.59
1993	Hagerstown	A	26	26	0	0	146.2	650	153	78	67	11	3	4	6	73	0	102	15	2	8	6	.571	0	0	4.11
1994	Dunedin	A	32	12	0	11	103.1	460	119	72	60	10	2	7	3	40	0	64	12	0	3	9	.250	0	2	5.23
1995	Knoxville	AA	14	0	0	6	30.2	140	42	25	20	2	1	1	1	11	0	16	3	0	0	3	.000	0	0	5.87
	Hagerstown	A	14	6	0	3	51	233	65	32	25	0	0	1	3	13	0	24	4	0	2	2	.500	0	1	4.41
	5 Min. YEARS		114	68	0	21	450.2	2013	503	283	234	28	9	16	17	201	0	287	55	4	17	29	.370	0	3	4.67

Brendan Donnelly

Pitches: Right **Bats:** Right **Pos:** P   **Ht:** 6'3" **Wt:** 200 **Born:** 7/4/71 **Age:** 24

			HOW MUCH HE PITCHED						WHAT HE GAVE UP											THE RESULTS					
Year	Team	Lg	G	GS	CG	GF	IP	BFP	H	R	ER	HR	SH	SF	HB	TBB	IBB	SO	WP	Bk	W	L	Pct.	ShO	Sv	ERA
1992	White Sox	R	9	7	0	1	41.2	191	41	25	17	0	0	2	8	21	0	31	6	0	0	3	.000	0	1	3.67
1993	Geneva	A	21	3	0	7	43	198	39	34	30	4	1	1	6	29	0	29	7	3	4	0	1.000	0	1	6.28
1994	Ohio Valley	IND	10	0	0	1	13.2	59	13	5	4	1	0	0	3	4	0	20	1	0	1	1	.500	0	0	2.63
1995	Charlstn-Wv	A	24	0	0	22	30.1	112	14	4	4	0	1	2	1	7	1	33	1	0	1	1	.500	0	12	1.19
	Winston-Sal	A	23	0	0	14	35.1	138	20	6	4	1	2	0	2	14	2	32	0	1	1	2	.333	0	2	1.02
	Indianapols	AAA	3	0	0	0	2.2	18	7	8	7	2	0	1	1	2	0	1	2	0	1	1	.500	0	0	23.63
	4 Min. YEARS		90	10	0	45	166.2	716	134	82	66	8	4	6	21	77	3	146	17	4	8	8	.500	0	16	3.56

Blake Doolan

Pitches: Right **Bats:** Right **Pos:** P   **Ht:** 6'0" **Wt:** 178 **Born:** 2/11/69 **Age:** 27

			HOW MUCH HE PITCHED						WHAT HE GAVE UP											THE RESULTS					
Year	Team	Lg	G	GS	CG	GF	IP	BFP	H	R	ER	HR	SH	SF	HB	TBB	IBB	SO	WP	Bk	W	L	Pct.	ShO	Sv	ERA
1992	Batavia	A	19	9	3	3	85.1	354	78	33	27	8	5	1	3	25	0	62	6	3	6	2	.750	2	1	2.85
1993	Spartanburg	A	8	8	1	0	58.1	228	50	16	11	2	1	1	0	9	1	34	2	0	2	2	.500	0	0	1.70
	Reading	AA	27	15	1	3	109.2	491	135	70	62	13	0	3	5	36	0	61	3	2	7	8	.467	0	0	5.09
1994	Clearwater	A	9	0	0	9	10.1	35	3	0	0	0	0	0	0	0	0	12	0	0	0	0	.000	0	5	0.00
	Reading	AA	50	0	0	22	67.1	297	70	45	40	5	5	3	3	28	3	42	8	1	3	2	.600	0	5	5.35
1995	Reading	AA	60	0	0	45	73	300	63	22	18	3	3	5	0	27	4	50	4	1	11	5	.688	0	16	2.22
	4 Min. YEARS		173	32	5	82	404	1705	399	186	158	31	14	13	11	125	8	261	23	7	29	19	.604	2	28	3.52

Aaron Dorlarque

Pitches: Right **Bats:** Right **Pos:** P   **Ht:** 6'3" **Wt:** 180 **Born:** 2/16/70 **Age:** 26

			HOW MUCH HE PITCHED						WHAT HE GAVE UP											THE RESULTS					
Year	Team	Lg	G	GS	CG	GF	IP	BFP	H	R	ER	HR	SH	SF	HB	TBB	IBB	SO	WP	Bk	W	L	Pct.	ShO	Sv	ERA
1992	Eugene	A	32	0	0	31	40.1	162	30	12	8	0	1	0	1	10	2	46	2	1	1	2	.333	0	13	1.79
1993	Rockford	A	28	0	0	26	49.1	198	37	12	8	3	3	3	3	12	0	51	4	0	2	3	.400	0	16	1.46
1994	Memphis	AA	50	0	0	33	75	388	88	41	33	5	5	6	2	26	6	51	4	0	7	4	.636	0	14	3.96
1995	Wichita	AA	20	1	0	4	47	179	37	8	6	2	2	0	3	10	4	32	2	0	1	1	.500	0	0	1.15
	Omaha	AAA	24	0	0	13	40.1	166	38	19	19	7	1	3	3	15	1	24	1	0	2	2	.500	0	4	4.24
	4 Min. YEARS		154	2	0	107	252	1041	230	92	74	17	12	12	12	73	13	204	13	1	13	12	.520	0	47	2.64

Brian Dorsett

Bats: Right **Throws:** Right **Pos:** C   **Ht:** 6'4" **Wt:** 222 **Born:** 4/9/61 **Age:** 35

								BATTING									BASERUNNING				PERCENTAGES		
Year	Team	Lg	G	AB	H	2B	3B	HR	TB	R	RBI	TBB	IBB	SO	HBP	SH	SF	SB	CS	SB%	GDP	Avg	OBP	SLG
1983	Medford	R	14	48	13	2	1	1	20	11	10	5	0	5	0	0	0	0	0	.00	1	.271	.340	.417
	Madison	A	58	204	52	7	0	3	68	16	27	17	1	35	0	0	2	2	1	.67	4	.255	.309	.333
1984	Modesto	A	99	375	99	19	0	8	142	39	52	23	1	93	2	0	7	0	1	.00	8	.264	.305	.379
1985	Madison	A	40	161	43	11	0	2	60	15	30	12	1	23	2	1	2	0	2	.00	5	.267	.322	.373
	Huntsville	A	88	313	84	18	3	11	141	38	43	38	1	61	0	3	0	2	0	1.00	11	.268	.348	.450
1986	Tacoma	AAA	117	426	111	33	1	10	176	49	51	26	1	82	0	0	5	0	0	.00	16	.261	.304	.413
1987	Tacoma	AAA	78	282	66	14	1	6	100	31	39	33	3	50	3	1	5	0	0	.00	12	.234	.316	.355

Year	Team	Lg	G	AB	H	2B	3B	HR	TB	R	RBI	TBB	IBB	SO	HBP	SH	SF	SB	CS	SB%	GDP	Avg	OBP	SLG
	Buffalo	AAA	26	86	22	5	1	4	41	9	14	3	1	21	0	0	1	0	0	.00	2	.256	.278	.477
1988	Edmonton	AAA	53	163	43	7	0	11	83	21	32	28	1	29	0	1	2	1	2	.33	3	.264	.368	.509
1989	Columbus	AAA	110	388	97	21	1	17	171	45	62	31	2	87	5	2	5	2	2	.50	10	.250	.310	.441
1990	Columbus	AAA	114	415	113	28	1	14	185	44	67	49	6	71	5	1	3	1	1	.50	12	.272	.354	.446
1991	Las Vegas	AAA	62	215	66	13	1	13	120	36	38	17	0	43	1	0	1	0	0	.00	2	.307	.359	.558
	Buffalo	AAA	29	103	28	6	0	2	40	17	18	8	1	19	1	0	4	0	0	.00	1	.272	.319	.388
1992	Buffalo	AAA	131	492	142	35	0	21	240	69	102	38	4	68	6	2	5	1	0	1.00	5	.289	.344	.488
1993	Indianapols	AAA	77	278	83	27	0	18	164	38	57	28	2	53	3	0	5	2	0	1.00	4	.299	.363	.590
1995	Indianapols	AAA	91	313	82	25	1	16	157	40	58	25	0	47	4	0	8	1	1	.50	11	.262	.317	.502
1987	Cleveland	AL	5	11	3	0	0	1	6	2	3	0	0	3	1	0	0	0	0	.00	0	.273	.333	.545
1988	California	AL	7	11	1	0	0	0	1	0	2	1	0	5	0	0	0	0	0	.00	0	.091	.167	.091
1989	New York	AL	8	22	8	1	0	0	9	3	4	1	0	3	0	0	0	0	0	.00	2	.364	.391	.409
1990	New York	AL	14	35	5	2	0	0	7	2	0	2	0	4	0	0	0	0	0	.00	0	.143	.189	.200
1991	San Diego	NL	11	12	1	0	0	0	1	0	1	0	0	3	0	0	0	0	0	.00	0	.083	.083	.083
1993	Cincinnati	NL	25	63	16	4	0	2	26	7	12	3	0	14	0	0	0	0	0	.00	1	.254	.288	.413
1994	Cincinnati	NL	76	216	53	8	0	5	76	21	26	21	7	33	1	1	2	0	0	.00	10	.245	.313	.352
	12 Min. YEARS		1187	4262	1144	271	11	157	1908	518	700	381	25	787	35	11	55	12	11	.52	113	.268	.330	.448
	7 Maj. YEARS		146	370	87	15	0	8	126	35	48	28	7	65	2	1	2	0	0	.00	13	.235	.291	.341

Bruce Dostal

Bats: Left   **Throws:** Left   **Pos:** OF   **Ht:** 6' 0"   **Wt:** 195   **Born:** 3/10/65   **Age:** 31

					BATTING													BASERUNNING				PERCENTAGES		
Year	Team	Lg	G	AB	H	2B	3B	HR	TB	R	RBI	TBB	IBB	SO	HBP	SH	SF	SB	CS	SB%	GDP	Avg	OBP	SLG
1987	Great Falls	R	62	201	56	6	1	1	67	27	27	23	1	38	1	6	2	14	9	.61	0	.279	.352	.333
1988	Bakersfield	A	122	367	92	14	2	1	113	59	34	58	2	78	5	5	4	32	9	.78	2	.251	.357	.308
1989	Vero Beach	A	118	348	86	10	5	2	112	58	24	43	2	49	3	1	1	41	6	.87	8	.247	.334	.322
1990	Vero Beach	A	58	192	58	9	2	6	89	43	29	24	1	20	2	1	1	31	5	.86	2	.302	.384	.464
	San Antonio	AA	53	127	33	3	4	0	44	16	16	18	2	29	3	4	1	10	8	.56	1	.260	.362	.346
1991	Reading	AA	96	364	114	11	5	5	150	69	34	58	5	55	5	1	4	38	16	.70	5	.313	.411	.412
1992	Reading	AA	33	122	29	3	1	2	40	19	6	17	2	20	0	0	1	9	4	.69	1	.238	.329	.328
	Scranton-Wb	AAA	65	168	37	7	0	1	47	32	7	45	4	35	1	2	0	10	4	.71	1	.220	.388	.280
1993	Scranton-Wb	AAA	6	13	3	0	0	0	3	0	1	2	1	5	0	1	1	1	1	.50	1	.231	.313	.231
	Rochester	AAA	88	297	88	12	5	3	119	46	29	39	3	73	2	3	2	13	7	.65	3	.296	.379	.401
1994	Rochester	AAA	87	230	66	10	2	1	83	47	36	46	0	48	3	4	5	8	3	.73	3	.287	.405	.361
1995	Okla. City	AAA	88	293	62	14	6	4	100	35	31	30	0	49	3	4	1	11	3	.79	7	.212	.291	.341
	9 Min. YEARS		876	2722	724	99	33	26	967	450	274	403	23	499	28	32	23	218	75	.74	34	.266	.364	.355

Dave Doster

Bats: Right   **Throws:** Right   **Pos:** 2B   **Ht:** 5'10"   **Wt:** 185   **Born:** 10/8/70   **Age:** 25

					BATTING													BASERUNNING				PERCENTAGES		
Year	Team	Lg	G	AB	H	2B	3B	HR	TB	R	RBI	TBB	IBB	SO	HBP	SH	SF	SB	CS	SB%	GDP	Avg	OBP	SLG
1993	Spartanburg	A	60	223	61	15	0	3	85	34	20	25	1	36	3	6	1	1	0	1.00	5	.274	.353	.381
	Clearwater	A	9	28	10	3	1	0	15	4	2	2	0	2	0	0	0	0	0	.00	1	.357	.400	.536
1994	Clearwater	A	131	480	135	42	4	13	224	76	74	54	3	71	11	3	8	12	7	.63	12	.281	.362	.467
1995	Reading	AA	139	551	146	39	3	21	254	84	79	51	2	61	7	8	4	11	7	.61	11	.265	.333	.461
	3 Min. YEARS		339	1282	352	99	8	37	578	198	175	132	6	170	21	17	13	24	14	.63	29	.275	.349	.451

Mariano Dotel

Bats: Both   **Throws:** Right   **Pos:** SS   **Ht:** 6'2"   **Wt:** 160   **Born:** 4/3/71   **Age:** 25

					BATTING													BASERUNNING				PERCENTAGES		
Year	Team	Lg	G	AB	H	2B	3B	HR	TB	R	RBI	TBB	IBB	SO	HBP	SH	SF	SB	CS	SB%	GDP	Avg	OBP	SLG
1991	Myrtle Bch	A	125	327	67	7	0	0	74	42	20	43	0	90	2	17	0	7	15	.32	3	.205	.301	.226
1992	Dunedin	A	116	372	71	8	1	1	84	48	19	26	0	99	1	19	1	7	4	.64	4	.191	.245	.226
1993	Hagerstown	A	99	270	56	10	4	0	74	31	16	20	0	91	1	10	3	6	9	.40	3	.207	.262	.274
1994	Rancho Cuca	A	46	86	14	1	0	2	21	11	9	7	0	36	0	4	0	6	0	1.00	1	.163	.226	.244
	Wichita	AA	12	27	4	1	0	0	5	3	2	3	0	4	0	1	0	1	0	1.00	1	.148	.233	.185
1995	Memphis	AA	8	25	7	2	0	0	9	7	5	2	0	10	0	0	0	0	1	.00	0	.280	.333	.360
	Corp. Chrsti	IND	66	206	38	5	2	3	56	26	21	19	0	62	2	12	2	4	7	.36	2	.184	.258	.272
	5 Min. YEARS		472	1313	257	34	7	6	323	168	92	120	0	392	6	63	6	31	36	.46	14	.196	.265	.246

Dee Dowler

Bats: Right   **Throws:** Right   **Pos:** OF   **Ht:** 5'9"   **Wt:** 175   **Born:** 7/23/71   **Age:** 24

					BATTING													BASERUNNING				PERCENTAGES		
Year	Team	Lg	G	AB	H	2B	3B	HR	TB	R	RBI	TBB	IBB	SO	HBP	SH	SF	SB	CS	SB%	GDP	Avg	OBP	SLG
1993	Geneva	A	75	291	79	26	2	5	124	49	38	24	0	54	8	2	2	21	11	.66	3	.271	.342	.426
1994	Daytona	A	126	481	136	17	3	9	186	80	62	36	2	83	6	10	3	15	7	.68	6	.283	.338	.387
1995	Orlando	AA	9	31	7	2	0	0	9	6	1	2	0	5	0	0	0	1	0	1.00	0	.226	.273	.290
	Daytona	A	112	415	104	12	2	3	129	70	59	45	0	51	8	7	4	26	15	.63	11	.251	.333	.311
	3 Min. YEARS		322	1218	326	57	7	17	448	205	160	107	2	193	22	19	9	63	33	.66	20	.268	.336	.368

Brian Drahman

Pitches: Right   **Bats:** Right   **Pos:** P   **Ht:** 6' 3"   **Wt:** 231   **Born:** 11/7/66   **Age:** 29

			HOW MUCH HE PITCHED						WHAT HE GAVE UP										THE RESULTS				
Year	Team	Lg	G	GS	CG	GF	IP	BFP	H	R	ER	HR	SH	SF	HB	TBB	IBB	SO	WP	Bk	W	L	Pct.	ShO	Sv	ERA
1986	Helena	R	18	10	0	5	65.1	0	79	49	43	4	0	0	0	33	1	40	4	0	4	6	.400	0	2	5.92

Year	Team	Lg	G	GS	CG	GF	IP	BFP	H	R	ER	HR	SH	SF	HB	TBB	IBB	SO	WP	Bk	W	L	Pct.	ShO	Sv	ERA
1987	Beloit	A	46	0	0	41	79	318	63	28	19	2	4	2	3	22	3	60	5	1	6	5	.545	0	18	2.16
1988	Stockton	A	44	0	0	40	62.1	266	57	17	14	2	1	0	1	27	3	50	3	0	4	5	.444	0	14	2.02
1989	El Paso	AA	19	0	0	8	31	151	52	31	25	3	3	0	1	11	1	23	3	0	3	4	.429	0	2	7.26
	Stockton	A	12	0	0	10	27.2	112	22	11	10	0	1	0	2	9	0	30	2	0	3	2	.600	0	4	3.25
	Sarasota	A	7	2	0	3	16.2	73	18	9	6	1	1	0	1	5	1	9	1	0	0	1	.000	0	1	3.24
1990	Birmingham	AA	50	1	0	31	90.1	383	90	50	41	6	9	4	3	24	2	72	12	1	6	4	.600	0	17	4.08
1991	Vancouver	AAA	22	0	0	21	24.1	106	21	12	12	2	4	0	0	13	1	17	1	1	2	3	.400	0	12	4.44
1992	Vancouver	AAA	48	0	0	44	58.1	242	44	16	13	5	3	2	0	31	1	34	2	0	2	4	.333	0	30	2.01
1993	Nashville	AAA	54	0	0	50	55.2	249	59	29	18	3	3	4	2	19	8	49	6	0	9	4	.692	0	20	2.91
1994	Edmonton	AAA	45	0	0	35	60.1	261	60	38	32	9	2	2	1	25	0	62	4	0	3	2	.600	0	13	4.77
1995	Charlotte	AAA	21	0	0	15	20	99	28	14	14	1	2	1	0	11	1	17	3	0	2	1	.667	0	4	6.30
	Okla. City	AAA	22	0	0	15	32	145	36	11	11	3	1	1	2	14	3	19	0	0	2	2	.500	0	4	3.09
	Indianapolis	AAA	2	0	0	0	3	12	3	0	0	0	0	0	0	1	0	3	0	0	0	0	.000	0	0	0.00
1991	Chicago	AL	28	0	0	8	30.2	125	21	12	11	4	2	1	0	13	1	18	0	0	3	2	.600	0	0	3.23
1992	Chicago	AL	5	0	0	2	7	29	6	3	2	0	0	0	0	2	0	1	1	0	0	0	.000	0	0	2.57
1993	Chicago	AL	5	0	0	4	5.1	23	7	0	0	0	0	0	0	2	0	3	0	0	0	0	.000	0	1	0.00
1994	Florida	NL	9	0	0	3	13	59	15	9	9	2	1	2	0	6	1	7	2	0	0	0	.000	0	0	6.23
	10 Min. YEARS		410	13	0	318	626	2417	632	315	258	41	34	16	16	245	25	485	46	3	46	43	.517	0	141	3.71
	4 Maj. YEARS		47	0	0	17	56	236	49	24	22	6	3	3	0	23	2	29	3	0	3	2	.600	0	1	3.54

Kirk Dressendorfer

Pitches: Right **Bats:** Right **Pos:** P **Ht:** 5'11" **Wt:** 190 **Born:** 4/8/69 **Age:** 27

			HOW MUCH HE PITCHED						WHAT HE GAVE UP												THE RESULTS					
Year	Team	Lg	G	GS	CG	GF	IP	BFP	H	R	ER	HR	SH	SF	HB	TBB	IBB	SO	WP	Bk	W	L	Pct.	ShO	Sv	ERA
1990	Sou. Oregon	A	7	4	0	0	19.1	78	18	7	5	0	1	1	1	2	0	22	1	0	0	1	.000	0	0	2.33
1991	Tacoma	AAA	8	7	0	0	24	120	31	29	29	4	1	2	1	20	0	19	2	0	1	3	.250	0	0	10.88
1992	Modesto	A	3	3	0	0	13	56	8	7	7	1	0	0	1	6	0	18	1	0	0	2	.000	0	0	4.85
1993	Modesto	A	5	5	0	0	11.1	51	14	5	5	2	0	0	0	5	0	15	0	0	0	0	.000	0	0	3.97
1994	Athletics	R	6	6	0	0	12.1	45	3	1	0	0	0	0	1	4	0	17	0	0	0	1	.000	0	0	0.00
1995	Modesto	A	27	16	0	2	37	171	39	24	19	5	2	2	2	18	0	50	6	0	0	6	.000	0	0	4.62
	Huntsville	AA	9	4	0	1	20	79	13	7	7	1	0	0	2	5	0	18	1	0	0	0	.000	0	0	3.15
1991	Oakland	AL	7	7	0	0	34.2	159	33	28	21	5	2	1	0	21	0	17	3	0	3	3	.500	0	0	5.45
	6 Min. YEARS		65	45	0	3	137	600	126	80	72	13	4	5	8	60	0	159	11	0	1	14	.067	0	0	4.73

Darren Dreyer

Pitches: Right **Bats:** Right **Pos:** P **Ht:** 6'0" **Wt:** 208 **Born:** 5/21/71 **Age:** 25

			HOW MUCH HE PITCHED						WHAT HE GAVE UP												THE RESULTS					
Year	Team	Lg	G	GS	CG	GF	IP	BFP	H	R	ER	HR	SH	SF	HB	TBB	IBB	SO	WP	Bk	W	L	Pct.	ShO	Sv	ERA
1992	Geneva	A	13	13	3	0	81.2	326	87	35	28	4	0	2	4	12	0	87	1	0	7	4	.636	1	0	3.09
1993	Geneva	A	3	3	0	0	19.2	80	22	9	8	1	0	2	1	4	1	10	0	1	2	1	.667	0	0	3.66
	Daytona	A	4	4	1	0	30	113	22	8	6	1	3	2	1	3	0	17	1	0	2	2	.500	1	0	1.80
1994	Orlando	AA	17	7	0	3	43.2	193	52	30	30	6	3	2	2	15	0	30	2	1	1	4	.200	0	0	6.18
	Daytona	A	15	14	3	0	89.1	379	99	51	49	7	0	2	4	18	1	57	5	0	2	9	.182	1	0	4.94
1995	Daytona	A	29	0	0	19	55.2	214	42	18	12	3	1	2	1	9	0	45	0	0	3	5	.375	0	7	1.94
	Orlando	AA	14	0	0	5	23.2	98	24	11	11	1	3	1	3	3	1	10	0	0	1	3	.250	0	0	4.18
	4 Min. YEARS		95	41	7	27	343.2	1403	328	162	144	23	10	13	16	64	3	256	9	2	18	28	.391	3	7	3.77

Steve Dreyer

Pitches: Right **Bats:** Right **Pos:** P **Ht:** 6'3" **Wt:** 188 **Born:** 11/19/69 **Age:** 26

			HOW MUCH HE PITCHED						WHAT HE GAVE UP												THE RESULTS					
Year	Team	Lg	G	GS	CG	GF	IP	BFP	H	R	ER	HR	SH	SF	HB	TBB	IBB	SO	WP	Bk	W	L	Pct.	ShO	Sv	ERA
1990	Butte	R	8	8	0	0	35.2	146	32	21	18	2	0	0	0	10	0	29	1	0	1	1	.500	0	0	4.54
1991	Gastonia	A	25	25	3	0	162	661	137	51	43	5	4	5	4	62	1	122	4	0	7	10	.412	1	0	2.39
1992	Charlotte	A	26	26	4	0	168.2	675	164	54	45	8	10	0	6	37	2	111	4	0	11	7	.611	3	0	2.40
1993	Tulsa	AA	5	5	1	0	31.1	128	26	13	13	4	0	1	0	8	1	27	0	0	2	2	.500	1	0	3.73
	Okla. City	AAA	16	16	1	0	107	445	108	39	36	5	4	3	2	31	1	59	4	0	4	6	.400	0	0	3.03
1994	Okla. City	AAA	4	4	0	0	23	103	26	14	9	2	0	0	0	9	0	16	1	0	0	1	.000	0	0	3.52
1995	Rangers	R	2	2	0	0	9	34	6	1	1	0	0	0	1	2	0	7	0	0	0	1	.000	0	0	1.00
	Tulsa	AA	10	10	1	0	62.1	252	56	22	20	6	2	1	2	19	1	48	4	0	2	4	.333	0	0	2.89
1993	Texas	AL	10	6	0	1	41	186	48	26	26	7	0	1	0	20	1	23	0	0	3	3	.500	0	0	5.71
1994	Texas	AL	5	3	0	0	17.1	80	19	15	11	1	0	1	1	8	0	11	1	0	1	1	.500	0	0	5.71
	6 Min. YEARS		96	96	10	0	599	2444	555	215	185	32	21	10	15	178	6	419	18	0	27	32	.458	5	0	2.78
	2 Maj. YEARS		15	9	0	1	58.1	266	67	41	37	8	0	2	1	28	1	34	1	0	4	4	.500	0	0	5.71

Sean Drinkwater

Bats: Right **Throws:** Right **Pos:** 3B **Ht:** 6'3" **Wt:** 195 **Born:** 6/22/71 **Age:** 25

			BATTING														BASERUNNING				PERCENTAGES		
Year	Team	Lg	G	AB	H	2B	3B	HR	TB	R	RBI	TBB	IBB	SO	HBP	SH	SF	SB	CS	SB%	GDP	Avg	OBP	SLG
1992	Huntington	R	19	44	6	2	0	2	14	14	6	11	0	16	2	0	0	0	0	.00	0	.136	.333	.318
	Spokane	A	66	256	77	12	2	4	105	35	41	25	0	27	0	1	6	7	4	.64	8	.301	.355	.410
1993	Rancho Cuca	A	121	486	131	29	1	10	192	69	84	35	1	78	2	1	12	2	0	1.00	6	.270	.314	.395
1994	Wichita	AA	91	299	71	17	3	5	109	34	39	21	1	40	1	1	6	4	0	1.00	11	.237	.284	.365
	Rancho Cuca	A	28	96	22	6	0	1	31	15	12	10	0	29	1	1	2	1	0	1.00	2	.229	.303	.323
1995	Memphis	AA	102	287	69	12	1	6	101	29	26	26	1	49	1	2	3	3	4	.43	6	.240	.303	.352
	4 Min. YEARS		427	1468	376	78	7	28	552	196	208	128	3	239	7	6	29	17	8	.68	33	.256	.313	.376

Travis Driskill

Pitches: Right **Bats:** Right **Pos:** P **Ht:** 6'0" **Wt:** 185 **Born:** 8/1/71 **Age:** 24

		HOW MUCH HE PITCHED						WHAT HE GAVE UP												THE RESULTS					
Year Team	Lg	G	GS	CG	GF	IP	BFP	H	R	ER	HR	SH	SF	HB	TBB	IBB	SO	WP	Bk	W	L	Pct.	ShO	Sv	ERA
1993 Watertown	A	21	8	0	7	63	276	62	38	29	4	3	6	5	21	0	53	6	0	5	4	.556	0	3	4.14
1994 Columbus	A	62	0	0	59	64.1	267	51	25	18	2	5	2	1	30	4	88	6	0	5	5	.500	0	35	2.52
1995 Canton-Akrn	AA	33	0	0	22	46.1	200	46	24	24	3	1	1	1	19	1	39	0	1	3	4	.429	0	4	4.66
Kinston	A	15	0	0	9	23	90	17	7	7	2	0	3	1	5	1	24	1	0	0	2	.000	0	0	2.74
3 Min. YEARS		131	8	0	97	196.2	833	176	94	78	11	9	12	8	75	6	204	13	1	13	15	.464	0	42	3.57

Michael Drumright

Pitches: Right **Bats:** Left **Pos:** P **Ht:** 6'4" **Wt:** 210 **Born:** 4/19/74 **Age:** 22

		HOW MUCH HE PITCHED						WHAT HE GAVE UP												THE RESULTS					
Year Team	Lg	G	GS	CG	GF	IP	BFP	H	R	ER	HR	SH	SF	HB	TBB	IBB	SO	WP	Bk	W	L	Pct.	ShO	Sv	ERA
1995 Lakeland	A	5	5	0	0	21	87	19	11	10	2	1	0	0	9	0	19	1	2	1	1	.500	0	0	4.29
Jacksonville	AA	5	5	0	0	31.2	137	30	13	13	4	0	0	2	15	0	34	1	5	0	1	.000	0	0	3.69
1 Min. YEARS		10	10	0	0	52.2	224	49	24	23	6	1	0	2	24	0	53	2	7	1	2	.333	0	0	3.93

Brian DuBois

Pitches: Left **Bats:** Left **Pos:** P **Ht:** 5'10" **Wt:** 194 **Born:** 4/18/67 **Age:** 29

		HOW MUCH HE PITCHED						WHAT HE GAVE UP												THE RESULTS					
Year Team	Lg	G	GS	CG	GF	IP	BFP	H	R	ER	HR	SH	SF	HB	TBB	IBB	SO	WP	Bk	W	L	Pct.	ShO	Sv	ERA
1985 Bluefield	R	10	9	2	1	57.2	231	42	23	16	1	3	1	2	20	0	67	5	0	5	4	.556	1	0	2.50
1986 Hagerstown	A	5	5	0	0	20.1	95	29	19	16	1	1	1	1	11	0	17	2	1	1	2	.333	0	0	7.08
Bluefield	R	3	1	0	0	9.1	37	8	2	1	0	0	0	0	2	0	8	1	1	1	1	.500	0	0	0.96
1987 Hagerstown	A	27	25	3	0	155	662	162	81	67	13	7	5	5	73	2	96	5	0	8	9	.471	0	0	3.89
1988 Virginia	A	9	9	0	0	48.2	228	66	42	30	2	1	1	0	20	0	35	2	1	2	5	.286	0	0	5.55
Hagerstown	A	19	19	7	0	135	556	129	71	55	5	4	2	0	30	0	112	6	3	12	4	.750	1	0	3.67
1989 Hagerstown	AA	15	15	6	0	112	440	93	36	31	5	6	1	1	18	0	82	4	0	6	4	.600	2	0	2.49
Rochester	AAA	4	4	0	0	30	121	24	8	6	3	0	0	0	12	0	16	2	0	3	1	.750	0	0	1.80
Toledo	AAA	3	3	0	0	24	93	17	6	6	3	0	1	0	6	0	13	0	0	1	1	.500	0	0	2.25
1990 Toledo	AAA	13	10	2	2	69.2	297	67	27	21	6	2	2	2	26	1	47	2	0	5	4	.556	1	0	2.71
1991 Orioles	R	1	1	0	0	0	0	0	0	0	0	0	0	0	0	0	0	0	0	0	0	.000	0	0	0.00
1993 Frederick	A	10	8	1	0	58	237	50	19	10	2	2	0	0	13	1	55	4	0	6	2	.750	1	0	1.55
Bowie	AA	13	13	0	0	75	316	71	36	21	2	4	5	1	29	0	37	5	0	6	1	.857	0	0	2.52
Rochester	AAA	3	3	0	0	13	62	20	13	13	3	2	0	1	4	0	10	0	0	0	2	.000	0	0	9.00
1994 Rochester	AAA	8	7	0	0	27.1	132	50	24	22	3	0	0	0	6	0	20	1	0	0	4	.000	0	0	7.24
Reading	AA	4	4	1	0	25.1	99	22	8	6	1	3	1	1	2	0	16	0	0	2	1	.667	1	0	2.13
Scranton-Wb	AAA	27	0	0	10	37.1	150	28	10	9	3	0	4	3	11	3	25	1	0	1	0	1.000	0	2	2.17
1995 Scranton-Wb	AAA	49	0	0	19	51.1	230	58	31	26	4	3	2	1	25	5	48	5	0	1	5	.167	0	0	4.56
1989 Detroit	AL	6	5	0	1	36	153	29	14	7	2	0	1	2	17	3	13	0	1	0	4	.000	0	1	1.75
1990 Detroit	AL	12	11	0	0	58.1	255	70	37	33	9	2	4	1	22	1	34	5	1	3	5	.375	0	0	5.09
10 Min. YEARS		223	136	22	32	949	3986	936	456	356	57	38	26	18	308	12	704	45	6	63	50	.558	7	3	3.38
2 Maj. YEARS		18	16	0	1	94.1	408	99	51	40	11	2	5	3	39	4	47	5	2	3	9	.250	0	1	3.82

Steve Duda

Pitches: Right **Bats:** Right **Pos:** P **Ht:** 5'11" **Wt:** 170 **Born:** 6/27/71 **Age:** 25

		HOW MUCH HE PITCHED						WHAT HE GAVE UP												THE RESULTS					
Year Team	Lg	G	GS	CG	GF	IP	BFP	H	R	ER	HR	SH	SF	HB	TBB	IBB	SO	WP	Bk	W	L	Pct.	ShO	Sv	ERA
1993 Helena	R	5	4	0	0	24.1	106	24	15	14	1	1	1	3	8	0	21	2	0	3	1	.750	0	0	5.18
Beloit	A	6	6	0	0	36.1	161	45	18	18	2	0	0	2	11	1	30	2	1	2	1	.667	0	0	4.46
Stockton	A	2	2	0	0	10	44	10	6	5	1	0	0	0	4	0	7	0	0	1	0	1.000	0	0	4.50
1994 Stockton	A	13	9	2	1	57	251	71	34	32	4	5	1	3	17	0	32	2	2	2	6	.250	0	0	5.05
Beloit	A	27	0	0	18	41.2	176	42	17	15	1	5	0	2	13	5	42	4	1	3	3	.500	0	10	3.24
1995 Stockton	A	12	12	2	0	79	343	87	48	38	7	5	2	6	20	0	59	0	3	1	3	.333	1	0	4.33
El Paso	AA	24	4	0	7	44.1	212	58	33	24	2	2	2	5	16	1	29	0	0	1	3	.250	0	1	4.87
3 Min. YEARS		89	37	4	26	292.2	1293	337	171	146	16	18	6	23	89	7	220	10	7	15	20	.429	1	11	4.49

Kyle Duey

Pitches: Right **Bats:** Right **Pos:** P **Ht:** 6'2" **Wt:** 215 **Born:** 11/8/67 **Age:** 28

		HOW MUCH HE PITCHED						WHAT HE GAVE UP												THE RESULTS					
Year Team	Lg	G	GS	CG	GF	IP	BFP	H	R	ER	HR	SH	SF	HB	TBB	IBB	SO	WP	Bk	W	L	Pct.	ShO	Sv	ERA
1990 Medicne Hat	R	15	11	0	1	72.1	325	72	38	31	4	2	2	4	34	0	54	8	0	4	6	.400	0	0	3.86
1991 Myrtle Bch	A	38	1	0	18	82.1	356	77	42	30	4	4	2	2	31	0	84	7	0	6	5	.545	0	5	3.28
Dunedin	A	9	0	0	4	15.2	77	19	10	5	0	3	0	0	12	2	8	2	0	1	3	.250	0	0	2.87
1992 Dunedin	A	48	0	0	21	77	341	84	31	22	4	5	2	1	33	7	51	17	0	7	3	.700	0	7	2.57
1993 Knoxville	AA	37	1	0	15	68	317	92	57	52	7	3	2	0	27	0	40	6	0	2	3	.400	0	0	6.88
Syracuse	AAA	11	0	0	4	20	83	19	10	9	1	0	1	0	7	1	13	3	0	1	2	.667	0	1	4.05
1994 Syracuse	AAA	12	0	0	3	17.2	87	26	17	13	2	1	1	1	6	1	9	0	0	0	0	.000	0	0	6.62
Knoxville	AA	12	2	0	3	33.2	147	37	17	16	4	1	2	2	9	1	15	1	0	1	1	.500	0	0	4.28
Jackson	AA	16	0	0	7	24.2	112	26	9	6	2	4	0	1	12	4	20	2	0	1	3	.250	0	0	2.19
1995 Jackson	AA	7	0	0	6	6.2	32	11	4	4	1	1	0	0	2	0	4	0	0	0	2	.000	0	2	5.40
Amarillo	IND	21	6	1	13	66.2	281	66	35	24	2	4	1	0	24	5	65	6	0	4	6	.600	1	3	3.24
6 Min. YEARS		226	21	1	95	484.2	2158	529	270	212	31	28	13	9	197	21	363	52	0	30	31	.492	1	18	3.94

Mike Dumas

Bats: Right **Throws:** Right **Pos:** OF-2B **Ht:** 5'9" **Wt:** 163 **Born:** 5/28/71 **Age:** 25

Year	Team	Lg	G	AB	H	2B	3B	HR	TB	R	RBI	TBB	IBB	SO	HBP	SH	SF	SB	CS	SB%	GDP	Avg	OBP	SLG
1992	Brewers	R	31	103	32	4	1	0	38	32	13	21	0	9	3	4	2	10	3	.77	1	.311	.434	.369
	Helena	R	14	48	11	3	0	0	14	5	5	2	0	6	0	2	0	5	1	.83	2	.229	.260	.292
1993	Beloit	A	76	174	40	3	0	0	43	28	9	27	0	30	0	2	0	13	11	.54	1	.230	.333	.247
1994	Beloit	A	100	331	102	7	0	0	109	66	36	62	0	59	3	10	1	41	16	.72	4	.308	.421	.329
1995	El Paso	AA	12	23	5	0	1	0	7	5	4	3	0	0	0	0	1	2	1	.67	0	.217	.296	.304
	Stockton	A	74	243	57	7	3	1	73	41	17	27	0	26	1	6	1	21	12	.64	8	.235	.313	.300
	Beloit	A	20	71	18	1	2	0	23	11	4	11	0	11	0	1	0	9	6	.60	0	.254	.354	.324
	4 Min. YEARS		327	993	265	25	7	1	307	188	88	153	0	141	7	25	5	101	50	.67	16	.267	.367	.309

Andres Duncan

Bats: Both **Throws:** Right **Pos:** SS **Ht:** 5'11" **Wt:** 155 **Born:** 11/30/71 **Age:** 24

Year	Team	Lg	G	AB	H	2B	3B	HR	TB	R	RBI	TBB	IBB	SO	HBP	SH	SF	SB	CS	SB%	GDP	Avg	OBP	SLG
1991	Clinton	A	109	347	77	6	5	1	96	49	24	31	1	106	3	8	2	36	8	.82	1	.222	.290	.277
1992	San Jose	A	109	308	71	7	3	1	87	46	32	35	2	76	9	13	4	19	9	.68	8	.231	.323	.282
1993	Shreveport	AA	35	75	11	2	1	1	18	4	9	5	1	25	1	1	1	2	0	1.00	1	.147	.207	.240
	Phoenix	AAA	5	4	2	0	0	0	2	1	0	1	0	0	0	0	0	0	0	.00	1	.500	.600	.500
	San Jose	A	36	111	25	1	2	1	33	17	12	12	0	28	2	2	2	14	3	.82	3	.225	.307	.297
	Fort Myers	A	5	22	8	0	0	1	11	3	1	3	0	6	0	0	0	4	2	.67	0	.364	.440	.500
1994	Nashville	AA	122	397	101	15	0	9	143	50	46	28	1	98	5	7	3	20	8	.71	5	.254	.309	.360
1995	Salt Lake	AAA	12	36	10	2	1	0	14	2	6	4	0	5	1	2	1	2	0	1.00	0	.278	.357	.389
	New Britain	AA	83	230	52	5	2	0	61	28	10	14	1	51	3	2	3	10	5	.67	2	.226	.276	.265
	5 Min. YEARS		516	1530	357	38	14	14	465	200	140	133	8	395	24	35	16	107	35	.75	23	.233	.302	.304

Chip Duncan

Pitches: Right **Bats:** Right **Pos:** P **Ht:** 5'11" **Wt:** 185 **Born:** 6/27/65 **Age:** 31

Year	Team	Lg	G	GS	CG	GF	IP	BFP	H	R	ER	HR	SH	SF	HB	TBB	IBB	SO	WP	Bk	W	L	Pct.	ShO	Sv	ERA
1987	Watertown	A	24	0	0	16	49.2	222	45	20	13	1	5	2	3	22	3	57	4	0	4	2	.667	0	4	2.36
1988	Salem	A	28	28	0	0	156.2	713	168	103	79	18	5	4	5	70	2	102	17	8	8	10	.444	0	4	4.54
1989	Salem	A	26	4	0	10	68.2	305	64	49	39	4	3	8	6	33	1	55	5	4	2	4	.333	0	2	5.11
1990	Salem	A	37	3	2	17	84.2	406	105	61	49	5	4	3	4	48	3	95	9	1	6	4	.600	0	1	5.21
1991	Carolina	AA	6	0	0	6	8	45	17	8	7	1	0	0	1	4	0	9	1	0	0	0	.000	0	1	7.88
	Memphis	AA	22	9	2	5	80.1	342	82	42	40	11	2	1	3	28	0	58	5	1	6	3	.667	1	0	4.48
1992	Memphis	AA	33	2	1	12	73.1	316	72	49	38	7	6	4	2	24	1	51	3	1	0	3	.000	0	3	4.66
1994	Reading	AA	17	11	0	2	77.2	339	79	40	36	9	1	3	4	34	2	62	3	4	4	2	.667	0	0	4.17
1995	Okla. City	AAA	3	0	0	1	5.1	22	6	2	2	0	1	1	0	1	0	3	0	0	0	0	.000	0	0	3.38
	Tulsa	AA	17	1	0	11	36	153	34	12	12	2	1	0	1	17	6	31	4	0	2	1	.667	0	1	3.00
	New Orleans	AAA	14	5	0	5	34.1	161	44	26	24	7	1	2	2	18	2	23	5	1	1	4	.200	0	0	6.29
	8 Min. YEARS		227	63	5	85	674.2	3024	716	412	339	65	29	28	31	299	20	546	56	20	33	33	.500	1	12	4.52

Mike Durant

Bats: Right **Throws:** Right **Pos:** C **Ht:** 6'2" **Wt:** 198 **Born:** 9/14/69 **Age:** 26

Year	Team	Lg	G	AB	H	2B	3B	HR	TB	R	RBI	TBB	IBB	SO	HBP	SH	SF	SB	CS	SB%	GDP	Avg	OBP	SLG
1991	Kenosha	A	66	217	44	10	0	2	60	27	20	25	0	35	3	2	1	20	5	.80	4	.203	.293	.276
1992	Visalia	A	119	418	119	18	2	6	159	61	57	55	0	35	5	3	8	19	15	.56	10	.285	.368	.380
1993	Nashville	AA	123	437	106	23	1	8	155	58	57	44	1	68	6	4	3	16	4	.80	2	.243	.318	.355
1994	Salt Lake	AAA	103	343	102	24	4	4	146	67	51	35	0	47	4	5	0	9	3	.75	7	.297	.369	.426
1995	Salt Lake	AAA	85	295	74	15	3	2	101	40	23	20	0	31	2	3	2	11	7	.61	13	.251	.301	.342
	5 Min. YEARS		496	1710	445	90	10	22	621	253	208	179	1	216	20	17	14	75	34	.69	36	.260	.335	.363

Leon Durham

Bats: Left **Throws:** Left **Pos:** DH **Ht:** 6'2" **Wt:** 210 **Born:** 7/31/57 **Age:** 38

Year	Team	Lg	G	AB	H	2B	3B	HR	TB	R	RBI	TBB	IBB	SO	HBP	SH	SF	SB	CS	SB%	GDP	Avg	OBP	SLG
1976	St. Louis	R	44	156	35	3	5	2	54	25	18	14	-	33	1	0	0	7	0	1.00	-	.224	.292	.346
1977	Gastonia	A	63	239	88	18	3	4	124	45	44	21	-	31	2	0	3	7	2	.78	-	.368	.419	.519
	St. Pete	A	63	209	60	3	6	0	75	26	25	28	-	31	0	1	2	7	4	.64	-	.287	.368	.359
1978	Arkansas	AA	102	367	116	21	5	12	183	72	70	53	-	61	4	0	4	13	8	.62	-	.316	.404	.499
1979	Springfield	AAA	127	449	139	33	4	23	249	84	88	65	-	61	4	0	2	16	4	.80	-	.310	.400	.555
1980	Springfield	AAA	32	128	33	5	5	5	63	20	23	15	-	27	0	0	0	10	3	.77	-	.258	.336	.492
1989	Louisville	AAA	59	178	51	10	0	10	91	31	30	20	-	38	4	0	2	0	0	.00	-	.287	.368	.511
1990	Salinas	A	36	114	26	5	1	8	57	20	26	19	2	25	0	0	1	0	1	.00	1	.228	.336	.500
	Salinas	A	36	114	26	5	1	8	57	20	26	19	-	25	0	0	-	0	1	.00	-	.228	.336	.500
1991	San Luis	AAA	7	23	5	1	0	0	6	2	8	1	-	6	0	0	2	0	0	.00	-	.217	.231	.261
1993	St. Paul	IND	65	226	66	12	1	11	113	44	59	45	5	50	1	0	4	4	2	.67	6	.292	.406	.500
1994	St. Paul	IND	52	166	40	2	0	8	66	27	31	31	3	42	1	0	0	3	1	.75	1	.241	.364	.398
1995	Vancouver	AAA	18	55	15	1	0	2	22	7	10	5	0	11	0	0	0	0	0	.00	1	.273	.333	.400
1980	St. Louis	NL	96	303	82	15	4	8	129	42	42	18	1	55	3	3	5	8	5	.62	3	.271	.309	.426

Year	Team	Lg	G	AB	H	2B	3B	HR	TB	R	RBI	TBB	IBB	SO	HBP	SH	SF	SB	CS	SB%	GDP	Avg	OBP	SLG
1981	Chicago	NL	87	328	95	14	6	10	151	42	35	27	6	53	0	0	0	25	11	.69	6	.290	.344	.460
1982	Chicago	NL	148	539	168	33	7	22	281	84	90	66	14	77	2	0	2	28	14	.67	11	.312	.388	.521
1983	Chicago	NL	100	337	87	18	8	12	157	58	55	66	12	83	3	0	3	12	6	.67	4	.258	.381	.466
1984	Chicago	NL	137	473	132	30	4	23	239	86	96	69	11	86	1	0	5	16	8	.67	8	.279	.369	.505
1985	Chicago	NL	153	542	153	32	2	21	252	58	75	64	24	99	0	0	1	7	6	.54	5	.282	.357	.465
1986	Chicago	NL	141	484	127	18	7	20	219	66	65	67	16	98	1	0	5	8	7	.53	6	.262	.350	.452
1987	Chicago	NL	131	439	120	22	1	27	225	70	63	51	9	92	0	0	2	2	2	.50	6	.273	.348	.513
1988	Chicago	NL	24	73	16	6	1	3	33	10	6	9	2	20	0	0	0	0	1	.00	0	.219	.305	.452
	Cincinnati	NL	21	51	11	3	0	1	17	4	2	5	1	12	0	0	0	0	0	.00	0	.216	.286	.333
1989	St. Louis	NL	29	18	1	1	0	0	2	2	1	2	0	4	1	0	1	0	1	.00	0	.056	.182	.111
	11 Min. YEARS		704	2424	700	119	31	93	1160	423	453	336	10	441	17	1	21	67	26	.72	9	.289	.376	.479
	10 Maj. YEARS		1067	3587	992	192	40	147	1705	522	530	444	96	679	9	3	24	106	61	.63	49	.277	.356	.475

Gabe Duross

Bats: Left **Throws:** Left **Pos:** 1B **Ht:** 6'1" **Wt:** 195 **Born:** 4/6/72 **Age:** 24

						BATTING												BASERUNNING				PERCENTAGES		
Year	Team	Lg	G	AB	H	2B	3B	HR	TB	R	RBI	TBB	IBB	SO	HBP	SH	SF	SB	CS	SB%	GDP	Avg	OBP	SLG
1993	Geneva	A	62	225	61	15	2	6	98	35	41	6	1	16	3	2	0	9	4	.69	3	.271	.299	.436
1994	Peoria	A	119	465	136	27	2	6	185	48	95	13	4	26	5	1	4	3	4	.43	16	.292	.316	.398
1995	Orlando	AA	68	244	64	10	1	3	85	23	40	10	3	20	1	0	2	3	2	.60	12	.262	.292	.348
	Daytona	A	60	224	54	9	0	3	72	20	34	11	2	12	2	0	3	4	4	.50	6	.241	.279	.321
	3 Min. YEARS		309	1158	315	61	5	18	440	126	210	40	10	74	11	3	9	19	14	.58	37	.272	.300	.380

Jermaine Dye

Bats: Right **Throws:** Right **Pos:** OF **Ht:** 6'0" **Wt:** 195 **Born:** 1/28/74 **Age:** 22

						BATTING												BASERUNNING				PERCENTAGES		
Year	Team	Lg	G	AB	H	2B	3B	HR	TB	R	RBI	TBB	IBB	SO	HBP	SH	SF	SB	CS	SB%	GDP	Avg	OBP	SLG
1993	Braves	R	31	124	43	14	0	0	57	17	27	5	0	13	5	0	1	5	0	1.00	5	.347	.393	.460
	Danville	R	25	94	26	6	1	2	40	6	12	8	1	10	0	0	2	4	1	.80	2	.277	.327	.426
1994	Macon	A	135	506	151	41	1	15	239	73	98	33	1	82	8	0	8	19	10	.66	10	.298	.346	.472
1995	Greenville	AA	104	403	115	26	4	15	194	50	71	27	2	74	1	2	4	4	8	.33	9	.285	.329	.481
	3 Min. YEARS		295	1127	335	87	6	32	530	146	208	73	4	179	14	2	15	32	19	.63	26	.297	.343	.470

Tommy Eason

Bats: Right **Throws:** Right **Pos:** C **Ht:** 6'0" **Wt:** 200 **Born:** 7/8/70 **Age:** 25

						BATTING												BASERUNNING				PERCENTAGES		
Year	Team	Lg	G	AB	H	2B	3B	HR	TB	R	RBI	TBB	IBB	SO	HBP	SH	SF	SB	CS	SB%	GDP	Avg	OBP	SLG
1991	Batavia	A	15	51	16	3	0	1	22	8	4	8	0	2	0	0	0	1	1	.50	0	.314	.407	.431
	Spartanburg	A	27	86	24	9	0	1	36	10	10	6	0	7	0	0	0	1	0	1.00	1	.279	.326	.419
1992	Spartanburg	A	73	262	78	20	1	7	121	41	37	24	1	21	2	1	2	2	1	.67	9	.298	.359	.462
1994	Clearwater	A	50	193	59	14	1	1	78	26	23	13	0	16	0	0	3	1	3	.25	3	.306	.344	.404
	Reading	AA	41	143	42	9	0	6	69	25	21	11	0	21	1	0	0	1	1	.50	8	.294	.348	.483
1995	Reading	AA	96	333	85	18	3	14	151	43	50	18	1	61	1	1	7	2	2	.50	3	.255	.291	.453
	4 Min. YEARS		302	1068	304	73	5	30	477	153	145	80	2	128	4	8	10	8	8	.50	24	.285	.334	.447

Angel Echevarria

Bats: Right **Throws:** Right **Pos:** OF **Ht:** 6'4" **Wt:** 215 **Born:** 5/25/71 **Age:** 25

						BATTING												BASERUNNING				PERCENTAGES		
Year	Team	Lg	G	AB	H	2B	3B	HR	TB	R	RBI	TBB	IBB	SO	HBP	SH	SF	SB	CS	SB%	GDP	Avg	OBP	SLG
1992	Bend	A	57	205	46	4	1	5	67	24	30	19	1	54	2	0	0	8	1	.89	5	.224	.296	.327
1993	Central Val	A	104	358	97	16	2	6	135	45	52	44	0	74	5	5	3	6	5	.55	7	.271	.356	.377
1994	Central Val	A	50	192	58	8	1	6	86	28	35	9	0	25	4	0	3	2	2	.50	6	.302	.341	.448
	New Haven	AA	58	205	52	6	0	8	82	25	32	15	1	46	2	0	2	2	4	.33	8	.254	.308	.400
1995	New Haven	AA	124	453	136	30	1	21	231	78	100	56	3	93	8	0	7	8	3	.73	8	.300	.382	.510
	4 Min. YEARS		393	1413	389	64	5	46	601	200	249	143	5	292	21	5	15	26	15	.63	34	.275	.347	.425

Tim Edge

Bats: Right **Throws:** Right **Pos:** C **Ht:** 6'0" **Wt:** 210 **Born:** 10/26/68 **Age:** 27

						BATTING												BASERUNNING				PERCENTAGES		
Year	Team	Lg	G	AB	H	2B	3B	HR	TB	R	RBI	TBB	IBB	SO	HBP	SH	SF	SB	CS	SB%	GDP	Avg	OBP	SLG
1990	Welland	A	63	149	32	5	0	1	40	6	12	19	1	27	2	0	1	4	3	.57	1	.215	.310	.268
1991	Salem	A	96	298	67	16	2	6	105	36	30	44	1	67	5	5	0	4	2	.67	7	.225	.334	.352
1992	Carolina	AA	4	9	1	0	0	0	1	1	0	2	1	5	0	0	0	0	0	.00	0	.111	.273	.111
	Salem	A	68	216	39	5	1	6	64	18	26	21	0	55	5	0	1	3	2	.60	3	.181	.267	.296
1993	Buffalo	AAA	1	2	0	0	0	0	0	0	0	0	0	0	0	0	0	0	0	.00	0	.000	.000	.000
	Carolina	AA	46	160	35	8	0	3	52	12	16	11	0	41	1	2	0	1	2	.33	5	.219	.273	.325
1994	Augusta	A	11	29	9	3	0	0	12	2	4	3	0	5	0	0	0	0	0	.00	0	.310	.375	.414
	Carolina	AA	6	20	3	1	0	0	4	1	2	1	0	9	0	0	0	0	0	.00	0	.150	.190	.200
	Buffalo	AAA	8	18	4	2	0	0	6	0	0	1	0	4	0	0	0	0	0	.00	0	.222	.263	.333
1995	Carolina	AA	45	126	27	5	0	4	44	15	19	10	0	33	0	0	1	0	0	.00	4	.214	.270	.349
	6 Min. YEARS		348	1027	217	45	3	20	328	91	109	112	3	246	13	7	3	12	9	.57	20	.211	.296	.319

Brian Edmondson

Pitches: Right Bats: Right Pos: P   Ht: 6'2" Wt: 165 Born: 1/29/73 Age: 23

		HOW MUCH HE PITCHED						WHAT HE GAVE UP										THE RESULTS					
Year	Team	Lg	G	GS	CG	GF	IP	BFP	H	R	ER	HR	SH	SF	HB	TBB	IBB	SO	WP	Bk	W	L	Pct.	ShO	Sv	ERA
1991	Bristol	R	12	12	1	0	69	289	72	38	35	7	1	2	3	23	1	42	5	2	4	4	.500	0	0	4.57
1992	Fayettevlle	A	28	27	3	0	155.1	665	145	69	58	10	5	3	6	67	0	125	6	2	10	6	.625	1	0	3.36
1993	Lakeland	A	19	19	1	0	114.1	483	115	44	38	6	1	0	3	43	0	64	7	0	8	5	.615	0	0	2.99
	London	AA	5	5	1	0	23	109	30	23	16	2	1	0	0	13	0	17	1	0	0	4	.000	0	0	6.26
1994	Trenton	AA	26	26	2	0	162	703	171	89	82	12	2	6	6	61	1	90	11	2	11	9	.550	0	0	4.56
1995	Binghamton	AA	23	22	2	0	134.1	601	150	82	71	17	5	5	6	59	2	69	7	0	7	11	.389	1	0	4.76
	5 Min. YEARS		113	111	10	0	658	2850	683	345	300	54	15	16	24	266	4	407	37	6	40	39	.506	2	0	4.10

Geoff Edsell

Pitches: Right Bats: Right Pos: P   Ht: 6'2" Wt: 195 Born: 12/12/71 Age: 24

		HOW MUCH HE PITCHED						WHAT HE GAVE UP										THE RESULTS					
Year	Team	Lg	G	GS	CG	GF	IP	BFP	H	R	ER	HR	SH	SF	HB	TBB	IBB	SO	WP	Bk	W	L	Pct.	ShO	Sv	ERA
1993	Boise	A	13	13	1	0	64	296	64	52	49	10	1	5	3	40	0	63	6	3	4	3	.571	0	0	6.89
1994	Cedar Rapds	A	17	17	4	0	125.1	538	109	54	42	10	5	0	6	65	1	84	10	4	11	5	.688	1	0	3.02
	Lk Elsinore	A	9	7	0	1	40	174	38	21	18	3	0	0	2	24	1	26	3	2	2	2	.500	0	0	4.05
1995	Lk Elsinore	A	23	22	1	0	139.2	600	127	81	57	11	7	3	7	67	0	134	6	1	8	12	.400	1	0	3.67
	Midland	AA	5	5	1	0	32	140	39	26	21	5	1	2	0	16	0	19	5	0	2	3	.400	0	0	5.91
	3 Min. YEARS		67	64	7	1	401	1748	377	234	187	39	14	10	18	212	2	326	30	10	27	25	.519	2	0	4.20

Mike Edwards

Bats: Right Throws: Right Pos: 3B   Ht: 6'1" Wt: 205 Born: 3/9/70 Age: 26

			BATTING														BASERUNNING				PERCENTAGES		
Year	Team	Lg	G	AB	H	2B	3B	HR	TB	R	RBI	TBB	IBB	SO	HBP	SH	SF	SB	CS	SB%	GDP	Avg	OBP	SLG
1991	Butte	R	66	217	68	11	1	10	111	56	42	38	1	45	2	1	3	9	4	.69	3	.313	.415	.512
1992	Gastonia	A	109	375	90	10	0	11	133	39	48	43	0	72	1	1	3	7	11	.39	9	.240	.318	.355
1993	Charlotte	A	130	458	128	26	2	12	194	73	79	82	2	70	4	1	3	11	6	.65	14	.279	.391	.424
1994	Tulsa	AA	104	342	89	16	5	6	133	39	37	43	2	56	10	3	3	2	5	.29	15	.260	.357	.389
1995	Tulsa	AA	38	111	24	3	1	3	38	11	13	15	0	13	2	1	1	0	0	.00	5	.216	.318	.342
	5 Min. YEARS		447	1503	399	66	9	42	609	218	219	221	5	256	19	7	13	29	26	.53	46	.265	.364	.405

Wayne Edwards

Pitches: Left Bats: Left Pos: P   Ht: 6'5" Wt: 185 Born: 3/7/64 Age: 32

		HOW MUCH HE PITCHED						WHAT HE GAVE UP										THE RESULTS					
Year	Team	Lg	G	GS	CG	GF	IP	BFP	H	R	ER	HR	SH	SF	HB	TBB	IBB	SO	WP	Bk	W	L	Pct.	ShO	Sv	ERA
1985	White Sox	R	11	11	3	0	68.2	274	52	26	19	0	1	1	3	18	0	61	2	0	7	3	.700	0	0	2.49
1986	Peninsula	A	24	21	0	2	128.1	574	149	80	60	10	6	2	2	68	1	86	8	2	8	8	.500	0	0	4.21
1987	Daytona Bch	A	29	28	15	0	199.2	862	211	91	80	4	5	6	9	68	3	121	17	0	16	8	.667	2	0	3.61
1988	Birmingham	AA	27	27	6	0	167	762	176	108	91	9	5	10	5	92	3	136	16	7	9	12	.429	1	0	4.90
	Vancouver	AAA	2	0	0	1	3	9	0	0	0	0	0	0	0	0	0	2	0	0	0	0	.000	0	0	0.00
1989	Birmingham	AA	24	19	5	1	158	660	131	69	56	6	4	1	5	65	1	122	6	4	10	4	.714	0	1	3.19
1991	Vancouver	AAA	14	12	0	1	64.2	304	73	50	45	4	3	2	5	37	0	35	4	0	3	9	.250	0	0	6.26
1992	Syracuse	AAA	41	12	0	10	130.2	583	127	71	65	13	6	3	4	76	3	108	22	0	4	6	.400	0	3	4.48
1994	Toledo	AAA	12	0	0	4	19.2	95	17	17	12	2	1	0	1	19	0	16	1	1	0	1	.000	0	0	5.49
1995	Albuquerque	AAA	14	0	0	3	16	82	17	16	9	1	2	1	0	17	3	12	2	0	1	2	.333	0	1	5.06
	Bakersfield	A	21	21	1	0	128.2	557	125	63	48	7	2	2	10	56	0	83	10	0	9	8	.529	0	0	3.36
1989	Chicago	AL	7	0	0	2	7.1	30	7	3	3	1	0	1	0	3	0	9	0	0	0	0	.000	0	0	3.68
1990	Chicago	AL	42	5	0	3	95	396	81	39	34	6	4	2	3	41	2	63	1	0	5	3	.625	0	2	3.22
1991	Chicago	AL	13	0	0	3	23.1	106	22	14	10	2	2	2	0	17	3	12	2	0	0	2	.000	0	0	3.86
	9 Min. YEARS		219	151	30	22	1084.1	4762	1078	591	485	56	35	28	44	516	14	782	88	14	67	61	.523	3	5	4.03
	3 Maj. YEARS		62	5	0	13	125.2	532	110	56	47	9	6	5	3	61	5	84	3	0	5	5	.500	0	2	3.37

Kurt Ehmann

Bats: Right Throws: Right Pos: SS   Ht: 6'1" Wt: 185 Born: 8/18/70 Age: 25

			BATTING														BASERUNNING				PERCENTAGES		
Year	Team	Lg	G	AB	H	2B	3B	HR	TB	R	RBI	TBB	IBB	SO	HBP	SH	SF	SB	CS	SB%	GDP	Avg	OBP	SLG
1992	Everett	A	64	215	57	9	0	2	72	25	20	31	0	51	4	4	0	6	3	.67	1	.265	.368	.335
1993	San Jose	A	123	439	115	20	1	5	152	81	57	75	2	69	11	3	4	12	9	.57	4	.262	.380	.346
1994	Shreveport	AA	124	426	104	20	0	1	127	46	40	27	1	85	11	13	6	9	3	.75	5	.244	.302	.298
1995	Phoenix	AAA	67	216	58	5	2	0	67	21	7	24	1	41	3	4	4	8	3	.73	1	.269	.344	.310
	Shreveport	AA	38	130	30	5	0	1	38	24	17	22	1	15	5	4	2	1	2	.33	5	.231	.358	.292
	4 Min. YEARS		416	1426	364	59	3	9	456	197	141	179	5	261	34	28	16	36	20	.64	16	.255	.349	.320

Paul Ellis

Bats: Left Throws: Right Pos: C   Ht: 6'1" Wt: 205 Born: 11/28/68 Age: 27

			BATTING														BASERUNNING				PERCENTAGES		
Year	Team	Lg	G	AB	H	2B	3B	HR	TB	R	RBI	TBB	IBB	SO	HBP	SH	SF	SB	CS	SB%	GDP	Avg	OBP	SLG
1990	Hamilton	A	15	58	18	4	0	3	31	8	18	6	3	13	0	0	2	0	0	.00	1	.310	.364	.534
	Springfield	A	50	183	43	5	0	5	63	18	25	26	1	34	2	0	0	0	1	.00	2	.235	.336	.344
1991	St. Pete	A	119	402	82	11	0	6	111	26	42	52	1	35	6	0	4	0	0	.00	8	.204	.302	.276
1992	St. Pete	A	84	308	67	17	0	2	90	22	29	26	1	22	3	0	4	0	1	.00	4	.218	.282	.292

Year Team	Lg	G	AB	H	2B	3B	HR	TB	R	RBI	TBB	IBB	SO	HBP	SH	SF	SB	CS	SB%	GDP	Avg	OBP	SLG
Arkansas	AA	25	79	18	2	0	2	26	9	8	13	2	14	1	0	1	0	1	.00	0	.228	.340	.329
1993 Arkansas	AA	24	78	26	3	0	1	32	5	11	16	0	2	3	0	0	0	2	.00	1	.333	.464	.410
Louisville	AAA	50	125	25	6	0	0	31	12	8	13	2	16	1	0	1	0	0	.00	3	.200	.279	.248
1994 Arkansas	AA	102	281	65	9	0	6	92	28	39	35	4	34	0	6	2	0	0	.00	11	.231	.314	.327
1995 Arkansas	AA	78	229	52	6	0	2	64	17	25	49	4	18	4	4	1	0	1	.00	9	.227	.371	.279
6 Min. YEARS		547	1743	396	63	0	27	540	145	205	236	18	188	20	10	15	0	6	.00	39	.227	.324	.310

Robert Ellis

Pitches: Right Bats: Right Pos: P   **Ht: 6'5" Wt: 220 Born: 12/15/70 Age: 25**

Year Team	Lg	G	GS	CG	GF	IP	BFP	H	R	ER	HR	SH	SF	HB	TBB	IBB	SO	WP	Bk	W	L	Pct.	ShO	Sv	ERA
1991 Utica	A	15	15	1	0	87.2	407	87	66	45	4	6	5	6	61	0	66	13	0	3	9	.250	1	0	4.62
1992 White Sox	R	1	1	0	0	5	24	10	6	6	0	0	0	0	1	0	4	0	0	1	0	1.000	0	0	10.80
South Bend	A	18	18	1	0	123	481	90	46	32	3	4	2	4	35	0	97	7	2	6	5	.545	1	0	2.34
1993 Sarasota	A	15	15	8	0	104	414	81	37	29	3	4	3	3	31	1	79	6	1	7	8	.467	2	0	2.51
Birmingham	AA	12	12	2	0	81.1	336	68	33	28	2	1	1	4	21	0	77	6	0	6	3	.667	1	0	3.10
1994 Nashville	AAA	19	19	1	0	105	483	126	77	71	19	5	6	2	55	1	76	1	4	4	10	.286	0	0	6.09
1995 Nashville	AAA	4	4	0	0	20.2	85	16	7	5	2	0	1	1	10	0	9	1	0	1	1	.500	0	0	2.18
5 Min. YEARS		84	84	13	0	526.2	2230	478	272	216	33	20	18	20	214	2	408	34	7	28	36	.438	5	0	3.69

Scott Emerson

Pitches: Left Bats: Both Pos: P   **Ht: 6'5" Wt: 175 Born: 12/22/71 Age: 24**

Year Team	Lg	G	GS	CG	GF	IP	BFP	H	R	ER	HR	SH	SF	HB	TBB	IBB	SO	WP	Bk	W	L	Pct.	ShO	Sv	ERA
1992 Bluefield	R	14	11	0	0	69	301	72	31	22	5	0	3	3	35	0	41	6	0	4	3	.571	0	0	2.87
1993 Albany	A	27	27	1	0	147.1	633	141	72	58	6	4	5	7	62	1	115	10	2	10	9	.526	0	0	3.54
1994 Frederick	A	28	22	2	0	129.2	573	141	78	61	6	5	5	4	62	1	87	4	1	8	8	.500	0	0	4.23
1995 Bowie	AA	4	4	0	0	16	82	19	18	9	3	0	1	0	14	0	13	3	0	0	2	.000	0	0	5.06
Trenton	AA	4	0	0	0	5.2	29	3	3	3	0	0	0	0	2	0	5	1	0	0	0	.000	0	0	4.76
Sarasota	A	16	11	1	1	60.1	273	66	38	32	2	2	2	6	29	2	47	6	0	2	5	.286	0	0	4.77
4 Min. YEARS		93	75	4	1	428	1891	450	240	185	22	11	16	20	204	4	308	30	3	24	27	.471	0	0	3.89

Tom Engle

Pitches: Right Bats: Right Pos: P   **Ht: 6'3" Wt: 220 Born: 2/14/71 Age: 25**

Year Team	Lg	G	GS	CG	GF	IP	BFP	H	R	ER	HR	SH	SF	HB	TBB	IBB	SO	WP	Bk	W	L	Pct.	ShO	Sv	ERA
1989 Kingsport	R	13	12	0	1	52.2	271	62	55	39	10	2	2	3	47	0	50	2	2	3	4	.429	0	0	6.66
1990 Kingsport	R	14	12	1	0	77.1	332	71	35	28	9	2	1	4	31	0	75	7	0	6	3	.667	0	0	3.26
1991 Columbia	A	7	5	0	2	30.2	128	22	13	11	1	0	1	2	17	0	32	2	1	3	2	.600	0	0	3.23
1993 Capital Cty	A	15	3	0	4	30	141	30	19	18	2	0	1	1	20	1	38	3	0	0	2	.000	0	1	5.40
Pittsfield	A	15	14	3	0	84	348	57	35	31	5	2	2	8	35	1	100	4	2	7	7	.500	1	0	3.32
1994 Mets	R	2	1	0	0	5.2	33	10	10	9	0	0	0	0	5	0	8	2	0	0	1	.000	0	0	14.29
Columbia	A	17	17	1	0	94	397	92	50	44	10	3	5	7	30	1	65	9	1	5	6	.455	0	0	4.21
1995 Norfolk	AAA	1	1	0	0	3	17	5	4	4	0	0	0	0	3	0	5	0	0	0	1	.000	0	0	12.00
Binghamton	AA	13	2	0	5	28.1	118	28	19	17	5	2	0	3	7	0	15	2	0	2	1	.667	0	0	5.40
St. Lucie	A	9	9	1	0	50	203	34	16	10	1	0	3	5	15	1	41	0	0	3	3	.500	0	0	1.80
6 Min. YEARS		106	76	6	12	455.2	1988	411	256	211	43	11	15	33	210	4	429	31	6	29	30	.492	1	1	4.17

Chad Epperson

Bats: Both Throws: Right Pos: C   **Ht: 6'3" Wt: 221 Born: 3/26/72 Age: 24**

Year Team	Lg	G	AB	H	2B	3B	HR	TB	R	RBI	TBB	IBB	SO	HBP	SH	SF	SB	CS	SB%	GDP	Avg	OBP	SLG
1992 Mets	R	37	97	16	2	0	1	21	7	12	12	0	20	3	0	3	1	1	.50	2	.165	.270	.216
1993 Kingsport	R	38	117	40	7	0	6	65	15	26	18	0	24	1	1	0	3	1	.75	4	.342	.434	.556
1994 St. Lucie	A	50	148	32	7	0	2	45	15	10	16	2	42	0	1	2	1	2	.33	2	.216	.289	.304
1995 Binghamton	AA	7	17	1	0	1	0	3	0	0	1	1	8	0	0	0	1	0	1.00	0	.059	.111	.176
St. Lucie	A	42	121	23	7	1	1	35	7	14	17	2	32	0	1	2	1	0	1.00	7	.190	.286	.289
4 Min. YEARS		174	500	112	23	2	10	169	44	62	64	5	126	4	3	7	7	4	.64	15	.224	.313	.338

Scott Epps

Bats: Right Throws: Right Pos: C   **Ht: 5'11" Wt: 180 Born: 12/8/69 Age: 26**

Year Team	Lg	G	AB	H	2B	3B	HR	TB	R	RBI	TBB	IBB	SO	HBP	SH	SF	SB	CS	SB%	GDP	Avg	OBP	SLG
1992 Oneonta	A	16	36	6	1	0	0	7	3	1	6	0	6	1	0	1	0	0	.00	1	.167	.302	.194
1993 Pr. William	A	34	92	18	4	0	1	25	12	17	9	0	24	1	0	1	0	0	.00	4	.196	.272	.272
1994 Columbus	AAA	3	2	0	0	0	0	0	0	0	0	0	2	0	0	0	0	0	.00	0	.000	.000	.000
Tampa	A	27	72	11	2	2	0	17	10	12	7	0	20	0	1	0	0	0	.00	2	.153	.289	.236
1995 Columbus	AAA	4	7	1	0	0	0	1	0	0	0	0	1	0	1	0	0	0	.00	0	.143	.143	.143
Norwich	AA	33	73	18	6	0	0	24	6	7	9	0	21	0	2	1	0	0	.00	0	.247	.325	.329
4 Min. YEARS		117	282	54	13	2	1	74	31	37	31	0	74	2	4	2	0	0	.00	8	.191	.274	.262

Brad Erdman

Bats: Right Throws: Right Pos: C Ht: 6'3" Wt: 190 Born: 2/23/70 Age: 26

BATTING / BASERUNNING / PERCENTAGES

Year	Team	Lg	G	AB	H	2B	3B	HR	TB	R	RBI	TBB	IBB	SO	HBP	SH	SF	SB	CS	SB%	GDP	Avg	OBP	SLG
1989	Geneva	A	26	85	15	2	0	0	17	6	3	6	1	26	0	0	1	1	1	.50	2	.176	.228	.200
1990	Peoria	A	37	119	23	3	0	0	26	9	4	12	0	42	1	1	0	0	0	.00	2	.193	.273	.218
	Geneva	A	34	111	25	4	0	0	29	12	15	11	0	31	1	3	0	2	0	1.00	0	.225	.301	.261
1991	Peoria	A	83	280	71	19	1	4	104	33	26	32	1	59	3	8	1	5	0	1.00	6	.254	.335	.371
1992	Winston-Sal	A	65	219	42	14	0	3	55	29	14	12	0	53	4	4	1	1	5	.17	5	.192	.246	.251
1993	Peoria	A	20	57	14	1	0	1	18	7	10	6	0	12	2	3	1	2	0	1.00	0	.246	.333	.316
	Orlando	AA	69	171	31	5	0	1	39	12	17	18	5	42	6	9	3	2	2	.50	2	.181	.278	.228
1994	Daytona	A	76	236	60	12	1	2	80	26	24	21	0	47	9	3	0	2	2	.50	8	.254	.338	.339
	Orlando	AA	1	0	0	0	0	0	0	0	0	0	0	0	0	0	0	0	0	.00	0	.000	.000	.000
1995	Daytona	A	8	26	4	1	0	0	5	6	3	4	0	6	0	1	0	0	0	.00	0	.154	.267	.192
	Orlando	AA	14	36	4	0	0	0	4	4	0	1	0	6	2	0	0	0	0	.00	4	.111	.179	.111
7 Min. YEARS			433	1340	289	51	2	11	377	144	116	123	7	324	28	32	7	15	10	.60	29	.216	.294	.281

Jaime Escamilla

Pitches: Left Bats: Right Pos: P Ht: 5'9" Wt: 165 Born: 5/25/72 Age: 24

HOW MUCH HE PITCHED / WHAT HE GAVE UP / THE RESULTS

Year	Team	Lg	G	GS	CG	GF	IP	BFP	H	R	ER	HR	SH	SF	HB	TBB	IBB	SO	WP	Bk	W	L	Pct.	ShO	Sv	ERA
1994	Hudson Vall	A	24	3	0	11	57.2	238	35	27	16	2	4	2	4	25	1	72	6	3	5	5	.500	0	3	2.50
1995	Tulsa	AA	4	0	0	0	5	23	6	4	1	1	0	0	0	2	0	5	1	0	0	0	.000	0	0	1.80
	Charlstn-Sc	A	32	5	0	10	71.1	305	59	38	35	8	3	3	2	38	1	76	8	1	3	4	.429	0	2	4.42
2 Min. YEARS			60	8	0	21	134	566	100	69	52	11	7	5	6	65	2	153	15	4	8	9	.471	0	5	3.49

Ramon Espinosa

Bats: Right Throws: Right Pos: OF Ht: 6'0" Wt: 175 Born: 2/7/72 Age: 24

BATTING / BASERUNNING / PERCENTAGES

Year	Team	Lg	G	AB	H	2B	3B	HR	TB	R	RBI	TBB	IBB	SO	HBP	SH	SF	SB	CS	SB%	GDP	Avg	OBP	SLG
1991	Pirates	R	19	63	15	2	0	0	17	7	5	2	0	7	0	0	0	3	0	1.00	3	.238	.262	.270
1992	Welland	A	60	208	56	12	5	4	90	27	22	9	0	23	0	0	2	10	5	.67	9	.269	.297	.433
1993	Augusta	A	70	266	79	9	3	2	100	32	27	12	2	51	2	1	3	17	5	.77	12	.297	.329	.376
	Salem	A	54	208	56	8	2	8	92	30	25	6	0	36	1	2	0	11	6	.65	6	.269	.293	.442
1994	Carolina	AA	82	291	78	16	3	2	106	44	40	11	1	38	1	2	4	12	10	.55	4	.268	.293	.364
1995	Carolina	AA	134	489	140	28	2	3	181	69	48	17	3	64	5	8	1	14	6	.70	15	.286	.316	.370
5 Min. YEARS			419	1525	424	75	15	19	586	209	167	57	6	219	9	13	10	67	32	.68	48	.278	.306	.384

Bobby Estalella

Bats: Right Throws: Right Pos: C Ht: 6'1" Wt: 200 Born: 8/23/74 Age: 21

BATTING / BASERUNNING / PERCENTAGES

Year	Team	Lg	G	AB	H	2B	3B	HR	TB	R	RBI	TBB	IBB	SO	HBP	SH	SF	SB	CS	SB%	GDP	Avg	OBP	SLG
1993	Martinsvlle	R	35	122	36	11	0	3	56	14	19	14	2	24	2	0	0	0	1	.00	6	.295	.377	.459
	Clearwater	A	11	35	8	0	0	0	8	4	4	2	0	3	0	0	0	0	0	.00	0	.229	.270	.229
1994	Spartanburg	A	86	299	65	19	1	9	113	34	41	31	0	85	1	1	4	0	1	.00	5	.217	.290	.378
	Clearwater	A	13	46	12	1	0	2	19	3	9	3	0	17	0	2	1	0	0	.00	0	.261	.300	.413
1995	Clearwater	A	117	404	105	24	1	15	176	61	58	56	2	76	2	3	4	0	3	.00	12	.260	.350	.436
	Reading	AA	10	34	8	1	0	2	15	5	9	4	1	7	1	0	0	0	0	.00	1	.235	.333	.441
3 Min. YEARS			272	940	234	56	2	31	387	121	140	110	5	212	6	6	9	0	5	.00	26	.249	.329	.412

Osmani Estrada

Bats: Right Throws: Right Pos: 3B Ht: 5'8" Wt: 180 Born: 1/23/69 Age: 27

BATTING / BASERUNNING / PERCENTAGES

Year	Team	Lg	G	AB	H	2B	3B	HR	TB	R	RBI	TBB	IBB	SO	HBP	SH	SF	SB	CS	SB%	GDP	Avg	OBP	SLG
1993	Erie	A	60	225	60	11	0	4	83	24	22	17	1	26	6	1	2	1	7	.13	4	.267	.332	.369
1994	Charlotte	A	131	501	128	29	4	4	177	64	30	57	0	60	11	7	5	8	10	.44	10	.255	.341	.353
1995	Tulsa	AA	120	410	109	23	3	3	147	44	43	35	2	49	9	5	4	2	2	.00	9	.266	.334	.359
3 Min. YEARS			311	1136	297	63	7	11	407	132	95	109	3	135	26	13	11	11	19	.32	23	.261	.337	.358

Roger Etheridge

Pitches: Left Bats: Left Pos: P Ht: 6'5" Wt: 215 Born: 5/31/72 Age: 24

HOW MUCH HE PITCHED / WHAT HE GAVE UP / THE RESULTS

Year	Team	Lg	G	GS	CG	GF	IP	BFP	H	R	ER	HR	SH	SF	HB	TBB	IBB	SO	WP	Bk	W	L	Pct.	ShO	Sv	ERA
1992	Princeton	R	17	5	0	5	35.1	165	37	33	27	3	0	0	1	25	1	35	5	1	1	1	.500	0	1	6.88
1993	Princeton	R	9	9	1	0	54.1	227	40	14	9	2	2	1	2	28	1	60	3	1	3	2	.600	0	1	1.49
	Charlstn-Wv	A	13	8	0	0	43.2	208	43	41	35	2	2	2	4	35	0	28	1	1	3	3	.500	0	0	7.21
1994	Charlstn-Wv	A	10	10	0	0	58.1	258	64	35	29	6	4	1	4	27	0	42	2	0	2	2	.500	0	0	4.47
	Macon	A	7	4	0	1	33	150	39	17	13	3	0	1	2	8	0	19	1	0	3	1	.750	0	0	3.55
	Durham	A	9	9	1	0	64.1	245	41	12	10	2	2	1	0	16	0	36	3	0	6	2	.750	1	0	1.40
1995	Greenville	AA	32	16	1	6	101.2	462	120	73	64	10	4	5	3	52	1	47	8	1	2	10	.167	0	0	5.67
4 Min. YEARS			97	61	3	12	390.2	1715	384	225	187	28	14	11	16	191	3	267	23	4	20	21	.488	1	1	4.31

Mark Ettles

Pitches: Right **Bats:** Right **Pos:** P **Ht:** 6'0" **Wt:** 185 **Born:** 10/30/66 **Age:** 29

Year Team	Lg	G	GS	CG	GF	IP	BFP	H	R	ER	HR	SH	SF	HB	TBB	IBB	SO	WP	Bk	W	L	Pct.	ShO	Sv	ERA
1989 Niagara Fal	A	5	0	0	3	17.2	66	12	3	2	0	0	0	0	2	0	21	1	1	3	0	1.000	0	1	1.02
Fayetteville	A	19	0	0	11	27.2	120	28	9	7	1	2	0	1	9	2	34	1	2	2	2	.500	0	4	2.28
1990 Lakeland	A	45	0	0	21	68	295	63	34	25	1	4	2	6	16	1	62	4	2	5	5	.500	0	3	3.31
1991 Lakeland	A	8	1	0	0	17	74	19	11	9	2	0	0	1	6	0	14	1	1	2	1	.667	0	0	4.76
Charlstn-Sc	A	29	0	0	23	45.2	193	36	15	12	2	5	2	2	12	2	57	2	0	2	1	.667	0	12	2.36
Waterloo	A	14	0	0	14	16	60	6	5	4	2	4	0	0	6	2	24	2	0	1	2	.333	0	8	2.25
1992 Wichita	AA	54	0	0	43	68.1	283	54	23	21	6	4	1	4	23	6	86	8	1	3	8	.273	0	22	2.77
1993 Las Vegas	AAA	47	0	0	41	49.2	224	58	28	26	2	3	1	2	22	6	29	13	0	3	6	.333	0	15	4.71
1994 Padres	R	7	0	0	6	6.2	29	7	3	2	0	1	1	0	1	0	9	0	0	0	1	.000	0	2	2.70
Wichita	AA	3	0	0	3	3	13	3	2	2	0	1	0	0	1	0	1	1	0	0	0	.000	0	0	6.00
1995 Padres	R	3	0	0	0	4.2	24	6	6	3	1	0	0	1	4	0	2	1	1	0	0	.000	0	0	5.79
Rancho Cuca	A	3	0	0	1	5.2	26	7	5	4	1	0	1	0	1	0	7	1	0	0	0	.000	0	0	6.35
Las Vegas	AAA	10	0	0	3	12.2	62	21	11	11	4	0	1	0	3	0	10	1	0	0	0	.000	0	0	7.82
1993 San Diego	NL	14	0	0	5	18	81	23	16	13	4	0	2	0	4	1	9	3	0	1	0	1.000	0	0	6.50
7 Min. YEARS		247	1	0	169	342.2	1469	320	155	128	22	24	8	18	106	19	356	37	8	21	26	.447	0	67	3.36

Bart Evans

Pitches: Right **Bats:** Right **Pos:** P **Ht:** 6'1" **Wt:** 190 **Born:** 12/30/70 **Age:** 25

Year Team	Lg	G	GS	CG	GF	IP	BFP	H	R	ER	HR	SH	SF	HB	TBB	IBB	SO	WP	Bk	W	L	Pct.	ShO	Sv	ERA
1992 Eugene	A	13	1	0	4	26	126	17	20	18	1	1	2	4	31	0	39	14	0	1	1	.500	0	0	6.23
1993 Rockford	A	27	16	0	4	99	439	95	52	48	5	1	2	4	60	0	120	10	1	10	4	.714	0	0	4.36
1994 Wilmington	A	26	26	0	0	145	587	107	53	48	7	1	0	4	61	0	145	10	0	10	3	.769	0	0	2.98
1995 Wichita	AA	7	7	0	0	22.1	123	22	28	26	3	1	0	1	45	0	13	7	1	0	4	.000	0	0	10.48
Wilmington	A	16	6	0	4	46.2	215	30	21	15	0	0	1	5	44	0	47	7	0	4	1	.800	0	2	2.89
4 Min. YEARS		89	56	0	12	339	1490	271	174	155	16	4	5	18	241	0	364	48	2	25	13	.658	0	2	4.12

Dave Evans

Pitches: Right **Bats:** Right **Pos:** P **Ht:** 6'3" **Wt:** 185 **Born:** 1/1/68 **Age:** 28

Year Team	Lg	G	GS	CG	GF	IP	BFP	H	R	ER	HR	SH	SF	HB	TBB	IBB	SO	WP	Bk	W	L	Pct.	ShO	Sv	ERA
1990 San Bernrdo	A	26	26	4	0	155	673	135	83	72	9	4	7	7	74	0	143	10	0	14	9	.609	0	0	4.18
1991 Jacksonvlle	AA	21	20	1	0	115.2	507	118	74	67	15	2	7	9	49	0	76	12	0	5	9	.357	0	0	5.21
1993 Appleton	A	5	5	0	0	27.2	117	21	9	7	0	0	0	2	15	0	23	5	2	2	1	.667	0	0	2.28
Riverside	A	8	8	1	0	41.2	187	41	22	21	5	1	1	5	23	0	42	2	0	3	2	.600	1	0	4.54
1994 Jacksonvlle	AA	31	6	0	8	81.1	354	86	59	50	11	3	4	5	31	2	62	4	0	3	5	.375	0	2	5.53
1995 Jackson	AA	49	0	0	37	67.2	278	50	29	25	2	5	3	4	28	6	54	0	1	2	9	.182	0	18	3.33
Tucson	AAA	2	0	0	0	3	12	2	0	0	0	0	0	0	1	0	4	0	0	0	0	.000	0	0	0.00
5 Min. YEARS		142	65	6	45	492	2128	453	276	242	42	15	22	32	221	8	404	33	3	29	35	.453	1	20	4.43

Sean Evans

Pitches: Right **Bats:** Right **Pos:** P **Ht:** 6'1" **Wt:** 185 **Born:** 11/6/70 **Age:** 25

Year Team	Lg	G	GS	CG	GF	IP	BFP	H	R	ER	HR	SH	SF	HB	TBB	IBB	SO	WP	Bk	W	L	Pct.	ShO	Sv	ERA
1991 Welland	A	10	6	0	0	38.2	177	42	26	19	1	0	2	5	20	0	32	3	0	1	1	.500	0	0	4.42
1992 Augusta	A	7	7	0	0	40.1	160	25	14	10	0	0	1	2	18	0	32	2	0	1	2	.333	0	0	2.23
Salem	A	15	10	0	2	60.2	266	68	42	39	8	2	2	5	25	0	37	6	3	4	4	.500	0	1	5.79
1993 Salem	A	45	3	0	10	66.1	303	67	50	41	8	1	2	6	33	0	70	11	0	1	4	.200	0	0	5.56
1994 Salem	A	51	0	0	34	55.2	273	55	40	24	1	4	2	7	34	3	49	7	0	3	7	.300	0	9	3.88
1995 Carolina	AA	29	2	0	10	49	218	47	35	29	1	0	1	3	25	1	44	5	0	5	2	.714	0	0	5.33
5 Min. YEARS		157	28	0	56	310.2	1397	304	207	162	19	7	10	28	155	4	264	34	3	15	20	.429	0	10	4.69

Darin Everson

Bats: Left **Throws:** Right **Pos:** 1B **Ht:** 6'3" **Wt:** 224 **Born:** 4/22/71 **Age:** 25

Year Team	Lg	G	AB	H	2B	3B	HR	TB	R	RBI	TBB	IBB	SO	HBP	SH	SF	SB	CS	SB%	GDP	Avg	OBP	SLG
1994 Burlington	A	39	117	31	10	1	7	64	23	32	12	1	30	2	1	1	0	0	.00	0	.265	.341	.547
1995 Harrisburg	AA	5	14	3	1	0	0	4	0	1	0	0	2	0	1	0	0	0	.00	0	.214	.214	.286
W. Palm Bch	A	38	105	23	2	0	1	28	7	13	12	2	22	6	0	1	0	0	.00	3	.219	.331	.267
2 Min. YEARS		82	236	57	13	1	8	96	30	46	24	3	54	8	2	2	0	0	.00	3	.242	.330	.407

Jeff Faino

Pitches: Left **Bats:** Right **Pos:** P **Ht:** 6'0" **Wt:** 185 **Born:** 11/22/72 **Age:** 23

Year Team	Lg	G	GS	CG	GF	IP	BFP	H	R	ER	HR	SH	SF	HB	TBB	IBB	SO	WP	Bk	W	L	Pct.	ShO	Sv	ERA
1992 Elmira	A	20	1	0	10	42.2	193	44	33	24	1	1	2	3	18	4	36	3	3	1	5	.167	0	2	5.06
1993 Lynchburg	A	40	8	0	12	105.1	437	93	45	37	6	7	4	4	37	6	79	4	1	6	3	.667	0	1	3.16
1994 Lynchburg	A	40	8	0	9	97.1	441	107	66	59	16	4	4	1	41	1	93	3	1	1	9	.100	0	3	5.46
1995 Trenton	AA	5	0	0	1	7.2	32	9	3	2	1	0	0	0	1	0	5	0	0	1	1	.500	0	0	2.35
Bowie	AA	31	0	0	14	43	175	34	18	13	2	3	3	2	15	1	17	2	0	0	2	.000	0	0	2.72

Team	Lg	G	GS	CG	GF	IP	BFP	H	R	ER	HR	SH	SF	HB	TBB	IBB	SO	WP	Bk	W	L	Pct.	ShO	Sv	ERA
Frederick	A	4	0	0	2	5.2	26	7	5	3	0	1	0	0	2	0	8	1	0	0	0	.000	0	0	4.76
4 Min. YEARS		140	17	0	48	301.2	1304	294	170	138	26	16	13	10	114	12	238	13	5	9	20	.310	0	6	4.12

Steve Falteisek

Pitches: Right Bats: Right Pos: P Ht: 6'2" Wt: 200 Born: 1/28/72 Age: 24

		HOW MUCH HE PITCHED						WHAT HE GAVE UP												THE RESULTS					
Year Team	Lg	G	GS	CG	GF	IP	BFP	H	R	ER	HR	SH	SF	HB	TBB	IBB	SO	WP	Bk	W	L	Pct.	ShO	Sv	ERA
1992 Jamestown	A	15	15	2	0	96	407	84	47	38	3	4	1	5	31	2	82	9	10	3	8	.273	0	0	3.56
1993 Burlington	A	14	14	0	0	76.1	345	86	59	50	4	4	1	2	35	0	63	4	1	3	5	.375	0	0	5.90
1994 W. Palm Bch	A	27	24	1	0	159.2	658	144	72	45	3	0	6	3	49	0	91	11	4	9	4	.692	0	0	2.54
1995 Harrisburg	AA	25	25	5	0	168	707	152	74	55	3	7	5	11	64	4	112	6	1	9	6	.600	0	0	2.95
Ottawa	AAA	3	3	1	0	23	86	17	4	3	0	0	0	1	5	0	18	0	1	2	0	1.000	1	0	1.17
4 Min. YEARS		84	81	9	0	523	2203	483	256	191	13	15	13	22	184	6	366	30	17	26	23	.531	1	0	3.29

Steve Fanning

Bats: Right Throws: Right Pos: DH Ht: 6'3" Wt: 180 Born: 5/16/67 Age: 29

		BATTING														BASERUNNING				PERCENTAGES		
Year Team	Lg	G	AB	H	2B	3B	HR	TB	R	RBI	TBB	IBB	SO	HBP	SH	SF	SB	CS	SB%	GDP	Avg	OBP	SLG
1988 Hamilton	A	60	175	39	8	0	0	47	22	2	28	0	58	4	1	0	5	1	.83	2	.223	.343	.269
1989 Savannah	A	112	407	108	13	2	5	140	59	40	44	1	94	5	5	0	7	1	.88	11	.265	.344	.344
1990 Arkansas	AA	126	404	91	23	4	4	134	50	34	59	3	91	5	0	2	0	2	.00	10	.225	.330	.332
1991 Arkansas	AA	60	162	39	7	0	1	49	19	15	29	1	45	4	2	0	3	5	.38	5	.241	.369	.302
St. Pete	A	53	189	42	7	1	2	57	19	14	29	1	27	1	3	0	1	3	.25	3	.222	.329	.302
1992 St. Pete	A	1	0	0	0	0	0	0	0	0	0	0	0	0	0	0	0	0	.00	0	.000	.000	.000
Louisville	AAA	19	49	9	1	2	0	14	8	4	8	1	14	0	0	0	0	0	.00	2	.184	.298	.286
Arkansas	AA	58	117	26	5	0	2	37	17	14	10	0	37	0	1	3	2	1	.67	4	.222	.277	.316
1993 Arkansas	AA	67	240	50	14	0	3	73	28	20	26	1	71	2	1	1	5	3	.63	5	.213	.291	.305
1994 Louisville	AAA	65	61	15	3	0	0	18	7	5	10	0	22	1	1	0	0	1	.00	1	.246	.361	.295
1995 Iowa	AAA	4	5	0	0	0	0	0	0	0	0	0	4	0	0	0	0	0	.00	0	.000	.167	.000
8 Min. YEARS		655	1818	422	81	9	17	572	229	148	244	8	463	22	14	6	23	17	.58	43	.232	.329	.315

Paul Faries

Bats: Right Throws: Right Pos: 2B Ht: 5'10" Wt: 165 Born: 2/20/65 Age: 31

		BATTING														BASERUNNING				PERCENTAGES		
Year Team	Lg	G	AB	H	2B	3B	HR	TB	R	RBI	TBB	IBB	SO	HBP	SH	SF	SB	CS	SB%	GDP	Avg	OBP	SLG
1987 Spokane	A	74	280	86	9	3	0	101	67	27	36	0	25	5	4	5	30	9	.77	7	.307	.390	.361
1988 Riverside	A	141	579	183	39	4	2	236	108	77	72	1	79	8	7	7	65	30	.68	14	.316	.394	.408
1989 Wichita	AA	130	513	136	25	8	6	195	79	52	47	0	52	2	2	1	41	13	.76	13	.265	.329	.380
1990 Las Vegas	AAA	137	552	172	29	3	5	222	109	64	75	1	60	6	7	1	48	15	.76	16	.312	.399	.402
1991 High Desert	A	10	42	13	2	2	0	19	6	5	2	1	3	0	1	1	1	0	1.00	2	.310	.333	.452
Las Vegas	AAA	20	75	23	2	1	1	30	16	12	12	0	5	0	2	1	7	3	.70	2	.307	.398	.400
1992 Las Vegas	AAA	125	457	134	15	6	1	164	77	40	40	1	53	3	4	2	28	9	.76	13	.293	.353	.359
1993 Phoenix	AAA	78	327	99	14	5	2	129	56	32	22	1	30	1	3	1	18	11	.62	8	.303	.348	.394
1994 Phoenix	AAA	124	503	141	21	4	2	176	77	50	28	0	53	6	7	3	31	10	.76	19	.280	.324	.350
1995 Edmonton	AAA	117	424	127	15	2	0	146	67	46	34	1	47	2	7	5	14	8	.64	12	.300	.351	.344
1990 San Diego	NL	14	37	7	1	0	0	8	4	2	4	0	7	1	2	1	0	1	.00	0	.189	.279	.216
1991 San Diego	NL	57	130	23	3	1	0	28	13	7	14	0	21	1	4	0	3	1	.75	3	.177	.262	.215
1992 San Diego	NL	10	11	5	1	0	0	6	3	1	1	0	2	0	0	0	0	0	.00	0	.455	.500	.545
1993 San Francisco	NL	15	36	8	2	1	0	12	6	4	1	0	4	0	1	1	2	0	1.00	1	.222	.237	.333
9 Min. YEARS		956	3752	1114	171	38	19	1418	662	405	368	6	407	33	44	27	283	108	.72	106	.297	.362	.378
4 Maj. YEARS		96	214	43	7	2	0	54	26	14	20	0	34	2	7	2	5	2	.71	6	.201	.273	.252

Monty Fariss

Bats: Right Throws: Right Pos: 1B Ht: 6'4" Wt: 205 Born: 10/13/67 Age: 28

		BATTING														BASERUNNING				PERCENTAGES		
Year Team	Lg	G	AB	H	2B	3B	HR	TB	R	RBI	TBB	IBB	SO	HBP	SH	SF	SB	CS	SB%	GDP	Avg	OBP	SLG
1988 Butte	R	17	53	21	1	0	4	34	16	22	20	2	7	2	0	0	2	0	1.00	1	.396	.558	.642
Tulsa	AA	49	165	37	6	6	3	64	21	31	22	0	39	0	1	1	2	0	1.00	2	.224	.314	.388
1989 Tulsa	AA	132	497	135	27	2	5	181	72	52	64	0	112	0	8	6	12	6	.67	13	.272	.351	.364
1990 Tulsa	AA	71	244	73	15	6	7	121	45	34	36	0	60	1	1	0	8	5	.62	9	.299	.391	.496
Okla. City	AAA	62	225	68	12	3	4	98	30	31	34	0	48	0	0	2	1	1	.50	7	.302	.391	.436
1991 Okla. City	AAA	137	494	134	31	9	13	222	84	73	91	1	143	0	3	2	5	7	.36	11	.271	.383	.449
1992 Okla. City	AAA	49	187	56	13	3	9	102	28	38	31	1	42	0	0	1	5	4	.56	5	.299	.397	.545
1993 Edmonton	AAA	74	254	65	11	4	6	102	32	37	43	0	74	2	1	2	1	5	.17	3	.256	.365	.402
1994 Edmonton	AAA	129	414	118	32	4	20	218	83	60	55	1	99	6	0	4	2	4	.33	10	.285	.374	.527
1995 Iowa	AAA	10	33	6	0	0	1	9	5	2	9	2	7	0	0	0	0	0	.00	0	.182	.357	.273
1991 Texas	AL	19	31	8	1	0	1	12	6	6	7	0	11	0	0	0	0	0	.00	0	.258	.395	.387
1992 Texas	AL	67	166	36	7	1	3	54	13	21	17	0	51	2	2	0	0	2	.00	3	.217	.297	.325
1993 Florida	NL	18	29	5	2	1	0	9	3	2	5	0	13	0	0	0	0	0	.00	2	.172	.294	.310
8 Min. YEARS		730	2566	713	148	37	72	1151	416	380	405	7	631	11	14	20	37	32	.54	61	.278	.376	.449
3 Maj. YEARS		104	226	49	10	2	4	75	22	29	29	0	75	2	2	0	0	2	.00	5	.217	.311	.332

Howard Farmer

Pitches: Right Bats: Right Pos: P Ht: 6' 3" Wt: 190 Born: 1/18/66 Age: 30

Year	Team	Lg	G	GS	CG	GF	IP	BFP	H	R	ER	HR	SH	SF	HB	TBB	IBB	SO	WP	Bk	W	L	Pct.	ShO	Sv	ERA
			HOW MUCH HE PITCHED						WHAT HE GAVE UP												THE RESULTS					
1987	Jamestown	A	15	15	3	0	96.1	404	93	42	35	4	1	2	3	30	0	63	4	2	9	6	.600	1	0	3.27
1988	Rockford	A	27	25	8	0	193.2	774	153	70	54	10	3	5	8	58	2	145	10	9	15	7	.682	2	0	2.51
1989	Jacksonville	AA	26	26	5	0	184	724	122	59	45	5	7	4	4	50	0	151	6	10	12	9	.571	2	0	2.20
	Indianapolis	AAA	1	1	0	0	7	28	3	1	0	0	0	0	0	3	0	3	0	0	1	0	1.000	0	0	0.00
1990	Indianapolis	AAA	26	26	4	0	148	640	150	84	64	12	4	4	6	48	2	99	5	2	7	9	.438	2	0	3.89
1991	Indianapolis	AAA	20	19	0	0	105	444	93	55	45	5	7	4	6	37	0	67	5	2	6	4	.600	0	0	3.86
1992	Indianapolis	AAA	30	6	0	9	84	360	89	41	35	8	5	0	1	24	2	64	10	2	3	2	.600	0	0	3.75
1993	Ottawa	AAA	2	0	0	1	4	20	7	5	5	1	0	0	1	0	0	1	0	0	0	1	.000	0	0	11.25
	New Orleans	AAA	20	13	1	1	75.1	340	93	52	48	8	1	4	1	24	1	55	2	1	4	3	.571	0	0	5.73
	El Paso	AA	4	4	1	0	24.1	95	14	9	9	2	2	0	2	10	0	16	0	2	2	1	.667	0	0	3.33
1995	Chattanooga	AA	1	1	0	0	4	21	5	6	3	1	0	0	0	1	0	2	0	0	0	1	.000	0	0	6.75
1990	Montreal	NL	6	4	0	0	23	99	26	18	18	9	2	1	0	10	1	14	1	0	0	3	.000	0	0	7.04
	8 Min. YEARS		172	136	22	11	925.2	3850	822	424	343	56	30	23	32	285	7	666	42	30	59	43	.578	7	0	3.33

Michael Farmer

Pitches: Left Bats: Both Pos: P Ht: 6'1" Wt: 175 Born: 7/3/68 Age: 27

Year	Team	Lg	G	GS	CG	GF	IP	BFP	H	R	ER	HR	SH	SF	HB	TBB	IBB	SO	WP	Bk	W	L	Pct.	ShO	Sv	ERA
			HOW MUCH HE PITCHED						WHAT HE GAVE UP												THE RESULTS					
1992	Clearwater	A	11	9	1	2	53	209	33	16	11	1	1	1	1	13	1	41	2	5	3	3	.500	1	0	1.87
1993	Reading	AA	22	18	0	3	102	455	125	62	57	18	5	5	1	34	2	64	8	4	5	10	.333	0	0	5.03
1994	Central Val	A	14	3	0	4	28.2	125	28	17	15	4	1	1	3	11	1	28	4	1	1	4	.200	0	1	4.71
	New Haven	AA	10	0	0	4	14	54	7	2	2	1	1	1	0	5	0	13	0	0	0	0	.000	0	2	1.29
1995	New Haven	AA	40	12	0	7	110.1	475	117	63	60	8	6	2	5	35	4	77	5	3	10	5	.667	0	0	4.89
	4 Min. YEARS		97	42	1	20	308	1318	310	160	145	32	14	10	10	98	8	223	19	13	19	22	.463	1	3	4.24

Jon Farrell

Bats: Right Throws: Right Pos: OF Ht: 6'2" Wt: 185 Born: 7/30/71 Age: 24

Year	Team	Lg	G	AB	H	2B	3B	HR	TB	R	RBI	TBB	IBB	SO	HBP	SH	SF	SB	CS	SB%	GDP	Avg	OBP	SLG
			BATTING															BASERUNNING				PERCENTAGES		
1991	Welland	A	69	241	61	20	3	8	111	37	35	31	1	71	4	0	2	9	6	.60	1	.253	.345	.461
1992	Augusta	A	92	320	71	11	5	8	116	44	48	39	2	93	4	1	6	8	7	.53	5	.222	.309	.363
1993	Salem	A	105	386	92	9	1	20	163	58	51	40	0	103	8	1	0	5	6	.45	5	.238	.323	.422
1994	Salem	A	123	445	120	21	4	11	182	67	42	41	1	91	4	0	1	11	2	.85	8	.270	.336	.409
1995	Carolina	AA	94	314	69	13	0	10	112	34	47	15	0	82	4	3	3	3	4	.43	9	.220	.262	.357
	5 Min. YEARS		483	1706	413	74	13	57	684	240	223	166	4	440	24	5	12	36	25	.59	28	.242	.316	.401

Mike Farrell

Pitches: Left Bats: Left Pos: P Ht: 6'2" Wt: 184 Born: 1/28/69 Age: 27

Year	Team	Lg	G	GS	CG	GF	IP	BFP	H	R	ER	HR	SH	SF	HB	TBB	IBB	SO	WP	Bk	W	L	Pct.	ShO	Sv	ERA
			HOW MUCH HE PITCHED						WHAT HE GAVE UP												THE RESULTS					
1991	Brewers	R	6	2	0	1	21.1	100	25	15	11	1	0	1	0	3	0	17	0	1	2	1	.667	0	0	4.64
	Helena	R	5	3	2	1	32	119	17	5	3	2	1	0	0	8	1	22	0	3	4	0	1.000	0	0	0.84
	Beloit	A	6	5	0	1	36.1	148	33	13	8	2	0	1	2	8	0	38	1	1	2	3	.400	0	0	1.98
1992	Stockton	A	13	13	3	0	92.2	371	82	28	24	6	5	3	5	21	0	67	1	3	8	4	.667	1	0	2.33
	El Paso	AA	14	14	5	0	106.1	435	95	42	31	5	7	0	7	25	4	66	0	1	7	6	.538	0	0	2.62
1993	New Orleans	AAA	26	26	3	0	152	637	164	92	82	22	2	2	6	32	1	63	2	2	9	9	.500	1	0	4.86
1994	El Paso	AA	5	5	0	0	29	127	39	18	18	5	1	1	1	5	0	16	1	2	3	0	1.000	0	0	5.59
	New Orleans	AAA	30	11	0	7	89	401	110	67	57	8	8	4	8	27	3	51	6	3	6	4	.600	0	0	5.76
1995	New Orleans	AAA	25	24	0	0	141.2	619	173	84	72	19	2	5	4	38	3	74	2	1	8	10	.444	0	0	4.57
	5 Min. YEARS		130	103	13	10	700.1	2957	738	364	306	70	26	17	33	167	12	414	13	17	49	37	.570	2	0	3.93

Sal Fasano

Bats: Right Throws: Right Pos: C Ht: 6'2" Wt: 220 Born: 8/10/71 Age: 24

Year	Team	Lg	G	AB	H	2B	3B	HR	TB	R	RBI	TBB	IBB	SO	HBP	SH	SF	SB	CS	SB%	GDP	Avg	OBP	SLG
			BATTING															BASERUNNING				PERCENTAGES		
1993	Eugene	A	49	176	47	11	1	10	90	25	36	19	2	49	6	0	2	4	3	.57	1	.267	.355	.511
1994	Rockford	A	97	345	97	16	1	25	190	61	81	33	4	66	16	0	5	8	3	.73	10	.281	.366	.551
	Wilmington	A	23	90	29	7	0	7	57	15	32	13	0	24	0	0	0	0	0	.00	3	.322	.408	.633
1995	Wilmington	A	23	88	20	2	1	2	30	12	7	5	0	16	1	0	0	0	0	.00	4	.227	.277	.341
	Wichita	AA	87	317	92	18	2	20	174	60	66	27	1	61	16	0	2	3	6	.33	8	.290	.373	.549
	3 Min. YEARS		279	1016	285	54	5	64	541	173	222	97	7	216	39	0	9	15	12	.56	26	.281	.363	.532

Ken Felder

Bats: Right Throws: Right Pos: OF Ht: 6'3" Wt: 220 Born: 2/9/71 Age: 25

Year	Team	Lg	G	AB	H	2B	3B	HR	TB	R	RBI	TBB	IBB	SO	HBP	SH	SF	SB	CS	SB%	GDP	Avg	OBP	SLG
			BATTING															BASERUNNING				PERCENTAGES		
1992	Helena	R	74	276	60	8	1	15	115	58	48	35	0	102	16	0	4	11	2	.85	3	.217	.335	.417
1993	Beloit	A	32	99	18	4	2	3	35	12	8	10	0	40	2	0	0	1	1	.50	5	.182	.270	.354
1994	Stockton	A	121	435	119	21	2	10	174	56	60	32	1	112	11	5	4	4	4	.50	6	.274	.336	.400

Year Team	Lg	G	AB	H	2B	3B	HR	TB	R	RBI	TBB	IBB	SO	HBP	SH	SF	SB	CS	SB%	GDP	Avg	OBP	SLG
1995 El Paso	AA	114	367	100	24	4	12	168	51	55	48	3	94	6	0	4	2	6	.25	10	.272	.362	.458
4 Min. YEARS		341	1177	297	57	9	40	492	177	171	125	4	348	35	5	12	18	13	.58	24	.252	.339	.418

Junior Felix

Bats: Both **Throws:** Right **Pos:** OF **Ht:** 5'11" **Wt:** 165 **Born:** 10/3/67 **Age:** 28

				BATTING													BASERUNNING				PERCENTAGES		
Year Team	Lg	G	AB	H	2B	3B	HR	TB	R	RBI	TBB	IBB	SO	HBP	SH	SF	SB	CS	SB%	GDP	Avg	OBP	SLG
1986 Medicne Hat	R	67	263	75	9	3	4	102	57	28	35	1	84	6	0	0	37	9	.80	4	.285	.382	.388
1987 Myrtle Bch	A	124	466	135	15	9	12	204	70	51	43	8	124	10	2	2	64	28	.70	2	.290	.361	.438
1988 Knoxville	AA	93	360	91	16	5	3	126	52	25	20	2	82	3	2	1	40	16	.71	4	.253	.297	.350
1989 Syracuse	AAA	21	87	24	4	2	1	35	17	10	9	0	18	0	1	1	13	3	.81	2	.276	.340	.402
1991 Palm Spring	A	18	64	23	3	0	2	32	12	10	16	1	11	0	0	0	8	2	.80	2	.359	.488	.500
1993 Edmonton	AAA	7	31	11	2	0	0	13	7	5	4	0	8	0	0	0	0	0	.00	1	.355	.429	.419
1995 Ottawa	AAA	51	160	36	7	3	3	58	22	24	15	1	48	3	1	0	1	2	.33	6	.225	.303	.363
1989 Toronto	AL	110	415	107	14	8	9	164	62	46	33	2	101	3	0	3	18	12	.60	5	.258	.315	.395
1990 Toronto	AL	127	463	122	23	7	15	204	73	65	45	0	99	2	2	5	13	8	.62	4	.263	.328	.441
1991 California	AL	66	230	65	10	2	2	85	32	26	11	0	55	3	0	2	7	5	.58	5	.283	.321	.370
1992 California	AL	139	509	125	22	5	9	184	63	72	33	5	128	2	5	9	8	8	.50	9	.246	.289	.361
1993 Florida	NL	57	214	51	11	1	7	85	25	22	10	1	50	1	0	0	2	1	.67	6	.238	.276	.397
1994 Detroit	AL	86	301	92	25	1	13	158	54	49	26	2	76	8	0	4	6	1	.14	6	.306	.372	.525
7 Min. YEARS		381	1431	395	56	22	25	570	237	153	142	13	375	22	6	4	163	60	.73	21	.276	.350	.398
6 Maj. YEARS		585	2132	562	105	24	55	880	309	280	158	10	509	19	7	23	49	40	.55	35	.264	.317	.413

Lauro Felix

Bats: Right **Throws:** Right **Pos:** SS **Ht:** 5'9" **Wt:** 160 **Born:** 6/24/70 **Age:** 26

				BATTING													BASERUNNING				PERCENTAGES		
Year Team	Lg	G	AB	H	2B	3B	HR	TB	R	RBI	TBB	IBB	SO	HBP	SH	SF	SB	CS	SB%	GDP	Avg	OBP	SLG
1992 Sou. Oregon	A	11	24	10	1	0	1	14	5	3	8	0	5	0	0	1	2	1	.67	0	.417	.545	.583
Madison	A	53	199	42	4	0	0	46	29	13	29	0	41	3	8	0	7	6	.54	2	.211	.320	.231
1993 Modesto	A	102	302	62	6	2	2	78	55	35	69	0	70	1	8	2	7	4	.64	10	.205	.353	.258
1994 Modesto	A	49	141	34	12	1	3	57	17	16	15	0	40	3	3	0	4	1	.80	0	.241	.327	.404
Tacoma	AAA	43	131	23	5	0	0	28	13	5	17	0	34	2	4	1	0	4	.00	5	.176	.278	.214
1995 Huntsville	AA	10	27	3	0	0	1	6	3	1	2	0	8	0	0	0	0	0	.00	1	.111	.172	.222
El Paso	AA	81	220	61	13	1	3	85	51	25	45	0	44	4	5	2	6	1	.86	4	.277	.406	.386
4 Min. YEARS		349	1044	235	41	4	10	314	173	98	185	0	242	13	28	6	26	17	.60	22	.225	.347	.301

Carlos Fermin

Bats: Right **Throws:** Right **Pos:** SS **Ht:** 5'9" **Wt:** 140 **Born:** 7/12/73 **Age:** 22

				BATTING													BASERUNNING				PERCENTAGES		
Year Team	Lg	G	AB	H	2B	3B	HR	TB	R	RBI	TBB	IBB	SO	HBP	SH	SF	SB	CS	SB%	GDP	Avg	OBP	SLG
1990 Bristol	R	67	203	45	4	4	0	57	22	15	21	0	36	2	9	1	7	2	.78	5	.222	.300	.281
1991 Fayetteville	A	73	224	48	3	0	0	51	24	19	27	0	37	1	5	3	6	5	.55	8	.214	.298	.228
Lakeland	A	7	15	3	0	0	0	3	3	4	0	0	1	0	0	0	0	0	.00	1	.200	.200	.200
1992 Niagara Fal	A	29	71	12	2	0	0	14	9	7	9	0	13	2	1	0	3	3	.50	3	.169	.280	.197
London	AA	14	40	6	0	0	0	6	3	0	1	0	10	1	4	0	0	2	.00	5	.150	.171	.150
1993 Lakeland	A	86	278	70	11	1	0	83	25	19	25	2	38	1	3	0	3	2	.60	6	.252	.316	.299
1994 Lakeland	A	39	114	19	0	0	0	19	8	8	5	0	16	0	1	0	1	2	.33	5	.167	.202	.167
1995 Jacksonville	AA	59	127	22	4	0	1	29	10	9	5	0	16	0	0	0	0	2	.00	2	.173	.205	.228
6 Min. YEARS		374	1072	225	24	5	1	262	104	81	93	2	167	6	23	4	20	18	.53	35	.210	.276	.244

Danny Fernandez

Bats: Right **Throws:** Right **Pos:** C **Ht:** 5'11" **Wt:** 180 **Born:** 6/6/66 **Age:** 30

				BATTING													BASERUNNING				PERCENTAGES		
Year Team	Lg	G	AB	H	2B	3B	HR	TB	R	RBI	TBB	IBB	SO	HBP	SH	SF	SB	CS	SB%	GDP	Avg	OBP	SLG
1988 Clinton	A	23	53	12	1	0	0	13	2	3	6	0	15	1	2	0	2	0	1.00	1	.226	.317	.245
1989 San Jose	A	50	136	24	0	0	1	27	17	11	25	0	35	2	1	0	3	3	.50	4	.176	.313	.199
1990 San Jose	A	36	76	20	2	0	1	25	19	14	13	0	21	0	3	2	0	1	.00	4	.263	.363	.329
1991 Phoenix	AAA	4	3	0	0	0	0	0	0	0	0	0	0	0	0	0	0	0	.00	0	.000	.000	.000
Shreveport	AA	7	12	3	0	0	0	3	1	6	1	3	1	1	0	0	0	0	.00	0	.250	.526	.250
San Jose	A	37	90	22	5	1	0	29	14	11	29	1	26	0	0	2	0	2	.00	2	.244	.421	.322
1992 Shreveport	AA	60	185	40	2	0	2	48	18	22	16	2	34	1	5	1	2	0	1.00	5	.216	.281	.259
1993 Shreveport	AA	48	128	24	5	1	1	34	12	13	14	2	32	0	4	1	1	2	.33	2	.188	.266	.266
Phoenix	AAA	42	118	31	3	1	0	36	17	7	17	0	24	1	2	2	1	2	.33	6	.263	.355	.305
1994 Phoenix	AAA	44	143	39	5	1	1	49	15	18	12	0	28	0	1	0	1	0	1.00	4	.273	.329	.343
1995 Jacksonville	AA	94	230	38	5	0	4	55	18	16	29	1	60	4	3	2	1	3	.25	3	.165	.268	.239
8 Min. YEARS		445	1174	253	28	4	10	319	135	116	167	7	278	10	22	10	11	13	.46	31	.216	.316	.272

Jared Fernandez

Pitches: Right **Bats:** Right **Pos:** P **Ht:** 6'2" **Wt:** 225 **Born:** 2/2/72 **Age:** 24

		HOW MUCH HE PITCHED						WHAT HE GAVE UP										THE RESULTS					
Year Team	Lg	G	GS	CG	GF	IP	BFP	H	R	ER	HR	SH	SF	HB	TBB	IBB	SO	WP	Bk	W	L	Pct.	ShO	Sv	ERA
1994 Utica	A	21	1	0	15	30	144	43	18	12	4	0	0	0	8	2	24	0	1	1	1	.500	0	4	3.60
1995 Utica	A	5	5	1	0	38	148	30	11	8	2	0	1	1	9	1	23	1	0	3	2	.600	0	0	1.89
Trenton	AA	11	10	1	0	67	290	64	32	29	4	3	1	5	28	1	40	2	0	5	4	.556	0	0	3.90
2 Min. YEARS		37	16	2	15	135	582	137	61	49	10	3	2	6	45	4	87	3	1	9	7	.563	0	4	3.27

Osvaldo Fernandez

Pitches: Left **Bats:** Left **Pos:** P　　　　**Ht:** 6'2" **Wt:** 193 **Born:** 4/15/70 **Age:** 26

		HOW	MUCH	HE	PITCHED			WHAT	HE	GAVE	UP					THE	RESULTS			
Year Team	Lg	G	GS	CG	GF	IP	BFP	H	R	ER	HR	SH	SF	HB	TBB	IBB	SO	WP	Bk	W	L	Pct.	ShO	Sv	ERA
1994 Riverside	A	14	13	1	0	84.2	353	67	33	27	8	1	2	3	37	0	80	3	4	8	2	.800	1	0	2.87
1995 Port City	AA	27	26	0	0	156.1	654	139	78	62	6	4	1	5	60	1	160	12	1	12	7	.632	0	0	3.57
2 Min. YEARS		41	39	1	0	241	1007	206	111	89	14	5	3	8	97	1	240	15	5	20	9	.690	1	0	3.32

Mike Ferry

Pitches: Right **Bats:** Right **Pos:** P　　　　**Ht:** 6'3" **Wt:** 195 **Born:** 7/26/69 **Age:** 26

		HOW	MUCH	HE	PITCHED			WHAT	HE	GAVE	UP					THE	RESULTS			
Year Team	Lg	G	GS	CG	GF	IP	BFP	H	R	ER	HR	SH	SF	HB	TBB	IBB	SO	WP	Bk	W	L	Pct.	ShO	Sv	ERA
1990 Billings	R	27	0	0	24	31.2	140	29	13	10	3	2	1	1	12	1	29	6	2	2	5	.286	0	11	2.84
1991 Cedar Rapds	A	16	0	0	12	25.2	122	25	19	19	1	2	1	1	21	2	27	2	0	2	2	.500	0	3	6.66
Charlstn-Wv	A	22	1	0	11	44.1	191	41	23	22	2	4	2	1	21	2	51	4	0	1	3	.250	0	4	4.47
1992 Cedar Rapds	A	25	25	6	0	162.2	665	134	57	49	6	4	5	9	40	1	143	10	1	13	4	.765	0	0	2.71
1993 Chattanooga	AA	28	28	4	0	186.2	749	176	85	71	17	5	9	5	30	1	111	8	1	13	8	.619	1	0	3.42
1994 Indianapols	AAA	7	7	0	0	31	152	47	32	23	5	1	0	1	14	0	15	2	0	1	4	.200	0	0	6.68
Chattanooga	AA	21	21	3	0	147	616	162	72	58	11	6	6	3	20	1	94	7	1	9	7	.563	0	0	3.55
1995 Indianapols	AAA	3	3	0	0	17.1	76	21	15	10	3	0	2	0	3	0	3	0	0	1	2	.333	0	0	5.19
Chattanooga	AA	24	24	1	0	155	660	191	75	65	8	10	6	5	23	1	74	3	0	9	5	.643	0	0	3.77
6 Min. YEARS		173	109	14	47	801.1	3371	826	391	327	56	34	32	26	184	9	547	42	5	51	40	.560	1	16	3.67

Sean Fesh

Pitches: Left **Bats:** Left **Pos:** P　　　　**Ht:** 6'2" **Wt:** 165 **Born:** 11/3/72 **Age:** 23

		HOW	MUCH	HE	PITCHED			WHAT	HE	GAVE	UP					THE	RESULTS			
Year Team	Lg	G	GS	CG	GF	IP	BFP	H	R	ER	HR	SH	SF	HB	TBB	IBB	SO	WP	Bk	W	L	Pct.	ShO	Sv	ERA
1991 Astros	R	6	0	0	2	12.1	53	5	4	3	0	0	0	0	11	0	7	4	0	0	0	.000	0	0	2.19
1992 Osceola	A	3	0	0	2	5.1	24	5	3	1	0	0	0	0	1	0	5	3	0	0	1	.000	0	0	1.69
Astros	R	18	0	0	12	36.1	142	25	7	7	0	3	0	4	8	0	35	4	0	1	0	1.000	0	6	1.73
1993 Asheville	A	65	0	0	58	82.1	353	75	39	33	4	11	6	5	37	8	49	4	1	10	6	.625	0	20	3.61
1994 Osceola	A	43	0	0	29	49.2	222	50	27	14	2	5	0	6	24	6	32	2	0	2	4	.333	0	11	2.54
Jackson	AA	20	1	0	5	25.2	122	34	17	12	2	2	1	0	11	0	19	2	0	1	2	.333	0	0	4.21
1995 Tucson	AAA	10	0	0	1	13.1	52	11	2	2	0	0	0	0	3	0	7	0	0	1	0	1.000	0	0	1.35
Las Vegas	AAA	30	0	0	11	38	185	53	21	14	2	4	0	3	16	5	18	1	1	2	1	.667	0	1	3.32
5 Min. YEARS		195	1	0	120	263	1153	258	120	86	10	25	7	18	111	19	172	20	2	17	14	.548	0	38	2.94

Todd Fiegel

Pitches: Left **Bats:** Left **Pos:** P　　　　**Ht:** 6'2" **Wt:** 195 **Born:** 10/16/69 **Age:** 26

		HOW	MUCH	HE	PITCHED			WHAT	HE	GAVE	UP					THE	RESULTS			
Year Team	Lg	G	GS	CG	GF	IP	BFP	H	R	ER	HR	SH	SF	HB	TBB	IBB	SO	WP	Bk	W	L	Pct.	ShO	Sv	ERA
1991 Kingsport	R	11	11	2	0	66.1	268	45	20	15	2	0	1	12	25	1	90	6	3	5	4	.556	0	0	2.04
Columbia	A	2	1	0	1	9	40	7	6	6	0	0	0	1	6	0	11	3	0	0	1	.000	0	0	6.00
1992 Columbia	A	26	18	1	6	128.2	557	118	80	55	9	2	5	6	55	0	83	14	2	5	6	.455	0	2	3.85
1993 St. Lucie	A	25	16	0	5	116.2	505	122	60	44	7	3	5	3	42	0	71	4	2	10	7	.588	0	0	3.39
1994 Norfolk	AAA	4	0	0	1	8	34	9	8	8	0	0	1	0	3	0	6	0	0	0	0	.000	0	0	9.00
St. Lucie	A	5	0	0	1	4	15	1	0	0	0	0	0	0	1	0	6	0	0	1	0	1.000	0	1	0.00
Binghamton	AA	29	8	1	8	79.2	355	93	44	36	6	3	3	4	28	3	66	6	2	3	3	.500	0	1	4.07
1995 Binghamton	AA	4	0	0	1	3	21	4	5	5	1	0	1	4	3	0	1	1	1	0	1	.000	0	0	15.00
5 Min. YEARS		106	54	4	23	415.1	1795	399	223	169	25	8	16	30	163	4	334	35	10	24	22	.522	0	5	3.66

Mike Figga

Bats: Right **Throws:** Right **Pos:** C　　　　**Ht:** 6'0" **Wt:** 200 **Born:** 7/31/70 **Age:** 25

		BATTING															BASERUNNING				PERCENTAGES		
Year Team	Lg	G	AB	H	2B	3B	HR	TB	R	RBI	TBB	IBB	SO	HBP	SH	SF	SB	CS	SB%	GDP	Avg	OBP	SLG
1990 Yankees	R	40	123	35	1	1	2	44	19	18	17	2	33	1	0	1	4	2	.67	2	.285	.373	.358
1991 Pr. William	A	55	174	34	6	0	3	49	15	17	19	0	51	0	2	1	2	1	.67	9	.195	.273	.282
1992 Pr. William	A	3	10	2	1	0	0	3	0	0	2	0	3	0	0	0	1	0	1.00	0	.200	.333	.300
Ft. Laud	A	80	249	44	13	0	1	60	12	15	13	1	78	2	3	0	3	1	.75	7	.177	.223	.241
1993 San Bernrdo	A	83	308	82	17	1	25	176	48	71	17	0	84	2	2	3	2	3	.40	7	.266	.306	.571
Albany-Colo	AA	6	22	5	0	0	0	5	3	2	2	0	9	0	0	0	1	0	1.00	0	.227	.292	.227
1994 Albany-Colo	AA	1	2	1	1	0	0	2	1	0	0	0	0	0	0	0	0	0	.00	0	.500	.500	1.000
Tampa	A	111	420	116	17	5	15	188	48	75	22	1	94	2	1	5	3	0	1.00	12	.276	.312	.448
1995 Norwich	AA	109	399	108	22	4	13	177	59	61	43	3	90	1	2	6	1	0	1.00	10	.271	.339	.444
Columbus	AAA	8	25	7	1	0	1	11	2	3	3	0	5	0	0	0	0	0	.00	0	.280	.357	.440
6 Min. YEARS		496	1732	434	79	11	60	715	207	262	138	7	448	8	11	16	17	7	.71	47	.251	.306	.413

Bien Figueroa

Bats: Right **Throws:** Right **Pos:** SS　　　　**Ht:** 5'10" **Wt:** 170 **Born:** 2/7/64 **Age:** 32

		BATTING															BASERUNNING				PERCENTAGES		
Year Team	Lg	G	AB	H	2B	3B	HR	TB	R	RBI	TBB	IBB	SO	HBP	SH	SF	SB	CS	SB%	GDP	Avg	OBP	SLG
1986 Erie	A	73	249	59	4	0	0	63	31	30	32	1	26	1	1	3	13	4	.76	9	.237	.323	.253
1987 Springfield	A	134	489	136	13	3	2	161	52	83	34	2	46	4	12	7	7	7	.50	16	.278	.326	.329

Year Team	Lg	G	AB	H	2B	3B	HR	TB	R	RBI	TBB	IBB	SO	HBP	SH	SF	SB	CS	SB%	GDP	Avg	OBP	SLG
1988 Arkansas	AA	126	407	113	17	2	0	134	48	32	22	1	49	3	7	1	2	6	.25	16	.278	.319	.329
1989 Louisville	AAA	74	221	48	3	0	0	51	18	14	12	0	22	0	5	1	0	1	.00	7	.217	.256	.231
1990 Louisville	AAA	128	396	95	19	2	0	118	41	39	24	2	37	3	7	2	5	1	.83	15	.240	.287	.298
1991 Louisville	AAA	97	269	55	8	2	0	67	18	14	20	2	27	2	5	0	1	4	.20	10	.204	.265	.249
1992 Louisville	AAA	94	319	91	11	1	1	107	44	23	33	0	32	2	6	3	2	0	1.00	8	.285	.353	.335
1993 Louisville	AAA	93	272	65	17	1	0	84	44	15	16	1	27	3	1	1	1	1	.50	6	.239	.288	.309
1994 Harrisburg	AA	13	40	10	1	0	0	11	6	4	6	0	3	2	1	0	0	0	.00	2	.250	.375	.275
Ottawa	AAA	72	223	54	13	1	1	72	22	26	14	0	28	0	0	3	2	0	1.00	9	.242	.283	.323
1995 Okla. City	AAA	9	20	2	0	0	0	2	1	2	0	0	2	0	1	1	1	0	1.00	0	.100	.095	.100
1992 St. Louis	NL	12	11	2	1	0	0	3	1	4	1	0	2	0	0	0	0	0	.00	0	.182	.250	.273
10 Min. YEARS		913	2905	728	106	12	4	870	325	282	213	9	299	20	46	22	34	24	.59	98	.251	.304	.299

Fernando Figueroa

Pitches: Left **Bats:** Left **Pos:** P **Ht:** 6'1" **Wt:** 170 **Born:** 8/19/64 **Age:** 31

	HOW MUCH HE PITCHED						WHAT HE GAVE UP										THE RESULTS					
Year Team	Lg	G	GS	CG	GF	IP	BFP	H	R	ER	HR	SH	SF	HB	TBB	IBB	SO	WP	Bk	W	L	Pct.	ShO	Sv	ERA
1986 Yankees	R	16	11	3	1	80.2	345	77	37	25	2	5	1	2	29	0	68	7	1	4	6	.400	0	0	2.79
1987 Pr. William	A	19	3	0	8	31.1	151	35	23	21	6	1	5	1	22	1	19	0	1	1	1	.500	0	1	6.03
Ft. Laud	A	3	0	0	2	7.1	40	11	12	10	4	0	1	0	9	0	4	1	0	0	0	.000	0	0	12.27
Yankees	R	14	6	5	4	61.2	235	44	22	19	1	0	1	2	11	0	51	3	0	4	4	.500	3	1	2.77
1988 Ft. Laud	A	30	0	0	18	47.2	206	49	23	19	4	1	1	1	15	1	33	0	0	1	2	.333	0	2	3.59
1989 Miami	A	13	3	1	5	41.1	170	34	13	11	1	0	2	2	17	0	15	2	0	1	5	.167	0	1	2.40
1990 Williamsprt	AA	37	4	0	15	61.1	269	65	34	27	5	7	4	2	21	0	32	2	1	2	10	.167	0	4	3.96
1991 Jacksonville	AA	41	2	0	21	64	270	57	22	18	3	5	4	3	24	2	55	4	0	6	3	.667	0	5	2.53
1992 Jacksonville	AA	53	1	0	19	94.1	395	72	33	31	7	7	2	5	33	2	65	9	1	4	5	.444	0	7	2.96
1995 Carolina	AA	6	0	0	1	8	37	12	5	3	2	0	0	0	2	0	4	1	0	0	0	.000	0	0	3.38
8 Min. YEARS		232	30	9	94	497.2	2118	456	224	184	35	26	21	18	183	6	346	29	4	23	36	.390	3	21	3.33

John Finn

Bats: Right **Throws:** Right **Pos:** OF-2B **Ht:** 5'8" **Wt:** 168 **Born:** 10/18/67 **Age:** 28

	BATTING																BASERUNNING				PERCENTAGES		
Year Team	Lg	G	AB	H	2B	3B	HR	TB	R	RBI	TBB	IBB	SO	HBP	SH	SF	SB	CS	SB%	GDP	Avg	OBP	SLG
1989 Beloit	A	73	274	82	8	7	1	107	49	20	38	0	27	4	5	2	29	11	.73	3	.299	.390	.391
1990 Stockton	A	95	290	60	4	0	1	67	48	23	52	0	50	1	6	6	29	15	.66	1	.207	.324	.231
1991 Stockton	A	65	223	57	12	1	0	71	45	25	44	1	28	9	6	3	19	9	.68	5	.256	.394	.318
El Paso	AA	63	230	69	12	2	2	91	48	24	16	0	27	2	5	2	8	4	.67	0	.300	.348	.396
1992 El Paso	AA	124	439	121	12	6	1	148	83	47	71	3	44	11	9	7	30	12	.71	7	.276	.384	.337
1993 New Orleans	AAA	117	335	94	13	2	1	114	47	37	33	1	36	6	9	0	27	9	.75	8	.281	.356	.340
1994 New Orleans	AAA	76	229	66	12	0	2	84	36	24	35	1	21	7	6	4	15	10	.60	3	.288	.393	.367
1995 New Orleans	AAA	35	117	38	4	1	3	53	20	19	13	2	7	2	4	0	9	2	.82	1	.325	.402	.453
7 Min. YEARS		648	2137	587	77	19	11	735	376	219	302	8	240	42	50	24	166	72	.70	28	.275	.372	.344

Gar Finnvold

Pitches: Right **Bats:** Right **Pos:** P **Ht:** 6'5" **Wt:** 200 **Born:** 3/11/68 **Age:** 28

	HOW MUCH HE PITCHED						WHAT HE GAVE UP										THE RESULTS					
Year Team	Lg	G	GS	CG	GF	IP	BFP	H	R	ER	HR	SH	SF	HB	TBB	IBB	SO	WP	Bk	W	L	Pct.	ShO	Sv	ERA
1990 Elmira	A	15	15	5	0	95	400	91	43	33	2	3	5	5	22	0	89	6	5	5	5	.500	1	0	3.13
1991 Lynchburg	A	6	6	0	0	38	157	30	16	14	3	2	1	1	7	1	29	2	0	2	3	.400	0	0	3.32
Pawtucket	AAA	3	3	0	0	15	71	19	13	11	4	0	0	0	7	0	12	0	0	1	2	.333	0	0	6.60
New Britain	AA	16	16	0	0	101.1	426	97	46	43	7	1	3	3	36	2	80	8	1	5	8	.385	0	0	3.82
1992 New Britain	AA	25	25	3	0	165	695	156	69	64	6	6	2	6	52	4	135	6	4	7	13	.350	0	0	3.49
1993 Pawtucket	AAA	24	24	0	0	136	581	128	68	57	21	2	2	4	51	0	123	3	0	5	9	.357	0	0	3.77
1994 Pawtucket	AAA	7	7	0	0	42.1	173	32	19	17	5	0	1	2	15	0	32	1	0	5	1	.833	0	0	3.61
1995 Pawtucket	AAA	1	1	0	0	3.2	15	1	0	0	0	0	0	0	1	0	3	0	0	0	0	.000	0	0	0.00
1994 Boston	AL	8	8	0	0	36.1	167	45	27	24	4	0	1	3	15	0	17	0	0	0	4	.000	0	0	5.94
6 Min. YEARS		97	97	8	0	596.1	2518	554	275	239	48	14	14	21	191	7	503	26	10	30	41	.423	1	0	3.61

David Fisher

Bats: Right **Throws:** Right **Pos:** SS **Ht:** 6'0" **Wt:** 160 **Born:** 2/26/70 **Age:** 26

	BATTING																BASERUNNING				PERCENTAGES		
Year Team	Lg	G	AB	H	2B	3B	HR	TB	R	RBI	TBB	IBB	SO	HBP	SH	SF	SB	CS	SB%	GDP	Avg	OBP	SLG
1992 Martinsville	R	50	188	57	14	1	3	82	31	42	30	2	27	0	1	1	6	1	.86	2	.303	.397	.436
Batavia	A	21	80	27	4	1	1	36	10	14	6	0	5	4	2	0	3	2	.60	2	.338	.411	.450
1993 Clearwater	A	126	430	103	25	2	6	150	54	54	52	1	42	8	8	10	11	16	.41	7	.240	.326	.349
1994 Reading	AA	118	412	103	24	3	7	154	57	42	57	0	65	7	4	5	5	6	.45	6	.250	.348	.374
1995 Reading	AA	79	204	47	18	1	1	70	18	20	14	0	29	3	2	4	4	4	.50	0	.230	.284	.343
4 Min. YEARS		394	1314	337	85	8	18	492	170	172	159	3	168	22	21	19	29	29	.50	17	.256	.342	.374

Doug Fitzer

Pitches: Left **Bats:** Left **Pos:** P **Ht:** 6'5" **Wt:** 210 **Born:** 7/2/69 **Age:** 26

	HOW MUCH HE PITCHED						WHAT HE GAVE UP										THE RESULTS					
Year Team	Lg	G	GS	CG	GF	IP	BFP	H	R	ER	HR	SH	SF	HB	TBB	IBB	SO	WP	Bk	W	L	Pct.	ShO	Sv	ERA
1990 Bellingham	A	25	0	0	21	43.1	174	24	15	13	3	2	0	0	21	0	62	0	0	5	1	.833	0	3	2.70
1991 San Bernrdo	A	30	0	0	6	55	256	59	39	34	6	1	8	6	30	1	52	10	0	3	0	1.000	0	1	5.56
1992 Peninsula	A	26	0	0	14	33.1	137	21	10	5	1	1	1	1	18	1	28	3	0	3	1	.750	0	6	1.35

Year	Team	Lg	G	GS	CG	GF	IP	BFP	H	R	ER	HR	SH	SF	HB	TBB	IBB	SO	WP	Bk	W	L	Pct.	ShO	Sv	ERA
1994	Riverside	A	20	0	0	7	37	150	30	12	9	1	0	0	0	13	0	19	3	0	2	0	1.000	0	0	2.19
1995	Riverside	A	25	0	0	7	27.1	123	26	15	14	3	0	2	0	15	1	13	3	0	0	0	.000	0	0	4.61
	Port City	AA	4	0	0	1	5	20	3	4	3	1	0	0	0	1	0	4	0	0	0	0	.000	0	0	5.40
	5 Min. YEARS		130	0	0	56	201	860	163	95	78	15	4	11	7	98	3	178	19	0	13	2	.867	0	10	3.49

Robert Fitzpatrick

Bats: Right **Throws:** Right **Pos:** C **Ht:** 6'0" **Wt:** 190 **Born:** 9/14/68 **Age:** 27

						BATTING												BASERUNNING				PERCENTAGES		
Year	Team	Lg	G	AB	H	2B	3B	HR	TB	R	RBI	TBB	IBB	SO	HBP	SH	SF	SB	CS	SB%	GDP	Avg	OBP	SLG
1990	Jamestown	A	62	209	56	14	0	6	88	23	34	28	2	53	0	0	1	1	0	1.00	3	.268	.353	.421
1991	Rockford	A	93	296	70	15	0	6	103	39	35	34	0	82	3	2	2	1	5	.17	4	.236	.319	.348
1992	W. Palm Bch	A	96	336	86	19	0	8	129	42	37	37	1	81	2	1	0	4	3	.57	8	.256	.333	.384
1993	Harrisburg	AA	99	341	77	10	1	11	122	44	46	36	0	82	5	2	2	6	7	.46	10	.226	.307	.358
1994	Harrisburg	AA	95	315	79	12	1	9	120	39	34	29	2	78	4	2	1	3	4	.43	7	.251	.321	.381
1995	Harrisburg	AA	15	42	7	1	0	1	11	3	3	6	0	11	2	1	0	0	0	.00	1	.167	.300	.262
	Expos	R	9	25	5	3	0	0	8	5	4	7	0	4	0	0	0	0	0	.00	1	.200	.375	.320
	W. Palm Bch	A	17	43	9	1	0	1	13	3	5	9	0	12	0	0	1	3	3	.50	0	.209	.340	.302
	6 Min. YEARS		486	1607	389	75	2	42	594	198	198	186	5	403	16	8	7	18	22	.45	34	.242	.325	.370

Carlton Fleming

Bats: Both **Throws:** Right **Pos:** 2B **Ht:** 5'11" **Wt:** 175 **Born:** 8/25/71 **Age:** 24

						BATTING												BASERUNNING				PERCENTAGES		
Year	Team	Lg	G	AB	H	2B	3B	HR	TB	R	RBI	TBB	IBB	SO	HBP	SH	SF	SB	CS	SB%	GDP	Avg	OBP	SLG
1992	Oneonta	A	3	11	2	0	0	0	2	2	2	1	0	2	1	0	0	1	0	1.00	0	.182	.308	.182
	Greensboro		68	236	78	1	1	0	81	35	24	31	0	20	0	1	0	9	7	.56	2	.331	.408	.343
1993	Pr. William	A	120	442	132	14	2	0	150	72	25	80	2	23	0	6	1	21	10	.68	14	.299	.405	.339
1994	Albany-Colo	AA	117	378	92	12	1	0	106	39	37	52	0	37	3	10	4	20	10	.67	8	.243	.336	.280
1995	Columbus	AAA	32	86	19	6	0	0	25	9	5	8	0	6	0	1	0	0	2	.00	3	.221	.287	.291
	Norwich	AA	40	125	38	3	1	0	43	15	16	12	0	10	0	2	1	5	3	.63	4	.304	.362	.344
	4 Min. YEARS		380	1278	361	36	5	0	407	172	109	184	2	98	4	20	6	56	32	.64	31	.282	.373	.318

Huck Flener

Pitches: Left **Bats:** Both **Pos:** P **Ht:** 5'11" **Wt:** 175 **Born:** 2/25/69 **Age:** 27

			HOW MUCH HE PITCHED						WHAT HE GAVE UP											THE RESULTS					
Year	Team	Lg	G	GS	CG	GF	IP	BFP	H	R	ER	HR	SH	SF	HB	TBB	IBB	SO	WP	Bk	W	L	Pct.	ShO	Sv	ERA
1990	St. Cathrns	A	14	7	0	3	61.2	258	45	29	23	4	3	0	1	33	0	46	4	3	4	3	.571	0	1	3.36
1991	Myrtle Bch	A	55	0	0	44	79.1	334	58	28	16	1	5	3	0	41	0	107	7	2	6	4	.600	0	13	1.82
1992	Dunedin	A	41	8	0	19	112.1	451	70	35	28	4	5	2	7	50	2	93	2	1	7	3	.700	0	8	2.24
1993	Knoxville	AA	38	16	2	10	136.1	556	130	56	50	9	6	4	3	39	1	114	9	8	13	6	.684	2	4	3.30
1994	Syracuse	AAA	6	6	0	0	37	155	38	22	19	6	0	3	0	8	0	20	2	1	0	3	.000	0	0	4.62
1995	Syracuse	AAA	30	23	1	3	134.2	572	131	70	59	20	1	6	6	41	2	83	2	2	6	11	.353	0	0	3.94
1993	Toronto	AL	6	0	0	1	6.2	30	7	3	3	0	0	0	0	4	1	2	1	0	0	0	.000	0	0	4.05
	6 Min. YEARS		184	60	3	79	561.1	2326	472	240	195	44	20	18	17	212	5	463	26	17	36	30	.545	2	26	3.13

Miguel Flores

Bats: Right **Throws:** Right **Pos:** 2B **Ht:** 5'11" **Wt:** 185 **Born:** 8/16/70 **Age:** 25

						BATTING												BASERUNNING				PERCENTAGES		
Year	Team	Lg	G	AB	H	2B	3B	HR	TB	R	RBI	TBB	IBB	SO	HBP	SH	SF	SB	CS	SB%	GDP	Avg	OBP	SLG
1990	Burlington	R	57	208	52	8	1	3	71	33	25	20	0	18	2	0	0	22	7	.76	3	.250	.322	.341
1991	Kinston	A	124	425	114	19	3	5	154	61	40	34	1	45	9	7	6	29	7	.81	13	.268	.331	.362
1992	Canton-Akrn	AA	126	456	124	20	4	1	155	45	43	35	3	39	5	3	5	25	11	.69	19	.272	.327	.340
1993	Canton-Akrn	AA	116	435	127	20	5	3	166	73	54	59	0	39	3	4	3	36	9	.80	11	.292	.378	.382
1994	Charlotte	AAA	87	248	68	10	1	2	86	35	31	23	0	30	2	5	1	9	6	.60	8	.274	.339	.347
1995	Buffalo	AAA	31	113	32	8	1	0	42	13	12	5	0	13	1	1	0	5	0	1.00	4	.283	.319	.372
	6 Min. YEARS		541	1885	517	85	15	14	674	260	205	176	4	184	22	20	15	126	40	.76	58	.274	.341	.358

Tim Florez

Bats: Right **Throws:** Right **Pos:** 3B-2B **Ht:** 5'10" **Wt:** 170 **Born:** 7/23/69 **Age:** 26

						BATTING												BASERUNNING				PERCENTAGES		
Year	Team	Lg	G	AB	H	2B	3B	HR	TB	R	RBI	TBB	IBB	SO	HBP	SH	SF	SB	CS	SB%	GDP	Avg	OBP	SLG
1991	Everett	A	59	193	48	8	4	0	64	33	25	12	1	33	1	2	1	7	1	.88	4	.249	.295	.332
1992	Clinton	A	81	292	68	12	2	2	90	39	25	30	2	53	3	0	2	20	5	.80	6	.233	.309	.308
	San Jose	A	38	131	32	6	1	1	43	15	17	4	0	21	0	4	4	3	3	.50	2	.244	.259	.328
1993	Shreveport	AA	106	318	81	17	2	1	105	33	26	16	4	43	2	3	2	3	5	.38	9	.255	.293	.330
1994	Phoenix	AAA	13	24	6	1	0	1	10	5	2	1	0	4	0	0	0	0	0	.00	1	.250	.280	.417
	Shreveport	AA	61	158	34	10	0	1	47	21	13	21	3	34	1	2	1	0	3	.00	4	.215	.309	.297
1995	Shreveport	AA	100	295	79	11	2	9	121	37	46	26	1	49	4	3	3	4	3	.57	7	.268	.332	.410
	5 Min. YEARS		458	1411	348	65	11	15	480	183	154	110	11	237	11	14	13	37	20	.65	33	.247	.304	.340

Bill Flynt

Pitches: Left **Bats:** Left **Pos:** P **Ht:** 6'5" **Wt:** 215 **Born:** 11/23/67 **Age:** 28

			HOW MUCH HE PITCHED						WHAT HE GAVE UP											THE RESULTS					
Year	Team	Lg	G	GS	CG	GF	IP	BFP	H	R	ER	HR	SH	SF	HB	TBB	IBB	SO	WP	Bk	W	L	Pct.	ShO	Sv	ERA
1991	San Bernrdo	A	22	0	0	7	38	186	46	27	19	1	2	2	4	25	0	40	5	1	1	0	1.000	0	0	4.50

Year	Team	Lg	G	GS	CG	GF	IP	BFP	H	R	ER	HR	SH	SF	HB	TBB	IBB	SO	WP	Bk	W	L	Pct.	ShO	Sv	ERA
1995	Calgary	AAA	12	1	0	3	21.2	103	27	15	13	4	1	1	0	12	0	12	1	0	1	0	1.000	0	0	5.40
	Carolina	AA	4	0	0	1	3.2	16	3	0	0	0	1	0	0	2	0	6	0	0	0	0	.000	0	0	0.00
	2 Min. YEARS		38	1	0	11	63.1	305	76	42	32	5	4	3	4	39	0	58	6	1	2	0	1.000	0	0	4.55

P.J. Forbes

Bats: Right Throws: Right Pos: 2B   Ht: 5'10" Wt: 160 Born: 9/22/67 Age: 28

			BATTING														BASERUNNING				PERCENTAGES		
Year	Team	Lg	G	AB	H	2B	3B	HR	TB	R	RBI	TBB	IBB	SO	HBP	SH	SF	SB	CS	SB%	GDP	Avg	OBP	SLG
1990	Boise	A	43	170	42	9	1	0	53	29	19	23	1	21	0	7	1	11	4	.73	5	.247	.335	.312
1991	Palm Spring	A	94	349	93	14	2	2	117	45	26	36	1	44	4	12	0	18	8	.69	7	.266	.342	.335
1992	Quad City	A	105	376	106	16	5	2	138	53	46	44	1	51	2	24	5	15	6	.71	4	.282	.356	.367
1993	Midland	AA	126	498	159	23	2	15	231	90	64	26	1	50	4	14	2	6	8	.43	13	.319	.357	.464
	Vancouver	AAA	5	16	4	2	0	0	6	1	3	0	0	3	0	1	0	0	0	.00	1	.250	.250	.375
1994	Angels	R	2	6	0	0	0	0	0	1	0	0	0	1	0	0	0	0	0	.00	0	.000	.000	.000
	Vancouver	AAA	90	318	91	21	2	1	119	39	40	22	0	42	2	7	5	4	2	.67	6	.286	.331	.374
1995	Vancouver	AAA	109	369	101	22	3	1	132	47	52	21	0	46	2	7	10	4	6	.40	4	.274	.308	.358
	6 Min. YEARS		574	2102	596	107	15	21	796	305	250	172	4	258	14	72	23	58	34	.63	40	.284	.338	.379

Curt Ford

Bats: Left Throws: Right Pos: OF   Ht: 5'10" Wt: 150 Born: 10/11/60 Age: 35

			BATTING														BASERUNNING				PERCENTAGES		
Year	Team	Lg	G	AB	H	2B	3B	HR	TB	R	RBI	TBB	IBB	SO	HBP	SH	SF	SB	CS	SB%	GDP	Avg	OBP	SLG
1984	Arkansas	AA	118	442	143	23	1	10	198	62	78	52	5	50	3	1	6	25	10	.71	5	.324	.394	.448
	Louisville	AAA	13	38	10	2	0	0	12	5	1	4	1	9	0	1	0	5	1	.83	0	.263	.333	.316
1985	Louisville	AAA	127	475	121	20	6	7	174	73	45	56	3	48	7	6	3	45	17	.73	11	.255	.340	.366
1986	Louisville	AAA	53	200	59	9	2	4	84	47	31	28	0	16	0	0	3	24	7	.77	4	.295	.377	.420
1990	Scranton-Wb	AAA	56	195	43	5	3	5	69	28	12	22	0	39	1	1	1	14	5	.74	5	.221	.301	.354
1991	Toledo	AAA	102	366	98	24	4	3	139	52	38	42	0	38	1	7	5	8	10	.44	11	.268	.341	.380
1992	Louisville	AAA	88	257	77	15	3	6	116	47	31	29	4	26	4	0	3	9	6	.60	5	.300	.375	.451
1993	Rochester	IND	69	248	58	5	1	5	80	48	30	46	2	26	4	0	0	31	11	.74	3	.234	.362	.323
1995	Charlotte	AAA	57	167	51	10	0	3	70	18	17	9	1	29	3	0	0	2	4	.33	4	.305	.352	.419
1985	St. Louis	NL	11	12	6	2	0	0	8	2	3	4	0	1	0	0	0	1	0	1.00	0	.500	.625	.667
1986	St. Louis	NL	85	214	53	15	2	2	78	30	29	23	2	29	0	1	2	13	5	.72	1	.248	.318	.364
1987	St. Louis	NL	89	228	65	9	5	3	93	32	26	14	0	32	1	1	3	11	8	.58	5	.285	.325	.408
1988	St. Louis	NL	91	128	25	6	0	1	34	11	18	8	1	26	0	1	2	6	1	.86	4	.195	.239	.266
1989	Philadelphia	NL	108	142	31	5	1	1	41	13	13	16	0	33	1	0	2	5	3	.63	4	.218	.298	.289
1990	Philadelphia	NL	22	18	2	0	0	0	2	0	0	1	0	5	0	0	0	0	0	.00	1	.111	.158	.111
	8 Min. YEARS		683	2388	660	113	20	43	942	380	283	288	16	281	23	16	21	163	71	.70	48	.276	.357	.394
	6 Maj. YEARS		406	742	182	37	8	7	256	88	89	66	3	126	2	3	9	36	17	.68	15	.245	.305	.345

Tom Fordham

Pitches: Left Bats: Left Pos: P   Ht: 6'2" Wt: 210 Born: 2/20/74 Age: 22

			HOW MUCH HE PITCHED						WHAT HE GAVE UP											THE RESULTS				
Year	Team	Lg	G	GS	CG	GF	IP	BFP	H	R	ER	HR	SH	SF	HB	TBB	IBB	SO	WP	Bk	W	L	Pct.	ShO	Sv	ERA
1993	White Sox	R	3	0	0	1	10	41	9	2	2	0	0	0	0	3	0	12	1	0	1	1	.500	0	0	1.80
	Sarasota	A	2	0	0	1	5	21	3	1	0	0	0	0	0	3	2	5	1	1	0	0	.000	0	0	0.00
	Hickory	A	8	8	1	0	48.2	194	36	21	21	3	1	6	0	21	0	27	3	2	4	3	.571	0	0	3.88
1994	Hickory	A	17	17	1	0	109	452	101	47	38	10	1	1	3	30	1	121	5	4	10	5	.667	1	0	3.14
	South Bend	A	11	11	1	0	74.2	315	82	46	36	4	4	3	0	14	0	48	4	0	4	4	.500	1	0	4.34
1995	Pr. William	A	13	13	1	0	84	340	66	20	19	7	2	1	2	35	2	78	1	0	9	0	1.000	1	0	2.04
	Birmingham	AA	14	14	2	0	82.2	348	79	35	31	9	2	2	0	28	2	61	3	0	6	3	.667	1	0	3.38
	3 Min. YEARS		68	63	6	2	414	1711	376	172	147	33	10	13	5	134	7	352	18	7	34	16	.680	4	0	3.20

Tim Forkner

Bats: Left Throws: Right Pos: 3B   Ht: 5'11" Wt: 180 Born: 3/28/73 Age: 23

			BATTING														BASERUNNING				PERCENTAGES		
Year	Team	Lg	G	AB	H	2B	3B	HR	TB	R	RBI	TBB	IBB	SO	HBP	SH	SF	SB	CS	SB%	GDP	Avg	OBP	SLG
1993	Auburn	A	72	267	76	14	9	0	108	32	39	38	0	29	3	1	1	3	3	.50	8	.285	.379	.404
1994	Quad City	A	124	429	128	23	4	6	177	57	57	57	3	72	7	10	8	6	8	.43	10	.298	.383	.413
1995	Kissimmee	A	89	296	84	20	4	1	115	42	34	60	2	40	5	2	4	4	2	.67	11	.284	.408	.389
	Jackson	AA	35	119	32	11	0	3	52	19	23	19	0	14	2	0	0	1	3	.25	3	.269	.379	.437
	3 Min. YEARS		320	1111	320	68	17	10	452	150	153	174	5	155	17	13	13	14	16	.47	32	.288	.389	.407

Rick Forney

Pitches: Right Bats: Right Pos: P   Ht: 6'4" Wt: 210 Born: 10/24/71 Age: 24

			HOW MUCH HE PITCHED						WHAT HE GAVE UP											THE RESULTS				
Year	Team	Lg	G	GS	CG	GF	IP	BFP	H	R	ER	HR	SH	SF	HB	TBB	IBB	SO	WP	Bk	W	L	Pct.	ShO	Sv	ERA
1991	Orioles	R	12	10	2	0	65.2	260	48	21	16	1	1	1	4	10	0	51	1	2	7	0	1.000	1	0	2.19
1992	Kane County	A	20	18	2	0	123.1	513	114	40	34	4	4	2	9	26	1	104	9	2	3	6	.333	1	0	2.48
1993	Frederick	A	27	27	2	0	165	704	156	64	51	11	4	4	7	64	0	175	12	2	14	8	.636	0	0	2.78
	Bowie	AA	1	1	0	0	7	24	1	1	1	1	0	0	1	1	0	4	0	0	0	0	.000	0	0	1.29
1994	Bowie	AA	28	28	4	0	165.2	715	168	105	85	17	4	7	3	58	1	125	9	2	13	8	.619	2	0	4.62
1995	Rochester	AAA	3	3	0	0	16	72	19	9	7	2	2	1	0	6	0	12	2	0	0	0	.000	0	0	3.94
	Bowie	AA	23	19	1	2	97	437	110	69	62	14	2	6	3	42	0	73	7	1	7	7	.500	1	0	5.75
	5 Min. YEARS		114	106	11	2	639.2	2725	616	309	256	50	17	21	27	207	2	544	40	9	44	29	.603	5	0	3.60

Mark Foster

Pitches: Left **Bats:** Left **Pos:** P   **Ht:** 6'1" **Wt:** 200 **Born:** 12/24/71 **Age:** 24

			HOW MUCH HE PITCHED					WHAT HE GAVE UP								THE RESULTS				
Year	Team	Lg	G	GS	CG	GF	IP	BFP	H	R	ER	HR	SH	SF	HB	TBB	IBB	SO	WP	Bk	W	L	Pct.	ShO	Sv	ERA
1993	Martinsvlle	R	13	13	0	0	69.1	330	77	55	38	3	1	4	6	42	1	50	6	4	1	9	.100	0	0	4.93
1994	Spartanburg	A	32	0	0	25	42.1	192	41	23	21	0	5	1	4	24	0	40	10	3	4	2	.667	0	11	4.46
	Clearwater	A	16	1	0	5	26.2	118	28	13	10	0	0	0	0	14	0	22	0	1	2	2	.500	0	1	3.38
1995	Reading	AA	25	0	0	4	20.2	106	25	15	13	1	2	1	1	17	3	15	2	4	1	1	.500	0	1	5.66
	Clearwater	A	24	0	0	6	23.1	108	30	17	14	1	1	0	4	10	0	13	1	1	0	1	.000	0	0	5.40
	3 Min. YEARS		110	14	0	40	182.1	854	201	123	96	5	9	6	15	107	4	140	19	13	8	15	.348	0	14	4.74

Andy Fox

Bats: Left **Throws:** Right **Pos:** 3B-SS   **Ht:** 6'4" **Wt:** 185 **Born:** 1/12/71 **Age:** 25

			BATTING														BASERUNNING				PERCENTAGES		
Year	Team	Lg	G	AB	H	2B	3B	HR	TB	R	RBI	TBB	IBB	SO	HBP	SH	SF	SB	CS	SB%	GDP	Avg	OBP	SLG
1989	Yankees	R	40	141	35	9	2	3	57	26	25	31	1	29	2	0	2	6	1	.86	1	.248	.386	.404
1990	Greensboro	A	134	455	99	19	4	9	153	68	55	92	5	132	4	1	2	26	5	.84	14	.218	.353	.336
1991	Pr. William	A	126	417	96	22	2	10	152	60	46	81	3	104	6	1	9	15	13	.54	7	.230	.357	.365
1992	Pr. William	A	125	473	113	18	3	7	158	75	42	54	1	81	6	4	0	28	14	.67	7	.239	.325	.334
1993	Albany-Colo	AA	65	236	65	16	1	3	92	44	24	32	1	54	0	2	0	12	6	.67	1	.275	.362	.390
1994	Albany-Colo	AA	121	472	105	20	3	11	164	75	43	62	3	102	2	4	1	22	13	.63	4	.222	.315	.347
1995	Norwich	AA	44	175	36	3	5	5	64	23	17	19	0	36	0	1	1	8	1	.89	3	.206	.282	.366
	Columbus	AAA	82	302	105	16	6	9	160	61	37	43	1	41	4	2	3	22	4	.85	5	.348	.432	.530
	7 Min. YEARS		737	2671	654	123	26	57	1000	432	289	414	15	579	24	15	18	139	57	.71	42	.245	.349	.374

Chad Fox

Pitches: Right **Bats:** Right **Pos:** P   **Ht:** 6'2" **Wt:** 180 **Born:** 9/3/70 **Age:** 25

			HOW MUCH HE PITCHED					WHAT HE GAVE UP								THE RESULTS				
Year	Team	Lg	G	GS	CG	GF	IP	BFP	H	R	ER	HR	SH	SF	HB	TBB	IBB	SO	WP	Bk	W	L	Pct.	ShO	Sv	ERA
1992	Princeton	R	15	8	0	4	49.1	238	55	43	26	2	1	1	2	34	1	37	6	2	4	2	.667	0	0	4.74
1993	Charlstn-Wv	A	27	26	0	0	135.2	638	138	100	81	7	6	8	13	97	0	81	15	1	9	12	.429	0	0	5.37
1994	Winston-Sal	A	25	25	1	0	156.1	674	121	77	67	18	5	5	9	94	0	137	20	1	12	5	.706	0	0	3.86
1995	Chattanooga	AA	20	17	0	1	80	363	76	49	45	2	2	2	3	52	1	56	14	0	4	5	.444	0	0	5.06
	4 Min. YEARS		87	76	1	5	421.1	1913	390	269	219	29	14	16	27	277	2	311	55	4	29	24	.547	0	0	4.68

David Francisco

Bats: Right **Throws:** Right **Pos:** OF   **Ht:** 6'0" **Wt:** 165 **Born:** 2/27/72 **Age:** 24

			BATTING														BASERUNNING				PERCENTAGES		
Year	Team	Lg	G	AB	H	2B	3B	HR	TB	R	RBI	TBB	IBB	SO	HBP	SH	SF	SB	CS	SB%	GDP	Avg	OBP	SLG
1991	Athletics	R	56	208	50	7	4	1	68	34	34	24	0	30	2	2	1	14	5	.74	6	.240	.323	.327
1992	Athletics	R	10	37	14	1	1	1	20	12	8	5	0	6	4	0	0	6	2	.75	0	.378	.500	.541
	Reno	A	7	15	3	0	0	0	3	5	0	3	0	5	0	1	0	1	0	1.00	0	.200	.333	.200
	Madison	A	43	133	26	5	1	0	33	9	11	16	0	32	2	7	0	3	1	.75	1	.195	.291	.248
1993	Madison	A	129	484	134	24	8	2	180	87	50	50	1	108	12	9	4	27	16	.63	7	.277	.356	.372
1994	Modesto	A	130	499	138	18	5	9	193	86	48	61	0	110	9	11	2	29	18	.62	1	.277	.364	.387
1995	Huntsville	AA	129	477	133	17	1	5	167	75	48	38	0	92	11	5	3	30	8	.79	10	.279	.344	.350
	5 Min. YEARS		504	1853	498	72	20	18	664	308	199	197	1	383	40	35	10	110	50	.69	25	.269	.350	.358

Micah Franklin

Bats: Both **Throws:** Right **Pos:** OF   **Ht:** 6'0" **Wt:** 195 **Born:** 4/25/72 **Age:** 24

			BATTING														BASERUNNING				PERCENTAGES		
Year	Team	Lg	G	AB	H	2B	3B	HR	TB	R	RBI	TBB	IBB	SO	HBP	SH	SF	SB	CS	SB%	GDP	Avg	OBP	SLG
1990	Kingsport	R	39	158	41	9	2	7	75	29	25	8	0	44	1	0	2	4	1	.80	2	.259	.296	.475
1991	Pittsfield	A	26	94	27	4	2	0	35	17	14	21	0	20	1	2	1	12	3	.80	3	.287	.419	.372
	Erie	A	39	153	37	4	0	2	47	28	8	25	0	35	2	0	1	4	5	.44	3	.242	.354	.307
1992	Billings	R	75	251	84	13	2	11	134	58	60	53	3	65	15	0	3	18	17	.51	3	.335	.472	.534
1993	Winston-Sal	A	20	69	16	1	1	3	28	10	6	10	1	19	2	1	0	0	1	.00	0	.232	.346	.406
	Charlstn-Wv	A	102	343	90	14	4	17	163	56	68	47	4	109	18	3	6	6	1	.86	4	.262	.374	.475
1994	Winston-Sal	A	42	150	45	7	0	21	115	44	44	27	5	48	6	0	1	7	0	1.00	1	.300	.424	.767
	Chattanooga	AA	79	279	77	17	0	10	124	46	40	33	3	79	13	0	3	2	2	.50	3	.276	.375	.444
1995	Calgary	AAA	110	358	105	28	0	21	196	64	71	47	8	95	1	0	5	3	3	.50	7	.293	.372	.547
	6 Min. YEARS		532	1855	522	97	11	92	917	352	336	271	24	514	59	6	22	56	33	.63	26	.281	.386	.494

Ryan Franklin

Pitches: Right **Bats:** Right **Pos:** P   **Ht:** 6'3" **Wt:** 160 **Born:** 3/5/73 **Age:** 23

			HOW MUCH HE PITCHED					WHAT HE GAVE UP								THE RESULTS				
Year	Team	Lg	G	GS	CG	GF	IP	BFP	H	R	ER	HR	SH	SF	HB	TBB	IBB	SO	WP	Bk	W	L	Pct.	ShO	Sv	ERA
1993	Bellingham	A	15	14	1	0	74	321	72	38	24	2	2	1	3	27	0	55	7	3	5	3	.625	1	0	2.92
1994	Appleton	A	18	18	5	0	118	493	105	60	41	6	3	1	17	23	0	102	6	3	9	6	.600	1	0	3.13
	Calgary	AAA	1	1	0	0	5.2	28	9	6	5	2	0	0	0	1	0	2	0	0	0	0	.000	0	0	7.94
	Riverside	A	8	8	1	0	61.2	261	61	26	21	5	1	3	4	8	0	35	0	1	4	2	.667	1	0	3.06
1995	Port City	AA	31	20	1	2	146	627	153	84	70	13	11	3	12	43	4	102	6	2	6	10	.375	1	0	4.32
	3 Min. YEARS		73	61	8	2	405.1	1730	400	214	161	28	17	8	36	102	4	296	19	9	24	21	.533	4	0	3.57

Dan Fraraccio

Bats: Right **Throws:** Right **Pos:** 3B **Ht:** 5'11" **Wt:** 175 **Born:** 9/18/70 **Age:** 25

						BATTING												BASERUNNING				PERCENTAGES		
Year	Team	Lg	G	AB	H	2B	3B	HR	TB	R	RBI	TBB	IBB	SO	HBP	SH	SF	SB	CS	SB%	GDP	Avg	OBP	SLG
1992	White Sox	R	52	149	31	5	1	0	38	19	8	5	0	18	4	1	1	5	7	.42	0	.208	.252	.255
	Sarasota	A	1	3	1	0	0	0	1	0	0	0	0	1	0	0	0	0	0	.00	0	.333	.333	.333
1993	Hickory	A	41	147	31	9	1	1	45	13	15	6	0	21	3	0	1	2	2	.50	2	.211	.255	.306
	South Bend	A	49	135	37	10	0	0	47	23	21	6	0	29	3	1	1	0	1	.00	4	.274	.317	.348
1994	Pr. William	A	26	80	19	1	1	1	25	10	7	3	0	19	0	1	1	1	0	1.00	1	.238	.262	.313
	White Sox	R	3	2	1	0	0	0	1	0	0	1	0	1	0	0	0	0	0	.00	0	.500	.667	.500
1995	Nashville	AAA	10	28	7	0	0	0	7	2	3	1	0	6	0	1	0	2	0	1.00	0	.250	.276	.250
	Pr. William	A	24	74	17	5	0	2	28	11	6	8	0	12	0	1	0	0	0	.00	1	.230	.305	.378
	4 Min. YEARS		206	618	144	30	3	4	192	78	60	30	0	107	10	5	4	10	10	.50	10	.233	.278	.311

Ron Frazier

Pitches: Right **Bats:** Right **Pos:** P **Ht:** 6'2" **Wt:** 185 **Born:** 6/13/69 **Age:** 27

				HOW MUCH HE PITCHED					WHAT HE GAVE UP									THE RESULTS						
Year	Team	Lg	G	GS	CG	GF	IP	BFP	H	R	ER	HR	SH	SF	HB	TBB	IBB	SO	WP	Bk	W	L	Pct.	ShO	Sv	ERA
1990	Oneonta	A	13	13	0	0	80.1	328	67	32	22	5	2	7	2	33	0	67	4	5	6	2	.750	0	0	2.46
1991	Greensboro	A	25	25	3	0	169	692	140	65	45	10	3	6	9	42	0	127	8	4	12	6	.667	1	0	2.40
1992	Pr. William	A	16	7	0	4	56.1	236	51	27	20	10	2	0	5	11	0	52	2	1	4	3	.571	0	0	3.20
1993	Pr. William	A	15	15	1	0	101	403	79	34	24	5	2	1	1	23	0	108	4	1	8	3	.727	0	0	2.14
	Albany-Colo	AA	12	12	0	0	79.2	341	93	43	34	5	1	6	1	16	0	65	3	1	4	3	.571	0	0	3.84
1994	Columbus	AAA	20	17	1	1	104	454	108	59	54	9	5	2	5	43	0	62	3	2	6	6	.500	1	0	4.67
	Albany-Colo	AA	10	10	1	0	60.1	257	53	30	21	5	3	1	3	21	3	29	2	0	3	4	.429	0	0	3.13
1995	Columbus	AAA	24	5	0	9	54	240	54	33	27	4	4	2	4	23	2	31	7	1	1	2	.333	0	0	4.50
	6 Min. YEARS		135	104	6	14	704.2	2951	645	323	247	53	22	25	30	212	5	541	33	15	44	29	.603	2	0	3.15

Scott Fredrickson

Pitches: Right **Bats:** Right **Pos:** P **Ht:** 6'3" **Wt:** 215 **Born:** 8/19/67 **Age:** 28

				HOW MUCH HE PITCHED					WHAT HE GAVE UP									THE RESULTS						
Year	Team	Lg	G	GS	CG	GF	IP	BFP	H	R	ER	HR	SH	SF	HB	TBB	IBB	SO	WP	Bk	W	L	Pct.	ShO	Sv	ERA
1990	Spokane	A	26	1	0	15	46.2	197	35	22	17	3	4	1	2	17	1	61	6	4	3	3	.500	0	8	3.28
1991	Waterloo	A	26	0	0	22	38.1	153	24	9	5	1	1	2	1	15	3	40	3	2	3	5	.375	0	6	1.17
	High Desert	A	23	0	0	19	35	154	31	15	9	2	2	1	1	18	2	26	6	0	4	1	.800	0	7	2.31
1992	Wichita	AA	56	0	0	22	73.1	303	50	29	26	9	2	5	2	38	3	66	11	0	4	7	.364	0	5	3.19
1993	Colo. Sprng	AAA	23	0	0	18	26.1	119	25	16	16	3	2	1	0	19	3	20	2	0	1	3	.250	0	7	5.47
1995	Colo. Sprng	AAA	58	0	0	20	75.2	348	70	40	29	2	8	3	5	47	5	70	15	2	11	3	.786	0	4	3.45
1993	Colorado	NL	25	0	0	4	29	137	33	25	20	3	2	2	1	17	2	20	4	1	0	1	.000	0	0	6.21
	5 Min. YEARS		212	2	0	116	295.1	1274	235	131	102	20	19	13	11	154	17	283	43	8	26	22	.542	0	37	3.11

Chris Freeman

Pitches: Right **Bats:** Right **Pos:** P **Ht:** 6'4" **Wt:** 205 **Born:** 8/27/72 **Age:** 23

				HOW MUCH HE PITCHED					WHAT HE GAVE UP									THE RESULTS						
Year	Team	Lg	G	GS	CG	GF	IP	BFP	H	R	ER	HR	SH	SF	HB	TBB	IBB	SO	WP	Bk	W	L	Pct.	ShO	Sv	ERA
1994	Dunedin	A	17	3	0	5	50.2	205	44	16	14	1	2	2	0	21	1	45	5	2	3	2	.600	0	1	2.49
1995	Knoxville	AA	39	5	0	16	81.1	354	78	53	49	12	5	5	1	38	0	80	1	0	2	3	.400	0	8	5.42
	2 Min. YEARS		56	8	0	21	132	559	122	69	63	13	7	7	1	59	1	125	6	2	5	5	.500	0	9	4.30

Mike Freitas

Pitches: Right **Bats:** Right **Pos:** P **Ht:** 6'1" **Wt:** 160 **Born:** 9/22/69 **Age:** 26

				HOW MUCH HE PITCHED					WHAT HE GAVE UP									THE RESULTS						
Year	Team	Lg	G	GS	CG	GF	IP	BFP	H	R	ER	HR	SH	SF	HB	TBB	IBB	SO	WP	Bk	W	L	Pct.	ShO	Sv	ERA
1989	Pittsfield	A	13	2	0	8	33.1	137	37	19	15	2	4	1	0	5	1	16	2	4	3	0	1.000	0	0	4.05
1990	Pittsfield	A	5	0	0	0	9.1	37	7	4	4	0	1	1	0	4	0	8	0	2	1	0	1.000	0	0	3.86
	Columbia	A	13	9	0	2	70	285	60	27	19	5	1	1	2	14	0	47	5	0	5	2	.714	0	0	2.44
1991	Columbia	A	25	12	4	11	114.1	475	115	48	42	4	2	3	6	31	0	111	4	1	5	8	.385	2	2	3.31
	St. Lucie	A	5	0	0	4	10.2	45	11	4	3	1	2	0	1	1	0	6	0	0	0	1	.000	0	0	2.53
1992	St. Lucie	A	45	0	0	39	57.2	231	51	17	8	2	1	6	4	9	1	30	0	2	6	3	.667	0	24	1.25
1993	Wichita	AA	8	0	0	7	7.2	43	13	14	9	1	0	1	0	2	0	4	2	0	0	2	.000	0	0	10.57
1994	Padres	R	4	0	0	2	6	23	2	1	1	0	0	0	0	3	0	7	1	0	1	0	1.000	0	1	1.50
1995	Memphis	AA	54	0	0	16	59	246	55	26	24	3	2	3	2	26	8	36	3	1	0	6	.000	0	3	3.66
	7 Min. YEARS		172	23	4	90	368	1522	351	160	125	18	13	16	15	95	10	265	17	10	21	22	.488	2	29	3.06

Hanley Frias

Bats: Both **Throws:** Right **Pos:** SS **Ht:** 6'0" **Wt:** 160 **Born:** 12/5/73 **Age:** 22

						BATTING												BASERUNNING				PERCENTAGES		
Year	Team	Lg	G	AB	H	2B	3B	HR	TB	R	RBI	TBB	IBB	SO	HBP	SH	SF	SB	CS	SB%	GDP	Avg	OBP	SLG
1992	Rangers	R	58	205	50	9	2	0	63	37	28	27	0	30	2	2	2	28	6	.82	1	.244	.335	.307
1993	Charlstn-Sc	A	132	473	109	20	4	4	149	61	37	40	0	108	3	4	4	27	14	.66	8	.230	.292	.315
1994	High Desert	A	124	452	115	17	6	3	153	70	59	41	1	74	2	5	3	37	12	.76	9	.254	.317	.338
1995	Charlotte	A	33	120	40	6	3	0	52	23	14	15	0	11	1	3	1	8	6	.57	0	.333	.409	.433

Tulsa	AA	93	360	101	18	4	0	127	44	27	45	0	53	1	8	2	14	12	.54	6	.281	.360	.353
4 Min. YEARS		440	1610	415	70	19	7	544	235	165	168	1	276	9	22	12	114	50	.70	24	.258	.329	.338

Jason Friedman

Bats: Left **Throws:** Left **Pos:** 1B   **Ht:** 6'1" **Wt:** 200 **Born:** 8/8/69 **Age:** 26

								BATTING										BASERUNNING				PERCENTAGES		
Year	Team	Lg	G	AB	H	2B	3B	HR	TB	R	RBI	TBB	IBB	SO	HBP	SH	SF	SB	CS	SB%	GDP	Avg	OBP	SLG
1989	Red Sox	R	32	116	29	4	2	0	37	8	9	5	1	13	2	1	0	0	2	.00	4	.250	.293	.319
	Winter Havn	A	21	62	12	0	2	0	16	5	5	2	0	12	0	0	0	0	0	.00	0	.194	.219	.258
1990	Winter Havn	A	50	163	26	5	0	1	34	12	11	16	1	26	0	1	2	1	0	1.00	3	.160	.232	.209
	Elmira	A	67	213	51	16	0	0	67	25	23	26	1	27	2	0	2	3	4	.43	3	.239	.325	.315
1991	Elmira	A	70	253	68	13	2	8	109	36	36	35	5	43	3	1	2	2	0	1.00	4	.269	.362	.431
1992	Lynchburg	A	135	495	132	26	1	14	202	68	68	46	5	61	4	1	2	5	4	.56	9	.267	.333	.408
1993	New Britain	AA	81	294	73	15	1	1	93	22	24	20	4	50	3	1	4	2	0	1.00	7	.248	.299	.316
1994	Sarasota	A	124	469	154	35	11	7	232	60	87	22	9	74	1	1	12	2	3	.40	3	.328	.351	.495
1995	Pawtucket	AAA	14	51	15	3	0	2	24	6	9	2	1	3	0	1	1	0	0	.00	1	.294	.315	.471
	Bowie	AA	63	228	53	11	0	3	73	22	27	16	2	23	2	1	1	1	1	.50	7	.232	.287	.320
	Rochester	AAA	25	61	23	4	0	4	39	9	9	6	0	8	1	0	0	0	0	.00	2	.377	.441	.639
7 Min. YEARS			682	2405	636	132	19	40	926	273	308	196	29	340	18	8	26	16	14	.53	43	.264	.321	.385

John Fritz

Pitches: Right **Bats:** Right **Pos:** P   **Ht:** 6'1" **Wt:** 170 **Born:** 3/6/69 **Age:** 27

			HOW MUCH HE PITCHED						WHAT HE GAVE UP										THE RESULTS					
Year	Team	Lg	G	GS	CG	GF	IP	BFP	H	R	ER	HR	SH	SF	HB	TBB	IBB	SO	WP	Bk	W	L	Pct.	ShO	Sv	ERA
1988	Bend	A	14	7	0	3	44.1	202	46	25	18	0	2	3	5	23	1	30	3	0	0	0	.000	0	0	3.65
1989	Angels	R	14	14	0	0	85	377	86	50	39	0	2	4	3	38	1	70	10	12	4	5	.444	0	0	4.13
1990	Palm Spring	A	31	21	1	2	131	588	131	80	61	13	3	6	5	75	3	64	13	1	8	7	.533	1	0	4.19
1991	Miami	A	14	0	0	7	22.2	99	21	7	6	1	1	2	0	10	1	24	1	1	0	2	.000	0	1	2.38
	Quad City	A	25	5	0	9	61.1	260	52	27	25	3	2	5	4	24	1	72	2	3	2	3	.400	0	0	3.67
1992	Quad City	A	27	25	6	0	172.1	705	129	65	58	10	3	0	3	69	1	143	16	4	20	4	.833	1	0	3.03
1993	Midland	AA	20	20	2	0	129.2	547	125	61	52	12	2	3	8	42	0	85	12	0	9	5	.643	1	0	3.61
	Vancouver	AAA	8	7	0	0	42	187	52	22	19	3	2	2	0	18	1	29	2	0	3	1	.750	0	0	4.07
1994	Vancouver	AAA	10	9	1	0	54.1	240	61	33	30	12	2	3	1	23	0	29	3	0	3	2	.600	0	0	4.97
	Midland	AA	13	11	1	0	61.1	275	70	46	38	8	1	4	3	27	0	48	11	1	2	5	.286	0	0	5.58
1995	New Orleans	AAA	41	6	0	6	81.2	348	70	38	36	11	1	0	4	42	4	56	5	0	6	3	.667	0	1	3.97
8 Min. YEARS			217	125	11	27	885.2	3828	843	454	382	73	21	32	36	391	13	650	78	22	57	37	.606	3	2	3.88

Todd Frohwirth

Pitches: Right **Bats:** Right **Pos:** P   **Ht:** 6'4" **Wt:** 205 **Born:** 9/28/62 **Age:** 33

			HOW MUCH HE PITCHED						WHAT HE GAVE UP										THE RESULTS					
Year	Team	Lg	G	GS	CG	GF	IP	BFP	H	R	ER	HR	SH	SF	HB	TBB	IBB	SO	WP	Bk	W	L	Pct.	ShO	Sv	ERA
1984	Bend	A	29	0	0	25	49.2	0	26	17	9	0	0	0	3	31	4	60	1	0	4	4	.500	0	11	1.63
1985	Peninsula	A	54	0	0	48	82	363	70	33	20	2	3	1	4	48	3	74	6	3	7	5	.583	0	18	2.20
1986	Clearwater	A	32	0	0	23	52	227	54	29	23	1	1	2	2	18	2	39	2	0	3	3	.500	0	10	3.98
	Reading	AA	29	0	0	23	42	175	39	20	15	1	2	0	2	10	4	23	1	0	0	4	.000	0	12	3.21
1987	Maine	AAA	27	0	0	18	32.1	141	30	12	9	3	2	3	0	15	7	21	0	1	1	4	.200	0	3	2.51
	Reading	AA	36	0	0	31	58	217	36	14	12	3	1	4	2	13	0	44	1	0	2	4	.333	0	19	1.86
1988	Maine	AAA	49	0	0	38	62.2	258	52	21	17	3	5	0	5	19	3	39	3	1	7	3	.700	0	13	2.44
1989	Scranton-Wb	AAA	21	0	0	17	32.1	134	29	11	8	1	2	0	1	11	3	29	0	0	3	2	.600	0	7	2.23
1990	Scranton-Wb	AAA	67	0	0	52	83	349	77	34	28	3	6	3	8	32	3	56	0	0	9	7	.563	0	21	3.04
1991	Rochester	AAA	20	0	0	16	24.2	97	17	12	10	1	2	2	2	5	0	15	1	0	1	3	.250	0	8	3.65
1994	Pawtucket	AAA	34	0	0	10	52	225	49	21	18	5	1	0	0	19	3	55	4	0	2	0	1.000	0	6	3.12
1995	Buffalo	AAA	26	0	0	11	32.1	137	31	13	12	4	1	1	1	12	1	33	0	0	0	1	.000	0	3	3.34
1987	Philadelphia	NL	10	0	0	2	11	43	12	0	0	0	0	0	0	2	0	9	0	0	1	0	1.000	0	0	0.00
1988	Philadelphia	NL	12	0	0	6	12	62	16	11	11	2	1	1	0	11	6	11	1	0	1	2	.333	0	0	8.25
1989	Philadelphia	NL	45	0	0	11	62.2	258	56	26	25	4	3	1	3	18	0	39	1	1	1	0	1.000	0	0	3.59
1990	Philadelphia	NL	5	0	0	0	1	12	3	2	2	0	0	0	0	6	2	1	1	0	0	1	.000	0	0	18.00
1991	Baltimore	AL	51	0	0	10	96.1	372	64	24	20	2	4	1	1	29	3	77	0	0	7	3	.700	0	3	1.87
1992	Baltimore	AL	65	0	0	23	106	444	97	33	29	4	7	1	3	41	4	58	1	0	4	3	.571	0	4	2.46
1993	Baltimore	AL	70	0	0	30	96.1	411	91	47	41	7	7	2	3	44	8	50	1	0	6	7	.462	0	3	3.83
1994	Boston	AL	22	0	0	8	26.2	141	40	36	32	3	4	0	2	17	2	13	1	0	0	3	.000	0	1	10.80
10 Min. YEARS			424	0	0	312	603	2323	510	237	181	27	26	16	30	233	33	488	19	5	39	40	.494	0	131	2.70
8 Maj. YEARS			280	0	0	90	412	1743	379	179	160	22	26	6	12	168	25	258	6	1	20	19	.513	0	11	3.50

Jason Fronio

Pitches: Right **Bats:** Right **Pos:** P   **Ht:** 6'2" **Wt:** 205 **Born:** 12/26/69 **Age:** 26

			HOW MUCH HE PITCHED						WHAT HE GAVE UP										THE RESULTS					
Year	Team	Lg	G	GS	CG	GF	IP	BFP	H	R	ER	HR	SH	SF	HB	TBB	IBB	SO	WP	Bk	W	L	Pct.	ShO	Sv	ERA
1991	Watertown	A	3	0	0	2	3.2	21	6	8	8	1	0	0	0	4	0	1	0	0	0	1	.000	0	0	19.64
	Bend	A	5	0	0	2	13.2	62	12	7	6	0	0	1	0	6	0	11	2	1	0	0	.000	0	1	3.95
1992	Watertown	A	5	0	0	1	10	43	8	5	5	1	0	0	0	4	1	13	0	0	1	2	.333	0	0	4.50
	Columbus	A	20	0	0	15	32.1	117	11	7	3	2	1	2	1	11	1	40	1	1	3	1	.750	0	4	0.84
1993	Kinston	A	32	20	2	3	138.1	574	95	46	37	6	5	3	15	66	0	147	11	2	7	9	.438	0	0	2.41
1994	Kinston	A	10	5	0	0	41	176	36	13	9	1	3	1	4	14	0	40	9	2	5	1	.833	0	0	1.98
	Canton-Akrn	AA	16	15	1	0	94	409	95	51	39	7	3	3	2	35	0	65	7	3	7	6	.538	1	0	3.73

		G	GS	CG	GF	IP	BFP	H	R	ER	HR	SH	SF	HB	TBB	IBB	SO	WP	Bk	W	L	Pct.	ShO	Sv	ERA
1995 Canton-Akrn	AA	8	5	1	1	28.2	137	32	25	23	2	0	3	4	16	0	23	5	0	1	3	.250	0	0	7.22
5 Min. YEARS		99	45	4	24	361.2	1539	295	162	130	20	12	13	26	156	2	340	35	9	24	23	.511	1	5	3.24

Chad Frontera

Pitches: Right **Bats:** Right **Pos:** P **Ht:** 6'2" **Wt:** 195 **Born:** 11/22/72 **Age:** 23

		HOW MUCH HE PITCHED						WHAT HE GAVE UP												THE RESULTS					
Year Team	Lg	G	GS	CG	GF	IP	BFP	H	R	ER	HR	SH	SF	HB	TBB	IBB	SO	WP	Bk	W	L	Pct.	ShO	Sv	ERA
1994 Everett	A	13	12	0	0	59.2	273	60	35	23	3	1	2	7	27	2	50	6	0	4	4	.500	0	0	3.47
1995 Shreveport	AA	20	13	0	2	82	368	88	45	38	9	2	3	6	39	0	52	2	0	3	5	.375	0	1	4.17
2 Min. YEARS		33	25	0	2	141.2	641	148	80	61	12	3	5	13	66	2	102	8	0	7	9	.438	0	1	3.88

Troy Fryman

Bats: Left **Throws:** Right **Pos:** 1B **Ht:** 6'4" **Wt:** 195 **Born:** 10/2/71 **Age:** 24

		BATTING													BASERUNNING				PERCENTAGES		
Year Team	Lg	G	AB	H	2B	3B	HR	TB	R	RBI	TBB	IBB	SO	HBP	SH	SF	SB	CS	SB%	GDP	Avg	OBP	SLG
1991 White Sox	R	7	26	6	3	0	0	9	2	3	4	0	7	0	0	1	1	0	1.00	1	.231	.323	.346
Utica	A	52	178	43	15	1	2	66	23	16	14	1	45	1	1	2	1	0	1.00	2	.242	.297	.371
1992 South Bend	A	129	432	75	26	2	8	129	45	34	60	5	130	5	3	2	7	2	.78	3	.174	.281	.299
1993 South Bend	A	51	173	55	7	6	7	95	34	41	33	5	45	3	0	4	2	0	1.00	1	.318	.427	.549
Sarasota	A	78	285	68	16	3	5	105	42	46	31	3	55	3	0	1	0	0	.00	0	.239	.319	.368
1994 Birmingham	AA	123	445	100	22	4	6	148	55	43	31	3	88	3	2	0	2	5	.29	11	.225	.280	.333
1995 Birmingham	AA	112	356	79	13	3	8	122	48	41	49	6	97	6	2	3	9	1	.90	4	.222	.324	.343
5 Min. YEARS		552	1895	426	102	19	36	674	249	224	222	23	467	21	8	13	22	8	.73	22	.225	.311	.356

Aaron Fuller

Bats: Both **Throws:** Right **Pos:** OF **Ht:** 5'10" **Wt:** 170 **Born:** 9/7/71 **Age:** 24

		BATTING													BASERUNNING				PERCENTAGES		
Year Team	Lg	G	AB	H	2B	3B	HR	TB	R	RBI	TBB	IBB	SO	HBP	SH	SF	SB	CS	SB%	GDP	Avg	OBP	SLG
1993 Red Sox	R	6	11	6	0	1	0	8	5	2	3	0	0	0	0	0	3	0	1.00	1	.545	.643	.727
Utica	A	53	176	44	3	0	1	50	31	17	20	0	26	4	5	3	24	4	.86	0	.250	.335	.284
1994 Sarasota	A	118	414	108	17	2	2	135	89	28	82	1	90	5	14	2	45	13	.78	7	.261	.388	.326
1995 Trenton	AA	58	204	40	7	4	0	55	27	10	15	0	45	2	3	1	16	4	.80	2	.196	.257	.270
Visalia	A	49	186	47	7	3	1	63	27	19	19	0	32	1	3	2	11	10	.52	0	.253	.322	.339
3 Min. YEARS		284	991	245	34	10	4	311	179	76	139	1	193	12	25	8	99	31	.76	10	.247	.344	.314

Mark Fuller

Pitches: Right **Bats:** Left **Pos:** P **Ht:** 6'6" **Wt:** 216 **Born:** 8/5/70 **Age:** 25

		HOW MUCH HE PITCHED						WHAT HE GAVE UP												THE RESULTS					
Year Team	Lg	G	GS	CG	GF	IP	BFP	H	R	ER	HR	SH	SF	HB	TBB	IBB	SO	WP	Bk	W	L	Pct.	ShO	Sv	ERA
1992 Pittsfield	A	26	0	0	18	50	207	39	15	9	0	2	0	3	10	0	44	4	2	2	1	.667	0	6	1.62
1993 St. Lucie	A	40	0	0	18	47.1	201	53	13	10	0	4	1	3	12	2	31	0	1	4	3	.571	0	2	1.90
1994 Binghamton	AA	19	0	0	2	30.1	140	35	23	20	2	1	3	7	9	0	24	0	0	0	2	.000	0	0	5.93
St. Lucie	A	27	0	0	16	41.2	165	31	9	8	2	1	0	1	15	3	31	1	0	5	4	.556	0	3	1.73
1995 Norfolk	AAA	4	0	0	4	4.1	18	7	2	1	0	0	0	0	0	0	2	0	0	0	0	.000	0	1	2.08
Binghamton	AA	47	1	0	12	79.1	330	83	33	26	7	2	3	5	22	5	34	0	1	4	3	.571	0	1	2.95
4 Min. YEARS		163	1	0	70	253	1061	248	95	74	11	10	7	19	68	10	166	5	7	15	13	.536	0	13	2.63

Edwards Fully

Bats: Right **Throws:** Right **Pos:** OF **Ht:** 5'11" **Wt:** 191 **Born:** 7/14/71 **Age:** 24

		BATTING													BASERUNNING				PERCENTAGES		
Year Team	Lg	G	AB	H	2B	3B	HR	TB	R	RBI	TBB	IBB	SO	HBP	SH	SF	SB	CS	SB%	GDP	Avg	OBP	SLG
1989 Mets	R	26	74	20	4	1	0	26	8	7	9	0	14	1	0	1	5	2	.71	2	.270	.353	.351
1990 Kingsport	R	66	235	66	17	1	0	85	29	35	16	0	57	3	0	2	14	5	.74	4	.281	.332	.362
1991 Columbia	A	122	448	124	27	5	5	176	69	56	40	0	71	3	4	0	17	15	.53	9	.277	.340	.393
1992 St. Lucie	A	127	397	100	20	2	6	142	58	36	29	1	76	4	5	3	14	15	.48	10	.252	.307	.358
1993 St. Lucie	A	117	393	94	12	5	2	122	49	29	17	1	66	2	6	3	15	9	.63	16	.239	.272	.310
1994 Binghamton	AA	83	217	54	10	2	5	83	27	22	8	0	35	1	0	1	4	5	.44	3	.249	.278	.382
1995 Binghamton	AA	18	36	7	1	0	1	11	4	3	0	0	5	0	1	0	0	2	.00	0	.194	.194	.306
High Desert	A	38	149	55	11	0	6	84	28	34	7	0	22	2	1	0	9	6	.60	3	.369	.405	.564
Bowie	AA	34	119	26	5	0	2	37	15	6	6	0	23	1	1	0	2	3	.40	0	.218	.262	.311
7 Min. YEARS		631	2068	546	107	16	27	766	287	228	132	3	369	17	18	10	80	62	.56	47	.264	.312	.370

Ed Fulton

Bats: Left **Throws:** Right **Pos:** C **Ht:** 6'0" **Wt:** 195 **Born:** 1/7/66 **Age:** 30

		BATTING													BASERUNNING				PERCENTAGES		
Year Team	Lg	G	AB	H	2B	3B	HR	TB	R	RBI	TBB	IBB	SO	HBP	SH	SF	SB	CS	SB%	GDP	Avg	OBP	SLG
1987 Johnson Cty	R	67	245	71	16	1	13	128	36	59	36	3	42	2	0	5	4	2	.67	6	.290	.378	.522
1988 Springfield	A	110	374	100	20	6	7	153	46	55	44	3	69	1	2	5	0	0	.00	8	.267	.342	.409
1989 St. Pete	A	125	432	105	23	2	6	150	38	75	51	5	64	0	0	15	0	2	.00	11	.243	.313	.347
1990 Arkansas	AA	48	148	39	9	1	3	59	24	25	19	2	26	3	0	4	0	0	.00	6	.264	.351	.399
Louisville	AAA	36	100	24	4	2	2	38	9	14	8	1	16	0	1	3	2	0	1.00	4	.240	.288	.380
1991 Louisville	AAA	45	132	26	8	0	0	34	10	15	15	1	35	0	0	4	0	0	.00	4	.197	.279	.258
1992 Arkansas	AA	9	23	6	2	0	0	8	3	3	3	1	8	0	0	0	0	0	.00	0	.261	.346	.348
Louisville	AAA	77	234	47	5	0	12	88	19	29	22	1	56	0	2	2	0	0	.00	7	.201	.267	.376

1993	Louisville	AAA	61	147	31	5	0	3	45	13	18	11	0	27	1	1	3	0	0	.00	5	.211	.265	.306
1994	Toledo	AAA	59	159	36	6	0	5	57	19	18	15	1	38	0	1	2	1	1	.50	3	.226	.290	.358
1995	Pawtucket	AAA	9	17	5	2	0	0	7	0	2	3	1	6	0	0	0	0	0	.00	0	.294	.400	.412
	9 Min. YEARS		646	2011	490	100	12	51	767	217	315	227	19	387	7	7	39	7	5	.58	52	.244	.317	.381

Aaron Fultz

Pitches: Left **Bats:** Left **Pos:** P   **Ht:** 5'11" **Wt:** 183 **Born:** 9/4/73 **Age:** 22

			HOW MUCH HE PITCHED						WHAT HE GAVE UP											THE RESULTS					
Year	Team	Lg	G	GS	CG	GF	IP	BFP	H	R	ER	HR	SH	SF	HB	TBB	IBB	SO	WP	Bk	W	L	Pct.	ShO	Sv	ERA
1992	Giants	R	14	14	0	0	67.2	282	51	24	16	0	4	1	4	33	0	72	7	0	3	2	.600	0	0	2.13
1993	Clinton	A	26	25	2	0	148	641	132	63	56	8	12	2	11	64	2	144	10	2	14	8	.636	1	0	3.41
	Fort Wayne	A	1	1	0	0	4	21	10	4	4	0	0	0	0	0	0	3	0	0	0	0	.000	0	0	9.00
1994	Fort Myers	A	28	28	3	0	168.1	745	193	95	81	9	6	4	7	60	5	132	9	2	9	10	.474	0	0	4.33
1995	New Britain	AA	3	3	0	0	15	64	11	12	11	1	0	2	0	9	0	12	0	0	0	2	.000	0	0	6.60
	Fort Myers	A	21	21	2	0	122	516	115	52	44	10	4	3	8	41	1	127	7	1	3	6	.333	2	0	3.25
	4 Min. YEARS		93	92	7	0	525	2269	512	250	212	28	26	12	30	207	8	490	33	5	29	28	.509	3	0	3.63

Mike Fyhrie

Pitches: Right **Bats:** Right **Pos:** P   **Ht:** 6'2" **Wt:** 190 **Born:** 12/9/69 **Age:** 26

			HOW MUCH HE PITCHED						WHAT HE GAVE UP											THE RESULTS					
Year	Team	Lg	G	GS	CG	GF	IP	BFP	H	R	ER	HR	SH	SF	HB	TBB	IBB	SO	WP	Bk	W	L	Pct.	ShO	Sv	ERA
1991	Eugene	A	21	0	0	13	39.1	176	41	17	11	0	3	0	1	19	1	45	1	2	2	1	.667	0	5	2.52
1992	Baseball Cy	A	26	26	2	0	162	670	148	65	45	6	10	6	7	37	1	92	4	6	7	13	.350	0	0	2.50
1993	Wilmington	A	5	5	0	0	29.1	124	32	15	12	3	0	2	0	8	0	19	1	0	3	2	.600	0	0	3.68
	Memphis	AA	22	22	3	0	131.1	579	143	59	52	11	0	4	9	59	0	59	7	1	11	4	.733	0	0	3.56
1994	Omaha	AAA	18	16	0	0	85	379	100	57	54	13	2	4	6	33	1	37	0	0	6	5	.545	0	0	5.72
	Memphis	AA	11	11	0	0	67	279	67	29	24	4	1	2	5	17	1	38	1	0	2	5	.286	0	0	3.22
1995	Wichita	AA	17	9	0	3	74	312	76	31	25	4	1	1	1	23	0	41	3	1	3	2	.600	0	1	3.04
	Omaha	AAA	14	11	0	2	60.2	259	71	34	30	7	0	2	4	14	0	39	0	0	3	4	.429	0	0	4.45
	5 Min. YEARS		134	100	5	18	648.2	2778	678	307	253	48	17	21	33	210	4	370	17	10	37	36	.507	0	6	3.51

Bob Gaddy

Pitches: Left **Bats:** Right **Pos:** P   **Ht:** 6'1" **Wt:** 202 **Born:** 1/11/67 **Age:** 29

			HOW MUCH HE PITCHED						WHAT HE GAVE UP											THE RESULTS					
Year	Team	Lg	G	GS	CG	GF	IP	BFP	H	R	ER	HR	SH	SF	HB	TBB	IBB	SO	WP	Bk	W	L	Pct.	ShO	Sv	ERA
1989	Batavia	A	16	11	1	3	75.2	302	61	29	25	9	1	3	0	22	0	72	1	1	4	6	.400	1	0	2.97
1990	Spartanburg	A	30	19	0	2	140.1	587	107	65	52	12	8	5	4	67	0	143	8	2	9	7	.563	0	2	3.33
1991	Reading	AA	10	2	0	3	21	98	20	12	11	2	0	3	2	15	0	16	1	1	1	1	.500	0	0	4.71
	Clearwater	A	34	0	0	17	52.1	222	48	19	13	0	1	1	4	22	0	34	2	1	4	1	.800	0	1	2.24
1992	Clearwater	A	44	0	0	17	64	273	58	30	25	3	0	3	5	21	2	54	4	0	5	5	.500	0	4	3.52
	Reading	AA	12	1	0	5	24.2	101	15	8	8	2	1	0	3	13	1	19	0	0	0	2	.000	0	1	2.92
1993	Scranton-Wb	AAA	23	3	0	10	48.1	232	54	35	30	4	5	4	3	29	5	40	2	0	1	4	.200	0	0	5.59
	Reading	AA	22	8	1	2	75.1	308	64	22	21	3	3	2	3	29	0	55	3	1	6	4	.600	1	0	2.51
1994	Scranton-Wb	AAA	27	25	5	1	165.1	723	161	86	66	7	7	6	4	74	1	117	12	0	9	12	.429	2	0	3.59
1995	Scranton-Wb	AAA	17	17	0	0	86	407	100	72	60	7	8	5	9	56	1	42	10	0	5	7	.417	0	0	6.28
	7 Min. YEARS		235	86	7	60	753	3253	688	378	311	49	34	32	37	348	10	592	43	6	44	49	.473	4	8	3.72

Eddy Gaillard

Pitches: Right **Bats:** Right **Pos:** P   **Ht:** 6'1" **Wt:** 180 **Born:** 8/13/70 **Age:** 25

			HOW MUCH HE PITCHED						WHAT HE GAVE UP											THE RESULTS					
Year	Team	Lg	G	GS	CG	GF	IP	BFP	H	R	ER	HR	SH	SF	HB	TBB	IBB	SO	WP	Bk	W	L	Pct.	ShO	Sv	ERA
1993	Niagara Fal	A	3	3	0	0	14.2	63	15	6	6	0	0	0	0	4	0	12	0	0	1	2	.333	0	0	3.68
	Fayetteville	A	11	11	0	0	61.2	261	64	30	28	8	2	0	4	20	0	41	1	1	5	2	.714	0	0	4.09
1994	Lakeland	A	30	9	0	8	92	389	82	37	29	3	1	2	10	29	0	51	3	1	6	1	.857	0	2	2.84
1995	Jacksonvlle	AA	8	0	0	2	8	42	11	5	5	0	2	1	0	5	1	4	0	0	0	1	.000	0	0	5.63
	Lakeland	A	43	0	0	38	55	227	48	13	8	1	1	3	0	18	2	51	2	1	2	4	.333	0	25	1.31
	3 Min. YEARS		95	23	0	48	231.1	982	220	91	76	12	6	6	14	76	3	159	6	3	14	10	.583	0	27	2.96

Jay Gainer

Bats: Left **Throws:** Left **Pos:** 1B   **Ht:** 6'0" **Wt:** 188 **Born:** 10/8/66 **Age:** 29

			BATTING														BASERUNNING				PERCENTAGES		
Year	Team	Lg	G	AB	H	2B	3B	HR	TB	R	RBI	TBB	IBB	SO	HBP	SH	SF	SB	CS	SB%	GDP	Avg	OBP	SLG
1990	Spokane	A	74	281	100	21	0	10	151	41	54	31	3	49	5	1	4	4	3	.57	4	.356	.424	.537
1991	High Desert	A	127	499	131	17	0	32	244	83	120	52	3	105	3	0	16	4	3	.57	8	.263	.326	.489
1992	Wichita	AA	105	376	98	12	1	23	181	57	67	46	6	101	0	1	6	4	2	.67	5	.261	.336	.481
1993	Colo. Sprng	AAA	86	293	86	11	3	10	133	51	74	22	2	70	1	1	4	4	2	.67	6	.294	.341	.454
1994	Colo. Sprng	AAA	94	283	70	13	2	9	114	38	34	25	2	62	0	1	1	2	3	.40	4	.247	.307	.403
1995	Colo. Sprng	AAA	112	358	104	19	1	23	194	57	86	42	9	64	0	0	6	2	3	.40	7	.291	.360	.542
1993	Colorado	NL	23	41	7	0	0	3	16	4	6	4	0	12	0	0	0	1	1	.50	0	.171	.244	.390
	6 Min. YEARS		598	2090	589	93	7	107	1017	327	435	218	25	451	9	4	37	20	16	.56	36	.282	.347	.487

Steve Gajkowski

Pitches: Right **Bats:** Right **Pos:** P   **Ht:** 6'2" **Wt:** 200 **Born:** 12/30/69 **Age:** 26

Year	Team	Lg	G	GS	CG	GF	IP	BFP	H	R	ER	HR	SH	SF	HB	TBB	IBB	SO	WP	Bk	W	L	Pct.	ShO	Sv	ERA
1990	Burlington	R	14	10	1	1	63.2	287	74	34	29	0	0	3	3	23	0	44	0	1	2	6	.250	0	0	4.10
1991	Columbus	A	3	0	0	2	6	24	3	2	2	0	0	0	0	5	0	5	0	0	0	0	.000	0	0	3.00
	Watertown	A	20	4	0	7	48	221	41	36	28	0	1	2	6	32	1	34	7	2	3	3	.500	0	0	5.25
1992	Utica	A	29	0	0	26	47	184	33	14	7	1	0	2	1	10	1	38	6	0	3	2	.600	0	14	1.34
1993	Sarasota	A	43	0	0	38	69.2	273	52	21	16	1	3	3	4	17	5	45	5	1	3	3	.500	0	15	2.07
	Birmingham	AA	1	0	0	0	2.1	8	0	0	0	0	0	0	0	0	0	2	0	0	0	0	.000	0	0	0.00
1994	Birmingham	AA	58	0	0	32	82.1	355	78	35	28	6	6	3	5	26	1	44	2	0	11	5	.688	0	8	3.06
1995	Nashville	AAA	15	0	0	5	24.2	103	26	15	7	2	0	1	1	8	1	12	1	0	0	1	.000	0	0	2.55
	Birmingham	AA	35	0	0	14	51.2	230	64	27	24	4	2	0	2	16	1	29	1	0	4	4	.500	0	2	4.18
	6 Min. YEARS		218	14	1	125	395.1	1685	371	184	141	14	12	14	22	137	10	253	22	4	26	24	.520	0	39	3.21

Dan Gakeler

Pitches: Right **Bats:** Right **Pos:** P   **Ht:** 6'6" **Wt:** 215 **Born:** 5/1/64 **Age:** 32

Year	Team	Lg	G	GS	CG	GF	IP	BFP	H	R	ER	HR	SH	SF	HB	TBB	IBB	SO	WP	Bk	W	L	Pct.	ShO	Sv	ERA
1984	Elmira	A	14	13	0	1	76.2	341	67	47	35	9	5	2	7	41	3	54	2	2	4	6	.400	0	0	4.11
1985	Greensboro	A	23	16	3	2	108	509	135	86	66	8	2	3	3	54	0	51	4	0	7	5	.583	1	0	5.50
1986	Greensboro	A	24	23	5	1	154.1	679	158	73	57	6	4	4	4	69	1	154	11	2	7	6	.538	1	1	3.32
1987	New Britain	AA	30	25	5	3	173	769	188	112	89	14	2	7	7	63	5	90	7	3	8	13	.381	1	0	4.63
1988	New Britain	AA	26	25	5	0	153.2	660	157	74	63	4	3	1	5	54	1	110	9	3	6	13	.316	2	0	3.69
1989	Jacksonville	AA	14	14	2	0	86.2	365	70	31	23	1	4	1	3	39	1	76	6	1	5	4	.556	1	0	2.39
	Indianapols	AAA	11	11	1	0	66.1	280	53	29	23	1	4	1	3	28	1	41	4	0	3	6	.333	0	0	3.12
1990	Indianapols	AAA	22	21	1	0	120	509	101	55	43	2	7	2	7	55	1	89	6	0	5	5	.500	1	0	3.23
1991	Toledo	AAA	23	2	0	12	43.2	187	44	22	17	0	2	1	1	13	1	32	3	0	2	3	.400	0	4	3.50
1992	London	AA	1	1	0	0	2	9	3	0	0	0	0	0	0	1	0	1	0	0	0	0	.000	0	0	0.00
	Toledo	AAA	3	3	0	0	12.2	57	14	10	10	3	0	0	1	4	0	11	2	0	0	1	.000	0	0	7.11
1993	Lynchburg	A	30	0	0	19	42.1	162	31	13	7	3	3	0	2	11	0	28	2	1	3	3	.500	0	9	1.49
	Pawtucket	AAA	6	0	0	3	12	66	21	11	10	1	2	0	0	9	0	8	2	0	0	1	.000	0	0	7.50
1994	Pawtucket	AAA	3	2	0	0	17	73	18	13	9	3	1	0	0	4	0	10	0	0	0	1	.000	0	0	4.76
	New Britain	AA	25	25	2	0	151.2	660	164	90	76	7	6	7	5	52	0	107	7	0	9	12	.429	0	0	4.51
1995	Pawtucket	AAA	4	4	0	0	20.2	97	24	14	14	2	1	2	2	9	1	13	3	0	0	2	.000	0	0	6.10
1991	Detroit	AL	31	7	0	11	73.2	331	73	52	47	5	3	3	1	39	6	43	7	0	1	4	.200	0	2	5.74
	12 Min. YEARS		259	185	24	41	1240.2	5423	1248	680	542	64	46	31	50	506	15	875	68	12	59	81	.421	7	14	3.93

Kevin Gallaher

Pitches: Right **Bats:** Right **Pos:** P   **Ht:** 6'3" **Wt:** 190 **Born:** 8/1/68 **Age:** 27

Year	Team	Lg	G	GS	CG	GF	IP	BFP	H	R	ER	HR	SH	SF	HB	TBB	IBB	SO	WP	Bk	W	L	Pct.	ShO	Sv	ERA
1991	Auburn	A	16	8	0	3	48	243	59	48	37	2	3	9	9	37	0	25	6	1	2	5	.286	0	0	6.94
1992	Osceola	A	1	1	0	0	6.1	26	2	2	2	1	0	0	0	3	0	5	1	0	0	1	.000	0	0	2.84
	Burlington	A	20	20	1	0	117	529	108	70	50	5	7	4	9	80	0	89	9	1	6	10	.375	0	0	3.85
1993	Osceola	A	21	21	1	0	135	586	132	68	57	7	3	3	4	57	1	93	8	3	7	7	.500	1	0	3.80
	Jackson	AA	4	4	0	0	24	95	14	7	7	3	1	2	2	10	0	30	6	0	0	2	.000	0	0	2.63
1994	Jackson	AA	18	18	0	0	106	468	88	57	46	5	1	2	8	67	1	112	13	0	6	6	.500	0	0	3.91
	Tucson	AAA	9	9	2	0	53.2	240	55	35	32	5	3	2	3	25	0	58	3	0	3	4	.429	0	0	5.37
1995	Kissimmee	A	7	7	0	0	17.1	86	8	11	11	0	0	0	3	24	0	21	2	0	1	1	.500	0	0	5.71
	Jackson	AA	6	6	1	0	42.1	179	31	18	16	1	3	1	0	23	1	28	4	0	2	2	.500	0	0	3.40
	Tucson	AAA	3	3	0	0	14	70	19	11	10	1	0	2	2	9	0	11	2	0	1	1	.500	0	0	6.43
	5 Min. YEARS		105	97	5	3	563.2	2522	516	327	268	30	21	25	40	335	3	472	54	5	28	39	.418	1	0	4.28

Bob Gamez

Pitches: Left **Bats:** Left **Pos:** P   **Ht:** 6'5" **Wt:** 185 **Born:** 11/18/68 **Age:** 27

Year	Team	Lg	G	GS	CG	GF	IP	BFP	H	R	ER	HR	SH	SF	HB	TBB	IBB	SO	WP	Bk	W	L	Pct.	ShO	Sv	ERA
1988	Rangers	R	2	0	0	0	2.2	10	0	0	0	0	0	0	0	4	0	1	0	0	0	0	.000	0	0	0.00
1989	Rangers	R	23	1	0	5	40.2	172	35	17	17	0	0	0	0	18	0	44	3	0	2	1	.667	0	2	3.76
1990	Boise	A	14	7	0	0	46.1	196	42	19	15	3	0	0	2	15	2	38	5	0	3	0	1.000	0	0	2.91
1991	Quad City	A	41	5	0	11	76.2	341	75	38	31	6	5	6	3	38	4	83	10	0	4	3	.571	0	1	3.64
1992	Palm Spring	A	38	13	0	8	98.1	431	106	63	54	4	7	6	2	44	5	70	10	0	8	8	.500	0	3	4.94
1993	Midland	AA	44	0	0	13	60.2	260	68	27	22	7	1	0	2	18	0	50	5	0	5	2	.714	0	0	3.26
	Vancouver	AAA	9	0	0	3	13.1	60	11	9	7	0	1	1	0	9	0	15	2	0	1	0	1.000	0	0	4.73
1994	Phoenix	AAA	39	14	0	13	98	459	130	73	66	11	4	4	2	51	2	60	9	0	5	10	.333	0	3	6.06
1995	Phoenix	AAA	36	0	0	5	66	292	76	46	41	6	4	1	0	27	4	41	7	0	3	5	.375	0	2	5.59
	8 Min. YEARS		246	49	0	58	502.2	2221	543	292	253	37	22	18	11	224	17	402	51	1	31	29	.517	0	11	4.53

Francisco Gamez

Pitches: Right **Bats:** Right **Pos:** P   **Ht:** 6'2" **Wt:** 185 **Born:** 4/2/70 **Age:** 26

Year	Team	Lg	G	GS	CG	GF	IP	BFP	H	R	ER	HR	SH	SF	HB	TBB	IBB	SO	WP	Bk	W	L	Pct.	ShO	Sv	ERA
1990	Brewers	R	11	7	1	1	50.2	211	44	21	15	5	0	2	3	20	0	32	0	6	2	3	.400	0	0	2.66
1991	Beloit	A	25	24	1	0	146.1	639	140	76	59	2	11	6	11	57	1	92	7	4	9	12	.429	0	0	3.63

Year	Team	Lg	G	GS	CG	GF	IP	BFP	H	R	ER	HR	SH	SF	HB	TBB	IBB	SO	WP	Bk	W	L	Pct.	ShO	Sv	ERA
1992	Stockton	A	23	23	2	0	134	578	134	64	54	5	3	4	1	69	1	95	4	1	9	5	.643	0	0	3.63
1993	El Paso	AA	15	14	1	0	68.1	315	92	45	41	3	2	2	8	25	1	26	0	0	2	8	.200	0	0	5.40
1994	El Paso	AA	27	27	2	0	168.1	740	193	104	90	13	3	6	12	62	6	87	10	2	10	7	.588	1	0	4.81
1995	El Paso	AA	27	8	0	6	68	316	79	46	40	8	5	2	4	39	5	32	6	0	2	1	.667	0	2	5.29
	Stockton	A	4	3	0	0	22.2	96	20	8	7	0	0	0	1	11	0	7	1	0	2	1	.667	0	0	2.78
	6 Min. YEARS		132	106	7	7	658.1	2895	702	364	306	36	24	22	40	283	14	371	28	13	36	37	.493	1	2	4.18

Gus Gandarillas

Pitches: Right Bats: Right Pos: P Ht: 6'0" Wt: 180 Born: 7/19/71 Age: 24

| | | | HOW MUCH HE PITCHED | | | | | | WHAT HE GAVE UP | | | | | | | | | | | | THE RESULTS | | | | |
Year	Team	Lg	G	GS	CG	GF	IP	BFP	H	R	ER	HR	SH	SF	HB	TBB	IBB	SO	WP	Bk	W	L	Pct.	ShO	Sv	ERA
1992	Elizabethtn	R	29	0	0	29	36	148	24	14	12	1	0	0	3	10	2	34	4	1	1	2	.333	0	13	3.00
1993	Fort Wayne	A	52	0	0	48	66.1	295	66	37	24	8	5	5	1	22	2	59	4	0	5	5	.500	0	25	3.26
1994	Fort Myers	A	37	0	0	34	46.2	190	37	7	4	0	3	2	2	13	4	39	5	0	4	1	.800	0	20	0.77
	Nashville	AA	28	0	0	20	37	163	34	13	13	1	2	1	4	10	0	29	6	0	2	2	.500	0	8	3.16
1995	Salt Lake	AAA	22	0	0	13	29.1	135	34	23	21	5	3	1	1	19	4	17	5	0	2	3	.400	0	2	6.44
	New Britain	AA	25	0	0	18	32.1	152	38	26	22	1	2	0	3	16	0	25	3	0	2	4	.333	0	7	6.12
	4 Min. YEARS		193	0	0	162	247.2	1076	233	120	96	16	15	9	14	90	12	203	27	1	16	17	.485	0	75	3.49

Joe Ganote

Pitches: Right Bats: Right Pos: P Ht: 6'1" Wt: 185 Born: 1/22/68 Age: 28

| | | | HOW MUCH HE PITCHED | | | | | | WHAT HE GAVE UP | | | | | | | | | | | | THE RESULTS | | | | |
Year	Team	Lg	G	GS	CG	GF	IP	BFP	H	R	ER	HR	SH	SF	HB	TBB	IBB	SO	WP	Bk	W	L	Pct.	ShO	Sv	ERA
1990	St. Cathrns	A	18	0	0	12	29.2	120	26	9	9	0	1	1	3	7	0	33	2	2	3	0	1.000	0	4	2.73
1991	Myrtle Bch	A	20	20	3	0	118.1	491	104	61	45	9	1	3	2	46	0	127	10	2	8	6	.571	1	0	3.42
	Dunedin	A	4	4	1	0	26.1	110	26	10	9	1	3	2	1	9	0	13	0	0	2	1	.667	1	0	3.08
1992	Dunedin	A	23	21	4	0	140.2	604	148	72	62	10	6	9	10	40	1	101	9	1	6	10	.375	1	0	3.97
1993	Knoxville	AA	33	19	1	6	138.2	589	150	70	64	11	3	10	5	52	0	88	13	0	8	6	.571	0	1	4.15
1994	Knoxville	AA	11	11	3	0	66	273	53	29	20	4	4	2	6	24	0	43	7	0	4	6	.400	1	0	2.73
	Syracuse	AAA	18	14	1	1	79	351	79	41	36	6	2	1	2	41	0	55	9	0	3	7	.300	0	0	4.10
1995	Syracuse	AAA	3	3	0	0	10.2	51	16	15	12	3	0	1	0	4	0	3	0	0	0	2	.000	0	0	10.13
	El Paso	AA	12	7	0	1	50.1	207	40	18	9	3	2	1	3	16	0	39	4	0	5	1	.833	0	1	1.61
	New Orleans	AAA	14	13	2	1	81.2	348	88	35	31	6	5	2	6	21	2	56	6	0	7	4	.636	1	0	3.42
	6 Min. YEARS		156	112	15	21	741.1	3144	730	360	297	53	27	32	38	260	3	558	60	5	46	43	.517	5	6	3.61

Jeff Garber

Bats: Right Throws: Right Pos: 3B Ht: 5'11" Wt: 180 Born: 9/27/66 Age: 29

| | | | BATTING | | | | | | | | | | | | | BASERUNNING | | | | PERCENTAGES | | |
Year	Team	Lg	G	AB	H	2B	3B	HR	TB	R	RBI	TBB	IBB	SO	HBP	SH	SF	SB	CS	SB%	GDP	Avg	OBP	SLG
1988	Eugene	A	65	243	61	14	2	1	82	31	25	30	1	45	5	4	3	12	9	.57	6	.251	.342	.337
1989	Appleton	A	117	407	107	18	3	7	152	63	50	54	1	77	13	9	8	4	1	.80	6	.263	.361	.373
1990	Baseball Cy	A	129	446	96	12	2	6	130	53	46	53	0	96	8	4	6	17	4	.81	6	.215	.306	.291
	Omaha	AAA	1	1	0	0	0	0	0	0	0	0	0	1	0	0	0	0	0	.00	0	.000	.000	.000
1991	Memphis	AA	61	200	50	4	1	0	56	24	19	26	0	44	4	7	0	7	2	.78	1	.250	.348	.280
	Omaha	AAA	34	94	26	3	3	1	38	12	13	6	0	21	0	2	1	0	2	.00	2	.277	.317	.404
1992	Memphis	AA	108	326	72	17	2	7	114	37	38	29	1	66	7	4	3	9	3	.75	7	.221	.296	.350
1993	Memphis	AA	81	253	71	13	0	12	120	40	32	26	2	61	5	2	0	1	3	.25	4	.281	.359	.474
1994	Omaha	AAA	23	58	15	4	0	0	19	7	10	6	0	18	0	0	0	1	0	1.00	0	.259	.328	.328
	Memphis	AA	54	181	55	10	2	7	90	29	29	31	2	37	1	1	2	6	5	.55	2	.304	.405	.497
1995	Omaha	AAA	6	14	2	0	0	0	2	1	0	0	0	5	0	0	1	0	0	.00	1	.143	.143	.143
	8 Min. YEARS		679	2223	555	95	15	41	803	297	262	261	7	471	43	33	23	57	29	.66	35	.250	.337	.361

Jose Garcia

Pitches: Right Bats: Right Pos: P Ht: 6'3" Wt: 146 Born: 6/12/72 Age: 24

| | | | HOW MUCH HE PITCHED | | | | | | WHAT HE GAVE UP | | | | | | | | | | | | THE RESULTS | | | | |
Year	Team	Lg	G	GS	CG	GF	IP	BFP	H	R	ER	HR	SH	SF	HB	TBB	IBB	SO	WP	Bk	W	L	Pct.	ShO	Sv	ERA
1993	Bakersfield	A	27	0	0	22	29	142	47	23	22	6	1	4	0	12	1	25	3	2	0	3	.000	0	4	6.83
	Yakima	A	36	0	0	30	44.2	188	40	14	12	1	0	2	3	19	2	19	2	0	2	2	.500	0	5	2.42
1994	Vero Beach	A	20	0	0	13	32.2	129	32	7	5	0	1	0	0	2	0	24	2	1	3	1	.750	0	4	1.38
	San Antonio	AA	7	0	0	7	11	40	7	2	2	0	1	1	0	6	2	8	0	1	2	0	1.000	0	3	1.64
	Albuquerque	AAA	37	0	0	7	57.2	258	66	39	33	6	2	3	3	26	5	38	2	0	4	1	.800	0	0	5.15
1995	Albuquerque	AAA	11	0	0	4	15.2	73	19	11	11	3	2	4	0	7	1	10	0	0	1	3	.250	0	0	6.32
	San Antonio	AA	38	0	0	15	58	242	50	32	26	4	4	4	6	24	0	36	6	2	2	6	.250	0	2	4.03
	3 Min. YEARS		176	0	0	98	248.2	1072	261	128	111	20	11	18	12	96	11	160	15	6	14	16	.467	0	18	4.02

Luis Garcia

Bats: Right Throws: Right Pos: SS Ht: 6'0" Wt: 174 Born: 5/20/75 Age: 21

| | | | BATTING | | | | | | | | | | | | | BASERUNNING | | | | PERCENTAGES | | |
Year	Team	Lg	G	AB	H	2B	3B	HR	TB	R	RBI	TBB	IBB	SO	HBP	SH	SF	SB	CS	SB%	GDP	Avg	OBP	SLG
1993	Bristol	R	24	57	12	1	0	1	16	7	7	3	0	11	0	1	0	3	1	.75	1	.211	.250	.281
1994	Jamestown	A	67	239	47	8	2	1	62	21	19	8	0	48	1	6	3	6	9	.40	4	.197	.223	.259
1995	Lakeland	A	102	361	101	10	4	2	125	39	35	8	0	42	1	4	4	9	10	.47	6	.280	.294	.346
	Jacksonville	AA	17	47	13	0	0	0	13	6	5	1	0	8	1	0	0	2	1	.67	0	.277	.306	.277
	3 Min. YEARS		210	704	173	19	6	4	216	73	66	20	0	109	3	11	7	20	21	.49	11	.246	.267	.307

108

Miguel Garcia

Pitches: Left **Bats:** Left **Pos:** P · **Ht:** 6' 1" **Wt:** 170 **Born:** 4/3/67 **Age:** 29

			HOW MUCH HE PITCHED						WHAT HE GAVE UP									THE RESULTS				
Year Team	Lg	G	GS	CG	GF	IP	BFP	H	R	ER	HR	SH	SF	HB	TBB	IBB	SO	WP	Bk	W	L	Pct.	ShO	Sv	ERA
1985 Quad City	A	29	1	0	10	65.1	273	60	25	21	6	3	2	4	21	2	50	4	1	3	2	.600	0	0	2.89
1986 Palm Spring	A	43	0	0	28	72.2	295	59	18	13	2	9	6	2	26	6	75	3	0	8	3	.727	0	9	1.61
1987 Midland	AA	50	0	0	25	87	373	86	35	25	3	3	2	0	34	7	67	9	0	10	6	.625	0	5	2.59
1988 Buffalo	AAA	25	1	0	14	66.1	284	71	26	19	3	2	0	0	21	2	34	9	2	6	2	.750	0	2	2.58
1989 Buffalo	AAA	31	1	0	10	59.2	271	64	39	29	3	2	2	0	29	1	54	4	0	6	2	.750	0	0	4.37
1990 Harrisburg	AA	21	20	0	0	131	569	143	76	58	6	6	5	7	38	1	49	5	2	8	10	.444	0	0	3.98
Buffalo	AAA	9	1	0	3	12	51	12	9	7	3	3	0	1	4	1	6	3	0	0	2	.000	0	0	5.25
1995 Ottawa	AAA	5	0	0	1	6.2	27	6	1	1	1	0	0	0	3	0	4	0	0	0	0	.000	0	0	1.35
1987 California	AL	1	0	0	1	1.2	11	3	4	3	0	0	0	0	3	0	1	0	0	0	0	.000	0	0	16.20
Pittsburgh	NL	1	0	0	1	0.2	2	0	0	0	0	0	0	0	0	0	0	0	0	0	0	.000	0	0	0.00
1988 Pittsburgh	NL	1	0	0	1	2	12	3	2	1	1	0	1	1	2	0	2	0	0	0	0	.000	0	0	4.50
1989 Pittsburgh	NL	11	0	0	6	16	78	25	15	15	2	1	0	0	7	3	9	1	0	0	2	.000	0	0	8.44
7 Min. YEARS		213	24	0	91	500.2	2143	501	229	173	27	28	17	14	176	20	339	37	5	41	27	.603	0	16	3.11
3 Maj. YEARS		14	0	0	9	20.1	103	31	21	19	3	1	1	1	12	3	11	2	0	0	2	.000	0	0	8.41

Omar Garcia

Bats: Right **Throws:** Right **Pos:** 1B · **Ht:** 6'0" **Wt:** 192 **Born:** 11/16/71 **Age:** 24

					BATTING												BASERUNNING				PERCENTAGES		
Year Team	Lg	G	AB	H	2B	3B	HR	TB	R	RBI	TBB	IBB	SO	HBP	SH	SF	SB	CS	SB%	GDP	Avg	OBP	SLG
1989 Mets	R	32	98	25	3	1	0	30	15	8	10	0	22	1	0	1	6	2	.75	1	.255	.327	.306
1990 Kingsport	R	67	246	82	15	2	6	119	42	36	24	1	24	0	0	2	10	5	.67	3	.333	.390	.484
1991 Columbia	A	108	394	99	11	4	4	130	63	50	31	0	55	0	1	3	12	5	.71	9	.251	.304	.330
1992 Columbia	A	126	469	136	18	5	3	173	66	70	55	1	37	1	0	11	35	11	.76	11	.290	.358	.369
1993 St. Lucie	A	129	485	156	17	7	3	196	73	76	57	2	47	2	2	5	25	8	.76	14	.322	.392	.404
1994 Binghamton	AA	64	246	88	14	4	5	125	38	42	22	1	31	1	0	4	3	5	.38	3	.358	.407	.508
Norfolk	AAA	67	227	55	9	2	0	68	28	28	19	1	35	0	1	5	7	4	.64	6	.242	.295	.300
1995 Norfolk	AAA	115	430	133	21	7	3	177	55	64	21	3	58	0	1	7	3	4	.43	13	.309	.336	.412
Binghamton	AA	5	19	10	1	1	0	13	4	1	4	1	0	0	0	0	0	0	.00	1	.526	.609	.684
7 Min. YEARS		713	2614	784	109	33	24	1031	384	375	243	10	309	5	5	38	101	44	.70	61	.300	.356	.394

Nomar Garciaparra

Bats: Right **Throws:** Right **Pos:** SS · **Ht:** 6'1" **Wt:** 175 **Born:** 7/23/73 **Age:** 22

					BATTING												BASERUNNING				PERCENTAGES		
Year Team	Lg	G	AB	H	2B	3B	HR	TB	R	RBI	TBB	IBB	SO	HBP	SH	SF	SB	CS	SB%	GDP	Avg	OBP	SLG
1994 Sarasota	A	28	105	31	8	1	1	44	20	16	10	0	6	1	3	2	5	2	.71	2	.295	.356	.419
1995 Trenton	AA	125	513	137	20	8	8	197	77	47	50	3	42	8	4	6	35	12	.74	10	.267	.338	.384
2 Min. YEARS		153	618	168	28	9	9	241	97	63	60	3	48	9	7	8	40	14	.74	12	.272	.341	.390

Mike Gardella

Pitches: Left **Bats:** Left **Pos:** P · **Ht:** 5'10" **Wt:** 195 **Born:** 1/18/67 **Age:** 29

				HOW MUCH HE PITCHED						WHAT HE GAVE UP									THE RESULTS				
Year Team	Lg	G	GS	CG	GF	IP	BFP	H	R	ER	HR	SH	SF	HB	TBB	IBB	SO	WP	Bk	W	L	Pct.	ShO	Sv	ERA
1989 Oneonta	A	28	0	0	26	37.2	153	23	8	7	2	2	2	0	15	0	66	1	0	2	0	1.000	0	19	1.67
1990 Pr. William	A	62	0	0	57	71.2	301	61	18	16	0	5	0	1	31	3	86	7	0	4	3	.571	0	30	2.01
1991 Albany-Colo	AA	53	0	0	27	77.2	344	70	37	33	1	10	3	1	55	6	76	3	0	4	5	.444	0	11	3.82
1992 Albany-Colo	AA	15	0	0	13	18	77	18	4	4	1	0	0	0	10	1	18	1	1	3	1	.750	0	5	2.00
Canton-Akrn	AA	33	3	0	14	55	241	43	30	22	5	1	2	4	32	0	45	3	1	2	2	.500	0	7	3.60
1993 Canton-Akrn	AA	21	0	0	7	22.2	114	26	14	11	2	3	0	1	22	2	14	0	0	2	1	.667	0	4	4.37
Shreveport	AA	5	0	0	3	8.2	32	4	1	1	0	1	0	0	3	0	11	0	0	0	0	.000	0	1	1.04
1994 Shreveport	AA	38	5	0	11	84	353	73	41	36	4	4	3	1	34	4	70	6	2	2	4	.333	0	3	3.86
1995 Phoenix	AAA	3	0	0	1	4	21	9	6	6	0	0	0	0	1	0	3	0	0	0	0	.000	0	0	13.50
7 Min. YEARS		258	8	0	159	379.1	1636	327	159	136	15	26	10	8	203	16	389	21	4	19	16	.543	0	80	3.23

Chris Gardner

Pitches: Right **Bats:** Right **Pos:** P · **Ht:** 6'0" **Wt:** 175 **Born:** 3/30/69 **Age:** 27

				HOW MUCH HE PITCHED						WHAT HE GAVE UP									THE RESULTS				
Year Team	Lg	G	GS	CG	GF	IP	BFP	H	R	ER	HR	SH	SF	HB	TBB	IBB	SO	WP	Bk	W	L	Pct.	ShO	Sv	ERA
1988 Astros	R	12	9	0	0	55.1	226	37	18	9	0	3	1	4	23	0	41	4	4	4	3	.571	0	0	1.46
1989 Asheville	A	15	15	2	0	77.1	360	76	53	33	5	1	3	1	58	0	49	8	10	3	8	.273	0	0	3.84
1990 Asheville	A	23	23	3	0	134	560	102	57	39	6	1	2	7	69	2	81	8	3	5	10	.333	1	0	2.62
1991 Jackson	AA	22	22	1	0	131.1	559	116	57	46	6	5	4	8	75	1	72	9	1	13	5	.722	1	0	3.15
1992 Tucson	AAA	20	20	0	0	110.2	515	141	80	70	1	9	5	5	63	1	49	6	3	6	9	.400	0	0	5.69
1994 Jackson	AA	10	10	0	0	51	214	44	25	20	1	2	4	1	21	0	34	7	0	3	2	.600	0	0	3.53
Tucson	AAA	18	12	0	2	72.1	339	95	53	49	6	3	1	5	32	1	33	3	0	3	4	.429	0	0	6.10
1995 Tucson	AAA	16	2	0	6	26.1	127	43	26	25	0	2	1	0	19	1	6	1	1	1	4	.200	0	0	8.54
1991 Houston	NL	5	4	0	0	24.2	103	19	12	11	5	2	0	0	14	1	12	0	0	1	2	.333	0	0	4.01
7 Min. YEARS		136	113	6	8	658.1	2900	654	369	291	25	26	21	31	360	6	365	46	22	38	45	.458	2	0	3.98

Jeff Gardner

Bats: Left **Throws:** Right **Pos:** 2B   **Ht:** 5'11" **Wt:** 175 **Born:** 2/4/64 **Age:** 32

Year	Team	Lg	G	AB	H	2B	3B	HR	TB	R	RBI	TBB	IBB	SO	HBP	SH	SF	SB	CS	SB%	GDP	Avg	OBP	SLG
1985	Columbia	A	123	401	118	9	1	0	129	80	50	142	1	40	5	10	1	31	5	.86	9	.294	.483	.322
1986	Lynchburg	A	111	334	91	11	2	1	109	59	39	81	3	33	4	8	3	6	4	.60	10	.272	.417	.326
1987	Jackson	AA	119	399	109	10	3	0	125	55	30	58	1	55	3	5	2	1	5	.17	7	.273	.368	.313
1988	Jackson	AA	134	432	109	15	2	0	128	46	33	69	7	52	1	14	1	13	8	.62	6	.252	.356	.296
	Tidewater	AAA	2	8	3	1	1	0	6	3	2	1	0	1	0	0	0	0	0	.00	0	.375	.444	.750
1989	Tidewater	AAA	101	269	75	11	0	0	86	28	24	25	1	27	0	4	3	0	0	.00	7	.279	.337	.320
1990	Tidewater	AAA	138	463	125	11	1	0	138	55	33	84	3	33	1	4	1	3	3	.50	12	.270	.383	.298
1991	Tidewater	AAA	136	504	147	23	4	1	181	73	56	84	4	48	3	7	5	6	5	.55	8	.292	.393	.359
1992	Las Vegas	AAA	120	439	147	30	5	1	190	82	51	67	6	48	2	7	2	7	2	.78	9	.335	.424	.433
1994	Ottawa	AAA	59	191	49	8	1	0	59	24	16	22	1	22	0	0	2	6	0	1.00	1	.257	.330	.309
1995	Iowa	AAA	65	235	76	11	0	3	96	35	24	23	0	27	1	2	1	1	2	.33	5	.323	.385	.409
1991	New York	NL	13	37	6	0	0	0	6	3	1	4	0	6	0	0	0	0	0	.00	0	.162	.238	.162
1992	San Diego	NL	15	19	2	0	0	0	2	0	0	1	0	8	0	0	0	0	0	.00	0	.105	.150	.105
1993	San Diego	NL	140	404	106	21	7	1	144	53	24	45	0	69	1	1	1	2	6	.25	3	.262	.337	.356
1994	Montreal	NL	18	32	7	0	1	0	9	4	1	3	0	5	0	0	1	0	0	.00	1	.219	.286	.281
	10 Min. YEARS		1108	3675	1049	140	20	6	1247	540	358	656	27	386	20	61	21	74	34	.69	74	.285	.395	.339
	4 Maj. YEARS		186	492	121	21	8	1	161	60	26	53	0	88	1	1	2	2	6	.25	4	.246	.319	.327

Scott Garrelts

Pitches: Right **Bats:** Right **Pos:** P   **Ht:** 6'4" **Wt:** 210 **Born:** 10/30/61 **Age:** 34

Year	Team	Lg	G	GS	CG	GF	IP	BFP	H	R	ER	HR	SH	SF	HB	TBB	IBB	SO	WP	Bk	W	L	Pct.	ShO	Sv	ERA
1984	Phoenix	AAA	21	19	2	0	97.2		97	75	64	8	0	0	2	82	2	69	9	0	5	7	.417	1	0	5.90
1992	San Jose	A	1	1	0	0	4	17	3	1	1	0	0	0	0	3	0	1	0	0	0	0	.000	0	0	2.25
	Shreveport	AA	2	2	0	0	9.2	36	4	2	2	0	0	1	0	3	0	15	1	0	0	0	.000	0	0	1.86
	Phoenix	AAA	4	4	0	0	11.2	55	14	14	11	2	1	0	1	5	0	7	1	0	0	2	.000	0	0	8.49
1993	Rancho Cuca	A	9	8	0	1	29.2	144	39	23	17	0	1	2	0	17	0	32	3	0	0	5	.000	0	1	5.16
	Las Vegas	AAA	1	1	0	0	3	20	10	7	7	0	0	1	0	2	0	1	3	0	0	0	.000	0	0	21.00
1995	Omaha	AAA	9	1	0	3	18.2	84	17	12	11	2	0	0	2	13	1	15	2	0	1	2	.333	0	1	5.30
1982	San Francisco	NL	1	0	0	1	2	11	3	3	3	0	0	0	0	2	0	4	0	0	0	0	.000	0	0	13.50
1983	San Francisco	NL	5	5	1	0	35.2	154	33	11	10	4	3	0	2	19	4	16	4	1	2	2	.500	1	0	2.52
1984	San Francisco	NL	21	3	0	5	43	206	45	33	27	6	5	2	1	34	1	32	3	0	2	3	.400	0	0	5.65
1985	San Francisco	NL	74	0	0	44	105.2	454	76	37	27	2	6	3	3	58	12	106	7	1	9	6	.600	0	13	2.30
1986	San Francisco	NL	53	18	2	27	173.2	717	144	65	60	17	10	7	2	74	11	125	9	1	13	9	.591	0	10	3.11
1987	San Francisco	NL	64	0	0	43	106.1	428	70	41	38	10	7	2	0	55	4	127	5	1	11	7	.611	0	12	3.22
1988	San Francisco	NL	65	0	0	40	98	413	80	42	39	3	9	2	2	46	10	86	6	4	5	9	.357	0	13	3.58
1989	San Francisco	NL	30	29	2	0	193.1	766	149	58	49	11	9	7	0	46	3	119	7	2	14	5	.737	1	0	2.28
1990	San Francisco	NL	31	31	4	0	182	786	190	91	84	16	10	5	3	70	8	80	7	0	12	11	.522	2	0	4.15
1991	San Francisco	NL	8	3	0	2	19.2	90	25	14	14	1	0	1	0	9	0	8	0	0	1	1	.500	0	0	6.41
	4 Min. YEARS		47	36	2	4	174.1	356	184	134	113	12	2	4	4	125	3	140	19	0	6	16	.273	0	2	5.83
	10 Maj. YEARS		352	89	9	162	959.1	4025	815	395	351	74	59	29	13	413	53	703	48	10	69	53	.566	4	48	3.29

Webster Garrison

Bats: Right **Throws:** Right **Pos:** 2B   **Ht:** 5'11" **Wt:** 170 **Born:** 8/24/65 **Age:** 30

Year	Team	Lg	G	AB	H	2B	3B	HR	TB	R	RBI	TBB	IBB	SO	HBP	SH	SF	SB	CS	SB%	GDP	Avg	OBP	SLG
1984	Florence	A	129	502	120	14	0	0	134	80	33	57	0	44	1	2	2	16	7	.70	9	.239	.317	.267
1985	Kinston	A	129	449	91	14	1	1	110	40	30	42	0	76	3	2	5	22	5	.81	6	.203	.273	.245
1986	Florence	A	105	354	85	10	0	3	104	47	40	56	3	53	2	0	3	4	7	.36	7	.240	.345	.294
	Knoxville	AA	5	6	0	0	0	0	0	0	0	0	0	2	0	0	0	1	0	1.00	0	.000	.000	.000
1987	Dunedin	A	128	477	135	14	4	0	157	70	44	57	0	53	0	0	5	27	9	.75	12	.283	.356	.329
1988	Knoxville	AA	138	534	136	24	5	0	170	61	40	53	0	74	1	2	4	42	15	.74	7	.255	.321	.318
1989	Knoxville	AA	54	203	55	6	2	4	77	38	14	33	0	38	0	4	1	18	6	.75	5	.271	.371	.379
	Syracuse	AAA	50	151	43	7	1	0	52	18	9	18	1	25	2	4	0	3	2	.60	5	.285	.368	.344
1990	Syracuse	AAA	37	101	20	5	1	0	27	12	10	14	0	20	0	3	1	0	3	.00	3	.198	.293	.267
1991	Tacoma	AAA	75	237	51	11	2	2	72	28	28	26	0	34	2	7	2	4	0	1.00	6	.215	.296	.304
	Huntsville	AA	31	110	29	9	0	2	44	18	10	16	0	21	1	0	1	5	2	.71	1	.264	.359	.400
1992	Tacoma	AAA	33	116	28	5	1	2	41	15	17	2	0	12	0	1	2	1	1	.50	5	.241	.250	.353
	Huntsville	AA	91	348	96	25	4	8	153	50	61	30	0	59	0	3	5	8	6	.57	12	.276	.329	.440
1993	Tacoma	AAA	138	544	165	29	5	7	225	91	73	58	2	64	2	2	5	17	9	.65	10	.303	.369	.414
1994	Col. Sprng	AAA	128	514	155	32	5	13	236	94	68	46	2	65	0	1	4	18	5	.78	11	.302	.356	.459
1995	Col. Sprng	AAA	126	460	135	32	6	12	215	83	77	46	3	74	3	6	1	12	4	.75	9	.293	.357	.467
	12 Min. YEARS		1397	5106	1344	237	37	54	1817	745	554	554	10	714	17	34	46	198	81	.71	115	.263	.335	.356

Dave Garrow

Bats: Right **Throws:** Right **Pos:** 3B   **Ht:** 6'3" **Wt:** 190 **Born:** 9/26/70 **Age:** 25

Year	Team	Lg	G	AB	H	2B	3B	HR	TB	R	RBI	TBB	IBB	SO	HBP	SH	SF	SB	CS	SB%	GDP	Avg	OBP	SLG
1991	Twins	R	42	145	32	4	0	0	36	11	18	12	0	16	1	1	4	5	3	.63	3	.221	.278	.248
	Elizabethtn	R	9	31	5	1	0	1	9	3	2	2	0	12	0	0	0	0	0	.00	1	.161	.212	.290
1992	Kenosha	A	119	397	94	22	4	2	130	41	44	20	0	70	3	7	3	12	6	.67	7	.237	.277	.327
1993	Fort Myers	A	109	351	73	15	0	2	94	33	25	25	0	62	0	3	2	11	4	.73	3	.208	.259	.268

110

Year Team	Lg	G	AB	H	2B	3B	HR	TB	R	RBI	TBB	IBB	SO	HBP	SH	SF	SB	CS	SB%	GDP	Avg	OBP	SLG
1994 Fort Myers	A	58	156	35	4	0	0	39	18	10	25	0	29	6	5	2	7	7	.50	1	.224	.349	.250
1995 New Britain	AA	6	14	2	0	0	0	2	0	1	2	0	2	0	0	0	0	0	.00	1	.143	.250	.143
5 Min. YEARS		343	1094	241	46	4	5	310	106	100	86	0	191	10	16	11	35	20	.64	16	.220	.281	.283

Sean Gavaghan

Pitches: Right **Bats:** Right **Pos:** P   **Ht:** 6'1" **Wt:** 185 **Born:** 12/19/69 **Age:** 26

		HOW MUCH HE PITCHED						WHAT HE GAVE UP									THE RESULTS					
Year Team	Lg	G	GS	CG	GF	IP	BFP	H	R	ER	HR	SH	SF	HB	TBB	IBB	SO	WP	Bk	W	L	Pct.	ShO	Sv	ERA
1992 Kenosha	A	20	6	0	8	57	243	63	22	13	2	5	4	2	18	1	39	3	3	2	3	.400	0	1	2.05
1993 Fort Wayne	A	11	0	0	5	22	89	14	5	3	0	2	0	0	7	0	25	2	1	3	1	.750	0	1	1.23
Fort Myers	A	19	0	0	13	31	134	37	10	9	1	1	0	0	8	1	24	2	0	1	3	.250	0	4	2.61
Nashville	AA	20	1	0	5	36.2	143	21	3	2	0	0	1	4	12	1	30	3	2	4	0	1.000	0	1	0.49
1994 Nashville	AA	56	0	0	35	85	366	59	35	22	5	6	4	1	56	1	63	3	0	5	5	.500	0	13	2.33
1995 New Britain	AA	21	0	0	21	28.2	119	18	10	7	0	2	2	2	10	2	30	0	1	2	1	.667	0	5	2.20
Salt Lake	AAA	35	0	0	15	47.1	221	53	32	29	3	6	1	3	31	3	28	3	0	1	4	.200	0	5	5.51
4 Min. YEARS		182	7	0	102	307.2	1315	265	117	85	11	22	12	12	142	9	239	16	7	18	17	.514	0	30	2.49

Dave Geeve

Pitches: Right **Bats:** Right **Pos:** P   **Ht:** 6'3" **Wt:** 190 **Born:** 10/19/69 **Age:** 26

		HOW MUCH HE PITCHED						WHAT HE GAVE UP									THE RESULTS					
Year Team	Lg	G	GS	CG	GF	IP	BFP	H	R	ER	HR	SH	SF	HB	TBB	IBB	SO	WP	Bk	W	L	Pct.	ShO	Sv	ERA
1991 Gastonia	A	14	14	1	0	79.1	323	74	40	38	7	2	2	1	20	1	69	0	1	6	4	.600	1	0	4.31
1992 Charlotte	A	25	24	0	1	139.1	572	138	61	52	8	4	3	6	22	1	97	6	0	8	8	.500	0	0	3.36
1993 Charlotte	A	24	23	1	1	132.2	539	141	52	42	7	3	2	3	19	0	80	8	1	11	8	.579	1	0	2.85
1994 Tulsa	AA	9	8	0	0	53	203	43	14	14	7	0	0	3	10	0	53	0	0	4	2	.667	0	0	2.38
1995 Okla. City	AAA	10	10	2	0	55.2	249	72	36	35	7	3	5	4	13	1	30	0	2	2	5	.286	0	0	5.66
Tulsa	AA	15	14	3	0	94	400	108	61	54	16	1	2	2	20	0	38	1	0	3	8	.273	1	0	5.17
5 Min. YEARS		97	93	7	2	554	2286	576	264	235	52	13	14	19	104	3	367	15	4	34	35	.493	3	0	3.82

Phil Geisler

Bats: Left **Throws:** Left **Pos:** OF   **Ht:** 6'3" **Wt:** 200 **Born:** 10/23/69 **Age:** 26

		BATTING													BASERUNNING				PERCENTAGES		
Year Team	Lg	G	AB	H	2B	3B	HR	TB	R	RBI	TBB	IBB	SO	HBP	SH	SF	SB	CS	SB%	GDP	Avg	OBP	SLG
1991 Martinsville	R	32	114	37	5	0	1	45	22	18	23	1	25	1	0	0	1	0	1.00	1	.325	.442	.395
Spartanburg	A	36	129	21	3	0	1	27	19	8	14	0	36	0	1	0	0	0	.00	2	.163	.245	.209
1992 Clearwater	A	120	400	87	10	3	6	121	39	33	41	1	88	4	1	2	4	9	.31	8	.218	.295	.303
1993 Clearwater	A	87	344	105	23	4	15	181	72	62	29	3	70	6	2	1	4	5	.44	5	.305	.368	.526
Reading	AA	48	178	48	14	1	3	73	25	14	17	2	50	3	1	0	4	2	.67	5	.270	.343	.410
1994 Scranton-Wb	AAA	54	183	36	5	1	0	43	14	11	18	3	48	1	1	2	2	2	.50	3	.197	.270	.235
Reading	AA	74	254	70	12	1	7	105	32	40	24	5	55	2	0	2	4	7	.36	5	.276	.340	.413
1995 Reading	AA	76	272	63	10	3	2	85	27	35	21	3	65	4	0	2	4	2	.67	5	.232	.294	.313
Scranton-Wb	AAA	20	43	8	5	0	1	16	2	7	2	0	13	0	1	0	0	0	.00	2	.186	.222	.372
5 Min. YEARS		547	1917	475	87	13	36	696	252	228	189	18	450	21	7	9	23	27	.46	34	.248	.321	.363

Brad Gennaro

Bats: Left **Throws:** Left **Pos:** OF   **Ht:** 6'1" **Wt:** 175 **Born:** 8/2/71 **Age:** 24

		BATTING													BASERUNNING				PERCENTAGES		
Year Team	Lg	G	AB	H	2B	3B	HR	TB	R	RBI	TBB	IBB	SO	HBP	SH	SF	SB	CS	SB%	GDP	Avg	OBP	SLG
1992 Charlstn-Sc	A	78	274	67	11	3	9	111	30	42	18	2	58	2	2	5	6	5	.55	6	.245	.291	.405
1993 Rancho Cuca	A	127	481	137	23	7	13	213	77	70	30	0	88	5	4	3	3	9	.25	11	.285	.331	.443
1994 Wichita	AA	128	500	139	19	7	16	220	71	60	38	6	88	6	1	1	8	4	.67	14	.278	.336	.440
1995 Memphis	AA	104	397	106	19	1	5	142	46	60	21	2	62	2	3	5	11	8	.58	9	.267	.304	.358
4 Min. YEARS		437	1652	449	72	18	43	686	224	232	107	10	296	15	10	14	28	26	.52	40	.272	.319	.415

Scott Gentile

Pitches: Right **Bats:** Right **Pos:** P   **Ht:** 5'11" **Wt:** 210 **Born:** 12/21/70 **Age:** 25

		HOW MUCH HE PITCHED						WHAT HE GAVE UP									THE RESULTS					
Year Team	Lg	G	GS	CG	GF	IP	BFP	H	R	ER	HR	SH	SF	HB	TBB	IBB	SO	WP	Bk	W	L	Pct.	ShO	Sv	ERA
1992 Jamestown	A	13	13	0	0	62.2	282	59	32	27	3	0	0	6	34	0	44	5	0	4	4	.500	0	0	3.88
1993 W. Palm Bch	A	25	25	0	0	138.1	592	132	72	62	8	4	5	7	54	0	108	6	0	8	9	.471	0	0	4.03
1994 Harrisburg	AA	6	2	0	1	10.1	72	16	21	20	1	1	0	0	25	0	14	6	0	0	1	.000	0	0	17.42
W. Palm Bch	A	53	1	0	40	65.1	255	44	16	14	0	3	0	1	19	0	90	4	2	5	2	.714	0	26	1.93
1995 Harrisburg	AA	37	0	0	26	49.2	202	36	19	19	3	2	1	4	15	2	48	1	0	2	2	.500	0	11	3.44
4 Min. YEARS		134	41	0	67	326.1	1403	287	160	142	15	10	6	18	147	2	304	22	2	19	18	.514	0	37	3.92

Ed Gerald

Bats: Both **Throws:** Right **Pos:** DH   **Ht:** 6'3" **Wt:** 205 **Born:** 7/18/70 **Age:** 25

		BATTING													BASERUNNING				PERCENTAGES		
Year Team	Lg	G	AB	H	2B	3B	HR	TB	R	RBI	TBB	IBB	SO	HBP	SH	SF	SB	CS	SB%	GDP	Avg	OBP	SLG
1989 Royals	R	61	217	40	1	6	1	56	30	24	30	0	80	1	1	0	15	5	.75	3	.184	.286	.258
1990 Royals	R	15	51	11	1	2	1	19	8	5	6	0	15	1	0	0	5	0	1.00	1	.216	.310	.373
Appleton	A	45	125	27	4	1	0	33	22	6	17	0	45	0	2	0	4	1	.80	2	.216	.310	.264
1991 Appleton	A	101	348	85	15	10	7	141	49	46	49	1	107	2	3	4	18	2	.90	6	.244	.337	.405
1992 Appleton	A	123	420	104	13	8	12	169	55	62	45	2	127	1	2	4	17	3	.85	3	.248	.319	.402

Year Team	Lg																					
1993 St. Pete	A	52	176	35	12	4	0	55	17	17	17	0	58	0	1	2	2	1	.67	8	.199	.267	.313
1994 Nashville	AA	112	393	107	15	6	13	173	64	52	42	1	107	0	3	2	14	5	.74	3	.272	.341	.440
1995 New Britain	AA	6	18	2	1	0	0	3	1	3	2	0	9	0	0	0	0	0	.00	1	.111	.200	.167
7 Min. YEARS		515	1748	411	62	37	34	649	246	212	208	4	548	5	12	12	75	17	.82	27	.235	.316	.371

Ron Gerstein

Pitches: Left **Bats:** Left **Pos:** P **Ht:** 6'1" **Wt:** 200 **Born:** 1/1/69 **Age:** 27

		HOW MUCH HE PITCHED						WHAT HE GAVE UP									THE RESULTS				
Year Team	Lg	G	GS	CG	GF	IP	BFP	H	R	ER	HR	SH	SF	HB	TBB	IBB	SO	WP	Bk	W	L	Pct.	ShO	Sv	ERA
1990 Salt Lake	R	2	1	0	0	4.1	25	7	7	7	1	0	1	0	5	0	3	0	0	0	1	.000	0	0	14.54
1991 Sumter	A	7	0	0	5	9.1	37	5	1	0	0	0	1	0	5	0	6	0	0	0	1	.000	0	1	0.00
1992 Rockford	A	33	5	0	17	51	236	62	37	32	2	2	2	1	28	1	40	5	3	4	8	.333	0	5	5.65
1993 Stockton	A	36	7	1	9	86.1	421	103	59	51	2	5	6	2	63	3	49	7	0	8	4	.667	0	0	5.32
1994 El Paso	AA	27	26	1	0	163.2	716	184	94	80	8	8	5	3	70	2	92	10	1	12	3	.800	1	0	4.40
1995 El Paso	AA	28	22	1	2	126.2	583	155	90	64	14	4	6	2	58	3	69	4	1	8	12	.400	0	1	4.55
6 Min. YEARS		133	61	3	33	441.1	2018	516	288	234	27	19	21	8	229	9	259	26	5	32	29	.525	1	7	4.77

Paul Gibson

Pitches: Left **Bats:** Right **Pos:** P **Ht:** 6'1" **Wt:** 195 **Born:** 1/4/60 **Age:** 36

		HOW MUCH HE PITCHED						WHAT HE GAVE UP									THE RESULTS				
Year Team	Lg	G	GS	CG	GF	IP	BFP	H	R	ER	HR	SH	SF	HB	TBB	IBB	SO	WP	Bk	W	L	Pct.	ShO	Sv	ERA
1984 Orlando	AA	27	12	3	7	121	529	125	71	52	9	4	2	1	54	0	64	6	0	7	7	.500	1	1	3.87
1985 Birmingham	AA	36	14	2	5	144.1	615	135	73	66	13	4	4	0	63	1	79	4	0	8	8	.500	2	1	4.12
1986 Glens Falls	AA	9	1	0	3	19.2	81	16	3	3	0	0	0	0	7	0	21	0	0	3	1	.750	0	1	1.37
Nashville	AAA	30	14	2	9	113.1	489	121	58	50	12	3	3	2	40	5	91	8	0	5	6	.455	0	2	3.97
1987 Toledo	AAA	27	27	7	0	179	753	173	83	69	14	2	5	3	57	6	118	6	1	14	7	.667	2	0	3.47
1992 Tidewater	AAA	2	0	0	1	3	14	3	1	1	0	2	0	0	2	1	1	0	0	0	0	.000	0	0	3.00
1993 Norfolk	AAA	14	0	0	11	21	79	10	2	2	0	1	0	0	5	0	29	0	0	1	1	.500	0	7	0.86
Columbus	AAA	3	1	0	1	7	25	4	0	0	0	0	0	0	1	0	7	0	0	1	0	1.000	0	0	0.00
1994 Columbus	AAA	5	0	0	4	5.1	24	5	2	2	1	0	0	0	4	0	3	0	0	0	0	.000	0	1	3.38
1995 Syracuse	AAA	26	0	0	8	24.1	106	24	16	13	0	1	0	2	6	2	28	1	0	0	1	.000	0	1	4.81
Calgary	AAA	19	0	0	9	19.1	86	21	11	8	1	0	2	0	9	1	17	3	0	0	2	.000	0	3	3.72
1988 Detroit	AL	40	1	0	18	92	390	83	33	30	6	3	5	2	34	8	50	3	1	4	2	.667	0	0	2.93
1989 Detroit	AL	45	13	0	16	132	573	129	71	68	11	7	5	6	57	12	77	4	1	4	8	.333	0	0	4.64
1990 Detroit	AL	61	0	0	17	97.1	422	99	36	33	10	4	5	1	44	12	56	1	1	5	4	.556	0	3	3.05
1991 Detroit	AL	68	0	0	28	96	432	112	51	49	10	2	2	3	48	8	52	4	0	5	7	.417	0	8	4.59
1992 New York	NL	43	1	0	12	62	273	70	37	36	7	3	1	0	25	0	49	1	0	0	1	.000	0	0	5.23
1993 New York	AL	20	0	0	9	35.1	142	31	15	12	4	0	3	0	9	0	25	0	0	2	0	1.000	0	0	3.06
New York	NL	8	0	0	1	8.2	42	14	6	5	1	0	0	0	2	0	12	1	0	1	1	.500	0	0	5.19
1994 New York	AL	30	0	0	15	29	130	26	17	16	5	0	2	1	17	3	21	1	1	1	1	.500	0	0	4.97
8 Min. YEARS		198	69	14	58	657.1	2801	637	320	266	50	17	16	9	248	16	458	28	1	39	33	.542	5	18	3.64
7 Maj. YEARS		315	15	0	116	552.1	2404	564	266	249	54	19	23	13	236	43	342	15	5	22	24	.478	0	11	4.06

Shawn Gilbert

Bats: Right **Throws:** Right **Pos:** SS **Ht:** 5'9" **Wt:** 170 **Born:** 3/12/65 **Age:** 31

		BATTING														BASERUNNING				PERCENTAGES		
Year Team	Lg	G	AB	H	2B	3B	HR	TB	R	RBI	TBB	IBB	SO	HBP	SH	SF	SB	CS	SB%	GDP	Avg	OBP	SLG
1987 Visalia	A	82	272	61	5	0	5	81	39	27	34	0	59	7	4	4	6	4	.60	8	.224	.322	.298
1988 Visalia	A	14	43	16	3	2	0	23	10	8	10	0	7	1	0	0	1	1	.50	0	.372	.500	.535
Kenosha	A	108	402	112	21	2	3	146	80	44	63	2	61	2	0	5	49	10	.83	6	.279	.375	.363
1989 Visalia	A	125	453	113	17	1	2	138	52	43	54	1	70	3	6	3	42	16	.72	11	.249	.331	.305
1990 Orlando	AA	123	433	110	18	2	4	144	68	44	61	0	69	5	4	3	31	9	.78	10	.254	.351	.333
1991 Orlando	AA	138	529	135	12	5	3	166	69	38	53	1	70	11	6	6	43	19	.69	18	.255	.332	.314
1992 Portland	AAA	138	444	109	17	2	3	139	60	52	36	2	55	4	5	2	31	8	.79	10	.245	.307	.313
1993 Nashville	AAA	104	278	63	17	2	0	84	28	17	12	0	41	2	2	1	6	2	.75	4	.227	.263	.302
1994 Scranton-Wb	AAA	141	547	139	33	4	7	201	81	52	66	3	86	7	3	3	20	15	.57	9	.254	.340	.367
1995 Scranton-Wb	AAA	136	536	141	26	2	2	177	84	42	64	0	102	6	4	4	16	11	.59	8	.263	.346	.330
9 Min. YEARS		1109	3937	999	169	22	29	1299	571	367	453	9	620	48	34	31	245	95	.72	84	.254	.336	.330

Joel Gilmore

Pitches: Right **Bats:** Right **Pos:** P **Ht:** 6'6" **Wt:** 230 **Born:** 12/16/69 **Age:** 26

		HOW MUCH HE PITCHED						WHAT HE GAVE UP									THE RESULTS				
Year Team	Lg	G	GS	CG	GF	IP	BFP	H	R	ER	HR	SH	SF	HB	TBB	IBB	SO	WP	Bk	W	L	Pct.	ShO	Sv	ERA
1991 Martinsvlle	R	11	9	0	2	59	230	45	16	10	3	1	2	1	14	1	51	2	7	4	3	.571	0	0	1.53
Spartanburg	A	2	1	0	0	7	26	3	0	0	0	0	0	2	0	8	0	0	1	0	1.000	0	0	0.00
1992 Spartanburg	A	10	9	1	0	61.1	240	47	21	18	3	3	0	2	17	1	60	2	0	2	4	.333	0	0	2.64
Clearwater	A	5	5	0	0	26.1	111	25	11	10	3	0	0	1	9	0	22	0	0	2	1	.667	0	0	3.42
1993 Clearwater	A	7	7	0	0	43.2	179	45	18	16	3	2	3	1	7	0	22	4	0	5	0	1.000	0	0	3.30
1994 Clearwater	A	20	19	1	1	119.1	495	121	57	43	11	0	4	4	20	3	72	4	1	9	6	.600	0	1	3.24
1995 Reading	AA	18	3	0	4	36	168	45	27	25	6	1	2	3	18	2	27	3	1	2	0	1.000	0	0	6.25
Sioux Falls	IND	11	11	2	0	71.2	310	86	43	37	8	0	0	3	21	0	28	5	1	3	5	.375	0	0	4.65
5 Min. YEARS		84	64	4	7	424.1	1759	417	193	159	37	7	11	15	108	7	290	20	10	28	19	.596	0	1	3.37

Tony Gilmore

Bats: Right **Throws:** Right **Pos:** C   **Ht:** 6'2" **Wt:** 195 **Born:** 10/15/68 **Age:** 27

Year	Team	Lg	G	AB	H	2B	3B	HR	TB	R	RBI	TBB	IBB	SO	HBP	SH	SF	SB	CS	SB%	GDP	Avg	OBP	SLG
1990	Auburn	A	33	106	23	8	0	0	31	9	7	6	0	23	0	1	1	2	1	.67	2	.217	.257	.292
1991	Burlington	A	82	276	75	12	0	1	90	25	27	25	2	45	3	5	1	2	2	.50	13	.272	.338	.326
1992	Osceola	A	80	266	55	7	0	1	65	26	21	17	2	46	4	1	1	1	5	.17	7	.207	.264	.244
1993	Jackson	AA	47	145	25	4	0	2	35	14	7	7	1	29	4	0	0	1	0	1.00	6	.172	.231	.241
1994	Tucson	AAA	2	5	0	0	0	0	0	1	0	0	0	0	0	1	0	0	0	.00	0	.000	.000	.000
	Jackson	AA	68	178	46	11	0	0	57	14	19	11	2	41	3	2	2	0	1	.00	5	.258	.309	.320
1995	Jackson	AA	53	145	31	3	0	1	37	10	15	10	0	26	0	1	2	0	0	.00	3	.214	.261	.255
	6 Min. YEARS		365	1121	255	45	0	5	315	99	96	76	7	210	14	11	7	6	9	.40	36	.227	.283	.281

Charles Gipson

Bats: Right **Throws:** Right **Pos:** OF   **Ht:** 6'2" **Wt:** 180 **Born:** 12/16/72 **Age:** 23

Year	Team	Lg	G	AB	H	2B	3B	HR	TB	R	RBI	TBB	IBB	SO	HBP	SH	SF	SB	CS	SB%	GDP	Avg	OBP	SLG
1992	Mariners	R	39	124	39	2	0	0	41	30	14	13	1	19	6	2	1	11	5	.69	0	.315	.403	.331
1993	Appleton	A	109	348	89	13	1	0	104	63	20	61	0	76	27	9	1	21	15	.58	5	.256	.405	.299
1994	Riverside	A	128	481	141	12	3	1	162	102	41	76	4	67	12	7	2	34	15	.69	8	.293	.401	.337
1995	Port City	AA	112	391	87	11	2	0	102	36	29	30	0	66	8	7	1	10	12	.45	13	.223	.291	.261
	4 Min. YEARS		388	1344	356	38	6	1	409	231	104	180	5	228	53	25	5	76	47	.62	24	.265	.372	.304

Jim Givens

Bats: Both **Throws:** Right **Pos:** 2B-SS   **Ht:** 6'1" **Wt:** 173 **Born:** 11/11/67 **Age:** 28

Year	Team	Lg	G	AB	H	2B	3B	HR	TB	R	RBI	TBB	IBB	SO	HBP	SH	SF	SB	CS	SB%	GDP	Avg	OBP	SLG
1991	Bristol	R	4	12	3	0	0	0	3	3	1	1	0	1	1	0	0	1	1	.50	0	.250	.357	.250
	Fayetteville	A	60	226	56	5	0	0	61	27	15	17	0	32	0	0	0	13	11	.54	7	.248	.300	.270
1992	Lakeland	A	124	456	110	15	3	0	131	51	29	27	2	50	1	12	3	18	13	.58	8	.241	.283	.287
1993	London	AA	82	262	69	8	3	3	92	24	28	16	2	45	2	5	4	17	8	.68	8	.263	.306	.351
	Toledo	AAA	44	148	38	4	2	0	46	18	13	10	0	18	1	2	1	6	3	.67	3	.257	.306	.311
1994	Toledo	AAA	105	283	66	7	4	0	81	25	11	30	0	64	1	4	0	16	10	.62	4	.233	.309	.286
1995	Toledo	AAA	79	219	52	5	1	0	59	23	14	26	0	40	1	0	1	7	5	.58	4	.237	.320	.269
	5 Min. YEARS		498	1606	394	44	13	3	473	171	111	127	4	250	7	23	9	78	51	.60	34	.245	.302	.295

Doug Glanville

Bats: Right **Throws:** Right **Pos:** OF   **Ht:** 6'2" **Wt:** 170 **Born:** 8/25/70 **Age:** 25

Year	Team	Lg	G	AB	H	2B	3B	HR	TB	R	RBI	TBB	IBB	SO	HBP	SH	SF	SB	CS	SB%	GDP	Avg	OBP	SLG
1991	Geneva	A	36	152	46	8	0	2	60	29	12	11	0	25	1	3	1	17	3	.85	1	.303	.352	.395
1992	Winston-Sal	A	120	485	125	18	4	4	163	72	36	40	0	78	4	9	2	32	9	.78	6	.258	.318	.336
1993	Daytona	A	61	239	70	10	1	2	88	47	21	28	0	24	3	4	0	18	15	.55	2	.293	.374	.368
	Orlando	AA	73	295	78	14	4	9	127	42	40	12	0	40	2	6	5	15	7	.68	1	.264	.293	.431
1994	Orlando	AA	130	483	127	22	2	5	168	53	52	24	4	49	5	10	7	26	20	.57	7	.263	.301	.348
1995	Iowa	AAA	112	419	113	16	2	4	145	40	37	16	0	64	3	7	4	13	9	.59	4	.270	.300	.346
	5 Min. YEARS		532	2073	559	88	13	26	751	291	198	131	4	280	18	39	19	121	63	.66	21	.270	.316	.362

Leon Glenn

Bats: Left **Throws:** Right **Pos:** 1B   **Ht:** 6'2" **Wt:** 200 **Born:** 9/16/69 **Age:** 26

Year	Team	Lg	G	AB	H	2B	3B	HR	TB	R	RBI	TBB	IBB	SO	HBP	SH	SF	SB	CS	SB%	GDP	Avg	OBP	SLG
1988	Brewers	R	55	212	72	13	10	8	129	54	53	24	2	29	2	2	3	5	4	.56	2	.340	.407	.608
1989	Helena	R	6	15	0	0	0	0	0	0	0	0	0	6	0	0	0	0	0	.00	0	.000	.000	.000
	Brewers	R	51	212	81	10	7	7	126	42	50	14	5	46	2	0	2	21	9	.70	2	.382	.422	.594
1990	Beloit	A	65	202	39	4	3	5	64	19	29	20	1	93	0	2	0	10	6	.63	1	.193	.266	.317
	Helena	R	42	153	36	6	2	4	58	19	26	29	1	41	1	1	1	12	3	.80	1	.235	.359	.379
1991	Beloit	A	51	161	28	2	2	6	52	23	27	13	0	60	0	3	2	18	3	.86	2	.174	.233	.323
	Bend	A	73	262	59	9	3	15	119	46	55	36	2	96	0	0	4	16	3	.84	3	.225	.315	.454
1992	Stockton	A	88	275	57	12	2	10	103	36	36	40	0	86	0	1	2	17	8	.68	0	.207	.306	.375
1993	Stockton	A	114	431	119	27	3	15	197	77	76	49	4	110	4	1	6	35	15	.70	9	.276	.351	.457
1994	El Paso	AA	67	219	56	12	3	8	98	40	32	20	2	67	1	1	0	8	7	.53	4	.256	.321	.447
	New Orleans	AAA	48	155	37	9	2	4	62	22	22	15	0	56	0	1	4	7	0	1.00	4	.239	.299	.400
1995	Midland	AA	120	433	110	19	11	17	202	68	65	34	1	126	2	3	3	16	11	.59	9	.254	.309	.467
	8 Min. YEARS		780	2730	694	123	48	99	1210	446	471	294	18	816	12	15	27	165	69	.71	37	.254	.326	.443

George Glinatsis

Pitches: Right **Bats:** Right **Pos:** P   **Ht:** 6'4" **Wt:** 195 **Born:** 6/29/69 **Age:** 27

			HOW MUCH HE PITCHED						WHAT HE GAVE UP										THE RESULTS					
Year	Team	Lg	G	GS	CG	GF	IP	BFP	H	R	ER	HR	SH	SF	HB	TBB	IBB	SO	WP	Bk	W	L	Pct.	ShO	Sv	ERA
1991	Mariners	R	12	12	0	0	74	322	62	35	18	1	0	1	8	32	0	80	17	8	10	2	.833	0	0	2.19
1992	San Bernrdo	A	28	18	1	5	125.2	564	123	83	64	14	3	4	3	67	1	117	19	1	3	12	.200	0	2	4.58
1993	Jacksonvlle	AA	9	5	0	0	34.2	152	39	26	26	4	0	1	0	15	0	25	1	1	5	2	.714	0	0	6.75
	Riverside	A	14	3	0	6	35.2	159	40	24	18	1	0	3	1	9	0	30	2	0	1	0	1.000	0	2	4.54

1994 Riverside	A	14	14	1	0	88.2	363	84	33	29	5	1	5	0	17	0	80	2	1	7	3	.700	0	0	2.94
Jacksonvlle	AA	9	8	3	1	54.1	218	44	17	14	2	2	2	3	16	2	44	4	0	5	2	.714	1	0	2.32
1995 Tacoma	AAA	8	8	0	0	30.2	138	39	25	25	4	0	2	1	13	0	13	0	0	1	2	.333	0	0	7.34
Port City	AA	18	18	1	0	93.1	427	104	63	55	6	2	4	13	44	1	68	7	1	6	7	.462	0	0	5.30
1994 Seattle	AL	2	2	0	0	5.1	28	9	8	8	2	0	1	0	6	0	1	0	0	0	1	.000	0	0	13.50
5 Min. YEARS		112	86	6	12	537	2343	535	306	249	37	8	22	29	213	4	457	52	12	38	30	.559	1	4	4.17

Barry Goetz

Pitches: Right **Bats:** Right **Pos:** P   **Ht:** 6'2" **Wt:** 195 **Born:** 8/28/68 **Age:** 27

		HOW MUCH HE PITCHED						WHAT HE GAVE UP												THE RESULTS					
Year Team	Lg	G	GS	CG	GF	IP	BFP	H	R	ER	HR	SH	SF	HB	TBB	IBB	SO	WP	Bk	W	L	Pct.	ShO	Sv	ERA
1990 Butte	R	4	0	0	2	5.2	22	2	1	1	0	1	0	1	3	0	2	0	0	0	1	.000	0	1	1.59
1991 Charlotte	A	46	0	0	33	56	248	56	24	15	1	6	3	0	24	2	42	6	0	3	1	.750	0	12	2.41
1992 Charlotte	A	33	0	0	28	33.1	138	21	10	10	1	2	0	1	19	0	38	1	1	4	5	.444	0	11	2.70
Tulsa	AA	10	0	0	5	14.1	59	10	2	1	0	2	0	0	6	0	7	1	0	2	1	.667	0	1	0.63
1993 Tulsa	AA	38	0	0	13	56.1	276	70	51	41	12	0	4	2	44	2	57	7	2	2	3	.400	0	1	6.55
1994 Okla. City	AAA	55	0	0	32	98.1	432	102	51	50	4	8	4	1	45	5	63	9	1	3	7	.300	0	9	4.58
1995 Okla. City	AAA	40	6	0	15	89.2	399	97	60	57	8	3	6	4	49	3	46	1	2	4	6	.400	0	1	5.72
6 Min. YEARS		226	6	0	128	353.2	1574	358	199	175	26	22	17	9	190	12	255	25	6	18	24	.429	0	36	4.45

Lonnie Goldberg

Bats: Right **Throws:** Right **Pos:** SS   **Ht:** 5'10" **Wt:** 170 **Born:** 8/1/70 **Age:** 25

		BATTING													BASERUNNING				PERCENTAGES		
Year Team	Lg	G	AB	H	2B	3B	HR	TB	R	RBI	TBB	IBB	SO	HBP	SH	SF	SB	CS	SB%	GDP	Avg	OBP	SLG
1993 Erie	A	72	283	72	11	1	1	88	39	37	32	0	40	1	3	3	22	10	.69	2	.254	.329	.311
1994 Charlstn-Sc	A	67	198	46	10	1	0	58	24	10	15	0	55	0	5	0	6	1	.86	2	.232	.286	.293
1995 Okla. City	AAA	10	30	7	3	0	1	13	2	5	2	0	4	0	0	0	1	0	1.00	1	.233	.281	.433
Charlstn-Sc	A	100	340	74	12	1	2	94	29	31	26	1	54	1	2	4	17	11	.61	3	.218	.272	.276
3 Min. YEARS		249	851	199	36	3	4	253	94	83	75	1	153	2	10	7	46	22	.68	8	.234	.295	.297

Gary Goldsmith

Pitches: Right **Bats:** Right **Pos:** P   **Ht:** 6'2" **Wt:** 205 **Born:** 7/4/71 **Age:** 24

		HOW MUCH HE PITCHED						WHAT HE GAVE UP												THE RESULTS					
Year Team	Lg	G	GS	CG	GF	IP	BFP	H	R	ER	HR	SH	SF	HB	TBB	IBB	SO	WP	Bk	W	L	Pct.	ShO	Sv	ERA
1993 Niagara Fal	A	21	5	0	12	54.2	231	43	21	14	3	2	0	4	20	3	64	4	0	4	2	.667	0	0	2.30
1994 Lakeland	A	23	19	1	3	120.2	499	105	50	44	4	4	4	7	51	2	81	7	2	7	7	.500	0	0	3.28
Trenton	AA	4	4	2	0	25.2	103	23	12	11	3	1	0	0	9	1	27	3	0	0	4	.000	0	0	3.86
1995 Jacksonvlle	AA	15	15	0	0	82	347	78	52	42	14	1	4	2	31	1	42	5	0	4	7	.364	0	0	4.61
3 Min. YEARS		63	43	3	15	283	1180	249	135	111	24	8	8	13	111	7	214	19	2	15	20	.429	0	0	3.53

Wayne Gomes

Pitches: Right **Bats:** Right **Pos:** P   **Ht:** 6'0" **Wt:** 215 **Born:** 1/15/73 **Age:** 23

		HOW MUCH HE PITCHED						WHAT HE GAVE UP												THE RESULTS					
Year Team	Lg	G	GS	CG	GF	IP	BFP	H	R	ER	HR	SH	SF	HB	TBB	IBB	SO	WP	Bk	W	L	Pct.	ShO	Sv	ERA
1993 Batavia	A	5	0	0	3	7.1	32	1	1	1	0	0	0	0	8	0	11	0	1	1	0	1.000	0	0	1.23
Clearwater	A	9	0	0	8	7.2	37	4	1	1	0	0	0	0	9	0	13	2	0	0	0	.000	0	4	1.17
1994 Clearwater	A	23	21	1	0	104.1	474	85	63	55	5	2	4	3	82	2	102	27	4	6	8	.429	1	0	4.74
1995 Reading	AA	22	22	1	0	104.2	462	89	54	46	8	3	1	1	70	0	102	6	6	7	4	.636	1	0	3.96
3 Min. YEARS		59	43	2	11	224	1005	179	119	103	13	5	5	4	169	2	228	35	11	14	12	.538	2	4	4.14

Fabio Gomez

Bats: Right **Throws:** Right **Pos:** 3B   **Ht:** 6'0" **Wt:** 185 **Born:** 5/12/68 **Age:** 28

		BATTING													BASERUNNING				PERCENTAGES		
Year Team	Lg	G	AB	H	2B	3B	HR	TB	R	RBI	TBB	IBB	SO	HBP	SH	SF	SB	CS	SB%	GDP	Avg	OBP	SLG
1987 Burlington	R	22	76	14	2	0	2	22	6	9	2	0	23	1	0	1	2	2	.50	3	.184	.213	.289
1988 Burlington	R	57	188	38	3	1	4	55	18	22	11	0	46	2	1	2	7	6	.54	3	.202	.251	.293
1989 Kinston	A	17	45	12	0	0	1	15	5	5	1	0	12	1	0	0	1	0	1.00	3	.267	.298	.333
Watertown	A	73	296	98	15	4	9	148	64	57	15	2	56	1	2	2	6	3	.67	6	.331	.363	.500
1990 Kinston	A	121	430	106	18	8	8	164	72	52	53	0	91	4	4	2	13	8	.62	9	.247	.333	.381
1992 Reno	A	130	503	154	16	12	19	251	101	115	62	6	92	2	2	5	7	9	.44	19	.306	.381	.499
1993 Huntsville	AA	60	220	57	10	1	7	90	26	33	17	0	43	2	3	1	5	3	.63	3	.259	.317	.409
Tacoma	AAA	67	252	71	10	1	2	89	28	29	20	1	47	3	0	5	5	9	.36	4	.282	.336	.353
1994 New Haven	AA	61	206	62	17	0	3	88	38	29	26	1	49	2	0	2	3	3	.50	6	.301	.381	.427
Colo. Sprng	AAA	29	44	7	3	0	1	13	6	5	4	0	16	0	1	0	0	0	.00	0	.159	.229	.295
1995 Port City	AA	29	93	22	4	0	1	29	7	11	12	0	20	0	1	2	1	3	.25	1	.237	.318	.312
Pueblo	IND	21	72	17	1	1	1	23	12	11	6	0	14	1	1	1	2	0	1.00	0	.236	.300	.319
8 Min. YEARS		687	2425	658	99	28	58	987	383	378	229	10	509	19	15	23	52	46	.53	57	.271	.336	.407

Rudy Gomez

Bats: Right **Throws:** Right **Pos:** 2B   **Ht:** 5'10" **Wt:** 165 **Born:** 6/8/69 **Age:** 27

		BATTING													BASERUNNING				PERCENTAGES		
Year Team	Lg	G	AB	H	2B	3B	HR	TB	R	RBI	TBB	IBB	SO	HBP	SH	SF	SB	CS	SB%	GDP	Avg	OBP	SLG
1991 Geneva	A	61	229	52	6	2	0	62	22	14	24	1	38	5	4	2	5	5	.50	8	.227	.312	.271
1992 Winston-Sal	A	112	363	84	13	1	1	102	43	25	28	0	60	4	7	2	8	6	.57	4	.231	.292	.281

Year	Team	Lg	G	AB	H	2B	3B	HR	TB	R	RBI	TBB	IBB	SO	HBP	SH	SF	SB	CS	SB%	GDP	Avg	OBP	SLG
1993	Daytona	A	40	147	39	4	1	0	45	20	12	19	0	24	0	3	3	3	5	.38	3	.265	.343	.306
	Iowa	AAA	9	20	3	0	0	0	3	0	0	1	0	8	0	0	0	0	0	.00	1	.150	.190	.150
	Orlando	AA	56	140	46	8	0	1	57	26	17	25	0	31	3	8	2	5	3	.63	4	.329	.435	.407
1994	Orlando	AA	91	229	58	10	0	2	74	26	16	18	0	45	2	1	0	4	7	.36	3	.253	.313	.323
1995	Orlando	AA	93	214	41	11	1	1	57	18	16	15	1	45	2	5	3	0	0	.00	8	.192	.248	.266
	5 Min. YEARS		462	1342	323	52	5	5	400	155	100	130	2	251	16	28	12	25	26	.49	31	.241	.313	.298

Frank Gonzales

Pitches: Left **Bats:** Right **Pos:** P **Ht:** 6'0" **Wt:** 185 **Born:** 3/12/68 **Age:** 28

			HOW MUCH HE PITCHED					WHAT HE GAVE UP										THE RESULTS					
Year	Team	Lg	G	GS	CG	GF	IP	BFP	H	R	ER	HR	SH	SF	HB	TBB	IBB	SO	WP	Bk	W	L	Pct.	ShO	Sv	ERA
1989	Niagara Fal	A	10	5	1	3	38	160	36	20	16	2	1	2	0	16	1	35	0	3	3	3	.500	1	0	3.79
1990	Fayetteville	A	25	25	0	0	143	606	123	54	48	2	1	7	4	66	0	101	9	1	10	6	.625	0	0	3.02
1991	Lakeland	A	25	25	1	0	146	603	130	62	55	3	5	9	3	55	0	99	3	1	11	5	.688	0	0	3.39
1992	London	AA	10	10	0	0	65.2	269	64	25	22	5	0	0	1	10	0	37	2	0	5	4	.556	0	0	3.02
	Toledo	AAA	18	17	2	0	98.1	421	100	48	47	7	3	2	3	36	0	65	5	0	4	6	.400	1	0	4.30
1993	Toledo	AAA	29	15	2	3	109.1	464	116	56	48	12	2	2	3	37	1	71	4	0	6	3	.667	0	0	3.95
1994	Toledo	AAA	34	17	0	1	117	535	142	79	62	11	1	8	3	58	3	86	7	1	6	11	.353	0	0	4.77
1995	Toledo	AAA	49	0	0	6	51.2	217	43	23	19	4	2	0	3	17	1	54	2	0	3	2	.600	0	0	3.31
	7 Min. YEARS		200	114	6	13	769	3275	754	367	317	46	15	30	20	295	6	548	32	6	48	40	.545	2	0	3.71

Javier Gonzalez

Bats: Right **Throws:** Right **Pos:** C **Ht:** 6'0" **Wt:** 193 **Born:** 10/3/68 **Age:** 27

			BATTING															BASERUNNING				PERCENTAGES		
Year	Team	Lg	G	AB	H	2B	3B	HR	TB	R	RBI	TBB	IBB	SO	HBP	SH	SF	SB	CS	SB%	GDP	Avg	OBP	SLG
1986	Kingsport	R	25	55	16	4	0	5	35	12	14	14	0	13	0	0	0	0	0	.00	1	.291	.435	.636
1987	Little Fall	A	40	145	38	6	1	3	61	10	25	14	1	00	0	1	3	2	1	.67	3	.262	.323	.421
1988	Columbia	A	79	250	50	4	2	3	67	21	21	15	0	58	2	6	1	0	1	.00	7	.200	.250	.268
1989	St. Lucie	A	56	175	43	7	0	3	59	26	16	10	0	39	5	4	3	1	0	1.00	4	.246	.301	.337
1990	Jackson	AA	45	137	23	4	0	4	39	16	15	13	1	42	0	3	2	0	1	.00	2	.168	.237	.285
1991	Tidewater	AAA	1	3	1	0	0	0	1	0	0	0	0	1	0	0	0	0	0	.00	0	.333	.333	.333
	Williamsprt	AA	48	150	23	7	0	4	42	7	14	12	0	45	2	1	1	0	1	1.00	4	.153	.224	.280
1992	Tidewater	AAA	39	120	25	4	0	4	41	9	12	4	0	33	2	2	0	0	0	.00	2	.208	.246	.342
1993	Binghamton	AA	94	257	59	7	0	10	96	30	36	24	0	65	5	0	3	0	0	.00	8	.230	.304	.374
1994	New Britain	AA	30	88	17	4	0	1	24	6	8	10	0	24	1	1	1	0	1	.00	4	.193	.280	.273
	Norfolk	AAA	17	43	10	1	0	1	14	5	1	1	0	10	0	1	0	0	0	.00	2	.233	.250	.326
1995	New Orleans	AAA	43	113	28	11	0	5	54	20	15	7	0	24	4	2	1	0	0	.00	0	.248	.312	.478
	10 Min. YEARS		517	1536	333	59	3	45	533	170	177	124	2	390	21	21	14	4	4	.50	34	.217	.282	.347

Mauricio Gonzalez

Bats: Both **Throws:** Right **Pos:** SS **Ht:** 5'11" **Wt:** 160 **Born:** 2/13/72 **Age:** 24

			BATTING															BASERUNNING				PERCENTAGES		
Year	Team	Lg	G	AB	H	2B	3B	HR	TB	R	RBI	TBB	IBB	SO	HBP	SH	SF	SB	CS	SB%	GDP	Avg	OBP	SLG
1992	Rockies/cub	R	35	148	51	4	5	0	65	19	14	6	0	19	1	0	0	3	4	.43	3	.345	.374	.439
	Bend	A	9	18	2	0	0	0	2	3	1	0	0	3	0	0	0	1	0	1.00	0	.111	.111	.111
1993	Central Val	A	83	263	74	8	2	3	95	30	27	19	3	37	2	2	1	1	5	.17	6	.281	.333	.361
1994	Central Val	A	104	358	92	14	2	4	122	42	41	18	1	58	0	9	5	5	0	1.00	13	.257	.289	.341
1995	New Haven	AA	73	164	44	5	3	0	55	20	12	7	0	29	1	1	0	0	1	.00	1	.268	.302	.335
	4 Min. YEARS		304	951	263	31	12	7	339	114	95	50	4	146	4	12	6	10	10	.50	23	.277	.314	.356

Paul Gonzalez

Bats: Left **Throws:** Right **Pos:** 3B **Ht:** 6'0" **Wt:** 185 **Born:** 4/22/69 **Age:** 27

			BATTING															BASERUNNING				PERCENTAGES		
Year	Team	Lg	G	AB	H	2B	3B	HR	TB	R	RBI	TBB	IBB	SO	HBP	SH	SF	SB	CS	SB%	GDP	Avg	OBP	SLG
1990	Spokane	A	1	4	1	1	0	0	2	0	2	1	0	1	0	0	0	0	0	.00	0	.250	.400	.500
	Charlstn-Sc	A	69	231	56	7	3	11	102	30	32	37	0	62	3	2	2	0	0	.00	4	.242	.352	.442
1991	High Desert	A	103	371	99	31	3	14	178	61	64	47	1	85	4	1	1	2	3	.40	5	.267	.355	.480
1992	Wichita	AA	120	432	110	18	2	15	177	59	54	48	3	124	4	0	3	7	3	.70	9	.255	.333	.410
1993	Wichita	AA	59	215	58	7	3	7	92	36	33	25	2	55	3	0	2	5	5	.50	2	.270	.351	.428
	Las Vegas	AAA	75	267	64	11	4	7	104	36	34	21	1	64	1	1	2	3	2	.60	7	.240	.296	.390
1994	Wichita	AA	73	215	52	9	4	6	87	23	24	27	6	63	3	0	3	3	2	.60	2	.242	.331	.405
	Las Vegas	AAA	4	13	2	0	0	0	2	0	2	2	0	2	0	0	0	0	0	.00	0	.154	.267	.154
	Pr. William	A	24	90	23	1	0	2	30	12	18	9	0	24	0	0	0	2	1	.67	3	.256	.323	.333
1995	Birmingham	AA	8	26	7	1	0	2	14	4	4	2	0	7	0	0	0	0	1	.00	0	.269	.321	.538
	Pr. William	A	92	290	60	10	0	7	91	25	34	31	3	85	3	1	3	1	1	.50	7	.207	.287	.314
	6 Min. YEARS		628	2154	532	96	19	71	879	286	301	250	16	572	21	5	16	23	18	.56	39	.247	.329	.408

Pete Gonzalez

Bats: Right **Throws:** Right **Pos:** C **Ht:** 6'0" **Wt:** 190 **Born:** 11/24/69 **Age:** 26

			BATTING															BASERUNNING				PERCENTAGES		
Year	Team	Lg	G	AB	H	2B	3B	HR	TB	R	RBI	TBB	IBB	SO	HBP	SH	SF	SB	CS	SB%	GDP	Avg	OBP	SLG
1989	Dodgers	R	34	94	23	5	0	0	28	16	13	14	0	16	0	0	0	3	1	.75	2	.245	.343	.298
1990	Vero Beach	A	90	198	43	12	0	2	61	31	21	42	2	40	11	5	3	2	2	.50	5	.217	.378	.308
1991	Vero Beach	A	74	207	45	12	0	1	60	26	14	31	0	32	6	5	1	1	0	1.00	4	.217	.335	.290
1992	Fayettevlle	A	42	110	25	5	0	0	30	17	19	38	0	23	6	1	3	5	2	.71	2	.227	.439	.273

Year Team	Lg	G	AB	H	2B	3B	HR	TB	R	RBI	TBB	IBB	SO	HBP	SH	SF	SB	CS	SB%	GDP	Avg	OBP	SLG
Toledo	AAA	9	17	2	2	0	0	4	1	0	1	0	3	0	1	0	0	0	.00	0	.118	.167	.235
Lakeland	A	32	81	24	7	0	1	34	15	13	19	0	9	2	1	0	1	0	1.00	0	.296	.441	.420
1993 Lakeland	A	63	200	50	4	1	2	62	20	25	31	4	28	2	2	3	7	2	.78	8	.250	.352	.310
London	AA	25	64	10	3	0	0	13	5	6	14	0	12	2	0	1	0	0	.00	0	.156	.321	.203
1994 Trenton	AA	16	55	15	3	0	0	18	3	8	4	0	7	1	0	0	2	1	.67	0	.273	.333	.327
Toledo	AAA	60	151	41	9	0	3	59	24	18	26	1	35	1	1	1	2	6	.25	1	.272	.380	.391
1995 Toledo	AAA	6	19	4	1	0	0	5	0	2	3	0	6	1	0	0	0	0	.00	0	.211	.348	.263
7 Min. YEARS		451	1196	282	63	1	9	374	158	139	223	7	211	32	16	12	23	14	.62	22	.236	.367	.313

Raul Gonzalez

Bats: Right Throws: Right Pos: OF Ht: 5'8" Wt: 175 Born: 12/27/73 Age: 22

Year Team	Lg	G	AB	H	2B	3B	HR	TB	R	RBI	TBB	IBB	SO	HBP	SH	SF	SB	CS	SB%	GDP	Avg	OBP	SLG
1991 Royals	R	47	160	47	5	3	0	58	24	17	19	0	21	0	1	2	3	4	.43	4	.294	.365	.363
1992 Appleton	A	119	449	115	32	1	9	176	82	51	57	1	58	2	4	6	13	5	.72	4	.256	.339	.392
1993 Wilmington	A	127	461	124	30	3	11	193	59	55	54	1	58	4	1	4	13	5	.72	8	.269	.348	.419
1994 Wilmington	A	115	414	108	19	8	9	170	60	51	45	2	50	2	2	4	0	4	.00	8	.261	.333	.411
1995 Wichita	AA	22	79	23	3	2	2	36	14	11	8	0	13	0	0	0	4	0	1.00	1	.291	.356	.456
Wilmington	A	86	308	90	19	3	11	148	36	49	14	3	34	2	3	7	6	4	.60	3	.292	.320	.481
5 Min. YEARS		516	1871	507	108	20	42	781	275	234	197	7	234	10	11	23	39	22	.64	28	.271	.340	.417

Keith Gordon

Bats: Right Throws: Right Pos: OF Ht: 6'2" Wt: 200 Born: 1/22/69 Age: 27

Year Team	Lg	G	AB	H	2B	3B	HR	TB	R	RBI	TBB	IBB	SO	HBP	SH	SF	SB	CS	SB%	GDP	Avg	OBP	SLG
1990 Billings	R	49	154	36	5	1	1	46	21	14	24	1	49	3	2	1	6	4	.60	2	.234	.346	.299
1991 Charlstn-Wv	A	123	388	104	14	10	8	162	63	46	50	2	134	5	7	1	25	9	.74	5	.268	.358	.418
1992 Cedar Rapds	A	114	375	94	19	3	12	155	59	63	43	2	135	3	1	4	21	10	.68	5	.251	.329	.413
1993 Chattanooga	AA	116	419	122	26	3	14	196	69	59	19	0	132	4	0	2	13	17	.43	15	.291	.327	.468
1994 Indianapls	AAA	18	58	12	1	0	1	16	3	4	4	0	25	0	1	0	0	0	.00	1	.207	.258	.276
Chattanooga	AA	82	254	71	16	2	8	115	46	38	21	0	74	1	0	2	11	7	.61	6	.280	.335	.453
1995 Indianapls	AAA	89	265	70	14	1	6	104	36	38	15	0	94	1	0	1	3	4	.43	3	.264	.304	.392
1993 Cincinnati	NL	3	6	1	0	0	0	1	0	0	0	0	2	0	0	0	0	0	.00	0	.167	.167	.167
6 Min. YEARS		591	1913	509	95	20	50	794	297	262	176	5	643	16	12	10	79	51	.61	37	.266	.331	.415

Clint Gould

Pitches: Right Bats: Right Pos: P Ht: 6'1" Wt: 230 Born: 8/18/71 Age: 24

Year Team	Lg	G	GS	CG	GF	IP	BFP	H	R	ER	HR	SH	SF	HB	TBB	IBB	SO	WP	Bk	W	L	Pct.	ShO	Sv	ERA
1994 Thunder Bay	IND	1	0	0	1	1	6	2	0	0	0	0	0	0	2	0	0	0	0	0	0	.000	0	0	0.00
1995 Wisconsin	A	25	0	0	15	34.1	164	34	24	22	4	1	0	2	28	1	20	1	0	0	0	.000	0	0	5.77
Tacoma	AAA	1	0	0	1	0.1	1	0	0	0	0	0	0	0	0	0	0	0	0	0	0	.000	0	0	0.00
2 Min. YEARS		27	0	0	17	35.2	171	36	24	22	4	1	0	2	30	1	20	1	0	0	0	.000	0	0	5.55

Sean Gousha

Bats: Right Throws: Right Pos: C Ht: 6'4" Wt: 200 Born: 9/19/70 Age: 25

Year Team	Lg	G	AB	H	2B	3B	HR	TB	R	RBI	TBB	IBB	SO	HBP	SH	SF	SB	CS	SB%	GDP	Avg	OBP	SLG
1992 Erie	A	20	62	15	2	0	0	17	4	6	5	0	19	0	0	1	3	0	1.00	0	.242	.294	.274
1993 High Desert	A	45	126	23	2	0	0	25	22	11	26	0	47	5	3	3	0	1	.00	3	.183	.338	.198
1994 Portland	AA	44	73	14	1	0	0	15	5	7	19	1	31	0	1	1	0	0	.00	2	.192	.355	.205
1995 Iowa	AAA	2	5	0	0	0	0	0	0	0	0	0	3	0	0	0	0	0	.00	0	.000	.000	.000
Daytona	A	5	8	2	2	0	0	4	1	0	1	0	0	0	0	1	0	0	.00	1	.250	.333	.500
Thunder Bay	IND	19	48	11	3	0	0	14	5	6	9	1	14	1	0	0	0	0	.00	1	.229	.362	.292
St. Paul	IND	51	158	35	6	0	2	47	24	15	27	1	49	0	2	1	3	1	.75	1	.222	.333	.297
4 Min. YEARS		186	480	100	16	0	2	122	61	45	87	3	163	6	6	6	3	1	.75	9	.208	.333	.254

Mauro Gozzo

Pitches: Right Bats: Right Pos: P Ht: 6'3" Wt: 212 Born: 3/7/66 Age: 30

Year Team	Lg	G	GS	CG	GF	IP	BFP	H	R	ER	HR	SH	SF	HB	TBB	IBB	SO	WP	Bk	W	L	Pct.	ShO	Sv	ERA
1984 Little Fall	A	24	0	0	8	38.1	176	40	27	24	3	0	2	0	28	4	30	7	1	4	3	.571	0	2	5.63
1985 Columbia	A	49	0	0	42	78	330	62	22	22	2	3	5	2	39	7	66	4	1	11	4	.733	0	14	2.54
1986 Lynchburg	A	60	0	0	46	78.1	341	80	30	27	3	5	2	2	35	3	50	4	1	9	4	.692	0	9	3.10
1987 Memphis	AA	19	14	1	2	91.1	400	95	58	46	13	1	2	4	36	2	56	3	3	6	5	.545	0	4	4.53
1988 Memphis	AA	33	12	0	9	92.2	430	127	64	59	9	2	7	1	36	1	48	14	3	4	9	.308	0	3	5.73
1989 Knoxville	AA	18	6	2	6	60.1	245	59	27	20	1	0	5	1	12	1	37	2	1	7	0	1.000	1	0	2.98
Syracuse	AAA	12	7	2	2	62	251	56	22	19	3	1	1	0	19	0	34	2	0	5	1	.833	1	2	2.76
1990 Syracuse	AAA	34	10	0	19	98	409	87	44	39	5	3	1	3	44	3	62	2	1	3	8	.273	0	7	3.58
1991 Colo. Sprng	AAA	25	20	3	4	130.1	588	143	86	76	9	3	7	6	68	3	81	7	4	10	6	.625	0	1	5.25
1992 Portland	AAA	37	19	3	11	155.2	644	155	61	58	11	6	0	3	50	3	108	2	0	10	9	.526	2	1	3.35
1993 Norfolk	AAA	28	28	2	0	190.1	798	208	88	73	10	4	5	9	49	7	97	6	0	8	11	.421	0	0	3.45
1994 Norfolk	AAA	4	4	2	0	29	112	22	7	6	2	1	1	1	4	0	12	0	0	2	2	.500	0	0	1.86
1995 Iowa	AAA	6	6	0	0	30.1	131	37	22	14	4	2	0	0	11	1	11	3	0	0	3	.000	0	0	4.15
1989 Toronto	AL	9	3	0	2	31.2	133	35	19	17	1	0	2	1	9	1	10	0	0	4	1	.800	0	0	4.83

Year	Team	Lg	G	GS	CG	GF	IP	BFP	H	R	ER	HR	SH	SF	HB	TBB	IBB	SO	WP	Bk	W	L	Pct.	ShO	Sv	ERA
1990	Cleveland	AL	2	0	0	1	3	13	2	0	0	0	0	0	0	2	0	2	0	0	0	0	.000	0	0	0.00
1991	Cleveland	AL	2	2	0	0	4.2	28	9	10	10	0	0	1	0	7	0	3	2	0	0	0	.000	0	0	19.29
1992	Minnesota	AL	2	0	0	0	1.2	12	7	5	5	2	0	0	0	0	0	1	1	0	0	0	.000	0	0	27.00
1993	New York	NL	10	0	0	5	14	57	11	5	4	1	0	0	0	5	1	6	0	0	1		.000	0	1	2.57
1994	New York	NL	23	8	0	5	69	323	86	48	37	5	6	5	1	28	10	33	5	0	3	5	.375	0	0	4.83
	12 Min. YEARS		349	126	15	149	1134.2	4855	1171	560	483	75	31	38	32	431	35	692	56	15	79	65	.549	4	39	3.83
	6 Maj. YEARS		48	13	0	13	124	566	150	87	73	9	6	8	2	51	12	55	8	0	7	7	.500	0	1	5.30

Rob Grable

Bats: Right Throws: Right Pos: OF   Ht: 6'2" Wt: 200 Born: 1/20/70 Age: 26

Year	Team	Lg	G	AB	H	2B	3B	HR	TB	R	RBI	TBB	IBB	SO	HBP	SH	SF	SB	CS	SB%	GDP	Avg	OBP	SLG
1991	Niagara Fal	A	73	251	76	18	2	7	119	48	46	46	0	55	2	3	0	2	4	.33	8	.303	.415	.474
1992	Fayettevlle	A	24	77	21	5	1	0	28	9	10	12	0	16	2	3	1	3	3	.50	3	.273	.380	.364
	Spartanburg	A	77	279	69	14	2	4	99	36	33	47	0	54	2	0	3	6	7	.46	8	.247	.356	.355
1993	Clearwater	A	98	351	110	27	5	5	162	60	55	49	3	72	7	0	5	16	9	.64	13	.313	.403	.462
	Reading	AA	37	120	28	4	1	1	37	10	10	18	1	27	1	0	1	2	1	.67	3	.233	.336	.308
1994	Reading	AA	42	161	43	6	3	2	61	19	18	13	0	34	4	1	4	7	4	.64	3	.267	.330	.379
1995	Scranton-Wb	AAA	26	83	19	4	0	3	32	7	11	7	0	34	1	1	0	3	0	1.00	1	.229	.297	.386
	Reading	AA	103	353	106	24	1	16	180	71	67	67	3	85	1	1	5	15	11	.58	8	.300	.408	.510
	5 Min. YEARS		480	1675	472	102	15	38	718	260	250	259	7	377	20	9	19	54	39	.58	47	.282	.381	.429

Tony Graffanino

Bats: Right Throws: Right Pos: 2B   Ht: 6'1" Wt: 200 Born: 6/6/72 Age: 24

Year	Team	Lg	G	AB	H	2B	3B	HR	TB	R	RBI	TBB	IBB	SO	HBP	SH	SF	SB	CS	SB%	GDP	Avg	OBP	SLG
1990	Pulaski	R	42	131	27	5	1	0	34	23	11	26	0	17	2	1	1	6	3	.67	3	.206	.344	.260
1991	Idaho Falls	R	66	274	95	16	4	4	131	53	57	27	0	37	3	2	2	19	4	.83	2	.347	.408	.478
1992	Macon	A	112	400	96	15	5	10	151	50	31	50	1	84	8	4	4	9	6	.60	6	.240	.333	.378
1993	Durham	A	123	459	126	30	5	15	211	78	69	45	1	78	4	2	4	24	11	.69	10	.275	.342	.460
1994	Greenville	AA	124	440	132	28	3	7	187	66	52	50	7	53	2	7	3	29	7	.81	8	.300	.372	.425
1995	Richmond	AAA	50	179	34	6	0	4	52	20	17	15	0	49	1	1	2	2	2	.50	4	.190	.254	.291
	6 Min. YEARS		517	1883	510	100	18	40	766	290	237	213	9	318	20	17	16	89	33	.73	33	.271	.348	.407

Greg Graham

Bats: Both Throws: Right Pos: 3B   Ht: 6'0" Wt: 175 Born: 1/30/69 Age: 27

Year	Team	Lg	G	AB	H	2B	3B	HR	TB	R	RBI	TBB	IBB	SO	HBP	SH	SF	SB	CS	SB%	GDP	Avg	OBP	SLG
1990	Winter Havn	A	15	39	2	0	0	0	2	0	1	2	0	16	0	1	0	0	0	.00	1	.051	.098	.051
	Red Sox	R	26	94	21	2	0	0	23	16	11	20	0	13	1	1	2	1	1	.50	1	.223	.359	.245
1991	Winter Havn	A	9	20	7	0	0	0	7	2	0	1	0	5	0	1	0	1	1	.50	1	.350	.381	.350
	Lynchburg	A	82	275	54	6	1	1	65	31	24	36	1	65	1		4	6	5	.55	9	.196	.291	.236
1992	New Britain	AA	104	347	78	6	1	0	86	32	19	30	1	62	3	5	1	9	10	.47	8	.225	.291	.248
1993	St. Lucie	A	26	56	11	1	0	0	12	10	4	13	0	10	1	0	0	2	2	.33	2	.196	.357	.214
1994	Binghamton	AA	48	137	34	6	0	0	40	19	19	11	0	25	0	2	1	2	1	.67	4	.248	.302	.292
	Norfolk	AAA	35	90	16	4	0	0	20	7	7	16	0	21	0	8	2	0	0	.00	3	.178	.206	.222
1995	Norfolk	AAA	47	122	24	5	0	0	29	14	9	15	1	23	1	2	1	1	2	.33	5	.197	.288	.238
	6 Min. YEARS		392	1180	247	30	2	1	284	131	94	144	3	243	7	24	8	21	22	.49	34	.209	.297	.241

Tim Graham

Bats: Left Throws: Right Pos: OF   Ht: 6'0" Wt: 185 Born: 9/4/71 Age: 24

Year	Team	Lg	G	AB	H	2B	3B	HR	TB	R	RBI	TBB	IBB	SO	HBP	SH	SF	SB	CS	SB%	GDP	Avg	OBP	SLG
1989	Red Sox	R	41	134	33	5	2	0	42	12	7	18	0	32	1	3	1	4	2	.67	2	.246	.338	.313
1990	Elmira	A	70	212	43	5	3	0	54	25	22	19	0	64	1	5	2	7	7	.50	3	.203	.269	.255
1991	Elmira	A	61	181	55	12	5	5	92	28	33	23	1	56	1	1	2	5	5	.50	0	.304	.382	.508
1992	Lynchburg	A	91	276	47	9	3	0	62	33	14	34	3	70	1	6	0	6	5	.55	4	.170	.264	.225
1993	Lynchburg	A	8	23	3	1	0	0	4	6	3	13	0	8	0	1	0	0	2	.00	0	.130	.444	.174
	Ft. Laud	A	53	162	42	5	7	0	61	34	11	32	4	31	0	3	2	8	3	.73	4	.259	.378	.377
1994	High Desert	A	117	417	127	23	7	18	218	77	65	61	1	114	1	4	1	13	10	.57	5	.305	.394	.523
1995	Trenton	AA	8	25	4	1	0	0	5	2	0	1	0	5	0	1	0	0	1	.00	0	.160	.192	.200
	7 Min. YEARS		449	1430	354	61	27	23	538	217	155	201	9	380	5	24	8	43	35	.55	18	.248	.341	.376

Jeff Granger

Pitches: Left Bats: Right Pos: P   Ht: 6'4" Wt: 200 Born: 12/16/71 Age: 24

Year	Team	Lg	G	GS	CG	GF	IP	BFP	H	R	ER	HR	SH	SF	HB	TBB	IBB	SO	WP	Bk	W	L	Pct.	ShO	Sv	ERA
1993	Eugene	A	8	7	0	0	36	146	28	17	12	2	1	0	1	10	1	56	1	0	3	3	.500	0	0	3.00
1994	Memphis	AA	25	25	0	0	139.2	615	155	72	60	8	3	3	0	61	0	112	14	3	7	7	.500	0	0	3.87
1995	Wichita	AA	18	18	0	0	95.2	439	122	76	63	9	3	4	1	40	0	81	10	0	4	7	.364	0	0	5.93
1993	Kansas City	AL	1	0	0	0	1	8	3	3	3	0	0	1	0	2	0	1	0	0	0	0	.000	0	0	27.00
1994	Kansas City	AL	2	2	0	0	9.1	47	13	8	7	2	0	1	0	6	0	3	0	0	0	0	.000	0	0	6.75
	3 Min. YEARS		51	50	0	0	271.1	1200	305	165	135	19	7	7	2	111	1	249	25	3	14	17	.452	0	0	4.48
	2 Maj. YEARS		3	2	0	0	10.1	55	16	11	10	2	0	1	0	8	0	4	0	0	0	1	.000	0	0	8.71

Mark Grant

Pitches: Right **Bats:** Right **Pos:** P   **Ht:** 6' 2" **Wt:** 215 **Born:** 10/24/63 **Age:** 32

Year	Team	Lg	G	GS	CG	GF	IP	BFP	H	R	ER	HR	SH	SF	HB	TBB	IBB	SO	WP	Bk	W	L	Pct.	ShO	Sv	ERA
1984	Phoenix	AAA	17	17	4	0	111.1	0	102	64	49	7	0	0	1	61	2	78	8	0	5	7	.417	1	0	3.96
1985	Phoenix	AAA	29	29	4	0	183	0	182	101	92	17	0	0	3	90	5	133	18	0	8	15	.348	3	0	4.52
1986	Phoenix	AAA	28	27	10	0	181.2	785	204	105	99	13	2	9	3	46	4	93	8	0	14	7	.667	3	0	4.90
1987	Phoenix	AAA	3	3	2	0	23	93	20	8	8	2	2	1	1	5	0	12	0	0	2	1	.667	0	0	3.13
1991	Richmond	AAA	1	1	0	0	3	10	2	0	0	0	0	0	1	1	0	3	0	0	0	0	.000	0	0	0.00
1992	Jacksonville	AA	5	5	0	0	32.2	125	25	10	7	2	0	0	1	4	0	21	0	0	1	2	.333	0	0	1.93
	Calgary	AAA	4	3	1	0	26	113	32	15	12	2	1	2	2	4	1	11	2	0	1	3	.250	0	0	4.15
1993	Tucson	AAA	4	0	0	1	8.1	34	5	1	1	0	1	0	0	4	0	10	0	0	1	0	1.000	0	0	1.08
	Vancouver	AAA	1	0	0	1	2	8	0	0	0	0	1	0	0	2	0	1	0	0	0	0	.000	0	0	0.00
1995	Iowa	AAA	11	11	2	0	69	276	58	28	24	6	0	2	2	10	0	39	1	0	5	2	.714	0	0	3.13
1984	San Francisco	NL	11	10	0	1	53.2	231	56	40	38	6	2	3	1	19	0	32	3	0	1	4	.200	0	1	6.37
1986	San Francisco	NL	4	1	0	3	10	39	6	4	4	0	0	0	0	5	0	5	0	1	0	1	.000	0	0	3.60
1987	San Diego	NL	17	17	2	0	102.1	456	104	59	53	16	8	0	0	52	3	58	6	1	6	7	.462	1	0	4.66
	San Francisco	NL	16	8	0	2	61	264	66	29	24	6	7	1	1	21	5	32	2	2	1	2	.333	0	1	3.54
1988	San Diego	NL	33	11	0	9	97.2	410	97	41	40	14	6	4	2	36	6	61	5	0	2	8	.200	0	0	3.69
1989	San Diego	NL	50	0	0	19	116.1	466	105	45	43	11	5	2	3	32	6	69	2	0	8	2	.800	0	2	3.33
1990	Atlanta	NL	33	1	0	16	52.1	231	61	30	27	4	2	2	1	18	3	40	1	0	1	2	.333	0	3	4.64
	San Diego	NL	26	0	0	5	39	180	47	23	21	5	4	3	0	19	8	29	1	1	1	1	.500	0	0	4.85
1992	Seattle	AL	23	10	0	4	81	352	100	39	35	6	5	1	2	22	2	42	2	0	2	4	.333	0	0	3.89
1993	Houston	NL	6	0	0	3	11	46	11	4	1	0	0	1	0	5	2	6	0	0	0	0	.000	0	0	0.82
	Colorado	NL	14	0	0	6	14.1	68	23	20	20	4	0	1	0	6	1	8	2	0	0	1	.000	0	1	12.56
	8 Min. YEARS		103	96	23	2	640	1444	630	332	292	49	7	14	14	227	12	401	37	0	37	37	.500	7	0	4.11
	8 Maj. YEARS		233	58	2	68	638.2	2743	676	334	306	72	39	18	10	235	36	382	24	5	22	32	.407	1	8	4.31

Danny Graves

Pitches: Right **Bats:** Right **Pos:** P   **Ht:** 5'11" **Wt:** 200 **Born:** 8/7/73 **Age:** 22

Year	Team	Lg	G	GS	CG	GF	IP	BFP	H	R	ER	HR	SH	SF	HB	TBB	IBB	SO	WP	Bk	W	L	Pct.	ShO	Sv	ERA
1995	Kinston	A	38	0	0	37	44	177	30	11	4	0	1	0	0	12	2	46	0	0	3	1	.750	0	21	0.82
	Canton-Akrn	AA	17	0	0	17	23.1	82	10	1	0	0	4	0	1	2	0	11	0	0	1	0	1.000	0	10	0.00
	Buffalo	AAA	3	0	0	3	3	16	5	4	1	0	0	0	0	1	0	2	1	0	0	0	.000	0	0	3.00
	1 Min. YEARS		58	0	0	57	70.1	275	45	16	5	0	5	0	1	15	2	59	1	0	4	1	.800	0	31	0.64

Dennis Gray

Pitches: Left **Bats:** Left **Pos:** P   **Ht:** 6'6" **Wt:** 225 **Born:** 12/24/69 **Age:** 26

Year	Team	Lg	G	GS	CG	GF	IP	BFP	H	R	ER	HR	SH	SF	HB	TBB	IBB	SO	WP	Bk	W	L	Pct.	ShO	Sv	ERA
1991	St. Cathrns	A	15	14	0	0	77	341	63	42	32	1	3	1	1	54	0	78	4	4	4	4	.500	0	0	3.74
1992	Myrtle Bch	A	28	28	0	0	155.1	659	122	82	66	8	2	5	6	93	0	141	13	4	11	12	.478	0	0	3.82
1993	Dunedin	A	26	26	0	0	141.1	607	115	71	56	7	7	6	7	97	1	108	6	0	8	10	.444	0	0	3.57
1994	Knoxville	AA	30	16	0	6	100.2	488	118	83	59	5	12	8	11	65	0	77	13	1	5	11	.313	0	0	5.27
1995	Syracuse	AAA	15	0	0	3	24.1	106	27	16	12	3	0	0	2	10	0	15	3	0	2	2	.500	0	0	4.44
	Knoxville	AA	24	0	0	10	32.2	143	29	25	23	2	2	0	1	20	0	22	5	0	0	3	.000	0	0	6.34
	5 Min. YEARS		138	84	0	19	531.1	2344	474	319	248	26	26	20	28	339	1	441	44	9	30	42	.417	0	0	4.20

Dave Graybill

Pitches: Right **Bats:** Right **Pos:** P   **Ht:** 6'2" **Wt:** 210 **Born:** 10/9/62 **Age:** 33

Year	Team	Lg	G	GS	CG	GF	IP	BFP	H	R	ER	HR	SH	SF	HB	TBB	IBB	SO	WP	Bk	W	L	Pct.	ShO	Sv	ERA
1984	W. Palm Bch	A	10	4	2	2	37.2	149	23	11	10	2	1	3	1	19	1	16	2	1	2	2	.500	0	1	2.39
1985	Jacksonville	AA	10	9	1	0	56.2	257	62	25	23	2	3	2	3	23	0	26	4	0	4	2	.667	0	0	3.65
1986	W. Palm Bch	A	18	17	0	0	77.1	315	62	28	26	4	2	4	1	32	0	46	4	1	5	5	.500	0	0	3.03
	Indianapolis	AAA	3	3	0	0	14	62	17	9	9	2	1	0	0	5	0	7	0	0	1	0	1.000	0	0	5.79
1987	Jacksonville	AA	11	11	1	0	66.1	284	66	34	31	10	1	1	2	22	0	29	0	0	5	4	.556	1	0	4.21
1989	Palm Spring	A	12	8	4	0	69	288	64	31	20	1	0	2	5	16	0	41	7	3	7	2	.778	1	0	2.61
	Midland	AA	17	6	0	5	61	275	76	39	32	3	3	1	3	19	3	32	1	3	4	4	.500	0	1	4.72
1995	Tacoma	AAA	6	0	0	4	9.1	43	12	8	7	1	0	2	0	6	0	1	0	0	0	0	.000	0	0	6.75
	6 Min. YEARS		87	58	8	11	391.1	1673	382	185	158	25	11	15	15	142	4	198	18	8	28	19	.596	2	2	3.63

Brian Grebeck

Bats: Right **Throws:** Right **Pos:** SS   **Ht:** 5'7" **Wt:** 160 **Born:** 8/31/67 **Age:** 28

Year	Team	Lg	G	AB	H	2B	3B	HR	TB	R	RBI	TBB	IBB	SO	HBP	SH	SF	SB	CS	SB%	GDP	Avg	OBP	SLG
1990	Boise	A	58	202	57	10	2	1	74	45	34	64	1	57	1	5	2	1	3	.25	3	.282	.454	.366
1991	Quad City	A	121	408	100	20	3	0	126	80	34	103	1	76	10	15	4	19	10	.66	8	.245	.406	.309
1992	Palm Spring	A	91	289	97	14	2	0	115	71	39	83	2	55	0	8	3	6	5	.55	10	.336	.480	.398
1993	Midland	AA	118	405	119	20	4	5	162	65	54	64	1	81	8	6	7	1	6	.86	8	.294	.395	.400
1994	Midland	AA	55	184	58	18	2	1	83	27	17	27	1	33	5	1	1	1	1	.50	7	.315	.415	.451
	Vancouver	AAA	38	127	38	7	0	2	51	23	18	16	0	14	3	2	3	1	2	.33	5	.299	.383	.402

1995 Vancouver	AAA	81	241	59	11	2	5	89	41	30	38	1	38	5	5	3	4	0	1.00	6	.245	.355	.369
6 Min. YEARS		562	1856	528	100	15	14	700	352	225	395	6	354	32	42	23	38	22	.63	47	.284	.414	.377

Gary Green

Bats: Right **Throws:** Right **Pos:** SS   **Ht:** 6' 3" **Wt:** 175 **Born:** 1/14/62 **Age:** 34

					BATTING											BASERUNNING				PERCENTAGES		
Year Team	Lg	G	AB	H	2B	3B	HR	TB	R	RBI	TBB	IBB	SO	HBP	SH	SF	SB	CS	SB%	GDP	Avg	OBP	SLG
1985 Beaumont	AA	119	409	105	17	1	1	127	44	51	27	2	54	1	15	4	8	7	.53	11	.257	.302	.311
1986 Las Vegas	AAA	129	416	104	11	3	0	121	42	41	29	1	46	1	5	3	3	0	1.00	6	.250	.298	.291
1987 Las Vegas	AAA	111	337	80	8	2	1	95	32	32	35	2	58	1	14	4	2	4	.33	9	.237	.308	.282
1988 Las Vegas	AAA	88	302	82	16	2	0	102	39	37	16	0	50	1	3	5	4	1	.80	7	.272	.306	.338
1989 Las Vegas	AAA	62	191	40	6	0	0	46	18	18	20	1	32	0	2	4	2	1	.67	4	.209	.279	.241
1990 Okla. City	AAA	55	167	39	11	0	4	62	19	25	22	0	43	0	2	2	1	2	.33	6	.234	.319	.371
1991 Okla. City	AAA	100	308	67	4	2	2	81	36	30	35	0	57	3	9	5	1	3	.25	6	.218	.299	.263
1992 Nashville	AAA	101	316	61	12	1	3	84	23	27	22	1	44	2	8	2	0	1	.00	6	.193	.249	.266
1993 Indianapolis	AAA	72	218	41	7	0	2	54	15	14	11	0	30	0	7	0	1	1	.50	2	.188	.227	.248
1995 Omaha	AAA	26	71	12	2	0	0	14	5	3	3	0	14	0	1	0	0	0	.00	1	.169	.203	.197
1986 San Diego	NL	13	33	7	1	0	0	8	2	2	1	0	11	0	1	0	0	0	.00	0	.212	.235	.242
1989 San Diego	NL	15	27	7	3	0	0	10	4	0	1	0	1	0	0	0	0	1	.00	0	.259	.286	.370
1990 Texas	AL	62	88	19	3	0	0	22	10	8	6	0	18	0	4	1	1	1	.50	2	.216	.263	.250
1991 Texas	AL	8	20	3	1	0	0	4	0	1	1	0	6	0	2	0	0	0	.00	0	.150	.190	.200
1992 Cincinnati	NL	8	12	4	1	0	0	5	3	0	0	0	2	0	0	0	0	0	.00	0	.333	.333	.417
10 Min. YEARS		863	2735	631	94	11	13	786	273	278	220	7	428	9	66	29	22	20	.52	64	.231	.287	.287
5 Maj. YEARS		106	180	40	9	0	0	49	19	11	9	0	38	0	7	1	1	2	.33	2	.222	.258	.272

Otis Green

Pitches: Left **Bats:** Left **Pos:** P   **Ht:** 6'2" **Wt:** 192 **Born:** 3/11/64 **Age:** 32

		HOW MUCH HE PITCHED						WHAT HE GAVE UP										THE RESULTS					
Year Team	Lg	G	GS	CG	GF	IP	BFP	H	R	ER	HR	SH	SF	HB	TBB	IBB	SO	WP	Bk	W	L	Pct.	ShO	Sv	ERA
1991 Stockton	A	12	11	2	0	75	300	41	18	16	1	1	2	5	33	0	106	4	0	9	1	.900	2	0	1.92
El Paso	AA	9	9	1	0	51	210	35	21	18	4	0	1	1	25	1	49	4	0	3	3	.500	0	0	3.18
1992 Denver	AAA	28	27	1	0	152.1	662	148	85	78	17	1	6	6	70	1	114	5	2	11	8	.579	0	0	4.61
1993 Vancouver	AAA	25	18	1	3	109	487	109	71	68	8	5	1	9	53	0	97	10	2	2	8	.200	0	0	5.61
1995 Tacoma	AAA	18	0	0	3	25	113	26	19	16	3	0	1	1	12	2	17	3	0	4	1	.800	0	0	5.76
4 Min. YEARS		92	65	5	6	412.1	1772	359	214	196	33	7	11	22	193	4	383	26	4	29	21	.580	2	0	4.28

Charlie Greene

Bats: Right **Throws:** Right **Pos:** C   **Ht:** 6'3" **Wt:** 170 **Born:** 1/23/71 **Age:** 25

					BATTING											BASERUNNING				PERCENTAGES		
Year Team	Lg	G	AB	H	2B	3B	HR	TB	R	RBI	TBB	IBB	SO	HBP	SH	SF	SB	CS	SB%	GDP	Avg	OBP	SLG
1991 Padres	R	49	183	52	15	1	5	84	27	39	16	0	23	3	2	6	6	1	.86	7	.284	.341	.459
1992 Charlstn-Sc	A	98	298	55	9	1	1	69	22	24	11	0	60	5	3	2	1	2	.33	7	.185	.225	.232
1993 Waterloo	A	84	213	38	8	0	2	52	19	20	13	0	33	3	6	3	0	0	.00	5	.178	.233	.244
1994 Binghamton	AA	30	106	18	4	0	0	22	13	2	6	1	18	1	0	1	0	0	.00	3	.170	.219	.208
St. Lucie	A	69	224	57	4	0	0	61	23	21	9	0	31	4	4	1	0	1	.00	3	.254	.294	.272
1995 Binghamton	AA	100	346	82	13	0	2	101	26	34	15	4	47	5	3	4	2	1	.67	10	.237	.270	.292
Norfolk	AAA	27	88	17	3	0	0	20	6	4	3	0	28	0	1	0	0	1	.00	1	.193	.220	.227
5 Min. YEARS		457	1458	319	56	2	10	409	136	144	73	5	240	21	19	17	9	6	.60	36	.219	.263	.281

Rick Greene

Pitches: Right **Bats:** Right **Pos:** P   **Ht:** 6'5" **Wt:** 200 **Born:** 1/2/71 **Age:** 25

		HOW MUCH HE PITCHED						WHAT HE GAVE UP										THE RESULTS					
Year Team	Lg	G	GS	CG	GF	IP	BFP	H	R	ER	HR	SH	SF	HB	TBB	IBB	SO	WP	Bk	W	L	Pct.	ShO	Sv	ERA
1993 Lakeland	A	26	0	0	11	40.2	184	57	28	28	1	6	0	4	16	1	32	5	2	2	3	.400	0	2	6.20
London	AA	23	0	0	11	29	135	31	22	21	1	3	3	1	20	3	19	3	2	2	2	.500	0	0	6.52
1994 Trenton	AA	20	0	0	14	19.1	92	17	17	17	0	3	2	0	21	2	5	2	0	1	1	.500	0	3	7.91
Lakeland	A	19	2	0	11	33.1	158	50	23	16	1	1	1	0	10	1	28	6	0	0	4	.000	0	4	4.32
1995 Jacksonville	AA	32	0	0	6	38.2	177	45	19	15	3	1	0	3	15	2	29	0	0	6	2	.750	0	0	3.49
3 Min. YEARS		120	2	0	53	161	746	200	109	97	5	14	6	5	82	9	113	16	4	11	12	.478	0	9	5.42

Todd Greene

Bats: Right **Throws:** Right **Pos:** C   **Ht:** 5' 9" **Wt:** 195 **Born:** 5/8/71 **Age:** 25

					BATTING											BASERUNNING				PERCENTAGES		
Year Team	Lg	G	AB	H	2B	3B	HR	TB	R	RBI	TBB	IBB	SO	HBP	SH	SF	SB	CS	SB%	GDP	Avg	OBP	SLG
1993 Boise	A	76	305	82	15	3	15	148	55	71	34	6	44	9	0	3	4	3	.57	3	.269	.356	.485
1994 Lk Elsinore	A	133	524	158	39	2	35	306	98	124	64	12	96	4	0	6	10	3	.77	12	.302	.378	.584
1995 Midland	AA	82	318	104	19	1	26	203	59	57	17	4	55	5	1	5	3	5	.38	6	.327	.365	.638
Vancouver	AAA	43	168	42	3	1	14	89	28	35	11	2	36	4	0	2	1	0	1.00	3	.250	.308	.530
3 Min. YEARS		334	1315	386	76	7	90	746	240	287	126	24	231	22	1	16	18	11	.62	24	.294	.361	.567

119

Kris Gresham

Bats: Right Throws: Right Pos: C Ht: 6'1" Wt: 193 Born: 8/30/70 Age: 25

Year	Team	Lg	G	AB	H	2B	3B	HR	TB	R	RBI	TBB	IBB	SO	HBP	SH	SF	SB	CS	SB%	GDP	Avg	OBP	SLG
1991	Bluefield	R	34	116	28	5	2	0	37	16	16	6	0	19	4	1	3	6	3	.67	6	.241	.295	.319
1992	Kane County	A	38	113	22	4	0	2	32	10	17	4	0	21	0	2	0	0	0	.00	1	.195	.222	.283
1993	Frederick	A	66	188	41	13	1	4	68	22	17	13	0	41	7	3	0	1	0	1.00	2	.218	.293	.362
1994	Bowie	AA	69	204	40	8	2	3	61	27	20	10	0	57	6	1	3	1	0	1.00	6	.196	.251	.299
1995	Bowie	AA	5	13	1	0	0	0	1	1	0	3	0	5	0	0	0	1	0	1.00	0	.077	.250	.077
	Rochester	AAA	21	64	16	2	1	0	20	5	4	4	0	15	2	0	0	0	0	.00	2	.250	.314	.313
	High Desert	A	47	140	36	8	0	5	59	25	15	12	1	31	4	2	2	1	3	.25	6	.257	.329	.421
	5 Min. YEARS		280	838	184	40	6	14	278	106	89	52	1	189	23	9	8	10	6	.63	23	.220	.281	.332

Craig Griffey

Bats: Right Throws: Right Pos: OF Ht: 5'11" Wt: 175 Born: 6/3/71 Age: 25

Year	Team	Lg	G	AB	H	2B	3B	HR	TB	R	RBI	TBB	IBB	SO	HBP	SH	SF	SB	CS	SB%	GDP	Avg	OBP	SLG
1991	Mariners	R	45	150	38	1	1	0	41	36	20	28	0	35	1	2	2	11	6	.65	0	.253	.370	.273
1992	Bellingham	A	63	220	55	6	1	1	66	30	21	22	0	35	3	2	2	15	8	.65	1	.250	.324	.300
1993	Appleton	A	37	102	26	7	0	2	39	14	20	12	0	18	1	1	3	9	3	.75	1	.255	.331	.382
	Riverside	A	58	191	46	4	4	3	67	30	25	17	3	25	2	3	7	10	2	.83	3	.241	.300	.351
1994	Jacksonvlle	AA	106	327	72	13	1	3	96	37	29	33	0	68	3	10	5	20	10	.67	3	.220	.293	.294
1995	Port City	AA	96	299	53	11	1	0	66	43	24	46	0	77	9	3	3	13	3	.81	5	.177	.303	.221
	5 Min. YEARS		405	1289	290	42	8	9	375	190	139	158	3	258	19	21	22	78	32	.71	13	.225	.314	.291

Ty Griffin

Bats: Both Throws: Right Pos: 2B Ht: 5'11" Wt: 185 Born: 9/5/67 Age: 28

Year	Team	Lg	G	AB	H	2B	3B	HR	TB	R	RBI	TBB	IBB	SO	HBP	SH	SF	SB	CS	SB%	GDP	Avg	OBP	SLG
1989	Peoria	A	82	296	85	15	6	10	142	45	64	49	9	74	5	1	2	16	4	.80	2	.287	.395	.480
	Charlotte	AA	45	143	33	6	0	3	48	25	21	25	1	29	2	0	1	8	5	.62	2	.231	.351	.336
1990	Charlotte	AA	78	249	52	9	1	8	87	34	27	57	1	55	3	1	1	7	4	.64	2	.209	.361	.349
	Winston-Sal	A	33	120	26	8	1	1	39	18	10	28	2	39	1	0	0	8	2	.80	3	.217	.369	.325
1991	Charlotte	AA	42	116	19	4	0	0	23	16	12	27	2	38	3	0	6	4	3	.57	1	.164	.322	.198
	Winston-Sal	A	88	314	76	21	3	3	112	71	25	72	2	80	1	0	3	24	4	.86	5	.242	.382	.357
1992	Chattanooga	AA	114	347	83	16	3	5	120	44	38	66	2	85	0	2	4	8	9	.47	7	.239	.357	.346
1993	Thunder Bay	IND	66	234	64	9	0	11	106	49	35	28	1	56	2	0	2	12	3	.80	6	.274	.353	.453
1994	Sioux City	IND	70	244	65	15	2	8	108	45	26	29	2	57	1	3	2	23	9	.72	1	.266	.344	.443
1995	Arkansas	AA	94	263	72	16	1	9	117	38	44	36	2	59	0	0	3	17	2	.89	5	.274	.358	.445
	7 Min. YEARS		712	2326	575	119	17	58	902	385	302	417	24	572	18	7	24	127	45	.74	34	.247	.363	.388

Pedro Grifol

Bats: Right Throws: Right Pos: C Ht: 6'1" Wt: 205 Born: 11/28/69 Age: 26

Year	Team	Lg	G	AB	H	2B	3B	HR	TB	R	RBI	TBB	IBB	SO	HBP	SH	SF	SB	CS	SB%	GDP	Avg	OBP	SLG
1991	Elizabethtn	R	55	202	53	12	0	7	86	24	36	16	0	33	2	0	4	0	1	.00	6	.262	.317	.426
	Orlando	AA	6	20	3	0	0	0	3	0	2	0	0	6	0	0	0	0	0	.00	0	.150	.150	.150
1992	Miracle	A	94	333	76	13	1	4	103	24	32	17	1	38	2	3	1	1	0	1.00	19	.228	.269	.309
	Orlando	AA	14	40	11	2	0	0	13	2	5	2	0	9	0	0	1	0	0	.00	2	.275	.302	.325
1993	Nashville	AA	58	197	40	13	0	5	68	22	29	11	0	38	2	5	3	0	1	.00	6	.203	.249	.345
	Portland	AAA	28	94	31	4	2	2	45	14	17	4	0	14	0	2	2	0	0	.00	5	.330	.350	.479
1994	Nashville	AA	20	55	7	0	0	1	10	4	4	10	0	7	1	0	1	0	0	.00	1	.127	.269	.182
1995	New Britain	AA	77	226	40	9	0	3	58	23	21	23	1	33	1	1	1	1	0	1.00	8	.177	.255	.257
	5 Min. YEARS		352	1167	261	53	3	22	386	113	146	83	2	178	8	11	13	2	2	.50	47	.224	.277	.331

Benji Grigsby

Pitches: Right Bats: Right Pos: P Ht: 6'1" Wt: 190 Born: 12/2/70 Age: 25

Year	Team	Lg	G	GS	CG	GF	IP	BFP	H	R	ER	HR	SH	SF	HB	TBB	IBB	SO	WP	Bk	W	L	Pct.	ShO	Sv	ERA
1992	Athletics	R	3	3	0	0	11	35	4	2	2	2	0	0	0	1	0	7	0	0	1	1	.500	0	1	1.64
1993	Modesto	A	39	10	0	10	90.1	396	90	49	48	12	2	1	3	42	2	72	9	1	5	6	.455	0	6	4.78
1994	Modesto	A	16	8	0	5	65.1	272	59	28	24	4	1	3	1	18	0	49	6	2	4	1	.800	0	4	3.31
	Huntsville	AA	17	7	0	5	47	205	43	17	15	2	1	1	2	23	2	30	1	0	3	2	.600	0	1	2.87
1995	Huntsville	AA	30	6	0	8	76.1	306	66	40	34	7	0	3	1	20	1	55	6	0	3	5	.375	0	3	4.01
	4 Min. YEARS		105	34	0	28	290	1214	262	136	123	27	4	8	7	104	5	213	22	3	16	15	.516	0	14	3.82

Kevin Grijak

Bats: Left Throws: Right Pos: 1B Ht: 6'2" Wt: 195 Born: 8/6/70 Age: 25

Year	Team	Lg	G	AB	H	2B	3B	HR	TB	R	RBI	TBB	IBB	SO	HBP	SH	SF	SB	CS	SB%	GDP	Avg	OBP	SLG
1991	Idaho Falls	R	52	202	68	9	1	10	109	33	58	16	1	15	1	2	4	4	1	.80	5	.337	.381	.540
1992	Pulaski	R	10	31	11	3	0	0	14	1	6	6	0	0	0	0	0	2	2	.50	1	.355	.459	.452
	Macon	A	47	157	41	13	0	5	69	20	21	15	2	16	3	0	2	3	1	1.00	5	.261	.333	.439
1993	Macon	A	120	389	115	26	5	7	172	50	58	37	4	37	6	2	12	9	5	.64	9	.296	.356	.442

Year	Team	Lg	G	AB	H	2B	3B	HR	TB	R	RBI	TBB	IBB	SO	HBP	SH	SF	SB	CS	SB%	GDP	Avg	OBP	SLG
1994	Durham	A	22	68	25	3	0	11	61	18	22	12	4	6	3	0	1	1	1	.50	1	.368	.476	.897
	Greenville	AA	100	348	94	19	1	11	148	40	58	20	1	40	6	0	7	2	3	.40	11	.270	.315	.425
1995	Greenville	AA	21	74	32	5	0	2	43	14	11	7	0	9	2	0	2	0	1	.00	0	.432	.482	.581
	Richmond	AAA	106	309	92	16	5	12	154	35	56	25	4	47	4	0	4	1	3	.25	10	.298	.354	.498
5 Min. YEARS			478	1578	478	94	12	58	770	211	290	138	16	170	25	4	32	22	16	.58	40	.303	.362	.488

John Grimm

Pitches: Right **Bats:** Right **Pos:** P   **Ht:** 5'11" **Wt:** 170 **Born:** 9/13/70 **Age:** 25

			HOW MUCH HE PITCHED						WHAT HE GAVE UP										THE RESULTS					
Year	Team	Lg	G	GS	CG	GF	IP	BFP	H	R	ER	HR	SH	SF	HB	TBB	IBB	SO	WP	Bk	W	L	Pct.	ShO	Sv	ERA
1992	Bristol	R	20	0	0	15	30.1	136	33	18	15	5	0	0	2	14	2	42	8	0	1	3	.250	0	6	4.45
1993	Fayetteville	A	23	0	0	15	37.1	144	18	7	6	1	1	1	1	14	2	58	4	0	0	2	.000	0	10	1.45
	Lakeland	A	16	0	0	15	18.1	79	12	7	5	2	0	2	0	11	0	17	0	0	2	1	.667	0	3	2.45
1994	Lakeland	A	44	0	0	37	53.2	222	37	19	15	3	2	0	1	31	2	65	2	1	4	3	.571	0	19	2.52
1995	Jacksonville	AA	13	0	0	5	15.2	82	23	17	15	5	0	0	1	10	0	9	0	0	2	1	.667	0	0	8.62
4 Min. YEARS			116	0	0	87	155.1	663	123	68	56	16	3	3	5	80	6	191	14	1	9	10	.474	0	38	3.24

Antonio Grissom

Bats: Right **Throws:** Right **Pos:** OF   **Ht:** 6'1" **Wt:** 195 **Born:** 1/11/70 **Age:** 26

			BATTING															BASERUNNING				PERCENTAGES		
Year	Team	Lg	G	AB	H	2B	3B	HR	TB	R	RBI	TBB	IBB	SO	HBP	SH	SF	SB	CS	SB%	GDP	Avg	OBP	SLG
1990	Martinsville	R	5	17	3	1	0	0	4	1	0	2	0	3	1	0	0	0	0	.00	0	.176	.300	.235
1991	Spartanburg	A	33	93	16	0	0	0	16	12	3	19	1	22	1	0	0	13	4	.76	1	.172	.319	.172
	Batavia	A	60	209	48	5	6	3	74	38	22	24	0	40	0	3	3	21	9	.70	5	.230	.305	.354
1992	Albany	A	136	490	132	21	5	4	175	89	47	79	1	87	5	3	4	62	20	.76	9	.269	.374	.357
1993	Burlington	A	73	271	68	13	5	5	106	40	27	35	2	60	3	4	1	21	11	.66	2	.251	.342	.391
	W. Palm Bch	A	40	138	31	3	1	2	42	16	7	19	0	20	1	2	0	9	6	.60	1	.225	.323	.304
1994	W. Palm Bch	A	101	309	69	9	1	0	80	35	27	36	1	93	1	0	3	17	12	.59	4	.223	.304	.317
1995	W. Palm Bch	A	8	20	4	1	0	0	5	3	1	4	0	6	0	0	0	2	1	.67	0	.200	.333	.250
	Harrisburg	AA	82	237	61	10	0	4	83	32	23	33	0	48	4	4	1	13	8	.62	6	.257	.356	.350
6 Min. YEARS			538	1784	432	63	18	24	603	270	157	251	5	339	16	16	12	158	71	.69	28	.242	.339	.338

Mike Groppuso

Bats: Right **Throws:** Right **Pos:** 3B   **Ht:** 6'3" **Wt:** 195 **Born:** 3/9/70 **Age:** 26

			BATTING															BASERUNNING				PERCENTAGES		
Year	Team	Lg	G	AB	H	2B	3B	HR	TB	R	RBI	TBB	IBB	SO	HBP	SH	SF	SB	CS	SB%	GDP	Avg	OBP	SLG
1991	Asheville	A	63	197	36	12	1	4	62	31	25	34	2	60	3	0	0	3	1	.75	3	.183	.312	.315
1992	Osceola	A	115	369	80	19	1	4	113	53	37	43	2	98	9	3	3	6	3	.67	4	.217	.311	.306
1993	Jackson	AA	114	370	89	18	0	10	137	41	49	35	4	121	5	0	1	3	3	.50	8	.241	.314	.370
1994	Jackson	AA	118	352	93	16	2	12	149	49	47	35	2	97	5	1	4	6	7	.46	10	.264	.336	.423
1995	Jackson	AA	24	79	17	3	1	1	25	5	5	16	3	17	1	1	1	2	1	.67	1	.215	.351	.316
5 Min. YEARS			434	1367	315	68	5	31	486	179	163	163	13	393	23	4	9	20	15	.57	26	.230	.321	.356

Ken Grundt

Pitches: Left **Bats:** Left **Pos:** P   **Ht:** 6'4" **Wt:** 195 **Born:** 8/26/69 **Age:** 26

			HOW MUCH HE PITCHED						WHAT HE GAVE UP										THE RESULTS					
Year	Team	Lg	G	GS	CG	GF	IP	BFP	H	R	ER	HR	SH	SF	HB	TBB	IBB	SO	WP	Bk	W	L	Pct.	ShO	Sv	ERA
1991	Everett	A	29	0	0	15	54	231	55	27	14	3	3	0	3	16	5	58	3	0	4	5	.444	0	4	2.33
1992	Clinton	A	40	0	0	28	57.2	226	39	11	4	2	3	0	3	11	2	59	1	0	5	3	.625	0	16	0.62
	San Jose	A	11	0	0	5	17.2	70	9	3	2	1	2	0	2	7	1	17	0	0	1	0	1.000	0	3	1.02
1993	Giants	R	4	0	0	0	4	17	5	1	1	0	0	0	0	0	0	2	0	0	0	0	.000	0	0	2.25
1994	Sioux Falls	IND	26	0	0	10	44	189	44	15	8	2	0	0	1	21	0	35	1	0	3	3	.500	0	2	1.64
1995	Asheville	A	20	0	0	11	30.1	111	18	1	1	0	1	1	1	7	1	38	2	0	0	0	.000	0	1	0.30
	New Haven	AA	28	0	0	8	38	146	26	14	9	1	2	0	1	10	2	27	2	0	2	2	.500	0	3	2.13
	Colo. Sprng	AAA	9	0	0	1	5.2	30	9	5	3	0	0	0	0	4	0	5	0	0	0	0	.000	0	0	4.76
5 Min. YEARS			167	0	0	78	251.1	1020	205	77	42	9	11	1	9	76	11	241	9	0	15	13	.536	0	29	1.50

Phillip Grundy

Pitches: Right **Bats:** Right **Pos:** P   **Ht:** 6'2" **Wt:** 195 **Born:** 9/8/72 **Age:** 23

			HOW MUCH HE PITCHED						WHAT HE GAVE UP										THE RESULTS					
Year	Team	Lg	G	GS	CG	GF	IP	BFP	H	R	ER	HR	SH	SF	HB	TBB	IBB	SO	WP	Bk	W	L	Pct.	ShO	Sv	ERA
1993	Eugene	A	15	13	0	0	69	301	68	31	25	7	2	1	5	37	1	61	5	1	3	5	.375	0	0	3.26
1994	Rockford	A	27	26	2	0	151.1	622	135	65	54	6	1	4	1	51	3	116	14	0	15	8	.652	0	0	3.21
1995	Wichita	AA	6	2	0	1	17.1	75	16	17	16	6	1	1	1	7	0	11	3	0	1	1	.500	0	0	8.31
	Wilmington	A	20	16	0	3	106	445	106	46	39	7	4	1	5	32	2	90	7	0	6	6	.500	0	1	3.31
3 Min. YEARS			68	57	2	4	343.2	1443	325	159	134	26	8	7	12	127	6	278	29	1	25	20	.556	0	1	3.51

Mike Grzanich

Pitches: Right **Bats:** Right **Pos:** P   **Ht:** 6'1" **Wt:** 180 **Born:** 8/24/72 **Age:** 23

			HOW MUCH HE PITCHED						WHAT HE GAVE UP										THE RESULTS					
Year	Team	Lg	G	GS	CG	GF	IP	BFP	H	R	ER	HR	SH	SF	HB	TBB	IBB	SO	WP	Bk	W	L	Pct.	ShO	Sv	ERA
1992	Astros	R	17	3	0	9	33.2	159	38	21	17	0	2	3	6	14	0	29	1	0	2	5	.286	0	3	4.54
1993	Auburn	A	16	14	4	1	93.1	409	106	63	50	11	3	3	3	27	0	71	7	1	5	8	.385	1	0	4.82
1994	Quad City	A	23	22	3	1	142.2	598	145	55	49	5	2	1	11	43	2	101	5	0	11	7	.611	0	0	3.09

Year	Team	Lg	G	GS	CG	GF	IP	BFP	H	R	ER	HR	SH	SF	HB	TBB	IBB	SO	WP	Bk	W	L	Pct.	ShO	Sv	ERA
1995	Jackson	AA	50	0	0	23	65.2	276	55	22	20	0	5	3	6	38	5	44	4	0	5	3	.625	0	8	2.74
	4 Min. YEARS		106	39	7	34	335.1	1442	344	161	136	16	12	10	26	122	7	245	17	1	23	23	.500	1	11	3.65

Creighton Gubanich

Bats: Right **Throws:** Right **Pos:** C   **Ht:** 6'3" **Wt:** 190 **Born:** 3/27/72 **Age:** 24

						BATTING													BASERUNNING				PERCENTAGES		
Year	Team	Lg	G	AB	H	2B	3B	HR	TB	R	RBI	TBB	IBB	SO	HBP	SH	SF	SB	CS	SB%	GDP	Avg	OBP	SLG
1991	Sou. Oregon	A	43	132	30	7	2	4	53	23	18	19	0	35	6	0	0	0	4	.00	2	.227	.350	.402
1992	Madison	A	121	404	100	19	3	9	152	46	55	41	1	102	16	8	1	0	7	.00	8	.248	.340	.376
1993	Madison	A	119	373	100	19	2	19	180	65	78	63	2	105	11	2	12	3	3	.50	7	.268	.379	.483
1994	Modesto	A	108	375	88	20	3	15	159	53	55	54	0	102	7	5	2	5	4	.56	9	.235	.340	.424
1995	Huntsville	AA	94	274	60	7	1	13	108	37	43	48	0	82	7	2	5	1	0	1.00	2	.219	.344	.394
	5 Min. YEARS		485	1558	378	72	11	60	652	224	249	225	3	426	47	17	20	9	18	.33	28	.243	.351	.418

Mark Guerra

Pitches: Right **Bats:** Right **Pos:** P   **Ht:** 6'2" **Wt:** 185 **Born:** 11/4/71 **Age:** 24

			HOW MUCH HE PITCHED						WHAT HE GAVE UP									THE RESULTS					
Year	Team	Lg	G	GS	CG	GF	IP	BFP	H	R	ER	HR	SH	SF	HB	TBB	IBB	SO	WP	Bk	W	L	Pct.	ShO	Sv	ERA
1994	Pittsfield	A	14	14	2	0	94	392	105	47	36	4	4	5	4	21	1	62	2	2	7	6	.538	0	0	3.45
1995	St. Lucie	A	23	23	4	0	160	644	148	55	47	5	4	4	4	33	1	110	2	3	9	9	.500	3	0	2.64
	Binghamton	AA	6	5	1	0	32.2	139	35	24	21	6	1	0	0	9	1	24	0	0	2	1	.667	0	0	5.79
	2 Min. YEARS		43	42	7	0	286.2	1175	288	126	104	15	9	9	8	63	3	196	4	5	18	16	.529	3	0	3.27

Juan Guerrero

Bats: Right **Throws:** Right **Pos:** 3B   **Ht:** 5'11" **Wt:** 160 **Born:** 2/1/67 **Age:** 29

						BATTING													BASERUNNING				PERCENTAGES		
Year	Team	Lg	G	AB	H	2B	3B	HR	TB	R	RBI	TBB	IBB	SO	HBP	SH	SF	SB	CS	SB%	GDP	Avg	OBP	SLG
1987	Pocatello	R	34	81	17	5	1	1	27	13	7	17	0	28	1	0	0	1	1	.50	1	.210	.354	.333
1988	Clinton	A	111	385	106	17	3	13	168	57	54	13	0	95	5	1	5	7	4	.64	5	.275	.304	.436
1989	San Jose	A	108	409	115	24	2	13	182	61	78	36	1	68	7	0	5	7	5	.58	13	.281	.346	.445
1990	Shreveport	AA	118	390	94	21	1	16	165	55	47	26	0	74	5	2	2	4	8	.33	9	.241	.296	.423
1991	Shreveport	AA	128	479	160	40	2	19	261	78	94	46	2	88	5	0	4	14	9	.61	12	.334	.395	.545
1994	Tucson	AAA	89	290	84	17	6	7	134	44	49	26	0	45	4	2	3	1	2	.33	11	.290	.353	.462
1995	Tucson	AAA	72	194	57	10	1	2	75	21	21	14	3	42	0	2	1	1	1	.50	3	.294	.340	.387
1992	Houston	NL	79	125	25	4	2	1	36	8	14	10	2	32	1	1	2	1	0	1.00	1	.200	.261	.288
	7 Min. YEARS		660	2228	633	134	16	71	1012	329	350	178	6	440	27	7	20	35	30	.54	54	.284	.342	.454

Mike Guerrero

Bats: Right **Throws:** Right **Pos:** SS   **Ht:** 5'11" **Wt:** 155 **Born:** 1/8/68 **Age:** 28

						BATTING													BASERUNNING				PERCENTAGES		
Year	Team	Lg	G	AB	H	2B	3B	HR	TB	R	RBI	TBB	IBB	SO	HBP	SH	SF	SB	CS	SB%	GDP	Avg	OBP	SLG
1987	Helena	R	52	181	40	3	1	0	45	22	14	16	0	43	0	4	0	8	6	.57	1	.221	.284	.249
1988	Brewers	R	8	29	8	1	0	0	9	9	7	5	0	5	0	1	0	0	0	.00	0	.276	.382	.310
	Helena	R	10	31	9	0	0	0	9	4	5	3	0	1	0	0	0	2	1	.67	1	.290	.353	.290
	Beloit	A	65	221	39	8	1	0	49	20	7	14	0	55	1	8	0	5	5	.50	5	.176	.229	.222
1989	Beloit	A	51	171	38	10	0	0	48	28	13	13	0	33	0	2	2	7	4	.64	1	.222	.274	.281
	Brewers	R	11	47	13	3	1	1	21	10	11	6	0	5	1	1	2	3	2	.60	0	.277	.357	.447
	Stockton	A	44	136	32	5	0	0	37	12	13	12	0	15	0	5	1	3	1	.75	2	.235	.295	.272
1990	Stockton	A	105	320	80	5	5	1	98	36	36	24	1	54	3	6	1	14	10	.58	13	.250	.307	.306
1991	El Paso	AA	37	117	24	2	0	0	26	23	13	18	1	16	0	2	0	2	1	.67	4	.205	.311	.222
	Stockton	A	59	204	48	4	1	1	57	22	18	28	1	28	1	4	5	6	2	.75	5	.235	.324	.279
1992	El Paso	AA	96	257	63	11	4	1	85	36	28	31	2	38	1	12	3	6	6	.50	1	.245	.325	.331
1993	Memphis	AA	24	68	18	6	0	0	24	7	4	4	0	7	0	4	0	0	2	.00	0	.265	.306	.353
	Wilmington	A	44	150	41	4	1	0	47	24	7	32	0	20	0	7	0	4	12	.25	0	.273	.401	.313
1994	El Paso	AA	8	11	3	1	0	0	4	2	3	0	0	2	0	0	0	0	0	.00	0	.273	.273	.364
	Stockton	A	27	86	30	3	0	2	39	13	15	5	0	12	1	0	2	1	2	.33	3	.349	.383	.453
1995	El Paso	AA	23	71	22	1	0	1	26	14	7	7	0	5	0	0	1	0	0	.00	1	.310	.367	.366
	9 Min. YEARS		664	2100	508	67	14	7	624	282	201	218	5	339	8	56	17	61	54	.53	37	.242	.313	.297

Pedro Guerrero

Bats: Right **Throws:** Right **Pos:** DH   **Ht:** 6'0" **Wt:** 199 **Born:** 6/29/56 **Age:** 40

						BATTING													BASERUNNING				PERCENTAGES		
Year	Team	Lg	G	AB	H	2B	3B	HR	TB	R	RBI	TBB	IBB	SO	HBP	SH	SF	SB	CS	SB%	GDP	Avg	OBP	SLG
1973	Cleveland	R	44	153	39	2	3	2	53	13	22	15	-	32	1	1	0	1	2	.33	-	.255	.325	.346
1974	Orangeburg	A	19	55	8	1	0	0	9	3	1	6	-	15	1	0	0	0	0	.00	-	.145	.242	.164
	Bellingham	A	82	297	94	23	2	3	130	49	55	20	-	52	1	0	2	4	0	1.00	-	.316	.359	.438
1975	Danville	A	104	351	121	25	5	10	186	81	76	63	-	57	3	1	5	10	4	.71	-	.345	.443	.530
1976	Waterbury	AA	132	495	151	30	10	5	216	73	66	52	-	72	0	0	1	23	7	.77	-	.305	.370	.436
1977	Albuquerque	AAA	32	129	52	11	4	4	83	30	39	15	-	24	1	0	0	0	1	.00	-	.403	.469	.643
1978	Albuquerque	AAA	134	492	166	28	4	14	244	92	116	58	-	69	5	1	15	17	5	.77	-	.337	.402	.496
1979	Albuquerque	AAA	113	453	151	33	9	22	268	94	103	31	-	84	2	0	5	26	8	.76	-	.333	.375	.592
1988	Albuquerque	AAA	5	12	5	0	0	1	8	3	4	5	2	5	0	0	0	0	0	.00	0	.417	.588	.667
1991	Louisville	AAA	3	11	5	0	0	1	8	2	2	0	0	0	0	0	0	0	0	.00	1	.455	.455	.727
1992	Louisville	AAA	18	55	14	5	0	3	28	5	7	6	1	7	0	0	0	0	0	.00	0	.255	.328	.509
1993	Sioux Falls	IND	42	151	42	5	0	3	56	23	33	21	2	20	0	0	4	3	0	1.00	2	.278	.358	.371

Year	Team	Lg	G	AB	H	2B	3B	HR	TB	R	RBI	TBB	IBB	SO	HBP	SH	SF	SB	CS	SB%	GDP	Avg	OBP	SLG
1994	Sioux Falls	IND	75	280	92	15	0	8	131	55	47	31	2	29	3	0	2	0	0	.00	5	.329	.399	.468
1995	Midland	AA	66	252	76	13	0	7	110	40	40	28	2	34	2	0	0	0	2	.00	16	.302	.376	.437
1978	Los Angeles	NL	5	8	5	0	1	0	7	3	1	0	0	0	0	0	0	0	0	.00	0	.625	.625	.875
1979	Los Angeles	NL	25	62	15	2	0	2	23	7	9	1	1	14	0	0	1	2	0	1.00	1	.242	.250	.371
1980	Los Angeles	NL	75	183	59	9	1	7	91	27	31	12	3	31	0	1	3	2	1	.67	2	.322	.359	.497
1981	Los Angeles	NL	98	347	104	17	2	12	161	46	48	34	3	57	2	3	1	5	9	.36	12	.300	.365	.464
1982	Los Angeles	NL	150	575	175	27	5	32	308	87	100	65	16	89	5	4	3	22	5	.81	7	.304	.378	.536
1983	Los Angeles	NL	160	584	174	28	6	32	310	87	103	72	12	110	2	0	6	23	7	.77	11	.298	.373	.531
1984	Los Angeles	NL	144	535	162	29	4	16	247	85	72	49	7	105	1	1	8	9	8	.53	7	.303	.358	.462
1985	Los Angeles	NL	137	487	156	22	2	33	281	99	87	83	14	68	6	0	5	12	4	.75	13	.320	.422	.577
1986	Los Angeles	NL	31	61	15	3	0	5	33	7	10	2	0	19	1	0	0	0	0	.00	1	.246	.281	.541
1987	Los Angeles	NL	152	545	184	25	2	27	294	89	89	74	18	85	4	0	7	9	7	.56	16	.338	.416	.539
1988	Los Angeles	NL	59	215	64	7	1	5	88	24	35	25	2	33	3	0	3	2	1	.67	2	.298	.374	.409
	St. Louis	NL	44	149	40	7	1	5	64	16	30	21	7	26	2	0	4	2	0	1.00	3	.268	.358	.430
1989	St. Louis	NL	162	570	177	42	1	17	272	60	117	79	13	84	4	0	12	2	0	1.00	17	.311	.391	.477
1990	St. Louis	NL	136	498	140	31	1	13	212	42	80	44	14	70	1	0	11	1	1	.50	14	.281	.334	.426
1991	St. Louis	NL	115	427	116	12	1	8	154	41	70	37	2	46	1	0	7	4	2	.67	12	.272	.326	.361
1992	St. Louis	NL	43	146	32	6	1	1	43	10	16	11	3	25	0	0	2	2	2	.50	4	.219	.270	.295
13 Min. YEARS			869	3186	1016	191	37	83	1530	563	611	351	9	500	19	3	34	84	29	.74	24	.319	.386	.480
15 Maj. YEARS			1536	5392	1618	267	29	215	2588	730	898	609	115	862	32	9	73	97	47	.67	122	.300	.370	.480

Wilton Guerrero

Bats: Right **Throws:** Right **Pos:** SS **Ht:** 5'11" **Wt:** 145 **Born:** 10/24/74 **Age:** 21

			BATTING															BASERUNNING				PERCENTAGES		
Year	Team	Lg	G	AB	H	2B	3B	HR	TB	R	RBI	TBB	IBB	SO	HBP	SH	SF	SB	CS	SB%	GDP	Avg	OBP	SLG
1993	Great Falls	R	66	256	76	5	1	0	83	44	21	24	1	33	3	5	0	20	8	.71	5	.297	.364	.324
1994	Vero Beach	A	110	402	118	11	4	1	140	55	32	29	0	71	1	10	2	23	20	.53	2	.294	.341	.348
1995	San Antonio	AA	95	382	133	13	6	0	158	53	26	26	3	63	1	4	1	21	22	.49	10	.348	.390	.414
	Albuquerque	AAA	14	49	16	1	1	0	19	10	2	1	1	7	0	0	0	2	3	.40	1	.327	.340	.388
3 Min. YEARS			285	1089	343	30	12	1	400	162	81	80	5	174	5	21	3	66	53	.55	18	.315	.364	.367

Michael Guilfoyle

Pitches: Left **Bats:** Left **Pos:** P **Ht:** 5'11" **Wt:** 187 **Born:** 4/29/68 **Age:** 28

			HOW MUCH HE PITCHED						WHAT HE GAVE UP											THE RESULTS				
Year	Team	Lg	G	GS	CG	GF	IP	BFP	H	R	ER	HR	SH	SF	HB	TBB	IBB	SO	WP	Bk	W	L	Pct.	ShO	Sv	ERA
1990	Bristol	R	16	7	0	3	64.2	278	54	35	22	6	3	1	1	25	0	80	4	3	4	6	.400	0	1	3.06
1991	Fayetteville	A	40	0	0	34	47.1	213	41	22	13	3	4	4	5	26	1	44	2	1	1	4	.200	0	8	2.47
1992	Lakeland	A	45	0	0	31	51	214	48	23	18	1	1	1	1	16	1	32	2	1	4	1	.800	0	11	3.18
1993	Lakeland	A	9	0	0	9	9.1	37	5	1	1	0	1	0	0	3	0	10	0	0	0	0	.000	0	1	0.96
	London	AA	49	0	0	18	41	181	43	19	17	2	5	2	2	16	0	35	0	1	1	2	.333	0	3	3.73
1994	Trenton	AA	42	0	0	32	50.1	227	60	27	25	4	4	2	1	25	0	36	1	1	7	8	.467	0	5	4.47
1995	Jacksonville	AA	56	0	0	14	59.1	256	55	23	19	2	2	0		31	3	50	1	0	5	1	.833	0	3	2.88
6 Min. YEARS			257	7	0	141	323	1406	306	150	115	18	20	12	10	142	5	287	10	7	22	22	.500	0	36	3.20

Mike Gulan

Bats: Right **Throws:** Right **Pos:** 3B **Ht:** 6'1" **Wt:** 190 **Born:** 12/18/70 **Age:** 25

			BATTING															BASERUNNING				PERCENTAGES		
Year	Team	Lg	G	AB	H	2B	3B	HR	TB	R	RBI	TBB	IBB	SO	HBP	SH	SF	SB	CS	SB%	GDP	Avg	OBP	SLG
1992	Hamilton	A	62	242	66	8	4	7	103	33	36	23	0	53	1	0	4	12	4	.75	7	.273	.333	.426
1993	Springfield	A	132	455	118	28	4	23	223	81	76	34	0	135	9	3	3	8	4	.67	4	.259	.321	.490
1994	St. Pete	A	120	466	113	30	2	8	171	39	56	26	2	108	2	0	6	2	8	.20	8	.242	.282	.367
1995	Arkansas	AA	64	242	76	16	3	12	134	47	48	11	1	52	6	0	1	4	2	.67	4	.314	.358	.554
	Louisville	AAA	58	195	46	10	4	5	79	21	27	10	1	53	3	0	2	2	2	.50	6	.236	.281	.405
4 Min. YEARS			436	1600	419	92	17	55	710	221	243	104	4	401	21	3	16	28	20	.58	29	.262	.312	.444

Jim Gutierrez

Pitches: Right **Bats:** Right **Pos:** P **Ht:** 6'2" **Wt:** 190 **Born:** 11/28/70 **Age:** 25

			HOW MUCH HE PITCHED						WHAT HE GAVE UP											THE RESULTS				
Year	Team	Lg	G	GS	CG	GF	IP	BFP	H	R	ER	HR	SH	SF	HB	TBB	IBB	SO	WP	Bk	W	L	Pct.	ShO	Sv	ERA
1989	Bellingham	A	13	11	0	1	57.2	268	68	44	25	4	0	1	1	24	0	33	1	0	1	5	.167	0	0	3.90
1990	Peninsula	A	28	28	4	0	186	758	171	82	71	9	6	11	6	41	0	95	6	1	11	13	.458	2	0	3.44
1991	San Bernrdo	A	17	14	1	0	82.2	377	100	65	60	11	0	3	2	37	0	66	4	0	4	4	.500	0	0	6.53
1992	Jacksonvlle	AA	15	11	0	1	54	234	58	34	30	7	1	2	3	17	0	44	0	0	1	5	.167	0	0	5.00
1993	Riverside	A	27	27	2	0	171.1	742	182	95	72	15	11	6	4	53	2	84	5	1	12	9	.571	0	0	3.78
1994	Jacksonvlle	AA	28	21	6	4	151.2	655	175	76	72	16	4	3	4	42	4	89	1	0	8	11	.421	1	0	4.27
1995	Jacksonvlle	AA	45	1	0	14	58.2	243	60	22	18	2	3	2	0	25	4	36	3	0	8	4	.667	0	0	2.76
7 Min. YEARS			173	113	13	20	762	3277	814	418	348	64	25	28	20	239	10	447	20	2	45	51	.469	3	4	4.11

Dave Haas

Pitches: Right **Bats:** Right **Pos:** P **Ht:** 6'1" **Wt:** 200 **Born:** 10/19/65 **Age:** 30

			HOW MUCH HE PITCHED						WHAT HE GAVE UP											THE RESULTS				
Year	Team	Lg	G	GS	CG	GF	IP	BFP	H	R	ER	HR	SH	SF	HB	TBB	IBB	SO	WP	Bk	W	L	Pct.	ShO	Sv	ERA
1988	Fayettevlle	A	11	11	0	0	54.2	243	59	20	11	0	1	1	6	19	1	46	2	4	4	3	.571	0	0	1.81
1989	Lakeland	A	10	10	1	0	62	247	50	16	14	1	0	1	6	16	0	46	1	1	4	1	.800	1	0	2.03
	London	AA	18	18	2	0	103.2	460	107	69	65	13	5	2	11	51	1	75	5	1	3	11	.214	1	0	5.64

1990 London	AA	27	27	3	0	177.2	740	151	64	59	10	4	3	10	74	1	116	14	1	13	8	.619	1	0	2.99
1991 Toledo	AAA	28	28	1	0	158.1	718	187	103	92	11	8	3	8	77	3	133	8	1	8	10	.444	0	0	5.23
1992 Toledo	AAA	22	22.	2	0	148.2	636	149	72	69	11	5	5	9	53	1	112	5	0	9	8	.529	0	0	4.18
1993 Toledo	AAA	2	2	0	0	4.1	27	8	9	9	0	0	0	1	6	0	2	1	0	0	0	.000	0	0	18.69
1994 Lakeland	A	5	3	0	0	20	90	23	9	8	0	2	3	3	8	0	4	0	0	1	0	1.000	0	0	3.60
1995 Orlando	AA	3	3	0	0	12.2	69	18	10	7	1	0	0	3	10	0	4	1	0	0	3	.000	0	0	4.97
Salinas	IND	18	16	0	0	99.2	424	103	63	51	12	4	3	9	24	1	63	3	0	7	5	.583	0	0	4.61
1991 Detroit	AL	11	0	0	0	10.2	50	8	8	8	1	2	2	1	12	3	6	1	0	1	0	1.000	0	0	6.75
1992 Detroit	AL	12	11	1	1	61.2	264	68	30	27	8	1	0	1	16	1	29	2	0	5	3	.625	1	0	3.94
1993 Detroit	AL	20	0	0	5	28	131	45	20	19	9	2	1	0	8	5	17	0	0	1	2	.333	0	0	6.11
8 Min. YEARS		144	140	9	0	841.2	3654	855	435	385	59	29	21	66	338	8	601	40	8	49	49	.500	3	0	4.12
3 Maj. YEARS		43	11	1	6	100.1	445	121	58	54	18	5	3	2	36	9	52	3	0	7	5	.583	1	0	4.84

Gary Hagy

Bats: Right **Throws:** Right **Pos:** SS   **Ht:** 6'3" **Wt:** 195 **Born:** 4/7/69 **Age:** 27

			BATTING													BASERUNNING				PERCENTAGES		
Year Team	Lg	G	AB	H	2B	3B	HR	TB	R	RBI	TBB	IBB	SO	HBP	SH	SF	SB	CS	SB%	GDP	Avg	OBP	SLG
1991 Boise	A	72	248	69	10	1	1	84	42	35	34	3	32	3	4	4	5	1	.83	7	.278	.367	.339
1992 Quad City	A	121	371	75	13	1	4	102	53	44	44	0	86	2	9	6	6	3	.67	3	.202	.286	.275
1993 Palm Spring	A	104	340	61	8	1	0	71	35	24	42	0	61	2	7	2	6	6	.50	4	.179	.272	.209
1995 Canton-Akrn	AA	6	17	5	2	0	0	7	2	3	1	0	2	0	0	0	0	0	.00	0	.294	.333	.412
Kinston	A	52	142	19	3	0	3	31	12	9	12	1	34	1	5	2	3	2	.60	1	.134	.204	.218
4 Min. YEARS		355	1118	229	36	3	8	295	144	115	133	4	215	8	25	14	20	12	.63	15	.205	.291	.264

Billy Hall

Bats: Both **Throws:** Right **Pos:** 2B   **Ht:** 5'9" **Wt:** 180 **Born:** 6/17/69 **Age:** 27

			BATTING													BASERUNNING				PERCENTAGES		
Year Team	Lg	G	AB	H	2B	3B	HR	TB	R	RBI	TBB	IBB	SO	HBP	SH	SF	SB	CS	SB%	GDP	Avg	OBP	SLG
1991 Charlstn-Sc	A	72	279	84	6	5	2	106	41	28	34	1	54	0	0	2	25	9	.74	2	.301	.375	.380
1992 High Desert	A	119	495	176	22	5	2	214	92	39	54	2	77	1	1	3	49	27	.64	2	.356	.418	.432
1993 Wichita	AA	124	486	131	27	7	4	184	80	46	37	1	88	3	4	4	29	19	.60	6	.270	.323	.379
1994 Wichita	AA	29	111	40	5	1	1	50	14	12	11	1	19	1	0	0	10	5	.67	5	.360	.423	.450
Las Vegas	AAA	70	280	74	11	3	3	100	43	21	32	0	61	1	5	1	24	6	.80	2	.264	.341	.357
1995 Las Vegas	AAA	86	249	56	3	1	1	64	42	22	20	1	47	1	1	3	22	5	.81	3	.225	.282	.257
5 Min. YEARS		500	1900	561	74	22	13	718	312	168	188	6	346	7	11	13	159	71	.69	20	.295	.359	.378

Shane Halter

Bats: Right **Throws:** Right **Pos:** SS   **Ht:** 5'10" **Wt:** 160 **Born:** 11/8/69 **Age:** 26

			BATTING													BASERUNNING				PERCENTAGES		
Year Team	Lg	G	AB	H	2B	3B	HR	TB	R	RBI	TBB	IBB	SO	HBP	SH	SF	SB	CS	SB%	GDP	Avg	OBP	SLG
1991 Eugene	A	64	236	55	9	1	1	69	41	18	49	0	59	3	2	1	12	6	.67	3	.233	.370	.292
1992 Appleton	A	80	313	83	22	3	3	120	50	33	41	1	54	1	5	3	21	6	.78	4	.265	.349	.383
Baseball Cy	A	44	117	28	1	0	1	32	11	14	24	0	31	0	5	4	5	5	.50	4	.239	.359	.274
1993 Wilmington	A	54	211	63	8	5	5	96	44	32	27	2	55	2	12	4	5	4	.56	3	.299	.377	.455
Memphis	AA	81	306	79	7	0	4	98	50	20	30	1	74	2	10	3	4	7	.36	3	.258	.326	.320
1994 Memphis	AA	129	494	111	23	1	6	154	61	39	39	0	102	3	15	6	10	14	.42	10	.225	.282	.312
1995 Omaha	AAA	124	392	90	19	3	8	139	42	39	40	0	97	1	19	1	2	3	.40	6	.230	.300	.355
5 Min. YEARS		576	2069	509	89	13	28	708	299	191	250	4	472	11	68	22	59	45	.57	33	.246	.327	.342

Chris Hancock

Pitches: Left **Bats:** Left **Pos:** P   **Ht:** 6'3" **Wt:** 205 **Born:** 9/12/69 **Age:** 26

		HOW MUCH HE PITCHED						WHAT HE GAVE UP										THE RESULTS				
Year Team	Lg	G	GS	CG	GF	IP	BFP	H	R	ER	HR	SH	SF	HB	TBB	IBB	SO	WP	Bk	W	L	Pct.	ShO	Sv	ERA
1988 Pocatello	R	12	11	0	0	42.2	241	60	54	42	2	2	3		43	0	31	12	1	2	5	.286	0	0	8.86
1989 Clinton	A	18	17	0	0	72	355	63	53	47	5	1	1	5	77	0	62	17	2	4	7	.364	0	0	5.88
Everett	A	11	11	0	0	52.2	262	47	52	33	3	1	7	2	53	0	50	13	0	2	5	.286	0	0	5.64
1990 Clinton	A	18	17	2	0	110.2	445	78	33	28	4	2	2	3	43	0	123	5	1	11	3	.786	1	0	2.28
San Jose	A	1	1	0	0	7.2	31	7	1	1	0	0	0	0	4	0	7	0	0	0	0	.000	0	0	1.17
1991 San Jose	A	9	9	0	0	53.1	227	42	16	12	4	0	0	1	33	1	59	5	0	4	3	.571	0	0	2.03
1992 San Jose	A	18	17	0	1	111.1	484	104	60	50	4	4	1	6	55	1	80	8	1	7	4	.636	0	0	4.04
Shreveport	AA	8	8	2	0	49.1	204	37	22	17	0	2	2	4	18	0	30	3	1	2	4	.333	0	0	3.10
1993 Shreveport	AA	23	23	0	0	124	544	126	71	56	13	7	3	7	52	2	93	8	0	8	8	.500	0	0	4.06
1994 Shreveport	AA	19	19	1	0	98	435	104	60	55	9	5	4	8	48	0	83	10	1	6	6	.500	1	0	5.05
Phoenix	AAA	9	4	0	2	16.1	86	27	17	14	2	1	1	0	14	2	12	1	0	1	0	1.000	0	0	7.71
1995 Portland	AA	1	0	0	0	0	2	2	1	1	0	0	0	0	0	0	0	0	0	0	0	.000	0	0	0.00
Charlotte	AAA	3	0	0	1	3.1	20	6	6	5	0	0	1	0	4	0	2	0	0	0	1	.000	0	0	13.50
Tyler	IND	6	6	0	0	34	164	40	28	24	2	1	1	5	22	0	30	1	0	1	3	.250	0	0	6.35
Alexandria	IND	10	10	0	0	45.1	207	55	29	27	4	6	2	4	28	0	32	4	0	3	3	.500	0	0	5.36
8 Min. YEARS		166	150	5	4	820.2	3707	798	503	412	50	32	28	45	494	6	694	87	7	51	52	.495	2	0	4.52

Ryan Hancock

Pitches: Right **Bats:** Right **Pos:** P   **Ht:** 6'2" **Wt:** 210 **Born:** 11/11/71 **Age:** 24

		HOW MUCH HE PITCHED						WHAT HE GAVE UP										THE RESULTS				
Year Team	Lg	G	GS	CG	GF	IP	BFP	H	R	ER	HR	SH	SF	HB	TBB	IBB	SO	WP	Bk	W	L	Pct.	ShO	Sv	ERA
1993 Boise	A	3	3	0	0	16.1	69	14	9	6	1	1	0	0	8	1	18	0	0	1	0	1.000	0	0	3.31

124

Year Team	Lg	G	GS	CG	GF	IP	BFP	H	R	ER	HR	SH	SF	HB	TBB	IBB	SO	WP	Bk	W	L	Pct.	ShO	Sv	ERA
1994 Lk Elsinore	A	18	18	3	0	116.1	494	113	62	49	10	1	5	5	36	1	95	2	5	9	6	.600	1	0	3.79
Midland	AA	8	8	0	0	48	219	63	34	31	1	1	1	6	11	0	35	0	2	3	4	.429	0	0	5.81
1995 Midland	AA	28	28	5	0	175.2	764	222	107	89	17	5	4	8	45	1	79	7	3	12	9	.571	1	0	4.56
3 Min. YEARS		57	57	8	0	356.1	1546	412	212	175	29	8	10	19	100	3	227	9	10	25	19	.568	2	0	4.42

Marcus Hanel

Bats: Right Throws: Right Pos: C — Ht: 6'4" Wt: 205 Born: 10/19/71 Age: 24

Year Team	Lg	G	AB	H	2B	3B	HR	TB	R	RBI	TBB	IBB	SO	HBP	SH	SF	SB	CS	SB%	GDP	Avg	OBP	SLG
1989 Pirates	R	28	78	18	3	1	0	23	11	8	6	0	18	0	4	0	2	1	.67	2	.231	.286	.295
1990 Welland	A	40	98	15	2	0	0	17	5	8	5	2	26	1	0	0	1	2	.33	2	.153	.202	.173
1991 Augusta	A	104	364	60	10	1	1	75	33	29	17	1	88	9	2	5	9	3	.75	8	.165	.218	.206
1992 Salem	A	75	231	43	8	0	3	60	12	17	11	0	53	2	6	1	4	0	1.00	6	.186	.229	.260
1993 Salem	A	69	195	36	6	2	2	52	18	16	18	2	65	4	9	2	5	3	.63	2	.185	.265	.267
1994 Salem	A	87	286	70	9	1	5	96	36	27	14	0	54	6	5	3	3	2	.60	5	.245	.291	.336
1995 Carolina	AA	21	60	11	1	0	0	12	1	3	4	0	18	1	1	1	0	1	.00	2	.183	.242	.200
Lynchburg	A	40	135	25	4	1	3	40	14	8	4	0	33	1	2	0	0	1	.00	1	.185	.214	.296
Calgary	AAA	2	8	1	0	0	0	1	0	0	0	0	0	1	0	0	0	0	.00	0	.125	.125	.125
7 Min. YEARS		466	1455	279	43	6	14	376	131	116	79	5	356	24	29	12	24	13	.65	28	.192	.243	.258

Carl Hanselman

Pitches: Right Bats: Left Pos: P — Ht: 6'5" Wt: 190 Born: 5/23/70 Age: 26

Year Team	Lg	G	GS	CG	GF	IP	BFP	H	R	ER	HR	SH	SF	HB	TBB	IBB	SO	WP	Bk	W	L	Pct.	ShO	Sv	ERA
1988 Pocatello	R	12	11	0	0	45.1	249	78	66	42	11	2	3	2	31	0	37	8	0	1	8	.111	0	0	8.34
1989 Clinton	A	15	15	1	0	86.1	391	81	55	46	5	3	4	3	56	1	37	6	3	1	11	.083	0	0	4.80
Everett	A	11	10	0	0	52.2	240	44	32	29	7	0	4	6	35	0	43	2	1	2	4	.333	0	0	4.96
1990 Clinton	A	25	24	2	0	145	620	120	71	52	12	4	3	7	75	1	120	15	0	0	10	.474	1	0	3.23
1991 San Jose	A	25	24	5	0	156.1	670	152	71	66	11	2	3	4	66	0	88	9	1	13	7	.650	1	0	3.80
1992 San Jose	A	16	16	5	0	106.1	445	102	44	30	3	3	2	5	32	0	62	5	2	8	5	.615	2	0	2.54
Shreveport	AA	11	11	2	0	80	323	73	31	22	1	1	3	1	17	1	42	2	0	6	4	.600	1	0	2.48
1993 Shreveport	AA	15	6	0	3	55.2	237	54	23	18	4	2	1	6	13	0	36	2	0	1	5	.167	0	2	2.91
Phoenix	AAA	21	13	0	5	87.1	398	115	66	58	8	5	5	2	35	3	45	7	1	2	6	.250	0	0	5.98
1995 Reading	AA	24	1	0	4	41	186	45	29	29	7	1	1	4	17	1	35	2	0	4	3	.571	0	2	6.37
7 Min. YEARS		175	131	15	12	856	3759	864	488	392	69	23	29	40	377	7	553	58	11	47	63	.427	5	4	4.12

Brent Hansen

Pitches: Right Bats: Right Pos: P — Ht: 6'2" Wt: 195 Born: 8/4/70 Age: 25

Year Team	Lg	G	GS	CG	GF	IP	BFP	H	R	ER	HR	SH	SF	HB	TBB	IBB	SO	WP	Bk	W	L	Pct.	ShO	Sv	ERA
1992 Red Sox	R	3	2	0	1	10	38	4	1	1	0	0	0	1	4	0	5	0	0	0	0	.000	0	0	0.90
Elmira	A	13	11	1	1	59	255	59	33	28	3	2	4	3	21	0	65	4	2	3	5	.375	1	0	4.27
1993 Ft. Laud	A	14	14	4	0	102.2	432	94	37	30	6	2	2	4	37	2	59	1	1	4	6	.400	2	0	2.63
New Britain	AA	15	15	1	0	93.1	398	99	55	51	9	1	5	4	30	2	56	2	0	2	11	.154	0	0	4.92
1994 Sarasota	A	8	7	0	1	40.1	167	37	15	13	0	0	1	0	15	0	27	3	0	2	2	.500	0	0	2.90
1995 Trenton	AA	11	11	2	0	77.1	327	70	32	28	5	3	2	12	17	1	52	1	2	4	5	.444	1	0	3.26
Pawtucket	AAA	14	14	2	0	92.1	385	90	48	44	12	0	3	5	23	0	50	1	0	7	5	.583	0	0	4.29
4 Min. YEARS		78	74	11	3	475	2002	453	221	195	35	8	17	29	147	5	314	12	5	22	34	.393	4	0	3.69

Terrel Hansen

Bats: Right Throws: Right Pos: OF — Ht: 6'3" Wt: 210 Born: 9/25/66 Age: 29

Year Team	Lg	G	AB	H	2B	3B	HR	TB	R	RBI	TBB	IBB	SO	HBP	SH	SF	SB	CS	SB%	GDP	Avg	OBP	SLG
1987 Jamestown	A	29	67	16	3	0	1	22	8	14	10	1	20	0	0	2	1	2	.33	3	.239	.329	.328
1988 W. Palm Bch	A	58	190	49	9	0	4	70	17	28	10	1	38	6	0	2	2	2	.50	5	.258	.313	.368
1989 Rockford	A	125	468	126	24	3	16	204	60	81	25	4	120	23	1	7	5	2	.71	8	.269	.333	.436
1990 Jacksonville	AA	123	420	109	26	2	24	211	72	83	43	2	88	24	1	3	3	4	.43	14	.260	.359	.502
1991 Tidewater	AAA	107	368	100	19	2	12	159	54	62	40	2	82	20	0	3	0	0	.00	20	.272	.371	.432
1992 Tidewater	AAA	115	395	98	18	0	12	152	43	47	24	1	96	7	1	4	4	2	.67	13	.248	.300	.385
1993 Ottawa	AAA	108	352	81	19	0	10	130	45	39	18	0	103	27	2	4	1	1	.50	7	.230	.314	.369
1994 Jacksonvlle	AA	110	404	128	21	1	22	217	57	78	18	0	88	16	0	2	2	4	.33	9	.317	.368	.537
Calgary	AAA	2	8	4	1	0	0	5	0	3	0	0	0	0	0	0	0	0	.00	0	.500	.500	.625
1995 Tacoma	AAA	20	50	11	1	0	3	21	5	10	2	0	12	1	0	1	0	0	.00	5	.220	.259	.420
Jacksonvlle	AA	55	179	40	8	0	9	75	22	22	10	1	40	8	0	2	0	1	.00	2	.223	.291	.419
9 Min. YEARS		852	2901	762	149	8	113	1266	383	467	200	12	687	132	5	30	18	18	.50	86	.263	.335	.436

Craig Hanson

Pitches: Right Bats: Right Pos: P — Ht: 6'3" Wt: 180 Born: 9/30/70 Age: 25

Year Team	Lg	G	GS	CG	GF	IP	BFP	H	R	ER	HR	SH	SF	HB	TBB	IBB	SO	WP	Bk	W	L	Pct.	ShO	Sv	ERA
1991 Spokane	A	13	10	1	2	61	284	76	56	44	3	2	5	0	24	0	39	11	2	1	3	.250	0	0	6.49
1992 Charlstn-Sc	A	28	17	0	4	118	509	115	60	43	7	3	8	5	49	4	75	7	0	2	10	.167	0	0	3.28
1993 Waterloo	A	28	16	1	3	112	511	120	78	61	10	7	5	6	62	2	90	8	1	7	14	.333	0	0	4.90
1994 Rancho Cuca	A	49	2	0	13	83	374	78	37	29	9	2	2	1	47	4	83	9	0	7	5	.583	0	3	3.14
1995 Memphis	AA	25	3	0	8	49	247	64	36	35	8	0	3	2	39	4	33	5	0	0	3	.000	0	1	6.43

Team	Lg																								
Rancho Cuca	A	9	9	0	0	36.2	175	43	29	25	6	1	2	6	19	1	31	3	1	3	4	.429	0	0	6.14
5 Min. YEARS		152	57	2	30	459.2	2100	496	296	237	43	15	25	20	240	15	351	43	4	20	39	.339	0	4	4.64

Mike Hardge

Bats: Right **Throws:** Right **Pos:** 2B **Ht:** 5'11" **Wt:** 183 **Born:** 1/27/72 **Age:** 24

Year	Team	Lg	G	AB	H	2B	3B	HR	TB	R	RBI	TBB	IBB	SO	HBP	SH	SF	SB	CS	SB%	GDP	Avg	OBP	SLG
1990	Expos	R	53	176	39	5	0	1	47	33	13	15	0	43	2	0	2	5	2	.71	1	.222	.287	.267
1991	Expos	R	60	237	60	17	3	3	92	44	30	23	0	41	2	0	4	20	7	.74	3	.253	.320	.388
1992	Rockford	A	127	448	97	21	2	12	158	63	49	47	0	141	3	4	2	44	13	.77	7	.217	.294	.353
	W. Palm Bch	A	4	15	5	1	0	0	6	3	0	2	0	5	0	0	0	2	0	1.00	0	.333	.412	.400
1993	W. Palm Bch	A	27	92	21	2	1	1	28	14	12	14	0	16	0	4	3	5	6	.45	1	.228	.321	.304
	Harrisburg	AA	99	386	94	14	10	6	146	70	35	37	0	97	3	3	1	27	8	.77	3	.244	.314	.378
1994	Harrisburg	AA	121	453	101	10	2	6	133	60	42	56	0	109	0	8	1	30	18	.63	8	.223	.308	.294
1995	Pawtucket	AAA	29	91	23	3	0	1	29	9	5	8	0	16	0	0	0	1	3	.25	2	.253	.313	.319
	Trenton	AA	40	127	31	4	1	0	37	18	12	11	0	26	0	1	2	3	4	.43	7	.244	.300	.291
	6 Min. YEARS		560	2025	471	77	19	30	676	314	198	213	0	494	10	20	15	137	61	.69	32	.233	.307	.334

Jason Hardtke

Bats: Both **Throws:** Right **Pos:** 2B **Ht:** 5'10" **Wt:** 175 **Born:** 9/15/71 **Age:** 24

Year	Team	Lg	G	AB	H	2B	3B	HR	TB	R	RBI	TBB	IBB	SO	HBP	SH	SF	SB	CS	SB%	GDP	Avg	OBP	SLG
1990	Burlington	R	39	142	38	7	0	4	57	18	16	23	0	19	2	0	0	11	1	.92	3	.268	.377	.401
1991	Columbus	A	139	534	155	26	8	12	233	104	81	75	5	48	7	6	6	22	4	.85	6	.290	.381	.436
1992	Kinston	A	6	19	4	0	0	0	4	3	1	4	0	4	0	0	0	0	0	.00	0	.211	.348	.211
	Waterloo	A	110	411	125	27	4	8	184	75	47	38	3	33	5	1	5	9	7	.56	9	.304	.366	.448
	High Desert	A	10	41	11	1	0	2	18	9	8	4	1	0	1	0	1	1	1	.50	1	.268	.340	.439
1993	Rancho Cuca	A	130	523	167	38	7	11	252	98	85	61	2	54	2	2	6	7	8	.47	12	.319	.389	.482
1994	Wichita	AA	75	255	60	15	1	5	92	26	29	21	1	44	0	2	4	1	2	.33	4	.235	.289	.361
	Rancho Cuca	A	4	13	4	0	0	0	4	2	0	3	0	2	0	0	0	1	0	.00	0	.308	.438	.308
1995	Norfolk	AAA	4	7	2	1	0	0	3	1	0	2	0	0	0	0	0	1	1	.50	0	.286	.444	.429
	Binghamton	AA	121	455	130	42	4	4	192	65	52	66	1	58	4	2	9	6	8	.43	7	.286	.375	.422
	6 Min. YEARS		638	2400	696	157	24	46	1039	401	319	297	12	266	21	13	31	58	33	.64	42	.290	.369	.433

Tim Harkrider

Bats: Both **Throws:** Right **Pos:** SS **Ht:** 6'0" **Wt:** 180 **Born:** 9/5/71 **Age:** 24

Year	Team	Lg	G	AB	H	2B	3B	HR	TB	R	RBI	TBB	IBB	SO	HBP	SH	SF	SB	CS	SB%	GDP	Avg	OBP	SLG
1993	Boise	A	3	10	4	2	0	0	6	4	1	5	0	0	0	0	0	0	0	.00	0	.400	.600	.600
	Cedar Rapds	A	54	190	48	11	0	0	59	29	14	22	0	28	1	8	0	7	4	.64	5	.253	.333	.311
1994	Midland	AA	112	409	111	20	1	1	136	69	49	64	2	51	5	17	5	13	12	.52	10	.271	.373	.333
1995	Midland	AA	124	460	134	22	4	2	170	66	39	48	3	36	2	14	4	3	5	.38	7	.291	.358	.370
	3 Min. YEARS		293	1069	297	55	5	3	371	168	103	139	5	115	8	39	9	23	21	.52	22	.278	.362	.347

Quentin Harley

Bats: Both **Throws:** Right **Pos:** 2B **Ht:** 5'11" **Wt:** 165 **Born:** 11/11/71 **Age:** 24

Year	Team	Lg	G	AB	H	2B	3B	HR	TB	R	RBI	TBB	IBB	SO	HBP	SH	SF	SB	CS	SB%	GDP	Avg	OBP	SLG
1990	Astros	R	35	109	35	6	1	0	49	19	12	23	1	11	2	0	0	17	2	.89	1	.321	.448	.394
1991	Asheville	A	114	345	82	9	2	2	101	46	21	30	0	86	10	6	4	8	8	.50	5	.238	.314	.293
1992	Burlington	A	83	279	74	12	2	1	93	33	19	23	1	65	4	6	0	13	6	.68	5	.265	.330	.333
1993	Osceola	A	121	391	89	12	8	1	120	42	51	36	2	67	8	2	6	20	13	.61	6	.228	.302	.307
1994	Rancho Cuca	A	96	333	105	17	5	8	156	74	35	55	0	45	5	4	2	19	6	.76	6	.315	.418	.468
1995	Memphis	AA	50	159	39	5	3	3	59	21	14	13	1	34	1	0	1	7	1	.88	2	.245	.305	.371
	6 Min. YEARS		499	1616	424	61	21	15	572	235	152	180	5	308	30	18	13	84	36	.70	25	.262	.345	.354

Kris Harmes

Bats: Left **Throws:** Right **Pos:** C-DH **Ht:** 6'2" **Wt:** 190 **Born:** 6/13/71 **Age:** 25

Year	Team	Lg	G	AB	H	2B	3B	HR	TB	R	RBI	TBB	IBB	SO	HBP	SH	SF	SB	CS	SB%	GDP	Avg	OBP	SLG
1990	Medicne Hat	R	50	165	43	8	1	1	56	18	18	24	1	21	1	0	0	2	4	.33	7	.261	.358	.339
	St. Cathrns	A	3	10	5	0	0	0	5	1	1	0	0	2	0	0	1	0	1	.00	0	.500	.455	.500
1991	Dunedin	A	16	44	11	3	0	0	14	4	3	9	1	7	0	3	0	2	0	1.00	0	.250	.377	.318
	St. Cathrns	A	68	230	45	16	0	6	79	31	31	37	2	38	1	7	1	6	6	.50	1	.196	.309	.343
1992	Dunedin	A	21	51	14	2	0	1	19	7	6	7	0	13	3	2	0	0	0	.00	2	.275	.373	.373
	St. Cathrns	A	66	229	56	7	0	5	78	20	25	23	2	41	0	1	3	0	4	.00	2	.245	.310	.341
	Knoxville	AA	7	23	7	1	0	0	8	2	4	1	0	1	0	0	0	0	0	.00	0	.304	.333	.348
1993	Hagerstown	A	130	482	133	29	1	14	206	68	73	69	0	86	4	2	2	3	4	.43	9	.276	.370	.427
1994	Dunedin	A	105	403	116	34	4	11	191	56	71	36	7	59	5	1	5	2	6	.25	4	.288	.350	.474
1995	Knoxville	AA	86	259	59	14	2	4	89	28	29	36	5	47	0	1	3	0	1	.00	8	.228	.319	.344
	6 Min. YEARS		552	1896	489	114	8	42	745	235	261	242	18	315	14	17	15	15	26	.37	33	.258	.344	.393

Doug Harrah

Pitches: Right **Bats:** Right **Pos:** P **Ht:** 6'0" **Wt:** 175 **Born:** 4/23/69 **Age:** 27

Year Team	Lg	G	GS	CG	GF	IP	BFP	H	R	ER	HR	SH	SF	HB	TBB	IBB	SO	WP	Bk	W	L	Pct.	ShO	Sv	ERA
1991 Pirates	R	5	1	0	0	12	49	8	4	3	0	0	0	0	6	0	10	0	2	1	2	.333	0	0	2.25
Welland	A	11	7	0	0	47	206	51	22	16	4	1	1	4	10	0	47	1	0	3	3	.500	0	0	3.06
1992 Salem	A	32	16	1	9	137.1	578	133	73	58	10	3	2	8	43	0	90	11	1	8	8	.500	0	3	3.80
1993 Carolina	AA	6	6	1	0	25.2	130	40	28	27	3	0	1	3	9	0	17	0	0	1	4	.200	0	0	9.47
Salem	A	24	19	0	1	115	500	125	61	54	14	4	6	6	26	0	85	4	3	8	5	.615	0	0	4.23
1994 Orlando	AA	55	0	0	35	80.2	332	70	38	27	4	8	4	4	18	4	43	6	1	7	4	.636	0	7	3.01
1995 Orlando	AA	44	0	0	21	69.2	296	58	21	15	6	4	1	5	34	6	49	4	0	5	2	.714	0	5	1.94
5 Min. YEARS		177	49	2	66	487.1	2091	485	247	200	41	20	15	30	146	10	341	26	7	33	28	.541	0	15	3.69

Denny Harriger

Pitches: Right **Bats:** Right **Pos:** P **Ht:** 5'11" **Wt:** 185 **Born:** 7/21/69 **Age:** 26

Year Team	Lg	G	GS	CG	GF	IP	BFP	H	R	ER	HR	SH	SF	HB	TBB	IBB	SO	WP	Bk	W	L	Pct.	ShO	Sv	ERA
1987 Kingsport	R	12	7	0	2	43.2	198	43	31	21	3	4	1	4	22	0	24	1	0	2	5	.286	0	0	4.33
1988 Kingsport	R	13	13	2	0	92.1	375	83	35	22	3	1	1	0	24	1	59	2	1	7	2	.778	1	0	2.14
1989 Pittsfield	A	3	3	1	0	21	84	20	4	4	0	2	0	1	0	0	17	0	0	2	0	1.000	1	0	1.71
St. Lucie	A	11	11	0	0	67.2	284	72	33	24	6	0	0	2	17	0	17	1	0	5	3	.625	0	0	3.19
1990 St. Lucie	A	27	7	1	9	71.2	293	73	36	28	0	0	0	1	20	0	47	2	1	5	3	.625	0	0	3.52
1991 Columbia	A	2	2	1	0	11	37	5	0	0	0	1	0	0	2	0	13	0	0	2	0	1.000	1	0	0.00
St. Lucie	A	14	11	2	1	71.1	286	67	20	18	2	4	2	1	12	0	37	1	0	6	1	.857	2	0	2.27
1992 Binghamton	AA	11	0	0	5	21.1	88	22	11	9	2	2	0	1	7	0	8	0	0	2	2	.500	0	0	3.80
St. Lucie	A	27	10	0	9	88.1	372	89	30	22	1	6	0	3	14	1	65	5	1	7	3	.700	0	3	2.24
1993 Binghamton	AA	35	24	4	4	170.2	716	174	69	56	8	6	2	7	40	0	89	9	1	13	10	.565	3	1	2.95
1994 Las Vegas	AAA	30	25	3	0	157.1	720	216	122	104	16	6	5	4	44	0	87	3	1	6	11	.353	0	0	5.95
1995 Las Vegas	AAA	29	28	7	0	177	776	187	94	80	12	6	5	4	60	2	97	4	1	9	9	.500	2	0	4.07
9 Min. YEARS		214	141	21	30	993.1	4229	1051	485	388	53	38	16	28	262	4	560	28	6	66	49	.574	10	6	3.52

Bryan Harris

Pitches: Left **Bats:** Left **Pos:** P **Ht:** 6'2" **Wt:** 205 **Born:** 9/11/71 **Age:** 24

Year Team	Lg	G	GS	CG	GF	IP	BFP	H	R	ER	HR	SH	SF	HB	TBB	IBB	SO	WP	Bk	W	L	Pct.	ShO	Sv	ERA
1993 Boise	A	16	16	1	0	105	419	80	29	22	4	1	0	8	29	1	96	5	3	8	3	.727	0	0	1.89
1994 Lk Elsinore	A	26	26	5	0	168.1	719	157	64	71	12	5	6	8	62	1	149	14	2	10	10	.500	1	0	3.80
1995 Midland	AA	39	4	0	10	78.1	359	105	50	43	9	4	3	4	32	1	60	9	2	6	5	.545	0	0	4.94
3 Min. YEARS		81	46	6	10	351.2	1497	342	173	136	25	10	9	20	123	3	305	28	7	24	18	.571	1	0	3.48

Donald Harris

Bats: Right **Throws:** Right **Pos:** OF **Ht:** 6'1" **Wt:** 185 **Born:** 11/12/67 **Age:** 28

Year Team	Lg	G	AB	H	2B	3B	HR	TB	R	RBI	TBB	IBB	SO	HBP	SH	SF	SB	CS	SB%	GDP	Avg	OBP	SLG
1989 Butte	R	65	264	75	7	8	6	116	50	37	12	0	54	6	0	3	14	4	.78	6	.284	.326	.439
1990 Tulsa	AA	64	213	34	5	1	1	44	16	15	7	0	69	3	3	0	7	3	.70	0	.160	.197	.207
Gastonia	A	58	221	46	10	0	3	65	27	13	14	0	63	2	4	0	15	8	.65	2	.208	.262	.294
1991 Tulsa	AA	130	450	102	17	8	11	168	47	53	26	1	118	7	7	2	9	6	.60	11	.227	.278	.373
1992 Tulsa	AA	83	303	77	15	2	11	129	39	39	9	1	85	7	3	1	4	3	.57	11	.254	.291	.426
1993 Okla. City	AAA	96	367	93	13	9	6	142	48	40	23	0	89	4	4	5	4	4	.50	5	.253	.301	.387
1994 Okla. City	AAA	127	478	116	14	5	16	188	59	59	26	1	107	8	3	2	6	12	.33	5	.243	.292	.393
1995 Okla. City	AAA	12	40	8	1	1	0	11	4	7	3	0	7	0	0	1	0	2	.00	2	.200	.250	.275
Bend	IND	18	81	28	4	0	7	53	19	27	7	0	14	1	0	0	1	0	.00	3	.346	.404	.654
1991 Texas	AL	18	8	3	0	0	1	6	4	2	1	0	3	0	0	0	1	0	1.00	0	.375	.444	.750
1992 Texas	AL	24	33	6	1	0	0	7	3	1	0	0	15	0	0	0	1	0	1.00	0	.182	.182	.212
1993 Texas	AL	40	76	15	2	0	1	20	10	8	5	0	18	1	3	1	0	1	.00	0	.197	.253	.263
7 Min. YEARS		653	2417	579	86	34	61	916	309	290	127	3	606	38	24	14	59	43	.58	45	.240	.287	.379
3 Maj. YEARS		82	117	24	3	0	2	33	17	11	6	0	36	1	3	1	2	1	.67	0	.205	.248	.282

Doug Harris

Pitches: Right **Bats:** Right **Pos:** P **Ht:** 6'4" **Wt:** 205 **Born:** 9/27/69 **Age:** 26

Year Team	Lg	G	GS	CG	GF	IP	BFP	H	R	ER	HR	SH	SF	HB	TBB	IBB	SO	WP	Bk	W	L	Pct.	ShO	Sv	ERA
1990 Eugene	A	15	15	0	0	69.1	309	74	46	34	5	3	2	4	28	0	46	6	2	4	5	.444	0	0	4.41
1991 Appleton	A	7	7	1	0	45	181	41	14	11	1	2	1	1	10	1	39	2	0	2	2	.500	1	0	2.20
Baseball Cy	A	19	18	3	0	116.2	466	92	38	32	3	4	3	3	27	4	84	4	1	10	6	.625	1	0	2.47
1992 Baseball Cy	A	7	7	0	0	29.1	122	25	11	7	3	0	0	2	6	0	22	2	0	0	2	.000	0	0	2.15
1993 Memphis	AA	22	12	1	4	86.2	367	99	54	45	6	3	2	3	13	0	38	3	0	3	6	.333	0	0	4.67
1994 Memphis	AA	30	13	0	9	100	449	122	70	53	8	4	10	9	28	2	43	6	0	3	9	.250	0	2	4.77
1995 Orioles	R	1	0	0	1	1	4	2	0	0	0	0	0	0	0	0	0	0	0	1	0	1.000	0	0	0.00
Bowie	AA	11	11	2	0	60.2	259	66	30	27	6	1	1	0	15	1	32	2	2	3	5	.375	0	0	4.01
6 Min. YEARS		112	83	7	14	508.2	2157	521	261	209	32	17	19	22	127	8	304	25	5	26	35	.426	2	2	3.70

Mike Harris

Bats: Left **Throws:** Left **Pos:** DH **Ht:** 5'11" **Wt:** 195 **Born:** 4/30/70 **Age:** 26

Year	Team	Lg	G	AB	H	2B	3B	HR	TB	R	RBI	TBB	IBB	SO	HBP	SH	SF	SB	CS	SB%	GDP	Avg	OBP	SLG
1991	Beloit	A	50	145	31	4	2	1	42	27	12	27	1	30	1	5	0	16	3	.84	4	.214	.341	.290
1992	Stockton	A	40	101	27	6	4	1	44	15	16	11	0	21	0	0	0	6	0	1.00	1	.267	.339	.436
1993	Stockton	A	104	363	112	17	3	9	162	64	65	63	4	56	6	8	4	19	7	.73	5	.309	.415	.446
1994	El Paso	AA	105	372	102	22	12	5	163	76	61	55	4	68	5	1	4	12	6	.67	8	.274	.372	.438
1995	New Orleans	AAA	21	56	13	3	0	0	16	3	5	4	1	9	0	0	0	1	1	.50	1	.232	.283	.286
	Beloit	A	12	41	14	1	1	0	17	8	5	4	0	5	0	0	0	7	1	.88	0	.341	.400	.415
	Brewers	R	6	23	7	2	1	0	11	5	4	2	0	7	0	0	0	0	1	.00	0	.304	.360	.478
	El Paso	AA	8	24	8	2	0	1	13	4	5	2	0	3	0	0	1	0	0	.00	0	.333	.370	.542
	5 Min. YEARS		346	1125	314	57	23	17	468	202	173	168	10	199	12	14	9	61	19	.76	19	.279	.376	.416

Pep Harris

Pitches: Right **Bats:** Right **Pos:** P **Ht:** 6'2" **Wt:** 185 **Born:** 9/23/72 **Age:** 23

Year	Team	Lg	G	GS	CG	GF	IP	BFP	H	R	ER	HR	SH	SF	HB	TBB	IBB	SO	WP	Bk	W	L	Pct.	ShO	Sv	ERA
1991	Burlington	R	13	13	0	0	65.2	292	67	30	24	7	4	2	3	31	0	47	5	0	4	3	.571	0	0	3.29
1992	Columbus	A	18	17	0	0	90.2	400	88	51	37	10	3	6	2	51	1	57	11	0	7	4	.636	0	0	3.67
1993	Columbus	A	26	17	0	4	119	510	113	67	56	7	4	1	4	44	0	82	6	0	7	8	.467	0	0	4.24
1994	Kinston	A	27	0	0	20	32.2	140	21	14	7	1	0	0	2	16	0	37	2	0	4	1	.800	0	8	1.93
	Canton-Akrn	AA	24	0	0	22	20.1	86	9	5	5	0	1	0	2	13	2	15	1	0	2	0	1.000	0	12	2.21
1995	Buffalo	AAA	14	0	0	3	32.2	141	32	11	9	2	0	0	0	15	0	18	0	0	2	1	.667	0	0	2.48
	Canton-Akrn	AA	32	7	0	20	83	346	78	34	22	4	8	4	4	23	3	40	2	2	6	3	.667	0	10	2.39
	5 Min. YEARS		154	54	0	69	444	1915	408	212	160	31	20	13	17	193	6	296	27	2	32	20	.615	0	30	3.24

Reggie Harris

Pitches: Right **Bats:** Right **Pos:** P **Ht:** 6'1" **Wt:** 190 **Born:** 8/12/68 **Age:** 27

Year	Team	Lg	G	GS	CG	GF	IP	BFP	H	R	ER	HR	SH	SF	HB	TBB	IBB	SO	WP	Bk	W	L	Pct.	ShO	Sv	ERA
1987	Elmira	A	9	8	1	0	46.2	212	50	29	26	3	1	1	6	22	0	25	3	0	2	3	.400	1	0	5.01
1988	Lynchburg	A	17	11	0	2	64	310	86	60	53	8	0	3	4	34	5	48	5	7	1	8	.111	0	0	7.45
	Elmira	A	10	10	0	0	54.1	237	56	37	32	5	1	3	2	28	0	46	1	2	3	6	.333	0	0	5.30
1989	Winter Havn	A	29	26	1	2	153.1	670	144	81	68	6	5	11	7	77	2	85	7	4	10	13	.435	0	0	3.99
1990	Huntsville	AA	5	5	0	0	29.2	131	26	12	10	3	1	1	4	16	0	34	4	0	2	2	.000	0	0	3.03
1991	Tacoma	AAA	16	15	0	0	83	380	83	55	46	11	0	4	3	58	0	72	5	0	5	4	.556	0	0	4.99
1992	Tacoma	AAA	29	28	1	0	149.2	676	141	108	95	12	3	5	6	117	0	111	20	6	6	16	.273	0	0	5.71
1993	Jacksonvlle	AA	9	8	0	1	37.2	167	33	24	20	4	1	1	3	22	0	30	3	2	1	4	.200	0	0	4.78
	Calgary	AAA	17	15	1	0	88.1	393	74	55	51	7	1	3	8	61	1	75	10	0	8	6	.571	0	0	5.20
1994	Calgary	AAA	20	18	0	0	98.2	481	137	99	89	21	0	3	8	51	1	73	5	2	6	9	.400	0	0	8.12
1995	Omaha	AAA	2	0	0	0	2	12	5	4	4	1	0	0	0	1	0	2	1	0	0	1	.000	0	0	18.00
1990	Oakland	AL	16	1	0	9	41.1	168	25	16	16	5	1	2	2	21	1	31	2	0	1	0	1.000	0	0	3.48
1991	Oakland	AL	2	0	0	1	3	15	5	4	4	0	0	1	0	3	1	2	2	0	0	0	.000	0	0	12.00
	9 Min. YEARS		163	144	4	5	807.1	3669	835	564	494	81	13	35	51	487	9	601	64	23	42	72	.368	1	0	5.51
	2 Maj. YEARS		18	1	0	10	44.1	183	30	20	20	5	1	3	2	24	2	33	4	0	1	0	1.000	0	0	4.06

Brian Harrison

Pitches: Right **Bats:** Right **Pos:** P **Ht:** 6'1" **Wt:** 175 **Born:** 12/18/68 **Age:** 27

Year	Team	Lg	G	GS	CG	GF	IP	BFP	H	R	ER	HR	SH	SF	HB	TBB	IBB	SO	WP	Bk	W	L	Pct.	ShO	Sv	ERA
1992	Appleton	A	16	15	1	0	98.2	419	114	47	40	5	1	5	1	16	0	54	2	1	5	6	.455	0	0	3.65
1993	Wilmington	A	26	26	1	0	173	707	168	76	63	16	7	6	2	38	0	98	6	1	13	6	.684	1	0	3.28
1994	Memphis	AA	28	28	1	0	172	717	180	87	69	11	5	9	5	31	0	94	2	0	9	10	.474	0	0	3.61
1995	Omaha	AAA	16	8	1	1	54.1	248	76	39	37	7	3	3	1	10	0	12	1	0	4	2	.667	0	0	6.13
	Wichita	AA	15	0	0	5	26.2	120	35	18	14	1	1	1	1	7	1	11	0	0	1	1	.500	0	2	4.73
	4 Min. YEARS		101	77	4	6	524.2	2211	573	267	223	40	17	24	10	102	1	269	11	2	32	25	.561	1	2	3.83

Brian Harrison

Pitches: Left **Bats:** Left **Pos:** P **Ht:** 6'1" **Wt:** 190 **Born:** 11/26/66 **Age:** 29

Year	Team	Lg	G	GS	CG	GF	IP	BFP	H	R	ER	HR	SH	SF	HB	TBB	IBB	SO	WP	Bk	W	L	Pct.	ShO	Sv	ERA
1986	Spokane	A	8	0	0	2	19.1	0	19	16	11	1	0	0	1	23	0	14	5	1	1	1	.500	0	0	5.12
	Tri-City	A	14	2	0	9	41.2	0	47	40	31	4	0	0	2	37	1	50	6	2	2	4	.333	0	2	6.70
1987	Charlstn-Sc	A	37	3	0	11	72.2	316	64	31	22	4	4	4	4	30	2	87	5	1	4	0	1.000	0	4	2.72
	Reno	A	1	1	0	0	3.2	22	6	5	3	0	0	0	0	5	0	2	0	0	0	0	.000	0	0	7.36
1988	Riverside	A	21	20	0	0	101.1	450	92	61	47	2	7	3	5	60	0	95	6	4	5	8	.385	0	0	4.17
1989	Riverside	A	42	2	0	28	71	323	69	42	33	3	4	1	4	43	4	81	9	1	2	7	.222	0	10	4.18
1990	Riverside	A	37	0	0	35	45.1	189	31	9	6	0	3	0	1	20	3	55	2	0	5	2	.714	0	18	1.19
1994	San Bernrdo	A	23	1	0	8	58.1	258	61	28	25	5	5	2	2	29	1	65	4	0	5	1	.833	0	3	3.86
1995	Memphis	AA	38	0	0	7	36	170	32	21	13	0	1	0	4	33	2	29	4	0	2	1	.667	0	0	3.25
	7 Min. YEARS		221	32	0	100	449.1	1728	421	253	191	19	24	10	23	280	13	478	41	9	26	24	.520	0	37	3.83

Tom Harrison

Pitches: Right Bats: Right Pos: P Ht: 6'2" Wt: 185 Born: 9/30/71 Age: 24

Year Team	Lg	G	GS	CG	GF	IP	BFP	H	R	ER	HR	SH	SF	HB	TBB	IBB	SO	WP	Bk	W	L	Pct.	ShO	Sv	ERA
1995 Durham	A	7	6	0	0	37.2	145	22	5	4	1	0	0	1	13	1	25	0	0	3	1	.750	0	0	0.96
Greenville	AA	14	14	1	0	88.1	370	87	50	43	9	7	1	2	27	3	57	5	0	6	4	.600	0	0	4.38
Richmond	AAA	9	6	0	1	42	182	34	17	15	2	4	3	2	20	1	16	0	1	2	1	.667	0	1	3.21
1 Min. YEARS		30	26	1	1	168	697	143	72	62	12	11	4	5	60	5	98	5	1	11	6	.647	0	1	3.32

Chris Hart

Bats: Right Throws: Right Pos: OF Ht: 6'0" Wt: 190 Born: 5/2/69 Age: 27

Year Team	Lg	G	AB	H	2B	3B	HR	TB	R	RBI	TBB	IBB	SO	HBP	SH	SF	SB	CS	SB%	GDP	Avg	OBP	SLG
1990 Sou. Oregon	A	67	239	63	14	2	6	99	50	32	37	0	85	11	1	3	15	3	.83	7	.264	.383	.414
1991 Sou. Oregon	A	9	21	3	1	0	0	4	3	1	1	0	5	1	0	0	0	0	.00	0	.143	.217	.190
Modesto	A	37	88	22	4	0	0	26	9	13	8	0	22	3	0	2	2	2	.50	2	.250	.327	.295
1992 Modesto	A	120	450	128	20	3	13	193	76	86	35	4	135	18	0	2	15	9	.63	14	.284	.358	.429
1993 Huntsville	AA	103	301	77	7	3	6	108	39	42	10	0	82	11	5	1	12	9	.57	5	.256	.303	.359
1994 Huntsville	AA	117	365	85	13	5	9	135	45	52	23	0	101	11	7	4	7	7	.50	7	.233	.295	.370
1995 Huntsville	AA	36	103	27	3	2	2	40	11	20	10	1	30	2	3	2	1	3	.25	1	.262	.333	.388
6 Min. YEARS		489	1567	405	62	15	36	605	233	246	124	5	460	57	16	14	52	33	.61	36	.258	.333	.386

Jason Hart

Pitches: Right Bats: Right Pos: P Ht: 6'0" Wt: 195 Born: 11/14/71 Age: 24

Year Team	Lg	G	GS	CG	GF	IP	BFP	H	R	ER	HR	SH	SF	HB	TBB	IBB	SO	WP	Bk	W	L	Pct.	ShO	Sv	ERA
1994 Peoria	A	20	0	0	10	37.1	149	29	17	15	4	1	1	0	7	0	33	3	0	4	2	.667	0	3	3.62
Daytona	A	26	0	0	23	37.1	150	26	11	7	1	0	2	2	6	0	39	3	0	3	3	.500	0	12	1.69
1995 Daytona	A	37	0	0	34	40.2	172	29	15	10	2	2	0	1	18	2	50	0	0	0	3	.000	0	24	2.21
Orlando	AA	14	0	0	10	17	69	14	5	4	0	1	3	1	4	0	20	1	0	0	1	.000	0	3	2.12
2 Min. YEARS		97	0	0	77	132.1	540	98	48	36	7	4	6	4	35	2	142	7	0	7	9	.438	0	42	2.45

Andy Hartung

Bats: Right Throws: Right Pos: 3B Ht: 6'1" Wt: 205 Born: 2/12/69 Age: 27

Year Team	Lg	G	AB	H	2B	3B	HR	TB	R	RBI	TBB	IBB	SO	HBP	SH	SF	SB	CS	SB%	GDP	Avg	OBP	SLG
1990 Geneva	A	74	263	87	19	2	11	143	48	70	45	3	55	6	1	3	1	1	.50	9	.331	.435	.544
1991 Peoria	A	28	101	22	3	2	1	32	9	11	8	0	16	2	0	0	0	1	.00	4	.218	.288	.317
Winston-Sal	A	53	159	44	3	0	7	68	20	22	17	0	43	4	2	1	0	2	.00	4	.277	.359	.428
1992 Winston-Sal	A	132	496	138	25	4	23	240	76	94	47	1	91	8	2	5	10	5	.67	9	.278	.347	.484
Charlotte	AA	2	9	3	1	0	1	7	1	3	0	0	1	0	0	0	0	0	.00	0	.333	.333	.778
1993 Daytona	A	44	173	51	10	1	4	75	24	32	23	0	33	0	0	0	1	1	.50	4	.295	.378	.434
1994 Daytona	A	32	110	21	5	0	3	35	14	15	18	0	19	0	1	1	3	0	1.00	4	.191	.302	.318
Duluth-Sup.	IND	60	225	61	14	2	8	103	34	35	28	1	47	1	0	3	5	0	1.00	8	.271	.350	.458
1995 New Haven	AA	12	31	3	2	0	0	5	4	0	2	0	7	0	0	0	1	0	1.00	0	.097	.152	.161
Winnipeg	IND	40	137	37	7	1	3	55	22	21	31	0	25	1	0	2	1	1	.50	1	.270	.404	.401
Lubbock	IND	34	110	29	7	0	3	45	12	19	17	0	14	0	2	3	1	0	.00	3	.264	.354	.409
6 Min. YEARS		511	1814	496	96	12	64	808	264	322	236	5	351	22	8	18	22	12	.65	46	.273	.361	.445

Raymond Harvey

Bats: Left Throws: Left Pos: DH-OF Ht: 6'1" Wt: 185 Born: 1/1/69 Age: 27

Year Team	Lg	G	AB	H	2B	3B	HR	TB	R	RBI	TBB	IBB	SO	HBP	SH	SF	SB	CS	SB%	GDP	Avg	OBP	SLG
1991 Columbus	A	129	443	124	22	7	10	190	75	80	71	6	66	10	2	9	7	4	.64	12	.280	.385	.429
1992 Kinston	A	97	331	94	18	0	2	118	35	45	36	4	43	4	1	2	2	1	.67	6	.284	.359	.356
1993 Canton-Akrn	AA	14	41	10	1	0	0	11	5	4	7	0	5	1	3	1	0	1	.00	1	.244	.360	.268
Kinston	A	88	335	95	19	2	3	127	36	39	28	1	43	3	3	1	3	6	.33	8	.284	.343	.379
1994 Canton-Akrn	AA	137	508	149	24	5	6	201	66	72	61	6	88	5	2	3	1	5	.17	14	.293	.373	.396
1995 Canton-Akrn	AA	122	444	115	20	1	3	146	52	32	43	1	75	3	7	2	1	4	.20	6	.259	.327	.329
5 Min. YEARS		587	2102	587	104	15	24	793	269	272	246	18	320	26	18	18	14	21	.40	47	.279	.359	.377

Chris Hatcher

Bats: Right Throws: Right Pos: 1B Ht: 6'3" Wt: 220 Born: 1/7/69 Age: 27

Year Team	Lg	G	AB	H	2B	3B	HR	TB	R	RBI	TBB	IBB	SO	HBP	SH	SF	SB	CS	SB%	GDP	Avg	OBP	SLG
1990 Auburn	A	72	259	64	10	0	9	101	37	45	27	3	86	5	0	5	8	2	.80	4	.247	.324	.390
1991 Burlington	A	129	497	117	23	6	13	191	69	65	46	4	180	9	0	4	10	5	.67	6	.235	.309	.384
1992 Osceola	A	97	367	103	19	6	17	185	49	68	20	1	97	5	0	5	11	0	1.00	5	.281	.322	.504
1993 Jackson	AA	101	367	95	15	3	15	161	45	64	11	0	104	11	0	3	5	8	.38	8	.259	.298	.439
1994 Tucson	AAA	108	349	104	28	4	12	176	55	73	19	0	90	4	0	6	5	1	.83	6	.298	.336	.504
1995 Jackson	AA	11	39	12	1	0	1	16	5	3	4	0	6	1	0	1	0	2	.00	3	.308	.378	.410
Tucson	AAA	94	290	83	19	2	14	148	59	50	42	2	107	4	1	2	7	3	.70	9	.286	.382	.510
6 Min. YEARS		612	2168	578	115	21	81	978	319	368	169	10	670	39	1	26	46	21	.69	39	.267	.327	.451

Hilly Hathaway

Pitches: Left **Bats:** Left **Pos:** P **Ht:** 6' 4" **Wt:** 195 **Born:** 9/12/69 **Age:** 26

Year Team	Lg	G	GS	CG	GF	IP	BFP	H	R	ER	HR	SH	SF	HB	TBB	IBB	SO	WP	Bk	W	L	Pct.	ShO	Sv	ERA
1990 Boise	A	15	15	0	0	86.1	337	57	18	14	1	1	3	2	25	0	113	7	5	8	2	.800	0	0	1.46
1991 Quad City	A	20	20	1	0	129	545	126	58	48	5	4	1	7	41	1	110	11	3	9	6	.600	0	0	3.35
1992 Palm Spring	A	3	3	2	0	24	98	25	5	4	1	0	0	0	3	0	17	0	0	2	1	.667	1	0	1.50
Midland	AA	14	14	1	0	95.1	378	90	39	34	2	1	1	8	10	0	69	2	2	7	2	.778	0	0	3.21
1993 Vancouver	AAA	12	12	0	0	70.1	291	60	38	32	5	1	2	2	27	0	44	4	1	7	0	1.000	0	0	4.09
1994 Las Vegas	AAA	26	15	0	1	95	453	121	82	66	15	2	5	5	48	0	68	6	2	2	9	.182	0	0	6.25
1995 Rancho Cuca	A	3	3	0	0	13	52	11	6	5	0	0	0	2	4	1	10	0	0	0	1	.000	0	0	3.46
Las Vegas	AAA	14	14	1	0	63.2	285	76	49	44	4	4	3	1	27	0	37	6	0	4	6	.400	0	0	6.22
1992 California	AL	2	1	0	0	5.2	29	8	5	5	1	1	1	0	3	0	1	0	0	0	0	.000	0	0	7.94
1993 California	AL	11	11	0	0	57.1	253	71	35	32	6	1	3	5	26	1	11	5	1	4	3	.571	0	0	5.02
6 Min. YEARS		107	96	5	1	576.2	2439	566	295	247	33	13	15	27	185	2	468	36	13	39	27	.591	1	0	3.85
2 Maj. YEARS		13	12	0	0	63	282	79	40	37	7	2	4	5	29	1	12	5	1	4	3	.571	0	0	5.29

Gary Haught

Pitches: Right **Bats:** Both **Pos:** P **Ht:** 6'1" **Wt:** 180 **Born:** 9/29/70 **Age:** 25

Year Team	Lg	G	GS	CG	GF	IP	BFP	H	R	ER	HR	SH	SF	HB	TBB	IBB	SO	WP	Bk	W	L	Pct.	ShO	Sv	ERA
1992 Sou. Oregon	A	19	4	0	9	68.1	266	58	18	15	3	1	1	2	14	0	69	1	2	8	2	.800	0	2	1.98
1993 Madison	A	17	12	2	1	83.2	333	62	27	24	8	3	1	2	29	2	75	1	2	7	1	.875	0	0	2.58
Modesto	A	12	0	0	4	23	106	25	14	13	3	0	2	1	17	2	15	0	0	1	1	.000	0	0	5.09
1994 Modesto	A	39	1	0	13	70.2	292	66	35	34	8	6	1	2	26	0	52	2	0	4	3	.571	0	2	4.33
1995 Modesto	A	34	4	0	6	86.2	355	76	29	25	10	10	0	6	24	1	81	0	0	9	5	.643	0	4	2.60
Huntsville	AA	9	3	0	3	23	97	23	14	11	4	1	0	1	8	1	20	0	0	1	1	.500	0	0	4.30
4 Min. YEARS		130	24	2	36	355.1	1449	310	137	122	36	21	5	14	118	6	312	4	4	29	13	.690	0	8	3.09

Ryan Hawblitzel

Pitches: Right **Bats:** Right **Pos:** P **Ht:** 6'2" **Wt:** 170 **Born:** 4/30/71 **Age:** 25

Year Team	Lg	G	GS	CG	GF	IP	BFP	H	R	ER	HR	SH	SF	HB	TBB	IBB	SO	WP	Bk	W	L	Pct.	ShO	Sv	ERA
1990 Huntington	R	14	14	2	0	75.2	322	72	38	33	8	0	0	6	25	0	71	2	0	6	5	.545	1	0	3.93
1991 Winston-Sal	A	20	20	5	0	134	552	110	40	34	7	5	7	7	47	0	103	8	1	15	2	.882	2	0	2.28
Charlotte	AA	5	5	1	0	33.2	141	31	14	12	2	5	2	3	12	3	25	0	0	1	2	.333	1	0	3.21
1992 Charlotte	AA	28	28	3	0	174.2	727	180	84	73	18	5	5	4	38	3	119	8	0	12	8	.600	1	0	3.76
1993 Colo. Sprng	AAA	29	28	0	0	165.1	764	221	129	113	16	10	9	4	49	0	90	3	0	8	13	.381	0	0	6.15
1994 Colo. Sprng	AAA	28	28	0	0	163	732	200	119	111	21	6	2	10	53	2	103	5	0	10	10	.500	1	0	6.13
1995 Colo. Sprng	AAA	21	14	0	1	83	352	88	47	42	7	3	5	3	17	1	40	2	0	5	3	.625	0	0	4.55
6 Min. YEARS		145	137	16	1	829.1	3590	902	471	418	79	34	30	37	241	9	551	28	1	57	43	.570	6	0	4.54

Kraig Hawkins

Bats: Both **Throws:** Right **Pos:** OF **Ht:** 6'2" **Wt:** 170 **Born:** 12/4/71 **Age:** 24

Year Team	Lg	G	AB	H	2B	3B	HR	TB	R	RBI	TBB	IBB	SO	HBP	SH	SF	SB	CS	SB%	GDP	Avg	OBP	SLG
1992 Oneonta	A	70	227	50	1	0	0	51	24	18	26	0	67	1	7	0	14	5	.74	1	.220	.303	.225
1993 Greensboro	A	131	418	106	13	1	0	121	66	45	67	1	112	1	9	3	67	18	.79	8	.254	.356	.289
1994 Tampa	A	108	437	104	7	1	0	113	72	29	61	0	105	2	3	0	37	19	.66	6	.238	.334	.259
1995 Norwich	AA	12	45	10	0	0	0	10	5	3	7	0	11	0	2	0	7	2	.78	0	.222	.327	.222
Tampa	A	111	432	105	9	3	1	123	56	19	66	0	95	2	11	1	28	14	.67	6	.243	.345	.285
4 Min. YEARS		432	1559	375	30	5	1	418	223	114	227	1	390	6	32	4	153	58	.73	21	.241	.339	.268

Dave Hayden

Bats: Right **Throws:** Right **Pos:** 3B **Ht:** 5'11" **Wt:** 170 **Born:** 12/1/69 **Age:** 26

Year Team	Lg	G	AB	H	2B	3B	HR	TB	R	RBI	TBB	IBB	SO	HBP	SH	SF	SB	CS	SB%	GDP	Avg	OBP	SLG
1991 Batavia	A	50	158	35	2	0	0	37	16	9	13	0	24	3	2	0	3	1	.75	5	.222	.293	.234
1992 Spartanburg	A	125	394	88	11	2	0	103	46	29	35	1	66	3	9	3	7	1	.88	8	.223	.290	.261
1993 Clearwater	A	97	290	90	13	0	0	103	42	27	39	1	38	6	1	2	8	9	.47	5	.310	.401	.355
1994 Reading	AA	87	234	59	9	1	4	82	27	24	27	1	56	1	3	1	3	1	.75	4	.252	.331	.350
1995 Reading	AA	68	192	45	6	0	3	60	22	11	26	3	39	1	0	2	0	3	.00	6	.234	.326	.313
Scranton-Wb	AAA	20	41	12	1	0	2	19	6	3	6	0	13	0	0	0	2	0	.00	1	.293	.383	.463
5 Min. YEARS		447	1309	329	42	3	9	404	159	103	146	6	236	14	15	8	21	17	.55	29	.251	.331	.309

Heath Haynes

Pitches: Right **Bats:** Right **Pos:** P **Ht:** 6' 0" **Wt:** 175 **Born:** 11/30/68 **Age:** 27

Year Team	Lg	G	GS	CG	GF	IP	BFP	H	R	ER	HR	SH	SF	HB	TBB	IBB	SO	WP	Bk	W	L	Pct.	ShO	Sv	ERA
1991 Jamestown	A	29	0	0	23	56.1	221	31	15	13	3	5	1	4	18	4	93	4	3	10	1	.909	0	11	2.08
1992 Rockford	A	45	0	0	36	57	239	49	19	12	0	4	1	4	15	3	78	1	3	3	1	.750	0	15	1.89
Harrisburg	AA	3	0	0	1	4.2	17	2	1	1	1	0	0	0	1	0	6	0	0	2	0	1.000	0	0	1.93
1993 Harrisburg	AA	57	0	0	22	66	270	46	27	19	2	5	3	2	19	4	78	4	2	8	0	1.000	0	5	2.59
1994 Ottawa	AAA	56	0	0	25	87	350	72	32	23	7	7	2	1	15	7	75	3	0	6	7	.462	0	4	2.38

Year	Team	Lg	G	GS	CG	GF	IP	BFP	H	R	ER	HR	SH	SF	HB	TBB	IBB	SO	WP	Bk	W	L	Pct.	ShO	Sv	ERA
1995	Edmonton	AAA	12	0	0	1	18.2	87	21	14	13	1	0	3	0	11	3	13	2	0	2	0	1.000	0	0	6.27
1994	Montreal	NL	4	0	0	2	3.2	17	3	1	0	0	0	1	0	3	0	1	0	0	0	0	.000	0	0	0.00
	5 Min. YEARS		202	0	0	108	289.2	1184	221	108	81	14	21	10	11	79	21	343	14	8	31	9	.775	0	35	2.52

Steve Hazlett

Bats: Right **Throws:** Right **Pos:** OF **Ht:** 5'11" **Wt:** 170 **Born:** 3/30/70 **Age:** 26

					BATTING												BASERUNNING				PERCENTAGES		
Year	Team	Lg	G	AB	H	2B	3B	HR	TB	R	RBI	TBB	IBB	SO	HBP	SH	SF	SB	CS	SB%	GDP	Avg	OBP	SLG
1991	Elizabethtn	R	64	210	42	11	0	4	65	50	24	63	0	53	6	1	1	13	7	.65	0	.200	.396	.310
1992	Kenosha	A	107	362	96	23	4	6	145	68	32	52	0	77	7	2	4	20	9	.69	5	.265	.365	.401
1993	Fort Myers	A	29	115	39	5	2	0	48	19	6	15	1	21	1	2	0	12	5	.71	0	.339	.420	.417
1994	Nashville	AA	123	457	134	31	1	14	209	63	54	37	1	99	8	6	3	9	3	.75	3	.293	.354	.457
1995	Salt Lake	AAA	127	427	128	25	6	4	177	71	49	41	1	65	4	2	3	8	10	.44	9	.300	.364	.415
	5 Min. YEARS		450	1571	439	95	13	28	644	271	165	208	3	315	26	13	11	62	34	.65	17	.279	.371	.410

Kurt Heble

Pitches: Right **Bats:** Right **Pos:** P **Ht:** 6'3" **Wt:** 205 **Born:** 2/9/69 **Age:** 27

			HOW MUCH HE PITCHED						WHAT HE GAVE UP											THE RESULTS					
Year	Team	Lg	G	GS	CG	GF	IP	BFP	H	R	ER	HR	SH	SF	HB	TBB	IBB	SO	WP	Bk	W	L	Pct.	ShO	Sv	ERA
1991	St. Cathrns	A	18	0	0	17	27	115	23	10	3	0	3	0	1	9	1	25	1	0	4	4	.500	0	3	1.00
1992	Myrtle Bch	A	8	0	0	5	9.2	42	7	5	4	0	0	1	0	7	0	13	3	0	0	0	.000	0	1	3.72
1993	Dunedin	A	41	0	0	21	50.2	217	35	16	14	1	2	1	3	34	1	66	4	1	6	1	.857	0	4	2.49
	Knoxville	AA	6	0	0	2	9.2	44	12	5	4	1	0	1	1	4	0	13	1	0	0	1	.000	0	0	3.72
1994	Knoxville	AA	46	1	0	20	71	339	77	46	38	8	2	5	2	48	2	63	5	0	5	3	.625	0	2	4.82
1995	Syracuse	AAA	4	0	0	1	4.2	23	6	4	3	0	0	0	0	2	0	5	1	0	0	0	.000	0	0	5.79
	Knoxville	AA	47	0	0	25	52.1	231	52	36	35	7	0	1	1	24	0	44	6	1	3	7	.300	0	6	6.02
	5 Min. YEARS		170	1	0	91	225	1011	212	122	101	17	7	9	8	128	4	229	21	2	18	16	.529	0	16	4.04

Steve Hecht

Bats: Left **Throws:** Right **Pos:** 2B-OF **Ht:** 5'9" **Wt:** 165 **Born:** 11/12/65 **Age:** 30

					BATTING												BASERUNNING				PERCENTAGES		
Year	Team	Lg	G	AB	H	2B	3B	HR	TB	R	RBI	TBB	IBB	SO	HBP	SH	SF	SB	CS	SB%	GDP	Avg	OBP	SLG
1988	Everett	A	13	44	7	1	0	0	8	8	4	6	0	7	0	0	0	7	3	.70	1	.159	.260	.182
	Fresno	A	52	204	52	7	1	1	64	40	12	25	0	32	0	0	0	42	14	.75	3	.255	.336	.314
1989	Phoenix	AAA	3	9	4	1	0	0	5	3	0	1	0	0	0	0	0	2	1	.67	0	.444	.500	.556
	San Jose	A	127	501	133	17	8	3	175	83	43	52	3	57	4	1	3	56	25	.69	5	.265	.338	.349
1990	Shreveport	AA	64	200	60	12	7	2	92	37	27	12	2	15	2	0	1	12	5	.71	0	.300	.344	.460
	Indianapols	AAA	58	197	50	12	2	2	72	21	13	7	1	32	0	2	0	11	5	.69	0	.254	.279	.365
1991	Indianapols	AAA	89	210	51	8	2	4	75	34	26	12	0	51	0	6	1	9	2	.82	2	.243	.283	.357
1992	Harrisburg	AA	100	269	69	13	5	1	95	46	17	31	0	35	5	8	0	17	7	.71	1	.257	.344	.353
1993	Shreveport	AA	49	168	50	8	6	3	79	25	11	11	1	25	1	1	0	5	3	.63	2	.298	.344	.470
	Phoenix	AAA	48	169	53	8	1	2	69	27	20	20	0	23	0	1	2	9	1	.90	2	.314	.382	.408
1994	Shreveport	AA	14	31	7	1	1	0	10	9	3	6	0	2	0	0	0	3	0	1.00	0	.226	.351	.323
	Phoenix	AAA	98	332	106	17	9	10	171	66	44	26	2	52	5	3	1	18	5	.78	4	.319	.376	.515
1995	Toledo	AAA	25	72	17	5	1	0	24	14	6	7	0	6	2	1	2	5	0	1.00	1	.236	.313	.333
	Okla. City	AAA	67	238	62	6	3	3	83	26	14	16	3	45	3	3	1	9	5	.64	1	.261	.314	.349
	8 Min. YEARS		807	2644	721	116	46	31	1022	439	240	232	12	382	22	26	11	205	76	.73	21	.273	.335	.387

Doug Hecker

Bats: Right **Throws:** Right **Pos:** 1B **Ht:** 6'4" **Wt:** 210 **Born:** 1/21/71 **Age:** 25

					BATTING												BASERUNNING				PERCENTAGES		
Year	Team	Lg	G	AB	H	2B	3B	HR	TB	R	RBI	TBB	IBB	SO	HBP	SH	SF	SB	CS	SB%	GDP	Avg	OBP	SLG
1992	Red Sox	R	8	28	6	1	0	0	7	1	1	5	0	3	0	0	0	0	0	.00	1	.214	.333	.250
	Winter Havn	A	59	209	50	12	0	6	80	22	32	18	0	47	3	2	1	0	0	.00	5	.239	.307	.383
1993	Lynchburg	A	127	490	116	23	3	21	208	57	73	36	0	149	6	0	2	0	0	.00	9	.237	.296	.424
1994	Sarasota	A	115	431	119	28	1	13	188	53	70	29	4	95	8	0	4	2	2	.50	8	.276	.331	.436
1995	Trenton	AA	61	221	45	16	0	5	76	20	32	18	2	43	2	4	3	2	0	1.00	8	.204	.266	.344
	Visalia	A	8	14	1	0	0	0	1	2	0	3	0	5	0	0	0	0	1	.00	0	.071	.235	.071
	Red Sox	R	2	0	0	0	0	0	0	0	0	0	0	0	0	0	0	0	0	.00	0	.000	.000	.000
	Sarasota	A	10	0	0	0	0	0	0	0	0	0	0	0	0	0	0	0	0	.00	0	.000	.000	.000
	4 Min. YEARS		390	1393	337	80	4	45	560	155	208	109	6	342	19	6	10	4	3	.57	31	.242	.304	.402

Bert Heffernan

Bats: Left **Throws:** Right **Pos:** C **Ht:** 5'10" **Wt:** 185 **Born:** 3/3/65 **Age:** 31

					BATTING												BASERUNNING				PERCENTAGES		
Year	Team	Lg	G	AB	H	2B	3B	HR	TB	R	RBI	TBB	IBB	SO	HBP	SH	SF	SB	CS	SB%	GDP	Avg	OBP	SLG
1988	Beloit	A	5	14	3	0	0	0	3	1	0	5	0	0	0	0	0	0	0	.00	1	.214	.421	.214
	Helena	R	65	196	55	13	0	4	80	47	31	61	1	40	0	2	4	14	5	.74	2	.281	.444	.408
1989	Beloit	A	127	425	126	20	1	4	160	53	59	70	1	57	4	3	4	9	8	.53	7	.296	.398	.376
1990	El Paso	AA	110	390	109	18	2	1	134	49	42	60	4	68	1	7	3	6	3	.67	16	.279	.374	.344
1991	Albuquerque	AAA	67	161	39	10	1	0	51	17	13	22	1	19	0	3	2	1	3	.25	7	.242	.330	.317
1992	Calgary	AAA	15	46	14	2	0	1	19	8	4	7	0	7	0	0	0	1	1	.50	1	.304	.396	.413
	Jacksonville	AA	58	196	56	9	0	2	71	16	23	29	0	28	2	2	2	4	7	.36	5	.286	.380	.362
1993	Shreveport	AA	33	98	23	2	0	0	25	8	7	10	1	14	3	0	1	1	1	.50	4	.235	.321	.255
	Phoenix	AAA	16	49	14	1	0	0	17	7	6	9	1	11	0	1	0	2	2	.50	0	.286	.397	.347

	Lg	G	AB	H	2B	3B	HR	TB	R	RBI	TBB	IBB	SO	HBP	SH	SF	SB	CS	SB%	GDP	Avg	OBP	SLG
Giants	R	7	25	8	0	0	0	8	3	4	6	1	2	0	0	0	2	1	.67	0	.320	.452	.320
1995 Ottawa	AAA	36	102	22	5	0	1	30	13	12	7	0	13	2	3	1	1	0	1.00	3	.216	.277	.294
1992 Seattle	AL	8	11	1	1	0	0	2	0	0	0	0	1	0	0	0	0	0	.00	1	.091	.091	.182
7 Min. YEARS		539	1702	469	80	5	13	598	222	201	286	13	259	12	21	17	41	31	.57	46	.276	.380	.351

Bronson Heflin

Pitches: Right Bats: Right Pos: P   Ht: 6'3" Wt: 195 Born: 8/29/71 Age: 24

		HOW MUCH HE PITCHED						WHAT HE GAVE UP										THE RESULTS					
Year Team	Lg	G	GS	CG	GF	IP	BFP	H	R	ER	HR	SH	SF	HB	TBB	IBB	SO	WP	Bk	W	L	Pct.	ShO	Sv	ERA
1994 Batavia	A	14	13	1	0	83	353	85	38	33	5	5	0	6	20	0	71	11	2	6	5	.545	0	0	3.58
1995 Clearwater	A	57	0	0	44	61	256	52	25	20	3	6	1	0	21	5	84	4	0	2	3	.400	0	21	2.95
Reading	AA	1	0	0	1	1	4	0	0	0	0	0	0	0	1	0	2	0	0	0	0	.000	0	0	0.00
2 Min. YEARS		72	13	1	45	145	613	137	63	53	8	11	1	6	42	5	157	15	2	8	8	.500	0	21	3.29

Dan Held

Bats: Right Throws: Right Pos: 1B   Ht: 6'0" Wt: 200 Born: 10/7/70 Age: 25

		BATTING															BASERUNNING				PERCENTAGES		
Year Team	Lg	G	AB	H	2B	3B	HR	TB	R	RBI	TBB	IBB	SO	HBP	SH	SF	SB	CS	SB%	GDP	Avg	OBP	SLG
1993 Batavia	A	45	151	31	8	1	3	50	18	16	16	0	40	6	1	2	3	.40	3	.205	.303	.331
1994 Spartanburg	A	130	484	123	32	1	18	211	69	69	52	2	119	9	1	11	2	0	1.00	11	.254	.331	.436
1995 Clearwater	A	134	489	133	35	1	21	233	82	82	56	1	127	19	1	4	2	1	.67	13	.272	.366	.476
Reading	AA	2	4	2	1	0	1	6	2	3	2	0	1	0	0	0	1	0	1.00	0	.500	.667	1.500
3 Min. YEARS		311	1128	289	76	3	43	500	171	170	126	3	287	34	3	17	7	4	.64	27	.256	.344	.443

Chris Henderson

Pitches: Right Bats: Right Pos: P   Ht: 6'2" Wt: 205 Born: 12/15/71 Age: 24

		HOW MUCH HE PITCHED						WHAT HE GAVE UP										THE RESULTS					
Year Team	Lg	G	GS	CG	GF	IP	BFP	H	R	ER	HR	SH	SF	HB	TBB	IBB	SO	WP	Bk	W	L	Pct.	ShO	Sv	ERA
1992 Bend	A	12	11	0	0	47.2	238	49	47	41	3	3	3	5	48	0	28	11	2	2	6	.250	0	0	7.74
1993 Bend	A	27	0	0	20	42	178	34	14	11	2	4	0	1	16	1	38	6	0	4	3	.571	0	8	2.36
1994 Central Val	A	51	4	0	26	73	340	72	47	44	6	2	4	0	50	3	72	15	0	5	3	.625	0	7	5.42
1995 New Haven	AA	3	0	0	3	4	15	1	0	0	0	1	0	0	2	0	2	1	0	0	0	.000	0	0	0.00
Asheville	A	17	0	0	10	27.2	119	20	6	5	1	0	1	4	18	0	28	4	0	1	1	.500	0	1	1.63
4 Min. YEARS		110	15	0	59	194.1	890	176	114	101	12	10	8	10	134	4	168	37	2	12	13	.480	0	16	4.68

Rodney Henderson

Pitches: Right Bats: Right Pos: P   Ht: 6'4" Wt: 193 Born: 3/11/71 Age: 25

		HOW MUCH HE PITCHED						WHAT HE GAVE UP										THE RESULTS					
Year Team	Lg	G	GS	CG	GF	IP	BFP	H	R	ER	HR	SH	SF	HB	TBB	IBB	SO	WP	Bk	W	L	Pct.	ShO	Sv	ERA
1992 Jamestown	A	1	1	0	0	3	13	2	3	2	0	0	0	0	5	0	2	0	0	0	0	.000	0	0	6.00
1993 W. Palm Bch	A	22	22	1	0	143	580	110	50	46	3	4	5	6	44	0	127	8	6	12	7	.632	1	0	2.90
Harrisburg	AA	5	5	0	0	29.2	125	20	10	6	0	1	0	0	15	0	25	2	1	5	0	1.000	0	0	1.82
1994 Harrisburg	AA	2	2	0	0	12	44	5	2	2	1	0	0	0	4	0	16	0	0	2	0	1.000	0	0	1.50
Ottawa	AAA	23	21	0	1	122.2	545	123	67	63	16	2	5	2	67	3	100	1	0	6	9	.400	0	1	4.62
1995 Harrisburg	AA	12	12	0	0	56.1	240	51	28	27	4	0	1	5	18	0	53	1	0	3	6	.333	0	0	4.31
1994 Montreal	NL	3	2	0	0	6.2	37	9	9	7	1	3	0	0	7	0	3	0	0	0	1	.000	0	0	9.45
4 Min. YEARS		65	63	1	1	366.2	1547	311	160	146	24	7	11	13	153	3	323	12	7	28	22	.560	1	1	3.58

Jon Henry

Pitches: Right Bats: Right Pos: P   Ht: 6'5" Wt: 215 Born: 8/1/68 Age: 27

		HOW MUCH HE PITCHED						WHAT HE GAVE UP										THE RESULTS					
Year Team	Lg	G	GS	CG	GF	IP	BFP	H	R	ER	HR	SH	SF	HB	TBB	IBB	SO	WP	Bk	W	L	Pct.	ShO	Sv	ERA
1990 Elizabethtn	R	14	13	1	1	87.1	365	82	40	35	11	0	2	7	28	0	89	1	3	7	2	.778	0	0	3.61
1991 Visalia	A	28	28	4	0	172.2	755	174	103	86	13	6	11	12	60	2	110	11	2	8	13	.381	0	0	4.48
1992 Orlando	AA	28	22	1	5	135.1	576	147	77	62	10	1	6	8	28	0	87	8	3	10	9	.526	0	0	4.12
1993 Nashville	AA	6	6	1	0	42.2	172	41	14	13	5	1	0	3	7	0	20	1	0	4	2	.667	1	0	2.74
Portland	AAA	26	13	0	4	94.2	432	122	68	60	13	2	4	5	30	0	62	2	2	6	5	.545	0	1	5.70
1994 Nashville	AA	12	9	0	1	58.1	242	57	22	19	3	0	1	4	12	0	46	0	2	8	1	.889	0	0	2.93
Salt Lake	AAA	10	10	0	0	57.1	254	72	42	36	7	0	1	6	17	0	27	2	0	4	4	.500	0	0	5.65
1995 Salt Lake	AAA	3	2	0	0	12	53	15	9	9	3	1	0	0	2	0	3	0	0	1	0	1.000	0	0	6.75
6 Min. YEARS		127	103	7	11	660.1	2849	710	375	320	65	11	25	45	184	2	444	25	12	48	36	.571	1	1	4.36

Santiago Henry

Bats: Right Throws: Right Pos: 2B   Ht: 5'11" Wt: 156 Born: 7/27/72 Age: 23

		BATTING															BASERUNNING				PERCENTAGES		
Year Team	Lg	G	AB	H	2B	3B	HR	TB	R	RBI	TBB	IBB	SO	HBP	SH	SF	SB	CS	SB%	GDP	Avg	OBP	SLG
1991 Blue Jays	R	59	220	44	10	3	0	60	23	14	11	0	44	0	1	2	7	5	.58	2	.200	.236	.273
1992 St. Cathrns	A	70	232	44	4	3	0	54	23	12	7	0	54	2	7	1	7	4	.64	1	.190	.219	.233
1993 Hagerstown	A	115	404	111	30	12	8	189	65	54	20	0	110	2	3	1	13	4	.76	7	.275	.311	.468
1994 Dunedin	A	109	408	103	22	6	6	155	56	46	19	2	99	7	2	4	9	4	.69	7	.252	.295	.380
1995 Knoxville	AA	138	454	100	25	4	2	139	47	30	10	0	91	5	7	5	16	6	.73	7	.220	.243	.306
5 Min. YEARS		491	1718	402	91	28	16	597	214	156	67	2	398	16	20	13	52	23	.69	24	.234	.267	.347

132

Julian Heredia

Pitches: Right **Bats:** Right **Pos:** P **Ht:** 6'1" **Wt:** 160 **Born:** 9/22/69 **Age:** 26

Year	Team	Lg	G	GS	CG	GF	IP	BFP	H	R	ER	HR	SH	SF	HB	TBB	IBB	SO	WP	Bk	W	L	Pct.	ShO	Sv	ERA
1989	Angels	R	14	13	3	1	92.1	402	109	55	44	5	2	2	1	21	0	74	2	11	3	4	.429	0	0	4.29
1990	Angels	R	5	5	0	0	26	114	26	14	11	1	0	1	0	10	0	18	0	1	2	2	.500	0	0	3.81
	Quad City	A	5	0	0	3	7	34	6	6	3	0	0	1	0	6	0	10	0	2	0	0	.000	0	0	3.86
1991	Boise	A	25	0	0	10	77	290	42	17	9	1	3	1	1	16	1	99	4	3	8	1	.889	0	5	1.05
1992	Quad City	A	29	0	0	25	43.1	162	27	8	8	0	2	1	0	11	1	45	3	1	6	1	.857	0	10	1.66
	Palm Spring	A	30	0	0	27	28.1	121	28	16	15	2	2	3	1	9	3	36	3	1	3	1	.750	0	10	4.76
1993	Midland	AA	46	1	0	19	89.1	361	77	42	31	10	0	1	8	19	0	89	3	2	5	3	.625	0	3	3.12
1994	Midland	AA	45	2	0	10	97.2	414	87	47	35	10	5	4	6	37	5	109	11	3	5	3	.625	0	5	3.23
1995	Vancouver	AAA	51	0	0	37	74.1	319	69	34	30	8	5	1	5	23	3	65	9	0	5	3	.625	0	10	3.63
	7 Min. YEARS		250	21	3	132	535.1	2217	471	239	186	37	19	15	22	152	13	545	35	24	37	18	.673	0	36	3.13

Matt Herges

Pitches: Right **Bats:** Right **Pos:** P **Ht:** 6'0" **Wt:** 200 **Born:** 4/1/70 **Age:** 26

Year	Team	Lg	G	GS	CG	GF	IP	BFP	H	R	ER	HR	SH	SF	HB	TBB	IBB	SO	WP	Bk	W	L	Pct.	ShO	Sv	ERA
1992	Yakima	A	27	0	0	23	44.2	194	33	21	16	2	1	0	3	24	1	57	2	3	2	3	.400	0	9	3.22
1993	Bakersfield	A	51	0	0	17	90.1	403	70	49	37	6	6	4	10	56	6	84	4	3	2	6	.250	0	2	3.69
1994	Vero Beach	A	48	3	1	12	111	476	115	45	41	8	8	2	4	33	3	61	3	3	8	9	.471	0	3	3.32
1995	San Antonio	AA	19	0	0	13	27.2	130	34	16	15	2	3	0	0	16	1	18	3	0	0	3	.000	0	8	4.88
	San Bernrdo	A	22	2	0	4	51.2	231	58	29	21	3	2	1	2	15	0	35	0	0	5	2	.714	0	1	3.66
	4 Min. YEARS		167	5	1	69	325.1	1434	310	160	130	21	20	7	19	144	11	255	12	9	17	23	.425	0	23	3.60

Fernando Hernandez

Pitches: Right **Bats:** Right **Pos:** P **Ht:** 6'2" **Wt:** 185 **Born:** 6/16/71 **Age:** 25

Year	Team	Lg	G	GS	CG	GF	IP	BFP	H	R	ER	HR	SH	SF	HB	TBB	IBB	SO	WP	Bk	W	L	Pct.	ShO	Sv	ERA
1990	Indians	R	11	11	2	0	69.2	289	61	36	31	3	2	2	1	30	0	43	2	7	4	4	.500	0	0	4.00
1991	Burlington	R	14	13	0	1	77	326	74	33	25	4	2	0	7	19	0	86	12	1	4	4	.500	0	0	2.92
1992	Columbus	A	11	11	1	0	68.2	268	42	16	12	4	1	0	6	33	1	70	4	1	4	5	.444	1	0	1.57
	Kinston	A	8	8	1	0	41.2	177	36	23	21	2	3	3	1	22	0	32	3	0	1	3	.250	0	0	4.54
1993	Kinston	A	8	8	0	0	51	200	34	15	10	1	2	1	2	18	0	53	1	0	2	3	.400	0	0	1.76
	Canton-Akrn	AA	2	2	0	0	7.2	40	14	11	10	1	0	1	1	5	0	8	0	0	0	1	.000	0	0	11.74
	Rancho Cuca	A	17	17	1	0	99.2	441	90	54	46	8	3	4	2	67	0	121	4	1	7	5	.583	0	0	4.15
1994	Wichita	AA	23	23	1	0	131.1	595	124	82	70	12	8	9	10	77	6	95	8	0	7	9	.438	1	0	4.80
1995	Las Vegas	AAA	8	8	0	0	37.2	186	43	32	32	3	0	2	3	31	3	40	4	0	1	6	.143	0	0	7.65
	Memphis	AA	12	12	0	0	66.1	303	72	46	38	4	0	0	3	42	1	74	8	1	4	6	.400	0	0	5.16
	6 Min. YEARS		114	113	6	1	650.2	2825	590	348	295	42	21	22	36	344	11	622	46	11	34	46	.425	2	0	4.08

Kiki Hernandez

Bats: Right **Throws:** Right **Pos:** C **Ht:** 5'11" **Wt:** 195 **Born:** 4/16/69 **Age:** 27

Year	Team	Lg	G	AB	H	2B	3B	HR	TB	R	RBI	TBB	IBB	SO	HBP	SH	SF	SB	CS	SB%	GDP	Avg	OBP	SLG
1988	Yankees	R	9	25	4	1	0	0	5	2	2	1	0	7	1	1	0	0	0	.00	1	.160	.222	.200
1989	Oneonta	A	29	94	21	4	0	2	31	12	7	15	0	21	1	0	0	1	1	.50	0	.223	.336	.330
1990	Pr. William	A	107	360	90	20	2	6	132	39	47	40	0	88	2	1	1	0	0	.00	11	.250	.328	.367
1991	Greensboro	A	108	385	128	27	2	15	204	54	78	64	5	50	9	1	8	2	6	.25	9	.332	.431	.530
	Pr. William	A	7	30	8	2	0	1	13	4	5	3	0	4	0	0	0	0	0	.00	1	.267	.333	.433
1992	Ft. Laud	A	3	9	1	0	0	0	1	1	1	2	0	2	0	0	0	0	0	.00	0	.111	.273	.111
	Albany-Colo	AA	99	328	92	18	0	4	122	46	40	38	1	45	3	2	3	0	0	.00	13	.280	.358	.372
1993	Columbus	AAA	22	54	13	4	0	1	20	8	8	6	1	12	1	1	2	0	0	.00	6	.241	.317	.370
1994	Albany-Colo	AA	4	11	1	0	0	0	1	0	0	3	0	2	0	0	0	0	0	.00	0	.091	.286	.091
	Columbus	AAA	48	134	36	7	1	4	57	17	22	12	0	29	1	1	1	1	3	.25	6	.269	.331	.425
1995	Charlotte	AAA	60	150	36	8	1	7	65	13	28	16	1	26	1	0	3	0	0	.00	5	.240	.312	.433
	8 Min. YEARS		496	1580	430	91	5	40	651	196	238	200	8	286	19	7	18	4	10	.29	47	.272	.357	.412

Willie Hernandez

Pitches: Left **Bats:** Left **Pos:** P **Ht:** 6'2" **Wt:** 185 **Born:** 11/14/54 **Age:** 41

Year	Team	Lg	G	GS	CG	GF	IP	BFP	H	R	ER	HR	SH	SF	HB	TBB	IBB	SO	WP	Bk	W	L	Pct.	ShO	Sv	ERA
1974	Spartanburg	A	26	26	13	0	190	-	169	82	58	11	-	-	5	49	0	179	15	0	11	11	.500	1	0	2.75
1975	Reading	AA	13	11	7	-	91	-	79	32	30	5	-	-	1	25	3	46	3	0	8	2	.800	1	0	2.97
	Toledo	AAA	13	13	4	0	80	-	86	43	29	3	-	-	0	26	4	46	4	0	6	4	.600	0	0	3.26
1976	Okla. City	AAA	25	23	3	-	135	-	154	82	68	18	-	-	2	30	5	88	1	0	8	9	.471	1	0	4.53
1981	Iowa	AAA	18	8	2	8	74	-	84	39	32	5	-	-	3	27	0	41	2	0	4	5	.444	0	2	3.89
1987	Toledo	AAA	2	0	0	0	3	14	4	1	1	0	0	0	0	1	0	2	0	0	0	0	.000	0	0	3.00
1995	Columbus	AAA	22	0	0	10	27	134	43	24	23	3	0	3	2	12	0	16	2	1	2	1	.667	0	0	7.67
1977	Chicago	NL	67	1	0	23	110	437	94	42	37	11	4	2	1	28	9	78	8	3	8	7	.533	0	4	3.03
1978	Chicago	NL	54	0	0	21	60	264	57	26	25	6	8	3	1	35	7	38	3	0	8	2	.800	0	3	3.75
1979	Chicago	NL	51	2	0	19	79	359	85	50	44	8	7	6	4	39	12	53	3	1	4	4	.500	0	0	5.01
1980	Chicago	NL	53	7	0	13	108	473	115	58	53	8	6	3	2	45	4	75	6	1	1	9	.100	0	0	4.42
1981	Chicago	NL	12	0	0	3	14	62	14	7	6	0	2	2	0	8	2	13	1	0	0	0	.000	0	2	3.86

Year	Team	Lg	G	GS	CG	GF	IP	BFP	H	R	ER	HR	SH	SF	HB	TBB	IBB	SO	WP	Bk	W	L	Pct.	ShO	Sv	ERA
1982	Chicago	NL	75	0	0	30	75	312	74	26	25	3	8	3	1	24	11	54	0	0	4	6	.400	0	10	3.00
1983	Chicago	NL	11	1	0	4	19.2	80	16	8	7	0	2	0	0	6	1	18	0	0	1	0	1.000	0	1	3.20
	Philadelphia	NL	63	0	0	27	95.2	398	93	39	35	9	5	0	1	26	7	75	5	0	8	4	.667	0	7	3.29
1984	Detroit	AL	80	0	0	68	140.1	548	96	30	30	6	9	3	4	36	8	112	2	0	9	3	.750	0	32	1.92
1985	Detroit	AL	74	0	0	64	106.2	415	82	38	32	13	4	5	1	14	2	76	2	0	8	10	.444	0	31	2.70
1986	Detroit	AL	64	0	0	53	88.2	376	87	35	35	13	1	3	5	21	1	77	2	1	8	7	.533	0	24	3.55
1987	Detroit	AL	45	0	0	31	49	217	53	27	20	8	2	3	0	20	7	30	1	0	3	4	.429	0	8	3.67
1988	Detroit	AL	63	0	0	38	67.2	284	50	24	23	8	6	3	4	31	6	59	3	3	6	5	.545	0	10	3.06
1989	Detroit	AL	32	0	0	25	31.1	141	36	21	20	4	1	0	1	16	2	30	0	1	2	2	.500	0	15	5.74
	6 Min. YEARS		119	81	29	18	600	148	619	303	241	45	0	3	13	170	12	418	27	1	39	32	.549	3	2	3.62
	13 Maj. YEARS		744	11	0	419	1045	4366	952	431	392	97	65	36	25	349	79	788	37	10	70	63	.526	0	147	3.38

Mike Hickey

Bats: Both **Throws:** Right **Pos:** 3B **Ht:** 6'2" **Wt:** 180 **Born:** 6/22/70 **Age:** 26

			BATTING															BASERUNNING				PERCENTAGES		
Year	Team	Lg	G	AB	H	2B	3B	HR	TB	R	RBI	TBB	IBB	SO	HBP	SH	SF	SB	CS	SB%	GDP	Avg	OBP	SLG
1992	Bellingham	A	15	57	14	2	0	0	16	8	11	4	0	14	0	0	0	3	0	1.00	1	.246	.295	.281
1993	Appleton	A	69	255	73	14	3	2	99	35	41	38	1	49	1	1	3	14	7	.67	6	.286	.377	.388
1994	Riverside	A	130	487	137	23	7	10	204	75	90	68	5	94	6	5	5	15	8	.65	12	.281	.373	.419
1995	Port City	AA	120	447	117	24	1	6	161	59	59	60	2	83	5	4	4	6	3	.67	9	.262	.353	.360
	4 Min. YEARS		334	1246	341	63	11	18	480	177	201	170	8	240	12	10	12	38	18	.68	28	.274	.363	.385

Richard Hidalgo

Bats: Right **Throws:** Right **Pos:** OF **Ht:** 6'2" **Wt:** 175 **Born:** 7/2/75 **Age:** 20

			BATTING															BASERUNNING				PERCENTAGES		
Year	Team	Lg	G	AB	H	2B	3B	HR	TB	R	RBI	TBB	IBB	SO	HBP	SH	SF	SB	CS	SB%	GDP	Avg	OBP	SLG
1992	Astros	R	51	184	57	7	3	1	73	20	27	13	0	27	3	1	3	14	5	.74	1	.310	.360	.397
1993	Asheville	A	111	403	109	23	3	10	168	49	55	30	0	76	4	2	5	21	13	.62	3	.270	.324	.417
1994	Quad City	A	124	476	139	47	6	12	234	68	76	23	1	80	7	1	4	12	12	.50	6	.292	.331	.492
1995	Jackson	AA	133	489	130	28	6	14	212	59	59	32	1	76	2	0	7	8	9	.47	11	.266	.309	.434
	4 Min. YEARS		419	1552	435	105	18	37	687	196	217	98	2	259	16	4	19	55	39	.59	21	.280	.326	.443

Mike Higgins

Bats: Right **Throws:** Right **Pos:** C **Ht:** 6'0" **Wt:** 205 **Born:** 6/3/71 **Age:** 25

			BATTING															BASERUNNING				PERCENTAGES		
Year	Team	Lg	G	AB	H	2B	3B	HR	TB	R	RBI	TBB	IBB	SO	HBP	SH	SF	SB	CS	SB%	GDP	Avg	OBP	SLG
1993	Bend	A	51	167	45	10	1	7	78	23	19	20	1	47	1	0	1	3	4	.43	1	.269	.349	.467
1994	New Haven	AA	1	1	0	0	0	0	0	0	0	0	0	0	0	0	0	0	0	.00	0	.000	.000	.000
	Asheville	A	56	205	55	14	0	3	78	29	15	18	0	35	2	0	1	1	2	.33	5	.268	.332	.380
	Central Val	A	45	157	34	4	0	0	38	15	16	15	0	37	1	1	1	2	1	.67	8	.217	.287	.242
1995	Salem	A	53	158	38	9	0	0	47	9	18	17	1	30	1	2	4	1	3	.25	1	.241	.311	.297
	New Haven	AA	17	49	12	0	0	0	12	4	6	3	0	10	0	3	1	0	0	.00	1	.245	.283	.245
	3 Min. YEARS		223	737	184	37	1	10	253	80	74	73	2	159	5	6	8	7	10	.41	15	.250	.318	.343

Erik Hiljus

Pitches: Right **Bats:** Right **Pos:** P **Ht:** 6'5" **Wt:** 225 **Born:** 12/25/72 **Age:** 23

			HOW MUCH HE PITCHED						WHAT HE GAVE UP												THE RESULTS				
Year	Team	Lg	G	GS	CG	GF	IP	BFP	H	R	ER	HR	SH	SF	HB	TBB	IBB	SO	WP	Bk	W	L	Pct.	ShO	Sv	ERA
1991	Mets	R	9	9	1	0	38	183	31	27	18	1	0	1	1	37	0	38	5	1	2	3	.400	1	0	4.26
1992	Kingsport	R	12	11	0	1	70.2	317	66	49	40	5	2	2	2	40	0	63	7	2	3	6	.333	0	0	5.09
1993	Capital Cty	A	27	27	1	0	145.2	640	114	76	70	8	2	7	4	111	1	157	17	4	7	10	.412	0	0	4.32
1994	St. Lucie	A	26	26	3	0	160.2	709	159	85	71	8	6	10	5	90	3	140	10	8	11	10	.524	1	0	3.98
1995	St. Lucie	A	17	17	0	0	111.1	453	85	46	37	4	6	5	3	50	2	98	10	6	8	4	.667	0	0	2.99
	Binghamton	AA	10	10	0	0	55.1	252	60	38	36	8	2	1	1	32	1	40	4	2	2	4	.333	0	0	5.86
	5 Min. YEARS		101	100	5	1	581.2	2554	515	321	272	34	18	26	16	360	7	536	53	23	33	37	.471	2	0	4.21

Chris Hill

Pitches: Left **Bats:** Left **Pos:** P **Ht:** 6'1" **Wt:** 175 **Born:** 4/13/69 **Age:** 27

			HOW MUCH HE PITCHED						WHAT HE GAVE UP												THE RESULTS				
Year	Team	Lg	G	GS	CG	GF	IP	BFP	H	R	ER	HR	SH	SF	HB	TBB	IBB	SO	WP	Bk	W	L	Pct.	ShO	Sv	ERA
1988	Little Fall	A	13	13	2	0	79.1	332	56	32	27	7	3	5	3	35	0	66	2	0	5	5	.500	1	0	3.06
1989	Columbia	A	29	25	2	1	165.2	705	140	74	56	5	7	2	4	78	1	157	9	1	11	7	.611	1	0	3.04
1990	St. Lucie	A	27	25	2	2	149.2	662	149	77	53	4	10	10	3	69	0	82	8	1	9	8	.529	0	1	3.19
1991	Williamsprt	AA	27	12	1	3	88.1	402	115	59	46	8	9	5	1	40	2	42	5	0	3	3	.500	0	1	4.69
	St. Lucie	A	6	4	0	1	32	110	18	6	4	1	1	1	0	4	0	24	0	0	4	0	1.000	0	1	1.13
1992	Osceola	A	30	26	1	0	159.2	677	154	73	52	4	4	3	5	58	1	126	11	1	16	7	.696	1	0	2.93
1993	Jackson	AA	58	3	0	27	105	453	90	54	45	9	4	2	7	53	6	93	8	0	6	4	.600	0	2	3.86
1994	Jackson	AA	45	8	0	15	100	446	95	55	42	11	2	3	7	57	3	83	3	0	5	3	.625	0	1	3.78
1995	Pawtucket	AAA	10	6	0	2	31	147	31	24	21	3	1	3	2	25	1	20	4	0	2	3	.400	0	0	6.10
	Trenton	AA	7	0	0	2	6	30	7	6	6	0	0	0	0	6	0	10	1	0	0	0	.000	0	0	9.00
	High Desert	A	5	1	0	2	13	66	20	13	13	5	0	3	1	7	0	10	1	0	0	2	.000	0	0	9.00
	Lubbock	IND	1	0	0	1	0.2	4	2	2	2	1	0	0	0	0	0	1	1	0	0	0	.000	0	0	27.00
	8 Min. YEARS		258	123	8	56	930.1	4034	877	473	367	58	41	37	33	432	14	714	53	3	61	42	.592	3	5	3.55

Eric Hill

Pitches: Right **Bats:** Right **Pos:** P Ht: 6'2" Wt: 190 Born: 11/19/67 Age: 28

		HOW MUCH HE PITCHED					WHAT HE GAVE UP									THE RESULTS					
Year Team	Lg	G	GS	CG	GF	IP	BFP	H	R	ER	HR	SH	SF	HB	TBB	IBB	SO	WP	Bk	W	L	Pct.	ShO	Sv	ERA

Year Team	Lg	G	GS	CG	GF	IP	BFP	H	R	ER	HR	SH	SF	HB	TBB	IBB	SO	WP	Bk	W	L	Pct.	ShO	Sv	ERA
1990 Batavia	A	10	8	2	1	53.2	219	49	27	24	9	2	1	0	10	0	34	5	0	2	4	.333	0	1	4.02
1991 Spartanburg	A	27	21	2	1	143	599	126	64	50	13	2	7	1	48	0	143	11	3	7	10	.412	1	0	3.15
1992 Clearwater	A	5	5	0	0	27.2	116	26	13	10	3	1	1	0	7	0	18	0	1	4	1	.800	0	0	3.25
Reading	AA	25	15	1	1	98	429	111	61	52	11	7	2	4	24	1	61	5	1	5	4	.556	0	0	4.78
1993 Reading	AA	21	7	0	3	68.2	303	72	44	35	10	2	4	1	30	2	37	5	3	2	3	.400	0	0	4.59
1994 Reading	AA	46	6	0	22	89.2	392	94	52	46	12	2	5	3	33	4	77	8	0	8	4	.667	0	2	4.62
1995 Reading	AA	38	0	0	16	59	251	55	23	19	1	3	3	0	27	6	52	2	1	4	3	.571	0	4	2.90
Scranton-Wb	AAA	21	0	0	7	23	99	24	13	11	4	1	0	0	9	0	16	2	0	4	3	.571	0	2	4.30
6 Min. YEARS		193	62	5	51	562.2	2408	557	297	247	63	20	23	9	188	13	438	38	9	36	32	.529	1	9	3.95

Lew Hill

Bats: Both **Throws:** Right **Pos:** OF Ht: 5'10" Wt: 190 Born: 4/16/69 Age: 27

		BATTING														BASERUNNING				PERCENTAGES		

Year Team	Lg	G	AB	H	2B	3B	HR	TB	R	RBI	TBB	IBB	SO	HBP	SH	SF	SB	CS	SB%	GDP	Avg	OBP	SLG
1987 Oneonta	A	14	39	11	0	2	0	15	9	0	3	0	16	0	0	0	0	0	.00	0	.282	.333	.385
Yankees	R	31	89	15	0	1	1	20	11	8	4	0	31	3	3	0	6	1	.86	1	.169	.229	.225
1988 Yankees	R	54	201	50	4	4	2	68	31	19	13	0	69	3	3	1	7	3	.70	1	.249	.303	.338
1989 Oneonta	A	48	164	35	5	3	4	58	36	24	14	0	60	13	0	1	7	2	.78	1	.213	.323	.354
1990 Greensboro	A	83	270	53	11	0	6	82	28	25	41	1	83	9	2	3	19	3	.86	4	.196	.319	.304
1991 Greensboro	A	125	426	97	17	3	6	138	69	45	67	0	112	14	1	1	36	16	.69	14	.228	.350	.324
1992 Greensboro	A	98	374	117	12	9	15	192	75	52	30	0	89	11	0	3	24	17	.59	3	.313	.378	.513
1993 Pr. William	A	116	460	115	22	3	13	182	66	57	29	0	124	18	3	4	12	7	.63	9	.250	.317	.396
1994 Albany-Colo	AA	82	257	59	13	2	9	103	36	33	24	3	75	8	2	4	3	5	.38	4	.230	.311	.401
1995 Columbus	AAA	54	144	39	5	0	4	56	15	20	5	1	36	1	0	0	6	5	.55	2	.271	.300	.389
9 Min. YEARS		705	2424	591	89	27	60	914	376	283	230	5	695	80	14	17	120	59	.67	39	.244	.328	.377

Milt Hill

Pitches: Right **Bats:** Right **Pos:** P Ht: 6'0" Wt: 180 Born: 8/22/65 Age: 30

		HOW MUCH HE PITCHED						WHAT HE GAVE UP										THE RESULTS					

Year Team	Lg	G	GS	CG	GF	IP	BFP	H	R	ER	HR	SH	SF	HB	TBB	IBB	SO	WP	Bk	W	L	Pct.	ShO	Sv	ERA
1987 Billings	R	21	0	0	19	32.2	125	25	10	6	1	1	0	1	4	2	40	5	0	3	1	.750	0	7	1.65
1988 Cedar Rapds	A	44	0	0	38	78.1	300	52	21	18	3	3	1	1	17	7	69	4	8	9	4	.692	0	13	2.07
1989 Chattanooga	AA	51	0	0	42	70	281	49	19	16	4	1	5	0	28	6	63	1	4	6	5	.545	0	13	2.06
1990 Nashville	AAA	48	0	0	11	71.1	276	51	20	18	4	1	5	2	18	1	58	4	2	4	4	.500	0	3	2.27
1991 Nashville	AAA	37	0	0	16	67.1	269	59	26	22	3	3	3	0	15	1	62	3	3	3	3	.500	0	3	2.94
1992 Nashville	AAA	53	0	0	39	74.1	292	56	30	22	7	3	1	1	17	4	70	4	1	0	5	.000	0	18	2.66
1993 Indianapolis	AAA	20	5	0	9	53	227	53	27	24	1	5	0	3	17	4	45	3	0	3	5	.375	0	2	4.08
1994 Jacksonvlle	AA	7	7	1	0	39.1	166	37	27	20	6	2	1	1	12	1	26	1	0	4	2	.667	0	0	4.58
1995 Carolina	AA	10	10	0	0	56	226	53	27	25	6	4	1	2	6	0	46	0	0	2	5	.500	0	0	4.02
Calgary	AAA	24	5	0	5	60.2	260	69	38	33	8	3	3	1	14	2	31	2	1	1	3	.250	0	0	4.90
1991 Cincinnati	NL	22	0	0	8	33.1	137	36	14	14	1	4	3	0	8	2	20	1	0	1	1	.500	0	0	3.78
1992 Cincinnati	NL	14	0	0	5	20	80	15	9	7	1	2	1	1	5	2	10	0	0	0	0	.000	0	1	3.15
1993 Cincinnati	NL	19	0	0	2	28.2	125	34	18	18	5	0	3	0	9	1	23	1	0	3	0	1.000	0	0	5.65
1994 Seattle	AL	13	0	0	2	23.2	111	30	19	17	4	1	1	0	11	3	16	0	0	1	0	1.000	0	0	6.46
Atlanta	NL	10	0	0	5	11.1	56	18	10	10	3	1	0	0	6	1	10	1	1	0	0	.000	0	0	7.94
9 Min. YEARS		315	27	1	179	603	2422	504	245	204	43	26	20	11	148	28	510	27	19	35	34	.507	0	59	3.04
4 Maj. YEARS		78	0	0	22	117	509	133	70	66	14	8	8	1	39	9	79	3	1	5	1	.833	0	1	5.08

Rob Hinds

Bats: Right **Throws:** Right **Pos:** 2B Ht: 6'1" Wt: 180 Born: 4/26/71 Age: 25

		BATTING														BASERUNNING				PERCENTAGES		

Year Team	Lg	G	AB	H	2B	3B	HR	TB	R	RBI	TBB	IBB	SO	HBP	SH	SF	SB	CS	SB%	GDP	Avg	OBP	SLG
1992 Oneonta	A	69	264	76	8	2	0	88	40	11	34	0	51	7	0	0	21	9	.70	3	.288	.384	.333
1993 Greensboro	A	126	503	114	14	3	0	134	80	50	72	0	101	13	1	2	51	22	.70	12	.227	.337	.266
1994 Tampa	A	110	405	118	10	3	1	137	63	32	31	0	76	4	7	3	24	11	.69	8	.291	.345	.338
1995 Norwich	AA	132	445	112	8	1	1	125	71	37	50	0	102	12	6	3	27	10	.73	4	.252	.341	.281
4 Min. YEARS		437	1617	420	40	9	2	484	254	130	187	0	330	36	14	8	123	52	.70	27	.260	.348	.299

Rich Hines

Pitches: Left **Bats:** Left **Pos:** P Ht: 6'1" Wt: 185 Born: 5/20/69 Age: 27

		HOW MUCH HE PITCHED						WHAT HE GAVE UP										THE RESULTS					

Year Team	Lg	G	GS	CG	GF	IP	BFP	H	R	ER	HR	SH	SF	HB	TBB	IBB	SO	WP	Bk	W	L	Pct.	ShO	Sv	ERA
1990 Yankees	R	11	9	0	0	61	242	44	18	12	0	0	3	2	19	0	73	9	1	5	2	.714	0	0	1.77
1991 Greensboro	A	26	26	6	0	155.1	667	147	76	55	8	5	2	2	68	1	126	7	3	8	9	.471	2	0	3.19
1992 Pr. William	A	25	24	0	1	140	610	131	75	56	12	3	3	7	61	3	84	10	0	11	7	.611	0	0	3.60
1993 Albany-Colo	AA	14	0	0	3	26	102	17	9	6	1	1	1	0	11	2	27	0	0	0	1	.000	0	0	2.08
Columbus	AAA	43	0	0	17	56	248	56	28	25	3	1	1	1	34	6	40	2	1	2	5	.286	0	4	4.02
1994 Columbus	AAA	49	2	0	12	84.1	367	87	48	43	11	1	2	0	41	4	54	6	0	3	2	.600	0	2	4.59
1995 Norwich	AA	54	0	0	28	62	283	58	38	25	2	1	4	5	34	7	50	7	2	3	5	.375	0	7	3.63
6 Min. YEARS		222	61	6	61	584.2	2519	534	292	222	37	12	16	17	268	23	454	41	7	32	31	.508	2	13	3.42

Larry Hingle

Pitches: Left   **Bats:** Left   **Pos:** P   **Ht:** 6'3"   **Wt:** 200   **Born:** 12/12/70   **Age:** 25

			HOW MUCH HE PITCHED						WHAT HE GAVE UP								THE RESULTS					
Year	Team	Lg	G	GS	CG	GF	IP	BFP	H	R	ER	HR	SH	SF	HB	TBB	IBB	SO	WP	Bk	W	L	Pct.	ShO	Sv	ERA
1992	Boise	A	15	15	0	0	76	339	83	52	33	8	2	3	1	29	1	56	9	7	6	4	.600	0	0	3.91
1993	Cedar Rapds	A	28	24	1	3	146.2	656	166	103	80	15	7	5	4	64	0	115	21	1	9	13	.409	0	1	4.91
1994	Lk Elsinore	A	15	0	0	9	26.1	121	28	15	11	2	0	3	0	15	0	13	3	0	0	0	.000	0	1	3.76
	Osceola	A	17	0	0	8	22	95	17	5	2	1	3	1	0	11	3	10	0	0	2	1	.667	0	4	0.82
1995	Jackson	AA	9	0	0	1	11.1	58	11	15	14	1	2	1	0	15	1	5	7	1	0	2	.000	0	0	11.12
	Kissimmee	A	10	0	0	6	7.2	48	15	18	16	1	0	0	0	11	0	2	1	0	0	0	.000	0	0	18.78
	4 Min. YEARS		94	39	1	27	290	1317	320	208	156	28	14	13	5	145	5	201	41	9	17	20	.459	0	6	4.84

Steve Hinton

Bats: Left   **Throws:** Left   **Pos:** 1B   **Ht:** 6'2"   **Wt:** 200   **Born:** 9/5/69   **Age:** 26

					BATTING											BASERUNNING				PERCENTAGES		
Year	Team	Lg	G	AB	H	2B	3B	HR	TB	R	RBI	TBB	IBB	SO	HBP	SH	SF	SB	CS	SB%	GDP	Avg	OBP	SLG
1991	Eugene	A	71	286	81	15	0	5	111	37	39	25	2	35	2	0	1	4	1	.80	7	.283	.345	.388
1992	Appleton	A	118	419	113	25	1	7	161	67	63	54	1	71	5	2	10	3	6	.45	10	.270	.352	.384
1993	Wilmington	A	104	344	85	11	1	8	122	43	42	46	1	79	1	1	4	4	5	.44	9	.247	.334	.355
1994	Burlington	A	41	147	42	9	1	10	83	28	26	18	2	22	2	0	4	1	0	1.00	3	.286	.363	.565
	W. Palm Bch	A	22	72	11	2	1	0	15	4	6	9	1	17	0	2	1	1	0	1.00	1	.153	.244	.208
	Duluth-Sup.	IND	46	171	43	2	3	0	51	18	17	11	0	32	3	1	1	6	2	.75	4	.251	.306	.298
1995	Harrisburg	AA	10	18	4	0	0	0	4	4	0	7	0	5	0	0	0	0	0	.00	0	.222	.440	.222
	5 Min. YEARS		412	1457	379	64	7	30	547	201	193	170	7	261	13	6	20	21	14	.60	34	.260	.339	.375

Tommy Hinzo

Bats: Both   **Throws:** Right   **Pos:** 2B   **Ht:** 5'10"   **Wt:** 175   **Born:** 6/18/64   **Age:** 32

					BATTING											BASERUNNING				PERCENTAGES		
Year	Team	Lg	G	AB	H	2B	3B	HR	TB	R	RBI	TBB	IBB	SO	HBP	SH	SF	SB	CS	SB%	GDP	Avg	OBP	SLG
1986	Batavia	A	55	219	73	7	3	1	89	35	15	12	1	44	4	3	0	24	8	.75	4	.333	.379	.406
1987	Kinston	A	65	266	74	11	1	0	87	64	25	32	0	44	3	0	0	49	10	.83	4	.278	.362	.327
	Williamsprt	AA	26	99	24	2	1	0	28	16	9	13	0	18	0	1	0	11	3	.79	1	.242	.330	.283
1988	Colo. Sprng	AAA	119	449	104	16	4	1	131	67	29	46	1	76	4	2	4	33	17	.66	7	.232	.306	.292
1989	Colo. Sprng	AAA	102	410	104	13	7	1	134	65	35	31	2	68	7	2	0	22	16	.58	2	.254	.317	.327
1990	Richmond	AAA	17	49	11	0	0	2	17	9	5	5	0	12	2	0	0	1	1	.50	2	.224	.321	.347
	Greenville	AA	25	73	19	2	2	1	28	12	12	10	0	12	2	2	1	3	1	.75	4	.260	.360	.384
	Memphis	AA	20	48	8	1	1	0	11	3	2	4	0	9	1	2	0	3	3	.50	1	.167	.245	.229
	Omaha	AAA	35	111	27	5	1	0	34	16	9	2	0	22	1	0	0	6	2	.75	0	.243	.261	.306
1991	Omaha	AAA	9	20	5	1	0	0	6	4	4	1	0	3	2	1	0	0	1	.00	0	.250	.348	.300
1993	Rochester	AAA	136	560	152	25	5	6	205	83	69	37	0	78	11	8	6	29	12	.71	8	.271	.326	.366
1994	Mariners	R	5	15	6	1	0	0	7	1	1	0	0	3	2	0	0	0	0	.00	0	.400	.471	.467
	Calgary	AAA	47	142	35	10	0	0	45	20	13	8	0	21	2	1	1	1	2	.33	2	.246	.294	.317
1995	Okla. City	AAA	82	254	64	10	1	0	76	33	20	13	1	38	4	3	3	8	3	.73	3	.252	.296	.299
1987	Cleveland	AL	67	257	68	9	3	3	92	31	21	10	0	47	2	10	1	9	4	.69	6	.265	.296	.358
1989	Cleveland	AL	18	17	0	0	0	0	0	4	0	2	0	6	0	2	0	1	2	.33	0	.000	.105	.000
	9 Min. YEARS		743	2715	706	104	26	12	898	428	248	214	5	448	45	25	16	190	79	.71	38	.260	.323	.331
	2 Maj. YEARS		85	274	68	9	3	3	92	35	21	12	0	53	2	12	1	10	6	.63	6	.248	.284	.336

Roy Hodge

Bats: Right   **Throws:** Right   **Pos:** OF   **Ht:** 6'2"   **Wt:** 191   **Born:** 6/22/71   **Age:** 25

					BATTING											BASERUNNING				PERCENTAGES		
Year	Team	Lg	G	AB	H	2B	3B	HR	TB	R	RBI	TBB	IBB	SO	HBP	SH	SF	SB	CS	SB%	GDP	Avg	OBP	SLG
1990	Bluefield	R	26	48	11	0	0	0	11	4	3	5	0	8	0	1	0	0	1	.00	1	.229	.302	.229
1991	Orioles	R	36	90	24	4	0	1	31	10	13	19	0	17	1	0	1	1	0	1.00	0	.267	.396	.344
1992	Kane County	A	25	52	13	1	0	0	14	3	7	9	0	12	0	0	0	5	4	.56	1	.250	.361	.269
	Bluefield	R	58	241	71	13	1	1	89	41	46	22	1	32	2	0	0	2	3	.40	1	.295	.358	.369
1993	Albany	A	29	97	25	3	2	0	32	25	11	13	0	21	0	0	0	1	0	1.00	2	.258	.345	.330
	Frederick	A	67	166	34	9	1	0	45	17	12	18	0	29	1	3	0	4	1	.80	7	.205	.286	.271
1994	Frederick	A	127	450	130	27	4	9	192	70	64	57	0	73	3	3	4	8	6	.57	12	.289	.370	.427
1995	Bowie	AA	29	99	17	1	1	0	20	11	9	18	0	15	1	0	2	2	0	1.00	5	.172	.300	.202
	High Desert	A	42	140	42	8	1	3	61	31	15	36	0	24	3	0	1	8	7	.53	3	.300	.450	.436
	Frederick	A	48	172	44	12	1	1	61	19	17	16	0	31	1	0	2	4	3	.57	3	.256	.319	.355
	6 Min. YEARS		487	1555	411	78	11	15	556	231	197	213	1	262	12	7	10	35	25	.58	45	.264	.355	.358

Steve Hoeme

Pitches: Right   **Bats:** Right   **Pos:** P   **Ht:** 6'6"   **Wt:** 230   **Born:** 11/2/67   **Age:** 28

					HOW MUCH HE PITCHED						WHAT HE GAVE UP								THE RESULTS					
Year	Team	Lg	G	GS	CG	GF	IP	BFP	H	R	ER	HR	SH	SF	HB	TBB	IBB	SO	WP	Bk	W	L	Pct.	ShO	Sv	ERA
1987	Royals	R	15	0	0	2	23.2	122	33	23	15	1	0	1	3	11	1	16	3	0	2	0	1.000	0	0	5.70
1988	Eugene	A	23	1	0	13	37.1	164	25	17	17	0	1	1	4	24	0	32	4	0	0	1	.000	0	1	4.10
1989	Appleton	A	29	12	0	1	89.1	402	83	47	33	9	4	1	7	57	0	73	10	2	4	5	.444	0	0	3.32
1990	Baseball Cy	A	33	1	0	7	60	268	49	28	22	2	1	2	5	40	0	51	13	2	2	2	.500	0	0	3.30
	Appleton	A	7	0	0	2	11.2	53	10	5	5	0	1	1	2	8	0	15	2	1	1	1	.500	0	0	3.86
1991	Charlstn-Sc	A	31	1	0	9	62.2	281	54	30	24	1	3	4	6	39	1	51	5	0	7	1	.875	0	0	3.45
1992	Waterloo	A	22	0	0	4	34.1	138	27	11	9	1	2	2	1	9	0	43	4	1	1	1	.500	0	1	2.36

136

		Lg	G	GS	CG	GF	IP	BFP	H	R	ER	HR	SH	SF	HB	TBB	IBB	SO	WP	Bk	W	L	Pct.	ShO	Sv	ERA
	High Desert	A	7	0	0	5	9	40	10	2	2	0	1	1	0	5	2	6	1	0	2	0	1.000	0	0	2.00
	Wichita	AA	20	1	0	6	35.2	171	48	27	25	1	1	2	1	19	1	24	3	0	1	1	.500	0	0	6.31
1993	Rancho Cuca	A	8	0	0	4	8.1	39	8	9	6	1	1	0	1	5	0	4	0	0	1	0	1.000	0	0	6.48
	Wichita	AA	44	0	0	37	48.1	198	41	17	13	2	3	0	1	16	3	47	3	0	2	3	.400	0	19	2.42
1994	Harrisburg	AA	33	1	0	5	58.1	235	43	20	15	1	2	1	3	23	0	51	2	1	6	2	.750	0	0	2.31
1995	Pawtucket	AAA	15	2	0	5	39	165	40	21	20	2	0	1	1	15	0	21	1	0	0	2	.000	0	1	4.62
	Trenton	AA	20	0	0	14	24.1	108	23	9	9	1	2	2	3	8	0	17	3	0	2	0	1.000	0	6	3.33
	9 Min. YEARS		307	19	0	114	542	2384	494	266	215	22	22	19	38	279	8	451	54	7	31	19	.620	0	30	3.57

Aaron Holbert

Bats: Right **Throws:** Right **Pos:** SS   **Ht:** 6'0" **Wt:** 160 **Born:** 1/9/73 **Age:** 23

			BATTING													BASERUNNING				PERCENTAGES		
Year	Team	Lg	G	AB	H	2B	3B	HR	TB	R	RBI	TBB	IBB	SO	HBP	SH	SF	SB	CS	SB%	GDP	Avg	OBP	SLG
1990	Johnson Cty	R	54	176	30	4	1	1	39	27	18	24	1	33	3	1	1	3	5	.38	2	.170	.279	.222
1991	Springfield	A	59	215	48	5	1	1	58	22	24	15	0	26	6	1	2	5	8	.38	3	.223	.290	.270
1992	Savannah	A	119	438	117	17	4	1	145	53	34	40	0	57	8	6	3	62	25	.71	4	.267	.337	.331
1993	St. Pete	A	121	457	121	18	3	2	151	60	31	28	2	61	4	15	1	45	22	.67	6	.265	.312	.330
1994	Cardinals	R	5	12	2	0	0	0	2	3	0	2	0	2	0	0	0	2	0	1.00	0	.167	.286	.167
	Arkansas	AA	59	233	69	10	6	2	97	41	19	14	0	25	2	4	1	9	7	.56	5	.296	.340	.416
1995	Louisville	AAA	112	401	103	16	4	9	154	57	40	20	1	60	5	3	5	14	6	.70	10	.257	.297	.384
	6 Min. YEARS		529	1932	490	70	19	16	646	263	166	143	4	264	28	30	13	140	73	.66	30	.254	.312	.334

David Holdridge

Pitches: Right **Bats:** Right **Pos:** P   **Ht:** 6'3" **Wt:** 195 **Born:** 2/5/69 **Age:** 27

			HOW MUCH HE PITCHED						WHAT HE GAVE UP											THE RESULTS					
Year	Team	Lg	G	GS	CG	GF	IP	BFP	H	R	ER	HR	SH	SF	HB	TBB	IBB	SO	WP	Bk	W	L	Pct.	ShO	Sv	ERA
1988	Quad City	A	28	28	0	0	153.2	686	151	92	66	4	5	4	13	79	1	110	8	4	6	12	.333	0	0	3.87
1989	Clearwater	A	24	24	3	0	132.1	610	147	100	84	11	2	6	8	77	0	77	16	1	7	10	.412	0	0	5.71
1990	Reading	AA	24	24	1	0	127.2	571	114	74	64	13	3	5	6	79	0	78	8	0	8	12	.400	0	0	4.51
1991	Reading	AA	7	7	0	0	26.1	135	26	24	16	3	2	3	1	34	0	19	3	0	0	2	.000	0	0	5.47
	Clearwater	A	15	0	0	4	25	126	34	23	21	2	0	2	1	21	0	23	4	0	0	0	.000	0	1	7.56
1992	Palm Spring	A	28	27	3	0	159	726	169	99	75	5	5	3	5	87	4	135	21	0	12	12	.500	2	0	4.25
1993	Midland	AA	27	27	1	0	151	700	202	117	102	13	4	2	11	55	0	123	13	1	8	10	.444	1	0	6.08
1994	Vancouver	AAA	4	0	0	1	7	36	12	7	4	1	0	1	1	4	0	4	0	0	0	0	.000	0	0	5.14
	Midland	AA	38	2	0	17	66.1	286	66	33	29	4	1	3	5	23	0	59	2	0	7	4	.636	0	2	3.93
1995	Lk Elsinore	A	12	0	0	8	18.1	74	13	3	2	0	1	1	2	5	1	24	3	0	3	0	1.000	0	1	0.98
	Midland	AA	14	0	0	11	25.1	100	20	8	5	1	1	0	1	8	0	23	2	0	1	0	1.000	0	1	1.78
	Vancouver	AAA	11	0	0	6	13.2	68	18	10	7	0	2	0	1	7	1	13	3	0	0	2	.000	0	1	4.61
	8 Min. YEARS		232	139	8	47	905.2	4118	972	590	475	57	26	30	55	479	7	688	83	6	52	64	.448	3	5	4.72

Rick Holifield

Bats: Left **Throws:** Left **Pos:** OF   **Ht:** 6'2" **Wt:** 165 **Born:** 3/25/70 **Age:** 26

			BATTING													BASERUNNING				PERCENTAGES		
Year	Team	Lg	G	AB	H	2B	3B	HR	TB	R	RBI	TBB	IBB	SO	HBP	SH	SF	SB	CS	SB%	GDP	Avg	OBP	SLG
1988	Medicne Hat	R	31	96	26	4	1	1	35	16	6	9	0	27	4	0	0	6	0	1.00	2	.271	.358	.365
1989	St. Cathrns	A	60	209	46	7	1	4	67	22	21	15	1	74	1	0	2	4	7	.36	2	.220	.273	.321
1990	Myrtle Bch	A	99	279	56	9	2	3	78	37	18	28	0	88	6	1	0	13	8	.62	7	.201	.288	.280
1991	Myrtle Bch	A	114	324	71	15	5	1	99	37	25	34	1	94	7	1	1	14	15	.48	0	.219	.306	.306
1992	Myrtle Bch	A	93	281	56	15	2	8	99	32	27	23	1	81	5	3	3	6	5	.55	2	.199	.269	.352
1993	Dunedin	A	127	407	112	18	12	20	214	84	68	56	6	129	16	6	4	30	13	.70	2	.275	.381	.526
1994	Knoxville	AA	71	238	59	10	9	4	99	31	31	24	2	64	3	1	1	23	5	.82	2	.248	.323	.416
	Scranton-Wb	AAA	18	55	7	1	0	0	8	5	0	3	0	19	2	0	0	0	1	.00	0	.127	.200	.145
	Reading	AA	42	155	44	8	3	7	79	29	19	18	0	34	3	1	0	21	7	.75	1	.284	.369	.510
1995	Scranton-Wb	AAA	76	223	46	6	3	3	67	32	24	24	0	52	6	1	3	21	5	.81	1	.206	.297	.300
	Reading	AA	30	93	23	3	1	1	31	18	5	22	3	18	1	2	0	5	2	.71	0	.247	.397	.333
	8 Min. YEARS		761	2360	546	96	39	52	876	343	244	256	14	680	54	16	14	143	68	.68	19	.231	.319	.371

Adrian Hollinger

Pitches: Right **Bats:** Left **Pos:** P   **Ht:** 6'0" **Wt:** 180 **Born:** 9/23/70 **Age:** 25

			HOW MUCH HE PITCHED						WHAT HE GAVE UP											THE RESULTS					
Year	Team	Lg	G	GS	CG	GF	IP	BFP	H	R	ER	HR	SH	SF	HB	TBB	IBB	SO	WP	Bk	W	L	Pct.	ShO	Sv	ERA
1991	Padres	R	8	0	0	3	12	76	21	20	17	1	1	0	0	16	2	14	1	2	1	1	.500	0	0	12.75
1992	Spokane	A	21	2	0	4	53.2	254	61	43	37	4	3	1	4	29	1	39	8	1	0	6	.000	0	1	6.20
1993	Waterloo	A	44	0	0	18	60.1	254	44	23	17	3	3	2	3	40	4	67	7	1	8	3	.727	0	5	2.54
1994	Rancho Cuca	A	19	0	0	9	23.2	111	20	17	15	3	1	0	3	19	0	32	3	2	0	1	.000	0	1	5.70
	Wichita	AA	25	0	0	10	46.2	218	47	32	25	4	0	2	3	33	2	42	7	0	1	3	.250	0	0	4.82
1995	Brevard Cty	AA	11	4	0	4	25	118	26	17	15	1	0	1	1	18	0	18	1	1	0	2	.000	0	2	5.40
	Sonoma Cty	IND	8	8	3	0	60	241	44	25	19	4	4	3	5	18	1	46	2	0	3	4	.429	0	0	2.85
	Greenville	AA	7	6	1	0	44.2	196	43	26	23	2	0	4	1	20	1	28	2	1	1	4	.200	0	0	4.63
	5 Min. YEARS		143	20	4	48	326	1468	306	203	168	22	12	14	20	193	11	286	31	8	14	24	.368	0	9	4.64

Damon Hollins

Bats: Right **Throws:** Left **Pos:** OF **Ht:** 5'11" **Wt:** 180 **Born:** 6/12/74 **Age:** 22

Year Team	Lg	G	AB	H	2B	3B	HR	TB	R	RBI	TBB	IBB	SO	HBP	SH	SF	SB	CS	SB%	GDP	Avg	OBP	SLG
1992 Braves	R	49	179	41	12	1	1	58	35	15	30	0	22	2	2	0	15	2	.88	3	.229	.346	.324
1993 Danville	R	62	240	77	15	2	7	117	37	51	19	0	30	1	0	3	10	2	.83	5	.321	.369	.488
1994 Durham	A	131	485	131	28	0	23	228	76	88	45	0	115	4	2	3	12	7	.63	9	.270	.335	.470
1995 Greenville	AA	129	466	115	26	2	18	199	64	77	44	6	120	4	0	6	6	6	.50	7	.247	.313	.427
4 Min. YEARS		371	1370	364	81	5	49	602	212	231	138	6	287	11	4	12	43	17	.72	24	.266	.335	.439

Stacy Hollins

Pitches: Right **Bats:** Right **Pos:** P **Ht:** 6'3" **Wt:** 175 **Born:** 7/31/72 **Age:** 23

Year Team	Lg	G	GS	CG	GF	IP	BFP	H	R	ER	HR	SH	SF	HB	TBB	IBB	SO	WP	Bk	W	L	Pct.	ShO	Sv	ERA
1992 Athletics	R	15	14	3	0	93	392	89	47	35	0	2	2	4	19	0	93	5	3	6	3	.667	2	0	3.39
1993 Madison	A	26	26	2	0	150.2	653	145	100	86	21	4	4	8	52	6	105	4	1	10	11	.476	1	0	5.14
1994 Modesto	A	29	22	0	3	143.1	610	133	57	54	10	4	2	8	55	1	131	7	1	13	6	.684	0	0	3.39
1995 Huntsville	AA	15	15	0	0	82.2	364	80	52	49	10	4	2	4	42	6	62	8	2	3	8	.273	0	0	5.33
Edmonton	AAA	7	7	0	0	29.2	156	47	43	34	4	0	1	1	21	3	25	6	0	0	7	.000	0	0	10.31
4 Min. YEARS		92	84	5	3	499.1	2175	494	299	258	45	14	11	25	189	16	416	30	7	32	35	.478	3	0	4.65

Brad Holman

Pitches: Right **Bats:** Right **Pos:** P **Ht:** 6'5" **Wt:** 200 **Born:** 2/9/68 **Age:** 28

Year Team	Lg	G	GS	CG	GF	IP	BFP	H	R	ER	HR	SH	SF	HB	TBB	IBB	SO	WP	Bk	W	L	Pct.	ShO	Sv	ERA
1990 Eugene	A	17	4	0	3	43.1	184	43	28	23	3	2	0	4	17	0	31	4	2	0	3	.000	0	0	4.78
1991 Peninsula	A	47	0	0	35	78.1	334	70	34	28	4	5	3	2	33	7	71	5	3	6	6	.500	0	10	3.22
1992 Peninsula	A	13	0	0	12	17.2	74	15	8	6	0	0	0	0	4	1	19	2	0	1	1	.500	0	5	3.06
Jacksonville	AA	35	0	0	15	73.2	305	67	24	21	6	0	2	4	21	3	76	3	0	3	3	.500	0	4	2.57
1993 Calgary	AAA	21	13	1	2	98.2	427	109	59	52	5	3	6	3	42	0	54	7	1	8	4	.667	0	0	4.74
1994 Calgary	AAA	24	2	0	8	38.2	209	65	54	48	3	1	4	4	27	0	19	4	0	0	1	.000	0	1	11.17
1995 Tacoma	AAA	5	0	0	0	6.2	31	9	6	6	0	0	0	0	3	0	1	0	0	1	0	1.000	0	0	8.10
Rochester	AAA	1	1	0	0	1.2	12	5	4	0	0	0	1	0	2	0	0	1	0	0	1	.000	0	0	0.00
New Haven	AA	7	1	0	4	16	58	8	6	6	0	0	1	0	5	0	9	1	1	0	0	.000	0	0	3.38
1993 Seattle	AL	19	0	0	9	36.1	152	27	17	15	1	1	0	5	16	2	17	2	0	1	3	.250	0	3	3.72
6 Min. YEARS		170	21	1	80	374.2	1634	391	223	190	21	11	17	17	154	11	280	27	7	19	19	.500	0	20	4.56

Craig Holman

Pitches: Right **Bats:** Both **Pos:** P **Ht:** 6'2" **Wt:** 200 **Born:** 3/13/69 **Age:** 27

Year Team	Lg	G	GS	CG	GF	IP	BFP	H	R	ER	HR	SH	SF	HB	TBB	IBB	SO	WP	Bk	W	L	Pct.	ShO	Sv	ERA
1991 Batavia	A	15	12	0	1	79.1	327	67	27	17	2	2	1	2	22	1	53	7	1	6	2	.750	0	0	1.93
1992 Spartanburg	A	25	24	3	1	143.1	611	153	72	59	9	4	4	4	39	0	129	10	2	9	6	.600	1	0	3.70
1993 Clearwater	A	7	1	0	2	18	71	17	7	5	1	0	0	0	1	0	7	1	0	0	0	.000	0	0	2.50
Reading	AA	24	24	4	0	139	586	134	73	64	5	3	2	12	43	1	86	6	1	8	13	.381	1	0	4.14
1994 Reading	AA	7	4	0	1	27.2	126	32	22	19	3	0	0	1	13	1	18	1	0	2	5	.286	0	0	6.18
1995 Reading	AA	32	1	0	13	56.2	235	55	27	22	10	2	2	2	16	2	40	2	1	1	1	.500	0	1	3.49
5 Min. YEARS		110	66	7	18	464	1956	459	228	186	30	11	9	21	134	5	333	27	5	26	27	.491	2	1	3.61

Shawn Holman

Pitches: Right **Bats:** Right **Pos:** P **Ht:** 6'2" **Wt:** 185 **Born:** 11/10/64 **Age:** 31

Year Team	Lg	G	GS	CG	GF	IP	BFP	H	R	ER	HR	SH	SF	HB	TBB	IBB	SO	WP	Bk	W	L	Pct.	ShO	Sv	ERA
1984 Macon	A	9	6	1	2	46.2	210	48	19	10	1	3	1	1	25	0	32	3	0	3	2	.600	1	0	1.93
Pr. William	A	15	14	1	0	77.2	345	74	46	35	4	1	2	2	49	0	47	9	0	7	4	.636	0	0	4.06
1985 Pr. William	A	24	23	4	0	142.1	596	123	69	56	11	3	8	6	53	2	65	11	2	10	11	.476	2	0	3.54
Nashua	AA	2	2	0	0	8	38	10	6	4	0	1	1	0	7	0	2	0	0	0	1	.000	0	0	4.50
1986 Nashua	AA	25	17	1	3	109.1	484	108	61	58	9	5	2	4	67	3	39	8	0	4	13	.235	1	0	4.77
1987 Harrisburg	AA	27	0	0	11	62	277	67	32	25	6	4	2	4	35	2	27	0	0	4	3	.571	0	2	3.63
Glens Falls	AA	18	5	0	5	42.1	201	49	33	29	4	0	1	4	25	2	22	6	0	1	3	.250	0	1	6.17
1988 Glens Falls	AA	52	0	0	26	91.2	377	82	36	19	3	7	2	7	26	1	44	7	2	8	3	.727	0	10	1.87
1989 Toledo	AAA	51	0	0	31	89.2	372	74	21	19	2	5	1	10	36	2	38	3	0	3	1	.750	0	11	1.91
1990 Toledo	AAA	17	0	0	3	20.1	110	27	22	17	3	0	1	3	14	0	10	0	0	2	1	.667	0	0	7.52
London	AA	28	0	0	14	31	147	35	26	21	2	1	0	5	15	0	26	1	0	0	3	.000	0	8	6.10
1993 Richmond	AAA	37	22	0	3	155	661	174	88	72	12	5	4	5	46	3	101	8	0	12	7	.632	0	0	4.18
1994 Ottawa	AAA	59	0	0	52	69.1	301	65	28	23	1	2	2	3	35	4	44	4	1	2	4	.333	0	31	2.99
1995 Albuquerque	AAA	49	1	0	22	79	386	107	58	45	3	5	5	5	39	7	60	7	0	5	6	.455	0	5	5.13
1989 Detroit	AL	5	0	0	3	10	50	8	2	2	0	0	1	0	11	1	9	0	0	0	0	.000	0	0	1.80
10 Min. YEARS		413	90	7	172	1024.1	4505	1043	545	433	61	42	32	59	472	26	557	67	5	61	62	.496	4	68	3.80

138

Chris Holt

Pitches: Right **Bats:** Right **Pos:** P — **Ht:** 6'4" **Wt:** 205 **Born:** 9/18/71 **Age:** 24

		HOW MUCH HE PITCHED						WHAT HE GAVE UP											THE RESULTS					
Year	Team	Lg	G	GS	CG	GF	IP	BFP	H	R	ER	HR	SH	SF	HB	TBB	IBB	SO	WP	Bk	W	L	Pct.	ShO	Sv	ERA
1992	Auburn	A	14	14	0	0	83	353	75	48	41	9	4	2	7	24	0	81	11	4	2	5	.286	0	0	4.45
1993	Quad City	A	26	26	10	0	186.1	775	162	70	47	10	8	2	3	54	1	176	9	3	11	10	.524	3	0	2.27
1994	Jackson	AA	26	25	5	0	167	679	169	78	64	11	6	4	9	22	2	111	5	1	10	9	.526	2	0	3.45
1995	Jackson	AA	5	5	1	0	32.1	126	27	8	6	2	1	0	0	5	1	24	1	0	2	2	.500	1	0	1.67
	Tucson	AAA	20	19	0	0	118.2	524	155	65	54	5	7	3	7	32	1	69	6	0	5	8	.385	0	0	4.10
	4 Min. YEARS		91	89	16	0	587.1	2457	588	269	212	37	26	11	26	137	5	461	32	8	30	34	.469	6	0	3.25

Dennis Hood

Bats: Right **Throws:** Right **Pos:** OF — **Ht:** 6'2" **Wt:** 180 **Born:** 7/3/66 **Age:** 29

			BATTING													BASERUNNING				PERCENTAGES		
Year	Team	Lg	G	AB	H	2B	3B	HR	TB	R	RBI	TBB	IBB	SO	HBP	SH	SF	SB	CS	SB%	GDP	Avg	OBP	SLG
1984	Braves	R	49	155	31	7	0	1	41	16	18	15	0	40	0	1	2	4	2	.67	1	.200	.267	.265
1985	Braves	R	59	204	49	14	0	1	66	19	17	21	1	59	6	3	3	7	3	.70	2	.240	.325	.324
1986	Sumter	A	135	562	142	25	3	7	194	104	42	62	1	146	8	10	4	43	17	.72	9	.253	.333	.345
1987	Durham	A	120	438	118	19	4	13	184	73	62	51	0	115	4	3	2	32	12	.73	8	.269	.349	.420
1988	Greenville	AA	141	525	135	15	8	14	208	85	47	52	5	139	8	1	2	31	8	.79	6	.257	.332	.396
1989	Greenville	AA	136	464	117	20	5	11	180	68	44	48	4	124	8	3	3	32	14	.70	5	.252	.331	.388
1990	Richmond	AAA	121	389	96	15	5	8	145	50	36	33	2	120	4	5	3	13	9	.59	3	.247	.310	.373
1991	Calgary	AAA	102	314	56	9	2	11	102	52	42	34	0	97	2	7	0	18	6	.75	2	.178	.263	.325
1993	Thunder Bay	IND	69	261	84	13	7	7	132	36	34	19	2	75	4	5	3	30	7	.81	2	.322	.373	.506
1994	Rochester	AAA	2	9	1	1	0	0	2	1	0	0	0	3	0	0	0	0	0	.00	0	.111	.111	.222
	Regina	IND	71	284	93	14	3	9	140	69	54	31	2	50	4	0	3	39	3	.93	2	.327	.398	.493
1995	Canton-Akrn	AA	8	23	5	1	0	0	6	6	2	2	0	7	0	0	0	1	0	1.00	0	.217	.280	.261
	Amarillo	IND	96	376	140	37	5	11	220	100	83	63	1	56	3	0	8	56	10	.85	5	.372	.458	.585
	11 Min. YEARS		1109	4004	1067	190	42	93	1620	679	481	431	18	1031	51	38	33	306	91	.77	45	.266	.343	.405

Jeff Horn

Bats: Right **Throws:** Right **Pos:** C — **Ht:** 6'1" **Wt:** 190 **Born:** 8/23/70 **Age:** 25

			BATTING													BASERUNNING				PERCENTAGES		
Year	Team	Lg	G	AB	H	2B	3B	HR	TB	R	RBI	TBB	IBB	SO	HBP	SH	SF	SB	CS	SB%	GDP	Avg	OBP	SLG
1992	Elizabethtn	R	41	144	35	6	0	1	44	20	26	25	1	25	4	0	2	2	0	1.00	5	.243	.366	.306
1993	Fort Wayne	A	66	200	39	7	0	5	61	19	23	18	0	51	4	1	4	1	2	.33	3	.195	.270	.305
1994	Fort Myers	A	34	100	28	3	0	0	31	10	9	8	1	11	3	0	1	0	2	.00	6	.280	.348	.310
1995	Salt Lake	AAA	3	10	5	1	0	0	6	0	2	0	0	1	0	0	0	0	0	.00	0	.500	.500	.600
	Fort Myers	A	66	199	53	5	1	0	60	25	20	38	1	30	4	1	3	2	3	.40	4	.266	.389	.302
	4 Min. YEARS		210	653	160	22	1	6	202	74	80	89	3	118	15	2	10	5	7	.42	18	.245	.344	.309

Tyrone Horne

Bats: Left **Throws:** Right **Pos:** OF — **Ht:** 5'10" **Wt:** 185 **Born:** 11/2/70 **Age:** 25

			BATTING													BASERUNNING				PERCENTAGES		
Year	Team	Lg	G	AB	H	2B	3B	HR	TB	R	RBI	TBB	IBB	SO	HBP	SH	SF	SB	CS	SB%	GDP	Avg	OBP	SLG
1989	Expos	R	24	68	14	3	2	0	21	7	13	11	0	29	0	0	0	4	4	.50	0	.206	.316	.309
1990	Gate City	R	56	202	57	11	2	1	75	26	13	24	1	62	2	2	2	23	8	.74	1	.282	.361	.371
	Jamestown	A	7	23	7	2	1	0	11	1	5	4	0	5	0	0	0	3	0	1.00	1	.304	.407	.478
1991	Sumter	A	118	428	114	20	3	10	170	69	49	42	1	133	2	1	4	23	12	.66	4	.266	.332	.397
1992	Rockford	A	129	480	134	27	4	12	205	71	48	62	5	141	1	2	2	23	13	.64	1	.279	.361	.427
	Harrisburg	AA	1	1	1	0	0	0	1	0	0	0	0	0	0	0	0	0	0	.00	0	1.000	1.000	1.000
1993	W. Palm Bch	A	82	288	85	19	2	10	138	43	44	40	1	72	0	1	3	11	10	.52	1	.295	.378	.479
	Harrisburg	AA	35	128	46	8	1	4	68	22	22	22	0	37	1	1	0	3	2	.60	3	.359	.457	.531
1994	Expos	R	7	29	7	1	0	1	11	3	7	4	0	9	0	0	0	1	0	1.00	1	.241	.333	.379
	Harrisburg	AA	90	311	89	15	0	9	131	56	48	50	1	92	1	1	2	11	13	.46	7	.286	.385	.421
1995	Harrisburg	AA	87	294	87	17	4	14	154	59	47	58	2	65	1	3	3	14	8	.64	3	.296	.410	.524
	Norwich	AA	46	166	47	16	1	2	71	23	22	26	1	36	0	0	3	4	2	.67	4	.283	.374	.428
	7 Min. YEARS		682	2418	688	139	20	63	1056	380	318	343	12	681	8	11	19	120	72	.63	25	.285	.373	.437

Steve Hosey

Bats: Right **Throws:** Right **Pos:** OF — **Ht:** 6'3" **Wt:** 225 **Born:** 4/2/69 **Age:** 27

			BATTING													BASERUNNING				PERCENTAGES		
Year	Team	Lg	G	AB	H	2B	3B	HR	TB	R	RBI	TBB	IBB	SO	HBP	SH	SF	SB	CS	SB%	GDP	Avg	OBP	SLG
1989	Everett	A	73	288	83	14	3	13	142	44	59	27	2	84	10	0	4	15	3	.83	3	.288	.367	.493
1990	San Jose	A	139	479	111	13	6	16	184	85	78	71	2	139	5	1	4	16	17	.48	7	.232	.335	.384
1991	Shreveport	AA	126	409	120	21	5	17	202	79	74	56	5	87	6	5	4	24	11	.69	7	.293	.383	.494
1992	Phoenix	AAA	125	462	132	28	7	10	204	64	65	39	4	98	6	0	5	15	15	.50	11	.286	.346	.442
1993	Phoenix	AAA	129	455	133	40	4	16	229	70	85	66	5	129	3	0	5	16	10	.62	7	.292	.382	.503
1994	Vancouver	AAA	112	374	97	22	2	17	174	67	60	47	1	113	6	3	8	9	7	.56	8	.259	.345	.465
1995	Midland	AA	30	88	21	4	0	2	31	16	16	12	1	31	2	0	1	5	4	.56	2	.239	.340	.352
	Vancouver	AAA	16	59	16	3	0	2	25	10	6	7	0	16	0	0	0	2	0	1.00	1	.271	.348	.424
1992	San Francisco	NL	21	56	14	1	0	1	18	6	6	0	0	15	0	0	2	1	1	.50	1	.250	.241	.321
1993	San Francisco	NL	3	2	1	1	0	0	2	0	1	0	0	1	0	0	0	0	0	.00	0	.500	.667	1.000
	7 Min. YEARS		750	2614	713	145	27	93	1191	435	443	325	20	697	38	9	29	102	67	.60	46	.273	.358	.456
	2 Maj. YEARS		24	58	15	2	0	1	20	6	7	0	0	16	0	0	2	1	1	.50	1	.259	.262	.345

Marcus Hostetler

Pitches: Right **Bats:** Right **Pos:** P   **Ht:** 6'3" **Wt:** 210 **Born:** 7/4/69 **Age:** 26

					HOW MUCH HE PITCHED				WHAT HE GAVE UP										THE RESULTS				
Year	Team	Lg	G	GS	CG	GF	IP	BFP	H	R	ER	HR	SH	SF	HB	TBB	IBB	SO	WP	Bk	W	L	Pct.	ShO	Sv	ERA
1993	Braves	R	3	0	0	3	9	32	2	1	1	0	0	0	1	2	1	12	0	4	2	0	1.000	0	0	1.00
	Danville	R	20	0	0	12	31.2	121	18	8	7	0	1	0	3	5	0	37	1	1	0	1	.000	0	5	1.99
1994	Macon	A	46	0	0	34	73.1	311	57	19	13	2	3	0	5	30	6	84	5	0	5	4	.556	0	9	1.60
1995	Greenville	AA	33	0	0	19	43.2	199	47	30	20	6	4	3	2	21	2	24	3	0	5	2	.714	0	2	4.12
	Durham	A	12	0	0	3	16.1	80	23	13	12	3	1	2	1	7	0	6	0	0	1	1	.500	0	0	6.61
	3 Min. YEARS		114	0	0	71	174	743	147	71	53	11	9	5	12	65	9	163	9	5	13	8	.619	0	16	2.74

Mike Hostetler

Pitches: Right **Bats:** Right **Pos:** P   **Ht:** 6'2" **Wt:** 195 **Born:** 6/5/70 **Age:** 26

					HOW MUCH HE PITCHED				WHAT HE GAVE UP										THE RESULTS				
Year	Team	Lg	G	GS	CG	GF	IP	BFP	H	R	ER	HR	SH	SF	HB	TBB	IBB	SO	WP	Bk	W	L	Pct.	ShO	Sv	ERA
1991	Pulaski	R	9	9	0	0	47	184	35	12	10	4	1	1	2	9	2	61	4	1	3	2	.600	0	0	1.91
1992	Durham	A	13	13	3	0	88	354	75	25	21	2	0	1	2	19	3	88	2	3	9	3	.750	2	0	2.15
	Greenville	AA	16	13	1	0	80.2	339	78	37	35	11	3	2	4	23	1	57	3	0	6	2	.750	0	0	3.90
1993	Richmond	AAA	9	9	0	0	48	212	50	29	27	5	1	0	4	18	2	36	0	0	1	3	.250	0	0	5.06
	Greenville	AA	19	19	2	0	135.2	559	122	48	41	9	6	2	7	36	3	105	6	0	8	5	.615	0	0	2.72
1994	Richmond	AAA	6	6	0	0	23.1	105	27	16	16	3	0	1	1	10	1	13	0	2	0	2	.000	0	0	6.17
1995	Greenville	AA	28	28	0	0	162.2	711	182	102	95	24	8	4	6	46	4	93	6	1	10	10	.500	0	0	5.26
	5 Min. YEARS		100	97	6	0	585.1	2464	569	269	245	58	19	11	26	161	16	453	21	7	37	27	.578	2	0	3.77

Tom Hostetler

Pitches: Right **Bats:** Right **Pos:** P   **Ht:** 5'10" **Wt:** 165 **Born:** 10/10/64 **Age:** 31

					HOW MUCH HE PITCHED				WHAT HE GAVE UP										THE RESULTS				
Year	Team	Lg	G	GS	CG	GF	IP	BFP	H	R	ER	HR	SH	SF	HB	TBB	IBB	SO	WP	Bk	W	L	Pct.	ShO	Sv	ERA
1987	Everett	A	14	13	2	0	90.2	386	77	37	31	10	2	3	2	34	0	89	4	0	9	2	.818	0	0	3.08
1988	Clinton	A	17	17	4	0	120.1	478	85	39	34	10	1	4	1	37	0	118	3	6	11	3	.786	2	0	2.54
	San Jose	A	6	6	0	0	29	120	29	11	9	1	0	1	0	11	0	27	4	1	2	0	1.000	0	0	2.79
1989	San Jose	A	16	16	2	0	111.1	463	99	44	32	5	6	4	1	26	0	103	1	5	9	4	.692	1	0	2.59
	Shreveport	AA	11	11	2	0	73.2	317	72	35	28	6	4	1	2	24	3	60	3	0	5	4	.556	1	0	3.42
1990	Shreveport	AA	23	22	1	1	130.1	545	119	55	44	5	6	1	3	40	3	112	5	3	5	8	.385	0	0	3.04
1991	Shreveport	AA	9	9	0	0	45.2	187	39	19	18	0	1	1	1	20	0	33	0	1	4	1	.800	0	0	3.55
1995	Edmonton	AAA	4	0	0	1	5	31	9	7	7	2	0	0	0	8	1	7	1	0	0	0	.000	0	0	12.60
	Winnipeg	IND	5	1	0	4	9.1	39	7	5	5	1	0	0	0	5	0	8	0	0	1	0	1.000	0	0	4.82
	6 Min. YEARS		105	95	11	6	615.1	2566	536	252	208	40	20	15	10	205	7	557	21	16	46	22	.676	3	0	3.04

Tyler Houston

Bats: Left **Throws:** Right **Pos:** 1B   **Ht:** 6'2" **Wt:** 210 **Born:** 1/17/71 **Age:** 25

						BATTING											BASERUNNING				PERCENTAGES		
Year	Team	Lg	G	AB	H	2B	3B	HR	TB	R	RBI	TBB	IBB	SO	HBP	SH	SF	SB	CS	SB%	GDP	Avg	OBP	SLG
1989	Idaho Falls	R	50	176	43	11	0	4	66	30	24	25	1	41	1	0	0	4	0	1.00	4	.244	.342	.375
1990	Sumter	A	117	442	93	14	3	13	152	58	56	49	1	101	2	2	7	6	2	.75	15	.210	.288	.344
1991	Macon	A	107	351	81	16	3	8	127	41	47	39	0	70	1	1	3	10	2	.83	8	.231	.307	.362
1992	Durham	A	117	402	91	17	1	7	131	39	38	20	0	89	1	3	5	5	6	.45	5	.226	.262	.326
1993	Greenville	AA	84	262	73	14	1	5	104	27	33	13	4	50	2	3	4	5	3	.63	12	.279	.313	.397
	Richmond	AAA	13	36	5	1	1	1	11	4	3	1	0	8	0	0	0	0	0	.00	1	.139	.162	.306
1994	Richmond	AAA	97	312	76	15	2	4	107	33	33	16	1	44	0	0	5	3	3	.50	12	.244	.276	.343
1995	Richmond	AAA	103	349	89	10	3	12	141	41	42	18	3	62	4	1	2	3	5	.38	6	.255	.298	.404
	7 Min. YEARS		688	2330	551	98	14	54	839	273	276	181	10	465	11	10	26	36	21	.63	63	.236	.292	.360

Chris Howard

Bats: Right **Throws:** Right **Pos:** C   **Ht:** 6'2" **Wt:** 220 **Born:** 2/27/66 **Age:** 30

						BATTING											BASERUNNING				PERCENTAGES		
Year	Team	Lg	G	AB	H	2B	3B	HR	TB	R	RBI	TBB	IBB	SO	HBP	SH	SF	SB	CS	SB%	GDP	Avg	OBP	SLG
1988	Bellingham	A	2	9	3	0	0	1	6	3	3	1	0	2	0	0	0	0	0	.00	0	.333	.400	.667
	Wausau	A	61	187	45	10	1	7	78	20	20	18	0	60	3	0	1	1	3	.25	4	.241	.316	.417
1989	Wausau	A	36	125	30	8	0	4	50	13	32	13	1	35	1	0	1	0	0	.00	2	.240	.314	.400
	Williamsprt	AA	86	296	75	13	0	9	115	30	36	28	0	79	5	2	1	0	1	.00	10	.253	.328	.389
1990	Williamsprt	AA	118	401	95	19	1	5	131	48	49	37	1	91	3	4	4	3	1	.75	16	.237	.303	.327
1991	Calgary	AAA	82	293	72	12	1	8	110	32	36	16	1	56	2	3	1	1	1	.50	10	.246	.288	.375
1992	Calgary	AAA	97	319	76	16	0	8	116	29	45	14	0	73	5	3	2	3	7	.30	9	.238	.279	.364
1993	Calgary	AAA	94	331	106	23	0	6	147	40	55	23	1	62	5	5	2	1	5	.17	4	.320	.371	.444
1994	Calgary	AAA	75	266	67	10	0	11	110	41	44	27	2	66	1	2	3	1	0	1.00	11	.252	.320	.414
1995	Tacoma	AAA	83	268	65	14	0	4	91	33	31	18	2	70	2	4	2	0	1	.00	9	.243	.293	.340
1991	Seattle	AL	9	6	1	1	0	0	2	1	0	1	0	2	0	0	0	0	0	.00	0	.167	.286	.333
1993	Seattle	AL	4	1	0	0	0	0	0	0	0	0	0	0	0	0	0	0	0	.00	0	.000	.000	.000
1994	Seattle	AL	9	25	5	1	0	0	6	2	2	1	0	6	1	1	1	0	0	.00	0	.200	.250	.240
	8 Min. YEARS		734	2495	634	125	3	63	954	289	351	195	8	594	27	23	16	10	19	.34	75	.254	.313	.382
	3 Maj. YEARS		22	32	6	2	0	0	8	3	2	2	0	8	1	1	1	0	0	.00	0	.188	.250	.250

Matt Howard

Bats: Right Throws: Right Pos: SS   Ht: 5'10" Wt: 170 Born: 9/22/67 Age: 28

Year	Team	Lg	G	AB	H	2B	3B	HR	TB	R	RBI	TBB	IBB	SO	HBP	SH	SF	SB	CS	SB%	GDP	Avg	OBP	SLG
1989	Great Falls	R	59	186	62	8	2	3	83	39	34	21	0	14	9	5	2	23	8	.74	3	.333	.422	.446
1990	Bakersfield	A	137	551	144	22	3	1	175	75	54	37	1	39	13	4	6	47	10	.82	8	.261	.320	.318
1991	Vero Beach	A	128	441	115	21	3	3	151	79	39	56	2	49	10	14	6	50	18	.74	6	.261	.353	.342
1992	San Antonio	AA	95	345	93	12	5	2	121	40	34	28	1	38	4	16	1	18	15	.55	12	.270	.331	.351
	Albuquerque	AAA	36	116	34	3	0	0	37	14	8	9	0	7	0	2	0	1	2	.33	2	.293	.344	.319
1993	Albuquerque	AAA	18	26	4	0	1	0	6	3	4	3	0	2	0	1	1	1	1	.50	1	.154	.233	.231
	San Antonio	AA	41	122	35	5	1	0	42	12	5	16	1	14	3	2	0	4	5	.44	4	.287	.383	.344
1994	Albuquerque	AAA	88	267	79	12	6	1	106	44	33	14	0	13	6	4	1	15	8	.65	12	.296	.344	.397
1995	Bowie	AA	70	251	76	8	2	1	91	42	15	29	1	27	5	3	1	22	4	.85	6	.303	.385	.363
7 Min. YEARS			672	2305	642	91	23	11	812	348	226	213	6	203	50	51	18	181	71	.72	54	.279	.350	.352

Tim Howard

Bats: Left Throws: Right Pos: OF   Ht: 5'10" Wt: 155 Born: 6/2/69 Age: 27

Year	Team	Lg	G	AB	H	2B	3B	HR	TB	R	RBI	TBB	IBB	SO	HBP	SH	SF	SB	CS	SB%	GDP	Avg	OBP	SLG
1988	Kingsport	R	68	243	68	14	4	3	99	39	46	27	2	43	3	1	6	7	3	.70	2	.280	.351	.407
1989	Columbia	A	15	57	16	1	0	0	17	8	4	1	0	9	1	0	0	3	1	.75	0	.281	.305	.298
	Pittsfield	A	63	228	64	6	8	0	86	35	31	19	2	22	2	2	3	13	9	.59	1	.281	.337	.377
1990	Columbia	A	128	505	163	18	11	10	233	80	89	46	7	44	0	1	9	30	10	.75	11	.323	.373	.461
1991	St. Lucie	A	60	235	61	6	3	5	88	20	37	14	3	16	1	2	8	7	7	.50	2	.260	.295	.374
	Williamsprt	AA	68	245	63	7	6	1	85	23	16	14	0	21	0	3	1	7	3	.70	5	.257	.296	.347
1992	Binghamton	AA	136	505	138	20	9	5	191	68	77	40	3	54	3	1	9	12	6	.67	4	.273	.325	.378
1993	Norfolk	AAA	64	197	52	7	2	3	72	18	16	10	2	13	1	0	1	2	1	.67	7	.264	.301	.365
	Binghamton	AA	28	100	30	6	1	2	44	13	15	23	1	8	0	0	3	2	0	1.00	0	.300	.421	.440
1995	Pawtucket	AAA	38	90	28	5	1	0	35	13	11	7	0	11	1	1	0	7	3	.70	3	.311	.367	.389
	Nashville	AAA	37	103	24	3	1	2	35	8	13	13	0	12	1	0	1	4	3	.57	3	.233	.322	.340
7 Min. YEARS			705	2508	707	93	46	31	985	325	355	214	20	253	13	11	41	94	46	.67	38	.282	.336	.393

Dann Howitt

Bats: Left Throws: Right Pos: OF-DH   Ht: 6'5" Wt: 205 Born: 2/13/64 Age: 32

Year	Team	Lg	G	AB	H	2B	3B	HR	TB	R	RBI	TBB	IBB	SO	HBP	SH	SF	SB	CS	SB%	GDP	Avg	OBP	SLG
1986	Medford	A	66	208	66	9	2	6	97	36	37	49	3	37	1	1	1	5	1	.83	7	.317	.448	.466
1987	Modesto	A	109	336	70	11	2	8	109	44	42	59	1	110	4	3	3	7	9	.44	8	.208	.331	.324
1988	Modesto	A	132	480	121	20	2	18	199	75	86	81	3	106	2	0	2	11	5	.69	9	.252	.361	.415
	Tacoma	AAA	4	15	2	1	0	0	3	1	0	0	0	4	0	0	0	0	0	.00	0	.133	.133	.200
1989	Huntsville	AA	138	509	143	28	2	26	253	78	111	68	7	107	3	2	6	2	1	.67	6	.281	.365	.497
1990	Tacoma	AAA	118	437	116	30	1	11	181	58	69	38	3	95	2	0	4	4	4	.50	16	.265	.324	.414
1991	Tacoma	AAA	122	449	120	28	6	14	202	58	73	49	2	92	2	1	5	5	2	.71	14	.267	.339	.450
1992	Tacoma	AAA	43	140	41	13	1	1	59	25	27	23	0	20	2	0	5	5	3	.63	3	.293	.388	.421
	Calgary	AAA	50	178	54	9	5	6	91	29	33	12	1	38	1	2	1	4	0	1.00	7	.303	.349	.511
1993	Calgary	AAA	95	333	93	20	1	21	178	57	77	39	2	67	1	1	7	7	5	.58	4	.279	.350	.535
1994	Nashville	AAA	66	231	59	15	1	8	100	30	36	19	1	48	2	0	1	4	0	1.00	4	.255	.316	.433
1995	Nashville	AAA	45	133	30	6	1	3	47	16	15	16	4	32	0	0	2	0	3	.00	5	.226	.305	.353
	Buffalo	AAA	41	119	36	8	3	4	62	19	18	14	2	30	0	0	0	0	0	.00	2	.303	.376	.521
1989	Oakland	AL	3	3	0	0	0	0	0	0	0	0	0	2	0	0	0	0	0	.00	0	.000	.000	.000
1990	Oakland	AL	14	22	3	0	1	0	5	3	1	3	0	12	0	0	0	0	0	.00	0	.136	.240	.227
1991	Oakland	AL	21	42	7	1	0	1	11	5	3	1	0	12	0	0	1	0	0	.00	0	.167	.182	.262
1992	Oakland	AL	22	48	6	0	0	1	9	1	2	5	1	4	0	1	0	0	0	.00	4	.125	.208	.188
	Seattle	AL	13	37	10	4	1	1	19	6	8	3	0	5	0	0	3	1	1	.50	2	.270	.302	.514
1993	Seattle	AL	32	76	16	3	1	2	27	6	8	4	0	18	0	0	0	0	0	.00	0	.211	.250	.355
1994	Chicago	AL	10	14	5	3	0	0	8	4	0	1	0	7	0	0	0	0	0	.00	1	.357	.400	.571
10 Min. YEARS			1029	3568	951	198	27	126	1581	526	624	467	29	786	20	10	37	54	33	.62	85	.267	.351	.443
6 Maj. YEARS			115	242	47	11	3	5	79	25	22	17	1	60	0	1	4	1	1	.50	8	.194	.243	.326

John Hrusovsky

Pitches: Right Bats: Right Pos: P   Ht: 6'1" Wt: 195 Born: 9/12/70 Age: 25

Year	Team	Lg	G	GS	CG	GF	IP	BFP	H	R	ER	HR	SH	SF	HB	TBB	IBB	SO	WP	Bk	W	L	Pct.	ShO	Sv	ERA
1991	Princeton	R	26	0	0	25	44.1	189	26	12	9	2	2	1	3	21	3	52	1	0	4	4	.500	0	7	1.83
1992	Charlstn-Wv	A	19	0	0	16	21.2	85	13	3	2	0	0	1	0	9	1	27	0	0	1	0	1.000	0	9	0.83
	Cedar Rapds	A	25	0	0	25	30.2	132	18	14	10	3	2	1	1	16	0	52	5	1	2	3	.400	0	7	2.93
1993	Winston-Sal	A	52	0	0	40	58.1	260	53	27	25	4	0	1	4	27	2	61	6	0	2	4	.333	0	25	3.86
1994	Chattanooga	AA	9	0	0	4	13.1	62	14	8	8	2	1	0	0	7	1	13	0	0	0	0	.000	0	0	5.40
	Canton-Akrn	AA	12	0	0	6	22	107	29	18	14	4	1	3	0	12	1	22	2	0	0	0	.000	0	1	5.73
	Kinston	A	19	1	0	15	23	113	28	19	16	2	0	1	1	16	0	16	4	0	0	3	.000	0	3	6.26
1995	Canton-Akrn	AA	35	4	0	11	69.2	323	77	64	55	12	4	6	2	35	3	59	1	0	1	7	.125	0	1	7.11
5 Min. YEARS			197	5	0	142	283	1271	258	165	139	29	10	14	11	143	11	302	19	1	10	21	.323	0	53	4.42

Mark Hubbard

Pitches: Left **Bats:** Left **Pos:** P   **Ht:** 6'2" **Wt:** 190 **Born:** 2/2/70 **Age:** 26

Year	Team	Lg	G	GS	CG	GF	IP	BFP	H	R	ER	HR	SH	SF	HB	TBB	IBB	SO	WP	Bk	W	L	Pct.	ShO	Sv	ERA
1994	Greensboro	A	26	26	2	0	149.1	642	162	69	59	11	1	5	7	46	0	139	4	3	13	7	.650	1	0	3.56
	Tampa	A	2	1	0	1	6.2	33	9	6	3	2	0	0	1	2	0	5	0	0	0	0	.000	0	0	4.05
1995	Tampa	A	13	11	1	0	68.1	269	52	22	14	2	1	2	4	21	0	40	2	0	4	3	.571	0	0	1.84
	Norwich	AA	13	12	0	1	72.2	310	81	38	34	2	2	2	6	25	1	39	1	1	4	4	.500	0	1	4.21
	2 Min. YEARS		54	50	3	2	297	1254	304	135	110	17	4	9	18	94	1	223	7	4	21	15	.583	1	1	3.33

Dan Hubbs

Pitches: Right **Bats:** Right **Pos:** P   **Ht:** 6'2" **Wt:** 200 **Born:** 1/23/71 **Age:** 25

Year	Team	Lg	G	GS	CG	GF	IP	BFP	H	R	ER	HR	SH	SF	HB	TBB	IBB	SO	WP	Bk	W	L	Pct.	ShO	Sv	ERA
1993	Great Falls	R	3	0	0	1	7.2	29	3	1	1	0	0	0	2	2	0	12	0	1	1	1	.500	0	0	1.17
	Bakersfield	A	19	1	0	8	44.2	181	32	20	18	4	1	2	0	15	1	44	3	1	2	1	.667	0	1	1.81
1994	Bakersfield	A	13	0	0	6	35.1	145	29	17	15	3	3	0	1	10	0	51	0	0	3	1	.750	0	2	3.82
	San Antonio	AA	38	1	0	13	80	340	82	34	28	3	1	6	4	27	7	75	5	0	5	5	.500	0	1	3.15
1995	San Antonio	AA	31	0	0	6	61	248	58	25	24	3	3	1	1	16	0	52	0	1	2	1	.667	0	0	3.54
	3 Min. YEARS		104	2	0	34	228.2	943	208	89	77	13	8	9	8	70	8	234	8	3	13	9	.591	0	4	3.03

Jeff Huber

Pitches: Left **Bats:** Right **Pos:** P   **Ht:** 6'4" **Wt:** 220 **Born:** 12/17/70 **Age:** 25

Year	Team	Lg	G	GS	CG	GF	IP	BFP	H	R	ER	HR	SH	SF	HB	TBB	IBB	SO	WP	Bk	W	L	Pct.	ShO	Sv	ERA
1990	Padres	R	9	7	0	1	35.2	153	32	20	12	0	0	2	0	15	0	20	2	2	1	4	.200	0	1	3.03
1992	Charlstn-Sc	A	46	0	0	30	77.1	309	66	31	25	3	2	0	4	21	2	59	6	5	8	3	.727	0	9	2.91
	Waterloo	A	9	0	0	6	15	58	15	4	4	0	1	1	0	1	0	13	0	0	1	2	.333	0	1	2.40
1993	Rancho Cuca	A	42	0	0	41	48.2	199	43	22	17	4	2	0	0	18	0	43	4	0	4	1	.800	0	18	3.14
	Wichita	AA	15	0	0	8	19.1	82	16	9	7	2	1	0	3	9	0	18	1	1	3	1	.750	0	3	3.26
1994	Wichita	AA	38	0	0	29	39.2	193	56	37	31	7	4	3	0	17	2	32	3	0	3	2	.600	0	12	7.03
1995	Memphis	AA	5	0	0	0	4.2	22	7	6	6	2	0	0	1	0	0	6	0	0	0	0	1.000	0	0	11.57
	Frederick	A	21	0	0	4	19	92	29	16	11	5	1	2	0	5	1	11	2	0	2	0	1.000	0	1	5.21
	Lubbock	IND	12	0	0	4	19	79	21	9	8	2	0	0	0	7	0	10	1	0	1	2	.333	0	1	3.79
	5 Min. YEARS		197	7	0	123	278.1	1187	285	154	121	25	11	8	8	93	5	212	19	8	23	15	.605	0	45	3.91

Ken Huckaby

Bats: Right **Throws:** Right **Pos:** C   **Ht:** 6'1" **Wt:** 205 **Born:** 1/27/71 **Age:** 25

Year	Team	Lg	G	AB	H	2B	3B	HR	TB	R	RBI	TBB	IBB	SO	HBP	SH	SF	SB	CS	SB%	GDP	Avg	OBP	SLG
1991	Great Falls	R	57	213	55	16	0	3	80	39	37	17	0	38	4	1	3	3	2	.60	4	.258	.321	.376
1992	Vero Beach	A	73	261	63	9	0	0	72	14	21	7	0	42	1	2	2	1	1	.50	5	.241	.262	.276
1993	Vero Beach	A	79	281	75	14	1	4	103	22	41	11	1	35	2	3	2	2	1	.67	3	.267	.297	.367
	San Antonio	AA	28	82	18	1	0	0	19	4	5	2	1	7	2	0	1	0	0	.00	0	.220	.253	.232
1994	San Antonio	AA	11	41	11	1	0	1	15	3	9	1	1	1	0	0	0	1	0	1.00	1	.268	.286	.366
	Bakersfield	A	77	270	81	18	1	2	107	29	30	10	0	37	2	0	1	2	3	.40	7	.300	.329	.396
1995	Albuquerque	AAA	89	278	90	16	2	1	113	30	40	12	1	26	4	3	1	3	1	.75	16	.324	.359	.406
	5 Min. YEARS		414	1426	393	75	4	11	509	141	183	60	4	186	15	9	10	12	8	.60	36	.276	.310	.357

Bobby Hughes

Bats: Right **Throws:** Right **Pos:** C   **Ht:** 6'4" **Wt:** 220 **Born:** 3/10/71 **Age:** 25

Year	Team	Lg	G	AB	H	2B	3B	HR	TB	R	RBI	TBB	IBB	SO	HBP	SH	SF	SB	CS	SB%	GDP	Avg	OBP	SLG
1992	Helena	R	11	40	7	1	0	0	10	5	6	4	0	14	2	0	0	0	0	.00	0	.175	.283	.250
1993	Beloit	A	98	321	89	11	3	17	157	42	56	23	0	77	6	5	0	1	3	.25	2	.277	.337	.489
1994	El Paso	AA	12	36	10	4	1	0	16	3	12	5	0	7	1	0	2	0	1	.00	1	.278	.364	.444
	Stockton	A	95	322	81	24	3	11	144	54	53	33	0	83	9	1	2	2	1	.67	2	.252	.336	.447
1995	Stockton	A	52	179	42	9	2	8	79	22	31	17	1	41	1	0	3	2	2	.50	10	.235	.300	.441
	El Paso	AA	51	173	46	12	0	7	79	11	27	12	1	30	2	0	2	0	2	.00	4	.266	.317	.457
	4 Min. YEARS		319	1071	275	61	10	43	485	137	185	94	2	252	21	6	9	5	9	.36	25	.257	.326	.453

Keith Hughes

Bats: Left **Throws:** Left **Pos:** OF   **Ht:** 6'3" **Wt:** 210 **Born:** 9/12/63 **Age:** 32

Year	Team	Lg	G	AB	H	2B	3B	HR	TB	R	RBI	TBB	IBB	SO	HBP	SH	SF	SB	CS	SB%	GDP	Avg	OBP	SLG
1982	Bend	A	55	179	46	10	2	3	69	29	26	30	1	42	1	1	2	2	0	1.00	2	.257	.363	.385
1983	Spartanburg	A	131	484	159	31	4	15	243	80	90	67	5	83	4	2	5	16	1	.94	8	.329	.411	.502
1984	Reading	AA	70	230	60	7	5	2	83	35	20	31	2	43	0	0	2	1	0	1.00	6	.261	.346	.361
	Nashville	AA	21	50	9	0	0	0	9	6	5	10	0	14	0	0	0	0	0	.00	0	.180	.317	.180
1985	Columbus	AAA	18	54	16	4	0	3	29	7	8	2	0	11	0	0	0	0	2	.00	0	.296	.321	.537
	Albany-Colo	AA	104	361	97	22	5	10	159	53	54	51	1	73	3	0	1	4	4	.50	4	.269	.363	.440
1986	Albany-Colo	AA	94	323	99	21	3	7	147	44	37	32	2	53	1	2	3	6	8	.43	8	.307	.368	.455
	Columbus	AAA	2	8	1	0	0	0	1	0	0	0	0	2	0	0	0	0	0	.00	1	.125	.125	.125
1987	Columbus	AAA	40	139	41	7	4	5	71	21	20	13	0	24	0	0	4	0	0	.00	4	.295	.353	.511

Year Team	Lg	G	AB	H	2B	3B	HR	TB	R	RBI	TBB	IBB	SO	HBP	SH	SF	SB	CS	SB%	GDP	Avg	OBP	SLG
Maine	AAA	50	177	52	8	0	12	96	27	37	24	2	34	3	0	1	4	2	.67	5	.294	.385	.542
1988 Rochester	AAA	77	274	74	13	2	7	112	44	49	43	5	57	2	0	4	11	3	.79	2	.270	.368	.409
1989 Rochester	AAA	83	285	78	20	4	2	112	44	43	44	3	47	1	0	2	4	5	.44	3	.274	.370	.393
1990 Tidewater	AAA	117	379	117	24	5	10	181	77	53	57	7	58	4	0	4	7	4	.64	9	.309	.401	.478
1991 Columbus	AAA	130	424	115	18	8	8	173	64	66	60	2	74	3	0	8	6	7	.46	9	.271	.360	.408
1992 Portland	AAA	89	221	60	11	3	5	92	37	26	25	2	39	0	0	1	6	4	.60	3	.271	.344	.416
1993 Indianapols	AAA	82	283	81	28	4	13	156	55	42	41	2	61	2	1	1	5	0	1.00	3	.286	.379	.551
1995 Omaha	AAA	103	342	99	22	2	11	158	51	46	30	3	41	1		4	4	2	.67	4	.289	.345	.462
1987 New York	AL	4	4	0	0	0	0	0	0	0	0	0	2	0	0	0	0	0	.00	0	.000	.000	.000
Philadelphia	NL	37	76	20	2	0	0	22	8	10	7	0	11	1	0	0	0	0	.00	1	.263	.333	.289
1988 Baltimore	AL	41	108	21	4	2	2	35	10	14	16	1	27	0	0	2	1	0	1.00	3	.194	.294	.324
1990 New York	NL	8	9	0	0	0	0	0	0	0	0	0	4	0	0	0	0	0	.00	0	.000	.000	.000
1993 Cincinnati	NL	3	4	0	0	0	0	0	0	0	0	0	0	0	0	0	0	0	.00	0	.000	.000	.000
13 Min. YEARS		1266	4213	1204	246	51	113	1891	674	622	560	37	756	25	7	39	76	42	.64	71	.286	.370	.449
4 Maj. YEARS		93	201	41	6	2	2	57	18	24	23	1	44	1	0	2	1	0	1.00	4	.204	.286	.284

Troy Hughes

Bats: Right **Throws:** Right **Pos:** OF   **Ht:** 6'4" **Wt:** 212 **Born:** 1/3/71 **Age:** 25

					BATTING												BASERUNNING				PERCENTAGES		
Year Team	Lg	G	AB	H	2B	3B	HR	TB	R	RBI	TBB	IBB	SO	HBP	SH	SF	SB	CS	SB%	GDP	Avg	OBP	SLG
1989 Braves	R	36	110	24	5	0	0	29	17	10	11	0	29	1	1	1	8	4	.67	0	.218	.293	.264
1990 Pulaski	R	46	145	39	7	1	1	51	22	17	16	0	39	0	2	1	5	1	.83	3	.269	.340	.352
1991 Macon	A	112	404	121	33	2	9	185	69	80	36	1	76	3	1	5	22	13	.63	6	.300	.357	.458
1992 Durham	A	128	449	110	21	4	16	187	64	53	49	3	97	1	2	6	12	7	.63	7	.245	.317	.416
1993 Greenville	AA	109	383	102	20	4	14	172	49	58	44	1	67	5	0	3	7	3	.70	10	.266	.347	.449
1994 Richmond	AAA	81	228	49	9	1	1	63	24	18	29	3	48	5	0	6	6	2	.75	7	.215	.310	.276
Greenville	AA	27	89	27	7	0	3	43	14	12	11	0	11	0	0	1	4	0	1.00	2	.303	.376	.483
1995 Greenville	AA	73	200	51	7	1	6	78	24	25	17	0	52	2	0	2	3	6	.33	1	.255	.317	.390
Norwich	AA	15	55	18	2	1	1	25	7	8	4	0	11	1	0	1	0	2	.00	3	.327	.377	.455
7 Min. YEARS		627	2063	541	111	14	51	833	290	281	217	8	430	18	6	26	67	38	.64	39	.262	.334	.404

Sean Hugo

Bats: Left **Throws:** Left **Pos:** OF   **Ht:** 6'1" **Wt:** 185 **Born:** 9/7/72 **Age:** 23

					BATTING												BASERUNNING				PERCENTAGES		
Year Team	Lg	G	AB	H	2B	3B	HR	TB	R	RBI	TBB	IBB	SO	HBP	SH	SF	SB	CS	SB%	GDP	Avg	OBP	SLG
1994 Albany	A	59	183	55	17	4	4	92	34	18	37	2	33	3	2	2	4	4	.50	3	.301	.422	.503
1995 Frederick	A	29	89	25	4	0	4	41	13	13	21	1	24	0	0	2	0	0	.00	4	.281	.411	.461
Bowie	AA	43	117	26	3	0	0	29	15	10	20	3	29	1	0	1	1	1	.50	0	.222	.338	.248
High Desert	A	28	75	18	3	1	1	26	8	13	12	0	21	1	0	2	1	1	.50	2	.240	.344	.347
2 Min. YEARS		159	464	124	27	5	9	188	70	69	90	6	107	5	2	7	6	6	.50	9	.267	.387	.405

Rich Humphrey

Pitches: Right **Bats:** Right **Pos:** P   **Ht:** 6'1" **Wt:** 185 **Born:** 6/24/71 **Age:** 25

			HOW MUCH HE PITCHED				WHAT HE GAVE UP											THE RESULTS				
Year Team	Lg	G	GS	CG	GF	IP	BFP	H	R	ER	HR	SH	SF	HB	TBB	IBB	SO	WP	Bk	W	L	Pct.	ShO	Sv	ERA
1993 Auburn	A	29	0	0	26	39.2	168	34	18	11	2	1	1	3	10	2	49	2	1	4	3	.571	0	9	2.50
1994 Astros	R	4	0	0	0	7	30	7	3	1	0	1	0	1	1	1	8	0	0	1	0	1.000	0	0	1.29
Osceola	A	3	0	0	0	6	32	8	8	7	0	1	0	2	3	0	5	0	0	0	0	.000	0	0	10.50
1995 Kissimmee	A	46	0	0	39	55	233	45	16	12	1	5	2	3	20	0	33	2	1	3	1	.750	0	14	1.96
Jackson	AA	9	0	0	1	16	66	11	5	3	0	2	1	0	9	2	9	1	0	1	1	.500	0	0	1.69
3 Min. YEARS		91	0	0	66	123.2	529	105	50	34	3	10	4	9	43	5	104	5	2	9	5	.643	0	23	2.47

Mike Humphreys

Bats: Right **Throws:** Right **Pos:** OF   **Ht:** 6'0" **Wt:** 185 **Born:** 4/10/67 **Age:** 29

					BATTING												BASERUNNING				PERCENTAGES		
Year Team	Lg	G	AB	H	2B	3B	HR	TB	R	RBI	TBB	IBB	SO	HBP	SH	SF	SB	CS	SB%	GDP	Avg	OBP	SLG
1988 Spokane	A	76	303	93	16	5	6	137	67	59	46	1	57	0	0	4	21	4	.84	0	.307	.394	.452
1989 Riverside	A	117	420	121	26	1	13	188	77	66	72	4	79	7	3	5	23	10	.70	9	.288	.397	.448
1990 Wichita	AA	116	421	116	21	4	17	196	92	79	67	4	79	5	2	4	37	9	.80	6	.276	.378	.466
Las Vegas	AAA	12	42	10	1	0	2	17	7	6	4	0	11	1	2	0	1	0	1.00	4	.238	.319	.405
1991 Columbus	AAA	117	413	117	23	5	9	177	71	53	63	3	61	3	1	6	34	9	.79	10	.283	.377	.429
1992 Columbus	AAA	114	408	115	18	6	6	163	83	46	59	0	70	1	3	5	37	13	.74	9	.282	.370	.400
1993 Columbus	AAA	92	330	95	16	2	6	133	59	42	52	2	57	3	2	2	18	15	.55	6	.288	.388	.403
1994 Columbus	AAA	135	487	121	25	1	8	172	83	51	64	0	92	5	6	8	28	12	.70	8	.248	.337	.353
1995 Tacoma	AAA	18	35	7	2	0	0	9	3	1	3	0	11	0	0	0	0	0	.00	0	.200	.256	.257
Buffalo	AAA	34	126	31	4	0	1	38	17	5	8	0	22	5	1	1	5	1	.83	0	.246	.314	.302
1991 New York	AL	25	40	8	0	0	0	8	9	3	9	0	7	0	1	0	2	0	1.00	0	.200	.347	.200
1992 New York	AL	4	10	1	0	0	0	1	0	0	0	0	1	0	0	0	0	0	.00	2	.100	.100	.100
1993 New York	AL	25	35	6	2	1	1	13	6	6	4	0	11	0	0	1	2	1	.67	0	.171	.250	.371
8 Min. YEARS		831	2985	826	152	24	68	1230	559	408	438	14	539	30	20	36	204	73	.74	61	.277	.371	.412
3 Maj. YEARS		54	85	15	2	1	1	22	15	9	13	0	19	0	1	1	4	1	.80	2	.176	.283	.259

Greg Hunter

Bats: Left **Throws:** Right **Pos:** SS **Ht:** 6'2" **Wt:** 180 **Born:** 1/17/68 **Age:** 28

Year	Team	Lg	G	AB	H	2B	3B	HR	TB	R	RBI	TBB	IBB	SO	HBP	SH	SF	SB	CS	SB%	GDP	Avg	OBP	SLG
1990	Bellingham	A	56	183	39	5	2	1	51	21	13	22	3	36	0	3	0	2	6	.25	5	.213	.298	.279
1991	San Bernrdo	A	129	413	100	12	0	2	118	65	32	74	6	62	1	9	4	21	11	.66	12	.242	.356	.286
1992	Peninsula	A	50	149	27	5	0	2	38	15	10	13	0	24	2	1	0	1	0	1.00	3	.181	.256	.255
	Jacksonvlle	AA	14	43	9	0	0	1	12	4	5	6	1	8	0	0	0	1	0	1.00	1	.209	.306	.279
	San Bernrdo	A	29	99	21	3	0	0	24	12	6	1	0	17	1	0	1	2	3	.40	2	.212	.225	.242
1995	New Britain	AA	6	13	1	0	0	0	1	1	0	1	0	1	0	0	0	1	0	1.00	0	.077	.143	.077
	4 Min. YEARS		284	900	197	25	2	6	244	118	66	117	10	148	4	13	5	28	20	.58	23	.219	.310	.271

Jim Hunter

Pitches: Right **Bats:** Right **Pos:** P **Ht:** 6'3" **Wt:** 205 **Born:** 6/22/64 **Age:** 32

Year	Team	Lg	G	GS	CG	GF	IP	BFP	H	R	ER	HR	SH	SF	HB	TBB	IBB	SO	WP	Bk	W	L	Pct.	ShO	Sv	ERA
1985	Jamestown	A	14	13	1	1	70.2	310	65	30	22	1	2	1	1	34	1	41	3	0	3	3	.500	0	0	2.80
1986	Burlington	A	9	9	1	0	45	210	52	28	23	1	0	1	2	25	0	28	2	1	2	3	.400	0	0	4.60
	Beloit	A	15	15	2	0	89.1	382	91	47	37	4	2	1	5	22	3	52	5	1	4	5	.444	0	0	3.73
1987	Stockton	A	8	8	0	0	51.1	214	39	16	14	1	1	2	5	20	0	44	2	0	6	1	.857	0	0	2.45
	El Paso	AA	16	15	1	1	95.2	421	117	60	49	14	1	2	2	33	1	62	4	0	5	5	.500	0	0	4.61
1988	El Paso	AA	26	26	2	0	147.2	666	163	107	93	15	3	4	8	77	2	103	4	3	8	11	.421	0	0	5.67
1989	El Paso	AA	19	19	4	0	124.2	547	149	70	58	9	3	4	4	45	1	68	5	0	7	10	.412	0	0	4.19
1990	El Paso	AA	9	9	2	0	62	258	64	31	27	9	0	0	1	15	0	37	1	0	6	3	.667	0	0	3.92
	Denver	AAA	20	20	2	0	117	512	138	76	61	5	4	8	5	45	1	57	1	0	6	8	.429	0	0	4.69
1991	Denver	AAA	14	14	0	0	87.1	374	94	38	32	6	4	1	5	27	0	43	2	0	7	4	.636	0	0	3.30
1992	El Paso	AA	3	3	0	0	18	69	18	6	6	0	0	1	1	3	0	9	0	1	1	1	.500	0	0	3.00
	Denver	AAA	34	18	3	9	134.2	590	144	68	55	13	4	4	4	46	2	56	2	2	6	7	.462	0	2	3.68
1993	New Orleans	AAA	39	3	0	8	68.2	301	82	40	32	8	2	1	6	25	2	35	1	0	5	2	.714	0	1	4.19
	El Paso	AA	14	0	0	2	22	89	20	8	6	1	1	1	2	6	1	10	0	0	3	1	.750	0	1	2.45
1994	Buffalo	AAA	5	5	0	0	22.2	96	22	11	11	1	3	1	2	6	0	9	1	0	0	1	.000	0	0	4.37
1995	Colo. Sprng	AAA	10	4	0	0	32.1	154	43	27	25	1	2	2	2	17	2	13	2	0	2	2	.500	0	0	6.96
1991	Milwaukee	AL	8	6	0	0	31	152	45	26	25	3	1	1	4	17	0	14	3	0	0	5	.000	0	0	7.26
	11 Min. YEARS		255	181	18	21	1189	5193	1301	663	551	89	32	34	53	446	16	667	35	8	71	67	.514	0	4	4.17

Rich Hunter

Pitches: Right **Bats:** Right **Pos:** P **Ht:** 6'1" **Wt:** 180 **Born:** 9/25/74 **Age:** 21

Year	Team	Lg	G	GS	CG	GF	IP	BFP	H	R	ER	HR	SH	SF	HB	TBB	IBB	SO	WP	Bk	W	L	Pct.	ShO	Sv	ERA
1993	Martinsvlle	R	13	9	0	1	49	254	82	61	52	9	1	6	4	27	0	36	4	1	0	6	.000	0	0	9.55
1994	Martinsvlle	R	18	0	0	8	38	153	31	19	19	3	1	2	0	9	1	39	1	0	3	2	.600	0	4	4.50
1995	Piedmont	A	15	15	3	0	104	404	79	37	32	9	1	1	2	19	0	80	0	0	10	2	.833	2	0	2.77
	Clearwater	A	9	9	0	0	58.1	242	62	23	19	3	3	2	5	7	0	46	3	3	6	0	1.000	0	0	2.93
	Reading	AA	3	3	0	0	22	86	14	6	5	1	0	1	0	6	0	17	2	0	3	0	1.000	0	0	2.05
	3 Min. YEARS		58	36	3	9	271.1	1139	268	146	127	25	6	12	11	68	1	218	10	4	22	10	.688	2	5	4.21

James Hurst

Pitches: Left **Bats:** Left **Pos:** P **Ht:** 6'0" **Wt:** 170 **Born:** 6/1/67 **Age:** 29

Year	Team	Lg	G	GS	CG	GF	IP	BFP	H	R	ER	HR	SH	SF	HB	TBB	IBB	SO	WP	Bk	W	L	Pct.	ShO	Sv	ERA
1990	Reno	A	25	21	1	1	131.2	613	165	102	80	19	6	3	4	68	0	90	8	2	4	11	.267	0	1	5.47
1991	Gastonia	A	11	8	0	1	51.2	207	41	18	13	0	3	2	2	14	1	44	0	2	3	3	.500	0	0	2.26
1992	Charlotte	A	32	1	0	11	54.1	232	60	29	23	2	5	1	2	12	0	49	3	0	3	2	.600	0	1	3.81
	Tulsa	AA	8	0	0	2	15.2	56	10	2	1	0	1	1	0	3	0	12	0	0	1	0	1.000	0	0	0.57
1993	Tulsa	AA	11	7	0	2	49.2	199	41	21	18	6	1	1	0	12	0	44	0	0	2	3	.400	0	1	3.26
	Okla. City	AAA	16	14	2	0	91.1	401	106	50	46	13	4	6	3	29	1	60	1	0	4	6	.400	0	0	4.53
1994	Okla. City	AAA	16	2	0	6	25.2	132	41	33	29	2	1	6	1	17	2	14	5	0	1	2	.333	0	0	10.17
	Tulsa	AA	12	12	2	0	80.1	340	83	46	41	10	3	1	2	26	1	59	8	0	4	6	.400	1	0	4.59
1995	Okla. City	AAA	28	7	0	11	46.2	236	71	40	38	6	2	0	3	25	0	42	4	0	1	5	.167	0	4	7.33
	Bowie	AA	1	0	0	0	1.1	8	2	3	0	0	1	0	0	1	0	1	0	0	0	0	.000	0	0	0.00
	Rochester	AA	10	0	0	2	19	74	17	8	8	2	0	1	0	4	1	17	4	0	1	1	.500	0	0	3.79
	Indianapols	AAA	3	0	0	2	3.1	13	2	2	2	0	1	0	0	1	0	1	0	0	0	0	.000	0	1	5.40
1994	Texas	AL	8	0	0	0	10.2	56	17	12	12	1	0	1	0	8	1	5	1	0	0	0	.000	0	0	10.13
	6 Min. YEARS		173	72	5	38	570.2	2511	639	354	299	61	27	22	17	212	6	433	33	4	24	39	.381	1	8	4.72

Jimmy Hurst

Bats: Right **Throws:** Right **Pos:** OF **Ht:** 6'6" **Wt:** 225 **Born:** 3/1/72 **Age:** 24

Year	Team	Lg	G	AB	H	2B	3B	HR	TB	R	RBI	TBB	IBB	SO	HBP	SH	SF	SB	CS	SB%	GDP	Avg	OBP	SLG
1991	White Sox	R	36	121	31	4	0	0	35	14	12	13	0	32	1	0	0	6	1	.86	3	.256	.333	.289
1992	Utica	A	68	220	50	8	5	6	86	31	35	27	1	78	4	2	5	11	3	.79	4	.227	.316	.391
1993	South Bend	A	123	464	113	26	0	20	199	79	79	37	3	141	8	0	5	15	2	.88	5	.244	.307	.429
1994	Pr. William	A	127	455	126	31	6	25	244	90	91	72	4	128	4	0	5	15	8	.65	9	.277	.377	.536
1995	Birmingham	AA	91	301	57	11	0	12	104	47	34	33	0	95	1	0	2	12	5	.71	5	.189	.270	.346
	5 Min. YEARS		445	1561	377	80	11	63	668	261	251	182	8	474	18	2	17	59	19	.76	30	.242	.325	.428

David Hutcheson

Pitches: Right Bats: Right Pos: P Ht: 6'2" Wt: 185 Born: 8/29/71 Age: 24

Year Team	Lg	G	GS	CG	GF	IP	BFP	H	R	ER	HR	SH	SF	HB	TBB	IBB	SO	WP	Bk	W	L	Pct.	ShO	Sv	ERA
1993 Peoria	A	15	12	1	1	89	357	71	26	23	2	5	2	5	29	0	82	9	1	4	3	.571	1	0	2.33
1994 Daytona	A	25	24	4	0	162	663	139	57	46	6	4	6	8	35	0	102	3	3	13	5	.722	3	0	2.56
Orlando	AA	3	3	1	0	19	80	12	10	7	2	0	0	1	7	0	12	0	0	1	2	.333	0	0	3.32
1995 Orlando	AA	28	27	1	1	168.1	708	178	84	75	23	5	3	8	45	3	103	6	0	8	10	.444	1	0	4.01
3 Min. YEARS		71	66	7	2	438.1	1808	400	177	151	33	14	11	22	116	3	299	18	4	26	20	.565	5	0	3.10

Jason Hutchins

Pitches: Right Bats: Right Pos: P Ht: 6'1" Wt: 185 Born: 3/20/70 Age: 26

Year Team	Lg	G	GS	CG	GF	IP	BFP	H	R	ER	HR	SH	SF	HB	TBB	IBB	SO	WP	Bk	W	L	Pct.	ShO	Sv	ERA
1992 Bend	A	34	0	0	26	41.2	176	24	15	12	4	4	2	6	24	2	65	3	3	0	3	.000	0	18	2.59
1993 Central Val	A	20	0	0	9	20.2	116	14	21	21	4	0	1	5	37	0	27	7	0	1	3	.250	0	1	9.15
Rockies	R	1	0	0	0	0	6	0	6	6	0	0	0	2	4	0	0	0	0	0	1	.000	0	0	0.00
1994 Central Val	A	19	0	0	18	24	99	15	6	5	1	0	1	1	14	0	29	5	0	1	1	.000	0	10	1.88
New Haven	AA	25	1	0	15	39.1	189	36	33	32	6	2	2	4	34	1	33	3	0	0	1	.000	0	1	7.32
1995 New Haven	AA	12	1	0	4	14	70	13	6	6	0	0	0	2	14	0	14	3	0	0	0	.000	0	1	3.86
4 Min. YEARS		111	2	0	72	139.2	656	102	87	82	15	6	6	20	127	3	168	21	3	1	9	.100	0	30	5.28

Mark Hutton

Pitches: Right Bats: Right Pos: P Ht: 6'6" Wt: 240 Born: 2/6/70 Age: 26

Year Team	Lg	G	GS	CG	GF	IP	BFP	H	R	ER	HR	SH	SF	HB	TBB	IBB	SO	WP	Bk	W	L	Pct.	ShO	Sv	ERA
1989 Oneonta	A	12	12	0	0	66.1	283	70	39	30	1	2	4	1	24	0	62	5	2	6	2	.750	0	0	4.07
1990 Greensboro	A	21	19	0	1	81.1	394	77	78	57	2	2	3	7	62	0	72	14	1	1	10	.091	0	0	6.31
1991 Ft. Laud	A	24	24	3	0	147	606	98	54	40	5	6	1	11	65	5	117	4	4	5	8	.385	0	0	2.45
Columbus	AAA	1	1	0	0	6	24	3	2	1	0	0	0	0	5	0	5	0	0	1	0	1.000	0	0	1.50
1992 Albany-Colo	AA	25	25	1	0	165.1	703	146	75	66	6	2	3	11	66	1	128	2	1	13	7	.650	0	0	3.59
Columbus	AAA	1	0	0	0	5	22	7	4	3	0	0	0	0	2	0	4	0	0	0	1	.000	0	0	5.40
1993 Columbus	AAA	21	21	0	0	133	544	98	52	47	14	2	0	10	53	0	112	2	1	10	4	.714	0	0	3.18
1994 Columbus	AAA	22	5	0	12	34.2	146	31	16	14	5	1	2	2	12	0	27	0	0	2	5	.286	0	3	3.63
1995 Columbus	AAA	11	11	0	0	52.1	243	64	51	49	7	0	3	4	24	1	23	2	0	2	6	.250	0	0	8.43
1993 New York	AL	7	4	0	2	22	104	24	17	14	2	2	2	1	17	0	12	0	0	1	1	.500	0	0	5.73
1994 New York	AL	2	0	0	1	3.2	16	4	3	2	0	0	0	0	0	0	1	0	0	0	0	.000	0	0	4.91
7 Min. YEARS		138	118	4	13	691	2965	594	371	307	40	15	16	46	313	7	550	29	9	40	43	.482	0	3	4.00
2 Maj. YEARS		9	4	0	3	25.2	120	28	20	16	2	2	2	1	17	0	13	0	0	1	1	.500	0	0	5.61

Rich Hyde

Pitches: Right Bats: Right Pos: P Ht: 6'0" Wt: 175 Born: 12/24/68 Age: 27

Year Team	Lg	G	GS	CG	GF	IP	BFP	H	R	ER	HR	SH	SF	HB	TBB	IBB	SO	WP	Bk	W	L	Pct.	ShO	Sv	ERA
1991 Everett	A	26	0	0	24	36.2	156	37	20	18	3	0	1	4	8	0	25	1	1	3	3	.500	0	7	4.42
1992 Clinton	A	8	0	0	7	7	24	3	0	0	0	0	0	0	1	0	1	0	0	0	0	.000	0	3	0.00
San Jose	A	37	4	0	12	82.2	352	81	42	37	4	2	6	3	33	2	43	2	1	6	2	.750	0	1	4.03
1993 Shreveport	AA	6	3	0	1	19.2	92	33	17	17	1	0	2	2	2	1	14	1	0	1	1	.500	0	0	7.78
San Jose	A	23	1	0	11	47	209	59	31	25	4	1	1	1	14	2	34	3	1	2	0	1.000	0	2	4.79
1994 Sioux Falls	IND	18	17	4	0	114.2	492	134	54	48	6	3	3	3	21	3	60	4	0	8	7	.533	1	0	3.77
1995 Sioux Falls	A	16	0	0	15	18	77	19	6	4	1	2	0	0	5	1	13	3	0	0	2	.000	0	7	2.00
Shreveport	AA	33	0	0	16	44	188	48	21	19	2	1	1	4	10	3	24	1	0	5	1	.833	0	7	3.89
5 Min. YEARS		167	25	4	86	369.2	1590	414	191	168	21	9	14	17	94	12	214	15	3	25	16	.610	1	27	4.09

Lou Hymel

Bats: Right Throws: Right Pos: C Ht: 6'2" Wt: 195 Born: 5/21/68 Age: 28

Year Team	Lg	G	AB	H	2B	3B	HR	TB	R	RBI	TBB	IBB	SO	HBP	SH	SF	SB	CS	SB%	GDP	Avg	OBP	SLG
1991 Sumter	A	34	116	23	5	1	2	36	7	15	5	0	46	1	0	0	1	1	.50	0	.198	.238	.310
1992 Albany	A	87	286	54	11	1	4	79	29	23	31	0	97	6	1	1	2	4	.33	3	.189	.281	.276
1993 Ottawa	AAA	3	3	0	0	0	0	0	0	0	0	0	2	0	0	0	0	0	.00	0	.000	.000	.000
Burlington	A	50	182	50	14	1	11	99	28	41	3	0	60	5	0	4	1	0	1.00	3	.275	.299	.544
W. Palm Bch	A	37	112	29	9	1	3	49	15	10	7	0	31	2	1	1	2	2	.50	0	.259	.311	.438
1994 Harrisburg	AA	77	233	58	16	0	12	110	36	36	9	0	67	3	2	7	1	0	1.00	7	.249	.278	.472
1995 Harrisburg	AA	95	302	57	10	2	11	104	35	36	22	0	97	8	1	2	3	2	.60	3	.189	.260	.344
5 Min. YEARS		383	1234	271	65	6	43	477	150	161	77	0	400	25	5	15	10	9	.53	16	.220	.276	.387

Adam Hyzdu

Bats: Right Throws: Right Pos: OF Ht: 6'2" Wt: 210 Born: 12/6/71 Age: 24

Year Team	Lg	G	AB	H	2B	3B	HR	TB	R	RBI	TBB	IBB	SO	HBP	SH	SF	SB	CS	SB%	GDP	Avg	OBP	SLG
1990 Everett	A	69	253	62	16	1	6	98	31	34	28	1	78	2	0	5	2	4	.33	4	.245	.319	.387
1991 Clinton	A	124	410	96	14	5	5	135	47	50	64	1	131	3	7	7	4	5	.44	10	.234	.340	.329

Year	Team	Lg	G	AB	H	2B	3B	HR	TB	R	RBI	TBB	IBB	SO	HBP	SH	SF	SB	CS	SB%	GDP	Avg	OBP	SLG
1992	San Jose	A	128	457	127	25	5	9	189	60	60	55	4	134	1	1	8	10	5	.67	6	.278	.351	.414
1993	San Jose	A	44	165	48	11	3	13	104	35	38	29	0	53	0	1	2	1	1	.50	3	.291	.393	.630
	Shreveport	AA	86	302	61	17	0	6	96	30	25	20	2	82	1	1	1	0	5	.00	5	.202	.253	.318
1994	Winston-Sal	A	55	210	58	11	1	15	116	30	39	18	0	33	2	0	2	1	5	.17	3	.276	.336	.552
	Chattanooga	AA	38	133	35	10	0	3	54	17	9	8	0	21	1	1	0	0	2	.00	1	.263	.310	.406
	Indianapolis	AAA	12	25	3	2	0	0	5	3	3	1	0	5	0	0	2	0	0	.00	0	.120	.143	.200
1995	Chattanooga	AA	102	312	82	14	1	13	137	55	48	45	2	56	4	2	1	3	2	.60	4	.263	.362	.439
	6 Min. YEARS		658	2267	572	120	16	70	934	308	306	268	10	593	14	13	23	21	29	.42	36	.252	.332	.412

Blaise Ilsley

Pitches: Left Bats: Left Pos: P Ht: 6' 1" Wt: 195 Born: 4/9/64 Age: 32

			HOW MUCH HE PITCHED						WHAT HE GAVE UP										THE RESULTS					
Year	Team	Lg	G	GS	CG	GF	IP	BFP	H	R	ER	HR	SH	SF	HB	TBB	IBB	SO	WP	Bk	W	L	Pct.	ShO	Sv	ERA
1985	Auburn	A	13	12	2	1	90	354	55	18	14	1	5	0	3	32	0	116	0	0	9	1	.900	0	0	1.40
1986	Asheville	A	15	15	9	0	120	453	74	27	26	11	2	2	2	23	0	146	2	2	12	2	.857	3	0	1.95
	Osceola	A	14	13	6	1	86.2	337	67	24	17	1	3	4	0	19	0	74	6	1	8	4	.667	2	0	1.77
1987	Columbus	AA	26	26	3	0	167.2	712	162	84	72	13	8	7	4	63	1	130	6	2	10	11	.476	0	0	3.86
1988	Columbus	AA	8	8	0	0	39.1	187	49	28	26	4	0	0	0	21	0	38	2	0	3	1	.750	0	0	5.95
1989	Osceola	A	2	2	0	0	7	28	8	5	5	2	0	0	0	0	0	6	0	0	0	0	.000	0	0	6.43
	Columbus	AA	4	4	0	0	20.2	87	19	10	3	2	1	0	0	5	0	11	2	1	1	1	.500	0	0	1.31
	Tucson	AAA	20	17	1	0	103	443	120	68	67	12	2	3	6	23	2	49	2	0	4	9	.308	0	0	5.85
1990	Columbus	AA	12	12	3	0	83.2	324	70	26	18	5	4	0	3	13	1	70	1	0	6	4	.600	3	0	1.94
	Tucson	AAA	20	6	1	4	62.2	295	87	50	45	4	1	2	3	24	0	39	8	0	2	1	.667	0	2	6.46
1991	Tucson	AAA	46	4	0	17	86.1	383	105	51	41	7	9	6	3	27	1	52	2	0	8	6	.571	0	0	4.27
1992	Louisville	AAA	33	10	1	10	98.1	429	114	56	47	15	7	4	4	23	2	56	3	0	5	4	.556	0	1	4.30
1993	Iowa	AAA	48	16	0	13	134.2	565	147	61	59	10	5	3	4	32	2	78	7	0	12	7	.632	0	4	3.94
1994	Iowa	AAA	22	16	2	0	116	487	120	68	57	11	1	7	3	21	0	51	2	1	10	4	.714	0	0	4.42
1995	Scranton-Wb	AAA	29	29	2	0	185.1	786	210	96	80	17	8	4	5	34	2	102	6	0	8	10	.444	1	0	3.88
1994	Chicago	NL	10	0	0	1	15	74	25	13	13	2	0	0	0	9	2	9	1	0	0	0	.000	0	0	7.80
	11 Min. YEARS		312	190	30	46	1401.1	5870	1407	672	577	115	56	42	40	360	11	1018	49	7	98	65	.601	9	7	3.71

Todd Ingram

Pitches: Right Bats: Right Pos: P Ht: 6'4" Wt: 200 Born: 4/1/68 Age: 28

			HOW MUCH HE PITCHED						WHAT HE GAVE UP										THE RESULTS					
Year	Team	Lg	G	GS	CG	GF	IP	BFP	H	R	ER	HR	SH	SF	HB	TBB	IBB	SO	WP	Bk	W	L	Pct.	ShO	Sv	ERA
1991	Sou. Oregon	A	17	12	1	1	81.1	355	72	39	31	4	2	2	6	39	0	64	5	3	6	5	.545	0	1	3.43
1992	Reno	A	41	9	0	23	67.1	332	91	69	54	8	0	3	3	40	4	44	12	2	1	7	.125	0	9	7.22
1993	Modesto	A	32	0	0	24	42.2	196	49	30	26	4	1	2	2	18	3	39	11	1	5	7	.417	0	9	5.48
1994	Huntsville	AA	48	0	0	28	59.1	278	63	40	36	4	5	0	1	37	4	55	7	0	3	8	.273	0	11	5.46
1995	Knoxville	AA	20	0	0	9	34	143	26	17	14	3	1	2	0	16	0	19	1	0	1	1	.500	0	3	3.71
	Trenton	AA	18	0	0	7	24.2	125	27	19	16	2	2	2	1	21	4	16	1	1	1	1	.500	0	0	5.84
	5 Min. YEARS		176	21	1	92	309.1	1429	328	214	177	25	11	11	13	171	15	237	37	7	17	29	.370	0	33	5.15

Jeff Innis

Pitches: Right Bats: Right Pos: P Ht: 6' 1" Wt: 170 Born: 7/5/62 Age: 33

			HOW MUCH HE PITCHED						WHAT HE GAVE UP										THE RESULTS					
Year	Team	Lg	G	GS	CG	GF	IP	BFP	H	R	ER	HR	SH	SF	HB	TBB	IBB	SO	WP	Bk	W	L	Pct.	ShO	Sv	ERA
1984	Jackson	AA	42	0	0	27	59.1	283	65	34	28	3	4	0	0	40	8	63	6	1	6	5	.545	0	8	4.25
1985	Lynchburg	A	53	0	0	39	77	311	46	26	20	2	6	2	1	40	1	91	3	0	6	3	.667	0	14	2.34
1986	Jackson	AA	56	0	0	48	92	359	69	30	25	2	3	6	1	24	3	75	2	0	4	5	.444	0	25	2.45
1987	Tidewater	AAA	29	0	0	18	44.1	171	26	10	10	3	2	0	0	16	4	28	1	0	6	1	.857	0	5	2.03
1988	Tidewater	AAA	34	0	0	19	48.1	213	42	22	19	3	3	1	0	25	8	43	1	0	0	5	.000	0	4	3.54
1989	Tidewater	AAA	25	0	0	18	29.2	127	28	9	7	0	3	1	1	8	2	14	1	0	3	1	.750	0	2	2.12
1990	Tidewater	AAA	40	0	0	33	52.2	209	34	11	10	1	4	1	3	17	5	42	0	0	5	2	.714	0	19	1.71
1994	Salt Lake	AAA	7	0	0	2	10	44	10	4	3	0	0	1	0	4	0	4	0	0	0	0	.000	0	0	2.70
	Las Vegas	AAA	33	0	0	8	36.1	176	41	32	16	4	1	1	0	23	3	34	0	0	1	2	.333	0	3	3.96
1995	Scranton-Wb	AAA	15	0	0	10	14.2	64	13	8	7	0	0	0	0	8	1	14	1	0	0	2	.000	0	6	4.30
1987	New York	NL	17	1	0	8	25.2	109	29	9	9	5	0	0	1	4	1	28	1	1	1	0	.000	0	0	3.16
1988	New York	NL	12	0	0	7	19	80	19	6	4	0	1	1	0	2	1	14	0	0	1	1	.500	0	0	1.89
1989	New York	NL	29	0	0	12	39.2	160	38	16	14	2	1	1	1	8	0	16	0	0	1	0	.000	0	3	3.18
1990	New York	NL	18	0	0	12	26.1	104	19	9	7	4	0	2	1	10	3	12	1	1	1	3	.250	0	1	2.39
1991	New York	NL	69	0	0	29	84.2	336	66	30	25	2	6	5	0	23	6	47	4	0	0	2	.000	0	0	2.66
1992	New York	NL	76	0	0	28	88	373	85	32	28	4	7	4	6	36	4	39	1	0	6	9	.400	0	1	2.86
1993	New York	NL	67	0	0	30	76.2	345	81	39	35	5	9	1	6	38	12	36	3	1	2	3	.400	0	3	4.11
	9 Min. YEARS		334	0	0	222	464.1	1957	375	186	145	18	26	14	6	205	35	408	15	2	31	26	.544	0	92	2.81
	7 Maj. YEARS		288	1	0	126	360	1507	337	141	122	22	24	14	15	121	27	192	10	3	10	20	.333	0	5	3.05

Damian Jackson

Bats: Right Throws: Right Pos: SS Ht: 5'10" Wt: 160 Born: 8/16/73 Age: 22

			BATTING														BASERUNNING				PERCENTAGES		
Year	Team	Lg	G	AB	H	2B	3B	HR	TB	R	RBI	TBB	IBB	SO	HBP	SH	SF	SB	CS	SB%	GDP	Avg	OBP	SLG
1992	Burlington	R	62	226	56	12	1	0	70	32	23	32	0	31	6	6	3	29	5	.85	1	.248	.352	.310
1993	Columbus	A	108	350	94	19	3	6	137	70	45	41	0	61	5	5	1	26	7	.79	1	.269	.353	.391
1994	Canton-Akrn	AA	138	531	143	29	5	5	197	85	46	60	2	121	5	10	5	37	16	.70	8	.269	.346	.371

Year	Team	Lg	G	AB	H	2B	3B	HR	TB	R	RBI	TBB	IBB	SO	HBP	SH	SF	SB	CS	SB%	GDP	Avg	OBP	SLG
1995	Canton-Akrn	AA	131	484	120	20	2	3	153	67	34	65	0	103	9	7	0	40	22	.65	6	.248	.348	.316
	4 Min. YEARS		439	1591	413	80	11	14	557	254	148	198	2	316	25	28	9	132	50	.73	16	.260	.349	.350

John Jackson

Bats: Left **Throws:** Left **Pos:** OF **Ht:** 6'0" **Wt:** 185 **Born:** 1/2/67 **Age:** 29

			BATTING															BASERUNNING				PERCENTAGES		
Year	Team	Lg	G	AB	H	2B	3B	HR	TB	R	RBI	TBB	IBB	SO	HBP	SH	SF	SB	CS	SB%	GDP	Avg	OBP	SLG
1990	Everett	A	26	92	28	2	2	1	37	26	7	27	0	11	4	1	1	14	4	.78	2	.304	.476	.402
1991	San Jose	A	14	44	13	0	2	0	17	8	3	8	0	5	1	0	0	1	2	.33	1	.295	.415	.386
1992	Midland	AA	40	151	44	4	3	0	54	19	16	17	0	20	3	3	0	12	5	.71	8	.291	.374	.358
1993	Midland	AA	70	243	79	18	2	3	110	43	34	40	1	43	10	6	4	12	8	.60	8	.325	.434	.453
	Vancouver	AAA	55	201	58	9	4	2	81	28	20	17	0	29	2	6	3	12	4	.75	3	.289	.345	.403
1994	Vancouver	AAA	102	358	105	16	5	2	137	62	38	46	1	37	7	3	4	18	11	.62	9	.293	.381	.383
1995	Vancouver	AAA	35	113	34	7	1	1	46	20	11	22	2	15	2	3	0	8	3	.73	3	.301	.423	.407
	New Britain	AA	16	57	17	2	1	3	30	8	8	11	0	7	1	0	0	3	4	.43	0	.298	.420	.526
	Salt Lake	AAA	55	194	54	14	3	4	86	39	21	22	0	20	3	3	3	8	2	.80	4	.278	.356	.443
	6 Min. YEARS		413	1453	432	72	23	16	598	253	158	210	4	187	33	25	15	88	43	.67	38	.297	.395	.412

Frank Jacobs

Bats: Left **Throws:** Left **Pos:** 1B **Ht:** 6'4" **Wt:** 250 **Born:** 5/22/68 **Age:** 28

			BATTING															BASERUNNING				PERCENTAGES		
Year	Team	Lg	G	AB	H	2B	3B	HR	TB	R	RBI	TBB	IBB	SO	HBP	SH	SF	SB	CS	SB%	GDP	Avg	OBP	SLG
1991	Pittsfield	A	74	287	67	12	5	9	116	52	50	46	3	56	0	0	2	5	2	.71	2	.233	.337	.404
1992	St. Lucie	A	123	434	108	23	3	12	173	55	55	35	2	78	4	0	5	3	3	.50	15	.249	.308	.399
1993	Binghamton	AA	109	346	93	17	3	9	143	50	46	42	3	72	4	0	0	2	3	.40	11	.269	.355	.413
1994	Binghamton	AA	121	431	123	26	4	13	188	64	67	51	3	65	1	0	7	2	1	.67	10	.285	.357	.436
1995	Norfolk	AAA	8	25	6	1	0	1	10	2	6	0	0	4	0	0	0	0	0	.00	1	.240	.240	.400
	Binghamton	AA	23	68	20	3	0	4	35	12	9	10	0	15	0	0	0	0	0	.00	3	.294	.385	.515
	Harrisburg	AA	78	269	85	19	0	9	131	44	51	48	7	41	5	0	2	1	3	.25	2	.316	.426	.487
	Ottawa	AAA	11	32	8	2	2	0	14	9	4	11	0	3	1	0	0	0	1	.00	1	.250	.455	.438
	5 Min. YEARS		547	1892	510	103	13	57	810	288	288	243	18	334	15	0	16	13	13	.50	45	.270	.355	.428

Angel Jaime

Bats: Right **Throws:** Right **Pos:** SS-OF **Ht:** 6'0" **Wt:** 160 **Born:** 3/6/73 **Age:** 23

			BATTING															BASERUNNING				PERCENTAGES		
Year	Team	Lg	G	AB	H	2B	3B	HR	TB	R	RBI	TBB	IBB	SO	HBP	SH	SF	SB	CS	SB%	GDP	Avg	OBP	SLG
1992	Great Falls	R	62	236	64	8	2	1	79	38	34	32	0	58	1	4	1	21	7	.75	6	.271	.359	.335
1993	Bakersfield	A	46	152	35	5	0	0	40	21	8	18	0	34	4	4	0	14	6	.70	3	.230	.328	.263
	Yakima	A	50	168	44	8	3	2	64	29	25	18	0	27	1	2	2	9	4	.69	6	.262	.333	.381
1994	Vero Beach	A	127	482	136	15	9	6	187	85	38	38	1	64	4	10	6	16	10	.62	8	.282	.336	.388
1995	San Antonio	AA	9	22	8	0	0	1	11	5	2	2	0	3	0	0	0	2	1	.67	1	.364	.417	.500
	4 Min. YEARS		294	1060	287	36	14	10	381	178	107	108	1	186	10	20	9	62	28	.69	24	.271	.341	.359

Pete Janicki

Pitches: Right **Bats:** Right **Pos:** P **Ht:** 6'4" **Wt:** 190 **Born:** 1/26/71 **Age:** 25

			HOW MUCH HE PITCHED						WHAT HE GAVE UP										THE RESULTS					
Year	Team	Lg	G	GS	CG	GF	IP	BFP	H	R	ER	HR	SH	SF	HB	TBB	IBB	SO	WP	Bk	W	L	Pct.	ShO	Sv	ERA
1993	Palm Spring	A	1	1	0	0	1.2	10	3	2	2	0	0	0	0	2	0	2	0	1	0	0	.000	0	0	10.80
1994	Midland	AA	14	14	1	0	70	327	86	68	54	4	3	1	6	33	1	54	15	3	2	6	.250	0	0	6.94
	Lk Elsinore	A	3	3	0	0	12	61	17	12	9	2	1	1	4	4	0	12	0	0	1	2	.333	0	0	6.75
1995	Lk Elsinore	A	20	20	0	0	123.1	532	130	66	42	7	3	6	5	28	0	106	6	1	9	4	.692	0	0	3.06
	Vancouver	AAA	9	9	0	0	48.2	227	64	38	38	8	1	4	1	23	0	34	0	0	1	4	.200	0	0	7.03
	3 Min. YEARS		47	47	1	0	255.2	1157	300	186	145	21	8	12	16	90	1	208	21	5	13	16	.448	0	0	5.10

Marty Janzen

Pitches: Right **Bats:** Right **Pos:** P **Ht:** 6'3" **Wt:** 197 **Born:** 5/31/73 **Age:** 23

			HOW MUCH HE PITCHED						WHAT HE GAVE UP										THE RESULTS					
Year	Team	Lg	G	GS	CG	GF	IP	BFP	H	R	ER	HR	SH	SF	HB	TBB	IBB	SO	WP	Bk	W	L	Pct.	ShO	Sv	ERA
1992	Yankees	R	12	11	0	0	68.2	277	55	21	18	0	3	2	5	15	0	73	3	3	7	2	.778	0	0	2.36
	Greensboro	A	2	0	0	2	5	20	5	2	2	0	0	0	0	1	0	5	2	0	0	0	.000	0	1	3.60
1993	Yankees	R	5	5	0	0	22.1	93	20	5	3	0	0	0	1	3	0	19	0	0	0	1	.000	0	0	1.21
1994	Greensboro	A	17	17	0	0	104	431	98	57	45	8	0	0	2	25	1	92	2	2	3	7	.300	0	0	3.89
1995	Tampa	A	18	18	1	0	113.2	461	102	38	33	4	1	2	4	30	0	104	3	4	10	3	.769	0	0	2.61
	Norwich	AA	3	3	0	0	20	85	17	11	11	2	0	0	2	7	0	16	2	0	1	2	.333	0	0	4.95
	Knoxville	AA	7	7	2	0	48	188	35	14	14	2	0	2	1	14	0	44	1	1	5	1	.833	1	0	2.63
	4 Min. YEARS		64	61	3	2	381.2	1555	332	148	126	16	4	6	15	95	1	353	13	10	26	16	.619	1	1	2.97

Matt Jarvis

Pitches: Left **Bats:** Right **Pos:** P **Ht:** 6'4" **Wt:** 185 **Born:** 2/22/72 **Age:** 24

			HOW MUCH HE PITCHED						WHAT HE GAVE UP										THE RESULTS					
Year	Team	Lg	G	GS	CG	GF	IP	BFP	H	R	ER	HR	SH	SF	HB	TBB	IBB	SO	WP	Bk	W	L	Pct.	ShO	Sv	ERA
1991	Orioles	R	11	5	0	2	37.1	163	44	22	18	2	1	2	0	17	0	30	2	1	3	1	.750	0	1	4.34
1992	Kane County	A	34	7	0	8	71.1	327	84	53	36	3	2	1	1	35	2	43	7	3	4	4	.500	0	0	4.54
1993	Albany	A	29	29	8	0	185.1	797	173	82	63	7	5	2	5	82	4	118	10	1	11	13	.458	1	0	3.06

Year	Team	Lg	G	GS	CG	GF	IP	BFP	H	R	ER	HR	SH	SF	HB	TBB	IBB	SO	WP	Bk	W	L	Pct.	ShO	Sv	ERA
1994	Frederick	A	31	14	0	3	103.2	459	92	58	48	7	5	2	9	48	0	67	3	0	10	4	.714	0	1	4.17
1995	Bowie	AA	26	21	0	1	118	531	154	71	67	11	4	4	4	42	1	60	5	3	9	8	.529	0	0	5.11
	5 Min. YEARS		131	76	8	14	515.2	2277	547	286	232	30	17	11	19	224	7	318	27	8	37	30	.552	1	2	4.05

Domingo Jean

Pitches: Right **Bats:** Right **Pos:** P   **Ht:** 6'2" **Wt:** 175 **Born:** 1/9/69 **Age:** 27

			HOW MUCH HE PITCHED						WHAT HE GAVE UP												THE RESULTS					
Year	Team	Lg	G	GS	CG	GF	IP	BFP	H	R	ER	HR	SH	SF	HB	TBB	IBB	SO	WP	Bk	W	L	Pct.	ShO	Sv	ERA
1990	White Sox	R	13	13	1	0	78.2	312	61	29	20	1	0	1	6	16	0	65	10	2	2	5	.286	0	0	2.29
1991	South Bend	A	25	25	2	0	158	680	121	75	58	7	3	7	10	65	0	141	17	5	12	8	.600	0	0	3.30
1992	Ft. Laud	A	23	23	5	0	158.2	637	118	57	46	3	7	6	6	49	1	172	4	1	6	11	.353	1	0	2.61
	Albany-Colo	AA	1	1	0	0	4	17	3	2	1	0	0	0	0	3	0	6	1	0	0	0	.000	0	0	2.25
1993	Albany-Colo	AA	11	11	1	0	61	257	42	24	17	1	1	1	5	33	0	41	4	0	5	3	.625	0	0	2.51
	Columbus	AAA	7	7	1	0	44.2	180	40	15	14	2	0	2	2	13	1	39	3	0	2	2	.500	0	0	2.82
	Pr. William	A	1	0	0	0	1.2	6	1	0	0	0	0	0	0	0	0	1	0	0	0	0	.000	0	0	0.00
1994	Tucson	AAA	6	3	0	1	19	88	20	13	12	3	0	1	2	11	1	16	0	0	0	0	.000	0	0	5.68
1995	Tucson	AAA	3	3	0	0	13.2	62	15	10	10	1	0	0	0	7	0	14	3	0	2	1	.667	0	0	6.59
	Okla. City	AAA	24	13	1	9	88	418	102	70	60	12	4	2	1	61	1	72	14	3	3	8	.273	0	1	6.14
	Indianapols	AAA	2	0	0	0	2	7	1	0	0	0	0	0	0	0	0	1	0	0	1	0	1.000	0	0	0.00
1993	New York	AL	10	6	0	1	40.1	176	37	20	20	7	0	1	0	19	0	20	1	0	1	1	.500	0	0	4.46
	6 Min. YEARS		116	99	11	10	629.1	2664	518	298	238	30	16	20	32	258	4	568	56	11	33	38	.465	1	1	3.40

Bernie Jenkins

Bats: Right **Throws:** Right **Pos:** OF   **Ht:** 6'4" **Wt:** 195 **Born:** 9/12/67 **Age:** 28

				BATTING													BASERUNNING				PERCENTAGES		
Year	Team	Lg	G	AB	H	2B	3B	HR	TB	R	RBI	TBB	IBB	SO	HBP	SH	SF	SB	CS	SB%	GDP	Avg	OBP	SLG
1988	Auburn	A	58	201	49	11	0	6	78	35	46	30	0	61	7	0	2	9	5	.64	5	.244	.358	.388
1989	Osceola	A	63	240	70	10	5	4	102	33	30	21	0	51	4	0	0	5	7	.42	1	.292	.358	.425
1990	Columbus	AA	51	162	37	6	2	5	62	19	20	20	0	45	1	2	1	6	3	.67	3	.228	.315	.383
1991	Jackson	AA	109	335	87	14	4	5	124	42	36	26	0	82	4	2	3	21	8	.72	8	.260	.318	.370
1992	Chattanooga	AA	22	48	15	3	2	0	22	7	4	6	0	12	2	0	0	2	1	.67	1	.313	.411	.458
	Cedar Rapds	A	71	258	74	16	2	8	118	53	32	31	0	60	5	1	0	26	9	.74	7	.287	.374	.457
1993	Chattanooga	AA	102	290	73	9	1	3	93	31	26	21	1	71	2	1	2	18	8	.69	8	.252	.305	.321
1995	Shreveport	AA	5	12	2	0	0	1	5	1	1	2	0	5	0	0	1	0	0	.00	1	.167	.286	.417
	7 Min. YEARS		481	1546	407	69	16	32	604	221	195	157	1	387	25	6	8	87	41	.68	34	.263	.339	.391

Demetrish Jenkins

Bats: Left **Throws:** Right **Pos:** 2B   **Ht:** 5'9" **Wt:** 175 **Born:** 6/28/73 **Age:** 23

				BATTING													BASERUNNING				PERCENTAGES		
Year	Team	Lg	G	AB	H	2B	3B	HR	TB	R	RBI	TBB	IBB	SO	HBP	SH	SF	SB	CS	SB%	GDP	Avg	OBP	SLG
1991	Princeton	R	59	230	60	6	4	1	77	31	18	8	0	30	1	7	1	2	7	.22	2	.261	.288	.335
1992	Billings	R	72	281	94	17	2	1	118	52	38	34	3	49	3	1	4	9	5	.64	3	.335	.407	.420
1993	Charlstn-Wv	A	133	480	140	32	4	8	204	93	58	73	2	104	3	4	4	27	6	.82	11	.292	.386	.425
1994	Winston-Sal	A	106	379	92	16	0	7	129	57	33	55	1	81	6	1	3	19	7	.73	9	.243	.345	.340
1995	Chattanooga	AA	8	17	1	1	0	0	2	1	1	3	0	7	0	0	0	0	1	.00	0	.059	.200	.118
	Charlstn-Wv	A	31	86	21	1	1	0	24	14	5	15	0	19	0	1	0	5	0	1.00	2	.244	.356	.279
	Winston-Sal	A	50	149	43	7	1	4	64	25	14	18	0	25	0	0	1	0	6	.00	1	.289	.363	.430
	5 Min. YEARS		459	1622	451	80	12	21	618	273	167	206	6	315	13	14	13	62	32	.66	28	.278	.361	.381

Geoffrey Jenkins

Bats: Left **Throws:** Left **Pos:** OF   **Ht:** 6'1" **Wt:** 195 **Born:** 7/21/74 **Age:** 21

				BATTING													BASERUNNING				PERCENTAGES		
Year	Team	Lg	G	AB	H	2B	3B	HR	TB	R	RBI	TBB	IBB	SO	HBP	SH	SF	SB	CS	SB%	GDP	Avg	OBP	SLG
1995	Helena	R	7	28	9	0	1	0	11	2	9	3	0	11	0	0	1	0	2	.00	0	.321	.375	.393
	Stockton	A	13	47	12	2	0	3	23	13	12	10	0	12	0	0	2	2	0	1.00	0	.255	.373	.489
	El Paso	AA	21	79	22	4	2	1	33	12	13	8	0	23	0	0	1	3	1	.75	1	.278	.341	.418
	1 Min. YEARS		41	154	43	6	3	4	67	27	34	21	0	46	0	0	4	5	3	.63	1	.279	.358	.435

Lance Jennings

Bats: Right **Throws:** Right **Pos:** C   **Ht:** 6'0" **Wt:** 195 **Born:** 10/3/71 **Age:** 24

				BATTING													BASERUNNING				PERCENTAGES		
Year	Team	Lg	G	AB	H	2B	3B	HR	TB	R	RBI	TBB	IBB	SO	HBP	SH	SF	SB	CS	SB%	GDP	Avg	OBP	SLG
1989	Royals	R	47	164	39	3	0	1	45	15	15	9	0	34	1	2	1	0	2	.00	3	.238	.280	.274
1990	Royals	R	15	48	14	4	0	0	18	4	5	4	0	12	1	0	0	0	4	.00	1	.292	.358	.375
	Eugene	A	31	92	17	3	1	4	34	8	9	6	0	21	0	2	1	0	0	.00	1	.185	.232	.370
1991	Appleton	A	82	284	67	22	0	5	104	25	42	20	1	65	3	1	2	0	2	.00	8	.236	.291	.366
	Baseball Cy	A	10	34	8	1	0	0	9	1	5	3	0	9	2	0	0	0	0	.00	2	.235	.333	.265
1992	Baseball Cy	A	51	174	45	7	0	7	73	16	24	15	0	44	2	1	1	0	0	.00	4	.259	.323	.420
	Memphis	AA	52	145	21	5	0	1	29	5	8	6	0	33	1	1	1	0	0	.00	4	.145	.183	.200
1993	Memphis	AA	98	327	67	11	0	4	90	27	33	21	0	83	6	1	2	0	1	.00	5	.205	.264	.275
1994	Wilmington	A	92	316	78	14	0	7	113	46	39	25	1	62	5	10	3	1	0	1.00	4	.247	.309	.358
1995	Wichita	AA	13	44	8	0	0	0	8	2	3	1	0	8	0	1	1	0	0	.00	1	.182	.196	.182
	Visalia	A	85	316	95	15	1	6	130	31	41	36	2	56	2	0	2	0	2	.00	6	.301	.374	.411
	7 Min. YEARS		576	1944	459	85	2	35	653	180	224	146	4	427	23	19	14	1	11	.08	41	.236	.295	.336

Robin Jennings

Bats: Left **Throws:** Left **Pos:** OF   **Ht:** 6'2" **Wt:** 200 **Born:** 4/11/72 **Age:** 24

Year Team	Lg	G	AB	H	2B	3B	HR	TB	R	RBI	TBB	IBB	SO	HBP	SH	SF	SB	CS	SB%	GDP	Avg	OBP	SLG
1992 Geneva	A	72	275	82	12	2	7	119	39	47	20	5	43	2	0	0	10	3	.77	7	.298	.350	.433
1993 Peoria	A	132	474	146	29	5	3	194	65	65	46	2	73	4	5	3	11	11	.50	9	.308	.372	.409
1994 Daytona	A	128	476	133	24	5	8	191	54	60	45	5	54	4	4	4	2	10	.17	13	.279	.344	.401
1995 Orlando	AA	132	490	145	27	7	17	237	71	79	44	5	61	4	0	5	7	14	.33	11	.296	.355	.484
4 Min. YEARS		464	1715	506	92	19	35	741	229	251	155	17	231	14	9	12	30	38	.44	40	.295	.356	.432

Marcus Jensen

Bats: Both **Throws:** Right **Pos:** C   **Ht:** 6'4" **Wt:** 195 **Born:** 12/14/72 **Age:** 23

Year Team	Lg	G	AB	H	2B	3B	HR	TB	R	RBI	TBB	IBB	SO	HBP	SH	SF	SB	CS	SB%	GDP	Avg	OBP	SLG
1990 Everett	A	51	171	29	3	0	2	38	21	12	24	0	60	5	0	0	0	1	.00	3	.170	.290	.222
1991 Giants	R	48	155	44	8	3	2	64	28	30	34	3	22	5	0	4	4	2	.67	2	.284	.419	.413
1992 Clinton	A	86	264	62	14	0	4	88	35	33	54	1	87	4	1	2	4	2	.67	5	.235	.370	.333
1993 Clinton	A	104	324	85	24	2	11	146	53	56	66	5	98	4	0	4	1	2	.33	5	.262	.389	.451
1994 San Jose	A	118	418	101	18	0	7	140	56	47	61	5	100	8	2	6	1	1	.50	9	.242	.345	.335
1995 Shreveport	AA	95	321	91	22	8	4	141	55	45	41	1	68	3	5	8	0	0	.00	4	.283	.362	.439
6 Min. YEARS		502	1653	412	89	13	30	617	248	223	280	17	435	29	8	24	10	8	.56	28	.249	.363	.373

Aaron Jersild

Pitches: Left **Bats:** Left **Pos:** P   **Ht:** 6'0" **Wt:** 180 **Born:** 6/28/69 **Age:** 27

Year Team	Lg	G	GS	CG	GF	IP	BFP	H	R	ER	HR	SH	SF	HB	TBB	IBB	SO	WP	Bk	W	L	Pct.	ShO	Sv	ERA
1992 St. Cathrns	A	22	0	0	17	35.1	140	26	11	8	0	0	0	1	8	0	36	1	1	0	1	.000	0	7	2.04
1993 Hagerstown	A	44	0	0	18	71	309	74	39	29	4	4	5	4	25	2	59	4	1	3	2	.600	0	3	3.68
1994 Dunedin	A	34	14	3	3	142	586	130	58	50	10	6	5	2	41	0	112	6	6	11	6	.647	1	0	3.17
1995 Knoxville	AA	14	5	0	4	40.2	184	47	28	27	6	1	0	1	21	1	29	2	1	2	2	.500	0	0	5.98
Dunedin	A	22	3	0	10	48.2	219	54	30	26	1	2	2	6	17	0	39	2	5	2	6	.250	0	1	4.81
4 Min. YEARS		136	22	3	52	337.2	1438	331	166	140	21	13	12	14	112	3	275	15	14	18	17	.514	1	11	3.73

Derek Jeter

Bats: Right **Throws:** Right **Pos:** SS   **Ht:** 6'3" **Wt:** 185 **Born:** 6/26/74 **Age:** 22

Year Team	Lg	G	AB	H	2B	3B	HR	TB	R	RBI	TBB	IBB	SO	HBP	SH	SF	SB	CS	SB%	GDP	Avg	OBP	SLG
1992 Yankees	R	47	173	35	10	0	3	54	19	25	19	0	36	5	0	2	2	2	.50	4	.202	.296	.312
Greensboro	A	11	37	9	0	0	1	12	4	4	7	0	16	1	0	0	0	1	.00	0	.243	.378	.324
1993 Greensboro	A	128	515	152	14	11	5	203	85	71	58	1	95	11	2	4	18	9	.67	9	.295	.376	.394
1994 Tampa	A	69	292	96	13	8	0	125	61	39	23	2	30	3	3	3	28	2	.93	4	.329	.380	.428
Albany-Colo	AA	34	122	46	7	2	2	63	17	13	15	0	16	1	3	1	12	2	.86	3	.377	.446	.516
Columbus	AAA	35	126	44	7	1	3	62	25	16	20	1	16	1	3	1	10	4	.71	6	.349	.439	.492
1995 Columbus	AAA	123	486	154	27	9	2	205	96	45	61	4	56	4	2	5	20	12	.63	9	.317	.394	.422
1995 New York	AL	15	48	12	4	0	0	18	5	7	3	0	11	0	0	0	0	0	.00	0	.250	.294	.375
4 Min. YEARS		447	1751	536	78	31	16	724	307	213	203	5	264	26	13	16	90	32	.74	35	.306	.383	.413

Miguel Jimenez

Pitches: Right **Bats:** Right **Pos:** P   **Ht:** 6'2" **Wt:** 205 **Born:** 8/19/69 **Age:** 26

Year Team	Lg	G	GS	CG	GF	IP	BFP	H	R	ER	HR	SH	SF	HB	TBB	IBB	SO	WP	Bk	W	L	Pct.	ShO	Sv	ERA
1991 Sou. Oregon	A	10	9	0	0	34.2	159	22	21	12	0	0	0	2	34	0	39	6	6	0	2	.000	0	0	3.12
1992 Madison	A	26	19	2	0	120.1	514	78	48	39	3	2	2	8	78	1	135	12	14	7	7	.500	1	0	2.92
Huntsville	AA	1	1	0	0	5	19	3	1	1	1	0	0	0	3	0	8	1	0	1	0	1.000	0	0	1.80
1993 Huntsville	AA	20	19	0	0	107	476	92	49	35	10	2	1	4	64	0	105	6	2	10	6	.625	0	0	2.94
Tacoma	AAA	8	8	0	0	37.2	164	32	23	20	4	2	1	0	24	0	34	3	0	2	3	.400	0	0	4.78
1994 Tacoma	AAA	23	15	0	0	74	372	82	83	75	9	1	4	4	79	0	64	12	2	3	9	.250	0	0	9.12
1995 Edmonton	AAA	6	3	0	2	7.1	43	12	10	10	0	1	0	1	10	0	4	0	0	0	0	.000	0	0	12.27
Modesto	A	4	4	0	0	18	83	14	13	12	5	0	1	2	14	0	11	4	0	1	2	.333	0	0	6.00
Huntsville	AA	6	6	0	0	30	124	25	12	12	3	1	0	1	11	0	28	1	0	3	2	.600	0	0	3.60
1993 Oakland	AL	5	4	0	0	27	120	27	12	12	5	0	0	1	16	0	13	0	0	1	0	1.000	0	0	4.00
1994 Oakland	AL	8	7	0	0	34	173	38	33	28	9	1	1	1	32	2	22	3	3	1	4	.200	0	0	7.41
5 Min. YEARS		104	84	2	4	434	1954	360	260	216	35	8	10	20	317	1	428	44	24	27	31	.466	1	0	4.48
2 Maj. YEARS		13	11	0	0	61	293	65	45	40	14	1	1	2	48	2	35	3	3	2	4	.333	0	0	5.90

Keith Johns

Bats: Right **Throws:** Right **Pos:** SS   **Ht:** 6'1" **Wt:** 175 **Born:** 7/19/71 **Age:** 24

Year Team	Lg	G	AB	H	2B	3B	HR	TB	R	RBI	TBB	IBB	SO	HBP	SH	SF	SB	CS	SB%	GDP	Avg	OBP	SLG
1992 Hamilton	A	70	275	78	11	1	1	94	36	28	27	0	42	1	1	3	15	10	.60	5	.284	.346	.342
1993 Springfield	A	132	467	121	24	1	2	153	74	40	70	0	68	4	9	5	40	20	.67	8	.259	.357	.328
1994 St. Pete	A	122	464	106	20	0	3	135	52	47	37	1	49	2	12	4	18	9	.67	7	.228	.286	.291
1995 Arkansas	AA	111	396	111	13	2	2	134	59	28	55	0	53	2	11	2	14	7	.67	11	.280	.369	.338

Year Team	Lg	G	AB	H	2B	3B	HR	TB	R	RBI	TBB	IBB	SO	HBP	SH	SF	SB	CS	SB%	GDP	Avg	OBP	SLG
Louisville	AAA	5	10	0	0	0	0	0	0	0	0	0	2	0	0	0	0	0	.00	0	.000	.000	.000
4 Min. YEARS		440	1612	416	68	4	8	516	231	143	189	1	214	9	33	14	87	46	.65	31	.258	.337	.320

Barry Johnson

Pitches: Right **Bats:** Right **Pos:** P   **Ht:** 6'4" **Wt:** 200 **Born:** 8/21/69 **Age:** 26

| | | HOW MUCH HE PITCHED | | | | | | WHAT HE GAVE UP | | | | | | | | | | | | THE RESULTS | | | | | |
Year Team	Lg	G	GS	CG	GF	IP	BFP	H	R	ER	HR	SH	SF	HB	TBB	IBB	SO	WP	Bk	W	L	Pct.	ShO	Sv	ERA
1991 Expos	R	7	1	0	3	12.2	55	10	9	5	0	0	0	4	6	0	10	2	0	0	2	.000	0	0	3.55
1992 South Bend	A	16	16	5	0	109.1	463	111	56	46	5	1	5	6	23	0	74	8	1	7	5	.583	1	0	3.79
1993 Sarasota	A	18	1	0	7	54.1	205	33	5	4	1	5	2	2	8	0	40	1	1	5	0	1.000	0	1	0.66
Birmingham	AA	13	1	0	8	21.2	97	27	11	8	2	1	1	0	6	0	16	2	1	2	0	1.000	0	1	3.32
1994 Birmingham	AA	51	4	0	12	97.2	427	100	51	35	7	8	3	2	30	3	67	2	0	6	2	.750	0	1	3.23
1995 Birmingham	AA	47	0	0	10	78	308	64	21	16	1	2	1	2	15	1	53	2	1	7	4	.636	0	0	1.85
5 Min. YEARS		152	23	5	40	373.2	1555	345	153	114	16	17	12	16	88	4	260	17	4	27	13	.675	1	3	2.75

Chris Johnson

Pitches: Right **Bats:** Right **Pos:** P   **Ht:** 6'8" **Wt:** 215 **Born:** 12/7/68 **Age:** 27

| | | HOW MUCH HE PITCHED | | | | | | WHAT HE GAVE UP | | | | | | | | | | | | THE RESULTS | | | | | |
Year Team	Lg	G	GS	CG	GF	IP	BFP	H	R	ER	HR	SH	SF	HB	TBB	IBB	SO	WP	Bk	W	L	Pct.	ShO	Sv	ERA
1987 Helena	R	12	11	0	0	60.1	257	55	32	27	8	3	3	3	21	0	54	5	2	5	0	1.000	0	0	4.03
1988 Beloit	A	26	26	0	0	130	566	137	66	57	9	4	4	4	42	3	99	5	9	8	10	.444	0	0	3.95
1989 Beloit	A	25	22	2	2	138.2	585	118	63	49	8	6	3	13	50	0	118	5	2	9	9	.500	1	0	3.18
1990 Stockton	A	23	23	1	0	142	592	121	56	47	7	5	5	9	54	1	112	4	1	13	6	.684	0	0	2.98
1991 El Paso	AA	13	12	0	1	66.2	322	85	56	48	4	6	3	4	40	4	43	5	0	4	4	.500	0	0	6.48
Harrisburg	AA	10	10	1	0	56.2	243	59	25	21	2	0	1	1	28	0	42	2	1	3	2	.600	1	0	3.34
1992 Harrisburg	AA	28	23	0	1	142.1	616	149	71	63	9	6	5	4	43	1	95	7	1	9	10	.474	0	0	3.98
1993 Harrisburg	AA	1	0	0	0	1.1	6	1	2	2	0	0	0	0	3	1	0	0	0	0	0	.000	0	0	13.50
Orlando	AA	15	1	0	3	27.1	133	31	12	9	1	3	1	4	15	2	14	3	0	0	1	.000	0	1	2.96
1994 Orlando	AA	20	1	0	9	38.1	146	33	15	13	2	4	1	0	8	1	28	0	0	1	1	.500	0	2	3.05
1995 Orlando	AA	46	0	0	21	70.1	296	68	34	27	6	4	3	1	24	7	49	3	0	5	4	.556	0	5	3.45
9 Min. YEARS		219	129	4	37	874	3762	857	432	363	56	41	29	43	328	20	654	39	16	57	47	.548	2	8	3.74

Dane Johnson

Pitches: Right **Bats:** Right **Pos:** P   **Ht:** 6'5" **Wt:** 205 **Born:** 2/10/63 **Age:** 33

| | | HOW MUCH HE PITCHED | | | | | | WHAT HE GAVE UP | | | | | | | | | | | | THE RESULTS | | | | | |
Year Team	Lg	G	GS	CG	GF	IP	BFP	H	R	ER	HR	SH	SF	HB	TBB	IBB	SO	WP	Bk	W	L	Pct.	ShO	Sv	ERA
1993 El Paso	AA	15	1	0	10	25.1	106	23	12	11	2	0	1	0	10	1	26	1	2	2	2	.500	0	1	3.91
New Orleans	AAA	13	0	0	8	15	56	11	4	4	2	1	0	0	4	1	10	1	0	0	0	.000	0	6	2.40
1994 Nashville	AAA	39	0	0	36	44	186	40	13	11	2	3	0	0	18	7	40	4	0	1	5	.167	0	24	2.25
1995 Nashville	AAA	46	0	0	28	56	240	48	24	15	2	5	1	1	28	6	51	3	1	4	4	.500	0	15	2.41
1994 Chicago	AL	15	0	0	4	12.1	61	16	9	9	2	0	1	0	11	1	7	0	0	2	1	.667	0	0	6.57
3 Min. YEARS		113	1	0	82	140.1	588	122	53	41	8	9	2	1	60	15	127	9	3	7	11	.389	0	46	2.63

Dom Johnson

Pitches: Right **Bats:** Right **Pos:** P   **Ht:** 6'5" **Wt:** 230 **Born:** 8/9/68 **Age:** 27

| | | HOW MUCH HE PITCHED | | | | | | WHAT HE GAVE UP | | | | | | | | | | | | THE RESULTS | | | | | |
Year Team	Lg	G	GS	CG	GF	IP	BFP	H	R	ER	HR	SH	SF	HB	TBB	IBB	SO	WP	Bk	W	L	Pct.	ShO	Sv	ERA
1987 Pocatello	R	18	2	0	5	35	174	42	35	28	2	1	3	4	26	1	30	5	0	1	2	.333	0	2	7.20
1988 Clinton	A	24	18	1	1	101	463	87	63	52	4	0	3	4	85	1	67	13	7	4	8	.333	0	0	4.63
1989 Clinton	A	8	7	0	0	37.1	179	42	29	24	2	0	3	2	28	0	30	3	2	0	0	.000	0	0	5.79
Salinas	A	17	14	1	1	87.1	393	75	42	37	4	1	0	5	63	0	60	15	5	6	4	.600	0	0	3.81
1990 San Jose	A	25	19	2	2	100	456	89	72	60	8	4	4	6	72	0	61	10	0	5	8	.385	0	0	5.40
1991 Reno	A	25	9	1	5	72	315	65	31	26	3	2	5	4	38	0	63	7	0	3	5	.375	0	2	3.25
1992 Palm Spring	A	22	4	0	6	40	196	44	32	30	4	1	0	3	35	1	23	10	1	0	4	.000	0	1	6.75
1993 Palm Spring	A	45	0	0	12	50.1	240	51	34	32	6	5	4	3	39	7	47	19	0	2	4	.333	0	5	5.72
1994 Midland	AA	31	16	0	3	128.2	580	136	84	67	11	2	3	7	64	0	116	12	2	7	9	.438	0	0	4.69
1995 Trenton	AA	5	2	0	1	14.1	74	19	16	15	2	0	0	1	12	0	11	2	1	1	2	.333	0	0	9.42
Mobile	IND	9	9	0	0	44.2	215	56	43	26	8	4	4	6	22	0	29	3	0	2	2	.500	0	0	5.24
9 Min. YEARS		229	100	5	36	710.2	3285	706	481	397	54	20	29	45	484	10	537	99	18	31	52	.373	0	5	5.03

Earl Johnson

Bats: Both **Throws:** Right **Pos:** OF   **Ht:** 5'9" **Wt:** 163 **Born:** 10/3/71 **Age:** 24

| | | BATTING | | | | | | | | | | | | | | | BASERUNNING | | | | PERCENTAGES | | |
Year Team	Lg	G	AB	H	2B	3B	HR	TB	R	RBI	TBB	IBB	SO	HBP	SH	SF	SB	CS	SB%	GDP	Avg	OBP	SLG
1992 Padres	R	35	101	17	1	0	0	18	20	1	10	0	28	1	0	0	19	5	.79	0	.168	.250	.178
1993 Spokane	A	63	199	49	3	1	0	54	33	14	16	0	49	1	5	1	19	3	.86	2	.246	.304	.271
1994 Springfield	A	136	533	149	11	3	1	169	80	43	37	0	94	3	13	4	80	25	.76	2	.280	.328	.317
1995 Rancho Cuca	A	81	341	100	11	3	0	117	51	25	25	0	51	1	5	0	34	12	.74	5	.293	.343	.343
Memphis	AA	2	10	2	0	0	0	2	0	0	1	0	0	0	0	0	0	1	.00	0	.200	.273	.200
4 Min. YEARS		317	1184	317	26	7	1	360	184	83	89	0	222	6	23	5	152	46	.77	9	.268	.321	.304

Erik Johnson

Bats: Right Throws: Right Pos: 2B Ht: 5'11" Wt: 165 Born: 10/11/65 Age: 30

Year	Team	Lg	G	AB	H	2B	3B	HR	TB	R	RBI	TBB	IBB	SO	HBP	SH	SF	SB	CS	SB%	GDP	Avg	OBP	SLG
1987	Pocatello	R	43	129	34	7	0	4	53	19	12	13	0	21	0	3	0	6	2	.75	1	.264	.331	.411
	Shreveport	AA	9	21	2	1	0	0	3	1	3	0	0	5	0	0	0	0	1	.00	0	.095	.095	.143
1988	Clinton	A	90	322	72	12	3	5	105	29	38	28	3	39	3	4	2	4	7	.36	6	.224	.290	.326
	San Jose	A	44	160	40	3	1	1	48	25	16	18	0	29	2	1	0	4	2	.67	5	.250	.333	.300
1989	Shreveport	AA	87	246	56	5	4	3	78	28	29	23	3	37	1	4	4	3	2	.60	10	.228	.292	.317
1990	Phoenix	AAA	2	3	0	0	0	0	0	0	0	1	0	1	0	0	0	0	0	.00	1	.000	.250	.000
	Shreveport	AA	91	270	60	6	0	1	69	35	15	22	3	38	3	3	0	6	6	.50	8	.222	.288	.256
1991	Phoenix	AAA	16	34	11	1	1	0	14	6	4	3	1	5	0	0	1	0	0	.00	0	.324	.368	.412
	Shreveport	AA	58	146	32	7	0	2	45	27	20	16	4	20	1	4	0	6	2	.75	3	.219	.301	.308
1992	Phoenix	AAA	90	229	55	5	1	0	62	24	19	20	2	38	2	5	1	8	10	.44	9	.240	.306	.271
1993	Phoenix	AAA	101	363	90	8	5	0	108	33	33	29	2	51	1	2	3	3	9	.25	13	.248	.303	.298
1994	Phoenix	AAA	106	384	112	19	3	1	140	43	45	35	3	57	3	1	5	2	6	.25	16	.292	.351	.365
1995	Calgary	AAA	123	455	135	35	6	3	191	64	58	39	6	40	0	3	6	5	4	.56	12	.297	.348	.420
1993	San Francisco	NL	4	5	2	2	0	0	4	1	0	0	0	0	1	0	0	0	0	.00	0	.400	.400	.800
1994	San Francisco	NL	5	13	2	0	0	0	2	0	0	0	0	4	0	0	0	0	0	.00	0	.154	.154	.154
	9 Min. YEARS		860	2762	699	109	24	20	916	334	292	247	27	381	16	30	22	47	51	.48	84	.253	.316	.332
	2 Maj. YEARS		9	18	4	2	0	0	6	1	0	0	0	4	0	0	0	0	0	.00	0	.222	.222	.333

J.J. Johnson

Pitches: Right Bats: Right Pos: P Ht: 6'6" Wt: 225 Born: 1/7/71 Age: 25

Year	Team	Lg	G	GS	CG	GF	IP	BFP	H	R	ER	HR	SH	SF	HB	TBB	IBB	SO	WP	Bk	W	L	Pct.	ShO	Sv	ERA
1993	Bend	A	8	4	0	4	34	142	20	10	3	2	2	0	2	10	0	27	4	4	4	1	.800	0	3	0.79
	Central Val	A	7	6	0	1	40.1	158	31	12	11	4	1	0	0	13	0	33	1	0	3	1	.750	0	0	2.45
1994	Central Val	A	21	20	2	0	103.2	435	98	57	41	7	5	4	5	37	3	70	8	4	5	11	.313	2	0	3.56
1995	New Haven	AA	19	12	0	1	67.2	297	77	43	40	2	1	4	3	29	1	37	6	0	6	3	.667	0	0	5.32
	Salem	A	5	4	0	0	22	94	23	6	5	0	1	0	1	5	0	9	1	0	1	2	.333	0	0	2.05
	3 Min. YEARS		60	46	2	6	267.2	1126	259	128	100	15	10	8	11	94	4	176	20	8	19	18	.514	2	3	3.36

J.J. Johnson

Bats: Right Throws: Right Pos: OF Ht: 6'0" Wt: 195 Born: 8/31/73 Age: 22

Year	Team	Lg	G	AB	H	2B	3B	HR	TB	R	RBI	TBB	IBB	SO	HBP	SH	SF	SB	CS	SB%	GDP	Avg	OBP	SLG
1991	Red Sox	R	31	110	19	1	0	0	20	14	9	10	0	15	2	0	0	3	1	.75	2	.173	.250	.182
1992	Elmira	A	30	114	26	3	1	1	34	8	12	4	0	32	1	4	1	8	0	1.00	2	.228	.258	.298
1993	Utica	A	43	170	49	17	4	2	80	33	27	9	1	34	7	2	3	5	3	.63	2	.288	.344	.471
	Lynchburg	A	25	94	24	3	0	4	39	10	17	7	0	20	2	2	2	1	2	.33	3	.255	.314	.415
1994	Lynchburg	A	131	515	120	28	4	14	198	66	51	36	3	132	4	1	1	4	7	.36	9	.233	.288	.384
1995	Sarasota	A	107	391	108	16	4	10	162	49	43	26	0	74	6	2	2	7	8	.47	9	.276	.329	.414
	Trenton	AA	2	6	3	0	0	0	3	1	1	0	0	0	0	0	0	0	0	.00	0	.500	.500	.500
	5 Min. YEARS		369	1400	349	68	13	31	536	181	160	92	4	307	22	11	11	28	21	.57	27	.249	.304	.383

Jack Johnson

Bats: Right Throws: Right Pos: C Ht: 6'3" Wt: 205 Born: 3/24/70 Age: 26

Year	Team	Lg	G	AB	H	2B	3B	HR	TB	R	RBI	TBB	IBB	SO	HBP	SH	SF	SB	CS	SB%	GDP	Avg	OBP	SLG
1991	Yakima	A	36	105	27	6	0	4	45	15	11	14	0	22	3	2	0	1	1	.50	2	.257	.361	.429
1992	Bakersfield	A	49	153	35	10	0	3	54	15	21	9	2	32	3	3	0	0	2	.00	2	.229	.285	.353
1993	Orlando	AA	33	82	19	6	0	0	25	9	5	12	0	22	1	3	1	0	1	.00	1	.232	.333	.305
	Daytona	A	3	9	1	0	0	0	1	0	0	0	0	3	0	0	0	0	0	.00	0	.111	.111	.111
	Peoria	A	39	96	18	7	0	0	25	10	10	23	0	33	1	4	2	3	0	1.00	4	.188	.344	.260
1994	Pr. William	A	22	57	9	2	0	1	14	6	5	1	0	17	0	1	1	0	0	.00	0	.158	.169	.246
1995	Rockford	A	24	71	15	2	0	2	23	5	14	8	2	17	0	0	1	0	0	.00	1	.211	.288	.324
	Daytona	A	4	8	3	0	0	1	6	1	2	1	0	4	0	0	0	0	0	.00	0	.375	.444	.750
	Pueblo	IND	11	32	7	4	0	0	11	5	5	4	0	9	0	0	0	0	0	.00	0	.219	.306	.344
	Orlando	AA	25	68	15	0	0	0	15	3	4	7	0	11	1	0	1	1	3	.25	1	.221	.299	.221
	5 Min. YEARS		246	681	149	37	0	11	219	69	77	79	4	170	9	13	6	5	7	.42	11	.219	.306	.322

Judd Johnson

Pitches: Left Bats: Right Pos: P Ht: 6'0" Wt: 185 Born: 5/4/66 Age: 30

Year	Team	Lg	G	GS	CG	GF	IP	BFP	H	R	ER	HR	SH	SF	HB	TBB	IBB	SO	WP	Bk	W	L	Pct.	ShO	Sv	ERA
1989	Sumter	A	11	0	0	6	25.2	103	20	7	6	0	4	0	0	7	1	25	4	0	3	2	.600	0	3	2.10
	Durham	A	32	3	0	10	77.2	329	79	22	15	2	4	4	0	16	3	41	3	0	6	2	.750	0	4	1.74
1990	Greenville	AA	28	24	3	1	149	638	159	75	68	17	9	1	1	43	1	59	3	2	5	10	.333	2	1	4.11
1991	Greenville	AA	47	9	0	19	98.1	411	108	42	39	4	2	1	2	15	0	66	7	0	10	7	.588	0	6	3.57
1992	Greenville	AA	43	0	0	16	68.1	276	56	21	13	6	3	0	2	14	3	40	1	0	6	0	1.000	0	2	1.71
	Richmond	AAA	1	0	0	1	1	3	0	0	0	0	0	0	0	1	0	0	0	0	0	0	.000	0	0	0.00
1993	Richmond	AAA	49	2	0	8	85	358	85	28	25	3	4	0	3	22	2	55	3	0	4	2	.667	0	0	2.65
1994	Richmond	AAA	40	0	0	5	76.1	319	77	38	31	3	3	4	2	22	5	46	2	1	6	5	.545	0	1	3.66

1995 Salt Lake	AAA	17	0	0	7	21	103	27	11	8	1	1	4	0	12	5	11	2	1	1	1	.500	0	1	3.43
7 Min. YEARS		268	38	3	73	602.1	2540	611	244	205	36	30	14	10	152	20	343	25	4	41	29	.586	2	18	3.06

Matt Johnson

Bats: Right Throws: Right Pos: 2B Ht: 5'10" Wt: 175 Born: 5/15/70 Age: 26

			BATTING														BASERUNNING				PERCENTAGES		
Year	Team	Lg	G	AB	H	2B	3B	HR	TB	R	RBI	TBB	IBB	SO	HBP	SH	SF	SB	CS	SB%	GDP	Avg	OBP	SLG
1992	Medicne Hat	R	67	234	60	10	2	2	80	33	28	38	0	36	6	3	2	6	6	.50	5	.256	.371	.342
1993	Dunedin	A	54	148	31	5	0	3	45	19	18	18	0	31	3	5	0	3	2	.60	3	.209	.308	.304
1994	Dunedin	A	82	243	62	15	0	4	89	33	35	28	0	47	5	3	1	4	2	.67	9	.255	.343	.366
	Knoxville	AA	5	10	0	0	0	0	0	0	1	2	0	2	0	0	0	0	1	.00	0	.000	.167	.000
1995	Syracuse	AAA	5	6	3	2	0	0	5	1	0	0	0	1	1	0	0	0	0	.00	0	.500	.571	.833
	Knoxville	AA	57	144	26	4	0	0	30	8	11	17	0	32	5	2	2	1	1	.50	5	.181	.286	.208
	4 Min. YEARS		270	785	182	36	2	9	249	94	93	103	0	149	20	13	5	14	12	.54	22	.232	.334	.317

Russ Johnson

Bats: Right Throws: Right Pos: SS Ht: 5'10" Wt: 185 Born: 2/22/73 Age: 23

			BATTING														BASERUNNING				PERCENTAGES		
Year	Team	Lg	G	AB	H	2B	3B	HR	TB	R	RBI	TBB	IBB	SO	HBP	SH	SF	SB	CS	SB%	GDP	Avg	OBP	SLG
1995	Jackson	AA	132	476	118	16	2	9	165	65	53	50	1	61	7	2	5	10	5	.67	11	.248	.325	.347

Sean Johnston

Pitches: Left Bats: Left Pos: P Ht: 6'0" Wt: 185 Born: 12/10/70 Age: 25

			HOW MUCH HE PITCHED					WHAT HE GAVE UP										THE RESULTS				
Year	Team	Lg	G	GS	CG	GF	IP	BFP	H	R	ER	HR	SH	SF	HB	TBB	IBB	SO	WP	Bk	W	L	Pct.	ShO	Sv	ERA
1992	Utica	A	14	14	1	0	80.2	325	78	44	25	4	0	2	2	21	0	56	4	0	4	4	.500	0	0	2.79
1993	South Bend	A	15	15	2	0	98	395	83	30	24	3	3	0	4	28	0	59	4	3	8	3	.727	2	0	2.20
	Sarasota	A	12	12	1	0	72	311	74	43	36	7	3	2	0	30	0	29	0	1	6	5	.545	0	0	4.50
1994	Pr. William	A	27	27	3	0	165	717	185	89	83	9	7	5	4	61	1	81	6	0	15	6	.714	1	0	4.53
1995	Birmingham	AA	34	13	0	8	98.1	432	120	53	46	6	2	2	2	36	0	44	2	1	5	2	.714	0	0	4.21
	4 Min. YEARS		102	81	7	8	514	2180	540	259	214	29	15	11	12	176	1	269	16	5	38	20	.655	3	0	3.75

Bobby Jones

Pitches: Left Bats: Right Pos: P Ht: 6'0" Wt: 175 Born: 4/11/72 Age: 24

			HOW MUCH HE PITCHED					WHAT HE GAVE UP										THE RESULTS				
Year	Team	Lg	G	GS	CG	GF	IP	BFP	H	R	ER	HR	SH	SF	HB	TBB	IBB	SO	WP	Bk	W	L	Pct.	ShO	Sv	ERA
1992	Helena	R	14	13	1	0	76.1	341	93	51	37	7	4	2	1	23	0	53	6	5	5	4	.556	0	0	4.36
1993	Beloit	A	25	25	4	0	144.2	661	159	82	66	9	1	6	9	65	1	115	4	4	10	10	.500	0	0	4.11
1994	Stockton	A	26	26	2	0	147.2	638	131	90	69	12	4	4	4	64	0	147	5	2	6	12	.333	0	0	4.21
1995	Colo. Sprng	AAA	11	8	0	0	40.2	204	50	38	33	5	4	1	2	33	1	48	4	1	1	2	.333	0	0	7.30
	New Haven	AA	27	8	0	9	73.1	315	61	27	21	4	3	3	8	36	2	70	7	0	5	2	.714	0	3	2.58
	4 Min. YEARS		103	80	7	9	482.2	2159	494	288	226	37	16	16	24	221	4	433	26	12	27	30	.474	0	3	4.21

Calvin Jones

Pitches: Right Bats: Right Pos: P Ht: 6'3" Wt: 185 Born: 9/26/63 Age: 32

			HOW MUCH HE PITCHED					WHAT HE GAVE UP										THE RESULTS				
Year	Team	Lg	G	GS	CG	GF	IP	BFP	H	R	ER	HR	SH	SF	HB	TBB	IBB	SO	WP	Bk	W	L	Pct.	ShO	Sv	ERA
1984	Bellingham	A	10	9	0	0	59.2	0	29	23	16	0	0	0	7	36	0	59	8	1	5	0	1.000	0	0	2.41
1985	Wausau	A	20	19	1	0	106	473	96	59	46	10	0	2	5	65	1	71	9	2	4	11	.267	0	0	3.91
1986	Salinas	A	26	25	2	0	157.1	680	141	76	63	9	4	4	4	90	2	137	15	2	11	8	.579	0	0	3.60
1987	Chattanooga	AA	26	10	0	12	81.1	372	90	58	45	5	5	1	2	38	0	77	4	0	2	9	.182	0	2	4.98
1988	Vermont	AA	24	4	0	0	74.2	312	52	26	22	1	4	2	0	47	2	58	4	3	7	5	.583	0	0	2.65
1989	San Bernrdo	A	5	0	0	4	12.1	49	8	1	1	0	0	1	0	7	0	15	0	2	2	0	1.000	0	1	0.73
	Williamsprt	AA	5	0	0	3	6.2	34	13	9	9	1	0	0	0	4	0	5	1	0	0	0	.000	0	0	12.15
1990	San Bernrdo	A	53	0	0	27	67	298	43	32	22	4	1	3	4	54	0	94	6	0	5	3	.625	0	8	2.96
1991	Calgary	AAA	20	0	0	15	23	109	19	12	10	1	0	0	2	19	1	25	6	2	1	1	.500	0	7	3.91
1992	Calgary	AAA	21	1	0	13	32.2	145	23	15	14	3	1	3	0	22	0	32	4	0	2	0	1.000	0	3	3.86
1993	Canton-Akrn	AA	43	0	0	36	62.2	253	40	25	23	1	3	1	1	26	2	73	9	1	5	5	.500	0	22	3.30
1994	Charlotte	AAA	55	0	0	35	62.2	275	64	30	27	4	1	3	1	27	2	47	10	0	3	3	.500	0	14	3.88
1995	Nashville	AAA	5	0	0	0	6.2	38	13	8	5	3	0	0	0	3	1	5	0	0	0	0	.000	0	0	6.75
	Pawtucket	AAA	33	0	0	27	38	165	37	23	17	5	3	2	0	15	1	36	6	0	5	2	.714	0	8	4.03
1991	Seattle	AL	27	0	0	6	46.1	194	33	14	13	0	6	0	1	29	5	42	6	0	2	2	.500	0	2	2.53
1992	Seattle	AL	38	1	0	14	61.2	275	50	39	39	8	1	4	3	47	1	49	10	0	3	5	.375	0	0	5.69
	12 Min. YEARS		346	68	3	178	790.2	3203	668	397	320	50	18	22	26	453	14	734	82	13	52	47	.525	0	65	3.64
	2 Maj. YEARS		65	1	0	20	108	469	83	53	52	8	7	4	3	76	6	91	16	0	5	7	.417	0	2	4.33

Dax Jones

Bats: Right Throws: Right Pos: OF Ht: 6'0" Wt: 170 Born: 8/4/70 Age: 25

			BATTING														BASERUNNING				PERCENTAGES		
Year	Team	Lg	G	AB	H	2B	3B	HR	TB	R	RBI	TBB	IBB	SO	HBP	SH	SF	SB	CS	SB%	GDP	Avg	OBP	SLG
1991	Everett	A	53	180	55	5	6	5	87	42	29	27	0	26	1	1	3	15	8	.65	4	.306	.393	.483
1992	Clinton	A	79	295	88	12	4	1	111	45	42	21	0	32	1	1	1	18	5	.78	6	.298	.346	.376
	Shreveport	AA	19	66	20	0	2	1	27	10	7	4	0	6	1	1	2	2	0	1.00	1	.303	.342	.409
1993	Shreveport	AA	118	436	124	19	5	4	165	59	36	26	6	53	4	3	2	13	8	.62	5	.284	.329	.378

152

Year	Team	Lg	G	AB	H	2B	3B	HR	TB	R	RBI	TBB	IBB	SO	HBP	SH	SF	SB	CS	SB%	GDP	Avg	OBP	SLG
1994	Phoenix	AAA	111	399	111	25	5	4	158	55	52	21	1	42	3	3	4	16	8	.67	14	.278	.316	.396
1995	Phoenix	AAA	112	404	108	21	3	2	141	47	45	31	1	52	2	2	5	11	10	.52	8	.267	.319	.349
	5 Min. YEARS		492	1780	506	82	25	17	689	258	211	130	10	211	12	11	17	75	39	.66	38	.284	.334	.387

Keith Jones

Bats: Left **Throws:** Left **Pos:** OF   **Ht:** 5'10" **Wt:** 160 **Born:** 1/28/71 **Age:** 25

							BATTING											BASERUNNING				PERCENTAGES		
Year	Team	Lg	G	AB	H	2B	3B	HR	TB	R	RBI	TBB	IBB	SO	HBP	SH	SF	SB	CS	SB%	GDP	Avg	OBP	SLG
1991	Johnson Cty	R	66	228	64	13	2	3	90	43	31	29	0	35	2	0	5	21	5	.81	4	.281	.360	.395
1992	Springfield	A	107	343	94	15	5	0	119	51	24	36	0	65	4	0	4	24	20	.55	4	.274	.346	.347
1993	St. Pete	A	102	324	79	12	4	0	99	40	25	14	2	40	0	5	0	21	9	.70	9	.244	.275	.306
1994	Madison	A	113	383	104	23	2	2	137	66	25	38	1	52	7	7	1	24	17	.59	4	.272	.347	.358
1995	Arkansas	AA	50	84	19	2	0	0	21	11	4	9	0	12	0	4	0	3	3	.50	3	.226	.301	.250
	5 Min. YEARS		438	1362	360	65	13	5	466	211	109	126	3	204	13	16	10	93	54	.63	24	.264	.330	.342

Stacy Jones

Pitches: Right **Bats:** Right **Pos:** P   **Ht:** 6'6" **Wt:** 225 **Born:** 5/26/67 **Age:** 29

			HOW MUCH HE PITCHED						WHAT HE GAVE UP										THE RESULTS					
Year	Team	Lg	G	GS	CG	GF	IP	BFP	H	R	ER	HR	SH	SF	HB	TBB	IBB	SO	WP	Bk	W	L	Pct.	ShO	Sv	ERA
1988	Erie	A	7	7	3	0	54.1	218	51	12	8	1	1	0	0	15	2	40	2	0	3	3	.500	2	0	1.33
	Hagerstown	A	6	6	3	0	37.2	156	35	14	12	2	1	4	1	12	0	23	2	0	3	1	.750	2	0	2.87
1989	Frederick	A	15	15	3	0	82.2	374	93	57	45	11	1	3	2	35	0	58	3	4	5	6	.455	1	0	4.90
1990	Frederick	A	15	0	0	11	26.2	119	31	13	10	0	0	1	1	7	1	24	1	1	1	2	.333	0	2	3.38
	Hagerstown	AA	19	0	0	11	40.1	176	46	27	23	1	4	1	1	11	1	41	2	0	1	6	.143	0	2	5.13
1991	Hagerstown	AA	12	0	0	4	30.1	130	24	6	6	1	2	0	1	15	1	26	1	0	0	1	.000	0	1	1.78
	Rochester	AAA	33	1	0	21	50.2	221	53	22	19	4	7	2	0	20	2	47	2	1	4	4	.500	0	8	3.38
1992	Frederick	A	7	6	0	0	33.2	134	32	15	12	3	0	0	1	4	0	30	0	0	2	1	.667	0	0	3.21
	Hagerstown	AA	11	9	0	0	69.2	290	62	30	27	1	1	3	1	25	0	45	0	2	2	5	.286	0	0	0.49
	Rochester	AAA	2	0	0	1	2.2	11	2	2	2	1	0	0	0	1	0	1	0	0	0	0	.000	0	1	6.75
1993	Frederick	A	4	2	0	0	12.2	60	24	17	14	4	1	0	0	1	0	7	0	1	0	2	.000	0	0	9.95
	Shreveport	AA	24	2	0	9	50.1	210	53	21	20	2	1	2	1	19	1	28	0	0	4	1	.800	0	1	3.58
1994	Shreveport	AA	56	0	0	53	64	270	73	21	17	2	5	0	2	12	2	64	1	1	3	6	.333	0	34	2.39
1995	Phoenix	AAA	4	0	0	0	6.1	35	8	9	6	0	0	2	0	6	1	4	0	0	0	1	.000	0	0	8.53
	El Paso	AA	8	0	0	5	13.1	58	12	7	3	0	1	0	0	4	0	14	1	0	1	1	.500	0	3	2.03
	New Orleans	AAA	34	0	0	25	47.2	197	51	16	16	3	1	1	2	12	2	39	3	0	3	2	.600	0	6	3.02
1991	Baltimore	AL	4	1	0	0	11	49	11	6	5	1	0	1	0	5	0	10	0	0	0	0	.000	0	0	4.09
	8 Min. YEARS		257	48	9	140	623	2659	650	289	240	36	26	19	13	199	13	491	18	10	32	42	.432	5	58	3.47

Terry Jones

Bats: Right **Throws:** Right **Pos:** OF   **Ht:** 5'10" **Wt:** 160 **Born:** 2/15/71 **Age:** 25

							BATTING											BASERUNNING				PERCENTAGES		
Year	Team	Lg	G	AB	H	2B	3B	HR	TB	R	RBI	TBB	IBB	SO	HBP	SH	SF	SB	CS	SB%	GDP	Avg	OBP	SLG
1993	Bend	A	33	138	40	5	4	0	53	21	18	12	1	19	0	2	0	16	6	.73	0	.290	.347	.384
	Central Val	A	21	73	21	1	0	0	22	16	7	10	0	15	1	1	0	5	0	1.00	4	.288	.381	.301
1994	Central Val	A	129	536	157	20	1	2	185	94	34	42	1	85	1	10	1	44	12	.79	12	.293	.345	.345
1995	New Haven	AA	124	472	127	12	1	1	144	78	26	39	0	104	3	3	3	51	19	.73	6	.269	.327	.305
	3 Min. YEARS		307	1219	345	38	6	3	404	209	85	103	2	223	5	16	4	116	37	.76	20	.283	.340	.331

Tim Jones

Bats: Left **Throws:** Right **Pos:** 2B-3B   **Ht:** 5'10" **Wt:** 175 **Born:** 12/1/62 **Age:** 33

							BATTING											BASERUNNING				PERCENTAGES		
Year	Team	Lg	G	AB	H	2B	3B	HR	TB	R	RBI	TBB	IBB	SO	HBP	SH	SF	SB	CS	SB%	GDP	Avg	OBP	SLG
1985	Johnson Cty	R	68	228	75	10	1	3	96	33	48	27	1	19	0	0	5	28	6	.82	1	.319	.382	.409
1986	St. Pete	A	39	142	36	3	2	0	43	19	27	30	0	8	1	0	3	8	6	.57	3	.254	.381	.303
	Arkansas	AA	96	284	76	15	1	2	99	36	27	40	2	32	2	3	2	7	5	.58	7	.268	.364	.349
1987	Arkansas	AA	61	176	58	12	0	3	79	23	26	29	4	16	2	3	3	16	10	.62	3	.330	.424	.449
	Louisville	AAA	73	276	78	14	3	4	110	48	43	29	1	27	0	2	0	11	3	.79	4	.283	.351	.399
1988	Louisville	AAA	103	370	95	21	2	6	138	63	38	36	3	56	3	5	1	39	12	.76	5	.257	.327	.373
1991	Louisville	AAA	86	305	78	9	1	5	104	34	29	37	1	59	0	4	3	19	5	.79	2	.256	.333	.341
1993	Louisville	AAA	101	408	118	22	10	5	175	72	46	44	1	67	2	2	4	13	8	.62	4	.289	.358	.429
1994	Charlotte	AAA	115	391	103	17	2	7	145	60	42	43	1	65	2	8	5	10	2	.83	8	.263	.336	.371
1995	Edmonton	AAA	2	6	3	1	0	0	4	1	1	0	0	0	0	0	0	0	0	.00	0	.500	.500	.667
1988	St. Louis	NL	31	52	14	0	0	0	14	2	3	4	0	10	0	0	0	4	1	.80	1	.269	.321	.269
1989	St. Louis	NL	42	75	22	6	0	0	28	11	7	7	1	8	1	1	2	1	0	1.00	2	.293	.353	.373
1990	St. Louis	NL	67	128	28	7	1	1	40	9	12	12	1	20	1	4	0	3	4	.43	1	.219	.291	.313
1991	St. Louis	NL	16	24	4	2	0	0	6	1	2	2	1	6	0	0	1	0	1	.00	0	.167	.222	.250
1992	St. Louis	NL	67	145	29	4	0	0	33	9	3	11	1	29	0	2	0	5	2	.71	1	.200	.256	.228
1993	St. Louis	NL	29	61	16	6	0	0	22	13	1	9	0	8	1	2	0	2	2	.50	0	.262	.366	.361
	8 Min. YEARS		744	2593	720	124	22	35	993	389	327	317	14	349	12	27	26	151	57	.73	37	.278	.356	.383
	6 Maj. YEARS		252	485	113	25	1	1	143	45	28	45	4	81	3	9	3	15	10	.60	5	.233	.300	.295

153

Ricky Jordan

Bats: Right Throws: Right Pos: DH Ht: 6' 3" Wt: 205 Born: 5/26/65 Age: 31

Year Team	Lg	G	AB	H	2B	3B	HR	TB	R	RBI	TBB	IBB	SO	HBP	SH	SF	SB	CS	SB%	GDP	Avg	OBP	SLG
1984 Spartanburg	A	128	490	143	23	4	10	204	72	76	32	2	63	4	0	5	8	2	.80	14	.292	.337	.416
1985 Clearwater	A	139	528	146	22	8	7	205	60	62	25	3	59	1	2	4	26	8	.76	10	.277	.308	.388
1986 Reading	AA	133	478	131	19	3	2	162	44	60	21	3	44	3	1	4	17	7	.71	5	.274	.306	.339
1987 Reading	AA	132	475	151	28	3	16	233	78	95	28	4	22	3	0	9	15	9	.63	18	.318	.353	.491
1988 Maine	AAA	87	338	104	23	1	7	150	42	36	6	0	30	0	0	1	10	0	1.00	15	.308	.319	.444
1990 Scranton-Wb	AAA	27	104	29	1	0	2	36	8	11	5	0	18	1	0	1	0	0	.00	6	.279	.315	.346
1992 Scranton-Wb	AAA	4	19	5	0	0	0	5	1	2	1	0	2	0	0	0	0	0	.00	0	.263	.300	.263
1995 Vancouver	AAA	19	63	14	2	0	2	22	5	9	3	0	7	1	0	0	0	0	.00	2	.222	.269	.349
1988 Philadelphia	NL	69	273	84	15	1	11	134	41	43	7	2	39	0	0	1	1	1	.50	5	.308	.324	.491
1989 Philadelphia	NL	144	523	149	22	3	12	213	63	75	23	5	62	5	0	8	4	3	.57	19	.285	.317	.407
1990 Philadelphia	NL	92	324	78	21	0	5	114	32	44	13	6	39	5	0	4	2	0	1.00	9	.241	.277	.352
1991 Philadelphia	NL	101	301	82	21	3	9	136	38	49	14	2	49	2	0	5	0	2	.00	11	.272	.304	.452
1992 Philadelphia	NL	94	276	84	19	0	4	115	33	34	5	0	44	0	0	3	3	0	1.00	8	.304	.313	.417
1993 Philadelphia	NL	90	159	46	4	1	5	67	21	18	8	1	32	1	0	2	0	0	.00	2	.289	.324	.421
1994 Philadelphia	NL	72	220	62	14	2	8	104	29	37	6	1	32	1	0	1	0	0	.00	7	.282	.303	.473
8 Min. YEARS		669	2495	723	118	19	46	1017	310	351	121	12	245	13	3	24	76	26	.75	70	.290	.323	.408
7 Maj. YEARS		662	2076	585	116	10	54	883	257	300	76	17	297	14	0	24	10	6	.63	61	.282	.308	.425

Terry Jorgensen

Bats: Right Throws: Right Pos: 3B Ht: 6' 4" Wt: 213 Born: 9/2/66 Age: 29

Year Team	Lg	G	AB	H	2B	3B	HR	TB	R	RBI	TBB	IBB	SO	HBP	SH	SF	SB	CS	SB%	GDP	Avg	OBP	SLG
1987 Kenosha	A	67	254	80	17	0	7	118	37	33	18	0	43	2	0	1	1	0	1.00	7	.315	.364	.465
1988 Orlando	AA	135	472	116	27	4	3	160	53	43	40	3	62	6	2	6	4	1	.80	11	.246	.309	.339
1989 Orlando	AA	135	514	135	27	5	13	211	84	101	76	4	78	5	0	9	1	1	.50	6	.263	.358	.411
1990 Portland	AAA	123	440	114	28	3	10	178	43	50	44	2	83	0	1	4	0	0	.00	11	.259	.324	.405
1991 Portland	AAA	126	456	136	29	0	11	198	74	59	54	1	41	4	2	2	1	0	1.00	22	.298	.376	.434
1992 Portland	AAA	135	505	149	32	2	14	227	78	71	54	3	58	4	3	5	2	0	1.00	22	.295	.364	.450
1993 Portland	AAA	61	238	73	18	2	4	107	37	44	19	2	28	1	1	0	1	0	1.00	11	.307	.360	.450
1994 Portland	AA	124	471	136	23	0	14	201	65	72	40	0	50	3	0	1	0	4	.00	14	.289	.348	.427
1995 Charlotte	AAA	99	356	94	14	0	7	129	38	52	39	1	40	1	1	4	3	3	.50	9	.264	.335	.362
1989 Minnesota	AL	10	23	4	1	0	0	5	1	2	4	0	5	0	0	0	0	0	.00	1	.174	.296	.217
1992 Minnesota	AL	22	58	18	1	0	0	19	5	5	3	0	11	1	0	1	1	2	.33	4	.310	.349	.328
1993 Minnesota	AL	59	152	34	7	0	1	44	15	12	10	0	21	0	0	1	1	0	1.00	7	.224	.270	.289
9 Min. YEARS		1005	3706	1033	215	16	83	1529	509	525	384	16	483	26	10	32	13	13	.50	113	.279	.348	.413
3 Maj. YEARS		91	233	56	9	0	1	68	21	19	17	0	37	1	0	2	2	2	.50	12	.240	.292	.292

Rob Juday

Bats: Both Throws: Right Pos: 2B Ht: 6'0" Wt: 180 Born: 12/29/70 Age: 25

Year Team	Lg	G	AB	H	2B	3B	HR	TB	R	RBI	TBB	IBB	SO	HBP	SH	SF	SB	CS	SB%	GDP	Avg	OBP	SLG
1992 Elmira	A	69	241	67	12	0	1	82	46	24	47	4	33	4	4	1	4	5	.44	6	.278	.403	.340
1993 Lynchburg	A	114	354	105	15	1	4	134	67	32	83	2	58	2	8	3	5	5	.50	9	.297	.430	.379
1994 Lynchburg	A	40	145	47	9	1	1	61	24	13	23	0	25	3	2	1	1	2	.33	3	.324	.424	.421
New Britain	AA	93	315	61	16	1	1	82	42	17	56	0	63	5	6	4	2	7	.22	6	.194	.321	.260
1995 Trenton	AA	3	10	1	0	0	0	1	0	0	2	1	4	0	0	0	0	0	.00	0	.100	.250	.100
4 Min. YEARS		319	1065	281	52	3	7	360	179	86	211	7	183	14	20	9	12	19	.39	24	.264	.390	.338

Jarod Juelsgaard

Pitches: Right Bats: Right Pos: P Ht: 6'3" Wt: 190 Born: 6/27/68 Age: 28

Year Team	Lg	G	GS	CG	GF	IP	BFP	H	R	ER	HR	SH	SF	HB	TBB	IBB	SO	WP	Bk	W	L	Pct.	ShO	Sv	ERA
1991 Everett	A	20	6	0	8	62	270	62	36	30	3	1	1	2	27	2	46	16	4	3	5	.375	0	3	4.35
1992 Clinton	A	35	9	1	11	76.2	368	86	58	45	2	4	4	3	52	6	60	12	1	6	9	.400	0	2	5.28
1993 Kane County	A	11	2	1	3	26	101	21	11	11	0	0	0	1	7	0	18	2	2	3	0	1.000	0	0	3.81
High Desert	A	17	16	0	1	79.1	359	81	57	49	8	1	1	1	58	0	58	4	1	6	5	.545	0	0	5.56
1994 Portland	AA	36	12	0	13	92.2	443	115	74	68	9	4	5	4	55	4	55	7	2	4	9	.308	0	0	6.60
1995 Portland	AA	48	0	0	13	71.2	313	65	35	31	3	1	2	2	44	2	44	5	0	3	1	.750	0	2	3.89
5 Min. YEARS		167	45	2	49	408.1	1854	430	271	234	25	11	13	13	243	14	281	46	10	25	29	.463	0	7	5.16

Mike Juhl

Pitches: Left Bats: Left Pos: P Ht: 5'9" Wt: 180 Born: 8/10/69 Age: 26

Year Team	Lg	G	GS	CG	GF	IP	BFP	H	R	ER	HR	SH	SF	HB	TBB	IBB	SO	WP	Bk	W	L	Pct.	ShO	Sv	ERA
1991 Spartanburg	A	25	0	0	13	49.1	197	43	23	16	5	1	0	1	7	0	45	0	0	3	2	.600	0	1	2.92
1992 Spartanburg	A	41	0	0	18	64	255	54	28	25	3	2	2	1	15	0	83	6	0	5	5	.500	0	1	3.52
1993 Clearwater	A	21	0	0	13	28	107	23	6	3	0	2	0	0	3	0	24	1	0	2	1	.667	0	4	0.96
1994 Clearwater	A	18	0	0	11	22.2	110	30	18	14	0	2	4	0	13	4	14	1	1	0	4	.000	0	0	5.56
1995 Scranton-Wb	AAA	1	0	0	1	0.1	0	0	0	0	0	0	0	0	0	0	0	0	0	0	0	.000	0	0	0.00
Reading	AA	49	0	0	16	46.1	208	43	32	22	4	4	1	1	28	1	39	2	1	1	8	.111	0	6	4.27
5 Min. YEARS		155	0	0	72	210.2	878	193	107	80	12	11	7	3	66	5	206	10	2	11	20	.355	0	12	3.42

Bob Kappesser

Bats: Right **Throws:** Right **Pos:** C **Ht:** 5'9" **Wt:** 180 **Born:** 2/14/67 **Age:** 29

Year	Team	Lg	G	AB	H	2B	3B	HR	TB	R	RBI	TBB	IBB	SO	HBP	SH	SF	SB	CS	SB%	GDP	Avg	OBP	SLG
1989	Helena	R	32	72	10	1	1	0	13	13	1	14	0	24	0	2	0	3	0	1.00	1	.139	.279	.181
1990	Stockton	A	63	147	27	2	1	0	31	17	12	15	0	39	2	2	1	2	6	.25	2	.184	.267	.211
	El Paso	AA	14	36	8	0	0	0	8	3	2	1	0	7	0	1	1	0	0	.00	0	.222	.237	.222
1991	Visalia	A	18	57	13	2	0	0	15	6	2	9	0	19	0	0	1	0	1	.00	3	.228	.328	.263
	Stockton	A	79	202	43	4	3	0	53	30	15	35	1	38	2	11	1	10	8	.56	3	.213	.333	.262
1992	El Paso	AA	88	233	55	7	1	1	67	32	33	22	0	49	3	2	2	6	7	.46	6	.236	.308	.288
1993	New Orleans	AAA	4	11	1	1	0	0	2	0	2	1	0	4	0	0	0	0	0	.00	1	.091	.167	.182
	El Paso	AA	67	173	43	9	1	2	60	25	23	20	0	29	2	3	2	7	3	.70	2	.249	.330	.347
1994	New Orleans	AAA	17	47	11	4	0	0	15	9	5	7	0	9	0	3	0	2	1	.67	1	.234	.333	.319
	El Paso	AA	53	140	33	0	1	0	35	15	10	16	0	32	0	1	0	4	2	.67	3	.236	.314	.250
1995	El Paso	AA	61	115	22	5	2	1	34	17	17	12	0	19	0	2	3	2	2	.50	4	.191	.262	.296
	7 Min. YEARS		496	1233	266	35	10	4	333	167	122	152	1	269	9	27	11	36	30	.55	26	.216	.304	.270

Robbie Katzaroff

Bats: Right **Throws:** Right **Pos:** OF **Ht:** 5'8" **Wt:** 170 **Born:** 7/29/68 **Age:** 27

Year	Team	Lg	G	AB	H	2B	3B	HR	TB	R	RBI	TBB	IBB	SO	HBP	SH	SF	SB	CS	SB%	GDP	Avg	OBP	SLG
1990	Jamestown	A	74	294	107	15	7	1	139	57	20	29	4	18	5	1	0	34	13	.72	3	.364	.430	.473
1991	Harrisburg	AA	137	558	162	21	2	3	196	94	50	54	3	61	5	9	1	33	18	.65	5	.290	.358	.351
1992	Binghamton	AA	119	450	127	18	7	0	159	65	29	40	1	45	5	6	4	24	18	.57	8	.282	.345	.353
1993	Phoenix	AAA	9	26	4	0	0	0	4	2	3	1	0	4	0	0	1	0	0	.00	0	.154	.179	.154
	Shreveport	AA	104	406	122	22	4	0	152	52	30	35	3	33	8	5	4	15	13	.54	3	.300	.364	.374
1994	Midland	AA	32	105	29	3	2	0	36	22	11	15	0	10	1	5	1	10	4	.71	2	.276	.369	.343
	Lk Elsinore	A	70	281	79	12	4	1	102	54	33	38	1	16	6	2	2	25	7	.78	4	.281	.374	.363
1995	Portland	AA	116	441	134	16	4	10	188	87	49	49	3	33	7	4	4	18	10	.64	4	.304	.379	.426
	6 Min. YEARS		661	2561	764	107	30	15	976	433	225	261	15	220	37	32	19	159	83	.66	29	.298	.369	.381

Brad Kaufman

Pitches: Right **Bats:** Right **Pos:** P **Ht:** 6'2" **Wt:** 210 **Born:** 4/26/72 **Age:** 24

			HOW MUCH HE PITCHED					WHAT HE GAVE UP									THE RESULTS					
Year	Team	Lg	G	GS	CG	GF	IP	BFP	H	R	ER	HR	SH	SF	HB	TBB	IBB	SO	WP	Bk	W	L	Pct.	ShO	Sv	ERA
1993	Spokane	A	25	8	1	11	53.2	264	56	56	41	8	0	3	3	41	2	48	4	2	5	4	.556	0	4	6.88
1994	Springfield	A	31	20	3	4	145.1	602	124	62	54	9	5	3	4	63	6	122	14	1	10	9	.526	0	0	3.34
1995	Memphis	AA	27	27	0	0	148.1	676	142	112	95	17	6	5	14	90	4	119	10	0	11	10	.524	0	0	5.76
	3 Min. YEARS		83	55	4	15	347.1	1542	322	230	190	34	11	11	21	194	12	289	28	3	26	23	.531	0	4	4.92

Greg Keagle

Pitches: Right **Bats:** Right **Pos:** P **Ht:** 6'2" **Wt:** 185 **Born:** 6/28/71 **Age:** 25

			HOW MUCH HE PITCHED					WHAT HE GAVE UP									THE RESULTS					
Year	Team	Lg	G	GS	CG	GF	IP	BFP	H	R	ER	HR	SH	SF	HB	TBB	IBB	SO	WP	Bk	W	L	Pct.	ShO	Sv	ERA
1993	Spokane	A	15	15	1	0	83	368	80	37	30	2	4	4	7	40	2	77	4	4	3	3	.500	0	0	3.25
1994	Rancho Cuca	A	14	14	1	0	92	377	62	23	21	2	1	3	5	41	1	91	1	0	11	1	.917	1	0	2.05
	Wichita	AA	13	13	0	0	70.1	321	84	53	49	5	5	2	2	32	1	57	3	1	3	9	.250	0	0	6.27
1995	Memphis	AA	15	15	1	0	81	365	82	52	46	11	1	3	6	41	2	82	8	3	4	9	.308	0	0	5.11
	Rancho Cuca	A	2	2	0	0	14	59	14	9	7	1	0	1	2	2	0	11	1	0	0	0	.000	0	0	4.50
	Las Vegas	AAA	14	13	0	1	75.2	351	76	47	36	3	6	5	6	42	2	49	2	0	7	6	.538	0	0	4.28
	3 Min. YEARS		73	72	3	1	416	1841	398	221	189	24	17	18	28	198	8	367	19	8	28	28	.500	1	0	4.09

Don Keister

Bats: Left **Throws:** Left **Pos:** DH-OF **Ht:** 5'9" **Wt:** 172 **Born:** 9/27/70 **Age:** 25

Year	Team	Lg	G	AB	H	2B	3B	HR	TB	R	RBI	TBB	IBB	SO	HBP	SH	SF	SB	CS	SB%	GDP	Avg	OBP	SLG
1992	Pittsfield	A	68	245	60	4	2	0	68	46	15	42	0	39	3	3	1	23	8	.74	1	.245	.361	.278
1993	St. Lucie	A	3	4	2	0	0	0	2	0	1	1	0	1	0	0	0	1	0	1.00	0	.500	.600	.500
	Capital Cty	A	101	314	86	11	2	1	104	60	39	91	0	60	3	8	4	33	17	.66	5	.274	.437	.331
1994	St. Lucie	A	75	237	69	8	0	0	77	36	22	46	4	21	1	2	1	14	14	.50	4	.291	.407	.325
1995	St. Lucie	A	28	94	31	5	2	0	40	15	14	14	0	11	2	0	1	5	4	.56	1	.330	.423	.426
	Binghamton	AA	66	146	32	7	1	1	44	23	10	29	1	26	5	2	0	3	4	.43	0	.219	.367	.301
	4 Min. YEARS		341	1040	280	35	7	2	335	180	100	223	5	158	14	15	7	78	48	.62	11	.269	.403	.322

Korey Keling

Pitches: Right **Bats:** Right **Pos:** P **Ht:** 6'5" **Wt:** 210 **Born:** 11/24/68 **Age:** 27

			HOW MUCH HE PITCHED					WHAT HE GAVE UP									THE RESULTS					
Year	Team	Lg	G	GS	CG	GF	IP	BFP	H	R	ER	HR	SH	SF	HB	TBB	IBB	SO	WP	Bk	W	L	Pct.	ShO	Sv	ERA
1991	Boise	A	15	14	0	1	83	340	71	31	28	3	5	1	3	30	0	96	5	4	6	2	.750	0	1	3.04
1992	Palm Spring	A	30	18	0	2	124	536	138	72	66	4	4	8	4	53	0	107	15	3	7	6	.538	0	0	4.79
1993	Palm Spring	A	31	21	2	1	158.2	667	152	69	58	9	3	7	3	62	1	131	7	2	8	8	.500	0	0	3.29
1994	Midland	AA	27	27	1	0	155	720	207	108	89	16	5	8	7	60	1	133	8	0	10	11	.476	0	0	5.17
1995	Vancouver	AAA	3	3	0	0	17.2	75	18	9	8	1	0	0	0	6	0	16	0	0	0	2	.000	0	0	4.08

155

		G	GS	CG	GF	IP	BFP	H	R	ER	HR	SH	SF	HB	TBB	IBB	SO	WP	Bk	W	L	Pct.	ShO	Sv	ERA
Midland	AA	29	12	1	7	122.1	518	113	53	47	7	0	1	1	52	3	101	9	2	8	5	.615	1	1	3.46
5 Min. YEARS		135	95	4	11	660.2	2856	699	342	296	40	17	25	18	263	5	584	44	11	39	34	.534	1	2	4.03

Rich Kelley

Pitches: Left **Bats:** Left **Pos:** P **Ht:** 6'3" **Wt:** 200 **Born:** 5/27/70 **Age:** 26

		HOW MUCH HE PITCHED						WHAT HE GAVE UP										THE RESULTS						
Year Team	Lg	G	GS	CG	GF	IP	BFP	H	R	ER	HR	SH	SF	HB	TBB	IBB	SO	WP	Bk	W	L	Pct.	ShO	Sv	ERA
1991 Niagara Fal	A	15	13	0	1	81.1	341	76	38	30	7	0	2	1	33	1	78	4	0	4	8	.333	0	0	3.32
1992 Fayetteville	A	28	26	2	0	162.2	664	140	62	51	15	2	4	6	63	0	117	12	9	13	5	.722	0	0	2.82
1993 Lakeland	A	26	9	0	10	85.2	350	78	31	29	2	2	2	4	31	1	45	5	4	4	5	.444	0	2	3.05
London	AA	7	0	0	0	5	25	7	5	5	1	0	0	0	5	0	3	3	1	0	0	.000	0	0	9.00
1994 Lakeland	A	13	0	0	10	38	156	32	15	10	2	2	5	0	15	1	23	0	0	4	2	.667	0	1	2.37
Trenton	AA	16	4	0	2	42.1	178	46	28	27	8	1	1	0	20	0	29	3	1	1	2	.333	0	0	5.74
1995 Jacksonvlle	AA	7	0	0	1	6	24	9	3	3	1	1	1	0	0	0	2	0	1	1	0	1.000	0	0	4.50
5 Min. YEARS		112	52	2	24	421	1738	388	182	155	36	8	15	11	167	3	297	27	16	27	22	.551	0	3	3.31

Frank Kellner

Bats: Both **Throws:** Right **Pos:** SS **Ht:** 5'11" **Wt:** 175 **Born:** 1/5/67 **Age:** 29

		BATTING														BASERUNNING				PERCENTAGES		
Year Team	Lg	G	AB	H	2B	3B	HR	TB	R	RBI	TBB	IBB	SO	HBP	SH	SF	SB	CS	SB%	GDP	Avg	OBP	SLG
1990 Osceola	A	109	369	91	9	7	0	114	43	34	65	2	65	1	9	3	14	7	.67	11	.247	.358	.309
Tucson	AAA	19	60	18	1	0	0	19	13	7	15	0	6	0	2	0	1	0	1.00	0	.300	.440	.317
1991 Osceola	A	53	204	44	8	1	1	57	27	15	20	2	24	0	4	0	8	1	.89	6	.216	.286	.279
Jackson	AA	83	311	84	7	4	2	105	47	25	29	2	37	0	2	2	6	5	.55	8	.270	.330	.338
1992 Jackson	AA	125	474	113	18	5	3	150	45	48	42	5	89	3	4	2	8	7	.53	9	.238	.303	.316
1993 Jackson	AA	121	355	107	27	2	4	150	51	36	38	5	51	2	2	6	11	12	.48	10	.301	.367	.423
1994 Tucson	AAA	106	296	88	13	5	1	114	32	35	46	3	40	0	3	2	5	4	.56	4	.297	.390	.385
1995 Jackson	AA	75	269	85	15	1	0	102	31	29	35	2	52	2	4	5	1	7	.13	2	.316	.392	.379
Tucson	AAA	28	89	16	3	1	0	21	11	7	15	0	12	0	1	1	1	0	1.00	2	.180	.295	.236
6 Min. YEARS		719	2427	646	101	26	11	832	300	236	305	21	376	8	31	21	55	43	.56	52	.266	.347	.343

John Kelly

Pitches: Right **Bats:** Right **Pos:** P **Ht:** 6'4" **Wt:** 185 **Born:** 7/3/67 **Age:** 28

		HOW MUCH HE PITCHED						WHAT HE GAVE UP										THE RESULTS						
Year Team	Lg	G	GS	CG	GF	IP	BFP	H	R	ER	HR	SH	SF	HB	TBB	IBB	SO	WP	Bk	W	L	Pct.	ShO	Sv	ERA
1990 Johnson Cty	R	25	0	0	22	34.1	145	22	7	3	1	1	1	2	12	3	41	1	3	1	2	.333	0	13	0.79
1991 Savannah	A	56	0	0	50	58.2	230	43	14	9	5	3	0	0	16	6	62	2	0	6	5	.545	0	30	1.38
1992 St. Pete	A	56	0	0	52	62	243	47	15	14	1	3	3	1	13	2	59	3	1	4	4	.500	0	38	2.03
1993 Arkansas	AA	51	0	0	45	58.1	245	53	28	23	4	8	0	1	12	5	40	1	0	2	4	.333	0	27	3.55
1994 Arkansas	AA	27	0	0	24	30.2	134	37	23	18	2	3	3	1	5	1	29	0	0	1	2	.333	0	16	5.28
Louisville	AAA	9	0	0	4	20.2	91	23	12	12	2	0	1	3	5	1	14	0	0	0	0	.000	0	0	5.23
1995 Arkansas	AA	66	0	0	58	77.1	322	76	24	18	4	6	2	0	21	5	47	3	1	7	7	.500	0	29	2.09
6 Min. YEARS		290	0	0	255	342	1409	301	123	97	19	24	10	8	84	23	292	10	5	21	24	.467	0	153	2.55

Pat Kelly

Bats: Right **Throws:** Right **Pos:** SS **Ht:** 5'11" **Wt:** 175 **Born:** 1/22/67 **Age:** 29

		BATTING														BASERUNNING				PERCENTAGES		
Year Team	Lg	G	AB	H	2B	3B	HR	TB	R	RBI	TBB	IBB	SO	HBP	SH	SF	SB	CS	SB%	GDP	Avg	OBP	SLG
1989 Pulaski	R	50	163	54	4	1	0	60	25	21	18	2	17	5	8	0	5	7	.42	4	.331	.414	.368
1990 Sumter	A	121	437	97	12	2	1	116	57	44	61	0	65	8	9	6	22	8	.73	10	.222	.324	.265
1991 Durham	A	54	120	30	5	0	0	35	14	12	14	0	18	1	1	1	4	4	.50	2	.250	.331	.292
Greenville	AA	30	90	27	6	2	0	37	14	5	13	1	10	0	2	1	5	1	.83	2	.300	.385	.411
1992 Greenville	AA	98	325	81	12	2	0	97	44	36	26	1	55	2	1	1	11	3	.79	6	.249	.308	.298
Richmond	AAA	6	15	7	0	0	0	7	1	4	3	0	2	0	0	0	0	0	.00	0	.467	.556	.467
1993 Durham	A	35	128	36	6	0	1	45	27	12	13	1	19	2	2	0	5	4	.56	3	.281	.357	.352
Greenville	AA	72	212	54	10	1	0	66	23	17	14	1	30	1	5	1	2	3	.40	4	.255	.303	.311
1994 Richmond	AAA	75	189	51	13	0	1	67	21	23	17	0	22	1	1	0	6	6	.50	3	.270	.333	.354
1995 Richmond	AAA	11	22	4	1	0	0	5	2	2	0	0	5	2	0	0	0	1	.00	1	.182	.250	.227
Syracuse	AAA	30	68	9	1	0	2	16	6	8	6	0	15	2	2	2	0	0	.00	1	.132	.218	.235
Knoxville	AA	47	161	39	6	1	2	53	22	14	13	1	30	1	5	0	1	1	.50	1	.242	.303	.329
7 Min. YEARS		629	1930	489	76	9	7	604	256	198	198	7	288	25	36	12	61	38	.62	37	.253	.329	.313

Jason Kendall

Bats: Right **Throws:** Right **Pos:** C **Ht:** 6'0" **Wt:** 170 **Born:** 6/26/74 **Age:** 22

		BATTING														BASERUNNING				PERCENTAGES		
Year Team	Lg	G	AB	H	2B	3B	HR	TB	R	RBI	TBB	IBB	SO	HBP	SH	SF	SB	CS	SB%	GDP	Avg	OBP	SLG
1992 Pirates	R	33	111	29	2	0	0	31	7	10	8	1	9	2	0	2	2	2	.50	3	.261	.317	.279
1993 Augusta	A	102	366	101	17	4	1	129	43	40	22	1	30	7	0	5	8	5	.62	17	.276	.325	.352
1994 Salem	A	101	371	118	19	2	7	162	68	66	47	1	21	13	0	7	14	3	.82	15	.318	.406	.437
Carolina	AA	13	47	11	2	0	0	13	6	6	2	0	3	2	0	0	0	0	.00	0	.234	.294	.277
1995 Carolina	AA	117	429	140	26	1	8	192	87	71	56	5	22	14	1	8	10	7	.59	10	.326	.414	.448
4 Min. YEARS		366	1324	399	66	7	16	527	211	193	135	8	85	38	1	22	34	17	.67	45	.301	.377	.398

156

Kenny Kendrena

Pitches: Right **Bats:** Right **Pos:** P | **Ht:** 5'11" **Wt:** 170 **Born:** 10/29/70 **Age:** 25

			HOW MUCH HE PITCHED					WHAT HE GAVE UP									THE RESULTS				
Year Team	Lg	G	GS	CG	GF	IP	BFP	H	R	ER	HR	SH	SF	HB	TBB	IBB	SO	WP	Bk	W	L	Pct.	ShO	Sv	ERA
1992 Erie	A	22	0	0	10	54.2	229	47	33	23	5	5	3	5	12	2	61	2	1	5	4	.556	0	3	3.79
1993 High Desert	A	40	0	0	25	66.2	307	78	50	49	16	2	4	4	26	1	63	7	0	6	0	1.000	0	2	6.62
1994 Brevard Cty	A	21	1	0	7	38	141	19	5	5	0	3	1	0	10	0	32	1	0	5	1	.833	0	0	1.18
Portland	AA	13	0	0	3	24.2	118	28	22	15	0	1	1	2	15	2	21	2	0	0	1	.000	0	0	5.47
1995 W. Palm Bch	A	16	0	0	5	23.2	102	23	9	8	2	1	1	0	11	2	19	3	0	3	3	.500	0	2	3.04
Harrisburg	AA	30	0	0	8	64.2	277	58	27	18	5	2	1	4	25	2	46	3	0	3	2	.600	0	1	2.51
4 Min. YEARS		142	1	0	58	272.1	1174	253	146	118	28	14	11	15	99	9	242	18	1	22	11	.667	0	8	3.90

Darryl Kennedy

Bats: Right **Throws:** Right **Pos:** C | **Ht:** 5'10" **Wt:** 170 **Born:** 1/23/69 **Age:** 27

					BATTING												BASERUNNING				PERCENTAGES		
Year Team	Lg	G	AB	H	2B	3B	HR	TB	R	RBI	TBB	IBB	SO	HBP	SH	SF	SB	CS	SB%	GDP	Avg	OBP	SLG
1991 Rangers	R	5	18	2	1	0	0	3	4	1	1	0	1	0	0	0	0	0	.00	0	.111	.158	.167
Charlotte	A	23	68	7	3	0	0	10	5	4	5	0	11	2	1	2	0	0	.00	2	.103	.182	.147
1992 Gastonia	A	13	33	3	1	0	0	4	2	2	6	1	6	1	0	1	0	2	.00	1	.091	.244	.121
Charlotte	A	13	28	13	4	0	0	17	3	6	3	0	3	0	0	0	0	1	.00	0	.464	.516	.607
Tulsa	AA	30	98	22	2	0	0	24	6	9	8	0	18	2	2	1	0	0	.00	4	.224	.294	.245
1993 Okla. City	AAA	6	16	1	0	0	0	1	2	0	3	0	4	0	1	0	0	0	.00	0	.063	.211	.063
Charlotte	A	106	347	97	23	0	1	123	47	30	47	0	38	1	5	2	5	7	.42	7	.280	.365	.354
1994 Charlotte	A	53	177	47	5	2	1	59	24	22	25	1	20	1	2	0	1	2	.33	7	.266	.360	.333
Tulsa	AA	23	70	16	3	0	1	22	5	5	8	0	10	0	2	0	1	1	.50	1	.229	.308	.314
1995 Tulsa	AA	61	195	49	9	1	3	69	26	26	17	0	22	3	3	4	0	0	.00	5	.251	.315	.354
Okla. City	AAA	3	11	2	0	0	1	5	1	3	0	0	2	0	0	0	0	0	.00	0	.182	.182	.455
5 Min. YEARS		336	1061	259	51	3	7	337	125	108	123	2	135	10	16	10	7	13	.35	27	.244	.326	.318

Dave Kennedy

Bats: Right **Throws:** Right **Pos:** 1B | **Ht:** 6'4" **Wt:** 215 **Born:** 9/3/70 **Age:** 25

					BATTING												BASERUNNING				PERCENTAGES		
Year Team	Lg	G	AB	H	2B	3B	HR	TB	R	RBI	TBB	IBB	SO	HBP	SH	SF	SB	CS	SB%	GDP	Avg	OBP	SLG
1993 Boise	A	74	248	59	14	2	10	107	53	49	65	7	63	0	0	2	5	0	1.00	1	.238	.394	.431
1994 St. Paul	IND	25	72	21	6	1	4	41	13	15	8	0	17	1	1	0	2	2	.50	4	.292	.370	.569
1995 New Haven	AA	128	484	148	22	2	22	240	75	96	48	1	131	5	0	4	4	1	.80	12	.306	.372	.496
3 Min. YEARS		227	804	228	42	5	36	388	141	160	121	8	211	6	1	6	8	3	.73	17	.284	.379	.483

Collin Kerley

Pitches: Right **Bats:** Right **Pos:** P | **Ht:** 6'3" **Wt:** 200 **Born:** 3/26/70 **Age:** 26

				HOW MUCH HE PITCHED					WHAT HE GAVE UP									THE RESULTS				
Year Team	Lg	G	GS	CG	GF	IP	BFP	H	R	ER	HR	SH	SF	HB	TBB	IBB	SO	WP	Bk	W	L	Pct.	ShO	Sv	ERA
1992 Geneva	A	23	2	1	16	48.1	200	37	13	11	2	4	0	1	15	1	46	4	1	3	1	.750	0	6	2.05
1993 Peoria	A	31	17	3	4	134.2	591	148	75	66	11	3	1	11	44	0	129	9	3	6	9	.400	0	0	4.41
1994 Daytona	A	40	1	0	21	68.1	297	68	37	35	1	1	4	2	24	4	63	11	0	1	4	.200	0	2	4.61
1995 Ottawa	AAA	5	0	0	1	8.1	39	11	3	2	0	1	0	0	3	0	3	0	0	2	0	1.000	0	0	2.16
Harrisburg	AA	2	0	0	0	6.2	26	5	0	0	0	0	0	0	1	0	3	1	0	0	0	.000	0	0	0.00
W. Palm Bch	A	19	0	0	8	27.1	119	28	16	12	0	0	0	1	11	1	17	2	0	1	3	.250	0	0	3.95
4 Min. YEARS		120	20	2	50	293.2	1272	297	144	126	14	9	5	15	98	6	261	27	4	13	17	.433	0	8	3.86

Keith Kessinger

Bats: Both **Throws:** Right **Pos:** SS-2B | **Ht:** 6'2" **Wt:** 185 **Born:** 2/19/67 **Age:** 29

					BATTING												BASERUNNING				PERCENTAGES		
Year Team	Lg	G	AB	H	2B	3B	HR	TB	R	RBI	TBB	IBB	SO	HBP	SH	SF	SB	CS	SB%	GDP	Avg	OBP	SLG
1989 Bluefield	R	28	99	27	4	0	2	37	17	9	8	0	12	1	2	0	1	0	1.00	1	.273	.333	.374
1990 Wausau	A	37	134	29	8	0	0	37	17	9	6	0	23	3	0	0	1	1	.50	2	.216	.266	.276
Frederick	A	64	145	22	4	0	0	26	18	8	20	0	36	3	5	0	0	0	.00	2	.152	.268	.179
1991 Frederick	A	26	56	10	3	0	0	13	5	4	8	0	12	0	1	0	2	1	.67	3	.179	.281	.232
Cedar Rapds	A	59	206	42	5	0	1	50	15	15	23	1	46	3	5	1	0	1	.00	4	.204	.292	.243
1992 Cedar Rapds	A	95	308	73	15	1	4	102	41	38	36	2	57	1	5	1	2	0	1.00	7	.237	.318	.331
1993 Chattanooga	AA	56	161	50	9	0	3	68	24	24	24	2	18	0	5	0	0	3	.00	4	.311	.400	.422
Indianapols	AAA	35	120	34	9	0	2	49	17	15	14	4	14	1	1	0	0	1	.00	0	.283	.363	.408
1994 Indianapols	AAA	115	393	98	19	3	3	132	37	48	36	4	60	0	4	1	3	1	.75	11	.249	.312	.336
1995 Orlando	AA	18	62	16	5	0	0	21	8	5	6	0	3	1	2	0	0	0	.00	1	.258	.333	.339
Iowa	AAA	68	210	48	11	0	2	65	21	20	25	2	23	1	7	2	1	1	.50	6	.229	.311	.310
1993 Cincinnati	NL	11	27	7	1	0	1	11	4	3	4	0	4	0	0	1	0	0	.00	1	.259	.344	.407
7 Min. YEARS		601	1894	449	92	4	17	600	220	199	206	15	304	14	37	5	10	9	.53	41	.237	.316	.317

Douglas Ketchen

Pitches: Right **Bats:** Right **Pos:** P | **Ht:** 6'1" **Wt:** 190 **Born:** 7/9/68 **Age:** 27

				HOW MUCH HE PITCHED					WHAT HE GAVE UP									THE RESULTS				
Year Team	Lg	G	GS	CG	GF	IP	BFP	H	R	ER	HR	SH	SF	HB	TBB	IBB	SO	WP	Bk	W	L	Pct.	ShO	Sv	ERA
1990 Auburn	A	19	12	1	2	92.2	393	81	43	35	4	7	2	4	40	2	76	8	2	6	5	.545	0	0	3.40
1991 Asheville	A	27	27	2	0	151.2	690	166	99	72	9	4	4	11	62	1	95	21	3	10	12	.455	1	0	4.27

Year Team	Lg	G	GS	CG	GF	IP	BFP	H	R	ER	HR	SH	SF	HB	TBB	IBB	SO	WP	Bk	W	L	Pct.	ShO	Sv	ERA
1992 Osceola	A	34	12	0	9	116	500	121	43	36	6	3	1	1	28	4	72	9	0	8	3	.727	0	5	2.79
1993 Jackson	AA	27	27	3	0	159.2	689	160	91	73	12	7	6	6	50	2	104	10	0	7	12	.368	1	0	4.11
1994 Jackson	AA	38	15	0	11	124.1	551	127	69	56	8	12	6	4	53	3	73	10	1	6	9	.400	0	6	4.05
Tucson	AAA	2	0	0	2	1.1	9	4	2	2	0	1	0	0	2	2	0	0	0	0	0	.000	0	0	13.50
1995 Jackson	AA	15	5	0	5	52.2	216	55	23	21	5	0	0	1	15	0	45	8	0	3	3	.500	0	1	3.59
Tucson	AAA	19	12	0	2	71.2	332	101	55	50	8	3	2	2	26	0	30	3	1	3	6	.333	0	1	6.28
6 Min. YEARS		181	110	6	31	770	3380	815	425	345	52	37	21	29	276	14	495	69	7	43	51	.457	2	13	4.03

Joe Keusch

Pitches: Right Bats: Left Pos: P   Ht: 6'1" Wt: 175 Born: 1/20/72 Age: 24

		HOW MUCH HE PITCHED						WHAT HE GAVE UP												THE RESULTS					
Year Team	Lg	G	GS	CG	GF	IP	BFP	H	R	ER	HR	SH	SF	HB	TBB	IBB	SO	WP	Bk	W	L	Pct.	ShO	Sv	ERA
1994 Hudson Vall	A	14	0	0	6	24	104	28	20	18	0	1	4	3	3	0	25	2	0	0	1	.000	0	0	6.75
1995 Charlotte	A	40	0	0	27	64.1	257	56	19	13	3	2	3	2	14	2	36	3	1	9	4	.692	0	8	1.82
Tulsa	AA	2	0	0	2	2.2	10	1	0	0	0	0	0	0	0	0	0	0	0	0	0	.000	0	0	0.00
2 Min. YEARS		56	0	0	35	91	371	85	39	31	3	3	7	5	17	2	61	5	1	9	5	.643	0	8	3.07

John Kiely

Pitches: Right Bats: Right Pos: P   Ht: 6'3" Wt: 215 Born: 10/4/64 Age: 31

		HOW MUCH HE PITCHED						WHAT HE GAVE UP												THE RESULTS					
Year Team	Lg	G	GS	CG	GF	IP	BFP	H	R	ER	HR	SH	SF	HB	TBB	IBB	SO	WP	Bk	W	L	Pct.	ShO	Sv	ERA
1988 Bristol	R	8	0	0	6	11.2	53	9	9	8	0	2	0	0	7	0	14	2	0	2	2	.500	0	1	6.17
1989 Lakeland	A	36	0	0	22	63.2	267	52	26	17	2	4	3	0	27	4	56	1	2	4	3	.571	0	8	2.40
1990 London	AA	46	0	0	25	76.2	321	63	17	15	2	2	4	2	42	6	52	2	0	3	0	1.000	0	12	1.76
1991 Toledo	AAA	42	0	0	27	72	301	57	25	17	3	4	2	3	35	3	60	2	0	4	2	.667	0	6	2.13
1992 Toledo	AAA	21	0	0	17	31.2	125	25	11	10	1	0	0	0	7	0	31	1	0	1	1	.500	0	9	2.84
1993 Toledo	AAA	37	0	0	16	58	261	65	34	25	8	1	2	1	25	1	48	2	0	3	4	.429	0	4	3.88
1994 Toledo	AAA	7	0	0	1	12.2	58	14	8	8	1	0	2	0	7	0	6	0	0	1	0	1.000	0	0	5.68
1995 Toledo	AAA	14	0	0	5	12.1	56	13	4	2	1	0	0	0	6	2	8	0	0	0	0	.000	0	0	1.46
1991 Detroit	AL	7	0	0	3	6.2	42	13	11	11	0	2	1	1	9	2	1	1	0	0	1	.000	0	0	14.85
1992 Detroit	AL	39	0	0	20	55	231	44	14	13	2	4	3	0	28	3	18	0	0	4	2	.667	0	0	2.13
1993 Detroit	AL	8	0	0	5	11.2	59	13	11	10	2	1	0	1	13	5	5	2	0	0	2	.000	0	0	7.71
8 Min. YEARS		211	0	0	119	338.2	1442	298	134	102	18	13	13	6	156	16	275	10	2	18	12	.600	0	40	2.71
3 Maj. YEARS		54	0	0	28	73.1	332	70	36	34	4	7	4	2	50	10	24	3	0	4	5	.444	0	0	4.17

Brooks Kieschnick

Bats: Left Throws: Right Pos: OF   Ht: 6'4" Wt: 228 Born: 6/6/72 Age: 24

		BATTING													BASERUNNING				PERCENTAGES		
Year Team	Lg	G	AB	H	2B	3B	HR	TB	R	RBI	TBB	IBB	SO	HBP	SH	SF	SB	CS	SB%	GDP	Avg	OBP	SLG
1993 Cubs	R	3	9	2	1	0	0	3	0	0	0	0	1	0	0	0	0	0	.00	0	.222	.222	.333
Daytona	A	6	22	4	2	0	0	6	1	2	1	0	4	0	0	0	1	0	.00	1	.182	.217	.273
Orlando	AA	25	91	31	8	0	2	45	12	10	7	1	19	0	0	0	1	2	.33	0	.341	.388	.495
1994 Orlando	AA	126	468	132	25	3	14	205	57	55	33	3	78	4	0	4	3	5	.38	10	.282	.332	.438
1995 Iowa	AAA	138	505	149	30	1	23	250	61	73	58	7	91	4	0	3	2	3	.40	11	.295	.370	.495
3 Min. YEARS		298	1095	318	66	4	39	509	131	140	99	11	193	8	0	7	6	11	.35	22	.290	.352	.465

Rusty Kilgo

Pitches: Left Bats: Left Pos: P   Ht: 6'0" Wt: 175 Born: 8/9/66 Age: 29

		HOW MUCH HE PITCHED						WHAT HE GAVE UP												THE RESULTS					
Year Team	Lg	G	GS	CG	GF	IP	BFP	H	R	ER	HR	SH	SF	HB	TBB	IBB	SO	WP	Bk	W	L	Pct.	ShO	Sv	ERA
1989 Jamestown	A	30	3	0	21	64.2	259	46	16	10	3	4	0	0	20	1	74	4	1	6	3	.667	0	8	1.39
1990 Rockford	A	45	0	0	31	88.2	347	62	26	22	1	2	1	3	20	1	85	6	2	4	4	.500	0	9	2.23
1991 W. Palm Bch	A	33	1	0	10	74	286	56	14	13	1	3	0	2	24	1	48	1	0	6	3	.667	0	5	1.58
Harrisburg	AA	14	0	0	10	25.2	105	24	11	10	1	3	1	1	4	1	20	3	0	1	0	1.000	0	1	3.51
1992 Rockford	A	4	0	0	2	8.2	28	3	0	0	0	0	0	0	0	0	8	0	0	0	0	.000	0	1	0.00
Cedar Rapds	A	25	0	0	21	33.2	125	18	4	3	0	3	1	1	6	0	34	2	0	3	1	.750	0	10	0.80
Chattanooga	AA	24	0	0	10	31.2	123	22	16	11	3	1	3	0	11	1	11	2	0	1	3	.250	0	3	3.13
1993 Chattanooga	AA	53	1	0	20	80.1	360	92	30	25	2	5	0	5	31	6	61	4	1	11	7	.611	0	6	2.80
1994 Indianapolis	AAA	50	0	0	11	62.1	274	75	32	28	6	4	2	0	17	5	30	2	0	5	6	.455	0	1	4.04
1995 Indianapolis	AAA	2	0	0	2	2	10	4	2	1	0	0	0	0	1	0	1	0	0	0	0	.000	0	0	4.50
Chattanooga	AA	54	0	0	47	66	273	67	21	17	0	2	0	0	13	5	61	4	0	8	2	.800	0	29	2.32
7 Min. YEARS		334	5	0	183	537.2	2190	469	172	140	17	27	8	12	147	21	433	28	4	45	28	.616	0	70	2.34

Tim Killeen

Bats: Left Throws: Right Pos: C   Ht: 6'0" Wt: 195 Born: 7/26/70 Age: 25

		BATTING													BASERUNNING				PERCENTAGES		
Year Team	Lg	G	AB	H	2B	3B	HR	TB	R	RBI	TBB	IBB	SO	HBP	SH	SF	SB	CS	SB%	GDP	Avg	OBP	SLG
1992 Sou. Oregon	A	39	119	28	7	0	3	44	20	12	17	1	30	2	0	0	5	3	.63	2	.235	.341	.370
1993 Madison	A	76	243	49	15	0	10	94	33	36	39	1	70	3	0	1	0	0	.00	11	.202	.318	.387
Tacoma	AAA	3	9	4	0	0	0	4	4	0	1	0	4	0	0	0	1	0	.00	0	.444	.500	.444
1994 Modesto	A	101	365	87	18	3	16	159	53	75	49	2	107	2	2	5	5	2	.71	5	.238	.328	.436
1995 Memphis	AA	77	230	54	14	0	9	95	27	40	27	6	71	0	0	1	2	0	1.00	5	.235	.314	.413
4 Min. YEARS		296	966	222	54	3	38	396	137	163	133	10	282	7	2	7	12	6	.67	23	.230	.325	.410

158

Jack Kimel

Pitches: Left **Bats:** Left **Pos:** P Ht: 6'1" Wt: 175 Born: 12/24/69 Age: 26

		HOW MUCH HE PITCHED						WHAT HE GAVE UP									THE RESULTS					
Year Team	Lg	G	GS	CG	GF	IP	BFP	H	R	ER	HR	SH	SF	HB	TBB	IBB	SO	WP	Bk	W	L	Pct.	ShO	Sv	ERA
1992 Butte	R	15	10	2	4	71	290	69	42	32	7	1	1	2	14	0	83	4	2	5	4	.556	0	1	4.06
1993 Charlstn-Sc	A	36	11	1	6	118	494	121	70	52	8	1	4	3	34	2	98	4	1	9	7	.563	0	0	3.97
1994 Tulsa	AA	10	0	0	3	11.1	69	27	21	19	1	0	0	1	8	0	8	2	0	1	0	1.000	0	0	15.09
Charlotte	A	38	0	0	20	45.2	191	41	17	13	2	3	1	0	19	3	31	2	0	3	1	.750	0	8	2.56
1995 Tulsa	AA	17	2	0	5	35.2	181	52	33	29	7	1	3	0	23	2	10	0	0	2	2	.500	0	0	7.32
4 Min. YEARS		116	23	3	38	281.2	1225	310	183	145	25	6	9	6	98	7	230	12	3	19	15	.559	0	9	4.63

Keith Kimsey

Bats: Right **Throws:** Right **Pos:** OF Ht: 6'7" Wt: 200 Born: 8/15/72 Age: 23

		BATTING														BASERUNNING				PERCENTAGES		
Year Team	Lg	G	AB	H	2B	3B	HR	TB	R	RBI	TBB	IBB	SO	HBP	SH	SF	SB	CS	SB%	GDP	Avg	OBP	SLG
1991 Bristol	R	53	164	26	3	0	3	38	10	17	14	0	60	1	1	1	2	3	.40	5	.159	.228	.232
1992 Niagara Fal	A	73	281	63	7	6	12	118	35	46	9	0	106	3	0	1	14	6	.70	4	.224	.255	.420
1993 Fayettevlle	A	120	469	115	19	6	19	203	79	85	50	2	168	2	0	3	2	0	1.00	16	.245	.319	.433
1994 Lakeland	A	121	448	100	19	3	12	161	47	58	29	0	136	3	0	3	4	3	.57	17	.223	.273	.359
1995 Jacksonvlle	AA	34	118	19	4	1	1	28	8	10	7	0	39	2	0	1	1	1	.50	6	.161	.219	.237
Lakeland	A	54	175	38	8	2	6	68	30	16	22	0	58	0	0	0	1	1	.50	4	.217	.305	.389
5 Min. YEARS		455	1655	361	60	18	53	616	209	232	131	2	567	11	1	9	24	14	.63	52	.218	.279	.372

Scott Kindell

Pitches: Left **Bats:** Left **Pos:** P Ht: 6'2" Wt: 198 Born: 11/18/72 Age: 23

		HOW MUCH HE PITCHED						WHAT HE GAVE UP									THE RESULTS					
Year Team	Lg	G	GS	CG	GF	IP	BFP	H	R	ER	HR	SH	SF	HB	TBB	IBB	SO	WP	Bk	W	L	Pct.	ShO	Sv	ERA
1990 Yankees	R	4	0	0	3	6.1	26	8	4	4	0	0	0	0	1	0	6	1	1	0	1	.000	0	0	5.68
1991 Yankees	R	21	4	0	13	41.2	190	53	28	17	2	1	2	1	10	0	27	2	0	0	4	.000	0	5	3.67
1993 Mets	R	14	0	0	3	24.1	99	16	6	4	0	2	1	1	6	0	21	2	0	1	0	1.000	0	1	1.48
St. Lucie	A	1	0	0	0	1	5	2	1	0	0	0	0	0	0	0	0	0	0	0	1	.000	0	0	0.00
1994 Kingsport	R	15	0	0	7	29.1	125	20	9	6	3	0	1	2	14	0	29	3	0	0	1	.000	0	2	1.84
St. Lucie	A	7	0	0	5	7.1	25	5	2	2	1	0	0	1	2	0	3	0	0	0	0	.000	0	0	2.45
1995 Binghamton	AA	1	0	0	0	1	5	2	0	0	0	0	0	0	0	0	0	0	0	0	0	.000	0	0	0.00
Pittsfield	A	20	0	0	9	26.2	109	25	11	7	1	2	2	1	6	0	14	2	0	4	1	.800	0	0	2.36
Columbia	A	1	0	0	1	0.1	1	0	0	0	0	0	0	0	0	0	0	0	0	0	0	.000	0	0	0.00
5 Min. YEARS		84	4	0	41	138	585	131	61	40	7	5	6	6	39	0	100	10	1	5	8	.385	0	8	2.61

Richard King

Pitches: Right **Bats:** Right **Pos:** P Ht: 6'4" Wt: 205 Born: 12/30/69 Age: 26

		HOW MUCH HE PITCHED						WHAT HE GAVE UP									THE RESULTS					
Year Team	Lg	G	GS	CG	GF	IP	BFP	H	R	ER	HR	SH	SF	HB	TBB	IBB	SO	WP	Bk	W	L	Pct.	ShO	Sv	ERA
1992 Sou. Oregon	A	15	14	1	0	69	309	81	52	46	6	3	3	5	22	0	71	10	5	3	7	.300	0	0	6.00
1993 Sou. Oregon	A	22	2	0	7	55.2	248	63	32	21	5	0	0	6	14	1	49	0	1	1	2	.333	0	3	3.40
1995 Richmond	AAA	14	0	0	5	14	63	13	8	4	1	0	0	0	6	0	3	0	0	1	1	.500	0	0	2.57
3 Min. YEARS		51	16	1	12	138.2	620	157	92	71	12	3	3	11	42	1	123	10	6	5	10	.333	0	3	4.61

Mark Kingston

Bats: Both **Throws:** Right **Pos:** 3B-1B Ht: 6'4" Wt: 210 Born: 5/16/70 Age: 26

		BATTING														BASERUNNING				PERCENTAGES		
Year Team	Lg	G	AB	H	2B	3B	HR	TB	R	RBI	TBB	IBB	SO	HBP	SH	SF	SB	CS	SB%	GDP	Avg	OBP	SLG
1992 Helena	R	39	122	32	7	1	1	44	21	14	12	0	32	1	1	1	0	0	.00	3	.262	.331	.361
1993 Geneva	A	3	9	2	0	0	0	2	0	0	0	0	3	1	0	0	0	0	.00	0	.222	.300	.222
Peoria	A	64	224	57	14	1	4	85	25	24	28	0	44	5	3	3	3	0	1.00	6	.254	.346	.379
1994 Daytona	A	109	370	83	14	1	4	111	42	35	34	1	79	6	1	4	1	2	.33	12	.224	.297	.300
1995 Daytona	A	49	170	40	8	0	2	54	23	23	14	2	33	1	0	3	1	1	.50	5	.235	.293	.318
Orlando	AA	66	199	53	13	0	5	81	17	24	22	5	41	1	2	2	0	1	.00	4	.266	.339	.407
4 Min. YEARS		330	1094	267	56	3	16	377	128	120	110	8	232	15	7	13	5	4	.56	26	.244	.318	.345

Jay Kirkpatrick

Bats: Left **Throws:** Right **Pos:** 1B Ht: 6'4" Wt: 210 Born: 7/10/69 Age: 26

		BATTING														BASERUNNING				PERCENTAGES		
Year Team	Lg	G	AB	H	2B	3B	HR	TB	R	RBI	TBB	IBB	SO	HBP	SH	SF	SB	CS	SB%	GDP	Avg	OBP	SLG
1991 Great Falls	R	50	168	54	11	1	2	73	25	26	13	0	23	3	0	0	1	2	.33	3	.321	.380	.435
1992 Vero Beach	A	114	385	108	22	2	6	152	32	50	31	4	82	4	1	6	2	2	.50	9	.281	.336	.395
1993 Bakersfield	A	103	375	108	21	0	8	153	42	63	35	2	78	4	1	3	1	4	.20	7	.288	.353	.408
San Antonio	AA	27	97	31	6	1	6	57	17	17	14	4	15	0	0	0	0	1	.00	4	.320	.405	.588
1994 San Antonio	AA	123	449	133	40	1	18	229	61	75	45	7	91	3	0	6	2	2	.50	12	.296	.360	.510
Albuquerque	AAA	3	5	1	1	0	0	2	0	1	1	0	1	0	0	0	0	0	.00	0	.200	.333	.400
1995 Albuquerque	AAA	13	40	10	1	1	1	16	4	6	2	1	6	0	0	0	0	0	.00	0	.250	.286	.400
San Bernrdo	A	71	267	72	19	0	15	136	38	50	40	3	75	0	0	2	3	0	1.00	3	.270	.362	.509
5 Min. YEARS		504	1786	517	121	6	56	818	219	288	181	21	371	14	2	17	9	11	.45	38	.289	.356	.458

Daron Kirkreit

Pitches: Right Bats: Right Pos: P Ht: 6'6" Wt: 225 Born: 8/7/72 Age: 23

			HOW MUCH HE PITCHED					WHAT HE GAVE UP									THE RESULTS					
Year	Team	Lg	G	GS	CG	GF	IP	BFP	H	R	ER	HR	SH	SF	HB	TBB	IBB	SO	WP	Bk	W	L	Pct.	ShO	Sv	ERA
1993	Watertown	A	7	7	1	0	36.1	156	33	14	9	1	1	0	0	11	0	44	1	1	4	1	.800	0	0	2.23
1994	Kinston	A	20	19	4	1	127.2	510	92	48	38	9	3	1	7	40	0	116	6	0	8	7	.533	0	0	2.68
	Canton-Akrn	AA	9	9	0	0	46.1	217	53	35	32	5	2	1	0	25	2	54	4	0	3	5	.375	0	0	6.22
1995	Canton-Akrn	AA	14	14	1	0	80.2	360	74	54	51	13	5	5	6	46	1	67	2	0	2	9	.182	0	0	5.69
	Kinston	A	3	3	0	0	13.2	63	14	9	9	1	1	1	2	6	0	14	1	0	0	1	.000	0	0	5.93
	3 Min. YEARS		53	52	6	1	304.2	1306	266	160	139	29	12	8	15	128	3	295	14	1	17	23	.425	0	0	4.11

Steven Kline

Pitches: Left Bats: Both Pos: P Ht: 6'2" Wt: 200 Born: 8/22/72 Age: 23

			HOW MUCH HE PITCHED					WHAT HE GAVE UP									THE RESULTS					
Year	Team	Lg	G	GS	CG	GF	IP	BFP	H	R	ER	HR	SH	SF	HB	TBB	IBB	SO	WP	Bk	W	L	Pct.	ShO	Sv	ERA
1993	Burlington	R	2	1	0	0	7.1	34	11	4	4	0	1	0	0	2	1	4	0	0	1	1	.500	0	0	4.91
	Watertown	A	13	13	2	0	79	332	77	36	28	3	3	2	4	12	0	45	5	0	5	4	.556	1	0	3.19
1994	Columbus	A	28	28	2	0	185.2	744	175	67	62	14	1	2	7	36	0	174	6	2	18	5	.783	1	0	3.01
1995	Canton-Akrn	AA	14	14	0	0	89.1	377	86	34	24	6	4	1	1	30	3	45	1	1	2	3	.400	0	0	2.42
	3 Min. YEARS		57	56	4	0	361.1	1487	349	141	118	23	9	5	12	80	4	268	12	3	26	13	.667	2	0	2.94

Joe Klink

Pitches: Left Bats: Left Pos: P Ht: 5'11" Wt: 175 Born: 2/3/62 Age: 34

			HOW MUCH HE PITCHED					WHAT HE GAVE UP									THE RESULTS					
Year	Team	Lg	G	GS	CG	GF	IP	BFP	H	R	ER	HR	SH	SF	HB	TBB	IBB	SO	WP	Bk	W	L	Pct.	ShO	Sv	ERA
1984	Columbia	A	31	0	0	27	38.2	172	30	19	15	1	4	3	1	28	0	49	5	1	5	4	.556	0	11	3.49
1985	Lynchburg	A	44	0	0	17	51.2	221	41	16	13	1	4	2	0	26	2	59	5	2	3	3	.500	0	5	2.26
1986	Orlando	AA	45	0	0	41	68	297	59	24	19	5	5	1	2	37	1	63	1	0	4	5	.444	0	11	2.51
1987	Portland	AAA	12	0	0	7	23	107	25	14	11	1	1	3	0	13	1	14	1	0	0	0	.000	0	0	4.30
1988	Huntsville	AA	21	0	0	12	34.2	143	25	6	3	0	0	0	0	14	1	30	3	4	1	2	.333	0	3	0.78
	Tacoma	AAA	27	0	0	15	38.2	185	48	29	22	0	5	3	1	17	1	32	3	6	2	1	.667	0	1	5.12
1989	Tacoma	AAA	6	0	0	5	6.2	23	2	0	0	0	0	0	1	2	0	5	0	0	0	0	.000	0	0	0.00
	Huntsville	AA	57	0	0	53	60.2	249	46	19	19	2	3	4	2	23	0	59	6	5	4	4	.500	0	26	2.82
1991	Modesto	A	3	3	0	0	5	19	4	2	2	0	0	0	0	1	0	1	0	0	0	0	.000	0	0	3.60
1994	Albuquerque	AAA	2	0	0	1	3	12	3	1	1	0	0	0	1	1	1	2	0	1	0	0	.000	0	0	3.00
1995	Buffalo	AAA	45	0	0	21	39	161	31	13	13	0	3	5	1	15	0	32	3	0	2	1	.667	0	8	3.00
1987	Minnesota	AL	12	0	0	5	23	116	37	18	17	4	1	1	0	11	0	17	1	0	0	1	.000	0	0	6.65
1990	Oakland	AL	40	0	0	19	39.2	165	34	9	9	1	1	0	0	18	0	19	3	1	0	0	.000	0	1	2.04
1991	Oakland	AL	62	0	0	10	62	266	60	30	30	4	8	0	5	21	5	34	4	0	10	3	.769	0	2	4.35
1993	Florida	NL	59	0	0	10	37.2	168	37	22	21	0	2	3	0	24	4	22	1	2	0	2	.000	0	0	5.02
	9 Min. YEARS		293	3	0	199	369	1589	314	143	118	12	25	21	9	177	7	346	27	19	21	20	.512	0	65	2.88
	4 Maj. YEARS		173	0	0	44	162.1	715	168	79	77	9	12	4	5	74	9	92	9	3	10	6	.625	0	3	4.27

Kevin Kloek

Pitches: Right Bats: Right Pos: P Ht: 6'3" Wt: 175 Born: 8/15/70 Age: 25

			HOW MUCH HE PITCHED					WHAT HE GAVE UP									THE RESULTS					
Year	Team	Lg	G	GS	CG	GF	IP	BFP	H	R	ER	HR	SH	SF	HB	TBB	IBB	SO	WP	Bk	W	L	Pct.	ShO	Sv	ERA
1992	Beloit	A	15	14	2	0	94	386	79	32	22	7	4	2	4	27	1	76	5	7	10	1	.909	1	0	2.11
1993	El Paso	AA	23	23	1	0	135.2	587	148	75	62	11	7	5	7	53	4	97	5	0	9	6	.600	1	0	4.11
1994	Brewers	R	3	3	0	0	19	71	9	3	3	0	0	0	0	3	0	19	1	0	2	0	1.000	0	0	1.42
	El Paso	AA	9	9	0	0	55.1	223	46	26	24	3	0	4	1	18	0	37	0	0	5	1	.833	0	0	3.90
1995	El Paso	AA	28	27	3	0	157	699	196	103	86	6	2	5	10	48	0	121	12	0	7	11	.389	1	0	4.93
	4 Min. YEARS		78	76	6	0	461	1966	478	239	197	27	13	16	22	149	5	350	23	7	33	19	.635	3	0	3.85

Chris Knabenshue

Bats: Left Throws: Right Pos: OF Ht: 6'1" Wt: 175 Born: 10/30/63 Age: 32

			BATTING														BASERUNNING				PERCENTAGES		
Year	Team	Lg	G	AB	H	2B	3B	HR	TB	R	RBI	TBB	IBB	SO	HBP	SH	SF	SB	CS	SB%	GDP	Avg	OBP	SLG
1985	Spokane	A	71	258	72	13	2	1	92	50	34	57	1	42	0	2	2	10	4	.71	3	.279	.407	.357
1986	Charleston	A	102	335	95	20	4	10	153	77	62	82	1	82	2	2	4	36	10	.78	7	.284	.423	.457
1987	Wichita	AA	128	473	146	31	3	15	228	91	65	66	11	99	1	0	0	20	14	.59	10	.309	.394	.482
1988	Wichita	AA	116	412	101	26	2	16	179	68	56	84	3	138	2	0	1	16	16	.50	6	.245	.375	.434
1989	Las Vegas	AAA	115	306	79	17	4	18	158	68	50	83	3	112	1	4	0	3	.00	5		.258	.418	.516
1990	Scranton-Wb	AAA	129	379	90	16	1	18	162	61	62	76	2	108	2	4	4	11	7	.61	7	.237	.364	.427
1991	Scranton-Wb	AAA	17	35	7	2	0	0	9	3	8	10	1	12	0	1	0	1	0	1.00	0	.200	.378	.257
	Denver	AAA	12	29	6	1	0	1	10	5	3	9	1	9	0	0	0	0	0	.00	0	.207	.395	.345
	Palm Spring	A	11	30	6	1	0	1	10	5	5	8	1	11	0	1	0	0	0	.00	0	.200	.368	.333
1992	Huntsville	AA	21	71	14	4	0	1	21	9	11	10	0	24	0	0	1	1	2	.33	0	.197	.293	.296
1994	Buffalo	AAA	45	131	38	8	1	2	54	17	18	24	2	27	0	0	1	0	0	.00	4	.290	.397	.412
1995	Pirates	R	4	17	3	0	0	1	6	1	2	0	0	1	0	0	0	0	0	.00	2	.176	.176	.353
	Calgary	AAA	4	10	0	0	0	0	0	2	1	4	0	3	0	0	0	0	0	.00	0	.000	.286	.000
	10 Min. YEARS		775	2486	657	139	17	84	1082	457	377	513	26	668	8	14	13	95	56	.63	44	.264	.390	.435

Brent Knackert

Pitches: Right **Bats:** Right **Pos:** P   **Ht:** 6'3" **Wt:** 195 **Born:** 8/1/69 **Age:** 26

Year Team	Lg	G	GS	CG	GF	IP	BFP	H	R	ER	HR	SH	SF	HB	TBB	IBB	SO	WP	Bk	W	L	Pct.	ShO	Sv	ERA
1987 White Sox	R	12	11	1	0	72.2	288	55	28	23	2	0	5	4	15	0	60	4	2	6	2	.750	1	0	2.85
1988 Tampa	A	23	23	4	0	142	591	132	58	50	4	2	5	4	46	3	78	11	5	10	8	.556	0	0	3.17
1989 Sarasota	A	35	12	2	22	98	407	85	41	32	3	0	2	4	35	0	80	4	2	8	5	.615	0	12	2.94
1991 San Bernrdo	A	2	2	0	0	4.1	20	3	1	1	0	0	0	1	3	0	7	0	0	0	0	.000	0	0	2.08
1992 Jacksonvlle	AA	21	19	2	1	117	495	123	62	53	15	3	4	3	41	0	74	0	0	7	8	.467	1	0	4.08
1993 Jacksonvlle	AA	4	2	0	1	14	55	6	4	4	1	0	0	3	4	0	10	0	1	0	0	.000	0	1	2.57
Binghamton	AA	15	6	0	2	43.2	193	59	30	27	2	1	1	4	13	0	27	1	3	1	3	.250	0	0	5.56
1995 Binghamton	AA	48	0	0	28	82.1	324	53	23	21	4	5	2	3	26	8	69	3	0	7	7	.500	0	11	2.30
1990 Seattle	AL	24	2	0	5	37.1	186	50	28	27	5	1	2	2	21	2	28	3	0	1	1	.500	0	0	6.51
7 Min. YEARS		160	75	9	54	574	2373	516	247	211	31	11	19	26	183	11	405	23	13	39	34	.534	2	24	3.31

Mike Knapp

Bats: Right **Throws:** Right **Pos:** C   **Ht:** 6'0" **Wt:** 195 **Born:** 10/6/64 **Age:** 31

Year Team	Lg	G	AB	H	2B	3B	HR	TB	R	RBI	TBB	IBB	SO	HBP	SH	SF	SB	CS	SB%	GDP	Avg	OBP	SLG
1986 Salem	A	64	224	66	12	1	1	89	31	39	31	1	37	3	1	3	4	4	.50	2	.295	.383	.397
1987 Quad City	A	91	327	84	14	3	1	107	34	31	27	0	48	4	0	7	1	6	.14	7	.257	.315	.327
1988 Midland	AA	100	327	86	12	1	3	109	34	33	35	0	64	2	6	5	1	3	.25	5	.263	.333	.333
1989 Midland	AA	20	64	21	2	0	2	29	7	6	3	0	8	2	1	0	0	0	.00	2	.328	.377	.453
Edmonton	AAA	51	144	38	8	0	1	49	15	22	15	0	27	4	3	1	0	4	.00	2	.264	.348	.340
1990 Midland	AA	57	193	50	8	0	2	64	16	21	16	0	29	0	0	1	1	1	.50	3	.259	.314	.332
Edmonton	AAA	12	39	8	0	0	0	10	3	4	4	0	6	0	0	0	0	0	.00	0	.205	.279	.256
1991 Charlotte	AA	92	266	68	12	0	1	83	19	33	19	3	53	1	7	1	4	0	1.00	8	.256	.307	.312
1992 Iowa	AAA	54	138	34	5	0	3	48	16	15	10	0	28	3	0	0	2	2	.50	1	.246	.311	.348
1993 Omaha	AAA	70	200	58	7	0	2	71	22	19	34	0	32	3	3	1	2	4	.33	6	.290	.399	.355
1994 Omaha	AAA	52	151	34	5	1	5	56	19	19	14	0	27	2	2	2	2	2	.50	1	.225	.296	.371
1995 Indianapolis	AAA	14	39	10	2	0	1	15	8	6	3	0	7	1	0	0	1	0	1.00	0	.256	.326	.385
High Desert	A	5	15	4	1	0	0	5	1	1	2	0	6	0	0	0	0	1	.00	0	.267	.333	.333
Rochester	AAA	40	126	23	1	1	1	29	10	12	12	0	26	1	0	1	1	1	.50	3	.183	.257	.230
10 Min. YEARS		722	2253	584	89	8	25	764	235	261	225	4	398	26	23	23	19	28	.40	40	.259	.330	.339

Greg Knowles

Pitches: Right **Bats:** Right **Pos:** P   **Ht:** 6'3" **Wt:** 196 **Born:** 1/9/69 **Age:** 27

Year Team	Lg	G	GS	CG	GF	IP	BFP	H	R	ER	HR	SH	SF	HB	TBB	IBB	SO	WP	Bk	W	L	Pct.	ShO	Sv	ERA
1991 Salt Lake	R	3	2	0	1	4.2	28	11	12	4	1	0	0	1	1	0	2	0	1	0	1	.000	0	0	7.71
1992 Savannah	A	39	0	0	23	44	188	37	17	15	1	5	2	2	15	3	30	1	1	6	4	.600	0	3	3.07
1993 Springfield	A	54	0	0	27	73.1	302	62	25	21	2	7	3	1	23	3	59	3	2	11	4	.733	0	2	2.58
1994 St. Pete	A	37	0	0	14	51.2	230	61	31	25	4	3	2	1	14	2	29	4	0	3	5	.375	0	0	4.35
1995 Bowie	AA	37	1	0	13	74	327	83	44	34	6	5	2	1	26	7	37	3	0	5	2	.714	0	2	4.14
5 Min. YEARS		170	3	0	78	247.2	1075	254	129	99	15	20	9	6	78	15	157	11	4	25	16	.610	0	8	3.60

Kerry Knox

Pitches: Left **Bats:** Left **Pos:** P   **Ht:** 6'0" **Wt:** 188 **Born:** 4/10/67 **Age:** 29

Year Team	Lg	G	GS	CG	GF	IP	BFP	H	R	ER	HR	SH	SF	HB	TBB	IBB	SO	WP	Bk	W	L	Pct.	ShO	Sv	ERA
1989 Spokane	A	12	12	1	0	75.1	306	74	30	22	7	1	3	1	10	0	76	1	3	8	2	.800	0	0	2.63
Charlstn-Sc	A	2	2	0	0	11	43	9	3	3	0	0	0	3	1	0	11	1	1	0	0	.000	0	0	2.45
1990 Riverside	A	27	27	3	0	179.2	768	188	97	73	14	9	6	3	49	2	111	8	4	11	12	.478	1	0	3.66
1991 Wichita	AA	28	15	1	1	113.2	504	133	72	62	13	2	2	4	36	1	51	5	2	4	4	.500	1	0	4.91
1992 Beloit	A	14	1	0	5	31	134	30	20	13	3	2	0	1	8	0	27	1	0	0	0	.000	0	4	3.77
El Paso	AA	13	1	0	2	15.2	76	16	14	12	1	1	1	2	12	1	12	1	1	0	1	.000	0	0	6.89
Stockton	A	5	4	0	0	24.2	99	26	6	6	1	1	1	0	5	0	15	1	0	1	1	.500	0	0	2.19
1993 Arkansas	AA	22	11	0	2	81	328	78	30	25	9	5	3	3	14	1	61	1	2	4	4	.500	0	0	2.78
Louisville	AAA	7	7	1	0	44	187	48	25	22	6	2	1	3	10	0	24	2	2	1	4	.200	1	0	4.50
1994 Louisville	AAA	32	24	1	0	149	673	185	104	95	21	8	9	10	43	4	83	4	5	8	9	.471	0	0	5.74
1995 Tyler	IND	11	7	0	1	48	196	49	16	13	2	3	0	3	4	0	32	0	0	4	2	.667	0	0	2.44
Tulsa	AA	5	4	0	1	29	124	28	12	11	2	1	0	1	9	1	14	2	0	2	2	.500	0	0	3.41
7 Min. YEARS		178	115	7	13	802	3438	864	429	357	79	35	26	34	201	12	517	27	20	43	41	.512	3	4	4.01

Kurt Knudsen

Pitches: Right **Bats:** Right **Pos:** P   **Ht:** 6'3" **Wt:** 210 **Born:** 2/20/67 **Age:** 29

Year Team	Lg	G	GS	CG	GF	IP	BFP	H	R	ER	HR	SH	SF	HB	TBB	IBB	SO	WP	Bk	W	L	Pct.	ShO	Sv	ERA
1988 Bristol	R	2	0	0	2	2.1	14	4	3	0	0	0	0	0	1	0	0	0	0	0	0	.000	0	0	0.00
Fayetteville	A	12	0	0	5	20	77	8	4	3	1	2	1	1	9	1	22	1	1	3	1	.750	0	1	1.35
Lakeland	A	7	0	0	5	9.1	39	7	2	1	0	0	0	0	7	0	6	2	0	0	0	.000	0	0	0.96
1989 Lakeland	A	45	0	0	26	54.1	225	43	16	13	5	2	1	0	22	7	68	2	3	3	2	.600	0	10	2.15
1990 Lakeland	A	14	8	0	0	67	253	42	18	17	2	2	1	0	22	0	70	5	2	5	0	1.000	0	3	2.28
London	AA	15	0	0	8	26	102	15	6	6	1	0	1	0	11	0	26	1	0	2	1	.667	0	1	2.08
1991 London	AA	34	0	0	18	51.2	226	42	29	20	1	4	1	1	30	0	56	4	1	2	3	.400	0	6	3.48

Year	Team	Lg	G	GS	CG	GF	IP	BFP	H	R	ER	HR	SH	SF	HB	TBB	IBB	SO	WP	Bk	W	L	Pct.	ShO	Sv	ERA
	Toledo	AAA	12	0	0	3	18.1	79	13	11	3	1	0	0	0	10	1	28	2	0	1	2	.333	0	0	1.47
1992	Toledo	AAA	12	0	0	8	21.2	82	11	5	5	1	1	1	1	6	0	19	1	0	3	1	.750	0	1	2.08
1993	Toledo	AAA	23	0	0	15	33.1	136	24	15	14	3	1	0	1	11	1	39	2	0	2	2	.500	0	6	3.78
1994	Toledo	AAA	37	7	0	22	67.1	299	56	38	30	8	1	4	3	42	1	64	0	1	2	5	.286	0	4	4.01
1995	Phoenix	AAA	11	1	0	4	19.2	86	18	13	11	2	0	2	0	11	0	20	0	0	0	1	.000	0	1	5.03
1992	Detroit	AL	48	1	0	14	70.2	313	70	39	36	9	4	2	1	41	9	51	5	0	2	3	.400	0	5	4.58
1993	Detroit	AL	30	0	0	7	37.2	171	41	22	20	9	2	3	4	16	2	29	2	0	3	2	.600	0	2	4.78
1994	Detroit	AL	4	0	0	0	5.1	34	7	8	8	2	0	0	0	11	1	1	0	0	1	0	1.000	0	0	13.50
	8 Min. YEARS		224	16	0	120	391	1618	283	160	123	21	16	17	10	182	13	418	21	9	23	18	.561	0	33	2.83
	3 Maj. YEARS		82	1	0	21	113.2	518	118	69	64	20	6	5	5	68	12	81	7	0	6	5	.545	0	7	5.07

Jim Koehler

Bats: Left **Throws:** Left **Pos:** OF　　**Ht:** 6'3" **Wt:** 215 **Born:** 11/5/70 **Age:** 25

							BATTING										BASERUNNING				PERCENTAGES		
Year	Team	Lg	G	AB	H	2B	3B	HR	TB	R	RBI	TBB	IBB	SO	HBP	SH	SF	SB	CS	SB%	GDP	Avg	OBP	SLG
1991	Butte	R	56	180	47	13	1	6	80	34	38	26	0	32	3	0	1	8	5	.62	5	.261	.362	.444
1993	Riverside	A	12	42	8	1	1	2	17	7	12	5	0	11	0	0	0	1	1	.50	1	.190	.277	.405
	Appleton	A	115	372	90	28	5	17	179	52	60	55	4	95	6	2	5	4	6	.40	11	.242	.345	.481
1994	Riverside	A	108	371	91	18	1	15	156	53	67	32	2	103	9	0	6	4	1	.80	8	.245	.316	.420
1995	Port City	AA	2	2	0	0	0	0	0	0	0	0	0	1	0	0	0	0	0	.00	0	.000	.000	.000
	Bend	IND	89	357	116	33	1	16	199	68	78	35	4	64	8	4	8	0	3	.00	5	.325	.390	.557
	4 Min. YEARS		382	1324	352	93	9	56	631	214	255	153	10	306	26	6	20	17	16	.52	30	.266	.349	.477

Brian Koelling

Bats: Right **Throws:** Right **Pos:** 2B-SS　　**Ht:** 6'1" **Wt:** 185 **Born:** 6/11/69 **Age:** 27

							BATTING										BASERUNNING				PERCENTAGES		
Year	Team	Lg	G	AB	H	2B	3B	HR	TB	R	RBI	TBB	IBB	SO	HBP	SH	SF	SB	CS	SB%	GDP	Avg	OBP	SLG
1991	Billings	R	22	85	30	7	1	2	45	17	12	14	0	23	1	0	0	6	2	.75	0	.353	.450	.529
	Cedar Rapds	A	35	147	38	6	0	1	47	27	12	14	0	39	3	0	1	22	6	.79	0	.259	.333	.320
1992	Cedar Rapds	A	129	460	121	18	7	5	168	81	43	49	0	137	1	9	2	47	16	.75	3	.263	.334	.365
1993	Chattanooga	AA	110	430	119	17	6	4	160	64	47	32	1	105	2	4	3	34	13	.72	2	.277	.328	.372
	Indianaplos	AAA	2	9	2	0	0	0	2	1	0	0	0	1	0	0	0	0	1	.00	0	.222	.300	.222
1994	Indianaplos	AAA	19	53	8	0	0	0	8	6	0	2	0	14	1	1	0	4	2	.67	0	.151	.196	.151
	Chattanooga	AA	92	343	96	11	5	3	126	54	31	24	1	64	4	7	1	27	18	.60	6	.280	.333	.367
1995	Chattanooga	AA	107	432	128	21	7	3	172	71	44	40	1	63	3	8	3	30	12	.71	9	.296	.358	.398
	Scranton-Wb	AAA	16	53	14	1	0	0	15	5	3	1	0	14	0	0	1	3	1	.75	1	.264	.273	.283
1993	Cincinnati	NL	7	15	1	0	0	0	1	2	0	0	0	2	1	0	0	0	0	.00	0	.067	.125	.067
	5 Min. YEARS		532	2012	556	81	26	18	743	326	192	176	3	460	16	29	11	173	71	.71	21	.276	.338	.369

Jerry Koller

Pitches: Right **Bats:** Right **Pos:** P　　**Ht:** 6'3" **Wt:** 190 **Born:** 6/30/72 **Age:** 24

			HOW MUCH HE PITCHED						WHAT HE GAVE UP										THE RESULTS					
Year	Team	Lg	G	GS	CG	GF	IP	BFP	H	R	ER	HR	SH	SF	HB	TBB	IBB	SO	WP	Bk	W	L	Pct.	ShO	Sv	ERA
1990	Braves	R	13	8	1	1	51	210	45	24	12	0	1	4		13	2	45	4	8	4	3	.571	1	0	2.12
1991	Braves	R	2	2	0	0	8	40	9	6	3	0	0	0		3	0	10	1	0	0	0	.000	0	0	3.38
	Idaho Falls	R	9	9	0	0	36	171	49	29	25	1	0	2	1	14	0	29	7	2	2	2	.500	0	0	6.25
1992	Macon	A	21	21	2	0	133	526	104	41	35	8	2	4	5	31	0	114	8	2	10	5	.667	0	0	2.37
1993	Durham	A	27	26	1	0	157.2	666	168	91	80	20	7	6	8	47	1	102	7	2	8	10	.444	0	0	4.57
1994	Greenville	AA	22	22	0	0	119.2	498	110	60	56	8	4	5	3	42	0	56	7	4	7	5	.583	0	0	4.21
1995	Greenville	AA	25	25	3	0	147.2	629	163	86	81	16	5	7	2	37	4	84	5	1	9	12	.429	0	0	4.94
	6 Min. YEARS		119	113	7	1	653	2740	648	337	292	53	18	25	23	187	7	440	39	19	40	37	.519	1	0	4.02

Rod Koller

Pitches: Right **Bats:** Right **Pos:** P　　**Ht:** 6'4" **Wt:** 195 **Born:** 7/13/70 **Age:** 25

			HOW MUCH HE PITCHED						WHAT HE GAVE UP										THE RESULTS					
Year	Team	Lg	G	GS	CG	GF	IP	BFP	H	R	ER	HR	SH	SF	HB	TBB	IBB	SO	WP	Bk	W	L	Pct.	ShO	Sv	ERA
1991	Burlington	R	2	0	0	0	3	13	3	1	1	0	0	1	0	3	0	0	0	0	0	0	.000	0	0	3.00
1992	Burlington	R	1	1	0	0	3	15	3	4	4	0	0	0	0	3	0	2	2	0	0	0	.000	0	0	12.00
	Watertown	A	15	7	0	3	52.2	238	71	35	30	1	1	1	2	14	0	24	2	3	3	7	.300	0	1	5.13
1993	Columbus	A	47	0	0	23	68.1	273	51	21	17	4	2	2	1	19	1	37	1	0	9	5	.643	0	9	2.24
1994	Canton-Akrn	AA	7	1	0	2	13	63	14	12	11	4	2	0	0	9	0	7	1	0	0	1	.000	0	0	7.62
	Kinston	A	37	0	0	15	57.2	243	55	32	19	4	2	3	1	16	0	33	5	0	4	4	.500	0	8	2.97
1995	Canton-Akrn	AA	9	1	0	2	18.2	89	26	17	15	2	0	1	2	4	0	3	0	0	0	0	.000	0	1	7.23
	5 Min. YEARS		118	10	0	45	216.1	934	223	122	97	15	7	8	6	65	1	106	11	3	16	18	.471	0	19	4.04

Dominic Konieczki

Pitches: Left **Bats:** Right **Pos:** P　　**Ht:** 6'1" **Wt:** 170 **Born:** 6/16/69 **Age:** 27

			HOW MUCH HE PITCHED						WHAT HE GAVE UP										THE RESULTS					
Year	Team	Lg	G	GS	CG	GF	IP	BFP	H	R	ER	HR	SH	SF	HB	TBB	IBB	SO	WP	Bk	W	L	Pct.	ShO	Sv	ERA
1991	Erie	A	24	0	0	19	31.2	139	25	15	11	1	3	0	3	16	1	46	5	0	2	5	.286	0	10	3.13
1992	Kenosha	A	49	0	0	31	56.1	230	44	14	11	2	6	0	0	19	2	79	3	0	5	3	.625	0	13	1.76
1993	Nashville	AA	42	0	0	23	48.2	221	65	47	36	4	3	2	1	16	1	39	5	0	2	6	.250	0	6	6.66
	Fort Myers	A	12	0	0	0	16.2	83	18	7	7	0	1	0	1	16	0	15	1	0	0	2	.000	0	2	3.78
1994	Fort Myers	A	47	0	0	15	74	336	74	44	29	1	3	2	3	36	5	74	10	1	3	5	.375	0	4	3.53

		G	AB	H	2B	3B	HR	TB	R	RBI	TBB	IBB	SO	HBP	SH	SF	SB	CS	SB%	GDP	Avg	OBP	SLG
1995 New Britain	AA	39	0	0	15	32.1	146	28	10	7	1	2	1	1	19	2	35	3	0	0	1	.000	0	1	1.95
5 Min. YEARS		213	0	0	112	259.2	1155	254	137	101	9	18	5	9	122	11	288	27	1	12	22	.353	0	34	3.50

Andy Kontorinis

Bats: Left **Throws:** Right **Pos:** DH-1B   **Ht:** 6'0" **Wt:** 198 **Born:** 11/18/69 **Age:** 26

					BATTING												BASERUNNING				PERCENTAGES		
Year Team	Lg	G	AB	H	2B	3B	HR	TB	R	RBI	TBB	IBB	SO	HBP	SH	SF	SB	CS	SB%	GDP	Avg	OBP	SLG
1992 Kenosha	A	75	273	77	12	0	5	104	26	44	28	2	39	4	0	5	2	4	.33	5	.282	.352	.381
1993 Fort Myers	A	114	408	104	24	3	3	143	44	59	40	5	42	6	3	4	4	5	.44	11	.255	.328	.350
1994 Fort Myers	A	100	344	99	19	5	6	146	49	51	57	3	39	1	1	4	7	4	.64	9	.288	.387	.424
Nashville	AA	9	31	5	0	0	1	8	5	2	2	1	6	0	1	0	0	0	.00	0	.161	.212	.258
1995 New Britain	AA	36	114	33	4	0	2	43	12	17	14	0	18	5	0	0	1	1	.50	3	.289	.391	.377
4 Min. YEARS		334	1170	318	59	8	17	444	136	173	141	11	144	16	5	13	14	14	.50	28	.272	.354	.379

Dan Kopriva

Bats: Right **Throws:** Right **Pos:** 3B   **Ht:** 5'11" **Wt:** 190 **Born:** 11/6/69 **Age:** 26

					BATTING												BASERUNNING				PERCENTAGES		
Year Team	Lg	G	AB	H	2B	3B	HR	TB	R	RBI	TBB	IBB	SO	HBP	SH	SF	SB	CS	SB%	GDP	Avg	OBP	SLG
1992 Princeton	R	24	89	23	3	0	3	35	11	11	10	0	13	1	0	0	3	1	.75	3	.258	.340	.393
Billings	R	51	196	60	15	2	11	112	37	38	21	0	23	3	0	0	5	2	.71	6	.306	.382	.571
1993 Charlstn-Wv	A	121	402	98	22	7	3	143	69	70	75	2	57	10	2	9	6	6	.50	19	.244	.369	.356
1994 Winston-Sal	A	90	290	90	15	1	11	140	57	36	49	0	39	9	3	2	7	5	.58	7	.310	.423	.483
1995 Winston-Sal	A	17	58	20	4	1	0	26	4	5	4	0	6	1	0	1	1	0	1.00	1	.345	.391	.448
Chattanooga	AA	51	121	34	8	0	1	45	14	11	11	0	14	2	2	0	1	1	.50	5	.281	.351	.372
4 Min. YEARS		354	1156	325	67	11	29	501	192	171	170	2	152	26	7	12	23	15	.61	42	.281	.382	.433

Bryn Kosco

Bats: Left **Throws:** Right **Pos:** 1B   **Ht:** 6'1" **Wt:** 185 **Born:** 3/9/67 **Age:** 29

					BATTING												BASERUNNING				PERCENTAGES		
Year Team	Lg	G	AB	H	2B	3B	HR	TB	R	RBI	TBB	IBB	SO	HBP	SH	SF	SB	CS	SB%	GDP	Avg	OBP	SLG
1988 Jamestown	A	63	229	65	19	2	8	112	26	42	18	4	48	1	0	3	1	0	1.00	5	.284	.335	.489
1989 Rockford	A	77	292	78	16	0	11	127	47	44	39	6	61	2	0	2	2	0	1.00	5	.267	.355	.435
W. Palm Bch	A	60	203	46	10	1	1	61	16	22	21	5	42	0	0	4	2	2	.50	4	.227	.294	.300
1990 Jacksonvlle	AA	33	113	28	8	0	0	36	7	15	11	2	23	0	2	1	0	0	.00	4	.248	.312	.319
1991 Harrisburg	AA	113	381	92	23	5	10	155	50	58	48	4	79	2	0	3	4	1	.80	9	.241	.327	.407
1992 Harrisburg	AA	106	341	78	17	0	5	110	35	41	31	2	75	1	1	5	2	0	1.00	6	.229	.291	.323
1993 High Desert	A	121	450	138	25	3	27	250	96	121	62	3	97	5	0	8	1	6	.14	13	.307	.390	.556
1994 New Haven	AA	132	479	116	24	3	22	212	64	90	59	6	124	4	1	6	2	2	.50	17	.242	.327	.443
1995 Iowa	AAA	119	363	91	24	3	15	166	50	52	30	5	85	1	2	3	2	2	.50	18	.251	.307	.457
8 Min. YEARS		824	2851	732	166	17	99	1229	391	485	319	37	634	16	6	35	16	13	.55	83	.257	.331	.431

John Kosenski

Pitches: Right **Bats:** Right **Pos:** P   **Ht:** 6'5" **Wt:** 195 **Born:** 1/28/69 **Age:** 27

		HOW MUCH HE PITCHED					WHAT HE GAVE UP										THE RESULTS					
Year Team	Lg	G	GS	CG	GF	IP	BFP	H	R	ER	HR	SH	SF	HB	TBB	IBB	SO	WP	Bk	W	L	Pct.	ShO	Sv	ERA
1991 Fayettevlle	A	37	1	0	9	73.2	323	59	32	22	3	4	2	5	42	1	42	4	2	4	2	.667	0	2	2.69
1992 Lakeland	A	27	20	4	2	120.2	524	135	61	55	4	7	3	7	31	0	67	7	4	5	8	.385	2	0	4.10
1993 Lakeland	A	35	2	0	8	65.2	276	45	24	20	3	2	2	2	43	2	42	7	0	3	3	.500	0	3	2.74
1994 Brainerd	IND	32	0	0	21	45.2	203	44	17	12	0	10	1	4	21	2	48	1	1	4	2	.667	0	6	2.36
1995 El Paso	AA	16	0	0	6	28.1	141	41	19	18	1	1	1	2	17	2	25	4	0	3	1	.750	0	0	5.72
5 Min. YEARS		147	23	4	46	334	1467	324	153	127	11	24	9	20	154	7	224	23	7	19	16	.543	2	11	3.42

Kevin Koslofski

Bats: Left **Throws:** Right **Pos:** OF   **Ht:** 5'8" **Wt:** 175 **Born:** 9/24/66 **Age:** 29

					BATTING												BASERUNNING				PERCENTAGES		
Year Team	Lg	G	AB	H	2B	3B	HR	TB	R	RBI	TBB	IBB	SO	HBP	SH	SF	SB	CS	SB%	GDP	Avg	OBP	SLG
1984 Eugene	A	53	155	29	2	2	1	38	23	10	25	0	37	0	1	1	10	2	.83	3	.187	.298	.245
1985 Royals	R	33	108	27	4	2	0	35	17	11	12	0	19	3	2	0	7	2	.78	1	.250	.341	.324
1986 Fort Myers	A	103	331	84	13	5	0	107	44	29	47	2	59	2	7	4	12	6	.67	6	.254	.346	.323
1987 Fort Myers	A	109	330	80	12	3	0	98	46	25	46	3	64	7	3	2	25	9	.74	4	.242	.345	.297
1988 Baseball Cy	A	108	368	97	7	8	3	129	52	30	44	5	71	4	4	2	32	11	.74	4	.264	.347	.351
1989 Baseball Cy	A	116	343	89	10	3	4	117	65	33	51	2	57	5	5	3	41	14	.75	9	.259	.361	.341
1990 Memphis	AA	118	367	78	11	5	3	108	52	32	54	1	89	2	7	3	12	7	.63	4	.213	.315	.294
1991 Memphis	AA	81	287	93	15	3	7	135	41	39	33	3	56	4	4	4	10	13	.43	2	.324	.396	.470
Omaha	AAA	25	94	28	3	2	2	41	13	19	15	0	19	1	2	1	4	3	.57	1	.298	.396	.436
1992 Omaha	AAA	78	280	87	12	5	4	121	29	32	21	3	47	2	7	1	8	3	.73	3	.311	.362	.432
1993 Omaha	AAA	111	395	109	22	5	7	162	58	45	43	2	73	2	3	2	15	7	.68	9	.276	.348	.410
1994 Omaha	AAA	93	307	66	8	3	6	98	43	39	37	4	90	1	4	3	10	4	.71	1	.215	.299	.319
1995 New Orleans	AAA	105	321	68	18	4	7	115	41	35	34	2	100	2	3	3	4	2	.67	1	.212	.289	.358
1992 Kansas City	AL	55	133	33	0	2	3	46	20	13	12	0	23	1	3	1	2	1	.67	2	.248	.313	.346
1993 Kansas City	AL	15	26	7	0	0	1	10	4	2	4	0	5	1	1	0	1	0	1.00	1	.269	.387	.385
1994 Kansas City	AL	2	4	1	0	0	0	1	2	0	2	1	1	0	0	0	0	0	.00	0	.250	.500	.250
12 Min. YEARS		1133	3686	935	137	50	44	1304	524	379	462	28	781	35	52	29	190	83	.70	47	.254	.340	.354
3 Maj. YEARS		72	163	41	0	2	4	57	26	15	18	1	29	2	4	1	2	2	.50	3	.252	.332	.350

Mike Kotarski

Pitches: Left **Bats:** Left **Pos:** P **Ht:** 6'1" **Wt:** 195 **Born:** 9/18/70 **Age:** 25

			HOW MUCH HE PITCHED				WHAT HE GAVE UP										THE RESULTS					
Year Team	Lg	G	GS	CG	GF	IP	BFP	H	R	ER	HR	SH	SF	HB	TBB	IBB	SO	WP	Bk	W	L	Pct.	ShO	Sv	ERA
1992 Bend	A	25	3	0	9	55.2	247	48	30	23	1	1	1	6	36	2	65	1	0	3	1	.750	0	0	3.72
1993 Central Val	A	52	0	0	32	88.1	396	87	44	38	9	11	2	3	37	3	81	3	1	6	2	.750	0	11	3.87
1994 New Haven	AA	18	0	0	12	21	109	29	29	23	7	0	3	0	13	0	14	3	0	0	1	.000	0	3	9.86
Central Val	A	41	1	0	11	62.1	278	69	39	27	8	1	3	3	29	3	58	7	4	1	3	.250	0	2	3.90
1995 Colo. Sprng	AAA	22	0	0	11	30	162	48	37	36	5	1	2	2	20	1	21	4	0	2	2	.500	0	2	10.80
New Haven	AA	31	0	0	10	50	234	43	25	18	4	4	2	1	36	4	54	3	5	2	3	.400	0	2	3.24
4 Min. YEARS		189	4	0	85	307.1	1426	324	204	165	34	18	13	15	171	13	293	21	10	14	12	.538	0	18	4.83

Chris Kotes

Pitches: Right **Bats:** Right **Pos:** P **Ht:** 6'3" **Wt:** 195 **Born:** 5/11/69 **Age:** 27

			HOW MUCH HE PITCHED				WHAT HE GAVE UP										THE RESULTS					
Year Team	Lg	G	GS	CG	GF	IP	BFP	H	R	ER	HR	SH	SF	HB	TBB	IBB	SO	WP	Bk	W	L	Pct.	ShO	Sv	ERA
1991 St. Cathrns	A	16	16	1	0	87	364	74	34	22	2	0	2	2	37	1	94	7	0	6	5	.545	0	0	2.28
1992 Myrtle Bch	A	25	25	0	0	132.1	554	110	63	52	11	1	5	4	68	1	100	7	1	12	5	.706	0	0	3.54
1993 Dunedin	A	10	8	0	0	42	169	37	17	12	1	0	1	0	12	0	41	1	1	2	2	.500	0	0	2.57
1994 Dunedin	A	26	24	2	0	148.2	616	134	54	50	7	5	4	5	55	0	91	5	1	10	6	.625	1	0	3.03
1995 Knoxville	AA	36	11	1	9	106.1	470	109	66	58	7	4	3	4	45	2	74	9	1	3	9	.250	0	1	4.91
5 Min. YEARS		113	84	4	9	516.1	2173	464	234	194	28	10	15	15	217	4	400	29	4	33	27	.550	1	1	3.38

Tony Kounas

Bats: Right **Throws:** Right **Pos:** C **Ht:** 6'2" **Wt:** 210 **Born:** 11/6/67 **Age:** 28

			BATTING														BASERUNNING				PERCENTAGES		
Year Team	Lg	G	AB	H	2B	3B	HR	TB	R	RBI	TBB	IBB	SO	HBP	SH	SF	SB	CS	SB%	GDP	Avg	OBP	SLG
1990 Bellingham	A	19	65	15	4	0	1	22	9	11	8	0	13	1	0	0	1	0	1.00	2	.231	.324	.338
1991 Peninsula	A	109	387	104	18	1	7	145	46	47	40	3	43	2	0	3	3	1	.75	11	.269	.338	.375
1992 San Bernrdo	A	111	378	99	23	2	10	156	51	55	40	1	43	1	1	1	2	5	.29	14	.262	.333	.413
1993 Jacksonvlle	AA	49	157	43	14	0	4	69	22	23	14	0	24	2	1	1	2	1	.67	3	.274	.339	.439
1994 Jacksonvlle	AA	68	212	54	14	0	7	89	26	23	15	0	32	2	1	1	1	0	.00	5	.255	.309	.420
1995 Harrisburg	AA	66	196	46	5	0	1	54	15	22	19	1	27	2	0	1	1	1	.50	7	.235	.307	.276
6 Min. YEARS		422	1395	361	78	3	30	535	169	181	136	5	182	10	3	7	9	9	.50	42	.259	.328	.384

Blaise Kozeniewski

Pitches: Right **Bats:** Right **Pos:** P **Ht:** 6'3" **Wt:** 185 **Born:** 11/2/69 **Age:** 26

			HOW MUCH HE PITCHED				WHAT HE GAVE UP										THE RESULTS					
Year Team	Lg	G	GS	CG	GF	IP	BFP	H	R	ER	HR	SH	SF	HB	TBB	IBB	SO	WP	Bk	W	L	Pct.	ShO	Sv	ERA
1993 Oneonta	A	24	0	0	11	37	175	45	29	20	3	0	1	1	17	0	21	4	0	2	1	.667	0	1	4.86
1994 Greensboro	A	39	0	0	15	62	264	55	31	17	3	2	3	3	22	0	45	4	0	2	4	.333	0	3	2.47
Albany-Colo	AA	2	0	0	0	4	14	1	0	0	0	0	0	0	1	1	4	1	0	0	0	.000	0	0	0.00
1995 Tampa	A	11	0	0	0	19	69	11	3	2	1	0	0	0	3	0	17	1	1	3	1	.750	0	0	0.95
Norwich	AA	29	0	0	13	55	250	53	35	30	2	1	2	6	27	0	33	3	0	1	0	1.000	0	0	4.91
3 Min. YEARS		105	0	0	39	177	772	165	98	69	9	3	6	10	70	1	120	13	1	8	6	.571	0	4	3.51

Tom Kramer

Pitches: Right **Bats:** Both **Pos:** P **Ht:** 6'0" **Wt:** 220 **Born:** 1/9/68 **Age:** 28

			HOW MUCH HE PITCHED				WHAT HE GAVE UP										THE RESULTS					
Year Team	Lg	G	GS	CG	GF	IP	BFP	H	R	ER	HR	SH	SF	HB	TBB	IBB	SO	WP	Bk	W	L	Pct.	ShO	Sv	ERA
1987 Burlington	R	12	11	2	1	71.2	292	57	31	24	2	0	1	1	26	0	71	0	0	7	3	.700	1	1	3.01
1988 Waterloo	A	27	27	10	0	198.2	814	173	70	56	9	10	3	3	60	3	152	5	3	14	7	.667	2	0	2.54
1989 Kinston	A	18	17	5	1	131.2	527	97	44	38	7	5	3	4	42	3	89	4	1	9	5	.643	1	0	2.60
Canton-Akrn	AA	10	8	1	0	43.1	202	58	34	30	6	3	4	0	20	0	26	3	0	1	6	.143	0	0	6.23
1990 Kinston	A	16	16	2	0	98	402	82	34	31	5	1	2	2	29	0	96	2	1	7	4	.636	1	0	2.85
Canton-Akrn	AA	12	10	2	0	72	287	67	25	24	3	2	1	0	14	1	46	1	0	6	3	.667	0	0	3.00
1991 Canton-Akrn	AA	35	5	0	13	79.1	320	61	23	21	5	6	1	1	34	3	61	3	0	7	3	.700	0	6	2.38
Colo. Sprng	AAA	10	1	0	6	11.1	45	5	1	1	1	0	0	0	5	0	18	1	0	1	0	1.000	0	0	0.79
1992 Colo. Sprng	AAA	38	3	0	11	75.2	344	88	43	41	2	4	3	1	43	2	72	0	0	8	3	.727	0	3	4.88
1994 Charlotte	AAA	13	0	0	6	19	85	15	11	10	2	2	1	0	11	1	20	2	0	1	3	.250	0	0	4.74
Indianapols	AAA	23	13	0	3	102.2	431	109	55	51	12	5	3	2	32	2	54	6	0	5	4	.556	0	0	4.47
1995 Toledo	AAA	6	5	0	0	27.1	116	23	15	14	6	0	2	0	16	0	15	0	0	3	1	.750	0	0	4.61
Chattanooga	AA	21	18	2	1	127	513	117	54	47	8	5	5	2	28	4	126	4	0	12	1	.923	0	0	3.33
1991 Cleveland	AL	4	0	0	1	4.2	30	10	9	9	1	0	3	0	6	0	4	1	0	0	0	.000	0	0	17.36
1993 Cleveland	AL	39	16	1	6	121	535	126	60	54	19	3	2	1	59	7	71	4	0	7	3	.700	0	0	4.02
8 Min. YEARS		241	134	24	42	1057.2	4376	952	440	388	68	43	29	16	360	19	846	31	5	81	43	.653	5	14	3.30
2 Maj. YEARS		43	16	1	7	125.2	565	136	69	63	20	3	5	2	65	7	75	1	0	7	3	.700	0	0	4.51

Frank Kremblas

Bats: Right **Throws:** Right **Pos:** 2B **Ht:** 5'11" **Wt:** 180 **Born:** 10/25/66 **Age:** 29

			BATTING														BASERUNNING				PERCENTAGES		
Year Team	Lg	G	AB	H	2B	3B	HR	TB	R	RBI	TBB	IBB	SO	HBP	SH	SF	SB	CS	SB%	GDP	Avg	OBP	SLG
1989 Reds	R	60	213	49	10	1	1	64	32	18	28	1	44	1	1	2	8	4	.67	5	.230	.320	.300

Year	Team	Lg	G	AB	H	2B	3B	HR	TB	R	RBI	TBB	IBB	SO	HBP	SH	SF	SB	CS	SB%	GDP	Avg	OBP	SLG
1990	Cedar Rapds	A	92	266	67	13	0	5	95	18	26	23	0	54	1	4	3	2	7	.22	7	.252	.311	.357
1991	Chattanooga	AA	102	320	77	17	0	3	103	35	41	29	1	61	2	4	2	3	4	.43	9	.241	.306	.322
1992	Chattanooga	AA	100	282	65	16	1	0	83	29	28	18	1	58	1	5	2	4	5	.44	2	.230	.277	.294
1993	Indianapols	AAA	108	341	83	15	4	8	130	38	46	42	2	78	0	3	0	7	4	.64	4	.243	.326	.381
1994	Chattanooga	AA	47	144	37	3	2	1	47	11	14	8	0	31	1	1	0	8	4	.67	3	.257	.301	.326
	Indianapols	AAA	43	150	36	9	2	1	52	21	11	10	0	42	0	2	1	2	3	.40	1	.240	.286	.347
1995	Indianapols	AAA	27	75	12	2	0	0	14	7	3	12	1	25	0	2	0	4	2	.67	2	.160	.276	.187
	Chattanooga	AA	19	67	10	2	0	1	15	8	6	7	0	10	1	0	2	1	1	.50	2	.149	.234	.224
7 Min. YEARS			598	1858	436	87	10	20	603	199	193	177	6	403	7	22	12	39	34	.53	35	.235	.302	.325

Jimmy Kremers

Bats: Left **Throws:** Right **Pos:** C **Ht:** 6' 3" **Wt:** 205 **Born:** 10/8/65 **Age:** 30

			BATTING															BASERUNNING				PERCENTAGES		
Year	Team	Lg	G	AB	H	2B	3B	HR	TB	R	RBI	TBB	IBB	SO	HBP	SH	SF	SB	CS	SB%	GDP	Avg	OBP	SLG
1988	Sumter	A	72	256	68	12	3	5	101	30	42	39	0	53	2	0	4	1	1	.50	3	.266	.362	.395
1989	Greenville	AA	121	388	91	19	1	16	160	41	58	34	5	95	0	2	2	5	5	.50	3	.235	.295	.412
1990	Richmond	AAA	63	190	44	8	0	6	70	25	24	35	1	47	1	0	1	1	0	1.00	4	.232	.352	.368
1991	Indianapols	AAA	98	290	70	14	0	11	117	34	42	40	6	97	0	5	4	2	1	.67	6	.241	.329	.403
1992	Indianapols	AAA	60	144	31	10	1	2	49	14	15	19	0	46	0	0	1	1	1	.50	4	.215	.305	.340
1993	Ottawa	AAA	4	15	3	0	0	1	6	1	2	1	1	2	0	0	0	0	0	.00	1	.200	.250	.400
	New Orleans	AAA	51	155	41	10	0	9	78	29	26	21	1	44	0	2	3	0	0	.00	1	.265	.346	.503
1994	El Paso	AA	1	1	1	1	0	0	2	0	0	0	0	0	0	0	0	0	0	1.000	0	1.000	1.000	2.000
	New Orleans	AAA	58	158	34	4	1	6	58	19	23	16	2	41	0	0	2	0	0	.00	3	.215	.287	.367
1995	Portland	AA	85	264	59	11	5	7	101	32	37	27	3	70	0	1	2	1	0	1.00	3	.223	.294	.383
1990	Atlanta	NL	29	73	8	1	1	1	14	7	2	6	1	27	0	0	0	0	0	.00	0	.110	.177	.192
8 Min. YEARS			613	1861	442	89	11	63	742	225	269	232	19	495	3	12	17	11	8	.58	28	.238	.320	.399

Jim Krevokuch

Bats: Right **Throws:** Right **Pos:** 3B **Ht:** 5'11" **Wt:** 175 **Born:** 5/13/69 **Age:** 27

			BATTING															BASERUNNING				PERCENTAGES		
Year	Team	Lg	G	AB	H	2B	3B	HR	TB	R	RBI	TBB	IBB	SO	HBP	SH	SF	SB	CS	SB%	GDP	Avg	OBP	SLG
1991	Welland	A	58	196	44	9	0	2	59	22	17	26	0	30	7	0	4	8	6	.57	4	.224	.330	.301
1992	Augusta	A	65	239	68	13	1	3	92	32	39	20	0	19	4	2	2	10	2	.83	5	.285	.347	.385
	Salem	A	51	158	48	13	0	4	73	30	20	20	1	13	4	1	1	1	1	.50	2	.304	.393	.462
1993	Carolina	AA	125	395	100	15	3	4	133	58	30	53	1	38	15	3	2	4	3	.57	10	.253	.361	.337
1994	Carolina	AA	107	335	80	17	1	4	111	35	41	22	0	42	4	2	6	2	3	.40	7	.239	.289	.331
1995	Carolina	AA	70	174	49	13	0	1	65	20	11	12	1	20	5	4	2	1	1	.50	6	.282	.342	.374
5 Min. YEARS			476	1497	389	80	5	18	533	197	158	153	3	162	39	12	17	26	16	.62	34	.260	.341	.356

Tim Kubinski

Pitches: Left **Bats:** Left **Pos:** P **Ht:** 6'4" **Wt:** 205 **Born:** 1/20/72 **Age:** 24

			HOW MUCH HE PITCHED					WHAT HE GAVE UP									THE RESULTS					
Year	Team	Lg	G	GS	CG	GF	IP	BFP	H	R	ER	HR	SH	SF	HB	TBB	IBB	SO	WP	Bk	W	L	Pct.	ShO	Sv	ERA
1993	Athletics	R	1	1	0	0	3	13	5	2	2	1	0	0	0	0	0	3	0	0	0	1	.000	0	0	6.00
	Sou. Oregon	A	12	12	1	0	70	294	67	36	22	4	2	2	6	18	0	51	2	2	5	5	.500	0	0	2.83
1994	W. Michigan	A	30	23	1	4	158.2	677	168	82	64	8	13	4	7	36	0	126	8	10	14	6	.700	0	0	3.63
1995	Edmonton	AAA	6	5	0	0	32	136	34	18	17	4	0	0	4	10	0	12	0	4	1	2	.333	0	0	4.78
	Modesto	A	25	17	0	4	109	485	126	73	60	12	6	5	8	24	0	83	10	1	6	10	.375	0	2	4.95
3 Min. YEARS			74	58	2	8	372.2	1605	400	211	165	29	21	11	25	88	0	275	20	17	26	24	.520	0	2	3.98

Jerry Kutzler

Pitches: Right **Bats:** Left **Pos:** P **Ht:** 6' 1" **Wt:** 175 **Born:** 3/25/65 **Age:** 31

			HOW MUCH HE PITCHED					WHAT HE GAVE UP									THE RESULTS					
Year	Team	Lg	G	GS	CG	GF	IP	BFP	H	R	ER	HR	SH	SF	HB	TBB	IBB	SO	WP	Bk	W	L	Pct.	ShO	Sv	ERA
1987	White Sox	R	4	3	0	0	20	83	14	13	11	1	1	1	2	7	0	16	1	0	1	1	.500	0	0	4.95
	Peninsula	A	10	9	2	1	63.2	268	53	34	29	1	2	4	3	24	1	30	2	0	5	2	.714	1	0	4.10
1988	Tampa	A	26	26	12	0	184	733	154	73	57	10	3	2	6	39	1	100	9	2	16	7	.696	4	0	2.79
1989	Birmingham	AA	14	14	4	0	99.1	423	95	50	40	5	6	2	4	27	0	85	2	1	9	4	.692	0	0	3.62
	Vancouver	AAA	12	12	2	0	80	333	76	37	34	6	6	2	7	20	1	36	0	0	5	5	.500	0	0	3.83
1990	Vancouver	AAA	19	19	2	0	113.2	491	124	64	53	8	4	6	6	34	0	73	2	1	5	7	.417	0	0	4.20
1991	Vancouver	AAA	29	24	5	2	158.1	730	199	98	89	9	7	6	9	62	4	64	5	0	5	10	.333	1	0	5.06
1992	Iowa	AAA	2	0	0	1	3	14	5	2	1	0	0	0	0	0	0	0	0	0	0	0	.000	0	0	3.00
	Winston-Sal	A	6	6	1	0	37.1	152	41	14	14	3	1	0	0	6	0	21	0	0	4	0	1.000	1	0	3.38
	Charlotte	AA	12	2	0	3	38.1	153	33	12	9	2	1	0	4	4	0	28	2	0	1	2	.333	0	0	2.11
1993	San Antonio	AA	2	0	0	0	5.2	20	3	1	1	0	1	0	0	3	1	1	1	1	1	0	1.000	0	0	1.59
	Albuquerque	AAA	35	11	0	5	100	442	124	70	62	10	6	9	2	31	1	50	4	0	5	6	.455	0	1	5.58
1994	Omaha	AAA	37	7	0	15	102.2	434	114	47	43	10	4	3	4	24	1	38	2	0	5	7	.417	0	2	3.77
1995	Omaha	AAA	37	7	0	12	103	449	128	48	46	8	3	2	5	27	2	45	0	0	8	5	.615	0	4	4.02
1990	Chicago	AL	7	7	0	0	31.1	141	38	23	21	2	1	1	0	14	1	21	1	0	2	1	.667	0	0	6.03
9 Min. YEARS			245	140	28	39	1109	4725	1163	563	489	73	44	38	48	305	11	589	30	5	70	56	.556	7	7	3.97

Kerry Lacy

Pitches: Right **Bats:** Right **Pos:** P **Ht:** 6'2" **Wt:** 195 **Born:** 8/7/72 **Age:** 23

Year	Team	Lg	G	GS	CG	GF	IP	BFP	H	R	ER	HR	SH	SF	HB	TBB	IBB	SO	WP	Bk	W	L	Pct.	ShO	Sv	ERA
1991	Butte	R	24	2	0	6	48	221	47	34	30	5	0	2	6	36	0	45	15	4	2	1	.667	0	1	5.63
1992	Gastonia	A	49	1	0	32	55.2	262	55	35	24	2	2	0	1	42	2	57	9	2	3	7	.300	0	17	3.88
1993	Charlstn-Sc	A	58	0	0	57	60	267	49	25	21	1	3	5	5	32	5	54	6	2	0	6	.000	0	36	3.15
	Charlotte	A	4	0	0	3	4.2	21	2	2	1	0	0	0	1	3	0	3	1	0	0	0	.000	0	2	1.93
1994	Tulsa	AA	41	0	0	35	63.2	270	49	30	26	4	3	2	3	37	4	46	3	1	2	6	.250	0	12	3.68
1995	Tulsa	AA	28	7	0	16	82	363	94	47	39	5	3	3	3	39	7	49	7	0	2	7	.222	0	9	4.28
	Okla. City	AAA	1	0	0	1	2.1	7	0	0	0	0	0	0	0	0	0	1	0	0	0	0	.000	0	1	0.00
	5 Min. YEARS		205	10	0	150	316.1	1411	296	173	141	17	11	12	19	189	18	255	41	9	9	27	.250	0	78	4.01

Jeff Ladd

Bats: Right **Throws:** Right **Pos:** DH **Ht:** 6'3" **Wt:** 200 **Born:** 7/10/70 **Age:** 25

Year	Team	Lg	G	AB	H	2B	3B	HR	TB	R	RBI	TBB	IBB	SO	HBP	SH	SF	SB	CS	SB%	GDP	Avg	OBP	SLG
1992	St. Cathrns	A	34	115	24	3	0	3	36	13	13	9	0	37	3	1	0	1	1	.50	4	.209	.283	.313
1993	Hagerstown	A	22	57	12	4	0	3	25	8	11	12	0	25	0	0	1	2	1	.67	0	.211	.343	.439
1994	St. Cathrns	A	59	203	66	13	0	12	115	43	44	44	2	60	3	0	1	2	1	.67	2	.325	.450	.567
	Hagerstown	A	41	140	37	4	0	8	65	20	25	21	0	48	5	1	0	4	1	.80	6	.264	.380	.464
1995	Hagerstown	A	94	311	95	17	3	19	175	54	58	78	5	94	9	0	3	6	3	.67	2	.305	.454	.563
	Knoxville	AA	9	24	7	1	1	0	10	1	2	5	0	8	1	1	0	0	0	.00	0	.292	.433	.417
	4 Min. YEARS		259	850	241	42	4	45	426	139	153	169	7	272	21	3	5	15	7	.68	14	.284	.412	.501

Cleveland Ladell

Bats: Right **Throws:** Right **Pos:** OF **Ht:** 5'11" **Wt:** 170 **Born:** 9/19/70 **Age:** 25

Year	Team	Lg	G	AB	H	2B	3B	HR	TB	R	RBI	TBB	IBB	SO	HBP	SH	SF	SB	CS	SB%	GDP	Avg	OBP	SLG
1992	Princeton	R	64	241	64	6	4	4	90	37	32	13	0	45	1	2	2	24	3	.89	1	.266	.304	.373
	Charlstn-Wv	A	8	30	6	0	0	0	6	3	0	3	0	14	0	0	0	3	1	.75	0	.200	.273	.200
1993	Winston-Sal	A	132	531	151	15	7	20	240	90	66	16	0	95	3	4	5	24	7	.77	13	.284	.306	.452
1994	Chattanooga	AA	33	99	16	4	1	1	25	9	9	4	0	26	0	0	1	4	1	.80	2	.162	.192	.253
	Winston-Sal	A	75	283	71	11	3	12	124	46	40	26	0	63	2	2	3	17	7	.71	3	.251	.315	.438
1995	Chattanooga	AA	135	517	151	28	7	5	208	76	43	39	1	88	2	4	2	28	15	.65	12	.292	.343	.402
	4 Min. YEARS		447	1701	459	64	22	42	693	261	190	101	1	331	8	12	13	100	34	.75	31	.270	.312	.407

David Lamb

Bats: Both **Throws:** Right **Pos:** SS **Ht:** 6'2" **Wt:** 165 **Born:** 6/6/75 **Age:** 21

Year	Team	Lg	G	AB	H	2B	3B	HR	TB	R	RBI	TBB	IBB	SO	HBP	SH	SF	SB	CS	SB%	GDP	Avg	OBP	SLG
1993	Orioles	R	16	56	10	1	0	0	11	4	6	10	0	8	0	0	0	2	0	1.00	1	.179	.303	.196
1994	Albany	A	92	308	74	9	2	0	87	37	29	32	0	40	2	6	0	4	1	.80	4	.240	.316	.282
1995	Bowie	AA	1	4	1	0	0	0	1	0	1	0	0	1	0	0	0	0	0	.00	0	.250	.250	.250
	Frederick	A	124	436	97	14	2	2	121	40	34	38	5	81	10	8	5	6	7	.46	10	.222	.297	.278
	3 Min. YEARS		233	804	182	24	4	2	220	81	70	80	5	130	12	14	5	12	8	.60	15	.226	.304	.274

Les Lancaster

Pitches: Right **Bats:** Right **Pos:** P **Ht:** 6' 2" **Wt:** 200 **Born:** 4/21/62 **Age:** 34

Year	Team	Lg	G	GS	CG	GF	IP	BFP	H	R	ER	HR	SH	SF	HB	TBB	IBB	SO	WP	Bk	W	L	Pct.	ShO	Sv	ERA
1985	Wytheville	R	20	10	7	8	102	433	98	49	41	6	4	3	1	24	5	81	4	0	7	4	.636	1	3	3.62
1986	Winston-Sal	A	13	13	3	0	97	396	88	37	30	4	3	4	2	30	2	52	1	1	8	3	.727	0	0	2.78
	Pittsfield	AA	14	14	2	0	88	389	105	46	41	4	2	4	5	34	2	49	2	1	5	6	.455	0	0	4.19
1987	Iowa	AAA	15	6	0	6	67	268	59	24	24	9	3	1	1	17	3	62	0	1	5	3	.625	0	4	3.22
1989	Iowa	AAA	17	14	3	0	91.1	389	76	38	27	6	4	4	3	43	0	56	2	4	5	7	.417	2	0	2.66
1990	Iowa	AAA	6	0	0	2	17.2	74	20	10	8	0	0	1	0	5	0	15	1	0	0	1	.000	0	1	4.08
1994	Syracuse	AAA	64	1	0	19	89.2	391	95	44	36	6	5	5	4	25	4	69	3	0	14	3	.824	0	3	3.61
1995	Buffalo	AAA	45	3	1	10	87.2	372	90	45	42	6	2	1	2	19	5	68	4	0	4	5	.444	0	0	4.31
1987	Chicago	NL	27	18	0	4	132.1	578	138	76	72	14	5	6	1	51	5	78	7	8	8	3	.727	0	0	4.90
1988	Chicago	NL	44	3	1	15	85.2	371	89	42	36	4	3	7	1	34	7	36	3	3	4	6	.400	0	5	3.78
1989	Chicago	NL	42	0	0	15	72.2	288	60	12	11	2	3	4	0	15	1	56	2	1	4	2	.667	0	8	1.36
1990	Chicago	NL	55	6	1	26	109	479	121	57	56	11	6	5	1	40	8	65	7	0	9	5	.643	1	6	4.62
1991	Chicago	NL	64	1	1	21	156	653	150	68	61	13	9	4	4	49	7	102	2	2	9	7	.563	0	3	3.52
1992	Detroit	AL	41	1	0	17	86.2	404	101	66	61	11	2	4	3	51	12	35	2	0	3	4	.429	0	0	6.33
1993	St. Louis	NL	50	0	0	12	61.1	259	56	24	20	5	5	1	1	21	5	36	5	0	4	1	.800	0	0	2.93
	7 Min. YEARS		194	61	16	45	640.1	2712	631	293	249	41	23	23	18	197	21	452	17	7	48	32	.600	3	11	3.50
	7 Maj. YEARS		323	39	3	110	703.2	3032	715	345	317	60	33	31	11	261	45	408	28	14	41	28	.594	1	22	4.05

Ced Landrum

Bats: Left **Throws:** Right **Pos:** OF **Ht:** 5' 7" **Wt:** 167 **Born:** 9/3/63 **Age:** 32

Year	Team	Lg	G	AB	H	2B	3B	HR	TB	R	RBI	TBB	IBB	SO	HBP	SH	SF	SB	CS	SB%	GDP	Avg	OBP	SLG
1986	Geneva	A	64	213	67	6	2	3	86	51	16	40	1	33	3	4	3	49	10	.83	1	.315	.425	.404

Year	Team	Lg	G	AB	H	2B	3B	HR	TB	R	RBI	TBB	IBB	SO	HBP	SH	SF	SB	CS	SB%	GDP	Avg	OBP	SLG
1987	Winston-Sal	A	126	458	129	13	7	4	168	82	49	78	3	50	6	1	4	79	18	.81	6	.282	.390	.367
1988	Pittsfield	AA	128	445	109	15	8	1	143	82	39	55	2	63	8	10	4	69	17	.80	4	.245	.336	.321
1989	Charlotte	AA	123	361	92	11	2	6	125	72	37	48	0	54	5	5	2	45	9	.83	4	.255	.349	.346
1990	Iowa	AAA	123	372	110	10	4	0	128	71	24	43	1	63	1	5	3	46	16	.74	4	.296	.368	.344
1991	Iowa	AAA	38	131	44	8	2	1	59	14	11	5	0	21	0	2	0	13	4	.76	2	.336	.360	.450
1992	Iowa	AAA	8	20	6	0	0	0	6	4	0	4	0	1	1	0	0	1	1	.50	0	.300	.440	.300
	Denver	AAA	43	144	45	7	0	1	55	20	19	13	0	16	0	4	2	15	9	.63	1	.313	.365	.382
1993	Portland	AAA	4	4	0	0	0	0	0	0	0	0	0	0	0	0	0	1	0	1.00	0	.000	.000	.000
	Norfolk	AAA	69	275	80	13	5	5	118	39	29	19	2	30	1	3	0	16	6	.73	5	.291	.339	.429
1995	Colo. Sprng	AAA	82	166	43	5	2	2	58	31	19	11	1	29	1	5	2	12	5	.71	2	.259	.306	.349
1991	Chicago	NL	56	86	20	2	1	0	24	28	6	10	0	18	0	3	0	27	5	.84	2	.233	.313	.279
1993	New York	NL	22	19	5	1	0	0	6	2	1	0	0	5	0	1	0	0	0	.00	0	.263	.263	.316
	9 Min. YEARS		808	2589	725	88	32	23	946	466	243	316	10	360	26	39	20	346	95	.78	29	.280	.362	.365
	2 Maj. YEARS		78	105	25	3	1	0	30	30	7	10	0	23	0	4	0	27	5	.84	2	.238	.304	.286

Tito Landrum

Bats: Right **Throws:** Right **Pos:** OF   **Ht:** 6'4" **Wt:** 210 **Born:** 8/26/70 **Age:** 25

			BATTING															BASERUNNING				PERCENTAGES		
Year	Team	Lg	G	AB	H	2B	3B	HR	TB	R	RBI	TBB	IBB	SO	HBP	SH	SF	SB	CS	SB%	GDP	Avg	OBP	SLG
1991	Great Falls	R	57	189	50	8	4	5	81	36	25	25	0	43	2	0	1	9	5	.64	1	.265	.355	.429
1992	Yakima	A	62	226	57	7	3	7	91	36	34	24	0	63	4	0	2	6	4	.60	6	.252	.332	.403
1993	Vero Beach	A	116	396	92	13	2	9	136	50	42	41	1	95	9	5	4	8	6	.57	5	.232	.316	.343
1994	Bakersfield	A	87	327	80	13	1	16	143	49	50	20	1	83	7	0	2	11	8	.58	3	.245	.301	.437
1995	San Antonio	AA	87	260	62	13	1	8	101	42	25	26	0	64	7	0	2	5	6	.45	9	.238	.322	.388
	5 Min. YEARS		409	1398	341	54	11	45	552	213	176	136	2	348	29	5	11	39	29	.57	24	.244	.321	.395

Todd Landry

Bats: Right **Throws:** Left **Pos:** 1B   **Ht:** 6'4" **Wt:** 215 **Born:** 8/21/72 **Age:** 23

			BATTING															BASERUNNING				PERCENTAGES		
Year	Team	Lg	G	AB	H	2B	3B	HR	TB	R	RBI	TBB	IBB	SO	HBP	SH	SF	SB	CS	SB%	GDP	Avg	OBP	SLG
1993	Helena	R	29	124	39	10	1	5	66	27	24	8	1	20	2	0	1	5	0	1.00	1	.315	.363	.532
	Beloit	A	38	149	45	6	0	4	63	26	24	4	0	36	0	0	2	4	4	.50	6	.302	.316	.423
1994	Stockton	A	105	356	95	12	6	8	143	55	49	28	0	53	5	4	4	4	1	.80	10	.267	.326	.402
1995	El Paso	AA	132	511	149	33	4	16	238	76	79	33	1	100	7	2	4	9	7	.56	21	.292	.341	.466
	3 Min. YEARS		304	1140	328	61	11	33	510	184	176	73	2	209	14	6	11	22	12	.65	39	.288	.335	.447

Aaron Lane

Pitches: Left **Bats:** Left **Pos:** P   **Ht:** 6'1" **Wt:** 180 **Born:** 6/2/71 **Age:** 25

			HOW MUCH HE PITCHED					WHAT HE GAVE UP												THE RESULTS				
Year	Team	Lg	G	GS	CG	GF	IP	BFP	H	R	ER	HR	SH	SF	HB	TBB	IBB	SO	WP	Bk	W	L	Pct.	ShO	Sv	ERA
1992	Bluefield	R	14	7	0	1	45	195	36	24	15	7	2	0	0	24	0	39	3	1	5	1	.833	0	0	3.00
1993	Albany	A	29	11	0	8	76	359	92	62	42	6	6	1	6	42	2	48	6	5	2	10	.167	0	0	4.97
1994	Albany	A	35	0	0	30	54.2	232	42	20	14	0	1	3	2	24	0	56	4	3	3	2	.600	0	11	2.30
	Frederick	A	5	0	0	5	7.1	32	10	3	3	1	0	0	0	3	0	6	1	0	1	1	.500	0	2	3.68
1995	Rochester	AAA	9	0	0	2	10	47	11	11	7	2	0	0	2	5	0	9	2	0	0	0	.000	0	0	6.30
	Bowie	AA	40	0	0	18	45.1	200	45	23	21	2	5	0	1	21	3	31	3	1	5	3	.625	0	2	4.17
	4 Min. YEARS		132	18	0	64	238.1	1065	236	143	102	18	14	4	11	119	5	189	19	10	16	17	.485	0	15	3.85

Dan Lane

Bats: Right **Throws:** Right **Pos:** SS   **Ht:** 6'2" **Wt:** 180 **Born:** 12/5/69 **Age:** 26

			BATTING															BASERUNNING				PERCENTAGES		
Year	Team	Lg	G	AB	H	2B	3B	HR	TB	R	RBI	TBB	IBB	SO	HBP	SH	SF	SB	CS	SB%	GDP	Avg	OBP	SLG
1992	Jamestown	A	56	182	49	16	2	6	87	36	27	16	0	32	2	1	0	3	1	.75	6	.269	.335	.478
1993	W. Palm Bch	A	66	193	44	9	0	2	59	25	24	26	3	31	2	4	1	2	2	.50	5	.228	.324	.306
1994	Harrisburg	AA	28	63	15	2	0	2	23	9	5	4	0	15	0	1	0	0	2	.00	2	.238	.284	.365
	W. Palm Bch	A	65	226	64	13	1	5	94	26	23	19	0	41	0	3	1	3	3	.50	6	.283	.337	.416
1995	Harrisburg	AA	39	81	10	1	0	0	11	5	1	3	0	21	3	1	0	0	1	.00	3	.123	.184	.136
	4 Min. YEARS		254	745	182	41	3	15	274	101	80	68	3	140	7	10	2	8	9	.47	22	.244	.313	.368

Gregg Langbehn

Pitches: Left **Bats:** Right **Pos:** P   **Ht:** 5'11" **Wt:** 182 **Born:** 11/14/69 **Age:** 26

			HOW MUCH HE PITCHED					WHAT HE GAVE UP												THE RESULTS				
Year	Team	Lg	G	GS	CG	GF	IP	BFP	H	R	ER	HR	SH	SF	HB	TBB	IBB	SO	WP	Bk	W	L	Pct.	ShO	Sv	ERA
1988	Kingsport	R	7	4	0	1	28.1	124	26	15	11	2	0	2	0	11	0	29	3	1	3	3	.500	0	0	3.49
1989	Pittsfield	A	14	14	3	0	100	406	76	33	20	1	8	3	2	35	3	70	2	0	10	3	.769	2	0	1.80
1990	Columbia	A	26	25	7	1	174	732	165	84	64	6	6	3	5	59	1	132	9	0	13	11	.542	2	0	3.31
1991	St. Lucie	A	27	27	1	0	175.1	702	149	53	49	7	5	4	4	44	3	106	7	1	10	12	.455	0	0	2.52
1992	Binghamton	AA	52	1	0	30	71	307	63	31	25	2	3	2	4	41	3	45	3	0	5	5	.500	0	9	3.17
1993	Norfolk	AAA	49	0	0	16	69.2	319	76	46	42	5	3	2	3	34	3	58	4	1	2	2	.500	0	2	5.43
1994	Norfolk	AAA	19	0	0	6	19	81	13	8	6	1	1	0	1	14	2	11	2	0	0	0	.000	0	0	2.84
	Binghamton	AA	32	0	0	10	46.1	213	45	31	28	2	1	2	5	28	2	42	0	0	3	3	.500	0	2	5.44
1995	Pawtucket	AAA	7	0	0	0	2	12	0	0	0	0	0	1	0	6	0	1	1	0	0	0	.000	0	0	0.00
	Trenton	AA	14	0	0	2	13.1	57	9	9	8	0	0	0	1	9	0	11	0	0	0	1	.000	0	0	5.40
	El Paso	AA	16	0	0	3	22.1	97	19	16	13	6	0	1	1	12	1	20	2	0	2	1	.667	0	0	5.24
	8 Min. YEARS		263	71	11	69	721.1	3050	641	326	266	32	27	21	26	293	18	525	33	3	48	43	.527	4	14	3.32

167

Eduardo Lantigua

Bats: Right **Throws:** Right **Pos:** OF **Ht:** 6'0" **Wt:** 198 **Born:** 9/4/73 **Age:** 22

Year	Team	Lg	G	AB	H	2B	3B	HR	TB	R	RBI	TBB	IBB	SO	HBP	SH	SF	SB	CS	SB%	GDP	Avg	OBP	SLG
1992	Dodgers	R	20	70	22	7	3	1	38	11	15	1	0	24	1	1	3	1	0	1.00	2	.314	.320	.543
	Great Falls	R	25	91	25	5	3	1	39	17	14	10	0	21	3	1	1	3	2	.60	1	.275	.362	.429
1993	Vero Beach	A	119	439	119	16	4	10	173	70	79	31	1	107	10	1	7	10	2	.83	15	.271	.329	.394
1994	Bakersfield	A	53	208	48	7	3	5	76	25	23	7	1	46	2	0	3	3	4	.43	3	.231	.259	.365
	Kinston	A	68	236	60	9	3	11	108	33	35	23	1	50	5	1	0	8	7	.53	6	.254	.333	.458
1995	Canton-Akrn	AA	13	46	9	2	0	1	14	5	4	1	0	14	1	1	0	0	0	.00	2	.196	.229	.304
	Columbus	A	23	87	21	5	0	1	29	13	10	4	1	20	2	0	1	2	1	.67	2	.241	.287	.333
	Sioux Falls	IND	40	135	36	6	1	5	59	19	15	10	1	31	1	1	0	4	0	1.00	3	.267	.322	.437
	4 Min. YEARS		361	1312	340	57	17	35	536	193	195	87	5	313	25	6	15	31	16	.66	34	.259	.314	.409

Andy Larkin

Pitches: Right **Bats:** Right **Pos:** P **Ht:** 6'4" **Wt:** 181 **Born:** 6/27/74 **Age:** 22

Year	Team	Lg	G	GS	CG	GF	IP	BFP	H	R	ER	HR	SH	SF	HB	TBB	IBB	SO	WP	Bk	W	L	Pct.	ShO	Sv	ERA
1992	Marlins	R	14	4	0	2	41.1	187	41	26	24	0	1	1	7	19	0	20	4	0	1	2	.333	0	2	5.23
1993	Elmira	A	14	14	4	0	88	368	74	43	29	1	1	3	12	23	0	89	9	1	5	7	.417	1	0	2.97
1994	Kane County	A	21	21	3	0	140	577	125	53	44	6	3	3	19	27	0	125	4	0	9	7	.563	1	0	2.83
1995	Portland	AA	9	9	0	0	40	160	29	16	15	5	4	0	6	11	2	23	1	0	1	2	.333	0	0	3.38
	4 Min. YEARS		58	48	7	2	309.1	1292	269	138	112	12	9	7	44	80	2	257	18	1	16	18	.471	2	2	3.26

Greg Larocca

Bats: Right **Throws:** Right **Pos:** SS **Ht:** 5'11" **Wt:** 185 **Born:** 11/10/72 **Age:** 23

Year	Team	Lg	G	AB	H	2B	3B	HR	TB	R	RBI	TBB	IBB	SO	HBP	SH	SF	SB	CS	SB%	GDP	Avg	OBP	SLG
1994	Spokane	A	42	158	46	9	2	0	59	20	14	14	0	18	2	2	0	7	2	.78	4	.291	.356	.373
	Rancho Cuca	A	28	85	14	5	1	1	24	7	8	7	0	11	2	1	1	3	1	.75	2	.165	.242	.282
1995	Rancho Cuca	A	125	466	150	36	5	8	220	77	74	44	0	77	12	0	2	15	4	.79	13	.322	.393	.472
	Memphis	AA	2	7	1	0	0	0	1	0	0	0	0	1	0	0	0	0	1	.00	1	.143	.143	.143
	2 Min. YEARS		197	716	211	50	8	9	304	104	96	65	0	107	16	3	3	25	8	.76	20	.295	.365	.425

Edgardo Larregui

Bats: Right **Throws:** Right **Pos:** OF **Ht:** 6'0" **Wt:** 185 **Born:** 12/1/72 **Age:** 23

Year	Team	Lg	G	AB	H	2B	3B	HR	TB	R	RBI	TBB	IBB	SO	HBP	SH	SF	SB	CS	SB%	GDP	Avg	OBP	SLG
1990	Huntington	R	34	102	19	3	0	2	28	13	16	7	0	12	0	2	3	3	0	1.00	1	.186	.232	.275
1991	Geneva	A	71	269	67	12	2	1	86	34	28	16	0	29	5	2	2	13	3	.81	10	.249	.301	.320
1992	Peoria	A	129	478	137	24	2	5	180	62	71	30	1	68	4	9	4	15	6	.71	12	.287	.331	.377
1993	Daytona	A	95	329	78	10	5	2	104	26	34	15	0	24	2	5	2	1	11	.08	13	.237	.273	.316
1994	Daytona	A	74	283	82	12	2	6	116	40	51	21	0	32	1	0	2	6	9	.40	10	.290	.339	.410
	Orlando	AA	35	111	32	2	1	0	36	14	7	5	0	13	1	2	1	3	6	.33	0	.288	.322	.324
1995	Orlando	AA	122	423	127	18	1	11	180	55	60	32	2	39	1	0	4	3	10	.23	15	.300	.348	.426
	6 Min. YEARS		560	1995	542	81	13	27	730	244	267	126	3	217	14	20	18	44	45	.49	61	.272	.317	.366

Chris Latham

Bats: Both **Throws:** Right **Pos:** OF **Ht:** 5'11" **Wt:** 174 **Born:** 5/26/73 **Age:** 23

Year	Team	Lg	G	AB	H	2B	3B	HR	TB	R	RBI	TBB	IBB	SO	HBP	SH	SF	SB	CS	SB%	GDP	Avg	OBP	SLG
1991	Dodgers	R	43	109	26	2	1	0	30	17	11	16	0	45	0	0	0	14	4	.78	0	.239	.333	.275
1992	Great Falls	R	17	37	12	2	0	0	14	8	3	8	0	8	0	0	1	1	1	.50	0	.324	.444	.378
	Dodgers	R	14	48	11	2	0	0	13	4	2	5	1	17	0	1	1	2	3	.40	0	.229	.296	.271
1993	Yakima	A	54	192	50	2	6	4	76	46	17	39	0	53	1	0	0	24	9	.73	2	.260	.388	.396
	Bakersfield	A	6	27	5	1	0	0	6	1	3	4	0	5	0	0	0	2	2	.50	2	.185	.290	.222
1994	Bakersfield	A	52	191	41	5	2	2	56	29	15	28	0	49	2	4	0	28	7	.80	2	.215	.321	.293
	Yakima	A	71	288	98	19	8	5	148	69	32	55	7	66	2	3	0	33	20	.62	1	.340	.449	.514
1995	Vero Beach	A	71	259	74	13	4	6	113	53	39	56	4	54	2	2	3	42	11	.79	2	.286	.413	.436
	San Antonio	AA	58	214	64	14	5	9	115	38	37	33	0	59	2	1	1	11	11	.50	2	.299	.396	.537
	Albuquerque	AAA	5	18	3	0	1	0	5	2	3	1	0	4	0	0	1	1	0	1.00	0	.167	.200	.278
	5 Min. YEARS		391	1383	384	60	27	26	576	267	162	245	13	360	9	11	7	158	68	.70	11	.278	.388	.416

Sean Lawrence

Pitches: Left **Bats:** Left **Pos:** P **Ht:** 6'4" **Wt:** 215 **Born:** 9/2/70 **Age:** 25

Year	Team	Lg	G	GS	CG	GF	IP	BFP	H	R	ER	HR	SH	SF	HB	TBB	IBB	SO	WP	Bk	W	L	Pct.	ShO	Sv	ERA
1992	Welland	A	15	15	0	0	74	330	75	55	43	10	2	2	2	34	1	71	6	3	3	6	.333	0	0	5.23
1993	Augusta	A	22	22	0	0	121	516	108	59	42	9	7	4	4	50	1	96	6	0	6	8	.429	0	0	3.12
	Salem	A	4	4	0	0	15	77	25	19	17	1	2	1	0	9	0	14	2	0	1	3	.250	0	0	10.20
1994	Salem	A	12	12	0	0	72	312	76	38	21	8	1	2	3	18	0	66	2	0	4	2	.667	0	0	2.63
1995	Carolina	AA	12	3	0	3	21.1	96	27	13	13	2	0	1	1	8	1	19	0	0	0	2	.000	0	0	5.48

Year	Team	Lg	G	GS	CG	GF	IP	BFP	H	R	ER	HR	SH	SF	HB	TBB	IBB	SO	WP	Bk	W	L	Pct.	ShO	Sv	ERA
	Lynchburg	A	20	19	0	0	111	465	115	56	52	16	3	3	1	25	0	82	3	0	5	8	.385	0	0	4.22
	4 Min. YEARS		85	75	0	3	414.1	1796	426	240	188	46	15	12	11	144	3	348	19	3	19	29	.396	0	0	4.08

Tim Layana

Pitches: Right **Bats:** Right **Pos:** P   **Ht:** 6' 2" **Wt:** 190 **Born:** 3/2/64 **Age:** 32

			HOW MUCH HE PITCHED						WHAT HE GAVE UP												THE RESULTS					
Year	Team	Lg	G	GS	CG	GF	IP	BFP	H	R	ER	HR	SH	SF	HB	TBB	IBB	SO	WP	Bk	W	L	Pct.	ShO	Sv	ERA
1986	Oneonta	A	3	3	0	0	19	71	10	5	5	1	1	0	1	5	0	24	1	0	2	0	1.000	0	0	2.37
	Ft. Laud	A	11	10	3	1	68.1	276	59	19	17	1	2	0	4	19	1	52	5	1	5	4	.556	1	1	2.24
1987	Albany-Colo	AA	8	7	1	1	46.1	195	51	28	26	4	2	1	2	18	0	19	1	1	2	4	.333	0	0	5.05
	Pr. William	A	7	3	0	2	22.2	111	29	22	16	3	1	2	1	11	0	17	5	2	2	1	.667	0	0	6.35
	Columbus	AAA	13	13	0	0	70	310	77	37	37	6	3	1	1	37	2	36	3	0	4	5	.444	0	0	4.76
1988	Albany-Colo	AA	14	14	1	0	87	378	90	52	42	3	3	3	6	30	2	42	2	8	5	7	.417	0	0	4.34
	Columbus	AAA	11	9	0	0	47.2	216	54	34	32	2	0	1	6	25	0	25	2	4	1	7	.125	0	0	6.04
1989	Albany-Colo	AA	40	1	0	37	67.2	261	53	17	13	2	5	1	3	15	3	48	2	4	7	4	.636	0	17	1.73
1991	Nashville	AAA	26	2	0	4	47.1	210	41	17	17	3	3	0	2	28	0	43	5	1	3	1	.750	0	1	3.23
1992	Rochester	AAA	41	3	0	28	72.1	323	79	45	43	4	4	4	4	38	6	48	14	0	3	3	.500	0	4	5.35
1993	Phoenix	AAA	55	0	0	38	67.1	306	80	42	36	5	4	6	5	24	4	55	8	2	3	2	.600	0	9	4.81
1994	San Bernrdo	A	11	0	0	11	15.1	71	10	11	4	0	1	0	2	9	1	17	2	0	1	3	.250	0	3	2.35
	Ottawa	AAA	42	0	0	19	59	280	72	47	33	6	6	3	2	28	6	35	4	1	1	5	.167	0	1	5.03
1995	Ottawa	AAA	26	0	0	9	36	178	56	35	34	7	1	2	2	20	1	27	4	0	1	1	.500	0	4	8.50
1990	Cincinnati	NL	55	0	0	17	80	344	71	33	31	7	4	3	2	44	5	53	5	4	5	3	.625	0	2	3.49
1991	Cincinnati	NL	22	0	0	9	20.2	95	23	18	16	1	1	0	0	11	0	14	3	0	0	2	.000	0	0	6.97
1993	San Francisco	NL	1	0	0	0	2	15	7	5	5	1	1	1	0	1	1	1	0	0	0	0	.000	0	0	22.50
	9 Min. YEARS		308	65	5	150	726	3186	761	411	355	47	36	24	41	307	26	488	58	24	40	47	.460	1	40	4.40
	3 Maj. YEARS		78	0	0	26	102.2	454	101	56	52	9	6	3	2	56	6	68	8	4	5	5	.500	0	2	4.56

Jalal Leach

Bats: Left **Throws:** Left **Pos:** OF   **Ht:** 6'2" **Wt:** 200 **Born:** 3/14/69 **Age:** 27

			BATTING													BASERUNNING				PERCENTAGES		
Year	Team	Lg	G	AB	H	2B	3B	HR	TB	R	RBI	TBB	IBB	SO	HBP	SH	SF	SB	CS	SB%	GDP	Avg	OBP	SLG
1990	Oneonta	A	69	257	74	7	1	2	89	41	18	37	3	52	0	4	0	33	13	.72	1	.288	.378	.346
1991	Ft. Laud	A	122	468	119	13	9	2	156	48	42	44	3	122	0	3	3	28	12	.70	5	.254	.317	.333
1992	Pr. William	A	128	462	122	22	7	5	173	61	65	47	2	114	0	3	5	18	9	.67	8	.264	.329	.374
1993	Albany-Colo	AA	125	457	129	19	9	14	208	66	79	47	3	113	1	0	4	16	12	.57	5	.282	.348	.455
1994	Columbus	AAA	132	444	116	18	9	6	170	56	56	39	3	106	1	3	4	14	12	.54	8	.261	.320	.383
1995	Columbus	AAA	88	272	66	12	5	6	106	37	31	22	1	60	2	1	4	11	4	.73	5	.243	.300	.390
	6 Min. YEARS		664	2360	626	91	40	35	902	307	291	236	15	567	4	14	20	120	62	.66	32	.265	.331	.382

Pat Leahy

Pitches: Right **Bats:** Right **Pos:** P   **Ht:** 6'6" **Wt:** 245 **Born:** 10/31/70 **Age:** 25

			HOW MUCH HE PITCHED						WHAT HE GAVE UP												THE RESULTS					
Year	Team	Lg	G	GS	CG	GF	IP	BFP	H	R	ER	HR	SH	SF	HB	TBB	IBB	SO	WP	Bk	W	L	Pct.	ShO	Sv	ERA
1992	Erie	A	26	0	0	18	37	153	37	11	7	3	2	2	2	12	0	27	3	1	2	0	1.000	0	5	1.70
1993	Kane County	A	25	25	2	0	139.2	594	124	68	50	6	9	3	23	43	2	106	12	7	8	11	.421	0	0	3.22
1994	Brevard Cty	A	13	12	0	0	84	340	72	32	29	4	1	4	7	18	0	59	7	1	7	3	.700	0	0	3.11
	Portland	AA	17	8	0	6	49.2	233	59	39	27	5	3	2	6	19	3	32	9	1	1	6	.143	0	0	4.89
1995	Portland	AA	13	6	0	1	42	175	32	24	21	5	5	1	1	20	3	37	2	0	3	1	.750	0	0	4.50
	Brevard Cty	A	11	11	0	0	46.1	200	41	29	20	6	1	2	5	22	1	43	2	0	4	4	.500	0	0	3.88
	4 Min. YEARS		105	62	2	25	398.2	1695	365	203	154	29	21	14	44	134	9	304	35	10	25	25	.500	0	5	3.48

Bob Leary

Bats: Left **Throws:** Left **Pos:** 1B   **Ht:** 6'3" **Wt:** 195 **Born:** 7/9/71 **Age:** 24

			BATTING													BASERUNNING				PERCENTAGES		
Year	Team	Lg	G	AB	H	2B	3B	HR	TB	R	RBI	TBB	IBB	SO	HBP	SH	SF	SB	CS	SB%	GDP	Avg	OBP	SLG
1991	Athletics	R	59	213	69	11	1	2	88	42	44	51	1	21	3	1	4	2	2	.50	4	.324	.454	.413
1992	Madison	A	116	365	93	18	3	4	129	47	48	66	4	64	4	3	3	3	3	.50	10	.255	.372	.353
1993	Madison	A	8	28	4	0	0	0	4	2	0	2	0	10	0	0	0	0	0	.00	0	.143	.200	.143
1994	Sioux City	IND	77	289	89	24	3	12	155	42	61	43	4	61	1	2	5	10	4	.71	3	.308	.393	.536
1995	Lynchburg	A	63	208	54	9	0	8	87	42	31	44	4	43	5	0	2	9	4	.69	3	.260	.398	.418
	Carolina	AA	67	243	74	14	3	6	112	38	42	40	2	38	3	0	3	3	3	.50	7	.305	.405	.461
	5 Min. YEARS		390	1346	383	76	10	32	575	213	226	246	15	237	16	6	17	27	16	.63	27	.285	.397	.427

Derek Lee

Bats: Left **Throws:** Right **Pos:** OF   **Ht:** 6' 1" **Wt:** 200 **Born:** 7/28/66 **Age:** 29

			BATTING													BASERUNNING				PERCENTAGES		
Year	Team	Lg	G	AB	H	2B	3B	HR	TB	R	RBI	TBB	IBB	SO	HBP	SH	SF	SB	CS	SB%	GDP	Avg	OBP	SLG
1988	Utica	A	76	252	86	7	5	2	109	51	47	50	5	48	3	3	4	54	15	.78	2	.341	.450	.433
1989	South Bend	A	125	448	128	24	7	11	199	89	48	87	4	83	9	4	2	45	26	.63	5	.286	.410	.444
1990	Birmingham	AA	126	411	105	21	3	7	153	68	75	71	5	93	6	3	5	14	10	.58	8	.255	.369	.372
1991	Birmingham	AA	45	154	50	10	2	5	79	36	16	46	5	23	6	0	1	9	7	.56	1	.325	.493	.513
	Vancouver	AAA	87	319	94	28	5	6	150	54	44	35	2	62	2	3	1	4	2	.67	1	.295	.367	.470
1992	Vancouver	AAA	115	381	104	20	6	7	157	58	50	56	7	65	6	4	2	17	7	.71	11	.273	.373	.412
1993	Portland	AAA	106	381	120	30	7	10	194	79	80	60	2	51	4	4	4	16	5	.76	10	.315	.410	.509
1994	Ottawa	AAA	131	463	139	35	9	13	231	62	75	66	9	81	2	0	6	12	6	.67	7	.300	.385	.499

Year	Team	Lg	G	AB	H	2B	3B	HR	TB	R	RBI	TBB	IBB	SO	HBP	SH	SF	SB	CS	SB%	GDP	Avg	OBP	SLG
1995	Norfolk	AAA	112	351	89	17	0	18	160	56	60	48	4	62	7	2	5	11	6	.65	11	.254	.350	.456
1993	Minnesota	AL	15	33	5	1	0	0	6	3	4	1	0	4	0	0	0	0	0	.00	0	.152	.176	.182
	8 Min. YEARS		923	3160	915	192	44	79	1432	553	495	519	43	568	45	23	30	182	84	.68	56	.290	.394	.453

Derrek Lee

Bats: Right Throws: Right Pos: 1B   Ht: 6'5" Wt: 205 Born: 9/6/75 Age: 20

					BATTING													BASERUNNING				PERCENTAGES		
Year	Team	Lg	G	AB	H	2B	3B	HR	TB	R	RBI	TBB	IBB	SO	HBP	SH	SF	SB	CS	SB%	GDP	Avg	OBP	SLG
1993	Padres	R	15	52	17	1	1	2	26	11	5	6	1	7	0	0	0	4	0	1.00	1	.327	.397	.500
	Rancho Cuca	A	20	73	20	5	1	1	30	13	10	10	0	20	1	0	0	0	2	.00	0	.274	.369	.411
1994	Rancho Cuca	A	126	442	118	19	2	8	165	66	53	42	2	95	7	0	6	18	14	.56	11	.267	.336	.373
1995	Rancho Cuca	A	128	502	151	25	2	23	249	82	95	49	2	130	7	0	7	14	7	.67	8	.301	.366	.496
	Memphis	AA	2	9	1	0	0	0	1	0	1	0	0	2	0	0	0	0	0	.00	0	.111	.111	.111
	3 Min. YEARS		291	1078	307	50	6	34	471	172	164	107	5	254	15	0	13	36	23	.61	20	.285	.354	.437

Phil Leftwich

Pitches: Right Bats: Right Pos: P   Ht: 6'5" Wt: 205 Born: 5/19/69 Age: 27

				HOW MUCH HE PITCHED						WHAT HE GAVE UP									THE RESULTS				
Year	Team	Lg	G	GS	CG	GF	IP	BFP	H	R	ER	HR	SH	SF	HB	TBB	IBB	SO	WP	Bk	W	L	Pct.	ShO	Sv	ERA
1990	Boise	A	15	15	0	0	92	373	88	36	19	0	0	4	1	23	1	81	3	2	8	2	.800	0	0	1.86
1991	Quad City	A	26	26	5	0	173	716	158	70	63	6	7	2	3	59	0	163	8	2	11	9	.550	1	0	3.28
	Midland	AA	1	1	0	0	6	27	5	2	2	0	0	0	0	5	0	3	0	0	1	0	1.000	0	0	3.00
1992	Midland	AA	21	21	0	0	121	546	156	90	79	10	6	3	4	37	1	85	2	1	6	9	.400	0	0	5.88
1993	Vancouver	AAA	20	20	3	0	126	552	138	74	65	8	3	4	2	45	1	102	4	0	7	7	.500	1	0	4.64
1994	Lk Elsinore	A	1	1	0	0	6	20	3	0	0	0	1	0	0	1	0	4	0	0	1	0	1.000	0	0	0.00
1995	Angels	R	4	4	0	0	20	76	13	4	1	0	0	2	0	2	0	32	0	0	1	1	.500	0	0	0.45
	Vancouver	AAA	6	5	1	0	36.2	142	28	13	13	4	2	1	0	9	0	25	3	0	2	0	1.000	0	0	3.19
1993	California	AL	12	12	1	0	80.2	343	81	35	34	5	3	1	3	27	1	31	1	0	4	6	.400	0	0	3.79
1994	California	AL	20	20	0	0	114	499	127	75	72	16	2	4	3	42	2	67	3	1	5	10	.333	0	0	5.68
	6 Min. YEARS		94	93	9	0	580.2	2452	589	289	242	28	19	16	10	181	3	495	20	5	37	28	.569	2	0	3.75
	2 Maj. YEARS		32	32	2	0	194.2	842	208	110	106	21	5	5	6	69	3	98	4	1	9	16	.360	0	0	4.90

Kevin Legault

Pitches: Right Bats: Right Pos: P   Ht: 6'1" Wt: 200 Born: 3/5/71 Age: 25

				HOW MUCH HE PITCHED						WHAT HE GAVE UP									THE RESULTS				
Year	Team	Lg	G	GS	CG	GF	IP	BFP	H	R	ER	HR	SH	SF	HB	TBB	IBB	SO	WP	Bk	W	L	Pct.	ShO	Sv	ERA
1992	Elizabethtn	R	17	2	0	6	55.2	221	38	20	13	0	4	2	1	11	0	53	1	0	7	0	1.000	0	2	2.10
1993	Fort Wayne	A	12	0	0	3	26.2	120	28	13	10	1	0	0	2	12	1	28	4	3	1	1	.500	0	2	3.38
	Fort Myers	A	18	18	3	0	110.1	493	142	80	70	4	1	4	4	32	1	60	4	0	3	9	.250	0	0	5.71
1994	Fort Myers	A	26	26	1	0	154.2	693	196	87	73	8	6	4	5	52	5	68	9	0	7	11	.389	0	0	4.25
1995	New Britain	AA	47	1	0	17	87	367	79	31	31	3	6	5	4	28	4	52	5	0	6	1	.857	0	3	3.21
	4 Min. YEARS		120	47	4	26	434.1	1894	483	231	197	16	17	15	17	135	11	261	23	3	24	22	.522	0	7	4.08

Keith Legree

Bats: Left Throws: Right Pos: OF   Ht: 6'2" Wt: 195 Born: 12/26/71 Age: 24

					BATTING													BASERUNNING				PERCENTAGES		
Year	Team	Lg	G	AB	H	2B	3B	HR	TB	R	RBI	TBB	IBB	SO	HBP	SH	SF	SB	CS	SB%	GDP	Avg	OBP	SLG
1991	Twins	R	45	165	49	5	5	1	67	33	17	21	0	38	2	0	2	15	3	.83	2	.297	.379	.406
1992	Elizabethtn	R	44	173	45	10	3	6	79	34	43	22	0	42	1	1	5	1	3	.25	1	.260	.338	.457
1993	Fort Wayne	A	49	178	43	6	2	3	62	28	14	21	2	51	3	0	0	1	2	.33	5	.242	.332	.348
1994	Fort Myers	A	55	186	45	8	1	4	67	16	15	23	1	52	1	0	2	8	3	.73	6	.242	.325	.360
1995	New Britain	AA	43	110	22	2	0	0	24	10	6	21	0	33	0	0	0	3	1	.75	3	.200	.328	.218
	5 Min. YEARS		236	812	204	31	11	14	299	121	95	108	3	216	7	1	9	28	12	.70	17	.251	.341	.368

Toby Lehman

Pitches: Right Bats: Right Pos: P   Ht: 6'0" Wt: 200 Born: 8/12/71 Age: 24

				HOW MUCH HE PITCHED						WHAT HE GAVE UP									THE RESULTS				
Year	Team	Lg	G	GS	CG	GF	IP	BFP	H	R	ER	HR	SH	SF	HB	TBB	IBB	SO	WP	Bk	W	L	Pct.	ShO	Sv	ERA
1992	White Sox	R	9	7	0	1	38	156	19	11	4	0	1	0	3	18	0	38	4	1	4	1	.800	0	1	0.95
1993	Hickory	A	39	7	1	25	102.2	455	84	49	40	6	3	7	12	57	1	91	9	2	4	3	.571	0	7	3.51
1994	South Bend	A	34	16	0	7	120.2	533	113	70	56	7	4	6	8	65	0	78	8	2	9	5	.643	0	4	4.18
1995	Bowie	AA	4	4	0	0	17	77	20	15	15	4	0	0	0	11	0	14	0	0	1	3	.250	0	0	7.94
	Frederick	A	19	10	1	2	55	237	44	30	26	9	3	1	3	27	1	48	6	0	0	5	.000	0	0	4.25
	4 Min. YEARS		105	44	2	35	333.1	1458	280	175	141	26	11	14	26	178	2	269	27	5	18	17	.514	0	12	3.81

Tim Leiper

Bats: Left Throws: Right Pos: OF   Ht: 5'11" Wt: 175 Born: 7/19/66 Age: 29

					BATTING													BASERUNNING				PERCENTAGES		
Year	Team	Lg	G	AB	H	2B	3B	HR	TB	R	RBI	TBB	IBB	SO	HBP	SH	SF	SB	CS	SB%	GDP	Avg	OBP	SLG
1985	Gastonia	A	31	106	30	4	2	1	41	16	14	9	0	17	0	2	1	4	3	.57	1	.283	.336	.387
	Lakeland	A	25	77	17	2	1	0	21	13	5	10	0	11	0	0	1	1	0	1.00	2	.221	.307	.273
	Bristol	R	61	211	65	16	0	3	90	37	47	15	1	18	1	0	2	7	4	.64	3	.308	.354	.427
1986	Lakeland	A	107	407	108	17	4	3	142	46	49	33	5	21	1	1	5	4	8	.33	23	.265	.318	.349
1987	Glens Falls	AA	46	176	56	12	0	4	80	31	26	12	2	12	0	1	4	4	1	.80	5	.318	.354	.455

Year	Team	Lg	G	AB	H	2B	3B	HR	TB	R	RBI	TBB	IBB	SO	HBP	SH	SF	SB	CS	SB%	GDP	Avg	OBP	SLG
1988	Toledo	AAA	22	48	8	1	0	0	9	6	4	6	0	7	0	1	0	0	1	.00	2	.167	.259	.188
	Glens Falls	AA	91	329	95	23	0	2	124	63	36	37	1	33	3	7	5	10	3	.77	10	.289	.361	.377
1989	London	AA	27	101	37	6	0	1	46	13	9	13	1	10	1	0	0	0	2	.00	0	.366	.443	.455
	Toledo	AAA	101	376	90	13	2	3	116	43	30	28	0	33	3	7	1	3	6	.33	1	.239	.297	.309
1990	London	AA	48	166	50	7	0	2	63	30	20	26	1	14	1	3	2	8	2	.80	3	.301	.395	.380
	Toledo	AAA	74	249	73	14	1	2	95	26	34	27	1	21	0	1	2	2	1	.67	2	.293	.360	.382
1991	Tidewater	AAA	93	282	71	11	1	2	90	33	30	35	5	32	1	4	4	0	3	.00	12	.252	.332	.319
1992	Memphis	AA	73	246	63	10	2	2	83	37	21	31	0	29	1	4	4	4	1	.80	6	.256	.337	.337
1993	Carolina	AA	44	132	34	4	0	1	41	11	11	10	0	6	2	1	0	0	1	.00	2	.258	.319	.311
	Buffalo	AAA	75	208	68	15	5	2	99	21	33	11	2	18	2	0	6	1	3	.25	3	.327	.357	.476
1994	Buffalo	AAA	114	349	92	20	2	4	128	36	39	21	5	39	1	7	1	3	3	.50	5	.264	.306	.367
1995	Toledo	AAA	18	66	14	1	0	0	15	3	6	4	0	8	0	0	1	0	0	.00	3	.212	.254	.227
	Jacksonville	AA	110	375	97	19	1	8	142	60	46	48	6	30	3	3	6	3	3	.50	11	.259	.343	.379
11 Min. YEARS			1160	3904	1068	195	21	40	1425	525	460	376	30	359	20	42	45	54	45	.55	94	.274	.337	.365

Steve Lemke

Pitches: Right Bats: Right Pos: P **Ht: 6'0" Wt: 185 Born: 1/4/70 Age: 26**

			HOW MUCH HE PITCHED				WHAT HE GAVE UP											THE RESULTS					
Year	Team	Lg	G	GS	CG	GF	IP	BFP	H	R	ER	HR	SH	SF	HB	TBB	IBB	SO	WP	Bk	W	L	Pct.	ShO	Sv	ERA
1992	Sou. Oregon	A	21	0	0	6	49.2	219	63	35	22	1	1	5	1	9	1	41	1	0	5	5	.500	0	1	3.99
1993	Sou. Oregon	A	8	0	0	4	14.1	65	13	11	7	2	1	0	0	6	0	11	1	0	1	0	1.000	0	1	4.40
	Madison	A	16	0	0	9	36	156	41	17	14	1	1	0	4	6	1	22	1	0	7	0	1.000	0	0	3.50
1994	W. Michigan	A	10	4	0	6	43.2	180	38	13	11	1	2	1	3	6	1	29	2	0	4	2	.667	0	1	2.27
	Huntsville	AA	1	1	0	0	4.2	21	9	3	3	0	0	0	0	1	0	1	0	0	0	0	.000	0	0	5.79
	Modesto	A	20	18	0	1	116.1	462	93	36	30	7	1	1	4	23	1	63	5	0	12	2	.857	0	1	2.32
1995	Huntsville	AA	25	19	0	1	125.1	544	144	72	61	5	7	3	8	29	4	65	9	0	4	9	.308	0	0	4.38
4 Min. YEARS			101	42	0	27	390	1647	401	187	148	17	13	10	20	80	8	232	19	0	33	18	.647	0	4	3.42

Don Lemon

Pitches: Right Bats: Right Pos: P **Ht: 6'4" Wt: 195 Born: 6/2/67 Age: 29**

			HOW MUCH HE PITCHED				WHAT HE GAVE UP											THE RESULTS					
Year	Team	Lg	G	GS	CG	GF	IP	BFP	H	R	ER	HR	SH	SF	HB	TBB	IBB	SO	WP	Bk	W	L	Pct.	ShO	Sv	ERA
1989	Idaho Falls	R	9	6	0	1	40.1	183	50	31	29	6	0	1	1	17	0	20	2	3	2	1	.667	0	0	6.47
1990	Sumter	A	4	4	0	0	21.1	95	29	20	15	2	0	0	0	5	0	3	2	0	1	2	.333	0	0	6.33
	Braves	R	2	2	1	0	12	49	14	5	3	1	0	0	0	1	0	13	0	1	1	0	1.000	0	0	2.25
	Idaho Falls	R	11	11	2	0	70.2	300	78	38	35	3	1	3	1	17	1	36	2	1	6	2	.750	1	0	4.46
1992	Erie	A	17	11	1	4	72.2	297	60	27	23	4	2	0	2	28	1	55	5	1	6	3	.667	1	2	2.85
1993	High Desert	A	5	5	0	0	24.1	108	35	17	10	2	1	3	0	2	0	17	4	0	1	0	.000	0	0	3.70
	Edmonton	AAA	21	11	0	1	74.1	331	89	48	43	10	2	3	1	20	1	52	2	0	3	3	.500	0	1	5.21
1994	Portland	AA	14	4	0	5	37.2	163	34	26	24	6	1	1	3	16	0	25	2	1	1	2	.333	0	1	5.73
	Edmonton	AAA	19	15	0	0	87.1	377	120	55	50	10	5	4	0	17	0	42	6	1	4	7	.364	0	0	5.15
1995	Charlotte	AAA	6	0	0	0	11.2	50	11	7	7	2	0	0	0	3	0	8	0	0	0	0	.000	0	0	5.40
	Portland	AA	30	3	0	11	62.1	263	60	30	25	3	4	4	0	19	3	47	0	2	1	6	.143	0	1	3.61
6 Min. YEARS			138	72	4	22	514.2	2216	580	304	264	49	16	19	8	145	6	318	25	10	25	27	.481	2	4	4.62

Chris Lemp

Pitches: Right Bats: Right Pos: P **Ht: 6'0" Wt: 175 Born: 7/23/71 Age: 24**

			HOW MUCH HE PITCHED				WHAT HE GAVE UP											THE RESULTS					
Year	Team	Lg	G	GS	CG	GF	IP	BFP	H	R	ER	HR	SH	SF	HB	TBB	IBB	SO	WP	Bk	W	L	Pct.	ShO	Sv	ERA
1991	Bluefield	R	25	0	0	23	39.1	161	22	14	9	0	0	4	2	24	0	43	6	1	0	1	.000	0	12	2.06
1992	Kane County	A	58	1	0	46	65	275	41	27	25	6	0	2	0	49	5	74	10	0	2	3	.400	0	26	3.46
1993	Frederick	A	52	0	0	33	60.2	278	51	32	24	5	3	1	4	35	1	51	5	2	4	1	.800	0	8	3.56
1994	Frederick	A	52	0	0	47	66.1	284	53	28	20	6	6	2	4	29	1	60	6	0	5	5	.500	0	21	2.71
1995	Rochester	AAA	3	0	0	1	4	21	7	5	5	1	0	1	0	3	0	4	1	0	0	1	.000	0	0	11.25
	Frederick	A	41	0	0	36	45.1	194	44	16	12	4	3	2	0	17	2	50	8	0	2	3	.400	0	19	2.38
	Bowie	AA	18	0	0	16	20	94	28	13	12	0	1	2	2	7	3	14	3	0	2	4	.333	0	4	5.40
5 Min. YEARS			249	1	0	202	300.2	1307	246	135	107	22	13	14	12	164	12	296	39	3	15	18	.455	0	90	3.20

Patrick Lennon

Bats: Right Throws: Right Pos: OF **Ht: 6'2" Wt: 200 Born: 4/27/68 Age: 28**

			BATTING															BASERUNNING				PERCENTAGES		
Year	Team	Lg	G	AB	H	2B	3B	HR	TB	R	RBI	TBB	IBB	SO	HBP	SH	SF	SB	CS	SB%	GDP	Avg	OBP	SLG
1986	Bellingham	A	51	169	41	5	2	3	59	35	27	36	0	50	0	1	1	8	6	.57	3	.243	.374	.349
1987	Wausau	A	98	319	80	21	3	7	128	54	34	46	1	82	1	1	2	25	8	.76	10	.251	.345	.401
1988	Vermont	AA	95	321	83	9	3	9	125	44	40	21	1	87	3	3	4	15	6	.71	9	.259	.307	.389
1989	Williamsprt	AA	66	248	65	14	2	3	92	32	31	23	2	53	0	0	5	7	4	.64	9	.262	.319	.371
1990	San Bernrdo	A	44	163	47	6	2	8	81	29	30	15	1	51	0	0	1	6	0	1.00	4	.288	.346	.497
	Williamsprt	AA	49	167	49	6	4	5	78	24	22	10	0	37	2	0	3	10	4	.71	2	.293	.335	.467
1991	Calgary	AAA	112	416	137	29	5	15	221	75	74	46	4	68	4	1	1	12	5	.71	9	.329	.400	.531
1992	Calgary	AAA	13	48	17	3	0	1	23	8	9	6	0	10	0	0	2	4	1	.80	1	.354	.426	.479
1993	Canton-Akrn	AA	45	152	39	7	1	4	60	24	22	30	1	45	1	0	2	4	2	.67	4	.257	.378	.395
1994	New Britain	AA	114	429	140	30	5	17	231	80	67	48	1	96	5	0	1	13	9	.59	10	.326	.400	.538
1995	Pawtucket	AAA	40	128	35	6	2	3	54	20	16	10	0	42	1	0	0	6	4	.60	6	.273	.356	.422
	Trenton	AA	27	98	39	7	0	1	49	19	8	14	0	22	1	0	0	7	2	.78	3	.398	.478	.500
	Salt Lake	AAA	34	115	46	15	0	6	79	26	29	12	2	29	1	0	1	2	1	.67	1	.400	.457	.687

Year	Team	Lg	G	AB	H	2B	3B	HR	TB	R	RBI	TBB	IBB	SO	HBP	SH	SF	SB	CS	SB%	GDP	Avg	OBP	SLG
1991	Seattle	AL	9	8	1	1	0	0	2	2	1	3	0	1	0	0	0	0	0	.00	0	.125	.364	.250
1992	Seattle	AL	1	2	0	0	0	0	0	0	0	0	0	0	0	0	0	0	0	.00	0	.000	.000	.000
	10 Min. YEARS		788	2773	818	158	29	82	1280	470	413	323	13	672	19	6	22	119	52	.70	71	.295	.370	.462
	2 Maj. YEARS		10	10	1	1	0	0	2	2	1	3	0	1	0	0	0	0	0	.00	0	.100	.308	.200

Brian Lesher

Bats: Right **Throws:** Left **Pos:** OF **Ht:** 6'5" **Wt:** 205 **Born:** 3/5/71 **Age:** 25

						BATTING												BASERUNNING				PERCENTAGES		
Year	Team	Lg	G	AB	H	2B	3B	HR	TB	R	RBI	TBB	IBB	SO	HBP	SH	SF	SB	CS	SB%	GDP	Avg	OBP	SLG
1992	Sou. Oregon	A	46	136	26	7	1	3	44	21	18	12	0	35	2	0	1	3	7	.30	3	.191	.265	.324
1993	Madison	A	119	394	108	13	5	5	146	63	47	46	0	102	9	6	6	20	9	.69	13	.274	.358	.371
1994	Modesto	A	117	393	114	21	0	14	177	76	68	81	5	84	8	0	8	11	11	.50	8	.290	.414	.450
1995	Huntsville	AA	127	471	123	23	2	19	207	78	71	64	2	110	2	0	1	7	8	.47	7	.261	.351	.439
	4 Min. YEARS		409	1394	371	64	8	41	574	238	204	203	7	331	21	6	16	41	35	.54	31	.266	.364	.412

Dana Levangie

Bats: Right **Throws:** Right **Pos:** C **Ht:** 5'10" **Wt:** 185 **Born:** 8/11/69 **Age:** 26

						BATTING												BASERUNNING				PERCENTAGES		
Year	Team	Lg	G	AB	H	2B	3B	HR	TB	R	RBI	TBB	IBB	SO	HBP	SH	SF	SB	CS	SB%	GDP	Avg	OBP	SLG
1991	Elmira	A	35	94	14	3	0	0	17	6	4	10	1	18	0	0	0	0	1	.00	1	.149	.231	.181
1992	Winter Havn	A	76	245	47	5	0	1	55	21	22	20	0	49	2	1	3	1	2	.33	6	.192	.256	.224
1993	Ft. Laud	A	80	250	47	5	0	0	52	17	11	26	0	46	0	2	0	0	2	.00	5	.188	.264	.208
1994	Lynchburg	A	79	239	56	8	2	3	77	19	21	25	2	36	3	6	0	1	2	.33	5	.234	.315	.322
	New Britain	AA	8	21	3	1	0	1	7	2	5	1	0	6	1	0	0	0	0	.00	0	.143	.217	.333
1995	Pawtucket	AAA	6	17	4	0	0	0	4	1	0	2	0	3	0	1	0	0	0	.00	0	.235	.316	.235
	Trenton	AA	42	129	23	3	1	0	28	10	7	11	0	30	1	0	1	1	3	.25	3	.178	.246	.217
	5 Min. YEARS		326	995	194	25	3	5	240	76	70	95	3	188	7	10	4	3	10	.23	20	.195	.269	.241

Alan Levine

Pitches: Right **Bats:** Left **Pos:** P **Ht:** 6'3" **Wt:** 180 **Born:** 5/22/68 **Age:** 28

			HOW MUCH HE PITCHED					WHAT HE GAVE UP										THE RESULTS					
Year	Team	Lg	G	GS	CG	GF	IP	BFP	H	R	ER	HR	SH	SF	HB	TBB	IBB	SO	WP	Bk	W	L	Pct.	ShO	Sv	ERA
1991	Utica	A	16	12	2	3	85	361	75	43	30	2	4	2	4	26	0	83	8	1	6	4	.600	1	1	3.18
1992	South Bend	A	23	23	2	0	156.2	650	151	67	49	6	6	2	8	36	1	131	9	1	9	5	.643	0	0	2.81
	Sarasota	A	3	2	0	0	15.2	68	17	11	7	1	3	2	0	5	1	11	0	1	0	2	.000	0	0	4.02
1993	Sarasota	A	27	26	5	0	161.1	696	169	87	66	6	11	3	7	50	3	129	11	3	11	8	.579	1	0	3.68
1994	Birmingham	AA	18	18	1	0	114.1	501	117	50	42	7	2	3	14	44	1	94	3	0	5	9	.357	0	0	3.31
	Nashville	AAA	8	4	0	1	24	116	34	23	21	2	1	3	2	11	0	24	0	0	0	2	.000	0	0	7.88
1995	Nashville	AAA	3	3	0	0	14	69	20	10	8	1	0	0	0	7	0	14	3	0	0	2	.000	0	0	5.14
	Birmingham	AA	43	1	0	31	73	305	61	22	19	2	2	2	2	25	5	68	7	1	4	3	.571	0	7	2.34
	5 Min. YEARS		141	89	10	35	644	2766	644	313	242	27	29	17	37	204	11	554	41	7	35	35	.500	2	8	3.38

Anthony Lewis

Bats: Left **Throws:** Left **Pos:** OF **Ht:** 6'0" **Wt:** 185 **Born:** 2/2/71 **Age:** 25

						BATTING												BASERUNNING				PERCENTAGES		
Year	Team	Lg	G	AB	H	2B	3B	HR	TB	R	RBI	TBB	IBB	SO	HBP	SH	SF	SB	CS	SB%	GDP	Avg	OBP	SLG
1989	Cardinals	R	51	187	46	10	0	2	62	32	27	11	1	45	0	0	4	11	3	.79	1	.246	.282	.332
1990	Savannah	A	128	465	118	22	4	8	172	55	49	24	6	79	1	2	1	10	13	.43	13	.254	.291	.370
1991	St. Pete	A	124	435	100	17	7	6	149	40	43	50	7	100	2	0	2	5	5	.50	7	.230	.311	.343
1992	St. Pete	A	128	454	101	18	2	15	168	50	55	46	6	105	5	1	4	2	4	.33	7	.222	.299	.370
1993	Arkansas	AA	112	326	86	28	2	13	157	48	50	25	3	98	0	1	3	3	4	.43	9	.264	.314	.482
1994	Arkansas	AA	88	335	85	18	1	17	156	58	50	27	0	69	0	0	2	2	1	.67	9	.254	.308	.466
	Louisville	AAA	21	74	9	0	1	0	11	3	6	0	0	27	0	0	0	0	0	.00	1	.122	.122	.149
1995	Arkansas	AA	115	407	102	21	3	24	201	55	85	44	5	117	2	0	1	0	2	.00	7	.251	.326	.494
	7 Min. YEARS		767	2683	647	134	20	85	1076	341	365	227	28	640	10	4	17	33	32	.51	50	.241	.301	.401

Jim Lewis

Pitches: Right **Bats:** Right **Pos:** P **Ht:** 6'4" **Wt:** 190 **Born:** 1/31/70 **Age:** 26

			HOW MUCH HE PITCHED					WHAT HE GAVE UP										THE RESULTS					
Year	Team	Lg	G	GS	CG	GF	IP	BFP	H	R	ER	HR	SH	SF	HB	TBB	IBB	SO	WP	Bk	W	L	Pct.	ShO	Sv	ERA
1991	Auburn	A	7	7	0	0	38.1	157	30	20	16	3	1	1	3	14	0	26	2	1	3	2	.600	0	0	3.76
1992	Tucson	AAA	1	1	0	0	1	4	0	0	0	0	0	0	0	2	0	0	0	0	0	0	.000	0	0	0.00
	Osceola	A	13	13	1	0	80.1	324	54	18	10	0	6	1	2	32	0	65	5	0	5	1	.833	0	0	1.12
	Jackson	AA	12	12	2	0	70	291	64	33	32	4	5	6	2	30	0	43	4	0	3	5	.375	1	0	4.11
1993	Osceola	A	4	4	0	0	7.2	34	8	4	2	1	0	0	0	2	0	3	0	0	0	0	.000	0	0	2.35
1994	Osceola	A	16	16	0	0	63	265	64	37	22	3	1	0	1	16	0	33	3	0	1	8	.111	0	0	3.14
	Jackson	AA	8	8	0	0	48	191	41	13	13	2	2	1	1	10	2	39	4	0	2	1	.667	0	0	2.44
1995	Buffalo	AAA	18	16	1	2	94	405	101	42	38	7	1	3	9	25	0	50	4	0	6	4	.600	0	1	3.64
	5 Min. YEARS		79	77	4	2	402.1	1671	362	167	133	20	16	12	18	131	2	259	22	1	20	21	.488	1	1	2.98

Scott Lewis

Pitches: Right Bats: Right Pos: P   Ht: 6' 3" Wt: 178 Born: 12/5/65 Age: 30

Year	Team	Lg	G	GS	CG	GF	IP	BFP	H	R	ER	HR	SH	SF	HB	TBB	IBB	SO	WP	Bk	W	L	Pct.	ShO	Sv	ERA
1988	Bend	A	9	9	2	0	61.2	262	63	33	24	3	1	3	5	12	0	53	3	2	5	3	.625	0	0	3.50
	Quad City	A	3	3	1	0	21.1	85	19	12	11	0	1	0	0	5	0	20	1	2	1	2	.333	0	0	4.64
	Palm Spring	A	2	1	0	0	8	37	12	5	5	3	0	0	0	2	0	7	0	0	0	1	.000	0	0	5.63
1989	Midland	AA	25	25	4	0	162.1	729	195	121	89	15	2	3	8	55	9	104	12	9	11	12	.478	1	0	4.93
1990	Edmonton	AAA	27	27	6	0	177.2	749	198	90	77	16	4	3	7	35	1	124	2	0	13	11	.542	0	0	3.90
1991	Edmonton	AAA	17	17	4	0	110	489	132	71	55	7	4	4	8	26	2	87	5	3	3	9	.250	0	0	4.50
1992	Edmonton	AAA	22	22	5	0	146.2	630	159	74	68	9	5	3	7	40	2	88	7	2	10	6	.625	0	0	4.17
1993	Midland	AA	1	1	0	0	6	25	6	1	1	0	0	1	0	0	0	2	0	0	1	0	1.000	0	0	1.50
	Vancouver	AAA	24	0	0	18	39.1	156	31	7	6	1	2	1	2	9	2	38	1	0	3	1	.750	0	9	1.37
1994	Lk Elsinore	A	2	0	0	1	4	19	5	3	2	0	0	0	0	1	0	5	0	0	0	0	.000	0	0	4.50
	Vancouver	AAA	4	0	0	1	6.2	23	2	2	2	1	1	0	0	1	0	4	1	0	2	0	1.000	0	1	2.70
	Tucson	AAA	8	0	0	4	8.1	41	11	7	6	0	0	1	0	5	2	8	1	0	1	1	.500	0	0	6.48
1995	Tacoma	AAA	3	2	0	0	9.1	47	13	10	10	1	1	1	3	4	0	11	0	1	1	1	.500	0	0	9.64
	Pawtucket	AAA	3	0	0	1	4.2	19	7	2	2	2	0	0	0	0	0	1	1	0	0	0	.000	0	0	3.86
1990	California	AL	2	2	1	0	16.1	60	10	4	4	2	0	0	0	2	0	9	0	0	1	1	.500	0	0	2.20
1991	California	AL	16	11	0	0	60.1	281	81	43	42	9	2	0	2	21	0	37	3	0	3	5	.375	0	0	6.27
1992	California	AL	21	2	0	7	38.1	160	36	18	17	3	0	3	2	14	1	18	1	1	4	0	1.000	0	0	3.99
1993	California	AL	15	4	0	2	32	142	37	16	15	3	2	7	2	12	1	10	1	0	1	2	.333	0	0	4.22
1994	California	AL	20	0	0	6	31	143	46	23	21	5	3	0	2	10	2	10	1	0	0	1	.000	0	0	6.10
	8 Min. YEARS		150	107	22	25	766	3311	853	438	358	58	21	20	40	195	18	552	34	19	51	47	.520	1	10	4.21
	5 Maj. YEARS		74	19	1	15	178	786	210	104	99	22	7	10	8	59	4	84	5	1	9	9	.500	0	0	5.01

T.R. Lewis

Bats: Right Throws: Right Pos: OF   Ht: 6'0" Wt: 180 Born: 4/15/71 Age: 25

Year	Team	Lg	G	AB	H	2B	3B	HR	TB	R	RBI	TBB	IBB	SO	HBP	SH	SF	SB	CS	SB%	GDP	Avg	OBP	SLG
1989	Bluefield	R	40	151	50	11	1	10	93	31	32	9	0	21	0	0	2	0	2	.00	2	.331	.364	.616
1990	Wausau	A	115	404	115	24	2	8	167	60	45	46	0	64	5	1	1	10	5	.67	14	.285	.364	.413
	Frederick	A	22	80	26	4	3	1	39	12	11	11	1	11	2	0	0	5	0	1.00	1	.325	.419	.488
1991	Frederick	A	49	159	33	7	2	0	44	18	7	19	2	25	1	2	1	1	1	.50	4	.208	.294	.277
1992	Kane County	A	45	134	40	10	0	2	56	26	22	13	0	22	3	1	4	5	4	.56	3	.299	.364	.418
	Frederick	A	84	313	96	27	6	7	156	58	54	36	0	46	2	0	5	5	2	.71	5	.307	.376	.498
1993	Bowie	AA	127	480	146	26	2	5	191	73	64	36	4	80	3	0	7	22	8	.73	12	.304	.352	.398
1994	Orioles	R	5	20	6	1	0	1	10	2	5	2	0	3	0	0	0	1	1	.50	0	.300	.364	.500
	Bowie	AA	17	72	18	5	0	3	32	13	8	6	0	15	0	0	1	1	0	1.00	1	.250	.304	.444
	Rochester	AAA	55	174	53	10	0	6	81	25	31	16	2	33	3	0	2	6	1	.86	1	.305	.369	.466
1995	Bowie	AA	86	309	91	19	1	5	127	57	44	40	2	43	1	1	6	12	3	.80	8	.294	.371	.411
	Rochester	AAA	22	78	23	7	0	4	42	12	19	7	0	14	1	0	1	1	1	.50	2	.295	.356	.538
	7 Min. YEARS		667	2374	697	151	17	52	1038	387	342	241	11	377	21	5	30	69	28	.71	53	.294	.360	.437

Cory Lidle

Pitches: Right Bats: Right Pos: P   Ht: 5'11" Wt: 175 Born: 3/22/72 Age: 24

Year	Team	Lg	G	GS	CG	GF	IP	BFP	H	R	ER	HR	SH	SF	HB	TBB	IBB	SO	WP	Bk	W	L	Pct.	ShO	Sv	ERA
1991	Twins	R	4	0	0	1	4.2	19	5	3	3	0	0	0	0	0	0	5	1	2	1	1	.500	0	0	5.79
1992	Elizabethtn	R	19	2	0	11	43.2	190	40	29	18	2	0	2	0	21	0	32	3	1	2	1	.667	0	6	3.71
1993	Pocatello	R	17	16	3	1	106.2	463	104	59	49	6	1	4	5	54	0	91	14	1	8	4	.667	0	1	4.13
1994	Stockton	A	25	1	0	12	42.2	200	60	32	21	2	0	0	1	13	1	38	1	0	1	2	.333	0	4	4.43
	Beloit	A	13	9	1	0	69	279	65	24	20	4	1	0	2	11	0	62	6	0	3	4	.429	1	0	2.61
1995	El Paso	AA	45	9	0	12	109.2	480	126	52	41	6	6	1	6	36	3	78	6	0	5	4	.556	0	0	3.36
	5 Min. YEARS		123	37	4	37	376.1	1631	400	199	152	20	8	7	14	135	4	306	31	4	20	16	.556	1	13	3.64

Kevin Lidle

Bats: Right Throws: Right Pos: C   Ht: 5'11" Wt: 170 Born: 3/22/72 Age: 24

Year	Team	Lg	G	AB	H	2B	3B	HR	TB	R	RBI	TBB	IBB	SO	HBP	SH	SF	SB	CS	SB%	GDP	Avg	OBP	SLG
1992	Niagara Fal	A	58	140	34	6	2	1	47	21	18	8	0	42	1	6	3	3	2	.60	1	.243	.283	.336
1993	Fayettevlle	A	58	197	42	14	1	5	73	29	25	34	0	42	1	0	1	2	0	1.00	0	.213	.330	.371
1994	Lakeland	A	56	187	49	13	2	6	84	26	30	19	0	46	4	1	1	1	1	.50	2	.262	.341	.449
1995	Jacksonvlle	AA	36	80	13	7	0	1	23	12	5	1	0	31	0	1	0	1	0	1.00	1	.163	.173	.288
	Fayettevlle	A	36	113	16	4	1	4	34	15	13	16	0	44	1	3	2	0	1	.00	1	.142	.250	.301
	4 Min. YEARS		244	717	154	44	6	17	261	103	91	78	0	205	7	11	7	7	4	.64	5	.215	.295	.364

Yfrain Linares

Pitches: Right Bats: Right Pos: P   Ht: 6'2" Wt: 180 Born: 12/7/69 Age: 26

Year	Team	Lg	G	GS	CG	GF	IP	BFP	H	R	ER	HR	SH	SF	HB	TBB	IBB	SO	WP	Bk	W	L	Pct.	ShO	Sv	ERA
1988	Reds	R	19	0	0	7	33.2	164	39	33	25	0	3	2	5	19	1	25	4	8	1	5	.167	0	0	6.68
1989	Reds	R	15	12	0	0	67	302	66	33	27	0	1	3	7	29	1	53	8	2	3	5	.375	0	0	3.63
1995	El Paso	AA	8	0	0	1	13.1	70	21	15	14	1	0	2	1	12	1	9	2	0	1	1	.500	0	0	9.45
	Stockton	A	7	3	0	1	23	98	20	7	3	1	1	0	0	16	1	17	3	0	2	0	1.000	0	0	1.17

Team		G	GS	CG	GF	IP	BFP	H	R	ER	HR	SH	SF	HB	TBB	IBB	SO	WP	Bk	W	L	Pct.	ShO	Sv	ERA
Beloit	A	19	12	0	3	71.1	324	75	42	34	2	1	3	5	43	0	63	5	3	3	3	.500	0	0	4.29
3 Min. YEARS		68	27	0	12	208.1	958	221	130	103	4	6	10	18	119	4	167	22	13	10	14	.417	0	0	4.45

Jim Lindeman

Bats: Right **Throws:** Right **Pos:** 1B **Ht:** 6' 1" **Wt:** 200 **Born:** 1/10/62 **Age:** 34

Year	Team	Lg	G	AB	H	2B	3B	HR	TB	R	RBI	TBB	IBB	SO	HBP	SH	SF	SB	CS	SB%	GDP	Avg	OBP	SLG
1984	Springfield	A	94	354	96	15	2	18	169	69	66	47	2	81	3	2	1	6	3	.67	6	.271	.360	.477
	Arkansas	AA	40	137	26	4	3	0	36	14	13	10	0	34	1	2	1	3	1	.75	2	.190	.248	.263
1985	Arkansas	AA	128	450	127	30	6	10	199	54	63	41	1	82	6	2	3	11	13	.46	13	.282	.348	.442
1986	Louisville	AAA	139	509	128	38	5	20	236	82	96	39	2	97	4	0	4	9	6	.60	9	.251	.308	.464
1987	Louisville	AAA	20	78	24	3	1	4	41	11	10	8	1	15	0	0	0	0	0	.00	1	.308	.372	.526
1988	Louisville	AAA	73	261	66	18	4	2	98	32	30	33	0	59	2	0	2	2	0	1.00	5	.253	.339	.375
1989	Louisville	AAA	29	109	33	8	1	5	58	18	20	14	2	17	0	0	0	3	0	1.00	5	.303	.382	.532
1990	Toledo	AAA	109	374	85	17	2	12	142	48	50	26	2	83	6	1	3	2	3	.40	16	.227	.286	.380
1991	Scranton-Wb	AAA	11	40	11	1	1	2	20	7	7	5	0	6	0	0	0	0	0	.00	1	.275	.356	.500
1992	Scranton-Wb	AAA	15	53	16	0	1	0	18	5	8	7	1	11	1	0	0	0	0	.00	2	.302	.393	.340
1993	Tucson	AAA	101	390	141	28	7	12	219	72	88	41	4	68	5	0	7	5	0	1.00	9	.362	.422	.562
1994	Norfolk	AAA	32	123	45	11	2	4	72	23	18	14	1	27	3	0	0	1	1	.50	3	.366	.443	.585
1995	Okla. City	AAA	83	294	74	16	3	12	132	52	36	33	4	54	5	0	3	0	1	.00	11	.252	.334	.449
1986	St. Louis	NL	19	55	14	1	0	1	18	7	6	2	0	10	0	0	1	1	1	.50	2	.255	.276	.327
1987	St. Louis	NL	75	207	43	13	0	8	80	20	28	11	0	56	3	2	4	3	1	.75	4	.208	.253	.386
1988	St. Louis	NL	17	43	9	1	0	2	16	3	7	2	0	9	0	1	0	0	0	.00	1	.209	.244	.372
1989	St. Louis	NL	73	45	5	1	0	0	6	8	2	3	0	18	0	1	1	0	0	.00	0	.111	.163	.133
1990	Detroit	AL	12	32	7	1	0	2	14	5	8	2	0	13	0	0	0	0	0	.00	0	.219	.265	.438
1991	Philadelphia	NL	65	95	32	5	0	0	37	13	12	13	1	14	0	2	1	0	1	.00	1	.337	.413	.389
1992	Philadelphia	NL	29	39	10	1	0	1	14	6	6	3	0	11	0	0	0	0	0	.00	1	.256	.310	.359
1993	Houston	NL	9	23	8	3	0	0	11	2	0	0	0	7	0	0	0	0	0	.00	0	.348	.348	.478
1994	New York	NL	52	137	37	8	1	7	68	18	20	6	2	35	1	0	1	0	0	.00	0	.270	.303	.496
	12 Min. YEARS		874	3172	872	189	38	101	1440	487	505	318	20	634	36	7	24	42	28	.60	83	.275	.345	.454
	9 Maj. YEARS		351	676	165	34	1	21	264	82	89	42	3	173	4	6	8	4	3	.57	11	.244	.289	.391

Joe Lis

Bats: Right **Throws:** Right **Pos:** 2B **Ht:** 5'10" **Wt:** 170 **Born:** 11/3/68 **Age:** 27

Year	Team	Lg	G	AB	H	2B	3B	HR	TB	R	RBI	TBB	IBB	SO	HBP	SH	SF	SB	CS	SB%	GDP	Avg	OBP	SLG
1991	St. Cathrns	A	66	206	60	12	1	5	89	36	27	41	0	19	4	9	4	3	3	.50	5	.291	.412	.432
1992	Myrtle Bch	A	125	434	130	25	0	13	194	70	79	68	5	54	7	2	7	5	11	.31	11	.300	.397	.447
1993	Knoxville	AA	129	448	130	29	3	8	189	66	64	42	1	58	16	2	5	6	9	.40	12	.290	.368	.422
1994	Syracuse	AAA	89	319	93	20	0	11	146	53	49	25	2	39	2	4	3	3	1	.75	14	.292	.344	.458
1995	Syracuse	AAA	130	485	127	33	4	17	219	68	56	46	1	54	2	0	5	6	2	.75	8	.262	.325	.452
	5 Min. YEARS		539	1892	540	119	8	54	837	293	275	222	9	224	31	17	24	23	26	.47	50	.285	.366	.442

Lew List

Bats: Right **Throws:** Right **Pos:** DH **Ht:** 6'3" **Wt:** 200 **Born:** 11/17/65 **Age:** 30

Year	Team	Lg	G	AB	H	2B	3B	HR	TB	R	RBI	TBB	IBB	SO	HBP	SH	SF	SB	CS	SB%	GDP	Avg	OBP	SLG
1987	Salem	A	13	18	0	0	0	0	0	2	0	4	0	7	0	0	0	0	0	.00	0	.000	.182	.000
1990	Mariners	R	14	44	11	1	3	1	21	7	8	12	1	5	1	0	0	1	2	.33	0	.250	.421	.477
1991	Augusta	A	12	33	9	3	0	1	15	7	10	7	1	10	0	0	2	1	0	1.00	0	.273	.381	.455
	Carolina	AA	7	20	3	0	1	0	5	1	2	0	0	6	0	0	0	0	0	.00	2	.150	.150	.250
	Salem	A	94	336	107	22	5	10	169	60	46	39	1	74	1	0	2	12	3	.80	6	.318	.389	.503
1992	Carolina	AA	9	24	5	1	0	0	6	3	1	3	1	3	0	0	0	0	0	.00	0	.208	.296	.250
	Gastonia	A	51	182	64	11	3	8	105	32	40	23	0	26	4	0	1	5	9	.36	2	.352	.433	.577
	Tulsa	AA	34	130	38	7	1	1	50	17	14	13	0	30	0	0	1	1	1	.50	1	.292	.357	.385
1993	Tulsa	AA	40	125	25	3	1	0	30	8	6	10	0	30	3	0	2	2	6	.25	6	.200	.271	.240
	Colo. Sprng	AAA	18	50	15	7	1	0	24	9	5	3	0	8	0	0	0	0	0	.00	5	.300	.340	.480
	Central Val	A	33	120	35	6	2	8	69	21	27	17	0	19	2	0	1	0	3	.00	5	.292	.386	.575
1994	New Haven	AA	81	271	68	13	1	8	107	45	40	32	5	69	5	1	0	1	2	.33	9	.251	.341	.395
1995	New Haven	AA	82	212	59	10	4	6	95	26	44	20	0	43	1	0	1	2	2	.50	4	.278	.342	.448
	7 Min. YEARS		488	1565	439	84	22	43	696	238	243	183	9	330	17	1	9	25	28	.47	37	.281	.360	.445

Martin Lister

Pitches: Left **Bats:** Left **Pos:** P **Ht:** 6'2" **Wt:** 210 **Born:** 6/12/72 **Age:** 24

			HOW MUCH HE PITCHED						WHAT HE GAVE UP											THE RESULTS					
Year	Team	Lg	G	GS	CG	GF	IP	BFP	H	R	ER	HR	SH	SF	HB	TBB	IBB	SO	WP	Bk	W	L	Pct.	ShO	Sv	ERA
1992	Billings	R	26	2	0	3	34.1	174	36	33	30	2	0	0	3	37	1	39	11	3	3	1	.750	0	1	7.86
1993	Charlstn-Wv	A	51	0	0	46	52	228	38	16	12	0	3	0	2	31	0	57	6	0	1	2	.333	0	32	2.08
1994	Winston-Sal	A	6	0	0	4	5	33	7	7	3	0	0	1	0	11	1	4	1	0	0	2	.000	0	2	5.40
	Quad City	A	46	0	0	32	47	207	31	18	15	0	1	1	0	37	1	54	2	1	2	4	.333	0	13	2.87
1995	Jackson	AA	15	13	1	1	69.2	299	80	35	31	2	3	2	1	24	0	27	6	0	4	3	.571	1	0	4.00
	4 Min. YEARS		144	15	1	86	208	941	192	109	91	4	7	4	6	140	3	181	26	4	10	12	.455	1	48	3.94

Bats: Right **Throws:** Right **Pos:** 1B

Greg Litton

Ht: 6' 0" **Wt:** 175 **Born:** 7/13/64 **Age:** 31

Year	Team	Lg	G	AB	H	2B	3B	HR	TB	R	RBI	TBB	IBB	SO	HBP	SH	SF	SB	CS	SB%	GDP	Avg	OBP	SLG
1984	Everett	A	62	243	57	12	2	4	85	29	26	27	0	47	1	0	0	2	1	.67	4	.235	.314	.350
1985	Fresno	A	141	564	150	33	7	12	233	88	103	50	0	86	3	2	7	8	4	.67	8	.266	.325	.413
1986	Shreveport	AA	131	455	112	30	3	10	178	46	55	52	4	77	4	5	2	1	2	.33	13	.246	.327	.391
1987	Shreveport	AA	72	254	66	6	3	8	102	34	33	22	2	51	2	2	2	2	4	.33	2	.260	.321	.402
	Phoenix	AAA	60	203	44	8	2	1	59	24	22	18	1	40	2	2	3	0	1	.00	5	.217	.283	.291
1988	Shreveport	AA	116	432	120	35	5	11	198	58	64	37	2	84	5	1	7	2	2	.50	8	.278	.337	.458
1989	Phoenix	AAA	30	89	16	4	2	2	30	6	6	8	0	24	0	0	2	1	3	.25	3	.180	.242	.337
1990	Phoenix	AAA	6	22	6	1	0	0	7	3	4	2	0	7	0	0	1	0	0	.00	0	.273	.320	.318
1991	Phoenix	AAA	8	27	11	1	0	4	24	9	9	8	0	5	0	0	0	0	0	.00	0	.407	.543	.889
1992	Phoenix	AAA	25	85	26	7	0	4	45	14	19	8	1	21	0	1	1	0	1	.00	2	.306	.362	.529
1993	Calgary	AAA	49	170	54	16	3	6	94	35	27	25	0	36	1	0	1	3	1	.75	3	.318	.404	.553
1994	Pawtucket	AAA	74	257	70	19	2	9	120	42	48	25	1	42	3	1	2	2	1	.67	9	.272	.341	.467
1995	Tacoma	AAA	117	388	120	25	1	9	174	58	56	43	1	69	3	4	6	2	2	.50	11	.309	.377	.448
1989	San Francisco	NL	71	143	36	5	3	4	59	12	17	7	0	29	1	4	0	0	2	.00	3	.252	.291	.413
1990	San Francisco	NL	93	204	50	9	1	1	64	17	24	11	0	45	1	2	2	1	0	1.00	5	.245	.284	.314
1991	San Francisco	NL	59	127	23	7	1	1	35	13	15	11	0	25	1	3	1	0	2	.00	2	.181	.250	.276
1992	San Francisco	NL	68	140	32	5	0	4	49	9	15	11	0	33	0	3	0	0	1	.00	2	.229	.285	.350
1993	Seattle	AL	72	174	52	17	0	3	78	25	25	18	2	30	1	5	1	0	1	.00	6	.299	.366	.448
1994	Boston	AL	11	21	2	0	0	0	2	2	1	0	0	5	0	0	1	0	0	.00	0	.095	.091	.095
	12 Min. YEARS		891	3189	852	197	30	80	1349	446	472	325	12	589	24	18	35	23	22	.51	68	.267	.336	.423
	6 Maj. YEARS		374	809	195	43	5	13	287	78	97	58	2	167	4	17	5	1	6	.14	18	.241	.293	.355

Bats: Right **Throws:** Right **Pos:** C

Jeff Livesey

Ht: 6'0" **Wt:** 185 **Born:** 5/24/66 **Age:** 30

Year	Team	Lg	G	AB	H	2B	3B	HR	TB	R	RBI	TBB	IBB	SO	HBP	SH	SF	SB	CS	SB%	GDP	Avg	OBP	SLG
1988	Oneonta	A	37	126	28	3	1	2	39	15	9	17	0	30	0	1	0	0	0	.00	4	.222	.315	.310
	Ft. Laud	A	9	25	5	2	0	0	7	2	2	1	0	11	0	1	0	0	0	.00	0	.200	.231	.280
1989	Pr. William	A	70	197	40	12	0	2	58	17	17	9	0	48	1	2	1	1	0	1.00	4	.203	.240	.294
1990	Ft. Laud	A	45	148	26	6	0	4	44	11	15	15	0	55	2	2	1	0	3	.00	4	.176	.259	.297
	Albany-Colo	AA	9	19	3	0	0	0	3	0	1	1	0	6	0	0	0	0	0	.00	0	.158	.200	.158
1991	Albany-Colo	AA	23	61	14	1	0	2	21	5	6	0	0	14	2	1	0	0	0	.00	0	.230	.254	.344
	Pr. William	A	20	73	18	5	0	2	29	8	9	3	0	13	0	1	1	0	0	.00	2	.247	.273	.397
1992	Columbus	AAA	3	9	1	0	0	0	1	0	1	0	0	2	0	0	0	0	0	.00	0	.111	.111	.111
	Albany-Colo	AA	18	42	8	3	0	0	11	1	5	6	0	13	0	2	0	0	0	.00	0	.190	.292	.262
1993	Albany-Colo	AA	32	104	16	4	0	0	20	6	6	7	0	22	0	4	0	0	0	.00	4	.154	.207	.192
	Columbus	AAA	34	89	22	5	0	2	33	9	8	2	0	19	0	2	0	0	0	.00	4	.247	.264	.371
1994	Albany-Colo	AA	31	106	32	6	1	2	46	13	16	0	0	20	0	1	2	1	0	1.00	3	.302	.296	.434
1995	Columbus	AAA	42	91	24	3	0	0	27	8	7	7	0	18	0	0	1	0	0	.00	5	.264	.313	.297
	8 Min. YEARS		373	1090	237	50	2	16	339	95	102	68	0	271	5	17	6	2	3	.40	26	.217	.265	.311

Bats: Right **Throws:** Right **Pos:** C

Paul Loduca

Ht: 5'10" **Wt:** 193 **Born:** 4/12/72 **Age:** 24

Year	Team	Lg	G	AB	H	2B	3B	HR	TB	R	RBI	TBB	IBB	SO	HBP	SH	SF	SB	CS	SB%	GDP	Avg	OBP	SLG
1993	Vero Beach	A	39	134	42	6	0	0	48	17	13	13	0	22	2	0	1	0	0	.00	2	.313	.380	.358
1994	Bakersfield	A	123	455	141	32	1	6	193	65	68	52	2	49	3	0	4	16	9	.64	5	.310	.381	.424
1995	San Antonio	AA	61	199	49	8	0	1	60	27	8	26	0	25	2	0	0	5	5	.50	12	.246	.339	.302
	3 Min. YEARS		223	788	232	46	1	7	301	109	89	91	2	96	7	0	5	21	14	.60	19	.294	.370	.382

Pitches: Right **Bats:** Both **Pos:** P

Carlton Loewer

Ht: 6'6" **Wt:** 220 **Born:** 9/24/73 **Age:** 22

			HOW MUCH HE PITCHED						WHAT HE GAVE UP												THE RESULTS					
Year	Team	Lg	G	GS	CG	GF	IP	BFP	H	R	ER	HR	SH	SF	HB	TBB	IBB	SO	WP	Bk	W	L	Pct.	ShO	Sv	ERA
1995	Clearwater	A	20	20	1	0	114.2	502	124	59	42	6	3	5	5	36	0	83	7	3	7	5	.583	0	0	3.30
	Reading	AA	8	8	0	0	50	212	42	17	12	3	1	0	1	31	0	35	4	0	4	1	.800	0	0	2.16
	1 Min. YEARS		28	28	1	0	164.2	714	166	76	54	9	4	5	6	67	0	118	11	3	11	6	.647	0	0	2.95

Bats: Right **Throws:** Right **Pos:** 2B

Rod Lofton

Ht: 5'11" **Wt:** 185 **Born:** 10/7/67 **Age:** 28

Year	Team	Lg	G	AB	H	2B	3B	HR	TB	R	RBI	TBB	IBB	SO	HBP	SH	SF	SB	CS	SB%	GDP	Avg	OBP	SLG
1988	Erie	A	72	251	75	13	1	0	90	40	37	35	0	29	3	8	4	37	7	.84	8	.299	.386	.359
1989	Frederick	A	127	473	115	9	2	0	128	65	29	56	1	72	2	7	3	62	21	.75	3	.243	.324	.271
1990	Frederick	A	2	9	5	1	0	0	6	1	2	0	0	1	0	0	0	2	0	1.00	0	.556	.556	.667
	Rochester	AAA	14	28	4	0	0	0	4	3	0	2	0	7	0	1	0	1	1	.50	1	.143	.200	.143
	Hagerstown	AA	89	294	80	7	2	0	91	35	34	23	0	50	2	10	2	24	4	.86	8	.272	.327	.310
1991	Rochester	AAA	3	3	0	0	0	0	0	0	1	0	0	0	0	0	0	0	0	.00	0	.000	.000	.000
	Hagerstown	AA	118	437	124	8	4	1	143	78	33	48	1	74	3	9	2	56	10	.85	3	.284	.357	.327
1992	Hagerstown	AA	50	172	43	7	0	0	50	17	8	7	0	22	2	3	0	11	6	.65	4	.250	.287	.291
	Rochester	AAA	52	132	31	3	1	0	36	24	8	8	0	26	0	0	1	10	3	.77	6	.235	.279	.273

Year	Team	Lg	G	AB	H	2B	3B	HR	TB	R	RBI	TBB	IBB	SO	HBP	SH	SF	SB	CS	SB%	GDP	Avg	OBP	SLG
1993	Indianapols	AAA	2	3	2	0	0	0	2	0	2	0	0	1	0	0	1	0	0	.00	0	.667	.500	.667
	Chattanooga	AA	10	27	3	0	0	0	3	1	2	7	0	11	0	1	1	2	0	1.00	0	.111	.286	.111
	El Paso	AA	67	200	53	8	5	2	77	39	21	13	0	40	5	5	1	16	1	.94	5	.265	.324	.385
1994	El Paso	AA	92	354	117	25	5	2	158	70	54	26	0	68	3	1	3	21	5	.81	5	.331	.378	.446
1995	New Orleans	AAA	102	240	52	7	0	1	62	30	18	15	1	48	1	2	2	9	3	.75	11	.217	.264	.258
	8 Min. YEARS		800	2623	704	88	20	6	850	403	249	240	3	449	21	51	19	251	61	.80	54	.268	.332	.324

Kevin Logsdon

Pitches: Left Bats: Both Pos: P Ht: 5'11" Wt: 215 Born: 12/23/70 Age: 25

			HOW MUCH HE PITCHED			WHAT HE GAVE UP												THE RESULTS					
Year	Team	Lg	G	GS	CG	GF	IP	BFP	H	R	ER	HR	SH	SF	HB	TBB	IBB	SO	WP	Bk	W	L	Pct.	ShO	Sv	ERA
1991	Watertown	A	13	11	0	0	59.1	272	58	42	28	2	5	3	1	41	3	38	6	0	2	5	.286	0	0	4.25
1992	Columbus	A	19	18	0	0	113.1	470	104	43	39	2	4	3	3	48	0	86	9	3	6	5	.545	0	0	2.94
1993	Kinston	A	31	20	1	10	124.2	566	146	94	85	11	10	6	5	57	0	105	6	2	6	7	.462	0	3	6.14
1994	Canton-Akrn	AA	39	0	0	20	64.1	268	45	24	18	3	3	3	3	34	1	34	5	0	4	2	.667	0	1	2.52
1995	Colo. Sprng	AAA	2	0	0	1	3	21	8	8	8	1	0	0	0	5	0	2	0	1	0	0	.000	0	0	24.00
	5 Min. YEARS		104	49	1	31	364.2	1597	361	211	176	18	21	15	14	185	4	265	26	6	18	19	.486	0	4	4.34

Rich Loiselle

Pitches: Right Bats: Right Pos: P Ht: 6'5" Wt: 225 Born: 1/12/72 Age: 24

			HOW MUCH HE PITCHED			WHAT HE GAVE UP												THE RESULTS					
Year	Team	Lg	G	GS	CG	GF	IP	BFP	H	R	ER	HR	SH	SF	HB	TBB	IBB	SO	WP	Bk	W	L	Pct.	ShO	Sv	ERA
1991	Padres	R	12	12	0	0	61.1	285	72	40	24	1	1	3	3	26	0	47	4	3	2	3	.400	0	0	3.52
1992	Charlstn-Sc	A	19	19	2	0	97	407	93	51	40	2	0	1	3	42	0	64	2	0	4	8	.333	2	0	3.71
1993	Waterloo	A	10	10	1	0	59.1	254	55	28	26	3	2	1	4	29	1	47	6	0	1	5	.167	1	0	3.94
	Rancho Cuca	A	14	14	1	0	82.2	380	109	64	53	5	3	3	5	34	1	53	1	0	5	8	.385	0	0	5.77
1994	Rancho Cuca	A	27	27	0	0	156.2	704	160	83	69	12	7	6	11	76	2	120	12	0	9	10	.474	0	0	3.96
1995	Memphis	A	13	13	1	0	78.2	357	82	46	31	5	1	1	6	33	2	48	3	1	6	3	.667	0	0	3.55
	Las Vegas	AAA	8	7	1	0	27.1	131	36	27	22	5	1	0	2	9	0	16	0	0	2	2	.500	1	0	7.24
	Tucson	AAA	2	1	0	0	10.1	44	8	4	3	0	0	0	2	4	0	4	0	1	0	0	.000	0	0	2.61
	5 Min. YEARS		105	103	6	0	573.1	2562	615	343	268	33	15	15	34	253	6	399	28	5	29	39	.426	4	0	4.21

Joe Long

Pitches: Right Bats: Right Pos: P Ht: 6'4" Wt: 200 Born: 6/23/71 Age: 25

			HOW MUCH HE PITCHED			WHAT HE GAVE UP												THE RESULTS					
Year	Team	Lg	G	GS	CG	GF	IP	BFP	H	R	ER	HR	SH	SF	HB	TBB	IBB	SO	WP	Bk	W	L	Pct.	ShO	Sv	ERA
1991	Oneonta	A	1	1	0	0	3	20	9	8	4	0	0	0	1	1	0	0	0	0	0	1	.000	0	0	12.00
	Yankees	R	8	6	0	1	38	164	39	23	11	0	0	2	3	7	0	27	4	1	3	2	.600	0	0	2.61
1992	Yankees	R	7	4	0	1	34.1	150	39	20	10	0	4	1	4	2	0	27	3	2	1	3	.250	0	0	2.62
	Ft. Laud	A	2	1	0	0	5.2	30	13	10	9	1	0	1	0	2	0	3	1	0	0	0	.000	0	0	14.29
1993	Greensboro	A	36	7	0	10	100.1	421	96	56	44	8	4	1	5	33	2	63	6	0	6	4	.600	0	4	3.95
1994	Tampa	A	32	1	0	7	49	221	61	27	19	2	1	3	3	20	2	21	4	1	1	3	.250	0	0	3.49
1995	Norwich	AA	43	1	0	15	81.2	391	103	54	44	4	2	6	6	48	3	34	3	0	4	2	.667	0	2	4.85
	5 Min. YEARS		129	21	0	34	312	1397	360	198	141	15	11	14	22	113	7	175	21	4	15	15	.500	0	6	4.07

Joey Long

Pitches: Left Bats: Right Pos: P Ht: 6'2" Wt: 195 Born: 7/15/70 Age: 25

			HOW MUCH HE PITCHED			WHAT HE GAVE UP												THE RESULTS					
Year	Team	Lg	G	GS	CG	GF	IP	BFP	H	R	ER	HR	SH	SF	HB	TBB	IBB	SO	WP	Bk	W	L	Pct.	ShO	Sv	ERA
1991	Spokane	A	13	11	0	0	56.2	282	78	57	44	2	1	3	2	39	0	40	8	4	1	9	.100	0	0	6.99
1993	Waterloo	A	33	7	0	7	96.1	415	96	56	52	7	3	1	3	36	2	90	8	3	4	3	.571	0	0	4.86
1994	Rancho Cuca	A	46	0	0	17	52	248	69	36	27	3	6	2	1	22	1	52	8	0	2	4	.333	0	3	4.67
1995	Las Vegas	AAA	25	0	0	9	31.1	143	38	22	16	1	0	4	0	16	2	13	0	0	1	3	.250	0	0	4.60
	Memphis	AA	25	0	0	3	21.2	104	28	15	8	0	1	1	1	10	2	18	0	0	0	2	.000	0	0	3.32
	4 Min. YEARS		142	18	0	36	258	1192	309	186	147	13	11	11	7	123	7	213	24	7	8	21	.276	0	3	5.13

Kevin Long

Bats: Left Throws: Left Pos: OF Ht: 5'9" Wt: 165 Born: 12/30/66 Age: 29

			BATTING														BASERUNNING				PERCENTAGES		
Year	Team	Lg	G	AB	H	2B	3B	HR	TB	R	RBI	TBB	IBB	SO	HBP	SH	SF	SB	CS	SB%	GDP	Avg	OBP	SLG
1989	Eugene	A	69	260	81	19	1	3	111	54	45	36	6	40	1	1	6	15	3	.83	7	.312	.389	.427
1990	Baseball Cy	A	85	308	87	17	5	2	120	53	33	32	0	28	0	7	2	22	6	.79	4	.282	.348	.390
1991	Memphis	AA	106	407	112	18	2	3	143	60	35	45	1	63	2	6	3	27	10	.73	8	.275	.348	.351
1992	Omaha	AAA	88	312	71	16	3	1	96	28	29	29	2	41	0	2	3	9	5	.64	4	.228	.291	.308
1993	Omaha	AAA	17	51	13	2	0	0	15	7	4	2	0	13	0	1	1	3	0	1.00	0	.255	.278	.294
	Memphis	AA	79	301	82	14	6	1	111	47	20	37	2	56	5	2	2	7	12	.37	4	.272	.359	.369
1994	Memphis	AA	10	24	5	3	0	0	8	5	1	5	0	2	0	0	0	2	0	1.00	2	.208	.345	.333
1995	Omaha	AAA	22	64	16	3	0	0	19	7	0	5	0	8	0	1	0	1	2	.33	3	.250	.304	.297
	Wichita	AA	67	250	73	14	1	1	92	38	26	41	2	29	2	0	0	9	6	.60	3	.292	.396	.368
	7 Min. YEARS		543	1977	540	106	18	11	715	299	193	232	13	280	10	20	17	95	44	.68	35	.273	.350	.362

R.D. Long

Bats: Both **Throws:** Right **Pos:** 2B   **Ht:** 6'1" **Wt:** 183 **Born:** 4/2/71 **Age:** 25

																	BASERUNNING				PERCENTAGES		
Year Team	Lg	G	AB	H	2B	3B	HR	TB	R	RBI	TBB	IBB	SO	HBP	SH	SF	SB	CS	SB%	GDP	Avg	OBP	SLG
1992 Oneonta	A	42	153	39	9	1	0	50	26	15	24	0	31	0	2	2	13	3	.81	2	.255	.352	.327
1993 Greensboro	A	58	170	41	4	4	3	62	21	20	33	0	45	0	4	1	6	4	.60	1	.241	.363	.365
1994 Tampa	A	94	257	61	9	2	6	92	44	33	43	1	66	2	0	2	37	9	.80	3	.237	.349	.358
1995 Norwich	AA	9	33	7	3	0	0	10	4	5	7	0	11	0	0	0	2	1	.67	1	.212	.350	.303
Tampa	A	110	384	96	15	10	4	143	70	36	72	1	100	2	9	2	28	13	.68	4	.250	.370	.372
4 Min. YEARS		313	997	244	40	17	13	357	165	109	179	2	253	4	15	7	86	30	.74	11	.245	.360	.358

Ryan Long

Bats: Right **Throws:** Right **Pos:** 3B   **Ht:** 6'2" **Wt:** 185 **Born:** 2/3/73 **Age:** 23

																	BASERUNNING				PERCENTAGES		
Year Team	Lg	G	AB	H	2B	3B	HR	TB	R	RBI	TBB	IBB	SO	HBP	SH	SF	SB	CS	SB%	GDP	Avg	OBP	SLG
1991 Royals	R	48	177	54	2	2	0	60	17	20	10	0	20	2	0	1	5	4	.56	3	.305	.347	.339
1992 Eugene	A	54	183	42	5	2	0	51	19	18	3	0	33	4	2	1	7	5	.58	4	.230	.257	.279
1993 Rockford	A	107	396	115	27	6	8	178	46	68	16	3	76	18	2	5	16	6	.73	6	.290	.343	.449
1994 Wilmington	A	123	494	130	25	5	11	198	69	68	16	0	72	8	3	3	7	3	.70	4	.263	.296	.401
1995 Wichita	AA	102	342	79	26	0	5	120	36	34	10	1	48	5	1	0	4	4	.50	9	.231	.263	.351
5 Min. YEARS		434	1592	420	85	15	24	607	187	208	55	4	249	37	8	10	39	22	.64	26	.264	.302	.381

Steve Long

Pitches: Right **Bats:** Right **Pos:** P   **Ht:** 6'4" **Wt:** 220 **Born:** 7/17/69 **Age:** 26

		HOW MUCH HE PITCHED						WHAT HE GAVE UP												THE RESULTS					
Year Team	Lg	G	GS	CG	GF	IP	BFP	H	R	ER	HR	SH	SF	HB	TBB	IBB	SO	WP	Bk	W	L	Pct.	ShO	Sv	ERA
1990 Jamestown	A	22	0	0	11	39.1	173	26	15	6	1	5	1	3	24	0	35	2	3	4	2	.667	0	2	1.37
1991 Sumter	A	63	0	0	53	76.1	335	72	34	27	2	5	1	5	31	1	79	15	2	3	3	.500	0	17	3.18
1992 W. Palm Bch	A	26	23	4	0	151.1	607	121	53	41	2	9	4	7	42	3	67	7	3	9	7	.563	0	0	2.44
1993 Binghamton	AA	38	19	4	4	156.2	682	165	87	70	9	5	7	7	58	0	70	6	1	12	8	.600	0	1	4.02
1994 Edmonton	AAA	29	29	2	0	172	781	224	119	101	15	5	7	17	59	1	85	14	0	10	11	.476	0	0	5.28
1995 Charlotte	AAA	33	6	0	10	74	344	71	57	49	7	1	2	8	46	1	46	14	0	5	4	.556	0	0	5.96
6 Min. YEARS		211	77	10	78	669.2	2922	679	365	294	36	30	22	47	260	6	382	58	9	43	35	.551	0	24	3.95

Tony Long

Pitches: Left **Bats:** Left **Pos:** P   **Ht:** 6'4" **Wt:** 220 **Born:** 11/20/69 **Age:** 26

		HOW MUCH HE PITCHED						WHAT HE GAVE UP												THE RESULTS					
Year Team	Lg	G	GS	CG	GF	IP	BFP	H	R	ER	HR	SH	SF	HB	TBB	IBB	SO	WP	Bk	W	L	Pct.	ShO	Sv	ERA
1990 Eugene	A	16	10	0	4	64.1	275	68	32	26	5	2	1	6	17	1	58	1	5	2	4	.333	0	1	3.64
1991 Baseball Cy	A	47	0	0	28	78	310	54	19	17	0	7	2	5	33	3	53	4	2	7	3	.700	0	10	1.96
1992 Baseball Cy	A	20	4	1	6	44.1	179	38	11	9	2	3	1	2	9	2	29	3	1	3	3	.500	0	1	1.83
1994 Winnipeg	IND	10	8	0	1	40.1	192	53	31	25	4	3	0	1	17	1	33	0	1	1	4	.200	0	1	5.58
Thunder Bay	IND	9	4	0	3	27.1	127	30	29	21	6	2	2	4	8	0	18	0	2	2	4	.333	0	0	6.91
1995 Arkansas	AA	32	0	0	8	55.1	241	58	28	23	5	3	3	2	14	0	35	0	1	4	4	.500	0	0	3.74
5 Min. YEARS		134	26	1	50	309.2	1324	301	150	121	22	20	9	20	98	7	226	8	12	19	22	.463	0	13	3.52

Luis Lopez

Bats: Right **Throws:** Right **Pos:** DH   **Ht:** 6'1" **Wt:** 190 **Born:** 9/1/64 **Age:** 31

																	BASERUNNING				PERCENTAGES		
Year Team	Lg	G	AB	H	2B	3B	HR	TB	R	RBI	TBB	IBB	SO	HBP	SH	SF	SB	CS	SB%	GDP	Avg	OBP	SLG
1984 Great Falls	R	68	275	90	15	5	6	133	60	61	27	1	15	5	1	2	4	4	.50	10	.327	.395	.484
1985 Vero Beach	A	120	382	106	18	2	1	131	47	43	25	3	41	6	3	3	2	2	.50	19	.277	.329	.343
1986 Vero Beach	A	122	434	124	21	3	1	154	52	60	33	3	25	2	2	4	5	7	.42	21	.286	.336	.355
1987 Bakersfield	A	142	550	181	43	2	16	276	89	96	38	3	49	9	5	6	6	6	.50	9	.329	.378	.502
1988 San Antonio	AA	124	470	116	16	3	7	159	56	65	32	5	33	13	5	7	3	4	.43	12	.247	.308	.338
1989 San Antonio	AA	99	327	87	17	0	10	134	46	51	38	4	39	5	0	2	1	0	1.00	14	.266	.349	.410
Albuquerque	AAA	19	75	37	7	0	2	50	17	16	6	0	7	1	0	2	1	0	1.00	1	.493	.524	.667
1990 Albuquerque	AAA	128	448	158	23	2	11	218	65	81	47	4	49	4	0	2	3	3	.50	12	.353	.417	.487
1991 Colo. Sprng	AAA	41	176	61	11	4	1	83	29	31	9	0	10	3	0	0	0	0	.00	4	.347	.388	.472
1992 Canton-Akrn	AA	20	82	21	1	0	0	22	4	7	3	0	8	0	0	0	0	1	1.00	4	.256	.282	.268
1993 Canton-Akrn	AA	60	231	64	16	0	2	86	30	41	13	0	16	5	2	3	0	3	.00	5	.277	.325	.372
Charlotte	AAA	67	242	76	15	0	12	127	36	37	6	2	17	1	0	2	0	0	.00	8	.314	.331	.525
1994 Richmond	AAA	133	521	159	33	3	18	252	67	79	34	5	43	5	0	4	4	2	.67	20	.305	.351	.484
1995 Buffalo	AAA	123	455	119	21	1	17	193	62	66	29	3	47	8	0	7	1	1	.50	15	.262	.313	.424
1990 Los Angeles	NL	6	6	0	0	0	0	0	0	0	0	0	2	0	0	0	0	0	.00	0	.000	.000	.000
1991 Cleveland	AL	35	82	18	4	1	0	24	7	7	4	1	7	1	1	1	0	0	.00	0	.220	.261	.293
12 Min. YEARS		1266	4668	1399	257	25	104	2018	660	734	340	33	399	67	18	44	31	32	.49	154	.300	.353	.432
2 Maj. YEARS		41	88	18	4	1	0	24	7	7	4	1	9	1	1	1	0	0	.00	0	.205	.245	.273

Pedro Lopez

Bats: Right **Throws:** Right **Pos:** C   **Ht:** 6'0" **Wt:** 160 **Born:** 3/29/69 **Age:** 27

																	BASERUNNING				PERCENTAGES		
Year Team	Lg	G	AB	H	2B	3B	HR	TB	R	RBI	TBB	IBB	SO	HBP	SH	SF	SB	CS	SB%	GDP	Avg	OBP	SLG
1988 Padres	R	42	156	44	4	6	1	63	18	22	10	0	24	0	0	0	9	4	.69	2	.282	.325	.404

Year	Team	Lg	G	AB	H	2B	3B	HR	TB	R	RBI	TBB	IBB	SO	HBP	SH	SF	SB	CS	SB%	GDP	Avg	OBP	SLG
1989	Waterloo	A	97	319	61	13	1	2	82	32	26	25	1	61	4	6	1	4	4	.50	12	.191	.258	.257
1990	Charlstn-Sc	A	32	101	20	2	0	0	22	9	5	7	0	18	4	0	2	0	1	.00	2	.198	.272	.218
1991	Waterloo	A	102	342	97	13	1	8	136	49	57	47	5	66	2	2	4	3	3	.50	4	.284	.370	.398
1992	Wichita	AA	96	319	78	8	4	6	112	35	48	13	0	68	7	2	6	4	3	.57	7	.245	.284	.351
1993	Rancho Cuca	A	37	103	26	10	0	1	39	25	9	24	1	19	2	0	0	0	1	.00	3	.252	.403	.379
	Wichita	AA	50	142	29	7	0	4	48	12	14	22	2	24	1	1	0	3	0	1.00	2	.204	.315	.338
1994	Wichita	AA	42	131	33	7	0	1	43	15	12	15	0	16	3	1	2	0	2	.00	2	.252	.338	.328
	Rancho Cuca	A	7	20	5	2	0	0	7	1	1	1	0	2	0	0	0	0	0	.00	1	.250	.286	.350
	Las Vegas	AAA	17	47	10	2	0	1	15	3	4	1	0	7	0	1	1	0	0	.00	1	.213	.224	.319
1995	El Paso	AA	84	218	68	15	2	4	99	32	28	18	1	45	4	3	0	0	3	.00	8	.312	.375	.454
	New Orleans	AAA	3	8	0	0	0	0	0	0	0	0	0	3	0	0	0	0	0	.00	0	.000	.000	.000
	8 Min. YEARS		609	1906	471	83	14	28	666	231	226	183	10	353	27	16	16	23	21	.52	44	.247	.319	.349

Rene Lopez

Bats: Right **Throws:** Right **Pos:** C   **Ht:** 5'11" **Wt:** 195 **Born:** 12/10/71 **Age:** 24

			BATTING															BASERUNNING				PERCENTAGES		
Year	Team	Lg	G	AB	H	2B	3B	HR	TB	R	RBI	TBB	IBB	SO	HBP	SH	SF	SB	CS	SB%	GDP	Avg	OBP	SLG
1993	Fort Wayne	A	92	340	85	12	1	3	108	26	44	45	0	57	2	1	5	0	1	.00	12	.250	.337	.318
1994	Fort Myers	A	109	383	101	12	1	7	136	48	48	46	1	66	2	0	7	3	3	.50	12	.264	.340	.355
1995	New Britain	AA	82	264	65	8	0	3	82	22	26	27	0	48	0	5	2	0	0	.00	5	.246	.314	.311
	3 Min. YEARS		283	987	251	32	2	13	326	96	118	118	1	171	4	6	14	3	4	.43	29	.254	.332	.330

Roberto Lopez

Bats: Both **Throws:** Right **Pos:** 2B   **Ht:** 5'9" **Wt:** 150 **Born:** 11/15/71 **Age:** 24

			BATTING															BASERUNNING				PERCENTAGES		
Year	Team	Lg	G	AB	H	2B	3B	HR	TB	R	RBI	TBB	IBB	SO	HBP	SH	SF	SB	CS	SB%	GDP	Avg	OBP	SLG
1994	Stockton	A	5	16	2	1	0	0	3	2	1	3	0	1	0	0	0	1	1	.50	0	.125	.263	.188
1995	El Paso	AA	114	417	130	22	8	1	171	80	44	77	2	63	4	6	5	9	4	.69	4	.312	.419	.410
	2 Min. YEARS		119	433	132	23	8	1	174	82	45	80	2	64	4	6	5	10	5	.67	4	.305	.414	.402

Billy Lott

Bats: Right **Throws:** Right **Pos:** OF   **Ht:** 6'4" **Wt:** 210 **Born:** 8/16/70 **Age:** 25

			BATTING															BASERUNNING				PERCENTAGES		
Year	Team	Lg	G	AB	H	2B	3B	HR	TB	R	RBI	TBB	IBB	SO	HBP	SH	SF	SB	CS	SB%	GDP	Avg	OBP	SLG
1989	Dodgers	R	46	150	29	2	4	0	39	18	9	10	0	48	1	1	0	5	1	.83	0	.193	.248	.260
1990	Bakersfield	A	38	133	27	1	1	2	36	11	14	6	0	46	1	1	1	3	2	.60	3	.203	.241	.271
	Yakima	A	65	240	66	13	2	4	95	37	38	10	0	62	3	0	4	4	0	1.00	1	.275	.307	.396
1991	Bakersfield	A	92	314	70	10	1	5	97	40	35	25	0	90	3	3	6	11	4	.73	8	.223	.282	.309
1992	Vero Beach	A	126	435	107	17	4	3	141	42	35	22	3	107	3	2	5	11	5	.69	18	.246	.284	.324
1993	San Antonio	AA	114	418	106	17	2	15	172	49	49	23	3	111	1	1	2	5	11	.31	8	.254	.293	.411
1994	San Antonio	AA	122	448	131	25	4	12	200	61	62	31	2	100	4	2	3	20	10	.67	7	.292	.342	.446
1995	Albuquerque	AAA	41	146	46	7	2	5	72	23	26	13	2	48	0	1	0	1	2	.33	1	.315	.371	.493
	7 Min. YEARS		644	2284	582	92	20	46	852	281	268	140	10	612	16	11	21	60	35	.63	50	.255	.300	.373

Torey Lovullo

Bats: Both **Throws:** Right **Pos:** 2B-3B   **Ht:** 6'0" **Wt:** 185 **Born:** 7/25/65 **Age:** 30

			BATTING															BASERUNNING				PERCENTAGES		
Year	Team	Lg	G	AB	H	2B	3B	HR	TB	R	RBI	TBB	IBB	SO	HBP	SH	SF	SB	CS	SB%	GDP	Avg	OBP	SLG
1987	Fayetteville	A	55	191	49	13	0	8	86	34	32	37	4	30	2	2	1	6	0	1.00	3	.257	.381	.450
	Lakeland	A	18	60	16	3	0	1	22	11	16	10	0	8	0	0	3	0	0	.00	0	.267	.356	.367
1988	Glens Falls	AA	78	270	74	17	1	9	120	37	50	36	3	44	1	0	6	2	0	1.00	5	.274	.355	.444
	Toledo	AAA	57	177	41	8	1	5	66	18	20	9	0	24	0	7	1	2	1	.67	1	.232	.267	.373
1989	Toledo	AAA	112	409	94	23	2	10	151	48	52	44	10	57	1	7	4	2	1	.67	10	.230	.303	.369
1990	Toledo	AAA	141	486	131	38	1	14	213	71	58	61	6	74	4	2	4	4	1	.80	12	.270	.353	.438
1991	Columbus	AAA	106	395	107	24	5	10	171	74	75	59	4	56	0	2	6	4	4	.50	10	.271	.361	.433
1992	Columbus	AAA	131	468	138	33	5	19	238	69	89	64	4	65	3	2	6	9	4	.69	8	.295	.379	.509
1994	Calgary	AAA	54	211	62	18	1	11	115	43	47	34	1	28	1	2	2	2	1	.67	3	.294	.391	.545
1995	Buffalo	AAA	132	474	121	20	5	16	199	84	61	70	7	62	2	1	5	3	1	.75	12	.255	.350	.420
1988	Detroit	AL	12	21	8	1	1	1	14	2	2	1	0	2	0	1	0	0	0	.00	1	.381	.409	.667
1989	Detroit	AL	29	87	10	2	0	1	15	8	4	14	0	20	0	1	2	0	0	.00	3	.115	.233	.172
1991	New York	AL	22	51	9	2	0	0	11	0	2	5	1	7	0	3	0	0	0	.00	1	.176	.250	.216
1993	California	AL	116	367	92	20	0	6	130	42	30	36	1	49	1	3	2	7	6	.54	8	.251	.318	.354
1994	Seattle	AL	36	72	16	5	0	2	27	9	7	9	1	13	0	0	0	1	0	1.00	1	.222	.309	.375
	8 Min. YEARS		884	3141	833	197	21	103	1381	489	500	424	39	448	14	25	38	34	13	.72	64	.265	.351	.440
	5 Maj. YEARS		215	598	135	30	1	10	197	61	45	65	3	91	1	8	4	8	6	.57	14	.226	.301	.329

Derek Lowe

Pitches: Right **Bats:** Right **Pos:** P | **Ht:** 6'6" **Wt:** 170 **Born:** 6/1/73 **Age:** 23

		HOW MUCH HE PITCHED						WHAT HE GAVE UP												THE RESULTS					
Year Team	Lg	G	GS	CG	GF	IP	BFP	H	R	ER	HR	SH	SF	HB	TBB	IBB	SO	WP	Bk	W	L	Pct.	ShO	Sv	ERA
1991 Mariners	R	12	12	0	0	71	295	58	26	19	2	1	4	2	21	0	60	4	6	5	3	.625	0	0	2.41
1992 Bellingham	A	14	13	2	1	85.2	349	69	34	23	2	3	1	4	22	0	66	5	4	7	3	.700	1	0	2.42
1993 Riverside	A	27	26	3	1	154	687	189	104	90	9	2	2	2	60	0	80	12	9	12	9	.571	2	0	5.26
1994 Jacksonvlle	AA	26	26	2	0	151.1	676	177	92	83	7	6	3	9	50	1	75	11	7	7	10	.412	0	0	4.94
1995 Mariners	R	2	2	0	0	9.2	35	5	1	1	0	0	0	0	2	0	11	0	0	1	0	1.000	0	0	0.93
Port City	AA	10	10	1	0	53.1	244	70	41	36	8	3	2	3	22	1	30	2	0	1	6	.143	0	0	6.08
5 Min. YEARS		91	89	8	2	525	2286	568	298	252	28	15	12	20	177	2	322	34	26	33	31	.516	3	0	4.32

Sean Lowe

Pitches: Right **Bats:** Right **Pos:** P | **Ht:** 6'2" **Wt:** 200 **Born:** 3/29/71 **Age:** 25

		HOW MUCH HE PITCHED						WHAT HE GAVE UP												THE RESULTS					
Year Team	Lg	G	GS	CG	GF	IP	BFP	H	R	ER	HR	SH	SF	HB	TBB	IBB	SO	WP	Bk	W	L	Pct.	ShO	Sv	ERA
1992 Hamilton	A	5	5	0	0	28	109	14	8	5	0	0	0	1	14	0	22	1	1	2	0	1.000	0	0	1.61
1993 St. Pete	A	25	25	0	0	132.2	594	152	80	63	6	2	5	6	62	1	87	4	5	6	11	.353	0	0	4.27
1994 St. Pete	A	21	21	0	0	114	488	119	51	44	6	3	2	5	37	0	92	3	0	5	6	.455	0	0	3.47
Arkansas	AA	3	3	0	0	19.1	76	13	3	3	0	2	0	0	8	0	11	0	0	2	1	.667	0	0	1.40
1995 Arkansas	AA	24	24	0	0	129	578	143	84	70	2	5	4	5	64	0	77	9	0	9	8	.529	0	0	4.88
4 Min. YEARS		78	78	0	0	423	1845	441	226	185	14	12	11	17	185	1	289	17	6	24	26	.480	0	0	3.94

Lou Lucca

Bats: Right **Throws:** Right **Pos:** 3B | **Ht:** 5'11" **Wt:** 210 **Born:** 10/13/70 **Age:** 25

		BATTING														BASERUNNING				PERCENTAGES		
Year Team	Lg	G	AB	H	2B	3B	HR	TB	R	RBI	TBB	IBB	SO	HBP	SH	SF	SB	CS	SB%	GDP	Avg	OBP	SLG
1992 Erie	A	76	263	74	16	1	13	131	54	44	33	0	40	5	0	2	6	3	.67	8	.281	.370	.498
1993 Kane County	A	127	419	116	25	2	6	163	52	53	60	0	58	9	2	7	4	10	.29	9	.277	.374	.389
1994 Brevard Cty	A	130	441	125	29	1	8	180	62	76	72	2	73	4	0	6	3	7	.30	18	.283	.384	.408
1995 Portland	AA	112	388	107	28	1	9	164	57	64	59	5	77	5	0	2	4	4	.50	18	.276	.377	.423
4 Min. YEARS		445	1511	422	98	5	36	638	222	237	224	7	248	23	2	17	17	24	.41	53	.279	.377	.422

Roger Luce

Bats: Right **Throws:** Right **Pos:** C | **Ht:** 6'4" **Wt:** 215 **Born:** 5/7/69 **Age:** 27

		BATTING														BASERUNNING				PERCENTAGES		
Year Team	Lg	G	AB	H	2B	3B	HR	TB	R	RBI	TBB	IBB	SO	HBP	SH	SF	SB	CS	SB%	GDP	Avg	OBP	SLG
1991 Gastonia	A	33	107	28	9	2	2	47	17	16	7	0	31	3	1	3	2	2	.50	1	.262	.317	.439
1992 Charlotte	A	91	303	70	9	0	1	82	18	20	19	1	77	3	1	2	3	4	.43	3	.231	.281	.271
1993 Tulsa	AA	101	321	62	14	2	8	104	35	29	17	0	107	4	0	1	2	1	.67	5	.193	.242	.324
1994 Tulsa	AA	59	191	54	11	2	6	87	27	22	16	0	56	0	1	0	2	2	.50	2	.283	.338	.455
Okla. City	AAA	49	169	40	9	1	1	54	20	14	4	0	40	0	1	0	0	0	.00	1	.237	.254	.320
1995 Okla. City	AAA	1	3	0	0	0	0	0	0	0	0	0	2	0	0	0	0	0	.00	0	.000	.000	.000
Jackson	AA	18	52	11	2	1	1	18	4	4	3	0	12	0	0	0	0	0	.00	3	.212	.255	.346
5 Min. YEARS		352	1146	265	54	8	19	392	121	105	66	1	325	10	4	6	9	9	.50	15	.231	.278	.342

Eric Ludwick

Pitches: Right **Bats:** Right **Pos:** P | **Ht:** 6'5" **Wt:** 211 **Born:** 12/14/71 **Age:** 24

		HOW MUCH HE PITCHED						WHAT HE GAVE UP												THE RESULTS					
Year Team	Lg	G	GS	CG	GF	IP	BFP	H	R	ER	HR	SH	SF	HB	TBB	IBB	SO	WP	Bk	W	L	Pct.	ShO	Sv	ERA
1993 Pittsfield	A	10	10	1	0	51	219	51	27	18	0	3	1	0	18	0	40	4	2	4	4	.500	0	0	3.18
1994 St. Lucie	A	27	27	3	0	150.1	671	162	102	76	6	1	12	6	77	1	77	3	5	7	13	.350	0	0	4.55
1995 Binghamton	AA	23	22	3	0	143.1	590	108	52	47	9	4	6	2	68	1	131	6	0	12	5	.706	2	0	2.95
Norfolk	AAA	4	3	0	0	20	88	22	16	13	3	0	0	1	7	0	9	1	0	1	1	.500	0	0	5.85
3 Min. YEARS		64	62	7	0	364.2	1568	343	196	154	18	8	19	9	170	2	257	14	7	24	23	.511	2	0	3.80

Larry Luebbers

Pitches: Right **Bats:** Right **Pos:** P   **Ht:** 6' 6" **Wt:** 205 **Born:** 10/11/69 **Age:** 26

			HOW MUCH HE PITCHED						WHAT HE GAVE UP											THE RESULTS					
Year	Team	Lg	G	GS	CG	GF	IP	BFP	H	R	ER	HR	SH	SF	HB	TBB	IBB	SO	WP	Bk	W	L	Pct.	ShO	Sv	ERA
1990	Billings	R	13	13	1	0	72.1	319	74	46	36	3	2	3	6	31	0	48	7	1	5	4	.556	1	0	4.48
1991	Cedar Rapds	A	28	28	3	0	184.2	781	177	85	64	8	12	6	10	64	5	98	11	4	8	10	.444	0	0	3.12
1992	Cedar Rapds	A	14	14	1	0	82.1	355	71	33	24	2	4	3	8	33	0	56	1	1	7	0	1.000	0	0	2.62
	Chattanooga	AA	14	14	1	0	87.1	368	86	34	22	5	2	1	4	34	1	56	5	2	6	5	.545	0	0	2.27
1993	Indianapols	AAA	15	15	0	0	84.1	380	81	45	39	7	6	2	6	47	5	51	1	0	4	7	.364	0	0	4.16
1994	Iowa	AAA	27	26	0	0	138.2	630	149	100	93	22	4	7	5	87	3	90	7	4	10	12	.455	0	0	6.04
1995	Chattanooga	AA	28	21	0	4	118	514	112	71	61	7	6	6	7	59	1	87	1	0	10	6	.625	0	0	4.65
1993	Cincinnati	NL	14	14	0	0	77.1	332	74	49	39	7	4	5	1	38	3	38	4	0	2	5	.286	0	0	4.54
	6 Min. YEARS		139	131	6	4	767.2	3347	750	414	339	54	36	28	46	355	15	486	33	12	50	44	.532	1	0	3.97

Rob Lukachyk

Bats: Left **Throws:** Right **Pos:** OF   **Ht:** 6'0" **Wt:** 185 **Born:** 7/24/68 **Age:** 27

					BATTING												BASERUNNING				PERCENTAGES		
Year	Team	Lg	G	AB	H	2B	3B	HR	TB	R	RBI	TBB	IBB	SO	HBP	SH	SF	SB	CS	SB%	GDP	Avg	OBP	SLG
1987	White Sox	R	17	54	12	1	1	0	15	6	7	9	2	13	0	0	0	5	1	.83	1	.222	.333	.278
1988	Utica	A	71	227	64	10	8	7	111	42	48	31	1	48	3	2	1	9	6	.60	2	.282	.374	.489
1989	South Bend	A	122	430	125	16	4	3	158	60	63	35	7	78	2	5	6	18	15	.55	5	.291	.342	.367
1990	Sarasota	A	118	428	104	23	9	4	157	56	36	31	4	88	2	4	4	17	8	.68	6	.243	.295	.367
1991	Sarasota	A	125	399	108	27	2	9	166	63	49	63	4	100	15	9	2	22	8	.73	2	.271	.388	.416
1992	Stockton	A	105	359	99	21	14	15	193	77	81	53	3	86	9	0	5	44	15	.75	0	.276	.378	.538
1993	New Orleans	AAA	8	24	4	1	0	2	11	5	6	3	0	6	0	2	0	0	0	.00	1	.167	.259	.458
	El Paso	AA	113	362	96	24	7	9	161	58	63	52	3	75	7	2	5	8	10	.44	10	.265	.364	.445
1994	Bowie	AA	108	371	107	19	6	10	168	68	54	47	9	60	5	1	5	33	6	.85	5	.288	.371	.453
1995	Toledo	AAA	104	346	88	24	7	7	147	43	26	33	0	75	2	3	3	8	5	.62	5	.254	.320	.425
	9 Min. YEARS		891	3000	807	166	58	66	1287	478	433	357	33	629	45	28	31	164	74	.69	36	.269	.352	.429

Matt Luke

Bats: Left **Throws:** Left **Pos:** OF   **Ht:** 6'5" **Wt:** 225 **Born:** 2/26/71 **Age:** 25

					BATTING												BASERUNNING				PERCENTAGES		
Year	Team	Lg	G	AB	H	2B	3B	HR	TB	R	RBI	TBB	IBB	SO	HBP	SH	SF	SB	CS	SB%	GDP	Avg	OBP	SLG
1992	Oneonta	A	69	271	67	11	7	2	98	30	34	19	3	32	2	0	3	4	1	.80	9	.247	.298	.362
1993	Greensboro	A	135	549	157	37	5	21	267	83	91	47	4	79	7	0	6	11	3	.79	9	.286	.346	.486
1994	Albany-Colo	AA	63	236	67	11	2	8	106	34	40	28	0	50	2	3	1	6	4	.60	6	.284	.363	.449
	Tampa	A	57	222	68	11	2	16	131	52	42	28	2	27	1	0	1	4	1	.80	7	.306	.385	.590
1995	Norwich	AA	93	365	95	17	5	8	146	48	53	20	2	68	2	3	4	5	4	.56	6	.260	.299	.400
	Columbus	AAA	23	77	23	4	1	3	38	11	12	2	0	12	1	1	0	1	1	.50	3	.299	.325	.494
	4 Min. YEARS		440	1720	477	91	22	58	786	258	272	144	11	268	15	7	15	31	14	.69	40	.277	.336	.457

Brent Lutz

Bats: Right **Throws:** Right **Pos:** C   **Ht:** 6'1" **Wt:** 185 **Born:** 5/7/70 **Age:** 26

					BATTING												BASERUNNING				PERCENTAGES		
Year	Team	Lg	G	AB	H	2B	3B	HR	TB	R	RBI	TBB	IBB	SO	HBP	SH	SF	SB	CS	SB%	GDP	Avg	OBP	SLG
1991	Medicne Hat	R	41	115	31	4	2	3	48	23	23	21	0	34	7	1	0	6	1	.86	0	.270	.413	.417
1992	Myrtle Bch	A	49	90	15	2	0	2	23	10	10	13	0	31	4	2	1	2	1	.67	0	.167	.296	.256
1993	Hagerstown	A	1	0	0	0	0	0	0	0	0	0	0	0	0	0	0	0	0	.00	0	.000	.000	.000
	Dunedin	A	84	246	65	12	3	4	95	38	33	31	1	60	5	3	2	16	8	.67	5	.264	.356	.386
1994	Knoxville	AA	111	372	101	16	5	8	151	56	41	34	0	100	17	2	2	19	10	.66	8	.272	.358	.406
1995	Syracuse	AAA	35	86	14	0	0	1	17	5	5	4	0	23	0	0	0	1	2	.33	3	.163	.200	.198
	Knoxville	AA	52	144	19	6	0	2	31	14	12	15	0	59	6	2	0	4	1	.80	1	.132	.242	.215
	5 Min. YEARS		373	1053	245	40	10	20	365	146	124	118	1	307	39	10	5	48	23	.68	17	.233	.331	.347

Ryan Luzinski

Bats: Right **Throws:** Right **Pos:** C   **Ht:** 6'0" **Wt:** 215 **Born:** 8/22/73 **Age:** 22

					BATTING												BASERUNNING				PERCENTAGES		
Year	Team	Lg	G	AB	H	2B	3B	HR	TB	R	RBI	TBB	IBB	SO	HBP	SH	SF	SB	CS	SB%	GDP	Avg	OBP	SLG
1992	Great Falls	R	61	227	57	14	4	4	91	26	29	22	2	47	2	0	1	2	1	.67	1	.251	.321	.401
1993	Bakersfield	A	48	147	41	10	1	3	62	18	9	13	0	24	5	0	0	2	2	.50	3	.279	.358	.422
	Yakima	A	69	237	61	10	3	4	89	32	46	41	4	44	4	3	3	6	1	.86	2	.257	.372	.376
1994	Vero Beach	A	112	379	99	18	3	11	156	48	61	33	1	91	5	1	5	2	1	.67	11	.261	.325	.412
1995	San Antonio	AA	44	144	33	5	0	1	41	18	9	13	1	32	3	2	1	1	1	.50	6	.229	.304	.285
	Vero Beach	A	38	134	45	12	0	5	72	15	23	9	3	21	0	0	1	1	0	1.00	4	.336	.375	.537
	4 Min. YEARS		372	1268	336	69	11	28	511	157	177	131	11	259	19	6	11	14	6	.70	27	.265	.340	.403

Mitch Lyden

Bats: Right Throws: Right Pos: C   Ht: 6' 3" Wt: 225 Born: 12/14/64 Age: 31

Year	Team	Lg	G	AB	H	2B	3B	HR	TB	R	RBI	TBB	IBB	SO	HBP	SH	SF	SB	CS	SB%	GDP	Avg	OBP	SLG
1984	Greensboro	A	14	32	7	1	0	1	11	3	2	1	1	9	0	0	0	0	0	.00	3	.219	.242	.344
	Yankees	R	54	200	47	4	0	1	54	21	21	13	1	36	4	1	2	3	1	.75	3	.235	.292	.270
1985	Ft. Laud	A	116	400	102	21	1	10	155	43	58	27	0	93	5	1	5	1	2	.33	15	.255	.307	.388
1986	Yankees	R	17	50	17	7	0	3	33	8	16	7	0	7	0	0	1	0	0	.00	0	.340	.414	.660
	Albany-Colo	AA	46	159	48	14	1	8	88	19	29	4	1	39	2	0	2	0	1	.00	5	.302	.323	.553
	Columbus	AAA	2	7	0	0	0	0	0	0	0	1	0	1	0	0	0	0	0	.00	0	.000	.125	.000
1987	Columbus	AAA	29	100	22	3	0	0	25	7	8	4	0	22	1	1	3	1	0	1.00	7	.220	.250	.250
	Albany-Colo	AA	71	233	59	12	2	8	99	25	36	11	0	47	2	1	1	0	0	.00	4	.253	.291	.425
1988	Pr. William	A	67	234	66	12	2	17	133	42	47	19	3	59	4	0	2	1	0	1.00	5	.282	.344	.568
	Albany-Colo	AA	20	78	32	7	1	8	65	16	21	5	1	15	0	0	1	0	2	.00	3	.410	.440	.833
1989	Albany-Colo	AA	53	160	43	2	0	6	63	24	21	12	3	51	2	1	0	1	0	1.00	5	.238	.292	.348
	Pr. William	A	30	105	29	2	1	7	54	17	28	8	0	26	8	0	1	1	0	1.00	2	.276	.369	.514
1990	Albany-Colo	AA	85	311	92	22	1	17	167	55	63	24	1	67	9	0	4	1	0	1.00	13	.296	.359	.537
	Columbus	AAA	41	147	33	8	0	7	62	18	20	7	0	34	4	0	1	0	0	.00	9	.224	.277	.422
1991	Toledo	AAA	101	340	76	11	2	18	145	34	55	15	3	108	0	0	7	0	0	.00	11	.224	.251	.426
1992	Tidewater	AAA	91	299	77	13	0	14	132	34	52	12	0	95	3	0	4	1	2	.33	11	.258	.289	.441
1993	Edmonton	AAA	50	160	49	15	1	8	90	34	31	5	0	34	0	0	2	1	1	.50	2	.306	.323	.563
1994	Edmonton	AAA	84	289	85	21	0	18	160	52	65	11	0	74	11	1	2	2	0	1.00	13	.294	.342	.554
1995	Omaha	AAA	71	237	60	8	1	12	106	26	44	11	2	66	2	3	6	0	0	.00	5	.253	.285	.447
1993	Florida	NL	6	10	3	0	0	1	6	2	1	0	0	3	0	0	0	0	0	.00	0	.300	.300	.600
	12 Min. YEARS		1042	3562	944	183	13	163	1642	478	617	197	16	883	57	9	44	13	9	.59	117	.265	.310	.461

Scott Lydy

Bats: Right Throws: Right Pos: OF   Ht: 6' 5" Wt: 195 Born: 10/26/68 Age: 27

Year	Team	Lg	G	AB	H	2B	3B	HR	TB	R	RBI	TBB	IBB	SO	HBP	SH	SF	SB	CS	SB%	GDP	Avg	OBP	SLG
1990	Madison	A	54	174	33	6	2	4	55	33	19	25	1	62	1	0	2	7	5	.58	1	.190	.292	.316
	Athletics	R	18	50	17	6	0	2	29	8	11	10	0	14	0	0	0	0	0	.00	1	.340	.450	.580
1991	Madison	A	127	464	120	26	2	12	186	64	69	66	5	109	5	0	4	24	9	.73	10	.259	.354	.401
1992	Reno	A	33	124	49	13	2	2	72	29	27	26	2	30	0	0	0	9	4	.69	1	.395	.500	.581
	Huntsville	AA	109	387	118	20	3	9	171	64	65	67	5	95	4	0	4	16	5	.76	4	.305	.409	.442
1993	Tacoma	AAA	95	341	100	22	6	9	161	70	41	50	3	87	1	2	3	12	4	.75	8	.293	.382	.472
1994	Tacoma	AAA	135	508	160	37	3	17	254	98	73	58	1	108	6	1	6	22	6	.79	14	.315	.388	.500
1995	Edmonton	AAA	104	400	116	29	7	16	207	78	65	33	3	66	6	3	5	15	4	.79	11	.290	.349	.518
1993	Oakland	AL	41	102	23	5	0	2	34	11	7	8	0	39	1	0	0	2	0	1.00	1	.225	.288	.333
	6 Min. YEARS		675	2448	713	159	25	71	1135	444	370	335	20	571	23	6	24	105	37	.74	50	.291	.378	.464

Dave Lynch

Pitches: Left Bats: Right Pos: P   Ht: 6'3" Wt: 205 Born: 10/7/65 Age: 30

Year	Team	Lg	G	GS	CG	GF	IP	BFP	H	R	ER	HR	SH	SF	HB	TBB	IBB	SO	WP	Bk	W	L	Pct.	ShO	Sv	ERA
1987	Rangers	R	13	9	1	0	55	221	38	18	14	1	2	2	3	29	0	55	5	4	4	3	.571	1	0	2.29
1988	Rangers	R	1	0	0	0	1.2	5	0	0	0	0	0	0	0	0	0	3	0	0	0	0	.000	0	0	0.00
	Charlotte	A	36	0	0	24	58	242	43	21	13	1	4	1	5	22	1	58	1	2	6	2	.750	0	6	2.02
1989	Okla. City	AAA	11	0	0	5	11.2	56	12	8	8	1	0	0	0	8	1	10	3	0	0	2	.000	0	0	6.17
	Tulsa	AA	39	0	0	24	51.2	209	39	7	5	2	0	0	2	24	0	53	3	2	8	0	1.000	0	7	0.87
1990	Okla. City	AAA	14	2	0	10	26.2	135	34	24	17	4	4	0	5	14	1	20	1	3	0	4	.000	0	1	5.74
	Tulsa	AA	21	6	0	10	59	242	60	25	25	5	3	1	3	21	1	37	2	1	4	4	.500	0	5	3.81
1991	Albuquerque	AAA	33	0	0	8	36.2	182	51	28	27	2	0	2	0	26	1	29	2	0	1	3	.250	0	0	6.63
	San Antonio	AA	11	0	0	7	13.1	62	17	11	10	2	0	1	0	6	0	10	0	0	0	1	.000	0	0	6.75
1992	Nashville	AAA	1	0	0	0	1.1	4	1	0	0	0	0	0	0	0	0	0	0	0	0	0	.000	0	0	0.00
	Chattanooga	AA	37	0	0	12	51	200	39	19	17	4	1	0	1	15	2	44	5	2	3	1	.750	0	2	3.00
1993	Chattanooga	AA	3	0	0	2	2.1	7	0	0	0	0	0	0	0	0	0	3	0	0	0	0	.000	0	1	0.00
	Indianapolis	AAA	59	0	0	27	84	370	73	41	30	3	8	2	2	48	8	76	3	1	9	4	.692	0	1	3.21
1994	Charlotte	AAA	57	0	0	21	57.2	256	62	32	30	5	7	1	3	22	6	50	3	0	2	7	.222	0	4	4.68
1995	Buffalo	AAA	14	0	0	3	14.2	66	16	8	7	0	1	1	0	7	1	14	0	0	1	2	.333	0	0	4.30
	9 Min. YEARS		350	17	1	153	524.2	2257	485	242	203	30	30	11	24	242	22	462	28	15	38	33	.535	1	28	3.48

Robert Machado

Bats: Right **Throws:** Right **Pos:** C **Ht:** 6'1" **Wt:** 150 **Born:** 6/3/73 **Age:** 23

Year Team	Lg	G	AB	H	2B	3B	HR	TB	R	RBI	TBB	IBB	SO	HBP	SH	SF	SB	CS	SB%	GDP	Avg	OBP	SLG
1991 White Sox	R	38	126	31	4	1	0	37	11	15	6	0	21	6	0	1	2	1	.67	2	.246	.309	.294
1992 Utica	A	45	161	44	13	1	2	65	16	20	5	0	26	0	0	1	1	5	.17	3	.273	.293	.404
1993 South Bend	A	75	281	86	14	3	2	112	34	33	19	0	59	4	2	4	1	2	.33	6	.306	.354	.399
1994 Pr.William	A	93	312	81	17	1	11	133	45	47	27	0	68	4	2	1	0	1	.00	10	.260	.326	.426
1995 Nashville	AAA	16	49	7	3	0	1	13	7	5	7	0	12	0	0	0	0	1	.00	1	.143	.250	.265
Pr.William	A	83	272	69	14	0	6	101	37	31	40	5	47	7	2	1	0	0	.00	6	.254	.363	.371
5 Min. YEARS		350	1201	318	65	6	22	461	150	151	104	5	233	21	6	8	4	10	.29	28	.265	.332	.384

Quinn Mack

Bats: Left **Throws:** Left **Pos:** OF **Ht:** 5'10" **Wt:** 185 **Born:** 9/11/65 **Age:** 30

Year Team	Lg	G	AB	H	2B	3B	HR	TB	R	RBI	TBB	IBB	SO	HBP	SH	SF	SB	CS	SB%	GDP	Avg	OBP	SLG
1987 Burlington	A	59	164	44	10	1	2	62	15	15	11	1	22	2	0	0	0	3	.00	7	.268	.322	.378
1988 W. Palm Bch	A	100	349	97	10	5	2	123	51	25	21	1	42	2	3	4	10	5	.67	8	.278	.319	.352
1989 Jacksonville	AA	122	378	97	19	3	6	140	46	40	27	2	55	1	4	4	5	7	.42	12	.257	.305	.370
1990 Indianapols	AAA	121	392	108	25	2	7	158	55	53	25	5	46	5	2	1	11	6	.65	20	.276	.326	.403
1991 Indianapols	AAA	120	416	113	19	8	5	163	35	49	12	0	42	3	1	3	4	6	.40	13	.272	.295	.392
1992 Indianapols	AAA	103	301	85	19	0	4	116	33	36	20	2	44	1	2	2	5	4	.56	10	.282	.327	.385
1993 Ottawa	AAA	8	21	2	0	0	0	2	1	0	1	0	3	0	1	0	0	0	.00	1	.095	.136	.095
Calgary	AAA	84	325	100	25	1	6	145	48	39	17	2	41	0	1	2	9	6	.60	12	.308	.340	.446
1994 Calgary	AAA	114	404	117	30	1	5	164	63	55	31	0	50	1	1	1	10	7	.59	19	.290	.341	.406
1995 Tacoma	AAA	70	204	54	11	0	1	68	30	17	24	5	21	1	1	0	9	2	.82	6	.265	.345	.333
Memphis	AA	20	63	15	1	0	2	22	6	6	8	1	8	2	1	0	2	1	.67	1	.238	.342	.349
1994 Seattle	AL	5	21	5	3	0	0	8	1	1	1	0	3	0	0	0	2	0	1.00	0	.238	.273	.381
9 Min. YEARS		921	3017	832	169	21	40	1163	383	331	197	19	374	18	17	17	65	47	.58	109	.276	.322	.385

Tony Mack

Pitches: Right **Bats:** Right **Pos:** P **Ht:** 5'10" **Wt:** 177 **Born:** 4/30/61 **Age:** 35

		HOW MUCH HE PITCHED						WHAT HE GAVE UP												THE RESULTS					
Year Team	Lg	G	GS	CG	GF	IP	BFP	H	R	ER	HR	SH	SF	HB	TBB	IBB	SO	WP	Bk	W	L	Pct.	ShO	Sv	ERA
1995 Vancouver	AAA	4	3	0	0	20	83	19	10	10	4	1	1	0	6	0	15	1	0	0	1	.000	0	0	4.50
Midland	AA	3	0	0	0	5.2	21	3	0	0	0	1	0	1	1	0	5	0	0	0	0	.000	0	0	0.00
Corp.Chrsti	IND	15	14	1	0	88	364	84	45	40	9	2	4	2	16	0	68	1	1	6	4	.600	1	0	4.09
1 Min. YEARS		22	17	1	0	113.2	468	106	55	50	13	4	5	2	23	0	88	2	1	6	5	.545	1	0	3.96

Dan Madsen

Bats: Both **Throws:** Left **Pos:** OF **Ht:** 6'0" **Wt:** 185 **Born:** 2/10/71 **Age:** 25

Year Team	Lg	G	AB	H	2B	3B	HR	TB	R	RBI	TBB	IBB	SO	HBP	SH	SF	SB	CS	SB%	GDP	Avg	OBP	SLG
1992 Geneva	A	70	235	57	8	1	4	79	33	31	42	0	65	12	3	2	12	13	.48	3	.243	.381	.336
1993 Peoria	A	80	265	56	16	4	0	80	39	32	37	2	60	10	7	2	9	8	.53	3	.211	.328	.302
1994 Peoria	A	33	116	36	6	2	3	55	22	14	15	1	17	2	3	2	11	3	.79	3	.310	.393	.474
Daytona	A	92	294	59	7	9	4	96	42	39	47	0	74	6	3	5	11	10	.52	10	.201	.318	.327
1995 Orlando	AA	15	26	5	0	1	0	7	6	6	6	0	2	0	0	0	0	1	.00	0	.192	.344	.269
Rockford	A	29	88	23	6	2	0	33	18	11	14	0	15	6	0	2	14	4	.78	6	.261	.391	.375
Daytona	A	13	36	7	1	0	1	11	7	3	3	0	11	1	1	0	4	2	.67	0	.194	.275	.306
Pueblo	IND	8	31	14	2	0	0	16	4	3	4	0	3	0	1	0	5	0	1.00	3	.452	.514	.516
Abilene	IND	48	163	42	6	3	4	66	22	28	14	2	47	3	0	2	9	2	.82	1	.258	.324	.405
4 Min. YEARS		388	1254	299	52	22	16	443	193	167	182	5	294	40	18	15	75	43	.64	28	.238	.349	.353

Calvin Maduro

Pitches: Right **Bats:** Right **Pos:** P **Ht:** 6'0" **Wt:** 175 **Born:** 9/5/74 **Age:** 21

		HOW MUCH HE PITCHED						WHAT HE GAVE UP												THE RESULTS					
Year Team	Lg	G	GS	CG	GF	IP	BFP	H	R	ER	HR	SH	SF	HB	TBB	IBB	SO	WP	Bk	W	L	Pct.	ShO	Sv	ERA
1992 Orioles	R	13	12	1	1	71.1	289	56	29	18	2	2	3	1	26	0	66	4	3	1	4	.200	1	0	2.27
1993 Bluefield	R	14	14	3	0	91	378	90	46	40	4	0	2	3	17	0	83	4	1	9	4	.692	0	0	3.96
1994 Frederick	A	27	26	0	1	152.1	636	132	86	72	18	3	3	4	59	0	137	10	4	9	8	.529	0	0	4.25
1995 Frederick	A	20	20	2	0	122.1	499	109	43	40	16	3	2	6	34	0	120	2	0	8	5	.615	2	0	2.94
Bowie	AA	7	7	0	0	35.1	165	39	28	20	3	1	2	0	27	0	26	3	0	0	6	.000	0	0	5.09
4 Min. YEARS		81	79	6	2	472.1	1967	426	232	190	43	9	12	14	163	0	432	23	8	27	27	.500	3	0	3.62

Ricky Magdaleno

Bats: Right **Throws:** Right **Pos:** SS **Ht:** 6'1" **Wt:** 170 **Born:** 7/6/74 **Age:** 21

Year Team	Lg	G	AB	H	2B	3B	HR	TB	R	RBI	TBB	IBB	SO	HBP	SH	SF	SB	CS	SB%	GDP	Avg	OBP	SLG
1993 Charlstn-Wv	A	131	447	107	15	4	3	139	49	25	37	0	103	1	6	1	8	8	.50	15	.239	.298	.311
1994 Winston-Sal	A	127	437	114	22	2	13	179	52	49	49	1	80	0	2	4	7	9	.44	9	.261	.333	.410
1995 Chattanooga	AA	11	40	7	2	0	1	12	2	2	4	0	13	0	0	0	0	0	.00	3	.175	.250	.300
Winston-Sal	A	91	309	69	13	1	7	105	30	40	15	0	69	2	3	3	3	1	.75	4	.223	.261	.340

		G	AB	H	2B	3B	HR	TB	R	RBI	TBB	IBB	SO	HBP	SH	SF	SB	CS	SB%	GDP	Avg	OBP	SLG
Indianapolis	AAA	4	8	1	0	0	1	4	1	1	0	0	3	0	1	0	0	0	.00	0	.125	.125	.500
3 Min. YEARS		364	1241	298	52	7	25	439	134	117	105	1	268	3	12	8	18	18	.50	31	.240	.299	.354

Bo Magee

Pitches: Left **Bats:** Right **Pos:** P   **Ht:** 6'4" **Wt:** 180 **Born:** 4/9/68   **Age:** 28

		HOW MUCH HE PITCHED						WHAT HE GAVE UP											THE RESULTS					
Year Team	Lg	G	GS	CG	GF	IP	BFP	H	R	ER	HR	SH	SF	HB	TBB	IBB	SO	WP	Bk	W	L	Pct.	ShO	Sv	ERA
1991 Butte	R	14	14	0	0	69.1	330	76	45	37	3	0	2	3	57	2	51	6	6	2	7	.222	0	0	4.80
1992 Gastonia	A	27	24	1	0	151	637	113	49	38	6	7	3	2	82	2	109	13	3	7	9	.438	1	0	2.26
1993 Charlotte	A	30	14	0	4	89	386	76	44	41	3	5	6	0	51	0	64	6	4	6	3	.667	0	0	4.15
1994 Kinston	A	28	0	0	13	44.1	200	35	31	25	5	0	3	0	29	0	51	4	0	0	0	.000	0	2	5.08
Canton-Akrn	AA	14	1	0	10	26.2	114	21	13	10	3	1	1	1	11	0	20	3	0	1	1	.500	0	2	3.38
1995 Canton-Akrn	AA	21	0	0	8	29.2	145	33	26	23	0	0	0	0	28	1	25	4	0	0	2	.000	0	1	6.98
Bowie	AA	5	1	0	3	8.1	40	10	8	5	2	0	2	0	6	1	7	1	0	1	1	.500	0	0	5.40
Frederick	A	5	5	0	0	26.2	111	28	15	12	4	2	0	2	5	0	28	2	0	2	1	.667	0	0	4.05
Rochester	AAA	2	0	0	1	2	11	4	3	3	0	0	0	0	1	0	1	0	0	0	0	.000	0	0	13.50
5 Min. YEARS		146	59	1	39	447	1974	396	234	194	26	15	17	8	270	6	356	39	13	19	25	.432	1	5	3.91

Wendell Magee

Bats: Right **Throws:** Right **Pos:** OF   **Ht:** 6'0" **Wt:** 225 **Born:** 8/3/72   **Age:** 23

		BATTING														BASERUNNING				PERCENTAGES		
Year Team	Lg	G	AB	H	2B	3B	HR	TB	R	RBI	TBB	IBB	SO	HBP	SH	SF	SB	CS	SB%	GDP	Avg	OBP	SLG
1994 Batavia	A	63	229	64	12	4	2	90	42	35	16	1	24	4	1	2	10	2	.83	5	.279	.335	.393
1995 Clearwater	A	96	388	137	24	5	6	189	67	46	33	3	40	4	1	5	7	10	.41	15	.353	.405	.487
Reading	AA	39	136	40	9	1	3	60	17	21	21	1	17	0	0	4	3	4	.43	3	.294	.379	.441
2 Min. YEARS		198	753	241	45	10	11	339	126	102	70	5	81	8	2	11	20	16	.56	23	.320	.379	.450

Joe Magrane

Pitches: Left **Bats:** Right **Pos:** P   **Ht:** 6'6" **Wt:** 230 **Born:** 7/2/64   **Age:** 31

		HOW MUCH HE PITCHED						WHAT HE GAVE UP											THE RESULTS					
Year Team	Lg	G	GS	CG	GF	IP	BFP	H	R	ER	HR	SH	SF	HB	TBB	IBB	SO	WP	Bk	W	L	Pct.	ShO	Sv	ERA
1985 Johnson Cty	R	6	5	2	0	30	113	15	4	2	0	0	0	1	11	0	31	0	2	2	1	.667	2	0	0.60
St. Pete	A	5	5	1	0	34.2	137	21	8	4	0	0	0	1	14	0	17	2	1	3	1	.750	1	0	1.04
1986 Arkansas	AA	13	13	5	0	89.1	353	66	29	24	3	4	1	2	31	0	66	8	0	8	4	.667	2	0	2.42
Louisville	AAA	15	15	8	0	113.1	457	93	34	26	4	2	5	5	33	1	72	7	4	9	6	.600	2	0	2.06
1987 Louisville	AAA	3	3	1	0	23.1	88	16	7	5	1	0	0	0	3	0	17	0	1	1	0	1.000	1	0	1.93
1988 Louisville	AAA	4	4	1	0	20	86	19	7	7	1	0	0	2	7	0	18	1	4	2	1	.667	0	0	3.15
1992 St. Pete	A	3	3	0	0	18	70	14	4	3	0	1	0	1	5	0	15	2	0	0	1	.000	0	0	1.50
Louisville	AAA	10	10	0	0	53.1	248	60	32	32	6	6	1	5	29	1	35	3	1	3	4	.429	0	0	5.40
1994 Lk Elsinore	A	2	2	0	0	10.2	47	9	3	3	0	1	1	0	4	0	8	1	0	0	0	.000	0	0	2.53
Vancouver	AAA	2	2	0	0	10	45	13	5	5	1	0	0	1	4	0	5	2	0	1	1	.500	0	0	4.50
1995 Ottawa	AAA	12	12	0	0	67	295	69	43	36	5	5	1	3	31	0	37	7	0	3	6	.333	0	0	4.84
1987 St. Louis	NL	27	26	4	0	170.1	722	157	75	67	9	9	3	10	60	6	101	9	7	9	7	.563	2	0	3.54
1988 St. Louis	NL	24	24	4	0	165.1	677	133	57	40	6	8	4	2	51	4	100	8	8	5	9	.357	3	0	2.18
1989 St. Louis	NL	34	33	9	1	234.2	971	219	81	76	5	14	8	6	72	7	127	14	5	18	9	.667	3	0	2.91
1990 St. Louis	NL	31	31	3	0	203.1	855	204	86	81	10	8	6	8	59	7	100	11	1	10	17	.370	2	0	3.59
1992 St. Louis	NL	5	5	0	0	31.1	143	34	15	14	2	3	1	2	15	0	20	4	0	1	2	.333	0	0	4.02
1993 California	AL	8	8	0	0	48	209	48	27	21	4	4	3	0	21	0	24	4	0	3	2	.600	0	0	3.94
St. Louis	NL	22	20	0	2	116	499	127	68	64	15	6	7	5	37	3	38	4	0	8	10	.444	0	0	4.97
1994 California	AL	20	11	1	4	74	357	89	63	60	18	0	3	6	51	0	33	7	0	2	6	.250	0	0	7.30
7 Min. YEARS		75	74	18	0	469.2	1939	395	176	147	21	19	9	21	172	2	321	33	13	32	25	.561	8	0	2.82
7 Maj. YEARS		171	158	21	7	1043	4433	1011	472	423	69	52	35	39	366	27	543	61	21	56	62	.475	10	0	3.65

John Mahalik

Bats: Right **Throws:** Right **Pos:** SS-3B   **Ht:** 6'2" **Wt:** 190 **Born:** 7/28/71   **Age:** 24

		BATTING														BASERUNNING				PERCENTAGES		
Year Team	Lg	G	AB	H	2B	3B	HR	TB	R	RBI	TBB	IBB	SO	HBP	SH	SF	SB	CS	SB%	GDP	Avg	OBP	SLG
1993 Butte	R	74	258	70	15	0	1	88	25	27	21	0	51	0	1	1	8	0	1.00	8	.271	.325	.341
1994 Burlington	A	9	30	5	0	0	0	5	1	3	1	0	5	0	1	0	0	1	.00	1	.167	.194	.167
W. Palm Bch	A	63	161	43	9	2	0	56	30	12	29	0	20	4	4	2	4	4	.50	4	.267	.388	.348
1995 Binghamton	AA	67	187	42	6	1	5	65	19	19	19	1	34	1	5	1	1	1	.50	6	.225	.298	.348
3 Min. YEARS		213	636	160	30	3	6	214	75	61	70	1	110	5	11	4	13	6	.68	18	.252	.329	.336

Scott Makarewicz

Bats: Right **Throws:** Right **Pos:** C   **Ht:** 6'0" **Wt:** 200 **Born:** 3/1/67   **Age:** 29

		BATTING														BASERUNNING				PERCENTAGES		
Year Team	Lg	G	AB	H	2B	3B	HR	TB	R	RBI	TBB	IBB	SO	HBP	SH	SF	SB	CS	SB%	GDP	Avg	OBP	SLG
1989 Auburn	A	61	216	52	17	0	4	81	22	24	14	0	43	4	5	1	2	0	1.00	1	.241	.298	.375
1990 Osceola	A	94	343	95	12	2	4	123	35	49	21	0	63	4	8	3	0	1	.00	11	.277	.323	.359
Columbus	AA	28	85	20	1	0	2	27	5	11	10	2	14	1	0	2	0	1	.00	3	.235	.316	.318
1991 Jackson	AA	76	229	53	9	0	2	68	23	30	18	5	36	8	0	3	1	4	.20	7	.231	.306	.297
1992 Jackson	AA	105	345	99	15	0	7	135	39	39	23	3	62	6	3	5	2	2	.50	6	.287	.338	.391
1993 Jackson	AA	92	285	70	14	1	7	107	31	35	17	2	51	8	1	3	1	1	.50	7	.246	.304	.375
1994 Tucson	AAA	63	171	49	10	1	3	70	24	32	13	0	28	4	6	1	0	0	.00	5	.287	.349	.409

Year Team	Lg	G	AB	H	2B	3B	HR	TB	R	RBI	TBB	IBB	SO	HBP	SH	SF	SB	CS	SB%	GDP	Avg	OBP	SLG
1995 Tucson	AAA	62	192	51	9	0	5	75	21	31	10	3	23	2	2	2	1	0	1.00	9	.266	.306	.391
7 Min. YEARS		581	1866	489	87	4	34	686	200	251	126	15	320	37	25	20	7	9	.44	49	.262	.318	.368

Mike Maksudian

Bats: Left **Throws:** Right **Pos:** C **Ht:** 5'11" **Wt:** 200 **Born:** 5/28/66 **Age:** 30

Year Team	Lg	G	AB	H	2B	3B	HR	TB	R	RBI	TBB	IBB	SO	HBP	SH	SF	SB	CS	SB%	GDP	Avg	OBP	SLG
1987 White Sox	R	34	109	38	11	3	1	58	23	28	19	4	13	1	0	2	7	2	.78	2	.349	.443	.532
1988 South Bend	A	102	366	111	26	3	4	155	51	50	60	9	59	3	0	2	5	3	.63	5	.303	.404	.423
Tampa	A	1	3	2	1	0	0	3	1	2	0	0	1	0	0	0	0	0	.00	0	.667	.667	1.000
St. Lucie	A	13	42	9	2	1	0	13	7	1	8	0	6	0	0	1	0	0	.00	1	.214	.333	.310
1989 Miami	A	83	288	90	18	4	9	143	36	42	28	2	42	0	0	2	6	4	.60	11	.313	.371	.497
1990 Knoxville	AA	121	422	121	22	5	8	177	51	55	50	6	66	2	0	1	6	4	.60	9	.287	.364	.419
1991 Syracuse	AAA	31	97	32	6	3	1	47	13	13	10	0	17	0	1	0	0	0	.00	2	.330	.393	.485
Knoxville	AA	71	231	59	12	3	5	92	32	35	37	5	43	0	0	5	2	2	.50	3	.255	.352	.398
1992 Syracuse	AAA	101	339	95	17	1	13	153	38	58	32	6	63	1	0	1	4	1	.80	7	.280	.343	.451
1993 Portland	AAA	76	264	83	16	7	10	143	57	49	45	3	51	0	0	4	5	1	.83	1	.314	.409	.542
1994 Iowa	AAA	58	198	63	18	2	8	109	45	38	33	5	39	0	1	3	1	1	.50	3	.318	.410	.551
1995 Edmonton	AAA	100	324	86	24	4	3	127	54	34	46	2	55	0	2	0	5	1	.83	7	.265	.357	.392
1992 Toronto	AL	3	3	0	0	0	0	0	0	0	0	0	0	0	0	0	0	0	.00	0	.000	.000	.000
1993 Minnesota	AL	5	12	2	1	0	0	3	2	2	4	0	2	0	0	1	0	0	.00	2	.167	.353	.250
1994 Chicago	NL	26	26	7	2	0	0	9	6	4	10	0	4	0	0	0	0	1	.00	0	.269	.472	.346
9 Min. YEARS		791	2683	789	173	36	62	1220	408	405	368	42	455	7	4	21	41	19	.68	51	.294	.378	.455
3 Maj. YEARS		34	41	9	3	0	0	12	8	6	14	0	6	0	0	1	0	1	.00	2	.220	.411	.293

Jose Malave

Bats: Right **Throws:** Right **Pos:** OF **Ht:** 6'2" **Wt:** 195 **Born:** 5/31/71 **Age:** 25

Year Team	Lg	G	AB	H	2B	3B	HR	TB	R	RBI	TBB	IBB	SO	HBP	SH	SF	SB	CS	SB%	GDP	Avg	OBP	SLG
1990 Elmira	A	13	29	4	1	0	0	5	4	3	2	0	12	0	0	1	1	0	1.00	0	.138	.188	.172
1991 Red Sox	R	37	146	47	4	2	2	61	24	28	10	0	23	1	0	3	6	0	1.00	3	.322	.363	.418
1992 Winter Havn	A	8	25	4	0	0	0	4	1	0	0	0	11	0	0	1	0	0	.00	0	.160	.160	.160
Elmira	A	65	268	87	9	1	12	134	44	46	14	3	48	3	0	1	8	3	.73	2	.325	.364	.500
1993 Lynchburg	A	82	312	94	27	1	8	147	42	54	36	3	54	3	0	5	2	3	.40	8	.301	.374	.471
1994 New Britain	AA	122	465	139	37	7	24	262	87	92	52	1	81	4	0	7	4	7	.36	12	.299	.369	.563
1995 Pawtucket	AAA	91	318	86	12	1	23	169	55	57	30	1	67	2	0	0	0	1	.00	4	.270	.337	.531
6 Min. YEARS		418	1563	461	90	12	69	782	257	280	144	8	296	13	1	17	21	14	.60	29	.295	.356	.500

Jay Maldonado

Pitches: Right **Bats:** Right **Pos:** P **Ht:** 6'0" **Wt:** 195 **Born:** 3/24/73 **Age:** 23

Year Team	Lg	G	GS	CG	GF	IP	BFP	H	R	ER	HR	SH	SF	HB	TBB	IBB	SO	WP	Bk	W	L	Pct.	ShO	Sv	ERA
1992 Blue Jays	R	9	0	0	3	15.2	65	10	2	0	0	0	0	1	7	0	10	2	0	0	0	.000	0	0	0.00
1993 St. Cathrns	A	13	0	0	4	36.1	143	16	7	4	2	1	1	1	15	0	38	2	1	1	1	.500	0	1	0.99
Hagerstown	A	8	0	0	2	12	53	11	4	4	0	0	0	1	6	0	9	1	0	1	0	1.000	0	0	3.00
1994 Hagerstown	A	40	0	0	16	75.1	323	69	44	33	6	6	4	4	24	1	65	8	1	6	5	.545	0	7	3.94
1995 New Britain	AA	5	0	0	1	5.1	28	7	8	7	0	1	0	0	3	0	4	0	3	0	0	.000	0	0	11.81
Fort Myers	A	5	0	0	1	4.1	23	6	4	3	0	0	0	0	4	1	4	1	1	0	1	.000	0	0	6.23
Corp.Chrsti	IND	6	2	0	4	18.1	88	20	18	16	6	0	3	1	16	0	14	2	0	0	3	.000	0	0	7.85
Laredo	IND	2	0	0	1	5.2	19	1	0	0	0	0	0	0	0	0	6	2	0	0	0	.000	0	0	0.00
4 Min. YEARS		88	2	0	32	173	742	140	87	67	14	8	8	9	75	2	150	18	6	8	10	.444	0	8	3.49

Rob Mallicoat

Pitches: Left **Bats:** Left **Pos:** P **Ht:** 6'3" **Wt:** 180 **Born:** 11/16/64 **Age:** 31

Year Team	Lg	G	GS	CG	GF	IP	BFP	H	R	ER	HR	SH	SF	HB	TBB	IBB	SO	WP	Bk	W	L	Pct.	ShO	Sv	ERA
1984 Auburn	A	1	1	0	0	5	25	8	3	3	1	0	0	0	3	0	6	2	0	0	0	.000	0	0	5.40
Asheville	A	11	11	2	0	64.1	276	49	30	28	5	1	1	4	36	0	57	7	2	3	4	.429	0	0	3.92
1985 Osceola	A	26	25	5	0	178.2	717	119	41	27	2	6	5	3	74	3	158	14	2	16	6	.727	2	0	1.36
1986 Tucson	AAA	3	3	0	0	14	68	18	14	10	1	1	0	0	8	0	9	0	1	0	2	.000	0	0	6.43
Columbus	AA	10	10	1	0	58	281	61	38	31	2	0	4	3	45	1	52	2	0	0	6	.000	0	0	4.81
1987 Columbus	AA	24	24	3	0	152.1	656	132	68	49	13	8	4	5	78	2	141	8	0	10	7	.588	0	0	2.89
Tucson	AAA	2	2	0	0	9.2	45	9	5	4	0	1	0	0	7	0	8	2	1	0	0	.000	0	0	3.72
1990 Astros	R	7	4	0	0	16.1	78	15	15	9	0	3	1	2	15	0	21	4	1	0	1	.000	0	0	4.96
Osceola	A	3	3	0	0	12	51	8	2	0	0	0	0	0	9	0	10	1	1	0	0	.000	0	0	0.00
1991 Jackson	AA	18	0	0	6	31	121	20	15	13	1	0	3	2	11	1	34	2	1	4	1	.800	0	1	3.77
Tucson	AAA	19	6	0	4	47.2	221	43	32	29	3	4	3	2	38	4	32	2	0	4	4	.500	0	1	5.48
1992 Tucson	AAA	37	0	0	15	50.1	204	36	17	15	0	3	1	2	21	3	53	3	2	1	3	.250	0	3	2.68
1994 Rancho Cuca	A	2	0	0	0	2.2	10	3	1	1	0	0	0	0	1	0	3	0	1	1	0	1.000	0	0	3.38
1995 Omaha	AAA	3	0	0	1	3	12	1	1	1	0	1	0	0	3	0	1	0	0	0	1	.000	0	0	3.00
Corp.Chrsti	IND	1	0	0	0	1.2	8	1	3	1	0	0	0	0	2	0	1	1	0	0	1	.000	0	0	5.40
1987 Houston	NL	4	1	0	0	6.2	31	8	5	5	0	0	0	0	6	0	4	0	0	0	0	.000	0	0	6.75
1991 Houston	NL	24	0	0	4	23.1	103	22	10	10	2	1	2	2	13	1	18	1	0	0	2	.000	0	1	3.86
1992 Houston	NL	23	0	0	6	23.2	120	26	19	19	2	3	1	5	19	2	20	2	0	0	0	.000	0	0	7.23

	G	GS	CG	GF	IP	BFP	H	R	ER	HR	SH	SF	HB	TBB	IBB	SO	WP	Bk	W	L	Pct.	ShO	Sv	ERA
9 Min. YEARS	167	89	11	26	646.2	2773	523	285	221	28	28	22	23	351	14	586	48	12	39	36	.520	2	5	3.08
3 Maj. YEARS	51	1	0	10	53.2	254	56	34	34	4	4	3	7	38	3	42	3	0	0	2	.000	0	1	5.70

Chuck Malloy

Pitches: Right **Bats:** Right **Pos:** P **Ht:** 6'4" **Wt:** 225 **Born:** 3/1/72 **Age:** 24

		HOW MUCH HE PITCHED					WHAT HE GAVE UP												THE RESULTS					
Year Team	Lg	G	GS	CG	GF	IP	BFP	H	R	ER	HR	SH	SF	HB	TBB	IBB	SO	WP	Bk	W	L	Pct.	ShO	Sv	ERA
1994 Utica	A	13	9	1	0	54.2	229	44	25	20	0	2	3	2	30	0	46	4	3	6	2	.750	1	0	3.29
1995 Sarasota	A	16	12	2	2	86.1	354	72	38	34	5	2	2	0	39	2	51	6	1	6	4	.600	1	0	3.54
Trenton	AA	1	1	0	0	5.2	28	9	5	3	0	0	2	2	1	0	1	1	0	0	0	.000	0	0	4.76
2 Min. YEARS		30	22	3	2	146.2	611	125	68	57	5	4	7	4	70	2	98	11	4	12	6	.667	2	0	3.50

Marty Malloy

Bats: Left **Throws:** Right **Pos:** 2B **Ht:** 5'10" **Wt:** 160 **Born:** 7/6/72 **Age:** 23

		BATTING													BASERUNNING				PERCENTAGES		
Year Team	Lg	G	AB	H	2B	3B	HR	TB	R	RBI	TBB	IBB	SO	HBP	SH	SF	SB	CS	SB%	GDP	Avg	OBP	SLG
1992 Idaho Falls	R	62	251	79	18	1	2	105	45	28	11	0	43	2	0	1	8	4	.67	2	.315	.347	.418
1993 Macon	A	109	376	110	19	3	2	141	55	36	39	3	70	2	3	3	24	8	.75	4	.293	.360	.375
1994 Durham	A	118	428	113	22	1	6	155	53	35	52	2	69	2	2	3	18	12	.60	9	.264	.344	.362
1995 Greenville	AA	124	461	128	20	3	10	184	73	59	39	1	58	0	7	8	11	12	.48	6	.278	.329	.399
4 Min. YEARS		413	1516	430	79	8	20	585	226	158	141	6	240	6	12	15	61	36	.63	21	.284	.344	.386

Sean Maloney

Pitches: Right **Bats:** Right **Pos:** P **Ht:** 6'7" **Wt:** 210 **Born:** 5/25/71 **Age:** 25

		HOW MUCH HE PITCHED					WHAT HE GAVE UP												THE RESULTS					
Year Team	Lg	G	GS	CG	GF	IP	BFP	H	R	ER	HR	SH	SF	HB	TBB	IBB	SO	WP	Bk	W	L	Pct.	ShO	Sv	ERA
1993 Helena	R	17	3	1	10	47.2	209	55	31	23	2	3	2	2	11	1	35	3	0	2	2	.500	0	0	4.34
1994 Beloit	A	51	0	0	41	59	272	73	42	36	3	2	5	4	10	5	53	6	1	2	6	.250	0	22	5.49
1995 El Paso	AA	43	0	0	27	64.2	292	69	41	30	4	4	4	3	28	9	54	5	0	7	5	.583	0	15	4.18
3 Min. YEARS		111	3	1	78	171.1	773	197	114	89	9	9	11	9	49	15	142	14	1	11	13	.458	0	37	4.68

John Malzone

Bats: Left **Throws:** Right **Pos:** 3B **Ht:** 5'10" **Wt:** 170 **Born:** 10/29/67 **Age:** 28

		BATTING													BASERUNNING				PERCENTAGES		
Year Team	Lg	G	AB	H	2B	3B	HR	TB	R	RBI	TBB	IBB	SO	HBP	SH	SF	SB	CS	SB%	GDP	Avg	OBP	SLG
1990 Lynchburg	A	65	187	48	4	1	2	60	18	15	27	0	63	1	1	0	3	1	.75	2	.257	.353	.321
1991 Winter Havn	A	103	266	66	11	2	1	84	40	28	60	4	58	4	3	4	2	5	.29	11	.248	.389	.316
1992 Lynchburg	A	117	386	118	24	6	4	166	49	52	29	0	53	2	2	2	1	2	.33	16	.306	.356	.430
1993 Pawtucket	AAA	75	207	49	7	0	2	62	14	15	12	0	24	1	0	0	2	1	.67	12	.237	.282	.300
1994 New Britain	AA	60	181	39	5	2	1	51	22	11	21	1	26	1	1	0	2	1	.67	7	.215	.300	.282
1995 Pawtucket	AAA	6	18	2	0	0	0	2	0	2	0	0	4	0	0	0	0	0	.00	1	.111	.111	.111
6 Min. YEARS		426	1245	322	51	11	10	425	143	123	149	5	228	9	7	6	10	10	.50	49	.259	.341	.341

Austin Manahan

Bats: Both **Throws:** Right **Pos:** OF **Ht:** 6'1" **Wt:** 185 **Born:** 4/12/70 **Age:** 26

		BATTING													BASERUNNING				PERCENTAGES		
Year Team	Lg	G	AB	H	2B	3B	HR	TB	R	RBI	TBB	IBB	SO	HBP	SH	SF	SB	CS	SB%	GDP	Avg	OBP	SLG
1988 Princeton	R	64	227	41	4	4	6	71	31	33	24	0	102	1	0	2	12	4	.75	1	.181	.260	.313
1989 Princeton	R	19	73	17	5	0	1	25	8	8	6	1	24	0	0	1	1	1	.50	0	.233	.288	.342
Welland	A	50	178	38	3	4	3	58	18	16	17	0	51	1	0	1	12	1	.92	3	.213	.284	.326
1990 Augusta	A	94	378	114	12	10	7	167	59	52	46	2	105	4	2	4	26	14	.65	4	.302	.380	.442
Salem	A	41	154	43	6	2	4	65	22	24	11	0	51	1	1	1	8	1	.89	4	.279	.329	.422
1991 Salem	A	113	369	78	14	1	9	121	53	35	47	0	127	3	1	2	16	10	.62	1	.211	.304	.328
1992 Carolina	AA	107	340	75	18	6	5	120	44	33	29	1	101	4	1	0	7	6	.54	5	.221	.290	.353
1993 W. Palm Bch	A	77	274	65	14	2	4	95	34	29	26	0	78	0	1	2	7	3	.70	4	.237	.301	.347
Rancho Cuca	A	43	145	42	8	4	2	64	17	22	11	0	38	1	1	2	7	2	.78	3	.290	.340	.441
1994 Rancho Cuca	A	11	27	8	1	0	0	9	9	3	3	0	10	0	0	0	2	1	.67	0	.296	.367	.333
Orlando	AA	55	128	37	7	2	2	54	11	10	6	0	37	0	1	1	2	2	.50	3	.289	.319	.422
1995 Orlando	AA	94	260	55	12	0	3	76	34	19	16	0	57	2	2	0	13	6	.68	9	.212	.263	.292
8 Min. YEARS		768	2553	613	104	35	46	925	340	284	242	4	781	17	10	16	113	51	.69	34	.240	.308	.362

Tony Manahan

Bats: Right **Throws:** Right **Pos:** 3B **Ht:** 6'0" **Wt:** 190 **Born:** 12/15/68 **Age:** 27

		BATTING													BASERUNNING				PERCENTAGES		
Year Team	Lg	G	AB	H	2B	3B	HR	TB	R	RBI	TBB	IBB	SO	HBP	SH	SF	SB	CS	SB%	GDP	Avg	OBP	SLG
1990 San Bernrdo	A	51	198	63	10	2	7	98	46	30	24	0	34	2	1	3	8	1	.89	4	.318	.392	.495
1991 Jacksonvlle	AA	113	410	104	23	2	7	152	67	45	54	0	81	6	2	3	11	5	.69	8	.254	.347	.371
1992 Jacksonvlle	AA	134	505	130	24	6	8	190	70	49	39	1	76	2	3	3	24	11	.69	12	.257	.311	.376
1993 Calgary	AAA	117	451	136	31	4	3	184	70	62	38	0	48	2	3	3	19	4	.83	12	.302	.356	.408
1994 Calgary	AAA	78	295	84	21	1	4	119	48	36	24	0	22	3	1	2	7	2	.78	5	.285	.343	.403
1995 Scranton-Wb	AAA	90	299	86	11	1	3	108	36	32	28	4	39	4	2	0	6	1	.86	7	.288	.356	.361
6 Min. YEARS		583	2158	603	120	16	32	851	337	254	207	5	300	19	12	14	75	24	.76	48	.279	.346	.394

185

Dwight Maness

Bats: Right **Throws:** Right **Pos:** OF   **Ht:** 6'3" **Wt:** 180 **Born:** 4/3/74 **Age:** 22

Year	Team	Lg	G	AB	H	2B	3B	HR	TB	R	RBI	TBB	IBB	SO	HBP	SH	SF	SB	CS	SB%	GDP	Avg	OBP	SLG
1992	Dodgers	R	44	139	35	6	3	0	47	24	12	14	0	36	8	3	3	18	9	.67	1	.252	.348	.338
1993	Vero Beach	A	118	409	106	21	4	6	153	57	42	32	0	105	15	8	7	22	13	.63	3	.259	.330	.374
1994	San Antonio	AA	57	215	47	5	5	5	77	32	20	25	0	54	6	2	0	15	16	.48	1	.219	.317	.358
	Bakersfield	A	74	248	62	13	1	3	86	38	26	29	3	67	11	5	5	21	9	.70	1	.250	.348	.347
1995	San Antonio	AA	57	179	40	2	3	5	63	29	24	20	0	44	5	5	2	4	6	.40	3	.223	.316	.352
	Vero Beach	A	43	143	33	3	0	3	45	16	23	11	0	29	6	2	5	13	5	.72	2	.231	.303	.315
	St. Lucie	A	14	44	9	4	0	0	13	4	5	7	0	6	0	1	0	1	2	.33	0	.205	.314	.295
	4 Min. YEARS		407	1377	332	54	16	22	484	200	152	138	3	341	51	26	22	94	60	.61	11	.241	.328	.351

Derek Manning

Pitches: Left **Bats:** Left **Pos:** P   **Ht:** 6'3" **Wt:** 220 **Born:** 7/21/70 **Age:** 25

			HOW MUCH HE PITCHED						WHAT HE GAVE UP									THE RESULTS					
Year	Team	Lg	G	GS	CG	GF	IP	BFP	H	R	ER	HR	SH	SF	HB	TBB	IBB	SO	WP	Bk	W	L	Pct.	ShO	Sv	ERA
1993	Sou. Oregon	A	15	13	2	0	79.1	322	71	35	32	5	2	3	3	21	2	63	3	4	5	4	.556	2	0	3.63
1994	W. Michigan	A	29	23	2	4	154	617	120	52	39	4	7	1	3	42	0	118	3	3	11	7	.611	1	2	2.28
1995	Huntsville	AA	5	5	0	0	28	114	26	14	14	4	1	0	0	7	0	22	0	0	1	2	.333	0	0	4.50
	Modesto	A	25	12	0	4	111	467	112	43	30	7	6	4	1	25	0	102	3	1	10	1	.909	0	3	2.43
	3 Min. YEARS		74	53	4	8	372.1	1520	329	144	115	20	16	8	7	95	2	305	9	8	27	14	.659	3	5	2.78

Henry Manning

Bats: Right **Throws:** Right **Pos:** C   **Ht:** 5'11" **Wt:** 185 **Born:** 7/3/68 **Age:** 27

Year	Team	Lg	G	AB	H	2B	3B	HR	TB	R	RBI	TBB	IBB	SO	HBP	SH	SF	SB	CS	SB%	GDP	Avg	OBP	SLG
1991	South Bend	A	23	67	19	3	0	0	22	5	10	1	0	4	2	2	0	0	2	.00	2	.284	.314	.328
	Sarasota	A	13	24	2	0	0	0	2	2	0	0	0	6	2	0	0	0	0	.00	0	.083	.154	.083
	Erie	A	12	44	7	1	0	0	8	3	8	2	0	7	0	0	2	0	0	.00	1	.159	.188	.182
1992	South Bend	A	66	213	60	9	0	1	72	26	30	14	1	22	5	0	1	4	2	.67	3	.282	.339	.338
1993	Birmingham	AA	30	106	19	3	1	2	30	7	9	3	0	25	3	0	0	0	1	.00	3	.179	.223	.283
	Sarasota	A	27	79	18	3	0	0	21	8	4	7	0	12	2	2	0	0	0	.00	1	.228	.307	.266
1994	Pr. William	A	31	105	27	5	0	2	38	10	10	1	0	22	2	2	0	0	0	.00	2	.257	.278	.362
	Nashville	AAA	21	46	13	0	0	1	16	5	9	1	0	4	2	3	1	0	0	.00	1	.283	.320	.348
1995	Birmingham	AA	11	30	9	1	0	2	16	3	11	1	0	1	0	0	3	0	0	.00	0	.300	.294	.533
	Winnipeg	IND	85	334	95	24	0	19	176	55	57	5	0	37	4	0	5	0	1	.00	11	.284	.299	.527
	5 Min. YEARS		319	1048	269	49	1	27	401	124	148	35	1	140	22	9	12	4	6	.40	24	.257	.292	.383

Jeff Mansur

Pitches: Left **Bats:** Left **Pos:** P   **Ht:** 5'11" **Wt:** 185 **Born:** 8/2/70 **Age:** 25

			HOW MUCH HE PITCHED						WHAT HE GAVE UP									THE RESULTS					
Year	Team	Lg	G	GS	CG	GF	IP	BFP	H	R	ER	HR	SH	SF	HB	TBB	IBB	SO	WP	Bk	W	L	Pct.	ShO	Sv	ERA
1992	Kenosha	A	11	10	1	0	65.1	266	69	27	21	6	3	2	1	8	1	46	1	2	6	3	.667	0	0	2.89
	Visalia	A	17	16	0	0	100.2	448	130	67	46	11	7	4	1	25	3	61	6	1	5	7	.417	0	0	4.11
1993	Nashville	AA	33	19	4	4	158.2	677	180	82	75	22	6	5	0	38	3	89	5	1	10	8	.556	0	0	4.25
1994	Nashville	AA	34	11	0	6	93.2	426	115	58	50	10	0	4	5	36	1	52	7	0	1	9	.100	0	0	4.80
1995	New Britain	AA	5	0	0	2	6.1	26	5	1	1	1	0	0	0	2	0	3	0	0	0	0	.000	0	1	1.42
	Orioles	R	3	0	0	1	5.1	27	11	5	2	1	0	1	1	0	0	2	0	0	0	0	.000	0	0	3.38
	Frederick	A	12	0	0	6	15.1	70	20	8	8	1	1	1	2	5	1	12	0	0	0	0	.000	0	0	4.70
	4 Min. YEARS		115	56	5	19	445.1	1940	530	248	203	52	17	17	10	114	9	265	19	4	22	27	.449	0	2	4.10

Barry Manuel

Pitches: Right **Bats:** Right **Pos:** P   **Ht:** 5'11" **Wt:** 185 **Born:** 8/12/65 **Age:** 30

			HOW MUCH HE PITCHED						WHAT HE GAVE UP									THE RESULTS					
Year	Team	Lg	G	GS	CG	GF	IP	BFP	H	R	ER	HR	SH	SF	HB	TBB	IBB	SO	WP	Bk	W	L	Pct.	ShO	Sv	ERA
1987	Rangers	R	1	0	0	0	1	7	3	2	2	0	0	0	0	1	0	1	2	0	0	0	.000	0	0	18.00
	Charlotte	A	13	5	0	3	30	138	33	24	22	2	1	2	3	18	0	19	4	0	1	2	.333	0	0	6.60
1988	Charlotte	A	37	0	0	22	60.1	259	47	24	17	4	6	1	4	32	0	55	8	3	4	3	.571	0	4	2.54
1989	Tulsa	AA	11	11	0	0	49.1	237	49	44	41	5	3	6	9	39	0	40	3	3	3	4	.429	0	0	7.48
	Charlotte	A	15	14	0	0	76.1	330	77	43	40	6	4	3	8	30	0	51	6	1	4	7	.364	0	0	4.72
1990	Charlotte	A	57	0	0	56	56.1	238	39	23	18	2	4	2	3	30	2	60	1	0	1	5	.167	0	36	2.88
1991	Tulsa	AA	56	0	0	48	68.1	300	63	29	25	5	4	2	5	34	1	45	0	1	2	7	.222	0	25	3.29
1992	Okla. City	AAA	27	0	0	22	27.1	143	32	24	16	1	1	2	2	26	0	11	1	0	1	8	.111	0	5	5.27
	Tulsa	AA	16	1	0	8	27	122	28	12	12	4	0	0	1	16	0	28	0	0	2	0	1.000	0	2	4.00
1993	Charlotte	A	3	0	0	1	4.2	20	6	0	0	0	0	0	0	2	0	4	0	0	0	0	.000	0	0	0.00
	Okla. City	AAA	21	0	0	10	23.2	109	29	21	21	0	0	1	0	16	1	19	3	0	2	2	.500	0	2	7.99
	Rochester	AAA	9	0	0	2	19.2	77	14	8	8	2	1	1	1	7	0	11	0	0	1	1	.500	0	0	3.66
1994	Rochester	AAA	35	20	1	10	139.2	629	161	87	85	21	2	7	3	58	2	107	7	1	11	8	.579	0	4	5.48
1995	Ottawa	AAA	35	22	1	8	127.1	554	125	71	65	4	4	9	14	50	1	85	6	2	5	12	.294	0	0	4.59
1991	Texas	AL	8	0	0	5	16	58	7	2	2	0	3	0	0	6	0	5	2	0	1	0	1.000	0	0	1.13
1992	Texas	AL	3	0	0	0	5.2	25	6	3	3	2	0	1	1	1	0	9	0	0	1	0	1.000	0	0	4.76
	9 Min. YEARS		336	73	2	190	711	3163	706	412	372	57	30	36	53	359	7	536	41	11	37	59	.385	0	79	4.71
	2 Maj. YEARS		11	0	0	5	21.2	83	13	5	5	2	3	1	1	7	0	14	2	0	2	0	1.000	0	0	2.08

Tony Marabella

Bats: Right Throws: Right Pos: 3B Ht: 5'11" Wt: 179 Born: 4/25/73 Age: 23

Year Team	Lg	G	AB	H	2B	3B	HR	TB	R	RBI	TBB	IBB	SO	HBP	SH	SF	SB	CS	SB%	GDP	Avg	OBP	SLG
1989 Expos	R	32	98	28	5	1	2	41	14	14	13	0	7	0	2	1	1	1	.50	3	.286	.366	.418
1990 Gate City	R	59	206	52	9	0	0	61	18	32	25	2	23	0	2	3	2	1	.67	6	.252	.329	.296
Jamestown	A	3	10	3	1	0	0	4	2	1	0	0	1	0	0	1	0	1	.00	0	.300	.273	.400
1991 Sumter	A	107	348	83	12	1	5	112	42	42	41	2	48	3	3	4	5	4	.56	8	.239	.321	.322
1993 Burlington	A	17	42	12	6	0	2	24	7	11	6	1	6	0	0	1	0	0	.00	0	.286	.367	.571
Jamestown	A	52	185	45	13	1	6	78	25	24	16	3	32	1	0	0	1	0	1.00	9	.243	.307	.422
1994 Expos	R	7	24	10	4	0	0	14	2	3	6	0	7	0	0	0	0	0	.00	0	.417	.533	.583
Burlington	A	38	137	35	6	0	4	53	22	18	16	0	16	0	1	1	0	2	.00	4	.255	.331	.387
1995 W. Palm Bch	A	60	201	52	6	1	0	60	22	21	13	0	23	0	0	3	1	1	.50	4	.259	.300	.299
Harrisburg	AA	30	89	20	1	0	1	24	10	11	7	0	11	0	3	1	0	1	.00	3	.225	.278	.270
6 Min. YEARS		405	1340	340	63	4	20	471	164	177	143	8	174	4	11	15	10	11	.48	37	.254	.324	.351

Marc Marini

Bats: Left Throws: Left Pos: OF Ht: 6'1" Wt: 185 Born: 3/17/70 Age: 26

Year Team	Lg	G	AB	H	2B	3B	HR	TB	R	RBI	TBB	IBB	SO	HBP	SH	SF	SB	CS	SB%	GDP	Avg	OBP	SLG
1992 Columbus	A	132	488	150	30	5	8	214	78	70	86	5	63	4	1	9	7	3	.70	10	.307	.409	.439
1993 Kinston	A	124	440	132	34	4	5	189	65	53	63	4	70	3	6	9	7	6	.54	9	.300	.384	.430
1994 Canton-Akrn	AA	91	331	91	21	2	17	167	58	65	50	3	62	0	2	3	2	4	.33	9	.275	.367	.505
1995 Canton-Akrn	AA	83	310	95	28	1	3	134	41	56	30	7	51	0	0	8	3	3	.50	9	.306	.359	.432
Buffalo	AAA	32	85	23	5	0	3	37	12	15	7	0	14	0	0	1	0	0	.00	3	.271	.323	.435
4 Min. YEARS		462	1654	491	118	12	36	741	254	259	236	19	260	7	9	30	19	16	.54	40	.297	.381	.448

Oreste Marrero

Bats: Left Throws: Left Pos: DH Ht: 6'0" Wt: 195 Born: 10/31/69 Age: 26

Year Team	Lg	G	AB	H	2B	3B	HR	TB	R	RBI	TBB	IBB	SO	HBP	SH	SF	SB	CS	SB%	GDP	Avg	OBP	SLG
1987 Helena	R	51	154	50	8	2	7	83	30	34	18	3	31	1	1	0	2	1	.67	1	.325	.399	.539
1988 Beloit	A	19	52	9	2	0	1	14	5	7	3	0	16	0	0	0	0	1	.00	0	.173	.218	.269
Helena	R	67	240	85	15	0	16	148	52	44	42	2	48	0	1	1	3	4	.43	4	.354	.449	.617
1989 Beloit	A	14	40	5	1	0	0	6	1	3	3	0	20	0	0	1	1	0	1.00	0	.125	.182	.150
Brewers	R	10	44	18	0	1	3	29	13	16	2	0	5	0	0	1	2	2	.50	0	.409	.426	.659
Boise	A	54	203	56	8	1	11	99	38	43	30	3	60	0	0	4	1	2	.33	3	.276	.363	.488
1990 Beloit	A	119	400	110	25	1	16	185	59	55	45	3	107	0	0	1	8	4	.67	12	.275	.348	.463
1991 Stockton	A	123	438	110	15	2	13	168	63	61	57	8	98	0	1	7	4	5	.44	5	.251	.333	.384
1992 El Paso	AA	18	54	10	2	1	1	17	8	8	4	0	13	0	0	1	1	0	1.00	5	.185	.237	.315
Stockton	A	76	243	67	17	0	7	105	35	51	44	6	49	1	1	1	3	2	.60	0	.276	.388	.432
1993 Harrisburg	AA	85	255	85	18	1	10	135	39	49	22	2	46	0	3	4	3	3	.50	2	.333	.381	.529
1994 Ottawa	AAA	88	254	62	14	7	7	111	41	31	29	1	56	0	0	2	1	1	.50	5	.244	.319	.437
1995 San Antonio	AA	125	445	115	25	3	21	209	60	86	64	5	98	3	0	3	5	2	.71	4	.258	.353	.470
Albuquerque	AAA	7	23	8	2	0	2	16	5	6	1	0	5	0	0	0	0	0	.00	0	.348	.375	.696
1993 Montreal	NL	32	81	17	5	1	1	27	10	4	14	0	16	0	0	0	1	3	.25	0	.210	.326	.333
9 Min. YEARS		856	2845	790	152	19	115	1325	449	494	364	33	652	5	8	26	34	27	.56	36	.278	.358	.466

David Marshall

Bats: Right Throws: Right Pos: SS Ht: 6'0" Wt: 175 Born: 6/27/70 Age: 26

Year Team	Lg	G	AB	H	2B	3B	HR	TB	R	RBI	TBB	IBB	SO	HBP	SH	SF	SB	CS	SB%	GDP	Avg	OBP	SLG
1992 Eugene	A	10	32	9	1	0	0	10	5	1	0	0	7	1	0	0	1	0	1.00	2	.281	.303	.313
Appleton	A	37	114	27	2	1	1	34	10	12	3	0	29	1	3	3	0	1	.00	3	.237	.256	.298
1993 Wilmington	A	92	279	67	13	2	1	87	34	27	18	0	49	2	2	3	0	2	.00	6	.240	.288	.312
1994 Wilmington	A	48	149	44	9	1	0	55	17	12	12	0	24	1	3	2	0	0	.00	5	.295	.348	.369
1995 Wichita	AA	60	146	33	1	1	0	36	14	9	4	0	23	1	5	0	0	0	.00	8	.226	.252	.247
4 Min. YEARS		247	720	180	26	5	2	222	80	61	37	0	132	6	13	8	1	3	.25	24	.250	.289	.308

Randy Marshall

Pitches: Left Bats: Left Pos: P Ht: 6'3" Wt: 170 Born: 10/12/66 Age: 29

Year Team	Lg	G	GS	CG	GF	IP	BFP	H	R	ER	HR	SH	SF	HB	TBB	IBB	SO	WP	Bk	W	L	Pct.	ShO	Sv	ERA
1989 Niagara Fal	A	6	0	0	2	12.2	57	18	11	11	3	1	0	0	3	0	14	0	2	0	2	.000	0	0	7.82
Fayettevlle	A	34	3	0	7	64.1	276	62	32	23	3	2	1	0	21	3	61	3	0	5	3	.625	0	0	3.22
1990 Fayetteville	A	14	14	5	0	101.2	377	64	17	15	3	2	1	0	14	1	81	0	0	13	0	1.000	0	0	1.33
Lakeland	A	13	13	2	0	72	293	71	29	24	3	2	3	1	14	1	40	3	0	7	2	.778	2	0	3.00
1991 London	AA	27	27	4	0	159	672	186	92	79	13	4	5	2	27	0	105	4	2	8	10	.444	1	0	4.47
Toledo	AAA	1	1	0	0	5	22	5	6	5	1	0	1	0	2	0	2	0	0	1	0	1.000	0	0	9.00
1992 Tidewater	AAA	26	25	3	0	151.2	641	170	75	68	15	8	6	3	31	0	87	0	0	7	13	.350	1	0	4.04
1993 Norfolk	AAA	4	1	0	1	7.1	47	19	18	16	2	0	0	0	4	1	3	1	0	0	2	.000	0	0	19.64
Binghamton	AA	7	7	0	0	35	173	61	39	33	3	1	2	0	8	0	21	1	0	0	3	.000	0	0	8.49
Colo. Sprng	AAA	11	1	0	5	21	101	35	20	9	2	0	1	0	6	0	12	2	1	1	1	.500	0	1	3.86
1994 Colo. Sprng	AAA	50	0	0	12	40.2	177	48	25	24	7	2	0	0	14	2	27	1	0	4	0	1.000	0	2	5.31

Year Team	Lg	G	GS	CG	GF	IP	BFP	H	R	ER	HR	SH	SF	HB	TBB	IBB	SO	WP	Bk	W	L	Pct.	ShO	Sv	ERA
1995 Toledo	AAA	20	17	2	0	109.1	445	99	38	28	7	4	3	2	29	3	67	2	0	7	3	.700	1	0	2.30
7 Min. YEARS		213	109	16	27	779.2	3281	838	402	335	62	26	23	8	168	11	520	21	5	53	38	.582	8	3	3.87

Ed Martel

Pitches: Right **Bats:** Right **Pos:** P   **Ht:** 6'1" **Wt:** 190 **Born:** 3/2/69 **Age:** 27

Year Team	Lg	G	GS	CG	GF	IP	BFP	H	R	ER	HR	SH	SF	HB	TBB	IBB	SO	WP	Bk	W	L	Pct.	ShO	Sv	ERA
1987 Oneonta	A	2	0	0	1	3	14	2	1	1	0	0	0	0	3	0	2	1	0	1	0	1.000	0	0	3.00
1988 Oneonta	A	9	8	0	1	41.2	181	53	20	14	0	5	2	1	8	0	24	4	0	2	2	.500	0	0	3.02
1989 Ft. Laud	A	26	24	4	1	144.2	617	151	76	65	4	6	6	5	39	0	86	8	2	10	8	.556	1	0	4.04
1990 Pr. William	A	25	25	2	0	143.1	614	134	77	65	8	5	2	6	65	0	95	2	3	8	13	.381	0	0	4.08
1991 Albany-Colo	AA	25	24	3	0	163.1	667	129	67	51	8	2	11	5	55	0	141	2	2	13	6	.684	2	0	2.81
1992 Columbus	AAA	26	25	3	0	150.2	652	159	98	93	17	2	2	6	59	2	94	2	1	10	9	.526	2	0	5.56
1995 Toledo	AAA	4	0	0	1	5.2	28	4	1	1	0	1	0	1	5	0	3	0	0	0	1	.000	0	0	1.59
Greenwood	IND	3	3	0	0	16.2	73	16	9	6	2	0	1	2	5	0	12	2	0	0	2	.000	0	0	3.24
Mobile	IND	7	7	0	0	34.1	165	40	27	21	3	0	3	3	29	1	11	5	0	2	4	.333	0	0	5.50
Thunder Bay	IND	5	4	0	1	9.1	58	12	22	21	1	0	1	0	20	0	3	2	0	0	2	.000	0	0	20.25
7 Min. YEARS		132	120	12	5	712.2	3069	700	398	338	43	21	28	29	288	3	471	28	8	46	47	.495	5	0	4.27

Chris Martin

Bats: Right **Throws:** Right **Pos:** SS-3B   **Ht:** 6'1" **Wt:** 170 **Born:** 1/25/68 **Age:** 28

Year Team	Lg	G	AB	H	2B	3B	HR	TB	R	RBI	TBB	IBB	SO	HBP	SH	SF	SB	CS	SB%	GDP	Avg	OBP	SLG
1990 W. Palm Bch	A	59	222	62	17	1	3	90	31	31	27	6	37	1	1	2	7	5	.58	4	.279	.357	.405
1991 Harrisburg	AA	87	294	66	10	0	6	94	30	36	22	0	61	4	2	5	1	4	.20	8	.224	.283	.320
1992 Harrisburg	AA	125	383	87	22	1	5	126	39	31	49	1	67	2	1	3	8	6	.57	15	.227	.316	.329
1993 Harrisburg	AA	116	395	116	23	1	7	162	68	54	40	2	48	6	7	3	16	6	.73	13	.294	.365	.410
1994 Ottawa	AAA	113	374	89	24	0	3	122	44	40	35	0	46	2	7	5	5	4	.56	17	.238	.303	.326
1995 Ottawa	AAA	126	412	106	19	1	3	136	55	40	46	1	59	4	8	3	30	5	.86	12	.257	.335	.330
6 Min. YEARS		626	2080	526	115	4	27	730	267	232	219	10	318	19	26	21	67	30	.69	69	.253	.327	.351

Jeff Martin

Bats: Right **Throws:** Right **Pos:** C   **Ht:** 6'4" **Wt:** 220 **Born:** 7/14/70 **Age:** 25

Year Team	Lg	G	AB	H	2B	3B	HR	TB	R	RBI	TBB	IBB	SO	HBP	SH	SF	SB	CS	SB%	GDP	Avg	OBP	SLG
1992 Red Sox	R	40	117	34	9	2	1	50	15	12	22	0	32	5	0	0	0	1	.00	3	.291	.424	.427
Elmira	A	12	38	6	0	0	2	12	4	5	3	0	16	1	2	1	0	0	.00	1	.158	.233	.316
1993 Pawtucket	AAA	9	19	4	1	0	1	8	5	2	4	0	9	1	1	0	1	0	1.00	0	.211	.375	.421
Lynchburg	A	62	192	35	7	2	6	64	25	22	23	0	78	3	4	0	0	0	.00	4	.182	.280	.333
1994 Lynchburg	A	34	99	24	4	0	3	37	14	12	8	0	37	2	0	1	1	0	1.00	2	.242	.309	.374
Sarasota	A	51	164	40	9	1	6	69	24	21	16	1	54	2	1	2	0	3	.00	1	.244	.315	.421
1995 Trenton	AA	78	254	55	10	1	4	79	25	30	16	0	83	5	6	3	3	3	.50	10	.217	.273	.311
4 Min. YEARS		286	883	198	40	6	23	319	112	104	92	1	309	19	14	7	5	7	.42	21	.224	.309	.361

Jerry Martin

Pitches: Right **Bats:** Right **Pos:** P   **Ht:** 6'3" **Wt:** 175 **Born:** 3/15/72 **Age:** 24

Year Team	Lg	G	GS	CG	GF	IP	BFP	H	R	ER	HR	SH	SF	HB	TBB	IBB	SO	WP	Bk	W	L	Pct.	ShO	Sv	ERA
1992 Rangers	R	9	6	0	1	38.1	148	31	12	11	0	0	2	3	8	0	26	1	2	3	0	1.000	0	1	2.58
Charlotte	A	5	2	1	1	16.2	65	12	6	6	3	1	0	1	4	0	12	0	1	1	1	.500	0	1	3.24
1993 Charlstn-Sc	A	28	28	1	0	161.2	680	157	83	75	18	1	4	4	61	2	109	7	7	8	10	.444	1	0	4.18
1994 Charlotte	A	28	27	1	0	164.2	665	133	52	38	6	2	4	4	68	0	80	8	7	13	6	.684	1	0	2.08
1995 Tulsa	AA	22	17	0	1	88.2	405	100	55	51	12	4	3	2	51	1	46	7	0	3	7	.300	0	0	5.18
4 Min. YEARS		92	80	3	3	470	1963	433	208	181	39	8	13	14	192	3	273	23	17	28	24	.538	2	2	3.47

Jim Martin

Bats: Left **Throws:** Right **Pos:** OF   **Ht:** 6'1" **Wt:** 195 **Born:** 12/10/70 **Age:** 25

Year Team	Lg	G	AB	H	2B	3B	HR	TB	R	RBI	TBB	IBB	SO	HBP	SH	SF	SB	CS	SB%	GDP	Avg	OBP	SLG
1992 Great Falls	R	56	204	63	5	7	5	97	37	30	28	2	52	7	0	3	8	2	.80	0	.309	.405	.475
1993 Bakersfield	A	118	441	114	17	3	12	173	60	50	45	2	131	13	0	4	27	12	.69	3	.259	.342	.392
1994 Bakersfield	A	93	360	96	15	8	12	163	50	58	36	3	90	7	0	2	37	16	.70	3	.267	.343	.453
San Antonio	AA	29	101	22	8	0	1	33	7	10	8	0	23	0	0	0	3	5	.38	1	.218	.275	.327
1995 San Antonio	AA	95	327	77	20	3	4	115	43	36	36	2	83	5	0	4	18	10	.64	4	.235	.317	.352
Albuquerque	AAA	25	75	19	3	1	1	27	8	7	8	0	20	0	0	0	3	3	.50	3	.253	.325	.360
4 Min. YEARS		416	1508	391	68	22	35	608	205	191	161	9	399	32	0	13	96	48	.67	14	.259	.341	.403

Tom Martin

Pitches: Left **Bats:** Left **Pos:** P   **Ht:** 6'1" **Wt:** 185 **Born:** 5/21/70 **Age:** 26

Year Team	Lg	G	GS	CG	GF	IP	BFP	H	R	ER	HR	SH	SF	HB	TBB	IBB	SO	WP	Bk	W	L	Pct.	ShO	Sv	ERA
1989 Bluefield	R	8	8	0	0	39	176	36	28	20	3	1	1	0	25	0	31	2	1	3	3	.500	0	0	4.62
Erie	A	7	7	0	0	40.2	190	42	39	30	2	0	2	1	25	1	44	11	2	0	5	.000	0	0	6.64
1990 Wausau	A	9	9	0	0	40	183	31	25	11	1	3	0	5	27	0	45	4	0	2	3	.400	0	0	2.48

Year	Team	Lg	G																						
1991	Kane County	A	38	10	0	19	99	442	92	50	40	4	6	4	3	56	3	106	13	0	4	10	.286	0	6	3.64
1992	High Desert	A	11	0	0	8	16.1	85	23	19	17	4	0	0	0	16	0	10	2	0	0	2	.000	0	0	9.37
	Waterloo	A	39	2	0	11	55	248	62	38	26	3	5	1	4	22	4	57	5	0	2	6	.250	0	3	4.25
1993	Rancho Cuca	A	47	1	0	16	59.1	290	72	41	37	4	1	7	7	39	2	53	9	0	1	4	.200	0	0	5.61
1994	Greenville	AA	36	6	0	9	74	324	82	40	38	6	7	1	4	27	3	51	3	0	5	6	.455	0	0	4.62
1995	Richmond	AAA	7	0	0	2	9	45	10	9	9	4	0	0	0	10	2	3	0	0	0	0	.000	0	0	9.00
	7 Min. YEARS		202	43	0	65	432.1	1983	450	289	228	31	23	16	24	247	14	400	49	3	17	39	.304	0	9	4.75

Ryan Martindale

Bats: Right **Throws:** Right **Pos:** C   **Ht:** 6'3" **Wt:** 215 **Born:** 12/2/68 **Age:** 27

			BATTING															BASERUNNING				PERCENTAGES		
Year	Team	Lg	G	AB	H	2B	3B	HR	TB	R	RBI	TBB	IBB	SO	HBP	SH	SF	SB	CS	SB%	GDP	Avg	OBP	SLG
1991	Watertown	A	67	243	56	7	0	4	75	34	25	20	3	51	7	1	1	7	4	.64	7	.230	.306	.309
1992	Kinston	A	99	331	75	8	1	5	100	38	40	25	1	74	12	1	2	8	2	.80	7	.227	.303	.302
1993	Canton-Akrn	AA	105	310	68	18	1	10	118	44	39	23	0	71	9	4	3	1	3	.25	4	.219	.290	.381
1994	Canton-Akrn	AA	86	276	81	14	3	6	119	41	41	26	1	54	7	2	2	3	2	.60	6	.293	.367	.431
1995	Buffalo	AAA	11	31	5	1	0	0	6	4	0	0	0	9	0	0	0	1	0	1.00	1	.161	.161	.194
	Canton-Akrn	AA	2	8	3	0	0	0	3	2	1	1	0	1	0	0	0	0	1	.00	1	.375	.444	.375
	5 Min. YEARS		370	1199	288	48	5	25	421	163	146	95	5	259	35	8	8	20	12	.63	26	.240	.313	.351

Carmelo Martinez

Bats: Right **Throws:** Right **Pos:** DH   **Ht:** 6'2" **Wt:** 225 **Born:** 7/28/60 **Age:** 35

			BATTING															BASERUNNING				PERCENTAGES		
Year	Team	Lg	G	AB	H	2B	3B	HR	TB	R	RBI	TBB	IBB	SO	HBP	SH	SF	SB	CS	SB%	GDP	Avg	OBP	SLG
1979	Chicago-NI	R	40	143	29	4	0	1	36	18	23	17	-	20	1	1	3	0	0	.00	-	.203	.287	.252
1980	Quad City	A	128	460	118	23	0	12	177	65	64	54	-	68	2	1	4	8	7	.53	-	.257	.335	.385
1981	Midland	AA	116	392	116	22	1	21	203	65	84	56	-	73	6	4	4	5	2	.71	-	.296	.389	.518
1982	Midland	AA	131	467	156	35	4	27	280	100	93	85	-	78	1	0	6	1	5	.17	-	.334	.433	.600
1983	Iowa	AAA	123	458	115	25	1	31	235	76	94	61	-	85	2	2	6	8	8	.50	-	.251	.338	.513
1993	Calgary	AAA	42	149	38	5	0	4	55	21	18	22	0	25	1	1	0	4	0	1.00	2	.255	.355	.369
1995	Buffalo	AAA	11	36	10	1	0	2	17	8	9	7	0	10	0	0	0	0	0	.00	1	.278	.395	.472
1983	Chicago	NL	29	89	23	3	0	6	44	8	16	4	0	19	0	0	1	0	0	.00	3	.258	.287	.494
1984	San Diego	NL	149	488	122	28	2	13	193	64	66	68	4	82	4	0	10	1	3	.25	7	.250	.340	.395
1985	San Diego	NL	150	514	130	28	1	21	223	64	72	87	4	82	3	2	4	0	4	.00	10	.253	.362	.434
1986	San Diego	NL	113	244	58	10	0	9	95	28	25	35	2	46	1	1	2	1	1	.50	9	.238	.333	.389
1987	San Diego	NL	139	447	122	21	2	15	192	59	70	70	5	82	3	1	4	5	5	.50	11	.273	.372	.430
1988	San Diego	NL	121	365	86	12	0	18	152	48	65	35	3	57	0	3	2	1	1	.50	10	.236	.301	.416
1989	San Diego	NL	111	267	59	12	2	6	93	23	39	32	3	54	0	0	0	0	0	.00	12	.221	.302	.348
1990	Philadelphia	NL	71	198	48	8	0	8	80	23	31	29	0	37	0	0	0	2	1	.67	3	.242	.339	.404
	Pittsburgh	NL	12	19	4	1	0	2	11	3	4	1	0	5	0	0	0	0	0	.00	0	.211	.250	.579
1991	Kansas City	AL	44	121	25	6	0	4	43	17	17	27	3	25	0	0	0	0	1	.00	4	.207	.351	.355
	Cincinnati	NL	53	138	32	5	0	6	55	12	19	15	1	37	0	0	3	0	0	.00	1	.232	.301	.399
	Pittsburgh	NL	11	16	4	0	0	0	4	1	0	1	0	2	0	0	0	0	0	.00	0	.250	.294	.250
	7 Min. YEARS		591	2105	582	115	6	98	1003	353	385	302	0	359	13	9	23	26	22	.54	3	.276	.367	.476
	9 Maj. YEARS		1003	2906	713	134	7	108	1185	350	424	404	25	528	11	7	28	10	16	.38	72	.245	.337	.408

Chito Martinez

Bats: Left **Throws:** Left **Pos:** OF   **Ht:** 5'10" **Wt:** 185 **Born:** 12/19/65 **Age:** 30

			BATTING															BASERUNNING				PERCENTAGES		
Year	Team	Lg	G	AB	H	2B	3B	HR	TB	R	RBI	TBB	IBB	SO	HBP	SH	SF	SB	CS	SB%	GDP	Avg	OBP	SLG
1984	Eugene	A	59	176	53	12	3	0	71	18	26	24	2	38	0	1	0	4	4	.50	3	.301	.385	.403
1985	Fort Myers	A	76	248	65	9	5	0	84	35	29	31	3	42	1	1	3	11	5	.69	8	.262	.343	.339
1986	Memphis	AA	93	283	86	16	5	11	145	48	44	42	4	58	2	2	1	4	4	.50	2	.304	.396	.512
1987	Omaha	AAA	35	121	26	10	1	2	44	14	14	11	0	43	0	0	0	0	0	.00	0	.215	.280	.364
	Memphis	AA	78	283	74	10	3	9	117	34	43	33	0	94	1	0	2	5	3	.63	4	.261	.339	.413
1988	Memphis	AA	141	485	110	16	4	13	173	67	65	66	4	130	1	2	6	20	3	.87	6	.227	.317	.357
1989	Memphis	AA	127	399	97	20	2	23	190	55	62	63	7	137	1	4	4	3	3	.50	8	.243	.345	.476
1990	Omaha	AAA	122	364	96	12	8	21	187	59	67	54	5	129	3	0	3	6	6	.50	3	.264	.361	.514
1991	Rochester	AAA	60	211	68	8	1	20	138	42	50	26	3	69	0	0	2	2	2	.50	3	.322	.393	.654
1993	Bowie	AA	5	13	1	0	0	0	1	1	5	2	0	2	0	0	1	0	0	.00	1	.077	.200	.077
	Rochester	AAA	43	145	38	11	0	5	64	14	23	11	0	34	0	2	0	0	0	.00	2	.262	.314	.441
1994	Columbus	AAA	94	300	83	16	5	16	157	47	47	48	5	80	0	2	4	0	1	.00	3	.277	.372	.523
1995	Colo. Sprng	AAA	42	110	17	8	0	4	37	18	6	12	0	32	0	0	2	0	0	.00	1	.155	.238	.336
1991	Baltimore	AL	67	216	58	12	1	13	111	32	33	11	0	51	0	0	1	1	1	.50	2	.269	.303	.514
1992	Baltimore	AL	83	198	53	10	1	5	80	26	25	31	4	47	2	0	0	1	0	.00	9	.268	.366	.404
1993	Baltimore	AL	8	15	0	0	0	0	0	0	0	4	2	4	0	0	0	0	0	.00	0	.000	.211	.000
	11 Min. YEARS		975	3138	814	148	37	124	1408	456	476	423	33	888	9	14	25	55	33	.63	43	.259	.347	.449
	3 Maj. YEARS		158	429	111	22	2	18	191	58	58	46	6	102	2	0	5	1	2	.33	11	.259	.330	.445

Domingo Martinez

Bats: Right **Throws:** Right **Pos:** 1B-DH   **Ht:** 6'2" **Wt:** 215 **Born:** 8/4/67 **Age:** 28

			BATTING															BASERUNNING				PERCENTAGES		
Year	Team	Lg	G	AB	H	2B	3B	HR	TB	R	RBI	TBB	IBB	SO	HBP	SH	SF	SB	CS	SB%	GDP	Avg	OBP	SLG
1985	Blue Jays	R	58	219	65	10	2	4	91	36	19	12	0	42	2	0	0	3	4	.43	3	.297	.339	.416
1986	Ventura	A	129	455	113	19	6	9	171	51	57	36	2	127	4	3	3	9	9	.50	15	.248	.307	.376

Year Team	Lg	G	AB	H	2B	3B	HR	TB	R	RBI	TBB	IBB	SO	HBP	SH	SF	SB	CS	SB%	GDP	Avg	OBP	SLG
1987 Dunedin	A	118	435	112	32	2	8	172	53	65	41	2	88	3	0	2	8	3	.73	9	.257	.324	.395
1988 Knoxville	AA	143	516	136	25	2	13	204	54	70	40	3	88	5	0	7	2	7	.22	13	.264	.319	.395
1989 Knoxville	AA	120	415	102	19	2	10	155	56	53	42	3	82	9	1	5	2	2	.50	7	.246	.325	.373
1990 Knoxville	AA	128	463	119	20	3	17	196	52	67	51	1	81	5	1	2	2	3	.40	24	.257	.336	.423
1991 Syracuse	AAA	126	467	146	16	2	17	217	61	83	41	0	107	6	5	6	6	4	.60	10	.313	.371	.465
1992 Syracuse	AAA	116	438	120	22	0	21	205	55	62	33	5	95	8	0	4	6	0	1.00	11	.274	.333	.468
1993 Syracuse	AAA	127	465	127	24	2	24	227	50	79	31	6	115	10	0	4	4	5	.44	11	.273	.329	.488
1994 Nashville	AAA	131	471	127	22	2	22	219	57	81	38	2	102	5	1	8	2	1	.67	12	.270	.326	.465
1995 Louisville	AAA	64	222	58	15	0	9	100	26	31	15	2	49	4	0	4	0	0	.00	7	.261	.314	.450
1992 Toronto	AL	7	8	5	0	0	1	8	2	3	0	0	1	0	0	0	0	0	.00	0	.625	.625	1.000
1993 Toronto	AL	8	14	4	0	0	1	7	2	3	1	0	7	0	0	0	0	0	.00	0	.286	.333	.500
11 Min. YEARS		1260	4566	1225	224	23	154	1957	551	667	380	26	976	61	11	45	44	38	.54	122	.268	.330	.429
2 Maj. YEARS		15	22	9	0	0	2	15	4	6	1	0	8	0	0	0	0	0	.00	0	.409	.435	.682

Felix Martinez

Bats: Both Throws: Right Pos: SS Ht: 6'0" Wt: 168 Born: 5/18/74 Age: 22

Year Team	Lg	G	AB	H	2B	3B	HR	TB	R	RBI	TBB	IBB	SO	HBP	SH	SF	SB	CS	SB%	GDP	Avg	OBP	SLG
1993 Royals	R	57	165	42	5	1	0	49	23	12	17	0	26	3	1	0	22	5	.81	2	.255	.335	.297
1994 Wilmington	A	117	400	107	16	4	2	137	65	43	30	0	91	3	12	2	19	8	.70	10	.268	.322	.343
1995 Wichita	AA	127	426	112	15	3	3	142	53	30	31	0	71	6	4	1	44	20	.69	5	.263	.321	.333
3 Min. YEARS		301	991	261	36	8	5	328	141	85	78	0	188	12	17	3	85	33	.72	17	.263	.324	.331

Francisco Martinez

Pitches: Right Bats: Right Pos: P Ht: 6'2" Wt: 180 Born: 4/24/68 Age: 28

Year Team	Lg	G	GS	CG	GF	IP	BFP	H	R	ER	HR	SH	SF	HB	TBB	IBB	SO	WP	Bk	W	L	Pct.	ShO	Sv	ERA
1990 Angels	R	17	3	0	0	33	168	31	40	24	0	1	1	3	32	0	29	8	0	3	2	.600	0	0	6.55
1992 Springfield	A	18	3	0	7	31	133	28	18	11	0	0	1	0	12	0	22	6	1	1	3	.250	0	0	3.19
1993 Savannah	A	14	14	2	0	95.1	371	70	28	20	4	1	2	1	23	1	79	2	0	7	3	.700	0	0	1.89
St. Pete	A	13	7	1	2	65.2	265	55	13	10	2	2	1	0	22	0	38	0	0	3	2	.600	1	0	1.37
Arkansas	AA	2	2	0	0	7	31	8	5	5	0	1	0	1	1	0	3	0	0	0	1	.000	0	0	6.43
1994 Arkansas	AA	45	0	0	31	58	249	48	25	19	5	4	0	2	25	1	34	4	1	5	4	.556	0	16	2.95
1995 Arkansas	AA	11	0	0	4	21	80	10	3	3	0	3	1	1	7	1	13	2	0	1	1	.500	0	1	1.29
Louisville	AAA	38	0	0	8	52.1	230	60	25	21	4	1	0	2	21	5	23	10	0	2	1	.667	0	0	3.61
5 Min. YEARS		158	29	3	52	363.1	1527	310	157	113	15	13	6	10	143	8	241	32	2	22	17	.564	1	17	2.80

Gabby Martinez

Bats: Right Throws: Right Pos: SS Ht: 6'2" Wt: 170 Born: 1/7/74 Age: 22

Year Team	Lg	G	AB	H	2B	3B	HR	TB	R	RBI	TBB	IBB	SO	HBP	SH	SF	SB	CS	SB%	GDP	Avg	OBP	SLG
1992 Brewers	R	48	165	43	7	2	0	54	29	24	12	0	19	3	2	2	7	5	.58	3	.261	.319	.327
1993 Beloit	A	94	285	69	14	5	0	93	40	24	14	0	52	1	15	4	22	10	.69	0	.242	.276	.326
1994 Stockton	A	112	364	90	18	3	0	114	37	32	17	1	66	4	4	4	19	11	.63	8	.247	.285	.313
1995 Stockton	A	64	213	55	13	3	1	77	25	20	10	0	25	2	9	3	13	6	.68	6	.258	.294	.362
El Paso	AA	44	133	37	3	2	0	44	13	11	2	0	22	2	3	1	5	1	.83	2	.278	.297	.331
4 Min. YEARS		362	1160	294	55	15	1	382	144	111	55	1	184	12	33	14	66	33	.67	19	.253	.291	.329

Jesus Martinez

Pitches: Left Bats: Left Pos: P Ht: 6'2" Wt: 145 Born: 3/13/74 Age: 22

Year Team	Lg	G	GS	CG	GF	IP	BFP	H	R	ER	HR	SH	SF	HB	TBB	IBB	SO	WP	Bk	W	L	Pct.	ShO	Sv	ERA
1992 Great Falls	R	6	6	0	0	18.1	112	36	30	27	4	0	0	2	21	0	23	9	0	0	3	.000	0	0	13.25
Dodgers	R	7	7	1	0	41	174	38	19	15	1	2	0	1	11	0	39	5	0	1	4	.200	0	0	3.29
1993 Bakersfield	A	30	21	0	2	145.2	653	144	95	67	12	5	11	5	75	0	108	6	5	4	13	.235	0	0	4.14
1994 San Antonio	AA	1	1	0	0	4	14	3	2	2	0	0	0	0	2	0	3	0	0	0	1	.000	0	0	4.50
Vero Beach	A	18	18	1	0	87.2	386	91	65	61	7	2	3	6	43	0	69	3	0	7	9	.438	1	0	6.26
1995 San Antonio	AA	24	24	1	0	139.2	603	129	64	55	6	7	4	7	71	0	83	16	4	6	9	.400	0	0	3.54
Albuquerque	AAA	2	0	0	0	4	20	4	2	2	0	1	1	1	4	2	5	0	0	1	1	.500	0	0	4.50
4 Min. YEARS		88	77	3	3	440.1	1962	445	277	229	30	17	19	22	227	2	330	39	9	19	40	.322	1	0	4.68

Jose Martinez

Pitches: Right Bats: Right Pos: P Ht: 6'2" Wt: 155 Born: 4/1/71 Age: 25

Year Team	Lg	G	GS	CG	GF	IP	BFP	H	R	ER	HR	SH	SF	HB	TBB	IBB	SO	WP	Bk	W	L	Pct.	ShO	Sv	ERA
1989 Mets	R	11	4	1	4	34.1	162	54	35	25	2	1	0	1	4	1	22	2	0	1	4	.200	0	0	6.55
1990 Mets	R	13	13	4	0	92	357	68	27	16	1	2	4	1	9	0	90	3	2	8	3	.727	2	0	1.57
1991 Columbia	A	26	26	9	0	193.1	754	162	51	32	3	5	2	0	30	1	158	4	1	20	4	.833	1	0	1.49
1992 St. Lucie	A	17	17	4	0	123	489	107	44	28	6	2	2	0	11	0	114	4	0	6	5	.545	1	0	2.05
Binghamton	AA	9	8	3	1	58	229	47	16	11	1	0	3	1	13	1	38	0	1	5	2	.714	1	0	1.71
1993 Edmonton	AAA	13	13	3	0	80	343	92	49	38	10	4	5	1	24	0	29	2	1	6	4	.600	0	0	4.28
Las Vegas	AAA	14	5	0	2	35.1	174	56	39	39	8	0	2	1	15	0	16	3	0	2	3	.400	0	0	9.93
1994 Wichita	AA	25	24	1	0	133.2	584	154	82	76	12	7	6	4	50	5	68	1	0	4	11	.267	1	0	5.12
1995 Las Vegas	AAA	27	25	2	0	151.2	646	156	86	80	9	9	5	7	44	2	64	5	0	6	10	.375	1	0	4.75

| 1994 San Diego | NL | 4 | 1 | 0 | 0 | 12 | 54 | 18 | 9 | 9 | 2 | 1 | 0 | 0 | 5 | 2 | 7 | 1 | 0 | 0 | 2 | .000 | 0 | 0 | 6.75 |
| 7 Min. YEARS | | 155 | 135 | 27 | 7 | 901.1 | 3738 | 896 | 429 | 345 | 52 | 30 | 29 | 16 | 200 | 10 | 599 | 24 | 5 | 58 | 46 | .558 | 7 | 0 | 3.44 |

Manuel Martinez

Bats: Right **Throws:** Right **Pos:** OF   **Ht:** 6'2" **Wt:** 169 **Born:** 10/3/70 **Age:** 25

					BATTING											BASERUNNING				PERCENTAGES		
Year Team	Lg	G	AB	H	2B	3B	HR	TB	R	RBI	TBB	IBB	SO	HBP	SH	SF	SB	CS	SB%	GDP	Avg	OBP	SLG
1990 Sou. Oregon	A	66	244	60	5	0	2	71	35	17	16	0	59	5	1	0	6	4	.60	5	.246	.306	.291
1991 Modesto	A	125	502	136	32	3	3	183	73	55	34	2	80	7	7	3	26	19	.58	7	.271	.324	.365
1992 Modesto	A	121	495	125	23	1	9	177	70	45	39	3	75	4	12	5	17	13	.57	7	.253	.309	.358
1993 San Bernrdo	A	109	459	148	26	3	11	213	88	52	41	2	60	5	6	4	28	21	.57	10	.322	.381	.464
Tacoma	AAA	20	59	18	2	0	1	23	9	6	4	0	12	0	1	0	2	3	.40	2	.305	.349	.390
1994 Tacoma	AAA	137	536	137	25	5	9	199	76	60	28	3	72	10	9	5	18	10	.64	14	.256	.302	.371
1995 Iowa	AAA	122	397	115	17	8	8	172	63	49	20	0	64	3	7	2	11	8	.58	3	.290	.327	.433
6 Min. YEARS		700	2692	739	130	20	43	1038	414	284	182	10	422	34	43	19	108	78	.58	48	.275	.326	.386

Pablo Martinez

Bats: Both **Throws:** Right **Pos:** SS   **Ht:** 5'10" **Wt:** 155 **Born:** 6/29/69 **Age:** 27

					BATTING											BASERUNNING				PERCENTAGES		
Year Team	Lg	G	AB	H	2B	3B	HR	TB	R	RBI	TBB	IBB	SO	HBP	SH	SF	SB	CS	SB%	GDP	Avg	OBP	SLG
1989 Spokane	A	2	8	2	0	0	0	2	3	0	0	0	0	0	0	0	1	0	1.00	1	.250	.250	.250
Padres	R	45	178	42	3	1	0	47	31	12	22	1	25	2	0	0	29	4	.88	1	.236	.327	.264
Charlstn-Sc	A	31	80	14	2	0	0	16	13	4	11	0	21	0	3	1	0	1	.00	2	.175	.272	.200
1990 Charlstn-Sc	A	136	453	100	12	6	0	124	51	33	41	0	104	4	7	2	16	10	.62	6	.221	.290	.274
1991 Charlstn-Sc	A	121	442	118	17	6	3	156	62	36	42	1	64	0	6	2	39	19	.67	8	.267	.329	.353
1992 High Desert	A	126	427	102	8	4	0	118	60	39	50	0	74	1	2	4	19	14	.58	16	.239	.317	.276
1993 Wichita	AA	45	130	36	5	1	2	49	19	14	11	1	24	1	1	1	8	5	.62	2	.277	.336	.377
Las Vegas	AAA	76	251	58	4	1	2	70	24	20	18	3	46	3	10	2	8	2	.80	5	.231	.288	.279
1994 Norfolk	AAA	34	80	12	1	0	0	13	8	5	4	0	22	0	3	0	1	1	.50	0	.150	.190	.163
Binghamton	AA	13	48	9	2	2	0	15	3	4	5	0	12	0	2	0	0	1	.00	3	.188	.264	.313
St. Lucie	A	49	177	42	5	0	1	50	19	10	13	0	29	0	3	1	7	7	.50	4	.237	.288	.282
1995 Greenville	AA	120	462	118	22	4	5	163	70	29	37	0	89	2	8	1	12	12	.50	7	.255	.313	.353
Richmond	AAA	14	48	11	0	2	0	15	5	4	2	0	7	0	0	0	1	1	.50	3	.229	.260	.313
7 Min. YEARS		812	2784	664	81	27	13	838	368	210	256	6	517	13	45	14	141	77	.65	58	.239	.304	.301

Ramiro Martinez

Pitches: Left **Bats:** Left **Pos:** P   **Ht:** 6'2" **Wt:** 185 **Born:** 1/28/72 **Age:** 24

		HOW MUCH HE PITCHED						WHAT HE GAVE UP										THE RESULTS					
Year Team	Lg	G	GS	CG	GF	IP	BFP	H	R	ER	HR	SH	SF	HB	TBB	IBB	SO	WP	Bk	W	L	Pct.	ShO	Sv	ERA
1992 Rangers	R	10	10	1	0	45.2	184	28	15	6	0	0	1	4	22	0	52	3	1	4	1	.800	1	0	1.18
1993 Charlstn-Sc	A	27	27	2	0	124.2	588	129	91	81	10	2	3	10	90	4	129	11	0	6	10	.375	2	0	5.85
1994 Tulsa	AA	23	23	2	0	139.1	589	126	79	70	21	1	3	4	69	0	107	2	1	6	10	.375	0	0	4.52
1995 Tulsa	AA	13	5	0	0	47	220	53	29	27	5	0	3	1	34	2	37	3	0	0	5	.000	0	0	5.17
Charlotte	A	14	6	0	6	46.1	192	45	21	21	3	3	3	0	15	0	30	3	0	2	2	.500	0	2	4.08
4 Min. YEARS		87	71	5	6	403	1773	381	235	205	39	6	13	19	230	6	355	22	2	18	28	.391	3	2	4.58

Ramon Martinez

Bats: Right **Throws:** Right **Pos:** 2B   **Ht:** 6'1" **Wt:** 170 **Born:** 10/10/72 **Age:** 23

					BATTING											BASERUNNING				PERCENTAGES		
Year Team	Lg	G	AB	H	2B	3B	HR	TB	R	RBI	TBB	IBB	SO	HBP	SH	SF	SB	CS	SB%	GDP	Avg	OBP	SLG
1993 Royals	R	37	97	23	5	0	0	28	16	9	8	0	6	2	2	2	3	0	1.00	5	.237	.303	.289
Wilmington	A	24	75	19	4	0	0	23	8	6	11	0	9	1	3	1	1	4	.20	2	.253	.352	.307
1994 Rockford	A	6	18	5	0	0	0	5	3	3	4	0	2	0	1	0	1	0	1.00	1	.278	.409	.278
Wilmington	A	90	325	87	13	2	2	110	40	35	35	0	25	4	20	5	6	3	.67	14	.268	.341	.338
1995 Wichita	AA	103	393	108	20	2	3	141	58	51	42	1	50	4	18	9	11	8	.58	11	.275	.344	.359
3 Min. YEARS		260	908	242	42	4	5	307	125	104	100	1	92	11	44	17	22	15	.59	33	.267	.341	.338

Ray Martinez

Bats: Right **Throws:** Right **Pos:** 3B   **Ht:** 6'0" **Wt:** 165 **Born:** 10/1/68 **Age:** 27

					BATTING											BASERUNNING				PERCENTAGES		
Year Team	Lg	G	AB	H	2B	3B	HR	TB	R	RBI	TBB	IBB	SO	HBP	SH	SF	SB	CS	SB%	GDP	Avg	OBP	SLG
1987 Salem	A	44	106	20	1	0	0	21	8	13	10	0	23	0	1	1	1	0	1.00	0	.189	.256	.198
1988 Bend	A	61	226	52	9	2	2	71	28	19	25	0	51	4	1	0	2	7	.22	5	.230	.318	.314
1989 Palm Spring	A	103	317	61	8	1	0	71	40	20	43	0	76	5	0	4	4	4	.50	11	.192	.295	.224
1990 Quad City	A	105	306	68	10	0	9	105	47	40	58	1	82	9	4	6	6	4	.60	5	.222	.356	.343
1991 Quad City	A	6	21	5	1	0	0	6	3	0	4	0	5	0	0	0	0	0	.00	2	.238	.360	.286
Palm Spring	A	106	371	100	13	5	2	129	58	41	66	3	64	6	7	0	10	7	.59	3	.270	.388	.348
1992 Midland	AA	30	111	25	4	3	3	44	16	14	6	0	31	2	0	0	1	0	1.00	3	.225	.277	.396
Edmonton	AAA	88	285	86	20	2	3	119	42	35	27	0	50	6	2	4	6	5	.55	9	.302	.370	.418
1993 Vancouver	AAA	114	357	90	24	2	3	127	54	35	35	4	64	7	4	4	5	6	.45	4	.252	.328	.356
1995 Ottawa	AAA	39	108	27	6	0	0	33	17	9	6	0	17	0	3	1	3	0	1.00	3	.250	.287	.306
Harrisburg	AA	48	152	36	6	0	1	45	18	13	20	2	24	1	0	0	3	2	.60	6	.237	.329	.296
8 Min. YEARS		744	2360	570	102	15	23	771	331	239	300	6	487	40	22	20	39	37	.51	51	.242	.335	.327

Tim Marx

Bats: Right **Throws:** Right **Pos:** C **Ht:** 6'2" **Wt:** 190 **Born:** 11/27/68 **Age:** 27

Year	Team	Lg	G	AB	H	2B	3B	HR	TB	R	RBI	TBB	IBB	SO	HBP	SH	SF	SB	CS	SB%	GDP	Avg	OBP	SLG
1992	Augusta	A	44	138	30	7	0	0	37	20	9	23	0	16	1	3	0	0	1	.00	4	.217	.333	.268
1993	Salem	A	13	43	10	0	0	0	10	2	5	7	0	9	0	1	1	1	1	.50	2	.233	.333	.233
	Augusta	A	53	162	45	8	0	3	62	28	21	34	0	18	2	2	2	3	4	.43	3	.278	.405	.383
	Buffalo	AAA	4	14	2	1	0	0	3	0	0	2	0	4	0	0	0	0	0	.00	1	.143	.250	.214
1994	Carolina	AA	77	239	71	11	2	7	107	32	42	20	1	29	1	2	5	1	3	.25	4	.297	.347	.448
1995	Calgary	AAA	61	185	55	11	1	1	71	27	12	19	2	16	0	1	3	2	3	.40	6	.297	.357	.384
	4 Min. YEARS		252	781	213	38	3	11	290	109	89	105	3	92	4	9	11	7	12	.37	20	.273	.357	.371

Damon Mashore

Bats: Both **Throws:** Right **Pos:** OF **Ht:** 5'11" **Wt:** 195 **Born:** 10/31/69 **Age:** 26

Year	Team	Lg	G	AB	H	2B	3B	HR	TB	R	RBI	TBB	IBB	SO	HBP	SH	SF	SB	CS	SB%	GDP	Avg	OBP	SLG
1991	Sou. Oregon	A	73	264	72	17	6	6	119	48	31	34	1	94	2	2	3	15	5	.75	6	.273	.356	.451
1992	Modesto	A	124	471	133	22	3	18	215	91	64	73	3	136	6	5	1	29	17	.63	6	.282	.385	.456
1993	Huntsville	AA	70	253	59	7	2	3	79	35	20	25	0	64	4	1	2	18	4	.82	5	.233	.310	.312
1994	Athletics	R	11	34	14	2	0	0	16	6	6	4	0	3	1	0	1	1	1	.50	3	.412	.475	.471
	Huntsville	AA	59	210	47	11	2	3	71	24	21	13	1	53	0	1	3	6	1	.86	3	.224	.265	.338
1995	Edmonton	AAA	117	337	101	19	5	1	133	50	37	42	0	77	5	3	3	17	5	.77	9	.300	.382	.395
	5 Min. YEARS		454	1569	426	78	18	31	633	254	179	191	5	427	18	12	13	86	33	.72	32	.272	.355	.403

Justin Mashore

Bats: Right **Throws:** Right **Pos:** OF **Ht:** 5'9" **Wt:** 190 **Born:** 2/14/72 **Age:** 24

Year	Team	Lg	G	AB	H	2B	3B	HR	TB	R	RBI	TBB	IBB	SO	HBP	SH	SF	SB	CS	SB%	GDP	Avg	OBP	SLG
1991	Bristol	R	58	177	36	3	0	3	48	29	11	28	1	65	0	2	0	17	6	.74	1	.203	.312	.271
1992	Fayetteville	A	120	401	96	18	3	4	132	54	43	36	2	117	3	9	1	31	8	.79	3	.239	.306	.329
1993	Lakeland	A	118	442	113	11	4	3	141	64	30	37	4	92	6	16	5	26	13	.67	9	.256	.318	.319
1994	Trenton	AA	131	450	100	13	5	7	144	63	45	36	0	120	3	8	3	31	7	.82	9	.222	.283	.320
1995	Toledo	AAA	72	223	49	4	3	4	71	32	21	14	1	62	3	9	2	12	9	.57	1	.220	.273	.318
	Jacksonville	AA	40	148	36	8	2	4	60	26	15	6	0	41	3	3	0	5	1	.83	2	.243	.287	.405
	5 Min. YEARS		539	1841	430	57	17	25	596	268	165	157	8	497	18	47	11	122	44	.73	25	.234	.298	.324

John Massarelli

Bats: Right **Throws:** Right **Pos:** OF **Ht:** 6'2" **Wt:** 200 **Born:** 1/23/66 **Age:** 30

Year	Team	Lg	G	AB	H	2B	3B	HR	TB	R	RBI	TBB	IBB	SO	HBP	SH	SF	SB	CS	SB%	GDP	Avg	OBP	SLG
1987	Auburn	A	23	56	9	1	2	0	14	7	3	7	0	10	0	0	1	3	0	1.00	2	.161	.250	.250
	Asheville	A	6	17	6	0	0	0	6	6	1	2	0	1	0	0	0	3	0	1.00	0	.353	.421	.353
1988	Auburn	A	59	179	54	8	1	0	64	29	26	32	0	31	3	1	4	25	5	.83	1	.302	.408	.358
1989	Asheville	A	90	246	61	13	2	3	87	43	21	35	0	42	3	2	2	25	6	.81	2	.248	.346	.354
1990	Osceola	A	120	396	117	8	3	2	137	55	50	41	4	73	2	5	7	54	6	.90	9	.295	.359	.346
1991	Osceola	A	51	194	60	9	0	1	72	27	22	16	2	34	4	2	2	18	8	.69	4	.309	.370	.371
	Jackson	AA	12	38	8	2	0	0	10	3	0	1	0	2	0	0	0	4	0	1.00	0	.211	.231	.263
	Tucson	AAA	46	127	34	7	1	0	43	19	16	15	1	18	0	1	1	10	2	.83	3	.268	.343	.339
1992	Jackson	AA	27	98	27	4	1	1	36	15	10	5	0	20	0	1	0	10	2	.83	2	.276	.311	.367
	Tucson	AAA	50	143	34	4	0	0	38	21	6	14	1	27	1	1	0	14	3	.82	2	.238	.310	.266
1993	Tucson	AAA	114	423	119	28	4	2	161	66	42	46	4	61	2	5	2	37	13	.74	14	.281	.353	.381
1994	Edmonton	AAA	120	414	108	18	10	4	158	67	36	34	1	72	0	0	3	39	7	.85	4	.261	.315	.382
1995	Charlotte	AAA	65	254	62	7	2	2	79	37	26	26	0	55	2	1	1	14	10	.58	2	.244	.318	.311
	Buffalo	AAA	3	1	0	0	0	0	0	0	0	0	1	0	0	0	0	0	0	.00	0	.000	.500	.000
	Canton-Akrn	AA	55	178	50	10	2	2	70	17	22	16	0	28	0	1	3	17	6	.74	5	.281	.335	.393
	9 Min. YEARS		841	2764	749	119	28	17	975	412	263	291	13	474	17	20	26	273	68	.80	46	.271	.341	.353

Billy Masse

Bats: Right **Throws:** Right **Pos:** OF **Ht:** 6'1" **Wt:** 190 **Born:** 7/6/66 **Age:** 29

Year	Team	Lg	G	AB	H	2B	3B	HR	TB	R	RBI	TBB	IBB	SO	HBP	SH	SF	SB	CS	SB%	GDP	Avg	OBP	SLG
1989	Pr. William	A	124	377	90	17	4	11	148	70	50	89	4	57	13	3	4	16	4	.80	6	.239	.398	.393
1990	Ft. Laud	A	68	230	63	15	0	6	96	42	33	33	2	28	6	0	5	9	0	1.00	2	.274	.372	.417
	Albany-Colo	AA	31	96	18	1	0	3	28	12	8	22	0	19	1	0	1	0	1	.00	2	.188	.342	.292
1991	Albany-Colo	AA	108	356	105	17	2	11	159	67	61	74	3	60	6	0	7	10	4	.71	11	.295	.418	.447
1992	Columbus	AAA	110	357	95	13	2	12	148	52	60	51	0	51	5	2	3	7	6	.54	13	.266	.363	.415
1993	Columbus	AAA	117	402	127	35	3	19	225	81	91	82	0	68	8	1	4	17	7	.71	9	.316	.438	.560
1994	Columbus	AAA	71	221	57	17	0	5	89	37	14	31	1	43	6	1	0	1	6	.14	7	.258	.364	.403
1995	Columbus	AAA	49	165	37	6	2	4	59	19	24	24	1	31	4	0	2	3	3	.50	7	.224	.333	.358
	7 Min. YEARS		678	2204	592	121	13	71	952	380	341	406	11	357	49	7	26	63	31	.67	57	.269	.390	.432

Mike Mathile

Pitches: Right **Bats:** Right **Pos:** P　　　　**Ht:** 6'4" **Wt:** 220 **Born:** 11/24/68 **Age:** 27

			HOW MUCH HE PITCHED				WHAT HE GAVE UP								THE RESULTS					
Year Team	Lg	G	GS	CG	GF	IP	BFP	H	R	ER	HR	SH	SF	HB	TBB	IBB	SO	WP	Bk	W	L	Pct.	ShO	Sv	ERA
1990 Jamestown	A	14	14	1	0	90	377	95	40	25	4	6	0	1	28	1	54	2	0	2	5	.286	0	0	2.50
1991 Rockford	A	17	17	5	0	116.2	465	100	45	32	3	2	0	4	19	0	66	4	6	9	3	.750	2	0	2.47
1992 Harrisburg	AA	26	26	7	0	185.2	741	175	61	59	6	3	3	5	28	0	89	6	1	12	5	.706	3	0	2.86
1993 Ottawa	AAA	31	21	2	6	140.1	594	147	74	65	9	3	4	6	41	1	56	7	0	9	9	.500	2	1	4.17
1994 Ottawa	AAA	2	0	0	1	5.2	26	9	1	1	0	0	0	0	2	1	1	0	0	0	1	.000	0	0	1.59
Indianapolis	AAA	2	2	0	0	3.2	20	10	8	8	3	0	0	0	0	0	2	0	0	0	1	.000	0	0	19.64
1995 Indianapolis	AAA	14	3	0	4	28.2	113	22	10	8	1	1	4	0	8	0	16	0	0	0	2	.000	0	0	2.51
6 Min. YEARS		106	83	15	11	570.2	2336	558	239	198	26	15	11	16	126	3	284	19	7	32	26	.552	7	1	3.12

Francisco Matos

Bats: Right **Throws:** Right **Pos:** 2B-SS　　　　**Ht:** 6'1" **Wt:** 160 **Born:** 7/23/69 **Age:** 26

		BATTING															BASERUNNING				PERCENTAGES		
Year Team	Lg	G	AB	H	2B	3B	HR	TB	R	RBI	TBB	IBB	SO	HBP	SH	SF	SB	CS	SB%	GDP	Avg	OBP	SLG
1989 Modesto	A	65	200	41	5	1	1	51	14	23	12	0	41	0	0	1	6	5	.55	5	.205	.249	.255
1990 Modesto	A	83	321	88	12	1	1	105	46	20	15	0	65	5	7	2	26	5	.84	2	.274	.315	.327
Huntsville	AA	45	180	41	3	3	0	50	18	12	9	1	18	1	2	1	7	4	.64	3	.228	.267	.278
1991 Huntsville	AA	55	191	37	1	2	0	42	18	19	17	1	28	2	5	0	12	2	.86	8	.194	.267	.220
Modesto	A	50	189	53	4	0	1	60	32	22	30	1	24	1	4	1	19	8	.70	5	.280	.380	.317
1992 Huntsville	AA	44	150	33	5	1	1	43	11	14	11	0	27	2	1	1	4	4	.50	4	.220	.280	.287
1993 Huntsville	AA	123	461	127	12	3	1	148	69	32	22	1	54	4	4	3	16	6	.73	6	.275	.312	.321
1994 Tacoma	AAA	86	336	103	10	1	0	115	40	30	14	0	32	0	4	3	16	9	.64	13	.307	.331	.342
1995 Calgary	AAA	100	341	110	11	6	3	142	36	40	5	0	25	2	3	1	9	2	.82	11	.323	.335	.416
1994 Oakland	AL	14	28	7	1	0	0	8	1	2	1	0	2	0	0	1	1	0	1.00	1	.250	.267	.286
7 Min. YEARS		651	2369	633	63	18	8	756	284	212	135	4	314	17	30	13	115	45	.72	57	.267	.310	.319

Jeff Matranga

Pitches: Right **Bats:** Right **Pos:** P　　　　**Ht:** 6'2" **Wt:** 170 **Born:** 12/14/70 **Age:** 25

			HOW MUCH HE PITCHED				WHAT HE GAVE UP								THE RESULTS					
Year Team	Lg	G	GS	CG	GF	IP	BFP	H	R	ER	HR	SH	SF	HB	TBB	IBB	SO	WP	Bk	W	L	Pct.	ShO	Sv	ERA
1992 Johnson Cty	R	19	1	0	12	36.1	158	34	17	12	1	0	1	3	13	1	47	3	0	3	0	1.000	0	2	2.97
1993 St. Pete	A	5	3	0	1	28.1	113	23	10	7	1	0	0	0	6	0	21	3	0	2	0	1.000	0	0	2.22
Savannah	A	15	15	3	0	103	387	74	24	17	8	1	0	4	13	0	90	4	0	11	3	.786	2	0	1.49
1994 St. Pete	A	63	0	0	26	87.1	367	76	30	23	4	5	2	3	30	7	76	1	1	5	3	.615	0	3	2.37
1995 St. Pete	A	53	0	0	17	65.2	272	49	27	20	2	3	3	9	20	3	71	2	0	3	4	.429	0	3	2.74
Arkansas	AA	7	0	0	4	8	27	1	0	0	0	0	0	0	3	0	4	0	0	0	0	.000	0	0	0.00
4 Min. YEARS		162	19	3	60	328.2	1324	257	108	79	16	9	6	19	85	11	309	13	1	27	12	.692	2	8	2.16

Mike Matthews

Pitches: Left **Bats:** Left **Pos:** P　　　　**Ht:** 6'3" **Wt:** 180 **Born:** 10/24/73 **Age:** 22

			HOW MUCH HE PITCHED				WHAT HE GAVE UP								THE RESULTS					
Year Team	Lg	G	GS	CG	GF	IP	BFP	H	R	ER	HR	SH	SF	HB	TBB	IBB	SO	WP	Bk	W	L	Pct.	ShO	Sv	ERA
1992 Burlington	R	10	10	0	0	62.1	245	33	13	7	1	2	1	3	27	0	55	3	1	7	0	1.000	0	0	1.01
Watertown	A	2	2	0	0	11	47	10	4	4	0	0	1	0	8	0	5	1	0	1	0	1.000	0	0	3.27
1994 Columbus	A	23	23	0	0	119.2	502	120	53	41	8	3	3	7	44	1	99	7	3	6	8	.429	0	0	3.08
1995 Canton-Akrn	AA	15	15	1	0	74.1	345	82	62	49	6	2	8	2	43	1	37	8	1	5	8	.385	0	0	5.93
3 Min. YEARS		50	50	1	0	267.1	1139	245	132	101	15	7	13	12	122	2	196	19	5	19	16	.543	0	0	3.40

Rob Mattson

Pitches: Right **Bats:** Left **Pos:** P　　　　**Ht:** 6'1" **Wt:** 190 **Born:** 11/18/66 **Age:** 29

			HOW MUCH HE PITCHED				WHAT HE GAVE UP								THE RESULTS					
Year Team	Lg	G	GS	CG	GF	IP	BFP	H	R	ER	HR	SH	SF	HB	TBB	IBB	SO	WP	Bk	W	L	Pct.	ShO	Sv	ERA
1991 Macon	A	23	7	3	4	76.2	312	61	29	24	1	1	4	4	17	1	51	5	1	5	2	.714	1	0	2.82
Durham	A	9	8	2	1	45.2	190	48	23	22	2	2	1	0	9	1	32	3	2	1	4	.200	0	0	4.34
1992 Beloit	A	8	1	0	2	17.1	76	15	8	8	1	1	1	0	7	1	16	0	2	1	0	1.000	0	0	4.15
1995 Memphis	AA	30	28	11	1	201.2	862	199	109	92	20	7	15	20	73	2	139	4	4	12	13	.480	3	0	4.11
3 Min. YEARS		70	44	16	8	341.1	1440	323	169	146	24	11	21	24	106	5	238	12	9	19	19	.500	4	1	3.85

Mike Maurer

Pitches: Right **Bats:** Right **Pos:** P　　　　**Ht:** 6'2" **Wt:** 185 **Born:** 7/4/72 **Age:** 23

			HOW MUCH HE PITCHED				WHAT HE GAVE UP								THE RESULTS					
Year Team	Lg	G	GS	CG	GF	IP	BFP	H	R	ER	HR	SH	SF	HB	TBB	IBB	SO	WP	Bk	W	L	Pct.	ShO	Sv	ERA
1994 Sou. Oregon	A	17	8	0	5	63.1	285	68	42	25	2	4	4	5	20	1	67	7	3	2	6	.250	0	3	3.55
1995 Huntsville	AA	17	0	0	14	20.2	100	34	18	15	0	2	1	0	5	2	19	2	0	0	2	.000	0	6	6.53
Modesto	A	39	0	0	37	40.1	157	27	9	8	3	2	2	2	9	0	44	2	0	2	2	.500	0	18	1.79
2 Min. YEARS		73	8	0	56	124.1	542	129	69	48	5	8	7	7	34	3	130	11	3	4	10	.286	0	27	3.47

193

Ron Maurer

Bats: Right **Throws:** Right **Pos:** 2B   **Ht:** 6'1" **Wt:** 185 **Born:** 6/10/68 **Age:** 28

Year	Team	Lg	G	AB	H	2B	3B	HR	TB	R	RBI	TBB	IBB	SO	HBP	SH	SF	SB	CS	SB%	GDP	Avg	OBP	SLG
1990	Great Falls	R	62	238	64	8	0	6	90	43	43	27	0	38	6	5	4	5	2	.71	4	.269	.353	.378
1991	Bakersfield	A	129	442	128	21	5	7	180	59	53	63	3	68	7	13	3	8	8	.50	15	.290	.384	.407
1992	San Antonio	AA	82	224	61	13	0	0	74	29	14	15	3	32	5	4	0	4	3	.57	6	.272	.332	.330
1993	San Antonio	AA	11	37	7	1	0	1	11	6	4	7	0	12	0	1	0	0	1	.00	0	.189	.318	.297
	Albuquerque	AAA	58	116	34	7	0	3	50	19	14	11	1	17	0	4	0	1	1	.50	6	.293	.354	.431
1994	Albuquerque	AAA	55	125	35	8	1	2	51	20	16	4	0	15	3	1	1	1	0	1.00	4	.280	.316	.408
1995	Albuquerque	AAA	84	185	48	14	2	5	81	29	25	19	2	34	3	1	1	1	2	.33	1	.259	.337	.438
	6 Min. YEARS		481	1367	377	72	8	24	537	205	169	146	9	216	24	29	9	20	17	.54	36	.276	.354	.393

Pat Maxwell

Bats: Left **Throws:** Right **Pos:** 3B   **Ht:** 6'0" **Wt:** 170 **Born:** 3/28/70 **Age:** 26

Year	Team	Lg	G	AB	H	2B	3B	HR	TB	R	RBI	TBB	IBB	SO	HBP	SH	SF	SB	CS	SB%	GDP	Avg	OBP	SLG
1991	Watertown	A	16	55	10	0	0	0	10	5	5	3	0	9	0	2	1	1	1	.50	0	.182	.220	.182
	Burlington	R	45	166	48	8	4	1	67	41	12	26	2	15	0	3	1	7	4	.64	1	.289	.383	.404
1992	Columbus	A	81	270	71	7	0	1	81	31	25	19	1	19	2	4	1	7	2	.78	4	.263	.315	.300
1993	Kinston	A	103	400	117	17	3	4	152	46	35	22	3	32	3	3	2	6	4	.60	5	.293	.333	.380
1994	Canton-Akrn	AA	75	256	67	8	0	0	75	30	19	16	1	32	2	9	2	8	4	.67	4	.262	.308	.293
1995	Canton-Akrn	AA	84	267	66	7	0	4	85	19	25	15	1	26	4	6	1	1	0	1.00	5	.247	.296	.318
	5 Min. YEARS		404	1414	379	47	7	10	470	172	121	101	8	133	11	27	8	30	15	.67	19	.268	.320	.332

Craig Mayes

Bats: Left **Throws:** Right **Pos:** C   **Ht:** 5'10" **Wt:** 195 **Born:** 5/8/70 **Age:** 26

Year	Team	Lg	G	AB	H	2B	3B	HR	TB	R	RBI	TBB	IBB	SO	HBP	SH	SF	SB	CS	SB%	GDP	Avg	OBP	SLG
1992	Everett	A	38	110	38	3	0	0	41	17	10	10	1	13	0	0	0	3	3	.50	5	.345	.400	.373
1993	Clinton	A	75	226	67	12	1	3	90	25	37	10	0	52	0	3	3	1	0	1.00	3	.296	.322	.398
1994	Clinton	A	49	155	32	5	1	1	42	13	14	11	1	33	0	2	1	0	2	.00	4	.206	.257	.271
	San Bernrdo	A	50	191	48	5	0	2	59	20	21	17	1	35	1	0	0	2	2	.50	3	.251	.316	.309
1995	Shreveport	AA	3	9	2	1	0	0	3	0	3	0	0	2	0	0	0	0	0	.00	0	.222	.222	.333
	San Jose	A	90	318	80	17	4	0	105	34	39	27	1	50	0	1	2	3	1	.75	7	.252	.308	.330
	4 Min. YEARS		305	1009	267	43	6	6	340	109	124	75	4	185	1	6	6	9	8	.53	27	.265	.314	.337

Scott Maynard

Bats: Right **Throws:** Right **Pos:** C   **Ht:** 6'2" **Wt:** 215 **Born:** 8/28/77 **Age:** 18

Year	Team	Lg	G	AB	H	2B	3B	HR	TB	R	RBI	TBB	IBB	SO	HBP	SH	SF	SB	CS	SB%	GDP	Avg	OBP	SLG
1995	Tacoma	AAA	1	1	0	0	0	0	0	0	0	0	0	0	0	0	0	0	0	.00	1	.000	.000	.000
	Mariners	R	21	72	17	2	0	1	22	6	12	9	0	21	0	1	2	0	0	.00	0	.236	.313	.306
	1 Min. YEARS		22	73	17	2	0	1	22	6	12	9	0	21	0	1	2	0	0	.00	1	.233	.310	.301

Matt Maysey

Pitches: Right **Bats:** Right **Pos:** P   **Ht:** 6'4" **Wt:** 225 **Born:** 1/8/67 **Age:** 29

Year	Team	Lg	G	GS	CG	GF	IP	BFP	H	R	ER	HR	SH	SF	HB	TBB	IBB	SO	WP	Bk	W	L	Pct.	ShO	Sv	ERA
1985	Spokane	A	7	4	0	2	29	0	27	18	15	3	0	0	1	16	0	18	5	0	0	3	.000	0	0	4.66
1986	Charleston	A	18	5	0	11	43	196	43	28	24	5	3	0	3	24	2	39	5	2	3	2	.600	0	1	5.02
1987	Charlstn-Sc	A	41	18	5	21	150.1	623	112	71	53	13	8	7	5	59	4	143	13	3	14	11	.560	0	7	3.17
1988	Wichita	AA	28	28	4	0	187	789	180	88	77	15	7	6	5	68	1	120	18	5	9	9	.500	0	0	3.71
1989	Las Vegas	AAA	28	28	4	0	176.1	773	173	94	80	19	3	1	2	84	3	96	12	3	8	12	.400	1	0	4.08
1990	Las Vegas	AAA	26	25	1	1	137.2	634	155	97	86	10	6	5	5	88	5	72	12	1	6	10	.375	0	0	5.62
1991	Harrisburg	AA	15	15	2	0	104.2	419	90	26	22	3	2	3	2	28	0	86	8	0	6	5	.545	2	0	1.89
	Indianapolis	AAA	12	12	0	0	63	272	60	45	36	7	0	1	2	33	2	45	6	0	3	6	.333	0	0	5.14
1992	Indianapolis	AAA	35	1	0	14	67	286	63	32	32	9	4	2	0	28	5	38	2	1	5	3	.625	0	5	4.30
1993	New Orleans	AAA	29	5	0	6	52.1	215	48	25	24	8	1	2	0	14	1	40	2	1	0	3	.000	0	2	4.13
1994	Buffalo	AAA	10	0	0	1	15	57	11	7	7	0	2	1	1	2	0	9	2	0	2	0	1.000	0	0	4.20
1995	Calgary	AAA	44	12	0	4	103	468	122	67	63	9	2	3	7	44	3	71	7	0	8	7	.533	0	1	5.50
1992	Montreal	NL	2	0	0	1	2.1	12	4	1	1	1	0	0	1	0	0	1	0	0	0	0	.000	0	0	3.86
1993	Milwaukee	AL	23	0	0	12	22	105	28	14	14	4	2	2	1	13	1	10	4	0	1	2	.333	0	1	5.73
	11 Min. YEARS		293	153	16	60	1128.1	4732	1084	598	519	101	38	31	33	488	26	777	92	16	64	71	.474	3	16	4.14
	2 Maj. YEARS		25	0	0	13	24.1	117	32	15	15	5	2	2	2	13	1	11	4	0	1	2	.333	0	1	5.55

Rod McCall

Bats: Left **Throws:** Right **Pos:** 1B-DH   **Ht:** 6'7" **Wt:** 220 **Born:** 11/4/71 **Age:** 24

Year	Team	Lg	G	AB	H	2B	3B	HR	TB	R	RBI	TBB	IBB	SO	HBP	SH	SF	SB	CS	SB%	GDP	Avg	OBP	SLG
1990	Indians	R	10	36	10	2	0	0	12	5	6	5	1	10	0	0	0	0	0	.00	0	.278	.366	.333
	Burlington	R	31	92	15	5	0	1	23	8	11	10	0	43	2	0	2	0	1	.00	1	.163	.255	.250
1991	Columbus	A	103	323	70	14	1	5	101	34	35	61	3	128	3	0	1	2	2	.50	5	.217	.345	.313
1992	Columbus	A	116	404	97	15	0	20	172	55	80	68	4	121	4	0	6	1	1	.50	9	.240	.351	.426

Year	Team	Lg	G	AB	H	2B	3B	HR	TB	R	RBI	TBB	IBB	SO	HBP	SH	SF	SB	CS	SB%	GDP	Avg	OBP	SLG
1993	Kinston	A	71	245	51	13	0	9	91	32	33	32	2	85	3	0	4	3	1	.75	3	.208	.303	.371
1994	Kinston	A	58	205	44	14	0	11	91	32	27	26	1	75	7	1	0	1	1	.50	2	.215	.324	.444
	High Desert	A	48	183	51	14	0	17	116	40	43	20	0	63	5	0	1	2	1	.67	4	.279	.364	.634
	Canton-Akrn	AA	20	66	13	4	0	3	26	8	9	2	0	27	2	1	1	0	0	.00	1	.197	.239	.394
1995	Bakersfield	A	96	345	114	19	1	20	195	61	70	40	7	90	8	2	4	2	5	.29	6	.330	.408	.565
	Canton-Akrn	AA	26	95	26	5	0	9	58	16	18	12	3	21	1	0	0	1	1	.50	3	.274	.361	.611
	6 Min. YEARS		579	1994	491	105	2	95	885	291	332	276	21	663	35	4	19	12	13	.48	34	.246	.345	.444

Greg McCarthy

Pitches: Left **Bats:** Left **Pos:** P **Ht:** 6'2" **Wt:** 193 **Born:** 10/30/68 **Age:** 27

			HOW MUCH HE PITCHED			WHAT HE GAVE UP												THE RESULTS					
Year	Team	Lg	G	GS	CG	GF	IP	BFP	H	R	ER	HR	SH	SF	HB	TBB	IBB	SO	WP	Bk	W	L	Pct.	ShO	Sv	ERA
1987	Utica	A	20	0	0	13	29.2	130	14	9	3	0	2	1	2	23	2	40	1	2	4	1	.800	0	3	0.91
1988	Spartanburg	A	34	1	0	20	64.2	297	52	36	29	3	3	3	10	52	0	65	8	3	4	2	.667	0	2	4.04
1989	Spartanburg	A	24	15	2	4	112	499	90	58	52	3	3	5	9	80	0	115	8	2	5	8	.385	1	0	4.18
1990	Clearwater	A	42	1	0	19	59.2	265	47	32	22	4	2	2	1	38	1	67	5	2	1	3	.250	0	5	3.32
1992	Kinston	A	23	0	0	21	27.1	105	14	0	0	0	1	0	5	9	0	37	8	0	3	0	1.000	0	12	0.00
1993	Kinston	A	9	0	0	6	10.2	51	8	4	2	0	0	0	0	13	0	14	2	0	0	0	.000	0	2	1.69
	Canton-Akrn	AA	33	0	0	19	34.1	156	28	18	18	1	0	3	2	37	2	39	5	0	2	3	.400	0	6	4.72
1994	Canton-Akrn	AA	22	0	0	19	32	133	19	12	8	0	0	0	1	23	2	39	2	0	2	3	.400	0	9	2.25
	Charlotte	AAA	18	0	0	11	23.1	118	17	22	18	1	1	2	6	28	1	21	5	0	1	0	1.000	0	0	6.94
1995	Birmingham	AA	38	0	0	13	44.2	195	37	28	25	4	4	2	2	29	3	48	3	1	3	3	.500	0	3	5.04
	8 Min. YEARS		263	17	2	145	438.1	1949	326	219	177	16	16	18	38	332	11	485	47	10	25	23	.521	1	42	3.63

Tom McCarthy

Pitches: Right **Bats:** Right **Pos:** P **Ht:** 6'0" **Wt:** 180 **Born:** 6/18/61 **Age:** 35

			HOW MUCH HE PITCHED			WHAT HE GAVE UP												THE RESULTS					
Year	Team	Lg	G	GS	CG	GF	IP	BFP	H	R	ER	HR	SH	SF	HB	TBB	IBB	SO	WP	Bk	W	L	Pct.	ShO	Sv	ERA
1984	New Britain	AA	38	1	0	27	79.1	356	71	35	27	0	8	2	1	56	1	65	3	0	8	5	.615	0	8	3.06
1985	Pawtucket	AAA	26	10	3	6	85.1	389	72	48	34	6	3	3	2	62	1	65	11	0	5	6	.455	1	0	3.59
1986	Tidewater	AAA	22	8	1	4	84.2	367	89	43	38	7	2	6	1	37	1	30	3	0	3	2	.600	0	3	4.04
1987	Tidewater	AAA	10	0	0	2	19	95	22	17	9	2	1	1	0	16	2	7	1	0	0	2	.000	0	0	4.26
	Jackson	AA	37	1	0	33	54.1	226	57	18	16	3	4	1	0	21	3	30	4	1	1	4	.200	0	21	2.65
1988	Tidewater	AAA	34	3	0	15	57.1	238	49	19	17	2	2	1	0	29	3	28	6	1	8	3	.727	0	3	2.67
	Vancouver	AAA	9	0	0	6	18.2	71	11	0	0	0	0	1	0	4	0	11	0	0	1	0	1.000	0	4	0.00
1989	Vancouver	AAA	17	0	0	14	26.2	113	27	17	16	1	4	0	0	10	1	17	4	0	2	4	.333	0	7	5.40
1991	Richmond	AAA	21	13	1	2	85	356	80	43	40	3	3	1	3	34	3	51	3	0	4	6	.400	0	4	4.24
1992	Richmond	AAA	48	3	0	34	92.2	391	95	45	33	2	7	2	4	21	5	52	5	0	4	6	.400	0	4	3.21
1993	Charlotte	AAA	45	2	0	11	105	440	104	55	48	15	5	4	5	26	4	61	5	0	6	5	.545	0	2	4.11
1995	Albuquerque	AAA	13	8	0	1	48	223	61	41	32	4	1	2	1	22	2	28	2	0	3	3	.500	0	0	6.00
1985	Boston	AL	3	0	0	2	5	25	7	6	6	1	0	1	0	4	0	2	1	0	0	0	.000	0	0	10.80
1988	Chicago	AL	6	0	0	4	13	51	9	2	2	0	0	0	2	2	0	5	0	0	2	0	1.000	0	1	1.38
1989	Chicago	AL	31	0	0	14	66.2	285	72	32	26	8	3	3	2	20	0	27	5	0	1	2	.333	0	0	3.51
	10 Min. YEARS		320	49	5	155	756	3271	734	381	310	45	40	24	17	338	26	445	47	2	45	46	.495	1	52	3.69
	3 Maj. YEARS		40	0	0	20	84.2	361	88	40	34	9	3	4	4	26	0	34	6	0	3	2	.600	0	1	3.61

Scott McClain

Bats: Right **Throws:** Right **Pos:** 3B **Ht:** 6'3" **Wt:** 209 **Born:** 5/19/72 **Age:** 24

			BATTING															BASERUNNING				PERCENTAGES		
Year	Team	Lg	G	AB	H	2B	3B	HR	TB	R	RBI	TBB	IBB	SO	HBP	SH	SF	SB	CS	SB%	GDP	Avg	OBP	SLG
1990	Bluefield	R	40	107	21	2	0	4	35	20	15	22	0	35	2	0	4	2	3	.40	1	.196	.333	.327
1991	Kane County	A	25	81	18	0	0	0	18	9	4	17	0	25	0	1	0	1	1	.50	4	.222	.357	.222
	Bluefield	R	41	149	39	5	0	0	44	16	24	14	0	39	3	0	1	5	3	.63	3	.262	.335	.295
1992	Kane County	A	96	316	84	12	2	3	109	43	30	48	1	62	6	6	1	7	4	.64	5	.266	.372	.345
1993	Frederick	A	133	427	111	22	2	9	164	65	54	70	0	88	6	3	2	10	6	.63	8	.260	.370	.384
1994	Bowie	AA	133	427	103	29	1	11	167	71	58	72	2	89	1	2	7	6	3	.67	14	.241	.347	.391
1995	Rochester	AAA	61	199	50	9	1	8	85	32	22	23	0	34	1	1	2	2	0	1.00	5	.251	.329	.427
	Bowie	AA	70	259	72	14	1	13	127	41	61	25	1	44	3	0	4	2	1	.67	13	.278	.344	.490
	6 Min. YEARS		599	1965	498	93	7	48	749	297	268	291	4	416	22	13	21	33	22	.60	53	.253	.353	.381

Paul McClellan

Pitches: Right **Bats:** Right **Pos:** P **Ht:** 6'2" **Wt:** 180 **Born:** 2/8/66 **Age:** 30

			HOW MUCH HE PITCHED			WHAT HE GAVE UP												THE RESULTS					
Year	Team	Lg	G	GS	CG	GF	IP	BFP	H	R	ER	HR	SH	SF	HB	TBB	IBB	SO	WP	Bk	W	L	Pct.	ShO	Sv	ERA
1986	Everett	A	13	13	2	0	86.1	0	71	39	32	2	0	0	0	46	0	74	8	0	5	4	.556	0	0	3.34
1987	Clinton	A	28	27	5	0	177.1	756	141	86	64	18	10	1	6	100	2	209	10	2	12	10	.545	2	0	3.25
1988	Shreveport	AA	27	27	4	0	167	701	146	89	75	11	7	5	4	62	4	128	3	22	10	12	.455	1	0	4.04
1989	Shreveport	AA	12	12	2	0	84.1	339	56	26	21	4	3	3	1	35	0	56	5	3	8	3	.727	0	0	2.24
	Phoenix	AAA	9	9	0	0	56.2	248	56	34	31	6	0	4	4	29	1	25	4	2	3	4	.429	0	0	4.92
1990	Phoenix	AAA	28	27	1	0	172.1	770	192	112	99	17	9	10	5	78	3	102	7	6	7	16	.304	0	0	5.17
1991	Shreveport	AA	14	14	1	0	95.2	384	75	33	30	4	1	2	2	30	1	63	8	2	11	1	.917	0	0	2.82
	Phoenix	AAA	5	5	2	0	38.1	160	27	12	12	2	3	1	0	21	2	18	2	1	2	2	.500	0	0	2.82
1992	Phoenix	AAA	20	7	0	4	64.1	293	85	46	42	9	5	1	1	21	0	43	7	3	2	6	.250	0	0	5.88
	Denver	AAA	9	5	0	1	31.2	137	36	19	15	4	1	3	1	14	0	14	0	0	1	1	.500	0	0	4.26
1995	New Orleans	AAA	3	3	1	0	16.1	71	19	11	11	0	0	0	0	8	0	8	0	1	0	3	.000	0	0	6.06

Year	Team	Lg					IP	BFP	H	R	ER	HR	SH	SF	HB	TBB	IBB	SO	WP	Bk	W	L	Pct.	ShO	Sv	ERA
1990	San Francisco	NL	4	1	0	2	7.2	44	14	10	10	3	1	0	1	6	0	2	0	0	0	1	.000	0	0	11.74
1991	San Francisco	NL	13	12	1	1	71	300	68	41	36	12	3	1	1	25	1	44	5	0	3	6	.333	0	0	4.56
	8 Min. YEARS		168	149	18	5	990.1	3859	904	507	432	77	39	30	24	444	12	740	54	42	61	62	.496	4	1	3.93
	2 Maj. YEARS		17	13	1	3	78.2	344	82	51	46	15	4	1	2	31	1	46	5	0	3	7	.300	0	0	5.26

Lloyd McClendon

Bats: Right **Throws:** Right **Pos:** OF   **Ht:** 6' 0" **Wt:** 208 **Born:** 1/11/59 **Age:** 37

									BATTING										BASERUNNING				PERCENTAGES		
Year	Team	Lg	G	AB	H	2B	3B	HR	TB	R	RBI	TBB	IBB	SO	HBP	SH	SF	SB	CS	SB%	GDP	Avg	OBP	SLG
1984	Vermont	AA	60	202	56	16	0	7	93	36	27	28	0	28	2	0	1	2	2	.50	5	.277	.369	.460
	Wichita	AAA	48	152	45	13	1	6	78	28	28	21	0	33	0	0	1	2	0	1.00	3	.296	.379	.513
1985	Denver	AAA	114	379	105	18	5	16	181	57	79	51	4	56	3	0	3	4	4	.50	6	.277	.365	.478
1986	Denver	AAA	132	433	112	30	1	24	216	75	88	70	1	75	2	0	4	2	4	.33	6	.259	.361	.499
1987	Nashville	AAA	26	84	24	6	0	3	39	11	14	17	0	15	2	0	2	1	1	.50	1	.286	.410	.464
1988	Nashville	AAA	2	7	1	0	0	0	1	0	0	1	0	1	0	0	0	0	0	.00	0	.143	.250	.143
1989	Iowa	AAA	34	109	35	10	0	4	57	18	13	21	1	19	0	0	1	4	1	.80	3	.321	.427	.523
1990	Iowa	AAA	25	91	26	2	0	2	34	14	10	8	1	19	2	0	1	3	1	.75	3	.286	.353	.374
1995	Buffalo	AAA	37	108	30	6	0	5	51	19	19	20	3	20	2	0	0	0	0	.00	5	.278	.400	.472
1987	Cincinnati	NL	45	72	15	5	0	2	26	8	13	4	0	15	0	0	1	1	0	1.00	1	.208	.247	.361
1988	Cincinnati	NL	72	137	30	4	0	3	43	9	14	15	1	22	2	1	2	4	0	1.00	6	.219	.301	.314
1989	Chicago	NL	92	259	74	12	1	12	124	47	40	37	3	31	1	1	7	6	4	.60	3	.286	.368	.479
1990	Chicago	NL	49	107	17	3	0	1	23	5	10	14	2	21	0	0	1	1	0	1.00	2	.159	.254	.215
	Pittsburgh	NL	4	3	1	0	0	1	4	1	2	0	0	1	0	0	0	0	0	.00	0	.333	.333	1.333
1991	Pittsburgh	NL	85	163	47	7	0	7	75	24	24	18	0	23	2	0	0	2	1	.67	2	.288	.366	.460
1992	Pittsburgh	NL	84	190	48	8	1	3	67	26	20	28	0	24	2	1	3	1	3	.25	5	.253	.350	.353
1993	Pittsburgh	NL	88	181	40	11	1	2	59	21	19	23	1	17	0	1	2	0	3	.00	4	.221	.306	.326
1994	Pittsburgh	NL	51	92	22	4	0	4	38	9	12	4	0	11	1	0	0	0	1	.00	1	.239	.278	.413
	8 Min. YEARS		478	1565	434	101	7	67	750	258	278	237	10	266	13	0	13	18	13	.58	32	.277	.374	.479
	8 Maj. YEARS		570	1204	294	54	3	35	459	150	154	143	7	165	8	4	16	15	12	.56	24	.244	.325	.381

Chad McConnell

Bats: Right **Throws:** Right **Pos:** OF   **Ht:** 6'1" **Wt:** 180 **Born:** 10/13/70 **Age:** 25

									BATTING										BASERUNNING				PERCENTAGES		
Year	Team	Lg	G	AB	H	2B	3B	HR	TB	R	RBI	TBB	IBB	SO	HBP	SH	SF	SB	CS	SB%	GDP	Avg	OBP	SLG
1993	Clearwater	A	90	300	72	17	3	6	113	43	37	51	2	98	4	0	2	9	5	.64	6	.240	.356	.377
1994	Clearwater	A	29	101	32	3	3	4	53	19	19	16	0	28	0	0	0	2	1	.67	4	.317	.410	.525
	Reading	AA	88	267	62	9	3	6	95	30	41	24	1	86	6	2	2	7	5	.58	6	.232	.308	.356
1995	Reading	AA	94	319	88	12	1	11	135	46	52	27	1	59	10	1	2	8	3	.73	8	.276	.349	.423
	3 Min. YEARS		301	987	254	41	10	27	396	138	149	118	4	271	20	3	6	26	14	.65	24	.257	.347	.401

Trey McCoy

Bats: Right **Throws:** Right **Pos:** DH   **Ht:** 6'3" **Wt:** 215 **Born:** 10/12/66 **Age:** 29

									BATTING										BASERUNNING				PERCENTAGES		
Year	Team	Lg	G	AB	H	2B	3B	HR	TB	R	RBI	TBB	IBB	SO	HBP	SH	SF	SB	CS	SB%	GDP	Avg	OBP	SLG
1990	Charlotte	A	45	160	37	11	0	3	57	19	18	23	0	35	1	0	0	0	0	.00	0	.231	.332	.356
	Gastonia	A	24	80	27	6	0	4	45	13	11	12	1	12	0	0	2	1	1	.50	0	.338	.415	.563
1991	Tulsa	AA	44	137	33	7	0	10	70	21	32	33	4	26	2	0	2	0	0	.00	6	.241	.391	.511
1992	Tulsa	AA	15	52	10	0	0	2	16	5	6	8	0	15	0	0	0	0	1	.00	0	.192	.300	.308
	Gastonia	A	32	99	35	6	0	8	65	17	30	23	0	19	7	0	2	3	0	1.00	0	.354	.496	.657
1993	Tulsa	AA	125	420	123	27	3	29	243	72	95	65	4	79	19	0	2	3	2	.60	9	.293	.409	.579
	Okla. City	AAA	8	28	7	1	1	3	19	6	11	5	0	5	1	0	0	0	0	.00	0	.250	.382	.679
1994	Okla. City	AAA	101	353	108	29	1	15	184	54	67	41	1	65	10	0	5	1	0	1.00	9	.306	.389	.521
1995	Okla. City	AAA	9	29	9	1	0	0	10	4	2	7	1	7	0	0	0	0	0	.00	1	.310	.444	.345
	Norfolk	AAA	25	67	14	5	0	3	28	6	7	5	0	11	2	0	0	0	0	.00	2	.209	.284	.418
	6 Min. YEARS		428	1425	403	93	5	77	737	217	279	222	11	274	42	0	13	8	4	.67	27	.283	.392	.517

Jim McCready

Pitches: Right **Bats:** Right **Pos:** P   **Ht:** 6'1" **Wt:** 177 **Born:** 11/25/69 **Age:** 26

							HOW MUCH HE PITCHED				WHAT HE GAVE UP											THE RESULTS			
Year	Team	Lg	G	GS	CG	GF	IP	BFP	H	R	ER	HR	SH	SF	HB	TBB	IBB	SO	WP	Bk	W	L	Pct.	ShO	Sv	ERA
1991	Mets	R	16	6	2	8	77.2	328	69	36	28	1	0	2	4	18	1	59	5	4	6	4	.600	0	1	3.24
1992	Columbia	A	35	9	1	17	87.1	362	85	35	24	3	3	0	5	23	0	54	4	0	5	3	.625	1	5	2.47
1993	St. Lucie	A	40	0	0	30	61.1	250	51	18	12	0	8	2	2	22	6	40	2	0	6	4	.600	0	16	1.76
	Binghamton	AA	14	0	0	4	18.1	73	18	7	7	0	2	0	0	4	1	12	0	0	1	1	.500	0	0	3.44
1994	Binghamton	AA	63	0	0	26	83.2	359	78	35	30	4	6	5	9	28	3	52	7	0	6	6	.500	0	7	3.23
1995	Binghamton	AA	32	0	0	16	39	178	42	21	14	4	3	2	2	14	1	17	5	0	1	1	.500	0	4	3.23
	Norfolk	AAA	28	0	0	4	40.1	175	41	14	9	0	5	1	0	20	1	21	1	0	0	0	.000	0	0	2.01
	5 Min. YEARS		228	15	3	109	407.2	1725	384	166	124	12	27	12	22	129	13	255	24	4	25	20	.556	1	33	2.74

Allen McDill

Pitches: Left **Bats:** Left **Pos:** P   **Ht:** 6'1" **Wt:** 160 **Born:** 8/23/71 **Age:** 24

							HOW MUCH HE PITCHED				WHAT HE GAVE UP											THE RESULTS			
Year	Team	Lg	G	GS	CG	GF	IP	BFP	H	R	ER	HR	SH	SF	HB	TBB	IBB	SO	WP	Bk	W	L	Pct.	ShO	Sv	ERA
1992	Kingsport	R	1	0	0	0	0.1	3	0	0	0	0	0	0	0	2	0	0	0	0	0	0	.000	0	0	0.00
	Mets	R	10	9	0	0	53.1	216	36	23	16	3	0	0	4	15	0	60	3	0	3	4	.429	0	0	2.70

196

Year	Team	Lg	G	GS	CG	GF	IP	BFP	H	R	ER	HR	SH	SF	HB	TBB	IBB	SO	WP	Bk	W	L	Pct.	ShO	Sv	ERA
1993	Kingsport	R	9	9	0	0	53.1	224	52	19	13	1	1	2	0	14	0	42	2	2	5	2	.714	0	0	2.19
	Pittsfield	A	5	5	0	0	28.1	132	31	22	17	0	2	2	1	15	0	24	3	0	2	3	.400			5.40
1994	Columbia	A	19	19	1	0	111.2	461	101	52	44	11	5	2	4	38	2	102	9	0	9	6	.600	0	0	3.55
1995	St. Lucie	A	7	7	1	0	49.1	190	36	11	9	2	1	0	1	13	0	28	3	0	4	2	.667	1	0	1.64
	Binghamton	AA	12	12	1	0	73	324	69	42	37	5	1	4	3	38	2	44	3	1	3	5	.375	0	0	4.56
	Wichita	AA	12	1	0	5	21.1	85	16	7	5	2	0	0	1	5	0	20	1	0	1	0	1.000	0	0	2.11
	4 Min. YEARS		75	62	3	5	390.2	1635	341	176	141	24	10	10	14	140	4	320	24	3	27	22	.551	1	1	3.25

Oddibe McDowell

Bats: Left **Throws:** Left **Pos:** OF   **Ht:** 5' 9" **Wt:** 165 **Born:** 8/25/62 **Age:** 33

			BATTING																BASERUNNING				PERCENTAGES		
Year	Team	Lg	G	AB	H	2B	3B	HR	TB	R	RBI	TBB	IBB	SO	HBP	SH	SF	SB	CS	SB%	GDP	Avg	OBP	SLG
1985	Okla. City	AAA	31	125	50	7	8	2	79	32	18	19	3	20	2	0	0	12	6	.67	1	.400	.486	.632
1988	Okla. City	AAA	18	70	20	3	1	1	28	9	6	8	0	10	0	0	0	4	0	1.00	0	.286	.359	.400
1992	Edmonton	AAA	6	14	3	1	0	0	4	1	2	5	1	4	0	0	0	0	1	.00	0	.214	.421	.286
1993	Tulsa	AA	34	114	39	7	1	8	72	26	31	19	2	24	1	3	1	3	3	.50	1	.342	.437	.632
1994	Okla. City	AAA	16	52	14	3	1	0	19	9	2	8	1	14	1	1	0	2	3	.40	0	.269	.377	.365
1995	Columbus	AAA	14	46	10	0	1	1	15	5	2	6	0	9	0	2	0	0	1	.00	1	.217	.308	.326
1985	Texas	AL	111	406	97	14	5	18	175	63	42	36	2	85	3	5	2	25	7	.78	6	.239	.304	.431
1986	Texas	AL	154	572	152	24	7	18	244	105	49	65	5	112	1	3	2	33	15	.69	12	.266	.341	.427
1987	Texas	AL	128	407	98	26	4	14	174	65	52	51	0	99	0	3	2	24	2	.92	8	.241	.324	.428
1988	Texas	AL	120	437	108	19	5	6	155	55	37	41	2	89	2	2	5	33	10	.77	3	.247	.311	.355
1989	Cleveland	AL	69	239	53	5	2	3	71	33	22	25	0	36	1	3	2	12	5	.71	3	.222	.296	.297
	Atlanta	NL	76	280	85	18	4	7	132	56	24	27	3	37	0	1	0	15	10	.60	0	.304	.365	.471
1990	Atlanta	NL	113	305	74	14	0	7	109	47	25	21	0	53	2	0	1	13	2	.87	3	.243	.295	.357
1994	Texas	AL	59	183	48	5	1	1	58	34	15	28	0	39	0	6	3	14	2	.88	3	.262	.355	.317
	6 Min. YEARS		119	421	136	21	12	12	217	82	61	65	7	81	4	6	1	21	14	.60	3	.323	.418	.515
	7 Maj. YEARS		830	2829	715	125	28	74	1118	458	266	294	12	550	9	23	17	169	53	.76	38	.253	.323	.395

Joe McEwing

Bats: Right **Throws:** Right **Pos:** 2B   **Ht:** 5'10" **Wt:** 170 **Born:** 10/19/72 **Age:** 23

			BATTING																BASERUNNING				PERCENTAGES		
Year	Team	Lg	G	AB	H	2B	3B	HR	TB	R	RBI	TBB	IBB	SO	HBP	SH	SF	SB	CS	SB%	GDP	Avg	OBP	SLG
1992	Cardinals	R	55	211	71	4	2	0	79	55	13	24	0	18	5	1	1	23	7	.77	1	.336	.415	.374
1993	Savannah	A	138	511	127	35	1	0	164	94	43	89	0	73	4	15	4	22	9	.71	7	.249	.362	.321
1994	Madison	A	90	346	112	24	2	4	152	58	47	32	4	53	1	5	3	18	15	.55	5	.324	.380	.439
	St. Pete	A	50	197	49	7	0	1	59	22	20	19	0	32	1	4	3	8	4	.67	4	.249	.314	.299
1995	St. Pete	A	75	281	64	13	0	1	80	33	23	25	3	49	1	6	4	2	3	.40	5	.228	.289	.285
	Arkansas	AA	42	121	30	4	0	2	40	16	12	9	2	13	1	6	0	3	2	.60	4	.248	.305	.331
	4 Min. YEARS		450	1667	453	87	5	8	574	278	158	198	9	238	13	37	15	76	40	.66	26	.272	.351	.344

Jason McFarlin

Bats: Left **Throws:** Left **Pos:** OF   **Ht:** 6'0" **Wt:** 175 **Born:** 6/28/70 **Age:** 26

			BATTING																BASERUNNING				PERCENTAGES		
Year	Team	Lg	G	AB	H	2B	3B	HR	TB	R	RBI	TBB	IBB	SO	HBP	SH	SF	SB	CS	SB%	GDP	Avg	OBP	SLG
1989	Everett	A	37	131	34	4	3	0	44	17	12	5	1	25	1	2	2	7	3	.70	3	.260	.288	.336
1990	Clinton	A	129	476	108	9	5	0	127	68	31	47	2	79	9	7	1	72	19	.79	7	.227	.308	.267
1991	San Jose	A	103	407	95	10	5	2	121	65	33	47	2	72	14	10	2	46	20	.70	6	.233	.332	.297
1992	San Jose	A	70	276	84	7	3	1	100	61	24	27	1	43	9	5	1	32	11	.74	4	.304	.383	.362
	Shreveport	AA	28	106	22	3	3	1	34	13	3	5	0	20	4	2	0	10	1	.91	0	.208	.270	.321
1993	Shreveport	AA	21	59	11	2	1	0	15	12	1	4	0	12	2	1	0	4	1	.80	0	.186	.262	.254
	San Jose	A	97	395	123	20	4	7	172	71	53	29	0	67	3	7	4	49	10	.83	5	.311	.360	.435
1994	Shreveport	AA	106	306	87	11	4	5	121	37	29	17	5	31	6	2	4	21	8	.72	6	.284	.330	.395
1995	Shreveport	AA	93	252	85	13	2	6	120	39	37	25	7	26	10	4	2	8	7	.53	8	.337	.415	.476
	7 Min. YEARS		684	2408	649	79	30	22	854	383	223	206	18	375	58	40	16	249	80	.76	39	.270	.340	.355

Terric McFarlin

Pitches: Right **Bats:** Both **Pos:** P   **Ht:** 6'0" **Wt:** 160 **Born:** 4/6/69 **Age:** 27

			HOW MUCH HE PITCHED						WHAT HE GAVE UP										THE RESULTS					
Year	Team	Lg	G	GS	CG	GF	IP	BFP	H	R	ER	HR	SH	SF	HB	TBB	IBB	SO	WP	Bk	W	L	Pct.	ShO	Sv	ERA
1991	Bakersfield	A	26	21	0	3	152	634	139	63	45	6	5	5	1	56	2	128	17	0	14	6	.700	0	0	2.66
1992	Bakersfield	A	6	5	0	1	27.1	115	16	10	8	2	0	0	1	19	0	30	1	0	2	0	1.000	0	0	2.63
1993	San Antonio	AA	52	0	0	24	95.1	407	87	37	30	2	6	2	3	37	4	77	7	0	4	7	.364	0	0	2.83
1994	Wichita	AA	30	0	0	10	41	169	30	16	10	3	3	0	0	17	3	38	5	1	1	2	.333	0	3	2.20
	Las Vegas	AAA	33	0	0	12	62.2	284	72	51	42	9	4	4	2	22	4	58	1	0	1	5	.167	0	2	6.03
1995	Las Vegas	AAA	58	2	0	20	122.2	535	120	67	54	11	6	3	2	59	4	85	18	0	7	6	.538	0	8	3.96
	5 Min. YEARS		205	28	0	70	501	2144	464	244	189	33	24	14	9	210	17	416	49	1	29	26	.527	0	16	3.40

Kevin McGehee

Pitches: Right **Bats:** Right **Pos:** P   **Ht:** 6' 0" **Wt:** 190 **Born:** 1/18/69 **Age:** 27

			HOW MUCH HE PITCHED						WHAT HE GAVE UP										THE RESULTS					
Year	Team	Lg	G	GS	CG	GF	IP	BFP	H	R	ER	HR	SH	SF	HB	TBB	IBB	SO	WP	Bk	W	L	Pct.	ShO	Sv	ERA
1990	Everett	A	15	14	1	0	73.2	333	74	48	39	6	3	2	4	38	0	86	16	5	4	8	.333	0	0	4.76
1991	San Jose	A	26	26	2	0	174	735	129	58	45	1	5	6	8	87	2	171	11	2	13	6	.684	0	0	2.33
1992	Shreveport	AA	25	24	1	0	158.1	654	146	61	52	10	3	7	5	42	0	140	8	1	9	7	.563	0	0	2.96

197

Year Team	Lg	G	GS	CG	GF	IP	BFP	H	R	ER	HR	SH	SF	HB	TBB	IBB	SO	WP	Bk	W	L	Pct.	ShO	Sv	ERA
1993 Phoenix	AAA	4	4	0	0	22	104	28	16	12	1	1	3	5	8	1	16	1	0	0	3	.000	0	0	4.91
Rochester	AAA	20	20	2	0	133.2	551	124	53	44	14	1	3	7	37	1	92	3	0	7	6	.538	0	0	2.96
1994 Rochester	AAA	25	24	2	0	149.1	638	165	85	79	24	2	7	9	35	2	89	7	1	10	8	.556	1	0	4.76
1995 Rochester	AAA	27	20	0	0	126.2	554	150	89	82	18	3	7	5	33	0	84	5	1	11	9	.550	0	0	5.83
1993 Baltimore	AL	5	0	0	1	16.2	75	18	11	11	5	1	1	2	7	2	7	1	0	0	0	.000	0	0	5.94
6 Min. YEARS		142	132	8	0	837.2	3569	816	410	353	74	18	35	43	280	6	678	51	10	54	47	.535	1	0	3.79

Tom McGraw

Pitches: Left **Bats:** Left **Pos:** P **Ht:** 6'2" **Wt:** 195 **Born:** 12/8/67 **Age:** 28

		HOW MUCH HE PITCHED						WHAT HE GAVE UP											THE RESULTS					
Year Team	Lg	G	GS	CG	GF	IP	BFP	H	R	ER	HR	SH	SF	HB	TBB	IBB	SO	WP	Bk	W	L	Pct.	ShO	Sv	ERA
1990 Beloit	A	12	12	1	0	70	299	49	33	15	1	1	2	2	34	0	61	4	4	7	3	.700	1	0	1.93
1991 El Paso	AA	9	7	0	2	35.2	163	43	28	23	1	2	1	1	21	0	28	0	0	1	1	.500	0	1	5.80
Stockton	A	11	7	0	1	47	183	35	15	12	2	2	1	2	13	0	39	3	1	3	0	1.000	0	0	2.30
1992 Stockton	A	15	15	1	0	97.1	414	97	44	29	1	4	3	2	31	5	70	5	0	6	4	.600	0	2	2.68
El Paso	AA	11	10	1	1	69.1	299	75	24	21	2	2	0	0	26	1	53	2	0	6	0	1.000	0	0	2.73
1993 High Desert	A	6	6	1	0	38	153	38	17	15	3	1	2	1	7	1	31	1	0	2	3	.400	0	0	3.55
Edmonton	AAA	5	2	0	1	9.2	45	12	7	6	1	0	1	0	4	0	8	1	0	2	0	1.000	0	0	5.59
1994 Portland	AA	37	7	0	11	74	327	81	44	38	9	3	1	5	35	3	56	6	0	3	5	.375	0	2	4.62
1995 Portland	AA	51	0	0	11	74.2	322	69	21	15	2	7	3	4	31	3	60	4	0	5	0	1.000	0	2	1.81
6 Min. YEARS		157	66	4	27	515.2	2205	499	233	174	22	22	14	17	202	12	406	26	5	35	16	.686	1	5	3.04

Terry McGriff

Bats: Right **Throws:** Right **Pos:** C **Ht:** 6'2" **Wt:** 195 **Born:** 9/23/63 **Age:** 32

		BATTING																BASERUNNING				PERCENTAGES		
Year Team	Lg	G	AB	H	2B	3B	HR	TB	R	RBI	TBB	IBB	SO	HBP	SH	SF	SB	CS	SB%	GDP	Avg	OBP	SLG
1984 Tampa	A	110	345	96	19	0	7	136	48	41	48	4	62	2	0	5	5	4	.56	13	.278	.365	.394
1985 Vermont	AA	110	363	92	10	4	13	149	52	60	54	2	81	3	0	1	1	0	1.00	6	.253	.354	.410
1986 Denver	AAA	108	340	99	22	1	9	150	54	54	41	4	71	2	2	6	0	0	.00	11	.291	.365	.441
1987 Nashville	AAA	67	228	62	11	3	10	109	36	33	25	5	47	0	0	5	0	0	.00	10	.272	.337	.478
1988 Nashville	AAA	35	97	21	3	1	1	29	8	12	10	2	15	0	0	1	0	0	.00	4	.216	.287	.299
1989 Nashville	AAA	102	335	94	24	1	5	135	42	28	29	3	68	1	1	0	1	1	.50	12	.281	.340	.403
1990 Nashville	AAA	94	325	91	17	0	9	135	44	54	38	1	46	2	2	6	2	2	.50	8	.280	.353	.415
1991 Tucson	AAA	51	146	42	15	1	0	59	18	24	16	0	20	3	0	2	0	1	.00	5	.288	.365	.404
1992 Syracuse	AAA	21	56	14	2	0	2	22	4	7	9	0	11	0	0	1	1	0	1.00	3	.250	.348	.393
1993 Edmonton	AAA	105	339	117	29	2	7	171	62	55	49	2	29	1	0	3	2	1	.67	10	.345	.426	.504
1995 Toledo	AAA	58	188	51	8	0	4	71	14	23	20	0	29	0	0	0	0	0	.00	9	.271	.341	.378
1987 Cincinnati	NL	34	89	20	3	0	2	29	6	11	8	0	17	0	0	0	0	0	.00	3	.225	.289	.326
1988 Cincinnati	NL	35	96	19	3	0	1	25	9	4	12	0	31	0	0	0	1	0	1.00	3	.198	.284	.260
1989 Cincinnati	NL	6	11	3	0	0	0	3	1	2	2	1	3	0	0	0	0	0	.00	0	.273	.385	.273
1990 Cincinnati	NL	2	4	0	0	0	0	0	0	0	0	0	1	0	0	0	0	0	.00	0	.000	.000	.000
Houston	NL	4	5	0	0	0	0	0	0	0	0	0	0	0	0	0	0	0	.00	0	.000	.000	.000
1993 Florida	NL	3	7	0	0	0	0	0	0	0	1	0	2	0	0	0	0	0	.00	0	.000	.125	.000
1994 St. Louis	NL	42	114	25	6	0	0	31	10	13	13	1	11	2	1	1	0	0	.00	8	.219	.308	.272
11 Min. YEARS		861	2762	779	160	13	67	1166	382	391	339	23	479	14	5	30	12	9	.57	90	.282	.360	.422
6 Maj. YEARS		126	326	67	12	0	3	88	26	30	36	2	65	2	1	2	1	0	1.00	14	.206	.287	.270

Ryan McGuire

Bats: Left **Throws:** Left **Pos:** 1B **Ht:** 6'1" **Wt:** 195 **Born:** 11/23/71 **Age:** 24

		BATTING																BASERUNNING				PERCENTAGES		
Year Team	Lg	G	AB	H	2B	3B	HR	TB	R	RBI	TBB	IBB	SO	HBP	SH	SF	SB	CS	SB%	GDP	Avg	OBP	SLG
1993 Ft. Laud	A	58	213	69	12	2	4	97	23	38	27	3	34	2	1	3	2	4	.33	11	.324	.400	.455
1994 Lynchburg	A	137	489	133	29	0	10	192	70	73	79	2	77	2	4	7	10	9	.53	19	.272	.371	.393
1995 Trenton	AA	109	414	138	29	1	7	190	59	59	58	5	51	0	4	1	11	8	.58	10	.333	.414	.459
3 Min. YEARS		304	1116	340	70	3	21	479	152	170	164	10	162	4	9	11	23	21	.52	40	.305	.392	.429

Walt McKeel

Bats: Right **Throws:** Right **Pos:** C **Ht:** 6'2" **Wt:** 200 **Born:** 1/17/72 **Age:** 24

		BATTING																BASERUNNING				PERCENTAGES		
Year Team	Lg	G	AB	H	2B	3B	HR	TB	R	RBI	TBB	IBB	SO	HBP	SH	SF	SB	CS	SB%	GDP	Avg	OBP	SLG
1990 Red Sox	R	13	44	11	3	0	0	14	2	6	3	0	8	0	0	1	0	2	.00	2	.250	.292	.318
1991 Red Sox	R	35	113	15	0	1	2	23	10	12	17	0	20	1	0	4	0	0	.00	5	.133	.244	.204
1992 Lynchburg	A	96	288	64	11	0	12	111	33	33	22	0	77	3	5	1	2	1	.67	3	.222	.283	.385
1993 Lynchburg	A	80	247	59	17	2	5	95	28	32	26	0	40	3	6	3	0	1	.00	6	.239	.315	.385
1994 Sarasota	A	37	137	38	8	1	2	54	15	15	8	1	19	1	0	0	1	0	1.00	1	.277	.322	.394
New Britain	AA	50	164	30	6	1	1	41	10	17	7	1	35	3	1	2	0	0	.00	5	.183	.227	.250
1995 Trenton	AA	29	84	20	3	1	2	31	11	11	8	0	15	0	0	2	2	1	.67	1	.238	.298	.369
Sarasota	A	62	198	66	14	0	8	104	26	35	25	0	28	3	0	5	6	3	.67	4	.333	.407	.525
6 Min. YEARS		402	1275	303	62	6	32	473	135	161	116	2	242	14	12	18	11	8	.58	27	.238	.304	.371

Mike McLain

Pitches: Right **Bats:** Right **Pos:** P **Ht:** 6'2" **Wt:** 205 **Born:** 3/18/70 **Age:** 26

		HOW MUCH HE PITCHED						WHAT HE GAVE UP											THE RESULTS					
Year Team	Lg	G	GS	CG	GF	IP	BFP	H	R	ER	HR	SH	SF	HB	TBB	IBB	SO	WP	Bk	W	L	Pct.	ShO	Sv	ERA
1992 Everett	A	6	0	0	1	9	42	10	6	5	0	1	1	1	4	0	7	1	1	0	1	.000	0	0	5.00

Year	Team	Lg																								
	Clinton	A	18	0	0	12	23.2	102	19	10	9	0	3	0	3	10	0	29	1	1	1	2	.333	0	5	3.42
1993	Clinton	A	36	1	0	20	73.2	322	66	36	24	5	4	2	9	23	4	78	1	1	4	3	.571	0	7	2.93
1994	San Jose	A	47	0	0	38	88	369	80	36	27	3	3	4	9	24	2	81	9	0	3	4	.429	0	13	2.76
1995	Shreveport	AA	11	0	0	4	17.1	66	13	7	6	1	1	0	1	3	0	11	0	0	2	1	.667	0	1	3.12
	San Jose	A	9	0	0	3	19.2	77	16	5	5	0	0	1	0	6	0	21	1	0	0	1	.000	0	2	2.29
	Lakeland	A	21	0	0	11	27.2	118	33	13	11	3	1	0	1	7	0	27	3	0			.500	0	6	3.58
	4 Min. YEARS		148	1	0	89	259	1096	237	113	87	12	13	8	24	77	6	254	16	3	11	13	.458	0	29	3.02

Billy McMillon

Bats: Left **Throws:** Left **Pos:** OF   **Ht:** 5'11" **Wt:** 172 **Born:** 11/17/71 **Age:** 24

			BATTING													BASERUNNING				PERCENTAGES		
Year	Team	Lg	G	AB	H	2B	3B	HR	TB	R	RBI	TBB	IBB	SO	HBP	SH	SF	SB	CS	SB%	GDP	Avg	OBP	SLG
1993	Elmira	A	57	227	69	14	2	6	105	38	35	30	4	44	4	0	0	5	4	.56	3	.304	.395	.463
1994	Kane County	A	137	496	125	25	3	17	207	88	101	84	2	99	10	1	9	7	3	.70	13	.252	.366	.417
1995	Portland	AA	141	518	162	29	3	14	239	92	93	96	5	90	7	1	5	15	9	.63	10	.313	.423	.461
	3 Min. YEARS		335	1241	356	68	8	37	551	218	229	210	11	233	21	2	14	27	16	.63	26	.287	.395	.444

Buck McNabb

Bats: Left **Throws:** Right **Pos:** OF   **Ht:** 6'0" **Wt:** 180 **Born:** 1/17/73 **Age:** 23

			BATTING													BASERUNNING				PERCENTAGES		
Year	Team	Lg	G	AB	H	2B	3B	HR	TB	R	RBI	TBB	IBB	SO	HBP	SH	SF	SB	CS	SB%	GDP	Avg	OBP	SLG
1991	Astros	R	48	174	51	3	3	0	60	34	9	12	0	33	4	3	2	23	8	.74	0	.293	.349	.345
1992	Burlington	A	123	456	118	12	3	1	139	82	34	60	0	80	10	3	2	56	19	.75	4	.259	.356	.305
1993	Osceola	A	125	487	139	15	7	1	171	69	35	52	2	66	6	4	1	28	15	.65	8	.285	.361	.351
1994	Jackson	AA	125	454	124	25	7	0	163	67	27	26	0	63	1	4	2	15	17	.47	10	.273	.313	.359
1995	Jackson	AA	15	50	13	1	0	0	14	4	3	5	0	11	0	0	0	1	0	1.00	1	.260	.327	.280
	Canton-Akrn	AA	19	48	8	0	0	0	8	3	1	6	0	14	1	2	0	0	1	.00	0	.167	.273	.167
	Bakersfield	A	63	237	71	8	1	0	81	34	27	38	1	38	0	4	2	11	1	.92	5	.300	.394	.342
	5 Min. YEARS		518	1906	524	64	21	2	636	293	136	199	3	305	22	20	9	134	61	.69	28	.275	.349	.334

Fred McNair

Bats: Right **Throws:** Right **Pos:** 1B   **Ht:** 6'4" **Wt:** 215 **Born:** 1/31/70 **Age:** 26

			BATTING													BASERUNNING				PERCENTAGES		
Year	Team	Lg	G	AB	H	2B	3B	HR	TB	R	RBI	TBB	IBB	SO	HBP	SH	SF	SB	CS	SB%	GDP	Avg	OBP	SLG
1989	Mariners	R	36	142	40	6	2	4	62	24	18	7	0	38	2	0	2	4	2	.67	2	.282	.320	.437
1990	Bellingham	A	50	176	36	8	0	3	53	16	17	15	1	55	3	1	0	7	3	.70	3	.205	.278	.301
1992	Bellingham	A	69	255	84	9	2	8	121	41	54	21	4	69	4	0	0	13	10	.57	9	.329	.389	.475
1993	Riverside	A	112	400	108	21	1	14	173	70	65	41	2	91	5	1	4	6	7	.46	11	.270	.342	.433
1994	Jacksonvlle	AA	57	200	44	11	0	4	67	17	21	12	1	47	1	0	1	3	1	.75	5	.220	.266	.335
	Appleton	A	60	222	67	15	3	9	115	34	49	11	0	48	2	0	3	7	0	1.00	6	.302	.336	.518
1995	Scranton-Wb	AAA	9	25	6	1	0	0	7	1	2	3	0	6	0	0	1	0	0	.00	1	.240	.310	.280
	Reading	AA	108	395	107	24	1	23	202	64	68	38	1	86	3	1	0	3	2	.60	12	.271	.339	.511
	6 Min. YEARS		501	1815	492	95	9	65	800	267	294	148	9	440	20	3	11	43	25	.63	49	.271	.331	.441

Jeff McNeely

Bats: Right **Throws:** Right **Pos:** OF   **Ht:** 6'2" **Wt:** 200 **Born:** 10/18/69 **Age:** 26

			BATTING													BASERUNNING				PERCENTAGES		
Year	Team	Lg	G	AB	H	2B	3B	HR	TB	R	RBI	TBB	IBB	SO	HBP	SH	SF	SB	CS	SB%	GDP	Avg	OBP	SLG
1989	Red Sox	R	9	32	13	1	1	0	16	10	4	7	0	3	0	0	1	5	1	.83	1	.406	.500	.500
	Elmira	A	61	208	52	7	0	2	65	20	21	26	0	54	4	1	0	16	8	.67	4	.250	.345	.313
1990	Winter Havn	A	16	62	10	0	0	0	10	4	3	3	0	19	0	0	0	7	1	.88	1	.161	.200	.161
	Elmira	A	73	246	77	4	5	6	109	41	37	40	5	60	3	8	2	39	10	.80	7	.313	.412	.443
1991	Lynchburg	A	106	382	123	16	5	4	161	58	38	74	3	74	4	4	1	38	21	.64	5	.322	.436	.421
1992	New Britain	A	85	261	57	8	4	2	79	30	11	26	0	78	2	4	0	10	5	.67	10	.218	.294	.303
1993	Pawtucket	AAA	129	498	130	14	3	2	156	65	35	43	1	102	3	10	2	40	7	.85	4	.261	.322	.313
1994	Pawtucket	AAA	117	458	106	15	5	4	143	60	34	49	0	100	9	5	3	13	17	.43	6	.231	.316	.312
1995	Louisville	AAA	109	271	64	6	1	0	72	31	19	23	0	53	0	0	1	5	8	.38	8	.236	.295	.266
1993	Boston	AL	21	37	11	1	1	0	14	10	1	7	0	9	0	0	0	6	0	1.00	0	.297	.409	.378
	7 Min. YEARS		705	2418	632	71	24	20	811	319	202	291	9	543	25	32	10	173	78	.69	46	.261	.345	.335

Tony Medrano

Bats: Right **Throws:** Right **Pos:** SS   **Ht:** 5'11" **Wt:** 155 **Born:** 12/8/74 **Age:** 21

			BATTING													BASERUNNING				PERCENTAGES		
Year	Team	Lg	G	AB	H	2B	3B	HR	TB	R	RBI	TBB	IBB	SO	HBP	SH	SF	SB	CS	SB%	GDP	Avg	OBP	SLG
1993	Blue Jays	R	39	158	42	9	0	0	51	20	9	10	0	9	3	0	0	6	2	.75	1	.266	.322	.323
1994	Blue Jays	R	6	22	8	4	0	1	15	2	5	1	0	0	0	0	0	0	0	.00	0	.364	.391	.682
	Dunedin	A	60	199	47	6	4	4	73	20	21	12	0	26	3	3	1	3	3	.50	4	.236	.288	.367
1995	Wichita	AA	1	5	0	0	0	0	0	0	0	0	0	3	0	0	0	0	0	.00	0	.000	.000	.000
	Wilmington	A	123	460	131	20	6	3	172	69	43	34	2	42	5	15	4	11	6	.65	10	.285	.338	.374
	3 Min. YEARS		229	844	228	39	10	8	311	111	78	57	2	80	11	18	5	20	11	.65	17	.270	.323	.368

Kevin Meier

Pitches: Right Bats: Right Pos: P Ht: 6'4" Wt: 200 Born: 2/20/66 Age: 30

Year	Team	Lg	G	GS	CG	GF	IP	BFP	H	R	ER	HR	SH	SF	HB	TBB	IBB	SO	WP	Bk	W	L	Pct.	ShO	Sv	ERA
1987	Pocatello	R	6	5	1	1	36.1	162	39	16	13	2	2	1	0	11	0	24	3	3	3	0	1.000	0	0	3.22
	Fresno	A	13	3	0	2	49.1	201	45	22	20	4	1	2	0	18	0	26	4	0	3	2	.600	0	1	3.65
1988	San Jose	A	17	17	0	0	99	450	112	64	53	4	3	4	2	44	0	59	1	2	7	6	.538	0	0	4.82
1989	San Jose	A	19	19	5	0	140.1	549	110	43	35	5	6	4	2	32	0	95	3	0	11	6	.647	4	0	2.24
	Shreveport	AA	6	6	1	0	38	158	34	24	20	7	1	1	0	7	0	23	1	0	3	2	.600	0	0	4.74
1990	Shreveport	AA	14	14	1	0	87.2	365	91	32	30	2	1	2	1	21	1	61	3	0	6	5	.545	1	0	3.08
	Phoenix	AAA	13	13	0	0	68.1	302	82	41	33	9	1	3	2	21	0	25	0	0	5	3	.625	0	0	4.35
1991	Shreveport	AA	33	18	2	3	135.2	595	157	86	76	15	6	8	1	38	2	79	10	0	9	6	.600	0	0	5.04
1992	Arkansas	AA	27	27	2	0	171	694	156	63	49	15	4	2	2	37	3	107	8	1	11	6	.647	1	0	2.58
1993	Louisville	AAA	27	24	1	0	135	597	156	95	87	21	0	5	7	44	0	98	5	1	8	6	.571	0	0	5.80
1994	Colo. Sprng	AAA	30	11	0	5	93.1	437	136	79	68	17	4	3	3	27	3	71	6	0	5	5	.500	0	2	6.56
1995	Orlando	AA	11	11	0	0	64.2	257	55	24	19	6	0	2	5	13	4	52	4	0	4	1	.800	0	0	2.64
	Iowa	AAA	3	2	0	0	10.2	51	18	10	10	6	0	0	0	3	0	7	1	0	1	2	.333	0	0	8.44
	9 Min. YEARS		219	170	13	11	1129.1	4818	1191	599	513	113	29	37	25	316	13	727	49	7	76	50	.603	6	3	4.09

Adam Meinershagen

Pitches: Right Bats: Right Pos: P Ht: 6'4" Wt: 190 Born: 7/25/73 Age: 22

Year	Team	Lg	G	GS	CG	GF	IP	BFP	H	R	ER	HR	SH	SF	HB	TBB	IBB	SO	WP	Bk	W	L	Pct.	ShO	Sv	ERA
1991	Blue Jays	R	11	8	0	3	41	178	39	28	16	1	0	1	2	19	0	21	9	3	3	2	.600	0	0	3.51
1992	St. Cathrns	A	11	8	0	0	44.1	199	44	24	22	6	1	3	3	20	0	36	8	6	1	7	.125	0	1	4.47
1993	Hagerstown	A	5	5	0	0	25.2	119	37	22	21	3	1	1	0	11	0	16	3	0	0	3	.000	0	0	7.36
	St. Cathrns	A	13	13	1	0	86	329	53	19	18	2	2	1	3	26	0	87	1	0	8	1	.889	1	0	1.88
1994	Dunedin	A	19	16	1	0	101.2	453	115	62	54	10	3	5	5	42	0	52	8	1	6	6	.500	0	0	4.78
1995	Knoxville	AA	3	3	0	0	11.2	55	17	14	14	2	1	0	1	2	0	4	0	0	1	1	.500	0	0	10.80
	Dunedin	A	21	13	1	2	98.1	430	115	59	41	13	3	8	6	23	1	53	3	0	5	9	.357	0	0	3.75
	5 Min. YEARS		83	66	3	6	408.2	1763	420	228	186	37	11	19	20	143	1	269	32	10	24	29	.453	1	1	4.10

Dan Melendez

Bats: Left Throws: Left Pos: 1B Ht: 6'4" Wt: 195 Born: 1/4/71 Age: 25

Year	Team	Lg	G	AB	H	2B	3B	HR	TB	R	RBI	TBB	IBB	SO	HBP	SH	SF	SB	CS	SB%	GDP	Avg	OBP	SLG
1992	Bakersfield	A	39	146	39	11	2	0	54	18	11	22	5	18	0	0	1	1	0	1.00	1	.267	.361	.370
1993	San Antonio	AA	47	158	38	11	0	7	70	25	30	11	0	29	1	0	5	0	0	.00	2	.241	.286	.443
1995	San Antonio	AA	128	464	121	28	1	7	172	46	59	51	5	66	1	0	6	0	3	.00	11	.261	.331	.371
	3 Min. YEARS		214	768	198	50	3	14	296	89	100	84	10	113	2	0	12	1	3	.25	14	.258	.328	.385

Jose Melendez

Pitches: Right Bats: Right Pos: P Ht: 6'2" Wt: 190 Born: 9/2/65 Age: 30

Year	Team	Lg	G	GS	CG	GF	IP	BFP	H	R	ER	HR	SH	SF	HB	TBB	IBB	SO	WP	Bk	W	L	Pct.	ShO	Sv	ERA
1984	Watertown	A	15	15	3	0	91	372	61	37	28	6	1	2	6	40	0	68	4	2	5	7	.417	1	0	2.77
1985	Pr. William	A	9	8	1	1	44.1	180	25	17	12	2	0	3	0	26	0	41	2	0	3	2	.600	0	1	2.44
1986	Pr. William	A	28	27	6	0	186.1	768	141	75	54	9	7	5	2	81	1	146	6	5	13	10	.565	1	0	2.61
1987	Harrisburg	AA	6	6	0	0	18.1	91	28	24	22	4	1	0	0	11	0	13	0	1	1	3	.250	0	0	10.80
	Salem	A	20	20	1	0	116.1	493	96	62	59	17	0	5	8	56	0	86	4	0	9	6	.600	1	0	4.56
1988	Salem	A	8	8	2	0	53.2	233	55	26	24	10	0	0	1	19	0	50	2	1	4	2	.667	1	0	4.02
	Harrisburg	AA	22	4	2	6	71.1	274	46	20	18	2	2	3	1	19	1	38	3	4	5	3	.625	2	1	2.27
1989	Williamsprt	AA	11	11	0	0	73.1	295	54	23	20	7	1	2	2	22	1	56	0	6	3	4	.429	0	0	2.45
	Calgary	AAA	17	2	0	4	40.2	184	42	27	26	6	2	3	3	19	2	24	1	0	1	2	.333	0	0	5.75
1990	Calgary	AAA	45	10	1	14	124.2	525	119	61	54	11	2	5	6	44	2	95	2	1	11	4	.733	0	2	3.90
1991	Las Vegas	AAA	9	8	1	1	58.2	238	54	27	26	8	1	4	3	11	0	45	0	0	7	0	1.000	0	0	3.99
1993	Pawtucket	AAA	19	0	0	10	35	156	37	24	21	7	2	2	2	7	0	31	2	0	2	3	.400	0	2	5.40
1994	Pawtucket	AAA	28	5	1	10	73.2	314	74	42	40	13	0	5	2	25	2	65	2	0	1	5	.167	0	4	4.89
1995	Scranton-Wb	AAA	2	0	0	0	3	19	6	4	2	0	1	1	1	2	0	1	0	0	0	0	.000	0	0	6.00
	Omaha	AAA	21	1	0	8	35	163	44	21	19	8	1	0	4	14	2	30	0	0	3	4	.429	0	0	4.89
1990	Seattle	AL	3	0	0	1	5.1	28	8	8	7	2	0	0	1	3	0	7	1	0	0	0	.000	0	0	11.81
1991	San Diego	NL	31	9	0	10	93.2	381	77	35	34	11	2	6	1	24	3	60	3	2	8	5	.615	0	3	3.27
1992	San Diego	NL	56	3	0	18	89.1	363	82	32	29	9	7	4	3	20	7	82	1	1	6	7	.462	0	0	2.92
1993	Boston	AL	9	0	0	5	16	63	10	4	4	2	0	2	0	5	3	14	0	0	2	1	.667	0	0	2.25
1994	Boston	AL	10	0	0	3	16.1	76	20	11	11	3	4	0	2	8	2	9	0	0	1	0	1.000	0	0	6.06
	11 Min. YEARS		260	125	18	54	1025.1	4305	882	490	425	110	21	40	41	396	11	789	28	20	68	55	.553	6	10	3.73
	5 Maj. YEARS		109	12	0	37	220.2	911	197	90	85	27	13	12	7	60	15	172	5	3	16	14	.533	0	3	3.47

Bob Melvin

Bats: Right Throws: Right Pos: C Ht: 6'4" Wt: 205 Born: 10/28/61 Age: 34

Year	Team	Lg	G	AB	H	2B	3B	HR	TB	R	RBI	TBB	IBB	SO	HBP	SH	SF	SB	CS	SB%	GDP	Avg	OBP	SLG
1984	Evansville	AAA	44	141	35	13	0	0	48	12	11	3	0	32	0	1	0	0	0	.00	3	.248	.264	.340
	Birmingham	AA	69	271	73	14	1	2	95	34	33	18	2	47	0	2	2	1	0	1.00	12	.269	.313	.351
1985	Nashville	AAA	53	177	48	7	1	9	84	27	24	16	0	38	1	1	2	3	1	.75	5	.271	.332	.475

Year	Team	Lg	G	AB	H	2B	3B	HR	TB	R	RBI	TBB	IBB	SO	HBP	SH	SF	SB	CS	SB%	GDP	Avg	OBP	SLG
1988	Phoenix	AAA	21	75	23	5	0	2	34	11	9	8	0	13	1	0	0	0	0	.00	4	.307	.381	.453
1994	Columbus	AAA	17	62	17	5	0	1	25	5	15	1	0	9	0	0	0	0	0	.00	1	.274	.286	.403
1995	Columbus	AAA	19	66	19	5	0	1	27	7	4	3	1	12	0	0	0	0	0	.00	3	.288	.319	.409
1985	Detroit	AL	41	82	18	4	1	0	24	10	4	3	0	21	0	2	0	0	0	.00	1	.220	.247	.293
1986	San Francisco	NL	89	268	60	14	2	5	93	24	25	15	1	69	0	3	3	3	2	.60	7	.224	.262	.347
1987	San Francisco	NL	84	246	49	8	0	11	90	31	31	17	3	44	0	0	2	0	4	.00	7	.199	.249	.366
1988	San Francisco	NL	92	273	64	13	1	8	103	23	27	13	0	46	0	1	1	0	2	.00	5	.234	.268	.377
1989	Baltimore	AL	85	278	67	10	1	1	82	22	32	15	3	53	0	7	1	1	4	.20	10	.241	.279	.295
1990	Baltimore	AL	93	301	73	14	1	5	104	30	37	11	1	53	0	3	3	0	1	.00	8	.243	.267	.346
1991	Baltimore	AL	79	228	57	10	0	1	70	11	23	11	2	46	0	1	5	0	0	.00	5	.250	.279	.307
1992	Kansas City	AL	32	70	22	5	0	0	27	5	6	5	0	13	0	0	2	0	0	.00	3	.314	.351	.386
1993	Boston	AL	77	176	39	7	0	3	55	13	23	7	0	44	1	3	3	0	0	.00	2	.222	.251	.313
1994	Chicago	AL	11	19	3	0	0	0	3	3	1	1	0	4	0	1	0	0	0	.00	1	.158	.200	.158
	New York	AL	9	14	4	0	0	1	7	2	3	0	0	3	0	0	0	0	0	.00	1	.286	.286	.500
	5 Min. YEARS		223	792	215	49	2	15	313	96	96	49	3	151	2	4	4	4	2	.67	28	.271	.314	.395
	10 Maj. YEARS		692	1955	456	85	6	35	658	174	212	98	10	396	1	21	20	4	13	.24	50	.233	.268	.337

Kirk Mendenhall

Bats: Right **Throws:** Right **Pos:** SS   **Ht:** 5'9" **Wt:** 160 **Born:** 9/17/67 **Age:** 28

			BATTING															BASERUNNING				PERCENTAGES		
Year	Team	Lg	G	AB	H	2B	3B	HR	TB	R	RBI	TBB	IBB	SO	HBP	SH	SF	SB	CS	SB%	GDP	Avg	OBP	SLG
1990	Niagara Fal	A	63	216	54	9	0	0	63	28	15	36	0	29	4	2	1	16	7	.70	3	.250	.366	.292
1991	Lakeland	A	111	354	89	10	4	1	110	38	38	36	0	57	2	12	3	9	8	.53	9	.251	.322	.311
1992	London	AA	105	362	87	17	2	4	120	54	36	52	0	61	4	4	2	9	7	.56	9	.240	.340	.331
1993	London	AA	97	275	56	5	1	1	66	41	18	30	0	45	5	4	3	21	4	.84	6	.204	.291	.240
1994	Trenton	AA	115	384	83	17	3	8	130	56	35	47	1	89	6	5	5	24	3	.89	4	.216	.308	.339
	Toledo	AAA	10	35	10	0	0	0	10	5	3	2	0	8	1	2	0	4	1	.80	2	.286	.342	.286
1995	Toledo	AAA	11	30	6	1	0	1	10	2	4	5	0	1	0	1	0	2	0	1.00	1	.200	.314	.333
	6 Min. YEARS		512	1656	385	59	10	15	509	224	149	208	1	290	22	30	14	85	30	.74	34	.232	.324	.307

Ramiro Mendoza

Pitches: Right **Bats:** Right **Pos:** P   **Ht:** 6'2" **Wt:** 154 **Born:** 6/15/72 **Age:** 24

			HOW MUCH HE PITCHED					WHAT HE GAVE UP										THE RESULTS					
Year	Team	Lg	G	GS	CG	GF	IP	BFP	H	R	ER	HR	SH	SF	HB	TBB	IBB	SO	WP	Bk	W	L	Pct.	ShO	Sv	ERA
1993	Yankees	R	15	9	0	3	67.2	275	59	26	21	3	0	1	4	7	0	61	3	0	4	5	.444	0	1	2.79
	Greensboro	A	2	0	0	1	3.2	18	3	1	1	0	0	0	0	5	0	3	0	0	1	0	.000	0	0	2.45
1994	Tampa	A	22	21	1	1	134.1	560	133	54	45	7	5	3	2	35	1	110	2	3	12	6	.667	0	0	3.01
1995	Norwich	AA	19	19	2	0	89.2	380	87	39	32	4	1	1	2	33	0	68	2	1	5	6	.455	1	0	3.21
	Columbus	AAA	2	2	0	0	14	51	10	4	4	0	0	1	0	2	0	13	1	0	1	0	1.000	0	0	2.57
	3 Min. YEARS		60	51	3	5	309.1	1284	292	124	103	14	6	6	8	82	1	255	8	4	22	18	.550	1	1	3.00

Reynol Mendoza

Pitches: Right **Bats:** Right **Pos:** P   **Ht:** 6'0" **Wt:** 215 **Born:** 10/27/70 **Age:** 25

			HOW MUCH HE PITCHED					WHAT HE GAVE UP										THE RESULTS					
Year	Team	Lg	G	GS	CG	GF	IP	BFP	H	R	ER	HR	SH	SF	HB	TBB	IBB	SO	WP	Bk	W	L	Pct.	ShO	Sv	ERA
1992	Erie	A	15	15	1	0	69.2	310	70	46	36	5	2	3	8	25	0	59	6	1	3	6	.333	1	0	4.65
1993	Kane County	A	26	23	3	3	163.2	647	129	59	52	5	6	0	9	45	3	153	13	3	12	5	.706	2	0	2.86
1994	Marlins	R	2	1	0	0	4.1	16	1	0	0	0	0	0	0	2	0	6	0	0	0	0	.000	0	0	0.00
	Brevard Cty	A	10	9	1	0	37	183	47	33	26	2	3	1	2	26	0	26	4	2	1	3	.250	0	0	6.32
1995	Portland	AA	27	27	1	0	168	715	163	73	64	6	10	4	9	69	3	120	15	0	9	10	.474	1	0	3.43
	4 Min. YEARS		80	75	6	3	442.2	1871	410	211	178	18	21	8	28	167	6	364	38	6	25	24	.510	2	2	3.62

Tony Menendez

Pitches: Right **Bats:** Right **Pos:** P   **Ht:** 6'2" **Wt:** 195 **Born:** 2/20/65 **Age:** 31

			HOW MUCH HE PITCHED					WHAT HE GAVE UP										THE RESULTS					
Year	Team	Lg	G	GS	CG	GF	IP	BFP	H	R	ER	HR	SH	SF	HB	TBB	IBB	SO	WP	Bk	W	L	Pct.	ShO	Sv	ERA
1984	White Sox	R	6	6	0	0	37	148	26	19	13	2	0	1	0	13	0	30	2	0	3	2	.600	0	0	3.16
1985	Buffalo	AAA	1	1	0	0	2.1	15	9	5	5	0	0	0	0	1	1	2	0	0	0	0	.000	0	0	19.29
	Appleton	A	24	24	2	0	148	620	134	67	45	8	6	3	4	55	0	100	11	1	13	4	.765	0	0	2.74
1986	Peninsula	A	11	10	1	1	63	279	58	35	32	9	1	6	4	29	0	43	6	0	4	4	.500	1	0	4.57
	Birmingham	AA	17	17	0	0	96.1	470	132	71	61	17	0	3	7	50	0	52	14	0	7	8	.467	0	0	5.70
1987	Birmingham	AA	27	27	4	0	173.1	776	193	111	93	19	3	7	7	76	1	102	12	2	10	10	.500	1	0	4.83
1988	Birmingham	AA	24	24	3	0	153	642	131	79	67	14	4	8	2	64	0	112	6	4	6	11	.353	0	0	3.94
1989	Birmingham	AA	27	18	2	6	144	596	123	61	51	14	5	1	4	53	2	115	7	2	10	4	.714	1	1	3.19
1990	Vancouver	AAA	24	9	2	2	72.2	307	63	34	30	6	3	5	6	28	1	48	1	0	2	5	.286	1	0	3.72
1991	Tulsa	AA	3	2	0	1	14	54	9	2	2	0	0	0	0	4	0	14	0	0	3	0	1.000	0	0	1.29
	Okla. City	AAA	21	19	0	1	116	504	107	70	67	6	5	8	6	62	3	82	8	1	5	5	.500	0	0	5.20
1992	Nashville	AAA	50	2	0	11	106.2	458	98	53	48	10	8	5	3	47	6	92	3	0	3	5	.375	0	1	4.05
1993	Buffalo	AAA	54	0	0	39	63.1	255	50	20	17	5	1	3	3	21	2	48	5	0	4	5	.444	0	24	2.42
1994	Phoenix	AAA	28	0	0	27	28.1	117	24	8	7	2	3	1	0	11	1	31	1	0	0	2	.000	0	12	2.22
1995	Phoenix	AAA	50	0	0	31	64.1	288	67	34	28	6	5	4	2	32	9	61	3	0	5	6	.455	0	13	3.92
1992	Cincinnati	NL	3	0	0	1	4.2	15	1	1	1	1	0	0	0	0	0	5	0	0	1	0	1.000	0	0	1.93
1993	Pittsburgh	NL	14	0	0	3	21	85	20	8	7	4	1	1	1	4	0	13	0	0	2	0	1.000	0	0	3.00
1994	San Francisco	NL	6	0	0	2	3.1	19	8	8	8	2	0	0	0	2	0	2	0	0	0	1	.000	0	0	21.60

	G	GS	CG	GF	IP	BFP	H	R	ER	HR	SH	SF	HB	TBB	IBB	SO	WP	Bk	W	L	Pct.	ShO	Sv	ERA
12 Min. YEARS	367	159	14	119	1282.1	5529	1224	669	566	118	44	55	48	546	26	932	79	10	75	72	.510	4	51	3.97
3 Maj. YEARS	23	0	0	6	29	119	29	17	16	7	1	1	1	6	0	20	0	0	3	1	.750	0	0	4.97

Hector Mercado

Pitches: Left **Bats:** Left **Pos:** P **Ht:** 6'3" **Wt:** 205 **Born:** 4/29/74 **Age:** 22

			HOW MUCH HE PITCHED						WHAT HE GAVE UP										THE RESULTS					
Year	Team	Lg	G	GS	CG	GF	IP	BFP	H	R	ER	HR	SH	SF	HB	TBB	IBB	SO	WP	Bk	W	L	Pct.	ShO	Sv	ERA
1992	Astros	R	13	3	0	4	30	140	22	17	14	0	1	0	3	25	0	36	7	6	1	2	.333	0	0	4.20
1993	Osceola	A	2	2	0	0	8.2	39	9	7	5	0	0	0	0	6	1	5	0	0	1	1	.500	0	0	5.19
	Astros	R	11	11	1	0	67	278	49	26	18	1	0	3	1	29	0	59	10	2	5	4	.556	1	0	2.42
1994	Osceola	A	25	25	1	0	136.2	601	123	75	60	5	11	4	1	79	4	88	9	3	6	13	.316	1	0	3.95
1995	Kissimmee	A	19	17	2	0	104	433	96	50	40	2	2	3	3	37	0	75	4	1	6	8	.429	0	0	3.46
	Jackson	AA	8	7	0	0	30	157	36	33	26	5	2	1	2	32	1	20	4	0	1	4	.200	0	0	7.80
4 Min. YEARS			78	65	4	4	376.1	1648	335	208	163	13	16	11	10	208	6	283	34	12	20	32	.385	2	0	3.90

Feliciano Mercedes

Bats: Both **Throws:** Right **Pos:** 2B **Ht:** 5'10" **Wt:** 145 **Born:** 7/9/73 **Age:** 22

			BATTING														BASERUNNING				PERCENTAGES		
Year	Team	Lg	G	AB	H	2B	3B	HR	TB	R	RBI	TBB	IBB	SO	HBP	SH	SF	SB	CS	SB%	GDP	Avg	OBP	SLG
1991	Orioles	R	53	185	41	4	5	0	55	34	15	29	0	45	2	1	0	12	5	.71	1	.222	.333	.297
1992	Kane County	A	53	166	40	4	1	0	46	23	10	18	0	38	2	8	1	9	9	.50	3	.241	.321	.277
	Bluefield	R	43	158	43	5	4	0	56	42	13	29	0	43	2	2	2	14	4	.78	4	.272	.387	.354
1993	Frederick	A	123	400	91	17	6	2	126	45	35	44	0	91	0	10	1	17	7	.71	9	.228	.303	.315
1994	Frederick	A	43	139	33	3	2	0	40	17	19	10	0	34	0	4	3	4	4	.50	2	.237	.283	.288
	Orioles	R	3	10	3	1	0	0	4	1	2	0	0	3	0	0	1	0	0	.00	0	.300	.273	.400
1995	Bowie	AA	28	80	12	1	0	0	13	10	7	6	0	14	1	1	1	2	3	.40	2	.150	.216	.163
	High Desert	A	31	107	25	4	1	0	31	10	10	5	0	24	0	1	0	5	0	1.00	1	.234	.268	.290
5 Min. YEARS			377	1245	288	39	19	2	371	182	111	141	0	292	7	27	9	63	32	.66	22	.231	.311	.298

Guillermo Mercedes

Bats: Both **Throws:** Right **Pos:** SS **Ht:** 5'11" **Wt:** 155 **Born:** 1/17/74 **Age:** 22

			BATTING														BASERUNNING				PERCENTAGES		
Year	Team	Lg	G	AB	H	2B	3B	HR	TB	R	RBI	TBB	IBB	SO	HBP	SH	SF	SB	CS	SB%	GDP	Avg	OBP	SLG
1992	Rangers	R	49	176	38	4	0	0	42	30	7	18	0	26	4	0	0	18	6	.75	1	.216	.303	.239
1993	Charlstn-Sc	A	127	457	109	12	2	0	125	55	30	47	0	60	2	8	3	41	17	.71	9	.239	.310	.274
1994	Charlotte	A	132	443	98	7	1	0	107	44	37	47	0	67	5	11	4	14	13	.52	9	.221	.301	.242
1995	Tulsa	AA	15	42	5	1	0	0	6	4	1	4	0	6	0	1	0	0	0	.00	2	.119	.196	.143
	Charlotte	A	33	110	24	2	0	0	26	10	5	7	0	12	1	2	1	1	2	.33	1	.218	.269	.236
	Columbus	A	55	183	35	5	1	2	48	23	8	18	0	19	3	1	0	6	3	.67	5	.191	.275	.262
4 Min. YEARS			411	1411	309	31	4	2	354	166	88	141	0	190	15	23	8	80	41	.66	27	.219	.295	.251

Luis Mercedes

Bats: Right **Throws:** Right **Pos:** OF **Ht:** 6'3" **Wt:** 195 **Born:** 2/20/68 **Age:** 28

			BATTING														BASERUNNING				PERCENTAGES		
Year	Team	Lg	G	AB	H	2B	3B	HR	TB	R	RBI	TBB	IBB	SO	HBP	SH	SF	SB	CS	SB%	GDP	Avg	OBP	SLG
1988	Bluefield	R	59	215	59	8	4	0	75	36	20	32	0	39	2	3	1	16	11	.59	6	.274	.372	.349
1989	Frederick	A	108	401	124	12	5	3	155	62	36	30	2	62	3	2	2	29	11	.73	7	.309	.360	.387
1990	Hagerstown	AA	108	416	139	12	4	3	168	71	37	34	2	70	6	6	2	38	14	.73	13	.334	.391	.404
1991	Rochester	AAA	102	374	125	14	5	2	155	68	36	65	0	63	5	6	4	23	14	.62	10	.334	.435	.414
1992	Rochester	AAA	103	409	128	15	1	3	154	62	29	44	2	56	1	3	3	35	14	.71	11	.313	.379	.377
1993	Phoenix	AAA	70	244	71	5	3	0	82	28	15	36	0	30	4	1	1	14	6	.70	5	.291	.389	.336
1995	Calgary	AAA	25	84	22	1	0	1	26	18	8	11	0	10	3	0	1	1	2	.33	2	.262	.367	.310
1991	Baltimore	AL	19	54	11	2	0	0	13	10	2	4	0	9	0	1	0	0	0	.00	1	.204	.259	.241
1992	Baltimore	AL	23	50	7	2	0	0	9	7	4	8	0	9	1	2	1	0	1	.00	2	.140	.267	.180
1993	Baltimore	AL	10	24	7	2	0	0	9	1	0	5	0	4	0	1	0	1	1	.50	1	.292	.414	.375
	San Francisco	NL	18	25	4	0	1	0	6	1	3	1	0	3	2	1	0	0	1	.00	0	.160	.250	.240
7 Min. YEARS			575	2143	668	67	22	12	815	345	181	252	6	330	24	21	13	156	72	.68	54	.312	.388	.380
3 Maj. YEARS			70	153	29	6	1	0	37	19	9	18	0	25	3	5	1	1	3	.25	4	.190	.286	.242

Mark Merchant

Bats: Both **Throws:** Right **Pos:** DH **Ht:** 6'2" **Wt:** 185 **Born:** 1/23/69 **Age:** 27

			BATTING														BASERUNNING				PERCENTAGES		
Year	Team	Lg	G	AB	H	2B	3B	HR	TB	R	RBI	TBB	IBB	SO	HBP	SH	SF	SB	CS	SB%	GDP	Avg	OBP	SLG
1987	Pirates	R	50	185	49	5	1	3	65	32	17	30	4	29	1	0	0	33	13	.72	0	.265	.370	.351
1988	Augusta	A	60	211	51	6	0	2	63	36	19	41	2	38	2	0	2	14	3	.82	5	.242	.367	.299
1989	Augusta	A	15	59	19	6	1	0	27	11	8	7	1	13	0	0	1	3	1	.75	1	.322	.388	.458
	San Bernrdo	A	119	429	90	15	2	11	142	65	46	61	1	101	2	0	4	17	6	.74	12	.210	.308	.331
1990	Williamsprt	AA	44	156	28	5	0	0	33	16	10	14	2	36	1	0	2	7	2	.78	8	.179	.249	.212
	San Bernrdo	A	29	102	32	3	0	4	47	22	19	20	0	34	0	0	0	8	2	.80	1	.314	.426	.461
1991	Peninsula	A	78	270	68	8	1	6	96	31	34	51	6	70	0	0	0	11	4	.73	7	.252	.371	.356
	Jacksonvlle	AA	51	156	44	10	0	5	69	22	17	21	4	37	1	0	1	3	4	.43	2	.282	.369	.442
1992	Jacksonvlle	AA	109	381	93	9	1	13	143	42	47	37	2	91	2	1	6	3	2	.60	11	.244	.310	.375
1993	Indianapols	AAA	3	6	1	1	0	0	2	2	0	2	0	3	0	1	0	0	0	.00	0	.167	.375	.333
	Chattanooga	AA	109	336	101	16	0	17	168	56	61	50	2	79	3	0	3	3	5	.38	9	.301	.393	.500
1994	Chattanooga	AA	106	329	102	14	2	5	135	31	56	39	8	46	0	1	5	1	2	.33	10	.310	.378	.410

Year Team	Lg	G	AB	H	2B	3B	HR	TB	R	RBI	TBB	IBB	SO	HBP	SH	SF	SB	CS	SB%	GDP	Avg	OBP	SLG
1995 Chattanooga	AA	25	53	11	0	0	1	14	4	6	7	1	15	0	0	0	0	0	.00	4	.208	.300	.264
Sioux City	IND	61	217	69	14	0	11	116	41	41	36	2	40	1	0	1	1	1	.50	2	.318	.416	.535
9 Min. YEARS		859	2890	758	112	8	78	1120	411	381	416	35	632	13	3	25	104	45	.70	72	.262	.355	.388

Lou Merloni

Bats: Right **Throws:** Right **Pos:** 2B **Ht:** 5'10" **Wt:** 188 **Born:** 4/6/71 **Age:** 25

Year Team	Lg	G	AB	H	2B	3B	HR	TB	R	RBI	TBB	IBB	SO	HBP	SH	SF	SB	CS	SB%	GDP	Avg	OBP	SLG
1993 Red Sox	R	4	14	5	1	0	0	6	4	1	1	0	1	1	0	0	1	1	.50	0	.357	.438	.429
Ft. Laud	A	44	156	38	1	1	2	47	14	21	13	1	26	1	0	4	1	1	.50	6	.244	.299	.301
1994 Sarasota	A	113	419	120	16	2	1	143	59	63	36	4	57	7	7	10	5	2	.71	11	.286	.345	.341
1995 Trenton	AA	93	318	88	16	1	1	109	42	30	39	3	50	11	11	2	7	7	.50	1	.277	.373	.343
3 Min. YEARS		254	907	251	34	4	4	305	119	115	89	8	134	20	18	16	14	11	.56	18	.277	.349	.336

Brett Merriman

Pitches: Right **Bats:** Right **Pos:** P **Ht:** 6'2" **Wt:** 215 **Born:** 7/15/66 **Age:** 29

Year Team	Lg	G	GS	CG	GF	IP	BFP	H	R	ER	HR	SH	SF	HB	TBB	IBB	SO	WP	Bk	W	L	Pct.	ShO	Sv	ERA
1988 Burlington	R	8	8	0	0	45.1	190	39	20	13	1	2	2	1	13	1	45	6	4	0	4	.000	0	0	2.58
1989 Miami	A	5	5	0	0	19	105	30	21	17	1	1	3	4	17	0	8	3	0	0	4	.000	0	0	8.05
Watertown	A	14	14	2	0	92	402	75	50	27	1	5	2	8	44	0	64	3	0	7	5	.583	2	0	2.64
1990 Palm Spring	A	24	16	0	0	100.2	460	106	60	42	2	3	1	9	55	2	53	8	0	3	10	.231	0	0	3.75
Midland	AA	2	0	0	1	4	18	7	1	1	0	0	0	0	0	0	1	0	0	1	0	1.000	0	0	2.25
1991 Palm Spring	A	34	0	0	17	41.1	188	36	20	9	0	3	1	2	30	5	23	4	0	4	1	.800	0	2	1.96
1992 Midland	AA	38	0	0	27	53.1	214	49	26	16	3	1	2	3	10	1	32	7	0	3	4	.429	0	9	2.70
Edmonton	AAA	22	0	0	14	31.2	136	31	10	5	0	0	1	2	10	3	15	2	0	1	3	.250	0	4	1.42
1993 Portland	AAA	39	0	0	33	48	206	46	19	16	0	1	2	3	18	0	29	2	0	5	0	1.000	0	15	3.00
1994 Salt Lake	AAA	17	0	0	8	20.1	100	18	18	16	1	1	0	4	16	0	12	3	0	0	1	.000	0	2	7.00
1995 Las Vegas	AAA	11	0	0	4	12	59	14	12	11	1	0	0	0	12	1	7	2	0	2	2	.500	0	0	8.25
1993 Minnesota	AL	19	0	0	10	27	135	36	29	29	3	2	2	3	23	2	14	1	0	1	1	.500	0	0	9.67
1994 Minnesota	AL	15	0	0	5	17	87	18	13	12	0	0	2	4	14	0	10	1	0	0	1	.000	0	0	6.35
8 Min. YEARS		214	43	2	104	467.2	2078	451	257	173	10	17	14	36	225	13	289	40	4	26	34	.433	2	32	3.33
2 Maj. YEARS		34	0	0	15	44	222	54	42	41	3	2	4	7	37	2	24	2	0	1	2	.333	0	0	8.39

Mark Mesewicz

Pitches: Left **Bats:** Left **Pos:** P **Ht:** 6'3" **Wt:** 195 **Born:** 10/13/69 **Age:** 26

Year Team	Lg	G	GS	CG	GF	IP	BFP	H	R	ER	HR	SH	SF	HB	TBB	IBB	SO	WP	Bk	W	L	Pct.	ShO	Sv	ERA
1992 Welland	A	29	0	0	17	47.1	197	43	19	13	1	2	0	1	16	2	55	5	0	5	3	.625	0	5	2.47
1993 Augusta	A	12	0	0	8	15.1	66	14	9	7	2	2	0	0	3	0	17	3	0	0	2	.000	0	0	4.11
Salem	A	48	0	0	12	65.1	265	57	24	20	7	3	0	3	15	0	75	6	0	4	4	.500	0	1	2.76
1994 Carolina	AA	55	0	0	12	72	311	74	41	34	5	2	2	7	17	0	52	5	0	6	2	.750	0	4	4.25
1995 Arkansas	AA	5	0	0	1	9.1	41	13	7	7	0	2	0	0	1	1	7	0	0	0	1	.000	0	0	6.75
Lynchburg	A	6	0	0	1	4.2	29	13	12	12	2	0	0	0	2	0	3	1	0	0	1	.000	0	0	23.14
Pirates	R	3	0	0	0	4.2	21	5	2	2	0	0	0	0	1	0	6	0	0	0	0	.000	0	0	3.86
4 Min. YEARS		158	0	0	51	218.2	930	219	114	95	17	11	2	11	55	3	215	20	0	15	13	.536	0	6	3.91

Mike Metcalfe

Bats: Both **Throws:** Right **Pos:** SS **Ht:** 5'10" **Wt:** 175 **Born:** 1/2/73 **Age:** 23

Year Team	Lg	G	AB	H	2B	3B	HR	TB	R	RBI	TBB	IBB	SO	HBP	SH	SF	SB	CS	SB%	GDP	Avg	OBP	SLG
1994 Bakersfield	A	69	275	78	10	3	0	88	44	18	28	0	34	1	4	2	41	13	.76	6	.284	.350	.320
1995 San Antonio	AA	10	41	10	1	0	0	11	10	2	7	0	2	0	1	1	1	2	.33	0	.244	.347	.268
Vero Beach	A	120	435	131	13	3	3	159	86	35	60	2	37	3	6	5	60	27	.69	8	.301	.386	.366
2 Min. YEARS		199	751	219	24	3	3	258	140	55	95	2	73	4	11	8	102	42	.71	14	.292	.371	.344

Jeff Michael

Bats: Right **Throws:** Right **Pos:** 1B **Ht:** 6'0" **Wt:** 174 **Born:** 8/8/71 **Age:** 24

Year Team	Lg	G	AB	H	2B	3B	HR	TB	R	RBI	TBB	IBB	SO	HBP	SH	SF	SB	CS	SB%	GDP	Avg	OBP	SLG
1993 Albany	A	49	163	44	6	0	0	50	20	14	14	0	21	3	5	1	5	1	.83	3	.270	.337	.307
1994 Frederick	A	80	258	73	12	1	1	90	28	24	12	1	33	1	0	0	7	7	.50	2	.283	.317	.349
1995 Bowie	AA	4	12	2	0	0	0	2	2	0	4	0	4	0	0	0	0	0	.00	0	.167	.375	.167
Frederick	A	66	203	50	12	0	0	62	19	17	24	1	46	1	5	3	3	4	.43	4	.246	.325	.305
3 Min. YEARS		199	636	169	30	1	1	204	69	55	54	2	104	5	10	4	15	12	.56	9	.266	.326	.321

Chris Michalak

Pitches: Left **Bats:** Left **Pos:** P **Ht:** 6'2" **Wt:** 195 **Born:** 1/4/71 **Age:** 25

Year Team	Lg	G	GS	CG	GF	IP	BFP	H	R	ER	HR	SH	SF	HB	TBB	IBB	SO	WP	Bk	W	L	Pct.	ShO	Sv	ERA
1993 Sou. Oregon	A	16	15	0	0	79	346	77	41	26	2	2	5	6	36	0	57	4	3	7	3	.700	0	0	2.85
1994 W. Michigan	A	15	10	0	2	67	291	66	32	29	3	4	2	8	28	0	38	2	3	5	3	.625	0	0	3.90
Modesto	A	17	10	1	3	77.1	310	67	28	25	13	2	3	3	20	1	46	4	3	5	3	.625	0	2	2.91
1995 Huntsville	AA	7	0	0	4	5.2	32	10	7	7	1	1	0	1	5	0	4	2	0	1	1	.500	0	1	11.12

	Lg	G	GS	CG	GF	IP	BFP	H	R	ER	HR	SH	SF	HB	TBB	IBB	SO	WP	Bk	W	L	Pct.	ShO	Sv	ERA
Modesto	A	44	0	0	16	65.1	266	56	26	19	3	4	3	4	27	1	49	2	1	3	2	.600	0	2	2.62
3 Min. YEARS		99	35	1	25	294.1	1245	276	134	105	22	13	13	22	116	2	194	14	10	21	12	.636	0	5	3.21

Pitches: Right **Bats:** Both **Pos:** P

Lincoln Mikkelsen

Ht: 6'0" **Wt:** 186 **Born:** 7/27/67 **Age:** 28

		HOW MUCH HE PITCHED						WHAT HE GAVE UP												THE RESULTS					
Year Team	Lg	G	GS	CG	GF	IP	BFP	H	R	ER	HR	SH	SF	HB	TBB	IBB	SO	WP	Bk	W	L	Pct.	ShO	Sv	ERA
1990 Erie	A	14	14	2	0	88.1	369	70	36	23	2	1	1	7	36	3	81	7	4	7	5	.583	0	0	2.34
1991 Stockton	A	27	16	0	5	121	521	116	51	46	3	2	2	14	42	0	103	5	4	5	5	.500	0	0	3.42
1992 Stockton	A	20	5	0	3	47.1	208	49	32	29	2	5	2	1	24	1	31	3	2	0	4	.000	0	0	5.51
1993 Duluth-Sup.	IND	18	17	1	1	105.1	449	112	57	49	6	4	3	10	37	2	86	2	1	2	6	.250	0	0	4.19
1994 Brainerd	IND	9	8	0	0	51.2	222	42	15	7	1	1	0	6	22	0	43	4	0	5	2	.714	0	0	1.22
1995 Harrisburg	AA	21	5	0	5	53.2	243	57	33	32	1	5	2	4	24	0	39	1	1	1	2	.333	0	0	5.37
Albany	A	12	0	0	5	23.1	107	24	14	5	0	1	0	3	8	0	17	1	0	0	1	.000	0	0	1.93
6 Min. YEARS		121	65	3	19	490.2	2119	470	238	191	15	19	10	45	193	6	400	23	12	20	25	.444	0	5	3.50

Pitches: Right **Bats:** Right **Pos:** P

Bob Milacki

Ht: 6'4" **Wt:** 230 **Born:** 7/28/64 **Age:** 31

		HOW MUCH HE PITCHED						WHAT HE GAVE UP												THE RESULTS					
Year Team	Lg	G	GS	CG	GF	IP	BFP	H	R	ER	HR	SH	SF	HB	TBB	IBB	SO	WP	Bk	W	L	Pct.	ShO	Sv	ERA
1984 Hagerstown	A	15	13	1	1	77.2	339	69	35	29	2	1	2	0	48	0	62	6	0	4	5	.444	0	0	3.36
1985 Daytona Bch	A	8	6	2	1	38.1	167	32	23	17	0	2	3	0	26	1	24	7	1	1	4	.200	0	0	3.99
Hagerstown	A	7	7	1	0	40.2	174	32	16	12	1	0	0	2	22	0	37	0	0	3	2	.600	0	0	2.66
1986 Hagerstown	A	13	12	1	0	60.2	292	69	59	32	4	1	4	1	37	2	46	6	1	4	5	.444	1	0	4.75
Miami	A	12	11	0	0	67.1	297	70	36	28	1	2	4	2	27	2	41	6	0	4	4	.500	0	0	3.74
Charlotte	AA	1	1	0	0	5.1	28	7	4	4	0	1	0	0	4	0	6	2	0	0	1	.000	0	0	6.75
1987 Charlotte	AA	29	24	2	2	148	662	168	86	75	10	2	3	3	66	0	101	10	0	11	9	.550	0	1	4.56
1988 Charlotte	AA	5	5	1	0	37.2	150	42	15	10	1	1	1	3	12	1	29	1	1	3	1	.750	0	0	2.39
Rochester	AAA	24	24	11	0	176.2	747	174	62	53	8	2	2	1	65	1	103	6	1	12	8	.600	3	0	2.70
1991 Hagerstown	AA	3	3	0	0	17	67	14	3	2	1	0	0	0	3	0	18	0	0	3	0	1.000	0	0	1.06
1992 Rochester	AAA	9	9	3	0	61	253	57	33	31	9	1	4	2	21	0	35	3	0	7	1	.875	0	0	4.57
1993 Charlotte	AAA	21	7	0	8	71.2	288	59	31	27	6	2	2	0	19	1	46	4	0	4	3	.571	0	4	3.39
1994 Omaha	AAA	16	14	1	1	86	386	91	54	48	11	5	5	6	42	0	59	2	0	4	3	.571	0	0	5.02
1995 Omaha	AAA	15	15	2	0	105.1	421	90	42	39	8	1	0	2	31	0	63	3	0	8	3	.727	2	0	3.33
Tacoma	AAA	12	12	1	0	71.2	322	94	50	42	5	2	3	0	23	1	31	0	0	6	4	.600	0	0	5.27
1988 Baltimore	AL	3	3	1	0	25	91	9	2	2	1	0	0	0	9	0	18	0	0	2	0	1.000	1	0	0.72
1989 Baltimore	AL	37	36	3	1	243	1022	233	105	101	21	7	6	2	88	4	113	1	1	14	12	.538	2	0	3.74
1990 Baltimore	AL	27	24	1	0	135.1	594	143	73	67	18	5	5	0	61	2	60	2	1	5	8	.385	0	0	4.46
1991 Baltimore	AL	31	26	3	1	184	758	175	86	82	17	7	5	1	53	3	108	1	2	10	9	.526	1	0	4.01
1992 Baltimore	AL	23	20	0	1	115.2	525	140	78	75	16	3	3	2	44	2	51	7	1	6	8	.429	0	1	5.84
1993 Cleveland	AL	5	2	0	0	16	74	19	8	6	3	0	0	0	11	0	7	0	0	1	1	.500	0	0	3.38
1994 Kansas City	AL	10	10	0	0	55.2	254	68	43	38	6	1	4	1	20	3	17	0	0	0	5	.000	0	0	6.14
10 Min. YEARS		190	163	26	13	1065	4593	1052	545	449	67	23	33	22	446	9	701	56	4	74	53	.583	6	5	3.79
7 Maj. YEARS		136	121	8	3	774.2	3318	787	395	371	82	23	23	6	286	14	374	13	5	38	43	.469	5	1	4.31

Pitches: Left **Bats:** Left **Pos:** P

Mike Milchin

Ht: 6'3" **Wt:** 190 **Born:** 2/28/68 **Age:** 28

		HOW MUCH HE PITCHED						WHAT HE GAVE UP												THE RESULTS					
Year Team	Lg	G	GS	CG	GF	IP	BFP	H	R	ER	HR	SH	SF	HB	TBB	IBB	SO	WP	Bk	W	L	Pct.	ShO	Sv	ERA
1989 Hamilton	A	8	8	1	0	41.1	165	35	11	10	2	1	2	2	9	0	46	0	5	1	2	.333	0	0	2.18
Springfield	A	6	6	1	0	42	167	30	14	10	3	3	1	0	10	1	44	2	1	3	2	.600	0	0	2.14
1990 St. Pete	A	11	11	1	0	68.1	277	57	25	21	1	2	0	1	20	0	66	4	2	6	1	.857	1	0	2.77
Arkansas	AA	17	17	4	0	102.1	444	103	62	49	8	7	5	1	47	3	75	6	1	6	8	.429	2	0	4.31
1991 Arkansas	AA	6	6	1	0	35.1	142	27	13	12	1	0	0	0	8	2	38	0	1	3	2	.600	1	0	3.06
Louisville	AAA	18	18	2	0	94	451	132	64	53	4	5	4	4	40	5	48	5	0	5	9	.357	1	0	5.07
1992 Louisville	AAA	12	12	1	0	65.1	299	69	46	43	8	3	4	1	31	5	37	5	3	2	6	.250	0	0	5.92
1993 Louisville	AAA	32	17	1	6	111.2	477	108	56	49	18	3	4	1	43	0	72	5	0	3	7	.300	0	0	3.95
1995 Albuquerque	AAA	18	17	2	0	83.1	359	94	43	40	2	1	2	0	30	1	50	5	0	8	4	.667	1	0	4.32
6 Min. YEARS		128	112	13	6	643.2	2781	655	334	287	47	24	21	10	238	17	476	32	13	37	41	.474	6	0	4.01

Bats: Right **Throws:** Right **Pos:** 1B

Adam Millan

Ht: 6'0" **Wt:** 195 **Born:** 3/26/72 **Age:** 24

		BATTING														BASERUNNING				PERCENTAGES		
Year Team	Lg	G	AB	H	2B	3B	HR	TB	R	RBI	TBB	IBB	SO	HBP	SH	SF	SB	CS	SB%	GDP	Avg	OBP	SLG
1994 Batavia	A	17	53	17	4	0	0	21	10	11	10	0	6	1	0	1	0	0	.00	1	.321	.431	.396
Spartanburg	A	48	153	41	12	0	4	65	20	29	33	1	21	1	0	1	1	1	.50	6	.268	.399	.425
1995 Reading	AA	10	20	7	3	0	1	13	3	7	4	0	3	1	0	1	0	0	.00	1	.350	.462	.650
Piedmont	A	107	394	116	25	2	10	175	69	64	44	3	45	7	1	3	1	4	.20	15	.294	.373	.444
2 Min. YEARS		182	620	181	44	2	15	274	102	111	91	4	75	10	1	6	2	5	.29	23	.292	.388	.442

Bats: Both **Throws:** Right **Pos:** 2B

Bernie Millan

Ht: 6'1" **Wt:** 202 **Born:** 12/27/70 **Age:** 25

		BATTING														BASERUNNING				PERCENTAGES		
Year Team	Lg	G	AB	H	2B	3B	HR	TB	R	RBI	TBB	IBB	SO	HBP	SH	SF	SB	CS	SB%	GDP	Avg	OBP	SLG
1990 Kingsport	R	57	184	57	5	1	0	64	14	20	12	1	17	1	2	2	2	2	.50	8	.310	.352	.348

Year	Team	Lg	G	AB	H	2B	3B	HR	TB	R	RBI	TBB	IBB	SO	HBP	SH	SF	SB	CS	SB%	GDP	Avg	OBP	SLG
1991	Pittsfield	A	20	62	12	0	0	0	12	5	11	2	0	6	0	1	2	0	1	.00	2	.194	.212	.194
	Columbia	A	60	179	51	4	1	0	57	21	21	9	1	27	0	7	2	2	4	.33	4	.285	.316	.318
1992	St. Lucie	A	77	262	71	8	2	1	86	26	23	12	2	21	0	1	0	4	2	.67	6	.271	.303	.328
1993	St. Lucie	A	122	459	124	12	0	0	136	33	54	22	2	28	1	6	5	2	9	.18	17	.270	.302	.296
1994	Stockton	A	126	489	147	21	3	1	177	56	51	22	1	39	0	13	3	8	6	.57	13	.301	.329	.362
1995	El Paso	AA	13	33	8	1	0	1	12	2	3	0	0	3	1	0	1	0	0	.00	6	.242	.257	.364
	Bend	IND	12	54	19	3	0	0	22	8	9	0	0	1	0	1	0	0	1	.00	0	.352	.352	.407
	6 Min. YEARS		487	1722	489	54	7	3	566	165	192	79	7	142	3	31	15	18	25	.42	57	.284	.314	.329

Jose Millares

Bats: Right **Throws:** Right **Pos:** DH **Ht:** 5'11" **Wt:** 190 **Born:** 3/24/68 **Age:** 28

			BATTING															BASERUNNING				PERCENTAGES		
Year	Team	Lg	G	AB	H	2B	3B	HR	TB	R	RBI	TBB	IBB	SO	HBP	SH	SF	SB	CS	SB%	GDP	Avg	OBP	SLG
1990	Bluefield	R	48	176	49	12	0	3	70	25	25	10	1	27	0	0	1	6	5	.55	1	.278	.316	.398
1991	Kane County	A	114	425	115	28	2	5	162	57	71	20	4	71	11	2	6	3	4	.43	6	.271	.316	.381
1992	Frederick	A	129	452	98	21	1	10	151	48	68	25	2	79	9	3	10	8	5	.62	6	.217	.266	.334
1993	Bowie	AA	30	50	14	1	2	0	19	6	5	1	0	9	7	2	0	1	1	.50	2	.280	.379	.380
	Frederick	A	85	299	75	11	0	9	113	38	36	23	0	44	12	2	2	4	4	.50	10	.251	.327	.378
1994	Bowie	AA	89	231	52	13	1	3	76	24	39	13	1	39	3	0	6	4	2	.67	10	.225	.269	.329
1995	Bowie	AA	120	411	102	30	3	4	150	50	50	20	0	62	19	2	6	7	6	.54	14	.248	.309	.365
	6 Min. YEARS		615	2044	505	116	9	34	741	248	294	112	8	331	61	11	31	33	27	.55	49	.247	.302	.363

Barry Miller

Bats: Left **Throws:** Left **Pos:** 1B **Ht:** 6'5" **Wt:** 210 **Born:** 7/10/68 **Age:** 27

			BATTING															BASERUNNING				PERCENTAGES		
Year	Team	Lg	G	AB	H	2B	3B	HR	TB	R	RBI	TBB	IBB	SO	HBP	SH	SF	SB	CS	SB%	GDP	Avg	OBP	SLG
1990	Everett	A	38	136	36	12	0	2	54	19	15	13	1	25	0	0	0	1	1	.50	1	.265	.329	.397
1991	Clinton	A	117	397	97	19	2	5	135	43	51	53	5	66	3	5	5	1	1	.50	10	.244	.334	.340
1992	San Jose	A	124	420	118	32	4	10	188	69	70	72	14	76	4	4	6	4	1	.80	9	.281	.386	.448
1993	Shreveport	AA	129	452	130	30	2	13	203	59	82	49	7	91	5	1	8	5	4	.56	5	.288	.358	.449
1994	Shreveport	AA	124	415	115	27	2	12	182	55	73	66	7	84	2	0	7	2	2	.50	12	.277	.373	.439
1995	Phoenix	AAA	71	156	35	8	1	2	51	18	21	23	0	35	0	0	1	0	2	.00	4	.224	.322	.327
	6 Min. YEARS		603	1976	531	128	11	44	813	263	312	276	34	377	14	10	27	13	11	.54	41	.269	.358	.411

Damian Miller

Bats: Right **Throws:** Right **Pos:** C **Ht:** 6'2" **Wt:** 190 **Born:** 10/13/69 **Age:** 26

			BATTING															BASERUNNING				PERCENTAGES		
Year	Team	Lg	G	AB	H	2B	3B	HR	TB	R	RBI	TBB	IBB	SO	HBP	SH	SF	SB	CS	SB%	GDP	Avg	OBP	SLG
1990	Elizabethtn	R	14	45	10	1	0	1	14	7	6	9	0	3	0	0	0	1	0	1.00	0	.222	.352	.311
1991	Kenosha	A	80	267	62	11	1	3	84	28	34	24	1	53	2	2	3	3	2	.60	4	.232	.297	.315
1992	Kenosha	A	115	377	110	27	2	5	156	53	56	53	1	66	7	2	4	6	1	.86	13	.292	.385	.414
1993	Fort Myers	A	87	325	69	12	1	1	86	31	26	31	0	44	0	1	0	6	3	.67	5	.212	.281	.265
	Nashville	AA	4	13	3	0	0	0	3	0	0	2	0	4	0	0	0	0	0	.00	0	.231	.333	.231
1994	Nashville	AA	103	328	88	10	0	8	122	36	35	35	2	51	1	2	5	4	6	.40	11	.268	.336	.372
1995	Salt Lake	AAA	83	295	84	23	1	3	118	39	41	15	1	39	3	5	2	2	4	.33	11	.285	.324	.400
	6 Min. YEARS		486	1650	426	84	5	21	583	194	198	169	5	260	13	12	14	22	16	.58	46	.258	.329	.353

Kurt Miller

Pitches: Right **Bats:** Right **Pos:** P **Ht:** 6'5" **Wt:** 205 **Born:** 8/24/72 **Age:** 23

			HOW MUCH HE PITCHED					WHAT HE GAVE UP										THE RESULTS					
Year	Team	Lg	G	GS	CG	GF	IP	BFP	H	R	ER	HR	SH	SF	HB	TBB	IBB	SO	WP	Bk	W	L	Pct.	ShO	Sv	ERA
1990	Welland	A	14	12	0	0	65.2	292	59	39	24	3	4	0	1	37	0	61	5	1	3	2	.600	0	0	3.29
1991	Augusta	A	21	21	2	0	115.1	492	89	49	32	6	1	3	4	57	0	103	12	6	6	7	.462	2	0	2.50
1992	Charlotte	A	12	12	0	0	75.1	294	51	23	20	2	1	2	2	29	0	58	5	2	5	4	.556	0	0	2.39
	Tulsa	AA	16	15	0	0	88	371	82	42	36	9	0	0	2	35	1	73	7	4	7	5	.583	0	0	3.68
1993	Tulsa	AA	18	18	0	0	96	438	102	69	54	8	2	5	5	45	2	68	8	0	6	8	.429	0	0	5.06
	Edmonton	AAA	9	9	0	0	48	201	42	24	24	2	1	3	0	34	0	19	5	1	3	3	.500	0	0	4.50
1994	Edmonton	AAA	23	23	0	0	125.2	592	164	105	96	18	3	7	2	64	1	58	10	0	7	13	.350	0	0	6.88
1995	Charlotte	AAA	22	22	0	0	126.2	563	143	76	65	13	5	3	7	55	0	83	6	0	8	11	.421	0	0	4.62
1994	Florida	NL	4	4	0	0	20	92	26	18	18	3	0	1	2	7	0	11	0	0	1	3	.250	0	0	8.10
	6 Min. YEARS		135	132	2	0	740.2	3243	732	427	351	61	17	23	23	356	4	523	58	14	45	53	.459	2	0	4.27

Roger Miller

Bats: Right **Throws:** Right **Pos:** C **Ht:** 6'0" **Wt:** 190 **Born:** 4/4/67 **Age:** 29

			BATTING															BASERUNNING				PERCENTAGES		
Year	Team	Lg	G	AB	H	2B	3B	HR	TB	R	RBI	TBB	IBB	SO	HBP	SH	SF	SB	CS	SB%	GDP	Avg	OBP	SLG
1989	Pocatello	R	57	199	66	8	3	6	98	39	38	19	1	14	4	2	4	8	5	.62	7	.332	.394	.492
1990	Clinton	A	111	319	82	11	1	3	104	31	41	28	3	30	1	8	3	1	3	.25	2	.257	.316	.326
	San Jose	A	3	7	4	0	0	0	4	1	2	1	0	0	0	0	0	0	0	.00	1	.571	.625	.571
1991	San Jose	A	108	369	101	10	1	9	140	59	59	52	5	38	6	9	3	4	0	1.00	10	.274	.370	.379
1993	Clinton	A	10	26	5	0	0	1	8	1	4	2	0	3	0	1	1	0	0	.00	1	.192	.241	.308
	Shreveport	AA	61	194	48	10	0	2	64	19	12	14	1	24	3	3	0	0	2	.00	6	.247	.308	.330
1994	San Jose	A	48	165	33	8	0	2	47	19	15	19	0	20	4	1	2	0	0	.00	4	.200	.295	.285
1995	Shreveport	AA	19	62	17	6	0	2	29	11	10	6	0	1	2	2	1	0	0	.00	1	.274	.352	.468

		G	AB	H	2B	3B	HR	TB	R	RBI	TBB	IBB	SO	HBP	SH	SF	SB	CS	SB%	GDP	Avg	OBP	SLG
Phoenix	AAA	43	137	29	4	1	1	38	14	10	9	0	15	0	4	0	0	0	.00	3	.212	.260	.277
6 Min. YEARS		460	1478	385	57	6	26	532	194	191	150	10	145	20	30	14	13	10	.57	35	.260	.334	.360

Ryan Miller

Bats: Right **Throws:** Right **Pos:** SS   **Ht:** 6'0" **Wt:** 175 **Born:** 10/22/72 **Age:** 23

			BATTING													BASERUNNING				PERCENTAGES		
Year Team	Lg	G	AB	H	2B	3B	HR	TB	R	RBI	TBB	IBB	SO	HBP	SH	SF	SB	CS	SB%	GDP	Avg	OBP	SLG
1994 Pittsfield	A	68	277	71	11	1	1	87	37	23	16	1	37	4	3	2	3	3	.50	0	.256	.304	.314
1995 St. Lucie	A	89	279	68	10	3	2	90	32	23	13	0	42	7	8	2	5	3	.63	7	.244	.292	.323
Binghamton	AA	9	19	1	0	0	0	1	3	0	2	0	4	0	1	0	1	0	1.00	0	.053	.143	.053
2 Min. YEARS		166	575	140	21	4	3	178	72	46	31	1	83	11	12	4	9	6	.60	7	.243	.293	.310

Travis Miller

Pitches: Left **Bats:** Right **Pos:** P   **Ht:** 6'3" **Wt:** 205 **Born:** 11/2/72 **Age:** 23

			HOW MUCH HE PITCHED					WHAT HE GAVE UP										THE RESULTS					
Year Team	Lg	G	GS	CG	GF	IP	BFP	H	R	ER	HR	SH	SF	HB	TBB	IBB	SO	WP	Bk	W	L	Pct.	ShO	Sv	ERA
1994 Fort Wayne	A	11	9	1	0	55.1	223	52	17	16	2	1	3	2	12	0	50	5	2	4	1	.800	0	0	2.60
Nashville	AA	1	1	0	0	6.1	23	3	3	2	0	0	0	0	2	0	4	1	0	0	0	.000	0	0	2.84
1995 New Britain	AA	28	27	1	1	162.2	723	172	93	79	17	6	3	4	65	2	151	5	0	7	9	.438	1	0	4.37
2 Min. YEARS		40	37	2	1	224.1	969	227	113	97	19	7	6	6	79	2	205	11	2	11	10	.524	1	0	3.89

Trever Miller

Pitches: Left **Bats:** Right **Pos:** P   **Ht:** 6'3" **Wt:** 175 **Born:** 5/29/73 **Age:** 23

			HOW MUCH HE PITCHED					WHAT HE GAVE UP										THE RESULTS					
Year Team	Lg	G	GS	CG	GF	IP	BFP	H	R	ER	HR	SH	SF	HB	TBB	IBB	SO	WP	Bk	W	L	Pct.	ShO	Sv	ERA
1991 Bristol	R	13	13	0	0	54	253	60	44	34	7	3	3	2	29	0	46	9	1	2	7	.222	0	0	5.67
1992 Bristol	R	12	12	1	0	69.1	331	75	45	38	4	3	3	1	27	0	64	4	1	3	8	.273	0	0	4.93
1993 Fayetteville	A	28	28	2	0	161	699	151	99	75	7	2	8	5	67	0	116	10	0	8	13	.381	0	0	4.19
1994 Trenton	AA	26	26	6	0	174.1	754	198	95	85	9	10	8	3	51	0	73	3	1	7	16	.304	0	0	4.39
1995 Jacksonville	AA	31	16	3	4	122.1	512	122	46	37	5	4	2	5	34	0	77	1	0	8	2	.800	2	0	2.72
5 Min. YEARS		110	95	12	4	581	2529	606	329	269	32	22	24	16	208	0	376	27	3	28	46	.378	2	0	4.17

Joe Millette

Bats: Right **Throws:** Right **Pos:** 2B   **Ht:** 6'1" **Wt:** 175 **Born:** 8/12/66 **Age:** 29

				BATTING												BASERUNNING				PERCENTAGES		
Year Team	Lg	G	AB	H	2B	3B	HR	TB	R	RBI	TBB	IBB	SO	HBP	SH	SF	SB	CS	SB%	GDP	Avg	OBP	SLG
1989 Batavia	A	11	42	10	3	0	0	13	4	4	4	0	6	0	0	0	3	0	1.00	0	.238	.304	.310
Spartanburg	A	60	209	50	4	3	0	60	27	18	28	0	36	7	3	3	4	2	.67	5	.239	.344	.287
1990 Clearwater	A	108	295	54	5	0	0	59	31	18	29	0	53	7	7	6	4	4	.50	5	.183	.267	.200
1991 Clearwater	A	18	55	14	2	0	0	16	6	6	7	0	6	1	3	2	1	2	.33	1	.255	.338	.291
Reading	AA	115	353	87	9	4	3	113	52	28	36	2	54	7	10	3	6	6	.50	5	.246	.326	.320
1992 Scranton-Wb	AAA	78	256	68	11	1	1	84	24	23	15	0	30	6	7	0	3	2	.60	8	.266	.321	.328
1993 Scranton-Wb	AAA	107	343	77	15	2	1	99	27	24	19	2	56	5	7	1	5	4	.56	9	.224	.274	.289
1994 Edmonton	AAA	118	406	107	22	3	4	147	41	38	13	3	73	6	6	2	5	5	.50	15	.264	.295	.362
1995 Charlotte	AAA	74	193	36	6	0	4	54	22	20	10	0	36	4	1	4	1	1	.50	4	.187	.237	.280
1992 Philadelphia	NL	33	78	16	0	0	0	16	5	2	5	2	10	2	2	0	1	0	1.00	1	.205	.271	.205
1993 Philadelphia	NL	10	10	2	0	0	0	2	3	2	1	0	2	0	3	0	0	0	.00	1	.200	.273	.200
7 Min. YEARS		689	2152	503	77	13	13	645	234	179	161	7	350	43	44	21	32	26	.55	52	.234	.297	.300
2 Maj. YEARS		43	88	18	0	0	0	18	8	4	6	2	12	2	5	0	1	0	1.00	9	.205	.271	.205

Ralph Milliard

Bats: Right **Throws:** Right **Pos:** 2B   **Ht:** 5'10" **Wt:** 160 **Born:** 12/30/73 **Age:** 22

				BATTING												BASERUNNING				PERCENTAGES		
Year Team	Lg	G	AB	H	2B	3B	HR	TB	R	RBI	TBB	IBB	SO	HBP	SH	SF	SB	CS	SB%	GDP	Avg	OBP	SLG
1993 Marlins	R	53	192	45	15	0	0	60	35	25	30	0	17	6	0	1	11	5	.69	8	.234	.354	.313
1994 Kane County	A	133	515	153	34	2	8	215	97	67	68	2	63	9	4	7	10	10	.50	6	.297	.384	.417
1995 Portland	AA	128	464	124	22	3	11	185	104	40	85	3	83	14	13	4	22	10	.69	5	.267	.393	.399
3 Min. YEARS		314	1171	322	71	5	19	460	236	132	183	5	163	29	17	12	43	25	.63	19	.275	.383	.393

Darren Milne

Bats: Right **Throws:** Right **Pos:** OF   **Ht:** 6'1" **Wt:** 190 **Born:** 3/24/71 **Age:** 25

				BATTING												BASERUNNING				PERCENTAGES		
Year Team	Lg	G	AB	H	2B	3B	HR	TB	R	RBI	TBB	IBB	SO	HBP	SH	SF	SB	CS	SB%	GDP	Avg	OBP	SLG
1992 Bristol	R	15	55	15	3	0	0	18	7	5	7	0	11	1	0	0	0	1	.00	3	.273	.365	.327
Fayetteville	A	46	137	31	5	0	2	42	16	18	20	1	34	6	4	1	9	5	.64	2	.226	.348	.307
1993 London	AA	5	20	1	0	0	0	1	2	1	2	0	7	0	0	0	0	0	.00	0	.050	.136	.050
Lakeland	A	71	204	40	6	1	3	63	19	18	23	0	33	0	2	2	6	5	.55	4	.196	.275	.309
1994 Trenton	AA	113	364	89	11	2	6	122	38	36	27	2	71	6	6	1	11	5	.69	10	.245	.307	.335
1995 Toledo	AAA	7	20	3	1	0	0	4	0	4	1	0	4	0	0	0	0	0	.00	1	.150	.190	.200
4 Min. YEARS		257	800	179	26	3	13	250	82	82	80	3	160	13	12	4	26	16	.62	20	.224	.303	.313

Dave Milstien

Bats: Right **Throws:** Right **Pos:** SS   **Ht:** 6'0" **Wt:** 170 **Born:** 9/11/68 **Age:** 27

Year Team	Lg	G	AB	H	2B	3B	HR	TB	R	RBI	TBB	IBB	SO	HBP	SH	SF	SB	CS	SB%	GDP	Avg	OBP	SLG
1986 Elmira	A	34	107	29	4	0	1	36	15	6	5	0	12	0	1	0	0	2	.00	4	.271	.304	.336
1987 Winter Havn	A	100	303	67	5	0	0	72	35	33	12	1	31	1	7	4	0	1	.00	9	.221	.250	.238
1988 Winter Havn	A	120	429	92	15	5	1	120	36	26	5	0	38	0	2	1	2	4	.33	10	.214	.223	.280
1989 New Britain	AA	106	345	87	10	0	0	97	34	27	23	0	50	2	10	2	5	5	.50	16	.252	.301	.281
1990 New Britain	AA	115	376	81	12	0	0	93	31	24	23	1	44	1	12	4	6	3	.67	13	.215	.260	.247
1991 New Britain	AA	86	309	86	6	1	4	106	36	31	46	1	38	1	2	5	3	5	.38	13	.278	.368	.343
Pawtucket	AAA	19	59	12	0	0	0	12	2	4	3	0	8	3	0	0	0	0	.00	1	.203	.277	.203
1992 Pawtucket	AAA	85	266	66	11	1	1	82	29	34	13	0	23	1	0	2	0	2	.00	9	.248	.284	.308
1993 Pawtucket	AAA	88	258	65	8	3	1	82	28	18	10	0	31	2	2	1	1	3	.25	8	.252	.284	.318
1994 Nashville	AAA	57	174	41	6	0	2	53	26	8	14	0	20	1	4	1	0	3	.00	8	.236	.295	.305
1995 Nashville	AAA	11	34	8	1	0	0	9	1	2	3	0	4	0	0	0	0	0	.00	1	.235	.297	.265
Beloit	A	53	196	64	12	1	2	84	47	21	23	1	15	6	1	0	8	4	.67	6	.327	.413	.429
Stockton	A	58	214	59	14	1	4	87	36	37	25	1	16	4	0	1	6	3	.67	5	.276	.361	.407
10 Min. YEARS		932	3070	757	104	12	16	933	356	271	205	5	330	22	41	21	31	35	.47	103	.247	.297	.304

Mark Mimbs

Pitches: Left **Bats:** Left **Pos:** P   **Ht:** 6'2" **Wt:** 180 **Born:** 2/13/69 **Age:** 27

Year Team	Lg	G	GS	CG	GF	IP	BFP	H	R	ER	HR	SH	SF	HB	TBB	IBB	SO	WP	Bk	W	L	Pct.	ShO	Sv	ERA
1990 Great Falls	R	14	14	0	0	78	325	69	32	28	3	0	0	1	29	0	94	4	3	7	4	.636	0	0	3.23
1991 Bakersfield	A	27	25	0	1	170	687	134	49	42	2	3	2	3	59	2	164	4	2	12	6	.667	0	0	2.22
1992 Albuquerque	AAA	12	7	0	0	48.2	217	58	34	33	4	1	1	0	19	1	32	4	0	0	4	.000	0	0	6.10
San Antonio	AA	13	13	0	0	82.1	340	78	43	33	3	5	2	2	22	4	55	3	0	1	5	.167	0	0	3.61
1993 Albuquerque	AAA	19	1	0	3	18.2	90	20	21	21	2	2	2	0	16	1	12	2	1	0	1	.000	0	1	10.13
San Antonio	AA	49	0	0	23	67.2	272	49	21	12	0	6	4	2	18	7	77	2	0	3	3	.500	0	10	1.60
1994 Bakersfield	A	1	0	0	0	1.2	7	3	0	0	0	0	0	0	0	0	0	0	0	0	0	.000	0	0	0.00
Albuquerque	AAA	6	0	0	3	6.2	28	8	3	3	1	0	0	0	0	0	9	1	0	1	0	1.000	0	0	4.05
1995 Albuquerque	AAA	23	16	1	2	106	433	105	40	35	7	3	3	1	22	0	96	7	1	6	5	.545	0	0	2.97
6 Min. YEARS		164	76	1	32	579.2	2399	524	243	207	20	20	14	9	185	15	539	27	7	30	28	.517	0	11	3.21

Nate Minchey

Pitches: Right **Bats:** Right **Pos:** P   **Ht:** 6'7" **Wt:** 215 **Born:** 8/31/69 **Age:** 26

Year Team	Lg	G	GS	CG	GF	IP	BFP	H	R	ER	HR	SH	SF	HB	TBB	IBB	SO	WP	Bk	W	L	Pct.	ShO	Sv	ERA
1987 Expos	R	12	11	2	0	54.2	252	62	45	30	1	0	0	3	28	0	61	6	0	3	4	.429	0	0	4.94
1988 Rockford	A	28	27	0	0	150.1	673	148	93	80	4	4	8	8	87	1	63	14	5	11	12	.478	0	0	4.79
1989 Rockford	A	15	15	0	0	87	395	85	51	46	2	4	2	3	54	0	53	14	1	3	6	.333	0	0	4.76
Burlington	A	11	11	1	0	69	294	69	37	35	6	2	5	2	28	0	34	8	0	2	6	.250	0	0	4.57
1990 Durham	A	25	24	2	0	133	579	143	75	56	11	4	3	5	46	0	100	13	2	4	11	.267	2	0	3.79
1991 Miami	A	13	13	4	0	95.1	378	81	31	20	1	2	1	4	32	0	61	1	2	5	3	.625	1	0	1.89
Durham	A	15	12	3	0	89	354	72	31	28	3	0	1	3	29	0	77	6	0	6	6	.500	0	0	2.83
1992 Greenville	AA	28	25	5	1	172	684	137	51	44	7	3	3	7	40	2	115	9	0	13	6	.684	4	0	2.30
Pawtucket	AAA	2	0	0	2	7	23	3	0	0	0	0	0	0	0	0	4	0	0	2	0	1.000	0	0	0.00
1993 Pawtucket	AAA	29	29	7	0	194.2	814	182	103	87	22	7	5	10	50	1	113	8	0	7	14	.333	2	0	4.02
1994 Pawtucket	AAA	23	22	6	1	151.1	622	128	65	51	14	1	4	5	51	0	93	7	1	11	5	.688	2	0	3.03
1995 Louisville	AAA	26	24	1	0	147.1	633	153	77	61	9	4	5	7	42	0	67	9	1	8	7	.533	0	0	3.73
1993 Boston	AL	5	5	1	0	33	142	35	16	13	5	1	0	0	8	2	18	2	0	1	2	.333	0	0	3.55
1994 Boston	AL	6	5	0	0	23	121	44	26	22	1	1	3	0	14	2	15	3	1	2	3	.400	0	0	8.61
9 Min. YEARS		227	213	31	4	1350.2	5701	1263	659	538	80	31	37	56	487	4	841	95	12	75	80	.484	11	0	3.58
2 Maj. YEARS		11	10	1	0	56	262	79	42	35	6	2	3	0	22	4	33	5	1	3	5	.375	0	0	5.63

Gino Minutelli

Pitches: Left **Bats:** Left **Pos:** P   **Ht:** 6'0" **Wt:** 185 **Born:** 5/23/64 **Age:** 32

Year Team	Lg	G	GS	CG	GF	IP	BFP	H	R	ER	HR	SH	SF	HB	TBB	IBB	SO	WP	Bk	W	L	Pct.	ShO	Sv	ERA
1985 Tri-City	A	20	10	0	7	57	57	61	57	51	3	0	0	6	57	0	79	6	0	4	8	.333	0	0	8.05
1986 Cedar Rapds	A	27	27	3	0	152.2	671	133	73	62	14	4	6	5	76	1	149	16	2	15	5	.750	2	0	3.66
1987 Tampa	A	17	15	5	1	104.1	461	98	51	44	4	10	3	5	48	4	70	13	1	7	6	.538	1	0	3.80
Vermont	AA	6	6	0	0	39.2	168	34	15	14	3	0	0	2	16	0	39	2	1	4	1	.800	0	0	3.18
1988 Chattanooga	AA	2	2	0	0	5.2	27	6	2	1	0	0	0	1	4	0	3	0	2	0	1	.000	0	0	1.59
1989 Reds	R	1	1	0	0	1	4	0	0	0	0	0	0	0	1	0	0	0	0	0	0	.000	0	0	0.00
Chattanooga	AA	6	6	1	0	29	140	28	19	17	1	0	1	6	23	0	20	8	4	1	1	.500	0	0	5.28
1990 Chattanooga	AA	17	17	5	0	108.1	467	106	52	48	9	5	2	2	46	1	75	5	13	9	5	.643	0	0	3.99
Nashville	AAA	11	11	3	0	78.1	315	65	34	28	5	1	1	1	31	0	61	1	0	5	2	.714	0	0	3.22
1991 Charlstn-Wv	A	2	2	0	0	8	28	2	0	0	0	0	0	0	4	0	8	0	0	1	0	1.000	0	0	0.00
Nashville	AAA	13	13	1	0	80.1	325	57	25	17	3	6	2	1	35	2	64	6	1	4	7	.364	1	0	1.90
1992 Nashville	AAA	29	29	1	0	158	722	177	96	75	18	13	5	5	76	1	110	11	1	4	12	.250	0	0	4.27
1993 Phoenix	AAA	49	0	0	34	53.2	235	55	28	24	1	1	3	0	26	0	57	6	0	2	2	.500	0	11	4.02
1994 Tucson	AAA	35	0	0	14	60.1	275	87	50	45	13	4	3	1	11	2	50	5	0	4	4	.500	0	0	6.71
Canton-Akrn	AA	4	3	0	1	20	83	16	8	7	1	1	1	0	8	0	11	2	0	0	1	.000	0	0	3.15
1995 Richmond	AAA	5	3	0	0	16.1	70	20	8	8	0	1	0	0	3	0	8	0	0	0	0	.000	0	0	4.41
1990 Cincinnati	NL	2	0	0	0	1	6	0	1	1	0	0	0	1	2	0	1	0	0	0	0	.000	0	0	9.00

Year	Team	Lg	G				IP	BFP	H	R	ER							SO			W	L	Pct.		Sv	ERA
1991	Cincinnati	NL	16	3	0	2	25.1	124	30	17	17	5	0	2	0	18	1	21	3	0	0	2	.000	0	0	6.04
1993	San Francisco	NL	9	0	0	4	14.1	64	7	9	6	2	1	2	0	15	0	10	1	0	0	1	.000	0	0	3.77
	11 Min. YEARS		244	145	19	57	972.2	3991	945	518	441	75	46	28	35	465	11	804	81	27	60	55	.522	4	11	4.08
	3 Maj. YEARS		27	3	0	6	40.2	194	37	27	24	7	1	4	1	35	1	31	5	0	0	3	.000	0	0	5.31

Doug Mirabelli

Bats: Right **Throws:** Right **Pos:** C **Ht:** 6'1" **Wt:** 205 **Born:** 10/18/70 **Age:** 25

						BATTING											BASERUNNING				PERCENTAGES		
Year	Team	Lg	G	AB	H	2B	3B	HR	TB	R	RBI	TBB	IBB	SO	HBP	SH	SF	SB	CS	SB%	GDP	Avg	OBP	SLG
1992	San Jose	A	53	177	41	11	1	0	54	30	21	24	0	18	4	2	2	1	3	.25	7	.232	.333	.305
1993	San Jose	A	113	371	100	19	2	1	126	58	48	72	1	55	4	2	4	0	4	.00	7	.270	.390	.340
1994	Shreveport	AA	85	255	56	8	0	4	76	23	24	36	5	48	0	2	0	3	1	.75	6	.220	.316	.298
1995	Phoenix	AAA	23	66	11	0	1	0	13	3	7	12	1	10	1	0	2	1	0	1.00	5	.167	.296	.197
	Shreveport	AA	40	126	38	13	0	0	51	14	16	20	1	14	0	2	0	1	0	1.00	3	.302	.397	.405
	4 Min. YEARS		314	995	246	51	4	5	320	128	116	164	8	145	9	8	8	6	8	.43	28	.247	.356	.322

Mike Misuraca

Pitches: Right **Bats:** Right **Pos:** P **Ht:** 6'0" **Wt:** 188 **Born:** 8/21/68 **Age:** 27

			HOW MUCH HE PITCHED						WHAT HE GAVE UP											THE RESULTS				
Year	Team	Lg	G	GS	CG	GF	IP	BFP	H	R	ER	HR	SH	SF	HB	TBB	IBB	SO	WP	Bk	W	L	Pct.	ShO	Sv	ERA
1989	Kenosha	A	9	9	0	0	46	204	47	32	27	9	3	0	5	15	0	30	1	4	1	5	.167	0	0	5.28
	Elizabethtn	R	13	13	9	0	103	424	92	34	29	3	4	4	5	33	0	89	8	6	10	3	.769	2	0	2.53
1990	Kenosha	A	26	26	1	0	167.1	718	164	81	62	6	5	4	12	57	1	116	6	8	9	9	.500	0	0	3.33
1991	Visalia	A	21	19	2	0	116	512	131	65	55	12	3	5	8	39	1	82	13	0	7	9	.438	1	0	4.27
1992	Miracle	A	28	28	3	0	157	687	163	84	63	7	7	4	9	63	1	107	4	0	7	14	.333	1	0	3.61
1993	Nashville	AA	25	17	2	2	113	483	103	57	48	9	6	1	5	40	0	80	7	1	6	6	.500	1	0	3.82
1994	Nashville	AA	17	17	0	0	106.2	450	115	56	43	10	1	2	5	22	0	80	4	0	8	4	.667	0	0	3.63
	Salt Lake	AAA	10	10	1	0	65.2	295	88	43	38	5	2	2	4	13	0	51	6	0	3	5	.375	0	0	5.21
1995	Salt Lake	AAA	31	19	1	2	143.1	628	174	93	85	15	0	6	8	36	1	67	7	0	9	6	.600	0	0	5.34
	7 Min. YEARS		180	158	19	4	1018	4401	1077	545	450	76	31	28	61	318	4	702	56	19	60	61	.496	5	0	3.98

John Mitchell

Pitches: Right **Bats:** Right **Pos:** P **Ht:** 6'2" **Wt:** 189 **Born:** 8/11/65 **Age:** 30

			HOW MUCH HE PITCHED						WHAT HE GAVE UP											THE RESULTS				
Year	Team	Lg	G	GS	CG	GF	IP	BFP	H	R	ER	HR	SH	SF	HB	TBB	IBB	SO	WP	Bk	W	L	Pct.	ShO	Sv	ERA
1984	Winter Havn	A	27	27	4	0	183.2	775	160	84	64	9	3	6	5	66	2	109	21	2	16	9	.640	0	0	3.14
1985	New Britain	AA	26	26	10	0	190.1	766	143	71	57	4	7	2	2	61	4	108	11	1	12	8	.600	1	0	2.70
1986	Tidewater	AAA	27	27	5	0	172.1	729	162	78	65	10	3	4	6	59	2	83	7	1	12	9	.571	2	0	3.39
1987	Tidewater	AAA	8	8	1	0	48.2	212	44	24	18	2	1	2	3	20	0	16	4	1	3	2	.600	1	0	3.33
1988	Tidewater	AAA	27	27	7	0	190	767	164	76	60	8	6	5	6	45	1	65	7	5	10	9	.526	2	0	2.84
1989	Tidewater	AAA	26	26	7	0	178.1	744	169	66	60	5	11	2	4	57	2	86	8	2	11	11	.500	2	0	3.03
1990	Rochester	AAA	8	7	3	0	46	178	39	9	8	3	0	0	1	9	0	15	0	0	5	0	1.000	2	0	1.57
1993	New Britain	AA	8	1	0	4	17.1	67	15	2	2	0	0	0	0	2	0	8	2	3	1	1	.500	0	1	1.04
1994	New Britain	AA	5	5	0	0	23.1	113	37	23	21	1	0	1	0	7	0	17	2	0	0	4	.000	0	0	8.10
	Okla. City	AAA	14	11	3	2	78.1	328	80	38	33	5	2	1	2	18	0	30	1	0	3	5	.375	2	0	3.79
1995	Ottawa	AAA	6	0	0	1	8.1	35	8	4	4	1	1	0	0	3	1	5	0	0	0	1	.000	0	0	4.32
1986	New York	NL	4	1	0	1	10	40	10	4	4	1	0	0	0	4	0	2	2	0	0	1	.000	0	0	3.60
1987	New York	NL	20	19	1	0	111.2	493	124	64	51	6	6	5	2	36	3	57	7	1	3	6	.333	0	0	4.11
1988	New York	NL	1	0	0	0	1	5	2	0	0	0	0	0	0	1	0	1	0	0	0	0	.000	0	0	0.00
1989	New York	NL	2	0	0	0	3	17	3	7	2	0	0	0	0	4	1	4	1	0	0	1	.000	0	0	6.00
1990	Baltimore	AL	24	17	0	2	114.1	509	133	63	59	7	6	8	3	48	3	43	3	0	6	6	.500	0	0	4.64
	10 Min. YEARS		182	165	40	7	1136.2	4714	1021	487	392	48	34	23	29	347	12	542	63	15	73	59	.553	12	1	3.10
	5 Maj. YEARS		51	37	1	3	240	1064	272	138	116	14	12	13	5	93	7	107	13	1	9	14	.391	0	0	4.35

Keith Mitchell

Bats: Right **Throws:** Right **Pos:** OF **Ht:** 5'10" **Wt:** 180 **Born:** 8/6/69 **Age:** 26

						BATTING											BASERUNNING				PERCENTAGES		
Year	Team	Lg	G	AB	H	2B	3B	HR	TB	R	RBI	TBB	IBB	SO	HBP	SH	SF	SB	CS	SB%	GDP	Avg	OBP	SLG
1987	Braves	R	57	208	50	12	1	2	70	24	21	29	0	50	2	0	2	7	2	.78	4	.240	.336	.337
1988	Sumter	A	98	341	85	16	1	5	118	35	33	41	0	50	4	3	2	9	6	.60	8	.249	.335	.346
1989	Burlington	A	127	448	117	23	0	10	170	64	49	70	1	65	5	0	4	12	7	.63	9	.261	.364	.379
1990	Durham	A	129	456	134	24	3	6	182	81	48	92	2	48	4	1	7	18	17	.51	16	.294	.411	.399
1991	Greenville	AA	60	214	70	15	3	10	121	46	47	29	0	29	1	3	5	12	8	.60	5	.327	.402	.565
	Richmond	AAA	25	95	31	6	1	2	45	16	17	9	0	13	1	2	3	0	2	.00	3	.326	.380	.474
1992	Richmond	AAA	121	403	91	19	1	4	124	45	50	66	2	55	4	2	4	14	9	.61	6	.226	.338	.308
1993	Richmond	AAA	110	353	82	23	1	4	119	59	44	44	0	48	2	3	3	9	5	.64	11	.232	.318	.337
1994	Calgary	AAA	9	39	10	0	0	4	22	6	12	2	0	4	0	0	1	0	0	.00	0	.256	.286	.564
1995	Indianapols	AAA	70	213	52	11	2	11	100	40	36	40	3	40	2	1	4	4	4	.50	7	.244	.363	.469
1991	Atlanta	NL	48	66	21	0	0	2	27	11	5	8	0	12	1	0	0	3	1	.75	1	.318	.392	.409
1994	Seattle	AL	46	128	29	2	0	5	46	21	15	18	0	22	1	1	1	0	0	.00	2	.227	.324	.359
	9 Min. YEARS		806	2770	722	149	13	58	1071	416	357	422	8	402	25	15	35	85	60	.59	69	.261	.359	.387
	2 Maj. YEARS		94	194	50	2	0	7	73	32	20	26	0	34	1	1	1	3	1	.75	3	.258	.347	.376

Larry Mitchell

Pitches: Right **Bats:** Right **Pos:** P **Ht:** 6'1" **Wt:** 200 **Born:** 10/16/71 **Age:** 24

			HOW MUCH HE PITCHED						WHAT HE GAVE UP									THE RESULTS				
Year	Team	Lg	G	GS	CG	GF	IP	BFP	H	R	ER	HR	SH	SF	HB	TBB	IBB	SO	WP	Bk	W	L	Pct.	ShO	Sv	ERA
1992	Martinsvlle	R	3	3	0	0	19	77	17	8	3	0	0	0	1	6	0	18	0	0	1	0	1.000	0	0	1.42
	Batavia	A	10	10	3	0	65	267	63	25	19	6	2	2	1	11	0	58	4	1	7	2	.778	1	0	2.63
1993	Spartanburg	A	19	19	4	0	116.1	505	113	55	53	3	2	7	3	54	0	114	14	0	6	6	.500	2	0	4.10
	Clearwater	A	9	9	1	0	57	234	50	23	19	0	5	2	0	21	1	45	4	1	4	4	.500	0	0	3.00
1994	Reading	AA	30	30	2	0	165.1	737	143	91	73	5	13	8	2	103	1	128	15	0	10	13	.435	0	0	3.97
1995	Reading	AA	25	24	1	1	128.1	584	136	85	79	13	2	2	4	72	4	107	7	1	6	11	.353	1	0	5.54
	4 Min. YEARS		96	95	11	1	551	2404	522	287	246	27	24	21	11	267	6	470	44	3	34	36	.486	4	0	4.02

Tony Mitchell

Bats: Both **Throws:** Right **Pos:** OF **Ht:** 6'4" **Wt:** 225 **Born:** 10/14/70 **Age:** 25

			BATTING														BASERUNNING				PERCENTAGES		
Year	Team	Lg	G	AB	H	2B	3B	HR	TB	R	RBI	TBB	IBB	SO	HBP	SH	SF	SB	CS	SB%	GDP	Avg	OBP	SLG
1989	Pirates	R	13	40	11	0	0	0	11	4	1	4	0	10	0	0	1	1	0	1.00	3	.275	.333	.275
1990	Pirates	R	44	102	30	4	2	3	47	18	13	8	0	21	1	0	0	3	4	.43	3	.294	.351	.461
1991	Welland	A	59	211	57	9	0	10	96	30	38	17	0	62	1	1	1	7	2	.78	4	.270	.326	.455
1992	Augusta	A	66	219	65	8	3	13	118	34	47	29	1	60	0	0	1	6	3	.67	3	.297	.378	.539
	Columbus	A	55	202	59	8	2	10	101	36	36	22	3	54	0	0	0	1	6	.14	5	.292	.362	.500
1993	Kinston	A	96	318	78	16	2	8	122	43	44	33	2	88	3	2	5	5	4	.56	8	.245	.318	.384
1994	Canton-Akrn	AA	130	494	130	24	0	25	229	70	89	41	0	114	5	0	5	6	1	.86	13	.263	.323	.464
1995	Jackson	AA	96	331	88	17	2	19	166	45	61	35	1	82	1	0	3	1	2	.33	10	.266	.335	.502
	7 Min. YEARS		559	1917	518	86	11	88	890	280	329	189	7	491	11	3	16	30	22	.58	49	.270	.337	.464

Greg Mix

Pitches: Right **Bats:** Right **Pos:** P **Ht:** 6'4" **Wt:** 210 **Born:** 8/21/71 **Age:** 24

			HOW MUCH HE PITCHED						WHAT HE GAVE UP									THE RESULTS				
Year	Team	Lg	G	GS	CG	GF	IP	BFP	H	R	ER	HR	SH	SF	HB	TBB	IBB	SO	WP	Bk	W	L	Pct.	ShO	Sv	ERA
1993	Elmira	A	17	1	0	8	45.1	205	51	26	21	4	0	1	4	17	0	38	6	0	3	3	.500	0	2	4.17
1994	Brevard Cty	A	44	0	0	22	78	314	65	29	27	2	4	4	2	20	2	51	1	0	6	2	.750	0	4	3.12
1995	Brevard Cty	A	5	4	1	0	29.2	119	27	13	13	1	0	0	3	10	0	17	1	1	3	1	.750	0	0	3.94
	Portland	AA	24	13	0	1	92.1	401	98	51	48	9	2	4	4	25	5	56	3	0	6	4	.600	0	0	4.68
	3 Min. YEARS		90	18	1	31	245.1	1039	241	119	109	16	6	9	13	72	7	162	9	1	18	10	.643	0	6	4.00

Doug Mlicki

Pitches: Right **Bats:** Right **Pos:** P **Ht:** 6'3" **Wt:** 175 **Born:** 4/23/71 **Age:** 25

			HOW MUCH HE PITCHED						WHAT HE GAVE UP									THE RESULTS				
Year	Team	Lg	G	GS	CG	GF	IP	BFP	H	R	ER	HR	SH	SF	HB	TBB	IBB	SO	WP	Bk	W	L	Pct.	ShO	Sv	ERA
1992	Auburn	A	14	13	0	0	81.1	330	50	35	27	4	1	3	6	30	0	83	9	2	1	6	.143	0	0	2.99
1993	Osceola	A	26	23	0	0	158.2	668	158	81	69	16	6	5	2	65	1	111	9	0	11	10	.524	0	0	3.91
1994	Jackson	AA	23	23	1	0	138.2	575	107	62	52	20	5	2	8	54	5	130	13	3	13	7	.650	0	0	3.38
1995	Jackson	AA	16	16	2	0	96.2	390	73	41	30	6	1	2	4	33	0	72	5	0	8	3	.727	0	0	2.79
	Tucson	AAA	6	6	0	0	34	155	44	27	21	3	2	1	2	6	0	22	1	0	1	2	.333	0	0	5.56
	4 Min. YEARS		85	81	3	0	509.1	2118	432	246	199	49	15	13	22	188	6	418	37	5	34	28	.548	0	0	3.52

Brian Moehler

Pitches: Right **Bats:** Right **Pos:** P **Ht:** 6'3" **Wt:** 195 **Born:** 12/31/71 **Age:** 24

			HOW MUCH HE PITCHED						WHAT HE GAVE UP									THE RESULTS				
Year	Team	Lg	G	GS	CG	GF	IP	BFP	H	R	ER	HR	SH	SF	HB	TBB	IBB	SO	WP	Bk	W	L	Pct.	ShO	Sv	ERA
1993	Niagara Fal	A	12	11	0	0	58.2	262	51	33	21	3	1	3	4	27	0	38	8	2	6	5	.545	0	0	3.22
1994	Lakeland	A	26	25	5	0	164.2	687	153	66	55	3	7	7	6	65	0	92	8	3	12	12	.500	2	0	3.01
1995	Jacksonvlle	AA	28	27	0	1	162.1	696	176	94	87	14	3	5	6	52	1	89	15	0	8	10	.444	0	0	4.82
	3 Min. YEARS		66	63	5	1	385.2	1645	380	193	163	20	11	15	16	144	1	219	31	5	26	27	.491	2	0	3.80

Jason Moler

Bats: Right **Throws:** Right **Pos:** 3B **Ht:** 6'1" **Wt:** 195 **Born:** 10/29/69 **Age:** 26

			BATTING														BASERUNNING				PERCENTAGES		
Year	Team	Lg	G	AB	H	2B	3B	HR	TB	R	RBI	TBB	IBB	SO	HBP	SH	SF	SB	CS	SB%	GDP	Avg	OBP	SLG
1993	Clearwater	A	97	350	101	17	2	15	167	59	64	46	3	40	3	0	4	5	7	.42	10	.289	.372	.477
	Reading	AA	38	138	39	11	0	2	56	15	19	12	0	31	2	0	1	1	1	.50	4	.283	.346	.406
1994	Scranton-Wb	AAA	44	144	35	9	1	2	52	16	16	18	1	26	1	2	2	2	2	.50	5	.243	.327	.361
	Reading	AA	78	285	81	13	3	4	112	37	37	29	1	21	2	0	1	7	6	.54	8	.284	.353	.393
1995	Reading	AA	22	83	22	3	0	2	31	17	14	12	2	13	0	0	1	2	2	.50	1	.265	.354	.373
	3 Min. YEARS		279	1000	278	53	6	25	418	144	150	117	7	131	8	2	9	17	18	.49	28	.278	.355	.418

Ben Molina

Bats: Right **Throws:** Right **Pos:** C **Ht:** 5'11" **Wt:** 190 **Born:** 7/20/74 **Age:** 21

			BATTING														BASERUNNING				PERCENTAGES		
Year	Team	Lg	G	AB	H	2B	3B	HR	TB	R	RBI	TBB	IBB	SO	HBP	SH	SF	SB	CS	SB%	GDP	Avg	OBP	SLG
1993	Angels	R	27	80	21	6	2	0	31	9	10	10	0	4	1	0	1	0	2	.00	0	.263	.348	.388
1994	Cedar Rapds	A	48	171	48	8	0	3	65	14	16	8	0	12	3	1	0	1	2	.33	3	.281	.324	.380

Year Team	Lg	G	AB	H	2B	3B	HR	TB	R	RBI	TBB	IBB	SO	HBP	SH	SF	SB	CS	SB%	GDP	Avg	OBP	SLG
1995 Vancouver	AAA	1	2	0	0	0	0	0	0	0	0	0	1	0	0	0	0	0	.00	0	.000	.000	.000
Cedar Rapds	A	39	133	39	9	0	4	60	15	17	15	0	11	1	1	1	1	1	.50	4	.293	.367	.451
Lk Elsinore	A	27	96	37	7	2	2	54	21	12	8	1	7	4	3	1	0	0	.00	2	.385	.450	.563
3 Min. YEARS		142	482	145	30	4	9	210	59	55	41	1	35	9	5	3	2	5	.29	10	.301	.364	.436

Izzy Molina

Bats: Right **Throws:** Right **Pos:** C **Ht:** 6'0" **Wt:** 200 **Born:** 6/3/71 **Age:** 25

								BATTING											BASERUNNING			PERCENTAGES		
Year Team	Lg	G	AB	H	2B	3B	HR	TB	R	RBI	TBB	IBB	SO	HBP	SH	SF	SB	CS	SB%	GDP	Avg	OBP	SLG
1990 Athletics	R	38	122	43	12	2	0	59	19	18	9	1	21	2	1	3	5	0	1.00	0	.352	.397	.484
1991 Madison	A	95	316	89	16	1	3	116	35	45	15	1	40	6	1	4	6	4	.60	9	.282	.323	.367
1992 Reno	A	116	436	113	17	2	10	164	71	75	39	0	57	7	7	6	8	7	.53	20	.259	.326	.376
Tacoma	AAA	10	36	7	0	1	0	9	3	5	2	0	6	0	0	0	1	0	1.00	1	.194	.237	.250
1993 Modesto	A	125	444	116	26	5	6	170	61	69	44	0	85	3	4	11	2	8	.20	11	.261	.325	.383
1994 Huntsville	AA	116	388	84	17	2	8	129	31	50	16	0	47	5	7	7	5	1	.83	10	.216	.252	.332
1995 Edmonton	AAA	2	6	1	0	0	0	1	0	0	0	0	2	0	0	0	0	0	.00	0	.167	.167	.167
Huntsville	AA	83	301	78	16	1	8	120	38	26	26	0	62	8	0	2	3	4	.43	6	.259	.332	.399
6 Min. YEARS		585	2049	531	104	14	35	768	258	288	151	2	320	31	20	33	30	24	.56	57	.259	.315	.375

Johnny Monell

Bats: Both **Throws:** Right **Pos:** DH **Ht:** 5'10" **Wt:** 180 **Born:** 10/31/65 **Age:** 30

								BATTING											BASERUNNING			PERCENTAGES		
Year Team	Lg	G	AB	H	2B	3B	HR	TB	R	RBI	TBB	IBB	SO	HBP	SH	SF	SB	CS	SB%	GDP	Avg	OBP	SLG
1985 Little Fall	A	67	211	45	9	2	2	64	17	25	20	3	25	0	1	4	7	7	.50	5	.213	.277	.303
1986 Columbia	A	86	258	67	9	2	6	98	50	46	21	1	38	0	0	2	11	4	.73	8	.260	.313	.380
1987 Columbia	A	100	358	101	21	5	4	144	61	41	33	2	40	5	1	5	20	8	.71	13	.282	.347	.402
Lynchburg	A	29	122	40	13	3	3	68	20	17	7	1	10	0	1	1	3	1	.75	4	.328	.362	.557
Tidewater	AAA	1	1	0	0	0	0	0	0	0	0	0	1	0	0	0	0	0	.00	0	.000	.000	.000
1988 Jackson	AA	13	40	10	2	0	1	15	4	5	2	0	4	0	0	1	0	0	.00	2	.250	.279	.375
St. Lucie	A	116	441	125	18	5	3	162	55	48	24	7	37	9	2	7	16	6	.73	9	.283	.328	.367
1989 Jackson	AA	80	232	72	6	2	6	100	27	29	13	4	28	1	1	2	6	1	.86	3	.310	.347	.431
1990 Tidewater	AAA	13	33	6	0	0	0	6	3	4	2	0	5	0	0	0	1	0	1.00	3	.182	.229	.182
Midland	AA	32	126	33	5	1	3	49	12	19	11	1	15	1	0	0	5	3	.63	4	.262	.326	.389
1995 Tulsa	AA	121	434	133	18	1	12	189	55	64	67	6	52	6	0	6	0	1	.00	10	.306	.402	.435
7 Min. YEARS		658	2256	632	101	21	40	895	304	298	200	25	255	22	6	28	69	31	.69	61	.280	.341	.397

Michael Mongiello

Pitches: Right **Bats:** Right **Pos:** P **Ht:** 6'2" **Wt:** 215 **Born:** 1/19/68 **Age:** 28

		HOW MUCH HE PITCHED						WHAT HE GAVE UP									THE RESULTS					
Year Team	Lg	G	GS	CG	GF	IP	BFP	H	R	ER	HR	SH	SF	HB	TBB	IBB	SO	WP	Bk	W	L	Pct.	ShO	Sv	ERA
1989 White Sox	R	8	4	0	3	32.2	135	28	16	13	2	0	0	2	13	0	28	3	1	1	3	.250	0	2	3.58
1990 South Bend	A	38	15	3	21	106.1	470	98	55	39	3	6	3	2	54	4	89	5	8	6	6	.500	1	13	3.30
1991 Sarasota	A	55	0	0	44	68	292	51	26	17	1	3	1	1	34	5	62	5	4	4	4	.500	0	23	2.25
1992 Birmingham	AA	44	3	0	25	82.1	351	76	38	35	3	2	2	5	38	3	73	12	0	5	2	.714	0	8	3.83
1993 Birmingham	AA	7	1	0	4	11.2	46	5	6	2	0	0	0	2	4	0	9	3	0	0	1	.000	0	1	1.54
Nashville	AAA	39	9	1	19	91	391	88	44	43	10	4	2	4	41	3	73	7	0	6	4	.600	0	7	4.25
1994 Nashville	AAA	45	5	0	13	86.1	393	94	39	35	6	10	1	3	49	7	77	7	0	4	6	.400	0	3	3.65
1995 Birmingham	AA	7	5	0	1	31.2	120	23	8	7	2	1	0	1	6	0	23	0	0	3	1	.750	0	0	1.99
Nashville	AAA	31	8	1	7	91	408	104	59	52	10	1	6	4	37	3	72	3	0	3	3	.500	0	1	5.14
7 Min. YEARS		274	50	5	137	601	2606	567	291	243	37	27	15	24	276	25	506	45	13	32	30	.516	1	55	3.64

Rafael Montalvo

Pitches: Right **Bats:** Right **Pos:** P **Ht:** 6'0" **Wt:** 185 **Born:** 3/31/64 **Age:** 32

		HOW MUCH HE PITCHED						WHAT HE GAVE UP									THE RESULTS					
Year Team	Lg	G	GS	CG	GF	IP	BFP	H	R	ER	HR	SH	SF	HB	TBB	IBB	SO	WP	Bk	W	L	Pct.	ShO	Sv	ERA
1984 San Antonio	AA	20	0	0	16	22.2	99	17	8	5	0	4	0	1	12	0	7	0	0	0	1	.000	0	7	1.99
Albuquerque	AAA	45	0	0	31	63.1	0	73	42	31	5	0	0	1	40	10	46	4	0	3	3	.500	0	12	4.41
1985 Albuquerque	AAA	30	0	0	22	36.1	0	42	16	12	1	0	0	1	28	8	17	3	0	1	5	.167	0	9	2.97
Tucson	AAA	22	0	0	8	38.2	0	55	23	23	5	0	0	0	25	5	25	2	1	1	2	.333	0	4	5.35
1986 Tucson	AAA	47	0	0	29	77	328	78	39	33	7	5	1	0	21	3	31	3	0	5	3	.625	0	9	3.86
1987 Tucson	AAA	59	2	0	27	94.2	440	113	56	37	0	3	5	2	41	4	43	8	0	8	4	.667	0	4	3.52
1988 Tucson	AAA	62	4	0	16	116.2	526	148	62	57	4	3	5	1	43	7	67	7	6	9	1	.900	0	3	4.40
1990 Edmonton	AAA	48	0	0	21	85.1	345	76	33	26	3	5	2	1	22	4	42	2	0	1	5	.167	0	9	2.74
1991 Edmonton	AAA	25	0	0	10	26.1	132	39	26	20	1	1	2	3	12	2	15	0	0	1	0	1.000	0	2	6.84
Midland	AA	22	2	0	1	57.2	269	89	39	36	4	2	3	1	15	1	30	2	0	5	1	.833	0	1	5.62
1995 Albuquerque	AAA	49	0	0	19	98.1	430	105	44	29	5	2	3	4	34	7	65	1	0	3	5	.375	0	4	2.65
1986 Houston	NL	1	0	0	0	1	6	1	1	1	0	0	0	0	2	0	0	0	0	0	0	.000	0	0	9.00
8 Min. YEARS		429	8	0	200	717	2569	835	388	309	35	25	21	15	293	51	388	32	7	37	30	.552	0	63	3.88

Rob Montalvo

Bats: Right **Throws:** Right **Pos:** SS **Ht:** 6'1" **Wt:** 165 **Born:** 3/25/70 **Age:** 26

								BATTING											BASERUNNING			PERCENTAGES		
Year Team	Lg	G	AB	H	2B	3B	HR	TB	R	RBI	TBB	IBB	SO	HBP	SH	SF	SB	CS	SB%	GDP	Avg	OBP	SLG
1988 St. Cathrns	A	62	190	32	4	0	0	36	19	18	25	0	48	0	4	1	4	5	.44	3	.168	.264	.189
1989 Dunedin	A	14	41	6	1	0	0	7	3	4	12	0	13	0	0	0	0	0	.00	0	.146	.340	.171

Team	Lg	G	AB	H	2B	3B	HR	TB	R	RBI	TBB	IBB	SO	HBP	SH	SF	SB	CS	SB%	GDP	Avg	OBP	SLG
Myrtle Bch	A	52	148	28	2	0	0	30	15	10	32	0	37	0	1	0	1	2	.33	2	.189	.333	.203
1990 St. Cathrns	A	38	115	21	2	0	0	23	11	5	21	1	19	1	1	1	1	2	.33	4	.183	.312	.200
Myrtle Bch	A	45	125	25	1	0	0	26	15	11	9	0	14	1	3	1	2	2	.50	2	.200	.257	.208
1991 Knoxville	AA	15	31	5	1	0	0	6	3	0	7	0	7	1	1	0	0	0	.00	0	.161	.333	.194
Dunedin	A	86	291	67	3	1	0	72	21	21	21	0	54	1	21	4	4	1	.80	6	.230	.281	.247
Syracuse	AAA	1	3	0	0	0	0	0	0	0	0	0	0	0	0	0	0	0	.00	0	.000	.000	.000
1992 Knoxville	AA	32	72	12	1	0	0	13	7	4	12	0	19	0	5	0	1	1	.50	3	.167	.286	.181
Syracuse	AAA	66	168	39	8	0	2	53	20	14	15	0	22	3	6	2	2	0	1.00	4	.232	.303	.315
1993 Syracuse	AAA	85	234	50	6	1	0	58	25	16	21	0	47	0	10	3	1	1	.50	7	.214	.275	.248
1994 Dunedin	A	7	17	7	1	0	0	8	5	1	3	0	2	0	0	0	0	0	.00	0	.412	.500	.471
Syracuse	AAA	74	179	41	8	0	1	52	24	16	12	1	43	0	6	1	3	3	.50	2	.229	.276	.291
1995 Syracuse	AAA	11	26	1	0	0	0	1	0	1	2	0	8	0	0	0	0	0	.00	1	.038	.107	.038
Thunder Bay	IND	39	124	28	8	1	1	41	19	10	23	0	23	1	5	2	4	3	.57	3	.226	.347	.331
8 Min. YEARS		627	1764	362	46	3	4	426	187	131	215	2	356	8	63	15	23	20	.53	37	.205	.292	.241

Ray Montgomery

Bats: Right Throws: Right Pos: OF   Ht: 6'3" Wt: 195 Born: 8/8/69 Age: 26

						BATTING												BASERUNNING				PERCENTAGES		
Year Team	Lg	G	AB	H	2B	3B	HR	TB	R	RBI	TBB	IBB	SO	HBP	SH	SF	SB	CS	SB%	GDP	Avg	OBP	SLG
1990 Auburn	A	61	193	45	8	1	0	55	19	13	23	1	32	1	4	1	11	5	.69	5	.233	.317	.285
1991 Burlington	A	120	433	109	24	3	3	148	60	57	37	1	66	8	11	2	17	14	.55	10	.252	.321	.342
1992 Jackson	A	51	148	31	4	1	1	40	13	10	7	2	27	0	1	1	4	1	.80	5	.209	.244	.270
1993 Tucson	AAA	15	50	17	3	1	2	28	9	6	5	0	7	1	1	0	1	2	.33	1	.340	.411	.560
Jackson	AA	100	338	95	16	3	10	147	50	59	36	1	54	6	1	6	12	6	.67	7	.281	.355	.435
1994 Tucson	AAA	103	332	85	19	6	7	137	51	51	35	6	54	2	2	3	5	3	.63	9	.256	.328	.413
1995 Jackson	AA	35	127	38	8	1	10	78	24	24	13	2	13	5	0	1	6	3	.67	3	.299	.384	.614
Tucson	AAA	88	291	88	19	0	11	140	48	68	24	1	58	2	1	8	5	3	.63	3	.302	.351	.481
6 Min. YEARS		573	1912	508	101	16	44	773	274	288	180	14	311	25	21	22	61	37	.62	43	.266	.333	.404

Steve Montgomery

Pitches: Right Bats: Right Pos: P   Ht: 6'4" Wt: 200 Born: 12/25/70 Age: 25

				HOW MUCH HE PITCHED					WHAT HE GAVE UP									THE RESULTS					
Year Team	Lg	G	GS	CG	GF	IP	BFP	H	R	ER	HR	SH	SF	HB	TBB	IBB	SO	WP	Bk	W	L	Pct.	ShO	Sv	ERA
1993 St. Pete	A	14	5	0	7	40.2	161	33	14	12	2	1	2	0	9	0	34	1	0	2	1	.667	0	3	2.66
Arkansas	AA	6	6	0	0	32	140	34	17	14	2	2	0	0	12	2	19	2	0	3	3	.500	0	0	3.94
1994 Arkansas	AA	50	9	0	19	107	447	97	43	39	10	4	4	3	33	3	73	5	0	4	5	.444	0	2	3.28
1995 Arkansas	AA	55	0	0	53	61	259	52	22	22	6	7	1	4	22	6	56	5	1	5	2	.714	0	36	3.25
3 Min. YEARS		125	20	0	79	240.2	1007	216	96	87	20	14	7	7	76	11	182	13	1	14	11	.560	0	41	3.25

Al Montoya

Pitches: Left Bats: Left Pos: P   Ht: 6'2" Wt: 168 Born: 6/10/69 Age: 27

				HOW MUCH HE PITCHED					WHAT HE GAVE UP									THE RESULTS					
Year Team	Lg	G	GS	CG	GF	IP	BFP	H	R	ER	HR	SH	SF	HB	TBB	IBB	SO	WP	Bk	W	L	Pct.	ShO	Sv	ERA
1991 Medicne Hat	R	15	14	5	1	82.1	359	94	46	37	4	2	2	2	21	0	56	10	9	5	7	.417	1	1	4.04
1992 Myrtle Bch	A	42	2	0	21	99	412	96	36	31	7	3	1	4	33	4	99	9	3	4	4	.500	0	10	2.82
1993 Dunedin	A	50	1	0	22	80.1	349	78	37	32	2	2	2	2	26	5	35	5	2	7	4	.636	0	6	3.50
Knoxville	AA	5	0	0	0	7	32	8	4	4	1	0	1	1	3	0	9	3	0	1	0	1.000	0	0	5.14
1994 Knoxville	AA	36	2	1	19	80.2	362	103	48	36	5	0	3	9	26	2	42	5	3	3	5	.375	0	2	4.02
1995 Syracuse	AAA	7	0	0	0	4.1	16	3	1	0	0	0	0	0	3	1	2	0	0	0	0	.000	0	0	0.00
Amarillo	IND	31	1	0	18	51.2	223	58	30	24	4	2	3	1	14	0	28	4	1	2	1	.667	0	4	4.18
5 Min. YEARS		186	20	6	81	405.1	1755	440	202	164	23	9	12	19	126	12	271	36	18	22	21	.512	1	22	3.64

Norm Montoya

Pitches: Left Bats: Left Pos: P   Ht: 6'1" Wt: 190 Born: 9/24/70 Age: 25

				HOW MUCH HE PITCHED					WHAT HE GAVE UP									THE RESULTS					
Year Team	Lg	G	GS	CG	GF	IP	BFP	H	R	ER	HR	SH	SF	HB	TBB	IBB	SO	WP	Bk	W	L	Pct.	ShO	Sv	ERA
1990 Angels	R	10	6	1	2	42	199	49	20	11	1	1	0	1	7	0	28	0	0	3	3	.500	0	1	2.11
Quad City	A	4	4	1	0	28.2	117	30	12	10	0	1	1	0	6	0	13	0	1	3	1	.750	0	0	3.14
1991 Quad City	A	8	8	0	0	40.1	186	55	27	23	2	1	1	0	12	0	22	4	1	4	1	.800	0	0	5.13
Palm Spring	A	17	17	1	0	105	455	117	64	48	10	3	2	2	26	4	45	3	1	4	7	.364	0	0	4.11
1992 Palm Spring	A	14	6	2	6	43.2	194	42	21	18	3	4	2	1	19	1	46	2	1	2	3	.400	0	0	3.71
1993 Palm Spring	A	28	4	0	8	63.2	286	83	38	34	0	3	4	3	21	5	35	6	0	1	3	.250	0	0	4.81
1994 Stockton	A	11	0	0	3	16.1	65	12	6	4	1	2	0	1	3	0	15	0	0	1	0	1.000	0	1	2.20
El Paso	AA	9	0	0	4	12.1	48	10	5	4	0	1	0	0	4	2	8	0	0	1	1	.500	0	1	2.92
1995 El Paso	AA	51	0	0	9	76.1	331	88	36	29	3	5	2	2	18	5	43	4	0	2	5	.286	0	2	3.42
6 Min. YEARS		152	45	5	32	433.1	1881	486	229	181	20	21	12	10	116	17	255	19	4	20	25	.444	0	5	3.76

Charlie Montoyo

Bats: Right Throws: Right Pos: 3B   Ht: 5'11" Wt: 170 Born: 10/17/65 Age: 30

						BATTING												BASERUNNING				PERCENTAGES		
Year Team	Lg	G	AB	H	2B	3B	HR	TB	R	RBI	TBB	IBB	SO	HBP	SH	SF	SB	CS	SB%	GDP	Avg	OBP	SLG
1987 Helena	R	13	45	13	1	2	0	18	12	2	12	0	3	0	0	1	2	1	.67	0	.289	.431	.400
Beloit	A	55	188	50	9	2	5	78	46	19	52	0	22	4	1	1	8	0	1.00	3	.266	.433	.415
1988 Stockton	A	132	450	115	14	1	3	140	103	61	156	0	93	5	6	2	16	6	.73	7	.256	.450	.311
1989 Stockton	A	129	448	111	22	2	0	137	69	48	102	3	40	11	6	4	13	9	.59	7	.248	.396	.306

Year	Team	Lg	G	AB	H	2B	3B	HR	TB	R	RBI	TBB	IBB	SO	HBP	SH	SF	SB	CS	SB%	GDP	Avg	OBP	SLG
1990	El Paso	AA	94	322	93	13	3	3	121	71	44	72	1	43	8	1	2	9	0	1.00	9	.289	.428	.376
1991	Denver	AAA	120	394	94	13	1	12	145	68	45	69	0	51	5	6	4	15	4	.79	6	.239	.356	.368
1992	Denver	AAA	84	259	84	7	4	2	105	40	34	47	0	36	1	2	1	3	5	.38	10	.324	.429	.405
1993	Ottawa	AAA	99	319	89	18	2	1	114	43	43	71	0	37	4	6	5	0	9	.00	11	.279	.411	.357
1994	Scranton-Wb	AAA	114	387	109	28	0	9	164	64	47	74	4	61	5	10	1	3	3	.50	10	.282	.403	.424
1995	Scranton-Wb	AAA	92	288	70	13	1	3	94	32	34	50	1	45	1	5	3	2	3	.40	4	.243	.354	.326
1993	Montreal	NL	4	5	2	1	0	0	3	1	3	0	0	0	0	0	0	0	0	.00	0	.400	.400	.600
	9 Min. YEARS		932	3100	828	138	18	38	1116	548	377	705	9	431	44	43	24	71	40	.64	68	.267	.407	.360

Jose Monzon

Bats: Right **Throws:** Right **Pos:** C   **Ht:** 6'1" **Wt:** 178 **Born:** 11/8/68 **Age:** 27

					BATTING													BASERUNNING				PERCENTAGES		
Year	Team	Lg	G	AB	H	2B	3B	HR	TB	R	RBI	TBB	IBB	SO	HBP	SH	SF	SB	CS	SB%	GDP	Avg	OBP	SLG
1987	Bristol	R	7	12	3	1	0	0	4	3	1	0	0	1	0	0	0	0	0	.00	1	.250	.250	.333
	Lakeland	A	4	5	0	0	0	0	0	0	0	0	0	4	0	2	0	0	0	.00	0	.000	.000	.000
	Fayettevlle	A	11	19	1	0	0	0	1	1	0	2	0	5	0	0	0	0	0	.00	0	.053	.143	.053
1989	Dunedin	A	16	48	12	2	1	0	16	4	7	5	0	11	0	0	0	0	0	.00	1	.250	.321	.333
	Myrtle Bch	A	50	165	39	7	0	1	49	18	10	19	0	31	0	0	0	3	2	.60	7	.236	.315	.297
1990	Dunedin	A	30	76	23	5	1	0	30	11	7	10	0	18	1	1	0	1	0	1.00	0	.303	.391	.395
	Knoxville	AA	1	3	1	0	0	0	1	1	0	0	0	0	0	0	0	0	0	.00	0	.333	.333	.333
1991	Dunedin	A	46	144	31	6	0	3	46	14	17	17	0	31	0	6	2	2	0	1.00	4	.215	.294	.319
	Knoxville	AA	44	116	31	5	0	0	36	12	11	13	1	23	0	1	1	1	1	.50	5	.267	.338	.310
1992	Knoxville	AA	65	178	41	9	1	0	52	17	10	12	0	42	2	3	1	3	2	.60	3	.230	.285	.292
	Syracuse	AAA	9	18	1	0	0	0	1	3	1	2	0	1	0	0	0	0	0	.00	1	.056	.150	.056
1993	Syracuse	AAA	71	197	47	7	0	3	63	14	21	11	0	37	0	4	0	0	1	.00	9	.239	.279	.320
1994	Midland	AA	83	283	71	18	3	4	107	41	35	24	0	52	2	3	0	1	1	.50	7	.251	.314	.378
1995	Vancouver	AAA	13	23	5	1	0	1	9	5	5	3	0	2	0	0	0	0	0	.00	1	.217	.308	.391
	Midland	AA	57	180	52	11	1	1	68	29	19	22	0	36	2	3	2	0	0	.00	6	.289	.369	.378
	8 Min. YEARS		507	1467	358	72	7	13	483	173	144	140	1	294	7	23	6	11	7	.61	45	.244	.312	.329

Ritch Moody

Pitches: Left **Bats:** Right **Pos:** P   **Ht:** 6'1" **Wt:** 185 **Born:** 2/22/71 **Age:** 25

			HOW MUCH HE PITCHED					WHAT HE GAVE UP										THE RESULTS					
Year	Team	Lg	G	GS	CG	GF	IP	BFP	H	R	ER	HR	SH	SF	HB	TBB	IBB	SO	WP	Bk	W	L	Pct.	ShO	Sv	ERA
1992	Gastonia	A	21	0	0	15	26.1	107	9	7	1	0	1	1	0	16	0	29	4	1	0	2	.000	0	11	0.34
	Tulsa	AA	7	0	0	7	6.1	26	3	2	1	0	0	0	1	2	0	6	1	0	0	0	.000	0	2	1.42
1993	Tulsa	AA	46	0	0	38	66	287	58	27	16	1	2	3	2	34	2	60	10	2	3	2	.600	0	16	2.18
1994	Okla. City	AAA	8	8	0	0	42	191	40	29	28	3	2	2	3	31	0	32	7	0	0	5	.000	0	0	6.00
1995	Rangers	R	2	2	0	0	10	46	10	3	3	0	0	0	0	6	0	10	1	0	0	0	.000	0	0	2.70
	Charlotte	A	1	1	0	0	4.1	22	3	3	3	0	1	0	0	8	0	0	1	0	0	1	.000	0	0	6.23
	Tulsa	AA	11	0	0	5	20.2	94	24	18	16	2	1	1	1	18	1	9	2	0	0	1	.000	0	0	6.97
	4 Min. YEARS		96	11	0	65	175.2	773	147	89	68	6	7	7	7	115	3	146	25	3	3	11	.214	0	29	3.48

Bobby Moore

Bats: Right **Throws:** Right **Pos:** OF   **Ht:** 5'9" **Wt:** 165 **Born:** 10/27/65 **Age:** 30

					BATTING													BASERUNNING				PERCENTAGES		
Year	Team	Lg	G	AB	H	2B	3B	HR	TB	R	RBI	TBB	IBB	SO	HBP	SH	SF	SB	CS	SB%	GDP	Avg	OBP	SLG
1987	Eugene	A	57	235	88	13	4	1	112	40	25	14	2	22	1	2	1	23	1	.96	5	.374	.410	.477
1988	Baseball Cy	A	60	224	52	4	2	0	60	25	10	17	0	20	2	4	0	12	7	.63	4	.232	.292	.268
1989	Baseball Cy	A	131	483	131	21	5	0	162	85	42	51	1	35	6	6	3	34	19	.64	6	.271	.346	.335
1990	Memphis	AA	112	422	128	20	6	2	166	93	36	56	0	32	2	8	4	27	7	.79	5	.303	.384	.393
1991	Omaha	AAA	130	494	120	13	3	0	139	65	34	37	0	41	3	13	2	35	15	.70	10	.243	.299	.281
1992	Richmond	AAA	92	316	79	13	3	0	98	41	25	21	0	26	0	6	3	14	6	.70	6	.250	.294	.310
1993	Richmond	AAA	1	3	2	0	0	0	2	2	0	1	0	0	0	0	0	1	0	1.00	0	.667	.750	.667
1994	Memphis	AA	27	97	23	2	1	2	33	10	7	8	0	15	1	2	1	1	2	.33	3	.237	.299	.340
	Richmond	AAA	60	216	79	6	3	5	106	37	18	18	1	16	0	1	2	10	6	.63	4	.366	.411	.491
1995	Richmond	AAA	108	329	85	18	2	3	116	45	27	27	4	27	4	3	2	9	7	.56	6	.258	.320	.353
1991	Kansas City	AL	18	14	5	1	0	0	6	3	0	1	0	2	0	0	0	3	2	.60	0	.357	.400	.429
	9 Min. YEARS		778	2819	787	110	29	13	994	443	224	250	5	234	19	45	18	166	70	.70	49	.279	.340	.353

Joel Moore

Pitches: Right **Bats:** Left **Pos:** P   **Ht:** 6'3" **Wt:** 200 **Born:** 8/13/72 **Age:** 23

			HOW MUCH HE PITCHED					WHAT HE GAVE UP										THE RESULTS					
Year	Team	Lg	G	GS	CG	GF	IP	BFP	H	R	ER	HR	SH	SF	HB	TBB	IBB	SO	WP	Bk	W	L	Pct.	ShO	Sv	ERA
1993	Bend	A	15	15	0	0	89.2	365	75	35	32	2	1	2	2	31	1	79	5	0	4	7	.364	0	0	3.21
1994	Central Val	A	25	24	0	0	133	607	149	78	67	8	6	1	8	64	1	89	12	1	11	8	.579	0	0	4.53
1995	New Haven	AA	27	26	1	0	157.1	682	156	69	56	8	6	6	8	67	2	102	5	1	14	6	.700	1	0	3.20
	3 Min. YEARS		67	65	1	0	380	1654	380	182	155	18	13	9	18	162	4	270	22	2	29	21	.580	1	0	3.67

Kerwin Moore

Bats: Both **Throws:** Right **Pos:** OF   **Ht:** 6'1" **Wt:** 190 **Born:** 10/29/70 **Age:** 25

					BATTING													BASERUNNING			PERCENTAGES		
Year	Team	Lg	G	AB	H	2B	3B	HR	TB	R	RBI	TBB	IBB	SO	HBP	SH	SF	SB	CS	SB%	GDP	Avg	OBP	SLG
1988	Royals	R	53	165	29	5	0	0	34	19	14	19	1	49	2	1	0	20	3	.87	2	.176	.269	.206
1989	Baseball Cy	A	4	11	4	0	0	1	7	3	2	1	0	2	0	0	0	0	0	.00	0	.364	.417	.636

Year	Team	Lg	G	AB	H	2B	3B	HR	TB	R	RBI	TBB	IBB	SO	HBP	SH	SF	SB	CS	SB%	GDP	Avg	OBP	SLG
	Eugene	A	65	226	50	9	2	2	69	44	25	36	0	75	2	1	0	20	6	.77	0	.221	.333	.305
1990	Appleton	A	128	451	100	17	7	2	137	93	36	111	2	139	3	6	1	57	19	.75	1	.222	.378	.304
1991	Baseball Cy	A	130	485	102	14	2	1	123	67	23	77	0	141	3	5	1	61	15	.80	5	.210	.322	.254
1992	Baseball Cy	A	66	248	59	2	1	1	66	39	10	40	1	67	2	4	1	26	9	.74	3	.238	.347	.266
	Memphis	AA	58	179	42	4	3	4	64	27	17	24	0	39	2	1	1	16	4	.80	2	.235	.330	.358
1993	High Desert	A	132	510	137	20	9	6	193	120	52	114	3	95	6	3	5	71	16	.82	3	.269	.405	.378
1994	Huntsville	AA	132	494	120	16	5	5	161	97	33	96	0	99	1	5	5	54	19	.74	11	.243	.364	.326
1995	Modesto	A	15	53	13	3	1	1	21	8	6	11	0	20	2	2	1	4	4	.50	2	.245	.388	.396
	Edmonton	AAA	72	265	74	14	4	2	102	53	26	47	1	67	1	3	1	10	3	.77	3	.279	.389	.385
	8 Min. YEARS		855	3087	730	104	34	25	977	570	244	576	8	793	24	31	16	339	98	.78	30	.236	.359	.316

Marcus Moore

Pitches: Right Bats: Both Pos: P **Ht: 6'5" Wt: 195 Born: 11/2/70 Age: 25**

			HOW MUCH HE PITCHED						WHAT HE GAVE UP												THE RESULTS				
Year	Team	Lg	G	GS	CG	GF	IP	BFP	H	R	ER	HR	SH	SF	HB	TBB	IBB	SO	WP	Bk	W	L	Pct.	ShO	Sv	ERA
1989	Bend	A	14	14	1	0	81.2	373	84	55	41	2	3	4	5	51	1	74	14	6	2	5	.286	1	0	4.52
1990	Quad City	A	27	27	2	0	160.1	717	150	83	59	6	2	7	3	106	0	160	13	9	16	5	.762	1	0	3.31
1991	Dunedin	A	27	25	2	1	160.2	694	139	78	66	3	9	5	4	99	3	115	12	9	6	13	.316	0	0	3.70
1992	Knoxville	AA	36	14	1	18	106.1	493	110	82	66	10	3	7	5	79	0	85	17	5	5	10	.333	0	0	5.59
1993	Central Val	A	8	0	0	8	12	53	7	3	1	0	1	0	0	9	0	15	1	0	1	0	1.000	0	2	0.75
	Colo. Sprng	AAA	30	0	0	14	44.1	209	54	26	22	3	3	1	1	29	0	38	4	0	1	5	.167	0	4	4.47
1994	Colo. Sprng	AAA	19	8	0	5	54	283	67	59	48	5	1	1	1	61	0	54	2	0	3	4	.429	0	0	8.00
1995	Indianapolis	AAA	7	1	0	2	12.2	62	13	8	7	0	1	0	0	14	2	6	0	0	1	0	1.000	0	1	4.97
	Chattanooga	AA	36	1	0	8	43.1	192	31	24	24	6	2	2	2	34	1	57	3	1	6	1	.857	0	2	4.98
1993	Colorado	NL	27	0	0	8	26.1	128	30	25	20	4	0	4	1	20	0	13	4	0	3	1	.750	0	0	6.84
1994	Colorado	NL	29	0	0	13	33.2	158	33	26	23	4	1	0	5	21	2	33	4	1	1	1	.500	0	0	6.15
	7 Min. YEARS		204	89	6	56	675.1	3076	655	418	334	35	25	27	21	482	7	604	66	30	41	43	.488	1	9	4.45
	2 Maj. YEARS		56	0	0	21	60	286	63	51	43	8	1	4	6	41	2	46	8	1	4	2	.667	0	0	6.45

Tim Moore

Bats: Both Throws: Left Pos: DH **Ht: 5'9" Wt: 215 Born: 8/27/71 Age: 24**

			BATTING														BASERUNNING				PERCENTAGES		
Year	Team	Lg	G	AB	H	2B	3B	HR	TB	R	RBI	TBB	IBB	SO	HBP	SH	SF	SB	CS	SB%	GDP	Avg	OBP	SLG
1989	Twins	R	37	95	16	3	0	0	19	10	10	24	0	26	0	0	0	19	1	.95	2	.168	.336	.200
1990	Twins	R	27	77	20	2	3	3	37	19	15	13	0	24	1	0	1	6	3	.67	0	.260	.370	.481
1991	Elizabethtn	R	57	197	52	17	1	12	107	33	37	28	3	57	2	0	1	7	2	.78	0	.264	.360	.543
1992	Kenosha	A	112	382	104	26	2	12	170	76	52	68	3	99	4	2	5	40	20	.67	11	.272	.383	.445
	Visalia	A	4	9	4	1	2	0	9	2	4	0	0	2	0	0	0	1	0	1.00	0	.444	.444	1.000
1993	Fort Myers	A	69	222	56	15	3	6	95	32	32	28	0	52	0	1	4	17	3	.85	0	.252	.331	.428
1994	Nashville	AA	123	436	108	25	0	18	187	50	67	38	3	130	8	2	4	9	10	.47	8	.248	.317	.429
1995	New Britain	AA	90	311	75	19	1	9	123	39	45	24	4	86	6	0	2	4	2	.67	7	.241	.306	.395
	7 Min. YEARS		519	1729	435	108	12	60	747	261	262	223	13	476	21	5	17	103	41	.72	31	.252	.341	.432

Tim Moore

Pitches: Right Bats: Right Pos: P **Ht: 6'4" Wt: 190 Born: 9/4/70 Age: 25**

			HOW MUCH HE PITCHED						WHAT HE GAVE UP												THE RESULTS				
Year	Team	Lg	G	GS	CG	GF	IP	BFP	H	R	ER	HR	SH	SF	HB	TBB	IBB	SO	WP	Bk	W	L	Pct.	ShO	Sv	ERA
1992	Utica	A	14	13	0	0	84.2	360	82	46	30	7	3	2	3	21	0	66	8	1	6	5	.545	0	0	3.19
1993	South Bend	A	26	26	4	0	165.1	692	156	89	83	21	6	7	12	52	0	108	8	1	11	9	.550	0	0	4.52
1994	Pr. William	A	27	0	0	13	66	279	59	24	19	4	6	1	2	24	0	77	3	1	2	2	.500	0	5	2.59
	Birmingham	AA	8	0	0	5	12.2	55	16	12	8	2	0	1	1	3	1	10	1	0	0	0	.000	0	0	5.68
1995	Birmingham	AA	29	19	0	3	120	521	118	58	49	10	7	6	4	40	1	78	6	2	7	5	.583	0	0	3.68
	4 Min. YEARS		104	58	4	21	448.2	1907	431	229	189	44	22	17	22	140	2	339	26	5	26	21	.553	0	5	3.79

Melvin Mora

Bats: Right Throws: Right Pos: OF **Ht: 5'10" Wt: 160 Born: 2/2/72 Age: 24**

			BATTING														BASERUNNING				PERCENTAGES		
Year	Team	Lg	G	AB	H	2B	3B	HR	TB	R	RBI	TBB	IBB	SO	HBP	SH	SF	SB	CS	SB%	GDP	Avg	OBP	SLG
1992	Astros	R	49	144	32	6	3	0	35	28	8	18	0	16	5	0	1	16	3	.84	2	.222	.327	.243
1993	Asheville	A	108	365	104	22	2	2	136	66	31	36	0	46	9	5	8	20	13	.61	7	.285	.356	.373
1994	Osceola	A	118	425	120	29	4	8	181	57	46	37	1	60	10	3	3	24	16	.60	8	.282	.352	.426
1995	Jackson	AA	123	467	139	32	4	3	180	63	45	32	1	57	9	7	7	22	11	.67	11	.298	.350	.385
	Tucson	AAA	2	5	3	0	1	0	5	3	1	2	0	0	0	0	0	1	0	1.00	0	.600	.714	1.000
	4 Min. YEARS		400	1406	398	86	13	13	537	217	131	125	3	179	33	15	19	83	43	.66	28	.283	.351	.382

Francisco Morales

Bats: Right Throws: Right Pos: C **Ht: 6'3" Wt: 180 Born: 1/31/73 Age: 23**

			BATTING														BASERUNNING				PERCENTAGES		
Year	Team	Lg	G	AB	H	2B	3B	HR	TB	R	RBI	TBB	IBB	SO	HBP	SH	SF	SB	CS	SB%	GDP	Avg	OBP	SLG
1992	Huntington	R	13	39	7	1	0	1	11	4	9	10	1	13	1	1	0	0	2	.33	1	.179	.360	.282
	Geneva	A	19	49	11	2	0	0	13	3	0	7	1	21	0	0	0	0	0	.00	2	.224	.321	.265
1993	Peoria	A	19	49	10	1	1	3	22	9	11	9	0	16	0	4	0	0	0	.00	2	.204	.328	.449
	Geneva	A	45	123	24	4	0	2	34	12	20	15	0	41	1	0	2	1	1	1.00	2	.195	.284	.276
1994	Orlando	AA	22	58	12	0	0	2	18	3	10	7	0	21	0	0	0	0	1	.00	1	.207	.292	.310
	Daytona	A	38	120	29	7	1	1	41	9	9	9	0	37	1	0	1	1	0	1.00	2	.242	.298	.342

Year	Team	Lg	G	AB	H	2B	3B	HR	TB	R	RBI	TBB	IBB	SO	HBP	SH	SF	SB	CS	SB%	GDP	Avg	OBP	SLG
1995	Orlando	AA	2	6	1	0	0	0	1	0	0	1	0	2	0	0	0	0	0	.00	0	.167	.286	.167
	Daytona	A	36	101	26	6	0	6	50	17	23	16	0	28	3	0	2	1	1	.50	2	.257	.369	.495
	Savannah	A	19	75	11	3	0	2	20	3	4	4	0	23	1	0	1		2	.00	2	.147	.198	.267
	St. Pete	A	28	87	17	5	0	2	28	10	10	11	0	29	1	0	0	1		1.00	3	.195	.293	.322
	4 Min. YEARS		241	707	148	29	2	19	238	70	97	89	1	231	8	5	6	5	6	.45	17	.209	.302	.337

Kevin Morgan

Bats: Right   Throws: Right   Pos: SS   **Ht: 6'1"   Wt: 170   Born: 3/3/70   Age: 26**

						BATTING												BASERUNNING				PERCENTAGES		
Year	Team	Lg	G	AB	H	2B	3B	HR	TB	R	RBI	TBB	IBB	SO	HBP	SH	SF	SB	CS	SB%	GDP	Avg	OBP	SLG
1991	Niagara Fal	A	70	252	60	13	0	0	73	23	26	21	0	49	3	4	4	8	6	.57	2	.238	.300	.290
1992	Fayettevlle	A	123	466	106	19	2	0	129	55	37	49	2	61	6	6	4	15	19	.44	10	.227	.307	.277
1993	Lakeland	A	112	417	99	12	2	2	121	45	34	32	2	84	2	3	4	7	6	.60	9	.237	.292	.290
1994	St. Lucie	A	132	448	122	8	3	1	139	63	47	37	0	62	7	9	3	7	7	.50	5	.272	.335	.310
1995	Binghamton	AA	114	430	119	21	1	4	154	63	51	44	4	52	5	7	2	9	9	.50	2	.277	.349	.358
	Norfolk	AAA	19	62	20	1	0	0	21	10	8	4	0	8	1	0	0	1	3	.25	1	.323	.373	.339
	5 Min. YEARS		570	2075	526	74	8	7	637	259	203	187	8	316	24	29	17	49	50	.49	29	.253	.320	.307

Mike Morland

Bats: Right   Throws: Right   Pos: C   **Ht: 6'0"   Wt: 190   Born: 8/17/69   Age: 26**

						BATTING												BASERUNNING				PERCENTAGES		
Year	Team	Lg	G	AB	H	2B	3B	HR	TB	R	RBI	TBB	IBB	SO	HBP	SH	SF	SB	CS	SB%	GDP	Avg	OBP	SLG
1991	St. Cathrns	A	46	146	38	8	1	2	54	10	21	22	0	33	0	2	4	0	1	.00	1	.260	.349	.370
1992	Myrtle Bch	A	104	265	45	9	0	4	66	21	26	29	0	60	2	1	4	2	1	.67	2	.170	.253	.249
1993	Knoxville	AA	45	112	26	4	1	0	32	7	15	10	0	31	0	3	0	1	1	.50	3	.232	.295	.286
1994	Syracuse	AAA	11	26	6	2	0	0	8	4	3	1	0	5	1	2	0	0	0	.00	0	.231	.286	.308
	Knoxville	AA	39	95	28	4	1	2	40	19	15	11	0	25	3	1	0	1	1	.50	3	.295	.385	.421
1995	Knoxville	AA	11	28	5	1	0	0	6	6	1	1	0	4	0	0	0	0	0	.00	1	.179	.207	.214
	5 Min. YEARS		256	672	148	28	3	8	206	67	81	74	0	158	6	9	8	4	4	.50	10	.220	.300	.307

Alvin Morman

Pitches: Left   Bats: Left   Pos: P   **Ht: 6'3"   Wt: 210   Born: 1/6/69   Age: 27**

						HOW MUCH HE PITCHED				WHAT HE GAVE UP										THE RESULTS				
Year	Team	Lg	G	GS	CG	GF	IP	BFP	H	R	ER	HR	SH	SF	HB	TBB	IBB	SO	WP	Bk	W	L	Pct.	ShO	Sv	ERA
1991	Astros	R	11	0	0	3	16.2	71	15	7	4	0	1	0	0	5	0	24	0	4	1	0	1.000	0	1	2.16
	Osceola	A	3	0	0	0	6	25	5	3	1	0	0	0	0	2	0	3	1	0	0	0	.000	0	0	1.50
1992	Asheville	A	57	0	0	37	75.1	313	60	17	13	3	3	1	3	26	2	70	2	0	8	0	1.000	0	15	1.55
1993	Jackson	AA	19	19	0	0	97.1	392	77	35	32	7	3	2	5	28	0	101	5	1	8	2	.800	0	0	2.96
1994	Tucson	AAA	58	0	0	23	74	327	84	51	42	7	5	9	2	26	4	49	3	0	3	7	.300	0	5	5.11
1995	Tucson	AAA	45	0	0	10	48.1	211	50	26	21	6	5	8	0	20	1	36	2	0	5	1	.833	0	3	3.91
	5 Min. YEARS		193	19	0	73	317.2	1339	291	139	113	23	17	20	10	107	7	283	13	5	25	10	.714	0	24	3.20

Geno Morones

Pitches: Right   Bats: Right   Pos: P   **Ht: 5'11"   Wt: 197   Born: 3/26/71   Age: 25**

						HOW MUCH HE PITCHED				WHAT HE GAVE UP										THE RESULTS				
Year	Team	Lg	G	GS	CG	GF	IP	BFP	H	R	ER	HR	SH	SF	HB	TBB	IBB	SO	WP	Bk	W	L	Pct.	ShO	Sv	ERA
1991	Huntington	R	22	0	0	16	35.1	166	37	18	17	2	1		3	24	1	36	7	0	2	3	.400	0	3	4.33
1992	Geneva	A	11	0	0	8	12.1	55	8	5	1	0	0		2	10	1	7	1	0	1	0	1.000	0	3	0.73
1993	Peoria	A	13	0	0	8	18.1	82	12	8	5	0	0	1	3	7	1	21	1	1	0	2	.000	0	0	2.45
	Daytona	A	13	6	1	1	51	206	44	10	10	0	2	1	3	16	2	27	3	0	5	1	.833	1	0	1.76
	Orlando	AA	4	4	1	0	24	108	29	14	13	2	0	2	2	9	0	14	1	0	2	2	.500	0	0	4.88
1994	Daytona	A	16	16	2	0	99.2	399	87	37	30	3	1	1	2	28	0	69	3	0	5	3	.625	2	0	2.71
1995	Wichita	AA	17	16	0	0	79	353	85	49	36	5	4	6	3	39	0	32	4	0	3	6	.333	0	0	4.10
	5 Min. YEARS		96	42	4	33	319.2	1369	302	141	112	12	9	14	16	133	5	206	19	1	18	17	.514	3	6	3.15

Keith Morrison

Pitches: Right   Bats: Right   Pos: P   **Ht: 6'4"   Wt: 190   Born: 11/22/69   Age: 26**

						HOW MUCH HE PITCHED				WHAT HE GAVE UP										THE RESULTS				
Year	Team	Lg	G	GS	CG	GF	IP	BFP	H	R	ER	HR	SH	SF	HB	TBB	IBB	SO	WP	Bk	W	L	Pct.	ShO	Sv	ERA
1990	Pulaski	R	13	13	2	0	79	348	77	46	36	4	1		2	37	0	79	5	8	6	6	.500	0	0	4.10
1991	Macon	A	8	8	1	0	42.2	174	41	23	14	2	2	1	2	6	0	25	0	2	4	3	.571	0	0	2.95
	Sumter	A	7	7	1	0	36	151	36	20	18	3	0	1	0	12	0	26	2	2	2	4	.333	0	0	4.50
1992	Albany	A	15	15	2	0	111	464	113	46	30	2	5	2	3	28	1	85	3	1	8	4	.667	1	0	2.43
	Rockford	A	15	3	0	7	35	158	46	24	20	2	4	1	1	7	0	29	2	1	1	2	.333	0	0	5.14
1993	Palm Spring	A	27	27	2	0	176	772	200	108	81	16	3	12	10	55	0	107	7	0	14	6	.700	1	0	4.14
1994	Midland	AA	12	12	3	0	83.2	355	78	39	33	4	3	1	7	28	1	61	1	1	6	3	.667	0	0	3.55
	Vancouver	AAA	16	14	2	2	85.1	394	111	68	62	17	3	3	0	27	2	50	1	0	4	6	.400	1	0	6.54
1995	Vancouver	AAA	28	26	4	1	160.2	685	178	97	88	16	2	11	6	40	0	84	4	0	14	9	.609	1	0	4.93
	6 Min. YEARS		141	125	17	10	809.1	3501	880	471	382	66	23	34	30	240	4	546	25	15	59	43	.578	4	0	4.25

Chris Morrow

Bats: Left **Throws:** Left **Pos:** OF **Ht:** 6'1" **Wt:** 190 **Born:** 11/8/69 **Age:** 26

Year	Team	Lg	G	AB	H	2B	3B	HR	TB	R	RBI	TBB	IBB	SO	HBP	SH	SF	SB	CS	SB%	GDP	Avg	OBP	SLG
1988	Great Falls	R	60	215	62	11	3	8	103	48	40	28	1	50	0	0	1	13	7	.65	4	.288	.369	.479
1989	Bakersfield	A	38	107	16	5	0	1	24	9	4	14	2	18	0	0	0	3	4	.43	0	.150	.248	.224
	Salem	A	27	93	30	3	3	2	45	20	16	12	2	11	1	0	0	4	2	.67	2	.323	.406	.484
1990	Bakersfield	A	95	325	78	17	2	5	114	37	40	20	3	53	2	1	3	8	6	.57	3	.240	.286	.351
1991	Vero Beach	A	85	273	83	13	5	3	115	29	29	14	3	32	3	1	2	6	6	.50	7	.304	.342	.421
	San Antonio	AA	24	89	32	6	0	2	44	13	8	4	0	14	0	0	0	1	1	.50	3	.360	.387	.494
1992	San Antonio	AA	84	245	57	5	4	5	85	22	30	6	0	41	1	1	3	4	3	.57	5	.233	.251	.347
	Albuquerque	AAA	24	67	19	2	1	1	26	6	7	5	2	9	0	0	0	1	0	1.00	3	.284	.333	.388
1993	Vero Beach	A	88	316	98	18	3	13	161	47	66	21	6	40	1	0	3	7	3	.70	5	.310	.352	.509
1995	Shreveport	AA	83	240	59	17	0	7	97	31	35	31	4	44	1	0	0	1	1	.50	8	.246	.335	.404
	7 Min. YEARS		608	1970	534	97	21	47	814	262	275	155	23	312	9	3	12	48	33	.59	40	.271	.325	.413

Kevin Morton

Pitches: Left **Bats:** Right **Pos:** P **Ht:** 6'2" **Wt:** 185 **Born:** 8/3/68 **Age:** 27

Year	Team	Lg	G	GS	CG	GF	IP	BFP	H	R	ER	HR	SH	SF	HB	TBB	IBB	SO	WP	Bk	W	L	Pct.	ShO	Sv	ERA
1989	Red Sox	R	2	1	0	1	6	22	2	0	0	0	0	0	1	1	0	11	0	0	1	1	1.000	0	1	0.00
	Elmira	A	3	3	2	0	24	90	11	6	5	0	2	2	1	6	0	32	1	0	1	1	.500	0	0	1.88
	Lynchburg	A	9	9	4	0	65	253	42	20	17	2	0	2	2	17	0	68	3	0	4	5	.444	2	0	2.35
1990	New Britain	AA	26	26	7	0	163	685	151	86	69	10	4	3	14	48	0	131	6	5	8	14	.364	2	0	3.81
1991	Pawtucket	AAA	16	15	1	0	98	412	91	41	38	8	2	2	2	30	1	80	3	2	7	3	.700	1	0	3.49
1992	Pawtucket	AAA	26	25	1	0	138.2	627	166	93	84	19	3	4	3	59	2	71	5	2	2	12	.143	0	0	5.45
1993	Memphis	AA	20	9	1	4	73	328	88	48	39	12	4	2	1	29	1	59	3	0	3	6	.333	0	1	4.81
1994	Norfolk	AAA	29	20	1	3	137	590	124	74	57	11	6	7	7	67	4	75	4	0	5	8	.385	1	1	3.74
1995	Iowa	AAA	28	12	1	5	92	405	97	52	49	13	4	4	2	42	3	49	3	0	1	7	.125	0	0	4.79
1991	Boston	AL	16	15	1	0	86.1	379	93	49	44	9	3	7	1	40	2	45	1	1	6	5	.545	0	0	4.59
	7 Min. YEARS		159	120	18	13	796.2	3412	772	420	358	75	25	26	33	299	11	576	28	9	32	56	.364	6	3	4.04

Joe Morvay

Pitches: Right **Bats:** Left **Pos:** P **Ht:** 6'4" **Wt:** 210 **Born:** 2/8/71 **Age:** 25

Year	Team	Lg	G	GS	CG	GF	IP	BFP	H	R	ER	HR	SH	SF	HB	TBB	IBB	SO	WP	Bk	W	L	Pct.	ShO	Sv	ERA
1993	Erie	A	18	2	0	0	38.1	160	32	18	12	0	1	2	2	14	1	42	1	0	2	3	.400	0	2	2.82
1994	Charlstn-Sc	A	37	1	0	11	71	303	50	27	22	4	4	1	9	30	1	85	4	0	2	4	.333	0	0	2.79
1995	Tulsa	AA	37	0	0	28	65.2	305	82	45	38	4	6	1	4	28	6	30	4	0	5	8	.385	0	8	5.21
	3 Min. YEARS		92	3	0	47	175	768	164	90	72	8	11	4	15	72	8	157	9	0	9	15	.375	0	10	3.70

Domingo Mota

Bats: Right **Throws:** Right **Pos:** 2B **Ht:** 5'8" **Wt:** 180 **Born:** 8/4/69 **Age:** 26

Year	Team	Lg	G	AB	H	2B	3B	HR	TB	R	RBI	TBB	IBB	SO	HBP	SH	SF	SB	CS	SB%	GDP	Avg	OBP	SLG
1990	Dodgers	R	61	213	73	12	2	1	92	46	34	36	3	19	8	2	1	23	15	.61	4	.343	.453	.432
1991	Bakersfield	A	104	408	112	20	2	8	160	75	44	44	1	83	6	10	4	37	19	.66	1	.275	.351	.392
1992	Memphis	AA	119	430	114	16	0	4	142	46	23	19	1	67	4	9	1	14	17	.45	7	.265	.302	.330
1993	Memphis	AA	56	196	42	7	3	1	58	22	16	11	0	48	1	3	3	10	9	.53	4	.214	.256	.296
	Wilmington	A	14	36	7	1	1	0	10	1	6	2	0	6	1	2	1	0	1	.00	5	.194	.250	.278
1994	Memphis	AA	48	156	37	3	2	3	53	23	11	8	1	26	3	4	0	6	3	.67	4	.237	.287	.340
1995	Chattanooga	AA	5	6	0	0	0	0	0	0	0	0	0	1	0	0	0	0	0	.00	1	.000	.000	.000
	6 Min. YEARS		407	1445	385	59	10	17	515	213	134	120	6	250	23	30	10	90	64	.58	22	.266	.330	.356

Gary Mota

Bats: Right **Throws:** Right **Pos:** OF **Ht:** 6'0" **Wt:** 195 **Born:** 10/6/70 **Age:** 25

Year	Team	Lg	G	AB	H	2B	3B	HR	TB	R	RBI	TBB	IBB	SO	HBP	SH	SF	SB	CS	SB%	GDP	Avg	OBP	SLG
1990	Auburn	A	69	248	64	12	4	3	93	39	19	26	2	74	2	3	2	12	1	.92	5	.258	.331	.375
1991	Osceola	A	22	71	14	2	2	0	20	10	3	8	0	19	0	0	0	4	1	.80	0	.197	.278	.282
1992	Asheville	A	137	484	141	21	5	23	241	92	89	58	5	131	3	0	6	22	10	.69	13	.291	.367	.498
1993	Jackson	AA	27	90	13	2	0	3	24	7	8	2	0	25	0	2	1	1	1	.50	2	.144	.161	.267
1994	Jackson	AA	108	314	75	13	4	10	126	46	54	57	2	80	3	0	4	12	7	.63	6	.239	.357	.401
1995	Reading	AA	33	110	25	4	2	1	36	13	9	8	2	23	0	1	0	0	2	.00	2	.227	.280	.327
	6 Min. YEARS		396	1317	332	54	17	40	540	207	182	159	11	352	8	6	13	51	22	.70	27	.252	.333	.410

Scott Moten

Pitches: Right **Bats:** Right **Pos:** P **Ht:** 6'1" **Wt:** 198 **Born:** 4/12/72 **Age:** 24

Year	Team	Lg	G	GS	CG	GF	IP	BFP	H	R	ER	HR	SH	SF	HB	TBB	IBB	SO	WP	Bk	W	L	Pct.	ShO	Sv	ERA
1992	Elizabethtn	R	13	12	1	0	78.2	334	60	31	21	1	1	1	6	32	0	71	2	2	8	1	.889	1	0	2.40
1993	Fort Wayne	A	30	22	0	4	140.2	627	152	99	79	8	6	3	11	63	2	141	7	2	7	11	.389	0	1	5.05
1994	Fort Myers	A	44	1	0	17	96	404	87	32	23	1	4	0	2	38	3	68	2	0	8	4	.667	0	7	2.16
	Nashville	AA	3	0	0	0	4.2	23	5	4	2	0	0	0	1	2	0	4	1	0	0	1	.000	0	0	3.86

Year	Team	Lg	G	GS	CG	GF	IP	BFP	H	R	ER	HR	SH	SF	HB	TBB	IBB	SO	WP	Bk	W	L	Pct.	ShO	Sv	ERA
1995	New Britain	AA	40	1	0	18	75.1	323	65	40	33	8	6	3	0	36	2	43	5	0	8	5	.615	0	3	3.94
	4 Min. YEARS		130	36	1	39	395.1	1711	369	206	158	18	17	7	20	171	7	327	17	4	31	22	.585	1	11	3.60

Chad Mottola

Bats: Right **Throws:** Right **Pos:** OF   **Ht:** 6'3" **Wt:** 215 **Born:** 10/15/71 **Age:** 24

Year	Team	Lg	G	AB	H	2B	3B	HR	TB	R	RBI	TBB	IBB	SO	HBP	SH	SF	SB	CS	SB%	GDP	Avg	OBP	SLG
1992	Billings	R	57	213	61	8	3	12	111	53	37	25	0	43	0	0	0	12	3	.80	4	.286	.361	.521
1993	Winston-Sal	A	137	493	138	25	3	21	232	76	91	62	2	109	2	0	3	13	7	.65	9	.280	.361	.471
1994	Chattanooga	AA	118	402	97	19	1	7	139	44	41	30	1	68	1	2	2	9	12	.43	12	.241	.294	.346
1995	Chattanooga	AA	51	181	53	13	1	10	98	32	39	13	0	32	1	0	1	1	2	.33	2	.293	.342	.541
	Indianapolis	AAA	69	239	62	11	1	8	99	40	37	20	0	50	0	1	1	8	1	.89	6	.259	.315	.414
	4 Min. YEARS		432	1528	411	76	9	58	679	245	245	150	3	302	4	3	7	43	25	.63	33	.269	.335	.444

Pat Moultrie

Bats: Left **Throws:** Left **Pos:** OF   **Ht:** 5'11" **Wt:** 160 **Born:** 4/27/73 **Age:** 23

Year	Team	Lg	G	AB	H	2B	3B	HR	TB	R	RBI	TBB	IBB	SO	HBP	SH	SF	SB	CS	SB%	GDP	Avg	OBP	SLG
1992	Blue Jays	R	47	125	29	3	0	0	32	12	12	20	0	35	0	4	0	7	8	.47	2	.232	.338	.256
1993	St. Cathrns	A	73	264	71	6	3	1	86	29	19	16	0	46	4	7	0	18	13	.58	1	.269	.320	.326
1994	Hagerstown	A	79	303	67	9	4	4	96	43	37	13	0	50	1	5	1	20	7	.74	2	.221	.255	.317
1995	Knoxville	AA	13	51	13	0	0	0	13	3	7	4	1	6	0	4	1	2	1	.67	0	.255	.304	.255
	Dunedin	A	92	349	86	8	4	1	105	40	29	27	1	65	3	3	3	15	4	.79	5	.246	.304	.301
	4 Min. YEARS		304	1092	266	26	11	6	332	127	104	80	2	202	8	23	5	62	33	.65	10	.244	.299	.304

Bill Mueller

Bats: Both **Throws:** Right **Pos:** 3B   **Ht:** 5'11" **Wt:** 173 **Born:** 3/17/71 **Age:** 25

Year	Team	Lg	G	AB	H	2B	3B	HR	TB	R	RBI	TBB	IBB	SO	HBP	SH	SF	SB	CS	SB%	GDP	Avg	OBP	SLG
1993	Everett	A	58	200	60	8	2	1	75	31	24	42	1	17	3	6	2	13	6	.68	3	.300	.425	.375
1994	San Jose	A	120	431	130	20	9	5	183	79	72	103	11	47	3	1	6	4	8	.33	15	.302	.435	.425
1995	Shreveport	AA	88	330	102	16	2	1	125	56	39	53	2	36	4	2	4	6	5	.55	9	.309	.407	.379
	Phoenix	AAA	41	172	51	13	6	2	82	23	19	19	0	31	0	6	1	0	0	.00	7	.297	.365	.477
	3 Min. YEARS		307	1133	343	57	19	9	465	189	154	217	14	131	10	15	13	23	19	.55	34	.303	.415	.410

Sean Mulligan

Bats: Right **Throws:** Right **Pos:** C   **Ht:** 6'2" **Wt:** 205 **Born:** 4/25/70 **Age:** 26

Year	Team	Lg	G	AB	H	2B	3B	HR	TB	R	RBI	TBB	IBB	SO	HBP	SH	SF	SB	CS	SB%	GDP	Avg	OBP	SLG
1991	Charlstn-Sc	A	60	215	56	9	3	4	83	24	30	17	0	56	6	1	1	4	1	.80	5	.260	.331	.386
1992	High Desert	A	35	118	19	4	0	4	35	14	14	11	1	38	3	0	1	0	0	.00	3	.161	.248	.297
	Waterloo	A	79	278	70	13	1	5	100	24	43	20	0	62	5	2	4	1	0	1.00	10	.252	.309	.360
1993	Rancho Cuca	A	79	268	75	10	3	6	109	29	36	34	0	33	3	0	4	1	3	.25	16	.280	.362	.407
1994	Rancho Cuca	A	66	243	74	18	1	9	121	45	49	24	1	39	5	1	8	1	0	1.00	4	.305	.368	.498
	Wichita	AA	56	208	73	14	0	1	90	29	30	11	2	25	5	0	3	2	3	.40	9	.351	.392	.433
1995	Las Vegas	AAA	101	339	93	20	1	7	136	34	43	27	2	61	8	1	3	0	0	.00	7	.274	.340	.401
	5 Min. YEARS		476	1669	460	88	9	36	674	199	245	144	6	314	35	5	24	9	7	.56	54	.276	.341	.404

Jarrod Munoz

Pitches: Left **Bats:** Left **Pos:** P   **Ht:** 5'9" **Wt:** 170 **Born:** 11/1/67 **Age:** 28

Year	Team	Lg	G	GS	CG	GF	IP	BFP	H	R	ER	HR	SH	SF	HB	TBB	IBB	SO	WP	Bk	W	L	Pct.	ShO	Sv	ERA
1990	Martinsvlle	R	14	14	3	0	95	383	70	35	29	12	1	1	1	48	0	126	12	0	6	7	.462	2	0	2.75
1991	Spartanburg	A	20	20	2	0	115.2	486	112	55	46	5	4	3	3	51	0	103	11	0	8	6	.571	0	0	3.58
	Clearwater	A	2	0	0	0	1.1	8	0	0	0	0	0	1	0	4	0	0	0	0	0	0	.000	0	0	0.00
1992	Clearwater	A	32	0	0	19	44.2	172	34	13	11	2	0	3	1	12	3	34	3	0	2	3	.400	0	6	2.22
1993	Clearwater	A	56	0	0	33	76	313	59	22	21	2	3	3	2	26	4	81	11	0	5	2	.714	0	9	2.49
1994	Reading	AA	9	0	0	0	13	67	19	11	11	5	1	0	0	11	1	11	0	1	0	0	.000	0	0	7.62
1995	Omaha	AAA	57	0	0	21	56	235	48	23	21	3	4	2	6	19	2	51	5	1	2	3	.400	0	6	3.38
	6 Min. YEARS		190	34	5	73	401.2	1664	342	159	139	29	13	13	13	171	10	406	42	2	23	21	.523	2	21	3.11

Jose Munoz

Bats: Both **Throws:** Right **Pos:** 2B   **Ht:** 5'11" **Wt:** 165 **Born:** 11/11/67 **Age:** 28

Year	Team	Lg	G	AB	H	2B	3B	HR	TB	R	RBI	TBB	IBB	SO	HBP	SH	SF	SB	CS	SB%	GDP	Avg	OBP	SLG
1987	Dodgers	R	54	187	60	7	0	0	67	31	22	26	3	22	3	2	1	6	5	.55	2	.321	.410	.358
1988	Bakersfield	A	105	347	86	6	0	0	92	35	24	42	0	54	3	5	1	7	2	.78	9	.248	.333	.265
1989	Vero Beach	A	105	300	77	15	1	0	94	39	24	14	0	31	1	5	3	6	2	.75	11	.257	.289	.313
1990	Bakersfield	A	14	39	7	1	0	0	8	3	6	6	0	7	0	0	0	2	1	.67	0	.179	.289	.205
	Vero Beach	A	113	397	117	18	3	2	147	57	47	34	3	43	2	8	4	28	8	.78	3	.295	.350	.370
1991	San Antonio	AA	31	123	39	6	2	0	49	25	13	12	1	14	1	3	0	4	2	.67	5	.317	.382	.398
	Albuquerque	AAA	101	389	127	18	4	0	153	49	65	20	0	36	2	6	5	15	10	.60	14	.326	.358	.393
1992	Albuquerque	AAA	131	450	137	20	3	2	169	48	45	25	6	46	1	7	0	7	4	.64	22	.304	.342	.376
1993	Albuquerque	AAA	127	438	126	21	5	1	160	66	54	29	3	46	1	8	3	6	3	.67	19	.288	.331	.365

216

Year Team	Lg	G	AB	H	2B	3B	HR	TB	R	RBI	TBB	IBB	SO	HBP	SH	SF	SB	CS	SB%	GDP	Avg	OBP	SLG
1994 Pawtucket	AAA	129	519	136	16	1	7	175	59	41	52	2	59	2	8	2	12	13	.48	16	.262	.330	.337
1995 Richmond	AAA	135	520	151	18	5	3	188	65	45	53	4	65	4	5	6	7	10	.41	18	.290	.357	.362
9 Min. YEARS		1045	3709	1063	146	24	15	1302	477	386	313	22	423	20	57	25	100	60	.63	119	.287	.343	.351

Omer Munoz

Bats: Right Throws: Right Pos: 2B   Ht: 5'9" Wt: 156 Born: 3/3/66 Age: 30

Year Team	Lg	G	AB	H	2B	3B	HR	TB	R	RBI	TBB	IBB	SO	HBP	SH	SF	SB	CS	SB%	GDP	Avg	OBP	SLG
1985 Clinton	A	47	121	25	4	0	0	29	9	11	7	0	7	0	4	0	3	2	.60	4	.207	.250	.240
1987 W. Palm Bch	A	5	7	0	0	0	0	0	0	0	1	0	1	0	0	0	0	1	.00	0	.000	.125	.000
Burlington	A	52	195	47	8	2	0	59	22	16	7	0	13	3	6	0	5	3	.63	4	.241	.278	.303
1988 W. Palm Bch	A	103	369	95	15	1	0	112	36	27	14	0	28	1	8	2	8	6	.57	3	.257	.285	.304
1989 W. Palm Bch	A	68	246	67	2	0	0	69	22	27	5	0	17	1	8	0	8	5	.62	12	.272	.290	.280
1990 Jacksonvlle	AA	70	197	50	5	0	1	58	19	18	5	0	18	2	1	1	3	0	1.00	1	.254	.278	.294
1991 Harrisburg	AA	63	214	66	7	1	1	78	27	21	3	0	17	0	11	1	1	0	1.00	4	.308	.317	.364
Indianapols	AAA	26	92	26	2	0	0	28	7	12	3	1	14	3	6	0	0	0	.00	2	.283	.327	.304
1992 Indianapols	AAA	116	375	94	12	1	1	111	33	30	10	0	32	4	9	4	7	2	.78	15	.251	.275	.296
1993 Buffalo	AAA	40	129	28	4	1	2	40	7	16	3	2	11	1	2	1	0	0	.00	2	.217	.239	.310
1994 Carolina	AA	79	287	90	15	1	5	122	30	38	12	2	29	2	3	3	2	4	.33	7	.314	.342	.425
1995 Carolina	AA	67	234	62	10	1	2	80	29	25	5	0	23	3	5	2	2	0	1.00	7	.265	.287	.342
10 Min. YEARS		736	2466	650	84	8	12	786	241	241	75	5	210	20	63	14	39	23	.63	61	.264	.289	.319

Orlando Munoz

Bats: Both Throws: Right Pos: 2B   Ht: 5'11" Wt: 175 Born: 5/4/71 Age: 25

Year Team	Lg	G	AB	H	2B	3B	HR	TB	R	RBI	TBB	IBB	SO	HBP	SH	SF	SB	CS	SB%	GDP	Avg	OBP	SLG
1989 Angels	R	39	135	30	4	2	0	38	18	18	10	0	21	1	2	1	5	5	.50	3	.222	.279	.281
1991 Palm Spring	A	36	122	33	4	0	0	37	16	10	15	0	23	3	7	0	3	3	.50	2	.270	.364	.303
1992 Palm Spring	A	103	329	77	9	1	0	88	50	43	50	1	53	4	4	2	21	4	.84	14	.234	.340	.267
1993 Palm Spring	A	64	237	64	8	3	0	78	38	24	47	0	25	2	3	5	23	14	.62	7	.270	.388	.329
Midland	AA	36	118	31	8	1	0	41	24	10	20	0	23	1	2	0	0	4	.00	4	.263	.374	.347
1994 Vancouver	AAA	63	187	62	8	0	0	70	26	20	23	0	27	1	7	3	2	5	.29	3	.332	.402	.374
1995 Vancouver	AAA	4	10	1	0	0	0	1	0	0	0	0	3	0	0	0	0	1	.00	1	.100	.100	.100
Midland	AA	87	309	97	19	4	1	127	39	44	33	2	33	2	5	6	9	5	.64	4	.314	.377	.411
6 Min. YEARS		432	1447	395	60	11	1	480	211	169	198	3	208	14	30	17	63	41	.61	38	.273	.362	.332

Danny Murphy

Pitches: Right Bats: Right Pos: P   Ht: 6'3" Wt: 215 Born: 9/18/64 Age: 31

		HOW MUCH HE PITCHED						WHAT HE GAVE UP											THE RESULTS					
Year Team	Lg	G	GS	CG	GF	IP	BFP	H	R	ER	HR	SH	SF	HB	TBB	IBB	SO	WP	Bk	W	L	Pct.	ShO	Sv	ERA
1984 Beloit	A	26	12	3	6	112.2	477	116	59	45	5	4	3	0	44	0	79	5	0	9	4	.692	1	2	3.59
1985 Stockton	A	24	21	3	2	132	0	114	65	58	1	0	0	4	84	2	157	10	0	9	7	.563	1	0	3.95
1986 El Paso	AA	18	18	1	0	116.1	505	126	63	57	10	0	5	3	40	0	89	4	0	9	2	.818	0	0	4.41
1987 El Paso	AA	22	22	5	0	135.1	614	152	88	77	18	1	9	1	69	3	107	8	2	10	7	.588	1	0	5.12
1988 Stockton	A	12	4	0	5	25.2	142	25	22	18	1	1	0	3	40	0	26	2	3	1	4	.200	0	2	6.31
1989 Las Vegas	AAA	27	21	3	3	133	603	129	75	62	9	10	4	3	78	1	93	12	6	6	9	.400	2	2	4.20
1990 Las Vegas	AAA	27	10	1	10	69.2	334	74	54	45	5	1	0	0	56	2	60	2	1	4	7	.364	0	3	5.81
1991 Okla. City	AAA	2	1	0	0	1	17	7	13	9	1	0	1	1	5	0	1	0	0	0	1	.000	0	0	81.00
1995 Edmonton	AAA	1	0	0	0	1.2	8	1	1	1	1	0	0	0	3	0	2	0	0	0	1	.000	0	0	5.40
1989 San Diego	NL	7	0	0	2	6.1	30	6	6	4	1	0	0	0	4	1	1	0	0	0	0	.000	0	0	5.68
9 Min. YEARS		159	109	16	26	727.1	2700	744	440	372	51	17	22	15	419	8	614	43	12	48	42	.533	5	9	4.60

Mike Murphy

Bats: Right Throws: Right Pos: OF   Ht: 6'2" Wt: 185 Born: 1/23/72 Age: 24

Year Team	Lg	G	AB	H	2B	3B	HR	TB	R	RBI	TBB	IBB	SO	HBP	SH	SF	SB	CS	SB%	GDP	Avg	OBP	SLG
1990 Martinsvlle	R	9	31	3	0	0	0	3	4	1	7	0	17	0	0	0	1	2	.33	1	.097	.263	.097
1991 Martinsvlle	R	44	156	34	3	0	0	37	15	7	11	1	40	1	2	0	9	2	.82	5	.218	.274	.237
1992 Batavia	A	63	228	58	6	2	2	74	32	27	21	0	48	4	3	0	15	8	.65	6	.254	.328	.325
1993 Spartanburg	A	133	509	147	29	6	3	197	70	60	35	1	91	9	9	2	33	14	.70	15	.289	.344	.387
1994 Dunedin	A	125	469	129	11	4	1	151	57	34	55	3	106	9	4	3	31	10	.76	9	.275	.360	.322
1995 Canton-Akrn	AA	10	23	1	0	0	0	1	3	0	4	0	3	0	0	0	0	1	.00	0	.043	.185	.043
Kinston	A	67	177	41	6	0	1	50	26	15	15	1	30	3	1	1	13	4	.76	2	.232	.301	.282
6 Min. YEARS		451	1593	413	55	12	7	513	207	144	148	6	335	26	19	6	102	41	.71	38	.259	.331	.322

Pat Murphy

Bats: Left Throws: Right Pos: 3B   Ht: 5'10" Wt: 160 Born: 3/24/72 Age: 24

Year Team	Lg	G	AB	H	2B	3B	HR	TB	R	RBI	TBB	IBB	SO	HBP	SH	SF	SB	CS	SB%	GDP	Avg	OBP	SLG
1993 Ft. Laud	A	54	186	55	4	2	0	63	28	21	24	0	23	1	1	2	9	9	.50	4	.296	.376	.339
1994 Lynchburg	A	117	456	113	19	4	0	140	64	26	45	1	72	3	2	2	27	19	.59	13	.248	.318	.307
Sarasota	A	2	7	1	0	0	0	1	0	0	0	0	2	0	0	0	1	0	1.00	0	.143	.143	.143
1995 Trenton	AA	35	114	26	4	0	0	30	17	11	6	1	21	1	1	1	10	6	.63	1	.228	.270	.263
Sarasota	A	54	189	38	4	0	2	48	18	15	8	0	26	1	2	0	12	5	.71	2	.201	.237	.254
3 Min. YEARS		262	952	233	31	6	2	282	127	73	83	2	144	6	6	5	59	39	.60	20	.245	.308	.296

Steve Murphy

Bats: Left **Throws:** Right **Pos:** OF   **Ht:** 5'8" **Wt:** 165 **Born:** 4/13/71 **Age:** 25

Year	Team	Lg	G	AB	H	2B	3B	HR	TB	R	RBI	TBB	IBB	SO	HBP	SH	SF	SB	CS	SB%	GDP	Avg	OBP	SLG
1993	Rockford	A	110	349	102	17	5	2	135	56	49	48	0	69	7	13	1	29	14	.67	4	.292	.388	.387
1994	Wilmington	A	102	353	87	15	7	1	119	57	37	45	0	63	4	9	4	23	4	.85	3	.246	.335	.337
1995	Wichita	AA	18	39	13	2	0	0	15	9	4	4	1	5	0	2	1	0	1	.00	2	.333	.386	.385
	3 Min. YEARS		230	741	202	34	12	3	269	122	90	97	1	137	11	24	6	52	19	.73	9	.273	.363	.363

Calvin Murray

Bats: Right **Throws:** Right **Pos:** OF   **Ht:** 5'11" **Wt:** 185 **Born:** 7/30/71 **Age:** 24

Year	Team	Lg	G	AB	H	2B	3B	HR	TB	R	RBI	TBB	IBB	SO	HBP	SH	SF	SB	CS	SB%	GDP	Avg	OBP	SLG
1993	Shreveport	AA	37	138	26	6	0	0	32	15	6	14	0	29	2	3	1	12	6	.67	0	.188	.271	.232
	San Jose	A	85	345	97	24	1	9	150	61	42	40	0	63	4	2	0	42	10	.81	4	.281	.362	.435
	Phoenix	AAA	5	19	6	1	1	0	9	4	0	2	0	5	0	0	0	1	1	.50	0	.316	.381	.474
1994	Shreveport	AA	129	480	111	19	5	2	146	67	35	47	0	81	5	8	4	33	13	.72	4	.231	.304	.304
1995	Phoenix	AAA	13	50	9	1	0	4	22	8	10	4	0	6	0	1	1	2	2	.50	2	.180	.236	.440
	Shreveport	AA	110	441	104	17	3	2	133	77	29	59	2	70	3	5	1	26	10	.72	5	.236	.329	.302
	3 Min. YEARS		379	1473	353	68	10	17	492	232	122	166	2	254	14	19	7	116	42	.73	15	.240	.321	.334

Glenn Murray

Bats: Right **Throws:** Right **Pos:** OF   **Ht:** 6'2" **Wt:** 200 **Born:** 11/23/70 **Age:** 25

Year	Team	Lg	G	AB	H	2B	3B	HR	TB	R	RBI	TBB	IBB	SO	HBP	SH	SF	SB	CS	SB%	GDP	Avg	OBP	SLG
1989	Expos	R	27	87	15	6	2	0	25	10	7	6	0	30	2	0	1	8	1	.89	1	.172	.240	.287
	Jamestown	A	3	10	3	1	0	0	4	1	1	1	0	1	0	0	0	0	0	.00	0	.300	.364	.400
1990	Jamestown	A	53	165	37	8	4	1	56	20	14	21	0	43	3	0	0	11	3	.79	3	.224	.323	.339
1991	Rockford	A	124	479	113	16	14	5	172	73	60	77	3	137	2	0	8	22	19	.54	8	.236	.339	.359
1992	W. Palm Bch	A	119	414	96	14	5	13	159	79	41	75	3	150	4	2	1	26	11	.70	4	.232	.354	.384
1993	Harrisburg	AA	127	475	120	21	4	26	227	82	96	56	1	111	8	0	2	16	7	.70	3	.253	.340	.478
1994	Pawtucket	AAA	130	465	104	17	1	25	198	74	64	55	4	134	4	0	2	9	3	.75	10	.224	.310	.426
1995	Pawtucket	AAA	104	336	82	15	0	25	172	66	66	34	1	109	11	1	5	5	6	.45	4	.244	.329	.512
	7 Min. YEARS		687	2431	570	98	30	95	1013	405	349	325	12	715	34	3	19	97	50	.66	33	.234	.331	.417

Heath Murray

Pitches: Left **Bats:** Left **Pos:** P   **Ht:** 6'4" **Wt:** 205 **Born:** 4/19/73 **Age:** 23

Year	Team	Lg	G	GS	CG	GF	IP	BFP	H	R	ER	HR	SH	SF	HB	TBB	IBB	SO	WP	Bk	W	L	Pct.	ShO	Sv	ERA
1994	Spokane	A	15	15	2	0	99.1	408	101	46	32	6	6	2	5	18	0	78	4	3	5	6	.455	1	0	2.90
1995	Rancho Cuca	A	14	14	4	0	92.1	381	80	37	32	5	3	2	4	38	1	81	6	3	9	4	.692	2	0	3.12
	Memphis	AA	14	14	0	0	77.1	363	83	36	29	1	3	3	4	42	1	71	7	1	5	4	.556	0	0	3.38
	2 Min. YEARS		43	43	6	0	269	1152	264	119	93	12	12	7	13	98	2	230	17	7	19	14	.576	3	0	3.11

Jim Musselwhite

Pitches: Right **Bats:** Right **Pos:** P   **Ht:** 6'1" **Wt:** 190 **Born:** 10/25/71 **Age:** 24

Year	Team	Lg	G	GS	CG	GF	IP	BFP	H	R	ER	HR	SH	SF	HB	TBB	IBB	SO	WP	Bk	W	L	Pct.	ShO	Sv	ERA
1993	Oneonta	A	5	4	0	0	20	84	15	7	5	0	1	1	0	8	0	18	1	0	1	1	.500	0	0	2.25
	Greensboro	A	11	10	0	1	67.2	285	60	29	21	4	3	2	2	24	0	60	4	2	5	3	.625	0	0	2.79
1994	Tampa	A	17	17	3	0	107.2	429	87	50	41	8	0	3	3	23	0	106	4	0	9	6	.600	2	0	3.43
	Albany-Colo	A	5	5	1	0	29.2	116	28	4	4	0	0	0	2	5	0	31	2	0	2	1	.667	1	0	1.21
1995	Norwich	AA	24	24	1	0	131.2	566	136	75	67	11	5	6	6	34	3	96	8	1	5	9	.357	0	0	4.58
	3 Min. YEARS		62	60	5	1	356.2	1480	326	165	138	23	9	12	13	94	3	311	19	3	22	20	.524	3	0	3.48

Jose Musset

Pitches: Right **Bats:** Right **Pos:** P   **Ht:** 6'3" **Wt:** 186 **Born:** 9/18/68 **Age:** 27

Year	Team	Lg	G	GS	CG	GF	IP	BFP	H	R	ER	HR	SH	SF	HB	TBB	IBB	SO	WP	Bk	W	L	Pct.	ShO	Sv	ERA
1990	Angels	R	13	13	0	0	62.2	298	63	54	42	2	1	1	6	41	2	49	7	1	2	7	.222	0	0	6.03
	Boise	A	1	0	0	1	0.2	3	0	0	0	0	0	0	0	1	0	0	0	0	0	0	.000	0	2	0.00
1991	Angels	R	10	0	0	10	14	63	14	7	5	0	0	1	1	5	0	10	1	0	1	1	.500	0	2	3.21
1992	Quad City	A	41	0	0	22	71.2	279	41	19	19	3	3	1	3	25	0	104	5	0	8	2	.800	0	6	2.39
1993	Midland	AA	59	0	0	49	62.1	278	59	38	38	9	0	4	5	32	2	59	4	0	2	6	.250	0	21	5.49
1994	Columbus	AAA	1	0	0	0	0.1	6	3	3	3	0	0	0	0	0	0	0	0	0	0	0	.000	0	0	81.00
1995	Columbus	AAA	5	0	0	1	4.1	19	4	4	3	2	0	0	0	2	0	4	1	0	0	0	.000	0	0	6.23
	Norwich	AA	34	0	0	12	48.2	217	43	21	18	2	3	3	7	24	2	42	4	0	4	1	.800	0	4	3.33
	6 Min. YEARS		164	13	0	95	264.2	1163	227	146	128	18	7	10	22	132	6	268	22	1	17	17	.500	0	33	4.35

Jeff Mutis

Pitches: Left **Bats:** Left **Pos:** P — **Ht:** 6'2" **Wt:** 195 **Born:** 12/20/66 **Age:** 29

Year	Team	Lg	G	GS	CG	GF	IP	BFP	H	R	ER	HR	SH	SF	HB	TBB	IBB	SO	WP	Bk	W	L	Pct.	ShO	Sv	ERA
1988	Burlington	R	3	3	0	0	22	79	8	1	1	0	0	0	0	6	0	20	1	2	3	0	1.000	0	0	0.41
	Kinston	A	1	1	0	0	5.2	24	6	1	1	0	1	0	0	3	0	2	1	0	1	0	1.000	0	0	1.59
1989	Kinston	A	16	15	5	1	99.2	406	87	42	29	6	1	4	2	20	0	68	3	2	7	3	.700	2	0	2.62
1990	Canton-Akrn	AA	26	26	7	0	165	702	178	73	58	6	3	2	3	44	2	94	5	1	11	10	.524	3	0	3.16
1991	Canton-Akrn	AA	25	24	7	0	169.2	682	138	42	34	0	8	4	6	51	2	89	3	1	11	5	.688	4	0	1.80
1992	Colo. Sprng	AAA	25	24	4	0	145.1	652	177	99	82	8	6	8	5	57	1	77	8	4	9	9	.500	0	0	5.08
1993	Charlotte	AAA	12	11	3	0	75.2	315	64	27	22	1	1	2	3	25	3	59	1	0	6	0	1.000	0	0	2.62
1994	Edmonton	AAA	13	4	0	5	26.2	127	36	26	25	1	0	2	0	13	0	18	1	1	0	3	.000	0	0	8.44
1995	Charlotte	AAA	27	0	0	5	36.1	153	31	18	15	2	2	4	1	14	2	21	1	0	0	1	.000	0	2	3.72
1991	Cleveland	AL	3	3	0	0	12.1	68	23	16	16	1	2	1	0	7	1	6	1	0	0	3	.000	0	0	11.68
1992	Cleveland	AL	3	2	0	0	11.1	64	24	14	12	4	0	2	0	6	0	8	2	0	0	2	.000	0	0	9.53
1993	Cleveland	AL	17	13	1	1	81	364	93	56	52	14	0	2	7	33	2	29	1	0	3	6	.333	1	0	5.78
1994	Florida	NL	35	0	0	7	38.1	177	51	25	23	6	5	2	1	15	3	30	0	1	1	0	1.000	0	0	5.40
	8 Min. YEARS		148	108	26	11	746	3140	725	329	267	24	22	26	20	233	10	448	24	12	48	31	.608	9	2	3.22
	4 Maj. YEARS		58	18	1	8	143	673	191	111	103	25	7	7	8	61	6	73	4	1	4	11	.267	1	0	6.48

Jimmy Myers

Pitches: Right **Bats:** Right **Pos:** P — **Ht:** 6'1" **Wt:** 190 **Born:** 4/28/69 **Age:** 27

Year	Team	Lg	G	GS	CG	GF	IP	BFP	H	R	ER	HR	SH	SF	HB	TBB	IBB	SO	WP	Bk	W	L	Pct.	ShO	Sv	ERA
1987	Pocatello	R	10	2	0	4	19.2	92	29	21	19	1	1	1	1	16	1	12	5	2	0	2	.000	0	0	8.69
1988	Pocatello	R	12	12	0	0	58.1	283	72	50	35	3	2	1	1	32	1	39	7	1	4	5	.444	0	0	5.40
1989	Clinton	A	32	21	0	5	137.2	592	139	71	57	6	8	5	9	58	5	63	11	0	4	12	.250	0	0	3.73
1990	San Jose	A	60	0	0	50	84	361	80	44	30	2	3	3	2	34	6	61	3	1	5	8	.385	0	25	3.21
1991	Shreveport	AA	62	0	0	55	76.1	325	71	22	21	2	6	0	2	30	5	51	4	0	6	4	.600	0	24	2.48
1992	Phoenix	AAA	25	0	0	19	23.2	114	32	20	15	1	2	1	0	13	5	11	0	0	0	4	.000	0	10	5.70
	Shreveport	AA	33	0	0	32	32	141	39	17	17	0	2	2	2	10	1	15	1	0	2	4	.333	0	18	4.78
1993	Shreveport	AA	29	0	0	14	49.1	210	50	14	11	1	2	0	2	19	3	23	4	0	2	2	.500	0	0	2.01
	Phoenix	AAA	31	3	0	5	58.2	259	69	35	24	2	3	0	3	22	2	20	5	0	2	5	.286	0	0	3.68
1994	Memphis	AA	33	2	0	12	64.1	286	68	38	35	3	7	2	4	32	4	35	7	1	4	4	.500	0	3	4.90
	Carolina	AA	11	0	0	5	11.2	49	7	3	3	0	0	1	3	7	1	7	1	0	1	1	.500	0	4	2.31
1995	Rochester	AAA	55	0	0	28	64.2	289	72	28	22	2	3	2	1	29	1	31	1	0	0	4	.000	0	6	3.06
	9 Min. YEARS		393	40	0	229	680.1	3001	728	363	289	23	39	18	30	302	35	368	49	5	30	55	.353	0	91	3.82

Rod Myers

Pitches: Right **Bats:** Right **Pos:** P — **Ht:** 6'1" **Wt:** 190 **Born:** 6/26/69 **Age:** 27

Year	Team	Lg	G	GS	CG	GF	IP	BFP	H	R	ER	HR	SH	SF	HB	TBB	IBB	SO	WP	Bk	W	L	Pct.	ShO	Sv	ERA
1990	Eugene	A	6	4	0	0	22.2	98	19	9	3	2	0	1	0	13	0	17	1	1	0	2	.000	0	0	1.19
1991	Appleton	A	9	4	0	1	27.2	127	22	9	8	0	1	1	1	26	0	29	1	1	1	1	.500	0	0	2.60
1992	Lethbridge	R	15	15	5	0	103.1	452	93	57	46	3	4	2	5	61	1	76	14	2	5	8	.385	0	0	4.01
1993	Rockford	A	12	12	5	0	85.1	322	65	22	17	3	2	2	1	18	0	65	3	1	7	3	.700	2	0	1.79
	Memphis	AA	12	12	1	0	65.2	294	73	46	41	8	2	2	10	32	0	42	3	3	3	6	.333	1	0	5.62
1994	Wilmington	A	4	0	0	2	9.1	37	9	6	5	1	0	0	0	1	0	9	1	0	1	1	.500	0	1	4.82
	Memphis	AA	42	0	0	30	69.2	284	45	20	8	3	2	4	5	29	2	53	3	0	5	1	.833	0	9	1.03
1995	Omaha	AAA	38	0	0	17	48.1	212	52	26	22	5	2	3	0	19	1	38	1	1	4	5	.444	0	2	4.10
	6 Min. YEARS		138	47	11	50	432	1826	378	195	150	25	13	15	22	199	4	329	27	9	26	27	.491	3	12	3.13

Rod Myers

Bats: Left **Throws:** Left **Pos:** OF — **Ht:** 6'0" **Wt:** 190 **Born:** 1/14/73 **Age:** 23

Year	Team	Lg	G	AB	H	2B	3B	HR	TB	R	RBI	TBB	IBB	SO	HBP	SH	SF	SB	CS	SB%	GDP	Avg	OBP	SLG
1991	Royals	R	44	133	37	2	3	1	48	14	18	6	1	27	5	0	1	12	2	.86	1	.278	.331	.361
	Baseball Cy	A	4	11	2	0	0	0	2	1	0	0	0	5	0	0	0	1	1	.50	1	.182	.182	.182
1992	Appleton	A	71	218	48	10	2	4	74	31	30	39	1	67	2	4	4	25	6	.81	3	.220	.338	.339
1993	Rockford	A	129	474	123	24	5	9	184	69	68	58	6	117	5	6	4	49	16	.75	7	.259	.344	.388
1994	Wilmington	A	126	457	120	20	4	12	184	76	65	67	3	93	6	12	1	31	11	.74	4	.263	.363	.403
1995	Wichita	AA	131	499	153	22	6	7	208	71	62	34	3	77	4	8	3	29	16	.64	7	.307	.354	.417
	5 Min. YEARS		505	1792	483	78	20	33	700	262	243	204	14	386	22	30	13	147	52	.74	23	.270	.349	.391

John Myrow

Bats: Right **Throws:** Right **Pos:** OF — **Ht:** 6'0" **Wt:** 177 **Born:** 2/11/72 **Age:** 24

Year	Team	Lg	G	AB	H	2B	3B	HR	TB	R	RBI	TBB	IBB	SO	HBP	SH	SF	SB	CS	SB%	GDP	Avg	OBP	SLG
1993	Bend	A	70	260	52	11	0	4	75	27	24	16	0	62	4	8	3	12	5	.71	3	.200	.254	.288
1994	Central Val	A	128	521	143	26	2	8	197	81	73	27	1	85	7	3	9	26	5	.84	16	.274	.314	.378
1995	New Haven	AA	96	353	87	18	1	3	116	52	50	25	2	67	8	3	3	16	5	.76	13	.246	.308	.329
	3 Min. YEARS		294	1134	282	55	3	15	388	160	147	68	3	214	19	14	15	54	15	.78	32	.249	.299	.342

Tyrone Narcisse

Pitches: Right **Bats:** Right **Pos:** P   **Ht:** 6'5" **Wt:** 205 **Born:** 2/4/72 **Age:** 24

Year Team	Lg	G	GS	CG	GF	IP	BFP	H	R	ER	HR	SH	SF	HB	TBB	IBB	SO	WP	Bk	W	L	Pct.	ShO	Sv	ERA
1990 Padres	R	7	1	0	3	10.2	52	13	11	6	0	0	0	2	6	0	6	3	2	0	0	.000	0	0	5.06
1991 Padres	R	11	10	0	0	37.1	193	43	41	31	1	1	1	4	37	0	23	5	3	2	3	.400	0	0	7.47
1992 Astros	R	11	6	0	2	34.2	158	31	25	19	0	1	3	2	24	0	32	5	1	3	2	.600	0	0	4.93
1993 Asheville	A	29	29	2	0	160.1	702	173	95	78	11	4	8	12	66	0	114	9	5	6	12	.333	0	0	4.38
1994 Osceola	A	26	26	2	0	146	633	153	91	79	7	5	5	11	57	2	86	9	4	7	11	.389	0	0	4.87
1995 Jackson	AA	27	27	2	0	163.2	686	140	76	59	8	11	7	10	60	5	93	8	0	5	14	.263	0	0	3.24
6 Min. YEARS		111	99	6	5	552.2	2424	553	339	272	27	22	24	41	250	7	354	39	15	23	42	.354	0	0	4.43

Dan Naulty

Pitches: Right **Bats:** Right **Pos:** P   **Ht:** 6'6" **Wt:** 202 **Born:** 1/6/70 **Age:** 26

Year Team	Lg	G	GS	CG	GF	IP	BFP	H	R	ER	HR	SH	SF	HB	TBB	IBB	SO	WP	Bk	W	L	Pct.	ShO	Sv	ERA
1992 Kenosha	A	6	2	0	1	18	83	22	12	11	3	1	0	1	7	0	14	1	1	0	1	.000	0	0	5.50
1993 Fort Myers	A	7	6	0	0	30	148	41	22	19	4	1	1	6	14	1	20	3	0	0	0	.000	0	0	5.70
Fort Wayne	A	18	18	3	0	116	478	101	45	42	5	3	1	2	48	0	96	7	5	6	8	.429	2	0	3.26
1994 Fort Myers	A	16	15	1	1	88.1	380	78	35	29	6	1	5	3	32	2	83	5	0	4	2	.667	0	0	2.95
Nashville	AA	9	9	0	0	47.1	208	48	32	31	4	2	5	1	22	1	29	3	0	0	7	.000	0	0	5.89
1995 Salt Lake	AAA	42	8	0	19	90.1	393	92	55	52	10	2	1	2	47	2	76	6	0	2	6	.250	0	4	5.18
4 Min. YEARS		98	58	4	21	390	1690	382	201	184	32	10	13	15	170	6	318	25	6	16	29	.356	2	4	4.25

Lipso Nava

Bats: Right **Throws:** Right **Pos:** 3B   **Ht:** 6'2" **Wt:** 175 **Born:** 11/28/68 **Age:** 27

Year Team	Lg	G	AB	H	2B	3B	HR	TB	R	RBI	TBB	IBB	SO	HBP	SH	SF	SB	CS	SB%	GDP	Avg	OBP	SLG
1990 Bellingham	A	46	171	43	12	0	0	55	11	15	15	2	31	2	3	0	2	2	.50	5	.251	.319	.322
San Bernrdo	A	7	23	4	1	0	0	5	1	1	0	0	9	2	1	0	0	0	.00	1	.174	.240	.217
1991 San Bernrdo	A	86	258	70	5	0	2	81	19	33	20	0	44	6	3	2	5	4	.56	4	.271	.336	.314
1992 Peninsula	A	102	346	78	16	2	3	107	32	35	18	1	56	8	4	1	7	3	.70	8	.225	.279	.309
1993 Jacksonvlle	AA	114	396	101	20	0	7	142	52	41	31	1	43	13	12	3	5	6	.45	11	.255	.327	.359
1994 Riverside	A	28	102	26	9	1	0	37	15	13	12	1	19	2	0	2	0	0	.00	5	.255	.339	.363
Jacksonvlle	AA	41	131	25	6	1	3	42	13	10	7	0	20	2	6	0	2	2	.50	1	.191	.243	.321
1995 Trenton	AA	20	51	11	3	0	1	17	7	7	1	0	5	3	1	1	1	0	1.00	1	.216	.268	.333
Sarasota	A	21	62	16	4	0	2	26	11	10	7	0	7	4	0	0	1	0	1.00	3	.258	.370	.419
6 Min. YEARS		465	1540	374	76	4	18	512	161	165	111	5	234	42	30	9	23	17	.58	39	.243	.310	.332

Mike Neal

Bats: Right **Throws:** Right **Pos:** 2B   **Ht:** 6'1" **Wt:** 180 **Born:** 11/5/71 **Age:** 24

Year Team	Lg	G	AB	H	2B	3B	HR	TB	R	RBI	TBB	IBB	SO	HBP	SH	SF	SB	CS	SB%	GDP	Avg	OBP	SLG
1993 Watertown	A	67	234	68	15	3	4	101	47	43	55	4	45	6	1	3	7	1	.88	2	.291	.433	.432
1994 Kinston	A	101	378	99	21	1	5	137	51	38	40	1	94	3	3	1	8	12	.40	6	.262	.336	.362
1995 Canton-Akrn	AA	134	419	112	24	2	5	155	64	46	71	3	79	9	4	8	5	6	.45	7	.267	.379	.370
3 Min. YEARS		302	1031	279	60	6	14	393	162	127	166	8	218	18	8	12	20	19	.51	15	.271	.377	.381

Chris Neier

Pitches: Right **Bats:** Right **Pos:** P   **Ht:** 6'4" **Wt:** 205 **Born:** 11/19/71 **Age:** 24

Year Team	Lg	G	GS	CG	GF	IP	BFP	H	R	ER	HR	SH	SF	HB	TBB	IBB	SO	WP	Bk	W	L	Pct.	ShO	Sv	ERA
1992 Rockies/cub	R	14	6	1	2	56.1	235	53	23	14	0	2	0	3	7	0	49	2	2	5	1	.833	0	0	2.24
1993 Bend	A	15	15	0	0	77	347	90	55	41	6	5	2	3	32	2	58	3	1	3	5	.375	0	0	4.79
1994 Asheville	A	31	0	0	6	56.1	247	61	28	23	4	1	5	3	19	1	49	1	0	2	2	.500	0	1	3.67
Central Val	A	19	0	0	10	27.2	113	28	10	9	1	0	1	0	4	1	23	4	0	1	0	1.000	0	4	2.93
1995 New Haven	AA	38	18	1	5	123.1	550	164	62	57	10	4	3	1	47	5	74	2	1	10	4	.714	0	0	4.16
4 Min. YEARS		117	39	2	26	340.2	1492	396	178	144	21	12	11	10	109	9	253	12	4	21	12	.636	0	5	3.80

Mike Neill

Bats: Left **Throws:** Left **Pos:** OF   **Ht:** 6'2" **Wt:** 189 **Born:** 4/27/70 **Age:** 26

Year Team	Lg	G	AB	H	2B	3B	HR	TB	R	RBI	TBB	IBB	SO	HBP	SH	SF	SB	CS	SB%	GDP	Avg	OBP	SLG
1991 Sou. Oregon	A	63	240	84	14	0	5	113	42	42	35	3	54	0	4	1	9	3	.75	1	.350	.431	.471
1992 Reno	A	130	473	159	26	7	5	214	101	76	81	2	96	5	6	2	23	11	.68	15	.336	.437	.452
Huntsville	AA	5	16	5	0	0	0	5	4	2	2	0	7	0	1	1	1	0	1.00	0	.313	.368	.313
1993 Huntsville	AA	54	179	44	8	0	1	55	30	15	34	0	45	1	0	1	3	4	.43	4	.246	.367	.307
Modesto	A	17	62	12	3	0	0	15	4	4	12	0	12	0	1	0	1	0	.00	0	.194	.324	.242
1994 Tacoma	AAA	7	22	5	1	0	0	6	1	2	3	0	7	0	0	0	0	0	.00	2	.227	.320	.273
Modesto	A	47	165	48	4	1	2	60	22	18	26	1	50	1	2	1	1	1	.50	4	.291	.389	.364
1995 Modesto	A	71	257	71	17	1	6	108	39	36	34	2	65	2	5	1	4	4	.50	6	.276	.364	.420
Huntsville	AA	33	107	32	6	1	2	46	11	16	12	1	29	0	0	1	1	0	1.00	1	.299	.367	.430
5 Min. YEARS		427	1521	460	79	10	21	622	254	211	239	9	365	9	19	8	42	24	.64	33	.302	.398	.409

Tom Nevers

Bats: Right Throws: Right Pos: 3B

Ht: 6'1" Wt: 175 Born: 9/13/71 Age: 24

Year	Team	Lg	G	AB	H	2B	3B	HR	TB	R	RBI	TBB	IBB	SO	HBP	SH	SF	SB	CS	SB%	GDP	Avg	OBP	SLG
1990	Astros	R	50	185	44	10	5	2	70	23	32	27	0	38	3	0	3	13	3	.81	3	.238	.339	.378
1991	Asheville	A	129	441	111	26	2	16	189	59	71	53	0	124	3	2	5	10	12	.45	11	.252	.333	.429
1992	Osceola	A	125	455	114	24	6	8	174	49	55	22	1	124	3	2	1	6	2	.75	10	.251	.289	.382
1993	Jackson	AA	55	184	50	8	2	1	65	21	10	16	2	36	2	1	1	7	2	.78	5	.272	.335	.353
1994	Jackson	AA	125	449	120	25	2	8	173	54	62	31	2	101	4	1	7	10	5	.67	8	.267	.316	.385
1995	Jackson	AA	83	298	72	7	3	8	109	36	35	24	2	58	2	0	2	5	2	.71	10	.242	.301	.366
	Stockton	A	4	14	4	0	0	0	4	2	3	0	0	6	2	0	0	1	0	1.00	0	.286	.375	.286
	El Paso	AA	35	118	30	5	0	1	38	19	12	11	0	21	3	0	0	2	1	.67	6	.254	.333	.322
	6 Min. YEARS		606	2144	545	105	20	44	822	263	280	184	7	508	22	6	19	54	27	.67	53	.254	.317	.383

Jim Newlin

Pitches: Right Bats: Right Pos: P

Ht: 6'2" Wt: 205 Born: 9/11/66 Age: 29

Year	Team	Lg	G	GS	CG	GF	IP	BFP	H	R	ER	HR	SH	SF	HB	TBB	IBB	SO	WP	Bk	W	L	Pct.	ShO	Sv	ERA
1989	San Bernrdo	A	19	0	0	9	28.2	110	13	6	5	1	1	0	3	15	1	25	1	1	1	2	.333	0	4	1.57
1990	San Bernrdo	A	36	0	0	28	45	192	35	24	18	2	2	3	4	21	5	56	3	2	1	5	.167	0	12	3.60
	Williamsprt	AA	20	0	0	12	38.2	174	45	22	15	2	3	2	2	15	0	23	0	3	1	1	.500	0	0	3.49
1991	Jacksonville	AA	47	0	0	37	64	275	58	24	16	4	9	2	5	29	5	48	3	1	6	5	.545	0	12	2.25
1992	Calgary	AAA	30	0	0	13	43.2	217	60	33	28	1	0	3	2	29	2	24	1	0	1	1	.500	0	3	5.77
	Jacksonvlle	AA	12	0	0	11	22	90	22	5	5	1	2	0	2	10	0	13	3	0	1	1	.500	0	1	2.05
1993	Jacksonville	AA	8	0	0	3	17.1	77	22	12	9	3	2	1	1	3	0	11	0	1	1	1	.500	0	0	4.67
	Knoxville	AA	13	2	0	4	26.1	133	41	28	26	2	3	3	0	13	1	19	3	4	0	2	.000	0	0	8.89
	Edmonton	AAA	4	0	0	1	6	35	11	9	9	1	0	2	2	4	0	3	1	1	0	0	.000	0	0	13.50
	High Desert	A	17	0	0	9	28.1	124	30	15	9	3	1	1	2	9	1	23	0	0	3	0	1.000	0	3	2.86
1994	Edmonton	AAA	21	0	0	6	38.2	186	60	36	34	3	3	1	3	17	2	23	3	0	2	4	.333	0	7	7.91
	Portland	AA	30	0	0	15	44.2	182	32	12	10	2	4	1	3	18	2	49	2	0	1	3	.250	0	4	2.01
1995	Charlotte	AAA	5	0	0	2	6.1	24	6	3	3	3	0	0	0	1	0	5	1	0	0	0	.000	0	0	4.26
	Bowie	AA	40	1	0	26	63.2	283	69	35	26	6	3	5	2	22	3	51	9	1	3	5	.375	0	11	3.68
	7 Min. YEARS		302	3	0	176	473.1	2102	504	264	213	34	33	24	31	206	22	373	30	14	21	30	.412	0	50	4.05

Andy Nezelek

Pitches: Right Bats: Left Pos: P

Ht: 6'6" Wt: 218 Born: 10/24/65 Age: 30

Year	Team	Lg	G	GS	CG	GF	IP	BFP	H	R	ER	HR	SH	SF	HB	TBB	IBB	SO	WP	Bk	W	L	Pct.	ShO	Sv	ERA
1986	Pulaski	R	12	12	2	0	66.1	308	69	36	20	4	2	4	9	22	1	55	7	0	2	4	.333	0	0	2.71
1987	Sumter	A	12	12	5	0	85	333	56	24	17	5	2	2	6	12	1	67	4	2	6	3	.667	0	0	1.80
1988	Greenville	AA	26	25	3	1	133.2	569	133	77	65	7	3	6	5	45	0	89	8	5	7	8	.467	0	0	4.38
1989	Richmond	AAA	48	0	0	37	77.1	324	65	25	21	0	8	3	3	35	6	30	8	0	4	5	.444	0	12	2.44
1990	Richmond	AAA	25	14	2	3	80.2	364	101	52	46	7	5	6	7	26	1	39	12	3	4	9	.308	0	0	5.13
1992	Greenville	AA	46	4	0	8	107.2	434	87	36	27	2	2	2	12	23	1	114	4	2	9	2	.818	0	1	2.26
	Richmond	AAA	2	0	0	0	6	20	3	0	0	0	0	0	1	0	0	5	0	0	0	0	.000	0	0	0.00
1995	Carolina	AA	6	0	0	1	14	64	16	9	8	3	0	0	0	3	0	14	0	0	1	0	1.000	0	1	5.14
	Pirates	H	4	0	0	4	7	34	12	7	6	0	1	0	0	2	1	6	2	0	1	1	.500	0	1	7.71
	7 Min. YEARS		181	67	12	54	577.2	2450	542	266	210	28	23	23	43	168	11	419	45	12	34	32	.515	0	15	3.27

Darrell Nicholas

Bats: Right Throws: Right Pos: OF

Ht: 6'0" Wt: 180 Born: 5/26/72 Age: 24

Year	Team	Lg	G	AB	H	2B	3B	HR	TB	R	RBI	TBB	IBB	SO	HBP	SH	SF	SB	CS	SB%	GDP	Avg	OBP	SLG
1994	Helena	R	15	61	23	3	2	0	30	18	13	10	0	10	1	0	0	11	3	.79	0	.377	.472	.492
	Beloit	A	59	221	63	8	3	1	80	33	35	22	1	54	1	2	4	17	4	.81	4	.285	.347	.362
1995	El Paso	AA	15	39	8	0	1	0	10	4	2	0	0	11	0	1	0	4	0	1.00	0	.205	.205	.256
	Stockton	A	87	350	112	16	3	5	149	54	39	23	1	75	1	1	11	26	8	.76	6	.320	.363	.426
	2 Min. YEARS		176	671	206	27	9	6	269	109	89	55	2	150	3	14	5	58	15	.79	10	.307	.360	.401

Jackie Nickell

Pitches: Right Bats: Right Pos: P

Ht: 5'10" Wt: 175 Born: 4/20/70 Age: 26

Year	Team	Lg	G	GS	CG	GF	IP	BFP	H	R	ER	HR	SH	SF	HB	TBB	IBB	SO	WP	Bk	W	L	Pct.	ShO	Sv	ERA
1992	Bellingham	A	1	1	0	0	5	23	5	4	4	1	0	0	1	1	0	3	0	1	0	1	.000	0	0	7.20
	San Bernrdo	A	13	4	0	4	40	185	45	33	31	8	1	3	4	23	0	30	3	6	0	4	.000	0	0	6.98
1993	Appleton	A	24	23	2	1	150	602	135	54	51	8	10	2	7	41	0	151	7	12	7	7	.500	0	0	3.06
1994	Riverside	A	15	14	1	0	90.1	370	77	42	38	9	3	0	4	21	0	71	3	7	9	4	.692	1	0	3.79
	Jacksonvlle	AA	3	2	1	0	14	62	16	10	7	2	1	0	1	3	0	11	2	0	1	0	1.000	0	0	4.50
1995	Port City	AA	27	9	0	7	89.1	367	74	40	37	11	2	4	8	30	0	81	4	4	5	8	.385	0	0	3.73
	4 Min. YEARS		83	53	4	12	388.2	1609	352	183	168	39	17	9	25	119	0	347	19	30	22	24	.478	1	0	3.89

Tony Nieto

Pitches: Right Bats: Both Pos: P Ht: 6'1" Wt: 170 Born: 4/19/73 Age: 23

Year Team	Lg	G	GS	CG	GF	IP	BFP	H	R	ER	HR	SH	SF	HB	TBB	IBB	SO	WP	Bk	W	L	Pct.	ShO	Sv	ERA
1994 Billings	R	21	2	0	11	44.1	175	33	21	11	1	1	0	4	10	0	31	2	1	1	1	.500	0	3	2.23
1995 Charlstn-Wv	A	13	8	2	0	55	246	55	37	21	1	6	1	8	21	6	35	1	0	3	4	.429	2	0	3.44
Bowie	AA	1	1	0	0	3	18	6	5	5	2	0	0	0	3	0	3	0	0	0	0	.000	0	0	15.00
Frederick	A	21	0	0	6	39	162	38	19	17	4	2	1	5	9	2	14	1	1	1	4	.200	0	0	3.92
2 Min. YEARS		56	11	2	17	141.1	601	132	82	54	8	9	2	17	43	8	83	4	3	5	9	.357	2	3	3.44

Ernie Nieves

Pitches: Right Bats: Right Pos: P Ht: 5'11" Wt: 183 Born: 8/26/70 Age: 25

Year Team	Lg	G	GS	CG	GF	IP	BFP	H	R	ER	HR	SH	SF	HB	TBB	IBB	SO	WP	Bk	W	L	Pct.	ShO	Sv	ERA
1989 Reds	R	25	0	0	24	31.2	132	27	12	8	1	1	0	2	10	2	30	3	4	0	3	.000	0	13	2.27
1990 Charlstn-Wv	A	20	0	0	11	25	114	19	14	10	3	6	1	3	16	3	21	1	0	1	3	.250	0	2	3.60
Billings	R	20	0	0	5	40.2	182	48	27	19	4	1	1	2	18	0	22	7	1	2	0	1.000	0	1	4.20
1991 Charlstn-Wv	A	27	10	0	7	87.2	377	96	38	29	1	2	1	7	32	2	53	3	1	6	1	.857	0	1	2.98
1992 Charlstn-Wv	A	37	0	0	14	74.2	322	71	37	31	5	4	4	1	38	6	35	5	3	11	6	.647	0	1	3.74
1994 Lk Elsinore	A	27	0	0	17	39.2	181	42	25	19	3	2	2	2	24	2	33	3	1	1	3	.250	0	1	4.31
1995 Midland	AA	6	1	0	1	13.1	62	15	7	6	1	2	1	1	10	1	3	1	0	0	1	.000	0	0	4.05
6 Min. YEARS		162	11	0	79	312.2	1370	318	160	122	18	18	10	18	148	16	197	23	10	21	17	.553	0	18	3.51

Jim Nix

Pitches: Right Bats: Right Pos: P Ht: 5'11" Wt: 175 Born: 9/6/70 Age: 25

Year Team	Lg	G	GS	CG	GF	IP	BFP	H	R	ER	HR	SH	SF	HB	TBB	IBB	SO	WP	Bk	W	L	Pct.	ShO	Sv	ERA
1992 Princeton	R	27	0	0	24	34.2	142	27	16	11	3	3	0	0	13	2	44	4	1	0	4	.000	0	13	2.86
Charlstn-Wv	A	2	0	0	1	3.1	15	3	0	0	0	0	0	1	1	1	5	0	0	0	0	.000	0	0	0.00
1993 Charlstn-Wv	A	26	5	1	18	60.2	237	28	19	15	1	2	1	5	24	3	75	5	1	7	2	.778	0	5	2.23
Winston-Sal	A	11	4	0	3	35.1	153	37	24	14	8	0	1	0	15	0	33	2	0	3	3	.500	0	0	3.57
1994 Winston-Sal	A	29	28	1	1	169	753	168	103	86	23	6	9	9	87	1	139	10	2	11	10	.524	0	0	4.58
1995 Chattanooga	AA	40	5	0	14	84.1	360	84	43	30	8	6	4	2	30	1	71	7	1	3	5	.375	0	2	3.20
4 Min. YEARS		135	42	2	61	387.1	1660	347	205	156	43	17	15	17	170	8	367	28	5	24	24	.500	0	20	3.62

Trot Nixon

Bats: Left Throws: Left Pos: OF Ht: 6'1" Wt: 195 Born: 4/11/74 Age: 22

Year Team	Lg	G	AB	H	2B	3B	HR	TB	R	RBI	TBB	IBB	SO	HBP	SH	SF	SB	CS	SB%	GDP	Avg	OBP	SLG
1994 Lynchburg	A	71	264	65	12	0	12	113	33	43	44	1	53	3	1	3	10	3	.77	5	.246	.357	.428
1995 Sarasota	A	73	264	80	11	4	5	114	43	39	45	3	46	1	0	2	7	5	.58	5	.303	.404	.432
Trenton	AA	25	94	15	3	1	2	26	9	8	7	0	20	0	2	2	2	1	.67	0	.160	.214	.277
2 Min. YEARS		169	622	160	26	5	19	253	85	90	96	4	119	4	3	7	19	9	.68	10	.257	.357	.407

Junior Noboa

Bats: Right Throws: Right Pos: 2B Ht: 5'10" Wt: 170 Born: 11/10/64 Age: 31

Year Team	Lg	G	AB	H	2B	3B	HR	TB	R	RBI	TBB	IBB	SO	HBP	SH	SF	SB	CS	SB%	GDP	Avg	OBP	SLG
1981 Batavia	A	50	162	49	8	0	0	57	15	6	11	0	19	2	2	1	11	4	.73	2	.302	.352	.352
1982 Waterloo	A	121	385	86	12	5	0	108	68	23	62	1	61	2	19	3	44	12	.79	7	.223	.332	.281
1983 Waterloo	A	132	449	115	22	3	1	146	64	29	48	1	71	5	18	2	47	20	.70	3	.256	.333	.325
1984 Buffalo	AA	117	383	97	18	4	1	126	55	45	31	0	28	2	17	3	12	7	.63	7	.253	.310	.329
1985 Maine	AAA	122	403	116	11	2	5	146	62	32	34	0	28	3	10	3	14	15	.48	3	.288	.345	.362
1986 Maine	AAA	108	399	114	21	1	4	149	44	32	15	0	33	2	8	3	10	14	.42	8	.286	.313	.373
1987 Buffalo	AAA	43	149	47	6	2	0	57	26	14	18	0	16	0	1	1	2	2	.50	3	.315	.387	.383
1988 Edmonton	AAA	50	159	47	6	1	0	55	24	17	11	0	12	0	3	0	5	5	.50	1	.296	.341	.346
1989 Indianapols	AAA	117	467	159	21	8	2	202	61	62	21	4	34	3	7	8	14	11	.56	2	.340	.367	.433
1992 Tidewater	AAA	6	20	4	0	0	0	4	1	3	0	0	4	0	0	0	0	0	.00	0	.200	.200	.200
1993 Indianapols	AAA	45	180	51	11	1	0	64	27	14	14	2	8	1	0	1	0	2	.00	5	.283	.337	.356
1994 Buffalo	AAA	67	240	69	9	1	0	80	26	18	14	5	11	1	3	0	4	6	.40	6	.288	.329	.333
1995 Rochester	AAA	6	20	2	0	0	0	2	1	2	0	0	0	0	0	1	0	0	.00	1	.100	.095	.100
1984 Cleveland	AL	23	11	4	0	0	0	4	3	0	0	0	2	0	1	0	1	0	1.00	1	.364	.364	.364
1987 Cleveland	AL	39	80	18	2	1	0	22	7	7	3	1	6	0	5	0	1	0	1.00	1	.225	.253	.275
1988 California	AL	21	16	1	0	0	0	1	4	0	0	0	1	0	0	0	0	0	.00	2	.063	.063	.063
1989 Montreal	NL	21	44	10	0	0	0	10	3	1	1	0	3	0	0	0	0	0	.00	2	.227	.244	.227
1990 Montreal	NL	81	158	42	7	2	0	53	15	14	7	2	14	1	3	4	4	1	.80	2	.266	.294	.335
1991 Montreal	NL	67	95	23	3	0	1	29	5	2	1	1	8	0	0	0	2	3	.40	2	.242	.250	.305
1992 New York	NL	46	47	7	0	0	0	7	7	3	3	0	8	1	0	1	0	0	.00	2	.149	.212	.149
1994 Oakland	AL	17	40	13	1	1	0	16	3	6	2	0	5	0	0	0	1	0	1.00	0	.325	.357	.400
Pittsburgh	NL	2	2	0	0	0	0	0	0	0	0	0	0	0	0	0	0	0	.00	0	.000	.000	.000
13 Min. YEARS		984	3416	956	145	28	13	1196	474	297	279	13	325	21	88	26	163	98	.62	54	.280	.336	.350
8 Maj. YEARS		317	493	118	13	4	1	142	47	33	17	4	47	2	9	5	9	4	.69	9	.239	.265	.288

J.D. Noland

Bats: Left **Throws:** Right **Pos:** OF-DH
Ht: 5'9" **Wt:** 173 **Born:** 12/5/68 **Age:** 27

Year	Team	Lg	G	AB	H	2B	3B	HR	TB	R	RBI	TBB	IBB	SO	HBP	SH	SF	SB	CS	SB%	GDP	Avg	OBP	SLG
1989	Waterloo	A	99	331	79	4	0	0	83	40	18	39	1	86	2	9	1	31	15	.67	4	.239	.322	.251
1990	Waterloo	A	125	456	112	20	6	4	156	75	51	71	3	84	1	4	6	48	24	.67	5	.246	.345	.342
1991	High Desert	A	128	495	137	23	12	4	196	114	68	78	5	96	2	5	4	81	23	.78	8	.277	.375	.396
1992	Wichita	AA	118	452	122	21	6	5	170	59	52	36	0	80	3	4	0	40	23	.63	5	.270	.328	.376
1994	New Haven	AA	55	212	62	6	3	3	83	28	44	18	1	27	2	3	4	24	8	.75	4	.292	.347	.392
	Colo. Sprng	AAA	53	214	74	13	2	3	100	37	34	9	0	32	2	1	1	11	8	.58	5	.346	.376	.467
1995	Tacoma	AAA	76	251	69	10	3	5	100	27	28	13	1	37	0	4	3	14	6	.70	7	.275	.307	.398
	6 Min. YEARS		654	2411	655	97	32	24	888	380	295	264	11	442	12	30	19	249	107	.70	38	.272	.344	.368

Rey Noriega

Bats: Both **Throws:** Right **Pos:** SS
Ht: 6'0" **Wt:** 175 **Born:** 3/15/68 **Age:** 28

Year	Team	Lg	G	AB	H	2B	3B	HR	TB	R	RBI	TBB	IBB	SO	HBP	SH	SF	SB	CS	SB%	GDP	Avg	OBP	SLG
1989	Yankees	R	39	125	37	4	6	0	53	29	16	33	0	27	1	3	3	7	2	.78	3	.296	.438	.424
1990	Ft. Laud	A	84	305	69	17	3	3	101	52	28	35	1	84	2	6	4	7	6	.54	5	.226	.306	.331
1991	Ft. Laud	A	126	429	107	19	7	14	182	67	68	78	7	134	2	0	2	12	4	.75	4	.249	.366	.424
1992	Albany-Colo	AA	22	78	8	2	0	0	10	2	3	5	0	31	0	0	0	1	0	1.00	2	.103	.157	.128
	Ft. Laud	A	99	338	75	19	6	5	121	41	38	41	5	86	1	1	1	12	2	.86	4	.222	.307	.358
1995	Birmingham	AA	42	100	19	5	0	0	24	9	5	11	0	27	1	2	0	1	2	.33	3	.190	.277	.240
	Nashville	AAA	20	55	9	4	0	1	16	6	3	4	0	20	0	1	0	0	0	.00	0	.164	.203	.291
	5 Min. YEARS		432	1430	324	70	22	23	507	206	161	206	13	409	7	13	11	40	16	.71	21	.227	.325	.355

Ken Norman

Bats: Both **Throws:** Right **Pos:** OF
Ht: 5'10" **Wt:** 180 **Born:** 7/13/71 **Age:** 24

Year	Team	Lg	G	AB	H	2B	3B	HR	TB	R	RBI	TBB	IBB	SO	HBP	SH	SF	SB	CS	SB%	GDP	Avg	OBP	SLG
1989	Twins	R	43	124	27	4	2	0	35	17	13	7	0	37	4	0	0	21	1	.95	0	.218	.281	.282
1990	Twins	R	44	131	33	6	2	1	46	22	9	9	0	46	2	1	1	23	2	.92	1	.252	.308	.351
1991	Elizabethtn	R	53	166	42	7	2	2	59	25	18	12	3	48	5	0	1	13	2	.87	2	.253	.321	.355
1992	Kenosha	A	20	51	3	0	0	0	3	2	3	0	0	15	0	0	0	1	0	1.00	0	.059	.059	.059
	Elizabethtn	R	35	129	32	4	1	2	44	32	11	10	1	30	4	1	2	8	3	.73	1	.248	.317	.341
1993	Fort Myers	A	84	237	49	9	0	1	61	27	8	11	0	67	4	0	0	12	7	.63	1	.207	.254	.257
1994	Fort Myers	A	106	368	86	12	3	2	110	49	30	34	1	83	6	1	2	32	6	.84	7	.234	.307	.299
1995	New Britain	AA	12	31	9	1	0	0	10	4	1	5	0	9	0	0	0	0	1	.00	1	.290	.389	.323
	Salinas	IND	86	312	78	9	8	5	118	55	34	25	1	76	3	1	2	36	6	.86	1	.250	.310	.378
	7 Min. YEARS		483	1549	359	52	18	13	486	233	127	113	6	411	28	4	8	146	28	.84	14	.232	.294	.314

Scott Norman

Pitches: Right **Bats:** Right **Pos:** P
Ht: 6'0" **Wt:** 195 **Born:** 9/1/72 **Age:** 23

Year	Team	Lg	G	GS	CG	GF	IP	BFP	H	R	ER	HR	SH	SF	HB	TBB	IBB	SO	WP	Bk	W	L	Pct.	ShO	Sv	ERA
1993	Bristol	R	13	13	1	0	77	355	100	54	45	7	1	1	6	18	0	43	9	5	3	6	.333	0	0	5.26
1994	Fayetteville	A	25	25	4	0	165	672	148	63	51	9	3	4	4	41	0	95	12	0	14	7	.667	2	0	2.78
	Lakeland	A	3	3	1	0	18.1	77	19	7	6	2	0	1	1	5	0	9	2	0	0	2	.000	1	0	2.95
1995	Jacksonvlle	AA	4	4	2	0	29	122	31	12	8	4	1	0	1	6	0	9	1	0	1	3	.250	0	0	2.48
	Lakeland	A	22	21	3	0	128.1	571	141	86	58	4	2	9	6	38	1	63	4	2	7	7	.500	0	0	4.07
	3 Min. YEARS		67	66	11	0	417.2	1797	439	222	168	26	7	15	18	108	1	219	28	7	25	25	.500	3	0	3.62

Joe Norris

Pitches: Right **Bats:** Right **Pos:** P
Ht: 6'4" **Wt:** 215 **Born:** 11/29/70 **Age:** 25

Year	Team	Lg	G	GS	CG	GF	IP	BFP	H	R	ER	HR	SH	SF	HB	TBB	IBB	SO	WP	Bk	W	L	Pct.	ShO	Sv	ERA
1990	Jamestown	A	13	13	1	0	62.1	290	63	48	36	2	1	2	4	43	0	72	9	5	3	7	.300	0	0	5.20
1991	Sumter	A	8	8	0	0	35	161	41	25	20	2	0	1	3	17	0	42	6	2	1	3	.250	0	0	5.14
1992	Rockford	A	27	27	1	0	163	723	160	88	68	5	11	5	10	79	2	143	21	3	5	15	.250	0	0	3.75
1993	W. Palm Bch	A	26	13	0	0	81	336	62	27	24	3	2	4	9	29	0	63	6	0	7	4	.636	0	0	2.67
1994	Nashville	AA	36	13	0	8	111	474	106	58	52	6	4	7	7	45	2	83	10	3	6	8	.429	0	1	4.22
1995	New Britain	AA	46	0	0	20	82.2	364	79	44	33	4	11	3	2	36	5	81	4	0	5	6	.455	0	5	3.59
	6 Min. YEARS		156	74	2	32	535	2348	511	288	233	22	29	22	35	249	9	484	56	13	27	43	.386	0	6	3.92

Kevin Northrup

Bats: Right **Throws:** Right **Pos:** OF
Ht: 6'1" **Wt:** 190 **Born:** 1/27/70 **Age:** 26

Year	Team	Lg	G	AB	H	2B	3B	HR	TB	R	RBI	TBB	IBB	SO	HBP	SH	SF	SB	CS	SB%	GDP	Avg	OBP	SLG
1992	Jamestown	A	18	72	21	4	1	4	39	14	15	8	0	17	3	0	0	8	1	.89	1	.292	.438	.542
1993	W. Palm Bch	A	131	459	136	29	0	6	183	65	63	70	7	76	3	4	5	10	7	.59	9	.296	.389	.399
1994	Harrisburg	AA	92	341	113	21	0	11	167	53	55	34	2	38	4	2	3	6	3	.67	14	.331	.395	.490
	Ottawa	AAA	33	102	29	7	1	3	47	19	16	16	0	16	1	0	0	2	0	1.00	4	.284	.387	.461
1995	St. Lucie	A	17	64	19	1	1	0	22	7	12	4	0	6	0	0	2	2	1	.67	2	.297	.329	.344
	Harrisburg	AA	40	152	47	14	0	1	64	23	27	10	1	16	0	0	0	0	1	.00	3	.309	.350	.421

		G	AB	H	2B	3B	HR	TB	R	RBI	TBB	IBB	SO	HBP	SH	SF	SB	CS	SB%	GDP	Avg	OBP	SLG
Edmonton	AAA	17	44	8	2	0	0	10	4	1	5	1	8	0	1	0	0	0	.00	0	.182	.265	.227
4 Min. YEARS		348	1234	373	78	3	25	532	185	189	147	11	177	11	7	11	28	13	.68	33	.302	.378	.431

Chris Norton

Bats: Right **Throws:** Right **Pos:** 1B   **Ht:** 6'2" **Wt:** 215 **Born:** 9/21/70 **Age:** 25

BATTING / BASERUNNING / PERCENTAGES

Year Team	Lg	G	AB	H	2B	3B	HR	TB	R	RBI	TBB	IBB	SO	HBP	SH	SF	SB	CS	SB%	GDP	Avg	OBP	SLG
1992 Watertown	A	1	4	0	0	0	0	0	1	0	0	0	2	0	0	0	0	0	.00	0	.000	.000	.000
Burlington	R	4	12	3	0	0	0	3	2	2	1	0	4	0	0	1	0	0	.00	0	.250	.286	.250
Jamestown	A	60	207	42	4	1	4	60	15	27	15	0	64	2	0	2	3	0	1.00	3	.203	.261	.290
1993 Cardinals	R	27	83	19	5	3	0	30	10	11	11	1	23	1	0	0	0	0	.00	2	.229	.326	.361
1994 Savannah	A	126	439	116	11	2	26	209	75	82	73	4	144	4	3	2	6	4	.60	11	.264	.373	.476
1995 Arkansas	AA	10	25	6	2	0	0	8	6	6	11	2	5	0	0	1	0	0	.00	0	.240	.459	.320
Lubbock	IND	97	327	95	16	3	21	180	61	61	75	7	87	1	0	2	6	2	.75	5	.291	.422	.550
4 Min. YEARS		325	1097	281	38	9	51	490	170	189	186	14	329	8	3	8	15	6	.71	21	.256	.366	.447

Greg Norton

Bats: Both **Throws:** Right **Pos:** 3B   **Ht:** 6'1" **Wt:** 182 **Born:** 7/6/72 **Age:** 23

BATTING / BASERUNNING / PERCENTAGES

Year Team	Lg	G	AB	H	2B	3B	HR	TB	R	RBI	TBB	IBB	SO	HBP	SH	SF	SB	CS	SB%	GDP	Avg	OBP	SLG
1993 White Sox	R	3	9	2	0	0	0	2	1	2	1	0	1	0	0	0	0	0	.00	0	.222	.300	.222
Hickory	A	71	254	62	12	2	4	90	36	36	41	1	44	1	1	4	0	2	.00	6	.244	.347	.354
1994 South Bend	A	127	477	137	22	2	6	181	73	64	62	4	71	2	2	3	5	3	.63	7	.287	.369	.379
1995 Birmingham	AA	133	469	117	23	2	6	162	65	60	64	7	90	5	3	10	19	12	.61	10	.249	.339	.345
3 Min. YEARS		334	1209	318	57	6	16	435	175	162	168	12	206	8	6	17	24	17	.59	23	.263	.352	.360

Rafael Novoa

Pitches: Left **Bats:** Left **Pos:** P   **Ht:** 6'1" **Wt:** 190 **Born:** 10/26/67 **Age:** 28

HOW MUCH HE PITCHED / WHAT HE GAVE UP / THE RESULTS

Year Team	Lg	G	GS	CG	GF	IP	BFP	H	R	ER	HR	SH	SF	HB	TBB	IBB	SO	WP	Bk	W	L	Pct.	ShO	Sv	ERA
1989 Everett	A	3	3	0	0	15	73	20	11	8	2	0	0	1	8	0	20	3	1	0	1	.000	0	0	4.80
Clinton	A	13	10	0	0	63.2	267	58	20	18	1	9	1	4	18	1	61	1	6	5	4	.556	0	0	2.54
1990 Clinton	A	15	14	3	0	97.2	397	73	32	26	6	2	3	4	30	0	113	2	2	9	2	.818	1	0	2.40
Shreveport	AA	11	10	2	1	71.2	297	60	21	21	3	1	2	3	25	0	66	1	0	5	4	.556	1	0	2.64
1991 Phoenix	AAA	17	17	0	0	93.2	450	135	83	62	16	5	6	5	37	3	46	3	1	6	6	.500	0	0	5.96
1992 El Paso	AA	22	21	6	1	146.1	617	143	63	53	6	4	3	9	48	3	124	8	1	10	7	.588	0	0	3.26
1993 New Orleans	AAA	20	18	2	0	113	471	105	55	43	20	1	3	5	38	3	74	4	1	10	5	.667	1	0	3.42
1994 Iowa	AAA	27	23	1	0	137.1	621	151	90	80	12	7	4	8	67	3	54	7	1	6	10	.375	0	0	5.24
1995 Nashville	AAA	3	3	0	0	10	58	17	13	12	0	0	1	2	9	0	3	0	0	0	1	.000	0	0	10.80
Binghamton	AA	4	0	0	2	8	34	6	2	2	0	1	0	0	5	0	6	0	0	0	1	.000	0	0	2.25
1990 San Francisco	NL	7	2	0	2	18.2	88	21	14	14	3	0	1	0	13	1	14	0	0	0	1	.000	0	1	6.75
1993 Milwaukee	AL	15	7	2	0	56	249	58	32	28	7	4	4	2	22	2	17	1	0	0	3	.000	0	0	4.50
7 Min. YEARS		135	119	14	4	756.1	3285	768	390	325	66	30	23	41	285	13	567	29	13	51	41	.554	3	0	3.87
2 Maj. YEARS		22	9	2	2	74.2	337	79	46	42	10	4	3	4	35	3	31	1	0	0	4	.000	0	1	5.06

Ramon Nunez

Bats: Right **Throws:** Right **Pos:** 1B   **Ht:** 6'0" **Wt:** 150 **Born:** 9/22/72 **Age:** 23

BATTING / BASERUNNING / PERCENTAGES

Year Team	Lg	G	AB	H	2B	3B	HR	TB	R	RBI	TBB	IBB	SO	HBP	SH	SF	SB	CS	SB%	GDP	Avg	OBP	SLG
1992 Pulaski	R	59	218	55	9	2	5	83	28	32	14	1	57	3	0	1	8	3	.73	7	.252	.305	.381
1993 Macon	A	115	377	108	18	5	7	157	57	40	37	2	73	4	6	2	6	5	.55	6	.286	.355	.416
1994 Durham	A	124	453	125	23	0	17	199	59	62	38	1	98	2	0	4	4	9	.31	9	.276	.332	.439
1995 Durham	A	17	54	20	4	0	5	39	13	15	8	0	9	0	1	1	0	0	.00	4	.370	.444	.722
Greenville	AA	81	241	63	15	2	9	109	34	34	15	0	63	3	0	3	1	1	.50	8	.261	.309	.452
4 Min. YEARS		396	1343	371	69	9	43	587	191	183	112	4	300	12	7	11	19	18	.51	34	.276	.335	.437

Rogelio Nunez

Bats: Both **Throws:** Right **Pos:** C   **Ht:** 6'0" **Wt:** 180 **Born:** 5/6/70 **Age:** 26

BATTING / BASERUNNING / PERCENTAGES

Year Team	Lg	G	AB	H	2B	3B	HR	TB	R	RBI	TBB	IBB	SO	HBP	SH	SF	SB	CS	SB%	GDP	Avg	OBP	SLG
1989 White Sox	R	38	106	24	1	0	0	25	8	10	1	0	21	0	3	1	8	4	.67	2	.226	.231	.236
1990 Utica	A	35	90	24	1	2	1	32	11	11	5	2	24	0	1	2	5	1	.83	1	.267	.299	.356
1991 South Bend	A	56	189	46	4	1	0	46	26	15	14	0	30	0	6	0	21	6	.78	4	.243	.291	.243
Sarasota	A	15	36	8	1	0	0	9	6	3	3	0	8	0	2	1	0	1	.00	1	.222	.275	.250
1992 Sarasota	A	101	282	61	3	3	0	70	24	32	23	0	68	1	5	1	19	13	.59	7	.216	.277	.248
1993 Birmingham	AA	83	257	55	10	3	0	71	22	21	5	0	53	1	6	2	2	4	.33	6	.214	.230	.276
1994 Birmingham	AA	66	210	62	7	2	0	73	23	21	8	0	38	0	4	0	7	3	.70	2	.295	.321	.348
1995 Tulsa	AA	82	263	59	4	0	2	69	27	17	10	0	43	8	8	1	0	7	.00	10	.224	.273	.262
7 Min. YEARS		476	1433	333	31	11	3	395	147	130	69	2	285	10	35	8	62	39	.61	33	.232	.271	.276

Kevin O'Connor

Bats: Left **Throws:** Right **Pos:** OF   **Ht:** 6'0" **Wt:** 180 **Born:** 6/8/69 **Age:** 27

Year	Team	Lg	G	AB	H	2B	3B	HR	TB	R	RBI	TBB	IBB	SO	HBP	SH	SF	SB	CS	SB%	GDP	Avg	OBP	SLG
1990	Idaho Falls	R	12	47	11	2	0	1	16	6	4	0	0	5	0	0	0	4	0	1.00	2	.234	.234	.340
1991	Macon	A	90	312	78	11	2	1	96	58	31	48	1	36	3	2	6	32	10	.76	3	.250	.350	.308
	Durham	A	28	79	16	1	0	3	26	14	10	8	0	13	0	0	2	1	4	.20	1	.203	.270	.329
1992	Durham	A	122	438	123	17	2	6	162	79	35	48	4	49	3	5	2	31	17	.65	2	.281	.354	.370
1993	Greenville	AA	122	355	67	15	2	7	107	63	30	62	1	63	7	4	0	18	10	.64	7	.189	.321	.301
1994	Greenville	AA	126	471	128	19	1	3	158	49	33	33	3	69	5	4	1	24	13	.65	1	.272	.325	.335
1995	Richmond	AAA	94	203	45	2	3	4	65	33	14	27	2	42	1	0	0	14	4	.78	3	.222	.316	.320
	6 Min. YEARS		594	1905	468	67	10	25	630	302	157	226	11	277	19	15	11	124	58	.68	19	.246	.330	.331

John O'Donoghue

Pitches: Left **Bats:** Left **Pos:** P   **Ht:** 6'6" **Wt:** 210 **Born:** 5/26/69 **Age:** 27

Year	Team	Lg	G	GS	CG	GF	IP	BFP	H	R	ER	HR	SH	SF	HB	TBB	IBB	SO	WP	Bk	W	L	Pct.	ShO	Sv	ERA
1990	Bluefield	R	10	6	2	3	49.1	200	49	13	11	2	2	0	1	10	0	67	2	1	4	2	.667	2	0	2.01
	Frederick	A	1	1	0	0	4	18	5	2	2	0	0	0	0	0	0	3	0	0	0	1	.000	0	0	4.50
1991	Frederick	A	22	21	2	1	133.2	567	131	55	43	6	0	2	2	50	2	128	8	1	7	8	.467	1	0	2.90
1992	Hagerstown	AA	17	16	2	1	112.1	459	78	37	28	6	4	2	4	40	0	87	7	4	7	4	.636	0	0	2.24
	Rochester	AAA	13	10	3	1	69.2	282	60	31	25	5	4	0	4	19	1	47	5	0	5	4	.556	1	0	3.23
1993	Rochester	AAA	22	20	2	1	127.2	543	122	60	55	11	8	3	3	41	0	111	3	0	7	4	.636	1	0	3.88
1994	Rochester	AAA	38	12	0	9	105.1	508	142	76	67	13	5	5	5	55	6	78	6	2	4	7	.364	0	1	5.72
1995	Albuquerque	AAA	25	18	1	3	92	394	97	58	39	10	1	1	0	25	0	59	3	0	5	6	.455	1	0	3.82
1993	Baltimore	AL	11	1	0	3	19.2	90	22	12	10	4	0	0	1	10	1	16	0	0	0	1	.000	0	0	4.58
	6 Min. YEARS		148	104	12	19	694	2971	684	332	270	53	24	13	15	240	9	580	34	8	39	36	.520	6	1	3.50

Greg O'Halloran

Bats: Left **Throws:** Right **Pos:** C   **Ht:** 6'2" **Wt:** 205 **Born:** 5/21/68 **Age:** 28

Year	Team	Lg	G	AB	H	2B	3B	HR	TB	R	RBI	TBB	IBB	SO	HBP	SH	SF	SB	CS	SB%	GDP	Avg	OBP	SLG
1989	St. Cathrns	A	69	265	75	13	2	5	107	31	27	21	2	33	1	0	0	7	4	.64	4	.283	.338	.404
1990	Dunedin	A	121	465	132	26	4	11	199	70	75	37	7	70	3	1	3	2	3	.40	4	.284	.339	.428
1991	Dunedin	A	20	74	21	3	1	0	26	7	4	7	1	8	0	0	0	1	1	.50	1	.284	.346	.351
	Knoxville	AA	110	350	89	13	3	8	132	37	53	27	3	46	0	2	6	11	6	.65	14	.254	.303	.377
1992	Knoxville	AA	117	409	111	20	5	2	147	44	34	31	2	64	0	2	5	7	7	.50	10	.271	.319	.359
1993	Syracuse	AAA	109	322	86	14	3	3	115	32	35	13	3	54	2	0	4	2	1	.67	13	.267	.296	.357
1994	Portland	AA	104	388	102	22	6	7	157	52	53	37	1	71	3	0	1	2	3	.40	9	.263	.331	.405
1995	Iowa	AAA	7	19	3	1	0	0	4	1	1	0	0	7	0	0	0	0	0	.00	1	.158	.150	.211
	Duluth-Sup.	IND	23	79	18	1	1	2	27	10	9	10	2	21	0	1	0	0	2	.00	1	.228	.315	.342
1994	Florida	NL	12	11	2	0	0	0	2	1	1	0	0	1	0	0	1	0	0	.00	0	.182	.167	.182
	7 Min. YEARS		680	2371	637	113	25	38	914	284	291	183	21	374	9	6	20	32	27	.54	56	.269	.321	.385

Rouglas Odor

Bats: Right **Throws:** Right **Pos:** SS   **Ht:** 5'11" **Wt:** 165 **Born:** 1/26/68 **Age:** 28

Year	Team	Lg	G	AB	H	2B	3B	HR	TB	R	RBI	TBB	IBB	SO	HBP	SH	SF	SB	CS	SB%	GDP	Avg	OBP	SLG
1988	Burlington	R	63	222	55	3	2	1	65	39	39	32	1	32	2	5	1	13	6	.68	2	.248	.346	.293
1989	Kinston	A	28	60	7	0	0	0	7	4	2	3	0	12	3	2	0	3	0	1.00	0	.117	.197	.117
	Watertown	A	52	195	53	9	2	4	78	30	24	17	1	34	2	2	2	10	1	.91	3	.272	.333	.400
1990	Kinston	A	114	445	116	21	1	2	145	64	42	42	2	99	2	11	2	30	10	.75	7	.261	.326	.326
1991	Canton-Akrn	AA	76	236	47	5	2	1	59	24	29	25	2	50	1	7	5	8	2	.80	1	.199	.273	.250
1992	Kinston	A	71	219	59	6	2	1	72	24	17	22	0	36	6	8	1	11	6	.65	5	.269	.351	.329
1993	Canton-Akrn	AA	86	263	55	8	2	3	76	39	18	22	0	65	1	3	3	10	4	.71	2	.209	.270	.289
1994	Canton-Akrn	AA	35	146	36	6	3	0	48	23	17	12	0	20	2	3	4	8	2	.80	2	.247	.305	.329
1995	El Paso	AA	6	17	5	0	0	0	5	2	2	2	0	2	0	0	0	0	0	.00	1	.294	.368	.294
	Laredo	IND	39	151	44	2	2	1	53	21	12	21	1	20	1	4	0	10	4	.71	0	.291	.382	.351
	Lubbock	IND	49	181	52	12	6	2	82	27	31	16	0	18	2	4	3	9	4	.69	1	.287	.347	.453
	8 Min. YEARS		619	2135	529	72	22	15	690	297	233	214	7	388	22	49	21	112	39	.74	24	.248	.320	.323

Dave Oehrlein

Pitches: Left **Bats:** Left **Pos:** P   **Ht:** 6'0" **Wt:** 190 **Born:** 9/1/69 **Age:** 26

Year	Team	Lg	G	GS	CG	GF	IP	BFP	H	R	ER	HR	SH	SF	HB	TBB	IBB	SO	WP	Bk	W	L	Pct.	ShO	Sv	ERA
1992	Hamilton	A	13	13	1	0	76	300	48	24	22	7	1	1	0	28	0	99	2	1	10	1	.909	1	0	2.61
1993	Springfield	A	13	13	0	0	60.1	270	70	38	33	6	2	1	0	21	0	52	0	0	3	4	.429	0	0	4.92
1994	Savannah	A	12	12	0	0	76.1	298	52	22	18	2	1	4	4	22	0	62	3	0	8	1	.889	0	0	2.12
	St. Pete	A	12	12	0	0	76	308	67	27	25	6	3	2	2	23	0	64	2	0	6	2	.750	0	0	2.96
1995	Arkansas	AA	23	10	1	4	77.2	338	80	48	42	6	5	2	4	28	1	52	5	0	4	7	.364	0	0	4.87
	4 Min. YEARS		73	60	2	4	366.1	1514	317	159	140	27	12	10	10	122	1	329	12	1	31	15	.674	1	0	3.44

Jamie Ogden

Bats: Left **Throws:** Left **Pos:** 1B **Ht:** 6'5" **Wt:** 215 **Born:** 1/19/72 **Age:** 24

Year Team	Lg	G	AB	H	2B	3B	HR	TB	R	RBI	TBB	IBB	SO	HBP	SH	SF	SB	CS	SB%	GDP	Avg	OBP	SLG
1990 Twins	R	28	101	20	1	2	0	25	11	5	7	0	41	0	0	0	2	0	1.00	2	.198	.250	.248
1991 Twins	R	37	122	39	9	7	2	68	22	25	11	0	30	0	0	4	7	4	.64	0	.320	.365	.557
1992 Kenosha	A	108	372	91	14	3	3	120	36	51	52	1	108	2	0	4	9	2	.82	9	.245	.337	.323
1993 Fort Myers	A	118	396	96	22	4	8	150	37	46	34	1	89	6	4	1	7	1	.88	11	.242	.311	.379
1994 Fort Myers	A	69	251	66	12	0	7	99	32	22	16	0	52	2	1	1	12	8	.60	6	.263	.311	.394
1995 New Britain	AA	117	384	109	22	1	13	172	54	61	48	5	90	1	0	5	6	5	.55	10	.284	.361	.448
6 Min. YEARS		477	1626	421	80	17	33	634	192	210	168	7	410	11	5	15	43	20	.68	38	.259	.330	.390

Kevin Ohme

Pitches: Left **Bats:** Left **Pos:** P **Ht:** 6'1" **Wt:** 175 **Born:** 4/13/71 **Age:** 25

Year Team	Lg	G	GS	CG	GF	IP	BFP	H	R	ER	HR	SH	SF	HB	TBB	IBB	SO	WP	Bk	W	L	Pct.	ShO	Sv	ERA
1993 Fort Wayne	A	15	4	0	6	46.1	184	38	19	13	1	2	2	1	15	1	45	4	1	3	2	.600	0	0	2.53
1994 Fort Wayne	A	2	2	0	0	7	29	7	2	2	0	0	0	1	0	0	8	0	0	0	1	.000	0	0	2.57
1995 New Britain	AA	35	11	0	7	101.1	427	89	51	39	5	7	7	3	45	1	52	7	0	3	4	.429	0	0	3.46
3 Min. YEARS		52	17	0	13	154.2	640	134	72	54	6	9	9	5	60	2	105	11	1	6	7	.462	0	0	3.14

Kirt Ojala

Pitches: Left **Bats:** Left **Pos:** P **Ht:** 6'2" **Wt:** 200 **Born:** 12/24/68 **Age:** 27

Year Team	Lg	G	GS	CG	GF	IP	BFP	H	R	ER	HR	SH	SF	HB	TBB	IBB	SO	WP	Bk	W	L	Pct.	ShO	Sv	ERA
1990 Oneonta	A	14	14	1	0	79	353	75	28	19	2	5	2	3	43	0	87	1	2	7	2	.778	0	0	2.16
1991 Pr. William	A	25	23	1	0	156.2	636	120	52	44	5	3	4	4	61	1	112	3	1	8	7	.533	0	0	2.53
1992 Albany-Colo	AA	24	23	2	0	151.2	642	130	71	61	10	3	7	0	80	0	116	10	0	12	8	.600	1	0	3.62
1993 Albany-Colo	AA	1	1	0	0	6.1	26	5	0	0	0	0	0	0	0	0	6	2	0	1	0	1.000	0	0	0.00
Columbus	AAA	31	20	0	3	126	575	145	85	77	13	4	5	3	71	2	83	13	1	8	9	.471	0	0	5.50
1994 Columbus	AAA	25	23	1	0	148	638	157	78	63	12	2	2	4	46	1	81	10	1	11	7	.611	1	0	3.83
1995 Columbus	AAA	32	20	0	5	145.2	619	138	74	64	15	6	2	3	54	3	107	7	1	8	7	.533	0	1	3.95
6 Min. YEARS		152	124	5	8	813.1	3489	770	388	328	57	23	22	17	357	7	592	46	6	55	40	.579	2	1	3.63

Jose Olmeda

Bats: Both **Throws:** Right **Pos:** OF **Ht:** 5'9" **Wt:** 155 **Born:** 6/20/68 **Age:** 28

Year Team	Lg	G	AB	H	2B	3B	HR	TB	R	RBI	TBB	IBB	SO	HBP	SH	SF	SB	CS	SB%	GDP	Avg	OBP	SLG
1989 Idaho Falls	R	61	230	57	5	6	1	77	36	27	31	0	40	0	0	1	9	4	.69	7	.248	.336	.335
1990 Sumter	A	103	367	93	14	6	7	140	60	40	55	2	49	2	4	4	17	9	.65	3	.253	.350	.381
Burlington	A	27	112	29	3	0	0	32	6	7	8	0	17	0	0	1	1	1	.50	1	.259	.306	.286
Greenville	AA	2	8	1	0	0	0	1	1	0	1	0	3	0	0	0	0	0	.00	0	.125	.222	.125
1991 Macon	A	81	305	84	16	8	3	125	66	30	38	0	38	1	2	1	34	7	.83	3	.275	.357	.410
Greenville	AA	50	173	35	10	1	3	56	18	16	15	0	36	2	5	2	9	2	.82	2	.202	.271	.324
1992 Durham	A	24	89	23	6	1	2	37	17	9	14	0	14	0	1	0	7	4	.64	0	.258	.359	.416
Greenville	AA	106	341	84	22	4	2	120	54	33	38	3	50	0	1	6	12	6	.67	4	.246	.317	.352
1993 Greenville	AA	122	451	126	33	2	9	190	61	51	29	2	63	0	5	9	15	7	.68	8	.279	.317	.421
1994 Richmond	AAA	109	387	89	19	6	4	132	49	39	30	6	74	1	8	1	17	4	.81	12	.230	.286	.341
1995 Richmond	AAA	80	241	61	11	3	1	81	22	24	16	2	41	1	3	2	2	1	.67	5	.253	.300	.336
Greenville	AA	31	108	27	5	1	4	46	16	10	7	0	18	0	0	0	1	0	1.00	4	.250	.296	.426
7 Min. YEARS		796	2812	709	144	38	36	1037	406	286	282	15	443	7	29	27	124	45	.73	49	.252	.319	.369

Steve Olsen

Pitches: Right **Bats:** Right **Pos:** P **Ht:** 6'4" **Wt:** 225 **Born:** 11/2/69 **Age:** 26

Year Team	Lg	G	GS	CG	GF	IP	BFP	H	R	ER	HR	SH	SF	HB	TBB	IBB	SO	WP	Bk	W	L	Pct.	ShO	Sv	ERA
1991 Utica	A	2	2	0	0	14	51	3	3	1	0	0	0	0	4	0	20	1	0	1	0	1.000	0	0	0.64
South Bend	A	13	13	0	0	81.2	352	80	44	33	4	2	4	3	28	1	76	3	3	5	2	.714	0	0	3.64
1992 Sarasota	A	13	13	3	0	88	363	68	22	19	4	2	1	3	32	0	85	3	2	11	1	.917	1	0	1.94
Birmingham	AA	12	12	1	0	77.1	320	68	28	26	5	0	2	0	29	1	46	2	0	6	4	.600	0	0	3.03
1993 Birmingham	AA	25	25	1	0	142	618	156	87	75	22	1	5	7	52	2	92	4	0	10	9	.526	1	0	4.75
1994 Birmingham	AA	16	16	1	0	102.2	432	100	47	42	8	2	2	3	28	1	69	9	0	5	7	.417	0	0	3.68
Nashville	AAA	11	11	2	0	71.1	289	69	30	26	4	2	1	0	18	0	58	0	1	7	2	.778	0	0	3.28
1995 Nashville	AAA	14	14	0	0	77	329	85	44	41	10	3	5	0	16	0	45	4	0	1	7	.125	0	0	4.79
Birmingham	AA	14	14	2	0	85.1	357	84	44	33	4	3	7	1	21	2	56	1	0	8	3	.727	1	0	3.48
5 Min. YEARS		120	120	10	0	739.1	3111	713	349	296	61	15	27	17	228	7	547	27	6	54	35	.607	3	0	3.60

Rey Ordonez

Bats: Both **Throws:** Right **Pos:** SS **Ht:** 5'9" **Wt:** 159 **Born:** 1/11/72 **Age:** 24

Year Team	Lg	G	AB	H	2B	3B	HR	TB	R	RBI	TBB	IBB	SO	HBP	SH	SF	SB	CS	SB%	GDP	Avg	OBP	SLG
1994 St. Lucie	A	79	314	97	21	2	2	128	47	40	14	0	28	0	6	2	11	6	.65	8	.309	.336	.408
Binghamton	AA	48	191	50	10	2	1	67	22	20	4	0	18	1	1	1	4	3	.57	2	.262	.279	.351

1995 Norfolk	AAA	125	439	94	21	4	2	129	49	50	27	2	50	3	10	7	11	13	.46	12	.214	.261	.294
2 Min. YEARS		252	944	241	52	8	5	324	118	110	45	2	96	4	17	10	26	22	.54	22	.255	.289	.343

Rafael Orellano

Pitches: Left **Bats:** Left **Pos:** P   **Ht:** 6'2" **Wt:** 160 **Born:** 4/28/73 **Age:** 23

		HOW MUCH HE PITCHED						WHAT HE GAVE UP										THE RESULTS					
Year Team	Lg	G	GS	CG	GF	IP	BFP	H	R	ER	HR	SH	SF	HB	TBB	IBB	SO	WP	Bk	W	L	Pct.	ShO	Sv	ERA
1993 Utica	A	11	0	0	7	18.2	84	22	15	12	4	2	1	1	7	0	13	1	0	1	2	.333	0	2	5.79
1994 Red Sox	R	4	3	0	0	13.1	50	6	3	3	0	0	0	0	4	0	10	1	2	1	0	1.000	0	0	2.03
Sarasota	A	16	16	2	0	97.1	375	68	28	26	5	1	0	4	25	0	103	2	3	11	3	.786	1	0	2.40
1995 Trenton	AA	27	27	2	0	186.2	772	146	68	64	18	4	1	11	72	0	160	9	4	11	7	.611	0	0	3.09
3 Min. YEARS		58	46	4	7	316	1281	242	114	105	27	7	2	16	108	0	286	13	9	24	12	.667	1	2	2.99

Eddie Oropesa

Pitches: Left **Bats:** Left **Pos:** P   **Ht:** 6'2" **Wt:** 200 **Born:** 11/23/71 **Age:** 24

		HOW MUCH HE PITCHED						WHAT HE GAVE UP										THE RESULTS					
Year Team	Lg	G	GS	CG	GF	IP	BFP	H	R	ER	HR	SH	SF	HB	TBB	IBB	SO	WP	Bk	W	L	Pct.	ShO	Sv	ERA
1994 Vero Beach	A	19	10	1	3	72	285	54	24	17	2	3	2	4	25	2	67	2	0	4	3	.571	1	0	2.13
1995 San Antonio	AA	16	0	0	7	17.1	87	22	8	6	2	1	2	3	12	1	16	0	1	1	1	.500	0	1	3.12
Vero Beach	A	19	1	0	7	28.1	120	25	12	12	0	1	2	3	10	0	23	4	2	3	1	.750	0	1	3.81
San Bernrdo	A	1	0	0	1	1	3	0	0	0	0	0	0	0	0	0	0	0	0	0	0	.000	0	1	0.00
2 Min. YEARS		55	11	1	18	118.2	495	101	44	35	4	5	6	10	47	3	106	6	3	8	5	.615	1	3	2.65

Bo Ortiz

Bats: Right **Throws:** Right **Pos:** OF   **Ht:** 5'11" **Wt:** 170 **Born:** 4/4/70 **Age:** 26

		BATTING													BASERUNNING				PERCENTAGES		
Year Team	Lg	G	AB	H	2B	3B	HR	TB	R	RBI	TBB	IBB	SO	HBP	SH	SF	SB	CS	SB%	GDP	Avg	OBP	SLG
1991 Bluefield	R	12	53	16	2	1	1	23	4	7	2	0	6	0	0	1	1	0	1.00	2	.302	.321	.434
Kane County	A	57	215	58	8	1	0	68	34	27	17	1	38	2	4	2	2	2	.50	4	.270	.328	.316
1992 Frederick	A	54	182	50	11	3	0	67	26	19	18	0	40	3	2	1	7	3	.70	4	.275	.348	.368
1993 Frederick	A	104	351	99	18	7	10	161	72	60	44	0	65	1	6	1	12	11	.52	7	.282	.372	.459
Bowie	AA	8	30	6	0	1	0	8	1	3	1	0	5	1	2	0	0	0	.00	0	.200	.250	.267
1994 Bowie	AA	85	320	99	21	3	10	156	58	54	28	2	47	4	1	0	13	4	.76	10	.309	.372	.488
Midland	AA	22	80	14	4	0	0	18	9	6	6	0	11	1	0	0	3	1	.75	2	.175	.241	.225
1995 Midland	AA	96	360	99	10	3	8	139	48	56	17	2	40	2	4	5	12	11	.52	6	.275	.307	.386
5 Min. YEARS		438	1591	441	74	19	29	640	252	232	133	5	252	20	19	10	50	32	.61	35	.277	.339	.402

Hector Ortiz

Bats: Right **Throws:** Right **Pos:** C   **Ht:** 6'0" **Wt:** 178 **Born:** 10/14/69 **Age:** 26

		BATTING													BASERUNNING				PERCENTAGES		
Year Team	Lg	G	AB	H	2B	3B	HR	TB	R	RBI	TBB	IBB	SO	HBP	SH	SF	SB	CS	SB%	GDP	Avg	OBP	SLG
1988 Salem	A	32	77	11	1	0	0	12	5	4	5	0	16	1	1	0	0	2	.00	1	.143	.205	.156
1989 Vero Beach	A	42	85	12	0	1	0	14	5	4	6	0	15	2	4	0	0	0	.00	1	.141	.215	.165
Salem	A	44	140	32	3	1	0	37	13	12	4	0	24	1	2	0	2	1	.67	6	.229	.255	.264
1990 Yakima	A	52	173	47	3	1	0	52	16	12	5	0	15	1	1	0	1	1	.50	6	.272	.296	.301
1991 Vero Beach	A	42	123	28	2	0	0	30	3	8	5	0	8	3	0	0	0	0	.00	2	.228	.275	.244
1992 Bakersfield	A	63	206	58	8	1	1	71	19	31	21	0	16	5	3	2	2	3	.40	8	.282	.359	.345
San Antonio	AA	26	59	12	1	0	0	13	1	5	11	0	13	1	1	0	0	0	.00	2	.203	.338	.220
1993 San Antonio	AA	49	131	28	5	0	1	36	6	6	9	2	17	0	3	0	0	2	.00	3	.214	.264	.275
Albuquerque	AAA	18	44	8	1	1	0	11	0	3	0	0	6	1	2	0	0	0	.00	1	.182	.200	.250
1994 Albuquerque	AAA	34	93	28	1	1	0	31	7	10	3	0	12	0	0	1	0	0	.00	7	.301	.320	.333
San Antonio	AA	24	75	9	0	0	0	9	4	4	2	0	7	1	0	2	0	0	.00	4	.120	.150	.120
1995 Orlando	AA	96	299	70	12	0	0	82	13	18	20	0	39	1	1	4	0	5	.00	10	.234	.281	.274
8 Min. YEARS		522	1505	343	37	6	2	398	92	117	91	2	188	17	18	9	5	14	.26	55	.228	.278	.264

Javier Ortiz

Bats: Right **Throws:** Right **Pos:** OF   **Ht:** 6'4" **Wt:** 220 **Born:** 1/22/63 **Age:** 33

		BATTING													BASERUNNING				PERCENTAGES		
Year Team	Lg	G	AB	H	2B	3B	HR	TB	R	RBI	TBB	IBB	SO	HBP	SH	SF	SB	CS	SB%	GDP	Avg	OBP	SLG
1983 Burlington	A	101	378	133	23	4	16	212	72	79	42	3	94	2	2	3	10	6	.63	14	.352	.416	.561
1984 Tulsa	AA	94	325	97	21	3	8	148	42	53	47	2	67	5	4	4	4	5	.44	8	.298	.391	.455
1985 Tulsa	AA	86	304	75	12	3	5	108	47	31	52	2	75	4	0	1	11	3	.79	10	.247	.363	.355
1986 Tulsa	AA	110	378	114	29	3	14	191	52	65	54	2	94	7	3	1	15	10	.60	7	.302	.398	.505
1987 Okla. City	AAA	119	381	105	23	7	15	187	58	69	58	2	99	4	1	10	5	2	.71	6	.276	.369	.491
1988 San Antonio	AA	51	182	53	13	2	8	94	35	33	22	0	38	5	0	5	6	3	.67	5	.291	.374	.516
1989 Albuquerque	AAA	70	220	59	10	0	11	102	42	36	34	1	54	4	1	0	2	2	.50	4	.268	.376	.464
Tucson	AAA	11	40	7	0	0	0	7	5	0	2	0	9	0	0	0	0	0	.00	1	.175	.214	.175
1990 Tucson	AAA	49	179	63	16	2	5	98	36	39	22	1	36	1	0	3	2	3	.40	6	.352	.420	.547
1991 Tucson	AAA	34	127	41	13	0	3	63	20	22	10	0	22	0	0	2	0	3	.00	4	.323	.367	.496
1993 Omaha	AAA	3	7	2	0	0	0	2	0	2	1	0	1	0	0	0	0	1	.00	1	.286	.333	.286
Pirates	R	8	23	7	3	0	0	10	5	6	8	0	7	0	0	0	0	0	.00	0	.304	.469	.435
Carolina	AA	33	109	37	10	1	5	64	17	24	15	3	18	2	0	3	1	1	.50	1	.339	.419	.587
1994 Nashville	AAA	111	346	95	20	2	16	167	49	55	36	2	56	2	1	3	8	1	.89	10	.275	.344	.483
1995 Nashville	AAA	7	24	4	0	0	1	7	3	1	1	0	5	0	0	0	0	0	.00	1	.167	.200	.292
St. Paul	IND	29	99	26	5	0	0	31	12	12	12	0	13	2	0	4	1	0	1.00	4	.263	.342	.313

227

Year	Team	Lg	G	AB	H	2B	3B	HR	TB	R	RBI	TBB	IBB	SO	HBP	SH	SF	SB	CS	SB%	GDP	Avg	OBP	SLG
1990	Houston	NL	30	77	21	5	1	1	31	7	10	12	0	11	0	0	1	1	1	.50	1	.273	.367	.403
1991	Houston	NL	47	83	23	4	1	1	32	7	5	14	0	14	0	0	0	0	0	.00	3	.277	.381	.386
	12 Min. YEARS		916	3122	918	198	27	107	1491	495	532	416	18	687	38	12	41	65	40	.62	81	.294	.379	.478
	2 Maj. YEARS		77	160	44	9	2	2	63	14	15	26	0	25	0	0	1	1	1	.50	4	.275	.374	.394

Junior Ortiz

Bats: Right **Throws:** Right **Pos:** C   **Ht:** 5'11" **Wt:** 185 **Born:** 10/24/59 **Age:** 36

			BATTING															BASERUNNING				PERCENTAGES		
Year	Team	Lg	G	AB	H	2B	3B	HR	TB	R	RBI	TBB	IBB	SO	HBP	SH	SF	SB	CS	SB%	GDP	Avg	OBP	SLG
1995	Nashville	AAA	64	172	32	9	0	1	44	13	16	12	0	27	4	2	1	0	0	.00	8	.186	.254	.256
1982	Pittsburgh	NL	7	15	3	1	0	0	4	1	0	1	0	3	0	0	0	0	0	.00	1	.200	.250	.267
1983	New York	NL	68	185	47	5	0	0	52	10	12	3	0	34	1	1	0	1	0	1.00	1	.254	.270	.281
	Pittsburgh	NL	5	8	1	0	0	0	1	1	0	1	0	0	0	1	0	0	0	.00	0	.125	.222	.125
1984	New York	NL	40	91	18	3	0	0	21	6	11	5	0	15	0	0	2	1	0	1.00	2	.198	.235	.231
1985	Pittsburgh	NL	23	72	21	2	0	1	26	4	5	3	1	17	0	1	0	1	0	1.00	1	.292	.320	.361
1986	Pittsburgh	NL	49	110	37	6	0	0	43	11	14	9	0	13	0	1	2	0	1	.00	4	.336	.380	.391
1987	Pittsburgh	NL	75	192	52	8	1	1	65	16	22	15	1	23	0	5	1	0	2	.00	6	.271	.322	.339
1988	Pittsburgh	NL	49	118	33	6	0	2	45	8	18	9	0	9	2	1	2	1	4	.20	6	.280	.336	.381
1989	Pittsburgh	NL	91	230	50	6	1	1	61	16	22	20	4	20	2	3	3	2	2	.50	9	.217	.282	.265
1990	Minnesota	AL	71	170	57	7	1	0	66	18	18	12	0	16	2	2	1	0	4	.00	4	.335	.384	.388
1991	Minnesota	AL	61	134	28	5	1	0	35	9	11	15	0	12	1	1	0	0	1	.00	6	.209	.293	.261
1992	Cleveland	AL	86	244	61	7	0	0	68	20	24	12	0	23	4	2	0	1	3	.25	7	.250	.296	.279
1993	Cleveland	AL	95	249	55	13	0	0	68	19	20	11	1	26	5	4	1	1	0	1.00	10	.221	.267	.273
1994	Texas	AL	29	76	21	2	0	0	23	3	9	5	0	11	1	4	0	0	1	.00	1	.276	.329	.303
	13 Maj. YEARS		749	1894	484	71	4	5	578	142	186	121	7	222	18	26	12	8	18	.31	58	.256	.305	.305

Ray Ortiz

Bats: Left **Throws:** Left **Pos:** OF   **Ht:** 6'2" **Wt:** 215 **Born:** 4/27/68 **Age:** 28

			BATTING															BASERUNNING				PERCENTAGES		
Year	Team	Lg	G	AB	H	2B	3B	HR	TB	R	RBI	TBB	IBB	SO	HBP	SH	SF	SB	CS	SB%	GDP	Avg	OBP	SLG
1989	Kenosha	A	51	175	43	8	1	3	62	19	21	24	2	32	3	1	2	4	0	1.00	4	.246	.343	.354
1990	Visalia	A	62	235	74	15	1	13	130	43	53	26	3	47	1	0	1	1	0	1.00	8	.315	.384	.553
	Orlando	AA	71	265	68	16	0	9	111	41	49	27	1	57	6	0	4	1	0	1.00	6	.257	.334	.419
1991	Orlando	AA	135	470	116	19	3	9	168	58	71	48	3	100	7	0	6	3	2	.60	10	.247	.322	.357
1992	Orlando	AA	78	266	70	16	1	10	118	40	47	21	1	46	1	0	2	0	1	.00	4	.263	.317	.444
	Portland	AAA	42	134	44	12	1	3	67	17	22	7	2	17	1	0	3	0	1	.00	5	.328	.359	.500
1993	Portland	AAA	111	357	101	18	2	5	138	42	53	14	2	58	1	0	6	2	1	.67	11	.283	.307	.387
1994	Phoenix	AAA	122	364	100	19	8	9	162	51	56	19	2	78	1	0	2	1	5	.17	7	.275	.311	.445
1995	Phoenix	AAA	66	190	46	10	2	4	72	22	29	13	3	36	0	0	1	1	0	1.00	9	.242	.289	.379
	Lubbock	IND	31	121	34	11	0	8	69	19	19	7	1	18	1	0	1	0	2	.00	2	.281	.323	.570
	7 Min. YEARS		769	2577	696	144	19	73	1097	352	420	206	20	489	22	1	28	13	12	.52	59	.270	.326	.426

John Orton

Bats: Right **Throws:** Right **Pos:** C   **Ht:** 6'1" **Wt:** 192 **Born:** 12/8/65 **Age:** 30

			BATTING															BASERUNNING				PERCENTAGES		
Year	Team	Lg	G	AB	H	2B	3B	HR	TB	R	RBI	TBB	IBB	SO	HBP	SH	SF	SB	CS	SB%	GDP	Avg	OBP	SLG
1987	Salem	A	51	176	46	8	1	8	80	31	36	32	1	61	7	1	2	6	2	.75	5	.261	.392	.455
	Midland	A	5	13	2	1	0	0	3	1	0	2	0	3	1	0	0	0	0	.00	0	.154	.313	.231
1988	Palm Spring	A	68	230	46	6	1	1	57	42	28	45	0	79	10	2	0	5	2	.71	4	.200	.354	.248
1989	Midland	AA	99	344	80	20	6	10	142	51	53	37	1	102	7	6	7	2	1	.67	5	.233	.314	.413
1990	Edmonton	AAA	50	174	42	8	0	6	68	29	26	19	1	63	0	1	1	4	2	.67	7	.241	.314	.391
1991	Edmonton	AAA	76	245	55	14	1	5	86	39	32	31	1	66	5	4	2	5	0	1.00	4	.224	.322	.351
1992	Edmonton	AAA	49	149	38	9	3	3	62	28	25	28	0	32	3	4	2	3	5	.38	3	.255	.379	.416
1993	Palm Spring	A	2	7	0	0	0	0	0	0	0	1	0	1	0	0	0	0	0	.00	0	.000	.125	.000
1994	Richmond	AAA	36	81	10	3	0	1	16	3	2	5	0	30	0	0	1	0	0	.00	3	.123	.172	.198
1995	Richmond	AAA	17	50	9	3	0	1	15	6	6	3	0	22	1	1	1	2	2	.50	1	.180	.236	.300
	Norfolk	AAA	56	170	49	8	0	3	66	20	20	14	0	45	3	0	0	1	3	.25	4	.288	.353	.388
1989	California	AL	16	39	7	1	0	0	8	4	4	2	0	17	0	1	0	0	0	.00	0	.179	.220	.205
1990	California	AL	31	84	16	5	0	1	24	8	6	5	0	31	1	2	0	0	1	.00	2	.190	.244	.286
1991	California	AL	29	69	14	4	0	0	18	7	3	10	0	17	1	4	0	0	1	.00	2	.203	.313	.261
1992	California	AL	43	114	25	3	0	2	34	11	12	7	0	32	2	2	0	1	1	.50	1	.219	.276	.298
1993	California	AL	37	95	18	5	0	1	26	5	4	7	0	24	1	2	0	1	2	.33	1	.189	.252	.274
	9 Min. YEARS		509	1639	377	80	12	38	595	250	228	217	4	504	37	19	16	28	17	.62	36	.230	.331	.363
	5 Maj. YEARS		156	401	80	18	0	4	110	35	29	31	0	121	5	11	0	2	5	.29	6	.200	.265	.274

Keith Osik

Bats: Right **Throws:** Right **Pos:** C   **Ht:** 6'0" **Wt:** 195 **Born:** 10/22/68 **Age:** 27

			BATTING															BASERUNNING				PERCENTAGES		
Year	Team	Lg	G	AB	H	2B	3B	HR	TB	R	RBI	TBB	IBB	SO	HBP	SH	SF	SB	CS	SB%	GDP	Avg	OBP	SLG
1990	Welland	A	29	97	27	4	0	1	34	13	20	11	1	12	2	1	3	2	6	.25	1	.278	.354	.351
1991	Carolina	AA	17	43	13	3	1	0	18	9	5	5	0	5	0	0	0	0	0	.00	1	.302	.375	.419
	Salem	A	87	300	81	13	1	6	114	31	35	38	0	48	3	3	2	2	3	.40	13	.270	.356	.380
1992	Carolina	AA	129	425	110	17	1	5	144	41	45	52	1	69	15	0	4	2	9	.18	12	.259	.357	.339
1993	Carolina	AA	103	371	105	21	2	10	160	47	47	30	1	47	9	4	1	0	2	.00	13	.283	.350	.431
1994	Buffalo	AAA	83	260	55	16	0	5	86	27	33	28	0	41	3	0	2	0	1	.00	5	.212	.294	.331

228

Year	Team		G	GS	CG	GF	IP	BFP	H	R	ER	HR	SH	SF	HB	TBB	IBB	SO	HBP	SH	SF	SB	CS	SB%	GDP	Avg	OBP	SLG
1995	Calgary	AAA	90	301	101	25	1	10	158	40	59	21	2	42	5	0	4		2	2	.50	5				.336	.384	.525
	6 Min. YEARS		538	1797	492	99	6	37	714	208	244	185	5	264	37	8	16		8	23	.26	50				.274	.351	.397

Al Osuna

Pitches: Left **Bats:** Right **Pos:** P **Ht:** 6' 3" **Wt:** 200 **Born:** 8/10/65 **Age:** 30

			HOW MUCH HE PITCHED						WHAT HE GAVE UP												THE RESULTS					
Year	Team	Lg	G	GS	CG	GF	IP	BFP	H	R	ER	HR	SH	SF	HB	TBB	IBB	SO	WP	Bk	W	L	Pct.	ShO	Sv	ERA
1987	Auburn	A	8	0	0	3	15.2	75	16	16	10	1	0	0	0	14	2	20	0	2	1	0	1.000	0	0	5.74
	Asheville	A	14	0	0	7	19.2	81	20	6	6	1	0	0	0	6	0	20	0	3	2	0	1.000	0	2	2.75
1988	Osceola	A	8	0	0	2	11.2	58	12	9	9	1	0	1	0	9	1	5	0	0	0	1	.000	0	0	6.94
	Asheville	A	31	0	0	19	50	212	41	19	11	1	1	0	2	25	2	41	4	9	6	1	.857	0	3	1.98
1989	Osceola	A	46	0	0	26	67.2	283	50	27	20	2	7	2	2	27	4	62	5	5	3	4	.429	0	7	2.66
1990	Columbus	AA	60	0	0	26	69.1	289	57	30	26	4	3	1	3	33	2	82	4	1	7	5	.583	0	6	3.38
1993	Tucson	AAA	13	4	0	3	30	133	26	16	15	1	0	1	5	17	0	38	4	0	3	1	.750	0	1	4.50
1994	Albuquerque	AAA	39	0	0	13	44.2	184	39	24	14	2	0	0	0	14	1	41	4	1	1	2	.333	0	3	2.82
1995	Rio Grande	IND	3	3	0	0	20	84	15	9	8	2	0	1	1	9	0	19	1	0	2	0	1.000	0	0	3.60
	Norfolk	AAA	14	4	0	2	42	175	39	14	14	5	0	3	1	12	0	31	1	0	3	1	.750	0	0	3.00
1990	Houston	NL	12	0	0	2	11.1	48	10	6	6	1	0	2	3	6	1	6	3	0	2	0	1.000	0	0	4.76
1991	Houston	NL	71	0	0	32	81.2	353	59	39	31	5	6	5	3	46	5	68	3	1	7	6	.538	0	12	3.42
1992	Houston	NL	66	0	0	17	61.2	270	52	29	29	8	5	6	1	38	5	37	3	1	6	3	.667	0	0	4.23
1993	Houston	NL	44	0	0	6	25.1	107	17	10	9	3	4	4	1	13	2	21	3	0	1	1	.500	0	2	3.20
1994	Los Angeles	NL	15	0	0	4	8.2	43	13	6	6	0	0	0	0	4	0	7	0	1	2	0	1.000	0	0	6.23
	7 Min. YEARS		236	11	0	101	370.2	1574	315	170	133	20	11	9	14	166	12	359	23	21	28	15	.651	0	22	3.23
	5 Maj. YEARS		208	0	0	61	188.2	821	151	90	81	17	15	17	8	107	13	139	12	3	18	10	.643	0	14	3.86

Willis Otanez

Bats: Right **Throws:** Right **Pos:** 3B **Ht:** 5'11" **Wt:** 150 **Born:** 4/19/73 **Age:** 23

			BATTING													BASERUNNING				PERCENTAGES		
Year	Team	Lg	G	AB	H	2B	3B	HR	TB	R	RBI	TBB	IBB	SO	HBP	SH	SF	SB	CS	SB%	GDP	Avg	OBP	SLG
1991	Great Falls	R	58	222	64	9	2	6	95	38	39	19	0	34	2	1	4	3	3	.50	7	.288	.344	.428
1992	Vero Beach	A	117	390	86	18	0	3	113	27	27	24	0	60	4	5	3	2	4	.33	10	.221	.271	.290
1993	Bakersfield	A	95	325	85	11	2	10	130	34	39	29	1	63	2	4	2	1	4	.20	9	.262	.324	.400
1994	Vero Beach	A	131	476	132	27	1	19	218	77	72	53	2	98	4	0	7	4	2	.67	10	.277	.350	.458
1995	Vero Beach	A	92	354	92	24	0	10	146	39	53	28	3	59	2	0	5	1	1	.50	15	.260	.314	.412
	San Antonio	AA	27	100	24	4	1	1	33	8	7	6	0	25	0	0	2	0	1	.00	3	.240	.278	.330
	5 Min. YEARS		520	1867	483	93	6	49	735	223	237	159	6	339	14	10	23	11	15	.42	54	.259	.318	.394

Billy Owens

Bats: Both **Throws:** Right **Pos:** 1B **Ht:** 6'1" **Wt:** 210 **Born:** 4/12/71 **Age:** 25

			BATTING													BASERUNNING				PERCENTAGES		
Year	Team	Lg	G	AB	H	2B	3B	HR	TB	R	RBI	TBB	IBB	SO	HBP	SH	SF	SB	CS	SB%	GDP	Avg	OBP	SLG
1992	Kane County	A	73	283	72	16	0	2	94	23	33	26	1	63	0	2	4	4	3	.57	2	.254	.313	.332
1993	Albany	A	120	458	136	23	2	11	196	64	66	49	6	70	2	1	5	3	5	.38	8	.297	.364	.428
	Frederick	A	17	60	21	4	0	0	25	8	8	3	0	8	0	0	1	0	0	.00	2	.350	.375	.417
1994	Bowie	AA	43	145	33	7	1	4	54	13	19	10	1	37	0	0	1	1	0	1.00	3	.228	.276	.372
	Frederick	A	80	324	74	16	0	10	100	60	50	44	5	73	1	0	1	1	1	.50	3	.228	.322	.398
1995	Rochester	AAA	9	28	4	0	0	0	4	2	1	1	0	6	0	0	0	0	0	.00	0	.143	.172	.143
	Bowie	AA	122	453	122	27	0	17	200	57	91	43	6	87	1	0	8	2	1	.67	13	.269	.329	.442
	4 Min. YEARS		470	1751	462	93	3	47	702	217	270	176	19	344	4	3	20	11	10	.52	31	.264	.329	.401

Scotty Pace

Pitches: Left **Bats:** Left **Pos:** P **Ht:** 6'4" **Wt:** 210 **Born:** 9/16/71 **Age:** 24

			HOW MUCH HE PITCHED						WHAT HE GAVE UP												THE RESULTS					
Year	Team	Lg	G	GS	CG	GF	IP	BFP	H	R	ER	HR	SH	SF	HB	TBB	IBB	SO	WP	Bk	W	L	Pct.	ShO	Sv	ERA
1994	Elmira	A	13	12	2	0	70.2	307	73	35	32	3	3	0	1	27	2	50	7	0	3	7	.300	0	0	4.08
1995	Hagerstown	A	11	6	2	2	57.2	211	32	8	7	2	1	0	2	12	0	57	4	0	4	2	.667	1	1	1.09
	Knoxville	AA	18	18	1	0	102.1	462	117	66	52	8	6	6	4	48	3	71	7	0	6	8	.429	1	0	4.57
	2 Min. YEARS		42	36	5	2	230.2	980	222	109	91	13	10	6	7	87	5	178	18	0	13	17	.433	2	1	3.55

Alexander Pacheco

Pitches: Right **Bats:** Right **Pos:** P **Ht:** 6'3" **Wt:** 170 **Born:** 7/19/73 **Age:** 22

			HOW MUCH HE PITCHED						WHAT HE GAVE UP												THE RESULTS					
Year	Team	Lg	G	GS	CG	GF	IP	BFP	H	R	ER	HR	SH	SF	HB	TBB	IBB	SO	WP	Bk	W	L	Pct.	ShO	Sv	ERA
1990	Expos	R	6	0	0	0	8.2	41	11	7	5	0	0	0	0	4	0	5	2	1	1	0	1.000	0	0	5.19
1991	Expos	R	15	4	0	3	44.1	209	56	32	25	0	1	2	1	26	0	19	6	0	3	0	1.000	0	0	5.08
1992	Jamestown	A	16	5	0	4	50.1	229	53	36	31	5	2	2	3	29	1	32	2	0	3	3	.500	0	0	5.54
1993	Jamestown	A	6	1	0	1	14	60	11	7	5	0	0	1	0	4	0	15	4	0	0	1	.000	0	0	3.21
	Burlington	A	13	7	0	2	43	194	47	31	20	3	2	2	3	12	0	24	3	0	3	5	.375	0	1	4.19
1994	Burlington	A	37	4	0	19	68.1	302	79	51	39	6	7	2	6	22	1	69	5	0	3	8	.273	0	5	5.14
	W. Palm Bch	A	9	0	0	0	12	47	9	3	3	1	0	1	0	4	0	12	2	0	1	0	1.000	0	0	2.25
1995	Harrisburg	AA	45	0	0	29	86.1	371	76	45	41	8	1	1	8	31	4	88	4	0	9	7	.563	0	4	4.27
	Ottawa	AAA	4	0	0	0	8.2	35	8	6	6	2	0	0	0	5	0	4	0	0	1	0	1.000	0	0	6.23
	6 Min. YEARS		151	21	0	58	335.2	1488	350	218	175	25	13	11	21	137	6	268	28	2	24	24	.500	0	11	4.69

Carey Paige

Pitches: Right **Bats:** Right **Pos:** P   **Ht:** 6'3" **Wt:** 175 **Born:** 3/2/74 **Age:** 22

| | | | HOW MUCH HE PITCHED | | | | | WHAT HE GAVE UP | | | | | | | | | THE RESULTS | | | | |
Year	Team	Lg	G	GS	CG	GF	IP	BFP	H	R	ER	HR	SH	SF	HB	TBB	IBB	SO	WP	Bk	W	L	Pct.	ShO	Sv	ERA
1992	Braves	R	13	7	0	1	40	170	32	19	17	1	0	2	3	17	0	39	5	0	0	3	.000	0	0	3.83
1993	Danville	R	13	13	0	0	66.1	298	59	37	31	3	2	1	3	32	0	58	6	0	2	4	.333	0	0	4.21
1994	Macon	A	19	19	1	0	105.2	440	87	32	20	3	2	2	5	33	2	119	3	2	8	6	.571	0	0	1.70
	Durham	A	6	6	0	0	28.2	130	31	19	15	2	0	2	2	13	0	25	0	0	2	2	.500	0	0	4.71
1995	Durham	A	10	10	1	0	64	252	53	24	24	8	2	3	1	15	1	37	1	0	5	3	.625	0	0	3.38
	Greenville	AA	7	7	0	0	41.1	182	45	30	23	5	1	0	2	11	0	26	2	0	1	4	.200	0	0	5.01
	4 Min. YEARS		68	62	2	1	346	1472	307	161	130	22	7	10	16	121	3	304	17	2	18	22	.450	0	0	3.38

Donn Pall

Pitches: Right **Bats:** Right **Pos:** P   **Ht:** 6'1" **Wt:** 180 **Born:** 1/11/62 **Age:** 34

| | | | HOW MUCH HE PITCHED | | | | | WHAT HE GAVE UP | | | | | | | | | THE RESULTS | | | | |
Year	Team	Lg	G	GS	CG	GF	IP	BFP	H	R	ER	HR	SH	SF	HB	TBB	IBB	SO	WP	Bk	W	L	Pct.	ShO	Sv	ERA
1985	White Sox	R	13	13	4	0	86	342	68	34	16	2	3	5	2	10	0	63	3	3	7	5	.583	2	0	1.67
1986	Appleton	A	11	11	3	0	78	317	71	29	20	2	2	0	4	14	1	51	4	0	5	5	.500	1	0	2.31
	Birmingham	AA	21	9	0	6	73	313	77	38	36	9	3	2	2	27	3	41	5	2	3	4	.429	0	1	4.44
1987	Birmingham	AA	30	23	3	3	158	718	173	100	75	18	3	8	8	63	4	139	9	2	8	11	.421	0	0	4.27
1988	Vancouver	AAA	44	0	0	25	72.2	293	61	21	18	2	2	1	3	20	2	41	2	1	5	2	.714	0	10	2.23
1989	South Bend	A	2	0	0	0	3.1	12	1	0	0	0	0	0	0	0	0	4	0	0	0	0	.000	0	0	0.00
1995	Nashville	AAA	44	0	0	13	86	365	89	40	38	10	5	3	4	20	7	79	3	0	4	3	.571	0	3	3.98
1988	Chicago	AL	17	0	0	6	28.2	130	39	11	11	1	2	1	0	8	1	16	1	0	0	2	.000	0	0	3.45
1989	Chicago	AL	53	0	0	27	87	370	90	35	32	9	8	2	8	19	3	58	4	1	4	5	.444	0	6	3.31
1990	Chicago	AL	56	0	0	11	76	306	63	33	28	7	4	2	4	24	8	39	2	0	3	5	.375	0	2	3.32
1991	Chicago	AL	51	0	0	7	71	282	59	22	19	7	4	0	3	20	3	40	2	0	7	2	.778	0	0	2.41
1992	Chicago	AL	39	0	0	12	73	323	79	43	40	9	1	3	2	27	8	27	1	2	5	2	.714	0	1	4.93
1993	Chicago	AL	39	0	0	9	58.2	251	62	25	21	5	6	1	2	11	3	29	3	0	2	3	.400	0	1	3.22
	Philadelphia	NL	8	0	0	2	17.2	69	15	7	5	1	0	1	0	3	0	11	0	1	1	0	1.000	0	0	2.55
1994	New York	AL	26	0	0	7	35	157	43	18	14	3	0	1	1	9	0	21	2	0	1	2	.333	0	0	3.60
	Chicago	NL	2	0	0	0	4	19	8	2	2	1	0	0	0	1	0	2	0	0	0	0	.000	0	0	4.50
	6 Min. YEARS		165	56	10	47	557	2360	540	262	203	43	18	19	23	154	17	418	26	8	32	30	.516	3	14	3.28
	7 Maj. YEARS		291	0	0	81	451	1907	458	196	172	43	26	10	20	122	26	243	15	4	23	21	.523	0	10	3.43

Jose Paniagua

Pitches: Right **Bats:** Right **Pos:** P   **Ht:** 6'1" **Wt:** 160 **Born:** 8/20/73 **Age:** 22

| | | | HOW MUCH HE PITCHED | | | | | WHAT HE GAVE UP | | | | | | | | | THE RESULTS | | | | |
Year	Team	Lg	G	GS	CG	GF	IP	BFP	H	R	ER	HR	SH	SF	HB	TBB	IBB	SO	WP	Bk	W	L	Pct.	ShO	Sv	ERA
1993	Expos	R	4	4	1	0	27	100	13	2	2	0	0	0	2	5	0	25	1	1	3	0	1.000	0	0	0.67
1994	W. Palm Bch	A	26	26	1	0	141	606	131	82	57	6	5	4	6	54	2	110	13	2	9	9	.500	0	0	3.64
1995	Harrisburg	AA	25	25	2	0	126.1	575	140	84	75	9	5	5	12	62	0	89	8	0	7	12	.368	1	0	5.34
	3 Min. YEARS		55	55	4	0	294.1	1281	284	168	134	15	10	9	20	121	2	224	22	3	19	21	.475	1	0	4.10

Jhonny Pantoja

Pitches: Right **Bats:** Right **Pos:** P   **Ht:** 6'3" **Wt:** 190 **Born:** 2/24/78 **Age:** 18

| | | | HOW MUCH HE PITCHED | | | | | WHAT HE GAVE UP | | | | | | | | | THE RESULTS | | | | |
Year	Team	Lg	G	GS	CG	GF	IP	BFP	H	R	ER	HR	SH	SF	HB	TBB	IBB	SO	WP	Bk	W	L	Pct.	ShO	Sv	ERA
1994	Albany-Colo	AA	12	12	0	0	65	285	73	44	33	5	0	3	1	24	0	52	3	3	3	7	.300	0	0	4.57
1995	Norwich	AA	11	2	0	2	25	119	29	23	18	1	1	1	2	14	0	19	0	0	1	2	.333	0	0	6.48
	2 Min. YEARS		23	14	0	2	90	404	102	67	51	6	1	4	3	38	0	71	3	3	4	9	.308	0	0	5.10

Erik Pappas

Bats: Right **Throws:** Right **Pos:** C   **Ht:** 6'0" **Wt:** 190 **Born:** 4/25/66 **Age:** 30

| | | | BATTING | | | | | | | | | | | | | | BASERUNNING | | | | PERCENTAGES | | |
Year	Team	Lg	G	AB	H	2B	3B	HR	TB	R	RBI	TBB	IBB	SO	HBP	SH	SF	SB	CS	SB%	GDP	Avg	OBP	SLG
1984	Salem	A	56	177	43	3	3	1	55	24	15	31	0	26	3	3	1	10	5	.67	1	.243	.363	.311
1985	Quad City	A	100	317	76	8	4	2	98	53	29	61	1	56	3	3	1	16	6	.73	3	.240	.366	.309
1986	Palm Spring	A	74	248	61	16	2	5	96	40	38	56	1	58	1	1	4	9	5	.64	7	.246	.382	.387
1987	Palm Spring	A	119	395	96	20	3	3	131	50	64	66	0	77	0	3	7	16	6	.73	8	.243	.346	.332
1988	Midland	AA	83	275	76	17	2	4	109	40	38	29	0	53	2	4	4	16	3	.84	6	.276	.345	.396
1989	Charlotte	AA	119	354	106	31	1	16	187	69	49	66	1	50	8	4	2	7	8	.47	8	.299	.419	.528
1990	Iowa	AAA	131	405	101	19	2	16	172	56	55	65	1	84	8	6	3	6	5	.55	13	.249	.362	.425
1991	Iowa	AAA	88	284	78	19	1	7	120	41	48	45	4	47	4	4	3	5	3	.63	12	.275	.378	.423
1992	Omaha	AAA	45	138	30	8	1	1	43	18	11	25	1	23	0	1	2	4	1	.80	3	.217	.333	.312
	Vancouver	AAA	37	98	27	4	0	4	43	17	17	14	0	17	2	1	2	4	0	1.00	3	.276	.371	.439
1993	Louisville	AAA	21	71	24	6	1	4	44	19	13	11	0	12	0	0	0	0	2	.00	1	.338	.427	.620
1994	Louisville	AAA	64	206	41	7	2	7	73	33	30	29	0	44	5	0	3	2	3	.40	5	.199	.309	.354
1995	Charlotte	AAA	122	389	86	28	3	10	150	48	52	61	0	78	6	1	4	10	7	.59	11	.221	.333	.386
1991	Chicago	NL	7	17	3	0	0	0	3	1	2	1	0	5	0	0	0	0	0	.00	0	.176	.222	.176
1993	St. Louis	NL	82	228	63	12	0	1	78	25	28	35	2	35	0	0	3	1	3	.25	7	.276	.368	.342
1994	St. Louis	NL	15	44	4	1	0	0	5	8	5	10	0	13	1	0	3	0	0	.00	1	.091	.259	.114
	12 Min. YEARS		1059	3357	845	186	25	80	1321	508	459	559	9	625	42	31	36	105	54	.66	81	.252	.362	.394
	3 Maj. YEARS		104	289	70	13	0	1	86	34	35	46	2	53	1	0	6	1	3	.25	8	.242	.342	.298

Clay Parker

Pitches: Right Bats: Right Pos: P   Ht: 6' 1" Wt: 175 Born: 12/19/62 Age: 33

			HOW MUCH HE PITCHED						WHAT HE GAVE UP								THE RESULTS					
Year	Team	Lg	G	GS	CG	GF	IP	BFP	H	R	ER	HR	SH	SF	HB	TBB	IBB	SO	WP	Bk	W	L	Pct.	ShO	Sv	ERA

Year	Team	Lg	G	GS	CG	GF	IP	BFP	H	R	ER	HR	SH	SF	HB	TBB	IBB	SO	WP	Bk	W	L	Pct.	ShO	Sv	ERA
1985	Bellingham	A	10	9	2	1	63.2	0	40	16	11	1	0	0	2	16	0	69	5	0	6	1	.857	0	0	1.55
1986	Wausau	A	26	26	4	0	178	738	171	77	57	11	3	5	7	39	1	154	13	1	8	7	.533	0	0	2.88
1987	Chattanooga	AA	16	16	5	0	112	451	103	47	34	7	1	3	1	14	1	60	2	0	7	5	.583	1	0	2.73
	Calgary	AAA	12	12	4	0	86	354	78	35	28	4	1	1	0	28	1	44	4	1	8	1	.889	0	0	2.93
1988	Columbus	AAA	10	10	0	0	49.2	204	49	21	18	3	1	2	3	9	0	51	2	2	2	2	.500	0	0	3.26
1989	Columbus	AAA	5	5	1	0	38	151	25	9	7	1	4	2	0	10	2	25	2	1	3	0	1.000	1	0	1.66
1990	Columbus	AAA	3	3	1	0	19	85	21	10	8	1	2	0	0	7	0	14	3	0	1	2	.333	0	0	3.79
	Toledo	AAA	6	6	1	0	35	142	37	13	12	2	1	2	0	6	0	20	0	0	1	3	.250	1	0	3.09
1991	Tacoma	AAA	25	20	3	2	132.1	555	123	65	54	6	2	4	2	44	0	78	5	2	7	6	.538	1	0	3.67
1992	Calgary	AAA	3	3	0	0	18	77	20	9	8	0	0	0	0	3	0	11	0	0	2	1	.667	0	0	4.00
1995	New Orleans	AAA	2	0	0	0	1.1	9	3	2	1	0	0	0	0	2	0	2	0	0	0	0	.000	0	0	6.75
1987	Seattle	AL	3	1	0	1	7.2	43	15	10	9	2	0	1	1	4	0	8	0	0	0	0	.000	0	0	10.57
1989	New York	AL	22	17	2	1	120	507	123	53	49	12	6	2	2	31	3	53	2	2	4	5	.444	0	0	3.68
1990	Detroit	AL	24	1	0	7	51	217	45	18	18	6	3	2	1	25	5	20	3	0	2	2	.500	0	0	3.18
	New York	AL	5	2	0	1	22	91	19	11	11	5	0	1	0	7	1	20	1	0	1	1	.500	0	0	4.50
1992	Seattle	AL	8	6	0	1	33.1	154	47	28	28	6	0	2	2	11	0	20	1	0	0	2	.000	0	0	7.56
	9 Min. YEARS		118	110	21	3	733	2766	670	304	238	36	13	19	15	178	5	528	36	7	45	28	.616	4	0	2.92
	4 Maj. YEARS		62	27	2	11	234	1012	249	120	115	31	9	8	6	78	9	121	7	2	7	10	.412	0	0	4.42

Franklin Parra

Bats: Both Throws: Right Pos: OF   Ht: 6'0" Wt: 165 Born: 7/8/71 Age: 24

			BATTING													BASERUNNING				PERCENTAGES		

Year	Team	Lg	G	AB	H	2B	3B	HR	TB	R	RBI	TBB	IBB	SO	HBP	SH	SF	SB	CS	SB%	GDP	Avg	OBP	SLG
1990	Rangers	R	37	116	30	2	1	0	34	11	9	4	0	28	1	0	1	8	3	.73	0	.259	.287	.293
1991	Butte	R	61	221	56	10	2	4	82	28	29	7	0	61	0	0	2	9	8	.53	3	.253	.274	.371
1992	Gastonia	A	45	157	33	7	1	1	45	15	7	9	0	40	3	3	1	13	6	.68	1	.210	.265	.287
	Butte	R	73	300	83	16	4	2	113	58	27	23	1	67	5	4	1	24	9	.73	6	.277	.337	.377
1993	Charlstn-Sc	A	125	446	95	13	6	5	135	52	25	37	0	99	3	3	3	18	13	.58	5	.213	.276	.303
1994	Charlotte	A	106	431	115	19	8	6	168	61	35	16	1	68	2	3	3	10	7	.59	5	.267	.294	.390
1995	Okla. City	AAA	6	18	3	1	0	0	4	0	1	2	0	4	0	0	1	1	0	1.00	1	.167	.238	.222
	Tulsa	AA	71	261	64	9	2	2	83	27	26	12	0	51	0	5	5	7	9	.44	5	.245	.273	.318
	6 Min. YEARS		524	1950	479	77	24	20	664	252	159	110	2	418	14	18	17	90	55	.62	26	.246	.288	.341

Tom Paskievitch

Pitches: Right Bats: Right Pos: P   Ht: 6'3" Wt: 210 Born: 7/19/68 Age: 27

			HOW MUCH HE PITCHED						WHAT HE GAVE UP								THE RESULTS					

Year	Team	Lg	G	GS	CG	GF	IP	BFP	H	R	ER	HR	SH	SF	HB	TBB	IBB	SO	WP	Bk	W	L	Pct.	ShO	Sv	ERA
1991	Erie	A	27	3	0	15	60	258	48	28	19	2	0	1	0	30	0	52	4	4	5	3	.625	0	3	2.85
1992	Waterloo	A	49	9	1	14	102.2	477	105	65	56	5	3	4	7	67	7	122	10	3	11	8	.579	0	4	4.91
1993	Rancho Cuca	A	31	0	0	10	45.1	182	26	9	6	1	2	0	4	18	4	45	5	0	3	0	1.000	0	1	1.19
	Wichita	AA	7	0	0	5	9	46	11	8	7	1	2	0	1	8	2	5	0	1	1	2	.333	0	0	7.00
1994	Kane County	A	7	0	0	7	6.1	30	8	3	3	0	0	0	1	2	0	13	3	0	0	0	.000	0	3	4.26
	Portland	AA	5	0	0	3	6.1	28	10	5	5	0	0	0	0	2	0	8	0	0	0	0	.000	0	0	7.11
	Duluth-Sup.	IND	21	14	3	3	115.1	476	109	50	41	3	6	1	8	26	0	82	3	0	3	7	.300	0	0	3.20
1995	Wichita	AA	5	0	0	1	5.1	21	6	3	3	1	0	1	0	2	0	3	1	0	1	1	.500	0	0	5.06
	St. Paul	IND	8	6	0	0	32.1	145	40	21	21	4	2	0	1	14	1	17	0	1	3	2	.600	0	0	5.85
	Winnipeg	IND	3	1	0	0	9	42	11	6	6	1	0	1	1	5	0	6	0	0	1	1	.500	0	0	6.00
	5 Min. YEARS		163	33	4	58	391.2	1705	374	198	167	18	15	8	23	175	14	347	26	9	28	24	.538	0	7	3.84

Bronswell Patrick

Pitches: Right Bats: Right Pos: P   Ht: 6'1" Wt: 205 Born: 9/16/70 Age: 25

			HOW MUCH HE PITCHED						WHAT HE GAVE UP								THE RESULTS					

Year	Team	Lg	G	GS	CG	GF	IP	BFP	H	R	ER	HR	SH	SF	HB	TBB	IBB	SO	WP	Bk	W	L	Pct.	ShO	Sv	ERA
1988	Athletics	R	14	13	2	0	96.1	390	99	37	32	7	1	2	2	16	1	64	1	2	8	3	.727	0	0	2.99
1989	Madison	A	12	10	0	1	54.1	238	62	29	22	3	2	0	0	14	0	32	3	2	2	5	.286	0	0	3.64
1990	Modesto	A	14	14	0	0	74.2	340	92	58	43	10	3	1	4	32	0	37	5	1	3	7	.300	0	0	5.18
	Madison	A	13	12	3	0	80	337	88	44	32	6	5	4	1	19	0	40	3	0	3	7	.300	0	0	3.60
1991	Modesto	A	28	26	3	1	169.2	716	158	77	61	9	4	4	1	60	4	95	7	0	12	12	.500	1	0	3.24
1992	Huntsville	AA	29	29	3	0	179.1	758	187	84	75	20	1	3	4	46	0	98	3	0	13	7	.650	0	0	3.76
1993	Tacoma	AAA	35	13	1	12	104.2	496	156	87	82	12	3	12	4	42	3	56	3	0	3	8	.273	0	1	7.05
1994	Huntsville	AA	7	3	0	1	27.2	120	31	11	9	2	1	0	2	10	0	16	1	1	2	0	1.000	0	0	2.93
	Tacoma	AAA	30	0	0	9	47.1	208	50	31	25	5	3	1	0	20	2	38	2	0	1	1	.500	0	2	4.75
1995	Tucson	AAA	43	4	0	10	81.2	352	91	42	38	3	2	3	1	21	1	62	4	0	5	1	.833	0	1	4.19
	8 Min. YEARS		225	124	12	34	915.2	3955	1014	500	419	77	25	30	19	280	11	538	32	6	52	51	.505	1	5	4.12

Danny Patterson

Pitches: Right Bats: Right Pos: P   Ht: 6'0" Wt: 168 Born: 2/17/71 Age: 25

			HOW MUCH HE PITCHED						WHAT HE GAVE UP								THE RESULTS					

Year	Team	Lg	G	GS	CG	GF	IP	BFP	H	R	ER	HR	SH	SF	HB	TBB	IBB	SO	WP	Bk	W	L	Pct.	ShO	Sv	ERA
1990	Butte	R	13	3	0	2	28.1	135	36	23	20	3	0	3	1	14	1	18	3	1	0	3	.000	0	1	6.35
1991	Rangers	R	11	9	0	0	50	201	43	21	18	1	1	0	3	12	0	46	2	3	5	3	.625	0	0	3.24

Year	Team	Lg	G	GS	CG	GF	IP	BFP	H	R	ER	HR	SH	SF	HB	TBB	IBB	SO	WP	Bk	W	L	Pct.	ShO	Sv	ERA
1992	Gastonia	A	23	21	3	0	105.1	447	106	47	42	9	2	2	4	33	3	84	5	13	4	6	.400	1	0	3.59
1993	Charlotte	A	47	0	0	24	68	286	55	22	19	2	5	1	1	28	4	41	5	0	5	6	.455	0	7	2.51
1994	Charlotte	A	7	0	0	4	13.2	57	13	7	7	1	0	1	0	5	0	9	1	0	1	0	1.000	0	0	4.61
	Tulsa	AA	30	1	0	19	44	181	35	13	8	2	3	3	1	17	1	33	5	2	1	4	.200	0	6	1.64
1995	Tulsa	AA	26	0	0	22	36.1	163	45	27	25	2	0	1	2	13	2	24	5	0	2	2	.500	0	5	6.19
	Okla. City	AAA	14	0	0	3	27.1	111	23	8	5	0	3	2	1	9	2	9	4	0	1	0	1.000	0	2	1.65
6 Min. YEARS			171	34	3	74	373	1581	356	168	144	20	14	13	13	131	13	264	30	19	19	24	.442	1	21	3.47

Ken Patterson

Pitches: Left Bats: Left Pos: P Ht: 6' 4" Wt: 222 Born: 7/8/64 Age: 31

			HOW MUCH HE PITCHED						WHAT HE GAVE UP												THE RESULTS					
Year	Team	Lg	G	GS	CG	GF	IP	BFP	H	R	ER	HR	SH	SF	HB	TBB	IBB	SO	WP	Bk	W	L	Pct.	ShO	Sv	ERA
1985	Oneonta	A	6	6	0	0	22.1	103	23	14	12	0	1	0	2	14	0	21	1	0	2	2	.500	0	0	4.84
1986	Ft. Laud	A	5	5	0	0	18.2	100	30	20	16	2	0	0	3	16	0	13	2	0	0	2	.000	0	0	7.71
	Oneonta	A	15	15	5	0	100.1	399	67	25	15	2	1	1	4	45	0	102	7	1	9	3	.750	4	0	1.35
1987	Ft. Laud	A	9	9	0	0	42.2	202	46	34	30	0	1	2	2	31	0	36	5	1	1	3	.250	0	0	6.33
	Albany-Colo	AA	24	8	1	14	63.2	272	59	31	28	2	3	3	2	31	1	47	4	0	3	6	.333	0	5	3.96
	Hawaii	AAA	3	0	0	3	3.1	14	1	0	0	0	0	0	0	3	0	5	0	0	0	0	.000	0	2	0.00
1988	Vancouver	AAA	55	4	1	23	86.1	349	64	37	31	4	5	4	2	36	7	89	7	2	6	5	.545	0	13	3.23
1989	Vancouver	AAA	2	2	0	0	9	35	6	2	1	0	1	1	1	1	0	17	2	0	0	1	.000	0	0	1.00
1992	Peoria	A	2	0	0	1	3	16	5	4	4	0	0	0	0	2	0	5	0	0	0	0	.000	0	0	12.00
	Iowa	AAA	1	0	0	0	1.2	11	4	4	4	2	1	0	1	1	0	1	0	0	0	1	.000	0	0	21.60
1994	Vancouver	AAA	3	0	0	1	5.2	30	5	7	6	0	0	1	0	6	0	5	0	0	0	0	.000	0	0	9.53
1995	Lk Elsinore	A	6	0	0	2	9.2	35	7	0	0	0	0	0	0	1	0	9	1	0	0	0	.000	0	0	0.00
	Angels	R	1	1	0	0	3	10	0	0	0	0	0	0	0	1	0	3	0	0	0	0	.000	0	1	0.00
	Vancouver	AAA	8	0	0	3	11	46	12	1	1	0	0	0	0	4	1	4	1	0	0	0	.000	0	1	0.82
1988	Chicago	AL	9	2	0	3	20.2	92	25	11	11	2	0	0	0	7	0	8	1	1	0	2	.000	0	1	4.79
1989	Chicago	AL	50	1	0	18	65.2	284	64	37	33	11	1	4	2	28	3	43	3	1	6	1	.857	0	0	4.52
1990	Chicago	AL	43	0	0	15	66.1	283	58	27	25	6	2	5	2	34	1	40	2	0	2	1	.667	0	2	3.39
1991	Chicago	AL	43	0	0	13	63.2	265	48	22	20	5	3	2	1	35	1	32	2	0	3	0	1.000	0	1	2.83
1992	Chicago	NL	32	1	0	4	41.2	191	41	25	18	7	6	4	1	27	6	23	3	1	2	3	.400	0	0	3.89
1993	California	AL	46	0	0	9	59	255	54	30	30	7	2	1	0	35	5	36	2	0	1	1	.500	0	1	4.58
1994	California	AL	1	0	0	0	0.2	2	0	0	0	0	0	0	0	0	0	1	0	0	0	0	.000	0	0	0.00
8 Min. YEARS			140	50	7	47	380.1	1622	329	179	148	12	13	12	17	192	9	357	30	4	21	23	.477	4	22	3.50
7 Maj. YEARS			224	4	0	62	317.2	1372	290	152	137	38	14	16	6	166	16	183	13	3	14	8	.636	0	5	3.88

Darrin Paxton

Pitches: Left Bats: Left Pos: P Ht: 6'4" Wt: 220 Born: 4/17/70 Age: 26

			HOW MUCH HE PITCHED						WHAT HE GAVE UP												THE RESULTS					
Year	Team	Lg	G	GS	CG	GF	IP	BFP	H	R	ER	HR	SH	SF	HB	TBB	IBB	SO	WP	Bk	W	L	Pct.	ShO	Sv	ERA
1991	Jamestown	A	13	6	0	1	58.1	230	37	13	13	2	1	1	3	27	1	62	2	0	5	1	.833	0	0	2.01
1992	Albany	A	33	15	2	5	129.1	545	102	56	43	8	2	1	1	62	4	120	9	3	6	9	.400	1	0	2.99
1993	Burlington	A	41	3	0	8	75	317	57	28	24	5	3	3	8	34	1	110	4	0	6	1	.857	0	1	2.88
1994	High Desert	A	12	12	0	0	76.2	311	64	38	37	9	2	3	1	18	0	70	3	1	5	3	.625	1	0	4.34
	Harrisburg	AA	17	15	1	0	83.2	360	83	39	35	7	2	1	2	37	0	80	2	0	4	6	.400	0	0	3.76
1995	Harrisburg	AA	7	0	0	2	7	30	5	2	1	0	0	0	0	3	1	7	0	0	0	1	.000	0	0	1.29
	Norfolk	AAA	1	0	0	0	2	10	3	2	2	0	0	0	0	2	0	0	0	0	0	0	.000	0	0	9.00
	Binghamton	AA	21	3	0	8	37	154	41	20	16	3	0	2	0	10	0	20	1	1	1	1	.500	0	1	3.89
5 Min. YEARS			145	54	5	24	469	1957	392	198	171	34	10	12	15	193	7	469	21	5	27	22	.551	2	1	3.28

Jay Payton

Bats: Right Throws: Right Pos: OF Ht: 5'10" Wt: 190 Born: 11/22/72 Age: 23

			BATTING													BASERUNNING				PERCENTAGES		
Year	Team	Lg	G	AB	H	2B	3B	HR	TB	R	RBI	TBB	IBB	SO	HBP	SH	SF	SB	CS	SB%	GDP	Avg	OBP	SLG
1994	Pittsfield	A	58	219	80	16	2	3	109	47	37	23	2	18	9	0	4	10	2	.83	1	.365	.439	.498
	Binghamton	AA	8	25	7	1	0	0	8	3	1	2	0	3	1	0	0	1	1	.50	1	.280	.357	.320
1995	Binghamton	AA	85	357	123	20	3	14	191	59	54	29	2	32	2	0	2	16	7	.70	11	.345	.395	.535
	Norfolk	AAA	50	196	47	11	4	4	78	33	30	11	0	22	2	4	2	11	3	.79	5	.240	.284	.398
2 Min. YEARS			201	797	257	48	9	21	386	142	122	65	4	75	14	4	8	38	13	.75	18	.322	.380	.484

Eddie Pearson

Bats: Both Throws: Right Pos: 1B-DH Ht: 6'3" Wt: 225 Born: 1/31/74 Age: 22

			BATTING													BASERUNNING				PERCENTAGES		
Year	Team	Lg	G	AB	H	2B	3B	HR	TB	R	RBI	TBB	IBB	SO	HBP	SH	SF	SB	CS	SB%	GDP	Avg	OBP	SLG
1992	White Sox	R	28	102	24	5	0	0	29	10	12	9	1	17	2	0	1	1	3	.25	3	.235	.307	.284
1993	Hickory	A	87	343	83	15	3	4	116	37	40	20	0	59	1	5	1	5	1	.83	8	.242	.285	.338
	South Bend	A	48	190	62	16	0	1	81	23	26	13	2	29	1	0	3	0	1	.00	1	.326	.367	.426
1994	Pr. William	A	130	502	139	28	3	12	209	58	80	45	1	80	3	0	3	0	0	.00	11	.277	.338	.416
1995	White Sox	R	6	20	6	2	0	1	11	7	6	3	0	2	0	0	0	0	0	.00	0	.300	.391	.550
	Birmingham	AA	50	201	45	13	0	2	64	20	25	7	0	36	1	0	2	1	0	1.00	9	.224	.251	.318
4 Min. YEARS			349	1358	359	79	6	20	510	155	189	97	4	223	8	5	10	7	5	.58	32	.264	.315	.376

Aldo Pecorilli

Bats: Right Throws: Right Pos: 1B Ht: 5'11" Wt: 185 Born: 9/12/70 Age: 25

Year	Team	Lg	G	AB	H	2B	3B	HR	TB	R	RBI	TBB	IBB	SO	HBP	SH	SF	SB	CS	SB%	GDP	Avg	OBP	SLG
1992	Johnson Cty	R	54	201	65	14	2	6	101	36	41	25	1	21	2	0	2	6	2	.75	4	.323	.400	.502
1993	Savannah	A	141	515	157	30	7	14	243	75	93	81	7	86	6	0	8	16	11	.59	5	.305	.400	.472
1994	St. Pete	A	135	508	141	26	3	18	227	76	78	56	4	69	4	1	3	13	9	.59	7	.278	.352	.447
1995	Greenville	AA	70	265	102	17	2	7	144	51	42	22	2	39	6	1	4	2	8	.20	4	.385	.438	.543
	Richmond	AAA	49	127	33	3	0	6	54	16	17	19	2	20	2	2	0	0	0	.00	5	.260	.365	.425
	4 Min. YEARS		449	1616	498	90	14	51	769	254	271	203	16	235	20	4	17	37	30	.55	25	.308	.388	.476

Tim Peek

Pitches: Right Bats: Right Pos: P Ht: 6'2" Wt: 210 Born: 1/23/68 Age: 28

Year	Team	Lg	G	GS	CG	GF	IP	BFP	H	R	ER	HR	SH	SF	HB	TBB	IBB	SO	WP	Bk	W	L	Pct.	ShO	Sv	ERA
1987	Utica	A	4	4	0	0	25.2	100	20	4	4	0	1	1	0	7	0	13	2	0	1	1	.500	0	0	1.40
	Spartanburg	A	10	9	1	0	56	228	50	24	20	6	3	1	1	16	0	39	2	1	2	3	.400	0	0	3.21
1988	Spartanburg	A	37	4	0	23	105.2	417	77	26	22	6	5	3	5	30	0	80	8	3	6	3	.667	0	9	1.87
1989	Clearwater	A	8	0	0	4	18.1	87	23	13	12	1	1	0	1	6	0	13	0	0	1	0	1.000	0	0	5.89
	Spartanburg	A	19	1	0	13	45.1	192	32	15	10	4	1	1	3	20	1	42	1	1	3	1	.750	0	3	1.99
1990	Madison	A	39	0	0	30	56.2	223	41	19	17	4	3	1	1	10	2	70	0	1	5	3	.625	0	7	2.70
1991	Huntsville	AA	56	0	0	49	66.1	279	65	31	24	5	7	2	1	15	3	52	2	0	2	4	.333	0	26	3.26
1992	Tacoma	AAA	57	0	0	23	87.2	379	87	38	29	7	7	1	4	37	9	52	1	0	4	3	.571	0	3	2.98
1993	Tacoma	AAA	60	0	0	25	86.2	389	103	46	38	8	7	6	5	28	5	63	0	1	9	6	.600	0	5	3.95
1994	Memphis	AAA	26	1	0	10	50	191	38	16	14	2	2	2	1	12	2	27	1	0	6	4	.600	0	2	2.52
	Omaha	AAA	9	2	0	1	21.2	97	25	18	15	5	1	0	2	8	0	9	1	0	0	2	.000	0	0	6.23
1995	Edmonton	AAA	12	0	0	3	21.2	87	20	11	11	3	0	1	0	7	0	6	2	0	0	0	.000	0	0	4.57
	9 Min. YEARS		337	21	1	181	641.2	2669	581	261	216	51	38	19	24	196	22	466	20	7	39	30	.565	0	53	3.03

Lloyd Peever

Pitches: Right Bats: Right Pos: P Ht: 5'11" Wt: 185 Born: 9/15/71 Age: 24

Year	Team	Lg	G	GS	CG	GF	IP	BFP	H	R	ER	HR	SH	SF	HB	TBB	IBB	SO	WP	Bk	W	L	Pct.	ShO	Sv	ERA
1992	Bend	A	11	8	0	2	43.1	180	44	18	14	2	1	2	2	10	0	48	3	0	3	2	.600	0	1	2.91
1993	Central Val	A	16	7	1	6	66.2	278	65	31	31	6	0	2	1	17	0	69	5	0	2	4	.333	1	4	4.19
1994	New Haven	AA	23	21	3	1	131.1	536	109	59	50	8	6	5	3	37	1	126	3	2	9	8	.529	2	1	3.43
1995	Colo. Sprng	AAA	8	8	0	0	42	185	45	26	25	5	0	3	1	16	0	25	3	0	3	2	.600	0	0	5.36
	4 Min. YEARS		58	44	4	9	283.1	1179	263	134	120	21	7	12	7	80	1	268	14	2	17	16	.515	3	6	3.81

Jose Peguero

Bats: Right Throws: Right Pos: 3B Ht: 6'0" Wt: 195 Born: 2/8/65 Age: 31

Year	Team	Lg	G	AB	H	2B	3B	HR	TB	R	RBI	TBB	IBB	SO	HBP	SH	SF	SB	CS	SB%	GDP	Avg	OBP	SLG
1990	Salinas	A	45	154	27	3	0	1	33	9	11	9	0	31	0	1	1	4	5	.44	2	.175	.220	.214
1994	San Bernrdo	A	129	533	154	18	0	25	247	91	76	21	1	104	8	4	3	11	5	.69	13	.289	.324	.463
1995	Vancouver	AAA	17	59	15	6	0	0	21	6	3	0	0	8	0	0	0	1	0	1.00	2	.254	.254	.356
	Palm Spring	IND	83	320	103	20	3	13	168	50	55	13	0	48	3	3	2	28	7	.80	2	.322	.352	.525
	3 Min. YEARS		274	1066	299	47	3	39	469	156	145	43	1	191	11	8	6	44	17	.72	19	.280	.313	.440

Julio Peguero

Bats: Both Throws: Right Pos: OF Ht: 6'0" Wt: 160 Born: 9/7/68 Age: 27

Year	Team	Lg	G	AB	H	2B	3B	HR	TB	R	RBI	TBB	IBB	SO	HBP	SH	SF	SB	CS	SB%	GDP	Avg	OBP	SLG
1987	Macon	A	132	520	148	11	6	4	183	88	53	56	3	76	1	1	4	23	9	.72	5	.285	.353	.352
1988	Salem	A	128	517	135	17	5	5	177	89	50	64	3	81	5	2	1	43	11	.80	11	.261	.348	.342
1989	Harrisburg	AA	76	284	70	14	1	2	92	34	21	29	0	39	2	1	0	14	12	.54	5	.246	.321	.324
1990	Harrisburg	AA	104	411	116	14	9	1	151	40	26	29	1	53	0	0	2	8	12	.40	17	.282	.328	.367
	Reading	AA	3	12	1	0	0	0	1	0	2	2	0	1	0	0	0	0	0	.00	0	.083	.214	.083
1991	Scranton-Wb	AAA	133	506	138	20	9	2	182	71	39	40	3	71	1	5	2	21	14	.60	12	.273	.326	.360
1992	Scranton-Wb	AAA	74	289	74	14	2	1	95	41	21	24	2	56	2	2	2	14	15	.48	5	.256	.315	.329
	Albuquerque	AAA	30	76	20	4	0	1	27	13	8	13	0	13	2	2	1	1	1	.50	1	.263	.380	.355
1993	Canton-Akrn	AA	65	177	40	6	5	0	56	19	14	17	1	32	1	4	1	4	1	.80	4	.226	.296	.316
1994	Riverside	A	28	99	38	2	1	2	48	16	23	11	0	17	1	4	1	3	4	.43	2	.384	.446	.485
1995	Port City	AA	71	256	81	15	1	3	107	42	18	16	1	34	1	4	1	12	8	.60	3	.316	.358	.418
	Tacoma	AAA	11	25	5	0	1	0	7	2	1	1	0	7	0	0	0	0	0	.00	0	.200	.231	.280
1992	Philadelphia	NL	14	9	2	0	0	0	2	3	0	3	0	3	0	1	0	0	0	.00	0	.222	.417	.222
	9 Min. YEARS		855	3172	866	117	40	21	1126	455	276	302	14	480	16	25	15	143	87	.62	65	.273	.338	.355

Jim Pena

Pitches: Left Bats: Left Pos: P Ht: 6'0" Wt: 175 Born: 9/17/64 Age: 31

Year	Team	Lg	G	GS	CG	GF	IP	BFP	H	R	ER	HR	SH	SF	HB	TBB	IBB	SO	WP	Bk	W	L	Pct.	ShO	Sv	ERA
1986	Everett	A	14	14	4	0	101.2	0	86	40	33	7	0	0	0	54	0	92	2	2	10	2	.833	0	0	2.92
1987	Clinton	A	26	26	6	0	161	690	158	90	71	15	6	5	3	80	0	142	6	2	10	11	.476	2	0	3.97

233

1989	Salinas	A	8	6	0	1	42.2	165	28	15	11	3	0	3	0	14	0	47	1	0	3	4	.429	0	0	2.32
	San Jose	A	16	15	1	0	97.1	408	84	45	33	9	1	2	2	35	0	71	2	4	4	8	.333	1	0	3.05
1990	Shreveport	AA	25	24	1	0	139	593	138	70	57	9	3	9	2	57	2	101	8	2	10	7	.588	0	0	3.69
1991	Shreveport	AA	45	3	1	16	83	362	84	56	44	9	3	5	0	41	5	51	3	2	7	4	.636	0	2	4.77
1992	Phoenix	AAA	33	2	0	12	39	174	45	22	18	4	4	0	0	20	6	27	0	0	7	3	.700	0	1	4.15
1993	Las Vegas	AAA	39	0	0	16	51.2	233	69	41	35	12	1	2	3	16	2	31	4	0	1	2	.333	0	0	6.10
	Wichita	A	10	1	0	4	16	60	10	5	3	0	1	5	0	2	0	12	2	0	2	0	1.000	0	0	1.69
1994	San Bernrdo	A	16	3	0	10	39	167	37	17	17	4	1	1	1	11	0	29	2	0	3	4	.429	0	0	3.92
1995	Ottawa	AAA	7	0	0	2	7.1	34	4	3	3	1	1	0	2	8	1	7	3	0	0	0	.000	0	0	3.68
1992	San Francisco	NL	25	2	0	4	44	204	49	19	17	4	8	1	1	20	5	32	0	0	1	1	.500	0	0	3.48
	9 Min. YEARS		239	94	13	61	777.2	2886	743	404	325	73	21	32	13	338	16	610	33	12	57	45	.559	3	6	3.76

Billy Percibal

Pitches: Right **Bats:** Right **Pos:** P   **Ht:** 6'1" **Wt:** 160 **Born:** 2/2/74 **Age:** 22

			HOW MUCH HE PITCHED						WHAT HE GAVE UP												THE RESULTS				
Year	Team	Lg	G	GS	CG	GF	IP	BFP	H	R	ER	HR	SH	SF	HB	TBB	IBB	SO	WP	Bk	W	L	Pct.	ShO	Sv	ERA
1992	Orioles	R	16	0	0	9	26.2	132	42	26	24	0	0	2	1	7	0	25	6	2	2	1	.667	0	0	8.10
1993	Bluefield	R	13	13	2	0	82.2	355	71	48	35	7	0	5	1	33	0	81	8	1	6	0	1.000	0	0	3.81
1994	Albany	A	28	28	3	0	169.1	744	160	80	67	9	1	3	1	90	0	132	13	4	13	9	.591	2	0	3.56
1995	High Desert	A	21	20	2	0	128	547	123	63	46	10	2	2	3	55	0	105	7	4	7	6	.538	0	0	3.23
	Bowie	AA	2	2	0	0	14	52	7	0	0	0	0	0	0	7	0	7	0	1	1	0	1.000	0	0	0.00
	4 Min. YEARS		80	63	7	9	420.2	1830	403	217	172	26	3	12	6	192	0	350	34	12	29	16	.644	2	0	3.68

Danny Perez

Bats: Right **Throws:** Right **Pos:** DH   **Ht:** 5'10" **Wt:** 188 **Born:** 2/26/71 **Age:** 25

			BATTING														BASERUNNING				PERCENTAGES		
Year	Team	Lg	G	AB	H	2B	3B	HR	TB	R	RBI	TBB	IBB	SO	HBP	SH	SF	SB	CS	SB%	GDP	Avg	OBP	SLG
1992	Helena	R	33	104	22	3	0	1	28	12	13	10	0	17	1	1	0	3	0	1.00	5	.212	.287	.269
1993	Beloit	A	106	377	113	17	6	10	172	70	59	56	0	64	5	1	2	23	8	.74	6	.300	.395	.456
	Stockton	A	10	24	7	3	1	0	12	4	0	2	0	5	0	0	0	2	1	.67	0	.292	.346	.500
1994	Stockton	A	9	33	9	0	0	0	9	7	3	7	0	7	0	0	0	2	2	.50	0	.273	.400	.273
	El Paso	AA	115	440	143	19	17	6	214	88	73	45	1	79	5	1	3	9	5	.64	11	.325	.391	.486
1995	El Paso	AA	22	76	21	1	1	0	24	16	7	4	0	14	1	0	1	1	0	1.00	0	.276	.317	.316
	New Orleans	AAA	12	34	10	1	0	0	11	5	0	5	1	9	0	0	0	0	0	.00	0	.294	.385	.324
	4 Min. YEARS		307	1088	325	44	25	17	470	202	155	129	2	195	12	3	6	40	16	.71	22	.299	.377	.432

David Perez

Pitches: Right **Bats:** Right **Pos:** P   **Ht:** 5'11" **Wt:** 170 **Born:** 5/23/68 **Age:** 28

			HOW MUCH HE PITCHED						WHAT HE GAVE UP												THE RESULTS				
Year	Team	Lg	G	GS	CG	GF	IP	BFP	H	R	ER	HR	SH	SF	HB	TBB	IBB	SO	WP	Bk	W	L	Pct.	ShO	Sv	ERA
1989	Butte	R	17	4	1	3	54	242	57	30	15	2	1	2	2	19	0	45	0	0	3	2	.600	0	1	2.50
1990	Charlotte	A	14	14	0	0	83.1	339	63	35	31	3	2	4	3	28	0	83	2	1	6	4	.600	0	0	3.35
1991	Tulsa	AA	25	24	4	0	147	619	130	76	69	11	5	2	4	69	3	97	5	3	5	14	.263	2	0	4.22
1992	Charlotte	A	13	7	1	5	59.1	227	44	14	14	3	1	0	1	15	2	31	2	1	5	2	.714	1	3	2.12
	Tulsa	AA	15	11	1	1	59.2	258	61	36	31	5	2	2	2	26	1	30	6	0	4	3	.571	0	0	4.68
1993	Tulsa	AA	33	14	1	6	125.1	520	119	64	56	11	3	8	3	34	7	111	3	1	9	10	.474	0	2	4.02
	Okla. City	AAA	2	1	0	0	7.1	34	8	10	10	1	0	1	0	4	0	3	2	0	1	0	1.000	0	0	12.27
1994	Okla. City	AAA	30	25	4	3	177	747	190	85	80	16	3	3	7	56	2	93	11	7	11	14	.440	1	0	4.07
1995	Tulsa	AA	8	7	0	0	46.1	204	49	30	27	5	5	0	1	18	2	25	1	0	3	2	.600	0	0	5.24
	Okla. City	AAA	20	20	1	0	103.1	461	120	71	64	16	0	0	13	34	1	74	5	0	5	12	.294	0	0	5.57
	7 Min. YEARS		177	127	13	18	862.2	3651	841	451	397	73	22	17	40	303	18	592	37	13	52	63	.452	4	6	4.14

Neifi Perez

Bats: Both **Throws:** Right **Pos:** SS   **Ht:** 6'0" **Wt:** 164 **Born:** 6/2/75 **Age:** 21

			BATTING														BASERUNNING				PERCENTAGES		
Year	Team	Lg	G	AB	H	2B	3B	HR	TB	R	RBI	TBB	IBB	SO	HBP	SH	SF	SB	CS	SB%	GDP	Avg	OBP	SLG
1993	Bend	A	75	296	77	11	4	3	105	35	32	19	2	43	2	4	3	19	14	.58	3	.260	.306	.355
1994	Central Val	A	134	506	121	16	7	1	154	64	35	32	1	79	2	19	5	9	7	.56	6	.239	.284	.304
1995	Colo. Sprng	AAA	11	36	10	4	0	0	14	4	2	0	0	5	0	1	0	1	1	.50	0	.278	.278	.389
	New Haven	AA	116	427	108	28	3	5	157	59	43	24	2	52	2	4	1	5	2	.71	6	.253	.295	.368
	3 Min. YEARS		336	1265	316	59	14	9	430	162	112	75	5	179	6	28	9	34	24	.59	15	.250	.293	.340

Tony Perezchica

Bats: Right **Throws:** Right **Pos:** 2B   **Ht:** 5'11" **Wt:** 165 **Born:** 4/20/66 **Age:** 30

			BATTING														BASERUNNING				PERCENTAGES		
Year	Team	Lg	G	AB	H	2B	3B	HR	TB	R	RBI	TBB	IBB	SO	HBP	SH	SF	SB	CS	SB%	GDP	Avg	OBP	SLG
1984	Everett	A	33	119	23	6	1	0	31	10	10	6	0	24	1	1	2	0	0	.00	4	.193	.234	.261
1985	Clinton	A	127	452	109	21	8	4	158	54	40	28	0	77	9	6	5	23	7	.77	9	.241	.296	.350
1986	Fresno	A	126	452	126	30	8	9	199	65	54	35	0	91	14	10	2	18	6	.75	11	.279	.348	.440
1987	Shreveport	AA	89	332	106	24	1	11	165	44	47	19	4	74	4	3	3	3	3	.50	10	.319	.360	.497
1988	Phoenix	AAA	134	517	158	18	10	9	223	79	64	44	1	125	3	7	3	10	13	.43	16	.306	.362	.431
1989	Phoenix	AAA	94	307	71	11	3	8	112	40	33	15	0	65	5	2	7	5	4	.56	8	.231	.272	.365
1990	Phoenix	AAA	105	392	105	22	6	9	166	55	49	34	3	76	7	0	4	8	5	.62	8	.268	.334	.423
1991	Phoenix	AAA	51	191	56	10	4	8	98	41	34	18	0	43	6	1	3	1	0	1.00	4	.293	.367	.513
1992	Colo. Sprng	AAA	20	70	12	1	0	2	19	8	9	4	0	20	1	3	0	1	1	.50	1	.171	.227	.271

Year	Team	Lg	G	AB	H	2B	3B	HR	TB	R	RBI	TBB	IBB	SO	HBP	SH	SF	SB	CS	SB%	GDP	Avg	OBP	SLG
1994	Albany-Colo	AA	44	166	56	11	5	8	101	32	33	14	1	35	5	1	5	1	2	.33	1	.337	.395	.608
	Columbus	AAA	28	102	30	6	2	3	49	19	9	7	2	19	1	1	0	2	1	.67	1	.294	.345	.480
1995	Columbus	AAA	101	358	92	12	4	7	133	43	44	18	2	74	5	7	5	3	3	.50	8	.257	.298	.372
1988	San Francisco	NL	7	8	1	0	0	0	1	1	1	2	0	1	0	0	1	0	0	.00	0	.125	.273	.125
1990	San Francisco	NL	4	3	1	0	0	0	1	1	0	1	0	2	0	0	0	0	0	.00	0	.333	.500	.333
1991	Cleveland	AL	17	22	8	2	0	0	10	4	0	3	0	5	0	0	0	0	0	.00	0	.364	.440	.455
	San Francisco	NL	23	48	11	4	1	0	17	2	3	2	0	12	0	0	0	0	1	.00	0	.229	.260	.354
1992	Cleveland	AL	18	20	2	1	0	0	3	2	1	2	0	6	0	0	0	0	0	.00	0	.100	.182	.150
	11 Min. YEARS		952	3458	944	172	52	78	1454	490	426	242	13	723	61	42	39	75	45	.63	81	.273	.328	.420
	4 Maj. YEARS		69	101	23	7	1	0	32	10	5	10	0	26	0	2		0	1	.00	0	.228	.295	.317

Donny Perigny

Pitches: Right **Bats:** Right **Pos:** P **Ht:** 5'11" **Wt:** 175 **Born:** 1/8/69 **Age:** 27

			HOW	MUCH	HE	PITCHED			WHAT	HE	GAVE	UP								THE	RESULTS			
Year	Team	Lg	G	GS	CG	GF	IP	BFP	H	R	ER	HR	SH	SF	HB	TBB	IBB	SO	WP	Bk	W	L	Pct.	ShO	Sv	ERA
1990	White Sox	R	7	1	0	5	16.2	64	9	1	1	0	1	0	0	6	0	19	0	0	1	1	.500	0	3	0.54
1991	South Bend	A	56	0	0	18	91.2	380	91	31	19	1	5	3	2	22	3	54	6	2	6	4	.600	0	6	1.87
1992	Sarasota	A	52	0	0	35	70.2	292	55	10	6	0	7	4	4	23	6	59	3	1	6	1	.857	0	20	0.76
1993	Birmingham	AA	48	0	0	25	70.1	297	69	38	33	9	2	4	5	15	1	57	7	1	3	4	.429	0	3	4.22
1994	Portland	AA	49	2	0	22	88.2	376	82	42	38	9	3	2	4	27	5	84	1	0	6	9	.400	0	11	3.86
1995	Charlotte	AAA	6	0	0	3	7	30	8	6	4	1	0	1	1	1	0	10	2	0	1	1	.500	0	0	5.14
	6 Min. YEARS		218	3	0	108	345	1439	314	128	101	20	18	14	16	94	15	283	19	4	23	20	.535	0	43	2.63

Joe Perona

Bats: Right **Throws:** Right **Pos:** 3B-C **Ht:** 6'0" **Wt:** 195 **Born:** 2/8/70 **Age:** 26

						BATTING											BASERUNNING				PERCENTAGES		
Year	Team	Lg	G	AB	H	2B	3B	HR	TB	R	RBI	TBB	IBB	SO	HBP	SH	SF	SB	CS	SB%	GDP	Avg	OBP	SLG
1991	Bristol	R	5	16	8	3	0	1	14	1	3	3	0	1	0	0	0	2	1	.67	1	.500	.579	.875
	Fayetteville	A	46	147	40	7	2	6	69	25	25	23	1	19	4	2	2	4	2	.67	3	.272	.381	.469
1992	Lakeland	A	94	286	63	6	0	4	81	28	37	24	0	27	5	6	4	2	2	.50	9	.220	.288	.283
1993	London	AA	102	349	94	17	2	5	130	34	29	28	1	56	4	3	2	2	5	.29	5	.269	.329	.372
1994	Trenton	AA	107	359	79	24	3	5	124	39	26	31	0	50	6	0	0	0	5	.00	9	.220	.293	.345
1995	Jacksonville	AA	13	34	5	3	0	0	8	2	3	2	0	5	0	0	1	0	0	.00	2	.147	.189	.235
	5 Min. YEARS		367	1191	289	60	7	21	426	129	123	111	2	158	19	11	9	10	15	.40	29	.243	.315	.358

Pat Perry

Pitches: Left **Bats:** Left **Pos:** P **Ht:** 6'1" **Wt:** 190 **Born:** 2/4/59 **Age:** 37

			HOW	MUCH	HE	PITCHED			WHAT	HE	GAVE	UP								THE	RESULTS			
Year	Team	Lg	G	GS	CG	GF	IP	BFP	H	R	ER	HR	SH	SF	HB	TBB	IBB	SO	WP	Bk	W	L	Pct.	ShO	Sv	ERA
1984	Arkansas	AA	25	0	0	11	48.2	196	34	8	6	2	2	1	0	17	3	51	4	0	4	2	.667	0	3	1.11
	Louisville	AAA	21	0	0	9	44.2	191	35	12	11	4	2	1	0	21	4	43	5	0	4	3	.571	0	2	2.22
1985	Louisville	AAA	45	2	0	24	91	364	56	33	24	2	6	5	3	39	3	63	3	0	4	3	.571	0	14	2.37
1986	Louisville	AAA	5	0	0	3	11	47	8	6	4	0	2	1	0	6	1	7	4	0	1	0	1.000	0	1	3.27
1988	Iowa	AAA	2	0	0	1	3	9	0	0	0	0	0	0	0	0	0	4	0	0	0	0	.000	0	0	0.00
1989	Iowa	AAA	5	0	0	1	4.1	22	3	3	3	1	0	0	1	6	0	4	1	0	1	0	1.000	0	0	6.23
1990	Bakersfield	A	3	3	0	0	5	20	3	3	2	0	0	1	0	1	0	7	1	0	0	0	.000	0	0	3.60
1991	Scranton-Wb	AAA	36	1	0	12	54.1	244	60	26	24	3	2	5	3	21	0	36	11	2	2	4	.333	0	4	3.98
1992	Las Vegas	AAA	16	0	0	2	12.2	55	19	11	9	0	0	1	0	1	1	1	3	0	0	0	.000	0	0	6.39
1995	Omaha	AAA	5	0	0	4	4.2	21	5	3	3	0	0	0	0	2	1	4	0	0	0	0	.000	0	3	5.79
1985	St. Louis	NL	6	0	0	1	12.1	42	3	0	0	0	0	0	0	3	1	6	1	0	1	0	1.000	0	0	0.00
1986	St. Louis	NL	46	0	0	20	68.2	288	59	31	29	5	0	7	0	34	9	29	5	0	2	3	.400	0	2	3.80
1987	Cincinnati	NL	12	0	0	3	15.1	55	6	0	0	0	1	0	1	4	1	6	0	0	1	0	1.000	0	1	0.00
	St. Louis	NL	45	0	0	13	65.2	269	54	34	32	7	2	1	2	21	3	33	3	0	4	2	.667	0	1	4.39
1988	Chicago	NL	35	0	0	13	38	158	40	15	14	5	0	2	1	7	0	24	2	0	3	2	.500	0	1	3.32
	Cincinnati	NL	12	0	0	5	20.2	93	21	17	13	4	1	3	0	9	4	11	1	1	2	2	.500	0	1	5.66
1989	Chicago	NL	19	0	0	6	35.2	141	23	8	7	2	1	1	0	16	3	20	1	0	0	1	.000	0	1	1.77
1990	Los Angeles	NL	7	0	0	2	6.2	36	9	7	6	0	0	1	1	5	1	2	2	0	0	0	.000	0	0	8.10
	9 Min. YEARS		163	6	0	67	279.1	1169	223	105	86	12	14	15	7	114	13	220	32	2	16	12	.571	0	27	2.77
	6 Maj. YEARS		182	0	0	63	263	1082	215	112	101	23	5	15	5	99	22	131	15	1	12	10	.545	0	6	3.46

Greg Perschke

Pitches: Right **Bats:** Right **Pos:** P **Ht:** 6'3" **Wt:** 180 **Born:** 8/3/67 **Age:** 28

			HOW	MUCH	HE	PITCHED			WHAT	HE	GAVE	UP								THE	RESULTS			
Year	Team	Lg	G	GS	CG	GF	IP	BFP	H	R	ER	HR	SH	SF	HB	TBB	IBB	SO	WP	Bk	W	L	Pct.	ShO	Sv	ERA
1989	Utica	A	14	0	0	14	17	61	5	3	3	0	0	0	1	4	0	20	0	3	0	0	.000	0	9	1.59
	South Bend	A	13	0	0	8	20.1	80	19	10	7	0	0	1	1	2	0	16	2	1	0	2	.000	0	1	3.10
1990	Sarasota	A	42	10	2	23	111.1	450	83	32	15	3	3	4	4	29	3	107	5	8	7	3	.700	0	9	1.21
	Birmingham	AA	4	4	1	0	27.2	110	20	9	8	3	0	1	3	6	0	18	1	0	3	1	.750	0	2	2.60
1991	Vancouver	AAA	27	27	3	0	176	759	170	104	91	18	7	10	7	62	0	98	8	3	7	12	.368	0	0	4.65
1992	Vancouver	AAA	29	28	1	0	165	692	159	83	69	13	1	7	7	44	0	82	4	2	12	7	.632	1	0	3.76
1993	Albuquerque	AAA	33	13	0	5	104.2	475	146	76	74	12	3	6	2	24	3	63	6	2	7	4	.636	0	0	6.36
1994	Orlando	AAA	25	0	0	14	41	158	28	9	7	2	3	0	1	10	4	26	0	1	4	3	.571	0	3	1.54
	Iowa	AAA	21	2	0	9	53	228	51	37	32	7	3	2	8	14	2	33	3	0	1	1	.500	0	5	5.43
1995	Buffalo	AAA	3	3	0	0	15.2	65	13	10	10	2	0	1	0	6	0	11	0	0	1	1	.500	0	0	5.74

		G	GS	CG	GF	IP	BFP	H	R	ER	HR	SH	SF	HB	TBB	IBB	SO	WP	Bk	W	L	Pct.	ShO	Sv	ERA
Canton-Akrn	AA	3	0	0	1	5.1	21	4	2	2	1	0	0	0	2	0	4	1	0	1	0	1.000	0	0	3.38
7 Min. YEARS		214	87	7	74	737	3099	698	375	318	61	20	32	34	203	12	478	30	20	43	34	.558	1	23	3.88

Chris Peters

Pitches: Left Bats: Left Pos: P   Ht: 6'1" Wt: 170 Born: 1/28/72 Age: 24

		HOW MUCH HE PITCHED						WHAT HE GAVE UP											THE RESULTS					
Year Team	Lg	G	GS	CG	GF	IP	BFP	H	R	ER	HR	SH	SF	HB	TBB	IBB	SO	WP	Bk	W	L	Pct.	ShO	Sv	ERA
1993 Welland	A	16	0	0	4	27.2	137	33	16	14	0	0	1	2	20	1	25	5	1	1	0	1.000	0	0	4.55
1994 Salem	A	3	0	0	1	3.1	16	5	5	5	2	0	0	1	1	0	2	1	0	1	0	1.000	0	0	13.50
Augusta	A	54	0	0	29	60.2	268	51	34	29	1	5	2	2	33	2	83	7	0	4	5	.444	0	0	4.30
1995 Lynchburg	A	24	24	3	0	144.2	586	126	57	39	5	7	4	5	35	2	132	12	1	11	5	.688	3	0	2.43
Carolina	AA	2	2	0	0	14	56	9	2	2	0	0	1	0	2	0	7	2	0	2	0	1.000	0	0	1.29
3 Min. YEARS		99	26	3	34	250.1	1063	224	114	89	8	12	8	10	91	5	249	27	2	19	10	.655	3	4	3.20

Chris Petersen

Bats: Right Throws: Right Pos: SS   Ht: 5'10" Wt: 160 Born: 11/6/70 Age: 25

		BATTING														BASERUNNING				PERCENTAGES		
Year Team	Lg	G	AB	H	2B	3B	HR	TB	R	RBI	TBB	IBB	SO	HBP	SH	SF	SB	CS	SB%	GDP	Avg	OBP	SLG
1992 Geneva	A	71	244	55	8	0	1	66	36	23	32	0	69	4	9	2	11	7	.61	4	.225	.323	.270
1993 Daytona	A	130	473	101	10	0	0	111	66	28	58	0	105	9	17	1	19	11	.63	10	.214	.311	.235
1994 Orlando	AA	117	376	85	12	3	1	106	34	26	37	0	89	2	16	1	8	11	.42	7	.226	.298	.282
1995 Orlando	AA	125	382	81	10	3	4	109	48	36	45	3	97	4	5	3	7	3	.70	14	.212	.300	.285
4 Min. YEARS		443	1475	322	40	6	6	392	184	113	172	3	360	19	47	7	45	32	.58	35	.218	.307	.266

Matt Petersen

Pitches: Right Bats: Right Pos: P   Ht: 6'4" Wt: 190 Born: 5/21/70 Age: 26

		HOW MUCH HE PITCHED						WHAT HE GAVE UP											THE RESULTS					
Year Team	Lg	G	GS	CG	GF	IP	BFP	H	R	ER	HR	SH	SF	HB	TBB	IBB	SO	WP	Bk	W	L	Pct.	ShO	Sv	ERA
1992 Erie	A	14	14	1	0	80.2	322	56	28	24	7	1	0	2	29	0	44	2	6	5	1	.833	0	0	2.68
1993 Kane County	A	30	22	1	3	141.2	608	139	85	77	15	4	2	10	46	2	118	9	3	9	11	.450	1	0	4.89
1994 Brevard Cty	A	13	11	1	1	78	311	57	28	25	3	1	2	4	28	0	61	2	3	9	3	.750	0	0	2.88
Portland	AA	16	14	0	0	81.2	351	74	49	44	10	2	7	6	39	1	64	3	1	4	5	.444	0	0	4.85
1995 Daytona	A	3	3	0	0	17.1	66	13	8	8	2	0	1	0	3	0	13	0	0	2	1	.667	0	0	4.15
Orlando	AA	24	15	1	2	89	414	107	66	58	15	5	4	7	39	5	59	2	2	3	9	.250	1	0	5.87
4 Min. YEARS		100	79	4	6	488.1	2072	446	264	236	52	13	16	29	184	8	359	18	15	32	30	.516	2	3	4.35

Charles Peterson

Bats: Right Throws: Right Pos: OF   Ht: 6'3" Wt: 200 Born: 5/8/74 Age: 22

		BATTING														BASERUNNING				PERCENTAGES		
Year Team	Lg	G	AB	H	2B	3B	HR	TB	R	RBI	TBB	IBB	SO	HBP	SH	SF	SB	CS	SB%	GDP	Avg	OBP	SLG
1993 Pirates	R	49	188	57	11	3	1	77	28	23	22	0	22	0	0	1	8	6	.57	4	.303	.374	.410
1994 Augusta	A	108	415	106	14	6	4	144	55	40	35	2	78	3	0	2	27	18	.60	7	.255	.316	.347
1995 Lynchburg	A	107	391	107	9	4	7	145	61	51	43	1	73	2	6	5	31	17	.65	11	.274	.345	.371
Carolina	AA	20	70	23	3	1	0	28	13	7	9	1	15	2	0	1	2	1	.67	1	.329	.415	.400
3 Min. YEARS		284	1064	293	37	14	12	394	157	121	109	4	188	7	6	9	68	42	.62	23	.275	.344	.370

Dean Peterson

Pitches: Right Bats: Right Pos: P   Ht: 6'3" Wt: 200 Born: 8/3/72 Age: 23

		HOW MUCH HE PITCHED						WHAT HE GAVE UP											THE RESULTS					
Year Team	Lg	G	GS	CG	GF	IP	BFP	H	R	ER	HR	SH	SF	HB	TBB	IBB	SO	WP	Bk	W	L	Pct.	ShO	Sv	ERA
1993 Red Sox	R	3	2	0	0	15	64	14	8	6	1	0	1	0	4	0	10	0	0	1	0	1.000	0	0	3.60
Utica	A	16	5	0	7	42	180	45	28	25	5	2	0	1	7	0	26	1	0	1	4	.200	0	2	5.36
1994 Sarasota	A	21	20	6	0	141	572	141	65	57	9	7	8	2	26	0	94	4	0	9	7	.563	3	0	3.64
1995 Trenton	AA	20	14	1	2	88.2	389	96	57	53	7	3	3	4	27	3	47	3	4	4	8	.333	0	0	5.38
Sarasota	A	4	4	0	0	17.1	90	25	17	13	2	1	1	3	10	0	15	1	0	1	3	.250	0	0	6.75
3 Min. YEARS		64	45	7	9	304	1295	321	175	154	24	13	13	10	74	3	192	9	4	16	22	.421	3	2	4.56

Mark Peterson

Pitches: Left Bats: Left Pos: P   Ht: 5'11" Wt: 195 Born: 11/27/70 Age: 25

		HOW MUCH HE PITCHED						WHAT HE GAVE UP											THE RESULTS					
Year Team	Lg	G	GS	CG	GF	IP	BFP	H	R	ER	HR	SH	SF	HB	TBB	IBB	SO	WP	Bk	W	L	Pct.	ShO	Sv	ERA
1992 Everett	A	20	5	0	7	53	226	58	23	19	5	2	0	1	17	1	47	0	4	3	2	.600	0	2	3.23
1993 San Jose	A	37	7	1	19	81.1	349	95	36	31	5	3	3	2	15	0	45	3	0	4	1	.800	1	0	3.43
1994 San Jose	A	9	4	0	2	36	139	36	16	16	4	2	2	0	6	1	27	1	0	3	3	.500	0	0	4.00
Shreveport	AA	28	3	1	11	55.2	223	58	24	21	1	2	2	1	6	1	31	0	0	3	2	.600	0	1	3.40
1995 Shreveport	AA	37	0	0	14	64	248	51	15	9	2	2	5	4	6	2	38	0	0	4	3	.571	0	5	1.27
4 Min. YEARS		131	19	2	53	290	1185	296	114	96	17	11	12	8	50	5	188	4	4	17	11	.607	1	5	2.98

Jose Pett

Pitches: Right Bats: Right Pos: P   Ht: 6'6" Wt: 190 Born: 1/8/76 Age: 20

		HOW MUCH HE PITCHED						WHAT HE GAVE UP											THE RESULTS					
Year Team	Lg	G	GS	CG	GF	IP	BFP	H	R	ER	HR	SH	SF	HB	TBB	IBB	SO	WP	Bk	W	L	Pct.	ShO	Sv	ERA
1993 Blue Jays	R	4	4	0	0	10	43	10	4	4	0	0	0	0	3	0	7	0	0	1	1	.500	0	0	3.60

Year	Team	Lg	G	GS	CG	GF	IP	BFP	H	R	ER	HR	SH	SF	HB	TBB	IBB	SO	WP	Bk	W	L	Pct.	ShO	Sv	ERA
1994	Dunedin	A	15	15	1	0	90.2	389	103	47	38	1	5	5	3	20	0	49	3	3	4	8	.333	0	0	3.77
1995	Knoxville	AA	26	25	1	0	141.2	602	132	87	67	16	4	4	4	48	0	89	8	0	8	9	.471	1	0	4.26
	3 Min. YEARS		45	44	2	0	242.1	1034	245	138	109	17	9	9	7	71	0	145	11	3	13	18	.419	1	0	4.05

Doug Pettit

Pitches: Right **Bats:** Left **Pos:** P **Ht:** 6'1" **Wt:** 220 **Born:** 4/10/70 **Age:** 26

			HOW MUCH HE PITCHED						WHAT HE GAVE UP												THE RESULTS					
Year	Team	Lg	G	GS	CG	GF	IP	BFP	H	R	ER	HR	SH	SF	HB	TBB	IBB	SO	WP	Bk	W	L	Pct.	ShO	Sv	ERA
1992	Erie	A	22	2	0	19	31.2	134	29	14	11	3	2	2	1	6	0	28	1	1	2	2	.500	0	11	3.13
1993	Kane County	A	52	0	0	38	77	313	67	26	21	7	6	1	2	16	5	63	1	1	5	10	.333	0	17	2.45
1994	Brevard Cty	A	40	0	0	31	46.2	194	37	13	13	4	4	1	2	13	1	38	1	1	3	3	.500	0	14	2.51
1995	Portland	AA	21	0	0	9	31.2	129	30	13	13	1	2	0	2	6	3	24	0	0	3	1	.750	0	2	3.69
	Brevard Cty	A	27	0	0	14	35	158	37	18	11	3	2	3	0	13	4	22	1	0	2	5	.286	0	4	2.83
	4 Min. YEARS		162	2	0	111	222	928	200	84	69	18	16	7	7	54	13	175	4	5	15	21	.417	0	48	2.80

Marty Pevey

Bats: Left **Throws:** Right **Pos:** C **Ht:** 6'1" **Wt:** 185 **Born:** 9/18/61 **Age:** 34

			BATTING														BASERUNNING				PERCENTAGES		
Year	Team	Lg	G	AB	H	2B	3B	HR	TB	R	RBI	TBB	IBB	SO	HBP	SH	SF	SB	CS	SB%	GDP	Avg	OBP	SLG
1984	St. Pete	A	128	441	136	16	4	2	166	53	60	48	7	47	1	6	4	7	7	.50	13	.308	.376	.376
1985	St. Pete	A	104	393	114	12	4	3	143	48	41	28	6	56	1	2	2	5	2	.71	9	.290	.337	.364
1986	Louisville	AAA	12	37	6	3	0	0	9	6	0	4	0	4	0	0	0	0	1	.00	0	.162	.244	.243
	Arkansas	AA	55	172	56	11	2	2	77	28	20	16	0	18	1	1	2	6	0	1.00	4	.326	.382	.448
1987	Louisville	AAA	16	38	9	2	0	1	14	5	5	0	0	10	0	0	1	0	0	.00	1	.237	.231	.368
	Arkansas	AA	80	197	55	11	1	3	77	28	16	10	2	33	1	1	1	6	1	.86	5	.279	.316	.391
1988	Jacksonville	AA	31	111	29	11	0	4	52	21	17	8	0	13	0	3	0	3	0	1.00	5	.261	.311	.468
	Indianapols	AAA	48	119	27	4	1	3	42	16	16	8	4	20	0	3	2	1	2	.33	4	.227	.271	.353
1989	Indianapols	AAA	34	108	28	4	2	1	39	12	14	8	1	20	0	2	0	3	3	.50	2	.259	.310	.361
1991	Syracuse	AAA	55	193	54	8	2	3	75	24	23	20	5	41	0	1	0	2	2	.33	4	.280	.347	.389
1992	Toledo	AAA	48	136	41	6	0	3	56	16	16	7	0	18	0	2	1	1	1	.50	1	.301	.333	.412
1993	Toledo	AAA	62	175	48	8	1	2	64	11	18	16	2	36	0	1	1	3	3	.50	3	.274	.333	.366
1994	Syracuse	AAA	96	259	70	13	2	6	105	29	31	20	3	55	1	4	3	2	3	.40	3	.270	.322	.405
1995	Tacoma	AAA	7	19	2	0	0	0	2	2	0	1	0	5	0	0	0	0	0	.00	0	.105	.150	.105
	Jacksonvlle	AA	20	58	15	2	0	1	20	2	7	4	0	17	0	2	2	0	2	.00	4	.259	.297	.345
1989	Montreal	NL	13	41	9	1	1	0	12	2	3	0	0	8	0	1	0	0	0	.00	1	.220	.220	.293
	11 Min. YEARS		796	2456	690	111	19	34	941	301	284	198	30	393	5	28	17	38	27	.58	58	.281	.334	.383

Randy Phillips

Pitches: Right **Bats:** Right **Pos:** P **Ht:** 6'3" **Wt:** 210 **Born:** 3/18/71 **Age:** 25

			HOW MUCH HE PITCHED						WHAT HE GAVE UP												THE RESULTS					
Year	Team	Lg	G	GS	CG	GF	IP	BFP	H	R	ER	HR	SH	SF	HB	TBB	IBB	SO	WP	Bk	W	L	Pct.	ShO	Sv	ERA
1992	Medicne Hat	R	15	13	1	0	91	390	88	48	34	9	1	2	9	25	0	69	4	3	2	4	.333	0	0	3.36
1993	Dunedin	A	17	17	0	0	110.1	453	99	51	47	12	4	2	5	30	3	87	5	6	7	6	.538	0	0	3.83
	Knoxville	AA	5	5	0	0	25	120	32	20	17	3	2	0	2	12	0	12	3	2	2	2	.500	0	0	6.12
1994	Knoxville	AA	8	8	0	0	48	192	37	16	13	4	1	2	1	12	0	31	2	2	3	2	.600	0	0	2.44
	Syracuse	AAA	22	19	0	1	108.2	493	126	81	73	16	1	4	7	45	1	81	4	2	6	9	.400	0	0	6.05
1995	Phoenix	AAA	25	24	2	0	132	574	155	83	75	11	4	6	4	40	2	66	8	2	4	13	.235	1	0	5.11
	4 Min. YEARS		92	86	3	1	515	2222	537	299	259	55	13	16	28	164	6	346	26	17	24	36	.400	1	0	4.53

Steve Phillips

Bats: Left **Throws:** Left **Pos:** OF **Ht:** 6'2" **Wt:** 205 **Born:** 1/12/68 **Age:** 28

			BATTING														BASERUNNING				PERCENTAGES		
Year	Team	Lg	G	AB	H	2B	3B	HR	TB	R	RBI	TBB	IBB	SO	HBP	SH	SF	SB	CS	SB%	GDP	Avg	OBP	SLG
1991	Oneonta	A	62	215	56	12	7	6	100	41	43	46	0	67	1	1	5	8	4	.67	1	.260	.386	.465
1992	Greensboro	A	129	461	114	26	3	7	167	63	67	71	2	146	2	2	2	6	7	.46	9	.247	.349	.362
1993	San Bernrdo	A	57	208	57	11	1	9	97	29	38	37	1	71	1	0	1	3	4	.43	2	.274	.385	.466
1994	San Bernrdo	A	66	233	69	15	1	8	110	44	42	46	2	79	2	0	2	1	4	.20	4	.296	.413	.472
1995	Norwich	AA	11	31	8	1	0	2	15	2	7	6	2	8	0	1	0	0	0	.00	0	.258	.378	.484
	5 Min. YEARS		325	1148	304	65	12	32	489	179	197	206	7	371	6	4	10	18	19	.49	16	.265	.377	.426

Tony Phillips

Pitches: Right **Bats:** Right **Pos:** P **Ht:** 6'4" **Wt:** 195 **Born:** 6/9/69 **Age:** 27

			HOW MUCH HE PITCHED						WHAT HE GAVE UP												THE RESULTS					
Year	Team	Lg	G	GS	CG	GF	IP	BFP	H	R	ER	HR	SH	SF	HB	TBB	IBB	SO	WP	Bk	W	L	Pct.	ShO	Sv	ERA
1992	San Bernrdo	A	37	0	0	29	51	227	44	23	18	1	4	4	2	28	2	40	3	3	4	3	.571	0	12	3.18
1993	Riverside	A	25	0	0	23	22	118	22	8	6	1	2	2	2	4	1	19	0	1	3	1	.750	0	15	1.80
	Jacksonvlle	AA	26	0	0	21	30.1	125	34	6	6	1	1	0	0	5	1	23	1	1	1	3	.250	0	5	1.78
1994	Jacksonvlle	AA	5	0	0	4	5.2	22	3	2	1	1	0	0	0	3	0	3	0	0	0	0	.000	0	1	1.59
	Calgary	AAA	55	1	0	29	98	438	132	66	61	11	2	5	2	23	5	51	2	4	6	3	.667	0	6	5.60
1995	Tacoma	AAA	47	1	0	19	87.1	370	98	44	40	6	3	7	6	14	7	44	0	2	3	2	.600	0	1	4.12
	4 Min. YEARS		195	2	0	125	302.1	1300	333	149	132	21	12	18	12	77	16	180	6	11	17	12	.586	0	40	3.93

Doug Piatt

Pitches: Right **Bats:** Left **Pos:** P
Ht: 6' 1" **Wt:** 185 **Born:** 9/26/65 **Age:** 30

Year	Team	Lg	G	GS	CG	GF	IP	BFP	H	R	ER	HR	SH	SF	HB	TBB	IBB	SO	WP	Bk	W	L	Pct.	ShO	Sv	ERA
1988	Burlington	R	2	0	0	1	1.1	9	4	2	2	0	0	0	0	1	0	1	0	0	0	0	.000	0	1	13.50
	Waterloo	A	26	0	0	22	36.2	153	33	18	9	2	1	1	0	11	1	40	1	1	2	1	.667	0	12	2.21
1989	Kinston	A	20	0	0	12	28.2	115	24	8	8	1	3	0	3	8	0	31	1	0	2	0	1.000	0	1	2.51
	Watertown	A	15	0	0	15	35	137	21	5	2	0	1	0	0	9	4	43	2	0	4	2	.667	0	6	0.51
	Rockford	A	11	0	0	6	19.2	86	19	7	7	1	1	0	1	11	1	24	2	0	2	2	.500	0	2	3.20
1990	W. Palm Bch	A	21	0	0	13	27.1	111	12	6	3	0	2	0	1	16	0	41	2	0	4	1	.800	0	9	0.99
	Jacksonville	AA	35	0	0	22	49	206	30	17	12	1	2	1	3	29	2	51	1	0	5	1	.833	0	6	2.20
1991	Indianapols	AAA	44	0	0	32	47	210	40	24	18	2	3	3	3	27	1	61	5	1	6	4	.600	0	13	3.45
1992	Harrisburg	AA	39	5	0	24	62.2	274	55	26	24	2	3	1	4	32	2	65	0	1	5	9	.357	0	7	3.45
	Indianapols	AAA	8	0	0	7	10.2	46	13	6	5	0	1	0	0	3	0	6	1	0	0	0	.000	0	3	4.22
1993	Memphis	AA	11	0	0	2	13.1	67	19	13	13	1	1	0	2	6	0	8	1	0	0	1	.000	0	0	8.78
	Carolina	AA	3	0	0	1	3.2	21	10	6	6	1	1	0	0	1	0	3	0	0	0	0	.000	0	0	14.73
	Buffalo	AAA	2	0	0	0	1	7	3	3	3	1	1	0	0	1	0	0	0	0	1	0	1.000	0	0	27.00
1995	Phoenix	AAA	6	0	0	2	7.2	34	7	5	5	0	1	1	0	5	1	3	0	0	0	1	.000	0	0	5.87
	Abilene	IND	37	0	0	36	51.2	225	52	28	21	5	5	3	2	18	3	45	5	1	4	6	.400	0	15	3.66
1991	Montreal	NL	21	0	0	3	34.2	145	29	11	10	3	2	0	0	17	0	29	1	0	0	0	.000	0	0	2.60
	7 Min. YEARS		280	5	0	195	395.1	1701	342	174	138	17	26	10	19	178	15	422	21	3	35	28	.556	0	75	3.14

Ricky Pickett

Pitches: Left **Bats:** Left **Pos:** P
Ht: 6'0" **Wt:** 185 **Born:** 1/19/70 **Age:** 26

Year	Team	Lg	G	GS	CG	GF	IP	BFP	H	R	ER	HR	SH	SF	HB	TBB	IBB	SO	WP	Bk	W	L	Pct.	ShO	Sv	ERA
1992	Billings	R	20	4	0	4	53.2	225	35	21	14	2	1	2	5	28	0	41	3	1	1	2	.333	0	2	2.35
1993	Charlstn-Wv	A	44	1	0	5	43.2	227	42	40	33	1	1	1	5	48	0	65	6	3	1	2	.333	0	0	6.80
1994	Charlstn-Wv	A	28	0	0	19	27.1	121	14	8	6	1	0	1	2	20	0	48	4	0	1	1	.500	0	13	1.98
	Winston-Sal	A	21	0	0	17	24	112	16	11	10	0	1	1	2	23	1	33	2	0	2	1	.667	0	4	3.75
1995	Chattanooga	AA	40	0	0	19	46.2	203	22	20	17	3	2	0	0	44	3	69	1	0	4	5	.444	0	9	3.28
	Shreveport	AA	14	0	0	9	21	82	9	5	4	1	0	1	0	9	0	23	2	0	2	0	1.000	0	3	1.71
	4 Min. YEARS		167	5	0	73	216.1	970	138	105	84	8	5	6	14	172	4	279	18	4	11	11	.500	0	31	3.49

Eddie Pierce

Pitches: Left **Bats:** Left **Pos:** P
Ht: 6' 1" **Wt:** 190 **Born:** 10/6/68 **Age:** 27

Year	Team	Lg	G	GS	CG	GF	IP	BFP	H	R	ER	HR	SH	SF	HB	TBB	IBB	SO	WP	Bk	W	L	Pct.	ShO	Sv	ERA
1989	Eugene	A	27	0	0	24	39	175	24	19	12	0	0	0	3	26	0	71	9	2	2	2	.500	0	4	2.77
1990	Baseball Cy	A	37	0	0	22	50	228	49	21	18	3	3	0	0	32	0	52	7	2	3	1	.750	0	5	3.24
	Memphis	AA	1	0	0	0	1	3	0	0	0	0	0	0	0	1	0	1	0	0	0	0	.000	0	0	0.00
1991	Memphis	AA	31	20	2	4	136	595	136	73	58	6	6	1	2	61	1	90	3	1	5	11	.313	0	0	3.84
1992	Memphis	AA	25	25	1	0	153.2	662	159	74	65	11	8	3	3	51	1	131	8	1	10	10	.500	1	0	3.81
1993	Memphis	AA	37	2	0	18	67.1	300	65	35	28	5	3	1	3	34	3	53	3	0	6	5	.545	0	1	3.74
	Omaha	AAA	12	2	0	3	34.2	153	40	24	21	6	3	1	1	13	1	20	0	0	0	2	.000	0	0	5.45
1994	Memphis	AA	13	13	1	0	74	318	80	38	32	5	2	1	2	22	0	52	5	0	5	3	.625	1	0	3.89
	Omaha	AAA	12	12	0	0	76	337	87	47	37	8	3	2	1	31	0	46	7	0	4	3	.571	0	0	4.38
1995	Omaha	AAA	3	0	0	1	3.2	22	9	4	3	0	0	0	0	1	0	1	0	0	0	0	.000	0	0	7.36
	Bowie	AA	7	4	0	1	21	102	32	16	15	2	1	2	0	9	0	16	2	0	0	2	.000	0	0	6.43
1992	Kansas City	AL	2	1	0	0	5.1	26	9	2	2	1	0	1	0	4	0	3	0	0	0	0	.000	0	0	3.38
	7 Min. YEARS		205	78	4	73	656.1	2894	681	351	289	46	29	11	15	281	6	533	44	6	35	39	.473	2	11	3.96

Rob Pierce

Pitches: Right **Bats:** Right **Pos:** P
Ht: 6'2" **Wt:** 200 **Born:** 12/17/70 **Age:** 25

Year	Team	Lg	G	GS	CG	GF	IP	BFP	H	R	ER	HR	SH	SF	HB	TBB	IBB	SO	WP	Bk	W	L	Pct.	ShO	Sv	ERA
1991	Athletics	R	20	2	0	5	53	254	59	48	33	4	0	4	5	29	2	34	9	1	2	2	.500	0	1	5.60
1992	Madison	A	34	0	0	19	59	272	62	33	29	3	5	5	3	30	2	56	6	1	2	3	.400	0	5	4.42
	Reno	A	15	1	0	4	30.2	158	45	33	25	2	2	2	1	22	0	22	4	0	1	0	.000	0	0	7.34
1993	Modesto	A	36	0	0	27	53	229	41	11	11	2	4	3	2	28	1	44	1	0	1	1	.500	0	14	1.87
1994	Huntsville	AA	37	1	0	16	56.1	254	58	43	38	5	2	2	3	30	2	39	6	0	3	6	.333	0	5	6.07
1995	Huntsville	AA	15	0	0	5	17.1	92	26	21	19	2	0	1	1	14	1	16	8	1	1	1	.500	0	0	9.87
	Lubbock	IND	11	11	1	0	66.1	291	70	45	37	4	4	3	3	27	0	49	5	0	4	5	.444	0	0	5.02
	5 Min. YEARS		168	15	1	76	335.2	1550	361	234	192	22	17	20	18	180	8	260	39	3	13	19	.406	0	25	5.15

Jason Pierson

Pitches: Left **Bats:** Right **Pos:** P
Ht: 6'0" **Wt:** 190 **Born:** 1/6/71 **Age:** 25

Year	Team	Lg	G	GS	CG	GF	IP	BFP	H	R	ER	HR	SH	SF	HB	TBB	IBB	SO	WP	Bk	W	L	Pct.	ShO	Sv	ERA
1992	Utica	A	15	15	1	0	87	358	90	34	23	5	0	3	1	18	2	62	2	4	8	2	.800	1	0	2.38
1993	South Bend	A	26	25	2	0	147.1	637	160	92	77	16	4	5	5	43	1	107	8	2	13	9	.591	0	0	4.70
1994	Pr. William	A	28	28	3	0	189.1	785	183	85	70	22	10	3	6	48	0	117	11	2	14	8	.636	1	0	3.33
1995	Birmingham	AA	4	4	0	0	23.1	102	29	22	21	6	0	1	2	6	0	15	0	1	0	2	.000	0	0	8.10
	Pr. William	A	21	12	0	5	91.2	382	91	48	45	9	1	4	2	22	0	69	1	0	5	4	.556	0	0	4.42
	4 Min. YEARS		94	84	6	5	538.2	2264	553	281	236	58	15	16	16	137	3	370	22	9	40	25	.615	2	0	3.94

Wander Pimentel

Bats: Right **Throws:** Right **Pos:** SS   **Ht:** 5'11" **Wt:** 185 **Born:** 9/18/72 **Age:** 23

								BATTING									BASERUNNING				PERCENTAGES		
Year	Team	Lg	G	AB	H	2B	3B	HR	TB	R	RBI	TBB	IBB	SO	HBP	SH	SF	SB	CS	SB%	GDP	Avg	OBP	SLG
1990	Hamilton	A	69	192	36	7	0	0	43	15	12	13	0	32	2	2	1	3	4	.43	1	.188	.245	.224
1991	Savannah	A	27	90	25	5	1	0	32	10	8	7	0	15	0	2	0	1	0	1.00	0	.278	.330	.356
	St. Pete	A	80	261	37	7	0	0	44	14	7	8	0	57	0	3	1	1	1	.50	11	.142	.167	.169
1992	Springfield	A	123	372	68	15	1	3	94	25	23	6	0	82	2	10	0	1	4	.20	7	.183	.200	.253
1993	Arkansas	AA	27	49	10	0	0	0	10	3	5	1	0	7	0	1	1	0	0	.00	2	.204	.216	.204
	St. Pete	A	23	58	11	0	0	0	11	3	4	3	0	8	0	1	0	0	0	.00	0	.190	.230	.190
1994	St. Pete	A	25	38	7	3	0	1	13	4	8	5	0	13	0	3	0	1	0	1.00	0	.184	.279	.342
1995	Arkansas	AA	2	2	0	0	0	0	0	0	0	0	0	0	0	0	0	0	0	.00	0	.000	.000	.000
	6 Min. YEARS		376	1062	194	37	2	4	247	74	67	43	0	214	4	22	3	7	9	.44	21	.183	.217	.233

Marc Pisciotta

Pitches: Right **Bats:** Right **Pos:** P   **Ht:** 6'5" **Wt:** 240 **Born:** 8/7/70 **Age:** 25

			HOW MUCH HE PITCHED					WHAT HE GAVE UP										THE RESULTS					
Year	Team	Lg	G	GS	CG	GF	IP	BFP	H	R	ER	HR	SH	SF	HB	TBB	IBB	SO	WP	Bk	W	L	Pct.	ShO	Sv	ERA
1991	Welland	A	24	0	0	21	34	143	16	4	1	0	2	1	3	20	1	47	7	1	1	1	.500	0	8	0.26
1992	Augusta	A	20	12	1	5	79.1	372	91	51	40	4	5	1	10	43	2	54	12	2	4	5	.444	0	1	4.54
1993	Augusta	A	34	0	0	28	43.2	188	31	18	13	0	5	0	5	17	1	49	5	0	5	2	.714	0	12	2.68
	Salem	A	20	0	0	18	18.1	88	23	13	6	0	1	1	0	13	0	13	2	0	0	0	.000	0	12	2.95
1994	Carolina	AA	26	0	0	17	25.2	121	29	21	16	2	6	2	3	15	2	21	1	1	3	4	.429	0	5	5.61
	Salem	A	31	0	0	30	29.1	134	24	14	5	1	2	1	3	13	1	23	4	0	1	4	.200	0	19	1.53
1995	Carolina	AA	56	0	0	27	69.1	313	60	37	32	2	7	3	6	45	8	57	4	0	6	4	.600	0	9	4.15
	5 Min. YEARS		211	12	1	146	299.2	1365	277	158	113	9	28	9	30	166	15	264	35	4	20	20	.500	0	66	3.39

Erik Plantenberg

Pitches: Left **Bats:** Right **Pos:** P   **Ht:** 6'1" **Wt:** 180 **Born:** 10/30/68 **Age:** 27

			HOW MUCH HE PITCHED					WHAT HE GAVE UP										THE RESULTS					
Year	Team	Lg	G	GS	CG	GF	IP	BFP	H	R	ER	HR	SH	SF	HB	TBB	IBB	SO	WP	Bk	W	L	Pct.	ShO	Sv	ERA
1990	Elmira	A	16	5	0	4	40.1	186	44	26	18	2	6	1	0	19	0	36	4	1	2	3	.400	0	1	4.02
1991	Lynchburg	A	20	20	0	0	103	461	116	59	43	3	4	2	4	51	1	73	8	0	11	5	.688	0	0	3.76
1992	Lynchburg	A	21	12	0	4	81.2	384	112	69	47	7	2	4	5	36	0	62	6	0	2	3	.400	0	0	5.18
1993	Jacksonville	AA	34	0	0	13	44.2	182	38	11	10	0	1	0	0	14	1	49	1	0	2	1	.667	0	1	2.01
1994	Jacksonville	AA	14	0	0	7	20.1	85	19	6	3	0	1	1	0	8	2	23	0	0	0	1	.000	0	4	1.33
	Calgary	AAA	19	19	1	0	101.2	480	122	82	66	10	2	3	2	62	1	69	14	0	6	7	.462	1	0	5.84
1995	Las Vegas	AAA	2	0	0	0	0.1	5	3	3	3	0	0	0	1	0	0	1	0	0	0	0	.000	0	0	81.00
	Memphis	AA	20	0	0	9	21.2	80	19	4	4	2	1	0	1	2	1	16	1	0	2	0	1.000	0	2	1.66
1993	Seattle	AL	20	0	0	4	9.2	53	11	7	7	0	1	0	1	12	1	3	1	0	0	0	.000	0	1	6.52
1994	Seattle	AL	6	0	0	2	7	31	4	0	0	0	0	0	0	7	0	1	0	0	0	0	.000	0	0	0.00
	6 Min. YEARS		146	56	0	37	413.2	1863	473	260	194	24	17	11	13	192	6	329	34	1	25	20	.556	1	8	4.22
	2 Maj. YEARS		26	0	0	6	16.2	84	15	7	7	0	1	0	2	19	1	4	1	0	0	0	.000	0	1	3.78

Allen Plaster

Pitches: Right **Bats:** Right **Pos:** P   **Ht:** 6'3" **Wt:** 210 **Born:** 8/13/70 **Age:** 25

			HOW MUCH HE PITCHED					WHAT HE GAVE UP										THE RESULTS					
Year	Team	Lg	G	GS	CG	GF	IP	BFP	H	R	ER	HR	SH	SF	HB	TBB	IBB	SO	WP	Bk	W	L	Pct.	ShO	Sv	ERA
1991	Bluefield	R	10	9	1	0	51.2	213	39	24	14	3	1	2	2	23	0	53	5	4	4	1	.800	1	0	2.44
	Frederick	A	4	2	0	1	9	50	13	14	11	2	1	0	0	8	0	10	0	0	0	3	.000	0	0	11.00
1992	Frederick	A	27	26	3	0	150.1	640	113	70	48	6	5	6	6	75	1	129	8	4	9	12	.429	1	0	2.87
1993	Modesto	A	21	18	0	0	95.2	422	89	55	50	11	0	2	3	61	1	89	3	0	4	4	.500	0	0	4.70
1994	Modesto	A	45	0	0	30	51.1	214	27	21	11	3	2	1	1	31	2	71	5	0	6	2	.750	0	13	1.93
1995	Huntsville	AA	43	0	0	14	68	290	63	26	24	4	4	2	0	26	0	47	7	0	1	0	1.000	0	2	3.18
	5 Min. YEARS		150	55	4	45	426	1829	344	210	158	29	13	13	12	224	4	399	28	8	24	22	.522	2	15	3.34

Kinnis Pledger

Bats: Left **Throws:** Right **Pos:** OF   **Ht:** 6'4" **Wt:** 215 **Born:** 7/17/68 **Age:** 27

								BATTING									BASERUNNING				PERCENTAGES		
Year	Team	Lg	G	AB	H	2B	3B	HR	TB	R	RBI	TBB	IBB	SO	HBP	SH	SF	SB	CS	SB%	GDP	Avg	OBP	SLG
1987	White Sox	R	37	127	32	6	3	1	47	18	13	13	3	46	0	0	1	20	0	1.00	1	.252	.319	.370
1988	South Bend	A	107	371	75	13	4	3	105	42	34	39	2	106	0	4	3	18	10	.64	2	.202	.276	.283
1989	South Bend	A	89	293	78	13	5	3	110	49	39	56	3	79	0	4	4	26	14	.65	0	.266	.380	.375
1990	Sarasota	A	131	460	114	18	4	3	149	72	40	94	3	134	8	6	3	26	14	.65	10	.248	.382	.324
	Vancouver	AAA	1	1	0	0	0	0	0	0	0	0	0	0	0	0	0	0	0	.00	0	.000	.000	.000
1991	Birmingham	AA	117	363	79	16	8	9	138	53	51	60	3	104	4	4	1	15	10	.60	2	.218	.334	.380
1992	Sarasota	A	59	217	70	11	2	7	106	42	38	28	4	47	3	0	1	13	9	.59	6	.323	.406	.488
	Birmingham	AA	60	191	34	5	2	1	46	18	14	19	0	65	0	5	3	2	4	.33	5	.178	.249	.241
1993	Birmingham	AA	125	393	95	10	6	14	159	70	56	74	0	120	3	5	4	19	6	.76	9	.242	.363	.405
1994	Daytona	A	11	37	8	1	1	1	14	5	3	10	0	12	0	0	0	0	0	.00	0	.216	.383	.378
	Orlando	AA	23	70	19	3	1	2	30	4	8	7	1	17	1	0	0	3	1	.75	4	.271	.346	.429
	Iowa	AAA	69	230	65	17	3	8	112	47	34	24	1	6	54	1	6	3	2	5	.29	2	.283	.349	.487
1995	Iowa	AAA	9	24	2	0	0	0	2	0	1	0	2	0	12	0	0	0	0	0	.00	0	.083	.154	.083

		G	AB	H	2B	3B	HR	TB	R	RBI	TBB	IBB	SO	HBP	SH	SF	SB	CS	SB%	GDP	Avg	OBP	SLG
Mobile	IND	85	299	80	17	3	21	166	57	61	53	4	76	2	2	3	14	7	.67	2	.268	.378	.555
9 Min. YEARS		923	3076	751	130	42	73	1184	478	391	479	27	872	22	36	26	158	80	.66	46	.244	.347	.385

Dale Plummer

Pitches: Right Bats: Right Pos: P   Ht: 6'4" Wt: 190 Born: 1/26/65 Age: 31

		HOW MUCH HE PITCHED						WHAT HE GAVE UP											THE RESULTS					
Year Team	Lg	G	GS	CG	GF	IP	BFP	H	R	ER	HR	SH	SF	HB	TBB	IBB	SO	WP	Bk	W	L	Pct.	ShO	Sv	ERA
1988 Little Fall	A	25	0	0	20	40.2	157	27	7	6	3	3	2	2	7	0	37	0	0	5	1	.833	0	10	1.33
1989 St. Lucie	A	10	0	0	8	13.2	67	20	10	9	2	2	1	1	7	1	8	1	0	1	0	1.000	0	3	5.93
Jackson	AA	25	5	2	8	71	281	60	17	16	5	8	1	1	21	3	36	1	0	5	0	1.000	1	2	2.03
1990 Tidewater	AAA	17	4	0	6	52.2	222	46	21	19	3	3	2	2	23	3	28	0	2	2	2	.500	0	1	3.25
Jackson	AA	4	0	0	2	9	33	5	2	2	1	1	0	0	3	1	3	0	0	1	1	.500	0	2	2.00
1991 Tidewater	AAA	46	4	0	14	97	414	95	49	43	8	4	5	6	32	6	33	3	0	4	3	.571	0	3	3.99
1992 Tidewater	AAA	31	0	0	14	58	248	59	26	23	8	2	2	4	19	1	29	0	0	4	0	1.000	0	3	3.57
1993 Norfolk	AAA	47	2	0	25	75	339	93	47	43	6	4	5	6	26	2	47	0	0	7	3	.700	0	4	5.16
1995 Pawtucket	AAA	34	10	1	9	100.2	457	140	73	58	13	5	5	6	18	2	47	0	1	9	9	.500	0	0	5.19
7 Min. YEARS		239	25	3	106	517.2	2218	545	252	219	49	32	23	28	156	19	268	5	3	38	19	.667	1	25	3.81

Charles Poe

Bats: Right Throws: Right Pos: OF   Ht: 6'0" Wt: 185 Born: 11/9/71 Age: 24

		BATTING															BASERUNNING				PERCENTAGES		
Year Team	Lg	G	AB	H	2B	3B	HR	TB	R	RBI	TBB	IBB	SO	HBP	SH	SF	SB	CS	SB%	GDP	Avg	OBP	SLG
1990 White Sox	R	46	147	26	3	2	0	33	13	16	16	0	38	4	0	4	10	5	.67	2	.177	.269	.224
1991 South Bend	A	117	418	89	29	6	5	145	57	59	38	1	136	2	4	5	20	5	.80	5	.213	.279	.347
1992 South Bend	A	67	228	41	9	3	3	65	26	26	23	0	64	2	2	3	4	1	.80	9	.180	.258	.285
Utica	A	47	164	49	8	1	5	74	27	29	18	0	39	2	0	2	10	2	.83	3	.299	.371	.451
1993 White Sox	R	3	13	4	3	0	1	10	2	2	1	0	3	0	0	0	0	1	.00	0	.308	.357	.769
Sarasota	A	95	313	78	16	6	11	139	45	47	33	0	91	4	2	0	5	8	.38	6	.249	.329	.444
1994 Pr. William	A	130	469	126	21	3	14	195	72	83	51	2	103	5	2	2	14	2	.88	9	.269	.345	.416
1995 Birmingham	AA	120	427	121	28	2	13	192	75	60	51	4	79	10	7	5	19	4	.83	7	.283	.369	.450
6 Min. YEARS		625	2179	534	117	23	52	853	317	322	231	7	553	29	17	21	82	28	.75	41	.245	.323	.391

Kevin Polcovich

Bats: Right Throws: Right Pos: SS   Ht: 5'9" Wt: 165 Born: 6/28/70 Age: 26

		BATTING															BASERUNNING				PERCENTAGES		
Year Team	Lg	G	AB	H	2B	3B	HR	TB	R	RBI	TBB	IBB	SO	HBP	SH	SF	SB	CS	SB%	GDP	Avg	OBP	SLG
1992 Carolina	AA	13	35	6	0	0	0	6	1	1	4	0	4	2	0	0	0	2	.00	1	.171	.293	.171
Augusta	A	46	153	40	6	2	0	50	24	10	18	0	30	8	3	0	7	7	.50	1	.261	.369	.327
1993 Augusta	A	14	48	13	2	0	0	15	9	4	7	0	8	0	2	1	2	1	.67	1	.271	.357	.313
Carolina	AA	4	11	3	0	0	0	3	1	1	1	0	1	2	0	0	0	0	.00	1	.273	.333	.273
Salem	A	94	282	72	10	3	1	91	44	25	49	0	42	12	6	3	13	6	.68	7	.255	.384	.323
1994 Carolina	AA	125	406	95	14	2	2	119	46	33	38	4	70	11	10	8	9	4	.69	6	.234	.311	.293
1995 Carolina	AA	64	221	70	8	0	3	87	27	18	14	1	29	5	3	1	10	5	.67	3	.317	.369	.394
Calgary	AAA	62	213	60	8	1	3	79	31	27	11	0	32	8	2	3	5	6	.45	7	.282	.336	.371
4 Min. YEARS		422	1369	359	48	8	9	450	183	119	142	5	216	46	28	16	46	31	.60	27	.262	.348	.329

Damon Pollard

Pitches: Right Bats: Right Pos: P   Ht: 5'9" Wt: 167 Born: 9/29/67 Age: 28

		HOW MUCH HE PITCHED						WHAT HE GAVE UP											THE RESULTS					
Year Team	Lg	G	GS	CG	GF	IP	BFP	H	R	ER	HR	SH	SF	HB	TBB	IBB	SO	WP	Bk	W	L	Pct.	ShO	Sv	ERA
1990 Eugene	A	14	14	1	0	70	292	46	35	26	4	0	3	6	42	0	77	7	1	3	3	.500	0	0	3.34
1991 Appleton	A	16	4	0	7	55.2	247	41	21	14	2	2	2	3	44	3	56	9	4	3	3	.500	0	1	2.26
Baseball Cy	A	13	2	0	3	25.1	117	22	14	12	0	0	5	1	22	0	23	8	0	1	1	.500	0	0	4.26
1992 Baseball Cy	A	49	0	0	35	71	297	46	30	21	2	2	6	1	43	3	51	6	1	4	3	.571	0	13	2.66
1993 St. Paul	IND	29	0	0	25	31.2	145	25	11	8	1	2	0	1	24	0	35	2	0	2	2	.500	0	14	2.27
1994 El Paso	AA	4	0	0	2	8.1	43	9	3	2	0	0	0	0	12	1	6	2	1	0	0	.000	0	0	2.16
Harrisburg	AA	21	0	0	7	32.1	172	47	44	38	10	1	3	1	32	1	31	5	0	3	0	1.000	0	0	10.58
W. Palm Bch	A	13	1	0	6	18	89	20	13	12	0	0	0	2	16	0	13	4	1	0	1	.000	0	0	6.00
1995 Harrisburg	AA	6	0	0	1	8.1	41	11	11	8	2	1	2	0	4	0	10	5	0	0	0	.000	0	0	8.64
W. Palm Bch	A	28	0	0	6	51	208	38	21	19	0	1	4	2	26	0	43	3	0	4	3	.571	0	1	3.35
6 Min. YEARS		193	21	1	92	371.2	1652	305	203	160	21	9	25	17	265	8	345	51	8	20	16	.556	0	29	3.87

Dale Polley

Pitches: Left Bats: Right Pos: P   Ht: 6'0" Wt: 165 Born: 8/9/65 Age: 30

		HOW MUCH HE PITCHED						WHAT HE GAVE UP											THE RESULTS					
Year Team	Lg	G	GS	CG	GF	IP	BFP	H	R	ER	HR	SH	SF	HB	TBB	IBB	SO	WP	Bk	W	L	Pct.	ShO	Sv	ERA
1987 Pulaski	R	13	1	0	8	25.2	103	18	7	5	1	0	1	0	9	0	37	1	0	0	2	.000	0	5	1.75
Sumter	A	7	6	1	1	40.2	167	37	16	13	2	3	1	0	9	0	32	1	1	3	1	.750	1	0	2.88
1988 Greenville	AA	36	16	0	10	128	531	102	56	45	18	5	3	1	49	0	67	4	2	9	6	.600	0	2	3.16
1989 Greenville	AA	28	26	3	0	163.2	681	142	75	61	11	10	3	4	58	1	106	6	2	6	15	.286	2	0	3.35
1990 Richmond	AAA	36	15	1	6	135	556	121	66	53	10	8	4	2	48	8	64	5	3	4	7	.364	1	0	3.53
1991 Richmond	AAA	50	1	0	27	66.1	294	70	24	24	2	5	4	4	30	5	38	0	0	2	3	.400	0	4	3.26
1992 Richmond	AAA	39	0	0	12	56.1	239	54	20	18	1	6	1	1	24	5	42	2	0	1	6	.143	0	2	2.88
1993 Greenville	AA	42	0	0	18	59	238	44	28	27	8	3	0	3	21	2	66	2	1	8	1	.889	0	2	4.12
Richmond	AAA	10	0	0	3	18.1	85	21	9	8	1	0	2	1	11	1	14	0	0	1	0	1.000	0	0	3.93

Year Team	Lg	G	GS	CG	GF	IP	BFP	H	R	ER	HR	SH	SF	HB	TBB	IBB	SO	WP	Bk	W	L	Pct.	ShO	Sv	ERA
1995 Richmond	AAA	47	0	0	22	63.1	261	51	15	11	2	2	3	2	20	5	60	2	0	3	2	.600	0	7	1.56
8 Min. YEARS		308	65	5	107	756.1	3155	660	316	265	56	42	22	18	279	27	526	23	9	37	43	.463	4	22	3.15

Tom Popplewell

Pitches: Right **Bats:** Right **Pos:** P **Ht:** 6'3" **Wt:** 225 **Born:** 8/3/67 **Age:** 28

		HOW MUCH HE PITCHED						WHAT HE GAVE UP												THE RESULTS					
Year Team	Lg	G	GS	CG	GF	IP	BFP	H	R	ER	HR	SH	SF	HB	TBB	IBB	SO	WP	Bk	W	L	Pct.	ShO	Sv	ERA
1987 Oneonta	A	16	9	0	5	65.1	309	79	53	37	3	5	4	2	38	2	54	4	0	4	6	.400	0	1	5.10
1988 Pr. William	A	22	20	1	1	113.1	541	127	89	70	5	7	3	9	63	2	58	8	1	4	12	.250	0	0	5.56
1989 Ft. Laud	A	32	14	0	5	119	522	119	67	53	6	2	8	3	60	1	70	9	0	3	5	.375	0	0	4.01
1990 Ft. Laud	A	15	15	3	0	101	408	82	38	25	2	2	1	1	23	0	59	4	1	6	5	.545	1	0	2.23
Albany-Colo	AA	14	12	0	0	64	275	56	31	29	4	0	0	3	36	0	34	2	0	8	2	.800	0	0	4.08
1991 Albany-Colo	AA	52	4	0	16	86	417	81	56	42	8	4	4	8	83	5	63	7	3	4	10	.286	0	3	4.40
1992 Albany-Colo	AA	28	2	0	11	50.2	242	52	46	41	4	1	4	3	34	2	33	4	1	2	1	.667	0	0	7.28
Columbus	AAA	4	0	0	0	6.1	38	6	5	5	0	0	0	0	11	0	7	0	0	1	0	1.000	0	0	7.11
1993 Albany-Colo	AA	34	4	1	12	64.1	301	60	45	42	3	1	3	5	48	2	59	11	0	1	3	.250	0	1	5.88
Columbus	AAA	1	0	0	0	2	8	2	1	1	0	0	0	0	1	0	2	0	0	0	0	.000	0	0	4.50
1994 El Paso	AA	36	0	0	20	36.1	181	36	34	33	4	2	3	5	41	1	30	7	0	2	4	.333	0	10	8.17
New Orleans	AAA	15	0	0	4	16	65	13	9	7	3	0	1	0	5	0	9	2	0	0	0	.000	0	0	3.94
1995 New Orleans	AAA	10	0	0	1	13.1	64	13	11	10	0	0	2	1	11	1	16	2	0	0	2	.000	0	0	6.75
El Paso	AA	4	0	0	0	3	21	7	5	5	0	0	0	1	6	0	1	2	0	0	0	.000	0	0	15.00
Canton-Akrn	AA	15	0	0	3	20.1	103	33	22	22	6	1	2	0	16	1	14	0	0	2	0	1.000	0	0	9.74
9 Min. YEARS		298	80	5	78	761	3495	766	512	422	48	25	35	41	476	17	509	62	6	37	50	.425	1	15	4.99

Scott Pose

Bats: Left **Throws:** Right **Pos:** OF **Ht:** 5'11" **Wt:** 165 **Born:** 2/11/67 **Age:** 29

		BATTING															BASERUNNING				PERCENTAGES		
Year Team	Lg	G	AB	H	2B	3B	HR	TB	R	RBI	TBB	IBB	SO	HBP	SH	SF	SB	CS	SB%	GDP	Avg	OBP	SLG
1989 Billings	R	60	210	74	7	2	0	85	52	25	54	3	31	1	1	1	26	3	.90	1	.352	.485	.405
1990 Charlstn-Wv	A	135	480	143	13	5	0	166	106	46	114	8	56	7	5	6	49	21	.70	5	.298	.435	.346
1991 Nashville	AAA	15	52	10	0	0	0	10	7	3	2	0	9	2	2	0	3	1	.75	0	.192	.250	.192
Chattanooga	AA	117	402	110	8	5	1	131	61	31	69	3	50	2	7	3	17	13	.57	7	.274	.380	.326
1992 Chattanooga	AA	136	526	180	22	8	2	224	87	45	63	5	66	4	4	3	21	27	.44	8	.342	.414	.426
1993 Edmonton	AAA	109	398	113	8	6	0	133	61	27	42	3	36	1	5	1	19	9	.68	8	.284	.353	.334
1994 New Orleans	AAA	124	429	121	13	7	0	148	60	52	47	2	52	2	9	4	20	8	.71	7	.282	.353	.345
1995 Albuquerque	AAA	7	16	3	1	0	0	4	5	1	2	0	0	0	0	0	2	0	1.00	0	.188	.278	.250
Salt Lake	AAA	77	219	66	10	1	0	78	46	20	31	2	28	1	3	3	15	4	.79	2	.301	.386	.356
1993 Florida	NL	15	41	8	2	0	0	10	0	3	2	0	4	0	0	0	0	2	.00	0	.195	.233	.244
7 Min. YEARS		780	2732	820	82	34	3	979	485	250	424	26	328	20	36	21	172	86	.67	39	.300	.395	.358

Lou Pote

Pitches: Right **Bats:** Right **Pos:** P **Ht:** 6'3" **Wt:** 190 **Born:** 8/27/71 **Age:** 24

		HOW MUCH HE PITCHED						WHAT HE GAVE UP												THE RESULTS					
Year Team	Lg	G	GS	CG	GF	IP	BFP	H	R	ER	HR	SH	SF	HB	TBB	IBB	SO	WP	Bk	W	L	Pct.	ShO	Sv	ERA
1991 Giants	R	8	8	0	0	42.1	184	38	23	12	0	0	1	0	18	0	41	5	0	2	3	.400	0	0	2.55
Everett	A	5	4	0	0	28.2	117	24	8	8	2	0	1	2	7	0	26	2	0	2	0	1.000	0	0	2.51
1992 Shreveport	AA	20	3	0	9	37.2	146	20	7	4	1	3	1	1	15	2	26	3	0	4	2	.667	0	0	0.96
San Jose	A	4	3	0	1	9.2	46	11	5	5	0	1	1	0	7	0	8	3	0	0	1	.000	0	0	4.66
1993 Shreveport	AA	19	19	0	0	108.1	453	111	53	49	10	1	3	0	45	1	81	3	1	8	7	.533	0	0	4.07
1994 Giants	R	4	4	0	0	19.2	73	9	0	0	0	1	0	0	6	0	30	0	0	1	0	1.000	0	0	0.00
Shreveport	AA	5	5	0	0	28.2	122	31	11	9	2	2	2	0	7	0	15	1	1	2	2	.500	0	0	2.83
1995 Shreveport	AA	28	0	0	11	50.2	226	53	41	30	8	4	1	0	26	1	30	4	0	2	2	.500	0	3	5.33
Harrisburg	AA	9	4	0	2	28.1	123	32	17	17	3	0	2	1	7	0	24	1	0	0	1	.000	0	0	5.40
5 Min. YEARS		102	50	0	23	354	1495	329	165	134	26	12	12	4	138	4	281	22	2	21	18	.538	0	3	3.41

Mike Potts

Pitches: Left **Bats:** Left **Pos:** P **Ht:** 5'9" **Wt:** 170 **Born:** 9/5/70 **Age:** 25

		HOW MUCH HE PITCHED						WHAT HE GAVE UP												THE RESULTS					
Year Team	Lg	G	GS	CG	GF	IP	BFP	H	R	ER	HR	SH	SF	HB	TBB	IBB	SO	WP	Bk	W	L	Pct.	ShO	Sv	ERA
1990 Braves	R	23	1	0	17	39	174	29	23	15	2	0	3	1	25	1	39	5	0	5	2	.714	0	4	3.46
1991 Macon	A	34	11	2	5	95.1	399	64	45	37	3	2	2	4	50	1	76	13	0	8	5	.615	2	1	3.49
1992 Durham	A	30	21	0	2	127.2	547	104	75	57	4	6	6	1	71	5	123	14	0	6	8	.429	0	1	4.02
1993 Greenville	AA	25	25	1	0	141.2	621	131	79	61	7	7	3	1	86	2	116	6	1	7	6	.538	0	0	3.88
1994 Richmond	AAA	52	0	0	18	85.2	369	75	41	35	3	3	2		43	6	66	6	0	6	3	.667	0	2	3.68
1995 Richmond	AAA	38	1	0	17	73.2	320	79	35	31	4	3	1	0	37	4	52	6	0	5	5	.500	0	1	3.79
6 Min. YEARS		202	59	3	59	563	2430	482	298	236	23	25	18	9	312	19	472	50	1	37	29	.561	2	9	3.77

Chop Pough

Bats: Right **Throws:** Right **Pos:** DH-1B **Ht:** 6'0" **Wt:** 173 **Born:** 12/25/69 **Age:** 26

		BATTING															BASERUNNING				PERCENTAGES		
Year Team	Lg	G	AB	H	2B	3B	HR	TB	R	RBI	TBB	IBB	SO	HBP	SH	SF	SB	CS	SB%	GDP	Avg	OBP	SLG
1988 Indians	R	52	173	45	11	0	3	65	28	21	24	1	52	1	2	0	1	3	.25	3	.260	.354	.376
1989 Burlington	R	67	225	58	15	1	8	99	39	37	36	1	64	3	0	2	9	5	.64	1	.258	.365	.440
1990 Reno	A	16	53	8	0	1	0	10	1	2	6	1	18	0	0	0	0	1	.00	1	.151	.237	.189
Watertown	A	76	285	72	15	1	9	116	47	49	40	2	71	2	0	4	21	4	.84	7	.253	.344	.407

Year	Team	Lg	G	AB	H	2B	3B	HR	TB	R	RBI	TBB	IBB	SO	HBP	SH	SF	SB	CS	SB%	GDP	Avg	OBP	SLG
1991	Kinston	A	11	30	5	1	0	0	6	2	2	1	0	9	1	0	0	1	0	1.00	1	.167	.219	.200
	Columbus	A	115	414	127	35	3	11	201	76	73	62	2	63	8	2	9	11	6	.65	6	.307	.400	.486
	Colo. Sprng	AAA	2	2	0	0	0	0	0	0	0	0	0	0	0	0	0	0	0	.00	0	.000	.000	.000
1992	Kinston	A	114	411	93	23	1	11	151	59	58	50	1	98	6	4	5	12	3	.80	13	.226	.316	.367
1993	Kinston	A	120	418	113	18	1	13	172	66	57	59	2	95	5	1	4	8	3	.73	8	.270	.364	.411
1994	Canton-Akrn	AA	105	379	113	24	3	20	203	69	66	43	3	86	5	0	6	3	2	.60	9	.298	.372	.536
	Charlotte	AAA	16	42	9	4	0	0	13	1	4	6	0	13	0	0	1	0	0	.00	0	.214	.306	.310
1995	Trenton	AA	97	363	101	23	5	21	197	68	69	50	8	101	7	0	4	11	5	.69	1	.278	.373	.543
	Pawtucket	AAA	30	99	23	8	1	5	48	12	23	7	1	27	1	0	1	0	0	.00	2	.232	.287	.485
	8 Min. YEARS		821	2894	767	177	17	101	1281	468	461	384	19	697	39	9	36	77	32	.71	52	.265	.355	.443

John Powell

Pitches: Right Bats: Right Pos: P   Ht: 5'10" Wt: 180 Born: 4/7/71 Age: 25

			HOW MUCH HE PITCHED						WHAT HE GAVE UP											THE RESULTS					
Year	Team	Lg	G	GS	CG	GF	IP	BFP	H	R	ER	HR	SH	SF	HB	TBB	IBB	SO	WP	Bk	W	L	Pct.	ShO	Sv	ERA
1994	Charlotte	A	17	12	2	0	81.1	327	61	38	32	4	6	0	4	28	1	85	2	4	2	8	.200	0	0	3.54
1995	Tulsa	AA	7	7	0	0	39.1	174	45	21	17	9	0	1	2	16	0	27	1	1	1	4	.200	0	0	3.89
	Charlotte	A	19	2	0	9	48	201	44	18	16	2	2	2	3	13	1	47	1	1	4	1	.800	0	2	3.00
	2 Min. YEARS		43	21	2	9	168.2	702	150	77	65	15	8	3	9	57	2	159	4	6	7	13	.350	0	2	3.47

Jose Prado

Pitches: Right Bats: Right Pos: P   Ht: 6'2" Wt: 195 Born: 5/9/72 Age: 24

			HOW MUCH HE PITCHED						WHAT HE GAVE UP											THE RESULTS					
Year	Team	Lg	G	GS	CG	GF	IP	BFP	H	R	ER	HR	SH	SF	HB	TBB	IBB	SO	WP	Bk	W	L	Pct.	ShO	Sv	ERA
1993	Vero Beach	A	12	9	0	0	55.2	233	45	31	27	2	1	3	1	29	3	31	1	4	3	4	.429	0	0	4.37
1994	Bakersfield	A	28	28	0	0	163.1	684	159	75	64	8	3	3	5	56	0	143	11	5	15	9	.625	0	0	3.53
1995	San Antonio	AA	28	22	0	3	144.2	621	126	70	56	9	7	9	7	64	0	93	13	2	7	11	.389	0	1	3.48
	3 Min. YEARS		68	59	0	3	363.2	1538	330	176	147	19	11	15	13	149	3	267	25	11	25	24	.510	0	1	3.64

Howard Prager

Bats: Left Throws: Left Pos: 1B   Ht: 6'2" Wt: 200 Born: 4/6/66 Age: 30

			BATTING															BASERUNNING				PERCENTAGES		
Year	Team	Lg	G	AB	H	2B	3B	HR	TB	R	RBI	TBB	IBB	SO	HBP	SH	SF	SB	CS	SB%	GDP	Avg	OBP	SLG
1989	Auburn	A	73	251	84	15	3	8	129	54	58	36	3	45	2	1	4	21	4	.84	2	.335	.416	.514
1990	Osceola	A	99	331	82	11	4	1	104	44	45	61	5	48	2	3	2	2	4	.33	9	.248	.366	.314
1991	Osceola	A	14	43	12	2	2	0	18	6	7	10	1	10	1	2	1	2	0	1.00	3	.279	.418	.419
	Jackson	AA	109	357	109	26	2	11	172	57	65	52	6	75	2	4	3	9	6	.60	15	.305	.394	.482
1992	Jackson	AA	113	326	84	13	0	5	112	36	48	45	4	75	6	2	3	1	4	.20	2	.258	.355	.344
1993	Arkansas	AA	59	158	50	8	1	7	81	31	21	28	5	34	0	2	2	4	2	.67	4	.316	.415	.513
	Louisville	AAA	63	209	55	17	0	4	84	27	28	24	1	37	2	0	1	0	0	.00	6	.263	.343	.402
1994	Louisville	AAA	86	176	42	8	0	7	71	24	23	32	4	36	1	0	2	3	1	.75	3	.239	.355	.403
1995	Louisville	AAA	54	102	26	5	0	6	49	9	15	19	0	25	0	0	0	1	1	.50	2	.255	.372	.480
	7 Min. YEARS		670	1953	544	105	12	49	820	288	310	307	29	385	16	14	18	43	22	.66	46	.279	.378	.420

Evan Pratte

Bats: Both Throws: Right Pos: 3B   Ht: 5'10" Wt: 175 Born: 12/18/68 Age: 27

			BATTING															BASERUNNING				PERCENTAGES		
Year	Team	Lg	G	AB	H	2B	3B	HR	TB	R	RBI	TBB	IBB	SO	HBP	SH	SF	SB	CS	SB%	GDP	Avg	OBP	SLG
1991	Niagara Fal	A	77	291	85	10	2	0	99	53	29	53	2	45	1	5	3	14	11	.56	8	.292	.399	.340
1992	Fayetteville	A	131	465	132	17	6	3	170	73	43	82	4	80	5	4	4	13	6	.68	13	.284	.394	.366
1993	London	AA	121	408	97	24	2	3	134	44	46	45	2	77	3	1	3	5	2	.71	12	.238	.316	.328
1994	Lakeland	A	9	30	12	3	0	0	15	8	5	6	0	3	0	2	0	0	1	.00	1	.400	.500	.500
	Trenton	AA	87	319	83	19	1	4	116	38	34	27	1	55	7	1	2	2	3	.40	6	.260	.330	.364
1995	Jacksonvlle	AA	18	52	13	2	0	0	15	2	1	7	3	9	2	0	0	0	3	.00	2	.250	.361	.288
	5 Min. YEARS		443	1565	422	75	11	10	549	218	158	220	12	269	18	13	12	34	26	.57	42	.270	.364	.351

John Pricher

Pitches: Right Bats: Both Pos: P   Ht: 5'10" Wt: 200 Born: 11/13/70 Age: 25

			HOW MUCH HE PITCHED						WHAT HE GAVE UP											THE RESULTS					
Year	Team	Lg	G	GS	CG	GF	IP	BFP	H	R	ER	HR	SH	SF	HB	TBB	IBB	SO	WP	Bk	W	L	Pct.	ShO	Sv	ERA
1992	Boise	A	32	0	0	30	43	169	34	8	5	1	1	1	0	8	3	65	1	4	2	1	.667	0	23	1.05
1993	Palm Spring	A	49	0	0	45	54	225	41	20	19	3	5	2	3	25	4	61	0	2	3	5	.375	0	26	3.17
1994	Midland	AA	40	0	0	19	49.1	225	60	33	30	6	2	1	1	22	1	30	3	0	2	3	.400	0	2	5.47
	Lk Elsinore	A	14	0	0	7	12.2	65	18	10	8	0	2	0	0	14	4	9	1	0	1	2	.333	0	1	5.68
1995	Midland	AA	8	0	0	6	10	48	16	7	5	1	0	1	0	6	0	7	0	0	0	0	.000	0	1	4.50
	Lk Elsinore	A	5	0	0	1	8	37	16	4	3	0	0	0	0	4	0	3	2	0	1	0	1.000	0	0	3.38
	Sioux City	IND	30	0	0	16	48	230	56	33	22	4	3	2	0	33	3	41	1	0	1	3	.250	0	1	4.13
	4 Min. YEARS		178	0	0	124	225	999	234	115	92	15	13	7	4	112	15	216	8	6	10	14	.417	0	53	3.68

Chris Pritchett

Bats: Left Throws: Right Pos: 1B   Ht: 6'4" Wt: 185 Born: 1/31/70 Age: 26

			BATTING															BASERUNNING				PERCENTAGES		
Year	Team	Lg	G	AB	H	2B	3B	HR	TB	R	RBI	TBB	IBB	SO	HBP	SH	SF	SB	CS	SB%	GDP	Avg	OBP	SLG
1991	Boise	A	70	255	68	10	3	9	111	41	50	47	3	41	2	0	3	1	0	1.00	7	.267	.381	.435

Year	Team	Lg	G	AB	H	2B	3B	HR	TB	R	RBI	TBB	IBB	SO	HBP	SH	SF	SB	CS	SB%	GDP	Avg	OBP	SLG
1992	Quad City	A	128	448	130	19	1	13	190	79	72	71	6	88	5	2	5	9	4	.69	7	.290	.389	.424
1993	Midland	AA	127	464	143	30	6	2	191	61	66	61	2	72	2	6	7	3	7	.30	17	.308	.386	.412
1994	Midland	AA	127	460	142	25	4	6	193	86	91	92	9	87	2	3	7	5	3	.63	8	.309	.421	.420
1995	Vancouver	AAA	123	434	120	27	4	8	179	66	53	56	6	79	5	2	1	2	3	.40	7	.276	.365	.412
	5 Min. YEARS		575	2061	603	111	18	38	864	333	332	327	26	367	16	13	23	20	17	.54	46	.293	.390	.419

Alan Probst

Bats: Right   Throws: Right   Pos: C   Ht: 6'4"   Wt: 205   Born: 10/24/70   Age: 25

			BATTING															BASERUNNING				PERCENTAGES		
Year	Team	Lg	G	AB	H	2B	3B	HR	TB	R	RBI	TBB	IBB	SO	HBP	SH	SF	SB	CS	SB%	GDP	Avg	OBP	SLG
1992	Auburn	A	66	224	53	14	1	5	84	24	34	23	1	48	3	1	2	1	0	1.00	5	.237	.313	.375
1993	Asheville	A	40	124	32	4	0	5	51	14	21	12	0	34	0	0	1	0	2	.00	5	.258	.321	.411
	Quad City	A	49	176	48	9	2	3	70	18	28	16	1	48	3	0	3	2	0	1.00	1	.273	.338	.398
1994	Quad City	A	113	375	87	14	1	9	130	50	41	37	3	98	2	3	3	2	5	.29	8	.232	.302	.347
1995	Quad City	A	51	151	39	12	1	7	74	23	27	13	0	28	1	1	1	2	0	1.00	3	.258	.319	.490
	Jackson	AA	28	89	21	5	0	1	29	11	8	7	0	25	1	0	2	0	0	.00	3	.236	.293	.326
	4 Min. YEARS		347	1139	280	58	5	30	438	140	159	108	5	281	10	5	12	7	7	.50	25	.246	.314	.385

Javier Puchales

Bats: Left   Throws: Left   Pos: OF   Ht: 6'0"   Wt: 170   Born: 3/29/72   Age: 24

			BATTING															BASERUNNING				PERCENTAGES		
Year	Team	Lg	G	AB	H	2B	3B	HR	TB	R	RBI	TBB	IBB	SO	HBP	SH	SF	SB	CS	SB%	GDP	Avg	OBP	SLG
1989	Dodgers	R	41	120	40	2	0	0	42	15	9	4	0	14	2	2	0	8	6	.57	0	.333	.365	.350
1990	Dodgers	R	29	55	11	0	0	0	11	7	3	7	0	20	0	0	0	4	2	.67	1	.200	.290	.200
1991	Great Falls	R	40	111	40	5	1	0	47	21	15	5	1	10	1	1	1	13	6	.68	4	.360	.390	.423
1993	Vero Beach	A	77	279	94	6	0	0	100	46	27	17	0	44	3	6	1	4	5	.44	9	.337	.380	.358
1994	San Antonio	AA	20	35	4	0	0	0	4	3	1	4	0	6	0	1	0	2	0	1.00	1	.114	.205	.114
1995	San Antonio	AA	31	57	13	1	0	0	14	4	1	3	1	6	0	1	1	0	2	.00	5	.228	.262	.246
	6 Min. YEARS		238	657	202	14	1	0	218	96	56	40	2	100	6	11	3	31	21	.60	20	.307	.351	.332

Benny Puig

Pitches: Left   Bats: Left   Pos: P   Ht: 5'10"   Wt: 183   Born: 10/16/65   Age: 30

			HOW MUCH HE PITCHED						WHAT HE GAVE UP												THE RESULTS					
Year	Team	Lg	G	GS	CG	GF	IP	BFP	H	R	ER	HR	SH	SF	HB	TBB	IBB	SO	WP	Bk	W	L	Pct.	ShO	Sv	ERA
1985	Reno	A	28	25	4	0	153.2	0	164	101	83	14	0	0	6	78	1	121	8	2	9	7	.563	2	0	4.86
1986	Reno	A	25	25	7	0	178.2	762	184	100	81	16	10	6	3	58	3	130	8	1	14	9	.609	2	0	4.08
1987	El Paso	AA	1	1	0	0	6.1	32	12	5	5	0	0	0	0	3	0	5	0	0	0	1	.000	0	0	7.11
	Stockton	A	27	23	7	0	167	702	161	78	61	10	6	4	9	64	3	123	11	1	11	8	.579	3	0	3.29
1988	El Paso	AA	54	0	0	23	92.1	394	92	55	45	12	3	3	3	31	1	62	7	9	8	4	.667	0	12	4.39
1989	El Paso	AA	47	0	0	43	64	269	62	30	26	5	1	3	1	22	0	47	3	0	1	3	.250	0	29	3.66
	Denver	AAA	12	0	0	4	13.1	79	30	13	10	1	2	1	1	8	2	12	1	0	1	1	.500	0	2	6.75
1990	Denver	AAA	19	0	0	9	26.2	124	35	12	10	3	1	3	3	9	0	24	0	0	2	0	1.000	0	3	3.38
	El Paso	AA	19	0	0	16	23.2	97	18	3	3	1	0	0	1	11	2	24	1	0	1	0	1.000	0	8	1.14
1992	Memphis	AA	68	0	0	59	75.2	289	45	17	17	4	6	5	1	21	1	64	1	0	4	2	.667	0	25	2.02
1993	Harrisburg	AA	14	0	0	3	18.1	75	16	5	5	1	0	1	2	7	0	10	0	1	1	0	1.000	0	1	2.45
1994	Ottawa	AAA	9	0	0	2	14.2	72	20	9	9	0	0	2	1	9	1	10	2	0	0	1	.000	0	0	5.52
	Sioux City	IND	4	4	0	0	24	105	24	11	10	1	0	0	1	14	0	16	1	0	2	1	.667	0	0	3.75
1995	Harrisburg	AA	1	0	0	0	1.2	9	3	2	0	0	0	0	0	1	0	0	0	0	0	0	.000	0	0	0.00
	10 Min. YEARS		328	78	18	159	860	3009	866	441	365	68	29	28	32	336	14	648	43	14	53	38	.582	7	77	3.82

Carlos Pulido

Pitches: Left   Bats: Left   Pos: P   Ht: 6'0"   Wt: 200   Born: 8/5/71   Age: 24

			HOW MUCH HE PITCHED						WHAT HE GAVE UP												THE RESULTS					
Year	Team	Lg	G	GS	CG	GF	IP	BFP	H	R	ER	HR	SH	SF	HB	TBB	IBB	SO	WP	Bk	W	L	Pct.	ShO	Sv	ERA
1989	Twins	R	22	0	0	11	36	143	22	9	9	0	0	2	3	14	0	46	6	3	3	0	1.000	0	2	2.25
1990	Kenosha	A	56	0	0	29	61.2	270	55	21	16	2	2	1	4	36	3	70	3	4	5	5	.500	0	6	2.34
1991	Visalia	A	57	0	0	32	80.2	334	77	34	18	2	5	2	0	23	2	102	3	1	1	5	.167	0	17	2.01
	Portland	AAA	2	0	0	2	1.2	10	4	3	3	1	0	0	1	0	2	0	0	0	0	0	.000	0	0	16.20
1992	Orlando	AA	52	5	0	20	100.1	432	99	52	49	7	1	6	3	37	0	87	4	1	6	2	.750	0	1	4.40
1993	Portland	AAA	33	22	1	5	146	625	169	74	68	8	3	4	2	45	1	79	8	1	10	6	.625	0	4	4.19
1995	Salt Lake	AAA	43	3	0	9	71.1	321	87	42	37	10	1	0	2	20	4	38	0	1	8	1	.889	0	3	4.67
1994	Minnesota	AL	19	14	0	1	84.1	366	87	57	56	17	2	4	1	40	1	32	3	2	3	7	.300	0	0	5.98
	6 Min. YEARS		265	30	1	108	497.2	2135	513	235	200	30	12	15	14	176	10	424	24	11	33	19	.635	0	29	3.62

Shawn Purdy

Pitches: Right   Bats: Right   Pos: P   Ht: 6'0"   Wt: 205   Born: 7/30/68   Age: 27

			HOW MUCH HE PITCHED						WHAT HE GAVE UP												THE RESULTS					
Year	Team	Lg	G	GS	CG	GF	IP	BFP	H	R	ER	HR	SH	SF	HB	TBB	IBB	SO	WP	Bk	W	L	Pct.	ShO	Sv	ERA
1991	Boise	A	15	15	1	0	95.2	394	87	37	32	3	3	2	4	27	2	78	6	0	8	4	.667	0	0	3.01
1992	Palm Spring	A	26	26	7	0	168	740	203	90	77	7	2	7	5	51	3	113	5	3	13	8	.619	0	0	4.13
1993	Angels	R	2	2	0	0	13	49	7	3	3	0	0	0	1	1	0	11	0	0	1	0	1.000	0	0	2.08
	Boise	A	1	1	0	0	6	25	2	2	0	0	0	1	0	5	2	1	0	0	1	0	1.000	0	0	0.00
	Palm Spring	A	5	3	0	2	27	120	30	12	11	2	1	0	3	5	2	17	1	0	1	1	.500	0	1	3.67
	Midland	AA	5	5	1	0	32	136	38	19	18	2	1	2	1	9	0	18	2	0	2	2	.500	0	0	5.06
1994	Midland	AA	10	5	1	0	36	170	48	39	35	2	2	2	2	15	1	19	6	1	1	6	.143	0	0	8.75

Year Team	Lg	G	GS	CG	GF	IP	BFP	H	R	ER	HR	SH	SF	HB	TBB	IBB	SO	WP	Bk	W	L	Pct.	ShO	Sv	ERA
Lk Elsinore	A	25	11	1	6	117.2	493	113	63	49	8	7	3	10	30	0	76	5	2	7	5	.583	0	0	3.75
1995 Shreveport	AA	52	1	0	40	62.1	260	61	31	26	1	1	3	1	18	2	33	3	0	6	3	.667	0	21	3.75
5 Min. YEARS		141	69	10	49	557.2	2387	589	296	251	31	17	20	27	161	12	366	28	6	40	29	.580	0	22	4.05

Dave Pyc

Pitches: Left **Bats:** Left **Pos:** P **Ht:** 6'3" **Wt:** 235 **Born:** 2/11/71 **Age:** 25

		HOW MUCH HE PITCHED						WHAT HE GAVE UP												THE RESULTS					
Year Team	Lg	G	GS	CG	GF	IP	BFP	H	R	ER	HR	SH	SF	HB	TBB	IBB	SO	WP	Bk	W	L	Pct.	ShO	Sv	ERA
1992 Great Falls	R	25	0	0	19	34.2	155	32	15	11	0	3	1	1	16	5	34	1	0	2	3	.400	0	9	2.86
1993 Vero Beach	A	23	15	1	2	113.1	469	97	41	30	1	6	3	1	47	2	78	5	4	7	8	.467	0	0	2.38
1994 San Antonio	AA	25	25	0	0	154.2	656	165	77	64	2	9	4	3	47	5	120	3	0	4	11	.267	0	0	3.72
1995 San Antonio	AA	26	26	1	0	157	676	170	72	59	6	6	4	3	49	1	78	3	1	12	6	.667	0	0	3.38
Albuquerque	AAA	1	1	0	0	7	31	7	5	3	1	0	1	0	2	1	3	0	0	0	1	.000	0	0	3.86
4 Min. YEARS		100	67	2	21	466.2	1987	471	210	167	10	24	13	8	161	14	313	12	5	25	29	.463	0	9	3.22

Tom Quinlan

Bats: Right **Throws:** Right **Pos:** 3B **Ht:** 6'3" **Wt:** 214 **Born:** 3/27/68 **Age:** 28

		BATTING														BASERUNNING				PERCENTAGES		
Year Team	Lg	G	AB	H	2B	3B	HR	TB	R	RBI	TBB	IBB	SO	HBP	SH	SF	SB	CS	SB%	GDP	Avg	OBP	SLG
1987 Myrtle Bch	A	132	435	97	20	3	5	138	42	51	34	0	130	6	3	6	2	0	.00	4	.223	.285	.317
1988 Knoxville	AA	98	326	71	19	1	8	116	33	47	35	1	99	5	3	2	4	9	.31	5	.218	.302	.356
1989 Knoxville	AA	139	452	95	21	3	16	170	62	57	41	0	118	9	3	4	6	4	.60	11	.210	.287	.376
1990 Knoxville	AA	141	481	124	24	6	15	205	70	51	49	2	157	14	7	1	8	9	.47	5	.258	.343	.426
1991 Syracuse	AAA	132	466	112	24	6	10	178	56	49	72	3	163	5	3	2	9	4	.69	7	.240	.347	.382
1992 Syracuse	AAA	107	349	75	17	1	6	112	43	36	43	0	112	10	1	2	1	3	.25	11	.215	.317	.321
1993 Syracuse	AAA	141	461	109	20	5	16	187	63	53	56	2	156	19	2	6	6	1	.86	7	.236	.339	.406
1994 Scranton-Wb	AAA	76	262	63	12	2	9	106	38	23	28	0	91	4	1	1	4	2	.67	7	.240	.322	.405
1995 Salt Lake	AAA	130	466	130	22	6	17	215	78	88	39	2	124	15	1	6	6	3	.67	11	.279	.350	.461
1990 Toronto	AL	1	2	1	0	0	0	1	0	0	0	0	1	1	0	0	0	0	.00	0	.500	.667	.500
1992 Toronto	AL	13	15	1	1	0	0	2	2	2	2	0	9	0	0	0	0	0	.00	0	.067	.176	.133
1994 Philadelphia	NL	24	35	7	2	0	1	12	6	3	3	1	13	0	0	0	0	0	.00	0	.200	.263	.343
9 Min. YEARS		1096	3698	876	179	33	102	1427	485	455	397	10	1150	87	24	30	44	37	.54	68	.237	.323	.386
3 Maj. YEARS		38	52	9	3	0	1	15	8	5	5	1	23	1	0	0	0	0	.00	0	.173	.259	.288

Rafael Quirico

Pitches: Left **Bats:** Left **Pos:** P **Ht:** 6'3" **Wt:** 170 **Born:** 9/7/69 **Age:** 26

		HOW MUCH HE PITCHED						WHAT HE GAVE UP												THE RESULTS					
Year Team	Lg	G	GS	CG	GF	IP	BFP	H	R	ER	HR	SH	SF	HB	TBB	IBB	SO	WP	Bk	W	L	Pct.	ShO	Sv	ERA
1989 Yankees	R	17	7	0	1	63.2	268	61	32	27	2	1	3	3	20	0	55	0	8	2	2	.500	0	1	3.82
1990 Greensboro	A	13	13	1	0	72	325	74	60	40	4	1	2	3	30	0	52	5	10	2	6	.250	0	0	5.00
Oneonta	A	14	14	1	0	87	359	69	38	31	2	2	4	4	39	0	69	9	9	6	3	.667	0	0	3.21
1991 Greensboro	A	26	26	1	0	155.1	641	103	59	39	5	1	2	7	80	0	162	12	9	12	8	.600	1	0	2.26
1992 Pr. William	A	23	23	2	0	130.2	570	128	84	46	11	8	1	1	50	1	123	7	7	6	11	.353	0	0	3.17
Columbus	AAA	1	1	0	0	6	27	6	3	2	0	0	0	0	4	0	1	1	0	1	0	1.000	0	0	3.00
1993 Albany-Colo	AA	36	11	0	15	94.2	403	92	46	37	15	5	1	1	33	2	79	6	1	4	10	.286	0	7	3.52
Columbus	AAA	5	2	0	0	11	53	12	10	9	3	0	0	0	7	0	16	1	0	2	0	1.000	0	0	7.36
1994 Columbus	AAA	37	0	0	12	63.2	289	63	41	33	6	1	2	3	36	1	49	9	1	0	4	.000	0	1	4.66
1995 Columbus	AAA	20	0	0	8	23	96	15	14	12	1	0	1	3	14	0	21	5	2	0	0	.000	0	0	4.70
7 Min. YEARS		192	97	5	36	707	3031	623	387	276	49	19	16	25	313	4	627	55	47	35	44	.443	1	9	3.51

Keifer Rackley

Bats: Left **Throws:** Right **Pos:** OF **Ht:** 6'1" **Wt:** 200 **Born:** 2/27/71 **Age:** 25

		BATTING														BASERUNNING				PERCENTAGES		
Year Team	Lg	G	AB	H	2B	3B	HR	TB	R	RBI	TBB	IBB	SO	HBP	SH	SF	SB	CS	SB%	GDP	Avg	OBP	SLG
1993 Bellingham	A	33	114	28	4	0	2	38	21	15	12	1	16	0	1	2	3	1	.75	3	.246	.313	.333
1994 Riverside	A	64	236	71	14	1	10	117	43	43	25	1	46	5	1	3	6	1	.86	6	.301	.375	.496
1995 Port City	AA	114	430	110	17	2	6	149	55	40	39	2	96	4	6	5	8	4	.67	11	.256	.320	.347
3 Min. YEARS		211	780	209	35	3	18	304	119	98	76	4	158	9	8	10	17	6	.74	20	.268	.336	.390

Mike Raczka

Pitches: Left **Bats:** Left **Pos:** P **Ht:** 6'0" **Wt:** 200 **Born:** 11/16/62 **Age:** 33

		HOW MUCH HE PITCHED						WHAT HE GAVE UP												THE RESULTS					
Year Team	Lg	G	GS	CG	GF	IP	BFP	H	R	ER	HR	SH	SF	HB	TBB	IBB	SO	WP	Bk	W	L	Pct.	ShO	Sv	ERA
1990 Las Vegas	AAA	4	2	0	0	11.2	52	11	10	10	2	1	0	0	9	0	7	1	0	1	0	1.000	0	0	7.71
Tacoma	AAA	42	0	0	18	55.2	238	48	27	22	3	5	1	3	35	3	54	2	0	6	5	.545	0	2	3.56
1992 Modesto	A	6	0	0	3	9.1	43	13	9	7	1	1	0	1	3	0	5	1	0	1	1	.500	0	0	6.75
Tacoma	AAA	31	1	0	11	48.2	196	38	22	19	3	3	4	0	24	6	26	2	1	0	0	.000	0	1	3.51
1993 Tacoma	AAA	55	0	0	11	60.1	269	65	39	36	6	3	2	3	30	2	40	3	0	2	1	.667	0	0	5.37
1994 New Britain	AA	34	0	0	6	41.2	162	34	20	16	2	1	1	0	16	0	25	4	0	3	1	.750	0	0	3.46
Pawtucket	AAA	24	1	0	4	26.2	114	19	7	6	1	2	2	0	14	1	14	5	0	1	1	.500	0	0	2.03
1995 Louisville	AAA	55	0	0	16	49	216	49	23	21	7	8	2	3	20	6	43	3	0	5	3	.625	0	1	3.86
1992 Oakland	AL	8	0	0	1	6.1	33	8	7	6	0	0	2	0	5	0	2	0	0	0	0	.000	0	0	8.53
5 Min. YEARS		251	4	0	69	303	1290	277	157	137	25	24	12	10	151	18	214	21	1	19	13	.594	0	4	4.07

Doug Radziewicz

Bats: Left **Throws:** Left **Pos:** 1B   **Ht:** 6'1" **Wt:** 195 **Born:** 4/24/69 **Age:** 27

						BATTING											BASERUNNING				PERCENTAGES		
Year Team	Lg	G	AB	H	2B	3B	HR	TB	R	RBI	TBB	IBB	SO	HBP	SH	SF	SB	CS	SB%	GDP	Avg	OBP	SLG
1991 Johnson Cty	R	62	201	58	15	2	4	89	31	28	25	2	18	2	0	2	1	0	1.00	4	.289	.370	.443
1992 Springfield	A	55	165	50	12	2	2	72	25	33	26	1	17	4	0	3	2	1	.67	3	.303	.404	.436
St. Pete	A	21	73	17	4	2	1	28	10	5	10	0	15	1	0	0	0	0	.00	2	.233	.333	.384
1993 St. Pete	A	123	439	150	36	2	4	202	66	72	73	11	58	5	1	5	6	8	.43	5	.342	.437	.460
1994 Arkansas	AA	121	342	76	16	2	8	120	33	40	43	2	65	3	1	6	1	0	1.00	8	.222	.310	.351
1995 Arkansas	AA	34	116	27	5	0	1	35	15	13	18	1	14	0	0	0	0	0	.00	2	.233	.336	.302
5 Min. YEARS		416	1336	378	88	10	20	546	180	191	195	17	187	15	2	16	10	9	.53	24	.283	.376	.409

Curtis Ralph

Pitches: Right **Bats:** Right **Pos:** P   **Ht:** 6'0" **Wt:** 205 **Born:** 8/6/68 **Age:** 27

			HOW MUCH HE PITCHED					WHAT HE GAVE UP											THE RESULTS					
Year Team	Lg	G	GS	CG	GF	IP	BFP	H	R	ER	HR	SH	SF	HB	TBB	IBB	SO	WP	Bk	W	L	Pct.	ShO	Sv	ERA
1988 Yankees	R	12	12	0	0	64.2	270	62	26	19	3	3	2	1	22	0	37	5	0	6	0	1.000	0	0	2.64
1989 Ft. Laud	A	15	10	0	3	59.1	274	66	42	26	4	1	3	6	37	0	31	11	0	6	2	.750	0	0	3.94
1990 Pr. William	A	43	0	0	16	80	345	69	30	28	3	5	2	5	40	3	75	5	1	4	3	.571	0	0	3.15
1991 Pr. William	A	47	0	0	24	65.1	264	51	28	24	5	3	3	4	22	4	60	1	0	5	7	.417	0	6	3.31
1992 Ft. Laud	A	12	0	0	6	22	102	23	10	6	2	2	0	3	7	1	22	1	2	1	2	.333	0	1	2.45
Pr. William	A	32	0	0	22	59	240	54	22	21	3	5	3	4	16	2	37	3	3	3	2	.600	0	4	3.20
1993 Pr. William	A	32	0	0	30	37	162	39	23	21	2	3	1	1	11	0	41	2	0	3	3	.500	0	15	5.11
1994 Albany-Colo	AA	43	0	0	14	65	273	56	17	17	3	1	1	4	31	2	54	5	1	7	2	.778	0	1	2.35
Columbus	AAA	1	0	0	0	1.2	7	0	0	0	0	0	0	0	2	0	1	0	0	0	0	.000	0	0	0.00
1995 Calgary	AAA	28	0	0	11	32	159	43	35	30	2	2	0	2	23	4	27	3	0	1	4	.200	0	1	8.44
Carolina	AA	18	1	0	2	26	105	23	8	7	3	0	0	0	10	0	17	1	0	1	1	.500	0	1	2.42
8 Min. YEARS		283	23	0	128	512	2201	486	241	199	30	25	15	30	221	16	402	37	7	37	26	.587	0	29	3.50

Kris Ralston

Pitches: Right **Bats:** Right **Pos:** P   **Ht:** 6'2" **Wt:** 205 **Born:** 8/8/71 **Age:** 24

			HOW MUCH HE PITCHED					WHAT HE GAVE UP											THE RESULTS					
Year Team	Lg	G	GS	CG	GF	IP	BFP	H	R	ER	HR	SH	SF	HB	TBB	IBB	SO	WP	Bk	W	L	Pct.	ShO	Sv	ERA
1993 Eugene	A	15	15	1	0	82	325	52	29	25	5	2	1	3	36	3	75	1	1	7	3	.700	0	0	2.74
1994 Wilmington	A	20	18	2	0	109.1	448	84	36	29	11	2	2	5	38	0	102	4	2	10	4	.714	1	0	2.39
1995 Wichita	AA	18	16	0	0	93.2	389	85	40	37	10	3	2	7	28	0	84	6	0	9	4	.692	0	0	3.56
3 Min. YEARS		53	49	3	0	285	1162	221	105	91	26	7	5	15	102	3	261	11	3	26	11	.703	1	0	2.87

Dan Rambo

Pitches: Right **Bats:** Right **Pos:** P   **Ht:** 6'0" **Wt:** 190 **Born:** 10/7/66 **Age:** 29

			HOW MUCH HE PITCHED					WHAT HE GAVE UP											THE RESULTS					
Year Team	Lg	G	GS	CG	GF	IP	BFP	H	R	ER	HR	SH	SF	HB	TBB	IBB	SO	WP	Bk	W	L	Pct.	ShO	Sv	ERA
1989 Pocatello	R	2	2	0	0	14	55	11	2	2	0	0	0	0	3	0	11	0	1	0	1	.000	0	0	1.29
Clinton	A	12	11	1	0	66.1	273	59	27	24	7	1	2	3	19	3	63	2	1	4	4	.500	0	0	3.26
1990 San Jose	A	26	17	2	3	143.2	575	104	47	35	8	6	2	4	42	1	142	3	2	12	2	.857	1	1	2.19
1991 Phoenix	AAA	3	2	0	0	13.2	63	18	8	7	1	2	0	0	6	0	10	0	0	0	1	.000	0	0	4.61
Shreveport	AA	26	21	1	1	147	618	146	71	60	12	7	4	4	43	2	103	7	2	12	6	.667	1	0	3.67
1992 Phoenix	AAA	20	1	0	4	41	181	47	28	27	1	3	2	3	15	2	32	0	1	1	2	.333	0	1	5.93
Shreveport	AA	28	2	0	11	60	255	56	23	19	2	3	0	2	19	5	45	6	2	6	3	.667	0	3	2.85
1993 Phoenix	AAA	18	5	0	2	51.2	266	77	44	41	6	2	4	0	33	7	31	10	0	1	3	.250	0	0	7.14
Shreveport	AA	15	15	1	0	102	413	98	46	36	1	0	5	4	27	1	61	2	1	7	5	.583	0	0	3.18
1994 Brainerd	IND	6	6	1	0	40	167	41	21	20	3	0	2	6	6	0	33	2	0	2	3	.400	0	0	4.50
El Paso	AA	13	1	0	3	25.1	100	24	7	6	2	1	1	0	4	1	20	2	0	1	3	.250	0	0	2.13
1995 New Orleans	AAA	7	6	0	1	36.1	155	39	23	21	6	2	0	2	9	1	22	1	0	0	4	.000	0	0	5.20
Tyler	IND	17	16	9	0	128	515	127	44	27	11	5	1	5	18	1	68	2	0	10	5	.667	0	0	1.90
7 Min. YEARS		193	105	15	25	869	3636	847	391	325	60	32	23	33	244	24	641	37	10	56	42	.571	2	4	3.37

Alex Ramirez

Bats: Right **Throws:** Right **Pos:** OF   **Ht:** 5'11" **Wt:** 176 **Born:** 10/3/74 **Age:** 21

						BATTING											BASERUNNING				PERCENTAGES		
Year Team	Lg	G	AB	H	2B	3B	HR	TB	R	RBI	TBB	IBB	SO	HBP	SH	SF	SB	CS	SB%	GDP	Avg	OBP	SLG
1993 Burlington	R	64	252	68	14	4	13	129	44	58	13	1	52	4	0	3	12	8	.60	4	.270	.313	.512
Kinston	A	3	12	2	0	0	0	2	0	1	0	0	5	0	0	0	0	1	.00	0	.167	.167	.167
1994 Columbus	A	125	458	115	23	3	18	198	64	57	26	0	100	4	0	4	7	5	.58	11	.251	.295	.432
1995 Bakersfield	A	98	406	131	25	2	10	190	56	52	18	1	76	3	0	1	13	9	.59	9	.323	.355	.468
Canton-Akrn	AA	33	133	33	3	4	1	47	15	11	5	1	24	0	1	1	3	5	.38	5	.248	.273	.353
3 Min. YEARS		323	1261	349	65	13	42	566	179	179	62	3	257	11	1	9	35	28	.56	29	.277	.314	.449

Hector Ramirez

Pitches: Right **Bats:** Right **Pos:** P   **Ht:** 6'3" **Wt:** 200 **Born:** 12/15/72 **Age:** 23

			HOW MUCH HE PITCHED					WHAT HE GAVE UP											THE RESULTS					
Year Team	Lg	G	GS	CG	GF	IP	BFP	H	R	ER	HR	SH	SF	HB	TBB	IBB	SO	WP	Bk	W	L	Pct.	ShO	Sv	ERA
1989 Mets	R	15	5	0	0	42	189	35	29	21	0	0	3	3	24	0	14	8	2	0	5	.000	0	0	4.50
1990 Mets	R	11	8	1	1	50.2	226	54	34	23	2	1	1	4	21	1	43	2	2	3	5	.375	0	0	4.09

Year	Team	Lg	G	GS	CG	SHO	IP														W	L	Pct			ERA
1991	Kingsport	R	14	13	1	0	85	364	83	39	24	5	0	5	4	28	2	64	9	0	8	2	.800	0	0	2.54
1992	Columbia	A	17	17	1	0	94.2	404	93	50	38	5	3	3	3	33	1	53	4	3	5	4	.556	0	0	3.61
1993	Mets	R	1	1	0	0	7	26	5	1	0	0	0	0	0	1	0	6	0	0	1	0	1.000	0	0	0.00
	Capital Cty	A	14	14	0	0	64	294	86	51	38	2	3	4	2	23	0	42	7	0	4	6	.400	0	0	5.34
1994	St. Lucie	A	27	27	6	0	194	802	202	86	74	10	10	6	5	50	2	110	6	8	11	12	.478	1	0	3.43
1995	Binghamton	AA	20	20	2	0	123.1	534	127	69	63	12	2	2	3	48	2	63	3	5	4	12	.250	0	0	4.60
	7 Min. YEARS		119	105	11	9	660.2	2839	685	359	281	36	19	24	24	228	8	395	39	20	36	46	.439	1	0	3.83

J.D. Ramirez

Bats: Right **Throws:** Right **Pos:** 2B **Ht:** 5'9" **Wt:** 160 **Born:** 11/19/66 **Age:** 29

Year	Team	Lg	G	AB	H	2B	3B	HR	TB	R	RBI	TBB	IBB	SO	HBP	SH	SF	SB	CS	SB%	GDP	Avg	OBP	SLG
1989	Salt Lake	R	38	150	55	11	1	2	74	23	26	11	0	13	2	1	2	2	3	.40	6	.367	.412	.493
	Jamestown	A	13	44	13	2	0	2	21	9	11	4	0	12	0	0	0	2	2	.50	0	.295	.354	.477
1990	Rockford	A	119	432	112	21	5	2	149	56	51	53	3	58	8	5	1	6	6	.50	8	.259	.350	.345
1991	W. Palm Bch	A	94	328	77	14	0	4	103	38	30	20	0	39	6	5	5	13	6	.68	10	.235	.287	.314
1992	Salt Lake	R	44	173	60	9	2	2	79	46	24	32	0	18	4	2	2	2	6	.25	2	.347	.455	.457
1993	Sioux City	IND	55	216	73	10	1	3	94	30	30	16	0	26	5	4	0	5	5	.50	2	.338	.397	.435
1994	Midland	AA	123	449	129	27	3	14	204	81	58	52	0	96	7	4	2	3	4	.43	8	.287	.369	.454
1995	Midland	AA	80	251	68	16	1	10	116	34	36	22	0	49	5	2	5	1	1	.50	5	.271	.336	.462
	Vancouver	AAA	1	4	0	0	0	0	0	0	0	0	0	1	0	0	0	0	0	.00	0	.000	.000	.000
	7 Min. YEARS		567	2047	587	110	13	39	840	317	266	210	3	312	37	23	17	34	33	.51	41	.287	.361	.410

Omar Ramirez

Bats: Right **Throws:** Right **Pos:** DH **Ht:** 5'9" **Wt:** 170 **Born:** 11/2/70 **Age:** 25

Year	Team	Lg	G	AB	H	2B	3B	HR	TB	R	RBI	TBB	IBB	SO	HBP	SH	SF	SB	CS	SB%	GDP	Avg	OBP	SLG
1990	Indians	R	18	58	10	0	0	0	10	6	2	11	0	11	0	0	0	2	4	.33	2	.172	.304	.172
1991	Watertown	A	56	210	56	17	0	2	79	30	17	30	0	30	1	3	1	12	2	.86	2	.267	.360	.376
1992	Kinston	A	110	411	123	20	5	13	192	73	49	38	1	53	3	8	2	19	12	.61	5	.299	.361	.467
1993	Canton-Akrn	AA	125	516	162	24	6	7	219	116	53	53	2	49	5	4	1	24	6	.80	9	.314	.383	.424
1994	Charlotte	AA	134	419	97	20	2	8	145	66	45	54	0	43	1	2	3	15	7	.68	11	.232	.319	.346
1995	Canton-Akrn	AA	10	34	11	0	0	0	11	6	3	3	0	3	0	1	0	0	0	.00	0	.324	.378	.324
	6 Min. YEARS		453	1648	459	81	13	30	656	297	169	189	3	189	10	18	7	72	31	.70	29	.279	.355	.398

Roberto Ramirez

Bats: Right **Throws:** Right **Pos:** OF **Ht:** 6'2" **Wt:** 180 **Born:** 3/18/70 **Age:** 26

Year	Team	Lg	G	AB	H	2B	3B	HR	TB	R	RBI	TBB	IBB	SO	HBP	SH	SF	SB	CS	SB%	GDP	Avg	OBP	SLG
1991	Clinton	A	17	55	10	0	1	0	12	4	5	2	0	18	0	0	2	0	1	.00	1	.182	.203	.218
	Everett	A	53	153	35	10	2	1	52	20	10	19	0	51	0	0	0	7	7	.50	5	.229	.314	.340
1992	Sou. Oregon	A	5	22	10	3	1	2	21	8	4	1	0	4	0	0	0	0	0	.00	0	.455	.478	.955
	Reno	A	55	190	65	13	3	7	105	31	29	15	2	45	2	2	2	3	5	.38	5	.342	.392	.553
1993	Madison	A	14	55	17	4	0	1	24	9	7	3	0	10	1	0	1	2	2	.50	2	.309	.350	.436
	Modesto	A	41	140	36	8	0	3	53	17	14	17	0	36	1	0	2	2	5	.29	3	.257	.338	.379
1994	Riverside	A	117	430	129	28	7	14	213	70	79	25	0	88	4	1	4	8	4	.67	9	.300	.341	.495
1995	Port City	AA	129	490	136	24	6	17	223	67	82	35	4	98	6	3	6	11	10	.52	14	.278	.330	.455
	5 Min. YEARS		431	1535	438	90	20	45	703	226	230	117	6	350	14	6	17	33	34	.49	39	.285	.338	.458

John Ramos

Bats: Right **Throws:** Right **Pos:** DH **Ht:** 6'0" **Wt:** 190 **Born:** 8/6/65 **Age:** 30

Year	Team	Lg	G	AB	H	2B	3B	HR	TB	R	RBI	TBB	IBB	SO	HBP	SH	SF	SB	CS	SB%	GDP	Avg	OBP	SLG
1986	Ft. Laud	A	54	184	49	10	1	2	67	25	28	26	0	23	1	4	2	8	3	.73	5	.266	.357	.364
	Oneonta	A	3	8	4	2	1	0	8	3	1	2	0	1	0	0	0	0	0	.00	0	.500	.600	1.000
1987	Pr. William	A	76	235	51	6	1	2	65	26	27	28	3	30	2	3	3	8	5	.62	10	.217	.302	.277
1988	Pr. William	A	109	391	119	18	2	8	165	47	57	49	1	34	7	2	5	8	2	.80	7	.304	.387	.422
	Albany-Colo	AA	21	72	16	1	3	1	26	11	13	12	0	9	1	0	2	2	1	.67	1	.222	.333	.361
1989	Albany-Colo	AA	105	359	98	21	0	9	146	55	60	40	2	65	7	2	2	7	5	.58	14	.273	.355	.407
1990	Columbus	AAA	2	6	0	0	0	0	0	0	1	0	0	0	0	0	0	0	0	.00	0	.000	.000	.000
	Albany-Colo	AA	84	287	90	20	1	4	124	38	45	36	0	39	3	0	5	1	0	1.00	10	.314	.390	.432
1991	Columbus	AAA	104	377	116	18	3	10	170	52	63	56	3	54	3	1	9	1	5	.17	15	.308	.393	.451
1992	Columbus	AAA	18	64	11	4	1	1	20	5	12	8	0	14	0	0	1	1	0	1.00	1	.172	.260	.313
1993	Columbus	AAA	49	158	41	7	0	1	51	17	18	19	1	32	0	0	2	1	2	.33	6	.259	.335	.323
1994	Las Vegas	AAA	114	312	102	25	1	10	159	51	46	40	1	41	1	2	3	0	0	.00	9	.327	.402	.510
1995	Syracuse	AAA	116	413	104	24	1	20	190	59	75	38	1	83	6	1	5	2	2	.50	11	.252	.320	.460
1991	New York	AL	10	26	8	1	0	0	9	4	3	1	0	3	0	0	2	0	0	.00	1	.308	.310	.346
	10 Min. YEARS		855	2866	801	156	15	68	1191	389	446	354	12	425	31	15	39	39	25	.61	89	.279	.360	.416

Ken Ramos

Bats: Left **Throws:** Left **Pos:** OF **Ht:** 6'1" **Wt:** 185 **Born:** 6/8/67 **Age:** 29

Year	Team	Lg	G	AB	H	2B	3B	HR	TB	R	RBI	TBB	IBB	SO	HBP	SH	SF	SB	CS	SB%	GDP	Avg	OBP	SLG
1989	Indians	R	54	193	60	7	2	1	74	41	14	39	1	18	3	3	2	17	7	.71	4	.311	.430	.383
	Kinston	A	8	21	3	0	0	0	3	6	0	5	0	2	0	1	0	2	0	1.00	0	.143	.308	.143

Year	Team	Lg	G	AB	H	2B	3B	HR	TB	R	RBI	TBB	IBB	SO	HBP	SH	SF	SB	CS	SB%	GDP	Avg	OBP	SLG
1990	Kinston	A	96	339	117	16	6	0	145	71	31	48	4	34	1	5	2	18	14	.56	4	.345	.426	.428
	Canton-Akrn	AA	19	73	24	2	2	0	30	12	11	8	0	10	0	0	1	2	1	.67	1	.329	.390	.411
1991	Canton-Akrn	AA	74	257	62	6	3	2	80	41	13	28	0	22	1	4	1	8	4	.67	3	.241	.317	.311
1992	Canton-Akrn	AA	125	442	150	23	5	5	198	93	42	82	6	37	0	5	1	14	11	.56	8	.339	.442	.448
1993	Charlotte	AAA	132	480	140	16	11	3	187	77	41	47	4	41	0	7	3	12	8	.60	10	.292	.353	.390
1994	Tucson	AAA	121	393	118	19	7	1	154	81	32	74	5	27	0	3	5	22	12	.65	9	.300	.407	.392
1995	Tucson	AAA	112	327	103	24	8	3	152	57	47	51	3	27	3	4	5	14	5	.74	3	.315	.407	.465
	7 Min. YEARS		741	2525	777	113	44	15	1023	479	231	382	23	218	8	32	20	109	62	.64	41	.308	.398	.405

Fernando Ramsey

Bats: Right **Throws:** Right **Pos:** OF **Ht:** 6' 1" **Wt:** 175 **Born:** 12/20/65 **Age:** 30

						BATTING												BASERUNNING				PERCENTAGES		
Year	Team	Lg	G	AB	H	2B	3B	HR	TB	R	RBI	TBB	IBB	SO	HBP	SH	SF	SB	CS	SB%	GDP	Avg	OBP	SLG
1987	Geneva	A	39	56	9	1	0	0	10	9	3	5	1	10	0	2	0	2	0	1.00	0	.161	.230	.179
1988	Charlstn-Wv	A	121	381	92	5	1	0	99	36	15	14	1	68	4	6	0	15	7	.68	4	.241	.276	.260
1989	Peoria	A	131	410	100	7	5	0	117	56	34	25	0	70	10	11	3	16	10	.62	6	.244	.301	.285
1990	Winston-Sal	A	124	428	109	12	4	5	144	52	48	19	0	50	3	9	2	43	7	.86	4	.255	.290	.336
1991	Charlotte	AA	139	547	151	18	6	6	199	78	49	36	0	90	3	7	2	37	17	.69	8	.276	.323	.364
1992	Iowa	AAA	133	480	129	9	5	1	151	62	38	23	0	78	2	11	0	39	12	.76	14	.269	.305	.315
1993	Iowa	AAA	134	545	147	30	7	5	206	76	42	25	2	72	2	9	0	13	13	.50	7	.270	.304	.378
1994	Norfolk	AAA	19	49	5	0	1	0	7	5	1	3	0	8	0	0	0	1	2	.33	0	.102	.154	.143
	Indianapols	AAA	14	51	18	4	0	0	22	9	4	0	0	7	0	0	0	3	1	.75	1	.353	.353	.431
1995	Nashville	AAA	98	406	126	19	3	5	166	61	45	13	2	47	3	4	2	26	8	.76	9	.310	.335	.409
1992	Chicago	NL	18	25	3	0	0	0	3	0	2	0	0	6	0	0	0	0	0	.00	0	.120	.120	.120
	9 Min. YEARS		952	3353	886	105	32	22	1121	444	279	163	6	500	27	59	9	195	77	.72	53	.264	.303	.334

Mark Ratekin

Pitches: Right **Bats:** Right **Pos:** P **Ht:** 6'4" **Wt:** 215 **Born:** 11/14/70 **Age:** 25

			HOW MUCH HE PITCHED					WHAT HE GAVE UP										THE RESULTS					
Year	Team	Lg	G	GS	CG	GF	IP	BFP	H	R	ER	HR	SH	SF	HB	TBB	IBB	SO	WP	Bk	W	L	Pct.	ShO	Sv	ERA
1991	Boise	A	14	13	1	1	70	287	59	31	26	1	1	2	3	22	0	49	3	2	5	2	.286	0	0	3.34
1992	Quad City	A	23	19	1	4	110	467	104	57	47	6	6	4	5	35	0	62	9	1	5	6	.455	0	0	3.85
1993	Palm Spring	A	21	21	6	0	143.1	618	151	78	62	5	5	6	6	46	0	66	5	1	7	7	.500	1	0	3.89
	Midland	AA	7	6	2	0	44.1	191	50	25	23	5	0	0	4	11	0	24	2	0	3	1	.750	0	0	4.67
1994	Midland	AA	8	8	2	0	56.2	233	54	36	31	5	0	1	2	14	4	37	1	0	3	4	.429	0	0	4.92
	Vancouver	AAA	21	20	1	0	123.2	549	159	78	69	10	1	4	4	40	2	55	8	0	12	5	.706	0	0	5.02
1995	Vancouver	AAA	19	3	0	3	50.2	223	62	35	30	7	6	3	1	18	2	14	3	0	3	2	.600	0	0	5.33
	Midland	AA	11	0	0	4	16.2	72	19	12	11	1	0	2	2	3	0	11	2	0	0	0	.000	0	0	5.94
	5 Min. YEARS		124	90	13	12	615.1	2640	658	352	299	40	19	22	27	189	8	318	33	4	35	30	.538	1	0	4.37

Gary Rath

Pitches: Left **Bats:** Left **Pos:** P **Ht:** 6'2" **Wt:** 185 **Born:** 1/10/73 **Age:** 23

			HOW MUCH HE PITCHED					WHAT HE GAVE UP										THE RESULTS					
Year	Team	Lg	G	GS	CG	GF	IP	BFP	H	R	ER	HR	SH	SF	HB	TBB	IBB	SO	WP	Bk	W	L	Pct.	ShO	Sv	ERA
1994	Vero Beach	A	13	11	0	0	62.2	261	55	26	19	3	3	3	2	23	0	50	4	0	5	6	.455	0	0	2.73
1995	San Antonio	AA	18	18	3	0	117	483	96	42	36	6	3	2	4	48	0	81	4	2	13	3	.813	1	0	2.77
	Albuquerque	AAA	8	8	0	0	39	178	46	31	22	4	1	1	2	20	0	23	2	0	3	5	.375	0	0	5.08
	2 Min. YEARS		39	37	3	0	218.2	922	197	99	77	13	7	6	8	91	0	154	10	2	21	14	.600	1	0	3.17

Daryl Ratliff

Bats: Right **Throws:** Right **Pos:** OF **Ht:** 6'1" **Wt:** 180 **Born:** 10/15/69 **Age:** 26

						BATTING												BASERUNNING				PERCENTAGES		
Year	Team	Lg	G	AB	H	2B	3B	HR	TB	R	RBI	TBB	IBB	SO	HBP	SH	SF	SB	CS	SB%	GDP	Avg	OBP	SLG
1989	Princeton	R	66	208	51	2	0	0	53	28	21	24	1	31	0	0	1	10	3	.77	2	.245	.322	.255
1990	Augusta	A	122	417	123	11	6	1	149	70	55	67	2	62	0	1	0	24	7	.77	12	.295	.393	.357
1991	Salem	A	88	352	103	8	4	2	125	60	23	27	0	43	0	2	1	35	9	.80	6	.293	.342	.355
	Carolina	AA	24	93	20	3	0	0	23	10	9	6	0	16	0	1	0	7	3	.70	1	.215	.263	.247
1992	Carolina	AA	124	413	99	13	3	0	118	45	26	41	0	50	0	5	4	25	11	.69	7	.240	.306	.286
1993	Carolina	AA	121	454	129	15	4	0	152	59	47	35	0	58	2	14	5	29	13	.69	9	.284	.335	.335
1994	Salem	A	36	138	44	9	2	1	60	25	19	12	0	18	0	1	0	5	5	.50	4	.319	.373	.435
	Carolina	AA	78	253	70	7	2	0	81	38	29	23	1	34	1	1	5	11	4	.73	8	.277	.333	.320
1995	Carolina	AA	16	63	18	4	0	1	25	10	5	8	1	10	0	2	0	2	1	.67	1	.286	.366	.397
	Calgary	AAA	95	286	98	11	1	0	111	41	37	18	2	30	2	4	0	9	6	.60	7	.343	.386	.388
	7 Min. YEARS		770	2677	755	83	22	5	897	386	271	261	7	352	5	31	16	157	62	.72	54	.282	.345	.335

Jon Ratliff

Pitches: Right **Bats:** Right **Pos:** P **Ht:** 6'5" **Wt:** 200 **Born:** 12/22/71 **Age:** 24

			HOW MUCH HE PITCHED					WHAT HE GAVE UP										THE RESULTS					
Year	Team	Lg	G	GS	CG	GF	IP	BFP	H	R	ER	HR	SH	SF	HB	TBB	IBB	SO	WP	Bk	W	L	Pct.	ShO	Sv	ERA
1993	Geneva	A	3	3	0	0	14	65	8	5	5	0	0	0	2	8	0	7	0	0	1	1	.500	0	0	3.21
	Daytona	A	8	8	0	0	41	194	50	29	18	0	2	3	5	23	0	15	3	1	2	4	.333	0	0	3.95
1994	Daytona	A	8	8	1	0	54	227	64	23	21	5	2	1	4	5	0	17	4	0	3	2	.600	0	0	3.50
	Iowa	AAA	5	4	0	0	28.1	131	39	19	17	7	1	1	2	7	0	10	3	0	1	3	.250	0	0	5.40
	Orlando	AA	12	12	1	0	62.1	292	78	44	39	4	4	5	8	26	1	19	5	0	1	9	.100	0	0	5.63

Year Team	Lg	G	GS	CG	GF	IP	BFP	H	R	ER	HR	SH	SF	HB	TBB	IBB	SO	WP	Bk	W	L	Pct.	ShO	Sv	ERA
1995 Orlando	AA	26	25	1	1	140	599	143	67	54	9	2	8	10	42	1	94	13	0	10	5	.667	1	0	3.47
3 Min. YEARS		62	60	3	1	339.2	1508	386	190	154	25	11	18	31	111	2	162	28	1	18	24	.429	1	0	4.08

Luis Raven

Bats: Right Throws: Right Pos: 3B Ht: 6'4" Wt: 230 Born: 11/19/68 Age: 27

Year Team	Lg	G	AB	H	2B	3B	HR	TB	R	RBI	TBB	IBB	SO	HBP	SH	SF	SB	CS	SB%	GDP	Avg	OBP	SLG
1989 Angels	R	43	145	30	6	2	1	43	15	20	8	0	43	1	0	3	3	0	1.00	3	.207	.248	.297
1991 Boise	A	38	84	23	2	0	2	31	13	13	9	0	19	1	0	0	1	1	.50	6	.274	.351	.369
1992 Palm Spring	A	107	378	109	16	2	9	156	59	55	24	2	81	2	0	4	18	7	.72	5	.288	.331	.413
1993 Midland	AA	43	167	43	12	1	2	63	21	30	5	1	45	1	1	0	4	2	.67	4	.257	.283	.377
Palm Spring	A	85	343	95	20	2	7	140	38	52	22	0	84	3	1	2	15	11	.58	6	.277	.324	.408
1994 Midland	AA	47	191	58	8	5	18	130	41	57	5	2	51	3	0	3	4	1	.80	9	.304	.327	.681
Vancouver	AAA	85	328	100	13	4	13	160	66	59	22	1	88	2	0	8	7	0	1.00	6	.305	.344	.488
1995 Lk Elsinore	A	6	24	10	2	1	2	20	5	6	5	0	7	1	0	0	1	0	1.00	1	.417	.533	.833
Vancouver	AAA	37	135	33	11	1	5	61	18	26	15	0	35	0	1	1	3	1	.75	6	.244	.318	.452
Midland	AA	21	86	23	2	1	5	42	9	15	4	0	30	1	0	1	1	0	.50	2	.267	.304	.488
6 Min. YEARS		512	1881	524	92	19	64	846	285	333	119	6	483	15	3	22	57	24	.70	47	.279	.323	.450

Kevin Rawitzer

Pitches: Left Bats: Left Pos: P Ht: 5'10" Wt: 185 Born: 2/28/71 Age: 25

Year Team	Lg	G	GS	CG	GF	IP	BFP	H	R	ER	HR	SH	SF	HB	TBB	IBB	SO	WP	Bk	W	L	Pct.	ShO	Sv	ERA
1993 Eugene	A	6	4	0	0	18	69	13	1	1	0	0	0	1	5	0	20	0	0	1	0	1.000	0	0	0.50
Rockford	A	5	5	0	0	30	126	23	7	5	0	0	0	1	11	0	34	0	0	3	0	1.000	0	0	1.50
1994 Rockford	A	15	15	0	0	76.1	329	80	27	21	5	0	4	3	27	1	75	6	1	5	2	.714	0	0	2.48
Wilmington	A	7	1	0	2	17.2	79	18	10	9	0	1	0	3	11	0	13	1	0	0	1	.000	0	1	4.58
1995 Wilmington	A	15	1	0	7	27	111	21	8	7	0	1	0	3	8	1	22	1	0	2	0	1.000	0	3	2.33
Wichita	AA	28	3	0	7	48	209	48	30	28	4	0	2	1	19	0	42	1	0	6	4	.600	0	1	5.25
3 Min. YEARS		76	29	0	16	217	923	203	83	71	9	2	6	9	81	2	206	9	1	17	7	.708	0	5	2.94

Ken Ray

Pitches: Right Bats: Right Pos: P Ht: 6'2" Wt: 160 Born: 11/27/74 Age: 21

Year Team	Lg	G	GS	CG	GF	IP	BFP	H	R	ER	HR	SH	SF	HB	TBB	IBB	SO	WP	Bk	W	L	Pct.	ShO	Sv	ERA
1993 Royals	R	13	7	0	3	47.1	204	44	21	12	1	1	3	0	17	0	45	6	0	2	3	.400	0	0	2.28
1994 Rockford	A	27	18	0	6	128.2	516	94	34	26	5	4	1	0	56	2	128	18	2	10	4	.714	0	3	1.82
1995 Wilmington	A	13	13	1	0	77	320	74	32	23	3	3	3	1	22	2	63	17	2	6	4	.600	0	0	2.69
Wichita	AA	14	14	0	0	75.1	342	83	55	50	7	1	0	1	46	0	53	8	1	4	5	.444	0	0	5.97
3 Min. YEARS		67	52	1	9	328.1	1382	295	142	111	16	9	7	2	141	4	289	49	5	22	16	.579	0	3	3.04

Tom Redington

Bats: Right Throws: Right Pos: 1B Ht: 6'1" Wt: 200 Born: 2/13/69 Age: 27

Year Team	Lg	G	AB	H	2B	3B	HR	TB	R	RBI	TBB	IBB	SO	HBP	SH	SF	SB	CS	SB%	GDP	Avg	OBP	SLG
1987 Sumter	A	18	56	18	2	0	0	20	9	5	13	0	14	0	0	0	1	2	.33	0	.321	.449	.357
1988 Sumter	A	129	429	84	13	1	11	132	45	60	75	2	71	5	0	4	4	5	.44	7	.196	.320	.308
1989 Burlington	A	85	298	89	14	0	17	154	49	52	53	5	47	7	0	4	4	1	.80	10	.299	.412	.517
Greenville	AA	33	110	27	4	0	3	40	9	13	7	0	22	0	0	2	1	1	.50	3	.245	.286	.364
1990 Greenville	AA	124	409	103	13	1	12	154	55	52	63	3	69	4	1	4	2	1	.67	2	.252	.354	.377
1991 Wichita	AA	116	394	112	23	0	5	150	54	57	67	2	66	3	0	6	2	3	.40	19	.284	.387	.381
1992 Birmingham	AA	88	255	59	7	0	5	81	21	29	26	0	41	3	2	2	0	1	.00	6	.231	.308	.318
1994 Lk Elsinore	A	129	469	139	31	1	13	211	72	66	71	1	85	5	1	4	6	4	.60	14	.296	.392	.450
1995 Midland	AA	9	32	8	2	0	0	10	5	3	6	0	5	1	0	1	0	0	.00	1	.250	.368	.313
Lk Elsinore	A	76	271	89	26	1	6	135	50	54	51	8	43	1	0	2	2	1	.67	4	.328	.434	.498
8 Min. YEARS		807	2723	728	135	4	72	1087	369	391	432	21	463	28	4	28	22	19	.54	73	.267	.370	.399

Mike Redmond

Bats: Right Throws: Right Pos: C Ht: 6'0" Wt: 190 Born: 5/5/71 Age: 25

Year Team	Lg	G	AB	H	2B	3B	HR	TB	R	RBI	TBB	IBB	SO	HBP	SH	SF	SB	CS	SB%	GDP	Avg	OBP	SLG
1993 Kane County	A	43	100	20	2	0	0	22	10	10	6	0	17	4	2	0	2	0	1.00	1	.200	.273	.220
1994 Kane County	A	92	306	83	10	0	1	96	39	24	26	0	31	9	6	2	3	4	.43	10	.271	.344	.314
Brevard Cty	A	12	42	11	4	0	0	15	4	2	3	0	4	1	0	0	0	0	.00	1	.262	.326	.357
1995 Portland	AA	105	333	85	11	1	3	107	37	39	22	2	27	3	4	3	2	2	.50	9	.255	.305	.321
3 Min. YEARS		252	781	199	27	1	4	240	90	75	57	2	79	17	12	5	7	6	.54	21	.255	.317	.307

Darren Reed

Bats: Right Throws: Right Pos: OF Ht: 6'1" Wt: 205 Born: 10/16/65 Age: 30

Year Team	Lg	G	AB	H	2B	3B	HR	TB	R	RBI	TBB	IBB	SO	HBP	SH	SF	SB	CS	SB%	GDP	Avg	OBP	SLG
1984 Oneonta	A	40	100	26	7	0	2	39	17	9	10	0	19	0	1	1	2	1	.67	2	.230	.290	.345
1985 Ft. Laud	A	100	369	117	21	4	10	176	63	61	36	3	56	7	0	7	13	3	.81	9	.317	.382	.477
1986 Albany-Colo	AA	51	196	45	11	1	4	70	22	27	15	0	24	1	1	5	1	0	1.00	2	.230	.281	.357

Year Team	Lg	G	AB	H	2B	3B	HR	TB	R	RBI	TBB	IBB	SO	HBP	SH	SF	SB	CS	SB%	GDP	Avg	OBP	SLG
1987 Columbus	AAA	21	79	26	3	3	8	59	15	16	4	0	9	0	0	0	0	2	.00	2	.329	.361	.747
Albany-Colo	AA	107	404	129	23	4	20	220	68	79	51	9	50	8	0	3	9	6	.60	10	.319	.403	.545
1988 Tidewater	AAA	101	345	83	26	0	9	136	31	47	32	2	66	3	3	4	0	3	.00	9	.241	.307	.394
1989 Tidewater	AAA	133	444	119	30	6	4	173	57	50	60	1	70	11	1	4	11	2	.85	15	.268	.366	.390
1990 Tidewater	AAA	104	359	95	21	6	17	179	58	74	51	4	62	6	0	4	15	4	.79	11	.265	.362	.499
1992 Indianapols	AAA	1	3	1	1	0	0	2	0	0	0	0	1	0	0	0	0	0	.00	0	.333	.333	.667
W. Palm Bch	A	10	40	10	4	0	2	20	6	12	1	0	14	4	0	1	0	0	.00	0	.250	.326	.500
1994 Buffalo	AAA	12	39	10	2	0	2	18	5	5	1	0	8	0	1	0	0	0	.00	1	.256	.275	.462
1995 Richmond	AAA	57	136	36	7	0	5	58	11	22	11	0	28	1	0	3	0	0	.00	4	.265	.318	.426
1990 New York	NL	26	39	8	4	1	1	17	5	2	3	0	11	0	0	0	1	0	1.00	0	.205	.262	.436
1992 Minnesota	AL	14	33	6	2	0	0	8	2	4	2	0	11	0	0	2	0	0	.00	0	.182	.216	.242
Montreal	NL	42	81	14	2	0	5	31	10	10	6	2	23	1	0	0	0	0	.00	3	.173	.239	.383
10 Min. YEARS		737	2527	697	156	24	83	1150	353	402	272	19	407	41	7	32	51	21	.71	65	.276	.352	.455
2 Maj. YEARS		82	153	28	8	1	6	56	17	16	11	2	45	1	0	2	1	0	1.00	3	.183	.240	.366

Pokey Reese

Bats: Right **Throws:** Right **Pos:** SS **Ht:** 6'0" **Wt:** 160 **Born:** 6/10/73 **Age:** 23

							BATTING										BASERUNNING				PERCENTAGES		
Year Team	Lg	G	AB	H	2B	3B	HR	TB	R	RBI	TBB	IBB	SO	HBP	SH	SF	SB	CS	SB%	GDP	Avg	OBP	SLG
1991 Princeton	R	62	231	55	8	3	3	78	30	27	23	0	44	0	0	2	10	8	.56	4	.238	.305	.338
1992 Charlstn-Wv	A	106	380	102	19	3	6	145	50	53	24	0	75	5	4	7	19	8	.70	2	.268	.315	.382
1993 Chattanooga	AA	102	345	73	17	4	3	107	35	37	23	1	77	1	3	7	8	5	.62	2	.212	.258	.310
1994 Chattanooga	AA	134	484	130	23	4	12	197	77	49	43	1	75	7	6	1	21	4	.84	6	.269	.336	.407
1995 Indianapols	AAA	89	343	82	21	1	10	135	51	46	36	0	81	4	1	3	8	5	.62	3	.239	.316	.394
5 Min. YEARS		493	1783	442	88	15	34	662	243	212	149	2	352	17	14	20	66	30	.69	17	.248	.309	.371

Derek Reid

Bats: Right **Throws:** Right **Pos:** OF **Ht:** 6'3" **Wt:** 195 **Born:** 2/4/70 **Age:** 26

							BATTING										BASERUNNING				PERCENTAGES		
Year Team	Lg	G	AB	H	2B	3B	HR	TB	R	RBI	TBB	IBB	SO	HBP	SH	SF	SB	CS	SB%	GDP	Avg	OBP	SLG
1990 Everett	A	62	215	62	15	1	5	94	35	40	20	2	49	3	4	3	21	3	.88	3	.288	.353	.437
1991 San Jose	A	121	454	122	23	6	4	169	72	65	37	2	91	1	6	10	27	9	.75	7	.269	.319	.372
1992 Shreveport	AA	2	6	1	1	0	0	2	1	0	0	0	1	0	1	0	0	0	.00	0	.167	.167	.333
1993 Clinton	A	15	57	17	2	0	0	19	5	7	1	0	6	0	1	0	3	2	.60	1	.298	.310	.333
San Jose	A	29	80	15	1	1	0	18	9	8	6	0	16	1	0	0	5	2	.71	1	.188	.253	.225
1994 San Bernrdo	A	59	238	70	18	1	6	108	34	38	21	2	60	1	2	2	15	1	.94	7	.294	.351	.454
Shreveport	AA	51	137	30	4	0	4	46	11	9	4	2	36	1	3	0	5	2	.71	6	.219	.246	.336
1995 Shreveport	AA	8	14	2	0	1	0	4	2	1	0	0	4	0	0	0	0	0	.00	0	.143	.143	.286
Burlington	A	95	354	101	15	4	13	163	74	55	31	0	55	4	3	1	22	4	.85	7	.285	.349	.460
6 Min. YEARS		442	1555	420	79	14	32	623	243	223	120	8	318	11	20	16	98	23	.81	32	.270	.324	.401

Desmond Relaford

Bats: Both **Throws:** Right **Pos:** SS **Ht:** 5'8" **Wt:** 155 **Born:** 9/16/73 **Age:** 22

							BATTING										BASERUNNING				PERCENTAGES		
Year Team	Lg	G	AB	H	2B	3B	HR	TB	R	RBI	TBB	IBB	SO	HBP	SH	SF	SB	CS	SB%	GDP	Avg	OBP	SLG
1991 Mariners	R	46	163	43	7	3	0	56	36	18	22	1	24	1	1	5	15	3	.83	0	.264	.346	.344
1992 Peninsula	A	130	445	96	18	1	3	125	53	34	39	1	88	1	4	6	27	7	.79	7	.216	.277	.281
1993 Jacksonvlle	AA	133	472	115	16	4	8	163	49	47	50	1	103	7	6	4	16	12	.57	4	.244	.323	.345
1994 Jacksonvlle	AA	37	143	29	7	3	3	51	24	11	22	0	28	0	2	2	10	1	.91	2	.203	.305	.357
Riverside	A	99	374	116	27	5	5	168	95	59	78	6	78	4	3	6	27	6	.82	7	.310	.429	.449
1995 Port City	AA	90	352	101	11	2	7	137	51	27	41	2	58	2	2	0	25	9	.74	4	.287	.365	.389
Tacoma	AAA	30	113	27	5	1	2	40	20	7	13	2	24	0	0	2	6	0	1.00	2	.239	.313	.354
5 Min. YEARS		565	2062	527	91	19	28	740	328	203	265	13	403	15	18	25	126	38	.77	26	.256	.341	.359

Mike Rendina

Bats: Left **Throws:** Left **Pos:** 1B **Ht:** 6'4" **Wt:** 215 **Born:** 9/28/70 **Age:** 25

							BATTING										BASERUNNING				PERCENTAGES		
Year Team	Lg	G	AB	H	2B	3B	HR	TB	R	RBI	TBB	IBB	SO	HBP	SH	SF	SB	CS	SB%	GDP	Avg	OBP	SLG
1988 Bristol	R	39	75	15	3	0	3	27	12	16	9	0	18	0	0	2	0	1	.00	3	.200	.279	.360
1989 Fayettevlle	A	28	86	10	4	0	0	14	9	5	11	1	19	0	3	0	0	0	.00	4	.116	.216	.163
Bristol	R	62	224	61	13	0	11	107	34	34	28	3	36	1	0	0	5	3	.63	6	.272	.356	.478
1990 Fayettevlle	A	137	475	121	23	3	11	183	59	77	76	7	90	3	0	4	4	4	.50	13	.255	.358	.385
1991 Lakeland	A	115	359	77	7	2	4	100	36	41	54	5	61	4	2	3	2	2	.50	11	.214	.321	.279
1992 Lakeland	A	121	397	106	23	1	9	158	48	69	46	5	59	2	1	7	2	0	1.00	9	.267	.341	.398
1993 London	AA	135	475	134	30	1	10	196	59	77	55	1	96	0	0	3	8	4	.67	6	.282	.355	.413
1994 Trenton	AA	116	387	88	15	0	11	136	46	46	29	2	77	2	0	2	2	1	.67	5	.227	.283	.351
1995 Jacksonvlle	AA	31	98	22	5	0	3	36	12	16	7	2	20	0	0	0	0	0	.00	3	.224	.276	.367
8 Min. YEARS		784	2576	634	123	7	62	957	315	381	315	26	476	12	6	21	23	15	.61	58	.246	.329	.372

Steve Renko

Pitches: Right **Bats:** Right **Pos:** P **Ht:** 6'3" **Wt:** 205 **Born:** 8/1/67 **Age:** 28

					HOW MUCH HE PITCHED			WHAT HE GAVE UP											THE RESULTS				
Year Team	Lg	G	GS	CG	GF	IP	BFP	H	R	ER	HR	SH	SF	HB	TBB	IBB	SO	WP	Bk	W	L	Pct.	ShO	Sv	ERA
1990 Expos	R	2	0	0	1	5	23	7	1	1	0	0	0	0	1	0	5	0	2	1	0	1.000	0	0	1.80
Gate City	R	11	10	2	0	59.2	263	56	32	26	4	2	0	2	23	1	68	6	1	3	4	.429	0	0	3.92

Year	Team	Lg	G	GS	CG	GF	IP	BFP	H	R	ER	HR	SH	SF	HB	TBB	IBB	SO	WP	Bk	W	L	Pct.	ShO	Sv	ERA
1991	W. Palm Bch	A	4	3	0	0	9	44	14	8	8	2	0	0	1	5	0	4	0	0	0	1	.000	0	0	8.00
	Rockford	A	16	16	1	0	99	431	95	43	35	3	3	3	4	34	0	102	16	1	4	5	.444	0	0	3.18
1992	Winter Havn	A	10	10	1	0	61.1	264	65	33	27	7	1	1	2	16	0	56	2	0	3	5	.375	0	0	3.96
	Lynchburg	A	6	6	0	0	34.1	153	39	18	15	6	2	4	0	14	0	23	6	0	1	1	.500	0	0	3.93
1993	Hagerstown	A	23	1	0	12	42.1	170	35	20	16	2	5	1	1	11	1	45	5	0	4	2	.667	0	5	3.40
	Knoxville	AA	12	5	0	1	34.2	149	38	21	14	1	6	2	1	8	0	30	7	0	1	3	.250	0	0	3.63
1994	Wichita	AA	42	0	0	16	78.2	375	90	56	44	4	7	5	1	49	8	59	10	1	3	8	.273	0	2	5.03
1995	Vancouver	AAA	10	9	0	0	51.1	226	53	29	24	2	0	3	0	18	0	22	5	0	2	5	.286	0	0	4.21
	Midland	AA	22	9	0	4	76.2	352	100	51	41	3	2	5	0	28	2	44	5	0	3	5	.375	0	1	4.81
	6 Min. YEARS		158	69	4	34	552	2450	592	312	251	34	28	24	12	207	12	458	62	5	25	39	.391	0	8	4.09

Dave Renteria

Bats: Right **Throws:** Right **Pos:** SS **Ht:** 6'0" **Wt:** 175 **Born:** 12/1/72 **Age:** 23

							BATTING											BASERUNNING				PERCENTAGES		
Year	Team	Lg	G	AB	H	2B	3B	HR	TB	R	RBI	TBB	IBB	SO	HBP	SH	SF	SB	CS	SB%	GDP	Avg	OBP	SLG
1992	Yankees	R	20	61	14	1	0	0	15	6	7	6	0	14	0	0	0	0	0	.00	1	.230	.299	.246
1993	Oneonta	A	43	129	30	7	0	0	37	19	16	14	0	25	0	3	1	1	3	.25	3	.233	.306	.287
1994	San Bernrdo	A	23	72	10	0	0	0	10	11	6	18	1	24	1	1	0	1	.00	1	.139	.315	.139
	Greensboro	A	38	101	23	3	0	1	29	12	11	12	0	16	0	1	1	1	2	.33	6	.228	.307	.287
	Tampa	A	3	8	0	0	0	0	0	3	0	1	0	0	0	0	0	0	0	.00	0	.000	.111	.000
	Columbus	AAA	2	1	0	0	0	0	0	0	0	0	0	0	0	0	0	0	0	.00	0	.000	.000	.000
	Albany-Colo	AAA	3	11	1	0	1	0	3	1	0	0	0	6	1	0	0	0	0	.00	1	.091	.167	.273
1995	Norwich	AA	15	38	4	0	0	0	4	4	0	3	0	13	0	1	0	1	0	1.00	0	.105	.171	.105
	Tampa	A	33	69	15	3	1	1	23	6	4	4	0	16	1	2	2	1	1	.50	1	.217	.263	.333
	4 Min. YEARS		180	490	97	14	2	2	121	62	44	58	1	114	3	8	5	4	7	.36	13	.198	.284	.247

Edgar Renteria

Bats: Right **Throws:** Right **Pos:** SS **Ht:** 6'1" **Wt:** 172 **Born:** 8/7/75 **Age:** 20

							BATTING											BASERUNNING				PERCENTAGES		
Year	Team	Lg	G	AB	H	2B	3B	HR	TB	R	RBI	TBB	IBB	SO	HBP	SH	SF	SB	CS	SB%	GDP	Avg	OBP	SLG
1992	Marlins	R	43	163	47	8	1	0	57	25	9	8	0	29	2	2	0	10	6	.63	1	.288	.329	.350
1993	Kane County	A	116	384	78	8	0	1	89	40	35	35	0	94	0	6	3	7	8	.47	3	.203	.268	.232
1994	Brevard Cty	A	128	439	111	15	1	0	128	46	36	35	2	56	0	2	2	6	11	.35	14	.253	.307	.292
1995	Portland	AA	135	508	147	15	7	7	197	70	68	32	2	85	2	8	8	30	11	.73	10	.289	.329	.388
	4 Min. YEARS		422	1494	383	46	9	8	471	181	148	110	4	264	4	18	13	53	36	.60	28	.256	.307	.315

Oscar Resendez

Pitches: Right **Bats:** Right **Pos:** P **Ht:** 6'1" **Wt:** 175 **Born:** 9/1/71 **Age:** 24

			HOW MUCH HE PITCHED						WHAT HE GAVE UP												THE RESULTS				
Year	Team	Lg	G	GS	CG	GF	IP	BFP	H	R	ER	HR	SH	SF	HB	TBB	IBB	SO	WP	Bk	W	L	Pct.	ShO	Sv	ERA
1991	Burlington	R	24	1	0	15	50.1	221	33	26	15	0	2	5	2	31	0	62	11	0	3	2	.600	0	6	2.68
1992	Columbus	A	5	1	0	2	11.2	47	9	2	2	0	0	0	0	7	0	13	1	0	0	1	.000	0	1	1.54
	Watertown	A	15	15	2	0	73.2	352	77	42	31	6	0	6	2	58	0	62	7	2	6	2	.750	0	0	3.79
1993	Columbus	A	32	2	1	9	66.1	300	61	43	35	5	5	1	2	45	3	49	8	0	7	3	.700	0	2	4.75
1994	High Desert	A	33	14	2	10	120.2	564	112	86	76	12	2	3	4	88	0	91	9	1	2	11	.154	1	2	5.67
1995	Port City	AA	11	0	0	3	17	76	16	8	8	0	0	0	0	8	0	15	2	0	0	2	.000	0	0	4.24
	5 Min. YEARS		120	33	5	39	339.2	1560	308	207	167	23	9	15	11	237	3	292	38	3	18	21	.462	1	10	4.42

Todd Revenig

Pitches: Right **Bats:** Right **Pos:** P **Ht:** 6'1" **Wt:** 185 **Born:** 6/28/69 **Age:** 27

			HOW MUCH HE PITCHED						WHAT HE GAVE UP												THE RESULTS				
Year	Team	Lg	G	GS	CG	GF	IP	BFP	H	R	ER	HR	SH	SF	HB	TBB	IBB	SO	WP	Bk	W	L	Pct.	ShO	Sv	ERA
1990	Sou. Oregon	A	24	0	0	14	44.2	176	33	13	4	2	4	1	0	9	2	46	1	2	3	2	.600	0	6	0.81
1991	Madison	A	26	0	0	22	28.2	109	13	6	3	1	3	0	0	10	2	27	1	1	1	0	1.000	0	13	0.94
	Huntsville	AA	12	0	0	6	18.1	68	11	3	2	1	0	1	2	4	0	10	0	0	1	2	.333	0	0	0.98
1992	Huntsville	AA	53	0	0	48	63.2	233	33	14	12	8	2	2	0	11	0	49	1	0	1	1	.500	0	33	1.70
1994	Athletics	R	4	4	0	0	7.2	33	7	4	3	1	1	0	0	2	0	6	0	0	0	0	.000	0	0	3.52
1995	Edmonton	AAA	45	0	0	30	54.1	230	53	32	26	5	3	3	2	15	1	28	2	0	4	5	.444	0	10	4.31
1992	Oakland	AL	2	0	0	2	2	7	2	0	0	0	0	0	0	0	0	1	0	0	0	0	.000	0	0	0.00
	5 Min. YEARS		164	4	0	120	217.1	849	150	72	50	18	13	7	4	51	5	166	5	3	10	10	.500	0	62	2.07

Harold Reynolds

Bats: Both **Throws:** Right **Pos:** 2B **Ht:** 5'11" **Wt:** 165 **Born:** 11/26/60 **Age:** 35

							BATTING											BASERUNNING				PERCENTAGES		
Year	Team	Lg	G	AB	H	2B	3B	HR	TB	R	RBI	TBB	IBB	SO	HBP	SH	SF	SB	CS	SB%	GDP	Avg	OBP	SLG
1981	Wausau	A	127	493	146	23	3	11	208	98	59	56	-	47	2	12	4	69	20	.78	-	.296	.368	.422
1982	Lynn	AA	102	375	102	14	4	2	130	58	48	36	-	41	3	8	3	39	20	.66	-	.272	.338	.347
1983	Salt Lake	AAA	136	534	165	20	9	1	206	84	72	47	-	43	5	14	6	54	19	.74	-	.309	.367	.386
1984	Salt Lake	AAA	135	558	165	22	6	3	208	94	54	73	2	72	3	9	3	37	17	.69	9	.296	.378	.373
	Salt Lake	AAA	135	558	165	22	6	3	208	94	54	73	-	72	3	9	3	37	17	.69	-	.296	.378	.373
1985	Calgary	AAA	52	212	77	11	3	5	109	36	30	28	1	18	1	3	4	9	13	.41	2	.363	.433	.514
1986	Calgary	AAA	29	118	37	7	0	1	47	20	7	20	0	12	0	1	0	10	8	.56	1	.314	.413	.398
1995	Omaha	AAA	38	109	22	6	1	1	33	12	11	13	1	10	0	0	2	2	3	.40	2	.202	.282	.303
1983	Seattle	AL	20	59	12	4	1	0	18	8	1	2	0	9	0	1	1	0	2	.00	1	.203	.226	.305
1984	Seattle	AL	10	10	3	0	0	0	3	3	0	0		1	1	0		1	1	.50	0	.300	.364	.300

Year	Team	Lg	G	AB	H	2B	3B	HR	TB	R	RBI	TBB	IBB	SO	HBP	SH	SF	SB	CS	SB%	GDP	Avg	OBP	SLG
1985	Seattle	AL	67	104	15	3	1	0	20	15	6	17	0	14	0	1	0	3	2	.60	0	.144	.264	.192
1986	Seattle	AL	126	445	99	19	4	1	129	46	24	29	0	42	3	9	0	30	12	.71	6	.222	.275	.290
1987	Seattle	AL	160	530	146	31	8	1	196	73	35	39	0	34	2	8	5	60	20	.75	7	.275	.325	.370
1988	Seattle	AL	158	598	169	26	11	4	229	61	41	51	1	51	2	10	2	35	29	.55	9	.283	.340	.383
1989	Seattle	AL	153	613	184	24	9	0	226	87	43	55	1	45	3	3	3	25	18	.58	4	.300	.359	.369
1990	Seattle	AL	160	642	162	36	5	5	223	100	55	81	3	52	3	5	6	31	16	.66	9	.252	.336	.347
1991	Seattle	AL	161	631	160	34	6	3	215	95	57	72	2	63	5	14	6	28	8	.78	11	.254	.332	.341
1992	Seattle	AL	140	458	113	23	3	3	151	55	33	45	1	41	3	11	4	15	12	.56	12	.247	.316	.330
1993	Baltimore	AL	145	485	122	20	4	4	162	64	47	66	3	47	4	10	5	12	11	.52	4	.252	.343	.334
1994	California	AL	74	207	48	10	1	0	60	33	11	23	0	18	1	3	1	10	7	.59	5	.232	.310	.290
	7 Min. YEARS		754	2957	879	125	32	27	1149	496	335	346	4	315	17	56	25	257	117	.69	14	.297	.371	.389
	12 Maj. YEARS		1374	4782	1233	230	53	21	1632	640	353	480	11	417	27	76	33	250	138	.64	68	.258	.327	.341

Bats: Both **Throws: Right** **Pos: C**

Lance Rice

Ht: 6'1" **Wt: 195** **Born: 10/19/66** **Age: 29**

Year	Team	Lg	G	AB	H	2B	3B	HR	TB	R	RBI	TBB	IBB	SO	HBP	SH	SF	SB	CS	SB%	GDP	Avg	OBP	SLG
1988	Great Falls	R	47	159	45	8	2	0	57	31	27	31	0	29	1	2	2	4	2	.67	2	.283	.399	.358
1989	Bakersfield	A	126	406	90	15	1	5	122	41	53	53	2	83	3	1	5	1	4	.20	9	.222	.313	.300
1990	San Antonio	AA	79	245	59	11	2	0	74	25	35	24	3	46	1	3	4	3	1	.75	6	.241	.307	.302
1991	San Antonio	AA	78	215	43	8	0	3	60	23	28	31	2	30	1	2	3	2	1	.67	7	.200	.300	.279
	Albuquerque	AAA	1	3	1	1	0	0	2	0	1	0	0	0	0	0	0	0	0	.00	0	.333	.333	.667
1992	San Antonio	AA	75	194	45	9	0	2	60	17	18	17	3	34	1	6	2	0	1	.00	2	.232	.294	.309
1993	Harrisburg	AA	46	136	32	10	0	1	45	12	20	16	0	22	0	2	2	0	1	.00	3	.235	.312	.331
1994	Harrisburg	AA	13	30	9	1	0	0	10	8	2	7	0	4	0	0	0	0	0	.00	2	.300	.432	.333
1995	Toledo	AAA	15	41	11	1	0	1	15	2	6	4	0	6	0	1	0	0	3	.00	0	.268	.333	.366
	Jacksonville	AA	65	154	19	1	1	3	31	8	11	11	0	23	0	2	0	0	0	.00	5	.123	.182	.201
	8 Min. YEARS		545	1583	354	65	6	15	476	167	201	194	10	277	7	19	18	10	13	.43	36	.224	.308	.301

Bats: Right **Throws: Right** **Pos: 2B**

Jeff Richardson

Ht: 6' 2" **Wt: 180** **Born: 8/26/65** **Age: 30**

Year	Team	Lg	G	AB	H	2B	3B	HR	TB	R	RBI	TBB	IBB	SO	HBP	SH	SF	SB	CS	SB%	GDP	Avg	OBP	SLG
1986	Billings	R	47	162	51	14	4	0	73	42	20	17	0	23	1	0	0	12	1	.92	0	.315	.383	.451
1987	Tampa	A	100	374	112	9	2	0	125	44	37	30	5	35	3	1	7	10	4	.71	16	.299	.350	.334
	Vermont	AA	35	134	28	4	0	0	32	24	8	5	0	25	1	2	0	5	0	1.00	4	.209	.243	.239
1988	Chattanooga	AA	122	399	100	17	1	1	122	50	37	23	0	56	9	12	4	8	1	.89	7	.251	.303	.306
1989	Nashville	AAA	88	286	78	19	2	1	104	36	25	17	4	42	1	6	3	3	1	.75	13	.273	.313	.364
1990	Buffalo	AAA	66	164	34	4	0	1	41	15	15	14	0	21	2	3	0	1	2	.33	6	.207	.278	.250
1991	Buffalo	AAA	62	186	48	16	2	1	71	21	24	18	7	29	2	9	3	5	3	.63	3	.258	.325	.382
1992	Buffalo	AAA	97	328	95	23	2	3	131	34	29	19	3	46	1	11	2	5	2	.71	12	.290	.329	.399
1993	Pawtucket	AAA	9	28	9	1	0	0	10	2	1	1	0	6	0	1	1	0	0	.00	1	.321	.333	.357
1994	Louisville	AAA	89	247	64	13	1	4	91	29	21	16	0	38	1	6	0	1	1	.50	10	.259	.307	.368
1995	Calgary	AAA	7	18	6	0	0	0	6	4	3	2	0	1	0	0	0	0	0	.00	1	.333	.381	.333
1989	Cincinnati	NL	53	125	21	4	0	2	31	10	11	10	0	23	1	3	1	1	0	1.00	4	.168	.234	.248
1991	Pittsburgh	NL	6	4	1	0	0	0	1	0	0	0	0	3	0	0	0	0	0	.00	0	.250	.250	.250
1993	Boston	AL	15	24	5	2	0	0	7	3	2	1	0	3	0	2	0	0	0	.00	0	.208	.240	.292
	10 Min. YEARS		722	2326	625	120	14	11	806	301	220	162	19	322	21	54	21	50	15	.77	73	.269	.319	.347
	3 Maj. YEARS		74	153	27	6	0	2	39	13	13	11	0	29	1	5	1	1	0	1.00	3	.176	.235	.255

Bats: Right **Throws: Right** **Pos: OF**

Scott Richardson

Ht: 6'1" **Wt: 175** **Born: 2/19/71** **Age: 25**

Year	Team	Lg	G	AB	H	2B	3B	HR	TB	R	RBI	TBB	IBB	SO	HBP	SH	SF	SB	CS	SB%	GDP	Avg	OBP	SLG
1992	Helena	R	69	289	83	10	5	2	109	58	36	35	1	43	4	1	0	22	5	.81	5	.287	.372	.377
1993	Beloit	A	125	475	131	26	7	3	180	76	64	42	0	85	1	6	5	50	12	.81	6	.276	.333	.379
1994	Stockton	A	131	495	131	25	3	2	168	76	33	73	0	64	1	9	0	49	12	.80	10	.265	.360	.339
1995	El Paso	AA	82	256	65	9	6	1	89	29	29	16	0	42	5	2	0	8	5	.62	13	.254	.310	.348
	Stockton	A	24	80	18	4	1	2	30	12	14	6	0	16	3	1	0	8	3	.73	3	.225	.303	.375
	4 Min. YEARS		431	1595	428	74	22	10	576	251	176	172	1	250	14	19	5	137	37	.79	37	.268	.344	.361

Pitches: Right **Bats: Right** **Pos: P**

Jeff Richey

Ht: 6'0" **Wt: 185** **Born: 9/30/69** **Age: 26**

Year	Team	Lg	G	GS	CG	GF	IP	BFP	H	R	ER	HR	SH	SF	HB	TBB	IBB	SO	WP	Bk	W	L	Pct.	ShO	Sv	ERA
1992	Everett	A	24	0	0	17	37.1	164	30	18	14	2	1	1	4	21	2	48	3	1	2	1	.667	0	7	3.38
1993	San Jose	A	21	0	0	16	29	131	34	13	11	2	2	1	1	11	1	30	1	0	3	1	.750	0	4	3.41
	Clinton	A	40	0	0	39	52.1	194	19	7	6	2	4	0	1	17	0	75	2	0	2	1	.667	0	28	1.03
1994	San Jose	A	49	0	0	40	84.1	350	70	30	20	4	7	6	6	32	2	87	1	2	3	4	.429	0	19	2.13
1995	Shreveport	AA	8	0	0	4	22	94	20	7	6	0	2	0	1	8	3	11	3	0	1	2	.333	0	1	2.45
	4 Min. YEARS		142	0	0	116	225	933	173	75	57	10	16	8	13	89	8	251	10	3	11	9	.550	0	59	2.28

Raymond Ricken

Pitches: Right Bats: Right Pos: P   Ht: 6'5" Wt: 225 Born: 8/11/73 Age: 22

			HOW MUCH HE PITCHED						WHAT HE GAVE UP								THE RESULTS					
Year Team	Lg	G	GS	CG	GF	IP	BFP	H	R	ER	HR	SH	SF	HB	TBB	IBB	SO	WP	Bk	W	L	Pct.	ShO	Sv	ERA
1994 Oneonta	A	10	10	0	0	50.1	206	45	25	20	1	1	1	2	17	1	55	6	3	2	3	.400	0	0	3.58
Greensboro	A	5	5	0	0	25	109	27	13	13	1	0	1	0	12	0	19	3	0	1	2	.333	0	0	4.68
1995 Greensboro	A	10	10	0	0	64.2	245	42	20	16	2	1	1	0	16	1	77	3	0	3	2	.600	0	0	2.23
Tampa	A	11	11	1	0	75.1	291	47	25	18	3	2	1	1	27	0	58	1	2	3	4	.429	0	0	2.15
Norwich	AA	8	8	1	0	53	217	44	21	16	2	2	0	1	24	2	43	3	0	4	2	.667	1	0	2.72
2 Min. YEARS		44	44	2	0	268.1	1068	205	104	83	9	6	4	4	96	4	252	16	5	13	13	.500	1	0	2.78

Kevin Riggs

Bats: Left Throws: Right Pos: DH   Ht: 5'11" Wt: 190 Born: 2/3/69 Age: 27

					BATTING													BASERUNNING				PERCENTAGES		
Year Team	Lg	G	AB	H	2B	3B	HR	TB	R	RBI	TBB	IBB	SO	HBP	SH	SF		SB	CS	SB%	GDP	Avg	OBP	SLG
1990 Billings	R	57	192	61	9	2	1	77	49	21	50	2	27	2	0	0		16	3	.84	5	.318	.463	.401
Charlstn-Wv	A	2	4	1	0	0	0	1	0	1	0	0	1	0	0	0		0	1	.00	0	.250	.250	.250
1991 Cedar Rapds	A	118	406	109	21	2	2	140	72	43	91	2	50	3	2	6		23	8	.74	11	.268	.401	.345
Charlstn-Wv	A	1	2	1	0	0	0	1	0	0	1	0	0	0	0	0		0	0	.00	0	.500	.667	.500
1992 Cedar Rapds	A	126	457	132	24	4	2	170	87	44	97	3	63	5	4	5		23	15	.61	10	.289	.415	.372
1993 Stockton	A	108	377	131	18	3	3	164	84	45	101	3	46	1	1	4		12	15	.44	8	.347	.482	.435
1994 El Paso	AA	66	230	68	10	2	1	85	38	22	46	1	39	1	0	0		3	7	.30	2	.296	.415	.370
1995 Norwich	AA	57	179	59	16	1	4	89	38	36	51	3	28	4	0	4		5	5	.50	4	.330	.479	.497
6 Min. YEARS		535	1847	562	98	14	13	727	368	212	437	14	254	16	7	19		82	54	.60	40	.304	.438	.394

Ernest Riles

Bats: Left Throws: Right Pos: DH   Ht: 6' 1" Wt: 180 Born: 10/2/60 Age: 35

					BATTING													BASERUNNING				PERCENTAGES		
Year Team	Lg	G	AB	H	2B	3B	HR	TB	R	RBI	TBB	IBB	SO	HBP	SH	SF		SB	CS	SB%	GDP	Avg	OBP	SLG
1984 Vancouver	AAA	123	424	113	19	7	3	155	59	54	67	8	67	1	1	8		1	2	.33	15	.267	.362	.366
1985 Vancouver	AAA	30	118	41	7	1	2	56	19	20	17	4	13	1	0	2		2	2	.50	1	.347	.428	.475
1987 El Paso	AA	41	153	52	10	0	6	80	45	24	28	1	24	0	0	2		1	1	.50	4	.340	.437	.523
1992 Tucson	AAA	60	202	62	17	3	1	88	37	35	30	4	33	0	1	4		2	1	.67	5	.307	.390	.436
1993 Pawtucket	AAA	6	18	5	0	0	2	11	4	6	3	0	0	0	0	2		0	0	.00	1	.278	.348	.611
1994 Vancouver	AAA	99	326	101	20	9	14	181	54	58	47	2	68	0	1	2		2	3	.40	2	.310	.395	.555
1995 Buffalo	AAA	6	18	5	0	0	1	8	5	7	3	0	1	1	0	1		0	0	.00	2	.278	.391	.444
1985 Milwaukee	AL	116	448	128	12	7	5	169	54	45	36	0	54	2	6	3		2	2	.50	16	.286	.339	.377
1986 Milwaukee	AL	145	524	132	24	2	9	187	69	47	54	0	80	1	6	3		7	7	.50	14	.252	.321	.357
1987 Milwaukee	AL	83	276	72	11	1	4	97	38	38	30	1	47	1	4	3		3	4	.43	6	.261	.329	.351
1988 Milwaukee	AL	41	127	32	6	1	1	43	7	9	7	0	26	0	1	0		2	2	.50	3	.252	.291	.339
San Francisco	NL	79	187	55	7	2	3	75	26	28	10	2	33	0	0	4		1	2	.33	5	.294	.323	.401
1989 San Francisco	NL	122	302	84	13	2	7	122	43	40	28	3	50	2	1	4		0	6	.00	7	.278	.339	.404
1990 San Francisco	NL	92	155	31	2	1	8	59	22	21	26	3	26	0	2	1		0	0	.00	2	.200	.313	.381
1991 Oakland	AL	108	281	60	8	4	5	91	30	32	31	3	42	1	4	4		3	2	.60	8	.214	.290	.324
1992 Houston	NL	39	61	16	1	0	1	20	5	4	2	0	11	0	0	1		1	0	1.00	4	.262	.281	.328
1993 Boston	AL	94	143	27	8	0	5	50	15	20	20	3	40	2	2	3		1	3	.25	3	.189	.292	.350
7 Min. YEARS		365	1259	379	73	20	29	579	223	204	195	19	206	3	3	21		8	9	.47	30	.301	.390	.460
9 Maj. YEARS		919	2504	637	92	20	48	913	309	284	244	15	409	9	25	29		20	28	.42	64	.254	.319	.365

Ed Riley

Pitches: Left Bats: Left Pos: P   Ht: 6'2" Wt: 195 Born: 2/10/70 Age: 26

			HOW MUCH HE PITCHED						WHAT HE GAVE UP								THE RESULTS					
Year Team	Lg	G	GS	CG	GF	IP	BFP	H	R	ER	HR	SH	SF	HB	TBB	IBB	SO	WP	Bk	W	L	Pct.	ShO	Sv	ERA
1988 R.S./marnrs	R	9	6	2	2	44.1	199	39	29	20	3	2	1	2	34	0	41	2	3	1	4	.200	0	1	4.06
1989 New Britain	AA	1	1	0	0	4.1	19	4	4	4	1	0	0	0	2	0	1	0	0	0	1	.000	0	0	8.31
Elmira	A	17	15	2	0	92	404	81	42	32	2	5	3	2	50	0	102	3	1	4	6	.400	1	0	3.13
1990 Winter Havn	A	31	24	0	4	159	682	152	79	55	5	6	3	1	64	0	107	5	9	4	9	.308	0	0	3.11
1991 Lynchburg	A	27	27	2	0	163	685	169	80	64	11	3	9	6	56	0	122	7	0	8	10	.444	1	0	3.53
1992 Pawtucket	AAA	1	1	0	0	6	25	7	3	3	1	0	0	0	1	0	4	0	0	0	0	.000	0	0	4.50
New Britain	AA	19	19	1	0	121	489	108	38	33	7	0	2	2	38	1	63	1	4	10	8	.556	1	0	2.45
1993 New Britain	AA	14	14	1	0	83.2	356	85	39	33	5	6	4	0	29	0	50	1	3	6	4	.600	0	0	3.55
Pawtucket	AAA	14	13	2	0	70	321	90	45	39	8	3	2	1	23	0	45	6	1	4	4	.500	0	0	5.01
1994 New Britain	AA	57	5	0	16	76	328	74	48	39	7	0	4	1	34	3	70	3	0	2	4	.333	0	2	4.62
1995 Trenton	AA	16	0	0	7	16.1	74	14	6	5	1	0	2	4	9	1	10	0	0	0	0	.000	0	0	2.76
8 Min. YEARS		206	125	10	29	835.2	3582	823	413	327	51	25	30	19	340	5	615	28	21	37	52	.416	2	4	3.52

Marquis Riley

Bats: Right Throws: Right Pos: OF   Ht: 5'10" Wt: 170 Born: 12/27/70 Age: 25

					BATTING													BASERUNNING				PERCENTAGES		
Year Team	Lg	G	AB	H	2B	3B	HR	TB	R	RBI	TBB	IBB	SO	HBP	SH	SF		SB	CS	SB%	GDP	Avg	OBP	SLG
1992 Boise	A	52	201	48	12	1	0	62	47	12	37	0	29	2	2	0		7	4	.64	3	.239	.363	.308
1993 Palm Spring	A	130	508	134	10	2	1	151	93	42	90	1	117	0	5	2		69	25	.73	3	.264	.373	.297
1994 Midland	AA	93	374	107	12	4	1	130	68	29	35	3	57	6	1	4		32	5	.86	10	.286	.353	.348
Vancouver	AAA	4	14	3	0	0	0	3	3	1	3	0	3	0	0	0		1	0	1.00	1	.214	.353	.214

252

Year	Team	Lg	G	AB	H	2B	3B	HR	TB	R	RBI	TBB	IBB	SO	HBP	SH	SF	SB	CS	SB%	GDP	Avg	OBP	SLG
1995	Vancouver	AAA	120	477	125	6	6	0	143	70	43	49	3	69	1	2	4	29	10	.74	11	.262	.330	.300
	4 Min. YEARS		399	1574	417	40	13	2	489	281	127	214	7	275	9	16	10	138	44	.76	28	.265	.354	.311

Eduardo Rios

Bats: Right **Throws:** Right **Pos:** 2B   **Ht:** 5'10" **Wt:** 160 **Born:** 10/13/72 **Age:** 23

						BATTING												BASERUNNING				PERCENTAGES		
Year	Team	Lg	G	AB	H	2B	3B	HR	TB	R	RBI	TBB	IBB	SO	HBP	SH	SF	SB	CS	SB%	GDP	Avg	OBP	SLG
1993	Great Falls	R	26	107	29	4	3	2	45	18	12	10	1	11	1	0	1	2	4	.33	1	.271	.336	.421
	Bakersfield	A	29	113	32	4	0	7	57	19	17	8	0	17	2	2	0	2	3	.40	1	.283	.341	.504
1994	Vero Beach	A	133	529	139	28	8	13	222	70	79	24	1	85	8	3	6	2	5	.29	15	.263	.302	.420
1995	San Antonio	AA	98	365	104	22	4	5	149	43	53	20	2	47	1	1	5	2	4	.33	8	.285	.320	.408
	3 Min. YEARS		286	1114	304	58	15	27	473	150	161	62	4	160	12	5	12	8	16	.33	25	.273	.315	.425

Brad Ripplemeyer

Bats: Right **Throws:** Right **Pos:** C   **Ht:** 6'2" **Wt:** 190 **Born:** 2/6/70 **Age:** 26

						BATTING												BASERUNNING				PERCENTAGES		
Year	Team	Lg	G	AB	H	2B	3B	HR	TB	R	RBI	TBB	IBB	SO	HBP	SH	SF	SB	CS	SB%	GDP	Avg	OBP	SLG
1991	Idaho Falls	R	37	120	43	12	2	5	74	28	22	24	1	29	3	2	0	1	2	.33	4	.358	.476	.617
1992	Durham	A	115	392	89	16	1	19	164	38	48	25	1	134	4	6	6	2	5	.29	2	.227	.276	.418
1993	Greenville	AA	95	277	53	14	0	4	79	25	27	31	4	74	6	3	3	0	2	.00	8	.191	.284	.285
1994	Durham	A	62	200	44	10	1	3	65	23	14	28	0	59	3	1	0	1	2	.33	6	.220	.325	.325
1995	Greenville	AA	53	165	30	8	0	2	44	8	16	11	0	54	0	5	2	1	0	1.00	5	.182	.230	.267
	5 Min. YEARS		362	1154	259	60	4	33	426	122	127	119	6	350	16	17	11	5	11	.31	25	.224	.303	.369

Greg Ritchie

Bats: Left **Throws:** Left **Pos:** OF   **Ht:** 6'0" **Wt:** 180 **Born:** 1/25/64 **Age:** 32

						BATTING												BASERUNNING				PERCENTAGES		
Year	Team	Lg	G	AB	H	2B	3B	HR	TB	R	RBI	TBB	IBB	SO	HBP	SH	SF	SB	CS	SB%	GDP	Avg	OBP	SLG
1986	Everett	A	40	100	25	3	1	0	30	36	11	47	0	3	0	0	3	18	2	.90	1	.250	.480	.300
1987	Clinton	A	124	416	140	19	11	4	193	102	49	90	8	80	3	5	3	41	21	.66	2	.337	.455	.464
1988	San Jose	A	131	507	145	29	5	6	202	118	65	116	0	119	3	1	7	40	17	.70	4	.286	.417	.398
1989	Shreveport	AA	97	332	79	14	4	0	101	53	35	46	0	61	1	7	7	30	7	.81	3	.238	.326	.304
1990	Phoenix	AAA	105	342	81	13	10	1	117	53	28	50	1	74	1	1	1	23	9	.72	1	.237	.335	.342
1991	Phoenix	AAA	67	157	45	8	0	0	53	23	16	19	2	29	0	0	2	13	4	.76	2	.287	.360	.338
1992	Phoenix	AAA	92	183	49	5	2	1	61	25	13	43	1	34	0	4	2	11	5	.69	3	.268	.404	.333
1995	Okla. City	AAA	9	28	5	0	0	1	8	5	4	6	1	4	0	0	0	1	0	1.00	0	.179	.324	.286
	8 Min. YEARS		665	2065	569	91	33	13	765	415	221	417	13	429	8	18	25	177	65	.73	16	.276	.395	.370

Todd Ritchie

Pitches: Right **Bats:** Right **Pos:** P   **Ht:** 6'3" **Wt:** 185 **Born:** 11/7/71 **Age:** 24

						HOW MUCH HE PITCHED				WHAT HE GAVE UP										THE RESULTS			
Year	Team	Lg	G	GS	CG	GF	IP	BFP	H	R	ER	HR	SH	SF	HB	TBB	IBB	SO	WP	Bk	W	L	Pct.	ShO	Sv	ERA
1990	Elizabethtn	R	11	11	1	0	65	261	45	22	14	5	2	2	6	24	0	49	2	3	5	2	.714	0	0	1.94
1991	Kenosha	A	21	21	0	0	116.2	498	113	53	46	3	4	1	7	50	0	101	10	1	7	6	.538	0	0	3.55
1992	Visalia	A	28	28	3	0	172.2	763	193	113	97	13	6	6	7	65	2	129	16	1	11	9	.550	1	0	5.06
1993	Nashville	AA	12	10	0	0	46.2	194	46	21	19	2	1	1	0	15	0	41	5	1	3	2	.600	0	0	3.66
1994	Nashville	AA	4	4	0	0	17	74	24	10	8	1	1	0	0	7	0	9	2	0	0	2	.000	0	0	4.24
1995	New Britain	AA	24	21	0	0	113	515	135	78	72	12	4	5	6	54	0	60	8	0	4	9	.308	0	0	5.73
	6 Min. YEARS		100	95	4	0	531	2305	556	297	256	36	18	15	26	215	2	389	43	6	30	30	.500	1	0	4.34

Lino Rivera

Pitches: Right **Bats:** Right **Pos:** P   **Ht:** 5'11" **Wt:** 173 **Born:** 12/2/66 **Age:** 29

						HOW MUCH HE PITCHED				WHAT HE GAVE UP										THE RESULTS			
Year	Team	Lg	G	GS	CG	GF	IP	BFP	H	R	ER	HR	SH	SF	HB	TBB	IBB	SO	WP	Bk	W	L	Pct.	ShO	Sv	ERA
1985	Rangers	R	16	0	0	8	34.2	153	30	18	11	2	1	1	2	17	0	30	2	2	0	1	.000	0	0	2.86
1986	Daytona Bch	A	1	0	0	0	2	13	6	6	6	0	0	0	0	2	0	2	0	0	0	0	.000	0	0	27.00
	Rangers	R	16	7	0	0	50.2	212	46	19	13	0	0	1	2	17	1	29	2	0	3	2	.600	0	0	2.31
1987	Gastonia	A	51	2	0	22	103.2	431	92	41	31	4	3	4	0	38	3	93	11	3	1	5	.167	0	5	2.69
1988	Charlotte	A	25	9	0	4	83.1	355	90	40	34	6	1	5	2	20	2	52	2	2	2	1	.667	0	2	3.67
1989	Fayetteville	A	38	0	0	33	56.2	250	57	28	18	1	5	1	5	24	0	50	4	1	4	1	.800	0	19	2.86
	Lakeland	A	13	0	0	8	19.2	79	10	3	0	0	0	0	0	9	1	13	0	0	3	0	1.000	0	1	0.00
1990	Lakeland	A	36	0	0	33	44	176	31	3	2	1	1	0	3	12	0	38	2	1	1	0	1.000	0	14	0.41
	Toledo	AAA	18	0	0	11	29.1	128	27	12	10	1	0	2	2	13	1	23	1	0	0	3	.000	0	1	3.07
1991	Lakeland	A	14	0	0	12	16	73	18	7	6	0	1	0	2	5	0	17	2	0	2	1	.667	0	3	3.38
	London	AA	17	0	0	6	26.2	114	25	13	11	5	2	0	2	11	0	19	1	1	2	2	.500	0	0	3.71
1992	Arkansas	AA	2	0	0	1	1.1	9	2	3	3	0	0	0	0	3	2	1	0	0	1	0	1.000	0	0	20.25
1995	Carolina	AA	4	0	0	1	6	31	10	6	4	0	0	0	0	3	0	4	0	0	0	0	.000	0	0	6.00
	9 Min. YEARS		251	18	0	139	474	2024	444	199	149	20	14	14	20	174	10	369	29	10	19	16	.543	0	45	2.83

Luis Rivera

Bats: Right **Throws:** Right **Pos:** SS   **Ht:** 5'10" **Wt:** 175 **Born:** 1/3/64 **Age:** 32

						BATTING												BASERUNNING				PERCENTAGES		
Year	Team	Lg	G	AB	H	2B	3B	HR	TB	R	RBI	TBB	IBB	SO	HBP	SH	SF	SB	CS	SB%	GDP	Avg	OBP	SLG
1984	W. Palm Bch	A	124	439	100	23	0	6	141	54	43	50	5	79	5	0	3	14	2	.88	16	.228	.312	.321

Year	Team	Lg	G	AB	H	2B	3B	HR	TB	R	RBI	TBB	IBB	SO	HBP	SH	SF	SB	CS	SB%	GDP	Avg	OBP	SLG
1985	Jacksonvlle	AA	138	538	129	20	2	16	201	74	72	44	1	69	7	3	6	18	15	.55	7	.240	.303	.374
1986	Indianapols	AAA	108	407	100	17	5	7	148	60	43	29	0	68	4	1	6	18	8	.69	12	.246	.298	.364
1987	Indianapols	AAA	108	433	135	26	3	8	191	73	53	32	2	73	2	3	3	24	11	.69	4	.312	.360	.441
1989	Pawtucket	AAA	43	175	44	9	0	1	56	22	13	11	0	23	1	4	0	5	3	.63	3	.251	.299	.320
1995	Okla. City	AAA	19	58	8	4	0	1	15	3	3	1	0	6	1	0	0	0	0	.00	1	.138	.167	.259
1986	Montreal	NL	55	166	34	11	1	0	47	20	13	17	0	33	2	1	1	1	1	.50	1	.205	.285	.283
1987	Montreal	NL	18	32	5	2	0	0	7	0	1	1	0	8	0	0	0	0	0	.00	0	.156	.182	.219
1988	Montreal	NL	123	371	83	17	3	4	118	35	30	24	4	69	1	3	3	3	4	.43	9	.224	.271	.318
1989	Boston	AL	93	323	83	17	1	5	117	35	29	20	1	60	1	4	1	2	3	.40	7	.257	.301	.362
1990	Boston	AL	118	346	78	20	0	7	119	38	45	25	0	58	1	12	1	4	3	.57	10	.225	.279	.344
1991	Boston	AL	129	414	107	22	3	8	159	64	40	35	0	86	3	12	4	4	4	.50	10	.258	.318	.384
1992	Boston	AL	102	288	62	11	1	0	75	17	29	26	0	56	3	5	0	4	3	.57	5	.215	.287	.260
1993	Boston	AL	62	130	27	8	1	1	40	13	7	11	0	36	1	2	1	1	2	.33	2	.208	.273	.308
1994	New York	NL	32	43	12	2	1	3	25	11	5	4	0	14	2	0	0	0	1	.00	1	.279	.367	.581
	6 Min. YEARS		540	2050	516	99	10	39	752	286	227	167	8	318	20	11	18	79	39	.67	43	.252	.312	.367
	9 Maj. YEARS		732	2113	491	110	11	28	707	233	199	163	5	420	14	39	11	19	21	.48	45	.232	.290	.335

Hector Roa

Bats: Both **Throws:** Right **Pos:** 3B   **Ht:** 5'11" **Wt:** 170 **Born:** 6/11/69 **Age:** 27

			BATTING															BASERUNNING				PERCENTAGES		
Year	Team	Lg	G	AB	H	2B	3B	HR	TB	R	RBI	TBB	IBB	SO	HBP	SH	SF	SB	CS	SB%	GDP	Avg	OBP	SLG
1990	Pulaski	R	21	92	32	3	2	3	48	23	14	5	1	17	1	1	0	6	0	1.00	2	.348	.388	.522
	Sumter	A	24	92	20	4	1	0	26	5	7	4	1	12	0	1	0	1	1	.50	3	.217	.250	.283
	Braves	R	13	43	9	1	0	1	13	7	2	5	1	5	1	3	0	4	0	1.00	2	.209	.306	.302
1991	Miami	A	87	280	57	3	5	1	73	32	18	15	1	51	3	3	1	17	9	.65	7	.204	.251	.261
	Macon	A	33	121	37	10	0	2	53	17	16	9	0	22	1	4	2	2	1	.67	1	.306	.353	.438
1992	Durham	A	110	377	105	27	7	8	170	52	46	16	2	55	2	6	2	14	4	.78	4	.279	.310	.451
	Greenville	AA	2	9	3	0	0	0	3	1	2	0	0	3	0	0	0	0	0	.00	0	.333	.333	.333
1993	Greenville	AA	123	447	110	28	4	6	164	50	58	24	0	72	8	2	2	6	7	.46	11	.246	.295	.367
1994	Durham	A	33	125	33	7	0	4	52	15	16	6	0	18	2	0	1	2	3	.40	3	.264	.306	.416
	Greenville	AA	40	146	39	6	1	5	62	17	22	3	0	24	2	1	4	2	4	.33	1	.267	.284	.425
1995	Richmond	AAA	40	120	31	5	0	2	42	15	7	3	1	23	1	1	1	0	1	.00	4	.258	.280	.350
	6 Min. YEARS		526	1852	476	94	20	32	706	234	208	90	7	302	21	22	13	54	30	.64	38	.257	.297	.381

Brett Roberts

Pitches: Right **Bats:** Right **Pos:** P   **Ht:** 6'7" **Wt:** 225 **Born:** 3/24/70 **Age:** 26

			HOW MUCH HE PITCHED						WHAT HE GAVE UP										THE RESULTS					
Year	Team	Lg	G	GS	CG	GF	IP	BFP	H	R	ER	HR	SH	SF	HB	TBB	IBB	SO	WP	Bk	W	L	Pct.	ShO	Sv	ERA
1991	Elizabethtn	R	6	6	1	0	28	112	21	8	7	0	0	0	0	10	0	27	2	4	3	0	1.000	0	0	2.25
1992	Kenosha	A	7	6	0	1	22.2	105	23	18	14	4	1	0	0	15	0	23	1	0	1	1	.500	0	0	5.56
1993	Fort Myers	A	28	28	3	0	173.2	772	184	93	84	5	5	5	4	86	5	108	10	2	9	16	.360	0	0	4.35
1994	Fort Myers	A	21	21	1	0	116.2	520	123	71	56	5	4	8	3	47	3	75	8	0	6	7	.462	0	0	4.32
	Nashville	AA	5	5	0	0	20	102	30	18	15	1	0	1	1	12	1	11	0	0	2	1	.667	0	0	6.75
1995	New Britain	AA	28	28	5	0	174	729	162	72	66	9	4	5	5	50	0	135	6	0	11	9	.550	1	0	3.41
	5 Min. YEARS		95	94	10	1	535	2340	543	280	242	24	14	19	13	220	9	379	27	6	32	34	.485	1	0	4.07

Chris Roberts

Pitches: Left **Bats:** Right **Pos:** P   **Ht:** 5'10" **Wt:** 185 **Born:** 6/25/71 **Age:** 25

			HOW MUCH HE PITCHED						WHAT HE GAVE UP										THE RESULTS					
Year	Team	Lg	G	GS	CG	GF	IP	BFP	H	R	ER	HR	SH	SF	HB	TBB	IBB	SO	WP	Bk	W	L	Pct.	ShO	Sv	ERA
1993	St. Lucie	A	25	25	3	0	173.1	703	162	64	53	3	2	4	7	36	0	111	2	1	13	5	.722	2	0	2.75
1994	Binghamton	AA	27	27	2	0	175.1	751	164	77	64	11	8	5	6	77	1	128	12	1	13	8	.619	2	0	3.29
1995	Norfolk	AAA	25	25	2	0	150	676	197	99	92	24	6	4	8	58	0	88	5	0	7	13	.350	0	0	5.52
	3 Min. YEARS		77	77	7	0	498.2	2130	523	240	209	38	16	13	21	171	1	327	19	2	33	26	.559	4	0	3.77

Lonell Roberts

Bats: Both **Throws:** Right **Pos:** OF   **Ht:** 6'0" **Wt:** 172 **Born:** 6/7/71 **Age:** 25

			BATTING															BASERUNNING				PERCENTAGES		
Year	Team	Lg	G	AB	H	2B	3B	HR	TB	R	RBI	TBB	IBB	SO	HBP	SH	SF	SB	CS	SB%	GDP	Avg	OBP	SLG
1989	Medicne Hat	R	29	78	11	1	0	0	12	2	6	7	0	27	1	1	0	3	3	.50	1	.141	.221	.154
1990	Medicne Hat	R	38	118	25	2	0	0	27	14	8	5	0	29	0	0	0	8	1	.89	3	.212	.244	.229
1991	Myrtle Bch	A	110	388	86	7	2	2	103	39	27	27	1	84	2	10	2	35	14	.71	0	.222	.274	.265
1992	St. Cathrns	A	62	244	50	3	1	0	55	37	11	19	1	75	3	4	0	33	13	.72	0	.205	.271	.225
	Knoxville	AA	5	14	0	0	0	0	0	1	0	1	0	4	0	0	0	1	0	1.00	0	.000	.067	.000
1993	Hagerstown	A	131	501	120	21	4	3	158	78	46	53	1	103	4	2	3	54	15	.78	8	.240	.316	.315
1994	Dunedin	A	118	490	132	18	3	3	165	74	31	32	3	104	3	2	4	61	12	.84	4	.269	.316	.337
1995	Knoxville	AA	116	454	107	12	3	1	128	66	29	27	1	97	3	4	4	57	18	.76	7	.236	.281	.282
	7 Min. YEARS		609	2287	531	64	13	9	648	311	158	171	7	523	16	23	13	252	76	.77	23	.232	.289	.283

Jason Robertson

Bats: Left **Throws:** Left **Pos:** OF   **Ht:** 6'2" **Wt:** 200 **Born:** 3/24/71 **Age:** 25

			BATTING															BASERUNNING				PERCENTAGES		
Year	Team	Lg	G	AB	H	2B	3B	HR	TB	R	RBI	TBB	IBB	SO	HBP	SH	SF	SB	CS	SB%	GDP	Avg	OBP	SLG
1989	Yankees	R	58	214	61	12	5	0	83	27	31	28	0	28	0	0	4	4	4	.50	2	.285	.362	.388
1990	Greensboro	A	133	496	125	22	5	6	175	71	44	67	2	110	2	4	1	21	13	.62	8	.252	.343	.353

1991	Pr. William	A	131	515	136	21	6	3	178	67	54	53	2	138	2	1	4	32	9	.78	8	.264	.333	.346
1992	Pr. William	A	68	254	61	6	4	5	90	34	34	31	0	55	1	1	3	14	6	.70	7	.240	.322	.354
	Albany-Colo	AA	55	204	44	12	1	3	67	18	33	10	0	44	2	2	2	9	3	.75	5	.216	.257	.328
1993	Albany-Colo	AA	130	483	110	29	4	6	165	65	41	43	3	126	4	3	2	35	12	.74	7	.228	.295	.342
1994	Albany-Colo	AA	124	432	94	10	7	11	151	54	53	50	3	120	3	5	4	20	10	.67	9	.218	.301	.350
1995	Norwich	AA	117	456	126	29	10	6	193	60	54	41	3	106	1	4	5	19	12	.61	5	.276	.334	.423
	7 Min. YEARS		816	3054	757	141	42	40	1102	396	344	323	13	727	15	20	25	154	69	.69	48	.248	.320	.361

Mike Robertson

Bats: Left **Throws:** Left **Pos:** 1B   **Ht:** 6'0" **Wt:** 180 **Born:** 10/9/70 **Age:** 25

			BATTING															BASERUNNING				PERCENTAGES		
Year	Team	Lg	G	AB	H	2B	3B	HR	TB	R	RBI	TBB	IBB	SO	HBP	SH	SF	SB	CS	SB%	GDP	Avg	OBP	SLG
1991	Utica	A	13	54	9	2	1	0	13	6	8	5	0	10	0	0	0	2	1	.67	0	.167	.237	.241
	South Bend	A	54	210	66	16	2	1	92	30	26	18	3	24	3	3	3	7	6	.54	5	.329	.385	.438
1992	Sarasota	A	106	395	99	21	3	10	156	50	59	50	3	55	7	1	3	5	7	.42	8	.251	.343	.395
	Birmingham	AA	27	90	17	8	1	1	30	6	9	10	1	19	0	1	1	0	1	.00	2	.189	.267	.333
1993	Birmingham	AA	138	511	138	31	3	11	208	73	73	59	4	97	3	0	8	10	5	.67	10	.270	.344	.407
1994	Birmingham	AA	53	196	62	20	2	3	95	32	30	31	4	34	2	0	2	6	3	.67	5	.316	.411	.485
	Nashville	AAA	67	213	48	8	1	8	82	21	21	15	4	27	3	0	0	0	3	.00	4	.225	.286	.385
1995	Nashville	AAA	139	499	124	17	4	19	206	55	52	50	7	72	11	3	2	2	4	.33	8	.248	.329	.413
	5 Min. YEARS		597	2168	566	123	17	53	882	273	278	238	26	338	29	8	19	32	30	.52	42	.261	.339	.407

Rod Robertson

Bats: Both **Throws:** Right **Pos:** OF   **Ht:** 5'9" **Wt:** 175 **Born:** 1/16/68 **Age:** 28

			BATTING															BASERUNNING				PERCENTAGES		
Year	Team	Lg	G	AB	H	2B	3B	HR	TB	R	RBI	TBB	IBB	SO	HBP	SH	SF	SB	CS	SB%	GDP	Avg	OBP	SLG
1986	Bend	A	65	248	60	5	2	1	72	40	25	28	0	51	4	5	0	18	7	.72	3	.242	.329	.290
1987	Spartanburg	A	92	300	63	10	3	1	82	39	20	12	2	65	6	5	1	14	4	.78	4	.210	.254	.273
1988	Spartanburg	A	124	430	104	12	1	8	142	54	39	13	0	83	9	5	2	29	14	.67	7	.242	.278	.330
1989	Clearwater	A	118	385	102	14	1	4	130	49	32	26	1	51	4	10	5	24	10	.71	8	.265	.314	.338
1990	Reading	AA	51	189	39	3	0	1	45	16	12	6	0	26	3	2	2	7	9	.44	2	.206	.240	.238
	Clearwater	A	58	204	44	7	1	2	59	17	21	18	1	30	2	5	2	8	3	.73	7	.216	.283	.289
1991	Reading	AA	117	416	102	19	0	9	148	52	51	33	0	74	2	6	4	20	6	.77	9	.245	.301	.356
1992	London	AA	64	243	58	12	0	7	91	26	34	15	0	34	3	4	1	13	5	.72	5	.239	.290	.374
	Toledo	AAA	70	222	46	6	1	5	69	23	22	15	2	41	2	3	2	8	5	.62	2	.207	.261	.311
1993	Toledo	AAA	121	409	96	13	2	12	149	54	48	27	1	77	3	5	4	15	7	.68	5	.235	.284	.364
1994	Orlando	AA	25	87	21	4	2	2	35	14	8	6	0	12	1	1	0	5	3	.63	1	.241	.298	.402
	Iowa	AAA	88	263	66	18	2	12	124	36	36	11	0	44	3	5	1	5	8	.38	4	.251	.288	.471
1995	Rochester	AAA	101	338	94	21	2	15	164	54	58	22	1	63	4	4	2	8	7	.53	6	.278	.328	.485
	10 Min. YEARS		1094	3734	895	144	17	79	1310	474	406	232	8	651	46	60	26	174	88	.66	65	.240	.290	.351

Don Robinson

Bats: Left **Throws:** Right **Pos:** DH   **Ht:** 6'0" **Wt:** 185 **Born:** 1/16/72 **Age:** 24

			BATTING															BASERUNNING				PERCENTAGES		
Year	Team	Lg	G	AB	H	2B	3B	HR	TB	R	RBI	TBB	IBB	SO	HBP	SH	SF	SB	CS	SB%	GDP	Avg	OBP	SLG
1990	Braves	R	41	118	23	3	2	0	30	13	15	13	0	36	1	5	0	5	2	.71	1	.195	.280	.254
1991	Pulaski	R	54	189	54	9	0	3	72	42	23	20	2	44	0	1	0	22	7	.76	1	.286	.354	.381
1992	Macon	A	113	399	98	17	2	1	122	42	41	28	0	118	5	6	3	20	10	.67	9	.246	.301	.306
1993	Durham	A	117	390	89	11	3	10	136	52	47	45	1	112	3	5	3	15	9	.63	10	.228	.311	.349
1994	Greenville	AA	120	358	90	23	2	13	156	49	46	32	5	74	5	2	4	11	10	.52	7	.251	.318	.436
1995	Greenville	AA	13	28	6	1	1	0	9	2	3	4	0	4	0	1	1	1	0	1.00	0	.214	.303	.321
	Long Beach	IND	86	332	96	26	3	7	149	68	61	48	2	52	1	4	3	20	6	.77	6	.289	.378	.449
	6 Min. YEARS		544	1814	456	90	13	34	674	268	236	190	10	440	15	24	14	94	44	.68	34	.251	.325	.372

Scott Robinson

Pitches: Right **Bats:** Right **Pos:** P   **Ht:** 6'2" **Wt:** 200 **Born:** 11/15/68 **Age:** 27

			HOW MUCH HE PITCHED					WHAT HE GAVE UP										THE RESULTS					
Year	Team	Lg	G	GS	CG	GF	IP	BFP	H	R	ER	HR	SH	SF	HB	TBB	IBB	SO	WP	Bk	W	L	Pct.	ShO	Sv	ERA
1990	Billings	R	12	12	0	0	58.2	278	63	53	35	3	0	3	1	35	1	38	7	0	4	3	.571	0	0	5.37
1991	Cedar Rapds	A	20	19	2	0	126.2	537	122	57	53	5	7	4	2	48	3	75	4	0	8	9	.471	1	0	3.77
1992	Charlstn-Wv	A	13	13	6	0	99.1	387	73	28	19	3	2	2	0	25	2	80	1	0	8	2	.800	3	0	1.72
	Chattanooga	AA	13	13	1	0	83	340	82	38	35	7	6	4	2	26	0	51	4	0	7	2	.778	1	0	3.80
1993	Indianapols	AAA	9	9	0	0	47.2	219	55	43	34	14	2	2	1	24	2	29	1	3	2	5	.286	0	0	6.42
	Chattanooga	AA	20	18	0	0	112	480	114	60	44	12	6	4	5	40	1	58	5	0	6	5	.545	0	0	3.54
1994	Phoenix	AAA	47	2	0	9	87.1	388	103	57	48	7	3	6	4	34	4	45	8	1	9	5	.643	0	0	4.95
1995	Phoenix	AAA	31	15	0	9	123.2	519	134	68	64	14	2	3	4	37	1	61	4	0	5	7	.417	0	0	4.66
	6 Min. YEARS		165	101	9	18	738.1	3148	746	404	332	65	28	28	19	269	14	437	34	4	49	38	.563	5	0	4.05

Raul Rodarte

Bats: Right **Throws:** Right **Pos:** 3B   **Ht:** 5'11" **Wt:** 190 **Born:** 4/9/70 **Age:** 26

			BATTING															BASERUNNING				PERCENTAGES		
Year	Team	Lg	G	AB	H	2B	3B	HR	TB	R	RBI	TBB	IBB	SO	HBP	SH	SF	SB	CS	SB%	GDP	Avg	OBP	SLG
1991	Peninsula	A	65	216	48	4	1	0	54	19	14	32	0	56	0	1	2	5	1	.83	5	.222	.320	.250
1992	Peninsula	A	94	290	72	8	6	2	98	37	22	35	2	37	1	3	2	15	10	.60	7	.248	.329	.338
1993	Riverside	A	106	402	116	19	1	5	152	79	48	51	0	66	0	6	2	13	14	.48	7	.289	.367	.378

1994 Jacksonvlle	AA	34	91	22	3	1	3	36	13	13	8	1	15	1	3	0	2	2	.50	2	.242	.310	.396
Riverside	A	39	156	50	6	4	4	76	29	37	15	1	31	2	1	1	5	2	.71	3	.321	.385	.487
1995 Lynchburg	A	104	346	99	18	2	12	157	57	48	35	2	49	4	2	1	19	13	.59	8	.286	.358	.454
Carolina	AA	16	54	20	5	1	0	27	8	11	10	3	14	0	2	0	2	2	.50	2	.370	.469	.500
5 Min. YEARS		458	1555	427	63	16	26	600	242	193	186	9	268	8	18	8	61	44	.58	34	.275	.353	.386

Boi Rodriguez

Bats: Left **Throws:** Right **Pos:** 1B   **Ht:** 6'0" **Wt:** 180 **Born:** 4/14/66 **Age:** 30

Year Team	Lg	BATTING															BASERUNNING				PERCENTAGES		
		G	AB	H	2B	3B	HR	TB	R	RBI	TBB	IBB	SO	HBP	SH	SF	SB	CS	SB%	GDP	Avg	OBP	SLG
1987 Jamestown	A	77	274	77	9	5	15	141	51	65	37	5	58	3	0	7	14	8	.64	2	.281	.364	.515
1988 W. Palm Bch	A	121	425	103	22	8	8	165	56	54	59	2	61	2	0	3	6	5	.55	6	.242	.335	.388
1989 Jacksonvlle	AA	130	388	96	19	6	9	154	53	50	53	3	58	2	1	5	6	3	.67	3	.247	.337	.397
1990 Jacksonvlle	AA	105	367	104	22	5	9	163	50	58	45	0	80	2	7	7	2	0	1.00	8	.283	.359	.444
1991 Greenville	AA	29	92	26	10	1	1	41	14	14	15	3	16	0	2	3	0	1	.00	2	.283	.373	.446
Richmond	AAA	105	392	110	25	1	8	161	50	49	34	5	100	2	2	5	1	3	.25	4	.281	.337	.411
1992 Richmond	AAA	93	278	77	8	3	16	139	40	40	32	5	61	1	0	0	0	0	.00	4	.277	.354	.500
1993 Richmond	AAA	88	236	63	13	1	10	108	34	22	26	3	55	1	0	0	4	1	.80	5	.267	.342	.458
1995 Calgary	AAA	11	39	10	2	0	2	18	10	10	3	1	5	0	0	0	1	0	1.00	0	.256	.310	.462
8 Min. YEARS		759	2491	666	130	30	78	1090	358	362	304	27	494	13	12	30	34	21	.62	34	.267	.346	.438

Frank Rodriguez

Pitches: Right **Bats:** Right **Pos:** P   **Ht:** 5'9" **Wt:** 160 **Born:** 1/6/73 **Age:** 23

Year Team	Lg	HOW MUCH HE PITCHED						WHAT HE GAVE UP									THE RESULTS					
		G	GS	CG	GF	IP	BFP	H	R	ER	HR	SH	SF	HB	TBB	IBB	SO	WP	Bk	W	L	Pct.	ShO	Sv	ERA
1992 Brewers	R	9	7	0	0	49	193	35	9	6	1	0	1	1	14	0	37	1	0	3	1	.750	0	0	1.10
Helena	R	6	1	0	2	10.2	46	14	6	3	1	0	0	1	3	0	3	3	0	1	1	.500	0	0	2.53
1993 Helena	R	18	1	0	9	41	176	31	19	11	0	2	0	1	17	3	63	8	1	2	1	.667	0	5	2.41
1994 Stockton	A	26	24	3	0	151	627	139	67	57	6	6	9	13	52	1	124	6	0	10	9	.526	1	0	3.40
1995 El Paso	AA	28	27	1	1	142.2	650	157	90	79	9	9	9	5	80	2	129	16	1	9	8	.529	0	0	4.98
4 Min. YEARS		87	60	4	12	394.1	1692	376	191	156	17	17	19	21	166	6	356	34	2	25	20	.556	1	5	3.56

Nerio Rodriguez

Bats: Right **Throws:** Right **Pos:** C   **Ht:** 6'0" **Wt:** 180 **Born:** 3/22/73 **Age:** 23

Year Team	Lg	BATTING															BASERUNNING				PERCENTAGES		
		G	AB	H	2B	3B	HR	TB	R	RBI	TBB	IBB	SO	HBP	SH	SF	SB	CS	SB%	GDP	Avg	OBP	SLG
1991 White Sox	R	26	89	20	1	0	0	21	4	8	2	0	24	0	0	0	3	2	.60	2	.225	.242	.236
1992 White Sox	R	41	122	33	8	1	2	49	18	13	10	0	31	1	1	3	1	5	.17	0	.270	.324	.402
1993 Hickory	A	82	262	54	9	2	4	79	31	32	27	0	70	3	0	2	4	0	1.00	5	.206	.286	.302
1994 South Bend	A	18	59	13	4	0	0	17	4	8	2	0	14	2	0	3	0	2	.00	1	.220	.258	.288
Pr. William	A	6	19	4	1	1	0	7	2	1	1	0	9	0	0	0	0	1	.00	0	.211	.250	.368
1995 Bowie	AA	3	4	0	0	0	0	0	0	0	2	0	2	0	0	0	0	0	.00	0	.000	.333	.000
High Desert	A	58	144	34	7	0	4	53	20	12	18	0	50	1	2	1	5	3	.63	0	.236	.323	.368
5 Min. YEARS		234	699	158	30	4	10	226	79	74	62	0	200	7	3	9	13	13	.50	8	.226	.292	.323

Tony Rodriguez

Bats: Right **Throws:** Right **Pos:** 3B   **Ht:** 5'11" **Wt:** 165 **Born:** 8/15/70 **Age:** 25

Year Team	Lg	BATTING															BASERUNNING				PERCENTAGES		
		G	AB	H	2B	3B	HR	TB	R	RBI	TBB	IBB	SO	HBP	SH	SF	SB	CS	SB%	GDP	Avg	OBP	SLG
1991 Elmira	A	77	272	70	10	2	1	87	48	23	32	0	45	3	2	4	29	4	.88	6	.257	.338	.320
1992 Lynchburg	A	128	516	115	14	4	1	140	59	27	25	0	84	3	7	3	11	6	.65	11	.223	.261	.271
1993 New Britain	AA	99	355	81	16	4	0	105	37	31	16	0	52	4	4	5	7	7	.50	8	.228	.266	.296
1994 Sarasota	A	15	49	11	0	0	0	11	4	5	4	0	9	0	2	0	1	0	1.00	3	.224	.283	.224
New Britain	AA	6	20	3	0	1	0	5	1	0	0	0	7	0	0	0	0	0	.00	1	.150	.150	.250
Pawtucket	AAA	64	169	43	4	1	4	61	16	18	5	0	22	0	7	2	3	3	.50	9	.254	.273	.361
1995 Pawtucket	AAA	96	317	85	15	2	0	104	37	21	15	0	39	6	11	4	11	5	.69	8	.268	.310	.328
5 Min. YEARS		485	1698	408	59	14	6	513	202	125	97	0	258	16	33	18	62	25	.71	46	.240	.285	.302

Vic Rodriguez

Bats: Right **Throws:** Right **Pos:** 3B   **Ht:** 5'11" **Wt:** 173 **Born:** 7/14/61 **Age:** 34

Year Team	Lg	BATTING															BASERUNNING				PERCENTAGES		
		G	AB	H	2B	3B	HR	TB	R	RBI	TBB	IBB	SO	HBP	SH	SF	SB	CS	SB%	GDP	Avg	OBP	SLG
1977 Bluefield	R	53	188	55	10	4	3	82	28	23	7	0	30	0	8	1	2	1	.67	7	.293	.316	.436
1978 Bluefield	R	59	209	67	4	2	2	81	26	28	8	0	23	0	1	4	0	0	.00	7	.321	.339	.388
1979 Miami	A	67	228	70	10	2	1	87	23	31	18	2	19	2	3	1	2	0	1.00	6	.307	.361	.382
1980 Alexandria	A	33	130	39	4	2	2	53	20	15	13	0	17	2	0	1	5	0	1.00	3	.300	.370	.408
Charlotte	AA	19	65	15	0	0	0	15	4	4	3	1	6	0	3	0	1	0	1.00	2	.231	.265	.231
Miami	A	49	184	60	10	2	2	80	21	21	18	1	16	0	1	3	1	2	.33	8	.326	.380	.435
1981 Charlotte	AA	138	553	169	22	1	9	220	68	65	37	0	51	1	7	3	5	4	.56	13	.306	.348	.398
1982 Charlotte	AA	47	165	48	13	0	3	70	17	18	14	2	14	1	1	2	0	1	.00	6	.291	.346	.424
Rochester	AAA	87	300	74	10	2	0	88	26	18	11	0	31	0	7	1	3	3	.50	11	.247	.272	.293
1983 Charlotte	AA	140	571	170	26	1	14	240	80	77	26	1	44	0	7	3	2	5	.29	21	.298	.327	.420
1984 Rochester	AAA	132	478	131	22	6	6	183	54	46	32	0	53	3	7	4	0	1	.00	23	.274	.321	.383
1985 Las Vegas	AAA	127	462	144	31	3	11	214	56	58	20	4	41	1	9	4	0	2	.00	10	.312	.339	.463
1986 Louisville	AAA	56	191	52	9	0	1	64	13	18	10	0	22	0	1	0	0	1	.00	5	.272	.308	.335

Year	Team	Lg	G	AB	H	2B	3B	HR	TB	R	RBI	TBB	IBB	SO	HBP	SH	SF	SB	CS	SB%	GDP	Avg	OBP	SLG
1987	Louisville	AAA	116	422	124	33	2	3	170	44	54	15	2	42	3	0	8	0	0	.00	18	.294	.317	.403
1988	Portland	AAA	139	562	162	27	8	9	232	67	69	34	1	48	2	6	5	2	2	.50	16	.288	.328	.413
1989	Portland	AAA	120	465	146	34	3	10	216	63	50	35	2	45	4	1	2	2	1	.67	18	.314	.366	.465
1990	Portland	AAA	12	39	11	1	0	1	15	4	2	2	0	5	0	0	0	0	0	.00	3	.282	.317	.385
1991	Portland	AAA	83	270	82	17	0	6	117	36	32	20	0	22	2	4	4	0	0	.00	7	.304	.351	.433
1992	Scranton-Wb	AAA	48	155	43	8	2	1	58	14	27	3	0	20	0	1	0	0	0	.00	4	.277	.291	.374
1993	Scranton-Wb	AAA	118	442	135	24	3	12	201	59	64	17	0	40	3	6	3	2	4	.33	18	.305	.333	.455
1994	Edmonton	AAA	84	273	76	13	0	6	107	28	46	11	0	23	5	1	5	1	2	.33	13	.278	.313	.392
1995	Pawtucket	AAA	31	116	32	5	0	0	37	10	8	2	0	13	0	3	1	1	1	.50	3	.276	.286	.319
1984	Baltimore	AL	11	17	7	3	0	0	10	4	2	0	0	0	0	0	0	0	0	.00	0	.412	.412	.588
1989	Minnesota	AL	6	11	5	2	0	0	7	2	0	0	0	1	0	0	0	0	0	.00	0	.455	.455	.636
	19 Min. YEARS		1758	6468	1905	333	43	102	2630	761	774	356	16	625	29	77	55	29	30	.49	222	.295	.331	.407
	2 Maj. YEARS		17	28	12	5	0	0	17	6	2	0	0	3	0	0	0	0	0	.00	0	.429	.429	.607

Bats: Right **Throws:** Right **Pos:** OF

Cecil Rodriques

Ht: 6'0" **Wt:** 175 **Born:** 9/3/71 **Age:** 24

			BATTING															BASERUNNING				PERCENTAGES		
Year	Team	Lg	G	AB	H	2B	3B	HR	TB	R	RBI	TBB	IBB	SO	HBP	SH	SF	SB	CS	SB%	GDP	Avg	OBP	SLG
1991	Brewers	R	29	111	26	3	0	0	29	19	7	25	0	19	1	0	1	11	5	.69	2	.234	.377	.261
1992	Helena	R	72	279	85	17	6	12	150	63	49	30	2	62	4	1	3	23	7	.77	1	.305	.377	.538
1993	Beloit	A	104	349	83	21	4	8	136	50	49	43	1	94	2	3	3	18	12	.60	4	.238	.322	.390
1994	Beloit	A	38	116	33	5	0	3	47	16	24	13	1	29	0	3	2	10	3	.77	1	.284	.351	.405
	Stockton	A	56	205	54	12	3	3	81	29	19	25	1	48	2	6	0	14	3	.82	1	.263	.349	.395
1995	Stockton	A	45	173	46	6	3	4	70	21	20	13	0	31	0	1	3	4	8	.33	4	.266	.312	.405
	El Paso	AA	72	244	65	9	7	2	94	36	24	15	0	51	1	0	4	5	2	.71	2	.266	.307	.385
	5 Min. YEARS		416	1477	392	73	23	32	607	234	192	164	5	334	10	14	16	85	40	.68	15	.265	.340	.411

Pitches: Right **Bats:** Right **Pos:** P

Bryan Rogers

Ht: 5'11" **Wt:** 170 **Born:** 10/30/67 **Age:** 28

			HOW MUCH HE PITCHED					WHAT HE GAVE UP										THE RESULTS					
Year	Team	Lg	G	GS	CG	GF	IP	BFP	H	R	ER	HR	SH	SF	HB	TBB	IBB	SO	WP	Bk	W	L	Pct.	ShO	Sv	ERA
1988	Kingsport	R	15	2	0	5	31.1	135	30	23	22	1	0	0	1	14	1	35	1	4	2	3	.400	0	0	6.32
1989	Columbia	A	14	4	0	6	43.1	181	36	16	15	1	5	0	2	14	0	36	0	1	3	2	.600	0	3	3.12
1990	St. Lucie	A	29	19	5	6	148.2	599	127	66	51	3	2	8	4	26	0	96	7	1	9	8	.529	0	4	3.09
1991	Williamsprt	AA	41	0	0	32	61	267	73	33	32	5	5	2	1	18	1	33	1	0	6	8	.429	0	15	4.72
1992	Binghamton	AA	22	0	0	10	35.1	152	37	21	17	4	2	1	1	7	0	20	0	0	3	2	.600	0	1	4.33
	St. Lucie	A	17	0	0	6	30.2	123	24	12	10	1	3	1	2	7	2	17	1	0	2	4	.333	0	2	2.93
1993	Binghamton	AA	62	0	0	40	84.2	347	80	29	22	4	5	4	0	25	2	42	4	0	5	4	.556	0	8	2.34
1994	Norfolk	AAA	20	0	0	4	30	133	35	19	18	4	1	2	1	10	2	8	0	0	2	2	.500	0	5	5.40
	Binghamton	AA	41	0	0	21	60	236	49	17	11	1	3	0	1	14	5	46	2	0	5	1	.833	0	11	1.65
1995	Norfolk	AAA	56	0	0	34	77.1	303	58	22	19	4	4	3	0	22	1	50	8	0	8	3	.727	0	10	2.21
	8 Min. YEARS		317	25	5	164	602.1	2476	549	258	217	28	30	21	13	157	14	383	24	6	45	37	.549	0	54	3.24

Pitches: Left **Bats:** Both **Pos:** P

Kevin Rogers

Ht: 6'2" **Wt:** 198 **Born:** 8/20/68 **Age:** 27

			HOW MUCH HE PITCHED					WHAT HE GAVE UP										THE RESULTS					
Year	Team	Lg	G	GS	CG	GF	IP	BFP	H	R	ER	HR	SH	SF	HB	TBB	IBB	SO	WP	Bk	W	L	Pct.	ShO	Sv	ERA
1988	Pocatello	R	13	13	1	0	69.2	314	73	54	48	4	0	3	2	35	0	71	5	4	2	8	.200	0	0	6.20
1989	Clinton	A	29	28	4	0	169.1	722	128	74	48	4	2	6	6	78	1	168	5	7	13	8	.619	0	0	2.55
1990	San Jose	A	28	26	1	1	172	731	143	86	69	9	6	8	11	68	1	186	19	3	14	5	.737	1	0	3.61
1991	Shreveport	AA	22	22	2	0	118	528	124	63	44	8	5	5	2	54	4	108	11	2	4	6	.400	0	0	3.36
1992	Shreveport	AA	16	16	2	0	101	413	87	34	29	3	2	1	4	29	0	110	7	0	8	5	.615	2	0	2.58
	Phoenix	AAA	11	11	1	0	69.2	287	63	34	31	0	5	3	1	22	1	62	2	1	3	3	.500	1	0	4.00
1995	San Jose	A	4	4	0	0	10	38	10	2	2	0	0	0	0	1	0	5	0	0	0	2	.000	0	1	1.80
	Phoenix	AAA	3	1	0	0	4.1	22	9	2	2	0	0	0	0	2	0	1	2	0	0	0	.000	0	0	4.15
1992	San Francisco	NL	6	6	0	0	34	148	37	17	16	4	2	0	1	13	1	26	2	0	0	2	.000	0	0	4.24
1993	San Francisco	NL	64	0	0	24	80.2	334	71	28	24	3	0	1	4	28	5	62	3	0	2	2	.500	0	0	2.68
1994	San Francisco	NL	9	0	0	2	10.1	46	10	4	4	1	0	0	0	6	0	7	0	0	0	0	.000	0	0	3.48
	6 Min. YEARS		126	121	11	1	714	3055	637	346	273	28	20	26	26	289	7	711	51	17	44	37	.543	4	0	3.44
	3 Maj. YEARS		79	6	0	26	125	528	118	49	44	8	2	1	5	47	6	95	5	0	2	4	.333	0	0	3.17

Bats: Right **Throws:** Right **Pos:** 2B

Lamarr Rogers

Ht: 5'8" **Wt:** 165 **Born:** 6/24/71 **Age:** 25

			BATTING															BASERUNNING				PERCENTAGES		
Year	Team	Lg	G	AB	H	2B	3B	HR	TB	R	RBI	TBB	IBB	SO	HBP	SH	SF	SB	CS	SB%	GDP	Avg	OBP	SLG
1992	Bend	A	66	231	67	13	3	2	92	41	21	53	0	31	2	3	2	22	7	.76	1	.290	.424	.398
1993	Central Val	A	112	406	107	14	2	2	131	68	33	68	1	54	4	7	4	29	15	.66	10	.264	.371	.323
1994	New Haven	AA	111	376	100	18	4	2	132	57	35	56	0	51	2	6	2	7	8	.47	8	.266	.362	.351
1995	New Haven	AA	109	371	105	15	0	0	120	68	31	64	1	50	1	8	3	21	7	.75	15	.283	.387	.323
	4 Min. YEARS		398	1384	379	60	9	6	475	234	120	241	2	186	9	24	11	79	37	.68	34	.274	.382	.343

Dave Rohde

Bats: Both **Throws:** Right **Pos:** SS   **Ht:** 6' 2" **Wt:** 180 **Born:** 5/8/64 **Age:** 32

Year Team	Lg	G	AB	H	2B	3B	HR	TB	R	RBI	TBB	IBB	SO	HBP	SH	SF	SB	CS	SB%	GDP	Avg	OBP	SLG
1986 Auburn	A	61	207	54	6	4	2	74	41	22	37	1	37	0	1	2	28	9	.76	2	.261	.370	.357
1987 Osceola	A	103	377	108	15	1	5	140	57	42	50	1	58	4	10	0	12	6	.67	4	.286	.376	.371
1988 Columbus	AA	142	486	130	20	2	4	166	76	53	81	1	62	5	4	7	36	4	.90	14	.267	.373	.342
1989 Columbus	AA	67	254	71	5	2	2	86	40	27	41	0	25	1	5	2	15	5	.75	6	.280	.379	.339
Tucson	AAA	75	234	68	7	3	1	84	35	30	32	1	30	1	7	5	11	5	.69	4	.291	.371	.359
1990 Tucson	AAA	47	170	60	10	2	0	74	42	20	40	0	20	1	1	0	5	2	.71	7	.353	.479	.435
1991 Tucson	AAA	73	253	94	10	4	1	115	36	40	52	3	34	5	2	5	15	6	.71	4	.372	.479	.455
1992 Colo. Sprng	AAA	121	448	132	17	14	4	189	85	55	57	1	60	4	8	2	13	8	.62	7	.295	.378	.422
1993 Buffalo	AAA	131	464	113	22	2	11	172	64	48	50	3	46	3	5	6	4	5	.44	11	.244	.317	.371
1994 Buffalo	AAA	101	273	62	11	1	1	78	24	23	38	4	35	1	4	4	7	4	.64	7	.227	.320	.286
1995 Tucson	AAA	73	170	47	8	2	0	59	27	20	32	1	17	0	6	2	2	2	.50	5	.276	.387	.347
1990 Houston	NL	59	98	18	4	0	0	22	8	5	9	2	20	5	4	1	0	0	.00	3	.184	.283	.224
1991 Houston	NL	29	41	5	0	0	0	5	3	0	5	0	8	0	2	0	0	0	.00	0	.122	.217	.122
1992 Cleveland	AL	5	7	0	0	0	0	0	0	0	0	2	1	3	0	0	0	0	.00	0	.000	.222	.000
10 Min. YEARS		994	3336	939	131	37	31	1237	527	380	510	16	424	25	53	35	148	56	.73	71	.281	.377	.371
3 Maj. YEARS		93	146	23	4	0	0	27	11	5	16	3	31	5	6	1	0	0	.00	4	.158	.262	.185

Dan Rohrmeier

Bats: Right **Throws:** Right **Pos:** OF   **Ht:** 6'0" **Wt:** 185 **Born:** 9/27/65 **Age:** 30

Year Team	Lg	G	AB	H	2B	3B	HR	TB	R	RBI	TBB	IBB	SO	HBP	SH	SF	SB	CS	SB%	GDP	Avg	OBP	SLG
1987 Peninsula	A	68	243	80	13	2	5	112	43	34	29	0	37	2	2	3	2	3	.40	3	.329	.401	.461
1988 Tampa	A	114	421	109	28	8	5	168	53	50	27	2	58	1	1	5	11	7	.61	4	.259	.302	.399
1989 Sarasota	A	25	74	16	2	0	1	21	11	4	12	0	15	0	1	1	1	0	1.00	2	.216	.322	.284
Charlotte	A	18	65	20	3	1	1	28	9	11	7	0	8	1	0	1	0	1	.00	1	.308	.378	.431
Tulsa	AA	57	210	67	3	4	5	93	24	27	11	0	20	1	4	0	5	8	.38	5	.319	.356	.443
1990 Tulsa	AA	119	453	138	24	7	10	206	76	62	37	0	51	0	1	4	13	11	.54	14	.305	.354	.455
1991 Tulsa	AA	121	418	122	20	2	5	161	67	62	60	1	57	4	4	7	3	2	.60	14	.292	.380	.385
1992 Memphis	AA	123	433	140	33	2	6	195	54	69	26	2	46	4	0	4	3	7	.30	11	.323	.364	.450
Omaha	AAA	8	29	7	1	0	1	11	4	5	3	0	4	0	0	0	0	1	.00	0	.241	.313	.379
1993 Omaha	AAA	118	432	107	23	3	17	187	51	70	23	0	59	3	1	7	2	1	.67	10	.248	.286	.433
1994 Memphis	AA	112	436	118	34	4	18	206	64	72	31	3	80	6	0	3	2	2	.50	15	.271	.326	.472
Chattanooga	AA	17	66	22	7	0	0	29	9	10	5	0	5	0	0	1	0	1	.00	5	.333	.375	.439
1995 Indianapols	AAA	10	34	6	3	1	0	11	5	3	0	0	4	0	0	0	0	0	.00	1	.176	.176	.324
Chattanooga	AA	118	426	139	31	0	17	221	77	76	41	5	63	7	1	7	0	1	.00	9	.326	.389	.519
9 Min. YEARS		1028	3740	1091	225	30	91	1649	547	555	312	13	507	29	15	43	42	45	.48	94	.292	.347	.441

Euclides Rojas

Pitches: Right **Bats:** Right **Pos:** P   **Ht:** 6'0" **Wt:** 190 **Born:** 8/25/67 **Age:** 28

		HOW MUCH HE PITCHED						WHAT HE GAVE UP												THE RESULTS					
Year Team	Lg	G	GS	CG	GF	IP	BFP	H	R	ER	HR	SH	SF	HB	TBB	IBB	SO	WP	Bk	W	L	Pct.	ShO	Sv	ERA
1995 Palm Spring	IND	5	5	1	0	35	141	24	18	13	2	0	2	2	12	0	29	6	2	1	4	.200	0	0	3.34
Marlins	R	2	2	0	0	10	35	6	1	1	0	1	0	0	1	0	7	0	1	2	0	1.000	0	0	0.90
Portland	AA	14	1	0	5	22	104	27	20	19	3	0	1	0	13	1	22	2	1	1	1	.500	0	0	7.77
Charlotte	AAA	2	0	0	1	3	13	2	1	1	0	0	0	0	2	0	2	0	0	0	1	.000	0	0	3.00
1 Min. YEARS		23	8	1	6	70	293	59	40	34	5	1	2	3	28	1	60	8	4	4	6	.400	0	1	4.37

Scott Rolen

Bats: Right **Throws:** Right **Pos:** 3B   **Ht:** 6'4" **Wt:** 210 **Born:** 4/4/75 **Age:** 21

Year Team	Lg	G	AB	H	2B	3B	HR	TB	R	RBI	TBB	IBB	SO	HBP	SH	SF	SB	CS	SB%	GDP	Avg	OBP	SLG
1993 Martinsvlle	R	25	80	25	5	0	0	30	8	12	10	0	15	7	0	1	3	4	.43	3	.313	.429	.375
1994 Spartanburg	A	138	513	151	34	5	14	237	83	72	55	4	90	4	1	7	6	8	.43	8	.294	.363	.462
1995 Clearwater	A	66	238	69	13	2	10	116	45	39	37	1	46	5	0	3	4	0	1.00	4	.290	.392	.487
Reading	AA	20	76	22	3	0	3	34	16	15	7	0	14	1	1	1	1	0	1.00	1	.289	.353	.447
3 Min. YEARS		249	907	267	55	7	27	417	152	138	109	5	165	17	2	12	14	12	.54	17	.294	.376	.460

David Rolls

Bats: Right **Throws:** Right **Pos:** C   **Ht:** 6'0" **Wt:** 195 **Born:** 10/1/66 **Age:** 29

Year Team	Lg	G	AB	H	2B	3B	HR	TB	R	RBI	TBB	IBB	SO	HBP	SH	SF	SB	CS	SB%	GDP	Avg	OBP	SLG
1988 Eugene	A	35	111	19	5	0	3	33	14	10	19	0	44	3	0	0	2	0	1.00	1	.171	.308	.297
1990 Eugene	A	45	128	36	5	0	5	56	24	13	21	0	27	6	1	2	1	1	.50	2	.281	.401	.438
1991 Salt Lake	R	66	224	73	21	1	4	108	58	47	48	0	37	8	0	6	4	3	.57	4	.326	.451	.482
1992 Charlotte	A	77	211	62	15	2	9	108	31	33	22	0	42	5	0	0	1	5	.17	4	.294	.374	.512
1993 Tulsa	AA	72	221	53	9	0	5	77	23	23	22	0	51	6	2	2	1	2	.33	4	.240	.323	.348
1994 Tulsa	AA	92	293	71	19	0	6	108	40	32	26	0	71	12	4	3	1	1	1.00	11	.242	.326	.369
1995 Okla. City	AAA	2	5	0	0	0	0	0	0	0	1	0	4	1	0	0	0	0	.00	0	.000	.286	.000
7 Min. YEARS		389	1193	314	74	3	32	490	190	159	159	0	276	41	7	13	11	11	.50	26	.263	.366	.411

Scott Romano

Bats: Right **Throws:** Right **Pos:** 3B **Ht:** 6'1" **Wt:** 185 **Born:** 8/3/71 **Age:** 24

Year Team	Lg	G	AB	H	2B	3B	HR	TB	R	RBI	TBB	IBB	SO	HBP	SH	SF	SB	CS	SB%	GDP	Avg	OBP	SLG
1989 Yankees	R	51	195	42	9	1	2	59	28	24	22	0	38	2	3	2	4	2	.67	2	.215	.299	.303
1990 Greensboro	A	58	189	38	8	0	0	46	17	11	23	0	43	3	4	0	12	5	.71	2	.201	.298	.243
Oneonta	A	57	178	43	8	2	1	58	30	19	30	1	38	6	2	2	18	2	.90	3	.242	.366	.326
1991 Greensboro	A	92	307	67	13	2	1	87	35	30	45	1	70	7	3	1	14	10	.58	5	.218	.331	.283
1992 Ft. Laud	A	106	358	86	17	2	3	116	30	24	27	0	62	3	4	1	11	6	.65	12	.240	.298	.324
1993 Greensboro	A	121	418	118	33	4	7	180	75	62	63	0	69	9	2	3	14	7	.67	10	.282	.385	.431
1994 Tampa	A	120	419	127	35	3	20	228	88	87	59	2	55	15	1	6	5	3	.63	3	.303	.403	.544
1995 Norwich	AA	100	353	87	15	1	7	125	43	51	48	1	57	7	4	2	7	2	.78	13	.246	.346	.354
7 Min. YEARS		705	2417	608	138	15	41	899	346	308	317	5	432	52	23	17	85	37	.70	50	.252	.349	.372

Paul Romanoli

Pitches: Left **Bats:** Left **Pos:** P **Ht:** 6'2" **Wt:** 182 **Born:** 9/22/69 **Age:** 26

Year Team	Lg	G	GS	CG	GF	IP	BFP	H	R	ER	HR	SH	SF	HB	TBB	IBB	SO	WP	Bk	W	L	Pct.	ShO	Sv	ERA
1991 Johnson Cty	R	8	0	0	1	11.2	46	7	0	0	0	1	0	1	4	0	19	1	1	2	0	1.000	0	0	0.00
Springfield	A	16	0	0	5	30.1	126	24	10	6	1	2	0	1	12	1	37	1	0	1	1	.500	0	0	1.78
1992 Springfield	A	62	0	0	11	79	313	46	21	13	4	3	1	11	17	0	112	5	0	5	2	.714	0	2	1.48
1993 St. Pete	A	17	0	0	7	21	108	21	14	10	2	3	3	2	21	2	17	1	0	0	0	.000	0	0	4.29
Canton-Akrn	AA	30	0	0	15	39.2	173	37	22	20	5	3	0	4	21	3	38	2	0	1	2	.333	0	0	4.54
1994 Duluth-Sup.	IND	29	0	0	24	54.2	238	47	29	26	5	6	3	5	26	1	57	3	1	3	5	.375	0	4	4.28
1995 Colo. Sprng	AAA	31	0	0	9	20	99	27	13	10	2	1	1	1	10	2	23	1	0	3	1	.750	0	3	4.50
5 Min. YEARS		193	0	0	72	256.1	1103	209	109	85	19	19	8	25	111	9	303	14	2	15	11	.577	0	9	2.98

Mandy Romero

Bats: Both **Throws:** Right **Pos:** DH **Ht:** 5'11" **Wt:** 196 **Born:** 10/19/67 **Age:** 28

Year Team	Lg	G	AB	H	2B	3B	HR	TB	R	RBI	TBB	IBB	SO	HBP	SH	SF	SB	CS	SB%	GDP	Avg	OBP	SLG
1988 Princeton	R	30	71	22	6	0	2	34	7	11	13	0	15	1	0	0	1	0	1.00	0	.310	.424	.479
1989 Augusta	A	121	388	87	26	3	4	131	58	55	67	4	74	6	3	6	8	5	.62	10	.224	.343	.338
1990 Salem	A	124	460	134	31	3	17	222	62	90	55	3	68	5	2	4	0	2	.00	10	.291	.370	.483
1991 Carolina	AA	98	323	70	12	0	3	91	28	31	45	4	53	1	2	2	1	2	.33	9	.217	.313	.282
1992 Carolina	AA	80	269	58	16	0	3	83	28	27	29	0	39	1	1	2	0	3	.00	10	.216	.292	.309
1993 Buffalo	AAA	42	136	31	6	1	2	45	11	14	6	1	12	0	1	1	1	0	1.00	5	.228	.259	.331
1994 Buffalo	AAA	7	23	3	0	0	0	3	3	1	2	0	1	0	1	0	0	0	.00	2	.130	.200	.130
1995 Wichita	AA	121	440	133	32	1	21	230	73	82	69	10	60	5	0	1	1	3	.25	15	.302	.402	.523
8 Min. YEARS		623	2110	538	129	8	52	839	270	311	286	22	322	19	10	16	12	15	.44	61	.255	.347	.398

Wilfredo Romero

Bats: Right **Throws:** Right **Pos:** OF **Ht:** 5'11" **Wt:** 158 **Born:** 8/5/74 **Age:** 21

Year Team	Lg	G	AB	H	2B	3B	HR	TB	R	RBI	TBB	IBB	SO	HBP	SH	SF	SB	CS	SB%	GDP	Avg	OBP	SLG
1993 Great Falls	R	15	58	16	5	0	0	21	12	9	2	0	9	0	0	0	2	1	.67	2	.276	.300	.362
Yakima	A	13	51	13	0	0	0	13	8	1	1	0	12	2	0	1	3	0	1.00	1	.255	.291	.255
Bakersfield	A	20	77	27	5	0	1	35	8	12	5	0	16	0	0	0	4	2	.67	2	.351	.390	.455
1994 Vero Beach	A	38	126	29	6	0	2	41	15	13	9	0	19	1	2	0	0	2	.00	2	.230	.287	.325
Bakersfield	A	70	260	71	19	1	7	113	36	36	19	0	53	3	1	0	15	5	.75	3	.273	.330	.435
1995 San Antonio	AA	105	376	100	20	1	7	143	46	44	40	1	69	5	0	6	10	12	.45	7	.266	.340	.380
3 Min. YEARS		261	948	256	55	2	17	366	125	115	76	1	178	11	3	7	34	22	.61	17	.270	.329	.386

Marc Ronan

Bats: Left **Throws:** Right **Pos:** C **Ht:** 6'2" **Wt:** 190 **Born:** 9/19/69 **Age:** 26

Year Team	Lg	G	AB	H	2B	3B	HR	TB	R	RBI	TBB	IBB	SO	HBP	SH	SF	SB	CS	SB%	GDP	Avg	OBP	SLG
1990 Hamilton	A	56	167	38	6	0	1	47	14	15	15	0	37	1	0	3	1	2	.33	3	.228	.290	.281
1991 Savannah	A	108	343	81	10	1	0	93	41	45	37	1	54	4	3	1	11	2	.85	13	.236	.317	.271
1992 Springfield	A	110	376	81	19	2	6	122	45	48	23	2	58	1	0	4	4	5	.44	11	.215	.260	.324
1993 St. Pete	A	25	87	27	5	0	0	32	13	6	6	0	10	0	3	2	0	0	.00	1	.310	.347	.368
Arkansas	AA	96	281	60	16	1	7	99	33	34	26	2	47	2	3	3	1	3	.25	4	.214	.282	.352
1994 Louisville	AAA	84	269	64	11	2	2	85	32	21	12	2	43	2	2	2	3	1	.75	9	.238	.274	.316
1995 Louisville	AAA	78	225	48	8	0	0	56	15	8	14	2	42	0	2	0	4	3	.57	10	.213	.259	.249
1993 St. Louis	NL	6	12	1	0	0	0	1	0	0	0	0	5	0	0	0	0	0	.00	0	.083	.083	.083
6 Min. YEARS		557	1748	399	75	6	16	534	193	177	133	9	291	10	13	15	24	16	.60	51	.228	.284	.305

Chad Roper

Bats: Right **Throws:** Right **Pos:** 3B **Ht:** 6'1" **Wt:** 212 **Born:** 3/29/74 **Age:** 22

Year Team	Lg	G	AB	H	2B	3B	HR	TB	R	RBI	TBB	IBB	SO	HBP	SH	SF	SB	CS	SB%	GDP	Avg	OBP	SLG
1992 Twins	R	20	76	25	5	3	1	39	16	11	5	1	16	1	0	1	1	0	1.00	1	.329	.373	.513
Elizabethtn	R	39	147	42	4	1	1	51	20	25	12	0	29	1	0	2	0	1	.00	3	.286	.340	.347
1993 Fort Myers	A	125	452	112	17	3	9	162	46	65	43	2	96	6	4	5	1	2	.33	10	.248	.318	.358

Year	Team	Lg	G	AB	H	2B	3B	HR	TB	R	RBI	TBB	IBB	SO	HBP	SH	SF	SB	CS	SB%	GDP	Avg	OBP	SLG
1994	Fort Myers	A	92	337	81	17	0	4	110	32	44	32	3	76	4	0	7	7	8	.47	8	.240	.308	.326
1995	New Britain	AA	120	443	100	22	3	11	161	41	61	27	3	86	3	1	4	2	3	.40	9	.226	.273	.363
	4 Min. YEARS		396	1455	360	65	10	26	523	155	206	119	9	303	15	5	19	11	14	.44	32	.247	.307	.359

Pete Rose

Bats: Left **Throws:** Right **Pos:** 3B **Ht:** 6'1" **Wt:** 180 **Born:** 11/16/69 **Age:** 26

			BATTING															BASERUNNING				PERCENTAGES		
Year	Team	Lg	G	AB	H	2B	3B	HR	TB	R	RBI	TBB	IBB	SO	HBP	SH	SF	SB	CS	SB%	GDP	Avg	OBP	SLG
1989	Frederick	A	24	67	12	3	0	0	15	3	7	0	0	15	1	0	0	1	1	.50	1	.179	.191	.224
	Erie	A	58	228	63	13	5	2	92	30	26	12	1	34	1	2	0	1	2	.33	3	.276	.315	.404
1990	Frederick	A	97	323	75	14	2	1	96	32	41	26	0	33	1	7	5	0	3	.00	6	.232	.287	.297
1991	Sarasota	A	99	323	70	12	2	0	86	31	35	36	3	35	2	8	3	5	6	.45	3	.217	.297	.266
1992	Columbus	A	131	510	129	24	6	9	192	67	54	48	2	53	6	8	3	4	3	.57	9	.253	.323	.376
1993	Kinston	A	74	284	62	10	1	7	95	33	30	25	0	34	2	6	1	1	3	.25	5	.218	.285	.335
1994	Hickory	A	32	114	25	4	1	0	31	14	12	13	2	18	2	3	2	0	0	.00	3	.219	.305	.272
	White Sox	R	2	4	2	0	0	0	2	1	1	0	0	0	0	0	0	0	0	.00	0	.500	.500	.500
	Pr. William	A	45	146	41	3	1	4	58	18	22	18	0	15	0	2	3	0	1	.00	2	.281	.353	.397
1995	Birmingham	AA	5	13	5	1	0	0	6	1	2	3	0	3	0	0	0	0	0	.00	0	.385	.500	.462
	South Bend	A	116	423	117	24	6	4	165	56	65	54	0	45	5	2	7	2	0	1.00	6	.277	.360	.390
	7 Min. YEARS		683	2435	601	108	24	27	838	286	295	235	8	285	20	38	24	14	19	.42	38	.247	.315	.344

Scott Rose

Pitches: Right **Bats:** Right **Pos:** P **Ht:** 6'3" **Wt:** 200 **Born:** 5/12/70 **Age:** 26

			HOW MUCH HE PITCHED					WHAT HE GAVE UP										THE RESULTS					
Year	Team	Lg	G	GS	CG	GF	IP	BFP	H	R	ER	HR	SH	SF	HB	TBB	IBB	SO	WP	Bk	W	L	Pct.	ShO	Sv	ERA
1990	Athletics	R	9	1	0	4	18.1	69	12	5	3	0	0	0	0	3	0	21	1	0	0	0	.000	0	2	1.47
	Modesto	A	6	0	0	3	14	61	14	5	2	0	0	0	0	6	1	10	2	0	0	0	.000	0	1	1.29
1991	Modesto	A	13	13	0	0	67.2	306	66	45	33	7	3	3	2	38	1	31	7	1	3	3	.500	0	0	4.39
1992	Madison	A	8	8	1	0	36	154	35	22	17	2	1	2	2	10	0	15	3	1	2	2	.500	0	0	4.25
	Reno	A	20	9	0	2	64	314	97	73	60	11	2	2	2	37	3	29	4	0	2	4	.333	0	0	8.44
1993	San Bernrdo	A	28	25	1	0	173.1	765	184	110	82	16	6	8	10	63	6	73	10	0	9	10	.474	1	0	4.26
1994	Huntsville	AA	41	0	0	25	73	328	87	44	38	2	9	4	2	24	8	43	9	0	6	10	.375	0	3	4.68
1995	Edmonton	AAA	5	1	0	2	10	45	13	7	7	0	1	0	0	7	0	0	0	0	0	2	.000	0	0	6.30
	Huntsville	AA	38	5	0	23	80	316	70	24	23	2	5	3	2	23	5	35	6	0	4	6	.400	0	13	2.59
	6 Min. YEARS		168	62	2	59	536.1	2358	578	335	265	40	27	22	20	211	24	257	42	2	26	37	.413	1	19	4.45

John Rosengren

Pitches: Left **Bats:** Left **Pos:** P **Ht:** 6'4" **Wt:** 190 **Born:** 8/10/72 **Age:** 23

			HOW MUCH HE PITCHED					WHAT HE GAVE UP										THE RESULTS					
Year	Team	Lg	G	GS	CG	GF	IP	BFP	H	R	ER	HR	SH	SF	HB	TBB	IBB	SO	WP	Bk	W	L	Pct.	ShO	Sv	ERA
1992	Bristol	R	14	3	0	3	23	113	16	21	20	2	0	5	0	30	0	28	6	2	0	3	.000	0	0	7.83
1993	Niagara Fal	A	15	15	0	0	82	333	52	32	22	3	1	4	6	38	0	91	6	1	7	3	.700	0	0	2.41
1994	Lakeland	A	22	22	4	0	135.2	569	113	51	38	4	2	4	7	56	0	101	3	2	9	6	.600	3	0	2.52
	Trenton	AA	3	3	0	0	17.1	79	21	15	14	2	1	1	0	11	0	7	0	1	0	2	.000	0	0	7.27
1995	Jacksonvlle	AA	14	13	0	0	67.2	308	73	39	34	7	2	2	5	40	0	59	12	2	2	7	.222	0	0	4.52
	Lakeland	A	13	8	0	1	56.1	253	46	33	25	6	2	2	7	36	0	35	2	0	3	3	.500	0	0	3.99
	4 Min. YEARS		81	64	4	4	382	1655	321	191	153	24	8	18	25	211	0	321	29	8	21	24	.467	3	0	3.60

Rico Rossy

Bats: Right **Throws:** Right **Pos:** SS **Ht:** 5'10" **Wt:** 175 **Born:** 2/16/64 **Age:** 32

			BATTING															BASERUNNING				PERCENTAGES		
Year	Team	Lg	G	AB	H	2B	3B	HR	TB	R	RBI	TBB	IBB	SO	HBP	SH	SF	SB	CS	SB%	GDP	Avg	OBP	SLG
1985	Newark	A	73	246	53	14	2	3	80	38	25	32	1	22	1	3	1	17	7	.71	13	.215	.307	.325
1986	Miami	A	38	134	34	7	1	1	46	26	9	24	0	8	1	6	1	10	6	.63	4	.254	.369	.343
	Charlotte	AA	77	232	68	16	2	3	97	40	25	26	0	19	2	8	1	13	5	.72	2	.293	.368	.418
1987	Charlotte	AA	127	471	135	22	3	4	175	69	50	43	0	38	3	3	1	20	9	.69	20	.287	.349	.372
1988	Buffalo	AAA	68	187	46	4	0	1	53	12	20	13	0	17	0	0	1	1	5	.17	4	.246	.294	.283
1989	Harrisburg	AA	78	238	60	16	1	2	84	20	25	27	0	19	3	0	2	2	4	.33	5	.252	.333	.353
	Buffalo	AAA	38	109	21	5	0	0	26	11	10	18	1	11	1	1	2	0	1.00	0	.193	.308	.239
1990	Buffalo	AAA	8	17	3	0	1	0	5	3	2	4	0	2	0	1	1	1	0	1.00	0	.176	.318	.294
	Greenville	AA	5	21	4	1	0	0	5	4	0	1	0	2	0	0	0	0	2	.00	1	.190	.227	.238
	Richmond	AAA	107	380	88	13	0	4	113	58	32	69	1	43	3	7	2	11	6	.65	12	.232	.352	.297
1991	Richmond	AAA	139	482	124	25	1	2	157	58	48	67	1	46	5	13	3	4	8	.33	12	.257	.352	.326
1992	Omaha	AAA	48	174	55	10	1	4	79	29	17	34	0	14	0	2	3	3	5	.38	5	.316	.422	.454
1993	Omaha	AAA	37	131	39	10	1	5	66	25	21	20	1	19	3	0	1	3	2	.60	1	.298	.400	.504
1994	Omaha	AAA	120	412	97	23	0	11	153	49	63	61	1	60	5	5	4	9	10	.47	14	.235	.338	.371
1995	Las Vegas	AAA	98	316	95	11	2	1	113	44	45	55	2	36	2	2	6	3	7	.30	13	.301	.401	.358
1991	Atlanta	NL	5	1	0	0	0	0	0	0	0	0	0	1	0	0	0	0	0	.00	0	.000	.000	.000
1992	Kansas City	AL	59	149	32	8	1	1	45	21	12	20	1	20	1	7	1	0	3	.00	6	.215	.310	.302
1993	Kansas City	AL	46	86	19	4	0	2	29	10	12	9	0	11	1	1	0	0	0	.00	0	.221	.302	.337
	11 Min. YEARS		1061	3550	922	177	15	41	1252	486	392	494	8	356	29	51	29	101	76	.57	110	.260	.352	.353
	3 Maj. YEARS		110	236	51	12	1	3	74	31	24	29	1	32	2	8	1	0	3	.00	6	.216	.306	.314

Mason Rudolph

Bats: Right Throws: Right Pos: C Ht: 6'1" Wt: 204 Born: 1/28/70 Age: 26

					BATTING											BASERUNNING				PERCENTAGES		
Year	Team	Lg	G	AB	H	2B	3B	HR	TB	R	RBI	TBB	IBB	SO	HBP	SH	SF	SB	CS	SB%	GDP	Avg	OBP	SLG
1988	Mets	R	31	106	18	4	0	0	22	8	13	5	1	28	1	1	1	2	0	1.00	4	.170	.212	.208
1989	Mets	R	21	62	11	2	0	0	13	3	1	0	0	24	0	3	0	1	0	1.00	1	.177	.177	.210
	Kingsport	R	20	51	8	2	0	2	16	7	4	0	0	22	0	0	1	0	0	.00	0	.157	.154	.314
1990	Kingsport	R	48	154	28	5	0	7	54	26	21	8	0	65	0	1	2	2	2	.00	1	.182	.224	.351
	Pittsfield	A	8	26	5	2	0	0	7	4	0	2	0	6	0	1	0	0	0	.00	0	.192	.250	.269
1991	Columbia	A	64	219	50	11	1	2	69	18	20	11	0	61	1	1	0	4	3	.57	3	.228	.268	.315
1992	St. Lucie	A	48	137	36	11	0	3	56	17	18	7	0	27	2	0	2	3	1	.75	1	.263	.304	.409
1993	St. Lucie	A	22	64	12	2	1	0	16	7	5	2	0	19	0	1	0	0	0	.00	1	.188	.212	.250
1994	St. Paul	IND	40	150	40	7	0	5	62	16	24	3	0	43	0	1	2	5	3	.63	1	.267	.277	.413
1995	Charlotte	AAA	2	4	1	0	0	0	1	1	0	0	0	1	0	0	0	0	0	.00	0	.250	.250	.250
	Portland	AA	41	76	15	4	1	4	33	9	16	1	0	29	2	0	1	0	1	.00	2	.197	.225	.434
	8 Min. YEARS		345	1049	224	50	3	23	349	116	122	39	1	325	7	10	9	15	10	.60	14	.214	.245	.333

Matt Ruebel

Pitches: Left Bats: Left Pos: P Ht: 6'2" Wt: 180 Born: 10/16/69 Age: 26

			HOW MUCH HE PITCHED					WHAT HE GAVE UP										THE RESULTS					
Year	Team	Lg	G	GS	CG	GF	IP	BFP	H	R	ER	HR	SH	SF	HB	TBB	IBB	SO	WP	Bk	W	L	Pct.	ShO	Sv	ERA
1991	Welland	A	6	6	0	0	27.2	113	16	9	6	3	0	1	4	11	0	27	2	3	1	1	.500	0	0	1.95
	Augusta	A	8	8	2	0	47	202	43	26	20	2	1	0	2	25	0	35	3	0	3	4	.429	1	0	3.83
1992	Augusta	A	12	10	1	1	64.2	268	53	26	20	1	3	0	5	19	0	65	2	1	5	2	.714	0	0	2.78
	Salem	A	13	13	1	0	78.1	344	77	49	41	13	6	5	3	43	0	46	6	1	1	6	.143	0	0	4.71
1993	Salem	A	19	1	0	4	33.1	168	34	31	22	6	3	0	3	32	3	29	8	2	1	4	.200	0	0	5.94
	Augusta	A	23	7	1	6	63.1	276	51	28	17	2	1	3	5	34	4	50	1	0	5	5	.500	1	0	2.42
1994	Carolina	AA	6	3	0	0	16.1	78	28	15	12	3	1	1	1	3	0	14	0	0	1	1	.500	0	0	6.61
	Salem	A	21	13	0	0	86.1	374	87	49	33	9	2	3	7	27	0	72	4	1	6	6	.500	0	0	3.44
1995	Carolina	AA	27	27	4	0	169.1	699	150	68	52	7	4	7	7	45	1	136	7	1	13	5	.722	3	0	2.76
	5 Min. YEARS		135	88	9	11	586.1	2522	539	301	223	46	21	20	37	239	8	474	33	9	36	34	.514	5	0	3.42

Tim Rumer

Pitches: Left Bats: Left Pos: P Ht: 6'3" Wt: 205 Born: 8/8/69 Age: 26

			HOW MUCH HE PITCHED					WHAT HE GAVE UP										THE RESULTS					
Year	Team	Lg	G	GS	CG	GF	IP	BFP	H	R	ER	HR	SH	SF	HB	TBB	IBB	SO	WP	Bk	W	L	Pct.	ShO	Sv	ERA
1990	Yankees	R	12	12	2	0	74	291	34	23	14	1	1	0	3	20	0	88	4	3	6	3	.667	0	0	1.70
1991	Ft. Laud	A	24	23	3	0	149.1	623	125	59	48	6	9	3	5	49	2	112	7	1	10	7	.588	2	0	2.89
1992	Pr. William	A	23	23	1	0	128	538	122	61	51	8	6	5	5	34	2	105	0	1	10	7	.588	0	0	3.59
	Columbus	AAA	1	1	0	0	1	3	0	0	0	0	0	0	0	0	0	1	0	0	0	0	.000	0	0	0.00
1994	Albany-Colo	AA	25	25	2	0	150.2	639	127	61	52	10	2	4	9	75	0	130	7	0	8	10	.444	1	0	3.11
1995	Columbus	AAA	28	25	0	1	141.1	654	156	98	82	13	7	5	16	76	1	110	5	1	10	8	.556	0	0	5.22
	5 Min. YEARS		113	109	8	1	644.1	2748	564	302	247	38	25	17	38	254	5	546	23	6	44	35	.557	3	0	3.45

Toby Rumfield

Bats: Right Throws: Right Pos: 1B Ht: 6'3" Wt: 190 Born: 9/4/72 Age: 23

					BATTING											BASERUNNING				PERCENTAGES		
Year	Team	Lg	G	AB	H	2B	3B	HR	TB	R	RBI	TBB	IBB	SO	HBP	SH	SF	SB	CS	SB%	GDP	Avg	OBP	SLG
1991	Princeton	R	59	226	62	13	3	3	90	22	30	9	0	43	5	2	3	1	7	.13	6	.274	.313	.398
1992	Billings	R	66	253	68	15	3	4	101	34	50	7	0	34	4	0	4	5	2	.71	4	.269	.295	.399
1993	Charlstn-Wv	A	97	333	75	20	1	5	112	36	50	26	1	74	3	0	4	6	4	.60	7	.225	.284	.336
1994	Winston-Sal	A	123	462	115	11	4	29	221	79	88	48	1	107	2	0	7	2	3	.40	9	.249	.318	.478
1995	Chattanooga	AA	92	273	72	12	1	8	110	32	53	26	2	47	3	3	5	0	3	.00	14	.264	.329	.403
	5 Min. YEARS		437	1547	392	71	12	49	634	203	271	116	4	305	17	5	23	14	19	.42	40	.253	.308	.410

Matt Rundels

Bats: Right Throws: Right Pos: 2B Ht: 5'11" Wt: 180 Born: 4/26/70 Age: 26

					BATTING											BASERUNNING				PERCENTAGES		
Year	Team	Lg	G	AB	H	2B	3B	HR	TB	R	RBI	TBB	IBB	SO	HBP	SH	SF	SB	CS	SB%	GDP	Avg	OBP	SLG
1992	Jamestown	A	75	277	71	6	2	6	99	43	28	25	0	43	5	2	3	32	11	.74	2	.256	.326	.357
1993	Burlington	A	64	203	55	7	4	4	82	36	17	38	1	36	5	3	1	14	7	.67	5	.271	.397	.404
	W. Palm Bch	A	8	26	3	0	1	0	5	2	2	3	1	4	0	0	1	3	1	.75	0	.115	.200	.192
	Harrisburg	AA	34	117	40	5	0	6	63	27	17	14	0	31	2	0	0	8	2	.80	1	.342	.421	.538
1994	Harrisburg	AA	112	330	73	9	6	6	112	53	31	51	4	79	2	2	3	19	7	.73	7	.221	.326	.339
1995	Ottawa	AAA	14	36	9	1	1	0	12	7	4	7	0	8	1	2	0	1	1	.50	1	.250	.386	.333
	Harrisburg	AA	120	462	114	30	4	11	185	72	55	47	1	112	8	8	1	19	11	.63	5	.247	.326	.400
	4 Min. YEARS		427	1451	365	58	18	33	558	240	154	185	7	313	23	17	9	96	40	.71	21	.252	.344	.385

Brian Rupp

Bats: Right Throws: Right Pos: 1B Ht: 6'5" Wt: 185 Born: 9/20/71 Age: 24

					BATTING											BASERUNNING				PERCENTAGES		
Year	Team	Lg	G	AB	H	2B	3B	HR	TB	R	RBI	TBB	IBB	SO	HBP	SH	SF	SB	CS	SB%	GDP	Avg	OBP	SLG
1992	Cardinals	R	56	207	80	20	1	0	102	34	40	21	5	16	1	0	7	10	7	.59	3	.386	.432	.493
1993	Savannah	A	122	472	151	31	7	4	208	80	81	48	2	70	3	1	5	3	2	.60	11	.320	.383	.441

Year	Team	Lg	G	AB	H	2B	3B	HR	TB	R	RBI	TBB	IBB	SO	HBP	SH	SF	SB	CS	SB%	GDP	Avg	OBP	SLG
1994	St. Pete	A	129	438	115	19	4	2	148	40	34	61	1	77	0	5	0	9	3	.75	20	.263	.353	.338
1995	St. Pete	A	90	325	90	12	2	0	106	30	23	27	1	43	1	4	0	0	0	.00	14	.277	.334	.326
	Arkansas	AA	23	77	25	3	0	0	28	10	6	6	0	12	0	1	0	0	1	.00	3	.325	.373	.364
	4 Min. YEARS		420	1519	461	85	14	6	592	194	184	163	9	218	5	11	12	22	13	.63	51	.303	.370	.390

Lee Russell

Pitches: Right **Bats:** Right **Pos:** P   **Ht:** 6'2" **Wt:** 175 **Born:** 8/20/70 **Age:** 25

			HOW MUCH HE PITCHED						WHAT HE GAVE UP									THE RESULTS					
Year	Team	Lg	G	GS	CG	GF	IP	BFP	H	R	ER	HR	SH	SF	HB	TBB	IBB	SO	WP	Bk	W	L	Pct.	ShO	Sv	ERA
1990	Mariners	R	19	5	0	3	55	251	50	33	19	1	0	3	6	27	1	51	1	1	5	1	.833	0	0	3.11
1991	Bellingham	A	15	15	0	0	95.1	414	85	48	31	6	3	1	1	43	1	77	13	0	6	7	.462	0	0	2.93
1992	Peninsula	A	27	26	2	1	157.1	665	132	76	55	4	6	3	8	59	4	130	5	1	7	10	.412	1	0	3.15
1993	Jacksonvlle	AA	17	17	0	0	89.2	400	115	67	55	14	2	2	2	32	1	52	5	0	4	9	.308	0	0	5.52
1994	Jacksonvlle	AA	36	3	0	19	71.2	314	82	44	36	8	3	2	0	25	5	39	5	0	1	9	.100	0	3	4.52
1995	Port City	AA	39	0	0	13	72.1	329	68	32	26	7	4	3	1	43	3	54	9	0	4	3	.571	0	1	3.24
	6 Min. YEARS		153	66	2	36	541.1	2373	532	300	222	40	18	14	18	229	15	403	38	2	27	39	.409	1	4	3.69

Paul Russo

Bats: Right **Throws:** Right **Pos:** 3B   **Ht:** 5'11" **Wt:** 215 **Born:** 8/26/69 **Age:** 26

			BATTING														BASERUNNING				PERCENTAGES		
Year	Team	Lg	G	AB	H	2B	3B	HR	TB	R	RBI	TBB	IBB	SO	HBP	SH	SF	SB	CS	SB%	GDP	Avg	OBP	SLG
1990	Elizabethtn	R	62	221	74	9	3	22	155	58	67	38	5	56	1	0	2	4	1	.80	3	.335	.431	.701
1991	Kenosha	A	125	421	114	20	3	20	200	60	100	64	4	105	7	0	10	4	1	.80	5	.271	.369	.475
1992	Orlando	AA	126	420	107	13	2	22	190	63	74	48	0	122	1	2	5	0	0	.00	17	.255	.329	.452
1993	Portland	AAA	83	288	81	24	2	10	139	43	47	29	0	69	0	0	6	0	1	.00	10	.281	.341	.483
1994	Salt Lake	AAA	35	115	34	7	0	3	50	18	17	12	0	28	2	0	3	0	3	.00	4	.296	.364	.435
	Nashville	AA	82	299	68	14	3	10	118	43	40	31	1	77	3	3	0	1	0	1.00	11	.227	.306	.395
1995	Memphis	AA	45	122	38	9	1	6	67	19	18	22	1	33	1	0	0	1	0	1.00	3	.311	.421	.549
	Las Vegas	AAA	44	148	44	10	0	4	66	17	19	9	2	31	0	1	2	0	1	.00	4	.297	.333	.446
	6 Min. YEARS		602	2034	560	106	14	97	985	321	382	253	13	521	15	6	28	10	7	.59	57	.275	.355	.484

Kevin Ryan

Pitches: Right **Bats:** Right **Pos:** P   **Ht:** 6'1" **Wt:** 187 **Born:** 9/23/70 **Age:** 25

			HOW MUCH HE PITCHED						WHAT HE GAVE UP									THE RESULTS					
Year	Team	Lg	G	GS	CG	GF	IP	BFP	H	R	ER	HR	SH	SF	HB	TBB	IBB	SO	WP	Bk	W	L	Pct.	ShO	Sv	ERA
1991	Bluefield	R	14	11	0	3	76.1	315	71	26	22	3	0	3	1	24	0	71	6	4	5	4	.556	0	1	2.59
	Kane County	A	1	1	0	0	9.1	35	6	1	1	0	1	0	1	2	0	8	0	0	0	0	.000	0	0	0.96
1992	Frederick	A	27	25	2	1	148.2	666	175	88	78	11	3	4	2	63	1	103	16	3	7	12	.368	0	0	4.72
1993	Bowie	AA	16	15	2	1	88.1	401	106	67	52	8	2	4	1	34	0	40	5	2	3	10	.231	0	0	5.30
	Frederick	A	15	2	0	4	33.1	136	28	11	9	3	1	0	2	9	0	23	0	0	0	3	.000	0	1	2.43
1994	Bowie	AA	41	4	0	14	81	351	86	40	33	8	7	2	2	30	2	37	9	0	8	2	.800	0	1	3.67
1995	Rochester	AAA	6	2	0	0	17.1	83	27	20	18	3	0	1	1	4	0	7	1	0	0	3	.000	0	0	9.35
	Bowie	AA	39	1	0	14	63	267	67	31	24	5	2	2	1	15	2	31	1	0	4	3	.571	0	5	3.43
	5 Min. YEARS		159	61	4	37	517.1	2254	566	284	237	41	16	16	11	181	5	320	41	9	27	37	.422	0	8	4.12

Matt Ryan

Pitches: Right **Bats:** Right **Pos:** P   **Ht:** 6'5" **Wt:** 190 **Born:** 3/20/72 **Age:** 24

			HOW MUCH HE PITCHED						WHAT HE GAVE UP									THE RESULTS					
Year	Team	Lg	G	GS	CG	GF	IP	BFP	H	R	ER	HR	SH	SF	HB	TBB	IBB	SO	WP	Bk	W	L	Pct.	ShO	Sv	ERA
1993	Pirates	R	9	0	0	5	19.1	81	17	8	5	0	1	0	1	9	0	20	0	0	1	1	.500	0	2	2.33
	Welland	A	16	0	0	12	17.1	84	11	10	3	0	0	1	1	12	1	25	5	0	0	1	.000	0	5	1.56
1994	Augusta	A	34	0	0	31	41	174	33	14	6	0	1	0	4	7	1	49	0	0	2	1	.667	0	13	1.32
	Salem	A	25	0	0	16	28.1	120	27	12	6	0	3	0	2	8	1	13	2	0	2	2	.500	0	7	1.91
1995	Calgary	AAA	5	0	0	4	4.2	20	5	1	1	0	0	0	1	1	1	2	0	0	0	0	.000	0	1	1.93
	Carolina	AA	44	0	0	38	46	188	33	10	8	0	4	0	2	19	2	23	3	0	2	1	.667	0	26	1.57
	3 Min. YEARS		133	0	0	106	156.2	667	126	55	29	0	9	1	11	56	6	132	10	0	7	6	.538	0	54	1.67

Kevin Rychel

Pitches: Right **Bats:** Right **Pos:** P   **Ht:** 5'9" **Wt:** 176 **Born:** 9/24/71 **Age:** 24

			HOW MUCH HE PITCHED						WHAT HE GAVE UP									THE RESULTS					
Year	Team	Lg	G	GS	CG	GF	IP	BFP	H	R	ER	HR	SH	SF	HB	TBB	IBB	SO	WP	Bk	W	L	Pct.	ShO	Sv	ERA
1989	Pirates	R	13	13	0	0	67	296	52	40	23	0	3	2	9	31	0	79	6	4	1	6	.143	0	0	3.09
1990	Augusta	A	27	23	0	0	129	615	127	79	59	3	5	4	8	87	0	105	26	6	10	4	.714	0	0	4.12
1991	Salem	A	11	11	0	0	49.1	230	48	44	33	7	1	4	3	27	0	34	10	3	1	7	.125	0	0	6.02
	Augusta	A	8	6	1	1	32.1	151	30	24	20	1	0	2	7	24	0	26	11	0	1	3	.250	1	0	5.57
1992	Augusta	A	13	0	0	8	16	74	12	12	8	0	2	0	0	12	1	16	0	0	1	3	.250	0	2	4.50
	Salem	A	37	0	0	25	39.1	182	37	22	17	4	3	2	4	27	3	35	9	0	2	3	.400	0	7	3.89
1993	Salem	A	53	2	0	11	73	333	68	41	32	3	1	2	10	44	2	86	27	0	5	4	.556	0	0	3.95
1994	Carolina	AA	36	3	0	11	74.2	331	69	45	39	5	2	3	8	42	0	52	12	0	5	3	.625	0	1	4.70
1995	Calgary	AAA	10	0	0	3	8.2	45	14	11	10	3	0	0	0	6	0	4	1	0	0	1	.000	0	0	10.38
	Carolina	AA	40	0	0	14	51.1	210	35	21	19	1	1	1	6	24	4	60	8	0	3	2	.600	0	1	3.33
	7 Min. YEARS		248	58	1	73	540.2	2467	492	339	260	27	18	20	55	324	10	497	110	13	29	36	.446	1	11	4.33

262

Paul Saccavino

Pitches: Right **Bats:** Right **Pos:** P   **Ht:** 6'4" **Wt:** 195 **Born:** 10/1/69 **Age:** 26

		HOW MUCH HE PITCHED						WHAT HE GAVE UP												THE RESULTS					
Year Team	Lg	G	GS	CG	GF	IP	BFP	H	R	ER	HR	SH	SF	HB	TBB	IBB	SO	WP	Bk	W	L	Pct.	ShO	Sv	ERA
1992 Elizabethtn	R	6	6	1	0	33	140	29	17	12	2	0	2	0	9	0	32	0	1	4	0	1.000	0	0	3.27
Kenosha	A	6	6	0	0	36.2	145	31	11	7	2	0	0	1	7	0	28	1	0	4	1	.800	0	0	1.72
1993 Fort Myers	A	23	19	2	4	105.1	479	122	63	55	2	3	3	6	49	3	55	6	1	5	8	.385	0	0	4.70
1994 Fort Myers	A	36	9	1	6	103.1	457	104	54	43	4	3	5	6	49	4	85	10	0	5	4	.556	0	2	3.75
1995 New Britain	AA	27	1	0	12	41.1	213	48	36	26	6	3	3	2	32	0	34	8	0	1	6	.143	0	1	5.66
4 Min. YEARS		98	41	4	22	319.2	1434	334	181	143	16	9	13	15	146	7	234	25	2	19	19	.500	0	3	4.03

Brian Sackinsky

Pitches: Right **Bats:** Right **Pos:** P   **Ht:** 6'4" **Wt:** 220 **Born:** 6/22/71 **Age:** 25

		HOW MUCH HE PITCHED						WHAT HE GAVE UP												THE RESULTS					
Year Team	Lg	G	GS	CG	GF	IP	BFP	H	R	ER	HR	SH	SF	HB	TBB	IBB	SO	WP	Bk	W	L	Pct.	ShO	Sv	ERA
1992 Frederick	A	5	3	0	0	10.1	55	20	15	15	3	0	1	0	6	0	10	4	0	0	3	.000	0	0	13.06
Bluefield	R	5	5	0	0	27.2	124	30	15	11	0	0	0	2	9	0	33	2	0	2	2	.500	0	0	3.58
1993 Albany	A	9	8	0	0	50.2	217	50	29	18	2	0	4	0	16	0	41	5	0	3	4	.429	0	0	3.20
Frederick	A	18	18	1	0	121	512	117	55	43	13	3	3	2	37	2	112	17	1	6	8	.429	0	0	3.20
1994 Bowie	AA	28	26	4	0	177	721	165	73	66	24	5	9	0	39	0	145	6	0	11	7	.611	0	0	3.36
1995 Rochester	AAA	14	11	0	0	62.2	260	70	33	32	6	1	4	1	10	0	42	4	0	3	3	.500	0	0	4.60
4 Min. YEARS		79	71	5	0	449.1	1889	452	220	185	48	9	21	5	117	2	383	38	1	25	27	.481	0	0	3.71

Olmedo Saenz

Bats: Right **Throws:** Right **Pos:** 3B   **Ht:** 6'0" **Wt:** 185 **Born:** 10/8/70 **Age:** 25

		BATTING															BASERUNNING				PERCENTAGES		
Year Team	Lg	G	AB	H	2B	3B	HR	TB	R	RBI	TBB	IBB	SO	HBP	SH	SF	SB	CS	SB%	GDP	Avg	OBP	SLG
1991 Sarasota	A	5	19	2	0	1	0	4	1	2	2	0	0	0	0	0	0	1	.00	1	.105	.190	.211
South Bend	A	56	192	47	10	1	2	65	23	22	21	0	48	5	1	2	5	3	.63	3	.245	.332	.339
1992 South Bend	A	132	493	121	26	4	7	176	66	59	36	4	52	11	2	3	16	13	.55	16	.245	.309	.357
1993 South Bend	A	13	50	18	4	1	0	24	3	7	7	0	7	0	0	1	1	1	.50	1	.360	.439	.480
Sarasota	A	33	121	31	9	4	0	48	13	27	9	0	18	2	1	1	3	1	.75	1	.256	.316	.397
Birmingham	AA	49	173	60	17	2	6	99	30	29	20	2	21	5	0	1	2	1	.67	7	.347	.427	.572
1994 Nashville	AAA	107	383	100	27	2	12	167	48	59	30	0	57	9	2	5	3	2	.60	5	.261	.326	.436
1995 Nashville	AAA	111	415	126	26	1	13	193	60	74	45	1	60	12	3	3	0	2	.00	11	.304	.385	.465
1994 Chicago	AL	5	14	2	0	1	0	4	2	0	0	0	5	0	0	1	0	0	.00	1	.143	.143	.286
5 Min. YEARS		506	1846	505	119	16	40	776	244	279	170	7	263	44	9	17	30	24	.56	45	.274	.347	.420

Jon Saffer

Bats: Left **Throws:** Right **Pos:** OF   **Ht:** 6'2" **Wt:** 200 **Born:** 7/6/73 **Age:** 22

		BATTING															BASERUNNING				PERCENTAGES		
Year Team	Lg	G	AB	H	2B	3B	HR	TB	R	RBI	TBB	IBB	SO	HBP	SH	SF	SB	CS	SB%	GDP	Avg	OBP	SLG
1992 Expos	R	36	139	38	2	0	0	40	18	11	11	0	23	1	2	1	7	5	.58	2	.273	.329	.288
1993 W. Palm Bch	A	7	24	5	0	0	0	5	3	2	2	0	5	1	1	0	1	3	.25	0	.208	.296	.208
Jamestown	A	61	225	58	17	5	0	85	31	18	31	1	46	2	3	1	11	5	.69	4	.258	.351	.378
1994 Vermont	A	70	263	83	18	5	3	120	44	43	33	1	47	1	1	1	14	3	.82	9	.316	.393	.456
1995 W. Palm Bch	A	92	324	103	10	6	4	137	60	35	53	1	49	2	4	1	18	9	.67	7	.318	.416	.423
Harrisburg	AA	20	76	18	4	0	0	22	9	4	6	0	14	0	0	0	2	1	.67	2	.237	.293	.289
4 Min. YEARS		286	1051	305	51	16	7	409	165	113	136	3	184	7	11	4	53	26	.67	24	.290	.374	.389

Marc Sagmoen

Bats: Left **Throws:** Left **Pos:** OF   **Ht:** 5'11" **Wt:** 180 **Born:** 4/6/71 **Age:** 25

		BATTING															BASERUNNING				PERCENTAGES		
Year Team	Lg	G	AB	H	2B	3B	HR	TB	R	RBI	TBB	IBB	SO	HBP	SH	SF	SB	CS	SB%	GDP	Avg	OBP	SLG
1993 Erie	A	6	23	7	1	1	0	10	6	2	3	0	7	1	0	1	0	0	.00	0	.304	.393	.435
Charlstn-Sc	A	63	234	69	13	4	6	108	44	34	23	0	39	3	3	3	16	4	.80	2	.295	.361	.462
1994 Charlotte	A	122	475	139	25	10	3	193	74	47	37	2	56	3	1	3	15	10	.60	15	.293	.346	.406
1995 Okla. City	AAA	56	188	42	11	3	3	68	20	25	16	0	31	2	1	4	5	2	.71	2	.223	.286	.362
Tulsa	AA	63	242	56	8	5	6	92	36	22	23	0	23	4	1	2	5	4	.56	2	.231	.306	.380
3 Min. YEARS		310	1162	313	58	23	18	471	180	130	102	2	156	13	6	13	41	20	.67	21	.269	.332	.405

John Salamon

Pitches: Right **Bats:** Right **Pos:** P   **Ht:** 6'1" **Wt:** 220 **Born:** 3/30/72 **Age:** 24

		HOW MUCH HE PITCHED						WHAT HE GAVE UP												THE RESULTS					
Year Team	Lg	G	GS	CG	GF	IP	BFP	H	R	ER	HR	SH	SF	HB	TBB	IBB	SO	WP	Bk	W	L	Pct.	ShO	Sv	ERA
1993 Augusta	A	47	0	0	14	61	282	43	37	24	1	5	5	9	42	2	59	5	2	1	2	.333	0	1	3.54
1994 Beloit	A	33	0	0	17	48	219	27	17	14	2	2	3	4	52	0	54	5	1	3	1	.750	0	6	2.63
1995 New Haven	AA	6	0	0	0	10.1	54	9	7	7	0	1	2	0	16	1	9	1	0	1	0	1.000	0	0	6.10
Salem	A	8	0	0	4	14.2	60	13	10	10	5	0	0	0	5	0	9	0	0	1	0	1.000	0	1	6.14
3 Min. YEARS		94	0	0	35	134	615	92	71	55	8	8	10	13	115	3	131	11	3	6	3	.667	0	8	3.69

Edwin Salcedo

Bats: Right **Throws:** Right **Pos:** DH-C **Ht:** 6'0" **Wt:** 214 **Born:** 7/8/70 **Age:** 25

								BATTING										BASERUNNING				PERCENTAGES		
Year	Team	Lg	G	AB	H	2B	3B	HR	TB	R	RBI	TBB	IBB	SO	HBP	SH	SF	SB	CS	SB%	GDP	Avg	OBP	SLG
1990	Yankees	R	16	33	5	2	1	0	9	0	2	1	0	16	1	0	0	1	0	1.00	0	.152	.200	.273
1991	Yankees	R	3	5	1	0	0	1	4	1	4	0	0	1	1	0	1	0	0	.00	0	.200	.286	.800
	Greensboro	A	33	98	18	3	0	1	24	9	10	4	0	40	3	0	2	2	0	1.00	2	.184	.234	.245
1992	Pr. William	A	44	132	33	6	1	7	62	15	29	8	0	47	3	1	1	1	1	.50	1	.250	.306	.470
1993	Pr. William	A	23	80	13	4	0	2	23	8	6	3	0	22	2	0	0	0	2	.00	5	.163	.212	.288
1994	Tampa	A	20	69	17	1	1	3	29	14	9	7	0	23	4	0	0	1	0	1.00	1	.246	.350	.420
	San Bernrdo	A	41	141	30	2	1	14	76	20	33	7	0	76	3	0	0	1	3	.25	1	.213	.265	.539
1995	Norwich	AA	3	2	0	0	0	0	0	0	0	0	0	2	0	0	0	0	0	.00	0	.000	.000	.000
	Spartanburg	IND	7	25	9	2	0	0	11	2	4	2	0	8	0	0	0	0	1	.00	1	.360	.407	.440
	Spartanburg	IND	10	27	9	2	0	0	11	2	4	2	0	10	0	0	0	0	1	.00	1	.333	.379	.407
	6 Min. YEARS		200	612	135	22	4	28	249	71	101	34	0	245	17	1	4	6	8	.43	12	.221	.279	.407

Roger Salkeld

Pitches: Right **Bats:** Right **Pos:** P **Ht:** 6'5" **Wt:** 215 **Born:** 3/6/71 **Age:** 25

			HOW MUCH HE PITCHED						WHAT HE GAVE UP									THE RESULTS					
Year	Team	Lg	G	GS	CG	GF	IP	BFP	H	R	ER	HR	SH	SF	HB	TBB	IBB	SO	WP	Bk	W	L	Pct.	ShO	Sv	ERA
1989	Bellingham	A	8	6	0	1	42	168	27	17	6	0	0	1	4	10	0	55	3	3	2	2	.500	0	0	1.29
1990	San Bernrdo	A	25	25	2	0	153.1	677	140	77	58	3	7	1	3	83	0	167	9	2	11	5	.688	0	0	3.40
1991	Jacksonville	AA	23	23	5	0	153.2	634	131	56	52	9	5	5	10	55	1	159	12	2	8	8	.500	0	0	3.05
	Calgary	AAA	4	4	0	0	19.1	90	18	16	11	2	1	0	4	13	0	21	1	0	2	1	.667	0	0	5.12
1993	Jacksonville	AA	14	14	0	0	77	334	71	39	28	8	3	5	5	29	1	56	2	1	4	3	.571	0	0	3.27
1994	Calgary	AAA	13	13	0	0	67.1	315	74	54	46	11	0	5	4	39	2	54	5	0	3	7	.300	0	0	6.15
1995	Tacoma	AAA	4	3	0	1	15	59	8	4	3	0	0	0	0	7	0	11	0	0	1	0	1.000	0	1	1.80
	Indianapols	AAA	20	20	1	0	119.1	497	96	60	56	13	3	4	2	57	1	86	3	0	12	2	.857	0	0	4.22
1993	Seattle	AL	3	2	0	0	14.1	61	13	4	4	0	0	0	1	4	0	13	0	0	0	0	.000	0	0	2.51
1994	Seattle	AL	13	13	0	0	59	291	76	47	47	7	0	3	1	45	1	46	2	0	2	5	.286	0	0	7.17
	6 Min. YEARS		111	108	8	2	647	2774	565	323	260	46	19	21	32	293	5	609	35	8	43	28	.606	0	1	3.62
	2 Maj. YEARS		16	15	0	0	73.1	352	89	51	51	7	0	3	2	49	1	59	2	0	2	5	.286	0	0	6.26

Todd Samples

Bats: Right **Throws:** Right **Pos:** OF **Ht:** 6'2" **Wt:** 185 **Born:** 8/1/69 **Age:** 26

								BATTING										BASERUNNING				PERCENTAGES		
Year	Team	Lg	G	AB	H	2B	3B	HR	TB	R	RBI	TBB	IBB	SO	HBP	SH	SF	SB	CS	SB%	GDP	Avg	OBP	SLG
1990	Jamestown	A	59	183	45	6	4	1	62	22	13	13	0	48	4	2	1	13	6	.68	3	.246	.308	.339
1991	Sumter	A	130	505	131	29	6	12	208	82	63	47	0	124	8	1	10	25	14	.64	5	.259	.326	.412
1992	Rockford	A	117	410	98	21	6	3	140	52	34	25	2	83	7	2	3	29	10	.74	7	.239	.292	.341
1993	Stockton	A	122	401	106	21	3	6	151	63	48	28	1	63	10	8	4	36	12	.75	7	.264	.325	.377
1994	Stockton	A	26	80	19	4	1	0	25	12	7	12	0	23	3	0	1	2	3	.40	2	.238	.354	.313
	El Paso	AA	80	218	55	16	6	1	86	31	26	20	1	46	4	1	2	7	7	.50	1	.252	.324	.394
1995	El Paso	AA	2	4	0	0	0	0	0	1	0	1	0	1	0	0	0	0	0	.00	0	.000	.200	.000
	Tyler	IND	47	142	28	5	2	2	43	17	22	5	0	25	1	7	3	8	4	.67	0	.197	.225	.303
	6 Min. YEARS		583	1943	482	102	28	25	715	280	213	151	4	413	37	21	24	120	56	.68	25	.248	.311	.368

Scott Samuels

Bats: Left **Throws:** Right **Pos:** OF **Ht:** 5'11" **Wt:** 190 **Born:** 5/19/71 **Age:** 25

								BATTING										BASERUNNING				PERCENTAGES		
Year	Team	Lg	G	AB	H	2B	3B	HR	TB	R	RBI	TBB	IBB	SO	HBP	SH	SF	SB	CS	SB%	GDP	Avg	OBP	SLG
1992	Erie	A	43	128	26	7	1	0	35	17	14	19	0	39	2	0	0	7	3	.70	2	.203	.315	.273
1993	High Desert	A	76	219	65	10	4	6	101	43	40	45	0	55	1	0	1	12	4	.75	7	.297	.417	.461
1994	Brevard Cty	A	89	281	65	11	0	3	85	35	25	46	1	70	4	1	1	11	5	.69	7	.231	.346	.302
1995	Orlando	AA	5	21	6	1	0	1	10	3	4	3	0	4	0	0	0	2	0	1.00	0	.286	.375	.476
	Daytona	A	112	388	127	29	12	2	186	92	42	69	7	63	8	3	4	38	14	.73	8	.327	.435	.479
	4 Min. YEARS		325	1037	289	58	17	12	417	190	125	182	8	231	15	4	6	70	26	.73	24	.279	.392	.402

Alex Sanchez

Pitches: Right **Bats:** Right **Pos:** P **Ht:** 6'2" **Wt:** 190 **Born:** 4/8/66 **Age:** 30

			HOW MUCH HE PITCHED						WHAT HE GAVE UP									THE RESULTS					
Year	Team	Lg	G	GS	CG	GF	IP	BFP	H	R	ER	HR	SH	SF	HB	TBB	IBB	SO	WP	Bk	W	L	Pct.	ShO	Sv	ERA
1987	St. Cathrns	A	17	17	0	0	95.1	401	72	33	28	3	0	0	5	38	0	116	6	0	8	3	.727	0	0	2.64
	Myrtle Bch	A	1	0	0	1	3	11	2	1	1	1	0	0	0	0	0	4	0	0	0	0	.000	0	1	3.00
1988	Knoxville	AA	24	24	2	0	149.1	622	100	56	42	8	1	2	3	74	0	166	5	7	12	5	.706	0	0	2.53
	Syracuse	AAA	10	10	1	0	57.2	258	47	26	23	8	3	2	0	43	1	57	4	3	4	3	.571	0	0	3.59
1989	Syracuse	AAA	28	27	1	0	169.2	697	125	68	59	14	1	5	1	74	0	141	11	5	13	7	.650	1	0	3.13
1990	Syracuse	AAA	22	22	1	0	112	521	111	77	71	15	7	8	4	79	1	65	5	0	5	9	.357	0	0	5.71
1991	Syracuse	AAA	14	5	0	8	28	153	33	33	32	2	1	2	1	35	0	12	14	0	1	4	.200	0	1	10.29
	Knoxville	AA	14	11	0	2	58.2	253	43	26	20	3	1	2	2	36	2	38	8	2	4	2	.667	0	0	3.07
1992	Baseball Cy	A	15	13	3	0	78.2	299	61	33	30	2	4	0	4	41	0	42	5	1	6	5	.545	2	0	3.43
	Memphis	AA	1	1	0	0	6	25	4	4	4	0	1	0	1	2	0	6	0	0	0	1	.000	0	0	6.00
1993	Memphis	AA	15	10	0	4	70	299	64	36	34	5	2	0	1	35	0	47	2	1	1	4	.200	0	0	4.37
	Omaha	AAA	16	9	1	3	51	231	62	46	46	7	2	1	0	28	1	31	6	0	2	8	.200	0	0	8.12
1994	Calgary	AAA	20	13	0	2	79	365	89	58	48	8	0	0	2	42	2	48	9	0	3	3	.500	0	0	5.47

		G	GS	CG	GF	IP	BFP	H	R	ER	HR	SH	SF	HB	TBB	IBB	SO	WP	Bk	W	L	Pct.	ShO	Sv	ERA
Wichita	AA	4	0	0	2	4	21	4	3	3	0	0	0	0	5	0	4	0	0	0	0	.000	0	0	6.75
1995 Edmonton	AAA	8	0	0	0	17.1	75	18	12	10	0	0	2	0	10	0	8	2	0	0	0	.000	0	0	5.19
1989 Toronto	AL	4	3	0	0	11.2	61	16	13	13	1	0	2	0	14	0	4	1	0	0	1	.000	0	0	10.03
9 Min. YEARS		209	162	9	22	979.2	4260	835	512	451	76	23	32	24	542	7	785	77	19	59	54	.522	3	2	4.14

Yuri Sanchez

Bats: Left **Throws:** Right **Pos:** SS **Ht:** 6'1" **Wt:** 165 **Born:** 11/11/73 **Age:** 22

		BATTING														BASERUNNING				PERCENTAGES		
Year Team	Lg	G	AB	H	2B	3B	HR	TB	R	RBI	TBB	IBB	SO	HBP	SH	SF	SB	CS	SB%	GDP	Avg	OBP	SLG
1992 Bristol	R	36	102	18	2	2	0	24	11	5	21	0	41	0	1	0	5	3	.63	1	.176	.317	.235
1993 Fayetteville	A	111	340	69	7	6	0	88	53	30	73	0	125	2	7	3	20	9	.69	3	.203	.344	.259
1994 Lakeland	A	89	254	59	5	5	1	77	41	19	39	0	75	4	5	1	21	8	.72	6	.232	.342	.303
Trenton	AA	28	78	16	2	2	0	22	7	2	11	0	25	0	2	0	4	1	.80	0	.205	.303	.282
1995 Jacksonville	AA	121	342	73	8	7	6	113	52	26	38	0	116	1	15	0	15	6	.71	3	.213	.294	.330
4 Min. YEARS		385	1116	235	24	22	7	324	164	82	182	0	382	7	30	4	65	27	.71	13	.211	.324	.290

Tracy Sanders

Bats: Left **Throws:** Right **Pos:** OF **Ht:** 6'2" **Wt:** 200 **Born:** 7/26/69 **Age:** 26

		BATTING														BASERUNNING				PERCENTAGES		
Year Team	Lg	G	AB	H	2B	3B	HR	TB	R	RBI	TBB	IBB	SO	HBP	SH	SF	SB	CS	SB%	GDP	Avg	OBP	SLG
1990 Burlington	R	51	178	50	12	1	10	94	38	34	33	0	36	2	0	1	10	3	.77	2	.281	.397	.528
Kinston	A	10	32	14	3	3	0	23	6	9	7	0	6	0	0	0	1	1	.50	0	.438	.538	.719
1991 Kinston	A	118	421	112	20	8	18	202	80	63	83	4	95	6	2	2	8	5	.62	9	.266	.393	.480
1992 Canton-Akrn	AA	114	381	92	11	3	21	172	66	87	77	3	113	3	4	3	3	6	.33	8	.241	.371	.451
1993 Canton-Akrn	AA	42	136	29	6	2	5	54	20	20	31	1	30	1	0	1	4	1	.80	1	.213	.361	.397
Wichita	AA	77	266	86	13	4	13	146	44	47	34	1	67	2	0	1	6	5	.55	2	.323	.403	.549
1994 Binghamton	AA	101	275	66	20	4	8	118	44	37	60	1	88	3	0	5	8	6	.57	1	.240	.376	.429
1995 Binghamton	AA	10	32	9	3	0	2	18	6	8	5	0	11	0	0	0	1	0	1.00	1	.281	.378	.563
Norfolk	AAA	64	110	25	6	0	4	43	21	14	34	0	34	4	0	0	3	1	.75	2	.227	.426	.391
6 Min. YEARS		587	1831	483	94	25	81	870	325	319	364	10	480	21	6	13	44	28	.61	25	.264	.389	.475

Chance Sanford

Bats: Left **Throws:** Right **Pos:** 2B **Ht:** 5'10" **Wt:** 165 **Born:** 6/2/72 **Age:** 24

		BATTING														BASERUNNING				PERCENTAGES		
Year Team	Lg	G	AB	H	2B	3B	HR	TB	R	RBI	TBB	IBB	SO	HBP	SH	SF	SB	CS	SB%	GDP	Avg	OBP	SLG
1992 Welland	A	59	214	61	11	3	5	93	36	21	35	4	39	0	0	3	13	4	.76	2	.285	.381	.435
Augusta	A	14	46	5	1	0	0	6	3	2	3	0	10	1	0	0	0	2	.00	0	.109	.180	.130
1993 Salem	A	115	428	109	21	5	10	170	54	37	33	0	80	1	3	2	11	10	.52	0	.255	.308	.397
1994 Salem	A	127	474	130	32	6	19	231	81	78	56	2	95	2	1	4	12	6	.67	7	.274	.351	.487
1995 Carolina	AA	16	36	10	3	1	3	24	6	10	5	1	7	1	0	0	3	1	.75	0	.278	.381	.667
Pirates	R	6	19	4	0	0	1	7	2	1	2	0	2	0	0	0	0	0	.00	0	.211	.286	.368
Lynchburg	A	16	66	22	4	0	3	35	8	14	7	0	13	0	0	1	1	0	1.00	1	.333	.392	.530
4 Min. YEARS		353	1283	341	72	15	41	566	190	163	141	5	246	5	4	10	40	23	.63	10	.266	.338	.441

Julio Santana

Pitches: Right **Bats:** Right **Pos:** P **Ht:** 6'0" **Wt:** 175 **Born:** 1/20/73 **Age:** 23

		HOW MUCH HE PITCHED						WHAT HE GAVE UP									THE RESULTS					
Year Team	Lg	G	GS	CG	GF	IP	BFP	H	R	ER	HR	SH	SF	HB	TBB	IBB	SO	WP	Bk	W	L	Pct.	ShO	Sv	ERA
1993 Rangers	R	26	0	0	12	39	153	31	9	6	0	0	0	1	7	0	50	1	0	4	1	.800	0	7	1.38
1994 Charlstn-Sc	A	16	16	0	0	91.1	383	65	38	25	3	0	4	7	44	0	103	7	1	6	7	.462	0	0	2.46
Tulsa	AA	11	11	2	0	71.1	290	50	26	23	1	1	2	2	41	0	45	2	0	7	2	.778	0	0	2.90
1995 Okla. City	AAA	2	2	0	0	3	25	9	14	13	3	0	0	0	7	0	6	1	1	0	2	.000	0	0	39.00
Charlotte	A	5	5	1	0	31.1	136	32	16	13	1	1	1	0	16	0	27	7	2	0	3	.000	0	0	3.73
Tulsa	AA	15	15	3	0	103	438	91	40	37	8	2	4	0	52	2	71	8	1	6	4	.600	0	0	3.23
3 Min. YEARS		75	49	6	12	339	1425	278	143	117	16	4	11	10	167	2	302	26	5	23	19	.548	0	7	3.11

Ruben Santana

Bats: Right **Throws:** Right **Pos:** 3B-2B **Ht:** 6'2" **Wt:** 175 **Born:** 3/7/70 **Age:** 26

		BATTING														BASERUNNING				PERCENTAGES		
Year Team	Lg	G	AB	H	2B	3B	HR	TB	R	RBI	TBB	IBB	SO	HBP	SH	SF	SB	CS	SB%	GDP	Avg	OBP	SLG
1990 Peninsula	A	26	80	17	1	0	0	18	3	5	1	0	22	1	0	0	6	1	.86	1	.213	.232	.225
Bellingham	A	47	155	39	3	2	4	58	22	13	18	2	39	6	0	1	10	9	.53	1	.252	.350	.374
1991 San Bernrdo	A	108	394	119	16	4	3	152	55	43	26	4	74	6	9	5	34	12	.74	4	.302	.350	.386
Jacksonvlle	AA	5	15	3	0	0	1	6	2	3	1	0	3	0	0	0	0	0	.00	0	.200	.250	.400
1992 Peninsula	A	113	401	118	19	4	8	169	54	61	21	0	54	9	6	1	17	16	.52	8	.294	.343	.421
1993 Jacksonvlle	AA	128	499	150	21	2	21	238	79	84	38	7	101	9	3	5	13	8	.62	2	.301	.358	.477
1994 Jacksonvlle	AA	131	501	148	25	4	7	202	62	68	28	1	62	11	3	4	10	7	.59	9	.295	.344	.403
1995 Chattanooga	AA	142	556	163	23	10	11	239	89	79	50	5	77	8	6	5	2	5	.29	17	.293	.357	.430
6 Min. YEARS		700	2601	757	108	26	55	1082	366	356	183	19	432	50	27	21	92	58	.61	42	.291	.347	.416

Henry Santos

Pitches: Left **Bats:** Left **Pos:** P **Ht:** 6'1" **Wt:** 175 **Born:** 1/17/73 **Age:** 23

Year	Team	Lg	G	GS	CG	GF	IP	BFP	H	R	ER	HR	SH	SF	HB	TBB	IBB	SO	WP	Bk	W	L	Pct.	ShO	Sv	ERA
1992	Bristol	R	12	0	0	7	15	74	17	18	11	3	0	1	0	12	0	16	4	0	0	1	.000	0	0	6.60
1993	Niagara Fal	A	7	7	0	0	42.1	172	29	15	11	3	1	0	2	17	0	50	0	0	2	1	.667	0	0	2.34
	Fayetteville	A	8	8	0	0	44	199	43	25	23	3	1	1	3	30	0	29	6	1	3	2	.600	0	0	4.70
1994	Fayetteville	A	15	15	0	0	82.2	356	76	44	36	11	1	1	3	42	0	57	3	0	4	8	.333	0	0	3.92
	Lakeland	A	11	11	0	0	52.2	276	88	52	45	11	6	1	4	34	0	35	5	2	1	6	.143	0	0	7.69
1995	Lakeland	A	35	10	0	7	97.2	434	111	59	46	3	5	4	6	40	0	80	10	0	5	6	.455	0	0	4.24
	Toledo	AAA	1	0	0	0	2.2	13	3	2	2	1	0	0	0	2	0	4	0	0	0	1	.000	0	0	6.75
	4 Min. YEARS		89	51	0	14	337	1524	367	215	174	35	14	8	18	177	0	271	28	3	15	25	.375	0	0	4.65

Jason Satre

Pitches: Right **Bats:** Right **Pos:** P **Ht:** 6'1" **Wt:** 180 **Born:** 8/24/70 **Age:** 25

Year	Team	Lg	G	GS	CG	GF	IP	BFP	H	R	ER	HR	SH	SF	HB	TBB	IBB	SO	WP	Bk	W	L	Pct.	ShO	Sv	ERA
1988	Reds	R	11	10	0	0	47	201	31	16	13	0	1	5	2	29	0	44	6	3	0	3	.000	0	0	2.49
1989	Greensboro	A	27	27	2	0	133.2	603	128	95	85	7	4	4	5	87	0	106	14	4	7	13	.350	0	0	5.72
1990	Charlstn-Wv	A	24	22	3	0	116	504	99	70	61	8	3	5	3	75	1	105	16	3	6	12	.333	1	0	4.73
1991	Cedar Rapds	A	21	20	4	1	132.2	551	101	48	38	5	6	4	2	67	1	130	6	0	8	6	.571	2	1	2.58
	Chattanooga	AA	8	8	0	0	44	195	37	26	25	7	1	0	2	26	0	44	6	1	1	7	.125	0	0	5.11
1992	Chattanooga	AA	14	11	0	2	58	247	56	42	35	7	1	2	1	26	1	36	4	0	3	5	.375	0	0	5.43
1993	Rochester	AAA	15	15	0	0	80	371	87	57	52	12	1	3	6	45	0	42	9	0	4	5	.444	0	0	5.85
	Bowie	AA	13	13	2	0	84	344	68	35	29	7	0	2	4	20	0	65	2	1	7	3	.700	0	0	3.11
1994	Rochester	AAA	37	15	1	5	130.1	578	126	80	72	21	2	6	9	67	5	73	8	0	6	7	.462	0	0	4.97
1995	Pawtucket	AAA	9	5	0	1	30.2	143	38	23	21	3	2	2	2	16	0	14	2	0	1	5	.167	0	0	6.16
	Rio Grande	IND	16	12	2	1	93.2	403	92	42	34	6	6	1	7	34	2	58	4	1	4	4	.500	0	1	3.27
	8 Min. YEARS		195	158	14	10	950	4140	863	534	465	83	27	34	43	492	10	717	77	13	47	70	.402	3	2	4.41

Chris Saunders

Bats: Right **Throws:** Right **Pos:** 3B **Ht:** 6'2" **Wt:** 200 **Born:** 7/19/70 **Age:** 25

Year	Team	Lg	G	AB	H	2B	3B	HR	TB	R	RBI	TBB	IBB	SO	HBP	SH	SF	SB	CS	SB%	GDP	Avg	OBP	SLG
1992	Pittsfield	A	72	254	64	11	2	2	85	34	32	34	0	50	1	1	5	5	2	.71	5	.252	.337	.335
1993	St. Lucie	A	123	456	115	14	4	4	149	45	64	40	4	89	1	1	4	6	7	.46	10	.252	.311	.327
1994	Binghamton	AA	132	499	134	29	0	10	193	68	70	43	0	96	4	2	7	6	6	.50	12	.269	.327	.387
1995	Norfolk	AAA	16	56	13	3	1	3	27	9	7	9	0	15	0	0	0	1	1	.50	1	.232	.338	.482
	Binghamton	AA	122	441	114	22	5	8	170	58	66	45	1	98	5	5	7	3	6	.33	7	.259	.329	.385
	4 Min. YEARS		465	1706	440	79	12	27	624	214	239	171	5	348	11	9	23	21	22	.49	35	.258	.325	.366

Doug Saunders

Bats: Right **Throws:** Right **Pos:** 3B **Ht:** 6'0" **Wt:** 172 **Born:** 12/13/69 **Age:** 26

Year	Team	Lg	G	AB	H	2B	3B	HR	TB	R	RBI	TBB	IBB	SO	HBP	SH	SF	SB	CS	SB%	GDP	Avg	OBP	SLG
1988	Mets	R	16	64	16	4	1	0	22	8	10	9	0	14	0	2	0	2	3	.40	0	.250	.342	.344
	Little Fall	A	29	100	30	6	1	0	38	10	11	6	0	15	0	1	0	1	4	.20	2	.300	.340	.380
1989	Columbia	A	115	377	99	18	4	4	137	53	38	35	2	78	3	4	3	5	5	.50	5	.263	.328	.363
1990	St. Lucie	A	115	408	92	8	4	1	111	52	43	43	0	96	2	7	2	24	10	.71	7	.225	.301	.272
1991	St. Lucie	A	70	230	54	9	2	2	73	19	18	25	0	43	4	5	0	5	6	.45	6	.235	.320	.317
1992	Binghamton	AA	130	435	108	16	2	5	143	45	38	52	0	68	1	5	4	8	12	.40	9	.248	.327	.329
1993	Norfolk	AAA	105	356	88	12	6	2	118	37	24	44	1	63	3	7	1	6	5	.55	13	.247	.334	.331
1994	Binghamton	AA	96	338	96	19	4	8	147	48	45	43	2	63	0	6	4	3	4	.43	6	.284	.361	.435
1995	Edmonton	AAA	5	16	3	2	1	0	7	2	4	0	0	2	0	0	0	0	0	.00	0	.188	.188	.438
	Tacoma	AAA	50	135	38	5	2	5	62	19	24	7	0	30	1	1	2	0	0	.00	3	.281	.317	.459
	Port City	AA	28	114	30	9	1	4	53	13	16	10	1	28	2	0	2	2	0	1.00	4	.263	.328	.465
1993	New York	NL	28	67	14	2	0	0	16	8	0	3	0	4	0	3	0	0	0	.00	2	.209	.243	.239
	8 Min. YEARS		759	2573	654	108	28	31	911	306	271	274	6	500	16	38	18	56	49	.53	55	.254	.328	.354

Rich Sauveur

Pitches: Left **Bats:** Left **Pos:** P **Ht:** 6'4" **Wt:** 185 **Born:** 11/23/63 **Age:** 32

Year	Team	Lg	G	GS	CG	GF	IP	BFP	H	R	ER	HR	SH	SF	HB	TBB	IBB	SO	WP	Bk	W	L	Pct.	ShO	Sv	ERA
1984	Pr. William	A	10	10	0	0	54.2	240	43	22	19	5	2	1	1	31	0	54	3	0	3	3	.500	0	0	3.13
	Nashua	AA	10	10	0	0	70.2	291	54	27	23	4	4	1	3	34	1	48	2	4	5	3	.625	2	0	2.93
1985	Nashua	AA	25	25	4	0	157.1	666	146	73	62	7	9	6	3	78	2	85	7	4	9	10	.474	2	0	3.55
1986	Nashua	AA	5	5	2	0	38	141	21	5	5	1	1	0	1	11	0	28	1	1	3	1	.750	1	0	1.18
	Hawaii	AAA	14	14	6	0	92	391	73	40	31	3	2	0	6	45	1	68	4	8	7	6	.538	1	0	3.03
1987	Harrisburg	AA	30	27	7	0	195	825	174	71	62	9	7	9	9	96	3	160	9	7	13	6	.684	1	0	2.86
1988	Jacksonville	AA	8	0	0	4	6.2	32	7	5	3	0	0	0	0	5	0	8	0	0	0	2	.000	0	1	4.05
	Indianapols	AAA	43	3	0	18	81.1	318	60	26	22	8	5	1	1	28	5	58	3	3	7	4	.636	0	10	2.43
1989	Indianapols	AAA	8	0	0	4	9.2	44	10	8	8	1	0	1	0	6	0	8	0	0	0	1	.000	0	1	7.45
1990	Miami	A	11	6	1	2	40.2	178	41	16	15	2	2	0	4	17	0	34	0	3	0	4	.000	0	0	3.32
	Indianapols	AAA	14	7	0	0	56	232	45	14	12	1	2	2	3	25	0	24	1	3	2	2	.500	0	0	1.93
1991	Tidewater	AAA	42	0	0	21	45.1	188	31	14	12	6	4	2	2	23	5	49	3	3	2	2	.500	0	6	2.38

Year	Team	Lg	G	GS	CG	GF	IP	BFP	H	R	ER	HR	SH	SF	HB	TBB	IBB	SO	WP	Bk	W	L	Pct.	ShO	Sv	ERA
1992	Omaha	AAA	34	13	1	7	117.1	467	93	54	42	8	3	5	2	39	1	88	4	4	7	6	.538	0	0	3.22
1993	Indianapols	AAA	5	5	0	0	34.2	146	41	10	7	2	2	0	2	7	2	21	0	0	2	0	1.000	0	0	1.82
1994	Indianapols	AAA	53	1	0	30	67	268	47	25	21	7	4	0	1	23	4	65	1	0	3	3	.500	0	12	2.82
1995	Indianapols	AAA	52	0	0	43	57	228	43	17	13	3	1	1	2	18	3	47	3	0	5	2	.714	0	15	2.05
1986	Pittsburgh	NL	3	3	0	0	12	57	17	8	8	3	1	0	2	6	0	6	0	2	0	0	.000	0	0	6.00
1988	Montreal	NL	4	0	0	0	3	14	3	2	2	1	0	0	0	2	0	3	0	0	0	0	.000	0	0	6.00
1991	New York	NL	6	0	0	0	3.1	19	7	4	4	1	2	0	0	2	0	4	0	0	0	0	.000	0	0	10.80
1992	Kansas City	AL	8	0	0	2	14.1	65	15	7	7	1	0	0	2	8	1	7	0	1	0	1	.000	0	0	4.40
	12 Min. YEARS		364	126	23	129	1123.1	4655	929	427	357	61	48	27	38	486	27	845	41	40	68	55	.553	7	45	2.86
	4 Maj. YEARS		21	3	0	2	32.2	155	42	21	21	6	3	0	4	18	1	20	0	3	0	1	.000	0	0	5.79

Warren Sawkiw

Bats: Both **Throws:** Right **Pos:** DH — **Ht:** 5'11" **Wt:** 180 **Born:** 1/19/68 **Age:** 28

			BATTING															BASERUNNING				PERCENTAGES		
Year	Team	Lg	G	AB	H	2B	3B	HR	TB	R	RBI	TBB	IBB	SO	HBP	SH	SF	SB	CS	SB%	GDP	Avg	OBP	SLG
1990	Niagara Fal	A	7	20	8	1	1	0	11	7	4	15	2	3	0	0	0	2	0	1.00	0	.400	.657	.550
	Fayettevlle	A	59	210	54	6	0	1	63	31	18	30	1	35	1	2	4	4	1	.80	6	.257	.347	.300
1991	Lakeland	A	112	420	114	20	7	2	154	58	42	42	2	87	3	3	3	2	9	.18	8	.271	.340	.367
1992	Lakeland	A	118	423	103	18	4	2	135	56	47	39	1	62	3	0	7	6	7	.46	13	.243	.307	.319
1993	Rochester	IND	70	272	89	21	2	9	141	42	45	31	2	53	1	0	2	14	2	.88	6	.327	.395	.518
1994	Winnipeg	IND	20	76	19	3	0	1	25	7	10	9	0	13	0	0	2	3	1	.75	0	.250	.322	.329
	Thunder Bay	IND	48	183	63	11	0	3	83	25	27	22	1	32	0	3	2	2	6	.25	2	.344	.411	.454
1995	Syracuse	AAA	11	42	8	1	0	0	9	3	0	5	0	8	0	0	0	2	0	1.00	1	.190	.277	.214
	Knoxville	AA	44	121	30	4	1	1	39	11	11	13	0	36	0	3	1	2	2	.50	2	.248	.319	.322
	6 Min. YEARS		489	1767	488	85	15	19	660	240	204	206	9	329	8	11	21	37	28	.57	38	.276	.351	.374

Will Scalzitti

Bats: Right **Throws:** Right **Pos:** C — **Ht:** 6'0" **Wt:** 190 **Born:** 8/29/72 **Age:** 23

			BATTING															BASERUNNING				PERCENTAGES		
Year	Team	Lg	G	AB	H	2B	3B	HR	TB	R	RBI	TBB	IBB	SO	HBP	SH	SF	SB	CS	SB%	GDP	Avg	OBP	SLG
1992	Bend	A	62	230	66	16	0	7	103	35	40	20	0	40	1	2	1	0	2	.00	9	.287	.345	.448
1993	Central Val	A	75	248	60	10	0	2	76	25	17	17	1	40	1	3	1	0	1	.00	6	.242	.292	.306
1994	Colo. Sprng	AAA	1	1	0	0	0	0	0	0	0	0	0	1	0	0	0	0	0	.00	0	.000	.000	.000
	Central Val	A	81	297	75	13	0	9	115	27	37	16	0	56	4	2	1	0	3	.00	8	.253	.299	.387
	New Haven	AA	10	30	7	0	0	1	10	2	6	0	0	4	0	0	0	0	0	.00	0	.233	.233	.333
1995	New Haven	AA	39	123	23	6	0	1	32	9	14	10	0	17	1	1	2	0	0	.00	0	.187	.250	.260
	Salem	A	11	35	7	1	0	0	8	4	0	4	1	5	1	1	0	0	1	.00	1	.200	.300	.229
	4 Min. YEARS		279	964	238	46	0	20	344	102	114	67	2	163	8	9	5	0	7	.00	24	.247	.300	.357

Jeff Schmidt

Pitches: Right **Bats:** Right **Pos:** P — **Ht:** 6'5" **Wt:** 190 **Born:** 2/21/71 **Age:** 25

			HOW MUCH HE PITCHED						WHAT HE GAVE UP												THE RESULTS					
Year	Team	Lg	G	GS	CG	GF	IP	BFP	H	R	ER	HR	SH	SF	HB	TBB	IBB	SO	WP	Bk	W	L	Pct.	ShO	Sv	ERA
1992	Boise	A	11	11	0	0	52.1	236	55	41	26	4	1	0	4	18	1	41	3	4	1	6	.143	0	0	4.47
1993	Cedar Rapds	A	26	25	3	0	152.1	696	166	105	83	16	9	6	16	58	3	107	11	4	3	14	.176	0	0	4.90
1994	Lk Elsinore	A	39	11	0	14	92	395	94	54	42	8	7	0	4	28	2	70	4	6	1	5	.167	0	12	4.11
1995	Midland	AA	20	20	0	0	100.1	466	127	75	65	12	2	4	5	48	1	46	17	1	4	12	.250	0	0	5.83
	4 Min. YEARS		96	67	3	14	397	1793	442	275	216	40	19	10	29	152	7	264	35	15	9	37	.196	0	12	4.90

Tom Schmidt

Bats: Right **Throws:** Right **Pos:** 3B — **Ht:** 6'3" **Wt:** 200 **Born:** 2/12/73 **Age:** 23

			BATTING															BASERUNNING				PERCENTAGES		
Year	Team	Lg	G	AB	H	2B	3B	HR	TB	R	RBI	TBB	IBB	SO	HBP	SH	SF	SB	CS	SB%	GDP	Avg	OBP	SLG
1992	Bend	A	68	249	64	13	1	7	100	39	27	24	1	78	4	0	1	17	3	.85	5	.257	.331	.402
1993	Central Val	A	126	478	117	15	1	19	191	61	62	40	2	107	4	1	5	5	3	.63	15	.245	.306	.400
1994	Central Val	A	99	334	81	8	1	9	118	36	50	52	2	100	8	2	2	3	4	.43	3	.243	.356	.353
1995	New Haven	AA	115	423	92	25	3	6	141	55	49	24	2	99	5	1	5	2	1	.67	13	.217	.265	.333
	4 Min. YEARS		408	1484	354	61	6	41	550	191	188	140	7	384	21	4	13	27	11	.71	36	.239	.311	.371

Todd Schmitt

Pitches: Right **Bats:** Right **Pos:** P — **Ht:** 6'2" **Wt:** 170 **Born:** 2/12/70 **Age:** 26

			HOW MUCH HE PITCHED						WHAT HE GAVE UP												THE RESULTS					
Year	Team	Lg	G	GS	CG	GF	IP	BFP	H	R	ER	HR	SH	SF	HB	TBB	IBB	SO	WP	Bk	W	L	Pct.	ShO	Sv	ERA
1992	Spokane	A	29	0	0	29	38	162	23	7	5	1	3	0	2	23	5	48	3	0	6	1	.857	0	15	1.18
1993	Waterloo	A	51	0	0	47	58.2	254	41	15	13	0	1	1	6	33	5	76	5	2	1	4	.200	0	25	1.99
1994	Rancho Cuca	A	53	0	0	50	50.2	215	43	15	11	2	5	1	2	24	1	45	2	1	2	4	.333	0	29	1.95
1995	Memphis	AA	26	0	0	24	27.2	108	18	4	4	2	0	1	1	11	2	27	0	0	0	0	.000	0	18	1.30
	Las Vegas	AAA	12	0	0	8	12.2	61	16	11	11	0	0	1	2	9	0	6	2	0	0	2	.000	0	2	7.82
	4 Min. YEARS		171	0	0	158	187.2	800	141	52	44	5	9	4	13	100	13	202	12	3	9	11	.450	0	89	2.11

Philip Schneider

Pitches: Left **Bats:** Left **Pos:** P **Ht:** 6'1" **Wt:** 215 **Born:** 4/26/71 **Age:** 25

					HOW MUCH HE PITCHED			WHAT HE GAVE UP										THE RESULTS				
Year	Team	Lg	G	GS	CG	GF	IP	BFP	H	R	ER	HR	SH	SF	HB	TBB	IBB	SO	WP	Bk	W	L	Pct.	ShO	Sv	ERA
1993	Bend	A	4	0	0	4	7	23	1	1	0	0	0	0	0	0	0	9	0	0	1	0	1.000	0	0	0.00
	Central Val	A	19	0	0	4	37.2	165	30	16	13	3	6	0	1	25	0	42	1	0	8	1	.889	0	0	3.11
1994	New Haven	AA	31	21	2	1	135.2	561	117	54	47	8	9	3	2	47	0	94	1	2	10	8	.556	1	0	3.12
1995	New Haven	AA	2	2	0	0	7	37	8	8	6	1	1	0	0	9	0	3	0	0	0	1	.000	0	0	7.71
	3 Min. YEARS		56	23	2	9	187.1	786	156	79	66	12	16	3	3	81	0	148	2	2	19	10	.655	1	0	3.17

Mike Schooler

Pitches: Right **Bats:** Right **Pos:** P **Ht:** 6'3" **Wt:** 220 **Born:** 8/10/62 **Age:** 33

					HOW MUCH HE PITCHED			WHAT HE GAVE UP										THE RESULTS				
Year	Team	Lg	G	GS	CG	GF	IP	BFP	H	R	ER	HR	SH	SF	HB	TBB	IBB	SO	WP	Bk	W	L	Pct.	ShO	Sv	ERA
1985	Bellingham	A	10	10	0	0	55.1	0	42	24	18	5	0	0	2	15	0	48	1	1	4	3	.571	0	0	2.93
1986	Wausau	A	26	26	6	0	166.1	700	166	83	62	20	3	3	4	44	0	171	10	2	12	10	.545	1	0	3.35
1987	Chattanooga	AA	28	28	3	0	175	748	183	87	77	14	2	5	6	48	1	144	4	7	13	8	.619	2	0	3.96
1988	Calgary	AAA	26	0	0	21	33.2	139	32	19	12	2	5	1	0	6	1	47	3	1	4	4	.500	0	8	3.21
1991	Jacksonvlle	AA	11	2	0	3	11.1	50	13	9	7	2	0	1	0	3	0	12	0	0	1	1	.500	0	0	5.56
1992	Calgary	AAA	1	1	0	0	2	8	2	0	0	0	0	0	0	0	0	0	0	0	0	0	.000	0	0	0.00
	Bellingham	A	2	1	0	0	3	12	1	2	0	0	0	0	0	0	0	3	0	0	0	0	.000	0	0	0.00
1993	Okla. City	AAA	28	0	0	20	45.2	205	59	33	30	3	1	1	0	11	3	31	5	2	1	3	.250	0	5	5.91
1994	Wichita	AA	22	9	0	7	57.2	261	82	37	30	1	6	3	0	12	3	37	2	0	0	8	.000	0	0	4.68
1995	Midland	AA	54	0	0	47	65.1	257	49	16	13	5	5	4	0	19	3	55	5	0	3	3	.500	0	20	1.79
1988	Seattle	AL	40	0	0	33	48.1	214	45	21	19	4	2	3	1	24	4	54	4	1	5	8	.385	0	15	3.54
1989	Seattle	AL	67	0	0	60	77	329	81	27	24	2	3	1	2	19	3	69	6	1	1	7	.125	0	33	2.81
1990	Seattle	AL	49	0	0	45	56	229	47	18	14	5	3	2	1	16	5	45	1	0	1	4	.200	0	30	2.25
1991	Seattle	AL	34	0	0	23	34.1	138	25	14	14	2	1	1	0	10	0	31	2	1	3	3	.500	0	7	3.67
1992	Seattle	AL	53	0	0	36	51.2	232	55	29	27	7	4	3	1	24	6	33	0	0	2	7	.222	0	13	4.70
1993	Texas	AL	17	0	0	0	24.1	111	30	17	15	3	2	0	0	10	1	16	1	0	3	0	1.000	0	0	5.55
	9 Min. YEARS		208	77	9	98	615.1	2380	630	310	249	52	22	18	12	158	11	548	30	13	38	40	.487	3	33	3.64
	6 Maj. YEARS		260	0	0	197	291.2	1253	283	126	113	23	15	10	5	103	19	248	14	3	15	29	.341	0	98	3.49

Brad Schorr

Pitches: Right **Bats:** Right **Pos:** P **Ht:** 6'2" **Wt:** 201 **Born:** 1/21/72 **Age:** 24

					HOW MUCH HE PITCHED			WHAT HE GAVE UP										THE RESULTS				
Year	Team	Lg	G	GS	CG	GF	IP	BFP	H	R	ER	HR	SH	SF	HB	TBB	IBB	SO	WP	Bk	W	L	Pct.	ShO	Sv	ERA
1990	Mets	R	12	8	0	4	57.2	221	44	23	19	0	1	1	2	7	0	47	2	2	2	3	.400	0	3	2.97
1991	Kingsport	R	11	11	3	0	71.2	293	53	40	25	6	0	2	9	16	1	69	5	0	5	6	.455	0	0	3.14
	Pittsfield	A	2	2	0	0	13.2	54	13	4	3	0	0	1	1	5	0	3	0	0	2	0	1.000	0	0	1.98
1992	Columbia	A	27	27	2	0	160	696	169	96	85	13	3	3	10	48	0	106	16	2	12	6	.667	1	0	4.78
1993	St. Lucie	A	27	26	4	1	181.2	770	192	87	75	8	9	8	10	52	1	75	7	4	11	10	.524	0	0	3.72
1994	St. Lucie	A	17	17	4	0	110.1	455	100	45	40	6	6	3	4	34	3	47	4	2	10	4	.714	3	0	3.26
	Binghamton	AA	10	9	0	0	51.1	229	59	36	32	6	1	1	2	19	0	22	2	0	4	4	.500	0	0	5.61
1995	Binghamton	AA	4	4	0	0	16.2	87	21	21	17	1	0	1	0	20	1	6	2	0	0	2	.000	0	0	9.18
	6 Min. YEARS		110	104	13	5	663	2805	651	352	296	40	20	20	38	201	6	375	38	10	46	35	.568	4	3	4.02

Rick Schu

Bats: Right **Throws:** Right **Pos:** SS **Ht:** 6'0" **Wt:** 190 **Born:** 1/26/62 **Age:** 34

						BATTING											BASERUNNING				PERCENTAGES		
Year	Team	Lg	G	AB	H	2B	3B	HR	TB	R	RBI	TBB	IBB	SO	HBP	SH	SF	SB	CS	SB%	GDP	Avg	OBP	SLG
1984	Portland	AAA	140	552	166	35	14	12	265	70	82	43	3	83	3	1	8	7	4	.64	9	.301	.350	.480
1985	Portland	AAA	42	150	42	8	3	4	68	19	22	14	0	20	2	0	1	1	6	.14	2	.280	.349	.453
1989	Rochester	AAA	28	94	21	6	1	1	32	11	10	16	1	21	1	0	2	3	2	.60	1	.223	.336	.340
1990	Edmonton	AAA	18	60	18	7	0	1	28	8	8	6	0	3	1	0	2	0	0	.00	2	.300	.362	.467
1991	Scranton-Wb	AAA	106	355	114	30	5	14	196	69	57	50	2	38	4	0	4	7	1	.88	9	.321	.407	.552
1992	Scranton-Wb	AAA	111	400	124	18	3	10	178	56	49	45	5	62	4	0	1	3	1	.75	9	.310	.384	.445
1995	Okla. City	AAA	110	398	108	19	3	12	169	49	57	40	1	63	5	0	2	5	3	.63	8	.271	.344	.425
1984	Philadelphia	NL	17	29	8	2	1	2	18	12	5	6	0	6	0	0	0	0	0	.00	0	.276	.389	.621
1985	Philadelphia	NL	112	416	105	21	4	7	155	54	24	38	3	78	2	1	0	8	6	.57	7	.252	.318	.373
1986	Philadelphia	NL	92	208	57	10	1	8	93	32	25	18	1	44	2	3	2	2	2	.50	1	.274	.335	.447
1987	Philadelphia	NL	92	196	46	6	3	7	79	24	23	20	1	36	2	0	1	0	2	.00	1	.235	.311	.403
1988	Baltimore	AL	89	270	69	9	4	4	98	22	20	21	0	49	3	0	0	6	4	.60	7	.256	.316	.363
1989	Baltimore	AL	1	0	0	0	0	0	0	0	0	0	0	0	0	0	0	0	0	.00	0	.000	.000	.000
	Detroit	AL	98	266	57	11	0	7	89	25	21	24	0	37	0	0	2	1	2	.33	6	.214	.278	.335
1990	California	AL	61	157	42	8	0	6	68	19	14	11	0	25	0	0	1	0	0	.00	4	.268	.314	.433
1991	Philadelphia	NL	17	22	2	0	0	0	2	1	2	1	0	7	0	0	1	0	0	.00	1	.091	.125	.091
	7 Min. YEARS		555	2009	593	123	29	54	936	282	285	214	12	290	20	1	19	26	17	.60	40	.295	.366	.466
	8 Maj. YEARS		579	1564	386	67	13	41	602	189	134	139	5	282	9	6	7	17	16	.52	27	.247	.311	.385

Lance Schuermann

Pitches: Left **Bats:** Left **Pos:** P **Ht:** 6'2" **Wt:** 200 **Born:** 2/7/70 **Age:** 26

					HOW MUCH HE PITCHED			WHAT HE GAVE UP										THE RESULTS				
Year	Team	Lg	G	GS	CG	GF	IP	BFP	H	R	ER	HR	SH	SF	HB	TBB	IBB	SO	WP	Bk	W	L	Pct.	ShO	Sv	ERA
1991	Butte	R	30	0	0	16	43.2	203	45	29	22	0	2	2	1	34	2	46	6	7	4	4	.500	0	4	4.53

Year	Team	Lg	G	GS	CG	GF	IP	BFP	H	R	ER	HR	SH	SF	HB	TBB	IBB	SO	WP	Bk	W	L	Pct.	ShO	Sv	ERA
1992	Miracle	A	51	5	0	17	86.1	390	87	51	45	1	5	9	2	56	1	68	7	2	4	7	.364	0	2	4.69
1993	Charlotte	A	46	0	0	24	65.1	256	40	20	15	1	3	5	1	28	2	59	2	0	1	4	.200	0	16	2.07
1994	Tulsa	AA	27	27	3	0	175.2	743	182	87	80	21	9	7	7	49	2	124	3	2	10	11	.476	0	0	4.10
1995	Okla. City	AAA	33	13	0	6	88.2	398	101	51	46	12	1	4	2	40	0	44	8	0	4	7	.364	0	0	4.67
	5 Min. YEARS		187	45	3	63	459.2	1990	455	238	208	35	20	27	13	207	7	341	26	11	23	33	.411	0	22	4.07

Jerry Schunk

Bats: Right **Throws:** Right **Pos:** SS   **Ht:** 5'11" **Wt:** 186 **Born:** 10/5/65 **Age:** 30

							BATTING									BASERUNNING				PERCENTAGES		
Year	Team	Lg	G	AB	H	2B	3B	HR	TB	R	RBI	TBB	IBB	SO	HBP	SH	SF	SB	CS	SB%	GDP	Avg	OBP	SLG
1986	St. Cathrns	A	71	272	75	12	0	7	108	39	33	21	2	25	2	6	3	18	6	.75	8	.276	.329	.397
1987	Dunedin	A	98	358	88	15	2	4	119	40	39	17	0	38	2	0	2	11	4	.73	9	.246	.282	.332
1988	Dunedin	A	87	343	88	17	2	5	124	36	28	19	0	30	2	8	1	11	7	.61	10	.257	.299	.362
1989	Knoxville	AA	95	270	65	13	4	4	98	32	31	17	0	19	3	8	5	6	3	.67	4	.241	.288	.363
1990	Knoxville	AA	85	274	79	13	1	3	103	32	31	9	0	25	3	14	3	8	7	.53	9	.288	.315	.376
	Syracuse	AAA	26	100	24	4	0	0	28	8	7	3	0	10	0	1	0	1	2	.33	3	.240	.262	.280
1991	Syracuse	AAA	92	327	81	9	0	5	105	34	29	8	0	26	4	10	0	0	3	.00	8	.248	.274	.321
1992	Syracuse	AAA	122	417	109	16	1	2	133	40	26	20	1	21	0	12	6	2	3	.40	13	.261	.291	.319
1993	Portland	AAA	118	397	107	28	1	2	143	53	47	18	1	23	5	13	4	5	3	.63	15	.270	.307	.360
1994	Portland	AAA	92	327	90	17	0	7	128	34	35	25	2	20	3	4	1	1	7	.13	8	.275	.331	.391
1995	Charlotte	AAA	101	343	77	13	0	6	108	36	33	19	2	31	2	4	4	8	0	1.00	16	.224	.266	.315
	10 Min. YEARS		987	3428	883	157	11	45	1197	384	339	176	8	268	26	80	29	71	45	.61	103	.258	.297	.349

Carl Schutz

Pitches: Left **Bats:** Left **Pos:** P   **Ht:** 5'11" **Wt:** 200 **Born:** 8/22/71 **Age:** 24

				HOW MUCH HE PITCHED						WHAT HE GAVE UP									THE RESULTS					
Year	Team	Lg	G	GS	CG	GF	IP	BFP	H	R	ER	HR	SH	SF	HB	TBB	IBB	SO	WP	Bk	W	L	Pct.	ShO	Sv	ERA
1993	Danville	R	13	0	0	9	14.2	57	6	1	1	0	1	0	0	6	0	25	1	0	1	0	1.000	0	4	0.61
	Greenville	AA	22	0	0	16	21.1	101	17	17	12	3	2	3	1	22	1	19	2	0	2	1	.667	0	3	5.06
1994	Durham	A	53	0	0	47	53.1	240	35	30	29	6	4	1	2	46	1	81	10	0	3	3	.500	0	20	4.89
1995	Greenville	AA	51	0	0	46	58.1	258	53	36	32	4	2	2	1	36	3	56	3	0	3	7	.300	0	26	4.94
	3 Min. YEARS		139	0	0	118	147.2	656	111	84	74	13	9	6	4	110	5	181	16	0	9	11	.450	0	53	4.51

Matt Schwenke

Bats: Right **Throws:** Right **Pos:** C   **Ht:** 6'2" **Wt:** 210 **Born:** 8/12/72 **Age:** 23

							BATTING									BASERUNNING				PERCENTAGES		
Year	Team	Lg	G	AB	H	2B	3B	HR	TB	R	RBI	TBB	IBB	SO	HBP	SH	SF	SB	CS	SB%	GDP	Avg	OBP	SLG
1993	Bakersfield	A	13	41	9	0	0	0	9	2	4	3	0	12	0	0	0	0	0	.00	0	.220	.273	.220
	Great Falls	R	29	79	18	4	0	0	22	6	4	10	0	21	0	2	0	0	0	.00	2	.228	.315	.278
1994	Bakersfield	A	42	131	22	3	0	1	28	7	14	6	0	41	3	2	0	0	0	.00	3	.168	.221	.214
1995	Clinton	A	36	100	19	5	1	1	29	3	8	2	0	34	1	2	1	0	0	.00	0	.190	.212	.290
	Rancho Cuca	A	22	56	10	2	0	0	12	7	7	2	0	20	0	1	1	0	0	.00	0	.179	.203	.214
	Memphis	AA	23	62	15	3	0	0	18	7	4	3	0	16	1	1	1	0	0	.00	0	.242	.284	.290
	3 Min. YEARS		165	469	93	17	1	2	118	32	41	26	0	144	5	8	3	0	0	.00	8	.198	.247	.252

Darryl Scott

Pitches: Right **Bats:** Right **Pos:** P   **Ht:** 6' 1" **Wt:** 185 **Born:** 8/6/68 **Age:** 27

				HOW MUCH HE PITCHED						WHAT HE GAVE UP									THE RESULTS					
Year	Team	Lg	G	GS	CG	GF	IP	BFP	H	R	ER	HR	SH	SF	HB	TBB	IBB	SO	WP	Bk	W	L	Pct.	ShO	Sv	ERA
1990	Boise	A	27	0	0	11	53.2	221	40	11	8	3	0	1	0	19	1	57	5	0	2	1	.667	0	5	1.34
1991	Quad City	A	47	0	0	36	75.1	285	35	18	13	2	2	0	1	26	4	123	9	1	4	3	.571	0	11	1.55
1992	Midland	AA	27	0	0	22	29.2	126	20	9	6	0	2	2	2	14	1	35	4	0	1	1	.500	0	9	1.82
	Edmonton	AAA	31	0	0	17	36.1	164	41	21	21	1	0	3	0	21	1	48	4	2	0	2	.000	0	6	5.20
1993	Vancouver	AAA	46	0	0	33	51.2	206	35	12	12	4	2	1	1	19	2	57	3	0	7	1	.875	0	15	2.09
1995	Colo. Sprng	AAA	59	1	0	27	95.2	429	113	63	50	7	4	7	3	41	7	77	7	0	4	10	.286	0	4	4.70
1993	California	AL	16	0	0	2	20	90	19	13	13	1	0	2	1	11	1	13	2	0	1	2	.333	0	0	5.85
	5 Min. YEARS		237	1	0	146	342.1	1431	284	134	110	17	10	14	7	140	16	397	32	3	18	18	.500	0	58	2.89

Gary Scott

Bats: Right **Throws:** Right **Pos:** 3B   **Ht:** 6' 0" **Wt:** 175 **Born:** 8/22/68 **Age:** 27

							BATTING									BASERUNNING				PERCENTAGES		
Year	Team	Lg	G	AB	H	2B	3B	HR	TB	R	RBI	TBB	IBB	SO	HBP	SH	SF	SB	CS	SB%	GDP	Avg	OBP	SLG
1989	Geneva	A	48	175	49	10	1	10	91	33	42	22	2	23	9	0	2	4	1	.80	2	.280	.385	.520
1990	Winston-Sal	A	102	380	112	22	0	12	170	63	70	29	4	66	14	5	6	17	3	.85	7	.295	.361	.447
	Charlotte	AA	35	143	44	9	0	4	65	21	17	7	1	17	0	0	3	3	4	.43	3	.308	.333	.455
1991	Iowa	AAA	63	231	48	10	2	3	71	21	34	20	2	45	6	3	2	0	6	.00	11	.208	.286	.307
1992	Iowa	AAA	95	354	93	26	0	10	149	48	48	37	1	48	6	4	5	3	1	.75	8	.263	.338	.421
1993	Indianapolis	AAA	77	284	60	12	1	3	83	39	18	21	0	33	4	2	2	2	1	.67	7	.211	.273	.292
	Portland	AAA	54	189	55	8	4	1	74	26	28	27	0	33	7	1	6	3	1	.75	8	.291	.389	.392
1994	Phoenix	AAA	121	426	122	24	3	9	179	55	58	35	3	61	10	1	4	4	7	.36	14	.286	.352	.420
1995	Phoenix	AAA	68	219	58	16	2	5	93	33	26	26	5	39	7	0	1	2	2	.50	3	.265	.360	.425
	Richmond	AAA	27	86	13	1	0	0	14	7	2	10	0	13	1	0	1	0	1	.00	0	.151	.245	.163
1991	Chicago	NL	31	79	13	3	0	1	19	8	5	13	4	14	3	1	0	0	1	.00	2	.165	.305	.241
1992	Chicago	NL	36	96	15	2	0	2	23	8	11	5	1	14	0	1	0	0	3	.00	3	.156	.198	.240

	G	AB	H	2B	3B	HR	TB	R	RBI	TBB	IBB	SO	HBP	SH	SF	SB	CS	SB%	GDP	Avg	OBP	SLG
7 Min. YEARS	690	2487	654	138	13	57	989	346	343	234	18	378	64	16	32	38	27	.58	63	.263	.338	.398
2 Maj. YEARS	67	175	28	5	0	3	42	16	16	18	5	28	3	2	0	0	2	.00	5	.160	.250	.240

Scott Scudder

Pitches: Right **Bats:** Right **Pos:** P **Ht:** 6'2" **Wt:** 190 **Born:** 2/14/68 **Age:** 28

		HOW MUCH HE PITCHED						WHAT HE GAVE UP												THE RESULTS					
Year Team	Lg	G	GS	CG	GF	IP	BFP	H	R	ER	HR	SH	SF	HB	TBB	IBB	SO	WP	Bk	W	L	Pct.	ShO	Sv	ERA
1986 Billings	R	12	8	0	1	52.2	0	42	34	28	1	0	0	3	36	0	38	8	0	1	3	.250	0	0	4.78
1987 Cedar Rapds	A	26	26	0	0	153.2	660	129	86	70	16	8	2	7	76	0	128	15	3	7	12	.368	0	0	4.10
1988 Cedar Rapds	A	16	15	1	0	102.1	405	61	30	23	3	2	1	2	41	0	126	5	0	7	3	.700	1	0	2.02
Chattanooga	AA	11	11	0	0	70	290	53	24	23	7	1	3	1	30	0	52	5	0	7	0	1.000	0	0	2.96
1989 Nashville	AAA	12	12	3	0	80.2	339	54	27	24	6	2	3	3	48	0	64	1	1	6	2	.750	3	0	2.68
1990 Nashville	AAA	11	11	1	0	80.2	315	53	27	21	1	0	1	0	32	0	60	0	3	7	1	.875	0	0	2.34
1992 Colo. Sprng	AAA	1	1	0	0	3	14	4	3	2	0	0	0	0	2	0	1	1	0	0	1	.000	0	0	6.00
1993 Charlotte	AAA	23	22	2	0	136	597	148	92	76	21	0	7	7	52	1	64	5	0	7	7	.500	0	0	5.03
1994 Buffalo	AAA	35	20	2	3	147.1	646	178	100	92	20	5	7	4	39	0	77	13	1	5	10	.333	0	1	5.62
1995 Indianapols	AAA	7	7	0	0	38.1	161	43	24	22	4	0	1	1	9	1	13	3	0	1	4	.200	0	0	5.17
1989 Cincinnati	NL	23	17	0	3	100.1	451	91	54	50	14	7	2	1	61	11	66	0	1	4	9	.308	0	0	4.49
1990 Cincinnati	NL	21	10	0	3	71.2	316	74	41	39	12	3	1	3	30	4	42	2	2	5	5	.500	0	0	4.90
1991 Cincinnati	NL	27	14	0	4	101.1	443	91	52	49	6	8	3	6	56	4	51	7	0	6	9	.400	0	1	4.35
1992 Cleveland	AL	23	22	0	0	109	509	134	80	64	10	6	4	2	55	0	66	7	0	6	10	.375	0	0	5.28
1993 Cleveland	AL	2	1	0	1	4	20	5	4	4	0	0	0	1	4	0	1	0	0	0	1	.000	0	0	9.00
9 Min. YEARS		154	133	9	4	864.2	3427	765	447	381	79	18	25	28	365	2	623	56	8	48	43	.527	4	1	3.97
5 Maj. YEARS		96	64	0	11	386.1	1739	395	231	206	42	24	10	13	206	19	226	16	3	21	34	.382	0	1	4.80

Scot Sealy

Bats: Right **Throws:** Right **Pos:** C **Ht:** 6'2" **Wt:** 200 **Born:** 2/10/71 **Age:** 25

		BATTING														BASERUNNING				PERCENTAGES		
Year Team	Lg	G	AB	H	2B	3B	HR	TB	R	RBI	TBB	IBB	SO	HBP	SH	SF	SB	CS	SB%	GDP	Avg	OBP	SLG
1992 Gastonia	A	56	175	42	8	0	3	59	16	16	14	0	46	0	0	2	1	2	.33	4	.240	.293	.337
1993 Charlstn-Sc	A	2	7	1	0	0	0	1	0	0	0	0	4	0	0	0	0	0	.00	0	.143	.143	.143
1995 Tacoma	AAA	4	10	3	0	0	0	3	1	0	0	0	0	0	0	0	0	0	.00	0	.300	.300	.300
Riverside	A	58	206	50	5	0	2	61	23	30	16	0	36	1	1	1	2	2	.50	4	.243	.299	.296
3 Min. YEARS		120	398	96	13	0	5	124	40	46	30	0	86	1	1	3	3	4	.43	8	.241	.294	.312

Kyle Sebach

Pitches: Right **Bats:** Right **Pos:** P **Ht:** 6'4" **Wt:** 195 **Born:** 9/6/71 **Age:** 24

		HOW MUCH HE PITCHED						WHAT HE GAVE UP												THE RESULTS					
Year Team	Lg	G	GS	CG	GF	IP	BFP	H	R	ER	HR	SH	SF	HB	TBB	IBB	SO	WP	Bk	W	L	Pct.	ShO	Sv	ERA
1991 Angels	R	13	11	1	0	64.2	296	62	49	45	4	2	3	7	39	1	58	7	2	3	5	.375	0	0	6.26
1992 Quad City	A	13	13	0	0	61.1	274	52	31	27	5	0	0	8	40	0	50	8	1	3	4	.429	0	0	3.96
Boise	A	13	8	0	3	40.2	215	50	42	34	0	0	6	8	34	0	41	9	1	1	5	.167	0	1	7.52
1993 Cedar Rapds	A	26	26	4	0	154	678	138	73	52	7	4	7	14	70	1	138	10	2	6	9	.400	0	0	3.04
1994 Lk Elsinore	A	10	10	3	0	73	306	67	35	28	5	2	2	4	24	1	39	5	0	3	4	.429	0	0	3.45
Midland	AA	16	16	4	0	112.2	494	129	69	58	11	2	4	9	40	0	85	3	0	5	5	.500	2	0	4.63
1995 Midland	AA	5	5	0	0	18.1	93	31	24	21	1	2	2	3	12	0	7	3	0	1	2	.333	0	0	10.31
Lk Elsinore	A	14	13	0	0	76.1	340	91	40	39	10	1	1	4	29	0	60	6	0	7	2	.778	0	0	4.60
5 Min. YEARS		110	102	12	4	601	2696	620	363	304	43	13	25	57	288	3	478	51	6	29	36	.446	2	1	4.55

Larry See

Bats: Right **Throws:** Right **Pos:** DH-1B **Ht:** 6'1" **Wt:** 195 **Born:** 6/20/60 **Age:** 36

		BATTING														BASERUNNING				PERCENTAGES		
Year Team	Lg	G	AB	H	2B	3B	HR	TB	R	RBI	TBB	IBB	SO	HBP	SH	SF	SB	CS	SB%	GDP	Avg	OBP	SLG
1995 Las Vegas	AAA	38	114	35	8	1	2	51	11	20	5	0	12	1	0	2	0	0	.00	5	.307	.336	.447
Rancho Cuca	A	49	171	59	10	0	14	111	34	50	14	1	31	4	0	2	0	2	.00	4	.345	.403	.649
1 Min. YEARS		87	285	94	18	1	16	162	45	70	19	1	43	5	0	4	0	2	.00	9	.330	.377	.568

Tate Seefried

Bats: Left **Throws:** Right **Pos:** 1B **Ht:** 6'4" **Wt:** 180 **Born:** 4/22/72 **Age:** 24

		BATTING														BASERUNNING				PERCENTAGES		
Year Team	Lg	G	AB	H	2B	3B	HR	TB	R	RBI	TBB	IBB	SO	HBP	SH	SF	SB	CS	SB%	GDP	Avg	OBP	SLG
1990 Yankees	R	52	178	28	3	0	0	31	15	20	22	0	53	2	0	1	2	1	.67	6	.157	.256	.174
1991 Oneonta	A	73	264	65	19	0	7	105	40	51	32	0	66	2	0	7	12	3	.80	6	.246	.325	.398
1992 Greensboro	A	141	532	129	23	5	20	222	73	90	51	2	166	2	1	3	8	8	.50	12	.242	.310	.417
1993 Pr. William	A	125	464	123	25	4	21	219	63	89	50	4	150	2	3	6	8	8	.50	8	.265	.335	.472
1994 Albany-Colo	AA	118	444	100	14	2	27	199	63	83	48	4	149	5	1	2	1	5	.17	12	.225	.307	.448
1995 Columbus	AAA	29	110	18	6	0	1	27	7	12	1	0	34	0	0	2	0	0	.00	2	.164	.168	.245
Norwich	AA	77	274	62	18	1	5	97	34	33	31	4	86	4	1	4	0	1	.00	6	.226	.310	.354
6 Min. YEARS		615	2266	525	108	12	81	900	295	378	235	12	704	17	6	25	31	26	.54	52	.232	.306	.397

Chris Seelbach

Pitches: Right Bats: Right Pos: P Ht: 6' 4" Wt: 180 Born: 12/18/72 Age: 23

			HOW MUCH HE PITCHED						WHAT HE GAVE UP											THE RESULTS					
Year	Team	Lg	G	GS	CG	GF	IP	BFP	H	R	ER	HR	SH	SF	HB	TBB	IBB	SO	WP	Bk	W	L	Pct.	ShO	Sv	ERA
1991	Braves	R	4	4	0	0	15	65	13	7	7	3	1	0	0	6	0	19	3	1	0	1	.000	0	0	4.20
1992	Macon	A	27	27	1	0	157.1	662	134	65	58	11	3	5	9	68	0	144	5	1	9	11	.450	0	0	3.32
1993	Durham	A	25	25	0	0	131.1	590	133	85	72	15	4	4	7	74	1	112	10	0	9	9	.500	0	0	4.93
1994	Greenville	AA	15	15	2	0	92.2	363	64	26	24	3	5	3	4	38	2	79	5	0	4	6	.400	0	0	2.33
	Richmond	AAA	12	11	0	0	61.1	273	68	37	33	6	2	3	0	36	2	35	3	0	3	5	.375	0	0	4.84
1995	Greenville	AA	9	9	1	0	60.1	249	38	15	11	2	5	3	4	30	0	65	3	1	6	0	1.000	1	0	1.64
	Richmond	AAA	14	14	1	0	73.1	314	64	39	38	7	0	3	2	39	0	65	3	0	4	6	.400	0	0	4.66
	5 Min. YEARS		106	105	5	0	591.1	2516	514	274	243	47	20	21	26	291	5	519	32	3	35	38	.479	1	0	3.70

Jose Segura

Pitches: Right Bats: Right Pos: P Ht: 5'11" Wt: 180 Born: 1/26/63 Age: 33

			HOW MUCH HE PITCHED						WHAT HE GAVE UP											THE RESULTS					
Year	Team	Lg	G	GS	CG	GF	IP	BFP	H	R	ER	HR	SH	SF	HB	TBB	IBB	SO	WP	Bk	W	L	Pct.	ShO	Sv	ERA
1984	Kinston	A	16	14	2	1	97.1	402	88	48	43	7	2	3	1	35	1	55	7	0	7	4	.636	1	0	3.98
	Knoxville	AA	12	12	1	0	69	322	75	47	34	4	2	1	0	47	1	26	8	1	4	6	.400	0	0	4.43
1985	Kinston	A	34	15	1	10	110.1	499	109	62	51	9	1	3	7	69	4	73	7	1	4	13	.235	1	1	4.16
1986	Knoxville	AA	24	17	1	3	106.2	491	101	72	50	7	0	7	6	72	1	55	11	1	4	7	.364	0	2	4.22
1987	Syracuse	AAA	43	12	0	12	107	499	136	90	78	13	2	10	1	59	2	54	14	1	5	8	.385	0	4	6.56
1988	Vancouver	AAA	20	19	0	0	111	507	127	69	56	4	5	7	0	60	0	39	3	6	6	6	.500	0	0	4.54
1989	Vancouver	AAA	44	0	0	32	66.2	263	50	21	17	0	1	3	0	19	2	52	1	3	1	2	.333	0	17	2.30
1990	Vancouver	AAA	40	0	0	27	54.2	246	49	34	31	0	2	5	1	35	1	47	6	0	1	3	.250	0	8	5.10
1991	Phoenix	AAA	32	0	0	27	39.1	177	46	15	15	4	3	3	1	17	2	21	3	0	5	5	.500	0	4	3.43
1992	Nashville	AAA	22	0	0	11	31.2	140	33	16	14	0	1	1	1	18	1	16	3	0	1	1	.500	0	1	3.98
1994	Columbus	AAA	5	0	0	3	4.2	22	5	5	1	0	0	0	0	3	0	3	0	0	0	1	.000	0	0	1.93
1995	Columbus	AAA	11	0	0	8	10.1	59	18	12	10	0	0	0	0	8	0	8	2	0	0	2	.000	0	4	8.71
1988	Chicago	AL	4	0	0	1	8.2	52	19	17	13	1	0	0	0	8	0	2	2	3	0	0	.000	0	0	13.50
1989	Chicago	AL	7	0	0	2	6	34	13	11	10	2	2	1	0	3	1	4	0	0	0	1	.000	0	0	15.00
1991	San Francisco	NL	11	0	0	2	16.1	72	20	11	8	1	1	0	0	5	0	10	2	0	0	1	.000	0	0	4.41
	11 Min. YEARS		303	89	5	134	808.2	3627	837	491	400	48	19	43	18	442	15	449	65	13	38	58	.396	2	41	4.45
	3 Maj. YEARS		22	0	0	5	31	158	52	39	31	4	3	1	0	16	1	16	4	3	0	2	.000	0	0	9.00

Bill Selby

Bats: Left Throws: Right Pos: 3B Ht: 5'9" Wt: 190 Born: 6/11/70 Age: 26

			BATTING														BASERUNNING				PERCENTAGES		
Year	Team	Lg	G	AB	H	2B	3B	HR	TB	R	RBI	TBB	IBB	SO	HBP	SH	SF	SB	CS	SB%	GDP	Avg	OBP	SLG
1992	Elmira	A	73	275	72	16	1	10	120	38	41	31	6	53	2	2	2	4	4	.50	3	.262	.339	.436
1993	Lynchburg	A	113	394	99	22	1	7	144	57	38	24	2	66	3	2	7	1	2	.33	6	.251	.294	.365
1994	Lynchburg	A	97	352	109	20	2	19	190	58	69	28	0	62	5	2	2	3	1	.75	7	.310	.367	.540
	New Britain	AA	35	107	28	5	0	1	36	15	18	15	0	16	0	0	6	0	1	.00	2	.262	.336	.336
1995	Trenton	AA	117	451	129	29	2	13	201	64	68	46	3	52	3	2	8	4	6	.40	14	.286	.350	.446
	4 Min. YEARS		435	1579	437	92	6	50	691	232	234	144	11	249	13	8	25	12	14	.46	32	.277	.337	.438

Rick Sellers

Bats: Right Throws: Right Pos: C Ht: 6'0" Wt: 210 Born: 2/22/67 Age: 29

			BATTING														BASERUNNING				PERCENTAGES		
Year	Team	Lg	G	AB	H	2B	3B	HR	TB	R	RBI	TBB	IBB	SO	HBP	SH	SF	SB	CS	SB%	GDP	Avg	OBP	SLG
1989	Niagara Fal	A	29	71	18	3	1	2	29	17	6	17	0	22	0	2	0	3	0	1.00	0	.254	.398	.408
1990	Fayetteville	A	130	430	100	13	4	7	142	48	57	61	2	102	2	1	8	5	3	.63	9	.233	.325	.330
1991	Lakeland	A	71	244	67	8	2	8	103	33	32	26	0	63	3	0	2	3	3	.50	3	.275	.349	.422
1992	London	AA	103	329	88	17	1	9	134	38	51	36	0	67	2	2	4	2	0	1.00	7	.267	.340	.407
1993	London	AA	72	239	63	11	0	6	92	31	31	45	2	55	0	0	0	5	3	.63	11	.264	.380	.385
	Toledo	AAA	18	46	13	4	1	2	25	6	7	3	0	8	1	0	0	0	0	.00	1	.283	.340	.543
1994	Indianapolis	AAA	58	180	47	13	0	1	63	23	18	25	1	41	0	1	2	0	1	.00	4	.261	.348	.350
1995	Indianapolis	AAA	5	19	5	1	0	3	15	3	7	1	0	3	0	0	0	0	0	.00	1	.263	.300	.789
	Chattanooga	AA	89	281	67	13	3	8	110	40	41	45	3	66	5	2	4	2	1	.67	8	.238	.349	.391
	7 Min. YEARS		575	1839	468	83	12	46	713	239	250	259	8	427	13	8	20	20	12	.63	43	.254	.347	.388

Frank Seminara

Pitches: Right Bats: Right Pos: P Ht: 6' 2" Wt: 205 Born: 5/16/67 Age: 29

			HOW MUCH HE PITCHED						WHAT HE GAVE UP											THE RESULTS					
Year	Team	Lg	G	GS	CG	GF	IP	BFP	H	R	ER	HR	SH	SF	HB	TBB	IBB	SO	WP	Bk	W	L	Pct.	ShO	Sv	ERA
1988	Oneonta	A	16	13	0	2	78.1	350	86	49	38	2	3	2	5	32	2	60	11	6	4	7	.364	0	1	4.37
1989	Pr. William	A	21	0	0	12	36.2	158	26	23	15	0	1	3	5	22	3	23	5	4	2	4	.333	0	2	3.68
	Oneonta	A	11	10	3	0	70	280	51	25	16	0	3	0	3	18	0	70	1	3	7	2	.778	1	0	2.06
1990	Pr. William	A	25	25	4	0	170.1	692	136	51	36	5	1	2	10	52	1	132	12	2	16	8	.667	2	0	1.90
1991	Wichita	AA	27	27	6	0	176	761	186	86	66	10	9	5	9	68	0	107	12	3	15	10	.600	1	0	3.38
1992	Las Vegas	AAA	13	13	1	0	80.2	357	92	46	37	2	2	4	3	33	3	48	2	5	6	4	.600	0	1	4.13
1993	Las Vegas	AAA	21	19	0	1	114.1	518	136	79	69	15	6	4	4	52	1	99	2	2	8	5	.615	0	1	5.43
1994	Norfolk	AAA	20	13	0	3	100.2	431	108	55	49	11	2	4	10	31	0	43	2	3	4	7	.364	0	0	4.38
1995	Rochester	AAA	29	0	0	5	35.2	149	31	13	13	2	3	2	1	14	0	20	3	1	1	0	1.000	0	0	3.28
	New Orleans	AAA	11	7	0	2	37.1	171	54	35	33	3	0	3	2	14	1	19	1	1	2	3	.400	0	0	7.96

Year	Team	Lg	G	GS	CG	GF	IP	BFP	H	R	ER	HR	SH	SF	HB	TBB	IBB	SO	WP	Bk	W	L	Pct.	ShO	Sv	ERA
1992	San Diego	NL	19	18	0	0	100.1	435	98	46	41	5	3	2	3	46	3	61	1	1	9	4	.692	0	0	3.68
1993	San Diego	NL	18	7	0	0	46.1	212	53	30	23	5	6	2	3	21	3	22	1	0	3	3	.500	0	0	4.47
1994	New York	NL	10	1	0	5	17	75	20	12	11	2	0	1	0	8	0	7	1	1	0	2	.000	0	0	5.82
	8 Min. YEARS		194	127	14	25	900	3867	893	462	372	50	30	29	52	336	11	621	51	30	65	50	.565	5	4	3.72
	3 Maj. YEARS		47	26	0	5	163.2	722	171	88	75	12	9	5	6	75	6	90	3	2	12	9	.571	0	0	4.12

Shawn Senior

Pitches: Left Bats: Left Pos: P   Ht: 6'1" Wt: 195 Born: 3/17/72 Age: 24

Year	Team	Lg	G	GS	CG	GF	IP	BFP	H	R	ER	HR	SH	SF	HB	TBB	IBB	SO	WP	Bk	W	L	Pct.	ShO	Sv	ERA
1993	Red Sox	R	3	2	0	0	14	60	10	7	3	0	1	0	1	6	0	17	0	0	3	0	1.000	0	0	1.93
	Utica	A	13	13	1	0	76.1	340	84	40	33	2	3	2	3	34	0	77	8	2	7	2	.778	0	0	3.89
1994	Lynchburg	A	13	13	0	0	76.1	338	73	45	30	6	3	2	2	34	1	62	5	1	4	4	.500	0	0	3.54
	Sarasota	A	14	13	0	0	83.1	360	82	33	28	6	2	0	2	47	0	58	8	2	8	3	.727	0	0	3.02
1995	Trenton	AA	27	27	0	0	151.1	673	154	91	76	15	5	11	9	68	2	90	10	4	11	7	.611	0	0	4.52
	Pawtucket	AAA	1	1	0	0	6	29	9	4	4	0	1	0	0	2	0	1	0	0	0	1	.000	0	0	6.00
	3 Min. YEARS		71	69	1	0	407.1	1800	412	220	174	29	15	15	17	191	3	305	31	9	33	17	.660	0	0	3.84

Jamie Sepeda

Pitches: Right Bats: Right Pos: P   Ht: 6'2" Wt: 200 Born: 12/8/70 Age: 25

Year	Team	Lg	G	GS	CG	GF	IP	BFP	H	R	ER	HR	SH	SF	HB	TBB	IBB	SO	WP	Bk	W	L	Pct.	ShO	Sv	ERA
1992	Batavia	A	5	5	0	0	32.1	126	22	7	4	0	1	0	1	9	0	31	0	4	0	0	.000	0	0	1.11
	Clearwater	A	6	6	0	0	35	145	33	14	14	0	3	0	1	12	0	27	1	0	2	3	.400	0	0	3.60
1993	Clearwater	A	26	26	2	0	160	694	165	81	64	8	5	7	5	63	3	97	7	5	9	9	.500	2	0	3.60
1994	Clearwater	A	5	5	1	0	32.1	133	32	13	11	2	0	0	0	6	0	20	1	0	2	1	.667	1	0	3.06
	Reading	AA	29	11	0	3	97.1	448	108	67	54	10	9	3	1	55	3	61	6	2	4	7	.364	0	0	4.99
1995	Tucson	AAA	8	8	0	0	40.1	178	52	22	22	1	4	0	2	12	0	19	1	2	3	2	.600	0	0	4.91
	Jackson	AA	1	1	0	0	4	21	7	4	4	0	0	1	0	2	0	1	0	0	1	0	.000	0	0	9.00
	Winnipeg	IND	4	4	0	0	18.2	98	31	24	21	3	3	1	1	10	0	6	2	0	0	3	.000	0	0	10.13
	Corp.Chrsti	IND	11	10	0	1	58.1	262	66	37	31	6	2	1	2	20	1	·39	7	0	4	3	.571	0	0	4.78
	4 Min. YEARS		95	76	3	4	478.1	2105	516	269	225	30	27	13	13	189	7	301	25	13	24	29	.453	3	0	4.23

Dan Serafini

Pitches: Left Bats: Both Pos: P   Ht: 6'1" Wt: 185 Born: 1/25/74 Age: 22

Year	Team	Lg	G	GS	CG	GF	IP	BFP	H	R	ER	HR	SH	SF	HB	TBB	IBB	SO	WP	Bk	W	L	Pct.	ShO	Sv	ERA
1992	Twins	R	8	6	0	0	29.2	130	27	16	12	0	1	1	1	15	0	33	3	1	1	0	1.000	0	0	3.64
1993	Fort Wayne	A	27	27	1	0	140.2	606	117	72	57	5	2	2	6	83	0	147	12	2	10	8	.556	1	0	3.65
1994	Fort Myers	A	23	23	2	0	136.2	600	149	84	70	11	7	5	6	57	1	130	7	1	9	9	.500	1	0	4.61
1995	New Britain	AA	27	27	1	0	162.2	692	155	74	61	7	3	4	12	72	0	123	3	4	12	9	.571	1	0	3.38
	Salt Lake	AAA	1	0	0	0	4	17	4	3	3	2	0	0	0	1	0	4	0	0	0	0	.000	0	1	6.75
	4 Min. YEARS		86	83	4	1	473.2	2045	452	249	203	25	13	12	25	228	1	437	25	8	32	26	.552	3	1	3.86

Chris Sexton

Bats: Right Throws: Right Pos: SS   Ht: 5'11" Wt: 180 Born: 8/3/71 Age: 24

Year	Team	Lg	G	AB	H	2B	3B	HR	TB	R	RBI	TBB	IBB	SO	HBP	SH	SF	SB	CS	SB%	GDP	Avg	OBP	SLG
1993	Billings	R	72	273	91	14	4	4	125	63	46	35	1	27	1	0	8	13	4	.76	6	.333	.401	.458
1994	Charlstn-Wv	A	133	467	140	21	4	5	184	82	59	91	3	67	2	6	6	18	11	.62	9	.300	.412	.394
1995	Winston-Sal	A	4	15	6	0	0	1	9	3	5	4	0	0	0	0	0	0	0	.00	0	.400	.526	.600
	Salem	A	123	461	123	16	6	4	163	81	32	93	2	55	1	12	1	14	11	.56	11	.267	.390	.354
	New Haven	AA	0	0	0	0	0	0	0	0	0	0	0	0	0	0	0	0	0	.00	0	.000	.000	.000
	3 Min. YEARS		333	1219	360	51	14	14	481	229	142	223	6	149	4	18	15	45	26	.63	26	.295	.402	.395

Basil Shabazz

Bats: Right Throws: Right Pos: OF   Ht: 6'0" Wt: 190 Born: 1/31/72 Age: 24

Year	Team	Lg	G	AB	H	2B	3B	HR	TB	R	RBI	TBB	IBB	SO	HBP	SH	SF	SB	CS	SB%	GDP	Avg	OBP	SLG
1991	Johnson Cty	R	40	117	24	3	0	0	27	18	11	16	0	38	2	1	1	4	7	.36	2	.205	.309	.231
1992	Johnson Cty	R	56	223	51	7	2	3	71	33	20	28	1	75	0	1	2	43	11	.80	1	.229	.312	.318
1993	Springfield	A	64	239	71	12	2	4	99	44	18	29	2	66	2	2	0	29	16	.64	1	.297	.378	.414
1994	St. Pete	A	80	308	72	8	2	0	84	50	27	50	1	99	3	4	0	44	18	.71	3	.234	.346	.273
	Arkansas	AA	45	171	30	5	1	3	46	18	10	15	1	60	0	0	0	13	6	.68	8	.175	.242	.269
1995	El Paso	AA	47	102	22	2	3	0	30	19	7	14	1	23	0	4	2	8	5	.62	2	.216	.305	.294
	5 Min. YEARS		332	1160	270	37	10	10	357	182	93	152	6	361	7	13	5	141	63	.69	17	.233	.324	.308

Bill Shafer

Pitches: Right Bats: Right Pos: P   Ht: 6'4" Wt: 215 Born: 10/6/72 Age: 23

Year	Team	Lg	G	GS	CG	GF	IP	BFP	H	R	ER	HR	SH	SF	HB	TBB	IBB	SO	WP	Bk	W	L	Pct.	ShO	Sv	ERA
1991	Braves	R	8	1	0	1	17.1	95	19	21	16	0	0	2	3	17	0	13	8	1	0	1	.000	0	0	8.31
1992	Pulaski	R	17	0	0	5	36.1	173	35	36	30	3	0	1	5	35	1	23	3	1	0	3	.000	0	1	7.43
1993	Danville	R	22	0	0	9	48.1	193	38	18	13	4	1	3	1	11	0	42	4	1	4	1	.800	0	6	2.42

Year	Team	Lg	G	GS	CG	GF	IP	BFP	H	R	ER	HR	SH	SF	HB	TBB	IBB	SO	WP	Bk	W	L	Pct.	ShO	Sv	ERA
1994	Macon	A	27	0	0	15	51.2	205	40	12	8	0	2	3	4	4	0	47	1	0	0	0	.000	0	8	1.39
	Durham	A	23	0	0	12	25.2	107	21	11	9	2	0	2	0	9	0	21	2	1	2	1	.667	0	2	3.16
1995	Greenville	AA	42	0	0	16	59.1	283	69	37	33	7	3	0	4	38	3	44	2	2	2	2	.500	0	1	5.01
	5 Min. YEARS		139	1	0	58	238.2	1056	222	135	109	13	9	9	19	114	4	190	20	5	8	8	.500	0	18	4.11

Jon Shave

Bats: Right **Throws:** Right **Pos:** 2B   **Ht:** 6'0" **Wt:** 180 **Born:** 11/4/67 **Age:** 28

			BATTING															BASERUNNING				PERCENTAGES		
Year	Team	Lg	G	AB	H	2B	3B	HR	TB	R	RBI	TBB	IBB	SO	HBP	SH	SF	SB	CS	SB%	GDP	Avg	OBP	SLG
1990	Butte	R	64	250	88	9	3	2	109	41	42	25	0	27	3	2	4	21	7	.75	8	.352	.411	.436
1991	Gastonia	A	55	213	62	11	0	2	79	29	24	20	0	26	1	3	0	11	9	.55	3	.291	.355	.371
	Charlotte	A	56	189	43	4	1	1	52	17	20	18	1	30	5	2	4	7	7	.50	3	.228	.306	.275
1992	Tulsa	AA	118	453	130	23	5	2	169	57	36	37	1	59	4	7	5	6	7	.46	10	.287	.343	.373
1993	Okla. City	AAA	100	399	105	17	3	4	140	58	41	20	0	60	2	9	1	4	3	.57	12	.263	.301	.351
1994	Okla. City	AAA	95	332	73	15	2	1	95	29	31	14	1	61	5	12	5	6	2	.75	6	.220	.258	.286
1995	Okla. City	AAA	32	83	17	1	0	0	18	10	5	7	0	28	1	1	0	1	0	1.00	1	.205	.275	.217
1993	Texas	AL	17	47	15	2	0	0	17	3	7	0	0	8	0	3	2	1	3	.25	0	.319	.306	.362
	6 Min. YEARS		520	1919	518	80	14	12	662	241	199	141	3	291	21	36	19	56	35	.62	43	.270	.324	.345

Cedric Shaw

Pitches: Left **Bats:** Left **Pos:** P   **Ht:** 5'11" **Wt:** 175 **Born:** 5/28/67 **Age:** 29

			HOW MUCH HE PITCHED						WHAT HE GAVE UP											THE RESULTS					
Year	Team	Lg	G	GS	CG	GF	IP	BFP	H	R	ER	HR	SH	SF	HB	TBB	IBB	SO	WP	Bk	W	L	Pct.	ShO	Sv	ERA
1988	Butte	R	12	12	0	0	56.1	241	54	28	25	1	2	2	3	32	0	50	4	2	5	2	.714	0	0	3.99
1989	Charlotte	A	25	24	4	0	148.2	610	135	60	45	8	6	6	9	54	2	82	5	2	10	6	.625	3	0	2.72
1990	Tulsa	AA	14	12	0	2	63	290	72	51	48	2	0	2	3	44	1	41	4	4	4	5	.444	0	0	6.86
	Charlotte	A	11	11	1	0	68	269	48	18	12	3	6	3	1	27	0	69	3	1	5	3	.625	0	0	1.59
1991	Tulsa	AA	26	23	1	1	142	606	142	76	64	9	4	3	3	66	0	111	11	9	9	8	.529	0	0	4.06
1992	Tulsa	AA	12	11	0	0	69.2	292	64	37	29	9	1	1	0	18	0	49	1	4	6	2	.750	0	0	3.75
	Okla. City	AAA	13	10	0	1	56.1	246	50	30	05	0	0	2	2	31	0	25	3	3	2	5	.286	0	0	5.50
1993	Okla. City	AAA	28	5	0	11	52.1	260	78	47	46	8	3	0	2	36	3	28	6	0	2	6	.250	0	0	7.91
1995	Harrisburg	AA	5	2	0	0	19.1	83	25	10	10	2	1	0	0	6	0	13	2	0	0	0	.000	0	0	4.66
	7 Min. YEARS		146	110	6	15	675.2	2897	676	366	314	51	23	19	23	314	6	468	39	25	43	38	.531	3	0	4.18

Curtis Shaw

Pitches: Left **Bats:** Left **Pos:** P   **Ht:** 6'2" **Wt:** 190 **Born:** 8/16/69 **Age:** 26

			HOW MUCH HE PITCHED						WHAT HE GAVE UP											THE RESULTS					
Year	Team	Lg	G	GS	CG	GF	IP	BFP	H	R	ER	HR	SH	SF	HB	TBB	IBB	SO	WP	Bk	W	L	Pct.	ShO	Sv	ERA
1990	Sou. Oregon	A	17	9	0	3	66.1	274	54	28	26	4	1	0	3	30	0	74	5	1	4	6	.400	0	0	3.53
1991	Madison	A	20	20	1	0	100.1	457	82	45	29	1	1	1	6	79	1	87	11	0	7	5	.583	0	0	2.60
1992	Modesto	A	27	27	2	0	177.1	749	146	71	60	5	7	7	6	98	0	154	12	1	13	4	.765	0	0	3.05
1993	Huntsville	AA	28	28	2	0	151.2	676	141	98	83	8	2	3	14	89	2	132	19	4	6	16	.273	1	0	4.93
1994	Huntsville	AA	7	7	0	0	42	181	39	22	21	1	4	1	1	20	0	33	3	0	2	1	.667	0	0	4.50
	Tacoma	AAA	32	8	0	7	82	396	98	69	63	10	5	6	7	61	0	46	11	2	2	6	.250	0	0	6.91
1995	Edmonton	AAA	42	3	0	11	98.1	454	91	60	51	4	5	6	6	88	8	52	17	1	6	5	.545	0	2	4.67
	6 Min. YEARS		173	102	5	21	718	3187	651	393	333	33	25	24	43	465	11	578	78	9	40	43	.482	1	2	4.17

John Shea

Pitches: Left **Bats:** Right **Pos:** P   **Ht:** 6'6" **Wt:** 210 **Born:** 6/23/66 **Age:** 30

			HOW MUCH HE PITCHED						WHAT HE GAVE UP											THE RESULTS					
Year	Team	Lg	G	GS	CG	GF	IP	BFP	H	R	ER	HR	SH	SF	HB	TBB	IBB	SO	WP	Bk	W	L	Pct.	ShO	Sv	ERA
1986	St. Cathrns	A	14	2	0	5	49	218	44	24	20	2	1	0	0	29	0	59	3	0	3	1	.750	0	0	3.67
1987	Myrtle Bch	A	26	23	1	1	140	604	147	67	54	13	3	3	5	42	1	92	2	3	11	5	.688	1	0	3.47
1988	Knoxville	A	13	0	0	5	18.1	92	23	14	11	1	2	2	1	12	0	14	3	2	1	3	.250	0	1	5.40
	Dunedin	A	24	18	1	2	122.2	498	115	43	30	4	8	1	1	25	0	83	5	15	4	6	.400	0	1	2.20
1989	Knoxville	AA	31	29	3	1	190.1	803	183	79	57	14	6	2	6	57	1	96	4	6	9	12	.429	1	0	2.70
1990	Syracuse	AAA	40	0	0	26	81.2	363	83	45	33	9	3	1	4	40	4	58	5	2	8	5	.615	0	3	3.64
1991	Syracuse	AAA	35	24	3	5	172	767	198	104	87	15	4	11	8	78	2	76	4	3	12	10	.545	0	2	4.55
1992	Syracuse	AAA	25	21	1	2	118	546	151	92	81	8	3	6	5	49	1	50	8	1	8	8	.500	1	0	6.18
1993	New Britain	AA	48	0	0	12	56.2	241	48	27	23	2	3	1	2	22	3	62	5	1	4	2	.667	0	1	3.65
	Pawtucket	AAA	12	3	0	1	36	170	51	31	28	6	1	2	0	19	0	20	1	0	2	2	.500	0	0	7.00
1994	El Paso	AAA	40	0	0	9	53.1	233	52	17	14	0	0	2	1	25	4	50	5	0	3	2	.714	0	3	2.36
1995	Rochester	AAA	38	0	0	19	39.2	172	38	16	13	8	1	1	1	17	2	37	2	0	0	0	.000	0	4	2.95
	10 Min. YEARS		346	120	9	88	1077.2	4707	1133	559	451	82	35	32	34	415	18	697	47	33	67	57	.540	3	15	3.77

Chris Sheehan

Pitches: Right **Bats:** Right **Pos:** P   **Ht:** 6'4" **Wt:** 205 **Born:** 1/5/69 **Age:** 27

			HOW MUCH HE PITCHED						WHAT HE GAVE UP											THE RESULTS					
Year	Team	Lg	G	GS	CG	GF	IP	BFP	H	R	ER	HR	SH	SF	HB	TBB	IBB	SO	WP	Bk	W	L	Pct.	ShO	Sv	ERA
1992	Eugene	A	19	4	0	7	56	250	67	36	26	5	2	0	1	14	0	38	7	7	2	3	.400	0	2	4.18
1993	Rockford	A	30	12	2	14	116.2	460	97	40	37	8	4	3	3	22	1	99	10	0	9	5	.643	0	5	2.85
1994	Wilmington	A	28	0	0	10	59.1	237	49	22	16	4	4	0	2	17	2	55	5	0	6	1	.857	0	4	2.43
1995	Wilmington	A	13	0	0	5	19.1	67	7	5	4	0	2	0	2	2	0	25	1	0	2	1	.667	0	3	1.86
	Wichita	AA	31	0	0	10	50.2	221	51	35	31	5	4	2	2	16	6	31	5	0	0	2	.000	0	2	5.51
	4 Min. YEARS		121	16	2	46	302	1235	271	138	114	22	16	5	9	71	9	250	28	7	19	12	.613	0	16	3.40

Andy Sheets

Bats: Right **Throws:** Right **Pos:** SS **Ht:** 6'2" **Wt:** 180 **Born:** 11/19/71 **Age:** 24

Year	Team	Lg	G	AB	H	2B	3B	HR	TB	R	RBI	TBB	IBB	SO	HBP	SH	SF	SB	CS	SB%	GDP	Avg	OBP	SLG
1993	Riverside	A	52	176	34	9	1	1	48	23	12	17	1	51	0	6	4	2	2	.50	4	.193	.259	.273
	Appleton	A	69	259	68	10	4	1	89	32	25	20	1	59	3	4	2	7	7	.50	3	.263	.320	.344
1994	Riverside	A	31	100	27	5	1	2	40	17	10	16	0	22	0	1	0	6	1	.86	1	.270	.371	.400
	Calgary	AAA	26	93	32	8	1	2	48	22	16	11	0	20	1	0	1	1	1	.50	7	.344	.415	.516
	Jacksonville	AA	70	232	51	12	0	0	63	26	17	20	0	54	2	6	1	3	5	.38	4	.220	.286	.272
1995	Tacoma	AAA	132	437	128	29	9	2	181	57	47	32	2	83	0	10	4	8	3	.73	9	.293	.338	.414
	3 Min. YEARS		380	1297	340	73	16	8	469	177	127	116	4	289	6	27	12	27	19	.59	28	.262	.323	.362

Chris Sheff

Bats: Right **Throws:** Right **Pos:** OF **Ht:** 6'3" **Wt:** 210 **Born:** 2/4/71 **Age:** 25

Year	Team	Lg	G	AB	H	2B	3B	HR	TB	R	RBI	TBB	IBB	SO	HBP	SH	SF	SB	CS	SB%	GDP	Avg	OBP	SLG
1992	Erie	A	57	193	46	8	2	3	67	29	16	32	1	47	1	1	1	15	2	.88	3	.238	.348	.347
1993	Kane County	A	129	456	124	22	5	5	171	79	50	58	2	100	2	3	5	33	10	.77	11	.272	.353	.375
1994	Brevard Cty	A	32	118	44	8	3	1	61	21	19	17	0	23	0	0	1	7	2	.78	2	.373	.449	.517
	Portland	AA	106	395	101	19	1	5	137	50	30	31	0	76	0	3	2	18	4	.82	13	.256	.308	.347
1995	Portland	AA	131	471	130	25	7	12	205	85	91	72	6	84	5	1	8	23	6	.79	10	.276	.372	.435
	4 Min. YEARS		455	1633	445	82	18	26	641	264	206	210	9	330	8	8	17	96	24	.80	44	.273	.355	.393

Scott Sheldon

Bats: Right **Throws:** Right **Pos:** 3B **Ht:** 6'3" **Wt:** 185 **Born:** 11/28/68 **Age:** 27

Year	Team	Lg	G	AB	H	2B	3B	HR	TB	R	RBI	TBB	IBB	SO	HBP	SH	SF	SB	CS	SB%	GDP	Avg	OBP	SLG
1991	Sou. Oregon	A	65	229	58	10	3	0	74	34	24	23	0	44	2	3	1	9	5	.64	5	.253	.325	.323
1992	Madison	A	74	279	76	16	0	6	110	41	24	32	1	78	1	3	4	5	4	.56	2	.272	.345	.394
1993	Madison	A	131	428	91	22	1	8	139	67	67	49	3	121	8	3	8	8	7	.53	8	.213	.300	.325
1994	Huntsville	AA	91	268	62	10	1	0	74	31	28	28	1	69	7	7	3	7	1	.88	4	.231	.317	.276
1995	Edmonton	AAA	45	128	33	7	1	4	54	21	12	15	0	15	2	4	1	4	2	.67	0	.258	.342	.422
	Huntsville	AA	66	235	51	10	2	4	77	25	15	23	0	60	1	3	1	5	0	1.00	7	.217	.288	.328
	5 Min. YEARS		472	1567	371	75	8	22	528	219	170	170	5	387	21	23	18	38	19	.67	26	.237	.316	.337

Ben Shelton

Bats: Right **Throws:** Left **Pos:** 1B **Ht:** 6'3" **Wt:** 210 **Born:** 9/21/69 **Age:** 26

Year	Team	Lg	G	AB	H	2B	3B	HR	TB	R	RBI	TBB	IBB	SO	HBP	SH	SF	SB	CS	SB%	GDP	Avg	OBP	SLG
1987	Pirates	R	38	119	34	8	3	4	60	22	16	12	1	48	2	0	1	7	2	.78	0	.286	.358	.504
1988	Augusta	A	38	128	25	2	2	5	46	25	20	30	0	72	2	0	1	3	2	.60	1	.195	.354	.359
	Princeton	R	63	204	45	7	3	4	70	34	20	42	1	82	5	0	3	8	3	.73	1	.221	.362	.343
1989	Augusta	A	122	386	95	16	4	8	143	67	50	87	1	132	3	0	2	18	4	.82	5	.246	.387	.370
1990	Salem	A	109	320	66	10	2	10	110	44	36	55	0	116	8	4	4	1	2	.33	5	.206	.333	.344
1991	Salem	A	65	203	53	10	2	14	109	37	56	45	4	65	5	1	0	3	2	.60	5	.261	.407	.537
	Carolina	AA	55	169	39	8	3	1	56	19	19	29	0	57	4	0	1	2	1	.67	2	.231	.355	.331
1992	Carolina	AA	115	368	86	17	0	10	133	57	51	68	1	117	8	0	3	4	3	.57	11	.234	.362	.361
1993	Buffalo	AAA	65	173	48	8	1	5	73	25	22	24	0	44	3	0	0	0	0	.00	2	.277	.375	.422
1995	Salt Lake	AAA	9	33	8	1	1	1	14	7	6	6	0	16	0	0	0	0	0	.00	0	.242	.359	.424
	New Britain	AA	56	176	42	5	0	13	86	37	30	40	0	58	3	0	2	4	0	1.00	6	.239	.385	.489
	Trenton	AA	35	118	22	2	0	4	36	23	13	27	4	31	3	0	1	1	1	.50	4	.186	.349	.305
1993	Pittsburgh	NL	15	24	6	1	0	2	13	3	7	3	0	3	0	0	0	0	0	.00	0	.250	.333	.542
	8 Min. YEARS		770	2397	563	94	21	79	936	397	339	465	12	838	46	5	18	51	20	.72	42	.235	.367	.390

Larry Shenk

Pitches: Right **Bats:** Right **Pos:** P **Ht:** 6'0" **Wt:** 185 **Born:** 6/13/69 **Age:** 27

			HOW MUCH HE PITCHED					WHAT HE GAVE UP												THE RESULTS					
Year	Team	Lg	G	GS	CG	GF	IP	BFP	H	R	ER	HR	SH	SF	HB	TBB	IBB	SO	WP	Bk	W	L	Pct.	ShO	Sv	ERA
1992	Bluefield	R	21	0	0	10	39.1	172	35	19	12	0	1	2	2	12	3	45	3	0	5	2	.714	0	1	2.75
1993	Albany	A	53	0	0	29	85.2	327	57	25	20	4	2	3	4	11	0	101	3	0	5	2	.714	0	9	2.10
1994	Frederick	A	49	0	0	22	66.1	292	62	42	35	9	5	1	1	32	0	76	4	0	8	3	.727	0	2	4.75
1995	Bowie	AA	6	0	0	1	9.2	45	6	8	7	1	4	1	0	8	0	8	2	0	0	0	.000	0	0	6.52
	High Desert	A	2	0	0	1	2.2	16	6	5	5	2	0	0	0	3	0	2	0	0	0	0	.000	0	1	16.88
	Winnipeg	IND	29	1	0	11	66	291	58	25	21	6	2	3	5	33	1	53	4	0	3	1	.750	0	2	2.86
	4 Min. YEARS		160	1	0	74	269.2	1143	224	124	100	22	11	9	13	99	4	285	16	0	21	8	.724	0	15	3.34

Darrell Sherman

Bats: Left **Throws:** Left **Pos:** OF **Ht:** 5'9" **Wt:** 160 **Born:** 12/4/67 **Age:** 28

Year	Team	Lg	G	AB	H	2B	3B	HR	TB	R	RBI	TBB	IBB	SO	HBP	SH	SF	SB	CS	SB%	GDP	Avg	OBP	SLG
1989	Spokane	A	70	258	82	13	1	0	97	70	29	58	2	29	1	3	2	58	7	.89	1	.318	.459	.376
1990	Riverside	A	131	483	140	10	4	0	158	97	35	89	2	51	12	6	2	74	26	.74	9	.290	.411	.327
	Las Vegas	AAA	4	12	0	0	0	0	0	1	1	1	0	2	0	0	0	1	0	1.00	0	.000	.077	.000

1991 Wichita	AA	131	502	148	17	3	3	180	93	48	74	1	28	9	2	6	43	21	.67	7	.295	.391	.359
1992 Wichita	AA	64	220	73	11	2	6	106	60	25	40	2	25	9	2	2	26	7	.79	6	.332	.450	.482
Las Vegas	AAA	71	269	77	8	1	3	96	48	22	42	0	41	3	1	1	26	5	.84	3	.286	.387	.357
1993 Las Vegas	AAA	82	272	72	8	2	0	84	52	11	38	0	27	2	7	1	20	10	.67	1	.265	.358	.309
1994 Colo. Sprng	AAA	28	49	11	0	0	0	11	5	5	8	2	8	2	0	0	1	3	.25	3	.224	.356	.224
1995 Tacoma	AAA	119	350	90	9	3	2	111	59	31	54	0	49	3	10	4	19	6	.76	6	.257	.358	.317
1993 San Diego	NL	37	63	14	1	0	0	15	8	2	6	0	8	3	1	1	2	1	.67	0	.222	.315	.238
7 Min. YEARS		700	2415	693	76	16	14	843	485	207	404	9	260	53	30	20	268	85	.76	34	.287	.398	.349

Steve Shifflett

Pitches: Right Bats: Right Pos: P   Ht: 6' 1" Wt: 210 Born: 1/5/66 Age: 30

		HOW MUCH HE PITCHED						WHAT HE GAVE UP										THE RESULTS					
Year Team	Lg	G	GS	CG	GF	IP	BFP	H	R	ER	HR	SH	SF	HB	TBB	IBB	SO	WP	Bk	W	L	Pct.	ShO	Sv	ERA
1989 Appleton	A	18	2	0	5	39	171	34	25	18	1	1	1	2	19	2	13	8	3	3	3	.500	0	0	4.15
1990 Appleton	A	57	0	0	34	82.2	330	67	35	27	3	6	2	3	28	4	40	1	1	6	5	.545	0	10	2.94
1991 Memphis	AA	59	1	0	35	113	460	105	34	27	4	8	3	5	22	6	78	1	3	11	5	.688	0	9	2.15
1992 Omaha	AAA	32	0	0	29	43.2	165	30	8	8	0	4	3	0	15	1	19	0	2	3	2	.600	0	14	1.65
1993 Omaha	AAA	43	0	0	27	56	257	78	34	31	7	4	5	0	15	3	31	2	0	3	3	.500	0	3	4.98
1994 Omaha	AAA	45	1	0	16	92.1	401	99	42	38	7	5	2	6	24	3	39	1	0	3	5	.375	0	2	3.70
1995 Iowa	AAA	26	0	0	8	27	116	30	18	16	2	3	4	1	6	1	10	0	0	5	1	.833	0	5	5.33
Colo. Sprng	AAA	23	0	0	9	38	184	61	33	29	6	1	4	0	13	2	21	0	2	4	3	.571	0	0	6.87
1992 Kansas City	AL	34	0	0	15	52	221	55	15	15	6	4	1	2	17	6	25	2	1	1	4	.200	0	0	2.60
7 Min. YEARS		303	4	0	163	491.2	2084	504	229	194	30	32	24	17	142	22	251	13	11	38	27	.585	0	40	3.55

Zak Shinall

Pitches: Right Bats: Right Pos: P   Ht: 6' 4" Wt: 220 Born: 10/14/68 Age: 27

		HOW MUCH HE PITCHED						WHAT HE GAVE UP										THE RESULTS					
Year Team	Lg	G	GS	CG	GF	IP	BFP	H	R	ER	HR	SH	SF	HB	TBB	IBB	SO	WP	Bk	W	L	Pct.	ShO	Sv	ERA
1987 Great Falls	R	1	0	0	0	1.1	15	4	8	7	1	0	0	1	5	0	0	0	1	0	0	.000	0	0	47.25
Dodgers	R	8	6	0	1	30.1	131	27	17	17	0	2	0	0	15	1	29	4	0	1	2	.333	0	0	5.04
1988 Bakersfield	A	28	19	1	3	113	526	90	65	53	1	3	6	4	104	0	63	20	3	7	8	.467	1	0	4.22
1989 Vero Beach	A	47	4	1	23	86	352	71	32	24	4	5	3	2	29	7	69	4	2	5	7	.417	0	7	2.51
1990 San Antonio	AA	20	15	0	3	91.1	390	93	44	36	2	5	0	1	41	1	43	6	1	6	3	.667	0	3	3.55
1991 San Antonio	AA	25	5	0	19	54.2	234	53	31	17	4	3	1	0	21	2	29	1	2	2	4	.333	0	9	2.80
Albuquerque	AA	29	0	0	11	41	176	48	15	14	3	2	0	2	10	0	22	3	0	2	0	1.000	0	1	3.07
1992 Albuquerque	AAA	64	0	0	32	82	363	91	38	30	7	7	2	1	37	11	46	4	0	13	5	.722	0	6	3.29
1993 Charlotte	AAA	1	0	0	0	0.2	6	3	4	4	0	0	0	0	1	0	0	0	0	0	0	.000	0	0	54.00
Calgary	AAA	33	0	0	19	46.2	211	55	29	26	6	2	1	4	18	3	25	4	0	2	1	.667	0	5	5.01
1995 New Orleans	AAA	9	0	0	1	13	58	15	11	11	4	0	0	1	7	1	5	2	0	0	0	.000	0	0	7.62
1993 Seattle	AL	1	0	0	0	2.2	14	4	1	1	1	0	0	0	2	0	0	0	0	0	0	.000	0	0	3.38
8 Min. YEARS		265	49	2	112	560	2462	550	294	239	32	29	13	16	288	26	331	48	9	38	30	.559	1	28	3.84

Steve Shoemaker

Pitches: Right Bats: Right Pos: P   Ht: 6'3" Wt: 195 Born: 2/24/70 Age: 26

		HOW MUCH HE PITCHED						WHAT HE GAVE UP										THE RESULTS					
Year Team	Lg	G	GS	CG	GF	IP	BFP	H	R	ER	HR	SH	SF	HB	TBB	IBB	SO	WP	Bk	W	L	Pct.	ShO	Sv	ERA
1991 Athletics	R	8	5	0	2	29.2	127	31	16	13	1	0	0	0	15	0	26	2	4	2	1	.667	0	0	3.94
1992 Madison	A	22	11	2	3	83.1	356	98	56	47	5	4	3	2	18	0	56	5	2	2	5	.286	0	1	5.08
Modesto	A	10	9	1	0	61.1	256	59	25	21	6	2	1	2	15	0	50	0	0	4	2	.667	0	0	3.08
1993 San Bernrdo	A	24	23	1	0	126.2	574	146	92	76	16	1	7	3	56	1	116	3	0	9	6	.600	1	0	5.40
1994 Huntsville	AA	36	2	0	11	62.2	273	65	30	23	2	4	2	1	21	3	47	3	0	2	2	.500	0	2	3.30
1995 Huntsville	AA	43	0	0	24	76	318	62	33	29	8	3	4	1	31	2	63	7	0	4	4	.500	0	5	3.43
5 Min. YEARS		143	50	4	40	439.2	1904	461	252	209	38	14	17	9	156	6	358	20	6	23	20	.535	1	8	4.28

Brian Shouse

Pitches: Left Bats: Left Pos: P   Ht: 5'11" Wt: 175 Born: 9/26/68 Age: 27

		HOW MUCH HE PITCHED						WHAT HE GAVE UP										THE RESULTS					
Year Team	Lg	G	GS	CG	GF	IP	BFP	H	R	ER	HR	SH	SF	HB	TBB	IBB	SO	WP	Bk	W	L	Pct.	ShO	Sv	ERA
1990 Welland	A	17	1	0	7	39.2	177	50	27	23	2	3	2	3	7	0	39	1	2	4	3	.571	0	2	5.22
1991 Augusta	A	26	0	0	25	31	124	22	13	11	1	1	1	3	9	1	32	5	0	2	3	.400	0	8	3.19
Salem	A	17	0	0	9	33.2	147	35	12	11	2	2	0	0	15	2	25	1	0	2	1	.667	0	3	2.94
1992 Carolina	AA	59	0	0	33	77.1	323	71	31	21	3	8	2	2	28	4	79	4	1	5	6	.455	0	4	2.44
1993 Buffalo	AAA	48	0	0	14	51.2	218	54	24	22	7	0	3	2	17	2	25	1	0	1	0	1.000	0	2	3.83
1994 Buffalo	AAA	43	0	0	20	52	212	44	22	21	6	4	2	1	15	4	31	0	0	3	4	.429	0	0	3.63
1995 Calgary	AAA	8	8	1	0	39.1	185	62	35	27	2	1	1	1	7	0	17	3	0	4	4	.500	0	0	6.18
Carolina	AA	21	20	0	0	114.2	480	126	64	57	14	5	3	4	19	2	76	1	1	7	6	.538	0	0	4.47
1993 Pittsburgh	NL	6	0	0	1	4	22	7	4	4	1	0	1	0	2	0	3	1	0	0	0	.000	0	0	9.00
6 Min. YEARS		239	29	1	108	439.1	1866	464	228	193	37	24	14	16	117	15	324	16	4	28	27	.509	0	19	3.95

Jose Silva

Pitches: Right Bats: Right Pos: P   Ht: 6'6" Wt: 180 Born: 12/19/73 Age: 22

		HOW MUCH HE PITCHED						WHAT HE GAVE UP										THE RESULTS					
Year Team	Lg	G	GS	CG	GF	IP	BFP	H	R	ER	HR	SH	SF	HB	TBB	IBB	SO	WP	Bk	W	L	Pct.	ShO	Sv	ERA
1992 Blue Jays	R	12	12	0	0	59.1	231	42	23	15	1	0	1	2	18	0	78	1	2	6	4	.600	0	0	2.28
1993 Hagerstown	A	24	24	0	0	142.2	581	103	50	40	4	0	4	4	62	0	161	9	1	12	5	.706	0	0	2.52

			G		H	2B	3B	HR	TB	R	RBI	TBB	IBB	SO	HBP	SH	SF				W	L	Pct.	ShO	Sv	ERA
1994	Dunedin	A	8	7	0	0	43	188	41	32	18	4	2	6	0	24	0	41	5	0	0	2	.000	0	0	3.77
	Knoxville	AA	16	16	1	0	91.1	381	89	47	42	9	2	2	3	31	0	71	4	0	4	8	.333	1	0	4.14
1995	Knoxville	AA	3	0	0	0	2	15	3	2	2	0	1	1	0	6	0	2	0	0	0	0	.000	0	0	9.00
	4 Min. YEARS		63	59	1	0	338.1	1396	278	154	117	20	5	14	9	141	0	353	19	3	22	19	.537	1	0	3.11

Brian Silvia

Bats: Right Throws: Right Pos: C-DH Ht: 6'0" Wt: 195 Born: 9/13/71 Age: 24

			BATTING															BASERUNNING				PERCENTAGES		
Year	Team	Lg	G	AB	H	2B	3B	HR	TB	R	RBI	TBB	IBB	SO	HBP	SH	SF	SB	CS	SB%	GDP	Avg	OBP	SLG
1992	Princeton	R	36	122	37	4	1	1	46	19	23	18	0	23	1	1	1	2	1	.67	2	.303	.394	.377
	Billings	R	5	13	2	0	0	0	2	4	1	4	0	7	0	0	0	0	0	.00	1	.154	.353	.154
1993	Princeton	R	5	17	3	0	0	0	3	1	1	2	0	1	0	0	0	1	1	.50	1	.176	.263	.176
	Charlstn-Wv	A	23	53	14	2	1	0	18	7	4	4	0	12	0	0	1	0	0	.00	2	.264	.310	.340
1994	New Jersey	A	67	218	66	18	4	6	110	35	42	34	3	44	13	0	3	4	2	.67	4	.303	.422	.505
1995	Savannah	A	59	198	49	14	2	8	91	25	33	31	1	39	8	0	3	4	2	.67	9	.247	.367	.460
	Arkansas	AA	12	29	7	1	0	0	8	4	3	4	0	9	1	0	0	0	0	.00	1	.241	.353	.276
	4 Min. YEARS		207	650	178	39	8	15	278	95	107	97	4	135	23	1	8	11	6	.65	20	.274	.383	.428

John Simmons

Pitches: Left Bats: Left Pos: P Ht: 6'6" Wt: 220 Born: 10/12/70 Age: 25

			HOW MUCH HE PITCHED					WHAT HE GAVE UP											THE RESULTS				
Year	Team	Lg	G	GS	CG	GF	IP	BFP	H	R	ER	HR	SH	SF	HB	TBB	IBB	SO	WP	Bk	W	L	Pct.	ShO	Sv	ERA
1992	Idaho Falls	R	27	0	0	17	40.1	179	40	25	16	2	1	3	1	13	0	44	4	2	3	1	.750	0	3	3.57
1993	Macon	A	35	0	0	10	67.2	283	49	25	20	6	7	1	3	25	2	59	2	0	1	5	.000	0	3	2.66
1994	Durham	A	40	0	0	11	67.2	295	67	35	33	8	2	3	2	31	2	47	5	1	3	2	.600	0	2	4.39
1995	Greenville	AA	48	0	0	15	60.1	266	67	35	31	9	1	0	0	22	2	54	3	0	1	5	.167	0	1	4.62
	4 Min. YEARS		150	0	0	53	236	1023	223	120	100	25	11	7	6	91	6	204	14	3	7	13	.350	0	9	3.81

Nelson Simmons

Bats: Both Throws: Right Pos: OF Ht: 6'1" Wt: 195 Born: 6/27/63 Age: 33

			BATTING															BASERUNNING				PERCENTAGES		
Year	Team	Lg	G	AB	H	2B	3B	HR	TB	R	RBI	TBB	IBB	SO	HBP	SH	SF	SB	CS	SB%	GDP	Avg	OBP	SLG
1984	Evansville	AAA	142	501	154	41	5	22	271	79	83	53	0	106	0	1	6	0	4	.00	15	.307	.370	.541
1985	Nashville	AAA	49	188	46	14	0	9	87	17	26	14	1	30	1	0	4	0	0	.00	4	.245	.295	.463
1986	Nashville	AAA	14	45	9	2	0	0	11	5	4	11	0	12	0	0	0	0	0	.00	4	.200	.357	.244
	Rochester	AAA	89	304	83	13	5	8	130	33	37	27	2	53	0	5	5	4	1	.80	10	.273	.327	.428
1987	Rochester	AAA	64	207	56	10	1	3	77	25	21	21	1	28	0	0	0	0	0	.00	9	.271	.333	.372
	Calgary	AAA	18	68	21	5	0	3	35	14	13	10	0	10	0	0	1	1	2	.33	1	.309	.392	.515
1988	Calgary	AAA	127	459	140	27	2	14	213	74	73	59	6	65	0	1	3	4	7	.36	14	.305	.382	.464
1989	Louisville	AAA	5	19	6	2	0	1	11	3	3	1	0	3	0	0	0	0	0	.00	0	.316	.350	.579
1990	Huntsville	AA	123	453	116	19	1	15	182	70	55	62	4	64	1	4	4	0	3	.00	13	.256	.344	.402
1991	Tacoma	AAA	118	427	116	18	2	8	162	48	67	48	6	56	0	0	7	0	1	.00	14	.272	.340	.379
1992	Denver	AAA	4	10	2	0	0	1	5	1	2	1	0	2	0	1	0	0	0	.00	0	.200	.273	.500
1993	Palm Spring	A	20	76	25	8	0	5	48	13	23	10	0	7	0	0	1	0	1	.00	0	.329	.402	.632
1995	Calgary	AAA	107	299	84	17	0	9	128	44	58	30	3	45	0	0	4	1	1	.50	5	.281	.342	.428
1984	Detroit	AL	9	30	13	2	0	0	15	4	3	2	1	5	0	0	0	1	0	1.00	2	.433	.469	.500
1985	Detroit	AL	75	251	60	11	0	10	101	31	33	26	5	41	0	0	4	1	0	1.00	4	.239	.306	.402
1987	Baltimore	AL	16	49	13	1	1	1	19	3	4	3	0	8	0	0	2	0	1	.00	3	.265	.296	.388
	11 Min. YEARS		880	3056	858	176	16	98	1360	426	465	347	23	481	2	12	38	10	20	.33	89	.281	.351	.445
	3 Maj. YEARS		100	330	86	14	1	11	135	38	40	31	6	54	0	0	6	2	1	.67	9	.261	.319	.409

Scott Simmons

Pitches: Left Bats: Right Pos: P Ht: 6'2" Wt: 200 Born: 8/15/69 Age: 26

			HOW MUCH HE PITCHED					WHAT HE GAVE UP											THE RESULTS				
Year	Team	Lg	G	GS	CG	GF	IP	BFP	H	R	ER	HR	SH	SF	HB	TBB	IBB	SO	WP	Bk	W	L	Pct.	ShO	Sv	ERA
1991	Hamilton	A	15	14	0	0	90.1	376	82	34	26	4	0	2	1	25	0	78	1	2	6	4	.600	0	0	2.59
1992	Springfield	A	27	27	2	0	170.1	699	160	63	53	10	9	3	2	39	0	116	10	2	15	7	.682	1	0	2.80
1993	St. Pete	A	13	12	1	1	78.2	326	70	38	30	1	4	4	0	31	0	54	6	1	4	5	.444	0	0	3.43
	Arkansas	AA	13	10	0	0	76.2	306	68	26	23	1	2	2	0	18	3	35	4	0	6	3	.667	0	0	2.70
1994	Arkansas	AA	26	26	2	0	162.1	663	148	63	49	4	10	4	3	39	1	115	4	1	7	11	.389	1	0	2.72
1995	Louisville	AAA	2	2	0	0	9	40	11	9	8	3	0	0	1	1	0	2	0	0	0	2	.000	0	0	8.00
	Arkansas	AA	22	22	1	0	139	569	145	66	53	9	5	6	1	28	1	73	5	0	11	9	.550	1	0	3.43
	5 Min. YEARS		118	113	6	1	726.1	2979	684	299	242	32	30	21	8	181	5	473	30	6	49	41	.544	3	0	3.00

Mitch Simmons

Bats: Right Throws: Right Pos: 2B Ht: 5'9" Wt: 170 Born: 12/13/68 Age: 27

			BATTING															BASERUNNING				PERCENTAGES		
Year	Team	Lg	G	AB	H	2B	3B	HR	TB	R	RBI	TBB	IBB	SO	HBP	SH	SF	SB	CS	SB%	GDP	Avg	OBP	SLG
1991	Jamestown	A	41	153	47	12	0	1	62	38	16	39	1	20	0	2	2	23	5	.82	1	.307	.443	.405
	W. Palm Bch	A	15	50	9	2	1	0	13	3	4	5	0	8	0	0	1	1	0	1.00	0	.180	.255	.260
1992	Albany	A	130	481	136	26	5	1	175	57	61	60	0	47	7	2	10	34	12	.74	6	.283	.364	.364
1993	W. Palm Bch	A	45	156	40	4	1	1	49	24	13	19	0	9	3	1	2	14	8	.64	3	.256	.344	.314
	Harrisburg	AA	29	77	18	1	1	0	21	5	5	7	0	14	0	2	1	2	0	1.00	1	.234	.294	.273
1994	Nashville	AA	102	391	124	26	3	1	159	46	48	39	0	38	6	3	5	30	9	.77	6	.317	.383	.407

Year Team	Lg	G	AB	H	2B	3B	HR	TB	R	RBI	TBB	IBB	SO	HBP	SH	SF	SB	CS	SB%	GDP	Avg	OBP	SLG
1995 Salt Lake	AAA	130	480	156	34	4	3	207	87	46	47	2	45	10	4	2	32	16	.67	9	.325	.395	.431
5 Min. YEARS		492	1788	530	105	12	9	686	260	193	216	3	181	26	14	22	136	50	.73	26	.296	.376	.384

Benji Simonton

Bats: Right **Throws:** Right **Pos:** 1B   **Ht:** 6'1" **Wt:** 225 **Born:** 5/5/72 **Age:** 24

						BATTING											BASERUNNING				PERCENTAGES		
Year Team	Lg	G	AB	H	2B	3B	HR	TB	R	RBI	TBB	IBB	SO	HBP	SH	SF	SB	CS	SB%	GDP	Avg	OBP	SLG
1992 Everett	A	68	225	55	10	0	6	83	37	34	39	0	78	3	2	3	9	4	.69	1	.244	.359	.369
1993 Clinton	A	100	310	79	18	4	12	141	52	49	40	2	112	6	0	2	8	7	.53	3	.255	.349	.455
1994 Clinton	A	67	237	64	16	4	14	130	47	57	52	3	73	5	1	0	10	3	.77	7	.270	.412	.549
San Jose	A	68	259	77	20	0	14	139	41	51	32	0	86	5	1	1	0	2	.00	5	.297	.384	.537
1995 San Jose	A	61	225	65	9	6	8	110	38	37	40	2	78	10	0	4	7	0	1.00	5	.289	.412	.489
Shreveport	AA	38	108	33	9	3	4	60	18	30	11	0	32	2	1	1	3	1	.75	1	.306	.377	.556
4 Min. YEARS		402	1364	373	82	17	58	663	233	258	214	7	459	31	5	11	37	17	.69	22	.273	.381	.486

Wesley Sims

Bats: Both **Throws:** Right **Pos:** SS   **Ht:** 6'0" **Wt:** 175 **Born:** 11/7/71 **Age:** 24

						BATTING											BASERUNNING				PERCENTAGES		
Year Team	Lg	G	AB	H	2B	3B	HR	TB	R	RBI	TBB	IBB	SO	HBP	SH	SF	SB	CS	SB%	GDP	Avg	OBP	SLG
1993 Erie	A	74	284	68	8	0	7	97	38	22	31	0	49	1	0	0	2	5	.29	9	.239	.316	.342
1994 Charlotte	A	92	312	68	8	3	3	91	26	32	36	4	51	2	5	2	9	3	.75	5	.218	.301	.292
1995 Tulsa	AA	12	43	10	1	1	0	13	4	5	6	0	3	0	0	0	0	1	.00	1	.233	.327	.302
Charlotte	A	5	11	3	1	0	0	4	2	1	2	0	5	0	0	0	0	0	.00	0	.273	.385	.364
3 Min. YEARS		183	650	149	18	4	10	205	70	60	75	4	108	3	5	2	11	9	.55	15	.229	.311	.315

Steve Sisco

Bats: Right **Throws:** Right **Pos:** 2B   **Ht:** 5'9" **Wt:** 180 **Born:** 12/2/69 **Age:** 26

						BATTING											BASERUNNING				PERCENTAGES		
Year Team	Lg	G	AB	H	2B	3B	HR	TB	R	RBI	TBB	IBB	SO	HBP	SH	SF	SB	CS	SB%	GDP	Avg	OBP	SLG
1992 Eugene	A	67	261	86	7	1	0	95	41	30	26	0	32	4	2	2	22	12	.65	7	.330	.396	.364
Appleton	A	1	4	1	0	0	0	1	1	0	0	0	1	0	0	0	0	0	.00	0	.250	.250	.250
1993 Rockford	A	124	460	132	22	4	2	168	62	57	42	2	65	2	4	5	25	10	.71	14	.287	.346	.365
1994 Wilmington	A	76	270	74	11	4	3	102	41	32	37	0	39	2	6	4	5	6	.45	7	.274	.361	.378
1995 Omaha	AAA	7	24	5	1	0	0	6	4	0	2	0	8	0	1	0	0	0	.00	0	.208	.269	.250
Wichita	AA	54	209	63	12	1	3	86	29	23	15	0	31	1	1	1	3	1	.75	5	.301	.350	.411
4 Min. YEARS		329	1228	361	53	10	8	458	178	142	122	2	176	9	14	12	55	29	.65	28	.294	.359	.373

Mark Small

Pitches: Right **Bats:** Right **Pos:** P   **Ht:** 6'3" **Wt:** 205 **Born:** 11/12/67 **Age:** 28

					HOW MUCH HE PITCHED				WHAT HE GAVE UP										THE RESULTS					
Year Team	Lg	G	GS	CG	GF	IP	BFP	H	R	ER	HR	SH	SF	HB	TBB	IBB	SO	WP	Bk	W	L	Pct.	ShO	Sv	ERA
1989 Auburn	A	10	3	0	4	19.2	87	17	13	11	3	0	1	1	11	0	23	3	0	0	1	.000	0	2	5.03
1990 Asheville	A	34	0	0	16	52	252	54	36	24	2	4	3	4	37	5	34	9	0	3	4	.429	0	6	4.15
1991 Osceola	A	26	0	0	10	44.2	172	30	10	8	2	1	0	1	19	1	44	2	0	3	0	1.000	0	2	1.61
1992 Osceola	A	22	20	1	2	105	435	97	56	45	8	3	3	0	38	0	69	5	1	5	9	.357	0	0	3.86
1993 Jackson	AA	51	0	0	18	84.2	361	71	34	30	8	8	3	3	41	6	64	8	2	7	2	.778	0	3	3.19
1994 Jackson	AA	16	0	0	9	21	97	22	16	9	1	1	2	1	10	2	14	4	0	3	1	.750	0	3	3.86
Tucson	AAA	41	0	0	12	70	321	88	48	41	9	3	3	2	34	2	30	13	0	8	5	.615	0	4	5.27
1995 Tucson	AAA	51	0	0	40	66	285	74	32	30	5	1	2	1	19	2	51	8	0	3	3	.500	0	19	4.09
7 Min. YEARS		251	23	1	111	463	2010	453	245	198	38	21	17	13	209	18	329	52	3	32	25	.561	0	36	3.85

Rueben Smiley

Bats: Left **Throws:** Left **Pos:** OF   **Ht:** 6'4" **Wt:** 195 **Born:** 8/27/68 **Age:** 27

						BATTING											BASERUNNING				PERCENTAGES		
Year Team	Lg	G	AB	H	2B	3B	HR	TB	R	RBI	TBB	IBB	SO	HBP	SH	SF	SB	CS	SB%	GDP	Avg	OBP	SLG
1988 Pocatello	R	50	185	53	3	3	1	65	40	16	31	3	33	0	0	1	7	6	.54	2	.286	.387	.351
1989 Clinton	A	125	451	94	13	3	0	113	53	26	30	0	72	5	7	2	22	9	.71	10	.208	.264	.251
1990 San Jose	A	135	455	121	9	5	3	149	78	48	40	0	105	10	7	4	25	7	.78	9	.266	.336	.327
1991 Shreveport	AA	104	318	73	8	4	5	104	57	31	55	9	58	2	5	0	37	7	.84	5	.230	.347	.327
1992 Shreveport	AA	93	316	81	12	5	6	121	38	35	21	8	71	4	1	1	19	6	.76	4	.256	.310	.383
Phoenix	AAA	17	37	8	3	0	0	11	5	2	3	0	9	1	1	0	0	2	.00	0	.216	.293	.297
1993 Phoenix	AAA	99	313	94	16	7	7	145	58	37	15	3	67	0	0	1	24	3	.89	6	.300	.331	.463
1994 Phoenix	AAA	69	227	68	8	4	2	90	36	20	14	3	35	1	0	0	10	6	.63	3	.300	.343	.396
1995 Las Vegas	AAA	34	96	21	4	1	3	36	10	17	8	1	19	0	0	2	6	3	.67	2	.219	.274	.375
Wichita	AA	41	104	25	3	1	2	36	16	13	8	0	20	0	0	2	1	3	.25	3	.240	.289	.346
8 Min. YEARS		767	2502	638	79	33	29	870	391	245	225	27	489	23	21	13	151	52	.74	42	.255	.321	.348

Bobby Smith

Bats: Right **Throws:** Right **Pos:** 3B   **Ht:** 6'3" **Wt:** 190 **Born:** 4/10/74 **Age:** 22

						BATTING											BASERUNNING				PERCENTAGES		
Year Team	Lg	G	AB	H	2B	3B	HR	TB	R	RBI	TBB	IBB	SO	HBP	SH	SF	SB	CS	SB%	GDP	Avg	OBP	SLG
1992 Braves	R	57	217	51	9	1	3	71	31	28	17	1	55	3	0	2	5	6	.45	5	.235	.297	.327
1993 Macon	A	108	384	94	16	7	4	136	53	38	23	1	81	5	8	0	12	8	.60	1	.245	.296	.354
1994 Durham	A	127	478	127	27	2	12	194	49	71	41	1	112	4	1	0	18	7	.72	19	.266	.329	.406

Year	Team	Lg	G	AB	H	2B	3B	HR	TB	R	RBI	TBB	IBB	SO	HBP	SH	SF	SB	CS	SB%	GDP	Avg	OBP	SLG
1995	Greenville	AA	127	444	116	27	3	14	191	75	58	40	2	109	7	4	1	12	6	.67	12	.261	.331	.430
	4 Min. YEARS		419	1523	388	79	13	33	592	208	195	121	5	357	19	13	3	47	27	.64	37	.255	.317	.389

Brandon Smith

Bats: Right **Throws:** Right **Pos:** C
Ht: 6'2" **Wt:** 200 **Born:** 3/9/73 **Age:** 23

			BATTING															BASERUNNING				PERCENTAGES		
Year	Team	Lg	G	AB	H	2B	3B	HR	TB	R	RBI	TBB	IBB	SO	HBP	SH	SF	SB	CS	SB%	GDP	Avg	OBP	SLG
1991	Athletics	R	36	111	21	3	0	1	27	16	10	16	0	24	3	1	2	1	3	.25	2	.189	.303	.243
1992	Athletics	R	11	19	5	1	0	0	6	1	4	1	0	1	0	1	0	0	0	.00	0	.263	.300	.316
1994	Norfolk	AAA	2	4	1	0	0	0	1	1	1	0	0	1	0	0	0	1	0	1.00	0	.250	.250	.250
	Pittsfield	A	18	54	8	2	0	1	13	2	3	0	0	18	1	0	2	0	0	.00	0	.148	.158	.241
1995	Binghamton	AA	2	2	0	0	0	0	0	0	0	0	0	1	0	0	0	0	0	.00	0	.000	.000	.000
	4 Min. YEARS		69	190	35	6	0	2	47	20	18	17	0	45	4	2	4	2	3	.40	2	.184	.260	.247

Bubba Smith

Bats: Right **Throws:** Right **Pos:** DH
Ht: 6'2" **Wt:** 225 **Born:** 12/18/69 **Age:** 26

			BATTING															BASERUNNING				PERCENTAGES		
Year	Team	Lg	G	AB	H	2B	3B	HR	TB	R	RBI	TBB	IBB	SO	HBP	SH	SF	SB	CS	SB%	GDP	Avg	OBP	SLG
1991	Bellingham	A	66	253	66	14	2	10	114	28	43	13	1	47	2	0	2	0	2	.00	9	.261	.300	.451
1992	Peninsula	A	137	482	126	22	1	32	246	70	93	65	7	138	5	0	5	4	10	.29	13	.261	.352	.510
1993	Jacksonvlle	AA	37	137	30	8	0	6	56	12	21	7	0	52	2	0	1	0	3	.00	1	.219	.265	.409
	Riverside	A	5	19	8	3	0	0	11	5	3	7	0	3	0	0	0	0	0	.00	0	.421	.577	.579
	Winston-Sal	A	92	342	103	16	0	27	200	55	81	35	1	109	7	0	4	2	0	1.00	8	.301	.374	.585
1994	Chattanooga	AA	4	9	0	0	0	0	0	0	0	0	0	7	0	0	0	0	0	.00	0	.000	.000	.000
	Charlstn-Wv	A	100	354	83	26	1	15	156	38	59	20	1	113	5	1	2	1	2	.33	9	.234	.283	.441
1995	Fort Myers	A	60	176	58	15	0	13	112	27	51	16	4	38	0	0	3	1	2	.33	8	.330	.379	.636
	New Britain	AA	42	148	36	11	0	6	65	20	21	6	1	41	0	0	1	0	0	.00	5	.243	.271	.439
	5 Min. YEARS		543	1920	510	115	4	109	960	255	372	169	15	548	21	1	18	8	19	.30	54	.266	.329	.500

Daryl Smith

Pitches: Right **Bats:** Right **Pos:** P
Ht: 6'4" **Wt:** 220 **Born:** 7/29/60 **Age:** 35

			HOW MUCH HE PITCHED						WHAT HE GAVE UP										THE RESULTS					
Year	Team	Lg	G	GS	CG	GF	IP	BFP	H	R	ER	HR	SH	SF	HB	TBB	IBB	SO	WP	Bk	W	L	Pct.	ShO	Sv	ERA
1984	Tulsa	AA	7	0	0	1	10.2	57	18	17	17	0	1	1	1	9	0	6	3	0	0	1	.000	0	0	14.34
	Salem	A	16	12	0	1	67	297	67	40	32	6	0	1	2	44	1	38	10	0	6	3	.667	0	0	4.30
1985	Waterloo	A	1	0	0	0	4.2	18	4	1	1	1	0	0	0	2	0	5	0	0	0	0	.000	0	0	1.93
	Waterbury	AA	16	6	1	8	53.2	231	42	25	21	5	1	2	1	37	1	38	5	0	2	2	.500	0	4	3.52
1986	Waterbury	AA	21	11	4	6	89	368	71	37	35	8	0	2	3	48	0	55	11	0	4	3	.571	1	0	3.54
1987	Williamsprt	A	2	2	0	0	8	37	11	8	7	1	0	1	0	3	0	5	1	0	1	1	.500	0	0	7.88
	Reading	AA	19	12	1	2	79.1	349	75	38	31	5	3	3	4	43	2	53	5	1	6	2	.750	0	1	3.52
	Maine	AAA	4	4	0	0	22.2	103	21	18	17	4	1	2	2	13	0	16	0	0	1	3	.250	0	0	6.75
1988	Birmingham	AA	40	0	0	33	53	226	42	25	19	0	2	4	0	27	3	44	6	6	1	4	.200	0	7	3.23
1990	Memphis	AA	21	0	0	5	48.1	211	46	27	17	1	3	6	0	23	0	48	10	0	2	1	.667	0	1	3.17
	Omaha	AAA	11	10	0	0	64	268	59	25	22	5	2	0	2	32	0	56	3	4	6	2	.750	0	0	3.09
1991	Omaha	AAA	23	14	0	4	93	389	82	38	35	10	3	1	4	33	1	94	4	2	4	5	.444	0	0	3.39
1993	Bowie	AA	3	3	0	0	22	91	14	7	6	1	1	0	1	11	0	23	0	0	0	0	.000	0	0	2.45
1995	Columbus	AAA	13	7	0	2	51.1	225	54	31	23	5	0	3	4	20	1	23	5	0	0	3	.000	0	0	4.03
1990	Kansas City	AL	2	1	0	1	6.2	27	5	3	3	0	0	2	0	4	0	6	0	0	0	1	.000	0	0	4.05
	9 Min. YEARS		197	81	6	60	666.2	2870	606	337	283	52	17	26	24	345	9	504	63	13	33	30	.524	1	13	3.82

Ed Smith

Bats: Right **Throws:** Right **Pos:** 3B
Ht: 6'4" **Wt:** 220 **Born:** 6/5/69 **Age:** 27

			BATTING															BASERUNNING				PERCENTAGES		
Year	Team	Lg	G	AB	H	2B	3B	HR	TB	R	RBI	TBB	IBB	SO	HBP	SH	SF	SB	CS	SB%	GDP	Avg	OBP	SLG
1987	White Sox	R	32	114	27	3	0	2	36	10	18	6	0	28	2	0	0	3	3	.50	1	.237	.287	.316
1988	South Bend	A	130	462	107	14	1	3	132	51	46	51	3	87	5	2	2	5	5	.50	9	.232	.313	.286
1989	South Bend	A	115	382	94	20	2	8	142	52	49	43	4	84	7	0	4	7	9	.44	10	.246	.330	.372
1990	Sarasota	A	63	239	46	10	3	4	74	22	23	11	1	61	7	1	3	0	3	.00	6	.192	.246	.310
	Birmingham	AA	72	247	61	14	3	1	84	22	23	22	0	49	0	3	4	2	1	.67	10	.247	.304	.340
1991	Sarasota	A	54	198	43	7	0	3	59	27	27	15	1	52	3	2	2	4	3	.57	2	.217	.280	.298
	Beloit	A	61	218	57	13	2	4	86	31	37	21	2	41	1	1	3	5	2	.71	5	.261	.325	.394
1992	Stockton	A	99	355	93	21	4	11	155	57	57	49	0	72	4	0	1	6	6	.50	8	.262	.357	.437
	El Paso	AA	22	86	25	5	0	2	36	11	15	8	0	20	1	0	1	0	1	.00	2	.291	.354	.419
1993	El Paso	AA	118	419	123	23	6	8	182	64	69	38	4	97	3	0	2	13	5	.72	13	.294	.355	.434
1994	Orlando	AA	115	401	104	17	5	16	179	51	60	37	1	75	4	0	3	4	11	.27	14	.259	.326	.446
1995	Buffalo	AAA	13	31	10	0	1	3	21	4	9	3	0	5	0	0	1	0	1	.00	0	.323	.371	.677
	Canton-Akrn	AA	103	365	88	18	2	11	143	41	52	36	4	93	1	1	3	0	2	.00	6	.241	.309	.392
	9 Min. YEARS		997	3517	878	165	29	76	1329	443	485	340	20	764	38	16	29	49	52	.49	86	.250	.320	.378

Eric Smith

Pitches: Right **Bats:** Right **Pos:** P
Ht: 6'3" **Wt:** 200 **Born:** 12/9/69 **Age:** 26

			HOW MUCH HE PITCHED						WHAT HE GAVE UP										THE RESULTS					
Year	Team	Lg	G	GS	CG	GF	IP	BFP	H	R	ER	HR	SH	SF	HB	TBB	IBB	SO	WP	Bk	W	L	Pct.	ShO	Sv	ERA
1992	Batavia	A	16	8	0	3	60.1	249	52	33	28	5	0	2	4	17	1	37	6	2	2	5	.286	0	2	4.18
1993	Spartanburg	A	35	1	0	25	55	244	51	19	16	1	3	3	5	30	1	52	7	0	2	7	.222	0	8	2.62

Year Team	Lg	G	GS	CG	GF	IP	BFP	H	R	ER	HR	SH	SF	HB	TBB	IBB	SO	WP	Bk	W	L	Pct.	ShO	Sv	ERA
1994 Clearwater	A	54	0	0	37	59	257	50	22	19	2	1	0	2	34	3	32	6	0	2	2	.500	0	15	2.90
1995 Reading	AA	4	0	0	0	4	28	11	9	9	1	0	0	1	4	1	5	2	0	0	1	.000	0	0	20.25
Clearwater	A	8	0	0	7	8	27	3	0	0	0	0	0	0	1	0	7	0	0	0	0	.000	0	4	0.00
4 Min. YEARS		117	9	0	72	186.1	805	167	83	72	9	4	5	12	86	6	133	21	2	6	15	.286	0	29	3.48

Greg Smith

Bats: Both **Throws:** Right **Pos:** SS **Ht:** 5'11" **Wt:** 170 **Born:** 4/5/67 **Age:** 29

									BATTING										BASERUNNING				PERCENTAGES		
Year Team	Lg	G	AB	H	2B	3B	HR	TB	R	RBI	TBB	IBB	SO	HBP	SH	SF	SB	CS	SB%	GDP	Avg	OBP	SLG
1985 Wytheville	R	51	179	42	6	2	0	52	28	15	20	1	27	2	3	1	8	1	.89	1	.235	.317	.291
1986 Peoria	A	53	170	43	6	3	2	61	24	26	19	1	45	1	2	0	9	2	.82	2	.253	.332	.359
1987 Peoria	A	124	444	120	23	5	6	171	69	56	62	5	96	4	7	5	26	9	.74	11	.270	.361	.385
1988 Winston-Sal	A	95	361	101	12	2	4	129	62	29	46	2	50	2	6	3	52	12	.81	5	.280	.362	.357
1989 Charlotte	AA	126	467	138	23	6	5	188	59	64	42	1	52	6	9	4	38	13	.75	8	.296	.358	.403
1990 Iowa	AAA	105	398	116	19	1	5	152	54	44	37	1	57	2	4	1	26	14	.65	8	.291	.354	.382
1991 Albuquerque	AAA	48	161	35	3	2	0	42	25	17	10	1	30	0	1	1	11	0	1.00	7	.217	.262	.261
1992 Toledo	AAA	128	445	104	15	3	7	146	56	46	46	0	72	3	4	2	24	3	.89	11	.234	.308	.328
1993 Iowa	AAA	131	500	141	27	1	9	197	82	54	53	1	61	3	9	8	25	11	.69	11	.282	.349	.394
1994 New Orleans	AAA	115	411	95	21	4	1	127	57	38	45	1	57	6	9	3	34	10	.77	8	.231	.314	.309
1995 New Orleans	AAA	59	170	36	3	1	0	41	18	9	17	1	22	2	2	1	11	7	.61	6	.212	.289	.241
Rochester	AAA	52	210	48	6	1	4	68	32	21	21	1	24	2	2	0	14	3	.82	2	.229	.305	.324
Indianapolis	AAA	4	14	3	0	0	0	3	1	0	2	0	3	0	0	0	0	0	.00	0	.214	.313	.214
1989 Chicago	NL	4	5	2	0	0	0	2	1	2	0	0	1	0	0	0	0	0	.00	0	.400	.500	.400
1990 Chicago	NL	18	44	9	2	1	0	13	4	5	2	0	5	0	1	1	1	0	1.00	1	.205	.234	.295
1991 Los Angeles	NL	5	3	0	0	0	0	0	1	0	0	0	1	0	0	0	0	0	.00	0	.000	.000	.000
11 Min. YEARS		1091	3930	1022	164	31	43	1377	567	419	420	16	596	33	58	29	278	85	.77	80	.260	.334	.350
3 Maj. YEARS		27	52	11	2	1	0	15	6	7	2	0	7	1	2	1	1	0	1.00	1	.212	.250	.288

Ira Smith

Bats: Right **Throws:** Right **Pos:** OF **Ht:** 5'11" **Wt:** 185 **Born:** 8/4/67 **Age:** 28

									BATTING										BASERUNNING				PERCENTAGES		
Year Team	Lg	G	AB	H	2B	3B	HR	TB	R	RBI	TBB	IBB	SO	HBP	SH	SF	SB	CS	SB%	GDP	Avg	OBP	SLG
1990 Great Falls	R	50	142	37	7	3	1	53	31	28	25	0	32	3	2	3	8	6	.57	3	.261	.376	.373
1991 Vero Beach	A	52	176	57	5	3	1	71	27	24	18	0	30	2	0	0	15	3	.83	7	.324	.393	.403
1992 Bakersfield	A	118	413	119	17	4	7	165	79	45	48	3	56	6	8	6	26	14	.65	12	.288	.366	.400
San Antonio	AA	6	11	4	0	1	0	6	3	1	1	0	2	0	0	0	0	0	.00	0	.364	.417	.545
1993 Rancho Cuca	A	92	347	120	30	6	7	183	71	47	55	1	41	5	2	3	32	16	.67	7	.346	.439	.527
Wichita	AA	13	39	9	0	1	0	11	7	4	4	0	9	0	1	0	0	2	.00	2	.231	.302	.282
1994 Wichita	AA	107	358	115	17	6	7	165	58	41	53	2	59	3	3	6	6	12	.33	5	.321	.407	.461
1995 Memphis	AA	64	238	72	13	3	5	106	40	36	23	0	32	2	0	3	11	4	.73	6	.303	.365	.445
Las Vegas	AAA	59	209	68	19	5	3	106	39	22	13	0	25	2	4	1	5	4	.56	3	.325	.369	.507
6 Min. YEARS		561	1933	601	108	32	31	866	355	248	240	6	286	23	20	22	103	61	.63	45	.311	.390	.448

John Smith

Bats: Right **Throws:** Right **Pos:** OF **Ht:** 5'9" **Wt:** 175 **Born:** 7/7/69 **Age:** 26

									BATTING										BASERUNNING				PERCENTAGES		
Year Team	Lg	G	AB	H	2B	3B	HR	TB	R	RBI	TBB	IBB	SO	HBP	SH	SF	SB	CS	SB%	GDP	Avg	OBP	SLG
1992 Pittsfield	A	68	254	61	13	3	8	104	46	35	36	0	66	3	0	1	18	11	.62	3	.240	.340	.409
1993 St. Lucie	A	110	365	98	19	8	11	166	66	56	48	1	86	11	1	4	22	13	.63	8	.268	.360	.455
1994 St. Lucie	A	111	390	97	17	2	18	172	59	70	45	3	113	6	3	2	13	9	.59	4	.249	.334	.441
1995 Binghamton	AA	9	12	1	1	0	0	2	2	1	2	0	6	1	0	0	0	0	.00	0	.083	.267	.167
Beloit	A	76	261	55	16	4	10	109	38	44	20	1	88	4	1	2	8	2	.80	4	.211	.275	.418
4 Min. YEARS		374	1282	312	66	17	47	553	211	206	151	5	359	25	5	9	61	35	.64	19	.243	.333	.431

Michael Smith

Pitches: Right **Bats:** Right **Pos:** P **Ht:** 6'3" **Wt:** 180 **Born:** 10/31/63 **Age:** 32

		HOW MUCH HE PITCHED						WHAT HE GAVE UP												THE RESULTS					
Year Team	Lg	G	GS	CG	GF	IP	BFP	H	R	ER	HR	SH	SF	HB	TBB	IBB	SO	WP	Bk	W	L	Pct.	ShO	Sv	ERA
1984 Reds	R	11	11	0	0	67	286	65	33	27	3	1	2	5	24	1	65	7	1	2	4	.333	0	0	3.63
1985 Billings	R	7	5	1	0	33.2	0	24	15	11	0	0	0	2	24	0	24	2	0	2	2	.500	1	0	2.94
Cedar Rapds	A	8	8	4	0	44.1	192	38	20	16	2	3	1	3	22	1	28	4	0	5	1	.833	3	0	3.25
1986 Cedar Rapds	A	28	27	4	1	191	807	155	88	71	12	4	2	6	106	1	172	19	0	10	10	.500	1	0	3.35
1987 Vermont	AA	27	27	6	0	171.1	740	152	78	64	5	6	3	3	117	3	104	15	2	8	12	.400	2	0	3.36
1988 Chattanooga	AA	28	28	5	0	194.1	822	160	90	69	10	5	5	10	98	2	141	10	3	9	10	.474	1	0	3.20
1989 Rochester	AAA	36	1	0	22	56	234	45	23	20	6	6	6	1	22	1	48	2	0	2	4	.333	0	7	3.21
1990 Rochester	AAA	29	20	1	3	123.1	551	118	76	68	14	3	3	8	73	1	112	12	2	9	6	.600	1	0	4.96
1991 El Paso	AA	11	10	1	1	50	234	52	44	29	0	0	1	4	29	1	44	5	0	3	3	.500	0	0	5.22
1995 Chattanooga	AA	3	2	0	0	5.2	37	11	13	11	0	0	0	1	5	0	5	1	0	0	2	.000	0	0	17.47
1989 Baltimore	AL	13	1	0	3	20	97	25	19	17	3	2	1	0	14	2	12	2	0	2	0	1.000	0	0	7.65
1990 Baltimore	AL	2	0	0	1	3	14	4	4	4	2	0	0	0	1	0	2	0	0	0	0	.000	0	0	12.00
9 Min. YEARS		188	139	22	27	936.2	3903	820	480	386	52	28	23	43	520	11	743	77	8	50	54	.481	9	7	3.71
2 Maj. YEARS		15	1	0	4	23	111	29	23	21	5	2	1	0	15	2	14	2	0	2	0	1.000	0	0	8.22

Mike Smith

Bats: Right **Throws:** Right **Pos:** 2B   **Ht:** 6'0" **Wt:** 180 **Born:** 12/1/69 **Age:** 26

																		BASERUNNING				PERCENTAGES		
Year Team	Lg	G	AB	H	2B	3B	HR	TB	R	RBI	TBB	IBB	SO	HBP	SH	SF	SB	CS	SB%	GDP	Avg	OBP	SLG
1992 Gastonia	A	81	302	61	15	3	4	94	30	23	37	1	48	1	2	4	3	11	.21	7	.202	.288	.311
1993 Charlotte	A	86	327	77	16	4	3	110	33	43	37	0	55	3	3	3	3	6	.33	7	.235	.316	.336
1994 High Desert	A	132	512	149	23	6	21	247	96	94	73	2	89	5	4	5	28	15	.65	13	.291	.382	.482
1995 Tulsa	AA	132	499	128	22	3	16	204	65	64	60	1	72	2	5	5	11	6	.65	13	.257	.336	.409
4 Min. YEARS		431	1640	415	76	16	44	655	224	224	207	3	264	11	14	17	45	38	.54	40	.253	.338	.399

Ottis Smith

Pitches: Left **Bats:** Right **Pos:** P   **Ht:** 6'1" **Wt:** 160 **Born:** 1/28/71 **Age:** 25

		HOW MUCH HE PITCHED						WHAT HE GAVE UP												THE RESULTS					
Year Team	Lg	G	GS	CG	GF	IP	BFP	H	R	ER	HR	SH	SF	HB	TBB	IBB	SO	WP	Bk	W	L	Pct.	ShO	Sv	ERA
1990 Mets	R	13	13	3	0	79.1	318	53	21	13	1	1	0	4	28	0	89	6	5	6	5	.545	1	0	1.47
1991 Pittsfield	A	15	15	2	0	103.1	437	89	49	30	5	0	3	5	42	0	79	4	1	7	2	.778	2	0	2.61
1992 Columbia	A	18	12	1	4	95.1	390	75	39	32	5	2	1	3	38	0	94	6	4	6	6	.500	0	2	3.02
St. Lucie	A	11	11	2	0	65.1	282	63	33	23	6	1	3	3	20	0	39	3	4	4	5	.444	1	0	3.17
1993 Norfolk	AAA	5	3	0	1	18.1	82	22	14	13	3	0	1	0	10	0	11	1	0	0	2	.000	0	0	6.38
St. Lucie	A	22	21	0	1	133.2	581	140	65	53	6	3	5	8	48	2	83	8	3	10	7	.588	0	0	3.57
1994 Orlando	AA	26	18	2	2	123	516	138	51	42	4	4	5	4	22	1	63	6	0	8	4	.667	2	0	3.07
1995 Orlando	AA	17	17	0	0	108.1	461	109	50	37	9	2	1	4	38	4	51	5	4	4	5	.444	0	0	3.07
Iowa	AAA	5	5	0	0	20.2	108	34	25	24	3	0	1	0	13	0	12	2	0	1	3	.250	0	0	10.45
6 Min. YEARS		132	115	10	8	747.1	3175	723	347	267	42	13	20	32	259	7	521	39	21	46	39	.541	6	2	3.22

Scotty Smith

Pitches: Right **Bats:** Right **Pos:** P   **Ht:** 6'3" **Wt:** 200 **Born:** 3/8/71 **Age:** 25

		HOW MUCH HE PITCHED						WHAT HE GAVE UP												THE RESULTS					
Year Team	Lg	G	GS	CG	GF	IP	BFP	H	R	ER	HR	SH	SF	HB	TBB	IBB	SO	WP	Bk	W	L	Pct.	ShO	Sv	ERA
1993 Erie	A	3	1	0	0	6.2	32	9	6	6	0	0	1	0	4	0	2	2	0	1	1	.500	0	0	8.10
1994 Charlotte	A	31	21	2	0	139.2	576	132	62	55	9	3	5	3	34	2	88	1	2	7	4	.636	0	0	3.54
1995 Tulsa	AA	29	13	1	12	101.2	469	144	83	69	15	3	6	2	31	4	38	5	0	5	8	.385	0	0	6.11
3 Min. YEARS		63	35	3	12	248	1077	285	151	130	24	6	12	5	69	6	128	8	2	13	13	.500	0	0	4.72

Tim Smith

Pitches: Right **Bats:** Right **Pos:** P   **Ht:** 6'2" **Wt:** 185 **Born:** 10/24/69 **Age:** 26

		HOW MUCH HE PITCHED						WHAT HE GAVE UP												THE RESULTS					
Year Team	Lg	G	GS	CG	GF	IP	BFP	H	R	ER	HR	SH	SF	HB	TBB	IBB	SO	WP	Bk	W	L	Pct.	ShO	Sv	ERA
1991 Sou. Oregon	A	14	13	1	0	75.1	330	78	52	27	5	1	4	2	17	1	79	7	2	5	2	.714	1	0	3.23
Madison	A	1	1	0	0	3.2	20	7	4	4	2	1	0	0	2	0	4	0	0	0	1	.000	0	0	9.82
1992 Reno	A	28	26	1	1	158	708	192	107	88	14	4	5	3	62	5	131	9	0	11	10	.524	0	0	5.01
Tacoma	AAA	2	2	1	0	11.1	47	10	9	9	1	0	0	0	4	0	7	0	0	1	1	.500	0	0	7.15
1993 San Bernrdo	A	16	15	2	0	88.1	371	84	47	43	13	3	2	2	45	3	72	2	1	6	4	.600	1	0	4.38
Tacoma	AAA	6	4	0	0	22.2	107	31	18	18	2	0	0	0	11	1	16	2	0	3	0	1.000	0	0	7.15
Huntsville	AA	9	6	1	1	43	184	46	22	16	5	1	1	1	18	0	31	4	0	1	3	.250	1	0	3.35
1994 Huntsville	AA	2	0	0	2	4.1	14	1	1	1	0	1	0	0	1	0	3	1	0	0	1	.000	0	0	2.08
Tacoma	AAA	24	5	0	9	51	233	54	37	33	11	2	2	1	25	0	36	4	1	4	4	.500	0	1	5.82
1995 Edmonton	AAA	9	7	0	0	37.1	174	44	27	25	2	2	2	1	22	2	22	4	0	3	2	.600	0	0	6.03
Winnipeg	IND	16	16	1	0	107	452	87	43	39	7	2	2	3	54	2	79	13	0	9	5	.643	0	0	3.28
5 Min. YEARS		127	95	7	13	602	2640	634	367	303	62	17	18	13	261	14	480	46	4	43	33	.566	3	2	4.53

Van Snider

Bats: Left **Throws:** Right **Pos:** OF   **Ht:** 6'3" **Wt:** 205 **Born:** 8/11/63 **Age:** 32

																		BASERUNNING				PERCENTAGES		
Year Team	Lg	G	AB	H	2B	3B	HR	TB	R	RBI	TBB	IBB	SO	HBP	SH	SF	SB	CS	SB%	GDP	Avg	OBP	SLG
1984 Memphis	AA	132	488	120	23	9	7	182	52	62	51	6	132	6	2	3	3	6	.33	5	.246	.323	.373
1985 Memphis	AA	85	292	69	15	4	8	116	43	39	43	6	63	1	1	4	4	8	.33	3	.236	.332	.397
1986 Memphis	AA	134	492	133	27	5	26	248	79	81	48	9	140	3	4	3	7	8	.47	7	.270	.337	.504
Omaha	AAA	4	13	4	2	1	0	8	5	3	2	0	3	0	0	0	0	0	.00	0	.308	.400	.615
1987 Omaha	AAA	70	244	50	9	1	9	88	26	27	13	4	69	2	0	1	2	1	.67	5	.205	.250	.361
Memphis	AA	45	174	57	10	7	9	108	25	40	10	0	34	1	0	0	2	5	.29	5	.328	.368	.621
1988 Nashville	AAA	135	525	152	22	8	23	259	72	73	22	9	96	5	1	3	5	7	.42	9	.290	.323	.493
1989 Nashville	AAA	119	442	98	17	9	12	169	48	64	32	2	117	4	0	8	7	0	1.00	5	.222	.276	.382
1990 Columbus	AAA	127	409	96	26	0	15	167	61	49	35	5	118	2	1	2	7	7	.50	7	.235	.297	.408
1992 Pawtucket	AAA	116	384	90	22	1	12	150	44	51	23	5	91	1	1	5	2	1	.67	9	.234	.276	.391
1993 Louisville	AAA	118	423	112	29	4	14	191	54	56	24	2	98	0	4	4	3	1	.75	9	.265	.302	.452
1995 Salt Lake	AAA	32	115	41	7	0	7	69	25	28	7	0	17	0	1	0	1	0	1.00	5	.357	.393	.600
1988 Cincinnati	NL	11	28	6	1	0	1	10	4	6	0	0	13	0	0	1	0	0	.00	0	.214	.207	.357
1989 Cincinnati	NL	8	7	1	0	0	0	1	1	0	0	0	5	0	0	0	0	0	.00	0	.143	.143	.143
10 Min. YEARS		1117	4001	1022	209	49	142	1755	534	573	310	48	978	25	15	33	43	44	.49	67	.255	.311	.439
2 Maj. YEARS		19	35	7	1	0	1	11	5	6	0	0	18	0	0	1	0	1	.00	0	.200	.194	.314

Cory Snyder

Bats: Right Throws: Right Pos: 3B   Ht: 6' 3" Wt: 205 Born: 11/11/62 Age: 33

Year Team	Lg	G	AB	H	2B	3B	HR	TB	R	RBI	TBB	IBB	SO	HBP	SH	SF	SB	CS	SB%	GDP	Avg	OBP	SLG
1985 Waterbury	AA	139	512	144	25	1	28	255	77	94	44	2	123	4	3	12	5	9	.36	12	.281	.336	.498
1986 Maine	AAA	49	192	58	19	0	9	104	25	32	17	1	39	1	1	3	2	3	.40	5	.302	.357	.542
1989 Canton-Akrn	AA	4	11	5	0	0	0	5	3	2	1	0	1	1	0	0	1	0	1.00	1	.455	.538	.455
1991 Syracuse	AAA	17	67	18	3	0	6	39	11	17	4	0	16	1	0	2	0	0	.00	0	.269	.311	.582
1995 Las Vegas	AAA	8	34	9	1	0	0	10	4	5	1	0	10	0	0	0	0	0	.00	0	.265	.286	.294
Pawtucket	AAA	20	66	15	4	0	3	28	9	8	5	0	25	0	0	0	0	0	.00	1	.227	.282	.424
1986 Cleveland	AL	103	416	113	21	1	24	208	58	69	16	0	123	0	1	0	2	3	.40*	8	.272	.299	.500
1987 Cleveland	AL	157	577	136	24	2	33	263	74	82	31	4	166	1	0	6	5	1	.83	3	.236	.273	.456
1988 Cleveland	AL	142	511	139	24	3	26	247	71	75	42	7	101	1	0	4	5	1	.83	12	.272	.326	.483
1989 Cleveland	AL	132	489	105	17	0	18	176	49	59	23	1	134	2	0	4	6	5	.55	11	.215	.251	.360
1990 Cleveland	AL	123	438	102	27	3	14	177	46	55	21	3	118	2	1	6	1	4	.20	11	.233	.268	.404
1991 Chicago	AL	50	117	22	4	0	3	35	10	11	6	1	41	0	3	0	0	0	.00	5	.188	.228	.299
Toronto	AL	21	49	7	0	1	0	9	4	6	3	0	19	0	1	1	0	0	.00	1	.143	.189	.184
1992 San Francisco	NL	124	390	105	22	2	14	173	48	57	23	2	96	2	2	3	4	4	.50	10	.269	.311	.444
1993 Los Angeles	NL	143	516	137	33	1	11	205	61	56	47	3	147	4	2	1	4	1	.80	8	.266	.331	.397
1994 Los Angeles	NL	73	153	36	6	0	6	60	18	18	14	4	47	1	1	2	1	0	1.00	5	.235	.300	.392
5 Min. YEARS		237	882	249	52	1	46	441	129	158	72	3	214	7	4	17	8	12	.40	21	.282	.335	.500
9 Maj. YEARS		1068	3656	902	178	13	149	1553	439	488	226	25	992	13	11	27	28	19	.60	74	.247	.291	.425

Jared Snyder

Bats: Right Throws: Right Pos: C   Ht: 6'2" Wt: 215 Born: 3/8/70 Age: 26

Year Team	Lg	G	AB	H	2B	3B	HR	TB	R	RBI	TBB	IBB	SO	HBP	SH	SF	SB	CS	SB%	GDP	Avg	OBP	SLG
1993 Geneva	A	51	148	31	7	0	2	44	15	22	16	0	29	10	5	1	5	1	.83	2	.209	.326	.297
1994 Cubs	R	10	29	5	2	0	0	7	3	4	1	0	5	1	1	1	0	0	.00	1	.172	.219	.241
1995 Orlando	AA	1	4	2	0	0	0	2	2	0	0	0	0	0	0	0	0	0	.00	0	.500	.500	.500
Rockford	A	24	65	12	2	0	1	17	7	6	6	0	15	4	1	0	0	0	.00	1	.185	.293	.262
Daytona	A	18	36	6	0	0	0	6	2	6	2	0	4	1	2	1	0	1	.00	2	.167	.225	.167
3 Min. YEARS		104	282	56	11	0	3	76	29	38	25	0	53	16	9	3	5	2	.71	6	.199	.298	.270

John Snyder

Pitches: Right Bats: Right Pos: P   Ht: 6'3" Wt: 185 Born: 8/16/74 Age: 21

Year Team	Lg	G	GS	CG	GF	IP	BFP	H	R	ER	HR	SH	SF	HB	TBB	IBB	SO	WP	Bk	W	L	Pct.	ShO	Sv	ERA
1992 Angels	R	15	0	0	7	44	195	40	27	16	0	2	5	3	16	1	38	1	4	2	4	.333	0	3	3.27
1993 Cedar Rapds	A	21	16	1	0	99	467	126	88	65	13	7	5	8	39	1	79	6	4	5	6	.455	1	0	5.91
1994 Lk Elsinore	A	26	26	2	0	159	698	181	101	79	16	5	5	6	56	0	108	11	2	10	11	.476	0	0	4.47
1995 Midland	AA	21	21	4	0	133.1	591	158	93	85	12	3	6	10	48	1	81	7	3	8	9	.471	0	0	5.74
Birmingham	AA	5	4	0	0	20.1	87	24	16	15	6	0	1	2	6	0	13	1	0	1	0	1.000	0	0	6.64
4 Min. YEARS		88	67	7	7	455.2	2038	529	325	260	47	17	22	29	165	3	319	26	13	26	30	.464	1	3	5.14

Randy Snyder

Bats: Right Throws: Right Pos: C   Ht: 6'2" Wt: 210 Born: 3/28/67 Age: 29

Year Team	Lg	G	AB	H	2B	3B	HR	TB	R	RBI	TBB	IBB	SO	HBP	SH	SF	SB	CS	SB%	GDP	Avg	OBP	SLG
1988 Beloit	A	29	92	18	4	0	0	22	7	6	8	0	27	1	3	0	3	3	.50	0	.196	.267	.239
1989 Stockton	A	34	101	19	4	1	0	25	10	9	15	2	31	1	3	4	2	1	1.00	3	.188	.289	.248
Brewers	R	19	60	17	2	1	0	21	14	8	11	2	14	0	1	1	5	2	.71	0	.283	.389	.350
Helena	R	24	79	25	2	0	2	33	13	13	12	1	13	0	0	1	0	1	.00	1	.316	.402	.418
1990 Beloit	A	101	319	64	17	0	4	93	43	29	30	2	71	2	7	2	7	2	.78	4	.201	.272	.292
1991 Stockton	A	82	223	57	11	2	6	90	33	33	37	1	67	9	4	3	7	2	.78	1	.256	.379	.404
El Paso	AA	8	24	5	1	0	0	6	7	1	5	0	5	0	0	1	1	0	1.00	1	.208	.333	.250
1992 Salt Lake	R	54	164	38	13	0	1	54	27	20	24	0	42	3	4	3	5	0	1.00	1	.232	.335	.329
1993 High Desert	A	20	68	20	5	1	3	36	13	17	9	0	11	1	0	3	0	0	.00	1	.294	.370	.529
Edmonton	AAA	38	94	25	6	0	1	34	12	10	7	1	28	0	0	1	0	1	.00	1	.266	.317	.362
1995 New Haven	AA	5	17	4	1	0	0	5	2	2	0	0	3	0	0	0	0	2	.00	0	.235	.222	.294
Salem	A	23	76	22	5	0	3	36	19	14	18	0	13	1	0	0	2	1	.67	3	.289	.432	.474
7 Min. YEARS		437	1317	314	71	5	20	455	200	162	176	9	325	18	22	19	32	14	.70	17	.238	.332	.345

Mark Sobolewski

Bats: Right Throws: Right Pos: 2B   Ht: 5'11" Wt: 185 Born: 2/10/70 Age: 26

Year Team	Lg	G	AB	H	2B	3B	HR	TB	R	RBI	TBB	IBB	SO	HBP	SH	SF	SB	CS	SB%	GDP	Avg	OBP	SLG
1992 Sou. Oregon	A	68	262	76	18	0	7	115	44	38	33	0	52	3	1	3	2	4	.33	8	.290	.372	.439
1993 Modesto	A	130	507	116	23	3	5	160	66	60	42	0	100	8	9	9	0	4	.00	12	.229	.293	.316
1994 Huntsville	AA	133	503	127	37	5	8	198	83	58	49	1	98	13	6	5	2	6	.25	11	.252	.332	.394
1995 Huntsville	AA	83	307	63	14	1	7	100	35	34	22	1	62	8	2	1	2	1	.67	11	.205	.275	.326
4 Min. YEARS		414	1579	382	92	9	27	573	228	190	146	2	312	32	18	18	6	15	.29	42	.242	.315	.363

Steve Soderstrom

Pitches: Right **Bats:** Right **Pos:** P   Ht: 6'3" Wt: 195 Born: 4/3/72 Age: 24

			HOW MUCH HE PITCHED					WHAT HE GAVE UP												THE RESULTS					
Year	Team	Lg	G	GS	CG	GF	IP	BFP	H	R	ER	HR	SH	SF	HB	TBB	IBB	SO	WP	Bk	W	L	Pct.	ShO	Sv	ERA
1994	San Jose	A	8	8	0	0	40.2	179	34	20	19	2	2	1	4	26	0	40	4	1	2	3	.400	0	0	4.20
1995	Shreveport	AA	22	22	0	0	116	508	106	53	44	6	5	2	10	51	0	91	12	2	9	5	.643	0	0	3.41
	2 Min. YEARS		30	30	0	0	156.2	687	140	73	63	8	7	3	14	77	0	131	16	3	11	8	.579	0	0	3.62

Steve Soliz

Bats: Right **Throws:** Right **Pos:** C   Ht: 5'10" Wt: 180 Born: 1/27/71 Age: 25

						BATTING										BASERUNNING				PERCENTAGES		
Year	Team	Lg	G	AB	H	2B	3B	HR	TB	R	RBI	TBB	IBB	SO	HBP	SH	SF	SB	CS	SB%	GDP	Avg	OBP	SLG
1993	Watertown	A	56	209	62	12	0	0	74	30	35	15	0	41	1	2	3	2	0	1.00	3	.297	.342	.354
1994	Kinston	A	51	163	43	7	1	3	61	26	19	16	0	32	1	2	1	3	0	1.00	0	.264	.331	.374
	Canton-Akrn	AA	18	54	10	1	0	0	11	4	0	2	0	9	1	1	0	0	0	.00	4	.185	.228	.204
1995	Bakersfield	A	44	159	39	5	0	1	47	9	11	15	0	34	2	0	0	2	1	.67	6	.245	.318	.296
	Canton-Akrn	AA	32	81	14	3	0	2	23	9	7	13	0	16	0	1	1	0	0	.00	3	.173	.284	.284
	3 Min. YEARS		201	666	168	28	1	6	216	78	72	61	0	132	5	6	5	7	1	.88	16	.252	.318	.324

Steve Solomon

Bats: Left **Throws:** Left **Pos:** OF   Ht: 6'0" Wt: 180 Born: 4/9/70 Age: 26

						BATTING										BASERUNNING				PERCENTAGES		
Year	Team	Lg	G	AB	H	2B	3B	HR	TB	R	RBI	TBB	IBB	SO	HBP	SH	SF	SB	CS	SB%	GDP	Avg	OBP	SLG
1992	Batavia	A	10	28	11	2	0	0	13	5	3	0	0	7	0	0	0	4	0	1.00	0	.393	.393	.464
1993	Spartanburg	A	81	306	88	16	4	1	115	59	33	39	0	49	8	7	1	14	3	.82	5	.288	.381	.376
1994	Clearwater	A	131	497	150	29	5	9	216	88	62	51	7	71	10	5	5	21	11	.66	12	.302	.375	.435
1995	Reading	AA	119	356	81	19	6	3	121	50	42	48	3	82	11	3	2	17	4	.81	11	.228	.336	.340
	4 Min. YEARS		341	1187	330	66	15	13	465	202	140	138	10	209	29	15	8	56	18	.76	28	.278	.365	.392

Don Sparks

Bats: Right **Throws:** Right **Pos:** 1B   Ht: 6'2" Wt: 185 Born: 6/19/66 Age: 30

						BATTING										BASERUNNING				PERCENTAGES		
Year	Team	Lg	G	AB	H	2B	3B	HR	TB	R	RBI	TBB	IBB	SO	HBP	SH	SF	SB	CS	SB%	GDP	Avg	OBP	SLG
1988	Pr. William	A	70	267	66	14	0	3	89	22	28	8	0	51	4	1	1	1	0	1.00	6	.247	.279	.333
1989	Pr. William	A	115	449	126	32	1	6	178	52	65	24	2	85	2	0	4	1	2	.33	20	.281	.317	.396
1990	Columbus	AAA	16	51	6	3	0	0	9	3	2	2	0	10	1	0	0	0	0	.00	3	.118	.167	.176
	Albany-Colo	AA	112	418	110	20	5	4	152	48	52	33	2	70	4	0	5	3	4	.43	14	.263	.320	.364
1991	Columbus	AAA	52	152	39	6	2	0	49	11	25	12	0	27	4	3	2	0	0	.00	7	.257	.324	.322
1992	Albany-Colo	AA	134	505	158	31	2	14	235	64	72	30	2	71	2	0	8	2	2	.50	14	.313	.349	.465
1993	Columbus	AAA	128	475	135	33	7	11	215	63	72	29	0	83	4	1	6	0	3	.00	14	.284	.327	.453
1994	Columbus	AAA	139	515	140	21	6	7	194	60	63	42	3	76	4	2	8	2	7	.22	17	.272	.327	.377
1995	Columbus	AAA	137	545	170	26	10	7	237	67	90	29	3	75	1	1	9	2	0	1.00	17	.312	.342	.435
	8 Min. YEARS		903	3377	950	186	33	52	1358	390	469	209	12	548	26	8	43	11	18	.38	114	.281	.324	.402

Greg Sparks

Bats: Left **Throws:** Left **Pos:** 1B   Ht: 6'0" Wt: 185 Born: 3/31/64 Age: 32

						BATTING										BASERUNNING				PERCENTAGES		
Year	Team	Lg	G	AB	H	2B	3B	HR	TB	R	RBI	TBB	IBB	SO	HBP	SH	SF	SB	CS	SB%	GDP	Avg	OBP	SLG
1984	Spokane	A	67	270	68	13	4	4	101	34	37	17	1	65	0	1	6	1	2	.33	2	.252	.290	.374
1985	Reno	A	123	436	123	23	1	7	169	57	73	36	0	89	1	2	3	4	4	.50	10	.282	.336	.388
1986	Charleston	A	105	344	81	18	1	10	131	40	59	35	1	61	1	1	2	4	3	.57	7	.235	.306	.381
1987	Madison	A	58	222	66	15	1	3	92	25	41	26	3	38	0	1	4	3	1	.75	6	.297	.365	.414
	Huntsville	AA	57	172	48	9	1	4	71	18	28	14	0	35	1	0	2	1	0	1.00	2	.279	.333	.413
1988	Huntsville	AA	124	421	98	21	0	8	143	47	50	48	6	117	3	3	4	5	5	.50	5	.233	.313	.340
1989	Salinas	A	108	356	92	24	1	9	145	38	54	44	4	92	1	0	5	1	5	.17	4	.258	.337	.407
1990	Albany-Colo	AA	129	455	112	24	1	19	195	66	77	42	1	118	5	1	3	0	2	.00	6	.246	.315	.429
1991	Carolina	AA	69	220	60	11	0	5	86	19	35	39	5	55	1	0	4	0	2	.00	3	.273	.379	.391
	Buffalo	AAA	55	128	23	7	0	3	39	13	16	12	0	31	0	2	2	1	0	1.00	4	.180	.246	.305
1992	London	AA	106	384	89	19	1	25	185	57	73	57	2	114	2	0	3	1	0	1.00	6	.232	.332	.482
	Toledo	AAA	23	72	13	1	0	2	20	6	4	4	0	26	0	1	1	0	1	.00	4	.181	.221	.278
1993	Pawtucket	AAA	58	198	34	6	0	4	52	7	21	14	0	54	2	1	2	0	3	.00	2	.172	.231	.263
	Canton-Akrn	AA	35	117	27	9	0	4	48	11	23	18	2	33	0	1	3	0	1	.00	4	.231	.326	.410
1994	New Haven	AA	88	243	45	8	0	8	77	27	28	33	4	80	1	0	3	0	1	1.00	1	.185	.282	.317
1995	Greenville	AA	65	145	31	6	0	5	52	15	21	17	1	41	2	2	2	0	0	.00	3	.214	.301	.359
	12 Min. YEARS		1270	4183	1010	214	11	120	1606	480	640	456	30	1049	20	16	49	22	29	.43	66	.241	.316	.384

Rodney Sparks

Bats: Right **Throws:** Right **Pos:** 2B   Ht: 6'0" Wt: 165 Born: 11/7/71 Age: 24

						BATTING										BASERUNNING				PERCENTAGES		
Year	Team	Lg	G	AB	H	2B	3B	HR	TB	R	RBI	TBB	IBB	SO	HBP	SH	SF	SB	CS	SB%	GDP	Avg	OBP	SLG
1994	Eugene	A	42	137	35	3	0	0	38	11	10	21	0	39	5	0	1	3	2	.60	3	.255	.372	.277
1995	Wichita	AA	1	0	0	0	0	0	0	0	0	0	0	0	0	0	0	0	0	.00	0	.000	.000	.000
	Springfield	A	43	96	21	4	0	1	28	11	7	8	0	14	0	1	0	0	0	.00	0	.219	.279	.292
	2 Min. YEARS		86	233	56	7	0	1	66	22	17	29	0	53	5	1	1	3	2	.60	3	.240	.336	.283

Vernon Spearman

Bats: Left **Throws:** Left **Pos:** OF **Ht:** 5'10" **Wt:** 160 **Born:** 12/17/69 **Age:** 26

Year Team	Lg	G	AB	H	2B	3B	HR	TB	R	RBI	TBB	IBB	SO	HBP	SH	SF	SB	CS	SB%	GDP	Avg	OBP	SLG
								BATTING									BASERUNNING				PERCENTAGES		
1991 Yakima	A	71	248	72	8	0	0	80	63	17	50	0	37	4	7	1	56	9	.86	1	.290	.416	.323
1992 Vero Beach	A	73	276	84	13	1	0	99	50	16	26	1	25	1	3	1	33	14	.70	5	.304	.365	.359
San Antonio	AA	48	185	52	3	3	0	61	24	11	15	0	16	1	6	1	18	9	.67	2	.281	.337	.330
1993 San Antonio	AA	56	162	42	4	2	0	50	22	13	11	0	21	1	5	0	13	4	.76	3	.259	.310	.309
Albuquerque	AAA	62	185	47	6	5	0	63	31	15	17	0	28	0	4	0	11	4	.73	4	.254	.317	.341
1994 San Antonio	AA	105	331	88	14	3	0	108	43	24	39	0	39	2	15	0	21	15	.58	2	.266	.347	.326
1995 Albuquerque	AAA	22	29	5	0	1	0	7	7	2	11	0	4	0	0	0	2	2	.50	2	.172	.400	.241
San Bernrdo	A	93	365	105	15	7	3	143	78	36	56	1	50	0	8	4	43	12	.78	5	.288	.379	.392
5 Min. YEARS		530	1781	495	63	22	3	611	318	134	225	2	220	9	48	7	197	69	.74	24	.278	.361	.343

Stan Spencer

Pitches: Right **Bats:** Right **Pos:** P **Ht:** 6'3" **Wt:** 195 **Born:** 8/2/68 **Age:** 27

Year Team	Lg	G	GS	CG	GF	IP	BFP	H	R	ER	HR	SH	SF	HB	TBB	IBB	SO	WP	Bk	W	L	Pct.	ShO	Sv	ERA
			HOW MUCH HE PITCHED								WHAT HE GAVE UP											THE RESULTS			
1991 Harrisburg	AA	17	17	1	0	92	389	90	52	45	6	4	2	4	30	0	66	2	3	6	1	.857	0	0	4.40
1993 High Desert	A	13	13	0	0	61.2	265	67	33	28	4	0	2	3	18	0	38	1	0	4	4	.500	0	0	4.09
1994 Brevard Cty	A	6	5	0	1	20	84	20	9	7	0	0	1	1	6	0	22	1	0	1	0	1.000	0	0	3.15
Portland	AA	20	20	1	0	124	505	113	52	48	12	4	6	2	30	2	96	3	1	9	4	.692	0	0	3.48
1995 Charlotte	AAA	9	9	0	0	41.1	198	61	37	36	9	0	0	3	24	1	19	0	0	1	4	.200	0	0	7.84
Portland	AA	8	8	0	0	39	193	57	39	32	9	4	4	2	19	0	32	0	0	1	4	.200	0	0	7.38
4 Min. YEARS		73	72	2	1	378	1634	408	222	196	40	8	15	15	127	3	273	7	4	22	17	.564	0	0	4.67

Scott Spiezio

Bats: Both **Throws:** Right **Pos:** 3B **Ht:** 6'2" **Wt:** 195 **Born:** 9/21/72 **Age:** 23

Year Team	Lg	G	AB	H	2B	3B	HR	TB	R	RBI	TBB	IBB	SO	HBP	SH	SF	SB	CS	SB%	GDP	Avg	OBP	SLG
								BATTING									BASERUNNING				PERCENTAGES		
1993 Sou. Oregon	A	31	125	41	10	2	3	64	32	19	16	0	18	0	0	0	0	1	.00	1	.328	.404	.512
Modesto	A	32	110	28	9	1	1	42	12	13	23	0	19	1	1	0	1	5	.17	4	.255	.388	.382
1994 Modesto	A	127	453	127	32	5	14	211	84	68	88	4	72	7	3	9	5	0	1.00	15	.280	.399	.466
1995 Huntsville	AA	141	528	149	33	8	13	237	78	86	67	2	78	4	2	14	10	3	.77	10	.282	.359	.449
3 Min. YEARS		331	1216	345	84	16	31	554	206	186	194	6	187	12	6	23	16	9	.64	30	.284	.381	.456

Paul Spoljaric

Pitches: Left **Bats:** Right **Pos:** P **Ht:** 6'3" **Wt:** 205 **Born:** 9/24/70 **Age:** 25

Year Team	Lg	G	GS	CG	GF	IP	BFP	H	R	ER	HR	SH	SF	HB	TBB	IBB	SO	WP	Bk	W	L	Pct.	ShO	Sv	ERA
			HOW MUCH HE PITCHED								WHAT HE GAVE UP											THE RESULTS			
1990 Medcne Hat	R	15	13	0	2	66.1	291	57	43	32	6	0	3	0	35	0	62	3	3	3	7	.300	0	1	4.34
1991 St. Cathrns	A	4	4	0	0	18.2	85	21	14	10	1	0	0	1	9	0	21	0	0	0	2	.000	0	0	4.82
1992 Myrtle Bch	A	26	26	1	0	162.2	647	111	68	51	7	4	4	5	58	0	161	7	1	10	8	.556	0	0	2.82
1993 Dunedin	A	4	4	0	0	26	99	16	5	4	1	0	0	2	12	0	29	2	0	3	0	1.000	0	0	1.38
Knoxville	AA	7	7	0	0	43.1	175	30	12	11	3	1	0	1	22	0	51	2	1	4	1	.800	0	0	2.28
Syracuse	AAA	18	18	1	0	95.1	424	97	63	56	14	1	6	2	52	0	88	8	1	8	7	.533	1	0	5.29
1994 Syracuse	AAA	8	8	0	0	47.1	224	47	37	30	7	1	3	0	28	1	38	4	0	1	5	.167	0	0	5.70
Knoxville	AA	17	16	0	0	102	446	88	50	41	12	2	5	7	48	0	79	4	1	6	5	.545	0	0	3.62
1995 Syracuse	AAA	43	9	0	27	87.2	382	69	51	48	13	3	1	2	54	3	108	8	0	2	10	.167	0	10	4.93
1994 Toronto	AL	2	1	0	0	2.1	21	5	10	10	3	0	0	0	9	1	2	0	0	0	1	.000	0	0	38.57
6 Min. YEARS		142	105	2	29	649.1	2773	536	343	283	64	12	22	20	318	4	637	38	7	37	45	.451	1	11	3.92

Jerry Spradlin

Pitches: Right **Bats:** Both **Pos:** P **Ht:** 6'7" **Wt:** 240 **Born:** 6/14/67 **Age:** 29

Year Team	Lg	G	GS	CG	GF	IP	BFP	H	R	ER	HR	SH	SF	HB	TBB	IBB	SO	WP	Bk	W	L	Pct.	ShO	Sv	ERA
			HOW MUCH HE PITCHED								WHAT HE GAVE UP											THE RESULTS			
1988 Billings	R	17	5	0	2	47.2	201	45	25	17	2	1	2	2	14	1	23	3	0	4	1	.800	0	0	3.21
1989 Greensboro	A	42	1	0	22	94.2	389	88	35	29	5	3	7	3	23	0	56	4	0	7	2	.778	0	2	2.76
1990 Cedar Rapds	A	5	0	0	0	12	57	13	8	4	1	1	0	0	5	1	6	0	0	0	1	.000	0	0	3.00
Charlstn-Wv	A	43	1	0	34	74.1	308	74	23	21	1	4	1	2	17	5	39	3	1	3	4	.429	0	17	2.54
1991 Chattanooga	AA	48	1	0	22	96	406	95	38	33	2	1	5	4	32	7	73	9	0	7	3	.700	0	4	3.09
1992 Cedar Rapds	A	1	0	0	0	2.1	11	5	2	2	0	0	0	0	0	0	4	0	0	1	0	1.000	0	0	7.71
Chattanooga	AA	59	0	0	53	65.1	248	52	11	10	1	6	1	0	13	3	35	3	0	3	3	.500	0	34	1.38
1993 Indianapls	AAA	34	0	0	8	56.2	239	58	24	22	4	2	0	0	12	2	46	2	0	3	2	.600	0	1	3.49
1994 Indianapls	AAA	28	5	0	7	73.1	319	87	36	30	5	3	2	5	16	1	49	3	1	3	3	.500	0	3	3.68
Edmonton	AAA	6	0	0	1	10.2	45	12	3	3	0	2	1	0	4	0	3	0	0	1	0	1.000	0	1	2.53
1995 Charlotte	AAA	41	0	0	14	59.1	244	59	26	20	6	2	3	3	15	1	38	5	0	3	3	.500	0	1	3.03
1993 Cincinnati	NL	37	0	0	16	49	193	44	20	19	4	3	4	0	9	0	24	3	1	2	1	.667	0	2	3.49
1994 Cincinnati	NL	6	0	0	2	8	38	12	11	9	2	0	2	0	2	0	4	0	0	0	0	.000	0	0	10.13
8 Min. YEARS		324	13	1	163	592.1	2467	588	231	191	27	25	22	19	151	21	372	32	2	35	22	.614	0	63	2.90
2 Maj. YEARS		43	0	0	18	57	231	56	31	28	6	3	6	0	11	0	28	3	1	2	1	.667	0	2	4.42

Steve Springer

Bats: Right **Throws:** Right **Pos:** 3B   **Ht:** 6' 0" **Wt:** 190 **Born:** 2/11/61 **Age:** 35

												BATTING							BASERUNNING				PERCENTAGES		
Year	Team	Lg	G	AB	H	2B	3B	HR	TB	R	RBI	TBB	IBB	SO	HBP	SH	SF	SB	CS	SB%	GDP	Avg	OBP	SLG
1984	Jackson	AA	103	362	99	21	3	5	141	41	40	24	3	50	2	0	0	6	4	.60	16	.273	.322	.390
1985	Tidewater	AAA	126	479	125	20	4	7	174	59	56	34	2	72	1	6	5	9	5	.64	16	.261	.308	.363
1986	Tidewater	AAA	117	440	120	19	6	4	163	52	46	30	0	74	1	5	0	10	5	.67	16	.273	.321	.370
1987	Tidewater	AAA	132	467	131	23	4	7	183	65	54	41	6	78	3	4	5	6	3	.67	10	.281	.339	.392
1988	Tidewater	AAA	97	337	88	15	0	2	109	42	25	29	0	66	0	2	1	4	0	1.00	7	.261	.319	.323
	Vancouver	AAA	27	105	28	4	1	2	40	15	9	4	1	17	0	2	0	1	2	.33	4	.267	.294	.381
1989	Vancouver	AAA	137	520	144	21	3	8	195	61	56	26	1	83	3	7	5	8	8	.50	11	.277	.312	.375
1990	Colo. Sprng	AAA	73	252	70	21	5	6	119	39	42	17	1	48	0	0	8	6	3	.67	6	.278	.314	.472
	Las Vegas	AAA	22	72	18	5	0	2	29	7	10	7	0	19	0	1	2	0	1	.00	2	.250	.309	.403
1991	Calgary	AAA	109	412	106	25	2	17	186	62	70	28	5	76	0	3	2	8	2	.80	14	.257	.303	.451
1992	Tidewater	AAA	117	427	124	16	0	16	188	57	70	22	1	85	0	0	3	9	4	.69	12	.290	.323	.440
1993	Norfolk	AAA	131	484	129	22	4	13	198	52	69	31	8	85	3	2	3	5	6	.45	13	.267	.313	.409
1994	Toledo	AAA	135	511	134	23	4	13	204	73	77	35	2	79	0	1	3	19	15	.56	9	.262	.308	.399
1995	Las Vegas	AAA	35	87	19	3	0	1	25	7	10	2	1	17	0	0	1	1	1	.50	5	.218	.233	.287
	Winnipeg	IND	8	31	5	0	0	0	5	4	0	1	0	11	0	0	0	0	0	.00	0	.161	.188	.161
	Toledo	AAA	25	102	27	7	1	2	42	14	10	4	1	18	0	0	2	1	1	.50	3	.265	.287	.412
1990	Cleveland	AL	4	12	2	0	0	0	2	1	1	0	0	6	0	0	1	0	0	.00	0	.167	.154	.167
1992	New York	NL	4	5	2	1	0	0	3	0	0	0	0	1	0	0	0	0	0	.00	0	.400	.400	.600
	12 Min. YEARS		1394	5088	1367	245	37	105	2001	650	644	335	32	878	13	33	40	93	60	.61	144	.269	.313	.393
	2 Maj. YEARS		8	17	4	1	0	0	5	1	1	0	0	7	0	0	1	0	0	.00	0	.235	.222	.294

Randy St. Claire

Pitches: Right **Bats:** Right **Pos:** P   **Ht:** 6' 2" **Wt:** 190 **Born:** 8/23/60 **Age:** 35

			HOW MUCH HE PITCHED						WHAT HE GAVE UP									THE RESULTS					
Year	Team	Lg	G	GS	CG	GF	IP	BFP	H	R	ER	HR	SH	SF	HB	TBB	IBB	SO	WP	Bk	W	L	Pct.	ShO	Sv	ERA
1990	Tucson	AAA	23	0	0	16	31.1	161	45	22	19	3	1	3	1	21	5	16	6	1	4	3	.571	0	0	5.46
	Okla. City	AAA	29	0	0	13	53.2	221	45	15	12	3	2	0	3	12	1	68	5	0	1	2	.333	0	1	2.01
1991	Richmond	AAA	29	0	0	14	68	245	39	10	9	2	3	1	4	11	2	60	7	0	6	2	.750	0	2	1.19
1992	Richmond	AAA	39	0	0	24	71.2	312	82	33	28	6	5	3	0	21	2	62	1	0	6	5	.545	0	4	3.52
1993	Richmond	AAA	6	0	0	0	9.2	47	14	6	3	0	0	1	0	2	0	3	0	0	0	0	.000	0	0	2.79
	Calgary	AAA	27	0	0	13	51.2	235	70	40	39	4	6	4	2	13	2	45	6	0	4	6	.400	0	3	6.79
	Syracuse	AAA	14	0	0	2	21	85	20	8	7	0	0	2	0	4	0	13	2	0	1	2	.333	0	0	3.00
1994	Syracuse	AAA	65	0	0	59	63	267	57	24	21	3	2	1	1	16	1	59	0	0	3	1	.750	0	33	3.00
1995	Calgary	AAA	54	0	0	40	54	258	72	31	30	5	8	3	3	21	5	43	1	0	3	5	.375	0	19	5.00
1984	Montreal	NL	4	0	0	4	8	38	11	4	4	0	1	2	1	2	1	4	0	0	0	0	.000	0	0	4.50
1985	Montreal	NL	42	0	0	14	68.2	294	69	32	30	3	6	1	1	26	7	25	1	0	5	3	.625	0	0	3.93
1986	Montreal	NL	11	0	0	2	19	76	13	5	5	2	0	0	0	6	1	21	1	0	2	0	1.000	0	1	2.37
1987	Montreal	NL	44	0	0	24	67	282	64	31	30	9	1	3	1	20	4	43	4	0	3	3	.500	0	7	4.03
1988	Cincinnati	NL	10	0	0	6	13.2	60	13	8	4	3	0	1	0	5	2	8	0	0	1	0	1.000	0	0	2.63
	Montreal	NL	6	0	0	3	7.1	38	11	5	5	2	0	1	0	5	1	6	0	1	0	0	.000	0	0	6.14
1989	Minnesota	AL	14	0	0	8	22.1	98	19	13	13	4	1	1	2	10	2	14	1	0	1	0	1.000	0	1	5.24
1991	Atlanta	NL	19	0	0	5	28.2	123	31	17	13	4	3	1	0	9	3	30	4	0	0	0	.000	0	0	4.08
1992	Atlanta	NL	10	0	0	1	15.1	68	17	11	10	1	0	0	0	8	3	7	0	0	0	0	.000	0	0	5.87
1994	Toronto	AL	2	0	0	2	2	12	4	4	2	0	1	0	0	2	1	2	0	0	0	0	.000	0	0	9.00
	6 Min. YEARS		286	0	0	181	424	1831	444	189	168	26	27	18	14	121	18	369	28	0	28	26	.519	0	62	3.57
	9 Maj. YEARS		162	0	0	69	252	1089	252	130	116	28	13	10	5	93	25	160	11	1	12	6	.667	0	9	4.14

Scott Standish

Pitches: Right **Bats:** Right **Pos:** P   **Ht:** 6'5" **Wt:** 225 **Born:** 10/5/72 **Age:** 23

			HOW MUCH HE PITCHED						WHAT HE GAVE UP									THE RESULTS					
Year	Team	Lg	G	GS	CG	GF	IP	BFP	H	R	ER	HR	SH	SF	HB	TBB	IBB	SO	WP	Bk	W	L	Pct.	ShO	Sv	ERA
1993	Oneonta	A	20	0	0	5	49.2	226	58	33	24	2	2	1	2	22	2	45	1	0	2	3	.400	0	1	4.35
1994	Greensboro	A	26	9	2	2	99	392	74	31	22	5	0	1	4	22	0	92	2	1	5	4	.556	0	0	2.00
	Tampa	A	5	4	0	0	29	113	18	7	7	4	1	2	2	5	0	36	2	0	2	1	.667	0	0	2.17
1995	Norwich	AA	17	9	0	0	60.1	280	73	43	38	3	2	3	5	30	3	47	4	2	4	3	.571	0	0	5.67
	Tampa	A	4	2	0	0	14	55	10	5	4	1	0	1	0	4	0	10	1	0	0	0	.000	0	0	2.57
	3 Min. YEARS		72	27	2	7	252	1066	233	119	95	15	5	8	13	83	5	230	10	3	13	11	.542	0	1	3.39

Chuck Stanhope

Pitches: Right **Bats:** Right **Pos:** P   **Ht:** 6'4" **Wt:** 185 **Born:** 3/23/64 **Age:** 32

			HOW MUCH HE PITCHED						WHAT HE GAVE UP									THE RESULTS					
Year	Team	Lg	G	GS	CG	GF	IP	BFP	H	R	ER	HR	SH	SF	HB	TBB	IBB	SO	WP	Bk	W	L	Pct.	ShO	Sv	ERA
1995	Edmonton	AAA	6	0	0	4	6	25	8	3	3	0	2	1	0	1	0	2	0	0	1	1	.500	0	0	4.50
	Mobile	IND	15	10	0	3	60.2	276	71	48	45	8	6	3	6	25	3	37	2	0	2	5	.286	0	1	6.68
	1 Min. YEARS		21	10	0	7	66.2	301	79	51	48	8	8	4	6	26	3	39	2	0	3	6	.333	0	1	6.48

Dave Staton

Bats: Right **Throws:** Right **Pos:** 1B-DH   **Ht:** 6' 5" **Wt:** 215 **Born:** 4/12/68 **Age:** 28

												BATTING							BASERUNNING				PERCENTAGES		
Year	Team	Lg	G	AB	H	2B	3B	HR	TB	R	RBI	TBB	IBB	SO	HBP	SH	SF	SB	CS	SB%	GDP	Avg	OBP	SLG
1989	Spokane	A	70	260	94	18	0	17	163	52	72	39	4	49	8	0	2	1	1	.50	13	.362	.456	.627

Year	Team	Lg	G	AB	H	2B	3B	HR	TB	R	RBI	TBB	IBB	SO	HBP	SH	SF	SB	CS	SB%	GDP	Avg	OBP	SLG
1990	Riverside	A	92	335	97	16	1	20	175	56	64	52	5	78	2	0	4	4	1	.80	11	.290	.384	.522
	Wichita	AA	45	164	50	11	0	6	79	26	31	22	0	37	1	0	1	0	0	.00	6	.305	.388	.482
1991	Las Vegas	AAA	107	375	100	19	1	22	187	61	74	44	4	89	3	0	3	1	0	1.00	12	.267	.346	.499
1992	Las Vegas	AAA	96	335	94	20	0	19	171	47	76	34	2	95	6	0	5	0	0	.00	14	.281	.353	.510
1993	Wichita	AA	5	12	5	3	0	0	8	2	2	2	0	3	0	0	0	0	0	.00	0	.417	.500	.667
	Rancho Cuca	A	58	221	70	21	0	18	145	37	58	30	1	52	1	0	0	0	0	.00	6	.317	.399	.656
	Las Vegas	AAA	11	37	10	0	0	7	31	8	11	3	0	9	0	0	1	0	0	.00	3	.270	.317	.838
1994	Las Vegas	AAA	79	271	75	10	2	12	125	39	47	44	3	62	5	0	5	0	0	.00	14	.277	.382	.461
1995	New Orleans	AAA	108	325	82	11	1	19	152	42	46	46	0	96	8	1	1	0	3	.00	6	.252	.358	.468
1993	San Diego	NL	17	42	11	3	0	5	29	7	9	3	0	12	1	0	0	0	0	.00	2	.262	.326	.690
1994	San Diego	NL	29	66	12	2	0	4	26	6	6	10	0	18	0	0	0	0	0	.00	3	.182	.289	.394
	7 Min. YEARS		671	2335	677	129	5	140	1236	370	481	316	19	570	34	1	23	6	5	.55	85	.290	.379	.529
	2 Maj. YEARS		46	108	23	5	0	9	55	13	15	13	0	30	1	0	0	0	0	.00	5	.213	.303	.509

David Steed

Bats: Right **Throws:** Right **Pos:** C   **Ht:** 6'1" **Wt:** 205 **Born:** 2/25/73 **Age:** 23

| | | | | | | BATTING | | | | | | | | | | BASERUNNING | | | | PERCENTAGES | | |
Year	Team	Lg	G	AB	H	2B	3B	HR	TB	R	RBI	TBB	IBB	SO	HBP	SH	SF	SB	CS	SB%	GDP	Avg	OBP	SLG
1994	Yakima	A	48	147	37	5	2	5	61	21	24	28	0	43	5	1	0	1	2	.33	4	.252	.389	.415
1995	Vero Beach	A	59	195	49	16	0	0	65	11	24	18	0	53	3	1	1	0	0	.00	5	.251	.333	.333
	San Antonio	AA	40	123	31	10	1	3	52	13	16	11	0	32	1	0	2	0	1	.00	2	.252	.314	.423
	2 Min. YEARS		147	465	117	31	3	8	178	45	64	57	0	128	9	2	3	1	3	.25	11	.252	.343	.383

Rick Steed

Pitches: Right **Bats:** Right **Pos:** P   **Ht:** 6'2" **Wt:** 185 **Born:** 9/8/70 **Age:** 25

| | | | HOW MUCH HE PITCHED | | | | | | WHAT HE GAVE UP | | | | | | | | | | THE RESULTS | | | | | |
Year	Team	Lg	G	GS	CG	GF	IP	BFP	H	R	ER	HR	SH	SF	HB	TBB	IBB	SO	WP	Bk	W	L	Pct.	ShO	Sv	ERA
1989	Medcne Hat	R	7	6	0	0	16	73	14	10	6	1	0	0	1	11	0	11	2	3	0	2	.000	0	0	3.38
1990	St. Cathrns	A	14	14	0	0	73.1	311	58	32	25	4	2	1	2	39	2	72	10	1	3	6	.333	0	0	3.07
1991	Myrtle Bch	A	28	27	4	0	172	743	101	90	77	11	7	3	5	82	0	122	13	2	12	13	.400	0	0	4.03
1992	Dunedin	A	20	19	2	1	104	451	106	56	44	4	3	5	9	40	0	57	11	1	6	6	.500	0	1	3.81
1993	Dunedin	A	22	20	2	0	111	502	120	81	62	10	2	4	3	62	1	66	9	1	4	9	.308	1	0	5.03
1994	Dunedin	A	30	0	0	17	44	195	33	14	13	1	2	1	1	30	1	55	10	1	3	1	.750	0	6	2.66
1995	Knoxville	AA	27	0	0	23	31.2	136	23	15	13	1	3	2	2	16	2	29	4	0	2	4	.333	0	9	3.69
	Syracuse	AAA	31	0	0	15	55.2	239	51	29	23	2	2	2	0	23	1	34	1	1	4	3	.571	0	1	3.72
	7 Min. YEARS		179	86	8	56	607.2	2652	566	333	263	34	21	20	23	283	7	446	62	10	34	44	.436	1	17	3.90

Kennie Steenstra

Pitches: Right **Bats:** Right **Pos:** P   **Ht:** 6'5" **Wt:** 220 **Born:** 10/13/70 **Age:** 25

| | | | HOW MUCH HE PITCHED | | | | | | WHAT HE GAVE UP | | | | | | | | | | THE RESULTS | | | | | |
Year	Team	Lg	G	GS	CG	GF	IP	BFP	H	R	ER	HR	SH	SF	HB	TBB	IBB	SO	WP	Bk	W	L	Pct.	ShO	Sv	ERA
1992	Geneva	A	3	3	1	0	20	76	11	4	2	0	0	0	0	3	0	12	0	1	3	0	1.000	0	0	0.90
	Peoria	A	12	12	4	0	89.2	364	79	29	21	5	2	1	3	21	1	68	4	3	6	3	.667	2	0	2.11
1993	Daytona	A	13	13	1	0	81.1	317	64	26	23	2	3	2	8	12	1	57	2	1	5	3	.625	1	0	2.55
	Iowa	AAA	1	1	0	0	6.2	32	9	5	5	2	0	0	0	4	0	6	0	0	1	0	1.000	0	0	6.75
	Orlando	AA	14	14	2	0	100.1	427	103	47	40	4	4	2	9	25	0	60	5	2	8	3	.727	2	0	3.59
1994	Iowa	AAA	3	3	0	0	13	68	24	21	19	2	0	2	2	4	0	10	0	0	1	2	.333	0	0	13.15
	Orlando	AA	23	23	2	0	158.1	654	146	55	46	12	9	3	9	39	4	83	4	1	9	7	.563	1	0	2.61
1995	Iowa	AAA	29	26	6	1	171.1	722	174	85	74	15	6	6	8	48	3	96	6	0	9	12	.429	2	0	3.89
	4 Min. YEARS		98	95	16	1	640.2	2660	610	272	230	42	24	16	39	156	9	392	21	8	42	30	.583	8	0	3.23

Mike Stefanski

Bats: Right **Throws:** Right **Pos:** C   **Ht:** 6'2" **Wt:** 202 **Born:** 9/12/69 **Age:** 26

| | | | | | | BATTING | | | | | | | | | | BASERUNNING | | | | PERCENTAGES | | |
Year	Team	Lg	G	AB	H	2B	3B	HR	TB	R	RBI	TBB	IBB	SO	HBP	SH	SF	SB	CS	SB%	GDP	Avg	OBP	SLG
1991	Brewers	R	56	206	76	5	5	0	91	43	43	22	0	22	5	0	6	3	2	.60	4	.369	.431	.442
1992	Beloit	A	116	385	105	12	0	4	129	66	45	55	1	81	4	3	3	9	4	.69	11	.273	.367	.335
1993	Stockton	A	97	345	111	22	2	10	167	58	57	49	2	45	5	1	2	6	1	.86	15	.322	.411	.484
1994	El Paso	AA	95	312	82	7	6	8	125	59	56	32	0	80	0	2	5	4	3	.57	5	.263	.327	.401
1995	El Paso	AA	6	27	11	3	0	1	17	5	6	0	0	3	0	0	0	1	0	1.00	2	.407	.407	.630
	New Orleans	AAA	78	228	56	10	2	2	76	30	24	14	0	28	1	5	5	2	0	1.00	8	.246	.286	.333
	5 Min. YEARS		448	1503	441	59	15	25	605	261	231	172	3	259	15	11	21	25	10	.71	43	.293	.367	.403

Rod Steph

Pitches: Right **Bats:** Right **Pos:** P   **Ht:** 5'11" **Wt:** 185 **Born:** 8/27/69 **Age:** 26

| | | | HOW MUCH HE PITCHED | | | | | | WHAT HE GAVE UP | | | | | | | | | | THE RESULTS | | | | | |
Year	Team	Lg	G	GS	CG	GF	IP	BFP	H	R	ER	HR	SH	SF	HB	TBB	IBB	SO	WP	Bk	W	L	Pct.	ShO	Sv	ERA
1991	Princeton	R	7	7	1	0	46.1	186	37	19	16	1	0	1	4	11	0	52	4	3	2	3	.400	1	0	3.11
	Cedar Rapds	A	8	7	3	0	56.2	229	46	19	16	5	2	0	4	15	1	46	3	4	4	3	.571	2	0	2.54
1992	Cedar Rapds	A	27	27	1	0	154.1	668	157	86	74	18	3	4	6	54	0	136	11	2	12	9	.571	1	0	4.32
1993	Winston-Sal	A	28	28	4	0	167.2	717	166	101	73	21	6	3	8	57	0	130	14	0	7	11	.389	2	0	3.92
1994	Thunder Bay	IND	13	13	3	0	88.1	354	68	30	24	5	3	1	4	17	0	76	5	0	8	1	.889	2	0	2.45
	Canton-Akrn	AA	3	3	1	0	20	89	27	13	12	2	1	0	0	4	0	6	1	0	1	2	.333	0	0	5.40
1995	Canton-Akrn	AA	32	20	1	5	137	595	150	74	58	6	7	2	9	33	1	82	5	0	8	10	.444	0	0	3.81
	5 Min. YEARS		118	105	14	5	670.1	2838	651	342	273	58	22	11	35	191	2	528	43	9	42	39	.519	8	0	3.67

285

Garrett Stephenson

Pitches: Right **Bats:** Right **Pos:** P | **Ht:** 6'4" **Wt:** 185 **Born:** 1/2/72 **Age:** 24

			HOW MUCH HE PITCHED						WHAT HE GAVE UP									THE RESULTS				
Year Team	Lg	G	GS	CG	GF	IP	BFP	H	R	ER	HR	SH	SF	HB	TBB	IBB	SO	WP	Bk	W	L	Pct.	ShO	Sv	ERA
1992 Bluefield	R	12	3	0	0	32.1	141	35	22	17	4	0	1	1	7	0	30	4	1	3	1	.750	0	0	4.73
1993 Albany	A	30	24	3	3	171.1	697	142	65	54	6	1	4	5	44	0	147	3	5	16	7	.696	2	1	2.84
1994 Frederick	A	18	17	1	0	107.1	450	91	62	48	13	2	5	5	36	2	133	2	4	7	5	.583	0	0	4.02
Bowie	AA	7	7	1	0	36.2	161	47	22	21	2	0	1	0	11	1	32	3	2	3	2	.600	1	0	5.15
1995 Bowie	AA	29	29	1	0	175.1	743	154	87	71	23	5	7	18	47	0	139	4	2	7	10	.412	0	0	3.64
4 Min. YEARS		96	80	6	3	523	2192	469	258	211	48	8	18	29	145	3	481	16	14	36	25	.590	3	1	3.63

Matt Stevens

Pitches: Right **Bats:** Right **Pos:** P | **Ht:** 6'1" **Wt:** 200 **Born:** 1/20/67 **Age:** 29

			HOW MUCH HE PITCHED						WHAT HE GAVE UP									THE RESULTS				
Year Team	Lg	G	GS	CG	GF	IP	BFP	H	R	ER	HR	SH	SF	HB	TBB	IBB	SO	WP	Bk	W	L	Pct.	ShO	Sv	ERA
1989 Batavia	A	16	4	0	6	45.2	185	35	11	10	2	2	0	2	13	2	48	2	0	5	1	.833	0	0	1.97
1990 Spartanburg	A	14	0	0	8	29	118	24	12	7	1	1	0	0	10	0	31	2	1	0	2	.000	0	2	2.17
Clearwater	A	10	0	0	8	12	43	4	1	1	1	0	0	0	4	1	9	0	0	1	1	.500	0	1	0.75
Reading	AA	25	0	0	12	44.1	196	43	23	14	5	4	2	0	20	6	34	4	0	3	3	.500	0	4	2.84
1991 Clearwater	A	38	0	0	32	39.2	154	16	7	4	0	3	0	0	18	1	49	1	0	3	0	.000	0	17	0.91
Reading	AA	25	0	0	11	40.1	162	35	16	16	5	1	1	0	11	1	31	2	0	5	1	.833	0	2	3.57
1992 Scranton-Wb	AAA	9	0	0	3	13	61	19	11	9	1	0	0	0	4	0	11	1	0	1	0	1.000	0	0	6.23
Reading	AA	46	0	0	37	58.2	250	65	31	26	3	3	3	0	16	4	43	3	0	4	4	.500	0	12	3.99
1993 Portland	AAA	53	0	0	16	81.2	352	75	27	18	2	2	3	1	35	3	60	6	1	5	3	.625	0	2	1.98
1994 Salt Lake	AAA	42	0	0	13	60.1	271	77	43	39	9	1	0	1	25	3	41	7	0	4	1	.800	0	2	5.82
1995 Salt Lake	AAA	7	0	0	3	7.2	34	9	4	3	1	0	1	1	2	0	5	0	0	0	0	.000	0	1	3.52
7 Min. YEARS		285	4	0	149	432.1	1826	402	186	147	30	17	10	5	158	21	362	28	2	28	19	.596	0	43	3.06

Andy Stewart

Bats: Right **Throws:** Right **Pos:** 1B-C | **Ht:** 5'11" **Wt:** 205 **Born:** 12/5/70 **Age:** 25

					BATTING												BASERUNNING				PERCENTAGES		
Year Team	Lg	G	AB	H	2B	3B	HR	TB	R	RBI	TBB	IBB	SO	HBP	SH	SF	SB	CS	SB%	GDP	Avg	OBP	SLG
1990 Royals	R	21	52	10	4	0	0	14	5	1	9	1	13	3	3	0	3	0	1.00	0	.192	.344	.269
1991 Baseball Cy	A	78	276	64	16	1	3	91	30	36	7	1	59	4	4	2	6	4	.60	6	.232	.260	.330
1992 Baseball Cy	A	94	283	73	13	1	4	100	31	38	21	1	45	2	4	1	3	8	.27	4	.258	.313	.353
1993 Wilmington	A	110	361	100	20	3	8	150	54	42	26	0	88	8	0	1	7	1	.88	6	.277	.338	.416
1994 Wilmington	A	94	360	114	24	3	17	195	53	66	30	4	56	13	2	4	0	2	.00	11	.317	.386	.542
Memphis	AA	20	72	17	1	0	0	18	10	5	3	1	5	4	1	1	0	0	.00	3	.236	.300	.250
1995 Wichita	AA	60	216	56	18	0	3	83	28	32	11	0	31	4	0	2	1	2	.33	9	.259	.305	.384
Omaha	AAA	44	156	47	11	0	3	67	24	21	12	1	18	8	0	0	0	1	.00	4	.301	.381	.429
6 Min. YEARS		521	1776	481	107	8	38	718	235	241	119	9	315	46	14	11	20	18	.53	43	.271	.331	.404

Phil Stidham

Pitches: Right **Bats:** Right **Pos:** P | **Ht:** 6'0" **Wt:** 180 **Born:** 11/18/68 **Age:** 27

			HOW MUCH HE PITCHED						WHAT HE GAVE UP									THE RESULTS				
Year Team	Lg	G	GS	CG	GF	IP	BFP	H	R	ER	HR	SH	SF	HB	TBB	IBB	SO	WP	Bk	W	L	Pct.	ShO	Sv	ERA
1991 Fayetteville	A	28	0	0	26	33.2	139	25	10	6	0	1	2	0	16	0	20	3	3	0	1	.000	0	8	1.60
1992 Lakeland	A	45	0	0	27	53.2	252	61	28	22	3	2	1	3	28	2	47	4	1	2	7	.222	0	6	3.69
1993 Lakeland	A	25	0	0	23	29.2	119	22	6	5	2	2	0	2	9	1	24	0	0	2	1	.667	0	9	1.52
London	AA	33	0	0	8	34	164	40	18	9	3	1	0	2	19	3	39	1	0	2	2	.500	0	2	2.38
1994 Trenton	AA	6	0	0	6	6	22	4	0	0	0	0	0	0	0	0	6	2	0	0	0	.000	0	3	0.00
Toledo	AAA	49	0	0	16	69	278	48	25	24	3	4	2	1	31	3	57	1	0	3	3	.500	0	3	3.13
1995 Binghamton	AA	7	0	0	4	9.2	47	9	6	5	0	1	0	0	9	0	7	0	0	0	0	.000	0	0	4.66
Norfolk	AAA	34	6	0	12	70	305	56	33	25	4	2	6	5	36	1	56	5	0	6	2	.750	0	1	3.21
1994 Detroit	AL	5	0	0	0	4.1	26	12	12	12	3	0	1	0	4	1	4	0	0	0	0	.000	0	0	24.92
5 Min. YEARS		227	6	0	122	305.2	1326	265	126	96	15	13	11	13	148	10	256	16	4	15	16	.484	0	32	2.83

Kurt Stillwell

Bats: Both **Throws:** Right **Pos:** SS | **Ht:** 5'11" **Wt:** 180 **Born:** 6/4/65 **Age:** 31

					BATTING												BASERUNNING				PERCENTAGES		
Year Team	Lg	G	AB	H	2B	3B	HR	TB	R	RBI	TBB	IBB	SO	HBP	SH	SF	SB	CS	SB%	GDP	Avg	OBP	SLG
1984 Cedar Rapds	A	112	382	96	15	1	4	125	63	33	70	1	53	1	3	5	24	9	.73	3	.251	.365	.327
1985 Denver	AAA	59	182	48	7	4	1	66	28	22	21	2	23	0	3	0	5	3	.63	3	.264	.340	.363
1986 Denver	AAA	10	30	7	0	0	0	7	2	2	2	0	4	0	0	0	2	0	1.00	2	.233	.281	.233
1994 Indianapols	AAA	93	337	91	22	5	8	147	46	49	30	2	55	3	1	7	1	1	.50	5	.270	.329	.436
1995 Indianapols	AAA	100	341	90	14	3	7	131	50	30	45	1	51	1	0	3	4	3	.57	6	.264	.349	.384
1986 Cincinnati	NL	104	279	64	6	1	0	72	31	26	30	1	47	2	4	0	6	2	.75	5	.229	.309	.258
1987 Cincinnati	NL	131	395	102	20	7	4	148	54	33	32	2	50	2	2	2	4	6	.40	5	.258	.316	.375
1988 Kansas City	AL	128	459	115	28	5	10	183	63	53	47	0	76	3	6	3	6	5	.55	7	.251	.322	.399
1989 Kansas City	AL	130	463	121	20	7	7	176	52	54	42	2	64	3	5	3	9	6	.60	3	.261	.325	.380
1990 Kansas City	AL	144	506	126	35	4	3	178	60	51	39	1	60	4	4	7	0	2	.00	11	.249	.304	.352
1991 Kansas City	AL	122	385	102	17	1	6	139	44	51	33	5	56	1	5	4	3	4	.43	8	.265	.322	.361
1992 San Diego	NL	114	379	86	15	3	2	113	35	24	26	9	58	1	4	6	4	1	.80	6	.227	.274	.298
1993 California	AL	22	61	16	2	2	0	22	2	3	4	0	11	0	1	2	2	0	1.00	2	.262	.299	.361

286

Year Team	Lg	G	AB	H	2B	3B	HR	TB	R	RBI	TBB	IBB	SO	HBP	SH	SF	SB	CS	SB%	GDP	Avg	OBP	SLG
San Diego	NL	57	121	26	4	0	1	33	9	11	11	2	22	1	2	0	4	3	.57	2	.215	.286	.273
5 Min. YEARS		374	1272	332	58	13	20	476	189	136	168	6	186	5	7	15	36	16	.69	19	.261	.346	.374
8 Maj. YEARS		952	3048	758	147	30	33	1064	350	306	264	22	444	17	33	27	38	29	.57	49	.249	.310	.349

Bob Stoddard

Pitches: Right **Bats:** Right **Pos:** P **Ht:** 6'1" **Wt:** 190 **Born:** 3/8/58 **Age:** 38

		HOW MUCH HE PITCHED						WHAT HE GAVE UP												THE RESULTS					
Year Team	Lg	G	GS	CG	GF	IP	BFP	H	R	ER	HR	SH	SF	HB	TBB	IBB	SO	WP	Bk	W	L	Pct.	ShO	Sv	ERA
1995 Norfolk	AAA	3	0	0	1	2.2	14	5	2	2	0	0	0	0	1	0	1	1	1	0	1	.000	0	0	6.75

Don Strange

Pitches: Right **Bats:** Right **Pos:** P **Ht:** 6'0" **Wt:** 195 **Born:** 5/26/67 **Age:** 29

		HOW MUCH HE PITCHED						WHAT HE GAVE UP												THE RESULTS					
Year Team	Lg	G	GS	CG	GF	IP	BFP	H	R	ER	HR	SH	SF	HB	TBB	IBB	SO	WP	Bk	W	L	Pct.	ShO	Sv	ERA
1989 Pulaski	R	27	0	0	20	33.0	136	27	9	9	1	0	1	0	6	2	39	4	1	3	0	1.000	0	5	2.45
1990 Sumter	A	46	0	0	41	54.1	208	34	6	4	0	1	3	3	12	3	53	2	0	4	1	.800	0	24	0.66
1991 Durham	A	38	0	0	32	40.1	172	39	13	8	1	2	2	1	8	1	51	7	0	0	0	.000	0	19	1.79
Greenville	AA	4	0	0	1	4.2	23	9	7	7	1	0	0	0	2	0	8	1	0	1	0	1.000	0	1	13.50
1992 Greenville	AA	48	0	0	41	60	234	43	19	16	3	0	1	1	19	3	58	3	0	5	3	.625	0	18	2.40
1993 Greenville	AA	27	0	0	24	24.2	109	27	11	10	3	0	2	0	9	1	27	2	0	1	1	.500	0	18	3.65
Richmond	AAA	34	0	0	19	46.1	200	45	24	20	1	2	1	0	19	6	34	4	0	1	2	.333	0	1	3.88
1994 Richmond	AAA	12	1	0	8	20.1	100	31	15	15	2	1	4	1	7	4	18	2	0	2	1	.667	0	0	6.64
Memphis	AA	14	0	0	11	21	80	11	4	4	3	1	0	1	6	1	18	0	0	0	0	.000	0	6	1.71
1995 Omaha	AAA	9	0	0	3	15.2	75	24	13	13	2	0	1	0	6	0	11	0	0	0	0	.000	0	0	7.47
Wichita	AA	24	0	0	17	36	136	28	7	6	2	0	1	0	7	0	36	5	0	0	1	.000	0	8	1.50
7 Min. YEARS		283	1	0	217	356.1	1473	318	128	112	19	7	16	7	101	21	353	30	1	17	9	.654	0	101	2.83

Chad Strickland

Bats: Right **Throws:** Right **Pos:** C **Ht:** 6'1" **Wt:** 185 **Born:** 3/16/72 **Age:** 24

		BATTING															BASERUNNING				PERCENTAGES		
Year Team	Lg	G	AB	H	2B	3B	HR	TB	R	RBI	TBB	IBB	SO	HBP	SH	SF	SB	CS	SB%	GDP	Avg	OBP	SLG
1990 Royals	R	50	163	36	7	0	3	43	14	12	11	0	24	0	2	4	6	2	.75	5	.221	.264	.264
1991 Appleton	A	28	81	14	4	0	1	21	5	5	2	0	12	0	1	1	2	1	.67	0	.173	.190	.259
Eugene	A	34	118	19	7	0	1	29	13	11	13	0	16	2	2	2	1	1	.50	1	.161	.252	.246
1992 Appleton	A	112	396	101	16	1	2	125	29	49	12	0	37	1	0	5	2	5	.29	6	.255	.275	.316
1993 Wilmington	A	122	409	102	16	6	2	136	51	46	23	0	46	3	7	9	4	3	.57	7	.249	.288	.333
1994 Memphis	AA	114	379	82	14	2	6	118	37	47	17	1	40	3	5	3	1	3	.25	8	.216	.254	.311
1995 Omaha	AAA	8	22	6	2	0	0	8	3	5	1	0	4	0	0	1	0	0	.00	0	.273	.292	.364
Wichita	AA	51	183	41	7	0	1	51	16	21	5	0	22	0	2	1	0	0	.00	9	.224	.243	.279
6 Min. YEARS		519	1751	401	73	9	13	531	168	196	84	1	201	9	19	26	16	15	.52	37	.229	.264	.303

Mark Strittmatter

Bats: Right **Throws:** Right **Pos:** C **Ht:** 6'1" **Wt:** 200 **Born:** 4/4/69 **Age:** 27

		BATTING															BASERUNNING				PERCENTAGES		
Year Team	Lg	G	AB	H	2B	3B	HR	TB	R	RBI	TBB	IBB	SO	HBP	SH	SF	SB	CS	SB%	GDP	Avg	OBP	SLG
1992 Bend	A	35	101	26	6	0	2	38	17	13	12	0	28	3	0	0	0	4	.00	2	.257	.353	.376
1993 Central Val	A	59	179	47	8	0	2	61	21	15	31	0	29	2	2	3	3	0	1.00	8	.263	.372	.341
Colo. Sprng	AAA	5	10	2	1	0	0	3	1	2	0	0	2	1	0	0	0	0	.00	2	.200	.273	.300
1994 New Haven	AA	73	215	49	8	0	2	63	20	26	33	1	39	9	3	4	1	2	.33	7	.228	.349	.293
1995 Colo. Sprng	AAA	5	17	5	2	0	0	7	1	3	0	0	3	0	0	0	0	0	.00	0	.294	.294	.412
New Haven	AA	90	288	70	12	1	7	105	44	42	47	1	51	6	1	2	1	1	1.00	5	.243	.359	.365
4 Min. YEARS		267	810	199	37	1	13	277	104	101	123	2	152	21	6	9	5	6	.45	24	.246	.356	.342

Everett Stull

Pitches: Right **Bats:** Right **Pos:** P **Ht:** 6'3" **Wt:** 195 **Born:** 8/24/71 **Age:** 24

		HOW MUCH HE PITCHED						WHAT HE GAVE UP												THE RESULTS					
Year Team	Lg	G	GS	CG	GF	IP	BFP	H	R	ER	HR	SH	SF	HB	TBB	IBB	SO	WP	Bk	W	L	Pct.	ShO	Sv	ERA
1992 Jamestown	A	14	14	0	0	63.1	303	52	49	38	2	2	3	3	61	0	64	18	4	3	5	.375	0	0	5.40
1993 Burlington	A	15	15	1	0	82.1	366	68	44	35	8	2	1	3	59	0	85	11	4	4	9	.308	0	0	3.83
1994 W. Palm Bch	A	27	26	3	0	147	627	116	60	54	3	7	3	12	78	0	165	15	6	10	10	.500	1	0	3.31
1995 Harrisburg	AA	24	24	0	0	126.2	569	114	88	78	12	5	5	9	79	2	132	7	1	3	12	.200	0	0	5.54
4 Min. YEARS		80	79	4	0	419.1	1865	350	241	205	25	16	12	27	277	2	446	51	15	20	36	.357	1	0	4.40

Grant Sullivan

Pitches: Left **Bats:** Left **Pos:** P **Ht:** 6'5" **Wt:** 210 **Born:** 3/19/70 **Age:** 26

		HOW MUCH HE PITCHED						WHAT HE GAVE UP												THE RESULTS					
Year Team	Lg	G	GS	CG	GF	IP	BFP	H	R	ER	HR	SH	SF	HB	TBB	IBB	SO	WP	Bk	W	L	Pct.	ShO	Sv	ERA
1991 Oneonta	A	15	15	2	0	94.1	414	92	56	45	2	3	3	5	38	2	45	5	5	6	6	.500	0	0	4.29
1992 Greensboro	A	13	13	3	0	82.1	351	87	35	20	3	3	6	3	21	0	53	7	1	4	6	.400	0	0	2.19
Ft. Laud	A	12	11	0	0	69.1	310	83	37	31	1	3	4	5	27	0	27	5	0	3	7	.300	0	0	4.02
1993 Pr. William	A	34	15	0	4	96.1	447	122	74	63	8	1	3	3	44	0	35	9	0	3	8	.273	0	1	5.89
1994 Tampa	A	22	0	0	6	38.2	183	43	28	22	2	2	3	2	27	1	27	1	1	1	0	1.000	0	0	5.12
Albany-Colo	AA	3	0	0	1	6.1	32	8	5	5	2	0	0	0	7	0	2	1	0	1	0	1.000	0	0	7.11
1995 Norwich	AA	1	0	0	0	0.2	6	4	4	4	2	0	0	0	0	0	0	1	0	0	0	.000	0	0	54.00

Team	Lg	G	GS	CG	GF	IP	BFP	H	R	ER	HR	SH	SF	HB	TBB	IBB	SO	WP	Bk	W	L	Pct.	ShO	Sv	ERA
Glens Falls	IND	12	3	0	2	23	105	26	16	14	2	1	0	5	8	0	24	2	0	1	2	.333	0	0	5.48
Glens Falls	IND	13	3	0	2	23.2	111	30	20	18	3	1	0	5	8	0	24	2	0	1	2	.333	0	0	6.85
5 Min. YEARS		125	60	5	15	434.2	1959	495	275	222	24	14	19	28	180	3	237	32	7	20	31	.392	0	1	4.60

Mike Sullivan

Pitches: Right **Bats:** Right **Pos:** P   **Ht:** 6'3" **Wt:** 195 **Born:** 1/27/68 **Age:** 28

		HOW MUCH HE PITCHED						WHAT HE GAVE UP												THE RESULTS					
Year Team	Lg	G	GS	CG	GF	IP	BFP	H	R	ER	HR	SH	SF	HB	TBB	IBB	SO	WP	Bk	W	L	Pct.	ShO	Sv	ERA
1989 Batavia	A	24	0	0	18	45.2	195	41	22	15	6	2	1	1	13	1	42	5	0	4	1	.800	0	5	2.96
1990 Spartanburg	A	22	0	0	18	36	164	39	19	18	1	4	2	0	17	0	28	5	2	4	3	.571	0	8	4.50
Clearwater	A	13	0	0	11	14.2	57	8	2	2	0	0	1	1	4	0	16	1	0	2	1	.667	0	3	1.23
1991 Clearwater	A	36	7	0	20	76	320	58	29	22	3	1	6	2	36	2	64	4	0	6	3	.667	0	11	2.61
1992 Reading	AA	34	0	0	13	44.2	204	56	34	24	5	2	1	1	18	2	27	3	2	2	1	.667	0	0	4.84
Clearwater	A	24	0	0	21	25.2	96	16	3	3	0	0	1	1	2	1	24	0	0	2	0	1.000	0	10	1.05
1993 Reading	AA	31	0	0	12	45.1	191	42	20	17	2	1	2	2	13	3	29	5	1	0	3	.000	0	4	3.38
1994 Reading	AA	11	0	0	3	14	65	12	10	8	2	2	1	2	13	2	11	1	1	0	1	.000	0	0	5.14
New Britain	AA	38	0	0	18	51.2	232	55	32	24	1	2	1	3	20	1	34	1	0	2	6	.250	0	3	4.18
1995 Trenton	AA	15	0	0	9	19.2	79	17	5	3	1	1	0	2	3	0	16	0	0	3	1	.750	0	2	1.37
7 Min. YEARS		248	7	0	143	373.1	1603	344	176	136	21	15	16	15	139	12	291	25	6	25	20	.556	0	46	3.28

Alex Sutherland

Bats: Right **Throws:** Right **Pos:** C   **Ht:** 5'11" **Wt:** 170 **Born:** 9/13/71 **Age:** 24

		BATTING													BASERUNNING				PERCENTAGES		
Year Team	Lg	G	AB	H	2B	3B	HR	TB	R	RBI	TBB	IBB	SO	HBP	SH	SF	SB	CS	SB%	GDP	Avg	OBP	SLG
1991 San Bernrdo	A	14	47	19	5	1	4	38	8	21	3	0	14	1	0	0	0	1	.00	0	.404	.451	.809
1992 San Bernrdo	A	31	90	23	1	0	2	30	10	9	5	0	28	1	0	0	0	1	.00	1	.256	.302	.333
1993 Appleton	A	103	325	78	20	0	6	116	40	31	20	2	62	1	2	2	5	4	.56	10	.240	.284	.357
1994 Appleton	A	94	330	84	17	2	3	114	24	40	19	0	70	3	2	2	2	6	.25	4	.255	.299	.345
1995 Port City	AA	13	44	9	3	0	0	12	1	3	5	0	7	0	0	0	1	0	1.00	3	.205	.286	.273
Wisconsin	A	90	303	68	17	2	1	92	36	35	19	2	56	2	2	1	2	0	1.00	5	.224	.274	.304
5 Min. YEARS		345	1139	281	63	5	16	402	119	139	71	4	237	8	6	5	10	12	.45	23	.247	.294	.353

John Sutherland

Pitches: Right **Bats:** Right **Pos:** P   **Ht:** 6'2" **Wt:** 185 **Born:** 10/11/68 **Age:** 27

		HOW MUCH HE PITCHED						WHAT HE GAVE UP												THE RESULTS					
Year Team	Lg	G	GS	CG	GF	IP	BFP	H	R	ER	HR	SH	SF	HB	TBB	IBB	SO	WP	Bk	W	L	Pct.	ShO	Sv	ERA
1991 Yankees	R	4	1	0	0	7.2	31	5	6	5	0	0	1	0	3	0	5	0	1	0	2	.000	0	0	5.87
1992 Oneonta	A	4	1	0	1	15.2	61	10	2	2	1	1	0	0	2	0	16	0	0	3	0	1.000	0	0	1.15
Greensboro	A	14	3	0	1	34	144	29	17	15	2	2	0	1	12	0	27	3	0	3	2	.600	0	0	3.97
1993 San Bernrdo	A	43	1	0	24	70.1	314	73	46	39	7	2	0	0	37	2	59	5	0	3	7	.300	0	4	4.99
1994 Albany-Colo	AA	31	4	0	11	63.2	276	62	35	27	6	1	1	2	25	2	49	1	0	6	4	.600	0	1	3.82
1995 Columbus	AAA	3	0	0	2	3	14	5	3	3	0	0	0	0	0	0	2	0	0	0	0	.000	0	0	9.00
Norwich	AA	13	0	0	6	13	51	12	5	4	3	0	1	1	3	0	12	0	0	1	0	1.000	0	2	2.77
5 Min. YEARS		112	10	0	45	207.1	891	196	114	95	19	6	3	4	82	4	170	9	1	16	15	.516	0	7	4.12

Glenn Sutko

Bats: Right **Throws:** Right **Pos:** C   **Ht:** 6'3" **Wt:** 225 **Born:** 5/9/68 **Age:** 28

		BATTING													BASERUNNING				PERCENTAGES		
Year Team	Lg	G	AB	H	2B	3B	HR	TB	R	RBI	TBB	IBB	SO	HBP	SH	SF	SB	CS	SB%	GDP	Avg	OBP	SLG
1988 Billings	R	30	84	13	2	1	1	20	3	8	14	0	38	1	3	2	3	1	.75	2	.155	.277	.238
1989 Greensboro	A	109	333	78	21	0	7	120	44	41	47	1	105	4	0	3	1	3	.25	5	.234	.333	.360
1990 Cedar Rapds	A	4	10	3	0	0	0	3	0	0	0	0	2	1	0	0	0	0	.00	1	.300	.364	.300
Chattanooga	AA	53	174	29	7	1	2	44	12	11	8	1	66	1	0	0	1	1	.50	2	.167	.208	.253
1991 Chattanooga	AA	23	63	18	3	0	3	30	12	11	9	2	20	0	2	0	0	0	.00	1	.286	.375	.476
Nashville	AAA	45	134	28	2	1	3	41	9	15	22	3	67	0	0	0	1	0	1.00	3	.209	.321	.306
1992 Chattanooga	AA	64	198	37	4	0	10	71	24	27	17	1	90	1	1	2	3	2	.60	1	.187	.252	.359
1993 Winston-Sal	A	31	1	0	0	0	0	0	1	0	0	0	0	0	0	0	0	0	.00	0	.000	.000	.000
1994 New Orleans	AAA	27	77	17	2	0	2	25	10	10	8	1	22	0	0	0	0	1	.00	1	.221	.294	.325
Beloit	A	59	186	41	9	2	4	66	28	21	35	2	80	1	1	2	3	1	.75	4	.220	.344	.355
1995 El Paso	AA	44	119	33	9	1	4	56	18	20	20	1	34	0	0	0	1	0	1.00	5	.277	.376	.471
New Orleans	AAA	42	101	21	8	0	3	38	7	14	7	0	35	0	0	0	0	0	.00	1	.208	.259	.376
1990 Cincinnati	NL	1	1	0	0	0	0	0	0	0	0	0	1	0	0	0	0	0	.00	0	.000	.000	.000
1991 Cincinnati	NL	10	10	1	0	0	0	1	0	1	2	0	6	0	0	0	0	0	.00	0	.100	.250	.100
8 Min. YEARS		531	1480	318	67	6	39	514	168	178	187	12	559	9	8	11	13	9	.59	26	.215	.305	.347
2 Maj. YEARS		11	11	1	0	0	0	1	0	1	2	0	7	0	0	0	0	0	.00	0	.091	.231	.091

Larry Sutton

Bats: Left **Throws:** Left **Pos:** 1B   **Ht:** 5'11" **Wt:** 175 **Born:** 5/14/70 **Age:** 26

		BATTING													BASERUNNING				PERCENTAGES		
Year Team	Lg	G	AB	H	2B	3B	HR	TB	R	RBI	TBB	IBB	SO	HBP	SH	SF	SB	CS	SB%	GDP	Avg	OBP	SLG
1992 Eugene	A	70	238	74	17	3	15	142	45	58	48	5	33	5	0	2	3	6	.33	3	.311	.433	.597
Appleton	A	1	2	0	0	0	0	0	1	0	2	0	1	0	0	0	0	1	.00	0	.000	.500	.000
1993 Rockford	A	113	361	97	24	1	7	144	67	50	95	5	65	8	0	8	3	5	.38	3	.269	.424	.399
1994 Wilmington	A	129	480	147	33	1	26	260	91	94	81	10	71	6	1	9	2	1	.67	7	.306	.406	.542

Year Team	Lg	G	AB	H	2B	3B	HR	TB	R	RBI	TBB	IBB	SO	HBP	SH	SF	SB	CS	SB%	GDP	Avg	OBP	SLG
1995 Wichita	AA	53	197	53	11	1	5	81	31	32	26	0	33	2	0	2	1	1	.50	3	.269	.357	.411
4 Min. YEARS		366	1278	371	85	6	53	627	235	234	252	20	203	21	1	21	9	14	.39	16	.290	.410	.491

Dale Sveum

Bats: Both **Throws:** Right **Pos:** 3B **Ht:** 6' 3" **Wt:** 185 **Born:** 11/23/63 **Age:** 32

		BATTING															BASERUNNING				PERCENTAGES		
Year Team	Lg	G	AB	H	2B	3B	HR	TB	R	RBI	TBB	IBB	SO	HBP	SH	SF	SB	CS	SB%	GDP	Avg	OBP	SLG
1984 El Paso	AA	131	523	172	41	8	9	256	84	84	43	1	72	0	1	6	6	3	.67	9	.329	.376	.489
1985 Vancouver	AAA	122	415	98	17	3	6	139	42	48	48	6	79	2	1	2	4	5	.44	17	.236	.317	.335
1986 Vancouver	AAA	28	105	31	3	2	1	41	16	23	13	0	24	1	0	3	0	0	.00	4	.295	.369	.390
1989 Beloit	A	6	15	2	1	0	0	3	0	2	5	2	6	0	0	0	0	0	.00	0	.133	.350	.200
Stockton	A	11	43	8	0	0	1	11	5	5	6	1	14	0	0	1	0	0	.00	2	.186	.280	.256
1990 Denver	AAA	57	218	63	17	2	2	90	25	26	20	3	49	0	2	0	1	2	.33	5	.289	.349	.413
1993 Tacoma	AAA	12	43	15	1	0	2	22	10	6	6	1	7	1	0	0	2	1	.67	1	.349	.440	.512
Calgary	AAA	33	120	36	11	1	6	67	31	26	24	0	32	0	0	1	0	1	.00	0	.300	.414	.558
1994 Calgary	AAA	102	393	111	21	3	22	204	71	78	49	4	98	2	0	5	1	0	1.00	12	.282	.361	.519
1995 Calgary	AAA	118	408	116	34	1	12	188	71	70	48	2	78	0	1	5	2	2	.50	8	.284	.356	.461
1986 Milwaukee	AL	91	317	78	13	2	7	116	35	35	32	0	63	1	5	1	4	3	.57	7	.246	.316	.366
1987 Milwaukee	AL	153	535	135	27	3	25	243	86	95	40	4	133	1	5	5	2	6	.25	11	.252	.303	.454
1988 Milwaukee	AL	129	467	113	14	4	9	162	41	51	21	0	122	1	3	3	1	0	1.00	6	.242	.274	.347
1990 Milwaukee	AL	48	117	23	7	0	1	33	15	12	12	0	30	2	0	2	0	1	.00	3	.197	.278	.282
1991 Milwaukee	AL	90	266	64	19	1	4	97	33	43	32	0	78	1	5	4	2	4	.33	8	.241	.320	.365
1992 Chicago	AL	114	245	59	9	0	2	40	15	12	12	0	29	0	2	3	1	1	.50	1	.219	.287	.351
Philadelphia	NL	54	135	24	4	0	2	34	13	16	16	4	39	0	0	2	0	0	.00	5	.178	.261	.252
1993 Oakland	AL	30	79	14	2	1	2	24	12	6	16	1	21	0	1	0	0	0	.00	0	.177	.316	.304
1994 Seattle	AL	10	27	5	0	0	0	8	3	2	2	0	10	0	0	0	0	0	.00	1	.185	.241	.296
8 Min. YEARS		620	2283	652	146	20	61	1021	363	368	262	20	459	6	5	23	16	14	.53	58	.286	.357	.447
8 Mai. YEARS		645	2057	481	95	11	53	757	253	272	183	9	525	6	21	20	10	15	.40	43	.234	.296	.368

Russ Swan

Pitches: Left **Bats:** Left **Pos:** P **Ht:** 6' 4" **Wt:** 210 **Born:** 1/3/64 **Age:** 32

		HOW MUCH HE PITCHED						WHAT HE GAVE UP												THE RESULTS					
Year Team	Lg	G	GS	CG	GF	IP	BFP	H	R	ER	HR	SH	SF	HB	TBB	IBB	SO	WP	Bk	W	L	Pct.	ShO	Sv	ERA
1986 Everett	A	7	7	2	0	46	0	30	17	11	2	0	0	1	22	0	45	1	1	5	0	1.000	0	0	2.15
Clinton	A	7	7	2	0	43.2	179	36	18	15	2	0	2	1	8	0	37	1	1	3	3	.500	1	0	3.09
1987 Fresno	A	12	12	0	0	64	274	54	40	27	5	4	0	1	29	0	59	4	0	6	3	.667	0	0	3.80
1988 San Jose	A	11	11	2	0	76.2	301	53	28	19	2	7	0	1	26	0	62	2	0	7	0	1.000	1	0	2.23
1989 Shreveport	A	11	11	0	0	75.1	304	62	25	22	2	1	1	1	22	1	56	3	2	2	3	.400	0	0	2.63
Phoenix	AAA	14	13	1	0	83	348	75	37	31	8	5	2	3	29	0	49	2	3	4	3	.571	0	0	3.36
1990 Phoenix	AAA	6	6	0	0	33.2	153	41	17	13	1	1	1	2	15	0	21	1	1	2	4	.333	0	0	3.48
Calgary	AAA	5	5	0	0	23	105	28	18	15	0	1	0	0	12	0	14	3	0	1	2	.333	0	0	5.87
1993 Calgary	AAA	9	0	0	3	10.2	51	14	11	10	1	0	0	0	8	0	7	0	0	2	1	.667	0	0	8.44
1994 Charlotte	AAA	21	2	0	1	39.1	186	53	34	31	4	4	1	1	18	2	13	5	0	1	3	.250	0	0	7.09
1995 Edmonton	AAA	17	0	0	12	18.2	85	23	9	9	2	1	1	0	11	4	10	4	0	3	3	.500	0	4	4.34
Amarillo	IND	7	0	0	4	6.2	37	10	7	5	1	2	0	0	6	2	4	2	0	1	2	.333	0	1	6.75
1989 San Francisco	NL	2	2	0	0	6.2	34	11	10	8	4	2	0	0	4	0	2	0	0	0	2	.000	0	0	10.80
1990 Seattle	AL	11	8	0	0	47	195	42	22	19	3	2	3	0	18	2	15	0	1	2	3	.400	0	0	3.64
San Francisco	NL	2	1	0	0	2.1	18	6	4	1	0	0	0	0	4	0	1	1	0	0	1	.000	0	0	3.86
1991 Seattle	AL	63	0	0	11	78.2	336	81	35	30	8	6	1	0	28	7	33	8	0	6	2	.750	0	2	3.43
1992 Seattle	AL	55	9	1	26	104.1	457	104	60	55	8	7	5	3	45	7	45	6	0	3	10	.231	0	9	4.74
1993 Seattle	AL	23	0	0	6	19.2	100	25	20	20	2	1	0	2	18	1	10	0	0	3	3	.500	0	0	9.15
1994 Cleveland	AL	12	0	0	2	8	43	13	11	10	1	2	0	0	7	1	2	0	0	0	1	.000	0	0	11.25
8 Min. YEARS		127	74	7	20	520.2	2023	479	261	208	30	26	8	11	206	9	377	28	8	37	27	.578	2	5	3.60
6 Mai. YEARS		168	20	1	45	266.2	1183	282	162	143	26	20	9	5	124	18	108	15	1	14	22	.389	0	11	4.83

Pedro Swann

Bats: Left **Throws:** Right **Pos:** OF **Ht:** 6'0" **Wt:** 195 **Born:** 10/27/70 **Age:** 25

		BATTING															BASERUNNING				PERCENTAGES		
Year Team	Lg	G	AB	H	2B	3B	HR	TB	R	RBI	TBB	IBB	SO	HBP	SH	SF	SB	CS	SB%	GDP	Avg	OBP	SLG
1991 Idaho Falls	R	55	174	48	6	1	3	65	35	28	33	0	45	2	1	2	8	5	.62	4	.276	.393	.374
1992 Pulaski	R	59	203	61	18	1	3	96	36	34	32	3	33	7	0	1	13	6	.68	6	.300	.412	.473
1993 Durham	A	61	182	63	8	2	6	93	27	27	19	0	38	1	0	0	6	12	.33	2	.346	.411	.511
Greenville	AA	44	157	48	9	2	3	70	19	21	9	0	23	1	1	0	2	2	.50	5	.306	.347	.446
1994 Greenville	AA	126	428	121	25	2	10	180	55	49	46	2	85	4	0	2	16	9	.64	14	.283	.356	.421
1995 Richmond	AAA	15	38	8	1	0	0	9	2	3	1	0	2	1	0	0	0	2	.00	0	.211	.250	.237
Greenville	AA	102	339	110	24	2	11	171	57	64	45	2	63	3	0	3	14	11	.56	8	.324	.405	.504
5 Min. YEARS		462	1521	459	91	10	38	684	231	226	185	7	289	19	2	8	59	47	.56	39	.302	.383	.450

Paul Swingle

Pitches: Right **Bats:** Right **Pos:** P **Ht:** 6' 0" **Wt:** 185 **Born:** 12/21/66 **Age:** 29

		HOW MUCH HE PITCHED						WHAT HE GAVE UP												THE RESULTS					
Year Team	Lg	G	GS	CG	GF	IP	BFP	H	R	ER	HR	SH	SF	HB	TBB	IBB	SO	WP	Bk	W	L	Pct.	ShO	Sv	ERA
1989 Bend	A	9	0	2	0	18.1	81	7	9	6	1	0	0	0	19	0	26	5	1	1	0	1.000	0	0	2.95
1990 Boise	A	14	0	0	12	13.2	51	5	1	1	0	1	0	0	3	1	24	0	0	0	1	.000	0	0	0.66
1991 Palm Spring	A	43	0	0	28	57	268	51	37	28	2	3	3	1	41	8	63	11	0	5	4	.556	0	10	4.42

Year	Team	Lg	G	GS	CG	GF	IP	BFP	H	R	ER	HR	SH	SF	HB	TBB	IBB	SO	WP	Bk	W	L	Pct.	ShO	Sv	ERA
1992	Midland	AA	25	25	2	0	149.2	648	158	88	78	14	3	6	6	51	1	104	8	2	8	10	.444	0	0	4.69
1993	Vancouver	AAA	37	4	0	11	67.2	318	85	61	52	4	2	4	1	32	1	61	3	1	2	9	.182	0	1	6.92
1995	New Orleans	AAA	35	0	0	9	43.1	185	42	25	22	7	1	0	1	15	2	41	5	0	1	4	.200	0	0	4.57
1993	California	AL	9	0	0	2	9.2	49	15	9	9	2	0	1	0	6	0	6	0	0	0	1	.000	0	0	8.38
	6 Min. YEARS		163	29	2	62	349.2	1551	348	221	187	27	11	13	9	161	13	319	32	4	17	28	.378	0	16	4.81

Jeff Tackett

Bats: Right **Throws:** Right **Pos:** C   **Ht:** 6' 2" **Wt:** 206 **Born:** 12/1/65 **Age:** 30

					BATTING												BASERUNNING				PERCENTAGES		
Year	Team	Lg	G	AB	H	2B	3B	HR	TB	R	RBI	TBB	IBB	SO	HBP	SH	SF	SB	CS	SB%	GDP	Avg	OBP	SLG
1984	Bluefield	R	34	98	16	2	0	0	18	9	12	23	0	28	0	0	2	1	1	.50	1	.163	.317	.184
1985	Daytona Bch	A	40	103	20	5	2	0	29	8	10	13	0	16	1	0	1	1	3	.25	6	.194	.288	.282
	Newark	A	62	187	39	6	0	0	45	21	22	22	0	33	2	3	1	2	2	.50	4	.209	.297	.241
1986	Hagerstown	A	83	246	70	15	1	0	87	53	21	36	0	36	5	0	1	16	5	.76	2	.285	.385	.354
1987	Charlotte	AA	61	205	46	6	1	0	54	18	13	12	0	34	2	1	1	5	5	.50	2	.224	.273	.263
1988	Charlotte	AA	81	272	56	9	0	0	65	24	18	42	0	46	2	0	1	6	4	.60	7	.206	.315	.239
1989	Rochester	AAA	67	199	36	3	1	2	47	13	17	19	0	45	1	2	2	3	1	.75	3	.181	.253	.236
1990	Rochester	AAA	108	306	73	8	3	4	99	37	33	47	0	50	7	3	0	4	8	.33	3	.239	.353	.324
1991	Rochester	AAA	126	433	102	18	2	6	142	64	50	54	0	60	2	4	3	3	3	.50	15	.236	.321	.328
1993	Rochester	AAA	8	25	8	2	0	0	10	1	2	3	0	8	2	0	1	0	0	.00	0	.320	.419	.400
1995	Toledo	AAA	96	301	81	15	0	6	114	32	30	35	0	46	1	7	5	2	1	.67	6	.269	.358	.379
1991	Baltimore	AL	6	8	1	0	0	0	1	1	0	2	0	2	0	1	0	0	0	.00	0	.125	.300	.125
1992	Baltimore	AL	65	179	43	8	1	5	68	21	24	17	1	28	2	6	4	0	0	.00	11	.240	.307	.380
1993	Baltimore	AL	39	87	15	3	0	0	18	8	9	13	0	28	0	2	1	0	0	.00	5	.172	.277	.207
1994	Baltimore	AL	26	53	12	3	1	2	23	5	9	5	0	13	2	0	0	0	0	.00	4	.226	.317	.434
	10 Min. YEARS		766	2375	547	89	10	18	710	280	228	306	0	402	31	18	14	43	33	.57	49	.230	.324	.299
	4 Maj. YEARS		136	327	71	14	2	7	110	35	42	37	1	71	4	9	5	0	0	.00	20	.217	.300	.336

Todd Takayoshi

Bats: Left **Throws:** Right **Pos:** C   **Ht:** 6'1" **Wt:** 190 **Born:** 10/4/70 **Age:** 25

					BATTING												BASERUNNING				PERCENTAGES		
Year	Team	Lg	G	AB	H	2B	3B	HR	TB	R	RBI	TBB	IBB	SO	HBP	SH	SF	SB	CS	SB%	GDP	Avg	OBP	SLG
1993	Pocatello	R	69	243	87	9	1	5	113	38	40	50	0	25	2	0	3	3	1	.75	4	.358	.466	.465
1994	Lk Elsinore	A	7	18	3	0	0	0	3	2	1	3	1	1	0	0	1	1	1	.50	1	.167	.286	.167
	Cedar Rapds	A	95	302	93	16	1	8	135	42	46	44	7	43	2	1	2	2	2	.50	8	.308	.397	.447
1995	Midland	AA	7	18	5	0	1	0	7	2	0	1	0	4	0	1	0	1	0	1.00	0	.278	.316	.389
	Lk Elsinore	A	60	157	38	6	1	3	55	19	30	42	1	30	0	2	0	1	1	.50	5	.242	.402	.350
	3 Min. YEARS		238	738	226	31	4	16	313	103	117	140	9	103	4	4	5	8	5	.62	18	.306	.417	.424

Scott Talanoa

Bats: Right **Throws:** Right **Pos:** DH   **Ht:** 6'5" **Wt:** 240 **Born:** 11/12/69 **Age:** 26

					BATTING												BASERUNNING				PERCENTAGES		
Year	Team	Lg	G	AB	H	2B	3B	HR	TB	R	RBI	TBB	IBB	SO	HBP	SH	SF	SB	CS	SB%	GDP	Avg	OBP	SLG
1991	Helena	R	37	127	37	10	0	6	65	24	29	29	2	32	3	0	2	1	2	.33	4	.291	.429	.512
1992	Beloit	A	106	357	82	18	0	13	139	57	56	49	1	109	2	3	2	7	4	.64	3	.230	.324	.389
1993	Beloit	A	87	258	74	12	0	25	161	55	66	71	6	86	8	0	4	5	3	.63	3	.287	.449	.624
1994	El Paso	AA	127	429	111	20	1	28	217	89	88	77	6	138	9	0	4	1	2	.33	11	.259	.380	.506
1995	New Orleans	AAA	31	98	14	4	0	1	21	9	3	6	0	26	2	0	1	0	0	.00	5	.143	.206	.214
	El Paso	AA	2	9	2	2	0	0	4	0	1	1	0	0	0	0	0	0	0	.00	1	.222	.300	.444
	5 Min. YEARS		390	1278	320	66	1	73	607	234	243	233	15	391	24	3	13	14	11	.56	27	.250	.373	.475

Jeff Tam

Pitches: Right **Bats:** Right **Pos:** P   **Ht:** 6'1" **Wt:** 185 **Born:** 8/19/70 **Age:** 25

			HOW MUCH HE PITCHED					WHAT HE GAVE UP										THE RESULTS					
Year	Team	Lg	G	GS	CG	GF	IP	BFP	H	R	ER	HR	SH	SF	HB	TBB	IBB	SO	WP	Bk	W	L	Pct.	ShO	Sv	ERA
1993	Pittsfield	A	21	1	0	13	40.1	180	50	21	15	0	0	1	1	7	0	31	1	3	3	3	.500	0	0	3.35
1994	Columbia	A	26	0	0	26	28	115	23	14	4	0	1	0	2	6	0	22	0	2	1	1	.500	0	18	1.29
	St. Lucie	A	24	0	0	22	26.2	99	13	0	0	0	0	0	3	6	1	15	1	2	0	0	.000	0	16	0.00
	Binghamton	AA	4	0	0	1	6.2	35	9	6	6	0	0	1	0	5	0	7	0	0	0	0	.000	0	0	8.10
1995	Mets	R	2	1	0	0	3	13	2	1	1	0	1	0	1	1	0	2	1	0	0	0	.000	0	0	3.00
	Binghamton	AA	14	0	0	7	18	83	20	11	9	1	2	1	4	4	2	9	3	0	0	2	.000	0	3	4.50
	3 Min. YEARS		91	2	0	69	122.2	525	117	53	35	1	5	2	12	29	3	86	6	7	4	6	.400	0	37	2.57

Andy Taulbee

Pitches: Right **Bats:** Right **Pos:** P   **Ht:** 6'4" **Wt:** 210 **Born:** 10/5/72 **Age:** 23

			HOW MUCH HE PITCHED					WHAT HE GAVE UP										THE RESULTS					
Year	Team	Lg	G	GS	CG	GF	IP	BFP	H	R	ER	HR	SH	SF	HB	TBB	IBB	SO	WP	Bk	W	L	Pct.	ShO	Sv	ERA
1994	San Jose	A	13	13	0	0	71	300	66	28	21	5	5	1	6	20	0	51	0	5	4	3	.571	0	0	2.66
1995	San Jose	A	10	9	1	0	62.2	251	50	27	21	7	4	0	4	22	0	33	2	0	3	2	.600	1	0	3.02
	Shreveport	AA	14	14	1	0	86.2	388	107	47	38	5	6	3	3	27	2	38	3	1	4	5	.444	1	0	3.95
	2 Min. YEARS		37	36	2	0	220.1	939	223	102	80	17	15	4	13	69	2	122	5	6	11	10	.524	2	0	3.27

Aaron Taylor

Pitches: Right **Bats:** Right **Pos:** P **Ht:** 6'4" **Wt:** 185 **Born:** 2/13/71 **Age:** 25

			HOW MUCH HE PITCHED					WHAT HE GAVE UP												THE RESULTS					
Year Team	Lg	G	GS	CG	GF	IP	BFP	H	R	ER	HR	SH	SF	HB	TBB	IBB	SO	WP	Bk	W	L	Pct.	ShO	Sv	ERA
1989 Wytheville	R	15	13	0	0	79.1	389	116	80	65	13	1	2	6	27	0	47	5	5	5	6	.455	0	0	7.37
1990 Huntington	R	26	0	0	25	44	171	32	13	9	3	5	2	1	10	0	50	2	0	4	4	.500	0	11	1.84
Winston-Sal	A	1	0	0	1	2	8	1	0	0	0	0	0	0	2	0	2	0	0	0	0	.000	0	0	0.00
1991 Peoria	A	15	14	1	1	78.1	362	99	60	45	4	3	4	5	27	1	42	8	3	2	4	.333	0	0	5.17
Geneva	A	21	1	0	14	34.2	145	32	15	14	2	1	1	2	9	1	30	2	0	1	3	.250	0	3	3.63
1992 Winston-Sal	A	62	0	0	51	85.2	347	74	29	21	4	6	5	2	17	1	59	5	0	10	7	.588	0	20	2.21
1993 Orlando	AA	28	3	0	16	55.2	258	73	37	30	6	2	2	5	15	2	37	3	1	5	4	.556	0	0	4.85
Daytona	A	15	1	0	8	23.2	104	21	13	12	1	3	0	3	8	0	17	0	0	1	0	1.000	0	2	4.56
1995 Huntsville	AA	5	4	0	0	25.1	106	26	7	6	3	1	1	1	6	0	24	1	1	1	1	.500	0	0	2.13
6 Min. YEARS		188	36	1	116	428.2	1890	474	254	202	36	22	17	25	121	5	308	26	10	29	29	.500	0	36	4.24

Bob Taylor

Pitches: Right **Bats:** Right **Pos:** P **Ht:** 6'3" **Wt:** 225 **Born:** 3/25/66 **Age:** 30

			HOW MUCH HE PITCHED					WHAT HE GAVE UP												THE RESULTS					
Year Team	Lg	G	GS	CG	GF	IP	BFP	H	R	ER	HR	SH	SF	HB	TBB	IBB	SO	WP	Bk	W	L	Pct.	ShO	Sv	ERA
1984 Paintsville	R	16	4	0	7	47.1	220	59	31	23	5	1	1	0	21	2	42	5	0	2	1	.667	0	0	4.37
1985 Helena	R	8	0	0	2	14	0	12	12	10	1	0	0	1	10	0	12	4	0	0	0	.000	0	0	6.43
1989 Pocatello	R	29	1	0	20	57.2	229	46	12	8	0	3	2	2	11	2	74	2	0	3	2	.600	0	10	1.25
1990 Clinton	A	31	0	0	30	35.1	156	29	13	6	2	1	2	4	16	0	42	2	0	5	2	.714	0	17	1.53
San Jose	A	13	0	0	9	20.1	100	24	19	16	1	2	2	1	15	2	18	1	0	3	2	.600	0	2	7.08
1991 San Jose	A	9	0	0	8	10.2	49	14	6	6	0	0	0	0	4	0	13	2	0	0	1	.000	0	4	5.06
Shreveport	AA	39	2	0	14	67.1	291	62	33	31	5	6	2	2	30	6	68	3	2	3	3	.500	0	2	4.14
1992 Shreveport	AA	34	1	1	10	60.1	253	60	22	17	1	3	3	0	17	4	56	3	1	4	2	.667	0	1	2.54
Phoenix	AAA	20	0	0	7	30	133	33	14	8	2	0	0	2	10	2	28	2	0	4	1	.800	0	0	2.40
1993 Phoenix	AAA	49	12	0	11	144.1	636	166	85	68	15	6	3	4	49	4	110	7	2	10	8	.556	0	2	4.24
1994 Phoenix	AAA	61	1	0	30	97.1	415	98	57	50	16	5	2	4	32	6	86	4	0	7	5	.583	0	10	4.62
1995 Iowa	AAA	54	0	0	40	57.2	241	42	20	18	3	5	3	2	28	2	48	4	0	4	2	.667	0	18	2.81
9 Min. YEARS		363	21	1	188	642.1	2723	645	324	261	51	32	20	22	243	30	597	39	5	45	29	.608	0	66	3.66

Jamie Taylor

Bats: Left **Throws:** Right **Pos:** 3B **Ht:** 6'2" **Wt:** 220 **Born:** 10/10/70 **Age:** 25

		BATTING														BASERUNNING				PERCENTAGES		
Year Team	Lg	G	AB	H	2B	3B	HR	TB	R	RBI	TBB	IBB	SO	HBP	SH	SF	SB	CS	SB%	GDP	Avg	OBP	SLG
1992 Watertown	A	60	208	61	13	1	1	79	25	35	30	1	36	1	0	3	4	0	1.00	2	.293	.380	.380
1993 Columbus	A	111	402	91	21	0	8	136	46	46	36	2	115	0	2	4	4	2	.67	2	.226	.287	.338
1994 Kinston	A	76	217	51	14	0	5	80	30	19	29	0	63	2	2	1	3	4	.43	2	.235	.329	.369
1995 Canton-Akrn	AA	4	11	0	0	0	0	0	0	0	0	0	4	1	1	0	0	0	.00	0	.000	.083	.000
Duluth-Sup.	IND	75	285	84	18	1	4	116	36	28	31	1	50	1	2	2	1	2	.33	9	.295	.364	.407
4 Min. YEARS		326	1123	287	66	2	18	411	137	128	126	4	268	5	7	10	12	8	.60	15	.256	.331	.366

Kerry Taylor

Pitches: Right **Bats:** Right **Pos:** P **Ht:** 6'3" **Wt:** 200 **Born:** 1/25/71 **Age:** 25

			HOW MUCH HE PITCHED					WHAT HE GAVE UP												THE RESULTS					
Year Team	Lg	G	GS	CG	GF	IP	BFP	H	R	ER	HR	SH	SF	HB	TBB	IBB	SO	WP	Bk	W	L	Pct.	ShO	Sv	ERA
1989 Elizabethtn	R	9	8	0	0	36	157	26	11	6	1	3	1	2	22	0	24	1	0	3	0	1.000	1	0	1.50
1990 Twins	R	14	13	1	1	63	275	57	37	25	2	0	4	4	33	0	59	5	4	3	1	.750	1	0	3.57
1991 Kenosha	A	26	26	2	0	132	586	121	74	56	4	2	5	10	84	1	84	11	1	7	11	.389	1	0	3.82
1992 Kenosha	A	27	27	2	0	170.1	733	150	71	52	3	6	2	10	68	0	158	11	1	10	9	.526	1	0	2.75
1994 Las Vegas	AAA	27	27	1	0	156	719	175	105	96	15	2	7	10	81	2	142	14	0	9	9	.500	0	0	5.54
1995 Las Vegas	AAA	8	8	0	0	37	174	44	21	18	3	4	0	2	21	1	21	0	0	2	2	.500	0	0	4.38
1993 San Diego	NL	36	7	0	9	68.1	326	72	53	49	5	10	3	4	49	0	45	4	0	0	5	.000	0	0	6.45
1994 San Diego	NL	1	1	0	0	4.1	24	9	4	4	1	0	0	1	1	0	3	0	0	0	0	.000	0	0	8.31
6 Min. YEARS		111	109	6	1	594.1	2644	573	319	253	28	17	19	38	309	4	488	42	6	34	32	.515	3	0	3.83
2 Maj. YEARS		37	8	0	9	72.2	350	81	57	53	6	10	3	5	50	0	48	4	0	0	5	.000	0	0	6.56

Sam Taylor

Bats: Left **Throws:** Left **Pos:** OF **Ht:** 5'11" **Wt:** 185 **Born:** 8/6/68 **Age:** 27

		BATTING														BASERUNNING				PERCENTAGES		
Year Team	Lg	G	AB	H	2B	3B	HR	TB	R	RBI	TBB	IBB	SO	HBP	SH	SF	SB	CS	SB%	GDP	Avg	OBP	SLG
1989 Batavia	A	47	147	39	7	2	1	53	17	20	20	1	9	1	0	2	2	1	.67	5	.265	.353	.361
1990 Spartanburg	A	75	289	89	13	5	5	127	46	36	24	4	30	3	0	1	10	3	.77	2	.308	.366	.439
1991 Clearwater	A	115	367	95	20	7	8	153	51	73	55	5	52	6	2	10	3	3	.50	7	.259	.356	.417
1992 Reading	AA	98	349	86	18	5	10	144	42	55	34	1	40	4	3	4	5	6	.45	9	.246	.317	.413
1993 Reading	AA	49	173	48	12	0	5	75	31	27	30	0	24	1	1	4	9	3	.75	3	.277	.364	.434
Scranton-Wb	AAA	67	191	46	7	1	6	73	24	25	20	3	36	3	0	2	4	2	.67	3	.241	.319	.382
1995 Scranton-Wb	AAA	3	7	1	0	0	0	1	3	1	1	0	2	0	0	0	0	0	.00	0	.143	.250	.143
Salinas	IND	89	332	88	16	8	17	171	65	55	48	2	56	3	3	1	9	5	.64	4	.265	.362	.515
6 Min. YEARS		543	1855	492	93	28	52	797	279	292	232	16	249	21	9	24	42	23	.65	33	.265	.349	.430

Scott Taylor

Pitches: Left   Bats: Left   Pos: P   Ht: 6'1"   Wt: 185   Born: 8/2/67   Age: 28

Year	Team	Lg	G	GS	CG	GF	IP	BFP	H	R	ER	HR	SH	SF	HB	TBB	IBB	SO	WP	Bk	W	L	Pct.	ShO	Sv	ERA
1988	Elmira	A	2	1	0	1	3.2	16	2	0	0	0	0	0	0	3	0	8	0	0	1	0	1.000	0	0	0.00
1989	Lynchburg	A	19	9	0	4	81	332	61	33	26	7	2	2	1	25	3	99	3	3	5	3	.625	0	1	2.89
1990	Lynchburg	A	13	13	1	0	89	372	76	36	27	2	3	0	2	30	2	120	7	3	5	6	.455	0	0	2.73
	New Britain	AA	5	5	1	0	27.1	117	23	8	5	0	3	0	1	13	1	27	1	0	0	2	.000	0	0	1.65
1991	New Britain	AA	4	4	0	0	29	109	20	2	2	0	0	0	0	9	0	38	1	0	2	0	1.000	0	0	0.62
	Pawtucket	AAA	7	7	1	0	39	161	32	19	15	3	0	2	1	17	0	35	1	1	3	3	.500	0	0	3.46
1992	Pawtucket	AAA	26	26	5	0	162	694	168	73	66	16	3	5	2	61	1	91	17	0	9	11	.450	0	0	3.67
1993	Pawtucket	AAA	47	8	0	10	122.2	533	132	61	55	12	7	2	3	48	0	88	2	1	7	7	.500	0	1	4.04
1995	Calgary	AAA	27	25	1	0	140	578	144	73	64	10	3	4	3	35	2	83	3	0	5	8	.385	0	0	4.11
1992	Boston	AL	4	1	0	1	14.2	57	13	8	8	4	0	0	0	4	0	7	0	0	1	1	.500	0	0	4.91
1993	Boston	AL	16	0	0	3	11	59	14	10	10	1	1	0	1	12	3	8	0	0	0	1	.000	0	0	8.18
	7 Min. YEARS		150	98	9	15	693.2	2912	658	305	260	50	21	15	13	241	9	589	35	8	37	40	.481	0	2	3.37
	2 Maj. YEARS		20	1	0	4	25.2	116	27	18	18	5	1	0	1	16	3	15	0	0	1	2	.333	0	0	6.31

Tommy Taylor

Pitches: Right   Bats: Right   Pos: P   Ht: 6'1"   Wt: 180   Born: 7/16/70   Age: 25

Year	Team	Lg	G	GS	CG	GF	IP	BFP	H	R	ER	HR	SH	SF	HB	TBB	IBB	SO	WP	Bk	W	L	Pct.	ShO	Sv	ERA
1989	Bluefield	R	11	10	0	0	41.2	208	56	42	30	4	1	3	0	29	1	36	1	0	1	3	.250	0	0	6.48
1990	Wausau	A	23	20	1	1	111	498	103	74	65	11	3	1	5	62	0	78	8	3	3	11	.214	1	0	5.27
1991	Kane County	A	26	14	1	2	96.1	443	110	70	56	1	5	2	1	54	6	59	9	2	4	11	.267	0	1	5.23
1992	Hagerstown	AA	1	0	0	0	0.2	4	1	1	1	0	0	1	0	1	0	0	0	0	0	0	.000	0	0	13.50
	Frederick	A	27	14	1	3	118.1	518	116	63	55	9	3	4	7	48	3	84	6	1	4	8	.333	1	0	4.18
1993	Bowie	AA	40	4	0	19	89.2	407	90	65	56	9	7	6	2	47	1	69	5	1	4	7	.364	0	4	5.62
1994	Frederick	A	32	0	0	16	43.1	207	54	29	21	5	2	1	2	18	1	48	3	0	4	1	.800	0	2	4.36
	Kinston	A	3	3	0	0	14.1	61	9	5	5	1	1	0	0	8	0	13	3	0	0	0	.000	0	0	3.14
1995	Canton-Akrn	AA	5	0	0	3	9.2	41	9	4	4	2	1	1	0	6	0	3	0	0	1	1	.500	0	0	3.72
	Amarillo	IND	7	4	0	2	25.1	119	31	20	14	1	2	3	0	12	1	13	1	0	0	3	.000	0	0	4.97
	7 Min. YEARS		175	69	3	46	550.1	2506	579	373	307	43	25	22	17	285	13	403	36	7	21	45	.318	2	6	5.02

Fausto Tejero

Bats: Right   Throws: Right   Pos: C   Ht: 6'2"   Wt: 205   Born: 10/26/68   Age: 27

Year	Team	Lg	G	AB	H	2B	3B	HR	TB	R	RBI	TBB	IBB	SO	HBP	SH	SF	SB	CS	SB%	GDP	Avg	OBP	SLG
1990	Boise	A	39	74	16	2	0	0	18	14	7	23	1	23	2	3	3	1	0	1.00	0	.216	.402	.243
1991	Quad City	A	83	244	42	7	0	1	52	16	18	14	0	52	4	3	1	0	1	.00	5	.172	.228	.213
1992	Edmonton	AAA	8	17	4	1	0	0	5	0	0	4	0	2	1	2	0	0	2	.00	0	.235	.409	.294
	Midland	AA	84	266	50	11	0	2	67	21	30	11	0	63	4	5	3	1	2	.33	6	.188	.229	.252
1993	Palm Spring	A	7	20	6	2	0	0	8	2	1	2	0	1	0	1	0	1	0	.00	0	.300	.364	.400
	Vancouver	AAA	20	59	9	0	0	0	9	2	2	4	1	12	1	2	1	1	1	.50	1	.153	.215	.153
	Midland	AA	26	69	9	1	1	1	15	3	7	8	0	17	2	1	1	0	0	.00	3	.130	.238	.217
1994	Midland	AA	50	150	32	3	0	5	50	17	24	15	0	31	1	1	2	2	2	.50	6	.213	.286	.333
	Vancouver	AAA	16	45	9	2	0	0	11	6	6	4	0	9	0	2	1	1	1	.50	1	.200	.260	.244
1995	Lk Elsinore	A	8	21	5	1	0	0	6	5	3	5	0	6	0	0	1	1	0	1.00	1	.238	.370	.286
	Vancouver	AAA	37	96	25	3	0	0	28	10	8	10	1	22	0	1	0	2	0	1.00	0	.260	.330	.292
	Midland	AA	16	53	12	3	0	0	18	7	11	1	0	13	1	0	1	0	1	.00	1	.226	.250	.340
	6 Min. YEARS		394	1114	219	36	1	10	287	103	117	101	3	251	16	21	14	9	11	.45	23	.197	.270	.258

Amaury Telemaco

Pitches: Right   Bats: Right   Pos: P   Ht: 6'3"   Wt: 180   Born: 1/19/74   Age: 22

Year	Team	Lg	G	GS	CG	GF	IP	BFP	H	R	ER	HR	SH	SF	HB	TBB	IBB	SO	WP	Bk	W	L	Pct.	ShO	Sv	ERA
1992	Huntington	R	12	12	2	0	76.1	318	71	45	34	6	2	1	2	17	0	93	7	0	3	5	.375	0	0	4.01
	Peoria	A	2	1	0	0	5.2	31	9	5	5	0	0	0	1	5	0	5	0	0	1	0	1.000	0	0	7.94
1993	Peoria	A	23	23	3	0	143.2	602	129	69	55	9	2	6	5	54	0	133	8	0	8	11	.421	0	0	3.45
1994	Daytona	A	11	11	2	0	76.2	313	62	35	29	4	4	2	4	23	0	59	3	3	7	3	.700	0	0	3.40
	Orlando	AA	12	12	2	0	62.2	264	56	29	24	6	4	2	4	20	0	49	3	0	3	5	.375	0	0	3.45
1995	Orlando	AA	22	22	3	0	147.2	587	112	60	54	13	8	3	4	42	3	151	7	1	8	8	.500	1	0	3.29
	4 Min. YEARS		82	81	12	0	512.2	2115	439	243	201	38	20	14	20	161	3	490	28	4	29	33	.468	1	0	3.53

Anthony Telford

Pitches: Right   Bats: Right   Pos: P   Ht: 6'0"   Wt: 184   Born: 3/6/66   Age: 30

Year	Team	Lg	G	GS	CG	GF	IP	BFP	H	R	ER	HR	SH	SF	HB	TBB	IBB	SO	WP	Bk	W	L	Pct.	ShO	Sv	ERA
1987	Newark	A	6	2	0	3	17.2	72	16	2	2	0	0	0	0	3	0	27	0	0	1	0	1.000	0	0	1.02
	Hagerstown	A	2	2	0	0	11.1	46	9	2	2	0	0	0	0	5	0	10	0	0	1	0	1.000	0	0	1.59
	Rochester	AAA	1	0	0	0	2	9	0	0	0	0	0	0	0	0	0	3	1	0	0	0	.000	0	0	0.00
1988	Hagerstown	A	1	1	0	0	7	24	3	0	0	0	0	0	0	0	0	10	0	0	1	0	1.000	0	0	0.00
1989	Frederick	A	9	5	0	2	25.2	116	25	15	12	1	1	2	2	12	0	19	2	0	2	1	.667	0	1	4.21
1990	Frederick	A	8	8	1	0	53.2	207	35	15	10	1	0	0	4	11	1	49	4	0	4	2	.667	0	0	1.68
	Hagerstown	AA	14	13	3	1	96	384	80	26	21	3	5	3	3	25	1	73	4	0	10	2	.833	1	0	1.97

Year	Team		G	GS	CG	GF	IP	BFP	H	R	ER	HR	SH	SF	HB	TBB	IBB	SO	WP	Bk	W	L	Pct.	ShO	Sv	ERA
1991	Rochester	AAA	27	25	3	0	157.1	666	166	82	69	18	5	3	4	48	2	115	7	1	12	9	.571	0	0	3.95
1992	Rochester	AAA	27	26	3	1	181	766	183	89	84	15	4	4	6	64	0	129	9	2	12	7	.632	0	0	4.18
1993	Rochester	AAA	38	6	0	12	90.2	397	98	51	43	10	2	4	3	33	3	66	6	0	7	7	.500	0	2	4.27
1994	Richmond	AAA	38	20	3	0	142.2	607	148	82	67	17	4	4	4	41	2	111	1	0	10	6	.625	1	0	4.23
1995	Edmonton	AAA	8	6	0	0	36.1	173	47	32	29	5	2	2	2	16	0	17	2	0	3	2	.600	0	0	7.18
	Canton-Akrn	AA	2	2	0	0	11	42	6	2	1	0	0	0	0	4	1	4	0	0	2	0	1.000	0	0	0.82
	Buffalo	AAA	16	2	0	4	39	161	35	15	15	1	1	4	2	10	3	24	1	0	4	1	.800	0	0	3.46
1990	Baltimore	AL	8	8	0	0	36.1	168	43	22	20	4	0	2	1	19	0	20	1	0	3	3	.500	0	0	4.95
1991	Baltimore	AL	9	1	0	4	26.2	109	27	12	12	3	0	1	0	6	1	24	1	0	0	0	.000	0	0	4.05
1993	Baltimore	AL	3	0	0	2	7.1	34	11	8	8	3	0	0	1	1	0	6	1	0	0	0	.000	0	0	9.82
	9 Min. YEARS		197	118	13	23	871.1	3670	851	413	355	71	24	26	31	275	13	657	37	3	69	37	.651	2	3	3.67
	3 Maj. YEARS		20	9	0	6	70.1	311	81	42	40	10	0	3	2	26	1	50	3	0	3	3	.500	0	0	5.12

David Tellers

Pitches: Right **Bats:** Right **Pos:** P **Ht:** 5'10" **Wt:** 175 **Born:** 3/13/68 **Age:** 28

			HOW MUCH HE PITCHED						WHAT HE GAVE UP												THE RESULTS					
Year	Team	Lg	G	GS	CG	GF	IP	BFP	H	R	ER	HR	SH	SF	HB	TBB	IBB	SO	WP	Bk	W	L	Pct.	ShO	Sv	ERA
1990	Welland	A	20	0	0	16	39.2	148	23	9	6	2	1	1	0	7	0	53	1	2	4	2	.667	0	5	1.36
1991	Carolina	AA	11	0	0	9	13.1	64	18	8	7	1	1	0	0	6	4	9	1	0	0	2	.000	0	1	4.73
	Salem	A	40	0	0	28	71	279	54	16	11	1	4	4	2	20	4	61	0	3	6	4	.600	0	10	1.39
1992	Carolina	AA	16	0	0	6	25.1	103	23	11	10	2	1	1	2	9	2	23	1	0	2	1	.667	0	2	3.55
	Salem	A	32	5	0	24	74	302	72	32	30	9	3	0	2	14	4	63	0	0	3	7	.300	0	10	3.65
1993	Duluth-Sup.	IND	38	0	0	20	51.1	225	57	17	14	2	2	0	3	19	6	40	1	1	7	3	.700	0	9	2.45
1994	New Haven	AA	41	1	0	22	71.2	285	57	31	27	8	2	0	3	12	2	56	2	2	1	6	.143	0	9	3.39
1995	New Haven	AA	33	3	0	4	69	278	60	29	22	3	2	3	4	14	1	63	3	0	2	5	.286	0	1	2.87
	6 Min. YEARS		231	9	0	129	415.1	1684	364	153	127	28	16	9	16	101	23	368	9	8	25	30	.455	0	47	2.75

Jose Texidor

Bats: Right **Throws:** Right **Pos:** OF **Ht:** 6'0" **Wt:** 150 **Born:** 12/14/71 **Age:** 24

			BATTING													BASERUNNING				PERCENTAGES		
Year	Team	Lg	G	AB	H	2B	3B	HR	TB	R	RBI	TBB	IBB	SO	HBP	SH	SF	SB	CS	SB%	GDP	Avg	OBP	SLG
1989	Rangers	R	8	11	0	0	0	0	0	0	0	2	0	2	0	0	0	0	1	.00	0	.000	.154	.000
1990	Rangers	R	50	168	39	5	3	1	53	29	20	20	1	24	1	0	1	3	3	.50	2	.232	.316	.315
1991	Charlotte	A	13	39	11	1	1	0	14	8	3	2	0	6	1	1	0	1	1	.50	2	.282	.333	.359
	Butte	R	37	130	49	6	1	3	66	26	23	9	1	23	0	1	0	5	2	.71	4	.377	.417	.508
1992	Gastonia	A	118	410	115	23	2	3	151	45	32	24	0	65	1	4	0	6	13	.32	5	.280	.322	.368
1993	Charlotte	A	19	72	23	4	0	0	27	14	4	5	1	11	0	0	0	2	0	1.00	1	.319	.364	.375
1994	Charlotte	A	131	501	129	24	5	5	178	69	68	48	0	80	3	1	4	3	11	.21	6	.257	.324	.355
1995	Tulsa	AA	129	494	133	33	1	5	183	55	64	31	3	61	3	2	2	1	1	.50	19	.269	.315	.370
	7 Min. YEARS		505	1825	499	96	13	17	672	246	214	141	6	272	9	9	7	21	32	.40	39	.273	.327	.368

John Thibert

Pitches: Right **Bats:** Right **Pos:** P **Ht:** 6'1" **Wt:** 190 **Born:** 1/9/70 **Age:** 26

			HOW MUCH HE PITCHED						WHAT HE GAVE UP												THE RESULTS					
Year	Team	Lg	G	GS	CG	GF	IP	BFP	H	R	ER	HR	SH	SF	HB	TBB	IBB	SO	WP	Bk	W	L	Pct.	ShO	Sv	ERA
1990	Yankees	R	13	11	0	0	54	245	51	44	28	1	3	1	4	29	0	35	7	3	1	5	.167	0	0	4.67
1991	Oneonta	A	3	1	0	0	3.1	26	9	11	10	0	1	0	1	6	0	2	2	0	1	0	1.000	0	0	27.00
	Yankees	R	8	6	0	0	39.2	166	29	13	4	0	1	1	0	11	0	40	9	4	3	2	.600	0	0	0.91
1992	Greensboro	A	6	0	0	6	7.2	39	9	7	7	1	0	0	0	6	0	11	3	0	0	0	.000	0	1	8.22
	Oneonta	A	21	0	0	7	50	209	43	24	20	0	1	2	3	19	0	48	7	0	0	4	.000	0	1	3.60
1994	Lk Elsinore	A	45	0	0	23	60	245	50	31	24	4	3	0	4	27	3	47	10	1	3	3	.500	0	2	3.60
1995	Midland	AA	12	0	0	5	23.2	104	19	12	11	1	0	1	2	17	0	15	3	0	0	0	.000	0	2	4.18
	5 Min. YEARS		108	18	0	41	238.1	1034	212	139	104	7	8	6	13	115	3	198	41	8	8	14	.364	0	6	3.93

Brian Thomas

Bats: Left **Throws:** Right **Pos:** OF **Ht:** 6'0" **Wt:** 185 **Born:** 5/6/71 **Age:** 25

			BATTING													BASERUNNING				PERCENTAGES		
Year	Team	Lg	G	AB	H	2B	3B	HR	TB	R	RBI	TBB	IBB	SO	HBP	SH	SF	SB	CS	SB%	GDP	Avg	OBP	SLG
1993	Charlotte	A	34	135	39	3	2	2	52	25	11	18	1	29	0	3	3	4	1	.80	4	.289	.365	.385
1994	Charlotte	A	124	450	127	26	9	5	186	60	61	55	4	122	5	5	8	23	9	.72	6	.282	.361	.413
1995	Tulsa	AA	131	458	123	24	9	4	177	61	35	50	6	87	2	5	5	8	4	.67	8	.269	.340	.386
	3 Min. YEARS		289	1043	289	53	20	11	415	146	107	123	11	238	7	13	16	35	14	.71	14	.277	.352	.398

Carlos Thomas

Pitches: Right **Bats:** Right **Pos:** P **Ht:** 6'4" **Wt:** 215 **Born:** 8/6/68 **Age:** 27

			HOW MUCH HE PITCHED						WHAT HE GAVE UP												THE RESULTS					
Year	Team	Lg	G	GS	CG	GF	IP	BFP	H	R	ER	HR	SH	SF	HB	TBB	IBB	SO	WP	Bk	W	L	Pct.	ShO	Sv	ERA
1991	Yakima	A	16	2	0	5	34.1	158	26	18	15	0	0	1	0	33	0	42	4	2	2	0	1.000	0	0	3.93
1992	Yakima	A	15	15	0	0	83	378	72	64	47	8	0	2	13	50	0	59	5	5	3	8	.273	0	0	5.10
1993	Bakersfield	A	38	8	0	7	97.2	444	89	51	47	8	2	5	4	75	0	82	12	0	5	9	.357	0	1	4.33
1994	San Antonio	AA	26	0	0	12	42	188	37	20	16	2	3	3	0	29	5	32	3	0	2	5	.286	0	3	3.43
	Bakersfield	A	15	1	0	8	28.2	129	27	21	17	1	4	1	1	22	0	17	6	0	2	2	.500	0	1	5.34
1995	Huntsville	AA	7	0	0	3	12.2	56	13	8	7	2	2	0	1	5	1	12	1	1	2	2	.500	0	0	4.97
	Corp.Chrsti	IND	21	0	0	8	27.1	116	16	9	8	2	0	1	3	16	0	36	4	2	3	0	1.000	0	2	2.63
	Memphis	AA	11	0	0	4	13.1	71	15	16	15	1	1	1	0	14	0	12	1	0	1	1	.500	0	0	10.13

293

		G	W	L	S	IP	BFP	H	R	ER	HR	SH	SF	HB	TBB	IBB	SO	WP	Bk	W	L	Pct.	ShO	Sv	ERA
Clinton	A	13	0	0	1	18.1	86	19	9	5	1	2	0	1	10	1	14	0	0	2	0	1.000	0	1	2.45
5 Min. YEARS		162	26	0	48	357.1	1626	314	216	177	25	14	14	23	254	7	306	36	10	22	27	.449	0	8	4.46

Keith Thomas

Bats: Both **Throws:** Right **Pos:** OF   **Ht:** 6'1" **Wt:** 180 **Born:** 9/12/68 **Age:** 27

					BATTING												BASERUNNING				PERCENTAGES		
Year	Team	Lg	G	AB	H	2B	3B	HR	TB	R	RBI	TBB	IBB	SO	HBP	SH	SF	SB	CS	SB%	GDP	Avg	OBP	SLG
1986	Reds	R	42	145	31	1	2	2	42	24	13	23	0	57	3	2	1	18	6	.75	1	.214	.331	.290
1987	Billings	R	45	142	36	6	2	4	58	22	24	7	1	45	0	1	0	11	4	.73	1	.254	.289	.408
1988	Greensboro	A	108	438	105	12	4	4	137	63	26	17	0	122	2	4	0	30	6	.83	2	.240	.271	.313
1989	Modesto	A	93	330	70	5	2	6	97	36	29	24	1	102	2	3	0	19	10	.66	5	.212	.270	.294
1990	Modesto	A	62	215	48	7	0	4	67	24	21	14	0	65	1	1	2	16	10	.62	4	.223	.272	.312
	Madison	A	44	142	30	3	1	3	44	21	20	10	0	43	0	1	2	12	1	.92	3	.211	.260	.310
1991	Madison	A	13	44	9	1	0	0	10	4	4	3	0	11	0	1	1	3	1	.75	1	.205	.255	.227
	Appleton	A	74	232	62	10	4	7	101	32	28	12	0	60	2	3	2	21	5	.81	1	.267	.306	.435
1992	Salem	A	104	372	103	24	8	16	191	54	51	18	2	90	5	1	6	30	7	.81	12	.277	.314	.513
	Carolina	AA	22	78	23	2	4	4	45	13	15	7	0	23	0	0	0	9	1	.90	2	.295	.353	.577
1993	Salem	A	25	94	25	8	0	4	45	17	11	7	0	30	2	1	0	8	1	.89	1	.266	.330	.479
	Carolina	AA	94	336	80	9	2	15	138	40	52	22	0	110	2	1	4	12	8	.60	2	.238	.286	.411
1994	Wichita	AA	109	307	73	13	4	7	115	38	33	32	1	82	5	1	1	46	10	.82	7	.238	.319	.375
1995	Memphis	AA	109	356	90	13	4	10	141	66	33	20	0	85	1	1	0	43	11	.80	6	.253	.294	.396
	10 Min. YEARS		944	3231	785	114	37	86	1231	454	360	216	5	925	25	21	18	278	81	.77	48	.243	.294	.381

Royal Thomas

Pitches: Right **Bats:** Right **Pos:** P   **Ht:** 6'2" **Wt:** 187 **Born:** 9/3/69 **Age:** 26

			HOW MUCH HE PITCHED						WHAT HE GAVE UP										THE RESULTS				
Year	Team	Lg	G	GS	CG	GF	IP	BFP	H	R	ER	HR	SH	SF	HB	TBB	IBB	SO	WP	Bk	W	L	Pct.	ShO	Sv	ERA
1987	Utica	A	19	6	0	7	76	308	67	23	16	1	2	2	0	18	3	62	3	1	6	0	1.000	0	2	1.89
1988	Clearwater	A	9	2	0	4	19	95	24	21	19	0	3	2	3	14	2	6	3	2	0	4	.000	0	2	9.00
	Spartanburg	A	22	22	7	0	145.2	611	134	74	49	7	6	3	7	47	0	67	7	1	6	13	.316	2	0	3.03
1989	Clearwater	A	27	21	11	0	154	630	141	70	57	7	6	6	1	39	1	49	1	0	11	9	.550	3	0	3.33
1990	Riverside	A	27	27	1	0	166	740	209	103	87	11	4	6	4	49	3	93	10	0	9	13	.409	0	0	4.72
1991	High Desert	A	27	27	4	0	155	699	178	108	81	15	4	6	5	61	2	99	9	1	8	13	.381	0	0	4.70
1992	Wichita	AA	41	14	0	6	125.1	573	151	104	88	12	5	5	6	51	3	91	8	1	7	7	.500	0	2	6.32
1993	San Antonio	AA	47	6	0	16	109.2	475	116	58	48	11	6	6	3	44	5	52	4	0	4	6	.400	0	2	3.94
1994	Greenville	AA	46	0	0	18	85.1	367	90	38	30	4	5	2	1	28	3	48	2	1	6	4	.600	0	2	3.16
1995	Richmond	AAA	39	8	1	12	88	389	103	43	34	6	3	2	2	24	2	39	1	0	7	7	.500	1	0	3.48
	9 Min. YEARS		304	133	24	63	1124	4887	1213	642	509	74	44	40	32	375	24	606	48	7	64	76	.457	6	10	4.08

Skeets Thomas

Bats: Left **Throws:** Right **Pos:** OF   **Ht:** 5'11" **Wt:** 195 **Born:** 9/9/68 **Age:** 27

					BATTING												BASERUNNING				PERCENTAGES		
Year	Team	Lg	G	AB	H	2B	3B	HR	TB	R	RBI	TBB	IBB	SO	HBP	SH	SF	SB	CS	SB%	GDP	Avg	OBP	SLG
1990	Hamilton	A	33	118	32	8	0	3	49	20	14	15	0	30	1	0	2	9	3	.75	1	.271	.353	.415
	Springfield	A	39	152	38	11	0	1	52	19	12	10	0	36	0	0	0	3	3	.50	4	.250	.296	.342
1991	St. Pete	A	115	429	128	13	10	3	170	51	46	35	0	71	5	0	3	8	8	.50	17	.298	.356	.396
1992	Arkansas	AA	115	408	111	18	5	10	169	49	49	21	0	91	1	0	3	3	6	.33	16	.272	.307	.414
1993	Louisville	AAA	108	377	104	15	1	9	148	30	40	15	4	75	3	0	1	1	0	1.00	9	.276	.308	.393
1994	Louisville	AAA	102	321	77	18	2	17	150	34	54	23	2	80	2	0	2	3	4	.43	12	.240	.293	.467
1995	Louisville	AAA	84	273	68	15	1	9	112	29	34	18	0	76	1	0	0	0	0	.00	14	.249	.298	.410
	6 Min. YEARS		596	2078	558	98	19	52	850	232	249	137	6	459	13	0	11	27	24	.53	73	.269	.316	.409

Fletcher Thompson

Bats: Left **Throws:** Right **Pos:** 3B   **Ht:** 5'11" **Wt:** 180 **Born:** 9/14/68 **Age:** 27

					BATTING												BASERUNNING				PERCENTAGES		
Year	Team	Lg	G	AB	H	2B	3B	HR	TB	R	RBI	TBB	IBB	SO	HBP	SH	SF	SB	CS	SB%	GDP	Avg	OBP	SLG
1990	Auburn	A	59	199	56	8	3	0	70	35	21	37	3	45	6	5	2	19	9	.68	2	.281	.406	.352
1991	Burlington	A	116	428	116	15	3	5	152	85	33	104	0	116	5	5	2	34	16	.68	2	.271	.417	.355
1993	Jackson	AA	98	316	93	15	2	4	124	64	29	55	2	83	1	7	1	23	12	.66	6	.294	.399	.392
1994	Jackson	AA	121	388	102	14	2	4	132	69	31	58	2	106	10	4	0	28	13	.68	5	.263	.373	.340
1995	El Paso	AA	11	26	5	0	0	0	5	3	3	1	0	9	0	0	0	0	0	.00	1	.192	.222	.192
	Alexandria	IND	99	353	121	28	2	15	198	106	66	97	5	101	4	1	3	47	6	.89	4	.343	.486	.561
	5 Min. YEARS		504	1710	493	80	12	28	681	362	183	352	12	460	26	22	8	151	56	.73	20	.288	.416	.398

Jason Thompson

Bats: Left **Throws:** Left **Pos:** 1B   **Ht:** 6'4" **Wt:** 200 **Born:** 6/13/71 **Age:** 25

					BATTING												BASERUNNING				PERCENTAGES		
Year	Team	Lg	G	AB	H	2B	3B	HR	TB	R	RBI	TBB	IBB	SO	HBP	SH	SF	SB	CS	SB%	GDP	Avg	OBP	SLG
1993	Spokane	A	66	240	72	25	1	7	120	36	38	37	6	47	1	0	5	3	2	.60	3	.300	.389	.500
1994	Rancho Cuca	A	68	253	91	19	2	13	153	57	63	37	4	58	3	0	3	1	1	.50	5	.360	.443	.605
	Wichita	AA	63	215	56	17	2	8	101	35	46	28	2	77	3	1	0	0	1	.00	5	.260	.352	.470
1995	Memphis	AA	137	475	129	20	1	20	211	62	64	62	4	131	0	0	5	7	3	.70	7	.272	.352	.444
	3 Min. YEARS		334	1183	348	81	6	48	585	190	211	164	16	313	7	1	14	11	7	.61	20	.294	.379	.495

John Thompson

Pitches: Right **Bats:** Right **Pos:** P **Ht:** 6'2" **Wt:** 200 **Born:** 1/18/73 **Age:** 23

Year	Team	Lg	G	GS	CG	GF	IP	BFP	H	R	ER	HR	SH	SF	HB	TBB	IBB	SO	WP	Bk	W	L	Pct.	ShO	Sv	ERA
1992	Mariners	R	14	11	1	1	70.2	301	54	35	29	1	1	1	2	32	1	65	13	4	6	3	.667	1	0	3.69
1993	Bellingham	A	17	1	0	8	34	165	31	23	16	3	0	0	1	33	2	28	9	0	0	2	.000	0	0	4.24
1994	Bellingham	A	15	15	1	0	82	354	63	40	33	6	0	4	3	44	0	78	19	3	4	5	.444	0	0	3.62
1995	Wisconsin	A	38	7	0	29	69.2	314	65	41	32	8	2	2	2	43	2	69	13	1	2	8	.200	0	19	4.13
	Tacoma	AAA	1	0	0	0	2.2	12	3	2	0	0	1	0	0	0	0	0	0	0	0	1	.000	0	0	0.00
	4 Min. YEARS		85	34	2	38	259	1146	216	141	110	18	4	7	8	152	5	240	54	8	12	19	.387	1	19	3.82

Justin Thompson

Pitches: Left **Bats:** Left **Pos:** P **Ht:** 6'3" **Wt:** 175 **Born:** 3/8/73 **Age:** 23

Year	Team	Lg	G	GS	CG	GF	IP	BFP	H	R	ER	HR	SH	SF	HB	TBB	IBB	SO	WP	Bk	W	L	Pct.	ShO	Sv	ERA
1991	Bristol	R	10	10	0	0	50	217	45	29	20	4	0	1	2	24	1	60	7	1	2	5	.286	0	0	3.60
1992	Fayettevlle	A	20	19	0	1	95	390	79	32	23	6	0	4	1	40	0	88	7	3	4	4	.500	0	0	2.18
1993	Lakeland	A	11	11	0	0	55.2	241	65	25	22	1	3	0	1	16	0	46	3	1	4	4	.500	0	0	3.56
	London	AA	14	14	1	0	83.2	376	96	51	38	9	0	4	2	37	0	72	4	1	3	6	.333	0	0	4.09
1995	Lakeland	A	6	6	0	0	24	107	30	13	13	1	0	2	2	8	0	20	0	0	2	1	.667	0	0	4.88
	Jacksonville	AA	18	18	3	0	123	502	110	55	51	7	4	2	3	38	2	98	3	0	6	7	.462	0	0	3.73
	4 Min. YEARS		79	78	4	1	431.1	1833	425	205	167	28	7	13	11	163	3	384	24	11	21	27	.438	0	0	3.48

John Thomson

Pitches: Right **Bats:** Right **Pos:** P **Ht:** 6'3" **Wt:** 170 **Born:** 10/1/73 **Age:** 22

Year	Team	Lg	G	GS	CG	GF	IP	BFP	H	R	ER	HR	SH	SF	HB	TBB	IBB	SO	WP	Bk	W	L	Pct.	ShO	Sv	ERA
1993	Rockies	R	11	11	0	0	50.2	228	43	40	26	0	0	2	3	31	0	36	14	1	3	5	.375	0	0	4.62
1994	Asheville	A	19	15	1	1	88.1	361	70	34	28	3	2	1	5	33	1	79	1	0	6	6	.500	1	0	2.85
	Central Val	A	9	8	0	0	49.1	201	43	20	18	0	0	2	1	18	1	41	3	1	3	1	.750	0	0	3.28
1995	New Haven	AA	26	24	0	0	131.1	572	132	69	61	8	2	7	2	56	0	82	3	2	7	8	.467	0	0	4.18
	3 Min. YEARS		65	58	1	1	319.2	1362	288	163	133	11	4	12	11	138	2	238	21	4	19	20	.487	1	0	3.74

Paul Thoutsis

Bats: Left **Throws:** Right **Pos:** OF **Ht:** 6'1" **Wt:** 185 **Born:** 10/23/65 **Age:** 30

Year	Team	Lg	G	AB	H	2B	3B	HR	TB	R	RBI	TBB	IBB	SO	HBP	SH	SF	SB	CS	SB%	GDP	Avg	OBP	SLG
1984	Winston-Sal	A	90	299	67	9	2	2	86	32	26	32	3	55	4	2	2	1	1	.50	6	.224	.306	.288
1985	Winter Havn	A	75	209	48	6	0	1	57	18	18	18	1	44	3	1	0	0	3	.00	2	.230	.300	.273
1986	Greensboro	A	106	364	105	16	3	15	172	83	77	77	3	57	6	1	11	0	0	.00	4	.288	.410	.473
1987	Winter Havn	A	105	336	83	14	2	7	122	47	41	35	3	50	7	2	2	2	1	.67	6	.247	.329	.363
	New Britain	AA	1	4	0	0	0	0	0	0	0	0	0	0	0	0	0	0	0	.00	0	.000	.000	.000
1988	Springfield	A	28	92	25	3	0	0	28	5	12	8	2	10	0	0	2	0	0	.00	4	.272	.324	.304
	Arkansas	AA	7	9	3	0	0	0	3	0	2	0	0	0	0	0	1	0	0	.00	0	.333	.300	.333
	St. Pete	A	30	91	25	4	0	0	29	14	8	14	3	7	0	0	1	0	1	.00	1	.275	.368	.319
1989	St. Pete	A	74	243	70	10	3	2	92	21	21	22	2	17	5	0	3	0	1	.00	6	.288	.355	.379
1990	Arkansas	AA	101	266	75	14	5	5	114	25	37	12	2	37	1	0	3	0	2	.00	3	.282	.312	.429
1992	New Britain	AA	108	327	79	21	3	4	118	31	47	24	2	46	4	1	4	0	5	.00	4	.242	.298	.361
1993	New Britain	AA	64	213	62	12	2	0	78	17	21	27	1	24	0	1	2	0	2	.00	4	.291	.368	.366
	Pawtucket	AAA	60	216	69	10	1	4	93	30	27	24	1	28	2	1	0	1	1	.50	9	.319	.393	.431
1994	Pawtucket	AAA	94	304	68	10	1	10	110	28	40	37	4	56	1	2	6	3	0	1.00	4	.224	.305	.362
1995	Columbus	AAA	52	130	28	4	1	0	34	10	15	4	0	16	1	1	1	1	0	1.00	5	.215	.243	.262
	11 Min. YEARS		995	3103	807	133	23	50	1136	361	392	334	27	447	34	12	38	8	17	.32	63	.260	.335	.366

Jerrey Thurston

Bats: Right **Throws:** Right **Pos:** C **Ht:** 6'4" **Wt:** 200 **Born:** 4/17/72 **Age:** 24

Year	Team	Lg	G	AB	H	2B	3B	HR	TB	R	RBI	TBB	IBB	SO	HBP	SH	SF	SB	CS	SB%	GDP	Avg	OBP	SLG
1990	Padres	R	42	144	33	6	1	0	41	22	16	14	0	37	0	2	0	4	1	.80	1	.229	.297	.285
1991	Charlstn-Sc	A	42	137	14	2	0	0	16	5	4	9	0	50	0	1	1	1	1	.50	3	.102	.156	.117
	Spokane	A	60	201	43	9	0	1	55	26	20	20	1	61	2	2	2	2	2	.50	2	.214	.289	.274
1992	Waterloo	A	96	263	37	7	0	0	44	20	14	12	0	73	2	6	2	1	0	1.00	4	.141	.183	.167
1993	Wichita	AA	78	197	48	10	0	2	64	22	22	14	0	62	6	3	0	2	0	1.00	3	.244	.313	.325
1994	Wichita	AA	77	238	51	10	2	4	77	30	28	19	1	73	8	2	1	1	4	.20	8	.214	.293	.324
1995	Las Vegas	AAA	5	20	4	1	0	0	5	2	0	0	0	5	1	0	0	0	0	.00	0	.200	.238	.250
	Rancho Cuca	A	76	200	44	9	0	1	56	24	13	21	0	64	7	4	3	1	0	1.00	2	.220	.312	.280
	6 Min. YEARS		476	1400	274	54	3	8	358	151	117	109	2	425	26	20	9	12	8	.60	23	.196	.265	.256

Tony Tijerina

Bats: Both **Throws:** Right **Pos:** C **Ht:** 6'0" **Wt:** 185 **Born:** 12/19/69 **Age:** 26

Year	Team	Lg	G	AB	H	2B	3B	HR	TB	R	RBI	TBB	IBB	SO	HBP	SH	SF	SB	CS	SB%	GDP	Avg	OBP	SLG
1991	Pittsfield	A	44	144	35	5	1	0	42	16	17	15	0	13	4	1	2	1	1	.50	3	.243	.327	.292
1992	St. Lucie	A	32	81	18	2	0	0	20	7	6	5	0	14	2	0	0	0	0	.00	1	.222	.284	.247

Year	Team	Lg	G	AB	H	2B	3B	HR	TB	R	RBI	TBB	IBB	SO	HBP	SH	SF	SB	CS	SB%	GDP	Avg	OBP	SLG
1993	Capital Cty	A	53	175	54	9	3	0	69	15	21	14	0	25	0	2	3	3	5	.38	3	.309	.354	.394
1994	Binghamton	AA	27	88	23	5	1	1	33	10	12	2	0	23	0	1	0	0	0	.00	3	.261	.278	.375
1995	Norfolk	AAA	1	0	0	0	0	0	0	0	0	0	0	0	0	0	0	0	0	.00	0	.000	.000	.000
	Binghamton	AA	32	118	21	5	0	0	26	3	9	1	0	22	3	0	2	0	0	.00	2	.178	.202	.220
	5 Min. YEARS		189	606	151	26	5	1	190	51	65	37	0	97	9	4	7	4	6	.40	12	.249	.299	.314

Pat Tilmon

Pitches: Right **Bats:** Right **Pos:** P **Ht:** 6'0" **Wt:** 177 **Born:** 5/4/66 **Age:** 30

			HOW MUCH HE PITCHED						WHAT HE GAVE UP											THE RESULTS					
Year	Team	Lg	G	GS	CG	GF	IP	BFP	H	R	ER	HR	SH	SF	HB	TBB	IBB	SO	WP	Bk	W	L	Pct.	ShO	Sv	ERA
1987	Pulaski	R	15	10	1	3	80.2	319	55	20	14	1	0	1	3	22	1	101	5	0	8	1	.889	1	0	1.56
1988	Burlington	A	18	18	4	0	117.2	494	102	54	44	11	1	5	3	35	0	101	10	2	8	5	.615	0	0	3.37
	Durham	A	8	8	0	0	37	171	45	26	22	3	1	1	0	19	3	29	1	1	1	3	.250	0	0	5.35
1989	Durham	A	33	23	0	6	144.1	615	145	63	52	6	1	4	9	44	2	92	5	0	11	4	.733	0	4	3.24
1990	Durham	A	38	7	0	10	101.2	451	105	54	44	7	3	3	4	37	3	104	14	0	6	5	.545	0	1	3.90
1993	Thunder Bay	IND	13	13	2	0	78.2	337	69	34	25	2	2	2	1	34	0	62	3	1	5	4	.556	1	0	2.86
1994	Thunder Bay	IND	17	17	6	0	111.2	457	97	55	43	6	5	2	3	30	1	89	3	0	5	8	.385	1	0	3.47
1995	Thunder Bay	IND	13	13	1	0	85.1	358	87	39	31	9	3	0	1	18	1	85	2	0	4	4	.500	0	0	3.27
	Syracuse	AAA	4	0	0	0	6	28	8	3	1	0	0	0	0	4	0	2	0	0	0	0	.000	0	0	1.50
	7 Min. YEARS		159	109	14	19	763	3230	713	348	276	45	16	18	24	243	11	665	46	4	48	34	.585	3	5	3.26

Aris Tirado

Pitches: Right **Bats:** Right **Pos:** P **Ht:** 5'8" **Wt:** 160 **Born:** 3/31/63 **Age:** 33

			HOW MUCH HE PITCHED						WHAT HE GAVE UP											THE RESULTS					
Year	Team	Lg	G	GS	CG	GF	IP	BFP	H	R	ER	HR	SH	SF	HB	TBB	IBB	SO	WP	Bk	W	L	Pct.	ShO	Sv	ERA
1995	Harrisburg	AA	8	0	0	4	11.2	48	8	1	1	1	0	1	0	5	0	10	0	0	1	0	1.000	0	1	0.77

Ken Tirpack

Bats: Left **Throws:** Right **Pos:** 1B **Ht:** 6'0" **Wt:** 186 **Born:** 10/3/69 **Age:** 26

			BATTING															BASERUNNING				PERCENTAGES		
Year	Team	Lg	G	AB	H	2B	3B	HR	TB	R	RBI	TBB	IBB	SO	HBP	SH	SF	SB	CS	SB%	GDP	Avg	OBP	SLG
1992	Elizabethtn	R	61	228	76	13	2	9	120	42	42	31	2	36	5	0	5	1	2	.33	1	.333	.416	.526
1993	Fort Wayne	A	127	473	139	34	3	9	206	71	70	68	4	103	6	0	6	1	4	.20	10	.294	.385	.436
1994	Nashville	AA	37	127	28	7	0	1	38	14	13	11	1	19	2	0	0	0	1	.00	4	.220	.293	.299
	Fort Myers	A	68	234	63	15	1	4	92	24	29	23	0	43	0	0	6	3	1	.75	7	.269	.327	.393
1995	New Britain	AA	7	16	4	2	0	2	12	4	3	5	1	3	0	0	0	1	0	1.00	1	.250	.429	.750
	4 Min. YEARS		300	1078	310	71	6	25	468	155	157	138	8	204	13	0	17	6	8	.43	25	.288	.370	.434

Dave Tokheim

Bats: Left **Throws:** Left **Pos:** OF **Ht:** 6'1" **Wt:** 185 **Born:** 5/25/69 **Age:** 27

			BATTING															BASERUNNING				PERCENTAGES		
Year	Team	Lg	G	AB	H	2B	3B	HR	TB	R	RBI	TBB	IBB	SO	HBP	SH	SF	SB	CS	SB%	GDP	Avg	OBP	SLG
1991	Batavia	A	40	158	51	12	3	2	75	28	21	9	0	20	1	2	1	6	2	.75	1	.323	.361	.475
1992	Clearwater	A	106	396	93	12	6	4	129	40	41	30	4	40	5	2	2	10	12	.45	6	.235	.296	.326
1993	Clearwater	A	41	155	51	8	2	0	63	27	11	14	4	17	2	1	1	7	5	.58	1	.329	.390	.406
	Reading	AA	65	257	75	11	6	2	104	30	25	12	0	36	0	3	0	8	6	.57	3	.292	.323	.405
1994	Reading	AA	126	438	132	17	6	13	200	56	47	27	2	70	4	1	3	12	10	.55	10	.301	.345	.457
1995	Scranton-Wb	AAA	127	450	122	18	8	11	189	64	66	18	2	55	5	3	7	6	7	.46	11	.271	.302	.420
	5 Min. YEARS		505	1854	524	78	31	32	760	245	211	110	12	238	17	12	14	49	42	.54	32	.283	.326	.410

Kevin Tolar

Pitches: Left **Bats:** Right **Pos:** P **Ht:** 6'3" **Wt:** 225 **Born:** 1/28/71 **Age:** 25

			HOW MUCH HE PITCHED						WHAT HE GAVE UP											THE RESULTS					
Year	Team	Lg	G	GS	CG	GF	IP	BFP	H	R	ER	HR	SH	SF	HB	TBB	IBB	SO	WP	Bk	W	L	Pct.	ShO	Sv	ERA
1989	White Sox	R	13	12	1	0	60	256	29	16	11	0	1	1	1	54	0	58	10	0	6	2	.750	0	0	1.65
1990	Utica	A	15	15	1	0	90.1	407	80	44	33	2	1	3	4	61	1	69	9	1	4	6	.400	0	0	3.29
1991	South Bend	A	30	19	0	6	114.2	510	87	54	35	3	5	5	8	85	0	87	6	0	8	5	.615	0	1	2.75
1992	Salinas	A	14	8	3	3	53.1	255	55	43	36	4	1	7	5	46	0	24	6	0	1	8	.111	0	0	6.08
	South Bend	A	18	10	0	6	81.1	339	59	34	26	5	7	4	2	41	0	81	5	1	6	5	.545	0	2	2.88
1993	Sarasota	A	23	11	0	8	77.1	358	75	55	46	1	5	7	6	51	1	60	8	0	2	6	.250	0	1	5.35
1995	Lynchburg	A	18	0	0	4	19.1	77	13	7	6	1	0	1	1	6	0	19	3	0	2	0	1.000	0	0	2.79
	Carolina	AA	12	0	0	3	12.1	59	16	5	5	0	0	2	0	7	0	9	2	0	1	0	1.000	0	0	3.65
	6 Min. YEARS		143	75	5	30	508.2	2261	414	258	198	16	20	30	27	351	2	407	49	2	30	32	.484	0	2	3.50

Paul Torres

Bats: Right **Throws:** Right **Pos:** 1B **Ht:** 6'3" **Wt:** 210 **Born:** 10/19/70 **Age:** 25

			BATTING															BASERUNNING				PERCENTAGES		
Year	Team	Lg	G	AB	H	2B	3B	HR	TB	R	RBI	TBB	IBB	SO	HBP	SH	SF	SB	CS	SB%	GDP	Avg	OBP	SLG
1989	Wytheville	R	54	191	45	9	1	7	77	34	38	32	0	55	6	0	2	2	4	.33	3	.236	.359	.403
1990	Peoria	A	36	123	30	4	1	5	51	18	18	13	0	33	2	1	0	1	1	.50	2	.244	.326	.415
	Geneva	A	77	271	72	23	1	10	127	46	45	39	1	72	10	2	5	9	3	.75	3	.266	.372	.469
1991	Winston-Sal	A	27	87	10	1	0	2	17	9	7	11	0	30	2	0	1	4	0	1.00	3	.115	.228	.195
	Peoria	A	99	352	75	24	2	13	142	60	50	48	2	91	9	3	0	6	2	.75	7	.213	.323	.403
1992	Winston-Sal	A	134	458	109	15	6	14	178	55	78	60	2	114	5	2	7	4	4	.50	10	.238	.328	.389

Year	Team	Lg	G	AB	H	2B	3B	HR	TB	R	RBI	TBB	IBB	SO	HBP	SH	SF	SB	CS	SB%	GDP	Avg	OBP	SLG
1993	Daytona	A	100	353	98	17	5	13	164	63	43	52	0	94	8	1	3	5	4	.56	5	.278	.380	.465
	Orlando	AA	19	55	14	4	0	3	27	10	10	7	0	18	0	0	0	3	0	1.00	1	.255	.339	.491
1994	Orlando	AA	61	160	38	2	1	10	72	21	26	31	1	41	2	1	2	2	6	.25	5	.238	.364	.450
	Daytona	A	26	90	28	6	3	4	52	12	20	11	2	26	0	0	1	4	1	.80	1	.311	.382	.578
1995	Orlando	A	63	228	68	14	1	10	114	38	45	29	4	40	1	0	2	0	3	.00	1	.298	.377	.500
	Arkansas	AA	66	231	52	11	0	10	93	24	33	21	0	56	5	1	0	2	1	.67	9	.225	.304	.403
	7 Min. YEARS		762	2599	639	130	21	101	1114	390	413	354	12	670	50	11	23	42	29	.59	50	.246	.345	.429

Ricky Torres

Pitches: Right **Bats:** Right **Pos:** P **Ht:** 6'2" **Wt:** 210 **Born:** 12/31/63 **Age:** 32

			HOW MUCH HE PITCHED						WHAT HE GAVE UP										THE RESULTS					
Year	Team	Lg	G	GS	CG	GF	IP	BFP	H	R	ER	HR	SH	SF	HB	TBB	IBB	SO	WP	Bk	W	L	Pct.	ShO	Sv	ERA
1984	Greensboro	A	20	19	3	1	117	504	97	59	48	11	4	2	2	49	0	110	9	2	8	4	.667	0	0	3.69
1985	Ft. Laud	A	17	17	1	0	92.1	408	103	56	48	7	3	1	1	36	0	107	7	0	6	6	.500	1	0	4.68
	Albany-Colo	AA	1	1	0	0	4	20	5	5	4	0	0	0	0	2	0	4	0	0	0	1	.000	0	0	9.00
	Oneonta	A	3	3	0	0	16	73	17	10	8	2	0	0	0	10	0	13	1	0	1	2	.333	0	0	4.50
1986	Yankees	R	2	2	1	0	17	64	7	2	2	0	0	0	1	5	0	12	0	0	2	0	1.000	1	0	1.06
	Ft. Laud	A	11	8	2	2	60	259	52	31	29	2	1	3	2	27	3	50	3	1	2	2	.500	1	1	4.35
1987	Pr. William	A	17	1	0	10	40.1	175	34	15	13	2	0	2	1	19	1	49	6	1	3	1	.750	0	4	2.90
	Albany-Colo	AA	34	0	0	16	64.2	280	60	29	24	2	1	0	1	22	4	71	9	0	8	3	.727	0	0	3.34
1988	Pr. William	A	19	0	0	19	28	110	17	4	1	2	0	1	0	10	0	32	4	0	2	0	1.000	0	8	0.32
	Albany-Colo	AA	19	0	0	11	61.1	255	53	27	24	1	3	4	1	23	0	46	3	5	2	2	.500	0	1	3.52
1989	Albany-Colo	AA	24	11	3	9	91.1	381	79	35	27	3	1	2	2	37	2	79	6	2	6	4	.600	2	1	2.66
1990	Albany-Colo	AA	9	3	0	3	26.2	115	20	12	7	1	0	2	1	17	1	16	0	0	2	2	.333	0	1	2.36
	Columbus	AAA	21	3	0	12	42.1	183	37	24	21	5	0	0	0	21	0	34	3	0	0	2	.000	0	1	4.46
1995	Ottawa	AAA	32	11	1	4	91.2	391	90	58	51	9	3	4	6	26	1	58	5	0	3	8	.273	0	0	5.01
	8 Min. YEARS		229	79	11	87	752.2	3218	671	367	307	47	16	21	18	304	12	681	56	11	44	37	.543	5	16	3.67

Tony Torres

Bats: Right **Throws:** Right **Pos:** 3B **Ht:** 5'9" **Wt:** 165 **Born:** 6/1/70 **Age:** 26

			BATTING													BASERUNNING				PERCENTAGES		
Year	Team	Lg	G	AB	H	2B	3B	HR	TB	R	RBI	TBB	IBB	SO	HBP	SH	SF	SB	CS	SB%	GDP	Avg	OBP	SLG
1992	Erie	A	40	157	46	9	1	0	57	31	16	20	0	26	4	0	2	13	5	.72	1	.293	.383	.363
1993	High Desert	A	89	287	66	9	3	1	84	45	25	24	0	69	2	5	3	14	8	.64	7	.230	.291	.293
1994	Brevard Cty	A	98	368	93	14	7	4	133	58	39	39	1	67	2	3	3	17	6	.74	6	.253	.325	.361
1995	Portland	AA	58	81	24	3	2	0	31	15	4	11	0	23	1	8	0	9	0	1.00	1	.296	.387	.383
	4 Min. YEARS		285	893	229	35	13	5	305	149	84	94	1	185	9	16	8	53	19	.74	15	.256	.331	.342

Dave Toth

Bats: Right **Throws:** Right **Pos:** C **Ht:** 6'1" **Wt:** 195 **Born:** 12/8/69 **Age:** 26

			BATTING													BASERUNNING				PERCENTAGES		
Year	Team	Lg	G	AB	H	2B	3B	HR	TB	R	RBI	TBB	IBB	SO	HBP	SH	SF	SB	CS	SB%	GDP	Avg	OBP	SLG
1990	Pulaski	R	26	82	22	0	0	0	22	9	10	11	0	12	1	1	2	2	0	1.00	1	.268	.354	.268
1991	Idaho Falls	R	47	160	34	3	0	4	49	27	22	18	1	21	4	1	2	1	0	1.00	6	.213	.304	.306
1992	Macon	A	87	310	80	15	2	3	108	32	41	21	0	44	4	0	2	3	3	.50	6	.258	.312	.348
1993	Macon	A	104	353	87	22	0	4	121	38	40	28	1	53	7	5	3	6	5	.55	11	.246	.312	.343
1994	Durham	A	72	165	40	11	0	2	57	23	20	19	0	28	1	1	1	1	0	1.00	4	.242	.323	.345
1995	Richmond	AAA	7	13	3	0	0	0	3	1	1	1	0	2	0	0	0	0	1	.00	1	.231	.286	.231
	Durham	A	85	257	63	6	0	6	87	20	26	25	1	42	6	0	1	3	3	.50	6	.245	.325	.339
	6 Min. YEARS		428	1340	329	57	2	19	447	150	160	123	3	202	23	8	11	16	12	.57	34	.246	.317	.334

Robert Toth

Pitches: Right **Bats:** Right **Pos:** P **Ht:** 6'2" **Wt:** 180 **Born:** 7/30/72 **Age:** 23

			HOW MUCH HE PITCHED						WHAT HE GAVE UP										THE RESULTS					
Year	Team	Lg	G	GS	CG	GF	IP	BFP	H	R	ER	HR	SH	SF	HB	TBB	IBB	SO	WP	Bk	W	L	Pct.	ShO	Sv	ERA
1990	Royals	R	7	7	0	0	38	148	34	8	7	1	0	0	2	4	0	22	3	0	2	2	.500	0	0	1.66
1991	Baseball Cy	A	13	10	0	0	63.2	263	53	24	20	1	5	1	2	23	2	42	0	0	2	3	.400	0	0	2.83
1992	Appleton	A	23	22	2	1	127.1	515	111	58	48	9	6	5	5	34	0	100	3	0	7	6	.538	0	0	3.39
1993	Wilmington	A	25	24	0	1	151.2	620	129	57	49	13	5	2	3	40	1	129	7	1	8	7	.533	0	0	2.91
1994	Wilmington	A	11	7	3	1	59.1	234	52	14	12	3	2	0	2	9	0	36	0	0	6	1	.857	2	0	1.82
	Memphis	AA	20	12	0	4	88.2	372	89	46	41	13	3	1	7	24	0	61	14	0	5	8	.385	0	1	4.16
1995	Wichita	AA	21	9	1	2	103.2	427	95	30	25	6	3	3	4	27	1	77	6	1	8	4	.667	0	0	2.17
	Omaha	AAA	8	8	1	0	47.1	205	53	25	19	7	3	2	2	8	0	31	0	0	1	2	.333	0	0	3.61
	6 Min. YEARS		128	99	7	9	679.2	2773	616	262	221	53	27	14	27	169	4	498	33	2	39	33	.542	2	1	2.93

Edgar Tovar

Bats: Right **Throws:** Right **Pos:** SS **Ht:** 6'1" **Wt:** 170 **Born:** 11/28/73 **Age:** 22

			BATTING													BASERUNNING				PERCENTAGES		
Year	Team	Lg	G	AB	H	2B	3B	HR	TB	R	RBI	TBB	IBB	SO	HBP	SH	SF	SB	CS	SB%	GDP	Avg	OBP	SLG
1992	Indianapolis	AAA	1	4	0	0	0	0	0	0	0	0	0	1	0	0	0	0	0	.00	0	.000	.000	.000
	Jamestown	A	72	281	75	7	1	4	96	38	31	10	0	14	3	2	0	13	9	.59	5	.267	.299	.342
1993	Harrisburg	AA	12	42	11	0	0	0	11	5	3	1	0	4	0	1	0	1	0	1.00	0	.262	.279	.262
	W. Palm Bch	A	116	467	107	21	2	2	138	52	32	16	2	33	3	11	2	4	5	.44	8	.229	.258	.296
1994	San Bernrdo	A	82	340	108	16	1	10	156	58	40	24	0	29	6	4	0	13	6	.68	3	.318	.373	.459
	W. Palm Bch	A	30	123	40	9	1	3	60	15	23	5	1	13	1	1	0	4	0	1.00	2	.325	.357	.488

Year Team	Lg	G	AB	H	2B	3B	HR	TB	R	RBI	TBB	IBB	SO	HBP	SH	SF	SB	CS	SB%	GDP	Avg	OBP	SLG
1995 Harrisburg	AA	81	247	50	7	2	3	70	28	21	16	2	24	4	9	1	1	3	.25	5	.202	.261	.283
4 Min. YEARS		394	1504	391	60	7	22	531	196	150	72	5	118	17	28	3	35	24	.59	23	.260	.301	.353

Bats: Right **Throws:** Right **Pos:** OF

Raul Tovar

Ht: 6'1" **Wt:** 183 **Born:** 11/14/58 **Age:** 37

							BATTING											BASERUNNING				PERCENTAGES		
Year Team	Lg	G	AB	H	2B	3B	HR	TB	R	RBI	TBB	IBB	SO	HBP	SH	SF	SB	CS	SB%	GDP	Avg	OBP	SLG
1995 Ottawa	AAA	20	56	17	2	0	0	19	8	7	8	0	5	0	0	0	0	0	.00	3	.304	.391	.339
Minnesota	IND	16	64	24	5	0	0	29	17	11	9	0	4	2	0	1	2	1	.67	4	.375	.461	.453
Minnesota	IND	16	64	24	5	0	0	29	17	11	9	0	4	2	0	1	2	1	.67	4	.375	.461	.453
Corp.Chrsti	IND	26	93	32	5	0	3	46	15	17	10	0	10	2	2	3	1	2	.33	2	.344	.407	.495
1 Min. YEARS		78	277	97	17	0	3	123	57	46	36	0	23	6	2	5	5	4	.56	13	.350	.429	.444

Bats: Right **Throws:** Right **Pos:** C

Jason Townley

Ht: 6'2" **Wt:** 220 **Born:** 6/18/69 **Age:** 27

							BATTING											BASERUNNING				PERCENTAGES		
Year Team	Lg	G	AB	H	2B	3B	HR	TB	R	RBI	TBB	IBB	SO	HBP	SH	SF	SB	CS	SB%	GDP	Avg	OBP	SLG
1987 St. Cathrns	A	60	177	31	4	1	6	55	21	17	27	0	47	2	0	3	1	1	.50	2	.175	.287	.311
1988 Dunedin	A	2	7	2	0	0	0	2	0	1	0	0	1	0	0	0	0	0	.00	1	.286	.286	.286
Myrtle Bch	A	5	15	6	2	0	1	11	4	3	1	0	4	0	0	0	0	0	.00	0	.400	.438	.733
St. Cathrns	A	64	225	49	4	0	5	68	19	18	30	1	65	1	1	1	2	4	.33	8	.218	.311	.302
1989 Dunedin	A	51	155	33	8	0	1	44	16	12	20	0	42	1	2	0	0	0	.00	5	.213	.307	.284
1990 Dunedin	A	119	397	116	22	1	11	173	58	63	41	0	82	3	5	3	1	2	.33	10	.292	.360	.436
1991 Knoxville	AA	81	213	42	8	0	0	50	12	13	31	0	56	1	10	1	0	4	.00	2	.197	.301	.235
1992 Knoxville	AA	56	185	43	11	0	2	60	7	20	14	0	48	1	4	0	1	1	.50	1	.232	.290	.324
1993 Dunedin	A	2	4	2	0	0	0	2	1	1	1	0	0	0	0	0	0	0	.00	0	.500	.600	.500
1994 Syracuse	AAA	78	187	51	6	0	3	66	25	27	24	3	54	0	2	1	2	0	1.00	8	.273	.354	.353
1995 Syracuse	AAA	96	264	69	11	0	8	104	25	30	38	0	71	0	3	8	0	0	.00	6	.261	.345	.394
9 Min. YEARS		614	1829	444	76	2	37	635	188	205	227	4	470	9	27	17	7	15	.32	43	.243	.327	.347

Bats: Left **Throws:** Left **Pos:** 1B

Chad Townsend

Ht: 6'5" **Wt:** 222 **Born:** 7/4/71 **Age:** 24

							BATTING											BASERUNNING				PERCENTAGES		
Year Team	Lg	G	AB	H	2B	3B	HR	TB	R	RBI	TBB	IBB	SO	HBP	SH	SF	SB	CS	SB%	GDP	Avg	OBP	SLG
1992 Burlington	R	44	133	36	8	0	7	65	19	26	15	1	31	2	3	1	0	0	.00	3	.271	.351	.489
1993 Columbus	A	104	314	74	15	3	10	125	43	40	23	1	84	2	1	3	1	0	1.00	4	.236	.289	.398
1994 High Desert	A	64	247	73	12	3	9	118	39	46	19	1	43	3	0	2	1	2	.33	6	.296	.351	.478
Kinston	A	64	229	52	6	0	10	88	29	43	27	3	49	5	0	1	2	1	.67	1	.227	.321	.384
1995 Canton-Akrn	AA	116	404	106	22	1	9	157	39	50	31	4	90	8	1	3	3	2	.60	6	.262	.325	.389
4 Min. YEARS		392	1327	341	63	7	45	553	169	205	115	10	297	20	5	10	7	5	.58	20	.257	.323	.417

Bats: Right **Throws:** Right **Pos:** DH

Todd Trafton

Ht: 6'2" **Wt:** 210 **Born:** 3/16/64 **Age:** 32

							BATTING											BASERUNNING				PERCENTAGES		
Year Team	Lg	G	AB	H	2B	3B	HR	TB	R	RBI	TBB	IBB	SO	HBP	SH	SF	SB	CS	SB%	GDP	Avg	OBP	SLG
1986 Peninsula	A	63	217	63	12	2	4	91	37	37	32	3	31	2	1	4	3	0	1.00	7	.290	.380	.419
1987 Daytona Bch	A	127	449	118	23	2	15	190	64	61	54	1	44	3	2	8	7	5	.58	10	.263	.340	.423
1988 Birmingham	AA	77	273	58	11	0	8	93	35	27	16	1	50	4	3	4	6	1	.86	4	.212	.263	.341
Tampa	A	47	154	40	9	2	5	68	22	24	17	0	29	3	1	2	0	0	.00	4	.260	.341	.442
1989 Birmingham	AA	107	351	91	17	3	12	150	57	56	38	4	82	8	4	3	10	4	.71	7	.259	.343	.427
1990 Vancouver	AAA	42	117	22	2	0	2	30	10	15	18	0	27	1	0	3	4	1	.80	2	.188	.295	.256
Birmingham	AA	35	116	30	5	1	5	52	21	25	18	0	28	1	0	3	0	3	.00	1	.259	.350	.448
1991 Chattanooga	AA	63	231	60	18	0	6	96	30	34	23	2	46	6	2	2	2	6	.25	6	.260	.340	.416
Nashville	AAA	75	263	75	16	1	9	120	37	41	28	0	46	3	2	3	1	0	1.00	6	.285	.357	.456
1992 Nashville	AAA	44	131	33	7	1	5	57	25	21	22	0	24	1	0	3	4	0	1.00	6	.252	.357	.435
Chattanooga	AA	67	242	68	18	2	9	117	34	38	28	2	47	3	0	0	1	1	.50	5	.281	.363	.483
1993 Tucson	AAA	8	20	5	1	1	0	8	3	2	2	0	4	1	0	0	0	1	.00	1	.250	.348	.400
1995 Indianapols	AAA	5	5	0	0	0	0	0	0	0	0	0	2	0	0	0	0	0	.00	0	.000	.000	.000
9 Min. YEARS		760	2569	663	139	15	80	1072	375	381	296	13	460	35	20	35	38	22	.63	53	.258	.339	.417

Pitches: Left **Bats:** Left **Pos:** P

Mark Tranbarger

Ht: 6'2" **Wt:** 205 **Born:** 9/17/69 **Age:** 26

			HOW MUCH HE PITCHED				WHAT HE GAVE UP											THE RESULTS					
Year Team	Lg	G	GS	CG	GF	IP	BFP	H	R	ER	HR	SH	SF	HB	TBB	IBB	SO	WP	Bk	W	L	Pct.	ShO	Sv	ERA
1991 Johnson Cty	R	4	0	0	0	8	37	11	7	2	0	0	0	2	0	0	6	1	1	1	0	1.000	0	0	2.25
Cardinals	R	23	0	0	4	29.1	115	22	5	4	0	1	2	0	4	0	37	3	1	3	0	1.000	0	1	1.23
1992 Springfield	A	42	0	0	17	49.2	220	47	27	20	4	1	3	3	24	0	38	2	1	1	0	1.000	0	2	3.62
1993 Savannah	A	56	1	0	11	66	276	56	25	23	3	3	2	3	29	0	50	2	0	5	2	.714	0	1	3.14
1994 Chattanooga	AA	12	0	0	6	10	46	12	6	6	0	0	1	1	4	0	9	1	0	0	1	.000	0	1	5.40
Winston-Sal	A	37	1	0	24	39.2	174	36	18	15	3	1	0	3	19	3	31	3	0	4	3	.571	0	12	3.40
1995 Chattanooga	AA	48	0	0	12	55.1	236	50	15	12	4	2	4	2	20	1	46	2	0	3	1	.750	0	0	1.95
5 Min. YEARS		222	2	0	74	258	1104	234	103	82	14	8	12	14	100	4	217	14	3	17	7	.708	0	16	2.86

Mark Tranberg

Pitches: Right **Bats:** Right **Pos:** P   **Ht:** 6'4" **Wt:** 210 **Born:** 2/28/69 **Age:** 27

			HOW MUCH HE PITCHED					WHAT HE GAVE UP									THE RESULTS					
Year	Team	Lg	G	GS	CG	GF	IP	BFP	H	R	ER	HR	SH	SF	HB	TBB	IBB	SO	WP	Bk	W	L	Pct.	ShO	Sv	ERA
1992	Batavia	A	11	0	0	4	20	103	23	20	18	5	0	0	2	15	1	25	4	1	0	2	.000	0	0	8.10
1993	Spartanburg	A	11	11	4	0	81.2	318	54	24	18	5	0	2	1	21	0	83	3	0	8	1	.889	1	0	1.98
	Clearwater	A	14	13	2	0	75.2	316	78	26	21	1	2	1	3	18	0	59	2	0	7	3	.700	0	0	2.50
1994	Clearwater	A	9	8	4	0	63.1	221	33	6	1	0	3	1	1	11	1	41	3	0	7	1	.875	3	0	0.14
	Reading	AA	24	15	0	3	94	441	122	76	63	15	3	4	5	37	1	60	4	2	3	12	.200	0	0	6.03
1995	Reading	AA	18	18	3	0	111	458	110	50	46	7	3	3	3	30	0	62	5	0	6	6	.500	3	0	3.73
	Scranton-Wb	AAA	11	2	0	3	23.2	107	32	19	19	3	2	1	2	6	0	15	4	0	1	4	.200	0	0	7.23
	4 Min. YEARS		98	67	13	10	469.1	1964	452	221	186	36	13	12	17	138	3	345	25	3	32	29	.525	7	0	3.57

Brian Traxler

Bats: Left **Throws:** Left **Pos:** 1B   **Ht:** 5'10" **Wt:** 203 **Born:** 9/26/67 **Age:** 28

			BATTING												BASERUNNING				PERCENTAGES		
Year	Team	Lg	G	AB	H	2B	3B	HR	TB	R	RBI	TBB	IBB	SO	HBP	SH	SF	SB	CS	SB%	GDP	Avg	OBP	SLG
1988	Vero Beach	A	72	260	76	14	0	2	96	30	34	30	0	35	0	0	1	1	1	.50	6	.292	.364	.369
1989	San Antonio	AA	63	228	79	7	0	9	113	37	44	22	1	20	0	3	4	1	0	1.00	4	.346	.398	.496
	Albuquerque	AAA	64	239	72	10	3	3	97	33	30	17	2	17	1	0	3	0	2	.00	4	.301	.346	.406
1990	Albuquerque	AAA	98	318	88	23	0	7	132	43	53	39	1	39	0	2	7	4	0	1.00	7	.277	.349	.415
1991	San Antonio	AA	103	379	97	24	0	7	142	50	61	53	8	44	3	0	5	1	2	.33	7	.256	.348	.375
	Albuquerque	AAA	18	28	10	3	1	1	18	3	8	3	0	5	0	0	0	0	0	.00	1	.357	.419	.643
1992	Albuquerque	AAA	127	393	119	26	4	11	186	58	58	36	9	34	1	1	5	1	1	.50	16	.303	.359	.473
1993	Albuquerque	AAA	127	441	147	36	3	16	237	81	83	46	14	38	2	0	3	0	2	.00	12	.333	.396	.537
1995	Albuquerque	AAA	110	353	100	24	1	11	159	46	50	24	3	27	0	1	0	1	3	.25	11	.283	.329	.450
1990	Los Angeles	NL	9	11	1	1	0	0	2	0	0	0	0	4	0	0	0	0	0	.00	0	.091	.091	.182
	7 Min. YEARS		782	2639	788	167	12	67	1180	381	421	270	38	259	7	7	28	9	11	.45	68	.299	.362	.447

Jody Treadwell

Pitches: Right **Bats:** Right **Pos:** P   **Ht:** 6'0" **Wt:** 190 **Born:** 12/14/68 **Age:** 27

			HOW MUCH HE PITCHED					WHAT HE GAVE UP									THE RESULTS					
Year	Team	Lg	G	GS	CG	GF	IP	BFP	H	R	ER	HR	SH	SF	HB	TBB	IBB	SO	WP	Bk	W	L	Pct.	ShO	Sv	ERA
1990	Vero Beach	A	16	8	2	5	80.1	316	59	17	16	2	3	1	1	22	6	80	2	3	9	1	.900	1	1	1.79
1991	San Antonio	AA	10	10	1	0	61	271	73	41	32	7	2	1	4	22	1	43	0	2	3	3	.500	0	0	4.72
	Bakersfield	A	17	14	0	0	91.1	392	92	46	38	8	2	0	4	34	2	84	7	1	5	4	.556	0	0	3.74
1992	San Antonio	AA	29	4	2	4	76	331	74	40	35	3	2	3	4	40	4	68	6	2	3	5	.375	1	1	4.14
1993	Albuquerque	AAA	39	10	0	6	105.1	481	119	58	55	7	3	2	7	52	7	102	11	2	5	4	.556	0	0	4.70
1994	Albuquerque	AAA	33	24	0	4	158.2	676	151	78	75	11	5	2	10	59	3	114	7	1	10	6	.625	0	2	4.25
1995	Albuquerque	AAA	30	15	1	4	125	510	121	61	55	15	2	5	2	32	4	79	9	1	7	5	.583	1	1	3.96
	6 Min. YEARS		174	85	6	23	697.2	2977	689	341	306	53	19	14	32	261	27	570	42	12	42	28	.600	3	5	3.95

Chad Tredaway

Bats: Both **Throws:** Right **Pos:** 3B   **Ht:** 6'0" **Wt:** 180 **Born:** 6/18/72 **Age:** 24

			BATTING												BASERUNNING				PERCENTAGES		
Year	Team	Lg	G	AB	H	2B	3B	HR	TB	R	RBI	TBB	IBB	SO	HBP	SH	SF	SB	CS	SB%	GDP	Avg	OBP	SLG
1992	Geneva	A	73	270	81	19	2	5	119	39	31	24	1	24	3	3	5	6	4	.60	3	.300	.358	.441
1993	Daytona	A	66	242	62	12	0	0	74	32	21	27	2	25	0	3	4	4	3	.57	1	.256	.326	.306
1994	Orlando	AA	45	146	28	3	0	1	34	13	15	10	0	20	1	1	3	2	0	1.00	3	.192	.244	.233
	Daytona	A	77	284	69	14	3	5	104	26	28	23	0	39	1	4	1	1	5	.17	6	.243	.301	.366
1995	Memphis	AA	10	30	8	1	0	0	9	5	4	3	1	5	0	0	0	1	0	1.00	0	.267	.333	.300
	Rancho Cuca	A	109	408	113	17	2	6	152	53	57	29	3	43	3	1	8	4	2	.67	10	.277	.324	.373
	4 Min. YEARS		380	1380	361	66	7	17	492	168	156	116	7	156	8	12	21	18	14	.56	23	.262	.318	.357

Mike Triessl

Bats: Right **Throws:** Right **Pos:** C   **Ht:** 6'1" **Wt:** 215 **Born:** 2/27/71 **Age:** 25

			BATTING												BASERUNNING				PERCENTAGES		
Year	Team	Lg	G	AB	H	2B	3B	HR	TB	R	RBI	TBB	IBB	SO	HBP	SH	SF	SB	CS	SB%	GDP	Avg	OBP	SLG
1993	Riverside	A	3	3	1	0	0	0	1	1	0	0	0	0	0	0	0	0	0	.00	0	.333	.333	.333
	Appleton	A	34	81	15	5	0	1	23	9	8	14	0	32	2	3	1	0	0	.00	0	.185	.316	.284
1994	Calgary	AAA	5	11	3	1	0	0	4	1	0	0	0	3	0	1	0	0	0	.00	0	.273	.273	.364
	Riverside	A	54	129	30	4	2	4	50	20	19	12	0	38	1	0	0	1	0	1.00	6	.233	.303	.388
1995	Riverside	A	22	74	27	2	0	3	38	15	14	12	1	15	1	0	1	0	0	.00	1	.365	.455	.514
	Memphis	AA	4	6	1	0	0	0	1	0	0	0	0	0	0	0	0	0	0	.00	0	.167	.167	.167
	Rancho Cuca	A	49	138	35	8	0	0	43	13	20	5	0	32	4	1	1	1	0	1.00	5	.254	.297	.312
	3 Min. YEARS		171	442	112	20	2	8	160	59	61	43	1	120	8	5	3	2	0	1.00	12	.253	.329	.362

Hector Trinidad

Pitches: Right **Bats:** Right **Pos:** P   **Ht:** 6'2" **Wt:** 190 **Born:** 9/8/73 **Age:** 22

			HOW MUCH HE PITCHED					WHAT HE GAVE UP									THE RESULTS					
Year	Team	Lg	G	GS	CG	GF	IP	BFP	H	R	ER	HR	SH	SF	HB	TBB	IBB	SO	WP	Bk	W	L	Pct.	ShO	Sv	ERA
1991	Huntington	R	12	10	2	1	69	286	64	28	22	4	0	1	3	11	0	61	0	0	6	3	.667	0	0	2.87
1992	Geneva	A	15	15	2	0	93.2	377	78	33	25	6	5	0	4	13	2	70	1	0	8	6	.571	0	0	2.40
1993	Peoria	A	22	22	4	0	153	622	142	56	42	6	5	7	4	29	1	118	7	1	7	6	.538	0	0	2.47

	Lg	G	GS	CG	GF	IP	BFP	H	R	ER	HR	SH	SF	HB	TBB	IBB	SO	WP	Bk	W	L	Pct.	ShO	Sv	ERA
Orlando	AA	4	4	1	0	24.2	108	34	19	18	5	1	0	1	7	0	13	2	0	1	3	.250	0	0	6.57
1994 Daytona	A	28	27	4	1	175.2	726	171	72	63	8	7	3	7	40	0	142	3	1	11	9	.550	1	0	3.23
1995 New Britain	AA	23	22	0	1	121	516	137	67	62	6	1	10	7	22	0	92	6	2	4	11	.267	0	0	4.61
5 Min. YEARS		104	100	13	3	637	2635	626	275	232	35	19	21	26	122	3	496	22	4	37	38	.493	1	0	3.28

John Trisler

Pitches: Right **Bats:** Right **Pos:** P **Ht:** 6'4" **Wt:** 235 **Born:** 3/19/70 **Age:** 26

		HOW MUCH HE PITCHED						WHAT HE GAVE UP												THE RESULTS					
Year Team	Lg	G	GS	CG	GF	IP	BFP	H	R	ER	HR	SH	SF	HB	TBB	IBB	SO	WP	Bk	W	L	Pct.	ShO	Sv	ERA
1991 Brewers	R	8	0	0	6	14.1	62	10	5	2	0	0	0	1	11	2	10	1	2	1	1	.500	0	1	1.26
1992 Beloit	A	26	8	1	5	91.1	391	77	41	36	4	3	4	6	40	2	67	7	4	7	1	.875	0	0	3.55
1993 Clearwater	A	27	22	0	1	117	532	138	74	61	6	5	3	4	49	0	71	6	2	10	6	.625	0	0	4.69
1994 Clearwater	A	27	22	4	1	156.2	641	148	68	57	12	7	8	8	36	0	72	4	2	8	10	.444	2	0	3.27
1995 Reading	AA	30	10	0	10	82	366	96	51	47	6	1	3	6	26	1	50	2	2	2	4	.333	0	0	5.16
5 Min. YEARS		118	62	5	23	461.1	1992	469	239	203	28	16	18	25	162	5	270	20	12	28	22	.560	2	1	3.96

Ricky Trlicek

Pitches: Right **Bats:** Right **Pos:** P **Ht:** 6'2" **Wt:** 200 **Born:** 4/26/69 **Age:** 27

		HOW MUCH HE PITCHED						WHAT HE GAVE UP												THE RESULTS					
Year Team	Lg	G	GS	CG	GF	IP	BFP	H	R	ER	HR	SH	SF	HB	TBB	IBB	SO	WP	Bk	W	L	Pct.	ShO	Sv	ERA
1987 Utica	A	10	8	1	0	37.1	177	43	28	17	2	0	0	1	31	2	22	5	1	2	5	.286	1	0	4.10
1988 Batavia	A	8	8	0	0	31.2	151	27	32	26	2	0	3	4	31	0	26	7	2	2	3	.400	0	0	7.39
1989 Sumter	A	15	15	0	0	93.2	385	73	40	27	7	3	3	4	40	1	72	3	3	6	5	.545	0	0	2.59
Durham	A	1	1	0	0	8	30	3	2	1	0	0	0	1	1	0	4	2	0	0	0	.000	0	0	1.13
1990 Dunedin	A	26	26	0	0	154.1	649	128	74	64	2	6	3	6	72	0	125	22	6	5	8	.385	0	0	3.73
1991 Knoxville	AA	41	0	0	38	51.1	218	36	26	14	3	2	3	0	22	3	55	4	0	2	5	.286	0	16	2.45
1992 Syracuse	AAA	35	0	0	23	43.1	195	37	22	21	2	2	2	0	31	1	35	8	1	1	1	.500	0	10	4.36
1994 New Britain	AA	6	6	0	0	24.2	88	12	3	2	0	1	1	0	6	0	13	0	0	0	1	.000	0	0	0.73
Pawtucket	AAA	11	3	0	1	27.1	112	19	11	8	2	0	2	0	13	0	19	2	0	2	1	.667	0	0	2.63
1995 Phoenix	AAA	38	0	0	19	63	279	72	44	37	7	4	3	0	21	6	43	6	1	5	4	.556	0	0	5.29
Canton-Akrn	AA	24	0	0	16	38.1	158	33	16	13	4	4	2	0	16	3	27	1	1	5	3	.625	0	0	3.05
1992 Toronto	AL	2	0	0	0	1.2	9	2	2	2	0	0	0	0	2	0	1	0	0	0	0	.000	0	0	10.80
1993 Los Angeles	NL	41	0	0	18	64	267	59	32	29	3	2	0	2	21	4	41	4	1	1	2	.333	0	1	4.08
1994 Boston	AL	12	1	0	2	22.1	113	32	21	20	5	0	0	0	16	2	7	1	2	1	1	.500	0	0	8.06
8 Min. YEARS		215	67	1	97	573	2442	483	298	230	31	22	22	16	284	16	441	60	15	30	36	.455	1	29	3.61
3 Maj. YEARS		55	1	0	20	88	389	93	55	51	8	2	0	2	39	6	49	5	3	2	3	.400	0	1	5.22

Keith Troutman

Pitches: Right **Bats:** Right **Pos:** P **Ht:** 6'1" **Wt:** 200 **Born:** 5/29/73 **Age:** 23

		HOW MUCH HE PITCHED						WHAT HE GAVE UP												THE RESULTS					
Year Team	Lg	G	GS	CG	GF	IP	BFP	H	R	ER	HR	SH	SF	HB	TBB	IBB	SO	WP	Bk	W	L	Pct.	ShO	Sv	ERA
1992 Yakima	A	26	0	0	19	37.1	163	33	19	14	2	2	2	1	15	3	43	2	2	4	1	.800	0	3	3.38
1993 Great Falls	R	27	0	0	23	42	166	52	12	8	2	1	3	2	12	1	48	2	0	1	1	.500	0	16	1.71
1994 Vero Beach	A	43	0	0	10	78.1	328	69	39	34	6	3	2	1	35	5	66	5	1	3	2	.600	0	0	3.91
1995 San Antonio	AA	38	0	0	22	65.2	268	64	24	23	3	1	3	1	18	1	50	3	0	1	2	.333	0	2	3.15
4 Min. YEARS		134	0	0	74	223.1	925	192	94	79	13	7	10	5	80	10	207	12	3	9	6	.600	0	21	3.18

George Tsamis

Pitches: Left **Bats:** Right **Pos:** P **Ht:** 6'2" **Wt:** 190 **Born:** 6/14/67 **Age:** 29

		HOW MUCH HE PITCHED						WHAT HE GAVE UP												THE RESULTS					
Year Team	Lg	G	GS	CG	GF	IP	BFP	H	R	ER	HR	SH	SF	HB	TBB	IBB	SO	WP	Bk	W	L	Pct.	ShO	Sv	ERA
1989 Visalia	A	15	13	3	1	94.1	387	85	36	32	10	3	0	2	34	0	87	9	3	6	3	.667	0	0	3.05
1990 Visalia	A	26	26	4	0	183.2	731	168	62	45	4	3	2	4	61	0	145	7	1	17	4	.810	3	0	2.21
1991 Orlando	AA	1	1	0	0	7	28	3	2	0	0	0	0	0	4	0	5	0	0	0	0	.000	0	0	0.00
Portland	AAA	29	27	2	0	167.2	716	183	75	61	11	8	6	5	66	0	75	7	1	10	8	.556	1	0	3.27
1992 Portland	AAA	39	22	4	6	163.2	700	195	78	71	12	4	5	5	51	1	71	2	0	13	4	.765	1	1	3.90
1993 Portland	AAA	3	3	0	0	14	74	27	15	13	2	0	1	0	5	0	10	0	0	1	2	.333	0	0	8.36
1994 Jacksonvlle	AA	13	5	0	3	43.1	181	41	24	20	5	2	1	2	14	1	18	1	0	3	3	.500	0	0	4.15
Calgary	AAA	2	0	0	0	2	18	7	5	4	1	0	0	0	0	0	0	0	0	0	0	.000	0	0	18.00
1995 Mohawk Val	IND	2	1	0	1	5	18	1	0	0	0	0	0	0	2	0	6	0	0	0	0	.000	0	0	0.00
Carolina	AA	12	0	0	2	11	46	12	5	5	1	0	0	1	5	1	7	2	0	0	0	.000	0	0	4.09
Port City	AA	7	0	0	4	10.1	51	11	4	3	0	0	0	1	11	2	3	0	0	0	0	.000	0	0	2.61
1993 Minnesota	AL	41	0	0	18	68.1	309	86	51	47	9	2	6	3	27	5	30	1	1	1	2	.333	0	1	6.19
7 Min. YEARS		149	98	13	17	702	2945	733	306	254	46	21	15	19	253	5	427	28	5	50	24	.676	5	1	3.26

Lee Tunnell

Pitches: Right **Bats:** Right **Pos:** P **Ht:** 6'0" **Wt:** 180 **Born:** 10/30/60 **Age:** 35

		HOW MUCH HE PITCHED						WHAT HE GAVE UP												THE RESULTS					
Year Team	Lg	G	GS	CG	GF	IP	BFP	H	R	ER	HR	SH	SF	HB	TBB	IBB	SO	WP	Bk	W	L	Pct.	ShO	Sv	ERA
1985 Hawaii	AAA	7	7	2	0	46.2	0	32	12	12	2	0	0	1	24	0	29	3	0	4	1	.800	2	0	2.31
1986 Hawaii	AAA	27	26	2	0	142.1	667	180	106	95	9	5	3	5	81	1	95	14	0	4	11	.267	0	0	6.01
1987 Louisville	AAA	6	6	1	0	37	156	33	16	14	3	0	0	0	19	0	32	2	2	4	1	.800	1	0	3.41
Springfield	A	1	1	0	0	2.2	11	4	1	1	0	0	0	0	0	0	3	0	0	0	1	.000	0	0	3.38
1988 Louisville	AAA	24	20	0	0	135.1	581	136	69	58	7	6	7	3	55	1	60	8	11	6	8	.429	0	0	3.86
1989 Portland	AAA	25	5	0	10	66.1	273	56	24	20	2	2	6	1	23	2	58	2	2	2	4	.333	0	4	2.71

Year	Team	Lg	G	GS	CG	GF	IP	BFP	H	R	ER	HR	SH	SF	HB	TBB	IBB	SO	WP	Bk	W	L	Pct.	ShO	Sv	ERA
1990	Tucson	AAA	33	20	2	6	124.1	556	144	76	66	5	8	1	0	48	4	59	4	0	6	7	.462	0	2	4.78
1994	New Haven	AA	17	0	0	5	29	116	23	7	6	0	1	0	1	7	1	25	3	1	3	1	.750	0	1	1.86
	Colo. Sprng	AAA	11	0	0	2	10.1	53	15	14	13	2	0	1	0	7	1	10	0	0	0	2	.000	0	0	11.32
1995	Toledo	AAA	7	0	0	1	14.1	53	9	5	5	0	2	0	1	2	0	7	0	0	0	1	.000	0	0	3.14
1982	Pittsburgh	NL	5	3	0	2	18.1	75	17	8	8	1	1	0	2	5	0	4	0	0	1	1	.500	0	0	3.93
1983	Pittsburgh	NL	35	25	5	4	177.2	731	167	81	72	15	2	6	2	58	3	95	11	5	11	6	.647	3	0	3.65
1984	Pittsburgh	NL	26	6	0	5	68.1	317	81	44	40	6	4	1	0	40	6	51	6	2	1	7	.125	0	1	5.27
1985	Pittsburgh	NL	24	23	0	1	132.1	565	126	70	59	11	3	2	1	57	4	74	3	0	4	10	.286	0	1	4.01
1987	St. Louis	NL	32	9	0	3	74.1	335	90	45	40	5	3	4	1	34	7	49	2	5	4	4	.500	0	0	4.84
1989	Minnesota	AL	10	0	0	4	12	59	18	8	8	1	0	0	0	6	1	7	0	0	1	0	1.000	0	0	6.00
	8 Min. YEARS		158	85	7	24	608.1	2466	632	330	290	30	24	18	12	266	10	378	36	16	29	37	.439	3	4	4.29
	6 Maj. YEARS		132	66	5	19	483	2082	499	256	227	39	13	13	6	200	21	280	22	12	22	28	.440	3	1	4.23

Brian Turang

Bats: Right **Throws:** Right **Pos:** OF   **Ht:** 5'10" **Wt:** 170 **Born:** 6/14/67 **Age:** 29

Year	Team	Lg	G	AB	H	2B	3B	HR	TB	R	RBI	TBB	IBB	SO	HBP	SH	SF	SB	CS	SB%	GDP	Avg	OBP	SLG
1989	Bellingham	A	60	207	59	10	3	4	87	42	11	33	0	50	12	2	0	9	6	.60	1	.285	.413	.420
1990	San Bernrdo	A	132	487	144	25	5	12	215	86	67	69	0	98	7	6	4	25	16	.61	8	.296	.388	.441
	Calgary	AAA	3	9	2	0	0	0	2	1	1	2	0	4	0	0	0	0	0	.00	0	.222	.364	.222
1991	Jacksonvlle	AA	41	130	28	6	2	0	38	14	7	13	1	33	2	2	0	5	2	.71	0	.215	.297	.292
	San Bernrdo	A	34	100	18	2	1	0	22	9	4	15	0	31	3	1	0	6	6	.50	1	.180	.305	.220
1992	Jacksonvlle	AA	129	483	121	21	3	14	190	67	63	44	1	61	12	2	3	19	9	.68	12	.251	.327	.393
1993	Calgary	AAA	110	423	137	20	11	8	203	84	54	40	2	48	3	5	4	24	8	.75	7	.324	.383	.480
1994	Jacksonvlle	AA	3	13	4	1	0	0	5	1	1	0	0	3	0	0	0	0	0	.00	0	.308	.308	.385
	Calgary	AAA	65	196	67	16	5	5	136	51	40	17	0	37	0	4	3	5	4	.56	7	.343	.377	.491
1995	Tacoma	AAA	59	196	47	4	1	1	56	22	18	13	0	35	0	3	3	7	4	.64	7	.240	.283	.286
1993	Seattle	AL	40	140	35	11	1	0	48	22	7	17	0	20	2	1	0	6	2	.75	3	.250	.340	.343
1994	Seattle	AL	38	112	21	5	1	1	31	9	8	7	0	25	1	3	0	3	1	.75	0	.188	.242	.277
	7 Min. YEARS		636	2325	655	105	31	44	954	377	266	246	4	400	39	25	17	100	55	.65	44	.282	.358	.410
	2 Maj. YEARS		78	252	56	16	2	1	79	31	15	24	0	45	3	4	0	9	3	.75	3	.222	.297	.313

Frank Turco

Bats: Right **Throws:** Right **Pos:** OF   **Ht:** 5'11" **Wt:** 165 **Born:** 7/3/68 **Age:** 27

Year	Team	Lg	G	AB	H	2B	3B	HR	TB	R	RBI	TBB	IBB	SO	HBP	SH	SF	SB	CS	SB%	GDP	Avg	OBP	SLG
1990	Rangers	R	5	10	3	1	0	0	4	1	1	1	0	1	0	0	0	0	1	.00	0	.300	.364	.400
	Gastonia	A	5	8	1	0	0	0	1	2	0	1	0	1	0	0	0	0	0	.00	0	.125	.222	.125
	Erie	A	29	83	18	5	0	3	32	12	9	8	0	16	1	2	1	1	0	1.00	1	.217	.290	.386
1991	Reno	A	38	104	18	3	1	0	23	7	4	7	0	28	2	3	1	3	0	1.00	3	.173	.237	.221
	Bend	A	60	215	51	14	3	1	74	33	26	27	0	36	2	0	0	9	8	.53	3	.237	.328	.344
1992	Charlotte	A	93	264	60	12	5	3	91	29	23	18	0	68	1	3	3	14	2	.88	2	.227	.276	.345
1993	Tulsa	AA	118	423	113	13	2	8	154	45	39	27	0	86	1	5	2	13	8	.62	8	.267	.311	.364
1994	Tulsa	AA	95	302	79	15	3	7	121	43	33	25	1	82	1	7	2	18	7	.72	4	.262	.318	.401
1995	Tulsa	AA	53	149	31	3	1	0	39	23	12	18	0	34	1	5	0	4	3	.57	2	.208	.298	.346
	6 Min. YEARS		496	1558	374	66	15	23	539	195	147	132	1	353	9	25	9	62	29	.68	23	.240	.302	.346

Brian Turner

Bats: Left **Throws:** Left **Pos:** OF   **Ht:** 6'2" **Wt:** 210 **Born:** 6/9/71 **Age:** 25

Year	Team	Lg	G	AB	H	2B	3B	HR	TB	R	RBI	TBB	IBB	SO	HBP	SH	SF	SB	CS	SB%	GDP	Avg	OBP	SLG
1989	Yankees	R	50	188	39	7	3	1	55	29	28	20	0	30	2	2	3	5	2	.71	4	.207	.286	.293
1990	Greensboro	A	37	118	24	5	1	0	31	14	5	16	0	29	0	1	0	3	2	.60	1	.203	.299	.263
	Oneonta	A	69	227	56	13	1	0	71	28	24	36	1	49	2	1	1	7	4	.64	1	.247	.353	.313
1991	Greensboro	A	123	424	113	17	2	8	158	58	63	59	1	93	2	2	4	10	11	.48	4	.267	.356	.373
1992	Ft. Laud	A	127	454	107	16	1	7	146	39	54	46	2	103	0	5	5	3	8	.27	13	.236	.303	.322
1993	San Bernrdo	A	109	406	132	23	3	21	224	69	68	49	4	75	2	2	3	4	2	.67	3	.325	.398	.552
1994	Albany-Colo	AA	2	4	2	0	0	0	2	1	1	1	1	0	0	0	0	1	0	1.00	0	.500	.600	.500
	Tampa	A	118	420	101	24	3	10	161	63	64	63	3	84	4	1	4	2	1	.67	7	.240	.342	.383
1995	Norwich	AA	86	311	92	21	3	4	131	39	43	25	2	72	1	2	4	3	2	.60	5	.296	.346	.421
	7 Min. YEARS		721	2552	666	126	17	51	979	340	350	315	14	535	13	16	24	38	32	.54	38	.261	.342	.384

Matt Turner

Pitches: Right **Bats:** Right **Pos:** P   **Ht:** 6'5" **Wt:** 215 **Born:** 2/18/67 **Age:** 29

Year	Team	Lg	G	GS	CG	GF	IP	BFP	H	R	ER	HR	SH	SF	HB	TBB	IBB	SO	WP	Bk	W	L	Pct.	ShO	Sv	ERA
1986	Pulaski	R	18	5	0	7	48.2	229	55	36	25	6	2	2	2	28	1	48	2	0	1	3	.250	0	2	4.62
1987	Sumter	A	39	9	0	17	93.2	423	91	61	49	8	5	4	5	48	2	102	8	6	2	3	.400	0	0	4.71
1988	Burlington	A	7	6	0	1	34.1	161	43	27	25	9	0	1	3	16	0	26	0	3	1	3	.250	0	0	6.55
	Sumter	A	7	0	0	4	15.2	65	17	8	8	0	0	0	2	3	0	7	1	0	1	0	1.000	0	0	4.60
1989	Durham	A	53	3	0	19	118	499	95	38	32	11	3	5	5	47	9	114	5	3	9	9	.500	0	2	2.44
1990	Greenville	AA	40	0	0	26	67.2	289	59	24	20	6	0	1	3	29	2	60	4	2	6	4	.600	0	4	2.66
	Richmond	AAA	22	1	0	11	42	175	44	20	18	6	1	1	2	16	1	36	6	1	2	3	.400	0	2	3.86
1991	Richmond	AAA	23	0	0	17	36	161	33	21	19	5	2	4	2	20	0	33	4	0	1	3	.250	0	5	4.75
	Tucson	AAA	13	0	0	5	26	115	27	12	12	0	0	1	1	14	2	25	1	2	1	1	.500	0	1	4.15

Year	Team	Lg	G	GS	CG	GF	IP	BFP	H	R	ER	HR	SH	SF	HB	TBB	IBB	SO	WP	Bk	W	L	Pct.	ShO	Sv	ERA
1992	Tucson	AAA	63	0	0	38	100	436	93	52	39	2	7	4	2	40	3	84	5	3	2	8	.200	0	14	3.51
1993	Edmonton	AAA	12	0	0	12	13.2	51	9	1	1	1	0	1	0	2	0	15	0	0	0	0	.000	0	10	0.66
1994	Charlotte	AAA	4	0	0	0	4.1	18	2	0	0	0	0	0	0	3	0	4	0	0	0	0	.000	0	0	0.00
1995	Buffalo	AAA	13	0	0	10	10.1	54	16	7	6	0	1	0	1	5	0	10	0	1	0	1	.000	0	3	5.23
1993	Florida	NL	55	0	0	26	68	279	55	23	22	7	6	4	1	26	9	59	6	1	4	5	.444	0	0	2.91
1994	Cleveland	AL	9	0	0	2	12.2	65	13	6	3	0	1	0	3	7	0	5	0	0	1	0	1.000	0	1	2.13
	10 Min. YEARS		314	24	0	167	610.1	2676	584	307	254	54	21	24	28	271	20	564	36	21	26	38	.406	0	42	3.75
	2 Maj. YEARS		64	0	0	28	80.2	344	68	29	25	7	7	4	4	33	9	64	6	1	5	5	.500	0	1	2.79

Aaron Turnier

Pitches: Left **Bats:** Left **Pos:** P   **Ht:** 6'3" **Wt:** 190 **Born:** 9/30/70 **Age:** 25

			HOW MUCH HE PITCHED						WHAT HE GAVE UP											THE RESULTS					
Year	Team	Lg	G	GS	CG	GF	IP	BFP	H	R	ER	HR	SH	SF	HB	TBB	IBB	SO	WP	Bk	W	L	Pct.	ShO	Sv	ERA
1992	Pulaski	R	6	4	0	0	16.2	74	17	8	6	2	0	0	1	10	0	15	1	0	0	1	.000	0	0	3.24
1993	Idaho Falls	R	9	3	0	3	30	124	27	15	15	3	0	1	0	9	0	24	2	1	4	0	1.000	0	0	4.50
	Macon	A	12	2	0	2	24	115	21	18	13	1	1	1	2	20	0	14	9	0	0	1	.000	0	1	4.88
1994	Macon	A	16	0	0	9	25.1	107	23	10	8	0	0	1	2	10	0	24	7	0	0	1	.000	0	0	2.84
	Durham	A	26	0	0	11	43	197	31	16	13	2	3	1	1	36	3	39	7	0	3	2	.600	0	3	2.72
1995	Greenville	AA	8	0	0	0	17.1	86	17	13	10	2	1	0	0	18	1	16	3	0	0	1	.000	0	0	5.19
	4 Min. YEARS		77	9	0	25	156.1	703	136	80	65	10	5	4	6	103	4	132	29	1	7	6	.538	0	4	3.74

Dave Tuttle

Pitches: Right **Bats:** Right **Pos:** P   **Ht:** 6'3" **Wt:** 190 **Born:** 9/29/69 **Age:** 26

			HOW MUCH HE PITCHED						WHAT HE GAVE UP											THE RESULTS					
Year	Team	Lg	G	GS	CG	GF	IP	BFP	H	R	ER	HR	SH	SF	HB	TBB	IBB	SO	WP	Bk	W	L	Pct.	ShO	Sv	ERA
1992	Charlstn-Wv	A	17	16	0	0	97.1	416	87	46	42	5	0	6	1	53	1	93	4	0	3	5	.375	0	0	3.88
1993	Charlstn-Wv	A	13	13	0	0	81.1	343	66	37	32	3	1	1	3	36	1	74	6	1	8	3	.727	0	0	3.54
	Winston-Sal	A	15	15	2	0	86.1	388	98	61	53	8	3	2	1	39	0	58	6	0	7	7	.500	1	0	5.53
1994	Chattanooga	AA	14	14	0	0	84	377	82	60	42	8	4	2	7	48	5	54	10	0	2	9	.182	0	0	4.50
	Winston-Sal	A	13	13	2	0	76.2	315	58	26	18	8	0	0	3	27	0	64	2	0	5	2	.714	0	0	2.11
1995	Chattanooga	AA	8	7	0	1	34.2	165	40	29	27	6	2	1	1	21	0	20	4	0	1	6	.143	0	0	7.01
	Winston-Sal	A	10	10	2	0	62.1	248	49	28	22	5	0	2	3	19	0	54	3	0	3	3	.500	1	0	3.18
	Lakeland	A	6	4	1	1	31	132	31	11	10	1	0	3	2	12	0	28	1	0	1	4	.200	0	0	2.90
	4 Min. YEARS		96	92	7	2	553.2	2384	511	298	246	44	10	17	21	255	7	445	36	1	30	39	.435	2	0	4.00

Mike Twardoski

Bats: Left **Throws:** Left **Pos:** 1B   **Ht:** 5'11" **Wt:** 185 **Born:** 7/13/64 **Age:** 31

			BATTING												BASERUNNING				PERCENTAGES		
Year	Team	Lg	G	AB	H	2B	3B	HR	TB	R	RBI	TBB	IBB	SO	HBP	SH	SF	SB	CS	SB%	GDP	Avg	OBP	SLG
1986	Batavia	A	63	202	62	12	0	6	92	33	17	43	2	25	0	2	1	11	3	.79	4	.307	.427	.455
1987	Kinston	A	85	267	77	16	2	3	106	45	38	73	5	50	2	0	5	3	3	.50	9	.288	.438	.397
1988	Kinston	A	132	450	145	26	3	6	195	80	87	117	6	59	0	0	10	21	8	.72	17	.322	.454	.433
1989	Canton-Akrn	AA	113	380	104	19	2	0	127	56	36	77	2	47	0	4	4	7	7	.50	12	.274	.393	.334
1990	New Britain	AA	127	413	121	34	3	1	164	72	45	95	4	46	0	7	2	4	3	.57	11	.293	.424	.397
1991	Winter Havn	A	4	14	2	1	0	0	3	2	2	0	0	1	0	0	1	0	0	.00	0	.143	.133	.214
	Pawtucket	AAA	110	367	93	20	2	4	129	52	26	62	4	65	3	14	1	0	1	.00	7	.253	.365	.351
1992	Pawtucket	AAA	121	389	113	23	4	13	183	55	49	92	4	56	1	9	6	1	5	.17	10	.290	.422	.470
1993	Norfolk	AAA	131	427	120	15	2	9	166	66	38	69	6	65	1	2	4	9	11	.45	10	.281	.379	.389
1994	Pawtucket	AAA	111	382	108	15	1	13	164	61	49	56	5	38	1	4	1	8	2	.80	11	.283	.375	.429
1995	Richmond	AAA	19	58	8	1	0	0	9	7	5	10	2	8	0	1	0	1	1	.50	0	.138	.265	.155
	10 Min. YEARS		1016	3349	953	182	19	55	1338	529	392	694	35	460	8	43	35	65	44	.60	91	.285	.405	.400

Brad Tyler

Bats: Left **Throws:** Right **Pos:** 2B   **Ht:** 6'2" **Wt:** 175 **Born:** 3/3/69 **Age:** 27

			BATTING												BASERUNNING				PERCENTAGES		
Year	Team	Lg	G	AB	H	2B	3B	HR	TB	R	RBI	TBB	IBB	SO	HBP	SH	SF	SB	CS	SB%	GDP	Avg	OBP	SLG
1990	Wausau	A	56	187	44	4	3	2	60	31	24	44	2	45	2	1	2	11	4	.73	2	.235	.383	.321
1991	Kane County	A	60	199	54	10	3	3	79	35	29	44	1	25	1	1	2	5	3	.63	0	.271	.402	.397
	Frederick	A	56	187	48	6	0	4	66	26	26	33	3	33	2	1	1	3	2	.60	0	.257	.372	.353
1992	Frederick	A	54	185	47	11	2	3	71	34	22	43	2	34	2	1	4	9	3	.75	2	.254	.393	.384
	Hagerstown	AA	83	256	57	9	1	2	74	41	21	34	2	45	2	1	0	23	5	.82	5	.223	.318	.289
1993	Bowie	AA	129	437	103	23	17	10	190	85	44	84	2	89	1	1	3	24	11	.69	2	.236	.358	.435
1994	Rochester	AAA	101	314	82	15	8	7	134	38	43	38	2	69	2	1	0	7	4	.64	4	.261	.345	.427
1995	Rochester	AAA	114	361	93	17	3	17	167	60	52	71	4	63	4	0	5	10	5	.67	3	.258	.381	.463
	6 Min. YEARS		653	2126	528	95	37	48	841	350	261	391	18	403	16	7	17	92	37	.71	18	.248	.367	.396

Joe Urso

Bats: Right **Throws:** Right **Pos:** 2B   **Ht:** 5'7" **Wt:** 160 **Born:** 7/28/70 **Age:** 25

			BATTING												BASERUNNING				PERCENTAGES		
Year	Team	Lg	G	AB	H	2B	3B	HR	TB	R	RBI	TBB	IBB	SO	HBP	SH	SF	SB	CS	SB%	GDP	Avg	OBP	SLG
1992	Boise	A	2	5	0	0	0	0	0	1	1	4	0	1	0	0	0	0	0	.00	0	.000	.444	.000
	Palm Spring	A	28	84	21	4	0	0	25	6	11	11	0	14	0	1	0	0	2	.00	1	.250	.337	.298
1993	Palm Spring	A	96	346	89	17	1	2	114	51	41	57	1	53	1	2	2	9	5	.64	4	.257	.362	.329
1994	Lk Elsinore	A	134	494	138	30	4	2	182	67	46	78	1	66	4	14	4	10	6	.63	8	.279	.379	.368
1995	Midland	AA	12	37	12	3	0	0	15	6	4	5	0	3	1	0	1	0	0	.00	0	.324	.409	.405

	Lg	G	AB	H	2B	3B	HR	TB	R	RBI	TBB	IBB	SO	HBP	SH	SF	SB	CS	SB%	GDP	Avg	OBP	SLG
Lk Elsinore	A	65	244	77	16	2	3	106	48	34	34	1	41	3	1	2	7	5	.58	6	.316	.403	.434
4 Min. YEARS		337	1210	337	70	7	7	442	179	137	189	3	178	9	18	9	26	18	.59	19	.279	.378	.365

Pitches: Left Bats: Right Pos: P

Sal Urso

Ht: 5'11" Wt: 175 Born: 1/19/72 Age: 24

		HOW MUCH HE PITCHED					WHAT HE GAVE UP											THE RESULTS					
Year Team	Lg	G	GS	CG	GF	IP	BFP	H	R	ER	HR	SH	SF	HB	TBB	IBB	SO	WP	Bk	W	L	Pct.	ShO	Sv	ERA
1990 Mariners	R	20	0	0	6	50.2	219	38	25	13	3	2	6	5	23	1	63	5	0	3	2	.600	0	1	2.31
1991 Peninsula	A	46	0	0	29	61.2	290	74	36	21	1	3	4	5	30	7	44	6	0	0	3	.000	0	8	3.06
1992 San Bernrdo	A	37	0	0	21	51.1	239	66	34	29	2	2	5	1	32	0	40	4	1	0	1	.000	0	1	5.08
1993 Appleton	A	36	1	0	18	53.2	226	57	24	20	2	4	2	1	24	1	50	7	1	4	4	.500	0	2	3.35
1994 Riverside	A	30	1	0	12	34.2	156	44	27	23	4	1	2	3	14	0	26	3	0	1	2	.333	0	4	5.97
1995 Port City	AA	51	0	0	8	45.2	185	41	13	11	0	0	0	0	21	0	44	7	1	2	0	1.000	0	1	2.17
6 Min. YEARS		220	2	0	94	297.2	1315	320	159	117	12	12	19	15	144	9	267	32	3	10	12	.455	0	13	3.54

Bats: Left Throws: Left Pos: OF

Pedro Valdes

Ht: 6'1" Wt: 160 Born: 6/29/73 Age: 23

		BATTING															BASERUNNING				PERCENTAGES		
Year Team	Lg	G	AB	H	2B	3B	HR	TB	R	RBI	TBB	IBB	SO	HBP	SH	SF	SB	CS	SB%	GDP	Avg	OBP	SLG
1991 Huntington	R	50	157	45	11	1	0	58	18	16	17	3	31	2	1	5	5	1	.83	1	.287	.354	.369
1992 Peoria	A	33	112	26	7	0	0	33	8	20	7	3	32	1	0	4	0	0	.00	1	.232	.268	.295
Geneva	A	66	254	69	10	0	5	94	27	24	3	1	33	3	2	2	4	5	.44	2	.272	.286	.370
1993 Peoria	A	65	234	74	11	1	7	108	33	36	10	4	40	0	5	4	2	2	.50	3	.316	.339	.462
Daytona	A	60	230	66	16	1	8	108	27	49	9	1	30	2	0	5	3	4	.43	8	.287	.313	.470
1994 Orlando	AA	116	365	103	14	4	1	128	39	37	20	3	45	2	2	1	2	6	.25	10	.282	.322	.351
1995 Orlando	AA	114	426	128	28	3	7	183	57	68	37	3	77	1	0	6	3	6	.33	7	.300	.359	.430
5 Min. YEARS		504	1778	511	97	10	28	712	209	250	103	18	288	14	10	27	19	24	.44	38	.287	.327	.400

Bats: Both Throws: Right Pos: OF

Trovin Valdez

Ht: 5'10" Wt: 163 Born: 11/18/73 Age: 22

		BATTING															BASERUNNING				PERCENTAGES		
Year Team	Lg	G	AB	H	2B	3B	HR	TB	R	RBI	TBB	IBB	SO	HBP	SH	SF	SB	CS	SB%	GDP	Avg	OBP	SLG
1993 Orioles	R	39	151	32	2	2	0	38	16	6	9	0	23	2	0	2	21	5	.81	1	.212	.256	.252
1994 Albany	A	20	65	17	0	2	0	21	10	4	1	0	17	2	0	1	9	1	.90	1	.262	.290	.323
Bluefield	R	55	184	53	7	3	3	75	43	18	11	1	26	5	5	5	20	6	.77	1	.288	.337	.408
1995 Bowie	AA	2	0	0	0	0	0	0	0	0	0	0	0	0	0	0	0	0	.00	0	.000	.000	.000
Frederick	A	112	375	92	12	4	0	112	51	13	18	0	77	5	6	1	34	21	.62	2	.245	.288	.299
3 Min. YEARS		228	775	194	21	11	3	246	120	41	39	1	143	12	13	7	84	33	.72	5	.250	.294	.317

Pitches: Right Bats: Right Pos: P

Julio Valera

Ht: 6' 2" Wt: 215 Born: 10/13/68 Age: 27

		HOW MUCH HE PITCHED					WHAT HE GAVE UP											THE RESULTS					
Year Team	Lg	G	GS	CG	GF	IP	BFP	H	R	ER	HR	SH	SF	HB	TBB	IBB	SO	WP	Bk	W	L	Pct.	ShO	Sv	ERA
1986 Kingsport	R	13	13	2	0	76.1	356	91	58	44	5	4	0	0	29	2	64	4	1	3	10	.231	1	0	5.19
1987 Columbia	A	22	22	2	0	125.1	522	114	53	39	7	2	1	4	31	0	97	6	0	8	7	.533	2	0	2.80
1988 Columbia	A	30	27	8	3	191	775	171	77	68	8	5	7	4	51	3	144	9	6	15	11	.577	0	1	3.20
1989 St. Lucie	A	6	6	3	0	45	173	34	5	5	1	2	0	0	6	1	45	0	0	4	2	.667	2	0	1.00
Jackson	A	19	19	6	0	137.1	566	123	47	38	4	7	3	8	36	2	107	10	0	10	6	.625	2	0	2.49
Tidewater	AAA	2	2	0	0	13	52	8	3	3	1	0	0	1	5	0	10	1	0	1	1	.500	0	0	2.08
1990 Tidewater	AAA	24	24	9	0	158	648	146	66	53	12	6	5	5	39	3	133	7	5	10	10	.500	2	0	3.02
1991 Tidewater	AAA	26	26	3	0	176.1	739	152	79	75	12	8	6	6	70	4	117	8	3	10	10	.500	1	0	3.83
1992 Tidewater	AAA	1	1	0	0	6	25	5	0	0	0	0	0	0	2	0	7	2	0	1	0	1.000	0	0	0.00
1994 Lk Elsinore	A	2	2	0	0	9.2	45	14	10	10	0	0	0	1	3	0	11	1	0	1	1	.500	0	0	9.31
Midland	A	3	3	0	0	19	79	17	8	8	2	0	1	0	9	0	15	0	0	1	0	1.000	0	0	3.79
Vancouver	AAA	11	11	0	0	59.2	269	70	40	35	9	2	3	3	20	1	43	4	1	1	3	.250	0	0	5.28
1995 Vancouver	AAA	13	13	2	0	71	314	85	54	45	2	0	0	2	21	0	43	1	0	2	5	.286	0	0	5.70
1990 New York	NL	3	3	0	0	13	64	20	11	10	1	0	0	0	7	0	4	0	0	1	1	.500	0	0	6.92
1991 New York	NL	2	0	0	1	2	11	1	0	0	0	0	0	0	4	1	3	0	0	0	0	.000	0	0	0.00
1992 California	AL	30	28	4	0	188	792	188	82	78	15	6	2	2	64	5	113	5	0	8	11	.421	2	0	3.73
1993 California	AL	19	5	0	8	53	246	77	44	39	8	4	1	2	15	2	28	2	0	3	6	.333	0	4	6.62
9 Min. YEARS		172	169	35	3	1087.2	4563	1030	500	423	63	36	26	34	322	16	836	53	16	67	66	.504	10	1	3.50
4 Maj. YEARS		54	36	4	9	256	1113	286	137	127	24	10	3	4	90	8	148	7	0	12	18	.400	2	4	4.46

Bats: Right Throws: Right Pos: SS

Ramon Valette

Ht: 6'1" Wt: 160 Born: 1/20/72 Age: 24

		BATTING															BASERUNNING				PERCENTAGES		
Year Team	Lg	G	AB	H	2B	3B	HR	TB	R	RBI	TBB	IBB	SO	HBP	SH	SF	SB	CS	SB%	GDP	Avg	OBP	SLG
1990 Twins	R	34	109	28	2	0	0	30	12	10	2	0	20	1	2	0	3	1	.75	3	.257	.277	.275
1991 Elizabethtn	R	25	74	11	2	0	0	13	7	1	6	0	24	0	0	1	1	0	1.00	5	.149	.210	.176
1992 Elizabethtn	R	44	140	28	6	0	0	34	21	11	15	0	34	1	1	3	6	0	1.00	1	.200	.277	.243
1993 Fort Wayne	A	112	382	91	20	0	6	129	46	38	23	0	89	4	2	4	12	7	.63	11	.238	.286	.338
1994 Fort Myers	A	122	404	97	21	1	4	132	50	49	22	0	80	5	3	1	19	7	.73	9	.240	.287	.327
1995 New Britain	AA	111	346	74	11	2	4	101	40	32	21	0	52	1	1	2	19	2	.90	14	.214	.259	.292
6 Min. YEARS		448	1455	329	62	3	14	439	176	141	89	0	299	12	9	11	60	17	.78	45	.226	.274	.302

Kerry Valrie

Bats: Right **Throws:** Right **Pos:** OF   **Ht:** 5'10" **Wt:** 195 **Born:** 10/31/68 **Age:** 27

Year	Team	Lg	G	AB	H	2B	3B	HR	TB	R	RBI	TBB	IBB	SO	HBP	SH	SF	SB	CS	SB%	GDP	Avg	OBP	SLG
1990	Utica	A	42	149	28	4	1	0	34	14	10	8	1	46	1	1	0	12	6	.67	4	.188	.234	.228
1991	South Bend	A	87	331	71	11	2	6	104	47	29	23	1	78	3	3	0	32	6	.84	3	.215	.272	.314
1992	South Bend	A	79	314	81	12	2	5	112	34	37	16	0	53	1	0	4	22	15	.59	6	.258	.293	.357
	Sarasota	A	51	174	41	9	0	1	53	13	23	14	0	42	1	0	2	13	1	.93	2	.236	.293	.305
1993	Sarasota	A	115	386	82	14	2	12	136	47	52	17	1	81	4	2	7	19	7	.73	3	.212	.249	.352
1994	Birmingham	AA	119	423	121	27	3	3	163	59	58	34	4	75	4	2	4	29	10	.74	3	.286	.342	.385
1995	Nashville	AAA	138	544	136	30	3	7	193	75	55	40	0	107	3	2	4	22	15	.59	15	.250	.303	.355
	6 Min. YEARS		631	2321	560	107	13	34	795	289	264	152	7	482	17	10	21	149	60	.71	36	.241	.290	.343

Ty Van Burkleo

Bats: Left **Throws:** Left **Pos:** 1B   **Ht:** 6'5" **Wt:** 225 **Born:** 10/7/63 **Age:** 32

Year	Team	Lg	G	AB	H	2B	3B	HR	TB	R	RBI	TBB	IBB	SO	HBP	SH	SF	SB	CS	SB%	GDP	Avg	OBP	SLG
1992	Edmonton	AAA	135	458	125	28	7	19	224	83	88	75	6	100	5	0	3	20	5	.80	10	.273	.379	.489
1993	Vancouver	AAA	105	361	99	19	2	6	140	47	56	51	3	89	2	1	4	7	3	.70	9	.274	.364	.388
1994	Colo. Sprng	AAA	128	428	116	28	3	21	213	90	86	82	2	111	4	0	5	4	4	.50	11	.271	.389	.498
1995	Colo. Sprng	AAA	76	231	66	14	0	14	126	43	57	29	2	57	1	1	2	2	1	.67	1	.286	.365	.545
1993	California	AL	12	33	5	3	0	1	11	2	1	6	0	9	0	0	0	1	0	1.00	0	.152	.282	.333
1994	Colorado	NL	2	5	0	0	0	0	0	0	0	0	0	1	0	0	0	0	0	.00	0	.000	.000	.000
	4 Min. YEARS		444	1478	406	89	14	60	703	263	287	237	13	357	12	2	14	33	13	.72	31	.275	.376	.476
	2 Maj. YEARS		14	38	5	3	0	1	11	2	1	6	0	10	0	0	0	1	0	1.00	0	.132	.250	.289

Doug Vanderweele

Pitches: Right **Bats:** Right **Pos:** P   **Ht:** 6'3" **Wt:** 200 **Born:** 3/18/70 **Age:** 26

			HOW MUCH HE PITCHED						WHAT HE GAVE UP										THE RESULTS					
Year	Team	Lg	G	GS	CG	GF	IP	BFP	H	R	ER	HR	SH	SF	HB	TBB	IBB	SO	WP	Bk	W	L	Pct.	ShO	Sv	ERA
1991	Everett	A	15	15	0	0	87	371	73	42	19	1	1	3	8	35	1	65	12	7	6	4	.600	0	0	1.97
1992	Clinton	A	9	9	0	0	51	228	61	33	28	5	2	2	2	24	1	39	7	3	3	3	.500	0	0	4.94
	San Jose	A	16	15	1	0	87.1	387	77	49	36	7	3	2	8	50	1	51	4	2	6	4	.600	0	0	3.71
	Phoenix	AAA	1	0	0	0	1.2	8	3	2	2	0	0	0	0	0	0	1	0	0	0	0	.000	0	0	10.80
1993	Shreveport	AA	1	0	0	0	2	7	0	0	0	0	0	0	0	0	0	3	0	0	0	0	.000	0	0	0.00
	San Jose	A	25	24	3	1	171	728	188	84	74	17	12	5	3	55	3	106	8	2	10	6	.625	0	0	3.89
1994	San Jose	A	8	8	0	0	51.2	215	46	21	16	3	4	1	5	10	0	33	0	0	3	3	.500	0	0	2.79
	Shreveport	AA	21	21	1	0	125.1	533	146	62	53	7	7	3	3	32	2	55	4	0	6	9	.400	0	0	3.81
1995	Phoenix	AAA	11	4	1	1	38.1	178	57	29	26	9	2	3	1	11	3	20	1	1	2	4	.333	0	0	6.10
	Shreveport	AA	13	9	0	0	64.1	253	61	18	18	3	1	0	2	13	0	22	3	0	5	2	.714	0	0	2.52
	5 Min. YEARS		120	105	6	2	679.2	2908	712	334	272	52	32	19	32	230	11	394	40	15	41	35	.539	0	0	3.60

Ben VanRyn

Pitches: Left **Bats:** Left **Pos:** P   **Ht:** 6'5" **Wt:** 195 **Born:** 8/9/71 **Age:** 24

			HOW MUCH HE PITCHED						WHAT HE GAVE UP										THE RESULTS					
Year	Team	Lg	G	GS	CG	GF	IP	BFP	H	R	ER	HR	SH	SF	HB	TBB	IBB	SO	WP	Bk	W	L	Pct.	ShO	Sv	ERA
1990	Expos	R	10	9	0	0	51.2	205	44	13	10	0	0	0	0	15	0	56	0	0	5	3	.625	0	0	1.74
1991	Sumter	A	20	20	0	0	109.1	506	122	96	79	14	3	7	6	61	0	77	10	4	2	13	.133	0	0	6.50
	Jamestown	A	6	6	1	0	32.1	143	37	19	18	1	0	0	2	12	0	23	4	0	3	3	.500	0	0	5.01
1992	Vero Beach	A	26	25	1	0	137.2	583	125	58	49	4	5	8	2	54	1	108	4	5	10	7	.588	1	0	3.20
1993	San Antonio	AA	21	21	1	0	134.1	557	118	43	33	5	4	1	3	38	1	144	2	4	14	4	.778	0	0	2.21
	Albuquerque	AAA	6	6	0	0	24.1	120	35	30	29	1	1	2	0	17	0	9	0	0	1	4	.200	0	0	10.73
1994	Albuquerque	AAA	12	9	0	1	50.2	251	75	42	36	6	3	1	0	24	1	44	0	1	4	1	.800	0	0	6.39
	San Antonio	AA	17	17	0	0	102.1	418	93	42	34	5	3	1	0	35	0	72	2	0	8	3	.727	0	0	2.99
1995	Chattanooga	AA	5	3	0	0	12.2	69	22	18	13	2	0	2	1	6	0	6	0	0	1	1	.000	0	0	9.24
	Vancouver	AAA	11	5	0	2	29.1	123	29	10	10	1	2	2	0	9	1	20	2	0	2	0	1.000	0	0	3.07
	Midland	AA	19	0	0	8	32.1	133	33	10	10	4	0	0	2	12	0	24	2	0	1	1	.500	0	1	2.78
	6 Min. YEARS		153	121	3	11	717	3108	733	381	321	43	21	24	18	283	4	583	26	14	50	40	.556	1	1	4.03

Hector Vargas

Bats: Right **Throws:** Right **Pos:** OF   **Ht:** 5'11" **Wt:** 155 **Born:** 6/3/66 **Age:** 30

Year	Team	Lg	G	AB	H	2B	3B	HR	TB	R	RBI	TBB	IBB	SO	HBP	SH	SF	SB	CS	SB%	GDP	Avg	OBP	SLG
1986	Yankees	R	61	212	50	6	0	0	56	27	25	33	0	28	3	3	2	10	11	.48	5	.236	.344	.264
1987	Pr. William	A	34	53	12	0	0	0	12	8	2	5	0	5	0	1	0	1	1	.50	3	.226	.293	.226
	Oneonta	A	15	43	12	4	1	0	18	4	7	2	0	6	1	0	2	1	2	.33	1	.279	.313	.419
	Albany-Colo	AA	44	130	29	3	0	1	35	18	10	15	0	30	0	5	0	3	2	.60	1	.223	.303	.269
1988	Ft. Laud	A	3	14	2	0	0	0	2	3	0	0	0	4	0	0	0	0	0	.00	0	.143	.143	.143
	Oneonta	A	46	143	37	5	2	0	46	24	16	13	0	23	0	0	2	11	0	1.00	7	.259	.316	.322
1989	Pr. William	A	5	11	2	1	0	0	3	2	0	3	0	4	0	1	0	0	0	.00	1	.182	.357	.273
	Peninsula	A	84	288	75	8	3	3	98	44	27	35	2	41	2	0	3	35	13	.73	11	.260	.341	.340
	Ft. Laud	A	19	53	17	2	1	0	21	6	3	3	0	15	0	0	1	2	2	.50	1	.321	.351	.396
1990	Ft. Laud	A	117	429	132	20	9	0	170	48	61	30	3	68	3	4	11	21	11	.66	8	.308	.349	.396
1991	Albany-Colo	AA	106	345	96	16	3	1	121	49	39	45	0	65	5	2	2	23	5	.82	10	.278	.368	.351

Year Team	Lg	G	AB	H	2B	3B	HR	TB	R	RBI	TBB	IBB	SO	HBP	SH	SF	SB	CS	SB%	GDP	Avg	OBP	SLG
1992 Albany-Colo	AA	116	417	125	26	9	1	172	64	41	48	0	73	2	2	0	25	13	.66	7	.300	.375	.412
1993 Ottawa	AAA	36	93	17	3	1	0	22	10	6	15	1	25	1	2	0	3	3	.50	2	.183	.303	.237
Canton-Akrn	AA	29	90	20	2	0	1	25	9	8	12	0	22	0	0	2	3	0	1.00	1	.222	.308	.278
1994 Bowie	AA	123	428	134	33	3	8	197	73	58	68	3	66	9	1	6	5	7	.42	9	.313	.413	.460
1995 Okla. City	AAA	98	305	84	10	2	0	98	38	27	30	1	54	2	4	2	6	1	.86	9	.275	.342	.321
10 Min. YEARS		936	3054	844	139	34	15	1096	426	333	357	8	529	28	25	33	149	71	.68	75	.276	.354	.359

Jason Varitek

Bats: Both **Throws:** Right **Pos:** C **Ht:** 6'2" **Wt:** 210 **Born:** 4/11/72 **Age:** 24

							BATTING										BASERUNNING				PERCENTAGES		
Year Team	Lg	G	AB	H	2B	3B	HR	TB	R	RBI	TBB	IBB	SO	HBP	SH	SF	SB	CS	SB%	GDP	Avg	OBP	SLG
1995 Port City	AA	104	352	79	14	2	10	127	42	44	61	4	126	2	3	3	0	1	.00	8	.224	.340	.361

Chris Vasquez

Bats: Left **Throws:** Right **Pos:** OF **Ht:** 5'11" **Wt:** 170 **Born:** 10/23/71 **Age:** 24

							BATTING										BASERUNNING				PERCENTAGES		
Year Team	Lg	G	AB	H	2B	3B	HR	TB	R	RBI	TBB	IBB	SO	HBP	SH	SF	SB	CS	SB%	GDP	Avg	OBP	SLG
1990 Billings	R	54	182	52	9	2	5	80	25	34	14	0	30	2	2	2	4	5	.44	1	.286	.340	.440
1991 Charlstn-Wv	A	51	163	41	6	0	1	50	15	15	9	0	40	1	1	1	3	1	.75	3	.252	.293	.307
Cedar Rapds	A	50	195	52	13	1	9	94	33	37	14	1	41	3	0	4	5	4	.56	4	.267	.319	.482
1992 Cedar Rapds	A	102	317	82	14	1	11	131	42	53	28	3	61	1	1	2	5	2	.71	8	.259	.319	.413
1993 Winston-Sal	A	67	233	61	10	1	10	103	29	31	11	1	52	1	0	0	1	1	.50	6	.262	.298	.442
1994 Charlstn-Wv	A	28	98	20	2	1	1	27	9	7	2	0	11	0	0	1	1	1	.50	2	.204	.218	.276
Winston-Sal	A	69	217	60	11	1	5	88	31	29	13	0	43	0	0	1	3	2	.60	4	.276	.316	.406
1995 Chattanooga	AA	7	15	6	1	0	1	10	3	1	2	0	3	0	0	0	0	0	.00	0	.400	.471	.667
Mohawk Val	IND	5	23	5	1	0	0	6	3	2	0	0	2	0	0	0	0	0	.00	2	.217	.217	.261
Sonoma Cty	IND	44	182	61	17	3	3	93	33	34	10	1	29	2	0	2	1	1	.50	2	.335	.372	.511
6 Min. YEARS		477	1625	440	84	10	46	682	223	243	103	6	312	10	4	13	23	17	.58	32	.271	.316	.420

Marcos Vasquez

Pitches: Right **Bats:** Right **Pos:** P **Ht:** 5'10" **Wt:** 170 **Born:** 11/5/68 **Age:** 27

						HOW MUCH HE PITCHED			WHAT HE GAVE UP										THE RESULTS				
Year Team	Lg	G	GS	CG	GF	IP	BFP	H	R	ER	HR	SH	SF	HB	TBB	IBB	SO	WP	Bk	W	L	Pct.	ShO	Sv	ERA
1987 Braves	R	12	12	1	0	70.1	308	68	35	29	1	1	4	4	35	2	46	5	1	3	5	.375	0	0	3.71
1988 Sumter	A	32	18	1	6	133	611	145	93	79	15	6	6	7	76	1	74	8	10	7	11	.389	0	0	5.35
1989 Sumter	A	25	25	4	0	156.2	661	144	78	57	9	2	7	4	56	0	98	4	2	10	10	.500	1	0	3.27
Burlington	A	2	2	0	0	11	52	13	11	8	1	1	1	0	4	0	10	1	0	0	0	.000	0	0	6.55
1990 Durham	A	12	11	1	0	57	255	60	33	24	6	0	0	5	29	1	28	6	0	4	2	.667	0	0	3.79
Burlington	A	15	13	5	1	87.2	366	89	50	37	2	2	2	1	20	0	41	8	2	6	5	.545	0	0	3.80
1991 Macon	A	14	14	3	0	92	373	61	35	26	2	2	0	5	40	0	75	10	0	7	4	.636	1	0	2.54
Durham	A	4	4	0	0	24	109	30	9	7	0	0	0	0	11	0	12	2	0	3	0	1.000	0	0	2.63
1992 Greenville	AA	14	14	1	0	73.1	319	81	38	35	6	2	4	2	30	0	38	7	0	6	4	.600	0	0	4.30
Durham	A	15	9	0	2	74.2	310	53	24	18	5	0	2	2	32	1	53	4	2	5	0	1.000	0	0	2.17
1993 Greenville	AA	43	4	0	16	82	366	96	47	42	1	9	2	2	37	7	61	3	2	4	5	.444	0	3	4.61
1994 Chattanooga	AA	29	19	1	3	131	558	121	60	51	8	8	4	4	52	2	71	8	2	8	7	.533	1	0	3.50
1995 Indianapols	AAA	2	0	0	1	4	13	1	0	0	0	0	0	0	0	0	1	0	0	0	0	.000	0	1	0.00
Chattanooga	AA	26	18	0	1	120	531	125	63	49	12	6	5	4	46	1	80	5	1	7	6	.538	0	1	3.68
9 Min. YEARS		245	163	17	30	1116.2	4832	1087	576	462	68	39	37	40	468	15	688	71	22	70	59	.543	3	5	3.72

Jim Vatcher

Bats: Right **Throws:** Right **Pos:** OF **Ht:** 5'9" **Wt:** 165 **Born:** 5/27/66 **Age:** 30

							BATTING										BASERUNNING				PERCENTAGES		
Year Team	Lg	G	AB	H	2B	3B	HR	TB	R	RBI	TBB	IBB	SO	HBP	SH	SF	SB	CS	SB%	GDP	Avg	OBP	SLG
1987 Utica	A	67	249	67	15	2	3	95	44	21	28	0	31	2	2	1	10	5	.67	5	.269	.346	.382
1988 Spartanburg	A	137	496	150	32	2	12	222	90	72	89	1	73	8	9	3	26	13	.67	10	.302	.414	.448
1989 Clearwater	A	92	349	105	30	5	4	157	51	46	41	0	49	2	0	2	7	3	.70	11	.301	.376	.450
Reading	AA	48	171	56	11	3	4	85	27	32	26	1	29	1	0	4	2	0	1.00	8	.327	.411	.497
1990 Scranton-Wb	AAA	55	181	46	12	4	5	81	30	22	32	1	33	0	1	2	1	4	.20	4	.254	.363	.448
1991 Las Vegas	AAA	117	395	105	28	6	17	196	67	67	53	3	76	3	3	2	4	12	.25	14	.266	.355	.496
1992 Las Vegas	AAA	111	280	77	15	3	8	122	41	35	39	4	60	3	6	2	2	6	.25	1	.275	.367	.436
1993 Las Vegas	AAA	103	293	93	17	2	7	135	36	45	35	0	46	4	5	2	3	4	.43	7	.317	.395	.461
1994 Norfolk	AAA	112	316	74	20	1	10	126	41	48	36	1	56	1	4	2	2	4	.33	4	.234	.313	.399
1995 Las Vegas	AAA	101	356	104	31	3	7	162	56	43	33	6	46	3	2	5	3	4	.43	6	.292	.353	.455
Scranton-Wb	AAA	9	24	9	1	0	0	10	4	2	1	0	4	0	0	0	1	0	1.00	1	.375	.400	.417
1990 Atlanta	NL	21	27	7	1	1	0	10	2	3	1	0	9	0	0	0	0	0	.00	0	.259	.286	.370
Philadelphia	NL	36	46	12	1	0	1	16	5	4	4	0	6	0	0	0	0	0	.00	1	.261	.320	.348
1991 San Diego	NL	17	20	4	0	0	0	4	3	2	4	0	6	0	0	0	1	0	1.00	0	.200	.333	.200
1992 San Diego	NL	13	16	4	1	0	0	5	1	2	3	0	6	0	0	1	0	0	.00	0	.250	.368	.313
9 Min. YEARS		952	3110	886	212	31	77	1391	487	433	413	17	503	27	32	25	61	55	.53	71	.285	.371	.447
3 Maj. YEARS		87	109	27	3	1	1	35	11	11	12	0	27	0	0	1	1	0	1.00	1	.248	.322	.321

Derek Vaughn

Bats: Right **Throws:** Right **Pos:** OF   **Ht:** 6'3" **Wt:** 180 **Born:** 1/11/70 **Age:** 26

Year	Team	Lg	G	AB	H	2B	3B	HR	TB	R	RBI	TBB	IBB	SO	HBP	SH	SF	SB	CS	SB%	GDP	Avg	OBP	SLG
1991	Spokane	A	49	192	52	5	2	1	64	21	17	15	0	47	2	1	0	15	7	.68	4	.271	.330	.333
1992	Waterloo	A	120	400	101	19	1	5	137	65	49	50	1	99	4	3	3	35	13	.73	5	.253	.339	.343
1993	Pocatello	R	72	299	93	14	3	5	128	60	43	24	3	52	4	2	8	40	13	.75	1	.311	.361	.428
1994	Lk Elsinore	A	13	36	6	2	0	0	8	5	1	2	0	9	0	1	0	2	0	1.00	0	.167	.211	.222
	Cedar Rapds	A	70	170	46	6	0	5	67	26	18	22	1	32	3	4	1	14	7	.67	5	.271	.362	.394
1995	Vancouver	AAA	1	3	2	0	0	0	2	0	0	0	0	0	0	0	0	1	0	1.00	0	.667	.667	.667
	Lk Elsinore	A	94	328	87	15	7	6	134	66	50	43	2	61	1	6	2	22	5	.81	9	.265	.350	.409
	5 Min. YEARS		419	1428	387	61	13	22	540	243	178	156	7	300	14	17	14	129	45	.74	24	.271	.346	.378

Jorge Velandia

Bats: Right **Throws:** Right **Pos:** SS   **Ht:** 5'9" **Wt:** 160 **Born:** 1/12/75 **Age:** 21

Year	Team	Lg	G	AB	H	2B	3B	HR	TB	R	RBI	TBB	IBB	SO	HBP	SH	SF	SB	CS	SB%	GDP	Avg	OBP	SLG
1992	Bristol	R	45	119	24	6	1	0	32	20	9	15	0	16	0	3	0	3	2	.60	1	.202	.291	.269
1993	Fayettevlle	A	37	106	17	4	0	0	21	15	11	13	0	21	3	0	2	5	0	1.00	3	.160	.266	.198
	Niagara Fal	A	72	212	41	11	0	1	55	30	22	19	0	48	0	3	2	22	4	.85	2	.193	.258	.259
1994	Lakeland	A	22	60	14	4	0	0	18	8	3	6	0	14	0	3	1	0	2	.00	0	.233	.299	.300
	Springfield	A	98	290	71	14	0	4	97	42	36	21	0	46	4	6	3	5	6	.45	8	.245	.302	.334
1995	Memphis	AA	63	186	38	10	2	4	64	23	17	14	2	37	1	1	1	0	2	.00	4	.204	.262	.344
	Las Vegas	AAA	66	206	54	12	3	0	72	25	25	13	1	37	2	7	2	0	0	.00	5	.262	.309	.350
	4 Min. YEARS		403	1179	259	61	6	9	359	163	123	101	3	219	10	23	11	35	16	.69	23	.220	.284	.304

Guillermo Velasquez

Bats: Left **Throws:** Right **Pos:** 1B   **Ht:** 6'3" **Wt:** 225 **Born:** 4/23/68 **Age:** 28

Year	Team	Lg	G	AB	H	2B	3B	HR	TB	R	RBI	TBB	IBB	SO	HBP	SH	SF	SB	CS	SB%	GDP	Avg	OBP	SLG
1987	Charlstn-Sc	A	102	295	65	12	0	3	86	32	30	16	0	65	0	1	0	2	0	1.00	13	.220	.260	.292
1988	Charlstn-Sc	A	135	520	149	28	3	11	216	55	90	34	9	110	1	3	9	1	1	.50	6	.287	.326	.415
1989	Riverside	A	139	544	152	30	2	9	213	73	69	51	4	91	2	0	10	4	3	.57	14	.279	.338	.392
1990	Wichita	AA	105	377	102	21	2	12	163	48	72	35	5	66	1	0	4	1	1	.50	9	.271	.331	.432
1991	Wichita	AA	130	501	148	26	3	21	243	72	100	48	6	75	1	0	7	4	2	.67	6	.295	.354	.485
1992	Las Vegas	AAA	136	512	158	44	4	7	231	68	99	44	8	94	1	0	9	3	1	.75	7	.309	.359	.451
1993	Las Vegas	AAA	30	129	43	6	1	5	66	23	24	10	1	19	1	0	2	0	0	.00	2	.333	.380	.512
1994	Charlotte	AAA	18	52	11	3	0	1	17	7	4	10	1	9	0	0	1	0	0	.00	1	.212	.333	.327
	New Britain	AA	23	70	15	2	0	0	17	6	9	12	1	15	0	0	2	0	1	.00	0	.214	.321	.243
1995	Ottawa	AAA	45	112	28	5	0	1	36	11	9	8	1	14	0	0	0	1	2	.33	3	.250	.300	.321
1992	San Diego	NL	15	23	7	0	0	1	10	1	5	1	0	7	0	0	0	0	0	.00	0	.304	.333	.435
1993	San Diego	NL	79	143	30	2	0	3	41	7	20	13	2	35	0	0	1	0	0	.00	3	.210	.274	.287
	9 Min. YEARS		863	3112	871	177	15	70	1288	395	506	268	36	558	7	4	44	16	11	.59	61	.280	.334	.414
	2 Maj. YEARS		94	166	37	2	0	4	51	8	25	14	2	42	0	0	1	0	0	.00	3	.223	.282	.307

Jose Velez

Bats: Both **Throws:** Left **Pos:** OF   **Ht:** 6'2" **Wt:** 165 **Born:** 3/6/73 **Age:** 23

Year	Team	Lg	G	AB	H	2B	3B	HR	TB	R	RBI	TBB	IBB	SO	HBP	SH	SF	SB	CS	SB%	GDP	Avg	OBP	SLG
1990	Cardinals	R	46	183	58	7	6	0	77	26	29	8	0	12	2	1	2	5	3	.63	1	.317	.349	.421
1991	Springfield	A	116	410	99	10	3	0	115	46	35	15	2	50	1	3	3	10	5	.67	4	.241	.268	.280
1992	Savannah	A	93	316	86	12	1	0	100	32	25	18	0	56	2	4	2	8	5	.62	2	.272	.314	.316
1993	St. Pete	A	81	178	42	3	2	0	49	12	15	6	1	32	0	3	0	0	1	.00	2	.236	.261	.275
1994	St. Pete	A	100	279	73	8	0	2	87	30	22	15	2	18	3	4	3	6	3	.67	8	.262	.303	.312
1995	Arkansas	AA	107	287	85	13	1	7	121	37	41	13	1	36	2	2	2	5	4	.56	8	.296	.329	.422
	6 Min. YEARS		543	1653	443	53	13	9	549	183	167	75	6	204	10	17	12	34	21	.62	29	.268	.302	.332

Leroy Ventress

Bats: Both **Throws:** Right **Pos:** OF   **Ht:** 6'0" **Wt:** 173 **Born:** 8/14/68 **Age:** 27

Year	Team	Lg	G	AB	H	2B	3B	HR	TB	R	RBI	TBB	IBB	SO	HBP	SH	SF	SB	CS	SB%	GDP	Avg	OBP	SLG
1986	Bend	A	38	115	30	2	0	1	35	15	14	13	0	34	0	2	1	6	4	.60	2	.261	.333	.304
1987	Utica	A	44	120	25	3	1	1	33	15	11	14	0	39	1	1	1	3	1	.75	2	.208	.294	.275
1988	Batavia	A	70	271	68	14	2	3	95	45	19	35	2	58	5	2	3	36	9	.80	2	.251	.344	.351
1989	Spartanburg	A	136	516	144	14	11	0	180	91	33	59	1	109	2	4	1	42	24	.64	4	.279	.355	.349
1990	Clearwater	A	39	140	27	2	0	0	29	24	9	26	0	30	0	2	1	12	5	.71	2	.193	.317	.207
1991	Clearwater	A	122	417	100	12	3	1	121	70	40	62	2	69	10	9	2	35	9	.80	9	.240	.350	.290
1993	Daytona	A	17	60	11	1	0	0	12	8	4	10	1	17	0	0	0	2	1	.67	1	.183	.300	.200
1994	Brainerd	IND	61	209	69	11	2	3	93	44	22	36	0	46	0	0	2	35	7	.83	2	.330	.425	.445
1995	Harrisburg	AA	11	41	9	0	0	0	9	4	0	5	0	19	0	0	0	3	0	1.00	0	.220	.304	.220
	9 Min. YEARS		538	1889	483	59	19	9	607	316	152	260	6	421	18	20	11	174	60	.74	24	.256	.349	.321

Dario Veras

Pitches: Right **Bats:** Right **Pos:** P **Ht:** 6'1" **Wt:** 155 **Born:** 3/13/73 **Age:** 23

		HOW MUCH HE PITCHED					WHAT HE GAVE UP									THE RESULTS					
Year Team	Lg	G	GS	CG	GF	IP	BFP	H	R	ER	HR	SH	SF	HB	TBB	IBB	SO	WP	Bk	W	L	Pct.	ShO	Sv	ERA
1993 Bakersfield	A	7	0	0	1	13.1	61	13	11	11	1	0	1	0	8	2	11	0	0	1	0	1.000	0	0	7.43
Vero Beach	A	24	0	0	8	54.2	229	59	23	17	2	3	1	1	14	5	31	3	0	2	2	.500	0	2	2.80
1994 Rancho Cuca	A	59	0	0	13	79	332	66	28	18	7	7	0	6	25	9	56	2	0	9	2	.818	0	3	2.05
1995 Memphis	AA	58	0	0	22	82.2	360	81	38	35	8	3	1	7	27	11	70	5	1	7	3	.700	0	1	3.81
3 Min. YEARS		148	0	0	44	229.2	982	219	100	81	18	13	3	14	74	27	168	10	1	19	7	.731	0	6	3.17

Steve Verduzco

Bats: Right **Throws:** Right **Pos:** OF **Ht:** 6'1" **Wt:** 185 **Born:** 9/10/72 **Age:** 23

		BATTING														BASERUNNING				PERCENTAGES		
Year Team	Lg	G	AB	H	2B	3B	HR	TB	R	RBI	TBB	IBB	SO	HBP	SH	SF	SB	CS	SB%	GDP	Avg	OBP	SLG
1993 Auburn	A	64	239	53	7	1	1	65	30	19	19	1	48	3	5	0	8	1	.89	6	.222	.287	.272
1994 Osceola	A	102	322	80	20	0	1	103	50	34	37	0	58	3	9	4	20	5	.80	8	.248	.328	.320
1995 Jackson	AA	18	29	7	3	0	1	13	4	1	0	0	8	0	0	0	0	1	.00	1	.241	.241	.448
Kissimmee	A	98	348	87	17	0	1	125	47	50	37	3	50	6	3	5	18	4	.82	10	.250	.328	.359
3 Min. YEARS		282	938	227	47	1	10	306	131	104	93	4	164	12	17	9	46	11	.81	25	.242	.316	.326

Jake Viano

Pitches: Right **Bats:** Right **Pos:** P **Ht:** 5'10" **Wt:** 170 **Born:** 9/4/73 **Age:** 22

		HOW MUCH HE PITCHED						WHAT HE GAVE UP										THE RESULTS					
Year Team	Lg	G	GS	CG	GF	IP	BFP	H	R	ER	HR	SH	SF	HB	TBB	IBB	SO	WP	Bk	W	L	Pct.	ShO	Sv	ERA
1993 Rockies	R	22	1	0	8	33	136	24	15	12	1	0	1	3	6	0	32	6	0	2	2	.500	0	1	3.27
1994 Asheville	A	41	0	0	35	53.1	219	36	11	8	3	4	0	2	24	4	58	9	0	4	1	.800	0	23	1.35
New Haven	AA	8	0	0	5	11.1	51	7	7	3	0	0	1	0	8	0	14	1	0	0	3	.000	0	0	2.38
1995 New Haven	AA	57	0	0	49	72	304	51	31	27	5	7	3	2	38	1	85	2	0	3	6	.333	0	19	3.38
3 Min. YEARS		128	1	0	97	169.2	710	118	64	50	9	11	5	7	76	5	189	18	0	9	12	.429	0	43	2.65

Jose Vidro

Bats: Both **Throws:** Right **Pos:** 2B **Ht:** 5'11" **Wt:** 175 **Born:** 8/27/74 **Age:** 21

		BATTING														BASERUNNING				PERCENTAGES		
Year Team	Lg	G	AB	H	2B	3B	HR	TB	R	RBI	TBB	IBB	SO	HBP	SH	SF	SB	CS	SB%	GDP	Avg	OBP	SLG
1992 Expos	R	54	200	66	6	2	4	88	29	31	16	1	31	0	1	2	10	1	.91	5	.330	.376	.440
1993 Burlington	A	76	287	69	19	0	2	94	39	34	28	3	54	5	4	2	3	2	.60	7	.240	.317	.328
1994 W. Palm Bch	A	125	465	124	30	2	4	170	57	49	51	4	56	5	3	3	8	2	.80	5	.267	.344	.366
1995 Harrisburg	AA	64	246	64	16	2	4	96	33	38	20	2	37	1	4	3	3	7	.30	5	.260	.315	.390
W. Palm Bch	A	44	163	53	15	2	3	81	20	24	8	0	21	2	2	2	0	1	.00	5	.325	.360	.497
4 Min. YEARS		363	1361	376	86	8	17	529	178	176	123	10	199	13	14	12	24	13	.65	27	.276	.339	.389

Jose Viera

Bats: Right **Throws:** Right **Pos:** 3B **Ht:** 6'1" **Wt:** 190 **Born:** 2/23/71 **Age:** 25

		BATTING														BASERUNNING				PERCENTAGES		
Year Team	Lg	G	AB	H	2B	3B	HR	TB	R	RBI	TBB	IBB	SO	HBP	SH	SF	SB	CS	SB%	GDP	Avg	OBP	SLG
1990 Huntington	R	65	245	80	22	1	8	128	34	36	18	2	30	1	0	3	3	1	.75	3	.327	.371	.522
1991 Peoria	A	132	513	136	37	0	6	191	52	55	48	3	78	2	1	7	3	3	.50	7	.265	.326	.372
1992 Winston-Sal	A	117	405	111	32	0	18	197	55	58	39	2	72	1	4	6	3	3	.50	10	.274	.335	.486
1993 Orlando	AA	3	11	1	0	0	0	1	0	1	1	0	1	0	0	0	0	0	.00	0	.091	.167	.091
1995 Orlando	AA	12	33	4	0	0	1	7	2	2	2	0	8	1	0	0	0	0	.00	0	.121	.194	.212
5 Min. YEARS		329	1207	332	91	1	33	524	143	152	108	7	189	5	5	16	9	7	.56	20	.275	.333	.434

Joey Vierra

Pitches: Left **Bats:** Left **Pos:** P **Ht:** 5'7" **Wt:** 170 **Born:** 1/31/66 **Age:** 30

		HOW MUCH HE PITCHED						WHAT HE GAVE UP										THE RESULTS					
Year Team	Lg	G	GS	CG	GF	IP	BFP	H	R	ER	HR	SH	SF	HB	TBB	IBB	SO	WP	Bk	W	L	Pct.	ShO	Sv	ERA
1987 Reds	R	14	0	0	11	21	78	11	4	2	0	1	1	0	5	0	29	0	0	1	2	.333	0	8	0.86
Tampa	A	9	0	0	6	8	40	14	11	9	3	1	0	1	3	0	7	0	0	1	1	.500	0	1	10.13
1988 Greensboro	A	34	0	0	24	41.1	162	30	13	11	0	3	0	1	8	2	42	6	3	2	1	.667	0	2	2.40
1989 Cedar Rapds	A	47	0	0	28	74.1	293	43	22	14	4	1	1	4	20	3	81	3	1	5	3	.625	0	7	1.70
1990 Nashville	AAA	49	0	0	17	57.2	246	55	25	21	6	7	4	0	25	2	37	1	0	3	3	.500	0	1	3.28
1991 Nashville	AAA	62	2	0	15	95.2	412	81	60	46	8	4	1	6	43	2	84	5	2	5	4	.556	0	2	4.33
1992 Chattanooga	AA	1	1	0	0	6	23	5	0	0	0	1	0	0	0	0	3	0	0	1	0	1.000	0	0	0.00
Nashville	AAA	52	0	0	19	81.2	336	65	29	27	6	2	2	2	28	2	62	6	1	4	1	.800	0	2	2.98
1993 San Antonio	AA	9	0	0	4	11.2	53	14	7	7	1	3	0	1	4	1	6	1	0	1	0	1.000	0	1	5.40
Albuquerque	AAA	29	0	0	15	33	155	38	22	18	3	4	0	2	18	6	24	4	1	0	4	.000	0	1	4.91
1994 Birmingham	AA	27	6	1	7	66.2	271	60	23	22	1	5	2	3	19	1	63	4	2	4	2	.667	1	1	2.97
Nashville	AAA	19	0	0	10	21.1	96	25	11	9	2	0	2	1	11	1	18	2	0	0	0	.000	0	3	3.80
1995 Nashville	AAA	56	1	0	22	58.1	237	47	28	27	6	1	5	1	19	4	57	4	0	2	2	.500	0	4	4.17
9 Min. YEARS		408	13	1	178	576.2	2402	488	255	213	40	33	18	22	203	24	513	36	10	29	23	.558	1	36	3.32

Hector Villanueva

Bats: Right **Throws:** Right **Pos:** 1B   **Ht:** 6' 1" **Wt:** 220 **Born:** 10/2/64 **Age:** 31

Year	Team	Lg	G	AB	H	2B	3B	HR	TB	R	RBI	TBB	IBB	SO	HBP	SH	SF	SB	CS	SB%	GDP	Avg	OBP	SLG
1985	Peoria	A	65	193	45	7	0	1	55	22	19	27	0	36	3	2	1	0	2	.00	7	.233	.335	.285
1986	Winston-Sal	A	125	412	131	20	2	13	194	58	100	81	3	42	2	2	12	6	4	.60	12	.318	.422	.471
1987	Pittsfield	AA	109	391	107	31	0	14	180	59	70	43	1	38	1	2	3	3	4	.43	8	.274	.345	.460
1988	Pittsfield	AA	127	436	137	24	3	10	197	50	75	71	6	58	4	2	8	5	4	.56	9	.314	.408	.452
1989	Iowa	AAA	120	444	112	25	1	12	175	46	57	32	2	95	1	1	2	1	1	.50	6	.252	.303	.394
1990	Iowa	AAA	52	177	47	7	1	8	80	20	34	19	2	36	1	1	0	0	1	.00	4	.266	.340	.452
1991	Iowa	AAA	6	25	9	3	0	2	18	2	9	1	1	6	0	0	1	0	0	.00	0	.360	.370	.720
1992	Iowa	AAA	49	159	38	8	0	9	73	21	35	20	0	36	0	1	2	0	1	.00	4	.239	.320	.459
1993	Louisville	AAA	40	124	30	9	0	5	54	13	20	16	1	18	1	0	1	0	0	.00	5	.242	.331	.435
1994	Ottawa	AAA	26	93	20	5	0	4	37	12	11	12	0	18	1	0	1	0	0	.00	4	.215	.308	.398
1995	Richmond	AAA	10	19	4	1	0	1	8	1	3	1	0	3	0	0	1	0	0	.00	0	.211	.238	.421
1990	Chicago	NL	52	114	31	4	1	7	58	14	18	4	2	27	2	0	0	1	0	1.00	3	.272	.308	.509
1991	Chicago	NL	71	192	53	10	1	13	104	23	32	21	1	30	0	0	1	0	0	.00	3	.276	.346	.542
1992	Chicago	NL	51	112	17	6	0	2	29	9	13	11	2	24	0	0	0	0	0	.00	5	.152	.228	.259
1993	St. Louis	NL	17	55	8	1	0	3	18	7	9	4	1	17	0	0	0	0	0	.00	3	.145	.203	.327
	11 Min. YEARS		729	2473	680	140	7	79	1071	304	433	323	16	386	14	11	32	15	17	.47	59	.275	.358	.433
	4 Maj. YEARS		191	473	109	21	2	25	209	53	72	40	6	98	2	0	1	1	0	1.00	14	.230	.293	.442

Julio Vinas

Bats: Right **Throws:** Right **Pos:** C   **Ht:** 6'0" **Wt:** 200 **Born:** 2/14/73 **Age:** 23

Year	Team	Lg	G	AB	H	2B	3B	HR	TB	R	RBI	TBB	IBB	SO	HBP	SH	SF	SB	CS	SB%	GDP	Avg	OBP	SLG
1991	White Sox	R	50	187	42	9	0	3	60	21	29	19	0	40	2	0	2	2	3	.40	5	.225	.300	.321
1992	South Bend	A	33	94	16	3	0	0	19	7	10	9	0	17	1	0	2	1	3	.25	1	.170	.245	.202
	Utica	A	47	151	37	6	4	0	51	22	24	11	0	29	2	1	5	1	2	.33	2	.245	.296	.338
1993	South Bend	A	55	188	60	15	1	9	104	24	37	12	1	29	1	2	2	1	1	.50	2	.319	.360	.553
	Sarasota	A	18	65	16	2	1	1	23	5	7	5	0	13	0	0	0	0	0	.00	2	.246	.300	.354
1994	South Bend	A	121	466	118	31	1	9	178	68	75	43	4	75	4	6	6	0	2	.00	9	.253	.318	.382
1995	Birmingham	AA	102	372	100	16	2	6	138	47	61	37	1	80	5	0	7	3	3	.50	6	.269	.337	.371
	5 Min. YEARS		426	1523	389	82	9	28	573	194	243	136	6	283	15	9	24	8	14	.36	27	.255	.318	.376

George Virgilio

Bats: Both **Throws:** Right **Pos:** 2B   **Ht:** 5'9" **Wt:** 170 **Born:** 2/15/71 **Age:** 25

Year	Team	Lg	G	AB	H	2B	3B	HR	TB	R	RBI	TBB	IBB	SO	HBP	SH	SF	SB	CS	SB%	GDP	Avg	OBP	SLG
1990	Pulaski	R	58	220	57	9	2	3	79	35	21	27	2	19	1	3	0	7	4	.64	9	.259	.343	.359
1991	Pulaski	R	15	54	19	5	0	0	24	8	7	3	0	6	2	1	1	3	0	1.00	1	.352	.400	.444
	Macon	A	46	148	28	4	2	1	39	17	17	13	0	19	1	0	1	4	2	.67	2	.189	.258	.264
1992	Macon	A	112	370	84	17	5	1	114	30	34	44	2	59	1	3	2	18	17	.51	12	.227	.309	.308
1994	Harrisburg	AA	89	243	63	16	1	5	96	29	41	26	0	36	2	1	2	1	1	.50	5	.259	.333	.395
1995	Harrisburg	AA	27	56	8	0	0	1	11	9	5	20	2	11	0	0	1	1	1	.50	2	.143	.364	.196
	Bowie	AA	41	107	25	3	0	1	31	11	13	13	0	11	2	1	1	0	0	.00	6	.234	.325	.290
	5 Min. YEARS		388	1198	284	54	10	12	394	139	138	146	6	161	9	9	8	34	25	.58	36	.237	.323	.329

Mark Voisard

Pitches: Right **Bats:** Right **Pos:** P   **Ht:** 6'5" **Wt:** 210 **Born:** 11/4/69 **Age:** 26

Year	Team	Lg	G	GS	CG	GF	IP	BFP	H	R	ER	HR	SH	SF	HB	TBB	IBB	SO	WP	Bk	W	L	Pct.	ShO	Sv	ERA
1992	Bend	A	26	1	0	5	53	233	51	28	26	5	2	2	3	29	2	65	4	0	5	2	.714	0	2	4.42
1993	Central Val	A	21	14	0	1	82.1	365	72	58	56	6	0	2	1	53	0	61	6	0	3	6	.333	0	0	6.12
1994	Central Val	A	18	4	0	4	46.2	197	29	18	9	2	3	0	3	22	2	38	3	2	3	2	.600	0	2	1.74
	New Haven	AA	30	1	0	27	43.1	174	34	9	8	1	2	2	0	17	5	36	3	1	3	2	.600	0	15	1.66
1995	Salem	A	6	0	0	2	7.1	33	8	6	6	4	0	1	1	4	0	5	0	0	0	0	.000	0	0	7.36
	New Haven	AA	27	0	0	10	30.2	132	31	12	11	1	0	1	2	14	0	22	4	0	2	0	1.000	0	2	3.23
	4 Min. YEARS		128	20	0	49	263.1	1134	225	131	116	19	7	8	10	139	9	227	20	3	16	12	.571	0	21	3.96

Scott Vollmer

Bats: Right **Throws:** Right **Pos:** C   **Ht:** 6'1" **Wt:** 175 **Born:** 2/9/71 **Age:** 25

Year	Team	Lg	G	AB	H	2B	3B	HR	TB	R	RBI	TBB	IBB	SO	HBP	SH	SF	SB	CS	SB%	GDP	Avg	OBP	SLG
1993	White Sox	R	43	132	36	9	0	0	45	19	11	17	0	11	2	1	2	3	4	.43	4	.273	.359	.341
1994	Hickory	A	110	420	115	24	4	7	168	52	81	39	2	63	4	4	6	0	1	.00	17	.274	.337	.400
1995	Birmingham	AA	81	258	61	5	0	6	84	35	39	42	1	39	1	4	4	0	1	.00	5	.236	.341	.326
	3 Min. YEARS		234	810	212	38	4	13	297	106	131	98	3	113	7	9	12	3	6	.33	26	.262	.342	.367

Derek Wachter

Bats: Right **Throws:** Right **Pos:** OF   **Ht:** 6'2" **Wt:** 195 **Born:** 8/28/70 **Age:** 25

Year	Team	Lg	G	AB	H	2B	3B	HR	TB	R	RBI	TBB	IBB	SO	HBP	SH	SF	SB	CS	SB%	GDP	Avg	OBP	SLG
1991	Brewers	R	51	186	59	16	5	6	103	52	42	40	1	59	0	0	4	3	0	1.00	1	.317	.433	.554

Year Team	Lg	G	AB	H	2B	3B	HR	TB	R	RBI	TBB	IBB	SO	HBP	SH	SF	SB	CS	SB%	GDP	Avg	OBP	SLG
1992 Beloit	A	111	363	98	17	9	10	163	53	61	43	1	113	1	5	3	6	5	.55	9	.270	.346	.449
1993 Stockton	A	115	420	123	20	4	22	217	75	108	64	2	93	6	3	11	3	3	.50	7	.293	.385	.517
1994 El Paso	AA	30	117	45	9	5	0	64	14	24	13	0	24	2	0	3	3	0	1.00	6	.385	.444	.547
New Orleans	AAA	65	221	63	15	1	5	95	33	39	24	1	57	3	4	3	3	0	1.00	6	.285	.359	.430
1995 New Orleans	AAA	112	382	98	23	1	8	147	44	45	39	2	67	5	0	3	2	2	.50	11	.257	.331	.385
5 Min. YEARS		484	1689	486	100	25	51	789	271	319	223	7	413	18	12	27	20	10	.67	36	.288	.371	.467

David Waco

Bats: Right **Throws:** Right **Pos:** 2B **Ht:** 6'0" **Wt:** 185 **Born:** 12/8/69 **Age:** 26

Year Team	Lg	G	AB	H	2B	3B	HR	TB	R	RBI	TBB	IBB	SO	HBP	SH	SF	SB	CS	SB%	GDP	Avg	OBP	SLG
1993 Sioux Falls	IND	55	203	50	5	0	7	76	34	25	24	0	33	6	3	1	0	2	.00	2	.246	.342	.374
1994 Spartanburg	A	31	90	22	4	0	2	32	13	10	15	0	20	3	3	1	0	3	.00	2	.244	.367	.356
Clearwater	A	40	115	39	12	2	3	64	20	31	17	0	14	1	3	2	0	0	.00	1	.339	.422	.557
1995 Reading	AA	5	10	3	0	0	0	3	1	1	0	0	2	0	0	0	0	0	.00	0	.300	.300	.300
Clearwater	A	59	193	43	8	1	0	53	22	13	23	0	27	5	5	0	2	2	.50	5	.223	.321	.275
3 Min. YEARS		190	611	157	29	3	12	228	90	80	79	0	96	15	14	4	2	7	.22	12	.257	.354	.373

Scott Wade

Bats: Right **Throws:** Right **Pos:** OF **Ht:** 6'2" **Wt:** 200 **Born:** 4/26/63 **Age:** 33

Year Team	Lg	G	AB	H	2B	3B	HR	TB	R	RBI	TBB	IBB	SO	HBP	SH	SF	SB	CS	SB%	GDP	Avg	OBP	SLG
1984 Winter Havn	A	48	157	38	10	0	2	54	24	15	26	0	36	1	0	1	3	2	.60	3	.242	.351	.344
1985 Winter Havn	A	104	320	67	13	3	7	107	42	37	49	5	80	4	1	3	12	8	.60	3	.209	.319	.334
1986 New Britain	AA	123	414	110	23	1	9	162	54	51	54	0	102	8	0	7	31	12	.72	4	.266	.356	.391
1987 Pawtucket	AAA	108	355	90	12	4	16	158	51	60	32	1	123	3	0	6	11	9	.55	3	.254	.316	.445
1988 Pawtucket	AAA	114	396	94	17	2	10	145	42	37	24	2	118	4	3	1	7	2	.78	8	.237	.287	.366
1989 Pawtucket	AAA	104	345	82	20	2	12	142	39	35	34	1	81	0	2	1	6	3	.67	8	.238	.305	.412
1990 Pawtucket	AAA	105	303	70	12	4	11	123	34	41	27	0	97	5	4	1	9	8	.53	6	.231	.304	.406
1991 Scranton-Wb	AAA	112	309	81	14	7	9	136	48	43	33	0	70	3	1	2	4	5	.44	8	.262	.337	440
1992 Syracuse	AAA	18	45	7	2	0	0	9	3	3	5	0	12	2	0	1	0	0	.00	2	.156	.264	.200
Iowa	AAA	72	227	54	14	0	14	110	38	38	28	2	57	4	3	7	5	3	.63	4	.238	.323	.485
1993 Iowa	AAA	47	147	25	8	0	3	42	14	15	12	0	42	2	1	2	9	3	.75	2	.170	.239	.286
Portland	AAA	11	37	12	3	1	0	17	6	4	2	0	10	2	0	0	0	1	.00	2	.324	.390	.459
Norfolk	AAA	23	79	15	3	1	6	38	10	13	5	0	32	0	0	0	0	0	.00	1	.190	.238	.481
1994 Scranton-Wb	AAA	31	75	14	5	0	3	28	6	9	7	0	29	1	0	0	1	0	1.00	3	.187	.265	.373
1995 Pawtucket	AAA	7	27	4	1	0	0	5	2	0	0	0	11	0	0	0	0	0	.00	0	.148	.148	.185
12 Min. YEARS		1027	3236	763	157	25	102	1276	413	401	338	11	900	39	15	32	98	56	.64	57	.236	.313	.394

Aubrey Waggoner

Bats: Left **Throws:** Right **Pos:** OF **Ht:** 5'11" **Wt:** 185 **Born:** 12/6/66 **Age:** 29

Year Team	Lg	G	AB	H	2B	3B	HR	TB	R	RBI	TBB	IBB	SO	HBP	SH	SF	SB	CS	SB%	GDP	Avg	OBP	SLG
1985 White Sox	R	49	142	27	6	2	1	40	33	10	49	3	40	1	3	2	12	7	.63	0	.190	.397	.282
1986 Appleton	A	60	188	34	2	0	3	45	25	7	23	1	46	3	3	0	29	4	.88	2	.181	.280	.239
White Sox	R	34	81	23	3	3	1	35	22	12	27	0	13	2	0	2	18	1	.95	0	.284	.464	.432
Peninsula	A	20	72	14	0	3	0	20	7	9	14	0	24	1	1	0	4	3	.57	2	.194	.333	.278
1987 Peninsula	A	115	426	113	15	4	12	172	82	51	87	2	88	5	4	2	52	23	.69	8	.265	.394	.404
1988 Birmingham	AA	13	40	8	2	2	0	14	6	1	11	0	11	1	0	1	4	5	.44	1	.200	.377	.350
Tampa	A	43	126	28	3	6	3	52	19	15	21	0	34	1	0	2	11	2	.85	2	.222	.333	.413
1989 Birmingham	AA	114	302	69	23	6	4	116	66	35	76	1	74	9	2	1	25	12	.68	1	.228	.397	.384
1990 Birmingham	AA	81	276	71	17	4	5	111	57	32	56	1	60	2	2	1	11	9	.55	1	.257	.385	.402
1991 Vancouver	AAA	50	156	32	4	4	1	47	23	10	19	0	39	2	1	1	5	3	.63	0	.205	.298	.301
Birmingham	AA	69	248	57	11	4	3	85	39	21	54	2	56	1	2	0	20	6	.77	1	.230	.370	.343
1992 Greenville	AA	90	237	64	14	3	14	126	51	45	70	1	81	1	0	3	21	12	.64	0	.270	.434	.532
Richmond	AAA	7	22	5	1	0	0	9	2	6	3	0	6	0	0	0	1	0	1.00	0	.227	.320	.409
1993 Calgary	AAA	13	38	10	2	1	2	20	9	4	15	0	17	0	0	0	3	0	1.00	0	.263	.472	.526
Jacksonville	AA	34	102	25	8	2	3	46	29	7	40	0	34	0	0	1	7	3	.70	0	.245	.455	.451
1994 Ottawa	AAA	11	17	4	0	0	1	7	4	5	5	0	5	0	0	0	1	1	.50	0	.235	.409	.412
Greenville	AA	53	158	44	5	3	4	67	28	14	33	1	57	0	1	3	10	6	.63	3	.278	.397	.424
1995 Pawtucket	AAA	16	48	9	1	0	0	10	3	8	10	1	22	0	0	0	2	2	.50	0	.188	.328	.208
11 Min. YEARS		872	2679	637	117	47	58	1022	505	292	613	13	707	29	20	19	236	99	.70	21	.238	.383	.381

Jimmy Waggoner

Bats: Left **Throws:** Right **Pos:** 2B **Ht:** 5'11" **Wt:** 185 **Born:** 4/17/67 **Age:** 29

Year Team	Lg	G	AB	H	2B	3B	HR	TB	R	RBI	TBB	IBB	SO	HBP	SH	SF	SB	CS	SB%	GDP	Avg	OBP	SLG
1989 Sou. Oregon	A	54	200	54	7	0	1	64	35	18	35	0	40	0	1	1	5	6	.45	0	.270	.377	.320
1990 Modesto	A	35	86	14	3	0	0	17	13	5	21	1	25	2	2	0	1	1	.50	0	.163	.339	.198
Madison	A	39	114	28	3	0	1	34	16	8	26	0	18	0	1	1	4	3	.57	3	.246	.383	.298
1991 Modesto	A	86	241	54	4	2	2	68	34	19	70	0	67	2	4	1	2	5	.29	4	.224	.401	.282
1992 Reno	A	93	317	98	18	0	11	149	75	57	87	2	50	4	1	3	2	5	.29	4	.309	.460	.470
Huntsville	AA	6	16	1	0	0	0	1	0	0	0	0	2	0	0	0	0	0	.00	1	.063	.063	.063
1993 Huntsville	AA	57	129	18	3	0	1	24	12	8	29	1	38	0	0	1	2	2	.50	5	.140	.296	.186
1994 Huntsville	AA	70	173	36	1	1	1	42	19	9	37	1	44	1	4	1	0	3	.00	4	.208	.349	.243

| 1995 Huntsville | AA | 51 | 110 | 22 | 5 | 1 | 0 | 29 | 18 | 15 | 34 | 0 | 29 | 2 | 3 | 0 | 1 | 2 | .33 | 1 | .200 | .397 | .264 |
| 7 Min. YEARS | | 491 | 1386 | 325 | 44 | 4 | 17 | 428 | 222 | 139 | 339 | 4 | 313 | 11 | 16 | 8 | 18 | 23 | .44 | 25 | .234 | .387 | .309 |

Bret Wagner

Pitches: Left **Bats:** Left **Pos:** P   **Ht:** 6'0" **Wt:** 190 **Born:** 4/17/73 **Age:** 23

| | | HOW MUCH HE PITCHED | | | | | WHAT HE GAVE UP | | | | | | | | THE RESULTS | | | | | |
Year Team	Lg	G	GS	CG	GF	IP	BFP	H	R	ER	HR	SH	SF	HB	TBB	IBB	SO	WP	Bk	W	L	Pct.	ShO	Sv	ERA
1994 New Jersey	A	3	3	0	0	12.1	53	10	9	7	0	0	0	0	4	0	10	3	0	1	1	.000	0	0	5.11
Savannah	A	7	7	0	0	44	161	27	8	6	2	0	1	0	6	0	43	3	1	4	1	.800	0	0	1.23
1995 St. Pete	A	17	17	1	0	93.1	373	77	36	22	3	3	2	2	28	0	59	4	0	5	4	.556	0	0	2.12
Arkansas	AA	6	6	0	0	36.2	161	34	14	13	1	1	1	0	18	0	31	3	0	1	2	.333	0	0	3.19
2 Min. YEARS		33	33	1	0	186.1	748	148	67	48	6	4	4	2	56	0	143	13	1	10	8	.556	0	0	2.32

Joe Wagner

Pitches: Right **Bats:** Right **Pos:** P   **Ht:** 6'1" **Wt:** 195 **Born:** 12/8/71 **Age:** 24

| | | HOW MUCH HE PITCHED | | | | | WHAT HE GAVE UP | | | | | | | | THE RESULTS | | | | | |
Year Team	Lg	G	GS	CG	GF	IP	BFP	H	R	ER	HR	SH	SF	HB	TBB	IBB	SO	WP	Bk	W	L	Pct.	ShO	Sv	ERA
1993 Helena	R	8	7	0	0	41.1	181	39	17	12	1	2	0	3	20	0	30	2	1	3	2	.600	0	0	2.61
1994 Beloit	A	28	28	7	0	185.1	793	178	99	81	10	8	3	6	71	3	137	20	1	13	9	.591	1	0	3.93
1995 El Paso	AA	5	5	0	0	19	109	32	31	21	7	0	0	2	22	0	8	4	0	0	4	.000	0	0	9.95
Stockton	A	20	18	0	1	107.2	494	124	62	52	8	8	3	4	53	0	76	7	0	7	6	.538	0	0	4.35
3 Min. YEARS		61	58	7	1	353.1	1577	373	209	166	26	18	6	15	166	3	251	33	2	23	21	.523	1	0	4.23

Matt Wagner

Pitches: Right **Bats:** Right **Pos:** P   **Ht:** 6'5" **Wt:** 215 **Born:** 4/4/72 **Age:** 24

| | | HOW MUCH HE PITCHED | | | | | WHAT HE GAVE UP | | | | | | | | THE RESULTS | | | | | |
Year Team	Lg	G	GS	CG	GF	IP	BFP	H	R	ER	HR	SH	SF	HB	TBB	IBB	SO	WP	Bk	W	L	Pct.	ShO	Sv	ERA
1994 Appleton	A	15	1	0	7	32.2	129	23	8	3	2	2	0	0	8	1	48	4	2	4	2	.667	0	1	0.83
1995 Port City	AA	23	23	0	0	137	566	121	57	43	9	3	4	4	33	1	111	5	1	5	8	.385	0	0	2.82
Tacoma	AAA	6	6	1	0	33	157	43	29	23	3	0	1	1	17	1	33	2	0	1	5	.167	0	0	6.27
2 Min. YEARS		44	30	1	7	202.2	852	187	94	69	14	5	5	5	58	3	192	11	3	10	15	.400	0	1	3.06

David Wainhouse

Pitches: Right **Bats:** Left **Pos:** P   **Ht:** 6'2" **Wt:** 185 **Born:** 11/7/67 **Age:** 28

| | | HOW MUCH HE PITCHED | | | | | WHAT HE GAVE UP | | | | | | | | THE RESULTS | | | | | |
Year Team	Lg	G	GS	CG	GF	IP	BFP	H	R	ER	HR	SH	SF	HB	TBB	IBB	SO	WP	Bk	W	L	Pct.	ShO	Sv	ERA
1989 W. Palm Bch	A	13	13	0	0	66.1	286	75	35	30	4	3	2	8	19	0	26	6	3	1	5	.167	0	0	4.07
1990 W. Palm Bch	A	12	12	2	0	76.2	327	68	28	18	1	0	3	5	34	0	58	2	3	6	3	.667	1	0	2.11
Jacksonville	AA	17	16	2	0	95.2	428	97	59	46	8	2	3	7	47	2	59	2	0	7	7	.500	0	0	4.33
1991 Harrisburg	AA	33	0	0	27	52	224	49	17	15	1	2	0	4	17	2	46	3	0	2	2	.500	0	11	2.60
Indianapols	AAA	14	0	0	8	28.2	127	28	14	13	1	2	1	3	15	1	13	3	0	2	0	1.000	0	1	4.08
1992 Indianapols	AAA	44	0	0	41	46	208	48	22	21	4	2	2	2	24	6	37	4	0	5	4	.556	0	21	4.11
1993 Calgary	AAA	13	0	0	10	15.2	62	10	7	7	2	2	2	1	7	1	7	2	0	0	1	.000	0	5	4.02
1995 Syracuse	AAA	26	0	0	21	24.1	111	29	13	10	1	1	2	1	11	3	18	4	0	3	2	.600	0	5	3.70
Portland	AA	17	0	0	5	25	122	39	22	20	3	0	1	1	8	1	16	1	0	2	1	.667	0	0	7.20
Charlotte	AAA	4	0	0	1	3.2	21	6	6	4	1	0	1	0	4	0	2	2	0	0	0	.000	0	0	9.82
1991 Montreal	NL	2	0	0	1	2.2	14	2	2	2	0	0	1	0	4	0	1	0	0	0	1	.000	0	0	6.75
1993 Seattle	AL	3	0	0	0	2.1	20	7	7	7	1	0	0	1	5	0	2	2	0	0	0	.000	0	0	27.00
6 Min. YEARS		193	41	4	113	434	1916	449	223	184	26	14	17	32	186	16	282	29	6	28	25	.528	1	43	3.82
2 Maj. YEARS		5	0	0	1	5	34	9	9	9	1	0	1	1	9	0	3	2	0	0	1	.000	0	0	16.20

Don Wakamatsu

Bats: Right **Throws:** Right **Pos:** C   **Ht:** 6'2" **Wt:** 210 **Born:** 2/22/63 **Age:** 33

| | | BATTING | | | | | | | | | | | | | | | BASERUNNING | | | | PERCENTAGES | | |
Year Team	Lg	G	AB	H	2B	3B	HR	TB	R	RBI	TBB	IBB	SO	HBP	SH	SF	SB	CS	SB%	GDP	Avg	OBP	SLG
1985 Billings	R	58	196	49	7	0	0	56	20	24	25	2	36	0	5	2	1	0	1.00	7	.250	.332	.286
1986 Tampa	A	112	361	100	18	2	1	125	41	66	53	2	66	5	0	8	6	1	.86	11	.277	.370	.346
1987 Cedar Rapds	A	103	365	79	13	1	7	115	33	41	30	1	71	3	2	3	3	3	.50	9	.216	.279	.315
1988 Chattanooga	AA	79	235	56	9	1	1	70	22	26	37	0	41	0	1	2	0	1	.00	5	.238	.339	.298
1989 Birmingham	AA	92	287	73	15	0	2	94	45	45	32	0	54	7	5	5	7	6	.54	4	.254	.338	.328
1990 Vancouver	AAA	62	187	49	10	0	0	59	20	13	13	1	35	7	1	1	2	2	.50	2	.262	.332	.316
1991 Vancouver	AAA	55	172	34	8	0	4	54	20	19	12	0	39	1	4	2	0	0	.00	3	.198	.251	.314
1992 Albuquerque	AAA	60	167	54	10	0	2	70	22	15	15	0	23	4	1	0	0	1	.00	5	.323	.392	.419
1993 Albuquerque	AAA	54	181	61	11	1	7	95	30	31	15	2	31	4	0	4	0	1	.00	3	.337	.392	.525
1994 Okla. City	AAA	1	2	0	0	0	0	0	0	0	0	0	1	0	0	0	0	0	.00	0	.000	.000	.000
1995 Tacoma	AAA	9	32	5	1	0	0	6	3	6	2	0	8	1	0	0	0	0	.00	0	.156	.229	.188
Canton-Akrn	AA	51	143	38	10	0	4	60	16	23	17	2	21	6	3	2	0	0	.00	7	.266	.363	.420
1991 Chicago	AL	18	31	7	0	0	0	7	2	0	1	0	6	0	0	0	0	0	.00	0	.226	.250	.226
11 Min. YEARS		736	2328	598	112	5	28	804	272	309	251	10	426	38	22	29	19	15	.56	60	.257	.335	.345

310

Joe Waldron

Pitches: Left **Bats:** Left **Pos:** P **Ht:** 6'0" **Wt:** 180 **Born:** 7/4/69 **Age:** 26

		HOW MUCH HE PITCHED						WHAT HE GAVE UP												THE RESULTS					
Year Team	Lg	G	GS	CG	GF	IP	BFP	H	R	ER	HR	SH	SF	HB	TBB	IBB	SO	WP	Bk	W	L	Pct.	ShO	Sv	ERA
1990 Spokane	A	21	1	0	4	46.2	244	61	45	32	2	3	1	3	40	0	42	5	2	1	4	.200	0	0	6.17
1991 Charlstn-Sc	A	38	16	0	13	147.1	628	135	72	61	9	5	7	2	59	4	141	4	9	10	6	.625	0	5	3.73
1992 Waterloo	A	49	2	0	15	94.2	416	113	63	52	9	3	2	2	32	3	73	7	2	7	3	.700	0	1	4.94
1993 Waterloo	A	16	1	1	5	32	132	19	11	9	1	2	2	1	19	2	30	3	0	3	3	.500	0	1	2.53
Rancho Cuca	A	30	0	0	8	35	155	43	28	23	6	0	0	1	11	0	31	0	2	1	2	.333	0	0	5.91
1994 Harrisburg	AA	2	0	0	0	2.1	8	1	0	0	0	0	0	0	0	0	0	0	1	0	0	.000	0	0	0.00
W. Palm Bch	A	34	0	0	13	51	202	42	10	9	2	2	1	3	15	0	56	2	2	4	3	.571	0	3	1.59
1995 Tucson	AAA	4	0	0	1	8.1	31	6	4	4	0	0	0	0	2	0	11	0	0	1	0	1.000	0	0	4.32
Jackson	AA	28	0	0	12	51	215	57	22	21	5	4	2	4	11	1	39	2	1	1	2	.333	0	2	3.71
Salem	A	9	0	0	3	14.1	64	23	5	4	0	0	0	0	1	0	17	0	0	1	2	.333	0	0	2.51
6 Min. YEARS		231	20	1	74	482.2	2095	500	260	215	34	19	15	16	190	10	440	23	19	29	25	.537	0	12	4.01

Dane Walker

Bats: Left **Throws:** Right **Pos:** DH-OF **Ht:** 5'10" **Wt:** 180 **Born:** 11/16/69 **Age:** 26

		BATTING												BASERUNNING				PERCENTAGES		
Year Team	Lg	G	AB	H	2B	3B	HR	TB	R	RBI	TBB	IBB	SO	HBP	SH	SF	SB	CS	SB%	GDP	Avg	OBP	SLG
1991 Athletics	R	29	118	43	3	0	2	52	37	22	24	1	11	2	1	0	12	1	.92	5	.364	.479	.441
Modesto	A	22	66	18	2	1	0	22	11	5	14	0	9	0	1	1	2	3	.40	2	.273	.395	.333
1992 Madison	A	82	287	85	13	2	3	111	56	23	42	0	57	1	4	2	23	10	.70	6	.296	.386	.387
Reno	A	31	122	34	6	0	0	40	24	3	23	1	23	1	0	0	8	7	.53	4	.279	.397	.328
1993 Modesto	A	122	443	131	22	1	9	182	94	67	94	0	55	0	7	1	16	16	.50	6	.296	.418	.411
1994 Modesto	A	9	27	11	4	0	1	18	6	16	10	0	5	0	1	1	0	0	.00	2	.407	.553	.667
Huntsville	AA	47	153	42	10	0	0	52	21	10	24	0	29	1	6	1	6	7	.46	3	.275	.374	.340
1995 Huntsville	AA	110	370	86	13	2	2	109	46	35	57	6	84	2	2	3	9	7	.56	9	.232	.336	.295
5 Min. YEARS		452	1586	450	73	6	17	586	295	181	288	8	273	7	22	9	76	51	.60	37	.284	.394	.369

Jamie Walker

Pitches: Left **Bats:** Left **Pos:** P **Ht:** 6'2" **Wt:** 190 **Born:** 7/1/71 **Age:** 25

		HOW MUCH HE PITCHED						WHAT HE GAVE UP												THE RESULTS					
Year Team	Lg	G	GS	CG	GF	IP	BFP	H	R	ER	HR	SH	SF	HB	TBB	IBB	SO	WP	Bk	W	L	Pct.	ShO	Sv	ERA
1992 Auburn	A	15	14	0	0	83.1	341	75	35	29	4	4	1	6	21	0	67	4	1	4	6	.400	0	0	3.13
1993 Quad City	A	25	24	1	1	131.2	585	140	92	75	12	10	5	6	48	1	121	12	0	3	11	.214	1	0	5.13
1994 Quad City	A	32	18	0	4	125	569	133	80	58	10	14	3	16	42	2	104	5	1	8	10	.444	0	1	4.18
1995 Jackson	AA	50	0	0	19	58	250	59	29	29	6	3	2	2	24	5	38	4	1	4	2	.667	0	2	4.50
4 Min. YEARS		122	56	1	24	398	1745	407	236	191	32	31	11	30	135	8	330	25	3	19	29	.396	1	3	4.32

Todd Walker

Bats: Left **Throws:** Right **Pos:** 2B **Ht:** 6'0" **Wt:** 180 **Born:** 5/25/73 **Age:** 23

		BATTING												BASERUNNING				PERCENTAGES		
Year Team	Lg	G	AB	H	2B	3B	HR	TB	R	RBI	TBB	IBB	SO	HBP	SH	SF	SB	CS	SB%	GDP	Avg	OBP	SLG
1994 Fort Myers	A	46	171	52	5	2	10	91	29	34	32	0	15	0	0	4	6	3	.67	4	.304	.406	.532
1995 New Britain	AA	137	513	149	27	3	21	245	83	85	63	1	101	2	1	8	23	9	.72	13	.290	.365	.478
2 Min. YEARS		183	684	201	32	5	31	336	112	119	95	1	116	2	1	12	29	12	.71	17	.294	.376	.491

Derek Wallace

Pitches: Right **Bats:** Right **Pos:** P **Ht:** 6'3" **Wt:** 200 **Born:** 9/1/71 **Age:** 24

		HOW MUCH HE PITCHED						WHAT HE GAVE UP												THE RESULTS					
Year Team	Lg	G	GS	CG	GF	IP	BFP	H	R	ER	HR	SH	SF	HB	TBB	IBB	SO	WP	Bk	W	L	Pct.	ShO	Sv	ERA
1992 Peoria	A	2	0	0	1	3.2	13	3	2	2	0	1	0	0	1	0	2	0	2	0	1	.000	0	0	4.91
1993 Daytona	A	14	12	0	1	79.1	342	85	50	37	6	6	2	2	23	2	34	5	11	5	6	.455	0	1	4.20
Iowa	AAA	1	1	0	0	4	20	8	5	5	0	0	1	0	1	0	2	0	0	0	0	.000	0	0	11.25
Orlando	AA	15	15	2	0	96.2	418	105	59	54	12	5	0	10	28	3	69	9	4	5	7	.417	0	0	5.03
1994 Orlando	AA	33	12	1	19	89.1	391	95	61	57	11	3	4	10	31	3	49	6	4	2	9	.182	0	8	5.74
Iowa	AAA	5	0	0	2	4.1	21	4	2	2	0	0	0	0	4	0	3	1	0	0	1	.000	0	0	4.15
1995 Wichita	AA	26	0	0	18	43	188	51	23	21	5	1	1	2	13	4	24	3	0	4	3	.571	0	6	4.40
Binghamton	AA	15	0	0	11	15.1	62	11	9	9	1	0	3	1	9	1	8	1	2	0	1	.000	0	2	5.28
4 Min. YEARS		111	40	3	52	335.2	1455	362	213	187	35	16	11	25	110	13	191	25	23	16	28	.364	0	18	5.01

Kent Wallace

Pitches: Right **Bats:** Left **Pos:** P **Ht:** 6'3" **Wt:** 192 **Born:** 8/22/70 **Age:** 25

		HOW MUCH HE PITCHED						WHAT HE GAVE UP												THE RESULTS					
Year Team	Lg	G	GS	CG	GF	IP	BFP	H	R	ER	HR	SH	SF	HB	TBB	IBB	SO	WP	Bk	W	L	Pct.	ShO	Sv	ERA
1992 Oneonta	A	14	14	1	0	81.1	336	72	36	23	2	1	3	0	11	0	55	3	0	8	4	.667	1	0	2.55
1993 Greensboro	A	13	10	2	2	66	277	63	31	22	2	0	2	2	12	0	49	3	2	4	2	.667	1	0	3.00
1994 Tampa	A	39	0	0	17	77.2	310	60	23	18	2	2	3	3	22	4	61	2	0	6	3	.667	0	7	2.09
1995 Norwich	AA	18	16	0	0	94.2	395	93	41	37	9	2	1	1	24	0	72	2	1	7	6	.538	0	0	3.52
Columbus	AAA	9	9	0	0	50.2	200	44	19	17	8	0	0	0	11	0	31	3	0	4	1	.800	0	0	3.02
4 Min. YEARS		93	49	3	20	370.1	1518	336	146	117	23	5	10	6	80	4	268	13	3	29	16	.644	2	9	2.84

Casey Waller

Bats: Both **Throws:** Right **Pos:** 2B   **Ht:** 5'11" **Wt:** 180 **Born:** 12/15/67 **Age:** 28

					BATTING												BASERUNNING				PERCENTAGES		
Year	Team	Lg	G	AB	H	2B	3B	HR	TB	R	RBI	TBB	IBB	SO	HBP	SH	SF	SB	CS	SB%	GDP	Avg	OBP	SLG
1989	Spartanburg	A	55	202	52	9	1	8	87	25	31	18	0	40	3	1	2	1	0	1.00	4	.257	.324	.431
1990	Reading	AA	67	236	57	11	2	3	81	24	24	15	1	32	10	1	2	1	1	.50	1	.242	.312	.343
	Clearwater	A	59	208	59	14	4	8	105	29	31	18	0	31	6	0	1	4	1	.80	4	.284	.356	.505
1991	Scranton-Wb	AAA	4	14	1	0	0	0	1	1	0	0	0	2	0	0	0	0	0	.00	0	.071	.071	.071
	Reading	AA	118	402	105	25	1	12	168	64	52	53	6	47	7	2	2	2	0	1.00	8	.261	.356	.418
1992	Reading	AA	91	314	80	14	3	5	115	42	31	31	2	49	3	1	4	5	3	.63	4	.255	.324	.366
	Scranton-Wb	AAA	23	61	18	4	0	0	22	11	8	6	3	11	0	1	3	1	1	.50	1	.295	.343	.361
1993	Scranton-Wb	AAA	58	170	30	7	1	1	42	19	13	10	1	20	1	0	1	2	0	1.00	3	.176	.225	.247
	Reading	AA	53	169	44	8	4	2	66	25	18	15	3	20	5	1	4	1	0	1.00	2	.260	.332	.391
1994	Brainerd	IND	68	247	71	11	3	5	103	45	39	29	5	23	5	0	5	17	4	.81	9	.287	.367	.417
1995	Portland	A	14	36	8	2	1	0	12	4	5	6	0	4	0	0	0	1	0	1.00	2	.222	.333	.333
	Thunder Bay	IND	41	171	51	11	0	6	80	27	26	12	0	27	3	1	0	3	0	.00	2	.298	.355	.468
	7 Min. YEARS		651	2230	576	116	20	50	882	316	278	213	21	306	43	7	24	35	13	.73	40	.258	.331	.396

Dan Walters

Bats: Right **Throws:** Right **Pos:** C   **Ht:** 6'4" **Wt:** 230 **Born:** 8/15/66 **Age:** 29

					BATTING												BASERUNNING				PERCENTAGES		
Year	Team	Lg	G	AB	H	2B	3B	HR	TB	R	RBI	TBB	IBB	SO	HBP	SH	SF	SB	CS	SB%	GDP	Avg	OBP	SLG
1985	Asheville	A	15	28	1	0	0	0	1	1	1	1	0	11	0	1	0	0	0	.00	1	.036	.069	.036
	Auburn	A	44	144	30	6	0	0	36	15	10	8	0	23	1	0	3	1	0	1.00	6	.208	.250	.250
1986	Asheville	A	101	366	96	21	1	8	143	42	46	14	0	59	1	1	2	1	1	.50	12	.262	.290	.391
1987	Osceola	A	99	338	84	8	0	1	95	23	30	33	2	42	0	5	5	2	4	.33	15	.249	.311	.281
1988	Tucson	AAA	2	7	0	0	0	0	0	0	0	0	0	2	0	0	0	0	0	.00	0	.000	.000	.000
	Columbus	AA	98	305	71	10	1	7	104	31	28	26	0	42	3	3	4	1	0	1.00	11	.233	.296	.341
1989	Wichita	AA	89	300	82	15	0	6	115	30	45	25	2	31	3	3	2	0	2	.00	5	.273	.333	.383
1990	Wichita	AA	58	199	59	12	0	7	92	25	40	21	2	21	1	0	2	0	0	.00	8	.296	.363	.462
	Las Vegas	AAA	53	184	47	9	0	3	65	19	26	13	0	24	0	0	3	0	0	.00	10	.255	.300	.353
1991	Las Vegas	AAA	96	293	93	22	0	4	127	39	44	22	5	35	0	0	2	0	0	.00	12	.317	.365	.433
1992	Las Vegas	AAA	35	127	50	9	0	2	65	16	25	10	1	12	2	1	2	0	0	.00	5	.394	.440	.512
1993	Las Vegas	AAA	66	223	64	14	0	5	93	26	39	14	0	26	1	0	1	1	2	.33	13	.287	.331	.417
1995	Colo. Sprng	AAA	52	155	44	9	2	3	66	15	23	7	1	20	1	1	1	0	0	.00	6	.284	.317	.426
1992	San Diego	NL	57	179	45	11	1	4	70	14	22	10	0	28	2	1	2	1	0	1.00	3	.251	.295	.391
1993	San Diego	NL	27	94	19	3	0	1	25	6	10	7	2	13	0	0	1	0	0	.00	2	.202	.255	.266
	10 Min. YEARS		808	2669	721	135	4	46	1002	282	357	194	13	348	13	15	25	6	9	.40	104	.270	.320	.375
	2 Maj. YEARS		84	273	64	14	1	5	95	20	32	17	2	41	2	1	3	1	0	1.00	5	.234	.281	.348

Chuck Wanke

Pitches: Left **Bats:** Right **Pos:** P   **Ht:** 6'5" **Wt:** 200 **Born:** 2/2/71 **Age:** 25

			HOW MUCH HE PITCHED						WHAT HE GAVE UP									THE RESULTS				
Year	Team	Lg	G	GS	CG	GF	IP	BFP	H	R	ER	HR	SH	SF	HB	TBB	IBB	SO	WP	Bk	W	L	Pct.	ShO	Sv	ERA
1990	Bend	A	6	6	0	0	27.2	138	27	22	15	2	0	0	2	26	0	25	5	1	0	3	.000	0	0	4.88
1991	Everett	A	13	0	0	5	22.2	107	18	19	13	7	1	0	2	17	0	25	5	1	0	1	.000	0	0	5.16
1992	Clinton	A	26	21	1	1	123	559	115	81	56	4	5	4	9	62	1	118	11	2	9	10	.474	0	0	4.10
1993	San Jose	A	27	20	0	4	131	594	137	91	74	9	3	6	9	75	2	98	4	2	6	7	.462	0	2	5.08
1994	Sioux Falls	IND	7	7	0	0	40.1	178	40	21	17	6	2	0	0	19	0	21	0	0	4	2	.667	0	0	3.79
1995	Shreveport	AA	43	0	0	17	41.1	183	35	23	20	1	0	1	5	22	0	40	2	0	2	3	.400	0	0	4.35
	6 Min. YEARS		122	54	1	27	386	1759	372	257	195	29	11	11	27	221	3	327	27	6	21	26	.447	0	2	4.55

Bryan Ward

Pitches: Left **Bats:** Left **Pos:** P   **Ht:** 6'2" **Wt:** 210 **Born:** 1/28/72 **Age:** 24

			HOW MUCH HE PITCHED						WHAT HE GAVE UP									THE RESULTS				
Year	Team	Lg	G	GS	CG	GF	IP	BFP	H	R	ER	HR	SH	SF	HB	TBB	IBB	SO	WP	Bk	W	L	Pct.	ShO	Sv	ERA
1993	Elmira	A	14	11	0	2	61.1	291	82	41	34	6	2	4	4	26	2	63	5	5	2	5	.286	0	0	4.99
1994	Kane County	A	47	0	0	40	55.2	235	46	27	21	4	3	4	2	21	2	62	2	0	3	4	.429	0	11	3.40
1995	Portland	AA	20	11	1	5	72	321	70	42	36	9	1	1	2	31	3	71	7	3	7	3	.700	1	2	4.50
	Brevard Cty	A	11	11	0	0	72	296	68	27	23	5	4	0	2	17	0	65	1	1	5	1	.833	0	0	2.88
	3 Min. YEARS		92	33	1	47	261	1143	266	137	114	24	10	9	10	95	7	261	15	9	17	13	.567	1	13	3.93

Jim Waring

Pitches: Right **Bats:** Left **Pos:** P   **Ht:** 6'2" **Wt:** 180 **Born:** 9/19/69 **Age:** 26

			HOW MUCH HE PITCHED						WHAT HE GAVE UP									THE RESULTS				
Year	Team	Lg	G	GS	CG	GF	IP	BFP	H	R	ER	HR	SH	SF	HB	TBB	IBB	SO	WP	Bk	W	L	Pct.	ShO	Sv	ERA
1991	Auburn	A	21	7	0	12	61	265	70	39	26	5	4	2	2	10	1	56	2	0	0	4	.000	0	3	3.84
1992	Burlington	A	20	20	2	0	122	476	100	42	30	9	2	0	4	19	0	104	5	3	11	7	.611	0	0	2.21
	Asheville	A	3	3	1	0	20	74	11	2	1	0	0	0	1	4	0	20	1	0	1	1	.500	0	0	0.45
1993	Osceola	A	4	0	0	0	17.1	72	16	5	5	0	0	0	0	6	0	16	1	0	1	1	.500	0	0	2.60
1994	Osceola	A	11	10	1	0	76.2	318	77	31	18	5	5	3	1	12	1	36	1	0	4	2	.667	1	0	2.11
	Jackson	AA	17	17	1	0	102.1	426	101	46	40	12	3	1	4	19	0	60	2	0	7	8	.467	1	0	3.52
1995	Tucson	AAA	5	5	0	0	22.1	108	30	24	21	1	0	2	5	8	0	5	0	0	2	2	.500	0	0	8.46
	Jackson	AA	17	5	0	5	51.2	243	77	49	46	7	3	2	3	15	2	27	2	0	1	4	.200	0	2	8.01

Team	Lg	G	GS	CG	GF	IP	BFP	H	R	ER	HR	SH	SF	HB	TBB	IBB	SO	WP	Bk	W	L	Pct.	ShO	Sv	ERA
Kissimmee	A	5	5	1	0	30.1	120	23	10	6	1	1	1	3	11	0	16	4	1	2	1	.667	0	0	1.78
5 Min. YEARS		103	72	6	17	503.2	2102	505	248	193	40	18	11	23	104	4	340	18	4	29	30	.492	2	5	3.45

Mike Warner

Bats: Left **Throws:** Left **Pos:** OF **Ht:** 5'10" **Wt:** 170 **Born:** 5/9/71 **Age:** 25

Year Team	Lg	G	AB	H	2B	3B	HR	TB	R	RBI	TBB	IBB	SO	HBP	SH	SF	SB	CS	SB%	GDP	Avg	OBP	SLG
1992 Idaho Falls	R	10	33	9	3	0	1	15	4	6	3	0	5	0	0	0	1	0	1.00	0	.273	.333	.455
Macon	A	50	180	50	7	2	1	64	40	8	34	0	28	0	3	0	21	4	.84	2	.278	.393	.356
1993 Durham	A	77	263	84	18	4	5	125	55	32	50	3	45	2	3	3	29	12	.71	4	.319	.428	.475
Greenville	AA	5	20	7	0	2	0	11	4	3	2	0	4	0	0	0	2	1	.67	0	.350	.409	.550
1994 Durham	A	88	321	103	23	4	13	181	80	44	51	1	50	2	1	1	24	10	.71	3	.321	.416	.564
Greenville	AA	16	55	18	5	0	1	26	13	3	9	0	5	1	0	0	3	0	1.00	0	.327	.431	.473
1995 Richmond	AAA	28	97	20	4	1	2	32	10	8	10	0	21	1	2	0	0	3	.00	0	.206	.287	.330
Greenville	AA	53	173	41	12	0	0	53	31	7	47	0	36	1	2	2	12	4	.75	1	.237	.399	.306
4 Min. YEARS		327	1142	332	72	17	23	507	237	111	206	4	194	7	11	6	92	34	.73	10	.291	.400	.444

Ron Warner

Bats: Right **Throws:** Right **Pos:** SS **Ht:** 6'3" **Wt:** 185 **Born:** 12/2/68 **Age:** 27

Year Team	Lg	G	AB	H	2B	3B	HR	TB	R	RBI	TBB	IBB	SO	HBP	SH	SF	SB	CS	SB%	GDP	Avg	OBP	SLG
1991 Hamilton	A	71	219	66	11	3	1	86	31	20	28	0	43	3	4	1	9	2	.82	4	.301	.386	.393
1992 Savannah	A	85	242	53	8	1	0	63	30	12	29	2	63	1	5	2	2	3	.40	1	.219	.303	.260
1993 St. Pete	A	103	311	90	8	3	4	116	42	37	31	2	39	5	7	4	5	1	.83	9	.289	.359	.373
1994 Arkansas	AA	95	233	56	14	1	4	84	28	25	39	5	57	1	2	0	1	1	.50	4	.240	.352	.361
1995 Arkansas	AA	47	98	24	3	0	0	27	9	8	16	1	15	1	3	2	0	0	.00	3	.245	.350	.276
5 Min. YEARS		401	1103	289	44	8	9	376	140	102	143	10	217	11	21	9	17	7	.71	25	.262	.350	.341

Brian Warren

Pitches: Right **Bats:** Right **Pos:** P **Ht:** 6'1" **Wt:** 165 **Born:** 4/26/67 **Age:** 29

Year Team	Lg	G	GS	CG	GF	IP	BFP	H	R	ER	HR	SH	SF	HB	TBB	IBB	SO	WP	Bk	W	L	Pct.	ShO	Sv	ERA
1990 Bristol	R	1	1	0	0	4	17	4	1	1	0	0	0	0	2	0	0	0	1	0	0	.000	0	0	2.25
Niagara Fal	A	12	10	1	2	62.1	258	53	26	15	3	0	2	4	15	0	62	2	0	2	6	.250	0	0	2.17
1991 Fayetteville	A	10	1	0	0	25.2	99	18	6	6	0	0	0	2	5	0	28	3	2	3	1	.750	0	0	2.10
Lakeland	A	17	16	4	0	103.1	406	86	34	29	3	6	1	1	15	1	75	6	3	8	2	.800	2	0	2.53
1992 London	AA	25	25	3	0	147.1	606	146	66	54	10	1	0	5	32	1	83	7	0	7	9	.438	2	0	3.30
1993 London	AA	22	1	0	13	29.1	125	36	19	19	6	0	1	0	9	0	21	1	0	3	3	.500	0	5	5.83
Toledo	AAA	24	1	0	11	36.2	160	40	17	14	3	0	1	2	11	2	26	3	0	2	2	.500	0	0	3.44
1994 Indianapolis	AAA	55	0	0	14	80.1	329	82	33	28	4	4	4	3	16	4	56	3	0	5	2	.714	0	1	3.14
1995 Indianapolis	AAA	41	0	0	9	56	234	56	18	10	2	1	1	5	9	2	35	2	1	2	1	.667	0	2	1.61
6 Min. YEARS		207	55	8	49	545	2234	521	220	176	31	12	10	22	114	10	386	27	7	32	26	.552	4	8	2.91

B.J. Waszgis

Bats: Right **Throws:** Right **Pos:** C **Ht:** 6'2" **Wt:** 210 **Born:** 8/24/70 **Age:** 25

Year Team	Lg	G	AB	H	2B	3B	HR	TB	R	RBI	TBB	IBB	SO	HBP	SH	SF	SB	CS	SB%	GDP	Avg	OBP	SLG
1991 Bluefield	R	12	35	8	1	0	3	18	8	8	5	0	11	1	0	0	3	0	1.00	1	.229	.341	.514
1992 Kane County	A	111	340	73	18	1	11	126	39	47	54	2	94	4	3	2	3	2	.60	8	.215	.328	.371
1993 Frederick	A	31	109	27	4	0	3	40	12	9	9	0	30	2	0	1	1	1	.50	2	.248	.314	.367
Albany	A	86	300	92	25	3	8	147	45	52	27	0	55	6	0	5	4	0	1.00	3	.307	.370	.490
1994 Frederick	A	122	426	120	16	3	21	205	76	100	65	2	94	5	3	4	6	1	.86	3	.282	.380	.481
1995 Bowie	AA	130	438	111	22	0	10	163	53	50	70	1	91	9	1	3	2	4	.33	5	.253	.365	.372
5 Min. YEARS		492	1648	431	86	7	56	699	233	266	230	5	375	27	7	15	19	8	.70	27	.262	.358	.424

Jason Watkins

Pitches: Right **Bats:** Right **Pos:** P **Ht:** 6'0" **Wt:** 195 **Born:** 3/26/70 **Age:** 26

Year Team	Lg	G	GS	CG	GF	IP	BFP	H	R	ER	HR	SH	SF	HB	TBB	IBB	SO	WP	Bk	W	L	Pct.	ShO	Sv	ERA
1992 Utica	A	26	0	0	7	43	180	37	14	10	2	2	3	1	16	1	57	3	0	2	3	.400	0	3	2.09
1993 South Bend	A	37	0	0	27	63	255	37	13	11	2	6	3	6	24	3	57	1	0	6	3	.667	0	16	1.57
1994 Pr. William	A	42	0	0	25	76.2	326	59	31	23	5	9	0	2	35	5	76	4	1	5	3	.625	0	5	2.70
1995 Birmingham	AA	10	0	0	3	13.2	64	18	7	6	1	0	0	1	3	0	10	1	1	0	0	.000	0	0	3.95
4 Min. YEARS		115	0	0	72	196.1	825	151	65	50	10	17	6	10	78	9	200	9	3	13	9	.591	0	24	2.29

Pat Watkins

Bats: Right **Throws:** Right **Pos:** OF **Ht:** 6'2" **Wt:** 185 **Born:** 9/2/72 **Age:** 23

Year Team	Lg	G	AB	H	2B	3B	HR	TB	R	RBI	TBB	IBB	SO	HBP	SH	SF	SB	CS	SB%	GDP	Avg	OBP	SLG
1993 Billings	R	66	235	63	10	3	6	97	46	30	22	0	44	2	1	1	15	4	.79	4	.268	.335	.413
1994 Winston-Sal	A	132	524	152	24	5	27	267	107	83	62	3	84	7	1	6	31	13	.70	8	.290	.369	.510
1995 Winston-Sal	A	27	107	22	3	1	4	39	14	13	10	0	24	0	1	2	1	0	1.00	5	.206	.269	.364
Chattanooga	AA	105	358	104	26	2	12	170	57	57	33	4	53	3	0	4	5	5	.50	7	.291	.352	.475
3 Min. YEARS		330	1224	341	63	11	49	573	224	183	127	7	205	12	3	13	52	22	.70	24	.279	.349	.468

Ron Watson

Pitches: Right **Bats:** Left **Pos:** P   **Ht:** 6'5" **Wt:** 240 **Born:** 9/12/68 **Age:** 27

			HOW	MUCH	HE	PITCHED			WHAT	HE	GAVE	UP						THE	RESULTS			
Year Team	Lg	G	GS	CG	GF	IP	BFP	H	R	ER	HR	SH	SF	HB	TBB	IBB	SO	WP	Bk	W	L	Pct.	ShO	Sv	ERA
1990 Angels	R	20	0	0	8	33	141	26	14	12	0	0	0	1	14	0	21	2	2	2	3	.400	0	0	3.27
1991 Boise	A	18	3	0	7	26	131	35	28	18	1	0	0	3	15	0	27	3	0	0	1	.000	0	0	6.23
1992 Quad City	A	40	0	0	25	70	298	43	20	10	2	6	4	4	42	3	69	11	1	8	5	.615	0	10	1.29
1993 Midland	AA	36	0	0	18	46.1	217	39	22	20	2	3	0	6	43	2	41	8	0	2	1	.667	0	3	3.88
1994 Midland	AA	52	0	0	44	57.1	259	54	29	24	2	3	1	3	37	1	53	6	0	0	6	.000	0	17	3.77
1995 Vancouver	AAA	5	0	0	2	5.2	26	3	3	3	0	1	0	0	6	1	3	0	0	0	1	.000	0	0	4.76
Midland	AA	3	0	0	0	3.2	17	2	2	2	0	0	0	0	6	0	3	3	0	0	0	.000	0	0	4.91
Lk Elsinore	A	10	0	0	6	11.1	50	6	6	6	0	1	0	2	6	0	8	1	1	1	0	1.000	0	0	4.76
6 Min. YEARS		184	3	0	110	253.1	1139	208	124	95	7	14	5	19	169	7	225	34	4	13	17	.433	0	30	3.38

Jim Wawruck

Bats: Left **Throws:** Left **Pos:** OF   **Ht:** 5'11" **Wt:** 185 **Born:** 4/23/70 **Age:** 26

									BATTING									BASERUNNING				PERCENTAGES		
Year Team	Lg	G	AB	H	2B	3B	HR	TB	R	RBI	TBB	IBB	SO	HBP	SH	SF	SB	CS	SB%	GDP	Avg	OBP	SLG
1991 Orioles	R	14	45	17	1	1	0	20	6	6	6	0	4	0	0	0	2	2	.50	0	.378	.451	.444
Frederick	A	22	83	23	3	0	0	26	15	7	7	0	14	1	1	0	10	0	1.00	1	.277	.341	.313
1992 Frederick	A	102	350	108	18	4	8	158	61	46	47	2	69	2	1	5	11	8	.58	9	.309	.389	.451
1993 Bowie	AA	128	475	141	21	5	4	184	59	44	43	3	66	1	5	2	28	11	.72	7	.297	.355	.387
1994 Rochester	AAA	114	440	132	20	7	9	193	63	53	32	1	77	4	1	2	17	2	.89	6	.300	.351	.439
1995 Bowie	AA	56	212	59	7	1	6	86	29	30	20	2	31	3	1	3	7	3	.70	7	.278	.345	.406
Rochester	AAA	39	149	45	12	3	1	66	21	23	13	0	23	2	1	2	5	4	.56	3	.302	.361	.443
5 Min. YEARS		475	1754	525	82	21	28	733	254	209	168	8	284	13	10	14	80	30	.73	34	.299	.362	.418

Eric Weaver

Pitches: Right **Bats:** Right **Pos:** P   **Ht:** 6'5" **Wt:** 230 **Born:** 8/4/73 **Age:** 22

			HOW	MUCH	HE	PITCHED			WHAT	HE	GAVE	UP						THE	RESULTS			
Year Team	Lg	G	GS	CG	GF	IP	BFP	H	R	ER	HR	SH	SF	HB	TBB	IBB	SO	WP	Bk	W	L	Pct.	ShO	Sv	ERA
1992 Vero Beach	A	19	18	1	0	89.2	394	73	52	41	7	5	6	1	57	0	73	17	2	4	11	.267	0	0	4.12
1993 Bakersfield	A	28	27	0	0	157.2	703	135	89	75	10	2	9	2	118	2	110	16	0	6	11	.353	0	0	4.28
1994 Vero Beach	A	7	7	0	0	24	109	28	20	18	3	0	0	1	9	1	22	1	0	1	3	.250	0	0	6.75
1995 San Antonio	AA	27	26	1	1	141.2	635	147	83	64	10	9	7	7	72	1	105	8	2	8	11	.421	0	0	4.07
4 Min. YEARS		81	78	2	1	413	1841	383	244	198	30	16	22	11	256	4	310	42	4	19	36	.345	0	0	4.31

Doug Webb

Pitches: Right **Bats:** Right **Pos:** P   **Ht:** 6'3" **Wt:** 195 **Born:** 8/25/73 **Age:** 22

			HOW	MUCH	HE	PITCHED			WHAT	HE	GAVE	UP						THE	RESULTS			
Year Team	Lg	G	GS	CG	GF	IP	BFP	H	R	ER	HR	SH	SF	HB	TBB	IBB	SO	WP	Bk	W	L	Pct.	ShO	Sv	ERA
1994 Brewers	R	1	0	0	1	1	3	0	0	0	0	0	0	0	0	0	1	0	0	0	0	.000	0	0	0.00
Stockton	A	29	0	0	12	35	179	38	33	21	2	1	4	2	27	0	34	5	4	0	2	.000	0	0	5.40
1995 Stockton	A	32	0	0	31	37	140	17	7	7	3	1	0	1	8	0	34	0	0	0	0	.000	0	22	1.70
El Paso	AA	18	0	0	16	18.1	77	11	9	9	3	1	1	0	13	1	11	2	0	2	1	.667	0	8	4.42
2 Min. YEARS		80	0	0	60	91.1	399	66	49	37	8	3	5	3	48	1	80	7	4	2	3	.400	0	30	3.65

Ben Weber

Pitches: Right **Bats:** Right **Pos:** P   **Ht:** 6'4" **Wt:** 180 **Born:** 11/17/69 **Age:** 26

			HOW	MUCH	HE	PITCHED			WHAT	HE	GAVE	UP						THE	RESULTS			
Year Team	Lg	G	GS	CG	GF	IP	BFP	H	R	ER	HR	SH	SF	HB	TBB	IBB	SO	WP	Bk	W	L	Pct.	ShO	Sv	ERA
1991 St. Cathrns	A	16	14	1	2	97.1	417	84	45	35	3	4	2	4	24	2	60	7	2	6	3	.667	0	0	3.24
1992 Myrtle Bch	A	41	1	0	23	98.2	406	83	27	18	1	2	3	7	29	3	65	7	0	4	7	.364	0	6	1.64
1993 Dunedin	A	55	0	0	36	83.1	355	87	36	27	4	9	0	7	25	5	45	7	1	8	3	.727	0	12	2.92
1994 Dunedin	A	18	0	0	14	26.1	110	25	8	8	1	6	0	1	5	3	19	1	0	3	2	.600	0	3	2.73
Knoxville	AA	25	10	0	6	95.2	400	103	49	40	8	3	1	2	16	0	55	4	0	4	3	.571	0	0	3.76
1995 Knoxville	AA	12	1	0	6	25.1	104	26	12	11	3	0	0	0	6	0	16	0	0	4	1	.800	0	0	3.91
Syracuse	AAA	25	15	0	3	91.2	403	111	62	55	10	2	1	3	27	1	38	5	0	4	5	.444	0	1	5.40
5 Min. YEARS		192	41	1	90	518.1	2195	540	237	194	30	26	7	24	132	14	298	31	3	33	24	.579	0	22	3.37

Neil Weber

Pitches: Left **Bats:** Left **Pos:** P   **Ht:** 6'5" **Wt:** 205 **Born:** 12/6/72 **Age:** 23

			HOW	MUCH	HE	PITCHED			WHAT	HE	GAVE	UP						THE	RESULTS			
Year Team	Lg	G	GS	CG	GF	IP	BFP	H	R	ER	HR	SH	SF	HB	TBB	IBB	SO	WP	Bk	W	L	Pct.	ShO	Sv	ERA
1993 Jamestown	A	16	16	2	0	94.1	398	84	46	29	3	0	4	4	36	0	80	3	3	6	5	.545	1	0	2.77
1994 W. Palm Bch	A	25	24	1	0	135	566	113	58	48	8	4	4	4	62	0	134	7	5	9	7	.563	0	0	3.20
1995 Harrisburg	AA	28	28	0	0	152.2	696	157	98	85	16	11	7	8	90	1	119	7	1	6	11	.353	0	0	5.01
3 Min. YEARS		69	68	3	0	382	1660	354	202	162	27	15	15	16	188	1	333	17	9	21	23	.477	1	0	3.82

Weston Weber

Pitches: Right Bats: Right Pos: P Ht: 6'0" Wt: 175 Born: 1/5/64 Age: 32

Year	Team	Lg	G	GS	CG	GF	IP	BFP	H	R	ER	HR	SH	SF	HB	TBB	IBB	SO	WP	Bk	W	L	Pct.	ShO	Sv	ERA
1986	Medford	A	13	13	0	0	68	0	64	42	26	4	0	0	4	28	0	69	5	1	5	5	.500	0	0	3.44
1987	Madison	A	9	8	0	0	46.2	203	44	21	18	4	0	2	1	27	0	38	2	1	4	1	.800	0	0	3.47
1988	Modesto	A	17	17	1	0	98	440	91	59	44	7	4	5	2	54	0	81	14	1	6	7	.462	0	0	4.04
1989	Huntsville	AA	15	2	0	4	34	161	34	25	20	2	1	3	1	29	0	17	0	3	3	2	.600	0	0	5.29
	Modesto	A	11	11	1	0	69	293	60	32	25	1	3	2	3	34	1	49	4	1	3	6	.333	0	0	3.26
	Tacoma	AAA	6	0	0	2	11	48	8	9	9	1	0	0	1	7	0	6	0	1	0	0	.000	0	0	7.36
1990	Tacoma	AAA	35	2	0	9	63	291	64	44	35	4	2	4	4	43	2	35	3	0	5	2	.714	0	1	5.00
	Portland	AAA	4	1	0	1	10	52	15	10	9	0	0	1	1	5	0	7	0	0	0	0	.000	0	0	8.10
1991	Huntsville	AA	34	0	0	17	54	240	57	23	13	1	1	2	4	18	1	26	4	1	2	3	.400	0	3	2.17
	Tacoma	AAA	15	0	0	11	31.2	129	28	14	7	0	1	1	2	7	0	15	1	1	2	0	1.000	0	1	1.99
1992	Tacoma	AAA	52	0	0	23	94	421	95	45	43	6	9	3	8	53	9	51	10	0	4	5	.444	0	2	4.12
1993	Jacksonvlle	AAA	17	0	0	8	26.2	109	25	6	5	1	0	1	1	7	1	12	2	0	2	1	.667	0	1	1.69
1994	Calgary	AAA	32	24	2	1	158.2	734	216	118	105	24	0	5	4	53	4	108	3	2	12	8	.600	0	0	5.96
1995	Tacoma	AAA	20	13	1	3	101.2	443	111	55	52	12	3	4	2	41	10	54	5	3	3	7	.300	0	0	4.60
	Las Vegas	AAA	9	8	1	0	48.2	220	59	37	26	4	2	2	2	9	0	32	1	0	3	4	.429	0	0	4.81
10 Min. YEARS			289	99	6	79	915	3784	971	540	437	71	26	35	40	415	28	600	54	15	54	51	.514	0	8	4.30

Eric Wedge

Bats: Right Throws: Right Pos: 1B Ht: 6'3" Wt: 230 Born: 1/27/68 Age: 28

Year	Team	Lg	G	AB	H	2B	3B	HR	TB	R	RBI	TBB	IBB	SO	HBP	SH	SF	SB	CS	SB%	GDP	Avg	OBP	SLG
1989	Elmira	A	41	145	34	6	2	7	65	20	22	15	0	21	0	0	0	1	1	.50	3	.234	.306	.448
	New Britain	AA	14	40	8	2	0	0	10	3	2	5	0	10	0	2	0	0	0	.00	1	.200	.289	.250
1990	New Britain	AA	103	339	77	13	1	5	107	36	48	51	2	54	1	0	5	1	3	.25	14	.227	.326	.316
1991	New Britain	AA	2	8	2	0	0	0	2	0	2	0	0	2	0	0	1	0	0	.00	0	.250	.222	.250
	Winter Havn	A	8	21	5	0	0	1	8	2	1	3	0	7	0	1	0	0	1	1.00	1	.238	.333	.381
	Pawtucket	AAA	53	163	38	14	1	5	69	24	18	25	0	26	1	2	5	1	2	.33	3	.233	.330	.423
1992	Pawtucket	AAA	65	211	63	9	0	11	105	28	40	32	3	40	1	0	3	0	0	.00	6	.299	.389	.498
1993	Central Val	A	6	23	7	0	0	3	16	6	11	2	1	6	0	0	0	0	0	.00	1	.304	.360	.696
	Colo. Sprng	AAA	38	90	24	6	0	3	39	17	13	16	1	22	2	0	0	0	0	.00	4	.267	.389	.433
1994	Pawtucket	AAA	77	255	73	14	0	19	144	44	59	51	5	48	2	0	2	0	1	.00	6	.286	.406	.565
1995	Pawtucket	AAA	108	376	88	17	1	20	167	52	68	63	4	96	2	0	3	1	3	.25	9	.234	.345	.444
1991	Boston	AL	1	1	1	0	0	0	1	0	0	0	0	0	0	0	0	0	0	.00	0	1.000	1.000	1.000
1992	Boston	AL	27	68	17	2	0	5	34	11	11	13	0	18	0	0	0	0	0	.00	1	.250	.370	.500
1993	Colorado	NL	9	11	2	0	0	0	2	2	1	0	0	4	0	0	0	0	0	.00	1	.182	.182	.182
1994	Boston	AL	2	6	0	0	0	0	0	0	0	1	0	3	0	0	0	0	0	.00	0	.000	.143	.000
7 Min. YEARS			515	1671	419	81	5	74	732	232	284	263	16	332	9	5	19	5	10	.33	48	.251	.352	.438
4 Maj. YEARS			39	86	20	2	0	5	37	13	12	14	0	25	0	0	0	0	0	.00	0	.233	.340	.430

Wes Weger

Bats: Right Throws: Right Pos: 2B-SS Ht: 6'0" Wt: 170 Born: 10/3/70 Age: 25

Year	Team	Lg	G	AB	H	2B	3B	HR	TB	R	RBI	TBB	IBB	SO	HBP	SH	SF	SB	CS	SB%	GDP	Avg	OBP	SLG
1992	Helena	R	36	133	57	9	1	5	83	36	31	22	0	9	0	2	5	7	2	.78	1	.429	.494	.624
	Stockton	A	32	120	31	7	2	1	45	26	18	20	0	17	3	0	0	3	3	.50	2	.258	.378	.375
1993	El Paso	AA	123	471	137	24	5	5	186	69	53	31	4	44	4	7	2	9	9	.50	6	.291	.339	.395
1995	El Paso	AA	45	160	41	9	2	0	54	22	19	10	1	14	0	1	1	1	1	.50	9	.256	.298	.338
	New Orleans	AAA	64	234	67	16	0	2	89	28	24	10	0	31	1	1	1	0	2	.00	5	.286	.317	.380
3 Min. YEARS			300	1118	333	65	10	13	457	181	145	93	5	115	8	11	9	20	17	.54	23	.298	.353	.409

Tom Wegmann

Pitches: Right Bats: Right Pos: P Ht: 6'0" Wt: 190 Born: 8/29/68 Age: 27

Year	Team	Lg	G	GS	CG	GF	IP	BFP	H	R	ER	HR	SH	SF	HB	TBB	IBB	SO	WP	Bk	W	L	Pct.	ShO	Sv	ERA
1990	Mets	R	1	0	0	1	1	3	0	0	0	0	0	0	0	0	0	3	0	1	0	0	.000	0	0	0.00
	Kingsport	R	14	12	4	1	84.1	342	53	34	24	8	1	2	1	30	0	103	10	7	5	4	.556	2	0	2.56
1991	Columbia	A	7	6	1	0	48	172	21	7	3	1	0	0	1	9	0	69	0	1	5	0	1.000	1	0	0.56
	St. Lucie	A	13	11	0	1	61	239	46	19	17	0	3	0	1	14	0	69	1	6	4	3	.571	0	1	2.51
1992	Tidewater	AAA	7	6	0	0	36.2	165	38	19	18	3	0	1	3	17	0	38	5	1	2	3	.400	0	0	4.42
	Binghamton	AA	27	11	2	4	97.2	384	73	29	28	5	2	1	4	27	1	93	3	2	9	2	.818	0	1	2.58
1993	Norfolk	AAA	44	2	0	14	86.1	356	68	33	31	8	7	1	1	34	8	99	4	1	5	3	.625	0	2	3.23
1994	Rochester	AAA	54	0	0	32	83	374	86	37	34	9	4	1	1	46	10	68	11	0	5	1	.833	0	10	3.69
1995	Rochester	AAA	9	5	1	2	34	140	30	15	13	3	3	1	3	9	0	23	0	0	3	2	.600	0	0	3.44
	Bowie	AA	14	11	0	0	64.2	272	56	35	30	8	2	2	2	22	2	49	0	2	2	3	.400	0	0	4.18
6 Min. YEARS			190	64	8	55	596.2	2447	471	228	198	42	19	12	16	208	21	614	34	21	40	21	.656	3	14	2.99

Chris Weinke

Bats: Left Throws: Left Pos: 1B Ht: 6'3" Wt: 205 Born: 7/31/72 Age: 23

Year	Team	Lg	G	AB	H	2B	3B	HR	TB	R	RBI	TBB	IBB	SO	HBP	SH	SF	SB	CS	SB%	GDP	Avg	OBP	SLG
1991	St. Cathrns	A	75	271	65	9	1	3	85	31	41	41	1	61	0	3	4	12	9	.57	1	.240	.335	.314

Year	Team	Lg	G	AB	H	2B	3B	HR	TB	R	RBI	TBB	IBB	SO	HBP	SH	SF	SB	CS	SB%	GDP	Avg	OBP	SLG
1992	Myrtle Bch	A	135	458	110	16	2	13	169	61	63	70	7	89	6	4	5	4	9	.31	6	.240	.345	.369
1993	Dunedin	A	128	476	135	16	2	17	206	68	98	66	8	78	2	1	4	8	6	.57	7	.284	.370	.433
1994	Knoxville	AA	139	526	133	23	2	8	184	61	87	45	6	121	0	4	5	12	4	.75	10	.253	.309	.350
1995	Syracuse	AAA	113	341	77	12	2	10	123	42	41	44	2	74	1	0	2	4	3	.57	10	.226	.314	.361
	5 Min. YEARS		590	2072	520	76	9	51	767	263	330	266	24	423	9	12	20	40	31	.56	34	.251	.336	.370

Mike Welch

Pitches: Right **Bats:** Left **Pos:** P   **Ht:** 6'2" **Wt:** 195 **Born:** 8/25/72 **Age:** 23

			HOW MUCH HE PITCHED						WHAT HE GAVE UP											THE RESULTS					
Year	Team	Lg	G	GS	CG	GF	IP	BFP	H	R	ER	HR	SH	SF	HB	TBB	IBB	SO	WP	Bk	W	L	Pct.	ShO	Sv	ERA
1993	Pittsfield	A	17	0	0	14	31	126	23	9	5	0	2	4	0	6	1	34	3	1	3	1	.750	0	9	1.45
1994	Columbia	A	24	24	5	0	159.2	667	151	81	64	14	7	5	11	33	0	127	5	0	7	11	.389	2	0	3.61
1995	St. Lucie	A	44	6	0	33	70	322	96	50	42	7	4	3	6	18	4	51	4	0	4	4	.500	0	15	5.40
	Binghamton	AA	1	0	0	1	1	3	0	0	0	0	0	0	0	0	0	2	0	0	0	0	.000	0	0	0.00
	3 Min. YEARS		86	30	5	48	261.2	1118	270	140	111	21	13	12	17	57	5	214	12	1	14	16	.467	2	24	3.82

Forry Wells

Bats: Left **Throws:** Right **Pos:** OF   **Ht:** 6'4" **Wt:** 205 **Born:** 3/21/71 **Age:** 25

			BATTING															BASERUNNING				PERCENTAGES		
Year	Team	Lg	G	AB	H	2B	3B	HR	TB	R	RBI	TBB	IBB	SO	HBP	SH	SF	SB	CS	SB%	GDP	Avg	OBP	SLG
1994	Bend	A	37	117	30	8	0	1	41	19	13	23	2	29	4	0	0	9	1	.90	2	.256	.396	.350
1995	Salem	A	119	402	102	23	4	18	187	60	67	56	6	105	7	3	1	6	3	.67	2	.254	.354	.465
	New Haven	AA	4	14	3	0	0	0	3	3	1	1	1	2	1	0	0	0	0	.00	1	.214	.313	.214
	2 Min. YEARS		160	533	135	31	4	19	231	82	81	80	9	136	12	3	1	15	4	.79	5	.253	.363	.433

Bill Wengert

Pitches: Right **Bats:** Right **Pos:** P   **Ht:** 6'5" **Wt:** 210 **Born:** 1/4/67 **Age:** 29

			HOW MUCH HE PITCHED						WHAT HE GAVE UP											THE RESULTS					
Year	Team	Lg	G	GS	CG	GF	IP	BFP	H	R	ER	HR	SH	SF	HB	TBB	IBB	SO	WP	Bk	W	L	Pct.	ShO	Sv	ERA
1988	Great Falls	R	14	6	0	1	45	202	44	28	18	4	2	1	0	23	0	42	2	1	3	3	.500	0	0	3.60
1989	Bakersfield	A	21	15	0	0	91.1	408	104	59	48	7	2	6	4	44	0	66	7	1	2	7	.222	0	0	4.73
1990	Vero Beach	A	22	7	0	6	74.2	320	66	40	32	5	0	4	4	36	1	47	4	0	5	1	.833	0	0	3.86
1991	Vero Beach	A	30	13	2	8	127	511	100	36	29	3	2	4	6	42	2	114	8	4	7	6	.538	2	3	2.06
1992	Vero Beach	A	5	5	0	0	22.2	104	31	14	13	5	1	2	1	6	0	15	2	0	1	0	1.000	0	0	5.16
	San Antonio	AA	10	7	0	0	50.1	212	48	20	18	3	2	0	0	13	0	43	2	0	2	3	.400	0	0	3.22
1993	Wichita	AA	28	25	3	1	162.1	693	167	86	74	16	8	8	8	43	3	106	15	2	7	7	.500	1	0	4.10
1994	Wichita	AA	35	16	0	10	112.2	516	145	81	68	10	6	4	5	35	2	85	9	0	6	7	.462	0	2	5.43
1995	Pawtucket	AAA	7	0	0	1	11.2	53	17	7	7	1	0	0	0	4	0	10	0	0	0	0	.000	0	0	5.40
	8 Min. YEARS		172	94	5	27	697.2	3019	722	371	307	54	23	29	28	246	8	528	49	8	33	35	.485	3	5	3.96

Bill Wertz

Pitches: Right **Bats:** Right **Pos:** P   **Ht:** 6'6" **Wt:** 220 **Born:** 1/15/67 **Age:** 29

			HOW MUCH HE PITCHED						WHAT HE GAVE UP											THE RESULTS					
Year	Team	Lg	G	GS	CG	GF	IP	BFP	H	R	ER	HR	SH	SF	HB	TBB	IBB	SO	WP	Bk	W	L	Pct.	ShO	Sv	ERA
1989	Indians	R	12	11	1	0	66	282	57	23	23	0	1	4	4	36	0	56	11	0	4	3	.571	1	0	3.14
1990	Reno	A	17	9	0	1	61.1	295	61	58	45	6	3	4	5	52	0	52	12	0	1	3	.250	0	0	6.60
	Watertown	A	14	14	2	0	100.2	431	81	39	32	3	2	3	4	48	0	92	6	0	10	2	.833	0	0	2.86
1991	Columbus	A	49	0	0	31	91	391	81	41	30	6	6	4	6	32	3	95	5	0	6	8	.429	0	9	2.97
1992	Canton-Akrn	AA	57	0	0	24	97.1	382	75	16	13	1	3	2	3	30	6	69	3	0	8	4	.667	0	8	1.20
1993	Charlotte	AAA	28	1	0	9	50.2	207	42	18	11	4	3	0	1	14	4	47	1	0	7	2	.778	0	1	1.95
1994	Charlotte	AAA	44	2	0	8	66	278	53	30	23	5	2	2	1	34	3	60	5	0	4	3	.571	0	1	3.14
1995	Pawtucket	AAA	29	6	0	12	63.2	298	74	47	41	11	4	4	1	31	1	55	7	0	4	5	.444	0	2	5.80
1993	Cleveland	AL	34	0	0	7	59.2	262	54	28	24	5	1	1	1	32	2	53	0	0	2	3	.400	0	0	3.62
1994	Cleveland	AL	1	0	0	0	4.1	23	9	5	5	0	0	0	0	3	0	5	0	0	0	0	.000	0	0	10.38
	7 Min. YEARS		250	43	3	85	596.2	2564	524	272	218	36	24	23	25	277	17	526	50	0	44	30	.595	1	20	3.29
	2 Maj. YEARS		35	0	0	7	64	285	63	33	29	5	1	1	1	33	2	54	0	0	2	3	.400	0	0	4.08

Barry Wesson

Bats: Right **Throws:** Right **Pos:** OF   **Ht:** 6'2" **Wt:** 195 **Born:** 4/6/77 **Age:** 19

			BATTING															BASERUNNING				PERCENTAGES		
Year	Team	Lg	G	AB	H	2B	3B	HR	TB	R	RBI	TBB	IBB	SO	HBP	SH	SF	SB	CS	SB%	GDP	Avg	OBP	SLG
1995	Astros	R	45	138	26	2	2	2	38	14	18	19	0	40	1	1	1	4	0	1.00	2	.188	.289	.275
	Jackson	AA	4	3	2	0	1	0	4	2	1	0	0	0	0	0	0	0	0	.00	0	.667	.667	1.333
	1 Min. YEARS		49	141	28	2	3	2	42	16	19	19	0	40	1	1	1	4	0	1.00	2	.199	.296	.298

Destry Westbrook

Pitches: Right **Bats:** Right **Pos:** P   **Ht:** 6'1" **Wt:** 195 **Born:** 12/13/70 **Age:** 25

			HOW MUCH HE PITCHED						WHAT HE GAVE UP											THE RESULTS					
Year	Team	Lg	G	GS	CG	GF	IP	BFP	H	R	ER	HR	SH	SF	HB	TBB	IBB	SO	WP	Bk	W	L	Pct.	ShO	Sv	ERA
1992	Auburn	A	12	2	0	5	17	105	29	33	29	5	0	2	4	19	0	19	6	2	0	3	.000	0	0	15.35
1993	Quad City	A	27	0	0	14	36.1	158	29	11	10	3	0	2	0	23	1	41	0	0	3	1	.750	0	2	2.48
1994	Quad City	A	27	0	0	12	46.1	205	48	25	23	3	2	2	2	23	1	50	3	0	0	2	.000	0	1	4.47
1995	Tucson	AAA	5	0	0	2	12.1	60	20	10	10	2	0	0	0	7	0	8	2	0	0	1	.000	0	0	7.30
	Kissimmee	A	10	0	0	2	19.2	106	34	24	22	2	1	0	0	13	1	22	2	0	0	1	.000	0	1	10.07

			G	GS	CG	GF	IP	BFP	H	R	ER	HR	SH	SF	HB	TBB	IBB	SO	WP	Bk	W	L	Pct.	ShO	Sv	ERA
Mobile	IND		8	1	0	1	13	66	13	13	10	1	0	1	0	13	2	11	1	0	0	1	.000	0	0	6.92
4 Min. YEARS			89	3	0	36	144.2	700	173	116	104	16	3	7	6	98	5	151	14	2	3	8	.273	0	4	6.47

Mickey Weston

Pitches: Right **Bats:** Right **Pos:** P **Ht:** 6' 1" **Wt:** 180 **Born:** 3/26/61 **Age:** 35

			HOW MUCH HE PITCHED						WHAT HE GAVE UP												THE RESULTS					
Year Team	Lg		G	GS	CG	GF	IP	BFP	H	R	ER	HR	SH	SF	HB	TBB	IBB	SO	WP	Bk	W	L	Pct.	ShO	Sv	ERA
1984 Columbia	A		32	2	0	20	63.2	272	58	27	13	2	6	1	2	27	6	40	5	0	6	5	.545	0	2	1.84
1985 Lynchburg	A		49	3	1	24	100.1	407	81	29	24	4	3	2	0	22	2	62	4	1	6	5	.545	1	10	2.15
1986 Jackson	AA		34	4	0	7	70.2	308	73	40	34	9	3	2	4	27	3	36	3	0	4	4	.500	0	2	4.33
1987 Jackson	AA		58	1	0	21	82	346	96	39	31	4	0	1	1	18	5	50	6	1	8	4	.667	0	3	3.40
1988 Jackson	AA		30	14	1	4	125.1	507	127	50	31	3	8	5	0	20	4	61	4	0	8	5	.615	0	0	2.23
Tidewater	AAA		4	4	2	0	29.2	115	21	6	5	0	3	0	1	5	1	16	1	0	2	1	.667	1	0	1.52
1989 Rochester	AAA		23	14	2	7	112	445	103	30	26	6	2	2	1	19	0	51	1	0	8	3	.727	1	4	2.09
1990 Rochester	AAA		29	12	2	13	109.1	432	93	36	24	3	1	2	0	22	0	58	3	0	11	1	.917	0	6	1.98
1991 Syracuse	AAA		27	25	3	1	166	710	193	85	69	7	4	5	3	36	1	60	10	0	12	6	.667	0	0	3.74
1992 Scranton-Wb	AAA		26	24	2	1	170.2	683	165	65	59	12	5	5	3	29	2	79	4	1	10	6	.625	1	1	3.11
1993 Norfolk	AAA		21	20	3	1	127.1	542	149	77	60	10	3	2	2	18	2	41	4	0	10	9	.526	0	0	4.24
1994 New Haven	AA		9	0	0	9	12	48	10	2	1	1	0	0	0	2	1	11	2	0	2	1	.667	0	2	0.75
Colo. Sprng	AAA		37	0	0	14	53.1	252	80	40	37	7	2	2	0	17	0	30	2	0	5	5	.500	0	1	6.24
1995 Toledo	AAA		28	27	2	0	180	734	170	68	58	14	2	5	7	41	1	69	4	0	11	7	.611	1	0	2.90
1989 Baltimore	AL		7	0	0	2	13	55	18	8	8	1	0	0	1	2	0	7	0	0	1	0	1.000	0	1	5.54
1990 Baltimore	AL		9	2	0	4	21	94	28	20	18	6	1	0	0	6	1	9	1	0	0	1	.000	0	0	7.71
1991 Toronto	AL		2	0	0	2	2	8	1	0	0	0	0	0	0	1	1	1	0	0	0	0	.000	0	0	0.00
1992 Philadelphia	NL		1	1	0	0	3.2	19	7	5	5	1	0	0	1	1	0	0	0	0	0	0	.000	0	0	12.27
1993 New York	NL		4	0	0	0	5.2	30	11	5	5	0	0	0	1	1	0	2	0	0	0	0	.000	0	0	7.94
12 Min. YEARS			407	150	18	122	1402.1	5801	1419	594	472	82	42	34	24	303	28	664	53	3	103	62	.624	5	31	3.03
5 Maj. YEARS			23	3	0	8	45.1	206	65	38	36	8	1	0	3	11	2	19	1	0	1	2	.333	0	1	7.15

Earl Wheeler

Pitches: Right **Bats:** Right **Pos:** P **Ht:** 6'2" **Wt:** 205 **Born:** 12/3/69 **Age:** 26

			HOW MUCH HE PITCHED						WHAT HE GAVE UP												THE RESULTS					
Year Team	Lg		G	GS	CG	GF	IP	BFP	H	R	ER	HR	SH	SF	HB	TBB	IBB	SO	WP	Bk	W	L	Pct.	ShO	Sv	ERA
1993 Charlstn-Sc	A		11	6	0	3	48	203	46	14	11	4	1	0	3	14	1	19	1	1	3	3	.500	0	0	2.06
1994 Charlotte	A		36	11	0	7	104	486	118	60	51	5	2	8	2	28	1	45	4	0	2	4	.333	0	4	4.41
1995 Tulsa	AA		5	0	0	3	8.1	41	14	8	5	1	0	1	0	2	0	6	2	0	1	1	.500	0	0	5.40
3 Min. YEARS			52	17	0	13	160.1	693	178	82	67	10	3	9	5	44	2	70	7	1	6	8	.429	0	0	3.76

Matt Whisenant

Pitches: Left **Bats:** Both **Pos:** P **Ht:** 6'3" **Wt:** 215 **Born:** 6/8/71 **Age:** 25

			HOW MUCH HE PITCHED						WHAT HE GAVE UP												THE RESULTS					
Year Team	Lg		G	GS	CG	GF	IP	BFP	H	R	ER	HR	SH	SF	HB	TBB	IBB	SO	WP	Bk	W	L	Pct.	ShO	Sv	ERA
1990 Princeton	R		9	4	0	2	15	85	16	27	19	3	0	1	3	20	0	25	7	0	0	0	.000	0	0	11.40
1991 Batavia	A		11	10	0	1	47.2	208	31	19	13	2	1	1	0	42	0	55	4	2	2	1	.667	0	0	2.45
1992 Spartanburg	A		27	27	2	0	150.2	652	117	69	54	9	5	6	10	85	0	151	10	6	11	7	.611	0	0	3.23
1993 Kane County	A		15	15	0	0	71	331	68	45	37	3	8	2	3	56	0	74	8	3	2	6	.250	0	0	4.69
1994 Brevard Cty	A		28	26	5	0	160	679	125	71	60	7	6	7	9	82	2	103	18	1	6	9	.400	1	0	3.38
1995 Portland	AA		23	22	2	0	128.2	544	106	57	50	8	7	4	9	65	3	107	8	0	10	6	.625	0	0	3.50
6 Min. YEARS			113	102	9	3	573	2499	463	288	233	32	27	21	34	350	5	515	55	12	31	29	.517	1	0	3.66

Steve Whitaker

Pitches: Left **Bats:** Left **Pos:** P **Ht:** 6'6" **Wt:** 225 **Born:** 4/15/70 **Age:** 26

			HOW MUCH HE PITCHED						WHAT HE GAVE UP												THE RESULTS					
Year Team	Lg		G	GS	CG	GF	IP	BFP	H	R	ER	HR	SH	SF	HB	TBB	IBB	SO	WP	Bk	W	L	Pct.	ShO	Sv	ERA
1991 San Jose	A		6	6	0	0	29.1	129	25	15	11	2	0	3	1	25	0	21	3	1	2	1	.667	0	0	3.38
1992 San Jose	A		26	26	3	0	148.1	648	157	80	69	7	6	5	6	86	2	83	10	0	8	9	.471	0	0	4.19
1993 San Jose	A		22	21	1	1	127.1	582	106	70	54	9	2	6	5	114	0	94	7	0	8	10	.444	0	0	3.82
Shreveport	AA		4	1	0	2	8.1	38	5	1	1	0	1	0	0	7	0	12	0	0	1	0	1.000	0	0	1.08
1994 Shreveport	AA		27	26	1	0	154.2	648	140	69	58	13	7	6	5	68	0	108	3	0	11	8	.579	1	0	3.38
1995 San Jose	A		2	0	0	0	6	26	7	3	3	0	0	0	0	2	0	2	0	0	0	0	.000	0	1	4.50
Shreveport	AA		4	3	0	0	16.1	70	17	8	7	0	1	0	0	10	0	10	1	0	2	0	1.000	0	0	3.86
Phoenix	AAA		16	10	0	3	54	261	72	47	42	2	6	4	0	36	2	30	3	1	0	5	.000	0	0	7.00
5 Min. YEARS			107	93	5	7	544.1	2402	529	293	245	33	23	24	17	348	4	360	27	2	32	33	.492	1	1	4.05

Billy White

Bats: Right **Throws:** Right **Pos:** 2B **Ht:** 6'0" **Wt:** 185 **Born:** 7/3/68 **Age:** 27

			BATTING														BASERUNNING				PERCENTAGES		
Year Team	Lg		G	AB	H	2B	3B	HR	TB	R	RBI	TBB	IBB	SO	HBP	SH	SF	SB	CS	SB%	GDP	Avg	OBP	SLG
1989 Geneva	A		68	254	82	19	1	3	112	44	29	43	0	36	3	2	1	16	5	.76	9	.323	.425	.441
1990 Winston-Sal	A		134	505	136	15	2	5	170	85	54	70	3	108	9	9	3	25	8	.76	13	.269	.366	.337
1991 Charlotte	AA		123	396	106	16	3	3	137	52	50	66	2	72	4	4	5	13	9	.59	9	.268	.374	.346
1992 Charlotte	AA		121	403	102	12	0	4	126	57	33	46	2	90	3	6	4	10	8	.56	9	.253	.331	.313
1993 Daytona	A		38	125	42	9	2	3	64	19	22	16	0	23	5	4	1	2	0	1.00	1	.336	.429	.512
Orlando	AA		40	120	29	11	1	2	48	14	14	15	1	28	0	2	2	1	2	.33	2	.242	.321	.400
1994 New Haven	AA		82	236	58	13	0	1	74	31	22	37	0	48	2	4	1	0	3	.00	11	.246	.351	.314

317

		G	AB	H	2B	3B	HR	TB	R	RBI	TBB	IBB	SO	HBP	SH	SF	SB	CS	SB%	GDP	Avg	OBP	SLG
1995 New Haven	AA	58	181	42	9	1	3	62	25	34	27	0	44	0	0	0	2	2	.50	3	.232	.332	.343
7 Min. YEARS		664	2220	597	104	10	24	793	327	258	320	6	449	26	31	17	69	37	.65	57	.269	.365	.357

Chad White

Bats: Both **Throws:** Right **Pos:** OF **Ht:** 6'2" **Wt:** 180 **Born:** 5/26/71 **Age:** 25

		BATTING															BASERUNNING				PERCENTAGES		
Year Team	Lg	G	AB	H	2B	3B	HR	TB	R	RBI	TBB	IBB	SO	HBP	SH	SF	SB	CS	SB%	GDP	Avg	OBP	SLG
1993 Auburn	A	66	247	72	12	2	2	94	47	29	34	2	33	1	2	1	15	8	.65	1	.291	.378	.381
1994 Osceola	A	94	286	66	8	1	1	79	29	29	25	2	43	6	7	2	8	9	.47	5	.231	.304	.276
1995 Quad City	A	75	242	59	14	0	0	73	36	18	37	3	35	1	4	2	12	4	.75	5	.244	.344	.302
Jackson	AA	32	77	21	4	0	0	25	11	3	8	1	9	0	3	0	2	1	.67	3	.273	.341	.325
3 Min. YEARS		267	852	218	38	3	3	271	123	79	104	8	120	8	16	5	37	22	.63	14	.256	.341	.318

Chris White

Pitches: Right **Bats:** Right **Pos:** P **Ht:** 6'0" **Wt:** 180 **Born:** 9/15/69 **Age:** 26

		HOW MUCH HE PITCHED						WHAT HE GAVE UP											THE RESULTS					
Year Team	Lg	G	GS	CG	GF	IP	BFP	H	R	ER	HR	SH	SF	HB	TBB	IBB	SO	WP	Bk	W	L	Pct.	ShO	Sv	ERA
1991 Auburn	A	26	0	0	17	46.2	205	46	25	19	3	1	1	3	18	2	38	3	5	2	3	.400	0	9	3.66
1992 Asheville	A	41	13	0	22	117.1	496	122	51	44	4	0	3	3	29	3	103	7	5	13	4	.765	0	8	3.38
1993 Osceola	A	13	12	1	0	88.1	364	88	37	33	8	0	3	2	19	1	51	1	2	6	3	.667	0	0	3.36
Jackson	AA	16	11	0	1	60	283	80	54	49	3	3	3	3	25	2	44	5	2	3	5	.375	0	1	7.35
1994 Jackson	AA	52	0	0	11	66.2	282	60	32	26	4	2	2	2	23	6	61	2	1	4	5	.444	0	2	3.51
1995 Tucson	AAA	5	1	0	2	10.1	44	16	10	10	1	1	0	0	2	0	6	0	0	1	1	.500	0	0	8.71
Jackson	AA	38	2	0	15	70.2	311	71	45	40	10	1	3	5	24	4	45	4	2	6	3	.667	0	0	5.09
5 Min. YEARS		191	39	1	68	460	1985	483	254	221	33	8	15	18	140	18	348	22	17	35	24	.593	0	20	4.32

Donnie White

Bats: Right **Throws:** Right **Pos:** OF **Ht:** 6'0" **Wt:** 170 **Born:** 3/13/72 **Age:** 24

		BATTING															BASERUNNING				PERCENTAGES		
Year Team	Lg	G	AB	H	2B	3B	HR	TB	R	RBI	TBB	IBB	SO	HBP	SH	SF	SB	CS	SB%	GDP	Avg	OBP	SLG
1991 Mets	R	54	196	47	10	2	0	61	32	13	24	0	37	3	0	3	30	7	.81	0	.240	.327	.311
1992 Kingsport	R	55	221	67	10	1	4	91	37	27	21	0	38	3	2	4	25	9	.74	1	.303	.365	.412
1993 Capital City	A	114	441	134	18	6	3	173	86	41	54	0	75	5	9	1	43	14	.75	4	.304	.385	.392
1994 St. Lucie	A	118	463	132	17	9	5	182	73	44	38	2	97	5	9	4	31	9	.78	7	.285	.343	.393
1995 Binghamton	AA	94	314	74	17	2	3	104	48	20	40	0	56	2	6	3	25	6	.81	10	.236	.323	.331
5 Min. YEARS		435	1635	454	72	20	15	611	276	145	177	2	303	18	26	15	154	45	.77	22	.278	.352	.374

Jason White

Bats: Right **Throws:** Left **Pos:** 1B **Ht:** 6'3" **Wt:** 215 **Born:** 2/26/70 **Age:** 26

		BATTING															BASERUNNING				PERCENTAGES		
Year Team	Lg	G	AB	H	2B	3B	HR	TB	R	RBI	TBB	IBB	SO	HBP	SH	SF	SB	CS	SB%	GDP	Avg	OBP	SLG
1992 Sou. Oregon	A	66	232	69	16	1	6	105	38	34	28	1	67	4	1	3	4	1	.80	4	.297	.378	.453
1993 Madison	A	119	382	102	24	0	14	168	61	55	36	0	100	7	6	6	1	4	.20	7	.267	.336	.440
1994 Modesto	A	113	379	78	14	2	22	162	53	62	47	4	138	3	5	0	1	1	.50	5	.206	.298	.427
1995 Huntsville	AA	48	167	39	4	1	8	69	20	27	24	2	49	2	0	3	2	1	.67	3	.234	.332	.413
Modesto	A	76	267	82	16	1	22	166	63	71	54	0	71	8	7	3	1	2	.33	9	.307	.434	.622
4 Min. YEARS		422	1427	370	74	5	72	670	235	249	189	7	425	24	19	15	9	9	.50	28	.259	.352	.470

Jimmy White

Bats: Left **Throws:** Right **Pos:** DH **Ht:** 6'1" **Wt:** 170 **Born:** 12/1/72 **Age:** 23

		BATTING															BASERUNNING				PERCENTAGES		
Year Team	Lg	G	AB	H	2B	3B	HR	TB	R	RBI	TBB	IBB	SO	HBP	SH	SF	SB	CS	SB%	GDP	Avg	OBP	SLG
1990 Astros	R	52	180	44	6	4	0	58	32	18	29	1	51	1	0	2	11	8	.58	2	.244	.349	.322
1991 Asheville	A	128	437	112	22	2	8	162	66	43	43	2	133	5	0	2	12	15	.44	8	.256	.329	.371
1992 Burlington	A	102	370	106	20	7	1	143	39	47	38	0	84	2	1	6	17	13	.57	7	.286	.351	.386
Asheville	A	24	83	28	6	1	2	42	12	14	7	1	15	0	0	0	5	0	1.00	0	.337	.389	.506
1993 Osceola	A	125	447	123	9	12	7	177	80	37	54	1	120	5	0	3	24	17	.59	1	.275	.358	.396
1994 Osceola	A	48	174	55	14	6	5	96	37	21	21	1	43	3	0	0	9	3	.75	2	.316	.399	.552
Jackson	AA	64	211	62	7	7	8	107	30	26	12	0	68	0	1	3	1	5	.17	7	.294	.327	.507
1995 Kissimmee	A	16	55	10	3	1	0	15	6	3	9	0	9	1	1	0	4	0	1.00	2	.182	.308	.273
Jackson	AA	2	1	0	0	0	0	0	1	0	1	0	0	0	0	0	0	0	.00	0	.000	.500	.000
Charlstn-Wv	A	20	65	11	3	1	1	19	7	8	6	0	27	1	1	1	1	1	.50	0	.169	.247	.292
Winston-Sal	A	31	111	29	5	1	7	57	15	18	4	0	33	2	1	1	1	1	.50	1	.261	.297	.514
6 Min. YEARS		612	2134	580	95	42	39	876	325	235	224	6	583	20	5	18	85	63	.57	30	.272	.344	.410

Wally Whitehurst

Pitches: Right **Bats:** Right **Pos:** P **Ht:** 6'3" **Wt:** 200 **Born:** 4/11/64 **Age:** 32

		HOW MUCH HE PITCHED						WHAT HE GAVE UP											THE RESULTS					
Year Team	Lg	G	GS	CG	GF	IP	BFP	H	R	ER	HR	SH	SF	HB	TBB	IBB	SO	WP	Bk	W	L	Pct.	ShO	Sv	ERA
1985 Medford	A	14	14	2	0	88	0	92	51	35	6	0	0	7	29	1	91	11	2	7	5	.583	0	0	3.58
Modesto	A	2	2	0	0	10	0	10	3	2	1	0	0	1	5	0	5	0	0	1	0	1.000	0	0	1.80
1986 Madison	A	8	8	5	0	61	234	42	8	4	1	0	1	1	16	0	57	4	0	6	1	.857	4	0	0.59
Huntsville	AA	19	19	2	0	104.2	468	114	66	54	4	5	2	7	46	3	54	12	3	9	5	.643	0	0	4.64
1987 Huntsville	AA	28	28	5	0	183.1	766	192	104	81	12	6	6	2	42	3	106	9	0	11	10	.524	3	0	3.98

Year	Team	Lg	G	GS	CG	GF	IP	BFP	H	R	ER	HR	SH	SF	HB	TBB	IBB	SO	WP	Bk	W	L	Pct.	ShO	Sv	ERA
1988	Tidewater	AAA	26	26	3	0	165	664	145	65	56	7	8	4	8	32	3	113	10	9	10	11	.476	1	0	3.05
1989	Tidewater	AAA	21	20	3	1	133	551	123	54	48	5	3	2	1	32	2	95	3	2	8	7	.533	1	0	3.25
1990	Tidewater	AAA	2	2	0	0	9	34	7	2	2	0	0	0	1	1	0	10	0	0	1	0	1.000	0	0	2.00
1993	Wichita	AA	4	4	0	0	21.1	80	11	4	3	1	0	0	0	5	0	14	4	1	1	0	1.000	0	0	1.27
1995	Phoenix	AAA	4	4	0	0	16.1	76	20	13	13	0	2	0	1	8	1	7	2	0	0	1	.000	0	0	7.16
	Pawtucket	AAA	6	6	0	0	27.2	123	36	21	20	3	1	0	0	5	0	13	3	0	1	3	.250	0	0	6.51
	Syracuse	AAA	6	4	0	0	28	119	32	16	12	4	1	0	0	7	0	21	1	0	3	1	.750	0	0	3.86
1989	New York	NL	9	1	0	4	14	64	17	7	7	2	0	1	0	5	0	9	1	0	0	1	.000	0	0	4.50
1990	New York	NL	38	0	0	16	65.2	263	63	27	24	5	3	0	0	9	2	46	2	0	1	0	1.000	0	2	3.29
1991	New York	NL	36	20	0	6	133.1	556	142	67	62	12	6	3	4	25	3	87	3	4	7	12	.368	0	1	4.19
1992	New York	NL	44	11	0	7	97	421	99	45	39	4	6	3	4	33	5	70	2	1	3	9	.250	0	0	3.62
1993	San Diego	NL	21	19	0	1	105.2	441	109	47	45	11	5	8	3	30	5	57	5	1	4	7	.364	0	0	3.83
1994	San Diego	NL	13	13	0	0	64	294	84	37	35	8	4	0	1	26	4	43	2	0	4	7	.364	0	0	4.92
8 Min. YEARS			140	137	20	1	847.1	3115	824	407	330	44	27	14	29	228	13	586	59	17	58	44	.569	9	0	3.51
6 Maj. YEARS			161	64	0	34	479.2	2039	514	230	212	42	24	15	12	128	19	312	15	6	19	36	.345	0	3	3.98

Casey Whitten

Pitches: Left **Bats:** Left **Pos:** P   **Ht:** 6'0" **Wt:** 175 **Born:** 5/23/72 **Age:** 24

			HOW MUCH HE PITCHED						WHAT HE GAVE UP												THE RESULTS					
Year	Team	Lg	G	GS	CG	GF	IP	BFP	H	R	ER	HR	SH	SF	HB	TBB	IBB	SO	WP	Bk	W	L	Pct.	ShO	Sv	ERA
1993	Watertown	A	14	14	0	0	81.2	331	75	28	22	8	0	4	3	18	0	81	5	0	6	3	.667	0	0	2.42
1994	Kinston	A	27	27	0	0	153.1	634	127	84	73	21	4	5	4	64	0	148	9	1	9	10	.474	0	0	4.28
1995	Canton-Akrn	AA	20	20	2	0	114.1	469	100	49	42	10	1	2	3	38	0	91	5	2	9	8	.529	1	0	3.31
3 Min. YEARS			61	61	2	0	349.1	1434	302	155	137	39	5	11	10	120	0	320	19	2	24	21	.533	1	0	3.53

Scott Wiegandt

Pitches: Left **Bats:** Left **Pos:** P   **Ht:** 5'11" **Wt:** 180 **Born:** 12/9/67 **Age:** 28

			HOW MUCH HE PITCHED						WHAT HE GAVE UP												THE RESULTS					
Year	Team	Lg	G	GS	CG	GF	IP	BFP	H	R	ER	HR	SH	SF	HB	TBB	IBB	SO	WP	Bk	W	L	Pct.	ShO	Sv	ERA
1989	Martinsvlle	R	9	9	0	0	45.2	187	44	22	13	4	2	0	1	15	0	47	0	0	2	5	.286	0	0	2.56
1990	Spartanburg	A	10	0	0	8	18.1	66	12	2	2	0	0	0	0	2	0	17	0	0	2	0	1.000	0	0	0.98
	Clearwater	A	33	4	0	16	75.2	316	70	33	22	4	4	3	3	37	2	52	6	3	4	8	.333	0	4	2.62
1991	Clearwater	A	11	0	0	5	10.1	47	14	7	4	0	0	0	0	3	0	11	2	0	1	0	1.000	0	1	3.48
	Reading	AA	48	0	0	5	81	341	66	26	24	4	3	2	1	40	2	50	5	1	2	3	.400	0	1	2.67
1992	Scranton-Wb	AAA	1	0	0	1	1	4	0	0	0	0	0	0	0	1	0	2	0	0	0	0	.000	0	0	0.00
	Reading	AA	56	0	0	12	81.2	354	66	31	27	3	5	1	1	48	5	65	8	1	6	3	.667	0	3	2.98
1993	Reading	AA	56	0	0	16	73.1	326	75	41	29	3	7	2	0	44	7	60	5	1	6	2	.750	0	5	3.56
1994	Scranton-Wb	AAA	6	0	0	1	4.2	30	11	8	7	0	1	1	1	3	0	3	0	0	0	0	.000	0	0	13.50
	Reading	AA	52	0	0	16	52.1	219	49	23	18	4	2	3	2	19	1	35	1	1	2	4	.333	0	0	3.10
1995	Scranton-Wb	AAA	47	0	0	15	54.1	234	55	19	18	0	1	0	2	27	8	41	5	2	1	3	.250	0	2	2.98
7 Min. YEARS			329	13	0	95	498.1	2124	462	212	164	22	25	12	11	239	25	383	32	9	25	29	.463	0	12	2.96

Johnny Wiggs

Pitches: Left **Bats:** Left **Pos:** P   **Ht:** 5'11" **Wt:** 165 **Born:** 3/13/67 **Age:** 29

			HOW MUCH HE PITCHED						WHAT HE GAVE UP												THE RESULTS					
Year	Team	Lg	G	GS	CG	GF	IP	BFP	H	R	ER	HR	SH	SF	HB	TBB	IBB	SO	WP	Bk	W	L	Pct.	ShO	Sv	ERA
1989	Bellingham	A	22	0	0	17	40	155	28	8	7	1	2	0	0	16	2	59	3	0	0	3	.000	0	9	1.58
1990	San Bernrdo	A	64	0	0	21	93.1	413	112	48	41	6	5	1	3	48	5	97	6	2	7	6	.538	0	8	3.95
1991	Peninsula	A	39	5	3	9	110	444	94	43	39	8	3	3	3	42	4	77	4	3	6	5	.545	1	2	3.19
	Jacksonvlle	AA	6	0	0	3	13.1	55	14	6	6	1	0	0	0	2	0	14	1	0	1	0	1.000	0	0	4.05
1992	Jacksonvlle	AA	8	0	0	2	10.1	48	17	14	13	4	1	0	0	6	1	14	0	1	2	1	.667	0	0	11.32
	Lakeland	A	14	1	0	6	18	78	17	5	4	1	3	1	0	8	1	24	1	0	1	1	.500	0	1	2.00
1995	Pawtucket	AAA	14	0	0	3	9.1	40	11	6	6	0	0	0	0	3	0	6	0	0	1	0	1.000	0	2	5.79
5 Min. YEARS			167	6	3	61	294.1	1233	293	130	116	21	14	5	6	125	13	291	15	6	18	16	.529	1	22	3.55

Chad Wiley

Pitches: Right **Bats:** Right **Pos:** P   **Ht:** 5'11" **Wt:** 175 **Born:** 11/20/71 **Age:** 24

			HOW MUCH HE PITCHED						WHAT HE GAVE UP												THE RESULTS					
Year	Team	Lg	G	GS	CG	GF	IP	BFP	H	R	ER	HR	SH	SF	HB	TBB	IBB	SO	WP	Bk	W	L	Pct.	ShO	Sv	ERA
1992	Butte	R	18	7	0	3	66.1	292	66	44	35	5	0	4	7	28	0	68	6	1	4	1	.800	0	1	4.75
1993	Charlstn-Sc	A	40	2	0	14	79.2	353	60	42	34	5	3	7	8	54	2	72	13	2	3	2	.600	0	2	3.84
1994	Charlotte	A	42	0	0	9	72	321	71	29	25	3	2	1	4	37	0	63	6	1	4	6	.400	0	1	3.13
1995	Tulsa	AA	26	23	0	2	159.2	672	165	78	69	19	5	3	6	52	3	69	6	4	6	9	.400	0	0	3.89
4 Min. YEARS			126	32	0	28	377.2	1638	362	193	163	32	10	15	25	171	5	272	31	8	17	18	.486	0	4	3.88

Curt Wilkerson

Bats: Both **Throws:** Right **Pos:** 2B   **Ht:** 5'9" **Wt:** 175 **Born:** 4/26/61 **Age:** 35

			BATTING														BASERUNNING				PERCENTAGES		
Year	Team	Lg	G	AB	H	2B	3B	HR	TB	R	RBI	TBB	IBB	SO	HBP	SH	SF	SB	CS	SB%	GDP	Avg	OBP	SLG
1994	Omaha	AAA	27	91	23	5	0	0	28	8	7	7	0	17	0	0	0	0	1	.00	3	.253	.306	.308
	Ottawa	AAA	13	43	9	3	0	0	12	3	5	2	0	7	0	0	1	0	0	.00	1	.209	.239	.279
1995	Tacoma	AAA	5	18	4	0	0	0	4	1	3	1	0	3	0	0	0	0	0	.00	0	.222	.263	.222
1983	Texas	AL	16	35	6	0	1	0	8	7	1	2	0	5	0	0	0	3	0	1.00	0	.171	.216	.229
1984	Texas	AL	153	484	120	12	0	1	135	47	26	22	0	72	2	12	2	12	10	.55	7	.248	.282	.279
1985	Texas	AL	129	360	88	11	6	0	111	35	22	22	0	63	4	6	3	14	7	.67	7	.244	.293	.308

Year Team	Lg	G	AB	H	2B	3B	HR	TB	R	RBI	TBB	IBB	SO	HBP	SH	SF	SB	CS	SB%	GDP	Avg	OBP	SLG
1986 Texas	AL	110	236	56	10	3	0	72	27	15	11	0	42	1	0	1	9	7	.56	2	.237	.273	.305
1987 Texas	AL	85	138	37	5	3	2	54	28	14	6	0	16	2	0	0	6	3	.67	2	.268	.308	.391
1988 Texas	AL	117	338	99	12	5	0	121	41	28	26	3	43	2	3	2	9	4	.69	7	.293	.345	.358
1989 Chicago	NL	77	160	39	4	2	1	50	18	10	8	0	33	0	1	1	4	2	.67	3	.244	.278	.313
1990 Chicago	NL	77	186	41	5	1	0	48	21	16	7	2	36	0	3	0	2	2	.50	4	.220	.249	.258
1991 Pittsburgh	NL	85	191	36	9	1	2	53	20	18	15	0	40	0	0	4	2	1	.67	2	.188	.243	.277
1992 Kansas City	AL	111	296	74	10	1	2	92	27	29	18	3	47	1	7	4	18	7	.72	4	.250	.292	.311
1993 Kansas City	AL	12	28	4	0	0	0	4	1	0	1	0	6	0	0	0	2	0	1.00	1	.143	.172	.143
2 Min. YEARS		45	152	36	8	0	0	44	12	15	10	0	27	0	0	1	0	1	.00	4	.237	.282	.289
11 Maj. YEARS		972	2452	600	78	23	8	748	272	179	138	8	403	12	32	17	81	43	.65	39	.245	.286	.305

Marc Wilkins

Pitches: Right **Bats:** Right **Pos:** P **Ht:** 5'11" **Wt:** 215 **Born:** 10/21/70 **Age:** 25

	HOW MUCH HE PITCHED						WHAT HE GAVE UP												THE RESULTS					
Year Team	Lg	G	GS	CG	GF	IP	BFP	H	R	ER	HR	SH	SF	HB	TBB	IBB	SO	WP	Bk	W	L	Pct.	ShO	Sv	ERA
1992 Welland	A	28	1	0	8	42	207	49	38	34	2	2	2	4	24	3	42	12	1	4	2	.667	0	1	7.29
1993 Augusta	A	48	5	0	14	77	360	83	52	36	4	1	2	13	31	1	73	10	0	5	6	.455	0	1	4.21
1994 Salem	A	28	28	0	0	151	657	155	84	62	15	6	3	22	45	0	90	14	1	8	5	.615	0	0	3.70
1995 Carolina	AA	37	12	0	1	99.1	436	91	47	44	8	5	3	11	44	2	80	9	0	5	3	.625	0	0	3.99
4 Min. YEARS		141	46	0	23	369.1	1660	378	221	176	29	14	10	50	144	6	285	45	2	22	16	.579	0	2	4.29

Jerry Willard

Bats: Left **Throws:** Right **Pos:** 1B **Ht:** 6' 2" **Wt:** 195 **Born:** 3/14/60 **Age:** 36

	BATTING															BASERUNNING				PERCENTAGES		
Year Team	Lg	G	AB	H	2B	3B	HR	TB	R	RBI	TBB	IBB	SO	HBP	SH	SF	SB	CS	SB%	GDP	Avg	OBP	SLG
1980 Central Ore	A	65	231	85	21	1	5	123	53	59	51	4	27	2	2	3	2	2	.50	4	.368	.481	.532
1981 Peninsula	A	107	334	87	17	1	12	142	43	60	49	5	66	2	3	5	6	4	.60	7	.260	.354	.425
1982 Reading	AA	81	281	82	10	1	12	130	43	51	38	3	48	4	0	2	1	3	.25	7	.292	.382	.463
Okla. City	AAA	36	95	22	5	0	2	33	13	14	27	1	18	2	0	1	1	1	.50	6	.232	.408	.347
1983 Charleston	AAA	127	396	119	22	2	19	202	61	77	80	7	76	5	4	3	0	4	.00	4	.301	.421	.510
1985 Maine	AAA	11	40	9	3	0	1	15	5	4	7	0	7	0	0	0	1	0	1.00	1	.225	.340	.375
1986 Tacoma	AAA	22	62	16	5	0	1	24	7	12	9	0	11	0	1	1	0	0	.00	0	.258	.347	.387
1987 Tacoma	AAA	67	215	64	15	0	6	97	42	38	56	3	33	0	3	3	0	1	.00	6	.298	.438	.451
1989 Birmingham	AA	5	10	3	1	0	0	4	5	1	7	1	2	0	0	0	0	0	.00	0	.300	.588	.400
Vancouver	AAA	90	283	78	18	1	7	119	32	38	43	5	56	4	0	1	2	0	.00	6	.276	.378	.420
1990 Vancouver	AAA	121	380	106	21	0	20	187	66	76	85	7	60	2	0	5	2	4	.33	11	.279	.409	.492
1991 Richmond	AAA	91	277	83	24	0	8	131	42	39	45	4	46	5	2	1	1	3	.25	2	.300	.405	.473
1992 Indianapolis	AAA	31	97	27	7	1	3	45	9	17	12	0	19	0	1	0	0	0	.00	2	.278	.358	.464
1993 Richmond	AAA	107	317	101	21	0	8	146	37	44	60	6	63	3	0	2	0	0	.00	5	.319	.429	.461
1994 Calgary	AAA	110	371	107	28	1	23	206	86	80	88	7	70	4	1	8	0	0	.00	14	.288	.423	.555
1995 Tacoma	AAA	85	228	61	16	0	9	104	33	47	45	6	43	3	0	3	0	0	.00	7	.268	.391	.456
1984 Cleveland	AL	87	246	55	8	1	10	95	21	37	26	0	55	0	0	3	1	0	1.00	6	.224	.295	.386
1985 Cleveland	AL	104	300	81	13	0	7	115	39	36	28	1	59	1	4	1	0	0	.00	3	.270	.333	.383
1986 Oakland	AL	75	161	43	7	0	4	62	17	26	22	0	28	2	4	4	0	1	.00	4	.267	.354	.385
1987 Oakland	AL	7	6	1	0	0	0	1	1	0	2	0	1	0	0	0	0	0	.00	0	.167	.375	.167
1990 Chicago	AL	3	3	0	0	0	0	0	0	0	0	0	2	0	0	0	0	0	.00	0	.000	.000	.000
1991 Atlanta	NL	17	14	3	0	0	1	6	1	4	2	0	5	0	0	0	0	0	.00	0	.214	.313	.429
1992 Atlanta	NL	26	23	8	1	0	2	15	2	7	1	1	3	0	0	0	0	0	.00	3	.348	.375	.652
Montreal	NL	21	25	3	0	0	0	3	0	1	1	0	7	0	0	0	0	0	.00	2	.120	.154	.120
1994 Seattle	AL	6	5	1	0	0	1	4	1	3	1	0	1	0	0	0	0	0	.00	1	.200	.333	.800
14 Min. YEARS		1156	3617	1050	234	8	136	1708	577	657	702	59	645	36	17	38	14	24	.37	82	.290	.407	.472
8 Maj. YEARS		346	783	195	29	1	25	301	82	114	83	2	161	3	8	8	1	1	.50	18	.249	.320	.384

Greg Williams

Pitches: Left **Bats:** Left **Pos:** P **Ht:** 6'1" **Wt:** 195 **Born:** 4/30/72 **Age:** 24

	HOW MUCH HE PITCHED						WHAT HE GAVE UP												THE RESULTS					
Year Team	Lg	G	GS	CG	GF	IP	BFP	H	R	ER	HR	SH	SF	HB	TBB	IBB	SO	WP	Bk	W	L	Pct.	ShO	Sv	ERA
1993 Watertown	A	1	0	0	0	0	4	1	1	0	0	0	0	0	2	1	0	0	0	0	1	.000	0	0	0.00
Burlington	R	11	4	0	2	41	188	31	30	20	2	1	2	3	29	2	48	6	2	3	1	.750	0	2	4.39
Kinston	A	2	1	0	0	3	15	6	3	3	1	0	0	0	1	0	2	1	0	0	1	.000	0	0	9.00
1994 Columbus	A	37	0	0	12	73.1	312	49	32	28	2	1	4	5	52	0	84	8	1	6	1	.857	0	1	3.44
1995 Kinston	A	30	0	0	8	22	88	15	9	6	1	1	0	2	8	0	18	5	0	2	1	.667	0	3	2.45
Canton-Akrn	AA	24	0	0	7	27.2	115	15	14	13	2	2	1	0	21	3	17	0	0	0	0	.000	0	0	4.23
3 Min. YEARS		105	5	0	30	167	722	117	89	70	8	5	7	10	113	6	169	20	3	11	5	.688	0	6	3.77

Jeff Williams

Pitches: Right **Bats:** Right **Pos:** P **Ht:** 6'4" **Wt:** 230 **Born:** 4/16/69 **Age:** 27

	HOW MUCH HE PITCHED						WHAT HE GAVE UP												THE RESULTS					
Year Team	Lg	G	GS	CG	GF	IP	BFP	H	R	ER	HR	SH	SF	HB	TBB	IBB	SO	WP	Bk	W	L	Pct.	ShO	Sv	ERA
1990 Bluefield	R	9	0	0	9	11.1	48	7	3	2	0	0	0	1	5	0	14	1	0	2	0	1.000	0	0	1.59
Frederick	A	16	0	0	13	25	115	23	17	13	2	0	2	2	17	0	31	1	0	2	1	.667	0	1	4.68
1991 Frederick	A	12	0	0	11	16.2	68	17	6	5	1	1	1	0	6	0	20	0	0	1	2	.333	0	6	2.70
Hagerstown	AA	39	0	0	29	55.1	247	52	23	16	1	2	3	0	32	1	42	6	0	3	5	.375	0	17	2.60
1992 Hagerstown	AA	36	15	3	16	123	579	148	91	66	9	5	6	6	70	0	82	15	1	8	10	.444	0	4	4.83
1993 Rochester	AAA	33	5	0	11	86	389	95	59	55	10	2	7	4	47	3	59	8	1	2	5	.286	0	1	5.76

Year	Team	Lg	G	GS	CG	GF	IP	BFP	H	R	ER	HR	SH	SF	HB	TBB	IBB	SO	WP	Bk	W	L	Pct.	ShO	Sv	ERA
1994	Albuquerque	AAA	3	0	0	0	4.1	21	7	4	4	0	0	0	0	3	0	4	0	0	0	1	.000	0	0	8.31
	Calgary	AAA	40	1	0	16	69.2	328	88	53	43	4	1	4	2	43	3	30	11	0	3	3	.500	0	0	5.56
1995	Tacoma	AAA	8	3	0	4	23	109	31	21	21	1	0	3	2	12	0	8	0	0	0	3	.000	0	0	8.22
	6 Min. YEARS		196	24	3	109	414.1	1904	468	277	225	28	11	26	17	235	7	290	42	2	21	30	.412	0	31	4.89

Juan Williams

Bats: Left Throws: Right Pos: OF **Ht: 6'0" Wt: 180 Born: 10/9/72 Age: 23**

									BATTING									BASERUNNING				PERCENTAGES		
Year	Team	Lg	G	AB	H	2B	3B	HR	TB	R	RBI	TBB	IBB	SO	HBP	SH	SF	SB	CS	SB%	GDP	Avg	OBP	SLG
1990	Pulaski	R	58	198	54	6	1	0	62	18	22	11	1	45	2	1	0	9	7	.56	6	.273	.318	.313
1991	Macon	A	106	347	81	13	2	1	101	44	32	39	1	100	3	6	2	12	11	.52	5	.233	.315	.291
1992	Macon	A	67	232	54	12	2	2	76	24	14	25	1	77	0	0	0	16	6	.73	2	.233	.307	.328
	Pulaski	R	47	169	47	6	4	6	79	26	31	13	1	46	0	1	1	9	3	.75	2	.278	.328	.467
1993	Durham	A	124	403	93	16	2	11	146	49	44	36	4	120	1	6	1	11	12	.48	9	.231	.295	.362
1994	Durham	A	122	394	86	14	0	19	157	55	57	54	1	131	1	0	4	7	10	.41	2	.218	.311	.398
1995	Greenville	AA	62	192	60	14	2	15	123	40	39	19	3	44	0	0	3	4	3	.57	5	.313	.369	.641
	Richmond	AAA	45	129	34	5	0	5	54	18	11	17	0	38	0	0	1	1	3	.25	5	.264	.347	.419
	6 Min. YEARS		631	2064	509	86	13	59	798	274	250	214	12	601	7	14	12	69	55	.56	36	.247	.318	.387

Keith Williams

Bats: Right Throws: Right Pos: OF **Ht: 6'0" Wt: 190 Born: 4/21/72 Age: 24**

									BATTING									BASERUNNING				PERCENTAGES		
Year	Team	Lg	G	AB	H	2B	3B	HR	TB	R	RBI	TBB	IBB	SO	HBP	SH	SF	SB	CS	SB%	GDP	Avg	OBP	SLG
1993	Everett	A	75	288	87	21	5	12	154	57	49	48	4	73	3	2	0	21	7	.75	5	.302	.407	.535
1994	San Jose	A	128	504	151	30	8	21	260	91	97	60	2	102	4	0	8	4	3	.57	8	.300	.373	.516
1995	Shreveport	AA	75	275	84	20	1	9	133	39	55	23	3	39	0	0	7	5	3	.63	5	.305	.351	.484
	Phoenix	AAA	24	83	25	4	1	2	37	7	14	5	0	11	1	4	2	0	0	.00	4	.301	.341	.446
	3 Min. YEARS		302	1150	347	75	15	44	584	194	215	136	9	225	8	6	17	30	13	.70	22	.302	.375	.508

Shad Williams

Pitches: Right Bats: Right Pos: P **Ht: 6'0" Wt: 185 Born: 3/10/71 Age: 25**

				HOW MUCH HE PITCHED					WHAT HE GAVE UP											THE RESULTS					
Year	Team	Lg	G	GS	CG	GF	IP	BFP	H	R	ER	HR	SH	SF	HB	TBB	IBB	SO	WP	Bk	W	L	Pct.	ShO	Sv	ERA
1992	Quad City	A	27	26	7	0	179.1	748	161	81	65	14	6	6	7	55	0	152	9	1	13	11	.542	0	0	3.26
1993	Midland	AA	27	27	2	0	175.2	758	192	100	92	16	6	6	3	65	1	91	9	1	7	10	.412	0	0	4.71
1994	Midland	AA	5	5	1	0	32.1	112	13	4	4	1	0	0	3	4	0	29	2	0	3	0	1.000	1	0	1.11
	Vancouver	AAA	16	16	1	0	86	386	100	61	44	14	3	2	3	30	0	42	6	0	4	6	.400	1	0	4.60
1995	Vancouver	AAA	25	25	3	0	149.2	627	142	65	56	16	3	3	4	48	2	114	7	1	9	7	.563	1	0	3.37
	4 Min. YEARS		100	99	14	0	623	2631	608	311	261	61	18	17	18	202	3	428	33	3	36	34	.514	3	0	3.77

Slim Williams

Pitches: Left Bats: Left Pos: P **Ht: 6'7" Wt: 232 Born: 5/18/65 Age: 31**

				HOW MUCH HE PITCHED					WHAT HE GAVE UP											THE RESULTS					
Year	Team	Lg	G	GS	CG	GF	IP	BFP	H	R	ER	HR	SH	SF	HB	TBB	IBB	SO	WP	Bk	W	L	Pct.	ShO	Sv	ERA
1984	Great Falls	R	8	0	0	3	11		10	14	11	0	0	0	0	16	0	9	1	0	0	1	.000	0	0	9.00
	Dodgers	R	2	0	0	0	3	20	4	4	0	0	0	0	0	4	0	1	1	0	0	0	.000	0	0	0.00
1985	Dodgers	R	13	13	1	0	66.2	306	54	35	28	1	3	2	2	55	0	59	5	4	4	4	.500	1	0	3.78
1986	Vero Beach	A	30	6	0	16	60	285	47	35	29	1	6	3	1	66	2	40	8	4	1	1	.500	0	0	4.35
1987	Visalia	A	13	13	2	0	85	373	66	38	21	5	6	1	5	62	2	81	10	0	7	4	.636	0	0	2.22
1988	Visalia	A	37	0	0	28	51	221	41	23	21	2	4	2	2	33	0	55	5	3	3	4	.429	0	12	3.71
1989	Orlando	AA	43	0	0	39	53.1	240	50	23	18	3	1	1	0	35	1	62	1	2	6	4	.600	0	14	3.04
	Portland	AAA	16	0	0	8	23.2	112	24	15	11	0	0	1	0	18	0	22	2	1	3	2	.600	0	3	4.18
1990	Portland	AAA	51	3	0	27	84	388	73	64	47	4	3	6	3	74	2	62	7	1	4	6	.400	0	3	5.04
1991	Phoenix	AAA	30	28	3	1	160	748	192	120	106	17	3	5	1	93	0	69	12	5	7	9	.438	0	0	5.96
1993	Orlando	AA	15	14	0	0	90.2	377	84	29	25	4	5	0	2	38	1	65	2	2	5	5	.500	0	0	2.48
	Iowa	AAA	17	13	0	1	78	329	74	32	30	5	5	2	1	37	0	49	3	2	5	3	.625	0	0	3.46
1994	Harrisburg	AA	1	1	0	0	4	18	3	1	0	0	0	0	0	2	0	5	0	0	0	0	.000	0	0	0.00
	Ottawa	AAA	27	11	1	3	99.1	448	105	60	50	5	2	3	1	53	1	57	7	0	9	2	.818	1	1	4.53
1995	Norfolk	AAA	27	13	0	6	106.1	453	89	42	36	3	1	5	1	56	0	88	5	2	11	4	.733	0	2	3.05
	Rochester	AAA	5	3	0	0	12.2	69	21	13	10	0	0	0	1	9	0	12	7	2	1	2	.333	0	0	7.11
	11 Min. YEARS		335	118	7	132	988.2	4387	937	548	443	50	39	31	20	651	9	736	75	28	66	51	.564	2	35	4.03

Ted Williams

Bats: Both Throws: Right Pos: DH **Ht: 6'1" Wt: 160 Born: 2/23/65 Age: 31**

									BATTING									BASERUNNING				PERCENTAGES		
Year	Team	Lg	G	AB	H	2B	3B	HR	TB	R	RBI	TBB	IBB	SO	HBP	SH	SF	SB	CS	SB%	GDP	Avg	OBP	SLG
1986	Bellingham	A	59	224	55	2	0	0	57	52	25	38	1	38	4	5	4	51	3	.94	1	.246	.359	.254
1987	Wausau	A	120	460	118	16	1	3	145	63	31	35	2	84	4	6	2	74	21	.78	4	.257	.313	.315
1988	San Bernrdo	A	135	525	130	14	3	6	168	82	50	34	0	137	8	5	6	71	18	.80	7	.248	.300	.320
1989	Williamsprt	AA	133	477	118	21	5	3	158	59	40	20	0	97	6	6	5	37	13	.74	4	.247	.283	.331
1990	Williamsprt	AA	81	321	73	11	2	1	91	37	18	14	0	59	8	0	1	34	11	.76	4	.227	.276	.283
	Calgary	AAA	43	143	38	3	4	6	67	30	20	8	0	22	1	1	1	9	4	.69	0	.266	.307	.469
1991	Jacksonvlle	AA	70	269	59	10	3	4	87	47	16	21	0	73	4	2	1	34	13	.72	1	.219	.285	.323
1992	Calgary	AAA	92	250	61	5	5	1	79	36	17	12	0	58	5	3	0	41	13	.76	4	.244	.292	.316
1993	Toledo	AAA	68	194	48	7	3	1	64	21	16	10	0	45	1	5	1	22	5	.81	2	.247	.286	.330

Year Team	Lg	G	AB	H	2B	3B	HR	TB	R	RBI	TBB	IBB	SO	HBP	SH	SF	SB	CS	SB%	GDP	Avg	OBP	SLG
London	AA	32	125	30	8	0	0	38	17	9	9	0	21	2	1	0	10	4	.71	8	.240	.301	.304
1994 Winnipeg	IND	36	151	41	7	1	0	50	26	9	9	0	25	1	1	1	17	3	.85	0	.272	.315	.331
Duluth-Sup.	IND	37	156	35	4	3	0	45	15	10	10	1	22	1	2	2	19	6	.76	2	.224	.272	.288
1995 Wichita	AA	1	0	0	0	0	0	0	0	0	0	0	0	0	0	0	0	0	.000	0	.000	.000	.000
10 Min. YEARS		907	3295	806	108	30	25	1049	486	261	220	6	681	45	37	24	419	114	.79	37	.245	.299	.318

Antone Williamson

Bats: Left **Throws:** Right **Pos:** 3B **Ht:** 6'1" **Wt:** 195 **Born:** 7/18/73 **Age:** 22

Year Team	Lg	G	AB	H	2B	3B	HR	TB	R	RBI	TBB	IBB	SO	HBP	SH	SF	SB	CS	SB%	GDP	Avg	OBP	SLG
1994 Helena	R	6	26	11	2	1	0	15	5	4	2	0	4	0	0	0	0	0	.00	1	.423	.464	.577
Stockton	A	23	85	19	4	0	3	32	6	13	7	0	19	0	1	3	0	0	.00	1	.224	.274	.376
El Paso	AA	14	48	12	3	0	1	18	8	9	7	0	8	0	0	1	0	0	.00	1	.250	.339	.375
1995 El Paso	AA	104	392	121	30	6	7	184	62	90	47	3	57	3	0	4	3	1	.75	10	.309	.383	.469
2 Min. YEARS		147	551	163	39	7	11	249	81	116	63	3	88	3	1	8	3	2	.60	13	.296	.366	.452

Travis Willis

Pitches: Right **Bats:** Right **Pos:** P **Ht:** 6'2" **Wt:** 185 **Born:** 11/28/68 **Age:** 27

Year Team	Lg	G	GS	CG	GF	IP	BFP	H	R	ER	HR	SH	SF	HB	TBB	IBB	SO	WP	Bk	W	L	Pct.	ShO	Sv	ERA
1989 Geneva	A	16	15	4	1	100.1	415	92	55	38	7	2	1	8	21	3	93	5	3	4	7	.364	0	0	3.41
1990 Peoria	A	31	22	6	4	163	682	152	78	59	6	8	7	14	41	1	93	9	6	10	11	.476	3	0	3.26
Winston-Sal	A	2	2	0	0	4.1	30	13	12	10	2	0	0	2	3	0	2	0	2	0	1	.000	0	0	20.77
1991 Winston-Sal	A	53	0	0	48	73.1	315	74	36	33	2	2	2	3	25	1	60	7	0	6	4	.600	0	26	4.05
1992 Iowa	AAA	3	0	0	2	7	32	9	6	6	4	1	0	0	3	0	1	1	0	1	1	.500	0	0	7.71
Charlotte	AA	46	0	0	22	61.2	252	55	23	20	2	2	2	1	16	3	34	5	0	5	3	.625	0	4	2.92
1993 Orlando	AA	61	1	0	57	82.1	357	91	37	26	2	10	3	2	22	6	56	8	0	8	6	.571	0	24	2.84
1994 Buffalo	AAA	56	0	0	10	76.1	329	89	42	36	7	1	3	0	26	3	42	3	0	6	3	.667	0	1	4.24
1995 Carolina	AA	16	0	0	6	21.2	101	23	10	7	0	1	1	3	10	2	12	2	0	1	1	.500	0	3	2.91
Calgary	AAA	22	0	0	7	39	188	57	35	31	4	2	0	4	15	4	13	2	0	2	2	.500	0	0	7.15
7 Min. YEARS		306	40	11	157	629	2701	655	334	266	36	29	19	37	182	23	406	42	11	43	39	.524	3	58	3.81

Brandon Wilson

Bats: Right **Throws:** Right **Pos:** SS **Ht:** 6'1" **Wt:** 175 **Born:** 2/26/69 **Age:** 27

Year Team	Lg	G	AB	H	2B	3B	HR	TB	R	RBI	TBB	IBB	SO	HBP	SH	SF	SB	CS	SB%	GDP	Avg	OBP	SLG
1990 White Sox	R	11	41	11	1	0	0	12	4	5	4	0	5	0	1	1	3	1	.75	1	.268	.326	.293
Utica	A	53	165	41	2	0	0	43	31	14	28	0	45	0	3	2	14	5	.74	1	.248	.354	.261
1991 South Bend	A	125	463	145	18	6	2	181	75	49	61	2	70	2	7	4	41	11	.79	3	.313	.392	.391
Birmingham	AA	2	10	4	1	0	0	5	3	2	0	0	2	0	0	0	0	0	.00	0	.400	.400	.500
1992 Sarasota	A	103	399	118	22	6	4	164	68	54	45	2	64	4	5	2	30	16	.65	4	.296	.371	.411
Birmingham	AA	27	107	29	4	0	0	33	10	4	4	0	16	0	0	0	5	0	1.00	1	.271	.297	.308
1993 Birmingham	AA	137	500	135	19	5	2	170	76	48	52	0	77	3	4	3	43	10	.81	7	.270	.341	.340
1994 Nashville	AAA	114	370	83	16	3	5	120	42	26	30	3	67	3	10	2	13	5	.72	4	.224	.286	.324
1995 Nashville	AAA	27	85	25	5	0	1	33	8	10	4	0	11	0	1	0	3	1	.75	3	.294	.326	.388
Indianapolis	AAA	4	12	2	0	0	0	2	3	0	2	0	1	0	0	0	0	0	.00	0	.167	.286	.167
Chattanooga	AA	75	308	101	29	1	9	159	56	50	28	0	52	3	2	2	12	6	.67	7	.328	.387	.516
6 Min. YEARS		678	2460	694	117	21	23	922	376	262	258	4	410	15	33	16	164	55	.75	31	.282	.352	.375

Craig Wilson

Bats: Right **Throws:** Right **Pos:** SS **Ht:** 6'1" **Wt:** 190 **Born:** 9/3/70 **Age:** 25

Year Team	Lg	G	AB	H	2B	3B	HR	TB	R	RBI	TBB	IBB	SO	HBP	SH	SF	SB	CS	SB%	GDP	Avg	OBP	SLG
1993 South Bend	A	132	455	118	27	2	5	164	56	59	49	2	50	8	7	6	4	4	.50	16	.259	.338	.360
1994 Pr. William	A	131	496	131	36	4	4	187	70	66	58	2	44	6	5	6	1	2	.33	16	.264	.345	.377
1995 Birmingham	AA	132	471	136	19	1	4	169	56	46	43	0	44	5	10	2	2	2	.50	21	.289	.353	.359
3 Min. YEARS		395	1422	385	82	7	13	520	182	171	150	4	138	19	22	14	7	8	.47	53	.271	.345	.366

Craig Wilson

Bats: Right **Throws:** Right **Pos:** 3B **Ht:** 5'11" **Wt:** 210 **Born:** 11/28/64 **Age:** 31

Year Team	Lg	G	AB	H	2B	3B	HR	TB	R	RBI	TBB	IBB	SO	HBP	SH	SF	SB	CS	SB%	GDP	Avg	OBP	SLG
1984 Erie	A	72	282	83	18	4	7	130	53	46	29	0	27	4	1	2	10	4	.71	8	.294	.366	.461
1985 Springfield	A	133	504	132	16	4	8	180	64	52	47	0	67	1	4	6	33	14	.70	12	.262	.323	.357
1986 Springfield	A	127	496	136	17	6	1	168	106	49	65	0	49	1	9	4	44	12	.79	11	.274	.357	.339
1987 St. Pete	A	38	162	58	6	4	0	72	35	28	14	0	5	0	0	0	12	8	.60	3	.358	.409	.444
Louisville	AAA	21	70	15	2	0	1	20	10	8	3	0	5	0	2	1	0	2	.00	1	.214	.243	.286
Arkansas	AA	66	238	69	13	1	1	87	37	26	30	1	19	1	3	2	9	6	.60	5	.290	.369	.366
1988 Louisville	AAA	133	497	127	27	2	1	161	59	46	54	0	46	0	6	4	6	4	.60	13	.256	.326	.324
1989 Arkansas	AA	55	224	71	12	1	1	88	41	40	21	1	14	1	3	1	8	5	.62	4	.317	.373	.393
Louisville	AAA	75	278	81	18	3	1	108	37	30	14	0	25	2	3	1	1	3	.25	5	.291	.329	.388
1990 Louisville	AAA	57	204	57	9	2	2	76	30	23	28	0	15	1	5	6	5	3	.63	3	.279	.360	.373
1992 Louisville	AAA	20	81	24	5	1	0	31	13	5	5	0	8	0	1	0	3	2	.60	2	.296	.337	.383
1993 Omaha	AAA	65	234	65	13	1	3	89	26	28	20	0	24	1	1	1	7	4	.64	6	.278	.336	.380
1994 Okla. City	AAA	65	227	59	6	0	4	77	23	27	23	4	24	1	6	2	1	2	.33	14	.260	.328	.339

Year	Team	Lg	G	AB	H	2B	3B	HR	TB	R	RBI	TBB	IBB	SO	HBP	SH	SF	SB	CS	SB%	GDP	Avg	OBP	SLG
1995	Toledo	AAA	121	468	123	31	0	9	181	56	65	37	0	61	3	3	7	8	2	.80	11	.263	.317	.387
1989	St. Louis	NL	6	4	1	0	0	0	1	1	1	1	0	2	0	0	0	0	0	.00	0	.250	.400	.250
1990	St. Louis	NL	55	121	30	2	0	0	32	13	7	8	0	14	0	0	2	0	2	.00	7	.248	.290	.264
1991	St. Louis	NL	60	82	14	2	0	0	16	5	13	6	2	10	0	0	2	0	0	.00	2	.171	.222	.195
1992	St. Louis	NL	61	106	33	6	0	0	39	6	13	10	2	18	0	2	1	1	2	.33	4	.311	.368	.368
1993	Kansas City	AL	21	49	13	1	0	1	17	6	3	7	0	6	0	1	0	1	1	.50	0	.265	.357	.347
	11 Min. YEARS		1048	3965	1100	193	29	39	1468	590	473	390	7	389	16	47	37	147	71	.67	98	.277	.342	.370
	5 Maj. YEARS		203	362	91	11	0	1	105	31	37	32	4	50	0	3	5	2	5	.29	13	.251	.308	.290

Desi Wilson

Bats: Left **Throws:** Left **Pos:** 1B **Ht:** 6'7" **Wt:** 230 **Born:** 5/9/68 **Age:** 28

				BATTING														BASERUNNING				PERCENTAGES		
Year	Team	Lg	G	AB	H	2B	3B	HR	TB	R	RBI	TBB	IBB	SO	HBP	SH	SF	SB	CS	SB%	GDP	Avg	OBP	SLG
1991	Rangers	R	8	25	4	2	0	0	6	1	7	3	0	2	0	0	1	0	0	.00	0	.160	.241	.240
1992	Butte	R	72	253	81	9	4	5	113	45	42	31	1	45	1	0	0	13	11	.54	1	.320	.396	.447
1993	Charlotte	A	131	511	156	21	7	3	200	83	70	50	4	90	7	0	2	29	11	.73	18	.305	.374	.391
1994	Tulsa	AA	129	493	142	27	0	6	187	69	55	40	5	115	2	0	1	16	14	.53	14	.288	.343	.379
1995	Shreveport	AA	122	482	138	27	3	5	186	77	72	40	2	68	1	0	7	11	9	.55	18	.286	.338	.386
	5 Min. YEARS		462	1764	521	86	14	19	692	275	246	164	12	320	11	0	11	69	45	.61	51	.295	.357	.392

Paul Wilson

Pitches: Right **Bats:** Right **Pos:** P **Ht:** 6'5" **Wt:** 235 **Born:** 3/28/73 **Age:** 23

			HOW MUCH HE PITCHED						WHAT HE GAVE UP										THE RESULTS					
Year	Team	Lg	G	GS	CG	GF	IP	BFP	H	R	ER	HR	SH	SF	HB	TBB	IBB	SO	WP	Bk	W	L	Pct.	ShO	Sv	ERA
1994	Mets	R	3	3	0	0	12	47	8	4	4	0	1	0	4	0	13	0	2	0	2	.000	0	0	3.00
	St. Lucie	A	8	8	0	0	37.1	160	32	23	21	3	0	1	3	17	1	37	0	5	0	5	.000	0	0	5.06
1995	Binghamton	AA	16	16	4	0	120.1	464	89	34	29	5	3	4	5	24	2	127	4	3	6	3	.667	1	0	2.17
	Norfolk	AAA	10	10	4	0	66.1	270	59	25	21	3	2	1	3	20	0	67	2	0	5	3	.625	2	0	2.85
	2 Min. YEARS		37	37	8	0	236	941	188	86	75	11	6	6	11	65	3	244	6	10	11	13	.458	3	0	2.86

Pookie Wilson

Bats: Left **Throws:** Left **Pos:** OF **Ht:** 5'10" **Wt:** 180 **Born:** 10/24/70 **Age:** 25

				BATTING														BASERUNNING				PERCENTAGES		
Year	Team	Lg	G	AB	H	2B	3B	HR	TB	R	RBI	TBB	IBB	SO	HBP	SH	SF	SB	CS	SB%	GDP	Avg	OBP	SLG
1992	Salt Lake	R	66	241	80	5	2	0	89	57	20	26	0	24	4	2	2	24	12	.67	6	.332	.403	.369
1993	Kane County	A	129	469	117	8	2	0	129	74	27	52	0	55	9	10	2	34	15	.69	6	.249	.335	.275
1994	Brevard Cty	A	125	483	129	12	4	1	152	81	29	50	1	49	3	8	3	26	14	.65	4	.267	.338	.315
1995	Portland	AA	107	348	95	13	5	3	127	51	44	18	2	51	11	5	4	9	4	.69	9	.273	.325	.365
	4 Min. YEARS		427	1541	421	38	13	4	497	263	120	146	3	179	27	25	11	93	45	.67	24	.273	.344	.323

Steve Wilson

Pitches: Left **Bats:** Left **Pos:** P **Ht:** 6'4" **Wt:** 224 **Born:** 12/13/64 **Age:** 31

			HOW MUCH HE PITCHED						WHAT HE GAVE UP										THE RESULTS					
Year	Team	Lg	G	GS	CG	GF	IP	BFP	H	R	ER	HR	SH	SF	HB	TBB	IBB	SO	WP	Bk	W	L	Pct.	ShO	Sv	ERA
1985	Burlington	A	21	10	0	4	72.2	317	71	44	37	11	1	4	2	27	1	76	1	3	3	5	.375	0	0	4.58
1986	Tulsa	AA	24	24	2	0	136.2	617	117	83	74	10	5	8	7	103	0	95	12	6	7	13	.350	0	0	4.87
1987	Charlotte	A	20	17	1	1	107	442	81	41	29	5	0	2	3	44	0	80	5	2	9	5	.643	1	0	2.44
1988	Tulsa	AA	25	25	5	0	165.1	698	147	72	58	14	6	4	8	53	1	132	3	1	15	7	.682	3	0	3.16
1991	Iowa	AAA	25	16	1	4	114	482	102	55	49	11	0	1	7	45	2	83	7	0	3	8	.273	0	0	3.87
1993	Albuquerque	AAA	13	12	0	0	51.1	220	57	29	25	5	4	1	2	14	0	44	4	2	0	3	.000	0	0	4.38
1994	New Orleans	AAA	51	3	0	15	76.2	332	78	39	37	5	1	2	4	33	5	67	5	1	8	6	.571	0	1	4.34
1995	Nashville	AAA	20	7	0	4	51.1	234	60	32	26	7	3	4	3	17	1	26	1	1	2	2	.500	0	1	4.56
1988	Texas	AL	3	0	0	1	7.2	31	7	5	5	1	0	0	0	4	1	1	0	0	0	0	.000	0	0	5.87
1989	Chicago	NL	53	8	0	9	85.2	364	83	43	40	6	5	4	1	31	5	65	0	1	6	4	.600	0	2	4.20
1990	Chicago	NL	45	15	1	5	139	597	140	77	74	17	9	3	2	43	6	95	2	1	4	9	.308	0	1	4.79
1991	Chicago	NL	8	0	0	2	12.1	53	13	7	6	1	0	1	0	5	1	9	0	0	0	0	.000	0	0	4.38
	Los Angeles	NL	11	0	0	3	8.1	28	1	0	0	0	0	0	0	4	0	5	0	0	0	0	.000	0	2	0.00
1992	Los Angeles	NL	60	0	0	8	66.2	301	74	37	31	6	5	4	1	29	7	54	7	0	2	5	.286	0	4	4.19
1993	Los Angeles	NL	25	0	0	4	25.2	120	30	13	13	2	1	0	1	14	4	23	3	0	1	0	1.000	0	1	4.56
	8 Min. YEARS		199	114	9	28	775	3342	713	395	335	68	20	26	36	336	10	603	38	16	47	49	.490	4	2	3.89
	6 Maj. YEARS		205	23	1	42	345.1	1494	348	182	169	33	20	12	5	130	24	252	12	2	13	18	.419	0	6	4.40

Thomas Wilson

Bats: Right **Throws:** Right **Pos:** C **Ht:** 6'3" **Wt:** 185 **Born:** 12/19/70 **Age:** 25

				BATTING														BASERUNNING				PERCENTAGES		
Year	Team	Lg	G	AB	H	2B	3B	HR	TB	R	RBI	TBB	IBB	SO	HBP	SH	SF	SB	CS	SB%	GDP	Avg	OBP	SLG
1991	Oneonta	A	70	243	59	12	2	4	87	38	42	34	2	71	3	0	5	4	4	.50	6	.243	.337	.358
1992	Greensboro	A	117	395	83	22	0	6	123	50	48	68	0	128	3	1	8	2	1	.67	8	.210	.325	.311
1993	Greensboro	A	120	394	98	20	1	10	150	55	63	91	0	112	4	3	8	2	5	.29	5	.249	.388	.381
1994	Albany-Colo	AA	123	408	100	20	1	7	143	54	42	58	2	100	6	4	4	4	6	.40	6	.245	.345	.350
1995	Columbus	AAA	22	62	16	3	1	0	21	11	9	9	0	10	0	2	0	0	0	1.00	0	.258	.352	.339
	Tampa	A	17	48	8	0	0	0	8	3	2	11	0	13	0	1	1	1	0	1.00	0	.167	.317	.167
	Norwich	AA	28	84	12	4	0	0	16	6	4	17	0	22	0	0	0	0	0	.00	3	.143	.287	.190
	5 Min. YEARS		497	1634	376	81	5	27	548	217	210	288	4	456	16	11	26	13	16	.45	28	.230	.346	.335

Randy Wilstead

Bats: Left Throws: Left Pos: DH Ht: 6'4" Wt: 200 Born: 4/5/68 Age: 28

Year	Team	Lg	G	AB	H	2B	3B	HR	TB	R	RBI	TBB	IBB	SO	HBP	SH	SF	SB	CS	SB%	GDP	Avg	OBP	SLG
1990	Jamestown	A	56	180	48	11	1	4	73	24	21	25	3	43	2	0	0	1	1	.50	0	.267	.362	.406
1991	Rockford	A	121	421	107	26	4	6	159	59	57	58	11	72	1	1	5	2	2	.50	7	.254	.342	.378
	W. Palm Bch	A	1	1	0	0	0	0	0	0	0	0	0	0	0	0	0	0	0	.00	0	.000	.000	.000
1992	W. Palm Bch	A	129	449	128	27	3	8	185	56	71	47	8	68	3	0	4	7	7	.50	12	.285	.354	.412
1993	W. Palm Bch	A	60	201	67	19	3	3	101	33	35	39	6	39	1	0	2	3	1	.75	3	.333	.440	.502
	Harrisburg	AA	45	108	28	7	0	4	47	10	15	12	2	21	0	0	1	1	1	.50	2	.259	.331	.435
1994	Harrisburg	AA	122	374	110	27	3	13	182	71	64	72	4	83	7	0	3	3	6	.33	7	.294	.414	.487
1995	Ottawa	AAA	9	24	7	2	1	0	11	6	3	6	0	3	2	0	2	0	0	.00	1	.292	.441	.458
	6 Min. YEARS		543	1758	495	119	15	38	758	259	266	259	34	329	16	1	17	17	18	.49	32	.282	.376	.431

Chris Wimmer

Bats: Right Throws: Right Pos: 2B Ht: 5'11" Wt: 170 Born: 9/25/70 Age: 25

Year	Team	Lg	G	AB	H	2B	3B	HR	TB	R	RBI	TBB	IBB	SO	HBP	SH	SF	SB	CS	SB%	GDP	Avg	OBP	SLG
1993	San Jose	A	123	493	130	21	4	3	168	76	53	42	1	72	8	7	6	49	12	.80	6	.264	.328	.341
1994	Shreveport	AA	126	462	131	21	3	4	170	63	49	25	2	56	8	5	4	21	13	.62	7	.284	.329	.368
1995	Phoenix	AAA	132	449	118	23	4	2	155	55	44	31	1	49	13	5	5	13	7	.65	10	.263	.325	.345
	3 Min. YEARS		381	1404	379	65	11	9	493	194	146	98	4	177	29	17	15	83	32	.72	23	.270	.327	.351

Darrin Winston

Pitches: Left Bats: Right Pos: P Ht: 6'0" Wt: 195 Born: 7/6/66 Age: 29

Year	Team	Lg	G	GS	CG	GF	IP	BFP	H	R	ER	HR	SH	SF	HB	TBB	IBB	SO	WP	Bk	W	L	Pct.	ShO	Sv	ERA
1988	Jamestown	A	14	7	0	5	44	194	47	28	24	3	3	2	0	19	0	29	2	4	2	4	.333	0	2	4.91
1989	Rockford	A	47	0	0	30	65	256	52	16	11	0	3	3	0	11	0	70	7	1	7	1	.875	0	16	1.52
1990	Jacksonville	AA	47	0	0	20	63	246	38	16	15	3	5	2	0	28	2	45	4	0	6	2	.750	0	7	2.14
1991	Indianapolis	AAA	27	0	0	4	31	143	26	10	5	3	6	2	1	21	5	23	2	0	1	0	1.000	0	1	1.45
1993	Harrisburg	AA	24	0	0	9	44.2	206	53	30	23	4	4	4	2	19	2	36	3	0	1	0	1.000	0	1	4.63
	W. Palm Bch	A	8	2	1	3	24.2	88	18	6	4	0	0	0	0	3	0	21	0	0	2	0	1.000	0	1	1.46
1994	Harrisburg	AA	25	0	0	11	35.1	144	32	12	6	3	3	0	2	9	3	27	0	0	4	2	.667	0	0	1.53
	Ottawa	AAA	23	0	0	9	28.1	116	27	15	12	6	1	0	0	10	1	17	0	0	2	0	1.000	0	1	3.81
1995	Calgary	AAA	53	0	0	20	50.2	226	59	33	27	8	0	2	0	17	2	40	2	0	4	6	.400	0	0	4.80
	7 Min. YEARS		268	9	1	111	386.2	1619	352	166	127	30	25	15	5	137	15	308	20	5	29	15	.659	0	28	2.96

Mark Wipf

Bats: Both Throws: Right Pos: OF Ht: 6'4" Wt: 195 Born: 1/11/73 Age: 23

Year	Team	Lg	G	AB	H	2B	3B	HR	TB	R	RBI	TBB	IBB	SO	HBP	SH	SF	SB	CS	SB%	GDP	Avg	OBP	SLG
1992	Kingsport	R	57	217	51	7	1	1	63	29	17	18	0	39	2	2	2	6	3	.67	5	.235	.297	.290
1993	Capital Cty	A	127	471	99	15	2	5	133	51	58	36	5	107	5	6	4	17	7	.71	5	.210	.271	.282
1994	Columbia	A	99	358	91	25	8	9	159	38	49	23	5	92	3	1	1	14	10	.58	6	.254	.304	.444
1995	St. Lucie	A	123	435	107	20	6	4	151	52	53	39	6	95	5	4	5	15	7	.68	4	.246	.312	.347
	Binghamton	AA	4	11	1	0	0	0	1	1	1	0	0	8	0	0	1	1	0	1.00	0	.091	.154	.091
	4 Min. YEARS		410	1492	349	67	17	19	507	171	178	117	16	341	15	13	13	53	27	.66	20	.234	.294	.340

Rob Wishnevski

Pitches: Right Bats: Right Pos: P Ht: 6'1" Wt: 215 Born: 1/2/67 Age: 29

Year	Team	Lg	G	GS	CG	GF	IP	BFP	H	R	ER	HR	SH	SF	HB	TBB	IBB	SO	WP	Bk	W	L	Pct.	ShO	Sv	ERA
1987	St. Cathrns	A	16	15	1	0	88	359	58	18	15	2	3	2	6	39	1	71	6	0	7	2	.778	0	0	1.53
1988	Dunedin	A	34	29	0	1	171.1	738	159	92	74	10	5	1	14	61	2	107	19	6	11	11	.500	1	0	3.89
1989	Knoxville	AA	14	11	0	2	66.1	278	50	23	17	4	2	3	4	26	0	36	4	0	6	1	.857	0	0	2.31
	Syracuse	AAA	16	12	2	2	89.1	372	83	44	39	6	2	3	9	25	0	32	8	1	5	5	.500	1	0	3.93
1990	Syracuse	AAA	9	8	0	0	48.2	229	65	40	36	6	0	1	0	23	1	28	2	0	2	5	.286	0	0	6.66
	Knoxville	AA	20	17	1	3	105.2	439	84	54	45	7	6	2	4	39	0	74	10	3	6	3	.667	1	1	3.83
1991	Knoxville	AA	31	10	0	11	101	439	78	46	33	2	3	3	9	53	5	58	11	1	6	8	.429	0	3	2.94
	El Paso	AA	7	0	0	3	16	71	17	8	7	1	2	1	1	6	3	9	1	0	4	0	1.000	0	3	3.94
1992	El Paso	AA	13	0	0	13	17.1	62	7	2	2	0	0	0	1	4	0	16	2	0	1	0	1.000	0	9	1.04
	Denver	AAA	44	1	0	27	77	357	87	49	43	4	6	3	3	39	7	64	7	0	9	6	.600	0	3	5.03
1993	New Orleans	AAA	52	0	0	33	70.1	296	68	34	32	9	3	2	9	17	2	72	3	1	5	3	.625	0	10	4.09
1994	Louisville	AAA	41	20	2	10	146.1	633	131	69	64	12	9	3	16	59	2	105	13	0	9	8	.529	1	3	3.94
1995	Okla. City	AAA	41	8	0	12	109	466	101	51	42	9	5	5	7	53	2	78	13	0	6	3	.667	0	3	3.47
	9 Min. YEARS		338	131	6	117	1106.1	4739	988	530	449	72	46	29	83	444	25	750	99	12	77	55	.583	3	31	3.65

Bill Wissler

Pitches: Right Bats: Right Pos: P Ht: 6'3" Wt: 205 Born: 8/27/70 Age: 25

Year	Team	Lg	G	GS	CG	GF	IP	BFP	H	R	ER	HR	SH	SF	HB	TBB	IBB	SO	WP	Bk	W	L	Pct.	ShO	Sv	ERA
1992	Kenosha	A	21	7	1	3	74	294	52	22	11	0	2	1	3	16	0	59	5	6	4	3	.571	1	0	1.34

Year	Team	Lg	G	GS	CG	GF	IP	BFP	H	R	ER	HR	SH	SF	HB	TBB	IBB	SO	WP	Bk	W	L	Pct.	ShO	Sv	ERA
	Orlando	AA	13	13	5	0	82.1	333	74	36	34	9	3	3	2	18	0	56	2	5	3	8	.273	1	0	3.72
1993	Nashville	AA	29	25	2	1	175.1	731	169	88	77	23	5	6	6	48	2	115	7	0	10	10	.500	0	0	3.95
1994	Salt Lake	AAA	53	3	0	24	92.1	434	125	68	65	14	5	3	4	37	7	64	2	1	5	6	.455	0	5	6.34
1995	Salt Lake	AAA	37	2	0	9	60.1	262	69	32	31	7	3	0	1	24	1	26	5	0	3	3	.500	0	1	4.62
	4 Min. YEARS		153	50	8	37	484.1	2054	489	246	218	53	18	13	16	143	10	320	21	12	25	30	.455	2	6	4.05

Jay Witasick

Pitches: Right **Bats:** Right **Pos:** P **Ht:** 6'4" **Wt:** 205 **Born:** 8/28/72 **Age:** 23

			HOW MUCH HE PITCHED						WHAT HE GAVE UP												THE RESULTS					
Year	Team	Lg	G	GS	CG	GF	IP	BFP	H	R	ER	HR	SH	SF	HB	TBB	IBB	SO	WP	Bk	W	L	Pct.	ShO	Sv	ERA
1993	Johnson Cty	R	12	12	0	0	67.2	288	65	42	31	8	4	1	0	19	0	74	5	1	4	3	.571	0	0	4.12
	Savannah	A	1	1	0	0	6	27	7	3	3	0	0	0	0	2	0	8	0	0	1	0	1.000	0	0	4.50
1994	Madison	A	18	18	2	0	112.1	443	74	36	29	5	5	3	2	42	0	141	5	0	10	4	.714	0	0	2.32
1995	St. Pete	A	18	18	1	0	105	425	80	39	32	4	1	4	0	36	1	109	5	1	7	7	.500	1	0	2.74
	Arkansas	AA	7	7	0	0	34	161	46	29	26	4	0	0	0	16	1	26	2	0	2	4	.333	0	0	6.88
	3 Min. YEARS		56	56	3	0	325	1344	272	149	121	21	10	8	2	115	2	358	17	2	24	18	.571	1	0	3.35

Shannon Withem

Pitches: Right **Bats:** Right **Pos:** P **Ht:** 6'3" **Wt:** 185 **Born:** 9/21/72 **Age:** 23

			HOW MUCH HE PITCHED						WHAT HE GAVE UP												THE RESULTS					
Year	Team	Lg	G	GS	CG	GF	IP	BFP	H	R	ER	HR	SH	SF	HB	TBB	IBB	SO	WP	Bk	W	L	Pct.	ShO	Sv	ERA
1990	Bristol	R	14	13	0	1	62	288	70	43	37	4	0	0	5	35	1	48	12	2	3	9	.250	0	0	5.37
1991	Fayetteville	A	11	11	0	0	47.2	241	71	53	45	2	2	0	0	30	0	19	8	0	2	6	.250	0	0	8.50
	Niagara Fal	A	8	3	0	2	27	115	26	12	10	0	0	2	2	11	0	17	2	0	1	2	.333	0	0	3.33
1992	Fayetteville	A	22	2	0	8	38	173	40	23	20	3	2	2	4	20	0	34	9	2	1	3	.250	0	2	4.74
1993	Lakeland	A	16	16	2	0	113	462	108	47	43	5	1	5	5	24	0	62	3	0	10	2	.833	1	0	3.42
1994	Trenton	AA	25	25	5	0	178	735	190	80	68	10	4	4	4	37	0	135	5	2	7	12	.368	1	0	3.44
1995	Jacksonville	AA	19	18	0	1	108	481	142	77	69	17	5	1	5	24	1	80	4	0	5	8	.385	0	0	5.75
	6 Min. YEARS		115	88	7	12	573.2	2495	647	335	292	41	14	14	25	181	2	395	43	6	29	42	.408	2	2	4.58

Mat Witkowski

Bats: Right **Throws:** Right **Pos:** 1B **Ht:** 6'0" **Wt:** 175 **Born:** 2/5/70 **Age:** 26

			BATTING														BASERUNNING				PERCENTAGES		
Year	Team	Lg	G	AB	H	2B	3B	HR	TB	R	RBI	TBB	IBB	SO	HBP	SH	SF	SB	CS	SB%	GDP	Avg	OBP	SLG
1988	Padres	R	51	201	65	5	3	0	76	37	25	16	1	32	3	2	1	17	6	.74	1	.323	.380	.378
	Spokane	A	1	1	0	0	0	0	0	1	0	0	0	1	0	0	0	0	0	.00	0	.000	.000	.000
1989	Charlstn-Sc	A	119	448	127	18	5	0	155	67	44	65	4	81	4	8	1	26	15	.63	4	.283	.378	.346
1990	Waterloo	A	128	470	119	24	2	1	150	75	55	59	3	104	6	5	7	19	14	.58	13	.253	.339	.319
1991	High Desert	A	129	485	129	17	8	6	180	80	56	60	2	81	6	6	3	24	11	.69	13	.266	.352	.371
1992	Wichita	AA	125	431	117	13	4	6	156	61	48	33	2	80	4	2	4	11	11	.50	8	.271	.326	.362
	Las Vegas	AAA	5	16	3	0	1	0	5	1	0	3	0	2	0	0	0	0	0	.00	1	.188	.316	.313
1993	Las Vegas	AAA	91	286	81	6	3	1	96	49	35	33	1	42	0	4	0	10	2	.83	8	.283	.357	.336
1994	Las Vegas	AAA	7	12	2	0	0	0	2	1	1	0	0	3	0	1	0	1	0	1.00	0	.167	.167	.167
	Wichita	AA	88	284	73	9	1	3	93	31	27	23	1	49	1	4	3	10	8	.56	8	.257	.312	.327
1995	Shreveport	AA	17	38	11	1	0	0	12	7	5	8	1	7	1	2	1	0	0	.00	0	.289	.417	.316
	8 Min. YEARS		761	2672	727	93	27	17	925	410	296	300	15	482	25	34	20	118	67	.64	56	.272	.349	.346

Trey Witte

Pitches: Right **Bats:** Right **Pos:** P **Ht:** 6'1" **Wt:** 192 **Born:** 1/15/70 **Age:** 26

			HOW MUCH HE PITCHED						WHAT HE GAVE UP												THE RESULTS					
Year	Team	Lg	G	GS	CG	GF	IP	BFP	H	R	ER	HR	SH	SF	HB	TBB	IBB	SO	WP	Bk	W	L	Pct.	ShO	Sv	ERA
1991	Bellingham	A	27	0	0	22	45	189	27	12	11	0	1	1	0	31	1	44	5	0	2	2	.500	0	8	2.20
1992	San Bernrdo	A	21	0	0	10	36.2	183	58	36	27	3	3	2	2	11	0	27	3	1	1	1	.500	0	1	6.63
1993	Appleton	A	28	14	1	3	101	425	111	57	48	8	4	8	9	22	0	62	3	0	3	9	.250	0	0	4.28
1994	Riverside	A	25	0	0	4	54.1	235	57	29	26	2	1	2	5	15	2	45	3	0	4	3	.571	0	0	4.31
1995	Port City	AA	48	0	0	34	62.1	250	48	17	12	0	6	3	5	14	0	39	0	1	3	2	.600	0	11	1.73
	5 Min. YEARS		149	14	1	73	299.1	1282	301	151	124	13	15	16	21	93	3	217	14	2	13	17	.433	0	20	3.73

Jerry Wolak

Bats: Right **Throws:** Right **Pos:** OF **Ht:** 5'10" **Wt:** 170 **Born:** 7/27/70 **Age:** 25

			BATTING														BASERUNNING				PERCENTAGES		
Year	Team	Lg	G	AB	H	2B	3B	HR	TB	R	RBI	TBB	IBB	SO	HBP	SH	SF	SB	CS	SB%	GDP	Avg	OBP	SLG
1988	White Sox	R	41	144	46	6	0	0	52	18	10	7	0	17	0	1	1	10	6	.63	2	.319	.349	.361
1989	Utica	A	57	223	61	13	5	0	84	28	24	12	0	35	4	1	0	12	4	.75	3	.274	.322	.377
1990	South Bend	A	121	352	98	17	0	1	118	48	28	37	1	68	6	4	2	11	15	.42	8	.278	.355	.335
1991	Sarasota	A	110	326	95	11	1	3	123	36	22	14	0	62	3	13	0	22	8	.73	3	.291	.327	.377
1992	Sarasota	A	90	332	96	23	5	5	144	47	39	14	4	54	5	9	2	17	14	.55	3	.289	.326	.434
	Birmingham	AA	46	169	50	13	1	0	65	18	13	8	0	25	2	1	0	5	2	.71	4	.296	.335	.385
1993	Birmingham	AA	137	525	160	35	4	9	230	78	64	26	2	95	8	2	4	16	12	.57	11	.305	.345	.438
1994	Nashville	AAA	111	394	101	21	2	8	150	42	35	15	0	75	4	7	2	6	4	.60	7	.256	.289	.381
1995	Nashville	AAA	108	385	88	21	1	14	153	43	63	20	1	83	7	5	2	5	3	.63	12	.229	.278	.397
	8 Min. YEARS		821	2850	795	166	19	40	1119	358	298	153	8	514	39	43	13	104	68	.60	53	.279	.323	.393

Joel Wolfe

Bats: Right **Throws:** Right **Pos:** 1B **Ht:** 6'3" **Wt:** 205 **Born:** 6/18/70 **Age:** 26

Year	Team	Lg	G	AB	H	2B	3B	HR	TB	R	RBI	TBB	IBB	SO	HBP	SH	SF	SB	CS	SB%	GDP	Avg	OBP	SLG
1991	Sou. Oregon	A	59	251	76	17	3	2	105	49	34	25	0	28	3	0	0	19	5	.79	8	.303	.373	.418
1992	Reno	A	122	463	118	18	5	1	149	80	44	59	1	72	0	4	2	19	13	.59	15	.255	.338	.322
1993	Modesto	A	87	300	105	29	1	6	154	54	56	51	0	42	6	0	6	18	14	.56	5	.350	.446	.513
	Huntsville	AA	36	134	40	6	0	3	55	20	18	13	1	24	0	1	0	6	3	.67	5	.299	.361	.410
1994	Huntsville	AA	121	436	120	26	3	5	167	65	57	61	2	79	4	6	7	26	10	.72	13	.275	.364	.383
1995	Edmonton	AAA	11	39	8	3	0	0	11	4	4	2	0	7	0	1	1	0	2	.00	1	.205	.238	.282
	Huntsville	AA	108	399	102	15	2	12	157	58	41	54	4	75	5	6	2	23	12	.66	5	.256	.350	.393
	5 Min. YEARS		544	2022	569	114	14	29	798	330	254	265	8	327	18	18	18	111	59	.65	52	.281	.367	.395

Mike Wolff

Bats: Right **Throws:** Right **Pos:** OF **Ht:** 6'1" **Wt:** 195 **Born:** 12/19/70 **Age:** 25

Year	Team	Lg	G	AB	H	2B	3B	HR	TB	R	RBI	TBB	IBB	SO	HBP	SH	SF	SB	CS	SB%	GDP	Avg	OBP	SLG
1992	Boise	A	68	244	66	12	1	11	113	49	39	32	1	60	6	1	2	5	5	.50	0	.270	.366	.463
1993	Cedar Rapds	A	120	407	100	18	5	17	179	63	72	74	1	104	2	5	5	8	8	.50	4	.246	.361	.440
1994	Midland	AA	113	397	115	30	1	13	186	64	58	54	3	91	6	5	6	10	9	.53	4	.290	.378	.469
1995	Midland	AA	127	445	135	28	3	14	211	76	70	65	3	83	3	4	7	10	9	.53	10	.303	.390	.474
	4 Min. YEARS		428	1493	416	88	10	55	689	252	239	225	8	338	17	15	20	33	31	.52	18	.279	.375	.461

Doug Wollenburg

Bats: Right **Throws:** Right **Pos:** 3B **Ht:** 6'2" **Wt:** 185 **Born:** 10/11/70 **Age:** 25

Year	Team	Lg	G	AB	H	2B	3B	HR	TB	R	RBI	TBB	IBB	SO	HBP	SH	SF	SB	CS	SB%	GDP	Avg	OBP	SLG
1992	Idaho Falls	R	69	257	78	10	1	4	102	43	43	24	1	29	4	1	2	11	5	.69	5	.304	.369	.397
1993	Durham	A	113	361	108	21	4	5	152	49	42	27	2	61	6	13	3	6	7	.46	4	.299	.355	.421
1994	Greenville	AA	91	246	57	15	2	2	82	31	19	20	0	44	7	7	4	3	4	.43	9	.232	.303	.333
1995	Greenville	AA	66	162	31	5	0	1	39	22	12	13	2	31	3	1	1	4	3	.57	6	.191	.263	.241
	4 Min. YEARS		339	1026	274	51	7	12	375	145	116	84	5	165	20	22	10	24	19	.56	24	.267	.332	.365

Tony Womack

Bats: Left **Throws:** Right **Pos:** SS **Ht:** 5'9" **Wt:** 153 **Born:** 9/25/69 **Age:** 26

Year	Team	Lg	G	AB	H	2B	3B	HR	TB	R	RBI	TBB	IBB	SO	HBP	SH	SF	SB	CS	SB%	GDP	Avg	OBP	SLG
1991	Welland	A	45	166	46	3	0	1	52	30	8	17	0	39	0	2	0	26	5	.84	1	.277	.344	.313
1992	Augusta	A	102	380	93	8	3	0	107	62	18	41	0	59	5	4	2	50	25	.67	2	.245	.325	.282
1993	Salem	A	72	304	91	11	3	2	114	41	18	13	0	34	2	2	1	28	14	.67	2	.299	.331	.375
	Carolina	AA	60	247	75	7	2	0	86	41	23	17	2	34	1	4	4	21	6	.78	3	.304	.346	.348
1994	Buffalo	AAA	106	421	93	9	2	0	106	40	18	19	2	76	0	12	2	41	10	.80	2	.221	.253	.252
1995	Calgary	AAA	30	107	30	3	1	0	35	12	6	12	1	11	0	0	0	7	5	.58	1	.280	.353	.327
	Carolina	AA	82	332	85	9	4	1	105	52	19	19	2	36	2	11	0	27	10	.73	2	.256	.300	.316
1993	Pittsburgh	NL	15	24	2	0	0	0	2	5	0	3	0	3	0	1	0	2	0	1.00	0	.083	.185	.083
1994	Pittsburgh	NL	5	12	4	0	0	0	4	4	1	2	0	3	0	0	0	0	0	.00	0	.333	.429	.333
	5 Min. YEARS		497	1957	513	50	15	4	605	278	110	138	7	289	10	35	9	200	75	.73	13	.262	.313	.309
	2 Maj. YEARS		20	36	6	0	0	0	6	9	1	5	0	6	0	1	0	2	0	1.00	0	.167	.268	.167

Jason Wood

Bats: Right **Throws:** Right **Pos:** 3B **Ht:** 6'1" **Wt:** 170 **Born:** 12/16/69 **Age:** 26

Year	Team	Lg	G	AB	H	2B	3B	HR	TB	R	RBI	TBB	IBB	SO	HBP	SH	SF	SB	CS	SB%	GDP	Avg	OBP	SLG
1991	Sou. Oregon	A	44	142	44	3	4	3	64	30	23	28	0	30	2	2	3	5	2	.71	0	.310	.423	.451
1992	Modesto	A	128	454	105	28	3	6	157	66	49	40	1	106	4	3	5	5	4	.56	15	.231	.296	.346
1993	Huntsville	AA	103	370	85	21	2	3	119	44	36	33	0	97	2	9	3	2	4	.33	7	.230	.294	.322
1994	Huntsville	AA	134	468	128	29	2	6	179	54	84	46	1	83	6	5	15	3	6	.33	9	.274	.336	.382
1995	Edmonton	AAA	127	421	99	20	5	2	135	49	50	29	3	72	3	6	12	1	4	.20	12	.235	.282	.321
	5 Min. YEARS		536	1855	461	101	16	20	654	243	242	176	5	388	17	25	38	16	20	.44	43	.249	.314	.353

Ted Wood

Bats: Left **Throws:** Left **Pos:** OF **Ht:** 6'2" **Wt:** 178 **Born:** 1/4/67 **Age:** 29

Year	Team	Lg	G	AB	H	2B	3B	HR	TB	R	RBI	TBB	IBB	SO	HBP	SH	SF	SB	CS	SB%	GDP	Avg	OBP	SLG
1989	Shreveport	AA	114	349	90	13	1	0	105	44	43	51	2	72	6	10	3	9	7	.56	8	.258	.359	.301
1990	Shreveport	AA	131	456	121	22	11	17	216	81	72	74	5	76	7	4	2	17	8	.68	8	.265	.375	.474
1991	Phoenix	AAA	137	512	159	38	6	11	242	90	109	86	4	96	4	0	10	12	7	.63	13	.311	.407	.473
1992	Phoenix	AAA	110	418	127	24	7	7	186	70	63	48	4	74	4	2	5	9	9	.50	5	.304	.377	.445
1993	Ottawa	AAA	83	231	59	11	4	1	81	39	21	38	3	54	2	2	1	12	2	.86	4	.255	.364	.351
1994	Ottawa	AAA	125	412	115	25	8	13	195	63	59	48	7	79	2	2	5	4	5	.44	13	.279	.353	.473
1995	Ottawa	AAA	98	326	87	16	1	8	129	35	49	37	6	63	2	1	3	9	2	.82	8	.267	.342	.396
1991	San Francisco	NL	10	25	3	0	0	0	3	0	1	2	0	11	0	1	0	0	0	.00	0	.120	.185	.120
1992	San Francisco	NL	24	58	12	2	0	1	17	5	3	6	0	15	1	2	0	0	0	.00	4	.207	.292	.293
1993	Montreal	NL	13	26	5	1	0	0	6	4	3	3	1	3	0	3	0	0	0	.00	0	.192	.276	.231

		G	AB	H	2B	3B	HR	TB	R	RBI	TBB	IBB	SO	HBP	SH	SF	SB	CS	SB%	GDP	Avg	OBP	SLG
7 Min. YEARS		798	2704	758	149	38	57	1154	422	416	382	31	514	27	21	29	72	40	.64	59	.280	.371	.427
3 Maj. YEARS		47	109	20	3	0	1	26	9	7	11	1	29	1	6	0	0	0	.00	4	.183	.264	.239

Chris Woodfin

Pitches: Right Bats: Right Pos: P   Ht: 6'1" Wt: 190 Born: 2/23/68 Age: 28

		HOW MUCH HE PITCHED						WHAT HE GAVE UP												THE RESULTS					
Year Team	Lg	G	GS	CG	GF	IP	BFP	H	R	ER	HR	SH	SF	HB	TBB	IBB	SO	WP	Bk	W	L	Pct.	ShO	Sv	ERA
1991 White Sox	R	13	1	0	10	26.1	104	19	7	7	0	1	0	0	7	0	24	0	0	1	0	1.000	0	4	2.39
South Bend	A	3	0	0	2	4.2	24	5	4	3	0	1	1	0	5	3	5	3	0	0	2	.000	0	1	5.79
1992 South Bend	A	36	0	0	19	59.1	258	53	27	18	1	6	0	4	27	1	82	6	0	3	6	.333	0	5	2.73
1993 White Sox	R	4	0	0	2	5	17	1	1	0	0	0	0	0	0	0	7	0	0	1	0	1.000	0	0	0.00
South Bend	A	11	0	0	7	16.2	63	10	3	3	1	0	0	1	3	0	34	0	0	0	0	.000	0	4	1.62
1994 Pr. William	A	29	0	0	26	28.2	130	21	16	6	1	1	2	1	18	1	43	4	0	2	4	.333	0	12	1.88
Birmingham	AA	13	0	0	13	15	63	9	5	5	0	0	0	0	9	1	19	1	0	1	1	.500	0	8	3.00
1995 Birmingham	AA	48	0	0	41	64	269	59	34	32	6	2	2	1	24	1	72	10	0	3	3	.500	0	20	4.50
5 Min. YEARS		157	1	0	120	219.2	928	177	97	74	9	11	5	7	93	7	286	24	0	11	16	.407	0	54	3.03

Ken Woods

Bats: Right Throws: Right Pos: OF   Ht: 5'9" Wt: 173 Born: 8/2/70 Age: 25

		BATTING															BASERUNNING				PERCENTAGES		
Year Team	Lg	G	AB	H	2B	3B	HR	TB	R	RBI	TBB	IBB	SO	HBP	SH	SF	SB	CS	SB%	GDP	Avg	OBP	SLG
1992 Everett	A	64	257	65	9	1	0	76	50	31	35	1	46	7	1	0	20	17	.54	2	.253	.358	.296
1993 Clinton	A	108	320	90	10	1	4	114	56	44	41	1	55	4	7	2	30	5	.86	13	.281	.368	.356
1994 San Jose	A	90	336	100	18	3	6	142	58	49	45	0	43	4	3	3	15	7	.68	9	.298	.384	.423
1995 Shreveport	AA	89	209	53	11	0	3	73	30	23	23	2	29	1	2	1	4	5	.44	4	.254	.329	.349
4 Min. YEARS		351	1122	308	48	5	13	405	194	147	144	4	173	16	13	6	69	34	.67	28	.275	.363	.361

Tyrone Woods

Bats: Right Throws: Right Pos: 1B-DH   Ht: 6'1" Wt: 190 Born: 8/19/69 Age: 26

		BATTING															BASERUNNING				PERCENTAGES		
Year Team	Lg	G	AB	H	2B	3B	HR	TB	R	RBI	TBB	IBB	SO	HBP	SH	SF	SB	CS	SB%	GDP	Avg	OBP	SLG
1988 Expos	R	43	149	18	2	0	2	26	12	12	7	0	47	0	0	2	2	4	.33	3	.121	.158	.174
1989 Jamestown	A	63	209	55	6	4	9	96	23	29	20	1	59	2	0	3	8	9	.47	5	.263	.329	.459
1990 Rockford	A	123	455	110	27	5	8	171	50	46	45	1	121	1	0	3	5	7	.42	13	.242	.310	.376
1991 W. Palm Bch	A	96	295	65	15	3	5	101	34	31	28	0	85	3	0	3	4	4	.50	5	.220	.292	.342
1992 Rockford	A	101	374	109	22	3	12	173	54	47	34	4	83	1	0	6	15	6	.71	6	.291	.347	.463
W. Palm Bch	A	15	56	16	1	2	1	24	7	7	6	0	15	1	0	1	2	1	.67	1	.286	.359	.429
Harrisburg	AA	4	4	0	0	0	0	0	0	0	0	0	3	0	0	0	0	0	.00	0	.000	.000	.000
1993 Harrisburg	AA	106	318	80	15	1	16	145	51	59	35	0	77	2	2	1	4	1	.80	8	.252	.329	.456
1994 Ottawa	AAA	88	294	66	12	0	6	96	34	30	26	4	76	2	0	3	2	1	.67	8	.224	.289	.327
Harrisburg	AA	38	133	42	16	2	5	77	23	28	13	2	29	1	0	2	2	1	.67	3	.316	.376	.579
1995 Rochester	AAA	70	238	62	17	1	8	105	30	31	24	1	68	1	0	2	2	3	.40	6	.261	.328	.441
8 Min. YEARS		747	2525	623	133	21	72	1014	318	320	238	13	663	14	2	26	46	37	.55	58	.247	.312	.402

Tracy Woodson

Bats: Right Throws: Right Pos: 3B   Ht: 6'3" Wt: 216 Born: 10/5/62 Age: 33

		BATTING															BASERUNNING				PERCENTAGES		
Year Team	Lg	G	AB	H	2B	3B	HR	TB	R	RBI	TBB	IBB	SO	HBP	SH	SF	SB	CS	SB%	GDP	Avg	OBP	SLG
1984 Vero Beach	A	76	256	56	9	0	4	77	29	36	27	2	41	6	0	4	7	4	.64	5	.219	.304	.301
1985 Vero Beach	A	138	504	126	30	4	9	191	55	62	50	6	78	9	5	8	10	5	.67	12	.250	.324	.379
1986 San Antonio	AA	131	495	133	27	3	18	220	65	90	33	7	59	5	1	1	4	1	.80	11	.269	.320	.444
1987 Albuquerque	AAA	67	259	75	13	2	5	107	37	44	17	0	22	2	0	4	1	1	.50	12	.290	.333	.413
1988 Albuquerque	AAA	85	313	100	21	1	17	174	46	73	39	4	48	2	1	4	1	3	.25	8	.319	.394	.556
1989 Albuquerque	AAA	89	325	95	21	0	14	158	49	59	32	2	40	4	0	3	2	1	.67	7	.292	.360	.486
1990 Vancouver	AAA	131	480	128	22	5	17	211	70	81	50	2	70	6	0	5	6	4	.60	18	.267	.340	.440
1991 Richmond	AAA	120	441	122	20	3	6	166	43	56	28	0	43	2	3	8	1	4	.20	18	.277	.317	.376
1992 Louisville	AAA	109	412	122	23	2	12	185	62	59	24	2	46	2	5	4	4	3	.57	12	.296	.335	.449
1994 Rochester	AAA	75	279	66	15	1	5	98	26	36	16	0	32	0	0	1	2	0	1.00	11	.237	.277	.351
Louisville	AAA	43	158	55	16	1	7	94	29	26	11	2	12	0	0	0	0	1	.00	4	.348	.391	.595
1995 Louisville	AAA	118	431	113	35	4	18	202	62	76	27	5	43	5	0	6	12	4	.75	18	.262	.309	.469
1987 Los Angeles	NL	53	136	31	8	1	1	44	14	11	9	2	21	2	0	1	1	1	.50	2	.228	.284	.324
1988 Los Angeles	NL	65	173	43	4	1	3	58	15	15	7	1	32	1	0	2	1	2	.33	4	.249	.279	.335
1989 Los Angeles	NL	4	6	0	0	0	0	0	0	0	0	0	1	0	0	0	0	0	.00	2	.000	.000	.000
1992 St. Louis	NL	31	114	35	8	0	1	46	9	22	3	0	10	1	1	0	0	0	.00	1	.307	.331	.404
1993 St. Louis	NL	62	77	16	2	0	0	18	4	2	1	0	14	0	0	1	0	0	.00	1	.208	.215	.234
11 Min. YEARS		1182	4353	1191	252	22	132	1883	573	698	354	32	534	43	15	48	50	31	.62	136	.274	.331	.433
5 Maj. YEARS		215	506	125	22	2	5	166	42	50	20	3	78	4	1	4	2	3	.40	10	.247	.279	.328

Shawn Wooten

Bats: Right Throws: Right Pos: 3B   Ht: 5'11" Wt: 205 Born: 7/24/72 Age: 23

		BATTING															BASERUNNING				PERCENTAGES		
Year Team	Lg	G	AB	H	2B	3B	HR	TB	R	RBI	TBB	IBB	SO	HBP	SH	SF	SB	CS	SB%	GDP	Avg	OBP	SLG
1993 Bristol	R	52	177	62	12	2	8	102	26	39	24	2	20	3	0	2	1	2	.33	7	.350	.432	.576
Fayetteville	A	5	16	4	0	0	1	7	2	5	3	0	3	0	0	0	0	0	.00	1	.250	.368	.438
1994 Fayetteville	A	121	439	118	25	1	3	154	45	61	27	0	84	11	3	4	1	3	.25	11	.269	.324	.351

		G	AB	H	2B	3B	HR	TB	R	RBI	TBB	IBB	SO	HBP	SH	SF	SB	CS	SB%	GDP	Avg	OBP	SLG
1995 Jacksonvlle	AA	20	70	9	1	0	2	16	4	7	1	0	17	1	0	1	0	0	.00	3	.129	.151	.229
Lakeland	A	38	135	31	10	1	2	49	11	11	10	0	28	2	0	1	0	1	.00	2	.230	.291	.363
3 Min. YEARS		236	837	224	48	4	16	328	88	123	65	2	152	17	3	8	2	6	.25	24	.268	.330	.392

Robert Worley

Pitches: Right **Bats:** Right **Pos:** P   **Ht:** 6'3" **Wt:** 185 **Born:** 2/15/71 **Age:** 25

		HOW MUCH HE PITCHED						WHAT HE GAVE UP												THE RESULTS					
Year Team	Lg	G	GS	CG	GF	IP	BFP	H	R	ER	HR	SH	SF	HB	TBB	IBB	SO	WP	Bk	W	L	Pct.	ShO	Sv	ERA
1992 Bellingham	A	18	0	0	6	28.2	136	31	23	19	2	3	1	3	17	1	20	3	1	1	5	.167	0	1	5.97
1993 Appleton	A	45	0	0	41	53	229	48	23	13	1	2	1	2	23	4	37	4	0	3	3	.500	0	22	2.21
1994 Riverside	A	40	0	0	35	48.1	218	47	29	23	3	3	0	1	32	2	37	3	1	2	2	.500	0	8	4.28
1995 Port City	AA	22	5	0	6	57	263	60	42	29	5	3	2	4	30	1	26	8	0	1	7	.125	0	0	4.58
Riverside	A	11	11	0	0	61	275	64	44	36	4	2	2	3	30	0	44	8	2	6	4	.600	0	0	5.31
4 Min. YEARS		136	16	0	88	248	1121	250	161	120	15	13	6	13	132	8	164	26	4	13	21	.382	0	31	4.35

Steve Worrell

Pitches: Left **Bats:** Left **Pos:** P   **Ht:** 6'2" **Wt:** 190 **Born:** 11/25/69 **Age:** 26

		HOW MUCH HE PITCHED						WHAT HE GAVE UP												THE RESULTS					
Year Team	Lg	G	GS	CG	GF	IP	BFP	H	R	ER	HR	SH	SF	HB	TBB	IBB	SO	WP	Bk	W	L	Pct.	ShO	Sv	ERA
1992 White Sox	R	2	0	0	2	3	10	1	0	0	0	0	0	0	0	0	5	0	0	0	0	.000	0	2	0.00
Utica	A	4	0	0	2	10	45	11	5	4	0	0	1	1	2	0	10	3	0	1	0	1.000	0	1	3.60
South Bend	A	14	0	0	5	22.1	91	17	2	0	0	1	0	0	7	0	21	0	0	1	1	.500	0	2	0.00
1993 South Bend	A	36	0	0	24	59	231	37	12	11	0	7	0	2	23	3	57	2	0	4	2	.667	0	10	1.68
1994 Pr. William	A	26	0	0	20	48	199	37	23	19	6	1	1	3	19	1	47	2	1	4	2	.667	0	3	3.56
1995 Birmingham	AA	7	0	0	1	10.1	35	2	0	0	0	0	0	0	0	0	6	0	0	1	0	1.000	0	0	0.00
Birmingham	AA	4	0	0	2	4.1	21	5	5	4	2	0	0	0	2	0	2	2	0	0	1	.000	0	0	8.31
Pr. William	A	29	0	0	18	47.1	180	32	10	8	3	3	1	1	7	2	52	1	0	3	1	.750	0	3	1.52
4 Min. YEARS		122	0	0	74	204.1	812	142	57	46	11	12	3	7	65	6	200	10	1	14	7	.667	0	21	2.03

Jamey Wright

Pitches: Right **Bats:** Right **Pos:** P   **Ht:** 6'6" **Wt:** 205 **Born:** 12/24/74 **Age:** 21

		HOW MUCH HE PITCHED						WHAT HE GAVE UP												THE RESULTS					
Year Team	Lg	G	GS	CG	GF	IP	BFP	H	R	ER	HR	SH	SF	HB	TBB	IBB	SO	WP	Bk	W	L	Pct.	ShO	Sv	ERA
1993 Rockies	R	8	8	0	0	36	158	35	19	16	1	0	0	5	9	0	26	7	0	1	3	.250	0	0	4.00
1994 Asheville	A	28	27	2	0	143.1	655	188	107	95	6	5	4	16	59	1	103	9	5	7	14	.333	0	0	5.97
1995 Salem	A	26	26	2	0	171	732	160	74	47	7	3	6	13	72	3	95	16	2	10	8	.556	1	0	2.47
New Haven	AA	1	1	0	0	3	20	6	6	3	0	0	0	1	3	0	0	0	0	0	1	.000	0	0	9.00
3 Min. YEARS		63	62	4	0	353.1	1565	389	206	161	14	8	10	35	143	4	224	32	7	18	26	.409	1	0	4.10

Rick Wrona

Bats: Right **Throws:** Right **Pos:** C   **Ht:** 6'1" **Wt:** 195 **Born:** 12/10/63 **Age:** 32

		BATTING															BASERUNNING				PERCENTAGES		
Year Team	Lg	G	AB	H	2B	3B	HR	TB	R	RBI	TBB	IBB	SO	HBP	SH	SF	SB	CS	SB%	GDP	Avg	OBP	SLG
1985 Peoria	A	6	16	4	1	0	0	5	2	2	2	0	5	0	0	0	0	0	.00	2	.250	.333	.313
Winston-Sal	A	20	49	11	4	0	0	15	4	2	3	0	15	0	0	0	0	1	.00	0	.224	.269	.306
1986 Winston-Sal	A	91	267	68	15	0	4	95	43	32	25	1	37	5	8	0	5	2	.71	9	.255	.330	.356
1987 Pittsfield	AA	70	218	48	10	3	1	67	22	25	7	3	32	1	2	3	5	1	.83	4	.220	.245	.307
1988 Pittsfield	AA	5	6	0	0	0	0	0	0	1	1	1	2	0	1	0	0	0	.00	0	.000	.125	.000
Iowa	AAA	83	193	51	9	0	2	66	28	23	17	1	34	0	0	0	0	0	.00	6	.264	.324	.342
1989 Iowa	AAA	60	189	41	8	3	2	61	15	13	7	2	40	1	0	0	1	1	.50	4	.217	.249	.323
1990 Iowa	AAA	58	146	33	4	0	2	43	16	15	10	1	35	1	3	0	0	2	.00	7	.226	.280	.295
1992 Nashville	AAA	40	118	29	8	2	2	47	16	10	5	0	21	1	1	0	1	1	.50	2	.246	.282	.398
1993 Nashville	AAA	73	184	39	13	0	3	61	24	22	11	0	35	2	4	3	0	1	.00	1	.212	.260	.332
1994 Indianaplos	AAA	6	21	6	0	0	0	6	2	0	0	0	6	2	0	0	0	0	.00	1	.286	.348	.286
New Orleans	AAA	53	158	39	8	3	1	56	20	21	7	0	33	2	2	1	2	1	.67	8	.247	.286	.354
1995 Buffalo	AAA	31	93	21	6	0	0	27	9	10	3	0	19	2	2	0	0	1	.00	0	.226	.263	.290
Louisville	AAA	16	31	7	1	1	1	13	1	2	2	0	6	0	0	1	0	0	.00	0	.226	.265	.419
1988 Chicago	NL	4	6	0	0	0	0	0	0	0	0	0	1	0	0	0	0	0	.00	0	.000	.000	.000
1989 Chicago	NL	38	92	26	2	1	2	36	11	14	2	1	21	1	0	2	0	0	.00	1	.283	.299	.391
1990 Chicago	NL	16	29	5	0	0	0	5	3	0	2	1	11	0	1	0	0	0	1.00	0	.172	.226	.172
1992 Cincinnati	NL	11	23	4	0	0	0	4	0	0	0	0	3	0	0	0	0	0	.00	2	.174	.174	.174
1993 Chicago	AL	4	8	1	0	0	0	1	0	1	0	0	4	0	0	0	0	0	.00	0	.125	.125	.125
1994 Milwaukee	AL	6	10	5	4	0	1	12	2	3	1	0	1	0	0	0	1	0	.00	0	.500	.545	1.200
10 Min. YEARS		612	1689	397	87	12	18	562	202	178	100	9	320	17	23	10	14	11	.56	52	.235	.283	.333
6 Maj. YEARS		79	168	41	6	1	3	58	16	18	5	2	41	1	2	2	1	0	1.00	3	.244	.267	.345

Julian Yan

Bats: Right **Throws:** Right **Pos:** 1B   **Ht:** 6'4" **Wt:** 190 **Born:** 7/24/65 **Age:** 30

		BATTING															BASERUNNING				PERCENTAGES		
Year Team	Lg	G	AB	H	2B	3B	HR	TB	R	RBI	TBB	IBB	SO	HBP	SH	SF	SB	CS	SB%	GDP	Avg	OBP	SLG
1986 St. Cathrns	A	73	282	77	7	2	15	133	40	49	25	1	72	2	0	1	2	1	.67	5	.273	.335	.472
1987 Myrtle Bch	A	132	481	111	21	2	17	187	67	71	41	1	129	8	0	5	3	3	.50	7	.231	.299	.389
1988 Dunedin	A	136	498	124	21	5	16	203	55	75	37	3	115	14	0	5	0	1	.00	12	.249	.316	.408
1989 Dunedin	A	133	460	115	21	5	24	218	68	72	47	5	130	10	1	4	2	4	.33	7	.250	.330	.474
1990 Knoxville	AA	113	389	95	18	3	15	164	55	48	25	1	108	6	0	4	2	1	.67	7	.244	.297	.422

Year	Team	Lg	G	AB	H	2B	3B	HR	TB	R	RBI	TBB	IBB	SO	HBP	SH	SF	SB	CS	SB%	GDP	Avg	OBP	SLG
1991	Knoxville	AA	103	351	98	16	3	16	168	45	61	22	0	108	5	3	2	2	4	.33	9	.279	.329	.479
1992	Knoxville	AA	111	392	106	23	4	16	185	51	49	28	6	93	6	0	5	1	5	.17	12	.270	.325	.472
1993	Syracuse	AAA	91	278	74	9	5	7	114	30	36	14	0	91	1	1	3	3	2	.60	6	.266	.301	.410
1994	Syracuse	AAA	34	81	21	4	2	2	35	13	11	9	0	17	0	0	0	2	1	.67	4	.259	.333	.432
1995	Ottawa	AAA	114	372	104	22	3	22	198	49	79	15	2	90	2	2	1	5	1	.83	10	.280	.310	.532
10 Min. YEARS			1040	3584	925	162	34	150	1605	473	551	263	19	953	54	7	30	22	23	.49	79	.258	.316	.448

Bruce Yard

Bats: Left **Throws:** Right **Pos:** SS   **Ht:** 6'0" **Wt:** 175 **Born:** 10/17/71 **Age:** 24

Year	Team	Lg	G	AB	H	2B	3B	HR	TB	R	RBI	TBB	IBB	SO	HBP	SH	SF	SB	CS	SB%	GDP	Avg	OBP	SLG
1993	Yakima	A	44	129	29	5	1	0	36	18	12	22	1	12	0	2	0	0	1	.00	9	.225	.338	.279
1994	Bakersfield	A	27	81	18	2	0	1	23	7	7	10	1	8	0	2	0	2	1	.67	5	.222	.308	.284
	Vero Beach	A	43	135	35	7	0	1	45	13	10	14	0	12	1	2	2	0	1	.00	2	.259	.329	.333
1995	Bakersfield	A	59	191	44	8	1	1	57	19	17	27	0	22	1	7	2	2	5	.29	10	.230	.326	.298
	San Antonio	AA	16	39	14	3	0	0	17	7	4	5	0	6	0	0	0	0	1	.00	0	.359	.432	.436
3 Min. YEARS			189	575	140	25	2	3	178	64	50	78	2	60	2	13	4	4	9	.31	26	.243	.334	.310

Eric Yelding

Bats: Right **Throws:** Right **Pos:** OF   **Ht:** 5'11" **Wt:** 165 **Born:** 2/22/65 **Age:** 31

Year	Team	Lg	G	AB	H	2B	3B	HR	TB	R	RBI	TBB	IBB	SO	HBP	SH	SF	SB	CS	SB%	GDP	Avg	OBP	SLG
1984	Medcine Hat	R	67	304	94	14	6	4	132	61	29	26	0	46	0	0	2	31	11	.74	3	.309	.361	.434
1985	Kinston	A	135	526	137	14	4	2	165	59	31	33	0	70	4	5	3	62	26	.70	4	.260	.307	.314
1986	Ventura	A	131	560	157	14	7	4	197	83	40	33	3	84	0	6	2	41	18	.69	6	.280	.319	.352
1987	Knoxville	AA	39	150	30	6	1	0	38	23	7	12	0	25	1	1	1	10	5	.67	4	.200	.262	.253
	Myrtle Bch	A	88	357	109	12	2	1	128	53	31	18	0	30	4	1	4	73	13	.85	5	.305	.342	.359
1988	Syracuse	AAA	138	556	139	15	2	1	161	69	38	36	3	102	0	2	0	59	23	.72	4	.250	.296	.290
1991	Tucson	AAA	11	43	17	3	0	0	20	6	3	4	0	4	2	0	0	4	2	.67	0	.395	.469	.465
1992	Tucson	AAA	57	218	63	8	5	0	81	30	23	13	0	50	0	2	1	17	9	.65	6	.289	.328	.372
	Vancouver	AAA	36	120	26	3	0	0	29	17	6	13	0	17	0	4	2	15	2	.88	2	.217	.289	.242
1994	Iowa	AAA	29	73	18	2	0	0	20	10	6	3	0	17	0	0	0	4	2	.67	2	.247	.276	.274
1995	Buffalo	AAA	29	81	28	7	0	1	38	13	9	6	0	12	0	1	0	3	1	.75	0	.346	.386	.469
	Canton-Akrn	AA	10	37	13	1	0	0	14	5	7	1	0	6	1	0	1	3	0	1.00	0	.351	.375	.378
	Abilene	IND	48	188	46	4	0	3	59	35	22	14	0	25	0	2	3	8	5	.62	4	.245	.293	.314
1989	Houston	NL	70	90	21	2	0	0	23	19	9	7	0	19	1	2	2	11	5	.69	2	.233	.290	.256
1990	Houston	NL	142	511	130	9	5	1	152	69	28	39	1	87	0	4	5	64	25	.72	11	.254	.305	.297
1991	Houston	NL	78	276	67	11	1	1	83	19	20	13	3	46	0	3	1	11	9	.55	4	.243	.276	.301
1992	Houston	NL	9	8	2	0	0	0	2	1	0	0	0	3	0	0	0	0	0	.00	0	.250	.250	.250
1993	Chicago	NL	69	108	22	5	1	1	32	14	10	11	2	22	0	4	0	3	2	.60	3	.204	.277	.296
9 Min. YEARS			818	3213	877	103	27	16	1082	464	252	212	6	488	12	23	20	330	117	.74	40	.273	.318	.337
5 Maj. YEARS			368	993	242	27	7	3	292	122	67	70	6	177	1	13	8	89	41	.68	20	.244	.292	.294

Mike York

Pitches: Right **Bats:** Right **Pos:** P   **Ht:** 6'1" **Wt:** 190 **Born:** 9/6/64 **Age:** 31

			HOW MUCH HE PITCHED					WHAT HE GAVE UP										THE RESULTS					
Year	Team	Lg	G	GS	CG	GF	IP	BFP	H	R	ER	HR	SH	SF	HB	TBB	IBB	SO	WP	Bk	W	L	Pct.	ShO	Sv	ERA
1984	White Sox	R	5	1	0	0	14.2	70	18	9	6	1	1	0	0	9	0	19	0	0	1	0	1.000	0	0	3.68
1985	Bristol	R	21	0	0	18	38	168	24	12	10	1	5	2	2	34	2	31	6	1	9	2	.818	0	2	2.37
1986	Lakeland	A	16	0	0	13	40.2	214	49	42	29	2	1	3	3	43	0	29	9	0	1	3	.250	0	1	6.42
	Gastonia	A	22	0	0	20	34	153	26	15	13	0	3	6	2	27	1	27	5	0	2	2	.500	0	9	3.44
1987	Macon	A	28	28	3	0	165.2	700	129	71	56	11	5	3	2	88	1	169	9	3	17	6	.739	2	0	3.04
1988	Salem	A	13	13	2	0	84	360	65	31	25	3	2	2	1	52	0	77	5	4	9	2	.818	1	0	2.68
	Harrisburg	AA	13	13	2	0	82.1	381	92	43	34	5	5	5	1	45	2	61	3	2	0	5	.000	0	0	3.72
1989	Harrisburg	AA	18	18	3	0	121	492	105	37	31	6	1	5	2	40	2	106	8	0	11	5	.688	2	0	2.31
	Buffalo	AAA	8	8	0	0	41	193	48	29	27	3	2	0	1	25	0	28	1	0	1	3	.250	0	0	5.93
1990	Buffalo	AAA	27	26	3	0	158.2	707	165	87	74	6	7	2	5	78	2	130	7	5	8	7	.533	1	0	4.20
1991	Buffalo	AAA	7	7	1	0	43.1	175	36	17	14	0	1	2	0	23	0	22	2	0	5	1	.833	0	0	2.91
	Colo. Sprng	AAA	5	5	0	0	26	130	40	19	17	2	0	1	1	16	0	13	1	0	0	1	.000	0	0	5.88
1992	Las Vegas	AAA	19	17	0	0	88.1	411	96	54	47	5	5	5	8	55	0	54	2	2	5	7	.417	0	0	4.79
	Buffalo	AAA	6	6	0	0	32.1	147	31	14	11	2	1	2	1	20	0	20	1	2	4	1	.800	0	0	3.06
1995	Syracuse	AAA	20	5	0	3	45	227	55	50	35	11	0	2	1	27	0	37	5	0	1	4	.200	0	0	7.00
1990	Pittsburgh	NL	4	1	0	0	12.2	56	13	5	4	0	2	1	1	5	0	4	0	0	1	1	.500	0	0	2.84
1991	Cleveland	AL	14	4	0	3	34.2	163	45	29	26	2	3	4	2	19	3	19	2	0	1	4	.200	0	0	6.75
10 Min. YEARS			228	147	14	54	1015	4534	979	530	429	58	39	40	30	582	10	823	64	19	74	49	.602	6	12	3.80
2 Maj. YEARS			18	5	0	3	47.1	219	58	34	30	2	5	5	3	24	3	23	2	1	2	5	.286	0	0	5.70

Dmitri Young

Bats: Both **Throws:** Right **Pos:** OF   **Ht:** 6'2" **Wt:** 215 **Born:** 10/11/73 **Age:** 22

Year	Team	Lg	G	AB	H	2B	3B	HR	TB	R	RBI	TBB	IBB	SO	HBP	SH	SF	SB	CS	SB%	GDP	Avg	OBP	SLG
1991	Johnson Cty	R	37	129	33	10	0	2	49	22	22	21	1	28	2	0	2	2	1	.67	1	.256	.364	.380
1992	Springfield	A	135	493	153	36	6	14	243	74	72	51	3	94	1	0	5	14	13	.52	9	.310	.378	.493
1993	St. Pete	A	69	270	85	13	3	5	119	31	43	24	3	28	2	0	5	3	4	.43	7	.315	.369	.441
	Arkansas	AA	45	166	41	11	2	3	65	13	21	9	1	29	2	0	0	4	4	.50	5	.247	.294	.392

Year	Team	Lg	G	AB	H	2B	3B	HR	TB	R	RBI	TBB	IBB	SO	HBP	SH	SF	SB	CS	SB%	GDP	Avg	OBP	SLG
1994	Arkansas	AA	125	453	123	33	2	8	184	53	54	36	14	60	5	1	3	0	3	.00	6	.272	.330	.406
1995	Arkansas	AA	97	367	107	18	6	10	167	54	62	30	3	46	3	0	3	2	4	.33	11	.292	.347	.455
	Louisville	AAA	2	7	2	0	0	0	2	3	0	1	0	1	0	0	0	0	0	.00	0	.286	.375	.286
	5 Min. YEARS		510	1885	544	121	19	42	829	250	274	172	25	286	19	1	17	25	29	.46	39	.289	.351	.440

Eddie Zambrano

Bats: Right **Throws:** Right **Pos:** OF **Ht:** 6' 3" **Wt:** 200 **Born:** 2/1/66 **Age:** 30

			BATTING															BASERUNNING				PERCENTAGES		
Year	Team	Lg	G	AB	H	2B	3B	HR	TB	R	RBI	TBB	IBB	SO	HBP	SH	SF	SB	CS	SB%	GDP	Avg	OBP	SLG
1990	Kinston	A	63	204	50	7	2	3	70	26	30	29	1	36	1	1	2	1	3	.25	6	.245	.339	.343
1991	Carolina	AA	83	269	68	17	3	3	100	28	39	22	0	57	4	2	7	4	2	.67	4	.253	.311	.372
	Buffalo	AAA	48	144	49	8	5	3	76	19	35	17	1	25	2	2	4	1	1	.50	1	.340	.407	.528
1992	Buffalo	AAA	126	394	112	22	4	16	190	47	79	51	2	75	4	3	5	3	2	.60	7	.284	.368	.482
1993	Iowa	AAA	133	469	142	29	2	32	271	95	115	54	11	93	6	2	7	10	7	.59	10	.303	.377	.578
1995	Trenton	AA	19	68	10	1	0	1	14	5	7	6	1	25	1	0	1	0	0	.00	1	.147	.224	.206
1993	Chicago	NL	8	17	5	0	0	0	5	1	2	1	0	3	0	0	0	0	0	.00	1	.294	.333	.294
1994	Chicago	NL	67	116	30	7	0	6	55	17	18	16	0	29	1	0	0	2	1	.67	3	.259	.353	.474
	5 Min. YEARS		472	1548	431	84	16	58	721	220	305	179	16	311	18	10	26	19	15	.56	29	.278	.355	.466
	2 Maj. YEARS		75	133	35	7	0	6	60	18	20	17	0	32	1	0	0	2	1	.67	4	.263	.351	.451

Jose Zambrano

Bats: Right **Throws:** Right **Pos:** OF **Ht:** 6'0" **Wt:** 165 **Born:** 3/18/71 **Age:** 25

			BATTING															BASERUNNING				PERCENTAGES		
Year	Team	Lg	G	AB	H	2B	3B	HR	TB	R	RBI	TBB	IBB	SO	HBP	SH	SF	SB	CS	SB%	GDP	Avg	OBP	SLG
1988	R.S./marnrs	R	28	99	31	5	0	4	48	15	14	4	0	16	1	2	1	6	5	.55	1	.313	.343	.485
1989	Red Sox	R	10	33	7	0	0	0	7	4	4	7	0	4	0	0	0	2	0	1.00	0	.212	.350	.212
	Winter Havn	A	49	146	32	4	3	1	45	12	14	15	0	36	2	2	2	4	2	.67	6	.219	.297	.308
1990	Winter Havn	A	88	307	83	14	3	4	115	30	32	23	0	72	3	4	0	6	4	.60	8	.270	.327	.375
1991	Lynchburg	A	3	9	1	0	0	0	1	0	0	0	0	5	0	0	0	0	1	.00	0	.111	.111	.111
1992	Red Sox	R	2	9	2	0	0	0	2	1	0	0	0	4	0	0	0	0	0	.00	0	.222	.222	.222
	Winter Havn	A	77	257	56	7	1	5	80	22	17	22	1	69	4	3	1	2	2	.50	3	.218	.289	.311
1993	Ft. Laud	A	23	57	9	3	0	1	15	6	5	6	0	24	0	3	0	0	1	.00	2	.158	.238	.263
	Lynchburg	A	72	233	57	16	2	9	104	32	27	20	1	70	4	5	0	0	2	.00	2	.245	.315	.446
1994	Lynchburg	A	70	247	69	12	1	7	104	36	31	29	0	61	3	3	2	1	1	.50	4	.279	.359	.421
1995	Sarasota	A	10	30	11	1	0	2	18	4	8	12	0	11	1	0	0	1	1	.50	0	.367	.558	.600
	Trenton	AA	22	62	15	6	0	2	27	7	7	11	0	15	3	0	0	2	1	.67	3	.242	.382	.435
	Red Sox	R	10	28	8	0	0	2	14	5	9	8	0	10	1	0	1	2	0	1.00	0	.286	.447	.500
	8 Min. YEARS		464	1517	381	68	10	37	580	174	168	157	2	397	22	22	7	26	20	.57	29	.251	.329	.382

Mike Zimmerman

Pitches: Right **Bats:** Right **Pos:** P **Ht:** 6'0" **Wt:** 180 **Born:** 2/6/69 **Age:** 27

			HOW MUCH HE PITCHED					WHAT HE GAVE UP										THE RESULTS					
Year	Team	Lg	G	GS	CG	GF	IP	BFP	H	R	ER	HR	SH	SF	HB	TBB	IBB	SO	WP	Bk	W	L	Pct.	ShO	Sv	ERA
1990	Welland	A	9	0	0	7	13.1	58	8	4	1	0	1	0	1	9	0	22	1	1	2	0	1.000	0	2	0.68
	Salem	A	19	0	0	13	25.2	122	28	19	17	1	1	1	5	16	3	24	3	2	1	1	.500	0	8	5.96
1991	Salem	A	49	1	0	44	70	344	51	47	34	1	2	1	14	72	2	63	20	1	4	2	.667	0	9	4.37
1992	Carolina	AA	27	27	1	0	153	673	141	82	65	10	8	7	7	75	2	107	13	4	4	15	.211	0	0	3.82
1993	Carolina	AA	33	0	0	23	45	198	40	26	18	2	1	1	4	21	2	30	2	1	2	3	.400	0	9	3.60
	Buffalo	AAA	33	0	0	8	46.1	199	45	23	21	5	4	2	0	28	3	32	2	0	3	1	.750	0	0	4.08
1994	Carolina	AA	16	0	0	15	16.1	72	13	6	5	1	1	0	1	8	0	9	2	0	2	2	.500	0	9	2.76
	Buffalo	AAA	19	0	0	4	23.1	99	25	10	9	0	2	0	2	13	1	14	3	0	0	1	.000	0	0	3.47
	Edmonton	AAA	9	7	0	1	38.2	179	33	19	15	0	1	3	5	29	0	23	7	1	5	1	.833	0	1	3.49
1995	Charlotte	AAA	31	7	0	9	69.2	319	84	46	41	6	3	3	4	41	0	30	10	0	2	2	.500	0	0	5.30
	6 Min. YEARS		245	42	1	124	501.1	2263	468	282	226	26	24	18	43	312	13	354	63	9	25	28	.472	0	39	4.06

Alan Zinter

Bats: Both **Throws:** Right **Pos:** 1B **Ht:** 6'2" **Wt:** 190 **Born:** 5/19/68 **Age:** 28

			BATTING															BASERUNNING				PERCENTAGES		
Year	Team	Lg	G	AB	H	2B	3B	HR	TB	R	RBI	TBB	IBB	SO	HBP	SH	SF	SB	CS	SB%	GDP	Avg	OBP	SLG
1989	Pittsfield	A	12	41	15	2	1	2	25	11	12	12	0	4	0	0	1	0	1	.00	0	.366	.500	.610
	St. Lucie	A	48	159	38	10	0	3	57	17	32	18	2	31	1	1	5	0	1	.00	5	.239	.311	.358
1990	St. Lucie	A	98	333	97	19	6	7	149	63	63	54	1	70	1	0	6	8	1	.89	10	.291	.386	.447
	Jackson	AA	6	20	4	1	0	0	5	2	1	3	0	11	0	0	0	1	0	1.00	1	.200	.304	.250
1991	Williamsprt	AA	124	422	93	13	6	9	145	44	54	59	1	106	3	2	2	3	3	.50	10	.220	.319	.344
1992	Binghamton	AA	128	431	96	13	5	16	167	63	50	70	5	117	4	0	0	0	0	.00	7	.223	.337	.387
1993	Binghamton	AA	134	432	113	24	4	24	217	68	87	90	7	105	1	0	5	1	0	1.00	4	.262	.386	.502
1994	Toledo	AAA	134	471	112	29	5	21	214	66	58	69	4	185	7	0	0	13	5	.72	3	.238	.344	.454
1995	Toledo	AAA	101	334	74	15	4	13	136	42	48	36	1	102	2	2	5	4	1	.80	5	.222	.297	.407
	7 Min. YEARS		785	2643	642	126	31	95	1115	376	405	411	21	731	19	5	24	30	12	.71	45	.243	.346	.422

330

Mike Zolecki

Pitches: Right **Bats:** Right **Pos:** P **Ht:** 6'2" **Wt:** 185 **Born:** 12/6/71 **Age:** 24

Year	Team	Lg	G	GS	CG	GF	IP	BFP	H	R	ER	HR	SH	SF	HB	TBB	IBB	SO	WP	Bk	W	L	Pct.	ShO	Sv	ERA
1993	Bend	A	14	8	1	3	55	247	47	35	27	7	0	3	2	30	1	78	5	1	4	3	.571	0	1	4.42
1994	Central Val	A	10	8	0	0	35.2	150	27	14	11	0	1	1	1	23	1	30	1	0	0	1	.000	0	0	2.78
1995	Salem	A	9	0	0	1	15	73	22	15	12	2	0	1	0	7	0	12	4	0	0	1	.000	0	0	7.20
	Asheville	A	9	9	0	0	42.2	187	34	20	18	3	1	0	3	29	0	33	6	1	3	2	.600	0	0	3.80
	New Haven	AA	9	7	0	1	55.1	229	56	25	20	2	1	1	1	20	1	32	0	2	3	4	.429	0	0	3.25
	3 Min. YEARS		51	32	1	5	203.2	886	186	109	88	14	3	6	7	109	3	185	16	4	10	11	.476	0	1	3.89

Steve Zongor

Pitches: Left **Bats:** Right **Pos:** P **Ht:** 5'11" **Wt:** 185 **Born:** 6/30/70 **Age:** 26

Year	Team	Lg	G	GS	CG	GF	IP	BFP	H	R	ER	HR	SH	SF	HB	TBB	IBB	SO	WP	Bk	W	L	Pct.	ShO	Sv	ERA
1993	Sou. Oregon	A	27	0	0	17	27.2	132	24	17	12	0	0	1	2	19	3	33	2	1	2	4	.333	0	3	3.90
1994	W. Michigan	A	22	0	0	19	22.2	93	11	6	6	0	1	0	3	13	1	26	3	0	2	1	.667	0	9	2.38
	Modesto	A	23	0	0	9	35.2	151	34	10	9	1	1	1	0	17	1	41	2	0	2	1	.667	0	1	2.27
1995	Modesto	A	37	0	0	9	55.1	238	57	29	25	3	5	3	1	21	1	55	2	0	7	2	.778	0	1	4.07
	Huntsville	AA	9	0	0	3	13	60	13	11	11	4	0	0	1	9	0	11	1	1	2	0	1.000	0	0	7.62
	3 Min. YEARS		118	0	0	57	154.1	674	139	73	63	8	7	5	7	79	6	166	10	2	15	8	.652	0	14	3.67

Jon Zuber

Bats: Left **Throws:** Left **Pos:** 1B **Ht:** 6'1" **Wt:** 175 **Born:** 12/10/69 **Age:** 26

Year	Team	Lg	G	AB	H	2B	3B	HR	TB	R	RBI	TBB	IBB	SO	HBP	SH	SF	SB	CS	SB%	GDP	Avg	OBP	SLG
1992	Batavia	A	22	88	30	6	3	1	45	14	21	9	1	11	1	0	1	1	1	.50	1	.341	.404	.511
	Spartanburg	A	54	206	59	13	1	3	83	24	36	33	1	31	1	0	1	3	1	.75	6	.286	.386	.403
1993	Clearwater	A	129	494	152	37	5	5	214	70	69	49	5	47	0	3	4	6	6	.50	15	.308	.367	.433
1994	Reading	AA	138	498	146	29	5	9	212	81	70	71	4	71	1	1	5	2	4	.33	11	.293	.379	.426
1995	Scranton-Wb	AAA	119	418	120	19	5	3	158	53	50	49	2	68	0	1	2	1	2	.33	12	.287	.360	.378
	4 Min. YEARS		462	1704	507	104	19	21	712	242	246	211	13	228	3	5	13	13	14	.48	45	.298	.373	.418

Dave Zuniga

Bats: Right **Throws:** Right **Pos:** 3B **Ht:** 5'8" **Wt:** 140 **Born:** 4/19/71 **Age:** 25

Year	Team	Lg	G	AB	H	2B	3B	HR	TB	R	RBI	TBB	IBB	SO	HBP	SH	SF	SB	CS	SB%	GDP	Avg	OBP	SLG
1993	Pittsfield	A	61	205	55	3	1	0	60	33	14	17	0	29	6	4	0	7	2	.78	6	.268	.342	.293
1994	Columbia	A	77	182	44	1	3	0	51	35	17	37	0	40	2	8	0	7	9	.44	2	.242	.376	.280
1995	Binghamton	AA	3	1	0	0	0	0	0	1	0	0	0	1	0	0	0	0	0	.00	0	.000	.000	.000
	Columbia	A	36	73	13	2	0	0	15	6	4	7	0	19	3	1	0	0	2	.00	2	.178	.277	.205
	St. Lucie	A	10	29	5	0	0	0	5	1	0	1	0	6	0	0	0	0	1	.00	1	.172	.200	.172
	3 Min. YEARS		187	490	117	6	4	0	131	76	35	62	0	95	11	13	0	14	14	.50	11	.239	.337	.267

Bob Zupcic

Bats: Right **Throws:** Right **Pos:** OF **Ht:** 6'4" **Wt:** 220 **Born:** 8/18/66 **Age:** 29

Year	Team	Lg	G	AB	H	2B	3B	HR	TB	R	RBI	TBB	IBB	SO	HBP	SH	SF	SB	CS	SB%	GDP	Avg	OBP	SLG
1987	Elmira	A	66	238	72	12	2	7	109	39	37	17	0	35	2	3	2	5	4	.56	5	.303	.351	.458
1988	Lynchburg	A	135	482	143	33	5	13	225	69	97	60	4	64	8	7	8	10	6	.63	6	.297	.378	.467
1989	Pawtucket	AAA	27	94	24	7	1	1	36	8	11	3	0	15	0	0	2	1	3	.25	2	.255	.273	.383
	New Britain	AA	94	346	75	12	2	2	97	37	28	19	0	55	1	7	2	15	1	.94	7	.217	.258	.280
1990	New Britain	AA	132	461	98	26	1	2	132	45	41	36	2	63	6	6	7	10	8	.56	7	.213	.275	.286
1991	Pawtucket	AAA	129	429	103	27	1	18	186	70	70	55	2	58	1	12	8	10	6	.63	5	.240	.323	.434
1992	Pawtucket	AAA	9	25	8	1	0	2	15	3	5	8	0	6	0	0	1	0	0	.00	0	.320	.471	.600
1994	Pawtucket	AAA	9	25	7	0	0	0	7	7	3	4	1	4	0	0	0	0	1	.00	0	.280	.379	.280
	Nashville	AAA	5	18	6	1	0	1	10	3	3	3	0	4	0	0	0	1	1	.50	1	.333	.429	.556
1995	Nashville	AAA	13	41	10	2	0	2	18	9	5	13	1	6	0	0	1	1	0	1.00	2	.244	.418	.439
	Duluth-Sup.	IND	9	35	11	3	0	1	17	4	5	5	2	3	0	0	0	1	1	.50	0	.314	.400	.486
	Charlotte	AAA	72	254	75	12	0	11	120	34	47	24	0	35	0	0	4	2	2	.50	3	.295	.351	.472
1991	Boston	AL	18	25	4	0	0	1	7	3	3	1	0	6	0	1	0	0	0	.00	0	.160	.192	.280
1992	Boston	AL	124	392	108	19	1	3	138	46	43	25	1	60	4	7	4	2	2	.50	6	.276	.322	.352
1993	Boston	AL	141	286	69	24	2	2	103	40	26	27	2	54	2	8	3	5	2	.71	7	.241	.308	.360
1994	Boston	AL	4	4	0	0	0	0	0	0	0	0	0	1	0	0	0	0	1	.00	0	.000	.000	.000
	Chicago	AL	32	88	18	4	1	1	27	10	8	4	0	16	0	4	0	1	0	.00	2	.205	.237	.307
	8 Min. YEARS		700	2448	632	136	12	60	972	328	352	247	12	348	18	36	35	56	34	.62	38	.258	.326	.397
	4 Maj. YEARS		319	795	199	47	4	7	275	99	80	57	3	137	6	20	8	7	5	.58	15	.250	.303	.346

Single-A & Rookie Stats

Over the past few years, Single-A and Rookie leagues have undergone a bit of a renaissance with baseball fans—making this section one of the most eagerly anticipated in our book. Look hard, and you can always find some hidden gems within these pages.

Note: Players from independent leagues are not included in this section.

1995 Batting -- Single-A and Rookie Leagues

Player	Lg	A	G	AB	H	2B	3B	HR	TB	R	RBI	TBB	IBB	SO	HBP	SH	SF	SB	CS	SB%	GDP	Avg	OBP	SLG
Abell,Tony,Savannah	A	21	17	49	6	1	0	0	7	1	2	4	0	18	1	1	0	1	1	.50	0	.122	.204	.143
Johnson Cty	R	21	55	190	49	10	2	0	63	27	16	22	1	76	5	2	3	8	8	.50	0	.258	.345	.332
Abernathy,Matt,Idaho Falls	R	22	63	256	75	12	5	9	124	52	45	26	1	64	5	1	3	6	4	.60	2	.293	.366	.484
Abreu,Nelson,Cubs	R	19	57	173	37	3	2	2	50	21	24	19	1	37	0	6	3	12	8	.60	8	.214	.287	.289
Acevedo,Juan,Rockies	R	19	29	90	19	2	1	0	23	10	8	9	0	25	1	2	1	2	4	.33	3	.211	.287	.256
Acosta,Eduardo,Albany	A	24	51	105	16	1	0	0	17	9	9	8	0	30	5	2	1	1	3	.25	2	.152	.242	.162
Adams,Jason,Auburn	A	23	51	181	39	6	0	0	45	28	18	27	1	19	3	1	0	3	1	.75	5	.215	.327	.249
Adamson,Jason,Erie	A	20	2	7	2	0	0	0	2	0	2	0	0	1	0	0	0	0	0	.00	0	.286	.286	.286
Pirates	R	22	42	145	37	9	0	1	49	20	16	17	0	21	3	0	0	1	1	.50	6	.255	.345	.338
Adolfo,Carlos,W. Palm Bch	A	20	28	81	15	1	0	1	19	6	7	5	0	22	0	0	0	1	0	1.00	1	.185	.233	.235
Albany	A	20	57	214	52	13	5	4	87	31	33	17	0	65	2	1	0	5	6	.45	4	.243	.305	.407
Afenir,Tom,Columbus	A	24	5	13	1	0	0	0	1	1	0	0	0	5	0	0	0	0	0	.00	0	.077	.077	.077
Watertown	A	24	6	15	3	2	0	0	5	2	3	0	0	3	1	1	0	0	0	.00	1	.200	.250	.333
Agnoly,Earl,Marlins	R	20	55	213	58	5	1	0	65	39	20	16	0	18	3	0	2	19	5	.79	3	.272	.329	.305
Aguila,Hector,Charlstn-Sc	A	21	13	33	5	1	0	0	6	4	3	5	0	13	0	1	0	1	0	1.00	2	.152	.263	.182
Rangers	R	21	53	182	35	7	5	0	52	20	17	12	0	27	3	1	2	6	2	.75	8	.192	.251	.286
Akers,Chad,Winston-Sal	A	24	103	361	94	14	1	2	116	41	29	27	1	49	1	7	3	25	8	.76	7	.260	.311	.321
Akins,Carlos,Orioles	R	21	42	138	39	9	1	3	59	35	20	22	0	28	3	0	2	9	3	.75	1	.283	.388	.428
Alamo,Efrain,Rockies	R	19	39	147	37	4	4	0	49	14	14	7	0	36	5	0	2	4	2	.67	2	.252	.304	.333
Alayon,Elvis,Red Sox	R	21	25	85	17	3	0	0	20	7	5	3	0	10	2	0	1	4	1	.80	2	.200	.242	.235
Albert,Chernan,Hickory	A	20	88	328	70	16	2	5	105	34	20	19	1	108	14	4	1	22	12	.65	4	.213	.285	.320
Bristol	A	20	38	152	41	5	3	5	67	27	14	9	1	37	3	1	0	12	8	.60	2	.270	.323	.441
Alderman,Kurt,Albany	A	25	55	161	40	8	1	2	56	21	17	11	0	40	1	0	0	2	1	.67	1	.248	.301	.348
Alexander,Chad,Auburn	A	22	70	273	78	13	5	5	116	44	42	25	1	36	7	1	5	7	1	.88	11	.286	.355	.425
Quad City	A	22	2	7	2	0	0	0	2	2	1	0	0	0	0	0	0	0	0	.00	0	.286	.286	.286
Alimena,Charles,San Jose	A	24	54	171	35	3	2	1	45	17	18	11	0	44	1	0	1	1	0	1.00	8	.205	.255	.263
Allen,Tony,Brewers	R	20	46	113	25	0	5	0	35	19	14	14	0	35	2	2	2	7	2	.78	2	.221	.313	.310
Allen,Dustin,Idaho Falls	R	23	29	104	34	7	0	4	53	21	24	21	0	19	0	0	2	1	2	.33	2	.327	.433	.510
Clinton	A	23	36	139	37	12	1	5	66	25	31	12	1	29	1	0	0	1	0	1.00	3	.266	.329	.475
Allen,Marlon,Charlstn-Wv	A	23	117	396	107	26	0	9	160	47	76	42	3	108	13	0	6	2	2	.50	10	.270	.354	.404
Alley,William,Orioles	R	19	12	30	9	4	0	0	13	10	3	11	0	4	1	0	2	0	0	.00	1	.300	.477	.433
Alleyne,Roberto,Astros	R	19	35	110	24	2	0	1	29	12	11	8	1	27	1	1	0	5	5	.50	4	.218	.277	.264
Allison,Chris,Michigan	A	24	87	298	94	8	4	0	110	46	22	52	1	39	7	4	0	36	4	.90	5	.315	.429	.369
Almanzar,Richard,Lakeland	A	20	42	140	43	9	0	1	55	29	14	18	0	20	4	5	0	11	9	.55	5	.307	.401	.393
Fayetteville	A	20	80	308	76	12	1	0	90	47	16	29	0	32	7	9	0	39	15	.72	5	.247	.326	.292
Almond,Greg,Savannah	A	25	18	56	9	2	0	0	11	2	3	8	0	16	1	0	0	0	1	.00	0	.161	.277	.196
Almonte,Wady,Bluefield	R	21	51	189	58	12	1	6	90	37	30	9	2	49	1	0	2	6	5	.55	4	.307	.338	.476
Altman,Heath,Burlington	A	25	20	24	3	0	0	1	6	4	2	4	0	15	1	0	0	1	0	1.00	0	.125	.276	.250
Alvarado,Basilio,W. Palm Bch	A	21	6	18	4	0	0	0	4	0	0	1	0	5	0	0	0	0	1	.00	1	.222	.263	.222
Expos	R	21	28	74	22	6	1	1	33	8	12	4	0	11	0	3	0	1	1	.50	3	.297	.333	.446
Alvarez,Luis,Cedar Rapds	A	26	42	123	24	7	1	2	39	14	13	12	3	15	1	0	1	2	2	.50	3	.195	.270	.317
Alvarez,Rafael,Fort Wayne	A	24	99	374	106	17	5	5	148	62	36	34	1	53	2	2	4	15	11	.58	5	.283	.343	.396
Alzualde,Daniel,Boise	A	24	24	67	19	3	0	1	25	3	8	5	0	19	1	1	0	0	0	.00	2	.284	.342	.373
Amado,Jose,Everett	A	21	57	215	57	15	1	8	98	33	33	24	6	19	6	0	5	15	5	.75	4	.265	.348	.456
Amador,Manuel,Piedmont	A	20	1	4	0	0	0	0	0	0	0	0	0	1	0	0	0	0	0	.00	0	.000	.200	.000
Clearwater	A	20	96	330	92	19	4	6	137	45	47	22	0	38	6	1	0	5	2	.71	6	.279	.335	.415
Amaya,Edilberto,White Sox	R	20	26	78	15	3	0	1	21	9	9	3	0	20	1	0	0	1	0	1.00	0	.192	.232	.269
Ambrosina,Pete,Savannah	A	22	129	464	111	10	2	1	128	55	36	69	3	100	11	4	2	20	12	.63	6	.239	.350	.276
Amerson,Gordie,Clinton	A	19	48	134	21	2	0	1	26	15	8	35	2	41	0	0	0	5	5	.50	2	.157	.331	.194
Idaho Falls	R	19	46	167	51	16	5	1	80	40	22	39	0	33	2	0	0	8	7	.53	4	.305	.442	.479
Amezcua,Adan,Quad City	A	22	46	142	35	8	2	4	59	13	12	5	0	28	1	1	1	2	3	.40	4	.246	.275	.415
Anderson,Cliff,Vero Beach	A	25	113	365	99	20	2	6	141	48	44	10	1	58	8	6	2	1	4	.20	4	.271	.304	.386
Anderson,Marlon,Batavia	A	22	74	312	92	13	4	3	122	52	40	15	2	20	4	2	4	22	8	.73	2	.295	.331	.391
Anderson,Milt,Burlington	R	23	58	210	54	7	3	3	76	45	19	41	1	44	4	0	1	38	6	.86	2	.257	.387	.362
Kinston	A	23	4	5	0	0	0	0	0	1	0	0	0	0	0	0	0	0	0	.00	0	.000	.000	.000
Anderson,Frank,Bristol	R	20	46	153	34	7	1	2	49	10	16	7	0	52	0	0	0	2	3	.40	0	.222	.253	.320
Andino,Luis,Martinsvlle	R	21	27	73	14	5	1	1	24	13	11	4	0	27	1	1	0	1	2	.33	1	.192	.241	.329
Andreopoulos,Alex,Helena	R	23	3	9	5	0	0	2	11	3	7	4	0	0	0	0	0	0	0	.00	0	.556	.692	1.222
Beloit	A	23	60	163	49	9	0	1	61	32	20	35	1	16	3	3	1	5	3	.63	2	.301	.431	.374
Andrews,Jeff,Huntington	R	24	34	112	12	0	0	1	15	10	12	6	0	31	2	0	1	1	1	.50	1	.107	.165	.134
Angeli,Doug,Clearwater	A	25	16	47	9	3	0	0	12	4	3	3	0	13	1	2	1	0	1	.00	0	.191	.250	.255
Anglen,Toby,Danville	R	22	63	221	56	11	0	3	76	32	35	24	1	33	1	0	3	14	4	.78	5	.253	.325	.344
Antczak,Chuck,Hickory	A	22	6	5	1	0	0	0	1	0	1	0	0	2	0	0	0	0	0	.00	0	.200	.200	.200
Bristol	R	22	24	59	18	4	0	1	25	11	10	6	0	16	7	0	1	2	1	1.00	1	.305	.425	.424
Antigua,Nilson,Pirates	R	20	27	98	24	3	1	0	29	6	10	2	0	19	0	0	2	1	0	1.00	5	.245	.255	.296
Antrim,Patrick,Oneonta	A	22	26	78	15	1	0	0	16	6	5	1	0	23	1	1	1	3	1	.75	1	.192	.210	.205
Yankees	R	22	16	52	13	2	1	0	17	9	4	4	0	13	1	2	0	3	0	1.00	1	.250	.316	.327
Arano,Eloy,Lakeland	A	22	102	353	100	9	1	0	111	35	33	9	1	55	0	3	1	5	6	.45	7	.283	.300	.314
Ardoin,Danny,Sou. Oregon	A	21	58	175	41	9	1	2	58	28	23	31	0	50	9	5	4	2	1	.67	2	.234	.370	.331
Arevalos,Ryan,Helena	R	23	47	137	33	11	0	3	53	40	18	39	0	38	4	2	0	5	4	.56	2	.241	.422	.387
Arias,David,Mariners	R	20	48	184	61	18	4	4	99	30	37	23	1	52	1	0	3	2	0	1.00	2	.332	.403	.538
Arias,Rogelio,Portland	A	20	13	43	12	1	0	0	13	4	3	1	0	3	0	0	1	3	1	.75	2	.279	.289	.302
Asheville	A	20	67	213	34	4	0	0	38	9	4	7	0	25	1	6	0	3	0	.00	2	.160	.190	.178
Arrollado,Courtney,Butte	R	21	62	216	58	11	0	0	69	34	21	19	0	38	2	2	0	9	2	.82	4	.269	.331	.319
Arvelo,Thomas,Columbia	A	22	16	40	5	2	0	0	7	2	4	0	3	0	7	0	0	0	1	0	1.00	0	.125	.163	.175
Pittsfield	A	22	67	279	85	8	7	0	107	41	17	16	0	63	5	2	1	24	6	.80	0	.305	.352	.384
Asche,Mike,Augusta	A	24	106	376	100	17	6	6	147	52	59	35	1	60	5	3	3	21	5	.81	6	.266	.334	.391

1995 Batting -- Single-A and Rookie Leagues

Player	Lg	A	G	AB	H	2B	3B	HR	TB	R	RBI	TBB	IBB	SO	HBP	SH	SF	SB	CS	SB%	GDP	Avg	OBP	SLG
Asencio,Fernando,San Bernrdo	A	22	29	105	27	1	4	2	42	15	18	6	0	31	2	1	0	2	0	1.00	0	.257	.310	.400
Vero Beach	A	22	58	184	49	8	3	2	69	24	21	6	0	22	1	1	4	4	3	.57	3	.266	.287	.375
Ashby,Chris,Greensboro	A	21	88	288	79	23	1	9	131	45	45	61	2	68	6	2	2	3	3	.50	9	.274	.409	.455
Astacio,Onofre,Twins	R	20	47	165	37	3	1	0	42	21	8	17	0	42	5	1	1	26	6	.81	3	.224	.314	.255
Augustine,Andy,Wisconsin	A	23	56	129	22	0	0	1	25	17	6	19	0	43	8	4	0	3	1	.75	5	.171	.314	.194
Austin,Lakevie,Utica	A	22	34	91	22	3	0	1	28	10	6	8	0	38	1	1	0	5	2	.71	1	.242	.310	.308
Avalos,Gilbert,Rockford	A	23	104	350	83	15	1	2	106	57	34	39	0	74	4	7	2	18	4	.82	8	.237	.319	.303
Aven,Bruce,Kinston	A	24	130	479	125	23	5	23	227	70	69	41	3	109	13	0	1	15	9	.63	7	.261	.335	.474
Aviles,Ronnel,Lethbridge	R	19	43	77	6	2	0	0	8	6	0	9	0	22	3	1	0	0	1	.00	4	.078	.202	.104
Aybar,Ramon,Tigers	R	20	38	112	27	2	1	0	31	22	10	18	0	38	5	4	2	16	5	.76	2	.241	.365	.277
Lakeland	A	20	3	8	1	0	0	0	1	1	0	1	0	5	0	0	0	0	0	.00	0	.125	.222	.125
Ayuso,Julio,Twins	R	19	25	71	12	0	0	0	12	5	3	7	1	20	1	1	0	0	1	.00	3	.169	.253	.169
Babin,Brady,Brevard Cty	A	20	32	105	26	3	2	2	39	15	19	9	0	20	1	1	2	0	1	.00	4	.248	.308	.371
Elmira	A	20	6	20	7	1	1	0	10	4	2	3	0	1	0	1	0	0	0	.00	0	.350	.435	.500
Backowski,Lance,Yakima	A	21	34	114	22	1	1	0	25	8	8	8	1	16	0	2	1	4	1	.80	7	.193	.244	.219
Bady,Edward,Vermont	A	23	72	295	97	15	3	2	124	51	25	24	3	52	5	2	0	34	19	.64	3	.329	.389	.420
Bagley,Sean,Bristol	R	20	35	64	13	1	1	0	16	8	5	8	0	25	1	2	0	9	3	.75	1	.203	.301	.250
Baker,Jason,Fort Myers	A	23	91	276	66	9	0	0	75	35	26	30	1	38	7	8	3	8	8	.50	5	.239	.326	.272
Baker,Jason,Great Falls	R	22	55	104	27	3	0	4	42	17	22	11	0	23	7	0	0	2	1	.67	3	.260	.369	.404
Bako,Paul,Winston-Sal	A	24	82	249	71	11	2	7	107	29	27	42	6	66	1	6	1	3	1	.75	6	.285	.389	.430
Balcazar,Carlos,Angels	R	22	35	93	28	5	1	1	38	11	11	12	1	20	2	0	0	2	0	1.00	1	.301	.393	.409
Bales,Taylor,Royals	R	22	8	14	0	0	0	0	0	2	0	4	0	6	1	0	0	0	0	.00	0	.000	.263	.000
Balfe,Ryan,Fayettevlle	A	20	113	398	104	20	2	10	158	53	49	48	0	85	9	0	1	1	1	.50	11	.261	.353	.397
Balint,Rob,Tigers	R	22	1	5	1	0	0	1	4	1	1	0	0	2	0	0	0	0	0	.00	0	.200	.200	.800
Fayettevlle	A	22	13	33	8	2	0	1	13	4	4	1	0	15	0	1	0	0	0	.00	0	.242	.265	.394
Ballara,Juan,Peoria	A	24	86	243	62	12	6	8	110	33	27	17	1	53	2	0	0	5	3	.63	5	.255	.309	.453
Banks,Tony,Modesto	A	24	28	81	16	3	0	1	22	10	10	13	0	17	0	4	1	3	0	1.00	1	.198	.305	.272
Barger,Mike,Riverside	A	25	82	344	109	10	1	2	127	77	41	38	1	45	2	5	1	33	14	.70	3	.317	.387	.369
Barkett,Andy,Butte	R	21	45	162	54	11	5	5	90	33	51	33	2	39	3	0	4	1	0	1.00	1	.333	.446	.556
Charlstn-Sc	A	21	21	78	17	6	0	0	23	7	12	10	0	27	0	0	3	0	3	.00	1	.218	.297	.295
Barksdale,Shane,Astros	R	19	47	159	41	9	1	3	61	19	25	20	1	61	3	0	0	7	11	.39	3	.258	.352	.384
Barlok,Todd,Great Falls	R	24	59	190	52	12	5	1	77	43	31	29	0	45	1	0	1	10	3	.77	1	.274	.371	.405
Barnes,Kelvin,Cubs	R	21	49	168	48	6	6	6	84	28	37	24	0	37	1	0	2	11	4	.73	4	.286	.374	.500
Rockford	A	21	5	12	2	0	0	0	2	1	0	1	0	3	1	0	0	0	0	.00	0	.167	.286	.167
Barnes,Larry,Angels	R	21	55	194	61	8	3	3	84	41	37	26	0	40	5	1	2	11	5	.69	1	.314	.405	.433
Barrett,Michael,Expos	R	19	50	183	57	13	4	0	78	22	19	15	1	19	0	0	1	7	6	.54	1	.311	.362	.426
Vermont	A	19	3	10	1	0	0	0	1	0	1	1	0	1	0	0	1	0	0	.00	0	.100	.167	.100
Barrios,Steven,Angels	R	20	29	74	15	1	1	0	18	12	2	18	0	9	0	1	1	4	1	.80	4	.203	.355	.243
Barthol,Blake,Portland	A	23	56	191	45	10	2	1	62	20	25	22	0	32	4	1	3	5	2	.71	5	.236	.323	.325
Barton,Scott,Williamsprt	A	22	16	45	10	5	2	0	19	3	13	4	0	13	0	1	1	0	1	.00	2	.222	.280	.422
Rockford	A	22	14	26	6	3	0	0	9	2	2	3	0	6	0	1	0	0	1	.00	0	.231	.310	.346
Basey,Marsalis,Kissimmee	A	24	91	317	73	6	0	0	79	37	16	18	1	35	4	2	3	12	5	.71	6	.230	.278	.249
Bass,Jayson,Fayettevlle	A	22	108	368	79	15	6	10	136	47	44	37	1	111	3	1	1	14	3	.82	3	.215	.291	.370
Bass,Jayson,Danville	R	20	64	268	60	17	4	0	85	38	17	28	2	61	4	0	2	24	8	.75	2	.224	.305	.317
Baugh,Gavin,Brevard Cty	A	22	81	250	47	11	2	1	65	24	21	26	0	70	4	2	3	10	3	.77	3	.188	.272	.260
Baughman,Justin,Boise	A	21	58	215	50	4	3	1	63	26	20	18	0	38	2	4	1	19	4	.83	2	.233	.297	.293
Bautista,Jorge,Marlins	R	19	42	126	26	6	1	0	34	16	4	12	0	23	1	1	0	0	0	.00	0	.206	.281	.270
Bautista,Juan,Peoria	A	23	84	189	42	4	1	2	54	31	22	4	0	43	2	3	3	18	8	.69	1	.222	.242	.286
Bazzani,Matt,Michigan	A	22	29	69	8	5	0	0	13	8	6	11	0	28	2	4	0	1	0	1.00	0	.116	.256	.188
Utica	A	22	29	74	18	4	3	3	37	15	17	4	0	17	6	3	0	1	0	1.00	0	.243	.333	.500
Bearden,Doug,Hickory	A	20	44	141	22	5	1	2	35	9	12	5	1	44	1	2	0	1	1	.50	6	.156	.190	.248
Bristol	R	20	46	167	39	10	1	3	60	26	22	6	0	40	3	3	2	5	0	1.00	1	.234	.270	.359
Beaumont,Hamil,Yankees	R	21	18	48	5	0	0	1	8	6	3	5	0	22	1	0	0	1	0	1.00	1	.104	.204	.167
Beeney,Ryan,Greensboro	A	23	57	227	63	6	0	0	69	32	21	29	0	48	4	2	3	9	8	.53	3	.278	.365	.304
Bejarano,Brian,Blue Jays	R	21	52	173	44	6	4	3	67	20	25	11	0	53	2	0	1	1	1	.50	3	.254	.305	.387
Bell,Mike,Charlotte	A	21	129	470	122	20	1	5	159	49	52	48	0	72	0	3	2	9	8	.53	11	.260	.327	.338
Bellhorn,Mark,Modesto	A	21	56	229	59	12	0	6	89	35	31	27	0	52	4	2	0	5	2	.71	9	.258	.346	.389
Belliard,Ronnie,Beloit	A	21	130	461	137	28	5	13	214	76	76	36	2	67	7	2	1	16	12	.57	10	.297	.356	.464
Bellum,Donnie,St. Pete	A	26	64	118	23	3	0	0	26	16	9	12	0	23	0	4	2	0	2	.00	5	.195	.265	.220
Beltran,Carlos,Royals	R	19	52	180	50	9	0	0	59	29	23	13	0	30	3	1	3	5	3	.63	1	.278	.332	.328
Bengoechea,Brandy,Modesto	A	24	134	467	122	19	4	5	164	60	44	47	1	96	9	11	3	7	10	.41	10	.261	.338	.351
Benner,Brian,Butte	R	20	67	245	74	15	5	2	105	42	40	44	1	83	4	0	3	5	2	.71	3	.302	.412	.429
Bellingham	A	20	2	8	1	1	0	0	2	0	1	1	0	4	0	0	0	0	0	.00	0	.125	.222	.250
Bentley,Kevin,Williamsprt	A	23	50	115	25	4	3	2	41	14	13	14	0	48	0	1	0	1	3	.25	1	.217	.302	.357
Berg,Dave,Brevard Cty	A	25	114	382	114	18	1	3	143	71	39	68	1	61	8	7	9	9	4	.69	5	.298	.407	.374
Bernhardt,Steve,Salem	A	25	59	180	39	3	2	4	58	18	16	8	0	38	5	5	2	2	3	.40	5	.217	.267	.322
Berry,Michael,W. Palm Bch	A	25	24	79	13	3	1	1	21	16	2	13	0	16	0	0	0	0	1	.00	1	.165	.283	.266
Visalia	A	25	98	368	113	28	4	9	176	69	61	57	1	70	5	1	3	12	6	.67	9	.307	.404	.478
Betances,Junior,Beloit	A	23	122	427	125	21	8	1	165	66	52	61	1	67	2	7	7	21	9	.70	9	.293	.378	.386
Betancourt,Rafael,Red Sox	R	21	51	168	43	5	0	0	48	18	19	13	0	31	1	4	3	8	5	.62	3	.256	.308	.286
Bethea,Larry,Great Falls	R	19	21	29	5	0	0	0	5	2	3	1	0	7	1	0	0	0	0	.00	2	.172	.226	.172
Betten,Randy,Boise	A	24	2	8	3	0	0	0	3	2	2	1	0	2	0	0	0	0	0	.00	0	.375	.444	.375
Cedar Rapds	A	24	36	60	14	2	0	0	16	8	4	13	0	8	0	2	0	2	2	.75	0	.233	.365	.267
Betts,Darrell,New Jersey	A	23	54	151	23	4	0	0	27	22	11	32	0	38	3	7	0	3	6	.33	2	.152	.312	.179
Betts,Todd,Kinston	A	23	109	331	90	15	3	9	138	52	44	88	2	56	6	1	1	2	3	.40	5	.272	.429	.417
Betzsold,Jim,Kinston	A	23	126	455	122	22	2	25	223	77	71	55	3	137	10	0	4	3	5	.38	0	.268	.357	.490
Beyna,Terry,Kissimmee	A	23	15	42	7	1	0	0	8	4	2	1	0	12	1	0	0	0	0	.00	4	.167	.222	.190

1995 Batting -- Single-A and Rookie Leagues

Player	Lg	A	G	AB	H	2B	3B	HR	TB	R	RBI	TBB	IBB	SO	HBP	SH	SF	SB	CS	SB%	GDP	Avg	OBP	SLG
Bierek,Kurt,Tampa	A	23	126	447	111	16	2	4	143	60	53	61	3	73	4	2	2	3	4	.43	11	.248	.342	.320
Biermann,Steve,Peoria	A	24	59	122	29	3	0	0	32	10	10	15	1	16	4	2	0	4	3	.57	5	.238	.340	.262
Bilderback,Ty,Boise	A	22	61	177	57	11	2	3	81	35	25	29	0	29	3	0	1	10	5	.67	4	.322	.424	.458
Biltimier,Mike,Vero Beach	A	25	127	422	95	14	0	14	151	62	50	48	1	109	5	3	4	0	1	.00	8	.225	.309	.358
Bishop,Steve,High Desert	A	25	12	43	5	1	1	0	8	5	3	4	0	12	1	0	0	1	0	1.00	1	.116	.208	.186
Bishop,Tim,Mets	R	22	47	156	37	6	5	2	59	31	15	13	0	38	3	0	3	4	2	.67	0	.237	.303	.378
Black,Brandon,Mets	R	21	30	105	37	12	3	1	58	16	25	10	0	11	1	0	1	1	1	.50	2	.352	.410	.552
Kingsport	R	21	31	106	31	5	0	3	45	17	20	8	0	23	3	0	1	7	1	.88	3	.292	.356	.425
Blair,Brian,Charlotte	A	24	69	264	59	5	3	0	70	34	9	34	3	42	1	2	1	14	6	.70	1	.223	.313	.265
Blakeney,Mo,Vermont	A	23	39	132	35	8	1	2	51	17	17	8	0	23	4	0	0	12	2	.86	3	.265	.326	.386
Bledsoe,Jim,Ogden	R	24	38	131	47	14	0	3	70	17	22	19	0	27	0	0	3	3	1	.75	3	.359	.440	.534
Blosser,Doug,Royals	R	19	50	161	41	10	1	7	74	18	33	32	0	39	1	0	2	0	0	.00	3	.255	.378	.460
Blum,Geoff,W. Palm Bch	A	23	125	457	120	20	2	1	147	54	62	34	1	61	3	1	7	6	5	.55	12	.263	.313	.322
Bocachica,Hiram,Albany	A	20	96	380	108	20	10	2	154	65	30	52	3	78	8	3	1	47	17	.73	4	.284	.381	.405
Bogle,Bryan,Rockford	A	23	36	97	20	3	0	2	29	13	11	8	0	20	0	0	1	4	1	.80	2	.206	.264	.299
Butte	R	23	2	9	3	1	0	0	4	0	2	1	0	4	0	0	0	0	0	.00	1	.333	.400	.444
Bluefield	R	23	10	31	14	2	0	1	19	11	4	4	0	2	2	0	1	1	0	1.00	1	.452	.526	.613
High Desert	A	23	19	64	11	2	1	0	15	7	4	8	0	18	0	0	0	3	1	.75	1	.172	.264	.234
Bokemeier,Mathew,Charlotte	A	23	105	385	91	16	1	8	133	42	34	26	1	76	2	4	0	7	7	.50	11	.236	.288	.345
Bonds,Bobby,Visalia	A	26	109	373	83	12	6	11	140	56	30	42	1	114	4	3	1	26	12	.68	5	.223	.307	.375
Bonifay,Ken,Lynchburg	A	25	116	375	92	22	2	10	148	57	54	63	4	88	11	0	4	3	5	.38	6	.245	.366	.395
Booty,Josh,Kane County	A	21	31	109	11	2	0	1	16	6	6	11	0	45	0	0	1	1	0	1.00	1	.101	.182	.147
Elmira	A	21	74	287	63	18	1	6	101	33	37	19	0	85	5	0	2	4	4	.50	12	.220	.278	.352
Borel,Jamie,Lakeland	A	24	16	41	5	1	0	0	6	8	1	6	0	6	1	1	0	2	1	.67	2	.122	.250	.146
Fayetteville	A	24	86	279	68	9	3	0	83	60	20	41	0	43	2	1	2	36	14	.72	2	.244	.343	.297
Borges,Mariano,Erie	A	23	17	45	5	0	0	0	5	4	2	3	0	11	2	0	0	1	1	.50	2	.111	.200	.111
Borges,Victor,Cubs	R	19	35	94	20	0	1	0	22	20	6	17	0	18	1	2	0	8	2	.80	1	.213	.339	.234
Borrero,Richie,Sarasota	A	23	34	98	20	5	0	0	25	9	4	5	0	22	2	1	2	0	1	.00	1	.204	.252	.255
Michigan	A	23	23	70	16	4	1	2	28	8	6	6	0	17	4	0	0	0	1	.00	2	.229	.325	.400
Boryczewski,Marty,Erie	A	23	10	32	3	0	0	0	3	0	0	1	0	6	0	0	0	0	0	.00	2	.094	.121	.094
Boulware,Ben,South Bend	A	24	129	476	123	19	5	2	158	68	60	32	2	78	8	2	3	24	13	.65	10	.258	.314	.332
Bourne,Charles,St. Cathrns	A	21	55	176	35	11	0	1	49	24	17	18	0	50	3	4	2	12	3	.80	2	.199	.281	.278
Bovender,Brent,Auburn	A	23	71	243	76	15	4	5	114	42	41	30	2	70	4	0	1	1	2	.33	7	.313	.396	.469
Bowen,Joe,Savannah	A	22	16	52	12	3	0	0	15	1	2	0	0	17	0	0	0	0	1	.00	0	.231	.231	.288
Bowers,Kevin,Mets	R	19	36	123	27	4	1	2	39	20	19	21	1	38	1	0	1	1	0	1.00	1	.220	.336	.317
Bowers,Ray,Quad City	A	22	110	372	90	19	1	12	147	52	58	35	1	119	13	0	6	10	9	.53	7	.242	.324	.395
Bowles,John,Michigan	A	21	106	352	85	18	0	4	115	48	46	46	1	70	9	5	3	5	8	.38	13	.241	.341	.327
Bowness,Brian,Bristol	R	22	54	202	45	4	0	1	52	20	23	12	0	37	2	0	1	0	1	.00	5	.223	.272	.257
Boyd,Quincy,Vero Beach	A	25	31	66	10	2	0	0	12	4	1	9	1	20	0	0	0	0	0	.00	0	.152	.253	.182
Boyette,Tony,Princeton	R	20	61	222	65	14	1	10	111	41	49	21	0	41	3	0	3	2	0	1.00	3	.293	.357	.500
Bracho,Darwin,Princeton	R	21	31	82	17	5	0	0	22	5	7	4	0	16	1	0	0	0	2	.00	1	.207	.253	.268
Braddy,Junior,Sarasota	A	24	114	413	109	12	5	2	137	41	36	31	0	99	5	2	4	13	12	.52	10	.264	.320	.332
Bragga,Matt,Charlstn-Wv	A	22	88	258	64	11	5	0	85	35	26	28	2	62	4	0	3	6	5	.55	2	.248	.328	.329
Brakebill,Mark,Lk Elsinore	A	26	2	7	1	0	0	0	1	0	1	0	1	2	0	0	0	0	0	.00	0	.143	.250	.143
Bramlett,Jeff,Great Falls	R	20	32	55	8	2	1	0	12	5	5	12	0	23	1	0	0	1	2	.33	1	.145	.300	.218
Brandon,Jelani,Springfield	A	22	74	230	56	12	1	3	79	32	37	35	0	37	2	2	3	6	2	.75	4	.243	.344	.343
Brannon,Tony,Utica	A	22	42	125	27	5	1	1	37	11	18	9	0	20	2	1	2	5	2	.71	5	.216	.275	.296
Branyan,Russ,Columbus	A	20	76	277	71	8	6	19	148	46	55	27	2	120	3	0	3	1	1	.50	6	.256	.326	.534
Bray,Notorris,Burlington	A	22	15	45	9	0	1	0	11	8	6	8	0	12	2	1	0	3	0	1.00	1	.200	.345	.244
Bellingham	A	22	2	4	2	0	0	0	2	3	0	3	0	1	0	0	0	0	0	.00	0	.500	.714	.500
Butte	R	22	60	188	48	9	1	1	62	50	14	46	0	35	12	1	1	27	10	.73	4	.255	.429	.330
Breuer,Jim,Bakersfield	A	22	10	21	1	0	0	0	1	0	3	2	0	13	1	0	2	0	0	.00	0	.048	.154	.048
Brewer,Doug,Macon	A	21	128	452	109	25	8	8	174	78	60	60	0	113	10	3	5	15	5	.75	6	.241	.340	.385
Bridgers,Brandon,Frederick	A	23	10	31	5	3	0	0	8	3	5	11	0	5	0	1	1	1	1	.50	0	.161	.372	.258
Brinkley,Josh,Albany	A	22	22	69	12	3	0	1	18	8	5	3	0	11	3	0	2	2	2	.50	1	.174	.240	.261
Vermont	A	22	38	122	27	2	0	0	29	14	11	14	0	26	6	0	2	6	1	.86	4	.221	.326	.238
Briones,Christopher,Hudson Vall	A	23	48	163	36	12	1	5	65	18	26	4	0	53	3	1	3	0	0	.00	2	.221	.249	.399
Brito,Domingo,Clearwater	A	20	1	1	0	0	0	0	0	0	0	0	0	1	0	0	0	0	0	.00	0	.000	.000	.000
Batavia	A	20	11	32	4	0	0	0	4	1	2	9	0	9	0	0	0	0	0	.00	2	.125	.317	.125
Martinsville	R	20	29	81	12	0	0	0	12	8	3	11	0	32	1	0	1	1	0	1.00	0	.148	.250	.148
Broach,Donald,Winston-Sal	A	24	117	460	120	23	4	8	175	74	34	50	2	73	5	5	2	16	14	.53	9	.261	.338	.380
Brooks,Eddie,Augusta	A	23	67	238	65	13	5	2	94	40	37	28	0	61	1	2	3	3	5	.38	2	.273	.348	.395
Lynchburg	A	23	27	68	8	1	0	0	9	6	2	8	0	21	1	1	1	0	1	.00	1	.118	.218	.132
Brooks,Rayme,Wilmington	A	26	94	326	71	16	0	8	111	41	30	25	1	82	6	1	1	2	1	.67	7	.218	.285	.340
Brown,Adrian,Augusta	A	22	76	287	86	15	4	4	121	64	31	33	0	23	1	3	2	25	14	.64	2	.300	.372	.422
Lynchburg	A	22	54	215	52	5	2	1	64	30	14	12	0	20	1	4	1	11	6	.65	3	.242	.284	.298
Brown,Armann,Fort Myers	A	23	23	63	12	2	3	0	20	6	9	3	0	15	1	0	1	1	0	1.00	1	.190	.235	.317
Fort Wayne	A	23	78	253	59	9	2	1	75	35	25	30	0	57	8	2	2	26	7	.79	8	.233	.333	.296
Brown,Derek,Orioles	R	19	49	146	34	5	0	0	39	15	11	23	0	32	1	0	1	3	3	.50	5	.233	.339	.267
Brown,Emil,W.Michigan	A	21	124	459	115	17	3	3	147	63	67	52	0	77	11	0	6	35	19	.65	15	.251	.337	.320
Brown,Eric,Great Falls	R	19	54	145	37	10	5	3	66	26	36	22	2	56	0	0	3	6	3	.67	3	.255	.343	.455
Brown,Jerome,Elizabethtn	R	20	17	71	13	2	0	0	15	10	1	5	0	25	1	0	0	5	0	1.00	0	.183	.247	.211
Brown,Nate,Albany	A	25	117	397	101	23	3	4	142	34	49	32	1	112	5	4	3	4	8	.33	6	.254	.316	.358
Brown,Ray,Winston-Sal	A	23	122	445	118	26	4	19	201	63	77	52	12	85	11	0	4	3	2	.60	8	.265	.354	.452
Charlstn-Wv	A	23	6	17	2	1	0	0	3	0	0	4	0	3	0	0	0	0	0	.00	0	.118	.286	.176
Brown,Ron,Brevard Cty	A	26	121	404	105	22	2	3	140	48	51	31	0	79	3	1	9	6	12	.33	14	.260	.311	.347
Brown,Roosevelt,Eugene	A	20	57	165	51	12	4	7	92	28	32	13	2	30	3	0	2	6	3	.67	1	.309	.366	.558

336

1995 Batting -- Single-A and Rookie Leagues

Player	Lg	A	G	AB	H	2B	3B	HR	TB	R	RBI	TBB	IBB	SO	HBP	SH	SF	SB	CS	SB%	GDP	Avg	OBP	SLG
Brown,Todd,Frederick	A	24	32	59	14	4	0	0	18	6	2	5	0	21	1	4	0	6	2	.75	1	.237	.308	.305
Brown,Vick,Greensboro	A	23	118	432	98	10	1	2	116	66	36	44	0	93	6	8	1	24	9	.73	11	.227	.306	.269
Brown,Willie,Brevard Cty	A	25	63	189	42	6	1	6	68	26	23	25	3	74	1	0	0	4	3	.57	1	.222	.316	.360
Brumbaugh,Cliff,Hudson Vall	A	22	74	282	101	19	4	2	134	44	45	39	4	51	2	0	2	15	3	.83	11	.358	.437	.475
Brunner,Mike,Auburn	A	24	26	83	16	6	0	2	28	7	11	5	0	25	0	0	0	2	1	.67	3	.193	.239	.337
Brunson,Matt,Lakeland	A	21	45	132	17	2	1	0	21	10	7	26	0	41	0	4	0	9	2	.82	1	.129	.272	.159
Fayettevlle	A	21	43	144	32	3	3	1	44	18	8	22	0	34	1	1	0	16	6	.73	1	.222	.329	.306
Bryan,Leonardo,Boise	A	23	42	80	16	3	1	0	21	8	6	16	0	18	0	0	0	3	2	.60	3	.200	.333	.263
Bryant,Chris,Bluefield	R	23	58	195	56	10	1	5	83	39	37	25	0	30	3	1	3	6	4	.60	10	.287	.372	.426
Brzozoski,Marc,Portland	A	22	66	240	56	6	2	2	72	22	25	25	3	71	4	1	2	7	4	.64	4	.233	.314	.300
Bucci,Carmen,Idaho Falls	R	23	50	113	21	2	0	0	23	22	7	14	0	32	5	0	2	7	2	.78	1	.186	.299	.204
Buchanan,Brian,Greensboro	A	22	23	96	29	3	0	3	41	19	12	9	1	17	1	0	0	7	1	.88	1	.302	.368	.427
Buchanan,Shawn,Pr. William	A	27	4	1	0	0	0	0	0	2	0	0	0	0	0	0	0	0	0	.00	0	.000	.000	.000
South Bend	A	27	103	350	94	16	4	2	124	45	35	46	0	72	10	1	3	10	8	.56	10	.269	.367	.354
Buckles,Matt,Martinsvlle	R	19	22	58	11	2	0	0	13	6	4	2	1	17	2	1	0	2	0	1.00	1	.190	.242	.224
Budzinski,Mark,Watertown	A	22	70	253	64	12	8	3	101	50	25	52	1	49	8	3	2	15	5	.75	3	.253	.394	.399
Buhner,Shawn,Wisconsin	A	23	87	292	70	14	3	2	96	24	36	16	2	65	6	0	4	0	2	.00	9	.240	.289	.329
Bunkley,Antuan,Twins	R	20	49	181	54	9	0	6	81	24	23	15	0	35	9	0	0	11	4	.73	3	.298	.380	.448
Burchel,Brad,Beloit	A	24	13	34	5	1	0	0	6	4	3	3	0	11	2	0	0	0	3	.00	0	.147	.256	.176
Burgos,Carlos,Springfield	A	24	27	72	13	2	0	0	15	8	8	7	0	11	3	0	1	0	0	.00	2	.181	.277	.208
Burke,Jamie,Lk Elsinore	A	24	106	365	100	15	6	2	133	47	56	32	1	53	9	11	4	6	4	.60	12	.274	.344	.364
Burks,Donny,Lethbridge	R	23	62	181	28	3	2	0	35	19	6	34	0	40	4	2	0	4	2	.67	6	.155	.301	.193
Burns,Kevin,Astros	R	20	42	136	34	4	1	3	49	17	23	12	1	24	0	0	1	8	3	.73	5	.250	.309	.360
Burress,Andy,Billings	R	18	35	103	27	9	2	2	46	17	18	6	0	16	3	0	1	2	2	.00	4	.262	.319	.447
Burrows,Mike,Everett	A	20	67	223	46	5	3	7	78	28	33	42	1	72	3	2	2	13	8	.62	1	.206	.337	.350
Bustos,Saul,Rockford	A	23	95	289	73	12	2	10	119	46	47	22	0	66	2	2	8	5	2	.71	8	.253	.302	.412
Butler,Garrett,Yankees	R	20	48	185	43	4	4	0	55	40	16	16	0	45	5	8	1	11	0	1.00	1	.232	.309	.297
Buxbaum,Danny,Boise	A	23	68	231	76	15	0	8	115	46	51	49	5	31	4	0	5	1	0	1.00	3	.329	.446	.498
Byington,Jimmie,Wilmington	A	22	92	273	61	6	1	0	69	24	23	13	0	33	4	3	2	12	6	.67	3	.223	.267	.253
Caballero,Craig,Jamestown	A	22	52	142	28	4	1	5	49	23	20	32	0	42	1	0	2	3	2	.60	10	.197	.345	.345
Cabrera,Alex,Daytona	A	24	54	214	63	14	0	2	83	26	35	9	0	36	4	0	2	2	4	.33	8	.294	.332	.388
Cabrera,Jairo,High Desert	A	24	14	39	8	0	0	0	8	2	3	3	0	7	1	2	1	1	0	1.00	1	.205	.273	.205
Frederick	A	24	25	60	11	1	0	0	12	7	1	7	0	13	1	2	0	0	1	.00	1	.183	.279	.200
Cabrera,Orlando,W. Palm Bch	A	22	3	5	1	0	0	0	1	0	0	0	0	1	0	0	0	0	0	.00	0	.200	.200	.200
Vermont	A	22	65	248	70	12	5	3	101	37	33	16	0	28	1	2	4	15	8	.65	3	.282	.323	.407
Cady,Todd,Kane County	A	23	115	387	97	23	1	11	155	47	66	47	3	104	9	0	4	0	0	1.00	4	.251	.342	.401
Calderon,Ricardo,Bellingham	A	20	67	216	49	9	0	6	76	23	35	22	6	73	4	1	2	1	2	.33	5	.227	.307	.352
Cameron,Ken,New Jersey	A	23	39	138	33	9	1	0	44	18	10	12	0	20	2	2	0	5	0	1.00	2	.239	.309	.319
Camfield,Eric,Oneonta	A	23	73	296	80	11	3	1	100	45	42	22	0	41	1	2	2	17	7	.71	1	.270	.321	.338
Camilli,Jason,Albany	A	20	53	181	34	5	0	3	48	28	16	38	0	50	3	0	2	13	10	.57	0	.188	.335	.265
Vermont	A	20	63	243	59	10	2	1	76	37	21	30	1	52	2	3	0	17	10	.63	4	.243	.329	.313
Camilo,Jose,Marlins	R	19	48	155	52	5	5	4	79	37	22	41	1	28	1	2	1	19	6	.76	2	.335	.475	.510
Campillo,Rob,Beloit	A	24	47	123	26	4	0	0	30	17	13	7	1	20	5	7	2	0	0	.00	2	.211	.277	.244
Stockton	A	24	35	106	32	3	0	0	35	10	17	7	0	13	1	3	2	0	0	.00	4	.302	.345	.330
Campos,Jesus,W. Palm Bch	A	22	107	326	72	6	2	0	82	32	21	25	0	40	2	5	5	18	7	.72	5	.221	.279	.252
Campos,Miguel,Cubs	R	20	36	115	24	6	0	3	39	21	13	8	0	37	3	2	0	5	1	.83	2	.209	.278	.339
Campusano,Carlos,Brewers	R	20	54	173	43	4	1	1	52	25	15	14	1	27	5	1	1	7	3	.70	6	.249	.321	.301
Cancel,David,Hickory	A	22	76	240	69	3	2	2	82	24	13	11	0	37	0	2	1	11	10	.52	3	.288	.317	.342
Cancel,Robby,Helena	R	20	46	154	37	9	0	0	46	18	24	9	0	20	2	1	2	8	3	.73	3	.240	.287	.299
Candelaria,Benjamin,Dunedin	A	21	125	471	122	21	5	5	168	66	49	53	1	98	0	3	5	11	4	.73	11	.259	.331	.357
Canetto,John,Erie	A	23	11	25	4	0	0	0	4	5	1	7	0	7	0	0	0	0	0	.00	1	.160	.344	.160
Lynchburg	A	23	13	28	7	2	0	0	9	5	2	3	0	13	0	0	1	0	0	.00	0	.250	.313	.321
Capallen,Rene,Tigers	R	18	33	101	32	3	1	0	37	17	13	13	0	14	2	4	0	6	4	.60	0	.317	.405	.366
Caraballo,Gary,Fort Myers	A	24	85	309	95	24	2	7	144	51	55	34	3	44	5	0	3	5	6	.45	10	.307	.382	.466
Cardenas,Epi,Columbus	A	24	125	513	149	28	4	7	206	69	56	30	0	64	2	6	5	11	7	.61	4	.290	.329	.402
Cardona,Alex,Johnson Cty	R	21	22	46	10	3	0	0	13	9	7	11	1	4	0	1	0	0	0	.00	0	.217	.368	.283
Cardona,Javier,Fayettevlle	A	20	51	165	34	8	0	3	51	18	19	13	0	30	1	0	0	1	0	1.00	5	.206	.268	.309
Cardona,Luis,Red Sox	R	18	42	136	29	6	0	1	38	14	15	8	0	35	5	0	1	0	1	.00	2	.213	.280	.279
Cardona,Paco,New Jersey	A	24	49	195	49	5	4	0	62	36	24	21	0	24	1	3	1	7	2	.78	3	.251	.326	.318
Carmona,Cesarin,Clinton	A	19	42	129	23	2	1	0	27	13	5	15	0	35	1	1	0	7	5	.59	2	.178	.269	.209
Padres	R	19	15	51	13	2	2	1	22	7	4	5	0	10	0	1	0	3	3	.50	0	.255	.321	.431
Carone,Richard,South Bend	A	25	111	347	88	16	1	9	133	56	51	84	0	91	9	5	2	0	0	.00	7	.254	.410	.383
Carpenter,Matt,Asheville	A	23	9	21	2	1	0	0	3	0	3	1	0	2	1	0	0	0	0	.00	0	.095	.136	.143
Salem	A	23	1	0	0	0	0	0	0	0	0	0	0	0	1	0	0	0	0	.00	0	.000	1.000	.000
Columbus	A	23	2	7	2	1	0	1	6	2	3	0	0	2	1	0	0	0	0	.00	0	.286	.375	.857
Watertown	A	23	12	31	10	3	0	0	13	4	4	4	0	7	0	0	0	0	0	.00	3	.323	.400	.419
Carpentier,Mike,Yakima	A	21	53	188	48	8	4	4	76	20	28	13	0	23	1	3	3	4	5	.44	2	.255	.302	.404
Great Falls	R	21	6	19	5	2	0	0	7	4	2	1	0	3	0	0	0	0	0	.00	0	.263	.300	.368
Carr,Jeremy,Wilmington	A	25	5	13	3	1	0	0	4	1	0	1	0	3	0	0	0	0	1	.00	0	.231	.286	.308
Bakersfield	A	25	128	499	128	22	2	1	157	92	38	79	0	73	11	6	0	52	21	.71	9	.257	.370	.315
Carranza,Pete,Salem	A	24	18	51	11	2	0	4	25	9	8	9	0	8	0	0	0	2	0	1.00	0	.216	.333	.490
Asheville	A	24	111	433	110	32	2	5	161	67	29	45	2	49	3	2	5	10	9	.53	4	.254	.325	.372
Carrasquel,Domingo,Stockton	A	24	67	160	43	10	0	0	53	19	20	18	0	21	0	10	1	2	5	.29	3	.269	.341	.331
Carroll,Doug,Wisconsin	A	22	90	276	62	18	0	5	95	29	40	18	3	60	14	0	3	3	0	1.00	7	.225	.302	.344
Carubelli,Gustavo,Braves	R	21	49	148	29	8	0	2	43	13	6	24	0	31	1	1	0	3	2	.60	6	.196	.312	.291
Carvajal,Jhonny,Charlstn-Wv	A	21	135	486	128	18	5	0	156	78	42	58	0	77	6	4	4	44	19	.70	4	.263	.347	.321
Carver,Steve,Batavia	A	23	56	217	66	13	2	7	104	35	41	17	1	29	0	1	1	2	1	.67	3	.304	.353	.479

337

1995 Batting -- Single-A and Rookie Leagues

Player	Lg	A	G	AB	H	2B	3B	HR	TB	R	RBI	TBB	IBB	SO	HBP	SH	SF	SB	CS	SB%	GDP	Avg	OBP	SLG
Casey,Sean,Watertown	A	21	55	207	68	18	0	2	92	26	37	18	4	21	1	0	3	3	0	1.00	6	.329	.380	.444
Casimiro,Carlos,Orioles	R	19	32	107	27	4	2	2	41	14	11	10	0	22	1	1	2	1	3	.25	3	.252	.317	.383
Castillo,Alberto,Burlington	A	20	34	103	17	4	0	4	33	7	13	7	0	43	0	0	0	2	0	1.00	0	.165	.218	.320
Bellingham	A	20	74	263	56	11	0	5	82	19	23	35	4	99	1	0	3	0	1	.00	2	.213	.305	.312
Castillo,Luis,Kane County	A	20	89	340	111	4	4	0	123	71	23	55	1	50	0	4	1	41	18	.69	1	.326	.419	.362
Castro,Dennis,Kane County	A	23	46	138	34	9	0	5	58	12	21	15	1	33	0	2	1	1	0	1.00	0	.246	.318	.420
Castro,Jose,W. Michigan	A	21	113	409	98	20	2	2	128	76	40	76	2	94	11	13	0	51	20	.72	2	.240	.373	.313
Castro,Nelson,Angels	A	20	55	190	37	1	2	0	42	34	22	27	0	50	4	4	1	15	7	.68	2	.195	.306	.221
Castro,Ramon,Kissimmee	A	20	36	120	25	5	0	0	30	6	8	6	0	21	1	0	1	0	0	.00	1	.208	.250	.250
Auburn	A	20	63	224	67	17	0	9	111	40	49	24	0	27	0	0	6	0	1	.00	6	.299	.358	.496
Cavanagh,Mike,San Jose	A	26	6	16	2	0	1	0	4	2	3	2	0	8	0	2	0	0	0	.00	0	.125	.222	.250
Cawhorn,Gerad,Kinston	A	24	85	262	55	12	0	1	70	23	22	29	2	60	2	5	2	4	1	.80	7	.210	.292	.267
Cedeno,Eduardo,Springfield	A	23	81	210	47	7	2	7	79	30	27	14	0	67	5	3	2	7	3	.70	1	.224	.286	.376
Cedeno,Jesus,Tigers	R	20	40	110	28	2	2	3	43	20	14	16	0	26	4	1	1	2	2	.50	1	.255	.366	.391
Cepeda,Jose,Royals	R	21	54	187	65	6	4	0	79	32	21	15	0	5	2	1	4	2	2	.50	0	.348	.394	.422
Cephas,Ben,Beloit	A	23	76	94	16	0	0	0	16	17	1	7	0	25	1	3	0	13	3	.81	0	.170	.235	.170
Cesar,Dionys,Athletics	R	19	48	171	55	11	4	2	80	41	21	23	0	29	2	3	2	17	10	.63	0	.322	.404	.468
Cespedes,Angel,Rockies	R	18	19	57	12	1	1	0	15	11	11	7	0	12	3	0	1	1	4	.20	0	.211	.324	.263
Chambers,Mack,Columbus	A	23	2	4	0	0	0	0	0	0	0	0	1	1	0	0	0	0	1	.00	0	.000	.200	.000
Chambers,Victor,Athletics	R	20	34	110	34	2	3	0	42	11	16	14	1	17	1	0	1	12	4	.75	3	.309	.389	.382
Chamblee,James,Utica	A	21	62	200	51	9	1	2	68	36	16	23	0	45	6	1	1	9	7	.56	5	.255	.348	.340
Champion,Jim,Fort Myers	A	22	99	308	70	14	4	3	101	38	33	26	0	88	12	5	3	3	1	.75	3	.227	.309	.328
Chapman,Eric,Columbus	A	24	54	199	48	9	3	0	63	27	8	19	1	42	0	2	0	23	6	.79	4	.241	.307	.317
Chapman,Scott,Astros	R	18	14	28	8	1	0	0	9	3	1	4	0	4	0	1	0	1	1	.50	2	.286	.375	.321
Charles,Curtis,Orioles	R	20	25	63	10	2	0	0	12	6	3	9	0	29	0	0	0	1	1	.50	1	.159	.264	.190
Charles,Steve,Blue Jays	R	21	48	145	31	4	2	0	39	17	15	24	1	47	4	1	1	7	2	.78	4	.214	.339	.269
Chastain,Dan,Marlins	R	23	4	10	2	0	0	0	2	0	0	0	0	1	0	0	0	1	0	1.00	1	.200	.200	.200
Chavez,Steve,Padres	R	20	55	197	51	7	5	0	68	30	24	24	0	48	5	1	1	5	6	.45	4	.259	.352	.345
Chevalier,Virgil,Utica	A	21	64	250	77	12	2	7	114	34	46	11	0	35	3	0	3	15	6	.71	6	.308	.341	.456
Michigan	A	22	2	6	4	1	0	0	5	2	0	1	0	0	0	0	0	1	0	1.00	0	.667	.714	.833
Choate,Jon,Watertown	A	22	59	196	43	10	2	2	63	28	24	24	0	36	1	0	2	2	3	.40	5	.219	.305	.321
Choi,Kyung,Boise	A	24	21	67	20	2	0	0	22	14	5	9	1	5	0	0	0	3	1	.75	0	.299	.377	.328
Cedar Rapds	A	24	36	123	28	4	2	1	39	14	14	9	0	12	1	1	2	4	1	.80	4	.228	.281	.317
Christenson,Ryan,Sou. Oregon	A	22	49	158	30	4	1	1	39	14	16	22	0	33	0	1	3	5	5	.50	3	.190	.286	.247
Christmon,Drew,Lakeland	A	24	79	273	60	8	6	9	107	34	39	14	1	96	4	1	2	7	2	.78	4	.220	.266	.392
Cisar,Ryan,Blue Jays	R	19	35	72	11	1	0	0	12	10	5	20	0	24	2	1	0	0	0	.00	1	.153	.344	.167
Clark,Howie,High Desert	A	22	100	329	85	20	2	5	124	50	40	32	0	51	4	3	3	12	6	.67	4	.258	.329	.377
Clark,John,Rockies	R	19	52	192	39	5	1	0	46	22	12	14	0	52	4	1	3	6	1	.86	4	.203	.268	.240
Clark,Kevin,Sarasota	A	23	84	293	66	11	0	4	89	23	31	21	0	63	2	1	0	2	5	.29	9	.225	.282	.304
Claudio,Patricio,Bakersfield	A	24	32	128	36	9	3	1	54	19	9	13	0	26	2	2	0	5	7	.42	3	.281	.357	.422
Kinston	A	24	89	298	79	7	4	5	109	37	27	26	2	73	0	5	1	27	11	.71	2	.265	.323	.366
Claybrook,Stephen,Billings	R	23	63	188	54	9	0	1	66	45	14	45	1	52	3	3	1	21	6	.78	2	.287	.430	.351
Clifford,Jim,Wisconsin	A	26	101	307	75	26	3	10	137	46	44	40	2	87	13	1	5	8	4	.67	3	.244	.351	.446
Cline,Pat,Rockford	A	21	112	390	106	27	0	13	172	65	77	58	3	93	11	0	5	6	1	.86	6	.272	.377	.441
Clyburn,Danny,Winston-Sal	A	22	59	227	59	10	2	11	106	27	41	13	1	59	4	0	2	2	4	.33	5	.260	.309	.467
Frederick	A	22	15	45	9	4	0	0	13	4	4	4	0	18	2	0	0	1	1	.50	0	.200	.294	.289
High Desert	A	22	45	160	45	3	1	12	86	20	37	17	1	41	4	0	3	2	1	.67	3	.281	.359	.538
Coach,Calvin,Savannah	A	23	65	218	43	2	1	0	47	15	10	20	1	58	1	2	0	8	4	.67	3	.197	.268	.216
Coats,Nathan,Watertown	A	22	12	29	8	2	1	0	12	2	3	4	0	11	0	0	0	0	0	.00	0	.276	.364	.414
Burlington	R	22	20	64	20	5	0	1	28	8	5	4	0	15	3	1	0	1	0	1.00	1	.313	.380	.438
Coburn,Todd,Huntington	R	24	62	228	64	12	3	4	94	37	39	22	1	47	1	0	0	7	1	.88	5	.281	.347	.412
Coca,Mark,Ogden	A	22	70	277	82	11	1	0	95	61	36	54	1	43	2	4	1	11	13	.46	7	.296	.413	.343
Coe,Ryan,Quad City	A	23	38	92	24	7	0	5	46	16	18	13	0	20	3	0	1	1	2	.33	4	.261	.367	.500
Coffee,Gary,Royals	R	21	52	189	62	9	3	11	110	30	45	28	0	38	0	0	0	2	0	1.00	3	.328	.415	.582
Colburn,Brian,Elizabethtn	R	20	11	40	7	0	0	0	7	3	4	3	0	8	2	0	0	2	0	1.00	1	.175	.267	.175
Cole,Ala,Kane County	A	20	56	122	15	3	0	1	21	10	7	17	0	48	6	3	2	3	1	.75	4	.123	.259	.172
Cole,Eric,Astros	R	20	39	122	33	3	1	0	38	17	12	7	0	21	2	3	0	7	5	.58	0	.270	.321	.311
Coleman,Michael,Michigan	A	20	112	422	113	16	2	11	166	70	61	40	1	93	6	6	3	29	5	.85	7	.268	.338	.393
Collier,Dan,Sarasota	A	25	67	242	62	12	1	12	112	30	44	20	0	83	5	0	3	5	9	.36	3	.256	.322	.463
Collier,Lou,Lynchburg	A	21	114	399	110	19	3	4	147	68	38	51	4	60	7	3	3	31	11	.74	13	.276	.365	.368
Collum,Gary,Columbia	A	24	9	24	6	0	1	0	8	2	7	2	0	7	0	0	2	2	0	1.00	0	.250	.286	.333
Colombino,Carlo,Columbus	A	31	2	2	0	0	0	0	0	0	0	0	0	1	0	0	0	0	0	.00	0	.000	.000	.000
Colon,Ariel,Braves	R	18	30	84	17	2	0	0	19	6	7	9	0	25	3	2	0	1	0	1.00	0	.202	.302	.226
Colon,Jose,Cubs	R	20	40	119	27	4	0	2	37	14	11	10	0	30	3	1	1	8	5	.62	4	.227	.301	.311
Colson,Jeremiah,Expos	R	20	23	48	3	0	1	0	5	4	4	2	0	24	1	1	0	1	2	.33	0	.063	.118	.104
Comeaux,Edward,Charlstn-Sc	A	22	90	243	51	7	1	0	60	38	19	39	0	58	2	3	3	10	7	.59	3	.210	.321	.247
Concepcion,David,Princeton	R	21	60	203	48	10	2	6	80	44	24	42	1	44	1	2	1	10	0	1.00	3	.236	.368	.394
Conley,Brian,Williamsprt	A	21	69	259	65	18	1	1	88	42	23	24	0	49	4	2	3	7	3	.70	4	.251	.321	.340
Connell,Jerry,Cubs	R	18	22	76	16	5	0	1	24	6	6	6	0	12	0	0	1	1	1	.50	3	.211	.268	.316
Conner,Decomba,Princeton	R	22	6	16	2	2	0	0	4	2	5	3	0	3	0	0	0	2	0	1.00	0	.125	.250	.250
Charlstn-Wv	A	22	91	308	81	10	7	5	120	55	40	39	1	77	3	4	6	22	5	.81	6	.263	.346	.390
Contreras,Efrain,Peoria	A	23	98	271	70	9	2	10	113	35	48	27	3	45	3	1	3	1	3	.25	12	.258	.329	.417
Conway,Jeff,Rancho Cuca	A	23	28	67	17	1	0	0	18	9	5	4	0	10	0	2	0	1	1	.50	3	.254	.296	.269
Cook,Hayward,Kane County	A	24	78	261	73	5	1	8	104	50	23	12	0	61	1	2	1	23	4	.85	4	.280	.313	.398
Cook,Jason,Riverside	A	24	6	21	4	1	0	0	5	9	3	5	0	4	0	0	0	0	0	.00	0	.190	.346	.238
Wisconsin	A	24	117	405	109	24	2	5	152	61	64	64	7	44	12	3	6	12	5	.71	8	.269	.380	.375
Cook,John,Lethbridge	R	23	58	220	58	10	2	1	75	26	29	18	1	32	1	4	2	4	3	.57	6	.264	.320	.341

338

1995 Batting -- Single-A and Rookie Leagues

Player	Lg	A	G	AB	H	2B	3B	HR	TB	R	RBI	TBB	IBB	SO	HBP	SH	SF	SB	CS	SB%	GDP	Avg	OBP	SLG
Cooney,James,Charlstn-Sc	A	24	18	46	4	0	0	1	7	2	2	3	0	14	0	0	0	1	0	1.00	1	.087	.143	.152
Cooney,Kyle,Vero Beach	A	23	105	356	99	11	2	6	132	44	54	17	1	50	23	1	2	4	3	.57	15	.278	.349	.371
Cooper,Steve,Savannah	A	26	48	156	39	7	0	0	46	13	12	22	0	51	1	0	1	2	0	1.00	4	.250	.344	.295
Cooper,Tim,Tampa	A	25	63	170	30	3	1	3	44	16	13	24	0	48	5	0	2	1	1	.50	3	.176	.294	.259
Coquillette,Trace,Albany	A	22	128	458	123	27	4	3	167	67	57	64	2	91	9	4	6	17	16	.52	8	.269	.365	.365
Cordero,Edward,Tigers	R	21	49	126	27	2	2	0	33	17	11	12	0	23	4	2	1	11	5	.69	2	.214	.301	.262
Cordero,Pablo,Burlington	A	23	59	190	46	9	2	2	65	21	21	14	0	38	2	3	1	2	1	.67	4	.242	.300	.342
Cornelius,Brian,Lynchburg	A	29	12	39	6	3	0	0	9	2	4	4	0	11	0	1	0	0	1	.00	1	.154	.233	.231
Cornelius,Jon,Batavia	A	22	68	263	69	11	4	3	97	29	41	22	0	59	5	3	2	4	2	.67	4	.262	.329	.369
Cornish,Tim,Ogden	R	23	13	42	5	1	0	0	6	3	2	4	0	19	0	0	0	1	0	1.00	0	.119	.196	.143
Corps,Erick,Rancho Cuca	A	21	73	183	35	6	0	1	44	21	13	22	0	54	2	4	2	1	1	.50	5	.191	.282	.240
Correa,Miguel,Durham	A	21	118	398	94	19	1	19	172	43	70	19	2	95	3	2	3	9	13	.41	6	.236	.274	.432
Corujo,Rey,Burlington	A	24	14	45	6	1	0	0	7	2	0	2	0	8	0	0	0	1	1	.50	2	.133	.170	.156
Bellingham	A	24	60	208	46	15	1	6	81	23	34	23	0	27	1	1	4	6	4	.60	8	.221	.297	.389
Corzo,Boanerge,Braves	R	18	27	87	18	3	0	3	30	7	7	5	0	22	2	0	1	0	0	.00	1	.207	.263	.345
Cossins,Tim,Rangers	R	26	2	4	0	0	0	0	0	0	0	0	0	1	0	0	0	0	0	.00	0	.000	.000	.000
Charlstn-Sc	A	26	22	59	12	5	0	1	20	8	8	9	0	13	1	0	0	2	0	1.00	0	.203	.319	.339
Charlotte	A	26	7	17	1	0	0	0	1	1	0	4	1	5	0	0	0	0	1	.00	0	.059	.238	.059
Costello,Brian,Clearwater	A	21	112	406	101	19	2	9	151	52	56	37	0	88	2	0	0	14	9	.61	9	.249	.315	.372
Cowsill,Brendon,Angels	R	21	34	113	29	5	3	0	40	18	13	18	0	28	0	2	2	7	0	1.00	1	.257	.353	.354
Cox,Chuck,Batavia	A	23	38	124	27	4	2	0	35	13	11	11	0	41	0	0	2	2	0	1.00	5	.218	.281	.282
Cox,Steven,Modesto	A	21	132	483	144	29	3	30	269	95	110	84	6	88	14	0	10	5	4	.56	12	.298	.409	.557
Cox,Rob,Kingsport	R	20	57	188	37	9	0	3	55	29	25	30	1	59	5	1	0	1	3	.25	2	.197	.323	.293
Crane,Todd,Batavia	A	22	27	69	17	3	0	0	20	15	8	13	0	25	1	1	0	2	0	1.00	2	.246	.373	.290
Crespo,Mike,Charlotte	A	25	28	74	12	2	0	0	14	6	3	6	0	23	0	0	0	0	0	.00	0	.162	.225	.189
Cromer,Brandon,Dunedin	A	22	106	329	78	11	3	6	113	40	43	43	3	84	5	5	3	0	5	.00	6	.237	.332	.343
Cromer,David,Modesto	A	21	108	378	98	18	5	14	168	59	52	36	1	66	4	6	6	5	7	.42	10	.259	.325	.444
Cropper,Roger,Lethbridge	R	23	65	243	69	11	7	1	97	38	24	24	1	53	4	6	4	16	5	.76	4	.284	.353	.399
Cross,Adam,Danville	R	22	50	181	55	15	0	1	73	21	16	11	0	16	2	0	1	15	11	.58	7	.304	.349	.403
Crutchfield,David,Cubs	R	21	31	104	24	5	4	0	37	19	8	11	0	33	2	3	1	13	1	.93	1	.231	.314	.356
Cruz,Andres,Twins	R	19	32	112	27	5	1	0	34	10	9	7	1	19	1	0	1	1	0	1.00	4	.241	.289	.304
Cruz,Cirilo,Mariners	R	21	39	146	45	8	0	0	53	22	20	16	0	37	3	2	0	0	2	.00	2	.308	.388	.363
Cruz,Deivi,Burlington	A	21	16	58	8	1	0	1	12	2	9	4	0	14	0	0	0	1	1	.50	1	.138	.194	.207
Bellingham	A	21	62	223	66	17	0	3	92	32	28	19	3	21	0	1	2	6	3	.67	5	.296	.348	.413
Cruz,Francis,Padres	R	21	1	2	0	0	0	0	0	0	0	0	0	1	0	0	0	1	0	1.00	0	.000	.333	.000
Cruz,Jose,Everett	A	22	3	11	5	0	0	0	5	6	2	3	0	3	0	0	0	1	0	1.00	0	.455	.571	.455
Riverside	A	22	35	144	37	7	1	7	67	34	29	24	1	50	0	0	2	3	1	.75	1	.257	.359	.465
Cuellar,Jose,Riverside	A	26	19	45	5	0	0	0	5	7	2	12	0	9	0	0	0	0	0	.00	0	.111	.298	.111
Cuevas,Eduardo,Rancho Cuca	A	22	43	140	34	5	2	1	46	14	24	7	1	16	0	0	3	5	1	.83	6	.243	.273	.329
Clinton	A	22	69	263	68	11	1	2	87	39	31	9	1	31	0	1	3	17	3	.85	5	.259	.280	.331
Cueves,Trent,Yakima	A	19	38	123	25	7	0	1	35	13	8	14	0	22	0	1	1	3	4	.43	3	.203	.283	.285
Culp,Brian,Salem	A	25	128	459	128	33	1	8	187	69	63	71	4	80	4	0	5	8	3	.73	8	.279	.377	.407
Culp,Matt,Watertown	A	23	33	85	11	3	0	1	17	7	8	14	0	26	3	0	1	1	0	1.00	1	.129	.275	.200
Culp,Randy,Vermont	A	21	1	3	0	0	0	0	0	0	0	0	0	0	0	0	0	0	0	.00	0	.000	.000	.000
Expos	R	21	10	33	5	2	0	0	7	2	1	1	0	9	0	0	1	0	1	.00	0	.152	.176	.212
Cunningham,Earl,Lk Elsinore	A	26	78	284	68	13	2	15	130	50	55	15	0	97	6	0	2	8	3	.73	7	.239	.290	.458
Curl,John,Medicne Hat	R	23	69	270	86	26	1	7	135	47	63	31	8	61	0	0	3	5	1	.83	11	.319	.385	.500
Current,Jeremy,Johnson Cty	R	20	23	63	16	3	0	0	19	5	6	8	0	23	3	1	1	0	0	.00	2	.254	.360	.302
Curtis,Kevin,High Desert	A	23	112	399	117	26	1	21	208	70	70	54	1	83	12	0	5	8	6	.57	7	.293	.389	.521
D'Amico,Jeffrey,W.Michigan	A	21	125	434	98	24	1	7	145	56	55	56	2	94	10	4	7	8	5	.62	12	.226	.323	.334
D'Aquila,Tom,High Desert	A	23	110	386	102	10	11	11	167	48	63	45	1	111	4	0	3	8	7	.53	11	.264	.345	.433
Daedelow,Craig,Orioles	R	20	49	170	44	9	0	1	56	35	11	24	0	19	3	1	0	7	2	.78	5	.259	.360	.329
Bluefield	R	20	5	13	0	0	0	0	0	1	1	4	0	3	0	0	0	0	1	.00	0	.000	.222	.000
Dalton,Dee,St. Pete	A	24	118	385	79	16	1	2	103	36	30	45	0	81	3	2	3	10	4	.71	7	.205	.291	.268
Dalton,Jed,Boise	A	23	48	126	33	8	1	0	43	10	10	8	1	20	0	1	0	1	1	.50	2	.262	.306	.341
Daniel,Mike,Lynchburg	A	26	50	169	48	11	1	10	91	31	35	29	1	36	1	2	1	0	2	.00	7	.284	.390	.538
Daniels,Ronney,Expos	R	19	20	74	12	4	2	0	20	6	3	4	0	27	0	0	0	3	1	.75	1	.162	.205	.270
Dantzler,Eric,Bellingham	A	23	6	17	2	1	0	1	6	2	1	0	0	5	0	0	0	1	0	1.00	0	.118	.118	.353
Burlington	A	23	30	84	14	1	0	1	18	6	7	12	0	24	0	1	0	2	0	1.00	5	.167	.263	.214
Darcuiel,Faruq,Wisconsin	A	23	83	282	73	10	3	1	92	29	20	22	0	50	5	4	2	27	6	.82	1	.259	.322	.326
Darden,Tony,Kane County	A	22	86	286	82	15	5	3	116	42	31	40	1	40	8	1	2	5	5	.50	6	.287	.387	.406
Darr,Mike,Fayetteville	A	20	112	395	114	21	2	5	154	58	66	58	2	88	4	0	7	5	2	.71	5	.289	.380	.390
Dasher,Melvin,Royals	R	19	16	35	7	2	0	1	12	3	5	1	0	15	0	0	0	0	0	.00	0	.200	.222	.343
Dasilva,Manny,W.Michigan	A	23	7	19	6	2	1	1	13	5	3	4	0	4	1	1	0	0	0	.00	1	.316	.458	.684
Sou. Oregon	A	23	55	195	48	14	4	3	79	31	33	26	1	25	6	1	3	3	1	.75	9	.246	.348	.405
Davalillo,David,Cedar Rapds	A	21	44	141	38	7	1	0	47	17	16	7	0	32	0	4	1	1	0	1.00	3	.270	.302	.333
Boise	A	21	36	112	25	9	1	1	39	17	12	6	0	21	1	1	0	1	0	1.00	4	.223	.269	.348
Davanon,Jeff,Sou. Oregon	A	22	57	167	42	6	2	1	55	29	17	34	0	49	0	5	1	6	5	.55	1	.251	.376	.329
Davenport,Jeff,Sarasota	A	25	10	22	0	0	0	0	0	1	3	1	0	8	0	0	2	0	0	.00	0	.000	.040	.000
Red Sox	R	25	5	13	1	0	0	0	1	0	0	0	0	3	0	0	0	0	0	.00	0	.077	.077	.077
Davidson,Cleatus,Twins	R	19	21	75	15	2	1	0	19	11	5	10	0	17	0	0	0	8	3	.73	0	.200	.294	.253
Elizabethtn	R	19	39	152	45	6	2	3	64	27	27	11	0	31	3	0	0	10	4	.71	2	.296	.355	.421
Davila,Victor,Dunedin	A	23	109	331	85	14	5	6	127	48	45	24	2	66	8	3	4	1	3	.25	4	.257	.319	.384
Davis,Albert,Pirates	R	19	10	43	13	3	0	3	25	8	9	1	0	6	0	0	0	1	0	1.00	0	.302	.318	.581
Erie	A	19	44	152	35	12	0	2	53	31	12	19	0	26	2	2	3	8	2	.80	3	.230	.318	.349
Davis,Doug,Lk Elsinore	A	33	1	3	1	0	0	0	1	0	0	1	0	1	0	0	0	0	0	.00	0	.333	.500	.333
Davis,James,Princeton	R	23	58	225	62	10	4	3	89	40	29	14	0	33	1	1	2	8	0	1.00	5	.276	.318	.396

339

1995 Batting -- Single-A and Rookie Leagues

																		BATTING	BASERUNNING				PERCENTAGES		
Player	Lg	A	G	AB	H	2B	3B	HR	TB	R	RBI	TBB	IBB	SO	HBP	SH	SF	SB	CS	SB%	GDP	Avg	OBP	SLG
Davis,Ben,Idaho Falls	R	19	52	197	55	8	3	5	84	36	46	17	1	36	1	3	1	0	0	.00	3	.279	.338	.426
Davis,Torrance,Expos	R	20	45	139	38	1	1	0	41	19	5	12	0	25	4	6	1	13	7	.65	2	.273	.346	.295
Dawkins,Walt,Batavia	A	23	58	203	64	11	4	1	86	46	31	27	0	36	4	2	3	15	6	.71	6	.315	.401	.424
Dawson,Charles,Macon	A	24	42	122	30	6	0	3	45	19	13	18	0	27	0	0	2	1	0	1.00	6	.246	.338	.369
De La Cruz,Jesus,Angels	R	22	31	79	19	4	1	0	25	6	10	3	1	17	3	2	0	1	2	.33	2	.241	.294	.316
De La Rosa,Elvis,Jamestown	A	21	14	42	10	2	0	0	12	3	5	1	0	15	0	0	1	1	1	.50	1	.238	.250	.286
Dean,Chris,Riverside	A	22	116	407	102	16	8	6	152	56	45	49	1	98	16	3	7	13	10	.57	6	.251	.349	.373
Dean,Mark,Peoria	A	25	75	190	39	2	2	0	45	19	12	14	0	42	7	5	0	4	3	.57	3	.205	.284	.237
Deares,Greg,St. Pete	A	25	20	51	12	1	0	0	13	3	6	2	0	8	0	0	0	0	0	.00	0	.235	.264	.255
Deboer,Rob,W. Michigan	A	25	104	339	82	25	2	6	129	57	50	58	1	110	4	1	4	11	6	.65	6	.242	.356	.381
Deck,Billy,Johnson Cty	R	19	59	205	53	12	0	1	68	27	30	30	0	52	7	1	2	4	6	.40	4	.259	.369	.332
DeJesus,Malvin,Lakeland	A	24	73	239	72	7	5	3	98	39	23	27	0	51	4	2	1	7	6	.54	1	.301	.380	.410
De La Cruz,Carlos,Tigers	R	20	47	155	51	7	1	2	66	24	17	20	1	45	0	0	0	28	4	.88	1	.329	.406	.426
Lakeland	A	20	2	3	0	0	0	0	0	0	0	0	0	2	0	0	0	0	0	.00	0	.000	.000	.000
De La Cruz,Wilfredo,Yankees	R	20	43	118	23	1	0	0	24	17	7	15	0	36	4	1	0	6	2	.75	2	.195	.307	.203
Delafield,Glenn,Tampa	A	24	7	26	7	1	0	1	11	4	6	2	0	11	1	0	0	1	0	1.00	0	.269	.345	.423
Greensboro	A	24	107	384	80	14	0	4	106	37	29	16	0	107	1	5	1	3	7	.30	12	.208	.241	.276
Delaney,Donnie,Wilmington	A	22	114	360	90	13	7	3	126	22	39	25	0	82	4	4	2	6	9	.40	8	.250	.304	.350
Delaney,Sean,Springfield	A	26	62	188	56	8	2	5	83	24	22	19	1	27	5	1	1	5	1	.83	5	.298	.376	.441
Deleon,Ray,Clinton	A	26	9	30	8	1	0	0	9	3	4	2	0	3	1	0	0	1	0	.00	1	.267	.324	.300
Deleon,Reymundo,Eugene	A	21	50	127	24	2	2	1	33	14	11	13	0	48	1	0	1	2	3	.40	3	.189	.268	.260
DeLeon,Santos,Wisconsin	A	22	9	19	2	0	0	0	2	0	3	0	0	5	0	2	0	1	0	1.00	0	.105	.227	.105
Delgado,Ariel,Angels	R	19	53	189	39	5	3	0	50	26	19	15	0	36	5	1	1	3	5	.63	7	.206	.281	.265
Delgado,Daniel,Pirates	R	19	33	106	19	2	0	0	21	15	7	15	0	16	1	0	0	6	0	1.00	1	.179	.287	.198
Delgado,Jose,Macon	A	21	45	169	40	5	3	3	60	19	16	11	0	28	0	4	2	4	4	.43	2	.237	.280	.355
Dellucci,David,Bluefield	R	22	20	69	23	5	1	2	36	11	12	6	1	7	1	0	1	3	1	.75	1	.333	.390	.522
Frederick	A	22	28	96	27	3	0	1	33	16	10	12	1	10	3	0	0	1	2	.33	3	.281	.378	.344
Deluca,Nic,New Jersey	A	24	3	8	2	0	0	0	2	1	0	0	0	2	0	0	0	0	0	.00	0	.250	.250	.250
Deman,Lou,New Jersey	A	23	52	186	41	8	0	2	55	22	24	12	0	60	5	1	1	2	3	.40	3	.220	.284	.296
Demetral,Scott,Ogden	R	23	60	231	63	11	1	1	79	37	27	22	1	42	3	6	0	3	4	.43	6	.273	.344	.342
Denbow,Don,Burlington	A	23	105	326	58	7	1	12	103	42	33	42	0	143	5	1	0	14	2	.88	2	.178	.282	.316
Denning,Wes,Vermont	A	23	56	168	33	0	2	0	37	30	17	23	0	45	4	4	3	16	5	.76	1	.196	.303	.220
Dennis,Brian,Rockford	A	24	51	102	21	3	0	2	30	10	16	13	0	28	16	1	3	1	1	.50	3	.206	.373	.294
Dennis,Les,Oneonta	A	23	48	148	39	6	2	1	52	24	13	14	0	40	3	0	2	5	2	.71	4	.264	.335	.351
Dent,Darrell,Orioles	R	19	36	125	35	7	3	0	48	24	6	21	0	22	2	0	1	6	2	.75	2	.280	.389	.384
Depastino,Joe,Michigan	A	22	98	325	90	20	4	10	148	47	53	30	1	70	8	1	4	3	3	.50	5	.277	.349	.455
Derosso,Tony,Michigan	A	20	106	382	89	20	1	13	150	57	50	38	2	93	11	1	2	9	1	.90	5	.233	.319	.393
Derotal,Francisco,Rancho Cuca	A	22	29	56	11	2	0	2	19	9	5	3	0	20	2	1	0	1	0	1.00	0	.196	.262	.339
Deschenes,Marc,Watertown	A	23	42	144	30	4	1	1	39	18	14	18	0	45	3	5	4	6	2	.75	3	.208	.302	.271
Desensi,Craig,Butte	R	23	29	72	15	2	1	0	19	10	5	6	0	14	4	0	2	2	0	1.00	3	.208	.305	.264
Deshazer,Jeremy,Astros	R	19	38	106	26	6	1	0	34	13	11	8	0	19	4	0	1	6	1	.86	2	.245	.319	.321
Diaz,Edwin,Charlotte	A	21	115	450	128	26	5	8	188	48	56	33	0	94	7	3	2	8	13	.38	10	.284	.341	.418
Diaz,Einar,Kinston	A	23	104	373	98	21	0	6	137	46	43	12	2	29	8	1	4	3	6	.33	6	.263	.297	.367
Diaz,Ivan,Johnson Cty	R	21	6	14	3	0	0	0	3	0	2	0	0	3	0	0	0	0	0	.00	0	.214	.214	.214
Diaz,Linardo,Batavia	A	21	22	75	18	4	1	1	27	13	7	3	0	17	6	4	0	4	1	.80	1	.240	.321	.360
Clearwater	A	21	11	33	7	1	0	0	8	1	1	3	0	7	0	0	1	0	0	.00	1	.212	.270	.242
Piedmont	A	21	9	12	1	1	0	0	2	0	0	0	0	2	0	0	0	0	0	.00	0	.083	.083	.167
Dieguez,Mike,Pittsfield	A	23	59	181	39	7	1	0	48	31	17	31	0	29	12	1	0	0	5	.00	5	.215	.366	.265
Dillingham,Dan,Lethbridge	R	22	51	161	28	7	0	3	44	21	16	15	2	49	2	2	2	4	2	.67	0	.174	.250	.273
Disalle,Javier,Orioles	R	20	4	12	4	0	0	0	4	0	1	0	0	1	0	0	0	1	1	.50	0	.333	.333	.333
Dishington,Nate,Savannah	A	21	124	444	95	17	5	11	155	56	44	62	4	154	17	0	6	13	7	.65	14	.214	.329	.349
Dobrolsky,Bill,Stockton	A	26	88	252	68	14	3	2	94	28	30	25	0	37	6	2	5	3	4	.43	4	.270	.344	.373
Doezie,Troy,New Jersey	A	22	23	84	16	5	2	1	28	15	12	10	0	18	1	0	0	1	0	1.00	5	.190	.284	.333
Domingo,Tyrone,Tigers	R	21	35	107	22	1	2	0	27	18	1	5	0	25	3	0	0	20	4	.83	1	.206	.261	.252
Donati,John,Cedar Rapds	A	23	116	381	109	24	2	16	185	63	75	57	1	92	10	1	4	5	3	.63	4	.286	.389	.486
Donato,Dan,Greensboro	A	23	108	387	123	30	1	7	176	55	69	37	5	46	4	0	3	7	6	.54	12	.318	.381	.455
Tampa	A	23	3	8	2	0	0	1	5	1	1	0	0	2	1	0	0	0	0	.00	0	.250	.333	.625
Doty,Derrin,Lk Elsinore	A	26	94	324	80	12	0	8	116	46	35	37	0	54	3	2	2	16	6	.73	4	.247	.328	.358
Dougherty,Keith,Eugene	A	22	2	8	1	0	0	0	1	0	0	0	0	3	0	0	0	0	0	.00	0	.125	.125	.125
Danville	R	22	25	85	25	1	5	4	47	14	14	3	0	14	1	1	0	1	1	.50	2	.294	.322	.553
Douglas,John,Blue Jays	R	22	55	179	42	6	0	2	54	21	26	24	1	35	18	3	4	6	4	.60	4	.235	.373	.302
Downs,Brian,White Sox	R	21	37	130	37	8	0	2	51	22	18	7	0	27	2	0	0	0	1	.00	2	.285	.331	.392
Drent,Brian,Bristol	R	22	49	161	39	13	0	5	67	31	26	39	1	58	3	0	3	16	2	.89	4	.242	.393	.416
Hickory	A	22	24	69	13	5	1	1	23	8	5	6	0	28	4	0	1	0	4	.00	0	.188	.288	.333
Driskell,Jeff,Lakeland	A	24	23	61	16	4	0	2	26	8	8	5	0	17	0	0	1	1	0	1.00	1	.262	.313	.426
Drizos,Justin,Portland	A	22	71	224	46	15	1	3	72	37	24	54	1	55	3	1	1	7	1	.88	3	.205	.365	.321
Ducasse,Luis,Athletics	R	19	6	16	1	0	0	0	1	1	1	5	0	8	0	0	1	0	0	.00	0	.063	.273	.063
Dukart,Derek,Greensboro	A	24	86	305	78	21	2	6	121	35	40	28	4	59	2	2	4	2	3	.40	11	.256	.319	.397
Duncan,Robbie,Danville	R	20	49	142	33	3	1	0	38	23	8	29	0	45	5	1	1	5	3	.63	1	.232	.379	.268
Dunn,Todd,Stockton	A	25	67	249	73	20	2	7	118	44	40	19	2	67	2	1	1	14	3	.82	5	.293	.347	.474
Dunwoody,Todd,Kane County	A	21	132	494	140	20	8	14	218	89	89	52	7	105	8	2	9	39	11	.78	7	.283	.355	.441
Durkin,Chris,San Bernrdo	A	25	57	164	44	10	1	8	80	24	31	28	0	48	1	1	3	9	6	.60	3	.268	.372	.488
Durrington,Trent,Boise	A	20	50	140	24	4	1	3	39	23	19	17	0	35	2	2	2	2	0	1.00	4	.171	.267	.279
Durso,Joe,Pr. William	A	25	58	178	38	3	2	4	57	16	22	16	1	31	2	1	1	0	0	.00	2	.213	.284	.320
Duverge,Salvadore,Rockies	R	20	46	164	47	9	3	1	65	22	18	20	1	36	6	0	3	11	4	.73	5	.287	.378	.396
Eaddy,Keith,High Desert	A	25	99	336	82	17	4	12	143	58	42	43	0	107	10	3	3	20	9	.69	8	.244	.344	.426
Eaglin,Mike,Macon	A	23	129	530	141	15	4	2	170	82	30	64	0	94	1	5	3	41	13	.76	8	.266	.352	.321

1995 Batting -- Single-A and Rookie Leagues

Player	Lg	A	G	AB	H	2B	3B	HR	TB	R	RBI	TBB	IBB	SO	HBP	SH	SF	SB	CS	SB%	GDP	Avg	OBP	SLG
									BATTING										BASERUNNING			PERCENTAGES		
Ealy,Tracey,San Jose	A	24	12	32	5	0	0	0	5	7	2	2	0	12	1	0	0	0	0	.00	2	.156	.229	.156
Savannah	A	24	101	370	90	18	1	7	131	38	35	41	3	103	2	3	3	8	5	.62	10	.243	.320	.354
Ebbert,Chad,Clinton	A	22	2	5	0	0	0	0	0	0	0	0	0	1	0	0	0	0	0	.00	0	.000	.000	.000
Padres	R	22	35	127	40	5	3	2	57	18	21	9	0	29	1	0	1	2	2	.50	4	.315	.362	.449
Idaho Falls	R	22	1	3	1	0	0	0	1	0	0	1	0	1	0	0	0	0	0	.00	1	.333	.500	.333
Echols,Mandell,Hudson Vall	A	22	58	215	61	8	3	1	78	31	21	14	0	48	5	0	1	15	13	.54	5	.284	.340	.363
Eddie,Steve,Charlstn-Wv	A	25	115	331	91	16	3	6	131	45	47	24	0	46	7	3	6	10	3	.77	9	.275	.332	.396
Edmondson,Tracy,Kingsport	R	21	44	155	41	11	0	3	61	36	25	27	1	34	2	2	1	8	1	.89	0	.265	.378	.394
Edwards,Aaron,Erie	A	22	15	53	14	0	0	0	14	10	3	6	1	10	0	1	0	7	2	.78	2	.264	.339	.264
Augusta	A	22	47	160	42	4	2	0	50	29	9	11	0	39	1	1	1	10	4	.71	2	.263	.312	.313
Edwards,Donald,Burlington	R	19	42	126	20	1	0	0	21	18	5	17	0	35	2	0	0	5	2	.71	2	.159	.269	.167
Elam,Brett,Portland	A	23	33	84	12	0	0	0	12	11	8	17	0	17	1	2	0	3	2	.60	3	.143	.291	.143
Asheville	A	23	1	2	0	0	0	0	0	0	0	0	0	1	0	0	0	0	0	.00	0	.000	.000	.000
Elliott,Dave,Helena	R	22	54	172	45	11	1	7	79	35	37	33	1	29	3	1	4	3	5	.38	3	.262	.382	.459
Elliott,Dawan,Pirates	R	19	34	109	24	1	2	0	29	8	9	6	0	30	0	0	2	3	0	1.00	3	.220	.261	.266
Elliott,Zach,Martinsvlle	R	22	45	151	54	10	4	2	78	46	19	32	1	30	7	1	2	13	5	.72	3	.358	.484	.517
Ellis,Kevin,Daytona	A	24	120	430	116	17	6	6	163	57	66	26	1	73	10	0	4	6	3	.67	11	.270	.323	.379
Ellison,Tony,Williamsprt	A	21	5	18	4	0	0	1	7	5	2	2	0	5	1	0	0	0	0	.00	0	.222	.333	.389
Ellison,Skeeter,Eugene	A	20	19	15	2	0	0	0	2	5	1	5	0	7	0	0	1	4	2	.67	0	.133	.333	.133
Braves	R	20	20	62	14	4	1	0	20	4	4	6	0	27	0	0	0	1	4	.20	0	.226	.294	.323
Emmons,Scott,Oneonta	A	22	67	242	48	15	3	2	75	24	25	25	0	62	3	2	5	1	1	.50	5	.198	.276	.310
Encarnacion,Anito,Cedar Rapds	A	23	42	86	18	3	0	0	21	4	6	2	0	12	0	1	0	0	0	.00	4	.209	.227	.244
Encarnacion,Juan,Fayettevlle	A	20	124	457	129	31	7	16	222	62	72	30	0	113	8	1	2	5	6	.45	10	.282	.336	.486
Encarnacion,Pedro,White Sox	R	21	10	24	8	0	0	0	8	1	1	1	0	4	0	1	0	2	1	.67	0	.333	.360	.333
Engle,Beau,Mets	R	21	10	28	5	2	1	0	9	3	1	2	0	3	0	0	0	0	0	.00	2	.179	.233	.321
Engleka,Matt,Jamestown	A	23	44	166	47	8	2	2	65	32	20	20	0	28	4	1	3	11	5	.69	5	.283	.368	.392
Ennis,Wayne,Princeton	R	19	10	21	1	0	0	0	1	4	2	0	0	8	0	1	0	0	0	.00	1	.048	.048	.048
Erickson,Corey,Mets	R	19	53	178	50	6	1	7	79	38	35	37	3	40	4	0	5	10	3	.77	2	.281	.406	.444
Kingsport	R	19	2	9	3	0	0	1	6	1	4	0	0	3	0	0	0	0	0	.00	0	.333	.333	.667
Erstad,Darin,Angels	R	22	4	18	10	1	0	0	11	2	1	1	0	1	0	0	0	1	0	1.00	0	.556	.579	.611
Lk Elsinore	A	22	25	113	41	7	3	5	69	24	24	6	0	22	0	0	1	3	0	1.00	1	.363	.392	.611
Erwin,Mat,Elmira	A	23	68	260	68	12	2	4	96	22	39	22	2	36	6	0	2	2	1	.67	10	.262	.331	.369
Escandon,Emiliano,Spokane	A	21	13	44	14	1	1	1	20	7	12	6	0	11	1	0	0	1	0	1.00	0	.318	.412	.455
Espada,Angel,Danville	R	21	33	113	34	0	1	1	39	17	8	12	0	16	0	1	0	16	4	.80	3	.301	.368	.345
Espinal,Juan,Clinton	A	21	116	336	70	11	0	7	102	28	46	47	2	79	4	6	7	3	3	.50	8	.208	.307	.304
Espiritu,Mike,Cedar Rapds	A	24	9	24	4	0	0	0	4	1	2	7	1	3	0	0	0	1	1	.50	2	.167	.355	.167
Estrada,Josue,Albany	A	21	70	235	50	11	1	2	69	27	17	24	3	70	2	3	0	2	3	.40	7	.213	.291	.294
Evans,Jason,South Bend	A	25	101	335	94	17	4	6	137	70	36	79	1	74	6	8	3	11	4	.73	3	.281	.423	.409
Evans,Kyle,Hudson Vall	A	22	57	189	45	11	1	4	70	31	25	27	1	39	7	0	2	4	1	.80	3	.238	.351	.370
Evans,Mick,Wilmington	A	23	96	317	69	15	1	8	110	26	36	27	3	79	2	4	1	0	2	.00	2	.218	.282	.347
Evans,Stan,Clearwater	A	25	89	286	71	5	3	0	82	34	32	29	0	33	0	4	3	10	5	.67	6	.248	.314	.287
Evans,Tom,Dunedin	A	21	130	444	124	29	3	9	186	63	66	51	0	80	8	3	7	7	2	.78	10	.279	.359	.419
Facione,Chris,Lakeland	A	25	110	400	117	17	6	5	161	44	56	35	3	76	2	2	4	20	10	.67	13	.293	.349	.403
Faggett,Ethan,Michigan	A	21	115	398	97	11	7	8	146	56	47	37	3	112	4	3	2	23	7	.77	9	.244	.313	.367
Fagley,Dan,Marlins	R	21	16	33	6	0	0	0	6	4	4	4	0	8	1	1	0	0	0	.00	1	.182	.289	.182
Failla,Paul,Cedar Rapds	A	23	129	459	116	23	4	2	153	77	48	66	0	102	2	7	3	30	19	.61	9	.253	.347	.333
Faircloth,Kevin,San Bernrdo	A	23	56	146	27	3	0	0	30	23	6	14	0	40	10	4	2	7	3	.70	2	.185	.297	.205
Falciglia,Anthony,Johnson Cty	R	23	33	118	37	14	0	4	63	18	26	12	0	34	1	0	0	1	0	1.00	4	.314	.373	.534
Savannah	A	23	23	71	12	2	0	0	14	4	5	9	0	17	1	0	1	1	1	.50	1	.169	.268	.197
Fana,Chico,Batavia	A	22	20	61	16	1	0	0	17	5	4	2	0	11	0	1	0	0	0	.00	1	.262	.286	.279
Fantauzzi,John,Asheville	A	24	107	329	70	20	0	8	114	38	44	51	2	79	3	1	2	1	1	.50	6	.213	.322	.347
Farner,Matt,Medicne Hat	R	21	45	142	39	3	3	2	54	28	24	26	3	48	1	0	0	9	5	.64	3	.275	.391	.380
Fauske,Joshua,White Sox	R	22	33	105	27	7	0	4	46	18	18	11	1	22	3	1	1	1	0	1.00	1	.257	.342	.438
Febles,Carlos,Royals	R	20	54	188	53	13	5	3	85	40	20	26	0	30	4	1	0	15	8	.65	5	.282	.381	.452
Fehrenbach,Todd,Billings	R	20	15	32	3	0	0	0	3	2	0	5	0	13	0	0	0	1	0	1.00	0	.094	.216	.094
Felix,Pedro,Bellingham	A	19	43	113	31	2	1	0	35	14	16	7	0	33	0	2	2	1	1	.50	2	.274	.311	.310
Feliz,Edgar,Pirates	R	18	17	55	13	4	0	0	17	4	8	2	0	14	0	0	1	0	2	.00	1	.236	.259	.309
Ferguson,Dwight,Red Sox	R	19	22	62	12	3	0	0	15	10	6	17	0	24	4	0	0	4	3	.57	0	.194	.398	.242
Fernandez,Antonio,Visalia	A	23	90	309	70	10	1	2	88	25	32	14	0	48	1	1	2	1	0	1.00	18	.227	.261	.285
Fernandez,Jose,Vermont	A	21	66	270	74	6	7	4	106	38	41	13	2	51	1	1	2	29	4	.88	2	.274	.308	.393
Fernandez,Randy,Huntington	R	22	15	39	12	0	0	0	12	2	3	5	0	16	1	0	2	2	4	.33	0	.308	.386	.308
Ferrier,Ross,St. Lucie	A	24	68	234	47	6	2	7	78	27	23	18	1	69	3	1	2	5	5	.29	6	.201	.265	.333
Columbia	A	24	23	70	13	1	0	2	20	6	5	8	0	20	1	0	0	5	0	1.00	4	.186	.278	.286
Feuerstein,Dave,Portland	A	22	70	269	72	10	3	5	103	40	44	23	2	41	2	3	3	20	8	.71	9	.268	.327	.383
Fick,Chris,St. Pete	A	26	113	348	102	25	3	13	172	56	52	38	2	79	10	0	3	1	2	.33	9	.293	.376	.494
Figueroa,Danny,Asheville	A	22	80	227	53	22	1	3	86	34	22	24	0	73	6	7	3	3	7	.30	2	.233	.319	.379
Figueroa,Luis,Mariners	R	19	32	120	35	2	0	0	37	14	11	12	0	9	2	0	1	1	2	.33	4	.292	.363	.308
Filchner,Duane,Sou. Oregon	A	23	62	189	52	4	0	6	74	34	34	35	2	28	3	1	2	12	8	.60	4	.275	.391	.392
Finnieston,Adam,Spokane	A	23	10	38	9	0	0	0	9	4	4	1	0	9	1	1	1	0	1	.00	0	.237	.268	.237
Fithian,Grant,Tampa	A	24	3	4	1	0	0	0	1	0	0	0	0	0	0	0	0	0	0	.00	0	.250	.250	.250
Greensboro	A	24	51	151	34	8	1	2	50	16	12	19	0	45	1	3	3	5	4	.56	5	.225	.310	.331
Fitzpatrick,Will,Stockton	A	25	13	29	6	1	0	1	10	5	4	8	0	16	0	0	0	0	0	.00	0	.207	.378	.345
Beloit	A	25	55	115	23	5	1	2	36	18	14	38	1	35	4	0	1	5	3	.63	0	.200	.411	.313
Flanigan,Steven,Erie	A	24	25	85	23	4	1	1	32	8	10	1	0	23	1	0	1	1	0	1.00	1	.271	.287	.376
Flores,Eric,Great Falls	R	19	40	83	19	5	1	0	26	12	9	16	0	28	0	1	0	3	1	.75	1	.229	.354	.313
Flores,Jose,Clearwater	A	23	49	185	41	4	3	1	54	25	19	15	0	27	4	7	1	12	5	.71	4	.222	.293	.292
Piedmont	A	23	61	186	49	7	0	0	56	22	19	24	0	29	3	5	4	11	8	.58	6	.263	.350	.301

341

1995 Batting -- Single-A and Rookie Leagues

Player	Lg	A	G	AB	H	2B	3B	HR	TB	R	RBI	TBB	IBB	SO	HBP	SH	SF	SB	CS	SB%	GDP	Avg	OBP	SLG
Flores,Oswaldo,Red Sox	R	18	14	33	9	0	0	1	12	8	6	3	0	11	0	0	0	1	1	.50	0	.273	.333	.364
Foote,Derek,Eugene	A	21	1	0	0	0	0	0	0	0	0	1	0	0	0	0	0	0	0	.00	0	.000	1.000	.000
Danville	R	21	17	58	21	4	0	3	34	10	9	3	0	21	1	0	0	0	0	.00	0	.362	.403	.586
Forkerway,Troy,Daytona	A	25	75	188	38	4	0	1	45	22	11	20	0	29	1	4	1	10	1	.91	5	.202	.281	.239
Fortin,Blaine,Blue Jays	R	18	42	112	23	4	1	1	32	13	14	5	0	16	3	0	2	0	2	.00	3	.205	.254	.286
Fortin,Troy,Fort Wayne	A	21	112	407	105	21	1	7	149	49	48	38	1	69	8	0	3	4	5	.44	7	.258	.331	.366
Foster,Jim,Frederick	A	24	128	429	112	27	3	6	163	44	56	51	5	63	8	0	5	2	3	.40	10	.261	.347	.380
Foster,Jeff,W. Palm Bch	A	24	65	179	37	7	3	4	62	22	26	10	1	42	1	3	1	10	3	.77	4	.207	.251	.346
Fowler,B.J.,Mariners	R	26	97	25	4	3	0	35	13	8	7	0	29	4	0	0	4	4	.50	0	.258	.333	.361
Francisco,Vicente,W. Michigan	A	23	85	277	68	8	2	1	83	41	25	30	0	48	1	12	1	4	8	.33	1	.245	.320	.300
Franco,Raul,Marlins	R	20	49	184	51	12	0	0	63	30	22	16	0	14	2	1	2	9	3	.75	5	.277	.338	.342
Franklin,Bo,Danville	R	21	51	148	36	5	2	0	45	30	17	28	1	51	0	1	1	9	5	.64	4	.243	.362	.304
Fraser,Joseph,Elizabethtn	R	21	46	184	48	4	0	4	64	29	21	20	0	22	2	2	2	5	4	.56	5	.261	.337	.348
Fort Wayne	A	21	5	15	3	0	0	0	3	0	2	0	0	5	0	0	1	1	0	1.00	0	.200	.188	.200
Frazier,Ty,Spokane	A	21	51	147	25	3	0	0	28	15	9	11	0	46	5	5	0	8	4	.67	3	.170	.252	.190
Freel,Ryan,St. Cathrns	A	20	65	243	68	10	5	3	97	30	29	22	0	49	7	7	5	12	7	.63	3	.280	.350	.399
Freeman,Ricky,Rockford	A	24	131	466	127	33	5	11	203	89	67	61	3	57	7	0	1	8	3	.73	11	.273	.364	.436
Freeman,Sean,Lakeland	A	24	119	414	120	21	2	6	163	42	65	49	3	98	2	0	7	3	4	.43	3	.290	.362	.394
Freeman,Terrance,Athletics	R	21	34	95	23	0	1	0	25	14	5	10	0	25	3	1	0	3	3	.50	3	.242	.333	.263
Freire,Alejandro,Quad City	A	21	125	417	127	23	1	15	197	71	65	50	1	83	6	2	7	9	5	.64	9	.305	.381	.472
Freitas,Joseph,New Jersey	A	22	14	47	9	6	0	0	15	8	9	5	0	18	1	0	2	2	0	1.00	1	.191	.273	.319
French,Anton,Peoria	A	20	116	417	114	19	5	10	173	71	37	37	2	98	6	7	0	57	16	.78	6	.273	.341	.415
Durham	A	20	7	26	7	1	0	0	8	3	2	3	0	2	1	0	0	4	1	.80	0	.269	.367	.308
Frias,Ovidio,Pirates	R	19	29	99	28	5	2	0	37	16	7	7	0	10	3	0	0	1	0	1.00	1	.283	.349	.374
Fric,Sean,Rockford	A	23	7	17	4	1	0	0	5	3	2	4	0	2	0	0	0	0	0	.00	1	.235	.381	.294
Friedrich,Steve,Hickory	A	23	136	532	134	24	6	6	188	56	50	16	0	107	5	2	4	19	16	.54	16	.252	.278	.353
Froschauer,Trevor,Kissimmee	A	23	102	325	64	8	1	12	110	32	40	49	0	121	13	0	3	2	0	1.00	10	.197	.323	.338
Frost,Robert,Kingsport	R	23	11	30	10	2	0	0	12	3	7	1	0	5	1	1	0	1	0	1.00	0	.333	.375	.400
Frye,Dan,Winston-Sal	A	26	7	11	2	1	0	1	6	3	2	5	0	4	0	0	0	0	0	.00	0	.182	.438	.545
Fuller,Brian,Jamestown	A	23	40	137	37	9	1	6	66	28	24	19	1	26	3	0	0	4	2	.67	0	.270	.371	.482
Fullmer,Brad,Albany	A	21	123	468	151	38	4	8	221	69	67	36	4	33	17	0	6	10	10	.50	9	.323	.387	.472
Funaro,Joe,Elmira	A	23	56	189	50	10	3	2	72	24	16	17	1	21	0	1	2	5	2	.71	3	.265	.322	.381
Fussell,Denny,Charlstn-Wv	A	25	20	44	11	2	0	0	13	4	7	4	1	10	0	0	1	1	0	1.00	0	.250	.306	.295
Gabriel,Denio,Bluefield	R	20	53	180	52	4	0	1	59	39	24	25	0	36	1	6	1	31	8	.79	1	.289	.377	.328
Gainey,Bryon,Columbia	A	20	124	448	109	20	5	14	181	49	64	30	1	157	9	0	2	1	3	.25	7	.243	.303	.404
Galarza,Joel,San Jose	A	22	58	209	61	13	1	7	97	28	44	11	0	35	2	4	5	6	2	.75	4	.292	.326	.464
Gallagher,Shawn,Rangers	R	19	58	210	71	13	3	7	111	34	40	19	0	44	1	0	3	17	4	.81	7	.338	.391	.529
Hudson Vall	A	19	5	20	3	2	0	0	5	1	4	1	0	4	1	0	0	0	0	.00	2	.150	.227	.250
Gallone,Santy,Clearwater	A	24	90	283	69	15	1	6	104	45	40	47	1	39	18	2	7	5	3	.63	11	.244	.377	.367
Gama,Rick,Idaho Falls	R	23	70	266	85	16	2	8	129	71	58	55	1	29	2	3	10	17	4	.81	2	.320	.426	.485
Gambill,Chad,Asheville	A	20	106	367	94	25	1	8	145	34	57	16	2	92	2	3	4	6	4	.60	9	.256	.288	.395
Gann,Steve,Winston-Sal	A	26	15	41	10	2	0	0	12	5	5	2	0	5	2	2	1	0	1	.00	0	.244	.304	.293
Charlstn-Wv	A	26	15	48	10	1	0	0	11	3	4	6	0	7	0	0	1	1	1	.50	1	.208	.291	.229
Garcia,Adrian,Durham	A	23	5	12	3	1	0	0	4	2	2	4	0	4	0	0	0	1	0	1.00	0	.250	.438	.333
Garcia,Amaury,Kane County	A	21	26	58	14	4	1	1	23	19	5	18	0	12	1	0	0	5	2	.71	1	.241	.429	.397
Elmira	A	21	62	231	63	7	3	0	76	40	17	34	2	50	4	3	0	41	12	.77	1	.273	.375	.329
Garcia,Apostol,Jamestown	A	19	60	200	47	8	3	0	61	25	21	10	0	36	3	7	1	10	6	.63	3	.235	.280	.305
Garcia,Carlos,Fort Wayne	A	20	34	95	18	5	0	0	23	13	10	7	0	13	0	3	0	11	0	1.00	0	.189	.245	.242
Elizabethtn	R	20	62	235	72	15	1	5	104	42	34	16	0	41	4	3	4	27	8	.77	5	.306	.355	.443
Garcia,Franklin,Beloit	A	21	26	61	14	2	0	0	16	7	6	5	0	14	0	1	1	5	2	.71	2	.230	.284	.262
Garcia,Guillermo,Winston-Sal	A	24	78	245	58	10	2	3	81	26	29	28	0	32	1	2	2	2	2	.50	7	.237	.315	.331
Garcia,Jaime,Vermont	A	24	50	149	36	7	2	2	53	22	16	27	2	30	4	2	1	1	1	.50	1	.242	.370	.356
Garcia,Jesse,Frederick	A	22	124	365	82	11	3	3	108	52	27	49	0	75	9	7	7	5	10	.33	5	.225	.329	.296
Garcia,Julio,Yankees	R	23	4	13	2	0	0	0	2	1	3	1	0	3	0	0	0	2	0	1.00	0	.154	.200	.154
Garcia,Luis,White Sox	R	20	45	161	37	5	2	0	46	33	12	20	0	29	0	3	3	9	3	.75	3	.230	.310	.286
Garcia,Manuel,Visalia	A	27	12	40	4	2	1	0	8	3	4	1	0	18	2	0	1	3	0	1.00	0	.100	.159	.200
Garcia,Miguel,Great Falls	R	21	59	171	38	7	2	1	52	32	20	18	0	47	5	2	1	22	4	.85	2	.222	.313	.304
Garcia,Neal,Fayettevlle	A	23	88	251	58	12	1	7	93	46	33	59	0	49	10	2	4	3	6	.33	5	.231	.392	.371
Garcia,Ozzie,St. Pete	A	22	105	315	55	4	0	0	59	37	13	28	0	66	6	7	0	24	11	.69	8	.175	.255	.187
Garcia,Vincente,Salem	A	21	119	457	111	26	1	10	169	62	41	53	1	73	1	5	2	5	0	1.00	10	.243	.322	.370
Gargiulo,Mike,Frederick	A	21	6	11	3	0	0	0	3	1	0	0	0	4	1	0	0	0	0	.00	0	.273	.333	.273
High Desert	A	21	14	34	7	1	0	0	8	2	4	1	0	9	0	1	0	0	1	.00	1	.206	.229	.235
Bluefield	R	21	48	180	52	7	4	3	76	24	21	10	1	35	0	1	1	1	2	.33	6	.289	.325	.422
Garman,Sean,New Jersey	A	22	50	133	26	5	0	0	31	20	8	21	0	25	1	3	1	1	0	1.00	4	.195	.308	.233
Garrett,Jason,Elmira	A	23	41	131	29	4	1	1	38	15	11	11	0	31	3	1	0	2	1	.67	5	.221	.297	.290
Gatti,Dom,Charlstn-Sc	A	24	96	335	77	8	4	0	93	50	32	53	0	38	4	3	4	39	15	.72	5	.230	.338	.278
Gavello,Tim,Ogden	R	24	8	26	7	3	0	0	10	3	4	8	0	5	0	0	0	0	0	.00	0	.269	.441	.385
Gazarek,Marty,Rockford	A	23	107	399	104	24	1	3	139	57	53	27	1	58	8	2	3	7	5	.58	8	.261	.318	.348
Gerteisen,Aaron,Peoria	A	23	73	218	47	6	1	2	61	24	17	25	0	29	0	3	1	7	5	.58	4	.216	.295	.280
Giallella,Brian,Butte	R	23	33	100	24	0	0	3	33	12	20	11	0	14	0	0	2	1	0	1.00	1	.240	.310	.330
Giardi,Rocco,Greensboro	A	23	46	101	17	4	0	1	24	10	5	15	0	17	3	0	1	3	4	.43	2	.168	.292	.238
Gibbs,Kevin,Yakima	A	22	52	182	57	6	4	1	74	36	18	36	1	46	5	2	3	38	5	.88	3	.313	.434	.407
Vero Beach	A	22	7	20	5	1	0	0	6	1	2	0	0	0	0	0	0	1	0	1.00	0	.250	.250	.300
San Bernrdo	A	22	5	13	3	1	0	0	4	1	0	0	0	2	0	0	0	1	0	1.00	0	.231	.231	.308
Gibralter,David,Michigan	A	21	121	456	115	34	4	16	199	48	82	20	2	79	8	3	4	3	4	.43	7	.252	.293	.436
Gibson,Derrick,Asheville	A	21	135	506	148	16	10	32	280	91	115	29	5	136	19	1	6	31	13	.70	10	.292	.350	.553
Gill,Sean,Kingsport	R	24	8	18	0	0	0	0	0	1	0	0	0	10	0	0	0	0	0	.00	0	.000	.053	.000

1995 Batting -- Single-A and Rookie Leagues

			BATTING															BASERUNNING				PERCENTAGES		
Player	Lg	A	G	AB	H	2B	3B	HR	TB	R	RBI	TBB	IBB	SO	HBP	SH	SF	SB	CS	SB%	GDP	Avg	OBP	SLG
Gipner,Mark,Greensboro	A	22	7	20	3	1	0	0	4	0	2	1	0	6	0	0	1	0	0	.00	0	.150	.182	.200
Oneonta	A	22	25	81	8	1	0	0	9	0	0	15	0	20	0	0	0	1	1	.50	4	.099	.240	.111
Giudice,John,Salem	A	25	99	356	92	21	4	7	142	49	48	24	2	81	4	0	3	7	4	.64	7	.258	.310	.399
Glass,Chip,Columbus	A	25	115	402	116	17	5	5	158	70	45	37	1	47	5	5	0	37	8	.82	5	.289	.356	.393
Glavine,Mike,Burlington	R	23	46	155	38	10	0	11	81	28	28	22	0	37	1	0	2	1	0	1.00	0	.245	.339	.523
Glenn,Darrin,Burlington	A	25	62	182	39	4	1	9	72	35	27	23	0	59	5	0	1	4	3	.57	8	.214	.318	.396
Goligoski,Jason,Pr.William	A	24	95	300	65	7	2	0	76	42	24	52	0	47	3	2	3	16	5	.76	4	.217	.335	.253
Gomez,Paul,Columbia	A	23	68	181	37	10	1	4	61	19	20	33	0	65	4	1	2	0	3	.00	4	.204	.336	.337
Gomez,Ramon,Hickory	A	20	76	231	53	6	0	0	59	26	9	18	0	64	2	3	0	17	9	.65	5	.229	.291	.255
White Sox	R	20	30	103	27	3	0	1	33	16	6	12	0	22	3	0	0	11	4	.73	2	.262	.356	.320
Gonzalez,Alexander,Brevard Cty	A	19	17	59	12	2	1	0	16	6	8	1	0	14	1	0	0	1	1	.50	2	.203	.230	.271
Marlins	R	19	53	187	55	7	4	2	76	30	30	19	0	27	2	1	4	11	2	.85	2	.294	.358	.406
Gonzalez,Jimmy,Quad City	A	23	35	78	19	3	1	1	27	4	14	9	0	13	1	0	1	1	2	.33	2	.244	.326	.346
Gonzalez,Manuel,Great Falls	R	20	59	197	71	9	3	4	98	35	30	9	1	27	0	1	3	16	7	.70	2	.360	.383	.497
Gonzalez,Mario,Charlstn-Sc	A	22	11	29	6	1	0	0	7	3	1	3	0	4	0	0	1	2	1	.67	0	.207	.273	.241
Gonzalez,Richard,Watertown	A	21	55	184	49	4	1	1	58	24	17	17	0	19	0	4	2	1	0	1.00	7	.266	.325	.315
Gonzalez,Wikleman,Augusta	A	22	84	278	67	17	0	3	93	41	36	26	0	32	2	2	5	5	4	.56	7	.241	.305	.335
Goodell,Steve,Elmira	A	21	69	253	64	14	4	7	107	42	30	36	0	50	14	1	2	4	5	.44	8	.253	.374	.423
Kane County	A	21	2	7	2	0	0	0	2	0	1	2	0	2	0	0	0	0	0	.00	0	.286	.444	.286
Goodhart,Steve,Billings	R	23	65	250	85	12	4	0	105	48	45	28	1	34	2	3	5	9	4	.69	1	.340	.404	.420
Goodman,Herb,Billings	R	23	37	79	16	3	0	0	19	10	4	9	0	24	1	0	0	3	1	.75	1	.203	.292	.241
Goodwin,Joseph,Hudson Vall	A	22	57	181	51	6	0	1	60	29	27	20	0	20	6	2	2	2	1	.67	7	.282	.368	.331
Goodwin,Keith,Red Sox	A	21	18	63	27	2	0	0	29	15	11	3	0	8	2	3	1	10	1	.91	1	.429	.464	.460
Utica	A	21	39	146	38	4	1	2	50	26	16	14	0	22	0	3	1	10	1	.91	5	.260	.323	.342
Gordon,Adrian,Fort Wayne	A	22	75	217	52	10	1	2	70	34	18	26	1	63	6	1	3	16	7	.70	3	.240	.333	.323
Gordon,Buck,Cubs	R	21	4	10	1	0	0	0	1	0	2	2	0	2	0	0	0	0	0	.00	1	.100	.250	.100
Gordon,Gary,Rockies	R	19	36	135	34	2	1	0	38	20	8	22	0	37	3	0	0	20	7	.74	1	.252	.369	.281
Gordon,Herman,Medicne Hat	R	21	51	181	42	2	1	5	61	26	20	10	0	57	1	1	4	2	1	.67	0	.232	.270	.337
Gorecki,Ryan,Hudson Vall	A	22	59	189	56	4	0	0	60	24	20	17	1	10	3	2	2	8	6	.57	9	.296	.360	.317
Graham,Johnny,Visalia	A	25	98	306	76	8	1	1	89	45	30	36	0	77	4	4	3	12	6	.67	2	.248	.332	.291
Grandizio,Steve,Peoria	A	24	117	379	106	18	4	1	135	65	33	42	1	63	10	2	5	21	8	.72	10	.280	.362	.356
Granzow,Judd,Yakima	A	19	50	156	35	5	2	4	56	12	13	15	4	53	3	0	1	3	1	.75	3	.224	.303	.359
Grass,Darren,Rancho Cuca	A	24	23	58	14	6	0	1	23	6	9	2	0	15	0	3	0	0	0	.00	1	.241	.267	.397
Graves,Bryan,Boise	A	21	32	53	11	2	0	1	16	9	5	17	0	12	0	0	0	0	0	.00	0	.208	.400	.302
Gray,Ricky,Jamestown	A	24	32	79	12	3	1	2	23	15	8	17	1	30	1	0	0	4	0	1.00	2	.152	.309	.291
Green,Bert,Savannah	A	22	132	429	98	7	6	1	120	48	25	55	3	101	3	9	1	26	9	.74	6	.228	.320	.280
Green,Raymond,Marlins	R	22	3	5	0	0	0	0	0	0	0	1	0	0	0	0	0	0	0	.00	2	.000	.167	.000
Green,Ron,Cubs	R	23	34	119	38	7	4	2	59	28	12	18	0	33	1	1	0	13	7	.65	0	.319	.407	.496
Grieve,Ben,W. Michigan	A	20	102	371	97	16	1	4	127	53	62	60	6	75	8	0	6	1	3	.79	10	.261	.371	.342
Modesto	A	20	28	107	28	5	0	2	39	17	14	15	1	22	0	0	2	2	0	1.00	3	.262	.347	.364
Griffin,Chad,Everett	A	22	36	82	15	2	0	1	20	11	5	16	1	36	0	1	0	1	0	1.00	0	.183	.316	.244
Griffin,Juan,Astros	R	20	26	64	11	1	1	0	14	11	10	6	0	22	3	3	0	5	1	.83	2	.172	.274	.219
Gronowski,Craig,Ogden	R	23	10	36	12	1	0	0	13	11	3	12	1	5	0	0	0	4	2	.67	0	.333	.500	.361
Groseclose,David,Portland	A	23	5	12	4	1	0	0	5	2	2	2	0	2	2	0	1	0	0	.00	0	.333	.471	.417
Rockies	R	23	31	119	30	4	1	0	36	19	8	15	0	26	0	0	0	4	0	1.00	3	.252	.336	.303
Gross,Rafael,Yakima	A	20	40	142	36	4	1	3	51	17	15	13	1	17	1	1	1	12	2	.86	3	.254	.318	.359
Vero Beach	A	21	35	115	29	4	1	0	35	18	8	3	0	15	3	1	2	5	4	.56	1	.252	.285	.304
Gruber,Nick,Red Sox	R	19	13	27	3	0	0	0	3	1	1	2	0	5	0	0	0	0	0	.00	1	.111	.172	.111
Grunewald,Keith,Salem	A	24	118	412	109	22	1	6	151	48	45	46	8	84	10	2	3	8	4	.67	8	.265	.350	.367
Guerrero,Diogene,Athletics	R	21	41	136	31	4	5	1	48	27	13	29	1	48	2	0	1	11	7	.61	0	.228	.369	.353
Guerrero,Rafael,Columbia	A	21	116	415	115	18	3	7	160	47	56	25	1	63	0	2	6	13	8	.62	15	.277	.314	.386
Guerrero,Sergio,Helena	R	21	44	129	39	10	1	4	63	26	17	13	0	12	2	3	1	5	1	.83	6	.302	.372	.488
Guerrero,Vladimir,Albany	A	20	110	421	140	21	10	16	229	77	63	30	3	45	7	0	4	12	7	.63	8	.333	.383	.544
Guevara,Giomar,Riverside	A	23	83	292	71	12	3	2	95	53	34	30	1	71	1	6	6	7	4	.64	4	.243	.310	.325
Gugino,Mark,Kane County	A	23	58	164	40	13	2	3	66	29	20	35	0	29	4	3	2	5	3	.63	4	.244	.385	.402
Guiel,Aaron,Lk Elsinore	A	23	113	409	110	25	7	7	170	73	58	69	0	96	7	4	4	7	6	.54	7	.269	.380	.416
Guiliano,Matthew,Piedmont	A	24	129	451	102	22	12	4	160	67	59	51	1	114	7	9	6	6	8	.43	7	.226	.311	.355
Guillen,Carlos,Astros	R	20	30	105	31	4	2	2	45	17	15	9	1	17	1	1	2	17	1	.94	0	.295	.350	.429
Guillen,Jose,Erie	A	20	66	258	81	17	1	12	136	41	46	10	0	44	12	0	1	1	5	.17	5	.314	.367	.527
Augusta	A	20	10	34	8	1	1	2	17	6	6	2	0	9	2	0	0	0	0	.00	0	.235	.316	.500
Guillen,Jose,Modesto	A	23	41	113	29	2	1	1	36	16	11	11	0	24	0	5	0	9	3	.75	3	.257	.323	.319
Gulseth,Mark,San Jose	A	24	22	64	15	4	1	0	21	8	6	10	2	16	0	0	0	1	0	1.00	0	.234	.338	.328
Burlington	A	24	41	137	38	7	0	4	57	15	19	18	0	30	2	0	2	3	3	.50	4	.277	.365	.416
Gunderson,Shane,Elizabethtn	R	22	37	139	43	11	2	7	79	32	30	20	0	24	2	0	1	4	0	1.00	3	.309	.401	.568
Fort Wayne	A	22	26	87	22	7	0	2	35	17	12	10	1	17	2	4	0	2	1	.67	0	.253	.343	.402
Guthrie,David,Princeton	R	22	55	181	37	11	0	0	48	28	13	18	1	41	3	4	1	7	1	.88	4	.204	.286	.265
Gutierrez,Rick,Kinston	A	26	117	439	115	21	7	4	162	63	46	67	3	62	4	7	4	43	16	.73	3	.262	.362	.369
Gyselman,Jeff,Clearwater	A	25	26	64	11	0	0	0	11	8	3	6	0	14	0	0	0	0	0	.00	4	.172	.243	.172
Haas,Chris,Johnson Cty	R	19	67	242	65	15	3	7	107	43	50	52	0	93	1	0	0	1	3	.25	8	.269	.400	.442
Haas,Matthew,Albany	A	24	52	186	39	7	0	0	46	18	15	18	1	30	2	3	1	5	1	.17	1	.235	.316	.277
Hacker,Steve,Eugene	A	21	16	57	12	3	0	2	21	4	9	1	0	13	2	0	1	0	0	.00	1	.211	.246	.368
Hacopian,Derek,Beloit	A	26	123	442	143	30	1	23	244	75	92	56	5	35	8	0	2	4	5	.44	20	.324	.407	.552
Hagge,Kirk,Tigers	R	20	43	96	17	0	0	0	17	8	3	16	1	32	0	0	0	3	2	.60	5	.177	.295	.177
Halemanu,Joshua,Kissimmee	A	22	6	15	2	0	0	0	2	1	0	1	0	7	0	0	0	0	0	.00	0	.133	.188	.133
Auburn	A	22	52	157	31	6	0	7	58	25	25	29	0	60	3	0	4	2	2	.50	0	.197	.326	.369
Hall,Andy,New Jersey	A	22	64	252	78	10	5	1	101	30	34	19	2	44	4	4	0	19	6	.76	2	.310	.367	.401
Hall,Darran,Billings	R	20	15	27	4	0	1	0	6	11	2	8	0	3	0	0	0	1	1	.50	2	.148	.343	.222

343

1995 Batting -- Single-A and Rookie Leagues

Player	Lg	A	G	AB	H	2B	3B	HR	TB	R	RBI	TBB	IBB	SO	HBP	SH	SF	SB	CS	SB%	GDP	Avg	OBP	SLG
Princeton	R	20	9	25	3	0	0	0	3	3	1	5	0	10	0	1	1	1	2	.33	0	.120	.258	.120
Hall,Ron,Asheville	A	20	130	448	134	20	4	4	174	64	46	44	4	78	17	1	4	26	13	.67	7	.299	.380	.388
Hall,Ryan,Peoria	A	24	108	317	86	24	0	7	131	38	44	49	2	70	4	3	5	1	2	.33	7	.271	.371	.413
Hallead,John,Portland	A	20	45	143	24	5	2	1	36	17	16	15	0	49	2	2	2	9	5	.64	1	.168	.253	.252
Hallmark,Patrick,Spokane	A	22	56	227	69	11	0	4	92	36	25	13	0	37	2	2	2	5	3	.63	5	.304	.344	.405
Ham,Kevin,Boise	A	21	69	238	75	7	3	7	109	39	43	40	2	57	8	0	1	2	2	.50	9	.315	.429	.458
Hamburg,Leon,W. Michigan	A	21	85	268	49	16	2	2	75	40	32	42	0	78	4	2	1	12	3	.80	5	.183	.302	.280
Hamilton,Joe,Michigan	A	21	119	405	88	15	2	16	155	65	59	73	3	124	5	2	6	8	7	.53	1	.217	.339	.383
Hamlin,Jonas,Stockton	A	26	99	388	129	32	5	16	219	65	69	17	2	86	4	1	6	5	4	.56	7	.332	.361	.564
Hammell,Al,Columbia	A	24	3	6	0	0	0	0	0	0	0	2	0	4	0	1	0	0	0	.00	0	.000	.250	.000
St. Lucie	A	24	34	70	11	1	0	1	15	7	3	16	0	19	1	1	0	2	1	.67	2	.157	.322	.214
Hampton,Michael,Charlstn-Wv	A	24	96	302	74	16	3	1	99	46	32	53	1	70	6	2	1	17	4	.81	6	.245	.367	.328
Hampton,Robby,Medicne Hat	R	20	55	187	44	14	1	7	81	28	27	11	0	73	6	0	2	2	3	.40	2	.235	.296	.433
Hansen,Elston,Tampa	A	24	61	187	36	12	1	2	56	28	19	23	0	45	4	5	3	0	1	.00	4	.193	.290	.299
Hansen,Jed,Springfield	A	23	122	414	107	27	7	9	175	86	50	78	0	73	7	6	1	44	10	.81	8	.258	.384	.423
Hardy,Bryan,Burlington	R	19	29	80	16	4	0	5	35	15	12	10	0	40	1	0	0	1	0	1.00	1	.200	.297	.438
Hare,Richie,Lakeland	A	24	9	20	3	0	0	0	3	3	2	1	0	4	0	0	0	0	0	.00	0	.150	.190	.150
Jamestown	A	24	27	57	11	4	0	0	15	6	3	2	0	13	1	0	0	4	1	.80	0	.193	.233	.263
Harmer,Frank,High Desert	A	21	6	12	3	1	0	1	7	3	1	5	0	5	0	0	0	0	0	.00	0	.250	.471	.583
Bluefield	R	18	58	11	3	0	0	0	14	5	10	9	0	14	0	0	2	1	0	1.00	0	.190	.290	.241
Harmon,Brian,Yakima	A	20	22	59	15	3	0	0	18	4	8	12	0	9	0	0	2	0	0	.00	3	.254	.370	.305
Harper,Rantie,Savannah	A	21	91	318	66	12	2	3	91	34	31	34	0	114	2	2	3	13	3	.81	6	.208	.286	.286
Harris,Eric,W. Michigan	A	23	70	202	34	9	2	7	68	29	29	26	0	73	7	0	2	5	0	1.00	5	.168	.283	.337
Harris,G.G.,Augusta	A	23	100	368	90	23	0	2	119	38	46	17	1	50	4	2	4	2	6	.25	9	.245	.282	.323
Harris,Robert,Sou. Oregon	A	24	63	230	58	14	1	1	77	31	16	32	0	32	3	1	4	9	5	.64	5	.252	.346	.335
Harris,Rodger,Johnson Cty	R	20	45	121	22	5	1	0	29	26	7	19	0	44	2	1	0	5	2	.71	3	.182	.303	.240
Harris,Ronrico,Brewers	R	21	48	172	48	6	3	0	60	40	22	37	1	22	4	0	1	26	10	.72	2	.279	.416	.349
Harrison,Adonis,Mariners	R	19	45	155	45	7	5	1	65	31	14	37	0	37	3	0	4	7	9	.44	0	.290	.427	.419
Harrison,Jamal,Twins	R	18	5	14	2	1	0	0	3	0	2	2	0	1	0	0	0	0	0	.00	0	.143	.250	.214
Harriss,Robin,Kinston	A	24	15	49	12	3	1	2	23	8	6	3	0	8	0	1	1	0	0	.00	1	.245	.283	.469
Columbus	A	24	51	179	40	6	0	2	52	18	18	11	0	30	3	3	0	0	3	.00	8	.223	.280	.291
Harvey,Aaron,Kane County	A	23	100	336	98	25	3	7	150	58	54	25	0	70	5	4	4	11	7	.61	4	.292	.346	.446
Hastings,Lionel,Brevard Cty	A	23	120	469	128	20	0	7	169	60	45	44	0	64	3	5	2	3	3	.50	14	.273	.338	.360
Hawkins,Wes,Frederick	A	24	78	199	42	10	2	0	56	13	16	11	0	49	4	4	1	4	1	.80	9	.211	.265	.281
Haws,Scott,Clearwater	A	24	2	1	0	0	0	0	0	0	0	0	0	1	0	0	0	0	0	.00	0	.000	.500	.000
Hayashi,Hiroyasu,Visalia	A	25	40	138	37	6	0	0	43	19	15	26	1	27	1	4	0	2	3	.40	4	.268	.388	.312
Hayes,Chris,St. Cathrns	A	22	70	271	83	17	3	2	112	39	36	24	0	50	7	1	1	8	7	.53	2	.306	.376	.413
Hayes,Darren,White Sox	R	23	6	20	6	0	0	0	6	2	2	2	0	1	1	0	0	0	0	.00	0	.300	.391	.300
Hickory	A	23	58	196	48	12	2	3	73	18	19	16	1	53	6	1	1	7	2	.78	6	.245	.320	.372
Hayes,Heath,Watertown	A	24	15	52	11	3	0	0	14	4	6	7	0	14	0	0	1	1	1	.50	1	.212	.300	.269
Heams,Shane,Everett	A	20	27	61	12	4	0	1	19	5	4	3	0	28	1	0	0	2	0	1.00	2	.197	.246	.311
Heath,Jason,Wisconsin	A	25	70	235	63	20	2	4	99	29	32	19	2	60	7	7	4	3	3	.50	4	.268	.336	.421
Heller,Brad,Charlstn-Sc	A	24	76	214	48	13	0	4	73	27	15	21	0	37	0	6	1	3	1	.75	4	.224	.292	.341
Helms,Ryan,Bristol	R	20	48	146	24	2	1	0	28	16	9	11	0	33	2	2	1	3	1	.75	3	.164	.231	.192
Helms,Wesley,Macon	A	20	136	539	149	32	1	11	216	89	85	50	0	107	10	0	3	2	2	.50	8	.276	.347	.401
Helton,Todd,Asheville	A	22	54	201	51	11	1	1	67	24	15	25	1	32	1	0	0	1	1	.50	7	.254	.339	.333
Hemphill,Bret,Lk Elsinore	A	24	45	146	29	7	0	1	39	12	17	18	0	36	3	0	3	2	1	.67	4	.199	.294	.267
Cedar Rapds	A	24	72	234	59	11	1	8	96	36	28	21	0	54	4	1	4	0	2	.00	7	.252	.319	.410
Hence,Sam,Bakersfield	A	25	4	8	1	0	0	0	1	1	0	0	0	1	0	1	0	0	0	.00	0	.125	.125	.125
Henderson,Juan,Cedar Rapds	A	22	123	402	92	12	1	2	112	61	28	36	0	79	3	10	2	47	12	.80	6	.229	.296	.279
Hendricks,Ryan,Huntington	R	23	58	178	46	12	0	11	91	38	36	46	3	50	0	0	2	8	1	.89	2	.258	.407	.511
Frederick	A	23	5	15	2	1	0	1	6	1	3	2	0	6	0	0	0	0	0	.00	1	.133	.235	.400
Henley,Bob,Albany	A	23	102	335	94	20	1	3	125	45	46	83	3	57	11	1	2	1	2	.33	11	.281	.436	.373
Henry,Antoine,Sarasota	A	23	16	62	14	0	1	2	22	14	8	8	0	7	0	0	0	5	2	.71	1	.226	.314	.355
Herdman,Eli,Elizabethtn	R	20	62	217	46	10	0	10	86	36	36	34	1	60	1	0	2	1	2	.33	4	.212	.319	.396
Herider,Jeremy,Charlstn-Wv	A	24	8	15	2	0	0	0	2	2	0	2	0	6	0	0	0	0	0	.00	0	.133	.235	.133
Hermansen,Chad,Pirates	R	18	24	92	28	10	1	3	49	14	17	9	1	19	0	0	1	0	0	.00	2	.304	.363	.533
Erie	A	18	44	165	45	8	3	6	77	30	25	18	0	39	4	0	2	4	2	.67	6	.273	.354	.467
Hernaiz,Juan,Vero Beach	A	21	50	156	33	1	1	2	42	17	9	9	1	39	1	4	0	5	1	.83	4	.212	.259	.269
Yakima	A	21	50	158	44	9	2	0	57	23	16	6	0	30	1	1	1	9	3	.75	1	.278	.307	.361
Hernandez,Alexander,Pirates	R	19	49	186	50	5	3	1	64	24	17	17	1	33	1	1	2	4	3	.57	3	.269	.330	.344
Hernandez,Carlos,Quad City	A	20	126	470	122	19	6	4	165	74	40	39	1	68	11	9	1	58	21	.73	4	.260	.330	.351
Hernandez,Ramon,Athletics	R	20	48	143	52	9	6	4	85	37	37	39	1	16	8	0	4	2	2	.75	3	.364	.510	.594
Hernandez,Rob,Elmira	A	23	8	25	1	0	0	0	1	0	0	5	0	7	0	1	0	1	0	1.00	0	.040	.200	.040
Hernandez,Victor,Athletics	R	19	21	46	7	0	0	0	7	5	3	5	0	21	1	0	0	2	0	1.00	1	.152	.250	.152
Herrera,Jesus,Princeton	R	19	46	149	36	8	0	1	47	18	9	7	0	38	4	1	1	6	5	.55	1	.242	.292	.315
Herrick,Jason,Cedar Rapds	A	22	104	358	102	21	4	11	164	54	57	38	2	84	2	3	3	19	3	.86	7	.285	.354	.458
Hicks,Jamie,Durham	A	24	41	105	23	6	0	0	29	9	14	5	2	18	0	0	1	0	2	.00	5	.219	.252	.276
Hightower,Vee,Rockford	A	24	64	238	63	11	1	7	97	51	36	39	1	52	6	0	1	23	6	.79	6	.265	.380	.408
Higman,Joe,Orioles	R	22	6	21	3	0	0	0	3	2	1	2	0	7	0	0	1	1	0	1.00	1	.143	.208	.143
Bluefield	R	22	11	24	5	0	0	0	5	2	3	3	0	8	0	0	0	2	0	1.00	1	.208	.296	.208
Huntington	R	22	13	45	12	1	0	0	13	4	4	3	0	18	1	0	0	1	0	1.00	0	.267	.327	.289
Hills,Rich,Idaho Falls	R	22	61	224	69	14	1	7	106	49	48	31	0	27	11	0	5	4	1	.80	5	.308	.410	.473
Hilo,Johnny,San Bernrdo	A	22	38	93	23	2	1	1	30	14	9	15	0	23	0	4	1	3	2	.60	1	.247	.352	.323
Yakima	A	22	50	168	42	10	0	3	61	18	22	23	2	33	3	0	0	5	2	.71	4	.250	.351	.363
Hilt,Scott,Fort Myers	A	23	19	42	7	0	0	1	10	3	3	3	0	12	1	0	0	0	0	.00	4	.167	.239	.238
Fort Wayne	A	23	30	92	17	5	1	1	27	13	15	11	0	28	1	0	0	0	0	.00	3	.185	.286	.293

344

1995 Batting -- Single-A and Rookie Leagues

Player	Lg	A	G	AB	H	2B	3B	HR	TB	R	RBI	TBB	IBB	SO	HBP	SH	SF	SB	CS	SB%	GDP	Avg	OBP	SLG
Hinds,Collin,Wisconsin	A	22	5	14	1	0	0	0	1	0	1	2	0	8	0	0	0	1	0	1.00	0	.071	.188	.071
Lethbridge	R	22	69	220	41	7	0	4	60	26	27	21	1	87	4	0	1	5	5	.50	9	.186	.268	.273
Hines,Pooh,Eugene	A	21	44	124	30	7	3	2	49	26	13	20	1	27	3	4	1	13	2	.87	3	.242	.358	.395
Hobbie,Matt,Huntington	R	21	60	211	48	12	5	2	76	25	24	23	0	49	1	0	5	17	5	.77	1	.227	.300	.360
Hodges,Randy,Danville	R	22	2	8	2	0	0	1	5	1	1	0	0	2	1	0	0	0	1	.00	1	.250	.333	.625
Eugene	A	22	61	206	60	7	5	2	83	29	28	12	1	35	7	3	1	10	6	.63	3	.291	.350	.403
Holdren,Nate,Salem	A	24	119	420	103	16	2	15	168	48	69	34	0	126	6	2	2	6	3	.67	7	.245	.310	.400
Holley,Jack,Hagerstown	A	19	23	79	16	4	0	0	20	6	7	3	0	18	1	1	0	0	2	.00	4	.203	.241	.253
St. Cathrns	A	19	65	246	59	2	1	3	72	33	26	22	0	47	5	7	0	3	3	.50	4	.240	.315	.293
Hollins,Darontaye,Bristol	R	21	62	222	55	7	2	0	66	24	14	20	1	75	4	2	2	14	5	.74	5	.248	.319	.297
Hooker,Kevin,Martinsvlle	R	23	49	179	60	16	1	9	105	38	46	21	0	34	7	0	3	2	3	.40	1	.335	.419	.587
Piedmont	A	23	16	46	8	2	0	0	10	4	6	9	0	13	3	0	1	1	0	1.00	0	.174	.339	.217
Hoover,Will,Kingsport	R	21	11	21	4	1	0	0	5	1	3	2	0	10	0	0	0	0	0	.00	0	.190	.261	.238
Horn,Marvin,White Sox	R	21	38	129	31	7	2	1	45	13	14	11	2	38	1	1	2	0	1	.00	3	.240	.301	.349
Hostetler,Brian,Stockton	A	26	3	7	0	0	0	0	0	0	0	0	0	3	0	0	0	0	0	.00	0	.000	.000	.000
House,Mitch,Lynchburg	A	24	16	50	9	3	0	1	15	7	6	9	1	13	1	0	1	0	1	.00	2	.180	.311	.300
Houser,Jeremy,Asheville	A	21	112	361	76	11	0	2	93	43	32	34	0	43	1	6	2	5	4	.56	7	.211	.279	.258
Huff,Lawrence,Piedmont	A	24	130	481	131	26	4	1	168	86	51	74	5	64	10	7	4	26	8	.76	9	.272	.378	.349
Hunt,Kenya,Idaho Falls	R	23	32	73	16	2	0	2	24	13	15	16	1	32	1	0	0	1	0	1.00	0	.219	.367	.329
Hunter,Andy,Padres	R	19	35	106	22	2	2	0	28	14	11	17	0	39	1	0	0	2	1	.67	2	.208	.323	.264
Hunter,Lanier,Huntington	R	23	62	216	54	12	2	4	82	36	18	32	0	64	8	2	2	15	10	.60	2	.250	.364	.380
Frederick	A	23	7	14	2	1	0	0	3	1	0	1	0	7	0	0	0	0	0	.00	0	.143	.200	.214
Hunter,Scott,San Bernrdo	A	20	113	379	108	19	3	11	166	68	59	36	1	83	6	4	1	27	8	.77	0	.285	.355	.438
Columbia	A	20	12	40	10	0	0	0	10	2	1	2	0	13	1	1	1	2	1	.67	2	.250	.295	.250
Hunter,Torii,Fort Myers	A	20	113	391	96	15	2	7	136	64	36	38	1	77	12	5	1	7	4	.64	8	.246	.330	.348
Hust,Gary,Modesto	A	24	128	467	111	20	2	27	216	85	87	61	3	169	4	4	3	10	4	.71	4	.238	.329	.463
Hutchins,Norm,Angels	R	20	14	59	16	1	0	1	19	9	7	4	0	10	1	2	1	8	4	.67	1	.271	.323	.322
Boise	A	20	45	176	44	6	2	2	60	34	11	15	0	44	2	4	1	10	6	.63	2	.250	.314	.341
Hutchison,Tom,Lethbridge	R	23	62	217	60	7	3	1	76	43	17	32	1	21	4	4	0	33	6	.85	3	.276	.379	.350
Iapoce,Anthony,Brewers	R	22	3	3	1	0	0	0	1	2	0	1	0	1	0	0	0	0	1	1.00	0	.333	.500	.333
Helena	R	22	39	146	44	7	0	0	51	43	13	28	0	24	2	2	2	19	3	.86	2	.301	.416	.349
Iatarola,Aaron,Cedar Rapids	A	24	115	388	101	20	1	16	171	62	69	44	1	92	5	1	7	7	4	.64	2	.260	.338	.441
Ibanez,Raul,Riverside	A	24	95	361	120	23	9	20	221	59	108	41	1	49	2	1	9	4	3	.57	7	.332	.395	.612
Ibarra,Jesse,Burlington	A	23	129	437	144	30	1	34	278	72	96	77	6	94	4	0	1	1	2	.33	8	.330	.434	.636
San Jose	A	23	3	9	3	2	0	0	5	1	4	1	0	1	0	0	0	0	0	.00	0	.333	.400	.556
Illig,Brett,Great Falls	R	18	23	42	7	1	0	0	8	4	1	3	0	14	0	1	0	0	0	.00	2	.167	.222	.190
Imrisek,Jason,Yankees	R	22	15	53	15	3	0	1	21	5	8	2	0	12	2	0	0	2	2	.50	1	.283	.333	.396
Oneonta	A	22	6	13	1	0	0	0	1	1	1	1	0	2	0	0	0	0	0	.00	0	.077	.143	.077
Ingram,Darron,Princeton	R	20	60	233	64	5	3	14	117	37	53	11	0	78	1	0	2	3	1	.75	5	.275	.308	.502
Insunza,Miguel,New Jersey	A	23	55	207	50	6	0	0	56	30	21	24	0	8	5	3	1	11	8	.58	8	.242	.333	.271
Isom,Daleon,Mariners	R	20	28	89	23	4	1	1	32	17	8	18	0	19	2	1	1	11	8	.58	2	.258	.391	.360
Isom,Johnny,Bluefield	R	22	59	212	73	14	4	6	113	47	56	25	0	27	1	2	7	8	2	.80	5	.344	.404	.533
Izquierdo,Sergio,Pr.William	A	23	10	32	6	2	0	0	8	6	2	2	0	3	2	0	0	0	0	.00	2	.188	.278	.250
Hickory	A	23	45	123	18	2	0	0	20	6	4	8	0	20	0	3	1	0	0	.00	4	.146	.197	.163
Jackson,Gavin,Sarasota	A	22	100	342	91	19	1	0	112	61	36	40	3	43	6	8	4	11	12	.48	8	.266	.349	.327
Jackson,Rod,Padres	R	21	45	150	38	6	0	0	44	16	6	9	0	39	2	1	0	11	3	.79	3	.253	.304	.293
Jackson,Ryan,Kane County	A	24	132	471	138	39	6	10	219	78	82	67	7	74	4	0	5	13	8	.62	9	.293	.382	.465
Jacobo,Roberto,Padres	R	20	46	166	40	2	3	0	48	18	15	12	2	49	1	0	0	10	7	.59	3	.241	.296	.289
Jacobus,Brian,Padres	R	20	44	144	28	7	0	0	35	12	11	8	0	32	2	0	1	0	1	.00	7	.194	.245	.243
James,Kennouth,Expos	R	19	43	156	33	1	0	0	34	20	3	20	0	43	3	0	0	11	8	.58	1	.212	.313	.218
Janke,Jared,Martinsvlle	R	22	46	149	36	11	0	3	56	24	27	26	0	25	3	0	0	5	1	.83	6	.242	.365	.376
Jaroncyk,Ryan,Mets	R	19	44	174	48	5	3	0	59	31	14	13	1	28	1	3	2	7	2	.78	3	.276	.326	.339
Pittsfield	A	19	4	13	3	0	0	0	3	5	0	3	0	5	1	0	0	5	0	1.00	0	.231	.412	.231
Jarrett,Link,Asheville	A	24	116	404	95	11	0	0	106	46	20	62	1	60	2	10	2	12	10	.55	5	.235	.338	.262
Jasco,Elinton,Cubs	R	21	34	124	47	6	3	1	62	28	17	16	1	18	2	2	4	29	9	.76	1	.379	.445	.500
Williamsprt	A	21	6	25	8	2	0	0	10	2	4	0	0	5	0	1	0	2	0	1.00	3	.320	.320	.400
Jefferson,Dave,Elmira	A	21	5	13	1	0	0	0	1	1	0	1	0	3	0	0	0	2	0	1.00	3	.077	.143	.077
Jelsovsky,Craig,Mets	R	20	18	43	10	2	0	0	12	6	6	3	0	4	3	2	1	2	0	.00	0	.233	.320	.279
Jenkins,Corey,Red Sox	R	19	35	124	18	1	0	1	22	12	6	11	0	43	2	0	0	5	2	.71	1	.145	.226	.177
Jensen,Blair,Burlington	R	20	21	47	9	1	0	0	10	3	2	6	0	21	0	1	0	2	1	1.00	3	.191	.283	.213
Jimenez,D'Angelo,Yankees	R	18	57	214	60	14	8	2	96	41	28	23	1	31	1	3	4	6	3	.67	4	.280	.347	.449
Jimenez,Elvis,Portland	A	20	37	123	22	0	2	1	29	8	9	8	0	36	0	1	0	7	4	.64	1	.179	.229	.236
Jimenez,Manny,Durham	A	24	121	375	92	16	2	2	118	40	23	17	1	71	5	3	0	8	6	.57	11	.245	.287	.315
Jimenez,Oscar,Wilmington	A	21	121	374	94	18	4	1	123	42	31	53	2	92	10	6	3	11	8	.58	3	.251	.357	.329
Jimenez,Ruben,Johnson Cty	R	20	41	116	19	0	4	0	27	13	20	16	0	27	3	1	3	5	6	.45	2	.164	.275	.233
Johnson,Andre,Daytona	A	26	5	14	1	0	0	0	1	2	2	0	0	4	0	0	0	0	0	.00	2	.071	.071	.071
Johnson,A.j.,Lethbridge	R	23	61	229	68	10	3	2	90	30	41	18	2	33	6	1	2	6	8	.43	9	.297	.361	.393
Johnson,Brian,Helena	R	23	34	87	21	2	0	2	29	24	10	9	0	18	1	3	2	3	4	.43	1	.241	.313	.333
Johnson,Carlisle,Twins	R	19	19	50	9	1	0	0	10	2	4	11	0	13	1	0	0	1	1	.50	1	.180	.339	.200
Johnson,Todd,Bakersfield	A	25	9	25	9	2	1	0	13	2	2	3	0	4	0	0	0	0	0	.00	1	.360	.429	.520
Kinston	A	25	21	56	13	2	1	0	17	4	9	0	0	13	0	0	0	0	0	.00	1	.232	.232	.304
Johnson,Damon,St. Cathrns	A	20	63	232	50	9	5	1	72	26	25	8	1	73	4	3	0	9	2	.82	4	.216	.253	.310
Johnson,Heath,Elizabethtn	R	19	59	201	42	10	0	1	55	31	16	41	1	51	3	0	1	4	5	.44	3	.209	.350	.274
Johnson,Jace,Athletics	R	21	17	38	5	1	0	0	9	4	4	4	0	16	1	0	0	1	1	.50	0	.132	.233	.237
Johnson,Jay,Clinton	A	23	8	17	2	0	0	0	2	0	0	1	0	3	0	1	0	0	0	.00	1	.118	.167	.118
Johnson,J.J.,Hudson Vall	A	20	46	150	36	7	3	5	64	27	16	12	0	38	5	0	2	10	6	.63	0	.240	.314	.427
Johnson,Jeffrey,Hickory	A	23	53	170	39	9	0	2	54	15	14	13	1	40	1	3	1	2	2	.50	2	.229	.286	.318

1995 Batting -- Single-A and Rookie Leagues

Player	Lg	A	G	AB	H	2B	3B	HR	TB	R	RBI	TBB	IBB	SO	HBP	SH	SF	SB	CS	SB%	GDP	Avg	OBP	SLG
Johnson,Duan,Mariners	R	20	40	162	56	9	3	0	71	32	27	8	0	14	2	0	2	3	2	.60	4	.346	.379	.438
Johnson,Keith,San Bernrdo	A	25	111	417	101	26	1	17	180	64	68	17	0	83	4	11	2	20	12	.63	4	.242	.277	.432
Johnson,Ledowick,Helena	R	23	35	93	24	3	0	1	30	18	18	20	0	24	2	1	2	5	6	.45	0	.258	.393	.323
Johnson,Mark,Hickory	A	20	107	319	58	9	0	2	73	31	17	59	1	52	3	2	2	3	5	.38	4	.182	.313	.229
Johnson,Rontrez,Red Sox	R	19	51	189	47	4	1	0	53	36	8	30	0	29	1	3	1	25	4	.86	1	.249	.353	.280
Johnson,T.J.,Twins	R	22	24	76	24	5	0	1	32	14	10	11	0	9	7	1	0	5	4	.56	1	.316	.447	.421
Elizabethtn	R	22	14	44	15	6	0	2	27	6	4	5	0	10	0	0	0	2	1	.67	0	.341	.408	.614
Jones,Andy,Macon	A	19	139	537	149	41	5	25	275	104	100	70	7	122	16	0	9	56	11	.84	9	.277	.372	.512
Jones,Ben,Fort Myers	A	22	109	335	80	10	2	0	94	60	31	41	2	53	6	16	1	19	6	.76	10	.239	.332	.281
Jones,Bryan,Tigers	R	21	33	93	23	2	0	0	25	13	7	11	0	34	0	2	1	7	1	.88	2	.247	.324	.269
Jones,Ivory,Elizabethtn	R	23	47	136	27	4	1	2	39	21	11	22	0	43	3	0	0	6	5	.55	0	.199	.310	.287
Jones,Jaime,Marlins	R	19	5	18	4	0	0	0	4	2	3	5	1	4	0	0	0	0	0	.00	0	.222	.391	.222
Elmira	A	19	31	116	33	6	2	4	55	21	11	9	0	30	0	0	1	5	4	.56	2	.284	.336	.474
Jones,Ken,Padres	R	24	1	4	2	1	0	0	3	0	1	0	0	1	0	0	0	0	0	.00	1	.500	.500	.750
Clinton	A	24	31	76	14	2	0	0	16	8	7	6	0	20	1	1	0	1	0	1.00	1	.184	.253	.211
Jones,Pookie,Asheville	A	24	16	63	22	6	2	0	32	16	8	2	0	14	0	0	0	3	0	1.00	1	.349	.369	.508
Salem	A	24	16	53	11	3	0	1	17	9	3	3	0	16	1	1	0	1	1	.50	4	.208	.263	.321
Jones,Ryan,Dunedin	A	21	127	478	119	28	6	18	201	65	78	41	3	92	7	0	5	1	1	.50	7	.249	.315	.421
Jones,Shane,Ogden	R	24	70	297	96	21	2	8	145	46	69	17	0	55	0	2	7	3	3	.50	6	.323	.352	.488
Jones,Timothy,Athletics	R	18	32	96	19	2	2	0	25	7	10	6	0	36	0	1	0	5	3	.63	1	.198	.245	.260
Jorgensen,Randy,Riverside	A	24	133	495	148	32	2	12	220	78	97	46	1	74	15	0	8	4	2	.67	13	.299	.371	.444
Jorgensen,Timothy,Watertown	A	23	73	295	96	19	9	8	157	44	52	32	4	63	2	1	1	4	1	.80	4	.325	.394	.532
Joseph,Terry,Williamsprt	A	22	70	260	76	8	10	1	107	49	34	30	1	33	7	1	0	18	6	.75	5	.292	.380	.412
Juarez,Raul,Twins	R	20	7	26	9	1	1	1	15	3	6	0	0	5	0	0	1	0	0	.00	1	.346	.333	.577
Elizabethtn	R	20	40	120	34	7	0	3	50	25	16	23	1	50	0	0	1	10	3	.77	0	.283	.396	.417
Judge,Mike,Brewers	R	24	16	41	12	2	1	0	16	8	6	8	0	9	3	0	0	2	1	.67	2	.293	.442	.390
Helena	R	24	30	112	39	13	1	0	54	28	25	11	0	12	6	1	0	1	2	.33	4	.348	.434	.482
Jumonville,Joe,Peoria	A	25	113	378	86	18	4	4	124	37	45	9	0	47	1	1	4	2	1	.67	12	.228	.245	.328
Kane,Ryan,Boise	A	22	74	283	78	14	2	14	138	39	59	25	4	57	5	0	5	0	0	.00	10	.276	.340	.488
Kapler,Gabriel,Jamestown	A	20	63	236	68	19	4	4	107	38	34	23	0	37	2	0	4	1	2	.33	4	.288	.351	.453
Katayama,Daika,Tigers	R	21	28	50	9	1	0	2	16	5	4	3	0	13	0	1	0	0	0	.00	0	.180	.226	.320
Kearney,Chad,Martinsvlle	R	20	29	80	18	1	0	1	22	9	5	10	0	32	1	0	0	1	2	.33	1	.225	.319	.275
Keech,Erik,Yankees	R	21	37	120	27	7	0	1	37	6	19	12	1	18	1	0	1	0	1	.00	6	.225	.299	.308
Keefe,Jamie,Clinton	A	22	67	175	42	3	1	1	50	28	10	23	0	42	2	3	0	12	3	.80	2	.240	.335	.286
Keel,David,Modesto	A	23	9	25	5	0	0	1	8	4	3	3	0	7	0	0	0	0	0	.00	0	.200	.286	.320
Keene,Andre,San Jose	A	25	103	323	82	15	1	15	144	62	62	76	2	101	9	0	6	7	6	.54	7	.254	.403	.446
Kehoe,John,Blue Jays	R	23	57	201	55	17	5	2	88	32	32	35	0	52	2	1	2	8	0	1.00	8	.274	.383	.438
Keifer,Greg,Burlington	A	23	6	14	2	1	0	0	3	3	2	2	0	4	0	0	0	1	0	1.00	0	.143	.250	.214
Bellingham	A	23	10	36	10	1	2	1	18	6	3	4	1	14	1	0	0	1	0	1.00	0	.278	.357	.500
San Jose	A	23	28	66	14	2	0	2	22	9	12	9	0	31	0	0	0	2	0	1.00	0	.212	.307	.333
Keighley,Chris,Ogden	R	23	47	133	25	5	0	2	36	21	21	36	1	31	1	5	4	1	1	.50	7	.188	.356	.271
Kelley,Erskine,Augusta	A	25	105	349	76	13	5	4	111	47	32	22	2	86	7	1	1	24	7	.77	10	.218	.277	.318
Kendall,Jeremey,Clearwater	A	24	36	135	29	1	2	3	43	18	10	14	0	40	6	1	2	15	5	.75	2	.215	.312	.319
Kennedy,Gus,Macon	A	22	128	439	111	29	5	24	222	83	76	95	10	151	2	0	3	20	6	.77	7	.253	.386	.506
Kennedy,Jed,Martinsvlle	R	18	43	146	29	7	1	0	38	11	15	7	0	36	1	0	2	10	0	1.00	2	.199	.237	.260
Kernan,Phil,Butte	R	23	59	200	55	9	7	4	90	24	39	26	0	57	4	0	2	0	2	.00	5	.275	.366	.450
Kerr,Brian,Bluefield	R	20	3	6	1	1	0	0	2	0	1	0	0	2	0	0	0	0	0	.00	0	.167	.167	.333
Orioles	R	20	10	38	7	2	1	1	14	4	7	2	0	10	1	1	2	1	0	1.00	1	.184	.233	.368
Kerr,Jim,Yankees	R	21	26	83	20	2	0	0	22	12	6	5	0	24	2	2	1	0	0	.00	2	.241	.297	.265
Key,Jeffrey,Piedmont	A	21	111	384	99	18	6	10	159	55	54	26	4	100	9	2	5	5	7	.42	8	.258	.316	.414
Kimbler,Douglas,Rockford	A	27	102	353	101	33	2	12	174	69	67	39	0	61	4	3	2	7	3	.70	8	.286	.362	.493
Kimm,Tyson,Batavia	A	23	14	37	10	2	0	0	12	8	6	6	0	6	1	0	2	0	0	.00	0	.270	.386	.324
King,Andre,Durham	A	22	111	421	106	22	3	9	161	59	33	39	1	126	10	5	4	15	13	.54	5	.252	.327	.382
Pr. William	A	22	9	32	5	1	1	0	8	4	3	6	0	9	0	1	0	1	0	1.00	0	.156	.289	.250
King,Brett,San Jose	A	23	107	394	108	29	4	3	154	61	41	41	1	86	5	5	6	28	8	.78	8	.274	.345	.391
King,Brion,Orioles	R	19	17	47	13	2	0	0	15	4	4	2	0	12	0	0	1	1	0	1.00	0	.277	.300	.319
King,Kevin,Expos	R	22	14	38	10	3	0	0	13	6	0	2	0	19	1	0	0	3	0	1.00	0	.263	.317	.342
King,Brian,Ogden	R	23	9	35	9	3	1	0	14	4	5	4	0	10	1	0	0	0	1	.00	0	.257	.350	.400
Kingman,Brendan,Brevard Cty	A	23	95	348	88	19	4	8	139	37	47	31	3	45	1	0	0	1	0	1.00	21	.253	.313	.399
Kingsale,Eugene,Bluefield	R	19	47	171	54	11	2	0	69	45	16	27	0	31	5	4	2	20	8	.71	0	.316	.420	.404
Kinkade,Mike,Helena	R	22	69	266	94	19	1	4	127	76	39	43	1	38	10	0	6	26	9	.74	6	.353	.452	.477
Kinnie,Donald,Cubs	R	22	35	120	30	6	4	0	44	20	14	12	0	36	3	0	1	12	1	.92	1	.250	.331	.367
Kirgan,Chris,Frederick	A	23	124	377	76	18	2	11	131	25	48	25	3	107	3	1	4	3	2	.60	7	.202	.254	.347
Kirkpatrick,Brian,Rockies	R	19	38	122	17	1	0	1	21	11	7	11	0	54	0	2	1	4	1	.80	4	.139	.209	.172
Klassen,Danny,Beloit	A	20	59	218	60	15	2	2	85	27	25	16	0	43	4	0	3	12	4	.75	4	.275	.332	.390
Klee,Charles,White Sox	R	19	44	155	33	8	0	0	41	24	19	19	0	41	2	0	2	3	2	.60	3	.213	.303	.265
Klostermeyer,Mike,Sou. Oregon	A	22	64	186	44	7	0	3	60	31	19	31	1	36	3	2	1	4	2	.67	4	.237	.353	.323
Knauss,Tom,Fort Myers	A	22	99	316	75	19	1	1	99	37	26	28	1	72	6	1	2	2	8	.20	4	.237	.310	.313
Knight,Brook,Helena	R	23	16	34	8	1	0	0	9	4	4	8	0	2	0	0	0	1	0	1.00	3	.235	.381	.265
Knight,Bill,Sou. Oregon	A	23	48	136	28	7	1	2	43	21	19	21	0	43	1	1	3	5	4	.56	3	.206	.313	.316
Knoblauh,Jay,Lynchburg	A	30	87	264	73	16	2	8	117	40	47	16	0	62	6	1	5	3	2	.60	9	.277	.326	.443
Knott,John,Durham	A	25	112	344	92	14	3	11	145	55	46	63	2	100	15	2	2	11	13	.46	5	.267	.401	.422
Knowles,Brian,Wilmington	A	24	9	25	0	0	0	0	0	1	0	0	0	5	0	0	0	0	0	.00	2	.000	.000	.000
Knowles,Eric,Tampa	A	22	115	390	106	24	4	1	141	45	33	45	0	58	3	3	2	7	3	.70	8	.271	.349	.361
Koerick,Tom,Hickory	A	23	73	200	37	10	1	2	55	15	20	15	0	85	7	0	1	2	2	.50	2	.185	.265	.275
Koeyers,Ramsey,W. Palm Bch	A	21	77	244	46	6	1	0	54	19	18	9	0	64	0	5	3	2	1	.67	10	.189	.215	.221
Kofler,Eric,Yankees	R	20	19	69	17	3	2	3	33	11	13	6	0	21	1	0	0	1	0	.50	2	.246	.288	.478

1995 Batting -- Single-A and Rookie Leagues

Player	Lg	A	G	AB	H	2B	3B	HR	TB	R	RBI	TBB	IBB	SO	HBP	SH	SF	SB	CS	SB%	GDP	Avg	OBP	SLG
Kominek,Toby,Helena	R	23	13	48	16	1	1	3	28	7	18	3	0	9	1	0	1	2	1	.67	0	.333	.377	.583
Beloit	A	23	55	187	52	14	2	7	91	38	30	18	1	56	10	0	2	12	2	.86	1	.278	.369	.487
Konerko,Paul,San Bernrdo	A	20	118	448	124	21	1	19	204	77	77	59	2	88	4	2	6	3	1	.75	12	.277	.362	.455
Koonce,Gray,Jamestown	A	21	73	289	81	16	1	3	108	37	34	35	0	63	2	0	1	8	3	.73	1	.280	.361	.374
Kopacz,Derek,Tigers	R	21	53	165	47	12	3	2	71	24	30	25	0	40	1	0	3	11	3	.79	2	.285	.376	.430
Kortmeyer,Scott,Spokane	A	22	21	64	9	2	0	0	11	6	2	5	0	26	3	0	2	0	0	.00	2	.141	.230	.172
Koscielniak,Dwain,Rancho Cuca	A	23	7	9	2	0	0	1	5	1	2	3	0	2	0	0	1	0	0	.00	0	.222	.385	.556
Koskie,Corey,Fort Wayne	A	23	123	462	143	37	5	16	238	64	78	38	3	79	9	1	5	2	4	.33	10	.310	.370	.515
Krause,Scott,Beloit	A	22	134	481	119	30	4	13	196	83	76	50	5	126	12	3	7	24	10	.71	7	.247	.329	.407
Kruger,Andy,Visalia	A	23	100	356	90	9	7	4	125	46	32	28	0	65	2	3	1	10	15	.40	4	.253	.310	.351
Kuilan,Robles,Marlins	R	20	48	153	38	8	0	0	46	14	27	17	1	20	1	2	2	4	1	.80	4	.248	.324	.301
Kane County	A	20	2	7	0	0	0	0	0	0	0	0	0	1	0	0	0	0	0	.00	0	.000	.000	.000
Kurek,Adam,Michigan	A	24	52	146	28	8	2	0	40	14	18	13	0	47	5	1	2	0	0	.00	2	.192	.277	.274
Lackey,Steve,Pittsfield	A	21	21	75	18	5	0	0	23	7	6	2	0	16	1	1	1	1	0	1.00	1	.240	.266	.307
Columbia	A	21	67	178	34	8	0	1	45	21	21	11	1	42	2	5	3	9	2	.82	2	.191	.242	.253
Ladjevich,Rick,Riverside	A	24	122	470	145	26	0	7	192	74	71	26	2	65	22	3	4	3	2	.60	8	.309	.370	.409
Laforest,Pierre,Expos	R	18	2	6	0	0	0	0	0	1	0	2	0	4	0	0	0	0	0	.00	0	.000	.250	.000
Lakovic,Greg,Elizabethtn	R	21	14	41	10	2	0	0	12	7	8	3	0	8	3	1	0	1	0	1.00	1	.244	.340	.293
Landaker,Dave,Kissimmee	A	22	96	287	59	7	2	0	70	30	18	42	0	47	10	4	5	8	10	.44	6	.206	.323	.244
Landers,Mark,St. Cathrns	A	24	74	271	63	11	0	10	104	43	52	45	4	86	4	0	4	1	2	.33	0	.232	.356	.384
Landry,Dan,Braves	R	23	38	122	29	5	0	2	40	16	7	11	0	25	3	3	0	4	1	.80	2	.238	.316	.328
Macon	A	23	13	53	12	1	0	0	13	4	6	6	0	16	3	0	1	2	0	1.00	0	.226	.333	.245
Landry,Lonny,Lakeland	A	23	19	56	9	1	0	0	10	2	4	2	0	16	0	1	0	0	0	.00	0	.161	.190	.179
Lane,Ryan,Fort Wayne	A	21	115	432	115	37	1	6	172	69	56	65	0	92	7	6	4	17	9	.65	9	.266	.368	.398
Langdon,Trajan,Idaho Falls	R	20	11	23	4	0	0	1	7	4	3	3	0	9	0	2	0	0	1	.00	0	.174	.269	.304
Langford,Derrick,Danville	R	21	27	85	29	3	0	1	35	7	16	9	0	18	1	0	1	1	2	.33	2	.341	.406	.412
Mets	R	22	6	16	2	0	0	0	2	0	1	1	1	6	0	0	0	0	0	.00	0	.125	.167	.125
Lantigua,Miguel,Kingsport	R	22	27	84	22	6	0	0	28	11	7	4	0	16	3	1	1	4	2	.67	3	.262	.315	.333
Lanza,Mike,Wisconsin	A	22	101	333	68	13	1	2	89	28	29	22	0	67	2	6	2	10	5	.67	7	.204	.256	.267
Lara,Edward,Athletics	R	20	47	184	53	6	6	1	74	42	26	22	0	19	2	1	2	23	9	.72	4	.288	.367	.402
Lariviere,Jason,New Jersey	A	22	33	100	28	3	1	0	33	13	9	14	0	10	0	2	0	8	2	.80	2	.280	.368	.330
Larkin,Stephen,Charlstn-Sc	A	22	113	369	94	19	1	5	130	50	45	54	4	80	1	3	5	18	10	.64	7	.255	.347	.352
Winston-Sal	A	22	13	50	11	1	0	0	12	2	4	3	1	12	0	0	1	2	2	.50	0	.220	.259	.240
Larue,Jason,Billings	R	22	58	183	50	8	1	5	75	35	31	16	2	28	12	2	2	3	5	.38	2	.273	.366	.410
Lauterhahn,Mike,Williamsprt	A	23	5	14	2	1	0	0	3	5	0	5	0	5	0	0	0	1	1	.50	0	.143	.368	.214
Law,Khris,Athletics	R	21	36	103	17	1	0	2	24	17	11	15	1	37	2	0	0	5	3	.63	2	.165	.283	.233
Lawrence,Mike,Angels	R	20	18	37	6	1	0	0	7	5	5	7	0	11	1	0	1	1	0	1.00	1	.162	.304	.189
Leaman,Jeff,Batavia	A	23	62	220	58	10	1	4	82	30	22	20	0	55	2	2	0	2	4	.33	3	.264	.331	.373
Lebron,Juan,Royals	R	19	47	147	26	5	2	2	41	17	13	10	0	38	2	0	4	0	3	.00	6	.177	.233	.279
LeBron,Ruben,Utica	A	20	52	150	43	6	3	1	58	30	15	11	0	28	2	4	2	16	7	.70	0	.287	.339	.387
Leclair,P.J.,Pittsfield	A	23	31	100	18	3	0	0	21	10	6	7	0	35	1	1	1	0	1	.00	0	.180	.239	.210
Lecronier,Jason,Bluefield	R	23	21	69	17	4	1	2	29	11	10	11	1	17	0	0	1	1	1	.50	1	.246	.346	.420
Frederick	A	23	40	131	37	8	1	6	65	17	19	12	2	40	0	0	0	1	0	1.00	3	.282	.343	.496
Ledee,Ricky,Greensboro	A	22	89	335	90	16	6	14	160	65	49	51	6	66	2	0	1	10	4	.71	3	.269	.368	.478
Lee,Carlos,Hickory	A	20	63	218	54	9	1	4	77	18	30	8	2	34	1	0	0	1	5	.17	7	.248	.278	.353
Bristol	R	20	67	269	93	17	1	7	133	43	45	8	3	34	2	0	3	17	7	.71	6	.346	.365	.494
Lee,Jason,Johnson Cty	R	19	28	76	8	1	0	0	9	10	4	8	0	38	1	1	0	2	4	.33	0	.105	.200	.118
Lemonis,Chris,Jamestown	A	22	57	191	45	7	2	0	56	19	21	18	0	32	2	3	1	5	1	.83	4	.236	.307	.293
Lemons,Rich,Kinston	A	24	5	12	3	1	0	0	4	1	0	2	0	4	0	0	0	1	0	1.00	1	.250	.357	.333
Bakersfield	A	24	36	124	35	5	0	4	52	18	16	13	1	42	1	1	0	4	2	.67	2	.282	.355	.419
Leon,Jose,Savannah	A	19	41	133	22	4	1	0	28	15	11	10	1	46	1	1	0	0	1	.00	6	.165	.229	.211
Leon,Donny,Yankees	R	20	16	41	7	1	0	0	8	3	5	3	0	14	0	0	0	0	0	.00	0	.171	.227	.195
Levias,Andres,South Bend	A	22	25	77	18	1	0	0	19	13	12	6	1	14	0	1	3	7	3	.70	2	.234	.279	.247
Butte	R	22	57	228	67	7	6	1	89	47	26	30	0	35	2	1	1	33	12	.73	3	.294	.379	.390
Lewis,Tyrone,Vero Beach	A	22	1	1	0	0	0	0	0	0	0	0	0	1	0	0	0	0	0	.00	0	.000	.000	.000
Lewis,Andreaus,Columbus	A	22	76	245	64	8	5	2	88	35	23	36	2	86	3	1	2	18	7	.72	0	.261	.360	.359
Lewis,Dwayne,Lethbridge	R	23	16	47	12	3	2	0	19	8	8	15	0	9	1	0	0	1	0	1.00	0	.255	.444	.404
Spokane	A	23	46	149	31	2	1	1	38	24	9	30	0	55	3	1	0	8	8	.50	2	.208	.352	.255
Lewis,Marc,Michigan	A	21	36	92	14	2	1	1	21	14	5	9	0	16	0	2	0	10	3	.77	1	.152	.228	.228
Utica	A	21	69	272	82	15	5	5	122	47	39	17	0	32	0	2	4	24	9	.73	6	.301	.339	.449
Lewis,Rob,Columbus	A	25	20	66	10	1	0	2	17	6	8	9	0	18	1	0	1	0	1	.00	3	.152	.260	.258
Lezeau,James,Salem	A	23	4	5	0	0	0	0	0	0	0	1	0	3	0	0	0	0	0	.00	1	.000	.167	.000
Light,Tal,Asheville	A	22	23	63	17	1	0	4	33	13	13	18	0	17	1	0	0	0	0	.00	0	.270	.417	.524
Lignitz,Jeremiah,Tigers	R	19	30	82	19	1	1	1	25	9	7	9	0	27	3	0	0	1	3	.25	1	.232	.330	.305
Lina,Estivinson,Rangers	R	19	31	89	16	1	0	1	24	10	7	8	0	19	4	0	0	0	1	.00	3	.180	.277	.270
Lindsey,John,Rockies	R	19	48	179	42	10	0	2	58	23	22	11	0	48	7	0	1	0	2	.00	4	.235	.303	.324
Lindsey,Rod,Idaho Falls	R	20	35	155	41	4	4	0	53	30	14	13	0	37	4	0	1	21	7	.75	1	.265	.335	.342
Liniak,Cole,Red Sox	R	19	23	79	21	7	0	1	31	9	8	4	0	8	1	2	0	2	0	1.00	1	.266	.310	.392
Little,Mark,Charlotte	A	23	115	438	112	31	8	9	186	75	50	51	1	108	14	2	2	20	14	.59	4	.256	.350	.425
Livingston,Clyde,Martinsvlle	R	23	33	104	22	5	2	2	37	15	25	8	0	22	0	0	1	0	1	1.00	0	.212	.265	.356
Livsey,Shane,Rockford	A	22	57	226	64	10	1	2	82	39	27	22	3	30	2	0	0	21	7	.75	0	.283	.352	.363
Llanos,Alexis,Angels	R	19	26	53	15	1	2	0	20	6	3	3	0	11	0	1	0	0	0	.00	0	.283	.321	.377
Llanos,Aurelio,Hagerstown	A	25	106	378	95	25	1	17	173	54	63	29	2	115	11	0	3	9	7	.56	5	.251	.321	.458
Llanos,Francisco,Expos	R	19	37	114	17	9	0	0	26	15	5	10	0	40	1	0	0	3	2	.60	1	.149	.224	.228
Llanos,Victor,Peoria	A	21	21	47	13	2	0	0	15	7	3	3	0	7	0	0	0	1	1	.00	0	.277	.320	.319
Llibre,Brian,Rangers	R	18	24	67	18	2	0	0	20	4	8	2	0	21	0	0	2	1	0	1.00	1	.269	.282	.299
Lobaton,Jose,Greensboro	A	22	60	185	45	6	5	0	61	26	23	22	0	58	2	11	2	11	6	.65	3	.243	.327	.330

347

1995 Batting -- Single-A and Rookie Leagues

Player	Lg	A	G	AB	H	2B	3B	HR	TB	R	RBI	TBB	IBB	SO	HBP	SH	SF	SB	CS	SB%	GDP	Avg	OBP	SLG
Oneonta	A	22	41	145	32	11	3	1	52	23	11	13	0	30	2	1	0	4	1	.80	2	.221	.294	.359
Loeb,Marc,Dunedin	A	26	64	193	43	12	0	1	58	17	23	24	0	46	2	3	0	1	1	.50	3	.223	.315	.301
Lofton,James,Winston-Sal	A	22	38	123	27	5	1	0	34	15	14	8	1	22	1	2	0	1	4	.20	0	.220	.273	.276
Charlstn-Wv	A	22	65	192	40	10	1	0	52	20	14	18	1	43	3	2	0	8	5	.62	2	.208	.286	.271
Lomasney,Steve,Red Sox	R	18	29	92	15	6	0	0	21	10	7	8	1	16	5	1	0	2	1	.67	0	.163	.267	.228
Lombard,George,Macon	A	20	49	180	37	6	1	3	54	32	16	27	3	44	5	1	0	16	4	.80	4	.206	.325	.300
Eugene	A	20	68	262	66	5	3	5	92	38	19	23	0	91	5	2	1	35	13	.73	0	.252	.323	.351
Lombardi,John,Sarasota	A	26	7	19	5	2	0	0	7	2	1	0	0	4	1	0	0	0	0	.00	0	.263	.300	.368
Long,Garrett,Pirates	R	19	20	63	22	2	1	1	29	13	8	17	0	10	0	0	0	0	1	.00	3	.349	.488	.460
Erie	A	19	29	108	30	4	0	2	40	17	16	15	0	25	1	0	2	2	2	.50	6	.278	.365	.370
Long,Justin,Brevard Cty	A	24	9	17	2	0	0	0	2	3	1	1	0	11	0	0	0	0	0	.00	0	.118	.167	.118
Elmira	A	24	56	186	39	6	1	5	62	25	17	17	0	54	1	1	1	13	3	.81	3	.210	.278	.333
Long,Terrence,Columbia	A	20	55	178	35	1	2	2	46	27	13	28	4	43	1	1	0	8	5	.62	3	.197	.309	.258
Pittsfield	A	20	51	187	48	9	4	4	77	24	31	18	2	36	1	1	1	11	4	.73	2	.257	.324	.412
Longueira,Tony,Royals	R	21	41	95	23	5	0	1	31	12	13	9	0	11	1	1	2	3	0	1.00	1	.242	.308	.326
Lopez,Edgar,Braves	R	21	38	117	25	4	0	0	29	14	5	20	0	13	0	1	0	5	5	.50	3	.214	.328	.248
Lopez,Jose,Columbia	A	20	82	280	65	17	4	5	105	37	38	35	3	76	4	2	7	7	2	.78	7	.232	.319	.375
St. Lucie	A	20	1	2	2	0	0	0	2	0	1	2	0	0	0	0	0	0	0	.00	0	1.000	1.000	1.000
Lopez,Louis,Ogden	R	23	46	182	65	15	0	7	101	36	39	16	0	20	2	3	2	1	1	.50	1	.357	.411	.555
Lopez,Mendy,Wilmington	A	21	130	428	116	29	3	2	157	42	36	28	0	73	5	7	2	18	10	.64	12	.271	.322	.367
Lopez,Mickey,Helena	R	22	57	225	73	19	2	1	99	66	41	38	3	20	5	2	4	12	8	.60	1	.324	.426	.440
Lopez,Victor,Charlstn-Sc	A	23	12	38	11	3	0	0	14	4	2	4	0	3	1	0	0	3	0	1.00	1	.289	.372	.368
Lopiccolo,Jamie,Ogden	R	23	70	260	101	11	3	12	154	74	55	55	4	40	8	0	3	15	7	.68	7	.388	.503	.592
Lorenzo,Juan,Twins	R	18	14	46	10	0	0	0	10	3	2	4	0	6	0	0	1	0	0	.00	0	.217	.275	.217
Lowell,Mike,Oneonta	A	22	72	281	73	18	0	1	94	36	27	23	0	34	3	0	6	3	1	.75	5	.260	.316	.335
Lowery,Terrell,Rangers	R	25	10	34	9	3	1	3	23	10	7	6	0	7	0	0	0	1	0	1.00	1	.265	.375	.676
Charlotte	A	25	11	35	9	2	2	0	15	4	4	6	0	6	1	0	0	1	0	1.00	2	.257	.381	.429
Lowry,Curt,Clinton	A	23	57	182	39	1	2	0	44	33	16	26	1	51	1	1	0	7	6	.54	2	.214	.314	.242
Luciano,Virgilio,Charlstn-Sc	A	20	104	285	62	14	1	2	84	30	31	26	2	76	3	3	4	18	9	.67	2	.218	.286	.295
Lugo,Jesus,Peoria	A	21	65	219	58	11	2	2	79	26	29	12	3	31	2	0	1	1	1	.50	8	.265	.309	.361
Lugo,Julio,Auburn	A	20	59	230	67	6	3	1	82	36	16	26	0	31	2	2	0	17	7	.71	7	.291	.368	.357
Lugo,Urbino,Burlington	R	21	32	94	23	0	0	0	23	13	5	3	0	20	0	1	0	9	4	.69	6	.245	.268	.245
Lunar,Fernando,Macon	A	19	39	134	24	2	0	0	26	13	9	10	0	38	3	3	0	1	0	1.00	3	.179	.252	.194
Eugene	A	19	38	131	32	6	0	2	44	13	16	9	0	28	0	2	0	0	1	.00	2	.244	.293	.336
Lutz,Manuel,White Sox	R	20	45	160	45	10	3	3	70	23	31	19	2	42	0	2	0	0	0	.00	3	.281	.361	.438
Luuloa,Keith,Lk Elsinore	A	21	102	380	100	22	7	5	151	50	53	24	0	47	6	7	1	1	5	.17	9	.263	.316	.397
Macero,Victor,Cubs	R	19	41	128	30	5	0	2	41	17	11	14	0	25	1	1	2	4	2	.67	2	.234	.310	.320
Macias,Jose,Vermont	A	22	53	176	42	4	2	0	50	24	9	19	0	19	2	2	0	11	7	.61	3	.239	.320	.284
Mackert,Jamie,Erie	A	22	35	101	22	4	4	2	40	18	17	22	0	46	1	1	0	0	4	.00	2	.218	.363	.396
Macon,Leland,Charlotte	A	23	119	405	105	15	3	2	132	52	38	41	1	85	22	2	7	14	12	.54	10	.259	.354	.326
Mader,Chris,Kinston	A	25	11	27	2	0	0	0	2	1	2	1	0	5	1	1	0	0	0	.00	0	.074	.138	.074
Madonna,Chris,St. Lucie	A	23	3	5	0	0	0	0	0	0	0	0	0	1	0	0	0	0	0	.00	0	.000	.000	.000
Madsen,Dave,St. Pete	A	24	121	388	109	20	3	4	147	48	64	70	1	62	2	0	9	1	0	1.00	14	.281	.386	.379
Magee,Danny,Durham	A	21	76	266	68	11	1	4	93	38	29	11	0	46	12	1	0	7	5	.58	5	.256	.315	.350
Mahoney,Mike,Eugene	A	23	43	112	27	6	0	1	36	14	15	15	1	17	3	1	1	6	2	.75	5	.241	.344	.321
Majeski,Brian,Vero Beach	A	21	69	147	33	3	1	2	44	22	11	26	2	34	2	3	0	9	8	.53	0	.224	.349	.299
Malave,Jaime,Yakima	A	21	44	137	37	13	2	1	57	12	15	6	0	41	1	1	2	1	1	.50	1	.270	.301	.416
Maleski,Tom,Williamsprt	A	18	40	112	26	8	1	0	36	13	14	19	0	25	2	1	0	1	1	.50	2	.232	.348	.321
Malin,Edgar,Huntington	R	21	21	63	11	1	0	1	15	12	8	10	0	27	0	0	0	3	2	.60	3	.175	.288	.238
Malone,Scott,Charlotte	A	25	100	314	74	14	1	2	96	33	40	45	1	41	2	5	3	5	2	.71	8	.236	.332	.306
Maloney,Jeffrey,Blue Jays	R	19	29	92	15	5	0	0	20	9	12	6	0	24	2	0	1	2	1	.67	4	.163	.228	.217
Manfredi,Joel,Great Falls	R	20	33	73	16	2	0	1	21	6	10	6	0	14	0	0	0	0	0	.00	3	.219	.278	.288
Mangham,Rodney,Kissimmee	A	24	42	134	28	7	1	0	37	19	12	22	0	31	0	3	1	5	3	.63	1	.209	.318	.276
Mapp,Eric,Princeton	R	18	61	210	47	11	0	5	73	32	23	18	0	58	3	2	0	10	1	.91	1	.224	.294	.348
Marine,Del,Lakeland	A	24	77	257	62	14	0	4	88	27	25	13	0	63	5	0	3	5	1	.83	5	.241	.288	.342
Markert,Joshua,Yakima	A	22	34	81	22	4	1	0	28	10	10	14	0	17	1	0	0	1	1	.50	2	.272	.385	.346
Marnell,Anthony,Idaho Falls	R	22	3	8	1	0	0	0	1	0	1	2	0	1	0	0	0	0	0	.00	0	.125	.300	.250
Padres	R	22	1	5	2	1	0	0	3	1	3	0	0	2	0	0	0	0	0	.00	0	.400	.400	.600
Rancho Cuca	A	22	16	23	1	0	0	0	1	3	1	1	0	13	0	0	0	0	0	.00	0	.043	.083	.043
Marquez,Jesus,Riverside	A	23	84	312	74	9	2	2	93	42	26	18	0	62	4	2	4	4	5	.44	5	.237	.284	.298
Marrero,Elieser,St. Pete	A	22	107	383	81	16	1	10	129	43	55	23	2	55	1	0	7	9	4	.69	10	.211	.254	.337
Marsh,Roy,Kissimmee	A	22	114	393	85	18	3	4	121	51	23	38	0	95	4	2	0	22	11	.67	6	.216	.292	.308
Martin,Lincoln,High Desert	A	24	54	150	36	7	2	1	50	27	12	28	0	37	0	4	2	7	4	.64	2	.240	.356	.333
Martin,Mike,Clinton	A	23	51	127	24	3	0	0	27	10	14	24	0	24	1	2	4	2	0	1.00	3	.189	.314	.213
Martin,Mike,Lakeland	A	24	6	17	3	0	0	0	3	1	1	3	0	1	0	1	0	0	0	.00	0	.176	.300	.176
Martin,Ryan,Danville	R	20	5	14	3	1	0	0	4	2	2	3	0	5	0	0	0	0	1	.00	0	.214	.353	.286
Martinez,Dalvis,Fayettevlle	A	22	36	102	26	7	0	3	42	17	15	16	0	35	0	1	0	1	0	1.00	1	.255	.356	.412
Lakeland	A	22	38	111	21	5	0	0	26	12	5	12	0	26	1	2	0	0	1	.00	6	.189	.274	.234
Martinez,Dave,Hudson Vall	A	22	44	124	31	6	0	0	37	19	17	13	1	25	3	0	2	1	1	.50	1	.250	.331	.298
Martinez,Eddy,Bluefield	R	18	57	185	57	11	3	1	77	42	35	23	0	42	5	1	0	5	5	.50	4	.308	.397	.416
Martinez,Erik,Clinton	A	24	29	59	6	0	0	0	6	4	2	3	0	10	1	1	0	2	0	1.00	1	.102	.159	.102
Ogden	R	24	34	116	30	9	0	1	42	21	13	11	0	26	6	6	1	1	0	1.00	4	.259	.351	.362
Martinez,Greg,Stockton	A	24	114	410	113	8	2	0	125	80	43	69	1	64	2	10	1	55	9	.86	7	.276	.382	.305
Martinez,Hipolito,Athletics	R	19	46	149	33	4	4	2	51	23	27	16	1	47	1	0	7	8	4	.67	1	.221	.289	.342
Martinez,Matt,Ogden	R	25	4	10	2	0	0	0	2	3	0	1	0	2	1	1	0	0	0	.00	0	.200	.333	.200
Martinez,Obed,Idaho Falls	R	20	53	193	53	7	1	1	65	31	31	15	0	33	3	1	0	3	3	.50	8	.275	.336	.337
Martinez,Rafael,Great Falls	R	20	58	183	50	13	3	4	81	30	30	23	0	36	1	0	3	5	3	.67	6	.273	.358	.443

1995 Batting -- Single-A and Rookie Leagues

Player	Lg	A	G	AB	H	2B	3B	HR	TB	R	RBI	TBB	IBB	SO	HBP	SH	SF	SB	CS	SB%	GDP	Avg	OBP	SLG
Martinez,Ramon,Brevard Cty	A	26	99	372	98	7	2	2	115	47	24	29	2	84	4	4	1	21	4	.84	0	.263	.323	.309
Martinez,Roger,Pittsfield	A	23	23	69	7	3	0	0	10	1	3	5	0	20	1	0	1	1	0	1.00	1	.101	.171	.145
Martinez,Tony,Johnson Cty	R	23	24	77	18	0	1	2	26	18	8	26	0	14	1	1	0	3	2	.60	2	.234	.433	.338
Martins,Eric,Modesto	A	23	106	407	118	17	5	1	148	71	54	62	0	74	4	18	4	7	8	.47	8	.290	.386	.364
Marval,Raul,San Jose	A	20	10	36	10	0	0	0	10	1	3	1	0	5	0	2	0	1	1	.50	0	.278	.297	.278
Burlington	A	20	88	296	79	8	2	1	94	42	19	10	0	32	6	3	1	4	6	.40	9	.267	.304	.318
Mason,Lamont,Princeton	R	23	26	78	13	3	1	0	18	11	3	16	0	21	0	0	0	6	4	.60	2	.167	.309	.231
Mastrullo,Mike,Huntington	R	21	46	134	24	5	2	0	33	20	14	25	0	43	3	10	4	5	4	.56	4	.179	.313	.246
Mata,Manuel,Martinsvlle	R	19	1	5	2	0	0	0	2	1	2	0	0	0	0	0	0	0	0	.00	0	.400	.400	.400
Mateo,Henry,Expos	R	19	38	122	18	0	0	0	18	11	6	14	0	47	5	5	1	2	7	.22	2	.148	.261	.148
Mateo,Jose,Great Falls	R	19	40	110	27	2	0	0	29	20	3	13	0	30	2	3	0	4	3	.57	2	.245	.336	.264
Mathews,Byron,South Bend	A	25	97	332	66	11	4	1	88	40	34	32	2	70	3	7	4	16	11	.59	6	.199	.272	.265
Mathis,Joe,Wisconsin	A	21	117	376	100	17	3	6	141	59	43	43	1	91	0	5	2	26	6	.81	7	.266	.340	.375
Matos,Julius,Columbus	A	21	52	155	38	7	3	0	51	16	13	11	1	21	3	1	0	2	2	.50	8	.245	.308	.329
Matos,Pascual,Macon	A	21	72	238	44	11	1	5	72	23	26	11	0	86	1	0	0	2	2	.50	4	.185	.224	.303
Matthews,Gary,Clinton	A	21	128	421	100	18	4	2	132	57	40	68	1	109	6	3	3	28	8	.78	7	.238	.349	.314
Matvey,Mike,St. Pete	A	24	87	304	83	15	4	0	106	32	20	40	1	67	3	2	1	1	5	.17	2	.273	.362	.349
Mauch,Dennis,Great Falls	R	22	28	79	20	2	0	0	22	10	9	10	0	19	6	1	1	4	2	.67	1	.253	.375	.278
Maxwell,Jason,Daytona	A	24	117	388	102	13	3	10	151	66	58	63	1	68	6	1	8	12	7	.63	6	.263	.368	.389
May,Freddie,Pirates	R	20	29	96	32	5	2	2	47	18	13	18	0	16	0	1	0	2	4	.33	2	.333	.435	.490
Erie	A	20	27	90	24	3	1	1	32	10	12	5	0	25	1	1	1	5	5	.50	2	.267	.309	.356
Mayber,Chan,Asheville	A	23	34	88	17	4	0	0	21	11	3	7	0	19	0	1	0	7	0	1.00	1	.193	.253	.239
Portland	A	23	27	78	16	2	1	0	20	13	8	13	0	22	2	2	0	6	3	.67	0	.205	.333	.256
Maynor,Tonka,Erie	A	24	11	31	4	1	0	1	8	2	3	4	0	2	2	0	0	0	0	.00	0	.129	.270	.258
Maysonet,Jose,Blue Jays	R	20	29	69	10	2	0	0	12	14	1	14	0	11	2	2	0	1	2	.33	3	.145	.306	.174
McAninch,John,Boise	A	22	42	112	28	9	0	2	43	16	12	11	0	24	2	1	0	0	0	.00	6	.250	.328	.384
McAulay,John,Hudson Vall	A	23	24	52	11	0	0	0	11	7	4	8	0	9	2	1	3	1	1	.50	1	.212	.323	.212
McBride,Charles,Durham	A	22	102	360	85	15	1	13	141	60	59	54	1	109	5	1	2	11	4	.73	5	.236	.342	.392
McCalmont,Jim,Fort Wayne	A	24	7	33	11	3	0	3	23	5	7	3	0	3	0	0	0	2	0	1.00	1	.333	.389	.697
Fort Myers	A	24	92	285	65	13	2	4	94	30	21	23	1	54	8	3	4	2	7	.22	8	.228	.300	.330
McCarthy,Kevin,Kingsport	R	19	26	91	12	2	1	1	19	11	4	17	1	18	1	0	0	1	2	.33	0	.132	.275	.209
Mets	R	19	22	75	10	1	0	1	14	5	5	2	0	13	1	0	2	0	0	.00	2	.133	.163	.187
McCartney,Sommer,Elmira	A	23	33	112	20	4	0	1	27	11	5	6	0	29	2	0	0	1	3	.25	1	.179	.233	.241
McCarty,Matt,Great Falls	R	20	16	22	5	0	0	0	5	3	1	1	0	4	1	0	0	1	0	.00	0	.227	.292	.227
Lethbridge	R	20	38	141	43	3	4	1	57	27	14	12	0	31	2	1	0	6	2	.75	5	.305	.365	.404
McClain,Terrence,Yakima	A	24	33	54	11	2	0	0	13	12	2	12	0	23	3	1	0	7	3	.70	1	.204	.377	.241
McClendon,Trav,New Jersey	A	23	50	161	46	9	1	1	60	25	18	10	1	25	5	1	1	6	3	.67	5	.286	.345	.373
McClure,Craig,Hickory	A	20	49	154	26	3	1	2	37	13	8	17	0	56	0	1	0	6	2	.75	4	.169	.251	.240
Bristol	R	20	64	223	52	6	2	4	74	26	26	22	0	65	3	4	1	7	8	.47	3	.233	.309	.332
McCormick,Andrew,Medicne Hat	R	23	69	258	76	8	2	5	113	64	37	64	0	67	3	1	1	15	5	.75	3	.295	.439	.438
McCormick,Cody,Oneonta	A	21	74	268	74	16	2	6	112	33	32	30	1	60	4	1	2	4	2	.67	2	.276	.355	.418
McCroskey,Jackie,Huntington	R	22	49	156	45	12	5	2	73	26	27	26	1	31	3	0	1	12	3	.80	0	.288	.398	.468
McDonald,Ashanti,Williamsprt	A	23	59	193	48	4	1	1	57	26	20	13	0	46	4	2	1	4	5	.44	5	.249	.308	.295
McDonald,Donzell,Yankees	R	21	28	110	26	5	1	0	33	23	9	16	0	24	2	0	1	11	2	.85	1	.236	.341	.300
McDonald,Jason,Modesto	A	24	133	493	129	25	7	6	186	109	50	110	0	84	6	8	2	70	20	.78	6	.262	.401	.377
McDonald,Keith,Peoria	A	23	65	179	48	6	0	1	57	22	20	22	0	38	6	4	0	0	1	.00	2	.268	.367	.318
McDougal,Mike,Savannah	A	21	15	50	4	0	0	0	4	2	4	2	0	17	0	0	0	1	1	.50	1	.080	.115	.080
Johnson Cty	R	21	32	97	17	3	1	3	31	8	12	6	0	27	0	0	0	0	2	.00	2	.175	.223	.320
McDougall,Matt,Mariners	R	19	27	101	24	3	0	0	27	17	9	12	0	21	1	0	0	9	4	.69	0	.238	.325	.267
McGonigle,Bill,Stockton	A	24	78	210	55	8	1	0	65	33	21	23	0	35	4	8	3	3	4	.43	3	.262	.342	.310
McHenry,Joe,Twins	R	20	34	114	25	8	0	0	33	9	7	9	0	38	0	2	1	2	3	.40	1	.219	.274	.289
McHugh,Ryan,New Jersey	A	22	26	98	19	4	0	1	26	7	14	8	0	39	1	1	1	2	0	1.00	3	.194	.259	.265
McKinnis,Leroy,Rancho Cuca	A	23	15	49	12	1	0	1	16	9	6	10	1	10	1	0	2	1	0	1.00	3	.245	.371	.327
McKinnon,Sandy,Pr. William	A	22	125	494	125	19	5	2	160	64	23	39	0	93	3	3	1	35	17	.67	6	.253	.311	.324
McKinnon,Tom,St. Pete	A	23	53	172	46	16	0	2	68	15	10	5	2	39	0	0	1	1	1	.50	4	.267	.287	.395
McLamb,Brian,Greensboro	A	23	81	252	57	11	0	6	86	34	32	25	2	61	6	2	0	11	4	.73	9	.226	.311	.341
McLendon,Craig,Rangers	R	20	25	66	16	2	0	0	18	7	4	5	0	10	1	0	0	1	0	1.00	2	.242	.306	.273
Hudson Vall	A	20	4	6	0	0	0	0	0	0	0	0	0	3	0	0	0	0	0	.00	0	.000	.000	.000
McMillan,Tommy,Savannah	A	20	85	262	56	8	1	7	87	21	21	35	2	91	2	3	2	5	4	.56	3	.214	.309	.332
McMullen,Jon,Clearwater	A	22	30	118	28	7	0	1	38	17	14	20	2	19	0	0	0	0	6	.00	2	.237	.348	.322
McNally,Jason,Rockies	R	24	41	141	30	2	0	2	38	18	18	18	0	39	4	1	1	2	1	.67	3	.213	.317	.270
McNally,Sean,Springfield	A	23	132	479	130	28	8	12	210	60	79	35	6	119	8	0	6	6	3	.67	10	.271	.328	.438
McNally,Shawn,New Jersey	A	22	24	90	23	5	0	1	31	11	10	8	0	18	5	1	0	5	1	.83	1	.256	.350	.344
Savannah	A	23	49	169	37	8	2	1	52	21	14	24	0	48	1	2	1	8	2	.80	2	.219	.318	.308
McNeal,Pepe,Burlington	R	20	27	89	25	7	0	1	33	4	15	4	0	20	2	0	1	2	0	1.00	2	.281	.323	.371
Johnson Cty	R	20	27	97	17	6	0	0	23	9	12	15	1	28	1	0	1	2	0	1.00	3	.175	.289	.237
McSparin,Paul,Pirates	R	22	23	72	21	5	0	3	35	14	13	4	0	19	1	0	1	1	1	.50	2	.292	.333	.486
McWhite,Moe,Danville	R	20	64	231	60	16	1	12	114	37	53	16	0	76	3	1	2	8	4	.67	5	.260	.313	.494
Mealing,Allen,Beloit	A	22	19	41	9	2	0	0	11	4	2	3	0	17	0	0	0	2	1	.67	0	.220	.273	.268
Helena	R	22	55	169	59	11	4	4	90	35	31	23	1	43	1	2	0	17	7	.71	3	.349	.430	.533
Medina,Tito,Rockford	A	26	61	12	1	0	1	0	16	8	8	7	0	15	2	0	0	6	1	.86	2	.197	.300	.262
Cubs	R	23	76	17	5	1	0	0	24	10	11	10	0	4	1	0	1	7	4	.64	1	.224	.318	.316
Medina,Robert,Blue Jays	R	20	30	62	11	1	1	2	20	5	8	4	0	23	0	0	0	1	1	.50	1	.177	.227	.323
Medrano,Teodoro,Everett	A	20	1	3	1	0	0	0	1	0	0	0	0	0	0	0	0	0	0	.00	0	.333	.333	.333
Mariners	R	20	1	1	0	0	0	0	0	0	0	0	0	0	0	0	0	0	0	.00	0	.000	.000	.000
Meggers,Mike,Winston-Sal	A	25	76	272	67	18	1	20	147	45	54	32	5	69	1	0	4	7	3	.70	5	.246	.324	.540
Meilan,Tony,Bakersfield	A	24	12	38	8	1	0	0	9	3	2	4	0	4	1	1	0	1	1	.50	0	.211	.268	.237

349

1995 Batting -- Single-A and Rookie Leagues

				BATTING														BASERUNNING				PERCENTAGES		
Player	Lg	A	G	AB	H	2B	3B	HR	TB	R	RBI	TBB	IBB	SO	HBP	SH	SF	SB	CS	SB%	GDP	Avg	OBP	SLG
Mejia,Marlon,Astros	R	21	34	98	23	1	0	0	24	19	5	8	0	21	2	6	0	2	3	.40	5	.235	.306	.245
Mejia,Miguel,High Desert	A	21	37	119	32	6	1	0	40	14	12	14	0	17	1	2	1	16	7	.70	3	.269	.348	.336
Bluefield	R	21	51	181	54	6	3	3	75	50	30	18	0	30	1	6	2	36	5	.88	5	.298	.361	.414
Melhuse,Adam,Dunedin	A	24	123	428	92	20	0	4	124	43	41	61	1	87	1	1	4	6	1	.86	7	.215	.312	.290
Melito,Mark,Spokane	A	24	61	200	50	7	1	3	68	24	20	27	0	30	6	5	2	2	2	.50	3	.250	.353	.340
Melo,Juan,Clinton	A	20	134	479	135	32	1	5	184	65	46	33	0	88	5	5	2	12	10	.55	11	.282	.333	.384
Meluskey,Mitch,Kinston	A	22	8	29	7	5	0	0	12	5	2	2	0	9	0	0	0	0	0	.00	0	.241	.290	.414
Kissimmee	A	22	78	261	56	18	1	3	85	23	31	27	2	33	1	2	4	3	0	1.00	12	.215	.287	.326
Mendez,Carlos,Wilmington	A	22	107	396	108	19	2	7	152	46	61	18	1	36	0	1	5	0	4	.00	17	.273	.301	.384
Mendez,Emilio,Beloit	A	23	7	17	1	0	0	0	1	0	1	1	0	9	0	1	0	0	0	.00	0	.059	.111	.059
Mendez,Rodolfo,Springfield	A	21	129	449	124	28	11	10	204	70	72	34	2	121	8	2	7	40	10	.80	13	.276	.333	.454
Mendez,Sergio,Lynchburg	A	22	65	236	58	13	0	8	95	30	35	9	1	49	3	2	2	9	4	.69	9	.246	.280	.403
Mendoza,Carlos,Kingsport	R	21	51	192	63	9	0	1	75	56	24	27	0	24	3	4	2	28	6	.82	3	.328	.415	.391
Mendoza,Francisco,Springfield	A	23	96	308	78	18	1	11	131	38	49	24	1	65	2	0	5	4	1	.80	7	.253	.307	.425
Mendoza,Jesus,Hickory	A	23	116	434	109	24	2	8	161	49	49	36	3	53	9	2	4	2	7	.22	11	.251	.319	.371
Menechino,Frankie,Pr. William	A	25	137	476	124	31	3	6	179	65	58	96	2	75	11	3	8	6	2	.75	17	.261	.391	.376
Mepri,Sal,Princeton	R	19	6	5	1	0	0	0	1	0	0	0	0	3	0	0	0	0	0	.00	0	.200	.200	.200
Mercado,Julio,Rangers	R	19	55	156	26	5	0	0	31	13	12	10	0	49	0	1	1	9	2	.82	1	.167	.216	.199
Merila,Mark,Idaho Falls	R	24	56	197	56	7	0	0	63	42	39	43	0	21	5	6	3	5	3	.63	5	.284	.419	.320
Meskauskas,John,Portland	A	23	9	29	10	3	0	1	16	4	9	8	1	7	1	0	2	2	2	.50	0	.345	.500	.552
Asheville	A	23	30	79	22	4	0	3	35	11	13	4	0	16	1	0	2	0	1	.00	4	.278	.314	.443
Messick,J.T.,Butte	R	23	40	130	26	5	1	0	33	16	14	21	0	23	0	1	3	0	0	.00	5	.200	.305	.254
Lethbridge	R	23	6	19	6	2	0	0	8	2	6	2	0	4	0	0	0	0	0	.00	1	.316	.381	.421
Messner,Jake,Burlington	R	19	46	144	32	2	4	0	42	17	9	14	0	40	1	0	1	7	5	.58	0	.222	.294	.292
Meyer,Bobby,Great Falls	R	21	25	40	6	0	1	0	8	4	4	3	0	14	0	1	0	0	0	.00	1	.150	.205	.200
Meyer,Travis,Yakima	A	22	36	83	17	7	0	0	24	9	5	11	0	22	1	0	2	0	1	.00	4	.205	.299	.289
Micucci,Mike,Daytona	A	23	23	41	8	2	0	0	10	4	3	4	0	9	0	2	0	0	0	.00	0	.195	.267	.244
Mientkiewicz,Douglas,Fort Myers	A	22	38	110	27	6	1	1	38	9	15	18	1	19	1	2	0	2	2	.50	1	.245	.357	.345
Mifflin,Brian,Mets	R	22	51	193	59	13	1	5	89	29	40	5	0	43	1	0	7	1	1	.50	7	.306	.316	.461
Kingsport	R	22	1	4	1	0	0	0	1	1	0	1	0	0	0	0	0	0	0	.00	0	.250	.400	.250
Miles,Aaron,Astros	R	19	47	171	44	9	3	0	59	32	18	14	0	14	0	4	1	9	6	.60	3	.257	.312	.345
Millar,Kevin,Brevard Cty	A	24	129	459	132	32	2	13	207	53	68	70	2	66	12	0	10	4	4	.50	8	.288	.388	.451
Milleding,Tony,Johnson Cty	R	20	31	87	24	7	1	3	42	14	12	7	0	15	1	0	0	1	0	1.00	1	.276	.337	.483
Miller,Kumandae,Elmira	A	22	47	154	31	4	3	0	41	9	15	8	0	40	2	2	3	2	4	.33	4	.201	.246	.266
Miller,Mike,Jamestown	A	23	64	197	45	9	1	3	65	39	27	60	0	66	10	0	0	10	7	.59	6	.228	.431	.330
Miller,Roy,Riverside	A	24	65	175	32	4	0	1	39	21	18	12	0	49	5	1	1	3	4	.43	4	.183	.254	.223
Millican,Kevin,Charlstn-Sc	A	24	88	270	58	17	0	5	90	27	28	31	1	81	2	1	2	2	4	.33	4	.215	.298	.333
Millwood,Terry,Twins	R	20	48	165	36	6	3	0	48	15	13	17	0	29	4	0	1	5	2	.71	1	.218	.305	.291
Milord,Clausel,Jamestown	A	22	34	87	18	3	1	1	26	13	12	20	0	21	1	0	2	6	4	.60	1	.207	.355	.299
Minici,Jason,Watertown	A	22	66	231	48	5	0	6	71	28	27	25	1	65	4	2	1	4	3	.57	3	.208	.295	.307
Miranda,Alex,W. Michigan	A	24	124	393	91	21	2	8	140	53	60	75	6	78	5	2	4	6	8	.43	3	.232	.358	.356
Miranda,Tony,Spokane	A	23	71	266	72	17	0	2	95	53	22	28	1	36	7	3	2	15	10	.60	8	.271	.353	.357
Mitchell,Donovan,Quad City	A	26	111	383	126	23	1	4	163	72	42	29	0	38	2	5	3	21	15	.58	10	.329	.376	.426
Mitchell,Mike,Tampa	A	23	102	368	98	16	1	8	140	40	61	29	1	52	2	1	6	1	0	1.00	10	.266	.319	.380
Mitchell,Rivers,Jamestown	A	24	60	234	66	8	6	0	86	28	17	13	0	35	3	7	0	15	7	.68	2	.282	.328	.368
Miyake,Chris,Erie	A	22	61	227	70	6	5	2	92	34	25	12	0	31	5	1	1	14	6	.70	3	.308	.355	.405
Miyauchi,Hector,Expos	R	29	16	43	10	2	0	1	15	9	2	7	0	8	3	0	0	3	1	.75	0	.233	.377	.349
Mobilia,Bill,Piedmont	A	25	55	150	36	5	2	0	45	17	17	13	0	39	2	7	1	1	0	1.00	1	.240	.307	.300
Moeder,Tony,Lk Elsinore	A	24	68	252	60	18	1	6	98	39	26	27	2	61	3	0	1	2	3	.40	7	.238	.318	.389
Cedar Rapds	A	24	48	168	45	11	1	15	103	32	47	19	0	36	4	0	3	2	2	.50	2	.268	.351	.613
Molina,Jose,Daytona	A	21	82	233	55	9	1	1	69	27	19	29	0	53	7	2	2	1	0	1.00	7	.236	.336	.296
Molina,Luis,Wisconsin	A	22	109	337	86	18	1	3	115	45	42	42	3	72	4	3	1	7	9	.44	5	.255	.345	.341
Monahan,Shane,Wisconsin	A	21	59	233	66	9	6	1	90	34	32	11	0	40	2	7	3	9	2	.82	4	.283	.317	.386
Monds,Wonder,Braves	R	23	4	15	2	0	0	0	2	1	1	1	0	8	0	0	0	2	1	.67	0	.133	.188	.133
Durham	A	23	81	297	83	17	0	6	118	44	33	17	1	63	1	1	1	28	7	.80	7	.279	.320	.397
Monroe,Craig,Rangers	R	19	54	193	48	6	2	0	58	22	33	18	0	25	2	1	2	13	2	.87	1	.249	.316	.301
Monroe,Darryl,Fayettevlle	A	24	104	382	99	21	2	3	133	55	28	23	1	76	16	8	3	23	12	.66	7	.259	.325	.348
Montas,Ricardo,Royals	R	19	22	28	2	0	0	1	5	2	3	3	0	6	1	0	0	0	0	.00	1	.071	.188	.179
Montgomery,Andre,Billings	R	22	44	122	31	2	1	1	38	18	9	8	0	20	1	1	2	4	4	.50	0	.254	.301	.311
Montiel,Dave,Beloit	A	23	74	100	16	1	0	0	17	20	11	11	0	19	8	4	3	19	10	.66	0	.160	.287	.170
Montilla,Julio,Royals	R	23	17	46	11	0	0	0	11	6	3	9	0	5	0	0	1	0	0	.00	1	.239	.357	.239
Wilmington	A	23	8	27	6	0	0	0	6	0	1	4	0	6	0	1	0	0	0	.00	0	.222	.323	.222
Moore,Donnie,Brewers	R	20	38	71	17	0	0	1	20	10	6	8	0	27	1	0	1	3	1	.75	0	.239	.318	.282
Moore,James,Padres	R	21	15	50	16	4	1	1	25	7	9	4	0	17	1	1	1	1	1	.50	2	.320	.375	.500
Idaho Falls	R	21	15	47	12	5	0	0	19	10	6	7	0	9	1	0	1	1	0	1.00	1	.255	.357	.404
Moore,Mark,Modesto	A	25	77	261	68	16	0	10	114	40	48	42	0	76	6	0	3	3	2	.60	9	.261	.363	.437
Moore,Mike,Vero Beach	A	25	7	22	6	1	0	0	7	3	1	6	0	8	0	0	0	0	1	.00	1	.273	.429	.318
Moore,Vince,Rancho Cuca	A	24	84	299	68	11	1	15	126	50	57	35	0	102	4	0	2	10	5	.67	5	.227	.312	.421
Moore,Brandon,South Bend	A	23	132	510	131	9	3	0	146	75	37	48	1	49	3	7	5	34	8	.81	15	.257	.322	.286
Morales,Erick,Columbia	A	22	38	109	30	4	0	0	34	12	11	12	0	18	1	3	0	2	1	.67	1	.275	.352	.312
Pittsfield	A	22	66	237	57	6	1	1	68	18	28	20	2	36	1	6	3	2	2	.50	4	.241	.299	.287
Morales,Alex,Bellingham	A	22	66	248	63	18	3	6	105	43	25	34	0	60	11	0	1	26	9	.74	1	.254	.367	.423
Morales,Rich,Ogden	R	31	1	0	0	0	0	0	0	0	0	0	0	0	0	0	0	0	0	.00	0	.000	.000	.000
Morales,Willie,Wisconsin	A	23	109	419	116	32	0	4	160	49	60	28	1	75	7	2	4	1	4	.20	13	.277	.330	.382
Moreno,Victor,Lethbridge	R	20	46	157	44	10	3	0	60	4	72	25	24	18	2	43	4	0	1	7	2	.78	2	.280	.367	.459
Spokane	A	20	7	24	4	1	0	0	5	3	0	2	0	10	1	0	0	0	0	.00	1	.167	.259	.208
Morenz,Shea,Oneonta	A	22	33	116	32	5	3	1	46	11	20	15	0	27	3	0	1	1	4	.20	4	.276	.370	.397

350

1995 Batting -- Single-A and Rookie Leagues

Player	Lg	A	G	AB	H	2B	3B	HR	TB	R	RBI	TBB	IBB	SO	HBP	SH	SF	SB	CS	SB%	GDP	Avg	OBP	SLG
Morgan,Dave,Hagerstown	A	24	67	249	66	14	1	4	94	26	26	18	1	53	2	1	2	1	0	1.00	4	.265	.317	.378
Morgan,Scott,Watertown	A	22	66	244	64	18	0	2	88	42	33	26	0	63	8	0	4	6	5	.55	11	.262	.348	.361
Moriarty,Michael,FortWayne	A	22	62	203	46	6	3	4	70	26	26	27	1	44	2	2	3	8	0	1.00	1	.227	.319	.345
Morillo,Cesar,Bakersfield	A	22	108	371	113	25	1	1	143	41	37	31	2	71	4	5	1	4	12	.25	6	.305	.364	.385
Morimoto,Ken,Yakima	A	21	55	178	48	4	2	0	56	27	14	19	1	40	0	3	2	19	4	.83	1	.270	.337	.315
Morreale,John,Stockton	A	24	30	88	21	2	1	0	25	13	8	8	0	16	0	1	1	0	3	.00	4	.239	.299	.284
Morris,Greg,Cedar Rapds	A	24	103	355	102	18	0	14	162	65	57	62	4	59	6	0	3	8	2	.80	6	.287	.399	.456
Morris,Bobby,Daytona	A	23	95	344	106	18	2	2	134	44	55	38	6	46	8	2	5	22	8	.73	5	.308	.385	.390
Morrison,Greg,Great Falls	R	20	55	164	53	8	2	2	71	29	30	12	1	15	2	0	5	1	3	.25	4	.323	.366	.433
Morrison,Ryan,Mets	R	21	38	110	28	7	0	1	38	20	11	17	1	21	4	0	3	3	0	1.00	0	.255	.366	.345
Morrow,Nick,Charlstn-Wv	A	24	139	467	117	28	8	9	188	67	54	77	2	123	2	2	1	41	17	.71	5	.251	.358	.403
Moschetti,Mike,W. Michigan	A	21	8	22	7	2	0	0	9	6	3	3	0	8	0	1	0	1	0	1.00	0	.318	.400	.409
Modesto	A	21	23	77	27	6	0	0	33	5	9	6	0	16	0	3	1	0	2	.00	2	.351	.393	.429
Sou. Oregon	A	21	39	141	34	4	1	0	40	21	15	20	0	27	6	0	1	13	1	.93	4	.241	.357	.284
Mosquera,Julio,Hagerstown	A	24	108	406	118	22	5	3	159	64	46	29	2	53	13	3	5	5	5	.50	13	.291	.353	.392
Mota,Alfonso,Boise	A	22	51	104	30	5	0	2	41	25	16	21	1	11	1	2	0	4	0	1.00	1	.288	.413	.394
Mota,Cristian,Burlington	R	20	59	234	66	17	3	2	95	37	36	6	1	55	2	0	2	7	3	.70	4	.282	.303	.406
Mota,Gleydel,Pittsfield	A	21	14	37	6	0	0	0	6	4	2	4	0	11	0	1	0	2	2	.50	0	.162	.244	.162
Mets	R	21	34	122	39	6	2	0	49	32	18	19	1	27	1	3	4	21	5	.81	1	.320	.404	.402
Kingsport	R	21	1	3	0	0	0	0	0	1	0	0	0	2	1	0	0	0	0	.00	0	.000	.250	.000
Mota,Guillermo,Columbia	A	22	123	400	97	24	3	4	139	45	45	32	1	127	4	6	1	8	3	.73	5	.243	.304	.348
Mota,Santo,St. Pete	A	24	64	173	27	8	0	1	38	27	11	15	0	40	0	2	0	6	0	1.00	2	.156	.223	.220
Motes,Jeff,St. Lucie	A	25	12	35	7	0	0	0	7	7	4	1	0	7	1	1	0	0	0	.00	1	.200	.243	.200
Pittsfield	A	25	52	169	39	7	3	0	52	14	15	21	0	33	1	4	3	1	1	.50	5	.231	.314	.308
Motte,James,Fort Myers	A	24	119	392	92	17	2	4	125	47	37	31	1	78	2	5	2	8	10	.44	13	.235	.293	.319
Motuzas,Jeff,Tampa	A	24	28	69	11	0	0	1	14	6	8	4	0	24	2	1	0	1	0	1.00	4	.159	.227	.203
Mowry,David,Rancho Cuca	A	24	50	142	34	10	0	3	53	19	23	21	1	38	0	0	1	0	0	.00	4	.239	.335	.373
Moyle,Mike,Columbus	A	24	73	227	46	7	0	6	71	19	31	35	0	46	1	3	6	2	3	.40	3	.203	.305	.313
Mucker,Kelcey,Fort Wayne	A	21	109	405	93	16	1	7	132	48	47	27	1	59	4	1	2	12	4	.75	8	.230	.283	.326
Mueller,Bret,New Jersey	A	23	70	267	70	5	8	2	97	39	39	20	0	61	4	0	1	7	3	.70	6	.262	.322	.363
Mullen,Adam,Danville	R	20	17	51	7	0	1	0	9	2	3	4	0	17	0	1	1	1	1	.50	0	.137	.196	.176
Mummau,Bob,Hagerstown	A	24	107	366	94	17	3	5	132	63	42	42	1	74	14	6	3	6	1	.86	7	.257	.353	.361
Munoz,Juan,Johnson Cty	R	22	57	190	66	12	1	7	101	43	31	27	0	17	0	0	2	13	2	.87	1	.347	.425	.532
Murphy,Jeff,St. Pete	A	25	50	122	22	3	1	2	33	9	14	19	0	36	2	0	0	0	0	.00	5	.180	.301	.270
Murphy,Quinn,Burlington	R	20	40	126	22	5	0	2	33	12	9	14	0	56	1	1	0	2	5	.29	1	.175	.262	.262
Myers,Aaron,Asheville	A	20	20	65	9	3	0	0	12	1	6	3	0	27	1	1	0	0	0	.00	1	.138	.188	.185
Portland	A	20	57	184	37	5	0	6	60	25	24	23	1	44	2	0	0	1	3	.25	6	.201	.297	.326
Nadeau,Mike,High Desert	A	22	22	57	14	0	0	0	14	5	4	6	0	12	5	3	0	3	2	.60	1	.246	.368	.246
Naples,Brandon,Kingsport	R	22	32	109	30	1	1	1	36	22	23	11	0	11	1	0	1	2	0	1.00	1	.275	.344	.330
Nathan,Joe,Bellingham	A	21	56	177	41	7	2	3	61	23	20	22	1	48	2	5	2	3	2	.60	5	.232	.320	.345
Nations,Joel,Spokane	A	23	40	140	30	6	1	0	38	15	16	20	0	26	1	0	0	1	1	.50	0	.214	.317	.271
Nava,Marlo,Fort Myers	A	23	112	376	91	18	0	1	112	47	37	22	1	45	2	11	2	5	9	.36	6	.242	.286	.298
Navas,Jesus,Hickory	A	21	79	202	46	7	0	1	56	23	16	28	0	36	5	3	3	3	6	.33	4	.228	.332	.277
Needham,Scott,Mariners	R	21	21	62	11	5	1	0	18	12	10	14	0	22	2	0	1	0	0	.00	1	.177	.342	.290
Nelson,Bryant,Kissimmee	A	21	105	395	129	34	5	3	182	47	52	20	0	37	1	1	6	14	10	.58	8	.327	.355	.461
Quad City	A	22	6	26	1	1	0	0	2	1	2	0	0	3	0	0	0	0	0	.00	2	.038	.038	.077
Nelson,Charlie,Vero Beach	A	24	80	277	75	13	2	0	92	37	30	46	2	50	0	3	1	33	13	.72	7	.271	.373	.332
San Bernrdo	A	24	1	4	1	0	0	0	1	0	0	0	0	0	0	0	0	0	0	.00	0	.250	.250	.250
Nelson,Kevin,Twins	R	19	45	138	20	8	0	1	31	7	11	11	1	36	0	1	2	1	1	.50	3	.145	.205	.225
Nelson,Tray,Oneonta	A	21	16	48	7	3	0	0	10	5	4	4	0	21	0	0	0	0	0	.00	0	.146	.204	.208
Neubart,Garrett,Portland	A	22	39	128	34	8	0	0	42	23	8	21	0	24	7	0	0	12	3	.80	0	.266	.392	.328
Newell,Brett,Macon	A	23	76	285	73	9	1	0	84	39	29	24	0	72	7	5	1	5	1	.83	5	.256	.328	.295
Durham	A	23	33	79	17	1	0	0	18	10	3	4	0	20	1	2	1	1	0	1.00	1	.215	.259	.228
Newhan,David,Sou. Oregon	A	22	42	145	39	8	1	6	67	25	21	29	1	30	1	1	3	10	5	.67	2	.269	.388	.462
W. Michigan	A	22	25	96	21	5	0	3	35	9	8	13	1	26	1	1	1	3	2	.60	1	.219	.315	.365
Newhouse,Andre,Pr. William	A	24	78	258	55	10	1	2	73	28	21	16	0	59	1	1	2	7	2	.78	6	.213	.260	.283
Newstrom,Doug,San Bernrdo	A	24	97	316	92	22	1	6	134	53	58	40	0	58	2	6	3	19	9	.68	7	.291	.371	.424
Niethammer,Marc,W. Palm Bch	A	22	96	315	59	11	3	10	106	34	31	31	3	105	4	1	2	4	6	.40	2	.187	.267	.337
Nieves,Jose,Williamsprt	A	21	69	276	59	13	1	4	86	46	44	21	1	39	6	0	3	11	10	.52	4	.214	.281	.312
Nihart,Tim,Fort Myers	A	23	4	10	2	2	0	0	4	1	2	1	0	3	0	0	0	0	0	.00	0	.200	.273	.400
Niles,Martin,Rockies	R	19	40	116	23	3	0	0	26	21	9	22	0	50	1	1	0	3	0	1.00	2	.198	.331	.224
Nitschke,Bear,Piedmont	A	25	2	4	0	0	0	0	0	0	0	0	0	0	0	0	0	0	0	.00	0	.000	.000	.000
Nobles,Ivan,Blue Jays	R	21	36	105	15	3	1	0	20	14	12	13	0	40	4	2	1	2	1	.67	1	.143	.260	.190
Nolte,Bruce,Huntington	R	22	61	209	46	6	2	3	65	30	21	21	0	46	2	5	1	16	5	.76	3	.220	.296	.311
Norman,Ty,Utica	A	22	49	159	40	5	0	3	54	23	15	8	0	28	2	2	4	8	4	.67	5	.252	.289	.340
Northeimer,Jamie,Piedmont	A	23	115	392	114	24	4	1	149	56	54	53	1	72	20	4	2	9	4	.69	13	.291	.400	.380
Clearwater	A	23	6	19	6	1	0	0	7	1	5	3	0	4	2	0	0	0	0	.00	0	.316	.458	.368
Norton,Andy,Bellingham	A	23	25	55	12	1	0	0	13	3	5	8	2	15	2	2	0	0	0	.00	3	.218	.338	.236
Nova,Fernando,White Sox	R	20	36	125	26	6	0	0	32	17	7	16	2	46	4	1	1	1	3	.25	0	.208	.315	.256
Nova,Geraldo,Red Sox	R	18	17	31	5	0	0	0	5	1	5	4	0	7	1	1	0	0	0	.00	0	.161	.270	.161
Nova,Felix,Williamsprt	A	21	52	172	38	7	1	0	47	25	13	21	0	48	1	1	2	2	1	.67	6	.221	.306	.273
Nuneviller,Tom,Clearwater	A	27	12	43	10	2	0	0	12	2	6	4	0	6	0	0	0	0	0	.00	4	.233	.286	.279
Nunez,Isaias,Peoria	A	22	120	378	82	19	6	2	119	37	43	25	1	66	1	1	5	1	6	.14	4	.217	.264	.315
Nunez,Juan,Rangers	R	19	43	137	33	2	1	1	40	16	7	15	0	46	2	3	0	26	9	.74	0	.241	.325	.292
Nunez,Sergio,Wilmington	A	21	124	460	109	10	2	4	135	63	25	51	4	66	3	13	1	33	19	.63	8	.237	.317	.293
O'Brien,Joe,Clearwater	A	23	13	50	7	1	0	1	11	6	7	3	0	13	1	0	0	1	0	1.00	4	.140	.204	.220
Piedmont	A	23	60	189	41	4	1	1	50	27	31	19	0	38	6	1	2	2	5	.29	6	.217	.306	.265

1995 Batting -- Single-A and Rookie Leagues

Player	**Lg**	**A**	**G**	**AB**	**H**	**2B**	**3B**	**HR**	**TB**	**R**	**RBI**	**TBB**	**IBB**	**SO**	**HBP**	**SH**	**SF**	**SB**	**CS**	**SB%**	**GDP**	**Avg**	**OBP**	**SLG**
O'Connor,Rick,Martinsvlle	R	22	53	174	39	4	1	0	45	27	11	26	1	52	4	4	0	13	8	.62	1	.224	.338	.259
O'Neal,Troy,Lethbridge	R	24	43	135	31	2	1	0	35	17	15	21	1	21	9	0	4	3	3	.50	6	.230	.361	.259
Helena	R	24	4	14	5	1	0	0	6	5	1	1	0	0	0	0	0	0	0	.00	0	.357	.400	.429
Oakland,Mike,Asheville	A	25	18	48	10	1	0	0	11	4	2	10	0	6	1	1	0	0	0	.00	1	.208	.356	.229
Ocasio,Willie,Asheville	A	25	14	39	12	0	0	0	12	3	2	3	0	7	0	0	0	0	2	.00	0	.308	.357	.308
Oglesby,Luke,Springfield	A	25	50	122	24	0	0	2	30	27	6	19	0	26	5	3	0	24	5	.83	0	.197	.329	.246
Wilmington	A	25	53	60	12	0	0	0	12	18	1	4	0	21	1	4	0	19	6	.76	0	.200	.262	.200
Ohmura,Iwao,Visalia	A	27	45	153	40	9	1	1	54	15	18	9	0	32	0	4	4	1	1	.50	5	.261	.295	.353
Olinde,Chad,Rockford	A	24	54	164	39	11	0	1	53	21	26	23	0	42	5	3	1	3	2	.60	0	.238	.347	.323
Oliveros,Leonardo,Martinsvle	R	20	48	155	44	9	0	2	59	17	18	14	1	18	2	0	2	0	0	.00	8	.284	.347	.381
Olmeda,Jose,Red Sox	R	18	42	129	28	4	1	4	46	15	14	11	0	42	3	5	2	3	3	.50	5	.217	.290	.357
Olmstead,Nate,Cedar Rapds	A	24	59	155	36	8	0	1	47	20	15	20	1	37	2	2	1	1	1	.50	7	.232	.326	.303
Olsen,D.c,Vermont	A	24	70	270	69	16	1	7	108	33	44	20	0	52	3	0	7	3	4	.43	5	.256	.307	.400
Oram,Jonny,Columbus	A	22	64	198	43	6	3	2	61	20	19	13	1	40	4	1	4	2	5	.29	9	.217	.274	.308
Ordaz,Luis,Charlstn-Wv	A	20	112	359	83	14	7	2	117	43	42	13	1	47	1	4	3	12	5	.71	10	.231	.267	.326
Ordonez,Magglio,Pr. William	A	21	131	487	116	24	2	12	180	61	65	41	0	71	3	0	7	11	5	.69	16	.238	.299	.370
Orie,Kevin,Daytona	A	23	119	409	100	17	4	9	152	54	51	42	2	71	15	0	6	5	4	.56	11	.244	.333	.372
Orndorff,Dave,Twins	R	18	23	67	14	0	0	1	17	12	3	13	0	11	2	0	0	5	0	1.00	1	.209	.354	.254
Oropeza,William,Expos	R	20	45	143	33	8	1	3	52	14	27	9	0	28	0	0	4	2	5	.29	3	.231	.269	.364
Ortega,Hector,Stockton	A	23	137	539	162	27	4	8	221	81	76	39	0	109	10	6	7	26	13	.67	8	.301	.355	.410
Ortega,Randy,Modesto	A	23	10	23	4	1	0	0	5	2	1	6	0	7	1	1	0	0	0	.00	0	.174	.367	.217
W. Michigan	A	23	48	162	35	4	0	0	39	8	13	13	0	27	1	1	0	0	2	.00	6	.216	.278	.241
Ortiz,Asbel,Rangers	R	20	43	128	39	10	1	3	60	18	23	8	0	26	3	2	1	4	2	.67	0	.305	.357	.469
Ortiz,Nicky,Sarasota	A	22	91	304	75	20	1	5	112	38	38	27	0	68	4	1	1	6	4	.60	3	.247	.315	.368
Ortiz,Pedro,Orioles	R	19	14	46	10	2	0	0	12	1	3	3	0	13	0	0	0	1	0	1.00	2	.217	.265	.261
Ortman,Ben,Asheville	A	25	14	38	6	1	0	1	10	7	4	4	0	9	0	0	1	1	1	.50	0	.158	.233	.263
Otero,Oscar,Braves	R	19	29	86	11	0	0	0	11	3	2	3	0	16	1	0	0	1	2	.33	0	.128	.165	.128
Ottavinia,Paul,W. Palm Bch	A	23	112	395	93	20	2	1	120	35	37	34	2	44	2	5	2	13	6	.68	10	.235	.298	.304
Ovalles,Homy,Expos	R	19	30	64	15	3	1	0	20	7	2	4	0	18	0	0	0	1	1	.50	1	.234	.279	.313
Owen,Andy,Yakima	A	22	56	165	40	12	1	0	54	16	17	9	0	35	3	1	2	6	1	.86	4	.242	.291	.327
Owen,Tom,Marlins	R	23	28	66	15	3	0	0	18	13	10	12	0	6	0	2	1	0	2	.00	7	.227	.342	.273
Owens,Walter,Watertown	A	23	23	44	12	1	0	0	13	9	3	6	0	10	0	2	0	2	1	.67	1	.273	.360	.295
Oyas,Danny,Winston-Sal	A	23	50	173	37	6	0	8	67	19	31	10	0	45	2	3	2	1	1	.50	6	.214	.262	.387
Ozario,Yudith,Columbia	A	21	123	456	99	12	2	2	121	59	33	34	3	113	3	9	2	40	15	.73	8	.217	.275	.265
Ozuna,Rafael,Great Falls	R	21	62	245	80	15	5	3	114	45	34	17	2	36	2	2	2	5	6	.45	8	.327	.372	.465
Pachot,John,W. Palm Bch	A	21	67	227	57	10	0	0	67	17	23	12	0	38	2	3	1	2	2	.33	4	.251	.293	.295
Paciorek,Pete,Padres	R	20	54	183	47	11	3	5	79	32	24	33	1	58	1	1	0	6	4	.60	1	.257	.373	.432
Paez,Isreal,Fort Wayne	A	19	113	388	101	12	2	2	123	47	45	35	1	55	1	3	1	12	11	.52	8	.260	.322	.317
Pagan,Angel,High Desert	A	22	35	115	18	3	1	1	26	12	10	4	0	29	3	2	1	3	2	.60	4	.157	.203	.226
Frederick	A	22	31	72	14	3	1	0	22	8	6	5	0	19	0	1	0	0	1	.00	4	.194	.247	.306
Pagano,Scott,Durham	A	25	110	354	94	12	1	1	111	47	26	38	5	75	5	7	1	41	21	.66	8	.266	.344	.314
Pagee,Shawn,Visalia	A	25	22	44	5	0	0	0	5	1	4	2	0	17	0	2	0	0	1	.00	1	.114	.152	.114
Palmer,Jim,Oneonta	A	21	15	43	3	0	0	0	3	4	4	7	0	16	1	0	0	0	0	.00	0	.070	.216	.070
Parent,Gerald,Helena	R	22	57	203	72	16	0	7	109	50	63	50	2	30	0	0	3	1	7	.13	6	.355	.477	.537
Parker,Allan,Visalia	A	24	121	395	91	18	2	0	113	40	36	27	0	81	1	9	6	6	7	.46	4	.230	.277	.286
Parker,Michael,Pittsfield	A	23	3	2	1	0	0	0	1	0	0	0	0	1	0	0	0	0	0	.00	0	.500	.500	.500
Parra,Jose,Rangers	R	19	45	135	21	4	2	0	29	16	7	24	0	41	4	2	0	12	6	.67	1	.156	.301	.215
Parsons,Jason,Billings	R	23	60	222	70	20	0	5	105	47	48	32	0	41	5	1	4	3	1	.75	2	.315	.407	.473
Parsons,Jeff,Pittsfield	A	22	49	172	39	4	0	0	43	31	10	37	0	33	0	3	0	25	7	.78	1	.227	.364	.250
Pasqual,Edison,Pirates	R	19	41	136	31	3	2	3	47	19	18	10	0	26	0	2	3	3	0	1.00	1	.228	.275	.346
Patel,Manny,Riverside	A	24	83	274	78	8	6	0	98	45	32	33	0	30	5	1	1	9	4	.69	5	.285	.371	.358
Patellis,Anthony,Princeton	R	22	46	166	42	7	1	11	84	21	32	11	1	58	3	0	1	4	2	.67	1	.253	.305	.506
Patterson,Jake,Fort Wayne	A	22	116	435	115	23	5	14	190	56	68	35	4	118	9	0	5	0	2	.00	5	.264	.329	.437
Patterson,Jarrod,Kingsport	R	22	64	240	67	17	3	13	129	45	57	28	2	50	0	0	3	3	1	.75	2	.279	.351	.538
Patton,Greg,Sarasota	A	24	8	23	5	0	0	0	5	1	0	2	0	6	0	0	0	0	0	.00	0	.217	.280	.217
Michigan	A	24	69	226	56	13	0	9	96	34	27	31	2	58	2	2	2	4	3	.57	2	.248	.341	.425
Patzke,Jeff,Dunedin	A	22	129	470	124	32	6	11	201	68	75	85	8	81	2	1	2	5	3	.63	10	.264	.377	.428
Paul,Kortney,Wilmington	A	24	8	9	1	0	0	0	1	1	0	1	0	2	0	0	0	0	0	.00	0	.111	.200	.111
Lethbridge	R	24	58	201	48	11	0	3	68	28	24	25	2	48	1	0	2	3	2	.60	0	.239	.323	.338
Paulin,Randy,Spokane	A	24	54	191	39	6	0	3	54	14	22	14	0	49	3	0	2	1	0	.00	0	.204	.267	.283
Paulino,Arturo,Modesto	A	21	5	9	1	0	0	0	1	2	0	4	0	4	0	0	1	1	0	1.00	1	.111	.385	.111
Athletics	R	21	30	113	30	2	4	0	40	18	13	14	0	33	2	0	0	14	2	.88	2	.265	.357	.354
Paxton,Chris,Orioles	R	19	11	31	7	1	0	0	10	1	6	1	0	4	0	0	0	0	0	.00	0	.226	.294	.323
Payano,Alexi,Cubs	R	19	29	91	27	4	1	2	39	20	14	11	1	16	5	0	1	0	0	1.00	1	.297	.398	.429
Pearson,Cory,Charlstn-Sc	A	21	61	183	38	8	0	1	49	21	13	18	1	53	5	0	0	13	6	.68	5	.208	.296	.268
Pearson,Kevin,Fort Wayne	A	23	29	78	11	1	1	1	17	10	7	6	0	30	3	1	0	1	0	1.00	0	.141	.230	.218
Peck,Tom,Blue Jays	R	21	59	215	58	12	2	2	80	42	22	40	0	39	4	4	2	10	6	.63	9	.270	.391	.372
Peeples,Michael,Medicne Hat	R	19	72	285	89	14	4	3	120	55	50	35	1	46	5	2	3	27	5	.84	14	.312	.393	.421
Pelis,Andy,Pittsfield	A	23	8	19	1	0	0	0	1	3	0	4	0	7	0	0	0	0	0	.00	2	.053	.217	.053
Pena,Adelis,Pirates	R	19	54	202	57	7	2	0	68	27	23	3	1	26	3	1	1	5	1	.83	9	.282	.301	.337
Pena,Alex,Pirates	R	18	48	172	41	7	3	1	57	15	20	6	0	26	0	1	0	3	4	.43	4	.238	.264	.331
Pena,Angel,Great Falls	R	21	49	138	40	11	1	4	65	24	15	21	2	32	3	0	1	2	1	.67	5	.290	.388	.471
Pena,Elvis,Asheville	A	19	48	145	33	2	0	0	35	27	4	28	0	32	4	3	0	23	6	.79	1	.228	.367	.241
Portland	A	19	58	215	54	6	3	0	66	29	18	26	0	45	1	3	0	28	7	.80	2	.251	.335	.307
Pena,Frank,Twins	R	19	21	69	13	6	0	1	22	9	7	5	1	18	0	1	1	0	0	.00	0	.188	.240	.275
Elizabethtn	R	19	10	21	4	2	0	0	6	4	2	2	0	10	0	0	0	0	0	.00	0	.190	.261	.286
Pena,Jose,Burlington	R	22	23	70	14	2	0	2	22	7	6	0	0	21	1	0	1	0	0	.00	0	.200	.208	.314

352

1995 Batting -- Single-A and Rookie Leagues

Player	Lg	A	G	AB	H	2B	3B	HR	TB	R	RBI	TBB	IBB	SO	HBP	SH	SF	SB	CS	SB%	GDP	Avg	OBP	SLG
Pena,Jose,Rangers	R	19	50	153	37	4	4	0	49	25	10	12	1	29	1	0	3	22	5	.81	2	.242	.296	.320
Pendergrass,Tyrone,Braves	R	19	52	188	34	4	0	1	41	19	7	15	0	51	1	0	0	8	4	.67	5	.181	.245	.218
Peniche,Fray,Tigers	R	19	28	83	13	1	0	1	17	8	4	2	0	31	2	0	1	2	0	1.00	1	.157	.193	.205
Pennyfeather,William,Princeton	R	28	1	3	0	0	0	0	0	0	0	0	0	1	0	0	0	0	0	.00	0	.000	.000	.000
Perez,Jhonny,Kissimmee	A	19	65	214	58	12	0	4	82	24	31	22	1	37	7	0	0	23	7	.77	5	.271	.358	.383
Perez,Joe,Charlstn-Sc	A	26	67	243	66	14	2	3	93	24	29	18	2	55	3	0	2	10	3	.77	2	.272	.327	.383
Charlotte	A	26	24	74	19	4	0	1	26	8	9	9	0	12	2	0	1	1	1	.50	0	.257	.349	.351
Perez,Mick,Williamsprt	A	24	7	17	5	0	1	0	7	2	3	3	0	3	3	0	1	0	0	.00	0	.294	.458	.412
Rockford	A	24	39	106	26	3	1	0	31	12	11	13	0	24	2	2	1	3	3	.50	5	.245	.336	.292
Perez,Nelson,Butte	R	20	61	215	48	5	5	2	69	24	20	9	0	44	2	1	0	2	2	.50	9	.223	.261	.321
Perez,Richard,Daytona	A	23	85	255	56	8	0	0	64	31	26	28	0	41	1	4	1	4	2	.67	5	.220	.298	.251
Perez,Santiago,Fayetteville	A	20	130	425	101	15	1	4	130	54	44	30	0	98	1	7	7	10	9	.53	6	.238	.285	.306
Pernell,Brandon,Padres	R	19	48	174	43	11	1	2	62	22	29	16	0	54	1	2	3	8	2	.80	2	.247	.309	.356
Perry,Chan,Columbus	A	23	113	411	117	30	4	9	182	64	50	53	1	49	2	2	4	7	2	.78	6	.285	.366	.443
Person,Wilt,Eugene	A	22	62	197	52	8	1	0	62	25	23	20	0	21	7	1	1	7	6	.54	4	.264	.351	.315
Peters,Tony,Brewers	R	21	51	172	42	8	2	2	60	25	24	29	0	55	2	1	0	9	3	.75	2	.244	.360	.349
Peterson,Nate,Kissimmee	A	24	76	257	72	17	0	4	101	34	22	21	2	42	4	0	1	3	1	.75	5	.280	.343	.393
Petillo,Bruce,Piedmont	A	25	2	9	1	0	0	0	1	0	2	0	0	3	0	0	0	0	0	.00	0	.111	.111	.111
Petrulis,Paul,St. Lucie	A	24	104	291	66	10	0	1	79	33	16	45	0	51	2	8	3	3	11	.21	8	.227	.333	.271
Pettiford,Torrey,Batavia	A	23	41	151	47	5	2	0	56	21	17	5	0	18	5	3	0	12	2	.86	4	.311	.354	.371
Phair,Kelly,Ogden	R	23	62	188	47	7	2	0	58	35	25	26	0	28	7	5	4	8	5	.62	5	.250	.356	.309
Phillips,Darren,Blue Jays	R	20	20	44	6	0	0	0	6	3	3	4	0	21	0	1	0	0	1	.00	0	.136	.208	.136
Phillips,Gary,San Jose	A	24	106	363	96	17	8	1	132	51	32	26	0	68	9	6	2	3	1	.75	6	.264	.328	.364
Pichardo,Sandy,St. Lucie	A	21	125	478	131	10	6	0	153	55	27	28	3	64	3	12	1	29	17	.63	6	.274	.318	.320
Pickering,Calvin,Orioles	R	19	15	60	30	10	0	1	43	8	22	2	0	6	1	0	0	0	0	.00	3	.500	.508	.717
Pickett,Eric,Danville	R	20	61	218	48	5	5	0	63	20	26	19	2	67	2	0	3	9	4	.69	2	.220	.285	.289
Pico,Brandon,Daytona	A	22	16	49	12	2	0	0	14	4	4	7	0	8	0	2	0	1	1	.50	0	.245	.339	.286
Rockford	A	22	96	383	115	27	4	4	162	59	47	34	0	53	2	4	3	7	7	.50	7	.300	.358	.423
Pierce,Kirk,Batavia	A	23	30	101	22	5	1	0	29	18	7	10	0	23	6	1	0	0	0	.00	4	.218	.325	.287
Pierzynski,A.J.,Fort Wayne	A	19	22	84	26	5	1	2	39	10	14	2	0	10	0	0	1	0	0	.00	1	.310	.322	.464
Elizabethtn	R	19	56	205	68	13	1	7	104	29	45	14	1	23	0	0	1	0	2	.00	6	.332	.373	.507
Pileski,Mark,Pittsfield	A	22	8	31	5	1	0	0	6	2	4	1	0	2	0	1	0	1	0	1.00	1	.161	.188	.194
Pinoni,Scott,Visalia	A	23	73	259	83	19	0	14	144	44	45	33	0	50	5	0	1	1	1	.50	8	.320	.406	.556
Spokane	A	23	11	38	7	2	0	0	9	4	4	5	0	9	1	0	0	0	0	.00	1	.184	.295	.237
Pinto,Rene,Yankees	R	18	15	49	9	0	1	0	11	2	4	7	0	11	1	0	0	0	0	.00	3	.184	.293	.224
Pitts,Rick,Royals	R	20	36	79	20	1	0	2	27	25	6	13	0	23	2	1	1	11	1	.92	0	.253	.368	.342
Podsednik,Scott,Hudson Vall	A	20	65	252	67	3	0	0	70	42	20	35	3	31	1	1	2	20	6	.77	9	.266	.355	.278
Pointer,Corey,Danville	R	20	46	158	44	5	3	8	79	33	27	19	1	60	0	1	0	8	4	.67	1	.278	.370	.500
Polanco,Enohel,Kingsport	R	20	62	205	47	5	2	2	62	28	21	18	0	60	2	3	3	7	6	.54	5	.229	.294	.302
Polanco,Juan,Athletics	R	21	48	179	53	11	5	2	80	41	23	17	0	35	2	1	1	18	8	.69	2	.296	.356	.447
Polanco,Placido,Peoria	A	20	103	361	96	7	4	2	117	43	41	18	0	30	1	11	2	7	6	.54	8	.266	.303	.324
Polidor,Wil,Pr. William	A	22	95	346	86	14	4	0	108	34	24	9	0	33	0	5	2	2	6	.25	18	.249	.266	.312
Pollock,Elton,Erie	A	23	43	174	52	7	1	2	67	29	21	12	1	30	1	1	1	12	5	.71	4	.299	.346	.385
Augusta	A	23	26	94	22	5	1	0	29	8	10	7	0	23	0	2	2	8	3	.73	5	.234	.282	.309
Pomierski,Joe,Everett	A	22	59	217	48	15	3	11	102	31	38	26	0	58	4	0	0	4	2	.67	2	.221	.316	.470
Pond,Simon,Albany	A	19	23	80	17	5	0	0	22	4	7	4	0	25	1	0	0	1	0	1.00	3	.213	.267	.275
Expos	R	19	45	133	20	6	1	0	28	13	12	22	0	34	1	0	0	2	3	.40	3	.150	.276	.211
Poor,Jeff,Burlington	A	22	101	322	78	23	1	4	115	33	38	27	1	68	7	2	3	1	0	1.00	9	.242	.312	.357
Porter,Kedric,Orioles	R	21	47	147	32	4	1	1	41	20	12	21	0	17	4	1	0	11	3	.79	2	.218	.331	.279
Porter,Bo,Daytona	A	23	113	336	73	12	2	3	98	54	19	32	0	104	2	4	3	22	10	.69	5	.217	.287	.292
Post,Dave,Vero Beach	A	22	52	114	27	2	1	0	31	16	11	23	0	11	2	3	1	3	0	1.00	5	.237	.371	.272
Powell,Chris,Lk Elsinore	A	27	13	40	8	2	1	1	15	7	2	13	0	10	3	0	0	0	2	.00	1	.200	.429	.375
Cedar Rapds	A	27	25	63	10	3	1	0	15	11	4	11	1	17	1	0	1	6	0	1.00	2	.159	.289	.238
Powell,Gordon,Stockton	A	25	111	389	99	19	5	12	164	58	48	21	1	85	0	3	5	22	6	.79	3	.254	.289	.422
Powell,Dante,San Jose	A	25	135	505	125	23	8	10	194	74	70	46	2	131	3	1	4	43	12	.78	8	.248	.312	.384
Pozo,Yohel,Asheville	A	22	40	139	30	3	0	1	36	7	15	4	0	32	0	1	1	0	3	.00	7	.216	.259	.259
Salem	A	22	43	135	23	4	0	0	27	7	3	2	0	21	1	4	0	0	1	.00	4	.170	.188	.200
Prada,Nelson,Twins	R	20	24	78	21	4	1	0	27	5	13	3	0	12	4	0	3	0	0	.00	3	.269	.318	.346
Prater,Andrew,Brevard Cty	A	23	73	173	26	5	0	2	37	18	16	18	0	49	4	5	4	0	0	.00	3	.150	.241	.214
Pratt,Wes,Union City	A	23	14	44	10	1	1	2	19	5	10	7	0	11	0	0	1	2	0	1.00	1	.227	.327	.432
Auburn	A	23	66	256	68	11	0	2	85	42	44	20	0	43	4	0	1	6	3	.67	9	.266	.327	.332
Prensi,Dagoberto,Hagerstown	A	23	104	361	75	18	5	4	115	40	33	18	0	106	0	1	1	10	6	.63	10	.208	.255	.319
Pressley,Kasey,Cubs	R	19	39	140	33	4	1	0	39	12	16	11	0	47	0	0	2	1	1	.50	5	.236	.288	.279
Preston,Doyle,Charlstn-Wv	A	23	7	16	2	1	0	0	3	1	2	4	0	5	0	0	0	1	0	1.00	1	.125	.300	.188
Billings	R	23	65	242	69	12	1	6	101	40	43	42	3	60	2	0	3	2	4	.33	7	.285	.391	.417
Price,Christopher,Springfield	A	21	52	159	42	7	1	3	60	22	14	23	0	32	2	1	1	6	2	.75	5	.264	.362	.377
Priest,Chris,Visalia	A	24	55	185	43	8	0	1	54	18	15	19	0	34	5	2	3	3	3	.50	6	.232	.316	.292
Prieto,Alejandro,Springfield	A	20	124	431	108	9	3	2	129	61	44	40	1	69	6	12	2	11	7	.61	10	.251	.322	.299
Prieto,Chris,Rancho Cuca	A	23	114	366	100	12	6	0	130	80	35	64	2	55	5	8	5	39	14	.74	10	.273	.384	.355
Prieto,Rick,Kinston	A	23	26	88	17	2	1	1	24	12	10	13	0	20	1	0	1	3	1	.75	2	.193	.297	.273
Bakersfield	A	23	74	248	55	12	2	2	77	34	22	29	0	46	3	6	0	15	2	.88	1	.222	.311	.310
Columbus	A	23	4	18	4	0	0	1	7	1	2	0	0	4	0	0	0	0	0	.00	0	.222	.222	.389
Prodanov,Peter,Utica	A	23	55	172	42	10	0	3	61	26	22	16	1	31	0	1	0	12	2	.86	2	.244	.304	.355
Prokopec,Luke,Great Falls	R	18	43	119	29	6	2	2	45	16	24	8	0	37	1	0	4	5	2	.71	1	.244	.288	.378
Prospero,Teodoro,Bellingham	A	19	41	109	15	2	0	0	17	6	6	6	0	45	2	3	0	1	0	1.00	1	.138	.193	.183
Pullen,Shane,Piedmont	A	23	118	435	109	26	4	7	164	65	57	34	3	70	3	2	5	4	2	.67	12	.251	.306	.377
Putko,Jim,Williamsprt	A	22	47	141	38	12	0	3	59	18	23	16	1	34	2	0	0	3	0	.00	3	.270	.352	.418

1995 Batting -- Single-A and Rookie Leagues

Player	Lg	A	G	AB	H	2B	3B	HR	TB	R	RBI	TBB	IBB	SO	HBP	SH	SF	SB	CS	SB%	GDP	Avg	OBP	SLG
Querecuto,Juan,Dunedin	A	26	53	140	25	4	1	1	34	16	10	8	1	31	3	0	0	0	0	.00	5	.179	.238	.243
Quezado,Dalmiro,Twins	R	19	31	99	15	5	0	0	20	5	4	1	0	17	1	4	1	1	1	.50	4	.152	.167	.202
Quillin,Ty,Frederick	A	24	16	41	5	0	0	0	5	4	3	4	0	15	0	0	0	0	1	.00	0	.122	.200	.122
Quinn,Mark,Spokane	A	22	44	162	46	12	2	6	80	28	37	15	0	28	5	0	3	0	1	.00	5	.284	.357	.494
Radcliff,Vic,Royals	R	19	38	123	32	8	2	4	56	25	15	12	0	24	7	0	1	3	6	.33	3	.260	.357	.455
Radmanovich,Ryan,Fort Myers	A	24	12	41	13	2	0	0	15	3	5	2	0	8	1	0	0	0	0	.00	0	.317	.364	.366
Raifstanger,John,Sarasota	A	23	102	326	88	19	1	2	115	52	24	34	1	63	3	2	2	6	1	.86	5	.270	.342	.353
Raio,Domenick,Martinsvlle	A	22	6	14	3	0	0	0	3	1	1	1	0	4	0	1	0	0	0	.00	0	.214	.267	.214
Raleigh,Matt,W. Palm Bch	A	25	66	179	37	11	0	2	54	29	18	54	1	64	6	1	3	4	2	.67	4	.207	.401	.302
Ramirez,Alonso,Burlington	R	22	10	18	3	0	0	0	3	3	1	3	0	6	0	0	1	0	1	.00	1	.167	.273	.167
Ramirez,Angel,Dunedin	A	23	131	541	149	19	5	8	202	78	52	21	0	99	5	0	2	17	12	.59	12	.275	.308	.373
Ramirez,Joel,Wisconsin	A	22	7	24	2	1	0	0	3	1	1	0	0	4	0	0	0	1	0	1.00	0	.083	.083	.125
Everett	A	22	70	243	61	12	0	1	76	31	31	37	0	39	9	2	0	9	6	.60	3	.251	.370	.313
Ramirez,Daniel,Kingsport	R	22	62	226	56	6	2	2	72	30	32	15	1	44	1	9	0	21	9	.70	5	.248	.298	.319
Ramirez,Francisco,Tigers	R	20	41	143	31	4	5	2	51	15	22	7	0	38	3	2	0	6	4	.60	3	.217	.263	.357
Ramirez,Hiram,Sarasota	A	23	40	140	26	2	0	2	34	13	12	3	0	29	0	2	1	3	2	.60	2	.186	.201	.243
Ramirez,Julio,Marlins	R	18	48	204	58	9	4	2	81	35	13	13	0	42	1	1	0	17	6	.74	2	.284	.330	.397
Ramos,Eddy,Kissimmee	A	23	30	105	12	3	1	0	17	5	8	4	1	27	0	0	3	0	0	.00	5	.114	.143	.162
Ramos,Jeff,Springfield	A	21	39	96	21	8	0	4	41	14	20	9	0	25	1	1	4	0	0	.00	3	.219	.282	.427
Royals	R	21	28	75	17	4	0	3	30	10	7	7	0	16	2	0	1	0	1	.00	1	.227	.306	.400
Ramos,Noel,Bluefield	R	19	31	107	21	5	1	5	43	18	18	10	0	43	2	0	0	1	0	1.00	0	.196	.277	.402
Orioles	R	19	4	15	3	1	0	0	4	1	5	2	0	6	0	0	1	0	1	.00	1	.200	.278	.267
Rand,Ian,Bellingham	A	19	23	47	6	0	0	0	6	4	1	4	0	25	2	0	0	0	0	.00	0	.128	.226	.128
Randolph,Ed,Mariners	R	21	41	135	38	11	4	3	66	22	25	12	0	30	3	1	2	5	5	.50	3	.281	.349	.489
Rascon,Rene,Elmira	A	22	34	114	25	4	1	0	31	12	11	20	3	34	0	2	1	3	3	.50	3	.219	.333	.272
Rasmussen,Nate,Bakersfield	A	21	23	71	14	4	0	0	18	12	6	12	0	23	0	0	1	0	0	.00	3	.197	.310	.254
Yakima	A	21	44	128	30	3	1	0	35	12	5	4	1	43	1	0	0	1	1	.50	4	.234	.263	.273
Rathmell,Lance,Utica	A	22	66	228	65	10	1	1	80	34	30	28	0	25	1	0	4	4	5	.44	7	.285	.360	.351
Rauer,Troy,Athletics	R	23	30	100	16	2	2	1	25	13	12	12	0	43	1	0	2	3	3	.50	1	.160	.252	.250
Raymondi,Mike,Huntington	R	20	28	75	18	3	0	1	24	8	8	5	0	27	2	0	0	1	0	1.00	3	.240	.281	.293
Raynor,Mark,Batavia	A	23	66	267	70	10	6	3	101	49	37	38	1	42	2	1	1	13	4	.76	1	.262	.357	.378
Reed,Billy,Hudson Vall	A	23	45	134	29	4	1	1	38	16	11	17	0	24	1	6	0	3	2	.60	5	.216	.309	.284
Reese,Mat,Modesto	A	25	15	50	10	4	0	1	17	4	6	4	0	23	0	0	0	0	2	.00	0	.200	.259	.340
Reeves,Glenn,Brevard Cty	A	22	117	415	112	22	2	1	141	68	33	78	0	78	6	2	3	6	7	.46	12	.270	.390	.340
Reilly,John,Hagerstown	A	23	1	2	0	0	0	0	0	1	0	0	0	1	0	0	0	0	0	.00	0	.000	.000	.000
St. Cathrns	A	23	32	77	20	2	2	1	29	8	10	6	0	20	10	2	1	0	0	.00	0	.260	.383	.377
Rendon,Miguel,Brewers	R	21	48	162	42	5	2	0	51	23	25	9	0	18	5	0	5	4	2	.67	5	.259	.309	.315
Rengifo,Daliene,White Sox	R	19	27	72	15	2	0	0	17	7	5	10	0	21	3	1	0	5	2	.71	1	.208	.329	.236
Rennhack,Mike,Quad City	A	21	100	299	81	14	1	1	100	46	47	39	1	37	1	4	8	15	4	.79	3	.271	.349	.334
Resetar,Gary,Asheville	A	29	2	5	0	0	0	0	0	0	0	0	0	1	0	0	0	0	0	.00	1	.000	.000	.000
Reyes,Freddy,Twins	R	20	6	21	5	1	0	1	9	2	4	1	0	6	0	0	0	0	0	.00	4	.238	.250	.429
Elizabethtn	R	20	40	130	36	10	1	5	63	17	21	6	0	28	3	0	1	0	0	.00	0	.277	.321	.485
Reyes,Michael,Kane County	A	24	14	37	7	3	0	0	10	8	4	7	0	11	1	0	0	2	0	.00	2	.189	.333	.270
Reyes,Winston,Piedmont	A	22	6	17	3	0	1	0	5	1	5	1	0	8	0	0	0	0	1	.00	0	.176	.222	.294
Huntington	R	22	20	68	18	4	0	0	22	5	8	3	0	17	0	1	0	3	2	.60	4	.265	.296	.324
Reynolds,Chance,Augusta	A	24	24	65	14	2	0	1	19	8	6	12	1	11	4	0	0	2	0	.00	1	.215	.370	.292
Lynchburg	A	24	5	15	3	0	0	0	3	0	2	3	0	2	2	0	0	0	1	.00	1	.200	.400	.200
Erie	A	24	37	120	29	2	0	0	31	17	18	14	0	18	3	1	4	0	2	.00	5	.242	.326	.258
Reynolds,Paul,Portland	A	23	45	135	28	7	1	1	40	15	6	5	1	43	3	0	1	9	3	.75	0	.207	.250	.296
Reynoso,Ismael,Marlins	R	18	25	68	15	0	0	0	15	12	8	12	0	18	1	0	0	1	0	1.00	0	.221	.346	.221
Ribaudo,Mike,Orioles	R	21	16	41	10	1	0	0	11	3	4	3	0	10	1	0	1	0	0	.00	1	.244	.304	.268
Rice,Charles,Augusta	A	20	14	54	12	3	0	1	18	8	8	2	0	14	2	0	0	0	0	.00	0	.222	.276	.333
Erie	A	20	70	269	85	15	2	8	128	44	33	19	0	59	8	0	1	7	5	.58	5	.316	.377	.476
Richard,Chris,New Jersey	A	22	75	284	80	14	3	3	109	36	43	47	3	31	6	0	2	6	6	.50	3	.282	.392	.384
Richardson,Brian,San Bernrdo	A	20	127	462	131	18	1	12	187	68	58	35	2	122	7	6	3	17	16	.52	11	.284	.341	.405
Richardson,Eric,Pr. William	A	23	9	18	3	0	0	0	3	2	1	1	0	3	0	0	0	0	1	.00	0	.167	.211	.167
South Bend	A	23	63	199	46	11	1	0	59	32	19	19	0	39	1	2	1	23	6	.79	3	.231	.300	.296
Riemer,Matt,Frederick	A	23	27	77	14	2	0	1	19	6	10	4	0	22	0	1	0	1	0	1.00	1	.182	.222	.247
Riggs,Adam,San Bernrdo	A	23	134	542	196	39	5	24	317	111	106	59	1	93	10	7	4	31	10	.76	9	.362	.431	.585
Rijo,Rafael,Charlotte	A	26	16	46	14	2	0	0	16	3	5	5	1	11	0	0	1	2	0	1.00	0	.304	.373	.348
Rincones,Wuarnner,South Bend	A	22	20	57	12	1	0	0	13	4	7	6	0	13	1	0	3	2	1	.00	0	.211	.284	.228
Bristol	R	22	61	189	60	10	4	1	81	25	25	32	0	29	4	0	2	2	0	1.00	5	.317	.423	.429
Rios,Armando,San Jose	A	23	128	488	143	34	3	8	207	76	75	74	3	75	1	4	7	51	10	.84	8	.293	.382	.424
Ritter,Ryan,Brewers	R	22	4	10	2	0	0	0	2	6	1	2	0	0	0	0	0	0	0	.00	0	.200	.200	.400
Helena	R	22	47	167	47	7	1	9	83	32	38	14	0	50	1	2	0	10	2	.83	3	.281	.341	.497
Rivera,Juan,Rangers	R	19	28	70	13	2	0	0	15	8	6	13	0	29	0	1	0	5	1	.83	1	.186	.313	.214
Rivera,Micky,Savannah	A	22	128	514	130	14	3	6	162	44	41	21	1	76	5	6	4	10	6	.63	15	.253	.287	.315
Rivera,Roberto,Orioles	R	19	42	150	44	7	3	3	66	21	26	10	0	38	2	0	2	6	3	.67	5	.293	.341	.440
Rivera,Santiago,Rancho Cuca	A	23	61	130	28	5	1	0	35	11	10	13	0	36	1	2	1	2	0	1.00	3	.215	.290	.269
Rivera,Wilfredo,Utica	A	22	44	138	29	3	1	0	40	14	15	5	0	35	5	0	0	3	1	.75	3	.210	.260	.290
Rivers,Jonathan,Hagerstown	A	21	123	429	126	16	6	6	172	54	48	40	0	104	6	1	4	18	5	.78	9	.294	.359	.401
Rives,Sherron,Fayetteville	A	24	56	150	34	8	0	0	42	15	19	11	0	36	3	2	3	1	1	.75	5	.227	.287	.280
Robbins,Lance,Cedar Rapds	A	25	38	81	19	4	0	0	23	18	6	8	0	16	2	0	0	1	3	.25	0	.235	.315	.284
Roberge,John,Vero Beach	A	23	3	9	0	0	0	0	0	1	0	0	0	2	0	0	0	0	0	.00	0	.000	.000	.000
San Bernrdo	A	23	116	450	129	22	1	17	204	92	59	34	0	62	8	2	3	31	8	.79	9	.287	.345	.453
Roberson,Gerald,Huntington	R	21	52	188	40	11	1	3	62	28	14	13	0	31	5	2	2	12	4	.75	3	.213	.279	.330
Roberts,David,Lakeland	A	24	92	357	108	10	3	3	137	67	30	39	2	43	1	3	2	30	8	.79	7	.303	.371	.384

1995 Batting -- Single-A and Rookie Leagues

Player	Lg	A	G	AB	H	2B	3B	HR	TB	R	RBI	TBB	IBB	SO	HBP	SH	SF	SB	CS	SB%	GDP	Avg	OBP	SLG
Roberts,John,Rancho Cuca	A	22	98	327	91	16	3	6	131	59	51	44	2	86	14	2	2	27	8	.77	9	.278	.385	.401
Robertson,Dean,Orioles	R	20	28	90	14	4	0	0	18	18	6	14	1	18	2	0	1	4	4	.50	2	.156	.280	.200
Robertson,Robbie,Winston-Sal	A	24	91	278	60	11	0	8	95	34	32	22	3	77	1	1	2	2	4	.33	7	.216	.274	.342
Robertson,Tommy,Lynchburg	A	24	61	161	44	7	0	1	54	16	23	20	2	41	1	1	2	3	7	.30	2	.273	.353	.335
Robinson,Tony,Augusta	A	20	96	297	68	9	0	2	83	34	37	38	1	60	11	1	1	21	11	.66	4	.229	.337	.279
Robinson,Daniel,Brevard Cty	A	25	105	354	84	17	3	7	128	38	52	35	0	81	1	2	3	10	6	.63	14	.237	.305	.362
Robinson,Darek,Peoria	A	23	113	363	87	15	0	2	108	36	23	37	2	60	2	7	1	2	5	.29	7	.240	.313	.298
Robinson,David,Batavia	A	23	56	201	44	9	3	2	65	27	26	20	0	45	2	0	1	9	3	.75	2	.219	.293	.323
Robinson,Hassan,Auburn	A	23	65	245	65	8	1	0	75	32	18	9	0	25	2	2	1	12	2	.86	9	.265	.296	.306
Robinson,Kerry,Johnson Cty	R	22	60	250	74	12	8	1	105	44	26	16	1	30	0	3	2	14	10	.58	3	.296	.336	.420
Robledo,Nilson,South Bend	A	27	135	537	153	24	3	20	243	71	108	30	4	100	3	1	16	2	2	.00	8	.285	.317	.453
Robles,Juan,Spokane	A	24	4	9	0	0	0	0	0	0	0	1	0	5	0	0	0	0	0	.00	0	.000	.100	.000
Royals	R	24	29	74	12	3	0	0	15	9	7	9	0	9	0	0	1	0	0	.00	1	.162	.250	.203
Robles,Oscar,Auburn	A	20	58	216	62	9	1	0	73	49	19	39	1	15	0	1	1	8	2	.80	5	.287	.395	.338
Robles,Rafael,Savannah	A	23	56	142	28	2	1	0	32	15	7	39	2	43	1	3	0	2	4	.33	2	.197	.374	.225
Rocha,Juan,Springfield	A	22	94	292	68	21	1	10	121	33	41	16	0	65	4	1	1	5	2	.71	4	.233	.281	.414
Roche,Marlon,Astros	R	21	29	92	30	5	0	0	35	20	11	10	0	19	2	1	3	9	8	.53	1	.326	.393	.380
Kissimmee	A	21	26	97	22	7	0	0	29	10	7	3	0	24	0	1	1	3	2	.60	2	.227	.248	.299
Roche,Mike,Helena	R	20	4	17	2	0	0	0	2	4	1	2	0	4	1	0	0	1	0	1.00	0	.118	.250	.118
Brewers	R	20	47	161	41	11	2	0	56	33	31	18	0	42	7	2	3	9	3	.75	3	.255	.349	.348
Rodriguez,Adam,Fayetteville	A	25	39	139	42	14	1	4	70	16	25	9	0	25	2	1	0	0	1	.00	5	.302	.353	.504
Lakeland	A	25	30	88	22	4	0	1	29	8	10	8	0	17	0	0	1	1	0	1.00	1	.250	.313	.330
Rodriguez,Franklin,Mariners	R	19	16	57	17	0	1	0	19	14	1	8	0	18	0	1	1	3	0	1.00	1	.298	.385	.333
Rodriguez,Javier,Everett	A	22	20	60	8	1	0	0	9	2	1	7	0	13	1	0	0	0	0	.00	1	.133	.235	.150
Rodriguez,John,Padres	R	20	31	94	19	1	1	1	25	12	11	2	0	27	1	0	0	0	3	.00	0	.202	.222	.266
Rodriguez,Juan,Angels	R	21	54	215	64	8	8	1	91	27	31	7	0	49	3	1	2	4	7	.36	1	.298	.326	.423
Rodriguez,Liubiemith,White Sox	R	19	36	119	27	6	1	1	38	18	11	23	0	19	0	2	0	4	2	.67	2	.227	.352	.319
Rodriguez,Luis,St. Cathrns	A	22	66	257	71	16	2	1	94	22	20	10	1	49	1	2	1	2	4	.33	7	.276	.305	.366
Rodriguez,Maximo,Kane County	A	22	72	236	45	7	1	5	69	18	30	18	0	65	2	1	2	0	1	.00	7	.191	.252	.292
Rodriguez,Miguel,Stockton	A	21	12	10	3	1	1	0	6	2	1	1	0	4	1	0	0	0	0	.00	0	.300	.417	.600
Brewers	R	21	49	163	51	12	1	1	68	24	18	11	0	34	4	1	1	9	2	.82	4	.313	.369	.417
Rodriguez,Noel,Quad City	A	22	109	386	120	26	5	8	180	48	71	28	1	49	4	0	4	4	5	.44	11	.311	.360	.466
Rodriguez,Roman,Lynchburg	A	27	44	130	33	4	0	0	37	11	9	7	0	25	2	3	1	1	0	1.00	9	.254	.300	.285
Rodriguez,Sammy,Mets	R	20	6	18	5	0	0	0	5	1	1	2	0	4	0	0	0	0	1	.00	0	.278	.350	.278
Butte	R	20	18	57	14	1	0	1	18	7	6	4	0	13	0	0	0	2	1	.67	0	.246	.295	.316
Rodriguez,Victor,Kane County	A	19	127	472	111	9	1	0	122	65	43	40	0	47	2	16	4	18	6	.75	17	.235	.295	.258
Rogue,Francisco,Brewers	R	20	19	62	14	3	1	0	19	10	10	1	0	9	0	0	0	0	0	.00	0	.226	.238	.306
Rojas,Christian,Billings	R	21	68	270	71	11	5	11	125	48	56	35	5	57	2	0	1	6	6	.50	3	.263	.351	.463
Rojas,Mo,Red Sox	R	19	42	140	29	5	0	1	37	22	16	20	0	34	5	2	3	5	3	.63	3	.207	.321	.264
Rojas,Roberto,Lakeland	A	25	4	12	3	0	0	0	3	1	2	1	1	4	0	0	0	1	0	1.00	0	.250	.308	.250
Rojas,Ron,Jamestown	A	23	17	47	10	1	0	1	14	8	8	8	1	9	2	1	0	1	0	1.00	0	.213	.345	.298
Roland,Will,Spokane	A	22	70	262	57	16	1	4	87	26	30	26	3	53	4	1	3	1	1	.50	13	.218	.295	.332
Rolison,Nate,Marlins	R	19	37	134	37	10	2	1	54	22	19	15	1	34	8	0	1	0	0	.00	1	.276	.380	.403
Roman,Felipe,Red Sox	R	19	50	175	39	8	3	1	56	15	18	7	0	39	2	1	1	1	1	.50	3	.223	.259	.320
Rondon,Alexander,W. Michigan	A	21	25	74	16	3	0	2	25	11	5	7	0	13	1	0	1	0	1	1.00	4	.216	.293	.338
Sou. Oregon	A	21	14	39	14	4	0	0	18	7	7	4	0	12	4	1	1	1	0	.00	0	.359	.458	.462
Root,Mitch,Clinton	A	22	89	309	85	20	1	3	116	37	42	37	1	52	2	0	2	3	1	.75	8	.275	.354	.375
Rosado,Juan,Albany	A	21	5	11	2	1	0	0	3	0	3	0	0	4	0	0	0	1	0	1.00	0	.182	.182	.273
Vermont	A	21	48	155	38	4	2	1	49	20	24	18	1	16	1	0	3	4	5	.44	2	.245	.322	.316
Rosado,Luis,Yankees	R	20	52	168	43	7	0	2	56	25	24	22	1	31	2	2	2	2	1	.67	4	.256	.349	.333
Rosario,Eliezer,Padres	R	20	7	27	7	0	0	0	7	3	3	5	0	6	1	0	0	1	0	1.00	0	.259	.394	.259
Idaho Falls	R	20	20	69	17	3	1	0	22	9	7	3	0	9	0	1	1	4	2	.67	1	.246	.274	.319
Rosario,Felix,St. Cathrns	A	24	64	217	49	6	0	1	58	24	21	18	1	44	1	5	3	9	3	.75	1	.226	.285	.267
Rosario,Juan,Marlins	R	20	5	7	0	0	0	0	0	1	0	4	0	2	0	0	0	1	0	1.00	1	.000	.364	.000
Rosario,Mel,South Bend	A	23	118	450	123	30	6	15	210	58	57	30	7	109	4	1	3	1	8	.11	0	.273	.322	.467
Rose,Carlos,Mariners	R	20	27	92	14	1	0	1	18	10	6	3	0	33	2	0	0	4	1	.80	5	.152	.196	.196
Rose,Damian,Rangers	R	19	13	31	3	0	0	0	3	5	2	4	0	16	3	0	0	3	1	.75	2	.097	.263	.097
Rose,Michael,Astros	R	19	35	89	23	2	1	1	30	13	9	11	0	18	3	0	0	2	1	.67	1	.258	.359	.337
Roskos,Johnny,Kane County	A	21	114	418	124	36	3	12	202	74	88	42	1	86	6	0	6	2	0	1.00	6	.297	.364	.483
Ross,Tony,Quad City	A	21	107	339	87	11	4	3	115	46	41	31	0	57	3	2	3	21	5	.81	4	.257	.322	.339
Rowson,James,Mariners	R	19	30	106	20	6	1	0	28	9	9	6	0	38	3	1	1	9	2	.82	1	.189	.250	.264
Royster,Aaron,Piedmont	A	23	126	489	129	23	3	8	182	73	58	39	1	106	7	0	4	22	9	.71	16	.264	.325	.372
Ruiz,Cesar,Tigers	R	21	45	132	38	6	5	1	57	17	19	11	0	35	3	1	2	4	2	.67	1	.288	.351	.432
Rupp,Chad,Fort Myers	A	24	107	376	100	23	1	12	161	44	52	38	1	77	2	0	3	14	3	.82	10	.266	.334	.428
Rushdan,Rasheed,Rockies	R	20	6	18	0	0	0	0	0	1	0	2	0	5	0	0	0	0	0	.00	2	.000	.100	.000
Russell,Jake,Batavia	A	22	40	141	27	8	1	2	38	9	18	11	0	25	5	1	3	0	2	.00	4	.191	.269	.270
Russin,Tom,Bluefield	R	22	57	215	67	21	1	5	105	42	41	18	2	27	4	0	1	1	1	.50	3	.312	.374	.488
Rust,Brian,Eugene	A	21	53	157	32	7	1	4	53	18	19	7	0	43	2	2	2	2	1	.67	2	.204	.244	.338
Rutherford,Daryl,Padres	R	20	47	186	62	12	4	5	97	29	27	11	1	28	0	0	3	13	7	.65	3	.333	.365	.522
Rutz,Ryan,Charlstn-Sc	A	23	133	491	108	20	1	1	133	60	22	55	0	88	2	7	2	36	26	.58	6	.220	.300	.271
Ryder,Derek,Cedar Rapds	A	23	17	21	2	0	0	0	2	1	2	5	0	7	0	0	3	0	1	.00	1	.095	.269	.095
Sachse,Matt,Everett	A	20	59	191	44	6	0	1	53	34	14	29	1	76	4	2	1	5	4	.56	3	.230	.342	.278
Sadler,Donnie,Michigan	A	21	118	438	124	25	8	9	192	103	56	79	0	85	6	3	3	41	13	.76	5	.283	.397	.438
Saffer,Jeff,Yankees	R	21	50	184	54	10	1	4	78	30	33	17	0	55	1	0	0	0	2	.00	1	.293	.356	.424
Sagers,Kory,Utica	A	22	25	66	12	1	1	0	15	11	7	5	0	18	0	1	1	1	1	.50	1	.182	.239	.227
Salano,Manuel,Princeton	R	18	31	74	16	4	0	1	23	12	14	7	0	20	1	1	0	2	2	.50	0	.216	.293	.311
Salazar,Juan,Cubs	R	18	36	130	37	7	1	2	52	12	24	9	0	12	0	1	0	3	1	.75	4	.285	.329	.400

1995 Batting -- Single-A and Rookie Leagues

Player	Lg	A	G	AB	H	2B	3B	HR	TB	R	RBI	TBB	IBB	SO	HBP	SH	SF	SB	CS	SB%	GDP	Avg	OBP	SLG
Salga,Andres,Rockies	R	18	21	67	12	2	0	0	14	7	5	5	0	29	1	1	1	1	1	.50	0	.179	.243	.209
Salzano,Jerry,Williamsprt	A	21	62	218	65	13	2	0	82	28	23	22	0	28	4	0	1	4	3	.57	6	.298	.371	.376
Rockford	A	21	6	21	6	1	1	0	9	0	2	1	0	1	0	0	0	0	1	.00	1	.286	.318	.429
Samboy,Nelson,Astros	R	19	55	192	60	12	2	1	79	39	22	26	0	19	3	4	1	21	8	.72	4	.313	.401	.411
Samuel,Quiva,Oneonta	A	22	37	124	34	7	1	4	55	15	17	10	0	42	2	0	3	2	0	1.00	3	.274	.331	.444
Sanchez,Marcos,Clinton	A	21	6	18	2	1	0	0	3	0	0	1	0	6	0	0	0	0	0	.00	0	.111	.158	.167
Idaho Falls	R	21	42	165	54	8	2	4	78	35	33	11	0	36	0	1	1	5	0	1.00	3	.327	.367	.473
Sanchez,Omar,Dunedin	A	25	39	120	30	5	0	0	35	25	8	21	0	22	3	2	1	6	4	.60	0	.250	.372	.292
St. Cathrns	A	25	74	292	88	16	6	3	125	62	23	39	1	50	8	2	0	26	10	.72	0	.301	.398	.428
Sanchez,Victor,Quad City	A	24	13	34	8	0	0	0	8	3	1	6	0	10	0	0	0	1	0	1.00	2	.235	.350	.235
Kissimmee	A	24	78	272	73	11	0	7	105	34	38	23	1	69	8	1	4	6	3	.67	5	.268	.339	.386
Sanders,Tony,Hagerstown	A	22	133	512	119	28	1	8	173	72	48	52	0	103	5	9	5	26	14	.65	8	.232	.307	.338
Sanders,Rod,Charlstn-Wv	A	21	81	152	31	7	2	1	45	22	11	12	0	45	1	3	0	4	8	.33	3	.204	.267	.296
Sanders,Pat,W. Michigan	A	24	11	24	5	0	0	0	5	4	3	4	0	6	0	0	1	0	0	.00	0	.208	.310	.208
Sanderson,David,Columbia	A	23	121	363	86	11	5	5	122	53	36	38	8	81	3	7	0	20	10	.67	6	.237	.314	.336
Santa,Roberto,Charlstn-Sc	A	24	99	295	77	11	1	5	105	35	46	55	1	37	2	1	8	0	6	.00	4	.261	.372	.356
Santana,Jose,Quad City	A	24	88	229	52	10	2	1	69	36	21	24	0	40	8	4	2	6	4	.60	7	.227	.319	.301
Santiago,Arnold,Burlington	R	21	35	123	35	5	1	0	42	15	11	4	0	22	0	0	1	3	1	.75	1	.285	.302	.341
Santos,Edgardo,Expos	R	22	23	68	15	2	1	0	19	4	4	3	0	6	0	1	1	2	2	.50	2	.221	.250	.279
Santucci,Steve,St. Pete	A	24	106	292	69	5	3	4	92	25	25	27	0	60	0	2	3	9	3	.75	8	.236	.298	.315
Sapp,Damian,Utica	A	20	37	111	22	5	1	1	32	19	14	14	0	34	5	2	1	0	2	.00	2	.198	.313	.288
Sasser,Rob,Danville	R	21	12	47	15	2	1	0	19	8	7	4	1	7	0	0	1	5	1	.83	1	.319	.365	.404
Eugene	A	21	57	216	58	9	1	9	96	40	32	23	1	51	3	0	2	14	4	.78	2	.269	.344	.444
Saturnino,Sherton,Eugene	A	24	8	21	5	0	0	1	8	4	1	1	0	7	0	0	0	2	0	1.00	0	.238	.273	.381
Macon	A	24	42	117	22	4	2	0	30	6	13	3	1	36	2	1	0	1	2	.33	1	.188	.221	.256
Saucedo,Roberto,Angels	R	20	30	75	21	1	1	1	27	13	9	12	0	11	1	0	2	3	1	.75	1	.280	.378	.360
Sauve,Erik,Charlotte	A	24	31	70	10	3	0	0	13	9	4	9	0	13	0	0	0	0	2	.00	1	.143	.241	.186
Saylor,Jamie,Kissimmee	A	21	89	289	66	4	1	2	78	38	19	22	1	58	6	0	2	13	6	.68	5	.228	.295	.270
Sbrocco,Jon,San Jose	A	25	120	425	128	14	5	2	158	66	46	55	3	43	10	17	1	12	10	.55	5	.301	.393	.372
Schaaf,Bob,Vero Beach	A	23	21	60	13	1	0	1	17	7	5	1	0	13	0	0	0	0	0	.00	2	.217	.230	.283
San Bernrdo	A	23	52	151	38	7	0	5	60	18	21	12	0	32	2	0	0	4	4	.50	4	.252	.315	.397
Schafer,Brett,Spokane	A	22	82	205	40	7	0	1	50	23	19	39	0	42	2	1	1	11	1	.92	4	.195	.328	.244
Scharrer,Jim,Braves	R	19	48	172	31	4	0	2	41	10	22	13	0	43	1	0	0	1	3	.25	3	.180	.242	.238
Schaub,Gregory,Brewers	R	19	33	95	26	4	3	0	36	12	11	5	0	20	0	1	1	5	4	.56	1	.274	.307	.379
Scheffer,Lawrence,Ogden	R	23	61	233	66	11	0	7	98	34	41	10	1	43	5	0	2	1	3	.25	8	.283	.324	.421
Scheker,Luis,Athletics	R	22	16	60	15	3	1	1	23	9	11	11	0	16	0	0	3	1	1	.50	2	.250	.351	.383
Schmitz,Mike,Tampa	A	25	4	13	3	1	0	0	4	2	0	0	0	1	0	0	0	0	0	.00	0	.231	.231	.308
Schneider,Brian,Expos	R	19	30	97	22	3	0	0	25	7	4	14	0	23	1	0	0	2	5	.29	1	.227	.330	.258
Schneider,Dan,Burlington	A	24	51	141	30	4	0	2	40	13	12	10	0	27	3	3	0	1	1	.50	6	.213	.279	.284
San Jose	A	24	13	36	6	1	0	0	7	3	2	1	0	7	0	1	0	0	0	.00	0	.167	.189	.194
Schock,Jared,Ogden	R	21	7	11	1	0	0	0	1	1	0	1	0	3	0	0	0	0	0	.00	2	.091	.167	.091
Schofield,Andy,Johnson Cty	R	22	40	119	27	8	0	0	35	22	11	19	0	30	3	0	0	6	1	.86	0	.227	.348	.294
Schreiber,Stanley,Erie	A	20	3	7	2	0	2	0	6	1	2	1	0	2	0	0	0	0	0	.00	0	.286	.375	.857
Pirates	R	20	38	128	33	1	2	0	38	16	10	21	0	23	2	3	1	8	2	.80	1	.258	.368	.297
Schreimann,Eric,Martinsvlle	R	21	38	127	38	7	0	2	51	12	18	10	2	20	13	2	1	3	1	.75	2	.299	.404	.402
Batavia	A	21	15	52	14	1	0	4	27	9	13	1	1	7	7	0	1	0	1	.00	1	.269	.361	.519
Piedmont	A	21	7	23	4	1	0	0	5	1	1	1	1	4	0	0	0	0	0	.00	0	.174	.200	.217
Schroeder,Johnny,Elizabethtn	R	20	62	236	62	7	2	10	103	44	39	18	0	59	3	0	2	2	1	.67	0	.263	.320	.436
Schwab,Chris,Albany	A	21	122	484	110	22	3	5	153	60	43	48	1	173	1	0	4	4	6	.40	4	.227	.296	.316
Scolaro,Donny,Kissimmee	A	24	23	63	19	3	0	0	22	9	3	7	0	12	0	2	2	1	0	1.00	1	.302	.361	.349
Auburn	A	24	49	159	38	6	0	0	44	14	25	11	0	27	2	2	2	1	3	.25	6	.239	.293	.277
Scott,Thomas,Billings	R	23	67	252	89	24	4	7	142	68	43	44	0	65	3	2	3	17	9	.65	0	.353	.450	.563
Secrist,Reed,Lynchburg	A	26	112	380	107	18	3	19	188	60	75	54	7	88	3	1	4	3	4	.43	9	.282	.372	.495
Seguignol,Fernando,Albany	A	21	121	457	95	22	2	12	157	59	66	28	3	141	6	1	6	12	8	.60	6	.208	.260	.344
Segura,Juan,Erie	A	22	26	105	27	2	3	2	41	10	9	3	1	24	0	2	0	1	1	.50	1	.257	.278	.390
Augusta	A	22	25	80	18	2	0	0	20	3	4	1	0	21	0	4	1	0	2	.00	2	.225	.232	.250
Seidel,Ryan,Williamsprt	A	23	64	203	60	8	5	0	78	27	20	17	2	37	1	1	3	13	2	.87	7	.296	.348	.384
Seitzer,Brad,Stockton	A	26	127	428	132	28	3	6	184	66	56	72	2	68	3	2	2	7	4	.64	10	.308	.410	.430
Selivanov,Andrei,Braves	R	19	23	52	8	3	0	0	11	4	4	7	0	7	0	0	0	0	0	.00	4	.154	.254	.212
Sell,Chip,Vero Beach	A	25	80	222	60	6	1	1	71	21	23	18	0	33	4	2	2	1	3	.25	5	.270	.333	.320
Serafin,Ricardo,Martinsville	R	19	22	53	10	1	0	1	14	8	4	1	0	20	2	0	0	4	0	1.00	2	.189	.232	.264
Serbio,Carmen,Martinsville	R	23	28	83	19	6	1	2	33	15	12	20	0	23	4	2	0	1	0	1.00	5	.229	.402	.398
Serra,Joaquin,Orioles	R	20	29	85	12	0	0	0	12	7	3	6	0	12	0	3	0	2	2	.50	2	.141	.198	.141
Serra,Jose,High Desert	A	23	76	234	61	6	1	0	69	30	22	18	0	30	6	3	1	11	5	.69	2	.261	.328	.295
Sexson,Richie,Kinston	A	21	131	494	151	34	0	22	251	80	85	43	5	115	10	0	7	4	6	.40	8	.306	.368	.508
Shanahan,Jason,Elmira	A	22	64	230	55	9	4	4	84	19	28	30	3	50	2	1	2	7	3	.70	5	.239	.330	.365
Shanks,Cliff,Butte	R	24	42	147	41	8	1	2	57	19	22	5	0	37	6	0	0	0	1	.00	0	.279	.329	.388
Shapiro,Tony,Butte	R	23	40	121	35	9	1	3	55	13	15	9	0	34	4	0	0	2	0	1.00	3	.289	.358	.455
Sharp,Scott,Charlstn-Wv	A	23	55	161	34	2	2	0	40	7	16	7	0	63	1	4	1	1	2	.33	4	.211	.247	.248
Shatley,Andy,Medcine Hat	R	20	70	261	59	12	2	2	81	32	30	29	2	66	4	0	1	3	5	.38	9	.226	.309	.310
Sheffer,Chad,Everett	A	22	56	193	54	9	1	0	65	31	18	27	0	38	2	6	4	28	8	.78	5	.280	.367	.337
Sheffield,Tony,Sarasota	A	22	103	315	75	17	3	1	101	45	25	28	0	109	2	4	1	9	11	.45	4	.238	.303	.321
Shelton,Barry,White Sox	R	22	33	103	29	5	0	2	40	10	13	10	0	16	7	1	0	1	0	1.00	1	.282	.383	.388
Shepherd,Brian,San Jose	A	23	13	32	5	0	0	0	5	2	1	11	0	6	1	2	0	0	2	.00	0	.156	.386	.156
Shipman,Nate,Tigers	R	19	30	60	11	2	0	1	16	8	10	10	0	21	3	0	0	4	0	1.00	0	.183	.329	.267
Shipp,Kemuel,Pirates	R	20	18	54	7	0	0	0	7	4	4	5	0	13	1	0	0	0	0	.00	2	.130	.213	.130
Shirley,Al,Mets	R	22	4	15	5	2	0	0	7	4	0	3	0	4	0	0	0	3	1	.75	0	.333	.444	.467

356

1995 Batting -- Single-A and Rookie Leagues

Player		Lg	A	G	AB	H	2B	3B	HR	TB	R	RBI	TBB	IBB	SO	HBP	SH	SF	SB	CS	SB%	GDP	Avg	OBP	SLG
	St. Lucie	A	22	59	183	34	6	3	5	61	27	18	23	1	94	5	0	1	8	4	.67	2	.186	.292	.333
Shockey,Greg,Lk Elsinore		A	26	114	441	144	32	3	20	242	85	88	42	2	88	6	0	2	2	2	.50	6	.327	.391	.549
Shores,Scott,Clearwater		A	24	133	460	117	23	5	7	171	74	52	55	1	127	10	3	2	30	16	.65	11	.254	.345	.372
Short,Rick,Frederick		A	23	5	13	1	0	0	0	1	1	2	1	0	2	0	0	1	1	0	1.00	0	.077	.143	.077
	Bluefield	R	23	11	39	11	2	0	2	19	9	12	2	0	1	1	0	1	2	1	.67	2	.282	.326	.487
	High Desert	A	23	29	98	41	3	0	4	56	14	12	10	0	5	2	0	0	1	2	.33	2	.418	.482	.571
Shugars,Shawn,Charlotte		A	24	10	23	8	1	1	0	11	4	3	3	0	4	1	0	0	0	0	.00	0	.348	.444	.478
	Charlstn-Sc	A	24	8	22	5	1	0	0	6	2	3	1	0	3	1	0	0	2	0	.00	0	.227	.292	.273
Shumpert,Derek,Greensboro		A	20	56	153	33	3	1	0	38	21	14	18	0	41	2	7	0	4	2	.67	2	.216	.306	.248
	Oneonta	A	20	62	196	41	7	3	0	54	25	11	29	0	58	2	2	0	13	3	.81	6	.209	.317	.276
Shy,Jason,Eugene		A	22	20	54	13	2	0	2	21	6	6	1	0	12	0	0	0	0	0	.00	0	.241	.255	.389
	Danville	R	22	8	13	3	0	0	0	3	1	0	2	0	3	0	0	0	0	0	.00	0	.231	.333	.231
Silverio,Richard,Rockies		R	19	35	136	37	4	4	1	52	19	19	8	0	34	6	0	1	2	3	.40	0	.272	.338	.382
Sime,Rafael,Marlins		R	19	55	204	49	7	6	2	74	26	22	20	1	48	3	0	3	7	1	.88	3	.240	.313	.363
Simmons,Brian,White Sox		R	22	5	17	3	1	0	1	7	5	5	6	0	1	0	0	0	0	0	.00	1	.176	.391	.412
	Hickory	A	22	41	163	31	6	1	2	45	13	11	19	0	44	2	0	0	4	4	.50	2	.190	.283	.276
Simmons,Mark,Lk Elsinore		A	23	81	238	48	7	1	1	60	35	25	32	0	61	2	2	0	10	8	.56	4	.202	.301	.252
Simon,Randall,Durham		A	21	122	420	111	18	1	18	185	56	79	36	14	63	5	0	5	6	5	.55	15	.264	.326	.440
Simonton,Cy,Everett		A	19	48	155	32	2	1	0	36	17	15	14	0	36	1	3	1	8	4	.67	3	.206	.275	.232
Simpson,Jeramie,Kingsport		R	21	59	229	74	11	10	0	105	50	28	20	0	37	6	1	3	25	5	.83	2	.323	.388	.459
Sims,Mike,Brevard Cty		A	25	89	260	48	6	0	1	57	24	20	15	0	52	2	5	1	4	2	.67	14	.185	.234	.219
Singleton,Christopher,San Jose		A	23	94	405	112	13	5	2	141	55	31	17	1	49	5	5	1	33	13	.72	5	.277	.313	.348
Singleton,Samuel,Brewers		R	20	47	139	34	4	3	0	44	28	19	20	0	33	1	1	2	2	3	.40	3	.245	.340	.317
Slemmer,Dave,Sou. Oregon		A	23	66	246	55	5	3	1	69	36	20	36	1	42	0	1	1	16	4	.80	9	.224	.322	.280
Smalley,Jevon,Princeton		R	23	39	97	25	5	1	2	38	17	14	16	0	31	2	0	0	3	2	.60	1	.258	.374	.392
Smith,David,Sarasota		A	24	23	67	20	5	1	0	27	12	6	9	0	10	3	1	0	1	5	.17	1	.299	.405	.403
	Michigan	A	24	61	187	41	11	0	1	55	18	23	20	0	46	5	1	4	1	1	.50	3	.219	.306	.294
Smith,Demond,Cedar Rapids		A	23	79	317	108	25	7	7	168	64	41	32	2	61	6	5	1	37	12	.76	3	.341	.410	.530
	Lk Elsinore	A	23	34	148	52	8	2	7	85	32	26	11	0	36	2	0	1	14	3	.82	1	.351	.401	.574
	W. Michigan	A	23	8	32	10	1	1	2	19	6	3	2	1	8	1	1	0	3	2	.60	0	.313	.371	.594
Smith,Frank,San Bernrdo		A	23	58	122	25	7	1	3	43	19	15	30	1	54	4	0	0	9	3	.75	0	.205	.373	.352
Smith,Jason,Asheville		A	25	24	80	8	3	0	1	14	7	8	8	0	40	2	0	0	0	1	.00	1	.100	.200	.175
	Salem	A	25	30	86	8	1	1	1	14	4	5	11	0	38	1	1	0	0	0	.00	1	.093	.204	.163
Smith,Joel,Visalia		A	27	67	262	75	12	3	9	120	32	43	15	0	65	3	2	3	0	1	.00	9	.286	.329	.458
	Lk Elsinore	A	27	30	88	18	4	0	3	31	12	9	11	0	15	0	0	3	0	1	.00	3	.205	.284	.352
Smith,John,Astros		R	19	23	67	10	3	2	1	20	9	5	3	0	23	3	0	0	2	2	.50	0	.149	.213	.299
Smith,Akili,Erie		A	20	14	40	5	0	0	1	8	6	1	4	0	13	1	1	0	1	0	1.00	0	.125	.222	.200
Smith,Matt,Springfield		A	20	117	412	93	18	1	6	131	49	46	24	4	96	1	1	1	8	5	.62	11	.226	.269	.318
Smith,Phil,Braves		R	19	38	114	14	1	0	0	15	5	5	4	0	37	0	2	0	0	1	.00	1	.123	.153	.132
Smith,Rick,Helena		R	24	61	218	67	19	1	8	112	42	44	36	3	40	4	0	3	0	4	.00	6	.307	.410	.514
Smith,Rod,Greensboro		A	20	62	235	57	5	6	0	74	31	9	34	1	41	2	2	0	17	12	.59	4	.243	.343	.315
	Oneonta	A	20	49	187	44	8	3	0	58	34	10	30	0	49	2	0	1	24	7	.77	1	.235	.345	.310
Smith,Scott,Riverside		A	24	56	179	42	6	0	2	54	28	20	21	1	60	2	1	0	2	1	.67	7	.235	.315	.302
	Wisconsin	A	24	34	107	35	12	1	3	58	13	17	11	0	21	2	1	0	7	1	.88	7	.327	.397	.542
Smith,Sean,Durham		A	22	32	93	26	8	0	3	43	10	13	9	1	22	0	1	0	1	0	1.00	3	.280	.343	.462
Smith,Sloan,Tampa		A	23	124	412	107	23	1	13	171	61	64	74	3	136	4	1	3	6	8	.43	8	.260	.375	.415
Snelling,Allen,Medicne Hat		R	23	35	115	26	2	0	1	31	9	11	7	0	31	3	2	0	1	2	.33	1	.226	.288	.270
Snook,Rob,Beloit		A	22	3	6	0	0	0	0	0	0	0	2	0	3	0	0	0	0	0	.00	0	.000	.250	.000
Snusz,Chris,Batavia		A	23	21	66	15	1	0	1	19	9	5	6	0	6	0	0	0	1	1	.50	0	.227	.292	.288
Solano,Angel,White Sox		R	20	44	151	35	5	1	1	45	20	13	9	1	23	0	0	1	7	3	.70	0	.232	.273	.298
Solano,Fausto,Dunedin		A	22	41	144	30	5	2	1	42	19	10	17	0	30	1	5	0	3	2	.60	4	.208	.296	.292
	Blue Jays	R	22	11	44	13	5	0	2	24	12	7	3	0	6	2	3	1	2	1	.67	4	.295	.360	.545
	St. Cathrns	A	22	57	207	59	17	1	2	84	28	24	30	1	28	3	4	1	14	4	.78	2	.285	.382	.406
Sorg,Jay,Billings		R	23	67	247	73	14	1	7	110	42	40	26	3	52	3	0	1	4	3	.57	5	.296	.368	.445
Soriano,Carlos,Mets		R	21	47	167	44	11	3	5	76	25	24	15	0	24	2	1	2	4	2	.33	4	.263	.328	.455
	Pittsfield	A	21	5	17	3	2	0	0	5	1	1	1	0	2	0	0	0	1	0	1.00	1	.176	.222	.294
Soriano,Fred,W. Michigan		A	21	108	309	80	7	3	3	102	68	32	51	1	75	8	18	2	40	6	.87	0	.259	.376	.330
Soriano,Jose,W. Michigan		A	22	122	409	88	12	2	6	122	64	43	33	3	100	8	15	5	35	12	.74	7	.215	.284	.298
Soriano,Juan,Mets		R	21	11	32	7	2	0	1	12	5	3	4	0	9	0	0	1	3	0	1.00	1	.219	.306	.375
	Kingsport	R	21	40	107	28	5	1	0	35	29	12	20	0	21	2	0	1	7	2	.78	1	.262	.385	.327
Sosa,Juan,Vero Beach		A	20	8	27	6	1	1	1	12	2	6	0	0	4	0	0	0	0	2	.00	0	.222	.222	.444
	Yakima	A	20	61	217	51	10	4	3	78	26	16	15	2	39	1	4	2	8	1	.89	4	.235	.285	.359
Southard,Scott,Brevard Cty		A	24	68	219	46	7	1	2	61	18	21	20	0	40	1	5	0	4	3	.57	2	.210	.279	.279
Sowards,Ryan,Vero Beach		A	22	75	196	56	13	0	3	78	36	34	47	2	32	3	2	4	1	0	1.00	6	.286	.424	.398
Speed,Dorian,Williamsprt		A	22	60	204	44	8	3	2	64	30	23	28	0	56	1	1	3	18	5	.78	3	.216	.309	.314
Spencer,Jeffrey,Braves		R	19	48	171	40	8	1	4	62	17	21	12	2	42	2	1	3	7	2	.78	1	.234	.287	.363
Spencer,Shane,Tampa		A	24	134	500	150	31	3	16	235	87	88	61	2	60	7	2	3	14	8	.64	7	.300	.382	.470
Spiegel,Rich,Eugene		A	22	7	14	2	0	0	0	2	0	0	2	0	3	1	0	0	0	0	.00	1	.143	.294	.143
Spinello,Joe,South Bend		A	24	7	14	3	0	0	0	3	2	1	2	0	3	0	0	0	0	0	.00	1	.214	.313	.214
	Pr. William	A	24	10	30	4	1	0	0	5	1	2	1	0	9	1	1	0	0	0	.00	1	.133	.161	.167
Springfield,Bo,Pirates		R	20	3	6	0	0	0	0	0	1	0	1	0	1	0	0	0	1	0	1.00	0	.000	.143	.000
	Erie	A	20	25	76	20	1	2	1	28	11	6	13	0	20	0	2	1	8	4	.67	2	.263	.367	.368
Spry,Shane,Bristol		R	20	15	43	10	2	0	0	12	5	6	10	0	7	0	2	0	0	0	.00	1	.233	.370	.279
Srebroski,Andy,Ogden		R	24	10	30	2	1	0	0	3	3	0	7	0	12	1	0	0	0	1	.00	1	.067	.263	.067
Stadler,Mike,Watertown		A	21	6	21	5	1	0	0	6	2	0	0	0	6	0	0	0	0	0	.00	0	.238	.227	.286
Stafford,Kimani,Royals		R	20	39	67	11	1	1	0	14	13	4	12	0	30	0	0	0	0	0	.00	1	.164	.291	.209
Stare,Lonny,Bakersfield		A	25	104	372	101	21	2	9	153	54	59	33	1	65	7	8	2	14	10	.58	9	.272	.341	.411

1995 Batting -- Single-A and Rookie Leagues

Player	Lg	A	G	AB	H	2B	3B	HR	TB	R	RBI	TBB	IBB	SO	HBP	SH	SF	SB	CS	SB%	GDP	Avg	OBP	SLG
Stasio,Chris,Michigan	A	25	87	315	96	22	1	7	141	44	47	25	0	78	4	1	3	1	0	1.00	7	.305	.360	.448
Staton,T.J.,Augusta	A	21	112	391	114	21	5	5	160	43	53	27	5	97	2	0	1	27	13	.68	6	.292	.340	.409
Steinkemper,Jake,Vermont	A	22	21	61	10	3	0	0	13	4	5	10	0	15	1	0	0	1	3	.25	0	.164	.292	.213
Stephens,Joel,Orioles	R	20	23	82	19	3	1	0	24	8	10	5	0	25	3	1	0	2	1	.67	3	.232	.300	.293
Stevens,Clayton,White Sox	R	20	42	143	32	1	4	5	56	19	21	20	3	40	3	1	0	3	2	.60	6	.224	.331	.392
Stevenson,Chad,Tigers	R	20	32	95	15	4	1	3	30	11	12	11	0	23	3	1	1	1	0	1.00	5	.158	.264	.316
Stewart,Keith,Mariners	R	22	15	46	9	0	1	1	14	12	6	11	0	23	0	1	0	3	0	1.00	1	.196	.351	.304
Stewart,Paxton,Medicne Hat	R	22	50	161	40	13	2	0	57	30	17	23	0	34	0	1	1	4	2	.67	6	.248	.341	.354
Stewart,Tommy,Kissimmee	A	23	52	167	42	4	1	1	51	9	15	17	0	48	3	3	1	0	2	.00	3	.251	.330	.305
Stingley,Derek,Piedmont	A	25	39	84	15	2	0	1	20	20	5	6	0	24	4	1	1	13	2	.87	2	.179	.263	.238
Stone,Craig,Hagerstown	A	20	96	355	98	20	4	8	150	47	52	34	0	104	8	0	5	3	2	.60	6	.276	.348	.423
Stone,Matt,Martinsvlle	R	21	40	111	28	8	0	0	36	15	13	29	0	37	2	0	1	3	0	1.00	5	.252	.413	.324
Stovall,Darond,W. Palm Bch	A	23	121	461	107	22	2	4	145	52	51	44	2	117	0	2	3	18	12	.60	4	.232	.297	.315
Strange,Mike,Hagerstown	A	22	96	290	68	9	2	1	84	51	27	61	0	92	4	2	0	13	3	.81	7	.234	.375	.290
Strasser,John,Bristol	R	21	46	159	36	3	2	0	43	24	10	20	0	38	4	4	0	6	1	.86	1	.226	.328	.270
Stratton,Kelly,Hudson Vall	A	24	30	58	12	2	0	1	17	10	8	7	1	6	2	0	0	1	1	.50	2	.207	.313	.293
Stricklin,Scott,FortMyers	A	24	65	166	31	1	0	0	32	20	8	41	2	25	0	5	0	4	4	.50	1	.187	.348	.193
Stuart,Rich,Angels	R	19	56	204	61	10	6	2	89	42	33	25	1	42	3	2	2	20	8	.71	5	.299	.380	.436
Stuckenschneide,Eric,SanBern	A	24	8	20	5	1	0	0	6	2	2	7	0	6	2	0	1	1	0	1.00	0	.250	.467	.300
Great Falls	R	24	40	118	37	8	2	4	61	32	16	32	0	26	5	0	1	10	7	.59	2	.314	.474	.517
Stumberger,Darren,Columbus	A	23	127	448	121	27	0	11	181	62	57	56	2	72	9	0	5	3	3	.50	13	.270	.359	.404
Sturdivant,Jack,Riverside	A	22	99	347	95	13	5	1	121	60	34	39	1	41	1	2	4	31	13	.70	3	.274	.345	.349
Sturges,Brian,Johnson Cty	R	23	17	42	6	1	0	0	7	5	6	2	0	7	3	1	0	0	0	.00	3	.143	.234	.167
Subero,Carlos,Augusta	A	24	31	97	18	2	0	0	20	8	6	2	0	24	0	3	0	1	0	1.00	2	.186	.202	.206
Charlotte	A	24	17	44	6	1	0	0	7	3	4	1	0	10	0	1	0	0	0	.00	1	.136	.136	.159
Suero,Reynaldo,Rangers	R	18	39	111	24	3	1	0	29	19	5	14	0	23	1	0	3	12	5	.71	1	.216	.302	.261
Sullivan,Davey,Orioles	R	20	38	125	29	6	0	1	38	13	12	10	0	23	1	2	2	1	1	.50	1	.232	.290	.304
Suplee,Ray,Tampa	A	25	98	317	74	9	1	7	106	33	37	33	1	94	7	3	4	4	2	.67	2	.233	.316	.334
Swafford,Derek,Augusta	A	21	119	447	113	15	5	3	147	69	48	33	1	101	8	6	2	52	16	.76	4	.253	.314	.329
Sweet,Jon,Augusta	A	24	87	267	76	9	1	1	90	28	22	18	2	31	5	2	2	5	4	.56	6	.285	.339	.337
Swift,Scott,Burlington	A	25	68	209	40	3	1	0	45	29	17	37	0	33	0	5	3	9	5	.64	4	.191	.309	.215
Tachikawa,Takashi,Visalia	A	20	47	119	21	2	1	1	28	10	14	8	0	28	0	0	1	1	1	.50	7	.176	.227	.235
Tackett,Tim,Visalia	A	24	105	370	89	17	3	0	112	51	27	47	1	35	4	9	3	14	9	.61	4	.241	.330	.303
Tardiff,Jeremy,Red Sox	R	19	10	23	3	0	1	1	8	2	4	1	0	2	0	0	0	0	0	.00	1	.130	.167	.348
Tatis,Fernando,Charlstn-Sc	A	21	131	499	151	43	4	15	247	74	84	45	4	94	7	1	4	22	19	.54	5	.303	.366	.495
Taylor,Avery,Orioles	R	20	13	30	1	0	0	0	1	2	2	3	0	12	0	1	0	0	0	.00	2	.033	.121	.033
Taylor,Byron,Savannah	A	23	14	29	3	0	0	0	3	2	0	1	0	10	1	0	0	0	0	.00	0	.103	.161	.103
Taylor,Jerry,Burlington	R	23	10	27	8	1	1	2	17	7	7	8	0	6	1	0	1	1	0	1.00	0	.296	.459	.630
Watertown	A	23	5	21	6	1	0	0	7	3	3	1	0	3	0	0	0	0	0	.00	1	.286	.318	.333
Taylor,Matthew,Eugene	A	22	10	24	0	0	0	0	0	1	0	5	0	8	1	0	0	0	1	.00	1	.000	.200	.000
Braves	R	22	35	112	18	2	0	0	20	9	6	10	0	11	2	2	0	1	4	.20	4	.161	.242	.179
Taylor,Mike,St. Pete	A	25	70	159	38	3	1	2	49	13	15	28	2	24	0	4	1	0	2	.00	2	.239	.351	.308
Taylor,Reggie,Martinsvlle	R	19	64	239	53	4	6	2	75	36	32	23	0	58	6	0	4	18	7	.72	5	.222	.301	.314
Tebbs,Nate,Sarasota	A	23	118	440	128	15	4	2	157	58	52	39	0	80	3	4	1	25	15	.63	7	.291	.352	.357
Teeters,Brian,Wilmington	A	23	64	162	37	7	0	6	62	25	26	19	1	51	1	2	0	11	5	.69	3	.228	.313	.383
Tejada,Miguel,Sou. Oregon	A	20	74	269	66	15	5	8	115	45	44	41	2	54	2	0	3	19	2	.90	3	.245	.346	.428
Tejcek,John,Riverside	A	24	105	416	108	22	3	10	166	72	54	32	1	116	4	4	2	23	3	.88	5	.260	.317	.399
Tena,Dario,Rancho Cuca	A	23	11	29	5	1	0	0	6	1	0	3	0	4	1	0	1	2	1	.67	1	.172	.273	.207
Clinton	A	23	99	295	54	6	0	0	60	30	19	25	0	41	1	5	2	33	10	.77	3	.183	.248	.203
Terrell,Matt,St. Lucie	A	24	86	193	38	6	2	0	48	24	9	18	0	53	1	3	1	11	2	.85	3	.197	.268	.249
Terry,Tony,Princeton	R	20	47	106	18	3	0	0	21	15	8	17	0	40	2	2	1	7	4	.64	0	.170	.294	.198
Terry,Reggie,Rangers	R	22	5	17	5	0	0	0	5	3	0	0	0	4	0	0	0	1	0	1.00	0	.294	.294	.294
Tessmar,Tim,Mets	R	22	56	196	41	5	4	0	54	20	28	30	1	27	4	0	2	4	1	.80	2	.209	.323	.276
Thielen,Duane,San Jose	A	24	91	282	60	13	1	8	99	38	34	38	1	81	3	3	2	4	5	.44	5	.213	.311	.351
Thobe,Steve,Augusta	A	24	84	291	87	12	2	6	121	43	38	29	6	71	5	0	0	1	3	.25	2	.299	.372	.416
Thomas,Greg,Kinston	A	23	102	329	72	21	0	11	126	32	43	25	4	98	3	1	7		2	.00	2	.219	.275	.383
Thomas,Juan,Pr. William	A	24	132	464	109	20	4	26	215	64	69	40	4	156	8	1	2	4	5	.44	16	.235	.305	.463
Thomas,Rod,Charlstn-Wv	A	22	29	82	12	3	0	1	18	8	6	7	1	25	0	0	0	3	0	1.00	3	.146	.209	.220
Winston-Sal	A	22	20	54	12	2	0	2	20	7	7	8	0	22	1	0	0	2	3	.40	0	.222	.333	.370
Thomasson,Shane,Everett	A	23	40	100	21	0	1	0	23	10	3	2	0	23	2	2	0	7	2	.78	1	.210	.240	.230
Thompson,Andrew,Hagerstown	A	20	124	461	110	19	2	6	151	48	57	29	2	108	8	1	3	2	3	.40	15	.239	.293	.328
Thompson,Bruce,Bellingham	A	23	66	241	56	7	2	2	73	49	13	43	1	75	0	1	0	18	6	.75	1	.232	.349	.303
Thompson,Karl,Everett	A	22	54	187	46	13	1	5	76	29	26	16	0	39	4	2	2	4	0	1.00	9	.246	.316	.406
Thompson,Leroy,Columbus	A	21	82	248	53	15	3	7	95	34	35	40	4	78	5	1	0	1	2	.33	4	.214	.334	.383
Thompson,Bliiy,Lakeland	A	25	73	223	54	13	1	5	84	26	28	15	0	45	1	1	3	4	0	1.00	2	.242	.289	.377
Thornhill,Chad,Watertown	A	23	55	164	41	8	1	0	51	34	16	37	1	31	1	1	1	0	0	.00	5	.250	.389	.311
Tidick,Mike,Hickory	A	25	56	132	28	9	2	2	47	17	9	21	2	41	5	0	2	5	4	.56	2	.212	.338	.356
Tiller,Brad,Burlington	R	20	55	195	46	10	1	1	61	24	23	11	0	49	3	2	2	11	5	.69	2	.236	.284	.313
Tillero,Ingmar,Royals	R	18	36	103	26	4	0	1	33	14	11	8	1	33	0	0	0	1	1	.50	3	.252	.306	.320
Timmons,Shayne,Medicne Hat	R	24	24	42	7	1	0	0	8	5	3	6	0	11	2	0	1	1	1	.00	1	.167	.294	.190
Tinoco,Luis,Everett	A	21	62	203	58	10	2	9	99	34	31	35	1	41	3	0	1	9	3	.75	6	.286	.397	.488
Tippin,Gregory,Utica	A	23	68	232	53	7	1	2	68	20	27	16	1	68	8	0	4	12	6	.67	1	.228	.296	.293
Tocco,Todd,Eugene	A	24	59	117	23	3	0	1	29	12	8	17	0	32	2	2	0	1	0	1.00	1	.197	.304	.248
Tohyama,Shoji,Visalia	A	28	51	155	46	9	2	2	65	15	24	8	0	38	3	1	1	1	1	.50	3	.297	.341	.419
Tolbert,Ernest,Mariners	R	20	26	91	16	3	2	1	26	16	7	9	0	24	2	0	0	2	2	.50	1	.176	.265	.286
Topham,Ryan,South Bend	A	22	14	48	12	3	0	0	15	4	2	4	0	12	0	1	0	0	0	.00	3	.250	.308	.313
Topping,Dan,Bellingham	A	20	57	180	48	5	0	5	68	15	31	14	4	24	8	0	0	0	0	.00	6	.267	.345	.378

1995 Batting -- Single-A and Rookie Leagues

Player	Lg	A	G	AB	H	2B	3B	HR	TB	R	RBI	TBB	IBB	SO	HBP	SH	SF	SB	CS	SB%	GDP	Avg	OBP	SLG
Torbett,Hanes,Kingsport	R	23	19	46	12	1	2	0	17	10	5	9	0	8	0	0	1	0	0	.00	0	.261	.375	.370
Torborg,Dale,St. Lucie	A	24	5	9	1	0	0	0	1	0	1	0	0	4	0	0	0	0	0	.00	1	.111	.111	.111
Tampa	A	24	2	1	0	0	0	0	0	0	0	0	0	1	0	0	0	0	0	.00	0	.000	.000	.000
Greensboro	A	24	33	81	16	4	0	1	23	10	11	7	0	28	1	0	0	1	0	1.00	0	.198	.270	.284
Torok,John,Piedmont	A	23	91	202	38	4	5	1	55	26	22	45	1	39	1	6	1	11	7	.61	2	.188	.337	.272
Torrealba,Steve,Braves	R	18	30	92	19	4	0	0	23	3	10	11	0	20	2	0	1	0	0	.00	3	.207	.302	.250
Torrealba,Yoruit,Bellingham	A	17	26	71	11	3	0	0	14	2	8	2	0	14	1	0	1	0	1	.00	1	.155	.187	.197
Torres,Jaime,Tampa	A	23	107	364	87	17	0	8	128	45	45	28	1	29	10	3	3	1	1	.50	14	.239	.309	.352
Totman,Jason,Clinton	A	23	61	229	66	19	3	0	91	32	32	26	0	27	4	1	2	6	1	.86	2	.288	.368	.397
Towle,Justin,Charlstn-Wv	A	22	107	343	92	22	2	8	142	54	60	44	0	95	1	1	3	3	6	.33	6	.268	.350	.414
Towner,Kyle,Wisconsin	A	23	104	301	68	12	0	1	83	64	24	63	1	59	4	5	3	34	11	.76	1	.226	.364	.276
Townsend,Terric,Martinsvlle	R	23	5	14	4	0	0	0	4	4	1	3	0	2	1	0	0	1	0	1.00	0	.286	.444	.286
Trammell,Gary,Quad City	A	23	102	336	100	12	3	2	124	44	33	32	0	62	1	5	3	14	8	.64	4	.298	.358	.369
Trammell,Bubba,Lakeland	A	24	122	454	129	32	3	16	215	61	72	48	2	80	4	0	4	13	3	.81	9	.284	.355	.474
Treanor,Matt,Springfield	A	20	75	211	39	6	2	3	58	17	19	21	0	59	4	2	2	1	1	.50	1	.185	.269	.275
Tribolet,Scott,Auburn	A	24	50	172	43	7	4	1	61	23	22	13	0	31	2	1	3	12	2	.86	1	.250	.305	.355
Trimble,Rob,Yankees	R	24	11	0	0	0	0	0	0	0	0	0	0	0	0	0	0	0	0	.00	0	.000	.000	.000
Greensboro	A	24	33	83	11	2	0	0	13	5	5	4	0	22	0	1	0	0	1	.00	0	.133	.172	.157
Trippy,Joe,Eugene	A	22	75	259	80	16	0	2	102	48	38	24	0	31	13	2	2	29	13	.69	1	.309	.393	.394
Troilo,Jason,Tampa	A	23	1	2	0	0	0	0	0	0	0	0	0	2	1	0	0	0	0	.00	0	.000	.333	.000
Greensboro	A	23	19	59	17	4	0	3	30	6	9	3	0	19	0	3	1	0	1	.00	0	.288	.317	.508
Truby,Chris,Quad City	A	22	118	400	93	23	4	9	151	68	64	41	0	66	3	3	3	27	8	.77	11	.233	.306	.378
Truitt,Theron,Marlins	R	20	24	67	12	0	0	0	12	8	8	7	0	13	3	0	3	6	1	.86	0	.179	.275	.179
Tucker,Jon,Yakima	A	19	41	115	19	3	0	1	25	6	5	13	0	35	1	0	0	0	0	.00	2	.165	.254	.217
Turner,Rocky,Columbia	A	24	12	17	3	0	0	0	3	2	1	2	0	5	0	2	0	0	2	.00	1	.176	.263	.176
Pittsfield	A	24	33	116	30	4	0	0	34	9	10	7	0	17	3	1	1	8	7	.53	0	.259	.315	.293
Twist,Jeff,Portland	A	23	27	79	11	3	0	0	14	6	6	9	0	18	1	0	1	0	2	.00	2	.139	.233	.177
Twitty,Sean,Tampa	A	25	1	4	1	0	0	0	1	0	0	0	0	1	0	0	0	0	0	.00	1	.250	.250	.250
Greensboro	A	25	80	293	83	25	1	10	140	49	58	29	1	83	6	0	2	6	2	.75	9	.283	.358	.478
Tyler,Joshua,Beloit	A	22	77	186	44	5	0	2	55	24	27	36	0	40	2	7	3	3	6	.33	4	.237	.361	.296
Tyrus,Jason,Clinton	A	24	65	159	36	5	1	2	49	15	17	10	0	53	1	3	0	4	5	.44	0	.226	.276	.308
Bakersfield	A	24	25	81	14	0	0	4	26	12	10	7	0	28	2	0	1	4	2	.67	1	.173	.253	.321
Ubaldo,Nelson,Astros	R	22	34	103	25	4	2	1	36	12	9	8	0	32	3	1	1	9	2	.82	3	.243	.313	.350
Ugueto,Hector,New Jersey	A	22	54	202	58	7	2	1	72	37	28	17	0	36	9	1	3	9	2	.82	4	.287	.364	.356
Ugueto,Jesus,St. Pete	A	23	37	77	10	1	0	0	11	3	3	3	0	18	1	1	1	0	1	.00	4	.130	.171	.143
Ullan,Dave,Clinton	A	23	43	96	20	1	0	1	24	8	11	20	1	16	3	2	1	0	2	.00	1	.208	.358	.250
Underwood,Devin,Butte	A	22	55	190	45	12	0	0	57	22	17	30	0	31	4	0	2	0	4	.00	6	.237	.350	.300
Unrat,Chris,Charlotte	A	25	66	172	43	8	1	1	56	22	17	23	1	38	0	4	2	1	2	.33	6	.250	.335	.326
Utting,Ben,Danville	R	20	55	189	45	8	1	0	55	30	15	27	2	34	2	1	1	12	4	.75	1	.238	.338	.291
Macon	A	20	21	55	12	2	0	0	14	5	6	7	0	13	0	0	0	1	1	.50	0	.218	.306	.255
Valdespino,Jose,Medicne Hat	R	22	35	105	20	3	2	3	36	14	13	18	0	34	2	1	1	1	1	.50	6	.190	.317	.343
Valdez,Mario,Hickory	A	21	130	441	120	30	5	11	193	65	56	67	2	107	5	0	3	9	7	.56	5	.272	.372	.438
Valencia,Victor,Yankees	R	19	25	58	14	1	0	1	18	5	8	6	0	22	0	0	0	0	0	.00	1	.241	.313	.310
Valenti,Jon,Sou. Oregon	A	22	35	110	23	5	0	2	34	13	16	8	0	18	1	1	2	2	0	1.00	1	.209	.264	.309
Valentin,Jose,Fort Wayne	A	20	112	383	123	26	5	19	216	59	65	47	7	75	2	1	0	0	5	.00	7	.321	.398	.564
Valera,Willy,Columbus	A	20	31	104	17	3	1	2	28	8	6	4	0	35	0	0	0	0	1	.00	3	.163	.194	.269
Watertown	A	20	65	240	61	13	3	3	89	33	29	14	0	57	2	2	2	4	2	.67	6	.254	.298	.371
Valera,Yojanny,Kingsport	R	19	56	204	60	13	0	3	82	30	36	11	0	33	5	2	1	2	1	.67	6	.294	.344	.402
Vallero,Rich,Ogden	R	22	46	127	29	6	0	0	35	17	9	16	0	35	0	2	0	1	2	.33	6	.228	.315	.276
Vallone,Gar,Boise	A	23	37	99	24	6	0	0	30	21	16	20	1	33	3	8	1	4	2	.67	3	.242	.382	.303
Van Oeveren,Ryan,Albany	A	23	49	135	22	4	0	1	29	11	7	14	0	44	0	1	2	1	1	.50	0	.163	.238	.215
Vandergriend,Jon,Boise	A	24	56	157	45	8	0	3	62	30	24	26	1	32	3	0	0	7	3	.70	2	.287	.398	.395
Varriano,Mark,Red Sox	R	23	18	49	8	1	0	0	9	4	6	6	0	10	2	0	0	0	0	.00	1	.163	.281	.184
Utica	A	23	4	11	1	0	0	0	1	2	1	2	0	3	0	0	0	0	0	.00	0	.091	.231	.091
Sarasota	A	23	8	16	0	0	0	0	0	0	0	1	0	9	0	0	0	0	0	.00	0	.000	.059	.000
Vaske,Terry,Macon	A	25	53	148	25	7	0	5	47	14	18	18	2	58	0	0	0	0	1	.00	1	.169	.259	.318
Vasquez,Danny,Charlstn-Sc	A	22	44	131	28	6	2	1	41	12	7	6	0	42	4	1	1	6	3	.67	4	.214	.268	.313
Hudson Vall	A	22	69	240	64	9	4	4	93	38	31	15	1	58	3	0	4	16	5	.76	4	.267	.313	.388
Vazquez,Ramon,Mariners	R	19	39	141	29	3	1	0	34	20	11	19	0	27	2	0	0	4	3	.57	2	.206	.309	.241
Vecchioni,Jerry,Braves	R	19	33	99	17	1	0	0	18	10	7	10	0	23	1	1	0	2	3	.40	2	.172	.255	.182
Velazquez,Andy,Salem	A	20	131	497	149	25	6	13	225	74	69	40	4	102	4	3	7	7	10	.41	17	.300	.352	.453
Velazquez,Jose,Yankees	R	20	58	209	60	9	2	3	82	33	34	30	2	20	1	0	3	4	4	.43	3	.287	.374	.392
Venezia,Danny,Fort Myers	A	24	16	49	12	1	1	0	15	5	4	7	0	8	0	1	0	1	0	1.00	1	.245	.333	.306
Venezia,Rich,Erie	A	22	38	108	22	2	0	1	27	11	10	13	0	24	0	4	2	5	1	.83	1	.204	.285	.250
Ventura,Wilfredo,Athletics	R	20	34	104	29	3	1	3	43	19	20	20	0	32	3	1	1	7	3	.70	0	.279	.406	.413
Veras,Iluminado,Angels	R	21	32	87	22	4	1	1	31	9	9	5	0	13	0	1	2	2	2	.50	2	.253	.287	.356
Veras,Juan,Charlstn-Sc	A	21	102	305	62	11	2	0	77	39	17	32	0	69	1	7	1	16	8	.67	1	.203	.280	.252
Veras,Wilton,Red Sox	R	18	31	91	24	1	0	0	25	7	5	7	0	9	3	0	0	1	2	.33	2	.264	.337	.275
Vessel,Andy,Charlotte	A	21	129	498	132	26	2	9	189	67	78	32	2	75	15	1	7	3	17	.15	11	.265	.324	.380
Vickers,Randy,Everett	A	20	68	266	68	13	2	12	121	35	37	20	2	102	3	0	0	5	2	.71	6	.256	.315	.455
Vida,James,Spokane	A	25	74	291	94	13	1	4	121	38	39	19	5	32	1	0	0	0	0	.00	5	.323	.367	.416
Vidal,Carlos,Rockies	R	21	39	136	39	11	1	1	55	19	20	23	0	20	1	0	3	3	3	.50	9	.287	.387	.404
Vieira,Scott,Williamsprt	A	22	61	214	68	8	2	6	98	35	46	25	1	37	9	0	4	3	1	.75	3	.318	.405	.458
Vigil,Scott,Ogden	R	24	20	60	17	2	0	0	19	16	8	16	0	13	5	0	0	2	1	.67	0	.283	.469	.317
Vilchez,Jose,Twins	R	20	45	142	32	6	0	0	38	14	6	1	0	29	0	4	0	7	5	.58	0	.225	.231	.268
Villa,Kahi,Blue Jays	R	20	40	138	25	6	2	0	35	20	11	14	0	28	1	1	0	2	1	.67	2	.181	.261	.254
Villalobos,Carlos,Wisconsin	A	21	110	389	101	16	4	9	152	64	53	35	1	76	3	4	5	16	4	.80	3	.260	.322	.391

1995 Batting -- Single-A and Rookie Leagues

Player	Lg	A	G	AB	H	2B	3B	HR	TB	R	RBI	TBB	IBB	SO	HBP	SH	SF	SB	CS	SB%	GDP	Avg	OBP	SLG
Viruet,Willie,Pittsfield	A	22	11	32	6	0	0	0	6	4	5	4	0	7	2	2	0	0	0	.00	0	.188	.316	.188
Vizcaino,Romulo,Fort Wayne	A	22	103	343	85	13	4	1	109	44	22	35	1	56	1	3	5	6	6	.50	6	.248	.315	.318
Vopata,Nathan,Hudson Vall	A	23	68	231	65	12	8	0	93	37	30	23	1	36	6	0	5	10	5	.67	7	.281	.355	.403
Waggoner,Jay,Jamestown	A	23	63	204	50	5	4	3	72	21	24	22	1	40	2	0	3	2	3	.40	2	.245	.320	.353
Wagner,Kyle,Boise	A	23	36	78	11	0	1	0	15	14	14	17	0	18	7	0	1	1	4	.20	1	.141	.340	.192
Waldrop,Tom,Macon	A	26	60	194	46	11	1	3	68	19	24	14	2	52	1	1	1	1	1	.50	3	.237	.294	.351
Walkanoff,A.J.,Yakima	A	22	38	112	25	5	0	0	30	7	15	17	0	21	0	0	2	1	0	1.00	1	.223	.321	.268
Walker,Joseph,Pr. William	A	24	1	3	1	0	1	0	3	1	2	1	0	1	0	0	0	0	0	.00	0	.333	.500	1.000
South Bend	A	24	6	6	0	0	0	0	0	0	0	4	0	4	0	0	0	0	0	.00	0	.000	.400	.000
Walker,Rod,Hudson Vall	A	20	13	26	2	0	0	0	2	2	1	0	0	10	0	0	1	1	0	1.00	2	.077	.074	.077
Lethbridge	R	20	39	125	33	4	1	0	39	21	8	20	0	31	4	2	0	7	4	.64	5	.264	.383	.312
Walker,Steve,Rockford	A	24	103	415	120	24	7	3	167	78	44	37	3	104	10	0	0	40	16	.71	1	.289	.361	.402
Walker,Shon,Augusta	A	22	110	358	82	20	0	6	120	49	51	68	3	127	0	1	4	10	9	.53	3	.229	.349	.335
Wallace,Brian,San Jose	A	24	25	81	18	1	0	2	25	15	8	9	1	18	1	2	0	3	0	1.00	1	.222	.308	.309
Burlington	A	24	97	338	72	12	0	9	111	48	38	34	0	65	6	7	5	7	5	.58	7	.213	.292	.328
Walls,Eric,Springfield	A	23	101	299	68	14	1	2	90	53	21	17	0	65	2	4	0	20	7	.74	8	.227	.274	.301
Walther,Chris,Brewers	R	19	50	174	45	3	2	0	52	28	19	10	0	9	1	1	0	4	3	.57	5	.259	.303	.299
Wambach,James,South Bend	A	26	9	27	6	0	0	0	6	1	2	2	0	6	0	0	0	0	0	.00	1	.222	.276	.222
Wampler,Sam,Piedmont	A	21	1	3	0	0	0	0	0	0	0	0	0	2	0	0	0	0	0	.00	0	.000	.000	.000
Martinsville	R	21	11	22	3	0	0	0	3	1	1	3	0	10	0	0	0	0	0	.00	2	.136	.240	.136
Ward,Daryle,Fayetteville	A	21	137	524	149	32	0	14	223	75	106	46	11	111	5	0	7	1	2	.33	13	.284	.344	.426
Ward,Jason,Lethbridge	R	24	11	24	3	0	0	0	3	3	2	6	0	6	0	0	0	0	0	.00	0	.125	.300	.125
Wardrop,Adam,Angels	R	20	49	146	37	4	2	0	45	26	10	30	0	36	6	5	1	8	7	.53	2	.253	.399	.308
Ware,Jeremy,Expos	R	20	38	116	28	4	2	2	42	18	15	18	0	28	3	0	1	5	4	.56	2	.241	.355	.362
Warner,Bryan,Columbus	A	21	119	393	94	14	4	8	140	47	58	25	3	73	2	4	0	8	2	.80	5	.239	.288	.356
Warner,Ken,Durham	A	22	51	137	31	11	1	2	50	12	13	12	1	32	0	3	2	1	2	.33	1	.226	.285	.365
Warner,Randy,St. Lucie	A	22	122	446	116	23	6	10	181	43	70	27	0	86	3	0	4	6	7	.46	9	.260	.304	.406
Wathan,Dusty,Wisconsin	A	22	5	11	1	0	0	1	4	1	3	0	0	3	1	0	0	0	0	.00	0	.091	.167	.364
Everett	A	22	53	181	49	9	1	6	78	32	25	17	0	26	7	1	0	2	1	.67	4	.271	.356	.431
Watkins,Sean,Idaho Falls	R	21	67	247	92	20	1	13	153	51	67	43	6	55	10	0	2	0	1	.00	13	.372	.480	.619
Watson,Jon,Bellingham	A	22	65	231	69	9	0	2	84	42	27	20	2	41	4	4	3	16	9	.64	3	.299	.360	.364
Watson,Kevin,Burlington	A	23	80	247	46	5	1	7	74	29	25	18	0	88	3	2	1	1	2	.33	4	.186	.249	.300
Watson,Marty,Pr. William	A	25	23	85	22	3	2	5	44	12	14	5	0	21	0	0	1	2	1	.67	4	.259	.297	.518
Watts,Josh,Piedmont	A	21	111	355	83	13	0	5	111	50	43	45	3	96	4	3	7	8	5	.62	6	.234	.321	.313
Weathersby,Len,Spokane	A	21	37	118	27	4	3	1	40	13	12	9	0	42	4	0	0	2	3	.40	4	.229	.305	.339
Weaver,Colby,Macon	A	23	14	37	9	0	0	1	12	4	6	5	0	8	2	0	0	1	0	1.00	1	.243	.364	.324
Durham	A	23	8	18	5	2	0	0	7	2	2	4	0	6	0	0	0	0	0	.00	0	.278	.409	.389
Weaver,Scott,Jamestown	A	22	65	236	71	11	2	5	101	33	34	38	5	33	3	0	2	16	4	.80	9	.301	.401	.428
Weaver,Terry,Bellingham	A	23	37	116	29	2	0	3	40	24	13	9	1	30	1	0	2	2	1	.67	0	.250	.310	.345
Webb,Kevin,Durham	A	26	43	121	22	4	0	5	41	17	11	18	0	39	4	0	1	0	1	.00	5	.182	.306	.339
Weisner,Randy,White Sox	R	24	5	7	2	1	0	0	3	1	4	1	0	0	0	0	0	2	0	1.00	0	.286	.375	.429
Welch,Brandon,Sou. Oregon	A	23	39	102	15	3	0	0	18	6	11	15	0	30	1	1	0	1	0	1.00	0	.147	.263	.176
Welch,Coby,Royals	R	22	16	43	12	2	0	0	14	7	9	3	0	8	0	0	0	0	0	.00	1	.279	.326	.326
Springfield	A	22	19	35	6	0	0	0	6	3	1	2	0	9	3	0	0	0	0	.00	0	.171	.275	.171
Wells,Mark,Asheville	A	24	40	115	33	6	3	8	69	21	23	9	2	38	1	1	2	1	3	.25	1	.287	.339	.600
Salem	A	24	66	236	46	8	0	10	84	24	31	13	3	83	1	1	1	0	3	.00	2	.195	.239	.356
Whatley,Gabe,Rockford	A	24	95	339	87	23	2	7	135	54	54	45	3	58	6	0	6	11	3	.79	6	.257	.348	.398
Daytona	A	24	15	42	11	3	0	1	17	8	5	7	0	5	0	0	0	2	0	1.00	1	.262	.367	.405
Whipple,Boomer,Erie	A	23	67	225	57	4	0	2	67	29	33	30	0	18	6	6	1	4	3	.57	8	.253	.355	.298
Whitaker,Chad,Burlington	R	19	47	181	43	13	1	5	73	20	27	14	1	59	1	0	2	3	4	.40	1	.238	.294	.403
White,Eric,Columbus	A	23	112	369	117	24	3	6	165	49	46	51	5	45	1	1	1	11	7	.61	12	.317	.400	.447
White,Mickey,Astros	R	20	1	4	0	0	0	0	0	1	0	0	0	0	0	0	0	0	0	.00	0	.000	.000	.000
White,Walt,Kane County	A	24	63	207	59	18	2	1	84	30	23	32	0	52	3	5	3	3	2	.60	3	.285	.384	.406
Whitehurst,Todd,St. Lucie	A	24	58	189	42	7	1	0	51	13	18	21	2	37	4	1	1	2	3	.40	1	.222	.312	.270
Columbia	A	24	21	61	10	3	0	1	16	10	1	11	0	19	4	1	0	2	1	.67	0	.164	.329	.262
Whitley,Matt,Portland	A	24	64	230	53	10	2	0	67	40	20	35	1	33	13	3	1	8	3	.73	5	.230	.362	.291
Whitlock,Michael,Blue Jays	R	19	54	168	43	10	3	3	68	27	22	41	3	48	6	0	1	5	0	1.00	4	.256	.417	.405
Whittaker,Jay,South Bend	A	22	67	227	50	14	3	5	85	29	31	26	0	58	3	1	2	14	5	.74	5	.220	.306	.374
Wieser,Mike,Durham	A	23	28	62	13	2	0	1	18	5	3	2	0	12	1	0	0	0	0	.00	0	.210	.246	.290
Wilcox,Chris,Oneonta	A	22	59	223	73	16	7	1	106	25	28	20	3	28	1	0	0	9	3	.75	4	.327	.382	.475
Wilhelm,Brent,Hickory	A	23	67	240	54	9	2	2	73	19	24	15	0	36	1	0	2	4	3	.57	6	.225	.271	.304
Wilkerson,Adrian,Brewers	R	21	55	160	53	1	1	0	56	22	28	16	0	28	2	3	3	18	7	.72	2	.331	.392	.350
Williams,Bryan,St. Cathrns	A	22	24	67	13	2	0	0	15	5	6	6	0	23	0	0	0	0	0	.00	0	.194	.257	.224
Williams,Curtis,Savannah	A	23	51	134	25	2	1	1	32	14	9	20	0	44	0	5	0	2	5	.29	2	.187	.292	.239
Williams,Ed,Lakeland	A	24	4	15	4	1	0	0	7	1	1	2	0	4	0	0	0	0	0	.00	0	.267	.267	.467
Williams,Ricky,Martinsvlle	R	19	36	113	27	1	0	0	28	19	11	6	0	32	2	0	0	13	2	.87	1	.239	.289	.248
Williams,Glenn,Macon	A	18	38	120	21	4	0	0	25	13	14	16	0	42	1	1	3	2	1	.67	3	.175	.271	.208
Eugene	A	18	71	268	60	11	4	7	100	39	36	21	1	71	5	0	2	7	4	.64	4	.224	.291	.373
Williams,Harold,Pr. William	A	25	129	472	133	30	1	14	207	56	72	48	11	98	11	1	2	4	2	.67	16	.282	.360	.439
Williams,Drew,Beloit	A	24	135	427	114	21	2	14	181	66	66	81	4	76	6	1	3	8	8	.50	9	.267	.390	.424
Williams,Jewell,Burlington	R	19	46	146	32	6	1	4	52	20	15	13	0	52	8	0	0	11	4	.73	3	.219	.317	.356
Williams,Marc,Mariners	R	19	22	88	20	7	1	0	29	6	6	0	0	23	0	0	1	4	2	.67	4	.227	.225	.330
Williams,Mark,Savannah	A	25	64	201	31	2	0	4	45	19	13	33	0	57	0	5	1	0	0	.00	10	.154	.272	.224
Williamson,Joel,High Desert	A	26	24	66	11	2	0	0	13	5	1	3	0	18	0	3	0	1	0	1.00	1	.167	.203	.197
Williamson,Matt,Piedmont	A	23	88	285	67	10	2	1	84	44	25	35	0	67	2	6	2	3	4	.43	5	.235	.321	.295
Wilson,Chris,Beloit	A	25	28	63	12	1	1	0	15	12	6	3	0	14	2	0	0	5	1	.83	0	.190	.250	.238
Wilson,Craig,Medicne Hat	R	19	49	184	52	14	1	7	89	33	35	24	1	41	3	0	1	8	2	.80	1	.283	.367	.484

1995 Batting -- Single-A and Rookie Leagues

Player	Lg	A	G	AB	H	2B	3B	HR	TB	R	RBI	TBB	IBB	SO	HBP	SH	SF	SB	CS	SB%	GDP	Avg	OBP	SLG
Wilson,Enrique,Kinston	A	20	117	464	124	24	7	6	180	55	52	25	2	38	2	4	10	18	19	.49	10	.267	.301	.388
Wilson,Brian,Charlstn-Wv	A	23	5	13	4	1	0	0	5	3	1	0	0	1	0	2	0	3	0	1.00	0	.308	.308	.385
Winston-Sal	A	23	20	58	13	1	0	2	20	10	8	7	0	16	0	0	0	1	2	.33	2	.224	.308	.345
Billings	R	23	62	209	60	14	1	0	76	32	36	35	0	49	1	3	4	7	7	.50	2	.287	.386	.364
Wilson,Preston,Columbia	A	21	111	442	119	26	5	20	215	70	61	19	2	114	9	1	3	20	6	.77	4	.269	.311	.486
Wilson,Todd,Burlington	A	24	30	105	27	5	0	2	38	8	11	6	0	12	4	0	0	1	0	1.00	1	.257	.322	.362
San Jose	A	24	37	117	28	7	1	0	37	14	13	6	0	19	2	3	0	1	0	1.00	5	.239	.288	.316
Wilson,Vance,Columbia	A	23	91	324	81	11	0	6	110	34	32	19	1	45	8	1	2	4	3	.57	6	.250	.306	.340
Wingate,Ervan,Bakersfield	A	22	121	445	104	23	1	8	153	51	59	42	0	86	6	4	4	5	8	.38	25	.234	.306	.344
Winget,Jeremy,Clinton	A	23	120	375	101	23	0	5	139	49	44	67	3	75	1	1	1	4	4	.50	7	.269	.381	.371
Winn,Randy,Elmira	A	22	51	213	67	7	4	0	82	38	22	15	0	31	3	0	2	19	7	.73	1	.315	.365	.385
Winn,Wess,Orioles	R	24	5	18	4	2	0	0	6	2	5	3	0	3	0	0	0	0	0	.00	1	.222	.333	.333
Bluefield	R	24	24	49	11	2	0	0	13	4	9	12	0	12	0	3	0	2	2	.50	0	.224	.377	.265
Winterlee,Scott,Columbia	A	25	4	7	3	0	0	0	3	0	0	2	0	0	0	0	0	0	0	.00	0	.429	.556	.429
Witt,Kevin,Hagerstown	A	20	119	479	111	35	1	14	190	58	50	28	2	148	4	3	0	1	5	.17	5	.232	.280	.397
Wittig,Paul,Bakersfield	A	22	93	331	92	17	1	7	132	44	53	20	0	66	6	5	5	6	3	.67	8	.278	.326	.399
Wojtkowski,Steve,Michigan	A	23	6	14	0	0	0	0	0	2	0	3	0	3	0	0	0	0	0	.00	1	.000	.176	.000
Wolff,Mike,High Desert	A	23	94	292	79	17	3	5	117	32	44	16	1	53	9	1	6	3	5	.38	5	.271	.322	.401
Wolger,Michael,Vermont	A	23	60	203	52	7	1	2	67	27	23	34	0	47	2	1	2	3	3	.50	5	.256	.365	.330
Wood,Tony,Huntington	R	23	56	205	55	5	2	0	64	26	19	15	0	55	2	1	1	5	2	.71	4	.268	.323	.312
Woodridge,Dickie,Rancho Cuca	A	25	116	358	101	9	3	3	125	67	58	71	1	40	2	2	5	9	4	.69	5	.282	.399	.349
Woodward,Chris,Medicne Hat	R	20	72	241	56	8	0	3	73	44	21	33	1	41	6	5	3	9	4	.69	1	.232	.336	.303
Woolf,Jason,Johnson Cty	R	19	31	111	31	7	1	0	40	16	14	8	0	21	1	1	3	6	3	.67	0	.279	.325	.360
Wright,Ron,Macon	A	20	135	527	143	23	1	32	264	93	104	62	1	118	2	0	3	2	0	1.00	11	.271	.348	.501
Wright,Terry,Charlstn-Wv	A	25	125	410	116	13	10	2	155	68	56	50	4	43	2	7	1	46	16	.74	8	.283	.363	.378
Wuerch,Jason,Greensboro	A	24	31	85	16	2	0	0	18	4	8	11	0	20	0	1	1	2	2	.50	5	.188	.278	.212
Wulfert,Mark,Clinton	A	23	48	147	36	10	1	1	51	17	16	17	0	34	1	1	1	9	2	.82	1	.245	.325	.347
Wyngarden,Brett,Visalia	A	25	76	270	71	14	0	3	94	21	24	12	0	81	3	1	3	1	2	.33	6	.263	.299	.348
Wyrick,Chris,St. Pete	A	24	55	139	33	6	1	1	44	20	15	10	0	25	5	1	0	3	1	.75	3	.237	.312	.317
Yedo,Carlos,Greensboro	A	22	117	435	107	22	1	13	170	65	57	53	5	126	0	0	2	2	1	.67	4	.246	.327	.391
Yoder,P.J.,Pittsfield	A	21	55	183	39	6	4	0	53	25	18	30	2	34	2	1	1	0	5	.00	6	.213	.329	.290
Young,Kevin,Cedar Rapids	A	24	119	395	115	22	2	2	147	58	46	37	0	42	15	7	4	17	12	.59	7	.291	.370	.372
Zahner,Kevin,Bakersfield	A	23	82	257	60	7	2	2	77	25	31	12	0	37	2	6	5	4	1	.80	10	.233	.268	.300
Zaletel,Brian,Burlington	A	25	27	97	22	4	0	2	32	9	5	4	0	19	3	0	1	0	0	.00	5	.227	.276	.330
Zambrano,Victor,Yankees	R	21	27	78	16	3	1	0	21	10	5	5	0	15	1	2	0	2	3	.40	2	.205	.262	.269
Zamora,Junior,Mets	R	20	20	56	13	2	2	0	19	9	4	5	0	10	1	1	1	0	0	.00	2	.232	.302	.339
Zapata,Ramon,Lynchburg	A	25	119	416	124	27	2	8	179	59	45	42	0	58	2	9	0	6	8	.43	13	.298	.365	.430
Zellers,Kevin,Bakersfield	A	23	96	332	80	16	1	5	113	39	27	39	1	106	8	2	3	5	6	.45	6	.241	.332	.340
Zerpa,Mauro,South Bend	A	21	41	87	19	1	0	0	20	5	5	6	0	20	1	2	0	1	0	1.00	3	.218	.277	.230
Zorrilla,Julio,Columbia	A	21	133	518	143	15	3	0	164	65	31	31	2	75	0	10	4	42	18	.70	9	.276	.315	.317
Zuleta,Julio,Williamsprt	A	21	30	75	13	3	1	0	18	9	6	11	1	12	2	0	0	0	1	.00	4	.173	.295	.240
Zumwalt,Russ,Butte	R	22	41	113	31	5	2	0	40	19	10	15	1	20	0	0	1	5	1	.83	2	.274	.357	.354
Zwisler,Joshua,Beloit	A	21	98	252	59	12	1	1	76	29	18	28	1	46	4	2	0	8	4	.67	4	.234	.320	.302

1995 Pitching -- Single-A and Rookie Leagues

Player	Lg	A	G	GS	CG	GF	IP	BFP	H	R	ER	HR	SH	SF	HB	TBB	IBB	SO	WP	Bk	W	L	Pct.	ShO	Sv	ERA
Abramavicius,Jason,Lynchburg	A	26	9	0	0	2	12.1	64	22	13	10	2	0	0	1	5	1	11	1	0	1	0	1.000	0	0	7.30
Abreu,Jose,Burlington	A	21	8	0	0	1	13	61	9	8	5	0	1	1	1	12	0	14	0	2	1	0	1.000	0	0	3.46
Bellingham	A	21	13	0	0	5	23.1	99	17	12	12	0	1	0	1	12	0	29	2	0	1	2	.333	0	1	4.63
Abreu,Juan,Butte	R	20	8	5	0	2	22.2	124	27	31	22	1	2	0	2	28	0	21	11	0	1	4	.200	0	0	8.74
Burlington	A	20	2	0	0	1	2	11	3	0	0	0	0	1	0	4	1	0	0	0	0	0	.000	0	0	0.00
Abreu,Oscar,Athletics	R	22	20	1	0	7	26	146	33	30	23	0	0	1	2	35	0	29	10	2	1	2	.333	0	0	7.96
Abreu,Winston,Danville	R	19	13	13	1	0	74	277	54	29	19	5	0	4	1	13	0	90	2	0	6	3	.667	0	0	2.31
Adair,Scott,Columbia	A	20	3	0	0	0	4.1	26	10	8	5	0	0	1	1	0	0	4	0	0	0	1	.000	0	0	10.38
Huntington	R	20	13	13	1	0	74.2	317	96	47	39	3	2	5	2	13	0	28	2	0	2	9	.182	0	0	4.70
Adam,Justin,Spokane	A	21	15	8	0	2	49.1	220	45	34	29	2	0	0	4	31	0	35	2	0	3	4	.429	0	1	5.29
Adge,Jason,Watertown	A	24	19	0	0	8	45.2	179	40	10	8	0	1	1	1	9	1	26	5	0	5	1	.833	0	1	1.58
Adkins,Tim,Dunedin	A	22	45	0	0	37	48	215	36	29	20	2	3	2	1	33	0	49	7	0	7	4	.636	0	17	3.75
Agostinelli,Pete,Clearwater	A	27	57	0	0	23	45.2	207	54	26	22	1	2	2	0	22	5	32	3	1	4	4	.500	0	6	4.34
Agosto,Stevenson,Angels	R	20	1	1	0	0	5	22	3	5	3	0	2	1	1	2	0	2	3	0	0	1	.000	0	0	5.40
Boise	A	20	13	11	0	1	52.1	224	39	20	17	1	0	3	5	30	2	34	12	0	6	2	.750	0	0	2.92
Aguiar,Douglas,Martinsvlle	R	19	15	7	0	4	45.1	195	46	28	28	3	0	1	3	21	0	42	5	1	2	2	.500	0	0	5.56
Aguilar,Alonzo,Royals	R	21	15	1	0	5	26.1	116	26	14	11	2	0	3	7	10	0	24	4	0	0	1	.000	0	1	3.76
Aguilar,Carlo,Yankees	R	20	18	0	0	6	39	159	36	11	9	0	3	0	0	13	1	34	8	1	6	0	1.000	0	1	2.08
Aguirre,Jose,Cedar Rapds	A	22	6	2	0	0	14	61	12	6	6	1	0	1	0	10	0	12	2	0	0	0	.000	0	0	3.86
Lk Elsinore	A	22	29	0	0	11	47	207	48	26	20	2	1	2	1	20	0	35	2	1	0	0	.000	0	0	3.83
Alazaus,Shawn,Greensboro	A	24	33	0	0	6	39	179	43	25	24	5	2	3	1	18	0	40	0	1	3	1	.750	0	1	5.54
Albaladejo,Randy,Kissimmee	A	23	7	0	0	4	8.2	51	13	13	11	0	1	1	3	10	0	5	2	0	0	0	.000	0	0	11.42
Auburn	A	23	9	0	0	6	10.1	48	12	6	6	0	0	2	2	5	0	7	2	0	0	0	.000	0	2	5.23
Albrecht,Jon,Spokane	A	24	17	0	0	13	21.1	89	14	8	8	1	0	0	3	12	1	15	2	0	2	2	.500	0	0	3.38
Alejo,Nigel,Kane County	A	21	48	0	0	38	52.2	233	48	17	14	5	2	0	2	25	2	47	5	0	4	1	.800	0	7	2.39
Alexander,Don,Ogden	R	24	19	1	0	6	32.2	164	43	32	23	0	4	1	3	26	1	30	7	3	2	4	.333	0	0	6.34
Alexis,Julio,Huntington	R	22	14	13	0	0	81.2	352	89	55	43	9	2	2	3	21	0	65	5	1	1	6	.143	0	0	4.74
Ali,Sam,Bellingham	A	25	5	0	0	4	8	38	10	7	7	1	1	0	0	4	0	3	2	1	0	2	.000	0	0	7.88
Burlington	A	25	3	0	0	2	4	16	4	1	1	0	0	0	0	0	0	2	0	0	0	0	.000	0	0	2.25
Alicea,Pat,Tigers	R	20	12	8	2	2	51.1	211	45	21	11	1	1	2	3	14	0	43	5	1	5	2	.714	1	1	1.93
Allen,Cedric,Charlstn-Wv	A	24	27	27	5	0	170.1	690	143	64	54	8	6	4	14	46	4	108	6	4	13	7	.650	2	0	2.85
Almanza,Armando,Savannah	A	23	20	20	0	0	108	476	108	62	47	13	5	4	3	40	1	72	6	1	3	9	.250	0	0	3.92
Alvarado,David,Pirates	R	18	9	2	0	4	15	66	15	8	8	1	0	0	2	4	0	15	3	2	1	0	1.000	0	1	4.80
Alvarado,Carlos,Pirates	R	18	2	0	0	0	3	15	1	2	2	0	0	1	0	5	0	2	3	0	0	0	.000	0	0	6.00
Alvarado,Luis,Fort Wayne	A	21	16	1	0	6	37	165	41	18	12	2	0	1	1	14	1	24	1	0	1	1	.500	0	2	2.92
Huntington	R	21	11	5	1	1	44	195	43	28	18	4	1	1	1	12	0	43	4	0	3	4	.429	0	0	3.68
Alvarez,Ivan,Burlington	A	26	4	2	0	0	13	59	17	12	7	2	1	0	0	5	0	12	3	0	1	2	.333	0	0	4.85
Alvarez,Juan,Boise	A	22	9	0	0	0	11.2	47	12	1	1	0	0	0	1	2	0	11	0	0	0	0	.000	0	0	0.77
Ambrose,John,Hickory	A	21	14	14	0	0	73	314	65	41	32	6	2	3	3	35	0	49	9	2	4	8	.333	0	0	3.95
South Bend	A	21	3	3	1	0	16.2	77	18	13	10	2	1	0	0	10	0	15	2	0	1	1	.500	0	0	5.40
Andersen,Mark,Brevard Cty	A	24	20	0	0	9	36.1	169	42	25	16	2	1	1	2	17	0	21	3	0	0	1	.000	0	0	3.96
Kane County	A	24	15	0	0	5	26	116	29	13	10	3	1	1	1	13	1	15	2	0	1	2	.333	0	1	3.46
Anderson,Eric,Springfield	A	21	21	14	1	2	92.2	391	89	39	35	4	0	2	4	34	1	52	8	0	9	5	.643	1	1	3.40
Wilmington	A	21	16	0	0	10	27.2	109	28	9	9	1	0	0	0	4	0	19	4	1	3	1	.750	0	2	2.93
Anderson,Eric,Elizabethtn	R	23	21	2	0	5	39.2	185	48	21	13	0	4	0	2	19	1	31	1	1	3	2	.600	0	0	2.95
Anderson,Gary,Burlington	A	22	14	0	0	12	17	81	18	12	12	2	0	0	4	8	0	22	2	0	1	2	.333	0	0	6.35
Anderson,Jimmy,Augusta	A	20	14	14	0	0	76.2	305	51	15	13	1	1	0	4	31	0	75	9	1	4	2	.667	0	0	1.53
Lynchburg	A	20	10	9	0	1	52.1	231	56	29	24	1	4	1	5	21	1	32	7	3	1	5	.167	0	0	4.13
Anderson,John,Astros	R	22	2	0	0	1	3	13	3	3	1	0	0	0	0	1	0	5	2	0	0	2	.000	0	0	3.00
Andrakin,Rob,San Jose	A	27	29	0	0	20	45.2	193	38	14	12	1	7	3	3	19	2	49	2	1	2	1	.667	0	7	2.36
Anez,Maycoll,Hickory	A	19	2	0	0	1	4	19	3	2	1	0	0	0	0	4	0	4	1	0	0	0	.000	0	0	2.25
White Sox	R	19	7	1	0	3	29	109	19	6	3	0	0	0	1	4	0	21	3	0	4	1	.800	0	1	0.93
Bristol	R	19	7	2	0	1	15.2	78	24	14	10	1	1	1	0	8	0	11	0	0	0	2	.000	0	1	5.74
Angerhofer,Chad,Princeton	R	20	13	7	0	2	38.2	189	52	37	31	5	0	2	1	17	0	38	6	1	2	4	.333	0	0	7.22
Antonini,Adrian,Batavia	A	23	3	3	0	0	5.2	30	12	6	6	0	0	0	1	1	0	8	0	0	0	0	.000	0	0	9.53
Piedmont	A	23	6	5	0	1	21.1	85	19	10	9	1	0	0	2	2	0	26	1	1	2	0	1.000	0	0	3.80
Antoszek,Chris,Sarasota	A	25	3	3	0	0	17.1	77	21	10	8	0	1	0	0	4	0	9	2	1	1	2	.333	0	0	4.15
Aquino,Julio,San Bernrdo	A	23	25	3	0	6	59.2	293	96	59	52	5	2	2	1	23	0	42	5	1	2	2	.500	0	0	7.84
Vero Beach	A	23	3	0	0	2	3	14	1	0	0	0	0	0	0	0	0	3	0	0	0	0	.000	0	0	0.00
Arellano,Carlos,Watertown	A	21	2	2	0	0	5	21	3	2	2	1	0	0	0	4	0	1	0	0	0	0	.000	0	0	3.60
Arias,Alfredo,Hagerstown	A	23	35	1	0	17	71.1	308	67	37	33	6	6	2	3	35	2	59	8	1	4	6	.400	0	1	4.16
Armas,Tony,Yankees	R	18	5	4	0	0	14	61	12	9	1	1	1	0	1	6	0	13	3	1	0	1	.000	0	0	0.64
Arroyo,Bronson,Pirates	R	19	13	9	0	0	61.1	275	72	39	29	4	2	0	4	9	0	48	5	0	5	4	.556	0	0	4.26
Arroyo,Luis,Rancho Cuca	A	22	26	24	0	0	128.2	599	158	97	75	9	8	6	12	62	6	102	7	3	7	10	.412	0	0	5.25
Asher,Ray,Red Sox	R	21	10	3	0	4	26	139	32	29	20	6	1	2	2	26	2	21	4	0	0	3	.000	0	0	6.92
Ashley,Antonio,Angels	R	19	5	0	0	2	8	31	6	3	2	0	0	0	0	1	0	4	0	0	0	0	.000	0	0	2.25
Ashworth,Kym,Vero Beach	A	19	24	24	1	0	120	515	111	56	47	8	6	5	1	64	0	97	24	2	7	4	.636	1	0	3.53
Atchley,Justin,Billings	R	22	13	13	0	0	77	327	91	33	30	4	2	1	2	20	2	65	2	1	10	0	1.000	0	0	3.51
Atkins,Dannon,Watertown	A	22	13	10	0	1	60.2	255	52	28	22	2	1	2	2	26	0	46	5	2	5	2	.714	0	1	3.26
Atwater,Joe,Pittsfield	A	21	1	1	0	0	8	33	8	2	2	0	0	0	0	3	0	6	0	0	1	0	1.000	0	0	2.25
Columbia	A	21	27	18	3	6	147.1	567	106	52	44	10	4	6	2	28	1	127	5	2	9	6	.600	2	1	2.69
Austin,Swan,Marlins	R	19	15	0	0	12	20.1	91	22	9	7	0	2	0	0	12	3	15	2	0	0	4	.000	0	4	3.10
Avila,Edwin,Boise	A	22	14	1	0	6	20	100	27	27	23	6	0	0	1	14	0	17	2	1	0	1	.000	0	0	10.35
Avrard,Corey,Boise	A	19	13	13	0	0	54.1	228	38	25	24	4	1	4	0	33	2	51	6	0	1	6	.143	0	0	3.98
Aybar,Manuel,Savannah	A	21	18	18	2	0	112.2	461	82	46	38	8	7	4	2	36	0	99	8	1	3	8	.273	1	0	3.04
St. Pete	A	21	9	9	0	0	48.1	202	42	27	18	4	0	1	1	16	0	43	7	1	2	5	.286	0	0	3.35
Babineaux,Darrin,Yakima	A	21	12	10	0	2	59.1	251	53	33	24	3	1	3	4	18	1	36	0	0	1	6	.143	0	0	3.64

1995 Pitching -- Single-A and Rookie Leagues

Player	Lg	A	G	GS	CG	GF	IP	BFP	H	R	ER	HR	SH	SF	HB	TBB	IBB	SO	WP	Bk	W	L	Pct.	ShO	Sv	ERA
Baez,Benito,Athletics	R	19	14	11	1	0	70	303	64	35	26	2	2	2	4	28	0	83	2	0	5	1	.833	0	0	3.34
Bailey,Ben,Billings	R	21	13	13	0	0	79	340	74	32	26	2	2	3	3	29	2	68	11	0	6	4	.600	0	0	2.96
Bailey,Phillip,Bellingham	A	22	19	4	0	0	59.2	237	51	15	9	3	0	0	3	15	0	39	1	1	6	1	.857	0	0	1.36
Baine,David,Charlotte	A	26	21	3	0	9	48.1	212	47	23	22	4	0	2	0	24	0	29	3	1	1	3	.250	0	0	4.10
Bair,Denny,Williamsprt	A	21	7	7	0	0	39.1	161	33	13	7	0	0	1	1	2	0	31	1	3	2	3	.400	0	0	1.60
Rockford	A	21	9	7	0	1	53.2	209	41	10	9	2	1	1	1	6	0	40	4	1	4	2	.667	0	0	1.51
Bair,Andy,Marlins	R	19	6	6	0	0	24.1	97	21	10	8	1	2	0	1	7	0	22	0	2	2	2	.500	0	0	2.96
Bajda,Mike,Fayettevlle	A	22	4	0	0	1	9	41	8	5	3	1	0	0	0	10	4	4	2	0	0	0	.000	0	0	3.00
Jamestown	A	22	13	3	0	0	23.2	123	35	26	21	2	2	1	3	17	0	14	3	3	2	2	.500	0	0	7.99
Baker,Derek,Columbia	A	23	36	0	0	24	62.2	267	52	25	23	5	2	4	6	35	0	44	5	1	2	8	.200	0	6	3.30
Baker,Jason,Vermont	A	21	14	14	0	0	72	317	59	40	33	2	1	0	5	47	1	57	11	0	6	5	.545	0	0	4.13
Baldwin,Scott,Modesto	A	26	5	3	0	0	13.1	75	16	11	9	1	1	3	0	19	0	10	5	0	0	1	.000	0	0	6.08
Bales,Joseph,White Sox	R	21	11	9	1	0	45.1	213	44	27	20	0	1	2	2	31	0	44	3	1	3	1	.750	0	0	3.97
Bales,Daniel,Idaho Falls	R	22	10	1	0	3	14.1	85	26	24	17	0	0	0	2	13	0	8	3	0	1	0	.000	0	1	10.67
Ballew,Preston,Mets	R	19	14	2	0	6	36	143	27	8	7	0	0	1	2	6	0	42	5	1	3	0	1.000	0	1	1.75
Pittsfield	A	19	1	1	0	0	5	20	2	0	0	0	0	0	0	3	0	4	1	0	1	0	1.000	0	0	0.00
Barbao,Joe,Piedmont	A	24	43	0	0	14	66.2	288	70	34	25	2	4	5	7	12	1	24	2	1	8	4	.667	0	1	3.38
Barcelo,Lorenzo,Bellingham	A	18	12	11	0	0	47	198	43	23	18	3	0	1	2	19	0	34	1	1	3	2	.600	0	0	3.45
Barfield,Rodney,Johnson Cty	R	21	10	10	0	0	36.2	199	52	50	40	3	3	2	8	30	0	18	4	2	2	7	.222	0	0	9.82
Barker,Jeff,Jamestown	A	22	14	0	0	2	16	70	15	10	7	2	2	0	2	8	0	14	0	0	2	2	.500	0	0	3.94
Barker,Richie,Rockford	A	23	32	0	0	15	43.2	196	45	20	18	2	1	0	2	20	1	23	5	0	2	0	1.000	0	1	3.71
Barkley,Brian,Sarasota	A	20	24	24	2	0	146.2	611	147	66	53	5	2	3	5	37	3	70	4	1	8	10	.444	2	0	3.25
Barksdale,Joe,Michigan	A	22	24	24	1	0	141	643	139	91	71	7	6	9	14	78	1	93	11	3	9	8	.529	0	0	4.53
Barnes,Keith,Salem	A	21	15	15	1	0	79	335	90	52	47	11	1	3	3	24	0	43	4	0	4	5	.444	0	0	5.35
Asheville	A	21	10	6	0	1	36.1	142	25	10	8	2	2	0	0	15	0	21	4	0	2	0	1.000	0	1	1.98
Barnes,Larry,Brewers	R	19	6	5	0	0	20.1	84	16	4	4	0	0	0	0	14	0	31	1	1	0	1	.000	0	0	1.77
Helena	R	19	3	2	0	0	12	49	5	5	3	0	0	1	1	6	0	15	6	0	2	0	1.000	0	0	2.25
Barnes,Monte,Oneonta	A	22	3	0	0	2	4.2	23	5	2	2	0	0	0	0	4	0	3	0	0	0	0	.000	0	0	3.86
Barnett,Marty,Batavia	A	22	10	10	0	0	49.1	228	67	45	34	3	2	4	5	10	1	32	9	3	1	6	.143	0	0	6.20
Baron,Jim,Rancho Cuca	A	22	3	0	0	1	2.2	22	7	8	5	1	1	0	0	6	0	3	2	0	0	0	.000	0	0	16.88
Clinton	A	22	11	9	1	1	50.2	232	65	42	35	4	3	2	1	16	2	31	4	0	0	8	.000	0	0	6.22
Idaho Falls	R	22	27	1	0	5	43	201	51	31	27	2	0	2	1	19	1	43	8	0	2	3	.400	0	0	5.65
Barrett,Mark,Rancho Cuca	A	24	32	0	0	11	32.2	149	39	18	13	2	2	1	2	11	1	29	0	0	1	0	1.000	0	1	3.58
Barrios,Manuel,Quad City	A	21	50	0	0	48	52	219	44	16	13	1	2	1	4	17	1	55	1	0	1	5	.167	0	23	2.25
Bartels,Todd,Elizabethtn	R	22	13	9	2	1	57	239	66	27	26	4	1	2	3	13	0	45	0	1	2	2	.750	0	0	4.11
Batchelder,Billy,Sou.Oregon	A	23	18	5	0	4	44	195	56	30	27	3	0	1	1	13	1	20	1	0	1	4	.200	0	0	5.52
Bates,Norm,Bluefield	R	21	14	2	0	5	25.2	113	22	13	7	1	1	0	2	16	0	31	5	1	2	0	1.000	0	3	2.45
Batista,Mario,Pirates	R	21	1	1	0	0	5	23	7	4	3	1	0	0	0	3	0	2	0	0	0	1	.000	0	0	5.40
Battaglia,Chuck,Lethbridge	R	21	4	3	0	0	20.1	90	24	11	9	2	1	1	0	6	0	9	1	0	0	3	.000	0	0	3.98
Rangers	R	21	10	8	0	1	41.2	186	46	31	23	2	0	2	1	13	0	35	5	0	4	3	.571	0	0	4.97
Bauer,Charles,Hudson Vall	A	23	15	15	0	0	82.1	357	81	42	29	0	1	1	8	32	0	62	13	6	4	3	.571	0	0	3.17
Bauldree,Joey,Braves	R	19	12	0	0	3	26.2	129	26	21	21	1	0	0	4	26	0	19	2	0	0	0	.000	0	0	7.09
Baxter,Herb,Modesto	A	24	29	14	0	3	91.1	434	104	75	67	10	4	4	3	64	0	73	20	6	4	7	.364	0	0	6.60
Beach,Scott,Erie	A	22	14	0	0	4	18	97	24	21	15	3	0	0	2	17	1	8	1	0	1	0	1.000	0	0	7.50
Beagle,Chad,Elmira	A	25	5	5	0	0	22	101	25	16	14	0	0	0	0	13	0	21	4	1	1	3	.250	0	0	5.73
Beaumont,Matt,Lk Elsinore	A	23	27	26	0	0	175.1	724	162	80	64	15	1	6	7	57	1	149	1	1	16	9	.640	0	0	3.29
Beck,Chris,Wisconsin	A	24	28	19	2	6	130	553	113	62	56	13	3	3	4	61	2	119	10	1	12	8	.600	2	2	3.88
Beck,Greg,Beloit	A	23	35	5	0	12	74.1	331	74	46	39	2	1	6	2	35	2	91	7	2	5	2	.714	0	2	4.72
Becker,Tom,Oneonta	A	21	15	15	0	0	77.2	353	83	55	46	0	4	4	2	40	0	65	12	2	6	6	.500	0	0	5.33
Beckerman,Andy,Astros	R	26	2	0	0	0	3	12	1	0	0	0	0	0	0	0	0	3	0	0	0	0	.000	0	0	0.00
Bedinger,Doug,Fort Wayne	A	21	46	0	0	35	66.1	301	74	37	34	8	7	5	4	28	3	62	5	0	6	6	.500	0	9	4.61
Beebe,Joey,Kingsport	R	21	9	7	0	1	44.1	182	43	16	16	3	2	1	1	12	0	34	5	0	5	1	.833	0	0	3.25
Beirne,Kevin,White Sox	R	22	2	0	0	2	3.2	15	2	1	1	0	0	0	0	1	0	3	0	0	0	0	.000	0	2	2.45
Bristol	R	22	9	0	0	7	9	35	4	0	0	0	0	0	0	4	0	12	0	0	1	0	1.000	0	0	0.00
Hickory	A	22	3	0	0	1	4	16	7	2	2	0	0	0	0	0	0	4	0	0	0	0	.000	0	0	4.50
Bell,Jason,Fort Wayne	A	21	9	6	0	2	34.1	139	26	11	5	0	3	0	1	6	0	40	6	2	3	1	.750	0	0	1.31
Bell,Mike,Vermont	A	23	7	0	0	4	16.2	59	7	5	1	0	1	0	1	5	2	12	0	0	0	0	.000	0	1	0.54
Albany	A	23	12	0	0	4	20.2	81	13	8	6	2	0	2	0	8	0	14	0	0	3	3	.500	0	0	2.61
Bell,Rob,Braves	R	19	10	8	0	0	34	154	38	29	26	2	0	2	2	14	0	33	7	0	1	6	.143	0	0	6.88
Benes,Adam,New Jersey	A	23	19	10	0	3	75	311	71	30	28	3	0	4	3	23	0	47	5	2	5	3	.625	0	0	3.36
Bennett,Jason,Watertown	A	21	16	12	0	2	79	333	86	36	33	5	2	0	9	20	3	53	2	1	3	3	.500	0	0	3.76
Bennett,Matt,New Jersey	A	22	23	0	0	7	47.1	203	49	30	18	0	2	2	2	13	1	43	3	0	3	0	1.000	0	0	3.42
Bennett,Thomas,Athletics	R	20	11	6	0	0	36.1	150	20	16	11	1	1	1	2	16	0	46	4	0	1	1	.500	0	0	2.72
Benny,Pete,Helena	R	20	11	7	0	1	46.1	205	48	25	20	2	0	0	4	24	0	47	4	1	5	0	1.000	0	0	3.88
Benson,Jeremy,Greensboro	A	23	3	0	0	0	4	14	1	0	0	0	0	0	0	0	0	0	0	0	0	0	.000	0	0	0.00
Benz,Jacob,W.Palm Bch	A	24	44	0	0	38	54	220	44	13	7	0	3	2	3	18	3	48	4	1	0	2	.000	0	22	1.17
Bermudez,Manuel,Bellingham	A	19	13	13	0	0	56.2	244	51	28	24	3	2	2	0	25	0	39	4	1	1	2	.333	0	0	3.81
Bernal,Manuel,Royals	R	22	6	6	0	0	33	130	29	9	5	1	0	1	1	4	0	25	3	0	3	0	1.000	0	0	1.36
Springfield	A	22	8	8	0	0	42.2	193	55	37	35	9	1	0	3	9	0	17	1	0	1	5	.167	0	0	7.38
Berninger,D.J.,Helena	R	23	21	0	0	4	28	159	45	28	24	4	1	1	2	34	2	11	2	0	3	1	.750	0	0	7.71
Berry,Jason,Oneonta	A	22	8	0	0	0	12.2	50	9	1	0	0	0	0	0	4	0	19	1	0	2	0	1.000	0	0	0.00
Tampa	A	22	7	0	0	1	19.2	78	14	3	2	0	0	0	1	10	0	14	1	0	2	0	1.000	0	0	0.92
Besser,Mike,Ogden	R	22	4	0	0	1	7	27	10	4	4	1	1	0	0	2	0	7	0	0	1	0	.500	0	0	5.14
Bettencourt,Justin,Jamestown	A	22	14	14	0	0	74.1	332	73	53	40	7	0	5	4	41	0	63	9	3	2	8	.200	0	0	4.84
Betti,Rick,Red Sox	R	22	3	1	0	2	7.1	30	7	3	2	0	0	0	0	3	0	13	1	0	1	0	1.000	0	1	2.45
Utica	A	22	12	0	0	5	17.2	65	9	2	2	1	0	0	0	2	0	25	1	0	2	1	.667	0	2	1.02
Michigan	A	22	1	0	0	0	2	7	1	0	0	0	0	0	0	0	0	0	0	0	0	0	.000	0	0	0.00

1995 Pitching -- Single-A and Rookie Leagues

			HOW MUCH HE PITCHED						WHAT HE GAVE UP												THE RESULTS					
Player	Lg	A	G	GS	CG	GF	IP	BFP	H	R	ER	HR	SH	SF	HB	TBB	IBB	SO	WP	Bk	W	L	Pct.	ShO	Sv	ERA
Bevel,Bobby,Portland	A	22	25	0	0	8	28	128	24	13	11	0	3	2	1	18	4	25	5	0	2	3	.400	0	1	3.54
Beverlin,Jay,W. Michigan	A	22	22	14	0	1	89	392	76	51	40	4	3	3	8	40	0	84	5	5	3	9	.250	0	0	4.04
Greensboro	A	22	7	7	1	0	51	198	49	15	15	1	0	0	0	6	0	31	6	4	2	4	.333	1	0	2.65
Biehl,Rod,Fort Myers	A	27	12	0	0	4	20	81	15	9	9	1	0	1	1	8	1	20	5	0	2	0	1.000	0	0	4.05
Bieniasz,Derek,Wisconsin	A	22	27	27	4	0	175.1	717	145	76	61	7	8	6	10	54	3	99	4	3	11	10	.524	2	0	3.13
Bigham,Dave,South Bend	A	25	25	23	1	1	153	651	176	62	56	9	10	5	11	35	0	101	10	2	8	7	.533	1	0	3.29
Bigler,Cory,Erie	A	23	10	4	0	3	29	135	34	21	15	2	2	1	2	13	1	13	1	1	0	6	.000	0	0	4.66
Binkley,Brett,Durham	A	24	24	0	0	6	28.2	138	34	20	19	2	2	1	1	21	1	20	4	1	2	2	.500	0	0	5.97
Binversie,Brian,Greensboro	A	23	31	0	0	12	45.1	206	53	30	25	7	0	5	2	18	1	32	2	0	0	4	.000	0	0	4.96
Birrell,Simon,Braves	R	18	13	3	0	6	37.2	184	47	37	25	2	3	2	4	23	0	18	4	1	2	3	.400	0	1	5.97
Birsner,Roark,Cubs	R	20	12	12	0	0	50	209	40	18	15	2	0	1	4	22	0	42	3	1	3	2	.600	0	0	2.70
Bishop,Joshua,Brewers	R	21	14	13	3	0	96	382	64	34	23	4	3	1	1	29	0	134	9	2	8	2	.800	1	0	2.16
Black,Jayson,Red Sox	R	20	12	9	3	0	65	293	83	42	32	3	2	1	7	14	0	50	7	0	4	5	.444	1	0	4.43
Blake,Todd,St. Pete	A	25	42	0	0	20	55.2	244	58	25	16	3	3	3	0	17	2	35	2	0	2	2	.500	0	0	2.59
Blanco,Alberto,Quad City	A	20	11	11	0	0	54.2	231	47	22	19	2	0	1	1	19	0	58	3	0	3	3	.500	1	0	3.13
Blanco,Roger,Mariners	R	19	12	12	0	0	54	247	60	43	33	2	1	6	7	24	0	27	5	2	1	6	.143	0	0	5.50
Bland,Nate,Bakersfield	A	21	27	23	0	1	122.1	562	155	89	71	13	5	3	1	55	0	46	12	4	4	9	.308	0	0	5.22
Blang,Michael,Kingsport	R	23	23	0	0	15	28.1	111	19	10	10	3	0	1	1	7	1	18	2	1	0	2	.000	0	7	3.18
Blank,John,Elizabethtn	R	22	15	5	0	2	35.2	159	40	21	18	3	0	0	0	16	1	32	5	2	3	0	1.000	0	0	4.54
Blasingim,Joseph,Bellingham	A	23	13	1	0	3	25.1	118	31	14	12	0	1	2	1	14	0	22	3	0	1	1	.500	0	0	4.26
Bledsoe,Randy,Savannah	A	24	28	0	0	7	33.2	167	41	25	24	0	1	3	4	22	1	28	4	0	2	1	.667	0	0	6.42
Blevins,Jeremy,Angels	R	18	11	9	0	0	51.1	224	39	20	14	0	2	0	4	32	0	48	4	1	5	1	.833	0	0	2.45
Bliss,Bill,Salem	A	26	34	0	0	17	44.2	193	38	24	21	4	2	1	1	25	6	23	9	2	3	2	.600	0	4	4.23
Blood,Darin,Bellingham	A	21	14	13	0	0	74.1	315	63	26	21	2	4	0	3	32	0	78	6	1	6	3	.667	0	0	2.54
Blythe,Billy,Macon	A	20	7	2	0	2	15.2	79	15	20	18	0	1	0	1	14	0	15	5	2	0	2	.000	0	1	10.34
Eugene	A	20	14	10	0	2	37.2	213	45	55	41	4	0	2	7	49	1	24	12	0	1	6	.143	0	0	9.80
Boardman,Eric,Oneonta	A	20	11	6	0	0	33	149	30	24	14	1	1	1	2	21	0	23	3	0	3	4	.429	0	0	3.82
Bock,Jeff,Durham	A	25	32	4	0	11	67	282	58	31	25	9	4	3	1	31	8	45	3	0	5	1	.833	0	2	3.36
Boggs,Harold,Elizabethtn	R	21	12	12	0	0	60.1	276	77	53	39	2	2	4	2	20	0	55	6	0	3	5	.375	0	0	5.82
Bogle,Sean,Williamsprt	A	22	12	0	0	5	22	99	22	12	5	0	2	1	1	8	0	15	2	1	1	0	1.000	0	0	2.05
Rockford	A	22	13	0	0	3	22.1	84	17	3	3	0	2	1	0	9	0	15	1	0	1	0	1.000	0	0	1.21
Boike,Todd,Expos	R	20	23	1	0	13	48	220	54	32	21	1	1	2	6	13	1	35	6	2	2	4	.333	0	2	3.94
Bonilla,Denis,Mariners	R	22	21	0	0	10	35.1	155	39	21	12	0	0	3	1	9	0	39	2	0	1	1	.500	0	2	3.06
Bonilla,Miguel,Pirates	R	22	2	0	0	2	4.2	20	5	1	1	0	0	0	0	1	0	2	0	0	0	0	.000	0	0	1.93
Bonilla,Welnis,Michigan	A	20	12	0	0	8	11.2	58	12	12	8	1	1	0	1	10	0	7	0	1	1	1	.500	0	0	6.17
Butte	R	20	27	2	0	13	39	202	46	34	19	4	0	0	3	33	2	30	3	4	2	2	.500	0	5	4.38
Booker,Chris,Cubs	R	19	13	7	0	2	42.1	173	36	22	13	0	0	2	0	16	0	43	4	1	3	2	.600	0	1	2.76
Borkowski,Dave,Tigers	R	19	10	10	1	0	51.2	212	45	24	17	2	1	0	5	8	0	36	1	2	3	2	.600	0	0	2.96
Lakeland	A	19	1	1	0	0	5	17	2	0	0	0	0	0	0	1	0	3	0	0	1	0	1.000	0	0	0.00
Borkowski,Rob,Mets	R	19	5	0	0	1	8	31	6	2	2	0	0	0	0	3	1	1	2	0	0	0	.000	0	0	2.25
Bost,Heath,Portland	A	21	10	0	0	1	16	63	15	6	6	1	0	0	0	0	0	25	1	0	1	0	1.000	0	0	3.38
Asheville	A	21	9	2	0	4	23.2	90	20	6	4	1	0	0	1	3	0	17	1	2	4	1	.800	0	0	1.52
Bourbakis,Mike,Great Falls	R	19	11	1	0	6	14	69	16	10	8	0	0	3	1	8	0	13	0	0	1	2	.333	0	0	5.14
Bowen,Mitch,Brevard Cty	A	23	41	3	0	17	88	381	87	36	25	3	5	1	3	32	2	51	6	0	0	2	.000	0	3	2.56
Bowers,Shane,Fort Myers	A	24	23	23	0	0	145.2	580	119	43	35	6	2	4	12	32	1	103	6	1	13	5	.722	0	0	2.16
Bowie,Micah,Macon	A	21	5	5	0	0	27.2	104	9	8	7	1	0	0	3	11	0	36	1	0	4	1	.800	0	0	2.28
Durham	A	21	23	23	1	0	130.1	561	119	65	52	8	13	3	8	61	3	91	4	3	4	11	.267	0	0	3.59
Bowles,Matt,Brewers	R	23	7	0	0	1	15	69	20	12	11	0	0	0	2	3	0	4	3	1	0	1	.000	0	0	6.60
Helena	R	23	6	3	0	0	10.2	66	17	18	18	2	0	0	5	18	0	10	7	0	1	0	1.000	0	0	15.19
Bowles,Brian,Blue Jays	R	19	8	0	0	2	15	70	18	12	4	2	0	1	1	3	0	11	2	1	1	2	.333	0	0	2.40
Bowman,Paul,Pittsfield	A	23	2	0	0	2	4.2	25	7	6	5	0	0	0	0	5	0	3	2	0	0	1	.000	0	0	9.64
Bowser,Bob,Martinsvlle	R	22	17	0	0	8	32.1	136	30	15	14	1	1	1	4	9	2	35	0	2	2	2	.500	0	1	3.90
Box,Shawn,Daytona	A	23	25	23	0	0	124	511	114	50	42	5	3	0	3	35	1	90	5	1	8	6	.571	0	0	3.05
Boyd,Bradley,Expos	R	20	17	0	0	9	23.1	111	27	17	13	0	1	2	1	13	0	10	5	1	1	1	.500	0	1	5.01
Boyd,Jason,Piedmont	A	23	26	24	1	1	151	638	151	77	60	8	5	3	4	44	0	129	18	2	6	8	.429	0	0	3.58
Brabant,Dan,Kinston	A	23	47	0	0	12	93.2	405	81	47	44	9	3	4	6	49	3	89	9	0	7	4	.636	0	4	4.23
Brabec,William,Medicne Hat	R	22	19	0	0	7	24.1	136	31	33	19	2	1	0	7	20	0	25	9	1	0	1	.000	0	0	7.03
Brand,Scott,Yankees	R	20	4	0	0	0	10	37	5	1	1	0	0	0	0	3	0	8	1	0	0	0	.000	0	0	0.90
Brandt,Dale,Oneonta	A	22	23	0	0	14	31.1	143	36	21	13	0	1	1	1	15	1	24	2	0	1	2	.333	0	0	3.73
Bray,Chris,Orioles	R	21	12	2	0	1	29.1	135	27	20	12	1	0	0	3	16	1	22	5	3	3	2	.600	0	0	3.68
Breitenstein,Keith,Kissimmee	A	24	4	0	0	1	6	29	7	2	2	0	1	1	0	3	1	4	0	0	0	1	.000	0	0	3.00
Brester,Jason,Bellingham	A	19	8	6	0	0	24	104	23	11	11	3	0	0	1	12	0	17	0	0	1	1	.500	0	0	4.13
Brewer,Brian,High Desert	A	24	17	15	1	0	80.2	376	96	66	49	2	4	0	5	42	1	65	5	2	1	9	.100	0	0	5.47
Frederick	A	24	14	8	0	3	67.2	263	49	22	19	2	3	2	3	19	1	48	5	2	2	4	.333	0	0	2.53
Briggs,Anthony,Macon	A	22	29	24	1	1	147.1	635	145	76	49	12	2	1	4	56	1	114	6	1	8	5	.615	1	0	2.99
Briscoe,Janos,Charlotte	A	23	1	0	0	1	2	10	3	0	0	0	0	0	0	0	0	2	0	0	0	0	.000	0	0	0.00
Brito,Juan,Mets	R	20	13	4	0	7	37	162	42	20	16	1	0	0	1	10	0	33	4	1	3	2	.600	0	0	3.89
Brixey,Dusty,Springfield	A	22	36	8	0	6	102	438	101	51	43	3	3	6	7	40	0	44	6	0	4	5	.444	0	2	3.79
Brizek,Seth,Everett	A	22	8	0	0	3	10.1	55	13	10	8	1	0	0	2	8	0	16	1	0	0	2	.000	0	0	6.97
Brohamer,Troy,San Jose	A	23	11	10	0	1	65.1	246	45	14	12	4	1	1	1	20	0	57	5	1	7	3	.700	0	0	1.65
Brooks,Antone,Eugene	A	22	15	0	0	5	17	67	9	5	1	1	0	0	0	8	1	26	0	0	2	0	1.000	0	0	0.53
Broome,Curtis,South Bend	A	24	28	4	1	10	89.1	392	98	50	42	9	3	2	2	39	0	62	5	1	5	8	.385	0	1	4.23
Broome,John,Hickory	A	23	4	0	0	3	4.2	25	8	5	5	1	0	1	0	4	0	3	0	0	0	0	.000	0	0	9.64
Brower,Jim,Charlotte	A	23	27	27	2	0	173.2	740	170	93	75	16	3	3	8	62	1	110	11	0	7	10	.412	1	0	3.89
Brown,Alvin,Lakeland	A	25	9	9	0	0	46.2	202	35	23	22	1	1	1	4	33	0	35	9	1	2	3	.400	0	0	4.24
Brown,Brett,Astros	R	22	12	0	0	9	11.1	52	12	7	4	0	1	0	0	6	1	12	0	0	0	0	.000	0	1	3.18
Kissimmee	A	22	1	0	0	1	0.2	3	1	0	0	0	0	0	0	0	0	0	0	0	0	0	.000	0	0	0.00

1995 Pitching -- Single-A and Rookie Leagues

Player	Lg	A	G	GS	CG	GF	IP	BFP	H	R	ER	HR	SH	SF	HB	TBB	IBB	SO	WP	Bk	W	L	Pct.	ShO	Sv	ERA
Brown,Charlie,Greensboro	A	22	45	2	0	22	57	252	57	31	28	6	3	3	2	23	5	69	11	1	4	4	.500	0	4	4.42
Brown,Cory,High Desert	A	23	30	10	0	8	94	417	104	66	56	15	5	5	6	32	0	80	3	1	2	7	.222	0	3	5.36
Brown,Darold,Eugene	A	22	3	3	0	0	17	77	18	16	8	3	1	0	0	6	1	13	1	0	0	3	.000	0	0	4.24
Macon	A	22	31	0	0	20	54.2	230	39	22	20	1	3	4	4	32	1	55	7	2	3	1	.750	0	5	3.29
Brown,Keith,Stockton	A	24	12	0	0	3	16.2	65	11	4	3	1	0	0	0	6	2	8	1	0	1	0	1.000	0	0	1.62
Brown,Shawn,Jamestown	A	25	18	0	0	11	19.1	97	27	16	13	1	0	1	3	6	0	10	2	1	1	2	.333	0	1	6.05
Brown,Tighe,White Sox	R	19	3	0	0	1	7.2	28	3	1	1	0	0	1	0	2	0	12	1	0	0	0	.000	0	0	1.17
Bruner,Clay,Tigers	R	19	5	4	0	0	16	77	15	12	7	1	3	0	3	10	0	15	1	0	0	1	.000	0	0	3.94
Bryant,Adam,Billings	R	24	29	0	0	26	37.1	157	39	13	13	3	0	1	2	5	1	30	4	4	4	2	.667	0	11	3.13
Bryant,Scooter,Rangers	R	19	1	0	0	1	1	4	0	0	0	0	0	0	0	1	0	1	0	0	0	0	.000	0	0	0.00
Bryant,Chris,Cubs	R	20	6	0	0	2	11	49	11	6	6	0	1	2	0	5	1	13	0	0	0	0	.000	0	0	4.91
Rockford	A	20	21	0	0	9	35	152	32	26	25	5	0	1	3	17	1	29	3	0	2	2	.500	0	0	6.43
Buckles,Brandall,Charlotte	A	23	48	0	0	43	69	293	70	29	24	5	5	2	0	21	3	43	4	2	2	9	.182	0	16	3.13
Buckman,Thomas,White Sox	R	22	18	0	0	15	26.1	113	26	15	9	1	1	1	1	6	0	18	1	2	1	2	.333	0	7	3.08
Bullock,Derek,Erie	A	23	11	11	0	0	65	270	65	21	17	0	1	0	2	15	0	27	1	0	4	4	.500	1	0	2.35
Burchart,Kyle,Blue Jays	R	19	13	2	0	2	35.1	186	55	45	30	2	1	4	4	20	0	27	11	5	1	3	.250	0	1	7.64
Burdick,Morgan,Asheville	A	21	17	0	0	7	26.2	110	26	13	13	1	0	0	0	10	1	19	2	0	0	1	.000	0	0	4.39
Burge,Jason,Lethbridge	R	23	23	0	0	15	34	151	27	17	13	2	2	1	4	13	0	49	0	1	2	4	.333	0	5	3.44
Burger,Rob,Martinsvlle	R	20	9	9	0	0	40.2	187	47	25	21	1	0	2	3	23	0	54	5	0	2	4	.333	0	0	4.65
Burgus,Travis,Elmira	A	23	15	15	0	0	88	369	84	45	34	7	3	3	4	29	0	63	4	1	7	5	.583	0	0	3.48
Burke,Ethan,Mets	R	20	13	0	0	12	18.2	83	19	9	9	0	0	1	0	5	0	14	2	0	1	2	.333	0	5	4.34
Burnett,A.J.,Mets	R	19	9	8	1	1	33.2	144	27	16	16	2	0	2	2	23	0	26	7	4	2	3	.400	0	0	4.28
Burt,Chris,Beloit	A	23	36	0	0	32	42.2	176	34	19	18	2	4	2	1	17	1	42	2	0	1	3	.250	0	27	3.80
Burton,Isaac,Mariners	R	23	2	0	0	0	3	15	1	2	1	0	1	0	1	4	0	2	0	1	0	0	.000	0	0	3.00
Burton,Jaime,Royals	R	21	6	1	0	1	12	60	13	11	11	1	0	1	0	10	0	14	5	1	0	0	.000	0	0	8.25
Bush,Craig,Michigan	A	22	34	2	0	18	75.1	320	68	37	32	8	2	0	3	30	0	78	4	0	7	3	.700	0	6	3.82
Dushart,John,Codar Rapds	A	25	19	3	0	7	36.2	179	47	34	30	6	0	0	4	17	0	24	3	0	2	2	.500	0	0	7.36
Bussa,Todd,Kane County	A	23	36	0	0	33	42	162	20	4	4	1	1	1	6	15	5	38	3	0	0	1	.000	0	14	0.86
Buteaux,Shane,Hickory	A	24	13	13	0	0	66.2	316	90	63	54	10	4	5	3	32	2	30	2	1	2	7	.222	0	0	7.29
Bristol	R	24	13	13	1	0	74	337	72	45	35	9	4	4	8	41	0	49	9	3	7	6	.538	0	0	4.26
Butler,Adam,Eugene	A	22	23	0	0	18	25.1	109	15	9	7	0	1	0	3	12	5	50	1	0	4	1	.800	0	8	2.49
Butler,Bobby,Red Sox	R	21	14	8	0	2	46.2	216	48	36	26	5	5	1	0	32	1	58	8	0	1	4	.200	0	0	5.01
Byrd,Matt,Durham	A	25	60	0	0	53	69.2	296	52	24	23	8	0	3	3	32	4	79	9	0	5	4	.556	0	27	2.97
Byrdak,Timothy,Wilmington	A	22	27	26	0	0	166.1	657	118	46	40	7	3	3	10	45	2	127	1	1	11	5	.688	0	0	2.16
Byrne,Earl,Rockford	A	23	13	11	0	0	60	269	54	36	31	2	3	6	3	38	0	51	8	1	4	3	.571	0	0	4.65
Cafaro,Rocco,High Desert	A	23	44	1	0	39	66.2	290	69	42	33	10	2	4	2	25	0	52	6	1	4	5	.444	0	8	4.46
Cain,Travis,Macon	A	20	14	2	0	4	26.1	136	25	23	22	2	0	0	6	31	0	32	7	0	1	2	.333	0	0	7.52
Cain,Chance,St. Pete	A	25	7	0	0	2	11	51	18	6	4	0	0	1	0	2	0	4	0	1	1	0	1.000	0	0	3.27
Caldwell,David,Columbus	A	21	27	27	0	0	151.1	655	162	87	74	12	4	2	4	58	0	104	6	2	11	10	.524	0	0	4.40
Call,Micheal,Pr. William	A	27	28	9	3	8	104.2	462	114	66	63	14	3	3	7	37	1	62	5	0	4	7	.364	1	1	5.42
Callahan,Damon,Charlstn-Wv	A	20	6	6	0	0	25	120	33	22	17	1	0	1	2	14	2	17	4	0	2	1	.667	0	0	6.12
Billings	R	20	14	14	0	0	80.1	347	82	36	26	1	2	3	4	30	2	50	7	0	9	2	.818	0	0	2.91
Callistro,Robby,Pr. William	A	26	8	0	0	1	18	79	19	8	8	3	1	0	0	7	0	18	1	1	1	1	.500	0	0	4.00
Camp,Jared,Helena	R	21	8	8	0	0	34.1	166	44	39	33	1	1	3	3	20	0	26	6	2	1	4	.200	0	0	8.65
Campbell,Tim,Idaho Falls	R	23	18	0	0	5	36.1	162	37	21	21	0	1	2	1	17	1	38	5	0	1	1	.500	0	1	5.20
Cannon,Kevin,Red Sox	R	21	5	3	1	0	26.2	107	14	6	2	1	0	0	0	9	0	38	0	1	2	1	.667	0	0	0.68
Utica	A	21	9	9	1	0	61	260	59	33	23	2	0	3	5	23	1	51	2	2	3	4	.429	0	0	3.39
Cardona,Isbel,Burlington	A	24	6	4	0	0	18	94	19	21	14	4	1	2	1	20	1	12	2	1	0	0	.000	0	0	7.00
Butte	R	24	3	3	0	0	15.1	73	26	13	12	1	0	0	0	7	0	9	0	0	0	2	.000	0	0	7.04
Caridad,Ron,Fort Myers	A	24	17	0	0	9	41.1	171	27	15	11	1	1	2	3	18	0	38	4	0	2	3	.400	0	3	2.40
Carl,Todd,Brevard Cty	A	23	15	7	0	3	52.1	224	44	26	23	3	1	2	2	27	0	19	3	0	3	4	.429	0	1	3.96
Kane County	A	23	12	7	0	2	39	192	69	37	37	8	0	1	5	11	0	22	7	0	0	5	.000	0	0	8.54
Carlson,Garret,White Sox	R	22	2	0	0	1	5	17	2	0	0	0	0	0	0	0	0	3	0	0	2	0	1.000	0	0	0.00
Hickory	A	22	3	0	0	1	1.2	11	2	6	6	1	0	0	0	4	0	2	0	0	0	0	.000	0	0	32.40
Carmano,Kevin,Royals	R	20	15	0	0	7	34	140	25	18	8	0	5	0	8	16	4	16	4	1	6	1	.857	0	2	2.12
Carrasco,Troy,Fort Myers	A	21	25	25	2	0	138	596	131	62	48	6	4	7	8	63	0	96	11	2	12	4	.750	0	0	3.13
Carroll,Dave,Peoria	A	23	24	6	0	5	51.1	230	53	33	25	3	2	0	3	24	0	41	6	1	2	2	.500	0	0	4.38
Carter,Lance,Springfield	A	21	27	24	1	0	137.2	584	151	77	61	14	2	4	8	22	0	118	11	1	9	5	.643	1	0	3.99
Caruthers,Clay,Charlstn-Wv	A	23	27	27	0	0	138.2	600	149	67	57	6	5	4	14	50	1	105	13	2	11	7	.611	0	0	3.70
Carvelli,Mike,Ogden	R	23	5	3	0	0	18	83	27	11	8	1	1	0	3	1	0	13	0	1	1	2	.333	0	0	3.93
Casey,Ryan,Rockford	A	23	16	0	0	8	19.1	89	19	15	13	1	1	1	1	11	0	12	3	1	0	2	.000	0	0	6.05
Castillo,Carlos,Hickory	A	21	14	12	2	2	79.2	343	85	42	33	11	1	3	3	18	0	67	0	0	5	6	.455	0	1	3.73
Castillo,Carlos,Lk Elsinore	A	25	52	0	0	52	52.1	223	55	18	14	2	1	0	5	15	0	40	2	1	2	1	.667	0	32	2.41
Castillo,Victor,Medicne Hat	R	22	2	0	0	0	2	14	5	5	0	0	0	0	0	1	0	2	0	0	0	0	.000	0	0	0.00
Castro,Antonio,Lk Elsinore	A	24	8	0	0	2	11.1	57	15	9	7	1	1	1	0	8	0	9	1	0	0	0	.000	0	0	5.56
Censale,Silvio,Piedmont	A	24	22	21	0	0	120	507	96	54	42	6	5	4	5	54	0	123	10	3	10	6	.625	0	0	3.15
Centeno,Jose,Expos	R	23	15	0	0	7	25.2	105	18	7	7	1	1	1	2	6	0	17	1	1	1	0	1.000	0	1	2.45
Vermont	A	23	6	0	0	4	10	39	8	2	1	1	0	0	0	0	0	6	1	0	0	0	.000	0	1	0.90
Cervantes,Peter,Yakima	A	21	13	10	0	1	50.1	226	55	32	26	3	1	2	3	16	0	35	1	0	3	5	.375	0	0	4.65
Challinor,John,Vero Beach	A	21	37	1	0	15	74.2	318	62	36	32	6	1	4	0	35	1	59	5	1	2	6	.250	0	1	3.86
Chambers,Scott,Yakima	A	20	20	1	0	6	28.2	130	31	20	17	1	1	1	1	13	0	37	4	0	1	2	.333	0	1	5.34
Chantres,Carlos,White Sox	R	20	11	11	2	0	61.2	257	65	32	22	2	1	1	1	14	0	47	1	2	2	3	.400	0	0	3.21
Chapa,Javier,Great Falls	R	20	13	9	0	1	49	177	54	36	31	4	0	3	2	17	0	37	5	0	2	2	.500	0	0	5.69
Chapman,Walker,Fort Wayne	A	20	14	11	0	2	53.1	249	59	41	37	4	2	3	2	36	0	31	3	1	2	6	.250	0	0	6.24
Elizabethtn	R	20	4	4	0	0	8	34	9	6	5	1	0	1	0	1	0	7	2	1	0	0	.000	0	0	5.63
Charbonneau,Marc,Great Falls	R	20	14	7	0	2	42.1	198	37	28	17	3	1	3	2	27	2	30	2	1	4	1	.800	0	0	3.61
Charles,Israel,Spokane	A	23	4	0	0	1	6	28	6	3	3	0	0	0	0	3	0	5	1	1	1	0	1.000	0	0	4.50

1995 Pitching -- Single-A and Rookie Leagues

Player	Lg	A	G	GS	CG	GF	IP	BFP	H	R	ER	HR	SH	SF	HB	TBB	IBB	SO	WP	Bk	W	L	Pct.	ShO	Sv	ERA
Charlton,Aaron,Burlington	A	23	16	0	0	6	24	105	18	13	11	2	0	1	4	13	0	16	4	0	0	1	.000	0	0	4.13
Chavarria,David,Charlstn-Sc	A	23	52	0	0	22	62	277	55	33	27	5	2	5	1	38	3	68	16	0	3	5	.375	0	6	3.92
Chaves,Rafael,Lynchburg	A	27	42	0	0	41	47.1	191	35	17	14	3	4	0	1	13	3	45	5	1	1	3	.250	0	22	2.66
Augusta	A	27	7	0	0	2	8.2	36	2	3	2	0	2	0	0	6	0	9	0	0	1	0	1.000	0	2	2.08
Chen,Bruce,Danville	R	19	14	13	1	0	70.1	310	78	42	31	3	1	4	3	19	1	56	3	1	4	4	.500	0	0	3.97
Chew,Greg,Erie	A	22	24	0	0	13	30.2	141	37	18	11	1	0	1	2	15	4	23	4	1	2	3	.400	0	3	3.23
Choi,Chang,Batavia	A	23	7	7	0	0	32.2	146	35	20	18	1	1	1	2	14	0	32	7	4	1	3	.250	0	0	4.96
Chrismon,Thad,Eugene	A	23	32	0	0	13	38	165	31	15	11	3	0	4	5	21	1	28	5	0	2	2	.500	0	3	2.61
Christmas,Mo,Durham	A	22	31	18	0	2	113.2	493	135	68	61	15	2	3	4	19	2	68	2	0	2	7	.222	0	0	4.83
Cindrich,Jeff,Tampa	A	25	24	0	0	9	39.1	177	50	28	19	4	0	3	0	17	1	32	5	0	1	4	.200	0	0	4.35
Cintron,Jose,Cedar Rapds	A	20	13	9	1	0	68	280	65	36	29	4	2	2	2	9	0	38	2	1	5	3	.625	1	0	3.84
Civit,Xavier,Albany	A	23	12	1	0	0	26	135	34	30	22	0	2	0	2	18	4	29	2	2	3	2	.400	0	0	7.62
Vermont	A	23	19	0	0	6	53.2	222	44	21	17	0	1	2	3	21	0	44	5	0	3	3	.500	0	1	2.85
Clark,Chris,Padres	R	21	13	12	1	0	73	313	52	30	17	1	1	1	7	38	0	82	5	5	5	5	.500	0	0	2.10
Idaho Falls	R	21	1	1	0	0	6	24	3	3	3	1	0	0	0	4	0	9	1	0	0	0	.000	0	0	4.50
Clark,Doug,Fayettevlle	A	25	4	0	0	2	4.2	27	10	11	6	2	0	0	0	3	0	3	0	1	0	1	.000	0	0	11.57
Clayton,Craig,Riverside	A	25	28	28	0	0	160.1	738	171	102	89	16	11	6	7	83	3	156	7	1	9	8	.529	0	0	5.00
Clelland,Rick,W. Palm Bch	A	24	35	5	0	10	70.1	316	59	30	21	3	3	5	8	46	1	66	10	0	2	4	.333	0	2	2.69
Clement,Matt,Rancho Cuca	A	21	12	12	0	0	57.1	267	61	37	27	1	2	4	5	49	0	33	12	0	3	4	.429	0	0	4.24
Idaho Falls	R	21	14	14	0	0	81	349	61	53	39	3	6	3	13	42	0	65	19	2	6	3	.667	0	0	4.33
Clemons,Chris,Pr.William	A	23	27	27	1	0	137	606	136	78	72	18	4	4	11	64	2	92	2	0	7	12	.368	0	0	4.73
Clifford,Eric,Everett	A	21	28	0	0	11	45	183	39	17	12	2	2	3	2	11	1	39	4	1	3	2	.600	0	4	2.40
Cloud,Antonia,Princeton	R	20	12	12	0	0	55.2	232	47	34	26	1	0	3	1	26	1	46	8	0	4	5	.444	0	0	4.20
Cloude,Ken,Wisconsin	A	21	25	25	4	0	161	677	137	64	58	8	1	7	8	63	4	140	10	1	9	8	.529	0	0	3.24
Cobb,Trevor,Twins	R	22	3	3	0	0	19	74	11	5	2	0	1	0	1	7	0	15	2	0	2	0	1.000	0	0	0.95
Fort Wayne	A	22	11	10	0	0	53.1	226	51	26	23	3	1	0	3	18	0	46	6	0	4	4	.500	0	0	3.88
Cochrane,Andrew,Danville	R	21	6	0	0	0	11.2	54	14	11	6	0	0	1	0	6	0	10	2	0	1	1	.500	0	0	4.63
Cochrane,Chris,W.Michigan	A	23	41	4	0	29	85	357	79	37	29	7	5	0	5	28	3	48	3	1	6	4	.600	0	9	3.07
Codd,Timothy,Hudson Vall	A	22	25	0	0	5	38	170	36	15	13	2	1	0	2	21	0	38	12	0	3	0	1.000	0	0	3.08
Coe,Brent,Blue Jays	R	21	2	2	0	0	8	35	8	4	3	0	1	0	0	3	0	6	2	0	0	1	.000	0	0	3.38
Coe,Keith,Boise	A	22	13	12	0	0	55.2	250	49	35	29	4	2	0	5	38	1	42	5	1	2	5	.286	0	0	4.69
Coggin,Dave,Martinsvlle	R	19	11	11	0	0	48	209	45	25	16	1	1	1	5	31	0	37	8	1	5	3	.625	0	0	3.00
Cole,Jason,Albany	A	23	32	4	0	11	57.2	257	67	33	28	3	2	2	4	22	2	51	2	1	3	3	.500	0	1	4.37
Collett,Andy,Everett	A	22	1	0	0	0	0.1	4	1	0	0	0	0	0	0	2	0	1	0	0	0	0	.000	0	0	0.00
Collie,Timothy,Erie	A	22	29	0	0	22	36	149	32	18	8	1	2	0	0	9	2	27	0	1	3	6	.333	0	11	2.00
Collins,E.J.,Helena	R	19	14	13	0	0	55.1	274	50	44	36	2	0	2	7	63	0	33	6	1	5	3	.625	0	0	5.86
Collins,Kenneth,Danville	R	22	18	1	0	10	32.1	153	36	31	15	2	2	2	4	15	0	29	6	1	1	0	1.000	0	0	4.18
Collins,Zach,Braves	R	23	3	0	0	3	7	27	6	2	2	0	1	0	0	1	0	2	0	0	0	0	.000	0	0	2.57
Macon	A	23	4	0	0	2	3.1	20	7	4	2	0	0	0	1	4	0	3	0	0	0	0	.000	0	0	5.40
Colmenares,Luis,Asheville	A	21	45	0	0	38	55	223	37	15	14	1	2	2	1	29	1	74	11	2	2	2	.500	0	21	2.29
Colon,Bartolo,Kinston	A	21	21	21	0	0	128.2	493	91	31	28	8	1	2	0	39	0	152	4	3	13	3	.813	0	0	1.96
Colon,Julio,San Bernrdo	A	23	49	0	0	30	79	343	68	47	38	7	1	1	2	37	2	75	12	0	6	3	.667	0	12	4.33
Conley,Curt,Salem	A	25	39	0	0	0	47.1	211	42	23	19	4	2	3	2	27	3	35	4	2	4	1	.800	0	3	3.61
Connelly,Steve,Sou. Oregon	A	22	17	0	0	10	28.1	133	29	17	12	1	3	2	4	14	4	19	6	0	2	4	.333	0	2	3.81
Contreras,Orlando,Rockies	R	19	16	0	0	5	28.1	144	40	27	19	0	1	2	2	17	0	18	0	0	2	2	.500	0	1	6.04
Conway,Keith,Savannah	A	23	60	0	0	26	74	297	49	14	12	1	5	3	3	26	3	87	3	0	7	2	.778	0	10	1.46
Conway,Robert,Everett	A	24	6	0	0	0	9	42	6	4	4	0	0	0	1	11	1	3	4	1	1	0	1.000	0	0	4.00
Cook,Jake,Michigan	A	21	21	11	0	3	76.1	333	68	48	41	3	5	1	2	39	0	50	12	2	5	3	.625	0	0	4.83
Cook,O.J.,Pirates	R	19	12	7	0	4	34.2	154	33	24	14	1	0	1	1	22	0	25	4	0	0	4	.000	0	2	3.63
Cook,Rodney,Charlstn-Sc	A	25	60	0	0	36	96	415	83	32	27	3	5	4	9	39	5	88	8	1	3	8	.273	0	11	2.53
Cooke,Alan,Ogden	R	24	16	5	0	2	40.1	194	52	26	23	5	0	1	6	32	1	23	4	1	0	5	.000	0	0	5.13
Cooper,Brian,Boise	A	21	13	11	0	1	62	264	60	31	27	5	4	1	6	22	1	66	4	1	3	2	.600	0	0	3.92
Cooper,Chadwick,Kingsport	R	21	22	1	0	14	29.2	123	21	12	10	2	0	0	2	12	0	38	1	0	0	0	.000	0	6	3.03
Cooper,David,Everett	A	21	17	2	0	7	33	166	36	31	27	5	1	0	3	31	0	20	8	0	1	2	.333	0	0	7.36
Cooper,Keith,Braves	R	23	2	0	0	1	3	12	2	1	1	0	0	0	0	1	0	3	0	0	1	0	1.000	0	0	3.00
Danville	R	23	17	0	0	14	27.1	106	20	9	5	1	1	1	1	5	0	23	2	0	1	0	1.000	0	4	1.65
Cope,Craig,Kingsport	R	20	12	0	0	7	10.2	54	9	12	10	0	0	1	1	12	0	10	5	0	0	0	.000	0	0	8.44
Cope,Robin,Riverside	A	23	11	5	0	0	31.2	162	50	31	26	2	0	1	0	18	1	13	3	2	2	4	.333	0	0	7.39
Corba,Lisandro,Braves	R	20	6	3	0	0	17	63	9	5	2	0	0	0	1	1	0	18	1	4	0	2	.000	0	0	1.06
Cordero,Francisco,Fayettevlle	A	18	4	4	0	0	20	92	26	16	14	1	1	2	2	12	0	19	4	0	0	3	.000	0	0	6.30
Jamestown	A	18	15	14	0	0	88	392	96	62	51	3	3	3	8	37	0	54	11	0	4	7	.364	0	0	5.22
Corey,Bryan,Jamestown	A	22	29	0	0	28	28	116	21	14	12	2	0	1	1	12	1	41	4	0	2	2	.500	0	10	3.86
Corey,Mark,Princeton	R	21	4	3	0	0	14.2	61	12	7	6	1	0	0	0	6	0	8	0	0	1	1	.500	0	0	3.68
Corn,Chris,Greensboro	A	24	49	0	0	39	82	317	54	20	16	3	1	2	2	22	0	101	5	1	8	7	.533	0	24	1.76
Tampa	A	24	4	0	0	1	5.2	25	3	2	2	0	0	0	0	3	0	9	2	0	0	1	.000	0	0	3.18
Corominas,Mike,Auburn	A	21	13	0	0	5	23.1	111	22	20	18	2	0	1	0	24	0	14	3	1	2	1	.667	0	0	6.94
Coronado,Osvaldo,Pittsfield	A	22	15	15	0	0	90.2	381	91	52	39	2	2	3	4	26	0	57	6	2	4	5	.444	0	0	3.87
Corral,Ruben,Medicne Hat	R	20	14	14	2	0	86	382	92	65	46	7	5	7	2	34	0	50	4	1	4	8	.333	0	0	4.81
Corrales,Ralph,Cubs	R	21	12	0	0	5	22.1	97	23	8	6	2	1	0	1	8	0	10	3	1	1	1	.500	0	2	2.42
Corrigan,Cory,Peoria	A	24	47	10	0	5	112.2	450	90	36	29	3	5	5	2	23	0	84	4	1	4	7	.364	0	0	2.32
Costa,Tony,Clearwater	A	25	25	25	2	0	145	631	155	75	62	5	6	5	10	39	0	71	11	4	9	10	.474	1	0	3.85
Costello,T.J.,Sou. Oregon	A	22	3	0	0	0	4.1	25	8	4	3	0	0	0	0	2	0	5	0	0	0	0	.000	0	0	6.23
Athletics	R	22	12	6	0	2	43.1	180	46	22	18	2	0	2	2	9	0	41	5	1	2	3	.400	0	1	3.74
Coyle,Bryan,Yakima	A	20	6	1	0	1	19.1	78	14	3	3	1	1	0	0	8	0	17	1	0	2	0	1.000	0	0	1.40
Craig,Casey,Mariners	R	20	2	0	0	0	3	14	5	2	2	0	0	0	0	2	0	0	0	0	1	0	1.000	0	0	6.00
Crawford,Chris,Astros	R	21	10	5	0	1	32.1	147	29	15	13	0	2	1	3	25	0	22	3	0	1	0	1.000	0	0	3.62
Crawford,Paxton,Red Sox	R	18	12	7	1	4	46	184	35	17	14	2	0	0	1	12	0	44	6	0	2	4	.333	0	2	2.74

1995 Pitching -- Single-A and Rookie Leagues

Player	Lg	A	G	GS	CG	GF	IP	BFP	H	R	ER	HR	SH	SF	HB	TBB	IBB	SO	WP	Bk	W	L	Pct.	ShO	Sv	ERA
Crills,Brad,High Desert	A	24	5	3	0	1	16.1	78	19	15	10	1	1	1	1	8	0	10	3	2	1	2	.333	0	0	5.51
Bluefield	R	24	4	4	0	0	20	78	15	3	2	0	0	0	5	5	0	15	1	0	3	0	1.000	1	0	0.90
Frederick	A	24	9	9	3	0	61.2	259	63	26	21	2	3	2	3	12	1	33	2	2	5	5	.286	1	0	3.06
Crine,Dennis,Hickory	A	21	15	11	0	1	60.1	276	74	52	41	7	2	4	5	20	2	20	5	1	3	6	.333	0	1	6.12
Crossley,Chad,Boise	A	24	2	0	0	1	1.1	9	3	4	3	1	0	0	0	1	0	0	0	0	0	0	.000	0	0	20.25
Cedar Rapds	A	24	12	0	0	7	16.1	85	18	16	14	2	2	2	8	15	0	9	5	1	0	0	.000	0	0	7.71
Croushore,Rich,St. Pete	A	25	12	11	0	0	59	250	44	25	23	2	3	1	4	32	0	57	5	0	6	4	.600	0	0	3.51
Crow,Paul,Riverside	A	23	51	0	0	47	61.2	249	54	21	18	1	3	2	3	13	0	46	2	0	3	4	.429	0	22	2.63
Crowell,Jim,Watertown	A	22	12	9	0	0	56.2	241	50	22	18	1	0	2	1	27	1	48	2	1	5	2	.714	0	0	2.86
Crowther,John,Hagerstown	A	22	11	11	0	0	38	189	52	36	23	3	0	0	3	27	0	21	10	2	1	3	.250	0	0	5.45
St. Cathrns	A	22	15	14	0	0	68.1	305	87	43	41	7	1	2	3	34	0	44	9	4	3	6	.333	0	0	5.40
Cruise,Mark,Savannah	A	23	6	0	0	0	7.1	37	8	5	3	1	0	0	0	1	0	5	1	0	0	0	.000	0	0	3.68
Crump,Jody,Peoria	A	23	25	0	0	7	36.1	167	40	25	25	3	1	1	0	26	0	16	3	1	1	1	.500	0	0	6.19
Cruz,Charlie,Eugene	A	22	15	15	0	0	81.1	348	68	34	23	2	2	3	4	36	2	90	2	1	6	7	.462	0	0	2.55
Cruz,Nelson,Bristol	R	23	1	0	0	1	1	6	2	1	1	0	0	1	1	0	0	0	0	0	0	0	.000	0	0	9.00
Hickory	A	23	44	0	0	29	66.2	285	65	31	20	6	3	1	4	15	2	68	5	0	2	7	.222	0	9	2.70
Pr. William	A	23	9	0	0	7	19.1	75	12	1	1	1	0	0	2	6	0	18	0	0	2	1	.667	0	1	0.47
Cubillan,Darwin,Greensboro	A	21	22	14	1	3	97	409	86	50	39	5	3	1	4	38	1	78	5	0	5	5	.500	1	0	3.62
Culberson,Don,Daytona	A	25	12	0	0	6	23.2	113	27	15	12	2	0	2	4	15	0	15	2	1	1	1	.500	0	0	4.56
Culp,Wes,Macon	A	21	39	5	0	14	104.2	456	100	56	41	7	8	5	6	44	2	56	7	1	4	6	.400	0	3	3.53
Cumberland,Chris,Yankees	R	23	4	4	0	0	7	26	3	1	1	0	0	0	0	1	0	7	0	0	1	0	1.000	0	0	1.29
Tampa	A	23	5	5	0	0	24.2	104	28	10	5	1	1	0	1	5	0	10	1	0	1	2	.333	0	0	1.82
Cummins,Brian,Jamestown	A	23	18	0	0	2	34.2	152	37	22	13	1	2	4	1	8	0	24	3	0	2	1	.667	0	1	3.37
Curran,Tighe,Peoria	A	22	24	0	0	7	40.1	174	35	18	13	0	2	0	2	21	0	21	2	1	3	0	1.000	0	0	2.90
Cushman,Scooter,Princeton	R	24	26	0	0	21	35	159	33	21	12	1	0	0	3	15	2	40	2	0	2	3	.400	0	8	3.09
D'Alessandro,Marc,Portland	A	20	16	15	2	0	97.1	397	82	34	32	9	0	4	3	28	0	64	2	3	9	3	.750	0	0	2.96
D'Amico,Jeffrey,Beloit	A	20	21	20	3	0	132	523	102	40	35	7	3	2	4	31	2	119	6	1	13	3	.813	1	0	2.39
Dace,Derek,Astros	R	21	11	10	2	1	69.1	274	60	20	15	2	3	1	1	6	0	77	5	2	3	4	.429	0	0	1.95
Kissimmee	A	21	1	1	0	0	2.2	17	4	5	5	0	0	1	0	5	0	1	0	0	0	1	.000	0	0	16.88
Dafun,Kekoa,Lk Elsinore	A	21	3	3	0	0	13	53	8	8	8	0	0	0	1	11	0	13	0	0	0	2	.000	0	0	5.54
Cedar Rapds	A	21	5	1	0	2	11	56	15	5	4	1	0	0	0	10	1	13	1	0	0	1	.000	0	0	3.27
Boise	A	21	16	12	0	2	59.1	271	57	40	35	5	4	1	8	33	1	61	4	0	4	4	.500	0	0	5.31
Daigle,Tim,Frederick	A	24	6	0	0	0	6.1	38	9	12	6	1	0	2	1	5	0	9	2	0	0	2	.000	0	0	8.53
High Desert	A	24	19	0	0	9	43.2	203	46	33	24	7	1	1	0	20	0	36	4	0	1	0	1.000	0	4	4.95
Dale,Carl,Peoria	A	23	24	24	2	0	143.2	613	124	66	47	8	3	2	1	62	0	104	6	1	9	9	.500	0	0	2.94
Dalton,Brian,Beloit	A	24	34	4	0	13	82	345	70	31	25	0	4	2	2	44	0	75	5	4	4	3	.571	0	4	2.74
Daniels,John,Wisconsin	A	22	39	0	0	19	74.1	315	63	28	22	5	0	2	6	22	2	60	2	0	4	5	.444	0	7	2.66
Daniels,Lee,Durham	A	25	21	0	0	7	23.1	102	26	13	11	1	3	0	1	14	1	24	0	4	1	4	.200	0	4	4.24
Darrell,Tom,Angels	R	19	18	5	0	7	63	254	51	18	12	1	1	3	4	14	0	49	3	1	4	3	.571	0	2	1.71
DaSilva,Fernando,W. Palm Bch	A	24	27	20	2	1	124	530	136	61	51	3	2	9	11	31	1	54	5	1	7	10	.412	0	0	3.70
Dault,Donnie,Kissimmee	A	24	41	5	0	16	108	445	95	52	37	2	4	0	5	36	0	95	8	5	4	7	.364	0	6	3.08
Davenport,Joe,Hagerstown	A	20	13	0	0	0	17.2	91	22	19	12	3	0	0	1	13	0	13	6	0	0	1	.000	0	0	6.11
Blue Jays	R	20	15	10	1	1	55.2	267	67	47	35	2	3	2	3	30	0	29	9	3	2	3	.400	0	1	5.66
Davey,Tom,St. Cathrns	A	22	7	7	0	0	38	160	27	19	14	2	0	2	3	21	0	29	3	1	4	3	.571	0	0	3.32
Hagerstown	A	22	8	8	0	0	37.1	167	29	23	14	2	1	1	2	31	0	25	9	0	4	1	.800	0	0	3.38
Davis,Eddie,San Bernrdo	A	23	5	1	0	2	14.1	68	17	10	6	1	1	0	3	6	0	6	0	1	0	0	.000	0	0	3.77
Yakima	A	23	20	4	0	5	53.1	248	61	33	29	2	1	1	3	32	2	36	5	0	2	3	.400	0	1	4.89
Davis,John,Great Falls	R	22	11	1	0	3	32	137	24	20	10	6	0	0	3	19	2	26	5	1	2	2	.500	0	0	2.81
Davis,Lance,Princeton	R	19	15	9	0	0	58	271	77	39	25	2	2	1	3	25	2	43	6	2	3	7	.300	0	0	3.88
Davis,Kane,Augusta	A	21	26	25	1	0	139.1	602	136	73	58	4	3	4	9	43	0	78	10	1	12	6	.667	0	0	3.75
Davis,Keith,Clinton	A	23	35	7	0	15	64.2	291	59	39	39	2	0	4	3	43	0	47	6	1	2	5	.286	0	2	5.43
Davis,Steve,Clinton	A	26	1	1	0	0	6	22	5	2	2	0	0	1	0	2	0	7	1	0	0	0	.000	0	0	3.00
Dawley,Joey,Frederick	A	24	24	0	0	8	32.2	163	41	28	23	4	1	1	3	22	1	29	5	1	1	2	.333	0	1	6.34
Dawsey,Jason,Helena	R	22	9	8	0	0	42.2	183	40	15	13	1	0	3	2	23	0	47	5	1	3	0	1.000	0	0	2.74
De Los Santos,Valerio,Brewers	R	20	14	12	0	0	82	341	81	34	20	3	5	4	6	12	2	57	6	2	4	6	.400	0	0	2.20
Deakman,Joshua,Boise	A	22	3	3	0	0	11.2	49	11	8	2	0	0	1	0	4	0	8	0	0	1	1	.500	0	0	1.54
Cedar Rapds	A	22	13	13	0	0	72.2	301	67	33	29	5	3	2	7	24	0	53	5	0	4	2	.667	0	0	3.59
Dean,Greg,Bluefield	R	22	10	6	0	3	37	159	34	22	16	3	1	1	2	17	0	33	4	1	6	2	.750	0	1	3.89
Debrino,Rob,Fort Myers	A	22	41	0	0	18	48.2	206	38	24	17	2	0	2	5	25	3	30	2	0	11	3	.786	0	4	3.14
Declue,Brian,Visalia	A	25	21	14	0	0	103	421	95	48	40	11	3	4	3	27	0	90	3	1	6	5	.545	0	0	3.50
Lk Elsinore	A	25	9	4	0	0	40.1	169	50	16	16	5	1	1	2	5	0	22	1	0	5	1	.833	0	0	3.57
De La Cruz,Fernando,Boise	A	21	1	0	0	0	1.1	11	3	6	2	1	0	0	1	2	0	4	0	0	0	0	.000	0	0	13.50
De La Cruz,Narciso,St. Cathrns	A	22	21	0	0	10	35	170	39	31	28	5	2	3	4	22	0	19	5	0	1	1	.500	0	0	7.20
Delahoya,Javier,Brevard Cty	A	26	5	0	0	1	10.1	40	6	2	2	1	0	0	2	2	0	8	0	0	1	0	1.000	0	0	1.74
De La Rosa,Raul,White Sox	R	20	11	2	0	5	27	116	22	9	5	0	0	2	1	16	1	22	4	0	4	1	.800	0	0	1.67
DeLeon,Elcilio,Lynchburg	A	24	13	0	0	3	17	74	12	9	8	2	1	1	3	11	0	9	0	0	2	0	1.000	0	0	4.24
Delgado,Ernesto,Brevard Cty	A	20	18	10	0	4	62.1	308	74	51	49	4	1	4	7	59	0	36	7	2	1	6	.143	0	0	7.07
De Los Santos,Luis,Yankees	R	18	2	0	0	1	5	23	5	2	0	0	0	0	1	2	0	6	0	0	0	0	.000	0	0	0.00
Delvalle,Henry,W. Michigan	A	23	3	0	0	0	5.1	24	4	4	2	0	0	0	0	4	0	8	1	0	1	1	.500	0	0	3.38
Demorejon,Pedro,White Sox	R	21	12	0	0	5	30	125	28	14	12	3	1	1	2	5	1	34	1	4	3	4	.429	0	1	3.60
Dempster,Ryan,Rangers	R	19	8	6	1	0	34.1	154	34	21	9	1	0	1	2	17	0	37	2	1	3	1	.750	0	0	2.36
Hudson Vall	A	19	1	1	0	0	5.2	24	7	2	2	0	1	0	0	6	0	6	0	0	1	0	1.000	0	0	3.18
Dennis,Shane,Clinton	A	24	14	14	3	0	86	364	68	51	37	5	4	0	2	35	3	80	5	0	3	9	.250	0	0	3.87
Rancho Cuca	A	24	11	11	2	0	79	316	63	27	22	8	3	2	0	22	1	77	1	0	8	2	.800	1	0	2.51
Derenches,Albert,Mariners	R	19	12	0	0	0	35.1	155	36	15	13	1	1	0	3	21	0	40	5	0	1	2	.333	0	0	3.31
Desabrias,Mark,Padres	R	20	19	2	0	13	55	234	52	28	19	2	1	1	7	20	0	28	3	0	2	1	.667	0	2	3.11
Desrosiers,Erik,Bristol	R	21	22	0	0	15	32	129	22	13	11	1	2	2	3	7	1	47	1	0	0	2	.000	0	2	3.09

1995 Pitching -- Single-A and Rookie Leagues

Player	Lg	A	G	GS	CG	GF	IP	BFP	H	R	ER	HR	SH	SF	HB	TBB	IBB	SO	WP	Bk	W	L	Pct.	ShO	Sv	ERA
Dessellier,Christopher,Tigers	R	22	1	0	0	1	1	5	0	0	0	0	0	0	0	1	0	3	0	0	0	0	.000	0	1	0.00
Detmers,Kris,St. Pete	A	22	25	25	1	0	146.2	606	120	64	53	12	3	7	2	57	0	150	3	2	10	9	.526	0	0	3.25
Deutsch,Curry,Pirates	R	23	14	0	0	10	35	149	40	17	11	1	3	1	2	11	1	19	3	0	2	4	.333	0	1	2.83
Devries,Andy,Daytona	A	23	21	1	0	9	45.1	203	45	21	18	2	2	2	5	22	0	21	6	0	1	0	1.000	0	0	3.57
Dewitt,Christopher,Kingsport	R	22	23	0	0	10	28	123	31	18	12	3	3	0	1	7	1	16	1	0	1	0	1.000	0	5	3.86
Dewitt,Matthew,Johnson Cty	R	18	13	12	0	0	62.2	305	84	56	49	10	0	3	1	32	0	45	5	2	2	6	.250	0	0	7.04
Dewitt,Scott,Marlins	R	21	11	10	1	0	63.2	245	48	15	14	1	3	2	2	9	0	70	1	1	5	3	.625	0	0	1.98
Kane County	A	21	1	1	0	0	3	10	0	0	0	0	0	0	1	1	0	2	0	0	0	0	.000	0	0	0.00
Diaz,Jairo,Williamsprt	A	20	30	0	0	6	45.1	188	39	21	15	2	5	0	3	10	1	55	4	1	1	7	.125	0	0	2.98
Dickens,John,Wilmington	A	25	48	0	0	27	76.1	296	57	17	15	1	4	2	3	17	3	59	5	0	3	1	.750	0	9	1.77
Dickson,Jason,Cedar Rapds	A	23	25	25	9	0	173	708	151	71	55	12	4	3	8	45	0	134	7	2	14	6	.700	1	0	2.86
Dickson,Lance,Cubs	R	26	2	1	0	0	3	14	2	0	0	0	0	0	0	3	0	3	0	0	1	0	1.000	0	0	0.00
Dietrich,Jason,Salem	A	23	6	0	0	1	7.1	39	9	7	7	2	0	0	1	8	0	9	0	0	1	0	1.000	0	0	8.59
Portland	A	23	10	1	0	5	13.1	48	5	0	0	0	0	0	0	5	0	24	0	0	0	0	.000	0	0	0.00
Dillinger,John,Lynchburg	A	22	27	22	0	1	123	540	111	62	55	10	5	5	7	67	4	97	9	7	6	6	.500	0	0	4.02
Dillon,Chad,Butte	R	20	15	7	0	0	41.1	228	60	58	47	2	0	5	7	39	0	26	11	0	0	5	.000	0	0	10.23
Dinnen,Kevin,Columbus	A	24	49	0	0	24	58.2	255	47	34	27	4	4	4	3	34	9	43	1	0	2	7	.222	0	1	4.14
Dinyar,Eric,Fayettevlle	A	22	42	0	0	16	86.2	356	77	34	24	1	1	4	8	25	0	71	2	1	4	3	.571	0	5	2.49
Diorio,Mike,Quad City	A	23	33	11	0	4	91.2	391	82	39	33	6	4	0	4	36	1	81	13	2	6	4	.600	0	1	3.24
Dixon,Bubba,Rancho Cuca	A	24	47	12	2	15	141.2	572	118	61	51	14	5	1	8	46	0	133	6	2	10	7	.588	0	0	3.24
Dixon,Jim,South Bend	A	23	11	1	0	6	17.2	88	28	19	12	2	1	1	4	11	1	11	3	1	1	2	.333	0	0	6.11
Hickory	A	23	35	0	0	17	51.1	220	43	23	11	1	4	2	1	16	5	56	6	1	4	1	.800	0	5	1.93
Dixon,Tim,Vermont	A	24	18	9	0	2	69	287	58	20	14	0	3	0	8	16	0	58	5	7	7	2	.778	0	1	1.83
Domenico,Brian,Michigan	A	23	6	1	0	1	9.1	48	11	12	3	3	3	0	0	11	1	5	0	0	0	2	.000	0	0	2.89
Done,Johnny,Medcine Hat	R	20	22	1	0	13	33.1	156	35	25	17	1	4	1	2	15	3	29	6	2	5	5	.500	0	1	4.59
Done,J.J.,Columbus	A	20	4	3	0	0	12	65	21	15	12	1	0	1	1	9	1	8	3	1	0	3	.000	0	0	9.00
Donnelly,Robert,New Jersey	A	22	36	0	0	13	48.1	210	37	21	19	1	4	1	3	30	4	63	5	0	1	3	.250	0	1	3.54
Donovan,Scot,Columbus	A	23	40	0	0	31	48.2	238	53	38	26	6	3	0	3	36	4	38	6	1	0	6	.000	0	10	4.81
Doorneweerd,Dave,Lynchburg	A	23	5	0	0	2	8	38	8	6	6	0	0	0	1	5	0	9	1	0	1	0	1.000	0	0	6.75
Dotel,Octavio,Mets	R	22	13	12	2	1	74.1	293	48	23	18	0	1	0	5	17	1	86	9	1	7	4	.636	0	0	2.18
St. Lucie	A	22	3	0	0	2	8	38	10	5	5	1	1	2	0	4	0	9	2	0	1	0	1.000	0	0	5.63
Dougherty,Anthony,Columbus	A	23	27	10	0	3	87.2	405	85	61	46	5	2	4	8	50	4	78	4	1	4	4	.500	0	0	4.72
Doughty,Brian,Wisconsin	A	21	32	3	0	12	84.1	360	83	50	37	4	4	3	6	26	3	54	5	0	5	7	.417	0	4	3.95
Douglas,Reggie,Rockies	R	19	15	0	0	9	27	135	37	29	28	1	2	0	2	19	0	17	11	11	0	1	.000	0	1	9.33
Dowhower,Deron,Fort Wayne	A	24	35	0	0	13	77	331	53	32	28	4	4	4	4	49	0	97	13	0	3	0	1.000	0	0	3.27
Downs,John,Wilmington	A	25	8	0	0	5	11.2	55	19	7	7	2	0	1	0	2	1	7	2	0	1	0	1.000	0	0	5.40
Doyle,Tom,Charlstn-Wv	A	26	14	12	1	0	62	272	57	34	30	3	2	1	7	30	3	66	9	0	6	4	.600	0	0	4.35
Winston-Sal	A	26	21	3	0	3	31.1	140	32	18	12	2	1	0	3	12	0	22	5	0	3	1	.750	0	1	3.45
Draeger,Mark,Hudson Vall	A	23	21	2	0	4	40	193	40	33	24	0	1	2	4	26	2	33	10	0	3	4	.429	0	1	5.40
Drewien,D.J.,Padres	R	23	1	0	0	0	2.2	11	2	1	0	0	0	0	0	0	0	2	0	0	0	0	.000	0	0	0.00
Rancho Cuca	A	23	17	0	0	1	28.1	127	30	20	20	3	1	1	2	11	1	26	2	0	1	2	.333	0	1	6.35
Drews,Matt,Tampa	A	21	28	28	3	0	182	748	142	73	46	5	5	5	17	58	0	140	8	2	15	7	.682	0	0	2.27
Droll,Jeff,South Bend	A	25	8	0	0	4	14	72	25	11	5	1	0	1	0	4	1	9	0	0	1	0	1.000	0	1	3.21
Druckrey,Christopher,Rockies	R	21	14	13	0	1	69.2	330	75	54	39	1	0	1	8	38	0	65	13	3	0	8	.000	0	0	5.04
Drumheller,Al,Tampa	A	24	32	0	0	10	40.1	158	24	11	6	1	2	2	1	14	2	45	1	0	3	3	.500	0	2	1.34
Drysdale,Brooks,Angels	R	25	4	0	0	3	3.1	16	4	4	3	0	0	0	0	1	1	7	0	0	0	0	.000	0	2	8.10
Lk Elsinore	A	25	8	0	0	2	9	41	8	3	2	1	1	1	0	4	1	8	2	0	1	0	1.000	0	0	2.00
Duffy,Ryan,Erie	A	23	19	8	0	4	51	223	59	33	27	1	0	0	1	14	0	31	2	0	1	2	.333	0	0	4.76
Duncan,Devohn,Padres	R	21	11	10	0	0	52	231	47	39	18	2	1	3	4	22	0	40	12	5	4	5	.444	0	0	3.12
Duncan,Sean,White Sox	R	23	3	0	0	1	6	25	5	3	0	0	0	0	0	1	0	6	1	0	0	0	.000	0	0	0.00
South Bend	A	23	12	0	0	7	11.1	44	8	2	1	0	0	0	0	3	0	8	0	0	0	0	.000	0	1	0.79
Dunn,Cordell,Pirates	R	20	5	0	0	2	10	46	13	9	6	0	0	0	0	4	0	5	2	0	1	1	.500	0	0	5.40
Dunne,Brian,Martinsvlle	R	22	16	6	0	1	48.1	229	67	39	23	7	1	2	2	10	0	33	3	2	2	3	.400	0	1	4.28
Duran,Roberto,Vero Beach	A	23	23	22	0	0	101.1	446	82	42	38	8	3	1	1	70	0	114	12	2	7	4	.636	0	0	3.38
Durkovic,Peter,Jamestown	A	22	14	1	0	0	24.1	115	28	17	16	4	0	0	1	10	0	10	2	1	0	0	.000	0	1	5.92
Durocher,Jayson,Albany	A	21	24	22	1	1	122	526	105	67	53	5	4	11	5	56	1	88	11	1	3	7	.300	0	0	3.91
Dutch,John,Michigan	A	23	32	0	0	16	51	257	80	50	45	5	3	6	3	20	1	23	3	1	2	4	.333	0	1	7.94
Duvall,Mike,Marlins	R	21	16	1	0	0	28.1	120	15	8	7	1	0	0	2	12	1	34	4	2	5	0	1.000	0	0	2.22
Dyess,Todd,Frederick	A	23	3	3	0	0	13.2	61	17	10	10	1	0	1	1	5	0	3	3	0	0	2	.000	0	0	6.59
High Desert	A	23	23	22	0	0	125.1	573	145	94	71	9	5	9	5	58	0	118	17	5	6	9	.400	0	0	5.10
Dykhoff,Radhames,High Desert	A	21	34	2	0	10	80.2	389	95	68	45	8	7	7	0	44	2	88	0	2	1	5	.167	0	3	5.02
Eaddy,Brad,Bakersfield	A	26	42	1	0	19	79.1	328	66	29	26	4	4	4	5	30	4	45	4	5	4	5	.444	0	5	2.95
Ebert,Derrin,Macon	A	19	28	28	0	0	182	766	184	87	67	12	5	4	7	46	0	124	3	2	14	5	.737	0	0	3.31
Eby,Mike,Jamestown	A	24	23	0	0	9	29.2	118	20	7	5	1	3	0	1	5	0	33	1	4	2	1	.667	0	2	1.52
Eden,Bill,Asheville	A	23	33	0	0	17	67.1	269	55	22	16	4	1	0	1	14	0	80	7	2	5	3	.625	0	9	2.14
Edwards,Jon,Burlington	R	23	19	1	0	5	37.1	172	44	28	22	2	0	0	1	16	1	31	3	0	3	2	.600	0	0	5.30
Ehler,Dan,Brevard Cty	A	21	16	15	0	0	88.1	380	88	46	35	2	4	3	8	26	1	66	0	1	5	6	.455	0	0	3.57
Eibey,Scott,Bluefield	R	22	14	6	0	3	43.2	196	51	32	27	4	2	0	2	24	0	26	6	1	3	1	.750	0	2	5.56
Einertson,Darrell,Oneonta	A	23	25	0	0	8	38.1	167	32	20	8	1	1	0	3	15	1	35	0	1	0	4	.000	0	0	1.88
Elarton,Scott,Quad City	A	20	26	26	0	0	149.2	668	149	86	74	12	8	4	8	71	2	112	12	0	13	7	.650	0	0	4.45
Ellison,Austin,Twins	R	20	11	0	0	6	16.2	78	17	10	7	0	0	1	0	15	0	11	3	0	0	0	.000	0	1	3.78
Emiliano,Jamie,Portland	A	21	28	0	0	22	38.2	165	31	18	15	0	2	1	4	12	2	41	5	0	4	1	.800	0	11	3.49
Enard,Tony,Elmira	A	21	15	0	0	8	30.2	149	33	36	26	1	0	5	4	22	0	27	10	4	0	5	.000	0	0	7.63
Endo,Masataka,Visalia	A	23	28	27	6	0	186.2	763	162	87	78	13	7	2	7	62	1	178	17	8	9	9	.500	3	0	3.76
Enloe,Mark,Mets	R	19	11	2	0	3	26	114	24	14	9	0	0	0	5	16	0	25	4	1	2	1	.667	0	0	3.12
Enoki,Yasuhiro,Visalia	A	24	13	13	2	0	74.1	335	104	52	45	8	1	3	2	11	0	51	2	0	4	7	.364	0	0	5.45
Epstein,Ian,W.Michigan	A	25	18	0	0	7	18.1	89	24	14	12	1	2	1	2	10	0	16	3	0	5	0	1.000	0	0	5.89

1995 Pitching -- Single-A and Rookie Leagues

Column groups: **HOW MUCH HE PITCHED** (G, GS, CG, GF, IP, BFP) · **WHAT HE GAVE UP** (H, R, ER, HR, SH, SF, HB, TBB, IBB, SO, WP, Bk) · **THE RESULTS** (W, L, Pct., ShO, Sv, ERA)

Player	Lg	A	G	GS	CG	GF	IP	BFP	H	R	ER	HR	SH	SF	HB	TBB	IBB	SO	WP	Bk	W	L	Pct.	ShO	Sv	ERA
Sou. Oregon	A	25	23	0	0	19	40.1	163	32	13	13	1	2	5	2	9	2	36	2	1	2	2	.500	0	1	2.90
Erdos,Todd,Rancho Cuca	A	22	1	0	0	0	2.2	13	5	4	4	0	0	1	0	4	0	4	0	0	0	0	.000	0	0	13.50
Clinton	A	22	5	1	0	1	5	27	4	4	3	0	0	0	0	8	1	1	2	0	0	0	.000	0	0	5.40
Idaho Falls	R	22	32	0	0	20	41.1	185	34	19	16	1	3	2	5	30	2	48	8	0	5	3	.625	0	1	3.48
Escobar,Kelvin,Medicne Hat	R	20	14	14	1	0	69.1	307	66	47	44	6	2	5	6	33	0	75	4	4	3	3	.500	1	0	5.71
Espino,Randy,Twins	R	18	4	2	0	1	10	50	11	10	1	0	1	0	0	6	0	3	3	2	0	1	.000	0	0	0.90
Estavil,Mauricio,Piedmont	A	24	42	0	0	18	44	202	33	20	18	0	0	0	2	37	1	58	6	0	3	5	.375	0	0	3.68
Estrada,Horacio,Brewers	R	20	8	1	0	3	17	73	13	9	7	1	1	1	0	8	0	21	4	2	0	1	.000	0	0	3.71
Helena	R	20	13	0	0	1	30	144	27	21	18	3	5	0	3	24	0	30	2	0	1	2	.333	0	0	5.40
Etler,Todd,Winston-Sal	A	22	24	23	3	0	153.2	628	148	71	63	13	4	5	2	49	2	78	3	2	6	12	.333	0	0	3.69
Evangelista,Alberto,Macon	A	22	24	2	1	12	54	224	42	29	21	4	4	3	2	16	0	51	6	2	4	4	.500	0	0	3.50
Eyre,Scott,White Sox	R	24	9	9	0	0	27.1	106	16	7	7	0	0	1	1	12	0	40	2	0	2	2	.500	0	0	2.30
Falls,Curt,Lethbridge	R	22	24	4	1	5	53.1	238	56	27	22	3	2	3	3	19	1	49	3	2	2	2	.500	0	1	3.71
Farfan,David,Boise	A	22	14	0	0	4	21.1	94	19	9	6	0	0	0	0	12	0	17	2	2	1	0	1.000	0	0	2.53
Farmer,Jon,Kane County	A	22	29	11	0	4	78.2	369	97	65	61	9	1	5	8	32	1	60	7	2	1	4	.200	0	0	6.98
Farnsworth,Kyle,Cubs	R	20	16	0	0	6	31	120	22	8	3	0	4	0	1	11	0	18	1	1	3	2	.600	0	0	0.87
Farr,Mark,Elmira	A	22	9	9	0	0	40	200	45	34	27	3	1	1	4	31	1	24	5	2	0	5	.000	0	0	6.07
Farrell,James,Red Sox	R	22	1	1	0	0	6	20	2	1	1	0	0	0	0	1	0	3	0	0	1	0	1.000	0	0	1.50
Michigan	A	22	13	13	1	0	69	291	62	34	28	10	1	1	5	23	0	70	3	1	3	2	.600	0	0	3.65
Farrow,Jason,Erie	A	22	20	4	0	2	48.1	213	44	18	12	0	6	2	6	20	2	50	4	2	3	1	.750	0	0	2.23
Farson,Bryan,Lynchburg	A	23	27	6	0	7	51	228	51	41	33	13	1	2	2	19	4	35	3	0	7	3	.700	0	0	5.82
Faulkner,Neal,Rockford	A	21	40	0	0	17	66	290	61	36	29	3	3	9	3	29	1	47	10	1	2	3	.400	0	1	3.90
Feingold,Leon,Burlington	R	23	1	0	0	0	0.1	11	2	8	8	0	0	0	0	8	0	1	0	0	0	0	.000	0	0	99.99
Feliciano,Pedro,Great Falls	R	19	6	0	0	3	6.2	43	12	12	10	0	0	0	0	7	1	9	4	2	0	0	.000	0	0	13.50
Felix,Ruben,Stockton	A	26	6	0	0	2	6.1	34	9	9	9	2	1	0	2	5	2	3	0	2	0	2	.000	0	0	12.79
Beloit	A	26	45	0	0	9	48.1	233	49	33	29	6	5	1	2	36	2	60	4	1	4	3	.571	0	0	5.40
Feliz,Bienvenido,Burlington	R	19	12	12	1	0	73	296	55	29	22	8	1	0	1	20	0	78	2	2	4	2	.667	1	0	2.71
Feliz,Jose,Cubs	R	19	13	5	0	6	36	158	29	20	7	0	2	1	4	10	0	27	2	0	3	2	.600	0	1	1.75
Fennell,Barry,Rockford	A	19	4	4	0	0	23	94	19	8	6	2	0	2	1	8	0	13	1	1	2	1	.667	0	0	2.35
Fereira,Marcos,Hickory	A	21	4	0	0	1	2.2	20	6	6	5	0	2	1	0	4	2	1	2	3	0	2	.000	0	0	16.88
White Sox	R	21	7	0	0	4	7.1	40	11	14	12	2	0	0	0	8	0	4	4	1	0	1	.000	0	0	14.73
Huntington	R	21	5	1	0	3	6.1	45	9	16	11	0	0	2	2	14	0	3	3	1	0	1	.000	0	0	15.63
Ferguson,Tim,Vermont	A	24	3	0	0	1	4.2	20	2	4	4	0	0	0	2	2	0	2	0	0	0	0	.000	0	0	7.71
Fernandes,Jamie,Butte	R	24	12	12	0	0	64.1	305	75	52	43	7	3	3	8	32	0	44	9	0	4	4	.500	0	0	6.02
Utica	A	24	3	1	0	1	9.2	41	9	5	5	0	0	1	0	3	0	7	1	0	0	1	.000	0	0	4.66
Fernandez,Omar,Great Falls	R	22	19	2	0	6	35.1	166	39	28	19	4	0	3	1	21	2	27	8	0	3	1	.750	0	0	4.84
Ferran,Alex,Sarasota	A	27	1	0	0	0	5		1	4	4	0	0	0	1	2	0	6	0	2	0	0	.000	0	0	0.00
Ferullo,Matt,Pittsfield	A	23	2	0	0	1	5	19	3	0	0	0	0	0	0	1	0	6	0	0	1	0	1.000	0	0	0.00
Fetchel,Tony,Visalia	A	24	18	1	0	5	24.1	132	22	20	18	0	0	0	11	32	0	11	7	0	0	1	.000	0	0	6.66
Fidge,Darren,Fort Wayne	A	21	39	17	1	20	134.1	572	126	62	55	11	4	2	9	37	1	106	15	1	6	5	.545	0	13	3.68
Figueroa,Julio,Expos	R	22	10	10	0	0	49.2	211	44	27	17	5	4	2	0	20	0	37	2	1	2	3	.400	0	0	3.08
Figueroa,Nelson,Kingsport	R	22	12	12	2	0	76.1	304	57	31	26	3	3	2	5	22	1	79	5	0	7	3	.700	2	0	3.07
Filbeck,Ryan,Kane County	A	23	25	0	0	6	41.2	182	40	19	17	0	2	3	3	17	3	28	7	0	5	0	1.000	0	0	3.67
Fiore,Tony,Clearwater	A	24	24	10	0	3	70.1	323	70	41	29	4	3	5	2	44	2	45	9	3	6	2	.750	0	0	3.71
Fisher,Louis,Orioles	R	19	9	7	2	0	39	167	27	23	8	0	3	0	0	24	0	29	4	2	4	3	.571	0	0	1.85
Fisher,Ryan,Pirates	R	22	1	0	0	0	1	4	1	0	0	0	0	0	0	0	0	1	0	0	0	0	.000	0	0	0.00
Fitterer,Scott,St.Cathrns	A	22	22	0	0	17	23.2	101	18	7	3	1	1	0	1	13	0	22	2	0	0	0	.000	0	9	1.14
Fitzpatrick,Ken,Springfield	A	21	12	7	0	1	43.2	187	36	26	19	3	1	1	1	17	0	29	4	1	2	2	.500	0	0	3.92
Fleetwood,Tony,Burlington	R	24	18	0	0	9	28.2	131	25	18	15	5	0	1	2	14	0	34	2	1	2	2	.500	0	0	4.71
Fletcher,Paul,South Bend	A	26	36	0	0	24	57.1	250	55	21	19	2	5	1	3	24	1	49	5	1	4	4	.500	0	5	2.98
Florentino,Osmin,Rockies	R	18	19	0	0	11	43.1	208	55	42	33	2	3	3	2	17	0	27	1	5	0	2	.000	0	2	6.85
Flores,Ignacio,Great Falls	R	21	16	12	0	1	68.2	301	66	42	36	3	0	1	4	38	0	76	4	2	6	4	.600	0	0	4.72
Flury,Pat,Wilmington	A	23	15	0	0	6	22	89	18	6	6	2	0	1	1	9	1	14	1	1	1	0	1.000	0	0	2.45
Springfield	A	23	34	0	0	19	54.1	246	65	32	26	5	4	1	1	24	0	35	2	0	2	6	.250	0	1	4.31
Foderaro,Kevin,Peoria	A	23	15	14	0	0	80	316	80	58	48	4	3	5	1	24	1	36	3	0	3	8	.273	0	0	6.20
Fonseca,Chad,Princeton	R	20	11	1	0	3	22.1	107	27	19	18	4	0	1	1	10	2	21	1	0	0	0	.000	0	0	7.25
Fontenot,Joseph,Bellingham	A	19	6	6	0	0	18.2	77	14	5	4	0	0	0	0	10	0	14	0	2	0	3	.000	0	0	1.93
Foran,John,Jamestown	A	22	14	0	0	4	17	79	17	15	11	1	0	1	0	6	0	18	3	3	1	2	.333	0	0	5.82
Forbes,Adam,Hickory	A	21	2	0	0	1	3.2	19	5	5	4	1	0	1	2	0	0	1	1	0	0	0	.000	0	0	9.82
Ford,Ben,Greensboro	A	20	7	0	0	2	7	31	4	4	4	1	1	0	0	5	0	5	2	0	0	0	.000	0	0	5.14
Oneonta	A	20	29	0	0	10	52	224	39	23	5	1	0	2	5	16	0	50	8	0	5	0	1.000	0	0	0.87
Ford,Brian,Batavia	A	23	29	0	0	26	38	143	24	8	5	1	2	2	0	5	0	44	2	0	3	1	.750	0	10	1.18
Ford,Jack,Hickory	A	24	27	27	3	0	173.2	738	174	86	75	14	8	5	6	66	3	157	5	0	8	14	.364	0	0	3.89
Forster,Pete,Twins	R	21	10	7	2	1	43.2	191	37	21	18	1	4	0	4	27	0	36	6	1	2	5	.286	0	0	3.71
Forster,Scott,W.Palm Bch	A	24	26	26	1	0	146.2	643	129	78	66	6	5	4	7	80	1	92	16	0	6	11	.353	0	0	4.05
Fortune,Peter,Expos	R	21	11	11	1	0	48	209	46	33	25	1	2	1	2	18	0	27	2	0	3	5	.375	0	0	4.69
Foster,Cliff,Athletics	R	24	1	1	0	0	1	8	4	4	3	0	0	0	0	0	0	0	0	0	0	0	.000	0	0	27.00
Foster,Kris,Yakima	A	21	15	0	0	5	56	241	38	27	18	2	2	4	2	38	3	55	8	1	2	3	.400	0	2	2.89
Foulke,Keith,San Jose	A	23	28	26	2	0	177.1	723	166	85	69	16	10	3	7	32	0	168	6	2	13	6	.684	5	0	3.50
Fowler,Ben,Braves	R	19	12	0	0	6	24.2	106	17	13	3	0	0	2	0	13	0	23	4	0	1	2	.333	0	1	1.09
Fox,Ryan,Ogden	R	22	2	0	0	1	2.1	16	7	6	2	1	0	0	1	0	0	2	1	0	0	0	.000	0	0	7.71
Frace,Ryan,Martinsvlle	R	24	14	0	0	7	29	121	20	14	7	1	0	0	0	9	1	31	4	2	3	2	.600	0	1	2.17
France,Kevin,Augusta	A	22	18	15	0	0	94.2	388	80	29	26	4	3	3	5	26	0	77	6	2	6	6	.500	0	0	2.47
Franek,Tom,Clearwater	A	25	9	0	0	5	12.2	54	12	6	5	2	0	0	0	3	1	9	0	0	0	0	.000	0	0	3.55
Franklin,Joel,Charlstn-Wv	A	23	14	1	0	5	50.2	221	49	28	28	2	2	3	4	22	2	58	6	0	3	3	.500	0	2	4.97
Frascatore,Steve,New Jersey	A	24	16	15	0	1	82.2	370	86	56	43	2	1	3	6	30	0	43	6	2	4	6	.400	0	0	4.68
Freehill,Mike,Cedar Rapds	A	25	54	0	0	49	55	234	54	25	16	4	3	0	7	12	5	47	10	1	4	5	.444	0	28	2.62

1995 Pitching -- Single-A and Rookie Leagues

Player	Lg	A	G	GS	CG	GF	IP	BFP	H	R	ER	HR	SH	SF	HB	TBB	IBB	SO	WP	Bk	W	L	Pct.	ShO	Sv	ERA
French,Jon,Sou. Oregon	A	23	20	0	0	12	26.2	132	34	21	19	3	1	0	5	17	1	18	3	0	1	2	.333	0	0	6.41
Friedman,Matt,Lethbridge	R	23	20	6	0	10	43.2	210	55	40	32	2	2	5	1	26	4	36	1	5	0	8	.000	0	4	6.60
Fuduric,Tony,Tigers	R	21	16	0	0	7	30.1	136	25	13	10	1	2	2	1	21	0	21	4	3	5	2	.714	0	0	2.97
Fuller,Stephen,Auburn	A	21	14	14	0	0	66.2	317	67	51	36	2	1	5	3	51	0	29	9	1	6	5	.545	0	0	4.86
Fussell,Chris,Bluefield	R	20	12	12	1	0	65.2	265	37	18	16	4	1	1	7	32	0	98	3	1	9	1	.900	1	0	2.19
Gaerte,Travis,Pirates	R	19	6	0	0	1	12	57	14	9	8	2	0	0	3	2	0	5	1	1	0	0	.000	0	0	6.00
Gaiko,Rob,Batavia	A	23	20	0	0	10	33	165	50	34	30	3	1	1	4	11	3	25	7	0	1	1	.500	0	0	8.18
Gamboa,Javier,Springfield	A	22	19	19	1	0	105.2	429	83	45	37	10	3	2	0	32	0	66	4	0	6	6	.500	0	0	3.15
Wilmington	A	22	8	8	0	0	49	202	42	23	22	6	3	0	1	13	0	33	2	0	3	4	.429	0	0	4.04
Gambs,Chris,Piedmont	A	22	9	0	0	2	19.2	95	24	17	15	2	0	2	1	14	0	15	3	0	0	0	.000	0	0	6.86
Batavia	A	22	7	7	0	0	34.1	148	31	21	21	0	1	1	0	22	0	21	4	0	3	2	.600	0	0	5.50
High Desert	A	22	3	0	0	2	3	16	4	4	4	0	0	0	0	4	0	1	0	0	0	0	.000	0	0	12.00
Gamez,Rene,Ogden	R	23	10	10	0	0	54.1	247	53	41	38	1	1	5	5	30	1	42	7	3	4	2	.667	0	0	6.29
Gandolph,Dave,Kissimmee	A	26	12	4	0	3	15.1	77	15	11	9	0	0	3	0	20	0	8	3	0	0	2	.000	0	0	5.28
Garber,Joel,Bristol	R	22	19	6	0	4	60	229	37	13	8	3	1	2	1	12	0	66	4	1	5	1	.833	0	0	1.20
Garcia,Al,Rockford	A	22	27	27	1	0	177	755	176	94	74	13	4	4	15	43	0	120	10	0	14	9	.609	1	0	3.76
Garcia,Ariel,South Bend	A	20	10	10	0	0	57.1	246	54	23	20	3	3	2	8	19	0	46	4	2	2	1	.667	0	0	3.14
Garcia,Eddy,Billings	R	20	15	5	0	3	48	193	38	20	14	0	0	0	0	12	1	45	2	2	3	2	.600	0	1	2.63
Garcia,Frank,Savannah	A	22	34	0	0	32	37	156	26	17	13	3	0	1	2	15	0	41	8	0	0	3	.000	0	24	3.16
St. Pete	A	22	16	0	0	8	16.2	98	27	22	19	1	0	1	1	18	0	8	3	0	0	1	.000	0	1	10.26
Garcia,Freddy,Astros	R	19	11	11	0	0	58.1	256	60	32	29	2	3	3	6	14	0	58	5	0	6	3	.667	0	0	4.47
Garcia,Jose,Eugene	A	21	14	14	0	0	70	307	64	43	30	7	1	0	0	35	0	62	2	3	3	3	.500	0	0	3.86
Garcia,Ricky,Elmira	A	22	15	15	0	0	75.1	341	80	56	50	3	1	2	5	46	0	53	5	2	1	7	.125	0	0	5.97
Garcia-luna,Francisco,Augusta	A	23	14	10	1	0	63	263	57	31	20	3	1	2	3	17	0	48	5	0	2	1	.667	0	0	2.86
Gardner,Scott,Lakeland	A	24	5	0	0	2	13	54	10	6	4	1	0	0	0	7	0	14	0	0	0	0	.000	0	0	2.77
Fayettevlle	A	24	49	1	0	22	87.1	351	62	26	20	5	1	0	2	24	1	112	8	2	6	3	.667	0	4	2.06
Garff,Jeff,Twins	R	20	15	6	0	6	45.2	175	34	12	9	1	4	0	4	5	0	30	1	0	4	2	.667	0	1	1.77
Garrett,Hal,Clinton	A	21	11	11	1	0	58	268	58	43	36	4	5	2	4	34	3	41	5	0	3	8	.273	0	0	5.59
Rancho Cuca	A	21	23	1	0	5	42	196	40	21	13	2	2	5	2	25	0	43	7	1	0	4	.000	0	0	2.79
Garrett,Neil,Salem	A	21	5	0	0	0	3.2	24	5	8	5	0	1	0	1	5	0	3	3	0	1	0	1.000	0	0	12.27
Garsky,Brian,Expos	A	20	14	6	0	2	43.1	199	48	25	15	1	1	3	2	19	0	43	6	3	2	3	.400	0	0	3.12
Gaskill,Derek,Helena	R	22	31	0	0	10	56	243	50	30	23	3	0	1	4	23	0	59	10	0	5	2	.714	0	1	3.70
Gaspar,Cade,Lakeland	A	22	23	23	0	0	99.1	422	95	48	43	5	1	3	9	44	0	97	13	3	7	6	.538	0	0	3.90
Gaston,Ryan,Rangers	R	19	10	1	0	5	22.2	95	19	9	5	0	0	2	2	6	0	9	1	0	0	0	.000	0	2	1.99
Gates,Sean,Rancho Cuca	A	24	1	0	0	0	2.2	10	1	0	0	0	0	0	1	0	0	0	0	0	0	0	.000	0	0	0.00
Clinton	A	24	29	0	0	12	39.2	178	39	23	22	3	2	2	5	19	3	27	1	0	0	2	.000	0	1	4.99
Gautreau,Mike,Peoria	A	22	45	0	0	9	63.1	278	62	42	32	3	3	1	2	29	1	55	2	2	4	3	.571	0	4	4.55
Genke,Todd,Piedmont	A	25	31	1	0	4	53	227	50	30	23	3	3	1	2	18	3	37	4	0	3	2	.600	0	1	3.91
Geraldo,Antonio,Blue Jays	R	21	2	2	0	0	6	24	6	1	1	0	0	0	0	1	0	6	2	0	0	0	.000	0	0	1.50
Gerland,Greg,Braves	R	23	2	0	0	2	4	14	1	0	0	0	0	0	1	0	0	3	0	0	1	0	1.000	0	0	0.00
Eugene	A	23	19	2	0	2	41.2	180	39	18	10	1	3	1	1	15	1	33	2	1	4	2	.667	0	0	2.16
Getz,Rodney,Marlins	A	20	6	6	0	0	29.1	112	25	12	11	2	0	1	1	4	0	30	3	0	1	1	.500	0	0	3.38
Giard,Ken,Eugene	A	23	25	0	0	7	34	137	31	9	9	3	2	0	1	5	1	44	3	0	3	0	1.000	0	2	2.38
Macon	A	23	5	0	0	3	13.1	51	7	1	1	0	1	0	0	5	0	19	2	0	1	0	1.000	0	0	0.68
Gil,Danny,Cubs	R	21	7	0	0	2	13	59	9	7	5	0	0	0	2	8	0	9	4	0	1	1	.500	0	0	3.46
Gillispie,Ryan,Pirates	R	19	4	0	0	4	7.1	37	8	4	2	0	0	1	1	6	0	4	1	0	0	1	.000	0	0	2.45
Giron,Emiliano,Winston-Sal	A	24	17	0	0	11	27.1	121	23	15	7	1	0	0	3	10	0	29	2	2	2	0	1.000	0	0	2.30
Charlstn-Wv	A	24	30	0	0	28	28.2	108	12	3	3	0	1	0	1	8	0	39	1	2	0	0	.000	0	20	0.94
Giron,Roberto,Princeton	R	20	24	0	0	12	36	159	33	23	22	3	1	3	4	14	1	41	6	1	1	1	.500	0	4	5.50
Giuliano,Joe,Danville	R	20	11	11	0	0	49.2	236	71	45	40	7	1	5	1	19	0	48	7	2	2	5	.286	0	0	7.25
Glauber,Keith,Savannah	A	24	40	0	0	3	62.2	277	50	29	26	2	2	3	5	36	3	62	9	1	2	1	.667	0	0	3.73
Glick,David,Brewers	R	20	18	0	0	4	25.1	115	24	13	12	0	1	0	1	14	0	29	4	4	2	0	1.000	0	0	4.26
Glover,Gary,Blue Jays	R	19	12	10	2	0	62.1	279	62	48	34	4	4	3	11	26	0	46	8	0	3	7	.300	0	0	4.91
Glynn,Ryan,Hudson Vall	A	21	9	8	0	0	44	192	56	27	23	0	0	1	3	16	1	21	10	3	3	3	.500	0	0	4.70
Gobert,Chris,Danville	R	23	3	0	0	0	5.2	23	7	0	0	0	0	0	0	3	0	1	1	0	0	0	.000	0	0	0.00
Goedde,Roger,Pirates	R	20	6	6	1	0	31	130	31	12	9	0	1	0	2	7	0	25	0	0	1	1	.500	0	0	2.61
Erie	A	20	5	5	0	0	20.1	110	31	23	18	1	2	4	0	17	0	8	13	0	1	3	.250	0	0	7.97
Gogolewski,Chris,Charlstn-Sc	A	22	30	19	2	5	140.1	627	169	93	66	5	4	5	12	38	1	84	12	2	5	13	.278	0	0	4.23
Golden,Matt,Savannah	A	24	64	0	0	24	90	355	71	22	20	2	2	2	0	21	4	94	4	2	7	3	.700	0	1	2.00
Goldman,Barry,Salem	A	27	8	0	0	0	9.1	41	8	7	6	0	0	0	0	7	1	6	2	0	0	0	.000	0	0	5.79
Gomez,Alexander,Angels	R	22	13	3	0	2	30.2	143	30	21	19	0	1	1	4	23	1	31	8	0	4	3	.571	0	0	5.58
Gomez,Augustine,South Bend	A	22	25	25	1	0	144	616	128	85	66	7	4	7	8	68	0	99	9	6	7	6	.538	0	0	4.13
Gomez,Dennys,Burlington	A	25	14	0	0	9	21.2	97	25	11	9	2	1	0	2	11	1	26	6	0	1	1	.500	0	1	3.74
Bellingham	A	25	4	0	0	2	6	31	8	6	5	2	0	0	0	3	0	6	1	0	0	1	.000	0	0	7.50
San Jose	A	25	13	0	0	5	30.1	136	27	13	7	0	3	2	2	15	0	23	1	0	2	0	1.000	0	1	2.08
Gomez,Marcial,Lk Elsinore	A	24	7	0	0	0	12.1	56	11	10	8	0	0	1	1	9	0	10	2	1	1	0	1.000	0	0	5.84
Gomez,Miguel,Medicne Hat	R	22	14	14	1	0	72.1	326	79	55	41	10	2	1	6	32	0	46	5	2	2	5	.286	0	0	5.10
Gonzalez,Gabe,Kane County	A	24	32	0	0	10	43.1	181	32	18	11	0	2	1	2	14	2	41	1	0	4	4	.500	0	2	2.28
Gonzalez,Generoso,Tigers	R	20	16	4	0	2	39.1	163	29	19	17	1	2	1	1	16	0	45	8	1	5	3	.625	0	1	3.89
Lakeland	A	20	1	0	0	0	2.2	8	1	0	0	0	0	0	0	1	0	1	1	0	0	0	.000	0	0	0.00
Gonzalez,Geremis,Rockford	A	21	12	12	1	0	65.1	297	63	43	37	4	1	4	8	28	0	36	8	1	4	4	.500	0	0	5.10
Daytona	A	21	19	2	0	7	44.1	178	34	15	6	0	1	2	1	13	1	30	4	2	5	1	.833	0	4	1.22
Gonzalez,Jhonny,Asheville	A	19	21	0	0	10	32.1	136	23	13	9	3	2	1	1	15	1	31	1	1	4	3	.571	0	3	2.48
Gonzalez,Jose,Mariners	R	19	12	10	0	0	56	250	56	40	33	1	2	2	2	31	0	66	8	5	4	4	.500	0	0	5.30
Gonzalez,Juan,Beloit	A	21	42	6	0	17	88.2	386	86	50	41	4	2	3	4	37	1	53	16	0	11	5	.688	0	6	4.16
Gonzalez,Laril,Portland	A	20	15	11	0	2	57.2	258	44	31	26	4	1	1	7	43	0	48	9	1	3	4	.429	0	2	4.06
Gooch,Arnie,Asheville	A	19	21	21	1	0	128.2	541	111	51	42	8	3	3	4	57	0	117	13	0	5	8	.385	1	0	2.94

370

1995 Pitching -- Single-A and Rookie Leagues

			HOW MUCH HE PITCHED						WHAT HE GAVE UP												THE RESULTS					
Player	Lg	A	G	GS	CG	GF	IP	BFP	H	R	ER	HR	SH	SF	HB	TBB	IBB	SO	WP	Bk	W	L	Pct.	ShO	Sv	ERA
Columbia	A	19	6	6	0	0	38.1	169	39	25	19	3	0	1	2	15	0	34	5	0	2	3	.400	0	0	4.46
Gooda,David,Beloit	A	19	3	3	0	0	14.1	61	13	8	6	1	1	0	1	7	0	9	0	0	0	0	.000	0	0	3.77
Helena	R	19	10	10	0	0	58.1	267	54	32	27	3	4	2	7	33	1	33	1	5	4	4	.500	0	0	4.17
Gordon,Mike,Tampa	A	23	21	21	1	0	124.1	521	111	54	42	6	3	1	4	49	0	96	9	2	4	6	.400	0	0	3.04
Dunedin	A	23	7	6	0	0	36.2	179	44	32	24	6	2	0	3	24	0	36	2	0	1	2	.333	0	0	5.89
Gorecki,Rick,Vero Beach	A	22	6	5	0	0	27	110	19	6	2	0	1	1	4	9	0	24	1	0	1	2	.333	0	0	0.67
Gosch,Grant,Astros	R	21	1	0	0	1	0.2	3	0	0	0	0	0	0	0	1	0	1	0	0	0	0	.000	0	0	0.00
Gourdin,Tom,Fort Wayne	A	23	41	0	0	19	89.2	384	90	49	44	10	3	3	9	32	0	74	11	2	6	6	.500	0	6	4.42
Graham,Steve,Macon	A	24	5	0	0	2	8.2	53	17	12	9	2	1	0	1	5	0	7	1	1	1	1	.500	0	0	9.35
Granata,Chris,Columbus	A	24	33	12	0	0	113	477	94	43	31	2	6	3	4	53	7	93	8	1	11	5	.688	0	0	2.47
Granger,Greg,Lakeland	A	23	27	25	1	0	142	639	176	93	79	7	6	7	15	46	0	91	8	2	9	12	.429	1	0	5.01
Grasser,Craig,St. Pete	A	26	26	0	0	7	33	133	26	5	5	2	0	0	2	12	1	27	2	0	4	2	.667	0	0	1.36
Graves,Jon,Idaho Falls	R	24	4	0	0	0	4	26	5	7	6	0	0	1	1	12	0	0	0	2	0	0	.000	0	0	13.50
Gray,Jason,White Sox	R	19	14	4	0	6	35.2	150	35	10	8	1	0	0	0	9	1	37	2	0	4	2	.667	0	1	2.02
Grebe,Brett,Augusta	A	25	32	0	0	15	37.1	165	42	19	15	3	1	2	0	16	1	36	2	1	2	2	.500	0	1	3.62
Green,Chris,Wisconsin	A	21	35	0	0	18	56.1	244	55	31	23	3	3	3	5	21	6	43	3	3	1	5	.167	0	2	3.67
Green,David,Auburn	A	21	14	14	2	0	82.2	365	82	48	35	1	4	0	10	29	0	48	5	0	8	2	.800	1	0	3.81
Green,Jason,Durham	A	22	39	1	0	14	50	248	31	31	31	1	2	4	1	79	1	59	13	1	2	4	.333	0	3	5.58
Greene,Brian,Williamsprt	A	22	18	5	0	3	46	203	52	28	17	1	2	1	2	16	0	25	4	1	3	2	.600	0	0	3.33
Grenert,Geoff,Cedar Rapids	A	25	27	4	0	7	72	317	76	43	33	4	1	4	9	23	1	55	3	1	3	4	.429	0	1	4.13
Grennan,Steve,St. Lucie	A	25	9	0	0	3	8.1	38	8	3	2	0	0	0	1	4	0	10	0	0	0	0	.000	0	0	2.16
Grife,Richard,Burlington	R	24	16	0	0	5	31	126	20	12	8	0	1	0	1	10	0	31	2	0	2	0	1.000	0	1	2.32
Watertown	A	24	5	0	0	2	10.2	44	10	5	3	0	1	0	0	5	0	8	1	0	1	2	.333	0	0	2.53
Griffin,Ryan,High Desert	A	22	31	25	0	4	143	686	182	129	108	14	4	10	17	80	0	96	21	2	6	15	.286	0	3	6.80
Groot,Frans,Vero Beach	A	25	14	1	0	10	29.1	127	28	21	19	4	2	5	3	18	0	15	2	1	0	0	.000	0	0	5.83
Grote,Jason,Burlington	A	21	6	0	0	2	8.2	41	10	10	9	2	0	0	2	5	0	5	1	0	0	1	.000	0	1	9.35
Butte	R	21	22	7	0	13	47.1	223	67	46	37	0	1	3	1	23	2	35	8	1	2	5	.286	0	4	7.04
Groves,Brian,Jamestown	A	23	16	0	0	6	24.1	111	21	17	12	0	0	0	2	17	0	15	5	0	0	1	.000	0	0	4.44
Gryboski,Kevin,Everett	A	22	25	0	0	14	36	156	27	18	14	2	3	1	3	18	2	25	3	0	1	5	.167	0	2	3.50
Gulin,Lindsay,Mets	R	19	10	4	0	3	47.1	182	36	11	9	4	0	1	1	13	0	48	2	1	6	0	1.000	0	0	1.71
Pittsfield	A	19	1	1	0	0	7	29	4	4	3	1	1	0	0	3	0	3	1	1	1	0	1.000	0	0	3.86
Gullard,Jack,Lethbridge	R	25	26	2	0	11	30	141	38	27	22	4	2	3	0	13	1	34	3	0	0	2	.000	0	1	6.60
Gunderson,Mike,Kissimmee	A	23	1	0	0	0	2.1	8	1	0	0	0	0	0	0	0	0	0	0	0	0	0	.000	0	0	0.00
Quad City	A	23	44	0	0	10	65.2	270	46	25	20	1	0	0	5	27	0	48	4	2	3	2	.600	0	1	2.74
Gunther,Kevin,Sou. Oregon	A	23	5	5	0	0	19	71	14	6	3	0	0	0	0	2	0	11	2	0	1	1	.500	0	0	1.42
W. Michigan	A	23	17	0	0	7	26.2	117	28	16	11	1	0	2	2	3	1	17	2	1	1	3	.250	0	2	3.71
Gutierrez,Alfredo,Brewers	R	20	7	0	0	4	8.1	44	10	9	6	0	0	1	2	8	0	7	1	0	0	0	.000	0	0	6.48
Gutierrez,Javier,Mariners	R	21	14	4	1	4	33.2	159	43	31	22	4	1	2	1	19	0	38	8	1	1	4	.200	0	0	5.88
Guzman,Domingo,Idaho Falls	R	21	27	0	0	23	25.2	127	25	22	19	2	3	1	1	25	1	33	6	3	2	1	.667	0	11	6.66
Guzman,Jonathan,Brewers	R	18	11	0	0	4	13	71	18	16	15	1	0	2	3	8	0	4	2	3	0	0	.000	0	0	10.38
Guzman,Jose,Cubs	R	33	2	0	0	0	6	24	5	1	1	1	0	0	0	0	0	3	0	0	0	0	.000	0	0	1.50
Hacen,Abraham,Orioles	R	25	13	8	0	2	46	201	34	21	13	2	1	3	4	32	0	37	3	1	2	3	.400	0	2	2.54
Hackett,Jason,High Desert	A	21	18	2	0	9	40	195	43	30	23	6	2	1	2	31	2	29	6	0	3	1	.750	0	1	5.18
Bluefield	R	21	13	6	0	4	50.2	226	45	28	17	3	1	1	3	28	2	54	13	1	3	1	.750	0	1	3.02
Hackman,Luther,Asheville	A	21	28	28	0	0	165	710	162	95	85	11	3	3	14	65	0	108	9	7	11	11	.500	0	0	4.64
Hagan,Danny,Winston-Sal	A	24	1	1	0	0	5	21	5	1	1	0	0	0	0	4	0	2	0	0	1	0	1.000	0	0	1.80
Halama,John,Quad City	A	24	55	0	0	26	62.1	241	48	16	14	7	2	1	3	22	1	56	1	0	1	2	.333	0	2	2.02
Hale,Chad,Michigan	A	24	42	0	0	14	69	280	68	27	19	4	2	5	2	13	1	49	3	0	6	3	.667	0	2	2.48
Hale,Shane,Frederick	A	27	6	2	0	0	14	69	21	18	17	1	1	3	1	6	2	6	1	0	0	0	.000	0	0	10.93
Orioles	R	27	2	2	0	0	7	32	6	2	1	0	0	0	0	4	0	6	0	0	0	0	.000	0	0	1.29
Hall,Billy,Quad City	A	22	36	0	0	20	50.1	199	29	18	12	3	0	0	2	18	0	36	3	1	4	2	.667	0	7	2.15
Hall,Yates,New Jersey	A	23	5	5	0	0	26.1	109	19	7	4	0	0	1	1	11	0	22	4	1	3	0	1.000	0	0	1.37
Peoria	A	23	9	8	0	0	45.2	197	45	25	23	4	0	1	0	24	0	47	5	0	2	5	.286	0	0	4.53
Halladay,Roy,Blue Jays	R	19	10	8	0	1	50.1	203	35	25	19	4	2	0	1	16	0	48	9	2	3	5	.375	0	0	3.40
Halley,Allen,Bristol	R	24	2	0	0	1	3	15	5	4	4	0	0	1	0	1	0	3	0	0	1	0	1.000	0	0	12.00
Hickory	A	24	13	9	0	2	60	234	46	21	17	6	1	0	2	12	2	58	2	1	2	1	.667	0	0	2.55
Halperin,Mike,Dunedin	A	22	14	12	0	0	69.2	298	70	36	28	4	1	0	3	29	1	63	2	0	3	5	.375	0	0	3.62
Hamada,Norihiro,Angels	R	22	1	0	0	0	0.2	4	1	1	1	0	0	0	0	1	0	2	0	0	0	0	.000	0	0	13.50
Hamilton,Paul,Piedmont	A	24	15	1	0	4	21	90	24	11	11	0	0	1	2	7	0	10	2	0	1	0	1.000	0	0	4.71
Batavia	A	24	14	13	1	0	83.2	348	73	30	24	2	3	0	5	23	0	62	10	1	7	2	.778	0	0	2.58
Hammack,Brandon,Williamsprt	A	23	27	0	0	17	32.1	151	32	20	15	3	2	1	2	14	1	40	2	2	1	5	.167	0	6	4.18
Hammerschmidt,Andy,Clinton	A	24	14	14	0	0	86	355	89	40	37	7	3	3	6	18	2	51	0	2	5	5	.500	0	0	3.87
Hammons,Matt,Cubs	R	19	10	8	0	1	46	186	35	14	12	1	1	3	2	16	0	32	2	1	3	1	.750	0	0	2.35
Hampton,Mark,Augusta	A	26	39	0	0	15	56.2	255	46	32	26	8	4	1	1	38	2	45	6	0	5	5	.500	0	0	4.13
Handy,Russell,Albany	A	21	30	5	0	6	71.2	340	78	50	34	4	3	6	3	37	1	57	14	1	2	7	.222	0	2	4.27
Hanson,Kris,Kinston	A	25	20	18	1	0	96.1	404	102	56	54	11	1	3	5	24	1	53	3	0	5	6	.455	0	0	5.04
Harper,Terry,Ogden	R	21	8	1	0	4	10.2	61	14	21	14	4	0	0	3	11	0	11	1	0	1	2	.333	0	0	11.81
Lethbridge	R	21	15	0	0	4	20.2	102	21	15	15	2	4	0	4	14	0	28	3	1	0	2	.000	0	0	6.53
Harris,D.J.,Dunedin	A	25	42	0	0	16	67	294	54	29	24	6	3	3	6	41	1	56	2	0	3	3	.500	0	2	3.22
Harris,Jeffrey,Elizabethtn	R	21	21	0	0	10	33	154	42	15	14	2	1	0	4	13	1	27	6	1	1	3	.250	0	0	3.82
Harrison,Scott,Burlington	R	18	5	5	0	0	16	81	22	19	16	3	2	2	1	13	0	13	1	0	1	0	.000	0	0	9.00
Hartgrove,Lyle,Sarasota	A	24	47	1	0	15	74.2	316	73	36	33	3	2	3	4	21	2	52	1	2	3	1	.750	0	2	3.98
Hartmann,Pete,Charlotte	A	25	15	2	0	9	35.2	180	46	34	29	7	4	2	0	26	0	30	3	4	2	4	.333	0	0	7.32
Stockton	A	25	12	0	0	5	14	61	9	7	7	1	1	0	0	11	0	9	1	1	2	0	1.000	0	1	4.50
Hartmann,Rich,St. Pete	A	23	13	0	0	7	16.1	65	13	5	3	2	0	0	0	3	0	12	3	0	0	0	.000	0	0	1.65
Savannah	A	23	31	0	0	10	41	182	35	26	23	8	2	1	3	20	2	52	3	0	1	2	.333	0	0	5.05
Hartnett,Bill,Kissimmee	A	25	32	2	0	7	74	346	87	52	33	3	2	4	4	32	1	61	6	1	1	1	.500	0	2	4.01

1995 Pitching -- Single-A and Rookie Leagues

Player	Lg	A	G	GS	CG	GF	IP	BFP	H	R	ER	HR	SH	SF	HB	TBB	IBB	SO	WP	Bk	W	L	Pct.	ShO	Sv	ERA
Hartshorn,Ty,Hagerstown	A	21	12	7	0	1	48.2	224	59	37	29	8	1	1	5	20	0	28	6	0	3	4	.429	0	0	5.36
St. Cathrns	A	21	13	13	1	0	69.2	307	83	45	33	6	3	1	3	25	0	25	6	1	3	4	.429	1	0	4.26
Hartvigson,Chad,San Jose	A	25	32	7	0	8	84	357	85	38	33	4	6	3	0	24	1	63	3	1	4	4	.500	0	4	3.54
Hartzog,Cullen,Lynchburg	A	26	43	1	0	17	59.1	254	49	23	22	5	1	1	2	30	2	45	8	0	6	4	.600	0	4	3.34
Harvell,Pete,Winston-Sal	A	24	4	0	0	1	5	28	9	7	7	1	0	1	0	4	0	1	1	0	0	1	.000	0	0	12.60
Charlstn-Wv	A	24	27	0	0	9	27.2	114	25	11	9	2	1	1	3	10	1	17	5	0	0	0	.000	0	0	2.93
Harvey,Terry,Watertown	A	23	8	8	0	0	54.1	205	36	13	11	1	0	3	1	6	1	33	0	0	6	2	.750	0	0	1.82
Hasselhoff,Derek,Bristol	R	22	12	11	0	1	66.1	281	66	32	27	4	1	1	2	14	0	46	2	2	7	3	.700	0	0	3.66
Hause,Brendan,W. Michigan	A	21	31	18	0	4	137.1	595	136	75	59	10	5	5	4	57	0	106	6	0	8	7	.533	0	0	3.87
Hausmann,Isaac,Charlstn-Sc	A	20	5	0	0	4	6.2	35	10	10	7	2	1	0	2	1	0	6	0	1	0	0	.000	0	0	9.45
Rangers	R	20	18	0	0	15	30.1	128	23	11	9	0	1	1	2	9	0	23	0	0	1	2	.333	0	6	2.67
Heathcott,Mike,Pr. William	A	27	27	14	1	4	88.2	387	96	56	46	8	2	7	2	36	3	68	18	0	4	9	.308	0	3	4.67
Hebbert,Allan,Kane County	A	23	5	2	0	2	8	46	9	12	11	1	0	1	2	15	0	3	2	0	0	1	.000	0	0	12.38
Heiserman,Rick,Kinston	A	23	19	19	1	0	113	470	97	55	47	13	3	4	9	42	1	86	6	1	9	3	.750	0	0	3.74
St. Pete	A	23	6	5	0	1	28	118	28	18	17	2	0	2	1	11	0	18	4	0	2	3	.400	0	0	5.46
Helvey,Rob,New Jersey	A	24	11	0	0	8	12.1	45	7	1	1	0	1	1	0	5	0	15	0	0	2	1	.667	0	2	0.73
Savannah	A	24	18	0	0	7	20.1	107	28	22	18	1	2	0	3	16	0	25	5	0	2	1	.667	0	1	7.97
Henderson,Kenny,Padres	R	23	3	1	0	0	7.2	40	12	8	7	0	0	0	1	6	0	12	1	3	0	1	.000	0	0	8.22
Idaho Falls	A	23	4	4	0	0	20	93	19	6	5	0	0	1	3	9	0	16	4	1	3	0	1.000	0	0	2.25
Henderson,Ryan,Vero Beach	A	26	39	6	0	10	104.1	453	98	53	45	1	6	1	5	58	3	86	9	2	11	5	.688	0	2	3.88
Henrikson,Dan,San Jose	A	27	7	0	0	7	32		8	6	6	0	0	0	0	4	0	6	0	0	0	5	.000	0	0	7.71
Henriquez,Oscar,Kissimmee	A	22	20	0	0	7	44.2	207	40	29	25	2	2	2	6	30	0	36	3	0	3	4	.429	0	1	5.04
Herbert,Russell,Hickory	A	24	18	18	1	0	114.2	474	83	48	34	9	3	3	8	46	0	115	5	2	3	8	.273	1	0	2.67
South Bend	A	24	9	9	0	0	53.2	224	46	25	21	3	1	0	3	27	0	48	1	2	2	4	.333	0	0	3.52
Herbison,Brett,Mets	R	19	9	9	0	0	41	170	31	13	10	3	1	2	0	16	0	31	4	0	3	0	1.000	0	0	2.20
Kingsport	R	19	1	1	0	0	5	23	6	4	4	2	1	0	0	2	0	4	1	0	1	0	1.000	0	0	7.20
Heredia,Felix,Brevard Cty	A	20	34	8	0	3	95.2	420	101	52	38	6	0	7	4	36	1	76	6	1	6	4	.600	0	1	3.57
Hermanson,Mike,Rancho Cuca	A	24	42	0	0	13	74.2	352	69	52	47	4	1	5	11	49	2	74	8	2	4	6	.400	0	0	5.67
Hernandez,Elvin,Erie	A	18	14	14	2	0	90.1	377	82	40	29	8	5	3	4	22	0	54	2	1	6	1	.857	1	0	2.89
Hernandez,Francis,Orioles	R	19	24	0	0	20	27.1	105	18	4	4	1	0	1	1	6	0	23	2	1	2	2	.500	0	11	1.32
Frederick	A	19	3	0	0	3	3	15	3	2	2	1	0	1	0	3	0	3	0	0	0	1	.000	0	1	6.00
Hernandez,Santos,Burlington	A	23	44	0	0	28	64.1	274	54	27	19	3	4	4	2	20	2	85	1	0	5	8	.385	0	9	2.66
Herr,David,Vermont	A	22	18	7	0	4	55	229	53	26	23	0	1	2	4	18	1	35	5	0	6	3	.667	0	1	3.76
Herrera,Ivan,Bellingham	A	19	1	0	0	0	2	7	0	0	0	0	0	0	0	1	0	1	0	0	0	0	.000	0	0	0.00
Herrmann,Gary,Clearwater	A	26	42	3	0	10	70	295	64	31	28	3	3	3	0	28	1	56	1	0	7	2	.778	0	3	3.60
Hibbard,Billy,Hagerstown	A	20	16	0	0	5	34.2	149	42	16	15	1	0	1	1	6	1	20	2	0	2	1	.667	0	0	3.89
Medicne Hat	R	20	4	3	0	0	17.2	70	14	8	7	1	0	1	0	4	0	15	0	0	1	1	.500	0	0	3.57
Hill,Jason,Cedar Rapds	A	24	48	0	0	17	59.1	276	59	38	30	4	8	1	5	41	6	49	2	1	2	1	.667	0	2	4.55
Hill,Shawn,Daytona	A	26	37	0	0	22	58.2	241	48	31	24	6	1	0	2	17	3	71	0	1	5	3	.625	0	3	3.68
Hill,Ty,Brewers	R	24	4	4	0	0	11.1		8	4	4	0	0	0	0	5	0	9	1	0	0	0	.000	0	0	3.18
Hilton,Willy,Sou. Oregon	A	23	16	1	0	6	30.2	143	37	22	15	1	3	2	0	12	1	31	4	1	1	4	.200	0	0	4.40
Hinchliffe,Brett,Riverside	A	21	15	15	0	0	77.2	373	110	69	57	10	5	3	8	35	3	68	4	0	3	8	.273	0	0	6.61
Hindy,Mark,Ogden	R	22	24	6	0	5	70.1	327	89	52	37	5	1	3	0	24	0	44	4	2	2	3	.400	0	1	4.73
Hinson,Dean,Visalia	A	24	23	0	0	14	34.1	150	30	18	15	1	3	0	4	16	0	35	9	2	1	1	.500	0	3	3.93
Lk Elsinore	A	24	5	0	0	4	6.2	36	8	9	4	1	0	1	1	6	0	4	1	0	0	0	.000	0	0	5.40
Hmielewski,Chris,W. Palm Bch	A	25	36	2	0	15	57.2	259	57	31	23	4	3	2	2	28	4	41	6	0	1	3	.250	0	1	3.59
Hoalton,Brandon,Huntington	R	22	6	6	0	0	28.2	127	31	23	17	4	1	1	2	11	0	26	5	0	1	3	.250	0	0	5.34
Hodge,Hal,Spokane	A	23	16	15	0	0	69.2	308	81	39	33	5	2	6	7	20	0	45	3	2	3	1	.750	0	0	4.26
Hodges,Kevin,Wilmington	A	23	12	10	0	1	53.2	232	53	31	27	1	1	1	2	25	1	27	4	0	2	3	.400	0	0	4.53
Hokanson,Don,Lethbridge	R	23	8	0	0	1	14.2	81	32	21	13	0	0	0	1	7	0	7	1	0	0	0	.000	0	0	7.98
Holden,Jason,Sou. Oregon	A	22	19	8	0	0	61	290	64	42	32	2	4	4	17	23	0	30	10	4	2	6	.250	0	0	4.72
Holding,Brook,Butte	R	23	27	0	0	10	42	191	36	26	24	1	2	2	0	33	1	49	6	1	4	3	.571	0	3	5.14
Hollis,Ron,Vero Beach	A	22	43	0	0	13	79	306	55	22	20	1	3	2	2	38	6	56	1	0	2	5	.286	0	2	2.47
Holobinko,Mike,Cubs	R	19	8	1	0	3	20.2	86	16	8	4	1	1	2	0	8	0	11	1	0	3	2	.600	0	0	1.74
Holtz,Mike,Lk Elsinore	A	23	56	0	0	19	82.2	341	70	26	21	7	5	4	5	23	3	101	2	0	4	4	.500	0	3	2.29
Hommel,Brian,Helena	R	23	15	0	0	8	20	86	7	3	1	0	2	0	4	14	0	32	2	1	2	0	1.000	0	2	0.45
Hook,Jeff,Astros	R	21	2	0	0	0	6	24	4	0	0	0	0	0	0	2	0	4	0	0	1	0	1.000	0	0	0.00
Horn,Keith,Watertown	A	22	8	8	0	0	44	180	39	18	14	4	0	1	0	12	0	36	0	2	2	2	.600	0	0	2.86
Horton,Aaron,Yankees	R	21	8	6	0	0	23	93	17	7	4	0	0	1	5	6	0	21	3	1	2	1	.667	0	0	1.57
Oneonta	A	21	6	3	0	1	22.1	96	19	13	8	2	0	0	3	4	0	12	0	1	0	2	.000	0	0	3.22
Horton,Eric,St. Cathrns	A	25	21	7	0	9	69.2	276	50	28	22	4	1	3	3	26	0	51	4	2	6	2	.750	0	3	2.84
Housely,Adam,Lakeland	A	24	19	1	0	3	30	141	39	23	20	0	1	0	3	11	0	23	1	0	0	1	.000	0	0	6.00
Fayettevlle	A	24	19	0	0	6	38	156	26	14	10	0	0	1	1	11	1	43	1	0	3	1	.750	0	1	2.37
Howard,Tom,Elmira	A	20	10	0	0	5	13.1	69	9	13	11	0	0	1	0	21	0	7	6	0	0	0	.000	0	0	7.43
Howatt,Jeffrey,Pittsfield	A	22	17	0	0	5	39	167	37	22	18	2	1	3	0	15	0	26	3	3	1	2	.333	0	0	4.15
Hower,Dan,Charlstn-Sc	A	23	22	17	0	3	82.2	404	96	88	67	5	4	3	5	59	1	55	13	0	4	7	.364	0	0	7.29
Howry,Bob,San Jose	A	22	27	25	1	1	165.1	695	171	79	65	6	12	4	8	54	0	107	7	3	12	10	.545	0	0	3.54
Hoy,Wayne,St. Cathrns	A	25	24	1	0	9	57	228	39	20	14	0	1	0	3	23	0	34	5	1	5	3	.625	0	3	2.21
Hritz,Derrick,Watertown	A	23	18	0	0	10	30	130	28	9	7	0	2	1	1	16	2	23	4	1	0	1	.000	0	1	2.10
Huber,Aaron,Modesto	A	23	4	0	0	1	5.1	27	7	3	0	0	0	0	0	3	0	5	0	0	0	0	.000	0	0	0.00
Huffman,Jeff,Sarasota	A	24	15	11	0	1	76.2	335	72	43	39	3	3	1	4	36	1	55	8	1	4	4	.500	0	0	4.58
Humphry,Trevor,Piedmont	A	24	28	20	2	4	119.1	532	122	67	48	7	2	4	6	63	0	102	13	0	5	7	.417	0	0	3.62
Hundley,Chanin,White Sox	R	22	3	0	0	0	4.1	22	7	5	4	1	0	3	0	2	0	2	0	0	0	0	.000	0	0	8.31
Hunt,Jon,Bristol	R	22	13	13	0	0	58.1	262	52	39	29	2	1	0	3	34	0	54	11	1	2	4	.333	0	0	4.47
Huntsman,Brandon,Orioles	R	20	13	12	1	0	65.1	286	53	38	28	4	2	2	3	33	0	64	4	0	6	3	.667	0	0	3.86
Huntsman,Scott,Beloit	A	23	43	0	0	14	49.2	229	42	17	15	3	2	1	5	34	2	49	5	0	4	3	.571	0	1	2.72
Hurst,Bill,Brevard Cty	A	26	39	4	0	29	50.2	228	33	20	17	1	3	1	8	41	4	35	4	0	1	4	.200	0	12	3.02

1995 Pitching -- Single-A and Rookie Leagues

			HOW MUCH HE PITCHED						WHAT HE GAVE UP												THE RESULTS					
Player	Lg	A	G	GS	CG	GF	IP	BFP	H	R	ER	HR	SH	SF	HB	TBB	IBB	SO	WP	Bk	W	L	Pct.	ShO	Sv	ERA
Hurtado,Victor,Marlins	R	19	7	7	1	0	33.1	134	14	5	3	0	2	1	2	16	0	28	2	0	3	1	.750	0	0	0.81
Hutzler,Jeff,Bellingham	A	23	7	7	0	0	31.1	130	35	9	6	0	1	0	3	8	0	19	2	2	2	2	.500	0	0	1.72
Burlington	A	23	9	9	0	0	51.2	223	51	34	20	4	3	2	2	17	1	44	4	1	3	5	.375	0	0	3.48
Iddon,Brent,Everett	A	20	14	14	1	0	74.1	326	86	49	36	8	1	0	6	25	0	67	3	0	3	5	.375	0	0	4.36
Idemoto,Kenichiro,Visalia	A	22	31	8	2	5	101	428	104	54	46	11	4	2	4	27	0	83	1	0	5	6	.455	0	2	4.10
Iglesias,Mike,Bakersfield	A	23	24	23	2	0	143.2	586	124	65	52	11	5	3	11	38	0	108	7	0	7	10	.412	1	0	3.26
San Bernrdo	A	23	4	3	0	0	15	74	26	14	11	1	0	0	2	2	0	12	3	0	1	2	.333	0	0	6.60
Ippolito,Robby,Riverside	A	23	35	0	0	11	60	272	59	41	28	4	4	1	6	31	2	43	8	0	1	3	.250	0	1	4.20
Irvine,Mike,Idaho Falls	R	22	28	0	0	9	52.1	238	59	40	34	6	1	2	3	28	1	52	6	0	2	1	.667	0	0	5.85
Ishee,Gabe,Brewers	R	21	15	12	1	1	79.1	344	78	41	32	0	1	6	5	41	1	90	12	2	9	2	.818	0	0	3.63
Isom,Jeff,Rancho Cuca	A	23	4	0	0	3	4	21	6	4	1	1	0	1	1	0	0	2	0	0	1	0	1.000	0	0	9.00
Clinton	A	23	35	15	2	8	116.1	501	123	56	44	7	7	5	6	42	5	94	5	1	8	8	.500	1	2	3.40
Izquierdo,Hansel,Marlins	R	19	1	0	0	0	2	10	3	3	0	0	1	0	0	2	0	1	0	0	0	0	.000	0	0	0.00
Jacob,Russell,Mariners	R	21	12	11	0	1	56.1	248	47	29	18	0	0	1	3	31	0	54	6	2	6	2	.750	0	0	2.88
Jacobs,Mike,Utica	A	23	13	13	2	0	86.1	371	83	35	26	1	2	0	1	37	2	51	1	0	8	3	.727	1	0	2.71
Jacobs,Ryan,Durham	A	22	29	25	1	3	148.2	640	145	72	58	12	6	5	3	57	3	99	10	0	11	6	.647	0	0	3.51
Jacobsen,Joe,Vero Beach	A	24	47	0	0	44	49	215	42	22	20	2	5	2	2	23	2	54	10	1	1	3	.250	0	32	3.67
San Bernrdo	A	24	4	0	0	3	3.2	17	4	2	0	0	0	0	0	2	0	5	1	0	0	0	.000	0	2	0.00
Jacobson,K.J.,Fayettevlle	A	25	25	12	0	5	68	317	72	52	44	3	2	3	6	44	1	64	9	2	5	7	.417	0	0	5.82
Jaime,Jorge,Ogden	R	25	10	0	0	6	16.2	74	22	8	8	1	1	0	1	4	0	12	1	0	0	0	.000	0	1	4.32
James,Jhon,Medicne Hat	R	21	2	0	0	1	1	8	2	2	2	1	0	0	0	3	0	1	1	0	0	0	.000	0	0	18.00
Jarvis,Jason,Greensboro	A	22	22	16	0	2	110.2	468	103	47	37	5	4	5	1	38	3	82	13	1	8	7	.533	0	0	3.01
Hagerstown	A	22	8	8	0	0	50	210	49	27	20	3	2	4	3	13	1	42	7	1	4	3	.571	0	0	3.60
Jaye,Jamie,Bakersfield	A	23	5	5	0	0	26.2	118	30	16	13	1	1	0	1	10	0	22	3	3	1	2	.333	0	0	4.39
Jenkins,A.J.,Clinton	A	24	33	13	2	5	91.1	437	109	80	67	10	3	6	5	55	5	54	10	0	1	12	.077	0	0	6.60
Jenkins,Scott,Lethbridge	R	23	15	6	0	4	47	239	56	49	34	8	0	2	7	40	0	43	9	1	1	3	.250	0	0	6.51
Jenkins,Jonathan,Visalia	A	28	33	1	0	22	47	223	43	34	29	3	2	5	5	38	0	38	5	1	1	1	.500	0	0	5.55
Jerzembeck,Mike,Tampa	A	24	2	0	0	0	3	17	5	4	3	1	0	0	0	2	0	1	1	0	0	1	.000	0	0	9.00
Jesperson,Bob,Winston-Sal	A	27	5	0	0	4	6.1	26	5	3	3	0	0	0	0	4	1	1	0	0	2	1	.667	0	1	4.26
Jimenez,Jhonny,Mariners	R	20	19	0	0	6	32	146	39	23	16	1	0	3	2	14	0	28	2	4	1	2	.333	0	0	4.50
Jimenez,Jose,Johnson Cty	R	22	14	14	1	0	90.1	380	81	48	35	3	3	1	5	25	0	85	7	1	5	7	.417	1	0	3.49
Johnson,Jason,Augusta	A	22	11	11	1	0	53.2	233	57	32	26	2	2	1	4	17	0	42	3	0	3	5	.375	0	0	4.36
Lynchburg	A	22	10	10	0	0	55	236	58	37	30	9	0	3	2	20	0	41	2	0	1	4	.200	0	0	4.91
Johnson,Joaquin,Braves	R	19	11	2	0	6	27	125	25	17	15	2	2	3	1	16	0	15	8	1	0	0	.000	0	0	5.00
Johnson,Jonathan,Charlotte	A	21	8	7	1	1	43.1	178	34	14	13	2	2	0	1	16	0	25	3	3	1	5	.167	0	0	2.70
Johnson,Mike,Blue Jays	R	20	3	3	0	0	15	74	20	15	12	1	0	0	3	8	0	13	7	0	0	2	.000	0	0	7.20
Medicne Hat	R	20	19	0	0	7	49	217	46	26	21	2	2	2	0	25	1	32	6	0	4	1	.800	0	3	3.86
Johnson,Ron,Peoria	A	24	22	19	0	0	102.1	449	105	56	36	9	4	4	4	36	0	61	1	0	5	7	.417	0	0	3.17
Johnson,Scott,Elmira	A	21	4	0	0	1	8.1	37	10	4	4	0	0	0	1	1	0	4	0	0	0	0	.000	0	0	4.32
Butte	R	21	20	0	0	4	39.2	191	59	31	29	2	0	2	0	11	1	31	2	4	0	2	.000	0	0	6.58
Johnson,Shelby,Mariners	R	22	9	0	0	3	17	82	24	16	10	0	1	1	2	9	0	14	2	0	1	1	.500	0	0	5.29
Johnston,Sean,Columbia	A	20	23	22	2	0	148.1	621	132	60	50	6	4	4	11	63	2	105	15	1	11	6	.647	0	0	3.03
Jolliffe,Brian,Braves	R	21	11	0	0	5	23	112	36	24	17	0	0	2	3	9	0	15	6	3	0	2	.000	0	1	6.65
Jones,Matt,Butte	R	24	21	0	0	9	35	181	54	40	31	4	0	3	2	17	1	30	2	2	0	1	.000	0	0	7.97
Jones,Scott,Utica	A	23	20	0	0	20	20	78	11	3	3	0	3	1	2	9	1	26	3	0	0	1	.000	0	13	1.35
Michigan	A	23	5	0	0	3	6.1	31	3	5	4	2	0	0	0	8	0	13	2	0	2	0	1.000	0	0	5.68
Jordan,Jason,Lakeland	A	23	4	4	0	0	19.2	94	32	20	13	1	0	4	1	7	0	8	1	0	1	3	.250	0	0	5.95
Fayettevlle	A	23	24	24	0	0	138	575	128	48	35	5	0	3	8	43	0	103	13	1	10	4	.714	0	0	2.28
Judd,Mike,Yankees	R	21	21	0	0	18	32.1	123	18	5	4	0	0	0	4	6	0	30	4	0	1	1	.500	0	8	1.11
Greensboro	A	21	1	0	0	1	2.2	11	2	2	0	0	0	0	0	2	0	2	1	0	0	0	.000	0	0	0.00
Judice,Bryan,Lethbridge	R	23	7	0	0	7	6	27	5	4	2	0	1	1	0	3	0	8	0	0	1	1	.500	0	3	3.00
Spokane	A	23	14	0	0	4	19.1	101	29	18	17	0	1	1	4	10	2	14	4	0	0	1	.000	0	1	7.91
Justiniano,Rene,Butte	R	22	12	12	0	0	60	285	86	58	50	7	0	5	1	26	1	40	3	7	0	8	.000	0	0	7.50
Kahlon,Harbrinder,Hudson Vall	A	23	30	0	0	16	54.1	220	35	16	14	3	5	0	1	21	5	76	10	1	5	5	.500	0	3	2.32
Kammerer,James,Rockies	R	22	6	0	0	5	9.1	43	11	5	1	0	0	0	0	3	0	14	1	0	1	0	1.000	0	0	0.96
Portland	A	22	11	5	0	0	35.1	135	24	8	6	0	1	1	0	11	0	17	1	0	2	1	.667	0	0	1.53
Karns,Tim,High Desert	A	24	7	0	0	2	15.1	67	10	6	1	0	0	0	0	9	0	9	2	0	1	0	1.000	0	0	0.59
Karvala,Kyle,Piedmont	A	25	20	0	0	10	18.1	75	13	9	7	0	0	2	0	7	0	17	1	0	5	1	.833	0	2	3.44
Kast,Nick,New Jersey	A	23	29	0	0	7	45.2	188	29	11	7	0	1	2	7	21	1	64	3	4	5	1	.833	0	0	1.38
Kauflin,Dave,Tigers	R	20	5	3	0	0	16.2	69	11	11	9	0	0	1	0	7	0	13	4	0	2	1	.667	0	0	4.86
Kawabata,Kyle,Batavia	A	22	18	0	0	4	32.2	140	34	16	13	3	2	1	3	5	1	30	2	1	1	0	1.000	0	0	3.58
Kaye,Justin,Mariners	R	20	12	0	0	4	19.1	111	33	28	23	1	0	2	1	19	0	13	4	0	0	1	.000	0	0	10.71
Kaysner,Brent,Spokane	A	22	19	0	0	11	34.2	147	15	7	6	1	1	0	7	24	0	37	4	0	0	0	.000	0	4	1.56
Kazama,Yuhito,Ogden	R	21	6	1	0	1	8.1	48	16	17	13	4	0	0	2	8	0	4	2	0	0	1	.000	0	0	14.04
Kazmirski,Robert,Athletics	R	24	28	0	0	25	38	155	36	13	9	0	0	1	1	6	2	32	2	1	1	0	1.000	0	10	2.13
Keehn,Drew,Portland	A	21	20	0	0	6	42.2	182	38	22	18	3	4	1	1	17	1	30	1	1	2	4	.333	0	0	3.80
Keith,Jeff,Burlington	A	24	47	0	0	38	66.1	275	35	26	22	1	4	3	6	42	4	74	6	0	1	3	.250	0	23	2.98
Kell,Rob,Charlstn-Sc	A	25	7	7	0	0	44	184	38	20	17	2	3	1	2	9	0	47	3	0	1	4	.200	0	0	3.48
Charlotte	A	25	11	0	0	5	20.2	93	16	9	7	1	0	0	2	15	0	21	2	0	1	0	1.000	0	1	3.05
Kelley,Jason,Cubs	R	21	7	5	0	1	25.2	110	10	11	2	0	0	0	2	19	0	20	2	2	1	1	.500	0	0	0.70
Williamsprt	A	20	3	3	0	0	16.2	70	14	3	3	0	0	0	1	7	0	17	1	1	1	1	.500	0	0	1.62
Kelly,Jeff,Augusta	A	21	26	26	0	0	142.2	608	134	68	55	8	6	5	4	51	0	114	12	0	6	11	.353	0	0	3.47
Kelly,John,Columbia	A	23	28	28	3	0	167	691	148	80	72	16	5	2	10	65	0	124	11	2	8	8	.500	0	0	3.88
Kenady,Jason,Bakersfield	A	22	23	16	0	1	87	419	107	76	65	7	1	3	3	68	0	69	10	1	4	10	.286	0	0	6.72
Kendrick,Scott,Williamsprt	A	20	5	5	0	0	27	117	26	14	10	2	1	2	3	8	0	15	3	0	1	2	.667	0	0	3.33
Kenny,Sean,St. Lucie	A	23	46	0	0	15	56.2	229	51	22	17	1	4	1	3	15	1	26	2	2	4	9	.308	0	2	2.70
Keppen,Jeffrey,Yakima	A	22	20	3	0	6	41.1	210	46	35	26	1	1	5	6	32	0	32	7	1	2	2	.500	0	0	5.66

1995 Pitching -- Single-A and Rookie Leagues

Player	Lg	A	G	GS	CG	GF	IP	BFP	H	R	ER	HR	SH	SF	HB	TBB	IBB	SO	WP	Bk	W	L	Pct.	ShO	Sv	ERA
Kershner,Jason,Martinsvlle	R	19	13	13	0	0	63	278	67	42	36	10	0	2	5	29	0	64	6	0	4	2	.667	0	0	5.14
Kessel,Kyle,Mets	R	20	7	7	0	0	40	160	29	12	8	1	1	1	2	11	0	47	3	0	3	0	1.000	0	0	1.80
Kingsport	R	20	5	5	0	0	30	134	33	11	6	1	0	0	4	10	1	23	0	0	4	0	1.000	0	0	1.80
Kester,Tim,Quad City	A	24	28	23	2	3	160.2	665	158	80	53	8	5	6	10	20	1	111	4	0	12	5	.706	0	0	2.97
Key,Bubba,Royals	R	19	16	0	0	11	28	118	17	13	8	0	4	0	4	12	1	34	3	1	1	2	.333	0	2	2.57
Khoury,Tony,Rockford	A	25	28	1	0	13	45	213	49	37	23	4	2	2	5	26	1	38	6	0	2	2	.500	0	0	4.60
Daytona	A	25	7	0	0	5	6.2	30	10	3	3	1	0	1	0	2	0	4	0	0	2	0	1.000	0	0	4.05
King,Curt,St. Pete	A	25	28	21	3	1	136	567	117	49	39	3	4	2	11	49	2	65	6	0	7	8	.467	0	0	2.58
King,Matt,Johnson Cty	R	20	1	0	0	0	0.2	8	2	5	5	0	0	0	0	4	0	2	1	0	0	0	.000	0	0	67.50
King,Raymond,Billings	R	22	28	0	0	15	43	169	31	11	8	1	2	0	0	15	3	43	1	1	3	0	1.000	0	5	1.67
King,Bill,W.Michigan	A	23	30	18	0	3	148.1	633	152	75	55	6	5	1	5	41	0	95	6	5	9	7	.563	0	2	3.34
Kinney,Matt,Red Sox	R	19	8	2	0	4	27.2	119	29	13	9	0	1	2	2	10	0	11	5	0	1	3	.250	0	2	2.93
Kirkman,Casey,Lethbridge	R	23	15	15	1	0	95	404	94	56	48	4	2	4	3	39	0	91	3	1	5	6	.455	0	0	4.55
Kitchen,Ron,Frederick	A	24	30	0	0	11	37.1	179	55	35	30	6	3	2	1	10	3	10	1	1	2	2	.500	0	0	7.23
Kjos,Ryan,Athletics	R	23	3	0	0	0	3.2	23	9	10	8	1	0	0	1	1	0	5	0	0	0	0	.000	0	0	19.64
Sou. Oregon	A	23	9	0	0	4	11	47	9	4	3	2	0	0	0	5	0	16	2	0	2	0	1.000	0	2	2.45
Kline,Jason,Ogden	R	23	25	6	0	10	58	273	80	45	35	7	2	4	3	25	1	37	2	1	3	4	.429	0	2	5.43
Knickerbocker,Tom,Athletics	R	20	17	7	0	1	43.2	193	39	27	19	0	0	0	5	25	0	40	7	0	4	3	.571	0	1	3.92
Knieper,Aaron,W. Palm Bch	A	24	32	6	0	10	70.2	317	67	38	31	0	3	4	4	46	2	48	12	4	2	4	.333	0	0	3.95
Knight,Brandon,Rangers	R	20	3	2	0	0	12	54	12	7	7	0	0	0	0	6	0	11	2	0	1	1	.500	0	0	5.25
Charlstn-Sc	A	20	9	9	0	0	54.2	218	37	22	19	5	0	4	0	21	0	52	4	1	4	2	.667	0	0	3.13
Knighton,Toure,Charlstn-Sc	A	20	22	19	1	1	107	482	121	64	58	5	2	3	8	46	0	100	8	1	1	9	.100	0	0	4.88
Knoll,Brian,Bellingham	A	22	22	2	0	5	57	232	44	22	13	1	4	1	3	17	0	35	2	1	5	2	.714	0	0	2.05
Knoll,Randy,Martinsvlle	R	19	6	6	0	0	17.1	83	21	18	17	1	0	1	2	9	0	22	7	0	0	3	.000	0	0	8.83
Knowland,Sammy,Danville	R	23	20	0	0	5	34.2	155	37	23	11	3	3	4	2	10	1	21	2	3	4	2	.667	0	1	2.86
Knox,Jeff,Cedar Rapids	A	23	25	17	0	1	108	481	125	69	59	4	4	3	13	24	0	56	6	6	7	6	.538	0	0	4.92
Koehler,P.K.,Eugene	A	22	2	2	0	0	4	27	4	10	10	1	0	0	1	12	0	5	0	1	0	2	.000	0	0	22.50
Danville	R	22	11	6	0	2	40.2	178	39	25	14	2	1	2	1	16	0	46	3	1	2	1	.667	0	1	3.10
Koenig,Matt,Pittsfield	A	23	15	12	0	1	78	334	81	47	37	6	1	1	3	23	0	43	6	0	4	5	.444	0	0	4.27
Kolb,Brandon,Idaho Falls	R	22	9	8	0	0	38.1	181	42	33	30	1	2	2	2	29	0	21	5	0	2	3	.400	0	0	7.04
Padres	R	22	4	4	1	0	23	100	13	10	3	0	0	0	3	13	0	21	4	0	1	1	.500	1	0	1.17
Kolb,Danny,Rangers	R	21	12	11	0	0	53	219	38	22	13	0	0	2	3	28	0	46	8	2	1	7	.125	0	0	2.21
Koppe,Clint,Charlstn-Wv	A	22	30	22	2	1	157.2	653	144	66	59	10	4	5	6	47	5	119	8	1	7	13	.350	0	0	3.37
Kosek,Kory,Martinsvlle	R	23	9	0	0	7	19	69	10	5	5	1	0	0	0	4	0	17	0	0	1	0	1.000	0	2	2.37
Piedmont	A	23	15	0	0	7	20.1	83	13	8	0	1	2	0	3	5	2	24	0	0	2	0	.333	0	3	0.00
Kostich,Bill,Lakeland	A	25	4	0	0	2	6	21	2	0	0	0	1	0	1	2	0	2	0	0	1	0	1.000	0	0	0.00
Kown,John,Johnson Cty	R	23	16	4	1	1	51	220	41	31	15	2	2	0	2	18	1	42	6	4	2	2	.500	0	0	2.65
Kramer,Dan,Sarasota	A	25	21	0	0	4	14.2	69	18	12	10	1	0	2	0	7	0	13	1	2	2	1	1.000	0	0	6.14
Kramer,Jeff,Stockton	A	22	32	24	0	2	149	662	174	87	74	9	8	4	12	58	0	108	9	6	12	7	.632	0	1	4.47
Kramer,Scott,Columbus	A	22	19	1	0	6	52	213	45	19	12	3	0	0	6	14	1	53	4	0	2	2	.500	0	0	2.08
Kraus,Timothy,Bristol	R	23	5	0	0	0	7.2	33	3	3	2	0	1	1	0	7	0	9	3	1	0	1	.000	0	1	2.35
Krause,Kevin,Rockford	A	22	30	13	0	5	99.1	431	96	53	42	7	2	1	5	41	0	58	10	1	6	7	.462	0	0	3.81
Krueger,Robert,Wisconsin	A	19	0	0	0	5	22	99	21	12	11	0	0	0	2	11	0	20	4	0	0	0	.000	0	0	4.50
Kruse,Kelly,White Sox	R	24	3	0	0	2	4	17	4	2	2	0	0	0	1	1	0	2	0	1	1	0	1.000	0	0	4.50
Bristol	R	24	15	0	0	8	19	107	33	22	26	5	2	0	4	16	0	21	2	2	0	1	.000	0	0	12.32
Kummerfeldt,Jason,Winston-Sal	A	26	37	3	0	14	77.2	326	78	37	30	7	1	1	7	19	5	51	1	0	4	6	.400	0	3	3.48
Kurtz,Danny,Everett	A	22	14	12	1	1	69.1	293	60	27	24	6	1	2	6	32	1	43	4	2	5	2	.714	0	0	3.12
Kusiewicz,Mike,Salem	A	19	1	1	0	0	6	26	7	1	1	0	0	0	2	0	0	7	0	1	0	0	.000	0	0	1.50
Asheville	A	19	21	21	0	0	122.1	484	92	40	28	6	2	0	6	34	0	103	9	1	8	4	.667	0	0	2.06
Kyslinger,Dan,Stockton	A	24	37	0	0	11	52.2	253	58	24	21	2	4	2	2	37	1	44	6	2	4	1	.800	0	1	3.59
Lacey,James,Expos	R	20	12	1	0	6	22.2	120	35	29	21	2	0	4	0	14	0	10	3	2	1	1	.500	0	0	8.34
Lachappa,Matt,Rancho Cuca	A	21	28	28	1	0	153.2	691	163	103	95	17	1	3	10	88	2	106	15	2	11	7	.611	0	0	5.56
LaGarde,Joseph,San Bernrdo	A	21	24	24	0	0	123.1	557	135	83	63	9	4	7	9	68	0	102	10	1	5	10	.333	0	0	4.60
Bakersfield	A	21	4	4	0	0	21.2	98	19	8	7	1	0	0	0	13	0	25	5	0	1	0	.500	0	0	2.91
Lail,Jerry,Oneonta	A	21	13	13	0	0	68	309	66	38	30	3	1	4	5	31	0	59	1	0	5	6	.455	0	0	3.97
Lake,Kevin,Burlington	A	23	28	21	0	2	119.1	544	136	75	59	10	2	3	6	61	3	85	9	0	10	7	.588	0	0	4.45
Lakman,Jason,White Sox	R	19	9	5	0	1	41.1	181	44	17	15	2	0	2	5	12	0	23	2	0	3	0	1.000	0	0	3.27
Lankford,Frank,Tampa	A	25	55	0	0	36	73	305	64	29	21	0	7	0	2	22	6	58	1	0	4	6	.400	0	15	2.59
Lapka,Rick,Billings	R	24	14	14	0	0	79	334	66	36	33	2	2	2	6	43	3	46	7	2	8	4	.667	0	0	3.76
LaPlante,Michel,Pirates	R	26	2	0	0	2	3	12	1	0	0	0	0	0	0	0	0	4	0	0	0	0	.000	0	1	0.00
Lynchburg	A	26	5	2	0	0	15.1	73	21	14	14	4	0	1	2	3	0	13	2	0	1	1	.500	0	0	8.22
Lapoint,Jason,Albany	A	25	33	0	0	12	61.1	272	72	34	24	1	1	2	1	20	0	52	3	0	5	2	.714	0	0	3.52
Lara,Nelson,Marlins	R	17	11	0	0	4	21.2	101	21	13	9	1	0	1	2	11	1	9	2	1	1	1	.500	0	0	3.74
Lara,Yovanny,Expos	R	20	11	4	0	1	30	139	35	21	17	4	0	3	2	19	0	16	0	1	1	2	.333	0	0	5.10
Largusa,Levon,Dunedin	A	25	16	7	1	1	59.1	268	68	32	27	2	1	1	0	28	0	37	1	0	4	4	.500	1	0	4.10
Larocca,Todd,High Desert	A	23	15	7	0	2	51	248	68	53	42	7	0	2	1	29	0	31	7	2	0	7	.000	0	1	7.41
Bluefield	R	23	8	6	1	0	44.1	181	38	17	15	5	0	0	3	14	0	38	1	0	4	1	.800	1	0	3.05
Frederick	A	23	5	5	0	0	30.2	132	22	7	6	1	0	2	0	16	0	24	4	0	3	1	.750	0	0	1.76
Larock,Scott,Salem	A	23	52	1	0	18	101.2	423	96	52	44	10	4	0	2	27	7	92	5	3	5	4	.556	0	4	3.90
Larson,Toby,Columbia	A	23	8	8	0	0	51.1	224	43	24	15	2	1	2	1	19	0	53	5	1	3	3	.500	0	0	2.63
St. Lucie	A	23	19	18	3	0	121.2	508	122	44	34	5	4	0	7	30	2	82	7	1	6	7	.462	1	0	2.52
Larue,Shaun,Lethbridge	R	24	26	0	0	8	36.1	163	30	13	12	1	1	2	2	24	2	42	3	0	2	2	.500	0	0	2.97
Lasbury,Bob,Asheville	A	23	6	0	0	1	8.1	43	10	11	8	1	0	0	0	6	0	5	1	0	0	2	.000	0	0	8.64
Lavenia,Mark,Macon	A	23	24	3	0	16	46.1	195	38	17	11	2	3	0	1	14	1	45	1	1	4	3	.571	0	4	2.14
Durham	A	23	6	0	0	0	11.1	51	14	8	7	1	0	1	0	5	0	9	3	0	0	1	.000	0	0	5.56
Lawrence,Clint,Blue Jays	R	19	12	9	0	3	45.1	202	40	33	23	1	0	1	1	26	0	40	9	1	1	5	.167	0	0	4.57
Lawrence,Rich,Billings	R	24	13	2	0	2	25	112	25	18	9	2	0	0	1	11	0	27	1	0	0	0	.000	0	0	3.24

1995 Pitching -- Single-A and Rookie Leagues

			HOW MUCH HE PITCHED						WHAT HE GAVE UP												THE RESULTS					
Player	Lg	A	G	GS	CG	GF	IP	BFP	H	R	ER	HR	SH	SF	HB	TBB	IBB	SO	WP	Bk	W	L	Pct.	ShO	Sv	ERA
Lawrie,Jason,Tigers	R	19	4	4	0	0	12	59	10	8	6	0	0	0	1	12	2	12	0	0	0	1	.000	0	0	4.50
Leach,Jumaane,Clinton	A	23	19	0	0	7	26.2	123	30	17	11	1	1	0	2	7	2	12	2	0	1	3	.250	0	0	3.71
LeBron,Jose,Expos	R	25	2	0	0	1	2	9	0	0	0	0	0	0	0	3	0	0	0	0	0	0	.000	0	0	0.00
Lee,Calvin,Ogden	R	22	5	5	0	0	20.1	102	21	23	17	1	0	0	2	21	0	15	3	0	1	2	.333	0	0	7.52
Lee,Jeremy,Hagerstown	A	21	26	26	1	0	148	626	160	82	69	11	1	8	8	29	0	118	4	0	7	11	.389	0	0	4.20
Legrow,Brett,Piedmont	A	25	8	2	0	4	14	64	16	10	8	2	0	0	0	5	0	8	2	0	0	1	.000	0	0	5.14
Lehoisky,Russ,Fort Myers	A	25	26	0	0	10	52	240	45	25	19	0	7	2	4	38	3	29	5	0	0	1	.000	0	0	3.29
Leibee,Skye,W. Michigan	A	22	9	0	0	1	7.2	48	9	13	10	0	0	1	3	13	0	5	2	0	0	1	.000	0	0	11.74
Sou. Oregon	A	22	2	0	0	0	2.1	10	1	1	1	0	0	0	1	1	1	3	0	0	0	0	.000	0	0	3.86
Leiber,Zane,South Bend	A	22	14	0	0	8	28.2	134	35	26	22	3	1	1	2	9	0	21	2	3	0	0	.000	0	0	6.91
Hickory	A	22	14	0	0	7	17.2	78	19	13	11	3	0	1	0	5	0	13	5	1	1	0	1.000	0	0	5.60
Lenhardt,Bruce,Brewers	R	22	2	0	0	0	4.2	23	8	2	2	0	1	0	2	1	0	3	1	0	1	0	1.000	0	0	3.86
Helena	R	22	9	0	0	6	9.1	46	7	6	2	1	0	0	1	11	1	10	1	0	0	1	.000	0	0	1.93
Leroy,John,Durham	A	21	24	22	1	0	125.2	545	128	82	76	17	2	5	5	57	1	77	5	1	6	9	.400	0	0	5.44
Leshnock,Donnie,Tampa	A	25	28	10	0	2	87.2	378	78	41	30	2	1	5	4	45	0	67	7	2	10	6	.625	0	2	3.08
Lewis,Mike,Brevard Cty	A	27	43	0	0	8	62	251	48	22	16	5	8	0	2	22	3	44	1	0	4	5	.444	0	1	2.32
Licciardi,Ron,Cubs	R	20	17	1	0	7	33.1	141	24	13	9	1	1	0	1	16	2	22	3	4	4	3	.571	0	0	2.43
Linares,Rich,Bakersfield	A	23	55	0	0	52	67.1	272	64	18	17	2	4	1	3	17	2	57	3	0	4	4	.500	0	20	2.27
Lindemann,Wayne,Pr. William	A	26	19	0	0	14	43	196	54	30	28	7	1	5	2	20	2	32	3	0	2	0	1.000	0	1	5.86
South Bend	A	26	7	6	0	1	22	117	32	21	18	5	1	1	2	16	0	15	0	0	0	4	.000	0	0	7.36
Linebarger,Keith,FortMyers	A	25	29	10	1	12	103	418	74	30	24	6	3	2	9	35	1	73	4	0	7	4	.636	1	4	2.10
Link,Bryan,Hudson Vall	A	23	15	15	1	0	90.1	370	79	39	35	5	5	2	3	25	0	88	7	1	5	3	.625	0	0	3.49
Lintern,Cory,Bellingham	A	24	3	0	0	1	10.1	41	6	2	1	0	1	0	0	2	0	6	0	0	2	0	1.000	0	1	0.87
Burlington	A	24	8	0	0	4	15	67	19	10	10	4	1	0	1	5	1	8	1	0	1	0	1.000	0	0	6.00
Liquet,Wilton,Vero Beach	A	23	4	1	0	1	6.2	29	5	3	3	0	1	0	0	5	0	3	1	0	0	0	.000	0	0	4.05
Lisio,Joe,Pittsfield	A	22	28	0	0	23	33.1	141	27	8	6	0	2	5	1	14	1	24	2	0	2	2	.500	0	12	1.62
Liz,Jesus,Spokane	A	21	9	0	0	4	12.2	70	19	15	10	0	0	2	0	12	0	11	3	0	0	0	.000	0	0	7.11
Lock,Dan,Quad City	A	23	27	27	1	0	143	642	152	94	66	13	8	4	10	58	0	90	5	0	8	15	.348	0	0	4.15
Locklear,Jeff,Salem	A	26	6	0	0	2	6.1	33	10	9	9	2	0	2	0	4	0	3	0	0	0	0	.000	0	0	12.79
Locklear,Dean,Visalia	A	26	9	9	0	0	52.2	225	50	29	23	4	1	1	5	21	0	27	6	0	3	3	.500	0	0	3.93
Loewe,Kevin,Danville	R	22	20	0	0	9	38	151	24	20	16	1	2	0	1	10	0	43	3	0	1	3	.250	0	5	3.79
Logan,Chris,Clinton	A	25	53	0	0	42	62	284	62	29	15	0	1	2	4	27	4	61	7	0	4	6	.400	0	17	2.18
Logan,Marcus,Savannah	A	24	34	7	0	2	86.2	373	73	42	32	3	1	5	2	38	0	83	11	1	3	6	.333	0	0	3.32
Loiz,Niuman,Kissimmee	A	22	13	13	0	0	56.2	271	71	48	35	2	2	3	2	30	0	33	10	0	0	8	.000	0	0	5.56
Auburn	A	22	3	3	1	0	13.2	56	7	5	4	0	0	0	0	8	0	11	2	1	1	1	.500	1	0	2.63
Lombardi,John,Frederick	A	23	6	3	0	0	16.1	75	22	13	13	2	0	1	2	6	0	13	2	0	0	4	.000	0	0	7.16
Lopez,Johann,Kissimmee	A	21	18	12	0	3	69	283	55	30	20	3	1	2	3	25	0	67	5	3	5	5	.500	0	1	2.61
Lopez,Jose,Angels	R	19	11	7	0	0	41.1	178	45	18	11	0	0	0	6	13	0	36	5	2	2	2	.500	0	0	2.40
Lopez,Orlando,Daytona	A	23	44	0	0	15	80.2	342	75	30	24	6	5	1	3	22	1	76	6	2	7	2	.778	0	8	2.68
Lopez,Rodrigo,Padres	R	20	11	7	0	3	34.2	162	41	29	21	0	1	2	2	14	0	33	3	1	1	1	.500	0	1	5.45
Lott,Brian,Charlstn-Wv	A	24	28	20	0	3	138	586	155	56	53	9	4	1	6	33	4	96	3	3	8	7	.533	0	1	3.46
Loudermilk,Darren,Burlington	R	21	21	1	0	0	41	195	40	27	23	1	0	1	6	23	1	38	8	0	2	2	.500	0	0	5.05
Lovingier,Kevin,Savannah	A	24	38	0	0	18	47	195	35	14	7	1	3	1	1	21	5	54	3	0	6	3	.667	0	1	1.34
St. Pete	A	24	22	0	0	6	21.2	82	9	4	4	0	1	1	2	10	1	14	1	0	1	0	1.000	0	1	1.66
Lowe,Benny,St. Cathrns	A	22	15	15	0	0	78.2	358	89	43	38	3	3	3	9	40	0	61	10	1	4	5	.444	0	0	4.35
Lowe,Jason,W. Michigan	A	23	7	0	0	4	9	50	17	14	11	4	0	0	0	6	0	7	2	0	0	0	.000	0	0	11.00
Lowry,Elliot,Burlington	R	21	10	0	0	0	9	50	26	15	13	1	1	1	0	10	0	15	8	0	0	0	.000	0	0	5.85
Lukasiewicz,Mark,Dunedin	A	23	31	13	0	11	88.1	383	80	62	55	13	1	2	7	42	0	71	7	0	3	6	.333	0	1	5.60
Lundquist,David,South Bend	A	23	18	18	5	0	118	492	107	54	47	3	7	3	5	38	0	60	3	0	8	4	.667	1	0	3.58
Lynch,Jim,Astros	R	20	17	1	0	12	34.2	148	14	12	6	1	0	0	5	26	0	49	10	2	2	1	.667	0	4	1.56
Lyons,Curt,Winston-Sal	A	21	26	26	0	0	160.1	672	139	66	53	10	6	2	15	67	3	122	9	3	9	9	.500	0	0	2.98
Maberry,Louis,Charlstn-Wv	A	25	4	0	0	2	5	21	2	1	0	1	0	0	0	3	1	0	0	0	0	1	.000	0	0	0.00
Winston-Sal	A	25	20	0	0	12	37.1	154	40	20	18	5	1	0	2	7	0	19	7	0	1	0	1.000	0	0	4.34
MacCa,Christopher,Portland	A	21	24	0	0	16	35.2	152	25	15	13	1	2	2	6	17	1	41	6	0	3	2	.600	0	5	3.28
Macdonald,Mike,Springfield	A	23	55	0	0	48	62.2	261	49	24	23	8	4	2	3	27	0	49	3	1	6	5	.545	0	12	3.30
Macey,Fausto,San Jose	A	20	28	25	1	0	171	709	167	84	74	17	7	5	6	50	1	94	6	4	8	9	.471	0	0	3.89
MacRae,Scott,Billings	R	21	18	0	0	4	27	135	32	24	17	0	0	5	3	20	4	9	2	1	0	1	.000	0	5	5.67
Maddox,Gene,Princeton	R	21	11	0	0	4	10.1	56	13	13	13	0	0	0	1	12	1	10	3	2	0	0	.000	0	0	11.32
Magnelli,Anthony,Visalia	A	25	29	0	0	25	40.1	161	40	20	19	2	4	1	0	6	0	30	5	1	2	5	.286	0	11	4.24
Magre,Peter,Winston-Sal	A	25	17	0	0	4	32	150	39	14	11	3	2	0	3	15	1	27	3	3	1	1	.500	0	2	3.09
Charlstn-Wv	A	25	21	0	0	2	28.1	119	34	16	16	2	1	2	2	8	2	19	3	0	2	1	.667	0	0	5.08
Mahaffey,Alan,Elizabethtn	R	22	13	12	1	0	70	308	66	42	27	4	6	2	3	20	0	73	4	7	5	6	.455	0	0	3.47
Mahlberg,John,Rockies	R	19	10	7	0	0	39	178	44	27	19	3	2	2	1	21	0	52	3	1	2	3	.400	0	0	4.38
Maine,Dalton,Frederick	A	24	19	0	0	10	22	98	20	10	9	2	0	1	2	11	0	21	5	0	1	1	.500	0	0	3.68
Bluefield	R	24	1	0	0	1	4	18	7	5	5	2	0	0	1	0	0	2	0	0	1	0	1.000	0	0	11.25
Orioles	R	24	18	0	0	6	30.1	122	24	7	7	0	0	1	0	9	1	32	1	0	1	0	1.000	0	2	2.08
Malko,Bryan,Twins	R	19	10	4	0	3	33	142	23	14	10	1	3	1	4	23	0	29	5	0	1	2	.333	0	1	2.73
Mallory,Trevor,Dunedin	A	24	37	3	0	10	70	326	80	53	39	4	1	3	3	41	0	46	7	0	0	5	.000	0	1	5.01
Marnott,Joe,Michigan	A	22	14	13	1	0	77	352	76	56	51	4	1	7	8	50	0	66	5	3	3	6	.333	0	0	5.96
Utica	A	22	9	6	0	3	32.1	173	40	35	24	1	0	3	11	28	0	36	10	0	0	4	.000	0	0	6.68
Manley,Kevin,Mets	R	20	2	0	0	0	1.1	11	1	1	1	0	0	0	0	3	0	0	1	0	0	0	.000	0	0	6.75
Mann,Jim,Medicne Hat	R	21	14	14	1	0	77.2	347	78	47	37	5	3	2	7	37	0	66	4	0	5	4	.556	1	0	4.29
Manning,David,Charlotte	A	24	26	20	0	2	128.2	545	127	56	50	7	3	3	3	46	0	66	6	0	5	3	.643	0	0	3.50
Manning,Len,Piedmont	A	24	27	26	1	0	160	658	130	68	47	10	7	5	7	58	0	154	4	2	10	10	.500	0	0	2.64
Manon,Julio,Huntington	R	22	16	8	2	3	74	319	75	34	30	4	0	3	2	30	2	77	8	0	3	4	.429	0	1	3.65
Manser,Chris,Tigers	R	20	6	5	0	1	29.1	120	24	10	8	1	1	2	0	5	0	26	6	0	3	2	.600	0	0	2.45
Marenghi,Matt,Frederick	A	23	30	16	0	8	113.1	475	108	73	64	14	1	8	9	41	2	85	6	1	4	13	.235	0	2	5.08

1995 Pitching -- Single-A and Rookie Leagues

Player	Lg	A	G	GS	CG	GF	IP	BFP	H	R	ER	HR	SH	SF	HB	TBB	IBB	SO	WP	Bk	W	L	Pct.	ShO	Sv	ERA
Marine,Justin,Billings	R	21	18	0	0	7	25.2	114	20	14	5	0	1	1	4	11	0	20	2	0	1	0	1.000	0	2	1.75
Markey,Barry,Cubs	R	19	17	1	0	9	41	168	43	11	8	0	1	0	0	7	0	24	1	1	4	1	.800	0	1	1.76
Markham,Andy,W. Palm Bch	A	23	24	23	1	0	121	532	129	62	53	8	4	6	9	44	1	58	4	1	7	11	.389	0	0	3.94
Marquardt,Scott,St. Pete	A	23	9	9	0	0	52.1	222	55	24	22	4	1	1	3	15	0	39	4	4	3	4	.429	0	0	3.78
Marquez,Ihosvany,Utica	A	24	12	0	0	3	20	84	13	8	6	0	0	1	4	13	0	23	4	0	0	0	.000	0	0	2.70
Michigan	A	24	3	0	0	0	4.2	21	3	4	4	0	0	0	0	4	0	7	0	0	1	0	1.000	0	0	7.71
Sarasota	A	24	12	0	0	4	15	70	10	6	5	1	1	0	2	13	1	18	0	0	1	1	.500	0	1	3.00
Marquez,Ralph,Twins	R	19	11	0	0	11	22	103	19	13	10	1	1	1	0	18	1	19	2	3	0	4	.000	0	1	4.09
Marquez,Robert,Vermont	A	23	29	0	0	29	32	122	15	5	3	0	1	0	1	11	0	32	1	0	1	1	.500	0	21	0.84
Marrero,Kenny,Lakeland	A	26	37	0	0	18	55.2	229	54	28	23	5	1	2	0	28	1	46	6	1	1	4	.200	0	5	3.72
Marriott,Michael,Marlins	R	19	2	2	0	0	8	32	2	2	1	0	0	0	1	7	0	6	1	0	0	0	.000	0	0	1.13
Marshall,Lee,Twins	R	19	6	1	0	0	11	57	16	10	6	1	1	1	2	8	0	7	2	0	0	1	.000	0	0	4.91
Marte,Damaso,Everett	A	22	11	5	0	1	36.2	141	25	11	9	2	1	1	1	10	0	39	3	0	2	2	.500	0	0	2.21
Martin,Chandler,Portland	A	22	7	7	0	0	38	153	20	10	7	0	2	0	2	21	0	34	3	3	4	1	.800	0	0	1.66
Asheville	A	22	8	8	0	0	49.1	216	48	23	21	0	2	0	3	27	0	32	6	1	4	3	.571	0	0	3.83
Martin,Cleburne,Expos	R	19	17	4	0	5	42.2	187	43	26	23	1	0	4	0	22	1	26	10	1	2	5	.286	0	2	4.85
Martin,Jeff,San Jose	A	23	36	0	0	28	71	305	60	34	26	5	5	2	3	25	3	63	1	0	5	6	.455	0	5	3.30
Martin,Jeff,Royals	R	22	11	10	1	0	55	216	35	12	9	1	0	2	7	11	0	53	2	3	3	1	.750	1	0	1.47
Martin,Jeremy,Ogden	R	24	9	2	0	2	17.2	79	23	16	15	2	1	1	4	11	0	11	3	0	1	1	.500	0	0	7.64
Martineau,Brian,Hudson Vall	A	21	30	0	0	26	41.2	166	30	10	6	1	5	0	3	10	1	39	4	5	5	2	.714	0	18	1.30
Martinez,Cesar,Sarasota	A	23	34	10	0	2	110.1	477	108	62	46	8	3	2	4	40	2	61	9	1	6	6	.500	0	0	3.75
Martinez,Humberto,Red Sox	R	21	14	0	0	6	27.1	119	25	14	11	3	0	2	2	17	0	19	2	0	0	3	.000	0	1	3.62
Martinez,Javier,Rockford	A	19	18	18	1	0	104.2	455	100	56	46	6	5	4	12	39	0	53	15	2	6	6	.500	0	0	3.96
Martinez,Johnny,Columbus	A	23	16	2	0	2	54	210	37	15	11	0	2	1	4	14	0	43	3	0	6	1	.857	0	0	1.83
Kinston	A	23	6	0	0	3	11	44	9	2	2	0	0	0	1	4	0	13	1	0	3	0	1.000	0	2	1.64
Martinez,Dennis,Burlington	R	22	15	2	0	6	27.1	139	35	31	24	1	0	1	2	18	1	22	7	1	0	1	.000	0	0	7.90
Martinez,Juan,Rangers	R	21	12	6	0	3	38.1	166	43	28	23	5	0	0	0	11	1	27	1	0	2	3	.400	0	0	5.40
Martinez,Ozzie,Fayettevlle	A	21	6	0	0	2	13	49	11	6	6	2	1	1	0	1	0	15	0	1	0	0	.000	0	0	4.15
Jamestown	A	21	15	15	1	0	90.2	384	85	46	38	10	3	1	6	30	1	56	2	4	4	4	.500	0	0	3.77
Martinez,Romulo,Tigers	R	19	16	0	0	3	24	115	27	22	20	0	1	0	1	13	3	14	3	5	0	0	.000	0	1	7.50
Martinez,Uriel,Clinton	A	21	11	0	0	2	17.1	84	27	15	10	2	0	1	0	3	0	8	5	2	0	0	.000	0	0	5.19
Martinez,William,Burlington	R	18	11	11	0	0	40	208	64	50	42	1	2	2	4	25	0	36	6	3	0	7	.000	0	0	9.45
Martino,Jay,Cubs	R	19	8	0	0	5	10.2	45	4	2	0	0	1	0	0	5	1	4	1	0	0	0	.000	0	2	0.00
Martino,Wilfredo,Rockies	R	18	16	3	0	6	44	203	48	27	26	2	0	2	4	23	0	44	7	2	3	1	.750	0	0	5.32
Masaoka,Onan,Yakima	A	18	15	7	0	5	49.1	225	28	25	20	2	1	0	4	47	0	75	12	4	2	4	.333	0	3	3.65
Maskivish,Joe,Augusta	A	24	26	0	0	26	29.2	122	23	9	7	0	1	0	3	9	4	33	2	0	2	1	.667	0	20	2.12
Mason,Roger,Pirates	R	37	1	0	0	0	1	5	2	0	0	0	0	0	0	0	0	1	0	0	1	0	1.000	0	0	0.00
Mathews,Del,Durham	A	21	33	16	1	8	112	478	117	53	44	6	4	1	10	38	2	77	6	0	7	8	.467	0	1	3.54
Mathis,Sammie,Watertown	A	23	18	0	0	4	33	153	39	22	16	1	0	3	4	15	1	21	1	2	4	1	.800	0	4	4.36
Matlack,Dan,Padres	R	20	16	0	0	5	27.2	122	20	15	11	1	1	2	3	14	0	16	0	1	0	2	.000	0	0	3.58
Mattes,Troy,Albany	A	20	4	4	0	0	19.2	92	21	12	11	0	2	0	0	12	1	15	1	1	0	2	.000	0	0	5.03
Vermont	A	20	10	10	0	0	46	209	51	34	19	3	5	4	5	25	0	23	7	0	3	4	.429	0	0	3.72
Expos	R	20	2	2	0	0	12	43	7	0	0	0	0	0	0	3	0	8	0	0	2	0	1.000	0	0	0.00
Mattson,Craig,Lynchburg	A	22	11	0	0	5	11.2	46	11	5	4	1	0	1	0	5	0	5	0	0	1	0	1.000	0	3	3.09
Matulevich,Jeff,St. Pete	A	26	51	0	0	48	58.2	253	50	20	18	3	2	1	0	30	3	61	4	0	1	5	.167	0	30	2.76
May,Scott,Rockford	A	34	8	3	0	0	26.1	108	20	7	5	0	1	0	1	9	0	24	0	0	3	0	1.000	0	0	1.71
Mayer,Aaron,Boise	A	21	20	1	0	1	35	159	38	29	21	4	1	0	2	22	0	32	11	0	3	1	.750	0	0	5.40
Mayhew,Keith,Eugene	A	24	24	1	0	3	39.2	185	46	29	20	2	2	1	3	17	0	35	4	2	0	1	.000	0	1	4.54
Mays,Joseph,Mariners	R	20	10	10	0	0	44.1	189	41	24	16	0	2	2	1	18	0	44	7	1	2	3	.400	0	0	3.25
Mays,Marcus,Kane County	A	22	8	0	0	5	11.2	56	15	8	8	1	0	0	1	7	1	6	1	0	1	2	.333	0	0	6.17
Mayse,Rob,Frederick	A	22	6	0	0	1	9.2	42	9	5	4	0	0	0	1	8	0	7	0	0	1	0	1.000	0	0	3.72
Mazzone,Tony,Eugene	A	23	25	0	0	7	44	200	50	24	19	3	2	4	7	12	1	38	1	0	3	1	.750	0	2	3.89
McAdams,Dennis,Asheville	A	22	5	0	0	3	7	29	7	4	3	1	0	0	0	2	0	7	0	0	0	0	.000	0	0	3.86
McBride,Chris,Hagerstown	A	22	19	19	2	0	107	461	121	61	51	4	5	3	5	27	1	52	3	1	5	10	.333	0	0	4.29
McBride,Rodney,Twins	R	21	12	11	1	0	61.1	275	63	38	21	3	4	5	3	34	0	36	8	1	3	7	.300	1	1	3.08
McCaffrey,Dennis,Johnson Cty	R	20	24	0	0	7	32	148	36	24	17	3	0	1	2	17	1	24	7	1	2	0	1.000	0	0	4.78
McCarter,Jason,Astros	R	19	16	0	0	9	22	97	16	8	7	2	5	0	2	16	0	21	6	0	1	0	1.000	0	0	2.86
McCaskey,Tom,White Sox	R	20	6	1	0	0	18	77	17	6	6	1	0	0	0	7	0	16	4	1	1	1	.500	0	0	3.00
McClinton,Patrick,Asheville	A	24	18	0	0	7	33.1	140	27	16	13	2	3	3	4	9	1	22	3	3	1	2	.333	0	2	3.51
McClurg,Clint,Batavia	A	22	10	5	1	1	37.2	171	41	26	18	2	3	2	4	21	0	14	4	0	2	2	.500	0	0	4.30
McCommon,Jason,W. Palm Bch	A	24	26	26	3	0	156	650	153	75	65	13	7	6	10	38	0	94	6	7	7	11	.389	1	0	3.75
McCormack,Andy,White Sox	R	22	1	1	0	0	6	21	4	1	1	1	0	0	0	0	0	4	0	0	1	0	1.000	0	0	1.50
South Bend	A	22	6	4	0	2	23.1	105	26	14	12	3	2	1	0	11	0	10	1	0	1	2	.333	0	0	4.63
McDonald,Matt,Athletics	R	22	5	1	0	2	16.1	71	16	7	4	1	0	2	1	9	0	23	1	1	0	0	.000	0	0	2.20
Sou. Oregon	A	22	13	9	0	0	51.2	211	42	22	18	4	2	0	1	18	0	47	2	1	4	3	.600	0	0	3.14
McEntire,Ethan,Columbia	A	20	6	6	1	0	32.1	146	26	14	12	4	3	0	4	23	0	31	3	0	3	2	.600	0	0	3.34
Pittsfield	A	20	13	13	0	0	69.1	325	81	43	39	2	1	2	5	46	0	41	7	0	4	2	.667	0	0	5.06
McFarlane,Joseph,Tigers	R	19	1	1	0	0	1.1	9	1	0	0	0	0	0	0	0	0	1	0	0	0	0	.000	0	0	0.00
McFerrin,Christian,Astros	R	20	20	0	0	12	34.2	153	28	20	11	0	3	0	5	17	2	39	6	1	4	4	.500	0	5	2.86
McGuire,Brandon,Angels	R	18	2	0	0	0	5.1	20	3	3	2	0	0	0	0	3	0	6	1	0	1	0	1.000	0	0	3.38
McHugh,Michael,Hudson Vall	A	23	10	0	0	3	15	85	26	17	14	0	0	0	0	14	0	9	4	0	0	0	.000	0	0	8.40
McKenzie,Scott,Winston-Sal	A	25	49	0	0	41	72	294	42	27	22	7	5	0	5	30	2	55	7	0	3	4	.429	0	20	2.75
McKnight,Chris,Danville	R	20	1	1	0	0	3	12	1	2	1	0	0	0	0	1	0	6	0	0	0	1	.000	0	0	3.00
Eugene	A	22	13	13	0	0	64.2	282	63	31	21	4	6	4	1	21	1	30	6	0	5	2	.714	0	0	2.92
McKnight,Tony,Astros	R	19	3	3	0	0	14	54	15	5	5	0	0	2	0	2	0	9	1	0	1	1	.500	0	0	3.21
McLaughlin,Denis,Sarasota	A	23	54	0	0	30	66.1	305	57	31	24	3	4	1	7	46	7	79	5	3	3	2	.600	0	6	3.26
McMillan,Leonard,Burlington	A	22	8	0	0	1	13.2	65	15	8	8	1	1	0	0	10	1	4	3	0	1	0	1.000	0	0	5.27

376

1995 Pitching -- Single-A and Rookie Leagues

Player	Lg	A	G	GS	CG	GF	IP	BFP	H	R	ER	HR	SH	SF	HB	TBB	IBB	SO	WP	Bk	W	L	Pct.	ShO	Sv	ERA
Butte	R	22	10	0	0	1	13.2	78	18	17	15	2	1	0	1	18	1	15	2	1	0	1	.000	0	0	9.88
McMullen,Jerry,Eugene	A	22	22	0	0	8	30.2	128	28	7	5	0	4	0	1	8	2	31	3	0	1	1	.500	0	1	1.47
McMullen,Mike,Burlington	A	23	29	11	2	6	83.2	410	98	76	51	5	2	4	9	54	3	53	9	2	4	10	.286	0	0	5.49
McNeely,Mitch,Yakima	A	22	24	3	0	8	53	226	53	30	25	1	2	2	0	15	2	31	6	5	3	4	.429	0	1	4.25
McNeese,John,Williamsprt	A	24	13	12	0	0	72.2	297	73	24	15	2	1	1	2	10	1	47	2	2	5	3	.625	0	0	1.86
McNeill,Kevin,Savannah	A	25	29	21	0	2	110.2	502	131	74	61	5	1	0	3	47	1	87	14	0	3	7	.300	0	0	4.96
McNichol,Brian,Williamsprt	A	22	9	9	0	0	49.2	215	57	28	17	1	1	1	2	8	0	35	1	1	3	1	.750	0	0	3.08
McWilliams,Matt,Eugene	A	23	24	4	0	10	49.1	208	34	21	11	1	1	1	0	7	1	42	4	2	2	3	.400	0	2	2.01
Meade,Paul,Bakersfield	A	27	24	0	0	9	53.2	253	70	47	45	15	3	3	5	25	1	32	4	2	2	2	.500	0	0	7.55
Meadows,Jimmy,Visalia	A	31	27	21	1	2	125.2	543	136	71	61	14	3	5	11	51	1	94	12	2	7	6	.538	1	0	4.37
Meadows,Brian,Kane County	A	20	26	26	1	0	147	646	163	90	69	11	8	4	12	41	0	103	3	2	9	9	.500	1	0	4.22
Meady,Todd,Royals	R	19	12	6	0	2	37.2	156	33	21	11	1	0	1	2	6	0	26	2	0	3	3	.500	0	2	2.63
Mear,Richard,Johnson Cty	R	20	14	14	0	0	78	338	68	37	29	4	3	1	3	40	1	75	10	1	7	3	.700	0	0	3.35
Medero,Gadiel,Bellingham	A	20	4	0	0	0	5.2	33	10	7	4	1	0	1	0	4	0	4	3	0	0	0	.000	0	0	6.35
Butte	R	20	8	1	0	5	10	59	22	19	17	0	0	0	1	7	0	4	1	1	0	0	.000	0	0	15.30
Medina,Rafael,Greensboro	A	21	19	19	1	0	98.2	418	86	48	44	8	0	5	6	38	0	108	6	3	4	4	.500	0	0	4.01
Tampa	A	21	6	6	0	0	30.1	131	29	12	8	0	0	0	1	12	0	25	0	2	2	2	.500	0	0	2.37
Medina,Tomas,Astros	R	21	11	1	0	0	22.1	115	37	26	21	0	1	0	1	14	0	23	7	0	1	0	1.000	0	0	8.46
Meiners,Doug,Hagerstown	A	22	18	18	3	0	117.1	477	121	52	39	5	2	2	3	14	0	73	4	1	8	4	.667	0	0	2.99
Mejia,Carlos,Utica	A	22	10	0	0	5	13.1	62	15	8	7	0	1	1	0	5	0	14	4	2	1	1	.500	0	1	4.72
Butte	R	22	10	7	0	2	38.1	164	37	16	16	4	1	5	2	17	1	28	2	1	2	1	.667	0	0	3.76
Mejia,Felix,Yankees	R	20	9	0	0	3	15.2	75	16	6	6	0	0	2	2	13	0	21	6	6	2	0	1.000	0	0	3.45
Mejias,Fernando,Hickory	A	24	30	16	0	4	111.2	497	128	78	57	6	3	3	5	38	4	76	11	2	2	9	.182	0	0	4.59
Mendes,Jaime,Batavia	A	23	30	0	0	14	41.1	177	50	23	18	3	2	2	2	6	0	35	4	0	1	1	.500	0	3	3.92
Mendez,Manuel,Johnson Cty	R	22	30	0	0	28	38	158	33	13	13	2	1	0	1	12	0	61	2	3	3	0	1.000	0	19	3.08
Mendoza,David,Blue Jays	R	20	12	10	0	0	48.2	225	58	37	27	0	2	1	4	14	0	39	4	3	2	5	.286	0	0	4.99
Mendoza,Geronimo,White Sox	R	18	10	0	0	8	14.2	59	8	9	7	3	0	2	1	7	0	11	1	0	0	1	.000	0	0	4.30
Mensink,Brian,Batavia	A	22	11	8	0	1	48.1	207	56	23	16	0	2	1	5	10	0	37	3	2	4	1	.800	0	0	2.98
Mercado,Gabriel,Beloit	A	23	24	23	0	1	129.1	565	138	89	77	18	3	3	5	50	1	89	6	3	11	6	.647	0	0	5.36
Mercedes,Carlos,Orioles	R	20	10	1	0	2	24.2	96	22	8	7	2	0	0	0	2	0	10	0	0	2	1	.667	0	0	2.55
Bluefield	R	20	1	0	0	1	1	6	2	1	1	0	0	0	0	1	0	1	0	0	0	0	.000	0	0	9.00
Merrick,Brett,Watertown	A	22	22	0	0	11	37.1	142	15	10	8	2	0	1	0	18	3	44	3	0	2	1	.667	0	4	1.93
Merrill,Ethan,Sarasota	A	24	27	25	1	2	150	672	155	86	63	11	3	5	11	67	2	78	7	0	11	7	.611	1	0	3.78
Mesa,Rafael,Kinston	A	22	35	1	0	24	52	206	34	19	17	5	4	3	4	20	2	29	4	0	4	3	.571	0	4	2.94
Metheney,Nelson,Clearwater	A	25	59	0	0	11	72	310	65	32	24	2	7	4	0	25	3	38	3	2	5	5	.500	0	1	3.00
Meyer,David,Tampa	A	24	12	11	0	0	58	281	84	49	42	3	2	3	4	29	0	29	6	4	3	4	.429	0	0	6.52
Greensboro	A	24	14	14	1	0	87	377	104	52	47	5	3	2	3	28	0	54	5	1	8	4	.667	1	0	4.86
Meyhoff,Jason,Fort Wayne	A	23	17	10	0	3	54.2	258	70	52	40	5	1	5	2	30	0	35	5	3	2	1	.667	0	0	6.59
Twins	R	23	2	0	0	1	2	9	3	3	1	0	0	1	0	0	0	3	1	0	0	0	.000	0	0	4.50
Micknich,Steve,Kane County	A	24	9	0	0	3	11.2	58	13	3	3	0	0	1	4	6	0	10	4	1	1	0	1.000	0	0	2.31
Elmira	A	24	4	0	0	4	5.1	20	1	0	0	0	0	0	1	2	0	6	0	0	0	0	.000	0	0	0.00
Miedreich,Kevin,New Jersey	A	23	15	15	0	0	74.2	340	84	47	39	2	2	7	8	33	0	39	5	1	2	6	.250	0	0	4.70
Miles,Chad,Kane County	A	23	19	0	0	4	27.1	145	35	33	22	3	4	4	4	23	1	14	2	1	1	1	.500	0	0	7.24
Elmira	A	23	14	0	0	4	21.2	105	29	18	16	2	1	1	1	10	0	10	5	1	1	1	.500	0	0	6.65
Militello,Sam,Brevard Cty	A	26	4	4	0	0	10.1	58	7	10	9	1	1	0	0	20	0	18	6	0	1	0	1.000	0	0	7.84
Miller,Brian,Martinsvlle	R	23	23	0	0	8	45.1	194	46	28	26	3	1	1	2	15	0	35	6	3	6	4	.600	0	3	5.16
Miller,David,Elmira	A	22	9	0	0	4	16.2	73	17	8	8	1	1	0	2	7	2	11	1	2	1	1	.500	0	1	4.32
Miller,Shawn,Helena	R	22	16	0	0	4	28	136	37	18	15	1	0	1	0	16	0	33	2	1	2	0	1.000	0	4	4.82
Miller,Shawn,Fort Myers	A	23	30	2	0	16	71	288	68	16	15	4	2	2	2	13	1	35	2	0	4	4	.500	0	4	1.90
Million,Doug,Salem	A	20	24	23	0	0	113	513	111	71	60	6	6	1	9	79	4	85	9	4	5	7	.417	0	0	4.62
Millwood,Kevin,Macon	A	21	29	12	0	5	103	458	86	65	53	10	3	1	5	57	0	89	10	0	5	6	.455	0	0	4.63
Mimnaugh,Scott,Sou. Oregon	A	25	3	3	0	0	8.1	43	10	8	3	1	1	0	2	4	0	8	0	1	0	2	.000	0	0	3.24
Minor,Tommy,Savannah	A	24	8	0	0	3	7.1	33	10	7	4	1	0	1	0	2	0	9	0	0	1	1	.500	0	0	4.91
Mirando,Walter,Kane County	A	21	25	25	1	0	128	562	102	68	58	9	7	4	9	88	2	106	11	2	8	7	.533	0	0	4.08
Mitchell,Alvin,Michigan	A	24	30	17	0	4	115.1	513	120	75	68	9	7	8	7	64	1	74	10	1	6	8	.429	0	1	5.31
Mitchell,Courtney,Piedmont	A	23	5	0	0	2	4.1	22	7	5	5	0	0	0	0	5	0	3	1	0	0	1	.000	0	0	10.38
Batavia	A	23	28	0	0	9	42.1	194	46	28	23	2	1	2	3	23	1	40	4	1	0	5	.000	0	1	4.89
Mitchell,John,Medicne Hat	R	21	25	0	0	23	36	150	20	15	10	1	3	1	1	17	1	50	5	1	2	2	.500	0	11	2.50
Mitchell,Kelvin,Everett	A	21	25	0	0	6	37	171	41	26	19	2	0	3	2	23	4	24	6	5	3	2	.600	0	1	4.62
Mitchell,Ken,Bakersfield	A	22	36	0	0	12	57.1	281	61	46	34	7	1	1	2	38	0	36	18	2	1	2	.333	0	0	5.34
Mitchell,Scott,Vermont	A	23	18	1	0	5	40.1	171	35	18	10	1	2	4	4	15	0	30	2	4	3	1	.750	0	1	2.23
Mittauer,Casey,Greensboro	A	23	49	0	0	22	74.1	294	60	26	16	3	6	4	3	14	4	59	5	0	3	6	.333	0	8	1.94
Mix,Derek,Clinton	A	22	35	0	0	18	49	247	34	42	28	1	2	3	12	54	2	40	29	0	1	0	1.000	0	5	5.14
Mlodik,Kevin,Sou. Oregon	A	21	20	10	0	1	60	273	62	35	21	3	0	3	8	20	0	43	4	2	2	2	.500	0	0	3.15
Montane,Ivan,Riverside	A	23	24	16	0	0	92.2	442	101	67	58	3	3	6	10	71	0	79	19	0	5	5	.500	0	0	5.63
Montelongo,Joseph,Rockford	A	22	20	20	1	0	118.1	512	109	62	56	8	4	5	6	49	0	82	8	1	10	7	.588	0	0	4.26
Montgomery,Joe,Princeton	R	23	13	3	0	4	45.1	190	45	19	12	1	0	1	2	14	0	27	5	3	3	0	1.000	0	0	2.38
Montoya,Wilmer,Kinston	A	22	1	0	0	0	3.1	15	4	2	2	0	1	0	0	1	0	2	0	0	1	0	1.000	0	0	5.40
Columbus	A	22	51	0	0	41	80.2	337	65	33	28	4	1	0	2	36	1	91	6	2	3	3	.500	0	31	3.12
Moody,Eric,Charlotte	A	25	13	13	2	0	88.1	353	84	30	27	2	3	1	5	13	0	57	0	0	5	5	.500	2	0	2.75
Moore,Sam,Elmira	A	24	15	0	0	9	29.1	124	23	8	6	1	1	0	1	4	0	22	3	1	1	2	.333	0	3	1.84
Moore,Dave,Royals	R	20	14	1	0	8	28	124	28	17	13	3	0	1	1	12	0	12	3	0	2	2	.500	0	0	4.18
Moore,David,Hickory	A	21	20	0	0	12	27.2	128	41	20	19	5	0	2	0	7	1	15	2	0	1	0	1.000	0	0	6.18
Bristol	R	21	15	0	0	5	29.2	136	34	22	17	3	0	1	0	11	0	37	3	0	1	0	1.000	0	0	5.16
Moore,Robert,Hudson Vall	A	23	13	13	0	0	63	280	77	45	38	5	2	5	4	13	0	45	10	3	2	3	.400	0	0	5.43
Moore,Trey,Riverside	A	23	24	24	0	0	148.1	605	122	65	51	6	2	5	2	58	1	134	6	1	14	6	.700	0	0	3.09
Moraga,David.W. Palm Bch	A	20	3	3	0	0	16	75	20	7	7	0	0	0	0	10	0	10	0	0	1	1	.500	0	0	3.94

377

1995 Pitching -- Single-A and Rookie Leagues

			HOW MUCH HE PITCHED						WHAT HE GAVE UP												THE RESULTS					
Player	Lg	A	G	GS	CG	GF	IP	BFP	H	R	ER	HR	SH	SF	HB	TBB	IBB	SO	WP	Bk	W	L	Pct.	ShO	Sv	ERA
Albany	A	20	25	24	1	0	147.2	620	136	63	44	6	6	4	1	46	0	109	10	0	8	8	.500	0	0	2.68
Moreno,Juan,Athletics	R	21	20	0	0	8	44.2	181	36	10	6	1	1	1	0	20	0	49	2	5	6	2	.750	0	0	1.21
Moreno,Julio,Orioles	R	20	5	5	1	0	34	131	17	9	6	0	1	2	1	7	0	29	1	1	3	2	.600	1	0	1.59
Bluefield	R	20	9	8	0	1	49.1	214	61	31	23	3	1	3	0	12	0	36	3	1	4	3	.571	0	0	4.20
Moreno,Orber,Royals	R	19	8	3	0	1	22	89	15	9	6	0	0	0	2	7	0	21	2	0	1	1	.500	0	0	2.45
Moreno,Ricardo,Rangers	R	20	4	1	1	2	15	56	13	3	3	1	2	0	0	1	0	8	0	1	1	0	1.000	0	0	1.80
Morgan,Eric,Wisconsin	A	23	7	0	0	4	13.1	54	5	6	2	1	1	1	2	7	0	7	1	0	0	0	.000	0	1	1.35
Morillo,Donald,Charlstn-Sc	A	22	18	0	0	13	25.2	115	22	7	6	1	0	0	3	17	2	28	1	0	1	4	.200	0	0	2.10
Morris,Chad,Vermont	A	23	9	0	0	6	15	65	11	4	4	1	0	1	1	9	0	19	5	3	1	0	1.000	0	0	2.40
Morris,Matt,New Jersey	A	21	2	2	0	0	11	45	12	3	2	1	0	0	0	3	0	13	0	3	2	0	1.000	0	0	1.64
St. Pete	A	21	6	6	1	0	34	134	22	16	9	1	2	0	0	11	0	31	0	2	3	2	.600	1	0	2.38
Morrison,Chris,Sou. Oregon	A	24	6	0	0	2	15	56	14	4	4	0	1	0	0	1	0	11	1	0	2	1	.667	0	0	2.40
W. Michigan	A	24	13	0	0	4	21.2	97	28	13	12	1	1	1	0	4	0	13	2	1	4	1	.800	0	0	4.98
Morse,Paul,Fort Myers	A	23	35	0	0	29	61.1	247	57	30	26	3	1	4	3	12	0	56	4	1	3	1	.750	0	15	3.82
Morseman,Bob,Bluefield	R	22	18	1	0	12	35.2	142	22	9	8	2	1	1	1	14	1	38	1	0	1	0	1.000	0	6	2.02
Mortimer,Michael,Charlstn-Sc	A	23	5	0	0	1	13.1	52	10	2	0	0	0	2	1	6	0	11	2	0	0	0	.000	0	0	0.00
Mosley,Tim,Williamsprt	A	21	23	0	0	6	33.2	161	40	23	16	0	2	2	4	16	0	26	2	0	2	0	1.000	0	1	4.28
Mosman,Marc,Bellingham	A	22	12	3	0	1	26.1	122	38	21	17	4	1	0	0	8	0	21	2	0	0	0	.000	0	0	5.81
Burlington	A	22	8	0	0	5	9	34	5	0	0	0	0	0	0	4	0	6	1	0	0	0	.000	0	0	0.00
Mosquea,Alberto,Martinsvlle	R	20	9	3	0	0	19.2	98	13	10	10	0	0	1	3	25	0	15	6	1	0	0	.000	0	0	4.58
Moss,Damian,Macon	A	19	27	27	0	0	149.1	653	134	73	59	13	0	2	12	70	0	177	14	5	9	10	.474	0	0	3.56
Mota,Daniel,Yankees	R	20	14	0	0	9	32.2	133	27	9	8	2	4	0	2	4	0	35	6	3	2	3	.400	0	0	2.20
Mott,Tom,Fort Wayne	A	22	25	25	1	0	129.2	567	123	67	58	6	6	3	10	48	0	64	14	0	13	4	.765	0	0	4.03
Mounce,Tony,Quad City	A	21	25	25	3	0	159	649	118	55	43	6	6	6	3	57	2	143	6	2	16	8	.667	1	0	2.43
Mudd,Scott,Hudson Vall	A	23	15	15	3	0	100.2	402	91	37	25	2	2	3	2	18	0	62	10	1	7	1	.875	1	0	2.24
Mull,Blaine,Springfield	A	19	25	25	0	0	125.1	564	142	79	68	12	9	7	6	50	1	71	14	0	4	10	.286	0	0	4.88
Mullins,Greg,Helena	R	24	4	4	0	0	23	98	22	7	7	0	0	0	2	6	0	14	0	2	4	0	1.000	0	0	2.74
Beloit	A	24	15	4	0	6	36.1	153	26	16	16	2	0	1	5	14	0	48	2	3	3	1	.750	0	2	3.96
Mullis,Steve,Royals	R	21	8	1	0	3	12.1	52	7	6	4	0	0	1	0	7	0	13	2	0	2	1	.667	0	1	2.92
Munro,Peter,Utica	A	21	14	14	0	0	90	389	79	38	26	3	3	3	7	33	1	74	4	0	5	4	.556	0	0	2.60
Murphy,Chris,Princeton	R	24	10	10	1	0	63.2	266	51	23	11	4	0	2	2	19	0	52	5	0	7	1	.875	1	0	1.55
Winston-Sal	A	24	4	3	0	1	20	75	13	7	6	2	1	1	0	5	0	22	1	0	2	1	.667	0	0	2.70
Murphy,Matt,Stockton	A	25	5	4	0	0	21.1	100	25	14	14	2	2	1	1	13	0	9	0	0	2	1	.667	0	0	5.91
Murphy,Sean,Portland	A	23	21	0	0	7	39.2	156	21	11	7	1	0	1	1	16	2	39	3	1	2	0	1.000	0	1	1.59
Murray,Dan,Pittsfield	A	22	22	0	0	19	32	145	24	17	7	1	2	0	1	16	3	34	3	0	0	6	.000	0	6	1.97
Muto,Junichiro,Visalia	A	27	17	0	0	10	38.1	149	33	16	15	1	1	1	2	5	0	35	1	0	1	2	.333	0	5	3.52
Myers,Jason,Burlington	A	22	16	16	1	0	95	413	109	64	53	14	3	5	2	26	0	85	4	0	2	9	.182	0	0	5.02
Myers,Tom,Visalia	A	26	30	13	0	5	85.1	406	108	81	61	6	3	6	10	45	0	34	7	1	3	8	.273	0	0	6.43
Mysel,David,Lakeland	A	25	20	0	0	8	29.1	141	36	22	19	3	3	0	3	14	0	32	2	0	1	1	.500	0	2	5.83
Najera,Noe,Columbus	A	25	43	0	0	15	42.2	189	34	20	16	3	2	1	6	24	3	53	4	2	3	1	.750	0	1	3.38
Kinston	A	25	8	3	0	2	20	78	10	6	5	0	1	0	2	9	1	14	0	0	0	1	.000	0	0	2.25
Nakashima,Tony,Great Falls	R	22	20	3	0	4	35.1	171	39	25	22	1	1	0	2	20	0	32	2	0	2	4	.333	0	0	5.60
Nartker,Steve,Fort Wayne	A	24	17	16	1	0	95.2	387	87	36	33	5	2	5	1	20	1	79	3	2	5	5	.500	1	0	3.10
Nash,Damond,Padres	R	20	15	3	1	2	44.1	212	55	42	36	2	2	2	3	27	0	32	4	0	1	3	.250	0	0	7.31
Nate,Scott,Helena	R	22	3	0	0	2	2	10	4	3	2	1	1	0	0	0	0	2	0	0	0	2	.000	0	1	9.00
Beloit	A	22	20	0	0	8	26	118	26	12	8	2	0	0	1	13	0	29	2	0	1	0	1.000	0	2	2.77
Neal,Billy,Great Falls	R	24	6	1	0	3	12.1	61	19	12	8	0	1	0	2	4	1	8	0	2	0	1	.000	0	0	5.84
Lethbridge	R	24	10	8	1	0	53	229	55	30	19	1	0	2	2	20	0	47	6	1	3	2	.600	0	0	3.23
Neese,Josh,Jamestown	A	24	20	2	0	5	36.1	153	29	15	15	2	4	3	4	14	2	38	4	4	3	1	.750	0	3	3.72
Negrette,Richard,Watertown	A	20	18	5	0	6	45.2	203	42	30	28	5	2	2	7	23	2	35	6	1	3	3	.500	0	3	5.52
Neiman,Josh,Padres	R	21	10	0	0	4	17	74	20	9	8	2	0	1	1	3	0	18	2	1	0	1	.000	0	1	4.24
Nelson,Chris,Sou. Oregon	A	23	16	6	0	3	54.1	218	43	25	21	5	3	3	3	13	1	52	1	1	2	3	.400	0	1	3.48
Modesto	A	23	2	2	0	0	10	37	4	1	1	0	0	0	0	4	0	8	1	0	2	0	1.000	0	0	0.90
Nelson,Earl,Durham	A	24	15	0	0	9	20	105	27	17	11	4	1	1	3	17	2	17	2	0	0	1	.000	0	2	4.95
Nelson,Rodney,Springfield	A	21	25	21	1	2	115.1	541	131	82	70	7	3	8	7	73	0	58	14	0	6	10	.375	0	0	5.46
Newell,Brandon,Mets	R	24	1	0	0	1	1	7	1	2	0	0	0	1	0	2	0	0	0	0	0	0	.000	0	0	0.00
St. Lucie	A	24	39	0	0	16	48.2	211	42	18	16	1	5	2	3	29	2	39	4	0	2	2	.500	0	3	2.96
Newman,Damon,W. Michigan	A	22	21	9	0	5	67.1	306	57	32	28	4	1	1	6	50	1	52	7	2	3	4	.429	0	1	3.74
Sou. Oregon	A	22	14	7	0	1	47.1	212	51	32	19	1	1	0	4	24	0	35	4	1	3	3	.500	0	1	3.61
Newman,Eric,Clinton	A	23	11	10	1	0	42.1	212	52	41	36	5	1	2	2	38	2	31	3	3	1	7	.125	0	0	7.65
Idaho Falls	R	23	15	14	0	0	81.2	365	91	49	40	3	5	4	3	35	0	65	3	1	8	4	.667	0	0	4.41
Newton,Chris,Fayettevlle	A	23	2	0	0	2	4.2	20	6	3	3	0	0	1	0	1	0	3	0	0	0	0	.000	0	0	5.79
Newton,Geronimo,Riverside	A	22	46	0	0	11	71.1	307	74	35	25	1	3	3	4	24	3	42	2	4	4	4	.500	0	2	3.15
Nichols,Jamie,White Sox	R	20	11	10	0	1	65.1	257	64	31	21	4	0	2	2	12	0	38	3	0	7	2	.778	0	0	2.89
Niedermaier,Brad,Elizabethtn	R	23	7	7	0	0	40.2	171	33	14	10	1	0	1	0	17	0	47	6	0	2	0	1.000	0	0	2.21
Niemeier,Todd,Everett	A	23	15	15	0	0	80	338	74	33	25	4	4	2	3	26	0	80	5	2	4	3	.571	0	0	2.81
Nivar,Amaury,Rockies	R	18	6	0	0	1	11.1	63	14	18	14	0	0	1	2	14	0	10	4	1	0	0	.000	0	0	11.12
Nix,Wayne,Athletics	R	19	6	3	0	0	14	57	15	10	9	3	1	0	1	4	0	14	1	0	0	2	.000	0	0	5.79
Noffke,Andrew,Utica	A	23	23	0	0	9	25.2	137	34	30	22	1	0	2	3	24	0	24	5	0	0	2	.000	0	0	7.71
Nogowski,Brandon,Mariners	R	20	20	0	0	17	27	124	31	10	8	0	1	0	1	13	1	27	4	0	0	0	.000	0	7	2.67
Noone,Billy,Batavia	A	23	6	0	0	2	5.2	35	14	11	9	1	0	1	0	3	0	2	1	0	1	0	1.000	0	0	14.29
Martinsvlle	R	23	1	1	0	0	4.1	17	3	1	1	1	0	0	0	1	0	5	0	0	0	0	.000	0	0	2.08
Norris,Mckenzie,Brewers	R	20	2	2	0	0	14.2	60	7	4	1	0	0	0	0	6	1	14	3	1	1	0	1.000	0	0	0.61
Novak,Troy,Ogden	R	24	15	15	2	0	97.1	416	101	50	42	5	1	3	4	41	0	71	5	0	5	1	.833	1	0	3.88
Nunez,Clemente,Brevard Cty	A	21	19	19	4	0	123.1	490	99	48	34	3	2	2	5	22	1	79	3	5	12	6	.667	2	0	2.48
Nunez,Maximo,Hagerstown	A	23	22	0	0	11	37.1	172	40	29	23	4	3	2	3	20	0	21	8	0	1	1	.500	0	0	5.54
St. Cathrns	A	23	7	0	0	4	7.2	42	11	10	8	1	0	2	0	7	0	6	1	0	1	0	1.000	0	0	9.39

1995 Pitching -- Single-A and Rookie Leagues

Player	Lg	A	G	GS	CG	GF	IP	BFP	H	R	ER	HR	SH	SF	HB	TBB	IBB	SO	WP	Bk	W	L	Pct.	ShO	Sv	ERA
Nuttle,Jamison,Augusta	A	24	6	0	0	0	7.2	38	5	3	1	0	0	0	0	8	0	10	0	0	0	0	.000	0	0	1.17
Erie	A	24	13	0	0	9	14.2	59	8	8	5	1	0	1	0	7	0	13	0	0	0	1	.000	0	1	3.07
Nyari,Pete,Piedmont	A	24	35	1	0	12	61.2	279	58	40	31	0	3	2	5	39	0	49	8	6	5	1	.833	0	1	4.52
Nye,Ryan,Clearwater	A	23	27	27	5	0	167	681	164	71	63	8	5	5	6	33	1	116	4	3	12	7	.632	1	0	3.40
Nygaard,Chris,Albany	A	24	41	0	0	18	56.2	241	60	25	18	5	3	0	2	8	0	43	3	0	6	4	.600	0	1	2.86
O'Brien,Brian,Fort Myers	A	24	24	0	0	17	34.1	147	31	20	11	2	2	1	0	15	1	20	4	0	0	3	.000	0	0	2.88
O'Connor,Brian,Pirates	R	19	14	5	0	5	43	183	33	22	9	1	0	1	0	13	0	43	4	2	2	2	.500	0	1	1.88
O'Flynn,Gardner,Charlstn-Sc	A	24	30	24	2	1	167	698	156	70	55	11	4	3	6	61	0	110	7	4	9	10	.474	1	0	2.96
O'Hearn,Paul,Ogden	R	25	11	7	0	1	32.1	176	41	45	32	0	0	1	14	26	0	27	3	3	1	4	.200	0	0	8.91
O'Malley,Paul,Kissimmee	A	23	27	27	0	0	147	661	148	86	59	7	3	3	18	62	0	80	13	2	8	10	.444	0	0	3.61
O'Quinn,Jimmy,Boise	A	22	23	0	0	9	22.1	106	22	12	12	1	1	2	3	18	2	26	6	0	0	0	.000	0	0	4.84
Oakley,Matt,Jamestown	A	22	1	0	0	0	1	7	3	2	2	0	0	0	0	1	0	0	0	0	0	0	.000	0	0	18.00
Ocando,Stiwar,Twins	R	18	14	0	0	8	22.2	118	26	25	15	2	1	4	4	22	0	20	7	4	0	1	.000	0	0	5.96
Ochsenfeld,Chris,Great Falls	R	19	14	7	0	2	42	209	50	45	32	1	0	4	1	33	0	32	5	0	1	4	.200	0	0	6.86
Ojeda,Erick,Kingsport	R	20	14	5	0	3	60	240	47	18	16	3	2	0	1	12	0	60	4	1	6	2	.750	0	0	2.40
Oldham,Bob,Burlington	R	22	18	8	0	4	52.1	249	55	43	32	3	2	1	9	32	2	55	4	0	3	6	.333	0	0	5.50
Olivier,Rich,Oneonta	A	21	12	12	0	0	60.1	264	63	36	26	2	3	2	4	21	0	50	8	0	3	3	.500	0	0	3.88
Olson,Philip,Mets	R	22	1	0	0	0	2	10	1	1	1	0	0	0	0	3	0	3	0	0	0	0	.000	0	0	4.50
Kingsport	R	22	12	10	2	1	67	271	47	24	18	1	1	1	8	23	0	45	4	1	6	2	.750	1	0	2.42
Olszewski,Eric,Macon	A	21	35	1	0	15	81.1	351	54	37	34	3	1	1	8	50	1	103	11	3	2	5	.286	0	5	3.76
Olszewski,Timothy,Bluefield	R	22	16	0	0	9	35.1	155	34	19	12	2	3	1	4	19	0	29	4	1	3	2	.600	0	3	3.06
Ormonde,Troy,Rockford	A	21	7	5	0	0	24.1	131	29	29	22	2	1	2	4	28	0	13	0	0	0	3	.000	0	0	8.14
Williamsprt	A	21	14	14	0	0	71.1	324	61	50	34	2	4	3	5	39	0	41	3	2	2	4	.333	0	0	4.29
Oropeza,Igor,Kinston	A	23	20	2	0	2	38	164	24	19	19	4	3	2	3	29	2	31	3	0	2	3	.400	0	1	4.50
Columbus	A	23	9	8	0	0	48.2	200	39	13	8	1	2	0	3	13	0	46	2	2	4	1	.800	0	0	1.48
Ortiz,Russell,Bellingham	A	22	25	0	0	20	34.1	131	19	4	2	1	0	1	0	13	0	55	2	1	2	0	1.000	0	11	0.52
San Jose	A	22	5	0	0	5	6	24	4	1	1	0	0	1	0	2	0	7	0	0	0	1	.000	0	0	1.50
Ortiz,Steve,Burlington	R	23	22	0	0	19	27.2	130	30	16	14	2	1	1	0	20	2	46	2	0	1	3	.250	0	7	4.55
Osteen,Gavin,Athletics	R	26	1	1	0	0	2	7	1	0	0	0	0	0	1	0	0	1	0	0	0	0	.000	0	0	0.00
Osting,Jimmy,Danville	R	19	11	10	0	0	39	190	46	34	31	1	0	1	0	25	0	43	12	0	2	7	.222	0	0	7.15
Ovalle,Bonnelly,Rangers	R	17	17	5	1	3	58	243	51	29	24	1	2	3	6	20	1	50	5	0	4	2	.667	1	1	3.72
Pacheco,Delvis,Braves	R	18	13	13	0	0	60	260	47	26	17	1	0	1	3	38	0	52	5	2	1	8	.111	0	0	2.55
Pack,Steve,St. Lucie	A	22	5	0	0	2	9.1	48	15	6	5	0	1	0	1	1	0	6	0	0	0	0	.000	0	0	4.82
Columbia	A	22	36	0	0	22	56	254	63	33	23	1	3	0	1	20	5	35	0	3	2	7	.222	0	12	3.70
Padilla,Roy,Michigan	A	20	4	1	0	2	8.1	46	10	9	6	0	0	0	0	7	0	7	2	0	0	0	.000	0	0	6.48
Butte	R	20	15	14	0	0	70	340	80	60	46	1	2	4	7	54	0	49	11	0	2	7	.222	0	0	5.91
Pailthorpe,Rob,Elmira	A	23	13	12	0	1	51.2	241	69	41	28	2	1	3	1	17	0	38	2	7	2	7	.222	0	1	4.88
Palki,Jeremy,Mariners	R	20	4	0	0	1	5.2	29	7	7	5	0	1	1	0	5	0	2	1	0	0	0	.000	0	0	7.94
Paluk,Jeff,San Bernrdo	A	23	41	0	0	19	52	255	65	34	33	2	4	3	7	30	2	52	1	0	6	3	.667	0	1	5.71
Vero Beach	A	23	2	0	0	0	4	19	5	3	3	0	0	0	0	2	0	4	0	0	1	0	1.000	0	0	6.75
Paredes,Carlos,Royals	R	20	10	10	0	0	51	221	56	28	20	2	2	2	2	17	0	37	4	0	4	2	.667	0	0	3.53
Parisi,Mike,Kane County	A	23	26	26	2	0	164.1	687	152	73	60	7	2	6	9	42	1	113	11	0	11	8	.579	1	0	3.29
Parotte,Frisco,Yankees	R	20	9	0	0	7	9.2	43	9	3	3	0	1	0	0	6	0	8	2	0	0	0	.000	0	1	2.79
Greensboro	A	20	22	0	0	8	35.1	161	40	20	11	3	2	1	2	16	1	35	3	0	3	1	.750	0	0	2.80
Parra,Julio,Vero Beach	A	21	22	1	0	12	41	176	39	21	13	2	1	2	1	20	1	36	4	0	7	3	.700	0	0	2.85
San Bernrdo	A	21	14	13	0	0	69.1	310	76	45	40	7	2	2	3	29	0	65	2	3	4	5	.444	0	0	5.19
Pasqualicchio,Michael,Helena	R	21	8	7	0	0	31.1	142	30	14	11	2	0	1	1	20	0	21	1	3	3	0	1.000	0	0	3.16
Patterson,Casey,Pittsfield	A	23	12	4	0	3	34	181	47	43	36	4	1	1	6	28	0	18	4	2	0	4	.000	0	0	9.53
Paugh,Richard,Augusta	A	24	52	0	0	25	59	252	60	23	17	3	4	1	0	17	5	61	6	1	6	2	.750	0	2	2.59
Paul,Andy,Stockton	A	24	38	13	0	11	106.1	473	116	59	48	7	5	1	8	42	4	87	6	3	7	5	.583	0	1	4.06
Paulino,Jose,Athletics	R	19	15	13	0	2	87.1	343	74	35	31	5	2	2	2	17	0	72	2	3	9	2	.818	0	0	3.19
Pauls,Matt,Charlstn-Sc	A	21	16	0	0	14	21.1	103	22	20	10	0	3	2	2	10	4	19	2	0	3	3	.500	0	2	4.22
Pavano,Carl,Michigan	A	20	22	22	1	0	141.1	591	118	63	54	7	6	7	6	52	0	138	9	0	6	6	.500	0	0	3.44
Pavicich,Paul,Fort Wayne	A	23	39	0	0	15	86.2	360	75	39	29	9	3	2	1	28	3	100	3	0	4	3	.571	0	5	3.01
Pavlovich,Tony,Brewers	R	21	19	0	0	18	18	78	20	10	8	0	2	1	0	3	0	20	1	0	0	2	.000	0	10	4.00
Helena	R	21	9	0	0	9	9.2	37	4	1	1	0	1	0	1	3	0	14	1	0	0	0	.000	0	4	0.93
Pearce,Jeffrey,Wisconsin	A	26	27	0	0	9	24.1	122	21	21	19	1	1	1	6	25	0	19	1	1	0	1	.000	0	0	7.03
Pearsall,J.J.,San Bernrdo	A	22	6	0	0	2	10.2	54	15	10	10	3	3	0	0	7	0	5	1	0	0	1	.000	0	0	8.44
Yakima	A	22	20	1	0	8	38.2	167	39	18	14	1	1	2	2	14	0	26	5	0	2	3	.400	0	1	3.26
Peguero,Jose,St. Cathrns	A	20	17	0	0	7	34	148	31	19	17	1	4	2	1	19	0	19	0	0	2	1	.667	0	0	4.50
Pelka,Brian,Augusta	A	24	26	0	0	7	40.2	193	46	31	27	3	4	2	5	29	1	29	4	1	1	3	.250	0	0	5.98
Pena,Alex,High Desert	A	23	34	6	0	20	77	363	97	68	57	4	7	1	4	28	2	44	6	3	3	4	.429	0	3	6.66
Pena,Jesus,Erie	A	21	3	3	0	0	10.2	56	18	16	15	1	1	0	2	7	0	5	0	0	0	3	.000	0	0	12.66
Pirates	R	21	7	6	0	0	35	138	20	11	10	0	0	0	1	19	0	36	4	0	0	0	.000	0	0	2.57
Pena,Juan,Red Sox	R	19	13	4	2	6	55.1	217	41	17	12	2	1	2	1	6	0	47	2	1	3	2	.600	1	1	1.95
Sarasota	A	19	2	2	0	0	7.1	35	8	4	4	0	0	0	2	3	0	5	1	1	1	1	.500	0	0	4.91
Penny,Tony,Royals	R	20	10	0	0	4	16	66	17	9	9	4	0	0	0	4	0	7	0	0	2	0	1.000	0	0	5.06
Peraza,Jose,Cubs	R	21	3	0	0	1	2.1	8	0	0	0	0	0	1	0	1	0	2	0	0	0	0	.000	0	0	0.00
Perez,Gil,Eerie	A	23	18	1	0	1	38.2	172	39	19	12	1	2	2	4	15	0	27	8	0	2	2	.500	0	0	2.79
Perez,Hilario,Utica	A	23	20	3	0	7	43	203	50	38	23	4	0	4	5	22	2	22	1	0	2	2	.500	0	1	4.81
Perez,Jayson,Clinton	A	22	13	1	0	2	20.2	110	31	28	15	2	0	2	2	15	2	17	1	0	0	1	.000	0	0	6.53
Idaho Falls	R	22	1	0	0	0	1	4	1	0	0	0	0	0	0	0	0	0	0	0	0	0	.000	0	0	0.00
Padres	R	22	2	0	0	1	2	11	3	2	2	0	0	0	0	2	0	1	0	0	0	0	.000	0	1	9.00
Perez,Jesse,Brewers	R	20	16	0	0	9	20	84	16	6	6	1	1	1	2	4	1	20	3	1	2	2	.500	0	4	2.70
Perez,Juan,W.Michigan	A	23	30	19	1	3	141	610	129	73	57	4	1	2	8	55	0	117	5	1	11	8	.579	1	0	3.64
Perez,Julio,Columbus	A	22	22	17	0	5	109.2	461	109	53	49	4	2	3	4	39	5	100	5	5	8	5	.615	0	1	4.02
Perez,Leo,Orioles	R	21	8	0	0	4	16.1	76	14	13	8	1	0	3	3	7	0	7	0	0	1	1	.500	0	0	4.41

379

1995 Pitching -- Single-A and Rookie Leagues

Player	Lg	A	G	GS	CG	GF	IP	BFP	H	R	ER	HR	SH	SF	HB	TBB	IBB	SO	WP	Bk	W	L	Pct.	ShO	Sv	ERA
Perez,Odaliz,Braves	R	18	12	12	1	0	65	264	48	22	16	0	3	0	3	18	0	62	7	3	3	5	.375	1	0	2.22
Perisho,Matt,Lk Elsinore	A	21	24	22	0	0	115.1	541	137	91	81	10	0	8	6	60	0	68	7	0	8	9	.471	0	0	6.32
Perkins,Dan,Fort Wayne	A	21	29	22	0	2	121.1	562	133	86	74	3	3	4	13	69	1	89	22	2	7	12	.368	0	0	5.49
Perkins,Paul,Lynchburg	A	25	25	0	0	14	29.2	135	34	15	13	1	0	0	2	10	3	28	1	0	0	3	.000	0	1	3.94
Perkins,Ron,Clearwater	A	28	6	0	0	3	6.1	30	6	3	2	1	0	0	1	5	0	3	1	0	1	1	.500	0	0	2.84
Perpetuo,Nelson,Charlotte	A	25	5	0	0	1	7	33	5	7	6	0	1	0	1	5	0	7	0	0	0	0	.000	0	0	7.71
Charlstn-Sc	A	25	32	10	1	13	103.2	439	80	47	37	11	3	2	5	51	5	125	5	1	6	4	.600	0	0	3.21
Persails,Mark,Tigers	R	20	11	10	0	0	51	237	50	37	25	4	5	3	4	25	0	30	8	1	1	4	.200	0	0	4.41
Petcka,Joe,Mets	R	25	1	0	0	1	2	7	1	0	0	0	0	0	0	0	0	0	0	0	0	0	.000	0	0	0.00
St. Lucie	A	25	30	1	0	12	46.2	213	39	35	31	1	2	0	3	35	0	28	7	0	1	1	.500	0	0	5.98
Peterman,Ernie,St. Cathrns	A	24	4	3	0	0	16.2	71	18	11	11	1	1	1	4	2	0	8	0	1	1	1	.500	0	0	5.94
Hagerstown	A	24	2	0	0	2	5	25	9	7	7	2	0	0	0	1	0	4	0	0	0	1	.000	0	0	12.60
Peters,Don,San Jose	A	26	20	13	0	5	68	284	68	33	32	6	1	3	4	24	0	38	1	1	3	3	.500	0	2	4.24
Peters,Brannon,Fort Wayne	A	24	11	1	0	5	24.2	115	29	17	12	1	2	0	1	16	1	24	3	0	1	1	.500	0	0	4.38
Peters,Timothy,Elizabethtn	R	22	27	0	0	7	32.2	134	27	16	6	1	0	0	0	5	2	36	4	0	2	3	.400	0	0	1.65
Peterson,Jay,Williamsprt	A	20	3	3	0	0	17	73	15	7	7	1	0	0	1	5	0	14	1	0	2	0	1.000	0	0	3.71
Rockford	A	20	13	13	0	0	65.1	312	67	56	47	5	1	2	0	47	0	45	9	1	4	7	.364	0	0	6.47
Petri,Thomas,Boise	A	23	10	1	0	1	23.2	105	27	12	11	0	1	4	1	13	0	9	5	1	1	0	1.000	0	0	4.18
Petroff,Dan,Cedar Rapids	A	22	27	27	2	0	146	635	153	86	75	9	5	4	14	47	0	98	9	2	9	10	.474	0	0	4.62
Pfaff,Jason,Lynchburg	A	26	35	10	0	4	114.1	488	115	56	41	6	5	2	8	31	3	95	8	0	5	6	.455	0	0	3.23
Phelps,Tom,W. Palm Bch	A	22	2	2	0	0	5	33	10	10	9	0	0	0	0	11	0	5	2	0	0	2	.000	0	0	16.20
Albany	A	22	24	24	1	0	135.1	597	142	76	50	6	0	4	5	45	0	119	5	1	10	9	.526	0	0	3.33
Phillips,Jason,Augusta	A	22	30	6	0	3	80	354	76	46	32	2	2	2	0	53	1	65	10	0	4	3	.571	0	0	3.60
Phillips,Jonny,Auburn	A	24	2	0	0	1	5.1	23	6	0	0	0	0	0	1	1	0	5	0	0	2	0	1.000	0	0	0.00
Phillips,Marc,Springfield	A	22	38	2	0	14	85.2	387	88	47	29	5	3	5	3	38	0	41	10	0	6	2	.750	0	3	3.05
Phipps,Chris,Piedmont	A	22	11	0	0	3	23	101	24	9	5	0	0	2	2	8	0	10	3	0	2	0	.000	0	1	1.96
Pickford,Kevin,Lynchburg	A	21	4	4	0	0	27.1	110	31	15	15	5	0	1	0	0	0	15	2	1	0	3	.000	0	0	4.94
Augusta	A	21	16	16	0	0	85.2	354	85	28	19	5	2	1	5	16	1	59	2	0	7	3	.700	0	0	2.00
Pierce,Drew,Huntington	R	21	22	0	0	17	33.1	159	46	29	23	2	3	2	4	10	0	42	9	1	2	4	.333	0	2	6.21
Pinango,Simon,Utica	A	22	20	0	0	6	28.2	135	30	27	22	2	0	3	1	16	1	27	4	0	2	4	.333	0	0	6.91
Pincavitch,Kevin,Vero Beach	A	25	32	13	2	5	124.2	504	83	37	23	7	5	1	5	48	0	103	12	1	10	7	.588	1	2	1.66
San Bernrdo	A	25	3	0	0	0	10	46	8	5	3	1	1	0	0	6	1	10	0	0	2	0	1.000	0	0	2.70
Pineda,Leonel,Kane County	A	19	5	5	1	0	33.1	142	44	14	13	0	2	2	0	6	1	10	3	0	2	2	.500	0	0	3.51
Pisciotta,Scott,W. Palm Bch	A	23	53	0	0	29	60.2	271	55	26	17	1	1	4	0	36	2	38	11	0	5	4	.556	0	2	2.52
Pivaral,Hugo,San Bernrdo	A	19	24	24	0	0	103	460	106	61	53	14	6	2	7	43	0	89	13	0	6	6	.600	0	0	4.63
Pizarro,Melvin,Martinsvlle	R	18	10	0	0	4	17.1	79	20	13	12	1	0	3	4	5	0	17	0	2	0	0	.000	0	0	6.23
Place,Mike,Durham	A	25	7	0	0	1	7.2	36	11	11	9	0	0	0	0	6	0	2	0	0	2	1	.667	0	0	10.57
South Bend	A	25	28	2	0	13	54.2	235	56	30	24	3	4	4	4	19	2	34	7	0	4	5	.444	0	3	3.95
Plant,David,Athletics	R	20	14	6	0	4	51	198	34	11	10	1	0	0	2	12	0	51	2	1	4	2	.667	0	0	1.76
Podjan,Jimmy,Rockies	R	21	17	5	0	3	45	231	71	58	45	3	2	3	3	27	0	30	14	1	2	7	.222	0	0	9.00
Ponson,Sidney,Bluefield	A	19	13	13	0	0	77.2	324	79	44	36	7	1	2	1	16	0	56	4	3	6	3	.667	0	0	4.17
Pontbriant,Matt,Lynchburg	A	24	27	17	1	4	108.2	476	137	67	61	16	5	2	14	28	3	60	2	1	7	7	.500	1	0	5.05
Pontes,Dan,Peoria	A	22	34	6	0	9	67.2	267	47	19	12	1	4	1	4	15	1	88	1	0	2	5	.286	0	1	1.60
Pool,Matt,Salem	A	22	28	28	2	0	165	705	191	90	88	18	5	2	6	50	5	95	16	1	9	9	.500	0	0	4.80
Portillo,Alex,South Bend	A	21	2	0	0	1	3.2	15	5	2	2	0	0	0	0	0	0	4	0	0	0	1	.000	0	0	4.91
Hickory	A	21	33	0	0	15	56	243	57	24	14	1	3	0	6	10	5	36	0	0	0	3	.000	0	2	2.25
Porzio,Mike,Ogden	R	23	8	8	2	0	48	220	66	39	34	4	0	3	2	15	0	26	6	0	4	3	.571	0	0	6.38
Poupart,Melvin,Kingsport	R	21	18	0	0	4	26.2	119	27	17	15	5	1	0	1	10	1	32	4	1	1	1	.500	0	1	5.06
Powell,Jeremy,Albany	A	20	1	1	0	0	5.2	20	4	1	1	0	0	0	0	1	0	6	1	0	1	0	1.000	0	0	1.59
Vermont	A	20	15	15	0	0	87	373	88	48	42	5	2	2	6	34	1	47	6	2	5	5	.500	0	0	4.34
Powell,Brian,Jamestown	A	22	5	5	0	0	26.1	108	19	12	9	1	0	1	5	8	0	15	3	0	2	1	.667	0	0	3.08
Fayettevlle	A	22	5	5	0	0	28	111	15	5	5	0	1	1	2	11	0	37	2	0	4	0	1.000	0	0	1.61
Prater,Pete,San Jose	A	23	5	4	0	0	22.2	90	18	8	8	0	1	1	1	7	0	14	0	0	2	0	1.000	0	0	3.18
Burlington	A	23	21	20	2	1	114.2	499	112	58	47	13	4	6	2	56	3	80	13	2	7	5	.583	0	0	3.69
Pratt,Richard,Pr. William	A	25	25	25	2	0	152	678	139	66	53	12	2	5	4	42	0	120	10	2	5	11	.313	1	0	3.14
Prejean,Alex,Huntington	R	21	14	3	0	2	31.2	164	37	36	33	2	0	3	3	31	0	23	11	1	3	2	.600	0	0	9.38
Prempas,Lyle,Brewers	R	21	13	6	0	2	50.2	226	49	33	23	1	2	2	1	28	0	67	4	0	6	5	.545	0	0	4.09
Presley,Kirk,Columbia	A	21	4	4	0	0	21	100	30	17	12	0	1	0	0	13	0	8	1	0	1	2	.333	0	0	5.14
Press,Gregg,Kane County	A	24	29	21	0	1	132.1	571	127	72	53	8	5	3	5	37	1	82	10	0	10	8	.556	0	0	3.60
Prestach,J.D.,Astros	R	20	11	11	0	0	51.1	225	48	18	15	0	2	1	5	24	0	56	4	6	4	3	.571	0	0	2.63
Preston,George,Brewers	R	22	2	0	0	0	7.2	30	5	1	0	0	0	0	0	3	0	15	1	1	1	0	1.000	0	0	0.00
Helena	R	22	3	2	0	1	6.2	36	11	9	6	3	0	1	0	4	0	5	0	0	0	1	.000	0	0	8.10
Price,Tom,San Bernrdo	A	24	42	13	2	9	151.2	605	145	49	37	5	5	1	3	14	4	82	5	0	10	5	.667	0	3	2.20
Priest,Eddie,Winston-Sal	A	22	12	12	1	0	67	275	60	32	27	7	2	2	0	22	0	60	2	0	5	5	.500	1	0	3.63
Prihoda,Steve,Spokane	A	23	14	13	1	0	69.1	293	65	36	25	7	3	1	5	18	0	63	4	0	1	6	.143	0	0	3.25
Puffer,Brandon,Twins	R	20	14	5	0	0	40.2	175	29	21	13	0	2	1	0	21	0	35	5	0	0	0	.000	0	1	2.88
Pumphrey,Kenny,Kingsport	R	19	12	12	0	0	65.1	283	50	32	28	3	3	0	6	42	0	76	7	0	7	3	.700	0	0	3.86
Putrich,Josh,Rockford	A	22	6	1	0	3	9.2	41	10	8	8	1	0	0	0	5	1	6	1	0	0	2	.000	0	0	7.45
Pyrtle,Joe,Pittsfield	A	22	17	0	0	7	31	140	32	18	12	1	1	1	0	12	0	17	2	3	0	1	.000	0	2	3.48
Quezada,Edward,Expos	R	21	12	10	0	0	52.1	221	52	36	29	2	1	1	5	10	0	36	10	1	0	7	.000	0	0	4.99
Quintana,Urbano,Huntington	R	21	19	1	0	11	34.2	162	43	26	22	4	1	1	5	12	0	35	5	5	1	2	.333	0	3	5.71
Quinteros,Steve,Angels	R	20	7	1	0	1	12.1	63	19	10	6	1	0	0	4	3	1	13	2	2	0	0	.000	0	0	4.38
Quirk,John,South Bend	A	25	22	1	0	9	52.1	244	52	32	23	4	1	6	1	36	0	30	4	0	3	2	.600	0	0	3.96
Radlosky,Robert,Fort Wayne	A	22	30	18	1	5	120.2	522	111	64	54	11	7	5	11	55	2	102	5	2	11	8	.579	0	0	4.03
Raggio,Brady,Peoria	A	23	8	8	3	0	48.2	181	42	13	10	1	1	0	1	7	0	46	1	0	3	0	1.000	2	0	1.85
St. Pete	A	23	20	3	0	4	47.1	195	43	24	20	2	3	1	1	13	2	35	2	1	2	3	.400	0	0	3.80
Rain,Steve,Rockford	A	21	53	0	0	51	59.1	234	38	12	8	0	3	2	1	23	3	66	8	0	5	2	.714	0	23	1.21

1995 Pitching -- Single-A and Rookie Leagues

Player	Lg	A	G	GS	CG	GF	IP	BFP	H	R	ER	HR	SH	SF	HB	TBB	IBB	SO	WP	Bk	W	L	Pct.	ShO	Sv	ERA
Raines,Ken,Durham	A	23	19	0	0	3	23.2	118	38	19	13	3	2	1	0	12	2	15	0	0	1	0	1.000	0	0	4.94
Danville	R	23	11	0	0	11	12.2	47	8	4	1	0	0	2	0	1	0	14	0	1	0	0	.000	0	6	0.71
Macon	A	23	14	0	0	12	18.2	70	11	4	4	0	0	0	0	5	1	22	1	1	1	1	.500	0	8	1.93
Rajotte,Jason,W. Michigan	A	23	44	0	0	37	52	242	51	27	18	1	3	1	3	38	3	52	3	0	2	2	.500	0	13	3.12
Rakers,Jason,Watertown	A	23	14	14	1	0	75	315	72	27	25	3	0	2	0	24	1	73	6	2	4	3	.571	1	0	3.00
Rama,Shelby,Clearwater	A	24	4	0	0	1	8.1	36	12	4	4	0	0	0	0	1	0	2	1	0	0	0	.000	0	0	4.32
Ramirez,Rafael,Savannah	A	21	26	25	0	0	147.1	645	160	81	64	8	4	9	7	42	1	91	9	2	6	15	.286	0	0	3.91
Ramos,Cesar,Bakersfield	A	22	24	4	0	6	60.2	257	63	28	24	2	6	2	1	17	0	35	7	1	6	3	.667	0	2	3.56
Kinston	A	22	8	0	0	2	12.1	56	16	6	5	0	2	0	2	3	1	4	0	0	1	2	.333	0	0	3.65
Ramos,Edgar,Quad City	A	21	2	2	0	0	4.2	27	5	9	8	0	0	0	1	7	0	5	1	0	0	0	.000	0	0	15.43
Astros	R	21	5	5	0	0	14.2	62	14	6	3	0	1	0	2	5	0	16	1	0	0	1	.000	0	0	1.84
Kissimmee	A	21	4	4	0	0	22	80	11	4	1	1	0	0	0	1	0	16	0	0	4	0	1.000	0	0	0.41
Randall,Scott,Portland	A	20	15	15	1	0	95	391	76	35	21	2	2	2	8	28	1	78	7	2	7	3	.700	0	0	1.99
Randolph,Stephen,Yankees	R	22	8	3	0	1	24.1	94	11	7	6	1	0	0	1	16	0	34	3	1	4	0	1.000	0	0	2.22
Oneonta	A	22	6	6	0	0	21.2	109	19	22	18	0	0	2	1	23	0	31	5	0	0	3	.000	0	0	7.48
Rangel,Julio,Yankees	R	20	14	0	0	5	28.2	123	20	18	14	2	1	0	4	16	1	30	2	0	1	3	.250	0	2	4.40
Rantz,Ronnie,Beloit	A	23	10	0	0	1	8.1	54	12	15	15	0	0	0	0	15	0	12	6	1	0	1	.000	0	0	16.20
Rath,Frederick,Elizabethtn	R	23	27	0	0	25	33.1	134	20	8	5	2	2	0	1	11	1	50	3	0	1	1	.500	0	12	1.35
Rathbun,Jason,Tampa	A	23	10	5	0	3	26.2	118	27	17	12	2	1	0	2	10	0	14	2	0	1	0	1.000	0	0	4.05
Ratliff,Chris,Burlington	A	23	15	14	1	0	61	281	74	49	43	7	1	2	1	32	5	33	5	0	2	6	.250	1	0	6.34
Rauch,Bob,Red Sox	R	23	7	0	0	6	5.2	27	8	4	3	0	2	0	0	2	1	6	0	0	0	1	.000	0	2	4.76
Reames,Britt,New Jersey	A	22	5	5	0	0	29.2	121	19	7	5	1	1	0	3	12	0	42	5	0	2	1	.667	0	0	1.52
Savannah	A	22	10	10	1	0	54.2	227	41	23	21	7	0	0	5	15	0	63	9	1	3	5	.375	0	0	3.46
Rector,Bobby,Burlington	A	21	27	24	0	0	135.2	589	135	78	62	7	4	5	6	59	3	102	9	2	9	11	.450	0	0	4.11
Redman,Mark,Fort Myers	A	22	8	5	0	0	32.2	134	28	13	10	4	1	2	1	13	0	26	2	0	2	1	.667	0	0	2.76
Reed,Brandon,Fayetteville	A	21	55	0	0	53	64.2	252	40	11	7	1	1	0	3	18	1	78	8	0	3	0	1.000	0	41	0.97
Reed,Brian,Peoria	A	24	63	0	0	30	90.1	357	55	29	18	5	5	3	6	25	2	119	3	1	11	3	.786	0	4	1.79
Reed,Daniel,Bluefield	R	21	6	1	0	1	14	53	10	5	4	1	0	0	0	5	0	11	0	0	1	0	1.000	0	0	2.57
Reed,Chris,Winston-Sal	A	22	24	24	3	0	149	613	116	63	55	11	3	1	4	68	1	104	3	1	10	7	.588	1	0	3.32
Reed,Jason,Vero Beach	A	23	21	0	0	9	23.2	102	18	9	9	3	0	0	1	11	1	17	0	0	0	0	.000	0	0	3.42
Great Falls	R	23	15	12	0	1	72.2	323	79	42	33	2	1	2	5	28	1	45	0	1	2	5	.286	0	1	4.09
Reed,Kenny,Martinsville	R	21	13	0	0	6	23	119	29	22	19	3	0	0	2	21	0	15	12	0	0	1	.000	0	0	7.43
Reed,Steve,Johnson Cty	R	20	31	0	0	19	42.2	194	48	24	21	2	0	1	0	15	0	41	3	2	2	2	.500	0	1	4.43
Reichstein,Derek,Elmira	A	23	22	2	0	8	51.2	234	52	37	30	2	2	4	5	27	1	37	5	4	1	4	.200	0	1	5.23
Reid,Rayon,Erie	A	22	8	7	0	0	47.2	189	37	16	13	2	0	0	3	11	0	47	4	1	3	3	.500	0	0	2.45
Augusta	A	22	12	11	1	0	61.2	268	52	36	30	6	1	1	5	28	0	47	4	1	2	5	.286	0	0	4.38
Reilly,Sean,Twins	R	19	6	0	0	1	13.2	65	19	12	8	1	0	0	0	6	0	11	0	0	0	1	.000	0	0	5.27
Reinfelder,Dave,Jamestown	A	22	16	14	0	0	78.1	334	85	48	40	6	5	3	6	17	0	55	5	0	2	5	.286	0	0	4.60
Reitzenstein,Brad,Portland	A	23	7	0	0	2	8	44	2	10	9	0	1	0	2	16	1	10	10	2	0	1	.000	0	0	10.13
Remington,Jake,Idaho Falls	R	20	15	15	1	0	87.1	379	106	62	50	3	2	3	5	29	0	54	5	1	5	5	.500	0	0	5.15
Renfroe,Chad,Michigan	A	22	12	3	0	6	31.2	138	28	16	11	1	0	1	2	15	2	25	4	0	1	3	.250	0	0	3.13
Renko,Todd,Boise	A	23	5	0	0	2	3.2	20	6	8	3	3	0	0	0	3	0	2	0	0	0	0	.000	0	0	7.36
Resz,Greg,Tampa	A	24	12	0	0	3	13.1	61	10	9	5	0	0	0	1	9	2	16	3	0	0	1	.000	0	1	3.38
Reyes,Dennis,Vero Beach	A	19	3	2	0	0	10	43	8	2	2	1	0	0	0	6	0	9	0	1	1	0	1.000	0	0	1.80
Reyes,Jose,Charlotte	A	26	30	2	0	11	61.1	274	67	38	30	7	0	3	4	22	0	41	5	0	1	3	.250	0	3	4.40
Charlstn-Sc	A	26	4	0	0	2	4	25	10	8	8	2	0	0	0	3	0	5	1	0	0	0	.000	0	0	18.00
Reyes,Jose,Erie	A	23	19	7	1	1	58.1	253	53	25	22	2	1	0	1	29	1	44	3	0	2	3	.400	0	0	3.39
Reynolds,Mark,Rangers	R	23	7	1	0	2	10	50	12	10	6	1	0	0	0	11	0	10	0	2	0	2	.000	0	0	5.40
Reynolds,Walker,Danville	R	22	20	0	0	4	38.1	166	26	19	17	3	1	2	6	19	1	30	3	0	1	3	.250	0	1	3.99
Rhine,Kendall,Hagerstown	A	25	42	0	0	36	55.1	230	41	20	16	2	4	0	3	28	1	49	8	0	3	3	.500	0	13	2.60
Rhodes,Joey,Orioles	R	21	13	11	0	0	71	311	72	36	24	0	3	1	2	28	1	43	2	0	4	2	.667	0	0	3.04
Frederick	A	21	2	1	0	1	6	28	8	3	3	0	1	0	2	2	0	2	1	0	0	1	.000	0	0	4.50
Rhodriguez,Rory,Albany	A	25	37	7	0	10	90	379	80	44	35	8	3	3	2	34	0	83	3	0	3	4	.429	0	2	3.50
Ricabal,Dan,San Bernrdo	A	23	43	0	0	13	72	315	63	35	31	7	0	2	5	33	1	62	2	1	4	1	.800	0	2	3.88
Richardson,Darrell,Lethbridge	R	24	15	15	1	0	84.2	393	106	63	47	6	1	1	5	38	0	85	10	1	5	4	.556	0	0	5.00
Richardson,Jesse,Helena	R	23	25	0	0	6	39	182	44	23	20	6	2	0	2	27	0	34	1	0	3	1	.750	0	2	4.62
Richardson,David,Marlins	R	22	9	0	0	6	15.2	62	8	5	4	1	0	1	2	5	0	8	1	0	0	2	.000	0	1	2.30
Richardson,Kasey,Twins	R	19	7	7	2	0	47	190	38	10	6	1	0	0	3	11	0	35	1	0	5	2	.714	2	0	1.15
Elizabethtn	R	19	3	3	0	0	19.1	79	12	8	5	0	3	1	1	13	1	11	1	0	1	0	1.000	0	0	2.33
Richmond,Terrance,Angels	R	19	1	0	0	0	1	5	1	1	1	1	0	0	0	1	0	0	0	0	0	0	.000	0	0	9.00
Ricketts,Chad,Cubs	R	21	2	2	0	0	9	32	1	1	0	0	0	0	1	1	0	5	0	0	1	0	1.000	0	0	0.00
Williamsprt	A	21	12	12	0	0	68.2	312	89	46	32	4	0	3	8	16	0	37	1	3	4	5	.444	0	0	4.19
Riedling,John,Billings	R	20	13	7	0	2	38.1	192	51	38	30	4	0	3	1	21	2	28	6	0	2	2	.500	0	1	7.04
Rigby,Brad,Modesto	A	23	31	23	0	0	154.2	653	135	79	66	5	2	7	12	48	0	145	8	2	11	4	.733	0	2	3.84
Riley,Brian,Angels	R	20	17	0	0	17	15	63	11	5	5	0	1	0	1	10	0	16	2	1	0	0	.000	0	9	3.00
Rios,Danny,Tampa	A	23	57	0	0	52	67.1	296	67	24	15	1	5	2	8	20	4	72	2	0	0	4	.000	0	24	2.00
Ritter,Jason,Springfield	A	21	7	0	0	2	11.2	65	19	20	16	1	0	1	2	6	0	12	3	0	1	0	1.000	0	0	12.34
Royals	R	21	2	0	0	1	3.2	16	3	1	0	0	1	0	0	1	0	2	1	0	0	0	.000	0	0	0.00
Spokane	A	21	10	4	0	0	33.2	135	25	12	12	1	0	1	3	15	0	29	1	1	3	1	.750	0	0	3.21
Rivera,Oscar,Great Falls	R	20	18	1	0	13	28.1	134	28	19	13	3	2	4	0	17	1	30	3	0	2	1	.667	0	1	4.13
Rivette,Scott,Sou. Oregon	A	22	9	1	0	3	19	83	16	5	2	0	1	1	1	11	2	22	1	0	2	0	1.000	0	0	0.95
W. Michigan	A	22	8	0	0	4	15.1	65	12	5	5	0	0	2	0	7	0	15	1	0	0	2	.000	0	2	2.93
Rizzo,Todd,Pr. William	A	25	36	0	0	10	68	307	68	30	21	2	2	1	3	39	8	59	13	0	3	5	.375	0	1	2.78
Roach,Petie,San Bernrdo	A	25	30	0	0	14	33	143	28	16	11	2	2	2	2	14	1	38	5	0	1	2	.333	0	8	3.00
Robbins,Jason,Winston-Sal	A	23	23	23	3	0	141	571	113	62	48	16	0	5	7	42	1	106	5	1	9	6	.600	1	0	3.06
Robbins,Mike,Spokane	A	22	5	5	0	0	27	109	23	9	7	1	1	0	2	6	0	16	1	1	1	3	.250	0	0	2.33
Springfield	A	22	8	8	0	0	40	172	47	22	20	4	0	1	1	9	0	26	2	0	2	3	.400	0	0	4.50

1995 Pitching -- Single-A and Rookie Leagues

Player	Lg	A	G	GS	CG	GF	IP	BFP	H	R	ER	HR	SH	SF	HB	TBB	IBB	SO	WP	Bk	W	L	Pct.	ShO	Sv	ERA
Robbins,Jacob,Yankees	R	20	14	3	0	3	37.1	159	32	26	23	2	2	1	1	18	1	17	4	0	2	3	.400	0	0	5.54
Oneonta	A	20	1	0	0	1	1	3	0	0	0	0	0	0	0	0	0	1	0	0	0	0	.000	0	0	0.00
Roberts,Frankie,Rangers	R	21	1	0	0	0	0.2	7	1	2	2	0	0	0	0	4	0	0	0	0	0	0	.000	0	0	27.00
Roberts,Grant,Mets	R	18	11	3	0	4	29.1	121	19	13	7	1	1	1	3	14	1	24	4	1	2	1	.667	0	0	2.15
Roberts,Randolph,Princeton	R	22	15	9	0	2	62.2	281	51	35	22	3	1	2	6	33	3	74	14	2	4	5	.444	0	0	3.16
Roberts,Ray,Wilmington	A	23	13	0	0	6	19	79	18	7	7	2	0	1	0	2	0	16	0	0	1	2	.333	0	4	3.32
Springfield	A	23	38	0	0	12	65.2	292	86	38	33	6	4	3	3	17	0	43	5	0	2	5	.286	0	1	4.52
Roberts,Willis,Fayettevlle	A	21	17	15	0	0	80	339	72	33	24	2	1	2	6	40	0	52	15	3	6	3	.667	0	0	2.70
Robins,Doug,Lethbridge	R	22	15	4	0	2	40.1	175	43	29	23	7	0	1	0	16	0	28	6	2	2	2	.500	0	0	5.13
Robinson,Marty,Yankees	R	19	11	8	2	0	61.2	236	54	20	17	4	2	0	3	13	0	56	7	2	6	1	.857	2	0	2.48
Greensboro	A	19	2	1	0	0	8.1	44	8	7	7	0	1	0	0	12	0	5	1	0	1	0	1.000	0	0	7.56
Rocker,John,Macon	A	21	16	16	0	0	86	375	86	50	43	5	1	1	4	52	0	61	5	1	4	4	.500	0	0	4.50
Eugene	A	21	12	12	0	0	59.1	260	45	40	34	4	1	1	2	36	0	74	7	2	1	5	.167	0	0	5.16
Rodriguez,Chris,Daytona	A	24	5	0	0	1	10.2	46	14	7	7	2	0	0	2	2	0	6	0	0	1	0	1.000	0	0	5.91
Rodriguez,Hector,Angels	R	21	9	2	1	2	24.2	99	21	9	8	1	1	1	2	9	0	21	8	0	2	2	.500	0	0	2.92
Rodriguez,Luis,Bellingham	A	20	4	0	0	1	6	33	6	5	4	0	0	1	0	8	0	8	1	0	0	0	.000	0	0	6.00
Butte	R	20	7	0	0	2	12.1	61	12	14	13	1	0	1	1	12	0	10	2	0	0	1	.000	0	0	9.49
Rodriguez,Salvador,Tampa	A	21	6	0	0	0	7.1	40	13	10	9	1	0	0	1	4	0	7	1	0	0	1	.000	0	0	11.05
Rodriguez,Tomas,Tigers	R	21	14	0	0	8	21.1	93	14	13	6	0	0	1	5	8	0	21	5	1	0	0	.000	0	1	2.53
Rodriguez,Victor,Medicne Hat	R	22	17	2	0	0	58	255	42	31	25	5	3	2	9	40	0	45	11	0	4	1	.800	0	0	3.88
Roettgen,Mark,Peoria	A	19	4	4	0	0	14	76	24	20	16	1	1	0	0	15	0	14	3	0	0	4	.000	0	0	10.29
Johnson Cty	R	19	13	13	0	0	66	302	63	48	41	11	4	3	6	40	0	60	4	4	4	5	.444	0	0	5.59
Rogan,Sean,Johnson Cty	R	22	12	0	0	6	28.2	134	30	22	18	4	2	3	3	17	0	22	2	0	1	0	1.000	0	0	5.65
Rogers,Jason,Frederick	A	23	15	14	1	0	66.2	309	64	38	32	1	2	2	3	45	3	39	6	2	1	3	.250	0	0	4.32
High Desert	A	23	5	5	0	0	23	121	32	26	20	2	1	0	0	18	0	10	5	0	1	3	.250	0	0	7.83
Rojano,Rafael,Greensboro	A	25	19	1	0	9	26	134	35	24	19	5	0	0	7	13	0	38	5	2	0	0	.000	0	1	6.58
Tampa	A	25	3	0	0	0	4.1	19	4	3	3	0	0	0	0	2	1	1	0	0	0	2	.000	0	0	6.23
Rojas,Miguel,Angels	R	20	9	0	0	4	9.2	47	10	6	5	0	0	2	6	5	0	7	3	4	1	0	1.000	0	0	4.66
Rolish,Chad,Sou. Oregon	A	23	4	0	0	4	6	26	6	3	2	0	2	0	0	4	2	1	0	0	1	0	1.000	0	1	3.00
Rolocut,Brian,San Bernrdo	A	22	11	3	0	2	12.2	70	15	10	8	0	2	3	1	16	0	10	0	0	1	0	1.000	0	0	5.68
Roman,Dan,Charlotte	A	25	7	5	0	1	25.2	126	30	22	22	2	1	2	6	19	1	21	2	2	2	2	.500	0	0	7.71
Romano,Mike,Dunedin	A	24	28	26	1	1	150.1	654	141	79	69	15	4	3	11	75	0	102	5	3	11	7	.611	1	0	4.13
Romboli,Curtis,Utica	A	23	14	6	2	3	51.1	225	60	32	26	1	1	1	1	16	0	34	4	1	2	3	.400	0	0	4.56
Romero,John,Angels	R	20	18	6	2	4	71	291	57	29	19	0	0	2	5	18	1	64	8	4	7	3	.700	1	1	2.41
Romine,Jason,Portland	A	21	4	3	0	0	12.2	58	14	9	9	0	0	2	0	7	0	5	0	0	0	1	.000	0	0	6.39
Romo,Gregory,Tigers	R	21	5	5	0	0	27.1	110	25	9	8	0	0	0	0	5	0	25	3	0	3	1	.750	0	0	2.63
Root,Derek,Kissimmee	A	21	5	0	0	1	6	29	10	3	3	0	0	0	0	2	0	3	0	0	0	0	.000	0	0	4.50
Auburn	A	21	17	3	0	5	38.1	165	28	14	14	0	2	1	2	24	0	37	4	1	2	0	1.000	0	1	3.29
Roque,Johnson Cty	R	21	14	0	0	3	19.1	81	15	11	11	4	1	1	2	9	1	22	0	3	2	0	1.000	0	0	5.12
Roque,Rafael,St. Lucie	A	24	24	24	2	0	136.2	582	114	65	54	7	2	4	4	72	1	81	11	4	6	9	.400	1	0	3.56
Rosa,Cristy,Rockies	R	18	12	12	0	0	58.2	273	77	56	35	0	2	4	2	16	0	42	8	2	0	9	.000	0	0	5.37
Rosado,Jose,Wilmington	A	21	25	25	0	0	138	562	128	53	48	9	2	7	3	30	6	117	1	5	10	7	.588	0	0	3.13
Rosario,Nelson,Medicne Hat	R	20	10	0	0	7	12.2	64	21	13	11	1	0	1	1	6	0	5	1	0	0	1	.000	0	0	7.82
Rose,Brian,Portland	A	23	5	0	0	1	8.2	40	10	5	5	1	2	1	2	6	1	11	0	0	1	1	.500	0	0	5.19
Asheville	A	23	10	1	0	5	14.2	62	14	8	8	0	0	0	4	2	0	15	1	0	1	0	1.000	0	0	4.91
Rose,Brian,Michigan	A	20	21	20	2	0	136	561	127	63	52	5	3	1	9	31	0	105	4	0	8	5	.615	0	0	3.44
Rosenbohm,Jim,Burlington	A	22	3	0	0	1	5	36	9	11	11	1	0	1	1	11	0	3	5	0	0	0	.000	0	0	19.80
Auburn	A	22	22	1	0	6	51.2	236	48	23	21	0	1	0	10	32	3	50	5	0	2	4	.333	0	1	3.66
Rosenkranz,Terry,Beloit	A	25	4	0	0	2	8	30	2	2	0	0	0	0	0	2	0	4	0	0	0	0	.000	0	0	0.00
Stockton	A	25	35	1	0	14	49.1	234	44	34	34	4	5	4	1	49	2	43	4	0	1	2	.333	0	0	6.20
Ross,Jeremy,Marlins	R	22	3	0	0	3	8	33	8	1	0	0	0	0	0	1	1	11	1	0	2	0	1.000	0	0	0.00
Elmira	A	22	20	0	0	3	42	184	38	17	14	0	1	2	2	20	1	40	6	1	1	0	1.000	0	2	3.00
Rossiter,Mike,Modesto	A	23	18	7	0	3	68.2	290	68	33	32	5	2	2	2	19	0	70	4	1	7	2	.778	0	0	4.19
Rowland,Thad,Visalia	A	25	7	0	0	3	11	53	18	8	6	1	0	0	1	4	0	5	1	0	0	1	.000	0	0	4.91
Ruch,Robert,Twins	R	23	7	2	0	4	23.1	98	16	13	10	0	0	0	1	16	0	30	3	0	1	3	.250	0	2	3.86
Fort Wayne	A	23	9	3	0	1	26.1	108	17	8	8	1	0	0	2	16	0	27	1	0	0	1	.000	0	1	2.73
Ruiz,Rafael,Hickory	A	21	5	0	0	1	4	25	7	8	7	0	0	0	1	5	0	5	2	0	1	0	1.000	0	0	15.75
Bristol	R	21	22	0	0	6	37.2	154	26	14	9	1	3	0	0	15	0	57	2	1	1	2	.333	0	1	2.15
Runion,Tony,Kinston	A	24	28	24	0	2	143	599	131	70	65	9	2	6	13	57	0	84	10	0	7	11	.389	0	0	4.09
Runion,Jeff,Charlstn-Sc	A	21	2	2	0	0	11.1	54	12	8	4	0	2	0	1	6	0	6	2	0	1	1	.500	0	0	3.18
Runyan,Paul,Charlstn-Wv	A	24	15	5	0	2	52.1	227	56	29	24	3	0	1	2	17	5	28	5	0	6	2	.750	0	0	4.13
Runyan,Sean,Quad City	A	22	22	11	0	2	76.1	327	67	37	31	10	1	2	3	29	0	65	4	0	4	6	.400	0	0	3.66
Rusch,Glendon,Wilmington	A	21	26	26	1	0	165.2	629	110	41	32	5	4	3	4	34	3	147	3	1	14	6	.700	1	0	1.74
Rushing,William,Fort Wayne	A	23	13	0	0	5	25.1	100	15	11	5	0	0	0	1	10	0	25	4	2	1	1	.500	0	1	1.78
Rushworth,Jim,Albany	A	24	6	0	0	4	8.2	44	10	9	8	0	0	1	0	6	3	5	3	0	1	2	.333	0	0	8.31
W. Palm Bch	A	24	10	0	0	4	12.1	54	11	5	5	0	1	1	1	6	0	9	0	0	1	0	1.000	0	1	3.65
Ruskey,Jason,Everett	A	23	3	3	0	0	13.1	62	15	13	9	3	0	0	1	9	0	7	2	0	0	3	.000	0	0	6.08
Ruyak,Todd,Winston-Sal	A	25	34	9	0	7	85.2	369	99	44	38	8	6	3	1	20	0	48	2	1	5	6	.455	0	0	3.99
Ryan,Jay,Daytona	A	20	26	26	0	0	134.2	579	128	61	52	10	3	2	9	54	0	98	13	1	11	5	.688	0	0	3.48
Ryan,Michael-sean,Rangers	R	20	17	0	0	8	38.1	159	36	15	10	1	1	1	2	12	0	41	2	0	2	5	.286	0	2	2.35
Ryan,Reid,Charlstn-Sc	A	25	22	5	0	0	47	250	64	57	49	3	1	1	6	40	2	39	4	0	0	4	.000	0	0	9.38
Visalia	A	25	12	5	0	4	31.2	170	51	43	33	3	1	4	7	26	0	14	2	3	0	6	.000	0	0	9.38
Sacharko,Mark,Astros	R	20	12	0	0	8	24	105	23	14	10	5	0	0	2	12	1	22	0	0	1	2	.333	0	0	3.75
Kissimmee	A	20	6	1	0	2	13.2	68	16	10	10	0	0	2	2	11	0	6	2	0	0	1	.000	0	0	6.59
Sadler,Alden,Stockton	A	24	37	14	1	10	114	501	122	62	56	9	3	2	8	59	0	82	6	2	4	9	.308	1	2	4.42
Sagedal,Brent,Hudson Vall	A	22	14	5	0	4	34.1	158	42	29	27	7	2	1	1	18	1	25	7	1	0	2	.000	0	1	7.08
Saier,Matt,Spokane	A	23	16	0	0	9	35.1	138	24	14	13	2	2	1	2	12	0	41	6	0	1	2	.333	0	4	3.31

1995 Pitching -- Single-A and Rookie Leagues

Player	Lg	A	G	GS	CG	GF	IP	BFP	H	R	ER	HR	SH	SF	HB	TBB	IBB	SO	WP	Bk	W	L	Pct.	ShO	Sv	ERA
Saipe,Mike,Salem	A	22	21	9	0	7	85.1	347	68	35	33	7	1	2	2	32	4	90	9	1	4	5	.444	0	3	3.48
Sak,James,Idaho Falls	R	22	13	0	0	3	32.2	123	15	9	6	1	1	0	0	12	1	55	1	1	3	1	.750	0	1	1.65
Clinton	A	22	7	7	3	0	50	200	42	12	11	2	1	2	0	14	0	37	0	3	6	1	.857	0	0	1.98
Salazar,Luis,Stockton	A	25	52	0	0	26	89.1	350	66	28	23	6	5	3	7	18	5	71	0	1	6	2	.750	0	10	2.32
Salazar,Michael,Lakeland	A	25	42	3	0	18	87.1	371	86	37	31	4	4	1	6	21	1	52	2	1	7	3	.700	0	5	3.19
Salmon,Fabian,South Bend	A	24	15	0	0	8	23.2	103	18	15	10	1	0	0	1	11	0	15	2	0	4	1	.800	0	3	3.80
Samboy,Juan,Mets	R	21	12	4	0	4	48.1	196	40	17	16	0	0	2	3	17	0	31	3	0	5	3	.625	0	1	2.98
Sampson,Benj,Fort Myers	A	21	28	27	3	1	160	664	148	71	62	11	8	8	4	52	0	95	5	0	11	9	.550	2	0	3.49
Sanchez,Bienvenido,Expos	R	20	16	1	0	9	37	153	27	7	6	0	2	0	3	12	0	29	4	3	1	2	.333	0	5	1.46
Sanchez,Jesus,Columbia	A	21	27	27	4	0	169.2	705	154	76	59	9	2	5	7	58	0	177	10	4	9	7	.563	0	0	3.13
Sanchez,Mike,Yakima	A	20	18	1	0	11	28.1	121	16	4	3	0	2	1	4	20	2	27	5	1	1	2	.333	0	5	0.95
Sanders,Frankie,Burlington	R	20	12	12	3	0	70	292	48	31	23	2	1	0	3	32	0	80	2	1	3	5	.375	0	0	2.96
Columbus	A	20	2	0	0	1	9	39	9	3	3	0	1	0	1	4	0	9	1	0	1	1	.500	0	0	3.00
Sanders,Allen,Royals	R	21	1	0	0	1	2	6	1	0	0	0	0	0	0	0	0	3	0	0	0	0	.000	0	1	0.00
Spokane	A	21	14	10	0	2	56.1	257	67	43	28	2	3	1	2	18	1	36	3	0	4	5	.444	0	0	4.47
Sanders,Craig,Spokane	A	23	22	0	0	12	46.1	197	32	11	10	2	2	1	2	24	0	32	2	1	3	1	.750	0	3	1.94
Saneaux,Francisco,High Desert	A	22	23	11	0	4	52.2	296	56	77	62	8	0	6	11	72	1	64	10	4	0	8	.000	0	1	10.59
Sangeado,Juan,Great Falls	R	21	16	3	0	4	46	207	47	28	22	4	4	1	1	25	3	46	4	0	1	3	.250	0	1	4.30
Santamaria,Juan,Tigers	R	19	12	0	0	2	20	104	26	17	12	2	1	1	4	11	1	17	4	3	2	0	1.000	0	1	5.40
Santamaria,Bill,Kingsport	R	20	13	13	1	0	71	303	62	37	33	8	1	3	3	29	0	55	3	0	5	3	.625	0	0	4.18
Santana,Marino,Wisconsin	A	24	15	15	2	0	96.2	368	57	26	19	5	2	2	1	25	0	110	6	0	8	3	.727	1	0	1.77
Riverside	A	24	9	9	0	0	48	214	44	47	33	10	3	4	2	25	0	57	2	3	3	5	.375	0	0	6.19
Santana,Pedro,Red Sox	R	18	12	6	0	2	39.1	182	51	40	28	6	2	3	0	20	0	14	3	1	2	4	.333	0	0	6.41
Santiago,Antonio,Utica	A	19	4	4	0	0	18.2	91	24	17	11	0	1	1	0	13	0	11	7	0	0	3	.000	0	0	5.30
Red Sox	R	19	6	3	0	2	25	107	30	17	12	0	0	0	0	3	0	24	1	2	2	2	.500	0	0	4.32
Santiago,Derek,Marlins	R	20	11	10	0	1	58	245	55	20	16	1	1	2	3	17	0	59	8	1	5	1	.833	0	0	2.48
Santiago,Jose,Spokane	A	21	22	0	0	10	48.2	227	60	26	17	1	1	2	5	20	4	32	3	0	2	4	.333	0	1	3.14
Santiago,Sandi,Tampa	A	26	34	3	0	12	57.2	251	54	28	25	1	1	3	0	29	1	55	6	0	3	2	.600	0	3	3.90
Santoro,Gary,Elmira	A	23	24	0	0	20	36	164	45	21	15	1	2	0	6	10	1	34	6	0	1	4	.200	0	6	3.75
Santos,Juan,Orioles	R	20	21	0	0	15	25.1	107	25	11	9	3	1	1	2	4	1	16	1	0	0	2	.000	0	3	3.20
Bluefield	R	20	1	0	0	0	3	10	1	0	0	0	0	0	0	0	0	2	1	0	0	0	.000	0	0	0.00
Santos,Rafael,Pirates	A	20	11	10	1	1	51.1	246	63	49	36	1	4	2	6	27	0	26	1	0	2	5	.286	0	0	6.31
Erie	A	20	2	0	0	1	5	5	0	0	0	0	0	0	0	2	0	1	0	0	0	0	.000	0	0	0.00
Sauerbeck,Scott,St. Lucie	A	24	20	1	0	4	26.2	116	26	10	6	0	0	2	0	14	1	25	2	2	0	1	.000	0	2	2.03
Columbia	A	24	19	0	0	13	33	139	28	14	12	2	2	0	1	14	1	33	3	1	5	4	.556	0	2	3.27
Saunders,Tony,Brevard Cty	A	22	13	13	0	0	71	275	60	29	24	6	1	4	7	15	0	54	3	0	6	5	.545	0	0	3.04
Sauritch,Chris,Frederick	A	24	1	0	0	1	1	4	1	1	1	0	0	0	0	0	0	1	0	0	0	0	.000	0	0	9.00
Bluefield	R	24	13	0	0	8	19.1	91	18	13	8	3	2	0	2	11	1	16	2	0	4	1	.800	0	3	3.72
High Desert	A	24	7	0	0	4	14.2	68	20	10	10	3	0	0	0	8	1	10	1	0	1	0	1.000	0	0	6.14
Sauve,Jeffrey,Utica	A	23	11	0	0	5	15.1	72	19	12	8	1	1	1	1	8	1	16	2	1	1	1	.500	0	1	4.70
Sawyer,Zack,Modesto	A	23	55	0	0	16	70	328	85	45	42	8	5	0	5	28	0	72	15	0	7	1	.875	0	3	5.40
Scafa,Bob,Bakersfield	A	23	42	5	0	13	78.2	349	92	56	37	13	2	3	4	26	1	61	4	0	5	8	.385	0	4	4.23
Schaffner,Eric,Yankees	R	21	11	7	0	1	43.2	182	31	17	8	1	4	1	4	16	0	48	4	2	2	2	.500	0	0	1.65
Greensboro	A	21	1	1	0	0	5.1	28	5	8	3	0	1	1	0	5	0	2	2	0	0	1	.000	0	0	5.06
Scheer,Greg,Everett	A	24	18	0	0	5	21.2	102	16	12	10	0	1	2	3	19	2	23	2	0	0	1	.000	0	1	4.15
Scheffer,Aaron,Wisconsin	A	20	9	0	0	6	13.2	65	17	14	10	2	1	0	0	5	1	8	2	0	0	1	.000	0	0	6.59
Everett	A	20	24	0	0	9	43.1	185	44	23	18	4	1	0	2	16	1	38	2	1	2	5	.286	0	1	3.74
Scheffler,Craig,Bakersfield	A	24	32	19	0	3	105.2	490	118	85	66	15	7	5	4	65	0	51	15	0	3	8	.273	0	0	5.62
Schenbeck,Tommy,Beloit	A	24	18	1	0	9	37.1	171	35	18	15	3	3	3	2	23	1	37	5	0	4	2	.667	0	5	3.62
Stockton	A	24	31	1	0	11	44.2	222	66	41	35	3	5	3	4	16	1	32	4	0	1	5	.167	0	2	7.05
Schiefelbein,Mike,Burlington	A	23	1	0	0	0	0	1	0	0	0	0	0	0	0	1	0	0	0	0	0	0	.000	0	0	0.00
Bellingham	A	23	3	0	0	0	0.2	6	1	0	0	0	0	0	0	3	0	1	0	0	0	0	.000	0	0	0.00
Schleuss,Del,Princeton	R	22	23	0	0	5	32	142	29	20	16	1	1	1	1	22	2	34	9	0	0	3	.000	0	1	4.50
Schlomann,Brett,Greensboro	A	21	25	25	1	0	147.2	639	144	76	64	10	2	1	9	54	1	140	8	1	10	7	.588	0	0	3.90
Tampa	A	21	2	2	0	0	11	44	10	6	2	2	0	0	0	3	0	8	0	0	2	0	1.000	0	0	1.64
Schlutt,Jason,Rancho Cuca	A	24	11	0	0	5	14.2	67	16	9	8	0	1	1	1	4	0	11	3	0	0	1	.000	0	2	4.91
Schneider,Jeff,Hagerstown	A	23	2	0	0	1	0.2	8	1	2	2	0	0	0	0	4	0	0	0	1	0	1	.000	0	0	27.00
Blue Jays	R	23	3	2	0	0	4.2	33	9	10	8	0	0	1	2	7	0	2	1	0	0	1	.000	0	0	15.43
Schneider,Tom,W. Palm Bch	A	23	4	0	0	1	3.1	21	8	5	4	0	0	0	1	2	0	3	0	0	0	1	.000	0	0	10.80
Schnur,Curt,Danville	R	23	18	0	0	7	31.1	159	34	24	20	0	3	5	4	22	0	31	5	3	1	4	.200	0	0	5.74
Schramm,Carl,San Jose	A	26	37	0	0	19	71	297	57	23	20	4	8	2	2	24	3	68	5	0	6	4	.600	0	3	2.54
Schrenk,Steve,White Sox	R	27	2	2	0	0	7	27	5	2	0	0	0	0	0	0	0	6	0	0	1	0	1.000	0	0	0.00
Schroeder,Rodney,Padres	A	21	2	2	0	0	7.1	38	12	7	6	0	0	0	2	2	0	8	1	0	0	1	.000	0	0	7.36
Schulte,Troy,Auburn	A	24	23	0	0	17	31.1	130	30	20	17	5	2	0	1	9	0	22	1	0	1	2	.333	0	6	4.88
Schultea,Mathew,Ogden	R	21	34	0	0	10	53.2	244	59	37	28	1	3	3	4	18	4	43	3	1	4	2	.667	0	1	4.70
Schultz,Scott,Watertown	A	23	9	5	0	3	30.2	141	39	24	16	2	0	1	2	11	0	20	2	3	1	3	.250	0	2	4.70
Scofield,Josh,Pirates	R	19	2	0	0	2	2	13	3	2	2	0	0	0	0	4	0	4	0	0	0	0	.000	0	0	9.00
Scott,Ron,Peoria	A	24	21	1	0	8	34	168	37	36	32	4	1	4	5	30	0	21	9	2	0	2	.000	0	0	8.47
Scutero,Brian,Boise	A	22	22	0	0	20	22	101	17	13	12	1	2	0	1	16	1	17	1	0	1	2	.333	0	12	4.91
Seabury,Jaron,Blue Jays	R	20	15	0	0	5	39.2	164	35	16	14	2	2	1	7	17	0	18	6	1	3	0	1.000	0	1	3.18
Secoda,Jason,Bristol	R	21	13	12	0	0	65.2	307	78	57	39	3	1	3	1	33	0	63	8	1	2	8	.200	0	0	5.35
Segura,Juan,Rockies	R	20	20	0	0	12	29.1	140	32	19	17	0	1	4	3	19	1	20	1	0	0	1	.000	0	1	5.22
Seip,Rod,Charlotte	A	22	6	4	0	1	27	116	26	9	6	1	0	2	1	6	1	23	1	0	2	1	.333	0	0	2.00
Seki,Kiyokazu,Visalia	A	31	35	3	0	16	85.2	360	79	53	47	11	1	0	1	29	0	84	1	0	5	6	.455	0	3	4.94
Sellner,Aaron,Elizabethtn	R	22	19	1	0	5	33.2	137	30	15	8	1	1	0	1	10	0	32	1	1	1	2	.333	0	2	2.14
Serna,Joe,Lakeland	A	22	5	0	0	3	9	44	10	4	2	1	2	0	1	5	2	3	1	2	0	1	.000	0	1	2.00
Fayetteville	A	22	12	0	0	4	26.2	105	14	13	7	1	3	0	2	11	0	21	2	0	4	0	1.000	0	0	2.36

Player	Lg	A	G	GS	CG	GF	IP	BFP	H	R	ER	HR	SH	SF	HB	TBB	IBB	SO	WP	Bk	W	L	Pct.	ShO	Sv	ERA
Settle,Brian,Pirates	R	18	11	0	0	5	20.2	105	25	22	19	4	2	3	1	20	0	11	4	1	0	2	.000	0	0	8.27
Severino,Edy,Blue Jays	R	20	24	0	0	12	24	121	31	25	15	0	2	2	2	13	0	13	8	2	1	3	.250	0	1	5.63
Severino,Jose,New Jersey	A	22	17	10	0	1	66.1	303	65	48	39	8	1	4	2	37	2	68	9	3	3	3	.500	0	0	5.29
Sexton,Jeff,Columbus	A	24	14	13	2	0	82.1	318	66	27	20	2	1	1	3	16	0	71	1	0	6	2	.750	2	0	2.19
Kinston	A	24	8	8	2	0	57	226	52	17	16	3	0	0	2	7	0	41	6	1	5	1	.833	1	0	2.53
Shannon,Bob,Royals	R	18	16	0	0	9	27.2	112	28	11	10	0	1	2	3	3	0	26	4	0	1	1	.500	0	2	3.25
Shaver,Tony,Quad City	A	24	35	0	0	9	56	222	35	15	10	2	2	0	2	19	1	40	2	1	2	0	1.000	0	1	1.61
Shelby,Anthony,Greensboro	A	22	27	13	0	3	89.2	381	87	54	40	5	2	4	6	28	0	81	6	0	3	8	.273	0	0	4.01
Sheldon,Shane,Helena	R	23	17	0	0	7	15.1	91	18	28	23	3	0	0	3	25	0	15	8	2	0	0	.000	0	0	13.50
Shiell,Jason,Braves	R	19	12	0	0	9	22.1	101	23	16	11	0	0	0	2	10	1	13	3	0	1	3	.250	0	2	4.43
Shoemaker,Stephen,Greensbro	A	23	17	17	0	0	81	347	62	33	28	5	2	2	4	52	0	82	4	0	4	4	.500	0	0	3.11
Tampa	A	23	3	2	0	0	16.2	73	9	5	2	1	2	1	0	13	0	12	2	0	0	1	.000	0	0	1.08
Short,Barry,Pittsfield	A	22	2	0	0	1	2	10	4	1	1	0	0	0	0	0	0	3	1	0	0	0	.000	0	1	4.50
Columbia	A	22	40	1	0	15	77.2	319	63	22	17	1	2	0	2	22	2	56	5	2	4	3	.571	0	4	1.97
Shrum,Dennis,Kissimmee	A	24	38	0	0	15	91.2	408	96	44	33	7	5	1	5	28	0	69	5	5	7	6	.538	0	5	3.24
Shumaker,Anthony,Martinsvlle	R	23	6	4	0	0	28	120	31	16	14	1	2	0	1	8	0	26	3	0	1	3	.250	0	0	4.50
Batavia	A	23	9	4	1	0	39	157	38	10	7	0	0	0	0	4	0	31	2	0	2	2	.500	1	0	1.62
Shumate,Jacob,Macon	A	20	17	14	0	0	56	296	38	56	45	7	1	3	9	87	0	57	19	2	0	8	.000	0	0	7.23
Danville	R	20	7	2	0	2	13.1	80	6	21	16	1	0	0	2	32	0	16	14	0	1	2	.333	0	0	10.80
Shurman,Ryan,Braves	R	19	10	7	0	0	34.2	158	37	31	26	1	0	0	2	21	0	26	9	3	1	6	.143	0	0	6.75
Sick,Dave,Cedar Rapds	A	24	50	0	0	12	73.2	331	72	41	30	5	5	2	10	27	3	64	5	1	6	5	.545	0	3	3.67
Sievert,Mark,Hagerstown	A	23	27	27	3	0	160.2	644	126	59	52	14	5	1	2	46	0	140	2	0	12	6	.667	0	0	2.91
Sikes,Jason,Martinsvlle	R	20	4	3	0	0	16.2	81	23	13	11	1	2	1	0	9	0	10	3	0	0	3	.000	0	0	5.94
Sikes,Ken,Vero Beach	A	23	14	12	0	1	64	291	64	44	36	4	0	2	2	36	0	50	4	1	3	4	.429	0	0	5.06
Sikorski,Brian,Auburn	A	21	23	0	0	19	34.1	137	22	8	8	1	0	1	0	14	2	35	1	0	1	2	.333	0	12	2.10
Quad City	A	21	2	0	0	1	3	11	1	1	0	0	0	0	0	0	0	4	0	0	1	0	1.000	0	0	0.00
Siler,Jeff,Lakeland	A	25	27	0	0	10	27.2	100	21	9	7	2	2	0	0	7	1	26	0	1	2	2	.500	0	1	2.28
Fayettevlle	A	25	21	0	0	4	22.2	86	16	2	1	0	2	0	1	11	0	25	1	1	1	1	.500	0	1	0.40
Silva,Luis,W. Michigan	A	21	10	1	0	1	21.1	102	31	16	16	2	1	1	2	7	0	24	2	3	1	0	1.000	0	0	6.75
Sou. Oregon	A	21	19	14	0	3	78	337	79	43	33	8	3	3	7	20	0	76	5	0	4	3	.571	0	1	3.81
Silva,Theodore,Charlstn-Sc	A	21	11	11	0	0	66.2	276	59	26	25	4	1	3	7	12	2	66	5	2	5	4	.556	0	0	3.38
Simmons,Carlos,Rangers	R	22	14	9	0	3	57.2	255	57	33	21	1	2	2	9	22	0	44	4	0	4	3	.571	0	0	3.28
Sinacori,Chris,Dunedin	A	25	12	0	0	11	12	53	13	9	9	1	0	0	3	4	1	11	1	0	0	1	.000	0	2	6.75
Sinclair,Steve,Dunedin	A	24	46	0	0	18	73	297	69	26	21	4	1	1	3	17	1	52	2	3	5	3	.625	0	2	2.59
Sinnes,Dave,Wilmington	A	25	18	0	0	11	23.2	115	15	12	8	0	1	1	5	24	1	34	6	0	0	2	.000	0	3	3.04
Skrmetta,Matt,Fayettevlle	A	23	44	2	0	15	89.2	371	66	36	27	9	6	1	3	35	2	105	2	0	4	2	.692	0	2	2.71
Skuse,Nick,Cedar Rapds	A	24	26	25	3	0	147	650	155	84	66	10	3	3	9	61	1	116	12	3	13	7	.650	1	0	4.04
Slade,Shawn,Lk Elsinore	A	25	15	0	0	6	14	65	15	11	8	1	2	0	1	5	0	15	0	2	1	0	1.000	0	0	5.14
Cedar Rapds	A	25	30	0	0	14	42.1	186	42	24	20	1	3	2	2	19	2	35	4	1	3	1	.750	0	3	4.25
Slamka,John,Asheville	A	22	6	1	0	2	11	46	9	5	5	0	0	1	1	4	0	7	1	1	1	1	.500	0	1	4.09
Slininger,Dennis,Peoria	A	24	3	3	0	0	10.2	54	16	13	13	5	0	0	0	7	0	12	0	0	0	3	.000	0	0	10.97
Smart,Jon,Expos	R	22	2	2	0	0	10.2	43	10	2	2	0	0	1	2	1	0	6	0	0	2	0	1.000	0	0	1.69
Vermont	A	22	5	5	0	0	27.2	118	29	9	7	1	1	3	3	7	0	21	0	0	0	1	.000	0	0	2.28
Smith,Andy,W. Michigan	A	21	30	22	0	4	122.2	554	117	71	53	3	2	3	10	72	1	68	6	1	4	10	.286	0	2	3.89
Smith,Brook,Burlington	A	23	39	4	0	12	88	414	85	67	49	7	7	3	3	72	7	70	19	2	3	2	.600	0	1	5.01
Smith,Hut,Frederick	A	23	20	2	0	7	32	162	39	23	23	4	2	1	4	31	1	28	7	1	3	2	.600	0	2	6.47
High Desert	A	23	11	9	0	1	46.1	216	58	54	47	10	2	5	8	15	0	38	4	1	3	4	.429	0	0	9.13
Smith,Cam,Fayettevlle	A	22	29	29	2	0	149	652	110	75	63	6	3	3	18	87	0	166	21	1	13	8	.619	2	0	3.81
Smith,Chuck,South Bend	A	26	26	25	4	1	167	688	128	70	50	8	7	2	13	61	0	145	21	11	10	10	.500	2	0	2.69
Smith,Dan,Rangers	R	20	4	3	0	0	19	81	19	9	9	0	0	0	2	5	0	12	0	0	0	3	.000	0	0	4.26
Charlotte	A	20	9	9	1	0	58	242	53	23	19	4	1	2	3	16	0	34	1	0	5	1	.833	1	0	2.95
Smith,Eric,Auburn	A	22	14	14	0	0	71	314	70	37	31	4	0	4	5	30	0	56	5	3	2	6	.250	0	0	3.93
Smith,John,W. Michigan	A	24	25	0	0	11	33.1	149	32	21	15	4	2	0	3	18	0	33	2	1	1	0	1.000	0	1	4.05
Smith,Josh,Padres	R	18	8	0	0	4	10.2	53	12	8	2	0	1	0	1	8	0	8	6	1	1	2	.333	0	1	1.69
Smith,Jake,Charlstn-Wv	A	24	44	0	0	14	62.1	275	66	28	25	3	4	1	2	24	5	43	3	1	4	5	.444	0	1	3.61
Smith,Justin,Batavia	A	24	15	10	0	0	61.1	266	71	35	29	5	1	2	5	20	0	37	5	2	4	3	.571	0	0	4.26
Smith,Keilan,Dunedin	A	22	26	24	1	1	149	663	164	83	68	11	6	2	15	53	1	85	16	3	11	6	.647	0	0	4.11
Smith,Mason,Burlington	A	23	8	4	0	2	23.1	109	26	18	18	1	0	1	0	12	1	19	2	1	0	4	.000	0	0	6.94
Smith,Ramon,Medicne Hat	R	22	19	0	0	9	22.1	104	15	16	9	2	0	0	0	24	0	26	6	0	1	4	.200	0	2	3.63
Smith,Brian,Hagerstown	A	23	47	0	0	36	104	402	77	18	10	1	5	0	5	16	1	101	2	2	9	1	.900	0	21	0.87
Smith,Randy,St. Cathrns	A	23	18	0	0	9	33	141	34	14	12	0	0	0	1	9	0	26	1	0	0	2	.000	0	2	3.27
Smith,Ryan,Riverside	A	24	23	23	2	0	141.2	609	142	68	49	7	7	5	10	50	1	108	5	3	10	7	.588	1	0	3.11
Smith,Shad,Burlington	A	29	2	2	0	0	8.2	42	10	8	6	1	1	0	0	6	1	4	1	0	1	0	1.000	0	0	6.23
Smith,Thomas,Rangers	R	19	5	0	0	1	3	33	6	14	9	0	0	0	0	17	0	4	17	2	0	0	.000	0	0	27.00
Smith,Toby,Wilmington	A	24	30	7	0	13	79	320	67	32	27	9	2	1	3	20	2	65	6	2	5	7	.417	0	4	3.08
Smith,Travis,Helena	R	23	20	7	0	11	56	224	41	16	15	4	0	0	7	19	0	63	4	2	4	2	.667	0	5	2.41
Smith,Roy,Wisconsin	A	20	27	27	1	0	149	669	179	100	89	9	6	1	3	54	2	109	10	2	7	14	.333	0	0	5.38
Smyth,Gregg,Auburn	A	23	14	14	1	0	75	332	87	48	38	2	2	6	2	25	0	48	6	0	6	6	.500	1	0	4.56
Snyder,Matt,Bluefield	R	21	17	0	0	15	34.2	150	35	9	4	1	0	0	3	13	0	46	1	0	0	0	.000	0	8	1.04
Sobik,Trad,Fayettevlle	A	20	18	18	0	0	101.2	430	100	68	47	4	2	4	5	43	0	58	1	2	8	5	.615	0	0	4.16
Sobkoviak,Jeff,Salem	A	24	40	5	0	10	86.1	371	96	52	46	13	3	4	5	37	5	44	7	0	5	3	.625	0	2	4.80
Soden,Chad,Everett	A	22	13	12	0	0	61.1	256	55	30	23	3	0	0	1	17	1	52	3	1	4	3	.571	0	0	3.38
Solomon,Dave,Charlstn-Wv	A	24	43	0	0	27	39.2	175	38	19	15	3	2	2	5	23	2	26	2	2	1	2	.333	0	6	3.40
Soriano,Jacobo,Angels	R	21	11	0	0	9	11.2	53	9	6	4	0	0	0	0	7	2	10	0	1	0	1	.000	0	4	3.09
Sorzano,Ronnie,Expos	R	20	4	4	0	0	19	86	24	13	11	0	0	0	1	6	0	10	1	0	1	2	.333	0	0	5.21
Sosa,Helpis,W. Michigan	A	23	21	6	0	5	53.2	255	59	47	28	5	3	4	4	26	0	37	5	1	3	5	.375	0	2	4.70
Sou. Oregon	A	23	6	2	0	2	13.1	65	21	11	10	2	0	2	1	6	1	17	1	0	0	1	.000	0	0	6.75

1995 Pitching -- Single-A and Rookie Leagues

			HOW MUCH HE PITCHED						WHAT HE GAVE UP												THE RESULTS					
Player	Lg	A	G	GS	CG	GF	IP	BFP	H	R	ER	HR	SH	SF	HB	TBB	IBB	SO	WP	Bk	W	L	Pct.	ShO	Sv	ERA
Sosa,Jose,Lynchburg	A	23	10	0	0	6	17	82	27	14	13	1	1	0	0	6	1	12	4	1	0	0	.000	0	0	6.88
Soto,Dan,Spokane	A	22	3	2	0	1	10.2	45	11	6	6	1	0	1	1	4	0	10	0	0	0	3	.000	0	0	5.06
Soto,Seferino,Yakima	A	20	15	6	0	1	36	189	30	37	31	1	0	2	1	54	2	34	9	2	0	2	.000	0	0	7.75
South,Carl,Yakima	A	21	13	10	0	1	55.2	257	72	47	38	4	1	3	1	19	0	30	12	0	3	6	.333	0	0	6.14
Spade,Matt,Augusta	A	23	51	1	0	21	71	289	50	23	23	4	1	0	6	19	3	71	5	1	6	5	.545	0	5	2.92
Spang,R.J.,Huntington	R	23	18	0	0	10	31.1	138	31	21	16	3	3	1	5	9	0	31	2	3	1	2	.333	0	3	4.60
Sparks,Jeff,Princeton	R	24	16	2	0	7	39	172	32	19	14	2	0	1	0	27	2	49	2	1	2	0	1.000	0	2	3.23
Spaulding,Scott,New Jersey	A	22	35	0	0	11	48.2	200	36	17	14	4	1	0	6	14	0	40	2	1	1	0	1.000	0	2	2.59
Spear,Russell,Idaho Falls	R	18	14	13	0	0	66.2	324	83	65	46	7	0	5	4	36	0	53	8	0	3	2	.600	0	0	6.21
Speier,Justin,Williamsprt	A	22	30	0	0	22	36.1	142	27	6	6	1	2	2	1	4	0	39	0	0	2	1	.667	0	12	1.49
Spiller,Derron,Visalia	A	26	32	11	0	8	88	390	114	64	59	6	6	3	5	16	1	52	5	2	5	8	.385	0	0	6.03
Splittorff,James,Elizabethtn	R	22	13	12	1	1	72.1	319	64	40	26	5	0	2	7	29	0	72	11	2	5	4	.556	1	0	3.24
Spring,Joshua,Dunedin	A	23	18	0	0	6	25.2	110	16	6	3	1	1	0	1	17	1	23	3	0	1	0	1.000	0	2	1.05
Hagerstown	A	23	19	4	0	4	45.1	198	44	23	21	5	2	2	3	19	0	33	4	0	1	4	.200	0	0	4.17
St. Pierre,Bobby,Oneonta	A	22	15	15	0	0	89	368	83	39	28	4	1	4	2	24	0	91	4	2	5	3	.625	0	0	2.83
Stachler,Eric,Auburn	A	23	18	0	0	5	36.1	179	47	35	34	2	2	2	1	27	2	32	4	0	1	2	.333	0	2	8.42
Stading,Kris,Cubs	R	19	11	0	0	1	13.2	66	8	4	1	0	0	1	1	14	0	12	1	1	0	0	.000	0	0	0.66
Stahl,Andy,Rockies	R	20	12	12	0	0	52	223	42	31	20	1	3	1	3	19	0	44	9	2	3	5	.375	0	0	3.46
Stallings,Ben,Red Sox	R	19	8	0	0	4	12.2	61	14	11	11	2	0	0	0	11	0	7	1	0	1	0	1.000	0	0	7.82
Stanifer,Robby,Brevard Cty	A	24	18	13	0	0	82.2	360	97	47	38	4	4	5	7	15	0	45	2	0	3	6	.333	0	0	4.14
Stark,Zac,Kane County	A	21	5	4	0	0	15.2	94	27	30	27	2	1	0	2	17	0	5	1	0	1	1	.500	0	0	15.51
Marlins	R	21	11	1	0	3	26	102	18	7	5	0	2	1	2	3	0	16	1	0	3	1	.750	0	2	1.73
Starling,Marcus,Huntington	R	23	13	3	0	4	21.1	130	36	39	36	2	0	1	6	25	0	22	11	0	0	2	.000	0	0	15.19
Steed,Sam,Springfield	A	27	8	0	0	6	14.2	64	14	4	4	1	0	0	0	6	0	14	2	0	2	0	1.000	0	0	2.45
Stein,Blake,Peoria	A	22	27	27	1	0	139.2	596	122	69	59	12	1	4	5	61	0	133	2	1	10	6	.625	0	0	3.80
Steinert,Rob,Dunedin	A	24	17	11	0	1	74.2	329	82	48	39	4	4	4	3	29	0	41	6	4	3	4	.429	0	0	4.70
Steinke,Brock,Kissimmee	A	21	8	5	0	0	32.2	160	48	28	24	0	0	4	1	16	0	15	5	1	0	3	.000	0	0	6.61
Quad City	A	21	21	1	0	7	37.1	168	30	20	18	2	0	4	3	27	0	18	4	2	2	1	.667	0	0	4.34
Auburn	A	21	6	0	0	3	8.2	38	11	2	2	1	0	0	0	3	0	6	0	0	1	0	1.000	0	0	2.08
Stentz,Brent,Tigers	R	20	24	0	0	24	26.2	107	21	7	7	1	1	1	1	12	1	28	4	1	2	1	.667	0	16	2.36
Lakeland	A	20	2	0	0	1	2	6	0	0	0	0	0	0	0	0	0	0	0	0	0	0	.000	0	0	0.00
Stephens,Shannon,Elmira	A	22	17	12	0	2	90.2	364	72	38	26	3	3	0	4	17	1	74	6	2	8	5	.615	0	0	2.58
Stephens,Bill,Albany	A	23	13	1	0	6	20.1	95	25	16	13	2	1	3	1	9	0	16	3	0	1	3	.250	0	0	5.75
Vermont	A	23	13	0	0	8	27.1	111	17	5	5	0	0	0	5	7	0	30	5	0	3	1	.750	0	3	1.65
Stephenson,Brian,Daytona	A	22	26	26	0	0	150	640	145	79	66	7	6	3	7	58	2	109	14	2	10	9	.526	0	0	3.96
Stern,Marty,Vermont	A	22	8	0	0	4	13.1	57	12	5	5	1	0	1	0	6	0	10	1	0	0	0	.000	0	0	3.38
Stevenson,Jason,Rockford	A	21	33	5	0	9	77.1	333	85	50	48	9	1	4	1	31	0	54	5	5	4	3	.571	0	2	5.59
Daytona	A	21	8	0	0	3	18.1	71	11	6	6	0	1	0	1	6	0	15	1	0	2	0	1.000	0	1	2.95
Stewart,Chris,St. Pete	A	24	30	0	0	7	33.2	150	29	22	20	2	2	2	1	25	1	36	2	1	0	1	.000	0	0	5.35
Salem	A	24	10	0	0	4	12.2	64	18	15	12	3	0	0	1	11	2	10	3	2	0	2	.000	0	0	8.53
Stewart,Chaad,Frederick	A	21	26	26	1	0	150.2	635	126	71	61	8	5	1	10	66	1	140	12	4	8	8	.500	1	0	3.64
Stewart,Scott,Charlstn-Sc	A	20	11	11	1	0	75.2	302	76	38	31	6	1	4	0	14	1	47	3	5	1	7	.125	0	0	3.69
Twins	R	20	3	1	0	0	5.2	29	7	4	4	0	0	0	0	4	0	9	0	0	0	0	.000	0	0	6.35
Stockstill,Jason,Angels	R	19	12	7	2	0	44.1	195	38	29	25	1	1	2	3	22	1	31	3	2	3	1	.750	1	0	5.08
Stone,Ricky,San Bernrdo	A	21	12	12	0	0	58	273	79	50	42	7	6	3	2	25	0	31	5	0	3	5	.375	0	0	6.52
Yakima	A	21	16	6	0	7	48	213	54	31	28	5	2	2	2	20	0	28	4	1	4	4	.500	0	2	5.25
Stoops,Jim,Bellingham	A	24	24	0	0	14	42	178	32	23	16	1	2	1	5	17	0	58	2	0	6	5	.545	0	4	3.43
Stubbs,Jerald,Albany	A	24	47	1	0	17	100.2	438	106	51	36	4	6	3	10	30	2	80	8	1	3	2	.600	0	3	3.22
Stumpf,Brian,Piedmont	A	24	55	0	0	47	61.2	258	59	20	16	2	5	2	0	19	0	66	7	0	3	3	.500	0	28	2.34
Styles,Bobby,Rangers	R	19	12	1	0	7	22	106	31	24	16	4	0	0	3	9	0	21	3	0	0	0	.000	0	1	6.55
Suazo,Rigoberto,Athletics	R	19	2	0	0	1	5.1	20	3	1	1	0	0	0	0	2	0	5	0	1	1	0	1.000	0	1	1.69
Sullivan,Dan,Riverside	A	26	53	0	0	26	85	383	98	49	39	3	2	4	3	38	3	59	4	0	4	4	.500	0	8	4.13
Sumter,Kevin,Boise	A	23	21	0	0	5	31.2	141	15	8	8	1	0	0	2	31	1	38	5	1	0	1	.000	0	0	2.27
Surratt,Jamie,Hickory	A	26	12	0	0	9	15.1	69	13	8	3	1	1	1	0	8	4	19	1	0	0	1	.000	0	3	1.76
South Bend	A	26	26	0	0	22	40.1	163	32	15	14	5	3	2	2	12	1	34	3	1	3	3	.500	0	11	3.12
Suzuki,Makoto,Mariners	R	21	4	0	0	0	4	19	5	4	3	1	0	0	1	3	0	5	0	0	1	0	1.000	0	0	6.75
Riverside	A	21	6	0	0	1	7.2	39	10	4	4	0	0	0	0	6	0	6	2	0	0	1	.000	0	0	4.70
Swan,Tyrone,Clearwater	A	27	37	0	0	10	47.2	208	50	25	18	5	2	2	1	19	1	46	6	0	2	3	.400	0	0	3.40
Swanson,Skeeter,Columbia	A	23	29	4	0	16	67.2	276	48	14	11	2	1	3	4	31	2	60	7	2	7	1	.875	0	3	1.46
Asheville	A	23	8	0	0	2	12.2	56	14	7	7	1	1	0	2	7	0	7	0	0	1	0	1.000	0	1	4.97
Sweezey,Gary,Great Falls	R	20	17	0	0	11	28	125	34	12	10	4	1	3	2	6	0	18	5	1	2	1	.667	0	3	3.21
Swenson,Mike,New Jersey	A	23	19	6	0	3	52.1	246	53	35	28	1	0	3	7	32	0	54	5	0	2	4	.333	0	0	4.82
Symmonds,Maika,Pirates	R	23	6	0	0	5	7.2	39	3	5	4	0	0	0	0	9	0	9	6	0	1	1	.500	0	4	4.70
Szimanski,Tom,Mariners	R	23	4	0	0	2	4.1	18	2	2	2	0	0	0	0	3	0	5	1	1	0	0	.000	0	0	4.15
Everett	A	23	16	0	0	11	21.1	79	13	4	4	0	0	0	0	6	0	32	0	0	2	0	1.000	0	5	1.69
Taczy,Craig,Great Falls	R	19	18	2	0	7	30.2	145	25	20	12	1	0	1	2	28	0	24	6	1	0	4	.000	0	0	3.52
Tagle,Hank,Pr. William	A	28	33	0	0	16	70	275	58	28	24	4	4	2	5	15	1	66	3	0	3	2	.600	0	3	3.09
Takahashi,Kurt,Bellingham	A	22	17	0	0	5	25.2	116	28	18	16	2	0	2	1	14	0	20	4	0	1	2	.333	0	0	5.61
Tanksley,William,Elizabethtn	R	22	11	0	0	4	15.1	67	16	13	7	3	2	0	1	5	0	17	0	1	0	2	.000	0	1	4.11
Tapia,Elias,Bakersfield	A	20	17	0	0	10	32.1	152	35	22	14	3	1	1	2	14	0	14	4	1	0	1	.000	0	1	3.90
Yakima	A	20	13	1	0	3	23.1	111	23	20	14	3	1	1	2	13	0	15	8	0	0	1	.000	0	0	5.40
Tatar,Jason,Fort Myers	A	21	21	15	0	4	82.2	339	64	33	24	3	0	4	2	36	0	60	3	2	4	5	.444	0	1	2.61
Tatis,Ramon,Pittsfield	A	23	13	13	1	0	79.1	341	88	40	32	2	1	1	3	27	0	69	8	3	4	5	.444	1	0	3.63
Columbia	A	23	18	2	0	9	32	141	34	27	20	1	2	1	1	14	0	27	5	0	2	3	.400	0	0	5.63
Taylor,Brien,Yankees	R	24	11	11	0	0	40	199	29	37	27	1	0	1	10	54	0	38	16	1	2	5	.286	0	0	6.07
Tebbetts,Scott,Martinsville	R	23	22	0	0	20	32	133	31	15	8	0	1	0	0	7	1	30	1	0	1	3	.250	0	9	2.25
Tejera,Michael,Marlins	R	19	11	3	0	4	34	142	28	13	10	2	4	1	2	16	1	28	0	2	3	1	.750	0	0	2.65

1995 Pitching -- Single-A and Rookie Leagues

			HOW MUCH HE PITCHED						WHAT HE GAVE UP												THE RESULTS					
Player	Lg	A	G	GS	CG	GF	IP	BFP	H	R	ER	HR	SH	SF	HB	TBB	IBB	SO	WP	Bk	W	L	Pct.	ShO	Sv	ERA
Telgheder,Jim,Sarasota	A	25	22	0	0	5	25	122	30	20	18	3	2	0	2	15	2	24	4	1	0	3	.000	0	0	6.48
Michigan	A	25	22	1	0	18	35	142	29	8	7	0	2	2	1	8	2	39	3	0	5	1	.833	0	4	1.80
Temple,Jason,Augusta	A	21	51	0	0	18	71.2	297	45	26	18	6	4	2	3	28	0	84	5	1	5	2	.714	0	5	2.26
Tessmer,Jay,Oneonta	A	23	34	0	0	33	38	156	27	8	4	0	0	0	3	12	2	52	3	2	2	0	1.000	0	20	0.95
Theodile,Robert,South Bend	A	23	7	4	0	0	26	130	45	30	22	1	1	1	1	13	0	16	5	0	1	2	.333	0	0	7.62
Hickory	A	23	20	17	1	1	107	470	103	61	45	8	3	5	5	53	2	77	13	4	6	9	.400	1	0	3.79
Theron,Greg,Riverside	A	22	40	0	0	20	68	299	72	44	38	8	4	2	7	23	0	45	8	0	4	2	.667	0	1	5.03
Thomas,Robbie,Yakima	A	24	7	2	0	1	20	89	15	11	8	0	1	2	1	11	0	17	2	0	0	1	.000	0	0	3.60
Bakersfield	A	24	26	6	0	4	49.1	247	55	51	41	8	4	4	5	36	0	39	6	0	1	6	.143	0	0	7.48
Thomas,Robert,Erie	A	22	15	0	0	7	15.2	71	9	10	8	2	2	2	1	17	1	9	4	0	1	1	.500	0	0	4.60
Thompson,Mark,Macon	A	25	13	0	0	8	21	82	13	12	11	1	2	4	1	4	1	15	0	1	3	2	.600	0	2	4.71
Thorn,Todd,Royals	R	19	11	10	0	0	47.1	201	43	23	17	1	1	1	6	14	0	58	4	1	4	2	.667	0	0	3.23
Thornton,Paul,Brevard Cty	A	26	42	1	0	27	71.2	311	66	34	26	5	5	1	8	27	2	56	3	0	4	5	.444	0	4	3.27
Thurman,Mike,Albany	A	22	22	22	2	0	110.1	482	133	79	67	4	3	7	4	32	0	77	7	0	3	8	.273	0	0	5.47
Thurmond,Travis,Cedar Rapids	A	22	14	2	0	4	39	172	36	25	23	4	2	0	1	20	4	55	3	0	2	5	.286	0	2	5.31
Boise	A	22	16	15	4	1	101.1	401	75	36	35	7	0	3	3	31	0	93	7	0	9	3	.750	1	0	3.11
Tickell,Brian,Auburn	A	21	13	11	2	0	72.2	310	79	47	45	6	1	2	4	18	0	31	5	0	5	3	.625	0	0	5.57
Tidwell,Jason,Brevard Cty	A	24	4	1	0	0	7	31	5	3	0	0	0	0	0	3	0	3	0	0	0	0	.000	0	0	0.00
Kane County	A	24	6	4	0	0	15.2	80	19	17	15	2	1	0	4	14	0	13	3	0	1	4	.200	0	0	8.62
Tijerina,Tano,Brewers	R	22	1	0	0	0	2	10	3	1	1	0	0	0	0	2	0	1	1	0	0	0	.000	0	0	4.50
Tillmon,Darrell,Red Sox	A	23	3	1	0	0	8	29	4	2	1	0	0	0	0	0	0	5	0	0	1	0	1.000	0	0	1.13
Michigan	A	23	13	10	2	2	76.1	293	56	25	19	8	2	0	0	12	0	53	1	0	6	3	.667	0	0	2.24
Tisdale,Warren,Mariners	R	19	13	0	0	3	22	88	17	5	4	0	0	1	0	10	0	9	3	0	1	1	.500	0	1	1.64
Tollberg,Brian,Beloit	A	23	22	22	1	0	132	529	119	59	50	10	2	5	6	27	0	110	5	4	13	4	.765	1	0	3.41
Tomko,Brett,Charlstn-Wv	A	23	9	7	0	0	49	192	41	12	10	1	1	1	1	9	1	46	4	2	4	2	.667	0	0	1.84
Toney,Mike,Dunedin	A	22	12	0	0	8	12.1	67	19	14	11	0	1	1	1	13	1	6	2	0	1	2	.333	0	3	8.03
Hagerstown	A	22	20	0	0	10	29	127	21	11	8	0	1	3	0	17	2	26	6	2	3	3	.500	0	4	2.48
Torres,Derek,Brewers	R	19	6	0	0	3	5.1	21	2	1	1	0	0	0	2	2	0	7	1	0	0	0	.000	0	0	1.69
Torres,Eric,Mets	R	19	11	0	0	6	20.2	83	11	5	1	1	1	0	1	6	0	8	4	2	0	2	.000	0	3	0.44
Torres,Luis,Clinton	A	20	3	0	0	0	2	16	5	3	3	0	0	0	0	5	0	1	0	2	0	0	.000	0	0	13.50
Padres	R	20	22	2	0	20	36	163	36	24	19	2	2	3	5	20	0	34	4	4	4	3	.571	0	8	4.75
Idaho Falls	R	20	1	0	0	0	1	7	3	3	3	0	0	0	0	2	0	2	0	0	0	1	.000	0	0	27.00
Torres,Yason,Great Falls	R	22	14	8	0	2	51	242	66	37	26	1	2	1	9	11	3	32	8	1	3	3	.500	0	1	4.59
Towns,Ryan,Wilmington	A	24	12	0	0	2	16	75	12	11	10	0	0	0	0	18	0	8	1	0	1	0	1.000	0	1	5.63
Springfield	A	24	18	1	0	7	30.2	141	33	24	19	6	1	0	2	17	0	31	4	1	0	0	.000	0	0	5.58
Trawick,Tim,Everett	A	24	16	13	3	1	86	350	66	34	30	11	0	0	9	31	0	63	1	2	6	2	.750	0	0	3.14
Treend,Patrick,Elmira	A	24	17	1	0	6	34.1	171	43	32	24	3	2	0	5	16	0	29	3	0	0	2	.000	0	0	6.29
Trimarco,Mike,High Desert	A	24	40	1	0	16	100.2	441	109	70	59	12	5	6	1	36	4	52	7	2	6	6	.500	0	2	5.27
Trumpour,Andy,Pittsfield	A	22	15	15	2	0	105	427	95	44	30	2	3	3	5	32	0	75	7	0	7	6	.538	1	0	2.57
Tucker,Ben,Bellingham	A	22	12	10	0	1	56.2	249	53	21	12	4	2	2	4	19	0	48	2	1	4	2	.667	0	0	1.91
Tucker,Julien,Kissimmee	A	23	19	15	0	0	68.1	327	86	61	38	3	1	6	5	27	0	28	5	3	2	11	.154	0	0	5.00
Turley,Jason,Astros	R	21	11	0	0	2	16	79	14	13	10	0	0	1	2	13	1	13	1	2	5	0	1.000	0	0	5.63
Turrentine,Rich,Columbia	A	25	26	14	0	8	104	437	70	38	29	3	6	4	6	60	1	111	16	1	4	4	.500	0	2	2.51
St. Lucie	A	25	4	4	0	0	19.1	92	17	14	13	3	1	0	2	17	0	14	3	0	0	3	.000	0	0	6.05
Tweedlie,Brad,Charlstn-Wv	A	24	19	7	0	4	49.2	226	46	36	34	3	0	4	3	34	0	40	5	1	2	4	.333	0	0	6.16
Twiggs,Greg,Daytona	A	24	18	13	1	1	89.1	355	64	30	14	3	1	1	5	28	0	80	4	0	8	3	.727	0	0	1.41
Tyner,Marcus,Macon	A	24	29	0	0	16	46.2	204	48	31	17	5	2	0	0	17	1	38	9	0	2	2	.500	0	3	3.28
Tyrrell,Jim,Michigan	A	23	16	0	0	7	25	114	17	17	10	3	3	2	4	15	1	37	2	1	2	3	.400	0	4	3.60
Upchurch,Wayne,Springfield	A	24	18	2	0	11	29.2	137	40	19	14	3	2	2	2	4	1	13	0	1	2	3	.400	0	1	4.25
Lethbridge	R	24	9	9	1	0	53	247	68	44	33	6	0	3	4	19	0	39	2	0	2	6	.250	1	0	5.60
Spokane	A	24	7	0	0	5	12.2	64	22	12	9	2	2	0	0	5	1	7	2	0	1	1	.500	0	0	6.39
Updike,Johnny,Brewers	R	23	4	0	0	1	3	19	2	4	4	0	0	0	0	8	0	3	2	0	0	0	.000	0	0	12.00
Urbina,Red,Modesto	A	22	30	0	0	11	41	185	51	28	24	4	0	1	4	16	0	18	4	0	2	0	1.000	0	1	5.27
Valdez,Ken,Boise	A	21	5	0	0	0	11.2	55	11	8	6	1	0	0	2	7	0	9	2	0	1	0	.000	0	0	4.63
Valencia,Enrique,Red Sox	R	19	14	0	0	7	34	154	51	25	18	3	0	1	0	9	0	19	0	2	1	2	.333	0	0	4.76
Valley,Jason,Clearwater	A	23	4	0	0	0	4.1	23	9	6	6	0	1	0	0	4	0	4	1	0	0	0	.000	0	0	12.46
Vandemark,John,Clearwater	A	24	24	0	0	6	27	127	24	21	17	4	1	1	0	21	1	18	2	1	1	2	.333	0	0	5.67
Vanderbush,Matt,Twins	R	22	8	6	0	1	36	153	37	23	16	2	1	2	3	9	0	28	3	3	2	3	.400	0	0	4.00
Vandeweg,Ryan,Clinton	A	22	15	15	1	0	91	400	92	56	42	5	3	2	7	32	3	89	3	1	6	4	.600	0	0	4.15
Vanhof,Dave,Riverside	A	22	4	4	0	0	17	88	26	25	20	3	1	2	0	12	0	12	2	1	1	1	.500	0	0	10.59
Wisconsin	A	22	15	13	1	1	62.2	291	52	42	29	4	4	3	3	50	2	27	8	0	4	5	.444	0	0	4.16
Vaninetti,Geno,Blue Jays	R	21	20	0	0	20	21.2	98	25	14	12	3	1	0	0	6	1	7	1	0	2	0	1.000	0	4	4.98
Vardijan,Daniel,Marlins	R	19	9	8	0	1	44	164	21	11	8	2	0	1	5	10	0	34	0	0	5	0	1.000	0	0	1.64
Kane County	A	19	1	1	0	0	3	17	5	3	2	0	0	0	1	2	0	2	1	0	0	0	.000	0	0	6.00
Vaught,Jay,Kinston	A	24	27	26	4	0	171	717	184	80	64	19	8	5	15	28	3	82	6	1	8	12	.400	0	0	3.37
Vavrek,Mike,Portland	A	22	3	3	0	0	14	52	8	0	0	0	0	0	0	3	0	14	0	0	0	0	.000	0	0	0.00
Asheville	A	22	12	12	1	0	76.2	322	64	24	17	3	0	1	5	25	0	54	4	5	5	4	.556	0	0	2.00
Vazquez,Archie,Pr.William	A	22	47	0	0	45	57.2	261	53	26	23	5	9	1	1	30	4	70	8	0	3	4	.429	0	20	3.59
Vazquez,Javier,Albany	A	20	21	21	1	0	102.2	459	109	67	58	8	1	2	9	47	0	87	2	2	6	6	.500	0	0	5.08
Vejil,Aaron,Huntington	R	21	14	0	0	10	19.2	91	19	15	13	2	1	1	2	10	0	21	5	1	1	0	1.000	0	2	5.95
Charlstn-Wv	A	21	6	0	0	3	3.1	15	2	0	0	0	0	0	0	3	1	5	0	0	2	0	1.000	0	0	0.00
Venafro,Michael,Hudson Vall	A	22	32	0	0	12	50.2	200	37	13	12	0	2	1	5	21	2	32	1	3	9	1	.900	0	2	2.13
Veniard,Jay,Blue Jays	R	21	3	1	0	2	11	39	4	2	1	0	0	0	0	2	0	18	2	0	1	0	1.000	0	0	0.82
Medicne Hat	R	21	11	10	0	0	63	280	67	34	19	2	2	3	3	21	0	43	6	2	4	1	.800	0	0	2.71
Verdin,Cesar,Yankees	R	19	11	5	0	0	26	114	26	15	10	1	0	0	1	10	0	35	1	0	2	2	.500	0	0	3.46
Vermillion,Grant,Boise	A	24	30	0	0	15	59.2	244	49	19	13	2	2	1	5	16	4	50	2	0	12	3	.800	0	6	1.96
Vicentino,Andy,Princeton	R	20	10	0	0	2	30	149	36	30	25	1	1	0	1	27	0	23	4	1	2	2	.500	0	0	7.50

1995 Pitching -- Single-A and Rookie Leagues

			HOW MUCH HE PITCHED						WHAT HE GAVE UP												THE RESULTS					
Player	Lg	A	G	GS	CG	GF	IP	BFP	H	R	ER	HR	SH	SF	HB	TBB	IBB	SO	WP	Bk	W	L	Pct.	ShO	Sv	ERA
Viegas,Randy,Pirates	R	20	6	4	0	2	28.1	119	28	13	8	0	0	0	1	5	0	24	0	0	3	2	.600	0	0	2.54
Erie	A	20	8	1	0	2	10	53	14	9	7	0	0	0	2	9	0	9	1	0	0	0	.000	0	0	6.30
Villafana,Jose,New Jersey	A	22	27	0	0	21	29.1	141	35	17	16	0	4	2	0	21	1	28	4	2	0	6	.000	0	13	4.91
Villafuerte,Brandon,Kingsport	R	20	20	0	0	6	32	144	28	21	20	0	1	1	1	26	0	42	6	0	5	1	.833	0	0	5.63
Villano,Mike,Burlington	A	24	16	0	0	7	25.1	120	20	12	8	1	2	1	4	21	0	29	5	0	3	1	.750	0	1	2.84
San Jose	A	24	21	0	0	16	32.2	137	27	7	6	2	0	1	3	11	0	42	3	0	0	1	.000	0	1	1.65
Villar,Maximo,Pirates	R	19	6	3	0	1	20	101	29	21	16	2	0	0	3	9	0	13	1	2	1	1	.500	0	1	7.20
Villarreal,Modesto,Spokane	A	20	16	11	0	1	80.2	330	73	30	26	4	2	3	3	23	2	57	5	2	8	2	.800	0	0	2.90
Villegas,Ismael,Cubs	R	19	11	10	0	0	41.1	168	33	17	11	1	2	6	2	11	0	26	3	2	3	2	.600	0	0	2.40
Virchis,Adam,Bristol	R	22	10	10	1	0	56	239	65	39	33	5	2	3	3	7	0	33	2	2	0	7	.000	0	0	5.30
Vizcaino,Ed,Cubs	R	19	14	0	0	6	16.2	77	15	10	5	1	5	2	2	6	2	11	0	0	1	1	.500	0	1	2.70
Volkert,Rusty,St. Cathrns	A	21	22	0	0	8	54	225	53	20	16	3	1	1	0	14	0	44	8	0	2	3	.400	0	2	2.67
Volkman,Keith,Angels	R	20	13	10	0	0	67.2	279	61	30	19	0	1	4	0	25	0	49	5	1	5	2	.714	0	0	2.53
Vota,Michael,Bristol	R	23	22	0	0	12	31.1	145	33	19	16	3	2	3	1	14	1	24	5	0	1	2	.333	0	4	4.60
Vukson,John,Yakima	A	20	11	0	0	5	7	57	9	20	13	1	0	4	3	26	0	6	6	0	0	0	.000	0	0	16.71
Wada,Takashi,Visalia	A	25	17	1	0	5	37	173	44	23	19	3	0	2	2	18	0	43	4	1	1	0	1.000	0	0	4.62
Wagner,Ken,Burlington	R	21	13	12	0	0	68.1	285	54	34	24	7	1	2	1	23	0	80	7	1	5	5	.500	0	0	3.16
Waites,Steve,Butte	R	23	28	0	0	8	43.1	209	60	33	23	3	3	2	2	22	4	26	3	1	2	5	.286	0	4	4.78
Waldrep,Art,Asheville	A	24	15	3	0	5	31.2	153	48	23	20	3	2	0	3	10	2	21	3	1	0	3	.000	0	1	5.68
Walker,Jim,Frederick	A	25	9	0	0	1	20.2	90	15	12	8	0	1	0	3	9	1	19	2	0	2	2	.500	0	0	3.48
Walker,Kevin,Padres	R	19	13	12	0	0	71.2	295	74	34	24	1	1	3	2	12	0	69	1	3	5	5	.500	0	0	3.01
Walker,Wade,Daytona	A	24	25	24	2	0	135	541	113	50	38	5	3	2	2	36	0	117	8	1	8	6	.571	1	0	2.53
Wallace,Jeff,Royals	R	20	12	7	0	3	44	177	28	20	6	0	1	1	1	15	0	51	3	2	5	3	.625	0	1	1.23
Walls,Doug,Salem	A	22	15	15	0	0	79.2	344	61	39	34	10	1	3	3	49	1	79	5	2	5	5	.500	0	0	3.84
Walsh,Matt,Modesto	A	23	44	9	0	21	100.2	445	98	64	52	11	5	3	6	45	4	108	5	2	2	7	.222	0	5	4.65
Walter,Mike,Kissimmee	A	21	41	0	0	23	71.1	338	78	58	44	4	5	9	10	42	1	42	9	2	4	3	.571	0	5	5.55
Walters,Brett,Clinton	A	21	32	19	4	4	146	598	133	58	44	9	6	1	10	27	3	122	4	2	8	7	.533	0	1	2.71
Ward,Jonathan,New Jersey	A	21	9	8	0	1	32.1	170	47	42	29	5	1	5	4	18	0	35	5	1	0	7	.000	0	0	8.07
Ward,Kerry,Pirates	R	21	11	6	0	2	44.1	204	59	33	24	2	1	1	0	13	0	27	3	1	2	6	.250	0	0	4.87
Warrecker,Teddy,Columbus	A	23	24	24	1	0	130.2	559	104	76	60	10	3	3	13	80	1	125	0	0	10	5	.667	1	0	4.13
Warren,Deshawn,Cedar Rapds	A	22	7	7	1	0	30.1	122	20	10	11	2	1	0	2	13	0	26	1	0	2	3	.400	1	0	3.26
Washburn,Jarrod,Boise	A	21	8	8	0	0	46	185	35	17	17	1	0	1	2	14	0	54	1	0	3	2	.600	0	0	3.33
Cedar Rapids	A	21	3	3	0	0	18.1	79	17	7	7	1	2	1	3	7	0	20	1	0	0	1	.000	0	0	3.44
Watts,Brandon,Vero Beach	A	23	13	8	0	1	49	215	46	29	22	5	0	2	1	22	0	42	4	1	5	3	.625	0	0	4.04
Weber,Dave,Williamsprt	A	21	22	2	0	9	34	165	51	38	30	3	1	0	2	15	0	28	2	2	2	3	.400	0	0	7.94
Weber,Eric,Jamestown	A	21	15	3	0	4	32.2	142	35	25	19	2	0	0	2	11	0	22	3	0	2	2	.500	0	0	5.23
Weber,Lenny,Watertown	A	23	5	0	0	3	9	37	5	2	2	0	1	0	0	6	1	11	1	0	1	0	1.000	0	0	2.00
Columbus	A	23	17	0	0	5	29.1	113	19	6	6	0	2	0	0	10	3	32	3	0	4	0	1.000	0	2	1.84
Wehn,Kevin,Asheville	A	23	5	0	0	3	10	42	9	7	7	1	0	0	0	4	0	5	1	0	0	2	.000	0	1	6.30
Weidert,Chris,Albany	A	22	3	3	0	0	10.1	55	16	14	9	3	0	1	0	5	0	17	0	0	1	2	.333	0	0	7.84
Vermont	A	22	15	15	1	0	95.1	378	67	31	19	4	0	2	4	21	0	52	8	0	11	1	.917	1	0	1.79
Weinberg,Todd,W. Michigan	A	24	36	9	0	5	87	392	86	52	46	3	2	1	13	56	2	54	19	2	4	5	.444	0	1	4.76
Weisner,Chad,Wisconsin	A	24	1	0	0	0	3	12	3	1	1	0	0	0	0	1	0	2	0	0	0	0	.000	0	0	3.00
Weiss,Marc,Charlstn-Wv	A	22	11	0	0	2	14.2	78	23	10	9	2	0	0	0	13	2	12	1	0	1	0	1.000	0	0	5.52
Billings	R	22	18	1	0	6	26	127	36	26	22	0	0	0	1	15	0	14	1	1	0	2	.333	0	0	7.62
Welch,David,Hickory	A	26	60	0	0	19	77.2	328	68	39	23	5	6	2	3	21	10	82	7	1	4	5	.444	0	5	2.67
Welch,Robb,Utica	A	20	12	12	1	0	65	303	76	45	41	1	1	3	5	39	0	35	7	1	4	4	.500	0	0	5.68
Welch,Travis,Peoria	A	22	46	0	0	46	46	203	40	26	23	6	5	0	3	18	1	45	5	1	3	4	.429	0	31	4.50
Wells,David,Durham	A	24	7	0	0	1	13.1	63	21	8	7	2	0	1	0	2	0	6	0	0	0	0	.000	0	0	4.72
Hickory	A	24	17	1	0	4	38.1	167	44	28	22	4	2	2	1	13	2	30	2	1	1	1	.500	0	0	5.17
West,Adam,Peoria	A	22	4	4	0	0	12.2	81	22	21	17	0	0	1	0	24	0	5	0	0	0	3	.000	0	0	12.08
Johnson Cty	R	22	18	1	0	1	41	187	41	26	13	1	2	4	3	19	1	41	2	0	1	1	.500	0	0	2.85
West,Ken,Marlins	R	20	13	0	0	7	29.1	125	32	17	8	2	2	0	1	6	2	9	0	0	2	1	.667	0	3	2.45
Weymouth,Marty,Mariners	R	18	9	4	0	1	31.2	144	37	23	14	2	1	1	2	10	0	26	3	1	2	3	.400	0	0	3.98
Whitaker,Ryan,Modesto	A	24	32	25	0	3	151	669	177	90	74	10	8	3	4	54	2	88	10	1	5	10	.333	0	0	4.41
White,Darell,Rancho Cuca	A	24	42	0	0	17	59.1	285	69	49	41	3	3	2	3	43	3	49	8	0	0	5	.000	0	0	6.22
White,Eric,Braves	R	18	13	1	0	8	32	161	39	37	24	1	1	3	1	22	0	10	9	0	1	1	.500	0	0	6.75
White,Gary,Orioles	R	23	12	10	2	0	66.1	262	52	26	16	1	1	1	2	16	1	56	5	1	5	4	.556	1	0	2.17
Frederick	A	23	1	1	0	0	6	23	3	2	2	1	0	0	0	2	0	4	0	0	1	0	1.000	0	0	3.00
Whiteman,Greg,Lakeland	A	23	4	4	0	0	19.1	87	18	16	13	0	0	2	0	15	0	20	1	1	1	2	.333	0	0	6.05
Fayetteville	A	23	23	23	1	0	125.2	547	108	68	59	9	5	4	9	58	0	145	4	1	6	8	.429	1	0	4.23
Whiteman,Tony,Fayetteville	A	25	28	0	0	4	25	117	25	16	11	1	2	1	2	18	0	23	2	0	0	1	.000	0	0	3.96
Whitman,Ryan,Rancho Cuca	A	24	14	0	0	5	16.1	79	23	13	9	0	1	0	0	7	0	13	0	1	1	2	.333	0	0	4.96
Whitson,Travis,Ogden	R	23	22	0	0	17	29.1	142	35	33	28	8	1	1	2	16	2	31	5	1	2	1	.667	0	4	8.59
Whitten,Mike,Brevard Cty	A	27	22	0	0	9	38.2	170	47	21	17	2	1	3	2	9	1	25	2	0	1	4	.200	0	1	3.96
Whitworth,Clint,Oneonta	A	24	12	1	0	2	27.1	136	31	23	18	0	0	2	5	15	0	15	9	0	2	0	.000	0	0	5.93
Wicks,Ross,Mets	R	19	12	1	0	6	18.2	75	15	7	7	1	0	1	0	6	0	15	1	0	0	0	.000	0	0	3.38
Widerski,Jonathan,Marlins	R	19	14	0	0	3	24.1	106	16	13	9	1	1	2	1	18	0	12	7	0	1	0	1.000	0	0	3.33
Wilkerson,Steven,Charlstn-Wv	A	23	16	0	0	8	19.2	97	21	13	12	0	0	1	3	18	0	15	4	0	1	1	.500	0	0	5.49
Wilkinson,Arrow,Oneonta	A	23	14	0	0	2	28.1	135	28	19	13	0	3	1	1	23	0	24	4	1	0	0	.000	0	0	4.13
Williams,Brad,Yankees	R	19	11	7	0	0	23.2	117	14	19	14	0	1	2	4	34	0	28	9	3	0	3	.000	0	0	5.32
Williams,Juan,Fort Wayne	A	22	3	0	0	3	6	29	7	4	3	0	2	0	0	3	0	4	0	0	0	0	.000	0	0	4.50
Williams,Matt,Bakersfield	A	25	7	7	0	0	34.1	150	34	9	9	1	3	2	3	14	0	30	1	1	2	0	1.000	0	0	2.36
Kissimmee	A	25	19	18	2	0	101	446	115	60	52	7	5	3	2	44	1	71	5	1	4	6	.400	0	0	4.63
Williams,Patrick,Rockies	R	20	5	3	0	0	14.1	78	21	16	9	0	0	1	1	10	0	6	0	0	0	2	.000	0	0	5.65
Williamson,Jeremy,Spokane	A	21	11	7	0	0	44	171	32	12	7	4	0	1	0	9	0	35	0	0	3	1	.750	0	0	1.43
Williard,Brian,Lk Elsinore	A	23	29	3	0	5	61.1	252	64	32	29	3	2	0	2	13	0	44	1	0	2	4	.333	0	0	4.26

1995 Pitching -- Single-A and Rookie Leagues

| | | | HOW MUCH HE PITCHED | | | | | | WHAT HE GAVE UP | | | | | | | | | | | | THE RESULTS | | | | | |
Player	Lg	A	G	GS	CG	GF	IP	BFP	H	R	ER	HR	SH	SF	HB	TBB	IBB	SO	WP	Bk	W	L	Pct.	ShO	Sv	ERA
Wilson,Mike,Oneonta	A	23	14	4	0	1	40.2	183	41	24	19	0	1	0	2	19	0	41	8	2	2	4	.333	0	0	4.20
Wilson,Mike,Fayettevle	A	23	17	8	0	3	49.1	211	43	29	24	2	1	0	7	19	0	36	8	1	4	3	.571	0	0	4.38
Jamestown	A	23	5	5	0	0	22	103	27	20	16	1	1	1	4	6	0	12	1	1	1	3	.250	0	0	6.55
Wilstead,Judd,Stockton	A	23	31	21	0	1	139.2	653	165	94	79	15	10	5	14	71	1	72	12	3	8	9	.471	0	0	5.09
Wimberly,Larry,Piedmont	A	20	24	24	0	0	135	542	99	48	40	9	1	3	9	44	0	139	8	4	10	3	.769	0	0	2.67
Winchester,Marty,Riverside	A	23	35	4	0	8	67	305	67	40	34	2	5	3	2	45	3	56	5	0	3	1	.750	0	0	4.57
Winchester,Scott,Watertown	A	23	23	0	0	22	28.2	116	24	10	9	0	1	2	2	6	2	27	2	2	3	1	.750	0	11	2.83
Winders,Brian,Spokane	A	23	2	1	0	0	3	23	10	10	10	2	0	0	1	3	0	2	0	0	0	1	.000	0	0	30.00
Windham,Mike,Savannah	A	24	26	25	0	0	132.2	581	133	73	60	11	2	2	10	60	1	115	16	1	6	9	.400	0	0	4.07
Winkle,Ken,Wilmington	A	23	11	0	0	5	13.2	67	16	18	16	5	1	1	1	10	1	14	1	0	1	1	.500	0	1	10.54
Springfield	A	24	9	0	0	3	12.1	56	16	13	13	3	0	0	1	2	0	8	2	0	1	1	.500	0	0	9.49
Winslett,Dax,Vero Beach	A	24	14	13	0	0	85	358	87	35	30	7	4	1	1	21	0	59	6	2	6	4	.600	0	0	3.18
Daytona	A	24	12	12	0	0	67	269	61	24	17	4	0	1	1	18	0	52	7	0	6	2	.750	0	0	2.28
Wise,Jamie,Danville	R	20	2	0	0	1	2.1	14	3	6	4	0	0	0	0	4	0	3	1	1	0	1	.000	0	0	15.43
Braves	R	20	4	0	0	3	6.2	35	1	8	5	0	0	0	0	3	0	6	1	0	0	2	.000	0	0	6.75
Wise,Will,Danville	R	20	10	10	0	0	46.1	201	42	33	29	2	2	2	7	23	0	24	4	2	0	3	.000	0	0	5.63
Wolff,Bryan,Rancho Cuca	A	24	54	0	0	43	57	262	39	23	21	4	4	3	3	54	0	77	15	0	2	7	.222	0	18	3.32
Wolff,Tom,Pittsfield	A	22	4	1	0	2	9	49	15	11	8	1	0	0	2	5	0	8	1	0	0	2	.000	0	0	8.00
Columbia	A	22	15	0	0	13	22.2	99	21	13	11	0	0	1	3	8	0	16	3	0	0	0	.000	0	0	4.37
Wood,Kerry,Cubs	R	19	1	1	0	0	3	9	0	0	0	0	0	0	0	1	0	2	0	0	0	0	.000	0	0	0.00
Williamsprt	A	19	2	2	0	0	4.1	23	5	8	5	0	0	0	0	5	0	5	1	0	0	0	.000	0	0	10.38
Woodard,Steven,Beloit	A	21	21	21	1	0	115	490	113	68	58	12	6	2	5	31	0	94	6	5	7	4	.636	0	0	4.54
Woodring,Jason,Albany	A	22	48	0	0	39	50.2	222	46	19	15	0	2	2	5	20	2	50	3	2	1	1	.500	0	16	2.66
Woodrow,Jim,Bellingham	A	23	27	0	0	14	44.1	192	35	18	18	3	2	3	2	25	2	34	3	1	4	4	.500	0	3	3.65
Woods,Brian,Pr. William	A	25	27	27	3	0	139.1	632	155	89	80	14	5	4	14	53	1	102	12	3	9	15	.375	0	0	5.17
Wright,Howard,Kissimmee	A	25	2	0	0	0	5	21	1	3	2	0	0	0	0	4	0	3	0	0	1	0	1.000	0	0	3.60
Wright,Jaret,Columbus	A	20	24	24	0	0	129	554	93	55	43	9	3	6	13	79	0	113	11	3	5	6	.455	0	0	3.00
Wright,Scott,Billings	R	23	17	0	0	4	27.1	123	28	15	11	1	1	0	2	7	0	29	0	2	2	0	1.000	0	0	3.62
Wuestenhoefer,Brady,Portland	A	23	14	14	1	0	77.2	343	88	50	40	5	1	2	3	23	0	50	5	2	1	9	.100	0	0	4.64
Wunsch,Kelly,Beloit	A	23	14	14	3	0	85.2	364	90	47	40	7	2	0	3	37	0	66	6	0	4	7	.364	1	0	4.20
Stockton	A	23	14	13	1	0	74.1	349	89	51	44	4	8	1	7	39	0	62	6	0	5	6	.455	1	0	5.33
Wyatt,Ben,Braves	R	19	12	8	1	3	42.1	194	36	25	14	1	0	4	3	27	0	24	6	2	1	3	.250	0	1	2.98
Wyatt,Cortez,Williamsprt	A	23	22	2	0	7	48	194	38	16	14	3	0	1	6	8	0	35	3	0	4	3	.571	0	0	2.63
Yan,Esteban,W. Palm Bch	A	22	24	21	1	1	137.2	580	139	63	47	3	7	5	10	33	0	89	8	3	6	8	.429	0	1	3.07
Yanez,Luis,Astros	R	18	11	11	0	0	61	253	52	29	20	4	2	1	0	15	1	63	8	0	2	5	.286	0	0	2.95
Ybarra,Jamie,Kane County	A	25	50	2	0	16	96	398	62	37	32	7	5	2	13	40	4	104	2	2	5	5	.500	0	2	3.00
Yeager,Gary,Batavia	A	22	19	8	1	4	81	327	74	33	23	2	0	0	3	16	0	57	7	4	9	4	.692	0	0	2.56
Yocum,David,Vero Beach	A	22	8	7	0	0	27.1	116	22	12	9	2	3	2	0	12	0	20	3	1	2	1	.667	0	0	2.96
Yoder,Jason,Martinsvlle	R	21	8	4	0	2	28.1	126	33	20	17	2	1	1	0	11	0	23	3	0	1	2	.333	0	0	5.40
Yonemura,Kazuki,Tigers	R	22	14	4	0	4	42.2	180	38	20	11	2	4	0	3	9	2	49	1	2	2	4	.333	0	1	2.32
York,Charles,Bakersfield	A	25	31	5	0	7	68	298	75	47	44	6	5	4	3	24	1	69	7	0	4	2	.667	0	1	5.82
Yoshida,Atsushi,Visalia	A	25	13	13	0	0	75	310	88	37	30	4	2	0	0	12	0	68	3	0	5	7	.417	0	0	3.60
Young,Christopher,Erie	A	23	16	10	1	2	67.2	288	62	34	21	5	5	1	3	17	0	38	0	1	5	2	.714	0	1	2.79
Young,Danny,Augusta	A	24	6	2	0	1	14.1	66	9	6	4	0	0	1	0	16	0	11	2	0	1	0	1.000	0	0	2.51
Lynchburg	A	24	24	2	0	7	41.1	196	52	37	34	3	1	2	2	27	1	34	5	0	2	4	.333	0	0	7.40
Young,Joe,St. Cathrns	A	21	15	15	0	0	83.2	349	72	29	19	4	3	4	5	35	0	73	5	3	6	5	.545	0	0	2.04
Young,Ty,Huntington	R	23	14	14	2	0	79	352	75	56	41	5	0	1	9	36	0	49	5	1	4	6	.400	1	0	4.67
Yount,Andy,Red Sox	R	19	5	5	0	0	16.1	69	13	8	5	1	1	0	2	6	0	17	1	1	0	1	.000	0	0	2.76
Zancanaro,Dave,W. Michigan	A	22	17	16	0	0	32.2	132	19	8	8	1	2	0	3	15	0	42	1	2	0	2	.000	0	0	2.20
Zanolla,Dan,Kane County	A	25	28	3	0	3	60.1	276	58	34	24	2	3	2	6	28	3	54	1	0	4	4	.500	0	0	3.58
Zavershnik,Mike,Blue Jays	R	20	19	0	0	8	36.1	170	44	29	22	1	1	2	3	11	1	26	5	0	1	1	.500	0	2	5.45
Zedalis,Craig,Eugene	A	23	8	0	0	1	13.1	62	16	6	4	0	0	1	1	4	0	10	0	0	0	0	.000	0	0	2.70
Macon	A	23	12	0	0	6	22.2	102	25	12	12	2	1	1	1	8	0	17	2	0	1	1	.500	0	0	4.76
Zerbe,Chad,San Bernrdo	A	24	28	27	1	0	163.1	718	168	103	83	15	10	5	3	64	0	94	4	0	11	7	.611	0	0	4.57
Zubiri,Jon,Columbus	A	21	1	1	0	0	3	12	3	0	0	0	0	0	0	0	0	3	0	0	0	0	.000	0	0	0.00

Team Stats

American Association Batting - AAA

Team	G	AB	H	2B	3B	HR	TB	R	RBI	TBB	IBB	SO	HBP	SH	SF	SB	CS	SB%	GDP	Avg	OBP	SLG
Indianapolis	144	4890	1344	286	29	193	2267	791	746	492	30	1001	54	25	39	93	50	.65	109	.275	.345	.464
Buffalo	144	4847	1338	261	41	129	2068	708	658	461	31	660	63	35	55	63	28	.69	119	.276	.343	.427
Omaha	144	4772	1305	266	31	144	2065	698	643	473	37	859	52	57	45	69	49	.58	101	.273	.343	.433
Nashville	144	4906	1288	239	25	113	1916	621	577	420	32	872	53	39	34	109	59	.65	123	.263	.325	.391
Louisville	144	4697	1217	245	27	122	1882	617	570	474	31	933	49	33	46	113	54	.68	118	.259	.330	.401
Oklahoma City	143	4696	1186	241	42	82	1757	572	529	401	31	856	49	28	41	68	37	.65	125	.253	.315	.374
New Orleans	142	4611	1166	206	30	85	1687	572	520	442	24	862	58	45	45	107	66	.62	98	.253	.323	.366
Iowa	143	4790	1285	226	32	92	1851	552	507	362	30	781	38	54	38	55	44	.56	109	.268	.322	.386
Total	574	38209	10129	1970	257	960	15493	5131	4750	3525	246	6824	416	316	343	677	387	.64	902	.265	.331	.405

American Association Pitching - AAA

Team	G	GS	CG	GF	IP	BFP	H	R	ER	HR	SH	SF	HB	TBB	IBB	SO	WP	Bk	W	L	Pct.	ShO	Sv	ERA
Buffalo	144	144	13	131	1251	5350	1278	604	543	91	27	48	61	396	15	820	44	4	82	62	.569	8	45	3.91
New Orleans	142	142	11	131	1213.2	5221	1274	606	537	113	29	32	50	445	29	806	67	10	63	79	.444	8	32	3.98
Iowa	143	143	13	130	1240.1	5329	1224	614	555	140	46	38	56	496	38	889	59	3	69	74	.483	8	32	4.03
Louisville	144	144	10	134	1241	5307	1208	623	522	106	47	40	45	406	41	840	60	5	74	70	.514	8	42	3.79
Indianapolis	144	144	12	132	1262	5348	1178	642	548	111	33	46	40	434	33	883	67	5	88	56	.611	8	41	3.91
Omaha	144	144	12	132	1238.1	5328	1301	660	586	132	43	44	53	423	25	820	51	8	76	68	.528	10	36	4.26
Nashville	144	144	8	136	1276.2	5502	1338	673	573	145	44	50	40	405	40	931	49	9	68	76	.472	11	39	4.04
Oklahoma City	143	143	11	132	1220.2	5427	1328	709	618	122	47	45	71	520	25	835	71	12	54	89	.378	7	26	4.56
Total	574	574	90	484	9943.2	42812	10129	5131	4482	960	316	343	416	3525	246	6824	468	56	574	574	.500	68	293	4.06

International League Batting - AAA

Team	G	AB	H	2B	3B	HR	TB	R	RBI	TBB	IBB	SO	HBP	SH	SF	SB	CS	SB%	GDP	Avg	OBP	SLG
Columbus	140	4730	1281	222	61	105	1940	687	629	456	20	911	36	38	46	104	57	.65	109	.271	.337	.410
Pawtucket	142	4732	1249	240	19	156	1995	676	630	456	21	951	45	32	36	94	63	.60	111	.264	.332	.422
Rochester	142	4735	1242	256	36	122	1936	669	616	446	21	823	48	27	46	125	65	.66	108	.262	.329	.409
Norfolk	142	4697	1219	229	40	90	1798	650	602	434	20	823	42	52	42	132	94	.58	110	.260	.325	.383
Scranton-WB	142	4734	1286	248	48	73	1849	645	602	459	19	777	72	58	50	95	55	.63	129	.272	.342	.391
Charlotte	140	4695	1220	218	17	101	1775	620	582	464	15	729	35	42	45	119	70	.63	97	.260	.328	.378
Ottawa	142	4644	1195	225	35	87	1751	618	566	454	31	824	44	65	30	161	53	.75	104	.257	.327	.377
Syracuse	141	4764	1227	243	41	128	1936	615	561	416	21	885	39	18	39	76	58	.57	104	.258	.320	.406
Toledo	142	4755	1222	224	35	108	1840	600	546	442	11	962	56	39	45	93	70	.57	107	.257	.325	.387
Richmond	141	4710	1222	194	33	78	1716	559	510	441	30	794	40	39	42	70	69	.50	115	.259	.325	.364
Total	707	47196	12363	2299	365	1048	18536	6339	5844	4468	209	8476	457	410	421	1069	654	.62	1094	.262	.329	.393

International League Pitching - AAA

Team	G	GS	CG	GF	IP	BFP	H	R	ER	HR	SH	SF	HB	TBB	IBB	SO	WP	Bk	W	L	Pct.	ShO	Sv	ERA
Norfolk	142	142	15	127	1258.2	5219	1153	493	421	79	52	34	39	419	7	921	47	10	86	56	.606	18	35	3.01
Richmond	141	141	4	137	1247.2	5283	1196	545	480	67	52	36	25	466	36	898	48	6	75	66	.532	14	41	3.46
Toledo	142	142	10	132	1253.1	5304	1241	571	483	108	38	40	41	411	31	735	52	2	71	71	.500	10	39	3.47
Ottawa	142	142	9	133	1224.1	5174	1190	611	533	87	51	48	50	410	13	761	53	6	72	70	.507	11	28	3.92
Rochester	142	142	9	133	1236.1	5265	1263	616	522	119	45	52	30	398	10	899	60	11	73	69	.514	5	36	3.80
Columbus	140	140	5	135	1223.2	5280	1220	643	553	84	33	36	62	478	18	822	84	11	71	68	.511	8	33	4.07
Scranton-WB	142	142	12	130	1236.1	5271	1211	646	554	96	49	40	61	435	38	882	74	6	70	72	.493	8	39	4.03
Pawtucket	142	142	6	136	1230.1	5368	1310	711	621	138	50	48	57	438	15	849	76	8	70	71	.496	1	33	4.54
Charlotte	140	140	6	134	1225.1	5363	1320	735	642	133	28	47	57	483	11	763	90	8	59	81	.421	9	29	4.72
Syracuse	141	141	1	140	1229.2	5437	1259	768	624	137	32	40	35	530	30	946	67	7	59	82	.418	4	29	4.57
Total	707	707	77	630	12365.2	52964	12363	6339	5433	1048	410	421	457	4468	209	8476	651	75	706	706	.500	88	342	3.95

Pacific Coast League Batting - AAA

Team	G	AB	H	2B	3B	HR	TB	R	RBI	TBB	IBB	SO	HBP	SH	SF	SB	CS	SB%	GDP	Avg	OBP	SLG
Salt Lake	144	4987	1516	332	45	107	2259	831	769	455	30	712	57	38	52	132	65	.67	132	.304	.365	.453
Colorado Springs	143	4819	1403	293	53	157	2273	821	770	444	49	829	34	46	50	105	50	.68	96	.291	.352	.472
Tucson	143	4816	1393	285	63	89	2071	786	726	555	48	848	34	54	54	134	68	.66	114	.289	.363	.430
Edmonton	144	4816	1340	295	43	86	1979	759	685	541	35	811	44	49	61	80	45	.64	126	.278	.352	.411
Albuquerque	144	4901	1396	277	52	111	2110	754	691	452	38	821	32	46	27	92	71	.56	134	.285	.347	.431
Calgary	141	4812	1451	306	35	106	2145	743	697	398	39	704	38	37	50	98	58	.63	110	.302	.356	.446
Vancouver	141	4726	1328	237	43	76	1879	723	648	504	40	755	39	42	46	114	52	.69	110	.281	.352	.398
Tacoma	144	4874	1358	240	49	114	2028	682	646	436	25	845	34	43	42	106	46	.70	119	.279	.339	.416
Las Vegas	144	4789	1300	254	32	83	1867	663	602	437	35	840	42	42	51	77	43	.64	126	.271	.334	.390
Phoenix	144	4871	1289	258	44	81	1878	658	604	525	38	791	54	63	62	66	58	.53	115	.265	.339	.386
Total	716	48411	13774	2767	459	1010	20489	7420	6838	4747	377	7956	408	460	495	1004	556	.64	1182	.285	.350	.423

Pacific Coast League Pitching - AAA

Team	G	GS	CG	GF	IP	BFP	H	R	ER	HR	SH	SF	HB	TBB	IBB	SO	WP	Bk	W	L	Pct.	ShO	Sv	ERA
Vancouver	141	141	14	127	1215.2	5223	1242	620	551	99	44	44	46	421	25	782	63	3	81	60	.574	11	26	4.08
Albuquerque	144	144	6	138	1248.2	5441	1340	688	571	98	40	42	31	490	47	919	60	8	75	69	.521	7	42	4.12
Tucson	143	143	1	142	1244.2	5468	1425	698	623	63	51	51	52	427	17	859	66	8	87	56	.608	8	41	4.50
Tacoma	144	144	10	134	1249	5469	1354	734	631	105	33	57	43	471	45	771	47	18	68	76	.472	8	40	4.55
Colorado Springs	143	143	4	139	1212	5408	1359	760	661	96	53	53	45	509	35	803	62	11	77	66	.538	11	32	4.91
Phoenix	144	144	8	136	1275.2	5609	1436	765	689	105	60	54	25	496	50	852	83	9	62	82	.431	5	28	4.86
Salt Lake	144	144	10	134	1249.2	5512	1446	773	698	116	39	44	34	448	39	754	60	11	79	65	.549	5	40	5.03
Las Vegas	144	144	15	129	1230.1	5544	1337	780	649	108	61	53	46	543	37	794	69	5	61	83	.424	8	29	4.75
Edmonton	144	144	6	138	1239.1	5499	1384	790	706	109	39	55	43	541	55	703	90	12	68	76	.472	5	32	5.13
Calgary	141	141	7	134	1195	5356	1451	812	707	111	40	42	43	401	27	719	50	7	58	83	.411	6	26	5.32
Total	716	716	81	635	12360	54529	13774	7420	6486	1010	460	495	408	4747	377	7956	650	92	716	716	.500	74	336	4.72

Eastern League Batting - AA

Team	G	AB	H	2B	3B	HR	TB	R	RBI	TBB	IBB	SO	HBP	SH	SF	SB	CS	SB%	GDP	Avg	OBP	SLG
Portland	142	4783	1286	223	45	93	1878	745	674	577	45	846	63	63	53	140	64	.69	104	.269	.352	.393
New Haven	142	4771	1243	226	27	87	1784	699	641	471	20	951	52	47	38	145	57	.72	100	.261	.331	.374
Reading	142	4712	1186	236	29	118	1834	672	621	494	30	853	69	50	42	100	66	.60	99	.252	.329	.389
Bowie	142	4678	1193	229	16	92	1730	663	605	542	22	838	70	29	49	126	51	.71	120	.255	.338	.370
Trenton	142	4829	1234	239	33	103	1848	649	584	529	36	935	64	51	52	135	84	.62	99	.256	.334	.383
Binghamton	142	4803	1231	247	35	74	1770	638	568	488	30	864	64	56	55	103	58	.64	87	.256	.330	.369
Norwich	141	4666	1206	237	46	89	1802	635	600	559	33	1066	71	38	50	116	59	.66	91	.258	.343	.386
New Britain	142	4717	1175	218	28	109	1776	627	575	507	22	965	44	24	43	139	58	.71	123	.249	.325	.377
Harrisburg	141	4591	1116	217	24	97	1672	587	544	469	37	940	51	66	33	89	66	.57	91	.243	.318	.364
Canton-Akron	142	4599	1158	228	21	84	1680	557	525	480	26	939	60	58	41	97	65	.60	82	.252	.328	.365
Total	709	47149	12028	2300	304	946	17774	6472	5937	5116	301	9197	608	482	456	1190	628	.65	996	.255	.333	.377

Eastern League Pitching - AA

Team	G	GS	CG	GF	IP	BFP	H	R	ER	HR	SH	SF	HB	TBB	IBB	SO	WP	Bk	W	L	Pct.	ShO	Sv	ERA
Portland	142	142	6	136	1255	5373	1184	592	528	93	61	35	59	497	41	979	59	11	86	56	.606	9	40	3.79
New Haven	142	142	3	139	1239.2	5332	1185	592	497	68	51	42	53	521	29	951	53	18	79	63	.556	14	37	3.61
Trenton	142	142	15	127	1279.2	5461	1197	624	538	97	42	46	90	452	22	905	57	24	73	69	.514	8	35	3.78
Binghamton	142	142	15	127	1259.1	5334	1162	625	547	103	42	48	52	487	33	897	57	21	67	75	.472	10	28	3.91
Reading	142	142	7	135	1247	5369	1211	634	553	112	45	29	41	513	33	991	56	24	73	69	.514	8	31	3.99
New Britain	142	142	7	135	1246.2	5430	1236	653	555	81	58	54	51	500	18	935	64	10	65	77	.458	12	26	4.01
Canton-Akron	142	142	9	133	1215.1	5280	1187	672	573	102	54	48	46	519	32	786	48	11	67	75	.472	9	33	4.24
Bowie	142	142	7	135	1231	5408	1225	681	565	125	43	56	55	530	32	892	75	17	68	74	.479	10	32	4.13
Harrisburg	141	141	7	134	1219.2	5354	1176	682	584	94	50	45	80	543	28	981	58	10	61	80	.433	6	26	4.01
Norwich	141	141	6	135	1231.2	5483	1265	717	591	71	36	53	81	554	33	880	81	12	70	71	.496	7	39	4.32
Total	709	709	82	627	12425	53824	12028	6472	5531	946	482	456	608	5116	301	9197	608	158	709	709	.500	93	327	4.01

Southern League Batting - AA

Team	G	AB	H	2B	3B	HR	TB	R	RBI	TBB	IBB	SO	HBP	SH	SF	SB	CS	SB%	GDP	Avg	OBP	SLG
Chattanooga	143	4885	1366	259	36	127	2078	730	680	480	38	808	53	45	40	91	58	.61	136	.280	.348	.425
Carolina	144	5023	1358	257	31	86	1935	689	629	445	42	826	67	67	48	129	72	.64	116	.270	.335	.385
Birmingham	144	4726	1249	225	23	83	1769	688	608	554	36	868	55	62	50	155	72	.68	104	.264	.345	.374
Greenville	142	4772	1278	263	29	132	1995	680	630	431	26	1006	39	47	48	90	87	.51	98	.268	.330	.418
Huntsville	144	4779	1200	202	30	119	1819	643	592	552	22	1027	59	34	45	113	68	.62	94	.251	.333	.381
Memphis	142	4753	1225	205	39	116	1856	624	573	389	26	1057	36	32	34	165	68	.71	90	.258	.317	.390
Jacksonville	144	4720	1091	214	25	132	1765	620	573	506	45	1053	69	56	33	103	61	.63	97	.231	.313	.371
Orlando	143	4736	1235	233	28	82	1770	617	560	454	30	786	34	50	39	83	73	.53	127	.261	.327	.374
Port City	142	4814	1216	229	24	93	1772	604	540	500	35	948	58	35	37	107	74	.59	117	.253	.328	.368
Knoxville	144	4619	1125	221	39	62	1610	577	502	442	21	989	67	43	32	181	98	.65	100	.244	.317	.349
Total	716	47827	12343	2308	304	1032	18355	6472	5887	4753	321	9370	537	471	406	1217	731	.62	1079	.258	.329	.384

Southern League Pitching - AA

Team	G	GS	CG	GF	IP	BFP	H	R	ER	HR	SH	SF	HB	TBB	IBB	SO	WP	Bk	W	L	Pct.	ShO	Sv	ERA
Orlando	143	143	6	137	1257.2	5274	1174	563	477	113	44	41	66	413	54	892	64	11	76	67	.531	14	43	3.41
Birmingham	144	144	8	136	1248.1	5282	1208	599	517	94	36	44	39	413	40	962	67	10	80	64	.556	9	35	3.73
Carolina	144	144	7	137	1322.1	5603	1267	611	511	86	57	34	63	418	40	979	71	5	89	55	.618	14	44	3.48
Port City	142	142	5	137	1264	5382	1179	617	508	89	52	33	78	475	18	989	79	13	62	80	.437	6	27	3.62
Jacksonville	144	144	13	131	1286.2	5476	1303	621	533	112	43	32	41	476	28	854	60	10	75	69	.521	8	36	3.73
Chattanooga	143	143	4	139	1258.1	5439	1239	633	528	85	60	49	39	488	29	1033	60	8	83	60	.580	9	44	3.78
Huntsville	144	144	4	141	1249	5299	1235	659	559	102	57	30	42	433	36	865	82	8	70	74	.486	7	39	4.03
Memphis	142	142	15	127	1236	5513	1191	704	593	103	31	43	88	652	51	1058	101	13	68	74	.479	5	32	4.32
Greenville	142	142	7	135	1234.2	5401	1303	726	638	134	52	46	44	477	35	819	66	8	59	83	.415	4	34	4.65
Knoxville	144	144	6	138	1222.1	5350	1249	761	646	114	39	54	37	508	12	919	84	7	54	90	.375	12	32	4.76
Total	716	716	72	644	12579.1	54019	12343	6472	5510	1032	471	406	537	4753	321	9370	734	93	716	716	.500	88	366	3.94

Texas League Batting - AA

Team	G	AB	H	2B	3B	HR	TB	R	RBI	TBB	IBB	SO	HBP	SH	SF	SB	CS	SB%	GDP	Avg	OBP	SLG
El Paso	136	4656	1331	274	67	84	1991	733	665	527	22	889	53	32	48	83	53	.61	131	.286	.362	.428
Shreveport	135	4644	1302	267	35	85	1894	733	663	546	40	742	54	58	47	108	66	.62	114	.280	.359	.408
Midland	136	4681	1328	235	50	136	2071	726	660	468	23	856	40	48	54	110	85	.56	93	.284	.350	.442
Wichita	136	4701	1328	243	34	99	1936	685	616	429	32	668	59	61	28	143	95	.60	109	.282	.348	.412
Arkansas	135	4387	1176	199	32	100	1739	617	570	492	31	787	47	52	26	86	63	.58	116	.268	.346	.396
San Antonio	136	4556	1209	228	34	86	1763	585	531	446	22	833	45	25	41	119	108	.52	98	.265	.334	.387
Jackson	135	4487	1174	203	24	86	1683	541	490	427	23	689	45	47	50	78	74	.51	114	.262	.329	.375
Tulsa	135	4513	1160	202	35	72	1648	540	501	424	18	683	46	53	42	54	50	.52	121	.257	.324	.365
Total	542	36625	10008	1851	311	748	14725	5160	4696	3759	211	6147	389	376	336	781	594	.57	896	.273	.344	.402

Texas League Pitching - AA

Team	G	GS	CG	GF	IP	BFP	H	R	ER	HR	SH	SF	HB	TBB	IBB	SO	WP	Bk	W	L	Pct.	ShO	Sv	ERA
Shreveport	135	135	6	129	1221	5164	1181	530	445	82	40	39	55	432	21	748	61	8	88	47	.652	14	44	3.28
San Antonio	136	136	6	130	1202	5184	1214	586	503	66	54	43	45	482	6	783	76	18	64	72	.471	5	38	3.77
Arkansas	135	135	7	128	1154	4953	1178	602	506	71	60	37	40	374	21	751	53	5	70	65	.519	7	41	3.95
Jackson	135	135	8	127	1185.2	5083	1123	607	514	85	58	43	59	495	36	815	81	9	62	73	.459	7	34	3.90
Wichita	136	136	3	133	1209.1	5230	1243	668	579	115	32	39	40	478	21	821	89	6	72	64	.529	5	44	4.31
Tulsa	135	135	9	126	1177.1	5188	1318	692	596	128	44	35	34	485	49	651	68	9	52	83	.385	6	24	4.56
Midland	136	136	13	123	1196.1	5254	1379	711	622	111	40	46	57	455	19	712	92	12	66	70	.485	3	29	4.68
El Paso	136	136	7	129	1199.1	5437	1372	764	613	90	48	54	59	558	38	866	86	4	68	68	.500	4	38	4.60
Total	542	542	59	483	9545	41493	10008	5160	4378	748	376	336	389	3759	211	6147	606	71	542	542	.500	51	292	4.13

California League Batting - A

Team	G	AB	H	2B	3B	HR	TB	R	RBI	TBB	IBB	SO	HBP	SH	SF	SB	CS	SB%	GDP	Avg	OBP	SLG
San Bernardino	139	4803	1362	250	29	154	2132	823	738	502	11	988	65	51	43	246	100	.71	82	.284	.356	.444
Lake Elsinore	139	4773	1312	275	51	108	2013	800	731	575	18	973	62	41	39	114	62	.65	108	.275	.358	.422
Riverside	139	4813	1319	213	44	85	1875	799	698	482	12	914	86	30	54	153	72	.68	81	.274	.347	.390
Modesto	140	4678	1251	245	30	138	1970	773	703	659	15	1064	72	80	44	137	79	.63	104	.267	.363	.421
Rancho Cucamonga	139	4733	1288	220	30	94	1850	742	676	522	14	980	73	36	50	169	62	.73	104	.272	.350	.391
Stockton	140	4778	1341	244	43	80	1911	730	626	458	11	872	47	74	49	220	97	.69	100	.281	.346	.400
San Jose	140	4835	1256	227	54	70	1801	695	602	528	19	1011	68	66	43	217	77	.74	90	.260	.338	.372
High Desert	140	4710	1218	215	39	120	1871	669	601	484	5	1033	91	44	41	181	103	.64	87	.259	.337	.397
Bakersfield	140	4690	1250	229	21	76	1749	626	551	475	14	952	68	60	33	149	97	.61	120	.267	.340	.373
Visalia	140	4756	1211	210	38	66	1695	591	529	459	6	1025	50	51	40	116	83	.58	105	.255	.324	.356
Total	698	47569	12808	2328	379	991	18867	7248	6455	5144	125	9812	682	533	436	1702	832	.67	981	.269	.346	.397

California League Pitching - A

Team	G	GS	CG	GF	IP	BFP	H	R	ER	HR	SH	SF	HB	TBB	IBB	SO	WP	Bk	W	L	Pct.	ShO	Sv	ERA
San Jose	140	140	5	135	1270	5236	1147	516	430	75	71	33	48	388	11	1013	56	14	77	63	.550	17	35	3.05
Lake Elsinore	139	139	5	134	1227.1	5292	1246	646	509	92	33	46	62	429	8	1022	58	10	82	57	.590	9	36	3.73
Modesto	140	140	0	140	1234.1	5387	1260	676	566	102	62	43	62	464	9	1077	98	15	78	62	.557	5	41	4.13
Stockton	140	140	5	135	1239.2	5523	1311	694	592	93	68	38	85	555	19	880	68	24	74	66	.529	7	40	4.30
Rancho Cucamonga	139	139	10	129	1216.1	5397	1212	718	601	95	41	48	87	605	21	1074	100	17	68	71	.489	8	30	4.45
San Bernardino	139	139	3	136	1248	5518	1311	719	589	101	60	40	60	493	14	980	80	9	85	54	.612	8	41	4.25
Bakersfield	140	140	3	137	1222	5431	1299	757	615	116	54	37	59	553	6	851	120	13	58	82	.414	4	33	4.53
Visalia	140	140	11	129	1243.1	5401	1322	759	644	102	42	38	81	447	3	974	92	22	58	82	.414	9	24	4.66
Riverside	139	139	2	137	1226.1	5483	1290	767	618	83	55	52	67	577	21	981	90	17	72	67	.518	6	34	4.54
High Desert	140	140	3	137	1227.2	5718	1410	996	789	132	47	61	71	633	13	960	115	31	46	94	.329	2	30	5.78
Total	698	698	47	651	12355	54386	12808	7248	5953	991	533	436	682	5144	125	9812	877	172	698	698	.500	75	344	4.34

Carolina League Batting - A

Team	G	AB	H	2B	3B	HR	TB	R	RBI	TBB	IBB	SO	HBP	SH	SF	SB	CS	SB%	GDP	Avg	OBP	SLG
Lynchburg	138	4483	1185	214	27	107	1774	655	577	501	31	880	59	45	40	156	107	.59	102	.264	.343	.396
Salem	140	4699	1186	231	29	109	1802	619	562	516	35	991	55	42	33	69	51	.58	101	.252	.331	.383
Kinston	137	4509	1145	222	31	119	1786	605	555	459	30	900	63	35	48	139	85	.62	63	.254	.328	.396
Winston-Salem	137	4508	1110	204	21	132	1752	601	562	458	43	961	53	40	35	105	72	.59	83	.246	.321	.389
Prince William	140	4576	1130	210	28	90	1666	572	520	477	26	878	57	24	35	96	48	.67	135	.247	.323	.364
Durham	139	4447	1109	197	14	109	1661	566	519	399	32	1007	77	32	25	150	100	.60	101	.249	.320	.374
Wilmington	138	4591	1173	204	33	75	1668	550	485	393	24	771	57	70	33	135	87	.61	89	.255	.320	.363
Frederick	137	4429	1038	197	26	67	1488	498	425	426	29	979	64	47	32	110	78	.59	96	.234	.309	.336
Total	553	36242	9076	1679	209	808	13597	4666	4205	3629	250	7367	485	335	281	960	628	.60	770	.250	.325	.375

Carolina League Pitching - A

Team	G	GS	CG	GF	IP	BFP	H	R	ER	HR	SH	SF	HB	TBB	IBB	SO	WP	Bk	W	L	Pct.	ShO	Sv	ERA
Wilmington	138	138	2	136	1232.2	5054	1017	459	389	63	35	29	57	405	33	1005	86	13	83	55	.601	17	46	2.84
Kinston	137	137	8	129	1214	5006	1056	500	437	98	44	35	74	408	23	943	69	7	81	56	.591	10	37	3.24
Winston-Salem	137	137	12	125	1198	4983	1065	538	443	102	34	24	60	427	19	850	57	14	69	68	.504	11	30	3.33
Prince William	140	140	12	128	1206	5147	1176	594	524	114	40	44	58	432	28	962	81	6	64	76	.457	11	32	3.91
Frederick	137	137	10	127	1190.2	5130	1123	617	518	101	45	38	68	487	25	1018	103	16	58	79	.423	11	32	3.92
Lynchburg	138	138	5	133	1182.2	5091	1213	640	547	106	44	36	51	393	34	893	83	16	67	71	.486	9	27	4.16
Durham	139	139	6	133	1186.2	5210	1188	650	560	109	51	40	60	541	34	825	74	9	63	76	.453	3	39	4.25
Salem	140	140	8	132	1237	5355	1238	668	563	115	42	35	57	536	54	871	114	22	68	72	.486	6	34	4.10
Total	553	553	63	490	9647.2	40976	9076	4666	3981	808	335	281	485	3629	250	7367	667	103	553	553	.500	78	277	3.71

Florida State League Batting - A

Team	G	AB	H	2B	3B	HR	TB	R	RBI	TBB	IBB	SO	HBP	SH	SF	SB	CS	SB%	GDP	Avg	OBP	SLG
Clearwater	138	4565	1192	219	33	90	1747	653	576	484	11	822	86	35	38	119	67	.64	129	.261	.341	.383
Daytona	135	4355	1114	187	32	53	1524	638	549	471	21	759	78	35	49	161	78	.67	98	.256	.336	.350
Dunedin	138	4616	1156	218	37	78	1682	621	546	504	20	930	50	40	38	79	44	.64	86	.250	.328	.364
Vero Beach	133	4280	1119	182	22	65	1540	583	507	451	23	755	68	41	42	184	87	.68	99	.261	.338	.360
Tampa	136	4438	1098	191	31	73	1570	580	512	557	15	911	56	44	35	98	56	.64	84	.247	.336	.354
Sarasota	134	4400	1146	198	26	65	1591	571	499	407	7	927	52	30	30	126	105	.55	80	.260	.328	.362
Brevard County	135	4492	1113	197	23	58	1530	556	490	502	11	891	52	39	52	83	53	.61	118	.248	.327	.341
Lakeland	135	4460	1162	190	38	65	1623	553	493	388	13	935	33	29	33	133	68	.66	83	.261	.322	.364
Fort Myers	131	4220	1045	196	22	54	1447	552	471	440	20	784	70	62	32	84	73	.54	99	.248	.327	.343
Charlotte	133	4375	1106	210	32	56	1548	543	483	449	12	839	78	34	33	96	96	.50	94	.253	.331	.354
West Palm Beach	136	4324	1045	182	29	37	1396	510	443	419	13	851	40	41	37	123	72	.63	81	.242	.312	.323
Kissimmee	136	4452	1073	205	21	48	1464	508	432	450	14	855	75	27	46	141	66	.68	109	.241	.318	.329
St. Lucie	135	4313	1034	154	40	42	1394	484	414	413	18	908	53	61	31	133	89	.60	83	.240	.312	.323
St. Petersburg	131	4175	975	173	20	46	1326	468	408	440	14	813	37	35	35	69	39	.64	107	.234	.310	.318
Total	943	61465	15378	2702	406	830	21382	7820	6833	6375	212	11980	828	543	531	1629	993	.62	1350	.250	.326	.348

Florida State League Pitching - A

Team	G	GS	CG	GF	IP	BFP	H	R	ER	HR	SH	SF	HB	TBB	IBB	SO	WP	Bk	W	L	Pct.	ShO	Sv	ERA
Fort Myers	131	131	10	121	1136	4719	978	450	360	60	36	44	62	409	13	823	66	9	75	55	.577	12	31	2.85
St. Petersburg	131	131	7	124	1121.1	4667	947	475	378	56	32	34	40	416	16	925	63	13	64	67	.489	12	34	3.03
Daytona	135	135	7	123	1173	4853	1020	484	388	60	33	20	49	382	12	980	77	11	87	48	.644	13	49	2.82
St. Lucie	135	135	18	117	1161.2	4875	1085	504	419	50	44	33	50	412	24	793	71	22	61	73	.455	16	27	3.25
Tampa	136	136	7	129	1187.2	4992	1054	513	371	42	35	32	58	439	17	939	67	19	72	64	.529	13	44	2.81
Vero Beach	133	133	3	130	1137	4889	990	521	429	64	43	38	35	563	14	939	115	23	74	59	.556	7	40	3.40
Charlotte	133	133	7	126	1154.1	4916	1120	538	449	77	38	33	50	394	9	758	55	23	65	67	.492	8	35	3.50
West Palm Beach	136	136	8	128	1146.1	4960	1110	550	445	43	41	53	70	478	18	745	92	17	54	81	.400	7	29	3.49
Brevard County	135	135	5	130	1191.1	5109	1123	582	456	65	44	40	79	462	20	828	57	12	61	74	.452	14	29	3.44
Clearwater	138	138	8	130	1201.2	5151	1202	583	474	59	49	43	40	416	20	891	67	29	79	59	.572	10	36	3.55
Sarasota	134	134	6	128	1153	5027	1142	606	488	57	35	33	66	466	28	819	82	25	65	68	.489	10	34	3.81
Lakeland	135	135	5	130	1156.2	5015	1181	617	498	56	36	46	72	450	8	887	75	19	64	69	.481	7	44	3.87
Dunedin	138	138	4	134	1200	5286	1205	668	536	93	37	33	79	541	8	840	77	22	63	74	.460	5	30	4.02
Kissimmee	136	136	5	131	1183.2	5315	1221	729	551	48	40	49	78	547	5	813	96	26	55	81	.404	7	30	4.19
Total	943	943	96	847	16303.2	69774	15378	7820	6222	830	543	531	828	6375	212	11980	1060	270	939	939	.500	141	492	3.43

Midwest League Batting - A

Team	G	AB	H	2B	3B	HR	TB	R	RBI	TBB	IBB	SO	HBP	SH	SF	SB	CS	SB%	GDP	Avg	OBP	SLG
Rockford	140	4678	1229	275	30	83	1813	764	662	524	19	894	98	26	40	184	71	.72	91	.263	.347	.388
Beloit	139	4491	1181	234	35	92	1761	723	620	560	24	860	90	44	37	194	99	.66	84	.263	.354	.392
Kane County	138	4550	1201	235	38	82	1758	706	616	535	21	935	60	43	47	171	70	.71	78	.264	.346	.386
Cedar Rapids	138	4497	1184	234	28	101	1777	697	597	525	16	880	65	47	43	195	82	.70	83	.263	.346	.395
Michigan	138	4601	1158	233	34	107	1780	684	607	534	16	1058	86	39	38	175	60	.74	75	.252	.338	.387
Ft. Wayne	140	4786	1251	253	38	93	1859	661	601	476	22	926	66	30	37	135	72	.65	84	.261	.334	.388
Quad City	137	4447	1195	226	33	78	1721	660	585	438	8	767	59	40	46	206	95	.68	94	.269	.339	.387
West Michigan	136	4304	1000	192	24	57	1411	650	533	606	23	996	82	72	40	226	96	.70	81	.232	.335	.328
Springfield	139	4503	1101	217	41	90	1670	638	563	425	15	980	68	40	37	187	59	.76	92	.245	.317	.371
South Bend	135	4507	1158	198	40	64	1628	630	563	511	18	857	57	41	55	143	72	.67	80	.257	.336	.361
Wisconsin	138	4444	1089	230	31	55	1546	593	529	452	24	926	89	60	48	166	59	.74	81	.245	.324	.348
Burlington	135	4255	1022	166	18	113	1563	569	497	429	8	960	61	37	24	103	46	.69	98	.240	.317	.367
Peoria	134	4271	1065	175	37	53	1473	534	454	356	16	738	52	50	29	131	72	.65	94	.249	.313	.345
Clinton	137	4316	1011	188	18	36	1343	521	451	510	13	910	38	39	31	160	72	.69	75	.234	.318	.311
Total	962	62650	15845	3056	445	1104	23103	9030	7878	6881	243	12687	971	608	552	2376	1025	.70	1190	.253	.334	.369

Midwest League Pitching - A

Team	G	GS	CG	GF	IP	BFP	H	R	ER	HR	SH	SF	HB	TBB	IBB	SO	WP	Bk	W	L	Pct.	ShO	Sv	ERA
Quad City	137	137	7	130	1166.1	4930	1011	533	414	73	38	31	59	427	11	922	63	10	76	61	.555	11	35	3.19
Wisconsin	138	138	14	124	1180	5062	1055	599	492	74	37	35	60	501	28	917	82	13	63	75	.457	8	35	3.75
Peoria	134	134	6	128	1131	4864	1039	605	478	72	41	33	39	466	6	937	55	15	62	72	.463	9	36	3.80
Beloit	139	139	8	131	1195.2	5142	1114	618	525	83	40	35	59	503	12	1064	89	28	88	51	.633	9	49	3.95
South Bend	135	135	13	122	1183.2	5119	1169	620	495	74	55	40	71	459	6	843	87	30	66	69	.489	8	27	3.76
Cedar Rapids	138	138	16	122	1184.2	5160	1184	655	535	79	48	31	104	425	23	907	81	21	76	62	.551	6	40	4.06
Ft. Wayne	140	140	4	136	1236.1	5365	1187	660	554	83	50	42	74	515	13	1029	120	20	75	65	.536	8	41	4.03
Rockford	140	140	4	136	1201	5226	1136	663	550	76	36	52	73	508	8	829	123	16	75	65	.536	5	29	4.12
West Michigan	136	136	1	135	1174.2	5209	1146	664	515	62	37	29	81	550	11	893	83	26	67	69	.493	9	36	3.95
Michigan	138	138	9	129	1208.2	5227	1130	665	544	81	50	55	71	502	13	975	82	13	75	63	.543	5	31	4.05
Kane County	138	138	5	133	1181.2	5230	1168	668	551	79	49	41	99	495	28	879	87	10	69	69	.500	8	26	4.20
Springfield	139	139	4	135	1175.1	5161	1248	680	564	103	41	45	54	429	3	729	95	7	65	74	.468	5	22	4.32
Clinton	137	137	19	118	1129	5035	1146	690	542	70	44	38	71	504	43	865	93	17	51	86	.372	4	25	4.32
Burlington	135	135	6	129	1103	4972	1112	710	545	95	42	45	56	597	38	898	114	13	54	81	.400	4	35	4.45
Total	962	962	116	846	16451	71702	15845	9030	7304	1104	608	552	971	6881	243	12687	1254	239	962	962	.500	99	467	4.00

Northwest League Batting - A

Team	G	AB	H	2B	3B	HR	TB	R	RBI	TBB	IBB	SO	HBP	SH	SF	SB	CS	SB%	GDP	Avg	OBP	SLG
Boise	75	2523	669	117	16	49	965	411	358	350	16	506	44	24	19	68	30	.69	59	.265	.362	.382
Southern Oregon	76	2488	589	109	20	36	846	372	311	385	8	509	40	26	31	107	44	.71	53	.237	.344	.340
Everett	76	2591	625	116	16	62	959	369	316	318	12	650	50	21	16	113	45	.72	48	.241	.334	.370
Eugene	76	2534	630	104	24	48	926	364	307	233	7	578	58	19	20	137	62	.69	34	.249	.324	.365
Bellingham	76	2563	613	111	11	44	878	334	290	276	25	654	40	20	24	79	42	.65	44	.239	.320	.343
Spokane	76	2575	623	110	11	30	845	333	281	271	9	546	50	19	18	54	36	.60	65	.242	.324	.328
Portland	75	2407	536	92	19	21	729	316	255	307	10	542	48	19	19	126	54	.70	46	.223	.320	.303
Yakima	76	2560	624	116	25	21	853	288	240	260	13	565	26	20	26	122	36	.77	53	.244	.317	.333
Total	303	20241	4909	875	142	311	7001	2787	2358	2400	100	4550	356	168	173	806	349	.70	402	.243	.331	.346

Northwest League Pitching - A

Team	G	GS	CG	GF	IP	BFP	H	R	ER	HR	SH	SF	HB	TBB	IBB	SO	WP	Bk	W	L	Pct.	ShO	Sv	ERA
Portland	75	75	4	71	662.1	2779	531	284	225	27	21	20	40	277	13	561	58	19	41	34	.547	4	23	3.06
Bellingham	76	76	0	76	685.1	2931	618	297	232	34	22	15	29	285	2	591	43	13	43	33	.566	8	21	3.05
Boise	75	75	4	71	653.2	2836	575	343	283	44	17	17	48	329	13	590	69	9	48	27	.640	5	20	3.90
Spokane	76	76	1	75	680.2	2952	653	345	276	38	20	21	52	269	11	522	44	9	36	40	.474	4	20	3.65
Everett	76	76	5	71	680	2919	622	346	274	55	15	14	44	294	14	572	54	15	37	39	.487	4	15	3.63
Eugene	76	76	0	76	667	2955	606	372	264	39	26	21	44	313	19	635	53	11	37	39	.487	2	19	3.56
Southern Oregon	76	76	0	76	669.1	2941	667	374	277	40	28	28	59	237	16	542	51	13	33	43	.434	3	13	3.72
Yakima	76	76	0	76	667.2	3039	637	426	337	34	19	37	40	396	12	537	95	16	28	48	.368	2	17	4.54
Total	303	303	14	289	5366	23352	4909	2787	2168	311	168	173	356	2400	100	4550	467	105	303	303	.500	32	148	3.64

New York-Penn League Batting - A

Team	G	AB	H	2B	3B	HR	TB	R	RBI	TBB	IBB	SO	HBP	SH	SF	SB	CS	SB%	GDP	Avg	OBP	SLG
Batavia	75	2592	680	106	31	31	941	389	336	236	5	474	50	22	17	88	35	.72	49	.262	.334	.363
Auburn	74	2444	653	112	18	32	897	383	331	258	5	410	29	10	24	71	27	.72	69	.267	.341	.367
Williamsport	76	2561	654	122	34	21	907	379	324	275	7	523	47	12	24	85	44	.66	51	.255	.336	.354
Hudson Valley	74	2512	670	105	25	24	897	376	306	252	13	465	50	13	31	107	51	.68	72	.267	.342	.357
New Jersey	76	2603	651	105	27	13	849	370	314	280	6	477	53	29	14	93	43	.68	54	.250	.334	.326
Erie	75	2503	661	92	25	46	941	368	307	232	3	502	50	23	20	81	50	.62	62	.264	.336	.376
Jamestown	76	2544	646	117	29	35	926	368	312	338	9	526	40	19	21	104	48	.68	50	.254	.348	.364
Watertown	73	2456	630	127	26	29	896	360	306	299	11	529	34	21	24	49	23	.68	61	.257	.342	.365
Utica	73	2425	622	98	23	33	865	358	304	191	2	479	41	21	30	125	55	.69	49	.256	.318	.357
Vermont	76	2505	643	94	28	24	865	354	287	257	9	457	36	17	27	152	72	.68	36	.257	.331	.345
St. Catharines	75	2557	658	119	25	28	911	344	289	248	9	570	53	40	20	96	45	.68	25	.257	.333	.356
Pittsfield	76	2498	623	101	32	14	830	325	270	274	7	487	36	26	23	103	50	.67	36	.249	.330	.332
Elmira	76	2534	616	106	30	34	884	316	261	253	11	552	42	14	17	111	52	.68	61	.243	.320	.349
Oneonta	75	2489	604	125	30	18	843	312	261	259	4	553	28	9	27	87	33	.73	42	.243	.318	.339
Total	525	35223	9011	1529	383	382	12452	5002	4208	3652	101	7004	589	276	319	1352	628	.68	717	.256	.333	.354

New York-Penn League Pitching - A

Team	G	GS	CG	GF	IP	BFP	H	R	ER	HR	SH	SF	HB	TBB	IBB	SO	WP	Bk	W	L	Pct.	ShO	Sv	ERA
Watertown	73	73	1	72	645.1	2695	580	268	222	27	11	21	30	228	18	508	41	17	46	27	.630	7	23	3.10
Vermont	76	76	1	75	667.2	2793	558	282	212	19	18	18	54	251	5	479	63	16	49	27	.645	9	30	2.86
Hudson Valley	74	74	4	70	660	2817	637	325	262	25	27	16	38	236	12	536	98	24	47	27	.635	3	24	3.57
St. Catharines	75	75	1	74	669.2	2887	652	341	276	38	23	22	41	292	0	461	59	14	38	37	.507	3	19	3.71
Erie	75	75	5	70	653	2861	648	350	255	31	27	17	35	256	12	434	48	9	34	41	.453	5	16	3.51
Williamsport	76	76	0	76	665.1	2905	678	362	250	25	23	19	44	193	3	494	34	18	37	39	.487	2	20	3.38
Auburn	74	74	6	68	621.2	2764	620	366	311	28	15	24	42	300	7	431	52	7	40	34	.541	5	24	4.50
Oneonta	75	75	0	75	646.2	2869	611	368	252	12	19	23	39	287	4	595	68	11	34	41	.453	2	20	3.51
Batavia	75	75	4	71	666	2882	716	369	291	28	21	20	42	194	6	507	71	18	41	34	.547	8	14	3.93
Pittsfield	76	76	3	73	659	2876	671	369	282	25	18	22	31	265	4	451	56	14	34	42	.447	4	22	3.85
New Jersey	76	76	0	76	682	3002	649	372	292	28	19	35	52	303	9	607	61	25	35	41	.461	5	17	3.85
Utica	73	73	7	66	636.1	2840	643	379	283	20	11	31	41	300	10	500	68	7	33	40	.452	2	19	4.00
Elmira	76	76	0	76	658	2937	675	424	333	30	19	22	46	293	7	507	71	30	25	51	.329	2	16	4.55
Jamestown	76	76	1	75	666.2	2936	673	427	340	46	25	29	54	254	4	494	61	24	32	44	.421	1	15	4.59
Total	525	525	33	492	9197.1	40064	9011	5002	3861	382	276	319	589	3652	101	7004	851	234	525	525	.500	58	279	3.78

South Atlantic League Batting - A

Team	G	AB	H	2B	3B	HR	TB	R	RBI	TBB	IBB	SO	HBP	SH	SF	SB	CS	SB%	GDP	Avg	OBP	SLG
Macon	141	4876	1197	231	31	127	1871	739	651	571	26	1225	73	24	34	172	54	.76	79	.245	.331	.384
Piedmont	140	4595	1146	213	46	50	1601	683	573	519	23	938	89	54	49	123	75	.62	106	.249	.334	.348
Fayetteville	141	4633	1169	234	30	85	1718	660	585	489	15	1025	73	37	38	158	79	.67	84	.252	.331	.371
Greensboro	140	4632	1154	223	26	86	1687	645	557	525	30	1077	49	49	28	127	80	.61	108	.249	.330	.364
Hagerstown	141	4678	1191	244	34	95	1788	638	557	461	15	1173	90	29	34	100	56	.64	95	.255	.331	.382
Albany	140	4757	1206	251	44	66	1743	633	550	510	24	1099	84	23	39	136	105	.56	75	.254	.334	.366
Charleston-WV	142	4551	1133	206	57	45	1588	633	549	513	17	1002	56	44	41	230	101	.69	82	.249	.330	.349
Columbus	142	4748	1207	221	45	93	1797	630	551	480	24	918	50	31	32	134	65	.67	102	.254	.327	.378
Augusta	138	4531	1158	203	37	48	1579	628	539	411	23	940	60	33	32	215	108	.67	74	.256	.324	.348
Asheville	139	4477	1086	210	24	81	1587	578	488	438	19	928	65	45	37	130	82	.61	78	.243	.317	.354
Columbia	140	4619	1111	183	34	73	1581	571	481	387	27	1118	57	54	36	187	85	.69	86	.241	.305	.342
Charleston-SC	139	4509	1054	220	20	46	1452	546	450	514	14	939	40	39	45	218	135	.62	64	.234	.315	.322
Hickory	138	4538	1030	198	29	57	1457	459	387	397	14	1047	71	28	27	118	101	.54	92	.227	.298	.321
Savannah	139	4534	977	138	28	50	1321	448	362	544	18	1243	60	46	29	124	71	.64	102	.215	.306	.291
Total	980	64678	15819	2975	485	1002	22770	8491	7280	6759	289	14672	917	536	501	2172	1197	.64	1227	.245	.322	.352

South Atlantic League Pitching - A

Team	G	GS	CG	GF	IP	BFP	H	R	ER	HR	SH	SF	HB	TBB	IBB	SO	WP	Bk	W	L	Pct.	ShO	Sv	ERA
Asheville	139	139	7	132	1212	5056	1060	505	423	69	27	19	64	450	7	1011	104	30	76	63	.547	13	42	3.14
Augusta	138	138	4	134	1199.1	5109	1059	533	419	60	40	28	57	460	18	1000	93	10	76	62	.551	8	36	3.14
Columbia	140	140	13	127	1235.2	5182	1067	542	434	65	35	37	58	488	14	1045	99	20	72	68	.514	11	30	3.16
Charleston-WV	142	142	10	132	1209	5154	1166	559	483	59	41	35	83	443	47	930	90	18	77	65	.542	11	42	3.60
Fayetteville	141	141	3	138	1231.2	5205	1035	571	440	55	34	33	81	524	6	1183	105	17	86	55	.610	10	54	3.22
Piedmont	140	140	7	133	1218.1	5150	1087	574	442	62	38	37	59	460	7	1074	93	19	82	58	.586	12	38	3.27
Greensboro	140	140	5	135	1226	5204	1137	595	488	79	34	40	52	450	19	1130	91	11	70	70	.500	11	38	3.58
Columbus	142	142	3	139	1242.1	5300	1085	598	472	66	38	29	78	569	39	1103	74	20	80	62	.563	17	48	3.42
Hagerstown	141	141	11	130	1216	5152	1178	599	476	76	39	31	56	391	9	906	97	11	73	68	.518	8	41	3.52
Savannah	139	139	3	136	1228.2	5307	1121	608	498	79	38	43	54	492	25	1118	120	11	56	83	.403	6	36	3.65
Charleston-SC	139	139	7	132	1201.1	5264	1179	683	548	78	39	45	72	509	27	1032	104	19	50	89	.360	4	23	4.11
Macon	141	141	2	139	1269.2	5548	1127	699	550	89	39	32	79	627	9	1136	122	24	71	70	.504	9	31	3.90
Hickory	138	138	7	131	1222	5315	1236	712	541	106	48	45	62	436	46	988	89	26	49	89	.355	9	27	3.98
Albany	140	140	6	134	1242.1	5465	1282	713	538	59	46	47	62	460	16	1016	82	12	62	78	.443	5	31	3.90
Total	980	980	88	892	17154.1	73411	15819	8491	6752	1002	536	501	917	6759	289	14672	1363	248	980	980	.500	134	517	3.54

Appalachian League Batting - R

Team	BATTING															BASERUNNING				PERCENTAGES		
	G	AB	H	2B	3B	HR	TB	R	RBI	TBB	IBB	SO	HBP	SH	SF	SB	CS	SB%	GDP	Avg	OBP	SLG
Bluefield	65	2174	637	120	22	42	927	437	370	241	7	416	27	24	27	127	46	.73	43	.293	.367	.426
Kingsport	66	2199	578	98	22	33	819	402	327	247	7	458	33	23	18	113	38	.75	29	.263	.344	.372
Elizabethton	64	2172	572	109	10	59	878	363	315	243	4	493	27	9	15	78	36	.68	36	.263	.343	.404
Johnson City	68	2261	562	119	23	28	811	357	300	304	4	583	33	14	20	70	51	.58	37	.249	.343	.359
Princeton	63	2098	497	98	13	53	780	330	286	210	3	546	25	15	14	71	26	.73	25	.237	.312	.372
Danville	67	2230	576	100	21	35	823	326	274	241	10	546	28	6	20	128	58	.69	37	.258	.335	.369
Martinsville	67	2131	526	97	17	27	738	325	279	257	6	531	58	13	17	91	32	.74	53	.247	.341	.346
Huntington	67	2134	505	96	22	32	741	307	255	255	5	552	30	23	19	108	44	.71	37	.237	.324	.347
Burlington	64	2133	508	92	15	40	750	298	236	194	3	598	31	6	15	103	39	.73	29	.238	.309	.352
Bristol	67	2209	559	91	18	29	773	296	251	210	6	546	38	18	19	95	39	.71	37	.253	.326	.350
Total	329	21741	5520	1020	183	378	8040	3441	2893	2402	55	5269	330	151	184	984	409	.71	363	.254	.335	.370

Appalachian League Pitching - R

Team	HOW MUCH THEY PITCHED						WHAT THEY GAVE UP											THE RESULTS					
	G	GS	CG	GF	IP	BFP	H	R	ER	HR	SH	SF	HB	TBB	IBB	SO	WP	Bk	W	L	Pct.	ShO	Sv	ERA
Kingsport	66	66	5	61	574.1	2414	480	263	223	38	18	10	35	226	5	532	48	4	48	18	.727	6	20	3.49
Bluefield	65	65	2	63	561	2381	511	269	201	41	14	10	36	227	4	531	50	10	49	16	.754	3	28	3.22
Elizabethton	64	64	4	60	551	2396	550	299	209	29	21	14	23	183	7	535	50	17	33	31	.516	5	13	3.41
Princeton	63	63	1	62	543.1	2434	538	339	253	29	6	18	24	267	16	506	71	13	31	32	.492	4	15	4.19
Bristol	67	67	2	65	566.1	2493	552	347	267	40	18	22	27	224	2	532	52	14	28	39	.418	2	10	4.24
Martinsville	67	67	0	67	557.2	2475	582	349	284	38	10	17	35	247	4	511	72	13	30	37	.448	1	17	4.58
Burlington	64	64	4	60	550	2491	538	373	298	38	12	12	35	272	7	582	56	9	26	38	.406	4	12	4.88
Danville	67	67	2	65	570.2	2515	540	378	276	31	17	37	33	243	3	536	70	14	27	40	.403	2	18	4.35
Johnson City	68	68	2	64	589	2666	599	399	311	50	21	20	36	279	5	539	35	33	.515	3	20	4.75	
Huntington	67	67	6	61	560.1	2551	630	425	342	44	14	24	46	234	2	465	75	14	22	45	.328	1	11	5.49
Total	329	329	28	301	5623.2	24816	5520	3441	2664	378	151	184	330	2402	55	5269	597	132	329	329	.500	31	164	4.26

Arizona League Batting - R

Team	BATTING															BASERUNNING				PERCENTAGES		
	G	AB	H	2B	3B	HR	TB	R	RBI	TBB	IBB	SO	HBP	SH	SF	SB	CS	SB%	GDP	Avg	OBP	SLG
Athletics	56	1847	473	61	44	20	682	329	253	262	5	481	31	8	28	134	65	.67	27	.256	.353	.369
Brewers	56	1899	504	68	28	5	643	315	254	203	2	376	38	13	19	106	45	.70	40	.265	.345	.339
Mariners	56	1959	510	93	28	13	690	304	228	224	1	477	32	8	18	71	47	.60	32	.260	.343	.354
Angels	56	1832	482	60	35	9	639	287	223	214	9	386	34	23	18	92	47	.66	32	.263	.348	.349
Padres	55	1822	469	78	27	18	655	254	212	177	4	482	21	9	12	69	45	.61	36	.257	.328	.359
Rockies	55	1819	418	60	17	8	536	237	182	194	1	503	42	8	18	63	33	.66	46	.230	.315	.295
Total	167	11178	2856	420	179	73	3853	1726	1352	1274	16	2705	198	69	113	535	282	.65	213	.256	.339	.345

Arizona League Pitching - R

Team	HOW MUCH THEY PITCHED						WHAT THEY GAVE UP											THE RESULTS					
	G	GS	CG	GF	IP	BFP	H	R	ER	HR	SH	SF	HB	TBB	IBB	SO	WP	Bk	W	L	Pct.	ShO	Sv	ERA
Angels	56	56	5	51	489	2073	422	222	160	5	10	14	47	193	7	429	57	21	35	21	.625	6	17	2.94
Brewers	56	56	5	51	493.2	2122	444	238	180	11	16	21	26	199	5	536	60	20	34	22	.607	2	16	3.28
Athletics	56	56	1	55	491.1	2073	436	238	184	17	7	10	26	190	2	496	42	25	37	19	.661	3	15	3.37
Padres	55	55	3	52	469.1	2083	457	292	196	14	11	18	43	205	0	406	49	20	24	31	.436	2	12	3.76
Mariners	56	56	1	55	493.2	2228	527	326	236	13	9	27	25	244	1	448	62	18	24	32	.429	1	10	4.30
Rockies	55	55	0	55	473.1	2257	569	410	306	13	16	23	31	243	1	390	72	28	13	42	.236	0	5	5.82
Total	167	167	15	152	2910.1	12836	2855	1726	1262	73	69	113	198	1274	16	2705	342	132	167	167	.500	14	75	3.90

Gulf Coast League Batting - R

Team	G	AB	H	2B	3B	HR	TB	R	RBI	TBB	IBB	SO	HBP	SH	SF	SB	CS	SB%	GDP	Avg	OBP	SLG
							BATTING									BASERUNNING				PERCENTAGES		
Mets	57	1875	487	92	26	25	706	306	256	205	8	360	30	12	35	63	23	.73	33	.260	.337	.377
Royals	57	1834	470	82	18	36	696	294	238	214	1	366	26	5	20	42	25	.63	32	.256	.339	.379
Marlins	56	1835	478	72	23	11	629	289	212	213	5	306	28	10	19	95	27	.78	33	.260	.343	.343
Yankees	58	1883	463	74	21	19	636	285	229	202	10	409	28	20	14	52	22	.70	36	.246	.326	.338
Cubs	57	1793	457	73	28	23	655	276	226	199	3	397	23	18	21	128	47	.73	39	.255	.333	.365
White Sox	58	1858	448	83	14	23	628	271	218	203	11	418	33	12	12	47	26	.64	36	.241	.325	.338
Astros	58	1784	449	68	19	15	600	268	205	173	4	381	31	26	13	114	58	.66	37	.252	.326	.336
Orioles	59	1856	448	85	13	14	601	260	198	212	1	375	28	10	20	59	31	.66	44	.241	.325	.324
Blue Jays	59	1819	402	82	21	17	577	259	215	258	5	467	52	19	16	47	23	.67	45	.221	.332	.317
Pirates	59	1898	487	72	21	20	661	245	212	163	3	331	15	8	14	38	20	.66	47	.257	.318	.348
Tigers	57	1715	411	50	24	19	566	237	185	189	2	467	36	18	12	122	39	.76	27	.240	.326	.330
Rangers	58	1783	414	68	20	15	567	230	188	170	1	417	25	10	17	135	40	.77	30	.232	.305	.318
Red Sox	57	1785	395	59	6	13	505	223	169	175	1	382	40	24	15	73	29	.72	31	.221	.303	.283
Expos	56	1727	375	75	15	8	504	195	137	175	1	425	24	16	9	62	58	.52	25	.217	.297	.292
Twins	55	1709	380	71	8	11	500	169	138	145	4	363	35	15	15	73	31	.70	28	.222	.294	.293
Braves	57	1721	326	53	2	14	425	141	116	161	2	401	19	13	6	36	32	.53	39	.189	.265	.247
Total	459	28875	6890	1159	279	283	9456	3948	3142	3057	62	6265	473	236	258	1186	531	.69	562	.239	.319	.327

Gulf Coast League Pitching - R

Team	G	GS	CG	GF	IP	BFP	H	R	ER	HR	SH	SF	HB	TBB	IBB	SO	WP	Bk	W	L	Pct.	ShO	Sv	ERA
		HOW MUCH THEY PITCHED					WHAT THEY GAVE UP												THE RESULTS					
Marlins	56	56	2	54	481.2	1966	367	167	123	15	21	13	27	158	9	401	40	8	40	16	.714	4	16	2.30
Mets	57	57	3	54	490.2	2012	381	175	138	14	7	12	21	173	4	439	57	12	38	19	.667	4	17	2.53
Cubs	57	57	0	57	483	2015	369	184	111	11	20	22	29	189	6	344	31	15	35	22	.614	5	11	2.07
Yankees	58	58	2	56	489.1	2052	372	215	157	16	19	9	43	241	3	483	79	21	32	26	.552	8	13	2.89
White Sox	58	58	3	55	482.2	2021	438	217	157	21	6	17	18	155	3	400	34	14	36	22	.621	5	13	2.93
Royals	57	57	1	56	483	2011	406	223	148	16	15	16	45	142	1	423	46	9	37	20	.649	5	15	2.76
Orioles	59	59	6	53	490.1	2073	407	223	145	16	9	20	21	190	5	377	28	10	34	25	.576	7	17	2.66
Astros	58	58	2	56	476.1	2066	429	228	170	16	23	12	29	199	6	492	59	13	32	26	.552	4	12	3.21
Tigers	57	57	3	54	462	2003	406	243	174	16	22	16	32	177	10	399	57	20	33	24	.579	5	23	3.39
Twins	55	55	5	50	453.1	1982	406	244	157	16	18	16	32	232	1	357	52	16	20	35	.364	6	9	3.12
Rangers	58	58	3	55	477.1	2082	456	274	195	18	8	18	32	196	3	385	51	7	24	34	.414	5	12	3.68
Expos	56	56	1	55	466.1	2056	470	281	207	18	13	24	26	179	2	310	51	16	21	35	.375	6	12	3.99
Red Sox	57	57	7	50	476.2	2084	494	287	208	37	12	14	18	181	4	400	42	7	21	36	.368	3	9	3.93
Braves	57	57	2	55	467	2099	448	314	225	11	10	20	27	244	1	342	72	19	14	43	.246	2	7	4.34
Pirates	59	59	2	57	488	2196	523	316	229	20	14	11	30	196	2	363	49	9	23	36	.390	3	9	4.22
Blue Jays	59	59	3	56	480	2196	518	363	260	22	19	18	43	205	2	350	86	20	19	40	.322	5	7	4.88
Total	459	459	45	414	7647.2	32914	6890	3954	2804	283	236	258	473	3057	62	6265	834	216	459	459	.500	77	202	3.30

Pioneer League Batting - R

Team	G	AB	H	2B	3B	HR	TB	R	RBI	TBB	IBB	SO	HBP	SH	SF	SB	CS	SB%	GDP	Avg	OBP	SLG
Helena	71	2428	739	160	14	55	1092	558	458	387	12	424	45	20	31	119	68	.64	49	.304	.405	.450
Idaho Falls	71	2525	741	133	26	55	1091	519	467	361	10	485	50	18	32	83	38	.69	53	.293	.388	.432
Billings	69	2426	702	138	21	45	1017	463	389	339	15	514	38	15	27	80	51	.61	31	.289	.381	.419
Ogden	70	2430	708	131	10	41	982	444	379	336	9	462	42	34	24	55	45	.55	65	.291	.383	.404
Medicine Hat	72	2434	636	130	19	45	939	415	351	317	16	611	36	13	27	84	35	.71	58	.261	.351	.386
Great Falls	69	2326	632	118	33	33	915	399	335	268	8	536	40	12	32	97	49	.66	51	.272	.353	.393
Butte	70	2394	638	113	35	23	890	372	322	309	4	521	47	6	21	88	38	.70	55	.266	.359	.372
Lethbridge	72	2404	580	92	28	20	788	340	261	290	13	531	49	22	19	98	46	.68	62	.241	.333	.328
Total	282	19367	5376	1015	186	317	7714	3510	2962	2607	87	4084	347	140	213	704	370	.66	424	.278	.370	.090

Pioneer League Pitching - R

Team	G	GS	CG	GF	IP	BFP	H	R	ER	HR	SH	SF	HB	TBB	IBB	SO	WP	Bk	W	L	Pct.	ShO	Sv	ERA
Billings	69	69	0	69	613	2670	613	316	244	20	12	20	29	239	22	474	48	14	49	20	.710	4	23	3.58
Helena	71	71	0	71	616	2854	608	388	321	44	16	16	61	411	4	559	69	21	49	22	.690	3	17	4.69
Medicine Hat	72	72	5	67	624.2	2816	613	422	308	46	27	26	44	312	5	510	70	14	35	37	.486	3	17	4.44
Great Falls	69	69	0	69	594.1	2748	635	426	309	37	13	29	37	309	16	485	61	12	31	38	.449	0	9	4.68
Lethbridge	72	72	5	67	632	2890	710	446	344	48	18	30	35	297	8	595	51	15	25	47	.347	2	14	4.90
Idaho Falls	71	71	1	70	634.2	2877	669	455	370	30	24	27	50	344	7	564	84	9	42	29	.592	3	17	5.25
Ogden	70	70	4	66	617.2	2893	759	506	401	51	15	30	53	313	10	443	57	16	32	38	.457	1	9	5.84
Butte	70	70	0	70	597.1	2930	769	551	444	41	15	35	38	382	15	454	76	23	19	51	.271	0	12	6.69
Total	282	282	15	267	4929.2	22678	5376	3510	2741	317	140	213	347	2607	87	4084	516	124	282	282	.500	16	118	5.00

Leader Boards

Players who split time between AAA and AA have combined numbers. The Batting Boards are for players with a minimum of 383 total plate appearances. The Pitching Boards are for pitchers who threw at least 112 innings.

Team Abbreviations

ABQ - Albuquerque	IWA - Iowa	PCY - Port City
ARK - Arkansas	JCK - Jackson	PHX - Phoenix
BIR - Birmingham	JAX - Jacksonville	PRT - Portland
BNG - Binghamton	KNX - Knoxville	REA - Reading
BOW - Bowie	LOU - Louisville	RMD - Richmond
BUF - Buffalo	LVG - Las Vegas	ROC - Rochester
CAN - Canton-Akron	MDL - Midland	SAN - San Antonio
CAR - Carolina	MEM - Memphis	SHR - Shreveport
CGY - Calgary	NBR - New Britain	SLK - Salt Lake
CHR - Charlotte	NHV - New Haven	SWB - Scranton-WB
CNG - Chattanooga	NO - New Orleans	SYR - Syracuse
COL - Columbus	NOR - Norfolk	TAC - Tacoma
CSP - Colorado Springs	NRW - Norwich	TCN - Tuscon
EDM - Edmonton	NVL - Nashville	TOL - Toledo
ELP - El Paso	OKC - Oklahoma City	TRE - Trenton
GRV - Greenville	OMA - Omaha	TUL - Tulsa
HRB - Harrisburg	ORL - Orlando	VAN - Vancouver
HVL - Huntsville	OTT - Ottawa	WCH - Wichita
IND - Indianapolis	PAW - Pawtucket	

League Abbreviations

AMAS - American Association	PCL - Pacific Coast League
EAST - Eastern League	SOU - Southern League
INT - International League	TEX - Texas League

Triple-A/Double-A Batting Leaders

Batting Average

Player	Team	League	
Coughlin, Kevin	**BIR**	**SOU**	**.372**
McCracken, Quinton	CSP	PCL	.359
Lennon, Patrick	SLK	PCL	.352
Ingram, Riccardo	SLK	PCL	.348
Guerrero, Wilton	ABQ	PCL	.346
Pecorilli, Aldo	RMD	INT	.344
Damon, Johnny	WCH	TEX	.343
Perez, Robert	SYR	INT	.343
Cookson, Brent	OMA	AMAS	.340
Hubbard, Trent	CSP	PCL	.340
Beamon, Trey	CGY	PCL	.334
McGuire, Ryan	TRE	EAST	.333
Ratliff, Daryl	CGY	PCL	.332
Pulliam, Harvey	CSP	PCL	.327
Hajek, Dave	TCN	PCL	.327

On-Base Percentage

Player	Team	League	
Coughlin, Kevin	**BIR**	**SOU**	**.439**
Damon, Johnny	WCH	TEX	.434
Grotewold, Jeff	OMA	AMAS	.434
Dodson, Bo	NO	AMAS	.425
Lennon, Patrick	SLK	PCL	.425
McMillon, Billy	PRT	EAST	.423
Lopez, Roberto	ELP	TEX	.419
McCracken, Quinton	CSP	PCL	.418
Giovanola, Ed	RMD	INT	.417
Berblinger, Jeff	ARK	TEX	.417
Hubbard, Trent	CSP	PCL	.416
Cookson, Brent	OMA	AMAS	.415
Schall, Gene	SWB	INT	.415
McGuire, Ryan	TRE	EAST	.414
Kendall, Jason	CAR	SOU	.414

Slugging Percentage

Player	Team	League	
Pulliam, Harvey	**CSP**	**PCL**	**.614**
Delgado, Carlos	SYR	INT	.610
Greene, Todd	VAN	PCL	.601
Cookson, Brent	OMA	AMAS	.585
Rivera, Ruben	COL	INT	.553
Huskey, Butch	NOR	INT	.548
Franklin, Micah	CGY	PCL	.547
Garcia, Karim	ABQ	PCL	.542
Gainer, Jay	CSP	PCL	.542
Cruz, Ivan	JAX	SOU	.538
Damon, Johnny	WCH	TEX	.534
Lennon, Patrick	SLK	PCL	.534
Yan, Julian	OTT	INT	.532
Pough, Chop	PAW	INT	.530
Schall, Gene	SWB	INT	.528

Home Runs

Player	Team	League	
Greene, Todd	**VAN**	**PCL**	**40**
Cruz, Ivan	JAX	SOU	31
Arias, George	MDL	TEX	30
Huskey, Butch	NOR	INT	28
Pough, Chop	PAW	INT	26
Pulliam, Harvey	CSP	PCL	25
Murray, Glenn	PAW	INT	25
Rivera, Ruben	COL	INT	24
Lewis, Anthony	ARK	TEX	24
Marrero, Oreste	ABQ	PCL	23
McNair, Fred	REA	EAST	23
Kieschnick, Brooks	IWA	AMAS	23
Gainer, Jay	CSP	PCL	23
Several tied at			22

Runs Batted In

Player	Team	League	
Arias, George	**MDL**	**TEX**	**104**
Canale, George	CAR	SOU	102
Echevarria, Angel	NHV	EAST	100
Kennedy, Dave	NHV	EAST	96
Cruz, Ivan	JAX	SOU	96
McMillon, Billy	PRT	EAST	93
Owens, Billy	BOW	EAST	92
Greene, Todd	VAN	PCL	92
Pough, Chop	PAW	INT	92
Marrero, Oreste	ABQ	PCL	92
Montgomery, Ray	TCN	PCL	92
Pulliam, Harvey	CSP	PCL	91
Bonnici, James	PCY	SOU	91
Garcia, Karim	ABQ	PCL	91
Sheff, Chris	PRT	EAST	91

Stolen Bases

Player	Team	League	
Burton, Essex	**BIR**	**SOU**	**60**
Roberts, Lonell	KNX	SOU	57
Jones, Terry	NHV	EAST	51
Carvajal, Jovino	VAN	PCL	49
Martinez, Felix	WCH	TEX	44
Buccheri, Jim	OTT	INT	44
McCracken, Quinton	CSP	PCL	43
Stewart, Shannon	KNX	SOU	42
Jackson, Damian	CAN	EAST	40
Barker, Glen	JAX	SOU	39
Hubbard, Trent	CSP	PCL	37
Garciaparra, Nomar	TRE	EAST	35
Womack, Tony	CAR	SOU	34
Bush, Homer	MEM	SOU	34
Several tied at			33

Triple-A/Double-A Batting Leaders

Catchers Batting Average

Player	Team	League	
Kendall, Jason	**CAR**	**SOU**	.326
Marzano, John	OKC	AMAS	.309
Greene, Todd	VAN	PCL	.300
Stewart, Andy	OMA	AMAS	.277
Figga, Mike	COL	INT	.271
Vinas, Julio	BIR	SOU	.269
Posada, Jorge	COL	INT	.255
Waszgis, B.J.	BOW	EAST	.253
Greene, Charlie	NOR	INT	.228
Varitek, Jason	PCY	SOU	.224
Pappas, Erik	CHR	INT	.221
Several tied at			.220

First Basemen Batting Average

Player	Team	League	
Pecorilli, Aldo	**RMD**	**INT**	.344
McGuire, Ryan	TRE	EAST	.333
Grijak, Kevin	RMD	INT	.324
Dodson, Bo	NO	AMAS	.322
Delgado, Carlos	SYR	INT	.318
Garcia, Omar	BNG	EAST	.318
Dunn, Steve	SLK	PCL	.316
Sparks, Don	COL	INT	.312
Litton, Greg	TAC	PCL	.309
Kennedy, Dave	NHV	EAST	.306
Grotewold, Jeff	OMA	AMAS	.294
Landry, Todd	ELP	TEX	.292
Gainer, Jay	CSP	PCL	.291
Hatcher, Chris	TCN	PCL	.289
Several tied at			.287

Second Basemen Batting Average

Player	Team	League	
Hajek, Dave	**TCN**	**PCL**	.327
Simons, Mitch	SLK	PCL	.325
Berblinger, Jeff	ARK	TEX	.319
Owens, Eric	IND	AMAS	.314
Lopez, Roberto	ELP	TEX	.312
Jordan, Kevin	SWB	INT	.310
Raabe, Brian	SLK	PCL	.305
Bridges, Kary	JCK	TEX	.301
Pozo, Arquimedez	TAC	PCL	.300
Faries, Paul	EDM	PCL	.300
Brady, Doug	NVL	AMAS	.298
Johnson, Erik	CGY	PCL	.297
Crespo, Felipe	SYR	INT	.294
Castleberry, Kevin	OTT	INT	.294
Several tied at			.293

Third Basemen Batting Average

Player	Team	League	
Williamson, Antone	**ELP**	**TEX**	.309
Mueller, Bill	PHX	PCL	.305
Saenz, Olmedo	NVL	AMAS	.304
Fox, Andy	COL	INT	.296
Santana, Ruben	CNG	SOU	.293
Ball, Jeff	TCN	PCL	.293
Selby, Bill	TRE	EAST	.286
Sveum, Dale	CGY	PCL	.284
Huskey, Butch	NOR	INT	.284
Batiste, Kim	ROC	INT	.283
Spiezio, Scott	HVL	SOU	.282
Franco, Matt	IWA	AMAS	.281
Arias, George	MDL	TEX	.279
Quinlan, Tom	SLK	PCL	.279
Gulan, Mike	LOU	AMAS	.279

Shortstops Batting Average

Player	Team	League	
Guerrero, Wilton	**ABQ**	**PCL**	.346
Snopek, Chris	NVL	AMAS	.323
Giovanola, Ed	RMD	INT	.321
Jeter, Derek	COL	INT	.317
Wilson, Brandon	CNG	SOU	.316
Aurilia, Rich	PHX	PCL	.302
Polcovich, Kevin	CGY	PCL	.300
Sheets, Andy	TAC	PCL	.293
Ripken, Billy	BUF	AMAS	.292
Harkrider, Tim	MDL	TEX	.291
Wilson, Craig	BIR	SOU	.289
Renteria, Edgar	PRT	EAST	.289
Loretta, Mark	NO	AMAS	.286
Hocking, Denny	SLK	PCL	.282
Kellner, Frank	TCN	PCL	.282

Outfielders Batting Average

Player	Team	League	
Coughlin, Kevin	**BIR**	**SOU**	.372
McCracken, Quinton	CSP	PCL	.359
Ingram, Riccardo	SLK	PCL	.348
Damon, Johnny	WCH	TEX	.343
Perez, Robert	SYR	INT	.343
Cookson, Brent	OMA	AMAS	.340
Hubbard, Trent	CSP	PCL	.340
Beamon, Trey	CGY	PCL	.334
Ratliff, Daryl	CGY	PCL	.332
Pulliam, Harvey	CSP	PCL	.327
Carter, Mike	IWA	AMAS	.325
Garcia, Karim	ABQ	PCL	.319
Carvajal, Jovino	VAN	PCL	.317
Rohrmeier, Dan	CNG	SOU	.315
Ramos, Ken	TCN	PCL	.315

Triple-A/Double-A Batting Leaders

Hits

Player	Team	League	
Perez, Robert	**SYR**	**INT**	172
Sparks, Don	COL	INT	170
Payton, Jay	NOR	INT	170
McCracken, Quinton	CSP	PCL	167
Ingram, Riccardo	SLK	PCL	166
Hajek, Dave	TCN	PCL	164
Santana, Ruben	CNG	SOU	163
Hubbard, Trent	CSP	PCL	163
Carvajal, Jovino	VAN	PCL	162
McMillon, Billy	PRT	EAST	162
Simons, Mitch	SLK	PCL	156
Jeter, Derek	COL	INT	154
Myers, Rod	WCH	TEX	153
Mueller, Bill	PHX	PCL	153
Several tied at			151

Doubles

Player	Team	League	
Hardtke, Jason	**BNG**	**EAST**	43
Ingram, Riccardo	**SLK**	**PCL**	43
Marzano, John	OKC	AMAS	41
Banks, Brian	ELP	TEX	39
Doster, Dave	REA	EAST	39
Perez, Robert	SYR	INT	38
Hajek, Dave	TCN	PCL	37
Bonnici, James	PCY	SOU	36
Woodson, Tracy	LOU	AMAS	35
Johnson, Erik	CGY	PCL	35
Several tied at			34

Triples

Player	Team	League	
Abreu, Bob	**TCN**	**PCL**	17
de la Cruz, Lorenzo	KNX	SOU	12
Thurman, Gary	TAC	PCL	12
Glenn, Leon	MDL	TEX	11
Fox, Andy	COL	INT	11
Arias, George	MDL	TEX	10
Banks, Brian	ELP	TEX	10
Sparks, Don	COL	INT	10
Robertson, Jason	NRW	EAST	10
Rivera, Ruben	COL	INT	10
Santana, Ruben	CNG	SOU	10
Garcia, Karim	ABQ	PCL	10
McCracken, Quinton	CSP	PCL	10
Several tied at			9

Extra Base Hits

Player	Team	League	
Greene, Todd	**VAN**	**PCL**	64
Pough, Chop	PAW	INT	63
Doster, Dave	REA	EAST	63
Pulliam, Harvey	CSP	PCL	61
Banks, Brian	ELP	TEX	61
Arias, George	MDL	TEX	59
Bonnici, James	PCY	SOU	59
Rivera, Ruben	COL	INT	58
Ingram, Riccardo	SLK	PCL	57
Canale, George	CAR	SOU	57
Garcia, Karim	ABQ	PCL	56
Payton, Jay	NOR	INT	56
Several tied at			54

Plate Appearances per Strikeout

Player	Team	League	
Raabe, Brian	**SLK**	**PCL**	**35.50**
Bridges, Kary	JCK	TEX	26.44
Kendall, Jason	CAR	SOU	23.09
Hajek, Dave	TCN	PCL	20.52
Pozo, Arquimedez	TAC	PCL	15.61
Katzaroff, Robbie	PRT	EAST	15.30
Cairo, Miguel	SAN	TEX	15.29
Harkrider, Tim	MDL	TEX	14.72
Ramos, Ken	TCN	PCL	14.48
Damon, Johnny	WCH	TEX	14.37
Garciaparra, Nomar	TRE	EAST	13.83
Palmeiro, Orlando	VAN	PCL	13.47
Leiper, Tim	JAX	SOU	13.32
Ripken, Billy	BUF	AMAS	12.95
Several tied at			12.58

Switch-Hitters Batting Average

Player	Team	League	
McCracken, Quinton	**CSP**	**PCL**	**.359**
Carvajal, Jovino	VAN	PCL	.317
Lopez, Roberto	ELP	TEX	.312
Banks, Brian	ELP	TEX	.308
Monell, Johnny	TUL	TEX	.306
Cedeno, Roger	ABQ	PCL	.305
Mueller, Bill	PHX	PCL	.305
Romero, Mandy	WCH	TEX	.302
Mashore, Damon	EDM	PCL	.300
Brady, Doug	NVL	AMAS	.298
Crespo, Felipe	SYR	INT	.294
Franklin, Micah	CGY	PCL	.293
Harkrider, Tim	MDL	TEX	.291
Young, Dmitri	LOU	AMAS	.291
Munoz, Jose	RMD	INT	.290

Triple-A/Double-A Pitching Leaders

Earned Run Average

Player	Team	League	
Rekar, Bryan	**CSP**	**PCL**	**1.89**
Isringhausen, Jason	NOR	INT	1.97
Coppinger, Rocky	ROC	INT	2.21
Schmidt, Jason	RMD	INT	2.25
Harris, Pep	CAN	EAST	2.41
Wilson, Paul	NOR	INT	2.41
Dessens, Elmer	CAR	SOU	2.49
Murray, Matt	RMD	INT	2.54
Toth, Robert	OMA	AMAS	2.62
Sodowsky, Clint	TOL	INT	2.65
Miller, Trever	JAX	SOU	2.72
Falteisek, Steve	OTT	INT	2.73
Ruebel, Matt	CAR	SOU	2.76
Andujar, Luis	BIR	SOU	2.85
Bolton, Rodney	NVL	AMAS	2.88

Wins

Player	Team	League	
Roa, Joe	**BUF**	**AMAS**	**17**
Wall, Donnie	**TCN**	**PCL**	**17**
Rath, Gary	ABQ	PCL	16
Kramer, Tom	CNG	SOU	15
Grace, Mike	SWB	INT	15
Dessens, Elmer	CAR	SOU	15
Chouinard, Bobby	HVL	SOU	14
Bolton, Rodney	NVL	AMAS	14
Andujar, Luis	BIR	SOU	14
Milacki, Bob	TAC	PCL	14
Murray, Matt	RMD	INT	14
Morrison, Keith	VAN	PCL	14
Moore, Joel	NHV	EAST	14
Several tied at			13

Saves

Player	Team	League	
Montgomery, Steve	**ARK**	**TEX**	**36**
Kilgo, Rusty	CNG	SOU	29
Kelly, John	JAX	SOU	29
Ryan, Matt	CAR	SOU	27
Bluma, Jamie	OMA	AMAS	26
Schutz, Carl	GRV	SOU	26
Ricci, Chuck	SWB	INT	25
Bailey, Cory	LOU	AMAS	25
Nichols, Rod	RMD	INT	25
Powell, Jay	PRT	EAST	24
Adams, Terry	IWA	AMAS	24
Purdy, Shawn	SHR	TEX	21
Christopher, Mike	TOL	INT	21
Several tied at			20

Games Pitched

Player	Team	League	
Ricci, Chuck	**SWB**	**INT**	**68**
Kelly, John	JAX	SOU	66
Trlicek, Ricky	CAN	EAST	62
Bluma, Jamie	OMA	AMAS	60
Czajkowski, Jim	CSP	PCL	60
McCready, Jim	NOR	INT	60
Doolan, Blake	REA	EAST	60
Scott, Darryl	CSP	PCL	59
DeJean, Mike	NRW	EAST	59
Hill, Eric	SWB	INT	59
Steed, Rick	SYR	INT	58
Veras, Dario	MEM	SOU	58
McFarlin, Terric	LVG	PCL	58
Fredrickson, Scott	CSP	PCL	58
Several tied at			57

Complete Games

Player	Team	League	
Mattson, Rob	**MEM**	**SOU**	**11**
Wilson, Paul	NOR	INT	8
Harriger, Denny	LVG	PCL	7
Sodowsky, Clint	TOL	INT	6
Steenstra, Kennie	IWA	AMAS	6
Falteisek, Steve	OTT	INT	6
Brooks, Wes	TRE	EAST	5
Hansen, Brent	PAW	INT	5
Hancock, Ryan	MDL	TEX	5
Roberts, Brett	NBR	EAST	5
Geeve, Dave	TUL	TEX	5
Several tied at			4

Shutouts

Player	Team	League	
Sodowsky, Clint	**TOL**	**INT**	**3**
Mattson, Rob	**MEM**	**SOU**	**3**
Isringhausen, Jason	**NOR**	**INT**	**3**
Wilson, Paul	**NOR**	**INT**	**3**
Tranberg, Mark	**SWB**	**INT**	**3**
Ruebel, Matt	**CAR**	**SOU**	**3**
Several tied at			2

Triple-A/Double-A Pitching Leaders

Strikeouts

Player	Team	League	
Wilson, Paul	**NOR**	**INT**	194
Orellano, Rafael	TRE	EAST	160
Fernandez, Osvaldo	PCY	SOU	160
Wagner, Billy	TCN	PCL	157
Miller, Travis	NBR	EAST	151
Telemaco, Amaury	ORL	SOU	151
Andujar, Luis	BIR	SOU	146
Wagner, Matt	TAC	PCL	144
Kramer, Tom	CNG	SOU	141
Haynes, Jimmy	ROC	INT	140
Ludwick, Eric	NOR	INT	140
Stephenson, Garrett	BOW	EAST	139
Mattson, Rob	MEM	SOU	139
Ruebel, Matt	CAR	SOU	136
Roberts, Brett	NBR	EAST	135

Strikeouts per 9 IP — Starters

Player	Team	League	
Hernandez, Fernando	**MEM**	**SOU**	9.87
Wagner, Billy	TCN	PCL	9.66
Kroon, Marc	MEM	SOU	9.60
Isringhausen, Jason	NOR	INT	9.42
Stull, Everett	HRB	EAST	9.38
Wilson, Paul	NOR	INT	9.35
Fernandez, Osvaldo	PCY	SOU	9.21
Telemaco, Amaury	ORL	SOU	9.20
Brandow, Derek	KNX	SOU	8.92
Gomes, Wayne	REA	EAST	8.77
Seelbach, Chris	RMD	INT	8.75
Baldwin, James	NVL	AMAS	8.40
Miller, Travis	NBR	EAST	8.35
Bertotti, Mike	NVL	AMAS	8.34
Rekar, Bryan	CSP	PCL	8.32

Strikeouts per 9 IP — Relievers

Player	Team	League	
Pickett, Ricky	**SHR**	**TEX**	12.24
Creek, Doug	LOU	AMAS	10.94
Viano, Jake	NHV	EAST	10.63
Woodfin, Chris	BIR	SOU	10.13
Alston, Garvin	NHV	EAST	9.86
Rychel, Kevin	CAR	SOU	9.60
Gonzales, Frank	TOL	INT	9.41
Watkins, Scott	SLK	PCL	9.38
Gibson, Paul	CGY	PCL	9.27
Ricci, Chuck	SWB	INT	9.14
Huisman, Rick	OMA	AMAS	9.05
Powell, Jay	PRT	EAST	9.00
Swartzbaugh, Dave	IWA	AMAS	8.88
Norris, Joe	NBR	EAST	8.82
Vierra, Joey	NVL	AMAS	8.79

Innings Pitched

Player	Team	League	
Mattson, Rob	**MEM**	**SOU**	201.2
Falteisek, Steve	OTT	INT	191.0
Orellano, Rafael	TRE	EAST	186.2
Wilson, Paul	NOR	INT	186.2
Ilsley, Blaise	SWB	INT	185.1
Farrell, John	BUF	AMAS	184.1
Sodowsky, Clint	TOL	INT	183.2
Weston, Mickey	TOL	INT	180.0
Bourgeois, Steven	PHX	PCL	180.0
Wall, Donnie	TCN	PCL	177.1
Milacki, Bob	TAC	PCL	177.0
Harriger, Denny	LVG	PCL	177.0
Hancock, Ryan	MDL	TEX	175.2
Stephenson, Garrett	BOW	EAST	175.1
Wasdin, John	EDM	PCL	174.1

Opponent Batting Average — Starters

Player	Team	League	
Coppinger, Rocky	**ROC**	**INT**	.192
Isringhausen, Jason	NOR	INT	.194
Rekar, Bryan	CSP	PCL	.200
Telemaco, Amaury	ORL	SOU	.211
Kroon, Marc	MEM	SOU	.211
Orellano, Rafael	TRE	EAST	.213
Seelbach, Chris	RMD	INT	.214
Salkeld, Roger	MDL	AMAS	.215
Ludwick, Eric	MEM	INT	.220
Wilson, Paul	NOR	INT	.220
Wagner, Billy	TCN	PCL	.224
Grott, Matt	BUF	AMAS	.228
Murray, Matt	RMD	INT	.229
Sodowsky, Clint	JAX	INT	.230
Gomes, Wayne	REA	EAST	.230

Opponent Batting Average — Relievers

Player	Team	League	
Pickett, Ricky	**SHR**	**TEX**	.135
Knackert, Brent	BNG	EAST	.184
Creek, Doug	LOU	AMAS	.190
Swartzbaugh, Dave	IWA	AMAS	.191
Alston, Garvin	NHV	EAST	.199
Viano, Jake	NHV	EAST	.200
Ricci, Chuck	SWB	INT	.203
Thobe, J.J.	COL	INT	.203
Rivera, Roberto	ORL	SOU	.206
Taylor, Bob	ABQ	AMAS	.206
Fletcher, Paul	NOR	INT	.206
DeJean, Mike	NRW	EAST	.207
Pavlas, Dave	COL	INT	.207
Evans, Dave	MDL	PCL	.208
Sauveur, Rich	TCN	AMAS	.208

1995 Park Data

1995 was the third season that STATS/Howe tracked park data for the minor leagues. As we've shown the last two years, the characteristics of certain minor league ballparks can have a *tremendous* effect on a hitter—even greater than with some major league parks. Debate on this subject usually centers around the Pacific Coast League, and once again, the data will show you why.

Simply put, the Index is a way of measuring each ballpark's effects on hitters and pitchers by comparing home and road performance, with an index of 100 indicating a neutral park. Any index over 100 favors the hitter in that category. Any index under 100 favors the pitcher. For example, a home-run index of 105 indicates that the team's home ballpark increases homers by about 5%.

Since dimensions in ballparks change from time to time, keep in mind that this data is for 1995 only.

American Association — AAA

Buffalo

	G	Avg	AB	R	H	2B	3B	HR	SO
Home	72	.263	4742	561	1247	242	41	65	708
Road	72	.278	4922	751	1370	270	42	155	773
Index	—	94	96	75	91	93	101	44	95

Indianapolis

	G	Avg	AB	R	H	2B	3B	HR	SO
Home	72	.259	4773	740	1234	254	23	170	933
Road	72	.262	4912	693	1287	284	36	134	951
Index	—	99	97	107	96	92	66	131	101

Iowa

	G	Avg	AB	R	H	2B	3B	HR	SO
Home	72	.263	4729	570	1243	244	21	119	860
Road	71	.266	4754	596	1266	213	34	113	809
Index	—	99	98	94	97	115	62	106	107

Louisville

	G	Avg	AB	R	H	2B	3B	HR	SO
Home	72	.257	4805	647	1237	251	44	133	907
Road	72	.255	4661	593	1187	242	32	95	866
Index	—	101	103	109	104	101	133	136	102

Nashville

	G	Avg	AB	R	H	2B	3B	HR	SO
Home	72	.261	5059	671	1320	241	25	135	955
Road	72	.272	4808	623	1306	258	31	123	849
Index	—	96	105	108	101	89	77	104	107

New Orleans

	G	Avg	AB	R	H	2B	3B	HR	SO
Home	70	.263	4604	582	1213	246	27	90	868
Road	72	.263	4672	596	1228	216	25	108	800
Index	—	100	101	100	102	116	110	85	110

Oklahoma City

	G	Avg	AB	R	H	2B	3B	HR	SO
Home	72	.269	4714	653	1267	245	50	93	834
Road	71	.264	4726	628	1247	228	25	111	856
Index	—	102	98	103	100	108	201	84	98

Omaha

	G	Avg	AB	R	H	2B	3B	HR	SO
Home	72	.286	4783	707	1368	247	26	155	759
Road	72	.260	4754	651	1238	259	32	121	920
Index	—	110	101	109	111	95	81	127	82

International League — AAA

Charlotte

	G	Avg	AB	R	H	2B	3B	HR	SO
Home	69	.272	4702	666	1279	187	24	134	729
Road	71	.266	4738	689	1261	239	31	100	763
Index	—	102	102	99	104	79	78	135	96

Columbus

	G	Avg	AB	R	H	2B	3B	HR	SO
Home	71	.271	4831	728	1307	246	63	101	865
Road	69	.261	4570	602	1194	230	31	88	868
Index	—	104	103	118	106	101	192	109	94

Norfolk

	G	Avg	AB	R	H	2B	3B	HR	SO
Home	71	.251	4578	562	1148	202	32	72	824
Road	71	.255	4793	581	1224	227	46	97	920
Index	—	98	96	97	94	93	73	78	94

Ottawa

	G	Avg	AB	R	H	2B	3B	HR	SO
Home	72	.256	4770	616	1222	259	34	73	818
Road	70	.259	4487	613	1163	204	36	101	767
Index	—	99	103	98	102	119	89	68	100

Pawtucket

	G	Avg	AB	R	H	2B	3B	HR	SO
Home	71	.274	4868	711	1334	259	16	178	900
Road	71	.263	4659	676	1225	242	58	116	900
Index	—	104	104	105	109	102	26	147	96

Richmond

	G	Avg	AB	R	H	2B	3B	HR	SO
Home	70	.255	4648	490	1185	195	20	47	811
Road	71	.259	4766	614	1233	230	39	98	881
Index	—	99	99	81	97	87	53	49	94

Rochester

	G	Avg	AB	R	H	2B	3B	HR	SO
Home	72	.272	4817	680	1309	269	35	124	929
Road	70	.257	4658	605	1196	213	28	117	790
Index	—	106	101	109	106	122	121	102	114

Scranton-WB

	G	Avg	AB	R	H	2B	3B	HR	SO
Home	70	.265	4690	646	1243	264	65	75	842
Road	72	.265	4730	645	1254	234	27	94	817
Index	—	100	102	103	102	114	243	80	104

Syracuse

	G	Avg	AB	R	H	2B	3B	HR	SO
Home	70	.254	4662	686	1186	228	45	133	911
Road	71	.265	4899	697	1300	256	40	132	920
Index	—	96	97	100	93	94	118	106	104

Toledo

	G	Avg	AB	R	H	2B	3B	HR	SO
Home	71	.248	4630	554	1150	190	31	111	847
Road	71	.268	4896	617	1313	224	29	105	850
Index	—	93	95	90	88	90	113	112	105

Pacific Coast League — AAA

Albuquerque

	G	Avg	AB	R	H	2B	3B	HR	SO
Home	72	.288	4989	758	1435	248	41	105	907
Road	72	.274	4749	684	1301	272	37	104	833
Index	—	105	105	111	110	87	105	96	104

Calgary

	G	Avg	AB	R	H	2B	3B	HR	SO
Home	71	.305	4797	802	1464	340	30	115	676
Road	70	.297	4845	753	1438	270	48	102	747
Index	—	103	98	105	100	127	63	114	91

Colorado Springs

	G	Avg	AB	R	H	2B	3B	HR	SO
Home	72	.297	4851	873	1439	315	54	152	813
Road	71	.281	4716	708	1323	266	48	101	819
Index	—	106	101	122	107	115	109	146	97

Edmonton

	G	Avg	AB	R	H	2B	3B	HR	SO
Home	72	.285	4790	771	1364	298	41	93	720
Road	72	.281	4843	778	1360	295	46	102	794
Index	—	101	99	99	100	102	90	92	92

Las Vegas

	G	Avg	AB	R	H	2B	3B	HR	SO
Home	73	.279	5051	786	1407	276	42	114	860
Road	71	.269	4577	657	1230	244	39	77	774
Index	—	104	107	116	111	102	98	134	101

Phoenix

	G	Avg	AB	R	H	2B	3B	HR	SO
Home	72	.275	4959	726	1365	269	57	100	847
Road	72	.278	4886	697	1360	272	44	86	796
Index	—	99	101	104	100	97	128	115	105

Salt Lake

	G	Avg	AB	R	H	2B	3B	HR	SO
Home	72	.300	4964	777	1487	300	55	110	698
Road	72	.297	4970	827	1475	300	39	113	768
Index	—	101	100	94	101	100	141	97	91

Tacoma

	G	Avg	AB	R	H	2B	3B	HR	SO
Home	72	.261	4716	609	1232	236	33	98	846
Road	72	.295	5023	807	1480	278	58	121	770
Index	—	89	94	75	83	90	61	86	117

Tucson

	G	Avg	AB	R	H	2B	3B	HR	SO
Home	72	.304	4956	808	1506	298	79	61	843
Road	71	.276	4746	676	1312	251	42	91	864
Index	—	110	103	118	113	114	180	64	93

Vancouver

	G	Avg	AB	R	H	2B	3B	HR	SO
Home	68	.248	4338	510	1075	187	27	62	746
Road	73	.296	5056	833	1495	319	58	113	791
Index	—	84	92	66	77	68	54	64	110

Eastern League — AA

Binghamton
	G	Avg	AB	R	H	2B	3B	HR	SO
Home	71	.254	4739	664	1204	236	38	96	918
Road	71	.249	4768	599	1189	231	26	81	843
Index	—	102	99	111	101	103	147	119	110

Bowie
	G	Avg	AB	R	H	2B	3B	HR	SO
Home	71	.261	4734	703	1234	237	14	114	875
Road	71	.254	4666	641	1184	240	23	103	855
Index	—	103	101	110	104	97	60	109	101

Canton-Akron
	G	Avg	AB	R	H	2B	3B	HR	SO
Home	70	.270	4601	615	1241	222	23	77	784
Road	72	.240	4608	614	1104	237	29	109	941
Index	—	113	103	103	116	94	79	71	83

Harrisburg
	G	Avg	AB	R	H	2B	3B	HR	SO
Home	70	.244	4502	595	1097	204	27	106	941
Road	71	.253	4722	674	1195	235	30	85	980
Index	—	96	97	90	93	91	94	131	101

New Britain
	G	Avg	AB	R	H	2B	3B	HR	SO
Home	70	.256	4592	607	1174	226	30	89	928
Road	72	.253	4890	673	1237	218	36	101	972
Index	—	101	97	93	98	110	89	94	102

New Haven
	G	Avg	AB	R	H	2B	3B	HR	SO
Home	72	.255	4785	658	1222	225	31	73	940
Road	70	.259	4650	633	1206	229	29	82	962
Index	—	98	100	101	99	95	104	87	95

Norwich
	G	Avg	AB	R	H	2B	3B	HR	SO
Home	71	.250	4724	628	1181	255	46	49	992
Road	70	.274	4700	724	1290	239	38	111	954
Index	—	91	99	86	90	106	120	44	103

Portland
	G	Avg	AB	R	H	2B	3B	HR	SO
Home	72	.260	4877	715	1266	220	37	111	999
Road	70	.260	4627	622	1204	213	36	75	826
Index	—	100	102	112	102	98	98	140	115

Reading
	G	Avg	AB	R	H	2B	3B	HR	SO
Home	71	.257	4718	675	1213	230	32	148	920
Road	71	.250	4736	631	1184	223	29	82	924
Index	—	103	100	107	102	104	111	181	100

Trenton
	G	Avg	AB	R	H	2B	3B	HR	SO
Home	71	.245	4878	612	1196	245	26	83	900
Road	71	.258	4783	661	1235	235	28	117	940
Index	—	95	102	93	97	102	91	70	94

Southern League — AA

Birmingham
	G	Avg	AB	R	H	2B	3B	HR	SO
Home	72	.262	4738	628	1242	216	26	60	860
Road	72	.257	4736	659	1215	199	22	117	970
Index	—	102	100	95	102	108	118	51	89

Carolina
	G	Avg	AB	R	H	2B	3B	HR	SO
Home	72	.269	4992	668	1344	275	30	85	885
Road	72	.253	5059	632	1281	238	26	87	920
Index	—	106	99	106	105	117	117	99	97

Chattanooga
	G	Avg	AB	R	H	2B	3B	HR	SO
Home	73	.271	4911	696	1333	259	34	94	946
Road	70	.266	4776	667	1272	241	34	118	895
Index	—	102	99	100	100	105	97	77	103

Greenville
	G	Avg	AB	R	H	2B	3B	HR	SO
Home	70	.272	4784	714	1303	223	29	156	924
Road	72	.268	4767	692	1278	256	38	110	901
Index	—	102	103	106	105	87	76	141	102

Huntsville
	G	Avg	AB	R	H	2B	3B	HR	SO
Home	72	.250	4747	638	1186	218	35	113	947
Road	72	.261	4768	642	1244	224	31	108	945
Index	—	96	100	99	95	98	113	105	101

Jacksonville
	G	Avg	AB	R	H	2B	3B	HR	SO
Home	72	.244	4750	575	1160	222	15	126	933
Road	72	.254	4852	666	1234	234	36	118	976
Index	—	96	98	86	94	97	43	109	98

Knoxville
	G	Avg	AB	R	H	2B	3B	HR	SO
Home	72	.266	4770	732	1268	259	59	83	923
Road	72	.243	4555	606	1106	199	24	93	985
Index	—	109	105	121	115	124	235	85	89

Memphis
	G	Avg	AB	R	H	2B	3B	HR	SO
Home	71	.249	4756	671	1184	227	33	126	1109
Road	71	.262	4696	657	1232	218	43	93	1006
Index	—	95	101	102	96	103	76	134	109

Orlando
	G	Avg	AB	R	H	2B	3B	HR	SO
Home	72	.256	4670	585	1195	214	22	104	820
Road	71	.254	4773	595	1214	252	21	91	858
Index	—	101	96	97	97	87	107	117	98

Port City
	G	Avg	AB	R	H	2B	3B	HR	SO
Home	70	.239	4710	565	1128	195	21	85	1023
Road	72	.261	4846	656	1267	247	29	97	914
Index	—	92	100	89	92	81	75	90	115

Texas League — AA

Arkansas
	G	Avg	AB	R	H	2B	3B	HR	SO
Home	66	.270	4238	623	1143	242	41	80	713
Road	69	.264	4589	596	1211	225	37	91	825
Index	—	102	97	109	99	116	120	95	94

El Paso
	G	Avg	AB	R	H	2B	3B	HR	SO
Home	69	.295	4752	814	1401	318	81	75	895
Road	67	.282	4620	683	1302	230	36	99	860
Index	—	105	100	116	104	134	219	74	101

Jackson
	G	Avg	AB	R	H	2B	3B	HR	SO
Home	69	.252	4547	569	1147	185	24	91	814
Road	66	.263	4368	579	1150	221	36	80	690
Index	—	96	100	94	95	80	64	109	113

Midland
	G	Avg	AB	R	H	2B	3B	HR	SO
Home	67	.308	4714	797	1453	284	44	144	797
Road	69	.271	4620	640	1254	217	44	103	771
Index	—	114	105	128	119	128	98	137	101

San Antonio
	G	Avg	AB	R	H	2B	3B	HR	SO
Home	68	.257	4607	524	1183	209	37	54	843
Road	68	.275	4509	647	1240	224	47	98	773
Index	—	93	102	81	95	91	77	54	107

Shreveport
	G	Avg	AB	R	H	2B	3B	HR	SO
Home	69	.257	4679	589	1201	222	30	70	730
Road	66	.281	4562	674	1282	225	27	97	760
Index	—	91	98	84	90	96	108	70	94

Tulsa
	G	Avg	AB	R	H	2B	3B	HR	SO
Home	67	.268	4539	570	1215	187	25	99	678
Road	68	.277	4564	662	1263	232	34	101	656
Index	—	97	101	87	98	81	74	99	104

Wichita
	G	Avg	AB	R	H	2B	3B	HR	SO
Home	67	.278	4549	674	1265	204	29	135	677
Road	69	.272	4793	679	1306	277	50	79	812
Index	—	102	98	102	100	78	61	180	88

California League — A

Bakersfield

	G	Avg	AB	R	H	2B	3B	HR	SO
Home	70	.279	4817	731	1344	220	11	105	920
Road	70	.262	4597	652	1205	231	29	87	883
Index	—	106	105	112	112	91	36	115	99

High Desert

	G	Avg	AB	R	H	2B	3B	HR	SO
Home	70	.286	4982	969	1423	259	62	169	970
Road	70	.260	4633	696	1205	235	44	83	1023
Index	—	110	108	139	118	102	131	189	88

Lake Elsinore

	G	Avg	AB	R	H	2B	3B	HR	SO
Home	70	.263	4729	680	1243	272	42	80	1014
Road	69	.276	4763	766	1315	233	37	120	981
Index	—	95	98	88	93	118	114	67	104

Modesto

	G	Avg	AB	R	H	2B	3B	HR	SO
Home	70	.253	4631	679	1171	242	24	135	1136
Road	70	.279	4802	770	1340	246	42	105	1005
Index	—	91	96	88	87	102	59	133	117

Rancho Cucamonga

	G	Avg	AB	R	H	2B	3B	HR	SO
Home	70	.270	4758	747	1285	229	50	88	1025
Road	69	.265	4588	713	1215	226	34	101	1029
Index	—	102	102	103	104	98	142	84	96

Riverside

	G	Avg	AB	R	H	2B	3B	HR	SO
Home	69	.276	4765	768	1317	216	30	55	911
Road	70	.270	4778	798	1292	210	49	113	984
Index	—	102	101	98	103	103	61	49	93

San Bernardino

	G	Avg	AB	R	H	2B	3B	HR	SO
Home	69	.279	4684	759	1308	248	23	162	982
Road	70	.274	4980	783	1365	256	40	93	986
Index	—	102	95	98	97	103	61	185	106

San Jose

	G	Avg	AB	R	H	2B	3B	HR	SO
Home	70	.242	4699	564	1137	182	49	54	1072
Road	70	.262	4832	647	1266	231	33	91	952
Index	—	92	97	87	90	81	153	61	116

Stockton

	G	Avg	AB	R	H	2B	3B	HR	SO
Home	70	.273	4714	672	1287	215	45	61	809
Road	70	.282	4837	752	1365	246	40	112	943
Index	—	97	97	89	94	90	115	56	88

Visalia

	G	Avg	AB	R	H	2B	3B	HR	SO
Home	70	.270	4790	679	1293	245	43	82	973
Road	70	.261	4759	671	1240	214	31	86	1026
Index	—	104	101	101	104	114	138	95	94

Carolina League — A

Durham

	G	Avg	AB	R	H	2B	3B	HR	SO
Home	71	.256	4610	630	1180	189	19	123	922
Road	68	.257	4354	584	1118	205	21	95	910
Index	—	100	101	103	101	87	85	122	96

Frederick

	G	Avg	AB	R	H	2B	3B	HR	SO
Home	67	.239	4446	566	1062	197	27	93	1051
Road	70	.246	4475	549	1099	210	25	75	946
Index	—	97	104	108	101	94	109	125	112

Kinston

	G	Avg	AB	R	H	2B	3B	HR	SO
Home	70	.240	4487	561	1078	191	19	112	922
Road	67	.251	4466	544	1123	218	33	105	921
Index	—	96	96	99	92	87	57	106	100

Lynchburg

	G	Avg	AB	R	H	2B	3B	HR	SO
Home	69	.268	4413	618	1181	258	30	102	839
Road	69	.262	4637	677	1217	215	30	111	934
Index	—	102	95	91	97	126	105	97	94

Prince William

	G	Avg	AB	R	H	2B	3B	HR	SO
Home	69	.251	4484	552	1126	225	32	79	904
Road	71	.253	4665	614	1180	194	31	125	936
Index	—	99	99	93	98	121	107	66	100

Salem

	G	Avg	AB	R	H	2B	3B	HR	SO
Home	70	.271	4677	681	1266	253	32	134	887
Road	70	.246	4706	604	1159	216	22	90	975
Index	—	110	99	113	109	118	146	150	92

Wilmington

	G	Avg	AB	R	H	2B	3B	HR	SO
Home	71	.237	4723	478	1121	185	36	31	963
Road	67	.243	4395	531	1069	207	23	107	813
Index	—	98	101	85	99	83	146	27	110

Winston-salem

	G	Avg	AB	R	H	2B	3B	HR	SO
Home	66	.241	4402	578	1063	180	14	134	879
Road	71	.245	4544	561	1112	213	24	100	932
Index	—	99	104	111	103	87	60	138	97

Florida State League — A

Brevard County

	G	Avg	AB	R	H	2B	3B	HR	SO
Home	69	.242	4520	549	1095	188	15	57	897
Road	66	.256	4455	589	1141	187	27	66	822
Index	—	95	97	89	92	99	55	85	108

Charlotte

	G	Avg	AB	R	H	2B	3B	HR	SO
Home	67	.247	4345	537	1074	214	29	62	851
Road	66	.260	4428	544	1152	208	30	71	746
Index	—	95	97	97	92	105	99	89	116

Clearwater

	G	Avg	AB	R	H	2B	3B	HR	SO
Home	72	.266	4766	657	1266	233	35	81	856
Road	66	.256	4402	579	1128	209	38	68	857
Index	—	104	99	104	103	103	85	110	92

Daytona

	G	Avg	AB	R	H	2B	3B	HR	SO
Home	66	.252	4289	578	1082	192	31	60	855
Road	69	.237	4435	544	1052	172	27	53	884
Index	—	106	101	111	108	115	119	117	100

Dunedin

	G	Avg	AB	R	H	2B	3B	HR	SO
Home	70	.256	4750	637	1218	225	36	102	908
Road	68	.257	4456	652	1143	212	36	69	862
Index	—	100	104	95	104	100	94	139	99

Fort Myers

	G	Avg	AB	R	H	2B	3B	HR	SO
Home	64	.233	4031	420	938	175	19	41	762
Road	67	.249	4355	582	1085	223	28	73	845
Index	—	93	97	76	91	85	73	61	97

Kissimmee

	G	Avg	AB	R	H	2B	3B	HR	SO
Home	67	.251	4508	596	1133	188	24	48	830
Road	69	.256	4540	641	1161	206	28	48	838
Index	—	98	102	96	101	92	86	101	100

Lakeland

	G	Avg	AB	R	H	2B	3B	HR	SO
Home	67	.260	4249	559	1105	153	62	57	837
Road	68	.268	4616	611	1238	241	30	64	985
Index	—	97	93	93	91	69	225	97	92

St. Lucie

	G	Avg	AB	R	H	2B	3B	HR	SO
Home	69	.248	4521	530	1121	166	38	44	875
Road	66	.242	4126	458	998	161	25	48	826
Index	—	103	105	111	107	94	139	84	97

St. Petersburg

	G	Avg	AB	R	H	2B	3B	HR	SO
Home	63	.234	4057	469	949	188	15	38	827
Road	68	.228	4262	474	973	177	19	64	911
Index	—	102	103	107	105	112	83	62	95

Sarasota

	G	Avg	AB	R	H	2B	3B	HR	SO
Home	68	.261	4619	626	1206	222	34	60	938
Road	66	.257	4208	551	1082	174	32	62	808
Index	—	102	107	110	108	116	97	88	106

Tampa

	G	Avg	AB	R	H	2B	3B	HR	SO
Home	65	.248	4247	544	1052	168	20	64	853
Road	71	.238	4617	549	1100	194	33	51	997
Index	—	104	100	108	104	94	66	136	93

Vero Beach

	G	Avg	AB	R	H	2B	3B	HR	SO
Home	68	.249	4301	585	1071	206	19	39	860
Road	65	.248	4185	519	1038	169	32	40	834
Index	—	100	98	108	99	119	58	216	100

West Palm Beach

	G	Avg	AB	R	H	2B	3B	HR	SO
Home	68	.251	4262	533	1068	184	28	27	831
Road	68	.248	4380	527	1087	169	20	53	765
Index	—	101	97	101	98	112	144	52	112

Midwest League — A

Beloit

	G	Avg	AB	R	H	2B	3B	HR	SO
Home	70	.259	4380	684	1133	212	30	90	960
Road	69	.252	4613	657	1161	234	39	85	964
Index	—	103	94	103	96	95	81	112	105

Burlington

	G	Avg	AB	R	H	2B	3B	HR	SO
Home	64	.253	4134	654	1045	172	15	126	929
Road	71	.250	4350	625	1089	200	34	82	929
Index	—	101	105	116	106	90	46	162	105

Cedar Rapids

	G	Avg	AB	R	H	2B	3B	HR	SO
Home	69	.263	4472	659	1177	226	26	110	898
Road	69	.260	4574	693	1191	218	32	70	889
Index	—	101	98	95	99	106	83	161	103

Clinton

	G	Avg	AB	R	H	2B	3B	HR	SO
Home	62	.250	4011	567	1001	184	20	43	835
Road	75	.247	4683	644	1156	213	26	63	940
Index	—	101	104	107	105	101	90	80	104

Ft. Wayne

	G	Avg	AB	R	H	2B	3B	HR	SO
Home	70	.261	4884	664	1274	259	48	67	1018
Road	70	.254	4578	657	1165	225	40	109	937
Index	—	103	107	101	109	108	112	58	102

Kane County

	G	Avg	AB	R	H	2B	3B	HR	SO
Home	74	.260	4876	753	1270	235	33	83	960
Road	64	.260	4218	621	1098	214	28	78	854
Index	—	100	100	105	100	95	102	92	97

Michigan

	G	Avg	AB	R	H	2B	3B	HR	SO
Home	68	.247	4516	710	1116	246	34	104	969
Road	70	.253	4633	639	1172	223	40	84	1064
Index	—	98	100	114	98	113	87	127	93

Peoria

	G	Avg	AB	R	H	2B	3B	HR	SO
Home	71	.250	4499	587	1123	213	43	63	886
Road	63	.242	4055	552	981	169	22	62	789
Index	—	103	98	94	102	114	176	92	101

Quad City

	G	Avg	AB	R	H	2B	3B	HR	SO
Home	71	.244	4478	585	1093	228	26	74	816
Road	66	.256	4342	608	1113	194	32	77	873
Index	—	95	96	89	91	114	79	93	91

Rockford

	G	Avg	AB	R	H	2B	3B	HR	SO
Home	70	.257	4612	694	1185	247	36	62	889
Road	70	.256	4615	733	1180	256	30	97	834
Index	—	100	100	95	100	97	120	64	107

South Bend

	G	Avg	AB	R	H	2B	3B	HR	SO
Home	66	.262	4319	577	1132	186	38	58	753
Road	69	.255	4678	673	1195	226	35	80	947
Index	—	103	97	90	99	89	118	79	86

Springfield

	G	Avg	AB	R	H	2B	3B	HR	SO
Home	70	.262	4630	687	1214	237	36	109	843
Road	69	.254	4464	631	1135	216	32	84	866
Index	—	103	102	107	105	106	108	125	94

West Michigan

	G	Avg	AB	R	H	2B	3B	HR	SO
Home	67	.262	4598	598	980	191	31	39	977
Road	69	.260	4484	716	1167	226	30	80	912
Index	—	87	99	86	86	87	107	50	111

Wisconsin

	G	Avg	AB	R	H	2B	3B	HR	SO
Home	70	.244	4508	611	1102	220	29	76	954
Road	68	.239	4363	581	1042	242	25	53	889
Index	—	102	100	102	103	88	112	139	104

South Atlantic League — A

Albany

	G	Avg	AB	R	H	2B	3B	HR	SO
Home	69	.261	4775	664	1245	262	55	33	1061
Road	71	.257	4831	682	1243	250	43	92	1054
Index	—	101	102	100	103	106	129	36	102

Asheville

	G	Avg	AB	R	H	2B	3B	HR	SO
Home	69	.247	4384	550	1083	205	13	86	921
Road	70	.232	4589	533	1063	194	29	64	1018
Index	—	107	97	105	103	111	47	141	95

Augusta

	G	Avg	AB	R	H	2B	3B	HR	SO
Home	69	.243	4552	585	1105	199	28	46	976
Road	69	.247	4501	576	1112	206	38	62	964
Index	—	98	101	102	99	96	73	73	100

Charleston-SC

	G	Avg	AB	R	H	2B	3B	HR	SO
Home	67	.246	4450	597	1096	232	34	61	949
Road	72	.244	4658	632	1137	233	31	63	1022
Index	—	101	103	102	104	104	115	101	97

Charleston-WV

	G	Avg	AB	R	H	2B	3B	HR	SO
Home	71	.254	4456	543	1131	213	42	23	936
Road	71	.251	4646	649	1168	206	43	81	996
Index	—	101	96	84	97	108	102	30	98

Columbia

	G	Avg	AB	R	H	2B	3B	HR	SO
Home	72	.231	4629	554	1069	218	26	61	1164
Road	68	.244	4551	559	1109	198	37	77	999
Index	—	95	96	94	91	108	69	78	115

Columbus

	G	Avg	AB	R	H	2B	3B	HR	SO
Home	73	.252	4816	631	1216	199	40	106	1002
Road	69	.238	4517	597	1076	198	33	53	1019
Index	—	106	101	100	107	94	114	188	92

Fayetteville

	G	Avg	AB	R	H	2B	3B	HR	SO
Home	70	.251	4575	657	1147	209	46	68	1050
Road	71	.230	4589	574	1057	199	20	72	1158
Index	—	109	101	116	110	105	231	95	91

Greensboro

	G	Avg	AB	R	H	2B	3B	HR	SO
Home	70	.243	4623	644	1122	199	27	84	1124
Road	70	.252	4636	596	1169	223	36	81	1083
Index	—	96	100	108	96	89	75	104	104

Hagerstown

	G	Avg	AB	R	H	2B	3B	HR	SO
Home	71	.250	4704	629	1176	225	28	90	1066
Road	70	.259	4606	608	1193	245	36	81	1013
Index	—	97	101	102	97	90	76	109	103

Hickory

	G	Avg	AB	R	H	2B	3B	HR	SO
Home	70	.245	4823	592	1181	244	37	93	1078
Road	68	.244	4438	579	1085	207	40	70	957
Index	—	100	106	99	106	108	85	122	104

Macon

	G	Avg	AB	R	H	2B	3B	HR	SO
Home	69	.241	4672	704	1126	191	26	130	1124
Road	72	.241	4972	734	1198	236	32	86	1237
Index	—	100	98	100	98	86	86	161	97

Piedmont

	G	Avg	AB	R	H	2B	3B	HR	SO
Home	69	.247	4509	641	1113	227	46	51	985
Road	71	.241	4641	616	1120	185	31	61	1027
Index	—	102	100	107	102	126	153	86	99

Savannah

	G	Avg	AB	R	H	2B	3B	HR	SO
Home	71	.214	4710	500	1009	152	37	70	1236
Road	68	.242	4503	556	1089	195	36	59	1125
Index	—	89	100	86	89	75	98	113	105

New York-Penn League — A

Auburn

	G	Avg	AB	R	H	2B	3B	HR	SO
Home	37	.255	2333	351	594	107	21	30	425
Road	37	.272	2494	398	679	121	18	30	416
Index	—	94	94	88	87	95	125	107	109

Batavia

	G	Avg	AB	R	H	2B	3B	HR	SO
Home	37	.267	2543	365	680	113	39	29	455
Road	38	.269	2654	393	715	122	22	30	526
Index	—	99	98	95	98	97	185	101	90

Elmira

	G	Avg	AB	R	H	2B	3B	HR	SO
Home	38	.243	2570	363	625	116	18	31	516
Road	38	.264	2521	377	665	104	35	33	543
Index	—	92	102	96	94	109	50	92	93

Erie

	G	Avg	AB	R	H	2B	3B	HR	SO
Home	38	.267	2575	375	688	115	21	37	477
Road	37	.253	2453	343	621	92	26	40	459
Index	—	106	102	106	108	119	77	88	99

Hudson Valley

	G	Avg	AB	R	H	2B	3B	HR	SO
Home	37	.257	2517	349	646	98	24	27	463
Road	37	.265	2494	352	661	103	23	22	538
Index	—	97	101	99	98	94	103	122	85

Jamestown

	G	Avg	AB	R	H	2B	3B	HR	SO
Home	38	.270	2586	431	697	117	34	54	489
Road	38	.246	2532	364	622	123	32	27	531
Index	—	110	102	118	112	93	104	196	90

New Jersey

	G	Avg	AB	R	H	2B	3B	HR	SO
Home	38	.259	2660	385	688	95	51	14	575
Road	38	.241	2536	357	612	89	26	27	509
Index	—	107	105	108	112	102	187	49	108

Oneonta

	G	Avg	AB	R	H	2B	3B	HR	SO
Home	37	.248	2487	327	616	113	41	11	576
Road	38	.239	2503	353	599	123	17	19	572
Index	—	103	102	95	106	92	243	58	101

Pittsfield

	G	Avg	AB	R	H	2B	3B	HR	SO
Home	38	.257	2493	333	641	100	26	10	445
Road	38	.257	2544	361	653	111	40	29	492
Index	—	100	98	92	98	92	66	35	92

St. Catharines

	G	Avg	AB	R	H	2B	3B	HR	SO
Home	38	.238	2504	295	595	118	9	30	559
Road	37	.279	2561	390	715	113	36	36	472
Index	—	85	95	74	81	107	26	85	121

Utica

	G	Avg	AB	R	H	2B	3B	HR	SO
Home	37	.265	2515	399	667	126	32	28	505
Road	36	.253	2367	338	598	95	23	25	474
Index	—	105	103	115	109	125	131	105	100

Vermont

	G	Avg	AB	R	H	2B	3B	HR	SO
Home	38	.234	2435	312	571	84	17	22	474
Road	38	.250	2522	324	630	113	31	21	461
Index	—	94	97	96	91	77	57	109	106

Watertown

	G	Avg	AB	R	H	2B	3B	HR	SO
Home	36	.245	2353	291	577	104	14	39	540
Road	37	.252	2507	337	633	115	31	17	497
Index	—	97	96	89	94	96	48	244	116

Williamsport

	G	Avg	AB	R	H	2B	3B	HR	SO
Home	38	.273	2652	426	724	123	36	20	504
Road	38	.239	2535	315	606	105	23	26	513
Index	—	114	105	135	119	112	150	74	94

Northwest League — A

Bellingham

	G	Avg	AB	R	H	2B	3B	HR	SO
Home	38	.221	2502	273	553	74	11	44	633
Road	38	.257	2640	358	678	134	19	34	612
Index	—	86	95	76	82	58	61	137	109

Boise

	G	Avg	AB	R	H	2B	3B	HR	SO
Home	37	.242	2399	323	580	95	19	40	510
Road	38	.261	2547	431	664	105	20	53	586
Index	—	93	97	77	90	96	101	80	92

Eugene

	G	Avg	AB	R	H	2B	3B	HR	SO
Home	38	.240	2533	352	608	101	18	40	656
Road	38	.246	2545	384	627	99	27	47	557
Index	—	97	100	92	97	103	67	86	118

Everett

	G	Avg	AB	R	H	2B	3B	HR	SO
Home	38	.244	2570	379	628	129	5	69	668
Road	38	.241	2572	336	619	117	25	48	554
Index	—	102	100	113	101	110	20	144	121

Portland

	G	Avg	AB	R	H	2B	3B	HR	SO
Home	38	.218	2472	315	538	102	24	24	565
Road	37	.225	2355	285	529	80	15	24	538
Index	—	97	102	108	99	121	152	95	100

Southern Oregon

	G	Avg	AB	R	H	2B	3B	HR	SO
Home	38	.256	2554	404	654	123	25	39	508
Road	38	.239	2519	342	601	121	13	37	543
Index	—	107	101	118	109	100	190	104	92

Spokane

	G	Avg	AB	R	H	2B	3B	HR	SO
Home	38	.263	2585	364	679	116	11	30	482
Road	38	.231	2579	314	597	114	11	38	586
Index	—	113	100	116	114	102	100	79	82

Yakima

	G	Avg	AB	R	H	2B	3B	HR	SO
Home	38	.255	2624	377	668	135	29	25	528
Road	38	.239	2482	337	593	105	12	30	574
Index	—	107	106	112	113	122	229	79	87

1995 AAA Lefty-Righty Stats

The following section includes batting splits for all hitters with 200 or more AAA at-bats in 1995, and pitching splits for all hurlers with 200 or more AAA batters faced.

AAA Batting vs. Left-Handed and Right-Handed Pitchers

Player - Team	vs Left H	AB	Avg	vs Right H	AB	Avg
Abreu,B. - Tucson	27	76	.355	98	339	.289
Alicea,E. - Norfolk	33	128	.258	74	308	.240
Amaro,R. - Buffalo	18	55	.327	47	158	.297
Aurilia,R. - Phoenix	20	62	.323	52	196	.265
Baez,K. - Toledo	33	134	.246	54	239	.226
Ball,J. - Tucson	28	77	.364	76	281	.270
Barker,T. - New Orleans	19	78	.244	49	186	.263
Basse,M. - New Orleans	16	58	.276	78	323	.241
Batiste,K. - Rochester	34	131	.260	67	251	.267
Battle,H. - Syracuse	42	150	.280	69	289	.239
Beamon,T. - Calgary	29	87	.333	122	365	.334
Bean,B. - Las Vegas	34	109	.312	95	336	.283
Bell,D. - Buffalo	26	85	.306	64	245	.261
Bell,J. - Pawtucket	26	93	.280	43	169	.254
Bellinger,C. - Phoenix	23	83	.277	53	194	.273
Benard,M. - Phoenix	17	58	.293	98	320	.306
Benavides,F. - Iowa	24	83	.289	52	232	.224
Benitez,Y. - Ottawa	47	161	.292	76	313	.243
Bieser,S. - Scranton-WB	14	57	.246	52	188	.277
Bowers,B. - Syracuse	10	57	.175	66	244	.270
Bowie,J. - Edmonton	27	115	.235	113	413	.274
Bradshaw,T. - Louisville	20	96	.208	90	293	.307
Brady,D. - Nashville	25	84	.298	109	366	.298
Bragg,D. - Tacoma	13	33	.394	52	179	.291
Bream,S. - Las Vegas	10	52	.192	63	251	.251
Brewer,R. - Charlotte	17	62	.274	59	174	.339
Brito,T. - Syracuse	32	108	.296	47	219	.215
Brooks,J. - Indianapolis	26	88	.295	66	237	.278
Brown,J. - Norfolk	25	68	.368	39	150	.260
Brown,R. - Pawtucket	25	95	.263	28	117	.239
Brumley,M. - Tucson	12	55	.218	74	273	.271
Bryant,S. - Edmonton	31	99	.313	86	305	.282
Buccheri,J. - Ottawa	54	161	.335	72	309	.233
Burnitz,J. - Buffalo	23	96	.240	103	347	.297
Busch,M. - Albequerque	30	99	.303	89	344	.259
Butler,R. - Scranton-WB	33	106	.311	65	221	.294
Byington,J. - New Orleans	25	80	.313	88	357	.246
Canate,W. - Syracuse	36	140	.257	44	201	.219
Candaele,C. - Buffalo	30	112	.268	60	252	.238
Cappuccio,C. - Nashville	11	45	.244	48	171	.281
Capra,N. - Charlotte	33	138	.239	71	268	.265
Caraballo,R. - Louisville	18	56	.321	60	189	.317
Carey,P. - Rochester	18	83	.217	49	201	.244
Carpenter,B. - Columbus	24	114	.211	68	260	.262
Carter,J. - Charlotte	41	123	.333	74	305	.243
Carter,M. - Iowa	36	102	.353	100	319	.313
Castellano,P. - Colo. Sprn	18	72	.250	71	262	.271
Castillo,A. - Norfolk	19	59	.322	39	158	.247
Castleberry,K. - Ottawa	35	123	.285	91	305	.298
Castro,J. - Albequerque	14	60	.233	77	281	.274
Cedeno,R. - Albequerque	18	65	.277	94	302	.311
Chimelis,J. - Phoenix	21	105	.200	82	293	.280
Cholowsky,D. - Louisville	13	65	.200	39	173	.225
Christopherson,E. - Pho	19	60	.317	43	222	.194
Cianfrocco,A. - Las Vegas	25	70	.357	75	252	.298
Clapinski,C. - Portland	10	43	.233	39	165	.236
Clark,T. - Portland	38	143	.266	97	356	.272
Clark,T. - Toledo	33	145	.228	65	260	.250
Cockrell,A. - Colo. Sprng	31	92	.337	80	263	.304
Colbert,C. - Las Vegas	10	48	.208	50	193	.259
Cole,S. - Colo. Sprng	10	46	.217	47	162	.290
Colon,C. - Iowa	24	115	.209	71	251	.283
Cookson,B. - Phoenix	18	63	.286	45	147	.306
Coomer,R. - Albequerque	18	60	.300	86	263	.327
Correia,R. - Vancouver	14	52	.269	66	212	.311
Costo,T. - Buffalo	20	97	.206	60	227	.264
Counsell,C. - Colo. Sprng	22	72	.306	90	327	.275
Crespo,F. - Syracuse	32	118	.271	69	224	.308
Cruz,F. - Edmonton	19	81	.235	105	363	.289
Cuyler,M. - Toledo	13	52	.250	49	151	.325
Dascenzo,D. - Charlotte	22	77	.286	47	188	.250
Deak,D. - Louisville	24	91	.264	57	245	.233
Deer,R. - Las Vegas	22	66	.333	66	237	.278
Delgado,C. - Syracuse	27	114	.237	77	215	.358
Denson,D. - Indianapolis	33	105	.314	66	252	.262

Player - Team	vs Left H	AB	Avg	vs Right H	AB	Avg
Devarez,C. - Rochester	31	103	.301	29	137	.212
Dodson,B. - New Orleans	8	29	.276	49	174	.282
Dorsett,B. - Indianapolis	27	80	.338	54	233	.232
Dostal,B. - Okla. City	9	41	.220	53	252	.210
Dunn,S. - Salt Lake	22	80	.275	105	322	.326
Durant,M. - Salt Lake	19	82	.232	55	213	.258
Eenhoorn,R. - Columbus	41	113	.363	39	205	.190
Ehmann,K. - Phoenix	22	72	.306	36	144	.250
Everett,C. - Norfolk	21	80	.262	57	180	.317
Faries,P. - Edmonton	24	89	.270	100	332	.301
Forbes,P. - Vancouver	22	72	.306	79	297	.266
Fox,A. - Columbus	28	101	.277	76	199	.382
Fox,E. - Okla. City	21	65	.323	76	284	.268
Franco,M. - Iowa	44	136	.324	84	319	.263
Franklin,M. - Calgary	33	98	.337	72	260	.277
Gainer,J. - Colo. Sprng	21	66	.318	83	292	.284
Garcia,K. - Albequerque	23	92	.250	128	382	.335
Garcia,O. - Norfolk	38	123	.309	95	307	.309
Gardner,J. - Iowa	17	58	.293	59	177	.333
Garrison,W. - Colo. Sprng	20	86	.233	115	374	.307
Giannelli,R. - Louisville	19	73	.260	96	317	.303
Gibralter,S. - Indianapolis	19	66	.288	64	197	.325
Gilbert,S. - Scranton-WB	35	144	.243	106	392	.270
Giles,B. - Buffalo	24	77	.312	104	336	.310
Giovanola,E. - Richmond	27	89	.303	76	232	.328
Givens,J. - Toledo	13	69	.188	39	147	.265
Glanville,D. - Iowa	32	90	.356	81	329	.246
Goff,J. - Tucson	8	34	.235	38	170	.224
Gordon,K. - Indianapolis	24	81	.296	46	184	.250
Grebeck,B. - Vancouver	7	46	.152	51	184	.277
Greene,W. - Indianapolis	21	85	.247	58	240	.242
Grijak,K. - Richmond	11	56	.196	81	253	.320
Grotewold,J. - Omaha	15	71	.211	88	279	.315
Gutierrez,R. - Tucson	17	40	.425	54	196	.276
Hajek,D. - Tucson	30	85	.353	133	415	.320
Hall,B. - Las Vegas	9	62	.145	47	187	.251
Hall,J. - Toledo	39	110	.355	63	209	.301
Halter,S. - Omaha	17	65	.262	69	305	.226
Haney,T. - Iowa	32	101	.317	70	225	.311
Hare,S. - Okla. City	14	41	.341	49	197	.249
Hatcher,C. - Tucson	18	50	.360	64	238	.269
Hatteberg,S. - Pawtucket	15	53	.283	53	194	.273
Hazlett,S. - Salt Lake	31	93	.333	97	334	.290
Hecht,S. - Okla. City	4	24	.167	58	214	.271
Hinzo,T. - Okla. City	12	44	.273	52	210	.248
Hocking,D. - Salt Lake	13	51	.255	67	249	.269
Holbert,A. - Louisville	25	119	.210	78	282	.277
Holifield,R. - Scranton-WB	10	62	.161	36	161	.224
Hosey,D. - Omaha	31	73	.425	49	198	.247
Houston,T. - Richmond	22	90	.244	67	259	.259
Howard,C. - Tacoma	13	67	.194	52	201	.259
Howitt,D. - Buffalo	8	41	.195	58	210	.276
Hubbard,M. - Iowa	22	73	.301	44	181	.243
Hubbard,T. - Colo. Sprng	28	94	.298	135	386	.350
Huckaby,K. - Albequerque	15	42	.357	75	236	.318
Hughes,K. - Omaha	23	73	.315	76	269	.283
Huskey,B. - Norfolk	28	108	.259	84	286	.294
Huson,J. - Rochester	12	84	.143	44	139	.317
Hyers,T. - Las Vegas	8	45	.178	67	214	.313
Ingram,G. - Albequerque	18	62	.290	39	170	.229
Ingram,R. - Salt Lake	28	85	.329	138	392	.352
Jackson,J. - Salt Lake	20	64	.313	68	243	.280
Jacobs,F. - Norfolk	1	7	.143	91	294	.310
Jeter,D. - Columbus	52	156	.333	102	330	.309
Johnson,E. - Calgary	31	102	.304	104	353	.295
Jones,D. - Phoenix	31	109	.284	77	295	.261
Jordan,K. - Scranton-WB	33	100	.330	94	310	.303
Jorgensen,T. - Charlotte	26	96	.271	68	260	.262
Katzaroff,R. - Portland	25	89	.281	109	352	.310
Kessinger,K. - Iowa	13	43	.302	35	167	.210
Kieschnick,B. - Iowa	32	143	.224	117	362	.323
Kosco,B. - Iowa	11	47	.234	80	316	.253
Koslofski,K. - New Orlean	12	50	.240	54	268	.201
Kowitz,B. - Richmond	29	104	.279	70	249	.281
Kremers,J. - Portland	6	38	.158	53	226	.235

Player - Team	vs Left H	AB	Avg	vs Right H	AB	Avg
Leach,J. - Columbus	17	80	.213	49	192	.255
Ledesma,A. - Norfolk	16	61	.262	44	140	.314
Lee,D. - Norfolk	17	92	.185	72	259	.278
Leonard,M. - Phoenix	23	88	.261	93	304	.306
Lieberthal,M. - Scranton	19	72	.264	59	206	.286
Lindeman,J. - Okla. City	8	46	.174	66	248	.266
Lis,J. - Syracuse	47	188	.250	80	292	.274
Litton,G. - Tacoma	28	87	.322	92	301	.306
Lofton,R. - New Orleans	15	57	.263	37	183	.202
Lopez,L. - Buffalo	36	118	.305	83	337	.246
Loretta,M. - New Orleans	32	100	.320	105	379	.277
Lovullo,T. - Buffalo	22	106	.208	99	368	.269
Lucca,L. - Portland	22	90	.244	85	298	.285
Lukachyk,R. - Toledo	22	84	.262	66	262	.252
Lyden,M. - Omaha	17	62	.274	43	175	.246
Lydy,S. - Edmonton	17	81	.210	99	317	.312
Lyons,B. - Nashville	13	54	.241	55	211	.261
Mack,Q. - Tacoma	6	27	.222	48	177	.271
Maksudian,M. - Edmonton	11	53	.208	73	267	.273
Malave,J. - Pawtucket	29	119	.244	56	198	.283
Manahan,A. - Scranton	19	89	.213	67	210	.319
Marsh,T. - Scranton-WB	28	66	.424	63	230	.274
Martin,C. - Ottawa	37	143	.259	69	269	.257
Martinez,D. - Louisville	25	82	.305	33	140	.236
Martinez,M. - Iowa	31	109	.284	84	288	.292
Marzano,J. - Okla. City	21	82	.256	111	345	.322
Mashore,D. - Edmonton	18	76	.237	83	259	.320
Mashore,J. - Toledo	22	99	.222	27	124	.218
Massarelli,J. - Charlotte	14	78	.179	48	176	.273
Matos,F. - Calgary	26	80	.325	84	261	.322
McCracken,Q. - Colo. Spr	13	40	.325	75	204	.368
McMillon,B. - Portland	37	139	.266	125	379	.330
McNeely,J. - Louisville	35	119	.294	29	152	.191
Mercedes,H. - Omaha	15	54	.278	44	221	.199
Miller,D. - Salt Lake	20	59	.339	64	236	.271
Milliard,R. - Portland	32	109	.294	92	355	.259
Mitchell,K. - Indianapolis	9	33	.273	43	180	.239
Montgomery,R. - Tucson	13	55	.236	72	232	.310
Montoyo,C. - Scranton	12	60	.200	58	228	.254
Moore,B. - Richmond	35	149	.235	50	180	.278
Moore,K. - Edmonton	13	43	.302	61	222	.275
Mottola,C. - Indianapolis	11	44	.250	51	195	.262
Mouton,L. - Nashville	20	74	.270	59	193	.306
Mulligan,S. - Las Vegas	34	97	.351	59	242	.244
Munoz,J. - Richmond	55	176	.313	96	344	.279
Murray,G. - Pawtucket	31	120	.258	49	210	.233
Nevin,P. - Tucson	9	41	.220	56	182	.308
Newfield,M. - Las Vegas	18	77	.234	61	191	.319
Noland,J. - Tacoma	9	31	.290	60	220	.273
Norman,L. - Omaha	25	61	.410	64	252	.254
O'Connor,K. - Richmond	9	36	.250	36	167	.216
Obando,S. - Rochester	38	107	.355	58	217	.267
Ochoa,A. - Norfolk	41	163	.252	89	296	.301
Olmeda,J. - Richmond	21	91	.231	40	150	.267
Ordonez,R. - Norfolk	27	122	.221	67	317	.211
Orton,J. - Norfolk	15	69	.217	42	148	.284
Osik,K. - Calgary	25	77	.325	76	224	.339
Otero,R. - Norfolk	20	75	.267	59	220	.268
Owens,E. - Indianapols	36	101	.356	98	326	.301
Owens,J. - Colo. Sprng	10	50	.200	55	171	.322
Palmeiro,O. - Vancouver	22	79	.278	100	319	.313
Pappas,E. - Charlotte	37	125	.296	49	264	.186
Pemberton,R. - Toledo	33	101	.327	44	123	.358
Penn,S. - Toledo	21	72	.292	33	146	.226
Perez,E. - Richmond	30	114	.263	56	210	.267
Perez,E. - Vancouver	16	46	.348	64	200	.320
Perez,R. - Syracuse	66	167	.395	106	335	.316
Perezchica,T. - Columbus	32	144	.222	60	214	.280
Polcovich,K. - Calgary	12	45	.267	48	168	.286
Posada,J. - Columbus	36	129	.279	58	239	.243
Pose,S. - Albequerque	8	33	.242	58	186	.312
Pozo,A. - Tacoma	32	104	.308	103	346	.298
Pritchett,C. - Vancouver	28	93	.301	92	341	.270
Pulliam,H. - Colo. Sprng	28	84	.333	105	323	.325
Pye,E. - Albequerque	18	60	.300	71	242	.293

AAA Batting vs. Left-Handed and Right-Handed Pitchers

Player - Team	vs Left H	AB	Avg	vs Right H	AB	Avg	Player - Team	vs Left H	AB	Avg	vs Right H	AB	Avg
Quinlan,T. - Salt Lake	30	106	.283	100	360	.278	Wolak,J. - Nashville	26	87	.299	62	298	.208
Raabe,B. - Salt Lake	29	93	.312	105	347	.303	Wood,J. - Edmonton	28	93	.301	70	325	.215
Ramos,J. - Syracuse	42	143	.294	59	265	.223	Wood,T. - Ottawa	20	85	.235	67	241	.278
Ramos,K. - Tucson	15	44	.341	88	278	.317	Woods,T. - Rochester	25	97	.258	37	141	.262
Ramsey,F. - Nashville	28	86	.326	98	320	.306	Woodson,T. - Louisville	33	115	.287	80	316	.253
Randa,J. - Omaha	6	34	.176	58	199	.291	Worthington,C. - Indianap.	18	68	.265	70	208	.337
Ratliff,D. - Calgary	16	65	.246	82	221	.371	Yan,J. - Ottawa	40	156	.256	64	216	.296
Redmond,M. - Portland	22	82	.268	63	251	.251	Young,E. - Edmonton	16	69	.232	80	278	.288
Reese,P. - Indianapolis	19	72	.264	63	271	.232	Zinter,A. - Toledo	28	127	.220	46	207	.222
Renteria,E. - Portland	35	124	.282	112	384	.292	Zosky,E. - Charlotte	26	98	.265	51	214	.238
Rhodes,K. - Pawtucket	18	58	.310	47	182	.258	Zuber,J. - Scranton-WB	32	130	.246	88	288	.306
Riley,M. - Vancouver	23	104	.221	102	373	.273	Zupcic,B. - Charlotte	27	78	.346	48	176	.273
Ripken,B. - Buffalo	38	111	.342	93	337	.276							
Robertson,M. - Nashville	20	112	.179	104	387	.269							
Robertson,R. - Rochester	54	140	.386	40	198	.202							
Rodriguez,A. - Tacoma	15	46	.326	62	168	.369							
Rodriguez,S. - Pawtucket	27	104	.260	50	218	.229							
Rodriguez,T. - Pawtucket	27	117	.231	57	197	.289							
Ronan,M. - Louisville	4	45	.089	44	180	.244							
Rossy,R. - Las Vegas	17	61	.279	78	255	.306							
Saenz,O. - Nashville	19	89	.213	107	326	.328							
Santangelo,F. - Ottawa	19	81	.235	49	186	.263							
Schall,G. - Scranton-WB	20	76	.263	80	244	.328							
Schu,R. - Okla. City	18	66	.273	90	332	.271							
Schunk,J. - Charlotte	23	89	.258	54	254	.213							
Scott,G. - Phoenix	22	64	.344	36	155	.232							
Sharperson,M. - Richmon	41	114	.360	54	184	.293							
Sheets,A. - Tacoma	23	86	.267	101	343	.294							
Sheff,C. - Portland	33	121	.273	97	350	.277							
Sherman,D. - Tacoma	11	44	.250	79	306	.258							
Siddall,J. - Ottawa	9	45	.200	44	199	.221							
Simmons,N. - Calgary	23	78	.295	61	221	.276							
Simms,M. - Tucson	17	51	.333	77	268	.287							
Simons,M. - Salt Lake	42	107	.393	114	373	.306							
Singleton,D. - New Orlean	18	71	.254	77	284	.271							
Smith,G. - Rochester	18	76	.237	30	134	.224							
Smith,I. - Las Vegas	14	46	.304	54	163	.331							
Smith,M. - Rochester	46	136	.338	55	228	.241							
Snopek,C. - Nashville	20	83	.241	106	308	.344							
Sparks,D. - Columbus	64	190	.337	106	355	.299							
Stairs,M. - Pawtucket	28	98	.286	49	173	.283							
Staton,D. - New Orleans	19	82	.232	63	243	.259							
Stefanski,M. - New Orlean	11	46	.239	45	182	.247							
Stillwell,K. - Indianapols	22	91	.242	68	250	.272							
Stynes,C. - Omaha	17	52	.327	67	254	.264							
Sveum,D. - Calgary	28	86	.326	88	322	.273							
Sweeney,M. - Vancouver	15	48	.313	63	178	.354							
Tackett,J. - Toledo	32	111	.288	49	190	.258							
Thomas,S. - Louisville	28	103	.272	40	170	.235							
Thurman,G. - Tacoma	27	97	.278	82	266	.308							
Tokheim,D. - Scranton	30	127	.236	92	323	.285							
Townley,J. - Syracuse	24	91	.264	44	170	.259							
Traxler,B. - Albequerque	12	42	.286	88	311	.283							
Tucker,M. - Omaha	14	55	.255	70	220	.318							
Turner,C. - Vancouver	9	48	.188	67	234	.286							
Tyler,B. - Rochester	18	104	.173	75	257	.292							
Unroe,T. - New Orleans	18	70	.257	79	301	.262							
Valrie,K. - Nashville	40	120	.333	96	424	.226							
Van Burkleo,T. - Colo. Spr	10	34	.294	56	197	.284							
Vargas,H. - Okla. City	31	75	.413	52	227	.229							
Vatcher,J. - Las Vegas	25	81	.309	79	275	.287							
Velandia,J. - Las Vegas	10	37	.270	44	169	.260							
Vitiello,J. - Omaha	14	54	.259	50	175	.286							
Wachter,D. - New Orleans	31	88	.352	67	296	.226							
Wedge,E. - Pawtucket	30	139	.216	58	232	.250							
Weger,W. - New Orleans	13	49	.265	54	185	.292							
Weinke,C. - Syracuse	23	94	.245	53	242	.219							
White,D. - Toledo	33	107	.308	49	202	.243							
Willard,J. - Tacoma	7	31	.226	54	197	.274							
Williams,G. - Edmonton	25	72	.347	65	218	.298							
Williams,R. - Albequerque	13	47	.277	60	185	.324							
Wilson,C. - Toledo	45	154	.292	78	314	.248							
Wilson,N. - Indianapolis	13	53	.245	82	251	.327							
Wilson,P. - Portland	40	118	.339	55	230	.239							
Wimmer,C. - Phoenix	23	101	.228	95	348	.273							

AAA Pitching vs. Left-Handed and Right-Handed Batters

	vs Left			vs Right		
Player - Team	H	AB	Avg	H	AB	Avg
Abbott,P. - Iowa	37	147	.252	67	282	.238
Adams,W. - Edmonton	24	99	.242	48	164	.293
Adamson,J. - Charlotte	18	84	.214	95	357	.266
Ahearne,P. - Toledo	85	252	.337	80	298	.268
Akerfelds,D. - Vancouver	14	45	.311	46	142	.324
Alberro,J. - Okla. City	28	127	.220	38	150	.253
Alfonseca,A. - Portland	33	142	.232	48	211	.227
Anderson,M. - Iowa	62	230	.270	94	398	.236
Anderson,S. - Omaha	27	112	.241	36	163	.221
Apana,M. - Tacoma	49	160	.306	72	246	.293
Archer,K. - New Orleans	15	69	.217	42	156	.269
Backlund,B. - Calgary	24	83	.289	35	118	.297
Bailey,C. - Louisville	10	76	.132	41	144	.285
Baker,S. - Edmonton	24	89	.270	99	332	.298
Baldwin,J. - Nashville	48	148	.324	72	250	.288
Baptist,T. - Syracuse	16	57	.281	67	260	.258
Barber,B. - Louisville	43	162	.265	62	251	.247
Barcelo,M. - Salt Lake	69	232	.297	145	377	.385
Bark,B. - Pawtucket	14	54	.259	49	201	.244
Barnes,B. - Pawtucket	15	68	.221	92	350	.263
Batchelor,R. - Louisville	31	118	.263	54	204	.265
Batista,M. - Charlotte	60	230	.261	58	223	.260
Baxter,R. - Ottawa	22	79	.278	103	313	.329
Beatty,B. - Indianapols	13	49	.265	67	221	.303
Bell,E. - Buffalo	26	110	.236	151	518	.292
Beltran,R. - Louisville	29	81	.358	127	445	.285
Benes,A. - Louisville	24	76	.316	13	124	.105
Bennett,E. - Tucson	26	77	.338	43	192	.224
Bennett,J. - Pawtucket	37	141	.262	54	164	.329
Birkbeck,M. - Norfolk	17	83	.205	35	115	.304
Blomdahl,B. - Toledo	19	80	.237	36	132	.273
Boehringer,B. - Columbus	36	153	.235	57	219	.260
Bolton,R. - Nashville	47	184	.255	75	284	.264
Bolton,T. - Nashville	20	85	.235	86	313	.275
Bottenfield,K. - Toledo	60	210	.286	88	322	.273
Boucher,D. - Ottawa	13	39	.333	52	178	.292
Boze,M. - New Orleans	45	166	.271	89	278	.320
Brandenburg,M. - Okla.	19	73	.260	33	141	.234
Brink,B. - Edmonton	23	90	.256	52	169	.308
Brock,C. - Richmond	28	89	.315	40	147	.272
Brock,R. - Edmonton	35	96	.365	40	133	.301
Brown,T. - Syracuse	40	133	.301	55	181	.304
Bruske,J. - Albequerque	41	134	.306	87	306	.284
Bryant,S. - Salt Lake	13	57	.228	49	143	.343
Buckley,T. - Indianapols	55	220	.250	86	298	.289
Bunch,M. - Omaha	27	98	.276	36	147	.245
Burgos,E. - Phoenix	20	61	.328	43	164	.262
Burke,J. - Colo. Sprng	26	114	.228	53	208	.255
Bustillos,A. - Colo. Sprng	52	176	.295	99	353	.280
Byrd,P. - Norfolk	37	168	.220	34	145	.234
Cadaret,G. - Las Vegas	15	48	.313	41	159	.258
Campbell,K. - Tacoma	14	57	.246	36	133	.271
Campbell,M. - Iowa	38	162	.235	55	217	.253
Carlson,D. - Phoenix	45	159	.283	88	318	.277
Carlyle,K. - Toledo	67	208	.322	72	277	.260
Carmona,R. - Tacoma	21	61	.344	31	126	.246
Carpenter,C. - Louisville	23	94	.245	35	150	.233
Carper,M. - Columbus	46	172	.267	68	240	.283
Carrara,G. - Syracuse	49	215	.228	67	284	.236
Castillo,J. - Tucson	24	53	.453	42	117	.359
Chergey,D. - Portland	18	101	.178	35	166	.211
Combs,P. - Scranton-WB	8	48	.167	63	173	.364
Converse,J. - Tacoma	32	94	.340	64	197	.325
Cook,A. - Columbus	19	82	.232	34	127	.268
Corbin,A. - Calgary	26	82	.317	50	164	.305
Cornelius,R. - Norfolk	35	149	.235	32	124	.258
Courtright,J. - Salt Lake	12	44	.273	96	292	.329
Cunnane,W. - Portland	50	191	.262	70	264	.265
Curtis,C. - Okla. City	28	109	.257	53	196	.270
Czajkowski,J. - Colo. Sprn	34	107	.318	56	207	.271
Daal,O. - Albequerque	8	41	.195	48	164	.293
Dabney,F. - Iowa	21	64	.328	47	158	.297
Darwin,J. - Tacoma	16	74	.216	35	154	.227
Daspit,J. - Edmonton	15	77	.195	54	184	.293
DeJesus,J. - Omaha	22	89	.247	32	127	.252

	vs Left			vs Right		
Player - Team	H	AB	Avg	H	AB	Avg
DeLaRosa,F. - Louisville	48	166	.289	56	272	.206
Delossantos,M. - Calgary	39	127	.307	46	161	.286
Deshaies,J. - Scranton	20	82	.244	85	358	.237
DeSilva,J. - Rochester	61	243	.251	95	338	.281
Dettmer,J. - Rochester	43	140	.307	55	196	.281
Diaz,R. - Ottawa	28	78	.359	23	105	.219
Dishman,G. - Las Vegas	7	41	.171	84	364	.231
DuBois,B. - Scranton-WB	16	79	.203	40	118	.339
Dunbar,M. - Columbus	14	42	.333	36	136	.265
Edenfield,K. - Vancouver	19	67	.284	37	156	.237
Eiland,D. - Columbus	64	210	.305	45	206	.218
Eversgerd,B. - Ottawa	14	55	.255	35	145	.241
Farrell,J. - Buffalo	72	269	.268	126	435	.290
Farrell,M. - New Orleans	22	85	.259	151	485	.311
Fesh,S. - Las Vegas	14	49	.286	50	162	.309
Flener,H. - Syracuse	21	85	.247	110	433	.254
Fletcher,P. - Scranton-WB	23	89	.258	24	133	.180
Frascatore,J. - Louisville	39	140	.279	50	186	.269
Fraser,W. - Ottawa	51	197	.259	43	209	.206
Frazier,R. - Columbus	24	73	.329	27	119	.227
Fredrickson,S. - Colo. Spr	34	93	.366	36	192	.188
Fritz,J. - New Orleans	27	94	.287	43	207	.208
Fyhrie,M. - Omaha	29	93	.312	42	146	.288
Gaddy,B. - Scranton-WB	22	77	.286	78	252	.310
Gamez,B. - Phoenix	19	68	.279	57	192	.297
Ganote,J. - New Orleans	46	141	.326	42	173	.243
Gavaghan,S. - Salt Lake	15	54	.278	38	126	.302
Geeve,D. - Okla. City	25	76	.329	47	148	.318
Givens,B. - New Orleans	11	38	.289	56	244	.230
Goetz,B. - Okla. City	36	107	.336	61	230	.265
Gonzales,F. - Toledo	15	84	.179	28	110	.255
Grant,M. - Iowa	29	107	.271	29	155	.187
Greer,K. - Phoenix	19	81	.235	46	163	.282
Grimsley,J. - Buffalo	18	99	.182	43	159	.270
Grott,M. - Indianapols	17	70	.243	82	364	.225
Hancock,L. - Calgary	32	80	.400	114	394	.289
Hansell,G. - Albequerque	23	67	.343	41	136	.301
Hansen,B. - Pawtucket	37	147	.252	53	207	.256
Harikkala,T. - Tacoma	45	178	.253	106	396	.268
Harriger,D. - Las Vegas	69	244	.283	118	457	.258
Harrison,B. - Omaha	32	100	.320	44	131	.336
Hartley,M. - Pawtucket	24	84	.286	24	113	.212
Hathaway,H. - Las Vegas	12	38	.316	64	212	.302
Hawblitzel,R. - Colo. Sprn	33	111	.297	55	213	.258
Hawkins,L. - Salt Lake	51	200	.255	99	353	.280
Haynes,J. - Rochester	50	269	.186	112	362	.309
Helling,R. - Okla. City	49	168	.292	83	266	.312
Henry,D. - Toledo	26	84	.310	17	97	.175
Heredia,J. - Vancouver	29	110	.264	40	170	.235
Hill,M. - Calgary	22	86	.256	47	153	.307
Holman,S. - Albequerque	26	94	.277	81	238	.340
Holt,C. - Tucson	42	123	.341	113	352	.321
Holzemer,M. - Vancouver	9	42	.214	36	154	.234
Hope,J. - Calgary	36	123	.293	40	181	.221
Huisman,R. - Tucson	20	59	.339	38	148	.257
Hurst,J. - Okla. City	12	33	.364	59	173	.341
Hutton,M. - Columbus	28	95	.295	36	117	.308
Ilsley,B. - Scranton-WB	40	152	.263	170	583	.292
Isringhausen,J. - Norfolk	32	145	.221	32	170	.188
Janicki,P. - Vancouver	19	79	.241	45	119	.378
Jarvis,K. - Indianapols	26	111	.234	36	131	.275
Jean,D. - Okla. City	36	137	.263	58	190	.305
Johns,D. - Edmonton	16	65	.246	132	451	.293
Johnson,D. - Nashville	11	61	.180	32	131	.244
Jones,B. - Colo. Sprng	13	35	.371	37	129	.287
Juden,J. - Scranton-WB	40	151	.265	33	154	.214
Juelsgaard,J. - Portland	28	94	.298	37	169	.219
Karp,R. - Scranton-WB	16	50	.320	65	268	.243
Keagle,G. - Las Vegas	27	110	.245	49	182	.269
Ketchen,D. - Tucson	32	100	.320	69	199	.347
Keyser,B. - Nashville	24	121	.198	25	136	.184
Kiefer,M. - New Orleans	31	121	.256	29	144	.201
Krivda,R. - Rochester	21	68	.309	75	317	.237
Krueger,B. - Tacoma	12	43	.279	40	157	.255
Kutzler,J. - Omaha	52	161	.323	76	251	.303

	vs Left			vs Right		
Player - Team	H	AB	Avg	H	AB	Avg
Lancaster,L. - Buffalo	38	130	.292	52	218	.239
Lemon,D. - Portland	27	98	.276	33	138	.239
Lewis,J. - Buffalo	30	135	.222	65	206	.316
Lewis,R. - Charlotte	30	104	.288	19	109	.174
Lieber,J. - Calgary	47	134	.351	75	211	.355
Lima,J. - Toledo	26	130	.200	35	115	.304
Linton,D. - Omaha	55	182	.302	74	251	.295
Lomon,K. - Richmond	21	78	.269	41	143	.287
Long,S. - Charlotte	27	133	.203	44	154	.286
Looney,B. - Pawtucket	18	86	.209	88	314	.280
Lopez,A. - Buffalo	38	146	.260	63	244	.258
Lorraine,A. - Vancouver	14	55	.255	91	325	.280
Magnante,M. - Omaha	8	43	.186	47	174	.270
Magrane,J. - Ottawa	16	58	.276	53	197	.269
Manuel,B. - Ottawa	56	203	.276	69	274	.252
Marquez,I. - Nashville	28	81	.346	51	185	.276
Marshall,R. - Toledo	13	76	.171	86	331	.260
Martinez,F. - Louisville	23	74	.311	37	132	.280
Martinez,J. - Las Vegas	45	192	.234	111	388	.286
Mathews,T. - Louisville	21	90	.233	39	175	.223
Mauser,T. - Las Vegas	20	63	.317	43	132	.326
May,D. - Richmond	7	28	.250	46	168	.274
Maysey,M. - Calgary	46	145	.317	76	267	.285
McAndrew,J. - New Orlea	37	161	.230	65	232	.280
McCarthy,T. - Albequerqu	23	65	.354	38	132	.288
McFarlin,T. - Las Vegas	40	158	.253	80	306	.261
McGehee,K. - Rochester	55	202	.272	95	304	.313
McGraw,T. - Portland	29	105	.276	40	172	.233
McMurtry,C. - Tucson	15	76	.197	39	172	.227
Mecir,J. - Tacoma	21	81	.259	38	163	.233
Mendoza,R. - Portland	75	259	.290	88	364	.242
Menendez,T. - Phoenix	15	69	.217	48	159	.302
Menhart,P. - Syracuse	32	86	.372	22	94	.234
Milacki,B. - Omaha	39	166	.235	51	221	.231
Milacki,B. - Tacoma	28	102	.275	66	192	.344
Milchin,M. - Albequerque	14	51	.275	80	275	.291
Miller,K. - Charlotte	60	215	.279	83	278	.299
Mimbs,M. - Albequerque	14	55	.255	90	349	.258
Minchey,N. - Louisville	56	209	.268	97	366	.265
Mintz,S. - Phoenix	14	62	.226	28	117	.239
Misuraca,M. - Salt Lake	69	216	.319	105	362	.290
Mix,G. - Portland	32	137	.234	66	229	.288
Mongiello,M. - Nashville	46	146	.315	58	214	.271
Montalvo,R. - Albequerqu	31	126	.246	74	261	.284
Morman,A. - Tucson	9	39	.231	40	132	.303
Morrison,K. - Vancouver	68	234	.291	110	392	.281
Morton,K. - Iowa	21	84	.250	76	269	.283
Munoz,J. - Omaha	16	64	.250	32	139	.230
Munoz,O. - Salt Lake	44	168	.262	77	273	.282
Murray,M. - Richmond	41	200	.205	67	259	.259
Myers,J. - Rochester	26	101	.257	46	153	.301
Myers,R. - Omaha	18	69	.261	34	119	.286
Naulty,D. - Salt Lake	32	114	.281	60	227	.264
Nichols,R. - Richmond	20	95	.211	34	128	.266
Nichting,C. - Okla. City	19	85	.224	39	163	.239
O'Donoghue,J. - Albeq.	13	52	.250	84	315	.267
Ojala,K. - Columbus	21	93	.226	115	458	.251
Olsen,S. - Nashville	34	131	.260	51	174	.293
Pall,D. - Nashville	24	108	.222	65	225	.289
Park,C. - Albequerque	28	128	.219	65	272	.239
Parra,J. - Albequerque	17	64	.266	45	144	.313
Patrick,B. - Tucson	24	81	.296	64	240	.267
Patterson,J. - Columbus	25	96	.260	31	136	.228
Pavlas,D. - Columbus	21	93	.226	22	114	.193
Perez,D. - Okla. City	39	126	.310	81	288	.281
Petkovsek,M. - Louisville	15	70	.214	23	128	.180
Phillips,R. - Phoenix	50	174	.287	105	346	.303
Phillips,T. - Tacoma	37	113	.327	61	227	.269
Phoenix,S. - Edmonton	22	82	.268	44	161	.273
Plummer,D. - Pawtucket	60	183	.328	77	235	.328
Polley,D. - Richmond	9	52	.173	42	182	.231
Potts,M. - Richmond	17	55	.309	62	224	.277
Powell,J. - Portland	19	76	.250	23	116	.198
Pulido,C. - Salt Lake	21	70	.300	66	228	.289
Pulsipher,B. - Norfolk	13	51	.255	71	284	.250

AAA Pitching vs. Left-Handed and Right-Handed Batters

Player - Team	vs Left H	AB	Avg	vs Right H	AB	Avg
Raczka,M. - Louisville	16	69	.232	33	114	.289
Rasmussen,D. - Omaha	13	41	.317	50	207	.242
Ratekin,M. - Vancouver	17	61	.279	45	134	.336
Reed,R. - Indianapols	45	199	.226	82	318	.258
Remlinger,M. - Indianapol	11	60	.183	29	111	.261
Renko,S. - Vancouver	21	72	.292	32	133	.241
Revenig,T. - Edmonton	19	75	.253	34	129	.264
Ricci,C. - Scranton-WB	20	94	.213	26	138	.188
Righetti,D. - Nashville	14	59	.237	67	256	.262
Roa,J. - Buffalo	61	250	.244	107	386	.277
Roberts,C. - Norfolk	37	104	.356	160	496	.323
Robinson,S. - Phoenix	47	159	.296	87	314	.277
Rodriguez,F. - Albeq.	16	62	.258	36	131	.275
Rogers,B. - Norfolk	23	108	.213	35	166	.211
Rogers,J. - Syracuse	18	100	.180	45	154	.292
Rosselli,J. - Phoenix	15	58	.259	79	256	.309
Rueter,K. - Ottawa	12	74	.162	108	387	.279
Ruffin,J. - Indianapols	6	52	.115	21	123	.171
Rumer,T. - Columbus	26	95	.274	130	455	.286
Sackinsky,B. - Rochester	35	106	.330	35	138	.254
Sager,A. - Colo. Sprng	54	191	.283	99	341	.290
Salkeld,R. - Indianapols	50	200	.250	46	231	.199
Sauveur,R. - Indianapols	13	56	.232	30	150	.200
Scheid,R. - Charlotte	14	50	.280	60	173	.347
Schmidt,C. - Ottawa	13	64	.203	27	119	.227
Schmidt,J. - Richmond	40	199	.201	57	218	.261
Schuermann,L. - Okla.	17	66	.258	84	285	.295
Scott,D. - Colo. Sprng	30	118	.254	83	256	.324
Seelbach,C. - Richmond	24	103	.233	40	167	.240
Shaw,C. - Edmonton	15	73	.205	73	266	.274
Sirotka,M. - Nashville	7	33	.212	44	165	.267
Slusarski,J. - Buffalo	16	69	.232	38	167	.228
Small,M. - Tucson	20	79	.253	51	172	.297
Smith,D. - Columbus	24	80	.300	30	118	.254
Smith,P. - Charlotte	27	100	.270	24	85	.282
Sodowsky,C. - Toledo	25	97	.258	22	115	.191
Spoljaric,P. - Syracuse	7	66	.106	62	253	.245
Spradlin,J. - Charlotte	29	98	.296	30	123	.244
Springer,D. - Scranton	79	307	.257	84	344	.244
St.Claire,R. - Calgary	21	83	.253	51	140	.364
Steed,R. - Syracuse	22	82	.268	29	130	.223
Steenstra,K. - Iowa	70	251	.279	104	403	.258
Stidham,P. - Norfolk	30	123	.244	24	129	.186
Sturtze,T. - Iowa	44	132	.333	64	212	.302
Sullivan,S. - Indianapols	20	71	.282	31	149	.208
Taylor,R. - Iowa	19	63	.302	23	140	.164
Taylor,S. - New Orleans	51	180	.283	81	323	.251
Taylor,S. - Calgary	25	93	.269	119	440	.270
Telgheder,D. - Norfolk	41	157	.261	36	183	.197
Thobe,J. - Ottawa	28	112	.250	49	210	.233
Thobe,T. - Richmond	10	63	.159	55	253	.217
Thomas,R. - Richmond	39	143	.273	64	215	.298
Thompson,M. - Colo. Sp.	25	90	.278	48	151	.318
Torres,R. - Ottawa	45	167	.269	45	185	.243
Toth,R. - Omaha	20	77	.260	33	113	.292
Treadwell,J. - Albeq.	38	138	.275	83	330	.252
Trlicek,R. - Phoenix	28	79	.354	42	174	.241
Trombley,M. - Salt Lake	30	109	.275	44	170	.259
Urbina,U. - Ottawa	23	108	.213	23	133	.173
Valdes,M. - Charlotte	97	323	.300	92	326	.282
Valdez,S. - Phoenix	34	155	.219	83	268	.310
Valera,J. - Vancouver	28	94	.298	52	165	.315
VanEgmond,T. - Pawtuck.	35	111	.315	31	140	.221
Vierra,J. - Nashville	17	78	.218	30	133	.226
Wade,T. - Richmond	16	69	.232	121	459	.264
Wagner,B. - Tucson	11	45	.244	59	241	.245
Walker,P. - Norfolk	23	86	.267	28	100	.280
Wall,D. - Tucson	69	242	.285	121	443	.273
Wallace,K. - Columbus	18	79	.228	26	110	.236
Ward,B. - Portland	15	65	.231	49	197	.249
Ware,J. - Syracuse	27	120	.225	35	150	.233
Warren,B. - Indianapols	23	78	.295	32	140	.229
Wasdin,J. - Edmonton	82	282	.291	111	406	.273
Watkins,S. - Salt Lake	7	40	.175	38	159	.239
Weber,B. - Syracuse	42	160	.262	69	210	.329

Player - Team	vs Left H	AB	Avg	vs Right H	AB	Avg
Weber,W. - Las Vegas	55	215	.256	115	383	.300
Wertz,B. - Pawtucket	32	116	.276	42	142	.296
Weston,M. - Toledo	77	320	.241	93	359	.259
Whisenant,M. - Portland	17	111	.153	89	348	.256
Whitaker,S. - Phoenix	14	35	.400	58	180	.322
White,G. - Ottawa	6	38	.158	52	200	.260
White,R. - Calgary	35	109	.321	62	212	.292
Whitehurst,W. - Pawtuck.	28	112	.250	40	116	.345
Wiegandt,S. - Scranton	10	66	.152	45	138	.326
Williams,J. - Norfolk	18	92	.196	92	357	.258
Williams,S. - Vancouver	55	221	.249	87	348	.250
Williams,T. - Albequerque	12	47	.255	47	138	.341
Wilson,P. - Norfolk	27	103	.262	32	141	.227
Wilson,S. - Nashville	9	37	.243	51	170	.300
Winston,D. - Calgary	16	54	.296	43	153	.281
Wishnevski,R. - Okla. City	45	136	.331	53	244	.217
Wissler,B. - Salt Lake	23	72	.319	43	157	.274
Wojciechowski,S. - Edm.	14	43	.326	61	250	.244
Wolcott,B. - Tacoma	30	100	.300	64	221	.290
Woodall,B. - Richmond	13	42	.310	57	211	.270
York,M. - Syracuse	28	89	.315	27	108	.250
Zimmerman,M. - Charlotte	51	135	.378	33	133	.248

Major League Equivalencies

"Yeah, but what do his MLE's look like?" That's the standard response around here when someone points out a minor-league player's gaudy batting stats. Sure, he might have hit .370 with 29 homers for Albuquerque, but what does it all *mean*?

Major League Equivalencies (MLE's) take a major step toward answering just that question: What do those minor-league stats mean? Invented by Bill James over a decade ago, MLE's take a minor leaguer's batting stats, adjust them for ballparks and leagues, and convert them to numbers representing what the hitter would have done, had he been in the majors.

Understand, MLE's are *not* projections. For all we know, a player here might have had his career year in 1995. All we're saying is, he'd have had a career year if he'd been in the majors, too. On the other hand, if given a chance in the majors most players will post numbers similar to their MLE's. Last year, for example, Marty Cordova's MLE's showed him with a .363 on-base percentage and .494 slugging percentage. He finished at .352 and .486.

We had our share of misses, too, but most of those came when players spent more time sitting on the bench than playing. One thing we've learned over the years: Don't ignore the MLE's.

Major League Equivalencies for 1995 AAA/AA Batters

Batter	Age	Avg	G	AB	R	H	2B	3B	HR	RBI	BB	SO	SB	CS	OBP	SLG
ATLANTA BRAVES																
Ayrault,Joe	24	.216	89	291	20	63	17	0	5	32	8	73	1	3	.237	.326
Dye,Jermaine	22	.254	104	386	38	98	22	2	12	54	17	77	2	7	.285	.415
Giovanola,Ed	27	.301	99	312	37	94	16	1	3	30	45	38	5	6	.389	.388
Grijak,Kevin	25	.304	127	372	39	113	18	3	12	55	24	57	0	2	.346	.465
Hollins,Damon	22	.220	129	450	49	99	22	1	14	59	28	125	3	5	.266	.367
Houston,Tyler	25	.240	103	342	34	82	9	1	11	35	14	63	2	4	.270	.368
Kowitz,Brian	26	.262	100	344	44	90	12	3	1	28	34	44	7	7	.328	.323
Malloy,Marty	23	.253	124	446	56	113	17	1	8	45	25	60	7	11	.293	.350
Martinez,Pablo	27	.226	134	492	57	111	19	3	4	25	24	99	7	11	.262	.301
Moore,Bobby	30	.238	108	320	37	76	16	1	2	22	22	27	6	6	.287	.313
Munoz,Jose	28	.269	135	505	54	136	16	2	2	37	43	65	4	9	.327	.321
Nunez,Ramon	23	.233	81	232	26	54	13	1	7	26	9	66	0	0	.261	.388
Olmeda,Jose	28	.230	111	339	30	78	14	1	3	27	17	59	1	0	.267	.304
Pecorilli,Aldo	25	.311	119	373	52	116	16	1	10	46	29	60	1	7	.361	.440
Perez,Eddie	28	.244	92	315	26	77	17	0	4	33	9	59	0	1	.265	.337
Scott,Gary	27	.196	95	291	27	57	13	1	3	18	25	53	1	1	.259	.278
Sharperson,Mike	34	.295	87	288	35	85	14	0	2	39	29	34	4	1	.360	.365
Smith,Bobby	22	.232	127	427	57	99	23	1	11	44	25	114	7	5	.274	.368
Swann,Pedro	25	.287	117	363	44	104	21	1	9	51	29	68	8	11	.339	.424
Warner,Mike	25	.202	81	262	31	53	13	0	1	11	38	58	7	5	.303	.263
Williams,Juan	23	.270	107	311	45	84	16	1	16	38	26	85	2	4	.326	.482
BALTIMORE ORIOLES																
Bartee,Kimera	23	.231	68	260	40	60	8	0	2	17	16	64	15	6	.275	.285
Batiste,Kim	28	.258	178	670	67	173	26	1	15	96	17	85	6	8	.277	.367
Berrios,Harry	24	.223	56	202	26	45	11	0	4	17	18	47	8	2	.286	.337
Brown,Jarvis	29	.262	120	423	76	111	24	3	5	36	47	103	12	7	.336	.369
Carey,Paul	28	.217	89	277	31	60	11	0	8	40	32	71	0	2	.298	.343
Castaldo,Gregg	25	.210	104	257	30	54	10	1	1	21	27	65	3	3	.285	.268
Devarez,Cesar	26	.224	67	232	25	52	10	0	0	17	5	26	1	2	.241	.267
Friedman,Jason	26	.243	102	329	29	80	14	0	6	36	16	35	0	1	.278	.340
Howard,Matt	28	.274	70	241	34	66	7	1	0	12	20	28	15	6	.330	.311
Huson,Jeff	31	.230	60	217	22	50	7	0	2	17	21	30	11	5	.298	.290
Lewis,T.R.	25	.266	108	372	55	99	22	0	7	51	32	60	8	4	.324	.382
McClain,Scott	24	.243	131	444	58	108	19	0	18	67	35	82	1	2	.299	.408
Millares,Jose	28	.224	120	398	40	89	26	1	3	40	13	66	4	6	.248	.317
Obando,Sherman	26	.267	85	311	34	83	22	3	8	42	23	59	0	1	.317	.434
Owens,Billy	25	.240	131	467	47	112	23	0	16	74	29	99	1	1	.284	.392
Robertson,Rod	28	.254	101	327	43	83	17	1	14	47	17	66	5	7	.291	.440
Smith,Mark	26	.251	96	351	44	88	21	1	10	53	19	72	5	3	.289	.402
Tyler,Brad	27	.236	114	351	48	83	14	1	15	42	57	66	7	5	.343	.410
Waszgis,B.J.	25	.231	130	425	43	98	19	0	9	40	48	97	1	4	.309	.339
Wawruck,Jim	26	.264	95	349	40	92	16	1	5	42	23	57	7	7	.309	.358
Woods,Tyrone	26	.235	70	230	24	54	14	0	7	25	19	71	1	3	.293	.387
BOSTON RED SOX																
Abad,Andy	23	.243	89	288	28	70	15	2	3	30	29	62	3	6	.312	.340
Bell,Juan	28	.258	68	260	37	67	21	0	4	20	18	48	2	4	.306	.385
Blosser,Greg	25	.232	66	228	28	53	14	0	9	35	14	57	2	1	.277	.412
Brown,Randy	26	.243	74	210	23	51	6	0	1	10	8	55	3	0	.271	.286
Carey,Todd	24	.272	76	228	29	62	12	0	7	34	23	47	2	3	.339	.417

Major League Equivalencies for 1995 AAA/AA Batters

Batter	Age	Avg	G	AB	R	H	2B	3B	HR	RBI	BB	SO	SB	CS	OBP	SLG
Fuller,Aaron	24	.196	58	204	26	40	8	3	0	9	12	48	11	3	.241	.265
Garciaparra,Nomar	22	.268	125	514	74	138	22	6	7	45	41	44	25	10	.323	.375
Hardge,Mike	24	.244	69	217	24	53	7	0	0	15	16	43	2	5	.296	.276
Hatteberg,Scott	26	.265	85	249	31	66	16	0	5	23	35	40	1	0	.356	.390
Hecker,Doug	25	.207	61	222	19	46	17	0	4	30	14	46	1	0	.254	.338
Hosey,Dwayne	29	.285	75	267	50	76	24	3	9	43	24	47	10	5	.344	.498
Mahay,Ron	25	.246	104	354	39	87	17	2	4	29	39	105	3	5	.321	.339
Malave,Jose	25	.261	91	314	48	82	12	0	19	50	26	70	0	0	.318	.481
Martin,Jeff	25	.217	78	254	24	55	11	0	3	29	13	88	2	2	.255	.295
McGuire,Ryan	24	.338	109	417	57	141	32	0	6	57	47	54	8	7	.405	.458
Merloni,Lou	25	.279	93	319	40	89	17	0	0	29	32	53	5	6	.345	.332
Murray,Glenn	25	.235	104	332	58	78	16	0	21	58	30	114	3	5	.298	.473
Pough,Chop	26	.267	127	461	75	123	33	4	23	86	47	136	8	4	.335	.505
Rhodes,Karl	27	.276	69	243	35	67	13	2	8	38	30	48	5	5	.355	.444
Rodriquez,Tony	25	.261	96	314	32	82	16	1	0	18	13	40	8	4	.291	.318
Selby,Bill	26	.289	117	453	61	131	32	1	11	65	37	55	2	5	.343	.437
Shelton,Ben	26	.208	100	322	60	67	7	0	14	43	57	111	2	0	.327	.360
Stairs,Matt	27	.276	75	268	35	74	18	0	10	49	25	43	2	2	.338	.455
Wedge,Eric	28	.226	108	372	46	84	18	0	17	60	55	100	0	2	.326	.411
CALIFORNIA ANGELS																
Arias,George	24	.248	134	499	70	124	15	5	25	81	41	128	1	1	.306	.449
Boykin,Tyrone	28	.239	62	201	26	48	8	1	5	19	13	38	1	1	.285	.363
Carvajal,Jovino	27	.286	120	489	66	140	11	3	1	25	13	64	32	20	.305	.327
Correia,Rod	28	.278	73	255	36	71	5	2	0	33	22	34	5	4	.336	.314
Forbes,P.J.	28	.249	109	357	40	89	18	1	0	44	18	48	2	6	.285	.305
Glenn,Leon	26	.224	120	416	52	93	15	5	14	50	22	136	10	12	.263	.385
Grebeck,Brian	28	.222	81	234	35	52	9	1	4	25	32	40	2	0	.316	.321
Greene,Todd	25	.272	125	467	69	127	17	0	33	74	20	97	2	5	.302	.520
Guerrero,Pedro	40	.270	66	241	31	65	10	0	5	31	18	36	0	2	.320	.373
Harkrider,Tim	24	.259	124	440	51	114	16	1	1	30	31	39	1	5	.308	.307
Munoz,Orlando	25	.271	91	303	30	82	14	1	0	34	21	38	5	6	.318	.323
Ortiz,Bo	26	.246	96	346	37	85	8	1	6	43	11	43	8	12	.269	.327
Palmeiro,Orlando	27	.281	107	384	56	108	17	2	0	40	35	36	11	7	.341	.336
Perez,Eduardo	26	.300	69	237	33	71	10	4	5	31	21	36	4	2	.357	.439
Pritchett,Chris	26	.254	123	421	56	107	23	2	7	45	48	83	1	3	.330	.368
Ramirez,J.D.	29	.237	81	245	26	58	12	0	8	28	14	54	0	1	.278	.384
Raven,Luis	27	.225	58	213	22	48	10	0	8	33	14	69	2	2	.273	.385
Riley,Marquis	25	.241	120	464	60	112	5	3	0	36	42	73	20	9	.304	.265
Turner,Chris	27	.242	80	273	37	66	17	1	2	41	29	57	2	0	.315	.333
Wolff,Mike	25	.271	127	425	59	115	22	1	11	54	43	89	6	9	.338	.405
CHICAGO CUBS																
Benavides,Freddie	30	.224	106	308	25	69	12	2	3	22	21	49	1	3	.274	.305
Bream,Scott	25	.192	116	370	31	71	5	0	1	17	34	82	4	5	.260	.214
Brown,Brant	25	.265	121	442	63	117	26	3	5	50	31	82	6	5	.313	.371
Burton,Darren	23	.257	105	381	48	98	22	1	4	35	30	73	9	10	.311	.352
Carter,Mike	27	.304	107	408	48	124	14	2	7	34	12	48	9	12	.324	.400
Coleman,Ken	29	.269	127	390	78	105	18	2	4	35	62	58	19	7	.369	.356
Colon,Cris	27	.241	106	357	29	86	16	0	3	30	14	53	0	0	.270	.311
Duross,Gabe	24	.256	68	242	21	62	9	0	2	38	8	21	2	2	.280	.318
Franco,Matt	26	.264	121	444	43	117	25	3	5	49	32	46	0	1	.313	.367

420

Major League Equivalencies for 1995 AAA/AA Batters

Batter	Age	Avg	G	AB	R	H	2B	3B	HR	RBI	BB	SO	SB	CS	OBP	SLG
Gardner,Jeff	32	.306	65	229	29	70	10	0	2	20	19	28	0	2	.359	.376
Glanville,Doug	25	.250	112	408	41	102	14	1	3	31	13	67	10	9	.273	.311
Gomez,Rudy	27	.184	93	212	17	39	10	0	1	15	12	48	0	0	.228	.245
Haney,Todd	30	.291	90	316	32	92	18	1	3	25	24	22	1	2	.341	.383
Hubbard,Mike	25	.242	75	248	23	60	5	2	4	19	22	62	4	1	.304	.327
Jennings,Robin	24	.289	132	485	67	140	26	5	16	75	36	65	5	14	.338	.462
Kessinger,Keith	29	.218	86	266	24	58	14	0	1	21	25	27	0	1	.285	.282
Kieschnick,Brooks	24	.276	138	492	52	136	27	0	19	62	50	95	1	3	.343	.447
Kosco,Bryn	29	.234	119	355	42	83	22	2	12	44	25	89	1	2	.284	.408
Larrequi,Edgardo	23	.292	122	418	52	122	17	0	11	57	26	41	2	10	.333	.411
Manahan,Austin	26	.205	94	258	32	53	11	0	3	18	13	61	10	6	.244	.283
Martinez,Manuel	25	.269	122	386	53	104	15	5	7	41	17	67	8	8	.300	.389
Ortiz,Hector	26	.226	96	296	12	67	11	0	0	17	16	41	0	5	.266	.264
Petersen,Chris	25	.204	125	378	45	77	9	2	4	34	36	103	5	3	.273	.270
Valdes,Pedro	23	.294	114	422	54	124	27	2	6	64	30	82	2	6	.341	.410
CHICAGO WHITE SOX																
Brady,Doug	26	.287	125	443	67	127	13	5	4	25	28	77	26	10	.329	.366
Burton,Essex	27	.246	142	548	90	135	14	1	0	40	63	82	46	17	.324	.276
Cameron,Mike	23	.238	107	345	60	82	18	4	10	56	43	109	16	6	.322	.400
Cappuccio,Carmine	26	.260	131	454	60	118	25	2	7	58	44	48	1	4	.325	.370
Coughlin,Kevin	25	.354	106	339	53	120	27	1	2	46	30	48	3	3	.407	.457
Fryman,Troy	24	.209	112	350	45	73	12	2	7	38	39	101	6	1	.288	.314
Hurst,Jimmy	24	.181	91	298	44	54	10	0	11	32	26	99	9	5	.247	.326
Lyons,Barry	36	.245	71	261	35	64	14	0	7	36	18	57	0	0	.294	.379
Mouton,Lyle	27	.285	71	263	37	75	15	0	7	38	21	59	8	4	.338	.422
Norton,Greg	23	.238	133	462	61	110	20	1	5	56	50	93	14	12	.313	.318
Poe,Charles	24	.273	120	421	71	115	26	1	12	56	40	82	14	4	.336	.425
Ramsey,Fernando	30	.300	98	400	57	120	17	2	4	42	12	48	21	8	.320	.383
Robertson,Mike	25	.235	139	490	52	115	15	3	16	49	47	74	1	4	.302	.376
Saenz,Olmedo	25	.293	111	409	56	120	24	0	12	70	42	61	0	2	.359	.440
Snopek,Chris	25	.313	113	387	53	121	21	3	11	52	47	74	1	5	.387	.468
Valrie,Kerry	27	.240	138	537	71	129	28	2	6	52	37	110	18	6	.289	.333
Vinas,Julio	23	.259	102	367	44	95	14	1	5	57	29	83	2	3	.313	.343
Vollmer,Scott	25	.227	81	255	33	58	4	0	5	36	33	40	0	1	.316	.302
Wilson,Craig	25	.280	132	465	53	130	17	0	3	43	34	46	1	2	.329	.335
Wolak,Jerry	25	.218	108	380	40	83	19	0	13	59	18	85	4	3	.254	.371
CINCINNATI REDS																
Brooks,Jerry	29	.258	90	314	33	81	17	1	11	42	18	38	2	0	.298	.424
Brown,Adam	29	.247	77	227	20	56	13	1	4	27	18	37	0	0	.302	.366
Denson,Drew	30	.252	107	345	48	87	19	0	14	56	29	69	0	0	.310	.429
Dismuke,Jamie	26	.263	112	373	52	98	10	0	18	60	35	49	0	0	.326	.434
Dorsett,Brian	35	.238	91	303	32	72	23	0	13	47	21	47	0	0	.287	.442
Gibralter,Steve	23	.289	79	253	40	73	17	1	14	51	21	71	0	1	.343	.530
Gordon,Keith	27	.238	89	256	29	61	12	0	4	31	12	95	2	3	.272	.332
Greene,Willie	24	.224	91	317	46	71	11	1	17	37	32	68	2	2	.295	.426
Hyzdu,Adam	24	.241	102	303	47	73	13	0	11	41	34	58	2	1	.318	.393
Ladell,Cleveland	25	.269	135	501	65	135	26	4	4	37	29	91	21	7	.309	.361
Mitchell,Keith	26	.218	70	206	32	45	10	1	9	29	34	40	3	3	.329	.408
Mottola,Chad	24	.249	120	406	59	101	22	0	14	63	26	83	6	1	.294	.406
Owens,Eric	25	.285	108	410	70	117	22	5	9	51	44	62	25	9	.355	.429

Major League Equivalencies for 1995 AAA/AA Batters

Batter	Age	Avg	G	AB	R	H	2B	3B	HR	RBI	BB	SO	SB	CS	OBP	SLG
Reese,Pokey	23	.216	89	333	42	72	19	0	8	37	30	82	6	4	.281	.345
Rohrmeier,Dan	30	.292	128	445	70	130	31	0	14	67	31	69	0	0	.338	.456
Rumfield,Toby	23	.242	92	265	27	64	11	0	6	45	19	48	0	2	.292	.351
Santana,Ruben	26	.270	142	538	76	145	21	6	9	68	38	79	1	4	.318	.381
Sellers,Rick	29	.219	94	292	36	64	12	1	8	40	34	71	1	0	.301	.349
Smith,Greg	29	.198	115	383	41	76	7	0	3	24	34	46	18	8	.264	.240
Stillwell,Kurt	31	.239	100	330	41	79	13	1	6	24	39	50	3	2	.320	.339
Watkins,Pat	23	.268	105	347	49	93	24	1	10	49	25	55	3	4	.317	.429
Wilson,Brandon	27	.292	106	391	57	114	31	0	7	51	25	66	11	5	.334	.425
Wilson,Nigel	26	.289	82	294	43	85	25	1	15	42	11	96	3	2	.315	.534
CLEVELAND INDIANS																
Amaro,Ruben	31	.299	54	211	41	63	15	2	6	21	17	29	4	1	.351	.474
Bryant,Pat	23	.248	127	415	56	103	22	2	16	55	40	121	12	8	.314	.427
Burnitz,Jeromy	27	.280	128	440	70	123	26	5	18	83	48	85	10	5	.350	.484
Candaele,Casey	35	.240	109	387	49	93	10	5	4	38	23	46	7	3	.283	.323
Costo,Tim	27	.240	105	321	40	77	11	1	10	58	25	66	1	0	.295	.374
Crosby,Mike	27	.158	75	222	16	35	5	0	4	18	7	62	0	1	.183	.234
Giles,Brian S.	25	.303	123	409	65	124	18	6	14	65	51	41	5	3	.380	.479
Harvey,Raymond	27	.251	122	439	49	110	20	0	2	30	33	78	0	4	.303	.310
Howitt,Dann	32	.256	86	250	33	64	14	2	5	31	28	62	0	3	.331	.388
Jackson,Damian	22	.237	131	477	63	113	20	1	2	32	51	108	30	11	.311	.296
Lopez,Luis	31	.255	123	451	60	115	21	0	16	64	27	48	0	1	.297	.408
Lovullo,Torey	30	.249	132	470	82	117	20	4	16	59	66	62	2	1	.341	.411
Marini,Marc	26	.290	115	390	49	113	33	0	4	66	29	67	2	3	.339	.405
Massarelli,John	30	.243	123	424	48	103	16	2	2	27	34	85	23	16	.299	.304
Maxwell,Pat	26	.239	84	264	17	63	7	0	3	23	11	27	0	0	.269	.299
Neal,Mike	24	.257	134	413	60	106	24	1	4	43	55	82	3	6	.344	.349
Ripken,Billy	31	.286	130	444	49	127	34	0	3	54	26	39	4	4	.326	.383
Smith,Ed	27	.236	116	390	41	92	18	1	12	57	30	102	0	3	.290	.379
Townsend,Chad	24	.253	116	399	36	101	22	0	8	47	24	94	2	2	.296	.368
COLORADO ROCKIES																
Case,Mike	27	.265	109	332	54	88	17	2	14	44	35	78	4	3	.335	.455
Castellano,Pedro	26	.260	99	331	29	86	21	1	10	35	17	57	1	0	.296	.420
Cockrell,Alan	33	.307	106	352	43	108	20	0	13	43	22	66	0	3	.348	.474
Cole,Stu	30	.263	76	205	20	54	14	1	2	17	12	19	0	2	.304	.371
Counsell,Craig	25	.268	118	392	44	105	20	5	4	39	25	47	6	2	.312	.375
Echevarria,Angel	25	.327	124	471	75	154	32	1	30	97	46	96	6	3	.387	.590
Gainer,Jay	29	.278	112	352	42	98	18	0	20	64	31	65	1	3	.337	.500
Garrison,Webster	30	.287	126	456	62	131	30	4	13	57	34	75	8	4	.337	.456
Hubbard,Trent	30	.333	123	475	76	158	27	5	13	49	45	60	25	10	.390	.493
Jones,Terry	25	.284	124	482	75	137	13	1	1	25	32	108	39	16	.329	.322
Kennedy,Dave	25	.333	128	504	72	168	23	2	32	93	39	136	3	1	.381	.577
List,Lew	30	.301	82	219	25	66	10	4	8	42	16	44	1	2	.349	.493
McCracken,Quinton	26	.362	116	467	73	169	26	11	4	45	34	61	30	14	.405	.490
Myrow,John	24	.261	96	360	50	94	19	1	4	48	20	69	12	5	.300	.353
Owens,Jayhawk	27	.294	70	221	35	65	12	4	13	35	14	62	1	1	.336	.561
Perez,Neifi	21	.268	127	471	59	126	36	4	7	42	19	56	3	3	.296	.406
Pulliam,Harvey	28	.327	115	407	67	133	28	4	28	68	36	60	4	2	.381	.622
Rogers,Lamarr	25	.298	109	379	65	113	16	0	0	30	52	51	15	6	.383	.340
Schmidt,Tom	23	.234	115	432	53	101	27	3	8	47	19	102	1	1	.266	.366

Major League Equivalencies for 1995 AAA/AA Batters

Batter	Age	Avg	G	AB	R	H	2B	3B	HR	RBI	BB	SO	SB	CS	OBP	SLG
Strittmatter,Mark	27	.263	95	312	42	82	14	1	10	42	38	55	0	0	.343	.410
Van Burkleo,Ty	32	.273	76	227	32	62	13	1	12	42	21	58	1	1	.335	.498
DETROIT TIGERS																
Baez,Kevin	29	.225	116	373	30	84	12	1	4	37	22	60	0	5	.268	.295
Barker,Glen	25	.231	133	502	73	116	24	3	10	48	28	154	32	12	.272	.351
Briley,Greg	31	.209	85	249	24	52	10	0	5	25	27	68	7	2	.286	.309
Catalanotto,Frank	22	.220	134	487	65	107	17	4	8	47	41	60	10	7	.280	.320
Clark,Tony	24	.238	110	403	51	96	15	1	17	64	54	137	0	1	.328	.407
Cooper,Gary	31	.269	99	334	65	90	20	0	19	65	50	89	6	3	.365	.500
Cruz,Ivan	28	.271	119	431	69	117	17	0	34	95	57	110	0	0	.357	.548
Cuyler,Milt	27	.299	54	201	33	60	9	3	7	28	20	42	5	6	.362	.478
Danapilis,Eric	25	.249	129	410	46	102	22	0	10	62	52	108	2	2	.333	.376
De La Nuez,Rex	28	.254	111	327	46	83	20	0	9	40	41	80	8	5	.337	.398
Fernandez,Danny	30	.158	94	228	17	36	4	0	4	15	24	64	0	2	.238	.228
Givens,Jim	28	.230	79	217	23	50	4	0	0	14	27	42	6	4	.316	.249
Hall,Joe	30	.313	91	316	53	99	18	1	12	48	37	53	3	0	.385	.491
Hansen,Terrel	29	.212	75	226	25	48	7	0	11	29	9	55	0	0	.243	.389
Leiper,Tim	29	.243	128	436	62	106	17	0	8	51	44	40	2	2	.313	.337
Lukachyk,Rob	27	.250	104	344	44	86	23	6	8	26	34	79	6	4	.317	.422
Mashore,Justin	24	.223	112	368	57	82	10	3	8	35	19	109	14	8	.261	.332
Nevin,Phil	25	.263	69	236	28	62	14	0	7	36	23	46	1	2	.328	.411
Pemberton,Rudy	26	.338	67	222	31	75	14	2	7	23	15	38	6	3	.380	.514
Penn,Shannon	26	.241	63	216	42	52	3	0	1	15	17	42	13	8	.296	.269
Rodriguez,Steve	25	.226	82	318	36	72	14	2	1	22	23	36	9	9	.279	.292
Sanchez,Yuri	22	.206	121	339	51	70	7	6	6	25	32	125	12	5	.275	.316
Tackett,Jeff	30	.262	96	298	32	78	14	0	6	30	36	48	1	0	.341	.369
White,Derrick	26	.261	87	307	51	80	14	2	15	50	30	68	5	5	.326	.466
Wilson,Craig	31	.256	121	464	57	119	29	0	9	66	38	64	6	1	.313	.377
Zinter,Alan	28	.219	101	333	43	73	13	3	15	49	37	108	3	0	.297	.411
FLORIDA MARLINS																
Brewer,Rod	30	.279	84	269	29	75	16	0	6	48	27	57	0	1	.345	.405
Capra,Nick	38	.230	119	392	47	90	14	0	7	40	42	47	15	6	.304	.319
Carter,Jeff	32	.244	124	414	61	101	17	2	0	17	48	90	15	6	.323	.295
Clapinski,Chris	24	.213	87	202	25	43	7	2	3	23	19	47	3	2	.281	.312
Clark,Tim	27	.245	134	482	49	118	30	1	6	70	40	92	0	5	.303	.349
Dascenzo,Doug	32	.234	75	256	40	60	7	0	2	20	19	31	10	9	.287	.285
Jorgensen,Terry	29	.238	99	344	29	82	12	0	5	40	30	42	2	3	.299	.317
Katzaroff,Robbie	27	.278	116	425	69	118	14	3	7	39	33	35	12	10	.330	.374
Kremers,Jimmy	30	.202	85	257	25	52	9	4	5	29	18	74	0	0	.255	.327
Lucca,Lou	25	.251	112	375	45	94	24	0	7	51	40	82	2	4	.323	.371
McMillon,Billy	24	.285	141	498	73	142	25	2	10	74	65	96	10	9	.368	.404
Milliard,Ralph	22	.243	128	449	83	109	19	2	8	31	57	88	14	5	.328	.347
Pappas,Erik	30	.198	122	378	37	75	24	2	7	40	47	81	7	7	.287	.328
Redmond,Mike	25	.232	105	323	29	75	9	0	2	31	14	28	1	2	.264	.279
Renteria,Edgar	20	.265	135	491	55	130	13	5	5	54	21	91	21	8	.295	.342
Schunk,Jerry	30	.201	101	333	28	67	11	0	4	25	14	32	5	0	.233	.270
Sheff,Chris	25	.252	131	456	67	115	22	5	9	72	48	89	15	6	.323	.382
Wilson,Pookie	25	.249	107	337	40	84	11	4	2	35	12	54	6	4	.275	.323
Zosky,Eddie	28	.222	92	302	21	67	13	1	2	33	5	50	1	3	.235	.291
Zupcic,Bob	29	.261	85	284	33	74	11	0	9	40	29	42	1	2	.329	.394

Major League Equivalencies for 1995 AAA/AA Batters

Batter	Age	Avg	G	AB	R	H	2B	3B	HR	RBI	BB	SO	SB	CS	OBP	SLG
HOUSTON ASTROS																
Abreu,Bob	22	.263	114	392	53	103	20	10	6	55	49	133	10	14	.345	.411
Ball,Jeff	27	.251	110	342	42	86	20	1	2	41	18	73	7	5	.289	.333
Bridges,Kary	24	.288	118	410	53	118	20	3	2	40	38	20	7	12	.348	.366
Brumley,Mike	33	.223	94	314	41	70	16	5	2	24	29	77	11	6	.289	.325
Chavez,Raul	23	.253	90	281	25	71	11	0	3	30	11	33	0	5	.281	.324
Colon,Dennis	22	.212	106	372	31	79	9	0	4	29	19	43	2	6	.251	.269
Gutierrez,Ricky	26	.260	64	223	34	58	10	2	0	19	20	31	6	7	.321	.323
Hajek,Dave	28	.282	131	471	73	133	30	2	2	58	28	30	8	7	.323	.367
Hatcher,Chris	27	.250	105	312	47	78	15	1	9	39	33	125	4	5	.322	.391
Hidalgo,Richard	20	.249	133	478	56	119	26	4	12	56	25	86	6	9	.286	.395
Johnson,Russ	23	.232	132	466	61	108	15	1	7	50	39	69	7	5	.291	.313
Kellner,Frank	29	.264	103	349	37	92	15	0	0	32	37	74	0	7	.334	.307
Mitchell,Tony	25	.248	96	323	42	80	15	1	14	57	27	96	0	2	.306	.430
Montgomery,Ray	26	.264	123	397	57	105	22	0	15	72	27	78	7	6	.311	.433
Mora,Melvin	24	.283	125	460	61	130	30	0	2	42	26	64	17	6	.321	.361
Ramos,Ken	29	.275	112	309	42	85	20	4	1	34	37	30	9	5	.353	.375
Simms,Mike	29	.252	85	301	41	76	21	4	8	48	25	72	6	2	.310	.429
KANSAS CITY ROYALS																
Chamberlain,Wes	30	.284	64	236	23	67	17	0	8	36	3	58	3	3	.293	.458
Cookson,Brent	26	.302	108	328	49	99	18	2	11	49	31	58	2	3	.362	.470
Damon,Johnny	22	.310	111	403	64	125	13	7	10	41	43	35	17	6	.377	.452
Diaz,Lino	25	.316	62	215	30	68	13	2	3	33	9	21	0	3	.344	.437
Fasano,Sal	24	.255	87	302	46	77	16	1	12	51	17	62	2	6	.295	.434
Grotewold,Jeff	30	.263	105	335	54	88	17	0	11	47	63	87	0	2	.379	.412
Halter,Shane	26	.205	124	380	32	78	17	2	5	30	31	96	1	3	.265	.300
Hughes,Keith	32	.259	103	328	40	85	19	1	7	36	23	40	2	2	.308	.387
Long,Kevin	29	.255	89	302	34	77	14	0	0	20	29	36	6	8	.320	.301
Long,Ryan	23	.205	102	331	27	68	23	0	3	26	6	48	2	4	.220	.302
Lyden,Mitch	31	.224	71	228	20	51	7	0	7	34	8	65	0	0	.250	.346
Martinez,Felix	22	.238	127	412	41	98	13	3	1	23	20	69	31	12	.273	.291
Martinez,Ramon	23	.248	103	379	44	94	17	1	1	39	27	50	7	8	.298	.306
Mercedes,Henry	26	.188	86	266	29	50	10	0	7	29	17	89	1	0	.237	.305
Myers,Rod	23	.278	131	479	55	133	19	5	4	48	22	78	20	8	.309	.363
Norman,Les	27	.256	83	301	36	77	17	2	5	25	13	47	3	3	.287	.375
Randa,Joe	26	.246	64	224	25	55	9	1	5	25	17	32	1	2	.299	.362
Romero,Mandy	28	.269	121	420	56	113	29	1	11	63	44	59	0	3	.338	.421
Sisco,Steve	26	.260	61	223	25	58	10	0	1	17	10	38	2	1	.292	.318
Stewart,Andy	25	.246	104	357	39	88	25	0	2	40	16	48	0	3	.279	.333
Stynes,Chris	23	.247	83	295	40	73	10	4	5	32	20	23	2	5	.295	.359
Tucker,Michael	25	.279	71	265	29	74	16	3	2	21	18	38	8	4	.325	.385
Vitiello,Joe	26	.247	59	219	25	54	12	1	7	32	9	49	0	1	.276	.406
LOS ANGELES DODGERS																
Blanco,Henry	24	.215	117	382	38	82	16	2	10	48	26	79	0	1	.265	.346
Busch,Mike	27	.219	121	415	44	91	22	0	11	40	27	108	1	2	.267	.352
Cairo,Miguel	22	.254	107	421	45	107	16	0	0	34	18	33	25	9	.285	.292
Castro,Juan	24	.219	104	320	33	70	12	1	1	28	13	44	2	4	.249	.272
Cedeno,Roger	21	.252	99	341	44	86	12	3	1	29	34	58	15	6	.320	.314
Garcia,Karim	20	.263	124	438	58	115	18	4	12	60	24	107	8	6	.301	.404
Guerrero,Wilton	21	.314	109	411	51	129	10	3	0	23	18	74	17	9	.343	.353

424

Major League Equivalencies for 1995 AAA/AA Batters

Batter	Age	Avg	G	AB	R	H	2B	3B	HR	RBI	BB	SO	SB	CS	OBP	SLG
Huckaby,Ken	25	.268	89	257	19	69	11	0	0	26	7	27	2	1	.288	.311
Ingram,Garey	25	.197	63	218	18	43	7	1	0	19	13	42	6	4	.242	.239
Landrum,Tito	25	.214	87	252	35	54	10	0	6	21	18	68	3	6	.267	.325
Latham,Chris	23	.257	63	222	33	57	10	2	7	32	23	67	8	11	.327	.414
Marrero,Oreste	26	.235	132	451	54	106	21	1	18	76	45	109	3	2	.304	.406
Martin,Jim	25	.207	120	386	41	80	18	1	3	34	30	109	15	13	.264	.282
Melendez,Dan	25	.234	128	448	39	105	22	0	5	50	36	70	0	3	.291	.317
Pye,Eddie	29	.242	84	281	32	68	14	0	1	21	19	37	7	2	.290	.302
Rios,Eduardo	23	.256	98	351	36	90	17	2	4	45	14	50	1	4	.285	.350
Romero,Wilfredo	21	.240	105	363	39	87	16	0	5	37	28	73	7	12	.294	.325
Traxler,Brian	28	.231	110	329	30	76	17	0	7	33	15	28	0	3	.265	.347
Williams,Reggie	30	.258	66	217	29	56	9	1	3	19	19	48	4	4	.318	.350
MILWAUKEE BREWERS																
Banks,Brian	25	.276	127	421	60	116	34	6	8	58	52	117	6	9	.355	.442
Barker,Tim	28	.249	80	261	40	65	8	3	0	22	27	40	8	8	.319	.303
Basse,Mike	26	.241	121	378	45	91	13	1	0	32	54	63	12	9	.336	.280
Dodson,Bo	25	.300	125	413	60	124	21	2	13	63	56	71	0	1	.384	.455
Felder,Ken	25	.241	114	352	38	85	20	2	8	41	30	98	1	6	.301	.378
Felix,Lauro	26	.228	91	237	40	54	11	0	2	18	29	54	4	1	.312	.300
Koslofski,Kevin	29	.204	105	318	38	65	17	3	6	32	31	102	3	2	.275	.333
Landry,Todd	23	.260	132	489	56	127	28	2	11	58	21	104	6	7	.290	.393
Lofton,Rod	28	.207	102	237	27	49	6	0	0	16	14	49	7	3	.251	.232
Lopez,Pedro	27	.269	87	216	23	58	13	1	2	20	11	50	0	3	.304	.366
Lopez,Roberto	24	.281	114	399	59	112	19	5	0	32	49	65	6	4	.359	.353
Loretta,Mark	24	.277	127	473	44	131	21	3	6	73	31	48	6	9	.321	.372
Nevers,Tom	24	.232	118	409	49	95	11	2	7	42	27	82	5	3	.280	.320
Richardson,Scott	25	.224	82	246	21	55	7	3	0	21	10	44	5	5	.254	.276
Rodriques,Cecil	24	.235	72	234	26	55	7	4	1	17	9	53	3	2	.263	.312
Singleton,Duane	23	.261	106	352	44	92	9	3	3	26	36	64	25	9	.330	.330
Staton,Dave	28	.241	108	320	39	77	10	0	16	42	43	98	0	3	.331	.422
Stefanski,Mike	26	.248	84	250	30	62	11	1	1	26	13	31	1	0	.285	.312
Sutko,Glenn	27	.221	86	213	19	47	14	0	4	27	18	71	0	0	.281	.343
Unroe,Tim	25	.251	102	366	40	92	20	1	5	41	16	96	3	3	.283	.352
Wachter,Derek	25	.247	112	377	40	93	22	0	6	41	36	68	1	2	.312	.353
Weger,Wes	25	.257	109	385	42	99	22	1	1	36	15	45	0	3	.285	.327
Williamson,Antone	22	.279	104	376	46	105	26	3	5	67	30	59	2	1	.333	.404
MINNESOTA TWINS																
Brede,Brent	24	.266	134	444	70	118	27	1	3	38	59	90	11	6	.352	.351
Byrd,Tony	25	.243	123	440	53	107	19	7	3	50	24	93	17	6	.282	.339
Coomer,Ron	29	.298	85	312	45	93	21	1	14	63	15	30	3	2	.330	.506
Duncan,Andres	24	.221	95	262	28	58	5	1	0	13	15	62	9	5	.264	.248
Dunn,Steve	26	.284	109	384	44	109	27	0	9	64	23	68	2	2	.324	.424
Durant,Mike	26	.225	85	285	31	64	13	2	1	17	15	33	8	7	.263	.295
Grifol,Pedro	26	.173	77	225	22	39	8	0	3	20	19	36	0	0	.238	.249
Hazlett,Steve	26	.271	127	410	55	111	22	4	3	38	32	70	5	10	.324	.366
Hocking,Denny	26	.254	117	382	39	97	21	1	6	58	20	45	9	8	.291	.361
Ingram,Riccardo	29	.316	122	455	62	144	38	1	9	66	32	64	2	5	.361	.464
Jackson,John	29	.264	106	352	55	93	19	2	6	33	46	44	13	9	.349	.381
Lawton,Matt	24	.262	114	408	74	107	18	4	13	53	48	77	21	8	.340	.422
Lennon,Patrick	28	.336	101	333	59	112	25	1	8	49	36	100	11	7	.401	.489

Major League Equivalencies for 1995 AAA/AA Batters

Batter	Age	Avg	G	AB	R	H	2B	3B	HR	RBI	BB	SO	SB	CS	OBP	SLG
Lopez,Rene	24	.240	82	262	21	63	7	0	3	25	23	52	0	0	.302	.302
Miller,Damian	26	.254	83	283	30	72	20	0	2	32	11	42	1	4	.282	.346
Moore,Tim	24	.236	90	309	38	73	18	0	9	44	20	96	3	2	.283	.382
Ogden,Jamie	24	.276	117	380	53	105	21	0	13	60	41	99	4	5	.347	.434
Pose,Scott	29	.259	84	224	39	58	8	0	0	15	25	30	12	4	.333	.295
Quinlan,Tom	28	.252	130	449	60	113	19	4	14	68	31	134	4	3	.300	.405
Raabe,Brian	28	.275	112	422	68	116	28	4	2	46	35	15	11	0	.330	.374
Roper,Chad	22	.222	120	441	40	98	21	2	11	60	23	94	1	3	.261	.354
Simons,Mitch	27	.294	130	459	67	135	30	2	2	35	37	48	23	9	.347	.381
Valette,Ramon	24	.209	111	344	39	72	10	1	4	31	18	57	15	2	.249	.279
Walker,Todd	23	.283	137	508	82	144	26	2	22	84	54	111	18	7	.352	.472
MONTREAL EXPOS																
Alcantara,Israel	23	.187	71	230	19	43	11	1	6	22	14	86	0	0	.234	.322
Barron,Tony	29	.227	88	264	33	60	13	0	13	36	18	48	0	1	.277	.424
Benitez,Yamil	23	.234	127	458	52	107	23	4	12	55	36	134	10	5	.289	.380
Buccheri,Jim	27	.242	133	454	51	110	15	2	0	24	40	60	33	12	.304	.284
Castleberry,Kevin	28	.267	118	412	52	110	17	2	5	44	42	61	6	6	.335	.354
Charbonnet,Mark	25	.224	120	393	26	88	13	2	5	44	13	111	2	5	.249	.305
Dauphin,Phil	27	.218	111	385	41	84	18	1	3	29	29	65	12	6	.273	.294
Grissom,Antonio	26	.228	82	228	25	52	9	0	2	18	22	51	9	7	.296	.294
Hymel,Lou	28	.164	95	293	27	48	9	1	7	28	15	103	2	1	.205	.273
Jacobs,Frank	28	.272	120	378	51	103	22	1	9	55	49	66	0	2	.356	.407
Martin,Chris	28	.233	126	399	44	93	18	0	2	32	38	61	22	8	.300	.293
Martinez,Ray	27	.215	87	251	27	54	10	0	0	17	17	42	4	1	.265	.255
Rundels,Matt	26	.220	134	481	61	106	28	2	7	46	37	127	13	10	.276	.331
Santangelo,F.P.	28	.232	95	259	29	60	15	2	1	20	26	23	5	3	.302	.317
Siddall,Joe	28	.194	83	242	20	47	13	1	0	18	19	44	2	2	.253	.256
Tovar,Edgar	22	.179	81	240	22	43	6	1	2	16	11	25	0	2	.215	.238
Vidro,Jose	21	.235	64	238	25	56	15	1	2	29	14	39	2	6	.278	.332
Wood,Ted	29	.241	98	315	28	76	15	0	6	39	30	66	6	1	.307	.346
Yan,Julian	30	.251	114	358	39	90	21	2	15	63	12	94	3	0	.276	.447
NEW YORK METS																
Agbayani,Benny	24	.246	88	284	30	70	9	1	0	20	26	54	8	3	.310	.285
Alicea,Ed	29	.230	122	427	56	98	14	3	2	34	38	81	16	7	.292	.290
Barry,Jeff	27	.238	92	320	41	76	15	4	8	47	22	71	2	1	.287	.384
Castillo,Alberto	26	.250	69	212	20	53	11	0	3	27	22	33	1	3	.321	.344
Daubach,Brian	24	.217	137	461	49	100	21	1	8	58	35	111	4	2	.272	.319
Davis,Jay	25	.227	126	454	51	103	14	4	2	42	17	74	7	6	.255	.289
Everett,Carl	26	.281	67	253	46	71	14	3	5	31	17	49	9	7	.326	.419
Garcia,Omar	24	.298	120	436	51	130	19	5	2	56	20	60	2	4	.329	.378
Greene,Charlie	25	.204	127	421	25	86	13	0	1	30	12	79	1	2	.226	.242
Hardtke,Jason	24	.257	125	444	52	114	35	2	3	41	44	62	4	10	.324	.365
Huskey,Butch	24	.266	109	384	58	102	16	0	24	77	33	92	6	6	.324	.495
Lee,Derek	29	.238	112	344	49	82	15	0	16	53	41	65	8	6	.319	.422
Morgan,Kevin	26	.255	133	474	58	121	18	0	3	48	32	63	6	12	.302	.312
Ochoa,Alex	24	.254	125	441	46	112	20	2	6	48	31	64	17	10	.303	.349
Ordonez,Rey	24	.200	125	431	43	86	18	3	1	44	23	52	8	15	.240	.262
Orton,John	30	.243	73	214	22	52	9	0	2	22	14	70	1	5	.289	.313
Otero,Ricky	24	.250	72	288	32	72	7	4	0	20	23	34	12	15	.305	.302
Payton,Jay	23	.281	135	533	76	150	26	5	13	69	28	57	19	10	.317	.422

426

Major League Equivalencies for 1995 AAA/AA Batters

Batter	Age	Avg	G	AB	R	H	2B	3B	HR	RBI	BB	SO	SB	CS	OBP	SLG
Saunders,Chris	25	.229	138	480	54	110	20	3	8	59	37	119	2	7	.284	.333
White,Donnie	24	.211	94	304	38	64	14	1	2	16	26	59	17	7	.273	.283
NEW YORK YANKEES																
Burnett,Roger	26	.202	104	347	27	70	12	0	2	25	20	67	2	2	.245	.254
Carpenter,Bubba	27	.234	116	368	50	86	11	2	10	43	34	72	9	5	.299	.356
Delvecchio,Nick	26	.245	125	421	57	103	21	2	17	64	51	141	1	0	.326	.425
Eenhoorn,Robert	28	.232	92	310	32	72	10	2	4	28	17	56	1	3	.272	.316
Figga,Mike	25	.248	117	411	52	102	20	2	11	54	32	100	0	0	.302	.387
Fleming,Carlton	24	.249	72	205	21	51	7	0	0	17	14	16	3	3	.297	.283
Fox,Andy	25	.277	126	465	73	129	16	7	12	47	50	80	21	6	.348	.419
Hinds,Rob	25	.231	132	433	61	100	7	0	0	32	35	108	19	7	.288	.247
Horne,Tyrone	25	.276	133	450	72	124	29	2	14	61	61	106	12	8	.362	.442
Hughes,Troy	25	.253	88	249	28	63	7	0	5	29	15	66	2	6	.295	.341
Jeter,Derek	22	.295	123	471	85	139	25	6	1	40	52	58	15	5	.365	.380
Leach,Jalal	27	.228	88	267	33	61	11	3	5	27	19	62	8	3	.280	.348
Luke,Matt	25	.250	116	432	50	108	18	3	9	56	15	84	3	3	.275	.368
Perezchica,Tony	30	.238	101	349	38	83	11	2	6	39	15	76	2	2	.269	.332
Posada,Jorge	24	.237	108	359	53	85	29	3	7	45	45	104	2	3	.322	.393
Rivera,Ruben	22	.260	119	416	75	108	21	6	20	64	48	145	17	10	.336	.483
Robertson,Jason	25	.257	117	444	52	114	26	6	5	46	29	112	13	11	.302	.376
Romano,Scott	24	.224	100	343	37	77	13	0	5	44	34	60	4	1	.294	.306
Seefried,Tate	24	.191	106	376	35	72	21	0	4	38	22	126	0	0	.236	.279
Sparks,Don	30	.290	137	528	59	153	24	6	6	80	25	77	1	0	.322	.392
Turner,Brian	25	.277	86	303	33	84	19	1	3	37	17	76	2	1	.316	.376
OAKLAND ATHLETICS																
Batista,Tony	22	.239	120	410	52	98	20	0	14	58	23	108	5	8	.279	.390
Bowie,Jim	31	.227	141	503	53	114	20	1	2	53	41	55	2	1	.285	.282
Bryant,Scott	28	.247	119	384	44	95	26	1	7	53	37	94	0	3	.314	.375
Cruz,Fausto	24	.244	114	426	55	104	18	1	8	51	26	72	5	5	.288	.347
Faries,Paul	31	.261	117	402	51	105	11	1	0	35	26	50	10	8	.306	.294
Francisco,David	24	.263	129	467	71	123	14	0	4	45	30	101	24	9	.308	.319
Gubanich,Creighton	24	.204	94	269	35	55	6	0	11	41	39	90	0	0	.305	.349
Herrera,Jose	23	.261	92	348	35	91	9	2	5	43	21	63	7	8	.304	.342
Lesher,Brian	25	.245	127	461	74	113	20	1	17	68	52	121	5	8	.322	.403
Lydy,Scott	27	.249	104	378	60	94	22	3	11	50	25	71	11	4	.295	.410
Maksudian,Mike	30	.222	100	306	41	68	18	2	2	26	35	59	3	1	.302	.314
Mashore,Damon	26	.258	117	318	38	82	14	2	0	28	32	84	12	5	.326	.314
Molina,Izzy	25	.237	85	299	36	71	14	0	7	24	21	70	2	4	.288	.355
Moore,Kerwin	25	.239	72	251	40	60	10	2	1	20	36	73	7	3	.334	.307
Sheldon,Scott	27	.207	111	352	39	73	13	1	5	23	29	82	6	2	.268	.293
Sobolewski,Mark	26	.189	83	301	33	57	12	0	6	32	17	68	1	1	.233	.289
Spiezio,Scott	23	.263	141	514	74	135	27	4	11	82	54	87	8	3	.333	.395
Walker,Dane	26	.213	110	361	44	77	11	1	1	33	46	92	7	7	.302	.258
Williams,George	27	.267	81	273	40	73	14	0	9	42	38	57	0	4	.357	.418
Wolfe,Joel	26	.234	119	428	58	100	15	1	11	42	44	89	18	9	.305	.350
Wood,Jason	26	.201	127	403	37	81	15	2	1	38	22	77	0	4	.242	.256
Young,Ernie	26	.237	95	329	53	78	16	2	11	55	37	78	1	2	.314	.398
PHILADELPHIA PHILLIES																
Bennett,Gary	24	.203	93	281	20	57	10	0	3	30	15	41	0	0	.243	.270
Bieser,Steve	28	.242	95	236	29	57	11	3	0	26	17	60	10	4	.292	.314

Major League Equivalencies for 1995 AAA/AA Batters

Batter	Age	Avg	G	AB	R	H	2B	3B	HR	RBI	BB	SO	SB	CS	OBP	SLG
Butler,Rob	26	.271	92	314	36	85	15	2	2	27	19	41	3	7	.312	.350
Doster,Dave	25	.239	139	532	64	127	36	1	16	60	33	66	7	6	.283	.400
Eason,Tommy	25	.227	96	321	33	73	16	1	10	38	11	66	1	1	.253	.377
Geisler,Phil	26	.200	96	305	21	61	13	1	1	31	14	84	2	1	.235	.259
Gilbert,Shawn	31	.237	136	518	66	123	24	1	1	33	50	109	11	10	.305	.293
Grable,Rob	26	.256	129	418	59	107	25	0	14	59	48	128	12	10	.333	.416
Hayden,Dave	26	.214	88	224	20	48	5	0	3	10	21	55	0	3	.282	.277
Holifield,Rick	26	.193	106	306	38	59	7	1	2	22	33	74	18	6	.271	.242
Jordan,Kevin	26	.282	106	394	48	111	27	2	3	47	22	38	2	0	.320	.383
Koelling,Brian	27	.266	123	467	59	124	20	4	2	37	27	82	23	7	.306	.338
Lieberthal,Mike	24	.254	85	268	34	68	19	1	4	33	34	27	0	3	.338	.377
Manahan,Tony	27	.260	90	288	28	75	10	0	2	25	22	41	4	0	.313	.316
Marsh,Tom	30	.281	78	285	36	80	20	3	7	37	10	41	6	2	.305	.446
McConnell,Chad	25	.245	94	306	35	75	11	0	8	40	17	64	5	2	.285	.359
McNair,Fred	26	.240	117	404	49	97	22	0	17	53	26	99	2	1	.286	.421
Montoyo,Charlie	30	.219	92	279	25	61	12	0	2	26	39	48	1	2	.314	.283
Schall,Gene	26	.286	92	308	41	88	23	2	9	49	38	57	2	2	.364	.461
Sefcik,Kevin	25	.246	135	513	55	126	21	2	3	39	26	53	9	10	.282	.312
Solomon,Steve	26	.203	119	345	38	70	17	3	2	32	31	89	11	3	.269	.287
Tokheim,Dave	27	.244	127	434	50	106	17	5	8	52	14	58	4	6	.268	.362
Vatcher,Jim	31	.254	110	358	40	91	27	1	4	30	22	53	2	3	.297	.369
Zuber,Jon	26	.261	119	403	42	105	18	3	2	39	38	72	0	1	.324	.335
PITTSBURGH PIRATES																
Allensworth,Jermaine	24	.253	107	388	59	98	23	3	1	17	25	67	17	10	.298	.335
Austin,Jake	26	.216	102	343	24	74	18	1	3	33	12	54	3	2	.242	.300
Beamon,Trey	22	.278	118	417	46	116	23	2	3	38	24	57	11	7	.317	.365
Beasley,Tony	29	.256	105	324	49	83	15	2	1	28	22	47	14	5	.303	.324
Brown,Michael	24	.217	60	217	24	47	12	0	6	27	19	66	0	2	.280	.355
Canale,George	30	.265	130	472	59	125	28	4	17	85	32	88	0	2	.312	.449
Cranford,Jay	25	.207	93	280	25	58	11	0	4	35	37	71	2	3	.300	.289
Espinosa,Ramon	24	.262	134	473	57	124	26	1	2	40	12	68	10	5	.280	.334
Farrell,Jon	24	.199	94	306	28	61	12	0	8	39	10	87	2	3	.225	.317
Franklin,Micah	24	.243	110	334	40	81	23	0	12	44	29	99	1	2	.303	.419
Johnson,Erik	30	.245	123	424	40	104	28	3	1	36	24	42	3	3	.286	.333
Kendall,Jason	22	.300	117	413	73	124	24	0	6	59	39	23	7	6	.361	.402
Leary,Bob	24	.278	67	234	31	65	13	2	4	35	28	40	2	2	.355	.402
Matos,Francisco	26	.267	100	315	22	84	9	3	1	25	3	26	5	1	.274	.324
Munoz,Omer	30	.242	67	227	24	55	9	0	1	20	3	24	1	0	.252	.295
Osik,Keith	27	.281	90	278	25	78	20	0	6	37	13	44	1	1	.313	.417
Polcovich,Kevin	26	.262	126	412	41	108	13	0	3	31	15	64	10	9	.288	.316
Ratliff,Daryl	26	.281	111	324	33	91	12	0	0	27	16	41	6	5	.315	.318
Simmons,Nelson	33	.229	107	279	27	64	14	0	5	36	18	47	0	0	.276	.333
Sveum,Dale	32	.236	118	382	44	90	28	0	7	44	30	81	1	1	.291	.364
Womack,Tony	26	.230	112	421	50	97	10	2	0	18	20	49	24	11	.265	.264
SAN DIEGO PADRES																
Bean,Billy	32	.242	119	417	46	101	26	1	10	52	31	57	1	2	.295	.381
Briggs,Stoney	24	.223	118	373	48	83	11	4	7	37	27	142	11	8	.275	.330
Bruno,Julio	23	.227	97	321	21	73	9	1	1	24	10	62	2	5	.251	.271
Bush,Homer	23	.254	108	417	43	106	10	3	4	30	10	88	23	10	.272	.321
Casanova,Papo	23	.247	89	296	34	73	15	0	11	35	17	54	2	1	.288	.409

Major League Equivalencies for 1995 AAA/AA Batters

Batter	Age	Avg	G	AB	R	H	2B	3B	HR	RBI	BB	SO	SB	CS	OBP	SLG
Cianfrocco,Archi	29	.265	89	302	35	80	15	1	7	39	11	64	3	0	.291	.391
Colbert,Craig	31	.210	74	229	20	48	6	0	0	16	14	46	0	0	.255	.236
Cotton,John	25	.224	121	392	48	88	15	4	9	38	26	108	10	6	.273	.352
Deer,Rob	35	.248	89	286	37	71	17	1	13	44	32	92	1	2	.324	.451
DeLeon,Roberto	25	.241	73	228	19	55	8	0	6	27	8	34	1	2	.267	.355
Drinkwater,Sean	25	.216	102	278	23	60	10	0	5	21	17	52	2	4	.261	.306
Gennaro,Brad	24	.238	104	382	37	91	15	0	4	48	14	66	7	8	.265	.309
Hall,Billy	27	.189	86	238	28	45	2	0	0	15	13	49	13	5	.231	.197
Hyers,Tim	24	.243	82	243	31	59	9	0	0	15	16	34	0	3	.290	.280
Killeen,Tim	25	.207	77	222	21	46	11	0	7	32	18	76	1	0	.267	.351
Mack,Quinn	30	.224	90	255	26	57	8	0	1	16	22	30	6	3	.285	.267
Mulligan,Sean	26	.234	101	321	23	75	15	0	5	29	18	64	0	0	.274	.327
Newfield,Marc	23	.256	73	254	28	65	11	0	6	30	16	42	1	0	.300	.370
Rossy,Rico	32	.256	98	297	30	76	8	1	0	30	37	37	1	7	.338	.290
Russo,Paul	26	.266	89	256	26	68	14	0	8	27	21	67	0	1	.321	.414
Smith,Ira	28	.276	123	424	58	117	24	3	6	44	23	60	10	8	.313	.389
Thomas,Keith	27	.227	109	344	53	78	10	2	9	26	13	91	28	12	.255	.346
Thompson,Jason	25	.243	137	457	50	111	16	0	16	52	42	140	4	3	.307	.383
Velandia,Jorge	21	.202	129	376	35	76	17	2	3	30	17	77	0	2	.237	.282
SAN FRANCISCO GIANTS																
Aurilia,Rich	24	.268	135	462	56	124	25	0	6	61	46	58	8	5	.335	.361
Bellinger,Clay	27	.236	97	263	25	62	13	0	1	24	20	55	2	2	.290	.297
Benard,Marvin	26	.263	111	357	53	94	11	3	4	24	38	69	6	13	.334	.345
Canizaro,Jason	22	.268	126	425	72	114	22	4	10	52	43	106	11	9	.335	.409
Chimelis,Joel	28	.224	118	380	36	85	26	0	5	50	21	56	0	2	.264	.332
Christopherson,Eric	27	.188	94	271	15	51	7	0	0	18	26	57	0	1	.259	.214
Cruz,Jake	23	.270	127	441	77	119	29	0	10	67	42	77	6	8	.333	.404
Ehmann,Kurt	25	.221	105	331	36	73	8	1	0	19	34	59	5	5	.293	.251
Florez,Tim	26	.245	100	286	32	70	9	1	8	40	19	53	2	3	.292	.367
Jensen,Marcus	23	.258	95	310	48	80	19	4	3	39	31	74	0	0	.326	.374
Jones,Dax	25	.231	112	385	35	89	17	1	1	34	23	55	7	10	.275	.288
Leonard,Mark	31	.254	112	370	55	94	20	1	9	60	62	66	2	2	.361	.386
McCarty,Dave	26	.303	74	274	48	83	23	1	9	39	25	59	0	1	.361	.493
McFarlin,Jason	26	.310	93	242	34	75	11	1	4	32	18	28	5	7	.358	.413
Morrow,Chris	26	.220	83	232	27	51	15	0	5	30	23	47	0	1	.290	.349
Mueller,Bill	25	.273	129	480	66	131	24	4	1	48	54	72	4	5	.346	.346
Murray,Calvin	24	.208	123	477	73	99	15	1	4	32	47	81	19	9	.279	.268
Williams,Keith	24	.274	99	343	39	94	20	0	9	58	20	53	3	3	.314	.411
Wilson,Desi	28	.262	122	466	67	122	24	1	3	63	30	73	8	9	.306	.337
Wimmer,Chris	25	.227	132	428	41	97	19	2	1	33	23	51	9	7	.266	.287
Woods,Ken	25	.232	89	203	26	47	9	0	2	20	17	31	2	5	.291	.305
SEATTLE MARINERS																
Bonnici,James	24	.282	138	507	73	143	39	2	19	89	65	108	1	1	.364	.479
Bragg,Darren	26	.290	53	207	20	60	13	1	3	26	20	42	7	2	.352	.406
Cora,Manuel	22	.223	80	260	16	58	9	2	0	14	7	43	0	4	.243	.273
Diaz,Eddy	24	.264	121	455	69	120	26	0	15	50	37	45	7	6	.319	.420
Gipson,Charles	23	.219	112	389	35	85	12	1	0	28	25	73	8	10	.266	.254
Griffey,Craig	25	.174	96	298	42	52	12	0	0	23	39	85	10	2	.270	.215
Hickey,Mike	26	.260	120	446	58	116	27	0	6	58	52	94	4	2	.337	.361
Howard,Chris	30	.228	83	263	28	60	14	0	3	26	16	76	0	0	.272	.316

Major League Equivalencies for 1995 AAA/AA Batters

Batter	Age	Avg	G	AB	R	H	2B	3B	HR	RBI	BB	SO	SB	CS	OBP	SLG
Litton,Greg	31	.293	117	379	50	111	25	0	7	48	38	75	1	1	.357	.414
Noland,J.D.	27	.257	76	245	23	63	10	1	4	24	11	40	10	5	.289	.355
Peguero,Julio	27	.301	82	279	42	84	17	0	3	17	14	45	9	6	.334	.394
Pozo,Arquimedez	22	.282	122	439	49	124	19	3	8	53	23	33	2	2	.318	.394
Rackley,Keifer	25	.254	114	429	54	109	18	1	6	39	33	106	6	3	.307	.343
Ramirez,Roberto	26	.275	129	488	66	134	26	4	16	80	30	109	8	8	.317	.443
Relaford,Desmond	22	.269	120	461	67	124	17	1	8	32	47	92	24	6	.337	.362
Rodriguez,Alex	20	.338	54	207	31	70	12	1	12	38	16	48	1	3	.386	.580
Saunders,Doug	26	.251	83	259	29	65	15	1	7	38	14	65	1	0	.289	.398
Sheets,Andy	24	.276	132	427	49	118	29	5	1	40	28	90	6	2	.321	.375
Sherman,Darrell	28	.240	119	342	50	82	9	1	1	26	48	53	14	5	.333	.281
Thurman,Gary	31	.280	93	353	56	99	10	7	4	39	17	67	17	5	.314	.382
Varitek,Jason	24	.222	104	351	41	78	16	1	10	43	53	144	0	0	.324	.359
Willard,Jerry	36	.254	85	224	28	57	16	0	8	40	40	46	0	0	.367	.433
ST. LOUIS CARDINALS																
Anderson,Charlie	26	.268	78	235	27	63	14	1	3	25	15	58	0	1	.312	.374
Bell,David	23	.252	88	321	36	81	12	0	6	36	19	48	3	2	.294	.346
Berblinger,Jeff	25	.302	87	324	58	98	14	3	4	25	35	42	11	15	.370	.401
Bradshaw,Terry	27	.262	111	378	53	99	22	5	6	34	43	62	14	5	.337	.394
Caraballo,Ramon	27	.292	69	236	31	69	9	0	6	20	15	43	10	3	.335	.407
Cholowsky,Dan	25	.240	130	417	58	100	19	0	10	51	46	109	12	8	.315	.357
Deak,Darrell	26	.220	106	327	34	72	20	1	5	28	42	92	1	1	.309	.333
Difelice,Mike	27	.249	83	233	18	58	12	0	0	23	21	41	0	1	.311	.300
Diggs,Tony	29	.249	101	265	32	66	11	6	1	18	30	47	6	5	.325	.347
Ellis,Paul	27	.213	78	225	15	48	5	0	1	22	36	19	0	0	.322	.249
Giannelli,Ray	30	.272	119	378	46	103	17	0	12	57	35	88	2	6	.334	.413
Griffin,Ty	28	.257	94	257	33	66	16	0	7	39	26	62	12	1	.325	.401
Gulan,Mike	25	.261	122	426	58	111	24	4	13	64	16	110	4	2	.287	.427
Holbert,Aaron	23	.234	112	389	46	91	15	2	7	32	16	62	10	5	.264	.337
Johns,Keith	24	.257	116	397	61	102	12	1	1	24	41	58	10	6	.326	.300
Lewis,Anthony	25	.238	115	400	48	95	20	2	20	75	32	124	0	1	.294	.448
Martinez,Domingo	28	.237	64	215	21	51	14	0	7	25	12	50	0	0	.278	.400
McNeely,Jeff	26	.216	109	264	25	57	5	0	0	15	18	55	3	7	.266	.235
Ronan,Marc	26	.195	78	220	12	43	7	0	0	6	11	43	2	2	.234	.227
Sweeney,Mark	26	.319	91	288	48	92	19	1	6	63	43	42	3	0	.408	.455
Thomas,Skeets	27	.229	84	266	23	61	14	0	7	28	14	79	0	0	.268	.361
Torres,Paul	25	.248	129	451	56	112	24	0	16	71	37	101	1	2	.305	.408
Velez,Jose	23	.279	107	280	32	78	13	0	5	36	9	37	3	3	.301	.379
Woodson,Tracy	33	.241	118	419	51	101	33	0	14	62	22	44	8	3	.279	.420
Young,Dmitri	22	.274	99	365	49	100	18	4	8	55	22	49	1	3	.315	.411
TEXAS RANGERS																
Byington,John	28	.245	122	429	44	105	13	1	1	28	18	42	4	1	.275	.287
Charles,Frank	27	.242	126	472	49	114	22	2	11	69	17	99	0	0	.268	.367
Dostal,Bruce	31	.201	88	289	32	58	12	5	3	28	27	51	8	2	.269	.308
Estrada,Osmani	27	.255	120	404	42	103	21	2	2	41	28	52	0	1	.303	.332
Fox,Eric	32	.263	92	342	47	90	19	4	5	46	27	71	3	4	.317	.386
Frias,Hanley	22	.270	93	355	42	96	16	3	0	25	36	56	10	11	.338	.332
Hare,Shawn	29	.252	68	234	24	59	11	2	3	27	21	49	2	0	.314	.355
Hecht,Steve	30	.243	92	305	36	74	9	2	2	17	20	53	10	4	.289	.305
Hinzo,Tommy	32	.237	82	249	30	59	8	0	0	18	11	39	6	2	.269	.269

Major League Equivalencies for 1995 AAA/AA Batters

Batter	Age	Avg	G	AB	R	H	2B	3B	HR	RBI	BB	SO	SB	CS	OBP	SLG
Horn,Sam	32	.293	82	246	37	72	14	1	16	53	32	73	0	1	.374	.553
Kennedy,Darryl	27	.233	64	202	25	47	8	0	2	27	13	25	0	0	.279	.302
Lindeman,Jim	34	.236	83	288	47	68	14	2	9	33	30	56	0	0	.308	.392
Marzano,John	33	.293	120	417	50	122	37	2	7	51	30	56	2	3	.340	.441
Monell,Johnny	30	.295	121	427	52	126	16	0	10	61	54	55	0	0	.374	.403
Nunez,Rogelio	26	.215	82	260	25	56	3	0	1	16	8	46	0	6	.239	.238
Parra,Franklin	24	.229	77	275	25	63	8	1	1	25	10	58	5	8	.256	.276
Sagmoen,Marc	25	.217	119	424	52	92	17	6	7	44	32	56	6	4	.272	.335
Schu,Rick	34	.256	110	390	45	100	17	2	9	52	36	66	3	2	.319	.379
Smith,Mike	26	.244	132	491	62	120	20	2	13	61	49	77	8	5	.313	.373
Texidor,Jose	24	.259	129	487	52	126	31	0	4	61	25	65	0	0	.295	.347
Thomas,Brian	25	.260	131	453	58	118	22	8	3	33	40	93	6	3	.320	.364
Vargas,Hector	30	.261	98	299	35	78	9	1	0	24	27	56	4	0	.322	.298
Worthington,Craig	31	.297	81	269	43	80	17	0	7	37	28	53	0	0	.364	.439
TORONTO BLUE JAYS																
Adriana,Sharnol	25	.267	75	255	28	68	16	0	3	28	23	69	9	12	.327	.365
Battle,Howard	24	.233	118	433	35	101	15	3	7	40	32	78	7	10	.286	.330
Boston,D.J.	24	.228	132	469	44	107	25	0	10	62	35	109	9	7	.282	.345
Bowers,Brent	25	.230	111	296	31	68	14	4	4	21	8	61	3	0	.250	.345
Brito,Tilson	24	.225	90	320	40	72	14	2	6	26	24	73	12	7	.279	.338
Butler,Rich	23	.199	127	407	39	81	14	3	4	39	25	92	9	4	.245	.278
Canate,Willie	24	.220	114	337	40	74	15	1	2	25	19	66	6	4	.261	.288
Coolbaugh,Mike	24	.228	142	492	62	112	30	1	9	49	27	120	5	10	.268	.348
Crespo,Felipe	23	.275	88	338	46	93	18	4	12	34	34	60	9	6	.341	.459
de la Cruz,Lorenzo	24	.261	140	499	55	130	19	10	8	53	26	140	8	10	.297	.387
Delgado,Carlos	24	.295	91	322	49	95	21	3	19	61	37	83	0	3	.368	.556
Harmes,Kris	25	.213	86	254	24	54	13	1	3	25	26	51	0	0	.286	.307
Henry,Santiago	23	.206	138	446	41	92	23	3	2	26	7	99	12	5	.219	.285
Kelly,Pat	29	.191	88	246	25	47	6	0	3	19	14	53	0	0	.235	.252
Lis,Joe	27	.245	130	474	56	116	30	3	16	46	38	57	4	1	.301	.422
Lutz,Brent	26	.128	87	226	16	29	5	0	2	14	14	88	2	1	.179	.177
Perez,Robert	27	.321	122	486	58	156	35	4	8	55	10	64	5	4	.335	.459
Ramos,John	30	.237	116	405	49	96	22	0	19	62	31	88	1	1	.291	.432
Roberts,Lonell	25	.220	116	445	57	98	11	2	1	25	20	107	44	15	.254	.261
Stewart,Shannon	22	.271	138	487	78	132	22	5	5	48	66	66	31	11	.358	.368
Townley,Jason	27	.241	96	257	20	62	10	0	7	25	31	76	0	2	.323	.362
Weinke,Chris	23	.205	113	332	35	68	11	1	8	34	36	79	3	2	.283	.316

About STATS, Inc. & Howe Sportsdata

STATS, Inc.

STATS, Inc. is the nation's leading independent sports information and statistical analysis company, providing detailed sports services for a wide array of clients.

One of the fastest-growing sports companies in the country, STATS provides the most up-to-the-minute sports information to professional teams, print and broadcast media, software developers and interactive srevice providers around the country. Some of our major clients are ESPN, Turner Sports, the Associated Press, *The Sporting News*, Electronic Arts and Motorola. Much of the information we provide is available to the public via America On-Line.

STATS Publishing, a division of STATS, Inc., produces 10 annual books, including the *STATS Major League Handbook*, the *Pro Football Handbook*, and the *Pro Basketball Handbook*. These publications deliver STATS expertise to fans, scouts, general managers and media around the country.

In addition, STATS offers the most innovative—and fun—fantasy sports games around, from *Bill James Fantasy Baseball* and *Bill James Classic Baseball* to *STATS Fantasy Football* and *STATS Fantasy Hoops*.

Information technology has grown by leaps and bounds in the last decade, and STATS will continue to be at the forefront as both a vendor and supplier of the most up-to-date, in-depth sports information available. If you haven't already, you will most certainly be seeing us at an infobahn rest stop in the near future.

For more information on our products, or on joining our reporter network, write us at:

STATS, Inc.
8131 Monticello Ave.
Skokie, IL 60076-3300

...or call us at 1-800-63-STATS (1-800-637-8287). Outside the U.S., dial 1-708-676-3383.

About Howe Sportsdata

Howe Sportsdata International has been keeping statistics on professional baseball since 1910. Currently, Howe is the official statistician for all all 17 U.S.-based National Association professional baseball leagues and seven independent leagues (though independent league stats are not contained in this book). Howe also compiles statistics for the Arizona Fall League, the Hawaiian Winter League, and winter leagues located in Mexico, Puerto Rico, the Dominican Republic, Venezuela and Australia. In addition, Howe keeps the official statistics of the Continental Basketball Association, all professional minor hockey leagues and the National Professional Soccer League.

Originally based in Chicago, Howe Sportsdata International is now located in Boston, Massachusetts on the historic Fish Pier, maintaining 24-hour/seven-days-per-week operation during the baseball season. Howe also maintains a satellite office in San Mateo, California. Howe is responsible for maintaining statistics for more than 250 teams who collectively play more than 13,000 games per year.

Howe also provides statistical information to all 28 major-league teams and to major media outlets such as *USA Today*, *The Sporting News*, *Baseball America*, the Associated Press and *Sports Illustrated*. Howe also counts as its customers many leading newspapers, of which the following are but a small representative sample: *The Los Angeles Times*, *The Detroit Free Press*, *The Miami Herald* and both *The Chicago Sun-Times* and *The Chicago Tribune*. For more information about Howe, write to:

Howe Sportsdata International
Boston Fish Pier, West Building #2, Suite 306
Boston, Massachusetts 02110

Appendix

Minor League Team	Organization	League	Level	Minor League Team	Organization	League	Level
Albany	Expos	South Atlantic League	A	Cubs (Fort Myers)	Cubs	Gulf Coast League	R
Albuquerque	Dodgers	Pacific Coast League	AAA	Danville	Braves	Appalachian League	R
Angels (Mesa)	Angels	Arizona League	R	Daytona	Cubs	Florida State League	A
Arkansas	Cardinals	Texas League	AA	Dunedin	Blue Jays	Florida State League	A
Asheville	Rockies	South Atlantic League	A	Durham	Braves	Carolina League	A
Astros (Kissimmee)	Astros	Gulf Coast League	R	Edmonton	Athletics	Pacific Coast League	AAA
Athletics (Scottsdale)	Athletics	Arizona League	R	El Paso	Brewers	Texas League	AA
Auburn	Astros	New York-Penn League	A	Elizabethton	Twins	Appalachian League	R
Augusta	Pirates	South Atlantic League	A	Elmira	Marlins	New York-Penn League	A
Bakersfield	Dodgers	California League	A	Erie	Pirates	New York-Penn League	A
Batavia	Phillies	New York-Penn League	A	Eugene	Braves	Northwest League	A
Bellingham	Giants	Northwest League	A	Everett	Mariners	Northwest League	A
Beloit	Brewers	Midwest League	A	Expos (W.Palm Beach)	Expos	Gulf Coast League	R
Billings	Reds	Pioneer League	R	Fayetteville	Tigers	South Atlantic League	A
Binghamton	Mets	Eastern League	AA	Frederick	Orioles	Carolina League	A
Birmingham	White Sox	Southern League	AA	Fort Myers	Twins	Florida State League	A
Blue Jays (Dunedin)	Blue Jays	Gulf Coast League	R	Fort Wayne	Twins	Midwest League	A
Bluefield	Orioles	Appalachian League	R	Great Falls	Dodgers	Pioneer League	R
Boise	Angels	Northwest League	A	Greensboro	Yankees	South Atlantic League	A
Bowie	Orioles	Eastern League	AA	Greenville	Braves	Southern League	AA
Braves (W.Palm Beach)	Braves	Gulf Coast League	R	Hagerstown	Blue Jays	South Atlantic League	A
Brevard County	Marlins	Florida State League	A	Harrisburg	Expos	Eastern League	AA
Brewers (Chandler)	Brewers	Arizona League	R	Helena	Brewers	Pioneer League	R
Bristol	Tigers	Appalachian League	R	Hickory	White Sox	South Atlantic League	A
Buffalo	Indians	American Association	AAA	High Desert	Orioles	California League	A
Burlington	Expos	Midwest League	A	Hudson Valley	Rangers	New York-Penn League	A
Burlington	Indians	Appalachian League	R	Huntington	Cubs	Appalachian League	R
Butte	Independent	Pioneer League	R	Huntsville	Athletics	Southern League	AA
Calgary	Pirates	Pacific Coast League	AAA	Idaho Falls	Braves	Pioneer League	R
Canton-Akron	Indians	Eastern League	AA	Indianapolis	Reds	American Association	AAA
Carolina	Pirates	Southern League	AA	Iowa	Cubs	American Association	AAA
Cedar Rapids	Angels	Midwest League	A	Jackson	Astros	Texas League	AA
Charleston-SC	Rangers	South Atlantic League	A	Jacksonville	Tigers	Southern League	AA
Charleston-WV	Reds	South Atlantic League	A	Jamestown	Tigers	New York-Penn League	A
Charlotte	Marlins	International League	AAA	Johnson City	Cardinals	Appalachian League	R
Charlotte	Rangers	Florida State League	A	Kane County	Marlins	Midwest League	A
Chattanooga	Reds	Southern League	AA	Kingsport	Mets	Appalachian League	R
Clearwater	Phillies	Florida State League	A	Kinston	Indians	Carolina League	A
Clinton	Padres	Midwest League	A	Kissimmee	Astros	Florida State League	A
Colorado Springs	Rockies	Pacific Coast League	AAA	Knoxville	Blue Jays	Southern League	AA
Columbia	Mets	South Atlantic League	A	Lake Elsinore	Angels	California League	A
Columbus	Yankees	International League	AAA	Lakeland	Tigers	Florida State League	A
Columbus	Indians	South Atlantic League	A	Las Vegas	Padres	Pacific Coast League	AAA

434

Minor League Team	Organization	League	Level
Lethbridge	Independent	Pioneer League	R
Louisville	Cardinals	American Association	AAA
Lynchburg	Pirates	Carolina League	A
Macon	Braves	South Atlantic League	A
Mariners (Peoria)	Mariners	Arizona League	R
Marlins (Melbourne)	Marlins	Gulf Coast League	R
Martinsville	Mets	Appalachian League	R
Medicine Hat	Blue Jays	Pioneer League	R
Memphis	Padres	Southern League	AA
Mets (St. Lucie)	Mets	Gulf Coast League	R
Michigan	Red Sox	Midwest League	A
Midland	Angels	Texas League	AA
Modesto	Athletics	California League	A
Nashville	White Sox	American Association	AAA
New Britain	Twins	Eastern League	AA
New Haven	Rockies	Eastern League	AA
New Jersey	Cardinals	New York-Penn League	A
New Orleans	Brewers	American Association	AAA
Norfolk	Mets	International League	AAA
Norwich	Yankees	Eastern League	AA
Ogden	Independent	Pioneer League	R
Oklahoma City	Rangers	American Association	AAA
Omaha	Royals	American Association	AAA
Oneonta	Yankees	New York-Penn League	A
Orioles (Sarasota)	Orioles	Gulf Coast League	R
Orlando	Cubs	Southern League	AA
Ottawa	Expos	International League	AAA
Padres (Peoria)	Padres	Arizona League	R
Pawtucket	Red Sox	International League	AAA
Peoria	Cardinals	Midwest League	A
Phoenix	Giants	Pacific Coast League	AAA
Piedmont	Phillies	South Atlantic League	A
Pirates (Bradenton)	Pirates	Gulf Coast League	R
Pittsfield	Mets	New York-Penn League	A
Port City	Mariners	Southern League	AA
Portland	Marlins	Eastern League	AA
Portland	Rockies	Northwest League	A
Prince William	White Sox	Carolina League	A
Princeton	Reds	Appalachian League	R
Quad City	Astros	Midwest League	A
Rancho Cucamonga	Padres	California League	A
Rangers (Pt. Charlotte)	Rangers	Gulf Coast League	R
Reading	Phillies	Eastern League	AA
Red Sox (Fort Myers)	Red Sox	Gulf Coast League	R
Richmond	Braves	International League	AAA
Riverside	Mariners	California League	A
Rochester	Orioles	International League	AAA
Rockford	Cubs	Midwest League	A
Rockies (Chandler)	Rockies	Arizona League	R
Royals (Fort Myers)	Royals	Gulf Coast League	R
Salem	Rockies	Carolina League	A
Salt Lake	Twins	Pacific Coast League	AAA
San Antonio	Dodgers	Texas League	AA
San Bernardino	Dodgers	California League	A
San Jose	Giants	California League	A
Sarasota	Red Sox	Florida State League	A
Savannah	Cardinals	South Atlantic League	A
Scranton-WB	Phillies	International League	AAA
Shreveport	Giants	Texas League	AA
South Bend	White Sox	Midwest League	A
Southern Oregon	Athletics	Northwest League	A
Spokane	Royals	Northwest League	A
Springfield	Royals	Midwest League	A
St. Catharines	Blue Jays	New York-Penn League	A
St. Lucie	Mets	Florida State League	A
St. Petersburg	Cardinals	Florida State League	A
Stockton	Brewers	California League	A
Syracuse	Blue Jays	International League	AAA
Tacoma	Mariners	Pacific Coast League	AAA
Tampa	Yankees	Florida State League	A
Tigers (Lakeland)	Tigers	Gulf Coast League	R
Toledo	Tigers	International League	AAA
Tucson	Astros	Pacific Coast League	AAA
Trenton	Red Sox	Eastern League	AA
Tulsa	Rangers	Texas League	AA
Twins (Fort Myers)	Twins	Gulf Coast League	R
Utica	Red Sox	New York-Penn League	A
Vancouver	Angels	Pacific Coast League	AAA
Vermont	Expos	New York-Penn League	A
Vero Beach	Dodgers	Florida State League	A
Visalia	Independent	California League	A
Watertown	Indians	New York-Penn League	A
Welland	Pirates	New York-Penn League	A
West Michigan	Athletics	Midwest League	A
West Palm Beach	Expos	Florida State League	A
White Sox (Sarasota)	White Sox	Gulf Coast League	R
Wichita	Royals	Texas League	AA
Williamsport	Cubs	New York-Penn League	A
Wilmington	Royals	Carolina League	A
Winston-Salem	Reds	Carolina League	A
Wisconsin Foxes	Mariners	Midwest League	A
Yakima	Dodgers	Northwest League	A
Yankees (Tampa)	Yankees	Gulf Coast League	R

Bill James Classic Baseb II

Joe Jackson, Walter Johnson, and Roberto Clemente are back on the field of your dreams!

If you're not ready to give up baseball in the fall, or if you're looking to relive its glorious past, then Bill James Classic Baseball is the game for you!

The Classic Game features players from all eras of Major League Baseball at all performance levels - not just the stars. You could see Honus Wagner, Josh Gibson, Carl Yastrzemski, Bob Uecker, Billy Grabarkewitz, and Dick Fowler...on the SAME team!

As owner, GM and manager all in one, you'll be able to...

- "Buy" your team of up to 25 players from our catalog of over 2,000 historical players (You'll receive $1 million to buy your favorite players)
- Choose the park your team will call home—current or historical, 63 in all!
- Rotate batting lineups for a right- or left-handed starting pitcher
- Change your pitching rotation for each series. Determine your set-up man, closer, and long reliever
- Alter in-game strategies, including stealing frequency, holding runners on base, hit-and-run, and much more!
- Select your best pinch hitter and late-inning defensive replacements (For example, Curt Flood will get to more balls than Hack Wilson!)

How to Play The Classic Game:

1. Sign up to be a team owner TODAY! Leagues forming year-round
2. STATS, Inc. will supply you with a catalog of eligible players and a rule book
3. You'll receive $1 million to buy your favorite major leaguers
4. Take part in a player and ballpark draft with 11 other owners
5. Set your pitching rotation, batting lineup, and managerial strategies
6. STATS runs the game simulation...a 154-game schedule, 14 weeks!
7. You'll receive customized in-depth weekly reports, featuring game summaries, stats, and boxscores

Order from STATS INC. Today!
Use Order Form in This Book, or Call 1-800-63-STATS or 708-676-3383!

STATS On-Line

Now you can have a direct line to a world of sports information just like the pros use with STATS On-Line. If you love to keep up with your favorite teams and players, STATS On-Line is for you. From Shaquille O'Neal's fast-breaking dunks to Ken Griffey's tape-measure blasts — if you want baseball, basketball, football and hockey stats, we put them at your fingertips!

STATS On-Line

- **Player Profiles and Team Profiles** — The #1 resource for scouting your favorite professional teams and players with information you simply can't find anywhere else! The most detailed info you've ever seen, including real-time stats. Follow baseball pitch-by-pitch, football snap-by-snap, and basketball and hockey shot-by-shot, with scores and player stats updated continually!

- **NO monthly or annual fees**

- **Local access numbers** — avoid costly long-distance charges!

- **Unlimited access** — 24 hours a day, seven days a week

- **Downloadable files** — get year-to-date stats in an ASCII format for baseball, football, basketball, and hockey

- **In-progress box scores** — You'll have access to the most up-to-the-second scoring stats for every team and player. When you log into STATS On-Line, you'll get detailed updates, including player stats and scoring plays while the games are in progress!

- **Other exclusive features** — transactions and injury information, team and player profiles and updates, standings, leader and trailer boards, game-by-game logs, fantasy game features, and much more!

Sign-up fee of $30 (applied towards future use), 24-hour access with usage charges of $.75/min. Mon.-Fri., 8am-6pm CST; $.25/min. all other hours and weekends.

Order from STATS INC. Today!
Use Order Form in This Book, or Call 1-800-63-STATS or 708-676-3383!

Bill James Fantasy Baseball

Bill James Fantasy Baseball enters its eighth season of offering baseball fans the most unique, realistic and exciting game fantasy sports has to offer.

You draft a 25-player roster and can expand to as many as 28. Players aren't ranked like in rotisserie leagues—you'll get credit for everything a player does, like hitting homers, driving in runs, turning double plays, pitching quality outings and more!

Also, the team which scores the most points among all leagues, plus wins the World Series, will receive the John McGraw Award, which includes a one-week trip to the Grapefruit League in spring training, a day at the ballpark with Bill James, and a new fantasy league named in his/her honor!

Unique Features Include:

• **Live fantasy experts** — available seven days a week

• **The best weekly reports in the business** — detailing who is in the lead, win-loss records, MVPs, and team strengths and weaknesses

• **On-Line computer system** — a world of information, including daily updates of fantasy standings and stats

• **Over twice as many statistics as rotisserie**

• **Transactions that are effective the very next day!**

"My goal was to develop a fantasy league based on the simplest yet most realistic principle possible. A league in which the values are as nearly as possible what they ought to be, without being distorted by artificial category values or rankings...."

- Bill James

All this, all summer long...for less than $5 per week!

Order from STATS INC. Today!
Use Order Form in This Book, or Call 1-800-63-STATS or 708-676-3383!

STATS Fantasy Hoops

Soar into the 1995-96 season with STATS Fantasy Hoops! SFH puts YOU in charge. Don't just sit back and watch Grant Hill, Shawn Kemp, and Alonzo Mourning - get in the game and coach your team to the top!

How to Play SFH:
1. Sign up to coach a team.
2. You'll receive a full set of rules and a draft form with SFH point values for all eligible players - anyone who played in the NBA in 1994-95, plus all 1995 NBA draft picks.
3. Complete the draft form and return it to STATS.
4. You will take part in the draft with nine other owners, and we will send you league rosters.
5. You make unlimited weekly transactions including trades, free agent signings, activations, and benchings.
6. Six of the 10 teams in your league advance to postseason play, with two teams ultimately advancing to the Finals.

SFH points values are tested against actual NBA results, mirroring the real thing. Weekly reports will tell you everything you need to know to lead your team to the SFH Championship!

STATS Fantasy Football

STATS Fantasy Football puts YOU in charge! You draft, trade, cut, bench, activate players and even sign free agents each week. SFF pits you head-to-head against 11 other owners.

STATS' scoring system applies realistic values, tested against actual NFL results. Each week, you'll receive a superb in-depth report telling you all about both team and league performances.

How to Play SFF:
1. Sign up today!
2. STATS sends you a draft form listing all eligible NFL players.
3. Fill out the draft form and return it to STATS, and you will take part in the draft along with 11 other team owners.
4. Go head-to-head against the other owners in your league. You'll make week-by-week roster moves and transactions through STATS' Fantasy Football experts, via phone, fax, or on-line!

Order from STATS INC. Today!
Use Order Form in This Book, or Call 1-800-63-STATS or 708-676-3383!

Get the Inside Scoop!

ONLY $16.95
Available 1/1/96

STATS Presents...

The Scouting Notebook: 1996

The Scouting Notebook:1996 builds upon seven years of tremendous success. STATS and its team of national scouts break new ground by covering every player who appeared last season in the majors, along with all the top prospects.

Unique Features:

☆ Extensive scouting reports on more than 700 Major League Baseball players

☆ Evaluations of nearly 200 minor league prospects

☆ Written by experts covering every team, including nationally-recognized analysts like Peter Gammons and John Benson

☆ Complete coverage of the strengths and weaknesses of each team's top players

"The STATS Scouting Notebook provides the most detailed and accurate player analyses. They're so good that opposing players should read them - and I'm sure some do."

— Chris Welsh, Color Commentator
SPORTSCHANNEL, WLWT-TV(OH)

Order from STATS INC. Today!
Use Order Form in This Book, or Call 1-800-63-STATS or 708-676-3383!

STATS INC.
Meet the Winning Lineup...

Bill James Presents:
STATS 1996 Major League Handbook
- Bill James' exclusive 1996 player projections
- Career data for every 1995 Major League Baseball player
- Complete lefty/righty pitcher and hitter breakdowns
- Leader boards, fielding stats and stadium data
- **Price: $17.95, Item #HB96, Available NOW!**

Bill James Presents:
STATS 1996 Minor League Handbook
- Year-by-year career statistical data for AA and AAA players
- Bill James' exclusive Major League Equivalencies
- Triple-A lefty/righty pitching and hitting splits
- Complete 1995 Single-A player statistics
- **Price: $17.95, Item #MH96, Available NOW!**

STATS 1996 Player Profiles
- Exclusive 1995 breakdowns for pitchers and hitters, over 30 in all: lefty/righty, home/road, clutch situations, ahead/behind in the count, month-by-month, etc.
- Complete breakdowns by player for the last five seasons
- Both team and league profiles
- **Price: $17.95, Item #PP96, Available NOW!**

STATS 1996 Minor League Scouting Notebook
- Evaluation of each organization's top prospects
- Essays, stat lines and grades for more than 400 prospects
- Top 50 prospects ranked
- **Price: $16.95, Item #MN96, Available 1/15/96**

ALSO...See STATS' *The Scouting Notebook: 1996,* located on the preceding page!

Bill James Presents:
STATS 1996 Batter Versus Pitcher Match-Ups!

- Complete stats for pitchers vs. batters (5+ career AB against them)
- Leader boards and stats for all 1995 Major League players
- **Price: $12.95, Item #BP96, Available 1/15/96**

STATS 1996 Baseball Scoreboard

- Entertaining essays interpreting baseball stats
- Easy-to-understand statistical charts
- Specific coverage of every major team
- Appendices that invite further reader analysis
- **Price: $16.95, Item #SB96, Available 3/1/96**

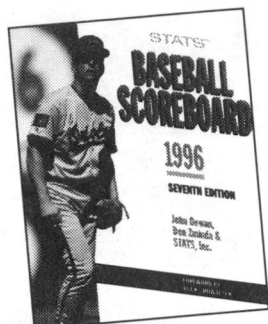

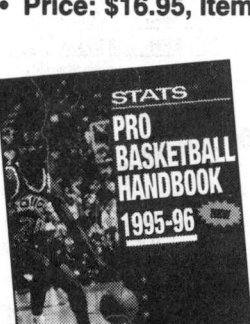

STATS 1995-96 Pro Basketball Handbook

- Career stats for every player who logged minutes during 1994-95
- Team game logs with points, rebounds, assists and much more
- Leader boards from points per game to triple doubles
- **Price: $17.95, Item #BH96, Available NOW!**

STATS 1996 Pro Football Handbook

- A complete season-by-season register for every active 1995 player
- Numerous statistical breakdowns for hundreds of NFL players
- Leader boards in a number of innovative and traditional categories
- **Price: $17.95, Item #FH96, Available 2/1/96**

Pro Football Revealed: The 100-Yard War (1996 Edition)

- Profiles each NFL team, complete with essays, charts and play diagrams
- Detailed statistical breakdowns on players, teams and coaches
- Essays about NFL trends and happenings by leading experts
- **Price: $16.95, Item #PF96 , Available 7/1/96**
- **1995 EDITION AVAILABLE NOW for ONLY $15.95!**

Order from STATS INC. Today!
Use Order Form in This Book, or Call 1-800-63-STATS or 708-676-3383!

STATS INC Order Form

Name_____ Phone_____
Address_____ Fax_____
City_____ State_____ Zip_____

Method of Payment (U.S. Funds Only):

❏ Check/Money Order ❏ Visa ❏ MasterCard

Cardholder Name_____

Credit Card Number_____ Exp. _____

Signature_____

BOOKS

Qty	Product Name	Item #	Price	Total
	STATS 1996 Major League Handbook	HB96	$17.95	
	1996 Major League Hndbk. (Comb-bnd)	HC96	$19.95	
	STATS 1996 Projections Update	PJUP	$9.95	
	The Scouting Notebook: 1996	SN96	$16.95	
	STATS 1996 Player Profiles	PP96	$17.95	
	1996 Player Profiles (Comb-bound)	PC96	$19.95	
	STATS 1996 Minor Lg. Scouting Ntbk.	MN96	$16.95	
	STATS 1996 Minor League Handbook	MH96	$17.95	
	1996 Minor League Hndbk. (Comb-bnd)	MC96	$19.95	
	STATS 1996 BVSP Match-Ups!	BP96	$12.95	
	STATS 1996 Baseball Scoreboard	SB96	$16.95	
	STATS 1995-96 Pro Basketball Hndbk.	BH96	$17.95	
	Pro Football Revealed (1996 Edition)	PF96	$16.95	
	STATS 1996 Pro Football Handbook	FH96	$17.95	

For previous editions, circle appropriate years:

Major League Handbook	91 92 93 94 95	$9.95
Scouting Report/Notebook	92 94 95	$9.95
Player Profiles	93 94 95	$9.95
Minor League Handbook	92 93 94 95	$9.95
Baseball Scoreboard	92 93 94 95	$9.95
Basketball Scoreboard	94 95	$9.95
Pro Football Handbook	95	$9.95
Pro Football Revealed	94 95	$9.95

FANTASY GAMES & STATSfax

Qty	Product Name	Item #	Price	Total
	Bill James Classic Baseball	BJCG	$129.00	
	How to Win The Classic Game (book)	CGBK	$16.95	
	The Classic Game STATSfax	CGX5	$20.00	
	Bill James Fantasy Baseball	BJFB	$89.00	
	BJFB STATSfax/5-day	SFX5	$20.00	
	BJFB STATSfax/7-day	SFX7	$25.00	
	STATS Fantasy Hoops	SFH	$85.00	
	SFH STATSfax/5-day	SFH5	$20.00	
	SFH STATSfax/7-day	SFH7	$25.00	
	STATS Fantasy Football	SFF	$69.00	
	SFF STATSfax/3-day	SFF3	$15.00	

STATS ON-LINE

Qty	Product Name	Item #	Price	Total
	STATS On-Line	ONLE	$30.00	

**For faster service, call
1-800-63-STATS or 708-676-3383,
or fax this form to STATS at
708-676-0821**

1st Fantasy Team Name (ex. Colt 45's):_____ _____
    What Fantasy Game is this team for?_____
2nd Fantasy Team Name (ex. Colt 45's):_____ _____
    What Fantasy Game is this team for?_____

NOTE: $1.00/player is charged for all roster moves and transactions.

For Bill James Fantasy Baseball
Would you like to play in a league drafted by Bill James?   ❏ Yes   ❏ No

TOTALS

	Price	Total
Product Total (excl. Fantasy Games and On-Line)		
For first class mailing in U.S. add:	+$2.50/book	
Canada—all orders—add:	+$3.50/book	
Order 2 or more books—subtract:	-$1.00/book	
IL residents add 8.5% sales tax		
Subtotal		
Fantasy Games & On-Line Total		
GRAND TOTAL		

FREE Information Kits:

❏ STATS Reporter Networks
❏ Bill James Classic Baseball
❏ Bill James Fantasy Baseball
❏ STATS On-Line
❏ STATS Fantasy Hoops
❏ STATS Fantasy Football
❏ STATS Year-end Reports
❏ STATSfax

BOOK

Mail to: STATS, Inc., 8131 Monticello Ave., Skokie, IL 60076-3300